THE ENCYCLOPAEDIA OF ISLAM
ENCYCLOPÉDIE DE L'ISLAM

INDEX OF PROPER NAMES/INDEX DES NOMS PROPRES
TO VOLUMES/DES TOMES
I-X

THE ENCYCLOPAEDIA OF ISLAM

NEW EDITION

ENCYCLOPÉDIE DE L'ISLAM

NOUVELLE ÉDITION

INDEX OF PROPER NAMES/
INDEX DES NOMS PROPRES

to Volumes I-X (Fascicules 1-178)
and to the Supplement, Fascicules 1-6

des Tomes I-X (Livraisons 1-176)
et du Supplément, Livraisons 1-6

COMPILED AND EDITED BY/
ÉTABLI ET PUBLIÉ PAR
E. VAN DONZEL

BRILL
LEIDEN · BOSTON · KÖLN
2002

The paper in this book meets the guidelines for permanence and durability of the Committee on Production Guidelines for Book Longevity of the Council on Library Resources.

Library of Congress Cataloging-in-Publication Data

Donzel, E. J. van.
The encyclopaedia of Islam, new edition. Index of proper names / compiled and edited by E. van Donzel = Encyclopédie de l'islam, nouvelle édition. Index des noms propres / établi et publié par E. van Donzel.
p. cm.
English and French
Issued in fascicles.
Description based on the index to v. I-X and to suppl., fasc. 1-6.
ISBN 9004121072 (pbk.)
1. Encyclopaedia of Islam—Indexes. 2. Islam—Indexes. 3. Islamic countries—Indexes. I. Title. II. Title: Encyclopédie de l'islam, nouvelle édition. Index des noms propres.
DS35.53.533D66 1993
909'.097671—dc20 93-28265
CIP

ISBN 90 04 12107 2

PRINTED IN THE NETHERLANDS

PREFACE TO THE SEVENTH EDITION

It has been considered opportune to publish, before the completion of the Encyclopaedia of Islam, still another bilingual version of the Index of Proper Names for Volume X. It should however be noted that the present volume does not contain references to French articles beyond the entry Türk Odjaghi down to the end of the letter U, since the final French fascicules of Volume X have not yet been published. Upon completion of the Encyclopaedia, including the Supplement, the Index will be published separately in English and French.

Leiden, October 2001 E. van Donzel

PRÉFACE À LA SEPTIÈME ÉDITION

Il a été jugé opportun de publier, avant que l'Encyclopédie de l'Islam soit achevée, encore une version bi-lingue de l'Index des Noms Propres du Volume X. Il faut pourtant noter que ce volume ne contient pas de renvois à des articles français au-delà de l'entrée Türk Odjaghi jusqu'à la fin de la lettre U, puisque les dernières livraisons françaises du Volume X n'ont pas encore été publiées. Lorsque l'Encyclopédie et son Supplément seront achevés, l'Index sera publié séparément en anglais et français.

Leyde, Octobre 2001 E. van Donzel

SYMBOLS USED

Small roman numerals denote the English version, and large roman numerals the French one. Bold type indicates the main article.

An arrow denotes 'see', an 'a' the first column on a page, a 'b' the second column, 's' the English, 'S' the French Supplement.

SYMBOLES EMPLOYÉS

Les petits chiffres romains renvoient à l'édition anglaise, les grands chiffres romains à l'édition française. Les gros caractères indiquent l'article principal.

Une flèche veut dire: «voir», tandis que les lettres 'a' et 'b' indiques les colonnes, les lettres 's' et 'S' les Suppléments anglais et français.

A

Aʿara → Dhu ’l-Sharā
Aʿarrās, Abu Muḥammad ʿAbd Allāh (VII) viii, 440b – VIII, 455a
Aaron → Hārūn b. ʿImrān
Aaron b. Elijah (the Younger/le Jeune) (1369) iv, 605b – IV, 630a
Aaron b. Jeshuah → Hārūn b. al-Faradj
Aaron b. Joseph (the Elder/l'Ancien) (XIV) iv, 605b, 607a – IV, 630a, 631b
al-Aʿazz, amīr (XII) i, 440a – I, 452b
Āb-i Diz (Lūristān) v, 830a, 867b – V, 836a, 874a
Āb-i Gargar v, 867a, b – V, 873b, 874a
Aba al-Khayl (Burayda, Āl) i, 1313a – I, 1353a
Aba ’l-Ḳiʿdān → Abḳayḳ
ʿAbābda (Bedja) i, **1a**, 1172a – I, **1a**, 1207a
Abad i, **2a**; v, 95a – I, **2a**; V, 97b
Ābādah i, **2b** – I, **2b**
Ābādān → Abbādān
Ābādeh → Ābādah
Ābādī Begum Umm Muḥammad ʿAlī (Rāmpūr, 1924) vii, 421a – VII, 422b
ʿAbādila → ʿAbdalī
ʿAbādila, Banū (Makka) iii, 263a; vi, 150a, 151a – III, 270a; VI, 149a, b, 150a
Abāḍites → Ibāḍiyya
Abʿādiyya → Ibʿādiyya
Abāʿir s, 117b – S, 116b
Abāḳā (Il-Khān) (1282) i, 1110a, 1188b, 1295a; ii, 606b, 607b; iii, 106a, 1122a, 1125a; iv, 30b, 31a, 88a, 620b, 817a, 1167b; v, 162a, 827a; vi, 16a, 231a, 322a, b, 420a, 482b, 494a; vii, 479b –
I, 1143b, 1223b, 1335a; II, 621b, 622b; III, 108a, 1149b, 1153a; IV, 32b, 33b, 92a, 645a, 850a, 1200a; V, 160a, 833a; VI, 14a, 225a, 306a, 307a, 405a, 468b, 479b; VII, 479a
ʿAbalāt (VII) ii, 1011b – II, 1035a
Aban, Ramdan (XX) iv, 362b – IV, 378b
Abān → Taʾrīkh
Abān b. ʿAbd Allāh al-Marwānī (Umayyad(e)), al-Andalus) (X) s, 153a – S, 153a
Abān b. ʿAbd al-Ḥamīd al-Lāḥiḳī (815) i, **2b**, 108a, 587a, 1216b; iii, 73a, 309a, 878b; iv, 54b, 504a, 822b;c vi, 276a; vii, 798b; viii, 376b –
I, **2b**, 111a, 606a, 1253a; III, 75b, 318b, 903a; IV, 57b, 526a, 855b; VI, 261a; VII, 800b; VIII, 384a
Abān b. Abī ʿAyyāsh (VIII) ix, 818b – IX, 854a
Abān b. Ṣadaḳa (VIII) i, 1034a – I, 1065b
Abān b. ʿUthmān b. ʿAffān (723) i, **2b**; s, 230b – I, **3a**; S, 230b
Abān b. ʿUthmān b. Yaḥyā (723) i, 3a – I, 3a
Abanūs i, **3a** – I, **3a**
Abarḳubādh i, **3a** – I, **3b**
Abarḳūh i, **3b**; vi, 366a – I, **3b**; VI, 350a
Abarshahr (Nīshāpūr) i, **3b** – I, **3b**
Abarwīz b. al-Maṣmughān (758) vi, 744b – VI, 734a
Abas (953) i, 637b; ii, 679b – I, 658a; II, 696b
Abaskūn i, **3b**; vii, 71a – I, **4a**; VII, 71b
Ābāza (Georgians/Géorgiens) i, **4a**, 1189a, 1190a – I, **4a**, 1224b, 1225a
Ābāza Aḥmed Pasha → Ābāza Meḥmed Pasha
Ābāza Ḥasan Pasha (1658) i, **4a**; iii, 88a, 318a, 1001b, 1248b; iv, 843b, 885a; v, 33a, b, 258a, b, 729a; vii, 707b –
I, **4b**; III, 90b, 327b, 1026b, 1281a; IV, 876b, 917b; V, 34a, b, 256a, 734a; VII, 708b
Ābāza Meḥmed Pasha (1634) i, **4a**; ii, 712b, 724a, 1090b; iii, 1248a; iv, 970a, 971b; v, 257a, b; vii, 600b –
I, **4a**; II, 731a, 742b, 1116a; III, 1280b; IV, 1002a, 1003b, 1004a; V, 255a; VII, 600b
Abāza Muḥammad Katkhudā (XVIII) s, 44a – S, 44b
Ābāza Muḥammad Pasha (1771) i, **4b**; iv, 869b – I, **4a**; IV, 903a
ʿAbazeed, Shaykh (Abū Yazīd al-Bistaāmī, 874) 71b – X, 74a
Abb → Ibb
ʿAbba → Libās
Abbā Djifār (XIX) ii, 545b – II, 558b
ʿAbbād, Banū → ʿAbbādid(e)s
ʿAbbād b. Akhdār al-Tamīmī (681) vii, 123b – VII, 125b
ʿAbbād b. Djulanda (ʿUmān) (VII) i, 451a – I, 464a
ʿAbbād b. Ḥusayn al-Ḥibatī (780) vi, 920b – VI, 912b
ʿAbbād b. Muḥammad → al-Muʿtaḍid bi-’llāh
ʿAbbād b. Sulaymān al-Ṣaymarī (864) i, **4b**; ii, 570a; iv, 985b; v, 576b, 806a; s, 226b, 391b –
I, **5a**; II, 584b; IV, 1018a; V, 581a, 811b; S, 226b, 392a
ʿAbbād b. Ziyād (VII) i, **5a**; iii, 882a; iv, 536a; vi, 545a – I, **5a**; III, 906a; IV, 559a; VI, 529b
ʿAbbād Ibn Djamāʿa (XIV) vii, 407b – VII, 409a
ʿAbbādān i, **5a**, 927b; iv, 6a, 7b, 674b, 906a, 1171b; v, 65b, 81a; vi, 664b; s, 32a, 48b, 57a, 291a –
I, **5a**, 955b; IV, 6b, 8b, 702a, 939a, 1205a; V, 67b, 83a; VI, 650b; S, 32b, 49a, 57b, 290b
al-ʿAbbādī, Abū ʿĀṣim (1066) i, **5b** – I, **5b**
ʿAbbādid(e)s/ʿAbbād, Banū (XI) i, **5b**, 862a, 1338b; v, 632b; vi, 606b; vii, 292b –
I, **5b**, 886b, 1379a; V, 636b; VI, 591a; VII, 294b
ʿAbbās, amīr (1146) ix, 437b – IX, 454a
ʿAbbās, Banū (Kabylia(e)) iv, 361a, b, 478a – IV, 377a, b, 499a
ʿAbbās I, Shāh (Ṣafawid(e)) (1629) i, **7b**, 15a, 95a, 190a, 228b, 240b, 267b, 553b, 625b, 643a, 685b, 701a, 707b, 904a, 942b, 1013a, 1066a, 1067a, 1068a, 1117a; ii, 16b, 104a, 283a, 976a, 1083b; iii, 157b, 210b, 214a, 348a,b, 1101b, 1190a; iv, 36a, 50a, 98a, 103a, 695a, 976b, 1041a, 1044a; v, 245a, 371a, 457b, 493a, 663b, 829b, 908b, 1113b; vi, 714b, 715a, b, 762b, 939a; vii, 224a, 317a, 600b, 928b;viii, 115b, 116a,b, 769a; s, 63a, 94b, 139a, b, 140a, b, 238a, 239a, 274b, 275a, 308a –
I, **7b**, 15a, 98a, 194b, 235b, 248a, 275b, 571b, 646b, 663b, 706a, 722b, 728b, 931b, 971b, 1044b, 1098a, 1099a, 1100a, 1151a; II, 17a, 106b, 801b, 998a, 1108b; III, 161a, 216b, 220a, 359a, b, 1128b, 1219b; IV, 38b, 53a, 102b, 107b, 723a, 1009a, 1072a, 1075b; V, 243a, 372a, 460b, 496a, 668b, 835b, 914b, 1110a; VI, 703b, 704b, 751b, 931a; VII, 225b, 226a, 319b, 600a, 929a;VIII, 118a,b, 7994b S, 63b, 94a, 138b, 139a, b, 140b, 238a, 239a, 274b, 308a
ʿAbbās II, Shāh (Ṣafawid(e)) (1666) i, 228b, 243a, 1068a; iii, 1102b; iv, 977a; v, 493b, 869a, 1089b, 1114a; vii, 61b, 224a, 318a, 476a;viii, 770b; s, 139a, 276a –
I, 235b, 252a, 1100b; III, 1129b; IV, 1009b; V, 496b, 875b, 1086b, 1110a; VII, 62a, 226a, 320b, 475b;VIII 796a; S, 138b, 275b
ʿAbbās III, Shāh (Ṣafawid(e)) (1749) ii, 310b; viii,771b – II, 319b, 310b; viii, 797b
al-ʿAbbās (al-Kūfa) (817) vi, 335b – VI, 319b
al-ʿAbbās b. ʿAbd al-Muṭṭalib (653) i, **8b**, 15a, 80a, 152b; ii, 726a; iii, 328a; iv, 320a; vi, 335a, 660a; vii, 369b, 371b; s, 92b –
I, **9a**, 15a, 82b, 157a; II, 744b; III, 338a; IV, 334b; VI, 319b, 645b; VII, 371b, 373a; S, 92b
ʿAbbās b. Abi ’l-Futūḥ (1154) i, **9a**, 196b, 198b; ii, 318a – I, **9a**, 202a, 204a; II, 327a
al-ʿAbbās b. Aḥmad b. Ṭūlūn (Ṭūlūnid(e)) (IX) i, 250b;

v, 49a; vi, 452b; s, **1a** – I, 258a; V, 50b; VI, 438a; S, **1a**
al-ʿAbbās b. al-Aḥnaf (808) i, **9b**, 587a, 1081b; ii, 1031b; iii, 1202b, 1262a; iv, 489a; vi, 253a, 468b; vii, 566b, 694b – I, **10a**, 606a, 1114a; II, 1055b; III, 1233a, 1294b; IV, 510a; VI, 237a, 454a; VII, 567a, 694b
al-ʿAbbās b. ʿAlī b. Abī Ṭālib (680) iii, 609b, 610a, 611a; v, 823a; s, 95a – III, 630b, 631a, b; V, 829a; S, 94b
al-ʿAbbās b. ʿAmr al-Ghanawī (917) i, **11a**; vii, 760b – I, **11a**; 762a
al-ʿAbbās b. Djaʿfar (VIII) s, 326b – S, 326a
al-ʿAbbās b. al-Faḍl, amīr (861) iv, 733a – IV, 762b
ʿAbbās b. Firnās (887) i, **11a**, 83a; ii, 1038a; viii, 616a, 632a,b – I, **11a**, 85b; II, 1062a; VIII, 635a, 651a
al-ʿAbbās b. al-Ḥasan al-Djardjarāʾī → al-Djardjarāʾī
al-ʿAbbās b. al-Ḥusayn al-Shīrāzī (973) i, **11b**; ii, 827a; iii, 730a – I, **11b**; II, 846b; III, 752b
al-ʿAbbās b. ʿĪsā b. Mūsā (IX) vi, 332b – VI, 317a
al-ʿAbbās b. al-Maʾmūn (838) i, **11b**; vi, 337b, 338a, b, 379a; vii, 776b – I, **11b**; VI, 322a, b, 363b; VII, 778a
al-ʿAbbās b. Mandīl (XIII) vi, 404a – VI, 388b
al-ʿAbbās b. Mirdās al-Sulaymī (VII) i, **12a**, 343b; ii, 1023b – I, **12a**, 354a; II, 1047a
al-ʿAbbās b. Muḥammad b. ʿAlī (802) i, **12b**; iv, 871a – I, **12b**; IV, 904a
al-ʿAbbās b. Mūsā b. ʿĪsā (813) vi, 334a – VI, 318b
al-ʿAbbās b. al-Musayyib (811) vi, 333a – VI, 317b
ʿAbbās b. Nāṣiḥ al-Thaḳafī (852) i, **12b** – I, **12b**
al-ʿAbbās b. Saʿīd (Saʿd) (VIII) vii, 629b – VII, 629b
ʿAbbās b. Shīth (Ghūrid(e)) (XI) ii, 1100a – II, 1126a
al-ʿAbbās b. al-Walīd I (Umayyad(e)) (750) i, **12b**, 57b, 1244a; ii, 715a; vi, 506a, 740a – I, **12b**, 59a, 1281b; II, 733b; VI, 491a, 729a
ʿAbbās Agha (XVIII) vii, 653a – VII, 653a
ʿAbbās Āḳā Ṣarrāf (XX) s, 365a – S, 365a
ʿAbbās Efendī → ʿAbd al-Bahāʾ
ʿAbbās Ḥamāda (XX) vi, 170a – VI, 160b
ʿAbbās Ḥilmī I Pasha, viceroy (1854) i, **13a**, 396a, 815a; ii, 149a, 423b; iv, 775b; vi, 75a; vii, 182b, 428b, 429b – I, **13a**, 407b, 838b; II, 153b, 434b; IV, 807a; VI, 73a; VII, 182b, 429b, 430b
ʿAbbās Ḥilmī II, Khedive (1944) i, **13a**, 817b; iii, 515a; vii, 438a, 715a; s, 39b, 123a, 300a – I, **13b**, 840b; III, 532b; VII, 439a, 716a; S, 39b, 122a, 300a
ʿAbbās Huwayda (amīr) (XX) vii, 450a – VII, 451a, b
ʿAbbās al-Ḳaṣṣāb, Shaykh (XX) vi, 614a – VI, 599a
ʿAbbās al-Ḳaṭṭān (XX) vi, 165b, 175b – VI, 158a
ʿAbbās Khān (Trākāne) (1822) s, 327b – S, 327a
ʿAbbās Ḳulī Khān Ādamiyyat (XX) s, 291a – S, 290b
ʿAbbās Ḳulī Khān Lārīdjānī Sartīp (XIX) v, 664a – V, 669a
al-ʿAbbās al-Maghrāwī (XIII) vi, 404a – VI, 388b
ʿAbbās Mīrzā (Ḳādjār) (1833) i, **13b**, 15a, 626a; ii, 839a, 952a; iii, 1103b, 1109a; iv, 163b, 391b, 392a, b, 462a, 861b, 1047b; v, 919a; vi, 484a, 502b, 551b, 715a – I, **14a**, 15a, 646b; II, 858b, 974a; III, 1130b, 1136b; IV, 170b, 408b, 409a, 482b, 895a, 1078b; V, 924b; VI, 470a, 488a, 536a, 704a
ʿAbbās Mīrzā III (Ḳādjār) (1735) vi, 56a – VI, 53b
ʿAbbās Mīrzā Mulk-ārā (Ḳadjār) (XIX) iv, 393b – IV, 410a
ʿAbbās Sarwānī (XVI) s, **1b** – S, **1b**
ʿAbbās al-Shihābī, amīr (XIX) ii, 444a, 636a – II, 455b, 652a
ʿAbbāsa (town/ville) i, **14b** – I, **14b**
ʿAbbāsa bint Aḥmad b. Ṭūlūn (IX) i, 14b – I, 14b
ʿAbbāsa bint al-Mahdī (VIII) i, **14a**; s, 263a – I, **14a**; S, 262b
ʿAbbāsābād i, **14b** – I, **15a**
ʿAbbāsī → Sikka
al-ʿAbbāsī, ʿAbd al-Laṭīf (XVII) ix, 4b – IX, 5a
al-ʿAbbāsī, Muḥammad al-Mahdī (XIX) s, 411b – S, 411b
ʿAbbāsid(e)s i, **15a**, 33a, 34a, 43a, 59a, 102a, 103b, 124b, 125a, 141a, 149a, 381a, 386b, 402b, 530a, 550b, 1352a; ii, 74b, 168b, 281a, 551b, 951a; iii, 265a, 984b; iv, 15b-17b, 44b-45b, 939a; v, 326a, 347b, 620b, 736a, 1233a; vi, 1b, 2a, 11a, 118b, 194a, 261a, 352a, 434a, 518a, b, 519a, b, 549b, 665a, 668b, 669b, 670a, 674b, 676a, 849b, 880b; vii, 43b, 160a, 191b; ix, 265a, b, 593b; s, 31b – I, **15a**, 34a, b, 44a, 61a, 105a, 106b, 128a, b, 145a, 153b, 392a, 397b, 414a, 546a, 568a, 1391a; II, 76a, 173b, 289b, 565a, 973a; III, 272b, 1009a; IV, 17a-19a, 47b-48b, 972a; V, 325b, 348b, 624b, 741b, 1223b; VI, 1b, 2a, 11a, 116b, 178a, 245b, 503a, b, 504a, 534a, 651a, 655a, 656a, 661a, 662b, 841a, 871b; VII, 43b, 161b, 192a; IX, 273a, b, 616a; S, 31b
—administration ii, 78a, 143a, 144a, 304b, 305a, 324a, 890b; iv, 755a, b, 939a-943a, 973b – II, 79b, 146b, 148a, 313a, b, 333b, 911a; IV, 785b, 786a, 972a-976a, 1006a
—art, architecture i, 561a, 616a; ii, 745b, 1054b; v, 216b – I, 578a, 636b; II, 764a, 1079a; V, 214a
—history/histoire i, 118a; iii, 899b, 925b; v, 488a – I, 121b; III, 923b, 950a; V, 491a
al-ʿAbbāsiyya → Ṭubna
ʿAbbāsiyya (Cairo/Caire) s, 208b – S, 208a
al-ʿAbbāsiyya (Ifrīḳiya) i, **24a**, 248a, 815b; iv, 829a; s, 144a – I, **24b**, 255b, 838b; IV, 862a; S, 144a
ʿAbbāsiyya (military academy/académie militaire) s, 5b – S, 4b
Abbotābād iii, 336a – III, 346b
Abbreviations s, **2a**
ʿAbbūd, Ibrāhīm (Sūdāb) (XX) v, 1064b; ix, 749a – V, 1062a; IX, 781b
ʿAbd/ʿabīd i, **24b**, 47a, 371a, 490b, 1060a; ii, 133b, 858b, 1079b, 1081a; iii, 3a, 277a, 345b; iv, 82b, 83a, 282b, 567a, 738a, 1116a; v, 58a, 358b, 359a, 856b, 942a, 1248b; viii, 879b – I, **25a**,48b, 381b, 505b, 1091b; II, 137a, 878b, 1104b, 1106a; III, 3b, 285a, 356a; IV, 86b, 87a, 295a, 589b, 767b, 1193b; V, 59b, 359b, 360a, 863b, 946a, 1239a; VIII, 909b
ʿAbd b. Ḥumayd (863) vii, 691b – VII, 691b
ʿAbd al-Aḥad Abū Aḥmad Sirhindī (1578) s, 313a – S, 312b
ʿAbd al-Aḥad Khān Mangit al-Bukhārī, Amīr (1910) i, 1296a; vi, 419a, 765a – I, 1335b; VI, 404a, 754a
ʿAbd al-ʿĀl (1332) i, 280b; x, 189a – I, 289a; X, 204b
ʿAbd al-ʿAlī al-Lakhnawī → Baḥr al-ʿUlūm, ʿAbd al-ʿAlī al-Lakhnawī
ʿAbd al-ʿĀlī Nizām al-Dīn b. Muḥammad Bīr Djandī (1527) x,146a – X, 157b
ʿAbd Allāh, A.H. (1973) v, 190a – V, 187b
ʿAbd Allāh, (king/le roi) → ʿAbd Allāh b. al-Ḥusayn
ʿAbd Allāh, Mawlāy → ʿAbd Allāh b. Ismāʿīl
ʿAbd Allāh, Sharīf (1877) vi, 151a – VI, 148b
ʿAbd Allāh I (Aghlabid(e)) (817) i, 248a, 250a; iii, 982a; ix, 584a – I, 256a, 258a; III, 1006b; IX, 666b
ʿAbd Allāh II (Aghlabid(e)) (903) i, 250b, 986b; iii, 982b – I, 258b, 1017a; III, 1007a
ʿAbd Allāh II (ʿAbd al-Wādid) → ʿAbd al-Wādid(e)s
ʿAbd Allāh III (Āl Ṣabāḥ) (1965) viii, 669a – VIII, 688b
ʿAbd Allāh III b. ʿAdjīb III (Ḳerrī) (1747) iv, 893a – IV, 925b

ʿAbd Allāh (Umayyad(e)) → ʿAbd Allāh b. Muḥammad b. ʿAbd al-Raḥmān
ʿAbd Allāh b. al-ʿAbbās (686) i, **40a**, 55b, 107a, 567b; ii, 219b, 359b, 416a, 480b, 888b, 1071a; iii, 235b, 241a, 242a, 370b, 608b, 649a, 1081b; iv, 767b; v, 406b; vi, 218a, 636a, 657b, 661a, 666b, 668b, 669b, 738a; vii, 75a, 100a, 262a, 293a, 758a; ix, 422a; s, 311a, b, 358a – I, **41a**, 57b, 110a, 585b; II, 226b, 369b, 427a, 492b, 909b, 1095b; III, 242b, 248a, 249a, 382a, 629a, 670a, 1108b; IV, 798a; V, 408a; VI, 202a, 621a, 643a, 647a, 652b, 654b, 656a, 727a; VII, 76a, 102a, 263b, 295a, 759b; IX, 436a; S, 311a, 358a
ʿAbd Allāh b. ʿAbbō (XVI) i, 1343a – I, 1383b
ʿAbd Allāh b. ʿAbd al-ʿAzīz b. ʿAbd al-Ḥaḳḳ (1159) v, 60b, 61a – V, 62b
ʿAbd Allāh b. ʿAbd al-ʿAzīz b. Musāʿad (XX) i, 1313a – I, 1353a
ʿAbd Allāh b. ʿAbd al-D̲j̲alīl vi, 264b – VI, 249a
ʿAbd Allāh b. ʿAbd al-Ḥakam → Ibn ʿAbd al-Ḥakam, ʿAbd Allāh
ʿAbd Allāh b. ʿAbd al-Ḳādir (1854) i, **41b** – I, **42b**
ʿAbd Allāh b. ʿAbd al-Karīm (Marʿas̲h̲ī) (1467) vi, 513b – VI, 499a
ʿAbd Allāh b. ʿAbd al-Malik (Umayyad(e)) (703) i, **42a**; v, 500a; vi, 774b; vii, 408b – I, **43b**; V, 503a; VI, 764a; VII, 410a
ʿAbd Allāh b. ʿAbd al-Muʾmin (XII) i, 160b; iii, 138b; s, 113b – I, 165a; III, 141b; S, 113a
ʿAbd Allāh b. ʿAbd al-Muṭṭalib (570) i, **42b**, 80a, 438b – I, **43b**, 82b, 450b
ʿAbd Allāh b. ʿAbd al-Raḥmān I (IX) iii, 74a, 495a; iv, 254b, 672b – III, 76b, 512a; IV, 265b, 700a
ʿAbd Allāh b. ʿAbd al-Raḥmān b. Abī Bakr (1513) ii, 730a – II, 748b
ʿAbd Allāh b. ʿAbd al-Ẓāhir → Ibn ʿAbd al-Ẓāhir
ʿAbd Allāh b. Abī ʿAmr b. Ḥafs b. al-Mug̲h̲īra (680) vi, 140a – VI, 138a
ʿAbd Allāh b. Abī Bakr (VII) i, 109b, 110a, 738a – I, 112b, 113a, 760a
ʿAbd Allāh b. Abī Bakr al-Miyānad̲j̲ī (1131) i, 840a, 841a; x, 322b; s, **2b**, **104b** – I, 863a, 864b; X, 347a; S, **2a**, **104a**
ʿAbd Allāh b. Abi ʾl-D̲j̲awād (IX) i, 249b – I, 257b
ʿAbd Allāh b. Abī Isḥāḳ (735) i, **42b**; iii, 1262a – I, **44a**, III, 1295a
ʿAbd Allāh b. Abī Rabīʿa b. al-Mug̲h̲īra Mak̲h̲zūmī (631) vi, 138b, 140b; vii, 862b – VI, 137a, 139a; VII, 864a
ʿAbd Allāh b. Abī Sarḥ → ʿAbd Allāh b. Saʿd
ʿAbd Allāh b. Abī Yūsuf, Amīr (Marīnid(e)) (1262) vi, 593a – VI, 577b
ʿAbd Allāh b. ʿAdī (976) vii, 576b; viii, 516b – VII, 577a; VIII, 534b
ʿAbd Allāh b. Aḥmad b. Ḥanbal i, 273b; iii, 158b; s, 16a – I, 281b; III, 162a; S, 16a
ʿAbd Allāh b. Aḥmad b. K̲h̲alīfa (1849) ii, 108b; iv, 953a – II, 111a; IV, 985b
ʿAbd Allāh b. ʿAlawī al-Haddād (1720) i, 829b – I, 852b
ʿAbd Allāh b. ʿAlī (ʿAbbāsid(e)) (764) i, 16a, 17a, **43a**, 103a, 108b, 773a; ii, 281a; iii, 292b, 398a, 991a; vi, 333b, 427b, 921b; vii, 910b – I, 16b, 17b, **44a**, 106a, 111b, 796a; II, 289b; III, 301b, 410b, 1015b; VI, 318a, 413a, 913a; VII, 911a
ʿAbd Allāh b. ʿAlī al-ʿAbs̲h̲amī (VII) s, 26a – S, 26b
ʿAbdallāh bin Alī bin Nassir, Sayyid (1820) iv, 886b, 887a; vi, 612b – IV, 919a, b; VI, 597b
ʿAbd Allāh b. ʿAlī al-ʿUyūnī (XI) iv, 664a – IV, 690b
ʿAbd Allāh b. ʿAlī b. Zannūn (1229) vi, 222b – VI, 216a
ʿAbd Allāh b. al-Amīn (IX) s, 116b – S, 116a
ʿAbd Allāh b. ʿĀmir (680) i, **43b**, 47b, 107a, 304a, 441a, 695b, 1130a; ii, 811b; iii, 304a; iv, 14b, 220a; v, 56b; vi, 620a; viii, 62b; ix, 34a – I, **44b**, 49a, 110a, 313b, 453b, 716b, 1164a; II, 831a; III, 313a; IV, 15b, 16a, 229b; V, 58a, b; VI, 605a; VIII, 64a; IX, 34b
ʿAbd Allāh b. ʿAmr b. al-ʿĀṣ viii,41a – VIII, 41b
ʿAbd Allāh b. ʿAmr al-Kindī (VIII) i, 48b; iv, 837b, 838a – I, 50a; IV, 870b, 871a
ʿAbd Allāh b. Asad → al-Yāfiʿī
ʿAbd Allāh b. ʿAṣim (1013) vii,82b – VII, 83b
ʿAbd Allāh b. ʿAṭāʾ al-Makkī (VIII) vii, 398a – VII, 399b
ʿAbd Allāh b. ʿAwn (767) ix, 771a – IX, 804b
ʿAbd Allāh b. ʿAwn b. Arṭabān (639) vi, 920a – VI, 911b
ʿAbd Allāh b. Abī Bakr al-Miyāmid̲j̲ī (ʿAyn al-ḳuḍāt al-Hamad̲h̲ānī) ix, 862b – IX, 898b
ʿAbd Allāh b. Barrī → Ibn Barrī, Abū Muḥammad
ʿAbd Allāh b. Bū G̲h̲āba (XIX) vi, 251a – VI, 235a
ʿAbd Allāh b. Budayl (VII) iv, 99b; v, 354b – IV, 104a; V, 356a
ʿAbd Allāh b. Bulayhid (XX) v, 998b; vi, 156b – V, 994a; VI, 152b
ʿAbd Allāh b. Buluggīn (Zīrid(e)) (1082) i, **43b**, 251a, 600a; ii, 1013a, 1016b; vi, 222b; vii, 553a – I, **45a**, 258b, 620a; II, 1036b, 1040a; VI, 216a; VII, 553b
ʿAbd Allāh b. Burayda (733) vii, 576a – VII,576b
ʿAbd Allāh b. Dīnār vi, 263a – VI, 247b
ʿAbd Allāh b. D̲j̲abala b. Ḥayyān al-Kinānī (834) iii, 1151a – III, 1179a
ʿAbd Allāh b. D̲j̲aʿfar b. Abī Ṭālib (699) i, **44a**; ii, 372b; iii, 608b, 819b, 889b; vi, 344b; s, 92b – I, **45b**; II, 382b; III, 629b, 843b, 913b; VI, 328b; S, 92b
ʿAbd Allāh b. D̲j̲aʿfar al-Ṣādiḳ (VIII) vii, 645b – VII, 645a
ʿAbd Allāh b. D̲j̲ahm (IX) viii, 89b – VIII, 92a
ʿAbd Allāh b. D̲j̲aḥs̲h̲ (VII) i, **44b**; v, 316a – I, **45b**; V, 315b
ʿAbd Allāh b. D̲j̲alwī Āl Saʿūd (XX) i, 1313a – I, 1353a
ʿAbd Allāh b. D̲j̲arīr al-Bad̲j̲alī (VII) iv, 1106b – IV, 1138a
ʿAbd Allāh b. D̲j̲udʿān (VI) i, **44b**, 115b; iii, 389b, 739a; iv, 821a; s, 247a, 380b – I, **45b**, 118b; III, 401b, 762a; IV, 854a; S, 247a, 380b
ʿAbd Allāh b. Fayṣal b. ʿAbd al-ʿAzīz (Āl Suʿūd) (XX) vi, 156a; s, 305b – VI, 152b; S, 305b
ʿAbd Allāh b. Fayṣal b. Turkī (Āl Suʿūd) (1887) ii, 176b; ix, 904a – II, 182a; IX, 942a
ʿAbd Allāh b. Fūdī (1828) v, 222b; vii, 435b – V, 220a; VII, 436b
ʿAbd Allāh b. G̲h̲aṭafān, Banū s, 225b – S, 225b
ʿAbd Allāh b. al-Ḥaḍramī → Ibn al-Ḥaḍramī
ʿAbd Allāh b. Ḥamdān (Ḥamdānid(e)) (902) ii, 453a; iii, 126b; v, 451b; vi, 900a – II, 464b; III, 129a; V, 454a; VI, 891b
ʿAbd Allāh b. Hammām b. al-Salūlī (715) i, **45a** – I, **46a**
ʿAbd Allāh b. Ḥamza → al-Manṣūr bi-ʾllāh
ʿAbd Allāh b. Ḥanẓala (683) i, **45a**, 50a, 55a; iii, 226b, 227a; v, 997a – I, **46b**, 51b, 57a; III, 233b, 234a; V, 992a
ʿAbd Allāh b. Ḥarb → ʿAbd Allāh b. ʿAmr al-Kindī
ʿAbd Allāh b. al-Ḥārit̲h̲ (VIII) s, 233a – S, 232b
ʿAbd Allāh b. al-Ḥārit̲h̲ b. Nawfal al-Hās̲h̲imī (Babba) (VIII) vii, 877b, 1045b – VII, 879a, 1047b
ʿAbd Allāh b. al-Ḥasan b. al-Ḥasan (ʿAlid(e)) (762) i, **45b**; iii, 615b, 786b, 984a; vi, 334b; vii, 348a – I, **46b**; III, 636b, 809b, 1008b; VI, 319a; VII, 349b
ʿAbd Allāh b. Ḥasan b. Ḥusayn b. ʿAlī b. Ḥusayn b.

Muḥammad b. ʿAbd al-Wahhāb (XX) vi, 156b – VI, 152b
ʿAbd Allāh b. Ḥasan Āl al-Shaykh (XX) vi, 157a – VI, 152b
ʿAbd Allāh b. Ḥātim (Ḥamdānid(e)) (1110) iii, 125b – III, 128a
ʿAbd Allāh b. Ḥaydara (XIX) i, 345a – I, 355b
ʿAbd Allāh b. Hilāl al-Ḥimyarī al-Kūfī (VIII) i, **45b** – I, **47a**
ʿAbd Allāh b. Ḥumayd b. Ḳaḥtaba (811) v, 855b; vi, 333b; x, 348b – V, 862b; VI, 318a; X, 374b
ʿAbd Allāh b. Ḥumayyid al-Sālimī (XX) i, 736a; s, 356a – I, 758a; S, 356a
ʿAbd Allāh b. Hurmuz (Baṣra) (780) vi, 878b – VI, 869b
ʿAbd Allāh b. Ḥusayn (Marāgha) (893) vi, 499a – VI, 484b
ʿAbd Allāh b. al-Ḥusayn, Amīr/King le roi (Hāshimite) (1951) i, **46a**, 447b; ii, 662b; iii, 264b, 605a, 606b, 1065b, 1066a; iv, 262a; v, 337b, 1053b, 1054b; vi, 31b, 262a; viii, 246a; x, 885b; s, 70a, 301a – I, **47a**, 460b; II, 679a; III, 272a, 626b, 627a, 1092b, 1093a; IV, 273b; V, 338a, 1050b, 1051b; VI, 30a, 246b; VIII, 252a; X, ;S, 70b, 301a
ʿAbd Allāh b. al-Ḥusayn b. ʿAbd Allāh (Amīr) b. al-Ḥusayn (Hashimite) (XXI) x, 886b – X,
ʿAbd Allāh b. al-Ḥusayn Rawāḥī (1166) viii, 459b – VIII, 475a
ʿAbd Allāh b. ʿIbāḍ (VII) i, 810a; iii, 648a, 651b; vii, 858b; s, 337b – I, 833a; III, 669b, 672b; VII, 860a; S, 337b
ʿAbd Allāh b. Ibrāhīm al-Aghlab → ʿAbd Allāh I/II (Aghlabid(e))
ʿAbd Allāh b. Ibrāhim b. Shāhrukh (Tīmūrid(e)) (1451) i, 91a, 135a, 147b, 227b; iii, 989b; s, 51a – I, 93b, 139a, 152a, 234b; III, 1014a; S, 51b
ʿAbd Allāh b. Ibrāhīm al-Mismaʿī → al-Mismaʿī
ʿAbd Allāh b. Ibrāhīm al-Nadjdī (XVII) iii, 677b – III, 699b
ʿAbd Allāh b. Idrīs II (Idrīsid(e)) (828) vi, 742b – VI, 731b
ʿAbd Allāh b. Idrīs al-Djaʿfarī (XI) i, 784a – I, 807a
ʿAbd Allāh b. Iskandar (Shaybānid(e)) (1598) i, **46b**, 1295b; ii, 45a, 446a; vi, 621a; ix, 429a; s, 340a, b – I, **47b**, 1335a; II, 45b, 457b; VI, 606a; IX, 445b; S, 339b, 340a
ʿAbd Allāh b. Ismāʿīl, Mawlāy (ʿAlawīd(e)) (1757) i, **47a**, 356a; ii, 510b, 820a; v, 1192a; vi, 595a; vii, 39a, 387a – I, **48b**, 367a; II, 523a, 839b; V, 1182a; VI, 580a; VII, 39a, 388a
ʿAbd Allāh b. ʿItbān (VII) iv, 99b – IV, 103b
ʿAbd Allāh b. Ḳaḥṭān (Yaʿfurid(e)) (X) ii, 854a; iv, 199b – II, 874a; IV, 208a
ʿAbd Allāh b. Ḳāsim al-Fihrī (al-Bunt) (XI) i, 1309b; iii, 496a – I, 1350a; III, 513a
ʿAbd Allāh b. Ḳāsim al-Ẓāhirī (885) i, 600a – I, 619b
ʿAbd Allāh b. Ḳawām al-Dīn (Marʿashī) (1360) vi, 511b – VI, 497a
ʿAbd Allāh b. Kerrīw al-Laghwāṭī (1921) vi, 251a – VI, 235a
ʿAbd Allāh b. Khālid b. Asīd (VII) s, 26a – S, 26a
ʿAbd Allāh b. Khaṭal (VII) iv, 821a – IV, 854a
ʿAbd Allāh b. Khāzim al-Sulamī (692) i, 3b, **47b**, 86a, 1293a; viii, 62b – I, 4a, **49a**, 88b, 1332b; VIII, 64a
ʿAbd Allāh b. Khurdhādhbah (IX) iv, 645b – IV, 672a
ʿAbd Allāh b. Kulayb b. Thaʿlaba (835) vi, 568a – VI, 553a
ʿAbd Allāh b. Lahīʿa (790) s, 87b – S, 87b
ʿAbd Allāh b. Maḥfūf al-Munadjdjim (1265) iv, 1130a – IV, 1161b
ʿAbd Allāh b. Maḥmūd al-Shāshī i, 147a – I, 151b
ʿAbd Allāh b. Mālik (XI) iv, 1127a – IV, 1158b
ʿAbd Allāh b. al-Maʾmūn (ʿAbbāsid(e)) (808) vi, 331b, 332b – VI, 316a, 317a
ʿAbd Allāh (ʿUbayd Allāh) b. Marwān II (Umayyad(e)) (746) i, 16a; ii, 90b, 234b; vi, 624a, 641b – I, 16b; II, 92a, 241a; VI, 609a, 627a
ʿAbd Allāh b. Masʿūd → Ibn Masʿūd, ʿAbd Allāh
ʿAbd Allāh b. Maṭar (Abū Rayḥāna) (VII) vii, 564b – VII, 564a
ʿAbd Allāh b. Maymūn (VIII) i, **48a**; ii, 170a, 301a, 850b, 851b; iii, 1072a – I, **49b**; II, 175a, 309a, 870b, 871b; III, 1099a
ʿAbd Allāh b. Mazdalī (XII) ii, 1013a – II, 1037a
ʿAbd Allāh b. Muʿāwiya (746) i, **48b**, 53b; ii, 441a; iii, 1266a; iv, 44b, 99b, 837a, 838a; v, 63b; vi, 427b, 624b; vii, 359b, 1016a; s, 233a – I, **50a**, 55a; II, 452b; III, 1298b; IV, 47a, 104a, 870a, 871a; V, 65b; VI, 412b, 609b; VII, 362a, 1018a; S, 232b
ʿAbd Allāh b. al-Mubārak → Ibn al-Mubārak, ʿAbd Allāh
ʿAbd Allāh b. al-Mughīra b. Saʿīd al-Badjalī vii, 348a – VII, 350a
ʿAbd Allāh b. Muḥammad, Sharīf → Makka
ʿAbd Allāh b. Muḥammad (Mīkālī) (915) vii, 26a – VII, 26a
ʿAbd Allāh b. Muḥammad b. ʿAbd Allāh (VIII) vii, 389a – VII, 390b
ʿAbd Allāh b. Muḥammad b. ʿAbd al-Laṭīf, Shaykh (XX) iii, 1065a – III, 1091b
ʿAbd Allāh b. Muḥammad b. Lubb (X) s, 80a – S, 80a
ʿAbd Allāh b. Muḥammad b. ʿAbd al-Raḥmān al-Marwānī (Umayyad(e), al-Andalus) (912) i, **49a**, 83b, 85b, 634a; iv, 665b; vi, 222a, 520b, 568a, 852a; vii, 569a; s, 153a – I, **50b**, 86a, 88a, 654b; IV, 692b; VI, 215b, 505b, 553a, 843b; VII, 570a; S, 153a
ʿAbd Allāh b. Muḥammad b. ʿAbd al-Salām → Abdullahi Sikka
ʿAbd Allāh b. Muḥammad b. ʿAbd al-Wahhāb (XIX) iii, 678b – III, 700b
ʿAbd Allāh b. Muḥammad b. Maslama → Ibn al-Afṭas
ʿAbd Allāh b. Muḥammad b. Saʿd (1146) i, 1083a – I, 1115b
ʿAbd Allāh b. Muḥammad Āl Muʿammar (ṣāḥib al-basīṭ) (1726) ii, 321a – II, 330b
ʿAbd Allāh b. Muḥammad Fūdī (XIX) ii, 942a, 1145a; iii, 276b – II, 963b, 1172a; III, 284b
ʿAbd Allāh b. Muḥammad Ghāzī (XX) vi, 175b
ʿAbd Allāh b. Muḥammad al-Kātib (X) i, 1309a; iv, 830a – I, 1349b; IV, 863a
ʿAbd Allāh b. Muḥammad Ḳuṭb Shāhī (1672) vii, 93b; s, 302a – VII, 95a; S, 301b
ʿAbd Allāh b. Muḥammad al-Māzandarānī (1363) ii, 81a; iv, 1035a – II, 82b; IV, 1066b
ʿAbd Allāh b. Muḥammad al-Nāshiʾ al-Akbar (906) viii, 378a – VIII, 390b
ʿAbd Allāh b. Muḥammad al-Taʿāʾishī (Abdullāhi) (Khalīfa) (1899) i, **49b**, 765a, 962a; ii, 124a; iv, 687a, 952b, 953a; v, 268a, 1249a-1251b; viii, 170b – I, **50b**, 788a, 991b; II, 127a; IV, 715b, 985a, b; V, 265b, 1239b – 1242b; VIII, 173a
ʿAbd Allāh b. al-Muʿizz (Zīride(e)) (XI) vii, 483b – VII, 483a
ʿAbd Allāh b. al-Muḳaffaʿ → Ibn al-Muḳaffaʿ, ʿAbd Allāh
ʿAbd Allāh b. Mūsā b. Nuṣayr (720) i, **50a**; vi, 221b, 926b – I, **51b**; VI, 215b, 918b
ʿAbd Allāh b. Muslim (VIII) i, 1033b – I, 1065a
ʿAbd Allāh b. al-Muʿtazz → Ibn al-Muʿtazz

ʿAbd Allāh b. Muṭīʿ (692) i, 45a, **50a**; iii, 226b, 227b; vii, 522a – I, 46b, **51b**; III, 233b, 234a; VII, 522b
ʿAbd Allāh b. Nāfiʿ al-Azraḳ (VIII) vii, 398b – VII, 400a
ʿAbd Allāh b. Nawf i, 850b – I, 874a
ʿAbd Allāh b. Nawfal, ḳāḍī (662) vi, 671a – VI, 657a
ʿAbd Allāh b. Rabīʿ (VIII) iii, 650b – III, 672a
ʿAbd Allāh b. Rabīʿa b. Riyāḥ al-Hilālī (VII) s, 92b – S, 92b
ʿAbd Allāh b. al-Rand ii, 463b; iv, 415b; v, 1181b – II, 475a; IV, 433b; V, 1171b
ʿAbd Allāh b. Ra<u>sh</u>īd → Ra<u>sh</u>īd, Āl
ʿAbd Allāh b. Rawāḥa (629) i, **50b**, 968b; ii, 372a; iii, 354a; iv, 835b, 1187b; v, 398b; vi, 604a; vii, 756b; viii, 118b, 459b – I, **52a**, 998b; II, 382b; III, 365a; IV, 868b, 1220a; V, 400a; VI, 588b; VII, 757b; VIII, 121a, 475a
ʿAbd Allāh b. Sabaʾ (VIII) i, **51a**, 382b; ii, 1094a; iii, 1164a; vii, 399a; viii, 387a; ix, 420b – I, **52b**, 393b; II, 1119b; III, 1192b; VII, 400a; VIII, 406a; IX, 434b
ʿAbd Allāh b. Saʿd b. Abī Sarḥ (656) i, **51b**, 115a, 451b, 966a, 1029a, 1157b; ii, 131a, 327b, 525b, 615a; iv, 825b; v, 90b; vii, 154a, 156b, 393a, 394b; viii, 38a, 84b, 862b – I, **53a**, 118a, 464b, 996a, 1060b, 1192a; II, 134b, 337a, 538b, 630b; IV, 858b; V, 93a; VII, 156a, 158a, 394a, 395b; VIII, 38b, 91b, 892b
ʿAbd Allāh b. Salām (663) i, **52a**, 1020b; ii, 363a; iii, 1232b; iv, 212a, 824b; vi, 636b – I, **53b**, 1052a; II, 373a; III, 1264b; IV, 221b, 857b; VI, 621a, b
ʿAbd Allāh b. Ṣāliḥ (XII) ix, 9b; s, 397a – IX, 9b; S, 397a
ʿAbd Allāh b. Salīm (VIII) vii, 807a – VII, 809a
ʿAbd Allāh b. Sālim (Āl Ṣabaḥ) (XX) v, 575a – V, 579b
ʿAbd Allāh b. Sayf al-Dawla (Ḥamdānid(e)) (949) vi, 930a – VI, 922a
ʿAbd Allāh b. <u>Sh</u>ay<u>kh</u> ʿAydarūs (1662) i, 781b – I, 804b
ʿAbd Allāh b. al-<u>Sh</u>ay<u>kh</u> (Marrāku<u>sh</u>) (1607) vi, 594b – VI, 579b
ʿAbd Allāh b. al-Simma ix, 777a – IX, 810b
ʿAbd Allāh b. Sinān (IX) iv, 117a – IV, 122a
ʿAbd Allāh b. Sulṭān Maḥmūd (Marʿa<u>sh</u>ī) (1530) vi, 514b, 515a – VI, 500a
ʿAbd Allāh b. Suʿūd (Āl Suʿūd) (1818) ii, 321a; iii, 362b, 999a; ix, 903b – II, 330b; III, 374a, 1024a; IX, 941b
ʿAbd Allāh b. Ṭāhir I b. al-Ḥusayn (Ṭāhirid(e)) (844) i, **52b**, 99b, 121b, 154a, 157b, 241a, 619a, 685a, 789b; ii, 524a; iii, 1083a; iv, 17a, 20b, 531a, 646a, b; v, 57b, 872b, 923a; vi, 336b, 337a, b, 707b, 775a; vii, 18b, 160b, 1016b; viii, 62b; x, 104b, 227b; s, 15a – I, **54a**, 102a, 125a, 158a, 162a, 248b, 637b, 706a, 812b; II, 537a; III, 1109b; IV, 18b, 22a, 554a, 672b, 673a; V, 59b, 878b, 928b; VI, 320b, 321b, 322a, 696a, 764b; VII, 18b, 162a, 1018b; VIII, 64a; X, 112b, 245b; S, 15a
ʿAbd Allāh b. Ṭarīf (VIII) iii, 659b – III, 680b
ʿAbd Allāh b. <u>Th</u>awr → Abū Fudayk, ʿAbd Allāh b. <u>Th</u>awr
ʿAbd Allāh b. <u>Th</u>unayyan (1943) ix, 904a – IX, 941b
ʿAbd Allāh b. Ubayy b. Salūl al-<u>Kh</u>azradjī (631) i, **53a**, 307b, 514b, 1283a; iv, 824b, 1187b; v, 996b; vii, 356b, 367a, 373b, 561b, 852b; s, 133b – I, **54b**, 317b, 530a, 1322b; IV, 857b, 1220a; V, 991b; VII, 359a, 369b, 374b, 562a, 854a; S, 133a
ʿAbd Allāh b. ʿUfayṣān (XIX) iv, 751a – IV, 781b
ʿAbd Allāh b. ʿUmar I b. al-<u>Kh</u>aṭṭāb (693) i, 40a, 50b, **53b**, 382b; iii, 65a; vi, 263a, 278b, 658a; vii, 522a, 783b; x, 33a – I, 41b, 51b, **55b**, 393b; III, 67b; VI, 247b, 263a, 643b; VII, 522a, 785b; X, 34b
ʿAbd Allāh b. ʿUmar II b. ʿAbd al-ʿAzīz (749) i, 49a, **53b**, 257b; ii, 90a, 744b; v, 731a; vi, 624a – I, 50a, **55a**, 265b; II, 92a, 763a; V, 736a; VI, 609a
ʿAbd Allāh b. ʿUmar al-ʿAr<u>dj</u>ī → al-ʿAr<u>dj</u>ī
ʿAbd Allāh b. ʿUmāra (921) s, 223a – S, 223a
ʿAbd Allāh b. Unays al-Anṣārī (VII) vi, 658b – VI, 644a
ʿAbd Allāh b. Unays al-<u>Dj</u>uhanī (VII) iii, 540b; v, 315b – III, 559b; V, 315a
ʿAbd Allāh b. ʿU<u>th</u>mān Faḍlī (XX) ii, 737a – II, 755b
ʿAbd Allāh b. Wahb al-Ḳura<u>sh</u>ī → Ibn Wahb ʿAbd Allāh al-Ḳura<u>sh</u>ī
ʿAbd Allāh b. Wahb al-Rāsibī (658) i, **54b**; iii, 235a; iv, 1074b, 1075a; vi, 280b; vii, 912b – I, **56a**; III, 242a; IV, 1106b; VI, 265a; VII, 913a
ʿAbd Allāh b. Yaḥyā al-Kindī → Ṭālib al-Haḳḳ
ʿAbd Allāh b. Yāsīn al-Gazūlī (Almoravid(e)) (1057) i, 762a, 864a, 1044b, 1176a; ii, 527a, 1121b; v, 653b, 654a, b; vi, 742b, 744a; vii, 584b, 613a; s, 27a – I, 785a, 888a, 1076a, 1211a; II, 540a, 1148a; V, 657b, 658b; VI, 731b, 733a; VII, 584b, 613a; S, 27a
ʿAbd Allāh b. Yazīd (Ibāḍī) (VIII) viii, 387b; s, 225b – VIII, 401a; S, 225b
ʿAbd Allāh b. Zaynab (Medina) (796) vi, 263b – VI, 248a
ʿAbd Allāh b. al-Ziʿbarā (mu<u>kh</u>aḍram) s, 91a – S, 90b
ʿAbd Allāh b. al-Zubayr (692) i, 41a, 45a, 50b, **54b**, 76b, 77a, 107a, 113b, 115a, 148b, 443b, 453b, 482a, 550a, 704a, 713b, 784b, 810a; ii, 89b, 197a, 360a, 415a; iii, 40a, 226b, 270b, 607b, 608b, 620b, 970a, 1254b; iv, 319a, 493a, 938a, 1075b; v, 997a, 1231a, 1232a; vii, 97b, 267b, 268a, b, 357a, 358b, 400b, 403a, 521a, b, 546a, 649b, 694a, 858b; viii, 119a; s, 26a, 230b, 311a, b, 357b; vi, 139a, 140a, b, 147a, 149a, 344a, 544b, 545a, 622a, 606b, 669a, 708b; x, 843a – I, 42a, 46a, 52a, **56b**, 78b, 79a, 110a, 116b, 118a, 153a, 456a, 466b, 496a, 567b, 725b, 735b, 807b, 833a; II, 91a, 203b, 370a, 425b; III, 41b, 233b, 278b, 628b, 629b, 641a, 994b, 1287b; IV, 333a, b, 514a, 971a, 1107a; V, 992a, 1221b, 1222b; S, 26b, 230b, 311a, b, 357b; VI, 137b, 138a, 139a, 145b, 147b, 328b, 529b, 607a, 646a, 655b, 697a; VII, 99b, 269b, 270a, b, 359b, 361a, 402a, 404a, 521b, 522a, 546a, 649b, 694a, 860a; VIII, 121b; X,
ʿAbd Allāh al-ʿAbdalkānī vii, 26a – VII, 26a
ʿAbd Allāh Abū <u>Dj</u>ābir b. ʿAbd Allāh (625) s, 230a – S, 230a
ʿAbd Allāh Abu 'l-<u>Dj</u>imāl, Sīdī v, 51a – V, 52b
ʿAbd Allāh Abū Yaʿḳūb b. Dāwūd (VIII) viii, 351a – VIII, 363b
ʿAbd Allāh Āl <u>Kh</u>alīfa → ʿAbd Allāh b. Aḥmad b. <u>Kh</u>alīfa
ʿAbd Allāh Āl Sulaymān Āl Ḥamdān (XX) vi, 156a – VI, 152b
ʿAbd Allāh Āl <u>Th</u>ānī (Ḳatar) (XX) ii, 177b – II, 183a
ʿAbd Allāh al-A<u>sh</u>ʿarī (720) vi, 493a – VI, 479a
ʿAbd Allāh al-A<u>sh</u>tar (VIII) vii, 389a – VII, 390a
ʿAbd Allāh Awwal al-Islām, Sulṭān (Makassar) (1605) vi, 116b – VI, 114a
ʿAbd Allāh al-Azraḳ b. al-Mu<u>gh</u>īra (VIII) vi, 140a – VI, 138a
ʿAbd Allāh al-Balʿamī → Balʿamī
ʿAbd Allāh al-Balansī → ʿAbd Allāh b. ʿAbd al-Raḥmān I
ʿAbd Allāh al-Bayyāsī (1226) i, 1150b; ii, 516a – I, 1184b; II, 528b
ʿAbd Allāh Bey (XVIII) s, 268a – S, 267b
ʿAbd Allāh Bosnevī (1644) i, 1271b – I, 1310b

ʿAbd Allāh Djammāʿ al-Ḳāsimī (XVI) iv, 892b – IV, 925b
ʿAbd Allāh Djewdet → Djewdet, ʿAbd Allāh
ʿAbd Allāh Dürri-zāde, Shaykh al-Islām (XX) vi, 984b – VI, 977a
ʿAbd Allāh Efendi, Shaykh al-Islām (1727) vi, 800b – VI, 790b
ʿAbd Allāh al-Ghālib bi-'llāh (Saʿdid(e)) (1574) i, **55b**, 245a, 859b, 1224b; ii, 619b; vi, 591b, 594b, 596a, b, 597a, b; s, 377b – I, **57b**, 252b, 883b, 1261a; II, 635a; VI, 576a, 579a, 580b, 581b, 582a; S, 377b
ʿAbd Allāh al-Ḥas, Shaykh (XX) s, 248a – S, 248b
ʿAbd Allāh Ilāhī → Ilāhī
ʿAbd Allāh Ḳādirī (XX) x, 961a – X,
ʿAbd Allāh Ḳarshe (Abdullahi Qarshe) ix, 726a – IX, 757b
ʿAbd Allāh al-Kātib → ʿAbd Allāh b. Muḥammad al-Kātib
ʿAbd Allāh al-Kāzarūnī (ʿālim) (1063) vi, 626b – VI, 611b
ʿAbd Allāh Khān → Ḥasan ʿAlī Bārha
ʿAbd Allāh Khān (Ghazīpūr) (XVIII) s, 325b – S, 325a
ʿAbd Allāh Khān, Özbeg (Khīwā) (1598) vi, 310a; vii, 317a, 677a, 925a; viii, 749b – VI, 295a; VII, 319b, 676b, 925b; VIII, 770a
ʿAbd Allāh Khān, Özbeg (Khīwa) (1855) s, 46a – S, 46b
ʿAbd Allāh Khān, Özbeg (Khīwa) (1920) iv, 1065b – IV, 1097a
ʿAbd Allāh Khān b. Iskandar (Shaybānid(e)) s, 340a, b – S, 339b, 340a
ʿAbd Allāh Khān Amīn al-Dawla (1847) vii, 453b, 454a – VII, 454b
ʿAbd Allāh Khān Brahoi (XVII) i, 1005b – I, 1036b
ʿAbd Allāh Khān-Ḳalʿa (town/ville) vi, 619a, 621a – VI, 604a, 606a
ʿAbd Allāh Khān Rohilla (XVIII) iii, 60a, b – III, 62b, 63a
ʿAbd Allāh Ḳuṭb al-Mulk → Ḥasan ʿAlī Bārha
ʿAbd Allāh Ḳuṭb Shāh (1672) iii, 318b, 319a, 427a; v, 549b; vi, 837b – III, 328a, 330a, 440b; V, 554b; VI, 828a
ʿAbd Allāh Marwārīd iii, 490b – III, 507b
ʿAbd Allāh Menou (Miṣr) (XIX) vii, 180b – VII, 182b
ʿAbd Allāh Mīrzā (Tīmūrid(e)) → ʿAbd Allāh b. Ibrāhīm b. Shāhrukh
ʿAbd Allāh Niyāzī Sirhindī (XVI) ii, 500a, b; iii, 492b – II, 512b, 513a; III, 509b
ʿAbd Allāh Pasha → Fikrī, ʿAbd Allāh Pasha
ʿAbd Allāh Pasha (ʿAkkā) (XIX) i, 1078b; ii, 210a, 636a; vii, 426b – I, 1111a; II, 216b, 652a; VII, 425a
ʿAbd Allāh Pasha Muḥsin-zāde Čelebi (1749) i, **56a**, 292a; iii, 132b – I, **58a**, 301a; III, 135a
ʿAbd Allāh Re'fet (poet(e)) (XVIII) vi, 1000a – VI, 992b
ʿAbd Allāh al-Riḍā → ʿAbd Allāh al-Shaykh al-Ṣāliḥ
ʿAbd Allāh Saʿd Djaʿalī (XIX) i, 765a; ii, 351b – I, 788a; II, 361b
ʿAbd Allāh al-Saksīwī (1350) vi, 593b – VI, 578b
ʿAbd Allāh Ṣāliḥ Fārsī (1982) x, 195b – X, 211a
ʿAbd Allāh Sari → Sari ʿAbd Allāh Efendī
ʿAbd Allāh Sarrādj (XX) vi, 152b – VI, 151b
ʿAbd Allāh Shaḳrūn (XX) vi, 755b – VI, 745a
ʿAbd Allāh Shaṭṭārī, Shaykh (1485) i, 1284a – I, 1323b
ʿAbd Allāh al-Shaybī (XX) vi, 156b – VI, 152b
ʿAbd Allāh al-Shaykh al-Ṣāliḥ iii, 262b – III, 270a
ʿAbd Allāh ʿUmar Balkhayr (XX) vi, 177b, 179a – VI, 162b
ʿAbd Allāh ʿUrayf (XX) vi, 176b
ʿAbd Allāh al-Wazīr (XX) vi, 566b – VI, 551a
ʿAbd Allāh Zākhir, Shammās (1734) vi, 796b – VI, 786b
ʿAbd al-ʿAllām Fayẓ Khān Oghlu (XIX) iv, 505a – IV, 527a
ʿAbd ʿAmr → ʿAbd al-Raḥmān b. ʿAwf
ʿAbd al-Ashhal i, 771b – I, 794b
ʿAbd al-ʿAẓīm b. Zayn al-ʿĀbidīn (Marʿashī) (1400) vi, 512b – VI, 497b
ʿAbd al-ʿAẓīm Mīrzā, Sayyid i, 262b – I, 270b
ʿAbd al-ʿAzīz → ʿAbd al-ʿAzīz b. al-Ḥasam
ʿAbd al-ʿAzīz (Banū ʿAbbās) (XVI) iv, 478a – IV, 499a
ʿAbd al-ʿAzīz (Ghalzay) (1715) i, 229a; iii, 603b – I, 236a; III, 624b
ʿAbd al-ʿAzīz I (Marīnid(e)) → Abū Farīs ʿAbd al-ʿAzīz I
ʿAbd al-ʿAzīz (Ottoman) (1876) i, **56b**, 285b, 286b, 397b, 836b, 948a; ii, 49a, 935b; iii, 250a, 621b; iv, 876a; vi, 68a, b, 69a, 342a, 372b, 758a; viii, 59b s, 281b – I, **58a**, 294a, 295a, 408b, 860a, 977b; II, 50a, 957b; III, 257a, 642a; IV, 909a; VI, 66a, b, 326a, 357a, 747a; VIII, 60b; S, 281b
ʿAbd al-ʿAzīz (amīr) (Marrākūsh) (1353) vi, 593b – VI, 578b
ʿAbd al-ʿAzīz, Mawlāy → ʿAbd al-ʿAzīz b. al-Ḥasan
ʿAbd al-ʿAzīz (Mountains/Montagnes de-) vi, 539b – VI, 524a
ʿAbd al-ʿAzīz, Özbeg Khān (1670) vi, 856a – VI, 847b
ʿAbd al-ʿAzīz b. ʿAbd al-Ḥaḳḳ (Khurāsān, Banū) (XI) v, 60a – V, 62a
ʿAbd al-ʿAzīz b. ʿAbd al-Ḳādir b. Ghaybī (XIX) i, 67a – I, 68b
ʿAbd al-ʿAzīz b. ʿAbd al-Muṭṭalib, ḳādī (VIII) vi, 140a – VI, 138b
ʿAbd al-ʿAzīz b. ʿAbd al-Raḥmān b. al-Fayṣal (Āl Suʿūd) (1953) i, 39a, 233b, 443b, 555b, 709b, 762a, 885b, 958a, 1299a, 1313a; ii, 77a, 108b, 175b, 176b, 354a, 569a, 573a, 626a, 660a; iii, 238a, 263b, 326b, 361b, 365a, 643b, 1062a, 1064b, 1066a, b; iv, 680b, 703b, 765b, 925b, 1073a; v, 63a, 574b, 575a, 998a, 999a; vi, 33a, 34a, 45b, 151b, 152b, 153a, 154b, 155a, 169b, 262a, 306b; vii, 422a, 782b; viii, 246a; ix, 904a; s, **3b**, 4b, 293b, 305b – I, 40a, 241a, 456b, 572b, 731a, 785a, 911b, 987a, 1339a, 1353a; II, 78b, 111a, 181a, 182a, 363b, 583a, 587a, 641b, 676b; III, 245a, 271b, 337a, 372b, 376b, 665a, 1088b, 1091a, 1092b, 1093a; IV, 708b, 732a, 796a, 958b, 1104b; V, 64b, 579a, b, 993b, 994a; VI, 31b, 32a, 44a, 150a, 151a, b, 152a, 160b, 246b, 344b; VII, 423b, 784b; VIII, 252a; IX, 942a; S, **2b**, 3b, 293a, 305b
ʿAbd al-ʿAzīz b. ʿAbd al-Raḥmān al-Azdī (817) vi, 335b – VI, 320a
ʿAbd al-ʿAzīz b. ʿAbd al-Raḥmān b. Abī ʿĀmir (Balansiya, ʿĀmirid(e)) (1041) i, 446a, 985b; vi, 344b, 576b – I, 459a, 1016a; VI, 329a, 561b
ʿAbd al-ʿAzīz b. ʿAbd al-Salām (1262) ix, 436a – IX. 454a
ʿAbd al-ʿAzīz b. Abī Dulaf (873) ii, 623b; iv, 100a – II, 639a; IV, 104a
ʿAbd al-ʿAzīz b. Abī Ḥāzim (798) vi, 280b – VI, 265b
ʿAbd al-ʿAzīz b. Djaʿfar → Ghulām al-Khallāl
ʿAbd al-ʿAzīz b. Fayṣal al-Dawīsh → ʿUzayyiz b. Fayṣal
ʿAbd al-ʿAzīz b. al-Ḥādjdj Ibrāhīm (1808) i, **57a** – I, **58b**
ʿAbd al-ʿAzīz b. al-Ḥadjdjādj (744) i, **57a**; iii, 990b – I, **59a**; III, 1015a
ʿAbd al-ʿAzīz b. al-Ḥasan (ʿAlawid(e)) (1907) i, **57b**, 357a, 1281b; ii, 820a; iii, 62a, 240a, 562a; v, 890a, 1193a, b; vi, 595b; s, 114a – I, **59b**, 368a, 1320b; II, 839b; III, 64b, 247a, 581b; V, 896b, 1183a, b; VI, 580a; S, 113b

'Abd al-'Azīz b. Ḥātim i, 1041a; ii, 679a – I, 1072b; II, 696a

'Abd al-'Azīz b. Marwān I (Umayyad(e)) (674) i, 42b, **58a**, 76b, 77b, 148b, 1242b; ii, 327b, 427b, 788a, 958a; iii, 271b, 572a, 819b; v, 552a, b; vi, 621b, 622a, b, 659a, 664a; s, 273a –
I, 43b, **60a**, 78b, 80a, 153a, 1280a; II, 337a, 438b, 807a, 980b; III, 279a, 591b, 843b; V, 557a, b; VI, 607a, b, 644b, 650a; S, 273a

'Abd al-'Azīz b. Marwān (Miṣr) (704) vii, 159b; x, 821a – VII, 161a; X,

'Abd al-'Azīz (II) b. Muḥammad (ṣadr) (1196) viii, 749a – VIII, 774a

'Abd al-'Azīz b. Muḥammad b. al-Nu'mān, ḳāḍī (XI) ii, 169b; iii, 78b, 79a – II, 174b; III, 81a, b

'Abd al-'Azīz b. Muḥammad b. Su'ūd (Āl Su'ūd) (1803) i, 554a; ii, 321a, 492b; iii, 678b; iv, 925a, b; vii, 410b; ix, 903n –
I, 571b; 330b, 504b; III, 700a; IV, 958a, b; VII, 411b; IX, 941a

'Abd al-'Azīz b. Muḥammad al-Fishtālī (1621) i, **58a**, 289a – I, **60a**, 298a

'Abd al-'Azīz b. Mūsā b. Nuṣayr (718) i, 50a, **58b**, 608b, 1054b, 1338b; ii, 485b. 1009a, 1012b; iii, 587b; iv, 115a, 672b; v, 367b; vii, 643b; x, 585a, 848a –
I, 51b, **60b**, 628a, 1086b, 1378b; II, 497b, 1032b, 1036a; III, 607b; IV, 120a, 700a; V, 368b; VII, 643a; X,

'Abd al-'Azīz b. Shu'ayb al-Ballūtī (961) i, 121b; iii, 1084b, 1085a – I, 125a; III, 1111b, 1112a

'Abd al-'Azīz b. 'Umar Māza (ṣadr) (XII) viii, 749a – VIII, 770a

'Abd al-'Azīz b. al-Walīd (728) i, **58b** – I, **60b**

'Abd al-'Azīz b. Yūsuf, Abu 'l-Ḳāsim (X) s, **4a**, 398a – S, **3b**, 398b

'Abd al-'Azīz al-Bakrī (Walba) (XI) i, 6a, 155b; ii, 1009a – I, 6a, 159b; II, 1032b

'Abd al-'Azīz al-Bawandī, Shaykh (XX) ii, 436a – II, 447b

'Abd al-'Azīz al-Dabbāgh (XIX) i, 277b; v, 647b; ix, 24b – I, 286a; V, 651b; IX, 26a

'Abd al-Aziz al-Dihlawī b. Walī Allāh, Mawlānā Shāh (1824) i, **59a**, 282a, 827b, 1193a; ii, 254b; iii, 431a; iv, 196a, 625b; vii, 442a; viii, 69a; s, 293a –
I, **60b**, 291a; 228a, 850a; II, 261b; III, 445a; IV, 204b, 650b; VII, 443a; VIII, 70b; S, 292b

'Abd al-Aziz Fahmī (XX) iii, 516a, 518b – III, 533b, 536a

'Abd al-'Azīz al-'Irāḳī (XX) vi, 110a – VI, 107b

'Abd al-'Azīz Ḵẖān (Buḵẖārā) (1680) i, 1295b; ii, 446a – I, 1335b; II, 458a

'Abd al-'Azīz al-Mālik al-Manṣūr (Mamlūk) (1405) ii, 781b – II, 800a

'Abd al-'Azīz al-Manṣūr → 'Abd al-'Azīz b. 'Abd al-Raḥmān

'Abd al-'Azīz Pasha (1725) vi, 502b – VI, 487b

'Abd al-'Azīz al-Shāwīsh, Shaykh (XX) vii, 439a – VII, 440a

'Abd al-'Azīz al-Tabbā', Sīdī (1508) vi, 591a, b – VI, 576a

'Abd al-'Azīz University/-é vi, 174a – VI, 161b

'Abd al-Bahā' (1920) i, 915b, 916b, 917a, 918a; s, 77a – I, 943b, 944a, b, 945b; S, 76b

'Abd al-Bāḳī (1821) vii, 685b – VII, 686a

'Abd al-Bāḳī (Farangī Maḥall) (XIX) s, 4b, 292a – S, 3b, 292a

'Abd al-Bāḳī, Maḥmūd → Bāḳī, Maḥmūd 'Abd al-Bāḳī

'Abd al-Bāḳī al-Fārūḳī → al-Fārūḳī, 'Abd al-Bāḳī

'Abd al-Bāḳī al-Ḥanbalī (1661) iii, 677b – III, 699b

'Abd al-Bāḳī Ḵẖān (1736) vi, 56a – VI, 54a

'Abd al-Bāḳī, Mīr Niẓām al-Dīn (Ni'mat-Allāhī) (XVI) viii, 46a – VIII, 47a

'Abd al-Bāḳī Nahāwandī (XVII) i, 857a – I, 880b

'Abd al-Bāḳī Naḳshbandī → Bāḳī bi-'llāh, Ḵẖʷādja

'Abd al-Bārī, Ḳiyām al-Dīn Muḥammad (Farangī Maḥall) (1926) vii, 354b; s, **4b**, 74a, b, 292a, b, 293b, 360b; – VII, 357a; S, **3b**, 74b, 75a, 292a, 293a, 360b

'Abd al-Bārī, Mawlānā (XX) vii, 354b – VII, 357a

'Abd al-Barr b. 'Anbasa (al-Ḳabḳ) (X) iv, 346b – IV, 361a

'Abd al-Bāsiṭ 'Abd al-Ṣamad (XX), Shaykh (XX) *74a – X,77a*

'Abd al-Dār, Banū iv, 320a; v, 581a, b; vi, 137b, 145a – IV, 334b; V, 586a, b; VI, 136a, 143a

'Abd al-Dār b. Ḳuṣayy (VI) vi, 145a – VI, 143a

'Abd al-Djabbār, Shaykh (XII) ii, 964a – II, 986a

'Abd al-Djabbār b. 'Abd al-Raḥmān al-Azdī (759) i, **59a**; vi, 428a; vii, 360a – I, **61a**; VI, 413b; VII, 362b

'Abd al-Djabbār b. Aḥmad (1025) i, **59b**, 343a; iii, 832a, 905b, 1019a, 1023a, 1071b, 1072a, 1144a, 1165b, 1171a; iv, 615b, 985b; v, 96a, 97a, 237a, 240a, 833b; vi, 376a; vii, 312a, 634a; viii, 534a, 981a; s, 13a, b, 14a, 25a, b, 31b, 225b, 343a, b, 346a, 348a, 392a, 393a –
I, **61b**, 353b; III, 856a, 929b, 1045a, 1049a, 1098b, 1172b, 1194b, 1200a; IV, 640a, 1018a; V, 98a, 99b, 235a, 238a, 839b; VI, 360b; VII, 314b, 634a; VIII, 552a, 1015a; S, 13b, 14a, 25b, 32a, 225b, 342b, 343a, 348a, 392b, 393a

'Abd al-Djabbār b. al-Ḥusayn b. Mu'ayya, Sayyid (XI) s, 19a – S, 19a

'Abd al-Djabbār b. Ḳays al-Murādī (Ibāḍī) (VIII) iii, 653b – III, 675a

'Abd al-Djalīl b. Ḥāfiẓ Abū Isḥāḳ (XVII) vii, 574a – VII, 574b

'Abd al-Djalīl Abu 'l-Maḥāsin → al-Dihistānī

'Abd al-Djalīl Djalīlī (XVII) ii, 402a – II, 412b

'Abd al-Djalīl al-Kazwīnī al-Rāzī (1170) vi, 549a – VI, 533b

'Abd al-Fattāḥ 'Amr (XX) s, 301a – S, 301a

'Abd al-Fattāḥ Fūmanī (XVII) i, **60a**, – I, **61b**

'Abd al-Ghaffār b. 'Abd al-Karīm → al-Ḳazwīnī

'Abd al-Ghaffār al-Akhras → al-Akhras

'Abd al-Ghaffār al-Dasūḳī → al-Dasūḳī, Ibrāhīm b. Ibrāhīm

'Abd al-Ghaffār al-Ḥimṣī (VIII) iv, 115b – IV, 120b

'Abd al-Ghaffār Ḵẖān (Kōhāt) → Ḵẖān, 'Abd al-Ghaffār

'Abd al-Ghāfir (Ghaffār) b. Husayn al-Kāshgharī (XI) iv, 699a – IV, 727a

'Abd al-Ghanī b. Ismā'īl al-Nābulusī (1731) i, **60a**, 596a, 795b, 1109b, 1235b; ii, 900a; iii, 935a; iv, 1006b; vi, 215a; vii, 724b, 812a –
I, **62a**, 615b, 819a,1143a, 1272b; II, 921a; III, 959b; IV, 1038b; VI, 199a; VII, 725a, 813b

'Abd al-Ghanī b. Sa'īd al-Miṣrī (X) s, 38a – S, 38a

'Abd al-Ghanī Maḥmūd (1875) vi, 614a – VI, 599a

'Abd al-Ghanī al-Maḳdisī → al-Maḳdisī, 'Abd al-Ghanī

'Abd Ḥadad (IV) vi, 378b – VI, 363a

'Abd al-Hādī, Banū iv, 834b – IV, 867b

'Abd al-Ḥāfiẓ, Mawlāy → Ḥāfiẓ, 'Abd al-

'Abd al-Ḥakam, Banū → Ibn 'Abd al-Ḥakam

'Abd al-Ḥakīm 'Āmir (XX) s, 5b, 8b, 9a – S, 4b, 8a, b

'Abd al-Ḥakīm al-Siyālkōtī → al-Siyālkōtī

'Abd al-Ḥaḳḳ, Shaykh (Dihlī) (1642) vii, 938a; s, 10b – VII, 938b; S, 10a

'Abd al-Ḥaḳḳ b. 'Abd al-'Azīz b. Ḵẖurāsān (XI) iii, 137b; v, 60a – III, 140b; V, 61b, 62a

ʿAbd al-Ḥaḳḳ b. Faḍl-i Ḥaḳḳ (XIX) ii, 735b, 736b – II, 754a, 755a
ʿAbd al-Ḥaḳḳ b. Sayf al-Dīn al-Dihlawī (1642) i, **60b**, 702b, 957a; ii, 296b; vi, 131b, 354a; vii, 988a; s, 299a –
I, **62b**, 724a, 986b; II, 304b; VI, 129b, 338a; VII, 989a; S, 353b
ʿAbd al-Ḥaḳḳ Abū Muḥammad → Marīnid(e)s
ʿAbd al-Ḥaḳḳ Ḥāmid (1937) i, **61a**, 1302a; ii, 692b; iii, 1199b; iv, 1153a; vi, 759a; s, 149b –
I, **63a**, 1342a; II, 709b; III, 1229b; IV, 1185a; VI, 748a; S, 150a
ʿAbd al-Ḥaḳḳ al-Hindī, Shaykh (XX) vi, 175b – VI, 162a
ʿAbd al-Ḥaḳḳ al-Ishbīlī s, 389b – S, 389b
ʿAbd al-Ḥaḳḳ Mollā (XIX) i, 61a, 921a; iv, 1153a – I, 63a, 948b; IV, 1185a
ʿAbd al-Ḥaḳḳ Muḥaddith, Shaykh i, 260a; iii, 430a, 435a – I, 268a; III, 444a, 449a
ʿAbd al-Ḥalīm Maḥmūd, Shaykh (XX) s, 224b – S, 225a
ʿAbd al-Ḥalīm Pasha b. Muḥammad ʿAlī Pasha (XIX) iii, 515a – III, 532b
ʿAbd al-Ḥalīm Sharar (1926) x, 879a – X,
ʿAbd al-Ḥamīd I (Ottoman) (1789) i, **62b**, 481b, 1004a; ii, 209b, 534a; iv, 946a; v, 314a; vi, 58a; vii, 387b; s, 401b –
I, **64a**, 496a, 1035a; II, 216a, 547a; IV, 978b; V, 313b; VI, 56a; VII, 388b; S, 402a
ʿAbd al-Ḥamīd II (Ottoman) (1918) i, **63b**, 286b, 289b, 294b, 298b, 431a, 657a, 736a, 776a, 948a, 958a, 1090a; ii, 104b, 289a, 354b, 418b, 430b, 474b, 489b, 513b, 532a, 533b, 642a, 682a, 878b; iii, 357b, 364a, 993a, 994a, 1199a, 1257b; iv, 168b, 681b, 872a, 876b, 946a; v, 61b, 905a, 949a, 1035a; vi, 8b, 89a, b, 92b, 93a, 286a, 304b, 531a, b, 614b, 733b, 758a, 759b, 760a; vii, 184b, 205b, 434b, 525b, 547a, 573b; viii, 59b, 248a; s, 100b, 161b, 179a, 211b, 282b, 296b, 330b, 359b –
I, 6**5b**, 295a, 298b, 303b, 307b, 443a, 678a, 758a, 799b, 977b, 987a, 1122b; II, 107a, 297a, 364b, 429b, 441b, 486b, 502a, 526b, 545a, 546b, 658a, 699a, 898b; III, 368b, 375b, 1018a, 1019a, 1229b, 1290b; IV, 176a, 709b, 905b, 909b, 979a; V, 63a, 911b, 952b, 1031b; VI, 8b, 87a, b, 90b, 271a, 290a, 515a, 516a, 599b, 722b, 747a, 748b, 749a; VII, 185a, 206b, 435b, 525b, 547b, 574a; VIII, 60b; S, 99b, 161b, 180a, 211b, 282b, 296a, 330a, 359b
ʿAbd al-Ḥamīd b. Bādīs → Ibn Bādīs
ʿAbd al-Ḥamīd b. Yaḥyā b. Saʿd (750) i, **65b**, 588a; ii, 304b; iii, 494b, 1242b, 1263a; iv, 755b; vii, 985a; viii, 533a –
I, **67b**, 607a; II, 313a; III, 511b, 1274b, 1296a; IV, 786a; VII, 985b; VIII, 550b
ʿAbd al-Ḥamīd Efendi (XIX) ii, 878b – II, 898b
ʿAbd al-Ḥamīd Khān (Kashmīr) (XX) iv, 711a – IV, 739b
ʿAbd al-Ḥamīd Lāhawrī (1654) i, **66a**; vii, 139b, 342b – I, **68a**; VII, 141b, 344b
ʿAbd al-Ḥamīd al-Manāzī (940) vi, 242b – VI, 226b
ʿAbd al-Ḥayy, Mawlawī iv, 196a; s, 4b – IV, 204b; S, 3b
ʿAbd al-Ḥayy, Shaykh (XVI) s, 312a – S, 312a
ʿAbd al-Ḥayy al-Lakhnawī (1886) i, **66a**, 282b; iii, 164a; s, 292b, 293a – I, **68a**, 291a; III, 167b; S, 292b
ʿAbd al-Ḥusayn, Mīrzā (XIX) iv, 979a – IV, 1011b
ʿAbd al-Ḥusayn Hazhīr (1949) ii, 882b; vii, 447a – II, 903a; VII, 448b
ʿAbd al-Ḥusayn Nūshīn (1970) vi, 764a – VI, 753a
ʿAbd al-Ilāh (Hāshimid(e)) (1882) ii, 872b; iii, 264a; vi, 151a, b, 615a, 616a – II, 892b; III, 271b; VI, 150a, 600a, 601a
ʿAbd al-Kaʿba → ʿAbd al-Raḥmān b. Abī Bakr; ʿAbd al-Raḥmān b. ʿAwf; ʿAbd al-Raḥmān b. Samura
ʿAbdelkader → ʿAbd al-Ḳādir
ʿAbd el-Kader → ʿAbd al-Ḳādir b. Muḥyī al-Dīn
ʿAbd al-Ḳādir (peninsula/presqu'île) vi, 641b – VI, 626b
ʿAbd al-Ḳādir b. ʿAlī → al-Fāsī, ʿAbd al-Ḳādir
ʿAbd al-Ḳādir b. ʿAmāra (Fundj) (1557) ii, 944a – II, 966a
ʿAbd al-Ḳādir b. Burhān Shāh (Niẓām Shāhī) (XVI) iii, 625b, 1161a – III, 646b, 1189a
ʿAbd al-Ḳādir b. Ghaybī (1435) i, **66b**; ii, 1074a – I, **68b**; II, 1098b
ʿAbd al-Ḳādir b. Muḥammad al-Maḳrīzī (1332) vi, 193b – VI, 177b
ʿAbd al-Ḳādir b. Muḥyī al-Dīn, Amīr (1883) i, 67a, 85a, 357a, 369a, 789a, 1177b, 1197b, 1247a; ii, 160b, 173a, 288b; iii, 561b, 806b; iv, 362a, 383a; v, 1160b, 1192b; vi, 252a; vii, 64b, 263a, 391a, 671a, 722a; s, 296a –
I, **69a**, 87b, 367b, 380a, 812b, 1212b, 1232b, 1285a; II, 165b, 178a, 296b; III, 581a, 829b; IV, 378a, 400a; V, 1150a, 1182b; VI, 236a; VII, 65a, 265a, 392a, 670b, 723a; S, 296a
ʿAbd al-Ḳādir Badāʾūnī → Badāʾūnī
ʿAbd al-Ḳādir al-Baghdādī (1682) i, **68a**, 712b; vi, 196a, 635a; vii, 580b; s, 388a, 407b –
I, **70a**, 734a; VI, 180a, 620a; VII, 581a; S, 388b, 407b
ʿAbd al-Ḳādir Dihlawī (1813) i, **68b**, 282b, 827b; ii, 735b; iii, 431a; iv, 196a; v, 803a – I, **70b**, 291a; II, 754a; III, 445a; IV, 204b; V, 809a
ʿAbd al-Ḳādir al-Djīlānī (al-Djīlī) (1166) i, **69a**, 91b, 137b, 595b, 903b, 904a, 1173a; ii, 535b; iii, 160b, 842b; iv, 380a-383a, 1134a; v, 475a, 1201a; vi, 178b, 251b, 280a, 354a, 463a, 644a; vii,189a, 726b; s, 182b, 223b, 323b –
I, **70b**, 94b, 141b, 615a, 931a,b; 1208a; II, 549a; III, 164a, 866b; IV, 396b-399b, 1165b; V, 478a, 1191a; VI, 163b, 236a, 264b, 338b, 449a, 629a; VII, 189b, 727b; S, 182b, 223b, 323a
ʿAbd al-Ḳādir al-Fāsī → al-Fāsī, ʿAbd al-Ḳādir
ʿAbd al-Ḳādir Ghiyāth al-Dīn b. Maḥmūd Khaldjī (1500) vi, 309b – VI, 295a
ʿAbd al-Ḳādir al-Gīlānī → ʿAbd al-Ḳādir al-Djīlānī
ʿAbd al-Ḳādir Khʷādja Sawda (1873) x, 65a – X, 67b
ʿAbd al-Ḳādir al-Ḳurashī (1373) i, **70b**; ix, 36a; s, 191b – I, **72b**; IX, 36b; S, 193a
ʿAbd al-Ḳādir al-Maghribī (XX) ii, 451b; iv, 159a; x, 240b – II, 463b; IV, 166a; X, 259b
ʿAbd al-Ḳādir Shāh → Ikhtiyār al-Dīn Abu 'l-Mudjāhid Ḳādir Khān
ʿAbd al-Ḳādir al-Shaybī, Shaykh (XX) vi, 153b – VI, 152a
ʿAbd al-Ḳādir al-Ṭubdjī (XIX) vi, 251b – VI, 236a
ʿAbd al-Ḳāhir b. Ṭāhir al-Baghdādī → al-Baghdādī
ʿAbd al-Ḳāhir al-Djurdjānī → al-Djurdjanī
ʿAbd al-Karīm (Bulái) (1626) ix, 637a – IX, 661b
ʿAbd al-Karīm (ḳāʾid, Marrākūsh) (1659) vi, 142b, 595a – VI, 141a, 579b
ʿAbd al-Karīm, Mawlānā (1450) vi, 70a – VI, 68a
ʿAbd al-Karīm, Mīr (XVII) i, 254a – I, 261b
ʿAbd al-Karīm b. ʿAbd Allāh (Marʿashī) (1467) vi, 514a, 516a – VI, 499a, 501a
ʿAbd al-Karīm b. ʿAdjarrad → Ibn ʿAdjarrad
ʿAbd al-Karīm b. ʿAlī Pérez (XVII) i, 405a – I, 416b
ʿAbd al-Karīm b. Mughīth (VIII) s, 92a – S, 92a
ʿAbd al-Karīm b. Muḥammad (Marʿashī) (1452) vi, 513b, 514b – VI, 498b, 499b
ʿAbd al-Karīm b. Muḥibb al-Dīn (1606) vii, 912a – VII, 912b

ʿAbd al-Karīm Bukhārī (1830) i, **71a** – I, **73a**
ʿAbd al-Karīm al-Djazārī, Banū iii, 961a – III, 986a
ʿAbd al-Karīm al-Djīlī (1428) i, **71a**, 596a; iii, 329a, 709a, 1240b; v, 525b; vi, 211a – I, **73a**, 615b; III, 339a, 731a, 1272b; V, 529b; VI, 195b
ʿAbd al-Karīm Kashmīrī (1784) i, **71b** – I, **73b**
ʿAbd al-Karīm Ḳāsim al-Khalīl (1915) iii, 519b, 1259a – III, 537b, 1291b
ʿAbd al-Karīm Khān (Ḳarakhānid(e)) (955) iii, 1113b; iv, 698b; v, 856b – III, 1141a; IV, 727a; V, 863a
ʿAbd al-Karīm Khān (Noghay) (1504) i, 721b – I, 743b
ʿAbd al-Karīm Khān b. Shāhrukh (1746) v, 29a – V, 30a
ʿAbd al-Karīm Lāhurī, Shaykh ii, 55a – II, 56a
ʿAbd al-Karīm Maʿmūr Khān (XVII) vii, 332a – VII, 333b
ʿAbd al-Karīm Munshī (1851) i, **72a** – I, **74a**
ʿAbd al-Karīm al-Sammān (1775) x, 257a -- X, 276a
ʿAbd al-Ḳawī (XVII) vii, 452b – VII, 454a
ʿAbd al-Ḳays, Banū i, **72b**, 529a, 545a, 942a; iv, 764a; v, 346a; vi, 441b, 649a; vii, 671a; s, 24b – I, **74b**, 545a, 562a, 971a; IV, 794b; V, 347a; VI, 427a, 634b; VII, 671a; S, 25a
ʿAbd al-Kerīm Pasha (XVIII) vii, 275b – VII, 277b
ʿAbd al-Khāliḳ Ḥassūna (1972) s, 240b – S, 241a
ʿAbd al-Khāliḳ b. Abi ʾl-Ṭalḥ al-Shihābī iii, 124b – III, 127a
ʿAbd al-Khāliḳ al-Sharḳī (XVIII) vi, 356b – VI, 340b
ʿAbd al-Khallāḳ Torres (Morocco/Maroc) (XX) vii, 416a – VII, 417b
ʿAbd el-Krīm (XX) vii, 416b – VII, 417b
ʿAbd al-Ḳuddūs al-Anṣārī (1983) v, 1005b; vi, 175b, 176b – V, 1001a
ʿAbd al-Laṭīf b. Ulugh Beg (Tīmūrid(e)) (1449) vi, 601b; x, 813a – VI, 586b; X,
ʿAbd al-Laṭīf al-Baghdādī (1231) i, **74a**, 595a; iii, 877a, 956b; v, 862a, 1129b, 1130a; vi, 204b, 367a, 410b, 412b, 413a, 637b, 845a, 1016b; vii, 140b, 141b, 165a; s, 115b, 408a – I, **76b**, 614a; III, 901a, 981a; V, 869a, 1125b, 1126a; VI, 188b, 351a, 395b, 397b, 398a, 622b, 836a, 1009b; VII, 142b, 143b, 166b; S, 115a, 408a
ʿAbd al-Laṭīf Čelebī → Laṭīfī
ʿAbd al-Laṭīf Ḳastamunilī → Laṭīfī
ʿAbd al-Laṭīf al-Ḳayātī (1842) vi, 355a – VI, 339a
ʿAbd al-Laṭīf Khān (Ḳazān) (XVI) iv, 849a – IV, 882a
ʿAbd al-Laṭīf Khān (Samarḳand) (XVI) i, 46b – I, 48a
ʿAbd al-Laṭīf Mīrzā (Tīmūrid(e)) (1450) i, 91a, 227b – I, 93b, 234a
ʿAbd al-Madān b. al-Dayyān (Balḥārith, Āl) iii, 223a, b – III, 229b, 230a
ʿAbd al-Madjīd I (Abdülmecid) (Ottoman) (1861) i, 37a, **74b**, 216b, 284b, 298a, 776a; 1226a; ii, 49a, 613a, 801a, 912a, 935a; iv, 143a; vi, 175a, 757a, b; vii, 428a; viii, 58b, 59a; x, 201a – I, 38a, **77a**, 223a, 293b, 307b, 799a, 1262b; II, 50a, 628a, 820a, 933b, 957a; IV, 149a; VI, 162a, 746b, 747a; VII, 429b; VIII, 59b, 60a; X, 217a
ʿAbd al-Madjīd II (Abdülmecid) (Ottoman) (1944) i, **75b**, ii, 119b; iv, 946b – I, **77b**, II, 122b; IV, 979b
ʿAbd al-Madjīd (Fāṭimid(e)) → al-Ḥāfiẓ
ʿAbd al-Madjīd Salīm, muftī (1954) x, 140a; s, 208b – X, 151a; S, 208b
ʿAbd al-Malik, Amīr (Sindjār) (1149) vi, 870b – VI, 861b
ʿAbd al-Malik I b. Nūḥ (Sāmānid(e)) (961) i, 421b, 984b; iii, 46b; v, 325a, 1162b; vi, 432b; viii, 1027b; s, 230b, 357b, 358a – I, 433b, 1015a; III, 48b; V, 324b, 1152a; VI, 418a; VIII, 1062b; S, 230b, 357b, 358a
ʿAbd al-Malik II (Sāmānid(e)) (1000) iii, 196b – III, 201a
ʿAbd al-Malik b. ʿAbd al-ʿAzīz → Ibn Djuraydj al-Makkī
ʿAbd al-Malik b. Abī ʿĀmir al-Maʿāfirī al-Muẓaffar (1008) i, 6a, **75b**, 242a, 446a, 494b, 1040b, 1096a; iii, 495b, 674a; 819a; iv, 632b; vii, **815b**; x, 853a – I, 6a, **77b**, 249b, 459a, 509b, 1072a, 1129a; III, 512b, 605b, 842b; IV, 657b; VII, **817a**; X,
ʿAbd al-Malik b. Abī Muḥammad Hudhayl (1103) ix, 307b – IX, 317a
ʿAbd al-Malik b. Aḥmad II b. Hūd → ʿImād al-Dawla b. Hūd
ʿAbd al-Malik b. ʿAlī b. ʿAbd al-Malik b. Abī Shayba (1210) vi, 381a – VI, 365b
ʿAbd al-Malik b. ʿAttāsh → Ibn ʿAttāsh
ʿAbd al-Malik b. Bishr b. Marwān al-Baṣra s, 52a – S, 52b
ʿAbd al-Malik b. Ghiṭrīf (faḳīh) (XI) vi, 436a – VI, 421b
ʿAbd al-Malik b. Ḥabīb (852) iv, 87a, b; vi, 374b; vii, 539b; viii, 515b; ix, 38a – IV, 91a, b; VI, 358b; VII, 539b; VIII, 533a; IX, 38b
ʿAbd al-Malik b. Hishām → Ibn Hishām, ʿAbd al-Malik
ʿAbd al-Malik b. Ḳaṭan al-Fihrī (741) i, **76a**, 991a; iv, 494b, 672b, 805a – I, **78a**, 1021b; IV, 515b, 700a, 837b
ʿAbd al-Malik b. Maḥammad al-Shaykh al-Mahdī (Saʿdid(e)) (XVI) i, 55b, 288b – I, 57b, 297b
ʿAbd al-Malik b. Makkī (XIII) iv, 338a – IV, 352a
ʿAbd al-Malik b. al-Manṣūr → ʿAbd al-Malik b. Abī ʿĀmir; ʿAbd al-Malik al-Muẓaffar
ʿAbd al-Malik b. Marwān (Umayyad(e)) (705) i, 2b, 45a, 47b, 55b, 58a, **76a**, 120a, 142a, 148b, 320b, 453b, 482a, 550a, 610a, 710b, 1038a, 1143b, 1242b, 1293a, 1349a; ii, 117b, 297b, 319b, 324a, 360a, 456b, 480a, 768b, 911a; iii, 40a, 648b, 717a; iv, 654b, 929b; vi, 139a, 140a, 147a, 230b, 336b, 338b, 428a, 505b, 621b, 622b, 623a, 625a, 626a, 640b, 659b, 660b, 665a, 669a, 676a, 677b, 774b; vii, 159b, 225b, 357a, 650a; x, 844b; s, 103b, 311a, b – I, 3a, 46a, 49a, 57a, 60a, **78b**, 123b, 146b, 153a, 330a, 466b, 496a, 567b, 613a, 732a, 1069b, 1178a, 1280a, 1332b, 1389a; II, 120a, 305b, 328b, 333b, 370a, 468b, 492a, 787a, 932b; III, 41b, 670a, 739a; IV, 681a, 962b; VI, 137b, 138a, 145b, 224b, 320b, 322b, 413a, 491a, 607a, b, 608a, 610a, 611a, 625b, 645a, 646b, 651a, 655a, 662b, 664a, 763b; VII, 161a, 227b, 359b, 649b; X, ;S, 103a, 310b, 311a, b
ʿAbd al-Malik b. Marwān, vizier (749) vii, 75a, 269b – VII, 76a, 271b
ʿAbd al-Malik b. Mughīth (VIII) i, 608b; ii, 485b; v, 1121a – I, 628a; II, 497b; V, 1117b
ʿAbd al-Malik b. al-Muhallab (VIII) vii, 359b – VII, 361b
ʿAbd al-Malik b. Muḥammad b. Djawhar (XI) ii, 389a – III, 399b
ʿAbd al-Malik b. Mundhir b. Saʿīd (979) vii, 570a – VII, 571a
ʿAbd al-Malik b. Mūsā b. Nuṣayr (720) i, **50a** – I, **51b**
ʿAbd al-Malik b. Nūḥ (Sāmānid(e)) (X) viii, 110a – VIII, 112b
ʿAbd al-Malik b. Sakardid (768) vi, 312a – VI, 297a
ʿAbd al-Malik b. Ṣāliḥ b. ʿAlī (811) i, **77b**, 761b; vi, 331a, 332a, 333b, 334a, 379a – I, **80a**, 784a; VI, 315b, 316b, 318a, b, 363b
ʿAbd al-Malik b. Shihāb al-Mismaʿī (780) vi, 640b – VI, 625b
ʿAbd al-Malik b. Yazīd (777) vi, 618a – VI, 602b
ʿAbd al-Malik b. Zaydān (Saʿdid(e)) (1631) vi, 594b – VI, 579b

ʿAbd al-Malik b. Zuhr → Ibn Zuhr
ʿAbd al-Malik Murād (XX) vi, 155a – VI, 152a
ʿAbd al-Malik al-Muẓaffar (1008) → ʿAbd al-Malik b. Abī ʿĀmir
ʿAbd al-Malik al-Muẓaffar (Afṭasid(e)) (1065) i, 6a, 242a. 446a, 985b, 1096a; ii, 1012a; iii, 674a – I, 6a, 249b, 459a, 1016b, 1129a; II, 1035b; III, 695b
ʿAbd Manāf, Banū i, 681a; iv, 320a; v, 435a, 581a; vi, 145a, 168b, 349a – I, 702a; IV, 334b; V, 436b, 586a; VI, 143b, 159b, 333a
ʿAbd al-Masīḥ (VI) vi, 726a; vii, 307b – VI, 715a; VII, 310a
ʿAbd al-Masīḥ b. ʿAmr → Ibn Buḳayla
ʿAbd al-Masīḥ b. Hāʿima al-Ḥimsī x, 228a – X, 246a
ʿAbd al-Matīn Khān (Dīr) (XX) ii, 317a – II, 326b
ʿAbd al-Muḥsin Saʿdūn (XX) vi, 616a; vii, 468b – VI, 601a; VII, 468b
ʿAbd al-Muʾmin b. ʿAbd Allāh Khān (Shaybānid(e)) (1589) i, 8a, 46b, 1001b; vi, 715a; s, 340b – I, 8a, 48a, 1032b; VI, 703b; S, 340a
ʿAbd al-Muʾmin b. Abi ʾl-Fayd (Djāhīd(e)) (1748) vi, 418b – VI, 403b
ʿAbd al-Muʾmin b. ʿAlī b. ʿAlwī (Almohad(e)) (1163) i, **78a**, 680a, 1044b, 1129b, 1148b, 1176a, 1205b; ii, 145b, 307b, 331b, 352b, 353a, 459a, 516a, 537a, 818b, 1009a; iii, 138b, 207b, 386b, 470b, 910a, 958b, 978b; iv, 415b, 479b, 827b, 943b; v, 61a, 379a, 626a, 1189b, 1245b; vi, 134a, 404a, 592a, 597a, 742b; vii, 247b, 585b, 802a; s, 113b, 376b – I, **80a**, 700b, 1076a, 1163b, 1183a, 1211a, 1241a; II, 149b, 316b, 341a, 362b, 471a, 529a, 550b, 838a, 1033a; III, 141b, 213a, 399a, 486b, 934a, 983a, 1003a; IV, 434a, 501a, 860b, 976b; V, 62b, 379b, 630a, 1179b, 1236a; VI, 132b, 388b, 577a, 581b, 732a; VII, 249a, 586a, 804a; S, 113a, 376b
ʿAbd al-Munʿim b. Idrīs (842) vii, 283b – VII, 285b
ʿAbd al-Munʿim Ayyūb II (Muḳaddam) (XV) i, 1280b – I, 1320a
ʿAbd al-Muṭṭalib, Sharīf (1856) vi, 151a – VI, 149b
ʿAbd al-Muṭṭalib b. Ghālib, Sharīf (1886) vi, 175a – VI, 162a
ʿAbd al-Muṭṭalib b. Hāshim (VII) i, 42b, **80a**, 115b, 136b, 851a; iii, 203b, 260a, 1093a; iv, 260a, 264a, 270b; vi, 168b – I, 43b, **82a**, 118b, 140b, 875a; III, 208b, 267b, 1120a; IV, 271b, 275b, 282b; VI, 159b
ʿAbd al-Muṭṭalib b. Riḍā al-Dīn (Marʿashī) (1400) vi, 512b – VI, 497b, 498a
ʿAbd al-Nabī (Mathurā) (1660) vi, 839a – VI, 829b
ʿAbd al-Nabī b. Aḥmad Sirhindī (1582) s, 313a – S, 312b
ʿAbd al-Nabī b. ʿAlī (XII) ii, 517a; v, 1244b, 1245a – II, 530a; V, 1235a, b
ʿAbd al-Nabī Fakhr al-Zamānī Ḳazwīnī (1619) vi, 834a; vii, 530a – VI, 824b; VII, 530b
ʿAbd al-Nāṣir, Djamāl (1970) ii, 649a, 674a; iii, 518a, 1069b, 1259a; iv, 125a, b, 719a, 781a, 783b; v, 1061b; vi, 24a; vii, 765a; viii, 247a, 717a; s, **5a**, 70a, 306a – II, 665a, 691a; III, 536a, 1096a, 1291b; IV, 130b, 131a, 748a, 812b, 815a; V, 1058b; VI, 22a; VII, 766b; VIII, 253a, 737b; S, **4a**, 70b, 305b
ʿAbd al-Nāṣir Ḥusayn → ʿAbd al-Nāṣir, Djamāl
ʿAbd Rabbih al-Kabīr (698) i, 810b; iv, 753a; vii, 357b – I, 834a; IV, 783b; VII, 359b
ʿAbd al-Raḥīm b. Aḥmad (Yemen) (IX) i, 402b – I, 414a
ʿAbd al-Raḥīm b. Aḥmad b. Ḥadjdjūn Ḳūnā (1196) v, 386b – V, 387b
ʿAbd al-Raḥīm b. ʿAlī → al-Ḳāḍī al-Fāḍil
ʿAbd al-Raḥīm b. Ilyās (X) ii, 857a; iii, 80a – II, 877a; III, 82b
ʿAbd al-Raḥīm b. Muḥammad → Ibn Nubāta
ʿAbd al-Raḥīm al-ʿAbbāsī (XVI) i, 1109b – I, 1143a
ʿAbd al-Raḥīm, Khān-i Khānān (1627) i, **80b**, 431a, 628a, 1136a, b, 1331a; ii, 597b; iii, 457b; iv, 1018a, 1127b; vi, 128a, 271b; vii, 129b, 328a, 331b, 332a, 343a, 458a, 478a, 938a, 1055a; ix, 396b – I, **82b**, 443b, 648b, 1170b, 1171a, 1371b; II, 612b; III, 473b; IV, 1050a, 1159a; VI, 126a, 256a; VII, 131b, 329a, 333a, b, 344b, 458a, 479b, 938b, 1057a; IX, 409b
ʿAbd al-Raḥīm al-Mutawakkil ʿalā ʾllāh (Karūkh) (IX) iv, 673a – IV, 700b
ʿAbd al-Raḥmān, Sharīf (Pontianak) (XVIII) s, 150b – S, 150b
ʿAbd al-Raḥmān I b. Muʿāwiya, al-Dākhil (Umayyad(e), al-Andalus) (788) i, **81b**, 86b, 493b, 497b, 618b, 1079b; ii, 1009a; iii, 12a, 702a; iv, 665b; v, 510b, 1160a, 1164b; vi, 221b, 428b, 520b, 568a; vii, 269a, 563b, 941b; x, 848a; s, 82a – I, **84a**, 89a, 508b, 512b, 637b, 1112a; II, 1032b; III, 12b, 724a; IV, 692b; V, 514a, 1149b, 1154b; VI, 215b, 413b, 505a, 53a; VII, 271a, 564a, 941b; X, ;S, 81b
ʿAbd al-Raḥmān II b. al-Ḥakam al-Mutawassiṭ (Umayyad(e), al-Andalus) (852) i, 11a, **82b**, 121b, 494a, 498a, 864b, 1012a, 1319b; ii, 515b, 1009a, 1038a; iii, 74a, 816a; iv, 672b, 822a; v, 510b, 1118b, 1119b; vi, 132a, 520b, 568a; vii, 275a, 633a ; x, 850a – I, 11a, **85a**, 125a, 509a, 513a, 888b, 1043a, 1360a; II, 528b, 1032b, 1062a; III, 76b, 839b; IV, 700a, 855a; V, 514a, 1115a, 1116b; VI, 130a, 505a, 553a; VII, 277a, 632b; X,
ʿAbd al-Raḥmān III al-Nāṣir (Umayyad(e), al-Andalus) (961) i, **83b**, 439b, 494a, 498a, 628b, 658a, 864b, 997a, 1012a, 1092a, 1150a, 1326a, 1343a; ii, 297b, 525a, 821b, 915b, 1009a; iii, 46a, 1042a; iv, 254b, 632b, 943a; v, 510b, 625b, 777b, 1008b; vi, 222a, 431b, 435a, 520b, 568a, 576a; vii, 45a, 248b, 486a, 569b, 641b; x, 849a, 851a; s, 80a, 153a – I, **85b**, 452a, 509a, 513a, 649a, 679a, 889a, 1027b, 1043a, 1124b, 1184b, 1366b, 1383b; II, 305b, 538a, 841a, 937a, 1032b; III, 48a, 1068a; IV, 265b, 657b, 976a; V, 514b, 629b, 783b, 1004a; VI, 215b, 417a, 420b, 505b, 553a, 561a; VII, 45a, 250a, 486a, 570a, 641a; X, , , S, 80a, 153a
ʿAbd al-Raḥmān IV al-Murtaḍā (Umayyad(e), al-Andalus) (1018) i, **84a**; ii, 1012b; iii, 147a, 496a, 791a; vi, 141b – I, **86b**; II, 1036a; III, 150b, 513a, 814b; VI, 139b
ʿAbd al-Raḥmān V al-Mustaẓhir (Umayyad(e)) (1024) i, **84a**; iii, 791a, 938b – I, **86b**; III, 814b, 963b
ʿAbd al-Raḥmān, Mawlāy → ʿAbd al-Raḥmān b. Hishām
ʿAbd al-Raḥmān b. ʿAbbās b. Rabīʿa Hāshimī (VII) iii, 716b, 717b – III, 739a, 740a
ʿAbd al-Raḥmān b. ʿAbd Allāh → Ibn ʿAbd al-Ḥakam, Abu ʾl-Ḳāsim
ʿAbd al-Raḥmān b. Abī ʿAlī (Marīnid(e)) (1353) vi, 593b – VI, 578b
ʿAbd al-Raḥmān b. Abī Bakr (VII) i, 109b, 110a, 145b; ii, 625b; s, 351b – I, 112b, 113a, 150a; II, 641a; S, 351b
ʿAbd al-Raḥmān b. Abī Ifellūsen (1374) vi, 593b, 594a – VI, 578b
ʿAbd al-Raḥmān b. Abī Nās Mandīl (XIII) vi, 404a – VI, 388b
ʿAbd al-Raḥmān b. Abī Nuʿaym al-Mulāʾī (IX) i, 143a – I, 147a
ʿAbd al-Raḥmān b. Aḥmad (822) vi, 337b – VI, 321b
ʿAbd al-Raḥmān b. ʿAlī → Ibn al-Daybaʿ
ʿAbd al-Raḥmān b. ʿAlī b. Bā Ḥassān (1415) iii, 270a – III, 278a

ʿAbd al-Raḥmān b. al-As̲h̲ʿat̲h̲ → Ibn al-As̲h̲ʿat̲h̲
ʿAbd al-Raḥmān b. ʿAwf al-Zuhrī (652) i, **84b**, 382a, 687a; ii, 366a, 625a, 846a; iii, 209b, 586b; iv, 521b; v, 110b; vi, 79a; vii, 254a, 364a; ix, 38a; s, 89b – I, **87a**, 393a, 708a; II, 376a, 640b, 865b; III, 215b, 607a; IV, 544a; V, 1106b; VI, 77a; VII, 255b, 366b; IX, 38b; S, 89b
ʿAbd al-Raḥmān b. al-Ḍaḥḥāk (VII) ii, 90a – II, 91b
ʿAbd al-Raḥmān b. D̲j̲abala (812) vi, 333b – VI, 318a
ʿAbd al-Raḥmān b. D̲j̲ābir b. ʿAbd Allāh (VIII) s, 231a – S, 230b
ʿAbd al-Raḥmān b. Fayṣal (Āl Suʿūd) (1889) iv, 925b; ix, 904a – IV, 958b; IX, 942a
ʿAbd al-Raḥmān b. Fayṣal b. ʿAbd al-ʿAzīz (Āl Suʿūd) (XX) s, 305b – S, 305b
ʿAbd al-Raḥmān b. Ḥabīb al-Fihrī (755) i, 81b, **86a**; iii, 654a; iv, 336b; viii, 688a; ix, 753b – I, 84a, **88b**; III, 675a; IV, 351a; VIII, 708a; IX, 786b
ʿAbd al-Raḥmān b. Ḥabīb al-Ṣiklabī (778) i, 86b – I, 89a
ʿAbd al-Raḥmān b. al-Ḥakam (VII) s, 10a – S, 9b
ʿAbd al-Raḥmān b. al-Ḥakam II al-Mustanṣir (969) ix, 740b – IX, 773a
ʿAbd al-Raḥmān b. al-Ḥārit̲h̲ b. His̲h̲ām al-Mak̲h̲zūmī (640) vi, 139a, 140b; viii, 853b – VI, 137a, 138b; VIII, 883a
ʿAbd al-Raḥmān b. Ḥassān b. T̲h̲ābit (722) s, **9b** – S, **9a**
ʿAbd al-Raḥmān b. His̲h̲ām, Mawlāy (ʿAlawid(e)) (1859) i, 67b, **84b**, 315b, 356b, 357a, 1224b, 1346b; ii, 117a, 160a, 173a, 510b, 823a; iii, 806a; iv, 634a; vi, 136a, 250b, 595b, 597a; vii, 39a, 391a – I, 69b, **87a**, 325a, 367b, 1261b, 1387a; II, 119b, 165a, 178a, 523a, 842b; III, 829b; IV, 660a; VI, 134a, 234b, 580a, 582a; VII, 39b, 392a
ʿAbd al-Raḥmān b. Ḥusayn Āl Saʿūd (XIX) iv, 1073a – IV, 1104b
ʿAbd al-Raḥmān b. ʿĪsā b. Dāʾūd (X) i, 387b; iv, 1094a – I, 398b; IV, 1125a
ʿAbd al-Raḥmān b. ʿĪsā al-Murs̲h̲idī i, 867b – I, 891b
ʿAbd al-Raḥmān b. Isḥāḳ b. Hayt̲h̲am i, 214a – I, 220b
ʿAbd al-Raḥmān b. Kaʿb al-Aṣamm (VII) i, 266b – I, 274b
ʿAbd al-Raḥmān b. al-Ḳāḍī vii, 622a – VII, 621b
ʿAbd al-Raḥmān b. al-Ḳāsim → Ibn al-Ḳāsim
ʿAbd al-Raḥmān b. Kaysān s, 88b, 90b – S, 88b, 90a
ʿAbd al-Raḥmān b. K̲h̲ālid b. al-Walīd b. al-Mug̲h̲īra (666) i, **85a**, 449b; iv, 928b; vi, 139a, b – I, **87b**, 462a; IV, 961b; VI, 137b, 138a
ʿAbd al-Raḥmān b. Mahdī al-Baṣrī (813) i, 272b; viii, 515a – I, 281a; VIII, 532b
ʿAbd al-Raḥmān b. Mahdī (Sudan/Soudan) v, 1252b – V, 1243b
ʿAbd al-Raḥmān b. al-Manṣūr b. Abī ʿĀmir (XI) vi, 842a – VI, 832b
ʿAbd al-Raḥmān b. Marwān b. Yūnus, Ibn al-D̲j̲illiḳī (889) i, **85b**, 494a, 1092a, 1339a; ii, 1009a; vi, 568a – I, **88a**, 509a, 1124b, 1379a; II, 1032b; VI, 553a
ʿAbd al-Raḥmān b. Mis̲h̲kam al-K̲h̲awlānī (VII) iv, 1135a – IV, 1166b
ʿAbd al-Raḥmān b. Muʿāwiya → ʿAbd al-Raḥmān I
ʿAbd al-Raḥmān b. Muḥammad b. Abī ʿĀmir (Sanchuelo) (1009) i, 76a, **84a**, 446a, 494b; iii, 495b, 739b, 746b, 819a; v, 743b, 1239a, b; x, 853a – I, 78a, **86b**, 459a, 509b; III, 512b, 762b, 769b, 842b; V, 749a, 1230a; X,
ʿAbd al-Raḥmān b. Muḥammad b. ʿAlī al-Barḳī (VIII) s, 127a – S, 126b
ʿAbd al-Raḥmān b. Muḥammad b. Murshid (Munḳid̲h̲, Banū) (1204) vii, 579b – VII, 580a
ʿAbd al-Raḥmān b. Muslim (VIII) viii, 67a – VIII, 68b
ʿAbd al-Raḥmān b. Muṣṭafā al-ʿAydarūsī i, 280b, 782a – I, 289b, 805a
ʿAbd al-Raḥmān b. Nāṣir (Safi) (XVIII) s, 401b – S, 402a
ʿAbd al-Raḥmān b. Rabīʿa → al-Bāhilī
ʿAbd al-Raḥmān b. Rustam b. Bahrām (768) i, 125a, 134b, 1175b; iii, 297a, 654a, b, 655a, 1041b; iv, 827a; v, 696a; vi, 312a; viii, 638a – I, 128b, 138a, 1210b; III, 306b, 675b, 676a, 1067b; IV, 860a; V, 701a; VI, 297a; VIII, 657a
ʿAbd al-Raḥmān b. Samura (670) i, 47b, **86a**, 1001a, 1344a; iv, 14b, 356b; v, 57a; viii, 595b; ix, 682b – I, 49a, **88a**, 1031b, 1384b; IV,15b, 16a, 372a; VIII, 614b; IX, 711a
ʿAbd al-Raḥmān b. S̲h̲ās̲h̲ū (XVII) vii, 470a – VII, 469b
ʿAbd al-Raḥmān b. Sulaymān al-Ahdal (1835) i, 255b, 782a – I, 263b, 805a
ʿAbd al-Raḥmān b. ʿUdays al-Balawī (VII) v, 318b – V, 318a
ʿAbd al-Raḥmān b. Umm al-Ḥakam (al-Kūfa) (VII) iii, 970a; vii, 269b – III, 994b; VII, 271b
ʿAbd al-Raḥmān b. ʿUtba al-Fihrī (685) vi, 622a, 742b – VI, 607a, 731b
ʿAbd al-Raḥmān b. Yazīd b. al-Muhallab (VII) vii, 359b – VII, 362a
ʿAbd al-Raḥmān ʿAbdī Pas̲h̲a → ʿAbdī Pas̲h̲a
ʿAbd al-Raḥmān al-ʿAmr (Dūra) (XIX) iv, 961a – IV, 993a
ʿAbd al-Raḥmān ʿAzzām Pas̲h̲a (XX) s, 240b – S, 240b
ʿAbd al-Raḥmān al-Barḳūḳī (XX) vi, 955b – VI, 948a
ʿAbd al-Raḥmān al-Fāsī → al-Fāsī, ʿAbd al-Raḥmān
ʿAbd al-Raḥmān al-G̲h̲āfiḳī (732) i, **86b**, 493a, 988b – I, **89a**, 508a, 1019a
ʿAbd al-Raḥmān G̲h̲āzī (XI) s, 280a – S, 280a
ʿAbd al-Raḥmān Harawī, Mīrzā (XIX) ii, 433b – II, 445a
ʿAbd al-Raḥmān Ismāʿīl (XX) vii, 903a – VII, 903b
ʿAbd al-Raḥmān Kahyā → ʿAbd al-Raḥman Katk̲h̲udā
ʿAbd al-Raḥmān Ḳaramānī, S̲h̲ayk̲h̲ (XVI) i, 1235a – I, 1272a
ʿAbd al-Raḥmān Katk̲h̲udā (Kiḥya) (1776) i, 815a; iv, 438a, 439b, 852b, 853a – I, 838a; IV, 457b, 459a, 885b, 886a
ʿAbd al-Raḥmān K̲h̲ān (Bārakzay) (1901) i, **87a**, 223b, 224b, 232a, 796b; ii, 1001b; iv, 411a; v, 1079a; vi, 765b, 807a; s, 237b, 368a – I, **89b**, 230a, 231a, 239a, 820a; II, 1024b; IV, 429a; V, 1076b; VI, 754b, 797a; S, 237b, 367b
ʿAbd al-Raḥmān K̲h̲ān (Nog̲h̲ay) (1538) i, 721b – I, 743b
ʿAbd al-Raḥmān Maẓhar, S̲h̲ayk̲h̲ (XX) vi, 171b
ʿAbd al-Raḥmān Mus̲h̲fiḳī → Mus̲h̲fiḳī
ʿAbd al-Raḥmān al-Nad̲j̲ūmī (XIX) i, 49b, 765a; v, 1250a, b – I, 51a, 788a; V, 1241a
ʿAbd al-Raḥmān al-Nāṣir → ʿAbd al-Raḥmān III
ʿAbd al-Raḥmān Pas̲h̲a (1684) i, 905a, 1284b – I, 932a, 1324a
ʿAbd al-Raḥmān Pas̲h̲a Bābān (1812) i, 845a – I, 868b
ʿAbd al-Raḥmān al-Ras̲h̲īd (Dār Fūr) (1800) ii, 123a – II, 126a
ʿAbd al-Raḥmān Rus̲h̲dī Pas̲h̲ā, Būlāḳ (XIX) i, 1299b – I, 1339b
ʿAbd al-Raḥmān Sanchuelo → ʿAbd al-Raḥmān b. Muḥammad b. Abī ʿĀmir
ʿAbd al-Raḥmān S̲h̲eref (XX) i, 1089b; iv, 297b; vi, 94a – I, 1122a; IV, 310b; VI, 92a
ʿAbd al-Raḥmān al-Ṣūfī (986) i, **86b**; ii, 300a; vi, 374b, 600b; s, 251a – I, **89a**; II, 308a; VI, 359a, 585a; S, 251a
ʿAbd al-Raḥmān al-Sūr (Ṣaydā) (XIX) i, 63b – I, 65b
ʿAbd al-Ras̲h̲īd b. Maḥmūd (G̲h̲aznawid(e)) (1051) i,

1130b, 1344b; ii, 1052a – I, 1165a, 1385a; II, 1076a
ʿAbd al-Rashīd b. Ṣāliḥ al-Bākuwī (XV) i, 967a – I, 997a
ʿAbd al-Rashīd Daylamī (XVII) iv, 1128a – IV, 1159b
ʿAbd al-Rashīd Khān Sulṭānī (Dihlī) (XIV) ii, 622b; iii, 317a; vi, 49a – II, 638a; III, 326b; VI, 47b
ʿAbd al-Rashīd al-Tattawī (1658) i, **88a**, iv, 526a – I, **90b**, 549a
ʿAbd al-Raʾūf al-Sinkilī (1693) i, **88a**, 742a; iii, 1220a, 1233b; v, 433a, 525b; vi, 235b – I, **90b**, 764a; III, 1251a, 1265b; V, 435b, 529b; VI, 208a
ʿAbd al-Rāziḳ, ʿAlī (XX) iii, 1168b; iv, 161a, 906b, 947a; s, 121b – III, 1197b; IV, 168a, 939b, 980a; S, 121a
ʿAbd al-Rāziḳ, Muṣṭafā (1947) i, 820a – I, 843a
ʿAbd al-Razzāḳ, vizier (XI) i, 1192a – I, 1227a
ʿAbd al-Razzāḳ (Ṣufrī) (IX) iii, 1036a – III, 1062a
ʿAbd al-Razzāḳ (Sabtawār) (1338) ix, 47b – IX, 48b
ʿAbd al-Razzāk, Abū Manṣūr Muḥammad (Ṭūs) (X) ii, 918b; x, 741b – II, 940a; X,
ʿAbd al- Razzāk. Shihåb al-Islām (vizier) (1122) ix, 16b – IX, 17a
ʿAbd al-Razzāḳ b. ʿAbd al-Ḳādir (1206) iv, 380b, 381a – IV, 397a, b
ʿAbd al-Razzāḳ b. Ḥammām al-Ṣanʿānī (827) → al-Ṣanʿānī
ʿAbd al-Razzāḳ b. Ḥasanwayh (X) iii, 258a – III, 265a
ʿAbd al-Razzāḳ (Bānsa) Sayyid (1724) vi, 354b; viii, 69a; s, 292b, 293a – VI, 339a; VIII, 70b; S, 292b, 293a
ʿAbd al-Razzāḳ Karabaka (XX) vi, 751a – VI, 740b
ʿAbd al-Razzāḳ al-Ḳāshānī (al-Ḳāshī) (1329) i, 88b, 347a, 351a; vi, 638a – I, 91a, 357b, 362a; VI, 623a
ʿAbd al-Razzāḳ al-Lāhidjī → Lāhidjī
ʿAbd al-Razzāḳ al-Samarḳandī (1482) i, **90b**; iii, 58a; s, 51a – I, **93b**; III, 60b; S, 51b
ʿAbd al-Razzāḳ al-Sanhūrī (XX) vi, 24a, 37a – VI, 22a, 35a
ʿAbd al-Reshīd ʿIṣmet Allāh (X) s, 82a – S, 82a
ʿAbd al-Saʿid Mir ʿĀlim → Mir ʿĀlim
ʿAbd al-Salām (Sokoto) (XIX) vii, 435b – VII, 436b
ʿAbd al-Salām II, Shaykh (1915) i, 1072a – I, 1104a
ʿAbd al-Salām, al-Ḥādjdj (XIX) iii, 395b – III, 408a
ʿAbd al-Salām b. Aḥmad → Ibn Ghānim
ʿAbd al-Salām b. Mashīsh al-Ḥasanī (1227) i, **91a**, 353a; v, 1201a; vi, 249b, 280a, 355a, 356a; s, 350b – I. **94a**, 363b; V, 1191b; VI, 234a, 264b, 339a, 340b; S, 350b
ʿAbd al-Salām ʿĀrif → ʿĀrif, ʿAbd al-Salām
ʿAbd al-Salām al-Ḳādirī (1698) vi, 356b – VI, 340b
ʿAbd al-Salām Khundjī, Shaykh (1345) v, 671a – V, 676b
ʿAbd al-Salām ʿUmar (XX) vi, 177b – VI, 163a
ʿAbd al-Salām Yazbak ʿAmād (XVIII) ii, 444a – II, 455b
ʿAbd al-Ṣamad b. al-Muʿadhdhal → Ibn al-Muʿadhdhal
ʿAbd al-Ṣamad Ibn Khazar (XII) v, 1179b – V, 1169b
ʿAbd al-Ṣamad al-Palimbānī (1776) i, **92a**; ii, 183a; iii, 1233b; vi, 235b; viii, 245a – I, **94b**; II, 189a; III, 1265b; VI, 208a; VIII, 251a
ʿAbd al-Ṣamad Zayn al-Dīn (1634) vi, 354b – VI, 338b
ʿAbd al-Sattār al-Bāsil (XX) vi, 219b – VI, 213b
ʿAbd Shams, Banū i, 9a, 55b, 136b, 151a; v, 435a; vi, 137b, 138a, 145a, 560a, 565b; x, 841a; s, 103b – I, 9a, 57a, 140b, 155a; V, 437a; VI, 135b, 136b, 143a, 544b, 550b; X, ; S, 102b
ʿAbd al-ʿUzza → ʿAbd al-Raḥmān b. Abī Bakr; Abū Lahab b. ʿAbd al-Muṭṭalib
ʿAbd al-Wādid(e)s (Banū ʿAbd al-Wād) i, **92a**, 129b, 168a, 367a, 1176b, 1205b; iii, 67b, 68b, 499a, 832a, 833b; v, 531a, 1180a, b, 1190a; vi, 142a, 404a, b, 405a, 440b, 441a, 572b, 728b; vii, 263a, 1022a; viii, 723b; s, 113a, 144b, 376b – I, **95a**, 133b, 172b, 378a, 1211b, 1241b; III, 70a, 71a, 516a, 855b, 857b; V, 535a, 1170a, b, 1180a; VI, 140a, 388b, 389a, b, 426a, b, 557b, 717b; VII, 265a, 1024a; VIII, 744a; S, 112b, 144b, 377a
ʿAbd al-Wahhāb (ḳāḍī) (1030) vi, 279a – VI, 264a
ʿAbd al-Wahhāb, Mawlānā (1903) s, 360b – S, 360b
ʿAbd al-Wahhāb, Muḥammad b. Ḥasanayn al-Ḥiṣāfī (1949) s, 371a – S, 371a
ʿAbd al-Wahhāb b. ʿAbd al-Raḥmān b. Rustum (ʿIbāḍī Imām) (811) i, 250a; ii, 441b; iii, 297b, 651a, 655a, 1041b; iv, 415b, 919b; vi, 840b, 946a; viii, 112b – I, 256a; II, 453a; III, 307a, 672a, 676a, 1067b; IV, 433b, 952b; VI, 831a, 938b; VIII, 115a
ʿAbd al-Wahhāb b. Abi ʾl-Faradj (1141) iii, 161a – III, 164b
ʿAbd al-Wahhāb b. Aḥmad, Nāʾib al-Ḥaram (XX) vi, 157a, 166a – VI, 153a, 158a
ʿAbd al-Wahhāb b. Bukht (731) i, 1103a, b; ii, 234b, 236a – I, 1136a, b; II, 241b, 242b
ʿAbd al-Wahhāb b. Dāwūd (Ṭāhirid(e)) (XV) i, 181b; vii, 996a – I, 186b; VII, 997b
ʿAbd al-Wahhāb b. Dhu ʾl-Himma ii, 234b – II, 241b
ʿAbd al-Wahhāb b. Faḍl Allāh (1317) ii, 732a – II, 750b
ʿAbd al-Wahhāb b. Ibrāhīm b. Muḥammad (750) vi, 230b – VI, 224b
ʿAbd al-Wahhāb b. Makkī (XIII) iv, 338a – IV, 352b
ʿAbd al-Wahhāb b. Muḥammad b. Ghālib b. Numayr al-Anṣārī (XII) s, 15b – S, 15b
ʿAbd al-Wahhāb b. Yūsuf al-Tudjībī (1968) s, **11a** – S, **10b**
ʿAbd al-Wahhāb Āshī (XX) vi, 176b, 177b – VI, 162b
ʿAbd al-Wahhāb Bukhārī, Shaykh (1525) s, **10b** – S, **10a**
ʿAbd al-Wahhāb al-Hamadānī (1540) i, 234a – I, 241a
ʿAbd al-Wahhāb al-Ḳazzāz (XX) vi, 165b – VI, 158a
ʿAbd al-Wahhāb al-Makkī iv, 338a – IV, 352b
ʿAbd al-Wahhāb al-Subkī → al-Subkī, Tādj al-Dīn
ʿAbd al-Wahhāb al-Sumādiḥī al-Tudjībī (1968) s, **11a** – S, **10b**
ʿAbd al-Wāḥid II al-Rashīd (Almohad(e)) (1241) iii, 338a, 705a, 921b, 1055a; v, 48b; s, 389a – III, 348a, 727a, 946a, 1081b; V, 50a; S, 389b
ʿAbd al-Wāḥid b. Ayman (VII) s, 357b – S, 357b
ʿAbd al-Wāḥid b. al-Muḳtadir bi-ʾllāh (X) vii, 414a – VII, 415b
ʿAbd al-Waḥīd b. al-Muwaffaḳ vii, 543a – VII, 543a
ʿAbd al-Wāḥid b. Sulaymān b. ʿAbd al-Malik (VIII) iii, 878a; v, 1156a – III, 902a; V, 1145b
ʿAbd al-Wāḥid b. Yazīd al-Hawwārī (VIII) iii, 169b, 297b, 1040b – III, 173a, 306b, 1066b
ʿAbd al-Wāḥid b. Zayd (793) viii, 354b – VIII, 367a
ʿAbd al-Wāḥid b. Ziyād b. al-Muhallab (VIII) vii, 359b – VII, 362a
ʿAbd al-Wāḥid al-Hāshimī (VII) s, 400b – S, 401a
ʿAbd al-Wāḥid al-Liḥyānī → Abu Darba al-Liḥyānī
ʿAbd al-Wāḥid al-Marrākushī (XIII) i, **94a**, 389b, ii, 72a; v, 1160b; s, 388a – I, **97a**, 400b; II, 73b; V, 1150a; S, 388b
ʿAbd al-Wāsiʿ Djabalī b.ʿAbd al-Djāmiʿ (1160) i, **94b**; viii, 971a – I, **97a**; VIII, 1005a
ʿAbd al-Wāsiʿ al-Niẓāmī i, 91a – I, 93b
ʿAbd Yaghūth b. Ṣalāt iii, 223a – III, 230a
ʿAbd al-Ẓāhir, Banū ii, 305b – II, 314a
ʿAbda, Banū vi, 595a, 741b – VI, 580a, 730b

ʿAbda b. al-Ṭabīb (VII) iv, 833a, 998b; vii, 308a – IV, 866a, 1031a; VII, 310b
Abdāl i, **94b**; s, 168b – I, **97b**; S, 169a
Abdāl, Shaykh → Bābā Walī
Abdāl Mūsā (XIV) iv, 811b – IV, 844b
Abdālān-i Rūm i, 1162a; iv, 473b – I, 1196b; IV, 494b
Abdālī (Durrānī), Banū i, 72b, **95a**, 229a, b, 295a; ii, 628b; iii, 177b, 604a; iv, 537b; vi, 714a; vii, 853a; viii, 771a – I, 74b, 97b, **98a**, 235b, 236a, 304b; II, 644b, III, 182a, 624b; IV, 560b; VI, 703b; VII, 854b; VIII, 797a
ʿAbdalī, ʿAbdiliyyūn (Laḥdj) i, **95b**, 345a – I, **98a**, 355b
ʿAbdallāb ii, 351b, 944a; iv, 892b – II, 361a, 965b; IV, 925b
ʿAbdallah → ʿAbd Allāh
ʿAbdallāhi → ʿAbdullāhi
ʿAbdān (Ḳarmaṭī) (IX) i, **95b**; ii, 851a; iii, 123b; iv, 198a, b, 660b; vi, 438b; viii, 922a – I, **98b**; II, 871a, III, 126a; IV, 206b, 207a, 687a; VI, 424a; VIII, 953b
al-ʿAbdarī, Abū ʿAbd Allāh b. al-Ḥādjdj → Ibn al-Ḥādjdj
al-ʿAbdarī, al-Ḥasan b. Muḥammad al-Iskandarī al-Kūshī viii, 51b – VIII,52b
al-ʿAbdarī, Muḥammad b. Muḥammad (XIV) i, **96a**, 602b; iii, 736b; vii, 186a – I, **98b**, 622a; III, 759a; VII, 186b
Ābdast → Wuḍūʾ
Abdelkader → ʿAbd al-Ḳādir b. Muḥyī al-Dīn al-Ḥasanī
Abderrahmane El-Mejdoub (XVI) vi, 254b – VI, 238b
ʿAbdī (XVII) i, **96b** – I, **99b**
al-ʿAbdī → Abu ʾl-Hudhayl; Djaʿfar b. al-Sammāk; al-Walīd
al-ʿAbdī, Abū Muḥammad vi, 633a – VI, 618a
ʿAbdī, Mawlawī ʿAbd Allāh (1664) v, 611a; viii, 256a – V, 615a; VIII, 258b
ʿAbdī Beg Nawīdī (1580) viii, 775b – VIII, 801b
ʿAbdī Čelebi Čiwi-zāde (1552) ii, 56b – II, 57b
ʿAbdī Efendi (XVIII) i, **97a** – I, **99b**
Abdī Ipekçi (XX) vi, 95b – VI, 93b
ʿAbdī Pasha (1692) i, **97a**; iv, 438a, 569a; vi, 990b – I, **99b**; IV, 457b, 591b; VI, 983b
ʿAbdillāh, Banū → Muṭayr, Banū
ʿAbdīn (palace) s, 301a – S, 300b
Abdjad i, **97a** – I, **100a**
Abdjar b. Djābir (641) i, 964a – I, 993b
ʿAbdūh al-Ḥamūlī(1901) vi, 103a; x, 144a – VI, 101a; X, 154b
Abdul Ghafoor, P.K. (XX) vi, 461a – VI, 446b
ʿAbdülḥaḳḳ Ḥāmid Tarhan (XIX) vi, 610a – VI, 595a
Abdul Kadiri (Gwandu) (XVIII) ii, 1146a – II, 1173b
Abdullah → ʿAbd Allāh
Abdullah bin Abdul Kadir Munshi → Munshi Abdullah
Abdullah Awlaniy (1934) vi, 769a, b – VI, 758a, b
Abdullah Badriy vi, 769b – VI, 758b
Abdullah Cevdet → Djewdet, ʿAbd Allāh
Abdullahi dan Fodio → ʿAbd Allāh b. Muḥammad Fūdī
Abdullah Haron, Imām (1995) ix, 731a – IX, 763a
Abdullah Kadi Abdus Salaam, Imām (1807) ix, 730b – IX, 762b
Abdullah Ḳadiriy (1839) vi, 767a, 769b – VI, 756b, 758b
Abdullahi Sikka (XVII) iv, 550a – IV, 574a
ʿAbdullāhi al-Taʿāʾishī → ʿAbd Allāh b. Muḥammad al-Taʿāʾishī
Abdullay Ba Demba (Fūta Djallon) (XVIII) ii, 960a, 1132b – II, 982a, 1159a
Abdur Ghafur Breshna (1974) vi, 768a – VI, 757a
Abdurähim Tiläsh Ötkür (XX) vi, 768a – VI,757b
Abdurrahiman Bafaki Tangal, Syed (1973) vi, 460a – VI, 446a
Abdurrauf Abdurahim-oghlî Fiṭrat (1937) vi, 767b – VI, 757a
Abdurrauf Shahidi (Shashudilin) vi, 767a – VI, 756b
Abéché → Abeshr
Ābeh → Āwa
Abel → Hābīl
Abencerages → Ibn al-Sarrādj
Abenguefith → Ibn Wāfid
Abenragel → Ibn Abi ʾl-Ridjāl
Abeshr (Abeche) i, **98a**; s, 164a, 165b – I, **100b**; S, 164a, 165b
Abhā i, **98a**, 707b, 709b; vi, 192a – I, **101a**, 729a, 731a; VI, 176a
Abhar i, **98b**; s, 22a – I, **101b**; S, 22b
al-Abharī (985) vi, 279a, 280b – VI, 264a, 265b
al-Abharī, Athīr al-Dīn Mufaḍḍal b. ʿUmar (1264) i, **98b**, 321a; ii, 949a; iii, 805a; iv, 92a; s, 414a – I, **101b**, 331a; II, 970b; III, 828b; IV, 96a; S, 414b
Abhay Singh (XVIII) i, 1053a; iii, 1010b – I, 1084b; III, 1035b
al-Ābī (1030) ii, 590b; vi, 820b; viii, 595a – II, 605a; VI, 811a; VIII, 614a
Abi ʾl-ʿĀfiya, Banū ii, 979a – II, 1001a
Abi ʾl-Ḥasan, Banū → Kalbid(e)s
Āb-i Istāda (lake/lac) s, 329b – S, 329a
Āb-i Mashhad → Kashaf Rūd
Abi ʾl-Shawārib, Banū iii, 691a; s, 386a – III, 713a; S, 386b
Abīb → Taʾrīkh
ʿAbīd → ʿAbd; Makhzan
ʿĀbid, Banū (Meknes) iv, 416a; v, 379a; vi, 595a – IV, 434a; V, 379b; VI, 580a
ʿAbīd b. al-Abraṣ (VI) i, **99a**, 1241b; iii, 1177b; vii, 254b; s, 272b – I, **101b**, 1279a; III, 1206b; VII, 256b; S, 272a
ʿAbīd b. ʿAlī (970) vi, 193a – VI, 177a
ʿAbīd b. Sharya → Ibn Sharya
ʿAbīd al-Bukhārī (Morocco/Maroc) i, 47a, 356a; v, 1191b, 1192a; vi, 891b – I, 48b, 367a; V, 1181b, 1182a; VI, 883a
ʿAbīd al-Mutaʿāl b. ʿAbd al-Mutaʿāl (1881) vi, 627a – VI, 612a
ʿAbīda, Banū vi, 566a – VI, 551a
ʿAbīda b. Hilāl (698) i, 811a; iv, 753a; v, 378a – I, 834a; IV, 783b; V, 379a
ʿĀbidīn Pasha (1908) iii, 1117a; s, 63a – III, 1144b; S, 63b
ʿAbidin Tadia Tjoessoep (South Africa/Afrique du Sud) (1699) ix, 730b – 762b
ʿĀbidiyya iv, 668a – IV, 695b
Abidjan ii, 63a – II, 64a
Ābiḳ → ʿAbd
Ābinūs → Abanūs
Ābish Khātūn (1263) ii, 812a; iv, 975b, 1046b, 1047a; vi, 482a – II, 831a; IV, 1008a, 1078a, b; VI, 468a
Abīward (Bāward) i, **99b** – I, **102a**
al-Abīwardī, Abu ʾl-Muẓaffar Muḥammad (1113) i, **100a**; s, 326b – I, **102b**; S, 326a
Abkarib Asʿad → Asʿad Kāmil
Abkarius → Iskandar Agha
Abḳayḳ (Buḳayḳ) i, **100a** – I, **103a**
Abkhāz i, **100b**, 1189b; iv, 351a; v, 488a, b, 496a – I, **103a**, 1224b; IV, 366a; V, 490b, 491b, 499a
ʿAbla i, 518b, 521b – I, 534a, 537a
al-Ablaḳ → Samawʾal
al-Ablaḳ al-Asadī i, 659b – I, 680b
al-Abnāʾ i, **102a**; v, 1111a; s, 115b, 116a – I, **104b**; V, 1107a; S, 115a, b

Abnāʾ al-Atrāk i, 102a – I, 105a
Abnāʾ al-dawla i, 102a; v, 57b – I, 105a; V, 59a
Abnūs → Abanūs
Abomey ii, 93b, 94a – II, 95b, 96a
Abou Chabakeh, Elias → Abū Shabaka, Ilyās
Aboukir → Abūḳīr
ʿAbr Muḥarram vi, 438b – VI, 424a
Abraha (VI) i, **102a**, 144b, 549a; ii, 895a; iv, 318b; vi, 145b, 358b, 561b, 563b; ix, 817b – I, **105a**, 149a, 566a; II, 916a; IV, 332b; VI, 143b, 342b, 546a, 548b; IX, 852b
Abraham → Ibrāhīm al-Khalīl
Abraham ben Ezra (1168) vii, 568a – VII, 569a
Abrash al-Kalbī (745) iii, 494b; vi, 624a – III, 511b; VI, 609a
al-ʿAbrī, Mādjid b. Khāmis (ʿUmān) (1927) viii, 993b – VIII, 1028a
ʿAbs, Banū i, 518b, 521b; ii, 71b, 873b, 1023a; iv, 1144a; s, 177a – I, 534a, 537a; II, 73a, 893b, 1046b; IV, 1175b; S, 178a
ʿAbsīs, Banū vi, 649a – VI, 634b
al-Abshīhī → al-Ibshīhī
al-Abṭaḥ (al-Muʿābada) vi, 154a, b – VI, 152a
Abtariyya iii, 244a; s, 129b – III, 251a; S, 129a
Abū → Kunya
Abu ʾl-ʿAbbās, amīr → Aḥmad II (Ḥafṣid(e))
Abu ʾl-ʿAbbās b. Abī Sālim (1374) vi, 593b, 594a – VI, 578b
Abu ʾl-ʿAbbās b. Wāsil (1006) s, 119a – S, 118b
Abu ʾl-ʿAbbās ʿAbd Allāh → ʿAbd Allāh I (Aghlabid(e))
Abu ʾl-ʿAbbās Aḥmad (Ḥafṣid(e)) → Aḥmad I, II
Abu ʾl-ʿAbbās Aḥmad (Marīnid(e)) (XIV) i, 167b; iii, 836a – I, 172b; III, 860a
Abu ʾl-ʿAbbās Aḥmad (Sharīf, Ceuta) s, 112b – S, 112a
Abu ʾl-ʿAbbās Aḥmad b. ʿAbd Allāh → Abū Maḥallī al-Sidjilmāsī
Abu ʾl-ʿAbbās Aḥmad b. al-ʿArūs → Ibn ʿArūs
Abu ʾl-ʿAbbās al-Aʿmā → al-Aʿmā al-Tuṭīlī
Abu ʾl-ʿAbbās al-Īrānshahrī i, 1031b – I, 1063a
Abu ʾl-ʿAbbās al-Ḳaṣṣāb (XI) i, 146a; iv, 1057b – I, 150b; IV, 1089a
Abu ʾl-ʿAbbās al-Maghribī (XII) ii, 528a – II, 541a
Abu ʾl-ʿAbbās Maʾmūn b. Maʾmūn (Khʷārazmshāh) (1017) vi, 726b – VI, 715b
Abu ʾl-ʿAbbās Muḥammad b. al-Aghlab → Muḥammad I (Aghlabid(e))
Abu ʾl-ʿAbbās al-Nabātī (XIII) i, 214b; iii, 737a; s, 114b – I, 220b; III, 759b; S, 114a
Abu ʾl-ʿAbbās Rabindjānī (942) vi, 608b – VI, 593a
Abu ʾl-ʿAbbās al-Saffāḥ (ʿAbbāsid(e)) (754) i, 12b, 16a, 17a, 42b, 43a, 45b, **103a**, 107b, 116b, 149a, 485a, 895a, 1033b; ii, 178a, 324a; iii, 265b, 988b; iv, 446b, 729a; v, 1233a; vi, 139b, 262b, 334b, 345a, 427b, 428a; vii, 396a; s, 31b, 198b – I, 12b, 16b, 17b, 43b, 44a, 46b, **106a**, 110b, 120a, 153a, 499b, 922a, 1065a; II, 183b, 333b; III, 273a, 1013a; IV, 466b, 758a; V, 1223b; VI, 137b, 247a, 319a, 329a, 412b, 413b; VII, 397a; S, 31b, 198b
Abu ʾl-ʿAbbās Ṣuʿlūk (X) s, 356b – S, 356a
Abu ʾl-ʿAbbās al-Ṭabīkhī (963) vii, 694b – VII, 695a
Abū ʿAbd al-ʿĀl → Aḥmad al-Badawī
Abū ʿAbd Allāh → Djaʿfar al-Ṣādiḳ
Abū ʿAbd Allāh b. al-Djannān (kātib) (XIII) viii, 573b – VIII, 592a
Abū ʿAbd Allāh b. Djarāda (XI) iii, 730b, 766a; s, 30a – III, 753b, 789a; S, 30a
Abū ʿAbd Allāh b. Mandah → Ibn Manda
Abū ʿAbd Allāh b. Mardanīsh (Martinez) (1185) vi, 339b – VI, 323b
Abū ʿAbd Allāh b. Muʿādh → Ibn Muʿādh
Abū ʿAbd Allāh b. Muḥsin al-Bashīr (XII) iii, 207b – III, 213a
Abū ʿAbd Allāh al-Andalusī (X) vi, 727b – VI, 716b
Abū ʿAbd Allāh Aṣbagh b. al-Faradj al-Faḳīh vii, 400b – VII, 401b
Abū ʿAbd Allāh al-Baṣrī al-Djuʿal (980) iii, 832a,b; vii, 312a; s, **12b** – III, 856a; VII, 314b; S, **13a**
Abū ʿAbd Allāh al-Dāmaghānī (XI) s, 29b – S, 29b
Abū ʿAbd Allāh al-Djayhānī → al-Djayhānī
Abū ʿAbd Allāh Ḥusayn (X) iii, 128b – III, 131b
Abū ʿAbd Allāh al-Ḥuṣrī (XI) i, 146a – I, 150a
Abū ʿAbd Allāh al-Māhānī → al-Māhānī
Abū ʿAbd Allāh al-Mahdī li-Dīn Allāh (X) s, 363a, b – S, 363a
Abū ʿAbd Allāh Muḥammad (amīr) iii, 68b, 826a,b – III, 10b, 850a
Abū ʿAbd Allāh Muḥammad I → al-Mustanṣir
Abū ʿAbd Allāh Muḥammad II → Abū ʿAṣīda
Abū ʿAbd Allāh Muḥammad III → al-Mustanṣir
Abū ʿAbd Allāh Muḥammad V (Ḥafṣid(e)) (1526) i, 678a; iii, 69a; iv, 1156a – I, 698b; III, 71b; IV, 1188a
Abū ʿAbd Allāh Muḥammad b. al-ʿAbbās (1513) s, 403a – S, 403b
Abū ʿAbd Allāh Muḥammad b. Abi ʾl-ʿUmar Ibn ʿAbd al-Barr (XII) ix, 309b – IX, 318a
Abū ʿAbd Allāh Muḥammad b. Aḥmad Djayhānī (IX) iv, 22a – IV, 24a
Abū ʿAbd Allāh Muḥammad b. ʿAlī al-ʿAlawī, Sayyid s, 19a, 401a – S, 19a, 401b
Abū ʿAbd Allāh Muḥammad b. ʿAnbasa (X) i, 159a – I, 163b
Abū ʿAbd Allāh Muḥammad b. Bakr al-Nafūsī, Shaykh (1048) ii, 141a; iii, 95b; vi, 948a – II, 145a; III, 98a; VI, 940b
Abū ʿAbd Allāh Muḥammad b. Ḥamawiya al-Djuwaynī (1135) i, 765b – I, 788b
Abū ʿAbd Allāh Muḥammad b. al-Ḥasan (970) s, 13a, b – S, 13a, b
Abū ʿAbd Allāh Muḥammad b. al-Ḥasan (Tripoli) (1022) vii, 482a, b – VII, 482a, b
Abū ʿAbd Allāh Muḥammad b. Ibrāhīm b. al-Sarrādj → Ibn al-Sarrādj
Abū ʿAbd Allāh Muḥammad b. Khālid al-Barkī (IX) s, 127b – S, 126b
Abū ʿAbd Allāh Muḥammad b. Muḥammad b. Yūsuf al-Sarrādj → Ibn al-Sarrādj
Abū ʿAbd Allāh Muḥammad Ādarrāḳ (1658) s, 40a – S, 40b
Abū ʿAbd Allāh Muḥammad al-Andalusī (1573) i, 56a – I, 57b
Abū ʿAbd Allāh Muḥammad al-Fāsī → Ibn al-Ḥādjdj
Abū ʿAbd Allāh Muḥammad al-Gharnāṭī → Ibn al-Sarrādj
Abū ʿAbd Allāh Muḥammad al-Ḥādjdj (Dilāʾī) (1729) s, 223b – S, 224a
Abū ʿAbd Allāh Muḥammad al-Ḥasan → al-Ḥasan
Abū ʿAbd Allāh Muḥammad al-Hazmīrī (XIV) iii, 339a,b – III, 349a,b
Abū ʿAbd Allāh Muḥammad Ibn ʿAbd al-Munʿim → Ibn ʿAbd al-Munʿim
Abū ʿAbd Allāh Muḥammad al-Mālaḳī → Ibn al-Sarrādj
Abū ʿAbd Allāh al-Shīʿī (911) i, **103b**, 249a, 863b, 1175b; ii, 98a, 852a, b; iii, 655b; iv, 198a, 361a; v, 540b, 1242b, 1243a; vi, 439a, 727b – I, **106b**, 257a, 888a, 1210b; II, 100a, 872a,b; III, 677a; IV, 206b, 377a; V, 545a, 1233b; VI, 424a, 716b
Abū ʿAbd Allāh al-Tamīmi (X) iv, 1134a – IV, 1165b
Abū ʿAbd Allāh Yaʿḳūb b. Dāʾūd (802) i, **103b**, 157b;

ii, 870a; v, 1238b; vii, 646b – I, **106b**, 162a; II, 890a; V, 1229a; VII, 646a
Abū ʿAdnān (VIII) s, 20a – S, 20b
Abū 'l-Aghlab Ibrāhīm (Aghlabid(e)) (851) ix, 584b – IX, 607a
Abū Aḥmad b. Djaʿfar (ʿAbbāsid(e)) (IX) vii, 390b – VII, 391b
Abū Aḥmad b. al-Mutawakkil → al-Muwaffaḳ (ʿAbbāsid(e))
Abū Aḥmad ʿAbd al-Salām (1014) ii, 127b; v, 928b – II, 130b; V, 933b
Abū Aḥmad al-ʿAskarī → al-ʿAskarī
Abū Aḥmad al-Ḥusayn b. Isḥāḳ Ibn Karnīb (X) vi, 844b – VI, 835b
Abū Aḥmad Khalaf (Ṣaffārid(e)) (1003) viii, 797b – VIII, 824a
Abū Aḥmad Muḥammad b. Maḥmūd b. Sebüktigin (Ghaznawid(e)) (1030) vi, 780a – VI, 770a
Abū Aḥmad al-Mūsawī (1004) iv, 378a – IV, 394b
Abu 'l-Aḥwas Maʿn b. Sumādiḥ al-Tudjībī (1024) vi, 576b – VI, 561b
Abu 'l-ʿAlāʾ b. Karnīb (X) i, 159a – I, 163b
Abu 'l-ʿAlāʾ Ibn Ḥassūl (1058) viii, 938a – VIII, 970a
Abu 'l-ʿAlāʾ al-Maʿarrī → al-Maʿarrī
Abu 'l-ʿAlāʾ Mawdūdī, Mawlānā (XX) ii, 437a; iii, 433b; vi, 461b – II, 448b; III, 447b; VI, 447a
Abu 'l-ʿAlāʾ al-Rabaʿī → Ṣāʿid al-Baghdādī
Abū ʿAlī b. Khalāṣ (XIII) s, 111b – S, 111a
Abū ʿAlī b. Marwān (Diyār Bakr) (X) ii, 344a; iii, 128b; v, 453a – II, 353b; III, 131b; V, 455b
Abū ʿAlī b. Muḥammad b. Sūrī (XI) ii, 1099b, 1100a – II, 1125b, 1126a
Abū ʿAlī b. al-Samḥ (XI) vi, 845b; s, 25a – VI, 836a; S, 25b
Abū ʿAlī b. ʿUthmān II, Abū Saʿīd (XIV) s, 112b – S, 112a
Abū ʿAlī b. al-Walīd (XI) s, 30a – S, 30a
Abū ʿAlī Aḥmad b. Muḥammad b. al-Muẓaffar (955) s, 386b – S, 387a
Abū ʿAlī al-Baghdādī → al-Ḳālī, Abū ʿAlī
Abū ʿAlī al-Balʿamī → al-Balʿamī
Abū ʿAlī al-Baṣīr s, 25a – S, 25a
Abū ʿAlī Čaghānī (X) iv, 22b, 23a, 100b; v, 76a; s, 125b – IV, 24b, 104b; V, 78b; S, 124b
Abū ʿAlī al-Djuzdjānī (IX) vi, 569b – VI, 554b
Abū ʿAlī al-Fārisī (987) vi, 634b – VI, 619b
Abū ʿAlī al-Fārmadī (1080) ii, 1038b; iii, 103a; iv, 1058a; s, **14b** – II, 1063a; III, 105b; IV, 1089a; S, **14b**
Abū ʿAlī al-Ḥākim → Muḥammad b. Aḥmad Abu 'l-Shalaʿlaʿ
Abū ʿAlī al-Ḥasan b. ʿAlī al-Djīlī i, 1237a; ii, 496a – I, 1274b; II, 508b
Abū ʿAlī al-Ḥasan b. Ismāʿīl b. Ḥammād (Ibn Dirham) (X) s, 385a – S, 385b
Abū ʿAlī al-Ḥasan b. Marwān (Diyār Bakr) (997) vi, 626a – VI, 611a
Abū ʿAlī Ḥasan b. Muḥammad (Mīkālī) (1032) → Ḥasanak
Abu ʿAlī Ḥasan b. Muḥammad b. Baṣo (1275) ix, 252b – IX, 260a
Abū ʿAlī al-Ḥasan b. Yaḥyā (XI) ix, 582b – IX, 605a
Abū ʿAlī al-Ḥasan al-Yūsī, Shaykh (XVII) vi, 591a – VI, 575b
Abū ʿAlī Ḥusayn b. Abi 'l-Ḥusayn (927) i, 688a; iii, 255a – I, 709a; III, 262b
Abū ʿAlī al-Ḥusaynī (1003) ii, 125b; v, 1126b – II, 129a; V, 1122b
Abū ʿAlī Ḳalandar Pānīpatī (1324) i, **104b**; iv, 666a – I, **107b**; IV, 693a
Abū ʿAlī al-Ḳālī → al-Ḳālī
Abū ʿAlī al-Masīlī (XII) vi, 728b – VI, 717b
Abū ʿAlī Muḥammad b. Arslān, Muntadjab al-Mulk (kātib) (1139) vi, 913b – VI, 905a
Abū ʿAlī Muḥammad b. Ilyās (955) ii, 1b; iii, 1156b; v, 158a, b, 352b – II, 1b; III, 1185a; V, 157b, 353b
Abū ʿAlī Muḥammad al-Khuzāʿī → Diʿbil
Abū ʿAlī al-Muḥassin (Ṣābī) (1010) viii, 674b – VIII, 694a
Abū ʿAlī Ṣāliḥ b. ʿAbd al-Ḥalīm (XIV) v, 1157a – V, 1146b
Abū ʿAlī Shādhān (1040) vi, 914b – VI, 906a
Abū ʿAlī Shatrandj (XII) iii, 355b – III, 366b
Abū ʿAlī Simdjūrī → Simdjūrī
Abū ʿAlī al-Sindī (IX) i, 162b – I, 167a
Abū ʿAlī Ṭāhir al-Mazdaḳānī (XII) ii, 282a – II, 290a
Abū ʿAlī Ṭarsūsī (X) i, 146b – I, 150b
Abu ʿAlī al-Yūsī → al-Yūsī
Abū ʿAlī Zāhir (998) i, 146a – I, 150a
Abu 'l-ʿĀliya al-Riyāḥī (708) i, **104b** – I, **107b**
Abu 'l-ʿAmaythal (854) ix, 454a; s, **15a** – IX, 469a; S, **15a**
Abū ʿĀmir b. Abī Yaʿḳūb Yūsuf (Marīnid(e)) (1288) vi, 593a – VI, 578a
Abū ʿĀmir al-Hinānī al-Laythī → ʿUrwa b. Udhrayna
Abū ʿĀmir Ibn Arḳam (vizier) (XII) vi, 110b – VI, 108b
Abū ʿĀmir al-Rāhib (VII) vi, 647a – VI, 632b
Abū ʿAmmār ʿAbd al-Kāfī al-Wardjlānī (XIII) iii, 96b; s, **15a** – III, 99a; S, **15b**
Abū ʿAmmār al-Aʿmā Nukkārī (X) i, 163a, 164a; iii, 95b, 659b – I, 167b, 168a, b; III, 98a, 680b
Abū ʿAmr b. al-ʿAlāʾ al-Māzinī → al-Māzinī
Abū ʿAmr ʿAbbād b. Muḥammad → al-Muʿtaḍid b. ʿAbbād
Abū ʿAmr Ismāʿīl b. Nudjayd (976) ix, 811b – IX, 846a
Abū ʿAmr al-Iṣṭakhrī iii, 823b – III, 847a
Abū ʿAmr al-Mughāzilī (X) i, 159a – I, 163b
Abū ʿAmr al-Shaybānī, Isḥāḳ b. Mirār (825) → al-Shaybānī, Abū ʿAmr Isḥāḳ b. Mirār
Abū ʿAmr Zabbān b. al-ʿAlāʾ (770) i, 42b, 104b, **105a**, 158a, 167a, 717b; iii, 136a, 742a; iv, 249a; v, 805a; vii, 114a; s, 24b –
I, 44a, 107b, **108a**, 162b, 172a, 739a; III, 139a, 764b; IV, 259b; V, 811a; VII, 116a; S, 24b
Abū ʿAmr al-Zāhid (X) s, 37b – S, 38a
Abū ʿAmra Kaysān → Kaysān
Abu 'l-ʿAnbas al-Ṣaymarī (888) iv, 1099b; ix, 453b s, **16a** – IV, 1130b; IX, 418b; S, **16b**
Abu 'l-ʿArab Muḥammad al-Tamīmī (945) i, 24a, **106a**; vi, 352b, 353b – I, 25a, **109a**; VI, 336b, 337b
Abū ʿArīsh i, **106b**; v, 808a; vi, 191b; s, 30a –
I, **109b**; V, 814a; VI, 175a; S, 30b
Abū ʿArūba (930) i, **106b** – I, **109b**
Abu 'l-ʿĀṣ, Banū vi, 621b, 622b – VI, 606b, 607a
Abu 'l-Asad al-Ḥimmānī (VIII) s, **17b** – S, **17b**
Abu 'l-ʿAsākir Sulṭān b. Sadīd al-Mulk ʿAlī (Munkidh, Banū) (1154) vii, 578a – VII, 578b
Abū 'l-ʿAshāʾir (Ḥamdānid(e)) (956) vi, 506b – VI, 491b
Abū ʿAṣīda (Ḥafṣid(e)) (1309) iii, 67b – III, 70a
Abū ʿĀṣim al-Nabīl (828) iii, 25a; s, **17b** – III, 26a; S, **18a**
Abu 'l-ʿAskar b. Maʿdān (1030) vi, 193a – VI, 177a
Abu 'l-Aswad al-Duʾalī (Dīlī) (688) i, **106b**, 565a, 566b, 1297b; iii, 173a; iv, 731b; v, 116b; vii, 280a, 913a; ix, 525a –
I, **110a**, 583b, 584b, 1337b; III, 176b; IV, 761a; V, 119a; VII, 281b, 913b; IX, 545a
Abu 'l-Aswār Shāwur (Shaddādid(e)) i, 638a, 660b; ii, 680b; iv, 347b, 348a, 815a – I, 659a, 681b; II, 697a; IV, 362b, 848a
Abū ʿAṭāʾ al-Sindī (VI) i, **107a** – I, **110a**

Abu 'l-ʿAtāhiya (825) i, **107b**, 569b, 587a, 751b, 1081b; iii, 618a, 996a, 1019b, 1262b; vi, 253a; vii, 694b; viii, 376b; s, 122b, 304a –
I, **110b**, 588a, 606a, 774a, 1114a; III, 638b, 1021a, 1045a, 1295b; VI, 237a; VII, 695a; VIII, 389a; S, 122a, 303b
Abu 'l-ʿAtāhiya (Ṭarīf, Āl) (Yemen) s, 335a – S, 334b
Abu 'l-Aṭbāḳ → Mubārak Abu 'l-Aṭbāḳ
Abu 'l-Aʿwar al-Sulamī (VII) i, **108a**; ix, 818a; s, 221b – IX, 853a; S, 221b
Abū ʿAwn ʿAbd al-Malik b. Yazīd al-Khurasānī (766) i, 16a, **108b**; iv, 447b; x, 926b – I, 16b, **111b**; IV, 467b; X,
Abu 'l-ʿAynāʾ (896) i, **108b**, 1082b; iii, 672b; s, 25a – I, **XIV**, 1114b; III, 694a; S, 25a
Abu 'l-ʿAysh Aḥmad (Idrīside(e)) (954) iii, 1036b – III, 1062b
Abū Ayyūb al-Anṣārī (672) i, **108b**, 312b; iv, 270b; v, 533a; vi, 354a, 645b, 646b, 862a –
I, **111b**, 322b; IV, 282b; V, 537a; VI, 338b, 630b, 631a, b, 853b
Abū Ayyūb al-Madīnī ii, 1011b; iii, 682a, 698b – II, 1035a; III, 704a, 720b
Abu 'l-ʿAzāʾim (1937) s, **18a** – S, **18a**
Abu 'l-Badr b. Nuṣrat Shāh (Bengal) → Fīrūz Shāh, ʿAlā al-Dīn (Bengal(e))
Abū Baghla (Kabylia/-e) (XIX) iv, 362a – IV, 378a
Abu 'l-Bahār b. Khalūf (XI) vii, 482a – VII, 482a
Abū Baḥr Ṣakhr → al-Aḥnaf b. Ḳays
Abū 'l-Baḳāʾ (Rubda) (1285) viii, 616a – VIII, 635a
Abu 'l-Baḳāʾ, Shaykh (XV) i, 841b – I, 864b
Abu 'l-Baḳāʾ b. Abī Zakariyyāʾ (Ḥafṣid(e)) (1311) iii, 67b; v, 531a; vi, 404b – III, 70a; V, 535a; VI, 389a
Abu Bakari b. Mwengo (XVIII) s, 351b – S, 351b
Abū Bakr (Ildeñizid(e)) (1205) vi, 500b – VI, 485b, 486a
Abū Bakr (Manding Bori, Mali) (XIII) vi, 421b – VI, 406b
Abū Bakr (al-Ṣiddīḳ) (634) i, **109b**, 114b, 127b, 158b, 381b, 382a, 443b, 549b, 697a, 1113b; ii, 601a, 725a, 842b, 844a, 845b; iii, 33a, 64a, b; iv, 927b, 937a; v, 404b, 777a; vi, 138b, 139a, 152b, 168b, 266b, 350b, 546b, 575a, 604a, 645b, 647a, b, 650a, 652a, 659a, 668b, 671a, 675a; ix, **534a**; s, 89b, 129b, 130a, 343a –
I, **112b**, 118a, 131a, 163a, 392b, 456a, 567a, 718a, 1147a; II, 616a, 743b, 862a, 864a, 865a; III, 35a, 66b, 67a; IV, 960b, 970a; V, 406a, 783a; VI, 137a, 151a, 160a, 251a, 335a, 531a, 560a, 588b, 630b, 632a, 633a, 635b, 637a, 645a, 654b, 657a, 661b; IX, **555a**; S, 89a, 128b, 129a, 343a
Abū Bakr (Ḥafsid(e)) → Abū Yaḥyā Abū Bakr
Abū Bakr (Salghūrid(e)) → Abū Bakr b. Saʿd b. Zangī
Abū Bakr Sayf al-Dīn (Mamlūk) (1341) ii, 285b – II, 293b
Abū Bakr b. ʿAbd Allāh → Ibn Abī 'l-Dunyā
Abū Bakr b. ʿAbd al-ʿAzīz (Balansiya) (1085) i, 446a, 986a – I, 459a, 1016b
Abū Bakr b. ʿAbd al-Karīm (ḳāʾid) (1668) vi, 595a – VI, 579b
Abū Bakr b. ʿAbd al-Raḥmān b. al-Mughīra (711) vi, 140a – VI, 138b
Abū Bakr b. ʿAbd al-Raḥmān ʿUbayd Allāh (716) s, 311b – S, 311a
Abū Bakr b. ʿAbd al-Ṣamad → ʿAbd al-Ṣamad
Abū Bakr b. Abī Djamra (1202) viii, 635b – VIII, 654b
Abū Bakr b. Abī Saʿīd (XV) i, 852b – I, 876a
Abū Bakr b. Abī Shayba → Ibn Abī Shayba
Abū Bakr b. Aḥmad → Ibn Ḳāḍī Shuhba
Abū Bakr b. Aḥmad b. Muḥammad b. Zayd Ṭūsī i, 423b – I, 435b
Abū Bakr b. ʿAlī al-Ḥamawī → Ibn Ḥidjdja
Abū Bakr b. ʿAlī al-Ṣinhādjī → al-Baydhāk
Abū Bakr b. al-ʿArabī → Ibn al-ʿArabī
Abū Bakr b. ʿAyyāsh (809) i,707a – I, 728a
Abū Bakr b. Bahrām al-Dimashḳī (1691) i, 698a; ii, 589a – I, 719a; II, 604a
Abū Bakr b. Eldiguz → Abū Bakr b. Pahlawān
Abū Bakr b. Fakhr al-Dīn (Maḳdishū) (XII) vi, 128b – VI, 126b
Abū Bakr b. Ḥammād iv, 662b – IV, 689a
Abū Bakr b. Ibrāhīm al-Sahrawī → Ibn Tifalwīt
Abū Bakr b. Ismāʿil b. ʿAbd al-Haḳḳ (XII) v, 60b – V, 62b
Abū Bakr b. Kīrān (1851) s, 390b – S, 391a
Abū Bakr b. al-Khamīs (XIII) s, 382a – S, 382a
Abū Bakr b. al-Maḳbūl al-Zaylaʿī (XVI) v, 807b – V, 813a
Abū Bakr b. Mīrānshāh b. Tīmūr (Timūrid(e)) (1404) vi, 105b – VI, 107b
Abū Bakr b. Mudjāhid → Ibn Mudjāhid, Aḥmad
Abū Bakr b. al-Mughīra al-Makhzūmī (712) s, **311a** – S, **310b**
Abū Bakr b. Muḥammad (Maḳdishū) (1322) vi, 128b – VI, 126b
Abū Bakr b. Muḥammad, Shaykh s, 223a – S, 223a
Abū Bakr b. Muḥammad, Sultan (Adal) (XVI) i, 286b; iii, 4a – I, 295b; III, 4a
Abū Bakr b. Muḥammad b. ʿAmr b. Ḥazm (ca. 730) x, 81a – X, 84b
Abū Bakr b. al-Nāṣir Muḥammad (Mamlūk) (1341) vi, 323b – VI, 307b
Abū Bakr b. Pahlawān Muḥammad (Ildeñizid(e)) (1210) i, 300b, 301a; iii, 1111b, 1112a; iv, 349a; vi, 501a; viii, 235a – I, 310a,b; III, 1139a, b; IV, 364a; VI, 486a; VIII, 240a
Abū Bakr b. Saʿd (I) b. Zangī (Salghurid(e)) (1260) i, 434a, 942b; iv, 498a, 764b; v, 671a; vi, 609a; viii, 701b, 720a, 978b – I, 446b, 971a; IV, 519b, 795a; V, 676a; VI, 593b; VIII, 721b, 740b, 1013a
Abū Bakr b. Shādhān (X) ix, 847b – IX, 882b
Abū Bakr b. Shāhūya (Ḳarmaṭī) iv, 664b – IV, 691b
Abū Bakr b. ʿUmar (Maḳdishū) (XIV) vi, 128b – VI, 126b
Abū Bakr b. ʿUmar al-Lamtūnī → al-Lamtūnī
Abū Bakr b. Ẓafar Khān (XIV) ii, 1077a – II, 1102a
Abū Bakr b. Zahr iv, 1007b – IV, 1039b
Abū Bakr b. Zayd al-Djirāʿī (1478) i, 759a – I, 781b
Abū Bakr al-Ādjurrī → al-Ādjurrī
Abū Bakr Aḥmad b. ʿAbd al-Raḥmān (1040) vi, 353b – VI, 337b
Abū Bakr Aḥmad b. ʿAlī b. Thābit → al-Khaṭīb al-Baghdādī
Abū Bakr Aḥmad b. Isḥāḳ b. Zayd b. Ṭāhir (Ṭāhirid(e), al-Andalus) (1063) x, 105b – X, 113b
Abū Bakr Aḥmad b. Kāmil (961) x, 11a – X, 11a
Abū Bakr al-Aṣamm → al-Aṣamm
Abū Bakr al-ʿAtīḳ (Sokoto) (1842) vii, 435b – VII, 436b
Abū Bakr al-ʿ Aydarus → al-ʿAydarus, Abū Bakr
Abū Bakr al-Bayṭār → Ibn al-Mundhir
Abū Bakr Djamālī Yazdī (1185) vi, 908a – VI, 899b
Abū Bakr Dughlat → Abū Bakr Mīrzā b. Sāniz
Abū Bakr al-Hirawī (1199) vi, 691b – VI, 679a
Abū Bakr Hishām → Hishām III
Abū Bakr Ibn Zaydūn b. al-Muʿtamid Ibn ʿAbbād (1091) vii, 766b – VII, 768a
Abū Bakr al-Ḳaffāl (1026) i, 146a – I, 150a
Abū Bakr al-Ḳaṭīʿī (978) i, 273b; iii, 158b – I, 282a; III, 162a
Abū Bakr al-Khallāl → al-Khallāl
Abū Bakr al-Kharāʾiṭī → al-Kharāʾiṭī

Abū Bakr al-Khʷārizmī → al-Khʷārizmī
Abū Bakr al-Marwazī → al-Marwāzī, Abū Bakr
Abū Bakr al-Mayūrḳī → al-Mayūrḳī, Abū Bakr
Abū Bakr Mīrzā (Tīmūrid(e)) (XV) iv, 586a, b – IV, 609a
Abū Bakr Mīrzā b. Sāniz (1514) ii, 622a; iv, 699a – II, 637b; IV, 727b
Abū Bakr Muḥammad b. Ayyūb → al-Malik al-ʿĀdil I
Abū Bakr Muḥammad b. Hāshim (Khālidī) (990) iii, 111a; iv, 936b – III, 113b; IV, 969b
Abū Bakr Muḥammad b. Isḥāḳ (Karrāmī) (XI) viii, 63b – VIII, 64b
Abū Bakr al-Rāzī → al-Rāzī
Abū Bakr Saʿd b. Zangī Rashīd al-Dīn (atabeg) (XIV) vi, 524a – VI, 509a
Abū Bakr Sayf al-Dīn b. Kāmil → al-Malik al-ʿĀdil II
Abū Bakr al-Shāshī (X) i, 126b; s, 194b, 384a – I, 130a; S, 193b, 384b
Abū Bakr al-Sidjistānī (928) iii, 158b – III, 162a
Abū Bakr Tādj al-Dīn , Sultan (XIX) viii, 1042a – VIII, 1078a
Abū Bakr Wafāʾī, Pīr (1496) i, 966a – I, 996a
Abū Bakr Yaʿḳūb b. Nāṣir al-Dīn, ḳāḍī (XIV) iv, 1127b – IV, 1159a
Abū Bakr al-Zubaydī → al-Zubaydī
Abū Bakra (671) i, **111a**; vi, 710a; s, 354b – I, **114b**; VI, 698b; S, 354b
Abū Barāʾ (VII) i, 1232b – I, 1269a
Abu ʾl-Barakāt al-ʿAlawī al-Zaydī (1145) s, **19a** – S, **19a**
Abu ʾl-Barakāt Hibat Allāh al-Baghdādī (1164) i, **111b**; ii, 774a; iv, 306a; vi, 450b; s, 273b – I, **114b**; II, 792b; iv, 319b; vi, 435b; 5, 273a
Abu ʾl-Barakāt al-Barbarī al-Maghribī (Maldives) vi, 245b – VI, 229b
Abu ʾl-Barakāt Muḥammad al-Balāfiḳī → lbn al-Ḥādjdj
Abū Barāḳish (1145) i, 131b; s, **19a** – I, 135a; S, **19b**
Abū Baṣīr (627) vi, 651b – VI, 636b
Abū Baṭṭa → al-Irdjānī
Abu ʾl-Bayḍāʾ al-Riyāḥī (VIII) s, **20a**, 73b – S, **20b**, 73b
Abū Bayhas al-Hayṣam b. Djābir (713) i, **113a**; ix, 766b – I, **116b**; IX, 799b
Abu Bekr Musaliar, T.K. (XX) vi, 462a – VI, 447b
Abū Bilal → Mirdās b. Udayya
Abū Bishr Mattā b. Yūnus → Mattā b. Yūnus
Abū Bukayr (1179) x, 303a – X, 226a
Abū Burda → al-Ashʿarī
Abū Dabbūs → Idrīs al-Maʾmūn
Abū Ḍabī → Abū Ẓabī
Abū Dahbal al-Djumaḥī (715) i,**113b** – I, **116b**
Abu ʾl-Daḳḳāḳ (XI) vi, 569b – VI, 554b
Abū Ḍamḍam i, **113b** – I, **116b**
Abū Ḍarba al-Liḥyānī (Ḥafṣid(e)) (1317) iii, 67b; iv, 338a; v, 1247a – III, 70a; IV, 352b; V, 1237b
Abu ʾl-Dardāʾ (652) i, **113b**, 959b – I, **117a**, 989a
Abū Dāʾūd, Zayn al-Dīn al-Ḳurashī (XIII) viii, 156b – VIII, 158b
Abū Dāʾūd al-Bakrī (VIII) i, 141b, 1001a – I, 145b, 1032a
Abū Dāʾūd al-Sidjistānī (889) i, **114a**; iii, 24a, 158b; vi, 346b, 634a, 658a; s, 232b – I, **117b**; III, 25a, 162a; VI, 330b, 619a, 643b; S, 232b
Abu ʾl-Dawāniḳ → al-Manṣūr, Abū Djaʿfar ʿAbd Allāh (ʿAbbāsid(e))
Abū Dāwūd Muḥammad b. Aḥmad (IX) s, 125b – S, 124b
Abū Dāwūdid(e)s → Bānīdjūrid(e)s
Abū Dhabī → Abū Ẓabī
Abu ʾl Dhahab → Muḥammad Abu ʾl-Dhahab
Abu ʾl-Dhahab, Muḥammad Bey (1775) i, 391b, 392a, 1033a; iii, 992a, iv, 853a; vii, 179a; s, **20b**, 44a – I, 403a, 1064b; III, 1016b, IV, 886a; VII, 181a; S, **20b**, 44b
Abū Dharr al-Ghifārī (652) i, **114b**, 266b, 382a, 549b; ii, 846b; vii, 264b, 517b, 780a; ix, 819b – I, **118a**, 274b, 393a, 567a; II, 866b; VII, 266b, 518a, 782a; IX, 854b
Abū Dharr al-Harawī (XI) i, 864b – I, 889a
Abu ʾl-Dhawwād Muḥammad b. al-Musayyab (ʿUkaylid(e) (996) x, 786b; s, 119a – X, ; S, 118b
Abū Dhuʾayb al-Hudhalī (649) i, **115a**; iii, 273a; iv, 252a; vi, 603b; vii, 308a, 843b, 980b, 981a; x, 2b – I, **118a**; III, 281a; IV, 263a; VI, 588b; vii, 310a, 844b, 981b; X, 2b
Abu ʾl-Ḍiyā Tewfīk → Ebüzziya Tevfik
Abū Djad → Abdjad
Abū Djaʿfar b. Aḥmad b. ʿAbd Allāh b. Ḥabash (al-ḥāsib) iii, 9a – III, 9b
Abū Djaʿfar Aḥmad (Ifrīḳiyya) (IX) viii, 844b – VIII, 874a
Abū Djaʿfar Aḥmad b. ʿAṭiyya (vizier) (XII) ii, 1014a – II, 1037b
Abū Djaʿfar Aḥmad b. Muḥammad (Sīstān) (963) i, 116a – I, 119b
Abū Djaʿfar Aḥmad b. Muḥammad b. Khalaf (Ṣaffārid(e)) (X) viii, 797a – VIII, 824a
Abū Djaʿfar Aḥmad b. Muḥammad al-Barḳī → al-Barḳī
Abū Djaʿfar al-Andalūsī → al-Ruʿaynī
Abū Djaʿfar al-Ḥadhdhāʾ (X) iii, 823b – III, 847a
Abū Djaʿfar Ḥamdīn → ʿAlī b. Aḍḥā
Abū Djaʿfar al-Hāshimī (1078) i, 1040a; iii, 160a, 699b, 700a, 766b – I, 1071b; III, 163b, 722a, 789b
Abū Djaʿfar Ibn Saʿīd (1165) iii, 66a – III, 68b
Abū Djaʿfar al-Khāzin → al-Khāzin
Abū Djaʿfar al-Manṣūr → al-Manṣūr (ʿAbbāsid(e))
Abū Djaʿfar Muḥammad b. ʿAbd Kān → lbn ʿAbd Kān
Abū Djaʿfar Muḥammad b. Abi ʾl-Ḥusayn Aḥmad (X) s, 357a – S, 357a
Abū Djaʿfar Muḥammad b. Abi ʾl-Ḥasan al-ʿAskarī (IX) vii, 459b – VII, 459b
Abū Djaʿfar Muḥammad b. al-Zubayr → lbn al-Zubayr
Abū Djaʿfar al-Ruʾāsī → al-Ruʾāsī
Abū Djaʿfar al-Ṭūsī → al-Ṭūsī
Abū Djaʿfar Ustādh-Hurmuz → Ustādh-Hurmuz
Abū Djahl ʿAmr b. Hishām b. al-Mughīra (624) i, **115a**, 136b, 151a, 868a; ii, 843b; iii, 152b; vi, 138a, 145b, 146b, 603b; vii, 369b – I, **118b**, 140b, 155b, 892a; II, 863a; III, 156a; VI, 136a, b, 144a, 145a, 588b; VII, 371b
Abū ʾl-Djarūd → al-Djārūdiyya
Abū ʾl-Djārūd Ziyād b. al-Mundhir (VIII) ii, 485a; vii, 399a; s, 48b – II, 497b; VII, 400a; S, 49a
Abū ʾl-Djaysh Mudjāhid → Mudjāhid al-Āmirī
Abū Djisrā (ʿIrāḳ) i, 865b – I, 890a
Abū Djubayla → Djabala b. al-Ḥārith
Abu ʾl-Djūd Muḥammad b. al-Layth (X) iv, 1182b – IV, 1215b
Abū Djummayza (1889) ii, 124a; iv, 953a; v, 1250b – II, 127a; IV, 985b; V, 1241a
Abu ʾl-Djunayd → Abū Nukhayla
Abū Duʿāba ʿAṭiyya (1063) vi, 379b – VI, 364a
Abū Duʾād al-Iyādī (VI) i, **115b**; iv, 289a, 919a – I, **119a**; IV, 302a, 952a
Abū Dulaf (Sāmarrā) i, 621a, 624a – I, 641a, 643b
Abū Dulaf al-Khazradjī (X) i, **116a**, 570b, 967a; iii, 106a; vi, 364b, 365a, 624b; vii, 495a; ix, 70b, 611b; x, 304b; s, 116a, 363a – I, **119a**, 589a, 996b; III, 108b; VI, 348b, 349a, 609b; VII, 494b; IX, 73a, 634b; X, 327b; S, 115b, 362b

Abū Dulaf al-Ḳāsim al-ʿIdjlī → al-Ḳāsim b. ʿĪsā
Abū Dulāma Zand b. al-Djawn (776) i, **116b**, 909b; iv, 1003b; vi, 475b – I, **120a**, 937a; IV, 1036a; VI, 461b
Abu ʾl-Dunyā Abu ʾl Ḥasan ʿAlī (928) i, **117a** – I, **120a**
Abū Duwād → Abū Duʿād
Abu ʾl-Faḍāʾil → Ḥamdānid(e)s
Abu ʾl-Faḍāʾil al-Sayyid Rukn al-Dīn → al-Astarābādhī, Rukn al-Dīn
Abu ʾl-Faḍl b. Abī Sālim (Marīnid(e)) (1370) vi, 593b – VI, 578b
Abu ʾl-Faḍl b. al-ʿAmīd (vizier) (970) vi, 199a, 637b – VI, 183b, 622b
Abu ʾl-Faḍl b. Idrīs Bidlīsī → Bidlīsī
Abu ʾl-Faḍl b. Mubārak Nāgawrī → Abu ʾl-Faḍl ʿAllāmī
Abū Faḍl b. al-Naḥwī → Ibn al-Naḥwī
Abu ʾl-Faḍl al-ʿAbbās b. ʿĪsā (faḳīh) (943) iv, 683b – IV, 711b
Abu ʾl-Faḍl al-ʿAbbās al-Shīrāzī → al-ʿAbbās b. al-Ḥusayn
Abu ʾl-Faḍl ʿAllāmī (1602) i, **117a**, 297a, 1331a; ii, 296a, 380a, 871a, b; iii, 423b; iv, 704a,759b, 1127b; vi, 131a, 456b; vii, 199b, 221a, 321b, 342b, 898a, 925a; s, 3b, 142b, 280a, 325a, 410b – I, **120b**, 306b, 1371b; II, 304a, 390b, 891a, b; III, 437b; IV, 732b, 790a, 1159a; VI, 129a, 442a; VII, 200a, 223a, 323b, 344b, 899a, 926a; S, 2b, 142a, 279b, 325a, 411a
Abu ʾl-Faḍl Djaʿfar b. ʿAlī al-Dimashḳī (XII) vi, 205a; s, 42b – VI, 189b; S, 43a
Abu ʾl-Faḍl Djaʿfar b. Muḥammad, al-Thāʾir fi-ʾllāh (966) iii, 255a; vi, 941b; s, 363a – III, 262b; VI, 933b; S, 363a
Abu ʾl-Faḍl Djaʿfar b. al-Muḳtadī (XI) vii, 540b – VII, 540b
Abu ʾl-Faḍl Djamāl al-Dīn Muḥammad → Djamāl Ḳarshī
Abu ʾl-Faḍl al-Djārūdī (XI) i, 515b – I, 531a
Abu ʾl-Faḍl Ismāʿīl → Ismāʿīl, Abu ʾl-Faḍl
Abu ʾl-Faḍl ʿIyāḍ → ʿIyāḍ
Abu ʾl-Faḍl Maʾmūrī vii, 322a – VII, 324a
Abu ʾl-Faḍl Mīrzā (Ḳādjār) vii, 432b – VII, 433a
Abu ʾl-Faḍl Muḥammad → Ibn al-ʿAmīd
Abu ʾl-Faḍl Muḥammad al-Baghdādī, vizier (XI) v, 929b – V, 934b
Abu ʾl-Faḍl Mūsā al-Iznīḳī → al-Iznīḳī
Abu ʾl-Faḍl Raydān → Raydān al-Saḳlabī
Abu ʾl-Faḍl ʿUbayd Allāh (Mīkālī) (1044) vii, 26a – VII, 26a
Abu ʾl-Faradj → Babbaghāʾ; Ibn al-Djawzī; Ibn al-ʿIbrī; Ibn al-Nadīm; Ibn al-Ṭayyib; al-Shīrāzī
Abu ʾl-Faradj b. Amarī (al-kabīr al-ḥilw) ix, 30, 199b
Abu ʾl-Faradj b. Masʿūd Rūnī (1106) iv, 61b; s, **21a** – IV, 64b; s, **21a**
Abu ʾl-Faradj b. al-Ṭayyib → Ibn al-Ṭayyib
Abu ʾl-Faradj Furḳān → Jeshuah b. Judah
Abu ʾl-Faradj Hārūn → Hārūn b. al-Faradj
Abu ʾl-Faradj al-Iṣbahānī (967) i, 10a, **118a**, 590a, 1354a; iii, 928a; v, 936b; vi, 99a, 604b; vii, 306b, 358b, 771a; viii, 14b; s, 24a, 35b, 64a, 116b, 183a, 310b, 311b, 401a, 409a –
I, 10a, **121b**, 609b, 1393a; III, 952b; V, 940b; VI, 96b, 589a; VII, 308b, 361a, 772b; VIII, 14b; S, 24a, 35b, 64b, 116a, 184b, 310b, 311a, 401b, 409a
Abu ʾl-Faradj Muḥammad Fasāndjus → Ibn Fasāndjus
Abu ʾl-Faradj Muḥammad al-Waʾwā (X) iv, 1005b – IV, 1038a
Abu ʾl-Faradj Sidjzī s, 21a – S, 21a
Abu ʾl-Faraḥ (Bārha) (XIV) s, 126b – S, 125b
Abū Fāris b. Abī Isḥāḳ (Ḥafṣid(e)) (1283) iii, 67a – III, 69b
Abū Fāris b. Aḥmad al-Manṣūr (Saʿdid(e)) (1603) vi, 591a, 594b – VI, 576a, 579a
Abū Fāris ʿAbd al-ʿAzīz al-Mutawakkil (Ḥafṣid(e)) (1434) i, 93a, 448b, 1225a, 1247a; ii, 459a; iii, **68b**, 778a, 843b; iv, 416a, 739b; v, 531a; s, 399a –
I, 95b, 461a, 1261b, 1284b; II, 471a; III, **71a**, 801b, 867b; IV, 434a, 769b; V, 535a; S, 399b
Abu Fāris ʿAbd al-ʿAzīz I (Marīnid(e)) (1372) iii, 832a, 836a – III, 855b, 859b
Abū Farrādj → Aḥmad al-Badawī
Abu ʾl-Fatḥ → Ibn al-ʿAmid; Ibn al-Furāt; al-Muẓaffar
Abu ʾl-Fatḥ b. Abi ʾl-Shawk (ʿAnnāzid(e)) (XI) i, 512b – I, 528a
Abu ʾl-Fatḥ al-Balaṭī → al-Balaṭī
Abu ʾl-Fatḥ Beg Bayāndur (1502) ii, 174a; s, 280b – II, 179a; S, 280b
Abu ʾl-Fatḥ al-Bustī → al-Bustī
Abu ʾl-Fatḥ Dāwūd b. Naṣr (Mulṭān) (1010) vi, 65b – VI, 63b
Abu ʾl-Fatḥ al-Daylamī, al-Nāṣir li-Dīn Allāh (1052) s, **22a** – S, **22b**
Abu ʾl-Fatḥ al-Ḥarrānī (1083) iii, 766b – III, 789b
Abu ʾl-Fatḥ al-Ḥulwānī (1112) iii, 766b – III, 789b
Abu ʾl-Fatḥ al-Ḥusaynī (XVI) s, 383a – S, 383a
Abu ʾl-Fatḥ Ibrāhīm → Ibrāhīm b. Shāhrukh
Abu ʾl-Fatḥ al-Iskandarī → al-Hamadhānī
Abu ʾl-Fatḥ Khān Bakhtiyārī (XVIII) iv, 104a, b – IV, 109a
Abu ʾl-Fatḥ Marzbān al-Sharḳī b. Ḳumādj vi, 14b – VI, 13a
Abu ʾl-Fatḥ Muḥammad b. ʿAnnāz → Muḥammad b. ʿAnnāz
Abu ʾl-Fatḥ Muḥammad Shāh → Maḥmūd I, Sayf al-Dīn, Begarha
Abu ʾl-Fatḥ al-Muẓaffar (X) vii, 414a – VII, 415b
Abu ʾl-Fatḥ al-Nāṣir al-Daylamī (Imām, Yemen) (1055) vii, 996a – VII, 997b
Abu ʾl-Fatḥ Naṣr b. Ibrāhīm (al-Ḳuds) (X) v, 330a – V, 330a
Abu ʾl-Fatḥ Yūsuf b. Khʷārazm-Shāh vi, 14b – VI, 13a
Abu ʾl-Fawāris Fanārūzī (Būyid(e)) (Kirmān) (1028) i, 131b; x, 232a– I, 135b; X, 250b
Abu ʾl-Fayd Khān (Djānid(e)), Bukhārā) (1747) ii, 446a; vi, 418b; vii, 854b – II, 458a; VI, 403b; VII, 856a
Abu ʾl-Fayyāḍ Sawwār (IX) s, 35b – S, 35b
Abu ʾl-Fidāʾ, al-Malik al-Muʾayyad ʿImād al-Dīn (Ayyūbid(e)) (1331) i, **118b**, 595a, 804b; ii, 585a; iii, 120a, 900b, 966b; iv, 485a; v, 925a, 1011b; vi, 231a, 283a, 377b, 381b, 429a, 439b, 544a, 580a; vii, 167b, 186a, 537a, 992a –
I, **122a**, 614b, 828b; II, 599b; III, 122b, 924b, 991a; IV, 506a; V, 930b, 1007a; VI, 225a, 268a, 362a, 365b, 414a, 425a, 528b, 564b; VII, 169a, 186b, 537a, 993b
Abū Firās al-Ḥamdānī (968) i, **119b**, 592a, 1249b; iii, 129b, 398a, 825a; iv, 55b; v, 647b; vi, 379a, b, 506b; vii, 577b, 770b –
I, **122b**, 611b, 1287b; III, 132a, 410b, 849a; IV, 58b; V, 651b; VI, 363b, 491b; VII, 578a, 772b
Abu ʾl-Fityān → Aḥmad al-Badawī
Abū Fudayk ʿAbd Allāh b. Thawr (693) i, **120a**, 550a, 942a; iv, 764a, 1076a; vii, 671a – I, **123b**, 567b, 971a; IV, 794b, 1107b; VII, 671a
Abū Futrus → Nahr Abī Futrus
Abu ʾl-Futūḥ Dāwūd b. Naṣr (XI) vii, 549a – VII, 549a
Abu ʾl-Futūḥ al-Ḥasan (Mūsāwī) (1039) i, 552a; iii, 262b; vi, 148b – I, 569b; III, 270a; VI, 147a
Abu ʾl-Futūḥ al-Rāzī (1131) i, **120a**; vii, 103a – I, **123b**; VII, 105a
Abu ʾl-Futūḥ Yūsuf → Buluggīn b. Zīrī

Abu 'l-Futūḥ Yūsuf b. ʿAbd Allāh (Kalbid(e)) (998) iv, 497a – IV, 518a
Abu 'l-Ghaḍanfar (1157) vi, 367a – VI, 351a
Abu 'l-Ghanāʾim Saʿd (fasandjus) (XI) ii, 827a – II, 847a
Abū Ghānim Bishr b. Ghānim al-Khurāsānī (IX) i, **120b**, iii, 653b, 656b – I, **124a**; III, 674b, 678a
Abū Ghānim Naṣr (Ḳarmaṭī) (VIII) iv, 494a, 661a – IV, 515a, 687b
Abu 'l-Gharānik → Muḥammad II (Aghlabid(e))
Abu 'l-Ghayth b. ʿAbda (ʿIdjl) (Ḳarmaṭī) (X) iv, 662a – IV, 689a
Abu 'l-Ghāzī Bahādur Khān (Khīwa) (1663) i, **120b**, 607b, 45a; ii, 1109b; iv, 1064a; v, 24a, 273b; vi, 416a, 418a, b; viii, 164a; s, 97b, 168b, 228a, 245b, 280b, 419b, 420a –
I, **124a**, 627b, 45b; II, 1135b; IV, 1096a; V, 24b, 271b; VI, 401a, 403a, b; VIII, 166a; S, 96b, 97a, 168b, 228a, 245b, 280b, 420a
Abū Ghosh, Banū v, 334a – V, 334b
Abū Ghubshān (Mecca) (IX) v, 78a; viii, 1003a – V, 80a; VIII, 1038a
Abū Ghufayl (Barghawāṭa) (913) i, 1044a – I, 1076a
Abū Ḥabasha vi, 1039b – VI, 1033a
Abū Ḥadīd, Muḥammad Farīd Wadjdī (XX) i, 598a; s, 244b – I, 617b; S, 244b
Abu 'l-Ḥadjdjādj b. al-Shaykh (1207) s, 381b – S, 382a
Abu 'l-Ḥadjdjādj Yūsuf b. Abi 'l-Ḳāsim → Ibn al-Sarrādj
Abu 'l-Ḥadjdjādj Yūsuf b. al-Sarrādj → Ibn al-Sarrādj
Abū Ḥafṣ, Shaykh (1163) vi, 521a – VI, 505b
Abū Ḥafṣ ʿAmrūs b. Fatḥ, Shaykh → ʿAmrūs b. Fatḥ
Abū Ḥafṣ al-Ḥaddād → Malāmatiyya (Nīshāpūr)
Abū Ḥafṣ al-Shiṭrandjī → al-Shiṭrandjī
Abū Ḥafṣ Sughdī iv, 55a, 525b – IV, 57b, 548a
Abū Ḥafṣ al-ʿUkbarī (998) v, 10a – V, 10b
Abū Ḥafṣ (ʿUmar b. Maslama al-Ḥaddād) (IX) vi, 569b – VI, 554b
Abū Ḥafṣ ʿUmar I (Ḥafṣid(e)) (1285) iii, 67a – III, 69b
Abū Ḥafṣ ʿUmar b. Djamīʿ (XIV) i, **121a** – I, **124b**
Abū Ḥafṣ ʿUmar al-Ballūṭī (IX) i, 83a, **121b**, 1249a; ii, 744b; iii, 1083a – I, 85b, **125a**, 1287a; II, 763a; III, 1109b
Abū Ḥafṣ ʿUmar b. al-Ḥādjdj (XII) iv, 116a – IV, 121a
Abū Ḥafṣ ʿUmar al-Hintātī (Īntī) (1175) i, 78b, 79a, b, **121b**, 161a; ii, 526b; iii, 66a, 461b; vi, 742b –
I, 80b, 81b, 82a, **125a**, 165b; II, 539b; III, 68b, 478a; VI, 732a
Abū Ḥafṣa Yazīd (684) vi, 625a – VI, 610a
Abu 'l-Hakam b. al-Mughīra → Abū Djahl
Abū Ḥāla al-Tamīmī (VII) iv, 898b – IV, 931a
Abū Ḥāmid al-Gharnāṭī (al-Andalusī) (1169) i, **122a**, 203b, 204a, 593b, 602b; v, 1012a, 1016a, 1018a; vi, 413b; vii, 140b, 474a; viii, 896b; ix, 582a –
I, **125b**, 209b, 210a, 613a, 622a; V, 1008, 1011b, 1012a, 1013b; VI, 398b; VII, 143a, 473b; VIII, 927b; IX, 605a
Abū Ḥāmid al-Marw al-Rūdhī (X) i, 126b – I, 130a
Abū Ḥammū I Mūsa b. Abī Saʿīd (ʿAbd al-Wādid(e)) (1318) i, 93a, 94a, **122b**; v, 1180a; vi, 728b – I, 95b, 96b, **126a**; V, 1170a; VI, 717b
Abū Ḥammū II (1389) i, 93a, **122b**, 155a; ii, 979a; iii, 826b, 831b, 832a – I, 95b, **126a**, 159b; II, 1001b; III, 850b, 855b
Abū Ḥamza → al-Mukhtār b. ʿAwf
Abū Ḥamza al-Khurasānī x, 377a – X, 404b
Abū Ḥamza Madjmaʿ b. Samʿān al-Ḥāʾik s, 341b – S, 341a
Abū Ḥanīfa al-Dīnawarī → al-Dīnawarī
Abū Ḥanīfa al-Nuʿmān (Fāṭimid(e)) → al-Nuʿmān
Abū Ḥanīfa al-Nuʿmān b. Thābit (767) i, 70b, **123a**, 164a, 481b, 692a, 730b, 904a; ii, 489a, 1022a; iii, 512a, 687b, 984b; iv, 855b; v, 239b, 731b; vi, 24a, 123b, 263b, 264b, 265b, 352b, 634b; vii, 606b, 663b; s, 232b, 303b, 304a, 401a–
I, 72b, **126b**, 169a, 495b, 713a, 752b, 913b; II, 501a, 1046a; III, 529b, 709a, 1009a; IV, 889a; V, 237b, 737a; VI, 21b, 121a, 248a, 249a, 250a, 336b, 619b; VII, 606a, 663b; S, 232b, 303b, 401b
—doctrine i, 164b, 332b; ii, 116a, 832a; iii, 162b, 209b, 1164b – I, 169b, 343a; II, 118b, 851b; III, 166a, 215b, 1193a
Abū Ḥanẓala → Abū Sufyān b. Ḥarb b. Umayya
Abū Ḥarb (Kākūyid(e)) (XI) iv, 465b – IV, 486b
Abū Ḥarb b. Manučihr (XII) v, 662a – V, 667b
Abū Ḥarb Bakhtiyār (XI) ix, 513b, 614a – IX, 637a
Abū Ḥarb al-Mubarḳaʿ (IX) v, 326b – V, 326b
Abū Ḥarb al-Ṣaffār (IX) vi, 605a – VI, 589b
Abū Ḥarb al-Yamanī → Abū Ḥarb al-Mubarḳaʿ
Abu 'l-Ḥārith Djummayn vii, 857a – VII, 858b
Abu 'l-Ḥārith Muḥammad b. Farīghūn (X) ii, 799a – II, 817b
Abu 'l-Ḥasan b. Āḳā Riḍā (painter/peintre) (XVII) vi, 425b, 426a, 534a; vii, 339a – VI, 410b, 411a, 518b; VII, 340b
Abu 'l-Ḥasan b. Bandār (X) vi, 224a – VI, 217b
Abu 'l-Ḥasan al-Aḥmar (810) s, **22b** – S, **22b**
Abu 'l-Ḥasan al-Akhfash (IX) i, 167b, 321b – I, 172b, 331b
Abu 'l-Ḥasan ʿAlī → ʿAzafī, Banū 'l-
Abu 'l-Ḥasan ʿAlī (Marīnid(e)) (1352) i, 93a, **124b**, 129b, 138a, 155a, 496a, 506b, 634a, 1149a, 1339b; ii, 146a, 525a, 822b; iii, 67b, 68a, 135a, 867b; iv, 828a; v, 531a, 1190a; vi, 124a, 258a, 356a, 404b, 422a, 441a, 572a, b, 573b, 593a, b, 597a; s, 45b, 376b, 377a –
I, 95b, **128a**, 133b, 142a, 159a, 510b, 521b, 655a, 1183a, 1379b; II, 150a, 538a, 842a; III, 70a, b, 137b, 890b; IV, 861a; V, 535a, 1180a; VI, 122a, 242b, 340a, 389a, 407a, 426b, 557a, b, 558a, 578a, b, 582a; S, 46a, 376b, 377a
Abu 'l-Ḥasan ʿAlī (Muley Hacén) (Naṣrid(e)) (1485) vii, 1020b, 1026b – VII, 1022b, 1028b, 1029a
Abu 'l-Ḥasan ʿAlī b. ʿAbd Allāh (1067) s, 343a – S, 342b
Abu 'l-Ḥasan ʿAlī b. Abī Fāris (Ḥafṣid(e)) (XV) iii, 69a – III, 71b
Abu 'l-Ḥasan ʿAlī b. Kaʿb al-Anṣārī (X) s, 13b – S, 14a
Abu 'l-Ḥasan ʿAlī b. Khalaf al-Zayyāt (1063) s, 390b – S, 391a
Abu 'l-Ḥasan ʿAlī b. al-Khalīl (VIII) iv, 1004a – IV, 1036b
Abu 'l-Ḥasan ʿAlī b. Maʾmūn b. Muḥammad (Khʷārazm-Shāh) (XI) vi, 340a – VI, 324a
Abu 'l-Ḥasan ʿAlī b. Muḥammad al-Ṣūfī al-Muzayyin (X) s, 350a – S, 350a
Abu 'l-Ḥasan ʿAlī b. Saʿīd al-Dawla (Ḥamdānid(e)) (X) iii, 130b – III, 133a
Abu 'l-Ḥasan ʿAlī b. Yūsuf al-Ḥakīm (XIV) viii, 818b – VIII, 847a
Abu 'l-Ḥasan ʿAlī al-Ḥuṣrī → al-Ḥuṣrī
Abu 'l-Ḥasan ʿAlī al-Maghribī → al-Maghribī
Abu 'l-Ḥasan ʿAlī al-Shādhilī → al-Shādhilī
Abu 'l-Ḥasan al-Anṣārī (1197) s, **23a** – S, **23a**
Abu 'l-Ḥasan Ardistānī (XIX) s, 23b – S, 23b
Abu 'l-Ḥasan al-Awwal (al-Māḍī) → Mūsā al-Kāẓim
Abu 'l-Ḥasan al-Battī (1015) s, **23a** – S, **23a**
Abu 'l-Ḥasan Djīlwa, Mīrzā (1897) s, **23b** – S, **23b**
Abu 'l-Ḥasan Fihr vi, 263a – VI, 247b
Abu 'l-Ḥasan Hilāl (Ṣābiʾ) viii, 674a – VIII, 693b
Abu 'l-Ḥasan Kharaḳānī → Kharaḳānī

Abu 'l-Ḥasan (Tānā) Ḳuṭb Shāhī (1686) i, 1210a; ii, 180b; iii, 427a; v, 549b; vi, 837b – I, 1246a; II, 186b; III, 441a; V, 554b; VI, 828a
Abu 'l-Ḥasan Hilāl (Ṣābī') viii, 674a – VIII, 693b
Abu 'l-Ḥasan Lārī (XVII) vii, 224a – VII, 225b
Abū 'l-Ḥasan Muḥammad b. Hilāl (Ṣābī') (1088) iii, 752b; vi, 198b, 243a; vii, 857b; viii, 674b – III, 775b; VI, 182b, 227a; VII, 859a; VIII, 694b
Abu 'l-Ḥasan Muḥammad b. Ibrāhīm b. Sīmdjūr → Sīmdjūr, Banū
Abu 'l-Ḥasan al-Maghribī (X) s, **24a** – S, **24a**
Abu 'l-Ḥasan al-Rabaʿī → al-Rabaʿī
Abu 'l-Ḥasan al-Rummānī → Rummānī
Abu 'l-Ḥasan al-Samlālī (XVII) i, 355b – I, 366b
Abu 'l-Ḥasan Shāh, Imām (1791) iv, 201b – IV, 210b
Abu 'l-Ḥasan Shīrāzī → al-Shīrāzī, Abu 'l-Ḥasan
Abu 'l-Ḥasan al-Tamgrūtī (XVI) i, 593b – I, 613a
Abu 'l-Ḥasan Thābit b. Abī Saʿīd Sinān (Ṣābī') (976) vii, 542a; viii, 673b – VII, 542a; VIII, 693a
Abu 'l-Ḥasan Thābit b. Ibrāhīm b. Hārūn (Zahrūn) (Ṣābī') (980) viii, 673b – VIII, 693b
Abu 'l-Ḥasanāt Muḥammad → ʿAbd al-Hayy
Abū Ḥāshid b. Yaḥyā b. Abī Ḥāshid (1052) s, 22b – S, 22b
Abū Hāshim (Sharīf) → Makka
Abū Hāshim b. al-Djubbāʾī (933) i, 4b, 411a; ii, 218b, 570a; iii, 171b, 832a, 1143a, 1165b; v, 702a; s, 12b, 13b, 25b, 32a, 226b, 343b, 346b, 348a – I, 5a, 423a; II, 225a, 584b; III, 175b, 856a, 1171b, 1194b; V, 707a; S, 13a, 14a, 25b, 32a, 226b, 343b, 346a, 348a
Abū Hāshim ʿAbd Allāh b. Muḥammad b. al-Ḥanafiyya (717) i, 15a, 48b, **124b**, 402a; ii, 441a; iii, 265a, 574a, 1265b; iv, 837a; vi, 332b; vii, 396a, 524a; ix, 412b; s, 357b – I, 15b, 50a, **128a**, 412b; II, 452b; III, 272b, 594a, 1298b; IV, 870a; VI, 317a; VII, 397b, 524b; IX, 437a; S, 357b
Abū Hāshim al-Bāwardī iv, 797a, 800b – IV, 829b, 833a
Abū Hāshim Muḥammad, Sharīf (Hāshimid(e)) (1094) vi, 148b – VI, 147a
Abū Ḥassūn ʿAlī al-Bādisī (Waṭṭāsid(e)) (1549) i, 859b, 860a; ii, 819b; vi, 1009b – I, 883b, 884a; II, 839a; VI, 1001b
Abū Ḥātim Aḥmad → ʿAzafī
Abū Ḥātim ʿAnbasa b. Isḥāḳ (856) ii, 72a – II, 73b
Abū Ḥātim al-Malzūzī, Yaʿḳūb b. Labīd (772) i, **125a**; iii, 297a, 654b; vi, 310b, 311a – I, **128b**; III, 306a, 676a; VI,295b, 296a
Abū Ḥātim al-Rāzī (890) iii, 158b – III, 162b
Abū Ḥātim al-Rāzī (933) i, **125a**, 160b, 694a; iii, 158b; iv, 661b; vii, 517a, 652a, 968b, 1006b; x, 391a – I, **129a**, 165a, 715a; III, 162a; IV, 688b; VII, 517b, 652a, 1008b; X, 419b
Abū Ḥātim al-Sidjistānī (869) i, **125b**, 158b, 167b, 718b; iii, 641b, 844b; vii, 258a, 279b, 281a – I, **129a**, 163a, 172b, 740; III, 662b, 868b; VII, 259b, 281b, 282b
Abū Ḥātim al-Warsinānī (X) v, 167a – V, 164b
Abū Ḥātim Yaʿḳūb b. Ḥabīb → al-Ibāḍiyya
Abū Ḥātim Yūsuf b. Muḥammad (Rustumid(e)) (907) vii, 895b – VII, 896a
Abū Ḥātim al-Zuṭṭī (X) iv, 661a – IV, 687b
Abu 'l-Hawl (Hōl) i, **125b**; vi, 414a; s, 408a – I, **129a**; VI, 399a; S, 408a
Abu 'l-Haydjā b, Rabīb al-Dawla (XI) x, 897b – X,
Abu 'l-Haydjāʾ b. Saʿd al-Dawla (Ḥamdānid(e)) (1011) iii, 130b; vii, 116a, 860a; s, 94a – III, 133a; VII, 118a, 861b; S, 93b
Abu 'l-Haydjāʾ ʿAbd Allāh b. Ḥamdān → ʿAbd Allāh b. Ḥamdān
Abu 'l-Haydjāʾ Hadhbānī (XII) v, 454a, 455a – V, 457a, b
Abu 'l-Haydjaʾ Ḥusayn b. Muḥammad (Rawwādid (e)) (988) ii, 680a; viii, 460b – II, 697a; VIII, 485b
Abu 'l-Haydjāʾ al-Rawwādī al-Kurdī, amīr (X) ii, 680a – II, 697a
Abū Ḥayyā al-Numayrī (760) viii, 120b; s, **24a** – VIII, 123a; S, **24b**
Abū Ḥayyān al-Gharnāṭī (1344) i, **126a**, 445b, 593a, 602b; iii, 698b, 801a, 861b; vii, 262a, 400a – I, **129b**, 458b, 612b, 622a; III, 720b, 824b, 885b; VII, 264a, 401b
Abū Ḥayyān al-Tawḥīdī (1023) i, **126b**, 130a, 151b, 159a, 176a, 427a, 590a, 1354a; ii, 387b, 766b, 774b; iii, 355a, 672b, 754b, 1071b, 1263b; v, 320a; vi, 443b, 845b; vii, 143b, 144a, 304b; viii, 615a; x, 67a; s, 13a, b, 72b, 88b, 119b, 289b, 389b, 398b – I, **130a**, 134a, 156a, 163b, 180b, 439a, 609a, 1393a; II, 397b, 785a, 793a; III, 366a, 694a, 777b, 1098a, 1296a; V, 319a; VI, 429a, 836b; VII, 145b, 146a, 306b; VIII, 152b, 634a; X, 69b; S, 13b, 73a, 88b, 119a, 289b, 390a, 398b
Abu 'l-Ḥazm b. Djahwar (vizier) (1031) ii, 389a; iii, 496a, 786a, 973bl vi, 189a – II, 399b; III, 513a, 809b, 998a; VI, 172b
Abū Hiffān, ʿAbd Allāh b. Aḥmad al-Mihzamī (869) iv, 1005a; vii, 660b; s, **24b** – IV, 1037b; VII, 660b; S, **25a**
Abū Hilāl al-ʿAskarī → al-ʿAskarī
Abū Ḥimāra → Bū Ḥmāra
Abu 'l-Hindī al-Riyāḥī iv, 1004a; viii, 884a – IV, 1036a, b; VIII, 914b
Abū Hubayra b. Rabīʿa b. Riyāḥ al-Hilālī (VII) s, 92b – S, 92b
Abu 'l-Hudā (XIX) i, 63b; ii, 418b, 419a; v, 949a – I, 65b; II, 429b; V, 953a
Abū Ḥudhayfa b. al-Mughīra (VII) vi, 139b – VI, 138a
Abu 'l-Hudhayl al-ʿAllāf (840) i, 2a, 4b, 10a, **127b**, 204b, 713b; ii, 449b; iii, 63b, 172a, 1143a, 1266a; v, 384a, 576b; vi, 335a, 336b, 458a, 468b, 636b; vii, 259a, 260a, 401a, 546b, 604a, 1031b, 1057a; s, 88b, 225b, 226a, 227a, 392a, 393b – I, 2a, 5a, 10a, **131a**, 210b, 735a; II, 461a; III, 66a, 175b, 1171b, 1299a; V, 385a, 581a; VI, 319b, 321a, 443b, 454a, 621b; VII, 261a, b, 402b, 546b, 603b, 1034a, 1059b; S, 88b, 225b, 226a, 227a, 392b, 394a
Abū Ḥulmān al-Fārisī (988) iii, 570b – III, 590a
Abū Hurayra al-Dawsī al-Yamānī (678) i, 52a, **129a**, 266b, 714a; iii, 242b; v, 1010a; vi, 79a, 674b; vii, 570b; s, 230b, 311a, b – I, 54a, **132b**, 274b, 736a; III, 249b; V, 1005b; VI, 77a, 661a; VII, 571b; S, 230b, 310b, 311a
Abū Hurayra al-Rāwandī (VIII) iv, 838a – IV, 871a
Abū Ḥusayn, Banū → Kalbid(e)s
Abu 'l-Ḥusayn b. Abī Yaʿlā (1131) i, 274a, b, 1039a; iii, 766b; iv, 990a – I, 282b, 1070b; III, 789b; IV, 1022b
Abu 'l-Ḥusayn b. Samʿun iii, 159b; v, 10a – III, 163a; V, 10b
Abu 'l-Ḥusayn Aḥmad b. al-Ḥasan al-Uṭrūsh (X) i, 688a; iii, 255a; s, 356b – I, 709a; III, 262b; S, 356b
Abu 'l-Ḥusayn al-Baṣrī (1044) iii, 1023b, 1025b, 1144a; s, 14a, **25a** – III, 1049a, 1051b, 1172b; S, 14a, **25b**
Abū Ḥuzāba, al-Walīd b. Ḥunayfa (704) s, **26a** – S, **26a**
Abu 'l-Ibar, Abu 'l-ʿAbbās Muḥammad (866) s, 16b, **26a** – S, 17a, **27b**
Abū Ibrāhīm Aḥmad b. Muḥammad (Aghlabid(e)) (863)

i, 24a, 248b, 250b, 621a; iii, 287b; iv, 829b – I, 25a, 256b, 258a, 641b; III, 296a; IV, 862a, b

Abū Ibrāhīm Isḥāḳ al-Fārābī → al-Fārābī

Abū ʿIḳāl al-Aghlab (Aghlabid(e)) (841) i, 248b, 250b; iv, 415b – I, 256a, 258a; IV, 433b

Abū ʿIkrima ʿĀmir b. ʿImrān al-Ḍabbī → al-Dabbī

Abū ʿIkrisha → Ḥādjib b. Zurāra

Abū ʿImrān Faḍl b. al-Djarrah (XII) ii, 484b – II, 497a

Abū ʿImrān al-Fāsī (1039) vi, 744a, 942b; vii, 483b; s, 26b – VI, 733a, 935a; VII, 483b; S, 26b

Abū ʿImrān Mūsā b. Muḥammad vi, 709b – VI, 698a

Abū ʿImrān Mūsā al-Ḥasan Muḥammad, Shaykh (1106) v, 247b – V, 245a

Abū ʿInān Fāris b. Abi 'l-Ḥasan ʿAlī (Marīnid(e)) (1359) i, 93a, 124b, 129b, 155a; ii, 822a, 979a; iii, 68a, 462a, 736a, 756a, 826a, 867a; iv, 635a, 729b; v, 531a, 626b, 1190a; vi, 142a, 572b, 593b; vii, 37a, 1024a –
I, 95b, 128a, 133b, 159b; II, 841b, 1001b; III, 70b, 478a, 758b, 779a, 849b, 890b; IV, 661b, 758b; V, 535a, 630b, 1180a; VI, 140a, 557b, 578b; VII, 37b, 1026a

Abu 'l-ʿIrmās → Abū Nukhayla

Abū ʿĪsā (Zandjī) (IX) vii, 526b – VII, 526b

Abū ʿĪsā al-Iṣfahānī (VII) i, 130a; iv, 96a, 603b, 604b, 606b – I, 133b; IV, 100a, 628a, 629a, 631a

Abū ʿĪsā Muḥammad b. Hārūn al-Warrāḳ (861) i, 130a; 905a; iv, 1132a; vi, 949a; vii, 459b; viii, 980b – I, 133b; III, 929a; IV, 1163b; VI, 941b; VII, 459b; VIII, 1015a

Abū Isḥāḳ → al-Shāṭibī

Abū Isḥāḳ I (Ḥafṣid(e)) (1283) iii, 48b, 67a – III, 50b, 69b

Abū Isḥāḳ II (Ḥafṣid(e)) (1369) iii, 68a, 867a – III, 70b, 891a

Abū Isḥāḳ, Sayyid (1207) vi, 840b – VI, 831b

Abū Isḥāḳ b. al-Rashīd (ʿAbbāsid(e)) (IX) i, 439b – I, 452a

Abū Isḥāḳ Čishtī (VII) ii, 50b – II, 51a

Abū Isḥāḳ Djamāl al-Dīn Īndjū (1350) iii, 1022a, 1208b; iv, 102b, 498b, 909b; v, 163a; vi, 908a; s, 415a –
III, 1048a, 1239a; IV, 107a, 520a, 942b; V, 161a; VI, 899bS, 415a

Abū Isḥāḳ al-Fārisī → al-Iṣṭakhrī

Abū Isḥāḳ al-Fārisī, Ibrāhīm b. ʿAlī (987) s, 27b – S, 27b

Abū Isḥāḳ al-Ḥuṣrī → al-Ḥuṣrī

Abū Isḥāḳ Ibrāhīm → Isḥāḳ b. Alp Takīn (Ghazna-wid(e))

Abū Isḥāḳ Ibrāhīm b. Abī ʿAbd Allāh b. al-Sarrādj → Ibn al-Sarrādj

Abū Isḥāḳ Ibrāhīm b. Abī 'l-Ḥasan Hilāl → al-Sābiʾ

Abū Isḥāḳ Ibrāhīm b. Abī Saʿīd Sinān (Sābiʾ) viii, 673a – VIII, 693a

Abū Isḥāḳ Ibrāhīm al-Adjdābī → al-Adjdābī

Abū Isḥāḳ Ibrāhīm al-Harawī (IX) i, 162b – I, 167a

Abū Isḥāḳ Ibrāhīm Ḳuwayrā (X) vi, 844b – VI, 835b

Abū Isḥāḳ Ibrāhīm al-Sāḥilī (1346) vi, 258b, 421b, 422a – VI, 243a, 407a

Abū Isḥāḳ al-Ilbīrī (1067) i, 130b, 602a – I, 134a, 621b

Abū Isḥāḳ Īndjū (1357) iii, 1208b; viii, 806b – III, 1239a; VIII, 833b

Abū Isḥāḳ Ismāʿīl b. al-Ḳāsim → Abu 'l-Atāhiya

Abū Isḥāḳ al-Kāzarūnī → al-Kāzarūnī

Abū Isḥāḳ Muḥammad b. Maʿmūn → al-Muʿtasim

Abū ʿIṣma (Zaydī) (805) vi, 438a – VI, 423b

Abū Kabīr al-Hudhalī (VII) i, 130b; vii, 309a – I, 134b; VII, 311b

Abū Kabrayn → Bū Ḳabrīn

Abū Kadr/Akdar (1179) x, 303a – X, 326a

Abu 'l-Kalām Āzād → Āzād

Abū Ḳalammas → Ḳalammas

Abū Ḳalamūn i, 131a – I, 135a

Abū Kalb → Sikka

Abū Kālīdjar al-Marzūbān, ʿImād al-Dīn (Būyid(e)) (1048) i, 131b, 512b, 1355a, b; ii, 194a, 391a, 856a, 962a; iii, 860a; iv, 294b, 379a, 457b, 911b; vi, 270b, 272b; vii, 270b, 731b, 1018a; viii, 945b –
I, 135b, 528a, 1394a, 1395a; II, 200a, 401b, 876a, 984a; III, 884a; IV, 307b, 395b, 477b, 944b; VI, 255b, 257b; VII, 272b, 732b, 1020a; VIII, 978a

Abū Kālīdjār Garshāsp → Garshāsp

Abu 'l-Kamāl Tamīm b. Zīrī (Īfranid(e)) (1054) i, 1044b; iii, 1043a; v, 1177b –
I, 1076a; III, 1069a; V, 1167b

Abū Kāmil Shudjāʿ b. Aslam (X) i, 132b; ii, 361b; viii, 555b – I, 136a; II, 371b; VIII, 573b

Abū Kārib Asʿad (ca. 400) x, 545b – X,

Abū Ḳarib Budayr b. Abī Ṣakhr (VII) s, 357b – S, 357b

Abū (Ibn) Karib (Kurayb/Karnab) al-Ḍarīr (VIII) i, 1116b; v, 433b – I, 1150b; V, 435b

Abu 'l-Ḳāsim i, 133b – I, 137b

Abu 'l-Ḳāsim → al-Zahrāwī

Abu 'l-Ḳāsim b. al-ʿAbbād vi, 204b – VI, 188b

Abu 'l-Ḳāsim b. Abi 'l-Zinād (VIII) s, 380b – S, 380b

Abu 'l-Ḳāsim b. ʿAddū vii, 585a – VII, 585b

Abu 'l-Ḳāsim b. Manda → Ibn Manda, ʿAbd al-Raḥmān

Abu 'l-Ḳāsim b. Maḥfūẓ, Djamāl al-Dīn iv, 810b – IV, 843b

Abu 'l-Ḳāsim b. ʿUbayd Allāh al-Mahdī (Fāṭimid(e)) (X) i, 207b; iii, 297b; v, 1175a, 1243b – I, 213b; III, 306b; V, 1165a, 1234a, b

Abu 'l-Ḳāsim b. Yūsuf b. al-Sarrādj → Ibn al-Sarrādj

Abu 'l-Ḳāsim ʿAlī (Mīkālī) (986) vii, 26a – VII, 26a

Abu 'l-Ḳāsim ʿAlī, Khʷādja (Mīkālī) (1032) vii, 26a – VII, 26a

Abu 'l-Ḳāsim Anūdjūr (Unūdjūr) → Unūdjūr

Abu 'l-Ḳāsim ʿĀrif (Ḳazwīn) (1934) vi, 71a – IV, 75a

Abu 'l-Ḳāsim Bābur b. Baysunghur (Tīmūrid(e)) (1457) i, 91a, 147b, 701a; iii, 603a; iv, 523b; vi, 513b; vii, 90a – I, 93b, 152a, 722a; III, 623b; IV, 546a; VI, 498b; VII, 92a

Abu 'l-Ḳāsim al-Barrādī → al-Barrādī

Abu 'l-Ḳāsim Bishr-i Yāsīn (990) i, 146a – I, 150a

Abu 'l-Ḳāsim Djaʿfar b. al-Uṭrūsh (925) i, 688a; iii, 255a; s, 356b – I, 709a; III, 262a; S, 356b

Abu 'l-Ḳāsim al-Djardjarāʾī → al-Djardjarāʾī

Abu 'l-Ḳāsim Farāhānī → Ḳāʾim-Maḳām, Abū l'-Ḳāsim

Abu 'l-Ḳāsim al-Fazarī → al-Fazarī

Abu 'l-Ḳāsim al-Ḥakkār → ʿAbd al-ʿAzīz b. Yūsuf

Abu 'l-Ḳāsim Ḥasan al-Shaddād (XIV) vii, 210b – VII, 212a

Abu 'l-Ḳāsim al-Ḥusayn b. ʿAlī al-Maghribī (vizier) → al-Maghribī

Abu 'l-Ḳāsim al-Kaʿbī al-Balkhī → al-Balkhī

Abu 'l-Ḳāsim Ḳāʾimmaḳām (Īrān) (XIX) s, 70b – S, 71a

Abu 'l-Ḳāsim Khalaf → al-Zahrāwī

Abu 'l-Ḳāsim Khān (ḳaʾim maḳām (1835) vii, 454a – VII, 454b

Abu 'l-Ḳāsim al-Ḳushayrī → al-Ḳushayrī

Abu 'l-Ḳāsim al-Madjrīṭī → al-Madjrīṭī

Abu 'l-Ḳāsim Maḥmūd → Maḥmūd b. Sebüktigin

Abu 'l-Ḳāsim al-Makkī (faḳīh) (XI) vii, 294b – VII, 296b

Abu 'l-Ḳāsim Muḥammad b. Yaḥyā → ʿAzafī

Abu 'l-Ḳāsim Muḥammad al-Sīmāwī al-ʿIrāḳī (XIII) v,112a; s, 270a – V, 114b; S, 269b

Abu 'l-Ḳāsim Rabīb al-Dīn (vizier) (1220) vi, 632a – VI, 617a

Abu ʾl-Ḳāsim Rāmis̲h̲t (1140) ix, 668a – IX, 694a
Abu ʾl-Ḳāsim Samd̲j̲ū al-Miknāsī (VIII) vi, 1038a – VI, 1031b
Abu ʾl-Ḳāsim S̲h̲ayk̲h̲ al-Raʾīs (Ḳād̲j̲ār) (XIX) iv, 164b – IV, 171b
Abu ʾl-Ḳāsim al-Wāsānī → al-Wāsānī
Abu ʾl-Ḳāsim Yazīd b. Mak̲h̲lad, S̲h̲ayk̲h̲ (X) iii, 95a, b, 656a; s, 48b – III, 97b, 98a, 677b; S, 49a
Abu ʾl-Ḳāsim al-Zayyānī → al-Zayyānī
Abū Ḳatāda, Anṣārī vi, 267b – VI, 252b
Abū Ḳays b. Abī Anas vii, 361b – VII, 364a
Abū Ḳays b. al-Aslat (wāʾil) (VI) i, 771b – I, 794b
Abū K̲h̲alaf al-Ḳuḍāʿī (1043) vi, 198a – VI, 182a
Abū K̲h̲ālid ʿAbd al-ʿAzīz (Asīd, Banū) i, 148b – I, 153a
Abū K̲h̲ālid Yazīd al-Wāsiṭī (al-D̲j̲ārūdiyya) ii, 485a; s, 48b – II, 497b; S, 49a
Abu K̲h̲alīfa al-D̲j̲umaḥī → al-Faḍl b. al-Ḥubāb
Abu ʾl-K̲h̲aṣīb (VIII) i, **133b** – I, **137b**
Abu ʾl-K̲h̲aṣīb Wuhayb b. ʿAbd Allāh (802) ix, 34a – IX, 34b
Abu ʾl-K̲h̲aṭṭāb al-Asadī (762) i, **134a**, 1156a; iv, 203a, 1132a; vi, 917b; vii, 517a – I, **137b**, 1190b; IV, 212a, 1163b; VI, 909a; VII, 517b
Abu ʾl-K̲h̲aṭṭāb al-Kalwad̲h̲ānī → al-Kalwad̲h̲ānī
Abu ʾl-K̲h̲aṭṭāb al-Maʿāfirī (Ibāḍī Imām) (757) i, **134a**, 1099a, 1175a; ii, 374b; iii, 296a, 297a, 654a, 1040b; iv, 827a; v, 696a; vi, 841a; viii, 638a – I, **138a**, 1132a, 1210b; II, 385a; III, 305b, 306a, 675b, 1066b; IV, 860a; V, 700b; VI, 831b; VIII, 657a
Abu ʾl-K̲h̲aṭṭār al-Ḥuṣām b. Dirār al-Kalbī (745) i, **134b**, 490a; ii, 1012b; iii, 601b; iv, 494b, 672b; vi, 221b – I, **138b**, 504b; II, 1036a; III 622b; IV, 515b, 700a; VI, 215b
Abu ʾl-K̲h̲ayr (Yemen) s, 354b – S, 354b
Abu ʾl-K̲h̲ayr ʿAbd al-Raḥmān (1786) vi, 112b – VI, 110a
Abu ʾl-K̲h̲ayr Abū Āzād (1868) i, 827b; s, 354b – I, 850b; S, 354b
Abu ʾl-K̲h̲ayr Ḥammād al-Dabbās (1106) i, 69a – I, 71a
Abu ʾl-K̲h̲ayr al-Ḥusayn al-Bag̲h̲dādī (XI) i, 1236b – I, 1274a
Abu ʾl-K̲h̲ayr al-Is̲h̲bīlī (XI) i, **135b**; ii, 901b – I, 13**9b**; II, 922b
Abu ʾl-K̲h̲ayr K̲h̲ān Özbeg (1469) i, 46b, **135a**, 147b, 148a; ii, 44b; vi, 417b; ix, 426a; s, 51a – I, 47b, **138b**, 152a; II, 45b; VI, 402b; IX, 442bS, 51b
Abu ʾl-K̲h̲ayrāt b. Ibrāhīm (XIX) ii, 124a – II, 127a
Abu ʾl-K̲h̲ayrid (e) → S̲h̲ībānid(e)s
Abū K̲h̲ayt̲h̲ama Zuhayr b. Ḥarb (857) iii, 687a; vii, 691b – III, 708b; VII, 691b
Abū K̲h̲azar Yag̲h̲lā b. Zaltāf, S̲h̲ayk̲h̲ (X) iii, 95a, b, 656a – III, 97b, 98a, 677b
Abū K̲h̲āzim Ibn Abī Yaʿlā (1133) iii, 766b – III, 789b
Abū K̲h̲āzim lbn al-Farrāʾ (1039) iii, 766b – III, 789b
Abū K̲h̲irās̲h̲ K̲h̲uwaylid (VII) i, **136a** – I, **140a**
Abu ʾl-K̲h̲uḍayb (Ṭabaristān) (VIII) ix, 54b – IX, 55b
Abuḳraṭ(īs) → Buḳrāṭ
Abū Ḳubays, D̲j̲abal i, **136a**, 178a; vi, 162a, 168b, 578b, 791b – I, **140a**, 183a; VI, 156a, 160a, 563b, 781b
Abū Kudāma Yazīd b. Fandīn al-Īfranī (803) iii, 1041b – III, 1067b
Abū Ḳuḥāfa (ʿUt̲h̲mān) b. ʿĀmir (VI) i, 109b, 110a – I, 112b, 113a
Abū Kurayb Muḥammad b. al-ʿAlāʾ (862) vii, 691a; x, 11b – VII, 691b; X, 11b
Abū Ḳurays̲h̲ (VIII) i, 1298a – I, 1338a
Abū Ḳurrā al-Īfranī al-Mag̲h̲īlī (Ṣufrī) (765) i, 367a, 1175b; iii, 1040b, 1041a; v, 1164b; vi, 311b, 312a; ix,768a – I, 378a, 1210b; III, 1066b, 1067a; V, 1154b; VI, 296b, 297a; IX, 801b
Abū Ḳurra, Theodore (820) i, **136b** – I, **140b**
Abū Lahab b. ʿAbd al-Muṭṭalib (624) i, 9a, 80a, 115b, **136b**, 152b; iii, 366b; vi, 146b – I, 9a, 82b, 118b, **140b**, 157a; III, 378a; VI, 145a
Abū Layla → al-Ḥārit̲h̲ b. ʿAbd al-ʿAzīz; Sulaymān Pas̲h̲a Misrāklī
Abū Layla Isḥāḳ b. Muḥammad (Awraba) s, 103a – S, 102b
Abu ʾl-Layt̲h̲ Naṣr → al-Ḥāfiẓ al-Samarḳandī
Abu ʾl-Layt̲h̲ al-Samarḳandī (983) i, 123b, **137a**; ii, 98b; iii, 163a; vii, 1052b; ix, 535a – I, 127a, **141a**; II, 100b; III, 166b; VII, 1054b; IX, 555b
Abū Layt̲h̲ al-Siḳillī (XII) iv, 118a – IV, 123a
Abū Leylī S̲h̲ayk̲h̲ Süleymān (Malāmī) (XVI) vi, 228a – VI, 222a
Abū Lubāba i, 266b – I, 274b
Abū Luʾluʾa (VII) iii, 586b; vii, 347a; x, 820a – III, 607a; VII, 349a; X,
Abu ʾl-Maʿālī → Muḥammad b. ʿAbd al-Bāḳī
Abu ʾl-Maʿālī (Mug̲h̲al) (XVI) s, 324b – S, 324a
Abu ʾl-Maʿālī b. Sayyid Mubārak (Bayhaḳī) (XVI) s, 132a – S, 131a
Abu ʾl-Maʿālī ʿAbd al-Malik → al-D̲j̲uwaynī
Abu ʾl-Maʿālī al-K̲h̲aṭīrī vii, 397a – VII, 398b
Abu ʾl-Maʿālī Muḥammad b. ʿUbayd Allāh (XI) i, **137a** – I, **141a**
Abu ʾl-Maʿālī al-Mus̲h̲arraf b. al-Murad̲j̲d̲j̲ā vii, 295a – VII, 297a
Abu ʾl-Maʿālī Naṣr Allāh iv, 704a – IV, 732b
Abu ʾl-Maʿālī Saʿd al-Dawla → Saʿd al-Dawla S̲h̲arīf
Abu ʾl-Maʿālī S̲h̲arīf I → Saʿd al-Dawla S̲h̲arīf
Abu ʾl-Maʿālī S̲h̲arīf II (Ḥamdānid(e)) (XI) iii, 130b – III, 133a
Abū Māḍī, Īliyyā (1957) v, 1254b, 1255a, b; s, **27b** – V, 1245b, 1246a, b; S, **28a**
Abū Madyan Hawwārī (Boumedienne, Houari) b. Muḥammad b. Sahla (XX) iii, 564a; iv, 363a; v, 1071a; vi, 250b – III, 583b; IV, 379a; V, 1068a; VI, 235a
Abū Madyan S̲h̲uʿayb al-Andalusī (1197) i, 91b, **137b**, 141a, 159b, 1205a; ii, 100b, 183a; iii, 339a, 701b, 800a, 844a, 866a; iv, 1006b; vi, 196b, 280a, 356a; ix, 316a; x, 124b; s, 403a – I, 94a, **141b**, 145a, 164a, 1241a; II, 102b, 189a; III, 349a, 723b, 823b, 868a, 890a; IV, 1038b; VI, 180b, 264b, 340a; IX, 326a; X, 134a; S, 403a
Abu ʾl-Mafāk̲h̲ir Yaḥyā (1335) ix, 111a – IX, 115a
Abu ʾl-Mag̲h̲rāʾ b. Mūsā b. Zurāra (IX) iv, 89a, b, 90a – IV, 93a, b, 94a
Abū Maḥallī al-Sid̲j̲ilmāsī (1613) vi, 594b; s, **28b** – VI, 579b; S, **28b**
Abu ʾl-Maḥāsin b. Tag̲h̲rībirdī (1470) i, **138a**, 595a; ii, 782a, 954a; iii, 188b, 775b; iv, 294b; vi, 194a; vii, 172b; s, 386b, 389a – I, **142a**, 614b; II, 800b, 976a; III, 193a, 798b; IV, 308a; VI, 178a; VII, 174b; S, 386b, 389a
Abu ʾl-Maḥāsin al-S̲h̲aybī (1433) vi, 824a – VI, 814b
Abū Maḥd̲h̲ūra (VII) vi, 677a – VI, 663b
Abū Maḥmūd b. D̲j̲aʿfar b. Falāḥ al-Kutamī (X) vii, 488b – VII, 488b
Abu ʾl-Makārim b. Muḥammad al-Abharī (XI) v, 930a – V, 934b
Abu ʾl-Makārim Aḥmad b. al-ʿAbbās, Tād̲j̲ al-Dīn (XII) ii, 333b; vi, 14b – II, 343b; VI, 13a
Abū Makārim Hibat Allāh (Rabīʿa, Banū) viii, 90b – VIII, 92b
Abū Mak̲h̲rama → Mak̲h̲rama, Bā
Abu ʾl-Malāḥim (dāʿī) (885) vi, 438b – VI, 424a
Abu ʾl-Malīḥ b. Mammati → Ibn Mammatī

Abū Manṣūr → al-Thaʿālibī
Abū Manṣūr b. Bahāʾ al-Dawla (1008) s, 119a – S, 118b
Abū Manṣūr b. Ṣāliḥān (X) viii, 694a – VIII, 713b
Abū Manṣūr b. Yūsuf (1067) iii, 699b, 766a; s, **29b**, 192a – III, 721b, 789a; S, **29b**, 193a
Abū Manṣūr al-Azdī (XI) i, 515b – I, 531a
Abū Manṣūr Farāmurz (Kākūyid(e)) (1051) iii, 471b; iv, 101a, 465b – III, 488a; IV, 105a, b, 486b
Abū Manṣūr Ilyās al-Nafūsī (IX) i, **139a**; ii, 369a; iv, 920a; vi, 452b – I, **143a**; II, 379a; IV, 953a; VI, 438a
Abū Manṣūr Kumrī s, 271b – S, 271b
Abū Manṣūr al-Maʿmarī (Muʿammarī) (X) iv, 63b – IV, 67a
Abū Manṣūr Muḥammad b. ʿAbd al-Razzāḳ (Ṭūs) (X) ii, 918b; x, 425b – II, 940a; X, 456a
Abū Manṣūr Muḥammad b. ʿAlī (1027) ii, 127b; v, 928b – II, 130b; V, 933b
Abū Manṣūr Ṭalḥa b. Ruzayḳ (808) vi, 333a – VI, 317b
Abū Marwān, Sīdī (1111) i, 512a – I, 527b
Abū Marwān b. Ḥayyān → Ibn Ḥayyān
Abū Marwān b. Razīn s, 81b – S, 81a
Abū Marwān ʿAbd al-Malik b. ʿAbd al-ʿAzīz (XIII) s, 81b – S, 81a
Abū Marwān ʿAbd al-Malik b. Djawhar (vizier) (IX) vii, 569a – 569b
Abū Maʿshar Djaʿfar b. Muḥammad al-Balkhī (886) i, **139a**, 589b; iii, 463b, 1072b, 1136b, 1137a; iv, 1182b; v, 130b, 297a, 950a; vii, 85b, 559a, 977a; viii, 100a, 103b, 106b, 107a, 108a; s, 17a –
I, **143b**, 608b; III, 480a, 1099a, 1164b, 1165a; IV, 1215b; V, 133b, 296b, 954a; VII, 87a, 559b, 977b; VIII, 102b, 105b, 106a, 108b, 109b, 110b; S, 17a
Abū Maʿshar Nadjīḥ al-Sindī (787) i, **140a** – I, **144a**
Abū Maslama, Shaykh (XI) i, 755a – I, 778a
Abū Masʿūd al-Anṣārī (720) vii, 27a – VII, 27a
Abū Matallī (Marabout) (XVII) ix, 545b – IX, 567a
Abu ʾl-Mawāhib → al-Ḥasan b. Sulaymān
Abu ı-Mawāhib (1628) viii, 425a – VIII, 439a
Abū Midfaʿ → Sikka
Abū Miḥdjān ʿAbd Allāh Mālik (ʿAmr) b. Ḥabīb al-Thaḳīfī (637) i, **140a**; iii, 850b; iv, 385b, 1002a; vi, 641b – I, **144a**; III, 874b; IV, 402b, 1031b; VI, 627a
Abū Miḥdjān Nuṣayb b. Rabāḥ → Nuṣayb
Abū Mikhnaf (774) i, **140b**; iii, 608a, 610a; v, 947b – I, **144b**; III, 628b, 631a; V, 951b
Abū Mismār, al-Sharīf Ḥammūd (1818) s, **30a** – S, **30b**
Abu ʾl-Muʿaskar al-Ḥusayn b. Maʿdān (Makrān) (XI) iii, 906a – III, 930b
Abū Mudar Ziyādat Allāh → Ziyādat Allāh III
Abū Mudjālid al-Baghdādī (882) iv, 1162a – IV, 1194a
Abu ʾl-Mughīra b. Ḥazm → Ibn Ḥazm
Abu ʾl-Mughīra ʿAmr b. Sharaḥīl al-ʿAnsī (Ḳadarī) iv, 370a – IV, 386b
Abu ʾl-Mughīth al-Rāfiḳī (IX) i, 153b – I, 157b
Abu ʾl-Muhādjir Dīnār al-Anṣārī (681) ii, 525b; iv, 826a; v, 518a; vi, 878a; x, 790a – II, 538b; IV, 859a; V, 521b; VI, 869b; X,
Abū Muḥammad (Sufyānid(e)) (744) vi, 624a – VI, 609a
Abū Muḥammad b. Abī Hafṣ (XIII) ii, 1007b, 1008a – II, 1031b
Abū Muḥammad b. Baraka (X) i, **140b**; iii, 731b – I, **144b**; III, 754b
Abū Muḥammad b. Djiyār al-Djayyānī (XII) ii, 516a – II, 529a
Abū Muḥammad b. ʿUbayd Allāh (1195) viii, 635b – VIII, 654b
Abū Muḥammad ʿAbd Allāh b. ʿAbd al-Muʾmin (Almohad(e)) (XII) iii, 386b; v, 61a – III, 399a; V, 62b
Abū Muḥammad ʿAbd Allāh b. ʿAbd al-Wāḥid (1228) iii, 66a – III, 68b
Abū Muḥammad ʿAbd Allāh b. Barrī → Ibn Barrī
Abū Muḥammad ʿAbd Allāh b. Manṣūr → Ibn Ṣulayḥa
Abū Muḥammad ʿAbd Allāh b. ʿUmar Tādj al-Dīn (Awlād al-Shaykh) (1244) i, 766a, b – I, 789a, b
Abū Muḥammad ʿAbd Allāh al-ʿĀdil (Almohad(e)) (1227) vi, 339b – VI, 323b
Abū Muḥammad ʿAbd al-Wahhāb b. Aḥmad → Ādarrāḳ
Abū Muḥammad ʿAbd al-Wāḥid (Almohad(e)) (1224) vi, 592b – VI, 577a
Abū Muḥammad ʿAbd al-Wāḥid b. Abī Ḥafs, Shaykh (1221) iii, 66a – III, 68b
Abū Muḥammad al-Ḥasan b. Ḥamdān, Nāṣir al-Dawla (1048) vii, 118b – VII, 121a
Abū Muḥammad Ḳāsim → ʿAzafī
Abū Muḥammad Ṣāliḥ b. Yanṣāran (1234) i, **141a**; iii, 339a – I, **145a**; III, 349a
Abū Muḥammad Ṭalḥa b. ʿAbd Allāh b. Khalaf al-Khuzāʿī → Ṭalhat al-Ṭalaḥāt
Abū Muḥammad al-Tamīmī (1095) iii, 766b – III, 789b
Abū Muḥammad Wislān b. Yaʿḳūb (X) iii, 95b – III, 98a
Abū Muḥammad Ziyādat Allāh → Ziyādat Allāh I
Abū Muḥammad al-Zubayr b. ʿUmar (1143) ii, 1013b – II, 1037a
Abū Muḥriz (ḳāḍī) (808) i, 685a – I, 706a
Abū Muḳātil Ḥafṣ b. Salm al-Samarḳandī (VIII) vi, 457b; vii, 606b – VI, 443a; VII, 606a
Abu ʾl-Mulūk → Bāwand
Abu ʾl-Munadjdjā (X) iv, 663b – IV, 690a
Abū Mūsā (island/île) i, 535b; iv, 778a, b; vii, 449b; s, 417b, 418a – I, 552a; IV, 809b, 810a; VII, 450b; S, 418a
Abū Mūsā al-Ashʿarī → al-Ashʿarī
Abū Mūsā al-Dabīlī → al-Dabīlī
Abū Mūsā I ʿĪsā b. Ādam (IX) i, 162a – I, 166b
Abū Mūsā ʿĪsā b. Ṣabīḥ → al-Murdār
Abū Mūsā al-Kharrāz iv, 801a – IV, 833a
Abū Musʿab Muḥammad b. Ayyūb → Muḥammad b. Ayyūb
Abu ʾl-Musāfir al-Fatḥ (Sādjid(e)) (929) vi, 499a – VI, 484b
Abū Musallam Musharraf b. ʿUbayd Allāh (XI) vii, 651a – VII, 650b
Abū Muslim b. Ḥammād (Ḳarmaṭī) (X) iv, 662b – IV, 689a
Abū Muslim al-Khurāsānī (754) i, 15b, 16a, 16b, 43a, 49a, 103a, 116b, **141a**, 149a, 755a, 1293a; ii, 78a, 86b, 110a, 505a, 739b, 966b; iii, 802b, 988a; iv, 15b, 16a, 45a, 411b, 446b, 718a, 838a; v, 57a, b, 63b, 64a, 69a, 618a, 855a; vi, 332a, 427b, 619b, 620a, b, 661a, 677a, 744b; vii, 94b, 500a, 664a, 1016a; ix, 423b, 874b; x, 845a –
I, 16a, 16b, 17a, 44b, 50b, 106a, 120a, **145a**, 153a, 778a, 1332b; II, 79b, 88b, 112b, 518a, 758a, 988b; III, 826a, 1012b; IV, 17a, b, 48a, 429b, 466b, 747a, 870b; V, 59a, 65b, 71a, 622a, 861b; VI, 316b, 412b, 413a, 604b, 605a, b, 646b, 663b, 733b; VII, 96a, 500a, 663b, 1018a; IX, 438a, 910b; X,
Abu ʾl-Muṭāʿ Dhu ʾl-Ḳarnayn (Ḥamdānid(e)) (XI) iii, 128b – III, 131b
Abu ʾl-Muṭahhar al-Azdī (XI) i, 133b; iii, 368a, 1264a; vii, 495a; s, **31a** – I, 137b; III, 379b, 1297a; VII, 495a; S, **31a**
Abu ʾl-Muṭarrif b. ʿAmīra → Ibn ʿAmīra

Abu 'l-Muṭarrif ʿAbd al-Raḥmān (917) vii, 941b – VII, 942a
Abu 'l-Muthannā → al-Sharḳī b. al-Kutāmī
Abu 'l-Muʾthir al-Bahlawī (IX) i, **141b** – I, **145b**
Abu 'l-Muẓaffar (amīr) (1021) iii, 799a – III, 822b
Abu 'l-Muẓaffar b. Yūnus (1197) iii, 751b – III, 774b
Abu 'l-Muẓaffar ʿAbd Allāh (Muḥtādjid(e)) (951) vii, 477b – VII, 477a
Abu 'l-Muẓaffar Ḥamdān b. Nāṣir al-Dawla (Ḥamdānid(e)) (X) vii, 983b; s, 36a – VII, 984a; S, 36b
Abu 'l-Muẓaffar Ḳāsim b. Djihāngīr (Aḳ-Ḳoyunlu) (1498) vi, 541a – VI, 525b
Abū Muẓaffar Naṣr b. Sebüktigin (Ghaznawid(e) (1021) x, 425b, 426a, 869a – X, 456a, 456b,
Abū Naḍḍāra, Yaʿḳūb b. Rafāʿīl Ṣanūʿ (1912) i, **141b**, 597a; ii, 466b; vi, 746b – I, **146a**, 616b; II, 478a; VI, 736a
Abū Nadjāḥ b. Ḳannāʾ (1129) i, 440a – I, 452b
Abu 'l-Nadjīb → ʿAmʿaḳ
Abu 'l-Nadjm → Badr b. Ḥasanwayh
Abu 'l-Nadjm al-ʿIdjlī (724) i, **142a**, 207b; viii, 377a; s, 259a – I, **146a**, 214a; VIII, 390a; S, 258b
Abū Nahshal b. Ḥumayd al-Ṭūsī (IX) i, 154a, 1289b; iii, 573a – I, 158a, 1329a; III, 593a
Abū Nās (Mandīl) (XIII) vi, 404a – VI, 388b
Abū Naṣr (vizier) (Bukhārā) (X) vi, 340a – VI, 324b
Abū Naṣr b. al-Ṣabbāgh (1085) vii, 781a – VII, 783a
Abū Naṣr Aḥmad b. Muḥammad (Farīghūnid(e) (1010) ii, 799b, 1011a; vii, 407a – II, 818a, 1034b; VII, 408a
Abū Naṣr Aḥmad al-Munāzī → al-Munāzī
Abū Naṣr Hārūn b. Saʿīd al-Tustarī (Sābīʾ) (1052) vii, 730a; viii, 674b – VII, 730b; VIII, 694b
Abū Naṣr Manṣūr b. ʿAlī → Ibn ʿIrāḳ
Abū Naṣr al-Miṣrī s, 267a – S, 266b
Abū Naṣr Mushkān (XI) i, 1130b; iv, 758b – I, 1164b; IV, 788b
Abū Naṣr Sābūr → Sābūr b. Ardashīr
Abū Naṣr Saʿd, al-Mustaʿīn bi-'llāh (Ciriza/Muley Zad) (Naṣrid(e)) (1463) vii, 1020b, 1026a – VII, 1022b, 1028b
Abū Naṣr Shāh-Fīrūz (X) s, 118b – S, 118a
Abū Naṣr-i Fārsī (XI) vi, 783a – VI, 773a
Abū Nātiḥ → al-Maʿlūf, Ibrāhīm
Abū Nuʿaym al-Faḍl b. Dukayn al-Mulāʾī (834) i, **143a;** viii, 515a – I, **147a;** VIII, 532b
Abū Nuʿaym al-Iṣfahānī (1038) i, **142b**; ii, 359b; iv, 212a; v, 1234b, 1235a; vi, 263a, b, 266b, 352b, 353a, 354a, 821a; vii, 95b; viii, 498a, 518a – I, **146b**; II, 369b; IV, 221b; V, 1225a, b; VI, 247b, 248a, 251b, 336b, 337b, 338a, 811b; VII, 97b; VIII, 515a, 536a
Abū Nūḥ (800) vi, 204a – VI, 188a
Abū Nukhayla al-Ḥimmānī (754) s, **31a** – S, **31b**
Abū Nukṭa (Wahhābī) (1809) s, 30b – S, 30b
Abū Numayy I, Muḥammad (Sharīf) (1301) i, 21a, 553a; iii, 262b; vi, 149b – I, 22a, 570b; III, 270a; VI, 148a
Abū Numayy II, Muḥammad (Sharīf) (1566) i, 1032b; ii, 517b, 572a, 788a; iii, 262b; v, 18a – I, 1064a; II, 530b, 586b, 806b; III, 270a; V, 18b
Abū Numayy b. Abi 'l-Barakāt (Mecca) (XVI) ix, 14a – IX, 14b
Abū Nūr b. Abī Ḳurra (Īfrānid(e)) (1058) iii, 1043b – III, 1069b
Abū Nuwās (813) i, 2b, 10b, 14a, 108a, 116b, 118b, **143b**, 150b, 158b, 196b, 438a, 587b, 751b, 1081b; ii, 437b, 591b, 1032a; iii, 156b, 328a, 618a, b, 745b, 1202b, 1262b; iv, 54b, 252a, 919a, 1004a, b, 1008b; v, 133a, 778b; vi, 253a, 468b, 604b, 641a; vii, 114a, 261b, 414b, 694b, 982a; viii, 884b; s, 25a, 58b, 253a, 352b –
I, 2b, 10b, 14a, 111a, 120a, 122a, **147b**, 155a, 163a, 202a, 450b, 606b, 774a, 1114a; II, 449a, 606a, 1056a; III, 159b, 338a, 638b, 639a, 768b, 1233a, 1295b; IV, 57b, 263a, 952a, 1036a, b, 1041a; V, 135b, 184b; VI, 237a, 454b, 589b, 626a; VII, 116a, 263a, 416a, 695a, 983a; VIII, 914b; S, 25a, 59a, 252b, 352b
Abu 'l-Rabīʿ (Marīnid(e)) (1310) s, 112b – S, 112a
Abu 'l-Rabīʿ b. Sālim → al-Kalāʿī
Abu 'l-Raddād (860) vii, 40a – VII, 40a
Abū Radjāʾ b. Ashhab (IX) vii, 409a – VII, 410b
Abū Rakwa Walīd b. Hishām (1007) ii, 858b; iii, 78b, 79b – II, 878a; III, 81a, 82a
Abū Rās (1823) ix, 20b – IX, 21b
Abū Rashīd al-Nīsābūrī (XI) s, **31b**, 345a, 346a, 393a – S, **32a**, 345a, 346a, 393b
Abu 'l-Rawāʾin (ʿĪsāwā) (1556) iv, 94a – IV, 98a
Abu 'l-Rayḥān al-Bīrūnī → al-Bīrūnī
Abū Rayyāsh (Aḥmad b. Abī Hāshim) vi, 167a, 268a – VI, 252a, 253a
Abū Ridjāʾ Muḥammad Zamān Khān (1872) ii, 500b – II, 513a
Abu 'l-Ridjāl b. Abī Bakkār (904) vi, 775b – VI, 765a
Abū Righāl (VI) i, **144b** – I, **149a**
Abū Riyāḥ Kaysānī iv, 837a – IV, 870a
Abū Riyāsh al-Ḳaysī (950) v, 374b; s, **32a** – V, 375a; S, **32b**
Abū Ruʾba (VII) vii, 606a – VII, 605b
Abū Ruḳayba → Bourguiba
Abū Rudaynī ʿUmar b. ʿAlī (IX) viii, 53a – VIII, 54a
Abu 'l-Saʿādāt Muḥammad → al-Nāṣir Abu 'l-Saʿādāt
Abu 'l-Ṣabbāh b. Yaḥyā al-Yaḥṣubī (VIII) iv, 115a – IV, 120b
Abū Saʿd al-Ḥasan b. Ḥamdūn (1211) iii, 784a – III, 807b
Abū Saʿd b. Muḥammad b. Mamā, Shabānkāra (XI) ix, 311a – IX, 320b
Abū Saʿd al-ʿAlāʾ b. Sahl (X) viii, 122a – VIII, 124b
Abū Saʿd al-Makhzūmī s, **32b** – S, **32b**
Abū Saʿd al-Mubārak al-Mukharrimī, ḳāḍī (XII) i, 69a – I, 71a
Abū Saʿd Saʿīd b. Abi 'l-Faḍl al-Maydānī (1145) vi, 914a – VI, 905b
Abū Saʿd al-Tustarī (1048) vii, 118b, 730a – VII, 121b, 730b
Abu 'l-Sādj Dīwdād b. Dīwdast (Sādjid(e)) (879) i, **145a**; vii, 395a; viii, 745a – I, **149b**; VII, 396a; VIII, 766b
Abū Safyān (VII) i, **145b** – I, **150a**
Abū Sahl b. Nawbakht (VIII) x, 226b – X, 244b
Abū Sahl Dūnash b. Tāmīm (X) iv, 304a – IV, 318a
Abū Sahl al-Harawī (X) s, 38a – S, 38a
Abū Sahl al-Ḳūhī (982) vi, 600b; s, 412b – VI, 585a; S, 412b
Abū Saʿīd (Īl-Khān) (1335) i, 91a, 510b, 764b, 908b, 1011a; ii, 68a, 401a, 706a; iii, 57b, 1122b; iv, 860a; vii, 170a, 189b, 404b, 462a, 820a, 928a; viii, 541b; s, 363b, 415a –
I, 93b, 526a, 787b, 936a, 1042a; II, 69a, 411b, 724a; III, 60a, 1150b; IV, 893a; VII, 171b, 190a, 405b, 461b, 822a, 928b; VIII, 559a; S, 363a, 415a
Abū Saʿīd (Marīnid(e)) (1331) i, 859b; ii, 146a, 822a, 979a; s, 45b – I, 883b; II, 150a, 841b, 1001b; S, 46a
Abū Saʿīd b. Abi 'l-Khayr (1049) i, **145b**, 162b; iii, 103a; iv, 63b, 1025b, 1057b; vi, 638a, 914b; vii, 550a, viii, 505a –
I, **150a**, 167a; III, 105b; IV, 67a, 1057b, 1088b; VI, 623a, 906a; VII, 550a; VIII, 522b
Abū Saʿīd b. al-Aʿrābī i, 114b – I, 117b
Abū Saʿīd b. Ḳarā Yūsuf, amīr (XV) iv, 587b – IV, 611a
Abū Saʿīd b. Muʿāwiya b. Yazīd b. al-Muhallab (VIII) vii, 359b – VII, 362a

Abū Saʿīd b. Sulṭān Muḥammad b. Mīrān<u>sh</u>āh (Tīmūrid(e)) (1469) i, 135a, **147b**, 227b, 311b, 852b; iii, 603a, 1100b; iv, 34a, 588a; vi, 54a, 193b, 309b, 456a, 482a, b, 501b, 505a; vii, 105b; x, 964b s, 50b, 51a – I, 139a, **151b**, 234b, 321a, 876a; III, 623b, 1127b; IV, 36b, 611b; VI, 52a, 177a, 295a, 441b, 468a, b, 487a, 490a; VII, 107b; X, ; S, 51b
Abū Saʿīd Abaḳ (Būrid(e)) (1154) i, 1332a, b; ii, 282a; iii, 399a – I, 1372b, 1373a; II, 290b; III, 411b
Abū Saʿīd al-Aflaḥ → al-Aflaḥ b. ʿAbd al-Wahhāb
Abū Saʿīd Āḳ-Sunḳur ʿAbd Allāh Ḳasīm al-Dawla(al-Ḥa<u>dj</u>ib) (1086) vi, 379b – VI, 364a
Abū Saʿīd Bahadur → Abū Saʿid al-Il<u>kh</u>ān
Abū Saʿīd al-<u>Dj</u>annābī → al-<u>Dj</u>annābī
Abū Saʿīd Efendi (<u>sh</u>ay<u>kh</u> al-Islām) (XVII) vi, 969a – VI, 961b
Abū Saʿīd Gurgān, Sultan (1469) vii, 78b – VII, 79b
Abū Saʿīd al-Ḳarmātī → al-<u>Dj</u>annābī
Abū Saʿīd <u>Kh</u>alafa al-Ba<u>dj</u>ī → Sayyidī Abū Saʿīd
Abū Sāʿīd al-<u>Kh</u>arrāz → al-<u>Kh</u>arrāz
Abū Saʿīd al-<u>Kh</u>aṭṭābī → al-<u>Kh</u>aṭṭābī
Abū Saʿīd al-Marwazī (IX) i, 153b – I, 158a
Abū Saʿīd Muḥammad b. Yūsuf (amīr) (841) vi, 506a – VI, 491b
Abū Saʿīd San<u>dj</u>ar al-<u>Dj</u>āwulī → ʿAlam al-Dīn San<u>dj</u>ar
Abū Saʿīd Sinān b. <u>Th</u>ābit b. Ḳurrā (Sābiʾ) (943) viii, 672a – VIII, 693a
Abū Saʿīd al-Sīrāfī → al-Sīrāfī
Abū Saʿīd ʿU<u>th</u>mān I (ʿAbd al-Wādid(e)) (1303) i, 93a; iii, 833a – I, 96a; III, 857a
Abū Saʿīd ʿU<u>th</u>mān II (ʿAbd al-Wādid(e)) (1352) i, 93a; iii, 867a – I, 96a; III, 890b
Abū Saʿīd ʿU<u>th</u>mān (Marīnid(e)) → ʿU<u>th</u>mān II (Marīnid(e))
Abū Saʿīd ʿU<u>th</u>mān b. ʿAbd al-Muʿmin, Sayyid (<u>Gh</u>arnāṭa) ii, 1013b, 1014a; iii, 66a, 755a, 772a – II, 1037b; III, 68b, 778a, 795a
Abū Saʿīd-zāde Feyḍ Allāh Efendi, <u>Sh</u>ay<u>kh</u> al-Islām (XVII) i, 394a – I, 405a
Abū Saʿīd Zayd (XI) i, 1310a – I, 1350a
Abū Ṣa<u>kh</u>r al-Hu<u>dh</u>alī (VII) i, **148b** – I, **153a**
Abū Salama b. ʿAbd al-Asad Ma<u>kh</u>zūmī (624) vi, 138a – VI, 136b
Abū Salama Ḥafs b. Sulaymān al-<u>Kh</u>allāl (vizier) (744) i, 15b, 16a, 16b, 103b, **149a**, 1293a; iii, 988a; vi, 334b, 620b; vii, 664a; ix, 423b – I, 16a, 16b, 17a, 106b, **153a**, 1332b; III, 1012b; VI, 319a, 605b; VII, 663b; IX, 437b
Abū Ṣāliḥ al-Armanī (XIII) vi, 411a, b; viii, 91a – VI, 396a, b; VIII, 92b
Abū Ṣāliḥ Mufliḥ, <u>Sh</u>ay<u>kh</u> (941) iii, 161a, 735a – III, 164b, 757b
Abū Sālim ʿAlī (Marīnid(e)) iii, 826a, 867a – III, 850a, 891a
Abu 'l-Ṣalt Umayya al-Andalūsī (1134) i, **149a**; vi, 450 b; viii, 42b – I, **153b**; VI, 435b; VIII, 43b
Abū Sammāl (Asad, Banū) vii, 564b – VII, 565a
Abu 'l-Sarāyā al-Ḥamdānī → Ḥamdānid(e)s
Abu 'l-Sarāyā al-Sarī b. Manṣūr al-<u>Sh</u>aybānī (815) i, **149b**, 402b; iii, 243b, 950b; iv, 17a; vi, 334b – I, **153b**; 414a, III, 250b, 975b; IV, 18a; VI, 318b
Abū 'l-Saydāʾ al-Dabbī → al-Dabbī, Abu 'l- Saydāʾ-
Abu 'l-Ṣaydāʾ Ṣāliḥ b. Ṭarīf (VIII) iii, 224a; iv, 15b, 44b; vii, 606a – III, 231a; IV, 16b, 47a; VII, 605b
Abū Sayyāra, ʿUmayla b. al-Aʿzal s, **33a** – S, **33b**
Abū Sekkine (Bagirmi) (XIX) i, 910b – I, 938a
Abū Seray → Ḳarḳīsiyā
Abū <u>Sh</u>abaka, Ilyās (1947) s, **33b** – S, **33b**
Abū <u>Sh</u>ādī, Aḥmad Zakī (1955) i, 598b; vii, 869a; s, **34a** – I, 618b; VII, 870a; S, **34a**
Abū <u>Sh</u>aḥma (VII) s, 230a – S, 230a
Abū <u>Sh</u>ākir al-Dayṣanī (zindīḳ) i, 48b; iii, 496b – I, 49b; III, 513b
Abū <u>Sh</u>akūr Bal<u>kh</u>ī (X) iv, 63a; viii, 885a; s, 35a – IV, 66b; VIII, 915a; S, 35a
Abu 'l-<u>Sh</u>alaʿlaʿ Muḥammad → Muḥammad b. Aḥmad
Abū <u>Sh</u>āma, <u>Sh</u>ihāb al-Dīn al-Maḳdisī (1268) i, **150a**, 1314b; iii, 268a, 693b, 753a, 934a, 1158a; vi, 430a; vii, 167a – I, **154a**, 1355a; III, 275b, 715b, 776a, 958b, 1186b; VI, 415b; VII, 168b
Abu 'l-<u>Sh</u>amaḳmaḳ (796) i, **150a**; iii, 966a – I, **154b**; III, 990b
Abū <u>Sh</u>amir al-Ḥanafī (IX) vii, 606b; s, 88b – VII, 606b; S, 88b
Abū <u>Sh</u>antūf (Hintāta) (XVI) vi, 734a – VI, 732a
Abu 'l-<u>Sh</u>awk Fāris (ʿAnnāzid(e)) (1045) i, 512b; iii, 258b, 571b; v, 453b, 454a – I, 528a; III, 266a, 591b; V, 456b
Abu 'l-<u>Sh</u>ay<u>kh</u> (979) vi, 821a – VI, 811a
Abu 'l-<u>Sh</u>ibl ʿĀṣim al-Bur<u>dj</u>ūmī (IX) iv, 1005a – IV, 1037b
Abu 'l-<u>Sh</u>īṣ al-<u>Kh</u>uzāʿī (915) i, **150b**; iv, 1004b; vii, 694b; s, 33a – I, **154b**; IV, 1037a; VII, 695a; S, 33a
Abū <u>Sh</u>uʿayb (island/île) → Lār (island/île)
Abū <u>Sh</u>uʿayb Ayyūb al-Ṣinhā<u>dj</u>ī (XII) i, 159b, 809b; iii, 339a – I, 164a, 832b; III, 349a
Abū <u>Shudj</u>āʿ Aḥmad b. Ḥasan (XII) i, **150b**, 867b; iii, 817a – I, **155a**, 891b; III, 841a
Abū <u>Shudj</u>āʿ Bā<u>dh</u> b. Dustāk → Bā<u>dh</u>
Abū <u>Shudj</u>āʿ Fātik b. ʿAbd Allāh al-Rūmī (1022) v, 929b, 933a,b; vii, 116b, 770b – V, 934b, 937a, b; VII, 118b, 772b
Abū <u>Shudj</u>āʿ Ru<u>dh</u>rawārī (XI) ii,384b; iii, 258b; s, 398a – II, 394b; III, 256b; S, 398b
Abū <u>Shudj</u>āʿ <u>Sh</u>īrawayh (1115) → <u>Sh</u>īrawayh, Abū <u>Shudj</u>āʾ
Abū <u>Sh</u>urāʿa (255) s, **35a** – S, **35b**
Abu Simbil → Abū Sinbil
Abu 'l-Simṭ Marwān b. Abi 'l-<u>Dj</u>anūb (X) vi, 625b – VI, 610b
Abu 'l-Simṭ Marwān b. Sulaymān (X) vi, 625a – VI, 610a
Abū Sinbil s, **35b** – S, **35b**
Abū Ṣufra Abu 'l-Muhallab (VII) iv, 1056b; vii, 357a – IV, 1087b; VII, 359a
Abū Sufyān b. Ḥarb b. Umayya (653) i, 9a, 115b, **151a**, 381b, 868a, 1283b; ii, 375b, 843b, 1020b; iii, 455a; vi, 138a, 145b, 146b; vii, 254a, 264a, 369b, 370a; x, 841a; s, 103b, 133b, 350a – I, 9a, 119a, **155a**, 392b, 892a, 1323a; II, 386a, 863b, 1044a; III, 471a; VI, 136b, 144a, 145a; VII, 255b, 265b, 266a, 371b; X, ; S, 103a, 133a, 350a
Abū Sufyān Maḥbūb b. al-Raḥīl → Maḥbūb b. al-Raḥīl
Abū Sulaymān Dāʾūd b. Ibrāhīm al-<u>Th</u>alātī i, 121b – I, 125a
Abū Sulaymān al-Si<u>dj</u>istānī al-Manṭiḳī (985) i, 127a, **151b**, 235b; ii, 359a; vi, 641a; s, 13b, 398b – I, 130b, **156a**, 243a; II, 369a; VI, 626a; S, 13b, 398b
Abū Sulaymān Muḥammad b. Maʿ<u>sh</u>ar → al-Maḳdisī, Abū Sulaymān
Abu 'l-Surrī → Sahl b. Maṣlīaḥ
Abu 'l-Surūr al-Mufarri<u>dj</u> → Ibn al-Sarrā<u>dj</u>
Abu 'l-Suʿūd, ʿAbd Allāh (XIX) ii, 466b – II, 478a
Abu 'l-Suʿūd Muḥammad b. Muḥyi 'l-Dīn al-ʿImādī (<u>Kh</u>o<u>dj</u>a Čelebi) (1574) i, **152a**, 1235a; ii, 32b, 56b, 687a; iii, 163b; iv, 375a, 376a, 557a, 560a, 881b; v, 682a; vi, 3b, 226b, 227a; vii, 546a, 912a; viii, 486b; ix, 401b – I, **156a**, 1272a; II, 33a, 57b, 704b; III, 167a; IV, 391b,

392b, 581a, 582b, 914a; V, 687b; VI, 3b, 220a, 221a; VII, 546a, 912b; VIII, 803a; IX, 414b
Abū Taghlib Faḍl Allāh al-Ghaḍanfar (Ḥamdānid(e)) (979) i, 211b, 824b, 954b; ii, 344a, 483a; iii, 127b, 128a, b, 246a, 841a; iv, 663b, 1084a; vi, 540a, 930a; vii, 910b, 911a, 995b; s, **36a** – I, 218a, 847a, 984a; II, 353b, 495a; III, 130b, 131a, 253a, 864b; IV, 690a, 1115b; VI, 524b, 922a; VII, 911a, b, 997a; S, **36a**
Abū Ṭāhir b. 'Alī, Atābeg (Lūr-i Buzurg) (XII) v, 826b – V, 832b
Abū Ṭāhir b. Ḥassūl (XI) vi, 638a – VI, 623a
Abū Ṭāhir 'Abd al-Raḥmān b. Aḥmad (Imām) (1091) ix, 86b – IX, 90a
Abū Ṭāhir Ibn 'Awfī (1185) iv, 137a; vi, 279a, 429a – IV, 142b; VI, 264a, 414a
Abū Ṭāhir Ibrāhīm al-Ḥamdānī (1010) iii, 128a,b – III, 130b, 131b
Abū Ṭāhir al-Khātūnī vi, 351b – VI, 336a
Abū Ṭāhir Sa'īd (1087) i, 147a – I, 151b
Abū Ṭāhir Sulaymān al-Karmaṭī → al-Djannābī
Abu 'l-Ṭāhir Tamīm → Tamīm b. Yūsuf
Abū Ṭāhir Ṭarsūsī i, **152b**; iv, 63b, 445a – I, **157a**; IV, 67a, 465a
Abū Ṭāḳa → Sikka
Abū Ṭālib b. 'Abd al-Muṭṭalib (619) i, 9a, 80a, 118b, **152b**, 381b; vi, 139b, 146a, b – I, 9a, 82b, 122a, **157a**, 392b; VI, 138a, 144b, 145a
Abū Ṭālib 'Abd Allāh → 'Azafī
Abū Ṭālib Aḥmad b. al-Ḳāsim (1656) vii, 779a – VII, 780b
Abū Ṭālib al-Akhīr (1128) s, 363a – S, 363a
Abū Ṭālib b. al-Ḥusayn, Sharīf (XVII) s, 407b – S, 407b
Abū Ṭālib b. Muḥammad Khudābanda (XVII) i, 8b; iii, 157b – I, 8b; III, 161a
Abū Ṭālib Fandaruskī iii, 114b – III, 116b
Abū Ṭālib Iṣfahānī, Mīrzā (XIX) s, 290a – S, 290a
Abū Ṭālib Kalīm → Kalīm
Abū Ṭālib Khān (1806) i, **153a**; iii, 1046a – I, **157b**; III, 1072a
Abū Ṭālib al-Makkī (998) i, **153a**, 274a, 351a; iii, 570b; iv, 470a, 486b; vii, 465a; viii, 993b; x, 9a – I, **157a**, 282b, 362a; III, 590b; IV, 491a, 507b; VII, 464b; VIII, 1028b; X, 9a
Abū Ṭālib al-Nāṭiḳ (1033) s, 335b – S, 335a
Abū Ṭālūt (Khāridjī) (VII) iv, 1076a – IV, 1107b
Abū Ṭālūt Sālim b. Maṭar (VII) iv, 1076a; vii, 858b – IV, 1107b; VII, 860a
Abu 'l-Ṭamaḥān al-Ḳaynī (634) i, 115b; iv, 820a; s, **37a** – I, 119a; IV, 853a; S, **37b**
Abū Tamīm Anṣārī (VII) vi, 837a – VI, 828a
Abū Tammām Ḥabīb b. 'Aws (845) i, 53a, 118b, **153a**, 331a, 386b, 449b, 592a, 822a, 857b, 1114b, 1289a, 1290a; ii, 248b; iii, 110b, 111b, 879a; v, 935a; vi, 107b, 625b, 635b; vii, 307b, 527a, 694b, 982a; viii, 892a; s, 15a, 26a, 32b, 33a, 277b – I, 54b, 122a, **157b**, 341b, 397b, 462b, 611a, 845a, 881b, 1148a, 1328b, 1329b; II, 256a; III, 113a, 114a, 903b; V, 939a; VI, 105b, 610b, 620b; VII, 309b, 527b, 695a, 982b; VIII, 922b; S, 15b, 26b, 32b, 33a, 277a
Abū Tāshufīn I (1337) i, 122b, **155a** – I, 126a, **159a**
Abū Tāshufīn II (1393) i, 122b, 123a, **155a**; iii, 832a – I, 126a, b, **159a**; III, 855b
Abū Tawwāma (XIII) vi, 131a – VI, 129b
Abū Tāyih (Tawāyihī) → 'Awda b. Ḥarb
Abū Ṭayyib → al-Mutanabbī; al-Ṭabarī
Abu 'l-Ṭayyib al-Lughawī (962) iii, 665a; s, **37b**, 361b – III, 686b; S, **38a**, 361a
Abu 'l-Ṭayyib Muḥammad al-Numayrī (X) iv, 1005b – IV, 1037b
Abū Ṭayyib al-Shawwā (X) vii, 492b – VII, 492b
Abū Ṭayyiba (cupper) (VII) s, 304a – S, 303b
Abū Thābit ('Abd al-Wādid) (XIV) i, 93a; iii, 867a; s, 377a – I, 95b; III, 890b; S, 377a
Abū Thābit 'Āmir (Marīnid(e)) (1308) v, 48b; vi, 441a, 593b; s, 103a – V, 50a; VI, 426b, 578a; S, 102b
Abu 'l-Thanā' Maḥmūd b. Ādjā i, 1109b – I, 1143a
Abū Thumāma (VII) iv, 472a – IV, 493a
Abū Thawr (854) i, **155a** – I, **159b**
Abū Ṭulayḥ → Abuklea
Abū Turāb → 'Alī b. Abī Ṭālib
Abū Turāb al-Athīrī (vizier) (XI) s, 29b – S, 29b
Abū Turāb Ḥaydar al-Din "Kāmil" (XVIII) iv, 544b – IV, 568a
Abū Turāb Mīrzā → Ismā'īl (III) (Safawid(e))
Abū Ṭurāb Nakhkhshābī (859) x, 377a – X, 404b
Abū Tuwayriḳ Badr (1570) ix, 435a – IX, 439b
Abū 'Ubayd b. Mas'ūd (VII) x, 819a – X,
Abū 'Ubayd b. Sallām x, 918a – X,
Abū 'Ubayd al-Bakrī (1094) i, 96a, **155b**, 345a, 488a, 511b, 600b, 862b; ii, 584b; iii, 991b; iv, 339a; v, 1011a, 1017b; vi, 257b, 258a, 359b, 639b, 640a; vii, 228a, b, 584a, 761a; viii, 17a; x, 346a; s, 304b, 376b – I, 99a, **159b**, 355b, 503a, 527a, 620a, 886b; II, 599a; III, 1016a; IV, 353a, b; V, 1006b, 1013b; VI, 242a, 343b, 624b, 625a; VII, 230a, b, 584b, 762b; VIII, 17a; X, 321b; S, 304a, 376b
Abū 'Ubayd al-Ḳāsim b. Sallām (838) i, 156a, **157b**, 158b, 718b; iv, 547b; v, 175a; vi, 194b, 344b, 654b, 816a, 822a; vii, 262a; viii, 150b, 672a; ix, 318a, 662a; x, 918a; s, 15b, 317b – I, 160a, **161b**, 163a, 740a; IV, 571b; V, 172a; VI, 178b, 328b, 640a, 806b, 812a; VII, 264a; VIII, 152b, 691b; IX, 328a, 688a; S, 16a, 317b
Abū 'Ubayd Allāh (786) i, 103b, **157b**, 1033b – I, 106b, **162a**, 1065a
Abū 'Ubayd al-Thaḳafī (634) ii, 555a – II, 569a
Abū 'Ubayda 'Āmir b. al-Djarraḥ (639) i, 110a, **158b**, 460b, 970b, 996a, 1137b, 1139a, 1215b; ii, 279b, 280a; iii, 397b; v, 923a; vi, 379a, 505b, 544b, 774a; vii, 570b; viii, 989b; ix, 263a; x, 820a – I, 113a, **163a**, 474a, 1000b, 1026b, 1172a, 1173b, 1251b; II, 288a; III, 410a; V, 928b; VI, 363a, 491a, 529b, 763b; VII, 571b; VIII, 1014b; IX, 271a: X,
Abū 'Ubayda al-Djanāwanī → al-Djanāwanī
Abū 'Ubayda Ma'mar b. al-Muthannā (824) i, 105b, 108b, 125b, 143b, **158a**, 167b, 588b, 717b, 718b, 794a; ii, 241a; iv, 1077a; vi, 786a, 828b; vii, 254b, 262a, 402a, 841a; s, 15b, 73b, 177a – I, 108b, 129a, 147b, **162a**, 172a, 607b, 739a, 817a; II, 248a; IV, 1109a; VI, 776a, 819a; VII, 256a, 264a, 402a, 842b; S, 16a, 74a, 178a
Abū 'Ubayda Muslim b. Abī Karīma al-Tamīmī (Ibāḍī) (VIII) i, 120b, 134a; iii, 649b, 650b, 651b, 654a, 658a; vii, 524b; viii, 638a; ix, 766a – I, 124a, 138a; III, 671a, b, 672b, 675b, 679b; VII, 524b; VIII, 657a; IX, 799b
Abū 'Udhba (1713) vi, 847b – VI, 838b
Abū 'l-'Uḳūl (1300) vii, 30a; x, 163a – VII, 30a; X, 175b
Abu 'l-'Ulā' b. 'Abd al-Mu'min (Almohad(e)) (XII) ii, 1072a – II, 1096b
Abu 'l-'Ulā' Idrīs → Idrīs al-Ma'mūn
Abū 'Ulāmā al-Mashdja'ī (1750) vi, 191b – VI, 175b
Abū Umāma As'ad (VII) vi, 645b – VI, 631a
Abū 'Umar b. Kawthar (XII) ix, 308b – IX, 318a
Abū 'Umar al-Djarmī → al-Djarmī, Abū 'Umar
Abū 'Umar Ibn Yūsuf (ḳāḍī 'l-ḳuḍāt) (922) iii, 101a, 692a; vi, 279b – III, 103b, 714a; VI, 264b
Abū 'Umar Inālū (XII) ii, 1013a – II, 1037a
Abū 'Umar Tāshufīn b. Abi 'l-Ḥasan (Marīnid(e)) (XIV) iii, 867a – III, 890b

Abū Umayma → Ismāʿīl Ṣabrī
Abū Usāma al-Harawī (1009) s, **38a** – S, **38a**
Abū ʿUtba → Abū Lahab b. ʿAbd al-Muṭṭalib
Abū ʿUthmān b. Saʿīd b. al-Ḥakam (Minūrḳa) (XIII) vii, 87a – VII, 88b
Abū ʿUthmān Saʿīd (1620) vi, 187a – VI, 170b
Abū ʿUthmān Saʿīd b. ʿAbd Allāh al-Tilimsānī → al-Tilimsānī, Abū ʿUthmān
Abū ʿUthmān Saʿīd b. Hāshim (1009) iii, 111a; iv, 936b – III, 113b; IV, 969b
Abū ʿUthmān Saʿīd b. Muḥammad b. al-Ḥaddād (914) i, 249b – I, 257b
Abū ʿUthmān Saʿīd b. Yaʿḳūb al-Dimashḳī (950) i, 1223b, 1340a; ii, 948b; vi, 902b – I, 1259b, 1380b; II, 970b; VI, 894a
Abū ʿUzaiyyiz → Ḳatāda b. Idrīs
Abu ʾl-Wafāʾ (vizier) (978) vi, 930a – VI, 922a
Abu ʾl-Wafāʾ, Shaykh (1491) iv, 230b – IV, 240b
Abu ʾl-Wafāʾ b. al-ʿAḳīl → Ibn al-ʿAḳīl
Abu ʾl-Wafāʾ al-Būz(a)djānī (998) i, 127a, **159a**, 1354a; iii, 1140a; vi, 119b, 600b; s, 398b, 412a, b, 413b, 414a –
I, 130b, **163b**, 1393a; III, 1168a; VI, 117b, 585b; S, 398b, 412a, 413a, b, 414a
Abū ʾl-Wafāʾ Ibrāhīm (1756) viii, 730a – VIII, 750b
Abū ʾl-Walīd b. al-Dabbāgh (1151) viii, 635b – VIII, 654b
Abu ʾl-Walīd b. al-Aḥmar (XV) i, 352a – I, 363a
Abu ʾl-Walīd al-Azraḳī → al-Azraḳī
Abu ʾl-Walīd al-Bādjī → Bādjī
Abu ʾl-Walīd Ḳurṭubī → Ibn Rushd, al-Djadd
Abu ʾl-Walīd Muḥammad b. Aḥmad b. Abī Duʾād i, 271b – I, 279b
Abu ʾl-Walīd Muḥammad b. Djahwar → Ibn Djahwar, Abu ʾl-Walīd
Abu ʾl-Ward b. al-Kawthar (750) i, 43a; iv, 493b – I, 44a; IV, 514b
Abū Yaʿazzā Yalannūr b. Maynūn al-Hazmīrī (1177) i, 137b, **159b**; vi, 356b; s, 38b – I, 141b, **164a**; VI, 340b; S, 29a
Abū Yaddās b. Dūnās (Īfrānid(e)) (1009) iii, 1043b – III, 1069b
Abū Yaḥyā b. al-Sakkāk (1413) ix, 347a – IX, 358a
Abū Yaḥyā Abū Bakr I al-Shahīd (Ḥafṣid(e)) (1309) iii, 67b – III, 70a
Abū Yaḥyā Abū Bakr II al-Mutawakkil (Ḥafṣid(e)) (1346) iii, 49a, 67b; iv, 416a; v, 531a – III, 50b, 70a; IV, 434a; V, 535a
Abū Yaḥyā al-Marwazī (X) i, 159a; vi, 844b – I, 163b; VI, 835b
Abū Yaḥyā al-Zadjdjālī (1294) vi, 824b – VI, 814b
Abū Yaḥyā Zakariyyāʾ → Ibn al-Liḥyānī
Abū Yaḥyā Zakariyyāʾ → al-Irdjānī
Abū Yaknī (amīr) (Ḥammādid(e)s) (1088) iii, 138a; vi, 427a – III, 141a; VI, 412a
Abū Yaʿḳūb b. ʿAbd al-Muʾmin (1163) vi, 521a – VI, 505b
Abū Yaʿḳūb al-Aḳtaʿ (X) iii, 100a – III, 102b
Abū Yaʿḳūb Ḳādī al-Khandaḳ (X) i, 816a – I, 839b
Abū Yaʿḳūb al-Khuraymī, Isḥāḳ b. Ḥassān b. Ḳūhī (821) i, **159b**; vi, 437b, 606a; s, 25a –
I, **164a**; VI, 423a, 591a; S, 25a
Abū Yaʿḳūb al-Shaḥḥām (871) vii, 784b – VII, 786b
Abū Yaʿḳūb al-Sidjzī (Sidjistānī) (X) i, **160a**; iii, 328b; iv, 199a, 508b, 662b; vii, 968b; s, 52b –
I, **164b**; III, 338b; IV, 207b, 530b, 689a; S, 53a
Abū Yaʿḳūb al-Sūsī (900) iv, 990b – IV, 1023a
Abū Yaʿḳūb Yūsuf I b. ʿAbd al-Muʾmin (Almohad(e)) (1184) i, **160b**, 1288a, 1339b; ii, 352b, 525a, 744b, 1014a; iii, 771b, 910a, 957a; iv, 116a; vii, 803b; ix, 308b; s, 112b, 307a –
I, **165a**, 1327b, 1379b; II, 362b, 538a, 763a, 1037b; III, 749b, 934a, 981b; IV, 121a; VII, 804b; IX, 318a; S, 112a, 306b
Abū Yaʿḳūb Yūsuf II al-Mustanṣir (Almohad(e)) (1224) vii, 1020b – VII, 1022b
Abū Yaʿḳūb Yūsuf I b. ʿAbd al-Ḥaḳḳ (Marīnid(e)) (1307) i, 92b; iii, 470b; vi, 142a, 356a, 440b, 441a, 521b, 572a, 593b, 596b; vii, 1022a; s, 377a –
I, 95b; III, 487a; VI, 140a, 340a, 426a, b, 505b, 556b, 557a, 577b, 578a; VII, 1024a; S, 377a
Abū Yaʿḳūb Yūsuf b. Abī Saʿīd (Ḳarmaṭī) (977) iv, 664a – IV, 691a
Abū Yaʿḳūb Yūsuf b. Ibrāhīm al-Sadrātī al-Wardjlānī (1174) viii, 756a; s, 15b – VIII, 780bl S, 16a
Abū Yaʿḳūb Yūsif b. Nūḥ → Yūsuf b. Nūḥ
Abū Yaʿḳūb Yūsuf al-Bādisī (XIV) i, 860a – I, 884a
Abū Yaʿḳūb Yūsuf al-Baṣīr → Yūsuf al-Baṣīr
Abu ʾl-Yakẓān Muḥammad b. Aflaḥ (894) i, 139a; vii, 402a – I, 143a; VII, 403a
Abū Yaʿla b. al-Farrāʾ → Ibn al-Farrāʾ
Abū Yaʿla b. Zurʿa (871) ix, 317b – IX, 327b
Abū Yasār ʿAbd Allāh al-Thaḳafī (748) iv, 371a – IV, 387b
Abū Yaʿzā Hazmīrī (1176) iii, 339a, 800b – III, 349a, b, 823b
Abū Yazīd → Makhdūm Shāh Dawlat
Abū Yazīd al-Bisṭāmī (874) i, **162a**, 1168a; ii, 32a; iv, 321a, 1057b; vi, 225a, b, 569b; vii, 95b; ix, 65b; x, 250a –
I, **166b**, 1202b; II, 32b; IV, 335b, 1089a; VI, 218b, 219a, 554a; VII, 97a; IX, 67a; X, 268b
Abū Yazīd Makhlad al-Nukkārī (947) i, **163a**, 699b, 770b, 863a, 1238a; ii, 852b, 977a; iii, 95b, 297b, 656a, 657b, 659b, 1040b, 1042a; iv, 459b, 479a, 740b, 827b; v, 696a, 1175a, b, 1246a, b; vi, 353b, 434a, b, 435a, 727b, 945a; vii, 485b; viii, 113b; s, 236b, 306b –
I, **167b**, 720b, 793b, 887a, 1275b; II, 872b, 999b; III, 98a 306b, 677a, 678b, 680b, 1066b, 1068a; IV, 480a, 501a, 770a, 860b; V, 701a, 1165a, b, 1237a; VI, 338a, 419b, 420a, 716b, 937a; VII, 485a; VIII, 120a, 658a; S, 236b, 306a
Abū Yazīd al-Sulamī → Yazīd b. Usayd al-Sulamī
Abu ʾl-Yumn al-ʿUlaymī → Mudjīr al-Dīn
Abū Yūsuf (Almohad(e)) → Abū Yaʿḳūb Yūsuf I
Abū Yūsuf Yaʿḳūb (Marīnid(e)) (1286) i, 1058a; ii, 819a, 822a, b; vii, 1021b, 1022a; viii, 808b; s, 112a, 113b –
I, 1089a; II, 838b, 841b, 842a; VII, 1023b, 1024a; VIII, 929b; S, 111b, 113a
Abū Yūsuf Yaʿḳūb (Rustamid(e)) (908) iii, 655b – III, 677a
Abū Yūsuf Yaʿḳūb b. Ibrāhīm al-Anṣārī al-Kūfī (798) i, 28a, 123a, 124a, **164a**, 588b, 773a; ii, 231b, 890b; iii, 162b, 512b; iv, 949a; vi, 2a, 24a, 264b, 352b, 495b, 659a; vii, 646a, 662b; viii, 497b; x, 917b –
I, 29a, 126b, 127b, **168b**, 281a, 607b, 796a; II, 238b, 911a; III, 166a, 529b; IV, 981b; VI, 2a, 21b, 249b, 336b, 481a, 645a; VII, 645b, 662b; VIII, 514b; X,
Abū Yūsuf Yaʿḳūb al-Ḳirḳisānī (Ḳarḳasānī) (Karaite) (X) iv, 605a – IV, 629a
Abū Yūsuf Yaʿḳūb al-Manṣūr (Almohad(e)) (1199) i, 137b, **165a**, 495b, 499b, 533b, 604b, 605b, 634a, 1224b; ii, 307b, 331b, 510a, 525a, 1007b; iii, 748b, 910b, 978b; iv, 118a, 461a, 614a, 729b; vi, 134a, 596b, 597a; vii, 211b, 579b, 802b; viii, 507a; s, 274a –
I, 141b, **169b**, 510b, 514b, 549b, 624b, 625a, 654b, 1261a; II, 316b, 341a, 522b, 538a, 1031a; III, 771b, 934b, 1003a; IV, 123a, 434a, 639a, 758b; VI, 132b,

581a, 582a; VII, 213a, 580a, 804b; VIII, 524b; S, 273b

Abū Zaʿbal   s, **38a** – S, **38a**

Abū Ẓabī   i, **166a**, 539b, 1313b, 1314a; ii, 557b, 619a; iv, 751b, 778a; v, 1058b; vi, 37b, 961b; s, 42a, 416b – I, **171a**, 556b, 1354a; II, 571b, 634b; IV, 781b, 809b; V, 1055b; VI, 35b, 954a; S, 42b, 417a

Abu ʾl-Zādjir Ismāʿīl   → Ismāʿīl b. Ziyād al-Nafūsī

Abū Ẓafar   → Bāhadur S̲h̲āh II

Abū ʾl-Ẓafar al-Hindī al-Sayyāḥ   vi, 112b -VII, 110a

Abū Zakariyyāʾ (Ḥafṣid(e)) (1279)   vi, 404a – VI, 388b

Abū Zakariyyāʾ b. K̲h̲aldūn   → Ibn K̲h̲aldūn

Abū Zakariyyāʾ al-Djanāwunī (XII)   i, **166b**, 1028a – I, **171b**, 1059b

Abū Zakariyyāʾ al-Farrāʾ   → al-Farrāʾ

Abū Zakariyyāʾ al-Mag̲h̲ribī, S̲h̲ayk̲h̲ (XII)   ii, 198a; v, 924b, 926b – II, 204b; V, 930a, 932a

Abū Zakariyyāʾ Yaḥyā b. al-K̲h̲ayr al-Wardj(a)lānī (XII)   i, 125a, **167a**; ii, 141a; iii, 95a; vi, 311a, b, 449a, 945a, 948b; viii, 112b; s, 15b – I, 128b, **171b**; II, 144b; III, 97b; VI, 296a, b, 434b, 937b, 940b; VIII, 115a; S, 15b

Abū Zakariyyāʾ Yaḥyā I (Ḥafṣid(e)) (1249)   i, 121b, 605b; ii, 1008a, 1014b; iii, 66a, 296b, 338a, 461b, 673a; iv, 337b; v, 1150a; s, 111b – I, 125a, 625a; II, 1031b, 1038a; III, 68b, 305b, 348a, 478a, 694b; IV, 352a; V, 1140b; S, 111a

Abū Zakariyyāʾ Yaḥyā II (Ḥafṣid(e)) (1279)   → al-Wāthiḳ

Abū Zakariyyāʾ Yaḥyā III (Ḥafṣid(e)) (1295)   iii, 67a; iv, 338a – III, 69b; IV, 352b

Abū Zakariyyāʾ Yaḥyā IV Ḥafṣid(e)) (1489)   iii, 69a – III, 71b

Abū Zakariyyāʾ al-Zamāmī, dāʿī (X)   iv, 661a – IV, 687b

Abū Zayd   → al-Balk̲h̲ī

Abū Zayd (Banū Hilāl)   i, **167b**; iii, 387a, b – I, **172a**; III, 399b, 400a

Abū Zayd b. Yūsuf al-Ḥardānī (Almohad(e)) (XII)   iii, 231a – III, 237b

Abū Zayd ʿAbd al-Raḥmān b. Igit   → Ibn Igit

Abū Zayd ʿAbd al-Raḥmān b. Maʿlā, S̲h̲ayk̲h̲ (XII)   iii, 96a – III, 99a

Abū Zayd ʿAbd al-Raḥman al-Hazmīrī (XIV)   iii, 339a, b, 731a – III, 349a, b, 754a

Abū Zayd al-Anṣārī, Saʿīd b. Aws (830)   i, 108b, 125b, 143b, **167b**, 717b, 1098a; s, 385b, 73b, 317b – I, 129a, 147b, **172a**, 739a, 1131a; S, 39a, 74a, 317a

Abū Zayd al-Fāzārī (XIII)   iv, 541a – IV, 564a

Abū Zayd al-Ḥasan al-Sīrāfī (X)   ii, 583b; s, 56a – II, 598a; S, 56b

Abū Zayd al-Ḳayrāwānī (996)   vi, 279a – VI, 264a

Abū Zayd al-Ḳuras̲h̲ī (X)   s, **38b** – S, **38b**

Abū Zayd al-Manāṭiḳī   vi, 354a – VI, 338a

Abū Zayd Muḥammad b. Abi ʾl-K̲h̲aṭṭāb al-Ḳuras̲h̲ī (X)   vii, 254b, 527a – VII, 256a, 527a

Abū Zayd al-Naḥwī   s, 286b – S, 286a

Abū Zayd al-Sarūdjī   → al-Ḥarīrī

Abū Zayd al-Sīrāfī   → Ak̲h̲bār al-Ṣīn waʾl-Hind

Abū Zayyān I (ʿAbd al-Wādid(e)) (1308)   i, **167b**; v, 1180a – I, **172b**; V, 1170a

Abū Zayyān II (1398)   i, **167b** – I, **172b**

Abū Zayyān III (1550)   i, **168a** – I, **172b**

Abū Zayyān Muḥammad   → Muḥammad IV (Marīnid(e))

Abū Z̲h̲ūr al-Markab, Banū   vi, 46a – VI, 44b

Abu ʾl-Zift al-Ḥasan (VIII)   iii, 616a – III, 636b

Abū ʾl-Zinād (751)   iii, 494b; vi, 263a; viii, 973b; s, 380a – III, 511b; VI, 247b; VIII, 1018a; S, 380b

Abū Ziyā Tewfiḳ Bey   → Tewfiḳ Bey

Abū Ziyād b. Salmā (718)   iv, 54a – IV, 57a

Abu ʾl-Zubayr   vi, 263a – VI, 247b

Abū Zurʿa (1423)   s, **39a** – S, **39a**

Abuʿam   → Tāfīlālt

Abubacer   → Ibn Ṭufayl

Abubakar Atiku (Kano)   iv, 550b – IV, 574b

Abubakar Imam (XX)   iii, 282b – III, 291b

Abūkārib Asʿad (ca.400)   x, 575b –

Abūk̲ir   i, **168a** – I, **172b**

Abuklea   i, **168b** – I, **173b**

Abulcasis   → al-Zahrāwī

Abulelizor, Albuleizor   → Ibn Zuhr, Abu ʾl-ʿAlāʾ

Abulpharagius Benattibus   → Ibn al-Ṭayyib

Abumeron   → Ibn Zuhr

al-ʿAbūr   → Nudjūm

Aburdja, Mudjīr al-Dīn (XIV)   s, 105b – S, 105a

Abūs̲h̲ahr   → Būs̲h̲ahr

Abus̲h̲ḳa   → Nawāʾī ʿAlī S̲h̲īr

Abūṣir   → Būṣir

al-Abwāʾ   i, **169a**; iii, 362b; vii, 645b; s, 312a – I, **173b**; III, 374a; VII, 645a; S, 311b

Abwāb   → Darband

Abyaḍ, Georges (1959)   vi, 746b, 750b, 751b, 755a; s, **39b** – VI, 735b, 739b, 741a, 744a; S, **39b**

Abyaḍ b. Ḥammāl al-Māribī (VII)   vi, 566a, b – VI, 551a, b

Abyan   i, **169a**, 538a; vi, 562b, 563a, b; s, 338a – I, **173b**, 555a; VI, 547a, 548a, b; S, 337b

al-Abyārī, S̲h̲ayk̲h̲ ʿAbd al-Hādī (1888)   s, **40a** – S, **40a**

al-Abzārī   → ʿAmīd al-Dīn

Ačalpur   → Eličpur

Accra (Ghana)   ii, 1003b – II, 1027a

Acheh   → Atjèh

Achehnese   → Malay

Achir   → As̲h̲īr

Acier   → Fūlād̲h̲

Açores   → al-Djazāʾir al-K̲h̲ālida

Acre   → ʿAkkā

ʿĀd, Banū   i, **169a**, 257a, iii, 537b, 1270a; iv, 820b; v, 497b, 811a; vi, 82a; ix, 91a – I, **174a**, 265a; III, 556a, 1303a; IV, 853b; V, 500b, 817a; VI, 80a; IX, 93b

ʿĀd b. ʿŪs b. Iram b. Sām b. Nūḥ   ix, 775a – IX, 808b

ʿĀd S̲h̲ayk̲h̲   vi, 628b – VI, 613b

ʿĀd Te-Mikāʾēl   vi, 628b – VI, 613b

Adāʾ   i, **169b** – I, **174b**

ʿĀda   i, **170a**, 173a, 277a, 741b, 744b, 980b, 1179a; ii, 22b, 890b; iv, 154b-156a – I, **174b**, 178a, 285b, 763b, 766b, 769a, 1011a, 1214a; II, 23a, 911b; IV, 161a-162a

Ada Ḳalʿe   i, **174b** – I, **179b**

Ada Pāzārī   i, **175a** – I, **180a**

Adab   i, 23a, 66a, 133b, **175b**, 326a, 328b, 345b, 588a; ii, 951b; iii, 884b, 893a, 1262a; iv, 510a; s, 93b – I, 22b, 68a, 137b, **180a**, 336a, 338b, 356b, 607a; II, 973b; III, 908b, 917a, 1295a; IV, 532a; S, 93a

ʿAdad   → Ḥisāb

Adal   i, **176b**, 763b, 1172b; iii, 3b, 4a – I, **181a**, 786b, 1207b; III, 3b, 4a

ʿAdāla   → ʿAdl

Adalar   → Kizil Adalar

Adʿalī, Banū   ii, 120b; x, 72a – II, 123a; X, 74b

Adalya   → Antalya

Ādam (Abu ʾl-Bas̲h̲ar)   i, **176b**; iv, 947b; v, 210a; vi, 218b – I, **181b**; IV, 980a; V, 207b; VI, 202b

Ādam, Mawlānā (XIV)   s, 353a – S, 353a

Adam, sultan (Banjarmasin) (1857)   s, 150b – S, 150b

ʿAdam   i, **178b**; v, 578b – I, **183b**; V, 583a

Adama   → Modibbo Adama

Adamiyyat, Ḥusayn Ruknzāda   iv, 72b; v, 198b – IV, 76b; V, 196a

Adamawa i, **179a**; ii, 9b, 10b, 941b, 942b – I, **183b**; 9b, 10b, 963b, 964a

ʿAdan i, 106b, 169a, **180b**, 536a, 539a, 552a, 554b, 781a, 976a; ii, 469a, 675a, 737a; iii, 881b; iv, 519a, 746a, 901b, 1188b; v, 71a, 1059b, 1244b; vi, 36a, 354b, 438b; vii, 66b; s, 338a –
I, 109b, 173b, **185b**, 552a, 556a, 570a, 572a, 804a, 1006b; II, 480b, 692a, 755b; III, 905b; IV, 541b, 775b, 934b, 1221b; V, 73a, 1056b, 1235a, b; VI, 34b, 339a, 424a; VII, 67a; S, 337b

ʿAdan Lāʿa vi, 438b – VI, 424a

Adana i, **182a**; v, 558a; vi, 59b, 69a; s, 138b – I, **187a**; V, 563a; VI, 57b, 67a; S, 138a

Ādār → Taʾrīk̲h̲

Adareñña → Harari

Adārisa → Idrīsid(e)s

Ādarrāk̲ s, **40a**, 399b – S, **40b**, 400a

Adāt → Nah̲w

Ādat → ʿĀda

al-ʿAdawī, Abu ʾl-Bak̲āʾ vi, 106b – VI, 104b

al-ʿAdawī, Muḥammad Ḥasanayn Mak̲h̲lūf (1936) vi, 279a; s, 40b – VI, 263b; S, 41a

ʿAdawiyya i, 195a – I, 201a

Aday, Banū vi, 416b, 417a – VI, 401b, 402a

al-ʿAḍaym i, **184a** – I, **189b**

Aḍḍād i, **184b**; v, 705a – I, **189b**; V, 710b

ʿAddās (Niniveh) viii, 677a – VIII, 696b

Addax → Mahāt

ʿAḍēm → al-ʿAḍaym

Aden → ʿAdan

Adfū i, **186a** ; vi, 672a – I, **191b**; VI, 658b

al-Adfūwī i, 186b; vi, 214b – I, 192a; VI, 198b

Adḥāʿ → ʿĪd al-adḥāʾ

ʿAdḥāb i, **186b** – I, **192a**

ʿAdḥāb al-K̲abr i, **186b**; iv, 667b; v, 236b – I, **192a**; IV, 694b; V, 234b

Adham K̲h̲ān (amīr) (1561) i, 1155a; vi, 310a, 407a – I, 1189b; VI, 295a, 391b

Adhamiyya → Ibrāhīm b. Adham

Adḥān i, **187b**; ii, 432b, 593b; iv, 181a; vi, 361b – I, **193a**; II, 444a, 608a; IV, 188b; VI, 345b

Ādḥār → Taʾrīk̲h̲

Ād̲h̲arbāydjān i, 8a, 13b, **188b**, 300b, 420b, 639a, 642b, 644a, 660a, 731b, 1052a, 1107b; ii, 680b, 903b; iii, 530a, 1099b; iv, 3a, 19b-20a, 347b, 392a; v, 496b, 497a, 729b, 730a, 1213b; vi, 15b, 56a, 64a, b, 120a, 130b, 200b, 202b, 274a, 334a, 335a, 337a, b, 338a, b, 420b, 438a, 482a, 492b, 495a, 498a, b, 499a, b, 500a, 501a, b, 502b, 504a, 512b, 514a, 516b, 539a, 541a, 553b, 623a, 670b; vii, 432a, 655b, 656a; viii, 642b; x, 41b; s, 23b, 47a, 70b, 71b, 116a, 135a, 147b, 170a, 239b, 274b, 282a, 326a, 366a, 378a –
I, 8a, 14a, **194a**, 310a, 432b, 659b, 663a, 664b, 680b, 753b, 1083b, 1141a; II, 697b, 924b; III, 1126b; IV, 3a-b, 21a-b, 362a, b, 409a; V, 499b, 500a, 734b, 735a, 1203a; VI, 14a, 54a, 62a, b, 117b, 128b, 184b, 187a, 259a, 318b, 319a, 321b, 322a, 322b, 405b, 406a, 423b, 468a, 478b, 480b, 483b, 484a, 484b, 485a, b, 486a, 487a, b, 488a, 489a, 490a, 497b, 499a, 501b, 524a, 525b, 538a, 608a, 657a; VII, 433a, 655a, b, 656a; VIII, 661b; X, 42b; S, 24a, 47b, 71b, 72a, 115b, 134b, 147b, 170a, 239b, 274b, 282a, 325b, 365b, 378b

Ād̲h̲arbāydjān (Russia/-e) → Azerbaydjān

Adhargūn i, **191b** – I, **197a**

Ād̲h̲arī (Azerī) i, 191a, **192a**, 756a, 1072b; ii, 89a, 938b; iv, 351a, 627b, 732a; v, 8a; vii, 352a, 353a; x, 710a; s, 415b –
I, 196b, **197b**, 778b, 1104b; II, 90b, 960b; IV, 366a, 652a, 761b; V, 8a; VII, 354a, 355a; X, 754a; S, 416a

Ād̲h̲arī literature x, **726b** – X, **772a**

Ad̲h̲aryūn → Ad̲h̲argūn

ʿAd̲h̲aym (river/rivière) v, 442a – V, 444b

ʿAd̲h̲rāʾ → Nud̲j̲ūm

ʿAd̲h̲rāʾ (Mard̲j̲ Rāhiṭ) vi, 545b – VI, 530a

Ad̲h̲rama x, 92b – X, 100a

Ad̲h̲rīʿāt i, **194a**; vi, 546a, 548a, 742a, b, 743a – I, **200a**; VI, 531a, 532b, 731b, 732b

Ad̲h̲ruḥ i, 55a, 108b, **194b**, 384a, b, 451b; ii, 535a; iv, 938a; vii, 373b; x. 883a; s, 230a –
I, 56b, 111b, **200a**, 395a, b, 464b; II, 548b; IV, 971a; VII, 374b; X, ;S, 230a

Ad̲h̲ur-Walās̲h̲ (VII) iv, 644b – IV, 671a

al-Ad̲h̲wāʾ i, **194b** – I, **200b**

ʿAdī, Banū iii, 386a, b; v, 1183a; vi, 137b, 145a, 649a – III, 398b, 399a; V, 1173a; VI, 136a, 143a, 634b

ʿAdī, Banū (village) s, 40b – S, 41a

ʿAdī b. ʿAmr, Banū v, 78b, 79a – V, 81a

ʿAdī b. Arṭāt (820) iv, 291a; s, **41a** – IV, 304a; S, **41a**

ʿAdī b. Ḥātim (687) i, **195a**; iii, 241a, 274b; v, 499b – I, **200b**, III, 248a, 282b; V, 502b

ʿAdī b. Musāfir al-Hakkārī (1162) i, **195a**; v, 209a, 475b, 644a – I, **201a**; V, 206b, 478b, 648b

ʿAdī b. al-Rik̲āʿ (VIII) i, **196a**, 436a; ii, 480a – I, **201b**, 448b; II, 492a

ʿAdī b. Zayd al-ʿIrādī (VI) i, 115b, **196a**, 565a, 584b; iii, 462b, 1261a; iv, 1002a; vii, 568b; viii, 119b, 884a –
I, 119a, **201b**, 583a, 603b; III, 479a, 1294a; IV, 1031b; VII, 569b; VIII, 122a, 914b

Ādi Granth iii, 456b – III, 472b

al-Adīb, Abu ʾl-Ḥasan (X) ix, 8b – IX, 8b

Adīb Isḥāk̲ → Isḥāk̲, Adīb

Adīb al-Mamālik → Amīrī, Muḥammad Ṣādik̲

Adīb Pīs̲h̲āwarī (1930) s, **41a** – S, **41b**

Adīb Ṣābir → Ṣābir b. Ismāʿīl al-Tirmid̲h̲ī

al-ʿĀḍid li-Dīn Allāh (Fāṭimid(e)) (1171) i, **196b**, 797a; ii, 318a, 856b, 857a; vi, 198a; vii, 163b; viii, 131b –
I, **202a**, 820b; II, 327a, 876b, 877a; VI, 182a; VII, 165b′ VIII, 134a

Adīg̲h̲es → Čerkes

al-ʿĀdil (vizier) (1041) vii, 270b – VII, 272b

al-ʿĀdil, Abū Muḥammad (Almohad(e)) → Abū Muḥammad ʿAbd Allāh

al-ʿĀdil I, al-Malik, Sayf al-Dīn (Ayyūbid(e)) (1193) → al-Malik al-ʿĀdil I

al-ʿĀdil II, al-Malik, Abū Bakr (Ayyūbid(e)) (1248) → al-Malik al-ʿĀdil II

ʿĀdil, Amīr ii, 401b; iv, 584b – II, 412a; IV, 608a

al-ʿĀdil b. al-Salār (vizier) (1153) i, 9a, **198b**; ii, 318a, 856b; iii, 868a; iv, 137a; vii, 579a –
I, 9a, **204a**; II, 327a, 876b; III, 892b; IV, 142b; VII, 579b

ʿĀdil Djabr (XX) vi, 615b – VI, 600a

ʿĀdil Girāy K̲h̲ān (Crimea/-ée) (1671) i, 311a; ii, 88a, 1113b; v, 140a – I, 320b; II, 89b; 1140a; V, 142b

ʿĀdil K̲h̲ān (Lāhawr) (1395) vi, 49b – VI, 48a

ʿĀdil K̲h̲ān I (Fārūk̲id(e)) (1441) ii, 814b – II, 834a

ʿĀdil K̲h̲ān II (Fārūk̲id(e)) (1501) ii, 814b; vi, 51a – II, 834a; VI, 49a

ʿĀdil K̲h̲ān III (Fārūk̲id(e)) (1509) ii, 815a, 1127b; iii, 422a; vi, 51a, 67b; vii, 105a –
II, 834a, 1154a; III, 435b; VI, 49b, 65b; VII, 107a

ʿĀdil Pas̲h̲a (Bahdīnān) (1808) i, 920a – I, 948a

ʿĀdil S̲h̲āh (Afs̲h̲ārid(e)) (1748) i, 246b; iii, 177b; iv, 104a; vii, 674b – I, 254b; III, 182a; IV, 109a; VII, 674b

ʿĀdil-S̲h̲āhs (Bīd̲j̲āpur) i, **199a**, 1048a, 1202b, 1203a, 1323a; ii, 220a, 1135a; iii, 425a, 426a, 447b, 1161a; vi, 68a, 269b, 369a, b, 536b, 610b, 695b; vii, 80a, 289a, 300a, 325b, 943a; ix, 483a –
I, **204b**, 1079b, 1238a, 1239a, 1363b; II, 227a,

1162a; III, 439a, 440a, 462b, 1189b; VI, 66a, 254a, 353b, 521a, 595b, 683b; VII, 81a, 291a, 302a, 327b, 943b; IX, 499b
ʿĀdila Khātūn (XVIII) i, **199a** – I, **204b**
ʿĀdilābād district i, 1322a; ii, 257b, 258a; iii, 481b; vi, 87a – I, 1362b; II, 264a, 265a; III, 498a; VI, 85a
Adilcevaz vi, 242b – VI, 227a
ʿĀdilī → Bāysonghor
Adīnā Beg Khān (XVIII) i, 296a; iii, 1158b; v, 598b – I, 305a; III, 1187a; V, 602b
Adivar, Adnan Bey (1955) i, 836b; iv, 933b, 934a, b; s, **41b** – I, 859b; IV, 966b, 967a, b; S, **42a**
Adiyaman i, **199b**; vi, 231a, 507a – I, **205b**; VI, 225a, 492b
ʿĀdj i, **200a**, 501a – I, **205b**, 516a
Adjaʾ wa-Salmā i, **203a**, 536b; s, 304b – I, **209a**, 553a; S, 304a
ʿAdjabshīr vi, 502b – VI, 488a
ʿAdjāʾib i, 122a, 157a, **203b**; ii, 77a, 583b, 586b – I, 125b, 161a, **209a**; II, 78b, 598a, 601a
Adjal i, **204a** – I, **210a**
ʿAdjala i, **205a** – I, **211a**
Adjall Shams al-Dīn ʿUmar Bukhārī, Sayyid (XIV) vi, 702b, 703a; viii, 159b – VI, 691a; VIII, 264b
ʿAdjam i, **206a**; iii, 212b; iv, 338b – I, **212a**; III, 218b; IV, 353a
ʿAdjamī oghlān i, **206b**, 1004a, 1256b, 1278a; ii, 986a, 996b, 1087a; iv, 242b – I, **212b**, 1034b, 1249b, 1317a; II, 1008b, 1019b, 1112b; IV, 253b
al-ʿAdjamiyya → Aljamía
ʿAdjārida i, **207a** – I, **213a**
Adjaristān i, 468b, 1108b – I, 482b, 1141b
al-Adjdābī, Abū Isḥāḳ i, **207a** – I, **213b**
al-Adjdābī, al-Ḥusayn b. ʿAbd Allāh (1040) vi, 353b – VI, 338a
Adjdābiya i, **207a**; v, 695b; s, 380b – I, **213b**; V, 700b; S, 380b
Adjdir s, 377b – S, 378a
al-ʿAdjdjādj, Abu ʾl-Shaʿthāʾ (715) i, 142a, **207b**, 1154b, 1310b; iii, 1262a; viii, 377a; x, 68b; s, 31b – I, 146b, **214a**, 1188b, 1350b; III, 1294b; VIII, 390a; X, 71a; S, 31b
ʿAdjīb s, 22a – S, 22b
ʿAdjīb al-Māndjilak (Fundj) (1607) ii, 944a; iv, 893a – II, 966a; IV, 925b
ʿAdjību b. ʿUmar Tal i, 297a – I, 306b
Adjirlū vi, 17a – VI, 15b
ʿAdjīsa vi, 727b – VI, 716b
ʿAdjlān b. Rumaytha, Sharīf (1375) i, 553a; vi, 149b – I, 570b; VI, 148a
ʿAdjlān Beg b. Ḳarasī (1335) iv, 628a – IV, 653a
ʿAdjlān al-Hamdānī (VII) s, 400b – S, 401a
ʿAdjlūn i, **208a**; vi, 345a, 547b; s, 391a – I, **214a**; VI, 329b, 532a; S, 391b
al-ʿAdjlūnī (1749) vi, 352b – VI, 337a
ʿAdjmān vi, 38a; vii, 782b; s, **42a**, 416b – VI, 36a; VII, 784b; S, **42b**, 417a
Adjmēr i, **208a**; ii, 50a, 274b; iii, 441a; v, 1218b, 1219b; vi, 53b, 369a, 691b; s, 5a, 55b, 293b, 353b, 420b – I, **214b**; II, 51a, 282b; III, 455b; V, 1208b, 1210a; VI, 51b, 353a, 679a; S, 4a, 56a, 293a, 353a, 421a
al-Adjnādayn i, **208b**; v, 323b, 800a; vi, 138b, 544b; s, 37a – I, **215a**; V, 323a, 806a; VI, 137a, 529a; S, 37b
Adjōdhān vi, 49b, 294b; s, 73b, 353a – VI, 48a, 280a; S, 74a, 353a
Adjr i, **209a**; iii, 1017a – I, **215a**; III, 1042b
ʿAdjrūd vi, 455b – VI, 441a
Adjūdānbāshī s, 108b, 290b – S, 108a, 290a
Adjurān (Sōmālī) vi, 128b – VI, 126b
al-Ādjurrī, Abū Bakr (971) iii, 159a, 735a; s, 83a – III, 162b, 757b; S, 82b
al-Adjurrī, Abū ʿUbayd (X) viii, 516a – VIII, 532b
Ādjurrūmiyya → Ibn Ādjurrūm
ʿAdjūz → Ayyām al-ʿAdjūz
al-ʿAdjūz al-Djurashiyya → Asmāʾ bint ʿUmays
Adjwad b. Zāmil al-Djabrī i, 553a, 942b; ii, 159b, 176a; iv, 764b; s, 234a – I, 571a, 971b; II, 164b, 181b; IV, 795a; S, 234a
Adjwaf → Taṣrīf
Adjyād vi, 155a, 160b, 167a, 178a – VI, 152a, 154b, 159a, 162a
ʿAdl i, **209a**, 334b, 410a, 415b; ii, 834a; iii, 1143b – I, **215b**, 344b, 422a, 427b; II, 854a; III, 1172a
ʿAdlī i, **210a** – I, **216a**
ʿAdn → Djanna
ʿAdnān i, **210a**, 544b; iv, 448a; vi, 472b – I, **216b**, 561b; IV, 467b; VI, 458b
Adowa → Adua
Adrar i, **210b**; v, 654a – I, **216b**; V, 658a
Adrār n-Deren (Atlas) i, 748a – I, 770b
Adrar Ifoghas i, 210b, iii, 1038b – I, 216b; III, 1064b
Adrar Tmar i, 210b, 733b – I, 217a, 755b
Adrianople → Edirne
Adriatic/Adriatique → Baḥr Adriyas
al-Adrīzī, Abu ʾl-ʿAbbās Aḥmad b. Ibrāhīm (1754) vi, 357a – VI, 341a
Adua vi, 643b – VI, 628b
ʿAḍud al-Dawla Fanā-Khusraw (Būyid(e)) (983) i, 87a, 151b, **211b**, 381a, 824a, 899b, 900a, 955a, 1005b, 1223b, 1350b, 1353a, 1354a, 1355b; ii, 127a, 144b, 344a, 487a, 748b, 802b, 812a, 856a, 893b, 905a, 925b; iii, 128a, 258a, 344b, 671a, 703a, 704a, 730a, 823b, 1157a, 1176a; iv, 24a, 222a, 358a, 675a, 859b, 975a; v, 153a, 158b, 229b, 353a, 452b, 867b, 873a, 896b, 1125a; vi, 117b, 120b, 193a, 198b, 199a, 261b, 519a, 521b, 522a, 600b, 626a, 634b, 637b, 658a, 676a; vii, 272b, 312b, 535b, 560b, 771a, 860a; s, 4a, 36b, 94a, b, 118a, 119a, 127a, 263b, 304b, 390a – I, 89b, 156a, **217b**, 392a, 847a, 926b, 984a, 1036b, 1260a, 1390b, 1392a, 1393a, 1394b; II, 130b, 148a, 353b, 499a, 767a, 821b, 831a, 875b, 914b, 926a, 947b; III, 131a, 265a, 355a, 629b, 725b, 726a, 753a, 847a, 1185b, 1204b; IV, 25b, 232a, 373b, 702b, 892b, 1007b; V, 154b, 157b, 227a, 353b, 455a, 874a, 879b, 903a, 1121b; VI, 115a, 118a, 177a, 182b, 183a, 246a, 503b, 506b, 585a, 611a, 619b, 622b, 643b; VII, 274b, 314b, 535a, 561b, 772b, 861b; S, 3b, 37a, 93b, 117b, 118b, 126a, 263b, 304b, 390b
ʿAḍud al-Dawla Shīrzād (XII) vi, 783a – VI, 773a
ʿAḍud al-Dīn → al-Īdjī
ʿAḍud al-Dīn Muḥammad b. ʿAbd Allāh (vizier) (1178) i, **212b**; iii, 891b; vii, 707a, 726b – I, **219a**; III, 915b; VII, 707b, 708a, 727a
ʿAḍudī Hospital/l' hôpital i, 900a, 901a, 1223b, 1224a – I, 927a, 928a, 1260a, b
Adulis vi, 641b, 643b – VI, 626b, 629a
al-ʿAdwa s, 305a – S, 304b
ʿAdwān, Banū iii, 363b; ix, 763b; s, 33a – III, 375a; IX, 796b; S, 33b
Adwiya i, **212b**, 1056a, 1057a; v, 251b – I, **219a**, 1087b, 1088b; V, 249b
Aegean Sea i, 464a; v, 505b, 506a, b
Aelius Gallus vi, 561a – VI, 545b
Afʿa i, **214b** – I, **221a**
Āfāḳ Pārsā (XX) vi, 486a – VI, 472a
Āfāḳīs (Gharībīs) (XV) iv, 908a; vi, 62b, 63a, 67b, 269a – IV, 941a; VI, 60b, 61a, 65a, 254a
Āfāḳiyya x, 250b – X, 269a
Afʿaluhū taʿālā i, 343a, 412b – I, 353b, 424a
Afāmiya (Apamea) i, **215a**; iv, 919b; vi, 578b; vii, 578a; viii, 128a – I, **221b**; IV, 952b; VI, 563b; VII, 578b; VIII, 130b

ʿAfār (Somali/-e) ii, 113b, 535b; iii, 1053a; v, 522a, 524a; x, 71b
– II, 116a, 549a; III, 1079a; V, 525b, 527b; X, 74b
ʿAfar (ʿUmān) → al-ʿIfār
ʿAfārīt → ʿIfrīt
Afāriḳa iv, 338b, 339a, b – IV, 353a, b, 354a
Afāwīh s, **42a** – S, **42b**
al-Afḍal → Rasūlid(e)s
al-Afḍal b. Amīr al-D̲j̲uyūs̲h̲ (Fāṭimid vizier) (1100) vi, 519b; viii, 832a – VI, 504b; VIII, 860b
al-Afḍal b. Badr al-D̲j̲amālī (1121) i, 149a, **215a**, 440a, 711a, 870b, 1091b; ii, 127a, 305a, 329a, 855b, 856b, 858a, 861b; iii, 545b, 932a; v, 328a; vii, 148a, 163a, 725a; s, 408a –
I, 203b, **221b**, 452b, 732b, 894b, 1124a; II, 130a, 313b, 338b, 875b, 876b, 878a, 881b; III, 564b, 956b; V, 328a; VII, 150a, 165a, 726a; S, 408a
al-Afḍal, al-Malik, b. Ṣalāḥ al-Dīn (Ayyūbid(e)) (1225) → al-Malik al Afḍal b. Ṣalāḥ al-Dīn
al-Afḍal al-ʿAbbās (Rasūlid(e)) (1377) vi, 452a; viii, 457a – VI, 336b; VIII, 472b
Afḍal al-Dawla Ḥaydarābād (1869) iii, 322b – III, 332a
Afḍal al-Dīn Kirmānī (XII) vi, 493b – VI, 479b
Afḍal al-Dīn Turka (1446) s, **43b** – S, **44a**
Afḍal K̲h̲ān (Bīd̲j̲āpūr) (1659) i, 199b, 1204a; vi, 126b, 534b – I, 205a, 1240a; VI, 124a, 519a
Afḍal K̲h̲ān Bārakzay (Afg̲h̲ānistān) (1867) i, 87a, 232a; ii, 638a – I, 89b. 239a; II, 654a
al-Afḍal Kutayfāt (1131) i, **216a**; ii, 857b; iii, 54b; iv, 200a – I, **222b**; II, 877b; III, 56b; IV, 209a
al-Afḍal Muḥammad b. Abi ʾl-Fidāʾ (XIV) i, 119a; iii, 120a, 900b – I, 122a; III, 123a, 924b
al-Afḍal al-Rasūlī → al-Afḍal al-ʿAbbās
Afḍal-i Ṣadr, K̲h̲ʷād̲j̲a → Afḍal al-Dīn Turka
al-Afḍal S̲h̲āhins̲h̲āh (vizier) vii, 510b – VII, 510b
Afendopolo, Caleb (1522) iv, 605b – IV, 630a
Āferīn → Taʾrīk̲h̲
ʿAffān Abū ʿUt̲h̲mān (VII) s, 103b – S, 103a
ʿAffān b. Muslim iv, 683a – IV, 711b
Afg̲h̲ān/Afg̲h̲an i, **216**, 1068a; iv, 1b, 37a-b; v, 72a, 461a, 782a; vi, 47b, 62a, 342b, 343a; vii, 674a; viii, 257b; s, 1b, 142a, 143b, 147a, 206b, 312a, 325a –
I, **223**, 1100b; IV, 1b, 39b; V, 74a, 464a, 788b; VI, 46a, 60a, 327a; VII, 674a; VIII, 259b; S, 1b, 141b, 143a, 147a, 206a, 312a, 325a
—literature/littérature i, 1123a; v, 72a – I, 1157a; V, 74a
—wars/guerres 1st: i, 72a, 962a; iv, 1143a; v, 102a, 580a; 2nd: i, 87b, 238a; v, 580b; 3rd: i, 238b; ii, 30b – Ière: I, 74a, 991b; IV, 1174b; V, 104b, 585a; 2ème: I, 90a, 245b; V, 585a; 3ème: I, 246a; II, 31a
al-Afg̲h̲ānī → D̲j̲amāl al-Dīn
Afg̲h̲ānī, ʿAlī Muḥammad (XX) iv, 73b – IV, 77a
Afg̲h̲ānistān i, **221a**, 853a, 676a; iii, 13a; iv, 535b; v, 501a; vi, 86a, b, 365b, 764b, 771b, 806a; vii, 12a; viii, 282a, b; ix, 446b; x, 685b;' s, 214b, 237a, 329b, 332b, 367a –
I, **227b**, 876b, 693a; III, 13b; IV, 558b; V, 504a; VI, 84a, b, 349b, 753b, 761a, 796a; VII, 12b; VIII, 290a, b; IX, 486b; X, ; S, 214a, 237a, 329a, 322b, 366b
—demography/-ie s, 214b – S, 214a
—ethnography/-ie i, 95a, 216-220, 224a, b; v, 245b – I, 98a, 223-226, 230b, 231a; V, 243a
—geography/-ie i, 71a, 221-223 – I, 73a, 227-230
—history/histoire i, 39a, 77a, 87a, b, 225b-233a, 295b; ii, 3a, 638a, 657a, 1100b; iii, 13a; iv, 357b, 917b; s, 270a – I, 40a, 79b, 89b, 90a, 232b-240a, 304b; II, 3a, 654a, 673b, 1126b; III, 13b; IV, 373a, 950b; S, 270a
—institutions ii, 426a; iii, 13b; v, 1079a – II, 437a; III, 14a; V, 1076a
—languages/langues i, 220a, b, 225a – I, 226b, 227a, 231b, 232a
—religion i, 225b, 1123-4 – I, 232a, 1157-8
ʿAfīf, S̲h̲ayk̲h̲ (Ṭāḳa) vi, 83b – VI, 81b
ʿAfīf al-Dīn → Boḍufenvalugē Sīdī
ʿAfīf al-Dīn al-Tilimsānī → al-Tilimsānī
Afīfan vi, 743b – VI, 732b
ʿAfīfī, Banū vi, 128b – VI, 126b
al-ʿAfīfī, ʿAbd al-Wahhāb (1758) s, **44a**, 408a – S, **44b**, 408b
al-ʿAfīfiyya s, 44a – S, 44b
ʿAfis (Alep(po)) vi, 230b – VI, 224a
Afk̲h̲āz → Abk̲h̲āz
al-Aflād̲j̲ i, **233a**, 538b, 546b; ii, 175b – I, **240a**, 555a, 564a; II, 180b
Aflaḥ b. ʿAbd al-Wahhāb b. Rustam (Rustumid(e)) (871) iii, 657a, 659b, 1041b; vi, 841a; vii, 895a; viii, 639a – III, 678a, 680b, 1067b; VI, 832a; VII, 896a; VIII, 658a
Aflaḥ (Marzūḳ) b. Yasār → Abū ʿAṭāʾ al-Sindī
Aflaḥ al-Nās̲h̲ib (Barka) (X) ii, 495a – II, 507b
ʿAflaḳ, Michel (XX) iv, 125a, b, 126a, 783a – IV, 130b, 131a, b, 814b
Aflākī, S̲h̲ams al-Dīn Aḥmad (XIV) i, **234a**; vi, 354b; viii, 972b; s, 83b – I, **241a**; VI, 338b; VIII, 1006b; S, 83a
Aflāṭūn i, **234a**, 350a, 631a; ii, 493a, 779b; iv, 329a – I, **241a**, 360b, 651b; II, 505b, 798a; IV, 343b
Aflīmūn (144) iv, 406a; s, **44b** – IV, 423b; S, **45a**
ʿAfrāʾ iii, 1038a – III, 1063b
Āfrāg i, **236a** – I, **243b**
Āfrāg (al-Manṣūra) s, **45b** – S, **45b**
Afrāg̲h̲a → Ifrāg̲h̲a
Afrāʾim b. al-Zaffān iii, 906b – III, 930b
Afrand̲j̲ Aḥmad (Miṣr) (1711) vi, 325a; vii, 179a – VI, 309b; VII, 180b
ʿAfrār, Banū vi, 82b, 83b – VI, 80b, 81b
Afrāsiyāb (Baṣra) (XVII) i, **236b**, 1087a; iii, 1257a; iv, 813b, 816a; vi, 511a, b, 764b –
I, **244a**, 1119b; III, 1289b; IV, 846a, 848b; VI, 496b, 497a, 754a
Afrāsiyāb II, Muẓaffar al-Dīn (XIV) v, 827a – V, 833b
Afrāsiyāb (Tūrānian/Touranien) i, **236a**, 1072b; iii, 112b, 813b, 816a; ix, 696b – I, **243b**, 1105; III, 115a, 846a, 848b; IX, 705a
Afrāsiyāb b. Kiyā Ḥasan (XIV) i, 237a – I, 244a
Afrāsiyāb I b. Yūsufs̲h̲āh (1296) iii, 337a, b; v, 827a – III, 347a, b; V, 833a
Afrāsiyābid(e)s (Kiyā-i Čulāb) (XIV) i, **237a**; vi, 938b – I, **244a**; VI, 930b
Afrīdī, Banū i, 217a, 219b, **237b**, 769a; ii, 1066a; iv, 1143a; vii, 548b – I, 223b, 226a, **245a**, 792a; II, 1090b; IV, 1174b; VII,548b
Afrīdūn → Farīdūn
Afrīdūn b. Farīburz (XI) iv, 348a – IV, 362b
Afrīg̲h̲id(e)s iv, 753b, 754a, 1062a, 1063b, 1065b – IV, 784a, b, 1093b, 1095a, 1097a
Āfrīg̲h̲ūnid(e)s → Farīg̲h̲ūnid(e)s
ʿAfrīn i, **239a**; viii, 128b – I, **246b**; VIII, 131a
Afrīnūh, Alexandra (XX) vii, 903a – VII, 903b
ʿAfrīt → ʿIfrīt
ʿAfṣ i, **239a** – I, **246b**
Afsantīn i, **239b** – I, **247a**
Afs̲h̲ār, Banū (Og̲h̲uz) i, **239b**; ii, 75b; iii, 1100a, 1102b, 1107a, 1109b; v, 154a, 825a; vi, 18a, 483b, 522b, 526a; vii, 673a; IX, 597b; s, 71a, 147b –
I, **247a**; II, 77a; III, 1127a, 1129b, 1134b, 1136b; V, 155a, 831a, b; VI, 16a, 469b, 507b, 510b; VII, 673a; IX, 620b; S, 71b, 147b
Afs̲h̲ār Urūmī Ḳulī K̲h̲ān (Imām) (XIX) vi, 484a – VI, 470a

Afshāri-Zand (1763) vi, 551a – VI, 535b
Afshīn (1080) vii, 122a – VII, 123b
al-Afshīn Ḥaydar (Khaydar) b. Ḳāwūs (Ushrūsana) (841) i, 52b, 145a, 154a, **241a**, 637a, 844a, 1072b, 1104a; iii, 471a; iv, 20b, 646a, 647a, 718b; v, 856a; vi, 337b, 338b, 499a; vii, 395a, 664a, 776a; viii, 501a; x, 925a; s, 116a –
I, 54b, 149b, 158b, **248b**, 658a, 867b, 1104b, 1137b; III, 487b; IV, 22a, 672b, 673b, 747a; V, 862b; VI, 321b, 323a, 484b; VII, 396b, 664a, 778a; VIII, 518a; X, ; S, 115b
Afshīn Kāwūs (Usrūshana) (IX) x, 925a – X,
Afşin (Kaza) vi, 509a – VI, 494b
Afsūn i, **241b** – I, **249a**
Afsūs (Afsōs) (1809) i, **241b** – I, **249a**
Afṣūs (Ephesus/Ephèse) → Aya Solūk
Aftakīn, Naṣr al-Dawla (XI) viii, 83a – VIII, 85a
Aftakīn al-Turkī (X) vii, 488b, 910b, 911a; viii, 832a – VII, 488b, 911a, b; VIII, 860b
Afṭasid(e)s (Banu ʾl-Afṭas) (XI) i, 6a, **242a**, 1092a, 1338b; iii, 680b; vi, 568a – I, 6a, **249b**, 1124b, 1379a; III, 702b; VI, 553a
Afughal vi, 591a – VI, 576a
al-Afwah al-Awdī (VI) i, **242b** – I, **250a**
Afyūn i, **243a**; ii, 904b – I, **251b**; II, 925b
Afyūn Ḳarā Ḥiṣār i, **243b**; iv, 578a; vi, 71b; s, 268b, 348b – I, **250b**; IV, 601b; VI, 69b; S, 268a, 348b
Afzar vi, 384b -VI, 368b
al-Afzārī, Asʿad b. Naṣr → ʿAmīd al-Dīn al-Abzārī al-Anṣārī
Aga → Agha
Agadès i, 307a; vi, 364b – I, 316b; VI, 348b
Agadir i, **244b** – I, **252a**
Agadir-Ighir i, 56a, **244b**, 357b, 1321a; iii, 62b; vi, 142b; ix, 900b – I, 58a, **252b**, 368a, 1361b; III, 65a; VI, 140b; VIII, 936b
Āgāh Efendi (XIX) iv, 875b, 876b; vi, 92a – IV, 908b, 909b; VI, 90a
Āgāh Efendī → Čapanzāde Agāh Efendī
Āgahī, Muḥammad Riḍā (1874) s, **46a**; vii, 574b – S, **46a**; VII, 575a
Agarsif → Garsīf
Agathodaemon → Aghāthūdhīmūn
Agau i, 1163a; v, 522a – I, 1197b; V, 525b
Agdāl (Marrākush) i, 85a, **245b**, 1346b; vi, 595b, 596b; s, 114a – I, 87b, **253a**, 1387a; VI, 580a, 581b; S, 113b
Āgehī (1577) i, **245b** – I, **253a**
Agēl → ʿUḳayl
Agha i, 35b, **245b**, 368a, 1256a; ii, 1121a; v, 472b – I, 36b, **253b**, 379a, 1294b; II, 1147a; V, 475a
Agha Faḍl Allāh (XVIII) vii, 444a – VII, 445a
Aghā Furṣat Shīrāzī, Mīrzā (XX) iv, 397b, 789a – IV, 415a, 820b
Āghā Ḥashar Kashmīrī (1935) i, 1166a; s, **46b** – 1200b; S, **47a**
Agha Ḥusayn Pasha → Ḥusayn Pasha, Agha
Agha Khān (title/titre) i, **246a**; ii, 140a; v, 942b – I, **254a**; II, 144a; V, 946a
Agha Khān I → Maḥallatī, Āghā Khān (1881)
Agha Khān II (1885) i, 246b; ix, 435b – I, 254a; IX, 453a
Agha Khān III (1957) i, 1196b; iii, 532b – I, 1231b; III, 551a
Agha Khān IV, Shāh Karīm (XX) ii, 129a; iv, 201b; viii, 84a – II, 132b; IV, 210b; VIII, 86b
Aghā Khān Kirmānī, Mīrzā ʿAbd al-Ḥusayn (1896) iv, 70b, 72a, 397b, 788b; vi, 292a; s, **53a**, 76b –
IV, 74b, 76a, 415a, 820b; vi, 277a; S, **53b**, 76b
Āghā Khān Nūrī, Mīrzā (1855) iii, 554b; iv, 394a, 978b; vi, 20a; s, 71a – III, 573b; IV, 411a, 1011a; VI, 18a; S, 71b
Aghā Mīr → Sayyid Muḥammad Khān (Awadh)
Aghā Mīrak (XV) i, 1211b, 1213a – I, 1247b, 1249b
Āghā Muḥammad Ḳāẓim Tunbākūfurūsh (XIX) x, 397b – X, 426a
Āghā Muḥammad Shāh → Aghā Ḥashar Kashmīrī
Āghā Muḥammad Shāh (Ḳādjār) (1797) i, 230a, b, **246b**, 701b, 720b, 1008b; ii, 335b, 812a, 838b; iii, 106a, 1103a; iv, 38a-b, 390a, b, 391a, 638a, 855b, 978b, 1091b; v, 156a, 164b, 495a, 663b, 825b, 835a; vi, 483b, 484a, 493a, 495a, 528a, 715a; s, 94b, 336a, 405b –
I, 237a, b, **254a**, 722b, 742a, 1039b; II, 345a, 831b, 858a; III, 108b, 1130b; IV, 40b, 407a, b, 408a, 664a, 888b, 1011a, 1123a; V, 162a, 498a, 669a, 831b, 841b; VI, 469b, 470a, 478b, 480b, 512a, 704a; S, 94a, 335b, 406a
Aghā Muṭahhar (XVIII) vii, 444a – VII, 445a
Aghā Sayyid Djamāl ii, 651a – II, 667a
Aghač i, **247a** – I, **254b**
Aghānī → Awghānī
al-Aghānī → Abu ʾl-Faradj al-Iṣfahānī
Aghaoghlu, Aḥmed (1939) s, **47a** – S, **47b**
Aghāthūdhīmūn i, **247a**; v, 111b – I, **254b**; V, 114a
al-Aghlab al-ʿIdjlī (641) i, **247b**; iii, 1262a; viii, 377a – I, **255a**; III, 1294b; VIII, 389b
Aghlabid(e)s (Banū ʾl-Aghlāb) i, 18a, 24a, 104a, **247b**, 439b, 532b, 862b, 986a, 1148b, 1175b, 1246b, 1319a, 1346a; ii, 145b; iii, 655b, 981b, 1041b; v, 220b; vi, 280b, 331a, 334a, 336b, 337b, 338a, 364a, 452b, 453a, 457a, 712b; x, 213a; s, 103a, 120b, 144b –
I, 18b, 24b, 107a, **255b**, 452a, 549a, 887a, 1017a, 1183a, 1210b, 1284b, 1359b, 1386b; II, 149b; III, 676b, 1006a, 1067b; V, 218a; VI, 265b, 316a, 318b, 321a, b, 322a, 348a, 438a, 442b, 701a; X, 230a; S, 102b, 120a, 144a
Āghmāt Aylān i, 7b, **250b**; v, 654b, 1178b; vi, 293b, 356a, 591b, 592a, 741a, b, 742b, 743b –
I, 7b, **258b**; V, 658b, 1168b; VI, 278b, 340a, 576a, b, 577a, 730b, 731a, b, 732b, 733a
Aghri̊ i, **251a**, 1117b; vi, 200b – I, **259a**, 1151a; VI, 184b
Aghri̊ Da i, **251b**; v, 441a, 465a; vi, 200b, 201b – I, **259a**; V, 443b, 467b; VI, 184b, 185b
Aghsartʿan → Akhsitān
al-Aghwāṭ → Laghouat
al-Aghzāz → Ghuzz
Āgrā i, **252b**, 757b, 1323a, 1324a, 1347b; ii, 271a; iii, 449b, 450a, 575b; v, 1135a, 1217a, 1218b, 1219a; vi, 53b, 128a, 343a, 369b; vii, 314a; s, 10b, 142b –
I, **260a**, 780a, 1363b, 1364b, 1388a; II, 279a; III, 465a, 595b; V, 1130b, 1206b, 1207a, 1208b, 1209a; VI, 51b, 126a, 327a, 353b; VII, 316a; S, 10a, 142a
Agrigento/-e → Djirdjent
Aguedal → Āgdāl
Agung, Sultan (Mataram) ii, 390b; iii, 1221b; ix, 852b; s, 150b – II, 400b; III, 1252b; IX, 888a; S, 150b
Aḥābīsh i, 24b, 891b; iii, 7b; vi, 266a – I, 25b, 918a; III, 8a; VI, 250b
Aḥadīs v, 686b; vii, 446a – V, 691b; VII, 447a
Ahaggar i, **254b**, 433b; iii, 298a – I, **262b**, 445b; III, 307b
Ahangarān ii, 1096b, 1099b; s, 411a – II, 1122b, 1125b; S, 411a
Ahar → Ḳaradja-Dagh
ʿAhd i, **255a**, 429b, 439b, 1143b; ii, 164b, 302b, 303a; iii, 396b; iv, 14b, 938b –
I, **263a**, 441b, 452a, 1178a; II, 169b, 311a, b; III, 409a; IV, 15b, 971b

al-Aḥdab → Ibrāhīm al-Aḥdab
al-Ahdab, Muḥammad b. Wāsil (XIV) viii, 987a – VIII, 1021b
al-Ahdal (Sayyids) i, **255b**; vi, 352a – I, **263b**; VI, 336a
al-Ahdal, Abū Bakr b. Abi 'l-Ḳāsim i, 255b – I, 263b
al-Ahdal, Abū Bakr b. ʿAlī, Ḳuṭb al-Yaman (1300) i, 255b – I, 263b
al-Ahdal, Ḥusayn b. al-Ṣiddīḳ (1497) i, 255b; vi, 354b – VI, 339a
Aḥdāth i, **256a**, 687a, 1332b; ii, 963a; v, 329b – I, **264a**, 708a, 1373a; II, 985a; V, 329b
ʿAhdī (Aḥmed of/de Baghdād) (1693) x, 55a – X, 56b
Āhī (1517) i, **257a** – I, **264b**
Aḥiḳar → al-Ḥayḳar
Āhinsa Bā'ī (1587) vi, 190a – VI, 173b
al-Aḥḳāf i, 169a, **257a**; vii, 496a; viii, 576a – I, 174a, **265a**; VII, 496a; VIII, 594b
Aḥkām i, **257a**; iii, 551b; iv, 151b; v, 870b, 878b – I, **265a**; III, 570a; IV, 157b; V, 877a, 884b
Ahl i, **257b**, 700b; iv, 785b – I, **265b**, 721b; IV, 817a
Ahl al-ahwā' i, **257b** – I, **265b**
Ahl Bārikalla v, 891b – V, 898a
Ahl al-bayt i, **257b**, 957b; ii, 169b, 843b; vi, 604b – I, **265b**, 987a; II, 174b, 863b; VI, 589a
Ahl al-buyūtāt i, **258b** – I, **266b**
Ahl al-dār i, **258b** – I, **266b**
Ahl al-dhimma i, **258b**, 338a, 855b; ii, 126b, 127b, 131b, 142b, 154a, 211a, 324a, 341b, 487b, 559b, 565a, 657b, 1075b; iii, 233b, 1180a, 1187a; iv, 240b; v, 179a, 736b – I, **266b**, 348b, 879a; II, 129b, 131a, 134b, 146b, 158b, 217b, 333b, 351b, 500a, 573b, 579a, 674a, 1100b; III, 240b, 1209a, 1216b; IV, 251a; V, 176b, 741b
Ahl al-farḍ → Mīrāth
Ahl al-ḥadīth i, **258b**, 692a, 1242a; ii, 889a; iii, 163a, 269b, 512b; s, 293a – I, **266b**, 713a, 1280a; II, 909b; III, 166b, 277b, 530a; S, 292b
Ahl-i ḥadīth i, **259a** – I, **267a**
Ahl-i Ḥaḳḳ i, **260a**, 840a, 841b; ii, 96a, 850a, 1140b; iv, 49a, 187b; v, 475b, 823a; vi, 201a, 502b; ix, 7a, 64a, 855a; x, 326a – I, **268a**, 863b, 865a; II, 98a. 870a, 1167a; IV, 52a,196a; V, 478b, 829a; VI, 185b, 488a; IX, 7a, 65b, 891a; X, 350b
Ahl al-ḥall wa'l-ʿaḳd i, **263b** – I, **272a**
Ahl al-kahf → Aṣḥāb al-kahf
Ahl al-kalām → Ahl al-naẓar
Ahl al-ḳibla i, **264a** – I, **272a**
Ahl al-kisā' i, **264a**; ii, 844a – I, **272a**; II, 863b
Ahl al-kitāb i, **264a**; ii, 1065b; iv, 408a, b – I, **272a**; II, 1090a; IV, 426a
Ahl al-naẓar i, **266a** – I, **274a**
Ahl al-ra'y → Aṣḥāb al-ra'y
Ahl al-ra'y → Aṣḥāb al-ra'y
Ahl al-Saḳīfa → Saḳīfa
Ahl al-ṣuffa i, 114a, 129a, **266a** – I, 117a, 133a, **274a**
Ahl al-sunna i, **267a**, 694a, 1039b; ii, 412a; iii, 248a, 846a; iv, 142a – I, **275a**, 715b, 1071a; II, 423a; III, 255a, 870a; IV, 148a
Ahlī (Shirāz) (1535) iv, 67a – IV, 70b
Ahl-i wāris i, **267a** – I, **275a**
Aḥlāf → Ḥilf
Aḥlāf, Banū (ʿAmārna) vi, 142b – VI, 141a
Aḥlāf, Banū (Ḳurashī) vi, 137b – VI, 136a
Ahlī (Shirāz) (1535) viii, 775a – VIII, 801a
Aḥmad (Aghlabid(e)) → Abū Ibrāhīm Aḥmad
Aḥmad I (Āl Sabāḥ) (1950) viii, 660a – IX, 688b
Aḥmad (Bahmanī) → Aḥmad Shāh
Aḥmad (Brunei XV) s, 152a – S, 152a
Aḥmad (Djalāyirid(e)) → Aḥmad b. Uways
Aḥmad (Ilkhānid(e)) → Aḥmad Takudār
Aḥmad, Imām (Zaydī) (1962) ix, 2a – IX, 2a
Aḥmad I (Ḥafṣid(e)) (1350) iii, 68a; iv, 416a – III, 70b; IV, 434a
Aḥmad II (Ḥafsid(e)) (1394) iii, 68b, 826b, 827b, 831b; v, 531a – III, 70b, 71a, 850a, b, 851a, 855b; V, 535a
Aḥmad III (Ḥafṣid(e)) (1569) iii, 69b – III, 71b
Aḥmad I (Ḳarakhānid(e)) → Aḥmad Khān b. Khiḍr
Aḥmad (Muḥammad) i, **267a** – I, **275a**
Aḥmad I al-Muḳtadir b. Hūd (Hūdid(e)) (1081) i, 499a, 865a, 1040b; ii, 112a; iii, 542a; iv, 478a; v, 683a; vii, 768a – I, 514a, 889a, 1072a; II, 114b; III, 561a; IV, 499a; V, 688a; VII, 770a
Aḥmad II al-Mustaʿīn (Hūdid(e)) (1110) i, 495b; iii, 542b; s, 383a – I, 510a; III, 561b; S, 383b
Aḥmad III al-Mustanṣir ((Hūdid(e)) (1142) i, 1083a; ii, 1013b; iii, 543a – I, 1115b; II, 1037a; III, 561
Aḥmad I (Ottoman) (1617) i, **267b**, 510b, 954b, 1226a, 1267a; ii, 208b, 543a, 684a; iii, 1185a; v, 18a, b, 272a; vi, 508b, 799a; s, 257b, 330b – I, **275b**, 526b, 983b, 1262b, 1305b; II, 215a, 556b, 701a; III, 1214b; V, 19a, 270a; VI, 494a, 789a; S, 257a, 330a
—mosque (Istanbul) iv, 233a – IV, 243b
Aḥmad II (Ottoman) (1695) ii, **268a**; v, 262a – I, **276a**; V, 260a
Aḥmad III (Ottoman) (1736) i, **268b**, 394b, 395a, 776a, 836b, 1076b; ii, 212b, 684a; iii, 1002a; iv, 874a, 969b; v, 18b, 19a, 641b, 642b, 643b; vi, 55a, 57a, 198b – I, **276b**, 406a, 799a, 859b, 1108b; II, 219a, 701a; III, 1027a; IV, 907b, 1001b; V, 19a, b, 645b, 646b, 647b; VI, 53a, 55a, 183a
Aḥmad, Shaykh (Bārzān) (XX) i, 1072a; v, 467a – I, 1104a; V, 470a
Aḥmad b. al-ʿAbbās b. ʿĪsā b. Shaykh (X) iv, 90b – IV, 94b
Aḥmad b. ʿAbd Allāh (ʿAbd al-Wādid(e)) → Abū Zayyān III
Aḥmad b. ʿAbd Allāh, Sulṭān (Faḍlī) (XX) ii, 737a – II, 755b
Aḥmad b. ʿAbd Allāh (Dilā'ī) (1680) vi, 891b; s, 223b – VI, 883a; S, 223b
Aḥmad b. ʿAbd Allāh b. Abi 'l-ʿAlā' (IX) vii, 518b – VII, 519a
Aḥmad b. ʿAbd Allāh al-Khūdjistānī (892) i, 452b; iii, 245a; v, 47a, 48a; vii, 76b; x, 741b – I, 465b; III, 252a; V, 48b, 49a; VII, 77b; X, 741b
Aḥmad b. ʿAbd Allāh Maʿn al-Andalusī (XVII) iv, 380a – IV, 396b
Aḥmad b. ʿAbd al-ʿAzīz b. Abī Dulaf (IX) i, 452b; ii, 301a, 623b; iv, 100a – I, 465b; II, 309a, 639a; IV, 104b
Aḥmad b. ʿAbd al-ʿAzīz al-Khurāsānī (XII) iii, 138b; v, 60b – III, 141a; V, 62a
Aḥmad b. ʿAbd al-Raḥīm → Abū Zurʿa
Aḥmad b. ʿAbd al-Raḥmān b. ʿAbd Allāh Rawāḥī (1312) viii, 459b – VIII, 475a
Aḥmad b. ʿAbd al-Raḥmān b. Nafāda (1204) viii, 376a – VIII, 389a
Aḥmad b. ʿAbd al-Raḥmān al-Djazā'irī ii, 183a – II, 189a
Aḥmad b. ʿAbd al-Ṣamad Shīrazī (vizier) (1030) vi, 453a; vii, 26b – VI, 438b; VII, 26b
Aḥmad b. Abi 'l-ʿAzā'im (1970) s, 18b – S, 18b
Aḥmad b. Abī Bakr → Muḥtādjid(e)s
Aḥmad b. Abī Du'ād (854) i, 153b, **271a**, 273a; ii,

385b; iii, 707a, 974b, 994b; iv, 289b, 718b; v, 647a; vi, 336a, 338b; vii, 4a, 392b, 401a, 776b, 777b; s, 17b, 25a, 90b –
I, 158a, **279b**, 281a; II, 396a; III, 729a, 999a, 1019b; IV, 302b, 747b; V, 651a; VI, 320b, 323a; VII, 4a, 394a, 402b, 778a, 779b; S, 18a, 25a, 90a
Aḥmad b. Abi 'l-Ḳāsim al-Ṣawmaʿī (1604) i, 159b – I, 164a
Aḥmad b. Abī Khālid al-Aḥwal (826) i, 241a, **271b**; vi, 334a, 336a, 337b – I, 248b, **280a**; VI, 318b, 320b, 321b
Aḥmad b. Abī Mismār (Abū ʿArīsh) (XIX) s, 30b – S, 31a
Aḥmad b. Abī Rabīʿa (X) ix, 208b – IX, 214b
Aḥmad b. Abi 'l-Saʿīd (al-Ḳarawiyyīn) (X) iv, 632b – IV, 657b
Aḥmad b. Abī Saʿīd b. Tīmūr (Aḥrār) (XV) s, 51a – S, 51b
Aḥmad b. Abī Ṭāhir Ṭayfūr → Ibn Abī Ṭāhir
Aḥmad b. Abī ʿUmāra → Ibn Abī ʿUmāra
Aḥmad b. ʿAdjlān, Sharīf (1396) vi, 149b – VI, 148a
Aḥmad b. ʿAlā' al-Dīn (Marāgha) (XII) vi, 500b – VI, 486a
Aḥmad b. ʿAlī (Rayy) (924) i, 125b; iv, 661b – I, 129a; IV, 688b
Aḥmad b. ʿAlī (Mai, Bornu) (XIX) i, 1260a – I, 1298a
Aḥmad b. ʿAlī b. Khayrān (1039) ii, 127b – II, 130b
Aḥmad b. ʿAlī b. Thābit → al-Khaṭīb al-Baghdādī
Aḥmad b. ʿAlī al-Hāshimī ii, 276a – II, 284a
Aḥmad b. ʿAlī, Sayyid, Karkiyā (1592) v, 603b – V, 607b
Aḥmad b. ʿAlī al-Ikhshīd (X) iv, 418b – IV, 436b
Aḥmad b. ʿAlī Zunbul (1653) iv, 1130a – IV, 1161b
Aḥmad b. ʿAmr al-Sulamī i, 697a – I, 718b
Aḥmad b. ʿAṭā' (922) x, 314b – X, 338b
Aḥmad b. al-Aṭrābulusī (IX) iii, 660a – III, 681a
Aḥmad b. Aṭṭāsh (Alamūt) (XII) i, 353a; iii, 725a; iv, 101b, 102a – I, 363b; III, 748a; IV, 106a, b
Aḥmad b. al-ʿAynī (XV) s, 38a – S, 38b
Aḥmad b. Bā Ḥmād (XIX) s, 114a – S, 113b
Aḥmad b. Baṣo (XII) iv, 118a – IV, 123a
Aḥmad b. Bāyazīd II (Ottoman) (XVI) i, 396a, 1120b; iv, 1159a; v, 677b; vii, 272b – I, 407b, 1154a, b; IV, 1191a; V, 682b; VII, 274b
Aḥmad b. Buwayh (Būya) → Muʿizz al-Dawla Aḥmad
Aḥmad b. Djābir → Aḥmad Āl Djābir
Aḥmad b. Djaʿfar, Amīr s, 125b – S, 124b
Aḥmad b. Djaʿfar al-Kattānī → al-Kattānī, Muḥammad b. Djaʿfar
Aḥmad b. Djamīl (1182) vi, 110b – VI, 108b
Aḥmad b. Faḍlān → Ibn Faḍlān
Aḥmad b. Fahd (1436) vii, 672a – VII, 672a
Aḥmad b. Faradj → Ibn Faradj al-Djayyānī
Aḥmad b. Farīghūn ii, 798b – II, 817b
Aḥmad b. al-Furāt → Ibn al-Furāt, Abu 'l-ʿAbbās Aḥmad
Aḥmad b. Ghālib (Djayzān) (XVII) ii, 517b – II, 530b
Aḥmad b. Ḥābiṭ (IX) i, **272a** – I, **280a**
Aḥmad b. al-Ḥādjdj (1697) s, 403b – S, 404a
Aḥmad b. al-Ḥādjdj ʿUmar (XIX) ix, 122a – IX, 126a
Aḥmad b. Ḥanbal (855) i, 114a, 155a, 259a, 271a, **272b**, 589b, 694b, 1242a, 1244b, 1245b; ii, 182b, 294b, 889b, 890a, 1093a; iii, 24a, 158a, 1266a; iv, 142a, 469b, 470a, 735a; v, 426a, 731b; vi, 123b, 351b, 352b, 353a, 627b, 636a; vii, 3a, 361b, 467a, 691b, 706a; s, 16a, 392a –
I, 117b, 159b, 267a, 279b, **280b**, 608b, 715b, 1280a, 1282b, 1283b; II, 188b, 302a, 910b, 1118b; III, 25a, 161b, 1299a; IV, 148a, 490b, 491a, 764b; V, 428b, 737a; VI, 121a, 335b, 336b, 337a, 612a, 621a; VII, 3a, 363b, 466b, 691b, 707a; S, 16b, 392b
Aḥmad b. Ḥarb (XII) iv, 668a; vi, 728b – IV, 695a; VI, 717b
Aḥmad b. al-Ḥasan, al-Mahdī li-Dīn Allāh, Imām → al-Mahdī li-Dīn Allāh Aḥmad b. al-Ḥasan b. al-Ḳāsim
Aḥmad b. Ḥasan al-Kalbī (969) iv, 496b – IV, 518a
Aḥmad b. al-Ḥusayn, al-Mahdī li-Dīn Allāh, Imām → al-Mahdī li-Dīn Allāh Aḥmad b. al-Ḥusayn
Aḥmad b. Ḥusayn, Sulṭān (Faḍlī) (XIX) ii, 737a – II, 755b
Aḥmad b. Ibrāhīm b. Ḥamdūn → Ibn Ḥamdūn
Aḥmad b. Ibrāhīm al-Uḳlīdisī → al-Uḳlīdisī
Aḥmad b. Idrīs, Sharīf (1837) i, **277b**, 709b; vi, 354b; viii, 990a; ix, 22b; x, 249a; s, 278b – I, **286a**, 731a; VI, 339a; VIII, 1024b; IX, 24a; X, 267b; S, 267b
Aḥmad b. al-Imām al-Manṣūr bi-'llāh al-Ḳāsim (Zaydī) (1650) vii, 270a – VII, 272a
Aḥmad b. ʿImrān, ḳāḍī (XII) iii, 125b – III, 128a
Aḥmad b. ʿĪsā b. Muḥammad b. ʿAlī al-Muhādjir (956) i, **277b**, 551b – I, **286a**, 569a
Aḥmad b. ʿIsā b. Shaykh al-Shaybānī (IX) vi, 540a; vii, 760a – VI, 761b; VII, 761b
Aḥmad b. ʿIsā b. Zayd (861) s, **48a** – S, **48b**
Aḥmad b. Isḥāḳ, Khwādja Pīr (XV) s, 84b – S, 84a
Aḥmad b. Ismāʿīl (Rasūlid(e)) (1424) i, 553a; iv, 642b – I, 570b; IV, 668b
Aḥmad II b. Ismāʿīl (Samānid(e)) (914) ii, 1082a; iii, 254b, 757b; iv, 22a, b; vi, 853a; viii, 797a, 1037a – II, 1107b; III, 261b, 780b; IV, 23b, 24a; VI, 844b; VIII, 823b, 1068b
Aḥmad b. Isrā'īl (vizier) (IX) vii, 793b – VII, 795b
Aḥmad b. al-Ḳāḍī (Kabyle) (XVI) ii, 537b; iv, 361b, 1155b, 1156a – II, 550b; IV, 377a, 1187b, 1188b
Aḥmad b. Ḳāsim, Sīdī s, 132b – S, 132a
Aḥmad b. Kayghulugh (X) iv, 100a – IV, 104b
Aḥmad b. Khālid → Aḥmad al-Nāṣirī
Aḥmad b. Khalīfa (Baḥrayn) (1796) i, 942b; iv, 751a, 953a – I, 971b; IV, 781b, 985b
Aḥmad b. al-Khaṣīb, Abū ʿAlī Aḥmad → Ibn al-Khaṣīb
Aḥmad b. al-Khaṣīb al-Djardjarā'ī → al-Djardjarā'ī
Aḥmad b. Khiḍr Khān b. Ibrāhīm (Ḳarakhānid(e)) (1095) vi, 274a – VI, 259a
Aḥmad b. Khiḍrōya (ṣūfī) (IX) i, 162b – I, 167a
Aḥmad b. Khūdja (XIX) vi, 251a – VI, 235a
Aḥmad b. Kurhub (916) ix, 585a – IX, 607b
Aḥmad b. Mādjid → Ibn Mādjid
Aḥmad b. Maḥmūd (XIII) iii, 1116a – III, 1143b
Aḥmad b. Makki (Ḳābis) (XIV) iv, 338a; x, 213b – IV, 352a; X, 230b
Aḥmad b. Maʿn (Duruz) (1697) ii, 635a – II, 651a
Aḥmad b. Marwān → Naṣr al-Dawla b. Marwān
Aḥmad b. Marzūḳ → Ibn Marzūḳ
Aḥmad b. Mīrānshāh b. Tīmūr (Tīmūrid(e)) (XV) vii, 105b – VII, 107b
Aḥmad b. al-Muʿadhdhal → Ibn al-Muʿadhdhal
Aḥmad b. Muʿāwiya → Ibn al-Ḳiṭṭ
Aḥmad b. al-Mubārak b. al-Walīd, dāʿī (XIII) s, 62a – S, 62b
Aḥmad b. Muḥammad (Maḥmūd) (XV) s, **49a** – S, **49b**
Aḥmad b. Muḥammad (Mūrītāniyā) (1891) vii, 614b – VII, 614b
Aḥmad b. Muḥammad (Sharwān-Shāh) (981) iv, 346a, 347a – IV, 361a, b
Aḥmad b. Muḥammad b. ʿAbd al-Ṣamad (XI) i, **278a** – I, **286b**
Aḥmad b. Muḥammad b. Ḥabīb Allāh → Amadu Bamba
Aḥmad b. Muḥammad b. Ilyās (Araghūn) (X) s, 80a – S, 80a
Aḥmad b. Muḥammad b. al-Ḳāsim (XII) ix, 899b – IX, 938a

Aḥmad b. Muḥammad b. Khayrāt (Djayzān) (XVIII) ii, 517b – II, 530b
Aḥmad b. Muḥammad Ādarrāķ → Ādarrāķ
Aḥmad b. Muḥammad al-Aghlab → Abū Ibrāhīm Aḥmad
Aḥmad b. Muḥammad al-Barķī → al-Barķī
Aḥmad b. Muḥammad al-Ḥabūḍī (1230) s, 338b – S, 338a
Aḥmad b. Muḥammad ʿIrfān → Aḥmad Brēlwī
Aḥmad b. Muḥammad al-Manṣūr → Aḥmad al-Manṣūr
Aḥmad b. Muḥammad al-Ṣāḥib (1386) vii, 537a – VII, 537a
Aḥmad b. Muḥammad b. Sālim al-Baṣrī (967) ix, 65b – IX, 67a
Aḥmad b. Muḥammad Zayn (1906) viii, 286a – VIII, 294a
Aḥmad b. Muḥriz (Marrākush) (1668) vi, 595a, 891b – VI, 579b, 883a
Aḥmad b. Muḥsin, Sharīf (XX) i, 1133a – I, 1167b
Aḥmad b. Mulḥim Maʿn (1697) vi, 343b, 344a – VI, 328a
Aḥmad b. Mūsā (1893) vi, 251a – VI, 235b
Aḥmad b. Mūsā b. Aḥmad al-Bukhārī → Bā Aḥmad
Aḥmad b. Mūsā b. Djaʿfar (IX) vii, 396b – VII, 397b
Aḥmad b. Mūsā b. Shākir (869) vi, 600a; s, 412a – VI, 585a; S, 412a
Aḥmad b. Mūsā al-Samlālī → Ḥmad u-Mūsā
Aḥmad b. Nāṣīr (Nāṣiriyya, Morocco/Maroc) i, 290a; vii, 1007a – I, 299a; VII, 1010a
Aḥmad b. Naṣr (Samānid(e)) (846) viii, 844b; s, 357a – VIII, 874a; S, 357a
Aḥmad b. Niẓām al-Mulk (vizier) (XII) vii, 735a – VII, 735b
Aḥmad b. Rusta → Ibn Rusta
Aḥmad b. Ṣadaķa iv, 929a – IV, 962a
Aḥmad b. Sahl b. Hāshim (919) i, **278a** – I, **286b**
Aḥmad b. Saʿīd (Āl Bū Saʿīd) (1783) vii, 227a; ix, 776a; x, 816b – VII, 228b; IX, 809b; X,
Aḥmad b. Saʿīd, Imām (Āl Bū Saʿīd) (1741) vi, 735a, 843a, 963a – VI, 724b, 834a, 955a
Aḥmad b. Saʿīd (961) i, 600a – I, 619b
Aḥmad b. Saʿīd (1783) i, 554a, 1098a, 1281b – I, 572a, 1131b, 1321a
Aḥmad b. Sālim (Aḥlāf) (XIX) v, 596b – V, 600a, b
Aḥmad b. Shādgeldi (Amasya) (XIV) i, 432a, 1117b, 1118a – I, 444a, 1151b, 1152a
Aḥmda b. Shāhīn (XVII) vi, 187a – VI, 171a
Aḥmad b. Sharķāwī al-Khalifī (1898) s, 40b – S, 41a
Aḥmad b. Shaykh Merkez (1500) vi, 1023a – VI, 1016a
Aḥmad b. Sīdī Aḥmad (Mūrītāniyā) (1899) vii, 614b – VII, 614b
Aḥmad b. Sulaymān, Zaydī Imām (1171) i, 552b; v, 954a – I, 570a; V, 958a
Aḥmad b. Sumayt al-Nakhlī (686) vi, 920a – VI, 912a
Aḥmad b. Tabarūya (1009) vii, 43b – VII, 44a
Aḥmad b. Ṭāhir vi, 438a – VI, 423b
Aḥmad b. Taymiyya → Ibn Taymiyya, Taķī al-Dīn Aḥmad
Aḥmad b. al-Ṭayyib (889) vi, 204b – VI, 188b
Aḥmad b. al-Trīkī (XVIII) vi, 250a – VI, 234b
Aḥmad b. Ṭūlūn (Ṭulūnid(e)) (884) i, 139a, 205a, **278a**, 341a, 517a, 551a, 621a, 990a, b, 1224a; ii, 36b, 129b, 130a, 281b, 305a, 328a, 958b, 1080b; iii, 86a, 398a, 745b, 880a; iv, 134a, 655a, 841b; v, 49a, 91a, b, 327a, 624a; vi, 195a, 365a, 379a, 413a, 455a, 654a, 657a, 669b, 672b, 676b, 677a; vii, 147b, 161a, 766a; viii, 91a, 464a; x, 616b; s, 120b –
I, 143a, 211a, **287a**, 351b, 532b, 568b, 641b, 1021a, 1260b; II, 37b, 133a, 289b, 313b, 337b, 980b, 1105b; III, 88a, 410b, 768b, 904a; IV, 139b, 681a, 874b; V, 50b, 93b, 326b, 628a; VI, 179a, 349a, 363b, 398a, 440b, 639a, 643a, 655b, 658b, 663a, 664a; VII, 150a, 162b, 767b; VIII, 479b; X, 662b; S, 120a
Aḥmad b. ʿUbayd Allāh b. al-Khaṣīb → al-Khaṣībī, Aḥmad b. ʿUbayd Allāh
Aḥmad b. ʿUbayda (941) ix, 819a – IX, 854a
Aḥmad b. ʿUķba al-Ḥaḍramī (1489) s, 208a – S, 208a
Aḥmad (Ḥabashī) b. ʿUmar b. ʿAbd Allāh b. Ibrāhīm b. al-Aghlab (870) vi, 295a – VI, 280b
Aḥmad b. Uways (Djalāyirid) (1410) i, 401b, 903b, 1051a, 1119a; ii, 401b; iv, 33b, 584b, 586a, b; vi, 324a; vii, 171b, 602b –
I, 930b, 1082b, 1152b; II, 412a; IV, 36a, 608a, b, 609a; VI, 308b; VII, 173b, 602a
Aḥmad b. Yaḥyā, Imām (1948) i, 555a – I, 572b
Aḥmad b. Yaḥyā b. Abī ʾl-Baghl (X) vii, 653a – VII, 652b
Aḥmad b. Yaḥyā b. al-Murtaḍā, al-Mahdī li-Dīn Allāh → al-Mahdī li-Dīn Allāh Aḥmad b. Yaḥyā
Aḥmad b. Yaḥyā al-Yaḥṣubī → Tādj al-Dawla (Labla)
Aḥmad b. Yūsuf (828) i, **279a** – I, **288a**
Aḥmad b. Yūsuf, Sīdī (XVII) i, 374b, 1300b; iv, 481b; vii, 64a – I, 385a, 1340b; IV, 502b; VII, 64b
Aḥmad b. Yūsuf al-Miṣrī → Ibn al-Dāya
Aḥmad b. Zaynī Daḥlān → Daḥlān
Aḥmad al-ʿAbbās b. Maḥammad al-Shaykh al-Aṣghar (Saʿdid(e)) (1659) vi, 595a – VI, 579b
Aḥmad ʿAbd al-Ḥaķķ, Shaykh (Ṣābiriyya) (XV) ii, 54a, 56a; s, 293a – II, 55a, 56b; S, 293a
Aḥmad Abu ʾl-Fatḥ (XX) s, 6a – S, 5a
Aḥmad Agha Ķarā ʿOthmān-oghlu (XVIII) iv, 593a – IV, 617a
Aḥmad al-Aḥsāʾī → al-Aḥsāʾī
Aḥmad Āl Djābir Āl Ṣabāḥ (XX) iii, 1066a; v, 575a; s, 50a – III, 1092b; V, 579b; S, 50b
Aḥmad ʿAlī (ķāḍī) (al-Mahdiyya) (XIX) v, 1252a, b – V, 1242b, 1243a
Aḥmad ʿAlī Khān Sulṭān Dulhā (Bhōpāl) (XIX) i, 1196a, 1197a – I, 1231b, 1232a
Aḥmad ʿAlī Khān, Nawwāb (XIX) iv, 666b; v, 779b – IV, 693b; V, 785b
Aḥmad ʿAlī Shawķ Ķidwāʾī (1925) vi, 838b – VI, 829a
Aḥmad Allāh, Mawlawī (Fayḍābād) (XIX) ii, 870b – II, 890b
Aḥmad Amīn (1954) i, **279b**; iv, 159b; vi, 408b; vii, 786b – I, **288a**; IV, 166a; VI, 393a; VII, 788a
Aḥmad al-ʿArabī (XX) v, 1005a – V, 1001a
Aḥmad al-Aʿradj al-Saʿdī (1523) ii, 527b; v, 119a; vi, 591a, 594a, b, 893a – II, 540b; V, 1181a; VI, 576a, 579a, 884b
Aḥmad Ashraf, Shāh (XX) s, 74a – S, 74b
Aḥmad Bā Djābir al-Ḥaḍramī (1592) i, 781b – I, 804b
Aḥmad Bābā (1523) vii, 625a – VII, 625a
Aḥmad Bābā al-Massūfī (1627) i, 96b, **279b**, 289a, 594b; iii, 763b, 844a; iv, 476b; vi, 187a, 258b, 280a; ix, 20b –
I, 99a, **288b**, 298a, 614a; III, 786b, 868a; IV, 497b; VI, 171a, 243a, 265a; IX, 21b
Aḥmad al-Badawī Abu ʾl-Fityān (1276) i, **280a**, 404a, 1127a; ii, 1009b; iii, 90b; vi, 87b, 354b, 454a, 652b; vii, 175b; x, 189a –
I, **289a**, 415b, 1161a; II, 1033b; III, 93a; VI, 85b, 338b, 439b, 637b; VII, 177b; X, 294a
Aḥmad Bakr b. Mūsā (Dār Fūr) ii, 123a – II, 126a
Aḥmad Barēlawī → Aḥmad Brēlwī
Aḥmad Beg (Ķarāmān-oghlu) → Fakhr al-Dīn Aḥmad
Aḥmad Bey (Ķusṭanṭīna) v, 532a – V, 536a
Aḥmad Bey (Tunis) (1855) i, 37a, **281b**; ii, 461b; iii, 94b, 561b, 636a, 684a, 720b; vi, 251a, 798a; vii, 436b, 717b –

I, 38a, **290a**; II, 473a; III, 97a, 581a, 657b, 705b, 743a; VI, 235b, 788a; VII, 437b; 718b
Aḥmad Bey (1942) iii, 636b – III, 658a
Aḥmad Bey Bosniak (1662) iv, 723a; vi, 325a – IV, 752a; VI, 309b
Aḥmad Bīdjān → Bīdjān
Aḥmad Brēlwī al-Mudjaddid, Sayyid (1831) i, **282a**, 432b; ii, 140a, 254b, 316b, 437a; iii, 119b, 335b, 431a; iv, 196a, b, 625b, 626a; vii, 290b, 442a, 555a, 939a – I, **291a**, 445a; II, 144a, 262a, 326a, 448b; III, 122a, 345b, 445a; IV, 204b, 205a, 650b, 651a; VII, 292b, 443b, 555b, 939b
Aḥmad al-Burnusī Zarrūḳ (1493) ii, 293a – II, 301a
Aḥmad Bushnāḳ Pasha (XVII) i, 904b, 905a – I, 932a
Aḥmad the Cameleer/le Chamelier (1545) vi, 226a, 227b, 228a, b – VI, 220a, 221a, 222a
Aḥmad Dghughī, Sīdī s, 53a – S, 53b
Aḥmad al-Dhahabī (ʿAlawid(e)) (XVIII) i, 47a, 356a – I, 48b, 367a
Aḥmad Djaʿfar Shīrāzī, Sayyid (XV) i, 1255a – I, 1293a
Aḥmad Djalāʾir → Aḥmad b. Uways
Aḥmad Djalāl al-Dīn Pasha (XIX) vii, 206a – VII, 207a
Aḥmad-i Djām (1141) i, **283a** – I, **291b**
Aḥmad Djazzār → Djazzār Pasha
Aḥmad Djewdet Pasha (1895) i, **284b**, 397a, 505a; ii, 474b, 702b, 935a; iii, 250a, b, 993a; iv, 168b, 872a; v, 837a, 1083a, 1084b; vi, 6b, 614b, 971b; vii, 546b – I, **293a**, 408b, 520b; II, 486b, 720b, 956b; III, 257b, 1017b; IV, 175b, 905b; V, 843b, 1080b, 1081b; VI, 6b, 599b, 964a; VII, 546b
Aḥmad Emīn Yalman (XX) ii, 475a, b; vi, 93a, b – II, 487b; VI, 91a, b
Aḥmad Faḍīl (Kasala) (1899) iv, 687a – IV, 715b
Aḥmad Fahmī Abu ʾl-Khayr (1960) s, 263a – S, 262b
Aḥmad Fāris al-Shidyāḳ → Fāris al-Dīn al-Shidyāḳ
Aḥmad al-Fayḍ Abādī (XX) vi, 176a
Aḥmad Fuʾād b. Fārūḳ (XX) s, 299b, 301b – S, 299a, 301b
Aḥmad al-Ganduz (XIX) vi, 250b – VI, 234b
Aḥmad Ghulām Khalīl → Ghulām Khaktk
Aḥmad Grāñ b. Ibrāhīm (1543) i, **286b**, 932b, 1172b; ii, 91a; iii, 4a, 176a; vi, 642a – I, **295b**, 961a, 1207b; II, 93a; III, 4a, 180a; VI, 627a
Aḥmad Ḥādjdjī Beg (1467) vii, 90b – VII, 92a
Aḥmad al-Hība (1919) v, 890b, 891a; vi, 595b; s, **47b** – V, 897a; VI, 580b; S, **48a**
Aḥmad Ḥikmet (1927) i, **287a**; iii, 260b – I, **295b**; III, 267b
Aḥmad Ibrāhīm al-Ghāzī → Aḥmad Grāñ
Aḥmad Ibrāhīm al-Ghazzāwī (XX) vi, 176b, 177a – VI, 162a
Aḥmad Iḥsān (1942) i, **287a**; ii, 474b – I, **296a**; II, 486b
Aḥmad Inaltigin (1033) vi, 780a – VI, 770a
Aḥmad ʿIzzet Pasha Furgaç → ʿIzzet Pasha, Aḥmed Furgaç
Aḥmad Kamal Bāshāzāda vii, 262a – VII, 264a
Aḥmad Ḳānṣawḥ (XVII) vii, 514b – VII, 514b
Aḥmad-i Ḳaraḥisārī (1556) iv, 1125a, b – IV, 1157a
Aḥmad Ḳaramānlī (Tarābulus al-Gharb) (XVIII) x, 214a – X, 231a
Aḥmad Katkhudā Mustaḥfiẓān Kharpūṭlū (1735) iv, 438a – IV, 457b
Aḥmad Ḳawām (XX) vii, 655a – VII, 654b
Aḥmad Khalīfa, Pasha (1694) x, 36b – X, 38a
Aḥmad Khān, Sayyid (Batuʾid) (1505) iii, 44b – III, 46a, b
Aḥmad Khān, Sir Sayyid (1898) i, 38b, **287b**, 403b, 443a, 505b, 827b; ii, 27b, 97a, 426b, 549b; iii, 93b, 358b, 431a, b, 433a, 458a, 1204b; iv, 170a, b; v, 202a; vi, 461b, 488b, 872a; vii, 534a, b; viii, 241a; ix, 433b; s, 74a, 106b, 107b, 247a – I, 39b, **296b**, 415a, 455b, 521a, 850b; II, 28a, 99a, 437a, 563a; III, 96a, 370a, 445a, b, 447a, 474a, 1235a; IV, 177b; V, 199b; VI, 447a, 474b, 863a; VII, 534a, b; VIII, 247a; IX, 458b; S, 74b, 105b, 107a, 247a
Aḥmad Khān b. Ḥasan Hārūn (Ilek-khān) (XII) iii, 1114b; iv, 581a – III, 1141b; IV, 604b
Aḥmad Khān b. Hūlāgū → Aḥmad Takūdār
Aḥmad Khān b. Hushang Shāh Ghūrī (1438) vi, 52b – VI, 51a
Aḥmad Khān b. Khiḍr Khān (Ilek-khān (XI) iii, 1114b, 1115b – III, 1142a, 1143a
Aḥmad Khān b. Muḥammad Zamān Khān → Aḥmad Shāh Durrānī
Aḥmad Khān ʿAlāʾ al-Dawla, Mīrzā (XX) s, 365a – S, 365a
Aḥmad Khān Bangash (Farrukhābād) (XVIII) ii, 808b; iii, 60a, 1158b – II, 827b; III, 62b, 1187a
Aḥmad Khān Nāṣir Djang (XVIII) vii, 446a – VII, 447a
Aḥmad Khān Sūr → Sikandar Shāh III Sūr
Aḥmad Khān Ūsmī (Dāghistān) (1587) ii, 87a – II, 88b
Aḥmad al-Khaṣībī (X) iv, 424a – IV, 442a
Aḥmad Khattū Maghribī → Maghribī, Aḥmad Khattū
Aḥmad Khayr al-Dīn (XX) vi, 751a, b – VI, 740b, 741a
Aḥmad al-Khudjistānī (IX) ix, 613b – IX, 636b
Aḥmad al-Ḳlībī (XIX) vi, 607a – VI, 591b
Aḥmad Köprülü → Köprülü
Aḥmad Lobo → Aḥmadu Lobbo
Aḥmad Māhir (XX) s, 58a – S, 58b
Aḥmad Maḥmūdī (1930) vi, 763b – VI, 753a
Aḥmad al-Maʿḳūr (Dār Fūr) ii, 122b – II, 125b
Aḥmad Mallāk (Sfax) (XIX) vi, 251a – VI, 235b
Aḥmad Maniklī Pasha (Kasala) (XIX) iv, 686b – IV, 714b
Aḥmad al-Manīnī (1759) viii, 718b – VIII, 749b
Aḥmad Mansūr b. Aḥmad, Shaykh (Manda) vi, 385b – VI, 370a
Aḥmad al-Manṣūr al-Dhahabī, Mawlāy (Saʿdid(e)) (1603) i, 58b, 279, **288b**, 1347a; ii, 134a, 308a, 510a, 819b; iii, 70a, 339b, 814a, 1047a; iv, 635a, b; v, 1119a; vi, 124a, 142b, 248b, 259a, 351a, 589b, 591a, 594b, 596b, 597b, 743a; viii, 724a; s, 28b, 223a – I, 60a, 288b, **297b**, 1387b; II, 137a, 317a, 522b, 839a; III, 72b, 349b, 837b, 1073a; IV, 661b; V, 1181a; VI, 122a, 141a, 233a, 243a, 335a, 574b, 576a, 579a, 581a, 582a, 732b; VIII, 745a; S, 29a, 223a
Aḥmad al-Masīlī (XIV) vi, 728b – VI, 717b
Aḥmad Midḥat Pasha (1913) i, **289a**, 975a; ii, 473b, 474a, b; iii, 357b, 375a, 622a, 630a, 1200a; iv, 602a, 682a, 930a, 931b; v, 194a, 195b; vii, 205b; s, 64b – I, **298a**, 1005b; II, 485b, 486a, b; III, 368b, 387a, 643a, 651a, 1230a; IV, 626b, 710a, 963a, 964b; V, 191a, 192b; VII, 206b; S, 65a
Aḥmad Mukhtār Pasha (1912) iv, 201a; v, 314a; vi, 192a, 983b; ix, 2a; s, 64b – IV, 210a; V, 314a; VI, 176a, 976a; IX, 2a; S, 64b
Aḥmad al-Muḳtadir → Aḥmad I (Hūdid(e))
Aḥmad Mumtāz Pasha (Sawākin) (XIX) iv, 687a – IV, 715a
Aḥmad Mürshidī i, 1202a – I, 1238a
Aḥmad Mūsā (painter/peintre) iii, 1127a, b – III, 1155a, b
Aḥmad Nadā (Filāha) (XIX) ii, 900b – II, 921a
Aḥmad al-Naḥḥās (X) i, 321b – I, 331b
Aḥmad Narāghī, Mullā (1829) vii, 298b – VII, 300b
Aḥmad al-Nāṣir b. al-Hādī ilā ʾl-Ḥaḳḳ (Zaydī Imām) (934) iii, 124b; vi, 436a; vii, 444b, 773a; s, 335b – III, 127b; VI, 421b; VII, 446a, 774b; S, 335a
Aḥmad al-Nāṣirī al-Salāwī (1897) i, **290a**, 315b; v, 1209b; vii, 1007a; s, 395a, b – I, **299a**, 325a; V, 1200a; VII, 1010a; S, 395b, 396a
Aḥmad Nayrīzī (Khaṭṭ) (XVIII) iv, 1123b – IV, 1155b

Aḥmad Niyāzī → Niyāzī Bey
Aḥmad Niẓām Shāh Baḥrī → Malik Aḥmad Baḥrī (Niẓām Shāhī)
Aḥmad-oghlu Shukr Allāh (XII) vii, 207b – VII, 208b
Aḥmad Pasha → al-Djazzār; Hersek-zāde; Miḳdād
Aḥmad Pasha (Ḳars) (1741) vi, 56b – VI, 54b
Aḥmad Pasha, Ḳara (1555) i, **291b**; ii, 704a; v, 67a – I, **300b**; II, 722a; V, 68a
Aḥmad Pasha (Ṣūfī) s, 49b – S, 50a
Aḥmad Pasha b. Ḥasan Pasha (Baghdād) (1747) i, 270a, **291a**, 905a; iii, 106a, 252a, 1257b; vi, 541b; vii, 853b – I, 278b, **300a**, 932b; III, 108b, 259a, 1290a; VI, 526a; VII, 855a
Aḥmad Pasha Abū Widān (Dār Fūr) (1843) ii, 123b; iv, 686b – II, 126b; IV, 714b
Aḥmad Pasha Bonneval (1747) i, **291b**, 395b, 1064b; ii, 511b; iii, 203b, 253a; iv, 738b; v, 52b – I, **300b**, 407a, 1096b; II, 524a; III, 209a, 260a; IV, 768a; V, 54a
Aḥmad Pasha Bursalỉ (1496) i, **292a**; vi, 609b – I, **301a**; VI, 594b
Aḥmad Pasha Gedik (1482) i, **292b**, 354b, 767b; ii, 337b, 530a; iii, 341b; iv, 656a, 868b, 892a; v, 726a, 764a – I, **301b**, 365b, 790b; II, 347b, 543a; III, 352a; IV, 682b, 902a, 924b; V, 731a, 769b
Aḥmad Pasha Khā'in (1524) i, **293a**; iii, 998a; vii, 177b, 721a – I, **302a**; III, 1023a; VII, 179b, 722a
Aḥmad Pasha Küčük → Kücük Aḥmad Pasha
Aḥmad Rafīḳ Altỉnay (1937) i, **293b**; vi, 94a – I, **302b**; VI, 92a
Aḥmad al-Raḳḳī i, 758b – I, 781b
Aḥmad Rāsim (1932) i, 287b, **293b**; v, 196a; vi, 94b; s, 64b – I, 296a, **303a**; V, 193a; VI, 92b; S, 65a
Aḥmad Rasmī (1783) i, **294b**; iii, 157a – I, **303b**; III, 161a
Aḥmad Rātib Pasha (XIX) vi, 151b – VI, 150a
Aḥmad al-Rāzī → al-Rāzī
Aḥmad Riḍwān (XVI) iv, 129a – IV, 134b
Aḥmad al-Rīfī Pasha (Tangier) (XVIII) i, 47b – I, 48b
Aḥmad Rỉzā (Riḍā) (XX) ii, 430b, 474b; iv, 285a; vii, 206a – II, 442a, 486b; IV, 207a, 297b; VII, 207a
Aḥmad Ṣābir (XX) vi, 153a – VI, 151b
Aḥmad Ṣa'lūk (923) iv, 100a – IV, 104b
Aḥmad al-Ṣāwī (1825) vi, 354b, 355a – VI, 339a
Aḥmad Shāh I, Shihāb al-Dīn (Bahmānid(e)) (1436) i, 923b, 924a, 925a, b, 1200a, b, 1323a; ii, 981a, 1115a, 1125b; iii, 15a, 417b, 420b, 638b; iv, 961b; v, 1215b – I, 951b, 952a, 953a, b, 1235b, 1236a, 1363b; II, 1003b, 1141a, 1153a; III, 15b, 431a, 434a, 659b; IV, 994a; V, 1205a
Aḥmad Shāh II, 'Alā' al-Dīn (Bahmānid(e)) (1458) i, 923b; ii, 814b; iii, 421a, 577a; iv, 962a; vi, 53b, 66b – I, 951b; II, 834a; III, 434b, 597a; IV, 994a; VI, 52a, 64b
Aḥmad Shāh III Niẓām al-Dīn (Bahmānid(e)) (1463) i, 923b; vi, 66b, 67a – I, 951b; VI, 64b
Aḥmad Shāh I (Gudjarāt) (1442) i, 295a, 299b, 506b; ii, 11a, 1125a; iii, 418b, 445a, 638a, 1010a; vi, 52b; vii, 957a – I, 304a, 308b, 522a; II, 11a, 1151b; III, 432a, 459b, 659b, 1035b; VI, 51a; VII, 958a
Aḥmad Shāh II (Gudjarāt) (1458) i, 295a; ii, 1125b – I, 304a; II, 1153a
Aḥmad Shāh III (Gudjarāt) (1561) ii, 1129a; vi, 52b – II, 1155b; VI, 50b
Aḥmad Shāh (Turcoman) (1074) vii, 121a – VII, 123a
Aḥmad Shāh, 'Alā' al-Dīn (Atjèh) (1735) i, 743b – I, 766a
Aḥmad Shāh b. Muḥammad 'Alī Shāh (Ḳadjār) (XX) ii, 652b; iv, 392a, 398b; v, 61b; vii, 432a; s, 342a – II, 668b; IV, 408b, 415b; V, 63a; VII, 432b; S, 342a
Aḥmad Shāh b. Muḥammad Shāh Shams al-Dīn (Bengal) → Rādjā Ganesh
Aḥmad Shāh Bahādur (Mughal) (1754/1775) i, **295a**; iii, 60a, 1158b; vi, 535b; vii, 316a, 457b, 869b – I, **304a**; III, 62b, 1187a; VI, 520a; VII, 318b, 457b, 871a
Aḥmad Shāh Durrānī (Abdālī, Afghān) (1773) i, 72b, 95b, 218b, 226b, 229b, 230a, 238a, **295a**, 432b, 454b, 970b, 1001b, 1005b, 1020a; ii, 488b, 628b, 1049b, 1131b; iii, 60b, 335b, 427b, 1158b; iv, 390a, 537b, 709b; v, 29a, 102a, 598b, 1079a; vi, 535b, 715a; vii, 220a, 290b, 316a, 457b, 549a, 869b; viii, 253b – I, 74b, 98a, 224b, 233a, 236b, 237a, 245a, **304b**, 445a, 467b, 1000a, 1032a, 1036b, 1051b; II, 501a, 644b, 1074a, 1158a; III, 63a, 346a, 441b, 1187a; IV, 407a, 560b, 738a; V, 30a, 104a, 602b, 1076b; VI, 520a, 703b, 704a; VII, 222a, 292b, 318b, 457b, 549b, 871a; VIII, 155b
Aḥmad Shāh Ganesh, Shams al-Dīn (Bengal(e)) (1442) i, 295a; iii, 419a – I, 304a; III, 432b
Aḥmad al-Shahīd Bā Faḍl (1523) ii, 730a – II, 748b
Aḥmad Shahīd, Sayyid (XIX) ii, 54b – II, 55b
Aḥmad Shāhis (Gudjarāt) vi, 126a, 368b, 369a – VI, 124a, 353a
Aḥmad Shāhs (India) i, **295a**, 1193a, 1329b; vi, 126a, 368b, 369a – I, **304a**, 1228b, 1370aVI, 124a, 353a
Aḥmad Shākir al-Karamī (XX) vi, 176a
Aḥmad Sharīf (Sanūsī) (XX) i, 277b, 1071a; v, 758a – I, 286a, 1103a; V, 763b
Aḥmad Shawḳī → Shawḳī Aḥmad
Aḥmad al-Shaykh (Amadu Sēku) (1898) i, **297a**; ii, 567b; iii, 39b – I, **306a**; II, 582a; III, 41a
Aḥmad Shihābī (Djānbulāt) (XVIII) ii, 444a, 635b – II, 455b, 651b
Aḥmad al-Sibā'ī (XX) vi, 176a, b, 177a – VI, 162a
Aḥmad Ṣiddīḳ, Khwādja (1259) ii, 1078a – II, 1103a
Aḥmad al-Sidjzī (1009) i, 725a; s, 412b – I, 747b; S, 413a
Aḥmad Sirhindī, Shaykh (1624) i, **297a**, 347a, 957a, 1022b; ii, 30a, 55a, 296b, 380b, 871b, 1144a; iii, 430a, 432b, 435b; vii, 290b, 297a, 327a, b, 432b; ix, 296a; x, 256a, 321a, 958b; s, 313a – I, **306b**, 357b, 986b, 1054a; II, 30b, 56a, 304b, 391a, 891b, 1171a; III, 444a, 446b, 449b; VII, 292b, 299a, 329a, b, 433b; IX, 304b; X, 274a, 345b, ; S, 312b
Aḥmad al-Subaḥī (XX) vi, 153b – VI, 152a
Aḥmad Sulṭān Bayat (XIX) vi, 202b – VI, 187a
Aḥmad al-Tābi'ī (XX) vi, 722b – VI, 711a
Aḥmad Tā'ib → 'Uthmān-zāde
Aḥmad Takūdār (Il-Khān) (1284) → Tegüder
Aḥmad Taymūr (XX) vi, 75a, b – VI, 73a, b
Aḥmad al-Ṭayyib wad (b.) al-Bashīr (1824) x, 248b – X, 267b
Aḥmad al-Ṭayyib al-'Aldj (XX) vi, 755b – VI, 744b
Aḥmad Ṭūsūn → Ṭūsūn b. Muḥammad 'Alī
Aḥmad ū-Mūsā, Awlād Sīdī (Tazerwalt) vi, 589b, 743a, 744a – VI, 574b, 732b, 733a
Aḥmad Wafīḳ Pasha (1891) i, 61b, 63b, 285b, **298a**, 473b; iii, 249b; iv, 791a; vi, 373a, 759a – I, 63b, 65b, 294b, **307a**, 485b; III, 256b; IV, 822b; VI, 357b, 748a
Aḥmad Wāṣif → Wāṣif
Aḥmad al-Waṭṭāsī (1545) vi, 594a, 893b – VI, 579a, 885a
Aḥmad Wehbī → Pīr Meḥmed Wehbī Khayyāṭ
Aḥmad Wuld 'Ayda (amīr) (1932) vii, 627a – VII, 626b
Aḥmad Yasawī (1167) i, **298b**, 1162a; iii, 76b, 1115a,

1116a; v, 264a, 859a; vii, 933b; x, 250a, 681a, 962b; s, 51a –
I, **308a**, 1196b; III, 79a, 1142b, 1143b; V, 262a, 866a; VII, 934a; X, 268b, ; S, 51b
Aḥmad Yuknakī, Adīb (XII) i, **299a** – I, **308b**
Aḥmad Zarrūḳ → Zarrūḳ, Aḥmad
Ahmad Zayn al-Dīn, Shaykh (1581) vi, 458b, 462a, 463a – VI, 444b, 447b, 449a
Aḥmad Zekī Welīdī → Togan, Zekī
Aḥmad Ziwar Pasha (1926) ii, 934b; iii, 516b – II, 956a; III, 534b
Ahmad Ziyaʾi (XX) vi, 768b – VI, 757b
Aḥmad Zog → Zog, King/le roi
Aḥmadābād i, **299b**; ii, 1125b; iii, 16a, 445a, b; v, 1210a; vi, 50b, 51b, 52a, 53b, 126a, 131a; s, 10b, 23b, 70b, 335b –
I, **308b**; II, 1153a; III, 16b, 459b, 460b; V, 1200b; VI, 49a, b, 50a, 51b, 124a, 129a; S, 10a, 23b, 71a, 335a
Aḥmadī → Sikka
Aḥmadī (town/ville) s, **50a** – S, **50b**
Aḥmad-i Rūmī (XIV) s, **49b** – s, **50a**
Aḥmadī, Tādj al-Dīn Ibrāhīm b. Khiḍr (1413) i, **299b**, 325a; ii, 98a; iii, 115a; iv, 128b; vi, 609b; vii, 567b; ix, 418a –
I, **309a**, 335a; II, 100b; III, 117b; IV, 134a; VI, 594b; VII, 568b; IX. 431b
Aḥmadīl b. Ibrāhīm b. Wahsūdān al-Rawwādī al-Kurdī (amīr) (1111) i, 300a; v, 454a; vi, 499b; viii, 470a – I, 309b; V, 456b; VI, 485a; VIII, 486b
Aḥmadīlīs i, 190a, **300a**; iii, 1112a; vi, 499b – I, 194b, **309b**; III, 1139a; VI, 485a
Aḥmadiyya i, 225b, **301a**; ii, 58b, 63b, 129a, 535b, 538b, 1004a; iii, 411b, 433b, 1228b; iv, 84b, 890a, 891a, 951a; s, 248b, 278b –
I, 232b, **310b**; II, 59b, 64b, 132b, 549a, 552a, 1027a; III, 424b, 447b, 1260b; IV, 88b, 922b, 923b, 983b; S, 248b, 278b
Aḥmadiyya (Derw(v)ish) i, 281a; ii, 164b – I, 289b; II, 170a
al-Aḥmadiyya (Khalwatiyya) iv, 992a, 993a – IV, 1024b, 1025b
Aḥmadnagar i, 81a, **303a**; ii, 99b, 158b; iii, 15b, 425b, 426b, 626a; iv, 202a; vi, 63a, b, 67a, 121b, 269a, b, 271b, 488b, 534b, 535b; viii, 73b; s, 246a –
I, 83b, **312b**; II, 101b, 163b; III, 16a, 439b, 440a, 646b; IV, 210b; VI, 61a, b, 65a, 119b, 254a, 256a, 474b, 518b, 520a; VIII, 75a; S, 246b
Aḥmadnagar (Gudjarāt) ii, 1125a; iii, 625b – II, 1151b, III, 646b
Aḥmadnagar (Uttar Pradesh) → Farrūkhābād
Aḥmadu I (Mūrītāniyā (1841) vii, 614b – VII, 614a
Aḥmadu (Ḥamadu) II (1852) i, 303b; ii, 941b; iii, 39a – I, 313a; II, 963b; III, 40b
Aḥmadu III (1862) i, 303b; ii, 941b – I, 313a; II, 963b
Ahmadū Bamba Mbacké ii, 63b, 568a – II, 64b, 582a
Aḥmadu Bello, Sir → Bello, Alhaji Aḥmadu
Aḥmadu Lobbo, Seku (1844) i, **303a**; ii, 251b, 252a, 941b; iii, 38b; v, 394b – I, **312b**; 259a, b, 963b; III, 40b; V, 395b
Aḥmadu Sheykhu → Aḥmad al-Shaykh
Aḥmadzay Khāns (Kilāt) v, 102a – V, 104a
al-Aḥmar → Abu ʾl-Ḥasan al-Aḥmar
Aḥmar, Banu ʾl- → Naṣrid(e)s
Aḥmed → Aḥmad
Aḥmed Aghaoghlu (XIX) vi, 94a – VI, 92a
Aḥmed Beg b. Ibrāhīm Beg (Menteshe) (1380) vi, 1018b – VI, 1011a
Aḥmed Čelebi, Zurnazen Edirneli Daghī (XVII) vi, 1007b – VI, 999b
Aḥmed of/de Edirne, Pīr (1591) vi, 228a – VI, 222a
Aḥmed Esʿad Efendi, Shaykh al-Islām (XVIII) vi, 1004b – VI, 997a
Aḥmed Faḳīh (Ḳonya) (XIII) viii, 972b; s, **50a** – VIII, 1007a; S **51a**
Aḥmed Fewzī Pasha (XIX) viii, 84b – VIII, 87a
Aḥmed Hāshim (XX) vi, 94b – VI, 92b
Aḥmed Iḥsān Bey (XX) vi, 93a – VI, 91a
Ahmed Kabaklî (XX) vi, 95b – VI, 93b
Aḥmed Khalīl → Fîndîḳoghlu
Aḥmed Midḥat Efendi (XIX) vi, 93a, b – VI, 90b, 91b
Ahmed Moulavi C.N. (XX) vi, 462b – VI, 448a
Aḥmed Nazīf (XIX) vii, 532a – VII, 532b
Aḥmed Pasha (mamlūk) (1747) vi, 1002a – VI, 994b
Aḥmed Riḍā Bey (1895) vi, 93a; vii, 206a – VI, 91a; VII, 207a
Aḥmed-i dāʿī (1421) viii, 211a, 212a, 544b – VIII, 215a, 216a, 562a
Aḥmed-oghlu Shükrullāh (XV) vii, 207b; viii, 806b – VII, 208b; VIII, 833b
al-Aḥnaf b. Ḳays (VII) i, **303b**, 343b, 1001a; ii, 415a, b; iii, 391b, 583a, 782a; iv, 14b; v, 56b; ix, 34a –
I, **313a**, 354a, 1031b; II, 426a, b; III, 404a, 603b, 805b; IV, 15b; V, 58a; IX, 34b
al-Ahnūm (Yemen) vi, 436b – VI, 422a
Aḥrām → Ḥaram
Aḥrār, Khwādja ʿUbayd Allāh (1490) i, 147b, 148a, 849a; iv, 113a; v, 859a; vii, 934a, 935a; viii, 800b; x, 250b; s, **50b**, 121b –
I, 152a, b, 872b; IV, 118a; V, 866a; VII, 934b, 935b; VIII, 827b; X, 269a; S, **51a**, 121a
Aḥrār al-Dustūriyyīn s, 18a – S, 18b
Aḥrārs v, 803a – V, 809a
Aḥruf → Ḳirāʾa
Ahrun b. Aʿyān al-Ḳass (VII) i, 213a; vi, 641a; s, **52a** – I, 219b; VI, 626a; S, **52b**
al-Aḥsāʾ → al-Ḥasā; Hufhūf
al-Aḥsāʾ (Shiʿites) ix, 904b, 905a – IX, 942b
al-Aḥsāʾī, Shaykh Aḥmad (1826) i, **304b**, 596a; iv, 51a, 854b; vi, 551b; ix, 403b; s, 305a –
I, **314a**, 615b; IV, 54a, 887b; VI, 536a; IX, 416b; S, 305a
Aḥsan → Djalāl al-Dīn
Aḥsanābād → Gulbargā
al-Ahtam iv, 832a, b – IV, 865a, b
Ahūsar vi, 514b – VI, 500a
Aḥwāḍ → Ḥawḍ
Aḥwāl → Ḥāl
al-Aḥwal, Muḥammad b. al-Ḥasan (873) vii, 282a; viii, 918b – VII, 283b; VIII, 950a
al-Ahwānī, ʿAbd al-ʿAzīz ii, 743b; v, 605b, 608b – II, 762a; V, 609b, 612b
al-Aḥwaṣ al-Ashʿarī (720) vi, 493a – VI, 479a
al-Aḥwaṣ al-Anṣārī (728) i, 10b, **305a**; ii, 91a, 428b, 1029b; iii, 2b; iv, 1002a; s, 10a –
I, 10b, **314b**; II, 92b, 439b, 1053a; III, 2b; IV, 1031b; S, 9b
al-Ahwāz i, 145a, 211b, **305b**, 695a, 1046b; ii, 383a, 426a; iii, 244b; iv, 6a, 7b, 675b; v, 80a, b, 81b, 867b; vi, 117b, 119b, 333b, 539a, 660b; vii, 26a, 271a; s, 35a, 118b, 119a –
I, 149b, 218a, **315a**, 716b, 1078a; II, 393a, 437a; III, 251b; IV, 6b, 8b, 703a; V, 82b, 83b, 874a; VI, 115b, 117b, 318a, 524a, 646a; VII, 26a, 273a; S, 35b, 118a, b
Aḥzāb → Ḥizb
ʿĀʾid, Āl i, 555a, 709b – I, 572b, 731a
ʿĀʾiḍ b. al-ʿAbbās b. Mandīl (1269) vi, 404a – VI, 388b
ʿĀʾiḍ b. Marʿī al-Mughaydī (XIX) i, 709b – I, 731a
ʿĀidh b. Saʿīd (657) vii, 463b – VII, 463a
Āʾidh, Banū (Makhzūm) vi, 633b – VI, 618b

ʿĀʾila i, **305b**, 700a – I, **315b**, 721b
Āʾīn i, **306b** – I, **316a**
Āʾīn al-Mulk (Khaldjī amīr) (1303) vi, 406b – VI, 391a
ʿAïr (Ayar) i, **307a; viii, 17b** – I, **316b; VIII, 17b**
ʿĀʾisha bint Abī Bakr (678) i, 107a, 109b, 110a, **307b**, 383a, 1048a; ii, 414a, 415b, 416a, 845b, 1059a; iii, 64a, 65a, 242b, 359b; v, 616a; vi, 467a, 475b, 575b, 621b, 640b, 646a, 652a, 659a, 669a; vii, 371a, 393a; s, 133a, 230a, 311a – I, 110a, 112b, 113a, **317a**, 394a, 1080a; II, 425a, 426b, 427a, 865a, 1083b; III, 66b, 67b, 249b, 371a; V, 620a; VI, 453a, 461b, 560a, 606b, 625b, 631a, 637a, b, 644b, 655b; VII, 373a, 394b; S, 132b, 230a, 311a
ʿĀʾisha bint ʿImrān → ʿĀʾisha al-Mannūbiyya
ʿĀʾisha bint Muʿāwiya b. al-Mughīra (VII) i, 76a; s, 103b – I, 78b; S, 103a
ʿĀʾisha bint Ṭalḥa (VII) i, **308b**; vi, 478a; vii, 650b – I, **318a**; VI, 464a; VII, 650a
ʿĀʾisha bint Yūsuf al-Bāʿūnī (XVI) i, 1109b – I, 1143a
ʿĀʾisha Ḳandīsha s, **52b**, 351a – S, **53a**, 351a
ʿĀʾisha al-Mannūbiyya (1257) i, **308b**; vi, 251a, 355a – I, **318a**; VI, 235a, 339a
ʿĀʾishe Sulṭān bint Murād III (Ottoman) (1586) vi, 865a – VI, 856a
Aïssaoua → ʿĪsāwa
Aït Aḥmad (Kabylia/-e) (XX) iv, 363a – IV, 379a
Ajarafe → al-Sharaf
Ajjer (Touareg) ii, 875a, 992a, 1022a – II, 895b, 1015a, 1046a
Aḳ Deniz → Baḥr al-Rūm
Aḳ Ḥiṣār i, **309a**; v, 284b – I, **319a**; V, 283a
Aḳ Ḥisārī i, **309b** – I, **319b**
Aḳ Kirmān i, **310a**, 1119b, 1252b; iv, 239a – I, **320a**, 1153a, b, 1290b; IV, 249b
Aḳ Ḳoyunlū i, 148b, 190a, 240a, 292b, **311a**, 639b, 666b, 861a, 903b, 1067a, 1117a, 1128b, 1133b, 1234a, 1328a; ii, 20b, 174a, 344b, 348a, 614a, 711b; iii, 198b, 315b, 507a, 1100b, 1257a; iv, 34a-35a, 267b, 475a; v, 54a, 457a, 492a; vi, 483a, 493a, 495a, 515b, 541a, 901a; x, 45b, 963b; s, 208a, 227b, 419b – I, 152b, 194b, 247b, 302a, **320b**, 660b, 687a, 885a, 930b, 1099a, 1150b, 1162b, 1167b, 1270b, 1368b; II, 21a, 179a, 354a, 357b, 629a, 730a; III, 203a, 325a, 524b, 1127b, 1289b; IV, 36b, 37a, 279b, 496a; V, 55b, 459b, 495a; VI, 469a, 478b, 480a, 500b, 525b, 892b; X, 46b, ; S, 208a, 227b, 419b
Aḳ Masdjid i, **312a** – I, **322a**
Aḳ Sarāy (town/ville) i, **312a**; iv, 578b; vi, 55b, 120b, 226b, 275b – I, **322a**; IV, 602a; VI, 53b, 118a, 220b, 260b
Aḳ Sarāy (palace) i, **312b**; s, 59a, 146a – I, **322a**; S, 59b, 146a
Aḳ Shams al-Dīn (1459) i, 109a, **312b**, 777a, 869b; iii, 43b, 131a; vi, 226a, 978b – I, 112a, **322a**, 800a, 893b; III, 45a, 133b; VI, 219b, 971a
Aḳ Shams al-Dīn, al-Mawlā (XVI) vi, 913b – VI, 905a
Aḳ Shehr i, **313a** – I, **322b**
Aḳ Ṣu (river/fleuve) i, 184a, **313b**, 454b; vi, 56a, 505b, 506a – I, 189b, **323a**, 467b; VI, 54a, 491a, b
Aḳ Ṣu (town/ville) i, **313b** – I, **323a**
Aḳ Ṣu (village) i, **314a** – I, **323b**
Aḳ Sunḳūr b. ʿAbd Allāh al-Ḥādjib (1094) i, **314a**, 1117a – I, **324a**, 1150b
Aḳ Sunḳūr I al-Bursuḳī, Ḳasīm al-Dawla (1133) i, 300a, **314a**, 664a, 1337a; iii, 86b, 87a, 1118b; iv, 201a; v, 921b; vi, 64a, 380a, 500a, 506b; vii, 408a, 733a, b, 983b; viii, 944a – I, 309b, **324a**, 684a, 1377a; III, 89a, 1146a; IV, 219b; V, 927a; VI, 62a, 364b, 485a, b, 492a; VII, 409b, 733b, 734a, 984a; VIII, 078b
Aḳ Sunḳūr II Nuṣrat al-Dīn (Aḥmadīlī) (XII) i, 300b; vi, 500a; viii, 239b – I, 310a; VI, 485b; VIII, 485b
Aḳ-Sunḳūr al-ʿĀdilī al-Sāḳī (1249) iv, 484a – IV, 505a
Aḳ Sunḳūr al-Ahmadīlī (1133) i, 300b – I, 310a
Aḳ Sunḳur al-Ṣarārī viii, 986a – VIII, 1020b
Āḳā → Āghā
Āḳā Mīrak (XVI) viii, 788a – VIII, 814b
Āḳā Muḥammad ʿAlī Khān Ḥādjdj Muḥammad (Niʿmat Allāhī) (1884) viii, 47b – VIII, 48a
Āḳā Muḥammad Khān (Ḳādjār) (1848) vi, 551b – VI, 536a
Āḳā Nadjafī, Muḥammad Taḳī Iṣfahānī (1931) v, 1087b; vii, 918b; s, **54a** – V, 1085a; VII, 919a; S, **54b**
Āḳā Riḍā (painter/peintre) (XVII) vi, 426a; vii, 339a – VI, 411a; VII, 340b
Āḳā Rustam (XVI) vi, 515a – VI, 500a
Āḳā Ṣādiḳ, Ḥādjdjī (XIX) s, 53a – S, 53b
al-ʿAḳaba (mountain road/route de montagne) i, **324b**; viii. 379b – I, **324b**; VIII, 392b
al-ʿAḳaba (port/Gulf/Golfe) i, 9a, 50b, 64b, **314b**, 534a, 548b, 783b; iii, 36a; v, 995b; vi, 151b, 154a; vii, 65a; s, 8b, 198b, 230a – I, 9a, 52a, 66b, **324b**; III, 37b; V, 991a; VI, 150a, 152a; VII, 65b; S, 8a, 198b, 230a
ʿAḳaba b. Muḥammad (Khuzāʿī) (850) vi, 900a – VI, 891a
ʿAḳabat al-Ḳibliyya vi, 545b – VI, 530a
ʿAḳabat al-Nisāʾ i, **315a** – I, **325a**
ʿAḳabi, Banū vi, 128b – VI, 126b
Āḳāʾī iv, 51b – IV, 54a
ʿAḳāʾid → ʿAḳīda
Akagündüz (1958) s, **55a** – S, **55b**
ʿAḳāl → ʿImāma
Akanṣūs, Abū ʿAbd Allāh (1877) i, **315a**; iii, 948b; vi, 113a; vii, 392a – I, **325a**; III, 973b; VI, 110b; VII, 393b
ʿAḳār s, **55a** – S, **55b**
Akara (Mālwā) vi, 309a – 294b
ʿAkārib → ʿAḳrabī
ʿAḳarḳūf i, **315b** – I, **325b**
Āḳāsī, Ḥādjdjī Mīrzā (XIX) v, 1222a; VII, 453a, 454a, 456a – V, 1212b; VII, 454a, b, 456a
al-ʿAkawwak, ʿAlī b. Djabala (828) i, **315b**; iv, 718b; s, 17b – I, **325b**; IV, 747a; S, 17b
Akbar (Mākū) (1642) vi, 202b – VI, 186b
Akbar I, Abu ʾl-Fatḥ Djalāl al-Dīn Muḥammad b. Humāyūn (Mughal) (1605) i, 8b, 80b, 117a, b, 208b, 228b, 229a, 238a, 252b, 253a, **316a**, 417b, 710b, 733a, 807b, 856b, 864b, 1069a, 1135a, b, 1136a, b, 1194a, 1323a, 1324a, 1331a, 1347b; ii, 50a, 121a, 155b, 156b, 162a, 271b, 272a, 296a, 336b, 379b, 503b, 814a, 840a, 871a, 973b, 1048a, 1085a, 1122b, 1129a, 1131a, 1144a; iii, 201b, 245b, 318b, 348a, 423b, 430a, 449b, 457a, 482b; iv, 219a, 523b, 709a, 910a, 922a, 1104a, 1159b; v, 598a, b, 599b, 635a, 686a, 689b, 1135b, 1217a; vi, 52b, 67a, 127a, 131a, 269b, 271b, 342b, 369b, 407a, 410a, 424b, 425a, 456b, 488b, 516b, 533b, 534a; vii, 133b, 134a, b, 139a, 195a, 221a, 314a, b, 317a, 320a, 327a, 329b, 337b, 345a, 573b, 932a; viii, 67b, 116b, 253b, 368a; ix, 846a s, 1b, 3a, b, 107b, 126b, 132a, 142b, 167a, 176b, 210b, 237b, 242b, 258a, 259b, 292a, 312a, 313a, 324b, 366b, 378a, 410b – I, 8b, 82b, 120b, 121a, 214b, 235b, 236a, 245a, 260b, 261a, **326a**, 429b, 731b, 831a, 755a, 880a, 888b, 1101a, 1157b, 1169b, 1170a, b, 1229a, 1364b, 1371b, 1387b; II, 51a, 124a, 160b, 161a, 167a, 280a, 304a, 346a, 390a, 516a, 833b, 860a, 891a, 916a,

931b, 943b, 995b, 1072b, 1110b, 1149a, 1156a, 1158a, 1171a; III, 206b, 252b, 328a, 358b, 437a, 444a, 465a, 473a, 499b; IV, 228b, 546a, 737a, b, 1135b, 1191b; V, 602a, 603b, 639a, 691a, 694b, 1135b, 1207a; VI, 50b, 65a, 125a, 129a, 254a, 256a, 326b, 353b, 391b, 395a, 410a, 442a, 474b, 501b, 518a; VII, 135b, 136a, b, 141a, 195b, 222b, 316b, 317a, 319b, 322b, 328b, 331a, 339b, 347a, 574b, 932b; VIII, 69a, 110a, 255b, 265a; IX, 881b; S, 1b, 2b, 107a, 125b, 131a, 142a, 167a, 177b, 210a, 237a, 242a, 257b, 259b, 291b, 312a, b, 324a, 366a, 378a, 411a
Akbar II (Mughal) (1837) ii, 221b; vii, 316b – II, 228b; VII, 318b
Akbar b. Awrangzīb (1688) i, 769a; vi, 132a, 534b, 856a; s, **55b** – I, 792a; VI, 130a, 519a, 847b; S, **56a**
Akbar, Sayyid Ḥusayn Allāhābādī (1921) i, **317b**; iii, 358b – I, **327a**; III, 370a
Akbarnagar → Rādjmahal
Akbar Shāh II ii, 221b; iv, 1102b – II, 228b; IV, 1133b
Aḳbughā ʿAbd al-Wāḥid, amīr (XIV) i, 814b – I, 838a
Aḳče i, **317b**; ii, 118a, 119a, b; v, 974a – I, **327b**; II, 121a, b, 122a; V, 976a
Aḳče Ḳodja (XIV) i, 468b – I, 482b
ʿAḳd i, **318a**; ii, 303a, b; iii, 1091b – I, **328a**; II, 311b, 312a; III, 1118a
Akdariyya i, **320a** – I, **330a**
al-Akfānī i, 1220b; iii, 1088a – I, 1257a; III, 1114b
al-Aḳfahsī (1405) vi, 720b; x, 586b – VI, 709b; X,
Akh → ʿĀʾila; Ikhwān; Muʾakhāt
al-Akhal (Sicily/Sicile) (IX) vii, 483b – VII, 483b
Ākhāl Tekke i, **320b** – I, **330b**
Akhalčikh → Akhiṣa
Akhalkhalaki (Armenia/-) i, 643a; v, 495a, b – I, 664a; V, 498a, b
Akharnar → Nudjūm
Akh(w)āsh, Banū v, 153b – V, 155a
Akhaweyn, Mullā i, 323a – I, 333a
Akhbār → Khabar; Taʾrīkh
Akhbār al-ʿAbbās iv, 446a – IV, 466a
Akhbār Madjmūʿa i, **320b**, 600b – I, **330b**, 620a
Akhbār al-Ṣīn wa 'l-Hind i, 991b; ii, 583b; iv, 648a; s, **55b** – I, 1022a; II, 598a; IV, 674b; S, **56a**
al-Akhbārī, Muḥammad b. ʿAbd al-Nabī al-Nīshābūrī (XIX) iv, 703b; vi, 551a; s, 57a – IV, 732a; VI, 535b; S, 57b
Akhbāriyya iv, 50a, 51a; vi, 549a, 550b, 551a; vii, 300b; viii, 779b; s, **56b**, 95b, 103b, 134b – IV, 53a, b; VI, 533b, 535a, b; VII, 302b; VIII, 805b; S, **57a**, 95a, 103a, 134a
Akh-čay (Mākū) vi, 200b, 201a, b – VI, 185a, b
al-Akhḍar i, **321a**; v, 700b, 706a – I, **331a**; V, 705b, 711a
Akhḍar, Djabal i, 207b, 1048b, 1049a, b; v, 759b, 760a – I, 213b, 1080a, b, 1081a; V, 765b, 766a
al-Akhḍarī, Abū Zayd (XVI) i, **321a**, 1019b – I, **331a**, 1051a
al-Akhfash i, **321a**; s, 22b, 361b – I, **331a**; S, 23a, 361a
al-Akhfash al-Akbar (927) i, 321b – I, 331a
al-Akhfash al-Aṣghar, Abu 'l-Ḥasan (927) i, 321b; vii, 279b, 280a, 526b – I, 331b; VII, 281b, 282a, 527a
al-Akhfash al-Awsaṭ (825) i, **321b**; iii, 758a; viii, 379a; x, 86a; s, 317b – I, **331b**; III, 781a; VIII, 392a; IX, 327b; X, 83b; S, 317b
Akhī i, **321b**, 347b, 468a, 510a, 510b; ii, 966b, 967b; iv, 621a, b; v, 254a; viii, 175a – I, **331b**, 358a, 482a, 526a; II, 988b, 989b; IV, 646a, b; V, 251b; VIII, 178a
Akhī Baba i, 323a, **323b**; ii, 968a; v, 173a – I, 333a, 333b; II, 990b; V, 170b
Akhī Čelebi (XV) iii, 340a – III, 350a
Akhī Ewrān i, 323a, **324a**, 510b; ii, 968a, 1138a; v, 173a – I, 333a, 333b, **334a**, 526a; II, 990a, 1165a; V, 170b
Akhī Faradj Zandjānī, Shaykh (1065) i, 322a; ii, 966b – I, 332a; II, 988b
Akhī Khazzām b. Ghālib (IX) iv, 215a, 216a – IV, 224b, 225b
Akhī Sirādj al-Dīn ʿUthmān, Shaykh (XIV) ii, 51b; v, 639a – II, 52b; V, 643a
Akhīdjūḳ (1359) i, 323b, **325a**; ii, 401a, 967a; vii, 820b – I, 333b, **335a**; III, 412a, 989a; VII, 822a
Ākhir → al-Asmāʾ al-Ḥusnā
Ākhir-i Čārshamba → Ṣafar
Ākhira i, **325a** – I, **335a**
Akhiskha i, 4a, **325a**; vi, 59b – I, 4a, **335b**; VI, 57a
Akhī-zāde, Āl i, 323a – I, 331b
Akhī-zāde Hüseyin Efendi, Shaykh al-Islām (1634) v, 272b; vii, 598a – V, 270a; VII, 598a
Akhī-zāde ʿAbdülḥalīm Efendi (XVII) i, 732b; iv, 900b – I, 754b; IV, 933b
Akhlāḳ i, **325b** – I, **335b**
Akhlāṭ (Khilāṭ) i, **329a**, 627a, 639a, 799a, 1206b; ii, 393a; iv, 354b, 817b; v, 455a; vi, 124b, 243b, 244a, 505a, 626a – I, **339a**, 647b, 659b, 822b, 1242b; II, 403b; IV, 370a, 850b; V, 457b; VI, 122b, 227b, 228a, 490a, 611a
Akhmīm/Ikhmīm i, **330a**, 1038b; vi, 119a, 413a, 912b – I, **340a**, 1070b; VI, 116b, 398a, 904a
al-Akhnas b. Sharīḳ i, 891a – I, 918a
Akhnūkh → Idrīs
al-Akhras (1874) i, **330a** – I, **340b**
Akhsatān b. Manūčihr b. Afrīdūn (Sharwān-shāh) (1159) iv, 348b, 915a – IV, 363a, 948a
al-Akhshabān i, 136a – I, 140a
Akhshām → Ṣalāt
Akhsīkath i, **330b**; ii, 791a; vi, 557b; s, 406b – I, **340b**; II, 810a; VI, 542a; S, 406b
Akhsitān b. Gagik (XI) v, 489a, b – V, 492a, b
al-Akhṭal (710) i, **331a**, 586a, 1241a; ii, 480a, 789a; iii, 354a; iv, 315b, 744b, 819a, 1002b, 1008b; vi, 379a, 475a, 545a, 671a; vii, 843a, 920b, 981a; viii, 110a, 130b; s, 10a, 394a, b – I, **341a**, 605a, 1278b; II, 492a, 807b; III, 365a; IV, 329b, 774b, 852a, 1035a, 1041a; VI, 363a, 461a, 529b, 657a; VII, 844a, 921a, 982a; VIII, 121a, 649b; S, 9b, 394b, 395a
Akhtarī (1561) i, **331b**; iv, 365a – I, **342a**; IV, 381a
Akhū Muḥsin (985) i, 95b, 96a, 403a; vi, 917b – I, 98b, 414b; VI, 909a
Akhū Ṭāz → Djardamur
Ākhūnd i, **331b** – I, **342a**
Akhund Bābā (Mullā Ilyās) (XVII) ii, 316b – II, 326a
Akhund Darwīza → Darwīza
Ākhund-zāda, Mīrzā Fatḥ ʿAlī (1878) i, **331b**; ii, 217a; iii, 358a; iv, 73b; v, 919b; vi, 291b, 758a, b, 763a, b; vii, 438b; viii, 116a; s, 53b, 76b, 109a, 290b – I, **342a**; II, 223b; III, 369b; IV, 77b; V, 925a; VI, 276b, 747b, 752b; VII, 439b; VIII, 118b; S, 54a, 76b, 108a, 290a
Akhūr → Amīr Ākhūr
Akhūremīrizāde Ḥāshimī (XVI) iii, 153b – III, 157a
Akhwakh i, 504a; iv, 631a – I, 519b; IV, 656a
al-ʿĀḳib b. ʿAbd Allāh (1550) viii, 18b – VIII, 18b
ʿĀkib al-Anuṣammānī of/de Takidda x, 122a – X, 132a
ʿAḳīda i, 121a, 195a, 310a, **332b**; iv, 279b – I, 124b, 201a, 319b, **342b**; IV, 291b
ʿĀkif Pasha → Muḥammad ʿĀkif Pasha
ʿAḳīḳ i, **336a** – I, **346b**
al-ʿAḳīḳ i, **336b**; iii, 121b; s, 199b – I, **347a**; III, 124b; S, 199b

ʿAḳīḳ al-Yamāma (Tamra) i, 336b – I, 347b
ʿAḳīḳ Dhāt ʿIrḳ i, 336b – I, 347a
ʿAḳīḳa i, **337a**; iv, 488a – I, **347b**; IV, 509a
al-ʿAḳīḳī, al-Ḥasan b. Muḥammad b. Djaʿfar (IX) vii, 418ba – VII, 419a
ʿAḳīl b. Abī Ṭālib (670) i, **337b**; vi, 650b, 828b; vii, 689a; ix, 715a – I, **348a**; VI, 636a, 818b; VII, 689a; VIII, 746a
ʿAḳīl b. Djābir b. ʿAbd Allāh (VIII) s, 231a – S, 230b
ʿAḳīl b. ʿUllafa al-Murrī vii, 629b – VII, 629a, b
ʿAḳīl Khān Rāzī, Mīr Muḥammad (1696) vi, 132a; s, **57b** – VI, 130a; S, **58a**
Āḳil al-Murār → Ḥudjr Āḳil al-Murār
ʿĀḳila i, **337b**; ii, 342a; iv, 334b – I, **348b**; II, 352a; IV, 349a
Aḳïndjï i, **340a**, 1302b; ii, 611b – I, **350b**, 1342b; II, 626b
Aḳīt, Āl vi, 259b – VI, 244a
ʿAkk, Banū i, **340b**; vi, 652b – I, **351a**; VI, 638a
ʿAkkā (Acre) i, 216a, **341a**, 946b, 1078a, b; ii, 63b, 129b; iii, 188a, 325a, b, 473a, 474b; iv, 485b, 965a; v, 594a, 595a; vi, 322a, b, 406a, 579a, 652a, b; vii, 168b, 817a, 998a; s, 20b, 120b, 121a, 162b, 205a, b, 268a, b – I, 222b, **351b**, 976a, 1110b; II, 65a, 133a; III, 192b, 335a, b, 489b, 491a; IV, 506a, 997a; V, 598a, 598b; VI, 306a, 307a, 390b, 564a, 638a; VII, 170a, 819a, 1000a; S, 21a, 120a, b, 162b, 205a, b, 268a
al-ʿAḳḳād, ʿAbbās Maḥmūd (1964) i, 598a; iii, 1207b; iv, 85b, 159b; v, 189a; vi, 91a, 409b, 414b; vii, 441a; viii, 88a; s, **57b** – I, 617b; III, 1238a; IV, 89b, 166b; V, 186b; VI, 89a, 394a, 399b; VII, 442a; 90b; S, **58a**
ʿAkkār vi, 345a, 579a; s, **58b** – VI, 329b; S, **59a**
ʿAkkāsbāshī (XX) s, 109b – S, 109a
Akkerman → Aḳ Kirmān
Aḳḳūsh al-Afram (Damas(cus)) vii, 991b – VII, 993a
ʿAḳl i, 341b, 1116a; iv, 157a, 487a, b – I, **352a**, 1149b; IV, 163b, 508a
ʿAḳliyyāt i, **342b**; iv, 469b – I, **353a**; IV, 490a
Aklub, Banū iv, 1106a – IV, 1137b
Aḳlūḳiyā vi, 420a – VI, 405a
Akmal al-Dīn al-Bābartī (XIV) i, 299b – I, 309a
Aḳmesdjid iv, 500a – IV, 521b, 522a
ʿAḳr (Wāsiṭ) (720) vi, 740a – VI, 729b
al-Aḳraʿ b. Ḥābis (VII) i, **343a**, 1247b; ii, 608b; iii, 169a; v, 109a; viii, 82b – I, **353b**, 1285b; II, 623b; III, 172b; V, 111b; VIII, 84b
ʿAḳrab i, **343b** – I, **354a**
ʿAḳrabāʾ i, **344a**, 628b; ii, 569a; vii, 402b – I, **354b**, 649b; II, 583b; VII, 404a
Aḳrābādhīn i, **344a** – I, **354b**
ʿAḳrabī i, **345a** – I, **355b**
Akrād → Kurd(e)s
Aḳrā-Rūdh vi, 498b – VI, 484a
ʿAks → Balāgha
al-Aḳṣā → Masdjid al-Aḳṣā
Aḳsarā → Aḳ Sarāy
al-Aḳsarāʾī, ʿIsā b. Ismāʿīl iii, 181a – III, 185b
Aḳsarayī → Djamāl al-Dīn
al-Aḳsarāyī, Karīm al-Dīn (1320) s, **59a** – S, **59b**
Aḳshehirli → Ḥasan Fehmī Efendi
Aḳ-Shehr vii, 1018a – VII, 1020a
Akstafa s, 146a – S, 146a
Aksu (Bug) vi, 56a – VI, 54a
Aḳsu (Khotan) s, 98a – S, 97b
Aksūm ii, 895b; iii, 9a, b, 10a – II, 916b; III, 9b, 10a, b
Aḳṭāʿ v, 152a – V, 154a
al-Aḳṭaʿ → Abū Yaʿḳūb; ʿAmr b. ʿUbayd Allāh
Aktau (Mangïstau mts) vi, 415a – VI, 400a
Aḳtaw (XIV) ii, 612b – II, 627b
Aḳṭāy (Mamlūk) (XIII) i, 944b – I, 973b
Aktham b. Ṣayfī i, **345a**; vi, 267a – I, **355b**; VI, 252a
al-ʿAḳūla → Dayr al-ʿĀḳūl
Aḳūniṭun s, **59b** – S, **59b**
Aḳūr → Athūr
Āḳūsh (Āḳ-ḳūsh) al-Burunlī (al-Barlī) (1261) vi, 322a; vii, 729b – VI, 306b; VII, 730a
Akūsha ii, 141b, 142a – II, 145b, 146a
al-Aḳwās → Arkush
Āl (clan) i, 258b, **345b**, 700b – I, 266b, **356a**, 721b
Āl followed by a family name, see also under that name/suivi d'un nom de famille, voir aussi sous le nom de cette famille
Āl (demon/démon) i, **345b** – I, **356a**
Āl → Sarāb
Āl Shaykh ix, 905a – IX, 943a
Āl Sulaymān, ʿAbd Allāh (XX) vi, 153a, 155b, 161a, 163b, 165b, 166a, b – VI, 151b, 152a, 154b, 156a, 157b, 158a, b
Āl-i Aḥmad, Sayyid Djalāl (1969) iv, 73b; v, 200b; s, **60a**, 135b – IV, 77a; V, 197b; S, **60b**, 135a
Āla i, **345b** – I, **356a**
al-ʿAlāʾ b. al-Ḥaḍramī (VII) i, 942a; ii, 811b; iv, 220a, 764a, 832b; vii, 570b – I, 971a; II, 831a; IV, 229b, 794b, 865b; VII, 571a
Ala Da i, **346a** – I, **356b**
ʿAlāʾ al-Dawla (Kākūyid(e)) → ʿAlāʾ al-Dawla Muḥammad b. Dushmanziyār
ʿAlāʾ al-Dawla (Timūrid(e)) (1459) i, 147b – I, 152a
ʿAlāʾ al-Dawla b. Sulaymān Beg (XV) i, 324a; ii, 240a; iv, 553a – I, 334a; II, 246b; IV, 576b
ʿAlāʾ al-Dawla ʿAlī b. Farāmurz → ʿAlī b. Farāmurz
ʿAlāʾ al-Dawla Ata-Khān (Kākūyid(e)) (1227) iv, 466b – IV, 487a
ʿAlāʾ al-Dawla Bozḳurd (Dhu ʾl-Ḳadr) (1515) vi, 509b, 510a, 541a – VI, 495a, 525b
ʿAlāʾ al-Dawla Farāmarz b. ʿAlī (XII) i, 113a – I, 116a
ʿAlāʾ al-Dawla Ḥasan Bāwandī (1171) v, 662a – V, 667b
ʿAlāʾ al-Dawla Muḥammad b. Dushmanziyār (Kākūyid(e)) (1041) i, 132a, 512b; iii, 331a, 942b; iv, 100b, 465a, b, 466b, 1103b; vi, 600b, 907a – I, 136a, 528a; III, 341a, 967a; IV, 105a, 465b, 486a, 487a, 1134b; VI, 585b, 898b
ʿAlāʾ al-Dawla al-Simnānī (1336) i, 88b, **346b**, 702b; v, 301a; viii, 408b; s, 122a – I, 91a, **357a**, 723b; V, 300b; VIII, 473b; S, 121b
ʿAlāʾ al-Dīn → Djahān-Sūz; Djuwaynī; Ghūrid(e)s; Ḳayḳubād I; Khwārazmshāhs; Saldjūḳs
ʿAlāʾ al-Dīn (Vize) (1562) vi, 228a – VI, 222a
ʿAlāʾ al-Dīn (engineer/ingénieur) (XIII) vi, 406a – VI, 390b
ʿAlāʾ al-Dīn (Marāgha) (XII) vi, 500b – VI, 485b, 486a
ʿAlāʾ al-Dīn, Sulṭān (Makassar) (1607) vi, 116b – VI, 114a
ʿAlāʾ al-Dīn b. Maḥmūd I Khaldjī (Mālwā) (1462) vi, 54a, 271a, 309b; vii, 957a – VI, 52a, 255b, 256a, 294b; VII, 957b
ʿAlāʾ al-Dīn b. Muḥammad Shāh IV (Sayyid, Dihlī) (1442) vi, 53a – VI, 51a
ʿAlāʾ al-Dīn Aḥmad Bahmanī → Aḥmad Shāh II
ʿAlāʾ al-Dīn ʿĀlam Shāh → ʿĀlam Shāh
ʿAlāʾ al-Dīn ʿAlī b. Faḍl Allāh → Faḍl Allāh
ʿAlāʾ al-Dīn ʿAlī b. Yūsuf Bālī (1497) ii, 879b – II, 899b
ʿAlāʾ al-Dīn ʿAlī Eretna → Eretna
ʿAlāʾ al-Dīn ʿAlī Karamān-Oghlu (XIV) vii, 593b – VII, 593a
ʿAlāʾ al-Dīn Beg (1333) i, **348a** – I, **358b**
ʿAlāʾ al-Dīn Dāwūd (Mengüček, Erzincan) (XIII) vii, 871a – VII, 872b

ʿAlāʾ al-Dīn Fīrūz → Fīrūz Shāh (Bengal(e))
ʿAlāʾ al-Dīn Ḥasan Bahman Shāh (1358) i, 923b, 924b, 1200a; ii, 51b, 99b, 180a, 270a, 1124b; vi, 67a; vii, 289a, 458a –
I, 951b, 952a, 1235a; II, 52b, 101b, 185b, 278a, 1151a; VI, 65a; VII, 291a, 458a
ʿAlāʾ al-Dīn Ḥusayn → Djahān-Sūz; Ḥusayn Shāh
ʿAlāʾ al-Dīn ʿImād Shāh (Berar) (1532) i, 914b; iii, 425a, 1159b, 1160a – I, 942a; III, 439a, 1188a, b
ʿAlāʾ al-Din Ḳara Sonḳor (1207) i, 300b; iii, 1112a – I, 310a; III, 1139a
ʿAlāʾ al-Dīn Karāba (Atabeg) (XII) vi, 501a – VI, 486a
ʿAlāʾ al-Dīn Khaldjī (Delhi) (1316) iv, 921a; vi, 691b, 1027a; viii, 5b – VI, 679a, 1020a; VIII, 5b
ʿAlāʾ al-Dīn Mudjāhid (Bahmānid(e)) (1378) vii, 458b – VII, 458b
ʿAlāʾ al-Dīn Muḥammad III Nizārī (1255) vii, 974a; viii, 598b – VII, 974b; VIII, 617b
ʿAlāʾ (Ḍiyāʾ) al-Dīn Muḥammad (Ghūrid(e)) (1215) ii, 1101b, 1103a – II, 1127b, 1129a
ʿAlāʾ al-Dīn Muḥammad (Khaldjī) → Muḥammad Shāh I Khaldjī (Delhi)
ʿAlā al-Dīn Muḥammad b. Tekish (Khʷārazm-Shāh) (1220) i, 4a, 1001b, 1010a, 1311a; ii, 43a, 329b, 393b, 571a, 606a, 752a, 894a, 1101b; iii, 114a, 195b, 196b, 197a, 198a; iv, 502b, 583a; v, 662b; vi, 77a, 482a, 717a, 939a; vii, 410a; viii, 63b, 432a; ix, 558a; s, 246a –
I, 4a, 1032a, 1041a, 1351b; II, 43b, 403a, 404a, 585b, 621a, 770a, 914b, 1127b; III, 116b, 200b, 201b, 203a; IV, 524b, 606b; V, 667b; VI, 75a, 468b, 705b, 931a; VII, 411a; VIII, 63a, 447a; IX, 586a; S, 246a
ʿAlā a;-Dīn Muḥammad (vizier, Sabzawār) ix, 47b, 48a – IX, 48b, 49a
ʿAlāʾ al-Dīn Pasha → ʿAlāʾ al-Dīn Beg
ʿAlāʾ al-Dīn Riʿāyat Shāh al-Ḳahhār (Atjèh) (1604) i, 743a; iii, 1220a; vii, 71b – I, 765b; III, 1250b; VII, 72b
ʿAlāʾ al-Dīn Ṣāḥib Andavār, Shaykh (Marakkayar) vi, 503b – VI, 489a
ʿAlāʾ al-Dīn (Sihālī) (XIV) i, 936b; s, 292a – I, 965b; S, 291a
ʿAlāʾ al-Dīn Tekish → Tekesh
ʿAlāʾ al-Mulk Ḥusaynī Shūshtarī Marʿashī (XVII) vi, 516b – VI, 501b
Ala Shehir i, **346a** – I, **356b**
Ālā Singh (Patiala) (XVIII) i, 1022b, 1194b; ii, 488b; iii, 485a – I, 1054a, 1229b; II, 501a; III, 502b
ʿAlā-yi Tabrīzī, ʿAbd Allāh (XIII) iv, 1045b, 1047b – IV, 1077a, 1079a
Ālaba wa ʾl-ḳilāʿ i, **348b** – I, **359a**
Alaca (Čorum) ii, 62b – II, 64a
Alačik iv, 1150b – IV, 1182b
Alacuas → Arkush
Aladdin → Alf Layla wa-Layla
Aladja i, **348b** – I, **359a**
Aladja Da i, **348b** – I, **359a**
Aladja Ḥiṣār i, **348b**; vi, 69b – I, **359a**; VI, 67b
Älägän (Mākū) vi, 201a – VI, 185a
Alaham, Banū s, 145a – S, 144b
Alahort → al-Ḥurr b. ʿAbd al-Raḥmān al-Thaḳafī
al-ʿAlāʾī s, 251b – S, 251b
ʿAlāʾī, Shaykh (XVI) ii, 500a; iii, 492b – II, 512b; III, 509b
Alain → Alān
ʿAlāʾiyya → Alanya
ʿAlāḳa → Nisba
ʿAlam i, **349a**; iii, 197a – I, **359b**; III, 201b
ʿĀlam i, **349b** – I, **360a**
ʿĀlam (poet/poète) (Hind) (XVIII) iii, 457b – III, 473b
ʿAlam, Queen/la reine (Nadjāhid(e)) (1150) i, 552b; v, 1244a – I, 570a; V, 1235a
ʿAlam al-Dīn, Āl ii, 749b, 751a; iv, 834b – II, 768a, 769b; Iv, 867a, b
ʿAlam al-Dīn Ḳayṣar (Mamlūk) (XIII) i, 780b; iii, 967a – I, 804a; III, 991b
ʿAlam al-Dīn al-Sakhāwī (1245) i, 150a – I, 154b
ʿAlam al-Dīn Sulaymān Maʿn (XVI) vi, 343a, b – VI, 327b, 328a
ʿAlam Khān → ʿAyn al-Mulk Multānī
ʿAlam Khān (Gudjārāt) (1545) vi, 52a – VI, 50b
ʿAlam Khān Fārūḳī (I) → Farūḳid(e)s
ʿAlam Khān Fārūkī (II) → Farūḳid(e)s
ʿĀlam Shāh ʿAlāʾ al-Dīn (Sayyidid(e) (Dihlī) (1478) i, 855b, 856a; ii, 270b; iii, 418a; v, 783b; vi, 62a; ix, 118b, 110a –
I, 879b, 880a; II, 279a; III, 431b; V, 789b; VI, 60a; IX, 122b, 126a
al-Aʿlam al-Shantamarī → al-Shantamarī
ʿAlāma i, **352a**; ii, 302a, 303a, 307b, 331b – I, **362b**; II, 310b, 311a, 316b, 341a
Alamak → Nudjūm
ʿAlambardār (1004) vii, 550a – VII, 550a
Alambic → al-Anbīḳ
ʿĀlamgīr I → Awrangzīb
ʿĀlamgīr II, ʿAzīz al-Dīn (Mughal) (1759) iii, 1158b; vi, 535b; vii, 316a, 869b – III, 1187a; VI, 520a; VII, 318b, 871a
al-ʿAlamī, Āl i, **352a** – I, **363a**
al-ʿAlamī, ʿAbd al-Ḳādir → Ḳaddūr al-ʿAlamī
al-ʿAlamī, Muḥammad b. al-Ṭayyib (1721) i, **352b** – I, **363a**
ʿĀlamiyān, Mīrzā, nazīr (XVII) iv, 1039b, 1044b – IV, 1071b, 1076a
ʿĀlamshāh Begum (XV) viii, 766b – VIII, 792a
Alamūt i, **352b**, 688b, 1359b; ii, 191a, 192a, 194a; iii, 253b, 254a, 501b; iv, 199b, 201b, 202a, 859b; v, 656b; vi, 64b, 494a, 512a, 789b; vii, 657a, 974a; viii, 72a; s, 356b –
I, **363b**, 709a, 1399b; II, 197a, 198a, 200a; III, 261a, 519a; IV, 208b, 210b, 211a, 892b; V, 660b; VI, 62b, 480a, 497a, 779b; VII, 656b, 974b; VIII, 74a; S, 356b
Alān (Alans/Alains) i, **354a**, 837a; ii, 86a; iv, 344a, 345a, b, 349a, b; v, 288a; vi, 420a; viii, 180a; x, 690a –
I, **365a**, 860; II, 87b; IV, 358b, 359b, 360a, 363b, 364b; V, 286b; VI, 405a; VIII, 182b; X, 732a
Äländ (Adharbāydjān) vi, 200b, 201a, 202a – VI, 185a, 186b
Aland (Djāgīr) vi, 63a, 369a – VI, 61a, 353b
Alangu, Tahir (1973) s, **61b** – S, **61b**
Alanya i, **354b**, 476b; iv, 817b – I, **365b**, 490b; IV, 850b
Alarcos → al-Arak
Alas (Atjèh) i, 740a – I, 762a
Alashehir ii, 989b; iii, 211b – II, 1012a; III, 217b
Ālāt → Āla
Alauddin, Sultan (Malacca) (XV) vi, 212b – VI, 196b
Alava → Ālaba wa ʾl-ḳilāʿ
Alavi of/de Mambram, Syed (1843) vi, 463a – VI, 449a
ʿAlawī (ʿAdan) i, **355a** – I, **366a**
ʿAlawī, Bā → Bā ʿAlawī
ʿAlawī, Buzurg (XX) iv, 73a; v, 199b, 200a – IV, 77a; V, 197a, b
al-ʿAlawī, al-Ḥasan b. Djaʿfar (XI) vii, 461a – VII, 461b
al-ʿAlawī, Muḥammad b. ʿUbayd Allāh (X) vii, 769b – VII, 771b
ʿAlawids, Alawites → ʿAlawīs; Nuṣayrīs
ʿAlawīs (ʿAlawiyya) i, 47a, 315b, **355a**, 689a, 1058a, 1149a; ii, 134a, 146a, 308a, 403, 823a; iii, 256b, 536a, 973a; iv, 634a; v, 592a, 656a; vi, 135a, 248b,

743a, 791b, 888b; viii, 147b; x, 698b; s, 48a, 336b, 339a –
I, 48b, 325a, **366a**, 710a, 1090a, 1183a; II, 137b, 150a, 316b, 414b, 842b; III, 263b, 554b, 997b; IV, 660a; V, 595b, 660a; VI, 133a, 232b, 732a, 781b, 880a; VIII, 149b; X, 742a; S, 48b, 336a, 338b
ʿAlawiyya (Mamlūks) iii, 992a – III, 1017a
Alay i, **358a** – I, **369a**
Alāy (river/fleuve) vi, 618b – VI, 603b
al-Alāya (ʿUmān) vi, 961b – VI, 954a
ʿAlāyā → Alanya
al-ʿAlāyilī, ʿAbd Allāh (XX) iv, 783a – IV, 814b
Alay-beyi-zāde → Muḥammad Emīn b. Hadjdjī Meḥmed
Albacete → al-Basīṭ
Albania(e) → Arnawutluḳ; Awlonya
Albarracin → Shanta Mariyyat al-Sharḳ
Albatenius, Albategni → al-Battānī
Albistān → Elbistān
Alboacen/Albohazen → (Abu 'l-Ḥasan) Ibn Abī 'l-Ridjāl al-Ḳayrawānī
Albohali → al-Khayyāṭ, Abū ʿAlī
Albū Muḥammad → Bū Muḥammad, Āl
Albubather → Ibn al-Khaṣīb, Abū Bakr
Albucasis → al-Zahrāwī
Albufera (lake/lac) → Balansiya
Album → Muraḳḳaʿ
Albumasar → Abū Maʿshar al-Balkhī
Albuquerque, Alfonso de i, 181b, 553b, 1038b; iii, 585a; vi, 51a, 459a; s, 234b – I, 186b, 571a, 1070a; III, 605a; VI, 49b, 444b; S, 234a
Alburz i, **358b**; iv, 1a, 4b-5a, 6b, 9b, 400b; v, 657b; vi, 337b, 492b, 494b; s, 309a –
I, **369a**; IV, 1a, 5a-b, 7a, 10b, 418a; V, 663a; VI, 321b, 478b, 480a; S, 308b
Alcabitius → al-Ḳabīṣī, ʿAbd al-ʿAzīz Abu 'l-Ṣaḳr
Alcacer do Sal → Ḳaṣr Abī Dānis
Alcala → al-Ḳalʿa
Alcantara → al-Ḳanṭara
Alcaraz s, 143a – S, 143a
Alcazar i, **358b** – I, **369b**
Alcazarquivir → al-Ḳaṣr al-Kabīr
Alcira → Djazīrat Shuḳr
Alcolea → al-Ḳulayʿa
Alcoran → al-Ḳur'ān
Aldamov → ʿAlibek Aldamov
Aldebaran → Nudjūm
Aledo → Alīṭ
Alekper ʿAlī Akbar Ṣābir
Alembic → al-Anbīḳ
ʿAlemdār Muṣṭafā Pasha (XIX) v, 1083a, 1084a – V, 1080b, 1081b
ʿAlem-i Nebewī → Sandjaḳ-i Sherīf
Alep(po) → Ḥalab
Alessio → Lesh
Alexander of Aphrodisias/Alexandre d'Aphrodise → al-Iskandar al-Afrūdīsī
Alexander the Great/Alexandre le Grand → al-Iskandar
Alexander of Damascus/Alexandre de Damas → al-Iskandar al-Dimashḳī
Alexander romance → Iskandar-nāma
Alexandretta/-e → Hatay; Iskandarūn
Alexandria/-e → al-Iskandariyya
Alexandropolis → Dede Aghač
Alf layla wa-layla i, 144b, **358b**, 359a, 574b, 595b, 1127a; ii, 356b, 547b; iii, 81a, 281b, 371a, 1050a; v, 951a –
I, 148b, **369b**, 370a, 593a, 615a, 1161a; II, 366a, 561a; III, 83b, 290a, 383a, 1076b; V, 955a
Alfa-graa → Ḥalfā'
Alfarabius → al-Fārābī
Alfard → Nudjūm
Alfraganus → al-Farghānī
Alfonso → Alfūnsho
Alfūnsho i, **364b** – I, **375b**
Alfūnsho (the Warrior/le Batailleur) (XII) i, 390a, 495b, 1150a; ii, 526b, 1007a, 1013a; iii, 543a, 771a; s, 81a, 397b –
I, 401a, 510a, 1184b; II, 539b, 1030b, 1037a; III, 561b, 794b; S, 80b, 398a
Alfūnsho III (IX) i, 85b, 1338b; ii, 1009a, b; iii, 842a; v, 498b, 1107b; s, 92a – I, 88a, 1378b; II, 1032b, 1033a; III, 865b; V, 501b, 1103b; S, 92a
Alfūnsho V (Naples) (XV) iv, 139b, 730a – IV, 145b, 759a
Alfūnsho VI (XI) i, 6b, 7a, 43b, 242b, 390a, 495a; ii, 243b, 1013a; iii, 706a; v, 392b, 498b, 1107b – I, 6b, 7a, 45a, 250a, 401a, 510a; II, 250b, 1036b; III, 728a; V, 393a, 501b, 1103b
Alfūnsho VII (XII) i, 1083a, 1150a; ii, 1009b, 1013b; iii, 771b; v, 498b – I, 1115b, 1184b; II, 1033a, 1037b; III, 794b; V, 501b
Alfūnsho VIII (XII) i, 161b, 165b, 495b, 605b, 1150a; iii, 1055a; iv, 482b; v, 392b –
I, 166a, 170b, 510b, 625a, 1184b; III, 1081a; IV, 503b; V, 393a
Alfūnsho XI (XIV) ii, 525a – II, 538b
Algarve → Gharb al-Andalus
Algazel → al-Ghazālī
Algeciras → al-Djazīra al-Khaḍrā'
Algedi → Nudjūm
Alger → al-Djazā'ir
Algeria i, **364b**, 661a, 1321a; ii, 172b; iii, 297b, 385a; iv, 1155b; v, 696a; vi, 248a, 250b, 789b, 947a, 1043a; viii, 901b; x. 155a; s, 215b
—demography s 215b
—geography i, 364b-366b
—history i, 37a, 85a, 356a, 366b-370b; iii, 524b, 561b, 562b, 564a, 727b, 1003b; iv, 362b; vi, 841a
—institutions i, 373a, 374a, 413a, 978a; ii, 425b; iii, 524b, 727b, 1003b; v, 916a
—languages, literature i, 374a-379b; ii, 469a; iii, 727b
—population i, 171a, 370b-373a, 1177a, b; v, 1164b
Algérie I, **375b**, 682a, 1361b; II, 178a; III, 307a, 397b; IV, 1187b; V, 701a; VI, 232a, 235a, 788b, 939a, 1036b; VIII, 932b; X, 166b; S, 215a
—démographie S, 215a
—géographie I, 375b-377b
—histoire I, 37b, 87a, 367a, 377b-384a; III, 542b, 581a, 582a, 583b, 750a, 1028b; IV, 378b; VI, 831b
—institutions I, 384a, 384b, 423b, 1008b; II, 436a; III, 542b, 750a, 1028b; V, 921b
—langues, littérature I, 384b-390b; II, 481a; III, 750a
—population I, 176a, 1212a, b; V, 1154a
Algeziras → al-Djazīra al-Khaḍrā'
Algiers → al-Djazā'ir
Algol → Nudjūm
Algomaiza → Nudjūm
Algorithmus i, **379b**; iv, 1070b – I, **390b**; IV, 1102a
Alhabor → Nudjūm
Alhagiag bin Thalmus → Ibn Ṭumlūs
Alhaiot → Nudjūm
Alhama → al-Ḥamma
Alhambra → Gharnāṭa
Alhān (Yemen) vi, 436a – VI, 421a
Alhazen → Ibn al-Haytham
Alhichante i, 405a – I, 416b
Alhidade → Asṭurlāb
Alhucemas → al-Ḥusayma; al-Khuzāmā
Āl-i Burhān x, 211b – X, 228b
al-ʿAlī (province) vi, 574b – VI, 559b

ʿAlī I b. Ibrāhīm (ʿĀdil Shāh) (1580) viii, 74a – VIII, 74b
ʿAlī II b. Muḥammad (ʿĀdil Shāh) (1672) viii, 154b – VIII, 157a
ʿAlī I b. Muḥammad (Idrīsid(e)) (849) iii, 1035b; s, 103a – III, 1061b; S, 102b
ʿAlī II b. ʿUmar (Idrīsid(e)) (IX) iii, 1035b, 1036a; s, 103a – III, 1061b; S, 102b
ʿĀlī II b. Yūsuf Pasha (XIX) x, 214b – X, 231b
Alī, Mai (Bornū) (1684) i, 1259b – I, 1298a
ʿAlī, Muṣṭafā b. Aḥmad Čelebī (1600) i, **380a**; ii, 895a; iii, 1200b; iv, 704a; vi, 351b, 412b; vii, 721a; viii, 3b; ix, 410a; s, 83a – I, **391a**; II, 916a; III, 1230b; IV, 732b; VI, 336a, 397b; VII, 722a; VIII, 3a; IX, 463b; S, 83a
ʿAlī, Shaykh (Ḳāḍī al-Ḳuḍāt) vi, 15b – VI, 14a
ʿAlī b. al-ʿAbbās al-Madjūsī (982) i, **381a**; ii, 60a, 481b; iv, 330a; s, 52b, 271b – I, **391b**; II, 61a, 494a; IV, 344a; S, 53a, 271b
ʿAlī b. ʿAbd Allāh, Sharīf (1908) iii, 605b; vi, 151b, 154a – III, 626a; VI, 150a, 152a
ʿAlī b. ʿAbd Allāh b. al-ʿAbbās (735) i, **381a**; iii, 574a – I, **392a**; III, 594a
ʿAlī b. ʿAbd Allāh (dāʿī) (XV) s, 407a – S, 407a
ʿAlī b. ʿAbd Allāh al-Ṭūsī (IX) i, 718b; s, 394b – I, 740a; S, 395a
ʿAlī b. ʿAbd al-ʿAzīz umm al-Walad-zāde (1514) iv, 471b – IV, 492b
ʿAlī b. ʿAbd al-Muʾmin (XII) i, 160b – I, 165a
ʿAlī b. ʿAbd al-Raḥmān (astronome/-r (XI) iii, 81a – III, 83a
ʿAlī b. ʿAbd al-Raḥmān b. Hudhayl al-Andalusī i, 1149b – I, 1184a
ʿAlī b. ʿAbd al-Raḥmān al-Djamal (Idrīsī Sharīf) (XIX) ii, 160a – II, 165a
ʿAlī b. Abī Bakr (Harāt) (1214) i, 593b – I, 613a
ʿAlī b. Abi ʾl-Faradj al-Baṣrī (1261) iii, 111b; vii, 527b – III, 113b; VII, 527b
ʿAlī b. Abi ʾl-Gharāt (Masʿūdid(e)) (1138) i, 1214b – I, 1251a
ʿAlī b. Abī Ḥafs Iṣfahānī (XIII) s, 35a – S, 35a
ʿAlī b. Abi ʾl-Ridjāl vi, 374b – VI, 359a
ʿAlī b. Abī Ṭālib (661) i, 44a, 152b, 181b, 212b, 260b, 337b, **381b**, 400b, 549b, 765a; ii, 218a, 414a, 625b, 725a, 726a, 842b, 846a, 848a, 993a; iii, 33a, 241a, 583b, 887a, 1254b, 1265a; iv, 277b, 836b, 1035a, 1074b, 1140a; v, 406b, 499a, 777a, 996b; vi, 11b, 107b, 139b, 267b, 279b, 337a, 350b, 351b, 374a, 604a, 605b, 621b, 645a, 650b, 652a, 657b, 659b, 664a, 669a, b; vii, 265a, 364a, 393a, 581b, 672b, 903b, 912b; ix, 410a; s, 89b, 92b, 94a, 119a, 130a, 157a, 270a, 351b, 357b, 358b, 401a – I, 45b, 157a, 186b, 218b, 268b, 348a, **392a**, 412a, 567a, 787b; II, 225a, 425a, 641a, 743b, 744b, 862a, 866a, 868a, 1016a; III, 35a, 248a, 603b, 911a, 1287a, 1298a; IV, 289b, 869b, 1067a, 1106a, 1171b; V, 408a, 502a, 783a, 992a; VI, 11a, 105b, 138a, 252a, 264b, 321b, 334b, 335b, 358b, 589a, 590b, 606b, 630b, 636a, 637a, b, 643a, 645b, 650a, 655b, 656a; VII, 266b, 366b, 394a, 582a, 672a, 904a, 913a; IX, 433b; S, 89b, 92b, 118b, 129a, 157a, 269b, 351b, 357b, 358b, 401b
—antagonist(e)s i, 52a, 54a, 108a, 308a, 1343b; iii, 235a, 583a, 887a – I, 53b, 56a, 111b, 317b, 1384a; III, 242a, 603b, 911a
—doctrines i, 263a, 275b; ii, 889a, 961a, 1098b; iii, 1163b – I, 271a, 284b; II, 909b, 983b, 1124b; III, 1192a
—supporters/partisans i, 51a, 107a, 109a, 117a, 195a, 431b, 704a; ii, 480b; iii, 123b, 235a, 583a – I, 52b, 110a, 111b, 120a, 200b, 443b, 725b; II, 492b; III, 126a, 242a, 603b
ʿAlī b. Abī Zayd (1122) ii, 490a – II, 502b
ʿAlī b. Aḍḥā al-Hamdānī (XII) ii, 1013b; iii, 850a, b – II, 1037a; III, 874a
ʿAlī b. Afrāsiyāb → ʿAlī Pasha Afrāsiyāb
ʿAlī b. Aḥmad b. Abī Saʿīd (Tīmūrid(e)) (1546) i, 1019a – I, 1050b
ʿAlī b. Aḥmad al-Ḍayf (XI) ii, 484a; vii, 544a – II, 496a; VII, 544a
ʿAlī b. Aḥmad al-Ḥabbāl ii, 137a – II, 140b
ʿAlī b. Aḥmad al-ʿAḳīḳ (911) ix, 819a – IX, 854a
ʿAlī b. Amādjūr (IX) vii, 28b – VII, 29a
ʿAlī b. ʿAsākir → Ibn ʿAsākir
ʿAlī b. Aybak al-Turkumānī (1257) vi, 321b, 327a – VI, 306a, 311b
ʿAlī b. Bakkār (823) viii, 498a – VIII, 515a
ʿAlī b. Burhān Niẓām Shāh (XVI) iii, 1161a – III, 1189b
ʿAlī b. Buwayh → ʿImād al-Dawla ʿAlī b. Būya
ʿAlī b. Dāʾūd (VIII) i, 103b – I, 106b
ʿAlī b. Dāwūd, Kurd(e) (892) vi, 900a – VI, 891b
ʿAlī b. Djabala → al-ʿAkawwak
ʿAlī b. Djaʿfar b. Falāḥ (XI) viii, 922b – VIII, 954a
ʿAlī b. al-Djahm (863) i, 153b, 154a, **386a**; iv, 491a; vi, 539a, 625b; viii, 376b – I, 157b, 158b, **397b**; IV, 512a; VI, 523b, 610b; VIII, 389a
ʿĀlī b. Djānbulāṭ (XVIII) x, 215b – X, 233a
ʿĀlī b. Djinnī (1065) x, 461b – X, 494b
ʿĀlī b. Djūdayʿ al-Kirmānī, Azdī x, 845a – X,
ʿĀlī b. Dubays (Mazyadid(e)) (XII) vii, 406b – VII, 408a
ʿAlī b. Dūstī (XIII) i, 347b – I, 358a
ʿAlī Ben ʿAyād (XX) vi, 751a, b – VI, 740a, b
ʿAlī b. al-Faḍl al-Djayshānī (881) i, 551b; iv, 198a, b, 661a; vi, 438b, 439a; s, 335a – I, 569a; IV, 206b, 207a, 687b; VI, 424a, b; S, 334b
ʿAlī b. Fakhr al-Dīn b. Ḳurḳumāz Maʿn (1633) vi, 343b – VI, 327b
ʿAlī b. Farāmurz (Kākūyid(e)) (1095) iv, 466a, b; vii, 489a – IV, 487a, b; VII, 489a
ʿAlī b. al-Furāt → Ibn al-Furāt, Abu ʾl-Ḥasan ʿAlī
ʿAlī b. Ghadhāhum (Ḳābis) (XIX) iv, 338b, 403b – IV, 352b, 421a
ʿAlī b. Ghāniya (1187) i, 165a, 1150a; ii, 463b, 1007a; iv, 337b, 614a, b – I, 170a, 1184b; II, 475a, 1030b; IV, 352a, 639a
ʿAlī b. al-Ḥaddād (XII) iv, 381a – IV, 397b
ʿAlī b. Ḥamdūn (927) iv, 459a; vi, 727b – IV, 479b; VI, 716b
ʿAlī b. Ḥamdush, Sīdī s, 53a – S, 53b
ʿAlī b. Ḥammūd (Ḥammūdid(e)) (1016) iii, 147a, 743a, 786a; vi, 222a, 852b; vii, 563b – III, 150a, 766a, 809b; VI, 216a, 844a; VII, 564a
ʿAlī b. Ḥamūd (Bū Saʿīd) (1918) i, 1283a – I, 1321b
ʿAlī b. Ḥamza al-Iṣfahānī (X) i, 154b; iii, 156b – I, 158b; III, 160a
ʿAlī b. Ḥanẓala b. Abī Sālim (1229) s, **61b** – S, **62a**
ʿAlī b. al-Ḥasan (Kilwa) (XII) v, 106b; vii, 250a – V, 108b; VII, 251b
ʿAlī b. al-Ḥasan al-Hāshimī (870) vi, 106a – VI, 104a
ʿAlī b. Ḥasan Bughra Khān → ʿAlī Tegīn
ʿAlī b. al-Ḥasan al-Mubārak → Abu ʾl-Ḥasan al-Aḥmar
ʿAlī b. Ḥātim → al-Ḥāmidī, ʿAlī b. Ḥātim
ʿAlī b. Ḥaydar (Ṣafawid(e)) (1494) iii, 316a; iv, 34b; viii, 237b, 766b – III, 325b; IV, 36b; VIII, 242b, 792a
ʿAlī b. Ḥazm → Ibn Ḥazm, Abū Muḥammad ʿAlī
ʿAlī b. Ḥirzihim → Ibn Ḥirzihim, ʿAlī
ʿAlī b. Hishām (829) i, 400a; vi, 337b, 338a; s, 116b, 252b – I, 411b; VI, 322a, b; S, 116a, 252b
ʿAlī b. Hudhayfa b. Māniʿ (XIII) iv, 87b – IV, 92a

ʿAlī b. Ḥudjr (858) vii, 691b – VII, 691b
ʿAlī b. Ḥumayd b. ʿAbd Allāh (Tanga) (XX) vi, 963b – VI, 955b
ʿAlī b. Ḥusām al-Dīn → al-Muttaḳī
ʿAlī b. Ḥusayn → Sīdī ʿAlī Reʾīs
ʿAlī b. al-Ḥusayn (Kilwa) v, 106b, 1157b – V, 108b, 1147b
ʿAlī b. al-Ḥusayn, Bey (1769) vi, 113a – VI, 110b
ʿAlī b. al-Ḥusayn b. Djaʿfar b. Ibrāhīm al-Walīd (1159) vii, 411a – VII, 412a
ʿAlī b. al-Ḥusayn b. al-Muslima → Ibn al-Muslima
ʿAlī b. Ḥusayn Zayn al-ʿĀbidīn → Zayn al-ʿĀbidīn
ʿAlī b. al-Ḥusayn b. ʿAbd al-ʿAlī al-Karakī → al-Muḥaḳḳiḳ al-T̲h̲ānī
ʿAlī b. al-Ḥusayn b. ʿAlī (Hāshimid(e)) (XX) ii, 572b; iii, 263b, 606b, 1067a – II, 587a; III, 271b, 627a, 1093b
ʿAlī b. al-Ḥusayn b. ʿAlī b. Abī Ṭālib (VII) iii, 227b, 610a, b – III, 234a, 630b, 631b
ʿAlī b. Ḥusayn b. Ḥusayn b. ʿAlī al-Ḳuras̲h̲ī (1284) s, **62a** – S, **62b**
ʿAlī b. Ḥusayn b. Idrīs (dāʿī muṭlaḳ) (XVI) s, 358b – S, 358b
ʿAlī b. al-Ik̲h̲s̲h̲īd (X) iv, 418a – IV, 436b
ʿAlī b. ʿĪsā b. Dāʾūd b. al-Djarrāḥ (vizier) (946) i, **386b**, 1046b, 1223b; ii, 79b, 195a, 197b, 325a, b, 383a, 388b, 453a, 1080b; iii, 100b, 133a, 153a, 619b, 692a, 739a, 886b, 949a; v, 319b, 953a; vi, 498a; vii, 542b, 1031a; s, 199a, 400b, 402a – I, **397b**, 1078a, 1259b; II, 81a, 201b, 204a, 334b, 335a, 393a, 399a, 464b, 1105b; III, 103a, 136a, 156b, 640b, 714a, 761b, 910b, 974a; V, 319a, 957a; VI, 483b; VII, 542a, 1033b; S, 199a, 401a, 402b
ʿAlī b. ʿĪsā b. Māhān → Ibn Māhān
ʿAlī b. ʿĪsā b. Maymūn (Ḳādis) iv, 383b – IV, 400b
ʿAlī b. ʿĪsā al-Ḥarrānī (843) vi, 600a – VI, 584b
ʿAlī b. ʿĪsā al-Kaḥḥāl (XI) i, **388a**, 449a, 785b – I, **399a**, 461b, 808b
ʿAlī b. Isḥāḳ b. G̲h̲āniya (1186) vi, 457a – VI, 442b
ʿAlī b. al-Ḳāḍī al-Nuʿmān (al-Azhar) (X) i, 816a – I, 839a
ʿAlī b. Kamāl al-Dīn, Sayyid (Marʿas̲h̲ī) (1400) vi, 512b, 513a, 516a – VI, 497b, 498a, 501a
ʿAlī b. Ḳara ʿUt̲h̲mān (Aḳ-Ḳirmān) (XV) i, 311b, 312a – I, 321b
ʿAlī b. Karmāk̲h̲ (XII) vii, 549b – VII, 550a
ʿAlī b. al-Karmānī (VIII) iii, 988b – III, 1013a
ʿAlī b. Ḳawām al-Dīn al-Marʿas̲h̲ī (1405) vi, 512b, 513a – VI, 498a
ʿAlī b. K̲h̲alaf (1063) vi, 423b, 543a; viii, 537b – VI, 408b, 527b; VIII. 555a
ʿAlī b. K̲h̲alīl (XV) iv, 221b – IV, 231a
ʿAlī b. K̲h̲as̲h̲ram (872) i, 1244a – I, 1282a
ʿAlī b. K̲h̲urs̲h̲īd (Daylamī) (X) i, 688a – I, 709a
ʿAlī b. Mahdī → Mahdid(e)s
ʿAlī b. Masʿūd I (G̲h̲aznawid(e)) (1049) ii, 1051b – II, 1076a
ʿAlī b. Maʿṣūm → ʿAlī K̲h̲ān
ʿAlī b. Maymūn (1511) i, **388b**; v, 625a – I, **399b**; V, 629a
ʿAlī b. Mazyad (XI) i, 684a; vii, 497a; s, 119a – I, 704b; VII, 497a; S, 118b
ʿAlī b. Muʿayyid (1384) vi, 13a – VI, 12a
ʿĀlī b. Mubāraks̲h̲āh (XV) x, 53b s̲ 55a
ʿAlī b. Mudjāhid al-ʿĀmirī Iḳbāl al-Dawla (1076) i, 1055a; ii, 112a; iii, 542b, 773a; vi, 926b; vii, 292b, 293a; viii, 880b – I, 1086b; II, 114b; III, 561a, 796b; VI, 918b; VII, 294b, 295a: VIII, 910b
ʿAlī b. Mudjat̲h̲t̲h̲il al-Mug̲h̲aydī (XIX) i, 709b – I, 731a
ʿAlī b. Muḥammad → Ṣulayḥid(e)s
ʿAlī b. Muḥammad b. ʿAbd Allāh b. al-Ḥasan (VIII) vii, 389a – VII, 390b
ʿAlī b. Muḥammad b. Barrī (1339) vii, 622a – VII, 621b
ʿAlī b. Muḥammad b. Djaʿfar al-Ḳaras̲h̲ī (1215) s, **62a** – S, **62a**
ʿAlī b. Muḥammad b. Tawba, ḳāḍī (XI) i, 130b – I, 134a
ʿAlī b. Muḥammad b. al-Walīd (dāʿī muṭlaḳ) (1215) iv, 200b; s, 61b – IV, 209b; S, 62a
ʿAlī b. Muḥammad al-Ḳūs̲h̲djī (1474) i, **393a**; vi, 601b, 980a – I, **404b**; VI, 586b, 972b
ʿAlī b. Muḥammad al-Sāmarrī (IX) vii, 443b – VII, 444b
ʿAlī b. Muḥammad al-Ṣulayḥī (dāʿī) (XI) i, 181b; ii, 517a; iii, 862b; vii, 732a – I, 186b; II, 530a; III, 886b; VII, 732b
ʿAlī b. Muḥammad al-Tūnisī al-Iyādī (976) s, **62b** – S, **63a**
ʿAlī b. Muḥammad al-Zandjī (883) i, **388b**, 551a, 942a, 1096a; vii, 526a; s, 49a – I, **400a**, 569a, 971a, 1129a; VII, 526b; S, 49b
ʿAlī b. Muḳarrab (ʿUyūnid(e)) i, 74a – I, 76a
ʿAlī b. Mūsā iii, 1114a – III, 1141a
ʿAlī b. Mūsā al-Kāẓim (al-Riḍā) (816) vi, 334b, 335a – VI, 319a, b
ʿAlī b. Mūsā al-Riḍā → ʿAlī al-Riḍā
ʿAlī b. Nāṣir Abu ʾl-Ḥārit̲h̲ī (XIX) s, 355b – S, 355b
ʿAlī b. Rabah b. Djanbulāt (1712) ii, 443b – II, 455b
ʿAlī b. Rabban al-Ṭabarī → al-Ṭabarī
ʿAlī b. Ras̲h̲īd b. Muḥammad (Mandīl) (1311) vi, 404b – VI, 389a
ʿAlī b. Rayṭa (760) vi, 745a – VI, 734a
ʿAlī b. Ridwān viii, 103a – VIII, 105b
ʿAlī b. Ṣalāḥ al-Dīn (Imām al-Djihād, Yemen) (1436) vii, 996a – VII, 997b
ʿAlī b. Ṣāliḥ iv, 505a – IV, 527a
ʿAlī b. Salmān al-Dāʿī iv, 78a – IV, 82a
ʿAlī b. Sayyid Muḥammad b. ʿAlī (XX) i, 277b – I, 286a
ʿAlī b. al-S̲h̲āh al-Fārisī → Bahnūd b. Saḥwān
ʿAlī b. S̲h̲ams al-Dīn (XVI) i, 60a, **389a** – I, 62a, **400b**
ʿAlī b. Sulaymān al-ʿAnṭakī (X) s, 38a – S, 38a
ʿAlī b. Sulaymān al-Damnātī (XX) ii, 109b – II, 112a
ʿAlī b. Ṭāhir (ʿAdan) (1497) vi, 132b – VI, 130b
ʿAlī b. al-Ṭāhir (Djelfa) vi, 254b – VI, 239a
ʿAlī b. Ṭaybug̲h̲ā al-Biklimis̲h̲ī (XIV) vi, 543a – VI, 527b
ʿAlī b. ʿUbayd Allāh b. Abī Rāfiʿ iii, 1151a – III, 1179a
ʿAlī b. ʿUbayd Allāh b. al-Ḥasan (IX) iii, 951a – III, 975b
ʿAlī b. ʿUmar (ḥādjib) (XII) iii, 47a – III, 49a
ʿAlī b. ʿUmrān (Ispahbad) (XI) iv, 100b – IV, 104b
ʿAlī b. Wafā iv, 283b – IV, 295b
ʿAlī b. Wahsūdān (919) ii, 191b, 192a; iv, 100a; viii, 472a; s, 356b – II, 197b, 198a; IV, 104b; VIII, 487b S, 356b
ʿAlī b. Waṣīf (dāʿī) (X) iv, 662b – IV, 689a
ʿAlī b. Yaddar (al-Sūs al-Aḳṣā) ix, 788b – IX, 935b
ʿAlī b. Yaḥyā b. Tamīm, amīr (XII) i, 149a; ii, 459a – I, 153b; II, 471a
ʿAlī b. Yaḥyā al-Armanī ix, 678a – IX, 706b
ʿAlī b. Yaḥyā al-Munadjdjim (X) ii, 127a; iv, 111a, 1005a; v, 1125a; vi, 625b; s, 17b, 25a – II, 130a; IV, 116a, 1037b; V, 1121b; VI, 610b; S, 18a, 25a
ʿAlī b. Yaḥyā al-Ṣūfī (XV) iv, 1125b – IV, 1157a
ʿAlī b. Yak̲h̲laf al-Nafūsī (ʿIbāḍī) (XII) iii, 657a – III, 678b
ʿAlī b. Yaḳṭīn (798) vii, 646a – VII, 646a
ʿAlī b. Yedder (Idder) (1254) vi, 141b – VI, 139b
ʿAlī b. Yūsuf b. Tās̲h̲ufīn (Almoravide)) (1143) i, 78b,

389a, 495b, 499b, 1347a; ii, 818b, 821b, 838a, 1007a, 1013a; iii, 542b, 712b, 771a, 959a, 977b; iv, 633a; vi, 590b, 591b, 592a, 596b; vii, 247b, 584a, 585b; viii, 690a; s, 397b –
I, 81a, **400b**, 510a, 514b, 1387b; II, 838a, 841a, 857b, 1030b, 1036b; III, 561b, 735a, 794b, 983b, 1002b; IV, 659a; VI, 575b, 576a, b, 577a, 581a; VII, 249a, 584b, 586a; VIII, 719a; S, 398a
ʿAlī b. Yūsuf al-Tūnisī s, 62b – S, 63a
ʿAlī b. Ẓāfir → Ibn Ẓāfir
ʿAlī b. al-Zandjī (X) v, 352b – V, 353b
ʿAlī b. Ziyād (709) viii, 843b – VIII, 873a
ʿAlī-Ābād vi, 384a – VI, 368b
ʿAlī ʿAbd al-Raḥmān al-Ḥusaynī (X) s, 18a – S, 18b
ʿAlī ʿAbd al-Rāziḳ → ʿAbd al-Rāziḳ
ʿAlī Abū ʿAbbās Sarwānī → ʿAbbās Sarwānī
ʿAlī Abū Ḥassūn (Īligh) (XVII) viii, 440a – VIII, 454b
ʿAlī ʿAdil-Shāh I (1579) i, 199a, 1047a, 1202b, 1203b, 1323b; iii,426a, 1161a; v, 938a –
I, 205a, 1079a, 1238a, 1239a, 1364a; III, 440a, 1189b; V, 942a
ʿAlī ʿAdil-Shāh II (1637) i, 199b; ii, 120b; iii, 119a, 426b; vi, 837a – I, 205a; II, 123b; III, 121b, 440b; VI, 827b
ʿAlī Agha (Modon) (XIX) vii, 217b – VII, 219a
ʿAlī Agha (Pinarhisar) (XIX) iv, 322b – IV, 337a
ʿAlī Agha b. Fatḥ ʿAlī Khān, Shaykh (XIX) v, 296b – V, 288a
ʿAlī al-Akbar → ʿAlī b. al-Ḥusayn b. ʿAlī
ʿAlī Akbar Dihkhudā (1956) iv, 71a – IV, 74b
ʿAlī Akbar Ḳawām al-Mulk (XIX) s, 336a – S, 335b
ʿAlī Akbar Khān Bahmān (XX) vi, 154b – VI, 152a
ʿAlī Akbar Khiṭāʾī (XVI) i, **390b**; ii, 588a – I, **402a**; II, 602b
ʿAlī Akbar Ṣābir (911) i, 194a; iii, 358a – I, 199b; III, 369b
ʿAlī al-Aʿlā, Sayyid (1419) iii, 600b; viii, 8b – III, 621a; VIII, 8b
ʿAlī al-Amīn (XV) s, 399a – S, 399a
ʿAlī Amīrī (1923) i, **391a** – I, **402a**
ʿAlī Āmulī → ʿAlī b. Ḳawām al-Dīn al-Marʿashī
ʿAlī al-ʿArabī Ilyās (XVI) i, 776b – I, 800a
ʿAlī al-Aʿradj (XVIII) i, 47b – I, 48b
ʿAli Ardobus Ibrahim (1959) vi, 768b – VI, 758a
ʿAlī al-Asʿad, Pasha (XIX) s, 162b – S, 162b
ʿAlī al-Armanī, amīr (863) i, 638b; ii, 235a – I, 659a; II, 242a
ʿAlī Aṣghar Khān Amīn al-Sulṭān, Mīrzā (1907) ii, 418a, 435a, 652a; iv, 394a, 979b; vii, 1004b; s, 365a –
II, 429a, 446b, 668b; IV, 411a, 1012a; VII, 1006a; S, 365a
ʿAlī al-Ashrafī al-Akhlāṭī, Ḥādjib (1226) vi, 505a – VI, 490a
ʿAli Askar Askar-Oghlī (XX) vi, 769a – VI, 758a
ʿAlī al-Aswārī (1193) vi, 636b – VI, 621b
ʿAlī ʿAzīz Efendi Giridli (1798) i, **391a**; iii, 375a – I, **402a**; III, 386b
ʿAlī al-Baghdādī (XVIII) vi, 249b – VI, 233b
ʿAlī Bār, Ḥādjib (1119) vi, 64a – VI, 62a
ʿAlī Barīd Shāh (1579) i, 1047a, 1200a, b; iii, 426a; v, 1215b – I, 1079a, 1235b, 1236a; III, 439b; V, 1205b
ʿAlī Beg (Aḳ-Ḳoyunlu) (1439) vi, 541a – VI, 525b
ʿAlī Beg (Turkman/Turkmène) (XIII) i, 243b; ii, 204b – I, 251a; II, 211a
ʿAlī Beg, Ḥādjdjī → Idrīs (the hidden/le caché)
ʿAlī Beg b. ʿAlāʾ al-Dīn (Ḳarāmānid(e)) (XIV) iv, 623a, b – IV, 648a, b
ʿAlī Beg b. Shahsuwār (Dhu ʾl-Ḳadrlī) (1515) ii, 240a; vi, 508a, 510a – II, 247a; VI, 493b, 495b
ʿAlī Beg Hersek-zāde (XVI) iii, 342a – III, 352a
ʿAlī Beg Ḳarāmān-oghlu (XIII) iv, 620a – IV, 644b
ʿAlī Ber → Sonni ʿAlī
ʿAlī Bey (Bulūṭ Ḳāpān) (1773) i, **391b**, 728b; ii, 233b; iii, 158a, 300a; iv, 723a, 852b, 853a; vi, 325b; vii, 420b, 709b; s, 20b, 268a –
I, **402b**, 750b; II, 240b; III, 161b, 309a; IV, 752a, 885b, 886a; VI, 310a; VII, 422b, 710a; S, 20b, 267b
ʿAlī Bey (Ḥusaynid(e)) (1756) iii, 605a, 635b – III, 625b, 657a
ʿAlī Bey (Ḥusaynid(e)) (1782) iii, 636a – III, 657a
ʿAlī Bey (Ḥusaynid(e)) (1902) iii, 636b – III, 658a
ʿAlī Bey (Miṣr) (1773) vii, 179a – VII, 181a
ʿAlī Bey (Trabzon) (1878) vi, 373a, 759a – VI, 357b, 748a
ʿAlī Bey, Amīr (Mombasa) (1589) v, 105a; vi, 128b, 129a; vii, 226a – V, 107a; VI, 127a; VII, 228a
ʿAlī Bey al-ʿAbbāsī (1818) i, **392a** – I, **403b**
ʿAlī Bey Eretnaoghlu → Eretna
ʿAlī Bey Evrenos-zāde (XV) ii, 703a, 721a – II, 721a, 739b
ʿAlī Bey Mikhāl-oghlu (XVII) i, 340b – I, 351a
ʿAlī Birādarān (XX) vii, 421b – VII, 423a
ʿAlī al-Bisṭāmī (1462) vi, 71a – VI, 69a
ʿAlī Burghul (Bulghūr) (XVIII) ii, 460a; iv, 617b – II, 471b; IV, 642b
ʿAlī Čelebī → ʿAlī, Muṣṭafā b. Aḥmad Čelebī; Ḳinalizāde ʿalā ʾl-Dīn ʿAlī
ʿAlī Dāya (1033) vi, 522b, 523a – VI, 507a, b
ʿAlī Dede, Pīr (1528) vi, 226b, 228a – VI, 220b, 222a
ʿAlī Dede al-Bosnawī (1598) i, 759a – I, 782a
ʿAlī Diara (XIX) iii, 39a – III, 41a
ʿAlī Dīnār (1916) ii, 124a, 125a – II, 127a, 128a
ʿAlī Djāh, Niẓām (Ḥaydarābād) (1803) iii, 322a – III, 331b
ʿAlī Djamālī → Djamālī
ʿAlī Djānbūlād (1605) vi, 343b – VI, 327b
ʿAlī Djanbulāṭ (1778) ii, 443b – II, 455b
ʿAlī Djānib (XX) vi, 93b, 94a – VI, 91b, 92a
ʿĀlī Efendi → ʿĀlī ʿAzīz
ʿAlī Ekber → ʿAlī Akbar Ṣābir
ʿAlī Emīrī (1924) vi, 542b; s, **63a** – VI, 527a; S, **63a**
ʿAlī Fethi (Okyar) → Okyar
ʿAlī Fuʿād Cebesoy (XX) ii, 700b – II, 718a
ʿAlī al-Hādī → al-ʿAskarī, Abu ʾl-Ḥasan ʿAlī
ʿAlī Ḥāfiẓ (XX) v, 1005b – V, 1001a
ʿAli Haji ibni Raja Ahmad (1870) vi, 237a – VI, 209b
ʿAlī Ḥakīm-Ilāhī, Āḳā (XIX) s, 24a – S, 24a
ʿAlī al-Hamādanī (1385) i, 347b, **392b**, 1004b; ii, 967a; iv, 708a; v, 301a; vii, 988a; x, 251a; s, 364b –
I, 358a, **403b**, 1035b; II, 989a; IV, 736b; V, 300b; VII, 988b; X, 270a; S, 364b
ʿAlī Ḥarāzim b. alʿArabī Barāda (XVIII) x, 464a – X, 497b
ʿAlī Ḥarfūsh (XVI) ii, 750a – II, 768a
ʿAlī Ḥazīn, Shaykh → Ḥazīn, Muḥammad ʿAlī b. Abī Ṭālib
ʿAlī Hüsaynzāde (XX) vi, 94a – VI, 92a
ʿAlī Ibn Ashkīlūlā (XIII) vii, 1021a – VII, 1023a
ʿAlī-Ilāhī i, 225b, 260a, **392b**; ii, 106b – I, 232a, 268b, **404a**; II, 109a
ʿAlī Ḳapu (Iṣfahān) vi, 17a – VI, 15a
ʿAlī Ḳarabāsh (1685) i, 965b; iv, 991b – I, 995b; IV, 1024a
ʿAlī al-Karakī (1531) x, 936a – X,
ʿAlī al-Ḳārī al- Harawī(1607) i, 1235b; ii, 500b; iii, 29a, 711a; v, 1235a, b; x, 916a – I, 1272b; II, 513a; III, 30a, 733b; V, 1225b, 1226a; X,
ʿAlī Ḳarīb b. Il-Arslan, ḥādjib (XI) iii, 47a; vii, 407a – III, 48b; VII, 408a
ʿAlī al-Kassār ii, 39b – II, 40b
ʿAlī Kathīr, Banū ix, 898b – IX, 935a

ʿAlī Kemāl Bey (XX) ii, 474b; iii, 595a; iv, 636a; vi, 94b – II, 486b; III, 615b; IV, 662a; VI, 92b
ʿAlī Khʷādja (Djand) (XIII) s, 246a – S, 246a
ʿAlī Khān → Mahdī ʿAlī Khān; Sayyid ʿAlī Khān
ʿAlī Khān (Ghuzz) (XI) vi, 416a – VI, 401a
ʿAlī Khān, Ḥādjdjī Mīrzā (1936) vi, 86b – VI, 84b
ʿAlī Khān, Nawwāb (1858) vi, 77b – VI, 75b
ʿAlī Khān, Shaykh (1666) vi, 526a – VI, 510b
ʿAlī Khān b. Agha Khān (XX) i, 246b – I, 254a
ʿAlī Khān b. Dawlat Khān (Pandjāb) (XVI) ii, 47b – II, 48b
ʿAlī Khān b. Ḥusayn Khān Bayat (1865) vi, 203a – VI, 187a
ʿAlī Khān Amīn al-Dawla, Mīrzā (1848) vi, 291b – VI, 277a
ʿAlī Khān Amīn al-Dawla, Mīrzā (1904) vii, 1004b – VII, 1006a
ʿAlī Khān al-Madanī (1705) i, **392b** – I, **404a**
ʿAlī Khān al-Marāghī, Ḥādjdjī (XIX) vii, 440a – VII, 441a
ʿAlī Khān Nuṣrat al-Mulk Ḳara Güzlü (1797) vi, 484a – VI, 470a
ʿAlī Khān Türe (1947) ix, 650a – IX, 674b
ʿAlī Khān Ẓahīr al-Dawla → Ẓahīr al-Dawla
ʿAlī Khān Zangana, Shaykh (XVII) v, 169b – V, 167a
ʿAlī al-Khaznī (1909) vi, 750a – VI, 739b
ʿAlī Khūrshīd, Fāshōda (XIX) ii, 828a – II, 847b
ʿAlī Khʷishāwand → ʿAlī Ḳarīb
ʿAlī Kiyā b. Iskandar-i Shaykhī (Marʿashī) (1402) i, 237b; v, 603a; vi, 512b – I, 244b; V, 607a; VI, 497b
ʿAlī Kiyā b. Sayyid Muḥammad (Marʿashī) (1476) vi, 514a, b, 515b – VI, 499b, 500b
ʿAlī Kolen Sonnī (Gao) (XIV) ii, 977a – II, 999b
ʿAlī Kücük, Zayn al-Dīn b. Begtegin (XII) i, 1160b; ii, 347b; iv, 76a – I, 1195a; II, 357b; IV, 80a
ʿAlī Ḳulī Khān (Bareilly) (XVII) i, 1042b – I, 1074a
ʿAlī Ḳulī Khān Afshār → ʿĀdil Shāh Afshār
ʿAlī Ḳulī Khān Istadjlū (Shīr Afkan) (1607) ii, 380b; s, 366b – II, 390b; S, 366a
ʿAlī Ḳulī Khān Khān-i Zamān (XVI) ii, 498b; s, 325a – II, 511a; S, 325a
ʿAlī Ḳulī Khān Shāmlū (XVI) i, 7b – I, 7b
ʿAlī Ḳulī Khān Wālih (XVIII) vii, 530b – VII, 530b
ʿAlī Ḳulī Ṣafarov → Ṣafarov, ʿAlī Ḳulī
ʿAlī Kūra (XVIII) vi, 249b – VI, 233b
ʿAlī Kurdī Ḳazwīnī, Mawlānā s, 51b – S, 52a
ʿAlī al-Ḳūshdjī (1474) i, **393a**, 776b; ii, 588a; viii, 541b, 542a – I, **404b**, 799b; II, 602b; VIII, 559b, 560a
ʿAlī Mahdī Muḥammad (Somalia/-e) ix, 721a – IX, 752b
ʿAlī Māhir (XX) s, 6b, 300a, 301b – S, 5b, 299b, 301a
ʿAlī Mardān i, **393b** – I, **404b**
ʿAlī Mardān Khaldjī (1213) i, **393b**; vi, 244b; vii, 433a – I, **404b**; VI, 228b; VII, 434a
ʿAlī Mardān Khān (Ḳandahār) (1657) i, 228b, 1347b; iv, 666a; v, 886a; vii, 318a, b, 333a, 632a; s, **63a** – I, 235b, 1388a; IV, 693a; V, 892a; VII, 320b, 321a, 334b, 631b; S, **63b**
ʿAlī Mardān Khān Bakhtiyarī (XVIII) i, **393b**; ii, 311a; iii, 1103a; iv, 104b, 639b; v, 825b – I, **405a**; II, 320a; III, 1130a; IV, 109a, 666a; V, 831b
ʿAlī Mardān Khān Faylī (XVIII) v, 825a – V, 831a
ʿAlī Mardān Khān Shāmlū (XVIII) i, 393b – I, 405a
ʿAlī Mīkālī (1032) vi, 522b – VI, 507a
ʿAlī Mīrzā Ẓill al-Sulṭān (Ḳādjār) (XIX) vii, 453b – VII, 454b
ʿAlī Mubārak Pasha vi, 412a – VI, 397a
ʿAlī al-Mudjāhid (Rasūlid(e)) i, 181b – I, 186b
ʿAlī al-Mudjāshiʿī al-Farazdaḳī (1086) vi, 913a – VI, 904b
ʿAlī Muftī (XX) vi, 165b – VI, 157b
ʿAlī Mughāyat Shāh (Atjèh) (1530) i, 742b; ii, 1220a – I, 765a; III, 1250b
ʿAlī Muḥammad b. Aḥmad al-Balkhī ii, 918b – II, 940a
ʿAlī Muḥammad Khān (Rohilla) (1749) i, 1042b; iii, 59b, 60a; vii, 316a, 457b; viii, 426a, 572a, b – I, 1074a; III, 62a, b; VII, 318b, 457b; VIII, 440a, 590b, 591a
ʿAlī Muḥammad Mukhliṣ i, 1123b – I, 1157b
ʿAlī Muḥammad Shīrāzī → Bāb, ʿAlī Muḥammad
ʿAlī Murād Khān (Zand) (XVIII) vii, 674b – VII, 674b
ʿAlī Murād Mamīwand Khān (XVIII) v, 825a, b – V, 831b
ʿAlī Murād, Mīr (XIX) iv, 1160a – IV, 1192a
ʿAlī Mushtāḳ, Mīr Sayyid (1757) v, 834b – V, 840b
ʿAlī al-Muttaḳī → al-Muttaḳī al-Hindī
ʿAlī al-Naḳī → al-ʿAskarī, Abu ʾl-Ḥasan ʿAlī
ʿAlī Nawrūz → Ḥasan Muḳaddam
ʿAlī Nūrī, Mollā (1820) viii, 695a – VIII, 715a
ʿAlī Pasha → Djanbulāt-oghlū; Djānīkli; Ferah; Hādjdji; Kemānkesh; Muʾadhdhinzāde
ʿAlī Pasha (Baghdād) (1762) i, 199a, 905a – I, 204b, 932b
ʿAlī Pasha (Ḥusaynid(e)) → ʿAlī Bey
ʿAlī Pasha b. Afrāsiyāb (Baṣra) (1652) i, 236b, 1087a; vi, 112a; vii, 673b – I, 244a, 1119b; VI, 110a; VII, 673b
ʿAlī Pasha ʿArabadji (1693) i, 268a, **394a**, 558a – I, 276b, **405a**, 575b
ʿAlī Pasha Čāndārli̊-zāde (1407) i, **394a**, 1303a; ii, 444b, 611a; vii, 594a; viii, 35b – I, **405b**, 1342b; II, 456b, 626a; VII, 593b; VIII, 36a
ʿAlī Pasha Čorlulu (1711) i, 56a, 268b, 269a, **394b**; ii, 1091a; iv, 233b – I, 58a, 276b, 277a, **405b**; II, 1116b; IV, 244a
ʿAlī Pasha Dāmād (1716) i, 268b, 269a, **395a**; iii, 1002a; iv, 969a; vii, 905b – I, 276b, 277b, **406a**; III, 1027a; IV, 1001b; VII, 906a
ʿAlī Pasha Güzeldje (1621) i, **395a**; iv, 572a; viii, 182a – I, **406b**; IV, 594b; VIII, 185a
ʿAlī Pasha Ḥakīm-oghlu (1758) i, 174b, **395b**, 1018a, 1267b; iv, 437b, 544a, 861b; s, 268a – I, 179b, **407a**, 1049b, 1306b; IV, 457b, 567b, 894b; S, 267b
ʿAlī Pasha Ḳaramānli̊ (1793) iv, 617b, 618a – IV, 642a, b
ʿAlī Pasha Khādim (1511) i, **396a**, 1120b, 1207b; iv, 231a, 1093a; v, 269a, b; vi, 72b, 1026a – I, **407a**, 1154a, 1243b; IV, 241a, 1124a; V, 267a; VI, 70a, 1019a
ʿAlī Pasha Moldowandji (XVIII) vii, 709a – VII, 710a
ʿAlī Pasha Mubārak (1893) i, 168a, **396a**, 596b; ii, 131b, 167a, 892a; v, 22b, 909a; vi, 602a, b; s, 369a – I, 173a, **407b**, 616a; II, 135a, 172b, 913a; V, 23b, 914b; VI, 587a; S, 369a
ʿAlī Pasha Muḥammad Amīn (1870) i, 298b, **396b**; ii, 642a, 934b, 996b; iii, 357a, 1187b, 1188a; vi, 758a, 759a – I, 307b, **408a**; II, 658a, 956b, 1019b; III, 368b, 1217b, 1218a; VI, 747a, 748a
ʿAlī Pasha Rizvanbegovič → Riḍwān Begovič
ʿAlī Pasha Semiz (1565) i, 291b, **398a**, 843b – I, 300b, **409b**, 866b
ʿAlī Pasha Silāḥdār (XIX) iii, 628b – III, 649a, b
ʿAlī Pasha Sürmeli (1695) i, 268a, **398a** – I, 276b, **409b**
ʿAlī Pasha Tepedelenli̊ (1822) i, **398b**, 653a, 657a; ii, 708b; iii, 91a, 628a; iv, 588b, 589a, 656b; v, 727b, 773b; vi, 58b; vii, 240b, 719b – I, **409b**, 673b, 677b; II, 727a; III, 93b, 648a; IV, 612a, b, 683a; V, 732b, 779b; VI, 56b; VII, 242a, 720b

Āli Rādjās Kannanūr iv, 547a – IV, 570b
ʿAlī Razmārā (XX) vii, 654b; s, 158a – VII, 654a; S, 158b
ʿAlī Reʾis b. Ḥüseyn ii, 588b, 589a – II, 603a, 604a
ʿAlī al-Riḍā, Abu ʾl-Ḥasan b. Mūsā b. Djaʿfar (Imām) (818) i, **399b**, 402b, 551a, 1250a; ii, 248b, 731b; iii, 1169b; iv, 17a, 45b; v, 59a; vi, 510b, 613b, 713b, 714a, 958b; vii, 396b, 450b, 605a; s, 127b – I, **411a**, 414a, 568b, 1288a; II, 256a, 750a; III, 1198b; IV, 18b, 48a; V, 60b; VI, 496b, 598b, 702b, 951a; VII, 397b, 451b, 604b; S, 126b
ʿAlī Riḍā b. Ḥādjdjī Ibrāhīm Khān (XIX) s, 336a – S, 335b
ʿAlī Riḍā b. Riḍā Khān (1954) vii, 447a – VII, 448a
ʿAlī Riḍā-i ʿAbbāsī (XVII) i, **400b**; iv, 1124a – I, **412a**; IV, 1155b
ʿAlī Riḍā Pasha (1919) ii, 813a; iv, 296b; vi, 984b – II, 832b; IV, 309b; VI, 977a
ʿAlī Riḍā Tabrīzī (XVI) viii, 788a, 789a – VIII, 814b, 815b
ʿAlī Sārī → ʿAlī b. Kamāl al-Dīn
ʿAlī Shāfiḳ Özdemir v, 145a – V, 147b
ʿAlī Shāh → Agha Khān II; ʿAlī ʿAdil-Shāh; ʿAlī Barīd Shāh; Wādjid ʿAlī Shāh;
ʿAlī Shāh (vizier) (XIV) i, 627a; iii, 1122b – I, 648a; III, 1150a, b
ʿAlī Shāh b. Fatḥ-ʿAlī Shāh (Ḳādjār) (XIX) vi, 481b – VI, 467b
ʿĀlī Shāh Čak (1578) s, 131b, 167a – S, 131a, 167a
ʿAlī Shahīd Pīr (Bīdjāpūr) i, 1203b – I, 1239a
ʿAlī Shanẓūrā (Mūrītāniyā) (1727) vii, 614b – VII, 614a
ʿAlī Shanẓūrā b. Haddī, amīr (Mūrītāniyā) (1757) vii, 624b – VII, 624a
ʿAlī Shaʿrāwī (XX) iii, 516a – III, 533b
ʿAlī Sharīʿatī (XX) vii, 762b – VII, 764b
ʿAlī al-Sharīf, Mawlāy vii, 392b; s, 114a – VII, 393b; S, 113b
ʿAlī Sharmarke (Zaylaʿ) (XIX) i, 1172b – I, 1207b
ʿAlī Shēr Ḳāniʿ → Ḳāniʿ
ʿAlī Shīr Beg → Mīr ʿAlī Shīr Hawāʾī
ʿAlī Shīr Khān (Baltistān) (XVI) i, 1004b – I, 1035b
ʿAlī Shīr Khurd Abū Malik Mughīth (XIV) vi, 272a – VI, 256b
ʿAlī Shīr Nawāʾī → Nawāʾī, Mīr ʿAlī Shīr
ʿAlī Shukr Beg (Bayram Khān) i, 1135a – I, 1169b
ʿAlī Suʿāwī (XIX) ii, 473b, 474a; vi, 92b; vii, 599b – II, 486a; VI, 90b; VII, 599b
ʿAlī al-Ṣulayḥī (1081) vii, 861a, 996a – VII, 862b, 997b
ʿAlī al-Ṭawīl (XII) i, 161b – I, 166a
ʿAlī Tegīn (ʿAlītigin) (Ilek-khān) i, 424b, 662a; ii, 4b; iii, 1114a; v, 76a; vi, 66a; s, 176b – I, 436b, 682b; II, 4b; III, 1141b; V, 78b; VI, 63b; S, 177b
ʿAlī Wāsiʿ → ʿAlī b. Ṣāliḥ
ʿAlī Werdī Khān (1756) i, **400b**; ii, 371a – I, **412a**; II, 381a
ʿAlī Yakan (XX) vii, 713b – VII, 714b
ʿAlī Yūsuf, Shaykh (1913) ii, 466b; iii, 516a; viii, 699a; s, 121b – II, 478b; III, 533b; VIII, 719a; S, 121a
ʿAlī al-Zaḳḳāḳ → al-Zaḳḳāḳ
ʿAlī-ābād iv, 1015a – IV, 1047a
ʿAlibek Aldamov ii, 18a – II, 18b
Alicante → Laḳant
Alidada(e) → Asṭurlāb
ʿAlid(e)s i, 45b, 48b, 73b, 103a, b, 125b, 143a, 149a, 290b, **400b**, 550b, 688a, 713a, 1035b, 1352a; ii, 168b, 191a, 192b, 851b; iii, 22a, 242a, 616a, 753a, 984b; iv, 88b; v, 1238b; vi, 627b, 669b, 938b – I, 46b, 50a, 75b, 106a, b, 129a, 147a, 153a, 299b, **412a**, 568a, 709a, 734b, 1067a, 1391a; II, 174a, 197a, 198b, 871b; III, 23a, 249a, 636b, 776a, 1009a; IV, 92b; V, 1229a; VI, 612b, 655b, 656a, 930b
Alif → Hidjāʾ
Aligaṙh i, 288a, **403a**, 1300a; ii, 97a, 132b, 426b; v, 283a; vi, 78a, 368b, 461b, 488b, 489a, 503b; viii, 241a; s, 4b, 106b, 247a – I, 297a, **414b**, 1340a; II, 99a, 136a, 437a; V, 281a; VI, 75b, 352b, 447a, 474b, 475a, 489a; VIII, 247a; S, 4a, 105b, 247b
—movement/mouvement d'- iii, 433a; iv, 793a; vi, 612a; s, 74a, 107b, 247a – III, 447a; IV, 825a; VI, 597a; S, 74b, 107a, 247b
—university/-é ii, 426b – II, 437a
ʿAliḳīn vi, 547b – VI, 532a
ʿAlīkozāy, Banū ii, 629a – II, 645a
Alilat → al-Lāt
ʿĀlim → ʿUlamāʾ
ʿĀlim, Mīr (Bukhārā) i, 1296a; ii, 700b – I, 1335b; II, 718b
ʿĀlima i, **403b**; ii, 1029b, 1048b – I, **415b**; II, 1053a, 1072b
Alimtu i, 419a – I, 430b
ʿAlim Allāh, Shaykh (XIX) s, 247a – S, 247a
ʿĀlim Khān (Khōḳand) (XIX) iv, 631b; v, 29b – IV, 656b; V, 30a, b
ʿAlīnagar ii, 7a – II, 7a
Alindjaḳ i, **404a**; v. 491b – I, **416a**; V, 494a
Aliou Faye, Cheikh (XX) vi, 705b – VI, 694a
Alip-manash → Alpamïsh
ʿAlishāh b. Būka Awbahī (XV) vii, 685a – VII, 685a
Alīsaʿ b. Ukhṭūb (Elisha) i, **404a** – I, **416a**
ʿAlīshān-zāde Ismāʿīl Ḥaḳḳi → Ismāʿīl Ḥaḳḳī Pasha
Alīṭ (Aledo) i, 7a, 43b; iii, 904b; iv, 672b; vii, 767b, 775b – I, 7b, 45a; III, 929a; IV, 700a; VII, 769a, 777b
ʿAlītigin ʿAlī Tegīn
Aliwāl Khān i, 1209b – I, 1245b
ʿAlīwiyya (Mostghanem) ii, 224b – II, 231b
ʿĀliya vi, 28a – VI, 26a
ʿAlīzāy (Mahsūd), Banū ii, 629a; vi, 86a – II, 644b; VI, 84a
Aljamía i, **404b**, 502b; iv, 317a; vii, 243a; s, 81a, 397a – I, **416a**, 517b; IV, 331a; VII, 244b; S, 81a, 397b
Aljamiado → Aljamía
Aljarafe → al-Sharaf
ʿAlḳa → ʿUḳūba
ʿAlḳama (VII) vii, 258b – VII, 260a
ʿAlḳama b. ʿAbada al-Tamīmī (VI) i, **405b**; iii, 1177b; iv, 998b, 1087b – I, **417a**; III, 1206b; IV, 1031a, 1118b
ʿAlḳama b. Dhī Djadan (al-Mathāmina) vi, 830b; viii, 979b, 980a – VI, 821a; VIII, 1019a
ʿAlḳama b. Ṣafwān b. Umayya ix, 440b – IX, 457b
ʿAlḳama b. ʿUlātha (VII) i, 441b, 442a, 690a – I, 454b, 455a, 711a
al-ʿAlḳamī i, **405b** – I, **417b**
Alkanna → al-Ḥinnāʾ
Alḳāṣ Mīrzā (Ṣafawid(e) (1549) i, **406a**; viii, 73a i, **417a**; VIII, 73a
Alkendi → al-Kindī, Abū Yūsuf Yaʿḳūb
All-India Muslim League v, 779b, 780a, 1080b; vii, 678b; viii, 241a; s, 4b – V, 785b, 786a, 1078a; VII, 678b; VIII, 247a; S, 3b
ʿAllāf b. Ḥassān (XI) ii, 484a, b – II, 496b
al-ʿAllāf, Isḥāḳ b. Wahb b. Ziyād (869) viii, 14a – VIII, 14a
Allāh i, 275a, 333a, 349b, **406a**, 773b, 776a; ii, 96a,

220b, 396a, 449a, 493b, 518a, 554a, 593b, 772b, 898b; iii, 28b, 82b, 497a, 870b, 917b, 1093b, 1196a; v, 3b, 411b –
I, 283b, 343b, 360a, **418a**, 796b, 819b; II, 98a, 227a, 406b, 460b, 505b, 513a, 567b, 608a, 791a, 919b; III, 30a, 85a, 514a, 894b, 941b, 1120b, 1226b; V, 4a, 413a
al-Allaḥ b. ʿAbd al-Wahhāb (Rustamid(e)) (872) iii, 655a; x. 100a – III, 676a; X, 108a
Allāh b. Sulaymān (ʿAzdī) (868) vi, 900a – VI, 891a
Allāh Akbar → Takbīr
Allāh Ḳulī Beg (XI) iv, 808a – IV, 840b
Allāh Ḳulī Khān (Gakkhaṙ) (1705) ii, 973b; vii, 574b – II, 996a; VII, 575a
Allāh Ḳulī Khān (Khīwa) (1842) iv, 1065a; vii, 574b; s, 46a, 228a – IV, 1096b; VII, 575a; S, 46b, 228b
Allah Temple of Islam vii, 702b – VII, 703b
Allāh Yār Kattaḳurghān (Ṣūfī) (1723) x, 65a – X, 67b
Allāh Yār Khān Āṣaf al-Dawla (XIX) vii, 454a – VII, 454b
Allāh Yār Thānī → Murtaḍā Ḥusayn
Allāhābād i, **417b**; ii, 426a; v, 1218b; s, 325b – I, **429b**; II, 437a; V, 1208b; S, 325a
Allāhdād, Mawlānā s, 74a – S, 74a
Allāhumma i, **418a** – I, **429b**
Allāhwardī (Allāh Wirdī) Khān (1613) i, 8a; ii, 1091b; iii, 585b; v, 672b, 825a; vii, 547b – I, 8a; II, 1117a; III, 605b; V, 677b, 831a; VII, 548a
ʿAllāḳa (X) ii, 483b; iii, 77a – II, 495b; III, 79b
al-ʿAllāḳī, wādī i, **418a**; ii, 214a; iv, 567b, 965b, 967a; viii, 90b, 863a – I, **430a**; II, 220b; IV, 590a, 969b; VIII, 92b, 894a
ʿAllāl al-Fāsī (1974) vii, 416a; s, **63b** – VII, 417a; S, **64a**
ʿAllaliyyīn s, 350b – S, 350b
ʿAllālū (XX) vi, 752a, 754b – VI, 741b, 744a
ʿAllama Kamāl al-Dīn (Čishtiyya) (XIV) ii, 54a – II, 55a
ʿAllāma-i Ḥillī → al-Ḥillī, Djamāl al-Dīn Ḥasan
ʿAllāmī → Abu ’l-Faḍl ʿAllāmī
ʿAllāmī, Shaykh → Abū ’l-Faḍl ʿAllāmī
Allān → Alān
ʿAllān al-Warrāḳ al-Shuʿūbī (IX) vi, 829a – VI, 819a
Allāt → al-Lāt
ʿAllawayh al-Aʿsar (850) i, 160a; s, 17b, **64a** – I, 164b; S, 17b, **64b**
Allidina Visram (1916) x, 781a – X,
ʿAllūya → ʿAllawayh
ʿAlma → ʿĀlima
Alma Ata i, **418b**; vi, 769b – I, **430a**; VI, 759a
Alma-da → Elma-dagh
Almada, almaden → al-Maʿdin
Almadia → Safīna
Almagest → Baṭlamiyūs
Almaḳah vi, 561a, 562a, b – VI, 545b, 546b, 547a
Almali̊ i, **418b**; iii, 1120b; v, 858b; ix, 621b; s, 240a – I, **430a**; III, 1148a; V, 865b; IX, 645a; S, 240a
Almanac/-h → Anwāʾ; Taʾrīkh
Almani Omar (Fūta Djallon) (1872) ii, 960a – II, 982b
Almanon → al-Maʾmūn b. Hārūn al-Rashīd (ʿAbbāsid(e))
Almanzor → al-Manṣūr bi-’llāh
Almās i, **419a**; v, 353b, 550a, 965a – I, **431a**; V, 354b, 555a, 969b
Almās Beg Ulugh Khān → Ulugh Khān
Almee → ʿĀlima
Almeria → al-Mariyya
Almicantarat → Muḳanṭarāt
Almodovar → al-Mudawwar
Almogávares i, **419b** – I, **431b**
Almohad(e)s → al-Muwaḥḥidūn
Almoravid(e)s → al-Murābiṭūn
Almuñecar → al-Munakkab
Alodia → ʿAlwa
Alōr s, 163a – S, 162b
Alp i, **419b** – I, **431b**
Alp Arghūn, Shams al-Dīn (Atabeg) (1271) iii, 1100a; v, 826b; vi, 494b – III, 1127a; V, 833a; VI, 480a
Alp Arslān, ʿAḍud al-Dawla Abū Shudjāʿ (Saldjūḳ) (1072) i, 329a, **420a**, 465b, 507b, 510a, 660b, 731a, 1041b, 1051b. 1336b; ii, 5a, 340a, 347b, 856a; iii, 86b, 196a, 197a, 471b, 1098b; iv, 27a, 291b, 347b, 348a, 458a, 807b, 840a; v, 388a, 489a; vi, 242b, 243a, 273b, 275a, 379b, 524a; vii, 120b, 693a; viii, 69b, 70a, 941a; s, 14b, 65a, 245b –
I, 339b, **432a**, 479b, 523a, 525b, 681b, 753a, 1073a, 1083a, b, 1376b; II, 5a, 350a, 357a, 876a; III, 88b, 200b, 202a, 488a, 1125b; IV, 29a-b, 304b, 362b, 363a, 478b, 840a, 873a; V, 389a, 492a; VI, 226b, 227a, 258a, 260a, 364a, 508b; VII, 122b, 693a; VIII, 71a,b, 973a; S, 15a, 65b, 245b
Alp Arslān b. Rigwān (Saldjūḳ) (1113) viii, 947b – VIII, 980a
Alp Khān (1316) ii, 695a, 1124a; iv, 419a; s, 105b – II, 712b, 1150b; IV, 437b; S, 104b
Alp Khān b. Dilāwar → Hūshang Shāh Ghūrī
Alp Ḳush Kūn-i Khar i, 865b – I, 890a
Alp Takīn (Alp Tigīn) (Fāṭimid vizier) (979) i, 823b, 824a; ii, 483a, 854a; iii, 246a, 841a; iv, 663b – I, 846b, 847a; II, 495a, 874a; III, 253a, 864b; IV, 690a
Alp Takīn (Alp Tigīn) (Ghaznawid(e)) (963) i, 226b, **421b**, 984b; ii, 1049a; iii, 46b; iv, 24a; vi, 65a, 433a; viii, 1037b –
I, 233b, **433a**, 1015a; II, 1073a; III, 48b, 864b; IV, 26a; VI, 62b, 418a; VIII, 1062b
Alp Tigin → Alp Takīn
Alp Yörük → Ḥusām al-Dīn Alp Yörük
Alpami̊sh i, **421b**; iii, 116a – I, **433b**; III, 118b
Alpetragius → al-Biṭrūdjī
Alpharas → Nudjūm
Alphonso → Alfūnsho
Alpī b. Timurtash (Artuḳid(e)) (1176) i, 664b; iii, 1119a, b – I, 684b; III, 1146b, 1147a
Alptakīn Bakdjur, amīr (X) iii, 398a – III, 410b
Alpuente → al-Bunt
Alpujarras → al-Busharrāt
Alruccaba → Rukba
Alsh i, **422b**, 492a; s, 144b – I, **434b**, 507a; S, 144a
Alṭāf Ḥusayn Ḥālī (1914) vi, 838a; vii, 662a, 668a; ix. 433b – VI, 829a; VII, 661b, 668a; IX, 456a
Altai(ï) i, **422b** – I, **434b**
Altaians i, **423a**; iii, 115a
Altair → Nudjūm
Altaïs I, **434b**; III, 117b
Altamġa ii, 14b, 157b – II, 14b, 162a
Altamish → Iltutmish
ʿAlth i, **423a** – I, **435a**
Alti̊ Parmak (1623) i, **423b** – I, **435a**
Alti Shahr (1623) i, **423b** – I, **435b**
Alti̊li̊k → Sikka
Alti̊n i, **423b** – I, **435b**
Alti̊n Köprü i, **424a** – I, **435b**
Alti̊n Ordu i, **424a**; iv, 280b – I, **436a**; IV, 292b
Alti̊ntash, (Anatolia(e)) i, **424a** – I, **436a**
Altıntash (Salkhad) (XII) viii, 128a – VIII, 130b
Alti̊ntash, Tādj al-Dīn b. Masʿūd II (Rūm Saldjūḳ)(XIV) i, 431b – I, 444a
Altun Djan (1063) vi, 482a – VI, 468a
Alṭūniya → Malik Alṭūniya
Altūntāsh al-Ḥādjib, Abū Saʿīd (Khʷārazm-Shāh) (1032) i, 278a, **424b**; iv, 1066b; vi, 780b; s, 176b – I, 286b, **436b**; IV, 1098b; VI, 770a; S, 177b
Aludel → al-ʿUthāl

Alughu Khān i, 1188a; ii, 3a, b; v, 38b – I, 1223a; II, 3a, b; V, 40a
ʿAlūk → al-Djinn
Alula (Somalia/-e) ix, 715b – IX, 746b
Alus, Sermed Mukhtār (1952) s, **64b** – S, **64b**
al-Ālūsī, Āl i, **425a** – I, **437a**
al-Ālūsī, Abu 'l-Thanā (1853) i, **425b**; vi, 113a – I, **437a**; VI, 111a
al-Ālūsī, Maḥmūd Shukrī (1924) i, **425b**, 596b vi, 614a – I, **437a**, 616a; VI, 599a
Alvand Dīv (1596) vi, 515a, b – VI, 500b, 501a
ʿAlwa i, **425b**; viii, 89a, b, 91a; ix, 698a – I, **437b**; VIII, 78a, b, 91a; IX, 727a
ʿAlwa bint Zurayḳa i, 1289b – I, 1329a
Alwāḥ → Lawḥ
Alwand b. Yūsuf b. Uzun Ḥasan (Aḳ-Ḳoyunlu) (1504) i, 311b, 312a; ii, 937a; iv, 186b, 1048b; viii, 767a – I, 321a, b; II, 959a; IV, 194b, 1080a; VIII, 792b
Alwand Kūh i, **426a** – I, **438a**
Alwār i, **426b** – I, **438b**
Ama → ʿAbd
al-Aʿmā al-Tuṭīlī (1130) i, **426b**, 595b, 602a; iii, 729b; vii, 811b – I, **438b**, 615a, 621b; III, 752a; VII, 813b
Amad, Banū i, 1078a – I, 1110b
ʿAmādiya i, **426b**; v, 460a – I, **438b**; V, 463a
Amādjūr, Banū i, 278b; iv, 89b; vi, 600b – I, 287a; IV, 93b; VI, 585a
Amadov Ḥamā Allāh Ḥaydara → Ḥamā Allāh
Amadu Bamba Mbacké (1927) vii, 609a; x, 575a; s, 182a – VII, 608b; X, ; S, 182a
Amadu Sēku → Aḥmad al-Shaykh
Amagdūl (Mogador) vi, 741b – VI, 731a
al-ʿAmāʾid vi, 562a – VI, 547a
al-Aʿmāḳ → al-ʿAmḳ
ʿAmʿaḳ, Shihāb al-Dīn Bukhārī (1147) vi, 276b; viii, 971a; s, **64b** – VI, 261b; VIII, 1005b; S, **65a**
ʿAmal i, 171a, **427a**; ii, 898a – I, 175b, **439a**; II, 919a
ʿAmala iii, 1106a, b – III, 1133a, b
ʿAmāla, Banū i, 439a – I, 451b
Amālī → Tadrīs
ʿAmālīḳ i, **429a**; ii, 917a; iii, 1270a; v, 994b – I, **441a**; II, 938b; III, 1303a; V, 989b
Amalric I ii, 318a, b – II, 327b
Amān i, **429a**; ii, 227b, 248a, 303b, 341b, 565a; iii, 197b, 547a, 1179b, 1180a, 1181b, 1182a; v, 179a – I, **441b**; II, 234b, 255b, 311b, 351b, 579a; III, 202b, 566a, 1208b, 1209a, 1210b, 1211a; V, 176b
Amān, Mīr (XIX) i, **430b**; iii, 376a; v, 201b – I, **442b**; III, 388a; V, 199a
Amān Allāh Khān (Kurdistān) (1825) vi, 484a; ix, 6b – VI, 470a; IX, 7a
Amān Allāh Khān, King/le roi (Afghānistān) (1960) i, 232b, 626b; ii, 531b, 657a, 658b; v, 37a, 1079a, b; vi, 86b, 169b, 262a, 768a; vii, 220b, 291a, 355a; s, **65b**, 237b – I, 239b, 647a; II, 544b, 673b, 675a; V, 38a, 1076b, 1077a; VI, 84b, 160b, 246b, 757a; VII, 222b, 293a, 357a; S, **66a**, 237b
Amān Allāh b. Khusraw Khān Nā-kām (1867) ix, 6b – IX, 7a
Amān al-Mulk (Chitral) (XIX) ii, 30b, 317a – II, 31a, 326a
Amānat (1858) i, **430b** – I, **443a**
Amānat Khān (Tādj Maḥall) (XVII) vii, 333b – VII, 335a
Amānī (Māzandarān) (1651) viii, 776a – VIII, 802a
Amanos ii, 982a; v, 810b; vi, 778a – II, 1004b; V, 816b; VI, 767b
Amantnāg iv, 177b – IV, 186a
ʿAmar, Mawlāy (1550) vi, 1009b – VI, 1001b
ʿAmāra i, **431a**; s, 179a – I, **443a**; s, 180a
ʿAmāra Dūnḳas (Fundj) (1533) ii, 943b, 944a; iv, 892b – II, 965b, 966a; IV, 925b
ʿAmārāt, Banū i, 483a – I, 497b
Amarkot i, **431a** – I, **443b**
al-ʿAmarrada (Muʿāwiya, Banū) vi, 473a – VI, 459a
al-Aʿmash, Sulaymān (765) i, 104b, **431b**; ii, 293a; iii, 843a; iv, 1112b; vi, 70b, 740a; vii, 607a; viii, 387a – I, 107b, **443b**; II, 301a; III, 867a; IV, 1144b; VI, 68b, 729a; VII, 607a; VIII, 400b
Amasya i, 12b, **431b**; iii, 215a; iv, 576b, 1159a; vi, 70b, 740a – I, 13a, **444a**; III, 221a; IV, 599b, 1191a; VI, 68b, 729a
Amasyalî Meḥmed Efendi → Memek Čelebi
Amasyawī, Maḥmūd b. Adham (XVI) viii, 544b – VIII, 562a
Ambāla i, **432b**, 1348a; s, 203a – I, **444b**, 1388b; S, 202b
Ambēr vi, 601b – VI, 586b
Ambon i, **433a** – I, **445a**
ʿAmda Ṣeyōn (Ṣion) (1344) i, 176b; ii, 175a; iii, 3b – I, 181a; II, 180b; III, 3b; IV, 797b, 798a, 799a, 800a
ʿAmdjad ʿAlī Shāh (Nawwāb) (1847) vii, 301a – VII, 303a
al-Amdjad Bahrāmshāh → Bahrām Shāh
Āmeddji i, **433a**; ii, 339a – I, **445b**; II, 348b
Ameer ʿAlī → Amīr ʿAlī
Amengku Rat I s, 201a – S, 201a
Aménokal i, **433b** – I, **445b**
Amēthī (Awadh) vi, 272a – VI, 257a
Amghar i, **433b**; – I, **446a**
Amghār, Banū vi, 592b; vii, 587a; ix, 507b – VI, 577a; VII, 587a; IX, 527a
Amhūrān vi, 81a – VI, 78b
Āmid → Diyār Bakr
ʿAmīd (title/titre) i, **434a**; vi, 275a – I, **446a**; VI, 260a
ʿAmīd al-Dawla lbn Djahīr ii, 384a, b – II, 394b, 395a
ʿAmīd al-Dīn al-Abzārī al-Anṣārī (1227) i, **434a** – I, **446b**
ʿAmīd al-Mulk al-Kundurī → al-Kundurī
Amīd Tūlakī Sūnāmī (XIII) s, **66b** – S, **67a**
al-Āmidī (981) i, 154a, b; vi, 438a, 709b; vii, 978b – I, 158b, 159a; VI, 423b, 698a; VII, 979a
al-ʿAmīdī, Abū Saʿd Muḥammad b. Aḥmad (1042) vii, 772a; s, 362a – VII, 774a; S, 361b
al-Āmidī, ʿAlī b. Abī ʿAlī al-Taghlabī (1233) i, **434b**; iii, 1025a, b; vii, 296b – I, **446b**; III, 1051a, b; VII, 298b
al-ʿAmīdī, Rukn al-Dīn (1218) i, **434b** – I, **446b**
ʿAmīḳ (lake/lac) s, 239a – S, 239a
ʿAmil (ʿawāmil) i, **436a** – I, **448a**
ʿĀmil (ʿummāl) i, 19b, **435a**, 1255a; ii, 118b, 328a; iii, 284a, b; iv, 941a – I, 20a, **447a**, 1293; II, 121b, 337b; III, 292b, 293b; IV, 974a
ʿĀmila, Banū i, **436a**; ii, 573b; v, 632a; vi, 477a; vii, 780a – I, **448b**; II, 588a; V, 636a; VI, 463a; VII, 781b
al-ʿĀmilī, ʿAlī b. Zayn al-Dīn (1557) vi, 550a – VI, 534b
al-ʿAmilī, Bahā al-Dīn (1621) i, **436b**; ii, 761a; iv, 725b; v, 872b, 873b; s, 308b – I, **448b**; II, 779b; IV, 754b; V, 878b, 879b; S, 308a
al-ʿĀmilī, al-Ḥurr → al-Ḥurr al-ʿĀmilī; Thaʿlaba b. Salāma
al-ʿAmilī, Muḥammad b. Ḥusayn Bahāʾ al-Dīn, Shaykh (1622) i, **436b**; ii, 761a; iv, 725b; v, 872b, 873b; vii, 94a, 132a, 203b, 475b; viii, 778a, 893b; s, 308b – I, **448b**; II, 779b; IV, 754b; V, 878b, 879b; VII, 96a, 134a, 204b, 475a, 547b; VIII, 138b, 804b, 924a; S, 308a
al-ʿĀmilī, Sayyid Aḥmad al-ʿAlawī (1633) vii, 94b – VII, 96b

(1384) vii, 169b; s, 56b – VII, 171a; S, 57a
al-ʿĀmilī, S̲h̲ahīd al-T̲h̲ānī Zayn al-Dīn → S̲h̲āhid al-Dīn
al-ʿĀmilī, S̲h̲ayk̲h̲ ʿAlī al-Karakī (1534) vi, 550a, b –
  VI, 534b, 535a
Amīn (poet/poète) (1620) vi, 837a – VI, 828a
al-Amīn → Abū Ḳubays
Amīn (āmēn) i, 436b – I, 449a
Amīn (umanā) i, 437a, 633a, 975b, ii, 105a –
  I, 449a, 654a, 1006a; II, 107a
Amīn, Ḳāsim → Ḳāsim Amīn
al-Amīn, Muḥammad b. Hārūn al-Ras̲h̲īd (ʿAbbāsid(e))
  (813) i, 18a, 77b, 143b, 160a, 437a, 897a, 899b,
  1034b, 1036a; ii, 235a, 730b, 731a; iii, 231b, 274a,
  360a, 618a; iv, 17a, 1091a; vi, 205b, 331a, 333a, b,
  379a, 606a, 668b; s, 22b, 116b –
  I, 18b, 80a, 147b, 164b, 449b, 924a, 926b, 1066a,
  1067b; II, 241b, 749b, 750a; III, 238a, 282a, 371b,
  638b; IV, 18a, 1122a; VI, 190a, 315b, 317b, 318a,
  363b, 591a, 654b; S, 23a, 116a
Amīn Arslān, amīr (XIX) iii, 593a III, 613b
al-Amīn Bey (Ḥusaynid(e), Tunisia/e) (XX) i, 1110b;
  iii, 637a; s, 11a – I, 1144a; III, 658a; S, 10b
Amīn b. ʿAḳīl vi, 177a – VI, 162b
al-Amīn b. Ḥamad, S̲h̲ayk̲h̲ (XIX) vi, 628b – VI, 613b
Amīn al-Dawla → Ibn al-Tilmīd̲h̲
Amīn al-Dawla b. Muḥammad Ḥusayn K̲h̲ān (Iṣfahān)
  (1834) iv, 104b, 105a, 476a – IV, 109b, 497a
Amīn al-Ḥusaynī, Muftī (1974) ii, 913b; iv, 961a; v,
  336b, 337a; vi, 31b, 388b; vii, 765a; viii, 445b; s, 67a –
  II, 934b; IV, 993b; V, 337b; VI, 30a, 372b; VII, 766b;
  VIII, 460b; S, 67b
Amīn K̲h̲ʷādja K̲h̲ānlî̄ḳ (Lukchun, Turfan) (1760) x,
  677a – X,
Amīn Rāzī (XVI) vii, 530a – VII, 530b
Amīn al-Sayyād (Demirdās̲h̲iya) s, 209a – S, 208b
Amīn al-Sulṭān (1907) vi, 292a; vii, 432a – VI, 277a;
  VII, 433a
Amīn Taḳī al-Dīn (XIX) s, 159b – S, 159b
Amīna Aḳdas (XIX) vi, 484b – VI, 470b
Amīna bint Wahb b. ʿAbd Manāf umm Muḥammad
  (576) i, 42b, 169a, 438a; iii, 362b; vi, 168b, 621b –
  I, 43b, 173b, 450b; III, 374a; VI, 159b, 606b
Āmina bint Wahb (576) i, 42b, 169a, 438a; iii, 362b –
  I, 43b, 173b, 450b; III, 374a
Amindivi (Islands/Îles) vi, 206b – VI, 191a
Amīndjī b. Djalāl b. Ḥasan (1602) s, 70b – S, 71a
Amīnī ʿAlī (XX) vii, 447b, 448a – VII, 449a
Amīr (title/titre) i, 19b, 438b, ii, 507b; iii, 45b; iv,
  941b, 942a; v, 686a, 1251b –
  I, 20a, 451a; II, 520a; III, 47b; IV, 974b, 975a; V,
  691a, 1242b
ʿĀmir s, 81b – S, 81b
ʿĀmir, Banū (Beni Amor) i, 1a, 440b; ii, 252b, 709a;
  iii, 6a, 7b; v, 522a – I, 1a, 453a; II, 260a, 728a; III, 6a,
  7b; V, 525b
ʿĀmir, Banū (Yamāma) vi, 625a – VI, 610a
ʿĀmir I (Ṭāhirid(e)) (1466) i, 440b; iii, 746a –
  I, 453b; III, 769a
ʿĀmir II (Ṭāhirid(e)) (1517) i, 441a; ii, 730a; iii, 746a;
  v, 807b – I, 453b; II, 748b; III, 769a; V, 813a
ʿĀmir ʿAbd Allāh (ʿAlī) Abu ʾl-Fazārī (X) s, 306a – S,
  306a
ʿĀmir (Djaʿda) → Djaʿda (ʿĀmir)
ʿĀmir b. ʿAbd al-Ḳays al-ʿAnbarī (VII) i, 441a, 960a –
  I, 453b, 989b
ʿĀmir b. ʿAbd al-Wahhāb → ʿĀmir II
ʿĀmir b. Dāwud (Aden) (1538) iv, 901b – IV, 934b
ʿĀmir n. Abī Djaws̲h̲an (929) ix, 363a – IX, 374b
ʿĀmir b. Dubāra (VII) i, 49a; iii, 802b; iv, 99b, 447a – I,
  50b; III, 826a; IV, 104a, 467a

ʿĀmir b. Fuhayra i, 110a; iii, 366b – I, 113a; III, 378b
ʿĀmir b. Kurayz s, 267b – S, 267a
ʿĀmir b. Luʾayy, Banū iii, 819b; vi, 139a, 145a, 334a,
  477b, 543b – III, 843a; VI, 137a, 143a, 318b, 463b,
  528a
ʿĀmir b. Miscaʿ (VII) vi, 640b – VI, 625b
ʿĀmir b. Rabīʿa b. ʿUḳayl (Djabrid(e)) s, 234a – S,
  234a
ʿĀmir b. Ṣaʿṣaʿa, Banū i, 441a, 544b; ii, 72a, 353b,
  895b, 1023a; iii, 168b; v, 101b, 526a, 583b, 640b,
  954a; vi, 543b, 918a; vii, 373b; s, 178a –
  I, 453b, 562a; II, 73a, 363b, 916b, 1047a; III, 172b;
  V, 103b, 529b, 589a, 644b, 958a; VI, 528a, 909b;
  VII, 375a; S, 179a
ʿĀmir b. S̲h̲ahr (VII) iii, 123a – III, 126a
ʿĀmir b. Ṭāhir → ʿĀmir I
ʿĀmir b. al-Ṭufayl (630) i, 441b, 442a, 690a, 1232b;
  iii, 136b; iv, 1106a –
  I, 454a, 455a, 711a, 1269a; III, 139a; IV, 1137b
Amīr Aḥmad K̲h̲ān (Maḥmudābād) (1940) vi, 78b –
  VI, 76a
Amīr Āk̲h̲ūr i, 442b; iv, 217b – I, 455b; IV, 227a
Amīr ʿAlī, Sayyid (1928) i, 38b, 442b; iii, 431b, 532b;
  iv, 170b; vi, 461b; s, 73b –
  I, 39b, 455b; III, 445b, 551a; IV, 178a; VI, 447a; S,
  74a
Amīr ʿAlī Barīd b. Ḳāsim Barīd (Barīd S̲h̲āhīs) (1517)
  i, 1047a, 1200a; ii, 1135a; iii, 425b, 1159b, 1160a, b;
  vi, 63b –
  I, 1078b, 1235b; II, 1162a; III, 439b, 1188a, b, 1189a;
  VI, 61b
Amīr ʿAlī Ḥusaynī (1526) vi, 514b – VI, 500a
Amīr-i Amīrān (XII) iii, 87a – III, 89b
Amīr Bas̲h̲kurt (XIV) i, 1075b – I, 1107b
al-Āmir bi-Aḥkām Allāh (Fāṭimid(e)) (1130) i, 215b,
  440a, 814b, 1091b; ii, 170b, 857b, 858a, b; iii, 54b;
  iv, 944a; vi, 143b; vii, 163b –
  I, 222a, 452b, 837b, 1124a; II, 175b, 877b, 878a; III,
  56b; IV, 976b; VI, 142a; VII, 165a
Amīr Buk̲h̲ārī, S̲h̲ayk̲h̲ (XV) vii, 595a – VII, 595a
Amīr Dād i, 443b – I, 456a
Amīr Doladay (Awnik) (XV) iv, 586a, b – IV, 608b, 609a
Amīr al-Ḥādjdj i, 443b; iv, 679a – I, 456a; IV, 706b
Amīr Ḥamza → Ḥamza b. ʿAbd al-Muṭṭalib
Amīr Ḥasan K̲h̲ān b. Nawwāb ʿAlī K̲h̲ān (1858) vi,
  77b – VI, 75b
ʿĀmīr al-Hintātī (1370) iii, 462a – III, 478a
Amīr Ḥusayn, a(d)miral (XVI) i, 441a; ii, 322a, 1127b;
  iv, 32b – I, 453b; II, 331b, 1154a; IV, 34b
al-Amīr al-Kabīr i, 444a; v, 792b – I, 456b; V, 798b
al-Amīr al-Kabīr, Muḥammad (XVIII) s, 411a – S, 411b
Amīr Kabīr, Mīrzā Muḥammad Taḳī K̲h̲ān (1852) i,
  833b; ii, 649b; iii, 554b, 1105b, 1107a; iv, 70b, 394a,
  395b, 396b, 398a, 787a, b, 1043a; v, 919a; vi, 20a;
  vii, 299a, 431b, 1003a; s, 70b –
  I, 856b; II, 666a; III, 573b, 1132b, 1134a; IV, 74a,
  411a, 412b, 413b, 415a, 819a, 1074b; V, 924b; VI,
  18a; VII, 301b, 432b, 1005a; S, 71a
Amīr K̲h̲ān (1834) i, 282b, 444a, 1195b; ii, 567a – I,
  291a, 456b, 1230b; II, 581b
Amīr K̲h̲ān Turkmān (XVI) iii, 157b – III, 161a
Amīr K̲h̲usraw Dihlawī (1325) i, 444a, 1212b, 1329a;
  ii, 56b, 504a, 794a; iii, 249a, 439a, 453a, 456b, 492a;
  iv, 66b, 759b, 1010a, 1136a; v, 937b, 1104b; vii,
  337b, 340b, 754b; ix, 241b; x, 113b; s, 46b, 105a,
  124a –
  I, 457a, 1249a, 1369b; II 57b, 517a, 813a; III, 256a,
  453a, 468b, 472a, 509a; IV, 70a, 789b, 1042a,
  1167b; V, 941b, 1100b; VII, 339a, 342b, 756a; IX,
  248a; X, 123a; S, 47a, 104b, 123b
Amīr Kiyāʾīs (Lāhīdjān) s, 363b – S, 363a

Amīr Kulāl (XIV) vii, 933b – VII, 934a
Amīr Madjlis i, **445a** – I, **457b**
Amīr Masʿūd → Masʿūd I b. Maḥmūd
Amīr Mīnāʾī (1900) v, 959a, 960b, 962a – V, 963a, 965a, 966a
Amīr Muḥammad Zamān (Kalāntar) iv, 475b – IV, 496b
Amīr Muʿizzī, hidjāʾ iii, 356a – III, 367a
Amir al-Mulk (Chitral) (XIX) ii, 30b – II, 31a
Amīr al-muʾminīn i, 21b, 79b, 83b, **445a**; ii, 676a – I, 22a, 82a, 86a, **458a**; II, 693a
Amīr al-muslimīn i, 79b, **445b** – I, 82a, **458b**
Amīr Niẓām, Ḥasan ʿAlī Khān (1899) s, **71a** – S, **71b**
ʿĀmir Rabīʿa, Banū (ʿUḳayl) i, 942a, b; iv, 664a,b – I, 971a; IV, 690b, 691b
Amīr Rūḥānī (XIII) iii, 1155b – III, 1184a
al-Amīr al-Ṣaghīr, Muḥammad (XIX) s, 411a – S, 411b
Amīr Sayyid Bayan (1294) ix, 621a – IX, 646b
Amīr Shāh Ḳāsim Bēglār (1547) iii, 1030a – III, 1056a
Amīr Shāhī (Sarbadarid(e)) vii, 442a; ix, 49a – VII, 443a; IX, 50a
Amīr Shāhī b. ʿAbd al-Karīm (Marʿashī) (1531) vi, 514b, 515a – VI, 500a
Amīr silāḥ i, **445b** – I, **458b**
Amīr Sultan (Bukhāra) (1429) viii, 136b – VIII, 139a
Amīr Sulṭān Muḥammad (Maklī) (XVII) vi, 190a – VI, 173b
Amīr al-umarāʾ i, 19a, 20a, b, **446a**, 899b, 1040a; ii, 507b; v, 622a – I, 20a, 21a, **458b**, 926b, 1071b; II, 520a; V, 626a
Amīr Wālī (Astarābadh) (1379) vi, 512a – VI, 497a
Amīr Yashbak ii, 172b – II, 178a
Amīr Zayn al-Dīn (Marʿashī) (1562) vi, 516b – VI, 501b
Amīra Ḳubād (XVI) i, 1066b – I, 1098b
Amīrān, ṣūfī (XIV) i, 195b – I, 201b
Amīrānshāh b. Ḳāwurd (XI) i, 827a – I, 850a
Amīrghaniyya → Mīrghāniyya
ʿĀmirī i, **446a** – I, **459a**
al-ʿAmirī (Meknès) (XIX) vi, 249b – VI, 233b
al-ʿĀmirī, Abu ʾl-Ḥasan Muḥammad b. Yūsuf (992) i, 235b; ii, 949a; vi, 351b; s, **72b** – I, 243a; II, 971a; VI, 335b; S, **72b**
al-ʿĀmirī, ʿĀlī b. ʿAbd al-Ḥadjdj al-Ghazzī (1777) vii, 470a – VII, 469b
ʿAmīrī, Muḥammad Ṣādiḳ Adīb al-Mamālik (1917) iv, 71a; vi, 114b; vii, 662a; s, **73a** – IV, 74b, VI, 112b; VII, 661b; S, **73b**
Amīr-i Aʿzam Sangsarī (XX) v, 664a – V, 669b
Amīr-i Niẓām → Taḳī Khān, Mīrzā
ʿĀmirid(e)s i, 76a, 84b, **446a**; iii, 495b, 743a; vi, 188b, 344b, 432a; vii, 590a – I, 78a, 86b, **459a**; III, 512b, 766a; VI, 172b, 329a, 417a; VII, 589b
Āmiriyya iii, 54b; iv, 200b, 201a – III, 56b; IV, 209a, b
Amirutzes, George (XV) vi, 69b, 71a – VI, 67b, 69a
Amizmiz vi, 142a – VI, 140b
al-ʿAmḳ i, **446b**; vi, 505b; s, 243a – I, **459a**; VI, 491a; S, 243a
ʿAmlūḳ, King/le roi i, 429a – I, 441a
ʿAmm, Banu ʾl- vi, 920b – VI, 912a
al-ʿAmma wa ʾl-Khāṣṣa → al-Khāṣṣa
ʿAmmān i, **447a**, 975b; vi, 31b, 32a, b, 546a; x, 887a – I, **460a**, 1006a; VI, 30a, b, 531a; X,
Amman, Mir → Amān, Mīr
ʿAmmār, Banū i, **448a**; ii, 353b, 568b; vii, 408a – I, **461a**; II, 363a, 582b; VII, 409b
ʿAmmār b. ʿAmr (VIII) iv, 1003b – IV, 1036a
ʿAmmār b. Yāsir, Abu ʾl-Yaḳẓān (657) i, **448b**, 704b; ii, 846a; iii, 29b, 241a, 874a; vi, 139b, 675b; ix, 554a; s, 354b – I, **461b**, 726a; II, 866a; III, 31a, 248a, 898a; VI, 137b, 662a; IX, 576a; S, 354b
ʿAmmār b. Yazīd → Khidāsh
ʿAmmār b. Yāsir (VII) ix, 555a – IX, 577a, b
ʿAmmār al-Baṣrī (IX) vi, 636b; vii, 517b – VI, 621b; VII, 518a
ʿAmmār al-Khāridjī (865) vii, 413b – VII, 415a
ʿAmmār al-Mawṣilī (XI) i, **448b**, 785b – I, **461b**, 805b
ʿAmmāra bint Ḥamza (VII) ii, 372a, – II, 382a
ʿAmmāriyya i, 371b, **449a** – I, 382a, **462a**
Ammī → Mūsā b. ʿĪsā
ʿAmmūn, Iskandar s, 159b – S, 159b
ʿAmmūriyya i, 154a, **449a**; ii, 237a; vi, 740a, 774b – I, 158a, **462a**; II, 243b; VI, 729a, 763b
Amorium → ʿAmmūriya
Amphila Bay vi, 642b – VI, 628a
Amr i, 414b, **449b**, 1170a – I, 426b, **462b**, 1205a
ʿAmr b. ʿAbd al-Mālik al-Warrāḳ ((IX) iv, 1005a – IV, 1037a
ʿAmr b. Abī Ṣayfī (VII) iv, 821a – IV, 854a
ʿAmr b. Abī Sufyān (VII) i, 151a – I, 155b
ʿAmr b.ʿAdī (III) i, **450b**; v, 633a – I, **463b**; V, 637a
ʿAmr b. al-Ahtam (676) i, **450b** – I, **463b**
ʿAmr b. ʿĀmir al-ʿAzdī (VI) vi, 564b – VI, 549b
ʿAmr b. al-ʿĀṣ al-Sahmī (663) i, 111a, 207a, 208b, 383b, 384a, **451a**, 531b, 659b, 812b, 932a, 966a, 1049a, 1098a, 1343b; ii, 306a, 327b, 372a, 625b, 910b, 957b, 1024b, 1056a; iii, 540b, 587a, 889b, 975b; iv, 132b, 424a, 514a, 841b, 1103b; v, 90b, 318a, 799b; vi, 362a, 411a, 452b, 648a, 649a, b, 656a, 666a, 669a, 671a, 672b, 674b, 677a, 740b; vii, 153b, 155b, 265a, 356b, 372b, 393b, 509b, 862b; ix, 554b; x, 816a; s, 157a, 267b – I, 114a, 213b, 215a, 394b, 395a, **464a**, 547b, 680b, 835b, 960b, 996a, 1080b, 1131a, 1384a; II, 314b, 337a, 382a, 641a, 932a, 980a, 1048b, 1080b; III, 559b, 607a, 913b, 1000a; IV, 138a, 442b, 536b, 874b, 1134b; V, 93a, 317b, 805b; VI, 346a, 395b, 438a, 633a, 634b, 635a, 641b, 652a, 655a, 657b, 658b, 661a, 663b, 729b; VII, 155b, 157b, 267a, 359a, 374a, 394b, 510a, 864a; IX, 576b; X, ; S, 157a, 267a
ʿAmr b. ʿAwf, Banū i, 771b; vi, 646b, 649a – I, 794b; VI, 632a, 634a
ʿAmr b. Bakr al-Tamīmī (VII) iii, 887a, b – III, 911a, b
ʿAmr b. Bāna (Bānata) → Ibn Bāna
ʿAmr b. Dīnār (742) vii, 398a, 758a – VII, 399b, 759b
ʿAmr b. Djamīl (VIII) s, 326b – S, 326a
ʿAmr b. al-Djamūḳ (VII) s, 230a – S, 230a
ʿAmr b. al-Djuʿayd iv, 421a – IV, 439b
ʿAmr b. al-Ḥadjdjādj al-Zubaydī (VII) iii, 609b, 610b – III, 630a, 631a
ʿAmr b. al-Ḥārith (VI) vii, 841a – VII, 842b
ʿAmr b. Ḥazm (Nadjrān) (VII) iv, 927b – IV, 960b
ʿAmr b. Hind (Lakhmid(e)) (568) i, **451b**, 772a; iii, 226b; v, 633b, 640a; vi, 477a; vii, 563a, 568b, 591b, 763b – I, **464b**, 795a; III, 229a; V, 637b, 644b; VI, 463a; VII, 563b, 569a, 591b, 765a
ʿAmr b. Ḥurayth al-Makhzūmī (VIII) i, 1242b; vi, 140b; ix, 823a – I, 1280b; VI, 138b; IX, 820b
ʿAmr b. Ḳamīʾa (530) i, **452a**, 963b; iii, 1177b, 1178a; vii, 580b, 581a – I, **465a**, 993a; III, 1206b, 1207a; VII, 581a, b
ʿAmr b. Ḳiʿās vii, 592a – VII, 592a
ʿAmr b. Kirkira (VIII) s, 20b, **73b** – S, 20b, **73b**
ʿAmr b. Kulthūm (VI) i, **452a**; iii, 222b; iv, 998a; v, 633b; vii, 254b – I, **465a**; III, 229a; IV, 1030b; V, 637b; VII, 256a
ʿAmr b. al-Layth (Ṣaffārid(e)) (902) i, 278a, **452b**, 1001a, 1294a; ii, 191b, 553b, 812a, 1048b; iii, 344b,

1202a; iv, 21a, b, 22a, 100a, 188b, 266a, 975a; v, 158a; vi, 661a; vii, 418a, 760a, 777b; viii, 63a, 796a; s, 125b –
I, 286b, **465b**, 1032a, 1333b; II, 197b, 567b, 831a, 1073a; III, 355a, 1232b; IV, 22b, 23a, b, 104b, 197a, 278a, 1007a; V, 157b; VI, 646b; VII, 419a, 761b, 779a; VIII, 64a, 823a; S, 124b
ʿAmr b. Luḥayy i, **453a**; ii, 572a; iii, 537a; iv, 91b, 421b; v, 76b, 77a, b, 692a; vi, 373b – I, **466a**; II, 586a; III, 555b; IV, 95b, 440a; V, 79a, b, 697a; VI, 358a
ʿAmr b. Maʿdīkarib (VII) i, **453a**; viii, 1051b – I, **466a**; VIII, 1087a
ʿAmr b. Masʿada (832) i, 279b, **453b** – I, 288a, **466b**
ʿAmr b. Muḥammad b. al-Ḳāsim (738) vi, 439b – VI, 425a
ʿAmr b. al-Mun<u>dh</u>ir III b. Māʾ al-Samāʾ (La<u>kh</u>mid(e)) vii, 591b – VII, 591b
ʿAmr b. al-Nuʿmān (VII) i, 53a, 771b, 1283a; iv, 1187b; v, 995a – I, 546, 794b, 1322b; IV, 1220a; V, 990b
ʿAmr b. Saʿd b. Mālik b. Ḍubayʿa → Muraḳḳi<u>sh</u> al-Aṣ<u>gh</u>ar
ʿAmr b. Saʿīd al-A<u>sh</u>daḳ (684) i, 58a, 76b, **453b**; ii, 360b; iii, 226b, 271a, 608b; vi, 622a, b –
I, 60a, 79a, **466b**; II, 370a; III, 233b, 278b, 629b; VI, 607a, b
ʿAmr b. Sālim al-Tu<u>dj</u>ībī (IX) i, 250b; v, 78a, b – I, 258a; V, 80b, 81a
ʿAmr b. <u>Sh</u>imr s, 233a – S, 232b
ʿAmr b. <u>Sh</u>uʿayb b. Muḥammad (736) vii, 576b – VII, 577a
ʿAmr b. Sufyān → Abu ʾl-Aʿwar al-Sulamī
ʿAmr b. ʿUbayd (761) i, 274a, **454a**; iii, 985a, 1142b; iv, 370b; vi, 458a; vii, 398b, 783a –
I, 282a, **467a**; III, 1009b, 1171a; IV, 387a; VI, 443b; VII, 400a, 785a
ʿAmr b. ʿUbayd Allāh al-Aḳṭaʿ (amīr) (863) i, 1103a, b; ii, 234b, 237a, b – I, 1136a, 1137a; II, 241b, 243b, 244b
ʿAmr b. ʿUmayr b. ʿAwf (VII) s, 355a – S, 354b
ʿAmr b. Umm Iyās i, 1241b – I, 1279b
ʿAmr b. Usāma (La<u>kh</u>mid(e)) vii, 591b – VII, 591b
ʿAmr b. al-Zubayr (681) i, 55a, 453b; iii, 970a – I, 56b, 466b; III, 994b
ʿAmr al-Ḍāʾīʿ → ʿAmr b. Ḳamīʾa
ʿAmr al-Ḳays b. ʿAmr (IV) i, 526a – I, 542a
ʿAmr Makkī (IX) iii, 100a, 102a – III, 102b, 104b
ʿAmr Muzayḳiyāʾ i, 771a – I, 794a
Amram → ʿImrān
al-ʿAmrāwī, Idrīs b. Muḥammad (1878) vii, 391b – VII, 393a
al-ʿAmrī → Muḥammad b. ʿU<u>th</u>mān; ʿU<u>th</u>mān b. Saʿīd
al-ʿAmrī, Abū ʿAmr ʿU<u>th</u>mān b. Saʿīd (880) viii, **812a** – VIII, **839a**
al-ʿAmrī, Abū <u>Dj</u>aʿfar Muḥammad b. ʿU<u>th</u>mān (917) viii, **812a** – VIII, **839a**
Amrī <u>Sh</u>īrāzī, Abu ʾl-Ḳāsim Muḥammad Ḳūhpāyaʾī (1591) viii, 115b – VIII, 118a
Amri Abedi (1965) vi, 612b, 613a – VI, 597b, 598a
Amritsar i, **454a**, 1348a; s, 242a – I, **467a**, 1388a; S, 242a
Amrōhā s, **73b** – S, **74a**
Amrōhāʾī, Maṣḥafī (XIX) s, 74a – S, 74b
ʿAmrūn al-Yaḥṣūbī (1007) iv, 289b – IV, 302b
ʿAmrūs b. Fatḥ (IX) i, 120b – I, 124a
ʿAmrūs b. Yūsuf (IX) iii, 74a; s, 82a – III, 76b; S, 81b
ʿAms → Nuṣayrīs
Āmū Daryā i, 222a, b, 313b, **454b**, 459b, 607a; 607a; ii, 1a, 2a; iv, 502b, 1060b; v, 24a, 388b, 581b, 868a; vi, 65a, 418a, 419a, 720a; s, 125a, 281a –
I, 228b, 229a, 323a, **467b**, 473a, 627a; II, 1a, 2a; IV, 524b, 1092a; V, 24b, 389b, 586b, 874b; VI, 63a, 403a, 404a, 709a; S, 124b, 281a
ʿAmūd i, **457b** – I, **470b**
ʿAmūdā the Great/la Grande (town/ville) ii, 235b – II, 242b
al-ʿAmūdayn vi, 778b – VI, 768b
al-ʿAmūdī, Āl ii, 173b – II, 179a
al-ʿAmūdī, Muḥammad Saʿīd (XX) vi, 175b, 176b, 177b – VI, 163a
al-ʿAmūdī, <u>Sh</u>ay<u>kh</u> vii, 515b – VII, 515b
ʿAmū<u>dj</u>a-zāde → Ḥusayn Pa<u>sh</u>a, ʿAmūdja-zāde
Āmul i, 237a, **459a**; ii, 746a; iv, 644a, 646b; vi, 433a, 510b, 511a, b, 512a, b, 513a, b, 514b, 515b, 516a, 618b; s, 298a, 363b –
I, 244b, **472a**; II, 764b; IV, 670b, 673a; VI, 418b, 496a, b, 497a, b, 498a, b, 499b, 500b, 501a, b, 603b; S, 297b, 363b
Āmul (Turkmen/-ène) i, 459**b**, iii, 255a; iv, 583b; s, 228a, 281a, 335a, 356b, 357a –
I, **472b**; III, 262a; IV, 607a; S, 228a, 281a, 334b, 356b
Āmulī → Awliyā Allāh; Karīm al-Dīn
al-Āmulī → Ḥaydar-i Āmulī
Āmulī, ʿAbd al-Munʿim (XVI) viii, 542a – VIII, 559b
Āmulī, Ṭālib ix, 141b – IX, 237b
ʿAmūr, Banū i, 371b, 460b – I, 382b, 473b
ʿAmūr, <u>Dj</u>abal→ <u>Dj</u>abal ʿAmūr
Amurath → Murād
Āmūya → Āmul, Turkmen/Turkmène
Āmūzagār, <u>Dj</u>am<u>sh</u>īd (XX) vii, 450b – 451b
ʿAmwās i, **460b** – I, **474a**
Āna → Sikka
ʿĀna i, **461a** – I, **474a**
Anadolu i, 292b, 322b, **461b**; ii, 8a, 83b, 966b; iii, 211a, 215b; v, 291b, 881a, 978a, 979a, 1144b; ix, 796b –
I, 302a, 332b, **475a**; II, 8a, 85a, 988b; III, 217a, 221b; V, 291a, b, 887b, 1137a; IX, 830b
Anadolu (eyālet) i, **480b**, 1160a; ii, 32b, 722a – I, **494b**, 1194b; II, 33a, 741a
Anadolu Ḥiṣārî i, **481a**, 1251b, 1318a; iii, 483a – I, **495a**, 1289b, 1358b; III, 500a
Anadolu Kavaghî i, 481a, 1252a – I, 495a, 1290a
Anāhīd → Zuhara
Anahilwada → Anhalwāra
ʿAnāḳ bint Ādam i, **481a** – I, **495b**
Anakkaza, Banū (Borkou) i, 1258a – I, 1296a
Anamur i, **481a** – I, **495b**
ʿĀnān b. David (VIII) i, 481b; iv, 604a, b, 606a – I, 495b; IV, 628a, 629a, 630b
Anand Ram Mu<u>kh</u>liṣ (1750) iv, 1127b, 1128a – IV, 1159a, b
Ananda b. Mangalay b. Ḳūbilay (1307) iv, 553b – IV, 577b
Anandpāl (XI) vi, 65b – VI, 63b
ʿAnāniyya i, **481b**; iv, 604a – I, **495b**; IV, 628a
Anapa i, 63a, **481b**; ii, 25b – I, 65a, **496a**; II, 26a
Anas b. Abī Unās (VII) iii, 224b – III, 231b
Anas b. Ḳays b. al-Muntafiḳ (VII) vii, 582a – VII, 582b
Anas b. Mālik (709) i, 52a, 431b, **482a**; iii, 40b, 586b, 947b; iv, 899a; vi, 266b, 651b –
I, 54a, 443b, **496a**; III, 42a, 606b, 972b; IV, 931b; VI, 251b, 637a
Anas b. Mudrik (<u>Kh</u>a<u>th</u>ʿm) (VII) iv, 1106a – IV, 1137b
ʿĀnāt s, 130a – S, 129b
Anatolia/-ie → Anadolu
Anavarza → ʿAyn Zarba
Anaw i, 701a – I, 722a
ʿAnaza (spear/lance) i, **482a**, 1215a – I, **496b**, 1251b
ʿAnaza, Banū i, **482b**, 528b, 545a, 873b, 1093b; ii, 184b; iii, 293a, 1253b; vi, 733b; vii, 782b; viii, 643a, 668b –

I, **496b**, 544b, 562a, 897b, 1126a; II, 190b; III, 302a, 1286a; VI, 722b; VII, 784b; VIII, 662b, 688a
Anazarba → ʿAyn Zarba
ʿAnazeh, Banū i, 1277a – I, 1316a
al-Anbābī, Muḥammad (XIX) i, 819b, 1019b – I, 842b, 1051a
Anbāduḳlīs i, 235b, **483b**; iii, 869a – I, 243a, **498a**; III, 893a
ʿAnbar i, **484a**, 837b – I, **498b**, 860b
al-Anbār i, 17a, **484b**, 1073b; ii, 195a, 946b; iv, 911b; vi, 333b, 633b; vii, 729b –
I, 17b, **499a**, 1105b; II, 201a, 968b; IV, 944a, b; VI, 318a, 618b; VII, 730a
ʿAnbar, Banū ʾl- → Tamīm
ʿAnbar al-Sak͟hartī (XIV) viii, 986a – VIII, 1020b
al-Anbārī → ʿĀmir b. ʿAbd al-Ḳays
al-Anbārī, Abū Bakr Muḥammad b. al-Ḳāsim (940) i, 185a, **485b**; vi, 634a, 822b; vii, 307a; viii, 14b, 646a – I, 190a, 500**a**; VI, 619a, 813a; VII, 309b; VIII, 14b, 665a
al-Anbārī, Abu ʾl-Barakāt Kamāl al-Dīn (1181) i, **485b**; iii, 550b, 706b, 934b; v, 242b; vi, 196a; vii, 914b –
I, **500a**; III, 569b, 728b, 959a; V, 240b; VI, 180a; VII, 915a
al-ʿAnbarī, Abu ʾl-Ḥasan ʿUmar b. Wāsil (924) viii, 840b – VIII, 869b
al-ʿAnbārī, Abū Muḥammad (916) i, **486a** – I, **500b**
al-ʿAnbarī, ʿUbayd Allāh b. al-Ḥasan (785) ix, 204a – IX, 210a
ʿAnbasa b. Isḥāḳ (856) vi, 674b – VI, 661a
ʿAnbasa b. Maʿdān (640) vi, 920b – VI, 912a
ʿAnbasa al-Aʿwar (al-Ḳabḳ) (X) iv, 346b – IV, 361a
al-Anbīḳ i, **486a** – I, **500b**
Anbiya v, 651b, 652b – V, 656a, 657a
Ancyra → Anḳara
ʿAndalīb → Mīrzā Ḥusayn K͟hān b. Ṣabā
al-Andalus i, 58b, 75b, 76a, 79b, 82a, 85b, 86b, 121b, 134b, 162a, 165b, 242a, 390a, 427b, **486b**, 1046a, 1148a, 1319b; ii, 129b, 130a, 331a, 601b; iii, 220a, 1055a; v, 877a, 1118b, 1119a, 1149b; vi, 280a, 428a, 430b, 469b, 520a, 601a, 841b, 851b, 881a, 1043b; vii, 590a; ix, 505b; x, 105b; s, 103a –
I, 60b, 77b, 78a, 81b, 84b, 88a, 89a, 125a, 138b, 166b, 170b, 249b, 401a, 440a, **501a**, 1078a, 1182b, 1360a; II, 132b, 133b, 341a, 616b; III, 226b, 1081a; V, 882b, 1115a, b, 1140b; VI, 264b, 413b, 416a, 455a, 505a, 585b, 832b, 843b, 872b, 1037a; VII, 589b; IX, 525a; X, 113b; S, 102b
—agriculture i, **491b**; ii, 901a; v, 878a – I, **506b**; II, 922a; V, 883b
—governors/gouverneurs i, **493a**, b; iii, 46a, 587b, 702a – I, **508a**, b; III, 48a, 607b, 724a
—history/histoire i, 44a, 320b; ii, 72a; iii, 762b, 789b, 805b, 848a; iv, 494b, 1156b – I, 45a, 330b; II, 73b; III, 785b, 812b, 829a, 872a; IV, 515b, 1188b
—literature, culture/littérature, culture i, 404b, **497a-503b**, 599a; ii, 729a, 988a; iii, 70a, b, 657b, 702a, 771b; iv, 1006b-1008a; v, 218b, 744b, 1128a – I, 416b, **512a-519a**, 619a; II, 747b, 1010b; III, 72b, 679a, 724a, 795a; IV, 1039a-1040a; V, 216a, 749b, 1124b
—in North Africa/en Afrique du Nord i, 92b, **496a**; ii, 161a; v, 1190b – I, 95b, **511a**; II, 166a; V, 1180b
Andaman isles/îles iii, 407a – III, 419b
Andarāb i, **504a** – I, **519a**
Andarāba s, 125b – S, 124b
Andarūn → Enderūn
Anḍawr vi, 80a – VI, 78a
Anday, Melih Cevdet iv, 545a – IV, 568b
Andelas (Sumatra) ix, 852a – IX, 887b
Andi, Banū i, **504a**, 756a; ii, 86b, 88b – I, **519b**, 778b; II, 88a, 90b
Andid͟jān i, **504b**, 847b; ii, 791b, 792a; v, 461a; vi, 557b, 769a – I, **520a**, 871a; II, 810b, 811a; V, 464a; VI, 542a, 758a
Andirin vi, 508b, 509a – VI, 494a, b
ʿAnd͟jar → ʿAyn al-D͟jarr
And͟judān iv, 201b – IV, 210b
And͟juman i, **505a**, xvi; ii, 429b, 433a, 434a, b; iv, 39b, 789b – I, **520b**; II, 440b, 444b, 445a, b; IV, 42a, 821a
And͟juman-i K͟huddām-i Kaʿba vii, 678b; s, 4b, **74a**, 293b – VII, 678b; S, 3b, **74b**, 293a
Andk͟h(ʷ)ūy i, **506a**, 530b; vi, 494b; ix, 431a; s, 281a – I, **521b**, 546b; VI, 480a; IX, 447b; S, 281a
Andrinople → Edirne
Âne → Ḥimār
Aneiza → ʿUnayza
al-Anf, Banū iv, 201a – IV, 209b, 210a
Anfā i, **506a**; vi, 573a – I, **521b**; VI, 558a
Angād vi, 141b – VI, 139b
Angeli → Amirutzes, George
Anglovič, Michael (1485) vi, 70a – VI, 68a
Angohrān s, 129a – S, 128a
Angora → Anḳara
Angres, Banū s, 246b – S, 246b
Anhalwāra i, **506b**; ii, 1123b, 1124a; vii, 911b – I, **522a**; II, 1149b, 1150a, b; VII, 912a
Ānī i, 421a, **507a**; 637b, 638a, 639a; iv, 347b, 670a; v, 452a; vi, 64b, 274a; ix, 169a –I, 432b, **522b**, 658b, 659a, b; IV, 362b, 697a, b; V, 454b; VI, 62b, 259a; IX, 174b
Ānis (Yemen) vi, 436b – VI, 422a
Anīs, Mīr Babar ʿAlī (1874) i, **508b**; ii, 73b; iii, 119b; vi, 610b, 611b; s, **74b**, 358b – I, **524a**; II, 74b; III, 122a; VI, 595b, 596a, b; S, **75a**, 358b
Anīs al-Dawla (XVIII) vi, 529b – VI, 513b
ʿAnḳāʾ i, **509a**; iii, 169a; iv, 928a; ix, 615b –
I, 5**24b**; III, 173a; IV, 961a; IX, 638b
ʿAnkā, Muḥammad (1962) x, 958b – X,
ʿAnkabūt i, **509a** – I, **524b**
Ankalāy (Zand͟j) (IX) vii, 526b – VII, 526b
Anḳara i, **509b**, 974b; vii, 776a; s, 47b, 318a – I, **525a**, 1004b; VII, 778a; S, 48a, 318a
—university/-é ii, 425b – II, 436b
Anḳārawī → Ismāʿīl Anḳārawī
al-Ankubarda (Lombardy/-ie) → Īṭaliya
Anmār, Banū i, 73a, 865a – I, 75a, 889b
Anna → Sikka
al-ʿAnnāba (Bône) i, **511b**; iv, 359b; vi, 427a, 741a; s, 103a, 156a – I, **527a**; IV, 375a; VI, 412a, 730a; S, 102b, 156b
Annam iii, 1210b, 1211a – III, 1241a, b
ʿAnnāzid(e)s i, **512a**; iii, 258b; v, 453b –
I, **527b**; III, 265b; 456b
Anniyya i, **513b** – I, **529a**; v, 456b
ʿAns, Banū vi, 566a; vii, 591b – VI, 551a; VII, 591a
Anṣāb → Nuṣb
ʿAnsabā (river/fleuve) vi, 628a – VI, 613a
Anṣār (Sudan/Soudan) v, 1249a, b, 1251a, 1252b – V, 1240a, b, 1241b, 1243b
al-Anṣār i, 45a, 55a, 110a, 305a, **514a**, 545a, 771a, 990b; ii, 728b; iii, 226b, 285b; iv, 1187a; v, 435a, 995a, 996b; s, 10a –
I, 46b, 57a, 113a, 314b, **529b**, 562a, 794a, 1021b; II, 747a; III, 233b, 294a; IV, 1220a; V, 437b, 990a, 991b, S, 9b
ʿAnsāra i, **515a** – I, **530b**
al-Anṣārī → ʿAbd al-Ḳuddūs; Abū Zayd; al-Awsī; Zakāriyyāʾ
al-Anṣārī (XV) s, 125a – S, 124a

al-Anṣārī, Abu 'l-Ḳāsim Sulaymān b. Nāṣir s, 346b – S, 346b
Anṣārī, Djābir b. ʿAbd Allāh → Djābir b. ʿAbd Allāh
Anṣārī, Muḥammad Amīn (XIX) s, 74a, 75a – S, 74b, 75b
al-AnsārL, Shaykh ʿAbd Allāh Ibrāhīm (XX) x, 147a- X, 159a
Anṣārī, Shaykh Ḥusayn s, 75a – S, 75b
Anṣārī, Shaykh Murtaḍā (1864) v, 1087b; vi, 552a, b; vii, 960b; s, **75a** – V, 1085a; VI, 536b, 537a; VII, 961b; S, **75b**
al-Anṣārī al-Harawī, ʿAbd Allāh (1089) i, 69b, 417a, **515b**, 936b; iii, 84a, 161a, 177b, 821b, 1148b; iv, 63b, 473a, 697a, 1057b; vi, 353a, 381a, 454b, 455b; viii, 539a, 574b; s, 292a –
I, 71b, 428b, 31a, 965b; III, 86a, 164b, 181b, 845b, 1176b; IV, 67a, 494a, 725b, 1089a; VI, 337a, 365a, 440a, 441a; VIII, 557a, 598b; S, 291b
al-Anṣārī al-Ḥusayn b. Yaḥyā (VIII) s, 82a – S, 81b
Anṣāriyya vi, 582a – VI, 567a
Anshary, Isa (XX) vi, 731b, 732a – VI, 721a
al-ʿAnsī → Abu 'l-Mughīra; ʿUmar b. Hāniʾ
al-ʿAnsī, al-Aswad (Yemen) (VII) vii, 592a – VII, 591b
ʿAnṣra → ʿAnṣāra
al-Anṭākī vi, 114a – VI, 111b
al-Anṭākī, Dāwūd (1599) i, **516a**, 594a; ii, 238a; iv, 1134a; s, 40b – I, **531b**, 613b; II, 244a; IV, 1165b; S, 40b
al-Anṭākī, Yaḥyā b. Saʿīd (1066) i, **516a**; iii, 81b – I, **531b**; III, 83b
Anṭākiya i, 182b, 466a, **516b**, 761b, 1125b; iii, 12b; v, 437a, 921b; vi, 3a, 322a, 379a, b, 381b, 505b, 506a, 507a, 544a, 578a, b ; viii, 128a –
I, 187b, 480a, **532a**, 784b, 1159b; III, 13a; V, 439b, 927a; VI, 3a, 306b, 363b, 364a, 365b, 491a, 492a, 528b, 563a, b; VIII, 131a
Antalya i, 476b, **517b**; iv, 816b; vi, 120b; x, 412a,b – I, 490b, **533a**; IV, 849a; VI, 118a; X, 441b, 442a
ʿAntar, Sīrat i, **518a**, 521b; ii, 236b, 238b; iii, 111b; v, 951b; vi, 78b, 752b –
I, **533b**, 537b; II, 243a, 245a; III, 114a; V, 955a; VI, 76b, 742a
ʿAntar b. Shaddād (VI) ii, 236b; vii, 254b; viii, 239a – II, 243a; VII, 256a; VIII, 244b
ʿAntara b. Shaddād (VI) i, 25a, **521a**; vi, 490a; vii, 254b; viii, 239a; s, 38b, 178b –
I, 26a, **537a**; VI, 476a; VII, 256a; VIII, 244b; S, 39a, 179b
ʿAntarī i, **522a** – I, **537b**
Anṭartūs → Ṭartūs
Antel → Djelāl, Ṣadreddīn
Antemuru, Banū i, **522a** – I, **538a**
Antep → ʿAyntāb
Antioch/-e → Antāḳiya
Anṭūn Faraḥ → Faraḥ Anṭūn
Anūdjūr → Unūdjūr
Anūsha b. Abi 'l-Ghāzī, Khān (Khīwa) (XVII) iv, 754a; vi, 417a; s, 281a, 420a – IV, 784b; VI, 402a; S, 281a, 420a
Anūsharwān (Chosroës I) i, **522b** – I, **538b**
Anūshirwān (Ilkhān) (1353) ii, 47a – II, 48a
Anūshirwān, Khusraw → Kisrā
Anūshirwān b. Ḳābūs iv, 100b – IV, 105a
Anūshirwān b. Khālid (1138) i, **522b**; iii, 221a, 327b, 1158a; iv, 265a; vi, 64a, b, 782a; vii, 735a – I, **538b**; III, 228a, 337b, 1186b; IV, 277a; VI, 62a, b, 772a; VII, 735b
Anūshirwān b. Khātūn (Saldjūḳ) (XI) v, 388a – V, 389a
Anūshirwān b. Ṭughrilbeg v, 388a – V, 389a
Anūshtekin → Anūshtigin
Anūshtigin al-Duzbarī (general) (XI) ii, 484a, 854b; vii, 117a, 1017b – II, 496a, 874a; VII, 119a, 1019b
Anūshtigin Gharčaʾī (Khwārazm-shāh) (1097) ii, 1011a, 1082a; iv, 1064a, 1067a; viii, 942b; ix, 16a; s, 279a –
II, 1034b, 1107a; IV, 1095b, 1098b; VIII, 975a; IX, 16b; S, 279a
Anūshtigin Shīrgīr, amīr (XII) i, 1359b – I, 1399b
Anwāʾ i, **523a**; iv, 518b; s, 380b – I, **538b**; IV, 541a; S, 380b
Anwākshūṭ → Nouakchott
Ānwar (XIX) ii, 222a – II, 228b
Anwār al-Ḥaḳḳ, shāh s, 293a – S, 293a
Anwār-i Suhaylī → Kalīla wa Dimna
Anwarī, Awḥad al-Dīn Khāwarānī (1189) i, **524a**, 1301a; ii, 1034a; iii, 1115a; vi, 608b; vii, 1019a; viii, 971a; s, 21b, 65a, 240a –
I, **540a**, 1341a; II, 1058a; III, 1142a; VI, 593a; VII, 1021a; VIII, 1005a; S, 21b, 65b, 240a
Anwarī, al-Ḥādjdj Saʿdullah → Enwerī
ʿAnz b. Wāʾil, Banū i, 709a – I, 729b
Anzarūt s, **77b** – S, **77b**
Apamea/-ée → Afāmiya
Apolaffar (Abū Djaʿfar) (amīr) (843) i, 1166a; iv, 275a – I, 1201a; IV, 287a
Apollonius of/de Tyana → Balīnūs
Aprīdīs → Afrīdī
ʿĀr iii, 396a; s, 53a, **78a**, 191a – III, 408b; S, 53b, **78a**, 192a
al-ʿĀra i, **524b** – I, **540a**
al-ʿArab i, **524b**; iii, 1098a – I, **540b**; III, 1125a
ʿArab, Djazīrat al- i, 102b, **533b**; s, 213b – I, 105b, **550a**; S, 213b
—administration i, **539a**, 976a – I, **555b**, 1006a
—demography/démographie s, 213b – S, 213b
—ethnography/-ie i, 39a, 436a, **543b**, 872a – I, 40a, 448b, **560b**, 896b
—flora and/et fauna i, **540a** – **I, 556b**
—geography/-ie i, 156a, 534b, 1230a, b; iii, 124a – I, 160b, **551a**, 1266b, 1267a, b; III, 127a
—history/histoire i, **547a-555a**; 773a, 881a – I, **564b-572b**; III, 796a, 905a
Arab League → al-Djāmiʿa al-ʿArabiyya
Arab Legion i, 46a; iii, 264b, 1258b
ʿArab Maḥmūd → Maḥmūd Shewḳat Pasha
ʿArab Muḥammad Khān (Shaybānid(e)) (XVII) i, 120b; v, 24a – I, 124a; V, 24b
Arab Revolt i, 46a; ii, 289a, 872a; iii, 263b, 643b
Arab Socialist Union s, 8a, 9a
Araba i, 205b, **556b**; v, 659a – I, 211b, **574b**; V, 663b
Ababnī, Arabaynī i, 176b; iii, 3b – I, 181a; III, 3b
Arabesque i, 498b, 501a, **558b**; ii, 557a, 777b, 864a; iii, 219b; v, 232b, 991a –
I, 513b, 516a, **576b**; II, 571a, 796a, 884a; III, 226a; V, 230b, 986a
ʿArabfaḳīh, Shihāb al-Dīn (XVI) i, **561a** – I, **579a**
ʿArabī Dafaʿ Allāh (XVII) i, 1157a; v, 1251a – I, 1191a; V, 1242a
ʿArābī Pasha → ʿUrābī Pasha
Arabia/-e → ʿArab, Djazīrat al-
Arabie Séoudite → al-Suʿūdiyya
ʿArabistān i, 561b; iii, 1102a; iv, 1171b; v, 80b, 81a; vi, 495a; vii, 673b, 675a –
I, 579a; III, 1129a; IV, 1204b; V, 82b, 83a; VI, 480b; VII, 673a, 674b
ʿArabiyya i, 157b, 501b, **561b**; ii, 167a, 280a, 306b; 468b, 472a, 490b; iii, 1216a, 1259a; v, 185b, 605b, 804a, 914a, 915b, 1091b, 1093a, 1203a, 1207a –
I, 162a, 516b, **579a**; II, 172b, 288b, 315b, 480b, 484a, 502b; III, 1247a, 1292a; V, 183a, 609b, 810a, 919b, 921a, 1088b, 1090a, 1193b, 1197b
al-ʿArabiyya (Ṭarīḳa) s, 411a – S, 411b
al-ʿArabiyya, Djazīrat i, 535b, **603a** – I, 552a, **622b**

'Arabkīr i, **603a** – I, **622b**
Arab(e)s → al-'Arab; Musta'riba
'Arabshāhid(e)s → Khʷārazm
'Arab-zāde vi, 971a – VI, 963b
'Araḍ i, 128b, **603b** – I, 132a, **623a**
'Arāḍ → al-Muḥarrak
al-A'rāf i, **603b** – I, **623b**
'Arafa, 'Arafāt i, 43b, **604a**; iii, 31b, 35b; vi, 45a,
    105b, 148a, 154a, 155a, 162a, 169b, 659a; s, 33a – I,
    44b, **623b**; III, 33a, 37a; VI, 44a, 103a, 146b, 152a,
    156a, 160b, 644b; S, 33b
'Arafa, Mawlāy → Muḥammad b. 'Arafa
'Arafa, Sīdī (al-Ḳayrawān) (XVI) iii, 69a; iv, 828a – III,
    71b; IV, 861a
Arafale vi, 643b – VI, 628b
Araghūn s, **80a** – S, **79b**
al-Arā'ish i, 356a, **604b**; v, 1245b; s, 29a –
    I, 367a, **624a**; V, 1236a; S, 29a
Arāk → Sultānābād
Arāk (Iran) s, 342a – S, 341b
al-Arak (Alarcos) i, 165b, **605b** – I, 170b, **625a**
Arakan i, **606a**, 1333a; ii, 32a – I, **625b**, 1272b; II, 32b
Arak'el of/de Tabrīz s, 275a – S, 274b
Arāḳim, Banū x, 91a – X, 98a
Aral Sea i, 456a, **606b**; s, 169a, 244b –
    I, 469a, **626b**; S, 169a, 244b
Ārām Shāh (Mu'izzī, Delhi) (1211) ii, 267a; iii,
    416a, 1155a; s, 360a – II, 275b; III, 429a, 1183b; S,
    359b
Arar → Harar
Ararat → Aghri Dagh
Aras, Araxes → al-Rass
Arat, Reshīd Raḥmetī (1964) s, **82a** – S, **82a**
Arayabnī → Arababnī
Arbā', Banū i, 371b – I, 382b
Arba'a (Mānd) vi, 384b – VI, 368b
Arbāb → Rabb
Arbad → Irbid
al-Arba'ī x, 141a – X, 151a
'Arbān i, **608a** – I, **628a**
Arba'ūn Ḥadīthᵃⁿ s, **82b** – S, **82b**
Arbela → Irbid
Arbeles → Irbil
al-'Arbī (Larbi) Bakkūsh, Banū s, 387a – S, 387a
Arbil v, 455b, 456a – V, 458a, b
'Arbīlī, Ibrāhīm (XIX) ii, 471a – II, 483a
Arbira → Irbil
Arbūna (Narbonne) i, **608b**; iii, 495a; v, 1121a – I,
    628a; III, 512a; V, 1117b
Archidona → Urḏjuḏhūna
Architecture i, 457b, **608b**; ii, 288a, 340b, 557a; iii,
    142, 143, 228b, 1123b, 1267a; iv, 236a, b; v, 12a,
    1136a –
    I, 470b, **628b**; II, 296a, 350a, 571a; III, 146, 147,
    235b, 1151b, 1300a; IV, 246b; V, 11a, 1131b
—al-Andalus i, **497b**; ii, 1014b-1019a – I, **512b**; II,
    1038a-1042b
—India/Inde, Indonesia/-ésie ii, 598a, 1103b; iii,
    148a, 440b, 1227b – II, 613a, 1129b; III, 151a, 454b,
    1259a
Arči i, **624b**, 756a; ii, 88b – I, **645a**, 778b; II, 90b
Arcos → Arkush
Arcot i, **624b**; iii, 320a; vi, 535b – I, **645a**; III, 331a;
    VI, 520a
Arctic/Arctique → Baḥr al-Ẓulma (al-Ẓulumāt)
Arḍ i, **625a**; ii, 93a, 900b – I, **645b**; II, 94b, 921b
'Arḍ → Isti'rāḍ
'Arḍ ḥāl i, **625a** – I, **646a**
Arḍ al-Sidra → Saḳḳāra
Arḍ al-Ṭibr, – al-Dhahab vii, 245b – VII, 247a
Arḍ al-Waḳwaḳ vii, 245b – VII, 247a

Ardabb → Kayl
Ardabīl i, **625a**, 837a; ii, 88a, 598b; iv, 7b, 49a, 1170a;
    v, 244a; vi, 120a, 498b, 499a, 500a, 633b; viii, 755a,
    b; s, 139a, 140a –
    I, **646a**, 860b; II, 89b, 613b; IV, 8b, 51b, 1203a; V,
    241b; VI, 117b, 483b, 484b, 485a, 618b; VIII, 777a;
    S, 138b, 139b
al-Ardabīlī, Aḥmad b. Muḥammad (1585) viii, 778b –
    VIII, 804b
Ardabīlī, Mīrzā Naṣr Allāh Ṣadr al-Mamālik (XIX) vii,
    453a – VII, 454a
Ardabīlī, Ṣafī al-Dīn → Ṣafī al-Dīn
al-Ardabīlī, Uways al-Laṭīfī (XV) viii, 542b – VIII,
    560a
Ardahān i, 468b, **626a**, 643b – I, 482b, **646b**, 664a
Ardakān i, **626a**; s, 342a – I, **646b**; S, 341b
Ardalān i, **626b**; v, 170a; vi, 495b – I, **647a**; V, 167b;
    VI, 480b
Ardashāt i, 645b – I, 666a
Ardashīr (Bāwandid(e)) → Ḥusām al-Dawla
Ardashīr I (Sāsānid(e)) (241) i, 2b, 305b, 528a, 548b,
    626b, 1341b; ii, 16b, 135b, 925b; iii, 112b, 113a,
    394a; iv, 809b; vi, 633a –
    I, 2b, 315a, 544a, 566a, **647a**, 1381b; II, 16b, 139a,
    947a; III, 115a, b, 406b; IV, 842a; VI, 618a
Ardashīr II (Sāsānid(e)) (383) i, 626b; ix, 74b – I,
    647a; IX, 78a
Ardashīr III (Sāsānid(e)) (629) i, 626b; ix, 80a – I,
    647a; IX, 83b
Ardashīr Khurra → Fīrūzābād
Ardibehisht → Ta'rīkh
Ardistān i, **626b**; iv, 99b; v, 1147b; vi, 365b; s, 23b – I,
    647b; IV, 104a; V, 1139a; VI, 349b; S, 23b
Ardjastānī, Muḥammad Ḥusayn b. 'Abd Allāh Shahrabī
    (XIX) vi, 609b – VI, 594a
al-'Ardjī, 'Abd Allāh b. 'Umar (738) i, 10b, 305a,
    626b; ii, 428b, 1011b, 1029b, 1030b –
    I, 10b, 314b, **647b**; II, 439b, 1035a, 1053a, 1054a
Ardjīsh i, **627a**; iv, 587a – I, **647b**; IV, 609b
Ardjīsh-Da → Erdjiyās Daghi
Ardjumand Bānū Bēgam (XVII) vii, 332b – VII, 334a
Ardjun Singh, Guru (Sikh) (1605) ii, 380b; iii, 424a;
    vii, 315a – II, 390b; III, 437b; VII, 317a
Ardjūna (Arjona) vii, 1021a – VII, 1023a
Ardumusht s, 36a, 37a – S, 36b, 37a
Ardzrunī i, 637a, b – I, 658a
Areg (Reg) → 'Irḳ
Areshgūl → Tafna
'Arfaḍja b. Harthama al-Bārikī (VII) ii, 811b – II, 831a
Argan i, **627b** – I, **648a**
Arghana → Ergani
Arghen → Hargha
Arghiyān s, **83a** – S, **83a**
Arghūn (Mongols) i, 148a, 227b, 228a, **627b**; iii,
    420a, 632b; vi, 189b – I, 152a, 234b, 235a, **648a**; III,
    433b, 654a; VI, 173a
Arghūn b. Abaḳa (Īlkhān) (1291) i, 346b; ii, 606b,
    607b; iii, 1122a; iv, 31a, 621a; v, 102b, 662b, 827a;
    vi, 16a, 494a, 502a; viii, 702b –
    I, 357a; II, 621b, 622b; III, 1150a; IV, 33b, 645b; V,
    105a, 668a, 833a; VI, 14a, 479b, 487b; VIII, 722b
Arghūn Āḳā (XIII) ii, 606a; iv, 30b – II, 621a; IV, 32b
Arghūn al-'Alā'ī (Miṣr) (XIV) vii, 170b; viii, 986a; ix,
    154b – VII, 172b; VIII, 1020b; IX, 159b
Arghūn al-Dawādār (1312) vi, 323a – VI, 307b
Arghūn al-Nāṣirī (1330) iii, 954b; vii, 992a – III, 979a;
    VII, 993b
Arghūn Shāh (1331) viii, 894b – VIII, 925b
Arghūn Shāh (1349) iii, 818a – III, 841b
Arghūn Shāh b. Kilidj Arslan II (XIII) i, 431b – I, 444a
Argungu (Gwandu) ii, 1146b – II, 1173b

Argyrocastro → Ergiri
al-Arḥabī, Mālik b. Kaʿb (VII) viii, 118b – VIII, 121a
al-Arḥabī, Yazīd b. Kays (VII) viii, 853b – VIII, 883a
ʿArīb (singer/chanteur) (IX) iv, 821b; x, 810b – IV, 854b; X,
ʿArīb b. Saʿd al-Kātib al-Ḳurṭubī (980) i, 491b, 600a, **628a**; viii, 352a, 822b – I, 506b, 620a, **649a**; VIII, 364b, 850b
al-ʿĀriḍ → Ibn Saʿdān
al-ʿĀriḍ (Nadjd) i, 72b, 126b, **628b** – I, 74b, 130b, **649a**
ʿArīda, Nasīb (XX) v, 1254b, 1255a, b; vi, 91a – V, 1245b, 1246a, b; VI, 89a
ʿArīf i, 438b, **629a**; iv, 532a – I, 451a, **649b**; IV, 555a
ʿĀrif → Djalāl al-Dīn; Muḥammad
ʿArīf, ʿAbd al-Bāḳī (1713) vi, 112b – VI, 110a
ʿĀrif, ʿAbd al-Raḥmān (XX) v, 469a – V, 471b, 472a
ʿĀrif, ʿAbd al-Salām (1963) iii, 1259a; iv, 719a; v, 468b, 469a; vi, 29a – III, 1292a; IV, 748a; V, 471a, b; VI, 27a
ʿĀrif, Abu ʾl-Ḳāsim (1934) iv, 789b – IV, 821b
ʿĀrif, Amīr → ʿĀrif Čelebī
ʿĀrif, Mīrzā Abu ʾl-Ḳāsim (1934) s, **83b** – S, **83b**
ʿĀrif al-ʿĀrif (XX) s, 67b – S, 68a
ʿĀrif Čelebī (1320) s, **83b** – S, **83a**
ʿĀrif Hikmet (calligraphe/-r) (1918) iv, 1126b – IV, 1158a
ʿArif Hikmet Bey (1859) i, 71a, **630a**; v, 263b, 1005a – I, 73a, **651a**; V, 261b, 1000b
ʿĀrif Ḥikmet Hersekli → Hersekli
ʿĀrif Pasha (XIX) iv, 876b – IV, 909b
ʿĀrif al-Shihābī (XX) iii, 519a, b – III, 537a, b
ʿĀrif, Ulu → ʿĀrif Čelebī
ʿĀrif al-Zayn (1960) vii, 780b – VII, 782a
ʿĀrifī, Mawlānā Maḥmūd (1449) iv, 67a; s, **84a** – IV, 70b; S, **84a**
Arïgh Böke b. Toluy b. Činghiz Khān (Mongol) (1266) i, 1188a; ii, 3a, 45b; iv, 811b; v, 38b, 300a; vii, 230a – I, 1223a; II, 3a, 46b; IV, 844b; V, 40a, 299b; VII, 232a
Arīn → Ḳubbat al-Arḍ
al-ʿArīsh i, **630b**; vi, 195a – I, **651a**; VI, 179a
Aristotle/Aristote → Arisṭūṭalīs
Aristotle, Theology of i, 349b, 416b, 449b, 514a, 631a; ii, 554b, 949a; iii, 644a, 942b; v, 701a, 842a
Aristote, Théologie d' I, 360b, 428a, 462b, 529b, 651b; II, 568b, 971a; III, 665b, 967b; V, 706a, 848b
Arisṭūṭālīs/Arisṭū i, 178b, 235b, 342a, 349b, 350a, 419b, 513b, **630b**, 736b, 795b, 1083b, 1155b, 1340a; ii, 101b, 249a, 358b, 493a, 550a, 740a, 765a, 770a, 779b, 948b; iii, 21b, 29b, 301b, 509a, 596b, 915b, 942b, 1130a; vi, 203b, 220a – I, 183b, 243a, 352b, 360b, 431a, 529a, **651b**, 758b, 819a, 1116a, 1190a, 1380b; II, 103b, 256a, 368b, 505b, 563b, 758b, 783b, 788b, 798a, 970b; III, 22b, 31b, 310b, 526b, 617a, 939b, 967b, 1158a; VI, 188a, 214a
Ariyaruk (XI) ii, 336a – II, 345b
ʿĀriyya i, **633a** – I, **654a**
Arḳa → ʿIrḳa
Arkalī Khān b. Fīrūz Shāh II Djalāl al-Dīn Khaldjī (XIV) i, 1036a; iv, 920b, 921a – I, 1067b; IV, 953b, 954a
al-Arḳam b. Abi ʾl-Arḳam Makhzūmī (624) i, **633b**; vi, 138a – I, **654a**; VI, 136b
Arkān → Rukn
Ārkāt → Arcot
Arkiko vi, 641b, 642a, b, 643a, b – VI, 626b, 627b, 628a, b, 629a
Arkush i, 6a, **633b**; vii, 761a – I, 6a, **654b**; VII, 762b
Armāʾīl (VIII) vi, 744a – VI, 733b
Armenia/-énie → Armīniya
Armenian/Arménien (language/langue) iv, 350b, 351b; v, 1a – IV, 365b, 366b; V, 1a
Armenians/Arméniens i, 470b, 638b, 666a; ii, 65b; iii, 214b; iv, 8a, 99a, 240b, 241b, 476a, 485b; v, 1a, 136b, 462b; ix, 163a, 167a; s, 274b, 275a, b – I, 484b, 659a, 686b; II, 66b; III, 220b; IV, 8b-9a, 103a, 251a, b, 252a, 497a, 506b; V, 1a, 139b, 465b; IX, 271b, 275b; S, 274b
Armīniya i, 10a, 18a, 64b, 77a, 465a, 470a, **634a**, 660a, 1052a; ii, 37a, 678b; iii, 12b; iv, 89b, 90a, 344b, 345b, 347b; v, 292a; vi, 230b, 274a, 334a, 335a, 337b, 338a, 427b, 499a, 670b; s, 225b, 365a – I, 10a, 18b, 66b, 79b, 478b, 484b, **655a**, 680b, 1084a; II, 37b, 695b; III, 13a; IV, 93b, 94a, 359a, 360b, 362a; V, 292a; VI, 224b, 259a, 318b, 319a, 322a, b, 412b, 484b, 657a; S, 225b, 365a
Armiyā → Irmiyā
Arnab s, **84b** – S, **84a**
Arnawutluḳ i, **650a**, 1090b, 1118b, 1162a; ii, 184a, 721a; iv, 342b, 1173b; v, 265a, 276b, 284b; vi, 59b, 71b, 74a; s, 149b – I, **670a**, 1123a, 1152a, 1196b; II, 190a, 739b; IV, 357a, 1206b; V, 262b, 274b, 283a; VI, 57b, 69b, 72a; S, 149b
Arnedo → Arnīṭ
Arnīṭ i, **658a** – I, **678b**
ʿArnūn → Ḳalʿat al-Shaḳīf
Aror → Arūr
Arpa i, **658a** – I, **679a**
Arpā Khān (Čingizid(e)) (1336) ii, 45b, 401a; iii, 1208a – II, 46b, 411b; III, 1239a
Arpalïḳ i, **658a** – I, **679a**
Arrabal iii, 74a – III, 76b
ʿArrāda i, 556b, **658b**; iii, 469b, 470a, 482a – I, 574b, **679b**; III, 486a, b, 499a
Arradjān i, **659a**; vi, 120a; s, 119a – I, **679b**; VI, 117b; S, 118b
al-Arradjānī, Abū Bakr Aḥmad (1149) i, **659b**; iv, 863b; s, 326b – I, **680a**; IV, 897a; S, 326a
al-Arradjānī, Naṣiḥ al-Dīn Abū Bakr Aḥmad (1149) viii, 971a – VIII, 1005a
ʿArrāf i, **659b**; iv, 421b – I, **680a**; IV, 440a
ʿArrām al-Sulāmī (IX) ix, 817b – IX, 852b
Arrān i, 639a, 642a, **660a**, 1041a; ii, 975b; iii, 1110b; iv, 344b, 345b, 347b, 573a; vi, 274a, 275b, 337a, 500a – I, 659b, 662b, **680b**, 1072b; II, 998a; III, 1138a; IV, 359a, b, 360b, 362b, 595b; VI, 259a, 260b, 321b, 485a, b
Arri(u)zafa → al-Ruṣāfa (al-Andalus)
ʿArṣat al-Nīl (Marrākush) vi, 596b – VI, 581b
Arsenius (patriarch(e)) (1010) iii, 79a – III, 81b
ʿArsh → Kursī
ʿArsh (Algeria/Algérie) i, **661a**; iv, 362a – I, **681b**; IV, 377b
Arshad al-Dawla (1911) vii, 432b – VII, 433b
Arshakawah vi, 201a – VI, 185a
Arshashdib → Arči
Arshgūl i, **661b**; s, 376b – I, **682a**; S, 377a
Arshīn → Dhirāʿ
Arslan i, **661b** – I, **682b**
Arslan b. Aḳ Sunḳur → Arslān Abīhī
Arslan b. Saldjūḳ (1034) i, **661b**, 1292a; ii, 4a, b, 1108b; iii, 1114a – I, **682b**, 1331b; II, 4b, 1134b; III, 1141b
Arslan b. Toghrïl b. Muḥammad, Muʿizz al-Dīn (Saldjūḳ) (1176) iii, 1110b; vi, 482a, 500a; viii, 239b – III, 1137b; VI, 468a, 485b; VIII, 245a
Arslan Āba, Atabeg → Āḳ-Sunḳur II
Arslan Abīhī, Nuṣrat al-Dīn (Marāgha) (1175) i, 300b; ii, 764b – I, 310a; II, 783a

Arslan Agha (XVII) vii, 319a – VII, 321b
Arslan Arghūn (Saldjūḳ) (1096) i, **662a**, 1051b, 1331b; iv, 1067a; vii, 489b – I, **683a**, 1083a, b, 1372b; IV, 1098b; VII, 489a
Arslan Beg (Abkhāz) (XIX) i, 101a – I, 104a
Arslan Beg b. Balangirī → Khāṣṣ Beg Arslān
Arslan Isrāʾīl → Arslān b. Saldjūḳ
Arslan Khān (Dihlī) (XIII) vi, 47b, 48a – VI, 46a, b
Arslan Khān (Ḳarlūḳ) (XIII) iii, 1115a, 1120a; iv, 808b; ix, 67a – III, 1142b, 1148a; IV, 841a; IX, 70a
Arslan Khān b. Kılıdj Arslan II (Saldjūḳ) (XII) viii, 15b – VIII, 15b
Arslan Khān Aḥmad → Aḥmad Khān b. Ḥasan
Arslan Khān Muḥammad b.ʿAlī (Ilek-Khān) (1024) v, 45b; s, 245b – V, 47a; S, 245b
Arslan Khān Muḥammad II (Samarḳand) ix, 15b – IX, 16a
Arslan Khātūn bint Čaghrī Beg Dāwūd (XI) iv, 26b, 466a – IV, 28b, 487a
Arslan Shāh b. Ḳïlïdj Arslān II (Rūm Saldjūḳ) (XII) viii, 15b – VIII, 15b
Arslan Shāh I b. Kirmān Shāh, amīr (Saldjūḳ) (Kirmān) (1142) iv, 466a; v, 159b; vii, 535b; viii, 945b – IV, 487a; V, 158b; VII, 535a; VIII, 978a
Arslan Shāh b. Masʿūd III (Ghaznawid(e)) (1118) i, 217b, 940a; ii, 893b, 1052a; vii, 535b; ix, 15b – I, 224a, 968b; II, 914b, 1076b; VII, 535b; IX, 16a
Arslan Shāh b. Masʿūd (Zangid(e)) → Zangid(e)s
Arslan Shāh b. Tughrïl Shāh II (Saldjūḳ) (1176) i, 940b; iii, 197b; v, 160a; viii, 944b – I, 969a; III, 202b; V, 158b; VIII, 977a
Arslan Tepe vi, 230a – VI, 224a
Arslanlï → Sikka
Arsūf i, **662b**; vi, 322a – I, **683b**; VI, 306b
Artena → Eretna
Artuḳ b. Ekseb (Artuḳid(e)) (1091) i, 662b; ii, 384b; v, 328a; vi, 274b; viii, 947a – I, 683b; II, 395a; V, 328a; VI, 259b; VIII, 979b
Artūḳ İnaḳ (1740) vi, 418a; s, 420a – VI, 403a; S, 420a
Artuḳid(e)s i, 466b, 467a, 639a, **662b**; ii, 344a, 613b; iii, 507a, 1099a, 1118a, 1197b; iv, 464b; v, 454b; vi, 274b, 540b, 542b, 930b; vii, 273b; ix, 68b; s, 266b – I, 480a, b, 659b, **683b**; II, 354a, 629a; III, 524a, 1126a, 1145b, 1228a; IV, 485a; V, 457a; VI, 259b, 525a, 527a, 922b; VII, 275b; IX, 71b; S, 266a
Artvin i, **667b**; ii, 62a – I, **688a**; II, 63b
ʿArūba → Taʾrīkh
ʿArūḍ i, **667b**; ii, 159b, 834b; iii, 672a; iv, 57a, 326b, 714b, 1187b – I, **688a**; II, 164b, 854a; III, 693b; IV, 60a, 340b, 743a, 1220b
Arūḍī → Niẓāmī Arūḍī
ʿArūdj (Barbarossa) (1518) i, 367b, 368a, **677b**; ii, 520a, 537b, 839b; iv, 361a, b, 1155b; v, 504a; vii, 64b; s, 80b – I, 378b, **698b**; II, 533a, 550b, 859a; IV, 377a, 1187b; V, 507a; VII, 65a; S, 80a
Arung Palakka (Sulawesi) (1696) ix, 813b – IX, 848b
Arūr i, **679a**; v, 817a – I, **699b**; V, 823a
ʿArūs, Banū i, 604b – I, 624b
ʿArūs resmi i, **679a**; ii, 147a – I, **700a**; II, 151a
al-ʿArūsī al-Tilimsānī → Ibn ʿArūs
ʿArūsiyya i, **679b**; iii, 713b; vi, 355a; x, 248a; s, 93a – I, **700a**; III, 735b; VI, 339a; X, 266b; S, 92b
Arwā bint Aḥmad al-Sayyida (Sulayḥid(e)) ix, 816a, b – IX, 851a, b
Arwād/Ruwād i, 935b; iii, 475a; vi, 538a; s, 120b – I, 964b; III, 491b; VI, 522b; S, 120a
Arwand-rūd → Shaṭṭ al-ʿArab
Arya Damar (Palembang) iii, 1219a – III, 1250a
Arya Dilah (ʿAbd Allāh) (Palembang) (1486) viii, 245a – VIII, 251a
Arya Kusuma ʿAbd al-Raḥīm, Susuhunan (Palembang) (1706) viii, 245a – VIII, 251a
Aryāṭ al-Ḥabashī viii, 979b – VIII, 1014a
Arzachel → al-Zarḳālī
Arzan i, **679b**; ii, 712a – I, **700a**; II, 730b
Arzan al-Rūm → Erzurum
Ārzāw i, **680a** – I, **700b**
Arzila → Aṣīla
Ārzū, Khān (1756) i, **680a**; iv, 526b – I, **701a**; IV, 549a
Ās → Alān
Ās (myrt(l)e) s, **87a** – S, **87a**
ʿAṣā i, **680b**; iv, 377b – I, **701a**; IV, 394a
al-Asʿāʾ (Mahra) vi, 81a – VI, 79a
ʿAṣaba → Mīrāth
ʿAṣabiyya i, **681a**; ii, 962b; iii, 830b; iv, 46a – I, 701b, II, 984b; III, 854a; IV, 48b
Asad → Minṭaḳat al-Burūdj; Nudjūm
al-Asad (lion) i, **681a** – I, **702a**
Asad, Banū i, 99a, 528a, b, **683a**, 1241a, 1358b; iii, 1177a; vi, 145a, 146a, 965a; vii, 373b – I, 101b, 544a, b, **704a**, 1279a, 1398b; III, 1206a; VI, 143a, 144a, 957b; VII, 375a
Asad, Banū (ancient tribe/tribu ancienne) i, **684b**; ii, 71b; iv, 820a; v, 348a; s, 19b, 20a, 304b – I, **705b**; II, 73a; IV, 853a; V, 349a; S, 19b, 20a, 304a
Asad b. ʿAbd Allāh al-Ḳasrī (738) i, **684b**, 760a, 1001a, 1033a, 1293a; ii, 1010b; iii, 223b, 493b; iv, 54b, 926b; v, 2a, b, 47b, 76a, 856a; vii, 1016a; x, 590b, 925a – I, **705b**, 782b, 1032a, 1065a, 1332b; II, 1034a; III, 230b, 510b; IV, 57b, 959b; V, 2a, b, 49a, 78a, 862b; VII, 1018a; X,
Asʿad b. Abī Yaʿfur (Yuʿfir) (Ḥiwālid(e)) (905) iv, 661a; vi, 439a; s, 335a – IV, 688a; VI, 424b; S, 334b
Asad b. al-Furāt (ḳāḍī) (828) i, 248b, 249b, 250a, **685a**; iii, 817a; iv, 733a, 829b; v, 1159b; vi, 279a, 280b, 751a; vii, 186b; viii, 843b; ix, 584a, 669b – I, 256a, 257a, 258a, **706a**; III, 840b; IV, 762b, 862b; V, 1149a; VI, 264a, 265b, 740b; VII, 187a; VIII, 873b; IX, 606b, 696b
al-Asʿad Ibn Mammātī → Ibn Mammātī
Asad b. Mūsā b. Ibrāhīm (827) s, **87b** – S, **87b**
Asʿad b. Shihāb (Ṣanʿāʾ) (XI) iii, 125b – III, 128a
Asʿad b. Zurāra (VII) vii, 649b – VII, 649a
Asʿad Abū Ḳarib al-Ḥimyarī (Tubbaʿ) iv, 318b – IV, 332b
Asad Allāh b. Ḥasan b. Riḍā al-Dīn (Marʿashī) (XV) vi, 513b, 514a – VI, 499a
Asad Allāh b. Mīr Zayn al-Dīn Marʿashī, Amīr (1555) vi, 516b – VI, 501b
Asad Allāh ʿAlam (1978) vii, 448a – VII, 449a
Asad Allāh Ḥusaynī Marʿashī, Sayyid (1576) vi, 516b – VI, 501b
Asad Allāh Iṣfahānī (XVII) i, **685b** – I, **706a**
Asad Allāh Mīrzā (XIX) viii, 100b – VIII, 102b
Asʿad al-ʿAẓm (1757) ix, 70a – IX, 278a
Asad al-Dawla → Ṣāliḥ b. Mīrdās
Asad al-Dīn → Shirkūh
Asad al-Dīn Muḥammad b. al-Ḥasan (Ṣanʿāʾ) (XIII) v, 1241a – V, 1231b
Asad Efendī → Esʿad Efendī
Asʿad Kāmil, Tubbaʿ i, 548b; iii, 540b; v, 895a – I, 566a; III, 559a; V, 901b
Asad al-Ḳasrī → Asad b. ʿAbd Allāh
Asad Khān Lārī (Berar) (XVI) iii, 1160b – III, 1189a
Asad al-Luḳaymī (1765) i, 60b; viii, 385a – I, 62b; VIII, 398a
Asʿad Pasha al-ʿAẓm, Khān (1752) ii, 287b, 288a; iii,

120b; v, 925b; vi, 455a – II, 295b, 296a; III, 123a; V, 931a; VI, 440b
Asʿad al-Shidyāḳ (1830) ii, 801a – II, 819b
Asadābādh i, **685b** – I, **706b**
Asadābādī, Sayyid Djamāl al-Dīn s, 53b, 290b – S, 54a, 290a
Asadī (dynasty/-ie), Ḥims) iii, 399b – III, 411b
al-Asadī, Abu 'l-Rūḥ ʿĪsā b. ʿAlī b. Ḥassān (XIII) s, 392b – S, 393a
Asadī, Abū Manṣūr ʿAlī b. Aḥmad al-Ṭūsī (XI) vii, 567b – VII, 568a
Asadī, Abū Naṣr Aḥmad b. Manṣūr al-Ṭūsī (XI) i, **685b**; ii, 439b; iv, 61b, 62b, 525b, 1123b – I, **706b**; II, 451a; IV, 65a, 66a, 548a, 1155a
Asadī, ʿAlī b. Aḥmad b. Manṣūr al-Ṭūsī (XI) i, **685b** – I, **706b**
al-Asadī, al-Ḥasan b. Dubays (1018) vi, 921a – VI, 913a
al-Asadī, Ḥusayn (ḳāḍī) (1300) vi, 15b – VI, 14a
al-Asadī, ʿĪsā (XIII) iv, 745a; v, 9a; vii, 948a; s, 175b – IV, 774b; V, 9b; VII, 948b; S, 170b
al-Asadī, Ismāʿīl b. Sammār (VIII) ix, 827b – IX, 861b
al-Asadī, Manṣūr b. al-Ḥusayn (amīr) (XI) vii, 271a – VII, 273a
al-Asadī, Manẓūr b. Marthad viii, 377a – VIII, 390a
Asadiyya (Shīrkūh) vi, 320a – VI, 304b
Āṣaf b. Barakhyā i, **686a**, 775a; ix, 823a – I, **707a**, 798a; IX, 857b
Āṣaf al-Dawla (Ḳādjār) iv, 393a, b – IV, 410a
Āṣaf al-Dawla, Nawāb (Awadh) (XVIII) i, 153a, 757a, b, 813b, 1095a; ii, 265a, 499a, 870b; iii, 1163a; v, 635a, 636a; ix, 90a; s, 358b, 359a – I, 157b, 779b, 780a, 836b, 1128a; II, 273a, 511b, 890b; III, 1191b; V, 639a, 640b; IX, 96a; S, 358b, 359a
Āṣaf Djāh I, Niẓām al-Mulk (Ḥaydarābād) → Niẓām al-Mulk Čin Ḳïlič Khān
Āṣaf Djāh VII → ʿUthmān ʿAlī Khān
Āṣāf-Djāhs (Ḥaydarābād) i, 686a, 1015b, 1170a; ii, 99b; iii, 318b – I, 707a, 1047a, 1205a; II, 101b; III, 328a
Āṣaf Khān (1554) ii, 1129a – II, 1155b
Āsaf Khān, Abu 'l-Ḥasan (1641) i, 686a, 1347b; ii, 381a, 813b; iv, 1020a; v, 601a; vi, 190a; vii, 574a; viii, 125a – I, **707a**, 1388a; II, 391a, 832b; IV, 1052a; V, 604b; VI, 173b; VII, 574b; VIII, 127b, 128a
al-Āṣafī al-Ulughkhānī → Ḥādjdjī al-Dabīr
ʿAsākir, Banū ii, 283a; iii, 713b – II, 291b; III, 736a
al-Aṣamm → Muḥammad b. ʿUmar
al-Aṣamm, Abu 'l-ʿAbbās Muḥammad b. Yaʿḳūb al-Nīsābūrī (957) i, **686b**; viii, 53a – I, **707b**; VIII, 54a
al-Aṣamm, Abū Bakr (Naṣr b. Abī Layth) (Miṣr) (VIII) s, 90b – S, 90a
al-Aṣamm, Abū Bakr ʿAbd al-Raḥmān b. Kaysān (Baṣra) (817) iii, 1166a; vi, 737b; vii, 546b, 784b; s, **88b**, 226b – III, 1194b; VI, 727a; VII, 546b, 786b; S, **88a**, 226b
al-Aṣamm, Abu 'l-ʿAbbās Muḥammad al-Nīsābūrī (957) i, 142b, **686b** – I, 146b, **707b**
al-Aṣamm, Muḥammad b. Abi 'l-Layth (840) vii, 4a – VII, 4a
al-Aṣamm, Sufyān b. al-Abrad al-Kalbī (VII) i, **686b**, 810b; ii, 809a; iii, 716b; iv, 753a – I, **707b**, 834a; II, 828b; III, 739a; IV, 783b
Asandamur Kurdjī (Tripoli) (XIV) vii, 991b – VII, 993a
Asar Kale → ʿAmmūriya
Asās → Ismāʿīliyya
ʿAsas i, **687a**; iv, 103b – I, **707b**; IV, 108a
Asas al-Sunna → Asad b. Mūsā b. Ibrāhīm
Asātigīn (Mosul) (870) vi, 900a – VI, 891a
Asāṭīr al-Awwalīn iii, 369a; s, **90b** – III, 381a; S, **90b**
Asāwira (Pers(i)ans) vi, 875b – VI, 866b
Aṣba → Iṣbaʿ
al-Aṣbagh (838) vi, 279a – VI, 264a
Aṣbagh b. al-ʿAbbās (1196) s, 382a – S, 382a
Aṣbagh b. ʿAbd Allāh b. Wānsūs (805) vi, 568a – VI, 553a
Aṣbagh b. Khalīl vii, 400a – VII, 401b
Aṣbagh b. Nabīl (XI) vii, 248b – VII, 250a
Asbagh b. Wakīl (IX) ix, 584b – IX, 667a
al-Aṣbagh (al-Asyaʿ) al-Kalbī (VII) i, 84b; ii, 625a; iv, 493b, 494a – I, 87a; II, 640b; IV, 515a
al-Aṣbaḥī (XIII) vi, 182b; vii, 28b – VI, 166b; VII, 28b
Asben → Aïr
Ascalon → al-ʿĀsḳalān
Aṣfar (yellow/jaune) i, **687b**; v, 700b, 706b – I, **708b**; V, 705b, 711b
al-Aṣfar al-Muntafiḳ (X) iv, 663b – IV, 690b
Aṣfar, Banu 'l- i, 688a – I, 709a
Asfār b. Kurdūya (Baghdād) (X) s, 398a – S, 398b
Asfār b. Shīrawayhī (Shīrōya) (931) i, **688a**; ii, 192a; iii, 255a; iv, 23a, 661b, 859b; vi, 115b, 539a; s, 357a – I, 70**9a**; II, 198a; III, 262a; IV, 24b, 688b, 892b; VI, 113a, 523b; S, 357a
Aṣfī (Safi) i, 85a, 141a, 687b, **688b**; vi, 573a, 589a, 594a, 741b; vii, 387a; s, 29a, 401b – I, 87b, 145a, 708b, **709b**; VI, 558a, 573b, 579a, 731a; VII, 388a; S, 29a, 402a
Asfizār → Sabzawār
al-Asfizārī, Abū Ḥākim al-Muẓaffar b. Ismāʿīl (1121) vii, 196b – VII, 196b
al-Aʿshā i, **689b** – I, **710b**
al-Aʿshā, Maymūn b. Ḳays (625) i, 196a, 442b, **689b**; 963b, 1081b; iv, 1002a, 1008b; vii, 190b, 208b, 254b, 980b; viii, 883b; ix, 9b; s, 197b – I, 202a, 455a, **710b**, 993a, 1113b; IV, 1031b, 1041a; VII, 191a, 210a, 256a, 981b; VIII, 914a; XI, 10a; S, 197b
Aʿshā Hamdān (702) i, **690b**; ii, 190b; iii, 123a, 354a, 716b; vi, 193a, 604a, 605a – I, **711a**; II, 196b; III, 126a, 365a, 738b; VI, 177a, 589a, 590a
Aṣḥāb → Ṣaḥāba
Ashʿab (771) i, **690b** – I, **711b**
Aṣḥāb al-ḥadīth → Ahl al-ḥadīth
Aṣḥāb al-kahf i, **691a**, 998a; iv, 724a – I, **712a**, 1028b; IV, 753a
Aṣḥāb al-rass i, 509a, **692a**; iii, 169a – I, 524b, **713a**; III, 172b
Aṣḥāb al-raʾy i, **692a**; ii, 889a – I, **713a**; II, 910a
Aṣḥāb al-ukhdūd i, 692a, **692b** – I, 713a, **713b**
al-Ashadjdj al-Muʿammar → Abu 'l-Dunyā
Ashāḳa Bāsh, Banū iv, 387b, 389a, 390b – IV, 404a, 406a, 407a
Ashām i, **692b**; iv, 460b – I, **714a**; IV, 480b
Aʿshār → ʿUshr
al-ʿAshara al-Mubashshara i, **693a** – I, **714a**
Ashʿarī, Banū vi, 221b, 493a – VI, 215a, 479a
al-Ashʿarī (1444) i, 1154a; ii, 740b – I, 1188a; II, 759a
al-Ashʿarī, Abū Burda (721) i, **693b**; vii, 635b – I, **714b**; VII, 635a
al-Ashʿarī, Abu 'l-Ḥasan (935) i, 129a, 204b, 275a, 589b, **694a**, 958b, 1039a; ii, 412a, 449b, 554a, 569b, 570a, 931a; iii, 767a, 1037b, 1063a, 1144a, b, 1164b, 1170b, 1173b; iv, 271b, 470a; v, 526b; vi, 353a, 376a, 846b; vii, 187b, 546b, 1051a; s, 347a, 392a – I, 132b, 210b, 283b, 609a, **715a**, 988a, 1070b; II, 422b, 461a, 568a, 584a, b, 952b; III, 790a, 1063a, 1089b, 1172b, 1193a, 1196b, 1202a; IV, 284a, 491a; V, 530b; VI, 337b, 360b, 837b; VII, 188a, 546b, 1053a; S, 347a, 392b

al-As̲h̲ʿarī, Abū Mūsā (662) i, 304a, 383b, 384a, 693b, **695a**, 704a; ii, 414b, 415b, 811b, 1120a; iii, 1015b; iv, 13b, 99b, 220a; v, 406b, 451a, 499b; vi, 565b, 647b, 649a, 920a; vii, 207a; ix, 98a; s, 89b – I, 313b, 394b, 395a, 714b, **716a**, 725b; II, 425a, 426a, 831a, 1146a; III, 1041a; IV, 14b, 103b, 229b; V, 407b, 453b, 502b; VI, 550b, 633a, 634b, 911b; VII, 208a; IX, 102a; S, 89b
al-As̲h̲ʿarī, Aḥmad b. Muḥammad (IX) viii, 387b – VIII, 401a
As̲h̲ʿariyya i, 179a, 333a, b, 334a, 335a, 410b, 411a, b, 412a, b, 413a, 415b, **696a**, 714a, 958b; ii, 102b, 365a, 449b, 493b, 605a, 608a, 618a, 833b, iii, 171b, 330a, 465b, 767a, 1072b, 1144b, 1146a; iv, 107b, 108a, 172b, 183a, 365b, 366a, 469a, 616a, 692a, 693a; v, 527a; vi, 218b, 447b, 448a; s, 30a, 343b, 346b – I, 183b, 343b, 344a, 345b, 422a, b, 423b, 424b, 425a, 427b, **717a**, 735b, 988a; II, 104b, 375a, 461b, 506a, 620a, 623a, 633b, 853a; III, 175b, 340a, 482a, 790a, 1099a, 1172b, 1174b; IV, 112b, 113a, 180a, 191a, 381b, 382a, 490a, 640b, 720b, 721a; V, 531a; VI, 202b, 433a, b; S, 30a, 343b, 346a
al-As̲h̲ʿat̲h̲ b. D̲j̲aʿfar al-K̲h̲uzāʿī → al-K̲h̲uzāʿī
al-As̲h̲ʿat̲h̲ b. Ḳays (661) i, 42b, 625b, **696b**, 864a; ii, 198b; iii, 242b, 715a, 888b; v, 119b; viii, 97a; ix, 553b; s, 337b – I, 43b, 646a, **718a**, 888a; II, 204b; III, 249b, 737b, 912b; V, 122a; VIII, 99b; IX, 571a; S, 337a
al-As̲h̲daḳ → ʿAmr b. Saʿīd al-As̲h̲daḳ
As̲h̲d̲j̲aʿ, Banū vii, 561b – VII, 562b
al-As̲h̲d̲j̲aʿ b. ʿAmr al-Sulamī (VIII) i, **697a** – I, **718a**
As̲h̲hab (Mālikī) (819) vi, 279a; viii, 844a – VI, 264a; VIII, 873b
ʿĀs̲h̲iḳ i, 193b, **697b**; ii, 990b; iii, 374a; iv, 706a; v, 275a – I, 199a, **718b**; II, 1013b; III, 386a; IV, 734b; V, 273b
ʿĀs̲h̲iḳ, Muḥammad b. ʿUt̲h̲mān b. Bāyezīd (XVI) i, **697b**; ii, 588a; v, 982a; s, 330b – I, **718b**; II, 602a; V, 978b; S, 330a
ʿĀs̲h̲iḳ Čelebi (Pīr Meḥmed of/de Prizrin) (1572) i, **698a**; iv, 1137a; v, 116a, 693a; x, 55a; s, 83a – I, **719a**; IV, 1169a; V, 118b, 698a; X, 56b; S, 83a
ʿAs̲h̲iḳ Pas̲h̲a (1333) i, 419b, **698b**; iii, 375a; v, 173a – I, 431b, **719b**; III, 387a; V, 170b
ʿĀs̲h̲ik Weysel (1973) s, **91a** – S, **91a**
ʿĀs̲h̲iḳ-pas̲h̲a-zāde (1484) i, **699a**; ii, 1044b; iii, 23a – I, **720a**; II, 1069a; III, 24a
ʿAs̲h̲iklu, Banū iv, 577b – IV, 601a
As̲h̲īr i, **699a**, 1319b; ii, 114b; iv, 459a; vi, 728a, b; ix, 18a – I, **720b**, 1359b; II, 117b; IV, 479b; VI, 717a; IX, 18b
ʿĀs̲h̲ir Efendi (XIX) ii, 474a – II, 486a
ʿAs̲h̲īra i, **700a**; iv, 334a, b, 595a; v, 472a – I, **721b**; IV, 348b, 349a, 619a; V, 474b
As̲h̲k (XIX) iii, 376a – III, 387b
ʿAs̲h̲ḳābād i, 320b, **700b**; vi, 621b, 720a; x, 686a – I, 330b, **722a**; VI, 606b, 709a; X,
As̲h̲ḳīlūla, Banū (Tud̲j̲ībid(e)s) iv, 729b; vi, 222b; vii, 1021a – IV, 758b; VI, 216b; VII, 1023a
As̲h̲kūd̲j̲a → Darg̲h̲in
As̲h̲lūn K̲h̲ātūn umm al-Nāṣir Muḥammad b. Ḳalawūn (Mamlūk) (XIV) vii, 990b – VII, 993a
al-As̲h̲mūnayn → Us̲h̲mūnayn
As̲h̲nās, vizier (IX) vii, 653a; s, 106a – VII, 652b; S, 105b
As̲h̲ot → As̲h̲ūṭ
As̲h̲rāf → S̲h̲arīf
As̲h̲raf (Čūbānid(e)) → Malik As̲h̲raf
As̲h̲rāf (faction) iii, 88a; v, 349b – III, 90b; V, 350b
As̲h̲rāf (India/Inde) iii, 411a – III, 423b
As̲h̲raf (town/ville, Māzandarān) i, 8b, 198a, 329a, 434b, **701a**, 780b, 799a, b. 940b, 971a; ii, 284a, 347b; iii, 504a; iv, 502b, 817b; vi, 516b, 528a; s, 140b – I, 8b, 203b, 339b, 446b, **722b**, 803b, 822b, 969a, 1001a; II, 292a, 357b; III, 521a; IV, 543a, b, 850b; VI, 501b, 512b; S, 140b
As̲h̲rāf (Sudan/Soudan) i, 49b, 765a; ii, 124a; v, 1250a, b – I, 50b, 788a; II, 127a; V, 1240b, 1241b
al-As̲h̲raf I Muẓaffar al-Dīn, al-Malik (Ayyūbid(e)) (1220) → al-Malik al-As̲h̲raf Mūsā I Muẓaffar al-Dīn (Ayyūbid(e))
al-As̲h̲raf (Rasūlid(e)) (1296) vi, 81b; vii, 30a – VI, 79b; VII, 30a
As̲h̲raf b. ʿAbd al-ʿAzīz (Afg̲h̲anistān) (1729) i, 229b, 270a, 291a; iii, 604b; v, 461a – I, 236b, 278b, 300a; III, 625a; V, 464a
al-As̲h̲raf b. al-ʿĀdil, al-Malik (Ayyūbid(e)) (1198) → al-Malikal-As̲h̲raf b. al-ʿĀdil
As̲h̲raf ʿAlī, Sayyid vii, 132b – VII, 134b
As̲h̲raf ʿAlī b. ʿAbd al-Ḥaḳḳ al-Fārūḳī (1943) i, **701b**; iii, 433b, 1174a, b – I, **723a**; III, 447b, 1203a, b
As̲h̲raf ʿAlī K̲h̲ān (1772) i, **702a** – I, **723a**
As̲h̲raf bint Riḍā S̲h̲āh Pahlawī (XX) vi, 486b – VI, 472b
As̲h̲raf al-Dīn Gīlānī (1934) iv, 71a; vii, 754b; s, **91b** – IV, 74b; VII, 756a; S, **91b**
As̲h̲raf D̲j̲ahāngīr al-Simnānī (1405) i, **702b**, 859a; ii, 51b, 392a, 1115a – I, **723b**, 883a; II, 52b, 402b, 1141a
al-As̲h̲raf Ismāʿīl (Rasūlid(e)) (1401) viii, 457a – VIII, 472b
al-As̲h̲raf K̲h̲alīl b. Ḳalawūn (Mamlūk) (1293) vi, 322b; vii, 461b, 991b – VI, 307a; VII, 461b, 993a
As̲h̲raf K̲h̲ān (K̲h̲aṭṭ) (1572) iv, 1127b – IV, 1159a
al-As̲h̲raf Mūsā b. Ibrāhīm (Ayyūbid(e)) (1262) iii, 399b, 989b; vi, 321b, 381a; vii, 273a, b – III, 412a, 1014b; VI, 305b, 365b; VII, 275a, b
As̲h̲raf-og̲h̲lu Rūmī (XIV) iii, 43b – III, 45a
As̲h̲raf Og̲h̲ullarï i, **702b**, 1256b; iv, 621a – I, **724a**, 1295a; IV, 646a, b
As̲h̲raf Rumī, ʿAbd Allāh (1493) i, 704a – I, 725a
al-As̲h̲raf S̲h̲aʿbān II b. Ḥusayn (Mamlūk) (1376) vi, 195a, 424a, 548a – VI, 179a, 409b, 532b
al-As̲h̲raf ʿUmar (Rasūlid(e)) (1296) viii, 457a – VIII, 472b
As̲h̲rafī → Sikka
al-As̲h̲rafī, Sayf al-Dīn Ḳaratāy Ibn ʿAbd al-ʿAzīz (1376) vi, 580b – VI, 565a
As̲h̲rafiyya (Mamlūk) i, **704a**; v, 73a; vi, 316b, 320a – I, **725a**; V, 75a; VI, 301a, 304b
As̲h̲ras b. ʿAbd Allāh al-Sulamī → al-Sulamī
al-ʿAs̲h̲s̲h̲āb i, **704a** – I, **725a**
al-As̲h̲tar, Malik b. al-Ḥārit̲h̲ (VII) i, 382b, **704a**; ii, 89b, 416a; iii, 1265a; iv, 1035a; v, 499b, 954a – I, 393b, **725b**; II, 91a, 427a; III, 1298a; IV, 1067a; V, 502b, 958a
As̲h̲tard̲j̲ān vi, 366a – VI, 350a
As̲h̲tark̲h̲ānid(e)s → D̲j̲ānid(e)s
Ās̲h̲tiyānīs (Irān) vii, 653b – VII, 653a
As̲h̲turḳa (Astorga) s, **92a** – S, **91b**
As̲h̲ur → At̲h̲ūr
As̲h̲ur Ada vii, 455a – VII, 455b
ʿĀs̲h̲ūrāʾ i, 265a, **705a**, 823b, 1352a; iii, 635a; s, 190a – I, 273a, **726a**, 846b, 1391b; III, 656a; S, 191b
As̲h̲ūṭ I (Armenia/-ie) (890) i, 507a, 637a; v, 488b – I, 522b, 657b; V, 491b
As̲h̲ūṭ II (Armenia/-ie) (929) i, 507a, 637b; ii, 679b – I, 522b, 658a; II, 696b
As̲h̲ūṭ III (Armenia/-nie) (977) i, 507a, 637b; ii, 680a; iv, 670a – I, 522b, 658b; II, 697a; IV, 697a

Ashūṭ IV (Armenia/-ie) (1040) i, 638a – I, 658b
Ashūṭ Msaker (Bagratid(e)) (IX) i, 507a – I, 522b
al-ʿĀṣī (Orontes) i, 239a, 706a; ii, 555b, 556a; s, 243a – I, 246b, **727a**; II, 569b, 570a; S, 243a
Āṣif al-Dawla (Iṣfahān) (XIX) iv, 105a – IV, 109b
Aṣīla i, **706a**; v, 1118b; vi, 573a – I, **727b**; V, 1115a; VI, 558a
ʿAsim → Čelebi-zāde Ismāʿīl ʿAsim
ʿĀṣim Aḥmad (1819) i, **707a**, 1327b; ii, 536b; v, 951b; vi, 340b – I, **728b**, 1368a; II, 366a; V, 955b; VI, 325a
Asim, Dj. (XX) vi, 768b – VI, 758a
ʿĀṣim b. ʿAbd Allāh al-Hilālī (VIII) ii, 601a; iii, 223b, 1202a – II, 615b; III, 230b, 1232a
ʿĀṣim b. Abi ʾl-Nadjdjūd (745) i, **706b**; iii, 63a; v, 127b, 128a – I, **728a**; III, 65b; V, 130b
ʿĀṣim b. Djamīl al-Yazdadjūmī (X) ii, 1095b – II, 1121a
ʿĀṣim b. Thābit al-Anṣārī (VII) v, 40b, 41a – V, 41b, 42a
ʿĀṣim b. ʿUmar b. al-Khaṭṭāb (VII) vi, 344b – VI, 328b
ʿĀṣim al-Aḥwal (VIII) i, 104b – I, 107b
Asim Bezirci (XX) vi, 95b – VI, 93b
Asim Degel (Kano) (XIX) iv, 550b – IV, 574a
ʿĀṣim Efendi Ismāʿīl → Čelebi-zāde
ʿĀṣim al-Sadrātī (VIII) iii, 654a, b; vi, 312a – III, 675b, 676a; VI, 297a
ʿAsīr (Arabia/-e) i, 98a, 106b, 539a, **707b**, 811b, 881b; v, 391b; vi, 151a, 156b, 192a; s, 3b, 30a, 278b – I, 101a, 109b, 555b, **729a**, 834b, 907a; V, 392a; VI, 149b, 152b, 176a; S, 3a, 30b, 278b
Asīr (Mānd) vi, 384b – VI, 368b
Asīr, Djalāl al-Dīn (1639) i, **707b**; iv, 69a; viii, 776a – I, **728b**; IV, 72b; VIII, 802a
Asīrgarh i, **710a**; ii, 815b; iv, 1023a – I, **731b**; II, 835a; IV, 1055a
Asīrī (XIX) s, 109b – S, 109a
Āsitāna → Istanbul
Asiuṭ → Asyūṭ
Āsiya (Pharaoh's wife/femme du Pharaon) i, **710b**; ii, 848a, 917b; vi, 629a, 652b – I, **731b**; II, 868a, 938b; VI, 614a, 637b
Ask (Damāwand) ii, 106b; v, 660b, 661a, 664a – II, 108b; V, 666a, b, 669a
ʿĀsḳalān i, 9b, **710b**, 946b; ii, 911a, 912a, 1056a; iv, 958b; v, 331a; vi, 230a, 652a; s, 121a – I, 9b, **732a**, 975b; II, 932b, 933b, 1081a; IV, 992a; V, 331a; VI, 224a, 637b; S, 120b
al-ʿAsḳalānī → Ibn Ḥadjar
al-ʿAsḳalānī, ʿAlāʾ al-Dīn b. Ẓāfir (XII) vii, 1040a – VII, 1042a
al-ʿAskar → Djaysh
al-ʿAskar → Sāmarrāʾ
al-ʿAskar (al-Fusṭāṭ) ii, 958b, 959a – II, 980b, 981a
ʿAskar Khān Afshār Arūmī (XIX) s, 290a – S, 290a
ʿAskar Mukram i, **711b**; s, 12b, 37b – I, **733a**; S, 13a, 38a
ʿAskarī i, **712a**; ii, 147a; iv, 231b, 242a, b, 563a, 564a – I, **733b**; II, 151b; IV, 242a, 253a, 585a, 586b
al-ʿAskarī, Abū Aḥmad al-Ḥasan (993) i, **712b**; viii, 14a; s, 38a – I, **734a**; VIII, 14b; S, 38a
al-ʿAskarī, Abu ʾl-Ḥasan ʿAlī b. Muḥammad al-Naḳī (X. Imām) (868) i, **713a**; iii, 246b; vii, 443a, 459b; viii, 1040b; s, 95a, 127b – I, **734b**; III, 253b; VII, 444a, 459b; VIII, 1076a; S, 94b, 127a
al-ʿAskarī, Abū Hilāl (1010) i, 590b, **712b**, 759a, 857b; ii, 386a; iv, 249a; vi, 438a, 823a; vii, 527b I, 609b, 7**34a**, 781b, 881b; II, 396b; IV, 260a; VI, 423b, 813a; VII, 527b
al-ʿAskarī, al-Ḥasan → al-Ḥasan al-ʿAskarī
ʿAskarī b. Bābur (Mughal) (XVI) i, 228b, 1135b; iii, 575b, 576a; iv, 523b – I, 235a, 1170a; III, 595a, 596a; IV, 546a
ʿAskerī → ʿAskarī
Askia al-Ḥādjdj Muḥammad → Muḥammad b. Abī Bakr (Songhay)
Aṣl → Uṣūl
al-Aslaʿ b. ʿAbd Allāh al-ʿAbsī s, 177b – S, 178b
al-Aṣlaḥ i, **713b** – I, **735a**
Aslam, Banū v, 78b; vii, 356b, 561b – V, 80b; VII, 359a, 562b
Aslam b. Zurʿa al-Kilābī (681) vi, 123b – VI, 125b
Aslam, Ēm (XX) v, 204a, b – V, 201b, 202a
Asmāʾ bint ʿAbd al-ʿAzīz b. Marwān (746) vi, 664a – VI, 650a
Asmāʾ bint Abī Bakr (693) i, 109b, 110a, **713b**; ix, 742a; s, 311a – 112b, 113a, **735b**; IX, 774b; S, 311a
Asmāʾ bint Mukharriba (VI) i, 115b; iii, 169a; vi, 145b – I, 118b; III, 172b; VI, 144a
Asmāʾ bint al-Nuʿmān → al-Djawniyya
Asmāʾ bint ʿUmays (659) i, 44a, 109b, 400b;ii, 372a, 844b, 846a; iv, 1106b; vii, 393a; S, **92b**, 172a – I, 45b, 112b, 412a; II, 382a, 864b, 866a; IV, 1138a; VII, 394a; S, **92a**; 173a
al-Asmāʾ al-Ḥusnā i, 408a, **714a**; ii, 753a – I, 420a, **735b**; II, 771b
al-Aṣmaʿī, Abū Saʿīd ʿAbd al-Malik (828) i, 105b, 108b, 115a, b, 125b, 158a, 167b, 338a, 520b, 521b, 588b, **717b**, 772a, 921a, 1241a; ii, 952b; iii, 136a; iv, 249a; vi, 625b; vii, 254b, 279b, 306b, 526b, 831b; s, 15b, 17b, 20a, 33a, 128b, 277a, 317b, 394b – I, 108b, 118b, 119a, 129a, 162b, 172a, 349a, 536a, 537b, 607b, **739a**, 795a, 949a, 1279a; II, 974b; III, 139a; IV, 260a; VI, 610b; VII, 256a, 281b, 308b, 527a, 833a; S, 16a, 18a, 20b, 33b, 127b, 276b, 317b, 395a
al-Aṣmaʿiyyāt → al-Aṣmaʿī
Āsmāngird Mountains/Mont vi, 384a – VI, 368a, b
al-Asmar, ʿAbd al-Salām al-Faytūrī (1574) vi, 355a; s, **93a** – VI, 339a; S, **92b**
al-Asnawī (1370) vi, 133a – VI, 131a
Asparukh (Bulghar) (VII) x, 692a – X, 734b
Asper → Aḳče
ʿAṣr i, **719a** – I, **740b**
Asrāfīl → Isrāfīl
Āṣṣ → Alān
Assab i, **719a**; ii, 113a; vi, 643b; ix, 715a – I, **740b**; II, 115b; VI, 628b, 629a; IX, 746a
Aṣṣāda, Banū vi, 741b, 742a, 744a – VI, 730b, 731a, 733a
ʿAssāf al-Naṣrānī (XIII) iii, 951b – III, 976a
al-ʿAssāl, Awlād → Ibn al-ʿAssāl
al-ʿAssālī, Aḥmad b. ʿAlī al-Ḥarīrī (1638) iv, 992a – IV, 1024b
al-ʿAssāliyya iv, 992a – IV, 1024b
Assam i, **719a**; vi, 489a – I, **741a**; VI, 475a
ʿAṣṣār, Muḥammad (1377) i, **720a**; iv, 67a – I, **741b**; IV, 70b
Assenid(e)s i, 1302a – I, 1342a
Assiout → Asyūṭ
Assuan → Uswān
Assyria → Athūr
Astarābādh i, **720a**; ii, 1141a; iii, 212b, 1102a; iv, 389a, b, 390a, b, 855b; vi, 14b, 494b, 495a, 512a, b, 513b, 514b, 515b; s, 139b, 356b, 357a, 363b, 380a – I, **741b**; II, 1168a; III, 218b, 1129a; IV, 406a, b, 407a, 888b; VI, 13a, 480a, 480b, 497a, 498a, 499a, b, 500b; S, 139a, 356b, 363b, 380a
al-Astarābādhī i, **720b** – I, **742b**
al-Astarābādhī, Muḥammad Yūsuf (XVI) vi, 516b – VI, 501b

al-Astarābā̲dh̲ī, Raḍī al-Dīn (1285) i, **721a**; iii, 781a, 861b; vii, 914b – I, **742b**; III, 804b, 885b; VII, 915a
al-Astarābā̲dh̲ī, Rukn al-Dīn (1317) i, **721a** – I, **743a**
al-Astarābādī, D̲j̲alāl al-Dīn Muḥammad Yūsuf (Ṣadr) (XVI) vi, 18a, 516b – VI, 16a, 501b
Astarābādī, Faḍl Allāh (1384) viii, 114b, 540a – VIII, 117a, 557b
Astarābādī, G̲h̲iyā̲th̲ al-Dīn Muḥammad b. Ḥusayn b. Muḥammad (amīr) (Ḥurūfī) ii, 733a, 735a – II, 751b, 753b
Astarābādī, Ibrāhīm b. Walī Allāh (XVI) viii, 540b – VIII, 558b
al-Astarābādī, Mīrzā Muḥammad b. ʿAlī (1619) vi, 550b; s, 56b – VI, 535a; S, 57a
al-Astarābādī, Muḥammad Amīn (1640) viii, 779b – VIII, 805b
Astarābādī, Muḥammad Bāḳir → al-Dāmād
al-Astarābādī, Mullā Muḥammad Amīn b. Muḥammad S̲h̲arīf (1626) vi, 550b; vii, 298a; s, 56b, 57a – VI, 535a; VII, 300a; S, 57a, b
Asṭarlāb → Asṭurlāb
Astarte → al-Lāt
Astorga → As̲h̲turḳa
Astra̲kh̲ān i, **721b**, 1108a; ii, 44a, 179a; iv, 280b, 576a; v, 138a, b; vi, 416b; s, 318a – I, **743a**, 1141a; II, 45a, 184b; IV, 292b, 599a; V, 140b, 141a; VI, 401b; S, 318a
Astra̲kh̲ānid(e)s → D̲j̲ānids
Asṭurlāb i, **722b**; iii, 808b, 924a, 928b, 1136b; v, 46a; vi, 374b – I, **744a**; III, 832a, 948b, 953a, 1165a; V, 47b; VI, 359a
al-Asṭurlābī, ʿAlī b. ʿĪsā (831) vi, 600a – VI, 584b
al-Asṭurlābī → al-Badīʿ
al-Aʿsūm (Yemen) vi, 474a – VI, 460a
al-Aswad b. Kaʿb al-ʿAnsī (632) i, 110b, **728a**, 738a; iii, 223b; iv, 1135b; viii, 94a; s, 116a – I, 113b, **749b**, 759b; III, 230a; IV, 1167a; VIII, 96a; S, 115b
al-Aswad b. al-Mun̲dh̲ir III (VI) ii, 71b – II, 73a
al-Aswad b. Yaʿfur (VI) i, **728b**; iv, 998b; s, 256a, 394b – I, **750a**; IV, 1031a; S, 255b, 395a
al-Aswad b. Yazīd vii, 258b – VII, 260a
Aswan → Uswān
al-Aṣyaʿ al-Kalbī → al-Aṣba̲gh̲ al-Kalbī
Asylum → Bast, Bīmāristān
Asyūṭ i, **728b**; ii, 424a; v, 515a; vi, 119a, 361a, 671b; s, 5a, 40b, 121b – I, **750b**; II, 434b; V, 519a; VI, 116b, 345a, 658a; S, 4a, 41a, 121a
al-Asyūṭī, S̲h̲ams al-Dīn (1416) ix, 539a – IX, 560b
Ata (father/père) i, **729a** – I, **751a**
ʿAṭāʾ i, **729a**; ii, 360a; vi, 205b – I, **751a**; II, 370a; VI, 190a
ʿAṭāʾ b. Abī Rabāḥ (732) i, 123a, **730a**; ii, 538b, 886b, 888b; vii, 631b, 636a; s, 232b, 386b – I, 126b, **752b**; II, 552a, 907a, 909a; VII, 631a, 635b; S, 232b, 386b
ʿAṭāʾ b. Yasār al-Hilālī (722) iv, 369a – IV, 385
ʿAṭāʾ Allāh Efendi (XVI) i, 1235a; iv, 322b – I, 1272a; IV, 337a
ʿAṭāʾ Allāh Efendi, S̲h̲ānī-zāde → Shānī-zāde
ʿAṭāʾ Allāh ʿO̲th̲mān-og̲h̲lu (1767) iv, 593a – IV, 617a
ʿAṭāʾ Bey, Meḥmed (1919) i, **730b** – I, **752a**
ʿAṭāʾ Bey, Ṭayyārzāde (1877) i, **730b** – I, **752a**
ʿAṭāʾ Ilāhī, Banū iii, 1107b – III, 1134b
ʿAṭāʾ al-Ḳasm, S̲h̲ay̲kh̲ (XX) vi, 538b – VI, 523a
ʿAṭāʾ, K̲h̲ʷā̲d̲j̲a (XIV) s, 105b – S, 105a
ʿAṭāʾ Malik D̲j̲uwaynī → al-D̲j̲uwaynī, ʿAlāʾ al-Dīn
ʿAtāba i, **730b** – I, **752b**
Atabak (Atabeg) i, 3b, 20b, 639a, **731a**, 1081a, 1276b; iii, 1016a; iv, 26a, 32a, 466b; v, 826a, 828a – I, 3b, 21b, 659b, **753a**, 1106a, 1316a; III, 1041b; IV, 28a, 34a, 487a; V, 832b, 834a
Atābak al-ʿAsākir i, **732b**; v, 73a – I, **754b**; V, 75a
ʿAtabāt s, **94a**, 104a – S, **93b**, 103b
Atabeg → Atabak
Atabia (Maprusi, Ghana) (1741) ii, 1003b – II, 1026b
Atač, Nūr Allāh (1957) s, **96a**, 98b – S, **95b**, 98a
ʿAṭāʾī, ʿAṭāʾ Allāh b. Yaḥyā (1635) i, **732b** – I, **754b**
ʿAṭāʾī, Newʿi-zāde (1635) viii, 8b, 164a – VIII, 9a, 166b
Atak i, **733a**; iv, 1102a, 1159b – I, **755a**; IV, 1133a, 1191b
Ātäk → Abīward
Atalîḳ i, 733b; s, **96b** – I, 755b; S, **96a**
ʿAtama i, **733b** – I, **755b**
At(a)man → ʿO̲th̲mān I
Atar i, **733b**; v, 654a – I, **755b**; V, 658a
Atargatis vi, 378b, 382a – VI, 363a, 366a
al-Ātāsī, M. Hā̲sh̲im (XX) iv, 138a – IV, 144a
Atatürk (Muṣṭafā Kemāl Pa̲sh̲a) (1938) i, 75b, 470b, 511a, 641b, **734a**, 777a, 783a, 1255b;ii, 104b, 392a, 430b, 432a, 466b, 475b, 497b, 531b,595b, 630a, 644b, 700a, 701b, 712b; iii, 526b, 622a; iv, 124a, 169a, 297b, 611b, 873a, 934a, b, 935b, 946b; v, 906a, 1099b; vi, 94b, 288a, 304b, 470a, 610a, 757b; vii, 188a, 284a, 677b, 764b; viii, 168b, 251a, 1053b; x, 694a; s, 41b, 63a, 98a, 282a, 329a – I, 77b, 484b, 527a, 662a, **756a**, 800a, 806a, 1294a; II, 107a, 402b, 442a, 443a, 478a, b, 510a, 544b, 610a, 646a, 660b, 718a, 719b, 731a; III, 545a, 642b; IV, 129a, 176b, 311a, 636a, 906b, 967a, b, 968b, 979a; V, 911b, 1095a; VI, 92b, 273b, 290a, 456a, 595a, 747a; VII, 188b, 286a, 677b, 766b; VIII, 171a, 1089a; X, 736b; S, 42a, 63b, 97b, 282a, 328b
ʿAṭawiyya vii, 859a – VII, 860b
Ātāy → Čay
Atay, Fāliḥ Rîfḳī (1971) s, **98a** – S, **97b**
Atbara i, **735a**, 1172a, 1239b; iv, 686a; v, 1251b – I, **757a**, 1207b, 1277b; IV, 714a; V, 1242a
Atbe̲d̲j̲ → A̲th̲bā̲d̲j̲
Ātbēgī → Atabak
Atchin, Atcheh → Atjèh
ʿAteiba → ʿUtayba
Atek i, **735a** – I, **757a**
Āte̲sh̲ → Mā̲d̲j̲ūs
Āte̲sh̲izāde Memi S̲h̲āh (1531) ii, 1042b – II, 1067a
ʿAṭf i, **735b** – I, **757b**
Aṭfar → D̲j̲abala b. al-Ḥāri̲th̲
Aṭfīḥ i, **735b** – I, **757b**
Aṭfiyā̲sh̲ (Aṭfayyi̲sh̲), Muḥammad b. Yūsuf (1914) i, **736a**; viii, 993b – I, **758a**; VIII, 1028b
Atga K̲h̲ān (XVI) vii, 331b – VII, 333a
A̲th̲āfit (Yemen) s, 22a, 335a – S, 22b, 334b
A̲th̲ar i, **736a**, 1199a – I, **758a**, 1234b
al-Ā̲th̲ār al-ʿUlwiyya i, **736b**; iii, 30a – I, **758b**; III, 31b
A̲th̲ā̲th̲ v, 1158a; s, **99a** – V, 1148a; S, **98a**
A̲th̲bā̲d̲j̲, Banū i, 533a, 1246b; iii, 138a, 386a; iv, 479a; v, 1179a; vi, 728b; vii, 994a; s, 62b – I, 549b, 1284b; III, 140b, 398b; IV, 501a; V, 1169a; VI, 717b; VII, 995b; S, 63a
Athens/Athènes → Atīna
A̲th̲īr, Banū iii, 723b, 961a – III, 746a, 985b
A̲th̲īr-i A̲kh̲sikatī (1174) iv, 62a; viii, 971a – IV, 65a; VIII, 1005b
ʿA̲th̲lī̲th̲ i, **737b** – I, **759b**
ʿA̲th̲r/ʿA̲th̲thar i, **737b**; vi, 436a- I, **759b**; VI, 421a
A̲th̲ūr s, **100a** – S, **99b**
ʿĀṭif Efendi (XVIII) iii, 590a – III, 610a
ʿAtīḳ b. ʿAbd al-Wāḥid b. Ziyād b. al-Muhallab (VIII) vii, 359b – VII, 362a
ʿAtīḳ b. Aslam b. Ya̲dh̲kur, Banū vi, 830b – VI, 821a

ʿĀtīḳa bint ʿAbd al-Malik b. al-Ḥāri<u>th</u> (VIII) vi, 140b – VI, 138b
ʿĀtīḳa bint Aḥmed III (Ottoman) (1724) vi, 860b – VI, 851b
ʿĀtīḳa bint Muʿāwiya i, 113b – I, 116b
ʿĀtīḳa bint <u>Sh</u>u<u>dh</u>a (IX) vii, 518a – VII, 518b
ʿĀtīḳa bint Zayd (VII) i, **738a** – I, **760a**
Atil i, 721b, **738a**; iv, 280a, 1173a, 1176a, 1177b, 1178b; v, 1013b – I, 743b, **760a**; IV, 292b, 1206b, 1209b, 1211a, 1212a; V, 1009a
Atīna i, **738b** – I, **760b**
ʿAtīra i, **739b**; s, 221b – I, **761b**; S, 221b
Āti<u>sh</u>, <u>Kh</u>ʷā<u>dj</u>a Ḥaydar ʿAlī (1847) ii, 84b; x, 878a; s, **102a** – II, 86a; X, ;S, **101b**
Āti<u>sh</u>ī (Kandahar) (1565) ix, 241a – IX, 247b
ʿAṭiyya (Mirdāsid(e)) (1065) vi, 544a – VI, 528b
ʿAṭiyya, Banū iii, 642b – III, 664a
ʿAṭiyya, Muḥammad (XX) viii, 727b – VIII, 748a
ʿAṭiyya b. al-Aswad al-Ḥanafī (688) iv, 534b; vii, 859a – IV, 558a; VII, 860b
Atjèh i, 88a, 92a, **739b**; iii, 1218b, 1220a, 1233a; v, 21b; vi, 43a, 234b, 235a, b, 236b, 239b, 240a, 732b; vii, 71b; s, 199b –
I, 90b, 94b, **761b**; III, 1249b, 1250b, 1265a; V, 22a; VI, 41b, 204b, 205a, 207b, 208a, b, 209b, 721b; VII, 72b; S, 199b
—war/la guerre d' i, 743b; iii, 1223a, 1228b – I, 766a; III, 1254a, 1260a
al-ʿAtk i, 538b, **747b** – I, 555a, **770a**
Atlagić Meḥmed Pa<u>sh</u>a (XVII) v, 775a – V, 781a
Atlami<u>sh</u> (Awnik) (XIV) iv, 586a – IV, 608b
Atlas i, 364b, 460a, **748a**; v, 1184b, 1186b – I,375b, 473b, **770b**; V, 1174b, 1176b
Aṭrābulus → Ṭarābulus
al-Aṭrash → al-Mā<u>dh</u>arāʾī
Atrek (river/fleuve) i, **749b**; vi, 495a, 716b – I, **772a**; VI, 480b, 705b
Atsiz b. Muḥammad b. Anū<u>sh</u>tigin (<u>Kh</u>ʷārazm<u>sh</u>āh) (1156) i, **750a**; ii, 603a; iii, 196b; iv, 29a, 1067a; v, 311b; vi, 415b, 620b; viii, 63b; ix, 16a; s, 245b –
I, **772b**; II, 618a; III, 201a; IV, 31b, 1099a; V, 311a; VI, 400b, 605b; VIII, 64b; IX, 16b; S, 245b
Atsiz b. Uvak (1079) i, **750b**, 870a; ii, 282a, 856b, 911b; iii, 160a; v, 328a; vii, 121a, 731a; viii, 946b –
I, **773a**, 894b; II, 290a, 876a, 932b; III, 163a; V, 328a; VII, 123a, 731b; VIII, 979a
ʿAttāb b. Asīd (634) i, **751a** – I, **773b**
Attāb b. Saʿd b. Zuhayr, Banū x, 91a – X, 98a
Attāb b. Warḳāʾ (Iṣfahān) (VII) i, 810b – I, 833b
al-ʿAttābī, Kul<u>th</u>ūm b. ʿAmr (835) i, **751a**, 857b; vi, 437b – I, **773b**, 881a; VI, 423a
al-ʿAṭṭār (1824) vi, 113a – VI, 111a
al-ʿAṭṭār (druggist/droguiste) i, **751b**; iv, 95b; s, 42b – I, **774a**; IV, 99b; S, 43a
ʿAṭṭār, Aḥmad ʿAbd al-<u>Gh</u>afūr (XX) vi, 175b
al-ʿAṭṭār → Dāwūd b. ʿAbd al-Raḥmān
al-ʿAṭṭār, Ḥasan b. Muḥammad (1835) i, **755a**, 819b; ii, 356b; viii, 523b – I, **777b**, 842b; II, 366a; VIII, 541a
ʿAṭṭār, Hā<u>sh</u>im (XIX) iv, 775b – IV, 806b
ʿAṭṭār, <u>Kh</u>ʷā<u>dj</u>a ʿAlāʾ al-Dīn (1393) vii, 934a – VII, 934b
ʿAṭṭār, <u>Sh</u>ay<u>kh</u> Farīd al-Dīn (1220) i, 146a, **752b**; ii, 98b, 1041b, 1138a; iii, 373a; iv, 62a, 63a, 65a, 402a; vi, 73a, b, 85b, 762a; vii, 440a, 528b; viii, 83b, 580a; ix, 862b; x, 958a –
I, 150a, **775a**; II, 101a, 1066a, 1165a; III, 385a; IV, 65b, 66b, 68b, 419b; VI, 71a, b, 83b, 751b; VII, 441a, 529a; VIII, 598b; IX, 898b; X,
ʿAṭṭār, <u>Sh</u>ay<u>kh</u> <u>Kh</u>ʷā<u>dj</u>a Ḥasan (XV) s, 50b – S, 51b
ʿAttāra (Yemen) vi, 192a – VI, 176a
ʿAṭṭārīn (Ḳurṭuba) vi, 188b – VI, 172b
ʿAṭṭā<u>sh</u>, ʿAbd al-Malik → Ibn ʿAṭṭā<u>sh</u>
Attila (Hun) (453) x, 691b – X, 734a
Attock → Atak
Aurès → Awrās
Ausa (Dakhan) vi, 63b – VI, 61a
Austria/Autriche → Nemče
Avars i, 504a, 624b, **755a**, 998b; ii, 86a, b, 141b, 251a; iii, 157a; iv, 342b, 343a, 344b, 351a, 571b, 631b, 1172a; v, 55b, 81b, 579b; x, 691b – I, 519b, 645a, **777b**, 1029a; II, 88a, 145a, 258b; III, 160b; IV, 357a, b, 359a, 366a, 594a, 656a, 1205b; V, 57a, 83b, 584a; X, 734a
Avaristān ii, 86a – II, 87b
Avempace → Ibn Bā<u>djdj</u>a
Avenetan, Avennathan → Ibn al-Hay<u>th</u>am
Avennasar → al-Fārābī
Avenzoar → Ibn Zuhr, Abū Marwān
Averroes → Ibn Ru<u>sh</u>d
Avesta i, 236a; iii, 112b; iv, 11a; v, 1110a – I, 243b; III, 115a; IV, 12a; V, 1106a
Avetis Sulṭān-Zāda (XX) s, 365b – S, 365b
Avicenna/-e → Ibn Sīnā
Avram Camondo → Camondo
Avroman → Hawrāmān
Av<u>sh</u>ar (Anatolia/-e) vi, 420b – VI, 405b
Āwa i, **756b** – I, **779a**
ʿAwaḍ b. Ṣāliḥ (ʿAwlaḳī, Banū) (XX) i, 767a – I, 790a
Awadh (Oudh) i, 153a, **756b**, 809a, 1330a; ii, 808b, 870b; iv, 276b, 908a; v, 635a, 1033b, 1240a; vi, 48a, 49b, 77b, 244b, 272a, 535b, 537a; vii, 300b, 412a, 433a; viii, 793b; s, 76b, 95a, 102b, 247a, 292a, 312b, 358b, 360a –
I, 157b, **779a**, 832b, 1371a; II, 827b, 890b; IV, 289a, 941a; V, 639a, 1029b, 1230b; VI, 46b, 48a, 75b, 228b, 257a, 520a, 521b; VII, 302b, 413b, 434a; VIII, 820b; S, 76b, 94a, 101b, 247a, 291b, 312b, 358b, 360a
—Nawwābs i, 856a, 1330a; iii, 61a, 451a, 1163a – I, 879b, 1370b; III, 63b, 466b, 1191b
Awadhī (Eastern Hindī) iii, 456b; vi, 272a – III, 472b; VI, 257a
ʿAwā<u>dh</u>il → ʿAw<u>dh</u>alī
Āwa<u>dj</u> → Āwa
Awa<u>dj</u>ïḳ vi, 200b, 201a – VI, 185a
Awāʿil i, **758a**, 772b – I, **780b**, 795b
Awāl (Baḥrayn) vi, 357b – VI, 341b
ʿAwāliḳ → ʿAwlaḳī
ʿAwālim → ʿĀlima
Awami League viii, 243a – VIII, 248b
ʿAwāmil → ʿĀmil
al-ʿAwāmir, Banū i, **759b** – I, **782a**
ʿAwāna b. al-Ḥakam al-Kalbī (764) i, **760a**; v, 947b; vii, 268b – I, **782b**; V, 951a; VII, 270b
Awar → Avars
al-Aʿwar → Abū Yaʿḳūb al-<u>Kh</u>uraymī
ʿAwāriḍ i, **760a**; ii, 147a; iv, 234b – I, **783a**; II, 151a; IV, 244b
al-ʿAwāṣim i, 145a, 239a, 465b, 517a, **761a**, 909b, 996a, 1292b; ii, 36a; vi, 230b, 332b; s, 243a, b –
I, 149b, 246b, 479a, 532b, **783b**, 937b, 1026b, 1332a; II, 36b; VI, 224b, 317b; S, 243a, b
al-Awāzim, Banū i, 546a, **762a**; iii, 642a, 1068a – I, 563b, **784b**; III, 663b, 1094b
ʿAwda b. Ḥarb Abū Tāyih (XX) iii, 643a – III, 664b
Awda Abū Tayyiʿ. <u>Sh</u>ay<u>kh</u> (XX) x, 885a – X,
Awda<u>gh</u>ost i, **762a**; 1002a; iii, 288b, 657a; v, 653a; vi, 742b; vii, 585a –
I, **785a**; II, 1025b; III, 297b, 678a; V, 657a; VI, 731b; VII, 585a
ʿAw<u>dh</u>alī i, **762b**; ii, 675b – I, **785b**; II, 692a

ʿAwdhila → ʿAwdhalī
Awdj → Nudjūm
Awdjila i, **763a**, 1049a, b – I, **758b**, 1081a, b
ʿAwf b. ʿAṭiyya iv, 998a – IV, 1030b
ʿAwf b. Badr al-Fazārī s, 177b – S, 178b
Awfāt i, 176b, **763b**; iii, 3b, 5b – I, 181a, **786b**; III, 3b, 5b
ʿAwfī, Muḥammad (1232) i, 94b, **764a**, 780a, 1131a; iii, 373a, 1155b; v, 385b; vii, 529b; s, 21a, 22a, 416a –
I, 97a, **786b**, 803a, 1156b; III, 385a, 1184a; V, 386b; VII, 530a; S, 21a, 22a, 416b
Awghānī, Banū i, 218a – I, 224b
Awḥad al-Dīn ʿAbd al-Wāḥid (1385) ii, 330a – II, 340a
Awḥad al-Zamān → Abu ʾl-Barakāt
al-Awḥadī (1408) vi, 194a – VI, 178a
Awḥadī Marāghaʿī (1338) iii, 635a; x,321b – III, 656b; X, 346a
Awḥadī, Rukn al-Dīn (1337) i, **764b**; iv, 67b – I, **787a**; IV, 71a
al-Awḥadī Taḳī al-dīn Muḥammad al-Ḥusaynī → Taḳī Awḥadī
Awḳāf → Waḳf
Awḳāt → Waḳt
ʿAwl i, 320a, **764b** – I, 330a, **787b**
Awlād → name of ancestor/le nom de l'ancêtre
Awlād al-Balad i, **765a**; v, 1250a, 1251b – I, **788a**; V, 1240b, 1241a, 1242b
Awlād Dulaym, Banū vi, 741b – VI, 730b
Awlād Ḥassān vii, 613b, 614a, 616a – VII, 613b, 616a, b
Awlād Khalīfa iv, 382b – IV, 399b
Awlād Mṭāʿ vi, 594a – VI, 579a
Awlād al-nās i, 102a, **765a**, 1060a; iii, 99b; iv, 552b – I, 105a, **788a**, 1091b; III, 102a' IV, 576a
Awlād Nāṣir vii, 613b – VII, 613b
Awlād Saʿd Allāh vi, 743a – VI, 732a
Awlād al-Shaykh i, **765b**, 802b – I, **788b**, 826a
Awlād Sīdī Shaykh vi, 252a; viii, 794b – VI, 236b; VIII, 821b
Awlād Sulaymān s, 164a, b – S, 164a, b
Awlād Yūnus vi, 743a – VI, 732a
ʿAwlaḳī i, **766b**; ii, 675b – I, **789b**; II, 692a
Āwlīl (island/île) ii, 1121b; vii, 57a – II, 1148a; VII, 58a
Awliyāʾ → Walī (Saint)
Awliyā Allāh Āmulī, Mawlānā (XIV) i, 871b; iii, 810b – I, 896a; III, 833b
Awliyā ata i, **767a** – I, **790a**
Awliyar, Shaykh iv, 723b – IV, 752b
Awlonya i, 656a, **767b** – I, 676b, **790b**
ʿAwn, Āl iii, 263a, 605b – III, 270b, 626a
ʿAwn Allāh Kāẓimī → al-Kāẓimī, Meḥmed
ʿAwn b. ʿĀlī x, 41b – X, 43a
ʿAwn b. Djaʿfar b. Abī Ṭālib (VII) s, 92b – S, 92b
ʿAwn al-Dīn al-Tutunčī, imām (XIII) vii, 9b – VII, 10a
ʿAwn al-Rafīḳ, Sharīf (1905) ii, 91a; vi, 151a – II, 93a; VI, 150a
Awraba, Banū i, 1037a; iii, 1031b; v, 517b, 518a; vi, 889b; s, **102b** – I, 1068b; III, 1057b; V, 521b; VI, 881a; S, **102a**
Awrangābād i, **768a**; ii, 55a, 99b, 262b; iii, 450b; vi, 53a, 369b – I, **791a**; II, 56a, 101b, 270b; III, 466b; VI, 51a, 354a
Awrangābād Sayyid i, **768a** – I, **791a**
Awrangābādī, ʿAbd al-Razzāḳ → Shāh Nawāz Khān
Awrangzīb ʿĀlamgīr I (Mughal) (1707) i, 199b, 218a, 229a, 253a, 432b, 624b, **768a**, 954a, 1069a, 1161a, 1166a, 1193b, 1202b, 1210a, 1219a, 1300a, 1329b, 1331a; ii, 99b, 121a, 132a, 134b, 162a, 379a, 488b, 504a, 558a, 566b, 1049b; iii, 199a, 200b, 202a, 308b, 424b, 427a, 430a, 450b, 453b, 492b; iv, 93a, 286b, 514a, 914b, 1128a; v, 47b, 598b, 1135b, 1259a; vi, 126b, 310a, 369b, 407a, 456b, 534b, 535a, 536a, 610b, 612a, 696b; vii, 194a, 315a, b, 318a, 333b, 339b, 346a, 443b; viii, 253b; s, 55b, 57b, 126b, 142b, 246b, 258a, b, 292a, 410b, 420b –
I, 205a, 224b, 235b, 260b, 445a, 645b, **791a**, 983b, 1101a, 1196a, 1200b, 1228b, 1238a, 1246a, 1255a, 1340a, 1370b, 1371b; II, 101b, 124a, 135b, 138a, 167a, 389a, 500b, 517a, 572a, 581a, 1074a; III, 204a, 205b, 207b, 328a, 438a, 441a, 444a, 466a, 469b, 509b; IV, 97b, 299a, 536a, 947b, 1159b; V, 48b, 602a, 1131a, 1250a; VI, 124b, 295a, 354a, 392a, 442a, 519a, 520b, 595b, 596b, 684b; VII, 194b, 317b, 320b, 335a, 341a, 348a, 444b; VIII, 255b; S, 56a, 58a, 125b, 142a, 246b, 257b, 258a, 291b, 411a, 420b, 421a
Awrangzīb Khān → Bādshāh Khān
Awrās (Aurès) i, 170a, 171b, 366a, 367a, 748b, **770a**, 1037a; iv, 383a, 459b; v, 696a; vi, 434b, 435a; s, 103a –
I, 175a, 176a, 377a, b, 771a, **793a**, 1068b; IV, 400a, 480a; V, 701a; VI, 420a, b; S, 102b
Awrigha, Banū i, 1049a – I, 1081a
al-Aws, Banū i, 514a, 544b, **771a**, 1283a; iii, 812a; iv, 835b, 1187a; v, 995a; vi, 373b, 374a, 472a; vii, 367a, 852b; s, 229b, 230a –
I, 529b, 561b, **794a**, 1322b; III, 835b; IV, 868b, 1220a; V, 990a, b; VI, 358a, 458a; VII, 369b, 854a; S, 229b, 230a
Aws b. Ḥadjar (VI) i, **772a**; vi, 605b; x, 586a – I, **795a**; VI, 590a: X,
Aws b. Ḥāritha b. Laʾm i, 1241a – I, 1279a
Aws b. Maghrāʾ vii, 843a – VII, 844a
Awsan iv, 746a – IV, 776a
Awshār → Afshār
Awsī, Āl vi, 646a – VI, 631b
al-Awsī al-Anṣarī, ʿUmar b. Ibrāhīm iii, 181a – III, 185b
Awtād i, 95a, **772a** – I, 97b, **795a**
al-ʿAwwāʾ → Nudjūm
ʿAwwād, Tawfīḳ Yūsuf (XX) v, 189b, 190b – V, 186b, 187b
Awwal i, **772a** – I, **795a**
al-ʿAwwām b. al-Zadjdjādj (Baḥrayn) (XI) iv, 764b – IV, 794b
al-ʿAwwām b. ʿAbd al-ʿAzīz al-Badjalī (VIII) i, 134b – I, 138b
al-ʿAwwānī, Ibrāhīm (1320) vi, 353b – VI, 337b
al-Awzāʿī, Abū ʿAmr ʿAbd al-Raḥmān (774) i, 164b, **772b**, 1137b; ii, 489a, 889b, 1026b; vi, 263b, 281a, 352b; vii, 398a; viii, 713a; ix, 7a; s, 384b –
I, 169a, **795b**, 1172a; II, 501a, 910a, 1050b; VI, 248b, 266a, 337a; VII, 399b; VIII, 733b; IX, 7b; S, 385a
Awzal → al-Hawzalī, Muḥammad b. ʿĀlī
Ay Khanum (1120) vi, 764b – VI, 754a
Ay Aba, Muʾayyad al-Dīn (Nīshāpūr) (1120) vi, 64a, b, 782a; vii, 408a; ix, 16b – VI, 62a, 771b; VII, 409b; IX, 17a
Ay Aba al-Muʾayyad (1172) x, 742b -
Ay Tak, Ikhtiyār al-Dīn (Rayy) (XII) ii, 253a; ix, 16b – II, 260b– IX, 17a
Āya, āyāt i, **773b**; iv, 616a; v, 422a – I, **796b**; IV, 641a; V, 424a
Aya Mavra → Levkas
Aya Sofya i, 75a, **774a**; iv, 225a, b, 226a –
I, 77a, **797a**; IV, 234b, 235b, 236a
Aya Solūk i, **777b** – I, **800b**
Aya Stefanos → Yeshilköy

Aʿyān i, 657a, **778a**, 1304a; ii, 33b, 640b, 724a; iii, 1187b – I, 677b, **801b**, 1344a; II, 34a, 657a, 742b; III, 1217a
ʿAyān Kāzarūnī, Shaykh s, 51b, S,52a
Aʿyāṣ (Umayya) vi, 626a; s, **103b** – VI, 611a; S, **102b**
Āyās (town/ville) i, **778b**, 946b; ii, 38a; iii, 475a – I, **802a**, 975b; II, 39a; III, 491b
Ayās, Mawlānā (1451) vi, 70a – VI, 68a
Ayās Pasha (1539) i, 293b, **779a**; ii, 203b – I, 302b, **802a**; II, 210a
Ayash vi, 226b – VI, 220b
Āyāt → Āya
Āyatullāh (Ayatollah) (title/titre) s, **103b** – S, **103a**
Āyātullāh Kāshānī → Kāshānī
Āyatullāh Ḳumī → Ṭabāṭabāʾī, Sayyid Āḳā Ḥusayn b. Muḥammad
Ayāz (1507) vi, 51a – VI, 49b
Ayāz, Abu ʾl-Nadjm (1057) i, **780a** – I, **803a**
Ayāz, Amīr (1105) i, **780a** – I, **803b**
Ayāz b. Alp Arslān (Saldjūḳ) (1072) vi, 273b – VI, 258a, b
Aybak, al-Muʿizz ʿIzz al-Dīn al-Muʿaẓẓamī (Mamlūk) (1248) i, 732a, **780b**;, 804a, 944b; ii, 284a; iv, 210a, 484b; v, 571a, 627b, 821a; vi, 321b, 668b; vii, 148a, 166b, 274a, 989b; viii, 989a, 995a; s, 250a – I, 754a, **803b**; 828b, 973b; II, 292a; IV, 219b, 505b; V, 575b, 631b, 827a; vi, 305b, 655a; VII, 150a, 168a, 276a, 990a; VIII, 1024a, 1030a; S, 250a
Aybak Ḳuṭb al-Dīn → Ḳuṭb al-Dīn Aybak
Aybak al-Turkumānī (1257) i, 732a, 804a, 944b; vi, 321b, 668n – I, 754a, 828b, 973b; VI, 305b, 655a
Aybar, Mehmet Ali (XX) iv, 124b – IV, 130a
Aybeg → Aybak
ʿAydarūs, Āl i, **780b** – I, **804a**
ʿAydarūs, ʿAbd Allāh (1461) i, 781a – I, 804a
al-ʿAydarūs, ʿAbd al-Ḳādir i, 255b, 594b, 781a; iv, 449b – I, 263b, 614a, 804b; IV, 469b
al-ʿAydarūs, Abū Bakr (1508) i, 181b, **781a**; iv, 450a; vi, 132b, 354b – I, 186b, **804a**; IV, 479a; VI, 130b, 339a
ʿAydarūs, ʿAlī Zayn al-ʿAbidīn (1632) i, 781b – I, 805a
ʿAydarūs b. ʿAlī (1948) i, 767a – I, 790a
ʿAydarūs b. ʿUmar al-Ḥabshī (1895) i, 782a – I, 805b
Aydemir, Colonel Talât (XX) iii, 204a – III, 209b
ʿAydhāb i, **782b**, 1158a; ii, 130b; v, 514b, 519a; vi, 195a, b; vii, 164b; viii, 863b; – I, **805b**, 1192b; II, 134a; V, 518a, 522b; VI, 179a, b; VII, 166a; VIII, 894a
Aydid, Muḥammad Faraḥ (general) ix, 721a – IX, 752b
Aydimur → ʿIzz al-Dīn Aydimur
Aydi̊n i, 467b, **782b**, 1234b; v, 505b, 506a, 557b; vi, 372b, 716b, 975a – I, 481b, **806a**, 1271b; V, 509a, b, 562b; VI, 357a, 705b, 967a
—Edict of/Édit d' vi, 496b – VI, 482a
Aydi̊n-oghlu i, 346a, 778a, **783a**, 807a; ii, 599a; vi, 1018b; vii, 939b – I, 356b, 801a, **806b**, 830a; II, 613b; VI, 1011a; VII, 940a
Aydin Reʿīs (Cacciadiavolo) (XVI) iv, 1156a, b – IV, 1188a, b
Ay-Doghmi̊sh (1205) vi, 500b – VI, 485b, 486a
Aydoghu b. Kushdoghan → Shumla
Ayesha Bai (Kerala) vi, 460b – VI, 446b
ʿAyhala b. Kaʿb → al-Aswad b. Kaʿb al-ʿAnsī
ʿĀyid, Banū i, 98b; vii, 921a – I, 101a; VII, 921b
ʿĀyisha Kargīli Diz → Ṭāḳ
al-Ayka → Madyan
Aykaç, Fāḍil Aḥmed (XX) iii, 357b – III, 368b
Ayla i, 558b, **783b;** x,883a– I, 576a, **807a; X,**
Aylūl → Taʾrīkh
Aymak i, **784a**; s, 367a – I, **807b**; S, 367a
Aymal Khān, Afghān (XVII) i, 970b – I, 1000a
Aymān → Ḳasam
Ayman b. Khuraym (VII) i, **784b**; s, 273a – I, **807b**; S, 273a
ʿAyn → Hidjaʾ
ʿAyn (eye/l'oeil) i, **785a**; iv, 954a – I, **808b**; IV, 986b
ʿAyn (evil eye/mauvais oeil) i, **786a**; iv, 1009a – I, **809a**; IV, 1041b
ʿAyn, aʿyān (sight/la vue) i, **784b**; ii, 486b – I, **808a**; II, 499a
ʿAyn, ʿuyūn (spring water/source d'eau) i, 538b, 1232a – I, 555b, 1269a
ʿAyn al-Baḳar vi, 652a – VI, 637b
ʿAyn Dārā iv, 834b – IV, 867b
ʿAyn al-Dawla (Ṣadr-i Aʿẓam)) (XX) ii, 650b, 651a; viii, 140a – II, 666b, 667b; VIII, 142b
ʿAyn Dilfa i, **786b** – I, **810a**
ʿAyn Djālūt (battle/bataille) (1260) i, 21b, **786b**, 1125a; ii, 284b; iii, 184a; v, 571b; vi, 314b, 321b, 543b; vii, 167a – I, 22a, **810a**, 1158b; II, 292b; III, 188a; V, 576a; VI, 299b, 306a, 528a; VII, 168b
ʿAyn al-Djarr i, **787b**; vi, 623b; s, 229b – I, **811a**; VI, 609a; S, 229b
ʿAyn Ḥunayn vi, 179b – VI, 163b
ʿAyn al-Ḳuḍāt al-Hamadhānī → ʿAbd Allāh b. Abī Bakr al-Mīyānadjī
Ayn al-Mulk Māhrū (XIII) s, 105b – S, 105a
ʿAyn al-Mulk Multānī (1322) i, 764a; ii, 12b, 218b; iii, 405b; iv, 759a, 922a; v, 635a; vi, 309b; s, **105a** – I, 787a; II, 12b, 225a; III, 416a; IV, 789b, 955a; V, 639a; VI, 294b; S, **104b**
ʿAyn Mūsā i, **788a** – I, **811a**
ʿAyn Shams i, **788a**; ii, 424a; vi, 75b, 411a, 412b, 413a – I, **811b**; II, 434b; VI, 73b, 395b, 397b, 398a
ʿAyn al-Tamr i, **788b**; x, 791a – I, **812a**; X,
ʿAyn Temushent i, **789a;** x, 791a– I, **812b;** X,
ʿAyn al-Warda i, **789a**; vii, 522a – I, **812b**; VII, 522b
ʿAyn Warḳa s, 159b – S, 159b
ʿAyn Yashīr i, 699b – I, 712a
ʿAyn Zarba i, **789a**; ii, 37b; vi, 505b, 775a – I, **812b**; II, 38a; VI, 491a, 764b
ʿAyn Zubayda vi, 164b, 177b, 179a – VI, 157b, 163b
Ayna Čāshnegīr, Sayf al-Dīn, amīr (XIII) i, 510a – I, 525b
Aynabakhtī i, **790a**; iv, 882a; v, 504a; s, 80b – I, **813b**; IV, 914b; V, 507b; S, 80b
Aynāl → Īnāl
Aynalu, Banū iv, 9b – IV, 10a
ʿAynayn → al-Djubayl
ʿAynayn, Āl Bū iv, 751b – IV, 781b
al-ʿAynī (1487) vii, 537a – VII, 537a
al-ʿAynī, Abū Muḥammad Badr al-Dīn (1451) i, 138a, 595a, **790b**, 1128a; iii, 488b; iv, 966b; v, 489b; vi, 194a; vii, 172b, 969b – I, 142a, 614b, **814a**, 1162a; III, 505b; IV, 998b; V, 492b; VI, 178a; VII, 174b, 969b
ʿAynī ʿAlī (1617) vi, 508b – VI, 494a
ʿAynī, Ḥasan Efendi (1837) i, **790b** – I, **813b**
ʿAyniyya i, 51a; ii, 1094b; v, 889b, 892a – I, 52b; II, 1120b; V, 896a, 898a
ʿAynṭāb i, 262a, **791a**; ii, 206; vi, 231a, 378a, 507a, 508b – I, 270a, **814b**; II, 21a; VI, 225a, 362b, 492b, 494a
al-ʿAynṭabī, Muḥammad Shākir b. al-Ḥādjdj Ibrāhīm Ḥilmī (1877) vi, 913b – VI, 905a
ʿAynṭūra s, 33b – S, 33b
Ayodhyā → Awadh
Ayr → Aïr
al-ʿAyrayn Mnt. vi, 745a – VI, 734a, b

Ayrumlu Khāns vi, 200b – VI, 185a
ʿAyshe → ʿĀʾisha
Ayt i, **792a** – I, **815a**
Ayt Atta, Banū x, 82b – X, 86a
Ayt Idrasen s, 113b – S, 113a
Ayt Immūr, Banū vi, 590a – VI, 575a
Ayt Isḥāḳ s, 223a – S, 223a
Ayt Mūsā s, 113b – S, 112b
Ayt Yūsī s, 113b – S, 113a
Aytākh al-Turkī (849) vii, 777b; s, 106a – VII, 779b; S, 105b
Ayth Zekrī (1914) s, 403b – S, 403b
Āytigīn, Ikhtiyār al-Dīn (XIII) vii, 915b – VII, 916a
Aytimish al-Badjasī, amīr (1400) ii, 781b – II, 800a
Ayudhya (XV) vi, 212b – VI, 196b
Ayuka (1724) vi, 416b – VI, 401b
Ayüke Khān (Kalmuk) (1678) i, 1076a – I, 1108b
Aywalîk i, **792a** – I, **815b**
Aywān → Iwān
Aywaz (ʿAywāḍ) i, **792a** – I, **815b**
Ayyām al-ʿAdjūz i, **792b** – I, **816a**
Ayyām al-ʿArab i, 566a, **793a** – I, 584b, **816b**
ʿAyyān (Yemen) vi, 438b – VI, 424a
Ayyār → Taʾrīkh
ʿAyyār (ʿayyārūn) i, 256b, **794a**, 900a, b, 902a, b, 955a, 1355b; ii, 961b, 962a, 1043b; iv, 445a – I, 264b, **817b**, 927a, b, 929a, b, 984a, 1394b; II, 983b, 984a, 1068a; IV, 465a
ʿAyyāsh b. Lahīʿa (IX) i, 153b – I, 157b
ʿAyyāsh b. Nadjāh → Zabīd
al-ʿAyyāshī (marabout) (1641) v, 48b; viii, 899a – V, 50a; VIII, 930a
al-ʿAyyāshī, Abu 'l-Naṣr Muḥammad (IX) i, **794b**; iv, 711b; vi, 188a – I, **818a**; IV, 740a, b; VI, 172a
al-ʿAyyāshī, Abū Sālim ʿAbd Allāh (1679) i, **795a**; ii, 161a; iii, 736b – I, **818a**; II, 166a; III, 759a
Ayyil i, **795a** – I, **818b**
Ayyūb (Job) i, **795b**; 242a – I, **819a**; II, 249a
Ayyūb, Rashīd (XX) v, 1254b, 1255a, b – V, 1245b, 1246a, b
Ayyūb (of Edessa/d'Édesse) (IX) i, 213a – I, 219a
Ayyūb b. Abi Yazīd al-Nukkārī (X) i, 163b; iii, 1042a; vi, 727b – I, 168a; III, 1068a; VI, 716b
Ayyūb b. Aḥmad al-Taghlibī (850) vi, 900a – VI, 891a
Ayyūb b. Ḥabīb al-Lakhmī (VIII) i, 58b; iv, 477b – I, 60b; IV, 498b
Ayyūb b. al-Raḳḳī iv, 92a – IV, 96a
Ayyūb b. Salama (VIII) vi, 139a – VI, 137b
Ayyūb b. Shādhī b. Marwān (XII) i, 796b – I, 820a
Ayyūb b. Tamīm b. al-Muʿizz (Zīrid(e)) (XII) iii, 788a – III, 811b
Ayyūb Anṣārī (VII) s, 292a – S, 291b
Ayyūb Khan (1914) i, 232a, **796b**; iv, 537b – I, 239a, **819b**; IV, 561a
Ayyūb Khān (1974) iii, 533b, 565b, 566a; v, 1081b; vi, 78b; viii, 242b – III, 552a, 585a, b; IV, 1079a; VI, 76a; VIII, 248a
Ayyūb Ṣabrī Pasha (1890) i, **796b** – I, **820a**
Ayyūb al-Sakhtiyānī iv, 370b – IV, 387a
Ayyūbid(e)s i, 197b, 215a, 435b, 439b, 552b, 666b, **796b**, 814b, 816a, 1125a, 1206b, 1276b, 1316b; ii, 65a, 283b, 305b, 329b, 344b, 506a, 858a; iii, 120b, 228b, 473a, 507a; iv, 429b, 816b, 817b; v, 454b, 627b, 739a, 1245a; vi, 149a, 194a, 231a, 261b, 326b, 327a, 429a, b, 433b, 673b, 931a; vii, 164a, 998a; ix, 596b; s, 154a, 338a, 387b, 396a – I, 203a, 221b, 448a, 452a, 570a, 687a, **820a**, 837b, 839b, 1159a, 1242b, 1316a, 1356b; II, 66b, 291b, 314a, 339a, 354a, 519a, 878a; III, 123a, 235b, 489b, 524b; IV, 448b, 849b, 850b; V, 457b, 631b, 744a, 1235b; VI, 147b, 148a, 178a, 224b, 246a, 311a, b, 414b, 415a, 418b, 660a, 923a; VII, 165b, 1000a; IX, 619a; S, 154b, 337b, 388a, 396a
—literature/littérature iii, 753a, 967a – III, 776a, 991b
al-ʿAyyūḳ → Nudjūm
ʿAyyūḳī (XI) iv, 57b, 62b; vi, 833 – IV, 61a, 66a; VI, 823b
ʿAzab i, **807a**; iv, 230b, 723a – I, **830a**; IV, 241a, 752a
Āzād, Abu 'l-Kalām (1958) iii, 431b; iv, 170b; v, 7a, b; vi, 461b; s, 4b, **106a**, 247b – III, 445b; IV, 178a; V, 7b, 8a; VI, 447a; S, 3b, **105b**, 247b
Āzād, Muḥammad Ḥusayn (1910) i, **807b**; ii, 222a; iii, 93b; vii, 556a, 668a; s, 74b, **107a** – I, **830b**; II, 229a; III, 96a; VII, 556a, 668a; S, 75b, **106b**
Āzād Bilgrāmī, Ghulām-ʿAlī (1786) i, **808a**, 1219b; vi, 271b; vii, 530b – I, **831a**, 1255b; VI, 256a; VII, 530b
Āzād Khān (Afghān) (XVIII) i, 190a; iii, 1103a; iv, 390a, 639b – I, 196a; III, 1130a; IV, 407a, 666a
Āzādī s, **107b** – S, **107a**
al-ʿAzafī, Abu 'l-Ḳāsim (XIII) viii, 690b – VIII, 710b
ʿAzafī, Banu 'l- iv, 355b; s, 45b, **111b** – IV, 371a; S, 46a, **110b**
Azahari, Shaykh A.M. (Brunei) (XX) s, 152a, b – S, 152b
Azaḳ (Azov) i, **808b**; vi, 56a, 1025b – I, **831b**; VI, 54a, 1018a
Azal → Ḳidam
Azalay i, **808b**, 1222a; ii, 368a, b – I, **832a**, 1258a; II, 378a, b
Azalī i, **809a**; vi, 292a – I, **832a**; VI, 277a
Aʿẓam b. Awrangzīb (Mughal) (1707) vii, 341b – VII, 343b
Aʿẓam Humāyūn → Malik Mughīth (Mālwā); Maḥmūd II Khaldjī
Aʿẓam-i Humāyūn b. Sayf al-Dīn Ghūrī, vizier iv, 908a – IV, 941a
Aʿẓam Khān I (Rādjpūt) (XVII) i, 809a; iv, 1018b; vii, 333b – I, 832b; IV, 1050b; VII, 335a
Aʿẓam Khān II (Rādjpūt) (1771) i, 809a – I, 832b
Aʿẓam Khān (Mālwa) (XVI) v, 1a – V, 1b
Aʿẓam Khān Bārakzay → Muḥammad Aʿẓam b. Dūst Muḥammad
Aʿẓam Shāh Ghiyāth al-Dīn (Bengal(e)) (1419) ii, 216b; v, 638a – II, 223a; V, 642b
Aʿẓam Shāh (Mughal) → Muḥammad Aʿẓam b. Awrangzīb
Aʿẓamgarh i, **809a**; iii, 433a; ix. 433b – I, **832a**; III, 447b; IX. 450a, b
ʿAzamiyya (Ṭarīḳa) → Abu 'l-ʿAzāʾim
Azammūr i, **809b**; vi, 573a, 594a, 740a, 741b – I, **832b**; VI, 558a, 579a, 730a, 731a
Āzar i, **810a**; iii, 980a – I, **833a**; III, 1004b
Azar Kaywan (1618) v, 1114a – V, 1110a
Azarbāydjān → Adharbāydjān; Azerbaydjān
al-Azarīfī, Abū Muḥammad ʿAbd Allāh (1800) vi, 113a – VI, 110b
Azāriḳa i, 77a, **810a**; iii, 40b, 657b; iv, 15a, 44b, 99b, 269a, 752b, 1075b; v, 157b; vii, 123b, 357a, 877b x, 762a – I, 79a, **833a**; III, 42a, 679a; IV, 16a, 47a, 104a, 281a, 783a, 1107b; V, 157a; VII, 125b, 359b, 879a; X,
Azarquîel → al-Zarḳālī
ʿAzāz (battle of/bataille de (1030)) i, 239a; v, 106a; vii, 117b – I, 246b; V, 108a; VII, 119b
ʿAzāzīl i, **811a** – I, **834b**
Azd, Banū i, 304a, 529b, 544b, 548b, **811b**, 1140b; ii, 246b; iii, 223a, 782a; v, 77a; vi, 564b, 640b; x, 3a; s, 222b – I, 313b, 545b, 565b, 566a, **834b**, 1175a; II, 253b; III,

230a, 805b; V, 79a; VI, 549b, 625b; X, 3a; S, 223a
al-Azd b. al-Ghawth vi, 565b – VI, 550b
Azda bint al-Ḥārith b. Kalada (VII) s, 354b – S, 354b
Azdadja → al-Barānis
al-Azdamūrī, Sayf al-Dīn Manku Bāy (1415) vi, 580b – VI, 565b
al-Azdī → Abū Manṣūr; Abu 'l-Muṭahhar; ʿĪsā b. Rayʿān; Yazīd b. Ḥātim
al-Azdī, ʿAbd al-ʿAzīz b. ʿAbd al-Raḥmān (IX) vi, 332a – VI, 316b
al-Azdī, Abu 'l-Khaṭṭab vi, 774a – VI, 763b
al-Azdī, Abū Muḥammad Yūsuf, ḳāḍī (X) s, 284a – S, 284a
al-Azdī, Abū Zakariyyāʾ (945) i, **813a**; viii, 518a – I, **836b**; VIII, 535b
al-Azdī, ʿAlī b. Aḥmad (IX) viii, 53a – VIII, 54a
al-Azdī, Djunada b. Abī Umayya (VII) viii, 569a – VIII, 587a
al-Azdī, Hārūn b. Mūsā viii, 818b – VIII, 846b
al-Azdī, Ismāʿīl b. Isḥaḳ b. Ḥammād al-Ḳāḍī (895) vi, 280b; s, **113a** – VI, 265b; S, **112b**
al-Azdī, Ismāʿīl b. Isḥāḳ al-Ḳāḍī (895) s, **113a**. 384a – S, **112b**, 384b
al-Azdī, Muḥammad b. al-Muʿallāʾ s, 394b – S, 395a
Azemmūr → Azammūr
Azerbāydjān (republic/république) i, 191b, ii, 595a; iii, 530a; v, 1213b – I, 197a; II, 609b; III, 548b; V, 1203a
Azerī → Adharī
Azfarī (1818) i, **813b** – I, **836b**
Azghār vi, 741b – VI, 730b
al-Azhar i, **813b**; ii, 495a, 854a, 863a; iii, 841a, 986b; iv, 144a, 444a, 907b; v, 910b, 1124a; vi, 87b, 170a, 237b, 361a, 414a; ix, 260b; s, 18a, 40b, 121b, 132b, 262b, 408a, 411a – I, **837a**; II, 507b, 873b, 883a; III, 865a, 1011a; IV, 150a, 464a, 940a; V, 916b, 1120b; VI, 85b, 160b, 210b, 345a, 399a; IX, 268b, 269a; S, 18a, 41a, 121a, 132a, 262a, 408b, 411b
al-Azharī (XI) vi, 634b – VI, 619b
al-Azharī, Abū Manṣūr Muḥammad (980) i, 719a, **822a**; iv, 524b; vi, 914a; vii, 209b; viii, 14a; s, 20a, 38a, 250b – I, 740b, **845a**; IV, 547a; VI, 905b; VII, 211a; VIII, 14b; S, 20a, 38a, 250b
al-Azharī, Aḥmad (1748) i, 821b – I, 844b
al-Azharī, Ibrāhīm (1688) i, 821b – I, 844b
al-Azharī, Ismāʿīl (XX) iii, 524a – III, 542a
al-Azharī, Khālīd (1499) i, 821b, 1314b – I, 844b, 1355a
ʿAẓīm Allāh Khān (1859) i, **822a** – I, **845a**
ʿAẓīm al-Shān b. Bahādur Shāh I (XVIII) i, 914a, 1025b; ii, 7a, 379a, 810a – I, 941b, 1057a; II, 7a, 389b, 829a
ʿAẓīma i, **822b**; ii, 545a – I, **846a**; II, 558b
ʿAẓīmābād → Bānkīpūr
Azimech → Nudjūm
al-Aẓīmī (1161) i, **823a** – I, **846a**
Azimut → al-Samt
al-ʿĀzir → Lazarus/Lazare
al-ʿAzīz (Ayyūbid(e)) → al-Malik al-ʿAzīz ʿUthmān
al-ʿAzīz (Hammādid(e)) (1121) iii, 138b – III, 141a
ʿAzīz b. Ḥātim (VII) vii, 922a – VII, 922b
ʿAzīz ʿAlī al-Maṣrī (XX) s, 299b – S, 299b
al-ʿAzīz bi-'llāh Nizār (Fāṭimid(e)) (996) vii, 162a, 357b, 910b – VII, 163b, 360a, 911a
al-ʿAzīz bi-'llāh Nizār (Fāṭimid(e)) (996) i, 533a, 788a, 814b, 816a, **823a**, 1153b, 1218a; ii, 854a, 855a, 860a; iii, 76b, 128b, 130a, 246a, 385b; iv, 663b; vi, 199b, 435b, 545a, 670a, 673b; vii, 162a, 357b, 910b – I, 549a, 811b, 837b, 839a, **846a**, 1188a, 1254b; II, 874a, 875a, 879b; III, 79a, 131b, 132b, 253a, 398a; IV, 690a, b; VI, 183b, 421a, 530a, 656a, 660a; VII, 163b, 360a, 911a
ʿAzīz Ḍiyāʾ al-Dīn b. Zāhid (1913) v, 1005b – V, 1001a
ʿAzīz Efendī → ʿAlī ʿAzīz Giridli
ʿAzīz Khammār (Amrohā) (XX) s, 73b – S, 74a
ʿAzīz Miṣr i, 825b – I, 848b
Aziz Nesin (XX) vi, 95b – VI, 93b
ʿAzīz Saghrūshnī (XX) vi, 755b – VI, 745a
al-ʿAzīz ʿUthmān b. al-Ādil b. Ayyūb (Ayyūbid(e)) (XIII) ix, 738a – IX, 771b
ʿAzīza bint al-Ghiṭrīf b. ʿAṭāʾ s, 326b – S, 326a
ʿAzīza ʿUthmāna (XVIII) iii, 605a – III, 626a
ʿAzīzat al-Dīn Akhshāwrā Khātūn bint Mawdūd b. ʿImād al-Dīn Zangī (1213) vi, 871b – VI, 862a
ʿAzīzī (1585) i, **825b** – I, **848b**
ʿAzīzī → Ḳaračelebi-zāde
ʿAzīziyya x, 259a – X, 269a
Azkūtigīn b. Asātigīn (IX) vi, 900a – VI, 891b
ʿAzl i, **826a** – I, **849a**
al-ʿAzm, Āl v, 925a – V, 930a
ʿAzmī Gedizī (XVI) v, 952a – V, 955b
ʿAzmī-zade, Muṣṭafā (1631) i, **826a**; iii, 91b – I, **849a**; III, 94a
Aẓnag → al-Sahnadjī, Ibrāhīm b. ʿAbd Allāh
Azophi → al-Ṣūfī, Abu 'l-Ḥusayn
Azores/Açores → al-Djazāʾir al-Khālida
Azougui → Atar
Azov → Azaḳ
Azov, Sea of/Mer d'- → Baḥr Māyuṭis
Azra Erhat (XX) vi, 95b – VI, 93b
ʿAzrāʾīl → ʿIzrāʾīl
al-Azraḳ ix, 673a – IX, 700b
al-Azraḳī s, 271b, 272a – S, 271b
al-Azraḳī, Abu 'l-Walīd (VII) i, 591a, 609a, **826b**; ii, 757b – I, 610b, 628b, **849b**; II, 775b
Azraḳī Harawī, Zayn al-Dīn (1130) i, **827a**; iv, 61b; viii, 970b – I, **850a**; IV, 65a; VIII, 1004b
Azraḳī Kurds → Zraḳī
Azraḳites → Azāriḳa
Azrū s, **113** – S, **112b**
Azuel → Abū Muḥammad al-Zubayr b. ʿUmar
Azūg(g)i (Azuḳḳī) vii, 587b, 613a – VII, 587b, 613a
Azulejo → Khazaf
Āzurda, Ṣadr al-Dīn (1868) i, **827b**; ii, 736a – I, **850a**; II, 754b
ʿAzza → Kuthayyir
ʿAzza al-Maylāʾ (VII) i, **828a**; ii, 1073b; iii, 812a; iv, 821b; viii, 853a – I, **851a**; II, 1098b; III, 835b; IV, 854b; VIII, 882b
ʿAzzāba iii, 95a, 96a – III, 97b, 98b
ʿAzzān b. Ḳays (ʿUmān) (1871) i, 554b, 1283a; iv, 1085a; viii, 993a; s, 355b, 356a – I, 572a, 1321b; IV, 1116a; VIII, 1028a; S, 355b
ʿAzzān b. Tamīm (893) i, 813a – I, 836a

B

Bāʾ → Hidjāʾ; Mawāzīn
Bā i, **828a** – I, **851a**
Bā ʿAbbād i, **828b** – I, **851b**
Bā Aḥmad → Bā Ḥmād
Bā ʿAlawī, Āl i,77b, 780b, **828b**; iv, 885b, 887b; x, 303a – I, 286b, 804a, **851b**; IV, 918b, 920a; X, 326a
Bā Faḍl → Faḍl, Bā
Bā Faḳīh → Faḳīh, Bā
Bā Ḥassān → Ḥassān, Bā
Bā Ḥmād, Aḥmad b. Mūsā, vizier (1900) i, 57b, 357a;

ii, 820a; iii, 562b; v, 1193a; vi, 589b; s, **114a**, 336b – I, 59b, 368a; II, 839b; III, 581b; V, 1183a; VI, 574a; S, **113b**, 336a
Bā Hurmuz → Hurmuz, Bā
Bā Kat͟hīr → Kat͟hīr, Āl
Bā Kāzim → Kāzim, Bā
Ba Lobbo i, 303b; ii, 914b; iii, 39b – I, 313a; II, 963b; III, 41a
Bā Mak͟hrama → Mak͟hrama, Bā
Bā Ṣurra ii, 173b – II, 179a
Baalbek → Baʿlabakk
Bāb (gate/porte) i, **830a**; v, 989b – I, **853a**; V, 984b
Bāb (s͟īʿa) i, **832b**; ii, 97b; iv, 39a, 51b, 70b, 854b – I, **855b**; II, 99b; IV, 41b, 54a, 74b, 887b
al-Bāb (Buṭnān) i, 1349a, 1357b, 1358a; vi, 378a – I, 1389b, 1398a; VI, 362b
Bāb, ʿAlī Muḥammad S͟hīrāzī, Sayyid (1850) i, **833a**, 1030b; iv, 39a, 51b, 70b, 696a; vii, 422a; viii, 679a; ix, 404a – I, **856a**, 1062a; IV, 41b, 54a, 74b, 724a; VII, 424a; VIII, 698b; IX, 417a
Bāb Abraz Bag͟hdād) s, 384a – S, 384b
Bāb al-Abwāb (Darband) i, 32a, **835b**; iv, 342a, 1173a; vi, 740a, b; vii, 71a – I, 33a, **858b**; IV, 356b, 1206b; VI 729a, b; VII, 72a
Bāb Ad͟jyād (Mecca) vi, 167a – VI 159a
Bāb Ag͟hmāt (Marrākus͟h) vi, 591a, 596a – VI, 576a, 581a
Bāb Agnaw (Marrākus͟h) vi, 596b – VI, 581a, b
Bāb al-Aḥmar (Marrākus͟h) vi, 596b – VI, 581b
Bāb ʿĀlī (Istanbul) i, **836a**; iv, 568a, 1126a – I, **859b**; IV, 590b, 1158a
Bāb Allāh (Damas(cus)) s, 49a – S, 50a
Bāb Allāh (Ternate) (XVI) vi, 116b – VI, 114a
Bāb Allān → Bāb al-Lān
Bāb Aylān (Marrākus͟h) vi, 590b, 591a, 592a, 596a; s, 124b – VI, 575b, 576a, 577a, 581a; S, 382b
Bāb al-Azad͟j (Bag͟hdād) s, 192b – S, 194a
Bāb Banī S͟hayba (Mecca) vi, 708b – VI, 697b
Bāb Banī Sulaym (Baṣra) vi, 709a – VI, 698a
Bāb Berrīma (Marrākus͟h) vi, 596b – VI, 581b
Bāb Dabbāg͟h (Marrākus͟h) vi, 592a, 596a – VI, 577a, 581a
Bāb al-D͟hahab (Bag͟hdād) i, 896a, 897a – I, 922b, 924a
Bāb al-D͟jābiya (Damas(cus)) vi, 122b, 548a – VI, 120b, 532b
Bāb D͟jamāʾiz (Mecca) vi, 160a – VI, 154b
Bāb al-D͟jīsa (Fès) s, 126a – S, 125a
Bāb Dukkāla (Marrākus͟h) vi, 590a, b, 596a – VI, 574b, 575b, 581a
Bāb al-Durayba (Mecca) vi, 175a, 177a – VI, 162a
Bāb al-Farādīs (Damas(cus)) vi, 122b – VI, 120b
Bāb Fās → Bāb al-K͟hamīs
Bāb Futūḥ (Fès) vi, 123b – VI, 121b
Bāb al-Futūḥ (Miṣr) vii, 149a, 150a – VII, 151a, 152a
Bāb al-G͟hadr iv, 685a – IV, 713a
Bāb al-Ḥadīd (Cairo/le Caire) vi, 414a – VI, 399a
Bāb al-Ḥamra (Fès) vi, 124a – VI, 121b
Bāb al-Ḥarb (Bag͟hdād) vi, 123b – VI, 121a
Bāb Hiṭṭa (al-Ḳuds) vi, 626b – VI, 611b
Bāb-i Humāyūn (Istanbul) i, **836b**; iv, 568a – I, **860a**; IV, 590b
Bāb Ibrāhīm (Mecca) vi, 154b – VI, 152a
Bāb Ig͟hlī (Marrākus͟h) vi, 596b – VI, 581b
Bāb Kaysān (Damas(cus)) vi, 122b – VI, 120b
Bāb al-K͟hamīs (Marrākus͟h) vi, 590a, 596a – VI, 574b, 581a
Bāb al-K͟hawḳa (Málaga) vi, 220b – VI, 214b
Bāb Ḳṣība (Marrākus͟h) vi, 596b – VI, 581b
Bāb Ḳubbat Zamzam (Mecca) vi, 166a – VI, 158a
Bāb al-Kuḥl (Marrākus͟h) vi, 596b – VI, 581a
Bāb al-Lān (Bāb Allān) i, **837a**; iv, 342b – I, **860a**; IV, 357a
Bāb al-Mak͟hzen (Marrākus͟h) vi, 596a – VI, 581a
Bāb Maʿlā (Mecca) vi, 122b – VI 120b
Bāb al-Malik (Saʿūd) (Mecca) vi, 167b – VI, 159a
Bāb al-Mandab i, **837b**, 932a – I, **860b**, 960b
Bāb-i Mas͟hīk͟hat (Istanbul) i, **837b** – I, **861a**
Bāb Messūfa (Marrākus͟h) vi, 596a – VI, 581a
Bāb Muḥriḳ (Marrākus͟h) vi, 596a – VI, 581a
Bāb Nfīs (Marrākus͟h) vi, 596a – VI, 581a
Bāb al-Rabb (Marrākus͟h) vi, 591a – VI, 576a
Bāb al-Raḥā (Marrākus͟h) vi, 596a – VI, 581a
Bāb al-Riyāḥ (Málaga) vi, 220b – VI, 214b
Bāb al-Sāʿāt (Damas(cus)) vi, 671a – VI, 657b
Bāb al-Ṣafā (Mecca) vi, 154b, 666b – VI, 152a, 652b
Bāb al-Ṣag͟hīr (Damas(cus)) vi, 122b, 538a – VI, 120a, 522b
Bāb al-Salām (Mecca) vi, 153a, 160b, 167a, 177a, 709a – VI, 151b, 154b, 159a, 697b
Bāb al-Saliḥa (Marrākus͟h) vi, 596a – VI, 581a
Bāb-i Serʿaskeri (Istanbul) i, **838a**; ii, 513a; iii, 552b – I, **861a**; II, 525b; III, 571b
Bāb al-S͟hammāsiyya (Bag͟hdād) vii, 485a – VII, 484b
Bāb Tag͟hzūt (Marrākus͟h) vi, 596a – VI, 581a
Bāb al-Ṭāḳ (Bag͟hdād) i, 897a, 898b, 900a, b; s, 192b, 194a, 381a – I, 923b, 925b, 927a; S, 193b, 381a
Bāb al-Ṭubūl (Marrākus͟h) vi, 596b – VI, 581a
Bāb Tūmā (S͟hayk͟h Raslān, Damas(cus)) vi, 122b, 545b – VI, 120a, 530a
Bāb Umm Hāniʾ (Mecca) vi, 167a – VI, 159a
Bāb al-ʿUmra (Mecca) vi, 160b – VI, 154b
Bāb al-Wādī (Málaga) vi, 220b – VI, 214b
Bāb Yīntān (Marrākus͟h) vi, 596a – VI, 581a
Bāb al-Zumurrud (Bag͟hdād) vi, 519b – VI, 504a
Bāb Zuwayla (Cairo/le Caire) vi, 367b; s, 408a – VI, 351b; S, 408a
Baba i, **838b** – I, **861b**
Baba b. Ḥamā Allāh (Ḥamālī) (XX) iii, 108a – III, 110b
Baba Ādam (1119) i, 1168a; ii, 216a – I, 1202b; II, 223a
Baba Afḍal al-Dīn Muḥammad (1256) i, **838b** – I, **862a**
Baba ʿAlī b. Ṣāliḥ b. Ḳuṭb al-Dīn (XIV) ii, 989b – II, 1012b
Baba ʿAlī Mest-i ʿAd͟jemī (XVI) iv, 1137a – IV, 1169a
Baba ʿAlī Nad͟jd͟jār (XV) s, 423b – S, 423b
Baba Ardalān i, 626b – I, 647a
Baba Ayyūb (Chitral) ii, 29b – II, 30a
Baba Beg (1898) i, **839b** – I, **862b**
Baba Dāg͟hī → Babadag͟hī
Baba G͟hor iii, 16a – III, 17a
Baba Girāy (1522) i, 838b – I, 861b
Baba Ḥasan → Ḥasan Baba
Baba Ḥasan, Amīr (1460) vi, 513b – VI, 499a
Baba Ḥātim → Sālār K͟halīl
Baba Ilyās vi, 354b – VI, 338b
Baba Isḥāḳ (XIII) i, 698b, 843b, 1161b; ii, 989a – I, 719b, 867a, 1196b; II, 1012a
Baba Ismāʿīl Kubrawī (XV) s, 353b, 423b – S, 353b, 423b
Baba K͟hān → Fatḥ ʿAlī S͟hāh
Bāba K͟hān b. ʿAbd al-Mad͟jīd K͟hān (XX) x, 961a
Baba K͟hos͟hīn (XI) i, 262b, 841b; v, 823a – I, 271a, 865a; V, 829a
Baba Nūr al-Dīn Ris͟hī (1438) s, **114a** – S, **113b**
Baba Ratan → Ratan, Bābā Ḥad͟jd͟jī
Baba Sāhib → Bhāskar Rāo
Baba Sawindīk (VII) x, 33b – X, 35a
Baba Ṭāhir ʿUryān (1010) i, 262b, **839b**; iii, 106a; iv, 62a; x, 377b – I, 270b, **862b**; III, 108a; IV, 65b; X, 404b

Baba Toma (XIX) iv, 352a – IV, 367a
Baba ʿUthmān (XV) s, 353b – S, 353b
Baba Walī Ṣaḥib i, 506a; iii, 245b – I, 521b; III, 252b
Babadaghi i, **842b**; ii, 612a, 613a – I, **865b**; II, 627a, 628a
Babadjān b. Pinchas, Solomon (XIX) iv, 310b – IV, 324b
Bäbädjik (canton) vi, 201a, b – VI, 185a, b
Babaeski i, **843a** – I, **866b**
Bābāʾī i, 698b, 838b, **843b**; iv, 817a; viii, 191b – I, 719b, 861b, **866b**; IV, 849b; VIII, 194b
Bābāʾī b. Farhād (XVII) iv, 310a – IV, 323b
Bābāʾī b. Luṭf (XVII) iv, 310a – IV, 323b
Bābak Yaḥyā b. Muʿādh al-Khurramī (838) i, 52b, 153b, 154a, 241a, 625b, 660b, **844a**, 1072b; ii, 228a, 623b, 893a; iii, 274b, 471a; iv, 17a, 344b, 646a; v, 64b, 856a; vi, 335a, 337a, b, 338a, b, 499a, 504b; vii, 497b, 776a, 777a; s, 116a – I, 54a, 158a, b, 248b, 646a, 681b, **867a**, 1104b; II, 235a, 639a, 914a; III, 282a, 487b; IV, 18b, 359b, 672b; V, 66a, 862b; VI, 319a, 321b, 322a, b, 484b, 489b; VII, 497b, 778a, 779a; S, 115b
Bābalyūn (Babylon, Egypt(e) i, **844b**; vii, 147b I, 8**67b**; VII, 149b
Bābān, Āl i, **845a**; v, 460b; ix, 830a – I, **868a**; V, 463a; IX, 865a
al-Bābānī, Aḥmad al-Faḳīh (XVII) i, 845a – I, 818a
Bābar → Bābur
Babari (Gobir) (1770) iv, 549a – IV, 572b
al-Bābartī → Akmal al-Dīn
Bābā-Ṭāhir viii, 579b – VIII, 598b
Babatu (XIX) ii, 1003b – II, 1027a
al-Babāwī → Shams al-Dīn Muḥammad
Babba Zakī iv, 549a – IV, 572b
Babbaghāʾ i, **845b** – I, **868b**
al-Babbaghā, Abu ʾl-Faradj (1007) i, 120a, **845b**; ii, 198a; vii, 770b; s, 119b – I, 123a, **868b**; II, 204b; VII, 772b; S, 119a
Bābil (Babylon) i, **846a**; vi, 218a, 413a, 633b – I, **869a**; VI, 202a, 398a, 618b
Bābīs i, 304b, 833a, **846b**, 1099b; v, 102a, 502a; vi, 485a, 552a, b, 939b; vii, 422a, b, 440b, 1003b; viii, 114a; ix, 741a; s, 53b, 54b, 71a, 77a I, 314a, 856a, 8**70a**, 1132b; V, 104a, 505a; VI, 471a, 536b, 537a, 931b; VII, 424a, 442a, 1005a; VIII, 116b; IX, 773b; S, 53b, 55a, 72a, 76b
al-Babr vii, 497b – VII, 497b
Babrak Karmal (XX) vii, 291a – VII, 293a
Baʿbūd al-ʿAlawī (1715) vi, 112b – VI, 110a
Bābul → Bārfurūsh
Bābūlā vi, 507a – VI, 492b
Bābulkānī, Sayyid Haybat Allāh (XV) vi, 514a – VI, 499a
Bābulkānī Sayyids (XV) vi, 513b – VI, 499a
Bābūnadj s, 114b – S, **114a**
Bābur b. ʿUmar Shaykh b. Abī Saʿīd, Zahīr al-Dīn (Mughal) (1530) i, 218a, 227b, 228a, 252b, 627b, **847b**, 864b, 970a, 1069a, 1139b, 1192b, 1212a, 1323b, 1347b, ii, 29a, 47b, 120b, 264b, 271a, 792a, 973a, 978a, 1049b, 1122b, 1144a; iii, 199b, 200b, 202a, 317a, 422b, 448b, 492b, 995b; iv, 186b, 357a, 410a, 536b, 914b, 1021b; v, 36b, 45b, 250b, 649a, 687a, 885a, 1135a; vi, 52a, 63b, 410a, 425a, 557b, 693a; vii, 105b, 135a, 138b, 218a, 313b, 316b, 329a; viii, 767b; x, 722b; s, 1b, 312a, 313a, 324b, 325a, 329b, 331b – I, 224b, 234b, 260b, 648b, **870b**, 888b, 1000a, 1101a, 1174a, 1228a, 1248a, 1364b, 1387b; II, 29b, 48a, 123b, 272b, 279a, 810b, 995b, 1000b, 1074a, 1149a, 1171a; III, 204b, 205b, 207a, 326b, 436a, 464a, 509b, 1020b; IV, 194b, 372b, 428a, 560a, 947b, 1053b; V, 38a, 47a, 248b, 653b, 692a, 891a, 1130b; VI, 50a, 61b, 395a, 410a, 542a, 680b; VII, 107b, 136b, 140b, 220a, 316a, 319a, 330b; VIII, 793a; X, 767b; S, 1b, 312a, 313a, 324a, b, 329a, 331a
Bābur Mīrzā → Abu ʾl-Ḳāsim Bābur
Bābur-nāma i, 80b, 607a, 848b; ii, 909b – I, 83a, 627a, 872a; II, 931a
Babylon (Egypt-e) → Bābalyūn
Babylon (Mesopotamia/-e) → Bābil
Bačča-yi Saḳāō (Saḳaw) (1928) i, 232b; ii, 658b; v, 1079a; vi, 86b; s, 66b – I, 239b; II, 675a; V, 1076b; VI, 84b; S, 67a
Bachtarzi (Bāsh Ṭarzī, Muhyī ʾl-Dīn) (XX) vi, 752a, 754b – VI, 741b, 744a
Bäčkām → Badjkam
Backergunge → Bāḳargandj
Bactria/Bactriane i, 226a; v, 229a – I, 232b; V, 226b
Bād-i Hawā i, 656b, **850a**; ii, 147a – I, 677a, **873b**; II, 151a
Badāʾ i, 265b, **850a** – I, 273b, **873b**
Badajoz → Baṭalyaws
Badakhshān i, 46b, 87a, 223b, **851b**; ii, 43a; iii, 575a; iv, 202b, 205b; vi, 612b; vii, 129b, 134b; s, 50b, 125a, b, 258b, 367b – I, 48a, 89b, 230a, **875a**; II, 43b; III, 595a; IV, 211b, 215a; VI, 603b; VII, 131b, 136b; S, 51b, 124a, b, 258a, 367a
Badakhshānī, Shams al-Dīn s, 73b – S, 74a
Badal (Bedel) i, 760b, **855a**; ii, 147a – I, 783b, **878b**; II, 151a
Badal → Abdāl; Naḥw
Badan Singh (XVIII) i, 1193a – I, 1228a
Bādarāya → Badrā
Badasht vii, 422a – VII, 424a
Badāʾūn (Budāʾūn) i, **855b**; ii, 274b; iii, 441b; iv, 749b; v, 1135a; vi, 47b, 48a, b, 62a; vii, 433a; viii, 571b; s, 73b, 74a – I, **879b**; II, 282b; III, 455b; IV, 779b; V, 1130b; VI, 46a, b, 47a, 60a; VII, 434a; VIII, 590a; S, 74a, b
Badāʾūnī, ʿAbd al-Ḳādir (1615) i, **856a**, 1136a, b; ii, 871a; vii, 342a; s, 21a, 117b, 206b, 378a – I, **880a**, 1170b, 1171a; II, 891a; VII, 344a; S, 21a, 117a, 206a, 378b
Badāʾūnī, Sayyid Mīr Muḥammad (XVIII) vi, 953a – VI, 945b
Badawī → Aḥmād al-Badawī
al-Badawiyya → Aḥmad al-Badawī
Badawlat → Yaʿḳūb Beg (Kāshghar)
Baddh Uwaysī → al-Dhawnpurī, Sayyid Muḥammad
Baddāyā vi, 544a – VI, 528b
Bādghīs / Bādhghīs i, **857a**; 253a; v, 47a; vi, 331a, 428a, 492b, 617b, 633b; x, 926b; s, 367b – I, **881a**; II, 260a; V, 48b; VI, 315b, 413b, 478b, 602b, 618b; X, ; S, 367a
Bādgīr v, 1148b; s, **115a** – V, 1139b; S, **114b**
Bādh (Marwānid(e)) (Diyār Bakr) (983) i, 329a, 637b; ii, 344a; iii, 128b; v, 452b, 453a; vi, 540b, 626a, 930b – I, 339b, 658b; II, 353b; III, 131b; V, 455a, b; VI, 525a, 611a, 922a
Bādhām (Khurāsān) vi, 618a – VI. 602b
Bādhām, Bādhān (Yemen) (632) i, 102a, 728a; vi, 565b; s, **115b** – I, 105a, 750a; VI, 550a; S, **115a**
Bādhān Fayrūz → Ardabīl
Badhandūn → Bozanti
al-Badhdh i, 844a; vi, 335a, 504b; vii, 777a; s, **116a** – I, 867b; VI, 319a, 489b; VII, 779a; S, **115b**
Badhl al-Kubrā (839) iv, 821b; s, 1**116b** – IV, 854b; S, **116a**
Badīʿ i, 587b, 592a, **857b**, 981b; iii, 663b, 665a, 799b; iv, 248b; v, 319a, 321b, 898a, 900a –

I, 606b, 611b, **881a**, 1012a; III, 658a, 686b, 823a; IV, 259b; V, 318b, 321a, 904b, 906b
al-Badīʿ (palace) (Marrākush) vi, 594b, 596b – VI, 579a, 581a
Bādī I-IV (Fundj) ii, 944a, b – II, 966a, b
Bādī II (Sinnār) ix, 650a – IX, 675b
Bādī III (Sinnār) (1716) ix, 650b – IX, 675b
Badīʿ, Ḥasan iv, 72b, v, 198a – IV, 76b; V, 195b
al-Badīʿ al-Asṭurlābī (1139) i, **858b**; iii, 780b – I, **882a**; III, 804a
Badīʿ al-Dīn Shāh Madār (1440) i, 702b, **858b**; s, 385b – I, 724a, **882b**; S, 358b
Badīʿ al- Zamān → al-Hamadhānī
Badīʿ al-Zamān b. Ḥusayn Bayḳarā (XV) i, 627b; iii, 603a; iv, 1020b – I, 648a; III, 623b; IV, 1052b
Badīʿ al-Zamān b. Shāhrūkh (XVII) i, 853a – I, 876b
Badīʿ al-Zamān Mīrzā (1493) i, 406a; vi, 514b – I, 418a; VI, 499b
Badia y Leblich → ʿAlī Bey al-ʿAbbāsī
Badīha → Irtidjāl
Badīl → Abdāl
Bādīnān → Bahdīnān
al-Badīnī, Abu ʾl-Ḥasan (X) viii, 615a – VIII, 634b
Bādis i, **859b** – I, **883a**
Bādīs b. Ḥabbūs (Zīrid(e)) (Gharnāṭa) (1073) i, 6a, 130b, 1310a; ii, 1012b, 1015a; iii, 147b; vi, 221a, 222a, b, 728b; vii, 761a, 766b – I, 6b, 134a, 1350a; II, 1036b, 1038b; III, 150b; VI, 215a, 216a, 717a; VII, 762b, 768a
Bādīs b. al-Manṣūr (Zīrid(e)) (Ifrīḳiyya) (1016) i, **860a**; iii, 137a; iv, 479a; v, 1179a, 1182a, b; vi, 841b; vii, 474a, 481b – I, **884a**; III, 139b; IV, 501a; V, 1169a, 1172a, b; VI, 832a; VII, 473b, 481a
al-Bādisī, ʿAbd al-Ḥaḳḳ (1312) i, 596a, **860a**; viii, 503b – I, 615b, **884a**; VIII, 520b
al-Bādisī, Abū Ḥassūn ʿAlī → Abū Ḥassan ʿAlī
al-Bādisī, Abū Yaʿḳūb Yūsuf (XIV) I, **860a** – I, **884a**
Bādiya s, **116b** – S, **116a**
Bādj (tax(e)) i, **860b**; ii, 147a; iii, 489b – I, **884b**; II, 151a; III, 506a
Bādj (Firdawsī) i, **862a** – I, **886a**
Bādja (al-Andalus) i, **862a**, 1092a; ii, 1009a – I, **886a**, 1124b; II, 1032b
Bādjaddā i, **863b** – I, **887b**
Bādjalān, Banū i, **863b** – I, **887b**
al-Badjalī → Budayl b. Ṭahfa; Djarīr b. ʿAbd Allāh
al-Badjalī, Abū Bakr b. ʿAbd Allāh (986) ix, 811b – IX, 846b
al-Badjalī, Djibrīl b. Yaḥyā al-Khurāsānī (757) vi, 775a – VI, 764b
al-Badjalī, al-Ḥasan b. ʿAlī b. Warsand i, **863b**; s, 402b – I, **888a**; S, 403a
Badjaliyya i, 863b; s, 402b – I, 888a; S, 402b
Badjanāk → Pečeneg
al-Bādjarbaḳī (1312) ii, 377a – II, 387b
Bādjarmā (Bādjarmaḳ) i, **864a** – I, **888a**
Bādjarwān i, **864a** – I, **888a**
al-Badjasī → Aytimish
Bādjat al-Zayt (Tunisia/Tunésie) i, 862a, 863a – I, 886b, 887a
Badjāwa → Bedja
Bādjawr i, **864a** – I, **888b**
Badjdjāna (Pechina) i, **864b**; vi, 575b – I, **888b**; VI, 560b
al-Bādjī, Abū Saʿīd Khalaf (1230) vi, 355a – VI, 339a
al-Bādjī, Abu ʾl-Walīd (1081) i, **864b**; iii, 542b; vi, 279a, 281b; vii, 293a; ix, 187b – I, **889a**; III, 561a; VI, 264a, 266a; VII, 295a; IX, 193a
Bādjī Rāo I (Marāthā) (1728) i, 710a, 1053a, 1195a; iii, 320a; vi, 535a; vii, 316a, 457a – I, 731b, 1084b, 1230b; III, 330b; VI, 519b; VII, 318a, 457a
Bādjī Rāo II (Marāthā) (1818) vi, 535b – VI, 520a
Bādjī Rāo, Raghunnāth (1761) vi, 535a – VI, 520a
Badjīla, Banū i, **865a**; iv, 925b, 1105b; v, 617a; vi, 441b, 447a; vii, 347b, 592a; x, 3a; s, 37b – I, **889b**; IV, 958b, 1137a; V, 621a; VI, 427a, 463a; VII, 349b, 591b; X, 3a; S, 37b
Badjimzā (Bagimzā) i, **865b** – I, **890a**
Bādjisrā i, **865b** – I, **890a**
Badjkam, Abu ʾl- Ḥusayn, amīr (941) i, **866a**, 1040a, 1046b; iii, 127a, 345a, 902b; vi,206a; vii, 484a, 994b – I, 89**0a**, 1071b, 1078b; III, 130a, 355b, 926b; VI, 190b; 484a, 996b; VII, 484a, 996b
al-Bādjurbaḳī vi, 216b – VI, 200b
Bādjūrī, Ibrāhīm b. Muḥammad (1860) i, 151a, 413a, 819b, **867b**; ii, 451a, 727b; iv, 173a, 693b, 1108a – I, 155a, 1425a, 842b, **891b**, 1355a; II, 463a, 746a; IV, 180b, 721b, 1139b
Badlīs → Bidlīs
Badr, Āl i, 759b – I, 782a
Badr, battle of/bataille de (624) i, **867b**; ii, 950b; v, 1162a; vi, 138a, 146b, 603b, 650a; vii, 369b; s, 44b, 230a, 351b – I, **892a**; II, 972b; V, 1152a; VI, 136b, 145a, 588b, 635b; VII, 371b; S, 44b, 230a, 351b
Badr (ḥādjib) (X) x. 851a – X,
Badr (pīr), Shaykh Badr al-Dīn (1440) i, **868b** – I, **892b**
Badr (slave of ʿAbd al-Raḥmān I) (VIII) x, 848a – X,
Badr b. Aḥmad (Zaydī) (1962) ix, 2a – IX, 2a
Badr b. ʿAmmar al-Asadī → Badr al-Kharshanī
Badr b. Hasan(a)wayh (Hasanūya) (1000) i, 512b, 1030b; ii, 749a; iii, 244b, 258a, b; iv, 294a; v, 229b, 452b, 1124b; vi, 653a; s, 118b, 119a – I, 528a, 1062a; II, 767b; III, 251b, 265a, b; IV, 307b; V, 227b, 455a, 1121a; VI, 638b; S, 118a, b
Badr b. Hilāl (ʿAnnāzid(e)) (XI) i, 513a – I, 528b
Badr b. Muhalhil (ʿAnnāzid(e)) (XI) i, 513a – I, 528b
Badr Bū Ṭuwayriḳ (1538) i, 553b; vi, 82b; ix, 439a – I, 571a; VI, 80b; IX, 456a
Badr al-Dawla Sulaymān (Artuḳid(e)), Alep(po)) (XIII) i, 663b, 983a – I, 685b, 1014a
Badr al-Dīn b. Djamāʿa → lbn Djamāʿa
Badr al-Dīn b. Ḳāḍī Samāwnā (1416) i, 312b, **869a**; ii, 599b; vi, 976a; vii, 594b – I, 322b, **893a**; II, 614a; VI, 968b; VII, 594a
Badr al-Dīn Awliyā (Arakan) i, 606b – I, 626a
Badr al-Dīn al-Ḥasan b. ʿAlī (Rasūlid(e)) (1214) vi, 433b – VI, 418b
Badr al-Dīn al-Ḥasan b. Ḥūd (1300) x, 320b – X, 345a
Badr al-Dīn al-Ḥasanī, Shaykh (XX) vi, 538b – VI, 523a
Badr al-Dīn al-Hāshimī (1423) vi, 353a – VI, 337a
Badr al-Dīn Ibrāhīm (Ḳarāmān-oghlu) (XIV) iv, 621b, 622a – IV, 646b, 647a
Badr al-Dīn Ibrāhīm b. Khuteni (Ermenak) (XIII) iv, 620a – IV, 644b
Badr al-Dīn Khurāsānī, Khʷādja (XIII) ii, 81a; s, 157b – II, 82b; S, 158a
Badr al-Dīn Luʾluʾ → Luʾluʾ
Badr al-Dīn Muḥammad I, II, III → Faḍl Allāh, Āl
Badr al-Dīn Muḥammad al-Hamdānī (XIII) iv, 1188b – IV, 1221b
Badr al-Djamālī (vizier) (1094) i, 638b, 832a, **869b**, 926b, 1228a, 1316a; ii, 484b, 857b, 863b; iii, 253b; iv, 424b, 568a; v, 91b, 328a, 514b; vi, 367a, 453b, 673b; vii, 149b, 163a, 510b, 725a, 730b; viii, 464a, 864a; s, 390a – I, 659a, 855b, **894a**, 954b, 1264b, 1356b; II, 497a,

877b, 883a; III, 261a; IV, 443a, 590a; V, 94a, 328a, 518a; VI, 351a, 439a, 660a; VII, 151b, 164b, 510b, 726a, 731a; VIII, 479b, 894b; S, 390b
al-Badr al-Ḥabashī (1221) x, 320b – X, 345a
Badr al-Ḥammāmī (Iṣfahān) (X) iv, 100a – IV, 104b
Badr al-Kabīr (IX) iv, 494a – IV, 515a
Badr Khān Djazīrī (XIX) v, 462a, b – V, 465a
Badr al-Kharshanī, amīr (942) i, **870b**; vii, 770a – I, **894b**; VII, 772a
Badr al-Muʿtaḍidī, Abu 'l-Nadjm (902) i, 11a, 1223a; ii, 1080a; vii, 395a, 760a; s, **117b** – I, 11a, 1259b; II, 1105a; VII, 396a, 761b; S, **117a**
Badr al–Saklabī (X) viii, 880a – VIII, 910a
Badra i, **870b** – I, **895a**
Badrān b. Muḥallid (ʿUḳaylid(e)) (XI) viii, 394a – VIII, 407b
Badrān b. Ṣadaḳa (Asadī) (XII) iv, 911b – IV, 944b
Badrashayn (Umm ʿĪsā) vi, 411a – VI, 396a
Badr-i Čāčī (1346) ix, 241bl s, **117b** – IX, 248a; S, **117a**
Badr-i Djahān Khanum (1797) vi, 484a – VI, 470b
al-Badrī (XV) ii, 900b – II, 921a
al-Badrī (1800) vi, 112b – VI, 110b
al-Badrī, Sayf al-Dīn Aynabak (1376) vi, 580b – VI, 565a
Badrkhānī, Djalādat (1951) i, **871a** – I, **895a**
Badrkhānī, Thurayyā (1938) i, **871a** – I, **895a**
Bādshāh Khān (1925) ii, 317a – II, 326b
Bādūrayā i, **871b**, 899b; v, 566b – I, **895b**, 926b; V, 571a
Bādūsbānid(e)s i, **871b**; iii, 255a; iv, 808a; v, 663a, b; vi, 938b; s, 297b, 298a – I, **896a**; III, 262b; IV, 840b; V, 668b; VI, 930b; S, 297a, b
Badw i, 14b, **872a**, 1049b, 1149b, 1230a, 1239b, 1288b; ii, 92b, 174b, 342b, 455a, 1005b, 1055a, 1059b; iii, 190b, 1261b; iv, 960b, 961a; v, 334a; vi, 32b, 33b, 478b, 490a – I, 15a, **896b**, 1081a, 1184a, 1266b, 1277a, 1328a; II, 94b, 180a, 352a, 467a, 1029a, 1079b, 1084a; III, 195a, 1294b; IV, 992b, 993a; V, 334b; VI, 30b, 31b, 464b, 476a
—language/langue v, 1205b, 1206a, b – V, 1195b, 1196b, 1197a
Baena → Bayyāna
Baeza → Bayyāsa
Baezay Mohmands vii, 220a – VII, 222a
Bāfaḳī, Sharaf al-Dīn (1570) viii, 542b – VIII, 560b
Bafilo → Kubafolo
Bafur (Adrār) i, 211a – I, 217a
Bagamoyo vi, 370a – VI, 354a
Bagauda (Kano) (X) iii, 275b; iv, 548b, 551a – III, 283b; IV, 572a, 574b
Bāgerhāt ii, 486b; iii, 444a – II, 498b; III, 459a
Baggāra → Baḳḳāra
Bā → Nikāpur
Bāghān vi, 384b – VI, 368b
al-Baghawī, ʿAbd Allāh b. Muḥammad (X) vi, 634a – VI, 619a
al-Baghawī, Abū Muḥammad al-Farrāʾ (Ibn al-Farrāʾ) (1122) i, **893a**; ii, 382a; iii, 24b – I, **919b**; II, 392a; III, 25b
al-Baghawī, ʿAlī b. ʿAbd al-ʿAzīz (870) vi, 822a – VI, 812a
Bāghāya iv, 422b – IV, 441a
Baghbūr → Faghfūr
Bāghčeköy vi, 57a – VI, 55a
Bāghče Sarāy i, **893a**; ii, 1113a; v, 138a, 140b – I, **919b**; II, 1139a; V, 140b, 143b
Baghdād i, 8a, 17a, 18a, b, 19a, 21a, 291a, 438a, 576a, 616a, 866b, **894b**, 975a, b. 1038a; ii, 128b, 184b, 391a, 579b, 964a; iii, 702b, 1255a, 1256b, 1258a; iv, 20a, 215a, 652b; v, 33a, b, 458a, 928b; vi, 16a, 28b, 45a, 55b, 56b, 59b, 73b, 113b, 118a, 119b, 123b, 149b, 198a, 199a, 205a, 269b,270b, 273a, 275a, 332b, 333b, 335a, b, 338b, 405b, 428a, b, 450a, 494a, 499b, 501a, 517a, 532b, 539b, 541b, 600a, 606a, 613b, 635a, 656b, 668a, 669b, 671b; 13a, b, 15b, 33a, 95a, 102a, 113a, 182b, 191b, 192a, 199a, 225b, 267b – I, 8a, 17b, 19a, 20a, 21b, 300a, 450a, 595a, 636b, 890b, **921a**, 1005b, 1006a, 1069b; II, 132a, 190b, 401b, 594a, 986a; III, 724b, 1287b, 1289a, 1290b; IV, 21b, 224b, 678b; V, 34a, 35a, 460b, 933b; VI, 14a, 26b, 43b, 53b, 54b, 57b, 71b, 111a, 115b, 117b, 121a, 148a, 182a, 183a, 190a, 254a, 255b, 257b, 260a, 317a, 318a, b, 319b, 322b, 390a, 413b, 435b, 479b, 485a, 486b, 502a, 516b, 524a, 526a, 585a, 590b, 598b, 620a, 642a, 654b, 655b, 657b; S, 13a, 14a, 16a, 33a, 94a, 101b, 112b, 182b, 193a, 199a, 225b, 267a
—commerce i, 905b, 907a; ii, 745b; iii, 218a, 1252b – I, 932b, 934b; II, 764a; III, 224b, 1285a
—history/histoire i, 1309b; iii, 692b, 756a, 897a – I, 1349b, III, 715a, 779a, 921a
—institutions i, 212b, 899a, 900a, 902a, 903a, 906b, 1223a; ii, 127a; iii, 140a, 159b, 160b; v, 1127a, 1148a – I, 218b, 926a, 927a, 929a, 930a, 934a, 1259b; II, 130b; III, 142b, 163a, 164a; V, 1123a, b, 1139a
—monuments i, 11b, 52b, 616b, 831a, 832b, 896a-904b, 1354a; iii, 1268a; iv, 378a – I, 11b, 54b, 636b, 854a, 855b, 922b-932a, 1393a; III, 1301a; IV, 394b
—university/-é ii, 424b – II, 435b
Baghdād Khātūn bint Amīr Čūbān (1335) i, **908b**; ii, 68a, 980b – I, **936a**; II, 69a, 1003a
Baghdād Yolu i, 475a – I, 489a
al-Baghdādī → ʿAbd al-Ḳādir; ʿAbd al-Latīf; Abu 'l-Khayr al-Ḥusayn; Bahāʾ al-Dīn; al-Khaṭīb; Madjd al-Dīn
al-Baghdādī, ʿAbd al-Ḳāhir Abū Manṣūr (1037) i, **909a**; ii, 96a, 296a; iii, 1140a; iv, 183a-b, 667b; vi, 636b; vii, 54b, 296b, 1051b; viii, 497b – I, **936b**; II, 98a, 303b; III, 1168a; IV, 191a, 694b; VI, 621b; VII, 55a, 298b, 1053b; VIII, 514b
al-Baghdādī, ʿAbd al-Wahhāb (1031) ix, 10a – IX, 19b
Baghdādī, Aḥmad Saʿīd (XIX) vii, 903a – VII, 903b
Baghdādī, Mawlānā Khālid (1827) vii, 935b, 936b – VII, 936a, 937a
al-Baghdādī, Muḥammad b. al-Mubārak b. Maymūn (XII) vii, 527a – VII, 527a
al-Baghdādī, Muḥammad b. al-Sukrān (XIII) viii, 860a – VIII, 890a
al-Baghdādī, Sīdī Maḥmūd (XVI) viii, 18b – VIII, 18b
Bāgh-i Firdaws vi, 51b – VI, 49b
Bāgh-i Nīlūfar (Dhōlpūr) vii, 329a – VII, 330b
Bāgh-i Shaʿbān vi, 51b – VI, 49b
Bāghistān s, 50b – S, 51a
Baghl i, **909a**; iv, 1146a – I, **936b**; IV, 1178a
Baghlī → Dirham
Baghrās (Pagrae) i, 239a, **909b**, 1134a; vi, 623b – I, 246b, **937a**, 1168b; VI, 608b
Baghyughu, Aḥmad (Mali) vi, 258b – VI, 243a
Baghyughu, Muḥammad (Mali) vi, 258b – VI, 243a
Bagirmi (Baghirmi) i, **910a**; v, 278b, 357b; s, 164a, b – I, **937b**; V, 276b, 359a; S, 164a, b
Bagrat III v, 489a – V, 492a
Bagrat IV iv, 346b; v, 489a – IV, 361a; V, 492a
Bagrat V v, 491a – V, 494a
Bagratid(e)s i, 100b, 101a, 466a, 507a, 637b, 638a; iv, 346b, 347b, 669b; v, 488b, 489a, 496a – I, 103b, 479b, 522b, 658a, b; IV, 361a, 362a, 697a; V, 491b, 492a, 499a

Bagulal, Banū i, 504a; iv, 630b – I, 519b; IV, 655b
Bagzāda, Āl iii, 292a – III, 301a
Bāh i, **910b**; ii, 552a – I, **938a**; II, 566a
Bahā᾽ Allāh, Mīrzā Ḥusayn ʿAlī Nūrī (1892) i, 833b, 834b, 846b, 847a, **911a**, 916a; iii, 325b; iv, 51b, 696a; v, 698b, 1172b; vii, 921b; s, 77a – I, 856b, 857b, 870a, 870b, **938b**, 944a; III, 335b; IV, 54b, 724a; V, 703b, 1162b; VII, 922a; S, 76b
Bahā᾽ al-Dawla (1507) viii, 783b – VIII, 809b
Bahā᾽ al-Dawla wa-Ḍiyā᾽ al-Milla, Abū Naṣr Fīrūz (Būyid(e)) (1012) i, 512a, 899b, 1354a; ii, 348b, 749a; iii, 219b, 244b, 258b, 388a, 671b; iv, 378a; v, 348a, 1028a; vi, 199a, 206a, 261b; vii, 270b, 497a; s, 4b, **118a** – I, 528a, 926b, 1393b; II, 358a, 767b; III, 225b, 251b, 265b, 400a, 693a; IV, 394b; V, 349a, 1024a; VI, 183a, 190b, 246a; VII, 272b, 497a; S, 3b, **117b**
Bahā᾽ al-Dīn (vizier Gudjarāt) (1482) vi, 50b – VI, 49a
Bahā᾽ al-Dīn al-ʿĀmilī → al-ʿĀmilī
Bahā᾽ al-Dīn Baghdādī (XII) iii, 1243a – III, 1275a
Bahā᾽ al-Dīn Ḳara ʿUthmān (Aḳ Ḳoyūnlū) (1400) vi, 901a, VI, 892b
Bahā᾽ al-Dīn Muḥammad b. Djuwaynī (1279) ii, 607b; iv, 102a – II, 622b; IV, 106b
Bahā᾽ al-Dīn Sām (Bāmiyān) (1205) i, 1001b; ii, 1101b, 1103a – I, 1032a; II, 1127b, 1129a
Bahā᾽ al-Dīn Sām I (Ghūrid(e)) (1149) ii, 382a, 928b, 1096b, 1100b – II, 392b, 950a, 1122a, 1126b
Bahā᾽ al-Dīn Sām II (Ghūrid(e)) 1213) ii, 1103a – II, 1129a
Bahā᾽ al-Dīn Shākir (XX) iv, 285a, 872b – IV, 297b, 906a
Bahā᾽ al-Dīn Sulṭān al-ʿUlamā᾽ Walad b. Ḥusayn (XIV) ii, 393b; vi, 887b – II, 404a; VI, 878b
Bahā al-Dīn Zakariyyā᾽ (Suhrawardī) (1262) i, **912a**; iii, 635a, 1269a; v, 26a; vii, 550a; ix, 298b; x, 255b; s, 10b, 353b – I, **939b**; III, 656b, 1302a; V, 27a; VII, 550a; IX, 307a; X, 274b; S, 10a, 353b
Bahā᾽ al-Dīn Zuhayr (1258) i, 570b, 595b, **912b**; ii, 1032b; iii, 875b – I, 589b, 614b, **940a**; II, 1056b; III, 899b
Bahā᾽ al-Ḥaḳḳ → Bahā᾽ al-Dīn Zakariyyā
Bāhā Lāl Dās Bayrāgī (XVII) ii, 134b – II, 138a
Bahā᾽ Walad (1231) x, 320b – X, 345a
al-Bahā᾽ Zuhayr → Bahā᾽ al-Dīn Zuhayr
Bahādur i, **913a** – I, **940b**
Bahādūr Gīlānī (1494) ii, 1127b; v, 1258a; vi, 63a,b – II, 1154a; V, 1249a; VI, 61a
Bahādur Girāy I (Crimea/-ée) (1641) iv, 178b – IV, 185b
Bahādur Khān Gīlānī → Bahādur Gīlānī
Bahādur Khān II (Dāwūdpōtra) (1617) ii, 185b – II, 191b
Bahādur Khān b. Muẓaffar Shāh (Gudjarāt) (1526) vi, 52a, 270b, 310a – VI, 50a, b, 255a, 295a
Bahādur Khān Rohilla (1658) viii, 572b – VIII, 591a
Bahādur Shāh → Niẓām Shāh
Bahādur Shāh I (Mughal) (1712) i, 781b, **913b**, 1012b, 1068b, 1195a, 1210a; ii, 30a, 558a; iii, 427a; iv, 507b, 598b; vii, 315b, 318b, 722b; viii, 48b – I, 805a, **941a**, 1043b, 1101a, 1230b, 1246a; II, 30b, 572a; III, 441a; IV, 529b, 602a; VII, 318a, 321a, 723b; VIII, 49a
Bahādur Shāh II (Mughal) (1862) i, **914a**, 953b, 1012b; ii, 221b; vii, 316b – I, **942a**, 983a, 1043b; II, 228b; VII, 318b
Bahādur Shāh (Fārūkid(e)) ii, 815b – II, 835a
Bahādur Shāh Gudjarātī (1537) i, **914b**, 1193b; ii, 322b, 815a, 1128b; iii, 16a, 199b, 421b, 422a, 425b, 575b, 1160a; vi, 52a, 407a, 535a; vii, 314a; s, 335b – I, **942a**, 1228b; II, 332a, 834a, 1155a; III, 16b, 205a, 435a, b, 439b, 595a, 1188b; VI, 50a, 391b, 519b; VII, 316a; S, 335a
Bahāedin Shākir → Bahā᾽ al-Dīn Shākir
Bahā᾽ī Meḥmed Efendi (1654) i, **915a** – I, **943a**
Bahā᾽īs i, 263b, 833a, 847a, **915b**; iii, 325b; iv, 39a, 51b; vi, 292a, 720a; vii, 921b – I, 272a, 856a, 870b, **943b**; III, 335b; IV, 41b, 54b; VI, 277a, 709a; VII, 922a
Bahākath (Banākath, Fahākath, Shāhrukhiyya) i, 148a, 1011a; x, 349a, 813a; s, 51a – I, 152a, 1042a; X, 374b, ; S, 51b
Baḥammou (Berber) s, 328a – S, 327b
Bahār, Muḥammad Taḳī (1951) i, **918b**; iv, 71a, b; vi, 276b, 609a; vii, 662a, 754b, 879b; s, 110a, 334a – I, **946b**; IV, 74b-75a, 75b; VI, 261b, 593b, 594a; VII, 661b, 756a, 880b; S, 109b, 333b
Bahār, Rāy Tēkčand iv, 526b – IV, 549a
Bahār Khān b. Daryā Khān Noḥānī (1524) s, 203a – S, 203a
Bahār-i Dānesh → ʿInāyat Allāh Kanbū
Bahāristān → Djāmī
Bahārlū, Banū i, **919a**; iii, 1109b; iv, 9b; v, 668b – I, **947a**; III, 1136b; IV, 10a; V, 672b
Bahasa Indonesia iii, 1215b, 1217a, 1213a – III, 1246b, 1248a, 1263a
Bahāshima s, 25b – S, 25b
Bahasnā (Marʿash) vi, 507a, b – VI, 492b, 493a
Bahāwal Khān I (Dāwūdpōtrā) (1749) i, 919b; ii, 186a – I, 947b; II, 192a
Bahāwal Khān II – V → Rāwūdpōtrās
Bahāwalpūr i, **919b**; ii, 185b, 186a, 669a – I, **947b**; II, 191b, 192a, 685b
Bahbūdh b. ʿAbd Allāh al-Wahhāb (Zandjī) (IX) vii, 526b – VII, 526b
Baḥdal b. Unayf (657) i, **919b**; vi, 545a, 924b; vii, 267b – I, **947b**; VI, 529b, 916a; VII, 269b
Bahdīnān i, 427a, **920a**; v, 460a – I, 439a, **948a**; V, 463a
Bahdjat Khān (Čandērī) (1514) ii, 12b; vi, 54b – II, 13a; VI, 52b
Bahdjat Muṣṭafā Efendi (1834) i, 707a, **921a**; ii, 356b – I, 728b, **948a**; II, 366a
Baḥḥāra i, 929a – I, 957b
Bāhila, Banū i, **920b**, 1096b; v, 541a; vi, 545a; s, 243a – I, **948b**, 1129a, b; V, 545b; VI, 529b; S, 243a
al-Bāhilī, ʿAbd al-Raḥmān (VII) i, **921b**; iv, 343b, 1173b – I, **949a**; IV, 358a, 1206b
al-Bāhilī, Abu ᾽l-Ḥasan Sallām (vizier) vi, 111a – VI, 108b
al-Bāhilī, Abū Naṣr Aḥmad (845) i, 717b, 718b, **921b**; vii, 831b – I, 739a, 740a, **949b**; VII, 833a
al-Bāhilī, Abū ʿUmar (X) vi, 846b – VI, 837a
al-Bāhilī, al-Ḥusayn → al-Ḥusayn b. al-Daḥḥāk
al-Bāhilī, Salmān → Salmān b. Rabīʿa
Bahīmiyya, Banū vi, 474a – VI, 460a
Baḥīra → Buḥayra
Baḥīra (she-camel/chamelle) i, **922a** – I, **949b**
Baḥīrā (monk/moine) i, **922a**, 1276b – I, **950a**, 1315b
al-Bāhirī, Bakr b. Ḥassād (Ḥammād) iii, 889b – III, 913b
Bahishī → Djanna
Bāḥithat al-Bādiya → Malak Ḥifnī Nāṣif
Bāhiya (Marrākush) vi, 589b; s, 114a – VI, 574a; S, 113b
Bahlā (Oman) i, 140b – I, 145a
al-Bahlawī → Abu ᾽l-Mu᾽thir
Bahlōlzay, Banū vi, 86a – VI, 84a
Bahlūl (Kurd(e)s) i, **923a** – I, **951a**
Bahlūl (Morocco/Maroc) vi, 773b, 815b – VI, 763a, 805b
Bahlūl b. Marzūḳ s, 82a – S, 81b

Bahlūl Gwāliyārī, Shaykh (XVI) vii, 440a – VII, 441a
Bahlūl Lōdī (Delhi) (1489) i, 218a, 1322a; ii, 47b, 48b, 270, 498b, 1131a, 1144a; iii, 418a, 419b, 420a, 485a, 632a, 633b; iv, 276b; v, 31b, 598a, 783a, b; vi, 62a; s, 1b, 10b, 203a –
I, 224b, 1362b; II, 48a, 49b, 279a, 511a, 1158a, 1171a; III, 431b, 433a, b, 502a, 653a, 654b; IV, 288b; V, 32b, 602a, 789a, b; VI, 60a; S, 1b, 10a, 202b
Bahlūl Pasha (1825) i, 923b – I, 951a
Bahmaʾī, Banū iii, 1107a – III, 1134a
Bahman → Taʾrīkh
Bahman b. Isfandiyār (Kayānid(e)) iv, 809b; ix, 70b – IV, 842a; IX, 73a
Bahman b. Kayūmarth (Kāwūs, Banū) iv, 808a; v, 663a – IV, 840b; V, 668b
Bahman Lārīdjānī, Malik (1596) vi, 515b – VI, 501a
Bahman Mīrzā (Ḳādjār) (XIX) iv, 393a, b, 398a; vii, 455b – IV, 410a, 415a; VII, 455b
Bahman Shāh → ʿAlāʾ al-Dīn Ḥasan Bahman
Bahmandīz iii, 501b; iv, 815b; v, 229a – III, 518b; IV, 848b; V, 227a
Bahmanid(e)s i, 768a, **923b**, 1047a, 1170a, 1200a, b, 1203b; ii, 99b, 120b, 158b, 180a; iii, 15a, 114a, 420b, 446b; iv, 514a; v, 1a, 1258a; vi, 50b, 53b, 54a, 62b, 63b, 66b, 67a, 87a, 127b, 269b, 369a, 407a, 692a, 695a; vii, 943a; viii, 73b; x, 895a; s, 280a-
I, 791a, **951b**, 1078b, 1205a, 1236a, b, 1239a; II, 101b, 123b, 163b, 185b; III, 15b, 116b, 434a, 461b; IV, 536a; V, 1a, 1249a; VI, 49a, 52a, 60b, 61b, 64b, 65a, 85a, 125b, 253b, 353a, 391b, 679b, 683a; VII, 943b; VIII, 75a; X, ; S, 279b
Bahmanyār, Abu ʾl-Ḥasan (1067) i, **926a** – I, **954a**
Bāḥmīn (Bohemians) viii, 4a; s, 170b – VIII, 4a; S, 171a
al-Bahnasā i, **926a**, 945a- I, **954a**, 974a
Baḥr → ʿArūḍ
Baḥr (river/fleuve) i, **926b**; v, 949b – I, **954b**; V, 953b
Baḥr al-Abyaḍ → Baḥr al-Rūm
Baḥr Adriyas i, 927a, 935b – I, 955a, 964a
Baḥt al-Aḥmar → Baḥr al-Ḳulzum
Baḥr al-Aswad → Baḥr Bunṭus,;Ḳarā Deniz
Baḥr Āzāk → Baḥr Māyuṭis
Baḥr al-Banāt i, **927a** – I, **955a**
Baḥr Bunṭus i, **927a**, 935b; iv, 575a; v, 313a – I, **955a**, 964a; IV, 598a; V, 312b
Baḥr al-Dardūs iv, 514b – IV, 537a
Baḥr al-Djabal i, 929a – I, 957a
Baḥr Fāris i, **927b**, 930a; ii, 577b; iii, 1251b; iv, 500b; v, 66a, 507a, 572a; s, 222b –
I, **955b**, 958a; II, 592a; III, 1284a; IV, 522a; V, 68a, 510b, 577a; S, 222b
Baḥr al-Ghazāl i, **929a**, 1156b; v, 1248b, 1249b, 1250b; vi, 304a; viii, 39b –
I, **957a**, 1191a; V, 1239a, 1240a, 1241b; VI, 289b; VIII, 40a
Baḥr al-Hidjdjāna vi, 546a – VI, 531a
Baḥr al-Hind i, **930a**; ii, 584a; iii, 856b; v, 940b – I, **958a**; II, 598b; III, 880b; V, 944a
Baḥr al-Khazar i, 3b, 191a, **931a**; iv, 1b; vi, 129b, 415a; vii, 71a; s, 245b –
I, 4a, 196b, **959b**; IV, 1b; VI, 127b, 400a; VII, 71b; S, 245b
Baḥr al-Khazar, provinces iv, 6b-7a, 19a – IV, 7a-b, 20a-b
Baḥr Khʷarizm → Aral Sea/Mer d'Aral
Baḥr al-Ḳulzum i, **931b**; iii, 856b; iv, 686b; v, 367b – I, **960a**; III, 880b; IV, 714b; V, 368b
Baḥr Lūṭ i, **933a** – I, **961b**
Baḥr al-Maghrib → Baḥr al-Rūm
Baḥr Māyuṭis i, **933b**; iv, 576b – I, **962b**; IV, 599b
Baḥr al-Muḥīṭ i, **934a** – I, **962b**
Baḥr al-Muẓlim → al-Baḥr al-Muḥīṭ
Baḥr al-Nīl → al-Nīl
Baḥr Nīṭas → Baḥr Bunṭus
Baḥr al-Rūm i, **934b**, 936b; ii, 577b; v, 503a – I, **963b**, 965a; II, 592a; V, 506a
Baḥr al-Shāmī → Baḥr al-Rūm
Baḥr Tīrān i, 935b – I, 964a
Baḥr Uḳiyānūs → al-Baḥr al-Muḥīṭ
Baḥr al-ʿUlūm, ʿAbd al-ʿAlī al-Lakhnawī (1810) i, **936b**; ii, 104a; viii, 69a; s, 292b, 293a, b –
I, **965b**; II, 106b; VIII, 70b; S, 292a, 293a, b
Baḥr al-ʿUlūm, Sayyid Mahdī (XIX) s, 135a – S, 134b
Baḥr Ushmūm vi, 440b – VI, 426a
Baḥr al-Warank i, 934a, 935b – I, 962b, 964b
Baḥr al-Zandj i, 484a, **937b** – I, 498b, **966b**
Baḥr al-Ẓulma (Ẓulumāt) → al-Baḥr al-Muḥīṭ
Baḥra (Mecca) vi, 152b – VI, 151a
Bahrāʾ, Banū i, **938a** – I, **967a**
Bahrāʾič vi, 47b, 48a, 49b, 783b; s, 280a – VI, 46a, b, 48a, 773b; S, 280a
Bahrāidj → Djawnpur
Baḥrain → al-Baḥrayn
Baḥrak, Djamāl al-Dīn (1524) i, **938a** – I, **967a**
Bahrām (1140) i, 638b, **939a**; ii, 858a; iii, 55a – I, 659b, **968a**; II, 878a; III, 57a
Bahrām I-IV (Sāsānid(e)s) i, 938b; v, 169a, 1113b; vi, 421a; ix, 72b, 75a – I, 967b; V, 166b, 1110a; VI, 406b; IX, 75b, 78a
Bahrām V Gūr (Sāsānid(e)) (438) i, 226a, 568b, 939a; iv, 53a; v, 816b; vi, 617b; ix, 75b –
I, 232b, 587a, 967b, 968a; IV, 55b; V, 823a; VI, 602b; IX, 78b
Bahrām b. Lashkarsitān iv, 807a – IV, 839b
Bahrām Bayḍāʾī (XX) vi, 764a – VI, 753a
Bahrām Čūbīn i, 939a; iii, 113a, 584b; vi, 502a, 608b, 745a; viii, 119b; ix, 78b –
I, 967b, 968a; III, 115b, 604b; VI, 487a, 593b, 734a; VIII, 122a; IX, 82a
Bahrām al-Ismāʿīlī i, 1017a – I, 1048b
Bahrām Khān Khʷādja (1873) vi, 484b – VI, 470b
Bahrām Khān Māzandarānī (XIV) ii, 814a; vii, 458b – II, 833b; VII, 458b
Bahrām Khān Turkbačča (1405) vi, 294b – VI, 279b
Bahrām-Lam → Ibrāhīm Ināl
Bahrām Pasha (Yemen) (1575) i, 920a; viii, 521a – I, 948a; VIII, 539a
Bähram Rähmanaw (1961) vi, 770b – VI, 759b
Bahrāmshāh, Fakhr al-Dīn (Mengüčekid(e)) (1220) vi, 1016b; viii, 77a – VI, 1009a; VIII, 79a
Bahrām Shāh (Ṣafawid(e) (XVI) viii, 775b – VIII, 801b
Bahrām Shāh, Muʿizz al-Dīn (Muʿizzī, Delhi) (1242) ii, 267b, 609a, 973a; vii, 195a –
II, 276a, 624b, 995a; VII, 195b
Bahrām Shāh b. Masʿūd, Yamīn al-Dawla (Ghaznāwid(e)) (1157) i, 94b, 217b, 227a, **940a**; ii, 382a, 1052a, 1100b; v, 159b, 501a; vi, 783a; vii, 535b, 1016b; ix, 15b, 116a –
I, 97a, 224a, 233b, **968b**; II, 392b, 1076b, 1126b; V, 158b, 504b; VI, 773a; VII, 535b, 1018b; IX, 16a, 120a
Bahrām Shāh b. Tughrıl Shāh (Saldjūḳid(e)) (1174) i, **940b**; v, 160a; viii, 945b – I, **969a**; V, 158b; VIII, 978a
Bahrām Shāh al-Malik al-Amdjad (Ayyūbid(e)) (1229) i, 803b, **940b**, 971a – I, 826b, **969a**, 1001a
Bahrām Sīs (723) vi, 633b – VI, 618b
al-Baḥrānī → Muḥammad b. ʿAlī
al-Baḥrānī, ʿAbd ʿAlī b. Aḥmad al-Dirāzī s, 57a – S, 57b
Al-Baḥrānī, ʿAbd Allāh b. Ḥādjdj Ṣāliḥ al-Samāhīdjī s, 57b – S, 57b

Baḥrānī, Sayyid Mādjid (1619) vii, 475b – VII, 475a
al-Baḥrānī, Yūsuf b. Aḥmad iii, 1152a; s, 57a – III, 1180a; S, 57b
al-Baḥrayn ("the Two Seas"/"les deux mers") i, **940b**; iv, 664a, 751b, 764a, 953a, 1130b; v, 1057b; s, 234b, 318a, 417a –
I, **969b**; IV, 690b, 691a, 782a, 794b, 985b, 1162a; V, 1054b; S, 234b, 317b, 417a
Baḥrayn (Baḥrain) i, 19a, 55a, 72b, 73a, b, 120a, 233b, 535b, 540a, 553b, **941a**, 976a; ii, 108b, 177a, 452b; vi, 37a, 148a, 333b, 357b, 439a, 551a, 621b, 625b; vii, 449b, 464a, 570b –
I, 19b, 57a, 75a, b, 123b, 241a, 552a, 556b, 571a, **969b**, 1006b; II, 111a, 183a, 464b; VI, 35a, b, 146b, 318a, 341b, 424a, 535b, 606b, 610b; VII, 450b, 463b, 571a
Baḥri Mamlūks → Mamlūks
Baḥriyya (navy/marine) i, **945b**; s, **119b** – **I**, **974b**; S, **119a**
Baḥriyya (Mamlūk re(é)giment) i, 804a, **944b**; iv, 424b, 428a, 430a; v, 571a, b; vi, 320a; s, 392b – I, 828b, **973b**; IV, 443a, 446b, 448b; V, 576a; VI, 305b; S, 392b
Baḥriyya (oasis) i, **945a** – I, **974a**
Baḥriyye vekāleti i, 948b – I, 978a
Baḥrūn (Kamarān) ii, 235b – II, 232a
Bahrūr → Bhakkar
Baḥshal, Allām b. Sahl al-Wāsiṭī (901) i, **949a;** viii, 518a – I, **978a;** VIII, 536a
Bahshamiyya ii, 570a – II, 584b
Baḥth i, **949a** – I, **978a**
Bahū Bēgum ii, 870b – II, 890b
Bahū (Bao) s, 242a – S, 242a
Bahurasīr → al-Madāʾin
Baḥūṣiyya i, 375b – I, 386b
al-Bahūtī al-Miṣrī (1641) i, **949a**; iii, 162a –
I, **978b**; III, 165b
Bahw i, **949b** – I, **979a**
Baḥya ibn Paḳūda iv, 487a – IV, 507b
Baikal i, **950b** – I, **979b**
Bāʾikbāk (IX) vii, 794a – VII, 795b
Bailo → Bālyōs
Bairam Ali vi, 618a, 621b – VI, 603a, 606b
al-Baʿīth (VIII) i, **950b** – I, **980a**
Bajazet → Bāyazīd
Bajun Islands/Îles de - vi, 370a; ix, 715a – VI, 354b; IX, 746a
Baḳāʾ wa-Fanāʾ i, **951a**; iii, 546a; iv, 1083b, 1163a – I, **980a**; III, 565a; IV, 1114b, 1195a
Baḳʿa → Buḳʿa
al-Baḳʿa → al-Biḳāʿ
Baḳāʾī i, 1104a – I, 1137b
Bākalamūn → Abū Ḳalamūn
Baḳar i, **951b** – I, **980b**
Bāḳar, Āghā i, 952a – I, 981a
Baḳar, ʿīd → Bayram; ʿĪd
Bāḳargandj i, **951b** – I, **981a**
Baḳāriṭṭa (Buḳraṭūn) → Buḳrāṭ
Bakāwalī iii, 376b – III, 388b
Baḳāyā i, 1145a – I, 1179b
Bākbāk i, 278b; iii, 955b – I, 287a; III, 980a
Bakdjūr (991) i, 824b; ii, 483a; iii, 129b, 841a; v, 1211a; vii, 115b – I, 847b; II, 495b; III, 132b, 864b; V, 1201a; VII, 117b
Bakhʿa vi, 308a, b – VI, 293b
Bākhamrā i, **952a**; vi, 428a – I, **981b**; VI, 413a
Bākharz i, **952a**; vi, 495b – I, **981b**; VI, 480b
al-Bākharzī, Abu 'l-Ḥasan ʿAlī b. al-Ḥasan (1075) i, **952b**, 1132a; vii, 527b; viii, 71b, 513b, 970b; s, 31a – I, **981b**, 1166b; VII, 528a; VIII, 73a, 602a, 1004b; S, 31a
al-Bākharzī, Sayf al-Dīn → Sayf al-Dīn al-Bakharzī
Bakhīt, Shaykh i, 821a – I, 844a
Bakhīt al-Muṭīʿī al-Ḥanafī (1935) s, 121b – S, 12**1a**
al-Bakhrāʾ i, 57b, **952b**; s, 117a – I, 59a, **982a**; S, 116b
Bakhshī i, **953a**; iv, 268b, 269a, 757b; v, 686b – I, **982a**; IV, 280b, 281a, 788a; V, 691b
Bakhshī Aḥmad Khān iii, 61b – III, 64a
Bakhshīsh i, **953a** – I, **982b**
al-Bakhshiyya iv, 992a – IV, 1024b
Bakht Buland (XVII) vii, 899a – VII, 899b
Bakht Girāy ii, 1114a – II, 1140a
Bakht Khān (1859) i, **953b**; ii, 809a – I, **982b**; II, 828a
Bakhtanaṣṣar → Bukht-naṣar
Bakhtariyya bint Khurshīd Maṣmughān vi, 745a – VI, 734a
Bakhtāwar Khān (1685) i, **954a**; vii, 322a – I, **983a**; VII, 324a
Bakhtī i, **954b** – I, **983b**
Bakhtī, amīr v, 1179a – V, 1169a
Bakhtigān i, **954b** – I, **983b**
Bakhtīshūʿ → Bukhtīshūʿ
Bakhtiyār → Muḥammad Ḳuṭb al-Dīn
Bakhtiyār Sandjabī → Sindjābī
Bakhtiyār, ʿIzz al-Dawla (Buwayhid(e)) (967) i, 11b, 211b, **954b**, 1350b; ii, 748b; iii, 46b, 128a, 246a, 258a, 704a, 730a, 1176a, 1201b; iv, 24a, 208b, 293b; vi, 540a; vii, 799a; s, 13a, 36a, 118b, 398a –
I, 11b, 217b, **984a**, 1309b; II, 767a; III, 48b, 130b, 253a, 265a, 726a, 752b, 1204b, 1232a; IV, 25b, 218a, 306b; VI, 524b; VII, 801a; S, 13b, 36b, 118a, 398b
Bakhtiyār-nāma i, **955a**; iii, 373a, 377a –
I, **984b**; III, 384b, 389a
Bakhtiyārī, Banū i, **955b**; iii, 1102a, b, 1103a, 1105a, 1110a; iv, 5b, 8a, 9a, 98b, 706a; v, 664a, 822a, 824a, 825a, 826a, 829b, 830a; vi, 495a; vii, 453b; viii, 1080b; s, 142b, 146a, 147b, 365b – I, **985a**; III, 1129a, b, 1130a, 1132b, 1137a; IV, 6a, 8b, 9b, 103a, 134b; V, 669b, 828b, 830a, 831a, 832a, 836a; VI, 480b; VII, 454b; VIII, 1086b; S, 142a, 145b, 147b, 365b
Bakhtūs (queen/reine) ii, 234a – II, 241a
al-Baḳīʿ s, 311b – S, 311a
Bāḳī, Maḥmūd ʿAbd al- (1600) i, 292b, **956a**; ii, 221a; iv, 1137b; vi, 609b; viii, 8b; s, 324a –
I, 301b, **985**; II, 227b; IV, 1169b; VI, 594b; VIII, 8b; S, 323b
Baḳī b. Makhlad, Abū ʿAbd al-Raḥmān (889) i, 600a, **956b**; iii, 692b; vi, 132a; vii, 400a –
I, 619b, **986a**; III, 714b; VI, 130a; VII, 401b
Bāḳī bi-'llāh, Khwādja (1603) i, **957a**; iii, 432b; vii, 937b, 938a; x, 256a; s, 121b – I, **986b**; III, 446b; VII, 938b; X, 274b; S, 121a
Baḳīʿ al-Gharḳad (cemetery/cimetière, Madīna) i, **957b**; vi, 168b, 263b, 651b; vii, 276a – I, **987a**; VI, 159b, 248a, 636b; VII, 278a
Baḳī Khān Čela Ḳalmāḳ ii, 1085a – II, 1110a
Bāḳī Muḥammad (calligraphe(r)) iv, 1127b – IV, 1159a
Bāḳi Muḥammad Khān i, 8a; ii, 44b, 446a – I, 8a; II, 45b, 457b
Bāḳikhanlî, Bākikhānov (1847) i, 193b, **958a** – I, 199b, **987b**
Bakīl → Ḥāshid wa-Bakīl
al-Bāḳillānī, Abū Bakr Muḥammad (1013) i, 212a, 413a, 696b, 858a, **958b**; ii, 294a, 570b, 765a, 774b; iii, 544a, 1020a, 1063a, 1144b; iv, 108a, 183a, 272a, 378b, 470b, 616a, 949a; v, 426b; vi, 280b, 351b, 447b, 448a; vii, 312a; ix, 887a; s, 26b, 343b, 345a, 346b –
I, 218b, 425a, 717b, 881b, **988a**; II, 302a, 584b, 783b, 793a; III, 562b, 1045b, 1089b, 1173a; IV, 112b,

113a, 191a, 284a, 395a, 491b, 640b, 982a; V, 429a; VI, 265b, 335b, 433a, b; VII, 314b; IX, 923aS, 27a, 343b, 344b, 346a
Bāķir b. Māhān iii, 988a – III, 1012b
Bāķir Khān Khurāskānī iv, 104b, 391a – IV, 109a, 408a
Baķish iii, 1106b – III, 1134a
al-Bāķiyat us-Ṣāliḥat College (Vellore) vi, 462a – VI, 447b
Baķķ → Ķaml
Baķķ iv, 522a – IV, 544b
Bakka → Makka
al-Baķķa i, 100a – I, 103a
Bakkā' i, **959a** – I, **988b**
al-Bakkā'ī, Aḥmad (1864) v, 394a; vi, 259b – V, 395a; VI, 244a
al-Bakkā'i, Ziyād iii, 801a – III, 824a
Baķķāl i, **961a** – I, **990b**
Baķķam i, **961b** – I, **991a**
Bakkār (island/île) i, **961b** – I, **991a**
Bakkār b. Ķutayba (883) ix, 547b – IX, 569a
Baķķāra, Banū i, 49b, **962a**; ii, 122a, 124a; v, 266b, 1249a, 1250a, 1251b; viii, 171b – I, 50b, 51a, **991b**; II, 125a, 127a; V, 264b, 1240a, 1241a, 1242b; VIII, 173b
B'aķlīn vi, 28a – VI, 26a
Baķliyya i, **962b**; iv, 661a – I, **992a**; IV, 687b
al-Bakr, Aḥmad Ḥasan v, 469a – V, 472a
Bakr, Banū i, 526b, 527a, 529b, 962b, 1339a; ii, 71b; iii, 222b; v, 116b, 346a, 362a; vi, 490a, 733b; vii, 266a, 373b – I, 542b, 543a, 545b, 992b, 1379b; II, 73a; III, 229a; V, 119a, 347a, 363a; VI, 476a, 722b; VII, 268a, 375a
Bakr b. 'Abd al-'Azīz b. Abī Dulaf iii, 126a, 619a; iv, 718b – III, 129a, 639b; IV, 747b
Bakr b. 'Abd Manāt v, 78a, b, 79a – V, 80a, b, 81a
Bakr b. Ḥassād (Ḥammād) al-Bāhirī iii, 889b – III, 913b
Bakr b. Ḥumrān al-Aḥmarī (VII) vii, 690a – VII, 690b
Bakr b. Khāridja iv, 1003b – IV, 1036a
Baka b. Khunays al-Kūfī (VIII) vi, 613b – VI, 598b
Bakr b. al-Mu'tamir (810) vi, 332a – VI, 316b
Bakr b. al-Naṭṭāḥ, Abu 'l-Wā'il (808) s, **122a** – S, **121b**
Bakr b. Ukht 'Abd al-Wāḥid b. Zayd (VIII) vi, 457b – VI, 443a
Bakr b. Wā'il, Banū i, 545a, **962b**; ii, 241a, 343b; iii, 166b, 1254a; iv, 321b; vi, 640b; ix, 381b; x, 406b; s, 122a – I, 562a, **992b**; II, 247a, 353b; III, 170a, 1287a; IV, 336a; VI, 625b; IX, 404a; X, 429b; S, 121b
Bakr b. Zadlafa, Banū ix, 306b – IX, 315b
Bakr al-A'war al-Hadjarī al-Ķattāt (VIII) vii, 348a – VII, 350a
Bakr Beg i, 845a – I, 868a
Bakr Ṣidķī (1917) ii, 1045a; iii, 1258b; viii, 141b – II, 1069b; III, 1291a; VIII, 144a
Bakr Ṣū Bāshī (XVII) i, 904a, **962b**; iii, 1257a – I, 931b, **992a**; III, 1290a
al-Bakradjī, Ķāsim b. Muḥammad b. 'Alī al-Ḥalabī (1756) vi, 913b – VI, 905a
Bakrān, Muḥammad vi, 415b – VI, 400b
al-Bakrī → 'Abd al-'Azīz; Abū 'Ubayd
al-Bakrī → Bakriyya; Ṣiddīķī
al-Bakrī b. Abi 'l-Surūr (1619) i, **965a** – I, **995a**
al-Bakrī, Abu 'l-Ḥasan Aḥmad b. 'Abd Allāh) (XIII) i, **964b**; ii, 159a; vii, 100b; x, 346a – I, **994b**; II, 164a; VII, 102b; X, 371b
al-Bakrī, Aḥmad Murād (XX) x, 324b – X, 349b
al-Bakrī, Muḥammad (poet/poète) viii, 425a – VIII, 430a
al-Bakrī, Muḥammad b. 'Abd al-Raḥmān al-Ṣiddīķī (1545) i, **965b**; iv, 451b, 505b – I, **995a**; IV, 471b, 527a
al-Bakrī, Muḥammad b. Ayyūb (Walba) (XI) i, 6a; vii, 761a – I, 6a; VII, 762b
al-Bakrī, Muḥammad b. Muḥammad b. Abi 'l-Surūr (1650) i, **965a** – I, **995a**
al-Bakrī, Muḥammad b. Yūsuf, Ibn al-Warrāķ vi, 946a – VI, 938a
al-Bakrī, Muḥammad Ṭawfiķ b. 'Alī (1932) vi, 113b; s, **122b**, 132b – VI, 111a; S, **122a**, 132a
al-Bakrī, Muṣṭafā b. Kamāl al-Dīn (1749) i, 60a, b, **965b**; iv, 991b, 992a; vi, 112b, 627a; s, 44a – I, 62a, b, **995b**; IV, 1024b; VI, 110a, 612a; S, 44b
al-Bakrī, Shaykh → Shaykh al-Bakrī
al-Bakrī al-Khʷārazmī, Diyā' al-Dīn (1172) vi, 352b – VI, 337a
Bakriyya i, **966a** – I, **996a**
Bakriyya → Bakr b. Ukht 'Abd al-Wāhid
al-Bakriyya i, **966a**; s, 122b – I, **995b**; S, 122a
Baķt i, 32a, **966a** – I, 33a, **996a**
Baktamur Djilliķ (1412) vii, 723a, b – VII, 724a, b
Baktāsh al-Fakhiri, Badr al-Dīn iv, 485a – IV, 506a
Baktimur al-Silāḥdār, amīr (1300) vi, 545b – VI, 530a
Bākū i, 191b, **966b**; iii, 530b; iv, 348a; vi, 129b, 769b; vii, 71a; s, 73a, 136a, 365a, b – I, 197a, **996b**; III, 548b; IV, 363a; VI, 127b, 759a; VII, 72a; S, 73b, 135b, 365a
Ba'ķūba i, **967b** – I, **997b**
Bāķūm (Bāķūl) i, 609a; vii, 74a – I, 628b; VII,75a
Bakumpai s, 151a – S, 151a
Bākusāyā i, 870b, **968a** – I, 895a, **998a**
al-Bākuwī, 'Abd al-Rashīd Ṣāliḥ (1402) vii, 71a – VII, 72a
Ba'l i, 491b, **968a** – I, 506b, **998a**
Bal-Faķih → Faķīh, Bal-
Bālā i, **969b** – I, **999b**
Ba'la v, 692b – V, 697b
Bal'ā' b. Ķays vi, 349a – VI, 333b
Bālā-ghāt i, **970a** – I, **1000a**
Bālā Ḥiṣār i, **970a**; ii, 978a, 1119a – I, **1000a**; II, 1000b, 1145a
Bālā Murghāb vi, 617b – VI, 602b
Bālā Pīr → Ghāzī Miyān
Balābādh → Balāwāt
Ba'labakk i, 940b, **970b**, 1051a, 1214b; vi, 193b, 303a; vii, 693a – I, 969a, **1000b**, 1083a, 1250b; VI, 177b, 288b; VII, 693b
Balaban iv, 140a – IV, 146a
Balabān al-Tabbākhī, amīr (1279) vi, 579b – VI, 564b
Balabān Zaynī, al-Dawādār, Sayf al-Dīn, amīr (1281) iv, 483b; vi, 579b – IV, 504b; VI, 564b
Balabanköy vi, 57a – VI, 55a
Balad 'Ans s, 22b – S, 22b
al-Balādhurī, Aḥmad b. Yaḥyā (892) i, 591a, 635b, 760a, **971b**; ii, 131b; iii, 608a; iv, 275a, 342b; vi, 359a, 363a, 493a – I, 610b, 656b, 782b, **1001b**; II, 135a; III, 628b; IV, 287b, 357a; VI, 343a, 347a, 479a
Baladiyya i, **972b** – I, **1002b**
Bālādjī Rāo II (Pēshwā) (1761) vi, 535b; vii, 446a – VI, 520a; VII, 447a
Bālādjī Rāo Visvanāth (1719) vi, 535a – VI, 519b
Balā iv, 203b – IV, 212b
Balāgha i, 858a, **981b**, 1114a, b, 1116a; ii, 824a – I, 881b, **1012a**, 1147b, 1148a, 1149b; II, 843b
Balaķ (Mts) vi, 559a – VI, 544a
Balak, Nūr al-Dawla Balak b. Bahrām (Artuķid(e)) (1124) i, 664b, 732a, **983a**, 1025a; ii, 110b; iii, 87a; iv, 1084a; v, 106a; vi, 380a – I, 684a, 754a, **1013b**, 1056b; II, 113a; III, 89a; IV, 1115b; V, 108a; VI, 364a

Bālaḳ b. Ṣāfūn → ʿŪdj b. ʿAnāḳ
Balakhsh i, 851b – I, 875a
Bālakī i, 1031a – I, 1062b
Balaklava i, **983b** – I, **1014a**
Balʿam i, **984a** – I, **1014b**
Balʿamī, Abū ʿAlī Muḥammad (974) i, 4216, **984b**; iv, 504a; vi, 433a; vii, 85b; x. 14a; s, 297b – I, 433b **1015a**; IV, 526a; VI, 418a; VII, 87a; X, 14b; S, 297b
Balʿamī, Abu 'l-Faḍl Muḥammad (940) i, **984b**; s, 265b – I, **1015a**; S, 265b
Bāl-ʿanbar → Tamīm
Balandjar i, 921b, **985a**; iv, 343b, 344a, 1173a – I, 949b, **1015b**; IV, 358a, b, 1206b
al-Balansī, ʿUbayd Allāh b. ʿAbd Allāh (IX) viii, 870b – VIII, 900a
Balansiya (Valencia) i, 446b, 495a, **985a**, 1288a; iii, 673a; iv, 468a; ix, 351a; s, 143a – I, 459a, 510a, **1016a**, 1327b; III, 694b; IV, 489a; JX, 362a; S, 143a
Bālāpur s, 280a – S, 279b
Balarm (Palermo) i, 250b, **986a**; ii, 115a, 864a; iv, 497a, 979b; vi,650a, 653a – I, 258b, **1017a**; II, 117b, 883b; IV, 518b, 1012a; VI, 635a, 638b
Balāsāghūn i, **987a**; iii, 1114b; iv, 581a, 582a; v, 858a; s, 240a – I, **1017b**; III, 1141b; IV, 604b; 605b; V, 865a; S, 240a
Bālāsarīs ix, 404n – IX, 417b
Balash (Sāsānid(e)) (488) ix, 76b – IX, 79b
Balāṭ (Miletus/Milète) i, 950a, **987b**; vi, 366a – I, 979b, **1018a**; VI, 350a
Balāṭ i, **987b** – I, **1018b**
Balaṭ (Balad) s, 123b – S, 123a
Balāt (road/voie) i, **988a** – I, **1018b**
Balāṭ al-Shuhadāʾ i, 86b, 493a, 988a, **988b** – I, 89a, 508a, 1018b, **1019a**
al-Balāṭa → Shantarīn
al-Balaṭī, Abu 'l-Fatḥ ʿUthman (1202) s, **123b** – S, **123a**
Balāṭunus i, **989b** – I, **1020a**
Balawī, Banū → Baliyy
al-Balawī, Abū Zamʿa vi, 712b – VI, 701a
Balāwāt i, **989b** – I, **1020b**
Balawhar → Bilawhar wa-Yūdāsaf
al-Balawī (X) i, 96b, **990a**; iii, 745b – I, 99a, **1020b**; III, 768b
Bālāy Miyān → Ghāzī Miyān
Balayeur → Kannās
Baʿlbak → Baʿlabakk
Balban, Ghiyāth al-Dīn Ulugh Khān (Muʿizzī, Dihlī) (1287) i, 217b, 1036a; ii, 12b, 120a, 260b, 268a, 272b, 973a, 1084a, 143b; iii, 168a, 416a, 441b, 492a; iv, 749b, 818a; v, 629b, 638a, 685a, 1135a; vi, 47b, 48a, b, 368b, 532b; vii, 193b; s, 66b, 73b, **124a** – I, 1067b; II, 12b, 123a, 269a, 276a, 281a, 995a, 1109b, 1171a; III, 171b, 429a, 456a, 509a; IV, 779b, 851a; V, 633b, 642a, 690b, 1130b; VI, 46a, b, 47a, 352b, 516b; VII, 194a; S, 67a, 74a, **123a**
Balban, Muḥammad b. Ghiyāth al-Dīn (1286) vi, 609a; s, 124b – VI, 594a; S, 123b
Balbār (Ḥammādid(e)) (XI) vi, 427a – VI, 412a
Bālčano (painter/peintre) (XVII) vii, 339a – VII, 340b
Baldj b. Bishr (742) i, 76a, 82a, 134b, 490a, **990b**; 524b; iii, 494a; iv, 494b; v, 367a – I, 78b, 84b, 138b, 504b, **1021a**; II, 538a; III, 511a; IV, 515b, V, 368a
Baldj b. ʿUḳba al-Azdī (748) vii, 524b – VII, 525a
Balearic Isles/Baléares → Mayurḳa
Balewa, Abubakar Tafawa iii, 282b; iv, 774a – III, 291a; IV, 805a
Balfour Declaration/Déclaration de - vi, 388a – VI, 372b
Bālfurūsh → Bārfurūsh
Bal-Ḥāf → Ibn al-Ḥāf
Balharā i, **991a**; ii, 352a – I, **1022a**; II, 362a
Balḥārith → Ḥārith b. Kaʿb
Balhīb vi, 877b – VI, 869a
Bāli (al-Ḥabash) i, 176b, **991b**; iii, 6a – I, 181a, **1022b**; III, 6b
Bali (Indonesia/Indonésie) iii, 1213b, 1214b, 1219b, 1223a; v, 785a – III, 1244b, 1245a, 1250a, 1254a; V, 791b
Balī → Baliyy
Balī, Banū vii, 921a; viii, 863a – VII, 921b; VIII, 894a
al-Baʿlī, ʿAbd al-Raḥmān iii, 162a – III, 165b
Bali Bey b. Yaḥyā Pasha (Mohács) (1526) i, 1163b; ii, 201b; vii, 219a – I, 1198b; II, 208a; VII, 221a
Bālī Efendi (Vize) vi, 228a; ix. 705b – VI, 222a; IX, 734a
Baliabadra i, **992a** – I, **1022b**
Bāli i, **993a** – I, **1024a**
Balîḳ i, 610b; ii, 971b – I, 626a; II, 993b
Bālik i, **993b** – I, **1024b**
Bālikesrī/Bālîkesīr i, **993b**; iv, 628b; vi, 588a – I, **1024b**; IV, 653b; VI, 573a
Balīkh (river/fleuve) vi, 378b, 733a – VI, 363a, 722b
Balîkhane i, 1279a – I, 1318a
Bālîm Sulṭān i, 1162a; viii, 12a – I, 1196b; IX, 12a
Balīnūs (of Perge/de Perga) → al-Nadjdjār
Balīnūs/Balīnās of/de Tyane (Apollonius) (VIII) i, 737a, **994a**, b; ii, 93b, 359a; iii, 464a; v,111b; vi, 637b; vii, 833b; s, 270a – I, 759a, **1025a**, b; II, 95a, 368b; III, 480a; V, 114a; VI, 622b; VII, 834b; S, 269b
Bālis i, **995b**; vi, 733a, b – I, **1026b**; VI, 722a, b
Bālis-Maskana vi, 378a, 379b, 380a, 381b, 382a – VI, 362b, 363b, 364a, 365b, 366b
Balisāna vi, 576a – VI, 561a
al-Bālisī → Muḥammad b. Musallam
Bālish i, **997b** – I, **1027a**
Bālish (Vélez) i, **996a**; vi, 576a – I, **1027b**; VI, 561a
Baliyy, Banū i, 990a; iii, 363b; v, 317b, 318a, b – I, 1020b; III, 375a; V, 317a, b, 318a
Baliyya i, **997b** – I, **1028a**
al-Balḳāʾ, Banū i, **997b**, 1149a; vi, 371b; s, 117a – I, **1028b**, 1183b; VI, 356a; S, 116b
Balkā Khaldjī iii, 1155b – III, 1184a
Balkā-takīn i, 226b – I, 233b
Balkan i, 468a, **998a**; ii, 33b; iv, 297a – I, 482a, **1029a**; II, 34a; IV, 310a
Balkar i, **1000a**; ii, 23a; iv, 325a, 596b – I, **1031a**; II, 24a; IV, 339b, 620b
Balḳar vii, 352a – VII, 354a
Balḳayn → Ḳayn
Balkh i, 8a, 17b, 46b, 147b, 223b, 296a, 662a, 684b, 768b, **1000b**, 1033a; ii, 4b, 43a, 201a; iii, 134b; iv, 809b; vi, 14b, 273b, 313b, 494b, 522a, 608b, 618b, 620b, 780b; s, 97a, 125b, 227b, 326a, 340b, 416b, 419b – I, 8a, 18b, 48a, 152a, 230a, 305a, 683a, 705b, 791b, **1031b**, 1064b; II, 4b, 44a, 207b; III, 137a; IV, 842a; VI, 13a, 258b, 299a, 480a, 507a, 593a, 603b, 605b, 770a; S, 96b, 124b, 227b, 325b, 340a, 416b, 419b
Balkha(r) iv, 323a – IV, 357b
Balkhān i, **1002a**; vi, 415b, 416a; s, 280b – I, **1032b**; VI, 400b, 401a; S, 280b
Balkhash i, **1002a** – I, **1033a**
al-Balkhī → Abū Maʿshar
al-Balkhī, Abū ʿAlī Muḥammad ii, 918b – II, 940a
al-Balkhī, Abu 'l-Ḳāsim (931) i, **1002b**; iii, 979b; iv, 1162b; v, 702a; vii, 312a, b, 784b; s, 14b, 335b –

I, **1033b**; III, 1004a; IV, 1194b; V, 707a; VII, 314b, 315a, 786b; S, 14b, 335a
Balkhī, Abu 'l-Muʾayyad (X) ii, 918b – II, 940a
al-Balkhī, Abū Muṭīʿ (799) i, 124a; vii, 606b – I, 127b; VII, 606a
al-Balkhī, Abū Zayd Aḥmad b. Sahl (934) i, **1003a**; ii, 579b, 581a; iii, 57b, 787b, 1077b; iv, 223a, 1079a; vi, 639b, 640a; vii, 493a, 538b; viii, 372b; s, 72b, 265a, 266a, 386b – I, **1033b**; II, 594a, 596a; III, 60a, 810b, 1104b; IV, 232b, 1110b; VI, 624b, 625a; VII, 493a, 538b; VIII, 385b, 535b; S, 72b, 264b, 265b, 387a
al-Balkhī, Burhān al-Dīn al-Sikilkandī (1153) vi, 847b – VII, 838b
al-Balkhī, Ḥamīd al-Dīn Abū Bakr (1164) vii, 567b – VII, 568a
al-Balkhī, Ḳawām (Ḳiwām) al-Mulk Abū ʿAlī vi, 932a – VI, 924a
Balkhī, Muẓaffar Shams (1401) vi, 131b – VI, 129b
al-Balkhī, Nuṣayr b. Yaḥyā (881) vi, 846a – VI, 837a
al-Balkhī, Shaḳīḳ b. Ibrāhīm (809) vii, 647a; viii, 254b – VII, 647a; VIII, 267a
al-Balkhī al-Warrāḳ, Abu 'l-Djaysh al-Muẓaffar b. Muḥammad (977) vii, 312a, b – VII, 314a, 315a
Balkis → Bilḳīs
Balkuwārā → Sāmarrā
Ballā, Sīdī, Abū Muḥammad Ibn ʿAzzūz (1789) s, **124b** – S, **382b**
Ballabh Rāyʾ, Rādja i, 952a – I, 981a
Ballahara → Balharā
al-Ballūtīn → Abū Ḥafṣ ʿUmar; Mundhir b. Saʿīd
Balōč → Baluč
Balshas, Balshiči i, 653b – I, 674a
Bālta Līmānī (treaty/traité) (1838) i, **1003b**; vii, 429a, 467b – I, **1034b**; VII, 430a, 467b
Baltadjī i, **1003b** – **I, 1034b**
Baltadjī Muḥammad Pasha → Muḥammad Pasha
Bālṭa-oghlū Sulaymān Beg i, 1003b – I, 1034b
Baltic Sea → Baḥr al-Warank
Baltistān i, **1004b**; vi, 696b; viii, 136a; s, 242a, 423b – I, **1035b**; VI, 684b; VIII, 138a; S, 242a, 423b
Balūč, Baluchis i, 211b, 225a, 546a, **1005a**, 1354b; iii, 633b, 1098a, 1107b; iv, 10b; v, 153a, 673b, 674b; vi, 50b, 193b, 342b; s, 143b, 147a, 270b, 331a, b, 332a, b – I, 217b, 231b, 563b, **1035b**, 1393b; III, 655a, 1124b, 1134b; IV, 11a; V, 154a, 678b, 679b; VI, 49a, 177b, 327a; S, 143a, 147a, 270a, b, 331a, b
Balūčistān i, **1005a**; ii, 669a, 1083b; iv, 3b, 8a, 364a; v, 101b, 520b, 580b; vi, 65b, 192b; viii, 240b; s, 71b, 222a, 270b, 329b – I, **1036a**; II, 658b, 1109a; IV, 3b, 8b, 380a; V, 103b, 524a, 585a; VI, 63b, 176a; VIII, 246b; S, 72a, 222a, 270a, 329a
Balwant Singh i, 1166a – I, 1200b; IV, 3b, 8b, 380a; V, 103b, 524a, 585a; S, 72a, 222a, 270a, 329a
Balyā b. Malkān iv, 904b – IV, 937a
Balyānī, Awḥad al-Dīn (1288) x, 320b – X, 345a
Balyemez i, **1007b**, 1062b – I, **1038b**, 1094b
Bālyōs i, **1008a**; ii, 60b – I, **1039a**; II, 61b
Balyūnash s, **124b** – S, **124a**
Bam i, **1008a**; iii, 502a; iv, 1052a; v, 148b, 149b, 151a; s, 127a, 327a – I, **1039b**; III, 519a; IV, 1083b; V, 150b, 151b, 153a; S, 126a, 326b
Bamako i, **1008b**; vi, 260a – I, **1040a**; VI, 244b
Bambāra i, 297a, 1009a; ii, 252a; iii, 39b; iv, 314a; vi, 258b, 259a, b, 260a, 402b; s, 295b – I, 306a, 1040b; II, 259b; III, 41a; IV, 328a; VI, 243a, b, 244a, 387a; S, 295a
Bāmiyān i, **1009a**; ii, 1101a; s, 367a, b – I, **1040b**; II, 1127a; S, 367a, b
Bampūr i, **1010a**; vi, 192b – I, **1041b**; VI, 176b
Bān i, **1010b** – I, **1041b**
Banādir iv, 885b, 886a – IV, 918a, b
Banākat (Fanākath/Shāhrrukhiyya) i, **1010b**; x, 349a, 813a – I, **1042a; X, 374b**
Banākitī i, **1011a** – I, **1042a**
Banāras → Benares
Banarsidas vii, 323a – VII, 324b
Bānās, Nahr i, 1029b – I, 1061a
Banat → Temesvar
Banāt Ḳayn iv, 493b – IV, 514b
Banāt Naʿsh → Nudjūm
Bānat Suʿād i, **1011b**; iv, 316a, b – I, **1042b**; IV, 330b
Banbalūna i, 83b, **1011b**, 1079b; v, 1119a; vii, 1039b – I, 86a, **1043a**, 1111b; V, 1115b; VII, 1041b
Band i, **1012a**; v, 862b, 867-9 – I, **1043a**; V, 869b, 873b-875b
Band, military → Naḳḳāra-Khāna
Band-i Amīr i, 212b, 1012a; v, 867b – I, 218b, 1043b; V, 874a
Band-i Bahman vi, 384a – VI, 368b
Band-i Ḳīr iv, 675b; v, 867b – IV, 703b; V, 874a
Band-i Mīzān v, 867a, b – V, 873b
Bāndā i, **1012b** – I, **1043b**
Banda Bayrāgī i, 432b, 914a, 1022b; ii, 28b, 380b – I, 445a, 941b, 1054a; II, 29a, 390b
Banda islands/îles de i, **1012b** – I, **1044a**
Banda Nawāz → Sayyid Muḥammad
Bandanīdjīn i, 968a – I, 998a
Bandar i, **1013a** – I, **1044a**
Bandar b. Fayṣal b. ʿAbd al-ʿAzīz Āl Suʿūd s, 305b – S, 305b
Bandar ʿAbbās i, 928a, **1013a**, 1172b, 1282a, 1283a; iii, 585a; iv, 1170b; v, 148a, 151b, 152a, 183b, 673a, 674a; viii, 773a – I, 956a, **1044a**, 1207b, 1321a, b; III, 605a; IV, 1203b; V, 150b, 153a, 154a, 181a, 678a, 679b; VIII, 798b
Bandar Kung → Kung
Bandar Linga → Linga
Bandar Nādiriyya → Būshahr
Bandar Pahlawī i, **1013b**; iv, 7a – I, **1045a**; IV, 7b
Bandar Seri Begawan (Bandar Brunei) s, 151b – S, 151b
Bandar Shāpūr i, 1342a – I, 1382a
Bandar Tawayih (Tawwāhī) i, 180b – I, 186a
Bandayr ii, 620b, 621a – II, 636a, b
Bandirma i, **1014a**; vi, 587b – I, **1045b**; VI, 572a
Bandj, bang i, **1014b**; ii, 1068b; iii, 266b – I, **1045b**; II, 1093b; III, 274a
Bandjarmasin i, **1014b**; s, 150a, b, 151a, 199b – I, **1046a**; S, 150b, 151a, 199b
Bandjī b. Nahārān Shansabānī ii, 1099b – II, 1125a
Bandjūtakīn (992) vi, 506b – VI, 491b
Bānegā ix, 727b – IX, 758b
Bangāla i, 400b, 606a, **1015a**; ii, 183b, 751b, 1092a; iii, 14b, 419a, 422a, 427b, 444a, 533a, 631b; iv, 210b; vi, 49b, 61b, 273a, 343a, 535b, 693a; vii, 79a; viii, 68a; s, 247a – I, 412a, 625b, **1046a**; II, 189a, 770a, 1118a; III, 15b, 432b, 436a, 441b, 458b, 551b, 652b; IV, 220a; VI, 48a, 59b, 258a, 327a, 519b, 681a; VII, 80b; VIII, 69b; S, 247a
Bangalore v, 1259b, 1260a, b – V, 1250a, b, 1251a, b
Banganapalle i, **1015b** – I, **1046b**
Bangash, Banū i, 218b, 219a; v, 250b; vii, 220a – I, 224b, 225b; V, 248b; VII, 222a
Bangka i, **1015b**; vi, 239a – I, **1047a**; VI, 204a
Bangla → Fayḍābād
Bangladesh v, 1082a; viii, 241b, 243a – V, 1079b; VIII, 247b, 248b
Banhā i, **1015b** – I, **1047a**

Bani (Annam) iii, 1210b, 1212a – III, 1241a, 1242b
Banī Suwayf i, **1016a** – I, **1047b**
Banians vi, 734b, 735b – VI, 723b, 724b
al-Bānīdjūrī → Dāwūd b. ʿAbbās
Bānīdjūrid(e)s i, 504a; v, 76a; vii, 477b; x, 602a; s, **125a** – I, 519a; V, 78a; VII, 477a; X, 646b; S, **124a**
Banīḳa i, **1016a** – I, **1047b**
Bāniyās (Buluniyās, Balanea)) i, **1016b**; vii, 198b; viii, 129a, 131a – I, **1048a**; VII, 199a; VIII, 132a, 133b
Baniyās (Paneas) i, **1017a**; iv, 200a; vi, 577b, 578a, b, 579b, 580b, 582a, b, 789b; vii, 198b, 274a, b; s, 204b – I, **1048a**; IV, 208b, 209a; VI, 562b, 563a, b, 564b, 565b, 566b, 567a, 771b; VII, 199a, 276a; S, 204b
Bāniyās, Nahr → Bānās
Banjaluka i, **1017b**, 1263b, 1265b, 1266b, 1270b – I, **1048b**, 1302a, 1304a, 1305a, 1309b
Banking → Djahbadh and Ṣayrafī
Bānkīpūr i, **1018a**; vi, 198b – I, **1049b**; VI, 182b
Banmana → Bambāra
Bannāʾ → Bināʾ
al-Bannāʾ, Aḥmad b. Muḥammad → al-Dimyāṭī
al-Bannāʾ, Ḥasan (1949) i, **1018b**; ii, 429b; iii, 518a, 1068b, 1070a – I, **1049b**; II, 440b; III, 535b, 1095b, 1096b
Bannāʾī, ʿAlī b. Muḥammad (XV) vii, 685a – VII, 685a
Bannāʾī, Kamāl al-Dīn (1513) i, **1019a**; ii, 208a – I, **1050a**; II, 215a
al-Bannānī, Abū ʿAbdallāh Muḥammad b. Ḥasan (1780) vi, 279a – VI, 263b
al-Bannānī, Āl i, **1019b**; s, 405a – I, **1050b**; S, 405a
Bannū i, **1020a**; v, 251a, 501a; vi, 86a; s, 329b – I, **1051a**; V, 249a, 504a; VI, 84a; S, 329a
Bannʿučīs i, 1020a – I, 1051a
Bantam iii, 1219b, 1223b; vi, 235a; s, 199b, 201a, 202a, 374b – III, 1250a, 1255a; VI, 208a; S, 199b, 201a, b, 374b
Banū, followed by the name of the eponymous ancestor of a tribe, see in general under the name of that ancestor/suivi du nom de l'ancêtre éponyme d'une tribu, voir en général sous le nom de cet ancêtre
Banu 'l-Afṭas → Afṭasid(e)s
Banū Isrāʾīl i, 264b, **1020a**; vi, 737a, b – I, 272b, **1051b**; VI, 726a, 727a
Banū Maslama → Afṭasid(e)s
Bañuelo ii, 1015a – II, 1038b
Banūr i, **1022a**; ii, 28b; s, 1b – I, **1053b**; II, 29a; S, 1b
al-Banūrī, Ādam (1643) i, **1022b** – I, **1054a**
Banwālī Dās Walī vii, 343b – VII, 345a
Banya i, 700a – I, 721a
Banyan v, 807b – V, 813b
Banyar i, **1023a** – I, **1055a**
Bānyās → Baniyās
Banzart i, **1023b**; vii, 269b; s, 145a – I, **1055a**; VII, 271b; S, 144b
Bāʾolī i, **1024a**; v, 884b, 888b – I, **1055b**; V, 890b, 894b
Bāonī i, **1024b** – I, **1056a**
Bar Bahlūl → Abu 'l-Ḥasan b. Bahlūl
Bar Dīṣān → Ibn Dayṣan
Bar Hebraeus → Ibn al-ʿIbrī
al-Bāra i, 145b, **1024b** – I, 150a, **1056a**
al-Barāʾ b. ʿĀzib (691) i, 98b, **1025a**; iv, 858b – I, 101b, **1056b**; IV, 891b
al-Barāʾ b. Maʿrūr (622) i, **1025a**, 1241b; v, 82b – I, **1057a**, 1279b; V, 84b
Bāra Sayyids i, **1025b** – I, **1057a**
Bārā Wafāt i, **1026a** – I, **1057b**
Barāʾa i, 207a, 811a, **1026b**; ii, 78b, 79b, 308a – I, 213a, 834a, **1058a**, II, 80a, 81a, 317a
Baraba i, **1028a** – I, **1059b**
Barābīsh, Banū vi, 741b – VI, 730b
Barābra i, **1028b**; viii, 92a – I, **1060a**; VIII, 94b
Baradā (river/fleuve) i, **1029a**; ii, 1105a; viii, 118b – I, **1060b**; II, 1131a; VIII, 131a
Baradā (Djayhūn) i, **1030a** – I, **1061b**
Baradān i, **1030a** – I, **1061b**
Barādhiʿī, Abū Saʿīd (X) vii, 538a – VII, 538a
Barādūst i, **1030b** – I, **1062a**
Barāghīth i, 1049b – I, 1081a
Baraghwāṭa → Barghawāṭa
Barāhima i, 173a, **1031a**, 1092b; ii, 166b; iii, 905a; v, 550a; s, 93a – I, 177b, **1062b**, 1125a; II, 171b; III, 929a; V, 554b; S, 92b
Barahūt → Barhūt
Barak i, 1233b – I, 1270a
Baraḳ Baba (1307) i, **1031b**; ii, 1085b – I, **1063a**; II, 1111a
Baraḳ Ḥādjib → Burāk Ḥādjib
Baraḳ Khāns → Būraḳ Khān
Baraka i, **1032a**; iii, 305b; v, 745a – I, **1063b**; III, 315a; V, 750b
Baraka (ṣūfī) s, 3a – S, 2a
Baraka Khān (Mamlūk(e)) → al-Saʿīd Nāṣir al-Dīn Baraka (Berke) b. Baybars
Baraka Khān (Mongol) → Berke Khān
Baraka Umm Ayman (VII) x, 813a – X,
Barakai i, 1190a – I, 1225a
Barakāt I b. Ḥasan b. ʿAdjlān, Sharīf (1455) i, **1032a**; vi, 149b – **I**, **1064a**; VI, 148b
Barakāt II b. Muḥammad b. Barakāt I, Sharīf (1525) i, **1032b**; ii, 527b; iv, 552b; vi, 150a – I, **1064a**; II, 530a; IV, 576b; VI, 148b
Barakāt III b. Muḥammad b. Ibrāhīm (1682) i, **1032b** – I, **1064a**
Barakāt IV b. Yaḥyā (1723) i, **1032b** – I, **1064b**
Barakāt b. Mūsā iv, 514a, 552a, 553a – IV, 536b, 576a, 577a
Barāḳish (Yathill) vi, 88b – VI, 86b
Bārakzay i, 87a, 95b, 231a; ii, 628b, 629a; s, 65b – I, 89b, 98a, 238a; II, 644b, 645a; S, 66a
Baramendana Keita ii, 1132a – II, 1158b
al-Barāmika i, 2b, 10a, 14a, 17b, 107b, 143b, 160a, 271b, 364a, 751b, 897a, **1033a**; ii, 40b, 78a, 305a, 576b; iii, 231a; iv, 221b, 447a, 756a; vi, 276a, 334b, 335b, 336a; vii, 518a; s, 130a, 225b – I, 2b, 10a, 14a, 18a, 111a, 147b, 164b, 280a, 375a, 773b, 924a, **1064b**; II, 41b, 79b, 313b, 591a; III, 238a; IV, 231a, 466b, 786b; VI, 261a, 319a, 320a, b; VII, 518b; S, 129b, 225b
Bārāmūla s, 167a – S, 167a
Baran → Bulandshahr
Barʾān (temple) vi, 562a – VI, 547a
al-Barandjār i, 1305b – I, 1345b
Barānī, Bārānlu → Ḳarā Ḳoyunlu
Baranī, Ḍiyāʾ al-Dīn (1357) i, **1036a**; iv, 210b; vi, 121b; vii, 988a; s, 105a, b, 409a, b – I, **1067b**; IV, 220a; VI, 119b; VII, 989a; S, 104b, 105a, 409b
al-Barānis i, **1037a**, 1349b; vi, 741a; s, 102b – I, **1068b**, 1390a, 730a; S, 102a
Baranta i, **1037b** – I, **1069a**
Barār → Berār
Baraṭ vi, 436b – VI, 422a
Barāthā i, **1038a**, 1040a; s, 400b – I, **1069b**, 1071b; S, 401a
Barawa (Brava) i, **1038a**; vi, 128b, 129a, 704a – I, **1069b**; VI, 126b, 127a, 692b
al-Barāwī, Masʿūd b. Sultān Shafiʿ ʿAlī b. Sulṭān Muḥammad (1888) vi, 967a – VI, 959a
al-Barāwī, Shaykh Muḥyī al-Dīn b. al-Shaykh al-Ḳaḥṭānī (Zanzibar) (XIX) vi, 964a – VI, 956b

al-Barāwī, Uways b. Muḥammad (1909) x, 249b – X, 268a
Barāz (banda) iv, 16a; v, 64a – IV, 17b; V, 66a
Barbā i, **1038b** – I, **1070a**
Bārbad iv, 53b, 730b; vi, 102b, 276a – IV, 56b, 759b, VI, 100b, 261a
al-Barbahārī, al-Ḥasan b. ʿAlī (941) i, 277a, **1039a**; iii, 159a, 734b; iv, 172b, 470a; vi, 446b, 627b; viii, 14b – I, 286a, **1070b**; III, 162b, 757b; IV, 180a, 490b; VI, 432a, 612b;VIII, 14b
Bārbak Shāh b. Bahlūl Lōdī ii, 47b, 270b, 498b; iii, 420a, 632a, 633b – II, 48a, 279a, 511a; III, 433b, 653b, 655a
Bārbak Shāh Ilyās iii, 14b; s, 203a – III, 15b; S, 202b
Barbarī, Barābira → Barābra
Barbarīs → Hazāras
Barbarossa → ʿArūdj; Khayr al-Dīn
Barbary → al-Maghrib
Barbashturu i, 83b, **1040b**; v, 1119b; x, 824a; s, 152b – I, 86a, **1072a**; V, 1116a; X. ; S, 152b
Barberousse → ʿArūdj; Khayr al-Dīn
al-Barbīr (1811) vi, 113a – VI, 110b
Barcelona/-e ' Barshalūna
Barčlīgh-kent s, 246a – S, 246a
Barčuk (Uyghur Ḳaghān) (1209) x, 676b – X,
Bardalla, Abū ʿAbd Allāh Muḥammad (1721) s, **125b** – S, **125a**
Bardas Sclerus i, 212a – I, 218b
Bardasīr/Guwāshīr ix, 667a – IX, 693a
Bardesanes → Ibn Dayṣān
Bardhaʿa (Barda) i, 660a, b, **1040b**; iv, 346b; v, 397a; vi, 499a – I, 681a, **1072b**; IV, 361b; V, 398a; VI, 484b
al-Bardhaʿī, Abū Saʿīd (1009) vi, 278b, 279a – VI, 263b, 264a
al-Bardīdjī, Abū Bakr (914) vii, 576a; viii, 516a – VII, 576b; VIII, 534a
Bardistān vi, 384b – VI, 368b
Bardja (Berja) vi, 576a – VI, 561a
Bardjalūna → Barshalūna
Bardjawān, Abu 'l-Futūḥ (1000) i, **1041b**; ii, 858a; iii, 77a; iv, 1091b – I, **1073a**; II, 878a; III, 79b; IV, 1122b
Bārdjīk iv, 1173b – IV, 1207a
Bardo → Tūnis
Bardsīr v, 150b, 152a, b – V, 152b, 154a
Bardsīrī → Āḳā Khān Kirmānī
Bareilly, Barēlī i, **1042b**; iii, 60b, 61b; viii, 571b; s, 73b, 420b – I, **1074a**; III, 63a, 64a; VIII, 590a; S, 74a, 421a
Bārfurūsh (Bābul) i, **1043a**; vi, 511a – I, **1074b**; VI, 497b
Bārfurūshī, Nadīm iv, 1035a – IV, 1067a
Barghash b. Saʿīd b. Aḥmad, Bū Saʿīd (1888) i, 37b, **1043b**, 1282b; v, 1030b, 1031a; vi, 129a; vii, 35a; s, 355b – I, 38b, **1075a**, 1321b; V, 1026b, 1027a; VI, 127a; VII, 35b; S, 355b
Barghawāṭa, Banū i, 157a, **1043b**; ii, 275b, 1008b; v, 654b, 1160a, 1189a, 1199b; vi, 134a, 741a, 743b; vii, 585a – I, 161a, **1075b**; II, 284a, 1032a; V, 658b, 1150a, 1179a, 1189b; VI, 132a, 730b, 733a; VII, 585b
al-Barghawāṭī, Saḳḳūt (1083) viii, 690a – VIII, 710a
Bārgīn-farākh → Ḳarā-köl
Bārgīr iv, 219a, b – IV, 229a
Barghūth → Ḳaml
Bārha Sayyids viii, 73a; s, **126a** – VIII, 74b; S, **125b**
Barhebraeus → Ibn al-ʿIbrī
Barhūt i, **1045a** – I, **1076b**
Bari iv, 275a – IV, 287a
al-Barʿī (XI) vi, 898a – VI, 889a
Bafī Bēgam iii, 336a – III, 346a
Bārī Ṣaḥiba (Bīdjāpūr) (XVII) vii, 514b – VII, 515a
Bariba ii, 94a; iv, 538b; v, 281a – II, 96a; IV, 561b; V, 279a, b
Barīd i, **1045a**, 1039b; ii, 487a, 969b; iii, 109b, 182a; iv, 215b; v, 1142b – I, **1077a**, 1126a; II, 499a, 991b; III, 112a, 186a; IV, 225a; V, 1135b
Barīd Shāhīs (Bīdar) i, **1047a**, 1200a, b, 1201a; iii, 421b, 425a, b, 447a; vi, 68a, 126a, 368a, 695b; vii, 289a – I, **1078b**, 1236a, b; III, 435a, 438b, 439b, 462a; VI, 66a, 124a, 352as, 683b; VII, 291a
al-Barīdī, Abū ʿAbd Allāh (941) i, 866a, b, 867a, **1046b**; ii, 454a; iii, 127b; vi, 921a; vii, 484a, b, 994b – I, 890b, 891a, **1078a**; II, 465b; III, 130a; VI, 913a; VII, 484a, b, 996b
al-Barīdī, Abu 'l-Ḥusayn i, 1046b, 1047a – I, 1078b
al-Barīdī, Abu 'l-Ḳāsim i, 1047a; iii, 1175b – I, 1078b; III, 1204b
al-Barīdī, Abū Yūsuf i, 1046b, 1047a – I, 1078a, b
Bāridjān → Bāriz
Bāriḥ i, **1048a** – I, **1079b**
al-Bāriḥ iv, 290b – IV, 303b
Bārimmā → Ḥamrīn, Djabal
Bārīn vi, 378b, 381a, 429a – VI, 363a, 365a, 414b
Barīra (680) i, **1048a** – I, **1080a**
Barisan Hizbullah (XX) vi, 730b – VI, 719b
Barishk vi, 404a, b – VI, 388b, 389a, b
Barito (river) s, 150b – S, 150b
Bariyya iv, 980b – IV, 1013a
Bāriz, Djabal s, **127a** – S, **126a**
al-Bārizī, Kamāl al-Dīn iii, 799b; iv, 642a – III, 823a; IV, 668b
Barḳa i, **1048b**, 1169a; ii, 160b, 161b; iii, 296b; v, 694b, 695b, 758a, 760a; vi, 455b, 945b; s, 1a – I, **1080a**; 1204a; II, 165b, 166b; III, 305b; V, 699b, 700b, 763b, 765b; VI, 441a, 937b; S, 1a
Barḳa (Ḳumm) s, 127a – S, 126b
Barḳaʿīd i, **1050a** – I, **1082a**
al-Barkat ii, 1022b – II, 1046a, b
al-Barḳī, Abū Djaʿfar Aḥmad b. Muḥammad (IX) s, **127a**, 266a – S, **126b**, 265b
Barḳiyya ii, 318a, b, 858b – II, 327a, b, 878b
Barḳūḳ b. Anaṣ, al-Malik al-Ẓāhir Sayf al-Dīn (Mamlūk) (1399) i, 14b, 138a, 816b, 869a, **1050a**, 1109a, 1138a; ii, 24a, 105b, 239b, 285b, 330a, 337b; iii, 48b, 185a, 187a, 188a, 190a, 299b, 756b, 799b, 1198a; iv, 432b, 642a; v, 628a, 1141a; vi, 195a, 231b, 323b, 324a, 326b, 327a, 541a, 547b, 548a, 674a; vii, 171b, 407b; viii, 987a – I, 15a, 142a, 839b, 893a, **1082a**, 1142b, 1172b; II, 24b, 108a, 246a, 293b, 339b, 347b; III, 50b, 189a, 191a, 192b, 194b, 309a, 779b, 823a, 1228a; IV, 451b, 668a; V, 632a, 1134a; VI, 179a, 225a, 308a, b, 311a, b, 525b, 532a, b, 660b; VII, 173b, 409a; VIII, 1022a
Barḳūt i, 950b – I, 979b
Barkyārūḳ b. Malik-Shāh (Saldjūḳ) (1105) i, 314a, 353a, 466a, 513a, 664a, 731a, 780a, **1051b**, 1070b, 1336b; ii, 282a, 384b; iii, 196a; iv, 28b, 101b, 102a; v, 437a; vi, 64a, 275a, 499b, 540b; vii, 408a, 489b, 541a, 755a; viii, 72a, 81b, 716a, 942a; s, 279a, 382b, 384a – I, 324a, 363b, 480a, 529a, 684a, 753a, 803b, **1083a**, 1103a, 1377a; II, 290a, 395a; III, 201a; IV, 30b, 106a, b; V, 439b; VI, 61b, 260a, 485a, 525a; VII, 409a, 489a, 541a, 756a; VIII, 74a, 736b, 974a; S, 279a, 382b, 384a

Barlaam and/et Josaphat → Bilawhar wa Yūdāsaf
Barlās, Banū v, 182a – V, 179b
Barmak i, 1001a, 1033a, b – I, 1031b, 1065a
al-Barmakī → Djaʿfar b. Yaḥyā
Barmakid(e)s → Barāmika
Barniḳ → Benghāzī
Barōda i, **1053a**; vi, 535b – I, **1084b**; VI, 520a
Bārōghil ii, 29a – II, 29b
Barr al-Djazāʾir → Algeria/Algérie
al-Barrāḍ b. Ḳays al-Kinānī ii, 883b; iii, 285b; v, 116b – II, 904a; III, 294b; V, 119a
al-Barrādī, Abu ’l-Faḍl (XIV) i, 120b, 167a, **1053a**; ii, 140b; iii, 235b – I, 124a, 171b, **1085a**; II, 144b; III, 242a
al-Barrādī, Abu ’l-Ḳāsim (XV) vi, 311a, 948b – VI, 296 b, 941a
Barrāḥ ii, 103a – II, 105a
Barrāk b. Ghurayr Āl Ḥumayd → Barrāk b. ʿUrayʿir
Barrāk b. ʿUrayʿir Āl Ḥamīd iv, 765a, 925a – IV, 795b, 958a
Barre, Muḥammad Siyad (XX) ix, 720a – IX, 751a
Bārs Ṭūghān iv, 911b – IV, 944b
Barṣawmā al-Zāmir, Isḥāḳ (804) s, **128a** – S, **127b**
Barsbāy, al-Malik al-Ashraf Abu ’l-Naṣr (Mamlūk) (1438) i, 138a, 354b, 945b, 1032b, **1053b**; ii, 6a, 286a; iii, 20a, 99b, 186a, 190a, 923a, 1198a; iv, 133b, 267b, 433b, 642a, 643a; v, 304a; vi, 324a, b; vii, 173a; s, 39a, 43b, 273b – I, 142a, 365b, 974b, 1064a, **1085b**; II, 6a, 294a; III, 21a, 102a, 190b, 194a, 947b, 1228a; IV, 139a, 279b, 452b, 668b, 669b; V, 303b; VI, 308a, b; VII, 174b; S, 39b, 43b, 273b
Bārsbīk → Bārdjīk
Barshalūna i, 75b, **1054b**; ii, 485b – I, 78a, **1086b**; II, 497b
Barshambū, Sayf al-Dīn ʿAbd Allāh (XIV) viii, 90b → VIII, 92b
Barshāna vi, 576a – VI, 561a
Barshawīsh → Nudjūm
Barṣīṣā i, **1055a** – I, **1086b**
Barṣān iv, 213a – IV, 222b
Barsṭoghan ii, 391a – II, 401b
Bartāʾīl ii, 486b – II, 498b
Bartang i, 853b, 854a – I, 877a, b
Bārūd i, **1055b**; iii, 191a; v, 687a, 979a – I, **1087a**; III, 195b; V, 692a
al-Bārūdī, Maḥmūd Sāmī Pasha (1904) i, 597b, **1069b**; vii, 184a, b, 528b, 903a; s, 132b – I, 617a, **1101b**; VII, 184b, 529a, 903b; S, 132a
Barūdjird (Burudjird) i, **1070b**; v, 828b, 829a, b; s, 75a, 157b, 384a – I, **1102b**; V, 835a, 836a; S, 75b, 158a, 384b
al-Bārūk (Shūf) vi, 343b – VI, 327b
al-Bārūnī, ʿAbd Allāh i, 1070b – I, 1103a
al-Bārūnī, Sulaymān (1940) i, **1070b**; ii, 595a – I, **1103a**; II, 609b
al-Bārūsī, Abu ’l-Ḥasan Sālim vi, 224b – VI, 218b
Barwānī → Ibrā
Barzakh i, 940b, **1071b**, 1093a; ii, 581b; iv, 120b – I, 969b, **1103b**, 1125b; II, 596a; IV, 125b
Barzamān vi, 507a – VI, 492b
Bārzān i, **1072a**; v, 467b; vii, 714a – I, **1104a**; V, 470a; VII, 714b
Barzand i, **1072a** – I, **1104b**
al-Barzandjī, Djaʿfar b. Ḥasan (1765) vi, 350b, 354b; vii, 100b, 103a – VI, 335a, 338b; VII, 102b, 105a
Barzandjī, Muṣṭafā (XX) ix, 831a – IX, 866b
Barzandjī, Shaykh Maḥmūd (XX) v, 466b, 467b; viii, 463b; ix, 831a – V,469b, 470a; VIII, 479a; IX, 866a
Bārzānī → Muṣṭafā Bārzānī
Barzbān, Prince/le prince ii, 85b – II, 87b
Barzikanī iii, 258a – III, 265a, b
Barzū-nāma i, **1072b** – I, **1104b**
Barzūya i, **1073a** – I, **1105a**
Basadar s, 145a – S, 145a
Basaraba (Voyvoda, Wallachia) (XIV) x, 693a – X, 735b
al-Basāsīrī, Abu ’l-Ḥārith Arslān al-Muẓaffar (1060) i, 20b, 513a, 900b, **1073a**, 1355a; ii,348b,856a;iii, 159b, 891b, 1255b; iv, 26b,457b,458a,911b; v, 73b; vi, 272b, 966a; vii, 270b, 730b, 731a; s, 29b – I, 21a, 528b, 927b, **1105b**, 1394a; II, 358a, 876a; III, 163a, 915b, 1288a; IV, 28b, 478a, 944b; V, 75b; VI, 257b, 958a; VII, 272b, 731a, 731b; S, 29b
Basbās s, **128b** – S, **127b**
Bāshā → Pasha
Bashan → ʿŪdj
Bashariyya vii, 647b – VII, 647b
Bashdefterdār → Daftardār
Bashdjirt i, **1075a**, 1305a; ii, 995b; v, 1011b, 1012a, 1019a, b, 1020b – I, **1107a**, 1345b; II, 1018b; V, 1007b, 1015a, b, 1016b
Bashdjirt Literature x, **731b** – X, **777b**
Bashi-bozuḳ i, **1077b**; v, 35b – I, **1109b**; V, 36b
Bashīr (general/général) (838) vi, 775b – VI, 765a
al-Bashīr b. al-Mundhir iii, 652a – III, 673b
Bashīr b. Saʿd (633) i, **1077b**; viii, 118b; **s I, 1109b**; VIII, 121a
Bashīr Čelebi (XV) i, **1078a** – I, **1110a**
Bāshīr Ibrāhīmī → Ibrāhīmī
Bashīr Ḳāsim Malḥam ii, 636a – II, 652b
Bashīr Kizlar-aghasi iii, 253a – III, 260a
Bashīr Shihāb I b. Ḥusayn (1706) ii, 635a; vi, 344a, 346a – II, 651a; VI, 328a, 330a
Bashīr Shihāb II, Amīr (Lebanon/Liban) (1840) i, **1078a**, 1138a, 1281a; ii, 444a, 635b; iii, 999b; v, 792b; vi, 303b; vii, 670b; s, 159b, 162b – I, **1110b**, 1172b, 1320a; II, 455b, 651b; III, 1024b; V, 799a; VI, 288b; VII, 670a; S, 159b, 162b
al-Bashīr al-Wansharīsī, Shaykh (1130) vi, 592a – VI, 577a
Bashīrā iv, 1019b – IV, 1051b
Bashkard, Bashākard, Bashkardia v, 352b; s, **129a** – V, 353b; S, **128a**
Bashkent (battle of/bataille de) (1473) vi, 72a, 979b – VI, 70a, 972a
Bashkirs → Bashdjirt
al-Bashkunish i, 82a, 1011b, **1079b**; v, 1121a – I, 84b, 1043a, **1111b**; V, 1117b
Bashkirt/Bashkurt → Bashdjirt
Bashḳut, Djewād Fehmī (1971) s, **129b** – S, **128b**
Bashlik, Bashluk iv, 706a – IV, 734b
Bashmaḳ → al-Naʿl al-Sharīf
Bashmaḳlik i, **1079b** – I, **1112a**
Bashmuḥāsaba → Māliyya
Bashshār b. Burd, Abū Muʿādh (VIII) i, 10a, 143b, 331b, 587b, 857b, **1080a**; ii, 551b, 1031b; iii, 135b, 1019b, 1262b; iv, 54b, 1003b; vi, 267a, 625b, 635b; vii, 694b, 982a; viii, 377b, 984b; s, 58b – I, 10a, 148a, 341b, 606b, 881a, **1112a**; II, 565b, 1055b; III, 138b, 1045a, 1295b; IV, 57b, 1036a; VI, 251b, 610b, 620a; VII, 695a, 982b; VIII, 390a, 1019a; S, 59a
Bashshār b. Muslim iii, 41b – III, 43b
Bashshār al-Shaʿīrī (VIII) i, **1082a**; vii, 517a – I, **1114b**; VII, 517b
al-Bashshārī → al-Muḳaddasī
Bashtak (1341) vi, 323a, b – VI, 307b, 308a
Bāshūra i, 831a – I, 854a
Bashyāči, Elijah iv, 605b, 606a, 607b – IV, 630a, b, 632a
Bashwakīl → Baṣvekil

Bāṣiʿ (Bāḍiʿ) → Maṣawwaʿ
Basil I i, 182b – I, 187b
Basil II i, 638a; ii, 855a; iii, 77a, 130b; v, 820b – I, 658b; II, 875a; III, 79b, 133a; V, 826b
Baṣinnā iv, 654a – IV, 680b
al-Baṣīr, Abū ʿAlī (1535) i, **1082a**; v, 118a – I, **1114b**; V, 120b
Baṣīrī (tribe/tribu) i, **1082b**; iv, 9b; v, 668b – I, **1115a**; IV, 10a; V, 672b
Bāsirī iii, 1106b, 1107a – III, 1133b
al-Basīt i, **1083a** – I, **1115b**
Basīṭ → ʿArūḍ
Basīṭ wa murakkab i, **1083b** – I, **1116a**
Basiyeh, el- vi, 582b – VI, 567b
Basmačis i, 1077a, **1084a**; ii, 366b, 700b; iv, 792b; vi, 557b – I, 1109a, **1116b**; II, 376b, 718b; IV, 824b; VI, 542b
Basmala i, **1084a**; ii, 303a; iii, 122b; v, 411b – I, **1116b**; II, 311a; III, 125a; V, 412b
Basmil, Banū i, 1240a; x, 689b – I, 1278a; X, 781b
Basques → al-Bashkunish
al-Baṣra i, 40b, 62b, 76b, 86a, 131b, 236b, 389a, 529b, 549b, 695a, 810b, 907a, **1085a**; ii, 385a, 391a, 414b; iii, 1254b, 1257a; iv, 640a; v, 57a, 646a, 950b; vi, 112a, 119b, 139b, 140a, 196a, 198a, 199a, 262b, 266b, 267a, 270b, 272b, 279b, 280b, 333b, 334b, 335b, 336b, 344b, 345b, 359a, 362a, 363a, b, 428a, 477a, 509a, 606a, 620a, 640b, 647b, 653a, 656b, 658a, 660a, b, 664a, 668a, 670b, 671a, 677a, 679a, b, 709a, 710b, 735a; vii, 67a; s, 12b, 15b, 17b, 18b, 20a, 24a, 26a, 27b, 31a, 32a, 35a, 41a, 88b, 113a, 119a, 122a, 179a, 198b, 225b, 243a, 284b, 352a, 354b, 384b, 385a, 389b –
I, 41b, 64b, 78b, 88b, 135b, 244a, 400a, 545b, 567a, 716b, 833b, 934a, **1117b**; 395b, 401b, 425b; III, 1287a, 1289b; IV, 666a; V, 58b, 650a, 954b; VI, 110a, 117b, 137b, 138a, 180b, 182a, 183a, 247a, 251b, 255b, 257b, 264b, 265b, 318a, 319a, b, 321a, 328b, 329b, 343a, 346a, 347a, b, 413a, b, 463a, 494b, 591a, 605a, 625b, 633a, 638b, 642a, 643b, 645b, 646a, 654a, 656b, 657a, 664a, 666a, b, 698a, 699b, 724a; VII, 68a; S, 13a, 16a, 18a, 20b, 24b, 26a, 27b, 31b, 32b, 35b, 41a, 88b, 112b, 118b, 121b, 180a, 198b, 225b, 243a, 284b, 352a, 354b, 385a, b, 390a
—commerce i, 1086a, 1087a, b; ii, 130b; iii, 1252b – I, 1118b, 1119b, 1120a; II, 134a; III, 1285a
—monuments i, 610a; iii, 1268a – I, 629b, 630b; III, 1301a
—school of/l'école de i, 4b, 569b, 587b, 717b – I, 5a, 588a, 606b, 739a
al-Baṣra (Morocco/Maroc) i, **1087b**; iii, 149a – I, **1120a**; III, 152a
al-Baṣrī → ʿAlī b. Abi 'l-Faradj
al-Baṣrī, Abu ʾl-Ḥasan Aḥmad b. Muḥammad b. Sālim (987) viii, 840b, 993b – VIII, 870a, 1028b
al-Baṣrī, ʿAbd al-Djalīl s, 162b – S, 162b
Bassein, treaty of/traité de - vi, 535b – VI, 520a
Bassorah → al-Baṣra
Bast i, **1088a**; iii, 1170a; iv, 51a – I, **1120b**; III, 1199a; IV, 54a
Basṭ i, **1088b**; iii, 361a; iv, 326a – I, **1121a**; III, 372b; IV, 340b
Basta i, **1089a**; s, 144b – I, **1121b**; S, 144b
Bastām vi, 201b – VI, 186a
Bastū vi, 574b – VI, 559b
al-Basūs bint Munḳidh i, 565a, **1089a**; v, 362a; vi, 490a, 640b; s, 234b – I, 583a, **1121b**; V, 363a; VI, 476a, 625b; S, 234a
Başvekalet Arşivi i, 626a, **1089b**; ii, 82b, 128a – I, 646b, **1122a**; II, 84a, 131a
Başvekil i, **1091a** – I, **1123b**
al-Baṭāḥira, Banū i, **1091a**; vi, 80a, 84b – I, **1123b**; VI, 78a, 82a
al-Baṭāʾiḥ → al-Baṭīḥa
al-Baṭāʾiḥī (1192) vii, 164a – VII, 165b
al-Baṭāʾiḥī, Abū ʿAbd Allāh (al-Maʾmūn) (vizier) (XII) i, 440a, **1091b**; ii, 127a, 130a, 858a, 859b; iv, 429a – I, 452b, **1124a**; II, 130a, 133a, 878a, 879a; IV, 447b
al-Baṭāʾiḥī, Muḥammad → Muḥammad al-Baṭāʾiḥī
al-Baṭāʾinī, ʿAlī b. Abī Ḥamza (IX) vii, 647b – VII, 647b
Batak iii, 1214b, 1220a, 1225b – III, 1245a, 1250b, 1257a
Baṭalyaws i, 6a, 161a, **1092a**; iii, 498b – I, 6a, 165b, **1124b**; III, 515b
al-Baṭalyawsī, Abū Muḥammad ʿAbd Allāh Ibn al-Sīd (1127) i, 602a, **1092b**; ii, 838a; iv, 1007b; v, 929b; vi, 111a; vii, 280b –
I, 622a, **1125a**; II, 857b; IV, 1039b; V, 934b; VI, 108b; VII, 282b
Batavia i, 980b; ii, 390b; iii, 1221b – I, 1011a; II, 400b; III, 1252b
Baʿth (re(é)surrection) i, **1092b** – I, **1125a**
Baʿth → Nabīʾ
Baʿth party/partie iv, 125a, b, 126a; v, 486a, b, 1048b; vi, 470b; viii, 247a; s, 7b –
IV, 130b, 131a, b; V, 471a, 1045a; VI, 456a; VIII, 253a; S, 7a
Batha s, 166a – S, 166a
al-Baṭḥāʾ (Algeria/Algérie) vii, 186b – VII, 187a
al-Baṭḥāʾ (Makka) vi, 144b, 147a – VI, 142b, 145b
al-Bathaniyya i, **1093a**; iii, 293a – I, **1126a**; III, 302a
Baṭharī i, 1091a – I, 1123b
Báthory ii, 704a – II, 722a
al-Baṭīḥa i, **1093b**; iii, 1175b; v, 865a; vii, 484b, 650a; s, 118b, 119a, 243a – I, **1126b**; III, 1204b; V, 871b; VII, 484b, 649b; S, 118a, b, 243a
Bāṭil → Fāsid wa bāṭil
Bāṭin i, 1039a, 1099a, b; ii, 97b, 169a; iii, 662a; iv, 203a, b – I, 1070b, 1132a, b; II, 99b, 174b; III, 683b; IV, 212a, b
al-Bāṭin i, **1097b** – I, **1130b**
al-Bāṭina (plain(e)) i, 536b, 541a, **1098a**; vi, 734b – I, 553a, 558a, **1131a**; VI, 723b
Bāṭina Yāl Saʿd s, 355b – S, 355b
Bāṭiniyya i, 256b, 839a, **1098b**, 1332b; ii, 169a, 282a, 733b, 734a, 1040b, 1094b; iv, 25b, 28b-29a, 47a, 101b-102a; vi, 547a; vii, 408a –
I, 264a, 862a, **1131b**, 1373a; II, 174b, 290a, 752a, b, 1064b, 1120b; IV, 27b, 31a, 49b-50a, 106a-b; VI, 531b; VII, 409b
al-Bātiya → Nudjūm
Batjan i, **1100a** – I, **1133a**
Baṭlamiyūs (Ptolemy/Ptolémée) i, **1100a**; ii, 357b, 577b, 578a, 763a; iii, 788b, 906b, 1135b, 1136b; iv, 517b, 1182b; v, 762a; vi, 377b, 639b – I, **1133a**; II, 367a, 592a, b, 781b; III, 811b, 931a, 1163b, 1164b; IV, 540a, 1216a; V, 768a; VI, 362a, 625a
Baṭn i, **1102a** – I, **1135b**
Baṭn al-Agharr s, 198b – S, 198b
Baṭrīḳ → Biṭrīḳ
Batriyya, Butriyya iii, 244a, 1166a; s, 48b, **129b** – III, 251a, 1195a; S, 49a, **128b**
Batrūn i, **1102b** – I, **1135b**
al-Batt s, 23a – S, 23a
Baṭṭāl v, 332b – V, 332b
al-Baṭṭāl, ʿAbd Allāh (740) i, 243b, **1102b**; iii, 493b – I, 250b, **1136a**; III, 510b
al-Baṭṭāl, Sayyid (840) i, **1103b**; ii, 110a, 234b, 237b; iii, 115a; iv, 845b; v, 951b –
I, **1137a**; II, 112b, 241b, 244b; III, 117a; IV, 878b; V, 955a

Baṭṭāl b. ʿAbd Allāh s, 223a – S, 223a
Baṭṭāl Ḥuseyin Pasha ii, 25b, 207b – II, 26a, 214a
al-Battānī, Abū ʿAbd Allāh (Albatenius) (929) i, 589b, 727a, **1104b**; iii, 228a, 1137a; v, 84b; vi, 374b, 377b, 600b; vii, 680a; viii, 101b; s, 412b, 413b –
I, 608b, 749a, **1137b**; III, 235a, 1165a; V, 86b; VI, 359a, 362a, 585a; VII, 680a; VIII, 104a S, 413a, b
al-Battī → Abu 'l-Ḥasan al-Battī
Bātū b. Djūčī b. Čingiz Khān (Mongol) (1255) i, 135a, 467a, **1105a**, 1106b, 1187b, 1308a; ii, 3a, 44a, 571b; iv, 849a; v, 491a; vi, 419b, 420a; vii, 230a; viii, 162b; s, 203b –
I, 139a, 481a, **1138a**, 1139b, 1222b, 1348b; II, 3a, 45a, 586a; IV, 882a; V, 494a; VI, 405a; VII, 231b; VIII, 165a; S, 203a
Bātūʾid(e)s i, 1105a, b, **1106b**, 1308a; ii, 315b, 1112a; iii, 1121b; iv, 349b, 1064a; v, 136b, 137a; vi, 457a, 492b; s, 203b –
I, 1138a, b, **1139b**, 1348a; II, 324b, 1138a; III, 1149a; IV, 364b, 1095b; V, 139a, b; VI, 442b, 478b; S, 203a
Batumi i, 468b, **1108a** – I, 482b, **1141b**
Baʿūḍ iv, 522a – IV, 544b
al-Bāʿūnī i, **1109a** – I, **1142b**
Bāvī iii, 1107a – III, 1134a
Bawānātī, Muḥammad Bāḳir iv, 70b – IV, 74b
Bāwand(id(e)s) i, 237a, 872a, **1110a**; iii, 254b, 810a; iv, 207b, 645b; vi, 511b, 632a, 745a, 938a; s, 298a, 309a, 356b, 416a –
I, 244a, 896a, **1143a**; III, 262a, 833b; IV, 217a, 672a; VI, 497a, 617a, 734b, 930b; S, 297b, 308b, 356b, 416a
al-Bawandī, Shaykh → ʿAbd al-ʿAzīz al-Bawandī
Bāward → Abīward
Bawāzīdj i, **1110b** – I, **1144a**
Bāwiyān v, 896a – V, 902b
Bāwiyya, Banū vii, 675a – VII, 675a
Bawraḳ (Būraḳ) s, **130b** – S, **129b**
Baxar s, 325a – S, 324b
Bay (Bey) i, **1110b**; ii, 146b, 638b – I, **1144a**; II, 150b, 654b
Bayʿ i, **1111a** – I, **1144b**
al-Bayʿa i, 1111a, **1113a**; ii, 302b, 308a; iv, 943b, 944a; vi, 205b – I, 1144a, **1146b**; II, 311a, 317a; IV, 976a, 977a; VI, 190a
al-Bayāḍ vi, 439a – VI, 424b
al-Bayāḍī, Kamāl al-Dīn (1687) vi, 848a – VI, 839a
al-Bayālika vi, 230b – VI, 224b
Bayān i, **1114a**; v, 898a, 899b – I, **1147b**; V, 904a, 906a
Bayān b. Samʿān al-Tamīmī (737) i, **1116b**; ii, 1094b; iv, 837a; vii, 348a, 388b – I, **1150b**; II, 1120a; IV, 870a; VII, 350a, 389b
Bayān al-adyān ii, 74a – II, 75a
Bayānā iii, 441b; vi, 53b, 368b – III, 455b, 456a; VI, 51b, 352b
Baya(u)ndur, Banū x, 689b – X, 782a
Bayāndur, Abu 'l-Fatḥ Beg → Abu 'l-Fatḥ Bayāndur
Bayāniyya iii, 1256b; iv, 837a – III, 1298b; IV, 870a
Bayar, Celâl (XX) ii, 204a, 432b, 596a; iii, 527a; vi, 1011b – II, 210b, 444a, 611a; III, 545a; VI, 1004a
Bayarku, Banū x, 687b – X, 729b
Bayās → Payas
al-Bayāsī, Yūsuf b. Muḥammad iii, 111a – III, 113b
Bayāt (Türkmen) i, **1117a**; iii, 1101b, 1102b, 1108a; iv, 387a; v, 828a, b; vi, 201a, 202b –
I, **1150b**; III, 1128b, 1130a, 1135a; IV, 404a; V, 834a, b; VI, 185b, 187a
Bayʿat al-ḥarb i, 314b; v, 995b – I, 324b; V, 991a
Bayʿat al-nisāʾ i, 314b; v, 995b – I, 324b; V, 990b
Bayʿat al-riḍwān s, 131a – S, 130a
Bāyazīd I Yïldïrïm (Ottoman) (1403) i, 21b, 313a, 346a, 394a, 432a, 468a, 481a, 510b, 517b, 640a, 783b, 842b, 947b, 988a, 999a, **1117b**, 1251b, 1263a, 1303a, 1334a; ii, 11b, 239b, 292a, 611a, 684a, 697a, 722a, 984a, 989b, 990a, 1086a; iii, 1183a, 1248a; iv, 586a, 600b, 623a; v, 539a, 677a; vi, 3b, 231b; vii, 348b; viii, 193a; s, 314b –
I, 22a, 323a, 356b, 405b, 444a, 482a, 495a, 526a, 533b,661a, 806b, 866a, 976b, 1018b, 1029b, **1151a**, 1289b, 1301b, 1343a, 1374a; II, 11b, 246a, 300a, 626b, 701a, 714b, 741a, 1006b, 1012b, 1111b; III, 1212a, 1280b; IV, 608b, 625a, 648a; V, 543b, 682a; VI, 3b, 225a; VII, 350b; VIII, 196a; S, 314b
Bāyazīd II (Ottoman) (1512) i, 293a, 310b, 432a,510b, 842b, 1061a, **1119a**, 1207b, 1225b, 1253a; ii, 26a, 62a, 118b, 291b, 420b, 529a, 530a, 612a, 685a, 715a, 879a, 1087b; iii, 213a, 341a; iv, 92a, 230b, 291b, 463a, 565a, 1159a; v, 269a, 589b, 677b; vi, 324b, 525b, 530a, b, 606b, 795a; vii, 272a; viii, 8a, 767b –
I, 302a, 320a, 444a, 526b, 866a, 1093a, **1153a**, 1243b, 1262a, 1291a; II, 26b, 63a, 121a, 299b, 431a, 542a, 543a, 627a, 702b, 733b, 899b, 1113a; III, 219a, 351a; IV, 96a, 240b, 304b, 483b, 587b, 1191a; V, 267a, 593b, 682b; VI, 309a, 510a, 514a, b, 591b, 785a; VII, 274a; VIII, 4b, 793b
Bāyazīd (town/ville) i, **1117b**; vi, 55b, 200b, 201a, b – I, **1151a**; VI, 53b, 184b, 185a,b
Bāyazīd b. Uways al-Djalāyir i, 1117b; ii, 4016 – I, 1151a; II, 412a
Bāyazīd n. ʿAbd Allāh Anṣārī (Kānīgurām) (1572) i, 220a, 225b, 238a, **1121b**;iii, 430a, 575b; vii, 327b; viii, 468a –
I, 226b, 227a, 232b, 245a, **1155a**; III, 444a, 595a; VII, 329b; VIII, 484a
Bāyazīd Bayāt (XVI) vii, 342b – VII, 344a
Bāyazīd al-Bisṭāmī → Abū Yazīd al-Bisṭāmī
Bāyazīd Khān Kararānī ii, 183b – II, 189a
Bāyazīd Khān Maḥmūdābād vi, 77b – VI, 75b
Bāyazīd Kötürüm iv, 108b – IV, 113b
Bāyazīd Pasha (XV) vii, 594b – VII, 594a
Bāyazīd Sarwānī → ʿAbbās Sarwānī
Baybars I, al-Malik al-Ẓāhir Rukn al-Dīn al-Bunduḳdārī (Mamlūk) (1277) i, 21a, 280b, 354a, 517a, 553a, 662b, 711a, 786b, 804b, 945b, 946a, 966b, 989b, 1017a, 1046a, **1124b**, 1126b, 1127b, 1188a; ii, 38a, 170b, 285a, 568b, 693b, 966a; iii, 20a, 48a, 109b, 184b, 189a, 399b, 402b, 473a, 504b, 506a, 679a, 832b, 1121a; iv, 87b, 216b, 402b, 431a, 432b, 483b, 484b, 609a, 655a, 842b, 843a, 944b; v, 571b, 801b; vi, 45a, 46a, 143b, 149b, 195a, 258a, 315b, 321b, 322a, 324a, 325b, 326a, 352a, 359b, 419b, 440b, 507b, 543b, 579b, 654a, b, 659b, 663a, 666a, 667b, 669a, 672b, 673b, 777b, 790b; vii, 148a, 166b, 167a, b, 168b, 479b, 729b, 990b; viii, 90b. 147a, 464a, 995b, 999b; s, 391a –
I, 22a, 289a, 364b, 532b, 570b, 683b, 732b, 810a, 828b, 974b, 975a, 996b, 1020a, 1048b, 1077b, **1158b**, 1160b, 1162a, 1223b; II, 38b, 176a, 293a, 582b, 711a, 988a;III, 21a, 50a, 112a, 189a, 193b, 412a, 415a, 490a, 521b, 523a, 701a, 856b, 1148b; IV, 92a, 226a, 420a, 450a, 451b, 504b, 505b, 634a, 681b, 875b, 876a, 977b; V, 576a, 807b; VI, 43b, 44b, 142a, 148a, 179a, 242a, 300b, 306a, 308a, 310a, b, 336a, 343b, 405a, 426a, 493a, 528a, 564b, 639b, 640a, 645b, 649a, 652a, 653b, 655a, 659a, 660a, 767a, 780b; VII, 150a, 168a, b, 169a, 170a, 479a, 729b, 992a; VIII, 91b, 149a, 479b, 1030b, 1034b S, 391b
Baybars II al-Malik al-Muẓaffar Djāshnikīr (Mamlūk) (1310) i, **1126b**, 1325a; iii, 952a; iv, 429a, 433b; vi, 359b; vii, 169b, 176a, 635b, 991b – I, **1160b**, 1365b; III, 977a; IV, 447b, 452b; VI, 343b; VII, 170a, 177b, 635b, 993a

Baybars (usurper/usurpateur) (1312) vi, 323a – VI, 307b
Baybars, Sīrat i, **1126b** – I, **1160b**
Baybars al-Djāshenkīr (Čāshnegīr) → Baybars II
Baybars al-Manṣūrī (Mamlūk ge(é)ne(é)ral) (1325) i, **1127b**; vi, 317b; s, 388b – I, **1162a**; VI, 302a; S, 389a
Baybughā (u) Rūs (amīr) (XIV) vi, 316b; vii, 993a – VI, 301b; VII,994b
Bāybūrd i, **1128a**; ii, 223b – I, **1162b**; II, 230b
al-Bayḍā (el-Beizā') (Fārs; Yemen) i, **1128b**; vii, 779a – I, **1163a**; VII, 781a
Baydaḳ → Shaṭrandj
Baydamūr iii, 818a – III, 841b
Baydarā (amīr) (Miṣr) (XIII) iv, 964b, 965b; v, 595a; vii, 169a – IV, 997a, b; V, 598b; VII, 170b
al-Bayḍāwī, ʿAbd Allāh (1286) i, **1129a**; ii, 95b; iv, 912b; vi, 218a, 219a – I, **1163a**; II, 97b; IV, 945b; VI, 202a, 203a
al-Baydhaḳ, Abū Bakr (XII) i, 78a, 122a, 389a, **1129b**; iii, 958b; v, 1209a; vi, 592a; x, 346a – I, 80b, 125b, 400b, **1163b**; III, 983a; V, 1199b; VI, 577a; X, 371b
Baydju Noyon (Mongol) (XIII) i, 467a; ii, 38a, 712a; iv, 814a, 843a; v, 271b; vii, 479a; viii, 949a – I, 481a; II, 38b, 730b; IV, 846b, 876a; V, 269b; VII, 479a; VIII, 981b
Baydu (1295) i, **1129b**; ii, 982a; iii, 1122b; v, 162b, 553b – I, **1164a**; II, 1004b; III, 1150a; V, 160b, 558b
Bayero ii, 1146b – II, 1173b
Bāyezīd → Bāyazīd
Bāyezīd Kötürüm → Djalāl al-Dīn Kötürüm
Bāyezīdli (XIX) vi, 508b – VI, 494a
Bayhaḳ i, **1130a**, 1131b; s, 343a – I, **1164a**, 1166a; S, 342b
al-Bayhaḳī → Abū Saʿīd
Bayhaḳī Sayyids s, **131b**, 329a – S, **130b**, 328b
al-Bayhaḳī, Abū Bakr Aḥmad (1066) i, **1130a**; iii, 24b; v, 1126b – I, **1164b**; III, 25b; V, 1123a
al-Bayhaḳī, Abū Djaʿfar (1149) vi, 914a – VI, 905b
al-Bayhaḳī, Abū Djaʿfar Aḥmad (1110) s, 289b – S, 289b
al-Bayhaḳī, Abu 'l-Faḍl Muḥammad (Dabīr) (1077) i, **1130b**; ii, 336a, 1053a; v, 1224b; vi, 108a, 115a, 193a, 353a, 410a, 433a, 780b, 987a; s, 245b – I, **1164b**; II, 345b, 1077b; V, 1215a; VI, 106a, 112b, 177a, 337a, 394b, 418b, 770b, 987b; S, 245b
al-Bayhaḳī, Abū Saʿīd i, 60a – I, 61b
al-Bayhaḳī, Aḥmad s, 354a – S, 354a
Bayhaḳī, Djaʿfarak iv, 525b – IV, 548b
al-Bayhaḳī, Ibrāhīm b. Muḥammad (X) i, 759a, 1**132a** – I, 781b, **1166b**
Bayhaḳī, Sayyid Muḥammad s, 423b – S, 423b
al-Bayhaḳī, Ẓahīr al-Dīn Abu 'l-Ḥasan ʿAlī (1169) i, 594b, **1131b**; vi, 824a, 913b; s, 245b – I, 614a, **1165b**; VI, 814a, 905a; S, 245b
al-Bayhaḳī, Zayd b. al-Ḥasan s, 236a – S, 236a
Bayḥān (wadi) i, **1132b**; iii, 208a; iv, 746a, b; s, 337a – I, **1166b**, III, 213b; IV, 776a, b; S, 336b
Bayḥān al-Kaṣāb i, **1133a**; ii, 675b; iv, 681a – I, **1167a**; II, 692a; IV, 709a
Bayhasiyya i, 113a; iii, 661a – I, 116b; III, 682b
Bayîldîm Ḳaṣrî vi, 57a – VI, 55a
Bayîndîr (tribe/tribu) i, 311a, **1133b**; ii, 200b; iii, 1100b; iv, 463a – I, 321a, **1168a**; II, 207a; III, 1127b; IV, 483b
Bāyirāt iv, 1036a – IV, 1068a
al-Baykandī, Abū ʿAmr ʿUthmān b. ʿAlī (1157) vi, 558a – VI, 542b
Bāyḳarā (Tīmūrid(e)) (1416) i, **1133b**; iv, 33a – I, **1168a**; IV, 35a
Bāyḳarā, Sultan Ḥusayn Mīrzā b. Manṣūr (Tīmūrid(e)) (1506) vii, 129b, 133b, 929a, 935a; viii, 750a, 1012a; x, 514a; s, 423a – VII, 131b, 135a, 929b, 935b; VIII, 770b, 1047b; X, 550b; S, 423b
Bāykbāk → Bākbāk
Baylaḳān i, **1134a**; vi, 337a; vii, 498a – I, **1168b**; VI, 321b; VII, 498a
al-Baylamān → Madjlis
Baylān i, **1134a** – I, **1168b**
Baynūn i, **1134b**; viii, 979b – I, **1169a**; VIII, 1014a
Bayra vi, 576a – VI, 561a
Bayraḳ → ʿAlam
Bayraḳdār i, **1134b**; iv, 679a – I, **1169a**; IV, 706b
Bayraḳdār Muṣṭafā Pasha → Muṣṭafā Pasha Bayraḳdār
Bayram → ʿĪd
Bayram, Muḥammad i, 597a – I, 616a
Bayram ʿAlī Khān (Ḳādjār Türkmen) (1785) i, **1135a**; vi, 621a – I, **1169b**; VI, 606a
Bayram ʿAlī Khān (1785) i, **1135a** – I, **1169b**
Bayrām Beg i, 1067a – I, 1099a
Bayram Khān, Khān-i Khānān Muḥammad (1560) i, 80b, 316a, **1135a**, 1194b; ii, 156a; iii, 423b; iv, 1020a; v, 629b; vi, 131a; vii, 314a, 320a; s, 312a – I, 82b, 326a, **1169b**, 1229b; II, 161a; III, 437a; IV, 1052a; V, 633b; VI, 129a; VII, 316b, 322b; S, 312a
Bayrām Khʷadja iii, 1100b; iv, 584a – III, 1127b; IV, 608a
Bayram Pasha (XVII) iii, 357a; iv, 573bL VIII, 3a – III, 368a; IV, 596b; VIII, 3a
Bayram al-Tūnusī v, 1160b – V, 1150a
Bayrām-i Walī → Ḥādjdji Bayrām
Bayrāmiyya i, 312b, 313a, 423b, 511a, **1137a**, 1235a; iii, 43a; vi, 226a; x, 252a; s, 283 – I, 322a, 435a, 526b, **1171b**, 1272a; III, 45a; VI, 219b; X, 270b; S, 282b
Bayrānwand v, 617a – V, 621a
Bayrūt i, **1137a**; ii, 129b, 635b; vi, 28a, 343b, 469b; viii, 131a – I, **1171b**; II, 133a, 651b; VI, 26a, 327b, 455b; VIII, 133b
—institutions ii, 424a – II, 435a
Baysān i, **1138b**; vi, 543b, 547a, b – I, **1173a**; VI, 528a, 531b, 532a
Bayṣar b. Ḥām vi, 411b – VI, 396b
Bāysonghor b. Shāh Rūkh, Ghiyāth al-Dīn (Tīmūrid(e)) (1433) i, **1139a**; ii, 919b, 1076a; iv, 1123a, 1124a; vii, 602b – I, **1173b**; II, 941a, 1101a; IV, 1155a, 1155b; VII, 602a
Bāysonghor b. Maḥmūd (1493) i, **1139b**; I, **1174a**
Bāysonghor b. Yaʿḳūb (Samarḳand) (XV) i, 312a, **1139b** – I, 3216, **1174a**
Bāysonghor, Muḥammad b. s, 43b, 84a – S, 44a, 84a
Bāysunkur → Bāysonghor
Bayt i, **1139b**; ii, 113b; iv, 1146b, 1148a – I, **1174a**; II, 116a; IV, 1178a, 1179b
Bayt, abyāt i, 668a – I, 688b
Bayt Asgedē vi, 628b – VI, 613b
Bayt Balḥāf vi, 80b – VI, 78a
Bayt Bāraʿfīt vi, 80b – VI, 78a
Bayt Djibrīn i, **1140a**; ii, 911b; s, 204b – I, **1174b**; II, 933a; S, 204b
Bayt Fā'is vi, 438b – VI, 424a
Bayt al-Faḳīh i, **1140b**; s, 30b – I, **1175a**; S, 30b
Bayt Grayza vi, 735b – VI, 724b
Bayt Ḥarāwīz vi, 80b – VI, 78a
Bayt al-Ḥikma i, 589a, 899a, **1141a**; iii, 872a; v, 1125a; vi, 336b – I, 608a, 926a, **1175b**; III, 896b; V, 1121b; VI, 321a
al-Bayt al-ḥarām i, 1139b – I, 1174a
Bayt Kalshāt vi, 80b – VI, 78a

Bayt Ḳamṣīt vi, 80b – VI, 78a
Bayt Ḳayʿāl i, 759b – I, 782b
Bayt Laḥm i, **1141a** – I, **1175b**
Bayt al-Maḳdis → al-Ḳuds
Bayt al-māl i, 729b, **1141b**; ii, 144b, 325a; v, 1251b, 1252a; s, 200a – I, 751b, **1176a**; II, 148b, 334b; V, 1242b, 1243a; S, 200b
al-Bayt al-Muḳaddas → al-Ḳuds
Bayt Rās i, **1149a**; s, 117a – I, **1183b**; S, 116b
Bayt Rayb vi, 438b – VI, 424a
Bayt Ṣamūdat vi, 80b – VI, 78a
Bayt T̲h̲uwār vi, 80b – VI, 78a
Bayt al-ṭirāz iii, 344b; iv, 216b – III, 355a; IV, 225b
Bayt Ziyād vi, 80b – VI, 78a
Bayt Zaʿbanāt vi, 80b – VI, 78a
Bayṭār i, **1149b** – I, **1184a**
al-Bayṭār, Ṣalāḥ al-Dīn iv, 161b – IV, 168b
Bāytūz i, 1348b; v, 691a – I, 1388b; V, 695b
Bayulî, Banū vi, 416b – VI, 401b
Bayundur → Bayîndîr
Bayyāna (Baena) i, **1150a** – I, **1184a**
Bayyāsa (Baeza) i, **1150a** – I, **1184b**
al-Bayyāsī, Abū Muḥammad (1127) iv, 116a; vi, 339b – IV, 121b; VI, 323b
Bayyina i, **1150b** – I, **1185a**
Bayyūmiyya i, 281a, **1151b** – I, 289b, **1186a**
Bayzara i, **1152a**; iv, 745a – I, **1186a**; IV, 774b
Bāz (Mānd) vi, 384b – VI, 368b
Bāz, Āl vi, 177a
Bāz Bahādur b. S̲h̲udjāʿ K̲h̲ān, Malik Bāyazīd (Mālwa) (1570) i, **1155a**; ii, 815a; iii, 421b, 453b; vi, 310a, 407a – I, **1189b**; II, 834b; III, 435a, 469b; VI, 295a, 391b
Bāz Bahādur (palace/palais de) vi, 407a, b – VI, 391b, 392b
Baza → Basta
Bāzabdā iv, 639a – IV, 665b
Bāzahr (Bezoar) i, **1155b**; v, 672a, 1229a – I, **1190a**; V, 677b, 1219a
Bāzār → Sūḳ
Bāzargān → Tidjāra
Bāzargān, Mahdī (XX) iv, 166a; vii, 450a, 762b, 763a – IV, 173a; VII, 451a, 764b
al-Bazdawī, b. Aḥmad al-Nasafī s, **132a**, 225b – S, **131a**, 225b
al-Bazdawī, ʿAbd al-Karīm b. Mūsā (X) vi, 846a – VI, 837a
al-Bazdawī, Abu ʾl-Yusr (1099) iii, 163b, 164a, 1024a, 1165a; vi, 846a – III, 167a, b, 1050a, 1193b; VI, 837a
Baz̲h̲ → Bādj
Bāziʿ (Baʾziʿ) b. ʿUrayʿir (XIX) iv, 925b – IV, 958b
Bazīg̲h̲ b. Mūsā (VIII) i, **1156a**; iv, 1132b – I, **1190b**; IV, 1164a
Bāzinḳir i, **1156b** – I, **1190b**
Bazirgan i, **1157a** – I, **1191b**
Bazmān, Kūh-i iv, 3b – IV, 3b
Bazm-i Ṣūfiyya-yi Hind s, 4b, 293b – S, 4a, 293a
Bāzūkiyyūn i, **1157a**; iii, 1108b; iv, 1029b; v, 459a – I, **1191b**; III, 1136a; IV, 1061b; V, 461b
Bāzyār i, 1152b, 1153a – I, 1187a, b
al-Bazzār (1349) i, 273b; vi, 353b – I, 282a; VI, 337b
al-Bazzāz (town/ville) vi, 921b – VI, 913a
al-Bazzāz, ʿAbd al-Raḥmān iv, 782b, 783a – IV, 814a, b
al-Bazzāz, Abū Bakr Muḥammad b. ʿAbd Allāh (965) vii, 648a – VII, 647b
Bazzāzistān → Ḳayṣariyya
Beaufort, Castle/Château → Ḳalʿat al-S̲h̲aḳīf
Beč i, **1157b** – I, **1191b**
Bécharré → Bs̲h̲arra
Bečkem → Badjkam
Bedel → Badal
Bédel → Bīdil
Bedestān → Bezzāzistān
Bedj → Beč
Bedja i, 1a, 782b, **1157b**, 1172a, 1239b; iii, 5b; iv, 686a, b, 687a; v, 99a, 368b; vi, 628a; viii, 90b, 863a; s, 243b – I, 1a, 805b, **1192a**, 1207a, 1277b; III, 5b; IV, 714a, b, 715a; V, 101b, 369a; VI, 613a; VIII, 894a; S, 243b
—language/langue v, 521b, 523a – V, 525b, 527a
Bedjkem (X) vii, 800a – VII, 802a
Bēdjwān i, 863b – I, 887b
Bedr al-Dīn, S̲h̲ayk̲h̲ (XVI) vii, 349a – VII, 351a
Bedr al-Dīn b. S̲h̲ayk̲h̲ Ḳāsim (1479) vii, 56b – VII, 57a
Bedrî Rahmî Eyuboğlu → Eyyūbog̲h̲lu, Bedrī Raḥmī
Beersheba → Bīr al-Sabʿ
Beg, Bey i, **1159a**; ii, 507b; v, 629b – I, **1193b**; II, 520a; V, 633b
Beg b. Yaḥyā Pas̲h̲a (XVI) vii, 239b – VII, 240b
Begam Anis Kidwai (XX) vi, 489a – VI, 475a
Begam Anwara Taimur (XX) vi, 489a – VI, 475a
Begam Ḥabībullāh (XX) vi, 489a – VI, 475a
Begam Liyāḳat ʿAlī K̲h̲ān (XX) vi, 489b – VI, 475b
Begam Mohammad Ali (XX) vi, 489a – VI, 475a
Begam Nasim Wali Khan (XX) vi, 489b – VI, 475b
Begam Nusrat Bhutto (XX) vi, 489b – VI, 475b
Bēgam Ṣāḥib ii, 378b – II, 389a
Bēgam Sulṭān ii, 922a – II 943a
Begdili i, **1159b**; iii, 1100a – I, **1194a**; III, 1127a
Bēglār iii, 1030a – III, 1055b
Beglerbegi i, 368a, 468b, 978a, **1159b**, 1191a; ii, 146a, 201b, 722a, 723b – I, 379a, 489b, 1008b, **1194a**, 1226a; II, 150a, 207b, 740b, 742a
Begteginid(e)s i, **1160b**; ii, 347b; v, 144b – I, **1195a**; II, 357b; V, 147a
Begtimur → S̲h̲āh-i Arman
Begtūzūn (998) vi, 65a, 433a – VI, 63a, 418b
Begum i, 1159a, **1161a** – I, 1193b, **1195b**
Bēhān → Bayḥān
Behāristān → Djāmī
Behdīn v, 1113a, b, 1114a – V, 1109b, 1110b
Beḥera → Buḥayra
Behesnī → Besni
Behis̲h̲t → Djanna
Behistūn → Bīsutūn
Behman → Bahman
Behnesā → Bahnasā
Behrām → Bahrām
Behrasīr v, 945a, 946a – V, 949a, b
Behzād → Bihzād
Beirut → Bayrūt
el-Beizāʾ → al-Bayḍāʾ
Béja → Badja
Bekaa → al-Biḳāʿ
Bekār odalarî iv, 236a – IV, 246b
Bekbulatovič, Simeon → Sāyin Bulāt
Bekči iv, 234b – IV, 245a
Bekeč/G̲h̲āzī Arslan Tegin (Karak̲h̲ānid(e)) x, 689b – X, 781b
Bekrī Bābā vi, 1015b – VI, 1008a
Bekrī Muṣṭafā Ag̲h̲a (XVII) i, **1161b**; iii, 375a; viii, 185b – I, **1196a**; III, 387a; VIII, 188a
Bektās̲h̲ al-Fāk̲h̲irī i, 571a – I, 590a
Bektās̲h̲ Walī → Ḥādjdjī Bektās̲h̲
Bektās̲h̲iyya i, 309b, 653a, 768a, 844a, **1161b**; ii, 202b, 292a, 968a; iii, 600b, 662b; iv, 168a, 811b, 951b; v, 283b, 285a; vi, 89a, 510a, 810a; viii, 2b, 210b, 244a; x, 251b; s, 95b – I, 319a, 673b, 791a, 867a, **1196a**; II, 209a, 300a,

990a; III, 621a, 684a; IV, 175b, 844b, 984a; V, 281b, 283b; VI, 87a, 495a, 800a; VIII, 2b, 214b, 250b; X, 270a; S, 95a
Bēla → Las Bēla
Belalcázar → Ghāfiķ
Belediye → Baladiyya
Beledjik → Bīredjik
Bēlen → Baylān
Belesh → Bālish
Belette, la → Ibn ʿIrs
Beleyn i, **1163a** – I, **1197b**
Belgrade i, 268a, 269b, 293a, 656a, **1163a**; iv, 239a, 969b; v, 262a, 263a; vi, 70a – I, 276b, 277b, 302a, 676b, **1197b**; IV, 249b, 1001b; V, 259b, 261a; VI, 68a
Belhūba, Belhīt → Abu 'l-Hawl
Belīgh, Ismāʿīl (1729) i, **1165b** – I, **1200a**
Belīgh, Meḥmed Emīn (1760) i, **1165b** – I, **1200a**
Belitung → Billiton
Belkasem Krim → Ibn al-Ķāsim Karīm
Bello, Alhaji Aḥmadu iii, 282b; iv, 549b, 550a, 774a – III, 291a; IV, 573b, 805a
Belomancy/Bélomancie → Istiķsām
Béloutchistan/Beluchistan → Balūčistan
Ben-ʿamma iii, 389a – III, 401b
Ben Ayed ii, 460a – II, 471b
Ben Badīs → Ibn Bādīs
Ben Bella, Aḥmad iii, 564a; v, 1070b – III, 583b; V, 1068a
Ben Cheneb (Shneb) → Ibn Abī Shanab
Ben Ganah i, 1247a – I, 1285a
Ben Ghedahem → Ibn Ghidhāhum
Ben Sedira iii, 689b, 690b – III, 711a, 712b
Benares/Bénarès i, **1165b**; vi, 369b, 602a; s, 47a – I, **1200b**; VI, 354a, 586b; S, 47a
Benavent i, **1166a** – I, **1201a**
Benavert (1068) i, **1166b** – I, **1201a**
Bender → Bandar
Bender (Bessarabia(e)) i, **1166b**; vi, 56a – I, **1201b**; VI, 54a
Beng → Bandj
Bengal/-e → Bangāla Tītū Mīr/miyan
Bengali i, **1167a** – I, **1201b**
Benghāzī i, 1049a, 1050a, **1169a**; v, 759b, 760a; s, 164b – I, 1081a, b, **1204a**; V, 765b, 766b; S, 164b
Beni Amer → Āmīr, Banū
Benī Mellāl s, **132a** – S, **131b**
Benī Menāser → Manāṣīr, Banū
Beni-Saf s, 376b – S, 376b
Beni Suef → Bani Suwayf
Benia → Banya
Benjamin → Binyāmīn
Benjamin b. Mishal iv, 310a – IV, 324a
Benlāk → Bennāk
Bennāk i, **1169b**; ii, 32b – I, **1204b**; II, 33a
Benue (river/rivière) i, 179a – I, 184a
Benyāmīn → Ibn Yāmīn
Beograd → Belgrade
Berār i, 924b, **1170a**; ii, 815b, 981b; iii, 425a, 1159a; v, 1a; vi, 63a, 68a, 87a, 536b; s, 279b, 280a – I, 952b, **1205a**; II, 834b, 1003b; III, 439a, 1187b; V, 1b; VI, 61a, 66a, 85a, 521a; S, 279b
Berāt i, **1170a**; ii, 32b, 119a; iii, 1180b, 1187a – I, **1205a**; II, 33a, 121b; III, 1209b, 1216b
Berātlî i, **1171b** – I, **1206b**
Berbe(è)r(e) (language/langue) i, 171a, 374b, 379a, 568b, 573b, 578b, 763a, 770a, 792a, 889a, 1044b, 1177a 1180-5; ii, 109b, 460a, 591b, 873b, 992b; iv, 307b, 1149a; v, 754b, 760a, 1206a; s, 397a – I, 175b, 385a, 390a, 587a, 592b, 597a, 786a, 793a, 815a, 915b, 1076b, 1212a, 1215-20; II, 112a, 472a, 606a, 894a, 1015b; IV, 321a, 1181a; V, 760b, 766a, 1196b; S, 397b
—territory/territoire i, **1171b**; v, 1249b – I, **1206b**; V, 1240b
Berberā i, **1172b; ix, 715a** – I, **1207b; IX, 746a**
Berberi i, **1173a** – I, **1222a**
Berbers/Berbères i, 32a, 47b, 79b, 86b, 92a, 125a, 163b, 167b, 171a, 207b, 244b, 245a, 254b, 355b, 367a, 374b, 379a, 532b, 699a, 770a, 990b, 1043b, 1049a, b, 1071b, **1173a**, 1238a, 1246b, 1321a; ii, 57b, 992b; iii, 494a, 982b; iv, 75a, b, 307b, 339a, 359a, 415a, b, 562a; v, 517b, 744a, 1156b, 1160a, 1187a; vi, 39b, 310b, 741a, 773b, 815a, 840a, 899a, 923a, 943b, 948a, 1038a, 1042a; vii, 611a; viii, 616a; ix, 844b; x, 118b; s, 145a, 153a, 376b – I, 32b, 48b, 82a, 88b, 95a, 128b, 168a, 172b, 175b, 213b, 252a, b, 262b, 366b, 377b, 385a, 390a, 548b, 720b, 793a, 1021b, 1075b, 1081a, b, 1103b, **1208a**, 1275b, 1284b, 1361b; II, 58b, 1015b; III, 511a, 1007a; IV, 79a, b, 321a, 353b, 374b, 433b, 584a; V, 521a, b, 749b, 1146b, 1149b, 1177a; VI, 37b, 295b, 730a, 763a, 805a, 831a, 839b, 890b, 915a, 935b, 940a, 1031a, 1035b; VII, 610b; viii, 635a; IX, 936b; X, 128a; S, 144b, 153a, 376b
—in/en al-Andalus i, 5b, 6a, b, 76a, 82a, b, 490b, 494a, b, 1176a, 1249a; ii, 505a, 541b; iii, 12a, 147a, 495b, 1043b; v, 1239b – I, 6a, b, 78b, 84a, 85a, 505a, 508b, 509b, 1211a, 1287a; II, 517b, 555a; III, 12b, 150a, 512b, 1069b; V, 1230a, b
—ethnography/-ie i, 370b, 1037a, **1173a**, 1349b; iii, 295b, 1039a; iv, 360b, 511b; v, 1196b – I, 381b, 1068b, **1208a**, 1390a; III, 305a, 1065a; IV, 376a, 533b; V, 1186b
—religion i, **1178a**; ii, 1079a; iii, 134b – I, **1213a**; II, 1104a; III, 137b
Berdī Beg Khān (Golden Horde) (1366) i, 325a, 1107b; ii, 401a; x, 560b – I, 335a, 1141a; II, 412a; X,
Berdi Khodja iv, 584a, b; s, 280b – IV, 608a; S, 280b
Bergama i, **1187a**; iv, 628a; vi, 740a; s, 137b – I, **1222a**; IV, 653a; VI, 729a; S, 137a
Berger → Čūpān
Berger, le (astronomie) S, 321a
Bergi → Birge
Berke b. Djūčī, Khān (Batuʾid(e)) (1266) i, 1106a, b, 1187b; ii, 44a; iii, 185a, 679a; iv, 30b, 349b; v, 301a; vi, 322a, b, 419b, 420a, b; vii, 168a, 974a – I, 1139a, 1140a, **1222b**; II, 45a; III, 189a, 701a; IV, 32b, 364b; V, 300a; VI, 306b, 405a; VII, 169b, 974b
Berkečār b. Djūčī (Mongol) (1269) vi, 420a – VI, 405a
Berk-yaruk → Barkyārūk
Béroia, Bérrhoia → Karaferye
Bertam (Malacca) vi, 207b – VI, 192a
Besermyans i, **1188b** – I, **1223b**
Beshike i, **1189a** – I, **1224a**
Beshiktāsh ii, 1042b; iv, 233a; v, 905a, 949a; vi, 57a – II, 1067a; IV, 243a; V, 911b, 952b; VI, 55a
Beshiktāsh Sāḥil Sarāyî vi, 57a – VI, 55a
Beshīr Agha (Ķizlar aghasî) (1730) vi, 55b, 56b – VI, 53b, 54b
Beshīr Agha (Malāmī) (1662) vi, 228a – VI, 221b
Beshlik ii, 28b – II, 28b
Beshparmak i, **1189a** – I, **1224a**
Besika Bay/Baie de → Beshike
Beskesek-Abaza i, **1189a** – I, **1224b**
Besleney ii, 21b, 22a – II, 22b, 23a
Besni (Bahasnā) i, **1190b**; vi, 505b – I, **1225b**; VI, 491a
Bessarabia/-ie → Budjāk
Bet (island/île; fort(e)ress(e)) vi, 50b – VI, 49a
Bēt → Bayt

Betelgeuze → Nudjūm
Bēth Aramāyē (IV) vi, 633a – VI, 618a
Bethlehem/Bethléem → Bayt Laḥm
Bēwarāsp vi, 744a, b – VI, 733b
Bey → Bay/Beg
Beyānī (Muṣṭafa of/de Rusčuk) (1597) x, 55a – X, 56b
Beyatlî → Yaḥyā Kemāl Beyatlî
Beyhan, Princess/la princesse ii, 999a – II, 1022a
Beylerbeyi → Beglerbegi
Beylik i, 368a, **1191a**; ii, 338b – I, 379a, **1226a**; II, 348b
Beyoghlu i, 973a, b; iii, 1181a; s, 314a, 315b – I, 1003a, b; III, 1210a; S, 314a, 315b
Beyrouth → Beirut
Beyshehir i, 703a, 703b, **1191b**; iv, 620b, 622a, 623a; s, 137a – I, 724a, 724b, **1226b**; IV, 645b, 647a, 648a; S, 136b
Bezzeta ii, 251a; iv, 571b – II, 258b; IV, 594a
Bezistān → Ḳayṣariyya
Bezm-i ʿĀlem → Walide Sultān
Bezoar → Bāzahr
Bezzāzistān iii, 212b, 213a; iv, 226b, 227a, b; v, 559b – III, 218b, 219a; IV, 236b, 237a, b; V, 564b
Bhagwān Dās iv, 709a – IV, 737b
Bhagwanis i, 173a – I, 177b
Bhagwant Rāy i, 1330a – I, 1371a
Bhakkar i, **1192a**; iii, 633a – I, **1227a**; III, 654a
Bhakti ii, 51b; iii, 435b, 456b – II, 52b; III, 450a, 472a
Bharatpūr i, **1192b**; s, 358b – I, **1228a**; S, 358b
Bharoč i, **1193a**; ii, 1129a; iii, 444b; s, 358b – I, **1228a**; II, 1155b; III, 459b; S, 358a
Bhāskar Rāo ii, 220a – II, 227a
Bhāskara i, 133a – I, 136b
Bhattā-Shāh s, 327b – S, 327a
Bhaṭṭi i, **1193b**; iii, 225b – I, **1229a**; III, 232a
Bhattinda i, **1193b**; vi, 47b, 48b; vii, 279a – I, **1229a**; VI, 46a, 47a; VII, 280b
Bhawāni Rām ii, 219a – II, 225b
Bhīkam Khān b. Maḥmūd Khān Sharḳī (Djawnpūr) (1458) vi, 62b – VI, 60b
Bhīls iv, 1023b – IV, 1055b
Bhīlsā vi, 55a, 309a – VI, 53a, 294b
Bhīm-Dēv (Radjpūt) (1423) vi, 50b; s, 242a – VI, 49a; S, 242a
Bhimpāl (Rādjā) (1026) vi, 65b – VI, 63b
Bhīra (Rabat) vi, 293b – VI, 279a
Bhitāʾī, Shāh ʿAbd al-Laṭīf (1752) i, **1194b**; vii, 328a, 376b; ix, 637a; x, 322a – I, **1230a**; VII, 329b, 377b; IX, 661b; X, 346b
Bhittanni vi, 86a – VI, 84a
Bhōdja, Rādja i, 1197a; ii, 218b, 219b – I, 1232a; II, 225a, 226a
Bhōdjpur iii, 638b – III, 660a
Bhōnslē, Raghudjī (1803) vi, 535b – VI, 519b, 520a
Bhōnslē, Shāhdjī (1664) vi, 534b – VI, 519a
Bhōnslēs vi, 534a, 515b, 536a – VI, 518b, 526a,b
Bhōpāl (town/ville) i, **1196b**; vi, 535b – I, **1232a**; VI, 519b
Bhōpāl (state/état) i, **1195a**; vii, 421a – I, **1230b**; VII, 423a
Bhūčar Mōrī (Sōraṭh) vii, 131b – VII, 133b
Bhutto. Benazir vi, 489b; viii, 243b – VI, 475b; VIII, 249b
Bhutto, Zulfiqar Ali (1979) v, 1081b; vi, 489b; viii, 243a – V, 1079a, b; VI, 475b; VIII, 248b
Bī Ammāñ → Ābādī Begum
Biʿa → Kanīsa
Bībān i, **1197a** – I, **1232b**
Bībī i, **1197b** – I, **1233a**
Bībī Aḳā Malik → al-Djawnpūrī
Bībī Djamāl ii, 49b – II, 50b
Bībī Khānım → Masdjid-i Djāmiʿ (Samarḳand)
Bībī Khātūn (Khʷārazm) (1257) vi, 482b – VI, 468b
Bībī Khʷunza iii, 632a – III, 653a
Bībī Rādjī Sharḳī (Djawnpur) (1452) vi, 62a, b – VI, 60a, b
Bibgha Arūs (amīr) (XIV) vii, 462a – VII, 461b
al-Biblāwī, ʿAlī b. Muḥammad (1905) s,123a, **132b** – S, 122b, **132a**
Bible i, 118a, 564b; iii, 1205a; iv, 303a, 308b, 312a – I, 121b, 582b; III, 1235b; IV, 316b, 322b, 326a
Bîčaḳdjî-zāde Mustafā Čelebī i, 775b – I, 799a
Bičitr (painter/peintre) (XVII) vii, 339a – VII, 340b
Bīd vi, 494a – VI, 480a
Bidʿ → al-Dawḥa (Ḳaṭar)
Bidʿa i, 277a, 1039a, **1199a**; iv, 141b – I, 286a, 1070b, **1234b**; IV, 147b
Bīdar i, 924a, 925a, b, 1047a, b, **1199b**, 1323a; iii, 425b, 447a; v, 295b, 888b, 1135a, 1215a, b; vi, 53b, 63a, b, 66b, 67b, 68a, 269a, 368b, 369a, 407a, b, 537a, 695b –
I, 952a, 953a, b, 1079a, **1235a**, 1363b; III, 439b, 462a; V, 295b, 895a, 1130b, 1205a; VI, 52a, 61a, 64b, 65b, 66a, 254a, 352b, 353b, 391b, 392a, b, 521b, 683b
Bidʿat ii, 147a – II, 151a
Bīdil, Mīrzā ʿAbd al-Ḳādir (1721) i, **1201a**; ii, 865b; vii, 341b, 529a – I, **1236b**; II, 885b; VII, 343b, 529b
Bīdjān, Aḥmed (XV) i, **1202a**; ii, 587b; iii, 43b – I, **1237b**; II, 602a; III, 45a
Bidjanagar → Vidjayanagara
Bīdjāpūr i, 199a, 768b, 769a, 913b, 924b, 1015b, **1202b**, 1323b; iii, 15a, 287b, 288a, 425a, b; v, 884b, 888b, 1259a, b; vi, 62b, 63b, 68a, 122a, 126a, b, 127a, 271b, 369a, b, 456b, 534b, 535a, b, 537b; vii, 404b; s, 246b –
I, 204b, 791b, 792a, 941a, 952b, 1046b, **1238a**, 1364a; III, 16a, 296b, 297a, 438b, 439b; V, 890b, 895a, 1250a, b; VI, 60b, 61b, 66a, 120a, 124a, 125a, 256a, 353b, 442a, 518b, 519a, 520a, 522a; VII, 406a; S, 246b
—monuments i, 1203b, 1204b; iii, 446b, 447b; v, 295a, 1216a – I, 1239a, 1240a; III, 461b, 462b; V, 295a, 1205b
Bidjār s, 142a, b – S, 142a
Bidjay Rāy i, 1194a – I, 1229b
Bidjāya (Bougie) i, 155a, 165a, 678a, 1204b; ii, 130a, 747b, 863b; iii, 67a, b, 138a, b, 500a; iv, 359b, 360b, 361b, 479b; v, 531a; vi, 320a, 404b, 426b, 573a; s, 113b –
I, 159a, 170a, 699a, **1240b**; II, 133b, 766a, 883b; III, 69b, 70a, 141a, b, 517a; IV, 375a, 376a, 377b, 501a; V, 535a; VI, 304b, 389a, 412a, 558a; S, 113a
Bīdjbehāra s, 114a – S, 113b
Bidjnawr i, 288a, **1206a**; s, 73b, 74a – I, 296b, **1241b**; S, 74a
Bidlīs (Bitlis) i, **1206a**; v, 457a, 458b, 459a; vi, 242b – I, **1242a**; V, 459b, 461a, b; VI, 227a
Bidlīsī, Abu 'l-Faḍl i, 1208a; iv, 704b – I, 1244a; IV, 733a
al-Bidlīsī, ʿAmmār (1194) ix, 778a – IX, 812a
Bidlīsī, Idrīs (1520) i, **1207b**; ii, 1136b; v, 457a, b, 481b – I, **1243b**; II, 1163a; V, 460a, b, 484b
Bidlīsī, Sharaf al-Din Khān (XVII) i, 1207a, **1208b**; v, 458a, b, 481b; vi, 931b; ix, 6b –
I, 1242b, **1244b**; V, 460b, 461b, 484b; VI, 923b; IX, 6b
Bidrī i, 1201a – I, 1236b
Biga s, 330a – S, 329b
Bigha i, **1209a** – I, **1245a**
Bigha → Misāḥa
Blāʾ ii, 551a, b; v, 778a; s, **133a** – II, 564b, 565b; V, 784a; S, **132b**

Bihādhīn → Muḥammad Iʿtimāzāda
Bihʾāfrīd b. Farwardīn (749) i, **1209a**; iv, 44b, 910a; v, 1111b – I, **1245a**; IV, 47b, 943a; V, 1107b
Bihāfarīd x, 926b – X,
Bihār i, **1209b**; iii, 423b; v, 783b; vi, 47a, b, 49a, 131a, 273a, 343a, 409b, 410a, 535b; vii, 314a; s, 167a, 203a, 325b – I, **1245b**; III, 437a; V, 790a; VI, 45b, 46a, 48a, 129b, 258a, 327a, 394b, 395a, 519b; VII, 316b; S, 167a, 202b, 325a
Bihār Sharīf vi, 131b, 410a – VI, 129b, 395a
Bihār-i Dānish → ʿInāyat Allāh Ḳanbū
al-Bihārī, Muḥibb Allāh (1707) i, 937a, b, **1210a**; iii, 435a – I, 966a, **1246a**; III, 449b
Bihāristān → Djāmī
Bihbihān i, 659a; iii, 1107a; v, 876a; s, 134b – I, 680a; III, 1134a; V, 882a; S, 134a
Bihbihānī, Āḳā ʿAbd al-Ḥusayn (XVIII) s, 135a – S, 134b
Bihbihānī, Āḳā Muḥammad ʿAlī (XVIII) s, 135a – S, 134b
Bihbihānī, Āḳā Sayyid Muḥammad Bākir Wahīd (1791) vi, 551a, 552a; viii, 46b, 541a– VI, 535b. 536b
Bihbihānī, Āḳā Sayyid Muḥammad Bāḳir Waḥīd (1793) vi, 551a, 552a; viii, 46b, 541a; s, 57a, **134b** – VI, 535b, 536b; VIII, 47a, 559a; S, 57b, **134a**
Bihbihānī, Muḥammad ʿAlī s, 135a – S, 134b
Bihbihānī, Sayyid ʿAbd Allāh (XX) viii, 140a; s, 104a, 365b – VIII, 142b; S, 103b, 365a
Bihbihānī, Sayyid Muḥammad (XX) vii, 300a – VII, 302a
Bihbūd Khān, *sardār* (XVIII) iv, 390a – IV, 406b
Bihisht → Djanna
Bihishtī, Aḥmed (1511) i, **1210b**; iv, 129a; v, 1105b; vi, 1023a – I, **1246b**; IV, 134b; V, 1101b; VI, 1016a
Bihḳubādh i, 789a, **1210b** – I, 812b, **1246b**
Bihrangī, Ṣamad (1968) v, 200b; s, **135a** – V, 198a; S, **134b**
Bihrūz al-Khādim (amīr) (XII) i, 797a; vii, 734b, 913b – I, 820a; VII, 735a, 913b
Bihrūz (amīr) (1577) i, **1211a** – I, **1247a**
Bihrūz Khān (1631) i, **1211a** – I, **1247a**
Bihzād, Kamāl al-Dīn (1533) i, 205b, **1211a**; vii, 602b; viii, 787b; s, 138b, 139a, b – I, 211b, **1247a**; VII, 602a; VIII, 813b; S, 138a, b, 139a
al-Biḳāʿ i, 787b, **1214a**; ii, 750a; v, 790a, 739b; s, 154a, 250a – I, 811a, **1250a**; II, 768a; V, 796a, 799b; S, 154a, 250a
al-Biḳāʿī, Burhān al-Dīn (1480) x, 394b – X, 423a
Bikbāshī → Biñbashï
Bikrami era/ère i, 1239a – I, 1277a
Biḳratīs → Buḳrāt
Bilād al-Barbarā (Barābara) vii, 245b – VII, 247a
Bilād al-Djarīd → Djarīd
Bilād al-Islām iv, 173a – IV, 180b
Bilād al-Shām x, 191a – X, 296b
Bilād Shāwir (Yemen) vi, 438b – VI, 424a
Bilād al-Sūdān i, 156b; ii, 121b, 137a; vi, 281b, 401a – I, 161a; II, 124b, 140b; VI, 266b, 385b
Bilād al-Sufāla vii, 245b – VII, 247a
Bilād -i thalātha i, **1214b** – I, **1250b**
Bilād Yāfiʿ (Yemen) vi, 439a – VI, 424b
Bilād al-Zandj iii, 653a; vii, 245b – III, 674b; VII, 247a
Bilāl b. Abī Burda al-Ashʿarī (739) i, 694a; ii, 232a, 245a; iii, 155a, 650a; iv, 919a, 926b – I, 715a; II, 239a, 252a; III, 158b, 671b; IV, 952a, 959b
Bilāl b. Djarīr al-Muḥammadī (1151) i, **1214b** – I, **1251a**
Bilāl b. al-Ḥārith (VII) i, 336b – I, 347a
Bilāl b. Rabāḥ (638) i, 24b, 110a, 188a, 482a, 1141b, **1215a**; ii, 846b; vi, 361b, 675a, 677a, 738b – I, 25b, 113a, 193b, 496b, 1176a, **1251a**; II, 866a; VI, 345b, 661b, 663b, 728a
Bilāl b. Tawʿa (VII) vii, 689 – VII, 690a
Bilāliyyūn → Muslimūn: Black Muslims
Bilʿam → Balʿam
Bilāwar v, 460b – V, 463b
Bilawhar wa-Yūdāsaf i, 2b, **1215b**; iv, 63a – I, 2b, **1251b**; IV, 66a-b
Bīlbak al-Khāzindār, amīr (XIII) i, 816b – I, 839b
al-Bilbālī, Makhlūf b. ʿAlī (Kano) (XVI) iv, 550a – IV, 573b
Bilban Tabakhī (amīr) (1297) vi, 507b – VI, 493a
Bilbās (confederation) i, 1217b; vi, 502b – I, **1254a**; VI, 488a
Bilbāy, al-Ẓāhir Sayf al-Dīn (Mamlūk) (1467) vii, 727a – VII, 727b
Bilbays i, **1218a**; s, 159a – I, **1254a**; S, 159a
Bilbīsī, Madjd al-Dīn (1399) viii, 635b – VIII, 654a
Bile → Bīredjik
Bileam → Balʿam
Biledjik i, **1218b**; iii, 215a; viii, 181a; s, 282a – I, **1254b**; III, 221a; VIII, 184a; S, 282a
Bilen vi, 643a – VI, 628a
`bilga Ḳaghān (734) x, 687b – X, 729b
Bilgā Takīn (Bilge Tegīn), amīr (974) i, 421b; ii, 978a; vi, 522b; s, 284b – I, 433b; II, 1000b; VI, 507b; S, 284b
Bilgrām i, **1218b**; vii, 445a – I, **1255a**; VII, 446a
Bilgrāmī → Ghulām Nabī
Bilgrāmī, ʿAbd al-Djalīl (1725) i, 808a, **1219a** – I, 831a, **1255b**
Bilgrāmī, ʿAbd al-Wāḥid vii, 956b – VII, 957b
Bilgrāmī, Sayyid ʿAlī (1911) i, **1219b** – I, **1255b**
Bilḳīs i, 262a, **1219b**; ii, 218a; iii, 541b; vi, 468a, 562a, 565b, 615a; viii, 665a, 979a,b; ix, 823a – I, 270a, **1256a**; II, 224b; III, 560b; VI, 453b, 547a, 550b, 600a; VIII, 684b, 1014a; IX, 857a
Billawr (Ballūr) i, **1220b**; v, 965a – I, **1256b**; V, 969b
Billiton i, **1221a**; vi, 293a – I, **1257b**; VI, 204a
Billūr Köshk i, **1221a**; iii, 375a – I, **1257b**; III, 387a
Bilma i, **1221b** – I, **1258a**
Bilmedje i, **1222a** – I, **1258b**
Bilmen, Ömer Nasuhī (XX) iii, 163b – III, 167a
Bīmāristān i, 899a, **1222b**; ii, 283b, 1015b, 1120a; iii, 195b; iv, 485b; v, 1006a; s, 273b, 274a, 381a – I, 926a, **1259a**; II, 291b, 1039b, 1146b; III, 200a; IV, 506b; V, 1001b; S, 273a, b, 381b
Bīmund (Bohemund) ii, 237b – II, 244a
Bin ʿAbd al-Krīm (Rīf) (XX) → Muḥammad b. ʿAbd al-Karīm
Bin ʿAlī (Mirbāṭ) vi, 83b – VI, 81b
Bin ʿArībat (Raysūt) vi, 83b – VI, 81b
Bināʾ i, **1226a** – I, **1262b**
Biñbashï i, **1229a** – I, **1265b**
Bingöl i, **1229a** – I, **1266a**
Bingöl Da i, **1229a** – I, **1266a**
Binkath x, 348b – X, 374b
Binn (Druze) s, **135b** – S, **135b**
Bint al-Khuss → Hind bint al-Khuss
al-Binya vi, 572a – VI, 557a
Binyāmīn i, 261a, 262a, **1229b** – I, 269a, 270a, **1266b**
Bīr (district) vi, 269a – VI, 254a
Biʾr i, 538b, **1230a**; s, 318b – I, 555a, **1266b**; S, 318a
Biʾr Ahmad (Yemen) i, 345a – I, 355b
Biʾr ʿAlālī (Čad) s, 165a – S, 165a
Biʾr ʿAlī (Mahra) vi, 81b – VI, 79b
Biʾr al-Hudhā (Arabia/-e) vi, 455b – VI, 441a
Biʾr Maʿūna (Arabia/-e) i, 442b, **1232b**; v, 41a; vi, 604a – I, 455a, **1269a**; V, 42a; VI, 588b

Biʾr Maymūn i, **1232b** – I, **1269b**
Biʾr Rūma (Medina) viii, 892a – VIII, 922b
Biʾr al-Sabʿ (Beersheba) i, **1233a** – I, **1269b**
Bīr Singh Dēv, Rādjā (1394) i, 117b; ii, 380a; vi, 49a, 534a – I, 121a; II, 390b; VI, 47b, 518b
al-Bīra i, **1233a**, b; viii, 128b – I, **1270a**, b; VIII, 131a
Biraima iv, 352a – IV, 367a
Bīrbal → Radja Bīrbal
Bīrbal Kāčrū s, 332a, 333a – S, 332a
Bīrdjand i, **1233a**; iv, 4a-b; V, 355a, b; vi, 495b – I, **1270a**; IV, 4b; V, 356b, 357a; VI, 480b
Bīrdjandī, Niẓām al-Dīn b. Muḥammad Ḥusayn (1527) viii, 541b – VIII, 559b
Bīredjik i, 1233b; vi, 378a, 509a, 539b – I, **1270b**; VI, 362b, 494b, 524b
Birge i, **1234b** – I, **1271b**
Birgewī (Birgili), Meḥmed (1573) i, 332b, **1235a**; iv, 560a – I, 343a, **1272a**; IV, 582b
Bîrghos → Lüleburgaz
Birkat al-Ḥabash (Cairo/le Caire) vi, 671b; vii, 509b – VI, 658a; VII, 510a
Birmali Sala Pate (Fulbe) (XVIII) ii, 942a – II, 964a
Birmanie I, 625b, **1272b**
Birnin-Katsina iv, 773b – IV, 804b
Birr i, **1235b** – I, **1273a**
Birs (- Nimrūd) i, **1235b** – I, **1273a**
Bīrūn i, **1236a**; ii, 15a, 1089a – I, **1273b**; II, 15b, 1114b
al-Bīrūnī, Abu ʾl-Rayḥān Muḥammad (al-Khwārazmī) (1050) i, 87a, 119a, 213a, 419a, 455b, 591b, 725a, 726b, 1014b, 1031a, b, 1131a, 1220b, **1236a**; ii, 584a; iii, 9a, 30b, 113b, 405a, 406a, 459a, 858a, 1206b; iv, 358b, 707a, 754a, 1061a, 1063a; v, 86a, b, 1025b; vi, 66a, 185a, 374b, 450b, 600b, 638a, 726b; vii, 199a, 977a; s, 56a, 59b, 249b, 251b, 253a, 327b, 363a, 413b – I, 89b, 122b, 219a, 220a, 431a, 468b, 610b, 747b, 748b, 1045b, 1062b, 1063a, 1165a, 1257a, **1273b**; II, 598b; III, 9b, 32a, 116a, 417b, 418b, 475a, 882a, 1237a; IV, 374a, 735b, 784b, 1092b, 1094b; V, 88a, b, 1021a; VI, 64a, 167b, 359a, 436a, 585b, 623a, 715b; VII, 199b, 977b; S, 56b, 60a, 250a, 252a, b, 327a, 362b, 414a
Birzāl, Banū i, **1238a**; iv, 254b, 665b; vi, 434b, 727a – I, **1275b**; IV, 265b, 692b; VI, 420a, 716a
al-Birzālī, ʿAlam al-Dīn al-Ḳāsim (1339) i, **1238a**; ii, 522b; iv, 863b; viii, 458b – I, **1276a**; II, 536a; IV, 897a; VIII, 474b
al-Birzālī, Muhammad b. ʿAbd Allāh (Ḳarmūna) (XI) i, 6a; vii, 761a – I, 6a; VII, 762b
Bisāṭ v, 1158b; vi, 664b; vii, 336a; s, **136a** – V, 1148a; VI, 650b; VII, 337b; S, **135b**
al-Bisāṭī, Muḥammad b. Aḥmad (*ḳāḍī*) (1438) vi, 280a – VI, 265a
Bisbarāy b. Harigarbhdās (Karkarni) (XVII) i, **1239a** – I, **1276b**
Bīsha (Yemen) i, 538a, b, **1239a**; vi, 435b; x, 10b – I, 554b, **1277a**; VI, 421a; X, 10b
Bīsharʿ i, **1239b** – I, **1277a**
Bishāra al-Khūrī s, 159b – S, 159b
Bishārīn, Banū i, 1b, 1172a, **1239b** – I, 1b, 1207a, **1277b**
Bishbalîk i, **1240a**; ix, 621b; x, 676b – I, **1277b;** IX, 645a; X,
Bishndās (painter/peintre) (XVII) vi, 425b, 426a; vii, 339a – VI, 410b, 411a; VII, 340b
al-Bishr (battle/bataille) i, **1240b** – I, **1278b**
Bishr b. Abī Khāzim (VI) i, **1241a**; vi, 349a – I, **1279a**; VI, 333b
Bishr b. al-Barāʾ (628) i, **1241b** – I, **1279b**
Bishr b. Dāwūd b. Yazīd b. Ḥātim b. Ḳabīsa b. al-Muhallab (IX) vii, 360a – VII, 362b
Bishr b. Ghiyāth al-Marīsī (833) i, **1241b**; ii, 373a, 388a; iv, 1163b; vii, 5b; s, 89a, 90a – I, **1279b**; II, 383b, 398b; IV, 1195b; VII, 6a; S, 88b, 90a
Bishr b. al-Ḥārith (846) ix, 866b – IX, 916b
Bishr b. Marwān (Umayyad(e))(693) i, **1242b**; ii, 788a; iii, 40b, 73a, 715a; vii, 145b, 357a – I, **1280a**; II, 807a; III, 42a, 75b, 737b; VII, 147b, 359b
Bishr b. al-Muʿtamir (825) i, 454a, 587a, **1243a**; iii, 1143b, 1266a; vi, 336b, 458a, 636b; vii, 259a, b, 546b, 604a; viii, 388a; ix, 454b; s, 89b, 225b, 226a, b – I, 467a, 606a, **1281a**; III, 1171b, 1299a; VI, 321a, 443b, 621b; VII, 260b, 261b, 546b, 603b; VIII, 401a; IX, 469b; S, 89b, 225b, 226a, b
Bishr b. Ṣafwān (VIII) i, 50a; ii, 327b; iii, 169b – I, 51b; II, 337a; III, 173a
Bishr b. al-Walīd (VIII) i, **1244a**; iii, 990b – I, **1281b**; III, 1015a
Bishr al-Ḥāfī, Abūnaṣr (840) i, **1244a**; vi, 350b; vii, 647a; s, 384b – I, **1282a**; VI, 334b; VII, 647a; S, 385a
Bishr-i Yāsīn → Abu ʾl-Kāsim
Bishtāsb b. Luhrāsb (Kayānid(e)) iv, 809b – IV, 842a
Biskra i, **1246b**; v, 1181a – I, **1284a**; V, 1171a
Bismillāh → Basmala
Bisṭām (Basṭam) i, **1247a**; s, 149a, 235a – I, **1285a**; S, 149a, 234b
Bisṭām b. Ḳays (615) i, 343a, 963b, **1247b**, ii, 72a – I, 353b, 993a, **1285b**; II, 73a
Bisṭām b. ʿUmar al-Ḍabbī → al-Ḍabbī, Bisṭām
al-Bisṭāmī, ʿAbd al-Raḥmān (1454) i, **1248a**; ii, 376a – I, **1286a**; II, 386b
al- Bisṭāmī, Abū Yazīd → Abū Yazīd
al-Bisṭāmī, ʿAlā al-Din → Muṣannifak
al-Bisṭāmī, ʿAlī b. Ṭayfūr (XVII) vii, 988b – VII, 989a
Bistī → Sikka
Bīsutūn (Bihistūn) i, **1248b**; v, 169a; vi, 494a – I, **1286a**; V, 166b; VI, 479b
Bīsutūn, Malik (1500) vi, 514b – VI, 499b
Bīsutūn b. Djihāngīr b. Kāwūs (1507) iv, 808a – IV, 840b
al-Biṭār, Ṣalāḥ al-Dīn (XX) iv, 125a – IV, 130b
Bitik, bitikči i, **1248b**; iv, 757a – I, **1286b**; IV, 787b
Bitlis → Bidlīs
Bitolja → Manastir/Monastir
Biṭrawsh i, **1249a**; ii, 744a; v, 510a – I, **1287a**; II, 762b; V, 513b
Biṭrīḳ (Patricius) i, 642b, **1249b**; v, 620a – I, 663a, **1287b**; V, 624a
al-Biṭrīḳ b. al-Nakā (VIII) viii, 423b – VIII, 437b
al-Biṭrūdjī, Nūr al-Dīn (Alpetragius) (XIII) i, **1250a**; iii, 957a; iv, 518a; viii, 102a – I, **1288a**; III, 982a; IV, 540b; VIII, 164b
Biyābānak i, **1250a** – I, **1288a**
Biya-pīsh → Gīlān-i Biyā Pas
Biyār, al-Biyār s, **149a** – S, **149a**
Biyārdjumand → Biyār
Bîyîḳlî ʿAlī Āghā (XVIII) i, 396a – I, 407a
Bîyîḳlî Meḥmed Pasha → Meḥmed Pasha Bîyîḳlî
Bizāʿā → Buzāʿā
Bizabān → Dilsiz
Bizerta/-e → Banzart
Bizye/Vize vi, 290b – VI, 275b
Black Sea → Baḥr Bunṭus; Ḳarā Deniz
Blida → Bulayda
Boabdil → Muḥammad XII (Naṣrid(e))
Bobastro → Bubashtru
Bodrum i, 476b, **1250b** – I, 490b, **1288b**
Bodufenvalugē Sīdī (1969) vi, 247a – VI, 231a
Boghā al-Kabīr → Bughā al-Kabīr

Boghā al-Sharābī → Bughā al-Sharābī
Boghā Ṭarkhān (VIII) iii, 493b – III, 510b
Boghaz → Boghaz-iči
Boghaz-iči i, **1251a**; v, 243a – I, **1289a**; V, 241a
Boghaz Kesen → Rūmeli Ḥiṣār
Boghdān (Moldavia) i, 4b, 310b, 1120a, **1252b**; v, 39b – I, 4b, 320a, 1153b, **1290b**; V, 40b
Bōgrā i, **1253b** – I, **1291b**
Bohemia → Čeh
Bohorās (Bohras) i, 172a, **1254a**; ii, 170b; iii, 381a, 434a, b, 544b; iv, 199b, 888a; v, 942b; vi, 246a; vii, 222b, 725a; x, 403a' s, 70b –
I, 176b, **1292a**; II, 175b; III, 393a, 448a, b, 563b; IV, 208a, 920b; V, 946a; VI, 230a; VII, 224a, 726a; X, 432a; S, 71a
Bohorās, Dāwūdī x, 103b – X, 111b
Bohtān → Kurd(e)s
Bokar Biro (Fūya Djallon) (XIX) ii, 960b, 1132b – II, 982b, 1159b
Bokar Salif Tall iii, 108a – III, 110b
Böke Budhrač (yabāku) x, 689a – X, 781b
Bokhārā → Bukhārā
Bolān Pass ix, 531a – IX, 551b
Bolēday Balūč s, 222a – S, 222a
Bolor Da → Pamir
Bolu i, **1255b**; s, 98b – I, **1293b**; S, 97b
Bölük i, 657a, 999b, **1256a**, 1278a; ii, 1098a, 1121a – I, 677b, 1030a, **1294a**, 1317a; II, 1124a, 1147a
Bölük-Bashi̊ i, **1256b** – I, **1294b**
Bölük-bashi̊, Aḥmed Durmush (XIX) s, 149b – S, 149b
Bölük-bashi̊, Riḍā Tewfīḳ (1949) iv, 933a; s, **149b** – IV, 966a; S, **149b**
Bolwadin i, **1256b**; s, 238b – I, **1294b**; S, 238b
Bombay City/la ville de- i, 979a, **1257a**; ii, 426a; vi, 536b; s, 47a, 247a – I, 1009a, **1295a**; II, 437a; VI, 521a; S, 47a, 247a
Bombay state/l'état de- i, **1257a** – I, **1295b**
Bondū → Senegal
Bône → al-ʿAnnāba
Bonneval, Comte de → Aḥmad Pasha Bonneval
Borāḳ x, 812b – X,
Bordj → Burdj
Böri b. Tughtigin (1132) x, 216b – X, 233b
Bori cult(e) (Hausa) iii, 278a – III, 286a
Böri Bars b. Alp Arslan (Saldjūḳ) (1095) viii, 81b – VIII, 83b
Böri Tigin → Ibrāhīm Tamghač Khān
Boris (Bulghar kaghan) (888) x, 692a – X, 734b
Börklüdje Muṣṭafā (XV) i, 869b; ii, 599b – I, 893b; II, 614a
Borkou i, **1257b** – I, **1295b**
Borku s, 165a, 116a – S, 164b, 166a
Borneo/-néo i, 1258b; iii, 1213a, b, 1215b, 1225b; v, 309b, 539b; s, **150a** – I, 1297a; III, 1243b, 1244b, 1246a, 1257a; V, 309a, 544a; S, **150a**
Bornū i, 35a, **1259a**; iii, 276a; iv, 541a, b, 548b, 567a; v, 278b; x, 122b; s, 164a, b – I, 36a, **1297a**; III, 284a; IV, 564b, 565a, 572a, b, 589b; V, 276b; X, 132a; S, 163b, 164a
Borsippa → Birs
Börte Fudjin ii, 41b, 42a, 571a – II, 42b, 585b
Borusu i, 1290b, 1291a, b – I, 1330a, b, 1331a, b
Bosna i, 4a, 97a, 285a, 310a, 656b, 1018a, **1261a**; ii, 211b, 681b; v, 32a, 263b, 774a; vi, 59b, 69a, 89b, 227b, 327b; vii, 244a; viii, 171b; ix, 28b; x, 697b; s, 281b –
I, 4b, 99b, 293b, 320a, 677a, 1049a, **1299a**; II, 218a, 698b; V, 33a, 261a, 780a; VI, 57b, 67a, 87b, 221b, 314a; VII, 245b; VIII, 174b; IX, 29a; X, ; S, 281b
Bosna-sarāy → Sarajevo
al-Bosnawī, ʿAlī Dede (1598) i, 759a – I, 782a
Bosnia/-e → Bosna
Bosphorus → Boghaz-iči
Boṣrā (Bostra) i, **1275b**, 1316a, b; v, 1138a, b, 1139a; vi, 123b, 364a, 546b; s, 117a –
I, **1314b**, 1356b, 1357b; V, 1132a, b, 1133a; VI, 121b, 347b, 531a; S, 116b
Bostān Čelebī iv, 190a – IV, 198a
Bostāndji̊ i, **1277b**; iv, 1100b – I, **1316b**; IV, 1131a
Bostāndji̊-bashi̊ i, **1278b** – I, **1318a**
Bostānzāde, Muṣṭafā Efendi (1570) i, **1279a** – I, **1318b**
Bostānzāde, Meḥmed Efendi (1598) i, 1279b; iv, 884a – I, 1319a; IV, 917a
Botlikh, Banū i, 504a; iv, 630b – I, 519b; IV, 655b
Boṭṭīwa, Banū i, 680a – I, 701a
Bou Regreg vi, 142b – VI, 140b
Bou Saada (Algeria/-e) s, 134a – S, 133b
Bouddha → Budd
Boudhistes → Sumaniyya
Bouira → Sūḳ Ḥamza
Boumedienne, Houari → Abū Madyan, Hawwārī
Bourguiba, Ḥabīb (XX) ii, 470b, 639a; iii, 524a, 563b, 636b; v, 915a, 1068b, 1161a; vii, 416a – II, 482b, 655b; III, 542a, b, 583a, 658a; V, 920b, 1066a, 1151a; VII, 417b
Bourguiba, Muḥammad (XX) vi, 750a – VI, 739b
Bourzey → Barzūya
Boyer Aḥmad, Banū iv, 5b – IV, 6a
Boynu-Yarali̊ Meḥmed Pasha (1649) v, 257a – V, 254b, 255a
Boz Aba (Atabeg) (1146) vi, 482a, 782a; vii, 406b; viii, 944a, 978b – VI, 468a, 772a; VII, 407b; VIII, 976b, 1013a
Bozan (al-Ruhā) (XI) viii, 947a – VIII, 979b
Bozanti i, **1280a**; v, 257a, b – I, **1319a**; V, 255a, b
Bozdja-ada (Tenedos) i, **1280b**; v, 257a, b – I, **1319b**; V, 255a, b
Bozo (Sudan) ii, 251b – II, 259a
Bozoḳ → Yozgat
Bozoḳlu Muṣṭafā Pasha (XVII) i, 268a – I, 276b
Boztepe, Khalīl Nihād (1949) iii, 357b; s, 324b – III, 368b; S, 324a
Brādōst, Banū v, 460a; x, 898a – V, 462b; X,
Brāhīm Lakudī (XX) vi, 750a – VI, 739b
Brahima bi Saidu (Fulbe) (1817) ii, 942a – II, 964a
Brahman(e)s → Barāhima
Brahōīs i, 1005a, b; ii, 388a; iv, 10b, 364b; v, 102a, 684b; s, 222a – I, 1036a, b; II, 398a; IV, 11b, 380b; V, 104b, 690a; S, 222a
Brahūʾī → Brahōīs
Braẓila → Ibrail
Brava → Barawa
Brechk → Barishk
Brēlwī → Aḥmad Brēlwī
Bridj Baratpūr (XVIII) i, 1193a – I, 1228a
Broach → Bharūč
Brousse → Bursa
Brunei vi, 241a; s, 150a, **151b** – VI, 212a; S, 150a, **151b**
Brusa → Bursa
Bryson → Tadbīr al-Manzil
Bsharrā i, **1280b** – I, **1320a**
Bteddīn i, **1281a** – I, 1320a
Bū → Kunya
Bū ʿAlī, Banū ii, 440b – II, 452a
Bū ʿAlī Čaghānī → Abū ʿAlī Čaghānī
Bū ʿAlī Ḳalandar → Abū ʿAlī Ḳalandar
Bū ʿAmāma (XIX) i, 369b, 1281b; ii, 885b – I, 380b, 1320b; II, 906a
Bū ʿAzza → Abū Yaʿazza
Bū Bakr b. Sālim, Shaykh (Ḥaḍramawt) s, 420b – S, 420b

Bū Dali (Djidjelli) ii, 538a – II, 551a
Bū Dhanayn, Āl (ʿAdjmān) s, 42a – S, 42b
Bū Djaʿd (Morocco/Maroc) vi, 890b – VI, 881b
Bū Falāḥ, Āl (Abū Ẓabī) i, 1313b – I, 1353b
Bū Falāsā, Āl ii, 618b – II, 634a
Bū Ḥanak (Ḥasan b. Ḥusaynī, (Ḳusṭanṭīna) (1754) v, 531b, 532a – V, 536a
Bū Ḥasan, Āl → ʿArab, Djazīrat al-
Bū Ḥmāra (1909) i, 57b, 357a, **1281a**; ii, 620a, 820a, 1116a; iii, 62b; v, 1193a –
I, 59b, 368a, **1320b**; II, 635b, 839b, 1142b; III, 65a; V, 1183a
Bū Ḳabrīn (1798) iv, 361a – IV, 376b
Bū Kamya (Kalyān Ḥasab Bey (Ḳusṭanṭīna) v, 531b – V, 535b
Bū Khuraybān, Āl (al-Būraymī) s, 42a – S, 42b
Bū Muḥammad, Āl (ʿAmāra) i, 431a, 1096a, b; vii, 582a; s, 243a – I, 443a, 1129a, b; VII, 582b; S, 243a
Bū Naṣr (1032) vi, 522a, b – VI, 507a, b
Bū Ngāb (1850) vi, 252a – VI, 236a
Bū Saʿāda (Algeria/-e) s, 224a – S, 224a
Bū Saʿīd (Algeria/-e) vi, 404b, 405a – VI, 389a, b
Bū Saʿīd, Āl (ʿUmān/Zanzibar) i, 539b, 554a, 1038b, **1281b**; iv, 887a, b; v, 507b, 655b; vi, 358a, 735a, b; s, 332b, 355b –
I, 556a, 572a, 1070a, **1321a**; IV, 919b, 920a; V, 511a, 659b; VI, 342a, 724a, b; S, 332a, 355b
Bū'l-Sbaʿ (Marrākush) vi, 595b – VI, 580a
Bū Shāmis, Āl (al-Buraymī) s, 42a – s, 42b
Bū Shenṭūf → Muḥammad b. Nāṣir
Buʿāth i, **1283a**; iv, 1187b; v, 436a, 995a; vii, 366b – I, **1322b**; IV, 1220a; V, 438b, 990b; VII, 369a
Bubakar Sori (Fulbe) (XIX) ii, 942b – II, 964a
Bubashtru (Bobastro) vii, 569a; s, **152b** – VII, 570a; S, **152b**
Bučaḳ → Budjāḳ
Bučāḳčī, Banū v, 154b – V, 155b
Bucharest/Bucarest → Bükresh
Buda → Budīn
Budapest → Budīn
Budayl b. Ṭahfa al-Badjalī (VIII) ii, 188a, 488a – II, 194a, 500b
Budayl b. Warḳāʾ al-Khuzāʿī (630) i, **1283b**; vii, 372b – I, **1322b**; VII, 374a
Budd i, **1283b** – I, **1323a**
Buddha → Budd
Buddhists → Sumaniyya
Buddūma (Buduma) (lake/lac, Čād) iv, 540b; s, 165a – IV, 564a; S, 165a
Būdh-Ardashīr → al-Mawṣil
Budhiya → Budha
Budhan, Shaykh (XVI) i, **1284a** – I, **1323b**
Būdhāsaf → Bilawhar wa-Yūdāsaf
Budīn i, 1164a, **1284b**; ii, 1133b, 1134a; iii, 998a; v, 1022a, b; s, 171a –
I, 1198b, **1324a**; II, 1160b, 1161a; III, 1023a; V, 1018a, b; S, 171a
Budja → Bedja
Budjāḳ i, 1253b, **1286b**; vi, 58b – I, 1291b, **1326a**; VI, 56b
Budjatlï → Bushatlïs
Budjayr b. Aws al-Ṭāʾī (VII) s, 37b – S, 37b
Budjnūrd i, **1287a**; vi, 495a; vii, 454a; s, 235a – I, **1326b**; VI, 480b; VII, 454b; S, 234b
Budūḥ ii, 370a; s, **153a** – II, 380a; S, **153a**
Budukh → Shāh Dagh
Buganda x, 778b – X,
Bughā al-Kabīr al-Turkī (862) i, 551a, 637a, 844a, **1287a**; ii, 1024a; iv, 345a, 1175a; v, 997a; vii, 778a, 794a; viii, 120b –
I, 568b, 657b, 867b, **1327a**; II, 1047b; IV, 359b, 1208b; V, 992b; VII, 780a, 795b; VIII, 122b
Bughā al-Sharābī al-Ṣaghīr al-Turkī (868) i, **1287b**; ii, 679a, 1080a; iv, 88b, 89a; v, 488b; vi, 504b; vii, 390a, 593a, 722b, 777b, 793b –
I, **1327a**; II, 696a, 1105a; IV, 92b, 93a; V, 491a; VI, 490a; VII, 391b, 583b, 723b, 779b, 795b
Bughdān → Boghdān
Bughrā Khān → Muḥammad II b. Sulaymān (Ḳarakhānid(e))
Bughra Khān (Yaghma) x, 684a – X, 781b
Bughrā Khān b. Balbān b. Mūsā (Ḳarakhānid(e) (992) i, 444a, 997a; ii, 268a; iv, 818a, 920b; v, 685b; s, 124b – I, 1017b, 457a; II, 276b; IV, 851a, 953b; V, 690b; S, 123b
Bughra Khān Hārūn (Ilek-Khān) (1102) i, 987a; ii, 254a; iii, 1113b, 1114a; viii, 110a – I, 1017b; II, 261a; III, 1141a; VIII, 112b
Bughračuḳ (Harāt) (X) iv, 189b – IV, 197b
al-Bughṭūri, Makrīn b. Muḥammad (XIII) i, **1287b** – I, **1327a**
Buginese/Buginais vi, 116a, b; s, 151a – VI, 113b, 114b; S, 151a
Bugfis (Kilāt) s, 332a – S, 331b
Buḥayra (lake/lac) i, **1288a** – I, **1327b**
Buḥayra (Beḥera, Egypt) i, **1288a**; iii, 299b; iv, 134a; s, 244a, 268a – I, **1327b**; III, 309a; IV, 140a; S, 244a, 267b
al-Buḥayra (Battle of/Bataille d') (1130) i, 1288a; vi, 592a, 945a – I, 1327b; VI, 577a, 937b
al-Buhriy, Hemedi b. Abdallah s, 351b – S, 351b
al-Buḥayra al-Mayyita al-Muntina → Baḥr Lūṭ
Buḥayrat Anṭākiyya i, 446b – I, 459b
Buḥayrat Khʷarazm → Aral
Buḥayrat Māyutis → Baḥr Māyutis
Buḥayrat Nastarāwa → Burullus
Buḥayrat Tinnīs viii, 38b – VIII, 39b
Buḥayrat Yaghrā → Buḥayrat Anṭākiyya
Buhlūl, al-Madjnūn al-Kūfī (X) i, **1288b** – I, **1328a**
Buhlūl b. Rāshid (799) viii, 843b – VIII, 873a
Buḥayrat Shaykh (XVI) iii, 455b – III, 471b
Buḥayrat b. Rāshid (799) i, 1289a; viii, 843b – I, 1328b; VIII, 873a
Buḥayrat Lōdi → Bahlūl Lōdī
al-Buḥturī, Abū ʿUbāda (897) i, 118b, 153b, 154a, 386b, 592a, **1289a**; iii, 111a, 573a, 693a; v, 935a; vi, 625b; vii, 527a, 982a; s, 16b, 25a, 26a, 277b –
I, 122a, 158a, b, 397b, 611a, **1328b**; III, 113b, 593a, 715a; V, 938b; VI, 610b; VII, 527b, 982b; S, 16b, 25a, 26b, 277a
Buḥturid(e)s ii, 634b; iv, 834b – II, 650b; IV, 867b
al-Buḥturiyya bint Khurshīd (Dābūyid(e)) (817) vi, 335a – VI, 319b
Būḳ i, **1290b** – I, **1330a**
Būḳʿa i, 1292a; s, **154a** – I, 1332a; S, **154a**
Buḳa (Oghuz) (XI) i, **1292a** – I, **1331b**
Buḳa Temür → Ṭughā Tīmūr
Būḳalā i, **1292b**; iii, 290a – I, **1332a**; III, 299a
Būḳalamūn → Abū Ḳalamūn
Bukar (Bāru) Dāʿū (Songhay) (XV) vii, 393b – VII, 395a
Bukar Garbai (Kanemi, Bornū) XX) i, 1260b; v, 359a – I, 1298b; V, 360a
Bukarest → Bükresh
al-Buḳayʿa i, **1292b**; vi, 579b; s, 154a – I, **1332a**; VI, 564b; S, 154a
Bukayḳ → Abḳayḳ
Bukayr b. Māhān (744) i, **1292b**; ii, 601a; iv, 446b, 837b; v, 2a, 3a; vii, 396a –
I, **1332b**; II, 616a; IV, 466b, 870b; V, 2a, 3a; VII, 397b
Bukayr b. Wishāḥ (696) i, 47b, **1293a** – I, 49a, **1332b**

Bukhār Khudāt (VII) i, 1293b, 1294a; s, 327a – I, 1333b; S, 326b
Bukhārā i, 320, 36a, 46b, 71a, 103a, 121a, 141b, 147b, 750a, 853a, **1293b**; ii, 2b, 43a, 446a, 932b, 1096a; iv, 188b, 189b, 310a; v, 28b, 541b, 853b, 856b, 858a, 859b, 966b, 1149a; vi, 77a, b, 115b, 130b, 333a, 340a, 365b, 418a, b, 419a, 433a, 621a, 764b, 766a, 769b; vii, 477b, 1015a; viii, 749a; ix, 427a; s, 49a, 50b, 65a, 66a, 97a, 107a, 145a, 227b, 228a, 261a, 265a, 281a, 326b, 340a, 419b, 420a – I, 33a, 37a, 48a, 73a, 106a, 124b, 145b, 152a, 772b, 877a, **1333a**; II, 2b, 44a, 457b, 954a, 1122a; IV, 196b, 197b, 324a; V, 29a, 546a, 860b, 863b, 865a, 866b, 971a, 1140a; VI, 75a, 113b, 128b, 317b, 324b, 349b, 403a, b, 404a, 418b, 606a, 754a, 755b, 759a; VII, 477a, 1017a; VIII, 779b; IX, 443b; S, 49b, 51b, 65a, b, 66b, 96b, 106b, 145a, 227b, 228a, 260b, 264b, 281a, 326a, 339b, 419b, 420b
al-Bukhārī → Ṣalāḥ al-Dīn b. Mubārak
al-Bukhārī, Aḥmad al-Faḍl (XI) vii, 199b – VII, 200a
Bukhārī, Amīr Aḥmad (1516) vii, 936a – VII, 936b
al-Bukhārī, Muḥammad b.ʿAbd al-Bāḳī (XVI) i, **1296b** – I, **1336a**
al-Bukhārī, Muḥammad b. Ismāʿīl (870) i, 791a, 808a, 892b, **1296b**; ii, 125b; iii, 24a, 27b, 512b, 778a, 803a, 862a, 909b, 948b; iv, 736b; vi, 112a, 353a; vii, 361b, 537b; s, 87b, 232b, 404b – I, 814b, 831b, 919a, **1336a**; II, 128b; III, 25b, 29a, 530a, 801b, 826b, 886a, 933b, 973a; IV, 766b; VI, 109b, 337b; VII, 363b, 537b; S, 87b, 232b, 404b
al-Bukhārī, Muḥammad ʿAlī Khān (XIX) ii, 618a – II, 633b
Bukhārī, Mullā Sayfī (1503) viii, 543a – VIII, 560b
al-Bukhārī, Nūr al-Dīn al-Ṣābūnī (1184) vi, 848a – VI, 838b
Bukhārī, Shaykh Muḥammad Murād (1729) vii, 936b – VII, 937a
al-Bukhārī al-Ghundjār, Muḥammad b. Aḥmad (1021) viii, 748b – VIII, 77a
Bukhārlïk (Bukharidīs) i, **1297a** – I, **1337a**
Bukhl i, **1297b** – I, **1337a**
Bukht-Naṣ(ṣ)ar (Nebuchadnezzar) i, 846a, **1297b**; ii, 112b; iv, 809b; vi, 412b – I, 869b, **1337b**; II, 115a; IV, 842a; VI, 397a, b
Bukhtīshūʿ i, 212b, **1298a**; iii, 872b; iv, 649a; s, 379b – I, 219a, **1338a**; III, 896b; IV, 675b; S, 379b
Būḳīr → Abūḳīr
Bukovina/-ne → Khotin
Buḳrāṭ (Hippocrate(s)) ii, 402b; iii, 897b; iv, 406b; s, **154b** – II, 413a; III, 921b; IV, 424a; S, **154b**
Bükresh i, **1298b** – I, **1338b**
Buḳūm, Banū i, **1299a** – I, **1339a**
Būlāḳ i, **1299b**; ii, 167a; iv, 425a, 442a, b; vi, 797b, 801b; vii, 69a – I, **1339a**; II, 172b; IV, 443b, 462a; VI, 787b, 791b; VII, 70a
Būlala (Kanem) iv, 541a; s, 164a – IV, 564b; S, 163b
Bulandshahr i, **1299b**; vi, 49b, 50a, 294b – I, **1339b**; VI, 48a, 279b
Būlātmūriyān, Banū iv, 860a – IV, 893b
Bulāy (Poley/Aguilar de la Frontera) i, **1300b** – I, **1340a**
Bulāy, battle of/bataille de (891) x, 850b – X,
Bulayda (Blida) i, **1300b** – I, **1340b**
al-Bulayṭī → al-Balaṭī
Bulbul i, **1301a**; ii, 1133a – I, **1340b**; II, 1160a
Bulbul Shāh (1327) iv, 708a; s, **156a** – IV, 736b; S, **156a**
al-Buldadjī (1289) iii, 163b – III, 167a
Buldur → Burdur
Bulgaria/-e i, 394a, **1302a**; ii, 610b, 611a; v, 534a, 1014b; x, 698a – I, 405b, **1342a**; II, 625b, 626a; V, 538a, 1010a; X, 741b
Bulghār i, 998b, 1000a, 1075b, 1105a, **1304b**; ii, 21a, 69b, 202b, 853b, 1107b; iii, 759a; iv, 280a, 648b, 1173a; v, 1011a; vi, 420a; vii, 352a; x, 691b – I, 1029a, 1031a, 1107b, 1138b, **1344b**; II, 21a, 71a, 209a, 873a, 1133b; III, 782a; IV, 292b, 675a, 1206a; V, 1007a; VI, 405b; VII, 354a; X, 734a
Bulghār-da → Toros
al-Bulghārī → Sharaf al-Dīn Husām al-Dīn; Yaʿḳūb b. Nuʿmān.
Bulghār-maʿden → Toros
Bulgur → Burghul
Bulkiah I (Brunei) (XVI) s, 152a – S, 152a
Bulkiah, Sultan Sir Hassanal (XX) s, 152b – S, 152b
al-Bulḳīnī, ʿAbd al-Raḥmān b. ʿUmar (1421) i, 138a, **1308b**; iii, 777b – I, 142a, **1349a**; III, 800b
al-Bulḳīnī, Muḥammad b. Muḥammad (1485) i, **1309a** – I, **1349a**
al-Bulḳīnī, Ṣāliḥ b. ʿUmar (1464) i, **1308b** – I, **1349a**
al-Bulḳīnī, Siradj al-Dīn ʿUmar (1403) i, **1308b**; iii, 699a – I, **1348b**; III, 721a
al-Bulḳīnī, ʿUmar b. Raslān (1403) vii, 692a – VII, 692b
Bullhē Shāh, ʿAbd Allāh (1758) vii, 328a; viii, 256a; x, 322a – VII, 329b; VIII, 258b; X, 346b
Bullū, Banū s, 148a – S, 148a
Buluggīn b. Bādīs b. Ḥabūs b. Zīrī (Zīrid(e)) (1057) i, 491b; vi, 222b – I, 506a; VI, 216a
Buluggīn b. Muḥammad (Ḥammādid(e)) (1062) iii, 137b – III, 140a
Buluggīn b. Zīrī b. Manād (Zīrid(e)) (984) i, 699b, 824a, 1044b, 1088a, **1309a**; ii, 520a, 821b, 854a; iii, 1036b, 1043a; v, 1010b, 1176a, b, 1177a; vi, 431b, 728a, 947a; vii, 64b, 486a; viii, 688b – I, 720b, 847a, 1076a, 1120b, **1349a**; II, 533a, 841a, 874a; III, 1062b, 1068b; V, 1006a, 1166a, b, 1167a; VI, 417a, 717a, 939b; VII, 64b, 485b; VIII, 708b
Bulū → Bāll
Būlūghān, amīr (Mongol) iv, 1047a – IV, 1078b
Buluḳḳīn → Banya
Buluniyās → Bāniyās
Buluwādīn → Bolwadin
Bumin (553) x, 687a – X, 729a
Būna (Bône) → al-ʿAnnāba
Bunān b. ʿAmr al-Ḍārib (IX) s, 284b – S, 284b
Bundār → Muḥammad b. Bashshār
Bundār al-Iṣbahānī → Ibn Lizza
al-Bundārī, al-Fatḥ b. ʿAlī (XIII) i, 523a, **1309b**; iii, 918b; iii, 1158a; vi, 430a – I, 538b, **1349b**; II, 940a; III, 1186b; VI, 415b
Bundēlas, Banū vii, 443b – VII, 445a
al-Bunduḳdārī → Baybars I
Bunduḳī → Sikka
al-Būnī, Abu 'l-Abbās (1225) ii, 376a; iii, 596a; iv, 1134a; v, 222b; s, 153a, **156a** – II, 386b; iii, 616b; IV, 1165b; V, 220a; S, 153a, **156b**
Bunkan, Muḥammad (1537) x, 36b – X, 38a
Bunn → Ḳahwa
Buñsuz (Ḳarāmān-oghlu) iv, 619b, 620a – IV, 644a
al-Bunt (Alpuente) i, **1309b** – I, **1350a**
Bunyāt (Bukhāra) (VIII) i, 1294a – I, 1333b
Būr → Baʿl
al-Burādiʿī ʿAlī (1737) iii, 162a – III, 165b
al-Burāḳ i, **1310a**; ii, 71a, 108a, 785b; vii, 376b – I, **1350a**; II, 72a, 110a, 804b; VII, 378a
al-Burāḳ b. ʿAbd Allāh (Ḳutlugh Khān) (VII) iii, 887a, b – III, 911a, b
Burāḳ (Baraḳ), *ḥādjib* (1235) i, **1311a**; ii, 393a; iv, 32a, 583b; v, 161b, 553a – I, **1351b**; II, 403b; IV, 34b, 607a; V, 159b, 558a
al-Burāḳ (Baraḳ) Khān (Čaghatay) (1271) i, **1311b**; ii,

1b, 3b, 45a, 791b; iv, 811b; v, 39a; vi, 420a – I, **1352a**; II, 1b, 3b, 46a, 810b; IV, 844b; V, 40a; VI, 405a
al-Burāḳ Reʾīs (1499) iv, 882a – IV, 914b
al-Burak al-Ṣarīmī (Ṣuraymī) (660) s, **157a** – S, **157a**
Būrān bint al-Ḥasan b. Sahl (884) i, 897b, **1312a**; ii, 731b; iii, 243b, 345b; vi, 335b – I, 924a, b, **1352b**; II, 750a; III, 250b, 356a; VI, 320a
Būrāniyya → Baḳliyya
Burayda i, 873a, **1312b**; iv, 717a – I, 897b, **1352b**; IV, 746a
Burayda b. al-Ḥuṣayb (680) i, **1313a**; v, 78b; vii, 983a – I, **1353b**; V, 80b; VII, 984a
Burayka/Bureka ii, 454b – II, 466b
Burayka (Banū Rabīʿa) (755) vi, 540a – VI, 524b
al-Buraymī i, 539b, **1313b**; s, 42a, 417b – I, 556b, **1353b**; S, 42b, 417b
Burd, Banū → Ibn Burd
Burda i, **1314b**; iii, 1232a; iv, 316a, 940a; v, 6b, 734a; s, 159a – I, **1354b**; III, 1264a; IV, 330b, 973a; V, 6b, 739b; S, 159a
Burdj i, 248b, **1315a**; iii, 475a – I, 256b, **1355a**; III, 491b
Burdj → Nudjūm
Burdj al-Ṣabī vi, 578b, 582b – VI, 563b, 567a
Burdjān (Bylghār) i, 1305a – I, 1345a
Burdjīs → Mamlūks
Burdjiyya (re(é)giment) i, 1050b, **1324b**; iv, 486a; vi, 316b, 322b – I, 1082a, **1365a**; IV, 507a; VI, 301b, 307a
al-Burdjumī (1033) i, 900b; ii, 962a – I, 927b; II, 984a
Burdur i, **1325a** – I, **1366a**
Bure (Amphila Bey) vi, 642b – VI, 628a
Burgas i, **1325b** – I, **1366b**
Burghaz, Būrghūs → Lüleburgaz
al-Burghāzī, Yaḥyā b. Khalīl i, 323b, 324b; ii, 968a – I, 333a, 334b; II, 990a
Burghush (Burgos) i, **1326a** – I, **1366b**
Burghūth → Muḥammad b. ʿĪsā (Burghūth)
Burghūthiyya i, **1326a**; vii, 868b – **I, 1367a**; VII, 870a
Burgos → Burghūth
Burhām(n)iyya i, 281a; ii, 166a – I, 289b; II, 171b
al-Burhān i, **1326b**; iii, 543b – I, **1367a**; III, 562b
Burhān I (Niẓām-Shahī) (1553) i, 914b, 1069a; iii, 425b, 426a, 1160 a, b; viii, 73a, b– I, 942a, 1101a; III, 439b, 1188b, 1189a; VIII, 75a
Burhān II (Niẓām-Shahī) (1595) ii, 815a, 921b; iii, 426b; vi, 271b; vii, 300a; viii, 73b – II, 834b, 943a; III, 440b; VI, 256a; VII, 302b; VIII, 75b
Burhān III (Niẓām Shāhī) (1632) viii, 74a – VIII, 76a
Burhān, Āl-i (Bukhārā) i, 1295a, **1327b**; iii, 1115a; v, 858a; viii, 749a – I, 1334b, **1368a**; III, 1142a; V, 865a; VIII, 779a
Burhān Muḥammad Ḥusayn b. Khalaf al-Tabrīzī (XVII) i, 1056b, **1327b**; iv, 526a – I, 1088b, **1368a**; IV, 549a
Burhān Burhān b. Abī Sharīf vi, 87b – VI, 85b
Burhān Asaf (XX) vi, 95a – VI, 93a
Burhān al-Dīn, Ḳādī Aḥmad (1398) i, 311b, 432a, 1117b, 1118a, **1327b**; ii, 706a; iv, 623a, 843a, 871a; viii, 581b; s, 324a – I, 321a, 444a, 1151b, 1152a, **1368a**; II, 724a; IV, 647b, 876a, 904b; VIII, 600a; S, 323b
Burhān al-Dīn Gharīb, Mawlānā (1337) i, **1328b**, 1331a; ii, 48a, 51b, 55a, b, 816a; s, 352b – I, **1369b**, 1371b; II, 49a, 52b, 56a, b, 835b; S, 352b
Burhān al-Dīn Ḳuṭb-i ʿĀlam (1453) i, **1329b**; ii, 1125b – I, **1370a**; II, 1153a
Burhān al-Din al-Marghīnānī → al-Marghīnānī
Burhān al-Dīn Muḥaḳḳiḳ, Sayyid (XIII) ii, 393b – II, 404a
Burhān al-Dīn Naṣr b. Aḥmad-i Djām (XII) i, 283a – I, 292a
Burhān ʿImād Shāh (ʿImād Shāhī) (XII) iii, 425a, 1161a – III, 439a, 1189b
Burhān al-Mulk (Nawwāb, Awadh) (1739) i, 757a, **1330a**; ii, 870a; iv, 666a; v, 635a; vii, 316a; viii, 793b; s, 325b – I, 779b, **1370b**; II, 890a; IV, 693a; V, 639a; VII, 318a; VIII, 820b; S, 325a
Burhānī, ʿAbd al-Malik (1073) vii, 489a – VII, 489a
Burhānī Abū Muʿizzi (1116) vi, 276b – VI, 261b
Burhānpūr i, **1330b**; ii, 816a; iii, 446b; vi, 52a, 67b, 369a, 535b, 690a – I, **1371b**; II, 835b; III, 461b; VI, 50b, 65b, 353a, 520a, 677b
al-Burhānpūrī, Muḥammad b. Faḍl Allāh (1590) ix, 296b – IX, 305a
al-Būrī s, 390b – S, 391a
Būrī → Tādj al-Mulūk
Būrī Takīn → Ibrāhīm Tamghač Khān
Buri-Bars (1095) i, 662a, **1331b** – I, 683a, **1372b**
Būrid(e)s i, 216a, **1332a**; ii, 282a – I, 222b, **1372b**; II, 290a
al-Būrīnī, al-Ḥasan (1615) i, **1333a**; vii, 469b – I, **1373b**; VII, 469a
Burḳat al-Amhār vi, 81a – VI, 78b
al-Burḳān (Kuwayt) i, 536b; s, 50a – I, 553a; S, 50b
Burke Sulṭān i, 135a – I, 139a
Bürklüdje Muṣṭafā → Dede Sulṭān
Burḳuʿ, Ḳaṣr s, **157a** – S, **157b**
Burma i, 606a, **1333a**
Burne (Mali) vi, 258a – VI, 242a
Būrrūdh (river/rivière) s, 356b – S, 356a
Bursa i, 4a, 298a, 1225b, **1333b**; ii, 746b; iii, 210b, 211b, 212b, 214a, 215a, 216a; iv, 574a, 1159b; v, 32b, 651a; vi, 3a, 120b, 228a, 366a, 530b; viii, 175b; s, 170a, 282b – I, 4a, 307b, 1262a, **1374a**; II, 765a; III, 216b, 217b, 218b, 220a, 221a, 222a; IV, 597a, 1191b; V, 33b, 655a; VI, 3a, 118a, 222a, 350a, 514b; VIII, 178a; S, 170b, 282b
Bursa Edict/Édit de - vi, 496b – VI, 482a
Bursalî → Aḥmad Pasha
Bursalî, Djelīlī Ḥamīd-zāde (1569) v, 1105b – V, 1101b
Bursalî Ṭāhir (XX) ii, 980b; iv, 284b – II, 1003a; IV, 296b
al-Bursawī, Muḥammad b. ʿAbd al-Ḥalīm (XVIII) vii, 469b – VII, 469a
Bursuḳ (1089) i, 1052b, **1336a** – I, 1084a, **1376b**
Bursuḳ b. Bursuḳ (XII) i, 1336b, 1337a; iii, 1118b; v, 924b – I, 1377a; III, 1146a; V, 930a
al-Bursukī → Aḳ Sunḳur
al-Burt i, **1337a** – I, **1377b**
Burṭās/Burdās i, 1305b, **1337b**; ii, 69b, 817a – I, 1345b, **1378a**; II, 71a, 836b
Burtuḳāl i, 58b, **1338b** – I, 60b, **1378b**
Burūdj → Minṭaḳat al-
Burūdjird → Barūdjird
Burūdjirdī, Muḥammad Ḥusayn Ṭabāṭabāʾī, Āyatullāh al-ʿUẓmā (1961) iv, 165b; vi, 548b, 552a, b, 553a; vii, 300a, 448a, 762b; s, 104a, **157b** – IV, 172b; VI, 533a, 536b, 537a, b; VII, 302a, 449b, 764a; S, 103a, **157b**
Burūdjirdī, Shaykh Asad Allāh s, 75a – S, 75b
Buruḳlus (Proclus) i, 234b, **1339b**; ii, 765a, 929b; iii, 1129b; iv, 129b – I, 241b, **1380a**; II, 783b, 951b; III, 1158a; IV, 135b
Burullus i, **1340b** – I, **1381a**
Burushaski s, **158b** – S, **158b**
Burūsho s, 158b – S, 158b
Burzōē (VI) i, 1359a; iv, 503a, b – I, 1399a; IV, 525a, b

al-Burzulī, Abu 'l-Ḳāsim (1438) i, **1341a**; vii, 1052b – I, **1381a**; VII, 1054b
Busayra → Ḳarḳīsiyā
Bū<u>sh</u>ahr (Bū<u>sh</u>īr) i, 928a, 1013b, **1341a**; iii, 1191a; iv, 851a; vi, 358a – I, 956b, 1044b, **1381b**; III, 1221a; IV, 884a; VI, 342a
Bushāḳ, Fa<u>kh</u>r al-Dīn Aḥmad b. Ḥallā<u>dj</u> (1424) i, **1342a**; iii, 355b; iv, 66a; vii, 567b; viii, 45b; s, 415b – I, **1382b**; III, 366b; IV, 69b; VII, 568b; VIII, 46a; S, 416a
Bushāḳ-i Aṭʿimma → Bushāḳ, Fa<u>kh</u>r al-Dīn
Bū<u>sh</u>an<u>dj</u> i, **1342b**; iv, 1073a – I, **1382b**; IV, 1105a
al-Bū<u>sh</u>an<u>dj</u>ī, Abu 'l-Ḥasan b. Sahl (X) vi, 224a – VI, 217b
al-Bu<u>sh</u>ārrāt i, **1343a** – I, **1383a**
Bu<u>sh</u>atlis i, 653a, 657a; iv, 588a; v, 276b, 775a – I, 673b, 677b; IV, 612a; V, 274b, 781a
al-Bū<u>sh</u>ikrī, Muḥammad b. ʿAbd Allāh (1865) x, 346b – X, 372a
Bū<u>sh</u>īr → Bū<u>sh</u>ahr
Bu<u>sh</u>ra iv, 459b – IV, 480a
al-Bu<u>sh</u>rawī, ʿAbd Allāh b. al-Ḥā<u>dj</u><u>dj</u> Muḥammad al-Tūnī (1666) s, 57a – S, 57b
Būṣīr, Abūṣīr i, **1343a**; iii, 961b; iv, 774a; vi, 411a, 624b; s, 159a – I, 1383b; III, 986a; IV, 805a; VI, 396a, 609b; S, 158b
al-Būṣīrī, <u>Sh</u>araf al-Dīn (1294) i, 595b, 821b, 1011b, 1070b, 1314b; iii, 720b; iv, 316a, 1134a; v, 958b; s, **158b**, 404b –
I, 615a, 844b, 1042b, 1102b, 1354b; III, 743a; IV, 330b, 1165b; V, 962b; S, **158b**, 404b
Busr b. Abī Arṭāt (VII) i, 109a, 695b, **1343b**; ii, 481a; iii, 782a; v, 532b, 533a; ix, 555a; s, 230b – I, 111b, 717a, **1384a**; II, 493a; III, 805b; V, 536b, 537a; IX, 577a; S, 230b
Busr al-Ḥarīrī v, 593b – V, 597a
Buṣrā → Boṣrā
Bust i, **1344a**; ii, 1054a, 1100b; v, 230a, 690b, 691a; vi, 345a, 523a; viii, 795b –
I, **1384a**; II, 1078b, 1126b; V, 228a, 695b, 696a; VI, 329a, 507b; VIII, 822b
Būstān i, **1345b**; ii, 908b, 1019a; v, 888b – I, **1385b**; II, 929b, 1042b; V, 895a
Būstān Efendi (1570) ii, 880b – II, 900b
al-Bustānī, Āl s, **159a** – S, **159a**
al-Bustānī, ʿAbd Allāh (1930) s, **159b** – S, **159b**
al-Bustānī, Buṭrus b. Būlus (1883) i, 596b; ii, 428b, 467a; iv, 525a; v, 794b; vi, 712a; vii, 902b; s, **159b** – I, 616a; II, 440a, 479a; IV, 547b; V, 800b; VI, 700b; VII, 903a; S, **159b**
al-Bustānī, Buṭrus b. Sulaymān (1969) s, **160a** – S, **160a**
al-Bustanī, Karam (1966) s, **160b** – S, **160b**
al-Bustānī, Saʿīd b. Salīm (1977) v, 188a; vii, 903a; s, **160b** – V, 185b; VII, 903b; S, **160b**
al-Bustānī, Salīm b. Buṭrus (1884) v, 188a; vii, 902a; s, 160a, **161a** – V, 185a; VII, 902b; S, 160a, **160b**
al-Bustānī, Sulaymān b. <u>Kh</u>aṭṭār (1925) i, 597b; iii, 112a; s, **161b** – I, 617a; III, 114b; S, **161a**
al-Bustānī, Wadīʿ (1954) vi, 615b; s, **162a** – VI, 600b; S, **162a**
al-Bustī, Abu 'l-Fatḥ (1010) i, **1348b**; iv, 61a – I, **1388b**; IV, 64b
al-Bustī, Abū Ḥātim Muḥammad b. Ḥibbān (965) v, 1126b; vii, 692a – V, 1122b; VII, 692b
al-Buṭāḥ (Baʿūḍa) vi, 267b – VI, 252b
Buṭāna (Kasala) iv, 686a, b – IV, 714a, b
Buṭayn → Nu<u>dj</u>ūm
Buṭnān, wādī i, **1348b**, 1357b; vi, 378a – I, **1389a**, 1398a; VI, 362b
Butr, Banū i, **1349b**; vi, 310b, 741a, 815a, 840a; ix, 894b – I, **1389b**; VI, 295b, 730b, 805a, 831a; IX, 930b
Butriyya → Abtariyya
Buṭrus <u>Gh</u>ālī (XX) vii, 715b – VII, 716b
Buṭrus Karāma (1851) s, **162b** – S, **162b**
Buṭrus al-Tūlawī (1745) ii, 795a – II, 814a
al-Buwayb (battle/bataille) (636) iv, 386a – IV, 403a
Buwayhid(e)s/Būyid(e)s i, 19a, 20a, 131b, 211b, 434a, 439b, 512b, 551b, 696a, 866b, 899b, 1045b, 1073b, **1350a**; ii, 144a, 178b, 192b, 214b, 326a, 487a, 506a, 748b, 1050b; iii, 46b, 159a, 1201b, 1255b; iv, 18a, 19a, 23a, b, 46b, 100b, 208b, 221b, 266a, 293b; v, 621b, 622a, 824a; vi, 66a, 148a, 261b, 272b, 275a, 433a, 440a, 549a, 600b, 669b, 941b; vii, 477b, 723b; viii, 472a; ix, 595b; s, 12b, 23a, 56b, 118a, b, 119a, b, 192a, 267b, 363a –
I, 20a, 21a, 135b, 217b, 446a, 452a, 528a, 569a, 717a, 891a, 926b, 1077b, 1105b, **1390a**; II, 148a, 184a, 198b, 221a, 335b, 499a, 518b, 767a, 1075a; III, 48b, 162b, 1232a, 1288a; IV, 19a-b, 20b, 25a, 49b, 104b, 217b, 231a, 278a, 307a; V, 626a, 830a; VI, 63b, 64a, 146b, 245b, 257b, 260a, 418a, 425a, 534a, 585a, 656a, 933b; VII, 477a, 724b; VIII, 488a; IX, 618a; S, 13a, 23b, 57a, 117b, 118a, b, 193a, 267a, 363a
Buwayr Aḥmadī iii, 1107a – III, 1134a
al-Buwayṭī, Yūsuf b. Yaḥyā (840) vii, 4a – VII, 4a
Buxar i, **1357b** – I, **1397b**
Būyids → Buwayhid(e)s
Büyük Ada vi, 588b – VI, 573a
Büyük Sulaymān Pa<u>sh</u>a → Sulaymān Pa<u>sh</u>a Büyük
Buyuruldu i, **1357b** – I, **1397b**
Buzāʿā i, 1349a, **1357b**; viii, 131a – I, 1389b, **1398a**; VIII, 134a
Būz-Abeh (1137) i, **1358a**; iv, 498a – I, **1398a**; IV, 519b
Būzači (Boz Ḥā<u>dj</u>ī) (pe(é)ninsula(e) vi, 415a, 416b; s, 168b, 169a – VI, 400a, 401b; S, 169a
Buzā<u>kh</u>a i, **1358b** – I, **1398b**
Būzān (XI) i, 1336b – I, 1376b
Buzan (1334) ii, 4a – II, 4a
Būzār → Ong <u>Kh</u>ān
al-Būz<u>dj</u>ānī → Abu 'l-Wafāʾ
Buz<u>gh</u>āla <u>Kh</u>āna ii, 116a – II, 118b
al-Būzīdī, Muḥammad (1814) iii, 696b, 697a, 700b – III, 718b, 719a, 723a
Buzur<u>dj</u>mihr → Buzurgmihr
Buzurg b. <u>Sh</u>ahriyār (956) i, 203b, 204a, 570b, **1358b**; ii, 583b; vi, 704a; vii, 245b; viii, 292b, 595a; ix, 698b –
I, 209b, 210a, 589a, **1398b**; II, 598a; VI, 692b; VII, 247a; VIII, 301a, 614a; IX, 727b
Buzurgmihr (Buzur<u>dj</u>mihr) (VI) i, **1358b**; iv, 53b, 503a, b; viii, 106b – I, **1399a**; IV, 56b, 525a, b; VIII, 108b
Buzurg-ummīd, Kiya (1138) i, 353b, **1359b**; v, 656b – I, 364a, **1399b**; V, 660b
Byblos → <u>Dj</u>ubayl
Byzantin(e)s → Rūm
Byzantion → Istanbul
Byzantium → Rūm
Bzz̤edu<u>kh</u> → Čerkes

C

Cabra → Ḳabra
Cachemire → Ka<u>sh</u>mīr
Čāč → Ta<u>sh</u>kent
Čāčī, Badr al-Dīn Muḥammad → Badr-i Čāčī

Čač-nāma iii, 459a; vii, 405b; s, **162a** – III, 475a; VII, 407a; S, **162a**
Čad, Chad iv, 540a, b, 566b; s, **163b**, 218a – IV, 563b, 564a, 589a; S, **163b**, 217b
Cádiz/Cadix → Ḳādis
Čādur (chador) v, 749b, 750a – V, 755a, 756a
Caesar → Ḳayṣar
Caesarea → Ḳaysariyya; Kayseri; S̲h̲ars̲h̲al
Caffa → Kefe
Čag̲h̲al-og̲h̲lu → Čig̲h̲ālazāde Sinān Pas̲h̲a
Čag̲h̲ānī, Abū ʿAlī Aḥmad b. Muḥtād̲j̲ (955) vi, 115b; vii, 477b; viii, 110a – VI, 113b; VII, 477a; VIII, 112a
Čag̲h̲āniyān ii, **1a**; vii, 477b; s, 50b, 386b – II, **1a**; VII, 477a; S, 51b, 387a
Čag̲h̲ān-rūd ii, **2a** – II, **2a**
Čag̲h̲atay K̲h̲ān b. Čingiz-K̲h̲ān (1241) i, 418b, 1105b; ii, **2a**, 3a, 43a, 44a, 269a, 571b; iii, 198a, 1120a; iv, 584a; vi, 77b, 494b, 518a – I, 430b, 1139a; II, **2a**, 3a, 44a, 45a, 277a, 586a; III, 203a, 1148a; IV, 607b; VI, 75a, 480a, 518a
Čag̲h̲atay K̲h̲ānat(e) i, 120b, 1295b, 1311b; ii, **3a**, 45b; iii, 1100a; iv, 274a, 587a; v, 858a, b; x, 511b; s, 96b, 98a, 227b, 240a, 246a – I, 124a, 1335a, 1352a; II, **3a**, 46b; III, 1127b; IV, 272a, 609b; V, 865a, b; X, 548a; S, 96a, 97a, 227b, 240a, 246a
—literature/littérature i, 813b; ii, 792a; iii, 317a; iv, 527a; v, 836a, 859b; x, 708a, **721a**; s, 46a, b – I, 836b; II, 811a; III, 327a; IV, 550a; V, 842b, 866b; X, 752b, **766b**; S, 46b
Čag̲h̲mīnī → al-D̲j̲ag̲h̲mīnī
Čag̲h̲rî-Beg Dāwūd (Sald̲j̲ūḳ) (1060) i, 662a, 1159a; ii, **4a**, 1108b; iii, 1114a; iv, 25a, 26b, 347b; v, 58a; vi, 620b; viii, 69b; s, 195a – I, 682b, 1193b; II, **4a**, 1134b; III, 1141b; IV, 26b, 28b, 362a; V, 60a; VI, 605b; VIII, 71a; S, 195a
Čahār Aymāḳ, Banū i, 224b; ii, **5b** – I, 231a; II, **5b**
Čahār Bāg̲h̲ (Iṣfahān) s, 275a – S, 275a
Čahār -Lang i, 955b; iii, 1105a, b; v, 822b – I, 985a; III, 1132b; V, 828b
Čahār Maḥall iv, 98a, b; s, 147b – IV, 102a, b; S, 147b
Čāhbār i, 1282a, 1283a – I, 1321a, b
Caïd → Ḳāʾid
Čāʾildā, S̲h̲ayk̲h̲ (XV) s, 73b – S, 74a
Caïn → Ḥābīl wa Ḳābīl
Cairo/le Caire → al-Ḳāhira
Čaka (Tzachas) (XI) i, 466a; ii, 686b; v, 505a; s, 168b – I, 480a; II, 704a; V, 508b; S, 168b
Čaḳa b. Nog̲h̲ay (XIV) i, 1302b; ii, 610b – I, 1342a; II, 625b
Čaḳa Bey (Sald̲j̲ūḳ) (1090) vii, 47a; viii, 890a; ix, 679b – VII, 47b; 920b; IX, 708b
Čakarsaz i, 424b – I, 436b
Čakîrd̲j̲î-bas̲h̲î ii, **6a**, 614b – II, **6a**, 629b
Čak, Tād̲j̲ī (XVI) s, 423b – S, 424a
Čaḳmaḳ, al-Malik al-Ẓāhir Sayf al-Dīn (Mamlūk) (1453) i, 138b, 281a, 1032b; ii, **6a**, 239b, 598b; iii, 187a, 1198a; vi, 195a; vii, 173b – I, 142b, 289b, 1064a; II, **6a**, 246b, 613b; III, 191b, 1228b; VI, 179a; VII, 175a
Čakmak Mustafa Fevzi (Kavaklî) (1950) ii, **6b**; iii, 527a – II, **6b**; III, 545a
Čaks, Banū iii, 420a; iv, 709a; vii, 300b; s, 131b, **167a**, 324b, 354a, 423b – III, 433b; IV, 737a,b; VII, 302b; S, 131a, **167a**, 324a, 353b, 424a
Čākur, Mīr (Balūcistān) i, 1005b – I, 1036b
Čala → Buk̲h̲ārā
Čalabī → ʿUnwān, Muḥammad Riḍā
Calabria/Calabre → Ḳillawriya
Calatayud → Ḳalʿat Ayyūb
Calatrava → Ḳalʿat Rabāḥ
Calcutta (Kalikātā) i, 979a; ii, **7a**, 426a; v, 201b; vi, 198b; s, 106a, 247a – I, 1009a; II, **7a**, 437a; V, 199a; VI, 183a; S, 105b, 247b
Čāldîrān (battle/bataille) (1514) i, 1030b, 1066b; ii, **7b**; iv, 35a, 186b; v, 35a, 457a; vi, 200b, 201a, b, 541a; viii, 768a; ix, 128b – I, 1062a, 1098b; II, **7b**; IV, 37b, 195a; V, 36a, 460a; VI, 185a, b, 526a; VIII, 793b; IX, 133b
Calender/Calendrier x, 258b – X, 277b
Čalî Bey (1416) i, 947b – I, 976b
Calicut → Kalikat
Caliz → K̲h̲alisioi
Čam ii, **8b**; iii, 1209a – II, **8b**; III, 1239b
Čamalal, Banū i, 504a; iv, 630b – I, 519b; IV, 655b
Čambāl (river/fleuve) vi, 536a – VI, 520b
Cambay → K̲h̲ambāyat
Cambodia/Cambodge → Ḳimār
Cameroons/Cameroun ii, **9a**; s, 218a – II, **9a**; S, 218a
Camieniec → Kaminča
Čamis̲h̲gezek v, 459a; vi, 71a – V, 462a; VI, 69a
Čamlîbel, Fārūḳ Nāfid̲h̲ (1973) s, **167b**, 324b – S, **167b**, 324a
Camondo, Avram (1873) s, **168a** – S, **168a**
Čampā (Champa) → Ṣanf
Čāmpānēr ii, **10b**, 1127a; iii, 445b, 482a, 575b; v, 1216b; vi, 50a, b, 51a, b, 52a, 53b, 270a, 310a; vii, 314a – II, **11a**, 1153b; III, 460b, 498b, 595b; V, 1206b; VI, 48b, 49a, b, 50a, 51b, 254b, 295a; VII, 316b
Campiña → Kanbāniya
Čʿan (Laz) v, 713b, 714a – V, 719a
Čanaḳ-ḳalʿe Bog̲h̲azî i, 4b, 1252a; ii, **11a**, 209a; iv, 628b, 884b, 1169b; v, 259a – I, 4b, 1290a; II, **11b**, 215b; IV, 653b, 917b, 1202b; V, 257a
Canary Islands/Canaries, Îles → al-D̲j̲azāʾir al-K̲h̲ālida
Čand Bībī bint Ḥusayn I (Niẓām S̲h̲āhī) (1604) viii, 74a – VIII, 75b, 76a
Čānd Mīnār vi, 368b, 369a – VI, 352b, 353b
Čandā Ṣāḥib → Ḥusayn Dūst K̲h̲ān
Čandarlî → D̲j̲andarlî
Čandar-og̲h̲lu → Isfendiyār-og̲h̲lu
Čānd Bībī bint Ḥusayn I (Niẓām S̲h̲āhī) (1604) i, 81a, 303a, 1202b; iii, 15b, 426b, 626a; viii, 74a – I, 83b, 312b, 1238a; III, 16a, 440b, 647a; VIII, 75b, 76a
Čandērī ii, **12b**; iii, 446a; v, 644b; vi, 52b, 53a, 54b, 55a, 62a, 126a; s, 331b – II, **12b**; III, 461a; V, 648b; VI, 51a, 52a, 52b, 60a, 124a; S, 331a
Candia/-e → Ḳandiya
Čandra Bhān Brahman (1663) vii, 343a – VII, 345a
Čandrā Sēn (Bulands̲h̲ahr) (1193) i, 1300a – I, 1339b
Čandragiri iii, 148b – III, 152a
Canea → Ḥānya
Čanēsar, Malik Sinān al-Dīn (XIII) iii, 1155b – III, 1183b
Canestrine → Ḳinnasrīn
Čangs̲h̲i (Čag̲h̲atay K̲h̲ānat(e)) (1334) ii, 4a – II, 4a
Canik → D̲j̲ānīk
Čankîrî ii, **13a**; v, 248a, 257a – II, **13b**; V, 245b, 254b
Cannanore → Kannanur
Čannēy K̲h̲ān (Dāwūdpōtr) ii, 185a – II, 191a
Cantemir → Ḳantimūr
Canton → K̲h̲ānfū
Čao i, 903a; ii, **14a**, 982a; iv, 31a – I, 930a; **14b**, 1004b; IV, 33b
Čapakčur → Bingöl
Čapan-og̲h̲lu → Derebey
Čapanog̲h̲lu Aḥmad → Aḥmad Pas̲h̲a
Čapanog̲h̲lu D̲j̲alāl al-Dīn Pas̲h̲a iii, 88b – III, 90b
Čapan-og̲h̲ullarî (Čoban-og̲h̲ullarî) i, 469a; ii, 206b,

207a; iv, 843b; s, **171b** – I, 483a; II, 213b; IV, 876b; S, **172a**
Čapan-zāde Agāh Efendi (1885) ii, 207b, 466a – II, 214a, 478a
Čapar b. Ḳaydu (Mongol) (XIV) ii, 3b, **14b**, 45b; vi, 783a; s, 240a – II, 3b, **14b**, 46b; VI, 772b; S, 240a
Capsa → Ḳafsa
Caracul → Karakay
Carcastillo → Ḳarḳastal
Čārdjūy → Āmul
Čārī (river/rivière) s, 327a – S, 326b
Čarkhī, Mawlānā Yaʿḳūb (1447) vii, 934a – VII, 934b
Čarlowicz → Ḳarlofča
Carmathians → Ḳarmaṭī
Carmona → Ḳarmūna
Carnatic → Karnātak
Carpenitze → Kerbenesh
Carthage/Carthagène → Ḳarṭādjanna
Casablanca → Dār al-Bayḍāʾ
Casbah → Ḳaṣaba (town/ville)
Casena → Katsina
Čāshna-gīr ii, **15a** – II, **15a**
Čashnagīr-bashi̊ ii, **15a** – II, **15a**
Caspian Sea/Caspienne, mer → Baḥr al-Khazar
Castamina, Castemol → Ḳasṭamūnī
Castilla → Ḳasṭīliya
Castille → Ḳashtāla
Castillo del Hierro → Firrīsh
Castriota, Georges → Iskender Beg
Castro giovanni → Ḳaṣryānnih
Cata → Ḳaṭā
Čatāldja ii, **15b** – II, **15b**
Catania/Catane → Ṣiḳilliya
Čātgām → Chittagong
Caucasus/-e → Ḳabḳ
Čāʾūsh (çavuş) ii, **16a** – II, **16a**
Cavalle → Ḳawāla
Čawdharī Khāliḳ al-Zamān (XX) vi, 78a – VI, 76a
Čawdor (Čawdi̊r), Banū ii, 16a; vi, 416a, b; s, 143b, **168b** – II, 16b; VI, 401a, b; S, 143a, **168b**
Čawgān ii, **16b**, 954a, 1035b; v, 688a – II, **16b**, 976a, 1059b; V, 693a
Čawhān ii, 1122b; iii, 167b, 168a, 225a; iv, 1023a – II, 1148b; III, 171b, 232a; IV, 1055a
Čawli → Fakhr al-Dawla; Mubāriz al-Dīn
Čawli̊ Saḳāwu (amīr) (XII) vii, 408a – VII, 409b
Cawnpore → Kānpur
Čawundur → Čawdor
Čay ii, **17b**, 904b; v, 1145b – II, **17b**, 925b; V, 1137a
Čāy-khāna s, **169a** – S, **169b**
Čaylaḳ Tewfīḳ (1892) ii, 474a; s, **169a** – II, 486b; S, **170b**
Čečens ii, **18a**; iii, 1235b, 1236a; iv, 351a; vii, 351b; x. 920b; – II, **18a**; III, 1267b, 1268a; IV, 366b; VII, 353b; X,
Čeh s, **170b** – S, **170b**
Celal Nuri Ileri → Ileri, Djelāl Nūrī
Celebes/Célèbes → Sulawesi
Čelebī ii, **19a**, 394b – II, **19a**, 405a
Čelebi Efendi → Djalāl al-Din Rūmī; Muḥammad b. Aḥmad Ṭāhā-zāde
Čelebi-zāde Ismāʿīl ʿĀṣim (1760) ii, **19b**, 1076a – II, **20a**, 1101a
Čeltükdji → Kürekčis
Cemalettin Mahir → Kemal Tahir
Cenap Şehabettin → Djanāb Shihāb al-Dīn
Čendereli → Djandarli̊
Čepni, Banū ii, **20b** – II, **20b**
Cercina, Cercinitis → Ḳarḳana
Čeremiss/Čeremisses ii, **20b** – II, **21a**
Cerigo → Čoka Adasi̊
Čerkes i, 32b, 64b, 470b, 732b, 1000a, 1050b, 1189b; ii, **21a**, 172b, 458a, 781b; iii, 316a; iv, 345b, 350a, 351a, 569a, 597a; v, 139a, 288a; vi, 315b, 325b, 382b; vii, 351a; x, 921a – I, 33b, 66b, 484b, 754b, 1031a, 1082a, 1224b; II, **22a**, 177b, 470a, 800a; III, 325b; IV, 360a, 365a, 366a, 591b, 621a; V, 141b, 286a, b; VI, 300b, 310a, 366b; VII, 353a; X,
Čerkes Edhem (1949) ii, **25b** – II, **21b**
Čerkes Ḥāfiẓ Meḥmed Pasha (XIX) vi, 232a; viii, 84b – VI, 226al VIII, 86b
Čerkes Ismāʿīl Pasha (1861) ii, 878b – II, 899a
Čerkes Meḥmed Tewfik (1949) ii, 25b, 26a – II, 21b
Čerkes Reshīd (1951) ii, 25b, 26a – II, 21b
Čerkeshī, Muṣṭafā (1814) ix, 155b – IX, 161a
Čerkeshiyya iv, 991b – IV, 1024a
César → Ḳayṣar
Césarée → Ḳaysariyya; Ḳayseri; Sharshal
Česhme (source) ii, **26a** – II, **26b**
Česhme (town/ville) vi, 69a – VI, 67a
Česhmīzāde, Muṣṭafā Rashīd (1770) ii, **26b** – II, **26b**
Çetin Altan (XX) vi, 95b – VI, 93b
Ceuta → Sabta
Cevat Rifat Atilhan s, 296b – S, 296b
Cevat Şaki̊r Kabaağackhli̊ → Haliḳarnas Bali̊ḳči̊si̊
Ceylon/Ceylan i, 177b; ii, **26b**, 577a; v, 297a – I, 182b; II, **27a**, 591b; V, 296b
Čeyrek ii, **28b** – II, **28b**
Chad → Čad
al-Chādirchī, Kāmil (XX) iv, 125a – IV, 130b
Chah → Shāh
Cham → Čam; Ḥām
Chamba → Djāba
Chamito-Sémitique → Ḥām; Sām
Chandax → al-Khandaḳ
Čhat ii, **28b**, 29a – II, **29a**, b
Čhatr, Čhattar → Miẓalla
Chaudhri Raḥmat ʿAlī (XX) viii, 241a – VIII, 246b
Chaul (naval battle/bataille navale) (1508) vi, 51a – VI, 49b
Chechaouen → Shafshāwan
Cheikh → Shaykh
Cheikho → Shaykhū Luwīs
Chélif v, 1173b, 1175a, 1179a, b, 1180a; vi, 404a, b – V, 1163b, 1165a, 1169a, b, 1170a; VI, 388b, 389a
Chella → Shāla
Cheng Ho (XX) v, 849b, 850a – V, 853b, 854a
Cherchell → Sharshāl
Chérif → Sharīf
China/-e → al-Ṣīn
Ch'in-chi-p'u v, 847a, b, 848a, b – V, 851b, 852a, b
Chinguetti → Shinḳīt
Chionites i, 225b, 226a; iii, 303b – I, 232b, 233a; III, 312b
Chio(s) → Saḳi̊z Ada
Chitral ii, **29a**, 317a; vi, 780a; s, 158b – II, **29b**, 326a; VI, 769b; S, 158b
Chittagong i, 606a, 1333a; ii, **31b**; iv, 177b – I, 625b, 1272b; II, **32b**; IV, 186a
Chleuh → Tashelḥīt
Chocim → Khotin
Chole (island/île) → Mafia
Chonae → Khōnās
Chorfa → Sharīf
Chosroës → Kisrā
Čhoti̊ Panḍuʾā vi, 368b – VI, 352b
Čhotī Begam (XIX) ii, 83b – II, 85a
Chum, Hajji (Zanzibar) s, 351b – S, 351b
Chypre → Ḳubrus
el-Cid → al-Sīd
Čift-resmi i, 999a, 1169b; ii, **32a**, 146b, 907a; iv, 211a

– I, 1030a, 1204b; II, **32b**, 150b, 928a; IV, 220b
Čiftlik   i, 1264b, 1266a, b, 1268b, 1269a; ii, **32b**, 907a
– I, 1303b, 1304b, 1305b, 1307b, 1308a; II, **33a**, 928a
Čighāla-zāde Sinān Pasha (1605)   i, 8a, 267b, 904a; ii, **33b**; iii, 1001a; s, 238b –
I, 8a, 275b, 931a; II, **34b**; III, 1026a; S, 238b
Čihil Sutūn palace/palais (Iṣfahān)   vi, 526b, 527b; s, 257a, 259b, 325b – VI, 511a, b; S, 256b, 259a, 325a
Čiḥrāzād   → Humāy
Cilicia/-e   i, 184a; ii, **34b**, 65b – I, 189a; II, **35b**, 67a
Čilla   → Khalwa
Čimkent   ii, **39a** – II, **39b**
Čīn   → al-Ṣīn
Cin   → Djinn
Činārūd   vi, 495a – VI, 480b
Čīn-Kālān   → Khānfū
Čīn Ḳilic Khān   → Āṣaf Djāh I
Čīn-Temūr (XIII)   ii, 606a; s, 246a – II, 621a; S, 246a
Čingāne   ii, **40b** – II, **41a**
Činghiz Khān (Mongol Great Khān) (1227)   i, 121a, 227a, 418b, 879b, 1295a; ii, 2a, 38a, **41a**, 393a, 571a, 607a, 894a; iii, 198a, 472a; iv, 30a; v, 391b, 858a; vi, 16a, 77a, 417b, 537a, 809b; vii, 232a, b, 997b; s, 176b –
I, 124b, 233b, 430b, 905a, 1335a; II, 2a, 38b, **42a**, 403a, 585b, 622a, 914b; III, 202b, 488b; IV, 32a; V, 392b, 865a; VI, 14a, 75a, 402b, 521b, 799b; VII, 234b, 999b; S, 177b
Činghiz Khān (Gudjarāt) (1567)   vii, 133b – VII, 135b
Čingizid(e)s   ii, **44a**; iv, 723b; s, 97a – II, **44b**; IV, 752b; S, 96b
Činī Darwāza (Māhūr)   vi, 87a – VI, 85b
Čīnīōt (Cīnyöt)   ii, **47a** – II, **48a**
Cintra   → Shintara
Čirāgh 'Alī (1895)   iii, 431b; iv, 170b – III, 445b; IV, 177b
Čirāgh-i Dihlī (1356)   ii, **47b**, 51a, 54a, 55a, b, 392a, 1114b; iii, 429b – II, **48b**, 52a, b, 56a, b, 402b, 1141a; III, 443b
Čirāghān (palace/palais, Istanbul)   ii, **49a**; vi, 531b – II, **49b**; VI, 515b
Circars   → Sarkārs
Circassians/Circassiens   → Čerkes
Circesium   → Ḳarḳīsiyā
Čirkīn, Bāḳir 'Alī   vii, 534a – VII, 534a
Čirmen   ii, **49a** – II, **50a**
Cirta   → Ḳusṭanṭīna
Čishtī, Khʷādja Ḳuṭb al-Dīn Mawdūd (1181)   vi, 872a – VI, 863a
Čishtī, Muʿīn al-Dīn Ḥasan (1236)   i, 72b, 208a, 912a, 1024a; ii, 48b, **49b**, 50b, 378b, 796b; iii, 429a; v, 546b; vi, 697b, 867a; vii, 932a; x, 255b; s, 5a, 293b, 353b –
I, 74b, 214b, 940a, 1055b; II, 49b, **50b**, 51a, 389a, 815b; III, 443a; V, 551a; VI, 685b, 857b; VII, 932b; 274b; S, 4a, 293a, 353a
Čishtī, Shaykh Ibban   s, 74a – S, 74a
Čishtī-Niẓāmī   s, 293a, 360b – S, 293a, 360b
Čishtī-Ṣābirī   → Ṣābiriyya
Čishtiyya   i, 95a; ii, **50b**, 137b, 296b, 421a, 796b, 1115b; iii, 167b, 429a, 433a, 1174b; iv, 48a, 507a, 1026b; vii, 898a; x, 322b; s, 5a, 312b, 313a, 353a –
I, 98a; II, **51a**, 141b, 304b, 431b, 815b, 1141b; III, 171a, 443a, 447a, 1203a; IV, 50b, 529a, 1058b; VII, 898b; S, 4a, 312b, 353a; X, 347a
Čishumī, Khʷādja Tādj al-Dīn 'Alī b. Shams al-Dīn Sarbadārid(e)) (1351)   ix, 48a – IX, 49a
Čitawr, Čitōr   iii, 457a, 482b; vi, 53a, b, 55a, 270a, 272a, 309b, 310a, 407a, 1027a; s, 105a – III, 473a, 499b; VI, 51b, 53a, 254b, 257a, 295a, 391b, 1020a; S, 104b

Čitr   → Ghāshiya
Čitrāl   → Chitral
Čittagong   → Chittagong
Čiwi Ilyāsii (XV)   ii, 56b – II, 57b
Čiwi-zāde, 'Abdī Čelebi (1552)   ii, **56b** – II, **57b**
Čiwi-zāde, Muḥammad (1587)   ii, **56b**; vii, 469a – II, **57b**; VII, 468b
Čiwi-zāde, Muḥyi al-Dīn Shaykh Muḥammad (1547)   ii, **56b** – II, **57b**
Cizrî, Melayê (XVII)   v, 482a – V, 484b
Claudias   → Ḳalāwdhiya
Čōbān   → Čūbān
Čoban Girāylar   ii, 1113b – II, 1139b
Čōbān-oghullari   → Čapan-oghullari
Čoghondur   i, 99b – I, 102b
Coilom   → Kūlam
Coïmbra/-e   → Ḳulumriyya
Čoka   → Ḳumāsh
Čoka Adasî   ii, **57a** – II, **58a**
Čökermish, amīr (XII)   vii, 408a – VII, 409b
Cölemerik   ii, **57a**; v, 456b – II, **58a**; V, 459a
Collyridia(e)ns   vi, 629b – VI, 614b
Colomb-Béchar   ii, **57b** – II, **58b**
Colonia   → Shābīn Ḳarā Ḥiṣār
Čomaḳ Baba (Marʿash)   vi, 510a, VI, 495a
Comania   → Dasht-i Ḳipčaḳ
Comans   → Ḳipčaḳ
Comnenus/Comnène, Alexis (1118)   v, 103b, 505a, 712b – V, 105b, 106a, 508b, 717b
Comnenus/Comnène, Isaac Ducas (XII)   v, 302b – V, 302a
Comnenus/Comnène, John/Jean (1143)   ii, 37a, 110b; v, 712b; vi, 380a – II, 38a, 113a; V, 717b; VI, 364b
Comnenus/Comnène, Manuel (1180)   i, 466b, 289b, 791b; ii, 37a, b, 111a, 715a; v, 104a – I, 480b, 813a, 815a; II, 38a, 113b, 733b; V, 106b
Comores   → Ḳumr
Conakry   → Ḳonakry
Congo (river-country/rivière-pays)   ii, **58a**; iv, 749b, 750b – II, **59a**; IV, 780a, b
Constantine III (al-Ḳurdj)(1414)   v, 492a, b – V, 495a, b
Constantine/Constantin   → Ḳusṭanṭīna
Constantinus Africanus   i, 381a; ii, **59b**; s, 271b – I, 392a; II, **60b**; S, 271b
Constantin(e) of/de Lampron (XIII)   ii, 37b, 38a – II, 38b
Constantinople   → Istanbul; Ḳusṭanṭīniyya
Constanza   → Köstendje
Consul   ii, **60b** – II, **61b**
Čōpān   → Čūbān
Čopan-ata   ii, **61a**, 69b – II, **62b**, 70b
Coptos   → Ḳifṭ
Copt(e)s   → Ḳibṭ
Coran   → al-Ḳurʾān
Čorbadjî   ii, **61b** – II, **62b**
Córdoba/-oue   → Ḳurṭuba
Coré   → Ḳārūn
Corea/Corée   → al-Sīlā
Corfu/Corfou   → Körfüz
Coria   → Ḳūriya
Corinth/-e   → Kordos
Čorlu   ii, **62a**; s, 282a – II, **63a**; S, 282a
Čorlulu 'Alī Pasha   → 'Alī Pasha Čorlulu
Cormaghun (XIII)   iv, 349b, 670a – IV, 364a, 697b
Corne d'Or   → Ghalaṭa; Istanbul; Takhtaḳalʿe
Coromandel   → Maʿbar
Coron   → Ḳoron
Corsica/Corse   s, 120b – S, 120a
Čoruh (Corukh)   ii, **62a** – II, **63b**
Čorum   ii, **62a**; s, 394b – II, **63b**; S, 395a
Cos   → Istanköy

Cosaques/Cossacks → Kazak̩
Cossacks → Kazak̲h̲
Côte d'Ivoire ii, **62b** – II, **64a**
Côte de l'or → G̲h̲āna
Côte des Pirates → al-Sāḥil
Cotonou → Kotonou
Couchitique → Kūs̲h̲
Čowdors → Čawdor, Banū
Crac → Karak
Crac des Chevaliers → Ḥiṣn al-Akrād
Črār (Srīnagar) s, 114b – S, 113b
Crete/Crète → Iḳrītis̲h̲
Crimea/-ée → Ḳīrīm
Croisades I, 203b, 222a, 351b, 480a, 532b, 535a, 570b, 683b, 732a, 759b, 801a, 806b, 807a, 822a, 823a, 937b, 1045b, 1048b, 1056b, 1077b, 1105a, 1135b, 1152b, 1159b, 1172a, 1173b, 1225b, 1254b, 1398a; II, 37b, **64b**, 133b, 168a, 876a, 933a, 1006a, 1080b; III, 89a, 301b, 334b, 489a, 491a, 521a, 1071a; IV, 304b, 504a, 506a, 875a, 991b; V, 105b, 302a, 330a, b, 806b, 929b; IX, 275a, b; S, 204b
Croia → Krujë
Crusades i, 197b, 198a, 215b, 341a, 466a, 517a, 519a, 552b, 662b, 710b, 737b, 778a, 783a, 784a, 798b, 799b, 910a, 1014a, 1017a, 1025a, 1045b, 1073a, 1102b, 1118b, 1125b, 1137b, 1139a, 1190b, 1218a, 1358a; ii, 37a, **63b**, 130a, 163a, 856a, 911b, 983b, 1056a; iii, 86b, 292b, 324b, 472b, 474b, 503b,504a, 1045a; iv, 291b, 483a, 485a, 842a, 958b; v, 103b, 303a, 330a, b, 800b, 924a; ix, 167a, b: s, 204b, 205a
Ctesiphon iii, 1254b; v, 945a, 946a; s, 298a – III, 1287a; V, 949a, 950a; S, 297b
Ču ii, **66b**; iv, 212b – II, **68a**; IV, 222a
Čūbak, Ṣādiḳ (XX) iv, 73a; v, 200a; s, 60a – IV, 77a; V, 197b; S, 60b
Čūbān, amīr (1327) i, 347a., 468a, 703a, 908b; ii, 68a, 69a; iii, 1122b; iv, 621b, 672a, 738a, 817b; v, 554b; vi, 482b; viii, 753a; ix, 821b – I, 357b, 481b, 724b, 936a; II, 69a, 70b; III, 1150b; IV, 646b, 699b, 767b, 850b; V, 559a; VI, 468b; VIII, 774b; IX, 867a
Čūbānid(e)s ii, **67b**, 401a; vi, 482b; x, 44a – II, **69a**, 411b; VI, 468b; X, 45b
Čūčak Bēgam (XVI) iii, 633b – III, 654b
Cuenca → Ḳūnka
Čufut Ḳalʿe i, 893a, b – I, 919b, 920a
Čūha Sulṭān Tekkelu (1525) vi, 514b – VI, 499b
Čuka → Ḳumās̲h̲
Čukurova → Cilicia
Čulābīs → Afrāsiyāb
Čulāḳ-Sūrk̲h̲ay-K̲h̲ān (XVIII) ii, 87b; v, 296b – II, 89b; V, 287b
Čulawī, Amīr Ḥusayn Kiyā (XVI) vi, 515b – VI, 500b
Čulīm ii, **68b** – II, **69b**
Cumania x, 693a – X, 735b
Cümhuriyet → D̲j̲ümhūriyyet
Čunār vi, 47a, 62a – VI, 45b, 60a
Čūpān ii, **69a**; s, 319b, 321a – II, **70a**; S, 319a, 321a
Čūpān-ata → Čopan-ata
Čūpān, Amīr → Čūbān
Čūpānbegī → Ḳubčūr
Čūrāman D̲j̲āt (XVIII) i, 1193a; ii, 810b – I, 1228a; II, 829b
Cuttack x, 894b – X,
Čuv(w)as̲h̲ i, 1307b, 1338a; ii, **69b**; iv, 281a, 608b; x, 691b – I, 1347b, 1378a; II, **70b**; IV, 293a, 633a; X, 734a
- Literature x, **732a** – X, **778a**
Cyprus → Ḳubrus
Cyrenaïca/Cyrénaïque → Barḳa
Cyrillus b. Laḳlaḳ (1243) s, 396a – S, 396b
Cyrus → al-Muḳawḳis
Cythère → Čoka Adasī
Czechoslovakia → Čeh

D

Daʿʿān, Treaty of/Traité de (1913) vi, 35b – VI, 34a
al-Daʿʿār, Banū s, 338a – S, 337b
Daʾb → Adab
al-Dabarān → Nud̲j̲ūm
Ḍabb ii, **70a**; s, 286b – II, **71a**; S, 286a
Dābba ii, **71a** – II, **72a**
Ḍabba, Banū ii, 71b; vi, 33a – II, 72b; VI, 317b
Ḍabba b. Muḥammad al-Asadī (X) iv, 637b – IV, 663b
Ḍabba b. Udd b. Ṭābīk̲h̲a ii, **71b** – II, **72b**
Dabbāg̲h̲ (tanne(u)r) s, **172a** – S, **173a**
al-Dabbāg̲h̲, Abū Zayd ʿAbd al-Raḥmān (1300) vi, 353b; s, **172b**, 395a – VI, 337b; S, **173b**, 395a
al-Dabbāg̲h̲ al-Fāsī (1719) vi, 356b – VI, 340b
al-Dabbāg̲h̲, Ḥusayn Ṭāhir (1927) vi, 157b – VI, 153a
Dabbāg̲h̲-zāde Meḥmed Efendi, S̲h̲ayk̲h̲ al-Islām (1687) vi, 983a – VI, 975a
al-Dabbās → Abu 'l-K̲h̲ayr Ḥammād
al-Ḍabbī, Abū 'l-ʿAbbās (1008) viii, 389b – VIII, 403a
al-Ḍabbī, Abū D̲j̲aʿfar (1203) i, 602b; ii, **72a** – I, 622a; II, **73b**
al-Ḍabbī, Abū ʿIkrima ʿAmir b. ʿImrān (864) iv, 446a; vi, 822b; vii, 306b – IV, 466a; VI, 812b; VII, 308b
al-Dabbī, Abū 'l-Ṣaydāʾ x, 844b – X,
al-Ḍabbī, Bisṭām b. ʿUmar (VII) iii, 649b, 658b – III, 670b, 680a
al-Ḍabbī, al-Mufaḍḍal b. Muḥammad (780) iii, 136b, 706b, 985a, 1178a; vii, 841a; s, 15b, 38b – III, 139a, 729a, 1009b, 1207a; VII, 842b; S, 16a, 39a
al-Ḍabbī, al-Mufaḍḍal (II) b. Salāma b. ʿĀsim (903) ii, 135b, 807b; vi, 215a,b, 822b; x, 32b; s, 177a – II, 139a, 826b; VI, 199a,b, 812b; X, 34a; S, 178b
al-Ḍabbī, al-Musayyab b. Zuhayr (791) vii, 645b ; s, 327a – VII, 645b; S, 326b
Dābiḳ ii, **72b**, 360b, 912a; vi, 544a – II, **73b**, 370a, 933b; VI, 528b
Dabīḳ ii, **72b** – II, **74a**
Dabīl → Dwīn
al-Dabīlī, Abū Mūsā (IX) i, 162b – I, 167a
Dabīr (scribe) iv, 758b, 759a; s, **173a** – IV, 788b, 789a; S,**174a**
Dabīr, Mīrzā Salāmat ʿAlī (1875) i, 508b; ii, **73a**; iii, 119b; vi, 610b, 611b; s, 74b – I, 524a; II, **74a**; III, 122a; VI, 595b, 596a, b; S, 75a
Dabistān al-Mad̲h̲āhib ii, **74a** – II, **75a**
Ḍābiṭ i, 975a; ii, **74a** – I, 1005a; II, **75b**
Ḍābiṭa K̲h̲ān (Rohilla) (1785) i, 1206a; ii, 1092b; iii, 61a; vii, 869b; viii, 572b – I, 1242a; II, 1118a; III, 63b; VII, 871a; VIII, 591a
Dābōē → Dābūya
Ḍabōt vi, 82a – VI, 79b
Ḍabṭ ii, **74b** 155b, 156a – II, **75b**, 160a, 161a
Ḍabṭiyya ii, **74b**; iv, 611b – II, **75b**; IV, 636a
Ḍabuʿ, Ḍabʿ s, **173b** – S, **174a**
Dābū vi, 510b, 511a – VI, 496a, b
Dābul vi, 63a, 66b – VI, 61a, 64b
Dabūsiyya s, **176b** – s, **177b**
Dābūya/Dābūyid(e)s i, 871b; ii, **74b**; iv, 207b, 644a; v, 69a; vi, 335a, 941a; s, 297b, 298a, b – I, 896a; II, **76a**; IV, 217a, 670b; V, 71a; VI, 319b, 933a; S, 297a, 298a
Dacca → Ḍhākā
Ḍād ii, **75a** – II, **76a**

Dada → Dede
Dadaloghlu (1870) ii, **75b** – II, **76b**
Dādhawayh (VII) i, 728a – I, 750a
Dād-Beg Ḥabashī (XI) s, 279a – S, 279a
Dādhburzmihr b. Farrukhān (734) ii, 74b, 809a; s, 299a – II, 76a, 828b; S, 298b
Dadjādja ii, **76a** – II, **77a**
al-Dadjdjāl i, 932a; ii, **76a**, 486b; iv, 408b; v, 800a – I, 960b; II, **77b**, 498b; IV, 426a; V, 806a
Dādū, Pīr (1593) v, 26b – V, 27b
Daff → Duff
Ḍafīr, Banū ii, **77a** – II, **78b**
Dafn → Dhunūb, Dafn al-
Daftar i, 1090a, b; ii, **77b**, 82a, b, 147b, 563a; iv, 1047b; viii, 149b – I, 1122b, 1124a; II, **78b**, 83b, 84a, 151b, 577a; IV, 1079a; VIII, 152a
Daftar-i Khāḳānī i, 999a; ii, **81b**, 147b – I, 1030a; II, **83b**, 151b
Daftardār i, 480b; ii, **83a**, 723b; iv, 560b – I, 495a; II, **84b**, 742a; IV, 583a
Dāgh, Nawwāb Mīrzā Khān (1905) ii, **83b**; iii, 119a; v 961b – II, **85a**; III, 121b; V, 966a
Dagh-Čufut ii, 86b, 88b, 89a – II, 88b, 90b
Dāgh u Taṣḥīḥa v, 685b, 686b; s, **176b** – V, 691a, b; S, **177b**
Daghfal vi, 828b – VI, 818b
Dāghistān i, 504a, 755a, 756a, 958a; ii, **85a**, 206a, 746b; iii, 157a; iv, 343a, b, 350a, 846b; v, 55b, 246a, 382a, 617b, 618a, 729b; vi, 55b, 56b; vii, 352a; viii, 642b; ix, 283b; x, 921b; s, 143a – I, 519b, 777b, 778b, 987b; II, **86b**, 212b, 765a; III, 160b; IV, 357b, 365a, 879b; V, 57a, 243b, 383a, 621b, 622a, 734b; VI, 53b, 54b; VII, 354a; VIII, 661b; IX, 292a; X, ;S, 143a
Daghūgh, Banū vi, 742a – VI, 731a
Dagno iv, 139b – IV, 145a
Dahak (Ghazna) vi, 783a – VI, 773a
Dāhār (VIII) iv, 534b – IV, 558a
Daḥdaḥ (Damas(cus)) vi, 122b – VI, 120b
Dahdam → Lamlam
al-Ḍaḥḥāḳ → Zuhāk
Ḍaḥḥāḳ, Azhd ii, 106b, 1099a; v, 449a – II, 109a, 1125a; V, 451b
al-Ḍaḥḥāk b. Ḳays al-Fihrī (684) i, 53b, 704b; ii, **89a**, 360a; iii, 270b, 687b; vi, 545a, 546b, 622a; vii, 268a, b, 464a; viii, 119a – I, 55b, 725b; II, **91a**, 370a; III, 278b, 709a; VI, 529b, 531a, 607a; VII, 270a, 463a; VIII, 121b
al-Ḍaḥḥāk b. Ḳays al-Shaybānī (746) ii, **90a**; iv, 1076a; vi, 624a; vii, 546a, 693b; ix, 767a – II, **92a**; IV, 1108a; VI, 609a, b; VII, 546a, 694a; IX, 800a
Daḥḥāk b. Muzāḥim (724) v, 1123a – V, 1119b
al-Daḥḥāḳ b. ʿUthmān (770) ix, 566b – IX, 588b
Dahhām b. Dawwās (XVIII) vii, 410a – VII, 411b
Dahhānī, Khwādja (XIII) viii, 972a,b – VIII, 1066b, 1007a
Daḥḥūn, Banū iii, 12a – III, 12b
Ḍāḥik, Mīr (XVIII) s, 358b – S, 358b
Dahinda (river/fleuve) vi, 294b – VI, 280a
Ḍāhir (Yemen) i, 762b – I, 785b
Dāhir (Sind) (VIII) vii, 405b; s, 163a – VII, 406b; S, 162a
Ḍāhir al-ʿUmar → Ẓāhir al-ʿUmar
Dāḥis ii, 873a, 1023a; s, 177a – II, 893b, 1046b; S, 178a
Dahistan → Dihistān
Dahlak islands/îles ii, **90b**, 709b; vi, 642a; vii, 861a – II, **92b**, 728b; VI, 627a; VII, 862b
Daḥlān, Aḥmad b. Zaynī (1886) i, 66a; ii, **91a**; vi, 176a, b – I, 68a; II, **93a**
al-Dahmānī, Sīdī Abū Yūsūf vi, 353b – VI, 337b
al-Dahnāʾ i, 537a; ii, **91b**; viii, 1048a – I, 553b; II, **93b**; VIII, 1084a
al-Dahnadj ii, **93a** – II, **95a**
Dahomey ii, **93b**; v, 279b – II, **95b**; V, 277b
Dahr ii, **94b** – II, **96b**
Dahriyya ii, **95a**, 770b; vi, 737b; s, 89a – II, **97a**, 789a; VI, 726b; S, 88b
Daḥshūr ii, **97b** – II, **99b**
Dāʿī i, 832b; ii, **97b** – I, 855b; II, **99b**
Dāʿī, Aḥmad b. Ibrāhīm (1472) ii, **98a**; iii, 1243a – II, **100a**; III, 1275a
Dāʾira → Dawāʾir
Dāʾira Saniyya s, **179a** – S, **180a**
Daḳahliyya ii, **99a**; vi, 440b – II, **101a**; VI, 426a
Dakar s, **179a** – S, **180b**
Dakhadayev, Muḥammad ʿAlī (1918) vi, 129b – VI, 127b
Dakhalieh → Daḳahliyya
Dakhan (Deccan) i, 81a, 117b, 923b; ii, **99a**; iii, 15a, 420b; v, 937a, 1214b, 1215a, b; vi, 50b, 53b, 54a, 62b, 126b, 271a, 309a, b, 406b, 488b, 534a, 536b; vii, 79b, 632a; viii, 67b; s, 74b, 335b – I, 83b, 121a, 951b; II, **101a**; III, 15b, 434a; V, 940b, 1204a, 1205a; VI, 48b, 51b, 52a, 60b, 124b, 255b, 294b, 295a, 391b, 474b, 518b, 521a; VII, 81a, 631b; VIII, 69b; S, 75a, 335b
Dakhanī (Dakhni) → Urdū
Dakhaw → ʿAlī Akbar Dihkhudā
Dakhīl ii, **100a**; iii, 1018a; iv, 412a – II, **1020a**; III, 1043b; IV, 430a
al-Dākhil → ʿAbd al-Raḥmān I; al-Ḥasan
Dākhla and/et Khārdja → al-Wāḥāt
Dakhtanūs vi, 603a – VI, 587b
Dakibyza → Gebze
Daḳīḳī, Abū Manṣūr Muḥammad (X) ii, **100a**, 918b, 1035b; iii, 113a; iv, 60b, 62b – II, **102a**, 939b, 1059b; III, 115b; IV, 64a, 65b
al-Daḳḳāḳ, Abū ʿAbd Allāh (XII) i, 137b; ii, **100b** – I, 141b; II, **102b**
al-Daḳḳāḳ, Abū ʿAli (1015) v, 526b – V, 530a, b
Dakkanī, Walī (1707) v, 959b, 961a, 1106a – V, 965a, 963b, 1102a, 1106a
Daḳūḳāʾ i, 184a, 512b; ii, **101a**; vi, 500b – I, 189b, 1528a; II, **103a**; VI, 486a
Dāl ii, **101a** – II, **103a**
al-Dalāl, Abū Zayd Nāḳid (762) iv, 1087b; s, **183a** – IV, 1118b; S, **184b**
Dalāṣī (al-Dalāṣīrī) → al-Buṣīrī
Dalhama → Dhu 'l-Himma
Ḍāliʿ i, 446a; ii, 675b – I, 459a; II, 692a
Dālī b. Aḥmad al-Maʿḳūr ii, 122b – II, 125b
Dalīl (sign(e)) ii, **101b**; iii, 543b – II, **103b**; III, 562a
Dalīl Baḥr → Dālī b. Aḥmad al-Maʿḳūr
Dalīpgarh i, 1020a – I, 1051b
Dallāl ii, **102b**; iii, 213a; v, 1004a, 1005a – II, **104b**; III, 219a; V, 1000a, b
Dalmā ix, 658b – IX, 684a
Dalmatia/-e s, **183b** – S, **184b**
Dalmāw vi, 49b – VI, 48a
Daltāwa ii, **103a** – II, **105b**
Dalūka, queen/la reine iii, 71b; vi, 412b, 413a – III, 73b; VI, 397b, 398a
al-Dalw → Minṭaḳat al-Burūdj; Nudjūm
Dām → Sikka
Dam (blood/sang) s, **188b**, 221b – S, **190a**, 221b
Damā (ʿUmān) vi, 735b – VI, 725a
Dāma al-ʿUlyā vi, 303a – VI, 288b
Dāmād ii, **103b** – II, **105b**
Dāmād ʿAlī Shehīd (1725) i, 268b; iv, 1039b; vii, 217a; ix, 14b – IV, 1124b; VII, 218b; IX, 15a
al-Dāmād al-Astarābādī, Mīr (1630) ii, **103b**; vi, 550a;

vii, 94a, 547b; viii, 541b; s, 308b – II, **106a**; VI, 534b; VII, 96a, 547b; VIII, 559a; S, 308a
Dāmād Ferīd Pasha (1923) ii, **104b**, 431b, 533b, 630b; iii, 595a; iv, 873a, b; vi, 984a – II, **107a**, 442b, 546b, 646a; III, 615b; IV, 906b, 907a; VI, 976b
Dāmād Pasha → ʿAlī Pasha; Ḥasan Pasha; Ibrāhīm Pasha; Sinān Pasha
Dāmād-zāde Fayḍ Allāh Efendi, Shaykh al-Islām (1758) vi, 1004b – VI, 997a
Dāmādjī (XVIII) i, 1053a – I, 1084b
al-Dāmaghānī, Abū 'l-Hasan ʿAlī (1119) s, **194a** – S, **193b**
al-Dāmaghānī, Āl s, **191b** – S, **193a**
al-Damāmīnī, Badr al-Dīn Muhammad b. ʿUmar (1423) iv, 135a – IV, 140b
al-Damāmīnī, Tādj al-Dīn (1331) iv, 641a – IV, 667b
Ḍamān i, 1144a; ii, **105a**; iv, 323b, 324a, 326a, 404b, 1046a, – I, 1178b; II, **107a**; IV, 337b, 338b, 340a, 422a, 1077b
Damanhūr (Buḥayra) i, 1288a, b; ii, **105b**; vii, 421a – I, 1327b, 1328a; II, **108a**; VII, 422b
Damanhūr al-Shahīd ii, **105b** – II, **107b**
Damas(cus) → Dimashḳ
Damāwand i, 358b; ii, **106a**; iv, 402; v, 89a, 657b, 659b, 660a; vi, 335a, 337b, 744a, b; s, 298a – I, 369a; II, **108b**; IV, 419b; V, 91a, 663a, 665a, b; VI, 319b, 321b, 733b; S, 297b
Damawiyya iv, 334b – IV, 349a
Dambat vi, 201a, b – VI, 185a, b
Damdam → Lamlam
Damēlī ii, 31a, 138b – II, 32a, 142a
Dāmghān ii, **107a**; iv, 701b; v, 377b, 378a; vi, 115b, 365a, 453a, 513a; s, 149a, 192a, 357a – II, **109b**; IV, 730a; V, 378a, b; VI, 113b, 349a, 438b, 498b; S, 149a, 193a, 356b
Dāmghānī, Ḥasan-i (Sardabārid(e)) (1361) ix, 48b – IX, 49b
Dāmghānī, Shams al-Dīn (XIV) ii, 1124b; iii, 14b; iv, 218b – II, 1151a; III, 15a; IV, 228a
Damietta/-e → Dimyaṭ
Ḍamīr → Naḥw
al-Dāmir iv, 686b – IV, 714b
Damir Ḳapu → Dar-i Āhanīn
al-Damīrī, Muḥammad b. Mūsā (1405) i, 509a, 594b; ii, **107b**; iii, 306b, 307b, 313a; vi, 218b, 904a; s, 392b – I, 524b, 613b; II, **109b**; III, 316a, 317a, 322b; VI, 203a, 895a; S, 393a
Ḍamīrī al-Iṣfahānī (1578) vi, 271a; viii, 775b – VI, 256a; VIII, 801b
al-Damlūdjī, ʿAbd Allāh (XX) vi, 153a, b – VI, 151b
Damḳōt vi, 81a – VI, 79a
Ḍamma → Ḥaraka
al-Dammām ii, **108a**, 175b, 569a; iii, 238b – II, **110b**, 181a, 583a; III, 245b
Dammār, Banū i, 6a; vi, 899a, 946b; vii, 761a – I, 6a; VI, 890b, 938b; VII, 762b
Damnāt (Demnate) ii, **109a**; vi, 741a – II, **111b**; VI, 730a
al-Damnātī → ʿAlī b. Sulaymān
al-Ḍamrī, ʿAmr b. Umayya (VII) vii, 517b, 863a – VII, 518a, 864a
al-Damurdāshī, Aḥmad (XVIII) ii, **109b** – II, **112a**
Dānā Shahīd, Shāh (1270) vii, 550a – VII, 550a
Danāgla viii, 92a,b – VIII, 94b
Dānaḳ → Sikka
Danāḳil/Danāḳla → Danḳalī
Danānīr al-Barmakī (IX) i, 1036a; s, 116b – I, 1067b; S, 116a
Dandānḳān, Dandānaḳān vi, 66a, 453a; vii, 407a; s, **195a**, 245b – VI, 64a, 438b; VII, 408b; S, **195a**, 245b
al-Dandarāwī, Abu 'l-ʿAbbās (1950) s, 279a – S, 278b
al-Dandarāwiyya x, 249a; s, 279a – X, 268a; S, 278b
Dāndēsh → Khāndēsh
al-Dānī, Abū ʿAmr (1053) ii, **109b**, 112a; iii, 753b; iv, 731b; v, 128a; vi, 188b, 189a; vii, 553a – II, **112a**, 114b; III, 776b; IV, 761a; V, 130b; VI, 172a, 173a; VII, 553b
al-Danī, Abū Bakr Muḥammad → Ibn al-Labbāna
Daniel → Dāniyāl
Dānish, Aḥmad Makhdūm (1897) s, 109b, 290a – S, 108b, 109b
Dānishgāh → Djāmiʿa
Dānishmend, Malik Aḥmad Ghāzī (XI) i, 465b, 466a, b, 1103b, 1104a; ii, 37a, 110a, 1044a; iii, 115a; viii, 36a – I, 479b, 480a, 1137a, b; II, 38a, 112b, 1068a; III, 117a; VIII, 36b
Dānishmend Khān (XVII) vii, 321b – VII, 323b
Dānishmend Tigin (XIII) i, 418b – I, 430b
Dānishmendid(e)s i, 431b, 466b, 510a, 639a, 665a, 666a; ii, 13b, **110a**; iv, 627b, 737b; v, 103b, 106a; vi, 231a; s, 154b – I, 444a, 480b, 525b, 659b, 684b, 686b; II, 13b, **112b**; IV, 652b, 767b; V, 106a, b; VI, 224b; S, 154b
Dāniya ii, **111b**; v, 631b – II, **114a**; V, 635b
Dāniyāl ii, **112b**, 377a; iv, 654a – II, **115a**, 387a; IV, 680b
Dāniyāl b. Akbar (Mughal) (1604) i, 80b, 1331a; ii, **113a**, 851b, 871a; iv, 1017b; vi, 814b; viii, 74a – I, 83a, 1371b; II, **115b**, 835a, 891a; IV, 1049b; VI, 805a; VIII, 75b
Dāniyāl b. Shaʿya i, 388b – I, 399b
Dāniyāl Biy Atalïḳ (Mangït) (1785) i, 230b, 1295b; iv, 310a; vi, 418b, 419a, 621a; s, 97a – I, 237b, 1335b; IV, 324a; VI, 403b, 404a, 606a; S, 96b
Dāniyār b. Ḳāsim Khān (1486) iv, 723b – IV, 752b
Danḳalī i, 176b, 765a, 1028b; ii, **113a**, 351a, 615a; iii, 4a, 5b; v, 1248b – I, 181a, 788a, 1060a; II, **115b**, 360b, 630b; III, 4a, 5b; V, 1239a
Dār ii, **113b**; iv, 236a, b, 1015a, 1016b; v, 23a – II, **116a**; IV, 246b, 247a, 1047a, 1048b; V, 24a
Dār-i āhanīn ii, **115b** – II, **118a**
Dār al-ʿahd i, 1253a; ii, **116a** – I, 1291a; II, **118b**
Dār-i Alān → Bāb al-Lān
Dār al-Baḥr s, 62b – S, 63a
Dār al-Bayḍāʾ, al- (Casablanca) i, 506a, 977b; ii, **116b**, 727a; vii, 387a; s, 63b, 134a, 145a, 223b – I, 521b, 1008a; II, **119a**, 745; VII, 388b; S, 64a, 133b, 144b, 223b
Dār al-Bayḍāʾ (Marrākush) vi, 596b – VI, 581b
Dār al-Ḍarb i, 24a, 1335b; ii, **117b**, 205b, 874b; iii, 41b; iv, 134b, 230b; v, 264b, 488b – I, 25a, 1375b; II, **120a**, 212a, 894b; III, 43a; IV, 140b, 241a; V, 262b, 491b
Dār al-Djihād i, 1163b – I, 1198a
Dār Fartīt i, 929a, b – I, 957b, 958a
Dār Firʿawn (Manf) vi, 413b – VI, 398a
Dār al-Funūn → Djāmiʿa
Dār al-Funūn (Tehran/Téhéran) vi, 291a – VI, 276b
Dār Fūr i, 35a, 49b, 929a, b, 962a; ii, **121b**, 351a; v, 267a, 1248b, 1249b; vi, 281b; s, 164a – I, 36a, 51a, 957b, 991b; II, **124b**, 361a; V, 264b, 265a, 1239a, 1240a; VI, 266b; S, 164a
Dār al-Ḥadīth ii, **125b**, 283a; v, 1129a; s, **195a** – II, **128b**, 291b; V, 1125a; S, **195a**
Dār al-Ḥadīth (Mecca) vi, 173b – VI, 161b
Dār al-Hamara iii, 149a – III, 152a
Dār al-Ḥarb i, 429b; ii, 116a, **126a**, 131b – I, 441b; II,

118b, **129b**, 135a
Dār al-Ḥikma i, 816a, 1141a; ii, **126b**, 169b, 859b; iii, 78b; v, 1033a, 1125b – I, 839b, 1175b; II, **130a**, 175a, 879a; III, 81a; V, 1029a, 1122a
Dār al-ʿIlm i, 899a; ii, **127a**, 169b; iii, 78b; v, 1125a, b, 1126a, 1129a; s, 95b – I, 926a; II, **130a**, 175a; III, 81a; V, 1121b, 1122a, b, 1125a; S, 95a
Dār al-Imāra (Bag͟hdād) i, 899b, 900a, 901a; ii, 128b – I, 926b, 927a, 928a; II, 131b
Dār al-Islām i, 116a, **127b**, 131b; iii, 546b; iv, 173a, b – II, 118b, **130b**, 134b; III, 565b; IV, 180b, 181a
Dār al-Ḳurʾān wa ʾl-Ḥadīt͟h ii, 126a – II, 129a
Dār al-Maḥfūzāt al-ʿUmūmiyya ii, **128a** – II, **131a**
Dār al-Mamlaka (Bag͟hdād) i, 901a, 1352b, 1354a – I, 928a, 1392a, 1393a
Dār al-Mizān vi, 384b – VI, 368b
Dār al-Muṣannifīn (Lak͟hnaw) ii, 132b – II, 135b
Dār al-Nadwa (Mecca) ii, **128b** – II, **131b**
Dār Runga (Čad) s, 164b – S, 164b
Dār al-Saʿāda → Saray
Dār al-Saʿāde Ag͟hasi̊ → Saray-ag͟hasi̊
Dār al-Ṣabbāg͟hīn viii, 985a – VIII, 1019b
Dār al-Salām ii, **128b** – II, **132a**
Dār al-Sawdāʾ vi, 563b – VI, 548a, b
Dār es-Salaam ii, **128b**; v, 1031a; vi, 370a – II, **132a**; V, 1027a; VI, 354b
Dār al-S͟hifāʾ (Turkey/-quie) i, 1225b – I, 1262a
Dār al-S͟hifāʾ (Srīnagar) s, 353b – S, 353b
Dār al-S͟hifāʾ (Tehran/Téhéran) s, 23b – S, 23b
Dār al-Ṣināʿa ii, **129b**; iii, 271b; s, 120a – II, **132b**; III, 279b; S, 119b
Dār Ṣīnī s, **197a** – S, **197a**
Dār al-Ṣulḥ ii, **131a** – II, **134b**
Dār al-Tablīg͟h al-Islāmī (Ḳum) iv, 166b – IV, 174a
Dār al-Takiyya al-Miṣriyya (Mecca) vi, 178a – VI, 163a
Dār al-Taḳrib bayna'l-Mad͟hāhib al-Islāmiyya (Cairo/-e) iv, 165b – IV, 172b
Dār al-Taḳrīb → Ik͟htilāf
Dār Tāma ii, 123b – II, 126b
Dār al-Ṭibāʿa → Maṭbaʿa
Dār Ṭirāz → Ṭirāz
Dār al-ʿUlūm i, 817b, 818a, 819a, 820a; ii, **131b**, 205a; v, 909a, 910b; vi, 602a; vii, 418b; s, 18a, 262b – I, 840b, 841a; 842a, 843a; II, **135a**, 211b; V, 915a, 916b; VI, 587a; VII, 420a; S, 18a, 262a
Dār al-ʿUmma (Marrākus͟h) vi, 596a – VI, 581a
Dār al-Wikāla iv, 136a – IV, 141b
Dāra (Abyssinia/-e) i, 176b – I, 181a
Darʿa → Ad͟hriʿāt
Darʿa (Draʿ) (town/ville; province) ii, **133b**; v, 1185a; vi, 540a, 589b, 590b; s, 29a, 402b – II, **137a**; V, 1175a; VI, 524b, 574b, 575a, b; S, 29a, 403a
Dārā, Dārāb (Dareios) ii, **132b**; iv, 809b – II, **136a**; 842a
Dārā S͟hukōh b. S͟hāh D͟jahān I (Mug͟hal) (1659) i, 229a, 768b, 769a, 781b, 1136a, 1166a; ii, 54b, **134a**, 378b; iii, 202a, b, 436a, 459a; iv, 69a; vi, 368b; vii, 189a, 327a, b, 343a, 452b; viii, 540b; s, 308b – I, 235b, 791b, 792a, 805a, 1170b, 1200b; II, 55b, **137b**, 389a; III, 207b, 450b, 475b; IV, 73a; VI, 353a; VII, 189b, 329a, 345a, 454a; VIII, 558a; S, 308a
Dārāb → Dārābd͟jird
Dārāb K͟hān (1625) i, 81b – I, 83b
Dārābd͟jird i, 43b, 896b; ii, **135b**; vi, 384a, 494a, 640b – I, 44b, 923a; II, **139a**; VI, 368b, 480a, 625b
al-Darabī, Abū 'l-Ṣaydāʾ x, 844b – X,
Dārābī, Ḥakīm ʿAbbās s, 308b – S, 308b
Darabukka ii, **135b** – II, **139a**
Dārādiz vi, 504a – VI, 489b
Daragaz vii, 454a – VII, 454b
Darak s, **198a** – S, **198a**
Darāk → Dawraḳ
Darak͟hs͟h i, 1233b – I, 1270a
al-Dāraḳuṭnī, Abu ʾl-Ḥasan ʿAlī b. ʿUmar (995) ii, **136a**; iii, 24b, 758a, 768b; viii, 517a; s, 400b – II, **139b**; III, 25b, 781a, 791b; VIII, 534b; S, 401a
Darandollä Nomad(e)s (Maḳdis͟hū) vi, 129a – VI, 127a
al-Darazī, Muḥammad (1019) ii, **136b**, 631b; iii, 80b, 154b – II, **140a**, 647b; III, 82b, 158a
Ḍarb → Dār al-Ḍarb; Sikka
Ḍarb → Madīna
Ḍarb Āl ʿAlī iii, 208a – III, 213b
Ḍarb al-Arbaʿīn ii, 122a, **137a** – II, 125a, **140b**
Ḍarb al-Fīl i, 707b – I, 729a
Ḍarb al-Ḥad͟jd͟j vi, 546a – VI, 531a
Ḍarb al-Kunhurī i, 748a – I, 770b
Ḍarb al-Saʿāda (Cairo/-e) vi, 75b – VI, 73a
Ḍarb Zubayda ii, 92a; s, **198b**, 304b – II, 94a; S, **198b**, 304b
Darband → Derbend
Darbkhāne → Dār al-Ḍarb
Darbukka → Darabukka
Darčīn s, 327a – S, 326b
Dard, K͟hʷād͟ja Mīr b. K͟hʷād͟ja Muḥammad Nāṣir (1785) ii, **137b**; vii, 555b, 939a; x, 878a; s, 358b – II, **141a**; VII, 555b, 939b; S, 358b
Dardanelles → Čanaḳ-kalʿe Bog͟hazi̊
Dardic and Kāfir Languages ii, **138a**; iv, 711b; v, 649a; s, 158b
Dardiques et Kāfires, Langues II, **142a**; IV, 740a; V, 653a; S, 158b
Dardīr (1786) vi, 279a – VI, 263b
al-Dardīr i, 867b – I, 891b
Dardīriyya ii, **139b** – I, **143b**
Dardistān ii, **140a**; s, 167a – II, **143b**; S, 167a
Dārd͟jān vi, 384b – VI, 368b
al-Dard͟jīnī, Abu ʾl-ʿAbbās Aḥmad b. Saʿīd (XIII) i, 167a, 1053b; ii, **140b**; iii, 96b, 656b; vi, 311a, 945a – I, 171b, 1085a; II, **144a**; III, 99a, 678a; VI, 296a, 937b
Dareios → Dārā
Dargāh ii, **141b**; iv, 26a – II, **145a**; IV, 27b
Darg͟hin i, 756a; ii, 86b, 89a, **141b**; iv, 846a, b; v, 285b – I, 778b; II, 88a, 90b, **145a**; IV, 879b, 880a; V, 283b
Darg͟hūt͟h viii, 763b – VIII, 788b
Darī (court language/langue de la cour) ii, **142a**; iv, 55a; vi, 768a – II, **146a**; IV, 58a; VI, 757a
al-Darʿī (XVIII) vi, 350a – VI, 334a
Darʿī, Moses (XII) iv, 605b – IV, 629b
Darial, Dariel → Bāb al-Lān
Ḍarība ii, **142b**; s, **199b** – II, **146a**; S, **199b**
Dārim → Tamīm
al-Dārimī, ʿAbd Allāh b. ʿAbd al-Raḥmān (869) ii, **159a**; iii, 24b; vii, 663a – II, **164a**; III, 25b; VII, 662b
al-Dārimī, Sufyān b. Mud͟jās͟hiʿ iv, 832b – IV, 865b
Dārin → Tārūt
al-Darīr, Ḥamid al-Dīn (1267) vii, 969a – VII, 969b
Ḍarīr, Muṣṭafā (XIV) ii, **159a** – II, **164a**
Ḍarīsa, Āl vi, 310b, 312a – VI, 295b, 297b
Darius, King/le roi → Dārā, Dārāb
Ḍariyya ii, **159b** – II, **164b**
al-Darʿiyya → al-Dirʿiyya
Darḳāwa i, 368b, 371a; ii, **160a**, 224a; iii, 261b, 696a, 701a, 968a; s, 371a – I, 379b, 382a; II, **165a**, 231a; III, 269a, 718b, 723a, 992b; S, 371a
al-Darḳawī, Abū Ḥāmid al-ʿArabī (1823) x, 247b – X, 266a

Darḳāwī Muḥammad al-Ḥarrāḳ (1845) vi, 250b, VI, 234b
Darna i, 1049a; ii, **160b** – I, 1081a; II, **165b**
Dārōd, Banū vii, 390a – VII, 391a
Darōhar s, 163a – S, 163a
Daron → al-Dārūm
Darra Gaz vi, 495b – VI, 480b
Darrās al-Fāsī iv, 341a; v, 1208b – IV, 355b; V, 1199a
Dars͟han ii, **162a** – II, **167a**
Darsim v, 465a – V, 468a
Dart → D͟jerīd
Dārūg͟ha ii, **162a**; iii, 491a; iv, 103b, 268b; s, 97a – II, **167a**; III, 508a; IV, 108a, 280b; S, 96b
Darul-Islam (Indonesia/-e) vi, 117a, 732a, b – VI, 114b, 721a, b
Darūliyya → Eskis͟hehir
al-Dārūm i, 1140a; ii, **163a** – I, 1174b; II, **168a**
Ḍarūra ii, **163b**; iii, 306b; iv, 692b – II, **168b**; III, 315b; IV, 720b
Darvīs͟h K͟husraw (1593) iv, 860b – IV, 894a
Darwāz vi, 618b – VI, 603b
Darwīs͟h ii, **164a**; iv, 49b; s, 154a – II, **169a** IV, 52a; S, 154a
Darwīs͟h ʿAbdi (1647) iv, 1126a – IV, 1157b
Darwīs͟h ʿAlī (Alep/-po) (XX) viii, 449a – VIII, 464a
Darwīs͟h ʿAlī, Cangī-yi K͟hāḳānī (XVII) viii, 543a – VIII, 560b
Darwīs͟h ʿAlī K͟hān (1556) i, 722a – I, 743b
Darwīs͟h K͟hēl Wazīrī, Banū vi, 86a; vii, 220a – VI, 84a; VII, 222a
Darwīs͟h K͟husraw (1593) viii, 115b – VIII, 118a
Darwīs͟h Muḥammad Naḳḳās͟h (XVI) i, 1211b – I, 1247b
Darwīs͟h Muḥammad Tark͟hān (1467) vii, 90b – VII, 92a
Darwīs͟h Riḍā (1631) viii, 116b – VIII, 119a
Darwīs͟h Waḥdatī (1909) vi, 614b – VI, 599b
Darwīza, Ak͟hund (XVI) i, 1121b, 1123a – I, 1155b, 1156b
Daryā ʿImād S͟hāh (ʿImād ṣahī) (1561) iii, 425a, 1160b, 1161a – III, 439a, 1188b, 1189b
Daryā K͟hān → Ẓafar K͟hān Lodī II
Daryā K͟hān Noḥānī (1524) ii, 1129a; v, 72a; s, **203a** – II, 1155b; V, 74a; S, **202b**
Daryā-begi ii, **165b** – II, **170b**
Daryā-yi S͟hāhī → Urmiya
Dās, Rād͟jā Bhagwān (XVI) s, 167a – S, 167a
Dāsenī → Ṭasinī
al-Das͟htakī, G͟hiyāt͟h al-Dīn Manṣūr b. Muḥammad (1541) iv, 610a; viii, 778a, 781b, 783a, 785b – IV, 634b; VIII, 804a, 807b, 809a, 811b
Das͟htakī, Ṣadr al-Dīn Muḥammad (1498) viii, 781b – VIII, 807b
Das͟htī → Muḥammad K͟hān (1881)
Das͟htī (Mānd) vi, 384b – VI, 368b
Das͟ht-i Arz͟han vi, 493b – VI, 479b
Das͟htī, ʿAlī (XX) iv, 73a; v, 199a – IV, 76b; V, 196a
Das͟ht-i Kavīr iv, 2a; s, 149a – IV, 2a; S, 149a
Das͟ht-i Ḳïpčaḳ vi, 314a, b, 315a, 322a, 417b; x, 562b; s, **203b** – VI, 299a, b, 300a, 306b, 402b; X, ; S, **203a**
Das͟ht-i Lūṭ iv, 2a,b, 4b; v, 147b, 352b – IV, 2a,b, 4b; V, 150a, 353b
Das͟ht-i Rūn vi, 496a – VI, 481a
Das͟htistān vi, 384b – VI, 368b
Daskara ii, **165b** – II, **171a**
Dastad͟jird ii, **166a** – II, **171b**
Dāstā-i Ḳahramān → Ḳahramān-nāma
al-Dāstānī, S͟hayk͟h Abū ʿAbd Allāh (X) i, 162b; iv, 1058a – I, 167a; IV, 1089a
Dast-i Mayṣan vi, 633b – VI, 618b
Dastūr → Dustūr
Dastūr Dīnār (Ḥabs͟hī) (1504) iii, 15a; vi, 63a, b – III, 16a; VI, 60b, 61a
Dasūḳ s, 18a – S, 18a
al-Dasūḳī, Ibrāhīm b. ʿAbd al-ʿAzīz (1287) ii, **166a** – II, **171b**
al-Dasūḳī, Ibrāhīm b. Ibrāhīm (1883) ii, **167a**; vi, 279a; x, 190a – II, **172b**; VI, 263b; X, 205b
al-Dasūḳī, Ibrāhīm b. Muḥammad (1513) ii, **167b** – II, **172b**
Dātā Gand͟j → Hud͟jwīrī
Datbūrd͟jmatūn (Dābūyid(e)) (737) vi, 941a – VI, 933a
Dat͟hīna ii, **167b**, 675b; iv, 746a, 747b – II, **173a**, 692a; IV, 776a, 777b
Datoʾ Patimang vi, 116b – VI, 114b
Datoʾri Bandang vi, 116b – VI, 114b
Datoʾri Tiro vi, 116b – VI, 114b
Dattū Sarwanī (XVI) s, 313a – S, 312b
Dāʾūd → Dāwūd
Dāʾū-Potra → Bahāwalpūr
David → Dāwūd
David II the Restorer/le Restaurateur → Dawid II Ag͟hmas͟henebeli
David b. al-Hītī (XV) iv, 605b – IV, 630a
Davudpaşa (Istanbul) vi, 529b – VI, 514a
Dawāʾ → Adwiya
Daʿwā ii, **170b** – II, **176a**
Daʿwa, daʿawāt i, 832b; ii, 97b, **168a**; iv, 203b; 815a – I, 855b; II, 99b, **173a**; IV, 212b; V, 521a
Dawā K͟hān → Duwā K͟hān
Dawādār ii, **172b**; iv, 759a – II, **177b**; IV, 789a
al-Dawādār, Sayf al-Dīn Aḥmad Aḳbug͟hā b. ʿAbd Allāh (1383) vi, 580b – VI, 565a
al-Dawādārī, Ibn Aybak (1336) vii, 167a – VII, 168b
Dawāʾir ii, **172b** – II, **178a**
Dawʿan, wādī ii, **173b** – II, **178b**
al-Dawʿanī, Muḥammad b. ʿAlī D͟jirfīl (1497) vi, 132b – VI, 130b
al-Daw(w)ānī, Muḥammad b. Asʿad D͟jalāl al-Dīn (1502) i, 326b, 329a; ii, **174a**; iv, 267b, 471b, 850b; v, 53b; vii, 143b, 272a, 478b; viii, 781a, 1047b – I, 337a, 339a; II, **179a**; IV, 279b, 492b, 883b; V, 55a; VII, 145b, 274a, 478a; VIII, 807a, 1083b
Dawār ii, **174b**; s, 318b – II, **180a**; s, 318a
Dāwar → Zamīn-i Dāwar
Dāwar Bak͟hs͟h b. K͟husraw b. D͟jahāngīr (XVII) i, 686b; v, 74a; vii, 315a – I, 707b; V, 76a; VII, 317b
Dawārō i, 176b; ii, **175a**; iii, 3b; vi, 128b – I, 181a; II, **180b**; III, 3b; VI, 126b
al-Dawāsir, Banū i, 233b, 545b, 873b; ii, 108b, **175b**; v, 40a; vi, 191b – I, 241a, 562b, 898a; II, 111a, **180b**; V, 41a; VI, 175b
Dawāt v, 988b; s, **203b** – V, 984a; S, **203a**
Dawāwida, Abū i, 1247a – I, 1285a
al-Dawḥa (Ḳaṭar) ii, **177a**; iv, 751a, b – II, **182b**; IV, 781b, 782a
Dawḥat Bilbūl (Arabia/-e) iv, 681a – IV, 708b
Dawid b. Georgi Las͟ha (Kurd͟j) (1273) v, 491a – V, 493b, 494a
Dawid b. Luarsab → Dāwūd K͟hān (Georgia/-e)
Dawid II Ag͟hmas͟henebeli v, 489b; vi, 64b – V, 492a; VI, 62a
Dawit I (Ḥabas͟h) (1411) iii, 4a – III, 4a
Dāwiyya and/et Isbitāriyya i, 293b, 1119b, 1250b; ii, 6a, 529b; iii, 325b, 504a, 1006b; iv, 483b; v, 342b; vi, 578b, 579a, b, 580a; viii, 569a; s, **204b** – I, 302b, 1153a, 1288b; II, 6a, 542b; III, 325b; 521b, 1032a; IV, 483b; V, 342b; VI, 563b, 564a, b, 564b; VIII, 587a; S, **204a**
Dawla ii, **177b**; iv, 293b; v, 621b, 623a – II, **183a**; IV, 306b; V, 625b, 627a
Dawlat-Begs s, 367b – S, 367a

Dawlat Čak (XVI) s, 324b – S, 324a
Dawlat Giray I (1577) ii, **178b**; v, 137a, 138a, b – II, **184b**; V, 139b, 141a
Dawlat Giray II (1713) ii, 1047a; iv, 569a; v, 140b – II, 1071b; IV, 591a; V, 143a
Dawlat Giray III (1717) i, 270b, 1287a – I, 279a, 1326b
Dawlat Ḳāḍī (Bengali) (XVII) i, 606b – I, 626a
Dawlat Khān (Rādjpūt) (XVII) i, 809a – I, 832a
Dawlat Khān (Rohilla) (1725) viii, 426a, 572a,b – VIII, 440a, 590a, 591a
Dawlat Khān b. Shudjāʿ (1555) i, 1155a – I, 1189b
Dawlat Khān Lōdī (1414) i, 218a; iii, 417b, 485a; vi, 49a, b, 50a; s, **206a** – I, 224b; III, 430b, 502a; VI, 47b, 48a, b; S, **206a**
Dawlat Khān Lōdī (1525) i, 848a; ii, 271a; iii, 420b, 995b; v, 598a – I, 871b; II, 224b; III, 434a, 1020a; V, 602a
Dawlat Muḥammad Āzādī (XVIII) vi, 130b – VI, 128b
Dawlat-Shāh (amīr) b. ʿAlāʾ al-Dawla (XV) ii, **179a**; vi, 276a; vii, 530a; x, 516a; s, 65a, 84a, 415a – II, **185a**; VI, 261a; VII, 530a; X, 553a; S, 65b, 84a, 415a
Dawlatābād i, 1322b, 1329a; ii, 99b, **179b**; iv, 922b; v, 884a; vi, 54a, 126a, 131b, 269a, 271a, 368b, 369a, 535b; vii, 412a; s, 57b, 105a, b, 279b, 352b – I, 1363a, 1369b; II, 101b, **185a**; IV, 955b; V, 890b; VI, 52a, 123b, 129b, 254a, 255b, 352b, 353b, 520a; VII, 413a; S, 58a, 104b, 105a, 279b, 352b
—monuments i, 1323b; ii, **180a**, 442a – I, 1364a; II, **186a**, 456b
al-Dawlatābādī, Shihāb al-Dīn (1445) i, 702b, 859a; ii, **180b** – I, 724a, 883a; II, **186b**
Dawlatyār s, 367a – S, 368a
Dawr s, **206b** – S, **206a**
Dawraḳ ii, **181a**; v, 89a – II, **186b**; V, 91a
Daws → Azd
Dawsa ii, **181b** – II, **187a**
Dāwūd (King David/ le roi -) i, 261a; ii, **182a**; iv, 947b – I, 269a; II, **187b**; IV, 980b
Dāwūd (Gudjarāt) (1459) vi, 50a – VI, 48b
Dāwūd b. ʿAbbās al-Bānīdjūrī (873) i, 1001a; s, 125a, b – I, 1032a; S, 124b
Dāwūd b. ʿAbd Allāh b. Idrīs al-Faṭānī (XIX) ii, **183a**; vi, 235b – II, **188b**; VI, 208a
Dāwūd b. ʿAbd al-Raḥmān al-ʿAṭṭār (IX) i, 827a – I, 850a
Dāwūd b. Abī Dāwūd (Khuttalan) (IX) s, 125b – S, 124b
Dāwūd b. al-ʿĀḍid (Fāṭimid(e)) (1207) iv, 200b – IV, 209b
Dāwūd b. Abū Hind (VIII) i, 104b – I, 107b
Dāwūd b. ʿAdjab Shāh (Bohorā) (1588) i, 1254b; iv, 201a; ix, 824b, 829a – I, 1292b; IV, 210a; IX, 859a, 864a
Dāwūd b. ʿAlī b. ʿAbbās (VIII) i, 43a; iv, 973b – I, 44a; IV, 1005b
Dāwūd b. Idrīs II (Idrīsid(e)) (VIII) iii, 1035b; iv, 632b – III, 1061b; IV, 657b
Dāwūd b. Khalaf al-Ẓāhirī (884) i, 337a; ii, **182b**, 889b, 890a; v, 239b; vii, 570a – I, 347b; II, **188a**, 910b; V, 237b; VII, 570b
Dāwūd b. Ḳuṭb Shāh (Bohorā) (XVI) i, 1254b, 1255a; iv, 201a; ix, 824b – I, 1292b, 1293a; IV, 210a; IX, 859a
Dāwūd b. Maḥmūd b. Muḥammad b. Malik-Shāh (Saldjūḳ) (1131) i, 300b, vi, 64a, 500a, 782a – I, 309b; VI, 61b, 485a, 771b
Dāwūd b. Marwān al-Raḳḳī → al-Muḳammiṣ
Dāwūd b. Rawḥ b. Ḥātim b. Ḳabīṣa b. al-Muhallab (VIII) vii, 360a – VII, 362b
Dāwūd b. Suḳmān (Artuḳid(e)) (XII) i, 664b, 983b; iii, 507a – I, 684b, 1014a; III, 524b
Dāwūd b. Sulaymān (Mikhlāf) (X) ii, 517a – II, 530a
Dāwūd b. Sulaymān (Kilwa) (1170) v, 106b, 1157b – V, 108b, 1147b
Dāwūd b. Yazīd b. Ḥātim b. Ḳabīṣa b. al-Muhallab (820) vii, 360a, 694a; VII, 362b, 694b; s, 326b – S, 326a
Dāwūd al-Anṭāḳī → al-Anṭāḳī
Dāwūd Atba, Ḥadjdj (XX) vi, 165b – VI, 157b
Dāwūd Barakāt (XX) s, 159b – S, 159b
Dāwūd Burhān al-Dīn → Dāwūd b. Ḳuṭb Shāh
Dāwūd al-Faṭānī → Dāwūd b. ʿAbd Allāh
Dāwūd Khākī, Bābā (Čak) (XVI) s, 167b – S, 167b
Dāwūd Khān (1549) vii, 721a – VII, 722a
Dāwūd Khān (1851) i, 330b, 905; ii, 184b, 813a, 1257b; s, 75a – I, 340b, 993a; II, 190a, 832a, 1290b; S, 75b
Dāwūd Khān (1875) ii, 184b, 637a – II, 190b, 653a
Dāwūd Khān (Carnatic/-que) (XVIII) i, 624b – I, 645b
Dāwūd Khān (Fārūḳī) ii, 814b – II, 834a
Dāwūd Khān (Rohilla) (1725) iii,59b; viii, 426a, 572a, b – III, 67a; VIII, 440a, 590a, 591a
Dāwūd Khān b. Luarsab (al-Kurdjī) v, 493a – V, 495b, 496a
Dāwūd Khān Ḳara (1623) ii, 183b; vii, 707b – II, 189b; VII, 708b
Dāwūd Khān Kararānī (1576) ii, **183a**; ii, 202b, 423b; vi, 342b – II, **189a**; III, 208a, 437a; VI, 327a
Dāwūd Khān Ḳodja (1498) ii, 184a; iv, 231a; vi, 3a, 72a – II, 190a; IV, 241b; VI, 3a, 70a
Dāwūd Khān Ḳurayshī i, 1210a – I, 1246a
Dāwūd Khān al-Kurdjī (1816) vi, 797a – VI, 787a
Dāwūd Khān Nawwāb (Maḥmūdābād) vi, 77b – VI, 75b
Dāwūd Pasha (1470) vi, 72a, 1025b – VI, 70a, 1018a
Dāwūd-Shāh Mengüček (XIII) iv, 817b, 818b, 871a – IV, 850b, 851b, 904b
Dāwūd al-Ṭāʾī (781) i, 124a – I, 127b
Dāwūdis i, 552b, 1255a; ii, 98a; iv, 201b – I, 570a, 1293a; II, 100a; IV, 210a
Dāwūdiyya → Ẓāhiriyya
Dāwūdiyya, Banū (Nasīla) vi, 728b – VI, 717b
Dāwūdpōtrās i, 230a; ii, **185a** – I, 237a; II, **191a**
al-Dawwānī (1501) i, 326b, 329a – I, 337a, 339a
Dāya → Rāzī, Nadjm al-Dīn
Ḍayʿa i, 1145b; ii, **187b** – I, 1180a; II, **193b**
Dayak s, 150b, 151a – S, 151a
Dayā Bahādur (1728) ii, 219a – II, 225b
Dayānat Khān (XVII) ii, 336b, 868b – II, 346a, 888b
al-Daybaʿ (1537) vii, 911b – VII, 912a
Daybul (Sind) ii, **188a**; iii, 441a; iv, 597b; vi, 405b, 691a; vii, 71a, 405b; ix, 75b; s, 243a – II, **194a**; III, 455a; IV, 621b; VI, 390a, 678b; VII, 72a, 407a; IX, 79a; S, 243a
Daydabān ii, **189a** – II, **195a**
Ḍayf ii, **189a**; iii, 1018a – II, **195a**; III, 1043b
Ḍayfa Khātūn (Ayyūbid(e)) (1242) iii, 87b; vii, 990a – III, 89b; VII, 991a
Dayi̊ i, 368a; ii, **189a** – I, 379a; II, **195a**
Dayi̊ Ḳarača Pasha (1456) viii, 10a – VIII, 10q
Dayla-rustāḳ vi, 511b, 513a – VI, 497a, 498a
Daylam i, 20a; ii, **189b**, 732a, 1111a; iv, 19a, 345b, 346a, 1078a; vi, 120a, 433b, 744a; vii, 655b; viii, 586a, 807b; s, 297b, 298a, 299a, 363a – I, 21a; II, **195b**, 750b, 1137a; IV, 20a, b, 360b, 1109b; VI, 117b, 419a, 733b; VII, 655a; VIII, 605a, 835a; S, 297a, b, 298b, 362b
Daylamān s, 335a – S, 334b
al-Daylamī, Abu ʾl-Ḥasan (XI) iii, 823a – III, 846b
al-Daylamī, Abū Ṭāhir Ilyās (1069) s, 192b – S, 193b
al-Daylamī, Muhadhdhab al-Dīn ʿAlī (1244) vii, 479a – VII, 479a

al-Daylamī, Muḥammad b. al-Ḥasan (1307) vi, 917b – VI, 909a
Daylamī, Banu 'l- (Yemen) s, 22b – S, 22b
Daylamīs i, 190a, 688a, 839b, 1350a, 1354a, 1355b; ii, **190a**, 506a, 1082b, 1111b; iii, 197a, 671b, 1201b; iv, 208a, 465a, 859a; vi, 115b, 499a; vii, 655b; x, 897b; s, 118b, 309a, 356b – I, 195b, 709a, 863a, 1390a, 1393b, 1394b; II, **196a**, 518b, 1108a, 1137b; III, 202a, 693a, 1232a; IV, 217a, 485b, 892a; VI, 113a, 484b; VII, 655a; X, ;S, 118a, 309a, 356a
al-Daymartī vi, 829a – VI, 819b
Dayn s, **207a** – S, **206b**
Dayr ii, **194b** – II, **200b**
Dayr ʿAbd al-Raḥmān ii, **195b** – II, **202a**
Dayr al-ʿĀḳūl ii, **196a**; vi, 728b; vii, 410b, 771a, 801b – II, **202a**; VI, 717b; VII, 412a, 772b, 803a
Dayr al-Aʿwar ii, **196b** – II, **202b**
Dayr al-Balaḥ vi, 31a – VI, 29b
Dayr al-Djamādjim i, 42b; ii, **196b**, 304b; iv, 289a, 495a, b; v, 639b; vii, 408b – I, 43b; II, **203a**, 313a; IV, 302a, 516a, 517a; V, 644a; VII, 410a
Dayr al-Djāthalīḳ ii, **197a**; vii, 408b, 650a – II, **203a**; 409b, 650a
Dayr Kaʿb ii, **197b** – II, **203b**
Dayr al-Ḳamar s, 159a, 160b – S, 159a, 160b
Dayr Ḳunnā ii, **197b** – II, **203b**
Dayr Ḳurra ii, **197b** – II, **204a**
Dayr Murrān ii, **198a**,b; vi, 599b – II, **204a**, b; VI, 584b
Dayr Mūsa ii, **198b** – II, **204b**
Dayr al-Rummān ii, 198b – II, 205a
Dayr Samʿān ii, **198b**; iii, 130a – II, **204b**; III, 132b
Dayr al-Suryānī (wādī al-Naṭrūn) i, 201a, 624a; ii, 195b – I, 206b, 643b; II, 201b
Dayr al-Zaʿfarān vi, 542a, b – VI, 527a
Dayr al-Zōr ii, **198b**; iv, 655a – II, **205a**; IV, 681b
Dayrī, Banū v, 333a – V, 333a
Daysam b. Ibrāhīm al-Kurdī (X) i, 190a; ii, 680a; v, 451a; vii, 656a; x, 42b, 897b – I, 194b; II, 697a; V, 454b; VII, 655b; X, 43b,
Daysam b. Isḥāḳ (X) vii, 633a – VII, 633a
Dayṣāniyya ii, **199a**; v, 384b – II, **205a** V, 385b
Dayyir vi, 384b – VI, 368b
Dayzan → al-Ḥaḍr
al-Ḍayzan b. Djabhala iii, 51a – III, 52b
Daza, Banū i, 1258a; s, 165a – I, 1296a; S, 165a
Dazā i, 1258a – I, 1296a
Dead Sea → Baḥr Lūṭ
Dēbal → Daybul
Debaroa → Debārwā
Debārwā vi, 642a; viii, 235b – VI, 627a; VIII, 241a
Debbeb, Fitawrāri (XIX) vi, 643a – VI, 628a
Debdou → Dubdū
Deccan → Dakhan
Dedan (al-ʿUlā) i, 547b; v, 761b, 762a; vi, 88b – I, 565a; V, 767b, 768a; VI, 86b
Dede ii, **199b** – II, **206a**
Dede Aghač ii, **200a** – II, **206a**
Dede Ḳorḳut i, 311a, 419b; ii, 75b, **200a**, 1109a; iii, 374a; viii, 163b – I, 321a, 431b; II, 77a, **206b**, 1135a; III, 385b; VIII, 166a
Dede Sulṭān i, 869b; ii, **200b** – I, 893b; II, **207a**
Dede ʿUmar Sikkīnī (XV) iii, 43b – III, 45a
Defter → Daftar
Defter Emini ii, **201a** – II, **207a**
Defterdār → Daftardār
Defterdār ʿAlī Pasha (1695) vii, 708a – VII, 708b
Dehās ii, **201a** – II, **207a**
Dehhānī, Khodja (XIII) ii, **201a** – II, **207b**
Dehkān → Dihḳan
Dehkhudā, ʿAlī Akbar s, **207b** – S, **207b**
Deir ez-Zor → Dayr al-Zōr
Deldoul s, 328b – S, 328a
Delhemma → Dhu 'l-Himma
Delhi → Dihlī
Deli ii, **201a** – II, **207b**
Deli Birader → Ghazālī, Meḥmed
Deli Ḥasan Pasha (XVII) ii, 208b; iv, 499a, 595a – II, 215a; IV, 520b, 619a
Deli Muṣṭafā (Bostandjî) (XIX) i, 1278b – I, 1317b
Deli-Orman ii, **202a** – II, **208b**
Delvina ii, **203a** – II, **209b**
Demak s, 150b, 199b, 201a, 202a – S, 150b, 199b, 201a, b
Demavend → Damāwand
Demesne → Ḍayʿa
Demetrius b. Sefer-beg (Abkhāz) (1822) i, 101a, 1132a – I, 104a, 1166a
Demetrius Cantwmir (Hospodar) → Kantimur
Demir → Kemal Tahir
Demir Baba (Bektāshī) ii, 202b – II, 209a
Demir Khān b. Ḳarāmān (1333) iv, 622a – IV, 646b
Demir Khān b. Karasî (XIV) iv, 628a – IV, 653a
Demir Kapî → Dar-i Āhanīn
Demirbāsh ii, **203b** – II, **210a**
Demirdāsh Bāshā, ʿAbd al-Raḥmān Muṣṭafā (1929) s, 208b – S, 208b
Demirdāshiyya i, 1152a; iv, 991b; vi, 88a; s, **208a** – I, 1186a; IV, 1024a; VI, 86a; S, **207b**
Demirel, Süleymān x, 695a – X,
Demirtash → Timurtash
Demnat → Damnāt
Demokrat Parti ii, **204a**, 569a, 645a; iv, 124b; v, 264a, 1038b – II, **210b**, 611a, 661b; IV, 129b; V, 261b, 1034b
Demokritos → Dīmuḳrāt
Demotika → Dimetoḳa
Denau (Āmū Dārya) s, 281a – S, 281a
Dendi (Songhai) ii, 94a – II, 96a
Deneb → Nudjūm
Denia → Dāniya
Deñizli ii, **204a** v, 557a, 588b; vi, 420b; s, 44b, 138a – II, **210b**; V, 562a, 592b; VI, 406a; S, 45a, 137b
Denktaş, Rauf (XX) v, 1078a – V, 1075b
Deoband ii, 55a, 132a, b, **205a**, 437a; v, 1135b; vi, 462a; x, 38b; s, 66b, 74a, 292b, 293b – II, 56a, 135b, 136a, **211b**, 448b; V, 1131a; VI, 447b; X, 39b; S, 67a, 74b, 292a, 293a
Deōgīri → Dawlatābād
Derʿa → Adhriʿāt
Dēra Fatḥ Khān ii, 205b; iii, 633b – II, 212a; III, 655a
Dēra Ghāzī Khān → Dēradjāt
Dēra Ismāʿīl Khān → Dēradjāt
Dēradjāt i, 1005b; ii, 185b, 186a, b, **205b**, 206a; iii, 633b; vi, 86a, b; viii, 253b; ix, 819b; s, 329b, 331b, 332a – I, 1036b; II, 191b, 192a, b, **212a**; III, 655a; VI, 84a, b; VIII, 256a; IX, 854b; S, 329a, 331a, b
Derbend (Bāb al-Abwāb) i, 32a, 835b, 921b, 1066b; ii, 85b, 87b, 88a, 115b, **206a** iv, 342b, 344a, b, 346a, 348a, b; vi, 129b, 740a; vii, 572b – I, 33a, 858b, 949a, 1098b; II, 87a, 89b, 90a, 118b, **212b**; IV, 357a, 358b, 359a, 361a, 362b, 363b; VI, 127b, 729a; VII, 573b
Derbouka → Darabukka
Derde Shay (Čad) (1939) s, 165a, b, 166b – S, 165a, b, 166b
Derdli, Ibrahim (1845) ii, **206b** – II, **212b**
Derdli Kātib (Bektāshī) ii, 202b – II, 209a
Derebey i, 469a; ii, **206b**, 446b – I, 483a; II, **213a**, 458b
Deren (Atlas) i, 748a – I, 770b

Dergāh → Dargāh
Derna → Darna
Dersim ii, **208a** – II, **214b**
Derwīsh Ḥasan Pasha → Derwīsh Pasha (1603)
Derwīsh Meḥmed (1512) vi, 125a – VI, 122b
Derwīsh Meḥmed Pasha (1655) ii, **209a**, 339a; iii, 1248a – II, **215b**, 348b; III, 1280b
Derwīsh Meḥmed Pasha (1777) ii, **209a** – II, **215b**
Derwīsh Meḥmed Pasha (1837) i, 241a, 1078b; ii, **209b** – I, 248b, 1111a; II, **216a**
Derwīsh Meḥmed Ẓillī (1648) ii, 717b; v, 18a – II, 736a; V, 18b
Derwīsh Pasha (1603) i, 1271a; ii, **208a** – I, 1310b; II, **214b**
Derwīsh Pasha (1606) ii, **208b**, 287b; iv, 572b; v, 641a – II, **215a**, 295b; IV, 595a; V, 645a
Derwīsh Pasha (Kozan) (XIX) vii, 525a – VII, 525a
Derwīsh Waḥdetī, *ḥāfiẓ* (XX) ii, 475a; iv, 283b – II, 487a; IV, 296a
Destour ii, 639a; iii, 524a – II, 655a; III, 542a
Devagiri → Dawlatābād
Deval Devi (XIX) ii, 269a, 695a, 1124a; iv, 922a – II, 277b, 712b, 1150b; IV, 955a
Deve Boynu ii, **210a** – II, **216b**
Devedji ii, **210b** – II, **217a**
Develi Ḳara Ḥiṣār → Ḳara Ḥiṣār
Develū, Banū (Ḳadjār) iv, 389a; vi, 483b – IV, 406a; VI, 469b
Devkoṭ ii, 297a – II, 305a
Devshirme i, 36a, 206b, 268b, 269b, 656b, 712a, 807a, 999b; ii, **210b**, 1086a, 1087a; s, 269b – I, 36b. 212b, 276b, 278a, 677a, 733b, 830b, 1030a; II, **217a**, 1111b, 1112b; S, 269a
Dēwal → Daybul
Dewal Dewi → Deval Devi
Dewlet → Dawlat
Dewlet-berdi (Girāy) (XV) iii, 44a – III, 45b
Dey → Dayi̊
Deymer → Hüsnü, Shefīḳ
Dghughī → Sīdī Abū 'l-Ḥasan ʿAlī b. Ḥamdūsh
Dghughiyyīn s, 350b – S, 350b
al-Dhabḥānī, Muḥammad b. Saʿīd (1470) iv, 449b – IV, 469b
Dhabīḥ Bihrūz (1971) vi, 764a – VI, 753a
Dhabīḥa ii, **213a**; s, 221b – II, **219b**; S, 221b
Dhafār → Ẓufār
Dhahab ii, **214a**, 1002a, 1003a; v, 964a, 965b, 967a, 970a, 977a – II, **220b**, 1025a, 1026b; V, 968b, 969b, 972b, 976a
al-Dhahabī → Aḥmad al-Dhahabī; Aḥmad al- Manṣūr
al-Dhahabī, Shams al-Dīn Abū ʿAbd Allāh (1348) i, 70a, 74b, 594b, 595a, 965a, 1238b; ii, 125b, **214b**, 522b, 523a; iii, 756a, 954b; vi, 349b, 350a, 352b, 353a; vii, 212b, 537b, 576b; viii, 458b, 517a; s, 225b, 311b, 386b, 400a –
I, 72a, 76b, 614a, b, 994b, 1276a; II, 128b, **221a**, 535b, 536a; III, 779a, 979a; VI, 334a, 336b, 337b; VII, 213b, 537b, 577a; VIII, 474a, 535a; S, 225b, 311b, 386b, 400b
al-Dhahabī, Shaykh (1977) vii, 291b – VII, 293b
Dhahabiyya → Kubrāwiyya
al-Dhahr → al-Ẓahr
Dhahran → Ẓahrān
Ḍhākā (Dacca) ii, 7a, **216a**, 426a; vi, 369b, 806a – II, 7a, **222b**, 437a; VI, 354a, 796a
Dhākir, Ḳāṣim Bey (1857) i, 193b; ii, **217a** –
I, 199b; II, **223b**
Dhakwān b. ʿAmr al-Fuḳaymī → al-Fuḳaymī, Dhakwān b. ʿAmr
Dhāl ii, **217b** – II, **224a**
Dhala → Ḍāliʿ
Dhalūl i, 541a – I, 558a
Dhamār ii, **218a**; vi, 433b, 436a; s, 335a – II, **224b**; VI, 418b, 419a, 421a, b; S, 334b
Dhamarʿalī Yuhabirr vi, 563b – VI, 548b
al-Dhammiyya ii, **218a**, 570a – II, **225a**, 584b
Dhanab → Nudjūm
Dhāndā (river/fleuve) vi, 49b – VI, 48a
Dhār ii, **218b**, 276b, 1124a; iii, 446a; vi, 309b; s, 105a – II, **225a**, 285a, 1150b; III, 460b; VI, 294b; S, 104b
Dharr b. ʿAbd Allāh (VII) vii, 605b – VII, 605a
Dharra ii, **219b** – II, **226b**
Dhārūr (district) vi, 269a – VI, 254a
Dharwān b. Thaʿlaba, Banū ix, 817a – IX, 852a
Dhārwār ii, **220a** – II, **226b**
Dhāt ii, **220a**; v, 1261a, 1262a – II, **227a**; V, 1252b, 1253a
Dhāt al-Himma → Dhu 'l-Himma
Dhāt al-Ṣawārī (naval battle) (655) i, 51b, 936a; vii, 155a; ix, 444b; s, 120b, **221b** – I, 53a, 964b; VII, 157a; IX, 461b; S, 120a, **221b**
Dhātī (1564) i, 956a; ii, **220b**, 737b; iv, 1137b – I, 985b; II, **227b**, 756a; IV, 1169a
Dhawḳ ii, **221a**, 1041a – II, **228a**, 1065b
Dhawḳ, Muḥammad (1854) i, 807b, 914b, 1116a; ii, 83b, 84a, **221b**; iii, 1095a; iv, 716b; v, 960a, b, 961b; s, 107a –
I, 831a, 942a, 1149b; II, 85b, **228b**; III, 1122a; IV, 745a; V, 964a, b, 965b; S, 106b
Dhawū ʿAbd Allāh iii, 263a – III, 270a
Dhawū Barakāt (Mecca) iii, 263a; vi, 150a, b – III, 270a; VI, 149a
Dhawū Ḥassān, Banū vi, 141b, 741a – VI, 139b, 730b
Dhawū Manṣūr, Banū vi, 141b, 142b, 143a – VI, 139b, 141a
Dhawū Masʿūd (Mecca) vi, 150b – VI, 149a
Dhawū ʿUbayd Allāh, Banū vi, 141b – VI, 139b
Dhawū Zayd (Mecca) iii, 263a; vi, 150a, b, 151a – III, 270a; VI, 149a, b
Dhawwāk → Čashna-gīr
al-Dhiʾāb ii, **222b**; iv, 79a – II, **229b**; IV, 83a
Dhiʾb ii, **223a** – II, **230a**
Dhiʾb, Banū ix, 84a – IX, 88a
Dhihnī, Bayburtlu (1859) ii, **223b** – II, **230b**
Dhikr i, 346b; ii, 55b, 160a, 164b, **223b**, 891b; iii, 1051a; iv, 94b, 487b, 992b; s, 313a –
I, 357a; II, 56b, 165a, 169b, **230b**, 912a; III, 1077b; IV, 99a, 508b, 1025a; S, 313a
Dhikrīs (Zikrīs) v, 1230b; s, **222a** – V, 1221a; S, **222a**
Dhimār → Dhamār
Dhimma i, 429b, 811a; ii, **227a**; iv, 1146b –
I, 441b, 834a; II, **234a**; IV, 1178a
Dhimma (capacity/-é) ii, **231a** – II, **238a**
Dhimmī → Ahl al-dhimma
Dhira i, 98b – I, 101a
Dhirāʿ ii, **231b** – II, **238b**
Dhiyāb b. Bādi (Ḳerrī) (XVIII) iv, 893a – IV, 925b
Dhofar → Ẓufār
Dhū Bīn s, 22a – S, 22b
Dhū, dhī, dhā i, 194b, 195a; ii, **232b** – I, 200b; II, **239a**
Dhu 'l-Aktāf → Shāpūr II
Dhū-Amīr vi, 563b – VI, 548b
Dhū Awān vi, 647a – VI, 632b
Dhū Djadan (Ḥimyar) vi, 829b; viii, 980a – VI, 820a; VIII, 1014a
Dhū Djibla ix, 1b – IX, 1b
Dhu 'l-Faḳār (sword/épée) i, 742a; ii, **233a**; vi, 528a, 537a – I, 764a; II, **239b**; VI, 512b, 521b
Dhu 'l-Faḳār al-Kurdī (XVI) i, 903b; iii, 1257a – I, 931a; III, 1289b
Dhu 'l-Faḳār Alī Khān b. Raḥmat Khān (XVIII) iii, 61b – III, 64a

Dhu 'l-Faḳār Bahādur (XIX) i, 1012b – I, 1044a
Dhu 'l-Faḳār Bey (XVIII) ii, 233b – II, 240a
Dhu 'l-Faḳāriyya ii, **233a**; iv, 723a, 852a; vi, 325a, b – II, **240a** IV, 752a, 885a; VI, 309b
Dhu 'l-Fiḳār Khān (Abdālī) (XVIII) i, 295b, 1025b; ii, 379a, 810a – I, 304b, 1057b; II, 389b, 829a
Dhū Ḥazfar, Banū (Mārib) vi, 561b – VI, 546b
Dhu 'l-Ḥidjdja → Ta'rīkh
Dhu 'l-Himma i, 1102b, 1103b, 1104a; ii, **233b** – I, 1136a, b, 1137a; II, **240b**
Dhū Ḥusā, Day of/Journée de s, 178a – S, 179a
Dhū Ḥusayn vi, 566a – VI, 551a
Dhu 'l-Ḳaʾda → Ta'rīkh
Dhu 'l-Ḳadr (Turkmen) i, 468a, b, 1190b; ii, 8a, **239a**, 724b; iii, 1105a; iv, 553a, 562b, 843a; vi, 231b, 324b, 507b, 508b; vii, 271b, 645a; ix, 129a – I, 482a, 1225b; II, 8a, **246a**, 743b; III, 1132b; IV, 576b, 585a, 876a; VI, 225a, 309a, 493a, 494a; VII, 273b, 644b; IX, 134a
Dhū Ḳār i, 690a, 964a; ii, **241a**; iv, 289a; v, 634a; viii, 120a – I, 711a, 993b; II, **247a**; IV, 302a; V, 638a; VIII, 122a
Dhū Ḳarad vii, 371a – VII, 373a
Dhu 'l-Ḳarnayn → Iskandar
Dhu 'l-Ḳarnayn b. ʿAyn al-Dawla (1162) ii, 111a – II, 113b
Dhu ʾl-Ḳaṣṣa (battle) x, 162a – X, 164b
Dhu 'l-Khalaṣa i, 865b; ii, **241b**; iv, 1106a – I, 889b; II, **248b**; IV, 1137b
Dhu 'l-Khimār → al-Aswad b. Kaʿb al-ʿAnsī
Dhu 'l-Kifl (Ayyūb/Job) i, 404b; ii, **242a**; vi, 652b; x, 542b – I, 416a; II, **249a**; VI, 638a; X,
Dhu ʾl-Madjāz (Mecca) x, 90a, 137a, 789a – X, 97b, 147b
Dhū Marmar iv, 201a – IV, 209b
Dhu 'l-Marwa v, 316b – V, 316a
Dhū Matāra vi, 473a – VI, 458b
Dhū Muḥammad (Mārib) vi, 566a – VI, 551a
Dhu 'l-Nūn (Dānishmendid(e)) (1173) ii, 111a; vi, 507a; viii, 132a – III, 113b; VI, 492b; VIII, 134b
Dhu 'l-Nūn, Abu 'l-Fayḍ al-Miṣrī (861) i, 274a, 718a; ii, **242a**; iii, 83b; iv, 990a; vi, 354a, 570a; viii, 892a – I, 282b, 739b; II, **249a**; III, 85b; IV, 1022b; VI, 338b, 555a; VIII, 923a
Dhu 'l-Nūn Ayyūb al-ʿIrāḳī vi, 91a – VI, 89a
Dhu 'l-Nūn Beg Arghūn (1507) i, 627b; iv, 536b; v, 579b – I, 648a; IV, 560a; V, 584b
Dhu 'l-Nūnid(e)s i, 7a, 202b; ii, **242b**; v, 392a; vii, 778b – I, 7a, 208a; II, **249b**; V, 393a; VII, 780b
Dhū Nuwās, Yūsuf Ashʿar (VI) i, 549a, 692b; ii, **243b**; v, 120b, 776b; vi, 829b; vii, 872a; s, 229b – I, 566a, 713b; II, **250b**; V, 123a, 782b; VI, 820a; VII, 873b; S, 229b
Dhū Raydān i, 548a, b; vi, 561a – I, 565b, 566a; VI, 546a
Dhu 'l-Riyāsatayn iv, 51b – IV, 54b
Dhu 'l-Ruḳayba v, 526a – V, 529b, 530a
Dhu 'l-Rumma (735) i, 586b; ii, 92b, **245a**; vii, 403b, 536b, 981b; viii, 377b; s, 42b – I, 605b; II, 94b, **252a**; VII, 405a, 536b, 982a; VIII, 390a; S, 42b
Dhu 'l-Shanātir (ʿUmān) vii, 551a – VII, 551b
Dhu 'l-Sharā ii, **246a**; iv, 321b; v, 1156b – II, **253a**; IV, 336a; V, 1146a
Dhū ʿUthkulān vi, 830b – VI, 820b
Dhū Yazan → Sayf
Dhuʾayb b. Mūsā (1151) iii, 134a; iv, 200b – III, 136b; IV, 209a
Dhubāb ii, **247b** – II, **254b**
Dhūbān, Shaykh s, 263a – S, 263a
Dhubyān, Banū ii, 71b, 873b, 1023a; vii, 841a; s, 177a, 178a – II, 73a, 893b, 1046b; VII, 842a; S, 178a, 179a
Dhūdhū Miyān b. Ḥādjdjī Sharīʿat Allāh (1860) vii, 291a – VII, 293a
Dhufār → Ẓufār
Dhuhl, Banū vi, 333a, 649a – VI, 317b, 634b
Dhuhl b. Thaʿlaba i, 963a – I, 992b
al-Dhulayḥ viii, 377a – VIII, 389b
Dhunnūnid(e)s → Dhu 'l-Nūnid(e)s
al-Dhunūb, Dafn ii, **248a**, 303b ; iv, 407a – II, **255a**, 312a; IV, 424b
Dhurr → Ḳamḥ
Diāgha (Mali) vi, 258b – VI, 243a
Ḍibāb → ʿĀmir b. Ṣaʿṣaʿa
Dībādj → Ḳumāsh
Dībādj b. Filshāh (Gīlān) (1300) vi, 907b, – VI, 899a
al-Dībadjāt → Maldives
Dibbiyya s, 159a, b, 161b, 162a – S, 159a, b, 161a, 162a
al-Dibdiba ii, **248b** – II, **255b**
Diʿbil (860) i, 154a, 1290a; ii, **248b**; iv, 929a; v, 375a; vi, 604a, b, 625b; vii, 694b; viii, 83a; s, 32b, 35b – I, 158b, 1329b; II, **255b**; IV, 962a; V, 376a; VI, 589a, 610b; VII, 695a; VIII, 85a; S, 32b, 35b
Dibir, *ḳāḍī* (1827) i, 756a – I, 778b
al-Dibsī → Yaʿḳūb
Ḍīdān b. Fahhād → Ibn Ḥithlayn
Ḍidd i, 184b; ii, **249a** – I, 189b; II, **256a**
Dīdebān → Daydabān
Didja al-ʿAwrāʾ → Shaṭṭ al-ʿArab
Didjla i, 184a, 191a, 634b, 1094b, 1095a, b; ii, **249a**; iii, 1251a; iv, 654a, 675a; v, 442a, 645b, 646b, 864b, 945a; s, 37a – I, 189b, 196b, 655a, 1127b, 1128a, b; II, **256b**; III, 1283b; IV, 680b, 702b; V, 444b, 649b, 650b, 871b, 948b; S, 37a
Dido i, 756a; ii, 86b, 88b, **251a**; iv, 571b; v, 55b – I, 778b; II, 88a, 90b, **258b**; IV, 594a; V, 57a
Dienné (Sudān) i, 303a; ii, **251b**; vi, 258b, 259a – I, 312b; II, **258b**; VI, 243a
Difrīgī → Diwrīgī
Diglal ii, **252b** – II, **260a**
Digurata → Ossetes
Dihātī → Muḥammad Masʿūd
Dihgāns i, 224a, b – I, 230b, 231a
Dih-i Khwāraḳān vi, 502 a, b – VI, 487a, b, 488a
Dih-i Naw → Djand
Dihistān ii, **253a**; vi, 415b, 493b, 717a; s, 299a – II, **260a**; VI, 400b, 479b, 706a; S, 298b
al-Dihistānī, ʿAbd al-Djalīl, vizier (XI) i, 1052b – I, 1084a
Dihḳan ii, **253b**; v, 853a, 854a – II, **261a**; V, 860a, 861a
Dihkhudā, ʿAlī Akbar (XX) iv, 72b, 527a – IV, 76b, 549b
al-Dihlawī, ʿAbd al-Ḥaḳḳ → ʿAbd al-Ḥaḳḳ b. Sayf al-Dīn
al-Dihlawī, Aḥmad Ḥasan s, 409a – S, 409b
al-Dihlawī, Nūr al-Ḥaḳḳ → Nūr al-Ḥaḳḳ al- Dihlawī
al-Dihlawī, Ghulām ʿAlī (1824) vii, 936b – VII, 937b
al-Dihlawī, Shāh ʿAbd al-ʿAzīz (1824) → ʿAbd al-ʿAzīz al-Dihlawī
al-Dihlawī, Shāh Walī Allāh (1762) i, 297b, 593a, 937a; ii, 138a, 205b, **254a**, 437a; iii, 324a, 358b, 430b, 432b, 435a, b; v, 833a; vii, 290b, 316a, 328a, 938b; s, 126b, 292b – I, 306b, 612b, 965b; II, 141b, 211b, **261b**, 448b; III, 334a, 369b, 444b, 446b, 449a, b; V, 839b; VII, 292b, 318b, 329b, 330a, 939a; S, 126a, 292b
al-Dihlawī, Shaykh ʿAbd Allāh (XX) vi, 164b – VI, 157b
al-Dihlawī, Shaykh ʿAbd al-Ḥaḳḳ → ʿAbd al-Ḥaḳḳ Sayf al-Dīn

Dihlī ii, 205a, **255b**; iii, 420a; v, 883b, 1135a; vi, 48b, 49a, 50a, 53a, 61b, 65b, 126a, 270b, 273a, 294b, 309a, b, 369b, 406b, 535b, 537a, 602a, 650a, 658b, 664b; vii, 314a, 854b; s, 57b, 66b, 74a, 102a, 247a, 353a, b, 358b –
II, 211b, **263a**; III, 433b; V, 890a, 1130b; VI, 47a, b, 48b, 51a, 59b, 63b, 123b, 255b, 257b, 279b, 294b, 353b, 391a, b, 520a, 521b, 586b, 635b, 644a, 650b; VII, 316a, 856a; S, 58a, 67a, 74b, 101b, 247a, 353a, 358b
—history/histoire i, 230a, 914a, 953b; ii, **255-9**; v, 6a – I, 237a, 942a, 983a; II, **263-7**; V, 6a
—monuments i, 1321b, 1324a, 1348a; ii, 254a, **259-66**; iii, 287b, 441a, 442a, b, 443a, 449a; iv, 268b; v, 1214b, 1219b – I, 1362a, 1364b, 1388b; II, 261b, **267-74**; III, 296b, 455b, 456b, 457a, b, 464b; IV, 280b; V, 1204b, 1210a
Dihlī Sultanat(e) i, 34a, 1036a, 1321b; ii, 153b, **266b**, 336a, 1124a; iii, 198b, 201a, 416a, 417a, 420a; iv, 218a, 759a; v, 598a, 685a, 1214b; vi, 368a, 488a; vii, 193b; viii, 67b; ix, 785b; x, 593b; s, 117b, 124a, 203a, 206a, b, 258a, 284b, 359b, 409a –
I, 34b, 1067b, 1362a; II, 158b, **274b**, 345b, 1150b; III, 203b, 206b, 429b, 430a, 433b; IV, 228a, 789b; V, 601b, 690b, 1204a, b; VI, 352a, 474a; VII, 194a; VIII, 69a; IX, 819b; X, 638a; S, 117a, 123a, 202b, 206a, 257b, 284b, 359b, 409b
—art ii, **274a** – II, **282b**
Dihm, Banū vi, 474b – VI, 460a
Dihram vi, 384b – VI, 368b
Dihwārs i, 224a – I, 230b
Diḥya b. Khalīfa al-Kalbī (670) ii, **274b**, 363b, 846a; iv, 492b, 839a; vii, 212a – II, **283a**, 373b, 866a; IV, 514a, 872a; VII, 213a
Diḥya b. Musʿab (Miṣr) (VIII) vii, 160b – VII, 162a
Dīk ii, **275a** – II, **283b**
Dīk al-Djinn al-Ḥimṣī (849) ii, **275b; ix, 453b** – II, **284a; IX, 468b**
al-Dīkdān s, **222b** – S, **222b**
al-Dikdikidjī (1775) vi, 215a – VI, 199a
Dikka ii, **276a** – II, **284b**
Dikwa (Bornū) (1259b) i, 1260a, b; ii, 10b – I, 1298b; II, 10b
Dil Hersek iii, 341b – III, 352a
al-Dilāʾ v, 1191b; vi, 356b, 607a; s, 29a, **223a** – V, 1181b; VI, 340b, 591b; S, 29a, **223a**
al-Dilāʾī, Maḥammad b. Abī Bakr (1636) vi, 112b; s, 223a – VI, 110a; S, 223a
al-Dilāʾī, Maḥammad al-Masnāwī (1724) vi, 112b, 350a – VI, 110a, 334a
al-Dilāʾī, Muḥammad b. Maḥammad b. Abī Bakr al-Murābiṭ (1678) s, 223b – S, 223b
Ḍilāl bint Lamak vii, 190a – VII, 190b
Dilāʾiyyūn s, 223a – S, 223a
al-Dilam iv, 1072b, 1073a – IV, 1104a, b
Dilāwar Khān (Ḥabshī, 1492) iii, 15a – III, 16a
Dilāwar Khān (Ḥabshī) (1588) ii, 921b, 922a; iii, 15b, 426b – II, 943a; III, 16a, 440b
Dilāwar Khān Ghūrī (Mālwā) (1405) ii, 218b, 219a, 270b, **276a**, 1125a; iii, 417a, 638a; vi, 52b, 309b, 406b, 407b –
II, 225b, 226a, 278b, **284b**, 1151b; III, 430b, 659a; VI, 51a, 294b, 391a, 392a
Dilāwar Khān Lōdī iii, 995b; iv, 1020a – III, 1020a; IV, 1052a
Dilāwar Pasha (1622) ii, **276b** – II, **285a**
Dilāzāk, Banū i, 218b – I, 224b
Dildār ʿAlī (1819) iii, 434a – III, 448b
Dilpasand Khān (1486) vi, 63a – VI, 61a
Dilras Bānū Begum (1657) vi, 131b – VI, 129b
Dilshād Khātūn (1352) i, 908b; ii, 68a; viii, 997b – I, 936a; II, 69b; VIII, 1032b
Dilsiz ii, **277a** – II, **285b**
Dimashḳ i, 153b, 256a, 551b, 824a, 870a, 975a, b, 1029a, b, 1332a; ii, **277b**, 360a, 541a, 1105a, 1106a; iii, 714a, 931b, 958a; iv, 174b, 214b; v, 993a; vi, 44b, 68b, 118b, 122b, 198a, 266b, 362b, 363b, 455a, 471a, 545a, 648a, 649b, 652a, 653a, 656b, 657a, 666b, 668a, 680b, 681a, 871b; viii, 128a,b, 728b; ix, 792b; s, 20b, 37a, 49a, 195a, b, 199a, 239a, 268a –
I, 157b, 264a, 569a, 847a, 894b, 1005b, 1006a, 1061a, 1372b; II, **286a**, 369b, 554b, 1131a, 1132a; III, 736b, 956a, 982b; IV, 182b, 224a; V, 988a; VI, 43b, 66b, 116b, 120a, 182a, 251a, 346b, 347b, 440b, 456b, 529b, 633b, 635a, 637b, 638b, 642b, 652b, 654a, b, 667b, 668a, 862a; VIII, 131a, b, 749a; IX, 827a; S, 20b, 37b, 49b, 195a, b, 199a, 239a
—the Great Mosque/la grande mosquée i, 610b, 622a; ii, 280b, 281a, 282a, b, 286a, 956a, b; iii, 286b, 921a – I, 631b, 643a; II, 289a, b, 290a, b, 294a, 978a, b; III, 295b, 945b
—institutions i, 1224a; ii, 283a, b, 286a, 288a, b, 289a, 290a, 424a; iii, 139b; v, 1127a – I, 1260b; II, 291a, b, 294a, 296a, b, 297a, 298a, 453a; III, 142b; V, 1123b
—monuments i, 831a, 1316a; ii, 280b, 283a, 284b, 285a, 286a, 287b, 1106a; iii, 142a; v, 217b, 1139a, 1140a – I, 854a, 1356a; II, 288b, 291a, 292b, 293a, 294a, b, 295b, 1132a; III, 146a; V, 215a, 1133a, 1133b
Dimashḳ Khodja b. Sālim (1404) ii, 614a – II, 629a
Dimashḳ Khʷādja (Čūbānid(e)) (1327) ii, 68a – II, 69a
al-Dimashḳī → Abū ʿUthmān; Ibn Isrāʿīl; Saʿīd b. Yaʿḳūb; Shams al-Dīn Muḥammad
al-Dimashḳī, Shams al-Dīn (1327) i, 594b; ii, **291a**; iv, 1081b; v, 1012b; vi, 111b; s, 45a, 130b – I, 613b; II, **299a**; IV, 1113a; V, 1008a; VI, 109a; S, 45b, 129b
al-Dimashḳī Sharīf ʿIzz al-Dīn (1315) viii, 156b – VIII, 158b
Dimdim vi, 502b – VI, 488a
Dimetoḳa (Dimotiḳa) ii, **291b**; vi, 290b – II, **299b**; VI, 276a
Dimlī → Zāzā
Dīmuḳrāt s, 154b – S, 155a
Dimurdāsh b. Djūbān → Tīmūrtāsh b. Čūbān
Dimyāṭ i, 946b; ii, 63b, 72b, **292a**; iv, 520b; v, 92a; vi, 440a, b, 547b; vii, 69b; s, 120b –
I, 976a; II, 65a, 74a, **300a**; IV, 543a; V, 94b; VI, 425b, 426a, 532a; VII, 70a; S, 120a
al-Dimyāṭī ʿAbd al-Muʾmin al-Shāfiʿī (1306) ii, **292b**; vi, 183b – II, **300b**; VI, 167a
al-Dimyāṭī, al-Bannāʾ (1705) ii, **293a** – II, **301a**
al-Dimyāṭī, Nūr al-Dīn (XIII) ii, **293a** – II, **301a**
Dīn ii, **293b**; iv, 171b, 174a; v, 621b, 622b, 623a, b, 629a; – II, **301b**; IV, 179a, 181b; V, 625b, 626b, 627a, b, 633a
Dīnādjpur ii, **297a** – II, **305a**
Dīnār ii, 120b, **297a**, 768b; v, 964a, 965b – II, 123a, **305a**, 787a; V, 968b, 969b
Dīnār, Malik (Oghuz) (1195) ii, **299a**, 1109a; iii, 1099b; v, 160b; viii, 946b; ix, 34b –
II, **307a**, 1135a; III, 1126b; V, 159a; VIII, 978b; IX, 35a
Dīnawar ii, **299a**; iv, 13b; v, 169b; vi, 493a, 502a, 539a; s, 17b – II, **307a**; IV, 14b; V, 167a; VI, 479a, 487a, 523b; S, 17b
al-Dīnawarī, Abū Bakr (1014) vi, 671b – VI, 657b
al-Dīnawarī, Abū Ḥanīfa Aḥmad (895) i, 135b, 213a, b, 718b; ii, **300a**; v, 1025a; vii, 83b, 831b; s, 42b, 128b, 249b, 277a, 314a –
I, 139b, 219a, 220a, 740a; II, **308a**; V, 1021a; VII, 85a, 833a; S, 42b, 128a, 250a, 276b, 313b

al-Dīnawarī, Abū Saʿīd Naṣr b. Yaʿḳūb (1009) ii, **300b**; iii, 772a; viii, 646a, b; s, 259a – II, **309a**; III, 795b; VIII, 665a, b; S, 258b
al-Dīnawarī al-Miṣrī (922) vi, 353a – VI, 337a
Dindān ii, **301a** – II, **309a**
Dinet, Alphonse s, **224a** – S, **224a**
Dīn-i Ilāhī (1581) i, 317a; ii, **296a**; iii, 423b, 459a; vi, 131a – I, 327a; II, **304a**; III, 437b, 475b; VI, 129a
Dionysos → Dhu 'l-Sharā
Dioula ii, 63a; v, 252b – II, 64b; V, 250b
Dioscoride(s) → Diyusḳuridīs
Dīpalpūr vi, 49a, b, 50a, 62a, 294a – VI, 47b, 48a, 60a, 279b
Dīr (Morocco/Maroc) s, 132a – S, 131b
Dīr (Pakistan) i, 864a; ii, 30b, **316b** – I, 888b, II, 31a, **325b**
Dir → Somali
Dīrač → Drac
Ḍirār b. ʿAmr al-Ghaṭafānī al-Kūfī (815) i, 333b; iii, 1037a, 1143a, 1166a; iv, 692b; vi, 458a; vii, 54b, 259a, 260a, 546b, 566a, 784b; s, 88b, 89a, **225b** – I, 344a; III, 1063a, 1171b, 1194b; IV, 720b; VI, 443b; VII, 55a, 261a, b, 546b, 566b, 786b; S, 88b, 89a, **225b**
Ḍirār b. Ḥusayn (VIII) ii, 72a – II, 73a
Ḍirār b. al-Azwar al-Asadī (833) vi, 268a – VI, 253a
Ḍirār b. al-Khaṭṭāb (633) ii, **317b**; iii, 975b; iv, 775a; vi, 603b; ix, 864b – II, **326b**; III, 1000b; IV, 806b; VI, 588b; IX, 900b
Dire Dawa ii, **317b** – II, **326b**
Ḍirghām b. ʿĀmir, Abu 'l-Ashbāl (1164) i, 197a; ii, **317b**, 856b; viii, 130b, 831b – I, 202b; II, **327a**, 876b; VIII, 133a, 860b
Dirham ii, 119a, 121a, **319a**, 991b; iii, 1116a; iv, 248b; v, 855a, 964a, 965b – II, 121b, 124a, **328b**, 1016a; III, 1143b; IV, 259b; V, 862a, 968b, 970a
Dirham b. Naṣr b. Ṣāliḥ (VII) iv, 20b; viii, 795b – IV, 22a; VIII, 822b
al-Dirʿiyya i, 628b; ii, 159b, **320b**; iii, 678b; iv, 925a, b, 1072b; v, 508a; vi, 150b; vii, 410a; ix, 903b; s, 30b – I, 649b; II, 165b, **329b**; III, 700a; IV, 958a, b, 1104b; V, 511b; VI, 149a; VII, 411b; IX, 941b; S, 30b
Dirlik ii, **322a** – II, **331b**
Diū ii, **322a**; vi, 51a, 52a, 233b, 270a – II, **331b**; VI, 49b, 50b, 206b, 254b
Divehi Rājjē → Maldives
Divittār → Dawādār
Dīw ii, **322b**, 1125a, 1128a, b; iv, 332a; vi, 938b – II, **332a**, 1151a, 1155a, b; IV, 346b; VI, 930b
Dīw Sulṭān Rūmlū (XVI) x, 108b, 137a – X, 118a, 147b
-Dīwān (administration) i, 19b, 279b, 316b, 382a, 729a, b, 801b, 905b, 1003b, 1141b, 1143a, 1145b; ii, 304b, 305b, **323a**, 360a, 505b;iv, 26a, 937b; v, 500b; s, 210a – I, 20a, 288a, 326b, 393a, 751b, 825a, 933a, 1034a, 1176a, 1177b, 1180a; II, 313a, 314a, **332b**, 370a, 518a; IV, 27b, 970b; V, 504a; S, 210a
Dīwān (collection) i, 143b, 1070a; ii, **323a**, 999b – I, 147b, 1102a; II, **332b**, 1023a
Dīwān-Begi s, 97a, **227b** – S, 96b, **227b**
Dīwān-i Humāyūn ii, **337b** – II, **347a**
Dīwān Sāwan Mal (XIX) s, 332a – S, 331b
Dīwān al-Shūrā → Madjlis al-Shūrā
Dīwān Shurfā Khān (1638) vi, 190b – VI, 174a
Dīwāna → Muẓaffar Shāh Shams al-Dīn Ḥabshī
Dīwāna Maḥmūd Čelebi (XVI) vi, 887b – VI, 879a
Dīwānī i, 1145b; ii, 128a, 332b; iv, 1125b, 1127b – I, 1180a; II, 131a, 342a; IV, 1157b, 1159a
Dīwāniyya ii, **339b** – II, **349a**
Dīwdād → Abu 'l-Sādj
Diwrīgī ii, **340a** – II, **349b**
Diwrīghī, Fakhr al-Dīn Muḥammad al-Salghūr (1236) viii, 1005b – VIII, 1040b
Diwrigli-zāde Shams al-Dīn Muʾayyad Čelebi (1447) vii, 272a – VII, 274a
Ḍiyāʿ → Ḍayʿa
Diya i, 29a, 31b, 171b, 338a, 892a; ii, 228a, **340b**; iv, 766b; v, 180a – I, 30a, 32a, 176a, 348b, 918b; II, 235a, **350b**; IV, 797a; V, 177b
Ḍiyā al-Dīn (Marand) vi, 504a – VI, 489b
Ḍiyā al-Dīn, Sayyid (XX) iv, 398b – IV, 416a
Ḍiyā al-Dīn b. al-Athīr → Ibn al-Athīr
Ḍiyā al-Dīn Abū Muḥammad Saʿīd b. Asʿad (XII) vi, 558a – VI, 542b
Ḍiyā al-Dīn Muḥammad → ʿAlāʾ al-Dīn Muḥammad
Ḍiyā al-Dīn Yūsuf (1513) vii, 935a – VII, 935b
Ḍiyā al-Dīn Yūsuf b. Muʿīn al-Dīn Djāmī (1394) viii, 749b – VIII, 770a
Ḍiyā Gökalp → Gökalp, Ziya
Ḍiyā al-Ḥaḳḳ → Zia ul-Haqq
Ḍiyā al-Mulk b. Niẓām al-Mulk (XI) viii, 72b – VIII, 74a
Ḍiyā Pasha → Ẓiyā Pasha
Ḍiyā al-Salṭana (XIX) vi, 484a – VI, 470a
Diyālā (river/fleuve) i, 184a; ii, **343a**; v, 442a; vi, 335b, 614a, 616a; vii, 912b – I, 189b; II, **352b**; V, 444b; VI, 320a, 599a, 601a; VII, 913a
Diyānat → Dayānat
Diyār Bakr i, 4b, 8a, 639a, 662b, 664a, 665b, 666a, 1054a; ii, 8a, **343b**, 384b, 523b, 707a; iii, 1197b; iv, 90b, 816b; v, 453a, 457b; vi, 3a, 242b, 270b, 341b, 366a, 420b, 539b, 541a, b, 626a, b, 627a, 633a, 667a; vii, 1017a; viii, 53b, 133a; s, 36b, 37a, 63a, 250a, 266b – I, 4b, 8a, 659b, 683b, 684a, 686a, 1085b; II, 8a, **353a**, 395a, 536b, 725a; III, 1227b; IV, 94b, 849b; V, 455b, 460a; VI, 3a, 226b, 255b, 326a, 350b, 406a, 524a, 525b, 526a, 611a, b, 618a, 653a; VII, 1019a; VIII, 54b, 135b; S, 36b, 37a, 63a, 250a, 266a
Diyār Muḍar i, 11a, 119b, 804a; ii, **347a**, 523b; vi, 379b, 380b – I, 11a, 123a, 828a; II, **357a**, 536b; VI, 363b, 365a
Diyār Rabīʿa ii, 344a, **348a**, 523b; vi, 379b, 539b, 540b, 781a; s, 37a – II, 353b, **357b**, 536b; VI, 364a, 524a, 525a, 770b; S, 37a
al-Diyārbakrī, Ḥusayn (1582) ii, **349a** – II, **358b**
Diyusḳuridīs i, 3a, 213a, b; ii, **349a**; iii, 147b, 259a, 737b, 928a; iv, 254b; s, 43a, 59b, 78a, 114b – I, 3a, 219a, 220a; II, **359a**; III, 150b, 266a, 760a, 952b; IV, 266a; S, 43b, 60a, 77b, 114b
Diz (river/rivière) v, 81a, 887a – V, 83b, 893b
Diza (castle/château) vi, 505a, 618a – VI, 490b, 602b
Dizai (Kurd(e)s) v, 471b, 473b – V, 474b, 476b
Dizfūl ii, **350a**; iv, 7b, 675a; v, 867b; vi, 494b; vii, 673a; s, 75a, b – II, **359b**; IV, 8b, 703a; V, 873b; VI, 480a; VII, 673a; S, 75b
Diz-gāh vi, 384b – VI, 368b
Dizi-i Pisar-i ʿUmāra → al-Dīkdān
Diz-i Siyāh v, 63a, 831b – V, 65a, 837b
Dizmār iv, 1044a, b – IV, 1075b
Djaʿāfira, Banū viii, 863b – VIII, 894b
al-Djaʿalī, Muḥammad (XVI) v, 267a – V, 264b
Djaʿaliyyūn ii, **351a**, 944b; v, 1248b; s, 164a – II, **360b**, 966b; V, 1239a; S, 164a
Djabā → Bennāk
Djaba → Djebe
Djāba (Chamba) ii, **352a** – II, **361b**
Djabaev → Djambul Djabaev
al-Djabal → al-Djibāl
Djabal Abān al-Aḥmar (Arabia/-e) viii, 613a – VIII, 632b

Djabal Abān al-Asmar viii, 613a – VIII, 632b
al-Djabal al-Aḥmar (Cairo/le Caire) vii, 519a – VII, 510a
Djabal al-Akhḍar i, 207b, 1048b, 1049a; v, 759b, 760a; viii, 566a, b; ix, 774b – I, 213b, 1080a,b, 1081a; V, 765b, 766a; VIII, 584b; IX, 808a
Djabal ʿĀmil vi, 550a; vii, 301b, 407b – VI, 534b; VII, 303b, 409a
Djabal ʿĀmila i, 463a; iv, 484a – I, 448b; IV, 504b
Djabal ʿAmmāriyya vii, 865a- VII, 866b
Djabal ʿAmūr i, **460a**; iv, 481b; s, 144b – I, **473b**; IV,502b; S, 144a
Djabal Anṣāriyya vi, 577b, 578b, 789a – VI, 562b, 563b, 778b
Djabal Aswad vi, 546a, 547a – VI, 531a, b
Djabal ʿAwf i, 208a – I, 214a
Djabal ʿAybān ix, 1a – IX, 1a
Djabal Babor iv, 359a, 360b, 361a – IV, 374b, 376a, 377a
Djabal Baḥrāʾ vi, 578b, 579a; vii, 117b – VI, 563a, 564a; VII, 119b
Djabal Balaḳ al-Awsaṭ vi, 562b, 563a – VI, 547b
Djabal Balaḳ al-Ḳiblī vi, 562b – VI, 547b
Djabal-i Barakāt → Yarpūz
Djabal Bāriz v, 148a, 153b; s, **127a** – V, 150b, 154b; S, **126a**
Djabal Bishrī vi, 378a – VI, 362b
Djabal Dana Ta vi, 382a – VI, 366a
Djabal Daran → Atlas
Djabal Dhukhār vi, 439a – VI, 424b
Djabal Djawshīn vii, 119a – VII, 121b
Djabal Djūdī → Djūdī, Djabal
Djabal al-Dukhkhān vi, 358a – VI, 342a
Djabal Ḍulāʿ iv, 779b – IV, 811a
Djabal Durūd vi, 170a – VI, 160b
Djabal al-Durūz vi, 31a, 1034b – VI, 29a, 1027b
Djabal Fāruh vi, 220b – VI, 214a
Djabal Gillīz vi, 589a, 591a, 592a, b, 593a, 594b, 596b – VI, 574a, 576a, 577a, b, 579b, 581a
Djabal al-Ḥadīd vi, 591a – VI, 575b
Djabal Ḥadjar viii, 436a,b – VIII, 450b, 451a
Djabal Ḥamrīn i, 184a; iii, **149a**; s, 100a – I, 189b; III, **152b**; S, 99b
Djabal al-Ḥarānīʿ x, 392a – X, 420b
Djabal al-Ḥārith → Aghridāgh; Djudī
Djabal Hindi vi, 155a – VI, 152a
Djabal Kabkāb vi, 179b – VI, 163b
Djabal Ḳalamūn vi, 308a – VI, 293a
Djabal al-Ḳarānīʿ x, 392a – X, 420b
Djabal Ḳāsiyūn → Ḳāsiyūn, Djabal
Djabal al-Ḳilāl i, 935b – I, 964b
Djabal al-Lukkām vi, 774b, 778b, 791a – VI, 764a, 768a, 780b
Djabal Maʿādid vi, 435a – VI, 420a
Djabal Madhrūb vi, 729a – VI, 718a
Djabal Masār s, 22a – S, 22b
Djabal Maswar vi, 436a, 438b, 439a – VI, 421a, 424a, b
Djabal Mūsā s, 124b – S, 124a
Djabal Nafūsa i, 139a, 1186a; ii, 369a, 441b; iii, 657b, 927b; iv, 78a, 919b; vi, 311a, 312a, 452b, 453a; vii, **894b**; ix, 289b – I, 143a, 1221a; II, 379a, 453a; III, 678b, 952a; IV, 82a, 952b; VI, 296a, 297b, 438a; VII, **895a;** IX, 298a
Djabal Nuḳum ix, 1a – IX, 1a
Djabal al-Nūr vi, 154b, 168b – VI, 152a, 160a
Djabal al-Raḥma i, 604a; iii, 35b; vi, 168b, 169b – I, 623b; III, 37a, b; VI, 160a, b
Djabal Ramm i, 169b – I, 174a
Djabal Rayyo i, 489a – I, 503b
Djabal Ṣabir vi, 474b; x, 118a – VI, 460a; X, 127b
Djabal Sablān vi, 494a – VI, 479b
Djabal Saʿd (Mecca) vi, 179b – VI, 163b
Djabal Ṣāfir vi, 566a – VI, 551a
Djabal Salmā vii, 865a – VII, 866b
Djabal Samaʿān vi, 382b – VI, 367a
Djabal Sarāt x, 3a – X, 3a
Djabal Says s, 117a, b, **228b** – S, 116b, **228b**
Djabal Shammar i, 536b; iii, 326b; ix, 290a; S, 3b, 304b, 407b – I, 553a; III, 336b; IX, 298b; S, 2b, 304a, 407b
Djabal al-Sikkīn → Djabal al-Lukkām
Djabal Sindjār viii, 147a – VIII, 149a
Djabal al-Sirādj ii, 817b – II, 837a
Djabal al-Summāḳ iv, 200a; vii, 117b – IV, 208b; VII, 119b
Djabal Taḳarbūst iv, 478b, 479a, b – IV, 499b, 501a, b
Djabal Ṭāriḳ i, 79b, 124b, 439a; ii, **352b** – I, 81b, 128a, 508a; II, **362a**
Djabal al-Ṭayr i, 535b – I, 551b
Djabal Tays vi, 436a, 438b – VI, 421a, 424a
Djabal Thabīr Thabīr, Djabal
Djabal Thawr iii, 760a; vi, 168b, 579b – III, 783a; VI, 160a, 564a
Djabal Timatrīn vii, 611a – VII, 611a
Djabal Titteri ix, 18a – IX, 18b
Djabal Tukhlā vi, 438b – VI, 424a
Djabal Ṭūr → Ṭūr ʿAbdīn
Djabal Ṭuwayḳ (Ṭuēḳ) → Tuwayḳ, Djabal
Djabal Yashkur (Cairo/le Caire) vii, 147b, 510a – VII, 149b, 510a
Djabal al-Zallādj vi, 355a – VI, 339a
Djabal Zarhūn s, 53a, 350b – S, 53b, 350b
Djabala (Nadjd) ii, **353b**; iii, 49a; v, 526a, 640a, b – II, **363a**; III, 51a; V, 529b, 644b
Djabala (Syria/-e) ii, **353a**; vi, 577b, 578a, 579b, 582a – II, **363a**; VI, 562b, 563a, 564a, b, 567a
Djabala b. al-Ayham (VII) i, 1339a; ii, 24b, **354a**; iv, 820b – I, 1379a; II, 25a, **364a**; IV, 853b
Djabala b. al-Ḥārith (VI) iv, 556b; s, **229b** – IV, 580b; S, **229b**
al-Djabanyānī (979) vi, 354a – VI, 338a
Djaʿbar, Ḳalʿat ii, **354a**; vi, 378a, 381b; vii, 118b – II, 364a; VI, 362b, 365b, 366a; VII, 121a
Djaʿbar b. Sābik (XI) ii, 354b – II, 364a
Djabarites → Djabrids/Djabrites
Djabart (Djabara) i, 763b; ii, **355a**, 709a, 710a; iii, 5a, b; v, 522a – I, 786b; II, **364b**, 728a, 729a; III, 5a, 6a; V, 525b
al-Djabartī, ʿAbd al-Raḥmān (1825) i, 707a, 819b; ii, 109b, **355a**; vi, 87b, 316b, 327a, 543a; s, 38b, 302a – I, 728b, 842b; II, 112a, **365a**; VI, 86a, 301b, 314a, 528b; S, 38b, 302a
Djabarūt → ʿĀlam
Djabbāna v, 23a, 347a – V, 24a, 348a
Djabbānat al-Sabīʿ vii, 523a – VII, 523b
al-Djabbār → Nudjūm
Djabbār b. Djazʾ viii, 377a – VIII, 389a
Djabbāra i, 942b; iv, 9b – I, 971b; IV, 10a
Djabbāriyya, Banū vi, 614a – VI, 599a
Djabbārlu vi, 201b – VI, 185b
Djabbul ii, **357a**; viii, 131a – II, **366b**; VIII, 134a
al-Djabbūl i, 1349a; ii, **357a**; iii, 85a; viii, 131a – I, 1389a; II, **367a**; III, 87b; VIII, 134a
Djabbūya → Yabghu
Djābir III (Āl Ṣabāḥ) (XX) viii, 669a – VIII, 688b
Djābir, Banū vi, 741b; s, 356a – VI, 730b; S, 356a
Djābir b. ʿAbd Allāh al-Anṣārī (697) vii, 398a, 757b; s, 75a, 94a, **230a** – VII, 399a, 759a; S, 75b, 93b, **230a**
Djābir b. Aflaḥ (Geber) (XII) i, 1250a; ii, **357a**; viii, 102a; x, 940b; s, 413b –
I, 1288a; II, **367a**; VIII, 104b; X, ; S, 414a
Djābir b. Ḥayyān (VIII) i, 131b, 235b, 247a, 995a, 1100b, 1156a; ii, **357a**, 370b, 375a, 949b; iii, 267a,

378a; v, 112a, 113a; vi, 204a; vii, 558a, 833b; viii, 52b; x, 147a; s, 270a – I, 135a, 242b, 255a, 1025b, 1133b, 1190a; II, **367b**, 380b, 385b, 971b; III, 274b, 389b; V, 114b, 115b; VI, 188b; VII, 558a, 835a; VIII, 53a; IX, 159b; S, 269b
Dj̲ābir b. Ḥunayy vii, 307b – VII, 310a
Dj̲ābir b. Malik b. Labīd (IX) vii, 633a – VII, 632b
Dj̲ābir b. Zayd (711) ii, **359b**; iii, 648b, 649a, b, 652a – II, **369a**; III, 669b, 670a, 671a, 673b
Dj̲ābir al-Dj̲uʿfī (745) vii, 348a, 399a; ix, 492a; s, **232b** – VII, 350a, 400a; IX, 511a; S, **232a**
al-Dj̲ābiya ii, 280a, **360a**; vi, 544a, 545a, 546b, 622a, b; s, 117a, 229b – II, 288b, **369b**; VI, 528b, 529b, 531a, 607a, b; S, 116b, 229b
Dj̲abr i, 371b; ii, 365a, 388b; s, **233a** – I, 382b; II, 375a, 399a; S, **233a**
al-Dj̲abr wa ʾl-Muḳābala ii, **360b**; iv, 1070a – II, **370b**; IV, 1102a
Dj̲abr b. ʿAtīḳ (VII) vii, 32b – VII, 32b
Dj̲abr b. al-Ḳāsim (X) ii, **362b** – II, **372b**
Dj̲abrāʾīl/Dj̲ibrīl ii, **362b**, 846a, 847a; v, 210a; vi, 217a, 219b, 629a, 675a; s, 231a – II, **372b**, 866a, b, 867a; V, 207b; VI, 201a, 203b, 614a, 661b; S, 231a
Dj̲abrāʾīl b. Bukh̲tīs̲h̲ūʿ (827) i, 1223a, 1298a – I, 1259b, 1338a
Dj̲abrāʾīl b. Yaḥyā (Samarḳand) (VIII) viii, 1032a – VIII, 1068a
Dj̲abrān Kh̲ālīl Dj̲abrān (1931) i, 597a; ii, **364a**, 404a, 471b; v, 188b, 1254b, 1255a, b, 1256b; vi, 75b, 91a; vii, 902a; viii, 88a – I, 616b; II, **373b**, 415a, 483b; V, 185b, 1245b, 1246a, b, 1247b; VI, 73b, 89a; VII, 902b; VIII, 90a
Dj̲abrī Saʿdallāh → Saʿd Allāh Dj̲abrī
Dj̲abrids/Djabrites i, 942b; ii, 176a; iv, 764b; x, 913b; s, **234a** – I, 971b; II, 181b; IV, 795a; X, ; S, **234a**
Dj̲abriyya i, 249b, 257b; ii, **365a**; iii, 1142b; iv, 271b – I, 257b, 265b; II, **375a**; III, 1171a; IV, 283b
Dj̲abuk (Türkmen) (1113) i, 983a – I, 1013b
Dj̲aʿd b. Dirham → Ibn Dirham
Dj̲aʿda (ʿĀmir), Banū i, 233b, 446a; ii, **365a**; iv, 745b – I, 240b, 495a; II, **375a** IV, 775b
Dj̲aʿda b. Kaʿb → ʿĀmir b. Ṣaʿṣaʿa
Dj̲add, Banu ʾl- iii, 748a – III, 771a
al-Dj̲add b. Ḳays s, 131a – S, 130b
Dj̲addāla (Gudāla), Banū vii, 584a – VII, 584b
Dj̲adh̲īma b. ʿĀmir, Banū ii, **365b**; vi, 268b, 649a; s, 189b – II, **375b**; VI, 253a, 634a; S, 190b
Dj̲adh̲īma b. ʿAwf, Banū iv, 764a – IV, 794b
Dj̲adh̲īma al-Abras̲h̲ (al-Waḍḍāḥ) (III) i, 14a, 196b, 450b; ii, **365b**; iv, 820a; vii, 850a; x, 191a; s, 272a – I, 14b, 202a, 463b; II, **375b**; IV, 853a; VII, 851b; X, 206a; S, 272a
al-Dj̲aʿdī → Marwān II (Umayyade(e))
al-Dj̲aʿdī (1190) ix, 187b – IX, 193a
Dj̲adīd ii, **366a**, 932b; iv, 792a, 848a; viii, 753a – II, **376a**, 954a; IV, 824a, 881a; VIII, 774b
Dj̲adīda → Manzil Bas̲h̲s̲h̲ū
al-Dj̲adīda (Morocco/Maroc) i, 56a, 85a, 291a, 356b, 809b; ii, **366b**; vi, 755b – I, 57b, 87b, 300a, 367a, 833a; II, **376b**; VI, 745a
Dj̲adīs → Ṭasm
Dj̲ādisiyya → al-Ḳādisiyya
Dj̲ādj̲arm s, 83a, **235a** – S, 83a, **234b**
al-Dj̲ādj̲armī, Badr al-Dīn b. ʿUmar (1287) s, **235b** – S, **235a**
al-Dj̲ādj̲armī, Muḥammad b. Badr (XIV) vii, 529b; s, **235b** – VII, 529b; S, **235b**
Dj̲adj̲nagar (Orissa) vi, 48a, 67a – VI, 46b, 65a
Dj̲ādū ii, **368a**; s, 15b – II, **378a**; S, 15b
Dj̲ādū (Tripolitania/Tripolitaine) ii, **368b** – II, **378b**
Dj̲adwal ii, **370a** – II, **380a**
al-Dj̲ady → Nudj̲ūm
Dj̲āf, Banū i, 512b; ii, **370b**, 481a – I, 528a; II, **380b**, 503b
Dj̲aʿfar (Ḳarmaṭī) (X) iv, 663b – IV, 690a, b
Dj̲aʿfar, Banū i, 441b, 442a; v, 489b; vii, 186a – I, 454a, b; V, 492b; VII, 186b
Dj̲aʿfar b. ʿAbd Allāh (X) i, 1306b, 1307b – I, 1346b, 1347b
Dj̲aʿfar b. ʿAbd al-Raḥmān (X) v, 1009b – V, 1005a
Dj̲aʿfar b. Abī Ṭālib (629) i, 109b, 118b, 152b; ii, **372a**; iii, 1266a; v, 398b; vi, 141b, 350b; vii, 372b, 374b, 393a, 756b, 862b; s, 92b – I, 112b, 122a, 157a; II, **382a**; III, 1298b; V, 400a; VI, 140a, 334b; VII, 374a, 376a, 394a, 757b, 864a; S, 92b
Dj̲aʿfar b. Abī Yaḥyā, S̲h̲ams al-Dīn Abu ʾl-Faḍl (1177) s, **236a** – S, **236a**
Dj̲aʿfar b. ʿAlī b. Ḥamdūn al-Andalusī (982) i, 1044b, 1238a, 1309a; ii, **372b**; iii, 1042b; v, 1176a, b, 1177a; vi, 727b, 728a, 1038a; vii, 487a – I, 1076a, 1275b, 1349b; II, **383a**; III, 1068b; V, 1166a, b, 1167a; VI, 716b, 717a, 1031a; VII, 487a
Dj̲aʿfar b. ʿAlī (Tiflīs) (XI) iv, 346b, 347b; v, 489a, b – IV, 361a, 362a; V, 491b, 492a, b
Dj̲aʿfar b. al-Faḍl (866) vi, 106a – VI, 104a
Dj̲aʿfar b. al-Faḍl b. al-Furāt → Ibn al-Furāt, Dj̲aʿfar
Dj̲aʿfar b. Fahardj̲is (IX) v, 451b – V, 454a
Dj̲aʿfar b. Falāḥ al-Kutāmī (X) vii, 488a – VII, 488a
Dj̲aʿfar b. al-Hādī (IX) s, 116b – S, 116a
Dj̲aʿfar b. Ḥarb (X) vii, 312a – VII, 314b
Dj̲aʿfar b. Ḥarb al-Hamadh̲ānī (850) ii, **373a**; iii, 1037a, 1266a; iv, 126b, 629b; vi, 636b; vii, 790a – II, **383a**; III, 1063a, 1299a; IV, 132a, 721a; VI, 621b; VII, 791b
Dj̲aʿfar b. Hārūn (803) iv, 645a – IV, 671b
Dj̲aʿfar b. al-Ḥasan b. al-Uṭrūs̲h̲ (X) vi, 115b; s, 356b, 357a – VI, 113a; S, 356b, 357a
Dj̲aʿfar b. Ḥinzāba (1001) iv, 419b – IV, 438a
Dj̲aʿfar b. Ismāʿīl (1899) vii, 100b – VII, 102b
Dj̲aʿfar b. Kh̲iḍr → Kās̲h̲if al-Gh̲iṭāʾ al-Nadj̲afī
Dj̲aʿfar b. Ḳudāma al-Kātib v, 319a, b – V, 318b, 319a
Dj̲aʿfar b. al-Manṣūr bi-ʾllāh (Zaydī) (1001) vi, 436a, 439a – VI, 421b, 424b
Dj̲aʿfar b. Manṣūr al-Yaman (X) ii, 861b; s, **236b** – II, 881b; S, **236b**
Dj̲aʿfar b. Mubas̲h̲s̲h̲ir (848) ii, **373a**; iii, 1266a; vii, 605a; ix, 824b; s, 89a – II, **383a**; III, 1299a; VII, 604b; IX, 859a; S, 89a
Dj̲aʿfar b. Muḥammad → Abū Maʿs̲h̲ar al-Balkh̲ī
Dj̲aʿfar b. Muḥammad (Kalbid(e)) (X) iv, 497a; ix, 670a – IV, 518a; IX, 696b
Dj̲aʿfar b. Muḥammad, S̲h̲arīf (Mūsāwid(e)) (X) iii, 262b; vi, 148a – III, 270a; VI, 146b
Dj̲aʿfar b. Muḥammad b. Aḥmad b. Hudh̲ār (IX) s, 1a – S, 1a
Dj̲aʿfar b. Muḥammad b. al-As̲h̲ʿath (VIII) vii, 646a – VII, 645b
Dj̲aʿfar b. Muḥammad b. Ḥamdān al-Mawṣilī (934) ii, 127a; v, 1125a; vi, 784b – II, 130b; V, 1121b; VI, 774a
Dj̲aʿfar b. Muḥammad b. Ḳūlūya al-Ḳummī (979) vii, 312a – VII, 314a
Dj̲aʿfar b. al-Muktafī biʾllāh viii, 103a – VIII, 105b
Dj̲aʿfar b. al-Sammāk al-ʿAbdī iii, 649b, 650a – III, 671a
Dj̲aʿfar b. Sulaymān (ʿAbbāsid(e)) (792) iii, 876a, 878a; vi, 263b; vii, 114a; viii, 536b, 996b – III, 900a, 902a; VI, 284a; VII, 116a; VIII, 554a, 1001b
Dj̲aʿfar b. Sulaymān al-Makramī (*dāʿī*) (XVII) vi, 190b, 191a – VI, 174b, 175a

Djaʿfar b. Yaḥyā al-Barmakī (803) i, 14a, 718a, 1034a, b, 1035b, 1045a, 1114b, 1298a; ii, 78a, 195a, 281b, 305a, 731a; iii, 233a; vi, 331a – I, 14a, 739a, 1065b, 1066a, 1067a, 1077a, 1148a, 1338a; II, 79b, 201a, 289b, 313b, 749b; III, 239b; VI, 315b, 316a
Djaʿfar b. Yūsuf (1019) iv, 497a – IV, 518b
Djaʿfar al-ʿAskarī (XX) x, 885b – X,
Djaʿfar Beg (1520) ii, **373b** – II, **383b**
Djaʿfar Čelebi (1515) ii, **374a**, 839b – II, **384a**, 859a
Djaʿfar al-Falāḥ (971) ii, 854a; iii, 246a – II, 874a; III, 253a
Djaʿfar Kāshif al-Ghiṭāʾ, Shaykh (XIX) vi, 13b, 551a, b – VI, 12a, 535b, 536a
Djaʿfar Khān Gakkhaŕ (1801) iii, 336a – III, 346a
Djaʿfar Khān Zand (1789) iii, 1191a; iv, 104b, 391a; v, 825b, 835a; s, 336a, 405b – III, 1221a; IV, 109a, 408a; V, 831b, 841a; S, 335b, 405b
Djaʿfar al-Khuldī (960) ix, 65b – IX, 67a
Djaʿfar Ḳulī Khān (Ḳādjār) (XVIII) iv, 104b, 391a – IV, 109a, 408a
Djaʿfar Mīr (1765) ii, **371a**, 1091b – II, **381a**, 1117a
Djaʿfar Mullā (XIX) s, 53a – S, 53b
aʿfaDjr Ḳulī Khān (Ḳādjār) (XVIII) iv, 104b, 391a – IV, 109a, 408a
Djaʿfar al-Namarī vi, 438a – VI, 423a
Djaʿfar Pasha (Yemen) (1616) vi, 437a – VI, 422a
Djaʿfar al-Ṣādiḳ b. ʿAlī Zayn al-ʿĀbidīn i, 781b – I, 805a
Djaʿfar al-Ṣādiḳ b. Muḥammad al-Bāḳir (Imām) (765) i, 48a, 134a, 402a, 402b, 1082a, 1116b, 1156a, 1245a; ii, 168b, 357b, 359a, **374a**, 377b, 761a, 857a; iii, 496b, 616b, 682b, 1061a, 1166b; iv, 114b, 1132a, b, 1134a; v, 1236b; vi, 12a, 219a, 334b; vii, 348a, 388b, 645b, 932a; ix, 423a, 770a; s, 231b, 232b, 233a, 401a – I, 49b, 137b, 412b, 414a, 1114b, 1150b, 1190b, 1283a; II, 174a, 367b, 368b, **384b**, 387b, 779a, 877a; III, 513b, 637a, 704b, 1087b, 1195b; IV, 119b, 1163b, 1164a, 1165b; V, 1227a; VI, 11b, 203b, 319a; VII, 350a, 389b, 645a, 934a; IX, 437a, 803b; S, 231b, 232b, 401b
Djaʿfar al-Sarrādj → al-Sarrādj, Abū Muḥammad
Djaʿfar Sharīf b. ʿAlī al-Ḳurayshī al-Nāgōrī (XIX) ii, **375a**; vi, 126b, 127a, 228b – II, **385b**; VI, 124b, 125a, 222b
Djaʿfar al-Ṭayyār → Djaʿfar b. Abī Ṭālib
Djaʿfar Zattallī (1713) iii, 358b; ix, 213b – III, 369b; IX, 219b
Djafāra (Libya/Libie) v, 759b; vi, 452b – V, 765b; VI, 438a
Djaʿfarābād s, 246b – S, 246b
al-Djaʿfarī (1744) vi, 354b – VI, 339a
Djaʿfarī, Abū ʿAlī Muḥammad (Ḳazwīn) (1033) iv, 859b – IV, 892b
Djaʿfarid(e)s (Ḥimyar) vi, 831b – VI, 822a
Djaʿfariyya ii, 375a; iv, 50b, 764a; vi, 27a, 28a, 37a, 56b; vii, 778a – II, 385a; IV, 53b, 794a; VI, 25a, 26a, 35b, 54b; VII, 779b
Djaff, Banū v, 471b – V, 474b
Djafna, Banū vii, 841a – VII, 842a
Djafr ii, **375b**; iii, 595b; iv, 1129a; vi, 216a – II, **386a**; III, 616a; IV, 1160b; VI, 200b
al-Djafūl → Mālik b. Nuwayra
al-Djāfūra i, 537a – I, 553b; IV, 1160b
Djagat → Dwārkā
Djagat Singh (XVII) iv, 543b – IV, 567a
Djaghatay → Čaghatay
Djaghatu vi, 502a, b – VI, 487a, b, 488a
al-Djaghbūb ii, **378a**; v, 759b, 760a; s, 165a – II, **388a**; V, 765b, 766a; S, 164b
al-Djaghmīnī, Maḥmūd ii, **378a** – II, **388b**
Djāghurī iii, 304a – III, 313b
Djāgīr ii, 155b, 156b, 158a, 272b, **378b**; s, 126b, 131b – II, 160a, 161b, 163a, 281a, **388b**; S, 125b, 130b
Djaḥādila, Banū iii, 363b, 541a – III, 375a, 560a
Djahān Ārā bint Shāh Djahān (XVI) ix, 195b, 196a – IX, 201a, 292a
Djahan Khān Pōpalzaʾi (XVIII) ii, 186a – II, 192a
Djahan Khānum bint Kāmrān Mīrzā (XX) vii, 432a – VII, 432b
Djahan Shāh b. Bahādur Shāh (Mughal) (XVIII) i, 914a; ii, 379a – I, 941b; II, 389b
Djahānābād v, 264b – V, 262b
Djahānārā Begam bint Shāh Djahān (1681) i, 253b, 1161a; ii, 50a, **378b**, 627b; vi, 126b, 488b; vii, 333a – I, 216b, 1195b; II, 51a, **389a**, 643b; VI, 124b, 474b; VII, 335a
Djahāndād Khān (1906) ii, 974a – II, 996a
Djahāndār Shāh (1713) i, 241b, 914a, 1025b; ii, **379a**, 810a – I, 249a, 941b, 1057b; II, **389b**, 829a
Djahāndār Shāh (1878) i, 853a – I, 876b
Djahāngīr b. Akbar (Mughal) (1627) i, 8b, 81a, 117b, 118a, 238a, 252b, 253a, 297b, 686a, 1331b, 1347b; ii, 54b, 121a, 157a, 162a, **379b**, 503b, 840a; iii, 424a, 434a, 450a, 492b; iv, 279a, 282a, 543a, 709a, 1017b; v, 598a, 600b, 1135b, 1214a; vi, 127a, 269b, 368b, 369b, 407a, 424b, 425b, 426a, 488a, 516b, 534a; vii, 139a, 189a, 194a, 204a, b, 221a, 315a, 317b, 331a, 338b, 343a, 345b; viii, 125a; s, 1b, 142b, 167b, 258a, 259b, 313b, 366b – I, 8b, 83b, 121a, 245b, 260b, 261a, 306b, 707a, 1372a, 1387b; II, 55b, 124a, 162a, 167a, **390a**, 516a, 860a; III, 437b, 448a, 465b, 509b; IV, 291a, 294b, 566b, 737b, 1050a; V, 602a, 604b, 1131a, 1203b; VI, 125a, 254a, 353a, b, 392a, 410a, b, 411a, 474b, 501b, 518a; VII, 141a, 189b, 194b, 205a, b, 222b, 317a, 320a, 332b, 340b, 344b, 347b; VIII, 127b; S, 2a, 142a, b, 167b, 258a, 259a, 313a, 366a
Djahāngīr b. Kāwūs Pādūspānī, Malik (XV) vi, 514a – VI, 499a
Djahāngir Djalīlī (1938) iv, 72b – IV, 76b
Djahāngir Khān (Kazakh) (1652) x, 681b – X,
Djahāngīr Muḥammad Khān (XIX) i, 1195b, 1197a – I, 1231a, 1232a
Djahāniyān-i Djahān Gasht, Makhdūm-i → Djalāl al-Dīn Ḥusayn al-Bukhārī
Djahannam i, 334b; ii, **381b** – I, 345a; II, **392a**
Djahānpanāh i, 1322b; ii, 258a, 259a; v, 888b, 1214b; vi, 49b, 294a, 532b, 692a – I, 1363a; II, 264a, 266b; V, 894b, 1204b; VI, 47b, 279b, 516b, 679b
Djahānshāh (Ḳara Ḳoyunlu) → Djihānshāh
Djahānshāh (Mughal) → Shāh Djahān
Djahān-Sūz, ʿAlāʾ al-Dīn Ḥusayn (Ghūrid(e)) (1161) i, 940a; ii, **382a**, 1049b, 1052b, 1100b, 1101a, 1103b; iii, 196a; v, 691a; vi, 198b – I, 969a; II, **392b**, 1074a, 1077a, 1126b, 1129b; III, 200b; V, 696a; VI, 182b
Djahān u Arghiyān s, 83b – S, 83a
Djahāz Maḥall vi, 407b – VI, 392b
Djahbadh i, 898b, 1144b; ii, 78b, 79b, 324b, 325a, **382b**; iv, 1032b – I, 925b, 1179a; II, 80a, 81a, 334a, b, **392b**; IV, 1064b
Djahḍam b. ʿAbd Allāh (VIII) iii, 986a – III, 1010b
Djaḥdar b. Ḍubayʿa vi, 640b – VI, 625b
al-Djaḥḥāf b. Ḥakīm (Ḥukaym) al-Sulamī (VII) i, 1241a; viii, 630b – I, 1278b; VIII, 649b)
Djāhidiyya → Khalwatiyya
Djāhiliyya i, 890a; ii, **383b**, 998b, 1073a; iii, 305b; iv, 998a; vi, 430a; s, 33a, 189a – I, 916a; II, **393b**, 1021b, 1097b; III, 314b; IV, 1030b; VI, 415b; S, 33a, 190a

Djaḥīm → Nār
Djahīr, Banū ii, 344a, **384a**; vi, 274b, 275a; vii, 540b, 693a, b, 755b; viii, 70b – II, 354a, **394b**; VI, 259b, 260a; VII, 540b, 693b, 756b; VIII, 72a
al-Djāḥiẓ, Abū ʿUthmān al- Baṣrī (868) i, 10b, 105b, 127a, 176a, 214b, 266a, 271b, 316a, 585a, 588b, 717b, 857b, 1115a, 1243b, 1297b; ii, 95b, 300a, **385a**, 536b, 552a, 590b, 824a, 951b, 1097a; iii, 312a, 354b, 367b, 389b, 990a, 1143a, 1263a; iv, 490b, 822b, 949a; v, 113b, 778b, 1224a, 1225a, b; vi, 109a, 115a, 313b, 346b, 351a, 539a, 605a, 607b, 634b, 636b, 640a, 903b; vii, 279b, 401a, 494a, 567a, 580b, 985b; viii, 95a, 535a, 839a; ix, 454b; s,13b, 24a, 25a, 35b, 45a, 73b, 85b, 88b, 124a, 263a, 273a, 286a, 294b, 316b, 318a, 392b, 402a – I, 10b, 108b, 131a, 180b, 221a, 274a, 279b, 325b, 604a, 608a, 739a, 881b, 1148b, 1281a, 1337b; II, 97b, 308a, **395a**, 550a, 565b, 605a, 843b, 973b, 1123a; III, 321b, 366a, 379a, 402a, 1014b, 1171b, 1296a; IV, 512a, 855b, 981b; V, 116a, 784b, 1214a, 1215b; VI, 107a, 113a, 298b, 330b, 335a, 523b, 589b, 592a, 619b, 621b, 625a, 895a; VII, 281b, 402b, 493b, 567b, 581a, 986b; VIII, 97a, 552b, 868a; IX, 470a; S, 14a, 24b, 25a, 35b, 45b, 74a, 85a, 88b, 123a, 263a, 272b, 286a, 294b, 316b, 318a, 393a, 402b
Djahlāwān ii, **387b** – II, **398a**
Djahm b. ʿAtiyya (VIII) iv, 447a – IV, 466b
Djahm b. Ṣafwān al-Samarkandī (746) i, 274a, 1242a; ii, **388a**; iii, 224a, 747b; vii, 784b; x, 343b; s, 225b – I, 282a, 1279b; II, **398a**; III, 231a, 770b; VII, 786b; X, 369a; S, 225b
Djahmiyya i, 124a, 275a, 976b, 333b, 334a, 335a, 410b; ii, 365a, **388a**; iii, 161b, 822a, 1143a, 1171a; iv, 469a, 1087a; vii, 604a; viii, 87b – I, 127b, 283b, 285a, 344a, b, 345a, 422b; II, 375a, **398b**; III, 165a, 846a, 1171a, 1200a; IV, 490a, 1118a; VII, 604a; VIII, 90a
al-Djahrāʾ (battle/bataille, 1920) iv, 680b, 681a – IV, 708b
Djahriyya (Kansu) iv, 554b – IV, 578b
Djahrum v, 671b – V, 676b, 677a
al-Djahshiyārī, Abū ʿAbd Allāh (942) i, 361a; ii, **388b**; iii, 371a; s, 48b – I, 372a; II, **399a**; III, 382b; S, 49a
Djahwarid(e)s i, 5b, 6a; ii, **389a**; vi, 189a; vii, 766b – I, 6a; II, **399b**; VI, 172b; VII, 768b
Djaḥẓa, Aḥmad b. Djaʿfar (936) i, 1036a; ii, **389b** – I, 1067b; II, **400a**
Djai Singh (XVII) i, 768b, 769a – I, 791b, 792a
Djaʾilda, Shaykh al-Islam (XV) vi, 53b, 62a – VI, 51b, 60a
Djāisī, Malik Muḥammad (XVI) iv, 922a – IV, 955a
Djāʾiz i, 2a; ii, **389b** – I, 2b; II, **400a**
Djāʾiza → Ṣila
Djakam, amīr (1407) ii, 781b – II, 800a
Djakarta i, 980b; ii, **390a**, 426b; iii, 1214a – I, 1011a; II, **400b**, 437b; III, 1244b
Djakat → Zakāt
Djakīm (Djakūn) (Alep(po)) vi, 541a – VI, 525b
Djaḳmaḳ → Čaḳmaḳ
Djaksu b. Tumbine Khān (Mangit) vi, 417b – VI, 402b
Djaʿl → Tazyīf
Djalāhima, Banū iv, 751a – IV, 781b
Djalāʾirid(e)s → Djalāyir
Djalāl, Muḥammad ʿUthmān → Muḥammad ʿUthmān Djalāl
Djalāl b. Abi 'l-Khayr Djazāʾirī, Shaykh (XV) vii, 672a – VII, 672a
Djalāl b. Shīr Shāh Sūrī (Bengal(e)) (XVI) vi, 47b – VI, 45b
Djalāl Āl-i Aḥmad (1969) viii, 116a – VIII, 118b
Djalāl al-Dawla (title/titre) ii, **390b** – II, **401a**
Djalāl Shīrzīl, Abū Ṭāhir (Būyid(e)) (1044) i, 131b, 512b, 1073a; ii, **391a**, 856a; iii, 860a; iv, 379a, 457a, b, 653a; vi, 261b, 270b, 272b, 965b; vii, 271a; s, 119a – I, 135b, 528a, 1105b; II, **401a**, 876a; III, 884a, b; IV, 395a, b, 477b, 679b; VI, 246a, 255b, 257b, 958a; VII, 273a; S, 118b
Djalāl al-Dīn b. Bayazīd Anṣārī (Rawshānī) (XVI) i, 238a, 1123a – I, 245a, 1157a
Djalāl al-Dīn Aḥsan (1339) ii, **391b**; vii, 412a – II, **402a**; VII, 413b
Djalāl al-Dīn ʿArif (1930) ii, **391b** – II, **402a**
Djalāl al-Dīn Bāyazīd (Isfendiyar-oghlu) (1385) iv, 108b; viii, 189b – IV, 113b; VIII, 192b
Djalāl al-Dīnal-Dawānī → al-Dawānī
Djalāl al-Dīn Ḥasan → Ḥasan III Rukn al-Dīn (Nizārī)
Djalāl al-Dīn Ḥasan b. ʿAlī b. Ṣadaḳa (vizier) (1128) vii, 735a – VII, 735b
Djalāl al-Dīn Ḥusayn al-Bukhārī (1384) i, 702b, 868b; ii, 186b, **392a**; iii, 434a; vi, 228b; vii, 1048b; x, 255b; s, 10b – I, 723b, 893a; II, 192b, **402b**; III, 448a; VI, 222b; VII, 1050b; X, 274b; S, 10a
Djalāl al-Dīn Iskandar b. ʿUmar Shaykh (Tīmūrid(e)) (XV) vii, 529a – VII, 529b
Djalāl al-Dīn Ḳaratāy i, 732a; iv, 813b; v, 1145a – I, 754a; IV, 846b; V, 1137a
Djalāl al-Dīn Khaldjī → Fīrūz Shāh II
Djalāl al-Dīn Khʷārazm-shāh Mangubirtī (1231) i, 190a, 227a, 301a, 329a,353b, 508a, 665a, 799a, 919b, 1010a, 1206b, 1311a; ii, 2a, 43b, 188b, 267b, 284a, **392b**, 606a, 680b, 711b, 975b, 1049b, 1083a; iii, 196b, 197a, 1112a; iv, 30a, 102a, 349a, 817b, 1068a; v, 31b, 455a, 490b; vi, 48b, 381a, 500b; vii, 231a, 273b, 498a, 549a, 666a, 727b, 871a, 973b, 990b, 998a; x, 43a, 898b – I, 194b, 233b, 310a, 339b, 364b, 523a, 686a, 822b, 947a, 1041a, 1242b, 1351b; II, 2a, 44b, 194b, 275b, 292a, **403a**, 621a, 697b, 729b, 998a, 1074a, 1108b; III, 201b, 202a, 1139b; IV, 32a-b, 106b, 364a, 850b, 1099b; V, 32b, 458a, 493b; VI, 46b, 365b, 486a; VII, 233a, 275b, 498a, 549a, 665b, 728a, 872b, 974a, 991a, 999b; X, 44b,
Djalāl al-Dīn Khʷārazmī, Sayyid (XIV) viii, 45a – VIII, 45b
Djalāl al-Dīn Mangubirtī → Djalāl al-Dīn Khʷārazm Shāh
Djalāl al-Dīn Mīrān Shāh b. Tīmūr (XV) vii, 133a – VII, 135a
Djalāl al-Dīn Mīrzā (Ḳadjār) (XIX) vii, 438b; s, 23b – VII, 439b; S, 24a
Djalāl al-Dīn Muḥammad → Muḥammad Shāh Gaṇeśa
Djalāl al-Dīn Pasha (Bosna) i, 1268a – I, 1307a
Djalāl al-Dīn Rūmī, Mawlānā (1273) i, 109b, 234a, 347a, 698b, 752b, 753b, 780a, 843b, 916b, 1194b; ii, 221a, **393b**; iii, 429b, 602a, 711a; iv, 65a, 67a, 190a, 570a; v, 255a, 676b; vi, 87a, 354b; vii, 480a, 754b, 1019a; s, 49b, 83b, 108a – I, 112b, 241a, 357b, 720a, 775a, 776a, 803a, 867a, 944b, 1230a; II, 228a, **404a**; III, 443b, 623a, 733b; IV, 68b, 70b, 198a, 592b; V, 253a, 682a; VI, 85a, 338b; VII, 479b, 756a, 1021a; S, 50b, 83a, 107a
Djalāl al-Dīn Surkh Bukhārī, Sayyid (XIV) x, 768a – X,
Djalāl al-Dīn Tabrīzī → Tabrīzī, Djalāl al-Dīn
Djalāl al-Dīn Ṭayyibshāh (Faḍlaqayh) (1282) ii, 737a – II, 755b
Djalāl al-Dīn Thanesarī → Thanesarī, Djalāl al-Dīn
Djalāl Ḥusayn Čelebi (XVII) ii, **397b** – II, **408a**
Djalāl Khān (Bahmānid(e)) (XV) iii, 577a – II, 597a

Djalāl al-Dīn (Bihār) (1534) vi, 47a – VI, 45b
Djalāl al-Dīn b. Maḥmūd Khān (Kālpī) (1437) vi, 61b, 66b – VI, 59b, 64b
Djalāl al-Dīn b. Shīr Shāh Sūrī (Bihār) (1536) ii, 271a; vi, 47a – II, 279b; VI, 45b
Djalāl al-Dīn Lōdī (XVI) ii, 271a; iii, 420b, 995a – II, 279a; III, 434a, 1020a
Djalāl Nūrī → Ileri, Djelāl Nūrī
Djalāl Redjāʿīzāde → Redjāʿīzāde
Djalālābād ii, **397b**; iv, 409b; vii, 407a; s, 66b, 237a – II, **408a**; IV, 427a, b; VII, 408b; S, 67a, 237a
Djalālakmār-parčīn vi, 511a – VI, 496b
Djalālī (brigands) i, 1334b; ii, 183b, 209a, 1046b; iii, 237b, 1002a, 1248b; iv, 499a, 594a, 843b; v, 258b, 270a, 677b; vi, 525b; s, **238a** – I, 1374b; II, 189b, 215b, 1071a; III, 244b, 1027a, 1281a; IV, 520b, 618a, 876b; V, 256b, 267b, 682b; VI, 510a; S, **238a**
Djalālī (calendar/calendrier) ii, **397b**; iv, 52a; vi, 275b; viii, 71b – II, **408a**; IV, 55a; VI, 260b; VIII, 73a
Djalālī (islet/îlot) vi, 734b, 735a – VI, 723b, 724a
Djalālī, Banū (Kurd(e)s) vi, 201b – VI, 185b
Djalāliyya (Suhrawardiyya) vi, 225b – VI, 219b
Djalāl-zāde Muṣṭafā Čelebi (1567) ii, **400a**; iii, 998b; iv, 565b, 566a – II, **410b**; III, 1023b; IV, 588a
Djalāl-zāde Ṣāliḥ Čelebi (1565) ii, **400b** – II, **411a**
Djalāl-zāde Ṭāhir Čelebi (XV) viii, 213b – VIII, 217b
Djaʿlān viii, 566a – VIII, 584b
Djālandhar/Čālandhar vi, 783a – VI, 773a
Djalaw Khān (Kart) (1327) iv, 672a – IV, 699b
Djalāyīn s, 357a – S, 357a
Djalāyir/Djalāyirid i, 66b, 190a, 311b, 508a, 861a, 903b, 1128b; ii, 348b, **401a**; iii, 1123a, 1256b; iv, 32a; v, 45b; vi, 482b, 494b, 502b, 901a; viii, 998a; x, 44a; s, 364a – I, 68b, 194b, 321a, 523b, 885a, 930b, 1162b; II, 358b, **411b**; III, 1150b, 1289a; IV, 34b; V, 47a; VI, 468b, 480a, 487b, 892b; VIII, 1032b; X, 45b; S, 363b
Djalī (calligraphy/-ie) iv, 1123a, b, 1125b, 1126a; v, 224a – IV, 1155a, b, 1157a, b; V, 222a
Djālī → Djawālī
Djalīlī, Āl (Mosul) ii, **402a** – II, **412b**
Djālīnūs (Galen/Galien) (199) i, 213a, 234a, 327a, b, 344b, 388a, 1198a; ii, 60a, 249a, **402b**, 765a, 771a, 780b, 929b; iii, 266b, 579a, 906b; iv, 129a, 329b, 330a, b, 406b; vi, 449a; s, 154b, 271a, 379b – I, 219a, 241b, 337a, b, 355a, 399b, 1233b; II, 61a, 256a, **413a**, 783b, 789b, 799b, 951a; III, 274a, 599a, 931a; IV, 134b, 344a, b, 345a, 424a; VI, 434b; S, 154b, 271a, 379b
Djāliya ii, **403b**, 470b; v, 1253a – II, **414a**, 482b; V, 1244a
Djaʿliyyīn, Banū i, 1a, 765a – I, 1a, 788a
Djallāb, Djallābiyya i, 1349b; ii, **404b** – I, 1390a; II, **415b**
Djallāba Hawwāra iii, 300a – III, 309b
Djāllandharī → Ḥafīz
Djalliḳiyya → Djilliḳiyya
Djālo i, 763a – I, 786a
Djālor ii, **405a**; iii, 441b; viii, 244b – II, **416a**; III, 456a; VIII, 250b
Djalūlāʾ (ʿIrāḳ) ii, **406a**; iv, 13b, 386a – II, **417a**; IV, 14b, 402b
Djalūlāʾ (al-Ḳayrawān) vii, 269b – VII, 271b
Djālūt (Goliath) ii, **406a** – II, **417a**
Djālwand v, 617a – V, 621a
Djalwatiyya i, 1137a – I, 1171b
Djalwī b. Turkī Āl Saʿūd (1853) i, 1313a – I, 1353a
Djām (Ghūr) ii, **406b**; v, 1148a; vi, 365b, 368b – II, **417b**; V, 1139a; VI, 349b, 352b
Djām (valley/vallée) vi, 495a – VI, 480b
Djām ʿAlī Khān III (1896) v, 684b, 685a – V, 690a
Djamʿ, djamāʿa ii, **406b** – II, **417b**
Djām Fīrūz (XVI) i, 627b; iii, 632b – I, 648b; III, 654a
Djām Mīr Khān I (1818) v, 684b – V, 690a
Djām Mīr Khān II (1888) v, 684b, 685a – V, 690a
Djām Nanda (XVI) i, 627b; iii, 420a, 634a – I, 648a; III, 433b, 655a
Djām Niẓām al-Dīn (Gudjārāt) (1473) vi, 50b, VI, 49a
Djāmaʿ al-Fnā (Marrākush) vi, 589b – VI, 574a, b
Djāmaʿ Ibn Ṣāliḥ (Marrākush) vi, 590b – VI, 575b
Djāmaʿ Niẓām al-Dīn Nindō (Rādjpūt) (1509) vi, 1896 – VI, 173b
Djamāʿa i, 171a, 276b, 373b, 770b, 1179b; ii, **411a**, 885b; iii, 98a; iv, 154b, 362a; v, 1198b – I, 176a, 285a, 384b, 793b, 1214b; II, **421b**, 906a; III, 100b; IV, 161a, 377b; V, 1189a
Djamāʿa, Banū iii, 749a – III, 772a
Djamāʿat-i Islāmī iii, 433a; vi, 461b, 462a; viii, 242b – III, 447b; VI, 447a, b; VIII, 248b
Djamādjim → Ḥumāḥim
Djāmakiyya ii, **413b**; vi, 276b – II, **424b**; VI, 261b
Djamal → Ibil
al-Djamal (battle/bataille) (656) i, 43b, 55a, 308a, 383b, 448b, 704b; ii, **414a** – I, 44b, 56b, 317b, 394a, 461b, 725b; II, **424b**
Djamāl → ʿIlm al-djamāl
al-Djamal al-Akbar (842) vii, 4a – VII, 4b
Djamāl al-Dīn b. Nubāta → Ibn Nubāta al-Miṣrī
Djamāl al-Dīn ʿAbd al-Ghānī (XIII) vii, 274a – VII, 276a
Djamāl al-Dīn Abū Bakr b. Mughulṭay (1389) vii, 350a – VII, 352a
Djamāl al-Dīn al-Afghānī (1897) i, 64b, 327a, 332a; ii, 97a, **416b**, 429a, 417a, 650a, 932b, 933b; iii, 250b, 514a, b, 1145b, 1149b, 1170a; iv, 112a, 159a, 162b, 164a, b, 397b, 720b, 946a; vi, 292a, 360a, 414a, 462a; vii, 184a, 418b, 716a, 813a; viii, 248a; s, 76a, 106b, 244b, 248a, 296a – I, 66a, 337a, 342a; II, 99a, **427b**, 440b, 483a, 666b, 954a, 955a; III, 257b, 531b, 532a, 1174a, 1178a, 1199a; IV, 117a, 165b, 169a, 171a, b, 415a, 749a, 979a; VI, 277a, 344a, 399a, 448a; VII, 184a, 419b, 717a, 815a; VIII, 262a; S, 76a, 106a, 244b, 248a, 296a
Djamāl al-Dīn Aḳḳūsh al-Afram al-Shāmī (1303) vi, 545b, 547b; viii, 156b, 157a – VI, 530a, 532a; VIII, 159a,b
Djamāl al-Dīn Aḳsarayī (1389) ii, **419b** – II, **430a**
Djamāl al-Dīn al-Ardistānī (XV) v, 53b – V, 55a
Djamāl al-Dīn Efendi (1919) ii, **420a** – II, **430b**
Djamāl Ḥamrīn x, 140a – X, 151b
Djamāl al-Dīn Hānsawī → Hānsawī
Djamāl al-Dīn Ibrāhīm, Shaykh al-Islām (1306) iv, 1040b, 1046b – IV, 1072a, 1077b
Djamāl al-Dīn Iṣfahānī, Muḥammad b. ʿAbd al-Razzāḳ (1192) iv, 62a, 515b; vi, 608b; s, **239b** – IV, 65b, 538a; VI, 593a; S, **239b**
Djamāl al-Dīn al-Ḥillī → al-Ḥillī, Djamāl al-Dīn
Djamāl al-Dīn al-Iṣfahānī → al-Djawād al-Iṣfahānī
Djamāl al-Dīn Ismāʿīl (Munḳidh, Banū) (1229) vii, 579b – VII, 580a
Djamāl al-Dīn al-Ḳāsimī → al-Ḳāsimī
Djamāl al-Dīn al-Khiḍr, Ḥākim (1315) vi, 231a – VI, 225a
Djamāl al-Dīn Maḥmūd b. ʿAlī, Ustādār (1397) iii, 773b; vi, 199b – III, 797a; VI, 184a
Djamāl al-Dīn Muḥammad (Būrid(e)) (1140) i, 1332a – I, 1372b
Djamāl al-Dīn Muḥammad b. Aḥmad b. ʿAbd Allāh (1498) ii, 730a – II, 748b

Djamāl al-Dīn Muḥammad Sām (XIV) ix, 112a – IX, 116a
Djamāl al-Dīn al-Ustādār (Miṣr) (XV) vii, 172a – VII, 174a
Djamāl al-Dīn Yāḳūt Ḥabshī) (1239) i, 1194a; ii, 1084a; iii, 14a – I, 1229b; II, 1109b; III, 15a
Djamāl al-Ḥusaynī (1520) ii, **420a** – II, **431a**
Djamāl Karshī (XIV) ii, 3b; v, 39a; s, **240a** – II, 3b; V, 40a; S, **240a**
Djamāl Khān, Ḥadjdjī (1770) i, 231a, 295b – I, 238a, 304b
Djamāl al-Mulk (vizier) (1104) i, 440a – I, 452b
Djamāl al-Mulk Muḥammad b. Niẓām al-Mulk (1082) viii, 72a, 81b – VIII, 73b, 83b
Djamāl Djamāl Pasha → Djemāl Pasha
Djamālī, ʿAlāʾ al-Dīn ʿAlī b. Aḥmad (1526) vii, 478b; ix, 401b – VII, 478b; IX, 414b
Djamālī, ʿAlī (1526) ii, **420a** – II, **431a**
Djamālī, Ḥāmid b. Faḍl Allāh (1536) ii, **420b** – II, **431b**
Djamālī, Kambo, Shaykh (1535) s, 312a – S, 312a
al-Djamāliyya (Ṭarīḳa) iv, 991b, 992a – IV, 1024a, b
Djamālzāda, Muḥammad ʿAli (XX) iv, 73a, 789b; v, 199a – IV, 77a, 821b; V, 196b
Djamar (Ḳum) vi, 493a – VI, 479a
Djambul → Awliyā ata
Djambul Djabaev (1945) i, 767a; ii, **421a** – I, 790a; II, **432a**
Djamdār ii, **421b** – II, **432a**
Djāmiʿ → Masdjid
Djāmiʿ, Banū iv, 337a – IV, 351b
Djāmī, Khʷādja Muḥammad Yūsuf (XIX) vii, 935b – VII, 936a
Djāmī, Mawlānā Nūr al-Dīn ʿAbd al-Raḥmān (1492) i, 88b, 146a, 347b, 753a, 1082b, 1211b; ii, **421b**; iii, 131b, 373a, 710b, 711a; iv, 64b, 66b, 650a, 1010a, 1073b; v, 482a, 650b, 1104b; vi, 225a; vii, 478b, 530a, 662a, 935a; viii, 540b, 704a, 800b; x, 322a; s, 46b, 83a, 415a – I, 91a, 150a, 358a, 775b, 1115a, 1247b; II, **432b**; III, 134a, 385a, 733a, b; IV, 68a, 70a, 676b, 1042b, 1105a; V, 484b, 654b, 1100b; VI, 218b; VII, 478a, 530b, 661b, 935b; VIII, 558a, 724a, 827b; X, 347a; S, 47a, 82b, 415b
al-Djāmiʿ al-Azhar → al-Azhar
Djāmiʿa i, 56b; ii, **422b**; iii, 250b; iv, 70b; v, 365a, 904b, 919a – I, 58b; II, **433b**; III, 257b; IV, 74a-b; V, 366a, 910b, 924b
al-Djāmiʿa al-ʿArabiyya i, 46a, 279b; iii, 264a; iv, 783a, 947a; viii, 246b; s, **240a** – I, 47b, 288a; III, 271b; IV, 814b, 979b; VIII, 252b; S, **240a**
Djāmiʿat Umm al-Ḳurā (Mecca) vi, 174a –VI, 161b
al-Djāmiʿayn vi, 965b; vii, 497a – VI, 958a; VII, 497a
Djāmid → Naḥw and/et Ṭabīʿa
Djamīl, Ṭanburī → Ṭanburī Djamīl
Djamīl b. ʿAbd Allāh al-ʿUdhrī (701) i, 10b; ii, **427b**, 1031a; vi, 468a; vii, 978a; s, 42b – I, 10b; II, **438b**, 1055a; VI, 453b; VII, 979a; S, 42b
Djamīl Nakhla al-Mudawwar (1907) ii, **428a** – II, **439a**
Djamīl Ṣadīḳī al-Dhahāwī vi, 609a – VI, 594a
Djamīl Ṣalībā (XX) vi, 538b – VI, 523a
Djamīla (singer/chanteuse) (VII) ii, **428b**, 1011b; iii, 931b; iv, 821b – II, **439b**, 1035a; III, 956b; IV, 854b
Djamīla bint al-Ḥasan Nāṣir al-Dawla (Ḥamdānid(e)) (X) s, 36b, 37a – S, 36b, 37a
Djamīla al-Ḥiṣāfiyya al-Khayriyya s, 371a – S, 371a
Djamīla al-Ḳaḥṭāniyya iii, 519b – III, 537b
Djamīla al-tashrīʿiyya v, 1060b, 1064a – V, 1057b, 1061a
Djamʿiyya ii, **428b**, 650b; iii, 514b; iv, 924a – II, **439b**, 666b; III, 532a; IV, 957a
Djamʿiyyat al-ʿahd iii, 520b – III, 538a
Djamʿiyyat al-djāmiʿa al-ʿarabiyya iii, 520b – III, 538b
Djamʿiyyat al-iṣlāḥ al-shaʿbī iii, 521b, 522a – III, 539b, 540a
Djamʿiyyat ittiḥād Miṣr al-fatāt ii, 429a; iii, 514b; vii, 852a – II, 440a; III, 532a; VII, 853a
Djamʿiyyat al-nahḍa iii, 519a – III, 537a
Djamʿiyyat-i ʿUlamāʾ-i Hind s, 4b, 106b – S, 3b, 105b
al-Djammāʿīlī, Taḳī al-Dīn (XIV) iii, 867b – III, 891b
Djammāl s, **241b** – S, **241b**
al-Djammāz, Abū ʿAbd Allāh (861) ii, **437b**; iii, 879a; vii, 847a – II, **449a**; III, 903b; VII, 858b
Djammū s, **241b** – S, **241b**
Djamnā ii, 255b, 265b, **437b**; s, 313a – II, 263a, 273b, **449a**; S, 312b
al-Djamra ii, **438a**; iii, 36a – II, **449b**; III, 37b
Djams (Sammā) ix, 634b – IX, 658b
Djamshīd ii, **438b**; iv, 12a, 220b, 221a, 1104b – II, **450a**; IV, 13a, 230a, b, 1135b
Djamshīd b. Sulṭān Aḥmad (Gilān-i Biyāpīsh) (XVI) vi, 483a – VI, 469b
Djamshīd Ḳarīn Ghawrī (1400) vi, 512b – VI, 497b
Djamshīdī, Banū i, 224b, 857a; ii, 5b; iii, 1107b – I, 231a, 881a; II, 5b; III, 1135a
Djamuḳa (Mongol) (XII) ii, 42a, 571a – II, 43a, 585b
Djamunā (river/fleuve) v, 885b – V, 891b, 892a
Djāmūs s, **242b** – S, **242b**
Djān b. Yār Muḥammad (Činglizid(e)) (XVI) ii, 44b – II, 45b
Djān ʿAlī Khān (Ḳāsimov) (1535) iv, 723b, 849b – IV, 752b, 882b
Djān Bābā (Maklī) (1608) vi, 190a – VI, 174a
Djān Begam bint ʿAbd al-Rahīm Khān, Khān-i Khānān (XVI) ii, 44b; vi, 488b – II, 45b; VI, 474b
Djān-i Djanān → Maẓhar
Djanāb Shihāb al-Dīn (Cenap Şehabettin) (1934) ii, **439b**, 474b; iii, 261b; vi, 93a, b – II, **451a**, 486b; III, 268b; VI, 91a, b
Djanāb-i Ṭāhira → Ḳurrat al-ʿAyn
al-Djanaba, Banū (ʿUmān) i, 1091b; ii, **440b**; iii, 270a; vi, 729a – I, 1124a; II, **452a**; III, 278a; VI, 718a
Djanāba ii, **440b** – II, **452a**
al-Djanad (Ḥaḍramawt) vi, 138b, 140b, 438b; s, 337b – VI, 137a, 139a, 424a; S, 337a
al-Djanad (Taʿizz) ix, 816a; x, 118a – IX, 851a; X, 127b
al-Djanadī, Abū ʿAbd Allāh (1332) i, 255b; ii, **441a**; viii, 458b – I, 263b; II, **452b**; VIII, 474a
Djanāḥ al-Dawla Ḥusayn (amīr) (1103) iii, 398b; viii, 519a – III, 411a; VIII, 537a
al-Djanāḥiyya i, 49a; ii, **441a**; iii, 1266a; iv, 44b, 838a – I, 50b; II, **452b**; III, 1298b; IV, 47a, 871a
al-Djanāwanī, Abū ʿUbayda (IX) ii, 369a, **441b**; iii, 657b; iv, 919b – II, 379a, **453a**; III, 678b; IV, 952b
al-Djanāwunī → Abū Zakariyyāʾ
al-Djanāwunī, Abū Yaḥyā Tawfīḳ (XIII) i, 1287b – I, 1327a
Djanāza ii, **441b** – II, **453b**
Djanb, Banū v, 954b – V, 958a, b
Djanbās Ḳalʿa i, 831a; iii, 502b – I, 854a; III, 519b
Djānbāz ii, **442b** – II, **454a**
Djānbāzān ii, **443a** – II, **454b**
Djānbeg Girāy Khān (1635) i, 310b; iii, 252a – I, 320b; III, 259a
Djanbī i, 125a; vi, 312a – I, 128b; VI, 297b
al-Djanbīhī, Muḥammad b. ʿAbd al-Nabī (1927) s, **244a** – S, **244a**

Djānbirdi al-Ghazālī → al-Ghazālī
Djānbulāṭ i, 1078a; ii, **443b**; v, 106a, 793a – I, 1110b; II, **455a**; V, 108a, 799a
Djānbulāṭ, Shaykh Ḳāsim (XVIII) i, 1078a; ii, 444a, 636a – I, 1110b; II, 455b, 652a
Djānbulāṭ-oghlu ʿAlī Pasha (1607) i, 4a, 182b, 267b; ii, 443b, 635a, 750a; iii, 88a; iv, 499a; vii, 600b; s, 239a – I, 4a, 188a, 276a; II, 455a, 651a, 768b; III, 90b; IV, 520b; VII, 600b; S, 239a
Djand ii, 571b; iii, 472a; iv, 542b; v, 247a; ix, 557b; s, **244b** – II, 585b; III, 488b; IV, 566a; V, 244b; IX, 580a; S, **244b**
Djandaba b. al-Ḥārith al-Kilābī ii, 234a – II, 241a
Djandal b. al-Rāʿī (VIII) viii, 120b – VIII, 123a
Djāndār ii, **444a**; v, 685a – II, **456a**; 690b
Djāndār (Anadolu) i, 467b – I, 481b
Djandārid(e)s (1400) vi, 975a – VI, 967a
Djandarlî i, 348a; ii, **444b**, 722a; iv, 292a; v, 1023b – I, 358b; II, **456a**, 740b; IV, 305a; V, 1019b
Djandarlî ʿAlī Pasha b. Khayr al-Dīn Khalīl Pasha → ʿAlī Pasha Čāndārlî-zāde
Djandarlî, Ibrāhīm Pasha (1429) ii, 445a, 721a – II, 456b, 739b
Djandarlî, Ibrāhīm Pasha b. Khalīl (1500) ii, 445a;iv, 231a; vi, 1025b; vii, 594b, 595a, 644b – II, 457a; IV, 241a; VI, 1018b; VII, 594a, b, 644b
Djandarlî, Khalīl Pasha b. Ibrāhīm (1453) → Khalīl Pasha Djandarlî
Djandarlî Khayr al-Dīn Khalīl Pasha (1387) ii, 444b; vii, 594a; viii, 192b, 193a – II, 456a; VII, 593b; VIII, 195b, 196a
Djandī, Baba Kamāl (1273) x, 251a – X, 270a
al-Djandī. Muʾayyad al-Dīn (1300) x, 320b – X, 345a
al-Djandī, Yaʿḳūb b. Shīrīn, *ḳāḍī* (XII) s, 246a –S, 246a
Djandjīra iii, 15b; s, **246a** – III, 16b; S, **246a**
Djandjis → Gangā
Djandjū ix, 440b – IX, 457b
Djandōl ii, 317a – II, 326b
Djandrāwar (river/fleuve) vii, 20b – VII, 20b
Djandūba → Djanbī
Djangalī ii, **445b**; v, 310b – II, **457a**; V, 310a
Djangī Yūsuf Dede (1669) iv, 190a – IV, 198b
Djānī Beg (Shaybānid(e)) (1528) i, 46b; iv, 391b – I, 47b; IV, 408b
Djānī Beg Abū Iskandar Khān (Tarkhān) (1601) i, 80b; vi, 190a – I, 83a; VI, 173b
Djānī Beg al-ʿAzīzī (amīr) (1485) i, 841a; vii, 173a – I, 864b; VII, 174b
Djānī Beg Maḥmūd Khān (Batuʾid(e)) (1357) i,325a, 808b, 1107b; ii, 401a; viii, 753a, 755b; ix, 42a; x. 88b – I, 335a, 831b, 1141a; II, 412a; VIII, 774b, 777a; IX, 43a; X, 96a
Djānī Beg Mīrzā (Arghūn) (1599) i, 628a; vii, 129b – I, 648b; VII, 131b
Djāni Bēgum bint ʿAbd al-Raḥīm Khān (XVII) i, 81a – I, 83b
Djānī Khān Ḳashḳāy (1823) iv, 706a – IV, 734b
Djānib ʿAlī Efendi (XVIII) vi, 56a – VI, 54a
Djānībāk al-Ṣūfī, amīr (XV) i, 1054b; iii, 923a – I, 1086a; III, 947b
Djānibak al-Ẓāhirī (1463) v, 73a – V, 75a
Djānibeg Girāy → Djānbeg Girāy
Djānībeg Khān i, 325a, 808b, 1107b; ii, 401a – I, 335a, 831b, 1141a; II, 412a
Djānid(e)s i, 1295b; ii, 44b, **446a**; v, 273b; viii, 232a; x, 681b; s, 97a, 227b, 419b – I, 1335a; II, 45b, **457b**; V, 271b; VIII, 237a; X. ; S, 96b, 227b, 419b
Djānīk ii, **446b** – II, **458a**
Djānīkli ii, 207a, 446b – II, 213b, 458b
Djānīkli Ḥādjdjī ʿAlī Pasha (1785) ii, 207b, **446b** – II, 214a, **458b**
Djānim al-Ashrafī, *kāshif* (Miṣr) (1522) v, 73a; vi, 325a; vii, 177b – V, 75a; VI, 309b; VII, 179b
Djānim al-Ashrafī (Syria(e)) (1462) vii, 727a – VII, 727b
Djānîm-Khodja Meḥmed Pasha (1730) vi, 55b – VI, 53b
Djān-Ḳalʿa s, 244b – S, 244b
Djānḳī ii, 334b; vi, 724b; s, 163a – II, 344a; VI, 713b; S, 163a
Djankirmān → Özı
Djanna i, 334b; ii, **447a** – I, 345a; II, **459a**
Djannāba ii, **452a** – II, **464a**
al-Djannābī, Abū Muḥammad Muṣṭafā (1590) ii, **452b**; iv, 406a – II, **464a**; IV, 424a
al-Djannābī, Abū Saʿīd Ḥasan (913) i, 11a, 73b, 551b; ii, **452b**; iv, 198a, 661a, 664a, 764a; vii, 760b – I, 11a, 76a, 569a; II, **464a**; IV, 206b, 687b, 691a, 794b; VII, 762a
al-Djannābī, Abū Ṭāhir (943) i, 485a, 551b; ii, **452b**; iii, 236a, 238a; iv, 198b, 661b, 662a, b, 664a; vii, 541b; s, 305a – I, 499b, 569a; II, **452b**; III, 243a, 245a; IV, 207a, 688b, 689b, 691a; VII, 541b; S, 304b
al-Djannābī, Aḥmad b. Abī Ṭāhir (951) vi, 435b – VI, 420b
al-Djannābī, Aḥmad b. Saʿīd (X) vii, 488a – VII, 487b
al-Djannābī, al-Ḥasan al-Aʿṣam b. Aḥmad b. Saʿīd (X) vii, 488a – VII, 487b
al-Djannābī, Saʿīd b. Abī Saʿīd (X) ii, 452b; iv, 664a – II, 464b; IV, 691a
Djanpulāt → Djanbulāt
Djānū → ʿUthmān Ādam
Djanza → Gandja
Djār → Djiwār
al-Djār ii, **454b**; vii, 42b, 69b – II, **466a**; VII, 43a, 70a
Djara iv, 335b, 338b, 340a – IV, 350a, 352b, 354b
Djarāblus vi, 378a, b – VI, 362b, 363a
Djarād ii, **455a** – II, **466b**
Djarāda → al-Djarādatān[i]
al-Djarādatān[i] iv, 820b; s, **246b** – Iv, 853b; S, **246b**
Djarādjima (Mardaïtes) i, 761a; ii, **456a**; vi, 505b – I, 784a; II, **468a**; VI, 491a
Djaralī and/et Datolī, Banū vi, 48a – VI, 46b
Djarār (peninsula/-e) vi, 641b – VI, 626b
Djarash i, 208a; ii, **458a** – I, 214a; II, **469b**
Djarāwa, Banū iii, 1039b, 1041b; iv, 422b, 479a, b; v, 1174b – III, 1065b, 1067a; IV, 440b, 501a, b; V, 1164b
al-Djarāwī, ʿAbd al-ʿAzīz (Miṣr) (IX) vii, 160b – VII, 162a
Djarba (Djerba) (island/île) ii, **458a**, 461a; iv, 1156a; v, 503b; s, 15b, 80b – II, **470a**, 473a; IV, 1188a; V, 507a; S, 15b, 80b
Djarba (battle/bataille) (1560) ii, **461a** – II, **473a**
al-Djarbāʾ ii, **461b**; x, 883a – II, **473a**; X,
Djarbādhakān → Gulpāyagān
Djardamur (XIV) vi, 580b – VI, 565a
al-Djardjarāʿī, al-ʿAbbās b. al-Ḥasan (908) ii, **461b**; iii, 619b, 767b, 892b; vii, 541b, 543a – II, **473b**; III, 640a, 790b, 916b; VII, 541b, 543a
al-Djardjarāʿī, Abu ʾl-Ḳāsim ʿAlī b. Aḥmad (1045) ii, **462a**; iii, 79a; vi, 198a; vii, 483a, 729b – II, **473b**; III, 81b; VI, 182a; VII, 482b, 730b
al-Djardjarāʿī, Aḥmad b. al-Khaṣīb (879) i, 1289b; ii, **461b**; iii, 835a, 1085a; vii, 583a, 653a – I, 1329a; II, **473b**; III, 858b, 1112a; VII, 583b, 652b
al-Djardjarāʿī, Muḥammad b. al-Faḍl (864) ii, **461b** – II, **473b**

al-Djarh wa 'l-taʿdīl i, 1199b; ii, **462a** – I, 1234b; II, **473b**
Djarhud (Ustāanawand) vi, 744b – VI, 733b
Djārī → Khaṭṭ
Djarīb → Kayl
Djarīd, Bilād al- ii, **462b**; iv, 739b, 740a; vii, 186b – II, **474b**; IV, 769a, b; VII, 186b
Djarīda i, 279b, 287a, b, 288a, 289b, 871a, b; ii, 288b, 289b, 364a, 403b, 404a, 417b, 418a, 428a, 429a, **464b**, 596b; iv, 73; iv, 70b, 71a, b, 112a, 124a, 681b, 857a, 876a; v, 438a, 484b, 838b, 1254b, s, **247a** –
I, 288a, 296a, b, 298b, 895b; II, 296b, 297a, 374a, 414a, b, 428a, b, 439a, 440a, **476a**, 611b; IV, 74a, b, 75b, 117a, 129a, b, 709b, 890a, 909a; V, 440b, 487b, 845a, 1245b; S, **247a**
Djarīda (military/-taire) ii, 78b, 79a, 80a – II, 80a, b, 81b
Djarīma ii, **479b** – II, **491b**
Djarīr, Awlād ii, 509b – II, 522a
Djarīr b. ʿAbd Allāh al-Badjalī (640) i, 865b; ii, 241b; vi, 710a; vii, 797b; viii, 82b; ix, 553b –
I, 889b; II, 248b; VI, 698b; VII, 799a; VIII, 84b; IX, 575b
Djarīr b. ʿAbd al-Ḥamīd (804) vii, 662b – VII, 662a
Djarīr b. ʿAbd al-Masīḥ → al-Mutalammis
Djarīr b. ʿAṭiyya (728) i, 158b, 196a, 331a, 436b, 586a, 950b, 1080a; ii, 245b, **479b**, 788b; iii, 42a, 354a, 853b; vi, 267a, 475a, 604b, 606a, 625a; vii, 114a, 145b, 261a, 402a, 546a, 920b; viii, 120b, 377b; s, 15a, 273a –
I, 162b, 201b, 341b, 448b, 605a, 980a, 1112b; II, 252b, **492a**, 807b; III, 43b, 365a, 877b; VI, 251b, 461a, 589a, 590b, 610a; VII, 116a, 147b, 262b, 403b, 546a, 921a; VIII, 123a, 390a; S, 15b, 273a
Djarīr b. Ḥammād b. Zayd (IX) s, 384b – S, 385a
Djarīr b. Yazīd (780) vi, 937b – VI, 929b
Djarīriyya x, 12b – X, 12b
Djāriya → ʿAbd
Djāriya b. Ḳudāma (VII) ii, **480b**; iii, 782a –
II, **492b**; III, 805b
Djarkent (Panfilov) vi, 768b – VI, 758a
Djarkh → Ḳaws
Djarm, Banū vi, 477b – VI, 463a
al-Djarmī, Abū ʿUmar (839) vii, 279b; ix, 317b – VII, 281b; IX, 327b
al-Djarmī, Muslim b. Abī Muslim (IX) viii, 874b – VIII, 904a
al-Djarmūzī, al-Ḥasan b. al-Muṭahhar (XVIII) vii, 514b – VII, 515a
Djarr → Naḥw
Djarrāḥ ii, **481b** – II, **493b**
al-Djarrāḥ, Banū → Djarrāḥid(e)s
al-Djarrāḥ b. ʿAbd Allāh al-Ḥakamī (730) i, 837a, 985a; ii, **482a**; iii, 493b; iv, 344a, 1173b; vi, 623a; ix, 254a –
I, 860a, 1015b; II, **494a**; III, 510b; IV, 358b, 1207a; VI, 608b; IX, 261a
al-Djarrāh b. ʿAmr ii, 236a – II, 243a
Djarrāḥid(e)s i, 386b, 784a; ii, 197b, **482b**, 854a; iii, 767b; v, 327b; vii, 461a, 760a –
I, 398a, 807a; II, 203b, **495a**, 874a; III, 790b; V, 327b; VII, 461a, 761b
al-Djarrāḳ b. ʿAbd Allāh al-Ḥakamī x, 844b – X,
Djarrūn (Djahrum) vi, 384a – VI, 368b
Djarshīḳ → Djirra
Djārsīf → Garsīf
al-Djārūd b. Abī Sabra ʿAbd al-Ḳays (630) i, 73a, 942a; vii, 114b – I, 75b, 971a; VII, 116b
al-Djārūdiyya ii, **485a**; iii, 1166a; vii, 459b; s, 129b, 130a, 400b – II, **497a**; III, 1195a; VII, 459b; S, 129a, 401a
Djarūmiyya, Banū vi, 371b – VI, 356a
Djarūn → Bandar ʿAbbās
Djarunda i, 82a; ii, **485a** – I, 84b; II, **497b**
Djarwal (Mecca) vi, 156b, 161a, 178b –
VI, 152b, 154b
Djarwānid(e)s s, 234a – S, 234a
Djāsak ii, **486a**; v, 675a – II, **498a**; V, 680b
Djasīm al-Dīn (XX) i, 1169a – I, 1204a
Djasīm b. Djābir (XIX) iv, 751b – IV, 782a
Djasīm b. Muḥammad (Āl Thānī) (1913) iv, 751b, 752a, 953b – IV, 782a, 986a
Djasrat b. Shaykhā (1442) v, 31b – V, 32b
Djasrath (Khokar) (XV) vii, 279a – VII, 280b
al-Djaṣṣāṣ, Aḥmad (981) ii, **486a**; vii, 562a; ix, 36a – II, **498a**; VII, 562b; IX, 36b
al-Djassāsa i, 932a; ii, **486b** – I, 960b; II, **498b**
Djassawr (Jessore) ii, **486b**; vi, 46b – II, **498b**; VI, 45a
Djastanid(e)s → Djustānid(e)s
Djāsūs ii, **486b**; iii, 181b – II, **499a**; III, 186a
Djaswant Rāo Holkar (XIX) i, 444a – I, 456b
Djaswant Singh (1678) i, 768b, 769a; ii, 567a; iii, 202a – I, 791b, 792a; II, 581b; III, 207b
Djāṭ, Banū (Zuṭṭ) i, 224b, 253a, 1005a, 1193a; ii, **488a**, 504a, 797b, 928b, 1122a, 1131b; iii, 197b; iv, 364b; vi, 50b; s, 163a –
I, 231b, 261a, 1036a, 1228a; II, **500a**, 516b, 816b, 950b, 1148b, 1158b; III, 202b; IV, 380b; VI, 49a; S, 163a
Djāta b. Sumar Rādja Pāl (Druze) vii, 544b – VII, 544b
Djāvuldur, Banū → Čāwdors
Djāwa → Djāwī
al-Djawād al-Iṣfahānī, Abū Djaʿfar (Djamāl al-Dīn) (1164) i, 604a, 1160b; ii, **489a**; vi, 870a – I, 623b, 1195a; II, **501b**; VI, 861a
Djawād Karbalāʾī, Sayyid (XIX) s, 53a – S, 53b
Djawād Pasha (1900) ii, **489b** – II, **502a**
Djawāhir → Djawhar
al-Djawāhirī, Muḥammad Mahdī (XX) ix, 230a – IX, 235b
Djawālī ii, 327a, 329a, **490a**, 561a – II, 336b, 338b, **502a**, 575a
al-Djawālī, Abū Manṣūr (al-Mawṣil) (XII) vi, 380a; vii, 983b – VI, 364a; VII, 984a
al-Djawālīḳī, Abū Manṣūr Mawhūb (1114) i, 485b, 593a; ii, **490a**; iii, 733a; iv, 913a; vii, 262a – I, 500a, 612a; II, **502b**; III, 755b; IV, 945b; VII, 264a
al-Djawālīḳī, Hishām b. Sāliḥ (VIII) viii, 387b: ix, 109a – VIII, 400b; IX, 423a
Djāwān (al-Baḥrayn) i, 941b – I, 970b
Djāwān, Mīrzā Kāẓim ʿAlī (815) ii, **490b**; v, 644b – II, **503a**; 648b
Djāwān Mardi → Futuwwa
Djāwānī Kurd(e)s → Djāf
Djawānrūd ii, **491a** – II, **503b**
Djāwars s, **249b** – S, **249b**
al-Djawāsim → Ḳawāsim
al-Djawāzir, Banū i, 1096b – I, 1129b
al-Djawbarī, ʿAbd al-Raḥīm (XIII) iii, 487b, 511a; vii, 495a; ix, 70a; s, 43a, **250a** – III, 504b, 528b; VII, 495a; IX, 73a; S, 43b, **250a**
Djawdhar (X) ii, **491a**, 1080b – II, **503b**, 1106a
Djawdhar, Pasha (XVI) i, 289a; ii, 977b – I, 298a; II, 1000a
Djawf i, 1313b; ii, **491b**; vi, 88b, 433a, 474b, 559b, 566a; ix, 90n – I, 1354a; II, **504a**; VI, 86b, 418b, 460a, 544a, 551a; IX, 93a
al-Djawf ii, **492a**, 624b – II, **504b**, 640a
Djawf Kufra ii, **492b**; s, 164b, 165a – II, **505a**; s, 164b
Djawhar (substance) i, 128b, 784b; ii, 220a, **493a** – I, 132a, 808a; II, 226b, **505a**

Djawhar (jewel/pierre précieuse) i, 1157b; ii, 1119b; iii, 30b; v, 965a; s, **250b** – I, 1192a; II, 1146a; III, 32a; V, 969b; S, **250b**
Djawhar Āftābačī (XVI) ii, **494a**; vii, 342b – II, **506b**; 344a
Djawhar b. ʿAbd Allāh al-Ṣiḳillī (992) i, 814a, 824a; ii, **494b**, 853a, b, 860a, 1080b; iii, 246a, 768b, 785b, 1036b, 1042b; iv, 275b, 663b, 1091b; v, 1160a, 1176a; vi, 650a, 673b; vii, 148b, 162a, 482b; viii, 40b, 90b, 879a, 880a, 1068b – I, 837b, 847a; II, **507a**, 873a, b, 879b, 1105al III, 253a, 701b, 808b, 1062b, 1068n; IV, 287b, 690b, 1122b; V, 1150a, 1166a; VI, 635a, 660a; VII, 150b, 163b, 486b; VIII, 41a, 92a, 909a, 910a
al-Djawhar b. Sakkum al-Gudālī (XI) vii, 584a, 621b – VII, 584b, 621b
Djawhar al-Adanī, Ṣfī (XII) vi, 133a – I, 131a
Djawhar al-Ḳanḳabāʾī (1440) i, 814b – I, 838a
Djawhar-Shādh (XV) vi, 714b – VI, 703b
Djawharī, Banū vi, 657b – VI, 643b
al-Djawharī, al-ʿAbbās b. Saʿīd (828) vi, 600a; s, 411b, 412b, 414a – VI, 584b; S, 412a, b, 414a
al-Djawharī, Abū Naṣr Ismāʿīl (1009) ii, **495b**, 926b; iii, 733a, 738b; iv, 524b, 527b; vii, 190a; viii, 378b, 661a; x, 33a; s, 38b, 240a, 289a, b – II, **508a**, 948a; II, 755b, 761b; IV, 547a, 550a; VII, 190a; VIII, 391b, 680b; X, 34b; S, 39a, 240a, 289a
al-Djawharī, Maḥammad s, 395b – S, 396a
al-Djawharī, Muḥammad Ibrāhīm Harawī Ḳazwīnī (1837) vi, 609b – VI, 594a
al-Djawharī, Ṭanṭāwī (1940) vi, 360b; vii, 439b; s, **262b** – VI, 344b; VII, 440b; S, **262a**
Djāwī ii, **497a**; vi, 151b – II, **509b**; VI, 150b
Djāwīd, Meḥmed ii, **497b**, 616a; iv, 285a, 297b – II, **510a**, 631b; IV, 297b, 310b
Djāwīdhān b. Sahl (1926) i, 844a; v, 64b – I, 867b; V, 66a
Djāwīdhān Khirad iv, 504b; s, **263a** – IV, 526b; S, **263a**
Djawkān → Čawgān
al-Djawl i, 536a – I, 552b
Djawlakiyya iv, 473a, b – IV, 494a, b
al-Djawlān ii, **498a**; vi, 455a, 546b; s, 229b – II, **510b**; VI, 440b, 531a; S, 229b
Djawn, Banu ʾl- v, 119a – V, 121b
Djawn al-Khaḍārim (Yamāma) vii, 858b – VII, 860a
Djawnā Khān → Muḥammad b. Tughluḳ
Djawnā Khān (Shamsābād) (1456) vi, 62b – VI, 60a
Djawnpūr ii, 270b, **498b**, 925a; iii, 419a, b, 420a, 442b, 444a, 632a, 1003a; iv, 276b; v, 783b, 889a, 1135a, 1216b; vi, 49a, b, 50a, 52a, 53b, 61b, 62a, b, 273a, 294b, 309b, 368a, 406b, 407b, 693b; vii, 79b, 314a, 573b; ix, 356a; s, 206b, 325a – II, 278b, **510b**, 946b; II, 432b, 433b, 457a, 459a, 653a, 1028a; IV, 288b; V, 789b, 895b, 1130b, 1206b; VI, 47b, 48a, 50a, 51b, 59b, 60a, b, 257b, 258a, 279b, 295a, 352a, 391b, 392a, 681b; VII, 80b, 316a, 574b; IX, 167b; S, 206a, 324b
al-Djawnpūrī, Maḥmūd (1652) i, 593a – I, 612b
al-Djawnpūrī, Sayyid Muḥammad (1505) ii, **499b**; v, 1230b; vii, 458a – II, **512a**; V, 1221a; VII, 458a
Djawsaḳ (Djawsat) vi, 541a – VI, 525b
Djawsaḳ al-Khāḳānī (Sāmarrāʾ) vii, 9a; viii, 1040b – VII, 9b; VIII, 1076a
Djawshakānī, Niʿmat Allāh (XVII) s, 139a – S, 138b
Dhawū Ḥassān, Banū vi, 741a – VI, 730b
al-Djāwulī, Abū Saʿīd ʿAlam al-Dīn Sandjar (amīr) (1344) iv, 960a; v, 628a – IV, 992b; V, 632a
Djāwuliyya iv, 960a – IV, 992b
Djaww → Djawf
al-Djawwād Yūnus b. Mawdūd b. al-ʿĀdil (1243) i, 766b – I, 789a
al-Djawwārī (1002) x, 33a – X, 34b
al-Djawwānī (1192) ii, **501a** – II, **514a**
Djawz s, **264a** – S, **263b**
al-Djawzāʾ → Minṭaḳat al-Burūdj; Nudjūm
al-Djawzahar ii, **501b** – II, **514b**
Djay iv, 98b, 99b, 100a, 106a – IV, 103a, b, 104b, 110b
Djāyasī → Malik Muḥammad Djāyasī
Djayb-i Humāyūn ii, **502b** – II, **515a**
Djayfar b. Djulanda i, 451a – I, 464a
Djayḥān (river/fleuve) ii, 35a, b, **502b**; vi, 505b, 507a, b – II, 36a, **515b**; VI, 490b, 492b, 493a
al-Djayhānī, Abū ʿAbd Allāh Aḥmad b. Muḥammad (978) s, **256b** – S, **265a**, b
al-Djayhānī, Abū ʿAbd Allāh Muḥammad b. Aḥmad b. Naṣr (922) i, 434a; ii, 581a; iv, 1079b; vi, 628a, 640a; viii, 1027a; s, **265a**, 376b – I, 446a; II, 595b; IV, 1111a; VI, 613a, 625a, b; VIII, 1062a; S, **264b**, 376b
al-Djayhānī, Abū ʿAlī Muḥammad b. Muḥammad (942) i, 984b, 1003a; iv, 847a; viii, 1027a; s, **265a**, b – I, 1015a, 1034a; IV, 880a; VIII, 1062a; S, **264b**, 265b
Djayḥūn → Baradā
Djayḥūn → Āmū Daryā
al-Djayla s, 356a – S, 356a
Djayn ii, **503a**, 1123b – II, **516a**, 1150a
Djaypāl, Rādjā (Hindū Shāhī) (986) ii, 1050b, 1123a; iii, 460b; vi, 65b; viii, 299b – II, 1075a, 1149a; III, 476b, VI, 63b; VIII, 308b
Djaypūr ii, **503b**; vi, 127b, 602a; s, 260a – II, **516b**; VI, 125b, 586b; S, 260a
Djayrūt vi, 82a – VI, 80a
Djaysalmer s, 312b – S, 312a
Djaysh ii, **504a**; v, 685a; vi, 142a – II, **517a**; V, 690a; VI, 140b
Djayshān s, 335a – S, 334b
Djaysh b. Ṣamṣāma (X) i, 1042a; ii, 483b; iii, 77a – I, 1073b; II, 495b; III, 79b
Djaysinha s, 163a – S, 163a
al-Djayṭālī (1329) ii, **515a**; iii, 95a, 97b – II, **528a**; III, 97b, 100a
Djayyān i, 1343a; ii, **515b**; iii, 498b – I, 1383b; II, **528b**; III, 515b
Djayyāsh b. Nadjāḥ → Nadjāḥid(e)s
Djayzān (Djāzān) i, 109a; ii, **516a** – I, 729b; II, **529a**
Djāz-Muryān s, 129a – S, 128a
Djazʾ b. Muʿāwiya (641) vi, 920b – VI, 912a
Djazāʾ ii, **518a** – II, **531a**
al-Djazāʾir (Algiers/Alger) i, 34b, 67b, 367b, 368b; ii, 115b, 425b, **519b**; iii, 251b, 606b; iv, 359b; vi, 58b, 59b, 134b, 573a; s, 325b – I, 35b, 69b, 378a, 379b; II, 118a, 436a, **533a**; III, 258b, 627b; IV, 375b; VI, 56b, 57b, 132b, 558a; S, 325a
al-Djazāʾir Banū → al-Djawāzir
al-Djazāʾir dey → Dayi
Djazāʾir-i Baḥr-i Safīd ii, **521b**; vi, 588b – II, **534b**; VI, 573b
Djazāʾir Ibn Khalfān → Khūriyā Mūriyā
al-Djazāʾir al-Khālida ii, **522a**; v, 755b – II, **535a**; V, 761b
Djazāʾir al-Saʿādāt → al-Djazāʾir al-Khālida
al-Djazāʿirī → Ḳaddūra al-Djazāʿirī
al-Djazāʿirī → Aḥmad b. ʿAbd al-Raḥmān
al-Djazāʿirī, ʿAlī b. Hilāl (XV) s, 380a – S, 380a
al-Djazāʿirī, Muḥammad b. Muḥammad (XIX) vi, 113b – VI, 111a
al-Djazāʿirī, Niʿmat b. Muḥammad (1718) vi, 112b – VI, 110a

al-Djazāʿirī, Sayyid Niʿmat Allāh (1700) vii, 476a – VII, 475b
al-Djazāʿirī, Shaykh Ṭāhir (1920) iii, 519a; iv, 159a; vii, 901a; viii, 906b, 908a – III, 536b; IV, 166a; VII, 901b; VIII, 937b, 939a
Djazā'irli Ghāzī Ḥasan → Djezā'irli Ghāzī Ḥasan Pasha
al-Djazarī (1429) vii, 1039b – VII, 1042a
al-Djazarī, Badīʿ al-Zamān Abu 'l-ʿIzz (XII) v, 861b; vi, 111a; s, **266b** – V, 868b; VI, 109a; S, **266a**
al-Djazarī, Shams al-Dīn Muḥammad b. Ibrāhīm (1338) ii, **522b**; iv, 965a; vii, 141a; viii, 458b; – II, **535b**; IV, 997a; VII, 143a; VIII, 474a
al-Djazarī, Shams al-Milla wa ʾl-Dīn (1301) s, **267a**, 371b, 372b, 373a, b, 400a – S, **266b**, 371b, 372b, 373a, b, 400b
Djazarī Ḳāsim Pasha (1483) vi, 1025b – VI, 1018a
Djazīra (island/île) ii, **523a** – II, **536a**
al-Djazīra (Djazīrat Aḳūr) i, 11b, 12b, 198a; ii, 64b, 249b, 344b, 347a, 348a, **523a**; iii, 933b, 1250b, 1252a; v, 453b, 457a, 458a; vi, 139a, 273b, 331a, 337a, 378a, 427b, 428b, 429b, 539b; s, 101a, 266b –
I, 12a, 12b, 203b; II, 65b, 256b, 354b, 357a, b, **536a**; III, 958a, 1283a, 1284b; V, 456a, 459b, 461a; VI, 137b, 258b, 316a, 321a, 362b, 412b, 413b, 415a, 524a; S, 100b, 266a
al-Djazīra al-Khaḍrāʾ (Algeciras) i, 6a, 12b, 58a, 1057b; ii, **524b**; v, 1119a; vi, 430b – I, 6a, 12b, 59b, 1089a; II, **537b**; V, 1115b; VI, 416a
Djazīrat al-ʿArab → ʿArab, Djazīrat al-
Djazīrat Banī Naṣr vi, 453b – VI, 439a
Djazīrat Firʿawn i, 784a – I, 807b
Djazīrat Ibn Kāwān → Kishm
Djazīrat Ibn ʿUmar → Ibn ʿUmar, Djazīrat
Djazīrat Ḳays → Ḳays, Djazīrat
Djazīrat al-Khiḍr → Abbādān
Djazīrat Sharīḳ ii, **525b**; vi, 457a – II, **538b**; VI, 442b
Djazīrat Shukr ii, **526a** – II, **539a**
Djazīrat Ṭarīf → Ṭarīfa
Djazm → Naḥw
al-Djazr (Syria/-e) v, 921a, b, 922a – V, 926b, 927a, b
al-Djazr wa 'l-madd → Madd
Djazūla, Banū ii, **526b**; vi, 741a, 742a, 744a – II, **539b**; VI, 730a, 731a, 733a
al-Djazūlī (al-Gazūlī), ʿAbd Allāh b. Yāsīn → ʿAbd Allāh b. Yāsīn
al-Djazūlī, Abū ʿAbd Allāh al-Samlāli (1465) i, **527a**; iii, 70a, 721b; vi, 743a, 773b; viii, 723a – II, **540a**; III, 72b, 743b; VI, 732a, 763a; VIII, 744a
al-Djazūlī, Abū Mūsā ʿIsā (1209) ii, **528a**; iii, 733a – II, **541a**; III, 755b
al-Djazūlī, Ibn Makhlūf al-Nuwayrī (1318) viii, 156a – VIII, 158b
al-Djazūlī, Muḥammad b. ʿAbd Allāh al-Ḥaḍīkī (1775) vi, 356b – VI, 341a
al-Djazūlī, Sīdī Muḥammad b. Slīmān vi, 591a, b – VI, 576a
al-Djazūliyya i, 245a; ii, 528a; iii, 339b; iv, 93b, 380a; vi, 356a; x, 247b; s, 223a –
I, 252b; II, 541a; III, 349b; IV, 97b, 396b; VI, 340b; X, 266a; S, 223a
al-Djazzār → Ibrāhīm b. Mūsā al-Ḳāẓim
Djazzār s, **267a** – S, **267a**
al-Djazzār Pasha, Aḥmad (1804) i, 341b, 1078a; ii, 444a, 635b, 912a; iii, 325b; iv, 842b; vi, 327b; viii, 75b; s, **268a** –
I, 352a, 1110b; II, 455b, 651b, 933b; III, 335b; IV, 875b; VI, 314a; VIII, 77a; S, **267b**
Djebe (Mongol) (XIII) i, 836a, 987a; ii, 43a – I, 859a, 1018a; II, 43b
Djebedji i, 807b, 1061b; s, **269b** – I, 830b, 1093a; S, **269a**
Djebel → Djabal
Djebeli, djebelü ii, **528b**, 1090a – II, **541b**, 1115b
Djeblé → Djabala
Djedda → Djudda
Djedīd → Djadīd
Djek → Shahdāgh
Djekermish al-Mawṣilī (XII) i, 1052a – I, 1084a
Djelal ed-Din Roumi → Djalāl al-Dīn Rūmī
Djelāl Meḥmed Ḳulī-zāde (XX) viii, 683b – VIII, 703a
Djelāl Sāhir (XX) vi, 94a; s, 98a – VI, 92a; S, 97b
Djelali → Djalālī
Djelālzāde → Djalālzāde
Djellāb, Banū x, 589b – X,
Djem b. Meḥemmed II (Ottoman Prince/ ()ttoman) (1495) i, 293a, 510b, 1119a, b, 1334b; ii, **529a**; iii, 341a; iv, 463a, 738a; vi, 324b, 1025a; viii, 569b –
I, 302a, 526b, 1153a, 1374b; II, **542a**; III, 351a; IV, 483b, 768a; VI, 309a, 1018a; VIII, 588a
Djemāʿa → Djamāʿa
Djemāl al-Dīn Bey (Derebey) (XIX) viii, 167a – VIII, 169b
Djemāl Pasha (Young Turk/Jeune Turc) (1922) ii, 289b, 431a, **531a**, 637b, 699b; iv, 284b, 872b, 906b; vi, 304a, b, 615a; s, 98a –
II, 297b, 442a, **544a**, 653b, 717b; IV, 297a, 906a, 939b; VI, 289a, 290a, 600a; S, 97b
Djemāl Pasha (Mecca) (1886) vi, 151b – VI, 150a
Djemalī Efendi → Djamālī, ʿAlī
Djemʿiyyet → Djamʿiyya
Djemʿiyyet-i ʿIlmiyye-i ʿOthmāniyye ii, **532a** – II, **545a**
Djemshīd → Djamshīd
Djenānī → ʿĀṣim, Aḥmad
Djenāze Ḥasan Pasha → Kaḥyā Ḥasan Pasha
Djendereli → Djandarlî
Djenné → Dienné
Djerba → Djarba
Djerīd ii, **532a**, 954a – II, **545b**, 976a
Djerīd → Djarīd, Bilād al-
Djerime → Djarīma
Djevrī vi, 836a – VI, 826b
Djewād Shākir → Halikarnas Balîḳčîsî
Djewān Bakht b. Bahādur Shāh II i, 914a – I, 942a
Djewānshīr line/dynastie (Mughal) iv, 573a – IV, 595b, 596a
Djewdet, ʿAbd Allāh (1932) ii, 430b, 474b, 475a, **533a**, 1117a; iii, 393a; iv, 168b, 169a; vi, 93a, 94a – II, 441b, 487a, **546a**, 1143a; III, 405b; IV, 176a; VI, 91a, 92a
Djewdet Pasha → Aḥmad Djewdet Pasha
Djewher Sulṭān bint Selīm II (XVI) viii, 316b – VIII, 327a
Djezāʾirli Ghāzī Ḥasan Pasha (1790) i, 63a; ii, 26b, **533b**; iii, 992b; iv, 455b, 588b, 853a; v, 764a, 1248a; vi, 325b; vii, 179a –
I, 65a; II, 26b, **547a**; III, 1017a; IV, 476a, 612a, 886a; V, 770a, 1238b; VI, 310a; VII, 181a
Djezzar → Djazzār
al-Djibāl i, 49a, 437b; ii, **534b**; vi, 64a, b, 66a, 117b, 120a, 332b, 333a, b, 337b, 338a, b, 539a, 574b, 653a, 781b –
I, 50b, 450a; II, **548a**; VI, 62a, b, 63b, 115b, 117b, 317a, b, 318a, 322a, b, 523b, 559b, 638b, 771a
Djibāl Ḳarīn i, 1350a; ii, **534b**; iv, 97b, 465a; v, 169a; vi, 937b; s. 43b – I, 1390b; II, **547b**; IV, 101b, 486b; V, 166b; VI, 930a; S, 44a
Djibāl Pādūspān vi, 938a – VI, 930a
Djibāliyya, Banū iii, 642a – III, 663b
Djibāliyyūn (Tunisia/-e) vi, 251a – VI, 235a

al-Djibāwī, Ḥasan (1504) viii, 729a – VIII, 750a
al-Djibāwī, Sa'd al-Dīn → Sa'd al-Dīn al-Djibāwī
Djibāya i, 533b; iv, 244b – I, 549b; IV, 255b
Djibbālī (language/langue) vi, 84a; s, 339b – VI, 82a; S, 339a
Djibrān → Djabrān
Djibrīl → Djabrā'īl
Djibrīl b. 'Umar (1785) viii, 18b – VIII, 18b
Djibūtī ii, **535b**; vi, 643b; ix, 717a; x, 71a; – II, **548b**; VI, 628b; IX, 748a; X, 74a
Djid'atī, Banū vi, 128b – VI, 126b
al-Djidd wa 'l-hazl ii, **536a** – II, **549b**
Djidda → Djudda
Djidjelli ii, **537a**; iv, 361a, 362a – II, **550a**; IV, 377a, 378a
Djīdjī Ānaga (Umm Mīrzā 'Azīz Kōka) (XVI) vii, 131a – VII, 133a
Djigdjla (Ogādēn) vii, 389b – VII, 391a
Djihād i, 7a, 31b, 179b, 250b, 276b, 314a, 445b, 664a; ii, 64a, 65a, 126a, 504b, **538a**; iii, 180a, 181b; iv, 772a, 796b; v, 1243b, 1250a –
I, 7b, 32b, 184b, 258b, 285a, 324a, 458a, 684a; II, 65a, 66a, 129b, 517a, **551b**; III, 184a, 185b; IV, 803a, 828b; V, 1234b, 1241a
Djihādiyya i, 1157a; v, 267b, 1252a – I, 1191a; V, 265b, 1242b
Djihān-Pahlawān Muḥammad b. Eldigüz (Ildeñizid(e)) (1186) i, 300b; iii, 47b, 1110b, 1111a, b; s, 416a – I, 310a; III, 49a, 1137b, 1138b; S, 416b
Djihāngīr (Mughal) → Djahāngīr
Djihāngīr b. 'Alī (Aḳ-ḳoyunlu) (1453) i, 311b, 312a; vi, 541a – I, 321b; VI, 525b
Djihāngīr b. 'Azīz (Banū Kāwūsh) (1004) iv, 808a – IV, 840b
Djihāngīr b. Süleymān II Ḳānūnī (Ottoman) (1553) iv, 232a; v, 727a – IV, 242b; V, 732a
Djihānshāh (Ḳara Ḳoyunlu) (1467) i, 147b, 311b; iv, 34a, 102b, 587b, 588a; vi, 513b; viii, 766b; x, 514a. 964b –
I, 152a, 321a; IV, 36b, 107a, 611a, b; VI, 498b, 499a; VIII, 792a; X, 550b,
Djihār (idol/-e) vii, 463b – VII, 462b
Djihinnām (VII) i, 690a – I, 711a
Djīl Djawbara b. Farrukhān Djīlānshāh (696) s, 298a – S, 297b
Djīl Djīlān → Djīl Djawbara
Djilāla, Djilālism(e) iv, 381b, 382b, 383a; s, 351a – IV, 398a, 399b; S, 351a
Djilālī b. Idrīs → Bū Ḥmāra
Djilālī Mthīred (XIX) vi, 250a – VI, 234b
al-Djīlālī al-Rūgī (1908) vi, 1009b – VI, 1001b
Djīlān s, 297b, 298a – S, 297a, b
Djilaw Khān (Čūbānid(e)) (1327) ii, 68a – II, 69a
Djild ii, **540a** – II, **553a**
al-Djildakī, 'Izz al-Dīn Aydamir (1342) iv, 1134a; V, 112a; S, **270a** – IV, 1165b; V, 114b; S, **269b**
al-Djīlī → 'Abd al-Ḳādir al-Djilanī
al-Djīlī, Ḳuṭb al-Dīn → 'Abd al-Karīm al-Djīlī
al-Djillī, Muḥammad b. 'Alī (994) viii, 146b – VIII, 148b
Djīlīs, Banū vi, 539a – VI, 523b
al-Djillī, Muḥammad b. 'Alī (994) viii, 146b – VIII, 148b
Djillik ii, **541a**, 1021a; s, 117a – II, **554a**, 1045a; S, 116b
Djilliḳiyya (Galicia(e)) ii, **541b**; v, 781b; vi, 221b; s, 92a – II, **554b**; V, 787b; VI, 215b; S, 92a
Djilwa ii, **542b** – II, **555b**
Djilwā, Mīrzā Abu 'l-Ḥasan (1896) vii, 132a – VII, 134a
Djilwatiyya ii, **542b**; iii, 538b; iv, 191b –
II, **555b**; III, 557a; IV, 199b
Djīm ii, **543b** – II, **556b**
Djimār vi, 105b – VI, 103a
Djimat ii, **545a** – II, **558b**
Djimmā ii, **545a** – II, **558b**
Djimrī (XIII) i, 467a; ii, 204b, 989a – I, 481a; II, 211a, 1012a
Djimri (rebel/-le) (XVII) viii, 831b – VIII, 860a
Djināḥ, Muḥammad 'Alī (1948) i, 1196b; ii, **545b**; iii, 532b, 1204b; iv, 299a; v, 780a; vi, 78a, b; viii, 241b, 254b –
I, 1231b; II, **559a**; III, 551a, 1235a; IV, 312a; V, 786a; VI, 76a; VIII, 247a, 256b
Djinās → Tadjnīs
Djināza → Djanāza
Djinbāwāy s, 244a – S, 244a
al-Djinbayhī/al-Djunbayhī → al-Djanbīhī
Djindjī vi, 535a – VI, 519a
Djindji Khwādja → Ḥusayn Djindji
Djinīn vi, 543b – VI, 528a
Djinn i, 187a; ii, 323a, 518b, **546b**; iii, 273b, 669a, 1050a; iv, 264b; v, 1101a, 1202a; s, 52b, 371a –
I, 192a; II, 332b, 531b, **560a**; III, 281b, 690b, 1076a; IV, 276b; V, 1097a, 1192b; S, 53a, 370b
Djinn 'Alī Pasha (XVIII) viii, 197a – VIII, 200b
Djins (genus/genre) ii, **550a** – II, **563b**
Djins (sex/-e) ii, **550b** – II, **564a**
Djirān, al-'Awd (VIII) viii, 120b – VIII, 123a
Djirab al-Dawla ii, 178b – II, 184a
Dji'rāna vi, 266a; vii, 373a – VI, 251a; VII, 374b
Djirdjā → Girgā
al-Djirdjāwī, 'Uthmān (XVIII) iv, 852b – IV, 885b
Djirdjent ii, **553a**; iv, 496b – II, **566b**; IV, 517b
Djirdjī Zaydān → Zaydān, Djirdjī
Djirdjīs ii, **553a** – II, **567a**
Djirga v, 1079a; s, **270a** – V, 1076b; S, **270a**
Djirm → Djism
Djirm (Badakhshān) i, 851b – I, 875b
Djirra (river/fleuve) ix, 310a – IX, 319b
Djīruft i, 810b; ii, **553b**; iv, 4a; v, 148b, 149a, 150b; vi, 493b; vii, 357a; s, 129a –
I, 834a; II, **567b**; IV, 4a; V, 150b, 151b, 152b; VI, 479b; VII, 359b; S, 128a
Djīsh → Gīsh
Djism ii, **553b** – II, **567b**
Djisr ii, **555a**, 716a; iv, 555a – II, **569a**, 734b; IV, 579a
al-Djisr, Shaykh Ḥusayn (1909) vi, 355a; viii, 446b – VI, 339a; VIII, 461a
Djisr Banāt Ya'ḳūb ii, **555a; viii, 757b** –
II, **569a; VIII, 782b**
Djisr al-Ḥadīd ii, **555b** – II, **569b**
Djisr al-Khashab vi, 547a – VI, 531b
Djisr Manbidj → Kal'at al-Nadjm
Djisr al-Shughr ii, **556a**; iv, 1015a – II, **570a**; IV, 1047a
Djisr al-Walīd vi, 774b – VI, 764a
Djisr-i Muṣṭafā Pasha s, 149b – S, 149b
Djiṣṣ ii, **556b** – II, **570b**
Djītal → Sikka; Wazn
al-Djiṭālī → al-Djayṭālī
Djiti Shahr → Altï Shahr
al-Djiwā' i, 539b; ii, **557b** – I, 556b; II, **571a**
Djīwan (1717) ii, **558a** – II, **572a**
Djiwār i, 429b, 890b; ii, **558b**; iii, 1017b –
I, 441b, 917b; II, **572b**; III, 1043a
Djīza (Gizeh) i, 125b; iii, 173b; vi, 195b, 411a, 652a; vii, 147a, 148a, b; s, 407b –
I, 129a; III, 177a; VI, 179b, 396a, 637b; VII, 149a, 150a, b; S, 407b
Djīzān → Djayzān
al-Djīzī, Abū Muḥammad (870) ii, **559a** – II, **573a**

Djizya i, 656a, b, 1090b, 1144a, 1146a; ii, 121a, 131a, 142b, 146b, 151b, 154a, 227a, 272a, 490a, **559a**; iii, 1181a; iv, 500a, 939a, 1033a, 1095a; v, 92b, 262b, 500b –
I, 677a, b, 1123b, 1178b, 1180b; II, 124a, 134b, 146a, 150b, 156a, 158b, 234a, 280b, 502a, **573a**; III, 1210a; IV, 521b, 972a, 1064b, 1126a; V, 94b, 260a, 503b
Djoči Khān → Djuči b. Čingiz Khān
Djōdhpur ii, **567a** – II, **581a**
Djogdjakarta ii, 426b, 427a – II, 437b, 438a
Djolof ii, **567a**; ix, 119a; x, 602a – II, **581b**; IX, 144a; X, 647a
Djowān Mīr (XIX) iv, 730b – IV, 759
Dju'ayl, Banū v, 318a – V, 317b
al-Djuba → al-Djawf
Djubar, Banū iv, 361a, b – IV, 377a
Djubārāt, Banū vii, 921a – VII, 921b
Djubayl (Lebanon/Liban) ii, **568a**; v, 789a, 793a; ix, 268a – II, **582b**; V, 796a, 799a; IX, 276b
al-Djubayl (Sa'ūdi Arabia/Arabie Séoudite) ii, **568b** – II, **583a**
al-Djubayla i, 628b; ii, **569a** – I, 649b; II, **583b**
Djubayla (island/île) vi, 729b – VI, 718b
Djubba → Libās
Djubba'dīn vi, 308a, b – VI, 293b
al-Djubbā'ī (Zandjī) (IX) vii, 526b – VII, 526b
al-Djubbā'ī, Abū 'Alī Muḥammad (915) i, 4b, 128b, 412a, 694a; ii, 449b, **569b**, 802b; iii, 465b, 1143a, 1165b; iv, 183a, 693a, 1162b, 1163a; vi, 846b; vii, 312a, 784a, 975b; ix, 551b; s, 13b, 88b, 90b, 344a, b, 345b, 347a –
I, 5a, 132b, 424a, 715a; II, 461b, **584a**, 821b; III, 481b, 1171b, 1194b; IV, 191a, 721a, 1194b, 1195a; VI, 837a; VII, 314b, 786a, 975b; IX, 573b; S, 14a, 88b, 90a, 344a, b, 345b, 346b, 347a
al-Djubbā'ī, Abū Hāshim 'Abd al-Salām (933) i, 4b, 411a; ii, 218b, 570a; iii, 171b, 832a, 1143a, 1165b; v, 702a; vii, 784a; viii, 534a; s, 12b, 13b, 25b, 32a, 226b, 343b, 346b, 348a –
I, 5a, 423a; II, 225a, 584b; III, 175b, 856a, 1171b, 1194b; V, 707a; VII, 784a; VIII, 551b; S, 13a, 14a, 25b, 32a, 226b, 343b, 346a, 348a
Djubūr ii, **570b**; s, 101b – II, **585a**; S, 101a
Djuči b. Čingiz Khān (Mongol) (1227) i, 1105a, 1106b, 1187b, 1188a; ii, 2a, 43a, 44a, **571a**; vi, 417b; s, 96b, 246a –
I, 1138a, 1139b, 1222b, 1223a; II, 2a, 44a, 45, **585b**; VI, 402b; S, 96a, 246a
Djučid(e)s s, 340a – S, 339b
Djudāla → Gudāla
Djuday' b. 'Alī al-Kirmānī (VIII) iii, 224a; vii, 1016a – III, 230b, 231a; VII, 1018a
Djudda i, 380b, 546b, 1032b, 1054b; ii, 91b, **571b**; iii, 11b, 362b, 760b, 1067a; v, 808a; vi, 33b, 34b, 35a, 144b, 148a, 150b, 151a, 157a, 163a, 195b, 324a, 641b; vii, 173a –
I, 391b, 564a, 1064a, 1086a; II, 93a, **586a**; III, 12a, 373b, 783b, 1093b; V, 813b; VI, 31b, 32b, 33a, 142b, 146b, 149a, b, 152b, 156a, 179b, 308b, 627a; VII, 175a
Djudhām, Banū i, 436a, 528b, 532a, 630b, 1140a; ii, **573b**; v, 594a, 632a, b, 897b; vi, 221b, 622a, 727b; vii, 372a, 921a; viii, 466a, 865a –
I, 448b, 544b, 548b, 651a, 1174b; II, **588a**; V, 597b, 636a, b, 903b; VI, 215b, 607a, 716b; VII, 374a, 921b; VIII, 481b, 895b
Djudhām (leprosy/lèpre) s, **270b** – S, **270b**
al-Djudhāmī, Abū 'Abd Allāh (XIII) s, 381b – S, 382a
al-Djudhāmī, al-'Alā' b. Mughīth (763) i, 82a, 862a; iv, 665b – I, 84b, 886a; IV, 692b
al-Djudhāmī, Ibn al-Ṣabbāgh (XIII) vii, 811b – VII, 813b
al-Djudhāmī, 'Uthmān b. 'Abd al-Ḥakam (779) vi, 280b – VI, 265a
Djudhayma al-Abrash i, 788b – I, 812a
Djūdī, Djabal i, 251b; ii, **573b**; s, 36a – I, 259a; II, **588a**; S, 36b
Djūdī al-Mawrūrī (813) ii, **574b** – II, **589a**
Djudjayn b. Thābit ii, 590b – II, 605b
Djufayna iii, 586b – III, 607a
al-Djufayna vi, 563b – VI, 548b
Dju'fī, Banū ii, 1059b, 1061b – II, 1084a, 1086a
al-Dju'fī, al-Mufaḍḍal b. 'Umar (Khaṭṭābī) (VIII) vii, 647b – VII, 647b
al-Dju'fī, Muḥammad b. Mūsā b. al-Ḥasan b. al-Furāt (ḳāī) (IX) viii, 146a – VIII, 148b
al-Djufra ii, **575a** – II, **589b**
Djufriyya vi, 640b – VI, 625b
Djughrāfiyā i, 1102a; ii, **575b**; iv, 1078a-1083a – I, 1135a; II, **590a**; IV, 1109b-1114b
Djuḥā ii, **590b**; vii, 1018a – II, **605a**; VII, 1020a
al-Djuhanī → 'Abd Allāh b. Unays; Ma'bad
al-Djuhanī, 'Abd al-Sharīḳ vii, 581a – VII, 581b
al-Djuhanī, 'Amr b. Murra (VII) viii, 82b – VIII, 84b
Djuhaymān → al-'Utaybī, Djuhaymān b. Muḥammad
Djuhayna → Ḳuḍā'a
al-Djuhaynī, Muḥammad b. Dīnār (798) vi, 280b – VI, 265b
Djuke-Tau → Zhukotin
Djūlāmerg → Čölemerik
al-Djulandā, Āl i, 812b, 813a, 1098a; viii, 85a; s, 222b, 223a – I, 835b, 836a, 1131a; VIII, 87a; S, 222b, 223a
al-Djulandā b. Mas'ūd b. Dja'far (752) i, 550b; ii, **592b**; iii, 652a; ix, 775a; x, 816a – I, 568a; II, **607a**; III, 673b; IX, 808b; X,
Djulbān (Alep(po) (XIV) vi, 381b – VI, 366a
Djulfā i, 8a, 643a; iv, 476a; vi, 291a; viii, 773b; s, **274b** – I, 8b, 663b; iv, 497a; VI, 276b; VIII, 799a; S, **274b**
Djulfār → Ra's al-Khayma
Djullanār s, **277a** – S, **276b**
al-Djulūdī, 'Abd al-'Azīz b. Yaḥyā iv, 927a – IV, 960a
Djum'a (Yawm al-) ii, **592b** – II, **607a**
Djum'a, Imām (Iṣfahān) (XIX) s, 169b – S, 169b
Djumādā → Ta'rīkh
Djumaḥ Banū vi, 137b, 145a; s, 284a – VI, 136a, 143a; S, 284a
al-Djumaḥī → Abū Dahbal; Ibn Sallām
al-Djumaḥī, Sa'īd b. 'Abd al-Raḥmān (790) s, 225b – S, 225b
Djumayla, Banū i, 233b – I, 241a
Djumblāṭ → Djānbulāṭ
Djumhūr b. al-'Idjlī (VIII) iv, 99b – IV, 104a
Djumhūriyya ii, **594a**, 644b – II, **608b**, 660b
al-Djumhūriyya al-'arabiyya al-muttaḥida ii, 649a, 674a; iii, 264b, 1259a; v, 1061a; vi, 36b, 280b; s, 2b, 7b –
II, 665a, 691a; III, 272a, 1291b; V, 1058b; VI, 35a, 265b; S, 7b, 12b
Djümhūriyyet Khalḳ Fïrkasï i, 734b; ii, 432b, **595b**; iii, 526b; iv, 124b, 791b, 988a; v, 1038a – I, 756b; II, 443a, **610a**; III, 545a; IV, 129b, 823b, 1020b; V, 1034a
Djumla → Naḥw
Djūnā Khān → Muḥammad b. Tughluḳ
Djūnāgaṛh (Ḳāṭhiawāṛ) ii, **597a**, 1127a; iii, 451a; vi, 50b, 190a, 270a, 419b; s, 246b –
II, **611b**, 1153b; III, 466b; VI, 49a, 147a, 254b, 404b; S, 246b
Djunayd, Shaykh (Ṣafawid(e)) (1460) ii, **598b**; iii,

315b, 1006b; vi, 613b; viii, 766b, 777a – II, **613b**; III, 325a, 1032a; VI, 598b; VIII, 791b, 803a
Djunayd (Aydînoghlu) (1425) i, 309a, 346a, 783b; ii, **599a**; vi, 975b; vii, 594b, 645a, 711a – I, 319a, 356b, 806b; II, **613b**; VI, 968a; VII, 594a, 644b, 712a
al-Djunayd, Abu 'l-Ḳāsim al-Baghdādī al-Nihāwandī (910) i, 162a, 415b; ii, **600a**; iii, 823b; iv, 114b; vi, 225a, 569b, 570a; vii, 871a; ix, 57a; x, 116b; s, 350a – I, 166b, 427b; II, **614b**; III, 847a; IV, 119b; VI, 218b, 554b, 555a; VII, 872b; IX, 60a; X, 126a; S, 350a
al-Djunayd b. ʿAbd Allāh al-Murrī (734) i, 1292b; ii, **600b**; iv, 708a – I, 1332b; II, **615a**; IV, 736b
al-Djunayd b. ʿAbd al-Raḥmān (VIII) vii, 629b; s, 252a – VII, 629a; S, 252a
al-Djunayd b. Ibrāhīm → Ṣafawid(e)s
Djunayd Khān (Turcoman) (XX) v, 24a, b – V, 25a
Djunaydib akhū Banī Rawāḥa s, 177b – S, 178b
Djunaydiyya i, 868b – I, 892b
Djunayr vi, 63a – VI, 61a
al-Djunbulānī al-Djannān, Abū Muḥammad ʿAbd Allāh (900) viii, 146a – VIII, 148b
Djunbulāṭ → Djānbulāṭ
Djund i, 76a, 82a, 134b, 248a, 490a, b, 729b, 991a; ii, 505a, **601a**; v, 685a – I, 78b, 84b, 138b, 255b, 504b, 505b, 751b, 1020b; II, 517b, **616a**; V, 690a
Djund (province) v, 125a – V, 127b
Djundab b. Khāridja al-Ṭā'ī i, 1241b; viii, 377a – I, 1279a; VIII, 389b
Djundaysābūr → Gondēshāpūr
Djundī → Ḥalḳa (soldiers/soldats)
Djundīsāpūr → Gondēshāpur
Djundub b. Djunāda → Abū Dharr al-Ghifārī
Djūnī vi, 303a – VI, 288b
Djungars x, 677a – X,
Djunnar ii, **602a**; vi, 269a – II, **616b**; VI, 254a
Djūr → Fīrūzābād
Djuradh s, **285b** – S, **285b**
Djurash s, 326b – S, 326a
Djurʾat (1810) ii, **602a** – II, **617a**
Djuraydj (Gregorius) i, 1021b; ii, **602b**; vi, 630b – I, 1053a; II, **617a**; VI, 615b
al-Djurayrī, Abū Muḥammad (924) viii, 840b – VIII, 869b
Djurbadhāḳān → Gulpāyagān
Djurd (Durūz) vi, 343b, 344a – VI, 328a
Djurdjān → Gurgān
Djurdjānī, Fakhr al-Dīn → Gurgānī
al-Djurdjānī, Abu 'l-ʿAbbās (1089) viii, 428a – VIII, 442a
al-Djurdjānī, Abū Bakr ʿAbd al-Ḳāhir (1078) i, 590b, 858a, 982a, 1115b; ii, 824b; iii, 834b, 1020a; iv, 250b, 251a, b, 864a; v, 899a, 900b, 1026a; vi, 218a, b, 340a, 348b; vii, 261a, 528a, 771b, 773b, 914b; ix, 455a; x, 129a; s, **277a** – I, 609b, 882a, 1012b, 1149a; II, 844a;III, 858b, 1045b; IV, 261b, 262a, b, 897b; V, 905b, 906b, 1022a; VI, 202a, b, 324b, 332b; VII, 263a, 528b, 773b, 775b, 915a; IX, 470b; X, 139a; S, **277a**
al-Djurdjānī, Abu 'l-Ḳāsim (XI) s, 14b – S, 15a
al-Djurdjānī, ʿAlī b. ʿAbd al-ʿAzīz Abu 'l-Ḥasan (1001) iv, 249b; vii, 772a; ix, 57a – IV, 260b; VII, 774a; IX, 60a
al-Djurdjānī, ʿAlī b. Muḥammad al-Sayyid al-Sharīf (1413) i, 342b, 343a, 351a, 714b, 715b, 1327a; ii, 294a, **602b**, 608a, 774a; iii, 330a, 664b, 1147b; iv, 123a, 272a; vi, 354b; vii, 821b; x. 89a – I, 353a, b, 362a, 736a, 737a, 1368a; II, 302a, **617b**, 623a, 792b; III, 340a, 686a, 1175b; IV, 128a, b, 284a; VI, 338b; VII, 823a; X, 96a
al-Djurdjānī, Ismāʿīl b. al-Ḥusayn (1136) i, 213b; ii, **603a**; s, 271b – I, 220a; II, **617b**; S, 271b
al-Djurdjānī, Mīr Sayyid Sharīf (1413) viii, 45b, 541b – VIII, 46a, 559a
al-Djurdjāniyya → Gurgandj
Djurdjīs b. Djibrīl (Djibrāʾīl) b. Bukhtīshū → Bukhtīshu
Djurdjūma ii, 456a, 457b – II, 468a, 469a
Djurdjura i, 369b; ii, **603a**; iv, 359a, 360a, 361a, 362b – I, 380b; II, **618a**; IV, 374b, 376a, 377a, 378b
Djurhum (Djurham), Banū i, 563a; ii, **603b**; iii, 389b, 739a; iv, 185a, 448b; v, 77a, b, 763a; vi, 145a, 738a – I, 581a; II, **618b**; III, 402a, 762a; IV, 193a, 468b; V, 79a, b, 769a; VI, 143a, 727b
al-Djurhumī, ʿIsam b. Shahbar (VI) vii, 841a – VII, 842b
Djurm ii, 479b, **604a** – II, 491b, **618b**
Djurmāghūn (XIII) iv, 102a – IV, 106b
Djurmāʾīs v, 163a – V, 161a
al-Djurr, Shukr Allāh (XX) v, 1256a, b – V, 1247a, b
al-Djurūmiyya v, 65a, 183a – V, 66b, 180b
Djurzān → al-Kurdj
Djusham (Djishum) s, 343a – S, 342b
Djusham b. Muʿāwiya, Banū ii, 626b; v, 48b; vi, 134a, b, 741b – II, 642b; V, 50a; VI, 132b, 133a, 730b
Djusnas Abū Farrukhān s, 298b – S, 298a
Djustān I b. Marzubān (Djustānid(e)) (960) ii, 191a; v, 452; vi, 499b; vii, 656b; x, 897b – II, 197a; V, 455a; VI, 484b; VII, 656a;
Djustān II (Djustānid(e) ii, 191a, b; iii, 245a – II, 197a, b; III, 252a
Djustān III (Djustānid(e) (IX) vii, 655b – VII, 655a
Djustān b. Sharmazan (X) x, 897b – X,
Djustān b. Wahsūdān ii, 192a – II, 198a
Djustānid(e)s ii, 191a, 193b; iii, 254b; v, 602b, 603a; vii, 655b; s, 356b – II, 197a, 199b; III, 261b; V, 606b, 607a; VII, 655a; S, 356b
Djūtid Shurafāʾ ix, 597a – IX, 527a
Djuwayn ii, **604b**; iv, 5a; s, 235a – II, **619b**; IV, 5b; S, 235a
al-Djuwaynī, ʿAbd Allāh b. Yūsuf (1047) i, 952b; ii, **605a**; iv, 149b; v, 526b – I, 981b; II, **620a**; IV, 155b; V, 530a
al-Djuwaynī, ʿAbu 'l-Maʿālī (Imām al-Ḥaramayn) (1085) i, 410b, 411a, 485a, 593a, 1130b; ii, 570b, **605a**, 1038b, 1040a; iii, 330a, 914a, 1019b, 1024b, 1145a; iv, 149b, 257b, 272a; vi, 376a, 448a, 456a, 739a; vii, 296b, 781a; viii, 63a; s, 343b, 346b, 347a, b, 348a, 403a – I, 422b, 423a, 499b, 612a, 1164b; II, 585a, **620a**, 1063a, 1064a; III, 340a, 938a, 1045a, 1050a, 1173b; IV, 155b, 268b, 284a; VI, 360b, 433b, 441b, 728a; VII, 298b, 783a; VIII, 64bS, 343b, 346a, 347a, b, 348a, 403b
al-Djuwaynī, Abū Muḥammad viii, 63a – VIII, 64a
al-Djuwaynī, ʿAlāʾ al-Dīn ʿAṭā-Malik (1283) i, 902b; ii, **606a**; iii, 738a; iv, 865a; v, 311b; vii, 234b; viii, 342b; s, 94b – I, 930a; II, **621a**; III, 760b; IV, 898a; V, 311b; VII, 236b; VIII, 354b; S, 94a
al-Djuwaynī, Bahāʾ al-Dīn Muḥammad (1279) ii, 607b; viii, 342b; s, 235b – II, 622b; VIII, 354b; S, 235a
Djuwaynī, Muntadjab al-Dīn Badīʿ (XII) ix, 16b – IX, 17a
al-Djuwaynī, Shams al-Dīn (Ṣāḥib dīwān) (1284) ii, 334a, **607a**; iii, 572b, 1269a; iv, 620b; v, 868b; vii, 234b; viii, 342b 702b, 806a; s, 235b – II, 343b, **622a**; III, 592b, 1302a; IV, 645a; V, 875a; VII, 236b; VIII,

354b, 722b, 833a; S, 235a
Djuwaynī Sharaf al-Din Harūn (1286) ii, 607b; viii, 806a – II, 622b; VIII, 833a
Djuwayra → Abū Du'ād al-Iyādī
Djuwayriyya bint Abī Djahl (VII) i, 751a – I, 773b
Djuwayriyya bint al-Ḥārith (VII) v, 78b – V, 80b
Djūybārī, Khwādja Muḥammad islam (1563) x, 250b – X, 269a
Djūybārīs s, 228a – S, 228a
Djuyum → Djuwayn
Djuyūsh Beg (XII) i, 300b; vi, 500a – I, 309b; VI, 485a
Djuz' (atom(e)) ii, 220a, **607b** – II, 226b, **623a**
Djuz' (Ḳur'ān) → Ḳur'ān
Djuz' (in poetry/en poésie) → 'Arūḍ
Djūzdjān ii, 1b, **608b**, 798b; vi, 65b, 618a; s, 125b, 367b, 376a, b, 386b – II, 1b, **623b**, 817b; VI, 63b, 602b; S, 124b, 367a, 376a, b, 387a
al-Djūzdjānī, Abū 'Amr Minhādj al-Dīn (1270) i, 1131a; ii, **609a**, 1099a; iii, 1155b – I, 1165b; II, **624a**, 1125a; III, 1184a
al-Djūzdjānī, Abū Sulaymān (890) vi, 846a – VI, 837a
al-Djūzdjānī, Abū 'Ubayd (XI) iii, 331a, 941a, b; vi, 638a; viii, 542a – III, 341a, 966a, b; VI, 623a; VIII, 560a
al-Djūzdjānī, Ibrāhīm b. Ya'ḳūb (873) viii, 515b – VIII, 533b
Dnieper → Özı
Dō'āb ii, **609b**, 868a; vi, 48a, 49a, 50a, 63b, 65b, 294b; x, 591b; s, 57b, 124a, 126a, 206b – II, **625a**, 888a; VI, 46b, 47b, 48b, 61b, 63b, 279b; X, 635b; S, 58a, 123b, 125b, 206a
Dō'ān → Daw'ān
Dob'a iii, 6a – III, 6a
Dobrotič (XIV) ii, 611a, 971b – II, 626a, 993b
Dobrudja i, 1302a; ii, **610a**, 909a, 971b; v, 277b; x, 699b – I, 1342a; II, **625a**, 930a, 993b; V, 275b
Dobrudja, Turks in - x, 699b –
Dōdāīs i, 1005b; s, 332a – I, 1036b; S, 331b
Dodecanese /- èse → On iki Ada
Ḍofār → Ẓafār
Dogali vi, 643b – VI, 628b
Doğan Avcioğlu (XX) vi, 95b – VI, 93b
Döger (Ghuzz) i, 666b; ii, **613b**, 1107b – I, 687a; II, **629a**, 1133b
Döger Sālim Beg (XIV) iv, 584b, 586a – IV, 608a, b
Doghandji ii, **614a** – II, **629b**
Dōgrās iv, 709b; s, 241b – IV, 738a; S, 242a
Doğu-Bayazit → Bāyazīd
Doha → al-Dawḥa
Doḳūz Khātūn (XIII) iii, 569b, 1122a; vii, 973a – III, 589a, 1149b; VII, 973b
Dolma Baghče → Istanbul
Dōmbkī → Balūčistān
Dome of the Rock/Dôme du Rocher → Ḳubbat al-Ṣakhra; Masdjid al-Aḳṣā
Donanma ii, **615a** – II, **630a**
Donbolī → Dumbulī, Banū
Dongola i, 50a; ii, **615a**; vi, 574b; vii, 425b; viii, 89b, 90b; ix, 155a; s, 278b – I, 51a; II, **630b**; VI, 559b; VII, 427a; VIII, 91b, 92b; IX, 160a; S, 278b
Dönme ii, **615b** – II, **631a**
Dönüm → Misāḥa
Dorylaion → Eskishehir
Dōsa → Dawsa
Dōst Muḥammad → Dūst Muḥammad
Douar → Dawār
Dra' /Draa → Dar'a
Drač ii, **616b** – II, **632a**
Drag(o)man → Tardjumān
Dragut → Ṭurghud 'Alī Pasha
Drīshak → Balūčistān
Druzes/Druses → Durūz
Du'ā' ii, 302a, 314b, **617a**; iv, 715b; v, 74a, b, 621b, 956b, 960a – II, 310a, 324a, **632b**; IV, 744a; V, 76a, b, 625b, 960a, 964b
Du'a Khān → Duwā Khān
Dū'an → Daw'an
Dubai → Dubayy
Dubays I b. 'Alī (Mazyadid(e)) (1081) i, 684a, 1073b, 1074a, 1075a; iii, 390a; iv, 911a; vi, 965b; vii, 118a – I, 704b, 1105b, 1106a, 1107a; III, 402a; IV, 944a; VI, 958a; VII, 120a
Dubays II b. Ṣadaḳa I (Mazyadid(e)) (1135) i, 300b, 314a, 684a; iv, 493b, 911b; vi, 64a, b, 544a; vii, 733a, b – I, 309b, 324a, 705a; IV, 515a, 944b; VI, 62a, b, 528b; VII, 734a
Dubayy i, 166b, 928b, 1313b; ii, **618b**; iv, 778a; vi, 37b; s, 416b – I, 171a, 956b, 1354a; II, **634a**; IV, 809b; VI, 36a; S, 417a
al-Dubb → Nudjūm
Dubdū ii, **619b** – II, **635a**
Dubrovnik → Raghūsa
Duče Meḥmed Pasha (XVII) i, 656b – I, 677b
Dūdāniyya → Dido
Dudekulas v, 648b – V, 652b
Dūdhū Miyān i, 952a; ii, 784a – I, 981a; II, 803a
Dudjayl → Kārūn
Dudlebs (Dūlāba), Banū s, 170b – S, 171a
Duero → Wādī Duwayro
Duff ii, **620a** – II, **635b**
Dūghāt ix, 649a – IX, 674a
Dughāgha → Daghūgh, Banū
Dūghlāt (Dūḳlāt) ii, 45b, **621b** – II, 46b, **637a**
Dūghlāt, Mīrzā Muḥammad (1534) viii, 136a – VIII, 138b
Ḍuḥā ii, **622b** – II, **638a**
al-Duhaym b. Khalīl, Aḥmad (949) s, 113a – S, 112b
Duhmān, Banū vi, 649a – VI, 634b
Duhn → Khazaf
Dukaginzade Yaḥyā Beg (1582) vi, 836a – VI, 826b
Duḳāḳ b. Tutush (Saldjūḳ) (1104) i, 664a, 731b, 1052a, 1332a; ii, 282a; iii, 398b; vi, 930b; viii, 947a; x, 600a – I, 683b, 753b, 1083b, 1372b; II, 290a; III, 411a; VI, 922b; VIII, 979b; X, 644b
al-Dūkālī, 'Abd al-Wāḥid s, 93a – S, 92b
Dukayn al-Rādjiz b. Radjā' al-Fuḳaymī (723) ii, **622b** – II, **638a**
Dukayn al-Rādjiz b. Sa'īd al-Dārimī (727) ii, **622b** – II, **638a**
Dukchi Ishān (XIX) iv, 113a – IV, 118b
Dukhān → Tütün
Dukhtar Khāṣṣa vi, 488a – VI, 474a
Dukkāla, Banū ii, **623a**; vi, 595a, 741a, b, 743a – II, **638b**; VI, 580a, 730b, 731a, 732a
al-Dukkālī, Abū Shu'ayb b. 'Abd al-Raḥmān (1937) iv, 159b ; viii, 905b – IV, 166b; VIII, 936b
Dūlāb → Nā'ūra
Dūlāb (Daylam) iv, 725a – IV, 754a
al-Dūlābī, Muḥammad b. Aḥmad (923) viii, 516a – VIII, 533b
Dulafid(e)s ii, **623a**; iv, 100a – II, **639a**; IV, 104a, b
Dūlanī bint Arghun b. Abaka (Īlkhān) (XIV) ii, 68a – II, 69a
Dulaym, Banū i, 461a; ii, **623b** – I, 474b; II, **639a**
Duldul ii, **624a** – II, **639b**
al-Dulfīn → Nudjūm
Dulghadir → Dhu 'l-Ḳadr
Dulūk i, 791b; ii, **624a**; vi, 506b, 507a – I, 815a; II, **639b**; VI, 491b, 492b

Dūmānlū vi, 384b – VI, 368b
Dūmat al-Djandal (al-Djawf) i, 55a, 384a, 525a, 882b, 969a; ii, **624b**; iv, 492b, 928a, b; vi, 544b; vii, 371a, 373b, 693b; x, 107b. 784a – I, 56b, 395a, 541a, 908a, 999a; II, **640a**; IV, 514a, 961a, b; VI, 529b; VII, 373a, 374b, 694a; X, 115b
Dumayr ii, 1021b – II, 1045a
Dumbulī, Banū ii, 193a; v, 460a – II, 199a; V, 462b
Dumbulī Khāns → Kurd(e)s
al-Dumistik Kurkāsh (X) vi, 230b – VI, 224b
Dūna, Banū vi, 310b – VI, 295b
Dunama b. Aḥmad (Bornu) (XIX) i, 1260a – I, 1298a
Dunama Dibbalemi (Kanem) (XIII) iv, 567a – IV, 589b
Dūnash b. Labrāṭ vii, 661a – VII, 660b
Dunaysir ii, **626a**; v, 248a; vi, 540a – II, **641b**; V, 246a; VI, 525a
Dunbāwand → Damāwand
Dunbulī → Dumbulī
Dündar Beg → Falak al-Dīn Dündar
Dungan (Dōngan, Tungan) → al-Ṣīn
Dungar Sen (XV) vi, 53a – VI, 51a
Dunghuzlum → Deñizli
Dungina → Kayalîk
Dun-huang x, 707a – X, 751b
Dunkulā → Dongola
Dunūh/Dumūya/Dumuwayh vi, 412b – VI, 397b
Dunyā i, 2a, 325a; ii, 295a, **626b** – I, 2b, 335a; II, 303a, **642a**
Dunyā Khātūn (Artukid(e)) (1367) vi, 540b – VI, 525a
Durač, Durrës → Drač
Dūrāh Pass ii, 29a – II, 29b
Durand Agreement/l'accord de – (1893) i, 87b – I, 90a
Durand Line vi, 86b; s, 66a, 270b – VI, 84b; S, 66a, 270a
al-Duraybī, Āl i, 1312b – I, 1353a
Durayd b. al-Ṣimma (630) ii, **626b**; iii, 578a; iv, 1027a; vi, 605a – II, **642b**; III, 598a; IV, 1059a; VI, 590a
Durazzo → Drač
Dūrbāsh ii, **627b** – II, **643a**
Durča'i, Sayyid Mahdī (1944) vii, 95b – VII, 97b
Durča'i, Sayyid Muḥammad Bāḳir (1923) vii, 95b; s, 157b – VII, 97b; S, 158a
Durgaras → Dōgrās
Durkānī → Balūčistān
Ḍurmā vi, 191b – VI, 175b
al-Durr i, 95b; ii, 557b, **628a**; iv, 764b; v, 572b, 675a, 819a – I, 98a; II, 571b, **643b**; IV, 795a; V, 577a, 680a, 82
Durrānī i, 72b, 95a, 217b, 219b, 230a, b, 295a; ii, **628b**, 1001b; iii, 202a, 428a; iv, 357a, 537b; s, 66b, 270a, 332b – I, 74b, 98a, 224a, 226a, 237a, b, 304b; II, **644b**, 1024b; III, 207b, 441b; IV, 372b, 561a; S, 67a, 270a, 331b
Dürrīzāde ʿAbd Allāh Bey (1923) ii, 105a, **630a** – II, 107a, **646a**
Dürrīzāde Meḥmed ʿĀrif Efendi (1800) ii, **629b**; iii, 604a, 1002b – II, **646a**; III, 624b, 1027b
Dürrīzāde Muṣṭafā Efendi (1775) ii, **629b** – II, **645a**
Dürrīzāde Seyyid ʿAbd Allāh (1828) ii, **630a** – II, **645b**
Dürrīzāde Seyyid Meḥmed ʿĀrif (1800) ii, **629b** – II, **645b**
Dürrīzāde Seyyid Meḥmed ʿAtā' Allāh (1785) ii, **629b** – II, **645b**
Dursun b. ʿAdjlān Karasî iv, 628a – IV, 653a
Dursun Beg (1461) vi, 70b, 71a – VI, 68b, 69a
Dursun Meḥmed Pasha (1691) i, 174b – I, 179b
al-Durūʿ, Banū ii, **630b**; iii, 1004b – II, **646b**; III, 1030a
Durūn (Darūn) i, 320b – I, 330b
Durūz i, 68a, 483a, 552a, 571a, 1042a, 1078b, 1093b; II, 98a, 136b, **631b**, 749b, 1026b; iii, 21a, 76b, 293a; iv, 199a, 332a, 484a, 834b; v, 791b, 793b; vi, 26a, b, 27b, 30b, 31a, 41b, 42a, 343a, 387b; vii, 117b; x, 192a,b; s, 49a, b, 135b, 206b, 268b, 269a, 371a – I, 69b, 497b, 569b, 589b, 1074a, 1110b, 1126a;II, 100a, 140a, **647b**, 768a, 1050a; III, 22a, 79a, 302a; IV, 207b, 346b, 504b, 867b; V, 797b, 799b; VI, 24a, b, 25b, 28b, 29a, 40a, 327b, 372a; VII, 119b; 207b; S, 49b, 50a, 135b, 206b, 268b, 370b
Dusares → Dhu 'l-Sharā
Dushanbe vi, 769a; x, 66a – VI, 758a; X, 68b
Dushmanziyār → Kākūyid(e)s
Dushmanziyārī, Banū iii, 1106b – III, 1134a
Dūst Bū Saʿd Dada (XI) i, 147b – I, 151b
Dūst Muḥammad (painter/peintre) (XVI) vii, 602b; viii, 787b, 788a – VII, 602b; VIII, 814a, b
Dūst Muḥammad Khān (1740) i, 1195a, 1197a – I, 1230b, 1232a
Dūst Muḥammad Khān (1863) i, 231a; ii, 417a, **637b**; iv, 537b; v, 48a; s, 237b, 367b – I, 238a; II, 428a, **653b**; IV, 561a; V, 49b; S, 237b, 367b
Dustūr i, 170a; ii, 79a, 151a, **638a**; iii, 186b – I, 174b; II, 80b, 155b, **654b**; III, 191a
Duwā Khān (Čaghatay) (1306) i, 504b; ii, 3b, 14b, 45a, 268b; iv, 31b, 32a – I, 520a; II, 3b, 15a, 46a, 277a; IV, 33b, 34b
Duwaydār → Dawādār
Duwayḥ (Dongola) s, 278b – S, 278b
al-Duwayhī → Iṣṭifān al-Duwayhī
al-Duwayḥī, Ibrāhīm al-Rashīd (1874) vi, 354b; s, **278b** – VI, 339a; S, **278b**
Duwayḥis (XVIII) iv, 925a – IV, 958a
Duyūn-i ʿUmūmiyye ii, **677a** – II, **694a**
Dūzakh → Djahannam
Düzmedje Muṣṭafā → Muṣṭafā Čelebi, Düzme
Dwārkā ii, **678a**, 1127a; vi, 50b – II, **695a**, 1153b; VI, 49a
Dwīn (Dabīl) i, 636a, 638a, 645a, b; ii, **678a**; vi, 504b, 648a; vii, 395a; ix, 169a – I, 656b, 658b, 665b, 666a; II, **695a**; VI, 490a, 633b; VII, 396a; IX, 174b
Dyābāt vi, 293b – VI, 279a
Dyallo i, 303a – I, 312b
Dyula (Mali) vi, 258b – VI, 243a
Džabić, A.F. (1918) i, 1271b, 1274a; ii, **681b** – I, 1311a, 1313b; II, **698b**
Džambul Džabaev → Djambul Djabaev
Dzhek iv, 1029a; v, 284b – IV, 1061a; V, 282b
Dzungharia ix, 648b, 648a, b – IX, 673b, 674a

E

ʿEbedyeshuʿ/ʿAbdīshūʿ vi, 115a – VI, 112b
Ebionites viii, 676a – VIII, 695b
Eblis → Iblīs
Ebu 'l-Suʿūd Efendi (ḳaḍī ʿasker) (XVI) vii, 545a – VII, 545a
Ebüzziya Tevfik (Abu 'l-Ḍiyā' Tewfīḳ) (1913) i, 289b; ii, 474b, **682a**; vi, 92b, 93a, 372b; vii, 532a – I, 298b; II, 486b, **699a**; VI, 90b, 91a, 357a; VII, 532b
Ecevit x, 696a – X,
Ecija → Istidjaʿ
Edebiyyāt-i Djedīde ii, **683a** – II, **700a**

Edessa/-e → al-Ruhā
Edfū/Edfou → Adfū
Edhem, Čerkes → Čerkes Edhem
Edhem, Khalīl → Eldem, Khalīl
Edhem Pasha → Ibrāhīm
Edigü (Noghay) (1419) i, 1108a; ii, 44a, 1112a; iii, 117a; vi, 417b; viii, 86a; x, 563a – I, 1141a; II, 45a, 1138b; III, 119b; VI, 402b; VIII, 88a; X,
Edindjik vi, 587b – VI, 572b
Ediou (Noghay) (XV) vi, 417b; viii, 86a – VI, 402b; VIII, 88a
Edirne i, 269a, 398b, 999a, 1078a, 1279a, 1334a; ii, **683a**; iii, 352a; iv, 590a; vi, 55a, 59b, 70a, 74a, 290b; s, 149b, 274a, 330b –
I, 277a, 410a, 1029b, 1110a, 1318b, 1374b; II, **700a**; III, 363a; IV, 614a; VI, 53a, 57a, 68a, 72a, 276a; S, 149b, 273b, 330a
—institutions i, 1225b; ii, 686a, 1133b – I, 1262a; II, 703a, b, 1160b
—monuments ii, 684a, b, 685a, b; iv, 592a, 722b, 1159a; v, 225a – II, 701b, 702a, b; IV, 616a, 751b, 1191a; V, 222b
Edirneli Naẓmī → Naẓmī
Edje Khalīl ii, 983b – II, 1006a
Edrei → Adhriʿāt
Edremit ii, **686b** – II, **703b**
ʿEdrūs → ʿAydarūs
Efe → Zeybek
Efendi i, 75a; ii, 19a, **687a** – I, 77a; II, 19b, **704a**
Eflāḳ (Wallachia/-e) i, 340b, 1118b, 1298b; ii, 611b, **687b**, 688b, 703a, 915; iii, 1004a; vi, 58b, 59b; viii, 609a –
I, 351a, 1152a, 1338b; II, 626b, **705a**, 721a, 936a; III, 1029a; VI, 56b, 57b; VIII, 628b
Egée, mer I, 477b; V, 509a, b, 510a
Egerdir → Eğridir
Egil vi, 541a – VI, 525b
Eğin ii, **689a** – II, **706a**
Eğri ii, **689b** – II, **707a**
Eğri Da → Aghrī Dagh
Eğriboz (Euboea) ii, **691a**; v, 722b; vi, 71b – II, **708b**; V, 778b; VI, 69b
Eğridir ii, **691b** – II, **709a**
Egypt/-e → Miṣr
Ekbez s, 171b, 172a – S, 172a, b
Ekdālā iii, 634b – III, 655b
Ekinči b. Ḳočḳar (1097) iv, 1067a; v, 385b; s, **279a** – IV, 1099a; V, 387a; S, **279a**
Ekrem Bey (1914) i, 287b, 558a; ii, 440a, **692a**; iii, 357b; iv, 930b; v, 195b; vi, 373a –
I, 296a, 576a; II, 451b, **709b**; III, 368b; IV, 963b; V, 192b; VI, 357b
Ekrem ʿÖmer Pasha (1854) vi, 68b – VI, 66b
Elam, Elamite v, 830b – V, 836b
Elath → Ayla
Elaziğ → Maʿmūrat al-ʿAzīz
Elbasan i, 652b, 655b; ii, **693a**; iv, 140a – I, 673a, 676a; II, **710a**; IV, 146a
Elbaz, Raphael Moise vi, 293a – VI, 278b
Elbistān ii, 239a, b, 240a, **693a**; iv, 463a; v, 73b; vi, 231b, 322a, 366a, 505b, 507a, b, 508a, b, 509a –
II, 246a, b, **710b**; IV, 483b; V, 75b; VI, 225a, 306b, 350a, 491a, 492a, 493a, b, 494a, b,
Elburz → Alburz
Elchasai(ī)tes → Ṣabi'; Ṣābi'a
Elche → Alsh
Elči ii, **694a**; iv, 31b – II, **711a**; IV, 34a
Eldem, Khalīl Edhem (1938) ii, **694b**; iii, 993b – II, **711b**; III, 1018a
Eldigüz, Eldigüzid(e)s → Ildeñiz, Ildeñizid(e)s
El-Erg → Djālo
Elesbaas i, 103a – I, 105b
El-Gāʿda i, 460b – I, 473b
El-Hajj Malik El-Shabazz → Malcolm X
Elias Andrawus s, 301a – S, 300b
Eličpur vi, 54a, 343a, 524a; s, **279b** – VI, 52a, 327a, 508b; S, **279b**
Elijah/Élie → Ilyās
Elijah Muhammad (1975) vii, 703a – VII, 703b
Elisha/Élisée → Alīsāʿ
El Ḳaghan (630) x, 687a – X, 729b
Elkass mirza → Alkāṣ mīrzā
Ellora → Elurā
Elma Daghi ii, **694b**, 982a; v, 810a, b – II, **712a**, 1004b; V, 816a, b
Elmali ii, **695a** – II, **712a**
Eloche → Alsh
El Tarish Ḳaghan → Tonyukuk
Eltüzer İnaḳ Khān (Khīwa) (1806) vii, 574b; s, 420a – VII, 575a; S, 420a
Elurā ii, **695a** – II, **712b**
Elvira → Ilbīra
Elwān Čelebi i, 698b; ii, 62b; vi, 354b – I, 719b; II, 63b; VI, 338b
Elwend → Alwand
Emānet i, 1090b; ii, 147b, 695b – I, 1123a; II, 152a, 713a → Emīn
Emanet-i Muḳaddese ii, **695b** – II, **712b**
Emba (river/fleuve) vi, 418a – VI, 403a
Ememik → al-Yamāmī
Emesa/Émèse → Ḥims
Emil Khʷādja (Ḳoca) (XIV) x, 590b – X,
Emīn ii, **695b** – II, **713a**
Emin, Mehmed → Yurdakul, Mehmed Emin
Emīn Pasha ii, 636b – II, 652b
Emīn Pasha (E.C. Schnitzer) (1892) ii, **696a**; v, 1250b – II, **713b**; V, 1241b
Emīne Sulṭān i, 394b; s, 282b – I, 406a; S, 282b
Eminek (1475) vi, 1016b – VI, 1009a
Emir → Amīr
Emīr Bukhārī, Sheykh (1421) vi, 530b – VI, 514b
Emir Efendi of/de Ḳāsim Pasha (XVI) vi, 228a – VI, 222a
Emīr Süleymān → Sulaymān Čelebi
Emīr Sulṭān (1429) ii, 103b, **697a**; s, 282b –
II, 105b, **714b**; S, 282b
Émirats Arabes Unis → al-Imārāt al-ʿArabiyya al-Muttaḥida
Emīrōf Murād, Ebu 'l-Fārūḳ → Mīzāndjī' Meḥmed Murād
Emniyyet-i ʿUmūmiyye ii, 74b – II, 75b
Empedocle(s) → Anbāduḳlīs
Emr → Amr
Emrāh s, 91b – S, 91a
Emreli ii, **697b**; vi, 588b – II, **715a**; VI, 573a
ʿEnbāḳōm i, 609a; vii, 74a; s, 396b – I, 628b; VII, 75a; S, 396b
Enderūn ii, **697b**, 1089a, 1091a; iv, 1097a – II, **715a**, 1114b, 1116b; IV, 1128a
Enderūn-i Hümāyūn Kütübkhānesi vi, 198b – VI, 183a
Endjümen → Andjuman
ʿEnesh vi, 506a – VI, 491b
Enez → Enos
Engürü → Ankara
Engürüs → Madjāristān; Ungurus
Enif → Nudjūm
Enīs ʿAwnī → Akagündüz
Enīs Behīdj s, 168a – S, 168a
Enīs Redjeb Dede, Shaykh (1734) vii, 575a – VII, 575b
Enna → Ḳaṣryānnih

Ennaya   vi, 582b – VI, 567a
Ennayer   → Yinnāyir
Ennedi   s, 165a, 166a – S, 165a, 166a
Enoch   → Idrīs
Enos   ii, **698a** – II, **715b**
Ents Behīdj   s, 168a – S, 168a
Enwer Pasha (1922)   i, 63b; ii, 431b, 531a, b, **698a**; iii,
   1199b; iv, 284b, 285b, 297a, b; v, 537b; vi, 983b; viii,
   251a –
   I, 65b; II, 442b, 544b, **716a**; III, 1229b; IV, 297a,
   298a, 310a, 311a; V, 542a; VI, 976a; VIII, 267b
Enwerī, Ḥādjdjī Saʿd Allāh (1794)   ii, **702b** – II, **720b**
Enzel   → Inzāl
Enzeli   → Bandar Pahlawī
Ephesus/Éphèse   → Aya Solūḳ
Ephthalites   → Hayāṭila
Erač   vi, 62a – VI, 60a
Erbakan, Necmettin   iv, 791b; x, 696b – IV, 823b; X,
Erbīl   → Irbīl
Erciyas   → Erdjiyas
Erdebīl   → Ardabil
Erdek (Gulf of/Golfe de)   vi, 587b, 588a – VI, 572b,
   573a
Erdel   ii, **703a** – II, **720b**
Erden ʿAlī   → ʿAlāʾ al-Dīn Beg
Erdjīsh   → Ardjīsh
Erdjiyas Daghî   ii, **705a**; iv, 845b – II, **723a**; IV, 878b
Ereğli   ii, **705a**; iv, 575b, 621a – II, **723a**; IV, 598b,
   646a
Erekle   → Iraklî II
Eretna   i, 432a, 510b; ii, 401a, **705b**; iv, 622b, 843a – I,
   444a, 526a; II, 411b, **724a**; IV, 647b, 876a
Erg   → Ṣaḥrāʾ
Erganí   ii, **707a** – II, **725a**
Ergen, Özbeg Khān   s, 246a – S, 246a
Ergene Khātūn   → Orkîna Khātūn
Ergenekon   ii, **707b** – II, **726a**
Ergin, Osman (1961)   ii, **708a** – II, **726a**
Ergiri   ii, **708b** – II, **726b**
Ergun, Saʿd al-Dīn Nüzhet   s, **280a** – S, **280a**
Eritrea   ii, **709a**; iii, 6a; vi, 628a – VI, 613a
Eriwan/Erivan   → Rewān
Ermenak, Ermenek   ii, **710a**; iii, 1006b; iv, 619a, 622a,
   b, – II, **727a**; III, 1032a; IV, 643b, 647a
Ermine   → Farw
Erota   vi, 628b – VI, 613b
Ersarî, Banū   i, 224a; v, 582a; vi, 416a, b; s, 143b,
   147a, **280b** – I, 231a; V, 587a; VI, 401a, b; S, 143a,
   147a, **280b**
Ersoy   → Mehmet Akif Ersoy
Ertoghrul   i, 329b, 340a; ii, **710b**, 715b ; viii, 180b,
   192a; ix, 706a – I, 340a, 350b; II, **727b**, 733b; VIII,
   183b, 195a; IX, 735a
Ertoghrul, Bursa   i, 1218b; ii, 711a – I, 1254b; II, 727b
Ertoghrul b. Bāyazīd (1392)   ii, **711a** – II, **728a**
Érythrée   II, **728a**; III, 6a; VI, 613a
Erzen   → Arzan
Erzerum   → Erzurūm
Erzindjān   i, 639a, 1328a; ii, 33a, **711a**; iv, 817b – I,
   659b, 1368b; II, 33b, **729b**; IV, 850b
Erzurūm   i, 4a, 465a, 636a, 639a; ii, 210a, 425b, 711b,
   712a, 945b; iii, 212b, 214b; iv, 394b, 817b; v, 33b; s,
   136a, 308a –
   I, 4a, 479a, 656b, 659b; II, 216b, 436b, 729b, **730a**,
   967b; III, 218b, 221a; IV, 411b, 850b; V, 34b; S,
   135b, 307b
Esad, Mehmed (Shaykh Muḥamad Asʿad) (1931)   vii,
   937a – VII, 937b
Esʿad Efendi, Aḥmed (1814)   ii, **712b** – II, **731a**
Esʿad Efendi, Meḥmed (1625)   ii, **713a**; iv, 900b – II,
   731b; IV, 933b

Esʿad Efendi, Meḥmed (1753)   ii, **713b**, 931b; iv, 527b
   – II, **731b**, 953a; IV, 550b
Esʿad Efendi, Meḥmed (1778)   ii, **713b** – II, **732a**
Esʿad Efendi, Meḥmed (1848)   i, 630a; ii, 465b, **714a**;
   vi, 59a – I, 651a; II, 477b, **732a**; VI, 57a
Esʿad Mukhliṣ Pasha, Saḳîzlî Aḥmed (1875)   ii, 636b;
   vi, 69a; vii, 205b – II, 652b; VI, 67a; VII, 206b
Esʿad Pasha (1932)   iv, 873b – IV, 907a
Esʿad Pasha, Saḳîzlî Aḥmed (1875)   s, **281b** – S, **281b**
Esāme   → Yeni Čeri
Esclavons   → Saḳāliba
Esdras   → Idrīs; ʿUzayr
Esen Bugha I   ii, 3b – II, 3b, 4a
Esen Bugha II   i, 148a; ii, 45b; v, 859a – I, 152a; II,
   46a; V, 866a
Esen Buḳa, Khān (1318)   x, 590b -
Esen Tayshi   iv, 512a – IV, 534a
Esendal, Memdūḥ Shewket (1952)   v, 194b, 197a; s,
   282a – V, 192a, 194b; S, **281b**
Eshām   → Ashām
Eshkindji   ii, 528b, **714b** – II, 541b, **733a**
Eshḳiyāʿ   iii, 317b – III, 327a
Eshref   → Ashraf
Eshref, Meḥmed (1912)   s, **282b** – S, **282a**
Eshref Edib (1910)   vi, 986a – VI, 978a
Eshref, Rüshen (Ünaydin)   iv, 874b – IV, 908a
Eshref-i Rūmī   → Eshrefoghlu
Eshrefiyye   s, 282b – S, 282b
Eshrefoghlu ʿAbd Allāh (1469)   s, **282b** – S, **282b**
Eski Baba   → Babaeski
Eski Ḳaplîdja   iv, 570a – IV, 593a
Eski Ḳarā Ḥiṣār   → Īsdje Ḳarā Ḥiṣār
Eski Malaṭya   vi, 232a – VI, 226a
Eski Sarāy   → Sarāy
Eski Üdjüm   s, 82a – S, 82a
Eskishehir   ii, **715a** – II, **733b**
Eṣnāf   → Ṣinf
Esne   → Isnā
Espagne   → al-Andalūs
Esrār Dede (1796)   ii, 999a; vi, 610a; s, **283a** – II,
   1022b; VI, 595a; S, **283a**
Estrangelo   iii, 963b – III, 988a
Eszék   ii, **715b** – II, **734a**
Esztergom   ii, **716a**; v, 641a, 1022a; vi, 75a; s, 171a –
   II, **734b**; V, 645a, 1018a; VI, 72b; S, 171a
Etājā, Etaya   → Iṭāwā
Etawah   → Iṭāwā
Ethiopia/-e   → al-Ḥabash
Ethiopians/-iens   → Ḥabasha
Etil   → Itil (river/rivière)
Et-Meydani   → Istanbul
Euboea   → Eğriboz
Euclid(e)   → Uḳlīdish
Eugène of Savoy/-de Savoie   i, 269b, 292a, 395a; iv,
   969b – I, 277b, 301a, 406b; IV, 1001b
Eunuchs/Eunuques (Mecca)   vi, 168a – VI, 159b
Euphrate(s)   → al-Furāt
Eutychius   → Saʿīd b. Biṭrīḳ
Eve   → Ḥawwāʾ
Ev-göčü   iv, 239b – IV, 250a
Evora   → Yābura
Evran   → Akhī Ewrān
Evren, Kenan   x, 696a – X.
Evrenos   → Ewrenos
Ewliyā Čelebi (1684)   i, 310b, 843a, 993a, 1076a; ii,
   589b, **717b**; iii, 7a; iv, 185b; v, 726b, 816a; vi, 411b;
   vii, 599a; s, 171b, 187a, 208b, 315b, 330b –
   I, 320a, 866a, 1023b, 1108a; II, 604a, **736a**; III, 7b;
   IV, 193b; V, 732a, 822a; VI, 396b; VII, 598b; S,
   171b, 188a, 208a, 315a, 330a
Ewrāḳ   i, 109a – I, 1122b

Ewrenos Beg, Ghāzī (1417) ii **720a**, 722a; iv, 628b; v, 772a; vi, 71a; vii, 237a, 645a; s, 330a, b, 331a – II, **738b**, 740b; IV, 653b; V, 778a; VI, 69a; VII, 238a, 644b; S, 329b, 330a, b
Ewrenos-oghullarî i, 340b, 1118b; ii, **720b** – I, 351a, 1152a; II, **739b**
Eyālet i, 468b, 469a, 640b, 906b, 974a, 1263b; ii, **721b** – I, 482b, 483a, 661a, 934a, 1004b, 1302a; II, **740a**
Eylūl → Taʾrīkh
Eymir (Eymür) ii, **724a** – II, **743a**
Eyvān → Īwān
Eyüp → Eyyūb
Eyyūb iv, 226a, 233a, 238b, 244a; vi, 3a, 55b, 125a, 530b; s, 315a – IV, 236a, 243a, 249a, 255a; VI, 3a, 53b, 122b, 514b; S, 315a
Eyyūb Agha Ḳara ʿOthmān-oghlu iv, 593b – IV, 617b
Eyyūb Ṣabrī iv, 284b – IV, 297a
Eyyūbī Aḥmad Pasha (1731) vi, 55b – VI, 53b
Eyyūboghlu, Bedrī Raḥmī s, 283a – S, 283a
Eyyūboghlu, Ṣabāḥ al-Dīn Raḥmī (1973) s, **283b** – S, **283a**
Ezafe → Iḍāfa
Ezan adî iv, 181a – IV, 188b
Ēzānā iii, 10a – III, 10b
Ezbek iv, 462b, 463a – IV, 483b
Ezbekiyya iv, 442a, b – IV, 462a, b
Ezekiel/Ezéchiel → Ḥizḳīl
Ezelī → Azalī
Ezra → Idrīs; ʿUzayr

F

Fāʾ ii, **725a** – II, **743a**
Faḍāʾil → Faḍīla
Fadak ii, **725a**, 844b; vi, 621b, 875a; vii, 398a – II, **743b**, 864a; VI, 606b, 866a; VII, 399a
Faḍāla ii, **727a**; vii, 387a – II, **745b**; VII, 388b
al-Faḍāli, Muḥammad (1821) i, 334a, 867b; ii, **727b** – I, 344a, 891b; II, **746a**
Fadʿān i, 483a – I, 497b
Faddāʿ, Āl (Mecca) vi, 177a
Faddān → Misāḥa
al-Faddaynī (IX) x, 883a – X.
Fadhlaka ii, **727b** – II, **746a**
al-Fāḍil → al-Ḳāḍī al-Fāḍil
Fāḍil Bey, Ḥüseyn (1810) ii, **727b** – II, **746a**
Fāḍil Ḥüsnī Dağlarca s, 150a – S, 150a
Fāḍil Khān → al-Bihārī
Fāḍil Pasha, Muṣṭafā, Mîṣîrlî (1875) ii, 474a, 642a, 682a, **728a**, 935b; iii, 357a, 593a; iv, 875b, 876a – II, 486a, 658a, 699a, **746b**, 957b; III, 368b, 613b; IV, 909a
Fāḍil Yuldash i, 422a – I, 434a
Faḍīla i, 327b; ii, **728b**; v, 331b; vi, 350a, 351a – I, 338a; II, **747a**; V, 331b; VI, 334b, 335b
Fāḍiliyya v, 889b, 892a – V, 896a, 898a
Fadjīdj → Figuig
al-Fadjīdjī i, 1154a – I, 1188a
Fadjr → Ṣalāt
Fadjr-i Ātī → Fedjr-i Ātī
Faḍl III b. Faḍl II (Shaddādid(e)) (1130) ii, 680b; vi, 274a – II, 697b; VI, 259a
Faḍl (poet/poétesse) iii, 1202b – III, 1233a
Faḍl, Āl iv, 87b; viii, 986b – IV, 91b; VIII, 1021a
Faḍl, Bā ii, **729b** – II, **748b**
al-Faḍl b. al-ʿAbbās i, 137a – I, 141a
al-Faḍl b. ʿAbd al-Ṣamad al-Raḳāshī (IX) vii, 414b – VII, 416a
Faḍl b. Abī Yazīd (948) i, 164a; vi, 435a – I, 168b; VI, 420b
al-Faḍl b. Aḥmad al-Isfarāʾinī (1013) ii, **730a**, 919a; iv, 107b – II, **749a**, 940a; IV, 112a
Faḍl b. ʿAlī al-ʿAbdalī i, 95b; v, 602a, b – I, 98a; V, 606a, b
Faḍl-i ʿAlī Khān i, 809a – I, 832b
al-Faḍl b. Djaʿfar b. al-Furāt → Ibn al-Furāt, Abu ʾl-Fatḥ
al-Faḍl b. al-Ḥubāb al-Djumāḥī (917) s, **284a** – S, **284a**
al-Faḍl b. Ḳārin iv, 493b – IV, 515a
al-Faḍl b. Marwān (vizier) (X) (864) ii, **730b**; iv, 929a; vii, 679a, 776b – II, **749a**; IV, 962a; VII, 678b, 778a
Faḍl b. Muḥammad b. Shaddādid iv, 1176b – IV, 1210a
Faḍl b. Nuʿayr, Āl iii, 400a – III, 412a
al-Faḍl b. al-Rabīʿ b. Yūnus (822) i, 107b, 143b, 437b, 438a, 1035a, 1298a; ii, **730b**; iii, 45b; iv, 17a; vi, 331b, 333b, 335a, 336a, 438a; vii, 646a; viii, 351a. 838b; s, 48a, 304b – I, 110b, 148a, 449b, 450a, 1066b, 1338a; II, **749a**; III, 47b; IV, 18a; VI, 316a, 318a, 319b, 320a, 423a; VII, 646a; VIII, 363b, 868a; S, 49a, 304b
al-Faḍl (al-Mufaḍḍal) b. Rawḥ al-Muhallab (794) vii, 360a – VII, 362b
al-Faḍl b. Sahl b. Zadhānfarūkh Dhu ʾl-Riyāsatayn (818) i, 271b, 400a, 437b, 1035b; ii, **731a**; iii, 231b, 243b; v, 621a; vi, 331b, 332b, 333b, 334a, b, 335b, 941a; vii, 215a, 404a, 558b, 694b; viii, 100b; s, 15a – I, 280a, 411b, 449b, 1067a; II, **749b**; III, 238a, 250b; V, 625a; VI, 316a, 317a, 318a, b, 319a, 320a, 933b; VII, 216b, 405b, 559a, 694b; VIII, 102b; S, 15b
al-Faḍl b. Ṣāliḥ (vizier) (X) i, 823b, 824a; ii, 483a; iii, 79b, 128b; vii, 910b – I, 846b, 847a; II, 495a; III, 82a, 131a; VII, 911a
al-Faḍl b. Shādhān iv, 660b, 661b; s, 89b – IV, 687a, 688a; S, 89b
al-Faḍl b. Yaḥyā b. Khālid al-Barmakī (808) i, 241a, 1033b, 1034a, b; ii, 191a, 540b, **732a**; iii, 233a, b; iv, 356b, 419b, 631b, 1164a, 1174b; v, 855b; vi, 331a, b, 437b, 438a; vii, 646a, b; viii, 145a; ix, 496a – I, 248b, 1065a, b, 1066a; II, 197a, 554a, **750b**; III, 239b, 240a; IV, 372a, 438a, 656b, 1196a, 1208a; V, 862b; VI, 315b, 316a, 423a; VII, 646a, b; VIII, 147a; IX, 515a
Faḍl al-Shāʿira, al-Yamāmiyya (871) s, **284b** – S, **284a**
Faḍl Allāh, Aḥmad → Ibn Faḍl Allāh al-ʿUmarī
Faḍl Allāh Āl i, 1046a; ii, 305b, **732a**; iii, 758b; iv, 509b – I, 1077b; II, 314a, **750b**; III, 781b; IV, 531b
Faḍl Allāh → Rashīd al-Dīn
Faḍl Allāh b. ʿĪsā Tashkandī iv, 505a – IV, 527a
Faḍl Allāh b. Muḥibb Allāh i, 1333a – I, 1373b
Faḍl Allāh b. Rabeh i, 1260a – I, 1298b
Faḍl Allāh b. Rūzbihān Khundjī (1521) → Khundjī, Faḍl Allāh b. Ruzbihān
Faḍl Allāh b. Saʿīd (947) vii, 569b – VII, 570a
Faḍl Allāh Balkhī → Iḳbāl Khān
Faḍl Allāh Dabbās iv, 966b – IV, 998b
Faḍl Allāh Djamālī → Djamālī
Faḍl Allāh Efendi iv, 194a – IV, 202a
Faḍl Allāh Ḥurūfī (1394) i, 1162a; ii, 685a, **733a**, 924a; iii, 600a, 601a; vi, 226b; vii, 105b, 226b; viii, 8a – I, 1196b; II, 702b, **751b**, 945b; III, 620b, 621b; VI, 220b; VII, 107b, 220b; VIII, 8a
Faḍl Allāh Nūrī, Shaykh (1909) vii, 299b – VII, 301b
Faḍl Allāh Zāhidī (XX) vii, 655a – VII, 654b
al-Faḍl al-Hadathī vii, 785a – VII, 787a
Faḍl-i Ḥaḳḳ (1862) i, 827b; ii, 104a, **735b**, 736a; iv, 196a, 197a – I, 850a; II, 106b, **754a, b**; IV, 204b, 205b

Faḍl al-Ḥaḳḳ (Bengal(e)) (XX) iii, 533a – 551b
al-Faḍl al-Ḳaṣabānī (1052) x, 461b – X, 494b
Faḍl al-Mawlā Muḥammad v, 1250b, 1251a – V, 1241b, 1242a
Faḍl al-Shāʿira al-Yamāniyya (871) viii, 856a – VIII, 885b
Faḍlawayh, Banū ii, **736b**; s, 326a – II, **755a**; S, 325b
Faḍlawayh b. ʿAlī Shabānkāra'ī (Kurd(e)s (1071) i, 420a; ii, 736b; iii, 1097b; iv, 222a, 807b; viii, 946a; ix, 157a – I, 432a; II, 755a; III, 1124a; IV, 232a, 840a; VIII, 978b; IX, 162b
Faḍlawī iii, 337a; v, 824b, 826b – III, 347a; V, 830b, 832b
Faḍlī (Fadhlī) ii, 675b, **737a** – II, 692a, **755b**
Faḍl-i Imām (1829) i, **736a** – II, **754b**
Faḍlī, Meḥmed (Ḳara Faḍlī) (1563) i, 1301b; ii, **737b**, 1133a; v, 957b – I, 1341b; II, **756a**, 1160a; V, 961b
Faḍlūn b. Abi 'l-Suvār iv, 773a – IV, 804a
Faḍlūn b. Minučihr iv, 670a – IV, 697b
Faḍlūn b. Shaddād iv, 346b; v, 489a – IV, 361a; V, 492a
Faḍlūya → Faḍlawayh b. ʿAlī
Fadu, Fadwa → Fidya
Faghfūr ii, **738a** – II, **756b**
Faghfūr (porcelain/-e) iii, 345b – III, 356b → Ṣīnī
Fahd ii, **738b** – II, **757a**
Fahd Banū iii, 759b – III, 783a
Fahd b. ʿAbd al-ʿAzīz (Āl Suʿūd) (XX) v, 1004a; vi, 158al ix, 905a – V, 999b; VI, 153b; IX, 943a
Fahd b. Ibrāhīm iii, 77a, 78a – III, 79b, 80b
al-Fāhikī i, 1154a; ii, 740b – I, 1188a; II, 759a
Fahīm, Aḥmad → al-Fār
Faḥl (Fiḥl) ii, **743a**; x, 883a – II, **761b**; X,
Faḥm v, 965a, 967b – V, 969b
Faḥm, Banū iii, 363b; s, 183a – III, 375a; S, 184b
Fahmī al-Mudarris (XX) vi, 615a – VI, 600a
Fahradj vi, 192b; s, 127a – VI, 176b; S, 126a
Fahrasa i, 70b, 96b, 1019b, 1092b; ii, **743b**; iii, 837b; vi, 406a; s, 303a – I, 72b, 99a, 1050b, 1125a; II, **762a**; III, 861b; VI, 391a; S, 302b
Faḥṣ al-Ballūṭ ii, **744a** – II, **762b**
Fā'ik, amīr (Harāt) (X) ii, 799a, – II, 818a
Fā'ik Khāṣṣa (994) vi, 65a, 340a, 433a; viii, 110a – VI, 63a, 324a, 418b; VIII, 112b
Fā'ik al-Niẓāmī al-Ṣaḳlabī (X) viii, 880a – VIII, 910a
Fā'ik Saʿīd v, 195a – V, 192a
Fāʿil → ʿIlla
Fāʿil → Naḥw
Fā'iz (1683) vi, 837b – VI, 828a
Fā'iẓ bi-Naṣr Allāh i, 9b; ii, 857a; iv, 944a – I, 9b; II, 877a; IV, 977a
Faizullah Khodja → Khodjaev
Faḳāriyya → Dhu 'l-Faḳāriyya
Faḳʿaṣ, Banū iv, 490b – IV, 511b
al-Faḳʿasī, al-Naẓẓār b. Hāshim viii, 376a – VIII, 389a
Fakhdh, Fakhidh i, 700a – I, 721b → ʿAshīra, Ḳabīla
Fākhita bint Abī Hāshim b. ʿUtba (VII) iv, 929b; vi, 139a – IV, 962b; VI, 137a
Fakhkh ii, **744b**; iii, 22a; vi, 147b – II, **763a**; III, 23a; VI, 146a
Fakhkhār i, 501a; ii, **745a**; iii, 1125b, 1267b; iv, 292a, 511b, 1164b; v, 942a – I, 516a; II, **763b**; III, 1153b, 1300b; IV, 305a, 533b, 1196b; V, 945b
Fakhr → Mufākhara
Fakhr Ārā'ī (1949) vii, 446b – VII, 448a
Fakhr al-Dawla Abū ʿAli (X) iv, 859a – IV, 892b
Fakhr al-Dawla Abu 'l-Ḥasan ʿAlī (Buwayhid(e)) (997) i, 59b, 211b, 212a; ii, **748b**; iii, 258a, 671b; iv, 100b, 358a; vi, 66a, 600b; vii, 272b; s, 118b, 323a – I, 61b, 218a; II, **767a**; III, 265b, 693a; IV, 104b, 373b; VI, 63b, 585b; VII, 274b; S, 117b, 322b
Fakhr al-Dawla Abū Manṣūr Kūfī (IX) iv, 859a – IV, 892a
Fakhr al-Dawla Čawlī i, 1012a; iii, 1097b; iv, 29a, 850b; v, 868a; s, 382b – I, 1043b; III, 1124a; IV, 31a, 883b; V, 874b; S, 383a
Fakhr al-Dawla Ḥasan b. Shāh (Bāwandid(e)) (1349) i, 237a, 1110a; vi, 511a; s, 363b, 364a – I, 244a, 1143b; VI, 496b; S, 363b
Fakhr al-Dawla Ibn Djahīr → Djahīr, Banū
Fakhr al-Dawla Muḥammad b. Djahīr i, 1206b; ii, 384a, b; v, 453a – I, 1242b; II, 394b, 395a; V, 455b
Fakhr al-Dīn I b. Maʿn (1544) ii, 634b, **749b**; iv, 483b – II, 650b, **768a**; IV, 504b
Fakhr al-Dīn II b. Ḳurḳumāz b. Maʿn (1635) i, 267b, 1138a; ii, 443b, 634b, **749b**, 912a; iii, 205b, 325a; iv, 834b; v, 792b; vi, 343b, 345a, 580b; vii, 600b, 911a; viii, 182b, 758b; ix, 99a; s, 49a, 159a – I, 276a, 1172b; II, 455a, 651a, **768a**, 933b; III, 211a, 335a; IV, 867b; V, 799a; VI, 327b, 329b, 565b; VII, 600b, 911b; VIII, 185b, 783a; IX, 103b; S, 49b, 159a
Fakhr al-Dīn (Maḳdishū) (XIII) vi, 128b – VI, 126b
Fakhr al-Dīn b. Abi 'l-Faradj (Ustādār) (XV) vii, 271b – VII, 273b
Fakhr al-Dīn b. Luḳmān (XIII) vii, 729b – VII, 730a
Fakhr al-Dīn b. Mīr-i Buzurg al-Marʿashī (1405) vi, 512a, b – VI, 497a, 498a
Fakhr al-Dīn b. al-Sāʿātī (XII) vi, 663a – VI, 648b
Fakhr al-Dīn ʿAbd Allāh b. al-Hādī iii, 685a – III, 707a
Fakhr al-Dīn ʿAdjemī (al-ʿAdjamī) (1468) ii, 685a, 879a – II, 702b, 899b
Fakhr al-Dīn Aḥmad Ḳarāmān-oghlu iv, 622a, b – IV, 647a
Fakhr al-Dīn ʿAlī (1288) viii, 831a – VIII, 860a
Fakhr al-Dīn ʿAlī Ṣafī (1532) iv, 704a – IV, 732b
Fakhr al-Dīn ʿAlī Tabrīzī → Ṣāḥib ʿAtāʿ
Fakhr al-Dīn Čishtī → Shāh Fakhr al-Dīn
Fakhr al-Dīn Gurgānī (XI) viii, 885b – VIII, 915b
Fakhr al-Dīn Harātī (ḳāḍī al-ḳuḍāt) *t* (1300) vi, 16a – VI, 14a
Fakhr al-Dīn Ibn Shaykh al-Shuyūkh (1250) vi, 321a – VI, 305b
Fakhr al-Dīn Ibrāhīm b. Lukmān iii, 679b – III, 701b
Fakhr al-Dīn ʿĪsā b. Ibrāhīm al-Mawṣil (XIII) vi, 628a – VI, 612b
Fakhr al-Dīn ʿIṣāmī → ʿIṣāmī
Fakhr al-Dīn Ḳara Arslan, amīr (Ḥiṣn Kayfā) (1149) vi, 870b – VI, 861b
Fakhr al-Dīn Kart iv, 672a – IV, 699b
Fakhr al-Dīn Mādjid iii, 774a – III, 797a
Fakhr al-Dīn al-Marāghī (1258) vi, 501a – VI, 486b
Fakhr al-Dīn Marʿashī, Sayyid v, 663a – V, 668a
Fakhr al-Dīn Masʿūd ii, 1100b, 1101a – II, 1126b, 1127a, b
Fakhr al-Dīn Mubārakshāh (XIV) ii, **751b** – II, **769b**
Fakhr al-Dīn Muḥammad b. Ḥasan b. ʿAllāma al-Ḥillī s, 364a – S, 363b
Fakhr al-Dīn Muḥammad (Kart) (1307) ix, 112a – IX, 116a
Fakhr al-Dīn Muḥammad b. ʿUmar al-Rāzī (1210) i, 113a, 342b, 411a, 594a, 1115b; ii, 393b, 449b, **751b**, 756b, 771a, 773b, 825b, 971a, 1025b; iii, 172a, 302a, b, 330a, 1020a, 1237b; iv, 120a, 183b, 251b, 367a, 406a, 669a; vi, 132a, 353a, 450a, 636b, 637b, 627b, 908a; vii, 55a, 199b; viii, 95a, 134a, 541a; ix, 887a; s,

25b, 90b, 343b, 396b –
I, 116a, 353a, 423a, 613b, 1149a; II, 404a, 461b, **770a**, 784a, 789b, 792b, 845b, 938b, 1049a; III, 175b, 311b, 340a, 1045b, 1269b; IV, 125a, 191b, 262b, 383a, 423b, 696b; VI, 130a, 337a, 435b, 612b, 621b, 622b, 899b; VII, 55b, 200a; VIII, 97b, 136b, 599a; IX, 923a; S, 25b, 26a, 90a, 343b, 397a
Fakhr al-Dīn Muḳrī, amīr (1285) vi, 580a – VI, 565a
Fakhr al-Dīn Pīrīoghlu iv, 671a – IV, 698b
Fakhr al-Dīn ʿUthmān b. al-Ḥādjdj Yūnis (Maʿn) (1506) vi, 343a – VI, 327b
Fakhr al-Dīn Yūsuf b. al-Shaykh i, 711a, 766a – I, 732b, 789a
Fakhr al-Dīn Zāhid i, 868b – I, 892b
Fakhr-i Ḳawwās v, 1027a – V, 1023a
Fakhr-i Mudabbir Mubārak Shāh (1236) iii, 181a, 196a, 197a, 344a, 481b, 1155b, 1202a; iv, 267a; v, 546b, 688a; vii, 193a, 679a, 988a; s, **284b** –
III, 185b, 200b, 202a, 354b, 498b, 1184a, 1232b; IV, 279a; V, 551a, 693a; VII, 193b, 679a, 989a; S, **284b**
Fakhr al-Muḥaḳḳiḳīn (1369) vi, 549b – VI, 534a
Fakhr al-Mulk → ʿAmmār, Banū
Fakhr al-Mulk ʿAmmār i, 448a – I, 461a
Fakhr al-Mulk Muḥammad b. ʿAlī → Ibn Khalaf, Abū Ghālib
Fakhr al-Mulk al-Muẓaffar b. Niẓām al-Mulk (1096) i, 1052b; ii, 1039b; vi, 14a, 489b; viii, 81b – I, 1084a; II, 1063b; VI, 12b, 489a; VIII, 83b
Fakhrā → Fakhr al-Dīn Mubārakshāh
Fakhr-i Mudabbir viii, 814b – VIII, 841b
Fakhrī (XIV) vi, 835b – VI, 826a
Fakhrī (1618) ii, **755b** – II, **774a**
Fakhrī, Shams al-Dīn Muḥammad (XIV) ii, **755b**; iv, 526a, b – II, **774a**; IV, 548b, 549a
Fakhrī Pasha v, 998a – V, 993a
Faḳīh i, 7a, 250a, 279b, 289a; ii, **756a**; v, 1124b, 1208a, 1248a – I, 7a, 258a, 288b, 298a; II, **774a**; V, 1121a, 1198b, 1239a
Fakhrī, Bā ii, **756a** – II, **774b**
Faḳīh, Bal (Bā ʿAlawī) ii, **756b** – II, **775a**
al-Faḳīh, Ibrāhīm v, 190a – V, 187a
al-Fākihī, Abū ʿAbd Allāh Muḥammad b. Isḥāḳ (IX) i, 591a, 827a; ii, **757a**; vi, 106a –
I, 610b, 850a; II, **775b**; VI, 104a
Faḳīr ii, **757b**; v, 1124b, 1208a, 1248a –
II, **776a**; V, 1121a, 1198b, 1239a
Faḳīr (well/puits) iv, 532b – IV, 555b
Faḳīr of/de Ipi (1960) vi, 86b; s, **285a** – VI, 84b; S, **285a**
Faḳīr Muḥammad Khān ii, **758a** – II, **776a**
Faḳīr Muḥammad Lahorī i, 827b – I, 850b
Faḳīrī, Ḳalḳandelì (XVI) ii, **758a**; ix, 410a – II, **776b**; IX, 423b
Faḳḳara → Foggara
Faḳr iv, 94b – IV, 98b
Faḳr-i ʿadjam iv, 52a – IV, 54b
Fāḳūdh vi, 630a – VI, 615a
Fāl v, 670b, 671b, 672a – V, 676a, 677a
Faʿl ii, **758b** – II, **777a**
Fāl-nāma ii, **760b** – II, **779a**
Faladj i, 233a, 539a, 1313b; iv, 531b – I, 240b, 555b, 1353b; IV, 554b
al-Faladj → al-Aflādj
Falak ii, **761b** – II, **780a**
Falakʿ Alā-i Tabrīzī ii, 81a – II, 82b
Falak al-Dīn b. Aḳ-Sunḳur II (XII) i, 300b; vi, 500b – I, 310a; VI, 485b
Falak al-Dīn Dündar ii, 692a; iii, 132b; iv, 622a – II, 709a; III, 136a; IV, 646b
Falak al-Maʿālī Manūčihr (Ziyārid(e)) (1029) vi, 453a – VI, 438b
Falaḳa ii, **763b** – II, **782a**
al-Falakī, Maḥmūd Pasha (1885) ii, **764a** – II, **782b**
Falakī Shirwānī (1155) ii, **764a**; iv, 62a, 348b; s, 333b – II, **782b**; IV, 65b, 363a; S, 333a
Falāsifa i, 351a, 414b, 415a; ii, **764b**; iii, 169b, 303a, 1146b, 1147b; iv, 366b, 469a, 794b; v, 237a, 238a, 702b; vi, 448b –
I, 362a, 426a, b; II, **783a**; III, 173b, 312a, 1174b, 1175b; IV, 382b, 490a, 827a; V, 235a, 236a, 707b; VI, 434a
Fālidj iii, 665b – III, 687a
Fāliḥ Rìfḳì Atay (XX) vi, 94b – VI, 92b
Falilu Mbacké (1968) vii, 609b – VII, 609a
Fallāḥiya → Dawraḳ
Fallāḳ ii, **767b**; iv, 954b – II, **786a**; IV, 987a
Fallāta ii, **767b** – II, **786a**
al-Fallātī, al-Ṭāhir b. Ibrāhīm iv, 773b – IV, 805a
Fallūdja (ʿIrāḳ) ii, **768a**; vi, 616a – II, **786b**; VI, 601a
al-Fallūdja (ʿIrāḳ) ii, **768a** – II, **786b**
Fallūdja (Miṣr) s, 6a – S, 5a
Fallūs b. Tutush (Saldjūḳ) (XII) viii, 995a – VIII, 1030a
Fals i, 203a; ii, **768a**; vi, 374a – I, 209a; II, **786b**; VI, 358b
al-Fals vi, 374a – VI, 358b
Falsafa i, 414b, 415a, 427b; ii, 450a, 618a, 752b, 764b, **769b**, 898a; iii, 75a, 329b; iv, 615b, 794b, 986b; v, 1129b –
I, 426a, b, 439b; II, 461b, 633b, 771a, 783a, **788a**, 919a; III, 77b, 339b; IV, 640a, 827a, 1019a; V, 1126a
Fālūghus ii, 236a – II, 242b
Famagusta/-gouste → Maghōsha
Fāmiya vi, 378b, 381a – VI, 363a, 365a
Fanāʿ → Baḳāʾ
Fanak ii, **775a**; iii, 809a – II, **794a**; III, 832a
Fanākatī, Aḥmad (1282) iv, 1020a – IV, 1052a
Fanār → Fener; Manār
al-Fanārī, Aḥmad i, 99a – I, 101b
al-Fanārī, Muḥammad → al-Fenārī
Fanar(a)ki (Istanbul) vi, 359b – VI, 344a
Fanduruskī → Abū Ṭālib
Fānī → Navāʾī
Fann ii, **775b**; iv, 528a – II, **794b**; IV, 551a
Fannā Khusraw → ʿAḍud al-Dawla
Fānnū bint ʿUmar b. Yīntān (Almoravid(e)) (1147) vii, 626b – VII, 626a
Fāo → al-Fāʿū
Faʾr s, **285b** – S, **285a**
Farʿ → Furūʿ (tax/impot)
al-Fār, Aḥmad Fahīm iii, 368a – III, 379b
al-Faraʿ s, 335a – S, 334b
Fārāb ii, **778a**; s, 244b, 245a, 289a, b – II, **797a**; S, 244b, 245a, 289a
al-Fārābī, Abū Ibrāhīm Isḥāḳ b. Ibrāhīm (961) ii, 496a; s, **289a** – II, 508a; S, **288b**
al-Fārābī, Abū Naṣr (950) i, 179a, 234b, 236a, 327b, 328a, 342a, b, 350b, 427a, 589a, 630b, 631b, 1102a; ii, 96a, 765b, 770b, **778b**, 949a; iii, 329b, 509b, 729a, 876b, 911b, 942b, 1148a; v, 113b, 702b; vi, 97b, 204b, 220a, 347a, 348b, 442b, 446b, 447b, 449a, b, 450a, 637a, 674a, 905a; vii, 682b, 683a, 1051a; viii, 123b, 421b; s, 289b, 408b –
I, 183b, 241b, 243a, 337b, 338b, 352a, 353a, 361a, 439b, 608b, 651b, 652 a, 1135a; II, 98a, 784a, 789a, **797a**, 971a; III, 339b, 527a, 751b, 900b, 935b, 967b, 1176a; V, 116a, 707b; VI, 95b, 188b, 214a, 331a, 332b, 428a, 432a, 433a, 434b, 435a, b, 622a, 660b, 896b; VII, 682b, 683a, 1053b; VIII, 126a, 436b; S, 289b, 409a
Faradj, al-Malik al-Nāṣir b. Barḳūk (Mamlūk) (1412) i, 138a; ii, 24a, 285b, **781a**; iii, 187a, 189b, 190a, 774a, 827b; iv, 428a; vi, 324a, 326b, 327a; vii, 168a, 172a –

I, 142a; II, 246b, 293b, **800a**; III, 191b, 194a,b, 797a, 851b; IV, 446b; VI, 308b, 311b; VII, 169b, 173b, 174a
Faradj, Muḥammad ʿAbd al-Salām (1982) vii, 291b – VII, 293b
Faradj, b. Sālim iii, 754a – III, 777a
al-Faradj baʿd al-Shidda → Nādira
Farāfra, Farāfira i, 945a; ii, **782a** – I, 974a; II, **801a**
Farāh ii, **782b**; s, 222a – II, **801a**; S, 222a
Faraḥ Anṭūn (1922) i, 597a; ii, **782b**; iii, 514b; vi, 414a, 598b; vii, 902a – I, 616b; II, **801b**; III, 532a; VI, 399a, 583b; VII, 902b
Farāh Dībā (XX) vii, 447a – VII, 448a
Faraḥābād i, 8b; ii, **783a**; vi, 526b – I, 8b; II, **801b**; VI, 511a
Farāhānī → Ḳāʾim-maḳām-i Farāhānī
Farāhānī, Mīrzā Ḥusayn Khān s, 109a – S, 108b
Farāʾiḍ ii, **783a** – II, **802a**
Farāʾiḍiyya i, 719b; ii, **783b**, 797b; iii, 433a; vii, 291a – I, 741b; II, **802b**, 816b; III, 447a; VII, 293a
al-Far(a)ma (port) i, 32a, 216a; vii, 43a – I, 33a, 222b; VII, 43b, 70a
Farāmarz, ʿImād al-Dawla → ʿImād al-Dawla
Farāmarz b. ʿAlī → ʿAlā al-Dawla
Farāmarz b. Muḥammad (Marʿashī) vi, 515a – VI, 500a
Farāmurz (Kākūyid(e)) → Abū Manṣūr Farāmurz
Farāmūsh-khāna ii, 433b; vi, 291b; s, **290a** – II, 445a; VI, 276b; S, **289b**
Farangī Maḥall → Lakhnaw (monuments)
Farangī Maḥall , Āl vii, 300b; viii, 68b; s, 4b, 5a, 74a, b, **292a**, 360b – VII, 302b; VIII, 70b; S, 3b, 4a, 74b, 75a, **291b**, 360b
Faras ii, **784b**; iii, 314b, 890b; iv, 214a-219b; v, 689a, b – II, **803b**; III, 324a, 914b; IV, 223b-229a; V, 694a, b
Faras (al-Marīs) vi, 574b – VI, 559b
Faras al-Māʾ s, **294a** – S, **293b**
Farasān i, 535a, 738a; ii, **787b**; x, 90b – I, 551b, 760a; II, **806b**; 97b
Farasnāma iv, 218b – IV, 228b
Farāwa vi, 780b; vii, 26a – VI, 770a, VII, 26a
al-Farawī, Muḥammad b. Muḥ. b. ʿAlī s, 83a – S, 82b
al-Farazdaḳ (728) i, 43a, 105a, 158b, 331a, 586a, 772a, 950b, 1248a; ii, 479b, **788a**, 998b; iii, 248a, 354a, 608b; iv, 819a; vi, 344b, 476a, 477b, 539a, 545a, 604b, 709b; vii, 114a, 144a, 261a, 402a, 920b, 981a, b – I, 44a, 108a, 162b, 341b, 605a, 795a, 980a, 1286a; II, 492a, **807a**, 1021b; III, 255a, 365a, 629b; IV, 852a; VI, 328b, 462a, 463b, 523b, 529b, 589a, 698a; VII, 116a, 147b, 262b, 403a, 921a, 982a, b
al-Fard → Nudjūm
Fard, afrād ii, **789b**; iii, 25b – II, **808b**; III, 26b
Farḍ, farīḍa ii, **790a**; iv, 141b – II, **809a**; IV, 147a
Fard, Wallace D. (1934) vii, 702b – VII, 703b
Fardoonji, Kavasji Mulla (XIX) vii, 222b – VII, 224b
al-Farfarūn → Farāfra
Farghalūs → Asbagh n. Wakīl
Farghānā i, 46b, 148a; ii, **790a**; iii, 1060b; iv, 632a; v, 29a, 31a, 45a, 966b; vi, 337a, 557a, b, 769b; vii, 313b, 477b; s, 51b, 97b, 327b, 406b – I, 48a, 152b; II, **809a**; III, 1087a; IV, 657a; V, 30a, 32a, 46b, 971a; VI, 321a, 542a, 758b; VII, 316a, 477a; S, 52a, 97a, 326a, 406b
al-Farghānī, Abū Manṣūr Aḥmad (1007) ii, **793a**; viii, 14b – II, **812a**; VIII, 14b
al-Farghānī, Abū Muḥammad ʿAbd Allāh (972) ii, **793a**; x, 11a – II, **812a**; X, 11a
al-Farghānī, Aḥmad b. Kathīr (Alfraganus) (861) i, 589b; ii, 763a, **793a**; iii, 1137a; vi, 374b; vii, 39b, 539b, 680a – I, 608b; II, 781b, **811b**; III, 1165b; VI, 358b; VII, 40a, 539b, 680a
Farhād Khān Ḳaramanlī (1596) iv, 808a; v, 663a; vi, 515b – IV, 840b; V, 668b; VI, 501a
Farhād Mīrzā (Ḳādjār) s, 95a – S, 94b
Farhād Mīrzā Muʿtamad al-Dawla s, 302a – S, 301b
Farhād Pasha → Ferhād Pasha
Farhād wa-Shīrīn ii, **793b**; iv, 601b, 730b; v, 650b – II, **812b**; IV, 625b, 759b; V, 654b
Farhang iv, 525b – IV, 548a
Farhangistān-i Irān i, 505a; v, 1095b, 1096a, b – I, 520b; V, 1092a, b, 1093a
Farḥāt, Djarmānūs (1732) i, 571b, 596b; ii, **795a** – I, 590a, 616a; II, **814a**
Farḥāt, Ilyās v, 1256b – V, 1247b
Farḥāt b. Saʿīd i, 1247a – I, 1285a
Farḥāt ʿAbbās iii, 525a; iv, 784b – III, 543a; IV, 816b
Farḥāt al-Mulk ii, 1124b – II, 1151a
Farīburz b. Garshāsp iv, 349a – IV, 364a
Farīburz b. Sāllār iv, 348a, b; s, 326a – IV, 362b, 363a; S, 325b
Farīd (pearl/perle) s, 253a – S, 252b
Farīd Bukhārī, Shaykh (XVII) vii, 938a; s, 122a – VII, 938b; S, 121b
Farīd al-Dīn → ʿAṭṭār
Farīd al-Dīn Masʿūd Gandj-i Shakar, Shaykh (1265) ii, 51a, **796b**; iii, 167b, 429a, 435b, 456b; v, 546b, 611a; viii, 68a, 240a; s, 73b, 353a – II, 52a, **815a**; III, 171a, 443a, 450a, 472b; V, 551a, b, 615a; VIII, 69b, 246aS, 74a, 353a
Farīd Murtaḍā Khān Bukhārī, Shaykh iv, 543b – IV, 567a
Farīd Pasha → Dāmād Ferīd Pasha
Farīd Wadjdī (1907) vi, 955b – VI, 948a
Farīḍa → Farāʾiḍ, Farḍ
Farīḍa (queen/reine) → Ṣafīnāz
Farīdkōṭ ii, **797b** – II, **816a**
Farīdpur ii, **797b** – II, **816b**
Farīdūn → Ferīdūn Aḥmed Beg
Farīdūn b. Abtiyān (Abtīn) ii, 106b, **798a**; iii, 105a; iv, 12a; v, 661a; vi, 744a – II, 109a, **816b**; III, 107a; IV, 13a; V, 666b; VI, 733b
Farīdūn, Djalāl al-Dīn → ʿĀrif Čelebī
Fārigh (1591) iv, 68a; viii, 776a – IV, 71b; VIII, 802a
Farīghūnid(e)s ii, 608b, **798b**; vi, 65b, 340a; s, 125b, 376a, 386b – II, 624a, **817b**; VI, 63b, 324a; S, 124b, 376a, 387a
Farīḳ → Abū Sinbil
al-Fāriḳī, Abu ʾl-Ḳāsim (1001) vii, 281b – VII, 283a
al-Fāriḳī , Shihāb al-Dīn iv, 642a – IV, 668a
Farīmān vi, 495b – VI, 480b
Fāris ii, **800a** – II, **818b**
Fāris (Marīnid(e)) (1415) vi, 594a – VI, 578b
Fāris b. ʿĪsā (X) iii, 103a – III, 105b
Fāris b. Muḥammad → Ḥusām al-Dīn Abū ʾl-Shawḳ
Fāris al-Dīn Aḳṭay al-Mustaʿrib al-Djamadār (1254) vi, 321b; vii, 166b – VI, 306a; VII, 168a
Fāris al-Dīn Ilbeki al-Sāḳī al-Ẓāhiri (Ṣafad) (1298) vi, 777b – VI, 767b
Fāris al-Dīn al-Shidyāḳ, Aḥmad (1887) i, 596b; ii, 464b, 466a, **800b**, 927a; iii, 665a; v, 1090a; vi, 598b; vii, 902a, b; ix, 229b; s, 40a – I, 616a; II, 476a, 477b, **819b**, 948b; III, 687a; V, 1087b; VI, 583b; VII, 902b, 903a; IX, 235a; S, 40b
Fāris Nimr → Nimr, Fāris
al-Fārisī → Abū Ḥulmān; Kamāl al-Dīn; Salmān
al-Fārisī, ʿAbd al-Ghāfir (1048) vi, 354a; s, 343a – VI, 338a; S, 343a
al-Fārisī , Abū ʿAlī al-Ḥasan (987) i, 87a; ii, **802b**; iii,

754b, 880b; iv, 182a; vi, 188b, 635b; vii, 914a; viii, 615a; s, 13a, 19a, 277a, 361b –
I, 89b; II, **821b**; III, 777b, 904b; IV, 190a; VI, 172b, 620b; VII, 915a; VIII, 634a; S, 13b, 19a, 277a, 361a
al-Fārisī, Abu 'l-Ṭāhir Muḥammad b. al-Ḥusayn (1058) vii, 474a – VII, 473a
al-Fārisī, ʿAlā' al-Dīn ʿAlī b. Balbān (1339) viii, 836a – VIII, 865a
al-Fārisī, Kamāl al-Dīn (1319) viii, 558a – VIII, 576a
al-Fārisī , Muḥammad b. al-Ḥasan s, 277a – S, 277a
al-Fārisī, ʿUmāra b. Wa<u>th</u>īma b. Mūsā b. al-Furāt (902) vii, 284a – VII, 285b
al-Fārisī , Wa<u>th</u>īma b. Mūsā b. al-Furāt (851) vii, 284a – VII, 285b
al-Fārisī al-Dima<u>sh</u>ḳī, Abū Ḥulmān (951) viii, 840b – VIII, 870a
Fārisiyya → Īrān
al-Fārisiyya i, 535b; ii, **803a** – I, 552a; II, **821b**
Far<u>j</u>a i, 705b – I, 726b
Fark → Faṣl
Farḳad al-Saba<u>kh</u>ī (VIII) vi, 613b – VI, 598b
al-Farḳadānī → Nu<u>dj</u>ūm
Fārkat (parkent) s, 51a – S, 51b
Fārmad s, 14b – S, 15a
al-Fārma<u>dh</u>ī → Abū ʿAlī al-Fārma<u>dh</u>ī
Farmān ii, 303b, 309a, **803a**; iii, 1189b; iv, 1131b – II, 312a, 317b, **822a**; III, 1219b; IV, 1163a
Farmān-Farmā, Ḥusayn ʿAlī Mīrzā (XIX) iv, 105a; vii, 453b – IV, 109b; VII, 454b
Fārmāsūn → Māsūniyya
Farmāsūniyya s, **296a** – S, **295b**
Farmūl ii, **806b** – II, 825b
Faro → <u>Sh</u>antamariyyat al-<u>Gh</u>arb
Farouk → Fārūḳ
al-Farrāʾ, Abū Zakariyyā' Yaḥyā b. Ziyād al-Kūfī (822) ii, **806b**; v, 174a, 351a; vii, 280a, 914a; viii, 573a; s, 22b –
II, **825b**; V, 171b, 351b; VII, 281b, 914b; VIII, 591b; S, 23a
al-Farrā', Muḥammad b. Aḥmad (X) vi, 224a – VI, 217b
Farra<u>kh</u>an, Minister Louis (XX) vii, 703b – VII, 704b
Farrān v, 41b, 42b – V, 42b, 44a
Farrā<u>sh</u> iv, 899a – IV, 931b
Farru<u>kh</u>-Hormizd i, 188b – I, 194a
Farru<u>kh</u> -<u>Sh</u>āh → ʿIzz al-Dīn Farru<u>kh</u>-<u>Sh</u>āh
Farru<u>kh</u> -Siyar, Abu 'l-Muẓaffar Muḥammad Muʿīn al-Dīn (Mu<u>gh</u>al) (1719) i, 1025b, 1026a; ii, 7a, 121a, 379b, 567a, 808a, **810a**; iii, 427a; iv, 279b; vi, 321b, 339b, 346a; vii, 443b; viii, 73a; s, 126b –
I, 1057b; II, 7a, 124a, 389b, 581b, 827b, **829a**; III, 441a; IV, 292a; VI, 323b, 341b, 348a; VII, 445a; VIII, 74b; S, 125b
Farru<u>kh</u> Beg (painter/peintre) (XVII) vi, 426a – VI, 411a
Farru<u>kh</u> <u>Kh</u>ān Amīn al-Dawla (1856) vi, 291b; vii, 1004a; s, 108b, 290b – VI, 276b; VII, 1005b; S, 108a, 290a
Farru<u>kh</u>ābād ii, **808a**; iii, 61a; vii, 443b; s, 106b – II, **827a**; III, 63b; VII, 445a; S, 106a
Farru<u>kh</u>ān b. al-Zaynabī (VII) vi, 745a, b; viii, 471a – VII, 734a, b; VIII, 487a
Farru<u>kh</u>ān Gīlān-shāh (680) iv, 207b; s, **297b** – IV, 217a; S, **297a**
Farru<u>kh</u>ān the Great/le Grand (Dābūyid(e) (728) ii, 74b, **809a** – II, 76a, **828b**
Farru<u>kh</u>ī, Muḥammad Ibrāhīm → Farru<u>kh</u>ī Yazdī
Farru<u>kh</u>ī Sīstānī, Abu 'l-Ḥasan (1037) i, 1301a; ii, **809b**; iv, 61a; vi, 66a, 453a, 608a, b, 609a; s, 108a –
I, 1341a; II, **828b**; IV, 64b; VI, 64a, 438b, 592b, 593b, 594a; S, 107a
Farru<u>kh</u>ī Yazdī, Muḥammad iv, 71a, 789b; s, 110a – IV, 75a, 821b; S, 109b
Farru<u>kh</u>rū Parsay iv, 1152a – IV, 1184a
Farru<u>kh</u>yasār iii, 316a; iv, 350a – III, 325b; IV, 365a
Farru<u>kh</u>zād b. Maḥmūd ii, 5a, 1052a – II, 5a, 1076a
Fārs i, 2b, 8a, 43b, 49a, 131b, 132a, 211b, 212a, 659a, 695b, 731b, 954b, 1350a, 1356a, 1358a; ii, **811a**; iii, 1097a; iv, 19b, 774a, 1046b; v, 450b, 665b; vi, 17b, 120a, 272b, 273a, 275b, 332a, 337b, 365a, 383b, 384a, b, 416a, 482a, 484b, 493b, 494a, 524a, 621b, 633b, 677a; s, 91a, 118b, 147b, 222b, 302a, 326a, 379b, 383b –
I, 2b, 8a, 44b, 50b, 135b, 136a, 217b, 218b, 679b, 716b, 753b, 984a, 1390b, 1395a, 1398b; II, **830b**; III, 1124a; IV, 21a, 805b, 1078a; V, 453a, 670b; VI, 15b, 16a, 118a, 257b, 257b, 260b, 316b, 322a, 349a, 367b, 368a, b, 401a, 468a, 470b, 479b, 480a, 509a, 606b, 618b, 663b; S, 90b, 117b, 147b, 223a, 301b, 325b, 379b, 384a
Fārs al-Liwāl<u>dj</u>ān vi, 384b – VI, 368b
Farsa<u>kh</u> (farsang) i, 247a; ii, **812b**; iii, 406a – I, 254b; II, **832a**; III, 418b
Far<u>sh</u> → Ḳālī
Far<u>sh</u> → Mafrū<u>sh</u>āt
Far<u>sh</u>ūṭ viii, 866a – VIII, 896b
Fārsī → Īrān
Fārsī, Abu 'l-<u>Kh</u>ayr (XVI) viii, 542a – VIII, 559b
Fārsistān → Īrān
al-Farsy, <u>Sh</u>ei<u>kh</u> Abdulla Salem (1982) ix, 917b – IX, 956a
Fartanā iv, 821a – IV, 854a
Far<u>th</u>iyya iii, 660a – III, 681a
Fārūḳ → Anṣārī, <u>Sh</u>ay<u>kh</u> Murtaḍā
Fārūḳ, Day of/Journée de s, 178a – S, 179a
Fārūḳ, King/le roi (1965) ii, 648b; iii, 517a, 572a; v, 1062a; vii, 904b, 905a; s, 5b, 6b, **299a** – II, 665a; III, 535a, 592a; V, 1059a; VII, 905b; S, 5a, b, **299a**
al-Fārūḳ → ʿUmar b. al-<u>Kh</u>aṭṭāb
al-Fārūḳī, ʿAbd al-Bāḳī (1862) i, 330b; ii, **813a** – I, 340b; II, **832a**
al-Fārūḳī, Kamāl iii, 1023b – III, 1049b
al-Fārūḳī, Mullā Maḥmūd (1652) ii, **813a** – II, **832b**
al-Fārūḳī, Rā<u>dj</u>ā → Malik Rā<u>dj</u>ā Fārūḳī
al-Fārūḳī, <u>Sh</u>ay<u>kh</u> <u>Dj</u>alāl al-Dīn (XVII) ii, 54b – II, 55b
al-Fārūḳī, <u>Sh</u>ay<u>kh</u> Muḥammad Maʿṣūm (XVII) vii, 602a – VII, 601b
al-Fārūḳī, <u>Sh</u>ay<u>kh</u> Niẓām al-Dīn (XVII) ii, 54b – II, 55b
Fārūḳid(e)s ii, **814a**, 1084b – II, **833b**, 1110a
Farw ii, **816b**; v, 752a, 857a – II, **836a**; V, 757b, 864a
Farwa(h) b. Musayk (VII) i, 728a; ii, 177b, 1096a; iv, 927b; v, 954a; vii, 592a – I, 750a; II, 183b, 1122a; IV, 960b; V, 958a; VII, 591b
Farwa b. Namfal iii, 1265b – III, 1298a
Farwān ii, **817b** – II, **837a**
Farwardīn → Taʾrī<u>kh</u>
Faryāb (Gūzgān) ii, **817b**; vi, 915a; ix, 431a – II, **837a**; VI, 906b; IX, 448a
Fāryāḳ → Fāris al-<u>Sh</u>idyāḳ
Faryūmadī, ʿIzz al-Dīn Ṭāhir (1270) viii, 342b – VIII, 354b
Fās i, 35a, 47a, 70b, 86a, 92b, 355b, 687b, 977b, 1225a; ii, **818a**, 835a; iii, 62b, 149a, 694b, 814a; iv, 774b; v, 877a, 1178a, 1189a; vi, 38a, 40a, 123b, 124a, 141b, 142b, 199b, 248a, 251a, 281a, 293a, 356a, 404a, b, 422a, 431b, 571b, 572a, b, 573a, b, 589a, 591a, 592a, 594a, b, 595a, b, 664a, 675a, 741b, 742b; vii, 641a; viii, 440b; s, 10a, 23a, 26b, 28b, 40a, 47b, 63b, 113b, 126a, 133b, 223b, 350b, 387b, 389a, 390b –
I, 35b, 48b, 72b, 88b, 366b, 708b, 1008a, 1261b; II,

837b, 854b; III, 65a, 152a, 717a, 837b; IV, 805b; V, 883a, 1168a, 1179a; VI, 36b, 38b, 121b, 122a, 140a, b, 183b, 232a, 235a, 266a, 278b, 340a, 388b, 389a, 407a, 417a, 556b, 557a, b, 558a, b, 573b, 575b, 576b, 577a, 578b, 579a, b, 580a, 650a, 662a, 730b, 731b; VII, 640b; VIII, 455a; S, 9b, 23a, 26b, 29a, 40b, 48a, 64a, 113a, 125a, 133a, 223b, 350b, 387b, 389b, 391a
—institutions i, 1224b; ii, 819a, 1822b; iii, 140a; v, 1190a, 1208a – I, 1261a; II, 839a, 842a; III, 142b; V, 1180a, 1198b
—monuments i, 85a, 499b, 1346b; ii, 818b, 821-823; iv, 632a; v, 1150a, b, 1151b, 1152a, 1153a – I, 87b, 514b, 1387a; II, 838a, 840-842; IV, 657a; V, 1140b, 1141a, b, 1142a, b
Fās al-Bālī ii, 819a, 822a, b, 823a – II, 838b, 841b, 842a, b
Fās al-Djadīd ii, 819a, 820b, 822a, b, 823a; iii, 499a – II, 838b, 840a, 841b, 842a, b; III, 516a
Fasā ii, **823b**; vi, 120a, 384a, 640b; s, 302a – II, **843a**; VI, 117b, 368b, 625b; S, 301b
Fasād → Fāsid, Kawn
Faṣāḥa i, 573b, 981b, 1114b; ii, **824a** – I, 592b, 1012a, 1148a; II, **843a**
Fasāʾī, Hādjdjī Mīrzā Ḥasan (XIX) s, **302a** – S, **301b**
Fasāna → Afsāna
Fasandjus, Banū ii, **827a** – II, **846b**
al-Fasāsīrī → al-Basāsīrī
al-Fasawī, Yaʿḳūb b. Sufyān (890) viii, 516a – VIII, 533b
al-Fāshir (el-Fasher/el-Facher) ii, 122a, **827b** – II, 125a, **847a**
Fāshoda ii, **828a** – II, **847b**
al-Fāsī → Ibn Abī Zarʿ
al-Fāsī, ʿAbd al-Kabīr (1879) s, **303a** – S, **303a**
al-Fāsī, ʿAbd al-Ḳādir b. ʿAlī (1680) i, **70b**, 86a, 139a, 795a; s, **302b**, 325b – I, **72b**, 88b, 143a, 818b; S, **302b**, 325a
al-Fāsī, ʿAbd al-Raḥmān b. ʿAbd al-Ḳādir (1685) vi, 255b, 350a, 356b; s, **302b** – VI, 239b, 334b, 340b; S, **302b**
al-Fāsī, ʿAbd al-Raḥmān b. Muḥammad (1626) i, **86a**, 139a, 428a; s, **302b** – I, **88b**, 143a, 440a; S, **302a**
al-Fāsī, ʿAbd al-Salām b. Muḥammad (1895) s, **10a** – S, **9b**
al-Fāsī, Abu ʿAbd Allāh Maḥammad → Mayyāra, Abū ʿAbd Allāh Maḥammad
al-Fāsī, Abū ʿAbd Allāh Muḥammad (1722) s, **303a**, 403b, 404b – S, **302b**, 404a, b
al-Fāsī, Abū ʿAbd Allāh Muḥammad (1765) s, **303a** – S, **302b**
al-Fāsī, Abū ʿAbd Allāh Muḥammad (1799) s, **303a** – S, **303a**
al-Fāsī, Abū Ḥafṣ ʿUmar (1774) s, **303a** – S, **303a**
al-Fāsī, Abū Ḥāmid Muḥammad s, 404b – S, 404b
al-Fāsī, Abū ʿImrān al-Ghafdjūmī (XI) vii, 584a – VII, 584b
al-Fāsī, Abū Madyan Muḥammad (1768) s, **303a** – S, **302b**
al-Fāsī, Abu ʾl-Maḥāsin (1604) i, **238b**, v, 1029a; s, **302b** – I, **143a**; V, 1025a; S, **302a**
al-Fāsī, Abū Mālik ʿAbd al-Wāḥid (1799) s, **303a** – S, **303a**
al-Fāsī, Aḥmad al-Ḥāfiẓ b. Abi ʾl-Maḥāsin (1612) s, **302b** – S, **302b**
al-Fāsī, Āl s, **302a** – S, **302a**
al-Fāsī, ʿAllāl iv, 159b – IV, 166b
al-Fāsī, al-ʿArabī (1642) i, 428a – I, 440a
al-Fāsī, David b. Abraham (X) iv, 305b, 605a; vii, 539b – IV, 319a, 629b; VII, 539b
al-Fāsī, Ḥamdūn Ibn al-Ḥadjdj (1817) vi, 113a – VI, 110b
al-Fāsī, Isaac (1103) vii, 540a – VII, 539b
al-Fāsī, Muḥammad b. ʿAbd al-Salām (1799) vi, 130b – VI, 128b
al-Fāsī, Muḥammad b. Muḥammad s, 371a – S, 371a
al-Fāsī, Muḥammad b. Sulaymān (1823) vi, 247b, 250b – VI, 232a, 234b
al-Fāsī, Muḥammad al-ʿArbī b. Abi ʾl-Maḥāsin (1642) i, 139a; s, **302b** – I, 143a; S, **302b**
al-Fāsī, Muḥammad al-Mahdī (1698) iii, 971b; vi, 350a, 351a, 356a; s, **302b** – III, 996a; VI, 334a, 335a, 340b; S, **302b**
al-Fāsī, Muḥammad al-Ṭāhir (1868) s, **303a** – S, **303a**
al-Fāsī, Muḥammad al-Ṭayyib (1701) ii, 1022a; s, **303a** – II, 1045b; S, **302b**
al-Fāsī, Sayyid Aḥmad b. Idrīs (1837) vi, 628b – VI, 613b
al-Fāsī, Sīdī ʿAbd al-Ḳādir s, 302b – S, 302a
al-Fāsī, Taḳī al-Dīn (1429) ii, **828b**; iii, 760a – II, **848a**; III, 783b
Fāsid wa-bāṭil i, 319a; ii, **829b** – I, 329a; II, **849a**
Faṣīḥ → Faṣāḥa
Faṣīh Dede (1699) ii, **833a** – II, **852b**
Faṣīḥī (1670) viii, 776a – VIII, 802a
Fāsiḳ ii, **833a** – II, **853a**
Fāṣila ii, **834b** – II, **854a**
Faṣīla ii, **835a** – II, **854b**
al-Fāsiyya (ṭarīḳa) vi, 454b – VI, 440a
al-Fāsiyyūn i, 70b, 138b, 139a; ii, **835a**; iv, 379b; s, 223b, 302a – I, 72b, 143a; II, **854b**; IV, 396a; S, 223b, 302a
Faskāt ū-Mzāl → Abū Ḥafs ʿUmar
Faskh ii, **836a**; iii, 1056b – II, **855b**; III, 1082b
Faṣl ii, **836b** – II, **856a**
Faṣl → Filāḥa, Mafṣūl
Faṣṣād s, **303b** – S, **303a**
Fatā i, 256b; ii, **837a**, 961a, 1043b; iv, 705a – I, 264b; II, **856b**, 983a, 1068a; IV, 733b
al-Fatāwā al-ʿĀlamgīriyya i, 1331a; ii, 157b, 736a, **837a**; iii, 163b, 435a – I, 1372a; II, 162b, 754b, **857a**; III, 167a, 449b
Fatḥ → Ḥaraka
al-Fatḥ b. Khāḳān (861) i, 1082b, 1289b; ii, 385b, **837b**; vi, 110b, 111a; vii, 528a, 559a, 777b, 985b – I, 1114b, 1329a; II, 396a, **857a**; VI, 108b; VII, 528a, 559b, 779b, 986b
al-Fatḥ b. Khāḳān al-Ishbīlī (1134) i, 602a; ii, **838a**; iii, 354b, 734a, 807b – I, 621b; II, **857b**; III, 365b, 756b, 831a
Fatḥ ʿAlī Khān (envoy) (1746) vi, 56b, 939b – VI, 54b, 931b
Fatḥ ʿAlī Khān (Ḳādjār) (1750) vii, 853a – VII, 854b
Fatḥ ʿAlī Khān (Ḳuba) (1765) ii, 206a; v, 296b – II, 212b; V, 288a
Fatḥ ʿAlī Khān Dāghistānī (1720) iii, 604a; iv, 389b; v, 663b – III, 624b; IV, 406a, b; V, 669a
Fatḥ ʿAli Khān Develū iv, 391b, 392a, 597b; vi, 483b – IV, 408b, 622a; VI, 469b
Fatḥ ʿAlī Khān Tālpūr iii, 323b; iv, 1160a – III, 333b; IV, 1192a
Fatḥ ʿAlī khund-zāda → Akhund-zāda, Mīrzā Fatḥ ʿAlī
Fatḥ ʿAlī Shāh (Ḳādjār) (1834) i, 13b, 246a, 304b, 682b, 1030b; ii, 335b, **838b**, 1083b; iii, 114a, 348b, 554a, 1103b, 1104a, 1191a; iv, 38b, 51a, 391a, b, 392a, b, 393a, 703b, 1040b; v, 371b, 750a, 1222a; vi, 276b, 483b, 484a, b, 516b, 524a, 525a, 528a, b, 529b, 551a, b, 715a, 803b; vii, 298b, 603a, 960b; viii, 58a, 665b; s, 57a, 94b, 108b, 336a, 405b – I, 14a, 254a, 314a, 703a, 1062a; II, 345a, **858a**,

1109a; III, 116b, 359b, 573a, 1130b, 1131a, 1221a; IV, 41a, 54a, 407b, 408b, 409a, b, 732a, 1072a; V, 372a, 755b, 1212a; VI, 261b, 469b, 470a, b, 502a, 508b, 510a, 512a, b, 513b, 535b, 536a, 793b; VII, 300b, 602b, 961b; VIII, 59a, 685a; S, 57b, 94a, 108a, 335b
Fatḥ ʿAlī Shāh b. ʿAbd al-Madjīd Khān (XX) x, 961a – X,
Fatḥ Allāh ʿImād al-Mulk, vizier (1482) ii, 981a; iii, 1159a; vi, 62b, 63a; vii, 459a – II, 1003b; III, 1187b; VI, 60b; VII, 459a
Fatḥ Allāh al-Shīrāzī, Mullā ii, 132a, 156b; s, 353b, 410b – II, 135b, 161b; S, 353b, 411a
Fatḥ Djang i, 231b – I, 238b
Fatḥ al-Dunyā wa'l-Dīn Djalāl Shāh Sulṭānī → Maḥmud Khān, Nāṣir al-Dīn (Kālpī)
Fatḥ Girāy I ii, 1046b, 1113b – II, 1071a, 1139b
Fatḥ Girāy II iv, 569a – IV, 591b
Fatḥ al-Ḳalʿī (Alep(po)) (1016) vii, 116b; – VII, 118b
Fatḥ Khān (Barakzay) i, 230b, 231a; ii, 637b – I, 237b, 238a; II, 653b
Fatḥ Khān (Dawūdpōtrā) ii, 187a – II, 192b
Fatḥ Khān (Gudjaratī) → Maḥmud I Begrā
Fatḥ Khān b. Malik ʿAmbar (XVII) iii, 15b, 626a; viii, 74b – III, 16b, 647a; VIII, 71a
Fatḥ Khān Ḥarāwī (1452) vi, 62a – VI, 60a
Fatḥ Shāh Djalāl al-Dīn ii, 797b; iii, 14b; vi, 46b; s, 131b – II, 816b; III, 15b; VI, 45a; S, 131a
Fatḥa iii, 172b – III, 176b
Fatḥābād ii, 32a, 180a; iii, 442b; v, 1216b – II, 32b, 185b; III, 457a; v, 1206b
Fatḥiyya → ʿAbd Allāh b. Djaʿfar al-Ṣādiḳ
Fatḥnāme ii, **839b** – II, **859a**
Fatḥpūr Sīkrī i, 252b, 1024a, 1324a; ii, **840a**; iii, 287b, 449b; v, 1135b, 1218a; vi, 127a, b, 190b, 294b, 368b; viii, 267b; ix, 46b; s, 378a – I, 260b, 1055b, 1364b; II, **860a**; III, 296b, 465a; V, 1131a, 1208a; VI, 125a, b, 174a, 280a, 352b; VIII, 275a; IX, 47b; S, 378a
Fātiḥ-Camii iv, 229a – IV, 239a
Fātiḥa ii, **841a**; v, 425a – II, **860b**; V, 427b
al-Fātik → Nadjāḥ, Banū
Fāṭima bint Abī Muslim v, 65a, b – V, 67a
Fāṭima bint ʿAmr b. Makhzūm i, 42b, 80a – I, 43b, 82b
Fāṭima bint Asad b. Hāshim i, 152b; ii, 850a – I, 157a; II, 870a
Fāṭima bint Barrī i, 280b – I, 289a
Fāṭima bint Djāsim (XIX) vi, 614a – VI, 599a
Fāṭima bint al-Ḥasan b. ʿAlī (VII) vii, 398a – VII, 399a
Fāṭima bint al-Ḥusayn s, 95a – S, 94b
Fāṭima bint Ḳays al-Fihriyya (VII) x, 913b – X,
Fāṭima bint Maẓlūm ii, 234a – II, 241a
Fāṭima bint Muḥammad (633) i, 15a, 187a, 381b, 382a, 400b; ii, 725a, **841b**; iii, 1232a; vi, 468a, 469a, 629a, 646a, 652a; s, 92b, 231a – I, 15b, 192b, 392b, 412a; II, 743b, **861a**; III, 1263b; VI, 454a, 455a, 614a, 631a, 637a; S, 92b, 231a
Fāṭima bint Muḥammad IX (Naṣrid(e)) s, 399a – S, 399b
Fāṭima bint Muḥammad al-Fihrī iv, 632a – IV, 657b
Fāṭima bint al-Mundhir III b. al-Nuʿmān (Lakhmid(e)) (VI) vii, 604a – VII, 603b
Fāṭima bint ʿUmar b. Ḥafṣ iii, 694a – III, 716a
Fāṭima Khānîm s, 331a – S, 330b
Fāṭima Khātūn vi, 367a – VI, 351b
Fāṭima Khātūn umm ʿĀrif Čelebi (XIII) s, 83b – S, 83a
Fāṭima Lärä i, 841b – I, 865a
Fāṭima al-Maʿṣūma v, 370b, 371b – V, 371b, 372a
Fāṭima Sulṭān bint ʿAbd al-Medjīd (Ottoman) (1854) vi, 860b – VI, 851b
Fāṭima Sulṭān bint Aḥmad III (Ottoman) (1731) i, 269b, 395a; ii, 49a; iii, 1002a; vi, 55b – I, 278a, 406a; II, 50a; III, 1027a; VI, 53b
Fāṭima Sulṭan bint Ibrāhīm (Ottoman) (1646) vi, 865a – VI, 855b
Fāṭima Sulṭān bint Selīm i, 291b – I, 300b
Fāṭimid(e)s i, 20a, 48b, 83b, 163a, 196b, 215b, 367a, 403a, 435b, 440a, 551b, 710b, 797b, 798a, 832b, 869b, 986a, 1074a, 1175b, 1354b; ii, 281b, 453b, 494b, 506a, **850a**, 911a; iii, 656a, 785a, 932a; iv, 198b, 200b, 204a, 378b, 458b; v, 327b, 620b, 623b, 738a, 1175b, 1243b; vi, 1b, 65b, 117b, 120b, 140b, 148a, 194a, 195a, 199b, 261b, 274b, 275a, 280b, 379b, 385b, 423b, 518a, b, 519a, b, 520a, 668b, 669b, 670a, 671a, 673b, 674b, 676a, 712b, 713a, 849a; vii, 160a, 162a; ix, 266a, 507a, 596b; s, 120b, 236b, 254b, 256b, 326a, 338a, 389a, b – I, 21a, 49b, 86a, 167b, 202a, 222a, 378a, 414b, 448a, 452b, 569a, 732a, 820b, 821b, 855b, 894a, 1017a, 1106a, 1210b, 1394a; II, 290a, 465b, 507a, 518b, **870a**, 932b; III, 677a, 808b, 956b; IV, 207b, 209b, 213a, 395a, 479a; V, 327a, 624b, 627a, 743a, 1165b, 1234a; VI, 1b, 63b, 115a, 118b, 139a, 146b, 178a, 179a, 183b, 246b, 259b, 260a, 265b, 364a, 369b, 408b, 503a, b, 504b, 655a, 656a, 657b, 660a, 661a, 662b, 701a, b, 841a; VII, 163a, b; IX, 274b, 526b, 618b; S, 120a, 236b, 254b, 256b, 325b, 337b, 389a, 390a
—administration i, 1148b; ii, 80a, 126b, 145b, 326a, 328a, **860a**; iii, 47b, 360a; iv, 943b, 1092a – I, 1183a; II, 81b, 130a, 149b, 335b, 337b, **879b**; III, 49b, 371b; IV, 976b, 1123a
—art, architecture i, 200b, 830a, 1319b; ii, 747a, 821b, **862b**; iv, 428b; v, 217a – I, 206b, 853a, 1183a; II, 765b, 841a, **882b**; IV, 447a; V, 214b
Fāṭin b. Tamzīt b. Ḍarī, Banū i, 1349b; vi, 310b, 815a – I, 1390a; VI, 295b, 831a
Fāṭin (Dāwūd) (1867) ii, **864b** – II, **884b**
Fatma ʿAliyye Khanîm i, 286a – I, 295a
Fatra ii, **865a** – II, **884b**
Fattāḥ Wālī vi, 751a – VI, 740b
Fattāḥī (1448) i, 257a; ii, **865a**; iv, 67a – I, 265a; II, **885a**; IV, 70b
al-Fattāl, al-Ḥasan b. ʿAbd al-Karīm s, 380a – S, 380a
Fatwā i, 40a, 176a, 399b; ii, 304a, 306a, **866a**, 890a; ix, 400a – I, 41a, 284b, 411a; II, 312a, 314b, **866a**, 911a; UX, 418a
Faṭwāka, Banū vi, 742a – VI, 731b
al-Fāʾū v, 66a – V, 68a
Fāʿw ii, **867b** – II, **887b**
Fawātiḥ al-suwwar (al-Ḳurʾān) v, **412a** – V, **413b**
Fawdj → Ḥarb, Lashkar
Fawdjdār ii, **868a**; s, 57b – II, **888a**; S, 58a
Fawrī, Aḥmad (1571) ii, **869a** – II, **889a**
Fawzī, Ḥusayn i, 598a – I, 617b
Fawzī al-Maʿlūf → Maʿlūf
Fawziyya bint Fuʾād al-Awwal (XX) ii, 654b; vii, 446b – II, 671a; VII, 447b
Fayʾ i, 704a, 1142a, 1144a; ii, **869a**; iv, 973a, 1031a, 1141b – I, 725b, 1176b, 1178b; II, **889a**; IV, 1005a, 1062b, 1173b
Fayḍ → Muḥsin-i Fayḍ-i Kāshānī
Fayḍ, Ḥiṣn s, 198b, 199b, **304b** – S, 198b, 199b, **304a**
al-Fayḍ b. Abī Ṣāliḥ (789) ii, **870a**; s, 17b – II, **890a**; S, 17b
Fayḍ b. Ḥām b. ʿAmalīḳ → Zayd al-Khayl al-Ṭāʾī
Fayḍ Aḥmad Fayḍ (1984) x, 879b – X,
Fayḍ Allāh, Ḥādjdj (XVIII) vii, 444a – VII, 445a
Fayḍ Allāh, Shaykh (1575) i, 1168a – I, 1203a

Fayḍ Allāh al-ʿAlamī i, 352b – I, 363a
Fayḍ Allāh Bey i, 1030b – I, 1062a
Fayḍ Allāh Efendi, Shaykh al-Islām (1702) ii, 19b; iii, 627a; vi, 55a; vii, 708a; viii, 752b; s, 63a – II, 20a; III, 649a; VI, 53a; VII, 709a; VIII, 206b, 774a; S, 63b
Fayḍ Allāh Khān iii, 60a, b, 61b – III, 62b, 63a, 64a
Fayḍ Athār vi, 18b – VI, 16b
Fayḍ al-Kashī i, 596a – I, 615b
Fayḍ Muḥammad Khān i, 1195a, 1197a – I, 1230b, 1232a
Fayḍābād ii, 1a, **870a**; s, 74b, 102a, 358b – II, 1a, **890a**; S, 75a, 101b, 358b
Fayḍī (Fayyāḍī) → Muḥsin-iFayḍ-i
Fayḍī Abu ʾl-Fayd b. Shaykh (1595) ii, **870b** – II, **890b**
Fayḍ-i Kāshānī (1680) vi, 550b; vii, **475b**. 548a; viii, 136a, 779b; s, 57a, **305a** – VI, 535a; VII, **475a**, 548a; VIII, 138b, 805a ; S, **305a**
al-Fayḍiyya iv, 992a; vi, 454b – IV, 1024b; VI, 440a
Faydj → Fuyūdj
Fayḍullāh → Fayḍ Allāh
Fāyiz, Awlād iv, 637b – IV, 664a
Faylaka island/île v, 573b, 574a – V, 578a, b
Faylasūf ii, **872a** – II, **892a**
Faylī iii, 1102b, 1106a; v, 823b, 829b – III, 1129b, 1133a; V, 829b, 835b
Fayoum → al-Fayyūm
Fayrūz → Fīrūz
Fayṣal I b. al- Sharīf al-Ḥusayn (Ḥāshimite) (1933) i, 46a, 684a; ii, 289b, 429b, 661a, **872a**; iii, 263b, 293a, 605b, 1258b; iv, 782b; v, 1044a, 1046b, 1091b; vi, 262a, 304a, 387a, 538a, 615a, b, 616a; vii, 442b; viii, 141a, 246a; x, 885a; s, 67b – I, 47b, 705a; II, 297b, 440b, 677b, **892b**; III, 271a, b, 302b, 626b, 1291a; IV, 814a; V, 1040b, 1043b, 1088b; VI, 246b, 289b, 371a, 522b, 600a, b; VII, 443b; VIII, 143b, 252a; X, ;S, 68a
Fayṣal II b. Ghāzī (Ḥāshimite) (1958) ii, 674b, **872b**; iii, 264a; viii, 141b – II, 691b, **892b**; III, 271b; VIII, 144a
Fayṣal b. ʿAbd al-ʿAzīz (Āl Suʿūd (1975) i, 98b; iii, 1066a; iv, 261a; vi, 34b, 155a, 156a, 166a, b, 169b; vii, 765a; ix, 904b; s, **305b** – I, 101b; III, 1092b; IV, 272b; VI, 32b, 152a, b, 158a, b, 160a; VII, 766b; IX, 942b; S, **305b**
Fayṣal b. Ḥusayn → Fayṣal I
Fayṣal b. Suʿūd (Āl Suʿūd) (1840) ii, 320b; vi, 151a – II, 330a; VI, 149b
Fayṣal b. Sulṭān al-Dawīsh (Mutayr chief) iii, 1065b, 1066a, 1067a, b; iv, 681a; v, 575a, 998a, b; vii, 782b – III, 1092a, b, 1093b, 1094a; IV, 708b; V, 579b, 993b; VII, 784a
Fayṣal b. Turkī (Āl Bū Saʿīd, Oman) (1913) i, 1282; vi, 729b; ix, 904a; s, 356a – I, 1322; VI, 718b; IX, 941b; S, 356a
Fayṣal b. Turkī (Āl Suʿūd) (1865) i, 98b, 554b; ii, 108b, 176b; iv, 751b, 765a, 1073a – I, 101a, 572a; II, 111a, 182a; IV, 782a, 795b, 1104b
Fayshān vi, 80b – VI, 78b
Faytūriyya s, 93a – S, 92b
al-Fayyāḍ b. ʿAlī b. Muḥammad b. al-Fayyāḍ (IX) vii, 460a, 905b – VII, 460a, 906b
Fayyāḍ Beg iii, 1198b – III, 1228b
Fayyāḍī → Fayḍī
al-Fayyūm i, 1145a; ii, **872b**; iv, 774a; vi, 88b, 119a, 219b, 671b, 674a; s, 379a – I, 1179a; II, **893a**; IV, 805a; VI, 86b, 116b, 213b, 658a, 660b; S, 379b
al-Fayyūmī → Saʿadya ben Yōsēf al-Fayyūmī
al-Fayyūmī (1333) x, 32b – X, 34a
al-Fayyūmī (1614) vi, 112a – VI, 110a
Fayyūmi, Nathanael iv, 304b – IV, 318a
Fayzabad → Fayḍābād
Fayẓī → Fayḍī
Faza vi, 129a – VI, 127a
Fazāra, Banū ii, 122a, b, **873a**, 1023b; iv, 493b; v, 267a; vii, 488a, 629b; x, 959b; s, 177a, b – II, 125a, b, **893b**, 1047a; IV, 514b; V, 264b; VII, 488a, 629a; X, ; S, 178a, b
al-Fazārī → Ibrāhīm b. Muḥammad
al-Fazārī, Abū Isḥaḳ (805) viii, 498b – IV, 515b
al-Fazārī, Abu ʾl-Ḳāsim Muḥammad (956) s, **306a** – S, **306a**
al-Fazārī, Muḥammad b. Ibrāhīm (790) iii, 1136a,b; iv, 517b; vii, 401b; viii, 874a – III, 1164b; IV, 540a; VII, 402b; VIII, 904a
al-Fazārī al-Ibāḍī, ʿAbd Allāh b. Yazīd viii, 112b; s, 225b – VIII, 115a; S, 225b
Fāzāz ii, **873b**; vi, 591b, 741a; s, 113b – II, **894a**; VI, 576b, 730a; S, 112b
Fāzil Ḥusayn Bey → Fāḍil Bey
Fazl, Fazlī → Faḍl, Faḍlī
Fazlullāh → Faḍl Allāh
Fāzūghlī ii, **874b** – II, **895a**
Fazyl → Fāḍil
Fazzān i, 35a, 39a; ii, **875a**; iii, 296b; iv, 542a; v, 759b; s, 163b, 164b – II, 36a, 40a; II, **895a**; III, 305b; IV, 565b; V, 765b; S, 163b, 164b
Fedākārān-i Millet Djemʿiyyeti iv, 857a – IV, 890a
Fedala → Faḍāla
Fedjr-i Ātī ii, **877b**; iii, 261a – II, **898a**; III, 268a
Fedū → Fidya
Fehīm-i Ḳadīm → Fehīm, Undjuzāde Muṣṭafā
Fehīm, Süleymān (1846) i, 284b; ii, **878a** – I, 293a; II, **898a**
Fehīm, Undjuzāde Muṣṭafā (1648) ii, **878a** – II, **898a**
Fehīm Pasha (1908) ii, **878a** – II, **898b**
Fehmī, Sheykh Ḥasan → Ḥasan Fehmī Efendi
Fehmī, Sheykh Muṣṭafā (1881) ii, **878b** – II, **898b**
Feisal → Fayṣal
Fellāgha → Fallāḳ
Fellani → Fulbe
Fellata → Fallāta
Fenārī, ʿAlāʾ al-Dīn ʿAlī b. Yūsuf Bālī (1497) ii, **879b** – II, **899b**
Fenārī, Muḥyi ʾl-Dīn Meḥmed (1548) ii, **879b**; vii, 225a – II, **899b**; VII, 226b
Fenārī, Shems al-Dīn Meḥmed (1431) i, 299b; ii, 602b, **879a**; v, 681a – I, 309a; II, 617b, **899a**; V, 686b
Fenārī-zāde ii, **879a** – II, **899a**
Fener ii, **879b**; iv, 241a – II, **900a**; IV, 252a
Fenerbāghčesi vi, 55b, 57a – VI, 53b, 55a
Fennec → Fanak
Feodosia → Kefe
Feraḥ ʿAlī Pasha ii, 25a – II, 26a
Ferdī ii, 880a – II, 900b
Ferdosi → Firdawsī
Ferghānā → Farghānā
Ferhād Pasha (1595) ii, 240a, **880b**; iii, 1001a; v, 493a; vi, 228a, 510a; s, 238b – II, 247a, **900b**; III, 1026a; V, 496a; VI, 221b, 495b; S, 238b
Ferhād u-Shīrīn → Farhād wa-Shīrīn
Ferhād Sokolović (Sokollu) i, 1017b, 1018a, 1263b; v, 775a – I, 1049a, 1302a; V, 781a
Ferhat → Farhat
Ferhat Hashed (Tunisia/-e) (XX) vii, 416b – VII, 418a
Ferīd Čelebi (engraver/graveur) (XVII) vii, 472b – VII, 472a
Ferīd Pasha → Dāmād

Ferīdūn Aḥmed Beg (1583) i, 312b; ii, 56b, 128a, 589a, 839b, **881a**; iii, 1045b, 1243a; vii, 7a, 596a; viii, 544b; s, 330a – I, 322b; II, 57b, 131a, 603b, 859a, **901b**; III, 1071b, 1275a; VII, 7a, 596a; VIII, 562a; S, 329b
Ferishte-oghlu i, 1162a – I, 1196b
Ferkhwān (Dābūyid(e)) (728) vi, 941a – VI, 933a
Fermān → Farmān
Fērōz → Fīrūz
Fērōz Mīnār (1490) vi, 368b – VI, 352b
Fērōzkōh → Fīrūzkūh
Fērōzshāh → Fīrūzshāh
Ferret → Ibn miḳraḍ
Fès → Fās
Fethi Naci vi, 95b – VI, 93b
Fethiye i, 476b – I, 490b
Fetoua → Fatwā
Fetwa → Fatwā
Fetwākhāne i, 837b; ii, 867a – I, 861a; II, 887a
Fevrī → Fawrī
al-Fewet ii, 1022b – II, 1046b
Fewzī i, 1271a – I, 1310b
Feyḍ Allāh → Abū Saʿīd-zāde Feyḍ Allāh
Feyzioğlu, Turhan ii, 646a – II, 662b
Fez (town/ville) → Fās
Fezzān → Fazzān
Fidāʾ iii, 183a; v, 647a; s, **306b** – III, 187b; V, 651a; S, **306b**
Fidāʾī (fidāwī) ii, **882a**; iii, 254a – II, **902b**; III, 261a
Fidāʾī Khān Kōka vii, 333b – VII, 335a
Fidāʾiyyān-i Islām ii, **882a**; iii, 529b; iv, 40b, 52a, 165a, 790a; s, 158a – II, **902b**; III, 548a; IV, 43a, 55a, 172b, 822a; S, 158a
Fiḍḍa ii, **883a**, 1139a; v, 964a, 965b, 966a, 967a, 970a, 977a – II, **903b**, 1166a; V, 968b, 970a, 973a, 976a
Fidjār, ḥarb al- (VI) ii, 627a, **883b**; iii, 285b, 389a; v, 3b, 434b; vi, 145b, 146a, 266a, 477b; – II, 642b, **904a**; III, 294b, 401b; V, 3b, 436b; VI, 144a, 250b, 463b;
Fidya ii, **884a** – II, **904b**
Fighānī, Shīrāzī (Bābā) (1519) ii, **884a**; iv, 69a; vii, 342a, 667b; viii, 776a – II, **905a**; IV, 72b; VII, 343b, 667b; VIII, 802a
Fighanī, Ramaḍān (1532) ii, **884b**; iii, 998a; iv, 715b – II, **904b**; III, 1023a; IV, 744a
Figuig (Fadjīdj) ii, **885a**; vi, 571b – II, **905b**; VI, 556b
Fiḥl → Faḥl
Fihr, Banū iv, 828b; vi, 145a; s, 302a – IV, 861b; VI, 143a; S, 302a
al-Fihrī, ʿAbd Allāh b. Ḥabīb (VIII) x, 848a – X,
al-Fihrī → ʿAbd al-Raḥmān; al-Daḥḥāk b. Kays
al-Fihrī, Abū Isḥāḳ (XIII) ii, **885b** – II, **906a**
al-Fihrī, Nāfiʿ b. ʿAbd al-Ḳays (VII) vii, 154a; viii, 89b – VII, 156a; VIII, 91b
al-Fihrī, Yūsuf b. ʿAbd al-Raḥmān (756) x, 848 a,b – X,
Fihrist → Bibliography/-ie); Fahrasa; Ibn al-Nadīm; Ṭūsī
Fiḳāriyya (Mamlūk) vi, 319a – VI, 303b
Fiḳh i, 26a, 86a, 106a, 142b, 169b, 170a, 272b, 274a, 338a, 428a, 436b, 910b; ii, 605b, **886a**, 1069a; iii, 103b, 435a, 647a, 901a; iv, 204a; v, 1129b – I, 27a, 88b, 109a, 146b, 174b, 280b, 282b, 348b, 440a, 449a, 938a; II, 620b, **906b**, 1093b; III, 105b, 449a, 668a, 925b; IV, 213a, b; V, 1126a
Fiḳh Akbar I i, 187b, 332b, 335a; iv, 172a – I, 192b, 343a, 345b; IV, 179b
Fiḳh Akbar II i, 411a; ii, 294a; iv, 172a, 470b – I, 423a; II, 302a; IV, 179b, 491a
al-Fiḳī, Muḥammad Ḥāmid (XX) vi, 897a – VI, 888a
Fikr ii, **891b** – II, **912a**
Fikret, Tevfik → Tewfīḳ Fikret
Fikrī, ʿAbd Allāh Pasha (1890) ii, **892a**; vi, 113b, 602b – II, **912b**; VI, 111a, 587a
Fikrī, Amīn Pasha ii, 892a – II, 913a
Fīl ii, **892b**, 1049b; iii, 201a, 345b; iv, 215a, 217b, 647b; v, 687a, 690a – II, **913a**, 1074a; III, 206a, 356b; IV, 224b, 227a, 674a; V, 692a, 694b
al-Fīl ii, **895a** – II, **916a**
Fiʿl ii, **895b**; v, 578a, b, 579a – II, **916b**; V, 582b, 583a, b
Fiʿl, afʿāl ii, **898a** – II, **919a**
Filāḥa ii, 32b, **899a**; iii, 964a – II, 33a, **920a**; III, 988b
Filʾakovo s, 171a – S, 171a
Filālīs → ʿAlawīs; Nuṣayrīs; Tāfīlālt
Filān iv, 343a – IV, 357b
Filardūs al-Rūmī vi, 506b – VI, 492a
Filasṭīn i, 111a, 197b, 216a, 451a, 975b; ii, 854a, **910b**; iii, 523b; iv, 834b; v, 912a; vi, 29a, 388a, 796b; vii, 9b; s, 67b – I, 114a, 203b, 222b, 464a, 1005b; II, 874a, **932a**; III, 541b; IV, 867b; V, 917b; VI, 27b, 372b, 786b; VII, 10a; S, 68a
—literature/littérature ii, 468a – II, 480a
Filibe ii, **914a**; s, 328b, 330a – II, **935b**; S, 328a, 329b
Filīmūn ii, 916b – II, 938a
Filkhāna → Pīlkhāna
Filori ii, **914b** – II, **936a**
Fils → Fals
Fīn iv, 694b, 695b – IV, 723a, b
Find al-Zimmānī vi, 477a – VI, 463a
Fi̊ndi̊ḳli̊ iv, 233a – IV, 243a
Fındıklılı Süleynān Efndi → Smer'danī-zāde
Fi̊ndi̊ḳoghlu, Diyāʾ al-Dīn Fakhrī (1974) s, **308a** – S, **307b**
Findiriskī, Mīrzā Abu ʾl-Ḳāsim (1640) vii, 452b, 547b; s, **308a** – VII, 453b, 547b; S, **308a**
Finike s, 221b – S, 221b
Finkenstein (treaty/traité) iv, 38b; v, 495b – IV, 41a; V, 498b
Finyāna, Fiñana ii, **915b** – II, **937a**
Firabr ii, **915b** – II, **937a**
Firandj → al-Ifrandj
Firārīs vi, 981b – VI, 974a
Firāsa i, 146b; ii, **916a**; v, 100a, 235a – I, 150b; II, **937b**; V, 102b, 233a
Firʿawn ii, **917a**; iii, 1175a; vi, 412a – II, **938b**; III, 1204a; VI, 397a
Firaydan iv, 98a, b – IV, 102a, b
Firda → Furḍa
Firdaws ii, 448b, 451a – II, 460b, 463a
Firdawsī (Ferdosi) (1020) i, 205b, 358b, 505a, 686a, 1072b, 1139b, 1309b, 1354a; ii, 132b, 740a, 794a, 798a, 894b, **918a**, 1050b; iii, 112b, 113a, 122a, 371a, 637b; iv, 62b; vi, 66a, 608b; viii, 76a, 77b, 80a; s, 108a – I, 211b, 369a, 520a, 706b, 1105a, 1174a, 1349b, 1393b; II, 136a, 758b, 812b, 816b, 915b, **939b**, 1075a; III, 115a, b, 124b, 383a, 659a; IV, 65b; VI, 64a, 593b; VIII, 78a, 79b, 82a; S, 107a
Firdawsī silsila vi, 131b – VI, 129b
Firdewsī rūmī (XV) ii, **921a** – II, **942b**
Firdousi → Firdawsī
Firīdun → Farīdūn
Firind v, 972a, b – V, 974b, 975a
Firishta → Malāʾika
Firishta, Muḥammad Ḳāsim Hindū Shāh Astarābādī (1623) i, 199a; ii, **921b**; vi, 121b, 294a; vii, 342b; s, 206b –

I, 204b; II, **943a**; VI, 119b, 279b; VII, 344a; S, 206a
Firishte-oghlu, ʿAbd al-Laṭīf (Ibn Malak) (XV) ii, **923b** – II, **945a**
Firishte-oghlu, ʿAbd al-Madjīd (1469) ii, **924a** – II, **945b**
Firḳa → Ḥizb, al-Milal wa ʾl-niḥal, Tariḳa
Firḳān al-Akhbār i, 260b, 261a, b, 263a – I, 268b, 269a, b, 271a
Firkovič, Abraham iv, 606a – IV, 630b
Firmān → Farmān
Firouz → Fīrūz
Firrīm (Pirrīm) iv, 644b; vi, 632b; s, **309a** – IV, 617a; VI, 617a; S, **308b**
Firrīsh (Castillo del Hierro) ii, **924a** – II, **945b**
Fīrūhā s, 154b – S, 155a
Fīrūz (ḍāʿī) vi, 438b – VI, 424a
Fīrūz (Gūr) i, 43b; ii, **925b**; vi, 365a, 384a,b – I, 44b; II, **947a**; VI, 349a, 368b
Fīrūz (Sāsānid(e)) (484) ix, 76a – IX, 79a
Fīrūz, (vizier) (1400) vii, 56a – VII, 56b
Fīrūz b. Daryā ʿImād al-Mulk (1574) iii, 1161b – III, 1190a
Fīrūz b. Kabk s, 125b – S, 124b
Fīrūz b. Radjab → Fīrūz Shāh III (Ṭughluḳ)
Fīrūz b. Yazdigird III (Sāsānid(e)) (VII) ix, 621b – IX, 645b
Fīrūz Bey i, 340b, 1118b; ii, 611b, 688a – I, 350b, 1152a; II, 627a, 705a
Fīrūz al-Daylamī i, 728a; iv, 1134b; s, 116a – I, 750a; IV, 1166b; S, 115b
Fīrūz Djang I, Ghāzī ʾl-Dīn Khān (XVII) vii, 446a – VII, 447a
Fīrūz Djang II → Muḥammad Panāh, Mīr
Fīrūz Ḥusayn iv, 571a – IV, 593b
Fīrūz Shāh Khaldjī → Khaldjīs
Fīrūz Shāh I Rukn al-Dīn (Muʿizzī, Dihlī) (1236) ii, 267b; vi, 488a – II, 276a; VI, 474a
Fīrūz Shāh II Djalāl al-Dīn (Khaldjī, Dihlī) (1296) i, 444b, 855b, 1036a, 1202b; ii, 179b, 256b, 268a; vi, 406b, 488a; vii, 457b – I, 457a, 879b, 1067b, 1238a; II, 185a, 263b, 276b; VI, 391a, 474a; VII, 457b
Fīrūz Shāh III Rukn al-Dīn (Tughluḳid(e), Dihlī) (1388) i, 432b, 855b, 1036a, b, 1156b; ii, 48a, 120b, 270a, 392a, 814a, **924b**, 1047b, 1124b; iii, 202b, 416b, 434a; iv, 218b, 276a, 368a, 543a, 749b, 1019a; vi, 273a, 294a, 368a, 532b, 533a, 537a, 692a, 693b, 866b; vii, 194a, 195a, 412a, 679b; viii, 1047b; x, 591b; s, 73b, 105b, 238a, 325a, 409b – I, 44b, 879b, 1067b, 1068a, 1200b; II, 49a, 123b, 278a, 402b, 833b, **946a**, 1027a, 1151a; III, 208a, 430a, 448a; IV, 228a, 288b, 384a, 566b, 779b, 1051a; VI, 257b, 279b, 352b, 517a, b, 521b, 679b, 681b, 857b; VII, 194b, 195b, 413a, 679b; VIII, 1083a; X, 637a; S, 74a, 105a, 238a, 324b, 409b
—administration ii, 154a, 336a, 566b, 924b, 1084b; iii, 492a – II, 158b, 346a, 580b, 946a, 1110a; III, 509a
—constructions i, 1322b; ii, 258a, 262a, b, 274b, 438a, 498b, 909b, 925a, 928b; iii, 225a, 442a, 485a; v, 549a, 884a, 885b, 1135a – I, 1363a; II, 264b, 270a, 271a, 283a, 449b, 511a, 931a, 946b, 950b; III, 232a, 456b, 502a; V, 553b, 890b, 891b, 1130b
Fīrūz Shāh (Mughal) ii, 809a – II, 828a
Fīrūz Shāh, ʿAlāʿ al-Dīn (Bengal(e)) (1533) i, 1168a; v, 639a; vi, 47a – I, 1203a; V, 643a; VI, 45b
Fīrūz Shāh, Sayf al-Dīn (Bengal(e)) (1490) iii, 14b, 422a; v, 639a; vi, 46b – III, 15b, 436a; V, 643a; VI, 45b
Fīrūz Shāh Tādj al-Dīn (Bahmānid(e)) (1422) i, 1200a; ii, 1114b; ii, 15a, 417b; vi, 67b; vii, 289a – I, 1235b; II, 1141a; III, 15b, 431a; VI, 65b; VII, 291a
Fīrūz Shāpūr (Anbār) i, 484b; vi, 633a – I, 499a; VI, 618a
Fīrūzābād (Adharbāydjān) iv, 989b – IV, 1022a
al-Fīrūzābādī, Abu ʾl-Ṭāhir al-Shīrāzī (1415) ii, 801b, **926a**; iii, 765a; iv, 524a, b; vi, 796a; vii, 445a – II, 820b, **947b**; III, 788a; IV, 546b, 547b; VI, 786a; VII, 446a
Fīrūz, Madjd al-Dīn (XIV) viii, 458b – VIII, 474a
Fīrūzadj ii, **927b** – II, **949a**
al-Fīrūzādjiyya i, 866a – I, 890a
Fīrūzānid(e)s ii, **928a**; iii, 255a – II, **949b**; III, 262b
Fīrūzkūh (Harāt) ii, **928a**, 1096b, 1101a – II, **950a**, 1122b, 1127a
Fīrūzkūh (Ṭabaristān) ii, **928b**; vi, 511b, 512b, 514b; s, 309b – II, **950a**; VI, 497a, b, 499b; S, 309a
Fīrūzkūhī i, 224b; ii, 5b; iii, 1107b – I, 231a; II, 5b; III, 1135a
Fīrūzpūr ii, **928b** – II, **950a**
Fishārakī, Sayyid Muḥammad s, 342a – S, 341b
Fishek → Shenlik
al-Fishtālī → ʿAbd al-ʿAzīz b. Muḥammad
Fisḳ → Fāsiḳ
Fiṭaḥl vi, 820a – VI, 810b
Fīthāghūras i, 235b; ii, 765b, **929a** – I, 243a; II, 784a, **951a**
Fitna ii, **930b**; iii, 494b, 495b; v, 1109b – II, **952a**; III, 511b, 512b; V, 1105a
Fiṭnat ii, 713b, **931b**; iii, 269a – II, 732a, **953a**; III, 277a
Fiṭr → ʿĪd al-fiṭr
Fiṭra ii, **931b** – II, **953b**
Fiṭrat, ʿAbd al-Raʾūf (XX) ii, **932a** – II, **954a**
al-Fītūrī Tlīsh (1943) vi, 252b – VI, 236b
Fityān → Fatā
Flores iii, 1219b – III, 1250b
Flori → Filori
Foča i, 476a, 1270b; iii, 214b – I, 490b, 1309b; III, 220b
Fodié Sylla iii, 108a – III, 110b
Foggāra ii, 875b; iv, 529a, 532b – II, 896a; IV, 552a, 555b
Folksong → Türkü
Fomalhaut → Nudjūm
Fondouk → Funduḳ
Fort Jesus → Mazrūʾī; Mombasa
Fortūn b. Mūsa iv, 713a – IV, 741b
Fortunate Islands → Djazāʾir al-Saʿādāt
Fostat → al-Fusṭāt
Fouad → Fuʾād
Foulbé → Fulbé
Fouta Djallon → Fūta Djallon
Fraga → Ifragha
Frāmarz Shāh ii, 30a – II, 30b
Franc-Maçonnerie → Farāmūsh-Khāna; Farmāsūniyya; Māsūniyya
Frankincense → Lubān; Mibkhara
Frasa → Ifrāgha
Frashëri i, 650b – I, 671a
Frāsiyāb → Afrāsiyāb
Fraxinetum ii, **933b**, v, 503a – II, **955b**; V, 506b
Frederick II (Hohenstaufen) vi, 413a, 579b, 637b, 638a; vii, 273b, 274a; ix, 582b – VI, 398a, 564a, 623a; VII, 275b; IX, 616a
Freetown ix, 550b – IX, 572b
Frères Musulmans → al-Ikhwān al-Muslimūn
Frīsa iv, 95a – IV, 99b
Frolinat s, 166a, b – S, 166a, b
Front national (Iran) IV, 43b, 44a, b
Frunze → Pishpek

Fu'ād al-Awwal (Egypt(e)) (1936) i, 13b; ii, **934a**; iii, 516a, 517a; v, 1061a; vi, 45a, 155b, 262a; vii, 765a; viii, 60a; s, 18b, 299a – I, 13b; II, **956a**; III, 533b, 534b; V, 1058a; VI, 43b, 152a, 246b; VII, 766b; VIII, 61a; S, 18b, 299a
Fu'ād al-Khaṭīb (XX) vi, 153b, 176a – VI, 152a
Fu'ād Pasha iv, 857a; v, 631a – IV, 890a; V, 635a
Fu'ād Pasha Kečedjizāde (1869) i, 284b, 286b, 397a, 397b; ii, 185a, 429a, 637a, **934b**; iii, 553a; iv, 295b, 460b; vi, 68b; s, 281b – I, 293b, 295a, 408a, 408b; II, 190b, 440a, 653a, **956b**; III, 572a; IV, 308b, 481a; VI, 66b; S, 281b
Fuat Köprülü → Köprülü
al-Fuḍayl b. ʿIyāḍ (803) i, 274a, 284a, 1246a; ii, **936a**; viii, 496a – I, 282b, 292b, 1283b; II, **958a**; VIII, 513a
Fuḍayl b. al-Zubayr al-Rassān ii, 485a – II, 497b
Fūdhandj s, **309b** – S, **309b**
al-Fudjā'a (VII) ix, 818a – IX, 853a
al-Fudjayra ii, **936b**; vi, 38a; s, 416b – II, **958b**; VI, 36a; S, 417a
al-Fūdūdī i, 129b – I, 133b
al-Fuḍūl iii, 389b – III, 402a
Fuḍūlī, Muḥammad b. Sulaymān (1556) i, 956b; ii, 206b, **937a**; iv, 704b, 1137b; v, 1105b; vii, 576b; viii, 581b, 775b; s, 83a, 324a – I, 986a; II, 213a, **958b**; IV, 732b, 1169a; V, 1101b; VII, 568b; VIII, 600b, 801b; S, 83a, 323b
Fughān → Ashraf ʿAlī Khān
Fujairah → al-Fudjayra
Fuḳahā' al-Madīna al-Sabʿa v, 997b; s, **310b** – V, 993a; S, **310a**
Fuḳarā' i, 1b, 483a – I, 2a, 497b
al-Fuḳaymī, Dhakwān b. ʿAmr ii, 998b – II, 1021b
al-Fuḳaymī, Muḥammad b. Dhu'ayb viii, 377a – VIII, 396a
Fula ii, 939a, 940b, 942b – II, 961a, 962a, 964b
Fūlād b. Shansab ii, 1099a – II, 1125a
Fūlād Khān s, 335b – S, 335b
Fūlād-Sutūn i, 132a; iii, 1201a; v, 73b; vi, 272b – I, 136a; III, 1231b; V, 75b; VI, 257b
Fūlād Turkbačča (XV) vii, 279a – VII, 280b
Fūlādh v, 971b, 978b – V, 974a, 977a
Fulani → Fulbe
Fulayḥ b. al-ʿAwrā' i, 118a; iii, 996a; s, 116b – I, 121b; III, 1021a; S, 116a
Fulaymūn → Aflīmūn
Fulayta, Banū ix, 807a – IX, 526b
Fulbe i, 179a, 303a, 910b, 1259a, 1260a; ii, 9b, 10a, 94a, 251b, 767b, **939a**, 959b, 960b, 1132a, 1144b; iii, 276b, 646a; iv, 549a; vi, 281b; vii, 435b; viii, 19b; x, 142a, 602a; s, 164a – I, 183b, 184a, 312b, 938a, 1297b, 1298a; II, 9b, 10a, 96a, 259a, 786a, **961a**, 981b, 982b, 1158b, 1172a; III, 284b, 667a; IV, 573a; VI, 266b; VII, 436b; VIII, 19b; X, 152a, 647a; S, 164a
Fulful b. Saʿīd i, 860a; v, 1176b, 1180b, 1182a – I, 884a; V, 1166b, 1170b, 1172a
Fulfulde → Fula
Fulk (king/roi) s, 204b – S, 204b
Fulūs → Fals
Fūman, Fūmin ii, 74b, **943b**; s, 298a – II, 76a, **965a**; S, 297b
Fūmanī → ʿAbd al-Fattāḥ Fūmanī
Fūmoluṭī, Aḥmad iv, 889a; vi, 385a – IV, 921b; VI, 369a
Fundj i, 425b, 1158a; ii, 252b, 615a, **943b**; iv, 686b, 891b; v, 267a; viii, 91a – I, 437b, 1192b; II, 260a, 630b, **965b**; IV, 714b, 925b; V, 264b; VIII, 93b
Funduḳ ii, **945a**; iv, 135b, 136a, 1015a – II, **966b**; IV, 141a, b, 1047a
Fünfkirchen → Pécs
Fung → Fundj
Fūr, Fūrāwī ii, 122a, 123a; v, 1250b – II, 125a, 126a; V, 1241a
al-Fūrakī, Abū Bakr iii, 1165a – III, 1193b
al-Furāt i, 405b, 467b, 468a, 634b, 994a, 1094b, 1095a; ii, 250a, 686b, **945a**; iii, 1251a; iv, 482a; v, 441b, 864b; s, 37a – I, 417b, 481b, 482a, 655a, 1024b, 1127b, 1128a; II, 257a, 704a, **967a**; III, 1283b; IV, 502b; V, 444a, 871b; S, 37a
al-Furāt, Banū iii, 767b; iv, 189a; v, 953a – III, 790b; IV, 197b; V, 957a
Furḍa ii, **948a** – II, **970a**
Furdat al-ruʿūs ii, 149a, 948a – II, 153a, 970a
Furfūriyūs (Porphyry(e)) i, 234b; ii, 550a, 780a, **948b**, 955a; iv, 92a – I, 241b; II, 563b, 798b, **970b**, 979b; IV, 96a
Furgač → ʿIzzet Pasha, Aḥmed
Furḳān ii, **949b** – II, **971b**
Furḳān (Iran) vii, 763a – VII, 764b
Furḳān b. Asad → Jeshuah b. Judah
Furḳān, Banū ii, 463a – II, 475a
Furn v, 41b, 42b – V, 42b, 43b
al-Furs ii, **950b** – II, **972b**
Fürstenspiegel → Siyāsa
Furūʿ (law/droit, doctrine) i, 257b, 277a; ii, 182b, 889b; iii, 162a, 182a – I, 265b, 285b; II, 188b, 910a; III, 165b, 186a
Furūʿ (poetic/poésie) i, 671a, b – I, 691b, 692b
Furūʿ (tax/impôt) i, 1144a; iv, 1041a – I, 1178b; IV, 1072b
Furūgh, Abu 'l-Ḳāsim Khān (XIX) ii, **951b** – II, **974a**
Furūgh, Muḥammad Mahdī b. Muḥammad Bāghir Iṣfahānī (XIX) ii, **952a** – II, **974a**
Furūgh al-Dīn → Furūgh
Furūgh Farrukhzād vi, 609a – VI, 594a
Furūghī, Mīrzā ʿAbbās (1858) ii, **952a**; iv, 69b – II, **974a**; IV, 73b
Furūghī, Mīrzā Muḥammad Iṣfahānī (XVIII) ii, **952a**; iv, 69b – II, **974a**; IV, 73b
Furūghī, Muḥammad ʿAli → Muḥammad ʿAli Furūghī
Furūghī, Muḥammad Ḥusayn (1043) ii, **952a** – II, **974a**
Furūḳ ii, 605a – II, 620a
Furūsiyya i, 520a; ii, **952b**; v, 688a, 689a, b – I, 536a; II, **974b**; V, 693a, 694a, b
Fusayfisā' i, 610b, 611b, 612a; ii, **955a**; iv, 1167b; v, 13b, 16b, 17a, 298b – I, 613a, 632a; II, **977b**; IV, 1200a; V, 14a, 17a, b, 298a
Fūshhandj → Būshandj
Fusṭāṭ (tent(e)) iv, 1147a – IV, 1179a
al-Fusṭāṭ i, 126a, 197a, 451b, 531b, 532a, 844b, 950b, 1346a; ii, 114b, 130a, 746a, **957b**, 1064b; iii, 79b, 675a; iv, 323b, 424a, b; vi, 186a, 195a, 362a, 363a, b, 410b, 647b, 648a, 649a, 660a, 666a, 668a, 670b, 671a; vii, 158b; s, 1a, 136b – I, 129b, 202b, 464b, 547b, 548a, 868a, 979b, 1386b; II, 117a, 133a, 764a, **979b**, 1089a; III, 81b, 696b; IV, 338a, 442b, 443a; VI, 169b, 179a, 346a, 347a, b, 395b, 633a, 634b, 645b, 652a, 654a, b, 656b, 657b; VII, 160a; S, 1a, 136a
—Djāmiʿ ʿAmr i, 610a, 619a, 624a, 814a; ii, 958a, 959a – I, 630a, 637b, 643b, 837b; II, 980a, 981a
Fuṣūṣ fī 'l-Ḥikma i, 414b; ii, 780a – I, 426b; II, 798b
Fūṭa v, 737b – V, 743a
Fūta Djallon ii, 941b, **959a**, 1131b; vi, 281b; viii, 16b; ix, 550b – II, 963b, **981b**, 1158b; VI, 266b; VIII, 16b; IX, 572b
Fūta Tōro vi, 259b, 281b; ix, 145b; x, 602a – VI, 244a, 266b; IX, 150b; X, 647a

Fūthāghūras → Fīthāghūras
Futūḥ b. Muḥammad b. Marwān al-Aṣghar vi, 625b – VI, 610b
Futūḥa (musician/musicienne) vi, 488a – VI, 474a
Futūḥāt → Ṭarābulus (al-Shaʿm)
al-Futūḥī, Tādj al-Dīn i, 949b – I, 978b
al-Futūḥī, Taḳī al-Dīn (1572) vii, 311b – VII, 313b
Futuwwa i, 21a, 256b, 277a, 321b, 322a, 520a, 794b, 900b; ii, 433a, **961a**, 1044a; iii, 671b, 1256a; iv, 705a; vi, 225a; vii, 998b – I, 21b, 264b, 285b, 331b, 332a, 536a, 817b, 927b; II, 444b, **983a**, 1068b; III, 693a, 1288b; IV, 733a; VI, 219a; VII, 1000b
Fütüwwetnāme i, 323a; ii, 967b, 968a, b – I, 333a; II, 989b, 990a, 991a
Futyā → Fatwā
al-Fuwaṭī, Hishām → Hishām b. ʿAmr al-Fuwaṭī
al-Fuwaṭī, Kamāl al-Dīn → Ibn al-Fuwaṭī
Fuwwa vi 119a – VI, 116b
Fuyūdj ii, **969b** – II, **991b**
Fuzūlī → Fuḍūlī
Fyzabad → Fayḍābād

G

Ğa Ssuling → Ma Chung-ying
Gaban ii, **970a** – II, **992a**
Gabès → Ḳābis
Gabon ii, **970a** – II, **992a**
Gabr ii, **970b** – II, **993a**
Gabrī (Mānd) vi, 384b – VI, 368b
Gabriel → Djabrāʾīl
Gadāʾī, Shaykh (Dihlī) (1568) ix, 241a – IX, 247b
Gadāʾī Kambō, Shaykh (1568) i, 1136a; s, **312a** – I, 1170b; S, **312a**
Gaddafi, Muʿammar → al-Ḳadhdhāfī
Gadjapatis vi, 67a – VI, 65a
Gadmīwa, Banū vi, 742a, b, 743a – VI, 731a, b, 732a
Gaeda i, 1258a – I, 1296a
Gāēkwār i, 1053a – I, 1084b
Gafinā (Marʿash) vi, 506b – VI, 492a
Gafsa → Ḳafṣa
Gafuri → Ghafūrī, Madjīd
Gagauz, Banū i, 1302b; ii, 610a, b, **971a**; iv, 600b, 814a; vi, 420b; x, 698b – I, 1342a; II, 625a, 626a, **993a**; IV, 625a, 847a; VI, 406a; X, 742a
Gagik I i, 507b, 638a; ii, 680a – I, 522b, 658b; II, 697a
Gagik II i, 638a; ii, 680b; iv, 670a – I, 659a; II, 697b; IV, 697a
Gagik-Abas i, 638b – I, 659a
Gagik Ardzrunī i, 637a – I, 658a
Gagrawn → Muṣṭafābād
Gāhāmbārs ii, 398a; vii, 15b – II, 408b; VII, 15b
Gāikwār ii, 1129b; vi, 535b – II, 1156b; VI, 520a
Gakkhaŕ ii, **972a**, 1131b, 1155b; v, 31b – II, **994b**, 1158a, 1184a; V, 32b
Galata → Ghalaṭa
Galata-Saray/Galata-Sérail → Ghalaṭa-Sarāyi̊
Gälbāghī v, 460b – V, 463a
Galen/Galien → Djālīnūs
Galena → al-Kuḥl
Galicia/Galice → Djillīḳiya
Galla → Oromo
Galla-dār (Mānd) vi, 384b – VI, 368b
Gallipoli → Gelibolu
Gamasāb, Gamasiyāb → Karkha
Gambia/-e ii, **974b** – II, **997a**
Gambīri ii, 138b – II, 142a
Gambra → Bandar ʿAbbās
Gamron (Gomron) → Bandar ʿAbbās
Gana, Banū x, 589b – X,
Ganāfa, Ganaveh → Djannāba
Gandamak s, 237b – S, 237a
Gandāpur ii, **975a** – II, **997b**
Gandāwa → Kandābīl
Gandhāra → Ḳandahār
Gandhi, M. K. i, 317b; v, 7b; s, 4b – I, 327b; V, 7b; S, 3b
Gandj ʿAlī Khān v, 164a – V, 161b
Gandja (Djanza, Elizavetpol) i, 8a, 191b, 660b, 1041b; ii, **975a**, iv, 1176b; v, 490a, 495b; vi, 55b, 56a, 64b, 85b, 274a; vii, 453a; ix, 169a; s, 143a – I, 8a, 197a, 681b, 1073a; II, **997b**, IV, 1210a; V, 492b, 498b; VI, 53b, 54a, 62b, 83b, 259a; VII, 454a; IX,, 174b; S, 143a
— (treaty/traité) (1735) viii, 771b – VIII, 797b
Gandjābā → Ḳandābil
al-Gandjī, Muḥammad b. Yūsuf v, 1236b, 1237a – V, 1227a, b
Gandj-i-Shakar → Fārīd al-Dīn Masʿūd
Gandjvar b. Isfandiyar s, 263b – S, 263a
Gando ii, 94a – II, 96a → Fulbe
Gandu iii, 277b – III, 285b
Ganfīsa, Banū vi, 742a – VI, 731a
Gangā, Ganges/Gange ii, **976a** – II, **998b**
Gangāwatī vi, 63a – VI, 61a
Gangōh s, 313a – S, 312b
Gangōhī, Shaykh ʿAbd al-Ḳuddūs (1537) ii, 54b, 55a, 56a; s, **312b** – II, 55b, 56a, b; S, **312b**
Gangōhī, Rukn al-Dīn Muḥammad b. ʿAbd al-Ḳuddūs (1537) s, 313a – S, 312b
Ganja iii, 266b – III, 274b
Ganza → Gandja
Gao (Mali) ii, **976b**; v, 222a; vi, 259a; vii, 393b; viii, 16b, 848a; ix, 753b, 756b; s, 295b – II, **999a**; V, 219b; VI, 243a; VII, 395a; VIII, 16b, 877a; IX, 786b, 789b; S, 295a
Gāon sabhā i, 758a – I, 780b
Gaourang i, 910b – I, 938a
Gardīz ii, **978a** – II, **1000b**
Gardīzī, Abū Saʿīd (XI) ii, **978b**; v, 1001a; vii, 21a; s, 136a, 245a, 266a, 326b – II, **1001a**; V, 1007a; VII, 21a; S, 135b, 245a, 265b, 326a
Gardīzī, Shāh Yūsuf vii, 550a – VII, 550a
Garĕbĕg → ʿĪd, Indonesia (Islam)
Gargar vi, 507a – VI, 492b
Gaŕhī vi, 47a – VI, 45b
Garmādūz s, 116a – S, 115b
Garmrūdī, ʿAbd Allāh s, 290b – S, 290a
Garmsīr → Ḳi̊shlaḳ
Garnāna, Banū vi, 742a – VI, 731b
Garrūs iii, 1102b, 1108b; s, 71a – III, 1129b, 1136a; S, 71b
Garrūsī, Amīr-i Niẓām s, 73a – S, 73b
Garshāsp II, Abū Kālīdjār (Kākūyid(e)) (1119) iv, 466a, b; vi, 908a – IV, 487a; VI, 899b
Garshāsp, ʿIzz al-Dīn v, 828a – V, 834b
Garshāsp b. Muḥammad iv, 466a – IV, 486b
Garsīf ii, **978b**; vi, 142b; vii, 642a – II, **1001a**; VI, 141a; VII, 641b
Gasprali̊ (Gasprinski), Ismāʿīl (1914) i, 894a; ii, 366a, 474b, **979a**; iv, 630b; vii, 764b; viii, 250b; s, 47a, 123a – I, 920b; II, 376a, 487a, **1001b**; IV, 655b; VII, 766a; VIII, 267a; S, 47b, 122b
Gasprinski → Gasprali̊
Gatha iv, 53a – IV, 56a
Gaṭṭāya iv, 95a – IV, 99a
Gāṭū, gaṭṭū iv, 743b – IV, 773b

Gavras i, 664b, 983a – I, 684a, 1013b
Gāvur → Kāfir
Gavur-Ḳalʿa (Marw) vi, 619a, b – VI, 604a, b
Gawakuke vii, 435b – VII, 436b
Gawālior → Gwāliyar
Gāwān, Maḥmūd → Maḥmūd Gāwān
Gāwar-Bātī i, 225a; ii, 31a, 138b – I, 231b; II, 32a, 142a
Gāwbāra → Gīl Gawbarā
Gāwdūk vi, 502a – VI, 487a
Gawhar Amān ii, 30a – II, 30b
Gawhar Amān b. Mulk Amān s, 327b – S, 327a
Gawhar Khātūn (XI) vii, 679b – VII, 679b
Gawhar Shād i, 147b, 148b; vi, 366a – I, 152a, 152b; VI, 350a
Gawhar-i Murād → Sāʿidī, Ghulām Ḥusayn
Gawhar-i Tādj ʿĀbida Sulṭān i, 1196b – I, 1232a
Gāwilgaṛh ii, **981a**; iv, 921a; vii, 314b; s, 280a – II, **1003b**; IV, 954a; VII, 317a; S, 279b
Gawr → Gaur
Gawṛ (Bengal(e)) iii, 444a, 634b; v, 638a' vi, 46b, 47a, b, 368b; vii, 314a – III, 459a, 655b; V, 642a; VI, 45a, b, 46a, 352b; VII, 316b
Gawur → Kāfir
Gāwur Daghlarï ii, **982a**; s, 171b – II, **1004b**; S, 172a
Gaykhātū b. Abaḳa (Il-Khānid(e)) (1295) i, 703a, 1129b; ii, 14a, **982a**, 1043a; iii, 284a, 1122a; iv, 31a, 621a; v, 162b, 553b, 827a; vi, 16a, 502a, 1017b; vii, 232a – I, 724b, 1164a; II, 14b, **1004b**, 1067a; III, 293a, 1150a; IV, 33b, 645b; V, 160b, 558b, 833a; VI, 14a, 487b, 1010a; VII, 234a
al-Gaylānī, Rashīd ʿĀlī → Rashīd ʿAlī
Gayō → Atjeh
Gayōmard, Shams al-Dīn ii, 268a, iii, 1270a; iv, 818b, 920b; vi, 513a, b; x, 110b – II, 276b; III, 1303a; IV, 851a, 953b; VI, 498a, b; X, 119b
Gaz (measure/mesure) s, **313b**
Gaza → Ghazza
Gaziantep → ʿAyntāb
Gaz-i-ilāhī iv, 1055b; s, 313b – IV, 1087a; S, 313a
Gazūla, Gazūlī → Djazūla, Djazūlī
Gāzurgāh viii, 267a – VIII, 274a
Gāzurgāhī vi, 73b – VI, 71b
Geben → Gaban
Geber → Gabr, Madjūs
Geber → Djābir b. Aflaḥ
Gebze (Dakibyza) ii, **982b**; vi, 366a – II, **1005a**; VI, 350b
Gečid resmi ii, 147a – II, 151a
Gedaref → al-Ḳaḍārif
Gedi, Gede ii, **983a**; vi, 283b, 704a – II, **1005b**; VI, 268a, b, 692b
Gedik → Ṣinf
Gedik Aḥmed → Aḥmad Pasha Gedik
Gediz Čayï ii, **983a** – II, **1005bb**
Geg i, 650a, 651a – I, 670a, 671b → Arnawutluḳ
Gehenna/Géhenne → Djahannam
Geladjo i, 303a – I, 312b
Gelenbe s, 282b – S, 282a
Gelibolu (Gallipoli) i, 947b; ii, 11b, **983a**; iv, 571b; vi, 71b, 587b; viii, 193a; s, 41b, 149b – I, 976b; II, 11b, **1005b**; IV, 594b; VI, 69b, 572b; VIII, 195b; S, 41b, 149b
Gemlik (Kios) ii, **987a**; vi, 588b – II, **1010a**; VI, 573a
Genāwah → Gnāwa
Genč ʿAlī Pasha (1736) vi, 56a – VI, 54a
Genč ʿOthmān ii, 75b – II, 77a
Genç Spor Klübü iv, 138a – IV, 144a
Genghis/Gengis Khan → Činghiz Khān
Genil → Shanīl
Geniza ii, **987b**; v, 738b – II, **1010a**; V, 743b
George(s), Saint → Djirdjīs
Georgia/-e → Abkhāz; al-Kurdj
Gerard of/de Cremona (1187) vii, 738b – VII, 739a
Gerasa → Djarash
Gerdek resmi → ʿArūs resmi
Geredelī Ḥadjdjī Khalīl (1831) ix, 156a – IX, 161a
Germany → Nemče
Germiyān i, 243b, 467b; ii, 204b; vi, 975a – I, 251a, 481b; II, 211a; VI, 967a
Germiyān-oghullarï i, 346a, 510b, 1256b; ii, **989a**; v, 359b, 539a; vii, 593b – I, 356b, 526a, 1295a; II, **1012a**; V, 360b, 543b; VII, 593a
Gerona/Gérone → Djarunda
Gerri → Ḳerrī
Gessi Pasha s, 164b – S, 164b
Gēsū Darāz vi, 369a – VI, 353b
Geṭna i, 733b – I, 755b
Gevele vi, 71b – VI, 696
Gevherī, Meḥmed (1737) ii, **990a** – II, **1013a**
Geygellis ii, 40b – II, 41b
Geyvān Ketkhudā (XVI) vii, 244b – VII, 246a
al-Ghāb (river/fleuve) ii, **990b**; vi, 578b – II, **1013b**; VI, 563b
Ghāba ii, **991a** – II, **1014a**
Ghabāghib vi, 546a, b, 548a – VI, 531a, 532b
Ghaban iv, 1165b – IV, 1198a
al-Ghabrā' s, 177b, 178a – S, 178b, 179b
Ghaḍā'irī iv, 61a – IV, 64b
Ghadāmès ii, 875a, 876b, **991b** – II, 895b, 897a, **1014b**
al-Ghaḍanfar → Abū Taghlib, Ḥamdanid(e)s
al-Ghadanfarī, Abū ʿAbd Allāh (1020) ix, 819a – IX, 854a
Ghaḍanfer Dede (1566) ii, 1088a; vi, 226b, 227a, 228a – II, 1113b; VI, 220a, 221a, 222a
Ghadār → Khazaf
Ghadīr Khumm i, 1025a, 1325b; ii, **993a**; vii, 276b; ix, 429b – I, 1056b, 1391b; II, **1015b**; VII, 278b; IX, 434b
al-Ghāḍirī ii, **994b** – II, **1017b**
Ghadjar ii, 40b – II, 41b
Ghaffārī, Aḥmad b. Muḥammad (1567) i, 423b; ii, **994b**; vii, 199b – I, 435b; II, **1017b**; VII, 200a
Ghaffūrī, ʿAlī iv, 166a – IV, 173b
Ghāfiḳ i, 1249a; ii, 744a, b; s, 313a – I, 1287a; II, 762b, 763a; S, 313b
Ghāfiḳī → ʿAbd al-Raḥmān al-Ghāfiḳī
al-Ghāfiḳī, Abū Djaʿfar Aḥmad (1146) i, 156a, 214a, 345a, 594b, 1156a; ii, 995a; iii, 737a; vi, 263a, 264b, 350b; s, **313b**, 383a, 397a – I, 160b, 220b, 355b, 613b, 1190b; II, 1018a; III, 760a; VI, 247b, 249a, 334b; S, **313b**, 383b, 397b
al-Ghāfiḳī, Abu 'l-Ḳāsim → al-Kabtawrī
al-Ghāfiḳī, Muḥammad b. Ḳassūm b. Aslam (XII) i, 449a; ii, **995a** – I, 462a; II, **1018a**
Ghāfirī, Banū i, 545b; ii, 630b; iii, 403b; viii, 993a; x, 816b; s, 355b, 356a – I, 562b; II, 646b; III, 415b; VIII, 1028a; X, ; S, 355a, b
Ghafūrī, Medjīd (1934) ii, **995a** – II, **1018a**
Ghaghauz → Gagauz
Ghā'ib ii, **995b** – II, **1018b**
Ghāʿita → Ghayta
Ghalāfiḳa ii, **996a** – II, **1019a**
Ghalaṭa i, 973a, b; ii, 833a, 999a; iv, 225b, 228b, 231b, 239a, 240b, 244a, 1158b; v, 313a, 533b; vi, 3a; s, 168a, **314a** – I, 1003a, b; II, 852b, 1022a; IV, 235a, 238b, 242a, 249b, 251a, 255a, 1191a; V, 312b, 537b; VI, 3a; S, 168b, **314a**

Ghalaṭa-Sarāyi̊ ii, **996b**; v, 904b; vi, 57a – II, **1019b**; V, 910b; VI, 55a
Ghalaṭāt-i Meshhūre ii, **997a** – II, **1020a**
Ghalča i, 225a; ii, **997b** – I, 231b; II, **1020b**
Ghaldan Khān iii, 1120b – III, 1148a
Ghaldjī → Ghalzay
Ghālī → Ghulāt
Ghālī, Rashīd v, 190a – V, 187a
Ghālib → Wahhābiyya
Ghālib (ʿAlīgaŕh) vi, 612a – VI, 597a
Ghālib, Ismāʿīl → Ismāʿīl Ghālib
Ghālib, Mīrzā Asad Allāh (1869) ii, 735b, **1000a**, 1036b; iii, 93b, 1095b; iv, 716b; v, 961b; vii, 341b, 376b; s, 334a, 360b – II, 754a, **1023a**, 1060b; III, 96a, 1122a; IV, 745a; V, 966a; VII, 343b, 378a; S, 333b, 360a
Ghālib, Sharīf (1813) i, 1299a; ii, 176b, 572b; v, 62b; vi, 150b – I, 1339a; II, 182a, 587a; V, 64b; VI, 149a
Ghālib b. ʿAbd al-Raḥmān al-Ṣiḳlabī (981) ii, **997b**; iii, 31a, 74b, 1036b; v, 626a, 1008a; vi, 431a – II, **1021a**; III, 32b, 77a, 1062b; V, 630a, 1004a; VI, 416a, b
Ghālib b. ʿAlī b. Hilāl iii, 403b – III, 415b
Ghālib b. Ṣaʿṣaʿa (VII) ii, 788a, **998a** – II, 807a, **1021a**
Ghālib Dede, Meḥmed Esʿad Shaykh (1799) ii, **999a**; iii, 90b; iv, 190b; vi, 610a; s, 283a – II, **1022a**; III, 93a; IV, 198b; VI, 594b; S, 283a
Ghālib Pasha → Meḥmed Saʿīd Ghālib Pasha
Ghaliev, Mīr Saʿīd Sulṭān (XX) vi, 585b, 586b – VI, 570b, 571a
Ghaliya i, 1299a – I, 1339a
Ghallābakhshī ii, 155b, 156a, 157b – II, 160a, b, 162b
Ghalzay (Afghān(e)) i, 88a, 95a, 217b, 219b, 229a, b, 1013b; ii, 812a, **1001a**; iii, 604b; iv, 537a, 917b; vii, 853b; s, 66b, 237b, 329b, 367a – I, 90b, 98a, 224a, 226a, 235b, 236b, 1044b; II, 831b, **1024a**; III, 625a; IV, 560b, 950b; VII, 854b; S, 67a, 237a, 329a, 368a
Ghamātiyyūn iii, 339a – III, 349a
Ghāmid ii, **1001b**; iii, 363b – II, **1024b**; III, 375a
al-Ghammād, Muḥammad b. ʿAlī al-Wadjdī (1624) vi, 350a – VI, 334a
al-Ghamr b. Yazīd (750) vii, 798a – VII, 800
Ghāna i, 211a, 762a; ii, 94a, **1003a**; iii, 288b; v, 386b, 387a, 653b; vi, 258a, 259b, 281b; vii, 612b; viii, 16b; ix, 754a; s, 217b – I, 217a, 785a; II, 96a, **1026a**; III, 297b; V, 387b, 388b, 657b; VI, 242a, 243b, 266b; VII, 612a; VIII, 16b; IX, 787a; S, 217a
Ghāna (Sudān) ii, **1001b**; iii, 657a – II, **1025a**; III, 678b
Ghanam i, 876a; s, **316b** – I, 900b; S, **316a**
Ghanānand iii, 457b – III, 473b
Ghanī, Muḥammad Ṭāhir Asha'ī (1688) ii, **1004a**, – II, **1027b**
Ghanī b. Aʿṣur b. Saʿd b. Ḳays ʿAylān, Banū ii, **1004b**; vi, 545a – II, **1028a**; VI, 529b
Ghānim, Khalīl → Khalīl Ghānim
Ghanīma i, 1142a, 1144a; ii, 146b, 154b, 504b, 869a, **1005a**; iii, 183a;iv, 1141b; v, 689b – I, 1176b, 1178b; II, 150b, 159b, 517b, 889a, **1028b**; III, 187a; IV, 1173a; V, 694b
Ghanīmat Kundjāhī, Muḥammad Akram (1690) ii, **1006b**; s, **322a** – II, **1030a** S, **321b**
Ghānimid(e)s ii, 517a; v, 333a – II, 530a; V, 333a
Ghāniya, Banū i, 92b, 161b, 165a, 367a, 533a, 798a, 1176a, 1205b; ii, 112a, 526a, **1007a**; iii, 1055b; iv, 337b, 416a, 479b; vi, 404a, 728b; vii, 897a, 989a; viii, 563a; s, 80b – I, 95a, 166a, 169b, 378a, 549b, 821b, 1211a, 1241a; II, 114b, 539a, **1030b**; III, 1081b; IV, 352a, 434a, 501b; VI, 388b, 717b; VII, 898a, 990a; VIII, 581a; S, 80b
Ghanm b. ʿAwf, Banū i, 683b; vi, 649a – I, 704b; VI, 634a
Ghār s, 327a – S, 326b
Ghār Ḥirā' vi, 168b – VI, 160a
Ghār Thawr vi, 168b – VI, 160a
Gharb (Durūz) vi, 343b, 344a – VI, 328a
Gharb (Morocco/Maroc) ii, **1008b**; iii, 300b; v, 1185b; s, 350b, 387b – II, **1032a**; III, 309b; V, 1175b; S, 350b, 387b
Gharb al-Andalus ii, **1009a** – II, **1032b**
al-Gharbiyya ii, **1009b**; vi, 453b, 580b; s, 18a, 40a – II, **1033a**; VI, 439a, 565b; S, 18a, 40a
Ghardaḳa vii, 53b – VII, 54a
Ghardāya ii, **1010a**; iii, 97b; viii, 794b – II, **1033b**; III, 100a; VIII, 821b
Ghardjistān, Gharshistān ii, **1010b**; vi, 65b, 617b, 618a; s, 376b – II, **1034a**; VI, 63b, 602b; S, 376b
Gharīb i, 157b, 275b; ii, **1011a**; iii, 25b – I, 162a, 284a; II, **1034b**; III, 26b
Gharībān ii, 921b, 1097b – II, 943a, 1123b
al-Ghāribī, Muḥammad b. Sulayyim s, 355b – S, 355b
Gharībīs → Āfāḳīs
al-Gharīḍ (VIII) ii, **1011b**; iii, 950a – II, **1035a**; III, 975a
Ghārim ii, **1011b** – II, **1035b**
Ghariyyān iii, 1064a – III, 1090b
Gharnāṭa (Granada) i, 6a, 43b, 84a, 491b, 495b, 1057b; ii, **1012a**; iii, 135a, 220a, 836b, 1110a; vi, 606b; vii, 1020a, 1028a – I, 6b, 45a, 86b, 506a, 510b, 1089b; II, **1035b**; III, 137b, 226b, 860b, 1137b; VI, 591a; VII, 1022a, 1030b
—Alhambra → al-Ḥamra
—monuments i, 1225a, 1320b; ii, **1014b**; iii, 144a, 498b – I, 1261b, 1361a; II, **1038a**; III, 145b, 515b
al-Gharnāṭī → Abū Ḥāmid; Abu Ḥayyān; al-Ḥādjdj
Ghars → Kars
Ghars al-Dawla b. Shumla i, 240a – I, 247a
Ghars al-Dīn Khalīl (Ramaḍān-oghlu) (1510) viii, 418b – VIII, 433a
Ghars al-Dīn-zāde iii, 340a – III, 350a
Ghars al-Niʿma → Abū 'l-Ḥasan Muḥammad b. Hilāl (Ṣābi')
Gharsiya b. Shandjuh s, 80b – S, 80b
Gharsiya b. Wanḳu i, 1079b – I, 1112a
Ghārūḳa s, **322b** – S, **322a**
Gharyān, ʿAbd al-Madjīd iv, 720b – IV, 749b
Ghaṣb ii, **1020a** – II, **1043b**
Ghāshiya ii, **1020a** – II, **1044a**
Ghaṣība ii, 321a – II, 330b
Ghasīl al-Malāʾika (623) ii, **1020b** – II, **1044a**
Ghassāl s, **322b** – S, **322b**
Ghassān b. ʿAbbād (Samarkand) i, 271b; vi, 335b; viii, 1026a, 1032a – I, 280a; VI, 320a; VIII, 1061a, 1068a
Ghassān b. Ḥāmid (VIII) viii, 536b – VIII, 554a
Ghassān al-Kūfī ii, 1022a – II, 1046a
al-Ghassānī, Abū ʿAbd Allāh (XVII) ii, **1021b**; s, 130b – II, **1045b**; S, 130a
al-Ghassānī, Abū ʿAlī (1104) viii, 635a – VIII, 654a
al-Ghassānī, Abu ʾl-Ḥasan Muḥammad b. Aḥmad b. Djumayʿ ix, 8b – IX, 8b
Ghassānid(e)s i, 405b, 526a, 548b, 890a, 1140b, 1249b; ii, **1020b**; iii, 272b, 292b; iv, 492b, 839a, 1145a; v, 633b; vi, 303a, 544b, 564b; vii, 840b; viii, 119b; s, 117a, 229b – I, 417a, 542a, 566a, 916b, 1175a, 1287b; II, **1044a**; III, 280a, 301b; IV, 514a, 872a, 1176b; V, 637b; VI, 288b, 529a, 549b; VII, 842a; VIII, 122a; S, 116a, 229b
Ghassāniyya ii, **1022a** – II, **1046a**
Ghassāsa, Banū vi, 1009a – VI, 1001b
Ghāt ii, 875a, 876b, **1022a** – II, 895b, 897a, **1046a**

Ghaṭafān, Banū ii, 627a, **1023a**; iii, 285b; iv, 1139a, 1144a; vii, 370b, 463b, 629b; s, 177a, 178a – II, 642b, **1046b**; III, 294b; IV, 1171a, 1175b; VII, 372b, 463a, 629a; S, 178a, 179a
al-Ghaṭafānī, Ḳaʿnab b. Ḍamra viii, 376a – III, 389a
Ghaṭān (Ḳaḥṭān), Banū vii, 782b – VII, 784b
Ghaṭaṭ iv, 743b – IV, 773b
Ghaṭghaṭ vi, 152b – VI, 151a
Ghāʾis vi, 67a, 421b – VI, 65a, 406b
Ghātwāls ii, 868b – II, 888b
al-Ghawār ii, **1024a** – II, **1048a**
Ghawāzī → Ghāziya
al-Ghawr i, 1138b; ii, **1024b** – I, 1173a; II, **1048a**
al-Ghawrī, Sultan → Ḳānsūh al-Ghawrī
Ghawth v, 543b; s, **323b** – V, 548a; S, **323a**
al-Ghawth s, 37b – S, 37b
Ghawth Muḥammad Khān i, 1195b – I, 1230b
Ghawthī Dede ii, 833a – II, 852b
Ghawwāṣī (poet/poète) (1650) iii, 376a; vi, 837b – III, 388a; VI, 828a
al-Ghayb ii, **1025a** – II, **1049a**
Ghayba ii, 996a, **1026a**; iii, 51b, 1167a; iv, 277b; v, 1236a – II, 1018b, **1049b**; III, 53a, 1195b; IV, 289b; V, 1226b
al-Ghayḍa (Mahra) vi, 81a – VI, 78b
Ghayghāya, Banū vi, 742a – VI, 731a
Ghaylān b. Muslim ii, **1026b**; iii, 1142b; iv, 271b, 370a, 371b – II, **1050a**; III, 1171a; IV, 283b, 386a, 388a
Ghaylān b. ʿUḳba → Dhu ʾl-Rumma
Ghayn ii, **1026b** – II, **1050b**
Ghayr, ghayra iv, 272b, 273a – IV, 284b, 285a
Ghayr Mahdī → Muḥammad al-Djawnpūrī
Ghayṭa ii, **1027b** – II, **1051a**
Ghayth (Mahra) vi, 82b – VI, 80a
al-Ghayṭī, Muḥammad b. Aḥmad b. ʿAlī (1576) vii, 100b – VII, 102b
al-Ghazāfī (1589) vi, 112a – VI, 110a
Ghazal i, 10b, 107b, 586a, 592a, 677b; ii, **1028a**; iv, 57b, 62a, 65a, 714b; v, 836a; vii, 96a; s, **323b** – I, 10b, 110b, 605a, 611b, 698a; II, **1051b**; IV, 60b-61a, 65b, 68b, 743a; V, 842b; VII, 98a; S, **323a**
Ghazāl ii, **1036b**; iv, 649a – II, **1060b**; IV, 675b
al-Ghazāl, Yaḥyā b. Ḥakam al-Bakrī (IX) i, 83a, 601a, 934b; ii, 516a, **1038a**; iii, 702a; v, 1119b; vii, 275a – I, 85b, 620b, 963a; II, 592a, **1062a**; III, 724a; V, 1116b; VII, 277a
al-Ghazālī, Abu ʾl-Futūḥ s, 384a – S, 384b
al-Ghazālī, Abū Ḥāmid Muḥammad al-Ṭūsī (1111) i, 25b, 92a, 274a, 326b, 327b, 333a, 347a, 350a, 351a, 390b, 411a, 412b, 414a, 416a, 427b, 513b, 593a, 595b, 696b, 714a, 715a, 826a, 839a, 1099b; ii, 96a, 144b, 225b, 451a, 605b, 765b, 767a, 773a, 834a, **1038b**, 1069b; iii, 254a, 512a, 544a, 683b, 712b, 915a, 958b, 1024b, 1029a, 1063b, 1148a, 1149a, 1168a, 1205b; iv, 25b, 149b, 257b, 279b, 487a, 697b, 895a; v, 54b, 329b; vi, 11b, 14a, 73b, 110b, 204b, 211a, 219a, 279b, 280a, 281a, 347a, 447a, 448b, 452a, 739a, 905b; vii, 143b, 296b, 445a, 465a, 585b, 591a, 755a, 986a; viii, 71b, 95b, 125a, 547b; x, 468a; s, 2b, 15a, 153a, 293a, 305b – I, 26b, 94b, 282b, 336b, 338a, 343a, 357b, 361a, 362a, 401b, 422b, 424b, 425b, 426a, 428a, 439b, 529a, 612a, 615a, 717b, 735b, 736b, 849a, 862b, 1133a; II, 98a, 148b, 232b, 462b, 620b, 784a, 785a, 791b, **1062b**, 1094a; III, 261a, 529b, 563a, 705b, 735a, 939b, 983a, 1050a, 1055a, 1090a, 1176a, 1177a, 1197a, 1236a; IV, 27a, 155b, 268b, 291b, 508a, 726a, 928b; V, 56a, 329b; VI, 11a, 12b, 71b, 108a, 188b, 195b, 203a, 264b, 265b, 331a, 432b, 433b, 434a, 437b, 728a, 897a; VII, 145b, 298b, 446a, b, 586a, 590b, 756a, 987a; VIII, 73a, 98a, 128a, 565a; X, 500a; S, 2a, 15a, 153b, 292b, 305a
al-Ghazālī, Aḥmad b. Muḥammad (1126) ii, 1038b, **1041b**; iv, 64a-b; viii, 539b; s, 2b – II, 1063a, **1066a**; IV, 67b; VIII, 557a; S, 2a
al-Ghazālī, Djānbirdī (1521) i, 779a; ii, 287a, **1042a**; iii, 88a, 400a; vi, 325a – I, 802b; II, 294b, **1066a**; III, 90b, 412b; VI, 309b
Ghazālī, Meḥmed (1535) ii, **1042a**; vi, 610a – II, **1066b**; VI, 594b
Ghazālī Mashhadī (1572) vii, 340b; viii, 775b – VII, 342b; VIII, 801b
Ghazan Khān (Hunza) iii, 581a – III, 601b
Ghazan Khān Maḥmūd (Il-Khānid(e)) (1304) i, 205b, 861a, 903a, 1011a, 1031b, 1126b, 1129b; ii, 47a, 285b, 311b, **1043a**, 1045b; iii, 189b, 198a, 284a, 399b, 490b, 951b, 1089b, 1099b, 1122b, 1124a, b; iv, 31a, b, 48b, 621a, 637b, 818a, 945a, 975b, 976a, 1038b, 1045b; v, 162b, 312a, 554b, 662b, 872b; vi, 15a, b, 16a, 19b, 117b, 120a, b, 483a, 494a, b, 501b, 502a, 524a, b, 545b, 547b, 601b, 714b; vii, 169a, 232a, 507a, 991b; viii, 156b; s, 59a, 94b – I, 211b, 885a, 930a, 1042a, 1063a, 1160b, 1164a; II, 48a, 293b, 320b, **1067a**, 1069b; III, 194a, 203a, 293a, 412a, 507b, 976b, 1116a, 1126b, 1150a, 1152a, b; IV, 33b, 34a, 51a, 646a, 664a, 851a, 978a, 1008a, b, 1070a, 1077a; V, 160b, 311b, 559a, 668a, 878b; VI, 13b, 14a, 17b, 115a, 117b, 118a, 469a, 479b, 480a, 487a, b, 509a, 530a, 532a, 586a, 703b; VII, 170b, 233b, 507a, 993a; VIII, 159a; S, 59b, 94a
Ghāzāniyye iii, 1124b, 1125a – III, 1152b, 1153a
Ghazāt → Ghazw
Ghazel (Ottoman) x, **718b** -X,
Ghāzī (ghuzāt) i, 322b; ii, 505b, **1043b**; iii, 196a – I, 332b; II, 518a, **1068a**; III, 201a
Ghāzī I, II (Zangid(e)s) → Sayf al-Dīn Ghāzī I, II
Ghāzī, Amīr → Gümüshtegin
Ghāzī b. Fayṣal (Hāshimite) (1939) ii, 872b, **1045a**; iii, 264a, 1258b; v, 1044b; viii, 141b – II, 892a, **1069b**; III, 271b, 1291a; V, 1041a; VIII, 144a
Ghāzī b. Ḥassān (1168) vi, 380b – VI, 364b
Ghāzī b. Ṣalāḥ al-Dīn → al-Ẓāhir Ghāzī
Ghāzī Beg b. Djānī Beg, Mīrzā (Arghūn) vii, 129b – VII, 131b
Ghāzī Čelebī ii, **1045a**; v, 505b; ix, 654a – II, **1069b**; V, 509a; IX, 679b
Ghāzī al-Dīn Ḥaydar i, 757b; ii, **1045b**; v, 635a, 637a – I, 780a; II, **1070a**; V, 639a, 641a
Ghāzī al-Dīn ʿImād al-Mulk (Haydarābād) vi, 535b – VI, 520a
Ghāzī al-Dīn Khān → ʿImād al-Mulk; Muḥammad Panāh, Mīr; Shihāb al-Dīn, Mīr
Ghāzī al-Dīn Khān iii, 320b – III, 331a
Ghāzī Evrenos Beg → Ewrenos
Ghāzī Girāy I (1524) ii, **1046a**, 1113b – II, **1070b**, 1139b
Ghāzī Girāy II (1607) ii, **1046a**; v, 138b – II, **1070b**; V, 141b
Ghāzī Girāy III (1708) ii, **1047a**; iv, 569a; v, 140b – II, **1071b**; IV, 591b; V, 143a
Ghāzī Ḥasan Pasha (XVIII) viii, 236a – VIII, 241b
Ghāzī Khān Čak (1566) iv, 709a; s, 167a, **324b**, 335b – IV, 737b; S, 167a, **324a**, 353b
Ghāzī Khunkʸār → Murād I (Ottoman)
Ghāzī Khusrew-bey → Khosrew beg
Ghāzī Ḳirān b. Sulṭān Aḥmad i, 1030b – I, 1062a
Ghāzī-Ḳumuḳ → Ḳumiḳ
Ghāzī Malik → Ghiyāth al-Dīn Tughluḳ I
Ghāzī Meḥmed Pasha → Muḥammad Pasha Bushatlī

Ghāzī Miyān, Sālār Masʿūd (1033) i, 756b, 855b; ii, **1047b**; iv, 210b; vi, **783b**; viii, 252a; s, 280a – I, 779a, 879b; II, **1071b**; IV, 220a; VI, **773b**; VIII, 254a; S, 280a
Ghāzī Muḥammad → Ḳāḍī Muḥammad
Ghāzīpūr vii, 314a; s, 203a, **325a** – VII, 316a; S, 202b, **324b**
Ghāziya i, 404a, 1036a; ii, **1048a** – I, 415b, 1067b; II, **1072b**
Ghāziyan i, 1014a – I, 1045a
Ghaziyya i, 528b – I, 544b
Ghazna i, 222b, 223a, 226b, 940a; ii, 382a, **1048b**, 1054a, 1103b; vi, 65a, b, 198b, 276b, 368b, 433a, 453a; s, 66b, 329b – I, 229a, 233b, 968b; II, 392b, **1073a**, 1078b, 1129b; VI, 62b, 63a, 182b, 261b, 352b, 418a, 438b; S, 67a, 329a
Ghaznawī, Shaykh Raḍiyy al-Dīn ʿAlī-yi Lālā (1244) viii, 458a – VIII, 423b
Ghaznawid(e)s i, 226b, 420a, 421b, 434a, 439b, 1130b, 1342b, 1344b; ii, 4b, 266b, 336a, 893b, **1050a**, 1083a, 1109a; iii, 47a, 197a, 415b, 438b, 471a; iv, 18b, 24a-25a, 61a, 189b, 208b, 217b, 266b, 357a, 696b, 758b; v, 58a, 597b, 691a, 956b; vi, 64a, 193a, 198b, 261b, 273b, 521b, 522a, 523a, b, 524a, 532b, 620b; vii, 193a, 477b, 653a, 679a; ix, 158b; s, 21a, b, 119a, 242a, 284b, 333a, 386b – I, 233b, 432a, 433a, 446a, 452a, 1165a, 1383a, 1385a; II, 4b, 274b, 345b, 914b, **1074b**, 1108a, 1135a; III, 48b, 202a, 428b, 453a, 487b; IV, 20a, 26a-b, 64a, 197b, 218a, 227a, 278b, 372b, 724b, 788b; V, 60a, 601b, 696a, 960b; VI, 62b, 177a, 182b, 246a, 258b, 506a, 516b, 605b; VII, 193b, 477a, 652b, 679a; IX, 164a; S, 21a, b, 118b, 242a, 284b, 332b, 387a
—art, architecture ii, 1053b, 1103b – II, 1078a, 1129b
Ghaznī s, 41a, 367a – S, 41b, 367b
Ghaznī Khān b. ʿĀdil Khān II (Khāndesh) (1508) vi, 51a – VI, 49a
Ghaznī Khān b. Hushang Shāh (Ghūrī, Mālwa) iv, 219a; vi, 52b, 309b – IV, 228b; VI, 51a, 294b
Ghaznī Khān Muḥammad b. Alp Khān Hūshang (Ghūrī, Mālwa) (1436) iii, 638b; iv, 1067b – III, 660a; IV, 1099b
Ghazw, Ghazwa i, 885b, 892a; ii, 64a, b, 509b, 1043b, **1055a**; v, 768a, 1161b – I, 911b, 918b; II, 65a, b, 522a, 1068a, **1079b**; V, 774a, 1151a
al-Ghazwānī, Sīdī ʿAbd Allāh (1528) vi, 591a, 597a – VI, 576a, 582a
Ghazza ii, **1056a**; iii, 187b; v, 801b; vi, 31a, 118b; ix, 210a, b; s, 20b, 326a – II, **1080b**; III, 192a; V, 807b; VI, 29b, 116b; IX, 216a, b; S, 20b, 325b
al-Ghazza (Mecca) vi, 161b – VI, 155b
al-Ghazzāl, al-Malakī (1777) vii, 387b; s, **325b** – VII, 388b; S, **325a**
al-Ghazzālī → al-Ghazālī
Ghazzan Khān b. Ḳāsim Khān ii, 316b – II, 326a
Ghazzāwī, Āl vi, 345b – VI, 329b
al-Ghazzāwī, ʿAlī Bey iv, 852b – IV, 885b
al-Ghazzī, Abū Isḥāḳ (1129) viii, 971a; s, **326a** – VIII, 1005a; S, **325b**
al-Ghazzī, Badr al-Dīn (1577) x, 5a – X, 5a
al-Ghazzī , Nadjm al-Dīn (1651) i, 100a, 594b; vi, 352a; vii, 469b – I, 103a, 614a; VI, 336b; VII, 469a
Gheghāya iii, 207a – III, 212b
Gheraba i, 371b – I, 382b
Ghība → Pandjāb
Ghidhāʿ ii, **1057a**; iii, 79a; s, 318b – II, **1081b**; III, 81b; S, 318b
Ghidjuwānī, Khʷādja ʿAbd al-Khāliḳ (1220) vii, 933b, 934a; viii, 933b, 934a – VII, 934a, b; VIII, 934a,b
Ghifār, Banū ii, **1072b**; v, 116b; vii, 561b – II, **1097a**; V, 119a; VII, 562a
al-Ghifārī, al-Ḥakam b. ʿAmr (VII) vii, 357a – VII, 359b
Ghīghāya vi, 590b – VI, 575b
Ghīlān, Ḳāʾid iv, 729b – IV, 758b
Ghilmān → Ghulām
Ghilzay → Ghalzay
Ghināʾ ii, **1072b**; iv, 821a; v, 480b – II, **1097b**; IV, 854a; V, 483b
Ghirbāl ii, 620b, 1074a – II, 636a, 1098b
Ghirbīb b. ʿAbd Allāh (797) ii, **1075b** – II, **1100a**
Ghirsh (Ghūrsh) → Sikka
Ghīṭa → Ghayṭa
al-Ghiṭaʾ, Shaykh ʿAlī Kāshif (1838) s, 75b – S, 76a
Ghīṭānī vi, 469a – VI, 454b
al-Ghiṭrīf b. ʿAṭāʾ al-Djurashī (VIII) v, 855a, b; s, **326b** – V, 862a, b; S, **326a**
Ghiṭrīf b. Ḳudāma (VIII) vii, 949a – VII, 949b
al-Ghiṭrīfī, Muḥammad b. Aḥmad s, 326b – S, 326a
Ghiyār ii, **1075b**; v, 736b, 744b – II, **1100b**; V, 741b, 750a
Ghiyāth (dāʿī) iv, 661b – IV, 688a
Ghiyāth b. Muḥammad s, 271b – S, 271b
Ghiyāth Beg i, 253b; ii, 380b – I, 261b; II, 390b
Ghiyāth al-Dīn (Ḳaraʾuna turk/-c) vi, 692b – VI, 680a
Ghiyāth al-Dīn b. Kamāl al-Dīn (Marʿashī) (1400) vi, 512a, b, 513a – VI, 497b, 498a
Ghiyāth al-Dīn b. Maḥmūd Khaldjī I (Mālwā) (1451) vi, 53b, 54a, 407a – VI, 51b, 52a, 391b
Ghiyāth al-Dīn b. Rashīd al-Dīn Faḍl Allāh (XIV) vii, 404b – VII, 405b
Ghiyāth al-Dīn Aʿẓam Shāh → Aʿẓam Shāh
Ghiyāth al-Dīn Balban → Balban
Ghiyāth al-Dīn Djāmī (1522) s, 139a – S, 138b
Ghiyāth al-Dīn Girāy ii, 1112b – II, 1138b
Ghiyāth al-Dīn al-Ḥādjdjī (Muẓaffarid(e)) vii, 820a – VII, 821b
Ghiyāth al-Dīn Iṣfahānī vi, 907b – VI, 899a
Ghiyāth al-Dīn Kaykhusraw → Kaykhusraw II
Ghiyāth al-Dīn Maḥmūd → Maḥmūd III (Bengal(e))
Ghiyāth al-Dīn Maḥmūd (Ghūrid(e)) (1212) ii, 752a, 1103a; iv, 917b – II, 770a, 1129a; IV, 950b
Ghiyāth al-Dīn Maḥmūd b. Meḥmed Beg (Menteshe) (1385) vi, 1018b – VI, 1011a
Ghiyāth al-Dīn Masʿūd b. ʿIzz al-Dīn Kay Kāʾwūs → Masʿūd II (Rūm Saldjūḳ)
Ghiyāth al-Dīn Muḥammad (1328) ix, 1a – IX, 6a
Ghiyāth al-Dīn Muḥammad I (Saldjūḳ) (1118) vii, 983b – VII, 984a
Ghiyāth al-Dīn Muḥammad b. Ḥusayn → Astarābādī
Ghiyāth al-Dīn Muḥammad b. Rashīd al-Dīn (1336) viii, 541b; s, 415b – VIII, 559a; S, 415b
Ghiyāth al-Dīn Muḥammad b. Sām I (Ghūrid(e)) (1202) → Muḥammad b. Sām I, Ghiyāth al-Dīn
Ghiyāth al-Dīn Muḥammad Eretna i, 1327b; ii, 239a, 706a, 712b – I, 1368b; II, 246a, 724a, 730b
Ghiyāth al-Dīn Muḥammad al-Kurtī i, 764b, 908b; ii, 68a; iii, 1022a; iv, 672a – I, 787b, 936a; II, 69a; III, 1048a; IV, 699b
Ghiyāth al-Dīn Naḳḳāsh (XV) ii, **1076a** – II, **1100b**
Ghiyāth al-Dīn Pīr ʿAlī iv, 672a – IV, 699b
Ghiyāth al-Dīn Pīrshāh (Khʷarazm) (1230) i, 1311a; ii, 393a; vi, 277b – I, 1351b; II, 403b; VI, 262b
Ghiyāth al-Dīn Shīrāzī iv, 1073b – IV, 1105a
Ghiyāth al-Dīn Tughluḳ I (Tughluḳid(e)), Dihlī) (1325)

i, 104b, 444b, 1322a; ii, 120a, 154b, 257a, 262a, 269b, 274b, 922b, **1076a**; iii, 201a, 416b, 441b, 492a; iv, 921b, 924a; v, 885a; vi, 126a, 127b; vii, 550a; s, 105b, 409a – I, 107b, 457b, 1362b; II, 123a, 159b, 263b, 269b, 277b, 283a, 944a, **1101a**; III, 206a, 429b, 456a, 509a; IV, 954b, 956b; V, 891b; VI, 124a, 125b; VII, 550a; S, 105a, 409b
Ghiyāth al-Dīn Tughluḳ Shāh II (Tughluḳid(e)), Dihlī) (1389) ii, **1077a**; vi, 61b – II, **1102a**; VI, 59b
Ghiyāth Mutaṭabbir → Sabzawārī, Muḥammad ʿAlāʾ al-Dīn
Ghiyāth al-Umma → Bahāʾ al-Dawla Fīrūz
Ghom → Ḳumm
Ghōr (Afghānistān) s, 367a – S, 367b
Ghōrāt (Afghānistān) vii, 218b; s, 367a – VII, 220a; S, 367b
Ghōrband s, 367b – S, 367a
Ghōriya Khēls i, 218b; vii, 220a – I, 224b; VII, 221b
Ghourides → Ghūrides
Ghouristan → Ghūr
Ghubār iii, 468b, 1140a; iv, 1124a, 1125b – III, 485a, 1168b; IV, 1155b, 1157a
Ghubayrā s, **327a** – S, **326b**
Ghubba i, 535b, 536a – I, 552a
Ghubrīnī ii, **1077b** – II, **1102a**
Ghudāna, Banū vi, 268a – VI, 253a
Ghudiyyāt v, 267a – V, 265a
Ghudjdāma, Banū vi, 742a – VI, 731b
Ghudjduwān ii, **1077b**; x, 88b – II, **1102b**; X, 96a
Ghudjdu(a)wānī, ʿAbd al-Khāliḳ (1220) ii, **1077b**; viii, 539b – II, **1102b**; VIII, 557b
Ghufrān ii, **1078a** – II, **1103a**
Ghufrān Maʿāb → Naṣīrābādī
Ghūl ii, **1078b**; s, 52b – II, **1103b**; S, 53a
Ghulām i, 7b, 8a, 1278a; ii, 507a, 551b, 837a, **1079b**, 1103a; iii, 195a; iv, 36a, 242a; v, 245a, 691b, 820a – I, 8a, b, 1317a; II, 519b, 565b, 856b, **1104b**, 1129a; III, 199b; IV, 38b, 253a; V, 243a, 696b, 826a
Ghulām-Ḥusayn Ṣādighī (1985) vi, 764a – VI, 753a
Ghulām Aḥmad i, 301a, 302b; iii, 433b – I, 310b, 312a; III, 447b
Ghulām ʿAlī Āzād → Āzād Bilgrāmī
Ghulām ʿAlī, Shāh (1824) iii, 433b; vii, 938b – III, 447b; VII, 939a
Ghulām Farīd v, 611a – V, 615a
Ghulām Ḥalim → ʿAbd al-ʿAzīz al-Dihlawī
Ghulām Haydar Khān ii, 638a – II, 654a
Ghulām Ḥusayn, Rādja (XX) vi, 78a – VI, 76a
Ghulām Ḥusayn Khān Tabāṭabāʾī (1815) ii, **1091b** – II, **1117a**
Ghulām Ḥusayn "Salīm" (1817) ii, **1092a** – II, **1118a**
Ghulām Isḥāḳ Khān viii, 243b – VIII, 249b
Ghulām Ḳadir Rohilla (1789) i, 813b; ii, **1092b**; iii, 428a – I, 836b; II, **1118a**; III, 442a
Ghulām Khalīl (IX) viii, 139b – VIII, 142a
Ghulām al-Khallāl (974) i, 274a, 274b; ii, **1093a**; iii, 158b, 735a; iv, 990a, 1083b; v, 10a – I, 282b, 283a; II, **1118b**; III, 162a, 757b; IV, 1022b, 1114b; V, 10a
Ghulām Khān (Rohilla) (XVIII) vii, 316b – VII, 318b
Ghulām Muḥammad iii, 565a, b; iv, 710b – III, 584b, 585a; IV, 739b
Ghulām Muḥammad b. Tīpū Sulṭān ii, 7b – II, 7b
Ghulām Nabī Bilgrāmī iii, 457b – III, 473b
Ghulām Naḳshband Lakhnawī i, 1219a – I, 1255b
Ghulām Shāh Kalhōrā ii, 186a; iii, 323b; iv, 544b – II, 192a; III, 333b; IV, 568a
Ghulām Shāhīs i, 295b – I, 304b
Ghulām Thaʿlab (957) ii, **1093a**; v, 608a; vi, 916b; s, 361a – II, **1119a**; V, 611b; VI, 908a; S, 361a
Ghulām Yaḥyā iii, 430b – III, 444b
Ghulām Zafariy vi, 768b – VI, 758a
Ghulāmī (XVIII) vi, 611a – VI, 596a
Ghulāt i, 51a, 1098b; ii, **1093b**; iii, 662a – I, 52b, 1132a; II, **1119b**; III, 683a
Ghulayfiḳa → Ghalāfiḳa
Ghuldja → Ḳuldja
Ghumāra, Banū i, 161a; ii, **1095a**; v, 1204a, b; vi, 741a, b, 743b – I, 165b; II, **1121a**; V, 1194b, 1195a; VI, 730a, b, 733a
Ghumdān ii, **1096a**; viii, 979b; ix, 1a – II, **1121b**; VIII, 1014a; IX, 1a
Ghumīk ii, 85b; iv, 348a – II, 87b; IV, 362b
Ghundjār (802) ii, **1096a** – II, **1122a**
Ghunm → Ghanīma
Ghūr ii, **1096b**; vi, 66a, 365b; s, 376b – II, **1122b**; VI, 64a, 349b; S, 376b
Ghurāb ii, **1096b** – II, **1122b**
al-Ghurāb (1771) vi, 113a – VI, 110b
Ghurāb → Safīna
al-Ghurāb → Nudjūm
Ghurabāʾ, Ghurebā ii, **1097b** – II, **1123b**
Ghurābiyya ii, **1098b** – II, **1124b**
Ghūrak (Ṣughd) (737) i, 241a; viii, 1032b – I, 248b; VIII, 1067b
al-Ghuraynī, ʿAbd al-Raḥmān b. Sulaymān s, 44a – S, 44b
Ghurbat → Ḳurbat
Ghūrī → Dilāwar Khān, Mālwā
al-Ghūrī (Mamlūk) → Ḳānsūh al-Ghawrī
Ghūrid(e)s i, 217b, 218a, 223b, 227a, 420a, 852a, 1010a, 1344b; ii, 266b, 382a, 894a, 1049b, 1052b, 1096b, **1099a**; iii, 197b, 415b, 471b; iv, 210a; v, 597b; vi, 193a, 198b, 309b, 618a; vii, 433a, 997a, b; viii, 253a; s, 242a, 284b – I, 224a, b, 230a, 233b, 432a, 876a, 1041a, 1385a; II, 275a, 392b, 914b, 1074a, 1077a, 1122b, **1125a**; III, 202a, 428b, 488a; IV, 219b; V, 601b; VI, 177a, 182b, 294b, 603a; VII, 434a, 999a; VIII, 255b; S, 242a, 284b
Ghurūsh → Sikka
Ghusl ii, **1104a**; iii, 1053a; iv, 264b – II, **1130a**; III, 1079a; IV, 276b
Ghūṭa i, 1029b; ii, 278a, 290b, 541a, **1104b**; vi, 378a, 544b, 545b, 546a, 566a; vii, 212a – I, 1061a; II, 286a, 298b, 554b, **1131a**; VI, 362b, 529a, 530a, b, 551a; VII, 213b
Ghuwaynim, Banū vi, 371b – VI, 356a
Ghuzāt → Ghāzī
Ghuzāt al-baḥr i, 1205b; ii, 521a, 526a, 678a; iii, 627b – I, 1241b; II, 534a, 539a, 695a; III, 648a
al-Ghuzūlī, ʿAlāʾ al-Dīn (1412) i, 361b; ii, **1106b**; vii, 1040a; s, 115b – I, 372b; II, **1132b**; VII, 1042a; S, 115a
Ghuzz (Aghzāz) i, 181b, 1029a; ii, **1110a**; x, 689b – I, 186b, 1060b; II, **1136a**; *X,*
Ghuzz (Oghuz) i, 147b, 190a, 227a, 239b, 311a, 512b, 524a, 607b, 660b, 661b, 662a, 729a, 1001b, 1073b, 1133b, 1292a; ii, 20b, 200a, 613b, 724a, 971a, 1101b, **1106b**; iii, 1098b, 1115a; iv, 18b, 26a-b, 29b, 101a, 347a, 614a, 1176a; v, 58b, 59a, 126a, 160a, b, 453b, 855b; vi, 243b, 272b, 415b, 416a, 493b, 499b, 620b, 714b; vii, 543b; viii, 943a, 1005a; x, 688b, 689b; s, 168b, 195a, 244b, 280b, 333b; – I, 151b, 194b, 233b, 247a, 321a, 528b, 540a, 627a, 681b, 682b, 683a, 751a, 1032a, 1106a, 1167b, 1331b; II, 20b, 206b, 629a, 743a, 993b, 1127b, **1132b**; III, 1125b, 1142a; IV, 20a, 28a, 31b, 105a,

362a, 638b, 1209b; V, 60a, b, 128b, 159a, 456a, 862a; VI, 227b, 257b, 400b, 401a, 479a, 485a, 605b, 703b; VII, 543b; VIII, 975a, 1040a; X, 730b, 781b; S, 168b, 195a, 244b, 280b, 333b
Giafar → Dja'far
Giālpō i, 1004b – I, 1035b
Giaour → Gabr, Kāfir
Gibel → Djabala
Gibralfaro → Djabal Fāruh
Gibraltar → Djabal Ṭāriḳ
Gibran → Djabrān
Gičkīs s, 222a, 332a – S, 222a, 331b
Gīl/Gīlī ii, 1111a; s, 356b, 363a – II, 1137a; S, 356a, b, 362b
Gīl Gawbarā ii, 74b; iv, 644b; s, 298a, 299a – II, 76a; IV, 671a; S, 297b, 298b
Gīlakī, Amīr i, 1250a – I, 1288a
Gīlān i, 8a, 46b, 60a, 91a, 389a, 1014a; ii, 189b, 190a, 445b, 903b, **1111a**; iii, 211a, 212a, 214b; v, 602b, 604a; vi, 66b, 433b, 483a, 499a, 512a, b, 513a, b, 514a, 515b, 516a; viii, 449b; s, 13a, 23b, 139b, 299a, 356b, 357a, 363a, 365b – I, 8a, 48a, 62a, 93b, 400b, 1045a; II, 195b, 196a, 457b, 924b, **1137a**; III, 216b, 218a, 221a; V, 606b, 608a; VI, 64b, 419a, 469b, 484b, 497a, b. 498a, b, 499a, 500b, 501a; VIII, 465a; S, 13b, 24a, 139a, 298b, 356b, 356b, 362b, 365a
Gīlān Shāh iv, 815a – IV, 848a
Gīlānī, Masīḥ al-Dīn Abu 'l-Fatḥ (1589) viii, 542b – VIII, 560a
Gilānī, Sayyid Muḥammad Makhdūm (1517) x, 255b – X, 274b
Gīlānī, Mullā Shamsa (1686) viii, 782a – VIII, 808a
Gīlān-i Biyāpīsh iv, 475b; v, 602b, 603a; vi, 18a, 483a, 515b, 516a – IV, 496b; V, 606b, 607a; VI, 16a, 469b, 500b, 501a
al-Gildakī → al-Djildakī
Gilgamesh iv, 902b – IV, 935b
Gilgit (Pakistan) ii, 30a, b, 1112a; iii, 581a; vi, 127a; viii, 240b; s, **327b** – II, 30a, 31b, 1138a; III, 601b; VI, 125a; VIII, 246bS, **327a**
Gilit iii, 1259b – III, 1292a
Gīlīz iii, 207a – III, 212b
Gimbri → Ḳonbur
Gindibu i, 524b – I, 540b
Ginukh → Dido
Giorgi III v, 490a – V, 493a
Giorgi V v, 491a – V, 494a
Giorgi VI v, 491b – V, 494a
Giorgi XI → Gurgīn Khān
Giorgi XII v, 495a – V, 498a
Girāy i, 893a; ii, 44b, 1046a, **1112a**; iv, 499b; v, 137a – I, 919b; II, 45a, 1070b, **1138a**; IV, 521a; V, 139b
Girdhār Bahādur ii, 219a – II, 225b
Girdkūh iii, 501b; viii, 599a – III, 518b; VIII, 618a
Giresün ii, **1114a** – II, **1140a**
Girgā ii, **1114a** – II, **1140b**
Girgenti → Djirdjent
Girishk ii, **1114b** – II, **1140b**
Girit → Iḳrītish
Girīz, girīzgāh iv, 715b – IV, 744a
Girnār (Gudjarāt) vi, 50a, b – VI, 48b
Gīsh i, 47a, 356a; ii, 146b, 509b, 510b – I, 48b, 366b; II, 150a, 522a, 523b
Gīsū Darāz, Muḥammad (1422) ii, 54a, 55a, 56a, **1114b**; iii, 418a, 429b, 434a, 436a; iv, 962a; s, 353a – II, 52b, 56a, b, **1140b**; III, 431a, 443b, 448a, 450a; IV, 994a; S, 353a
Giwa i, 956a – I, 985a
Gižduvan → Ghudjduwān
Gīza, Gizeh → al-Ḳāhira
Gjinokastër → Ergiri
Glāwa, Banū ii, **1116a**; vi, 742a, 743a – II, **1142a**; 731a, 732b
Glāwī Madanī ii, 1116a; iii, 62a – II, 1142a; III, 64b
Glāwī Tihāmī ii, 1116b – II, 1142b
Gnāns iii, 1163b; iv, 206a – III, 1192a; IV, 215a
Gnāwa iv, 381b – IV, 398a
Goa i, 924a, 978b; ii, 1128a; iii, 422a; vi, 63a, b, 67a – I, 951b, 1009a; II, 1154b; III, 435b; VI, 61a, 65a
Gobān → Ḳobān
Göbek adi̊ iv, 181a – IV, 188b
Godāvarī vi, 67b, 87a, 269a – VI, 65a, 85a, 254a
Godoberi, Banū i, 504a; iv, 630b – I, 519b; IV, 655b
Gogo → Gao
Gōgul Prashād Rasā (XIX) vii, 475b – VII, 475a
Goha → Djuḥā
Gök Tepe ii, **1116b** – II, **1143a**
Gokalā Djāt iv, 177b – IV, 186a
Gökalp, Ziyā (Ḍiyā') (1924) i, 327a; ii, 345b, 475b, **1117a**; iv, 123b, 169a, 791a; v, 264a, 271b; vi, 6b, 94a; viii, 251a; s, 47b, 150a, 167b – I, 337a; II, 355b, 487b, **1143a**; IV, 129a, 176a, 823a; V, 261b, 269a; VI, 6b, 91b; VIII, 267bS, 48a, 150a, 168a
Gökbürī, Muẓaffar al-Dīn → Muẓaffar al-Dīn Gökbürī
Gökčay → Gökče
Gökče Mūsā ii, 614a – II, 629a
Gökče-Tengiz ii, **1118a** – II, **1144a**
Göklän ii, **1118a**; iii, 1108a – II, **1144b**; III, 1135a
Göksu ii, **1118b**; vi, 539b – II, **1144b**; VI, 524a
Göksün ii, **1118b**; vi, 505b, 509a; s, 239a – II, **1145a**; VI, 491a, 494b; S, 239a
Golan → al-Djawlān
Golconda/Golconde → Golkonḍā
Gold Coast → Ghana
Golden Horde → Bātūid(e)s; Ḳipčaḳ; Sarāy
Golden Horn → Ghalaṭa; Istanbul; Takhtaḳal'e
al-Golea → al-Ḳulay'a
Goletta → Ḥalḳ al-wādi
Golfe Persique → Baḥr Fāris
Goliath → Djālūt
Golkonḍā i, 768b, 769b, 924a, 1323b; ii, 158b, **1118b**; iii, 318b, 426b, 448a; v, 549b; vi, 126b, 369b, 535a; vii, 458b – I, 791b, 792b, 951b, 1364a; II, 163b, **1145a**; III, 328a, 440b, 463a; V, 554a; VI, 124a, 353b, 519b; VII, 458b
Golubac vi, 70b – VI, 68b
Gōmal vi, 86a – VI, 84a
Gombroon/Gombrun → Bandar 'Abbās
Gomut/Gomit vi, 128b – VI, 126b
Gondar i, 49b; iii, 7a – I, 51a; III, 7b
Gondēshāpūr i, 212b, 516b, 1223a; ii, 577a, **1119b**; iii, 872b; v, 919a; vi, 599b; x, 452b; s, 354a – I, 219a, 532a, 1259b; II, 591b, **1146a**; III, 897a; V, 924b; VI, 584a; X, 485a; S, 354a
Gonduruḥmaan, Shaykh x, 71b – X, 74a
Gondwāna vi, 50b, 54a – VI, 48b, 52a
Gongo (Kankan) vi, 422a – VI, 407a
Gönüllü ii, **1120b** – II, **1146b**
Gora, Abdallāh Suleymān v, 483a – V, 485b
Gōrgān → Gūrgān
Gördes ii, **1121a**; s, 136b, 138a, 282b – II, **1147b**; S, 136a, 137b, 282b
Gorein, Djabal iv, 478b, 479b – IV, 499b, 501b
Görele s, 283a – S, 283a
Gorgan → Gurgān
Göridje → Korča; Manastir
Göridjeli Ḳoči Beg → Ḳoči Beg
Gorno- Badakhshān i, 853a – I, 877a
Gorwekht s, 285a – S, 285a

Gōsiōs s, 52a – S, 53a
Goule → Ghūl
La Goulette → Ḥalḳ al-Wādī
Goum → Gūm
Gourara (Gurāra) s, **328a**; vi, 141a – S, **327b**; VI, 139b
Govind Singh, Guru (Sikh) (1708) i, 913b; ii, 928b; vii, 315b – I, 941b; II, 950b; VII, 318a
Govindapur ii, 7a – II, 7a
Gövsa, Ibrāhīm ʿAlāʾ al-Dīn (1949) s, **328b** – S, **328a**
Gowardhan (painter/peintre) (XVII) vii, 339a – VII, 340b
Gowde, Aḥmad (Aḳ-Ḳoyunlu) (1397) i, 312a, 1082b; ii, 184a – I, 321b, 1115a; II, 190a
Goyum → Djuwayn
Gözgān → Djuzdjān
Grabadin i, 345a – I, 355b
Grain (Grane, Kuwayt) x, 956a – X,
Gran → Esztergom
Grañ → Aḥmad Grañ
Granada → Gharnāṭa
Grande Horde, la I, 1141a; II, 45a; V, 140a, b
Great Horde i, 1108a; ii, 44a; v, 137a, b
Greece/Grèce, Turks/Turcs in/en x, 699a – X,
Grenade → Gharnāṭa
Gresik s, 201b – S, 201b
Guadalajara → Wādī 'l-Ḥidjāra
Guadalquivir → al-Wādī 'l-Kabīr
al-Gūdālī, Yaḥyā b. Ibrāhīm → al-Djawhar b. Sakkum
Guadarrama → al-Sharrāt
Guadelmedina → Wādī 'l-Madīna
Guadiana → Wādī Yāna
Guadix → Wādī Āsh
Guanche i, 1180b – I, 1215b
Guardafui ii, **1121b** – II, **1147b**
Gudāla ii, **1121b**; v, 653b – II, **1148a**; V, 658a
Gūdarz iv, 815b, 816a – IV, 848b
Gūdjar i, 224b; ii, **1122a**, 1123a; iii, 335b – I, 231b; II, **1148b**, 1149b; III, 345b
Gudjarāt i, 506b, 561b, 924a, 1053a, 1254b; ii, 11a, 814b, 816a, **1123a**; iii, 16a, 421b, 444b, 857a, 1010a; iv, 199b, 202b, 901b; v, 26b, 1117a, 1216b; vi, 47a, 49b, 50b, 51a, b, 53a, 126b, 127a, b, 233b, 271a, 294b, 309b, 342b, 368b, 369a, b, 406b, 407b, 410b, 535a, b, 536a, 642a, 694a; vii, 79b, 133a, b; viii, 68a; ix, 785b; s, 105a, 200a, 312a, 335b – I, 522a, 579a, 952a, 1084b, 1292b; II, 11a, 834a, 835b, **1149b**; III, 16b, 17a, 435b, 459a, 881a, 1035b; IV, 208a, 211b, 934b; V, 27a, 1113b, 1206b; VI, 45b, 48a, b, 49a, 50a, 51a, 124b, 125a, b, 206b, 255b, 279b, 295a, 326b, 353a, b, 391b, 392a, 395a, 519b, 520a, 627a, 682a; VII, 80b, 135a, b; VIII, 69b; IX, 819b; S, 104b, 200a, 312a, 335a
Gudjarātī i, 1255a; ii, **1130b** – I, 1293a; II, **1157a**
Gudjarī, Gudjurī ii, 31a, 1122b – II, 32a, 1149a
Gudjrān'wāla ii, **1130b**; iii, 63a – II, **1157b**; III, 65b
Gudjrāt i, 80b; ii, **1131a** – I, 83a; II, **1158a**
Gudmanā → ʿAfīfī
Guellala → Ḳallala
Guerara → Ḳarāra
Guergour s, 144b, – S, 144a
Guers(c)if → Garsīf
Guezebida i, 1221b – I, 1258a
Guinea/Guinée ii, **1131b**; v, 252a – II, **1158b**; V, 250a
Gujarat, Gujerat → Gudjarāt
Gujarati, Guzarati → Gudjarātī
Guklān → Göklān
Gul ii, **1133a** – II, **1159b**
Gül ii, 1133b, 1134a – II, 1160b
Gul Khātūn s, **329a** – S, **328b**
Gulāb Sīngh ii, 30a, 140a; iii, 336a; iv, 709b; s, 242a – II, 30b, 144a; III, 346a; IV, 738a; S, 242a
Gulʿanbar → Shahrizūr
Gülbaba i, 1286a; ii, **1133b** – I, 1325b; II, **1160b**
Gulbadan Bēgum (1603) ii, **1134b**; vi, 488b; vii, 342b – II, **1161a**; VI, 474b; VII, 344a
Gulbāng ii, **1135a** – II, **1161b**
Gulbargā i, 924b, 925a, 1323a; ii, 54a, **1135a**; iii, 15a, 442a, 446b; v, 295b; vi, 127b, 369a – I, 952b, 953a, 1363b; II, 52b, **1162a**; III, 16a, 456b, 461b; V, 295b; VI, 125b, 353b
Gülek Boghaz ii, 1135b – II, 1162a
Gulia, Dimitri i, 101b – I, 104b
Gulistān i, 241b, 680a, 1212b; ii, 839a, **1135b**; iv, 392b, 394b; x, 88b – I, 249a, 701a, 1249a; II, 858b, **1162a**; IV, 409a, 411a; X, 96a
Gulistān (treaty/traité) v, 495b, 657a – V, 498b, 661a
Gülkhāne i, 74b; ii, 147b, **1135b** – I, 77a; II, 152a, **1162b**
Gülkhāne Decree/Décret de vi, 285b – VI, 270b
Gulkunda → Golkonḍā
Güllü (Agop Vartovian) vi, 758a, 759a – VI, 747b, 748a
Gülnūsh Sulṭān iv, 233b, 1100a – IV, 244a, 1131a
Gulpāyagān ii, **1135b**; vi, 14a – II, **1162b**; VI, 12b
Gulpāyagānī, Muḥammad Riḍāʾ (Āyatullāh) (XX) vi, 553b; vii, 762b – VI, 538a; VII, 764a
Gulrukh Bēgum bint Mīrzā Kāmrān (XVI) iv, 523b; vii, 133a, 134a – IV, 546a; VII, 135a, 136a
Gulshanī, Ibrāhīm b. Muḥammad (1534) ii, 345b, **1136a**; iii, 393a; iv, 991b – II, 355b, **1162b**; III, 405b; IV, 1024a
Gulshanī Ṣarūkhānī (XV) ii, **1137b** – II, **1164b**
Gülshaniyya ii, 1137b; vi, 886a – II, 1164b; VI, 877b
Gülshehrī (1317) ii, **1138a**; v, 173a; viii, 972a – II, **1164b**; V, 170b; VIII, 1006b
Gulshīrī, Hūshang v, 201a – V, 198a
Gūm ii, **1138b**; iv, 784b – II, **1165b**; IV, 816a
Gūmāl (Gomal) s, **329b** – S, **329a**
Gumi, Abū Bakr b. Maḥmūd (1992) x, 122b – X, 132a
Gümrük → Maks
Gumukh → Kemākh
Gümüldjine s, **329b** – S, **329a**
Gümüshāne, Gümüshkhāne i, 645b, 1128b; ii, **1139a**; v, 966a, 977a – I, 666a, 1162b; II, **1166a**; V, 970a
Gümüshkhānewī, Shaykh Ḍiyāʾ al-Dīn (1894) vii, 937a – VII, 937b
Gümüshtegin b. Dānishmend, Amīr Ghāzī (1134) i, 466a, b, 664b, 983a, 1276b; ii, 110b, 1139b; vi, 231a, 506b – I, 480a, 684a, 1013b, 1316a; II, 113a, 1166a; VI, 224b, 492a
Gunabādī, Sulṭān ʿAlī Shāh (Niʿmat Allāhī) (1909) i, 841a; viii, 47a – I, 864b; VIII, 47b
Gunābādīs x, 327b – X, 352a
Gunābādiyya iv, 51b – IV, 54b
Gunbad-i ʿAlawiyān (Hamadān) (1220) vii, 12b – VII, 13b
Gunbad-i Ghaffāriyya vi, 501b – VI, 487a
Gunbadh → Ḳubba
Gunbadh-i Ḳābūs ii, **1139b**, 1141b; iv, 6b, 358a – II, **1166a**, 1168b; IV, 7a, 373b
Gunḍāfa, Banū vi, 743a – VI, 732b
Güneri Bey i, 703a; iv, 620b, 621a, b; v, 677a – I, 724a; IV, 645a, b, 646a; V, 682a
Güntekin, Reşat Nuri → Reshād Nūrī
Gunzalī → Khunzal
Gūr → Fīrūzābād
Gura vi, 643a – VI, 628a
Gūrān ii, **1139b**; iii, 292a, 1109a; v, 168b – II, **1166b**; III, 301a, 1136a; V, 166a
Gūran, Shaykh Abu 'l-Fatḥ (1536) s, **331b** – S, **331a**

Gūrānī, Sharaf al-Dīn (1488) ii, **1140b** – II, **1167b**
Gūrānī language/langue i, 262b, 840a, 863b; ii, 1140a; iii, 1261a – I, 270b, 863b, 887b; II, 1167a; III, 1293b
Gurāra → Gourara
Gurčānī s, **331b** – S, **331a**
Gurdjistān → Kurdj
Gurdjü ʿAbd al-Nabī iv, 766a – IV, 796b
Gürdjü Meḥmed Nedjib Pasha (1850) v, 257a; vi, 68a – V, 255a; VI, 66a
Gürdjü Muṣṭafā Pasha iv, 723a – IV, 752a
Gurgān i, 3b, 40a; ii, 253a, 746a, 1139b, **1141a**; iii, 501b; iv, 6b, 10a, 19a; vi, 66a, 115b, 130b, 334b, 336a, 415b, 493a, b, 494a, 495a, 539a, 726b, 780a; s, 13a, 86b, 235a, 277a, 298a, 326b, 356b – I, 4a, 41b; II, 260b, 764b, 1166b, **1168a**; II, 519a; IV, 7a, 10b, 20b; VI, 64a, 113a, 128b, 319a, 320a, 400b, 478b, 479a, b, 480a, b, 523b, 715b, 770a; S, 13b, 86b, 235a, 277a, 297b, 326a, 356b
Gurgandj i, 120b, 456a, b; ii, 2a, 43b, 571b, **1141b**; iv, 1061b, 1063b, 1064a, b, 1066a; v, 858a; vi, 65b, 340a; x, 88b, 892b; s, 246a, 280b – I, 124a 469a, b; II, 2a, 44a, 586a, **1168b**; IV, 1093a, 1095a, b, 1096a, 1098a; V, 865a; VI, 63b, 324a; X, 96a, ; S, 246a, 280b
Gurgānī → Djurdjānī
Gurgānī, Abu ʾl-Haytham iv, 60b – IV, 64a
Gurgānī, Fakhr al-Dīn Asʿad (XI) ii, **1142b**; iv, 62b; vi, 632b, 833a; viii, 100a; s, 108a – II, **1169b**; IV, 66a; VI, 617b, 823a; VIII, 102a; S, 107a
Gurgīn, King/le roi → Giorgi
Gurgīn Khān i, 229a; iii, 603b; v, 493b – I, 236a; III, 624b; V, 496b
Gurgīn Milād v, 661a, 670a – V, 666b, 675b
Gurieli i, 1108b – I, 1141b
Gūrjara-Pratīhāras → al-Djurz
Gūrkhān (Kara-Khitāy) i, 987a, 11311a; ii, 791b, **1143a**; iii, 1114b; iv, 581b, 582a; vii, 410a – I, 1017b, 1351b; II, 810b, **1170b**; III, 1142a; IV, 605a, b; VII, 411a
Gürpinar → Ḥusayn Raḥmī
Gürsel, General/général ii, 433a, 646a – II, 444a, 662a
Gurush ii, 119a, b – II, 122a
Gurz v, 691b – V, 696b
Güwāhī (XVI) vi, 826b, 836a – VI, 817a, 826b
Guwākharz → Bākharz
Guwayn → Djuwayn
Gūyān → Djuwayn
Güyük b. Ögedey b. Činghiz Khān (Mongol Great Khān) (1248) i, 1105b; ii, 3a, 45b; vi, 77b, 524a; vii, 230a – I, 1139a; II, 3a, 46b; VI, 75a, 508b; VII, 232a
Guyum iv, 9b – IV, 10a
Güzel Ḥiṣār → Aydīn
Güzeldje Hisar → Anadolu Ḥiṣārī
Gūzgān → Djūzdjān
Gwādar i, 1282a; v, 684b; vi, 192b; s, **332a** – I, 1321a; V, 690a; VI, 176b; S, **331b**
Gwāliyār ii, **1143b**; iii, 995b; v, 1216a; vi, 49a, 53a, 65b, 127b, 535b; s, 331b – II, **1170b**; III, 1020a; V, 1206a; VI, 47b, 51a, 63b, 125b, 520a; S, 331a
Gwandu ii, **1144b**; vii, 435b – II, **1171b**; VII, 436b
Gwaris (Nigeria/-e) viii, 21a – VIII, 21a
Gwāṭar Bay s, 332b – S, 332a
Gyromancy → Raml

H

Hāʾ iii, **1a** – III, **1a**
Ḥāʾ iii, **2a** – III, **2a**
al-Habāʾa, Day of/Journée de s, 177a, 178a, b – S, 178a, 179a, b
al-Ḥabāb (1232) vi, 592b – VI, 577b
Ḥabāba (723) i, 1149a; ii, 428b, 1011b; iii, **2b**; iv, 821b – I, 1183b; II, 439b, 1035a; III, **2b**; IV, 854b
Ḥabābiḍ (Mārib) vi, 563a, b – VI, 548a, b
Habar Awal i, 1173a – I, 1208a
Ḥabash, Ḥabasha i, 39a, 44a, b, 80a, 84b, 102b, 111a, 286b, 547b, 561a, 763b, 991b; ii, 91a, 535b, 545a; iii, **2b**, 950b, 1137a; iv, 1088a; v, 116b, 950b, 1137a, 1250a; vi, 137b, 144b, 146b, 152a, b, 161a, 194a, 269b, 560a, 564a, b, 646b, 677b, 829b, 1002a ; viii, 808b; ix. 535b – I, 40a, 45b, 82b, 87a, 105a, 114b, 295b, 565a, 579a, 786b, 1022b; II, 93a, 548b, 558b; III, **3a**, 975b, 1165a; IV, 1119a; V, 119a, 1241a; VI, 136a, 143a, 145a, 150b, 151b, 154b, 178a, 254a, 545a, 549a, b, 631b, 664b, 820a, 840a, 994b; VIII, 835b; IX, 556a
Ḥabash (musician/musicien) s, 64a, 183a – S, 64b, 184b
Ḥabash ʿAmīd, Ḳuṭb al-Dīn (XIII) ii, 2b, 3b; viii, 893b – II, 2b, 3b; VIII, 924b
Ḥabash al-Ḥāsib al-Marwazī (IX) i, 159b; ii, 577a; iii, **8a**, 1137a; v, 85a; vi, 543a, 600a; vii, 29a; ix, 179b; x, 267a; s, 413b – I, 164a; II, 591b; III, **8b**, 1165a; V, 87a; VI, 527b, 584b; VII, 29a; IX, 185b; X, 284b; S, 413b
Ḥabash, Ikhtiyār al-Mulk Rashīd al-Dīn Abū Bakr (XIII) viii, 814b – VIII, 841b
Ḥabash Khān (XV) vi, 47a – VI, 45b
Ḥabasha i, 24b, 102a; ii, 244b, 940a; iii, **2b** – I, 25b, 105a; II, 251b, 962a; III, **3a**
Ḥabashat iii, **9a** – III, **9b**
Ḥabashī, Abū Shudjāʿ Yaḥyā (XI) vii, 489b – VII, 489a
Ḥabashī, Ḳaṣr vi, 295a – VI, 280b
al-Ḥabashī b. Muʿizz al-Dawla (X) vii, 485a – VII, 485a
Ḥabashī b. ʿUmar → Aḥmad b. ʿUmar
Ḥabaṭ iii, **10b** – III, **11a** → Ḥawṭa
Ḥabawnā i, 538a – I, 554b
Ḥabba iii, **10b** – III, **11a**
Habba Khātūn (XVI) s, **332a** – S, **332a**
al-Ḥabbāl, Abū Isḥāḳ (XI) viii, 707b – VIII, 727b
al-Habbāl al-Miṣrī s, 390b – S, 391a
Ḥabbān iii, **11a** – III, **11b**
Habbāniyya, Banū x, 4b – X. 4b
Habbāniyya, Lake/lac ii, 947b; iii, 1250b – II, 969b; III, 1283a
Ḥabbūs → Ḥabūs
Ḥabesh iii, **11a**; viii, 183b, 235a,b – III, **12a**; VIII, 186b, 240b, 241a
Ḥabeshī ʿAlī Agha (1678) vi, 991a – VI, 983b
Ḥabeshī Meḥmed Agha ii, 1088a; iii, 175b – II, 1113b; III, 179a
Ḥabīb b. ʿAbd al-Malik (VIII) iii, **11b** – III, **12b**
Ḥabīb b. Abī Thābit al-Kūfī (738) ix, 553a – IX, 575a
Ḥabīb b. Abī ʿUbayda al-Fihrī (VII) i, 86a, b, 990b; v, 367a; vi, 923a, ix, 584a, 753b; x, 848a – I, 88b, 89a, 1021b; V, 368a, VI, 915a; IX, 606b, 786b; X,
Ḥabīb b. Aws → Abū Tammām
Ḥabīb b. Gannūn (Benguennoun) (1864) vi, 250b – VI, 235a
Ḥabīb b. Ḥabīb b. Yazīd b. al-Muhallab (VIII) vi, 311b

– VI, 296b
Ḥabīb b. Maslama al-Fihrī (662) i, 325a, 635b, 636a, 660a, 1349a; ii, 276a, 456a, 678b; iii, **12b**, 20a; iv, 343b, 654b, 870b; v, 487b; vi, 230b; vii, 922a – I, 335b, 656b, 681a, 1389a; II, 284a, 468a, 695b; III, **13a**, 21a; IV, 358a, 681a, 904a; V, 490b; VI, 224b; VII, 922b
Ḥabīb b. al-Muhallab (VIII) vii, 359a – VII, 361b
Ḥabīb b. Murra (VIII) vii, 629b – VII, 629b
Ḥabīb b. Muẓāhir iii, 610a – III, 631a
Ḥabīb b. ʿUmar Tal i, 297a – I, 306a
Ḥabīb b. Yazīd b. al-Muhallab s, 41a – S, 41a
Ḥabīb Allāh b. Khalīl Allāh iv, 961b, 962a – IV, 994a
Ḥabīb Allāh II → Bačča-i Saḳaw
Ḥabīb Allāh Khān, Amīr (Afghanistān) (1919) i, 88a, 232a; iii, **13a**; v, 1079a; vi, 807a; s, 65b, 237b – I, 90b, 239b; III, **13b**; V, 1076b; VI, 797a; S, 66a, 237b
Ḥabīb Boulares (Bu 'l-ʿArīs) vi, 751b – VI, 740b
Ḥabīb Hassan Touma vi, 103a – VI, 100b
Ḥabīb Iṣfahānī iv, 72a – IV, 76a
Ḥabīb Khān Huwayda vi, 154b – VI, 152a
Ḥabīb al-Nadjdjār i, 517a; iii, **12b** – I, 532b; III, **13a**
Ḥabīb al-Raḥmān v, 803a – V, 809a
Ḥabīb Ṣāliḥ b. Ḥabīb ʿAlawī v, 655b, 656a – V, 660a
Ḥabīb Shāh s, 167a, 324b – S, 167a, 324a
Ḥabība bint Khāridja i, 109b – I, 112b
Ḥabība Saldjūḳ-Khātūn i, 1328a – I, 1368b
Ḥabībī i, 193a – I, 199a
Ḥabībīs iii, 12a – III, 12b
Hābīl wa-Ḳābīl i, 178a, 181a; iii, **13b**; iv, 724a – I, 183a, 186a; III, **14a**; IV, 753a
Hābil-oghlu i, 431b – I, 444a
Ḥābiṭiyya → Aḥmad b. Ḥābiṭ
Habitude → ʿĀda
Ḥabla Rud iv, 1030a – IV, 1061b
Habous → Waḳf
Ḥabsān → Djadjīra
Ḥabshī(s) ii, 816a, 1084b, 1129a; iii, **14a**, 419a, 422a, 631b; v, 687b; vi, 63a, 269a – II, 835b, 1110a, 1155b; III, **15a**, 432b, 436a, 652b; V, 692b; VI, 60b, 254a
al-Ḥabshī, Aḥmad b. Zayn (1732) i, 829b – I, 852b
Ḥabsiyya s, **333a** – S, **332b**
Habṭ vi, 741b – VI, 730b
Ḥabūda s, 338b – S, 338a
Ḥabūdīs s, 338b – S, 338a
Ḥabūs b. Ḥumayd iii, 688a – III, 709b
Ḥabūs b. Māksan ii, 516a, 1012b, 1015a; iv, 355a – II, 528b, 1036b, 1038b; IV, 370b
Ḥāč Ovasî → Mezö-Keresztes
Hacîlar s, 171b, 172a – S, 172a, b
al-Hada (plain(e)) vi, 160b – VI, 154b
Ḥadabas i, 536b – I, 553a
Ḥaḍāna iii, **16b** – III, **17b**
Hadanduwa i, 1158a,b; iv, 686b – I, 1192b, 1193a; IV, 714b
Ḥadārib i, 1157b, 1158a – I, 1192a,b
Ḥādārim vi, 734b – VI, 723b
Ḥadath iii, **19b** – III, **20b**
al-Ḥadath i, 1190b; iii, **19b**; v, 1239a; vi, 505b, 506a – I, 1225b; III, **20b**; V, 1229b; VI, 491a, b
Hadāyā ii, 146a – II, 150a
Ḥadd i, 382a, 383a; ii, 632a; iii, **20a**, 204b; iv, 770b, 771b; v, 730b, 731b – I, 393a, 394a; II, 648a; III, **21a**, 210a; IV, 801b, 802b; V, 735b, 736b
Hadda s, 237a – S, 237a
Ḥaddād, ʿAbd al-Masīḥ v, 1254b, 1255a, b – V, 1245b, 1246a, b
al-Ḥaddād, Abū Ḥafṣ vi, 225a – VI, 218b, 219a
Ḥaddād Banū iv, 540b – IV, 564a
Ḥaddād, Marie Anṭūn (XX) vii, 903a – VII, 903b
Ḥaddād, Nadjīb i, 597a – I, 616b
Ḥaddād, Niḳūlā (XX) vii, 903a – VII, 903b
Ḥaddād, Nudra v, 1254b, 1255a, b – V, 1245b, 1246a, b
Ḥaddād, al-Ṭāhir (1935) iv, 161a; s, **334a** – IV, 168a; S, 333b
Haddūḳa, A.H. ben v, 191a – V, 188a
Hadendoa → Bedja
Ḥādha s, 198b – S, 198b
Hadhbānīs (Kurd(e)s) v, 451b, 453b; vi, 499b – V, 454a, 456a; VI, 485a
Ḥadhf → Naḥw
Ḥadhw iv, 412a – IV, 430a
al-Hādī, Ibrāhīm b. ʿAlī b. Aḥmad vi, 113b – VI, 111b
al-Hādī ilā 'l-Ḥaḳḳ (ʿAbbāsid(e)) (786) i, 14a, 17b, 402b, 1034a, 1045b, 1298a; iii, 20a, **22a**, 29a, 231a, 232b, 617a, 742a, 996a; iv, 645a, 858b, 1164a; vi, 140b, 331a, b, 332a; s, 22a, 326b – I, 14a, 18a, 414a, 1065b, 1077a, 1338a; III, 21a, **23a**, 30b, 238a, 239b, 637b, 764b, 1021a; IV, 671b, 892a, 1196a; VI, 138b, 315b, 316a, b; S, 22b, 326a
al-Hādī ilā 'l-Ḥaḳḳ Yaḥyā al-Rassī (Zaydī) (911) i, 551b; iii, 617b; v, 1241a; vi, 433a, 435b, 436b, 439a; vii, 773a, 786a; s, **334b**, 358a – I, 569a; III, 638a; V, 1231b; VI, 418b, 421a, b, 422a, 424b; VII, 774b, 787b; S, **334b**, 358a
al-Hādī ʿIzz al-Dīn b. al-Ḥasan (Yemen) (XV) vii, 996a – VII, 997b
Hādī Sabzawārī → Sabzawārī
al-Ḥadīd iii, **22b**; iv, 819b; v, 964b, 966a, 967b, 971a, 978a, 1166b – III, **23b**; IV, 852a; V, 969a, 970b, 973b, 1156a, b
Ḥadīd → Nudjūm
Ḥadīd, Shaykh vi, 733b – VI, 722b
Ḥadīd (Djadīd) al-Ḳāra (Ḥudjūr) vi, 436b – VI, 422a
Ḥadīdī (XVI) iii, **22b** – III, **23b**
Ḥadīdīn, Banū vi, 733b – VI, 722b
al-Ḥādina iii, **23a** – III, **24a**
Ḥādir s, 48b – S, 49a
al-Ḥādira (VII) iii, **23a** – III, **24b**
Ḥadīth i, 25b, 258b, 326a, 410a, 566a, 589b, 1021a, b; ii, 71a, 125b, 448a, 729a, 889a; iii, **23b**, 369b, 435a; iv, 148a, b, 172a, 767b, 983b, 995a, 1107a, 1112a, 1135b; v, 1123b, 1132b, 1232a, b – I, 26b, 266b, 336a, 421b, 584b, 608b, 1052b, 1053a; II, 72a, 128b, 460a, 747b, 909b; III, **24b**, 381a, 449a; IV, 154a, b, 179b, 798a, 1016a, 1027b, 1138b, 1143b, 1167b; V, 1120a, 1128b, 1222b
—literature/littérature i, 59a, 60b, 106b, 158b, 273b; ii, 159a; iii, 927a – I, 61a, 62b, 109b, 163a, 281b; II, 164a; III, 951b
—scholars/spécialistes i, 104b, 129a, 143a, 272b, 275b, 485b, 791a, 1130a, 1296b; ii, 136a, 292b, 301a; iii, 82a, 821a, 848b, 860b, 874a – I, 107b, 133a, 147a, 280b, 284a, 500a, 814b, 1164b, 1336a; II, 139b, 300b, 309a; III, 84b, 844b, 872b, 884b, 898a
Ḥadīth Ḳudsī i, 88b; iii, **28b**, 101b; s, 83a – I, 91a; III, **30a**, 104a; S, 82b
Ḥadītha iv, 855b – IV, 888b
Ḥadītha b. al-Faḍl b. Rabīʿa (XIII) vii, 461b – VII, 461b
Ḥadīthat al-Furāt iii, **29b** – III, **31a**
Ḥadīthat al-Mawṣil iii, **29a** – III, **30b**
Ḥadīthat al-Nūra → Hadīthat al-Furāt
Hadiyya iii, 343a, 346b, 347b, 350a – III, 353a, 357a, 358a, 361a

Hadj → Ḥadjdj
Hadjar → al-Ḥasā
Hadjar (district) vi, 633b, 875a; vii, 374a, 570b – VI, 618b, 866a; VII, 375b, 571a
Hadjar (town/ville) iii, **29b** – III, **31a**
Ḥadjar (stone/pierre) iii, **29b**; iv, 1128b; v, 117b – III, **31a**; IV, 1160a; V, 120a
al-Hadjar, Djabal i, 536b – I, 552b
al-Ḥadjar al-Aswad i, 178a, 551b, 867a; ii, 453a; iv, 317a, b, 319a, b, 321b, 662a, b; v, 10a, 77b, 78a – I, 182b, 569a, 891b; II, 465a; IV, 331b, 332a, 333a, b, 335b, 688b, 689b; V, 10a, 79b, 80a
Ḥadjar Bādis i, 859b – I, 883b
Hadjar Ḥinū al-Zarīr iii, 208a; iv, 747a – III, 214a; IV, 777a
Ḥadjar Ismāʿīl vi, 165b – VI, 157b
Ḥadjar al-Nasr iii, **30b**; vii, 641b – III, **32a**; VII, 641a
Ḥadjar Shughlān vi, 507b – VI, 493a
Ḥadjar Tarbiyat vi, 486b – VI, 472b
Hadjarayn iii, **31a**; vi, 132b – III, **32b**; VI, 130b
al-Ḥadjarī 'l-Andalūsī, Aḥmad b. Ḳāsim (XVII) vii, 243b – VII, 245a
Hadjbūn al-Randāḥī, Abu 'l-ʿAbbās s, 112a – S, 111a
Ḥadjdj i, 178a, 443b; iii, **31b**, 927a, 1052b; iv, 320b, 322a; v, 424b, 897a, b, 1003a, 1004a; vi, 169a, 195a; vii, 65b – I, 182b, 456a; III, **33a**, 951b, 1078b; IV, 334b, 336b; V, 427a, 903b, 998b, 1000a; VI, 160a, 179b; VII, 66a
Ḥadjdj(ī) iii, 38b – III, 40a
al-Ḥadjdj ʿAmmār (XIX) viii, 399b – VIII, 413b
al-Ḥadjdj, Baʿl ii, 730a – II, 748b
al-Ḥadjdj al-ʿArbī v, 596b – V, 600a, b
al-Ḥadjdj Bashīr (1843) viii, 399b – VIII, 413b
al-Ḥadjdj al-Gharnāṭī ii, 901b – II, 922b
al-Ḥadjdj Ḥammūda (1787) iii, **38b** – III, **40a**
al-Ḥadjdj Masʿūd vi, 593b – VI, 578a
Ḥadjdj Muḥammad Ṭrīḳī iii, 247a – III, 254a
al-Ḥādjdj Sālim Suwarī (XV) ix, 757a – IX, 790a
al-Ḥadjdj ʿUmar b. Saʿīd Tāl (Tukulor) (1864) i, 297a, 303b; ii, 63a, 252b, 941b, 1132b; iii, **38b**, 107b, 289a; ix, 122a, 141b – I, 306a, 313a; II, 64a, b, 259b, 963b, 1159a,b; III, **40a**, 110a, 298a
Ḥadjdja vi, 436b – VI, 422a: IX, 126a, 146b
Ḥadjdjādj → Ḳutlugh Khāns
Ḥadjdjādj, Banū iv, 115b – IV, 120b
al-Ḥadjdjādj, Abū Djaʿfar (X) vii, 497a – VII, 497a
al-Ḥadjdjādj b. ʿAbd al-Malik b. Marwān ii, 280b, 304b, 480a; iii, 73a, 573b – II, 289a, 313a, 492a; III, 75b, 593a
Ḥadjdjādj b. Arṭāt i, 896b – I, 923a
Ḥadjdjādj b. Hurmuz i, 512b – I, 528a
Ḥadjdjādj b. Yūsuf b. Maṭar vii, 83a, 1050a; viii, 550b, 559a; s, 411b – VII, 84a; VIII, 568b, 577a; S, 412a
al-Ḥadjdjādj b. Yūsuf al-Ḥāsib (IX) iii, **43a**, 1136b, 1138b – III, **45a**, 1164b, 1166b
al-Ḥadjdjādj b. Yūsuf al-Thaḳafī (714) i, 42b, 54a, 55b, 76b, 77b, 105a, 142a, 482a, 485, 550a, 690b, 714a, 810b, 1005b, 1094b; ii, 27a, 195b, 197a,b, 561b, 788b; iii, **39b**, 247b, 649a, 715a,b, 716a, 717a, 841b, 970a, 1255a, 1267a; iv, 15a, 99b, 319b, 531b, 724b, 753a, 1075b, 1076a; v, 541a, 735b, 947b; vi, 44b, 139a, 147a, 336b, 656a, 660b, 669a, b, 691a, 967b; vii, 114b, 357b, 359a, 405b, 652b, 1030b; x, 816a, 843b; s, 230b, 243a, 354b – I, 43b, 56a, 57a, 79a, 79b, 108a, 146b, 496a, 499a, 567b, 711b, 735b, 833b, 1036a, 1127a; II, 27b, 202a, 203a, 204a, 574b, 807a; III, **41b**, 254b, 670b, 737b, 738a, 739a, b, 865b, 994b, 1287b, 1300a; IV, 16a, b, 104a, 333b, 554b, 753b, 783b, 1107b; V, 545b, 740b, 951b; VI, 43a, 137b, 145b, 320b, 642a, 646a, b, 655b, 678b, 959b; VII, 116b, 359b, 361a, 406b, 652a, 1033a; X, ; S, 230b, 243a, 354b
Ḥadjdjādj Sulṭān b. Terken Khātūn (Kirmān) (XIII) vi, 482b – VI, 468b
Ḥadjdjām → Faṣṣād
al-Ḥadjdjām → al-Ḥasan b. Muḥammad b. al-Ḳāsim (Idrīsid(e))
Ḥadjdjī I, al-Muẓaffar ii, 24a; iii, 48a, 239b – II, 24b; III, 50a, 246b
Ḥadjdjī II, al-Malik al-Ṣāliḥ Ṣalāḥ al-Dīn (Mamlūk) (1412) i, 1050b, 1051a; ii, 159a; vii, 171b – I, 1082a,b; II, 164a; VII, 173b
Ḥādjdjī ʿAbd Allāh vi, 354a – VI, 338b
Ḥādjdjī Aḥmad iv, 1082b – IV, 1114a
Ḥādjdjī ʿAlī-ḳulī Khān Bakhtiyarī s, 291a – S, 290b
Ḥādjdjī ʿAlī Pasha i, 268a, 394a – I, 276b, 405a
Ḥādjdjī ʿårif Beg (Haci Ārif Bey) (1885) ix, 418a – IX, 431b
Ḥādjdjī Bayrām Walī (1429) i, 312b, 509b, 511a, 869a, 1137a, 1202a; ii, 542b; iii, **43a**; vi, 226a; s, 282b – I, 322b, 525a, 526b, 893b, 1171b, 1237b; II, 556a; III, **45a**; VI, 219b; S, 282b
Ḥādjdjī Beg → Riḍwān Begovič
Ḥādjdjī Bektāsh Walī (XIII) i, 299a, 1161b, 1162a; ii, 20b; iii, 315a; iv, 811b; viii, 12a – I, 308a, 1196a, 1197a; II, 20b; III, 324b; IV, 844b; VIII, 12a
Ḥādjdjī al-Dabīr (XVII) s, **335b** – S, **335a**
Ḥādjdjī Dāwūd ii, 87b; v, 296b – II, 89b; V, 288a
Ḥādjdjī Djābir Khān (Kaʿb) (XIV) vii, 675a – VII, 675a
Ḥadjdjī Gerey → Ḥadjdjī Girāy
Ḥādjdjī Ghulām Ḥusayn (1840) vii, 454b – VII, 455a
Ḥadjdjī Girāy (1466) i, 1252b; ii, 44b, 1112b, 1113a; iii, **43b**; iv, 868b; v, 137a- I, 1290b; II, 45a, 1138b, 1139a; III, **45b**; IV, 902a; V, 140a
Ḥādjdjī Hāshim s, 336a – S, 335b
Ḥādjdjī Ibrāhīm Khān Kalāntar (XIX) iii, 1106a; iv, 391b, 392a, 394a, 476a, 706a; v, 835a; s, **336a** – III, 1133b; IV, 408a, b, 410b, 497a, 734b; V, 841a, b; S, **335b**
Ḥādjdjī Ilbegi (XIV) ii, 291b; vi, 290b; vii, 593a – II, 299b; VI, 276a; VII, 592b
Ḥādjdjī Ismāʿīl Agha i, 284b – I, 293a
Ḥādjdjī Kamāl (Čanderī) (XV) vi, 52b; vii, 531b – VI, 51a; VII, 531b
Ḥādjdjī Ḳawām al-Dīn Shīrāzī s, 336a – S, 335b
Ḥādjdjī Khalīfa → Kātib Čelebi
Ḥādjdjī Khān (Mālwā) (XVI) vi, 310a – VI, 295a
Ḥādjdjī Maḥmūd ʿAlī s, 336a – S, 335b
Ḥādjdjī Mawlá iv, 922a – IV, 955a
Ḥādjdjī Mīrzā Āghāsī i, 833b; iii, 554b; iv, 393a, b, 394a, 395b, 978b; v, 876a, 1222a – I, 856b; III, 573b; IV, 410a, 411a, 412b, 1011a; V, 882a, 1212b
Ḥādjdjī Mīrzā ʿAlī Khān → Faḳīr of/de Ipi
Ḥādjdjī Muḥammad i, 1124a – I, 1158a
Ḥadjdjī Mullā Sulṭān Gunābādī (1909) x, 397a – X, 426a
Ḥādjdjī Mullā Taḳi Barakānī i, 304b – I, 314a
Ḥādjdjī Muṣliḥ al-Dīn (XVII) vii, 349a – VII, 351a
Ḥādjdjī Nasīm Oghlu → Nasīm Oghlu
Ḥādjdjī Niʿmat Allāh → Niʿmat Allāh
Ḥādjdjī Pasha (XV) i, 299b; iii, **45a** – I, 309a; III, **46b**
Ḥādjdjī Raʾīs Djamāl, Āl (Mānd) (1725) vi, 384b – VI, 369a
Ḥādjdjī Ṣāḥib Turangzay vii, 220b – VII, 222a

Ḥādjdjī Shādgeldī i, 432a – I, 444a
Ḥādjdjī Shāh b. Yūsuf Shāh (Yazd) (XIV) vii, 820a – VII, 822a
Ḥadjdjī Shaykh ʿAbbās ʿAlī Kayman (XX) x, 397b – X, 426a
Ḥadjdjilu iv, 577b – IV, 601a
Ḥādjdjiyān vi, 384b – VI, 369a
Hadji → Ḥādjdjī
Hadji Abdul Malik Karim Amrullah → Hamka
Ḥādjib i, 5b, 94a; ii, 507b; iii, **45a**, 360a; iv, 421b; s, **336b** – I, 6a, 96b; II, 520a; III **47a**, 371b; IV, 439b; S, **336a**
Ḥādjib b. Zurāra (VII) ii, 354a; iii, **49a**; v, 640b – II, 363b; III, **51a**; V, 644b
Ḥādjib b. Begtoghdï (1035) vi, 780b – VI, 770a
Ḥādjib al-Tāʿī iii, 650b – III, 671b
Ḥādjib Tatar, amīr (XI) x, 897b – X,
Hadjiewad → Karagöz
Ḥādjīpūr vi, 47a – VI, 45b
al-Ḥādjir s, 198b – S, 198b
Hādjir, Banū iii, **49b** – III, **51b**
Ḥādjiz i, 940b – I, 969b
Ḥādjiz b. ʿAwf i, 812a – I, 835a
Ḥādjō Agha i, 871b – I, 895b
Ḥadjr i, 993b; iii, **50a** – I, 1024a; III, **52a**
Ḥadjr, Wādī s, 337a – S, 337a
al-Ḥadjūn (Mecca) vi, 122b, 123a – VI, 120b
Hadjw iii, 358b – III, 369b
Ḥadn i, 536a – I, 552b
al-Ḥaḍr (Hatra) i, 196b; iii, **50b**; vi, 921b – I, 202a; III, **52b**; VI, 913a
Ḥaḍra iii, **51a**; iv, 942a; s, 93a – III, **53a**; IV, 975a; S, 93a
al-Ḥadrabī i, 782b – I, 805b
Ḥaḍramawt i, 39b, 55a, 110b, 257a, 538a, 546b, 547b, 549b, 551b, 554a, 780b, 828b; iii, **51b**; vi, 132b, 191b, 194a, 473a, b; s, **336b**, 420b – I, 40b, 57a, 113b, 265a, 555a, 563b, 565a, 567a, 569a, 571b, 804a, 851b; III, **53b**; VI, 130b, 175b, 178a, 459a, b; S, **336b**, 420b
Ḥaḍramawt, Banū vi, 472a – VI, 458a
Ḥaḍramawt b. Ḥimyar s, 337a – S, 337a
al-Ḥaḍramī, Abū ʿAbd Allāh (XIV) vi, 356a – VI, 340a
al-Ḥaḍramī, Ḳāḍī Muḥammad b. al-Ḥasan al-Mūrādī (1095) vii, 587b – VII, 587b
Ḥaḍrat Bēgam i, 296a – I, 305a
Ḥaḍrat Maḥall, Bēgam i, 953b – I, 983a
Ḥaḍrat al-mallūk iv, 382b – IV, 399b
Ḥaḍrat Mīrzā Bashīr al-Dīn Maḥmūd Aḥmad i, 302a – I, 311a
Ḥaḍrat Tādj Faḳīh (1180) vi, 110a – VI, 394b
Ḥaḍrat-i Rāz iv, 51b – IV, 54b
Ḥaḍūr Shuʿayb i, 536a; iii, **53a** – I, 552b; III, **55a**
Hady iii, **53b** – III, **55b**
Hadyā i, 176b; iii, 3b – I, 181a; III, 3b
al-Ḥāf b. Ḳuḍāʿa b. Mālik b. Ḥimyar b. Ḳaḥṭān (Mahra) vi, 81b – VI, 79b
Ḥafar al-Bāṭin → Bāṭin
Ḥaffār (Hafar) iv, 675a; v, 65b, 66a – IV, 702b; V, 67b
al-Ḥāfī → Bishr
Hafik v, 248a – V, 246a
Ḥāfiẓ → Ḳurʾān
Ḥāfiẓ Tanïsh v, 859b – V, 866b
al-Ḥāfiẓ (Fāṭimid(e)) (1146) i, 814b, 939b, 1215a; ii, 170b, 855a, 857b; iii, **54b**; iv, 200a, b; vii, 163a – I, 837b, 968,b, 1251a; II, 175b, 875a, 877a; III, **56b**; IV, 209a; VII, 164b
Ḥāfiẓ, ʿAbd al- (ʿAlawī) (1937) i, 58a, 357b, 1281b; ii, 820a, 1116a; iii, **62a**, 562b; v, 890b, 1193b; vi, 249a, 595b, 596b; vii, 39a; s, 47b – I, 59b, 368a, 1320b; II, 839b, 1142b; III, **64b**, 581b; V, 897a, 1183b; VI, 233a, 580b, 581b; VII, 39b; S, 48a
al-Ḥāfiẓ, Mawlāy → Ḥāfiẓ, ʿAbd al-Ḥāfiẓ, Mullā s, 292a – S, 291b
Ḥāfiẓ, Shams al-Dīn Muḥammad Shīrāzī (1389) i, 153a, 1301a; ii, 439b, 760b, 1034a; iii, **55a**; iv, 56b, 65b, 909b; v, 671a; vi, 956b; vii, 458b, 480b, 821b; s, 35a, 415a – I, 157b, 1341a; II, 451a, 779a, 1058a; III, **57b**; IV, 59b, 69a, 942b; V, 676b; VI, 948b; VII, 458b, 480b, 823a; S, 35a, 415a
Ḥāfiẓ ʿAbd Allāh i, 1023a – I, 1054b
Ḥāfiẓ-i Abrū (1430) i, 607a, 1131a; iii, **57b**, 574b; iv, 1082a – I, 627a, 1165b; III, **59b**, 594a; IV, 1113a
Ḥāfiẓ ʿAfīfī Pasha iii, 515b; s, 301a – III, 533a; S, 301a
Ḥāfiẓ Agha i, 289b – I, 298a
Ḥāfiẓ Aḥmad, Mawlawī iv, 626a – IV 650b
Ḥāfiẓ Aḥmed Agha (XVIII) viii, 570b – VIII, 589a
Ḥāfiẓ Aḥmed Pasha (1632) i, 4a, 962b; ii, 635a, 750b; iii, **58a**; iv, 483b; v, 33a, 34a, b, 458a; vii, 598a – I, 4a, 992a; II, 651a, 769a; III, **60b**; IV, 504b; V, 34a, 35a, b, 460b; VII, 597b
Ḥāfiẓ al-Asad v, 1049a – V, 1045b
Ḥāfiẓ al-Dimashḳī → Ibn ʿAsākir
Ḥāfiẓ al-Dīn → al-Nasafī
Ḥāfiẓ Djāllandharī (1982) iii, 119b; vi, 838b – III, 122a; VI, 829a
Ḥāfiẓ Djawnpūrī i, 1284a – I, 1323b
Ḥāfiẓ Ghulām Rasūl Shawḳ ii, 221b – II, 228b
Ḥāfiẓ Ibrāhīm, Muḥammad (1932) i, 597b; iii, **59a**; iv, 159b, 967b; vi, 113b, 414a, 538b, 955b; s, 57b – I, 617a; III, **61b**; IV, 166b, 999b; VI, 111a, 399a, 523a, 948a; S, 58a
Ḥāfiẓ Ismāʿīl Haḳḳī ii, 637b, 698b, 699b – II, 653b, 716a, 717b
Ḥāfiẓ Muṣṭafā s, 282b – S, 282a
Ḥāfiẓ ʿOthmān (1699) iv, 1125a; vii, 905a – IV, 1157a; VII, 906a
Ḥāfiẓ Raḥmat Khān (Rohilla) (1774) i, 1042b, 1043a; iii, **59b**; vii, 707a; viii, 426b, 572b – I, 1074b; III, **62a**; VII, 708a; VIII, 440b, 591a
Ḥāfiẓ Ramaḍān iii, 515b – III, 533a
Ḥāfiẓ al-Samarḳandī, Abū al-Layth Naṣr (X) → Abu 'l-Layth
Ḥāfiẓ sh. Äbdusämätaw vi, 770a – VI, 759a
Ḥāfiẓ Tanïsh s, 227b, 340a – S, 227b, 339b
Ḥāfiẓ Wahba, Shaykh (XX) vi, 153a, b, 155b, 159b, 161a – VI, 151b, 152a, 154a, b
Ḥāfiẓa Maryam umm ʿInāyat Allāh Khān (XVIII) vi, 131b – VI, 129b
Ḥāfiẓābād iii, **62b** – III, **65a**
Ḥāfiẓī, Mawlūd b. Mawhūb (XX) viii, 902a,b – VIII, 932b, 933a
Ḥāfiẓiyya iv, 200b – IV, 209a, b
Ḥafiẓ-uddīn iv, 505a – IV, 526b
al-Ḥafnāwī Muḥammad b. Sālim (1767) viii, 399a – VIII, 413a
Ḥafrak iii, **63a** – III, **65b**
Ḥafṣ b. Sulaymān → Abū Salama
Ḥafṣ b. Sulaymān (796) i, 707a; iii, **63a** – I, 728a; III, **65b**
Ḥafṣ al-Fard, Abū ʿAmr (IX) iii, **63b**; s, 88b, 225b – III, **66a**; S, 88b, 225b
Ḥafṣa bint al-Ḥādjdj (1190) iii, **66a** – III, **68b**
Ḥafṣa bint ʿUmar b. al-Khaṭṭāb (665) i, 308a; ii, 414b; iii, **63b**; vi, 575b, 652a – I, 317b; II, 425a; III, **66a**; VI, 560a, 637b
Ḥafṣid(e)s i, 92b, 121b, 122b, 124b, 155a, 445b, 533a, 770b, 863a, 1027b, 1046a, 1148b, 1176b, 1205b,

1246b, 1341a; ii, 145a, 146a, 307b, 459b, 463b, 537a, 1077b; iii, 38b, **66a**; iv, 338a; v, 530b, 626a, b, 1190a, 1247a; vi, 216b, 281a, 355a, 404a, 572b, 593b, 728b, 742b; vii, 1023b; s, 93a, b, 111b, 307b – I, 95b, 125a, 126a, 128a, 159a, 458a, 549b, 793b, 887a, 1059a, 1078a, 1183a, 1211b, 1241a, 1284b, 1381b; II, 149a, b, 316b, 471b, 475b, 550b, 1102b; III, 40a, **68b**; IV, 352b; V, 531a, 630a, 1180a, 1237b; VI, 200b, 266a, 339b, 388b, 557b, 578a, 717b, 732a; VII, 1025b; S, 92b, 93a, 111a, 307a
Ḥafsiyya iii, 660a – III, 681a
Haft Gunbad vi, 127b – VI, 125b
Haft-Lang i, 955b; iii, 1105a,b; v, 825b – I, 985a; III, 1132b; V, 832a
Haft Sīn vi, 528b – VI, 513a
Hagar iv, 184b, 185a – IV, 193a
Haggada iv, 307b, 308a – IV, 321b
Ḥāḥā, Banū iii, **69b**; vi, 741a, b, 742a, b, 743a, b – III, **72a**; VI, 730b, 731a, b, 732a, b, 733a
al-Ḥāḥī, ʿAbd Allāh b. Saʿīd (1602) x. 346a – X, 372a
Ḥāḥiyyūn iii, 339a – III, 349a
Haifa → Ḥayfā
Ḥāʾik → Libās
Ḥāʾik s, **340b** – S, **340b**
al-Ḥāʾik, Muḥammad (XVIII) iii, **70a** – III, **72b**
Ḥāʾil → Ḥāyil
Ḥāʾir i, 535b, 613b; iii, **71a** – I, 552a, 633b; III, **73b**
al-Ḥāʾir (Nadjd) vi, 191b; ix, 739a – VI, 175b; IX, 771a
Ḥāʾirī, ʿAbd al-Karīm Yazdī (1937) iv, 1028b; vi, 553a, b; vii, 919a; s, 157b, 158a, **342a** – IV, 1060b; VI, 537b, 538a; VII, 919b; S, 158a, **341b**
Ḥaʾirī, Mīrzā Muḥammad Taḳī (XX) vi, 553a – VI, 537b
Ḥāʾiṭ al-ʿAdjūz iii, **71a** – III, **73b**
Haji, M.K. (Mappila) vi, 462b – VI, 448a
Haji Miskin (Padri) (XIX) viii, 238a – VIII, 243b
Hajira Begam (XX) vi, 489a – VI, 475a
Hajira Masroor (XX) vi, 489b – VI, 475b
Ḥaḳāʾiḳ iii, **71b**, 134a – III, **74a**, 136b
Ḥaḳāḳiyya iv, 668a – IV, 695b
Ḥakam iii, **72a** – III, **74b**
al-Ḥakam I b. Hishām (Umayyad(e), Cordova) (822) i, 11a, 12b; ii, 1038a; iii, **73b**; iv, 216b; vi, 139b, 568a; vii, 160b; x, 849b; s, 82a – I, 11a, 12b; II, 1062a; III, **76a**; IV, 226a; VI, 138a, 553a; VII, 162a; X, ;S, 81b
al-Ḥakam II al-Mustanṣir bi-'llāh (Umayyad(e), Cordova) (976) i, 156b, 494a, 498b, 601b, 628a, 864b, 950a, 1088a, 1291a; ii, 956a, 957a; iii, 30b, 46a, **74b**, 762b; v, 71b, 511a, 1119a; vi, 198a, 199a, 431a, b, 432a, 728a; vii, 208a, 487a, 569b; viii, 632a; ix, 740b; x, 852a – I, 161a, 509a, 513b, 621a, 649a, 889a, 979a, 1120b, 1330b; II, 978a, 979a; III, 32b, 48a, **77a**, 785b; V, 73b, 514b, 1115b; VI, 182b, 183b, 416b, 417a, b, 717a; VII, 208b, 486b, 570b; VIII, 651a; IX, 773a; X,
al-Ḥakam b. ʿAbdal (VII) iii, **72b**; s, 52a – III, **75a**; S, 52b
al-Ḥakam b. Abi 'l-ʿĀṣ ii, 811b; vi, 622b – II, 831a; VI, 607b
Hakam b. ʿAmr al-Ghifarī ii, 1072b – II, 1097a
al-Ḥakam b. Ḳanbar (VIII) iii, **73a**; vii, 694b – III, **75b**; VII, 694b
al-Ḥakam b. al-Muṭṭalib b. ʿAbd Allāh b. al-Muṭṭalib (VIII) vi, 381a – VI, 365a
Ḥakam b. Saʿd (1287) ii, 516b – II, 529b
Ḥakam b. Saʿd, Banū → Tihāma
Ḥakam b. Saʿīd al-Ḳazzāz iii, 496a – III, 513a
al-Ḥakam b. al-Ṣalt (VII) vii, 394b – VII, 396a
al-Ḥakam b. ʿUtayba s, 129b – S, 129a
al-Ḥakam b. al-Walīd II iii, 990b – III, 1015a
al-Ḥakam Abū Marwān I s, 103b – S, 103a
Ḥakam al-Wādī (singer/chanteur) (VIII) vii, 798a – VII, 800a
al-Ḥakamī → Abū Nuwās; al-Djarrāḥ b. ʿAbd Allāh; ʿUmāra b. ʿAlī
Hakari → Ḥakkārī
Ḥakhām, Simon iv, 310b – IV, 324b
Ḥaḳīḳa iii, **75a**, 1240b; v, 1261a, 1262a – III, **77b**, 1272b; V, 1252b, 1253a
Ḥaḳīḳat, Shāh Ḥusayn (XIX) vii, 475a – VII, 474b
Ḥakīm → Ṭabīb
Ḥakīm, Banu 'l- viii, 616a – VIII, 635a
Ḥakīm, Mīrzā → Muḥammad Ḥakīm
al-Ḥākim, Tawfīḳ i, 598a, b; v, 189a, b, 191b, 192b – I, 617b, 618a; V, 186b, 187a, 188b, 189b
al-Ḥakīm I bi-Amr Allāh (ʿAbbāsid(e), Cairo/le Caire) (1302) ii, 966a, iii, 679a; iv, 944b; vi, 322a; vii, 167b, 729b – II, 988a; III, 701a; IV, 977b; VI, 306b; VII, 169b, 730a
al-Ḥakīm bi-Amr Allāh (Fāṭimid(e)) (1021) i,620a, 814b, 816a, 1029a, 1042a, 1141a, 1218a; ii, 125b, 126b, 127a, 136b, 169b, 229a, 232b, 483b, 495b, 631b, 854a, 855a, 857a, 859b, 911b; iii, **76b**, 130b, 154a; iv, 199a, 944a; v, 91b, 327b, 1125b; vi, 148b, 198a, 199b, 366b, 367a, 600b, 626a, 650a, 653a, 663b, 665b, 671b, 672b, 673b; vii, 162a, 295a, 482b, 510a; s, 136a, 267b, 323a – I, 640b, 837b, 839b, 1060b, 1073b, 1175b, 1254b; II, 129a, 130a,b, 140a, 174b, 236a, 239a, 496a, 508a, 647b, 874a, 875a, 877a, 879a, 932b; III, **79a**, 133a, 157b; IV, 207b, 977a; V, 94a, 327b, 1122a; VI, 147a, 182a, 183b, 351a, 585b, 611a, 635a, 638b, 649b, 651b, 653b 658a, b, 660a; VII, 163b, 297a, 482a, 510a; S, 135b, 267a, 322b
Ḥakīm b. Djabala al-ʿAbdī vi, 193a – VI, 177a
Ḥakīm b. Ḥizām i, 151b; iv, 898b – I, 155b; IV, 931b
Ḥakīm Abu 'l-Fatḥ (1588) vii, 341a; viii, 123b – VII, 342b; VIII, 126b
Ḥakīm Adjmal Khān (Dihlī) (1886) vi, 488b – VI, 474b
Ḥakīm Ata (1186) i, 299a; iii, **76b**; x, 250a – I, 308a; III, **78b**; X, 269a
Ḥakīm ʿAyn al-Mulk i, 856b, – I, 880a
Ḥakīm-Bashi̊ → Hekīm – Dashi̊
al-Ḥakīm al-Djushāmī (1101) s, 14b, 90b, **343a** – S, 14b, 90a, **342b**
Ḥakīm Ghulām Nabī (XIX) vii, 555a – VII, 555b
Ḥakīm Idrīs → Bidlīsī, Idrīs
Ḥakīm Maysarī iv, 63a; vi, 833b – IV, 66b; VI, 824a
al-Ḥakīm al-Naysābūrī, Ibn al-Bayyiʿ (1014) ii, 136a; iii, 25a, 27a, 28a, **82a**; viii, 63a – II, 139b; III, 26a, 28b, 29b, **84b**; VIII, 64b
Ḥakīm Rukna Kāshī (XVI) x, 164b – X, 177a
al-Ḥakīm al-Shahīd iii, 163a – III, 166b
al-Ḥakīm al-Tirmidhī (930) vi, 821a; viii, 746b, 747a – VI, 811a; VIII, 768a
Ḥakīmoff, Karīm Khān (XX) vi, 153b – VI, 152a
al-Ḥaḳīr → Maysara
Ḥaḳīrī al-Ādharbāydjānī v, 1105b – V, 1101b
Ḥaḳḳ i, 60b, 275a; ii, 294b; iii, **82b** – I, 62b, 283b; II, 302b; III, **84b**
Ḥaḳḳ al-Dīn i, 763b – I, 786b
Hakkārī iii, **83a**, 1109a; v, 452b, 454b, 456b, 459b, 462b – III, **85b**, 1136b; V, 455a, 457a, 459a, 462b, 465a
al-Hakkārī, ʿAdī → ʿAdī b. Musāfir
al-Hakkārī, ʾAlāʿ al-Dīn ii, 966a; iii, 680a – II, 988a; III, 702a
al-Hakkārī, Ibn ʿAbd Allāh iv, 137a – IV, 143a
al-Hakkārī, ʿIsā iv, 613a – IV, 638a

Ḥaḳḳī → ʿAbd al-Ḥaḳḳ b. Sayf al-Dīn; Ibrāhīm Ḥaḳḳī; Ismāʿīl Ḥaḳḳī
Ḥaḳḳī, Maḥmūd Ṭāhir (XX) vii, 903a – VII, 903b
Ḥaḳḳī, Yaḥyā v, 190b, 191a, 192a – V, 187b, 188b, 189a
Ḥāl (attribut(e)) s, **343b** – S, **343a**
Ḥāl (grammar, grammaire) → Naḥw
Ḥāl, aḥwāl (Ṣūfī) i, 411a, 603b, 1088b; ii, 570a; iii, **83b** – I, 423a, 623a, 1121a; II, 584b; III, **85b**
Ḥalab i, 256a, 824b, 983b; ii, 795a; iii, **85a**, 120a, 129a,b, 130b, 212b, 1118b; v, 561a, 923b, 925b, 1211a; vi, 117b, 118b, 198a, 231a, b, 323a, 345b, 372b, 377b, 378b, 379a, b, 381b, 429a, 505b, 507b, 508b, 544a, 547b, 578a, 598a, 667a; viii, 127b, 729b; ix, 795a; s, 19a, 36a, 37b, 49a, 197a, 239a – I, 264a, 847b, 1014a; II, 814a; III, **87a**, 122b, 131b, 132a, 133a, 218b, 1146a; V, 566a, 929a, 931a, 1201a; VI, 115b, 116b, 182a, 225a, 307a, 329b, 357a, 362a, 363a, b, 364a, 365b, 366a, 414b, 491a, 493a, 494a, 528b, 532a, 563a, 583a, 653a; VIII, 130b, 750b; IX, 829a; S, 19a, 36b, 38a, 49b, 197a, 239a
—history/histoire i, 823a; iii, 695b – I, 846a; III, 717b
—institutions i, 1224a; ii, 83b, 424a; iii, 89a, 139b – I, 1260b; II, 85a, 435a; III, 91b, 142b
—monuments i, 830a, 1317b; iii, 87a, b, 88a, b; v, 1139a – I, 853a, 1358b; III, 89b, 90a, b, 91a; V, 1133a
Ḥalabdja ii, 371a – II, 381a
al-Ḥalabī, Abu 'l-Ṣalāḥ (XI) vii, 313a – VII, 315b
al-Ḥalabī, Abū 'l-Ṭayyib ʿAbd al-Munʿim b. Ghalbūn vi, 188b – VI, 172a
al-Ḥalabī, Aḥmad (1708) vi, 356b – VI, 340b
al-Ḥalabī, Burhān al-Dīn (1549) iii, **90a**, 163b, 711a – III, **92b**, 167a, 733b
al-Ḥalabī, Nūr al-Dīn (1635) iii, **90b** – III, **93a**
Ḥalaḳat Dimashḳ al-saghīra iii, 519a – III, 536b
Ḥalāl wa-Ḥarām → Sharīʿa
Ḥalam b. Shaybān (X) vii, 549a – VII, 549a
Halāward s, 125a – S, 124b
Ḥalbas al-Rabīʿī (Marand) (VII) vi, 504a – VI, 489b
Ḥālet Efendi (1822) i, 399a, 399b; ii, 209b; iii, **90b**, 628b; iv, 295a – I, 410b, 411a; II, 216a; III, **93a**, 649b; IV, 308b
Ḥaletī, ʿAzmi-zāde Muṣṭafā (1631) i, 826a; iii, **91b; viii,** 581b, 582a – I, 849a; III, **94a**; VIII, 600a, b
Ḥaletī ʿAlī Aʿlā, Ḥasan iv, 991b – IV, 1024a
Halevi, Judah iv, 304b – IV, 318a
Halevi, Moses ben Joseph iv, 305a – IV, 318b
al-Ḥalf iv, 687b, 689a – IV, 715b, 717a
Ḥalfāʾ iii, **92a** – III, **94b**
Ḥalfa al-Djadīda viii, 92b – VIII, 94b
al-Ḥalfawī, Ḳāsim (1591) vi, 350a – VI, 334b
Ḥālī → Bannāʾī
Ḥālī → Ḥaly
Ḥālī (ʿAligaṙh) vi, 612a – VI, 597a
Ḥālī, Alṭāf Ḥusayn (1914) i, 807b; iii, **93b**, 119b, 433a; iv, 170b; v, 202a, 962a; vi, 838a' vii, 662a, 668a; s, 74b, 106a, 107a, b – I, 851a; III, **96a**, 122a, 447a; IV, 178a; V, 199b, 966a; VI, 829a; VII, 661b, 668a; S, 75b, 105b, 106b, 107a
Halide Edīb → Khālide Edīb
al-Ḥalīfān → Tayyiʾ, Banū
Halikarnas Balîkcîsî (1973) v, 195a, 197a; s, **348b** – V, 192a, 194b; S, **348b**
Halil Kut → Khalīl Pasha
Halīladj iv, 357a; s, **349a** – IV, 372b; S, **349a**
Ḥalīm b. Muḥammad ʿAlī i, 142a; s, 296a – I, 146a; S, 296a
Ḥalīma iii, **94a** – III, **96b**
Ḥalīma bint Abī Dhuʾayb (VI) i, 957b; iii, **94a**; viii, 362b, 697b – I, 987a; III, **96b**; 375a, 717a
Ḥalīma Begī Āghā → ʿAlamshāh Begum
Ḥalīmī, Luṭf Allāh, Ḳāḍī (XV) iv, 526a; vii, 272a – IV, 548b; VII, 274a
Halḳ Fîrkasî → Khalḳ Fîrkasî
Ḥalḳ al-Wādī i, 281b; iii, **94b**; s, 80b – I, 290b; III, **97a**; S, 80b
Ḥalḳa (councils, conseils) i, 817a; ii, 141a; iii, **95a**; v, 1129a, 1134a, 1158b – I, 840a; II, 145a; III, **97b**; V, 1125b, 1129b, 1148a
Ḥalḳa (soldiers, soldats) i, 765b, 947a; iii, **99a**, 185b – I, 788b, 976a; III, **101b**, 189b
Ḥalḳa (sūfism(e)) → Taṣawwuf
Ḥalḳa (tactic/tactique) iii, 187b – III, 192a
Halkevi → Khalḳevi
Halkevleri i, 734b; ii, 596b – I, 756b; II, 611b
Halkodalarî ii, 596b; iv, 988a – II, 611b; IV, 1020b
al-Ḥallādj, al-Ḥusayn b. Manṣūr b. Maḥammā (922) i, 46a, 324b, 387b, 416a, 753a, 754a, 951a, 1128b; ii, 197b, 223b, 734a, 891b; iii, 83a, **99b**, 165b, 620a, 669b, 700a, 1207a; iv, 114b, 615b, 616b; v, 543b; vi, 279b; vii, 94b; s, 385b – I, 47a, 334b, 399a, 428a, 775b, 776b, 980a, 1163a; II, 204a, 230b, 752b, 912a; III, 85a, **102a**, 169a, 640b, 691a, 722a, 1237b; IV, 119b, 640a, 641a; V, 548a; VI, 264b; VII, 96b; S, 386a
Ḥallādjīn v, 559a – V, 564a
Ḥallādjiyya ii, 224b; iii, 103a, 823b – II, 231b; III, 105b, 847a
Ḥallāḳ s, **350a** – S, **350a**
al-Ḥallāniyya i, 535b; iii, 270a – I, 551b; III, 278a
Ḥālūmat al-ṭibāʿ al-tāmm iv, 260a – IV, 271b
Halvetiyye → Khalwatiyya
Ḥalwa → Ghidhāʾ
Ḥaly (Yaʿḳūb) iii, **104b**; vi, 150a – III, **106b**; VI, 148b
Ḥaly Abbas → ʿAli b. al-ʿAbbās
Haly Imrani → al-ʿImrānī, ʿAlī b. Aḥmad
Halys (river, fleuve) → Kîzîl-Irmāk
Ḥām b. Nūḥ iii, **104b**; v, 521a, b; vi, 411b – III, **107a**; V, 525a; VI, 396b
Ḥamā(h) → Ḥamāt
Ḥamā Allāh Ḥaydara iii, 107a, b, 108a, 289a – III, 109b, 110a, b, 298a
al-Ḥamād i, 536b; iii, 1253a – I, 553a; III, 1285b
al-Ḥamād (plain(e)) iv, 954a; vi, 546b – IV, 986a; VI, 531b
Ḥamad b. Aḥmad (Āl Bū SaÚīd (1792) x, 817a – X,
Ḥamad b. Aḥmad (Āl Bū Saʿīd) (1822) vi, 963b – VI, 956a
Ḥamad ʿImrān i, 1239b – I, 1277b
Ḥamāda, Banū ii, 568b – II, 583a
al-Hamadānī→ ʿAlī al-Hamadānī
Hamadānī, ʿAbd al-Samad (XIX) vii, 453a – VII, 454a
Hamadānī, Abū Yaʿḳūb Yūsuf (1140) 1, 299a, 515b; ii, 1078a; vii, 933b; viii, 539b x, 250a – I, 308a, 531b; II, 1103a; VII, 934a; VIII, 557b; X, 268b
Hamadānī, Mīr Sayyid ʿAlī (1385) viii, 539b – VIII, 557b
Hamadhān (Hamadān) i, 426a, 840a; iii, **105a**, 761b; iv, 3a, 7b, 13b, 465a; v, 171a; vi, 332a, b, 333a, 482a, 484a, b, 493a, 500a, 539a, 600b, 653b; s, 2b, 84a, 118b, 142b – I, 438a, 863a; III, **107b**, 784b; IV, 3b, 8b, 14b, 486a; V, 168b; VI, 316b, 317a, b, 468a, 470a, b, 479a, 485b, 523b, 585b, 639a; S, 2a, 83b, 142a
al-Hamadhānī, Abū Saʿd ʿAlī s, 119b – S, 119a
al-Hamadhānī, Aḥmad Badīʿ al-Zamān (1008) i, 116a, 331b, 590b; ii, 246a; iii, **106a**, 368a, 373a, 764a, 1264a; iv, 1069b; v, 132b, 768b, 1010a; vi, 107b,

108b, 379a, 756a; vii, 495a; viii, 735b; s, 17a, 31a – I, 119b, 341b, 610a; II, 253a; III, **108b**, 379b, 384b, 787b, 1297a; IV, 1101a; V, 135b, 774b, 1005b; VI, 105b, 106b, 363b, 745a; VII, 495a; VIII, 756b; S, 17b, 31a
al-Ḥamadhānī, Muḥammad b, ʿAbd al-Malik x, 14a – X, 14b
al-Hamadhānī, ʿAyn al-Ḳuḍāt → ʿAbd Allāh b. Abī Bakr al-Miyānadjī
al-Hamadhānī → Ibn al-Faḳīh; Yūsuf
Ḥamādisha (*ṭarīḳa*) vi, 250b; s, 53a, **350b** – VI, 234b; S, 53b, **350b**
Ḥamadu → Aḥmadu
Ḥamāhullāh vi, 260a – VI, 244b
Ḥamāʾil → Siḥr; Tamāʾim; Ṭilasm
al-Ḥamal → Minṭaḳat al-Burūdj; Nudjūm
Ḥamal b. Badr al-Fazārī s, 177b, 178a – S, 178b, 179a
Ḥamāliyya i, 1009a; ii, 63a, 94b; iii, **107a**; vi, 260a, 705a – I, 1040a; II, 64b, 96b; III, **109b**; VI, 244b, 693b
Ḥamāllāh, Shaykh → Ḥamā Allāh Ḥaydara
Ḥamām iii, **108b**; v, 924b – III, **111a**; V, 930a
Ḥamāma s, 144b – S, 144a, b
Ḥamāma b. al-Muʿizshz b. ʿAṭiyya v, 1177b – V, 1167b
Hāmān iii, **110a**; iv, 673a – III, **112b**; IV, 700b
Ḥamar-wēn (Maḳdishu) vi, 129a – VI, 127a
Hāmarz iii, **110b**, 586a – III, **113a**, 606a
Ḥamāsa i, 154b, 584b, 586a, 892a; iii, **110b**; s, 32b, **351a** – I, 159a, 603a, 605a, 918b; III, **113a**; S, 32b, **351a**
Hamasāla iv, 1045a – IV, 1076a
Ḥamāt i, 118b, 609b; iii, **119b**; v, 923a, 925a; vi, 118b, 230b, 321b, 323a, 378b, 379b, 380b, 429a, b, 545b, 547b, 577b, 578a, 681a; viii, 127b – I, 122a, 629b; III, **122a**; V, 928b, 930b; VI, 116a, 224a, 306a, 307a, 362b, 364a, 365a, 414a, b, 415a, 530a, 532a, 562b, 563a, 668a; VIII, 130b
Hamawand iii, **121b** – III, **124a**
Ḥamawī → Saʿd al-Dīn Ḥamawī
Ḥamawī, Ḳāḍī b. Kāshif al-Dīn (XVI) viii, 783b – VIII, 809b
al-Ḥamawī → Ibn Ḥidjdja; Yāḳūt
Ḥamawiya, Banū → Awlād al-Shaykh
Ḥamawiyya (*ṭarīḳa*) vii, 620a – VII, 620a
al-Hamaysaʿ b. Ḥimyar iii, 124a – III, 127a
Ḥamḍ, Wādī al- i, 538a; iii, **121b** – I, 554b; III, **124a**
Ḥamd Allāh, Shaykh (1520) iv, 1125a – IV, 1156b
Ḥamd Allāh Musṭawfī al-Ḳazwīnī (1339) i, 358b, 903a; iii, 114a, **122a**; iv, 859a, b, 863a, 1051b, 1052a, 1081b, 1082a; vi, 202a, 505a, 901a, 907b; vii, 754a; s, 235a, 382b – I, 369a, 930b; III, 116b, **124b**; IV, 892a, b, 896a, 1083a, b, 1113a; VI, 186a, 490b, 892a, 899a; VII, 755b; S, 234b, 383a
Ḥamdala iii, **122b** – III, **125a**
Ḥamdallāhi (Mali) i, 303a; ii, 941b; iii, 39b; vi, 259b – I, 312b; II, 963b; III, 41a; VI, 244a
Hamdān, Banū i, 544b, 548a; iii, **123a**; v, 346a; vi, 191a; vii, 591b, 592a, 777a; ix, 1b – I, 561b, 565b; III, **125b**; V, 347a; VI, 175a; VII, 591b, 778b; IX, 1b
Ḥamdān b. Ḥamdūn (Ḥamdānid(e)) (IX) iii, 126a; iv, 89b; vi, 540a, 900a; vii, 760a – III, 129a; IV, 93b; VI, 524b, 891b; VII, 761b
Ḥamdān b. al-Ḥasan Nāṣir al-Dawla (X) iii, 127b, 128a; vi, 540a – III, 130b, 131a; VI, 524b
Ḥamdān Abū ʿAndja iv, 687a – IV, 715a
Ḥamdān Ḳarmaṭ b. al-Ashʿath (IX) iii, **123b**, 198a, b, 660b; vi, 157b; viii, 922a – III, **126a**, 206b, 207a, 687a; VI, 153a; VIII, 953b
al-Hamdānī → (ʿĪsā) b. ʿUmar
al-Ḥamdānī, Abū Muḥammad al-Ḥasan (Ibn al-Ḥāʾik) (971) i, 534a; iii, 123b, **124a**, 1077a; iv, 335a; v, 110b, 113b; vi, 81a, 829b; s, 341b – I, 550b; III, 126a, **126b**, 1103b; IV, 350a; V, 113a, 116b; VI, 79a, 819b; S, 341b
Ḥamdānid(e)s (Syria/Syrie) i, 19a, 119b, 215a, 439b, 637b, 679b, 824b, 1046b, 1354b; ii, 281b, 348b, 524a; iii, **126a**, 398a; iv, 23b, 24a; vi, 379a, 626a, 900b, 930a; vii, 484b, 656b, 723b – I, 20a, 123a, 221b, 452a, 658b, 700b, 847b, 1078b, 1394a; II, 290a, 358a, 537a; III, **128b**, 410b; IV, 25b; VI, 363b, 611a, 891b, 922a; VII, 484b, 655b, 724b
Hamdānid(e)s (Yemen/Yémen) iii, **125a**, 259b; v, 820a, b; s, 62a – III, **128a**, 267a; V, 826b; S, 62b
Ḥamdawayh b. ʿAlī b. ʿĪsā b. Māhān vi, 334b – VI, 319a
al-Ḥamdawī, Abū ʿAlī Ismāʿīl s, **352a** – S, **352a**
Ḥamdī (1911) iv, 806b – IV, 839a
Ḥamdī, Ḥamd Allāh (1503) iii, **131a** – III, **133b**
Ḥamdī Bey → ʿOthmān Ḥamdī Bey
Ḥamdīs b. ʿAbd-al-Raḥmān al-Kindī i, 248a – I, 255b
Ḥamdūn, Abū ʿĀlī → Abū ʿAbd Allāh al-Andalusī
Ḥamdūn, Banū → Ibn Ḥamdūn
Ḥamdūn b. al-Ḥādjdj (1817) vi, 196b – VI, 180b
Ḥamdūn b. Ismāʿīl b. Dāwūd al-Kātib (IX) vii, 518b – VII, 519a
Ḥamdūn al-Ḳaṣṣār, Abū Ṣāliḥ (884) iii, **132a**; vi, 223b, 224b – III, **134b**; VI, 217a, 218b
Ḥamdūn Shalbī (XIX) vi, 251a – VI, 235b
Ḥamdūn al-Ṭāhirī (1777) vi, 356b – VI, 340b
al-Ḥamdūnī → al-Ḥamdawī, Abū ʿAlī Ismāʿīl
al-Ḥamdūniyya vi, 224b – VI, 218b
Ḥamdūshiyya x, 148a – X, 266b
Hamengku Buwono IX (Yogyakarta) ix, 852b, 892b – IX, 888a, 928b
Ḥāmī (Ḥaḍramaut) iii, **132a** – III, **135a**
Ḥāmī-i Āmidī (1747) iii, **132b** – III, **135a**
Ḥāmī 'l-Ḥaramayn → Khādim al-Ḥaramayn
Hamian i, 372a – I, 382b
Ḥamīd, Ḥamīd-oghullari̊ i, 467b, 468a; ii, 692a; iii, **132b**; iv, 210b; vii, 593a – I, 481b, 482a; II, 709a; III, **135b**; IV, 220a; VII, 593a
Ḥamīd, Sayyid s, 1b – S, 1b
Ḥāmid, Shaykh (1412) vi, 226a – VI, 219b
Ḥamīd, Shaykh Ḥādjdjī (Khalīfa) (XVI) vii, 440a – VII, 441a
Ḥāmid b. al-ʿAbbās (923) i, 387a; iii, 100b, 101a, **133a**, 739a, 767b; iv, 100a; v, 737a – I, 398a; III, 103a, b, **136a**, 761b, 791a; IV, 104b; V, 742a
Hāmid b. Djamālī Dihlawī → Djamālī, Hāmid b. Faḍl Allāh
Ḥāmid b. Muḥammad al-Murdjibī → al-Murdjibī
Ḥāmid b. Mūsā al-Ḳayṣarī i, 869a; iii, 43b – I, 893b; III, 45a
Ḥāmid b. Saʿīd i, 1281b – I, 1321a
Ḥāmid ʿAbd al-Mannān, Shaykh (XX) vi, 171b
Ḥamīd Allāh Khān i, 1195b, 1196a, b – I, 1231a, b
Ḥamīd al-Anṣārī s, 247b – S, 247b
Ḥamīd al-Dawla Ḥātim iii, 125b – III, 128b
Ḥamīd al-Dawla Ḥātim (Hamdānid(e), Yemen) (XII) vi, 433a – VI, 418b
Ḥamīd al-Dīn, Āl (Zaydī) ix, 2a; x, 228b – IX, 2a; X, 128a
Ḥamīd al-Dīn b. ʿAmʿaḳ → Ḥamīdī b. ʿAmʿaḳ
Ḥamīd al-Dīn Balkhī (1156) vi, 114b – VI, 112a
Ḥamīd al-Dīn Ḳāḍī Nāgawrī (1244) vii, 925a; s, **353a** – VII, 926a; S, **353a**
Ḥamīd al-Dīn al-Kirmānī → al-Kirmānī, Ḥamīd al-Dīn

Ḥamīd al-Dīn Ṣūfī Nāgawrī Siwālī (1276) ii, 51a, 55b; s, **353b** – II, 52a, 56b; S, **353a**
Ḥāmid Efendi ii, 56b – II, 57b
Ḥamīd Ḳalandar i, 1329a; ii, 48b, 55b; s, 352b – I, 1369b; II, 49a, 56b; S, 352b
Ḥamīd Kas̲h̲mīrī i, 72a – I, 74a
Ḥamīd K̲h̲ān (vizier) (Dihlī, D̲j̲awnpūr) (XV) v, 783b; vi, 62a – V, 789b; VI, 60a
Ḥamīd K̲h̲ān (Ḥabs̲h̲ī) iii, 15b; iv, 1018b – III, 16a; IV, 1050b
Ḥamīd al-Maḥallī (1254) vi, 351b, 352a – VI, 335b, 336a
Ḥamīd Pas̲h̲a → K̲h̲alīl Ḥamīd
Ḥamīda Bānū Begam i, 316a, 1135b; iii, 455b – I, 326a, 1170a; III, 471b
Ḥamīda (Ḥumayda) bint Ṣāʿid al-Barbariyya (VIII) vii, 645b – VII, 645a
Ḥamīdābād → Isparta
Ḥāmidī (1485) iii, **133b** – III, **136a**
al-Ḥāmidī, ʿAlī b. Ḥātim (Ḥamdānid(e), Yemen) (1209) iii, 125b, **134a**; v, 954b; vii, 411a; s, 62a – III, 128b, **137a**; V, 958a; VII, 412a; S, 62a
al-Ḥāmidī, ʿAlī b. Ḥātim (Ḥamdānid(e), Yemen) (1174) vi, 433a – VI, 418b
al-Ḥāmidī, Ḥamīd al-Dīn (1164) iii, **134b**; vi, 632b – III, **137a**; VI, 617b
al-Ḥāmidī, Ḥātim b. Ibrāhīm (1199) iii, **134a**; vii, 411a – III, **137a**; VII, 412a
al-Ḥāmidī, Ibrāhīm b. al-Ḥusayn (1162) iii, 72a, **134a**; iv, 200b, 204b; v, 894a; vi, 439b; vii, 411a – III, 14b, **136b**; IV, 209a, 213b; V, 900b; VI, 424b; VII, 412a
Ḥāmidī b. ʿAmʿaḳ s, 65a – S, 65b
Ḥamīdīya v, 462b; vi, 155a, 156b, 778b – V, 465b; VI, 152a, b, 768b
Ḥamīdīzāde Muṣṭafā Efendi → Muṣṭafā Efendi
Ḥamīd-og̲h̲ullari̊ → Ḥamīd
Ḥamīdū i, 368b; ii, 538a – I, 379b; II, 551a
Ḥā-Mīm b. Mann al-Muftarī (927) i, 1178b, 1186a; ii, 1095b; iii, **134b**; vi, 741b, 743b – I, 1213b, 1221a; II, 1121a; III, **137b**; VI, 730b, 733a
Hamīrat s, 42a – S, 42b
Hamka vi, 240b – VI, 205b
Ḥamlad̲j̲i̊ i, 1278a – I, 1317a, b
al-Ḥamma (Alhama) i, 492b; ii, 463a, 464a; iii, **135a**; vi, 221b, 431a – I, 507a; II, 475a, 476a; III, **137b**; VI, 215a, 416b
Ḥammād, Banū → Hammādid(e)s
Ḥammād b. Abī Ḥanīfa al-Nuʿmān i, 124a; iii, 512a – I, 127b; III, 529b
Ḥammād b. Abī Sulaymān (738) i, 123a; ii, 888b; v, 239b; x, 29a – I, 126b; II, 909a; V, 237b; X, 30a
Ḥammād b. Buluggīn (Zīrid(e)) (1028) i, 860a; iii, 137a; iv, 479a; vi, 841b; vii, 474a; ix, 18a – I, 884a; III, 139b, 140a; IV, 501a; VI, 832a; VII, 473b; IX, 18b
Ḥammād b. Isḥāḳ iii, 820a; iv, 111a – III, 843b; IV, 116a
Ḥammād b. Isḥāḳ b. Ismāʿīl (881) s, **384b** – S, **385a**
Ḥammād b. Salama (783) vii, 662b – VII, 662a
Ḥammād b. ʿUdayy s, 305a – S, 304b
Ḥammād b. Zayd b. Dirham (Mālikī) (795) vi, 263b; s, **384b** – VI, 248b; S, **385a**
Ḥammād b. al-Zibriḳān (VIII) iii, 135b, 136a; iv, 1003b; vii, 798b – III, 138b, 139a; IV, 1036a; VII, 800b
Ḥammād ʿAd̲j̲rad (777) i, 160a, 1080b; iii, **135a**, 136a; iv, 1003b; vii, 798b; viii, 884a, 996b – I, 164b, 1113a; III, **138a**, 139a; IV, 1036a; VII, 800b; VIII, 914b, 1031b
Ḥammād al-Barbarī iii, 233a – III, 240a
Ḥammād al-Dabbās (1139) ix, 778a – IX, 812a
Ḥammād al-Rāwiya (772) i, 718b; iii, 135b, **136a**, 641b, 1177b; iv, 316b, 919a, 1003b; vi, 442a; vii, 254a, 305b, 661a, 798b; viii, 545b – I, 740a; III, **138b**, 662b, 1206b; IV, 330b, 952a, 1036a; VI, 427b; VII, 256a, 307b, 660b, 800b; VIII, 563b
Ḥammāda iii, **136b**; v, 1185a – III, **139b**; V, 1175a
al-Ḥammādī, Yaḥyā b. Lamak b. Mālik (*dāʿī*) (X) vii, 725b – VII, 726b
Ḥammādid(e)s i, 79a, 165a, 533a, 699b, 860a, 1176a, 1204b, 1246b, 1319b; ii, 115a, 145b, 537a, 747b; iii, **137a**, 386a; iv, 478b; v, 59b, 60a, 1179a; vi, 426b, 427a, 728b; vii, 481b – I, 81b, 170a, 549b, 720b, 884a, 1211a, 1240b, 1284b, 1359b; II, 117b, 149b, 550b, 765b; III, **139b**, 398b; IV, 499b; V, 61b, 62a, 1169a; VI, 412a, b, 717b; VII, 481b
Ḥammāl iii, **139a** – III, **141b**
Ḥammām iii, **139b**, 148b; v, 13b, 14a, b, 16a – III, **142a**, 151b; V, 13b, 14b, 16a, b
Ḥammām b. Munabbih (749) viii, 657a; ix, 7b – VIII, 676a; IX, 8a
Hammam Ali s, 101b – S, 101a
Ḥammām Bourguiba v, 52a – V, 53b
Ḥammām Ḳarā Ḥiṣār iv, 580b – IV, 604a
Ḥammām Mask̲h̲ūṭīn vi, 738b – VI, 727b
Ḥammām al-Ṣarak̲h̲ iii, 141b, **146a**; s, 229a – III, 144b, **149a**; S, 229a
Ḥammām Sittī Maryam vi, 631b – VI, 631b
Ḥammāma b. Zīrī iii, 1043a – III, 1069a
Ḥammār, lake/lac i, 1095b – I, 1128b
Ḥammū b. Malīl (XI) viii, 763b – VIII, 788b
Ḥammu Ḳiyu s, 53a – S, 53b
Ḥammūda Bey (1659) ii, 459b; iv, 825b, 828a – II, 471b; IV, 858b, 861a
Ḥammūda Bey (Pas̲h̲a) (1814) iii, 94b, 636a; iv, 403a; viii, 763a – III, 97a, 657a; IV, 420b; VIII, 788a
Ḥammūdid(e)s i, 403a, 495a; ii, 525a; iii, **147a**, 938b, 1037a; vi, 222a, 842a; s, 398b – I, 414b, 509b; II, 538a; III, **150a**, 963b, 1062b; VI, 216a, 832b; S, 399a
Hammūya, Muḥammad b. (1135) s, 3a – S, 2a
Hāmōn (1554) iii, **147b** – III, **150b**
Ḥamrāʾ al-Asad s, 230a – S, 230a
Hampī iii, **147b**, 451a – III, **151a**, 466b
Ḥamrāʾ (Pers(i)ans) vi, 875b – VI, 866b
al-Ḥamrāʾ iii, **148b** – III, **152a**
al-Ḥamrāʾ, G̲h̲arnāṭa i, 459a, 495b, 497b, 500a, 682a, 1321a, 1347a; ii, 115a, 556b, 1012b, **1016b**, 1019a, b; iii, 973a; v, 219b – I, 472a, 510b, 512b, 515a, 703a, 1361a, 1387b; II, 117b, 570b, 1036a, **1040a**, 1042b, 1043a; III, 997b; V, 217a
Ḥamrīn, D̲j̲abal → D̲j̲abal Ḥamrin
Hams̲h̲in v, 713a – V, 718a
Ḥamūd b. ʿAbd Allāh, S̲h̲arīf (XVII) vii, 782b – VII, 784b
Ḥamūd b. Muḥammad Abū Mismār i, 709a; ii, 517b; v, 808a – I, 729b; II, 530b; V, 814a
Ḥamūda b. Murād ii, 189b – II, 195b
Ḥamūda Pas̲h̲a → Ḥammūda Bey (1814)
Ḥamūla iii, **149b** – III, **153a**
Hāmūn i, 222a; iii, **150a** – I, 229a; III, **153b**
Ḥamūs vi, 507b – VI, 493a
Ḥamūya, Muḥammad b. (1135) viii, 703b – VIII, 723b
Ḥamūya, Saʿd al-Dīn v, 301a – V, 300b
Hamza iii, **150a** – III, **153b**
Ḥamza, Amīr → Ḥamza b. ʿAbd al-Muṭṭalib
Ḥamza (Malāmī) (1561) vi, 227b, 228a – VI, 221a, b, 222a

Ḥamza b. ʿAbd Allāh → Ḥamza b. ʿAbd al-Muṭṭalib
Ḥamza b. ʿAbd Allāh (Khāridjī) → Ḥamza b. Adrak
Ḥamza b. ʿAbd Allāh b. al-Zubayr (VIII) vi, 262b – VI, 246b
Ḥamza b. ʿAbd al-Muṭṭalib (625) i, 80a, 115b; iii, 114b, **152b**, 455a, 1234b; iv, 896b, 994b, 1106b; v, 197b, 1161b; vi, 240a, 604a, 650b; x, 782b; s, 92b, 103b –
I, 82b, 119a; III, 116b, **156a**, 471a, 1266b; IV, 929a, 1027a, 1138a; V, 195a, 1151a; VI, 205a, 588b, 636a; X, ; S, 92b, 103a
Ḥamza b. Ādarak (Khāridjī) (828) i, 207a; ii, 978a; iii, 153a, 233b; v, 158a; vi, 331b, 337b; viii, 795b; ix, 683a –
I, 213a; II, 1000b; III, 156b, 240a; V, 157a; VI, 316a, 322a; VIII, 822b; IX, 711b
Ḥamza b. Aḥmad b. ʿUmar b. Ṣāliḥ → Ibn Asbāṭ al-Gharbī
Ḥamza b. ʿAlī b. Aḥmad (1018) ii, 136b, 632a; iii, 80b, **154a**; iv, 199a; vii, 544a –
II, 140a, 647b; III, 82b, **157b**; IV, 207b; VII, 544a
Ḥamza b. ʿAlī b. Rāshid (Mandīl) (XIV) vi, 404b – VI, 389b
Ḥamza b. Asad → Ibn al-Ḳālānisī
Ḥamza b. Bīḍ (734) iii, **154b** – III, **158a**
Ḥamza b. Ḥabīb (772) iii, **155a** – III, **158b**
Ḥamza b. Muḥammad al-Ḥanafī iii, 155b – III, 159a
Ḥamza b. Turghūd (1554) vii, 537a – VII, 537a
Ḥamza b. ʿUmāra (ʿAmmāra) i, 1116b; iv, 837a; v, 433b – I, 1150b; IV, 869b; V, 436a
Ḥamza b. ʿUthmān i, 311b, 312a; iii, 156b – I, 321b; III, 160a
Ḥamza Beg (Aḳ-ḳoyunlu) iii, **156b**; vi, 541a – III, **160a**; VI, 525b
Ḥamza Beg (Imām) (1834) i, 755b; ii, 88b; iii, **157a** – I, 778a; II, 90a; III, **160b**
Ḥamza Fanṣūrī (XVI) i, 742a; iii, **155b**, 1220a, 1233a; vi, 235b – I, 764a; III, **159a**, 1251a, 1265a; VI, 208a
Ḥamza Fatḥ Allāh (XIX) vii, 434a – VII, 435a
Ḥämzä Häkimzadä Niyaziy (Ḳoḳan) (1929) vi, 767b, 769b – VI, 756b, 758b
Ḥamza Ḥāmid Pasha (1770) iii, **157a** – III, **160b**
Ḥamza al-Ḥarrānī iii, **155b** – III, **159a**
Ḥamza al-Iṣfahānī, al-Muʾaddib (961) i, 144b; iii, **156a**, 371a; vi, 823a; ix, 100b; x, 226a; s, 382b – I, 148b; III, **159b**, 382b; VI, 813a; IX, 105a; X, 244a; S, 383a
Ḥamza Makhdūm (1578) s, **353b** – S, **353b**
Ḥamza Mīrzā (Ṣafawid(e)) (1586) iii, **157b**; iv, 861a; vii, 600b – III, **161a**; IV, 894a; VII, 600a
Ḥamza Mīrzā Hishmat al-Dawla (XIX) vii, 675a – VII, 675a
Ḥamza Pasha (1768) iii, **157b** – III, **161a**
Ḥamza Pasha Nishandjī iv, 566a – IV, 588a
Ḥamzat Tsadasa i, 756a – I, 778b
Ḥamzawīs Ḥamzawiyya ii, 98a; iii, 153b; iv, 128b; vi, 224a, 227b; x, 252a – II, 100b; III, 157a; IV, 134a; VI, 218a, 221b; X, 270b
Ḥamzāwī, Rashād v, 190b – V, 187b
Ḥamzevī → Ḥamzawī
Ḥamziyya i, 207a; iii, 153a, 653b, 658b – I, 213a; III, 156b, 674b, 679b
Ḥanābila i, 272b, 696a, 900a, 949a, 1040a; ii, 388a; iii, **158a**, 677b, 699b, 731a, 752a, 766a, 784b; iv, 173a; v, 9b; vi, 446b; s, 29b –
I, 280b, 717a, 927a, 978b, 1071b; II, 398b; III, **161b**, 699a, 721b, 753b, 775a, 789a, 807b; IV, 180b; V, 10a; VI, 432a; S, 29b
—doctrine i, 333b, 338b, 339a, 414a; ii, 411b; iii, 17a, 1144b, 1148a, 1149a, 1164b, 1171b; iv, 172b, 183b, 691a, 990a –
I, 344a, 349a, b, 425b; II, 422b; III, 17b, 1173a, 1176b, 1177b, 1193a, 1200b; IV, 180a, 191b, 719a, 1022b
al-Ḥanafī, Abu ʾl-ʿAlāʾ Aḥmad b. Abī Bakr al-Rāzī (XII) vi, 111a – VI, 109a
al-Ḥanafī, Abu ʾl-Ḳāsim b. ʿAbd al-ʿAlīm vi, 352b – VI, 337a
al-Ḥanafī, Aḥmad b. Muḥammad Rūmī s, 49b – S, 50a
Ḥanafī Aḥmad (XX) vii, 439b – VII, 440b
Ḥanafī-Māturīdī iii, 1149b, 1171a, 1172b, 1173a; iv, 172a, 470a, b, 693b – III, 1177b, 1200a, 1201b, 1202a; IV, 179b, 491a, 721b
Hanafites → Ḥanafiyya
Ḥanafiyya i, 70b, 123a, 164a, 332b, 338a, b, 340a, 803a; ii, 829b; iii, 6b, 17a, 90a, **162b**, 350b, 756b, 848b, 1024b; iv, 404a, b, 690a; vi, 2a, 3a, 557b; s, 23a –
I, 72b, 126b, 168b, 343a, 349a, 350b, 826a; II, 849b; III, 6b, 17b, 92b, **166a**, 361b, 779b, 872b, 1050a; IV, 422a, b, 718a; VI, 2a, 3a, 542b; S, 23b
Ḥanbal b. Hilāl i, 272b – I, 280b
al-Ḥanbalī (1503) vi, 353a – VI, 337a
Ḥanbalīs, Ḥanbalites → Ḥanābila
Ḥanbalī-zāde vi, 971a – VI, 963b
Ḥanbīl i, 689a – I, 710a
Handasa → ʿIlm al-handasa
Handjām vi, 358a – VI, 342a
Ḥandūs → Sikka
Handžič (al-Khāndjī) (1944) s, **354a** – S, **354a**
al-Ḥanfāʾ s, 177b – S, 178b
Hāniʾ b. Hāniʾ s, 298b – S, 298b
Hānī b. ʿUrwa al-Murādī (680) iii, **164b**, 609b; vii, 400b, 592a, 689b, 690a – III, **168a**, 629b; VII, 402a, 592a, 689b, 690a, b
Ḥanīf iii, **165a**; vi, 146a – III, **168b**; VI, 144b
Ḥanīfa b. Ludjaym, Banū i, 545a,b, 963a; ii, 569a; iii, **166b**; vi, 648b; s, 122a, 178a –
I, 562a, b, 992b; II, 583b; III, **170a**; VI, 634a; S, 121b, 179a
Ḥanīfa, Wādī → Wādī Ḥanīfa
Ḥanīna (comédienne) vi, 750a – VI, 739b
Ḥannā (Alep(po)) (XVIII) i, 359a – I, 370a
Ḥanna bint Djaḥsh (VII) vii, 649b – VII, 649b
Ḥanna umm Maryam vi, 630a – VI, 615a
Hanṣaliyya iii, **167a**; x, 247b – III, **170b**; X, 266a
Hānsawī, Djamāl al-Dīn (1260) iii, **167b**, 168b; s, 67a – III, **171a**, 172a; S, 67b
al-Ḥansh (Idrīs b. ʿAlī) (1901) vi, 250b – VI, 234b
Hanshīr i, 661a – I, 682a
Hānsī iii, **167b**, 225b; vi, 780b – III, **171b**, 232a; VI, 770a
Hānswī → Hānsawī
Ḥantama bint Hāshim b. al-Mughīra vi, 139a – VI, 137a
Hantīfa, Banū vi, 742a – VI, 731b
Ḥanūt iii, 404a – III, 416a
Ḥānya iii, 983b, 1086a, b; iv, 539b – III, 1008a, 1113a; IV, 563a
Ḥanẓala b. Abī ʿĀmir → Ghasīl al-Malāʾika
Ḥanẓala b. Abī Sufyān i, 151a; ii, 1020b – I, 155b; II, 1044a
Ḥanẓala b. Ḳatāda (Mecca) (XIII) vi, 149a – VI, 147b
Ḥanẓala b. Mālik, Banū iii, **168b**; v, 640a; vi, 267a, b, 268a – III, **172b**; V, 644b; VI, 252a, b
Ḥanẓala b. Ṣafwān iii, **169a** – III, **172b**
Ḥanẓala b. Ṣafwān al-Kalbī (VIII) i, 86b, 509a; iii, **169a**, 494a; iv, 826a – I, 88b, 524b; III, **173a**, 511a; IV, 859a

Ḥanẓala b. al-Sharḳī i, 115b – I, 119a
Ḥanẓala b. Thaʿlaba iii, 1022b – III, 1048b
Ḥanẓala Bādghīsī iv, 55a – IV, 58a
Haoussa → Hausa
Haouz → Ḥawz
Ḥāra ii, 230a; iii, **169b** – II, 237a; III, **173b**
al-Ḥāra (Marrākush) vi, 590a – VI, 575a
Harābī i, 1049b – I, 1081a
Ḥaraḍ vi, 191b – VI, 175b
Ḥarāfīsh → Ḥarfūsh
Ḥaraka wa-Sukūn iii, **169b**; iv, 731b – III, **173b**; IV, 761a
Ḥarakta s, 144b – S, 144a, b
Haram (pyramid(e)) iii, **173a** – III, **177a**
Ḥarām (Mamlūks) vi, 327b – VI, 314a
Ḥarām, Banū vi, 649a – VI, 634a
Ḥaram (enclos(ure)) i, 892b; iii, 294a,b, 1018a; iv, 37a, 322a; v, 810a, 1003a, 1201a – I, 919a; III, 303b, 1043b; IV, 39b, 336a; V, 815b, 816a, 999a, 1191b
Ḥaram Bilḳīs vi, 562a – VI, 546b
al-Ḥaram al-Sharīf iii, **173b**; v, 341b, 343b, 344a, 1143b, 1144a; vi, 153a, 707a – III, **177b**; V, 342b, 344b, 345a, 1136a, b; VI, 151b, 695b
al-Ḥaramayn iii, **175a**; iv, 956b; vi, 153a, 155b; vii, 466a; s, 304b – III, **179a**; IV, 990a; VI, 151b, 695b; VI, 151b, 152a; VII, 465b; S, 304b
Hārand s, 116a, 332a – S, 115b, 331b
Harar i, 976a; iii, 3b, 4b, **176a**; viii, 161b – I, 1006b; III, 3b, 4b, **179b**; VIII, 164a
Ḥarari iii, 7b, 176a – III, 8a, 180a
Ḥaras → Ḳaṣr
al-Ḥarāsīs, Banū iii, **176a**; vi, 84b – III, **180a**; VI, 82b
Harāt (Herāt) i, 7b, 8a, 47b, 91a, 147b, 222b, 223a, 227b, 228b, 1067b; ii, 1101b; iii, **177a**, 471b, 603a; iv, 39a, 394b, 523b, 672a; v, 58b, 59a, b, 873a, 993a; vi, 54a, 408a, 512a, b, 513a, b, 514b, 627b, 633b, 715a, 765a, 780a; vii, 92a, 453a, 455a, 481b, 1052b; viii, 704a, 1012b; s, 38a, 41a, 50b, 71a, 138b, 139b, 140a, 142a, 340a, 380a, 423b – I, 7b, 8a, 49a, 94a, 152a, 229a, 230a, 234b, 235b, 1100a; II, 1127b; III, **181a**, 488a, 624a; IV, 41a, b, 411b, 546b, 699b; V, 60b, 61a, 879a, 988a; VI, 52a, 392b, 497a, 498a, b, 499b, 612b, 618b, 704a, 769a; VII, 93b, 454a, 455b, 481a, 1055a; VIII, 724a, 1047b S, 38a, 41b, 51a, 71b, 138a, 139a, b, 142a, 340a, 380a, 423b
Ḥarāṭīn → Ḥarṭānī
al-Harawī → al-Anṣārī al-Harawī
al-Harawī, Abu 'l-Faḍl (950) vi, 600b – VI, 585a
al-Harawī, Abū ʿUbayd al-Ḳāsim b. Sallām (837) vi, 924a – VI, 916a
al-Ḥarawī, ʿAlī b. Abī Bakr (1215) ix, 262b, 582a – IX, 271a, 605a
Harawī, Ibn Ḥusām (1355) vii, 754b – VII, 756a
al-Harawī, Maḥmūd b. Muḥammad s, 406b – S, 406b
al-Harawī, Mīr ʿAlī (calligraphe(r)) (XVI) viii, 787b – VIII, 814a
Harawī, Mīrzā → ʿAbd al-Raḥmān Harawī
al-Harawī, Mollā Miskīn (XV) vii, 969b – VII, 969b
al-Harawī, Muḥammad iv, 801a – IV, 833a
al-Harawī al-Mawṣilī, ʿAlī (1215) i, 89a; iii, 71b, **178a**, 181a, b, 511a; iv, 958b; v, 214b – I, 91b; III, 74a, **182a**, 185b, 186a, 528a; IV, 991b; V, 212a
Ḥarāz (Yaman) iii, **178b**; iv, 201a; vi, 191b, 192a; ix, 816a; s, 407a – III, **182b**; IV, 209b, 210a; VI, 175a, b, 176a; IX, 851a; S, 407a
Harāz (river/fleuve) v, 659b, 660a – V, 665a
Ḥarāzem, Sīdī → Ibn Ḥirzihim
Ḥarāzim (1815) vi, 356b – VI, 340b
Ḥarb, Banū iii, **179b**, 363b, 1065b; v, 998a – III, **183b**, 375a, 1092a; V, 993b
Ḥarb (war/la guerre) iii, **180a**; v, 687a – III, **184a**; V, 692a
Ḥarb b. Umayya i, 1241b; ii, 883b; iii, **203a**; s, 103b – I, 1279a; II, 904a; III, **208b**; S, 103a
Ḥarb Akademisi iii, 204a – III, 209b
Ḥarba → ʿAnaza; ʿAṣā; Ḳaḍīb; Silāḥ
Ḥarbāʾ iii, **203b** – III, **209a**
Harbaḳa iv, 726a – IV, 755a
Ḥarbī i, 429b – I, 441b
al-Ḥarbī → Ibrāhīm
Harbin s, 82a – S, 82a
al-Ḥarbiyya iii, 1265b; iv, 837b; vi, 335a, b – III, 1298b; IV, 870a; VI, 319b
Ḥarbiye ii, 425b, 513b; iii, **203b**; v, 903b – II, 436b, 526b; III, **209a**; V, 909b
Ḥareket Ordusu iii, **204a** – III, **209b**
Ḥarf i, 345b; iii, 172a, **204b**, 597b, 598a, b; iv, 867b – I, 356a; III, 176a, **210a**, 618a, b, 619a; IV, 900b
Ḥarfūsh (amīrs) i, 971a; iii, **205b** – I, 1001a; III, **211a**
Ḥarfūsh, Muḥammad (amīr) (1850) vi, 308a – VI, 293b
Ḥarfūsh, ḥarāfīsh ii, 963a; iii, **206a** – II, 985a; III, **211b**
Hargeisa iii, **206b** – III, **212a**
Hargha, Banū iii, **207a**; vi, 742a, b, 744a – III, **212b**; VI, 731a, 732a, 733a
Hari Čand iii, 225a – III, 231b
Hari Čand, Diwān ii, 140a – II, 144a
Harī Rūd iii, **207b**; v, 872b, 873b; vi, 713b; s, 367a – III, **213a**; V, 878b, 879b; VI, 702b; S, 368a
Harī Singh (Kashmīr) iv, 710a – IV, 738b
Harī Singh Nalwa i, 970b; ii, 1131a; iii, 336a – I, 1000b; II, 1157b; III, 346a
Ḥarīb (district/wādī) iii, **207b**; iv, 747a – III, **213b**; IV, 777a
Ḥārik → Ḥurrāk
Ḥārim i, 239a; iii, **208b** – I, 246b; III, **214a**
Ḥarīm i, 35b; ii, 114b; iii, **209a**; v, 871b, 1149a – I, 36b; II, 117a; III, **214b**; V, 877b, 1180b
Ḥarim b. Ḥayyān i, 73b – I, 75b
Ḥarim b. Sinān ii, 1023a; vii, 629a – II, 1047a; VII, 628b
Ḥarīmī v, 269b – V, 267b
Harīpur iii, 336a – III, 346a
Ḥarīr ii, 904b; iii, **209b**, 400b; iv, 135a, 339b, 676b; v, 39a, 604b; s, 340b – II, 925b; III, **215a**, 413a; IV, 140b, 353b, 704b; V, 40b, 608b; S, 340b
al-Ḥarīrī, Abū Muḥammad ʿAlī (1247) iii, 811b; viii, 525b – III, 835a; VIII, 543b
al-Ḥarīrī, Abū Muḥammad al-Ḳāsim al-Baṣrī (1122) i, 523a, 570b, 591a, 669b; iii, **221a**, 733a, 834b, 1264a; iv, 913a; v, 207b, 608b; vi, 109a, b, 110a, 132b, 199a; vii, 388a; viii, 736a; s, 31a, 123b – I, 538b, 589a, 610a, 690b; III, **227b**, 755b, 858b, 1297a; IV, 945b; V, 205a, 612b; VI, 107a, 108a, 130b, 183a; VII, 389a; VIII, 757a; S, 31a, 122b
Ḥarīriyya iii, **222a**; vi, 88a – III, **228b**; VI, 86a
Ḥarīsh → Karkaddan
al-Ḥārith, Banū vi, 436a; ix, 817a; s, 335a – VI, 421b; IX, 852a; S, 334b
al-Ḥārith, Djabal i, 251b; ii, 574a – I, 259b; II, 588b
al-Ḥārith b. ʿAbd al-ʿAzīz b. Abī Dulaf ii, 623b – II, 639a
al-Ḥārith b. ʿAbd al-Muṭṭalib i, 80a; vi, 350b – I, 82b; VI, 334b

al-Ḥārith b. Abi 'l-ʿAlāʾ Saʿīd al-Taghlibī → Abū Firās
al-Ḥārith b. Abī Ḍirār (VII) v, 78b – V, 80b
al-Ḥārith b. Abī Rabīʿa ii, 196a – II, 202a
al-Ḥārith b. Abī Shām (Ghassānid(e)) (634) vi, 546b; – VI, 531a
al-Ḥārith b. ʿAmr (Kinda) (1528) i, 526b; iii, 1177a; v, 118b; vi, 951a; ix, 77a – I, 542b; III, 1206a; V, 121a; VI, 943b; IX, 80a
al-Ḥārith b. Asad → al-Muḥāsibī
al-Ḥārith b. ʿAwf → al-Ḥārith b. Ẓālim
al-Ḥārith b. Badr al-Fazārī s, 177b – S, 179a
Ḥārith b. Bazīʿ iv, 713a – IV, 741b
Ḥārith b. Djabala (Ghassānid(e)) (569) i, 102b, 405b, 548b, 1249b; ii, 1020b; iii, 94a, **222a**; iv, 726a, 1138a; v, 633a, b; s, 229b – I, 105b, 417a, 566a, 1287b; II, 1044b; III, 96b, **228b**; IV, 755a, 1170a; V, 637b; S, 229b
al-Ḥārith b. Fihr, Banū vi, 145a – VI, 143a
al-Ḥārith b. Ḥammām i, 115b – I, 119a
al-Ḥārith b. Ḥilliza al-Yashkurī iii, **222b**; vii, 254b; s, 272b – III, **229a**; VII, 256a; S, 272a
al-Ḥārith b. Hishām b. al-Mughīra Makhzūmī (VII) i, 115b; vi, 138b, 139a; s, 32b – I, 118b; VI, 136b, 137a; S, 33a
Ḥārith b. Kaʿb, Banū 'l- iii, **223a**; vii, 276a, 872a – III, **229b**; VII, 278a, 873b
al-Ḥārith b. Kalada b. ʿAmr al-Thakafī (634) ii, 1120a; iv, 820b; vi, 637b; x, **452a**; s, 133b, **354a** – II, 1146b; IV, 853b; VI, 622b; X, **484b**; S, 133a, **354a**
al-Ḥārith b. Khālid al-Makhzūmī (VII) i, 308b; vi, 140a – I, 318a; VI, 138a
al-Ḥārith b. Miskīn (ḳāḍī) (864) vi, 279a, 663b, 673a – VI, 264a, 649b, 659b
al-Ḥārith b. Ṣabīra s, 172a – S, 173a
al-Ḥārith b. Sharīd ix, 864a – IX. 900a
al-Ḥārith b. Suraydj (746) i, 530a, 684b; ii, 388a, 1026b; iii, **223b**, 471a, 1202a; iv, 44b, 370a; v, 57a, 76a, 854a; vii, 606a, 664a, 1016a – I, 546a, 705b; II, 398a, 1050b; III, **230b**, 487b, 1232a; IV, 47a, 386b; V, 59a, 78a, 861a; VII, 606a, 663b, 1018a
al-Ḥārith b. Talid al-Ḥaḍramī iii, 653b – III, 675a
al-Ḥārith b. Thaʿlaba s, 229b – S, 229b
al-Ḥārith b. Tirmāḥ s, 136a – S, 135b
al-Ḥārith b. Waʿla i, 690a – I, 711a
al-Ḥārith b. Ẓālim al-Kilābī ii, 234b – II, 241b
al-Ḥārith b. Ẓālim al-Murrī (VII) ii, 1023a, b; iii, 812a; vii, 629a; s, 178a – II, 1047a; III, 835b; VII, 628b; S, 179a
al-Ḥārith al-Ḥaffār (VIII) viii, 350b – VIII, 363b
al-Ḥārith al-Ḳubāʿ b. ʿAbd Allāh b. Abī Rabīʿa b. al-Mughīra vi, 140a – VI, 138a
Ḥārith al-Muḥāsibī → al-Muḥāsibī
Ḥāritha, Banū x, 211b – X, 228b
Ḥāritha b. Badr al-Ghudānī (684) iii, **224b**, 1261b; iv, 1002b – III, **231b**, 1294b; IV, 1035a
Ḥāritha b. Djanāb, Banū i, 771b; vi, 649a; vii, 267b – I, 794b; VI, 634a; VII, 269b
Ḥāritha b. al-Ḥadjdjādj → Abū Duʾād al-Iyādī
Ḥāritha b. Ḳaṭan i, 969a – I, 999a
al-Ḥāritha b. al-Nuʿmān ii, 843a – II, 863a
al-Ḥārithī, Muḥammad b. Ṭāhir s, 62a – S, 62b
al-Ḥārithī, Abūshiri b. Salim (XIX) x, 195a – X, 210b
al-Ḥārithī, Ṣāliḥ b. ʿAlī (ʿUmān) (1896) viii, 993a; s, **355a** – viii, 1028a; S, **355a**
al-Ḥārithī, Ziyād b. ʿAbd Allāh (VIII) viii, 531a – VIII, 363b
al-Ḥārithiyya iii, 659a, 1266a; iv, 837b, 838a; v, 63b, 945b – III, 680b, 1298b; IV, 870a, 871a; V, 65b, 949b
Hariyānā iii, 168a, **225a** – III, 171b, **231b**
Ḥarka ii, 509b; v, 1221a – II, 522a; V, 1211b
Harkand (Bangladesh) ix, 877b – IX, 913a
Harkarn b. Mathurādās (XVII) iii, **225b** – III, **232b**
Ḥarmala b. Yaḥyā (858) vii, 691b – VII, 691b
Harmas, Harmīs → Hirmis
Ḥarra i, 535a; iii, **226a**, 362a – I, 551b; III, **232b**, 373b
al-Ḥarra i, 50b, 55a; iii, **226a**; v, 997a – I, 51b, 57a; III, **233a**; V, 992b
Ḥarrān i, 16b, 106b, 119b, 136b; ii, 347b, 348a; iii, **227b**, 287a; v, 593b; vi, 338a, 380b, 539b, 623b, 624a, 667a, 670b, 781b; viii, 672b; x, 845a; s, 36b – I, 16b, 109b, 123a, 140b; II, 357b; III, **234b**, 295b; V, 597a; VI, 322a, 365a, 524b, 608b, 609a, 653a, 657a, 771b; VIII, 692a; X, ; S, 36b
al-Ḥarrānī → Abu 'l-Fatḥ; Ḥamza; Ibrahīm b. Dhakwān; ʿĪsā b. ʿAlī; Nadjm al-Dīn
al-Ḥarrānī, Muḥammad b. Salama (867) ix, 661a – IX, 686b
Ḥarrānians, Ḥarrāniens → Ṣābiʾa
Harrar → Harar
Ḥarrat Rahaṭ s, 198b – S, 198b
Harsusī (language, la langue) i, 575a; iii, 176b – I, 593b; III, 180b
Ḥarsūsī → al-Ḥarāsīs
Ḥarṭānī i, 371a; ii, 133b, 877a; iii, **230b**; v, 1197a; s, 328b – I, 381b; II, 137a, 897a; III, **237b**; V, 1187a; S, 328a
Harthama b. ʿArfadja al-Bāriḳī (650) iii, 29a; VI, 899b – III, 30b; VI, 891a
Harthama b. Aʿyan (816) i, 149b, 437b; ii, 196b, 886a; iii, **231a**, 233a, 243b, 982a; iv, 16b; vi, 333a, b, 334a, b; vii, 227b – I, 154a, 450a; II, 202b, 906b; III, **238a**, 240a, 250b, 1006b; IV, 18a; VI, 317b, 318a, b; VII, 229b
Harthama b. Naṣr s, 106a – S, 105b
Harūd → Harī Rūd
Hārūn b. ʿAbd Allāh (890) vi, 900a – VI, 891b
Hārūn b. Altūntāsh i, 424b; iv, 1067a – I, 436b; IV, 1098b
Hārūn b. al-Faradj (XI) iv, 605a; vii, 539b – IV, 629b; VII, 539b
Hārūn b. Gharīb (934) i, 688b, 962b; iii, 126b; vii, 414a – I, 709b, 992a; III, 129b; VII, 415b
Hārūn b. ʿImrān iii, **231b**; vi, 630a – III, **238b**; VI, 615a
Hārūn b. Khumarawayh (Ṭulūnid(e)) (905) iii, 745b; vii, 543a – III, 768b; VII, 543a
Hārūn b. al-Mahdī → Hārūn al-Rashīd
Hārūn b. Mūsā (Multān) ii, 892b – II, 913a
Hārūn b. Sayf al-Dīn b. Muḥammad Faḍl ii, 123b – II, 126b
Hārūn b. Sulaymān (892) vi, 900a – VI, 891b
Hārūn b. Yaḥyā i, 775a, 1033b; iii, **232a**, 1044b; vi, 89a – I, 798a, 1065a; III, **238b**, 1070b; VI, 87a
Hārūn b. al-Yamanī al-Mukhālif iii, 659b – III, 680b
Hārūn Bughra Khān → Bughra Khān Hārūn
Hārūn (Ḥasan) Khān b. Sulaymān (Ḳarakhānid(e)) vi, 274a – VI, 259a
Hārūn al-Rashīd (ʿAbbāsid(e)) (809) i, 14a, 18a, 107b, 118a, 144b, 164b, 247b, 364a, 437a, 485a, 510a, 550b, 697a, 1034a, 1035, 1298a; ii, 191a; iii, 22b, 231a, **232b**, 344b, 345b, 996a, 1044b; iv, 16b, 97b, 858b, 940b, 1164a; v, 174b, 533b, 1239a; vi, 2a, 140b, 147b, 205b, 263b, 264b, 331a, 379a, 437a, 468b, 499a, 506a, 544a, 578a, 660b, 665a, 714a, 744b, 752b; vii, 518a, 646a; viii, 411a, 412a; s, 22b, 26a, 48a, 64a, 122a, 128a, 198b, 199a, 225b, 251b, 252a, 263a, 304a, 326b, 372a – I, 14a, 18b, 110b, 121b, 148b, 169a, 255b, 375a, 449b, 499b, 525b, 568a, 718b, 1065b, 1066b, 1338a;

II, 197a; III, 23b, 238a, **239a**, 355a, 356a, 1021a, 1070b; IV, 17b-18a, 101b, 892a, 973b, 1196a; V, 172a, 537b, 1229b; VI, 2a, 138b, 146a, 190a, 248a, 249b, 315b, 363b, 423a, 454a, 484b, 491b, 528b, 563a, 646a, 651a, 702b, 733b, 742a; VII, 518b, 645b; VIII, 425b, 426a S, 23a, 26b, 49a, 64b, 121b, 127b, 198b, 199a, 225b, 252a, 262b, 304a, 326a, 372a
—constructions i, 182b, 199b, 616b, 761a, 789b; ii, 36a, 1120a; iii, 228a, 235a – I, 187b, 205b, 637a, 784a, 812b; II, 36b, 1146b; III, 235a, 241b
Hārūn al-Shārī ii, 524a; iii, 126a, 619a – II, 537a; III, 129a, 639b
al-Hārūniyya iii, **234b**; vi, 506a – III, **241b**; VI, 491b
Ḥarūnum vi, 562b – VI, 547a
Ḥarūrā᾽ i, 40b; iii, **235a**; vii, 523b – I, 41b; III, **242a**; VII, 524a
Ḥarūrites i, 384a, 385b; iii, 235a; iv, 1074b – I, 395a, 396b; III, 242a; IV, 1106b
Harūsindān b. Tīrdādh s, 357a – S, 357a
Hārūt wa-Mārūt i, 811b; iii, **236b**; vi, 216b, 218a, 737a, 738a – I, 834b; III, **243b**; VI, 201a, 202a, 726a, 727b
Ḥarz iv, 1038a – IV, 1069b
Harzam vi, 540b – VI, 525a
al-Ḥasā i, 72b, 100a, 538b, 539a; iii, **237b**; iv, 663b, 664a, b, 764b, 925a, b; v, 684a; vi, 157b, 274b, 435b, 734b; vii, 301b, 782b; s, 135b, 234a, 380a – I, 75a, 103a, 555a, 555b; III, **244a**, 567b; IV, 690a, b, 691b, 795a, 958a, b; V, 689a; VI, 153a, 259b, 420b, 724a; VII, 303b, 784b; S, 135b, 234a, 380a
Ḥasab wa-nasab i, 892b; iii, **238b** – I, 919a; III, **245b**
Ḥasab Allāh b. Muḥammad Faḍl ii, 123b – II, 126b
Ḥasan iii, 25a – III, 26b
al-Ḥasan I, Mawlāy (ʿAlawī) (1895) i, 290b, 356b, 357a, 1281a; ii, 109a, 820a, 823a, 885b, 1116a; iii, **240a**, 256a, 536a, 562a; v, 890a, 1192b, 1193a; vi, 134b, 135a, b, 589b, 595b, 743a; s, 114a – I, 299b, 367b, 368a, 1320b; II, 111b, 839b, 842b, 906a, 1142b; III, **247a**, 263b, 554b, 581b; V, 896b, 1182b, 1183a; VI, 132b, 133b, 574a, 580a, 732b; S, 113b
al-Ḥasan II (ʿAlawid(e)) ii, 673b; iii, 564a; v, 1072b, 1073a, 1195a – II, 690a; III, 583a; V, 1070a, b, 1185a
Ḥasan I (Nizārī) → Ḥasan-i Ṣabbāḥ
Ḥasan II (Nīzārī) (1193) i, 353b; iv, 28a, 200a, 205a; viii, 442a – I, 364b; IV, 30a, 208b, 214a; VIII, 457a
Ḥasan III Rukn al-Dīn (Ismāʿīlī) (1221) i, 353b; iv, 205b, 860a; vii, 1000b – I, 364b; IV, 214b, 893a; VII, 1002a, b
al-Ḥasan, Abū ʿAbdallāh Muḥammad iii, 69a; iv, 1157a – III, 71b; IV, 1189a
Ḥasan, Bayhaḳī Sayyid s, 131b – S, 130b
Ḥasan, al-Malik al-Nāṣir Nāṣir al-Dīn (Mamlūk) (1361) i, 765b, 1050b; iii, **239b**, 900b; iv, 431b, 940a; v, 1141a; vii, 171a, 992b – I, 788b, 1082a; III, **246b**, 925a; IV, 450a, b, 992b; V, 1134a; VII, 172b, 994b
al-Ḥasan, Mawlāy → al-Ḥasan (ʿAlawid(e)); al-Ḥasan, Abū Abdullāh
Ḥasan, Mīr Ghulām (1786) vi, 838a; s, **358b** – VI, 828b; S, **358b**
Ḥasan, Mullā (Farangī Maḥall) s, 292a – S, 292a
Ḥasan, Pīr v, 27a – V, 27b
Ḥasan, Shaykh (Čūbānid(e)) vi, 482b – VI, 468b
Ḥasan b. ʿAbd Allāh → Nāṣir al-Dawla Ḥasan
al-Ḥasan b. ʿAbd al-Raḥmān (XI) vii, 413a – VII, 414b
Ḥasan b. Abi 'l-Ḥasan → Japheth al-Barḳamānī
al-Ḥasan b. Abī 'l-Haydjā᾽ → Nāṣir al-Dawla Ḥasan
al-Ḥasan b. Abī Numayy II, Sharīf ii, 517b; s, 234b – II, 530a; S, 234b
Ḥasan b. Aḥmad al-Karmaṭī v, 368b – V, 369b
Ḥasan b. ʿAdī i, 195b – I, 201a
Ḥasan b. ʿAdjlān, Sharīf (1426) vi, 149b – VI, 148a
al-Ḥasan b. Aḥmad (Mombasa) (XVII) v, 105a; VII, 226b – V, 107a; VII, 228a
Ḥasan b. Aḥmad Bahmanī iii, 577a – III, 597a
Ḥasan b. ʿAlī → al-Ḥasan al-Utrūsh; Ibn Makūlā; Niẓām al-Mulk
Ḥasan b. ʿAlī (Ḥamdānid(e)) (896) vi, 900a – VI, 891b
al-Ḥasan b. ʿAlī (Zanzibar) vii, 250a – VII, 251b
al-Ḥasan b. ʿAlī (Zīrid(e)) iii, 138b, 933a – III, 141b, 958a
al-Ḥasan b. ʿAlī b. Abi 'l-Ḥusayn iv, 496b; v, 105b – IV, 517b, 518a; V, 107b
al-Ḥasan b. ʿAlī b. Abī Ṭālib (Imām) (669) i, 40b, 43b, 86a, 163b, 194b, 385a, 550a, 697a; ii, 843a, 848b; iii, **240b**, 607b, 889b; v, 945b; vi, 334a, 652a, 668b; vii, 265b, 688b; s, 401a – I, 41b, 44b, 88b, 168a, 200b, 396b, 567b, 718a; II, 863a, 868b; III, **247b**, 628a, 913a; V, 949b; VI, 318b, 637b, 654b; VII, 267b, 689a; S, 401b
Ḥasan b. ʿAlī al-Baṣrī → Japheth b. Eli
al-Ḥasan b. ʿAlī al-Kalbī i, 986b; ii, 853a; ix, 585a – I, 1017a; II, 873a; IX, 608b
al-Ḥasan b. ʿAlī al-Ma᾽mūnī i, 149b – I, 154a
Ḥasan b. ʿAlī Shāmma ii, 167a – II, 172a
al-Ḥasan b. ʿAlī ʿUmar al-Marrākushī i, 727a; ii, 586b; v, 1209b; s, 413b – I, 749a; II, 601a; V, 1200a; S, 414a
al-Ḥasan b. ʿAmmār i, 1042a; ii, 858b; iii, 76b, 77a; iv, 497a; v, 1160a – I, 1073b; II, 878b; III, 79a, b; IV, 518a; V, 1150a
Ḥasan b. Asad Allāh (Marʿashī) (1476) vi, 514a – VI, 499a
al-Ḥasan b. Ayyūb (X) vi, 636b – VI, 621b
Ḥasan b. al-Bāḳir iv, 859a – IV, 892b
Ḥasan b. Bālī Efendi (Malāmī) (XVI) vi, 228a – VI, 222a
Ḥasan b. Buwayh (Būya) → Rukn al-Dawla Ḥasan
Ḥasan b. al-Faḍl iv, 637b – IV, 664a
Ḥasan b. Faraḥ b. Ḥawshab b. Zādān al-Kūfī → Manṣūr al-Yaman
Ḥasan b. Farīghūn ii, 799b – II, 818b
al-Ḥasan b. Fīrūzān (Daylamī) (X) ii, 928a; vi, 115b – II, 949b; VI, 113b
Ḥasan b. Gannūn (Djannūn) (Idrīsid(e) (985) i, 1088a; iii, 30b, 74b, 1036b; vi, 431a, b; vii, 942b – I, 1120a; III, 32a, 77a, 1062b; VI, 416a, 417a; VII, 942b
Ḥasan b. Ḥabīb vi, 196b – VI, 180b
Ḥasan b. al-Ḥāfiẓ i, 939b; iii, 55a – I, 968a; III, 57a
al-Ḥasan b. Hānī᾽ → Abū Nuwās
Ḥasan b. Ḥārūn i, 866a – I, 890a
Ḥasan b. Ḥassūna iv, 686b – IV, 714b
al-Ḥasan b. Ḥayy → al-Ḥasan b. Ṣāliḥ b. Ḥayy
al-Ḥasan b. Hibat Allāh Ibn Asākir iii, 713b; iv, 201a – III, 736a; IV, 210a
Ḥasan b. Hibat Allāh Makramī (1775) vi, 191b, VI, 175b
al-Ḥasan b. al-Ḥusayn iv, 646b, 647a – IV, 673a, b
Ḥasan b. Idrīs, *dāʿī muṭlaḳ* s, 358b – S, 358b
al-Ḥasan b. al-Imām al-Manṣūr bi-'llāh al-Ḳāsim (Zaydid(e)) (1639) vii, 270a – VII, 272a
al-Ḥasan b. Ismāʿīl, Mawlāy (ʿAlawid(e)) vii, 387a – VII, 388a
al-Ḥasan b. Ismāʿīl Āl Shibām al-Makramī iv, 201a – IV, 210a
Ḥasan b. Ḳaḥṭaba (754) i, 16a, 103a, 449b; ii, 196b,

679a, 715a; iii, 802b; iv, 447a, b; vi, 417b; ix. 612b – I, 16b, 106a, 462b; II, 202b, 696a, 733b; III, 826a; IV, 466b, 467b; VI, 412b; IX, 636b
Ḥasan b. Ḳāsim (Idrīsid(e)) → Ḥasan b. Gannūn
Ḥasan b. al-Ḳāsim al-Dāʿi ilā ʾl-Ḥaḳḳ (Ḥasanid(e)) (928) i, 688a; ii, 191b, 192a, b; iii, 254b; vi, 115b, 941b; s, **356a** – I, 709a; II, 197b, 198a, b; III, 262a; VI, 113a, 933b; S, **356a**
Ḥasan b. Ḳatāda b. Idrīs, Sharīf (XIII) vi, 149b – VI, 148a
al-Ḥasan b. Khālid al-Ḥāzimī, Sharīf s, 30b – S, 30b
al-Ḥasan b. al-Khaṣīb → Ibn al-Khaṣīb
Ḥasan b. Khayr al-Dīn → Ḥasan Pasha (Algiers/ Alger)
al-Ḥasan b. Maḥbūb (XI) i, 758b; vii, 732a – I, 781b; VII, 733a
al-Ḥasan b. Makhlad → Ibn Makhlad
al-Ḥasan b. al-Manṣūr bi-ʾllāh al-Ḳāsim b. Muḥammad (Zaydī) (1613) vi, 437a – VI, 422a, b
al-Ḥasan b. Marwān v, 453a – V, 455b
al-Ḥasan b. Muḥammad (ʿAlawid(e)) → al-Ḥasan I, II
al-Ḥasan b. Muḥammad (Buwayhid(e)) → al-Muhallabī
al-Ḥasan b. Muḥammad (Khayrātid(e)) i, 709b – I, 731a
al-Ḥasan b. Muḥammad (Nizārī) → al-Ḥasan II, III
al-Ḥasan b. Muḥammad Āl ʿĀʾiḍ i, 709b – I, 731a
Ḥasan b. Muḥammad al-ʿAṭṭār → al-ʿAṭṭār, Ḥasan b. Muḥammad
al-Ḥasan b. Muḥammad b. al-Ḥanafiyya (705) v, 1026b; vi, 636b; s, **357b** – V, 1022b; VI, 621b; S, **357b**
Ḥasan b. Muḥammad b. Ḳalāwūn (Mamlūk) (1350) vi, 413b – VI, 398b
al-Ḥasan b. Muḥammad b. al-Ḳāsim (Idrīsid(e)) vii, 641b – VII, 641a
al-Ḥasan b. Muḥammad b. Samāʿa al-Sayrafī (Wāḳifī) (876) vii, 647b – VII, 647a
Ḥasan b. Muḥammad Abī Numayy, Sharīf (1601) vi, 150a – VI, 148b
Ḥasan b. Muḥammad Naẓẓām al-Nīsābūrī s, 413a – S, 413b
al-Ḥasan b. Mūsā (923) vii, 786a – VII, 788a
Ḥasan b. Nāmāwar ii, 194a – II, 200a
Ḥasan b. Nūḥ al-Hindī (1533) s, **358b** – S, **358a**
Ḥasan b. al-Nuʿmān (VII) vi, 751a – VI, 740b
al-Ḥasan b. Rabāḥ s, 352a – S, 352a
Ḥasan b. al-Ṣabbāḥ → Ḥasan-i Ṣabbāḥ
al-Ḥasan b. Ṣafī (1173) vi, 110b – VI, 108b
al-Ḥasan b. Sahl (850) i, 149b, 271b, 316a, 897b, 1298a, 1312a; ii, 731a, b; iii, **243b**, 345b, 951a, 987b; iv, 17a; vi, 334a, b, 335a, b, 336a; vii, 404a; s, 15a, 263b –
I, 154a, 280a, 325b, 924a, 1338a, 1352b; II, 749b, 750a; III, **250b**, 356a, 975b, 1012a; IV, 18a; VI, 318b, 319b, 320b; VII, 405b; S, 15b, 263a
al-Ḥasan b. Ṣāliḥ b. Ḥayy (784) iii, **244a**; s, 48a, 130a – III, **251a**; S, 48b, 129a
al-Ḥasan b. Sanbar (Shanbar) iv, 664a – IV, 691a
Ḥasan b. Sulaymān (Ilek-khān) (1102) iii, 1114a – III, 1141b
al-Ḥasan b, Sulaymān (Kilwa) (1333) ix, 699a, 700b – IX, 729a
al-Ḥasan b. Suwār (1017) i, 631b, 632a; vi, 204a, 347a, 845b – I, 652b; VI, 188a, 331a, 836a
Ḥasan b. Tīmūrtāsh (Čūbānid(e)) → Ḥasan Küčük
al-Ḥasan b. ʿUbayd Allāh b. Tughdj iv, 663a – IV, 690a
Ḥasan b. Ustādh-Hurmuz, ʿAmīd al-Djuyūsh (1011) iii, **244b**; vi, 965b – III, **251b**; VI, 957b
Ḥasan b. Wahb i, 153b – I, 158a
al-Ḥasan b. Yūsuf → al-Ḥillī
al-Ḥasan b. Zayd b. al-Ḥasan (783) i, 45b; iii, **244b**, 786b – I, 46b; III, **251b**, 809b
al-Ḥasan b. Zayd b. Muḥammad (al-ḍāʿī al-kabīr) (884) i, 352b; ii, 191a; iii, **245a**; iv, 46b; v, 662a; vi, 745b, 941a; vii, 390a, 410b, 418a, 723a, 786a, 794a; viii, 625b; x, 105a –
I, 363b; II, 197a; III, **252a**; IV, 49b; V, 667a; VI, 734b, 933b; VII, 391b, 412a, 419a, 724a, 787b, 795b; VIII, 644b; X, 113a
al-Ḥasan b. Zayn al-Dīn (1602) vii, 298a; viii, 777b – VII, 300a; VIII, 804b
Ḥasan b. Ziyād al-Luʾluʾī i, 124a; iii, 163a – I, 127b; III, 166b
Ḥasan ʿAbd al-Shukūr, Shaykh (XX) vi, 175b
Ḥasan Abdāl iii, **245a** – III, **252a**
Ḥasan Aghā (1545) i, 1247a; iii, **245b** – I, 1285a; III, **252b**
Ḥasan Agha (author, auteur) v, 261a – V, 259a
Ḥasan Agha (Aydinoghlu) ii, 599a – II, 614a
Ḥasan Akhmīnī i, 330a – I, 340b
Ḥasan al-Akhram iii, 80b, 154a – III, 82b, 157b
al-Ḥasan ʿalā dhikrihi ʾl-salām → Ḥasan II (Ismāʿīlī)
Ḥasan ʿAlī b. Djahānshāh i, 148a; iv, 588a – I, 152b; IV, 611b
Ḥasan ʿAlī b. Fatḥ ʿAlī Shāh (Ḳādjār) (XIX) vi, 484b – VI, 470b
Ḥasan ʿAlī Bārha i, 1025b, 1026a; ii, 379a, 810a; iv, 279b; s, 126b – I, 1057b; II, 389b, 829a; IV, 292a; S, 125b
Ḥasan ʿAlī Manṣūr (1965) iv, 42a; vii, 448b – IV, 44b; VII, 449b
Ḥasan ʿAlī Mīrzā Shudjāʿ al-Salṭana (Shīrāz) (XIX) iv, 313a, 393a; vii, 453b, 454a – IV, 327a, 409b; VII, 454b
Ḥasan ʿAlī Munshī (XVI) vii, 988a – VII, 989a
Ḥasan ʿAlī Shāh → Agha KhānI
al-Ḥasan Amīrkā b. Abi ʾl-Faḍl al-Thāʾir s, 363a – S, 363a
al-Ḥasan al-Aʿṣam (977) i, 551b; ii, 854a; iii, **246a**; iv, 663a, b; s, 36b – I, 569a; II, 874a; III, **253a**; IV, 690a; S, 36b
Ḥasan al-ʿAskarī, Abū Muḥammad (XI. Imām) (874) iii, **246b**; vii, 443a; viii, 146a, 1040b; s, 95a – III, **253b**; VII, 444a; VIII, 148b, 1076a S, 94b
Ḥasan Baba, dey (1683) iii, **247a**, 629a – III, **254a**, 650a
Ḥasan Balfiyya iv, 852a – IV, 885a
al-Ḥasan al-Bannāʾ → al-Bannāʾ
al-Ḥasan al-Bashīr (Sūdān) (XX) ix, 750b – IX, 788b
al-Ḥasan al-Baṣrī (728) i, 105a, b, 454a, 718a, 1080b; ii, 293a, 729a, 891b; iii, **247b**, 682b, 947b, 948a; iv, 142a, 212a, 369a, 486a, 734a, b; v, 209b, 936a, 1231b; vi, 266b, 351a, 457b, 709b; vii, 783a, b; s, 230b, 323b, 350a, 358a –
I, 108a, b, 467a, 739b, 1113a; II, 301a, 747b, 912b; III, **254b**, 704a, 972a, b; IV, 148a, 221b, 385a, 507a, 763b, 764a; V, 207a, 940a, 1222a; VI, 251b, 335b, 443a, 698a; VII, 785a, b; S, 230b, 323a, 350a, 358a
Ḥasan Bāwand → Fakhr al-Dawla Ḥasan
Ḥasan al-Bawwāb i, 195b – I, 201a
Ḥasan Bāyḳarā → Bāyḳarā
Ḥasan Bedr al-Dīn, Pasha (1912) vi, 372b, 373a; s, **359b** – VI, 357a, b; S, **359a**
Ḥasan Bey al-Djuddāwī iii, 992a, b – III, 1017a
Ḥasan Bey-zāde (1636) iii, **248b** – III, **255b**
Ḥasan Bey Melikor Zerdabi → Zerdabi
Ḥasan Buzurg, Shaykh (Djalāyirid(e)), (1337) i, 903b, 908b; ii, 68a, b, 401a, 706a; iii, 1122b, 1208b; vi, 502b –

I, 930b, 936a; II, 69a, b, 411b, 724a; III, 1150b, 1239a; VI, 487b

Ḥasan Čelebi   → Ḳinalîzāde

al-Ḥasan al-Dāk̲h̲il, s̲h̲arīf   iii, 256b – III, 263b

Ḥasan Dihlawī (1336)   iii, **249a** – III, **256a**

Ḥasan D̲j̲alāyir   → Ḥasan Buzurg

Ḥasan D̲j̲ūrī, S̲h̲ayk̲h̲ (Marʿas̲h̲ī) (XIV)   vi, 511a – VI, 496b

Ḥasan Esīrī (XVII)   viii, 5a – VIII, 5a

Ḥasan Fak̲h̲r al-Dawla (Bāwandid(e)) (1349)   vi, 511b – VI, 497a

Ḥasan al-Faḳī (XX)   vi, 176b

Ḥasan al-Fārūḳī   ii, 814b; iii, 638a – II, 834a; III, 659b

Ḥasan Fasāʾī (Kawār)   vi, 384a – VI, 368b

Ḥasan Fehmī (1909)   iii, **251a**; iv, 284a – III, **258a**; IV, 296a

Ḥasan Fehmī Efendi (1881)   iii, **250a**; iv, 168b – III, **257a**; IV, 176a

Ḥasan Fehmī Pas̲h̲a (1910)   ii, 473b; iii, **249b** – II, 485b; III, **256b**

Ḥasan Gangū   → Muḥammad I (Bahmānid(e))

Ḥasan G̲h̲aznawī As̲h̲raf   s, 416b – S, 416b

Ḥasan al-Ik̲h̲nāʿī   i, 280b – I, 289a

Ḥasan-ili   s, 168b – S, 169a

Ḥasan ʿIzzet Pas̲h̲a   ii, 699b – II, 717b

Ḥasan Kabīr al-Dīn, Pīr   iv, 202b; v, 26a – IV, 211b; V, 27a

Ḥasan Kāfī   i, 310a, 1271b – I, 319b, 1310b

Ḥasan Ḳāʾimī (1690) ix, 39b – IX, 30b

Ḥasan Karlug̲h̲, Sayf al-Dīn (Multān) (1249)   i, 227a; vi, 48a, b – I, 234a; VI, 46b, 47a

al-Ḥasan al-Kātib (XI)   vii, 683b, 976a – VII, 684a, 976b

Ḥasan K̲h̲ān (Ḳarak̲h̲ānid(e))   → Ḥasan b. Sulaymān

Ḥasan K̲h̲ān Bāyburdī   iv, 1044b – IV, 1076a

Ḥasan K̲h̲ān Ḳās̲h̲ḳāy   iv, 706a – IV, 734b

Ḥasan K̲h̲ān Sālār (Mas̲h̲had) (1849)   vi, 715a – VI, 704a

Ḥasan el-K̲h̲eyūn   i, 684a – I, 705a

Ḥasan Kücük (Čūbānid(e)) (1343)   ii, **68a**, 401a, 706a; iii, 1122b, 1208b – II, **69b**, 411b, 724a; III, 1150b, 1239a

Ḥasan Malik of/de Čadura   s, 366a – S, 366a

Ḥasan Mīrzā b. Muḥammad K̲h̲udābanda (1576)   vi, 515a – VI, 500a

Ḥasan Muḳaddam (1925)   vi, 764a – VI, 753a

al-Ḥasan al-Mustanṣir (Ḥammūdid(e))   vi, 222a – VI, 216a

al-Ḥasan Nāṣir al-Dawla, Amīr   s, 36a – S, 36a

Ḥasan Nit̲h̲ārī   s, 340a – S, 339b

Ḥasan Niẓāmī (XIII)   v, 546b; s, **359b** – V, 551a; S, **359b**

Ḥasan Pas̲h̲a   → D̲j̲ezāʾirli G̲h̲āzī; Kāhya; K̲h̲ādim; Kücük; Ṣoḳolli; Tiryāḳī; Yemenli; Yemis̲h̲d̲j̲i;

Ḥasan Pas̲h̲a (Algiers, Alger) (1572)   iii, **251a**; iv, 1158a; v, 362a – III, **258a**; IV, 1190a; V, 363a

Ḥasan Pas̲h̲a (Bag̲h̲dād) (1723)   i, 905a; iii, **252a**, 1257b – I, 932b; III, **259a**, 1290a

Ḥasan Pas̲h̲a (Mora) (XVII)   vii, 239b – VII, 241a

Ḥasan Pas̲h̲a (Yemen) (1604)   vi, 436b – VI, 422a

Ḥasan Pas̲h̲a, Dāmād (1713)   iii, **252b** – III, **259b**

Ḥasan Pas̲h̲a, Sayyid (1748)   iii, **253a**; iv, 233b – III, **260a**; IV, 244a

Ḥasan Pas̲h̲a, S̲h̲erīf (1791)   ii, 534a; iii, **253a** ; s, 331a – II, 547b; III, **260a**; S, 330b

Ḥasan Pas̲h̲a Čatald̲j̲alî (1631)   iii, **252a**; iv, 92a – III, **259a**; IV, 96a

Ḥasan Pas̲h̲a Predojevič   i, 1266a; ix, 681a – I, 1305a; IX, 708a

Ḥasan al-Rammāḥ (1294)   i, 1056a; vii, 885b – I, 1087b; VII, 886b

Ḥasan al-Rayyī   s, 252b – S, 252b

Ḥasan-i D̲j̲ūrī, S̲h̲ayk̲h̲ (1842) ix, 98a – IX, 48b

Ḥasan-i Rūmlū (XVI)   iii, **253b** – III, **260b**

Ḥasan-i Ṣabbāḥ (1124)   i, 215b, 352b, 353a,b, 1359b; ii, 98a, 194a, 858b; iii, **253b**, 544b, 725a; iv, 199b, 200a, 205a; vi, 918a; vii, 541a; viii, 72a, b, 84a – I, 221b, 363b, 364a, 1399b; II, 100a, 200a, 878a; III, **260b**, 563b, 747b; IV, 208b, 214a; VI, 909b; VII, 541a; VIII, 74a, 86a

Ḥasan Ṣabrī   iii, 515b; s, 300b – III, 533a; S, 300a

Ḥasan Sezāʾī (1738)   viii, 167a – VIII, 169b

Ḥasan S̲h̲āh b. Gul K̲h̲ātūn (Kas̲h̲mīr)   s, 131b, 242a, 329a, 423b – S, 130b, 242a, 328b, 423b

Ḥasan S̲h̲āh Bahmanī   → ʿAlāʾ al-Dīn Ḥasan

Ḥasan S̲h̲āh Bahmanī (1484)   s, 353b – S, 353b

Ḥasan S̲h̲īrāzī, Mīrzā   s, 54a – S, 54b

Ḥasan the Tailor/le Tailleur   vi, 228a, b – VI, 222a

Ḥasan al-Turābī (Sūdān) (XX)   ix, 750b – IX, 780b

Ḥasan al-Uṭrūs̲h̲ Abū Muḥammad b. ʿAlī Zayn al-ʿĀbidīn, Imām (917)   i, 688a, 1350b; ii, 191b; iii, **254a**; iv, 19a; v, 603a; vi, 516a, 941b; vii, 542b, 645b, 995b; s, 356b, 363a – I, 709a, 1391a; II, 197b; III, **261b**; IV, 20b; V, 607a; VI, 501a, 933b; VII, 542b, 645a, 997b; S, 356a, 362

Ḥasanābād ix, 6b – IX, 7a

Ḥasanak, Abū ʿAlī Ḥasan (1032)   iii, **255b**; vi, 916a; vii, 26b; viii, 63a – III, **263a**; VI, 907b; VII, 26b; VIII, 64b

Ḥasanayn al-Ḥiṣāfī   → al-Ḥiṣāfī

Ḥasanī   iii, **256a** – III, **263b**

Ḥasan-ī Buzurg (1356)   viii, 997b – VIII, 1032b

Ḥasanī, Ḥasaniyyūn (Ḥasanid(e)s)   i, 403a; ii, 572b; iii, **256b**; v, 1191b; vi, 140b, 148a; ix, 507a – I, 414b; II, 586b; III, **263b**; V, 1181b; VI, 138b, 146b; IX, 526b

Ḥasanī, Ibrāhīm al-   v, 133a – V, 135b

Ḥasanī Rūmlū (XVI)   viii, 776b – VIII, 802b

al-Ḥasaniyya   iii, 660a – III, 681a

Ḥasankeyf   → Ḥiṣn Kayfā

Ḥasanmat (Sawādkūh) (1545)   vi, 515a – VI, 500a

Ḥasanwayh al-Barzikānī   i, 211b; ii, 299b, 748b; iii, **258a**, 703b; v, 452b; s, 118b – I, 218a; II, 307b, 767a; III, **265a**, 725b; V, 455a; S, 118a

Ḥasanwayhid(e)s   i, 1030b; iii, **258a**; v, 824a – I, 1062a; III, **265a**; V, 830a

Ḥasanzāde Meḥmed Efendi   iv, 737a – IV, 766b

Ḥāṣbayyā   vi, 28a, 31a – VI, 26a, 29a

Ḥasdāy b. S̲h̲aprūṭ (975)   ii, 349b; iii, **259a**; viii, 626a, 813b – II, 359a; III, **266a**; VIII, 644b, 841a

Ḥas̲h̲ā   iv, 272b, 273a – IV, 284b, 285a

Ḥas̲h̲arāt al-arḍ   iii, 307b – III, 317a

Ḥās̲h̲id wa-Bakīl, Banū   iii, **259a**; v, 807b; vi, 436a – III, **266b**; V, 813b; VI, 421a, b

Hās̲h̲im, Abū Ibrāhīm S̲h̲īrāzī   s, 405b – S, 405b

Hās̲h̲im, Aḥmed (1933)   iii, **260a** – III, **267b**

Hās̲h̲im, Banū   → Hās̲h̲imid(e)s; Hās̲h̲imiyya; Ḥid̲j̲āz; Makka; Muḥammad

Hās̲h̲im, Labība (XX)   vii, 903a – VII, 903b

Hās̲h̲im, S̲h̲ehu   i, 1260a; v, 358b – I, 1298b; V, 359b

Hās̲h̲im b. ʿAbd al-ʿAzīz (IX)   i, 85b; vii, 569a – I, 88a; VII, 569b

Hās̲h̲im b. ʿAbd Manāf   i, 15a, 80a, 115b; ii, 1056a; iii, **260a**, 262b, 265a, 1093a; v, 41b – I, 15b, 82a, 118b; II, 1080b; III, **267a**, 270a, 272b, 1120a; V, 43a

Hās̲h̲im b. Sulaymān (Mecca) (XX)   vi, 165b – VI, 157b

Hās̲h̲im b. ʿUrwa   vi, 263a – VI, 247b

Hās̲h̲im b. ʿUtba   iii, **260a** – III, **267a**

Hāshim ʿAlī (1756) vi, 611a – VI, 596a
Hāshim al-Atāsī (XX) v, 1047a; vi, 538a – V, 1043b, 1044a; VI, 522b
Hāshim (Sayyid) b. Ḥasan (Bayhaḳī) s, 131b – S, 131a
Hāshim Baba ii, 543b – II, 556b
Hāshim Bey (XIX) vii, 685b – VII, 686a
Hāshim Khān (1933) vi, 86b – VI, 84b
Hāshim Khodjandī iv, 505a – IV, 527a
Hāshim Musabbaʿāwī ii, 123a; v, 267a – II, 126a; V, 265a
Hāshim al-Ṭaʿʿān vii, 145b – VII, 147b
Hāshim Ushkūrī s, 23b – S, 24a
Hāshim al-Zawāwī (1947) vi, 176b
al-Hāshimī, ʿAlī b. Sulaymān viii, 101b – VIII, 104a
al-Hāshimī, Shaykh (1961) iii, **261b** – III, **269a**
Hāshimid(e)s (Bāb al-Abwāb) i, 835b; iv, 345a – I, 859a; IV, 359b
Hāshimid(e)s (Ḥidjāz, ʿIrāḳ, Jordan) i, 41a; iii, **263a**, 1065b, 1066b; vi, 31b; s, 3b – I, 42a; III, **270b**, 1092a, 1093b; VI, 30a; S, 3b
Hāshimid(e)s (al-Hawāshim, Mecca) i, 552a; iii, **262b**; vi, 137b, 138a, 145a, 146a, 148b, 149a, 441b; ix, 507a – I, 569b; III, **269b**; VI, 135b, 136a, 143a, 144b, 147a, b, 427a: IX, 526b
Hāshimiyya (ʿAbbāsid(e)s) i, 15a, 17a, 258a; iii, **265a**; iv, 446a, 837a; v, 1b-2b; vi, 624b; x, 841a; 845a – I, 15b, 17b, 266a; III, **272b**; IV, 466a, 870a; V, 1b-2b; VI, 609b
al-Hāshimiyya (capital(e)) i, 17a, 895b; iii, **265b**; iv, 729a; vi, 345a – I, 17b, 922a; III, **273a**; IV, 758a; VI, 329a
Hāshimiyya (Djilwatiyya) ii, 543b – II, 556b
al-Ḥashīr i, 233b – I, 240b
Ḥashīsh i, 1014b; iii, **266a** – I, 1045b; III, **273b**
Ḥashīshiyya (Nizārīs) i, 353a; ii, 170b, 882a; iii, **267b**; v, 922a; vi, 577b – I, 364a; II, 176a, 902b; III, **275b**; V, 927b; VI, 562b
Ḥāshiya i, 816b; iii, **268b** – I, 840a; III, **276b**
Ḥāshiya (entourage) → Ḳaṣr
Ḥashm-i Ḳalb iii, 199a – III, 204a
Ḥashmet (1768) iii, **269a**, 357a – III, **277a**, 368a
Ḥashr → Ḳiyāma
Hashtād-Sar s, 116a – S, 115b
Hashtarūd vi, 498b, 502a, b – VI, 483b, 487a
al-Ḥashw i, 671b; iii, 269b – I, 692a; III, 277b
Ḥashwiyya i, 410b; iii, **269b**, 905b; iv, 470a – I, 422b; III, **277b**, 929b; IV, 491a
Ḥāsib → ʿIlm al-ḥisāb
Ḥāsik iii, **269b**; vi, 80a – III, **277b**; VI, 78a
al-Ḥāsikiyya i, 535b; iii, 270a – I, 551b; III, 277b
Ḥasʾirān vi, 80b – VI, 78b
al-Ḥaṣkafī iii, 163b – III, 167a
Haskūra (Hasākira), Banū vi, 741a, 742a, 743a, b – VI, 730a, 731a, b, 732a, b
Ḥasrat Mohānī (1951) v, 7a; s, **360a** – V, 7b; S, **359b**
Ḥāssa → Ḥiss
Ḥassān, Bā iii, **270a** – III, **278a**
al-Ḥassān b. al-Djarrāḥ al-Ṭaʾī (1024) ii, 482b; iii, 246a; vii, 117a – II, 495a; III, 253a; VII, 118b
Ḥassān b. Gümüshtigin, amīr (1123) vi, 380a – VI, 364a
Ḥassān b. Mālik b. Baḥdal al-Kalbī (688) ii, 89b, 360a; iii, **270b**; iv, 493a, 929b; vi, 622a; vii, 267b – II, 91b, 370a; III, **278a**; IV, 514a, 962b; VI, 607a; VII, 269b
Ḥassān b. Mufarridj (688) ii, 483b, 484a, 855b; iii, 80a; iv, 842a; v, 1211b – II, 496a,b, 875a; III, 82a; IV, 875a; V, 1201b
Ḥassān b. al-Nuʿmān (699) i, 77b, 862b, 1023b; ii, 130a; iii, **271a**; iv, 336b, 415b, 422a, b, 423a, 739b, 829b; vii, 643a – I, 79b, 886b, 1055a; II, 133b; III, **279a**; IV, 351a, 433b, 440b, 441a, b, 769b, 862b; VII, 643a
Ḥassān b. Thābit b. al-Mundhir (659) i, 50b, 145a, 828b, 1149a; ii, 541a, 993b, 1020b; iii, **271b**, 354a, 975b; iv, 835b, 1002a; vi, 475a, 575a, 605a; vii, 361b; s, 9b – I, 52a, 149a, 851b, 1183b; II, 554a, 1016b, 1044b; III, **279b**, 365a, 1000a; IV, 868b, 1031b; VI, 461a, 560a, 589b; VII, 364a; S, 9a
Hassani → Ḥasanī
Hassū Taylī (1603) s, **361a** – S, **360b**
Ḥassūn, Rizḳ Allāh ii, 471a – II, 483a
Ḥassūna, Banū v, 352a – V, 353a
Ḥassūna al-Laylī vi, 251a – VI, 235b
Hastādān vi, 495b – VI, 480b
Ḥātam Khān i, 444b – I, 457a
Hatay (Alexandretta/-e) i, 468b, 517a; iii, **273a**; iv, 138b; vi, 387b, 538a – I, 482b, 532b; III, **281a**; IV, 144a; VI, 372a, 522b
Hataylā Pir → Ghāzī Miyān
Hātī Khān ii, 973a – II, 995b
Ḥāṭib b. Abī Baltaʿa iv, 821a; vii, 511b – IV, 854a; VII, 512a
Hātif iii, **273a**, 668b – III, **281a**, 690
Hātif Iṣfahānī, Aḥmad (1783) iii, **273b**; viii, 448b – III, **281b**; VIII, 463b
Hātifī, ʿAbd Allāh (1521) iii, 114a, **274a**; iv, 1010a, 1073b; v, 1105a; viii, 775a – III, 116b, **281b**; IV, 1042b, 1105a; V, 1100b; VIII, 801a
Ḥaṭīm → Kaʿba
Ḥaṭīm, Banū s, 61b, 387b, 388a – S, 62a, 388a
Ḥaṭīm b. Aḥmad al-Ḥātimī v, 954b; s, 263a – V, 958a; S, 236a
Ḥaṭīm b. ʿAlī al-Zurayʿid v, 954b, 1244b – V, 958a, b, 1235a
Ḥaṭīm b. al-Ghashīm al-Mughallasī iii, 125b – III, 128a
Ḥaṭīm b. Harthama b. Aʿyan (IX) i, 844a; iii, 231b, **274a**; v, 297b; vi, 333a, 335a – I, 867b; III, 238a, **282a**; V, 297a; VI, 317b, 319a
Ḥaṭīm b. al-Ḥumās iii, 125b – III, 128b
Ḥaṭīm al-Ahdal i, 255b, 781a – I, 263b, 804b
Ḥaṭīm al-Ṭāʾī b. ʿAbd Allāh (VI) i, 195a, 364a, 1241b; ii, 961a; iii, **274b**, 343a; iv, 705a; vi, 474b; s, 234b – I, 200b, 375a, 1279b; II, 983b; III, **282b**, 353b; IV, 733a; VI, 460b; S, 234a
al-Ḥātimī, Abū ʿAlī Muḥammad (998) iv, 249b; vii, 772a; s, **361a** – IV, 260a; VII, 774a; S, **361a**
Ḥatimid(e)s s, 236a – S, 236a
Hatra → al-Ḥaḍr
Hatta ii, 663a, 664a, 665b – II, 679b, 680b, 682a
Ḥaṭṭin → Ḥiṭṭīn
Hausa i, 179b, 1259a; ii, 10a, 479a; iii, **275a**; iv, 773b; viii, 20a; ix, 761a – I, 184a, 1297b; II, 10a, 491b; III, **283a**; IV, 804b; VIII, 20a; IX, 794a
—language, literature/langue, littérature i, 179b; ii, 479a; iii, 278b; iv, 567b; v, 222b – I, 184b; II, 491b; III, 287a; IV, 589b; V, 220a
Havāyī i, 1063a – I, 1095a
Ḥawāla ii, 147b; iii, **283a, b**; iv, 405b – II, 151b; III, **292a, b**; IV, 423a
al-Ḥawānīt vi, 728b, 775b – VI, 717b, 765a
Ḥawār i, 535b – I, 552a
Ḥawārī iii, **285a** – III, **294a**
Ḥawāshī → Ḥāshiya
Ḥawāshib → Ḥawshabī
al-Hawāshim → Hāshimid(e)s
Hawāwīr iii, 300a – III, 309b

Hawāzin, Banū i, 12a, 544b; ii, 627a, 883b; iii, **285b**, 578a; vi, 266a, b; vii, 373a; viii, 697b; x, 788a, 789a; s, 177b –
I, 12a, 562a; II, 642b, 904a; III, **294a**, 598a; VI, 250b, 251a; VII, 374b; VIII, 717a; X, ; S, 178a
Hawbas vi, 561a – VI, 545b
Ḥawḍ (basin) ii, 461b; iii, **286a** – II, 473a; III, **295a**
Ḥawḍ (cistern) iii, **286b**; v, 884a, 888a – III, **295b**; V, 890a, b, 894b
Ḥawḍ (Mauritania(e)) iii, **288b**; v, 890a, 892a – III, **297b**; V, 896a, b, 898b
al-Ḥawḍ (Almería) vi, 576a – VI, 561a
Hawdha b. ʿAlī (VII) i, 689b, 690a, 964a; iii, 166b; vii, 664b; x, 57a – I, 710b, 711a, 993b; III, 170b; VII, 664a; X, 59a
Ḥawdhān vi, 191b – VI, 175a
al-Ḥawf viii, 39a – VIII, 39b
Ḥawfī iii, **289b**; vi, 248a – III, **298b**; VI, 232a
Ḥāwī iii, **291a**, 335a – III, **300a**, 345b
Ḥāwī iii, **291a** – III, **300a**
Ḥawīza (Ḥuwayza) i, 1096a; iii, **291b**; v, 80b; vii, 672a; ix, 856a – I, 1129a; III, **300b**; V, 82b; VII, 672a' IX, 891b
Hawr al-Hammār s, 243a – S, 243a
Ḥawra iii, **291b** – III, **300b**
Ḥawra → al-Dhiʾāb
Hawrāmān iii, **292a** – III, **301a**
Ḥawrān i, 1079a, 1093b, 1277a; ii, 1021a; iii, **292a**; vi, 303a, 349a, 545b, 547a –
I, 1111a, 1126a, 1316a; II, 1045a; III, **301a**; VI, 288b, 333a, 530a, 531b
Hawsam (Rūdisar, Gilān) vi, 513a; s, **363a** – VI, 498b; S, **362b**
al-Hawsamī, Abū Djaʿfar s, 363a – S, 363a
Ḥawshabī iii, **293b** – III, **302b**
Hawshanī vi, 216b – VI, 200b
Ḥawṭa iii, **294a**; s, 420b – III, **303a**; S, 420b
al-Ḥawṭa iii, **294b** – III, **303b**
Ḥawwāʾ iii, **295a**, 330b – III, **304b**, 340b
Ḥawwāʿ → Ḥāwī; Rukya
al-Ḥawwāʾ → Nudjūm
Hawwāra, Banū i, 250a, 254b, 1049a; ii, 979a, 1114b; iii, 66b, **295b**, 653b; iv, 481b, 568a; v, 515b; vi, 311a, 312a, 324a, 434b, 727a; vii, 186a, 420b; viii, 865a –
I, 258a, 262b, 1081a; II, 1001b, 1140b; III, 69a, **305a**, 675a; IV, 502b, 590a; V, 519a; VI, 296a, 297b, 308b, 420a, 716a; VII, 186a, 422a; VIII, 896a
al-Ḥawwārī, Abu 'l-Ḥasan (XIII) vi, 355a – VI, 339a
al-Ḥawwārī, Muḥammad b. Aḥmad vi, 196b – VI, 180b
Ḥawwārīn → Ḥuwwārīn
Ḥawz iii, **300b**; vi, 589a, b; s, 48a, 144b – III, **309b**; VI, 574a, b; S, 48b, 144b
al-Hawzālī, Muḥammad b. ʿAlī (1749) x, 346a – X, 372a
Hayākil i, 835a – I, 858a
Hayʾa (astronomy, astronomie) → ʿIlm al-hayʾa
Hayʾa iii, **301a** – III, **310a**
Ḥayāt iii, **302a** – III, **311a**
Ḥayāt, Shaykh iii, 230a – III, 237a
Ḥayāt b. Mulāmis → Ḥaywa b. Mulāmis
Ḥayāt Allāh Khān ii, 973b – II, 996a
Ḥayāt Muḥammad Khān i, 1195a – I, 1230b
Ḥayātī → ʿAbd al-Ḥayy, Shaykh
Ḥayātī, Shaykh Meḥmed (XVIII) viii, 166b – VIII, 169b
Ḥayātī-zāde iii, **303a** – III, **312b**
Hayāṭila (White Huns) i, 226a, b, 852a, 857a; ii, 1a; iii, 177a, **303b**, 584b; iv, 356a, 536a, 1172a, 1173b; v, 56b, 57a, 76a, 354b; vi, 633b, 720a; x, 303a, 691a; s, 327a –
I, 232b, 233a, 875b, 881a; II, 1a; III, 181a, **312b**, 604b; IV, 371b, 559a, 1205b, 1207a; V, 58a, b, 78a, 356a; VI, 618b, 709a; X, 326b; S, 326b
Ḥayawān iii, **304b**, 311b; v, 991b – III, **313b**, 321a; V, 986b
Hawwārī, Abū Madyan (Boumédienne) → Abū Madyan, Hawwārī
Haybat Khān Niyāzī s, 324b – S, 324a
Ḥayḍ iii, **315b** – III, **325a**
Ḥaydar iii, **315b** – III, **325a**
Ḥaydar (clan) s, 105b – S, 105a
Ḥaydar (general/général) s, 301a – S, 301a
Ḥaydar, Āl iv, 857a – IV, 890a
Ḥaydar, Amīr (Bukhārā) i, 1295b – I, 1335b
Ḥaydar, Ghāzi 'l-Dīn → Ghāzi 'l-Dīn
Ḥaydar, Malik al-ʿUlamāʾ Mullā s, 4b, 292b – S, 3b, 292a
Ḥaydar, Mīr i, 530b – I, 546b
Ḥaydar, Naṣīr al-Dīn (Nawwāb) (1837) vii, 301a – VII, 303a
Ḥaydar b. ʿAlī (XVII) iii, **316a** – III, **325b**
Ḥaydar b. Djunayd, Shaykh (Ṣafawid(e)| (1488) i, 923a; iii, **315b**; iv, 34a,b, 573a; v, 243b; viii, 237b, 766b, 777a –
I, 951a; III, **325a**; IV, 36b, 595b; V, 241b; VIII, 242b, 792a, 802a
Ḥaydar b. Kāʾus → al-Afshīn
Ḥaydar al-Afshīn → al-Afshīn
Ḥaydar ʿAlī Khān Bahādur (Mappila) (1782) i, 296b, 625a, 1015b; iii, **316b**, 428a; iv, 547a; v, 1259a, b, 1260a; vi, 459b, 535b; vii, 897b –
I, 305b, 645b, 1047a; III, **326a**, 442a; IV, 571a; V, 1250a, b, 1251b; VI, 445a, 520a; VII, 898b
Ḥaydar Bāmātōf (1872) vii, 205b – VII, 206b
Ḥaydar Beg i, 153a – I, 157b
Ḥaydar Mīrzā Dūghlāt Muḥammad (1551) i, 1002a; ii, 621b; iii, **317a**; iv, 213b, 410a, 612a, 708b; vii, 218a; s, 131b, 167a, 324b, 366a –
I, 1033a; II, 637b; III, **326b**; IV, 223a, 428a, 637a, 737a; VII, 220a; S, 131a, 167a, 324a, 366a
Ḥaydar Ḥaydar (Syria/-e) vi, 469a – VI, 454b
Ḥaydar Khān ʿAmū Ughlī (1921) s, **365a** – S. **364b**
Ḥaydar Ḳuli Sulṭān (Afshār) (XVI) i, 240a; vii, 673a – I, 247b; VII, 673a
Ḥaydar Malik (VII) s, 332b, **366a** – S, 332a, **366a**
Ḥaydar Pasha (Yemen) (XVII) iv, 828a; vii, 270a – IV, 861a; VII, 272a
Ḥaydar Shāh b. Zayn al-ʿĀbidīn (Kashmīr) s, 131b, 329a – S, 130b, 328b
Ḥaydar Shihāb (Maʿn, XVIII) v, 792b; vi, 344a – V, 799a; VI, 328a
Ḥaydar al-Shihābī (1835) vi, 345b, 346a – VI, 330a
Ḥaydar-i Āmulī, Bahāʾ al-Dīn (1385) iv, 49b, 698a; s, **363b** – IV, 52a, 726b; S, **363b**
Ḥaydar-oghlu Meḥmed (XVII) i, 4a; iii, **317b**; iv, 766a – I, 4b; III, **327a**; IV, 796b
Ḥaydara b. Mahdī i, 345a – I, 355b
Ḥaydarābād (Deccan) i, 924a, 1170a; ii, 99b, 426b, 1119a; iii, **318a**; iv, 219b; v, 550b; vi, 87a, 369b, 489b, 535b, 536a, b, 696a; viii, 67a, 73a; s, 4b, 47a, 280a –
I, 951b, 1205a; II, 101b, 437b, 1145a; III, **328a**; IV, 229a; V, 555a; VI, 85a, 353b, 475b, 520a, b, 521a, 684a; VIII, 68b, 74b; S, 3b, 47b, 279b
—institutions ii, 426b; iii, 318b, 322b – II, 437b; III, 328b, 332b
—monuments iii, 319a, 448a – III, 328b, 463a
—Niẓām of/de i, 1170a, 1202b; iii, 318b, 322a – I, 1205a, 1238b; III, 328a, 332a

Ḥaydarābād (Sind) iii, **323b** – III, **333b**
Ḥaydarān iii, **324b**; vi, 712b – III, **334b**; VI, 701a
Ḥaydarānlu (Mākū) vi, 201b – VI, 185b
Ḥaydarī, Ḥaydar Ba<u>kh</u>s<u>h</u> iii, 376b – III, 388a
Ḥaydarī<u>kh</u>āna s, 336a – S, 335b
Ḥaydarīs iv, 99a, 860b – IV, 103b, 893b
Ḥaydariyya iv, 474a; x, 250a – IV, 495a; X, 269a
Hay<u>dj</u> (Baḥrayn) x, 90a – X, 97a
Haydut i, 1267a – I, 1305b
Ḥayfā i, 946b; iii, **324b**, 365a; vi, 45b, 322a – I, 976a; III, **334b**, 376b; VI, 44a, 306b
al-Ḥayfī, ʿAbd al-<u>D</u>jalīl b. Muḥammad b. al-Musallam vii, 491a – VII, 490b
Ḥāyil, Ḥāʾil iii, **326b**; s, 3b, 305a – III, **336b**; S, 2b, 304b
al-Ḥayḳ, Hayākil i, 181a – I, 186a
Haykal, Muḥammad Ḥusayn i, 597b, 598a; ii, 467a; iv, 173a; v, 188b, 189b; vi, 956a; s, 6b, 58a – I, 617a, 617b; II, 478b; IV, 180b; V, 185b, 187a; VI, 948b; S, 5b, 58b
Haykal al-Zahra i, 488b – I, 503b
al-Ḥaykār (Aḥiḳar) v, 811b, 812a, 813a – V, 817b, 818a, 819a
al-Ḥayḳutān ix, 777a – IX, 811a
Haylāna, Banū vi, 592a, 742a – VI, 576b, 731a
al-Ḥaymā iii, **327a**; vi, 84b, 192a, 436b – III, **337a**; VI, 82b, 175b, 422a
Haymana vi, 226b – VI, 220b
Ḥayr → Ḥāʾir
Ḥayra iv, 95a – IV, 99a
Hayrabolu vi, 227b – VI, 221a
Ḥayratī (1553) iv, 68a; viii, 775b – IV, 71b; VIII, 801b
Ḥayrī<u>dj</u> s, 337a – S, 337a
Ḥays s, **366b** – S, **366b**
al-Ḥays s, 30b – S, 30b
Ḥayṣa Bayṣa (1179) iii, **327b**, 819b; vi, 64b – III, **337b**, 843a; VI, 62b
al-Hayṣam al-Hamdānī iii, 233a – III, 240a
Hayṣamiyya iv, 668a – IV, 695b
Hayṭal → Hayāṭila
al-Haytham (ḍāʿī) vi, 439a – VI, 424a
Hay<u>th</u>am b. ʿAbd Allāh (870) vi, 900a – VI, 891b
al-Hay<u>th</u>am b. ʿAdī (821) iii, 136a, **328a**; vi, 828b; vii, 258a; s, 38b – III, 139a, **338a**; VI, 819a; VII, 260a; S, 39a
al-Hay<u>th</u>am b. al-Hay<u>th</u>am (Ibāḍī) (IX) vii, 546b – VII, 546b
al-Hay<u>th</u>am b. Muḥammad (IX) ix, 488a – IX, 507a
al-Hay<u>th</u>am b. al-Rabīʿ b. Zurāra → Abū Ḥayyā al-Numayrī
al-Hay<u>th</u>amī (1563) vii, 191b – VII, 191b
Haythūm → Hethum
Hayūlā iii, **328a** – III, **338b**
Haywa b. Mulāmis al-Ḥaḍramī iv, 115a – IV, 120b
Ḥayy i, 306a; iii, **330a** – I, 315b; III, **340b**
Ḥayy b. Yaḳẓān iii, **330b**, 944a, 957a, 974b – III, **341a**, 968b, 981b, 999a
Ḥayya iii, **334b**; iv, 95a – III, **334b**; IV, 99a
Ḥayya b. Turkī b. <u>D</u>jalwī s, 305b – S, 305b
Ḥayyān b. <u>D</u>jabala iv, 646b – IV, 673a
Ḥayyān b. <u>Kh</u>alaf → Ibn Ḥayyān
Ḥayyān al-Sarrādj iv, 837a – IV, 870a
Haza<u>dj</u> → ʿArūḍ
Hazār Afsāna i, 361a, b; iii, 313b – I, 371b, 372b; III, 323a
Hazār Sutūn (palace/palais) vi, 532b – VI, 516b
Hazāras (Af<u>gh</u>ānistān) i, 88a, 224a, b, 229a, 857a, 1010a, 1173a; ii, 5b; iii, 335a, 1100b, 1107b; s, **367a**, b – I, 90b, 231a, 236a, 881a, 1041a, 1222a; II, 5b; III, 345b, 1127b, 1135a; S, **366b**, 367a
Hazāras (Pakistān) iii, **335b** – III, **345b**
Hazāra<u>dj</u>āt s, **367a** – S, **367b**
Hazārasp i, 421a, 872a; ii, 194a; iii, **336b**; s, 228b, 420a – I, 433a, 896a; II, 200a; III, **346b**; S, 228b, 420a
Hazārasp, Malik iii, 337a, b; v, 826b – III, 347a,b; V, 832b
Hazārasp Muḥammad (XV) vi, 512b – VI, 497b
Hazāraspid(e)s iii, **336b**,; iv, 32a; v, 824b, 826b – III, **347a**, 1041b; IV, 34a; V, 830b, 832b
Hazārāt i, 139b – I, 143b
Hazār<u>dj</u>arīb vi, 512a, b, 515a; s, 140b, 309b – VI, 497a, 498a, 500b; S, 140b, 309a
Hazārfann → Ḥusayn Hezārfenn
Hazāristān i, 223b – I, 230a
Hazārmard → ʿUmar b. Ḥafṣ b. ʿU<u>th</u>mān b. Ḳabīṣa
Hazārnao i, 238b – I, 245b
Hazhīr → ʿAbd al-Ḥusayn
Ḥāzī i, 659b; iv, 421b – I, 680b; IV, 439b
Ḥāzim b. ʿAlī ii, 484b – II, 497a
Ḥāzim b. Muḥammad al-Ḳarṭā<u>dj</u>annī (1285) iii, **337b**; iv, 672b; vi, 196b, 348b – III, 348a; IV, 700a; VI, 180b, 332b
Ḥāzim b. Zayd al-<u>D</u>jahḍamī s, 384b – S, 385a
Ḥazīn, Muḥammad b. Abī Ṭālib (<u>Sh</u>ay<u>kh</u> ʿAlī) (1766) i, 680b, 1166a, 1301a; iii, 313b, **338b**; iv, 69b; vii, 300b, 530a; s, 108a – I, 701a, 1200b, 1341a; III, 323a, **348b**; IV, 73a; VII, 302a, 530b; S, 107b
Hazīrān → Taʾrī<u>kh</u>
Hazmīra, Banū vi, 592a, 741b – VI, 576b, 731a
al-Hazmīrī → Abū ʿAbd Allāh Muḥammad; Abū Zayd ʿAbd al-Raḥmān; Abū Yaʿazzā; Abū Zayd
al-Hazmīrī al-Marrāku<u>sh</u>ī (1280) vi, 356a – VI, 340a
Hazmīriyyūn iii, **338b** – III, **349a**
Hazra<u>dj</u>a, Banū vi, 742a, 743b – VI, 731a, 732b
Hazrat, Āl s, 66b – S, 67a
Hazzāʿ b. Muḥammad i, 1032b – I, 1064a
Hebron → al-<u>Kh</u>alīl
Hedjaz → al-Ḥi<u>dj</u>āz
Ḥefeṣ ben Yaṣlīaḥ iv, 306a – IV, 320a
Hegira/-e → Hi<u>dj</u>ra
Heis (Somalia/-e) ix, 715a – IX, 746b
Hejar, ʿAbd al-Raḥmān v, 483a – V, 486a
Ḥekīm-Ba<u>sh</u>ï iii, **339b** – III, **350a**
Ḥekīm-o<u>gh</u>lu ʿAlī Pa<u>sh</u>a → ʿAlī Pa<u>sh</u>a Ḥakīm-o<u>gh</u>lu
Heliopolis iv, 442b – IV, 462b
Hellènes → Yūnān
Helmand, Helmend → Hilmand
Hélouan → Ḥulwān
Helphand, Alexander Israël (XX) vi, 94a – VI, 91b
Ḥelvā v, 642a, b – V, 646b
Hemedi al-Buhriy (XX) vi, 612b – VI, 597b
Hēmū i, 316a, 1136a; ii, 271b; iii, 423a – I, 326a, 1170a; II, 279b; III, 437a
Henoch → Idrīs
Hephthalites → Hayāṭila
Heraclea → Ereğli
Herat → Harāt
Herātī iv, 10b – IV, 11b
Hercule(s) → Hirḳil
Hercules, Pillars of/Hercule, Colonnes d'- → Ḳādis
Hereke → Ḳālī
Hergan Kale → ʿAmmūriya
Herī Rūd → Harī Rūd
Heriz s, 142b – S, 142a
Hermes/-ès → Hirmis
Hersek → Bosna

Hersekli ʿĀrif Ḥikmat i, 1302a; iii, 1200b – I, 1342a; III, 1230b
Hersek-og͟hlu → Hersek-zāde
Hersek-zāde Aḥmed Pas͟ha (1517) i, 244a, 1264b; iii, **340b**; iv, 565a; v, 774b; vi, 1025b – I, 251a, 1303a; III, **351a**; IV, 587b; V, 780b; VI, 1018b
Herzegovina → Bosna
Ḥesene i, 483a – I, 497b
Hes͟hdek i, 1075b – I, 1107b
Hethum I i, 639b; ii, 37b, 38a – I, 660a; II, 38a, b
Heybeli Ada → Marmara
Hezārfenn → Ḥusayn Hezārfenn
Hezārg͟hrad iii, **342a** – III, **352b**
Hezārpāre Aḥmed Pas͟ha (1648) iii, 318a, 983b; v, 272b – III, 327b, 1088a; V, 270b
Hiba (gift/cadeau) iii, **342b**; iv, 217b – III, **353a**; IV, 227a
Hiba (gift/donation entre vifs) iii, **350a** – III, **361a**
al-Hība → Aḥmad al-Hība
al-Hiba ii, 1116a – II, 1142b
Hibat Allāh b. ʿAbd al-Wāḥid vi, 349b – VI, 333b
Hibat Allāh b. ʿAlī → Ibn Mākūlā
Hibat Allāh b. D̲j̲amiʿ → Ibn D̲j̲amīʿ
Hibat Allāh b. al-Ḥusayn s, 267a, 372a – S, 266b, 372a
Hibat Allāh b. Ibrāhīm (1747) vi, 191b – VI, 175a
Hibat Allāh b. Mākūlā → Ibn Mākūlā, Hibat Allāh
Hibat Allāh b. Malkā → Abu 'l-Barakāt
Hibat Allāh b. Muḥammad (XII) iii, **351b**; v, 815a – III, **362b**; V, 821a
Hibat Allāh b. al-S͟had̲j̲arī (1148) vii, 527a – VII, 527a
Ḥibr → Kitāba
Ḥibrī (1676) iii, **351b** – III, **362b**
Ḥidāʾ → Ḥudāʾ
Ḥidād → ʿIdda, Libās
al-Hidāya al-Islāmiyya iv, 907a – IV, 940a
ʿHidayatʾ → Riḍā Ḳulī K͟hān
Hidāyat (Borneo) s, 150b – S, 150b
Hidāyat, Ṣādiḳ (1951) iii, **352a**; iv, 73a, b; v, 199b – III, **363a**; IV, 77a, b; V, 197a
Ḥid͟hāʾ → Libās
Hid̲j̲āʾ i, 442b, 584b, 586a; iii, **352b**; iv, 56a; s, 394a – I, 455a, 603a, 605a; III, **363b**; IV, 59a; S, 394b
al-Hid̲j̲āʾ, Ḥurūf → Ḥurūf al-hid̲j̲āʾ
Ḥid̲j̲āb i, 306b; iii, **359a**; v, 740a – I, 316a; III, **370b**; V, 745a
Ḥid̲j̲āba → Ḥād̲j̲ib
al-Hid̲j̲ar iii, **361b**, 1064b – III, **372b**, 1091b
al-Hid̲j̲ārī, Abū Muḥammad ʿAbd Allāh b. Ibrāhīm (1188) i, 602b; iii, 926a; vii, 492a, 811a – I, 622a; III, 950b; VII, 492a, 813a
al-Ḥid̲j̲āz i, 25a, 37a, 46a, 77a, 103a, 268b, 272b, 315a, 443b, 539a, 554b; ii, 572b, 660a, 1030a; iii, 34b, 263b, **362a**, 606a, 1066b; iv, 1002a; v, 519a, b, 1127b; vi, 9a, 33a, b, 34a, 45b, 87b, 139b, 144b, 150b, 156a, 264a, 266a, 280a, b, 332a, 334a, b, 336a, 360b, 433b, 435b; s, 3a, b, 4b, 10a, 20a, 198b, 305b – I, 25b, 38a, 47a, 79a, 106a, 276b, 281a, 324b, 456b, 555b, 572b; II, 587a, 676b, 1053b; III, 36a, 271a, **373a**, 626b, 1093b; IV, 1031b; V, 522b, 523a, 1124a; VI, 9a, 31a, b, 32a, 44a, 85b, 137b, 142b, 149b, 152b, 248b, 251a, 265a, b, 316b, 318b, 319a, 320b, 344b, 418b, 421a; S, 2b, 3a, b, 9b, 20a, 198b, 305b
—dialect(e) i, 573b, 574a – I, 592b
Ḥid̲j̲āz railway/chemin-de fer i, 64b, 315a; ii, 289a; iii, 34b, 293a, 326a, 363a, **364a**, 605b; v, 998a; vi, 361a; x, 885a – I, 66a, 324b; II, 297a; III, 36a, 302a, 336a, 374b, **375b**, 626b; V, 993a, b; VI, 345a; X,
Ḥid̲j̲āzī, Muḥammad iv, 73a; v, 199a – IV, 76b; V, 196a
Hid̲j̲d̲j̲āna vi, 544b – VI, 529a
Ḥid̲j̲r iv, 317a, 319b; vi, 147a – IV, 331b, 333b; VI, 145b
al-Ḥid̲j̲r (Saudi Arabia/Arabie Séoudite) iii, **365b**; vi, 455a – III, **377a**; VI, 440b
Hid̲j̲ra (emigration) iii, **366a** – III, **378a**
Hid̲j̲ra (fiḳh) s, **368a** – S, **369a**
Hid̲j̲ra, hud̲j̲ra → Hid̲j̲ar
Hid̲j̲ris v, 131b – V, 134a, b
Hid̲j̲wiyya iv, 715b – IV, 744b
Hidrellez → K͟hiḍr-ilyās
al-Ḥifnī, Yūsuf b. Sālim (1764) vi, 112b – VI, 110b
Ḥifnī Nāṣif (XIX) vi, 219b, 602b – VI, 213b, 587a
Hīfūḳraṭīs (Īfūḳraṭīs) → Buḳrāṭ
Ḥifẓ → Ḳirāʾa, Ḳurʾān
Ḥifẓī (XVIII) vi, 826b – VI, 817a
Ḥikāya iii, **367a**; v, 187a, 812a, 951b – III, **379a**; V, 184b, 818a, 955b
Ḥikma iii, **377b**; iv, 120a; s, 324a – III, **389a**; IV, 125a; S, 323b
Ḥikmān, Banū vi, 729a – VI, 718a
Ḥikmat Abū Zayd iv, 1152a – IV, 1184a
Ḥikmat Sulaymān iii, 521b, 1258b – III, 539b, 1291a
Ḥikmet, Aḥmad → Aḥmad Ḥikmet
Ḥikr s, **368b** – S, **368a**
Ḥīla → Ḥiyal
al-Hilāl ii, 403b, 466b, 472b – II, 414a, 478b, 484b
Hilāl iii, **379a** – III, **390b**
Hilāl, Banū i, 93b, 167b, 367a, 374a, b, 441a, 532b, 533a, 770b, 863a, 1049a, 1176a, 1204b; ii, 526a; iii, 138a, 324b, **385b**; iv, 337a, 739b, 827b, 830b; v, 60a, 760a, 1182b, 1196b; vi, 134a, b, 141a, 606a, 712b, 741a, b; vii, 482b, 483a, 731b; viii, 863b; ix, 16a, 895a; s, 62b, 328a – I, 96a, 172a, 378a, 385a, b, 454a, 548b, 549a, 793b, 887a, 1081a, 1211a, 1240b; II, 539a; III, 140b, 334b, **398a**; IV, 351b, 769b, 860b, 863b; V, 61b, 766a, 1172b, 1187a; VI, 132b, 133a, 139b, 591a, 701a, 730a, b; VII, 482b, 483a, 732a; VIII, 894b; IX, 18b, 911a S, 63a, 327b
Hilāl b. Abī Hilāl al-Ḥimṣī (883) ix, **481a**; s, 412a – IX, **499b**; S, 412a
Hilāl b. al-Aḥwāz al-Tamīmī (720) iv, 535a; vi, 954b – IV, 558a; VI, 946b
Hilāl b. Asʿar (700) vi, 954b – VI, 947a
Hilāl b. Badr i, 512b; iii, 258b – I, 528a; III, 266a
Hilāl b. Mardanīs͟h i, 161a; iii, 865a – I, 165b; III, 889a
Hilāl b. al-Muḥassin b. Ibrāhīm al-Ṣābiʾ (1056) i, 1354a, 1356b; ii, 80a; iii, 46a, 344a, **387b**, 741b; v, 624b; vi, 520b, 522a; viii, 674b – I, 1393a, 1395b; II, 81b; III, 48a, 354b, **400a**, 764a; V, 628b; VI, 505a, 506b; VIII, 694a
Hilāl b. Umayya v, 730b – V, 736a
Hilāl, Badr al-Dīn (1529) i, 1301b; iii, **388a**; s, 46b – I, 1341a; III, **400b**; S, 47a
al-Hilālī, Abu 'l-Abbās al-Sid̲j̲ilmāssī (1761) s, **370a** – S, **370a**
Ḥilf iii, **388b**; v, 581a, b, 596b – III, **401a**; V, 586a, b, 600a
Ḥilf al-Fuḍūl i, 44b, 110a; iii, **389a**; v, 435a; vi, 137b, 145a, b, 146a – I, 46a, 113a; III, **401b**; V, 437a; VI, 136a, 143b, 144b
Ḥilla, Banū iii, 578a – III, 598a
al-Ḥilla i, 684a; iii, **389b**; v, 34a; vi, 64b, 270b, 966a; vii, 297b; viii, 716a; s, 179a, 326a – I, 705a; III, **402a**; V, 35a; VI, 62a, 255b, 958a; VII, 299b; VIII, 736b; S, 180a, 325b

al-Ḥillī, Djamāl al-Dīn Ḥasan b. Yūsuf (ʿAllāma-i Ḥillī) (1325) ii, 774a; iii, **390a**, 1152a; iv, 277b; vi, 13a, 549a, b; vii, 132a, 297b, 417b, 1043b; viii, 777b; s, 56b, 380a –
II, 792b; III, **402b**, 1180a; IV, 290a; VI, 12a, 533b, 534a; VII, 134a, 299b, 408b, 1046a; VIII, 803b; S, 57a, 380a
al-Ḥillī. Muʿizz al-Dīn Muḥammad (891) x, 135b – X, 146a
al-Ḥillī, Nadjm al-Dīn Djaʿfār b. al-Ḥasan (Muḥakkik-i awwal) (1277) iii, **390b**; vi, 549a; vii, 297b; viii, 777b – III, **403a**; VI, 533b; VII, 299b; VIII, 803b
al-Ḥillī, Naṣīr al-Dīn al-Kāshānī s, 364a –
S, 363b
al-Ḥillī, Niʿmat Allāh (1533) viii, 778a –
VIII, 804a
al-Ḥillī, Ṣafī al-Dīn → Ṣafī al-Dīn al-Ḥillī
al-Ḥillī, Shumaym (1204) vi, 352a – VI, 336a
al-Ḥillī, Takī al-Dīn Ḥasan iii, 1152a – III, 1180a
al-Ḥillī al-Wāsiṭī vi, 434a – VI, 419a
Ḥilm ii, 536a; iii, **390b**; v, 435a – II, 549b; III, **403a**; V, 436b
Hilmand i, 222a; iii, **392a**; v, 690b, 868a; s, 367a – I, 228b; III, **404b**; V, 695b, 874b; S, 368a
Ḥilmī, Aḥmed Shehbenderzāde (1913) iii, **392b** – III, **405a**
Ḥilmī, Ḥüseyn → Ḥusayn Ḥilmī Pasha
Ḥilmī, Refīq v, 483b – V, 486b
Ḥilmī, Tunalî (1928) iii, **393a** – III, **405b**
Ḥilmī Bey (XIX) vii, 191b – VII, 192a
Ḥilmī Efendi, Aḥmed (1878) iii, **392b** – III, **405a**
Ḥilmī Pasha → Ḥusayn; Kečiboynuzu Ibrāhīm
al-Ḥilmiyya (Cairo/le Caire) vi, 75b, 434a –
VI, 73b, 419a
Ḥimā i, 442a; iii, 294b, **393a**; iv, 488a, 1143b; s, 304b – I, 454b; III, 303b, **405b**; IV, 509a, 1175b; S, 304a
Ḥimā Ḍariyya ii, 159b; s, 234b – II, 164b; S, 234a
Ḥimā Kulayb ii, 159b – II, 164b
Ḥimār iii, **393b** – III, **406a**
Ḥimār al-Djazīra → Marwān II (Umayyad(e))
Himatnagar ii, 1125a; iii, 1010a – II, 1151b; III, 1035b
Ḥimāya i, 1144a; ii, 143b; iii, **394a**; 1113a – I, 1178b; II, 147a; III, **406b**; 1140a
Ḥimṣ i, 57b, 85a, 119b, 609b, 1125a; ii, 590b; iii, **397a**, 1118b; vi, 139a, 221a, 321b, 322a, b, 406a, 506a, 545a, b, 578a, 580a, 623b, 648a; s, 154a, 162b –
I, 59a, 87b, 123a, 629b, 1159a; II, 605a; III, **409a**, 1146a; VI, 137b, 215a, 306a, b, 307a, 390b, 491a, 530a, 563a, 564b, 609a, 633b; S, 154a, 162b
—buildings/bâtiments iii, 401a, b, 402a – III, 413b, 414a, b
Ḥimṣ, battle of/bataille de (1280) iii, **402b** –
III, **415a**
Ḥimṣ (Morocco/Maroc) vi, 293a – VI, 278b
al-Ḥimsī → Dīk al-Djinn
al-Ḥimsī, ʿAbd al-Masīḥ b. ʿAbd Allāh b. Nāʾima (IX) x, 954b – X,
Himū → Hēmū
Ḥimyar → Yaman
Ḥimyar (language, langue) i, 564a; iii, 124b –
I, 582a; III, 127a
Ḥimyar, Banū i, 195a, 544b, 1259b; ii, 223a, 244a; iii, 52a; iv, 448a; v, 119a, 120b, 315a; s, 337b –
I, 200b, 561b, 1297b; II, 229b, 251a; III, 54a; IV, 468a; V, 121b, 123a, 314b; S, 337a
Ḥimyar b. Sabaʾ vi, 565b – VI, 550b
al-Ḥimyarī → Ibn ʿAbd al-Munʿim; al-Sayyid al-Ḥimyarī; Nashwān b. Saʿīd;
al-Ḥimyarī, Abu ʾl-Walīd Ismāʿīl b. Āmir (1048) vii, 528a, 1046a – VII, 528b, 1048b
al-Ḥimyarī, ʿAlī b. Nashwān b. Saʿīd vi, 433b – VI, 419a
al-Ḥimyarī, Ṣāliḥ b. Manṣūr (VIII) vii, 991a; viii, 522a – VII, 941b; VIII, 539b
Hinā, Banū iii, **403b**; vi, 735a; s, 355a, b –
III, **415b**; VI, 724a; S, 355a, b
Ḥināṭa iii, **403b** – III, **416a**
Hināwī, Banū x, 816a – X,
Hind (India/Inde) i, 91a, 172a, 177b, 287b, 295b, 435b, 978b, 1068b; ii, 119b, 336a, 566a, 1084a; iii, 198b, **404b**, 481a; iv, 170a-b; v, 562a, 888a; vi, 49b, 131a, 368a, 439a, 532b, 688b, 804b; vii, 13b, 79a; s, 21a, 219b –
I, 93b, 176b, 182b, 296b, 304b, 448a, 1009a, 1100b; II, 122b, 345b, 580a, 1109a; III, 203b, **417a**, 498a; IV, 177b; V, 566b, 894a; VI, 48a, 129a, 352a, 424b, 516b, 676b, 856b; VII, 14b, 80a; S, 21a, 219b
—agriculture ii, 909a; iii, 407b, 410a; iv, 1055b; v, 883b – II, 930b; III, 420a, 423a; IV, 1087a; V, 889b
—architecture i, 830b, 1321b; v, 294b – I, 853b, 1362a; V, 294b
—ethnography/-phie iii, 409b; vi, 489a –
III, 422a; VI, 475a
—geography/géographie ii, 576b; iii, 404b; v, 938b – II, 591a; III, 417a; V, 942a
—institutions ii, 426a, 437a; iii, 491b, 532a, 1204a; iv, 268a, b; v, 1080b, 1101a, 1134b –
II, 437a, 448b; III, 508b, 550b, 1234b; IV, 280a, b; V, 1078a, 1096b, 1130a
—languages, literature/langues, littérature i, 808a; ii, 1092a; iii, 164a, 412a; v, 232a –
I, 831a; II, 1117b; III, 167b, 425a; V, 229b
—music/musique iii, 452b – III, 468a
Hind bint Abī ʿUbayda iii, 984a – III, 1008b
Hind bint ʿAwf b. Zubayr s, 92b – S, 92a
Hind bint al-Khuss iii, **454b**; iv, 472a – III, **470b**; IV, 493a
Hind bint al-Nuʿmān b, al-Mundhir ix, 565b –
IX, 588a
Hind bint ʿUtba b. Rabīʿa (VII) iii, 152b, **455a**; iv, 332a; vi, 145b, 477a; vii, 145a; 264a; x, 944b –
III, 156a, **471a**; IV, 346b; VI, 144a, 463a; VII, 147a, 265b; X,
Hinda Gilan vi, 489b – VI, 475b
Hindāl b. Bābur (Mughal) (1551) i, 228b; iii, **455b**, 575a, b; vii, 130b, 131a –
I, 235a; III, **471a**, 595a, b; VII, 132b, 133a
Hindī iii, 1b, 413b, **456a**, 460b – III, 1b, 426b, **472a**, 477a
al-Hindī → al-Shiblī, Abū Ḥafs
Hindī, Sabk-i → Sabk-i Hindī
Hindibāʾ s, **370b** – S, **370a**
Hindiyya ii, 339b – II, 349b
Hindū i, 756b; iii, **458b**; iv, 794a – I, 779a; III, **474b**; IV, 826b
Hindūka al-Astarābādī (amīr) (XV) vi, 513b –
VI, 498b
Hindū-Kush i, 221b, 223a, 1009b; ii, 29a; iii, **459b**; iv, 409b, 410b; vi, 621a –
I, 228a, 229b, 1040b; II, 29b; III, **476a**; IV, 427a, 428b; VI, 606b
Hindū-shāh b. Sandjar Gīrānī vii, 404b –
VII, 405b
Hindūshāhīs iii, **460b**; v, 649a; vi, 65b; viii, 253a – III, **476b**; V, 653a; VI, 63a; VIII, 255a
Hindūstān → Hind
Hindustānī i, 1167a; iii, **460b**; v, 644b – I, 1202a; III, **476b**; V, 648b
Hindustānī Beg → Gūran, Shaykh
Hinglādj → Las-Bēla
Hinn s, **371a** – S, **370b**

Ḥinnāʾ iii, **461a**; v, 1b – III, **477a**; V, 1b
Ḥinṭa → Ḳamḥ
Hintāta, Banū iii, **461b**; vi, 593b, 594a, 742a, 743a – III, **478a**; VI, 578b, 579a, 731a, 732a
al-Hintātī → ʿAmīr al-Hintātī
al-Hintātī, ʿAbd al-Wāḥid b. Abī Ḥafs (XIII) vii, 989a – VII, 990a
Hippocrate(s) → Buḳrāṭ
Ḥirāʾ, Ḥarāʾ iii, **462a**; x, 98b – III, **478b**; X, 106a
al-Ḥīra i. 450b, 451b, 452a, 526a, 564b, 610a, 890a; iii, **462b**, 1254a; iv, 13b, 14a, 998b; v, 119a, 632a, b, 634a, b; vi, 145b, 633b,90a 660a; vii, 840b, 841a; viii, 121b; x, 90a, 191a; s, 91a, 272b – I, 463b, 464b, 465a, 542a, 582b, 630a, 916b; III, **478b**, 1287a; IV, 14b, 15a, 1031a; V, 121b, 636a, b, 638a, b; VI, 143b, 618b, 646a; VII, 842a, b; VIII, 121b; X, 97b, 206a; S, 90b, 272a
Hiraḳla → Eregli
Hiran Mīnār vi, 368b – VI, 353a
Ḥirār → Ḥarra
Ḥirbāʾ iii, **463a** – III, **479b**
Ḥirfa → Ṣinf
al-Ḥīrī, Abū ʿUthmān vi, 225a – VI, 218b, 219a
Hirḳil iv, 383b – IV, 400a
Hirmis i, 247a; iii, **463b**; iv, 120b; v, 111b; s, 270a, 407b – I, 255a; III, **479b**; IV, 126a; V, 114a; S, 269b, 408a
Ḥirth s, 355a, b – S, 355a
Ḥirz → Tamāʾim
Ḥisāb → ʿIlm al-ḥiisāb; Muḥāsaba
Ḥisāb iii, **465a**; v, 224b – III, **481a**; V, 222a
Ḥisāb al-ʿaḳd iii, **466a** – III, **482b**
Ḥisāb b. al-djummal iii, **468a**; v, 224b – III, **484a**; V, 222a
Ḥisāb b. al-ghubār iii, **468b** – III, **485a**
al-Ḥiṣāfī, Ḥasanayn (1910) vi, 355a, 454b; s, 18a, **371a** – VI, 339a, 440a; S, 18b, **371a**
al-Ḥiṣāfiyya al-Shādhiliyya s, 371a – S, 371a
Ḥiṣār (fortress/forteresse) iii, **483a** – III, **499b**
Ḥiṣār (Mā warāʾ al-Nahr) iii, **483a** – III, **500a**
Ḥiṣār (sie(è)ge) iii, **469a**; iv, 798b – III, **485b**; IV, 830b
Ḥiṣār, Abdülhak Şinasi (1963) iii, 260a, **484a**; v, 197a – III, 267b, **501a**; V, 194b
Ḥiṣār-Fīrūza ii, 134a; iii, 168a, 225b, 442b, **484b**; v, 884a, 855b; vi, 50a; s, 206b – II, 137b; III, 171b, 232a, 457a, **501b**; V, 890b, 891b; VI, 48b; S, 206a
Ḥiṣār-i Muḥammad → Narwar
Ḥisba i, 972b, 1335a; ii, 1064a; iii, 140a, **485b**, 489a, 491b, 681a, 960b; iv, 245a, 1161b; vi, 136a – I, 1002b, 1375b; II, 1088b; III, 143a, **503a**, 505b, 508b, 702b, 985a; IV, 256a, 1193b; VI, 134a
Ḥisbān x, 884a – X,
Hishām I, Abu ʾl-Walīd, al-Riḍā (Umayyad(e), Cordoba) (796) i, 493b, 494a, 497b; iii, **495a**; x, 849a; s, 92a – I, 508b, 512b; III, **512a**; X, ; S, 92a
Hishām II, al-Muʾayyad bi-ʾllāh (Umayyad(e), Cordoba) (1013) i, 6a, 75b, 84b, 494a,b; ii, 389a; iii, 46a, 74b, 147a, 220a, **495b**, 746b, 755b; v, 1239a, b; vi, 222a, 431a, 852a; vii, 292b; x, 848b; s,183a – I, 6a, 76b, 86b, 509a,b; II, 399b; III, 48a, 77a, 150a, 226b, **512b**, 769b, 778b; V, 1230a, b; VI, 216a, 416b, 844a; VII, 294b; X, ; S, 184b
Hishām III al-Muʿtadd bi-ʾllāh (1036) i, 1309b; iii, **496a**, 542a, 938b – I, 1350a; III, **513a**, 561a, 963b
Hishām, Mawlāy (Fīlālī) (1793) ii, 510b; vi, 595a, b – II, 523a; VI, 580a
Hishām, Sayyidī (Sīdī, marabout) (XIX) vi, 743a – VI, 732b
Hishām b. ʿAbd al-Malik (Umayyad(e)) (743) i, 142a, 613a,b, 1102b, 1292b; ii, 85b, 117b, 327b, 600b, 1026b; iii, **493a**, 747b; iv, 726a, 727a; v, 16b; vi, 139b, 230b, 428a, 623b, 676a, 740a, 829a; vii, 269a, 398a; s, 10a, 31b, 251b, 252a – I, 146b, 633a,b, 1136a, 1332a; II, 87a, 120a, 337a, 615a, 1050b; III, **510a**, 770b; IV, 755a, 756a; V, 17a; VI, 137b, 224b, 413a, 608b, 662b, 729b, 819a; VII, 271a, 399a; S, 9b, 31b, 251b, 252a
Hishām b. ʿAbd al-Djabbār iii, 819a – III, 843a
Hishām b. ʿAbd al-Malik al-Aṣghar (800) vi, 140b – VI, 138b
Hishām b. ʿAbd Manāf iv, 839a – IV, 872a
Hishām b. ʿAmr al-Fuwaṭī (842) i, 4b; iii, **496b**, 1266a; vii, 259a, 784b; x, 83b; s, 89a, 226b – I, 5a; III, **513b**, 1299a; VII, 260b, 786b; X, 83b; X, 90b; S, 89a, 226b
Hishām b. ʿAmr al-Taghlibī iv, 535a, 536a, 708a – IV, 260b, 786b
Hishām b. al-Ḥakam, Abū Muḥammad (kalām) (795) i, 128a, 850a; ii, 374b, 554a; iii, **496b**, 1037a, 1063a; iv, 182b, 271b, 692b, 1132a; v, 384b; vi, 737b; vii,259a, b, 312b, 645b, 646a; viii, 387b; s, 89a, 225b, 392a, 393b – I, 131b, 873b; II, 385a, 567b; III, **513b**, 1063a, 1089b; IV, 190b, 283b, 721a, 1163b; V, 385b; VI, 727a; VII, 261a, b, 315a, 645b; VIII, 400b; S, 88b, 225b, 392b, 394a
Hishām b. al-Ḥakam II al-Mustanṣir (Umayyad(e), Cordova) (X) ix, 740b – IX, 773a
Hishām b. Ismāʿīl (Medina) (IX) vi, 139b, 140a – VI, 137b, 138a
Hishām b. Ḳubayb b. Rusaḥ iii, 125b – III, 128b
Hishām b. al-Mughīra, Banū vi, 140b – VI, 138b
Hishām b. al-Mughīra al-Makhzūmī (VI) vi, 137b – VI, 136a
Hishām b. Muḥammad al-Kalbī → al-Kalbī
Hishām b. ʿUrwa b. al-Zubayr (763) iii, 810b; vi, 107a; x, 29b – III, 834a; VI, 105a; X, 30b
Hishām b. al-Walīd b. al-Mughīra vi, 139a, b – VI, 137b
al-Hishamī (musician/musicien) s, 64a, 183a – S, 64b, 184b
Ḥishna, Banū v, 317b – V, 317a
Ḥisn iii, **498a**; iv, 1139b – III, **515a**; IV, 1171a
Ḥisn b. ʿUmāra → al-Dīkdān
Ḥisn al-Akrād i, 1292b; iii, **503a**; vi, 322a, 579a, b, 581b, 582a; s, 204b – I, 1332a; III, **520b**; VI, 306b, 564a, b, 566a, b; S, 204b
Ḥisn Arkanāʾ vi, 231a – VI, 225a
Ḥisn Banī Bashīr vi, 221b – VI, 215a
Ḥisn Daī s, 132a – S, 131b
Ḥisn Dikbāya → al-Dīkdān
Ḥisn al-Faradj i, 165b – I, 170a
Ḥisn al-Ghurāb iii, **506a** – III, **523a**
Ḥisn al-Kawkab ii, 234a – II, 241a
Ḥisn Kayfā i, 664b, 665a, 666b, 804b, 1067a, 1068a; ii, 344b; iii, **506b**; v, 459a; vi, 626a; vii, 579a; viii, 133a, b; s, 250a – I, 684b, 686a, 687a, 828b, 1099a, 1100a; II, 354a; III, **524a**; V, 462a; VI, 611a; VII, 579b; VIII, 135b, 136a S, 250a
Ḥisn Liyyīṭ → Alīṭ
Ḥisn al-Mahdī iv, 674b – IV, 702a, b
Ḥisn Manṣūr → Adiyaman
Ḥisn al-Ṭāḳ iii, 502a – III, 519a
Ḥisn al-ʿUḳāb vi, 742b – VI, 732a
Ḥisn al-Wād vi, 221b – VI, 215a
Ḥisn Ziyād → Kharpūt
Ḥiṣnī (ṣūfī) (1426) vi, 350a – VI, 334b
Ḥiss iii, **509a** – III, **526a**
Ḥiṣṣa, Ḥiṣṣe → Tīmār, Waḳf

Hissar → Ḥiṣār
Hīt ii, 947a; iii, **510a** – II, 969a; III, **527a**
Ḥiṭṭān b. Kāmil b. ʿAlī (Munkidh, Banū) (1183) vii, 579b – VII, 580a
Ḥiṭṭīn, Ḥaṭṭīn (1187) i, 798a, 946b; iii, **510b**; vi, 578b; s, 205b – I, 821a, 975b; III, **528a**; VI, 563b; S, 205a
Ḥiwālid(e)s vi, 438b, 439a – VI, 424a, b
Ḥiyāḍ → Ḥawḍ
Ḥiyal iii, 159b, **510b**; iv, 253b; s, **371b** – III, 163a, **528a**; IV, 265a; S, **371a**
Ḥizām b. Ghālib iv, 215a – IV, 224b
Ḥizb, aḥzāb ii, 224a; iii, **513a** – II, 231a; III, **530b**
Ḥizb (political, politique) ii, 429b; iii, **514a** – II, 440b; III, **531b**
Ḥizkīl i, 404b; ii, 242a; iii, **535a** – I, 416a; II, 249a; III, **554a**
Hizzān, Banū i, 482b – I, 497a
Hlivne → Livno
Ḥmad u-Mūsā, Sīdī (1563) i, 35a; ii, 527a; iii, **535b**; v, 132b – I, 35b; II, 540a; III, **554a**; V, 135b
Ḥmādsha → Ḥamādisha
Ḥnayshiyya iv, 95a – IV, 99a
Hobyo Sultanate (Somalia/-e) ix, 717b – IX, 748b
Hōbyōt (Mahrī) vi, 84b; ix, 439b; s, 339b – VI, 82b; IX, 456a; S, 339a
Hoca → Khwādja
Hochow v, 847b, 848a, 851b – V, 851b, 852a, 855b
Hodh → Ḥawḍ
Hodja Aḥmed Sulṭān i, 1076b – I, 1108b
Hodna → Ḥuḍna
Hoesein Djajadiningrat (1960) s, **374b** – S, **374b**
Hofuf → al-Hufūf
Ḥogariyya → → Ḥudjriyya
Hoggar Ahaggar
Holkar, Djaswant Rāo (Marāthā) vi, 535b, 536a – VI, 520a
Holkar, Malhar Rāo (Marāthā) vi, 535b – VI, 520a
Holkar, Tukodjī Rāo (Marāthā) vi, 535b – VI, 520a
Homs → Ḥimṣ
Honaz → Khōnās
Hongrie (Madjar, Madjaristān) I, 275b, 300b, 409b, 719a, 1107b, 1198b; II, 576b, 734b; III, 1026a; IV, 615a, b; V, 374a, **1006b**
Hor → Khawr
Horde iii, **536a**; viii, 174b – III, **555a**; VIII, 177a
Horde Blanche I, 1140a; II, 45a,b
Horde d'Or → Bātūʾides; Ḳipčaḳ; Sarāy
Hormizd II (Sāsānid(e)) (309) ix, 73b – IX, 76b
Hormizd III (Sāsānid(e)) (459) ix, 76a – IX, 79b
Hormizd IV (Sāsānid(e)) (590) ix, 78b – IX, 83a
Hormuz → Hurmuz
Hormuzd Ardashīr → al-Ahwāz
Hoshangshāh Ghōrī → Ghūrid(e)s
Hōt → Balūčistān
Hotin → Khotin
Houri → Ḥūr
Hubal iii, **536b**; iv, 263b, 264a, 320a, 321a; v, 77b; vi, 373b – III, **555b**; IV, 275b, 334a, 336a; V, 79b; VI, 358a
Hubayra b. ʿAbd Yaghuth (al-Makshūḥ) vii, 592a – VII, 591b
Hubayra b. Abī Wahb iii, 975b – III, 1000a
Ḥubaysh b. Duldja (684) vi, 622b – VI, 607b
Ḥubaysh b. al-Ḥasan al-Dimashḳī (IX) s, **375b** – S, **375b**
Ḥubaysh b. Mubashshir ii, 373b – II, 383b
Ḥubaysh, Muḥammad s, 411a – S, 411b
Ḥubb → ʿIshḳ
Ḥubbā ii, 551b – II, 565a
Ḥubus → Waḳf
al-Ḥubūs, Banū iii, **537a** – III, **556a**
Hūd (prophet/prophète) i, 169a, 828b, 1045a; iii, **537b**; iv, 448b; v, 421a; vi, 81a, b, 83b, 106a, 652b – I, 174a, 851b, 1076b; III, **556a**; IV, 468b; V, 423a; VI, 79a, b, 81b, 103b, 638a
Hūd, Banū → Hūdid(e)s
Hūd b. Muḥkim (IX) x, 86b – X, 93b
Hudā ii, 294a – II, 302a
Hudā Shaʿrāwī Pasha, Madame (XX) iii, 360a; v, 740a; vi, 470a – III, 371b; V, 745b; VI, 456a
Hüdāʾī, ʿAziz Maḥmūd (1628) ii, 542b, 543a; iii, **538a**; iv, 191b, 972a – II, 555b, 556b; III, **557a**; IV, 199b, 1004a
al-Huḍaybī, Ḥasan iii, 518a, 1069a, b; iv, 160a – III, 535b, 1096a; IV, 166b
al-Ḥudaybiyya (628) iii, **539a**; iv, 320a; vi, 146b; vii, 371b; s, 131a – III, **557b**; IV, 334a; VI, 145a; VII, 373a; S, 130a
al-Ḥudayda (628) i, 709b; iii, **539b**; vi, 192a; s, 30b – I, 731a; III, **558a**; VI, 175b; S, 30b
al-Hudaylī Ṣāḥib al-Ḳāra (1627) vi, 132b – VI, 131a
al-Ḥuḍayn of/de Ūḳ s, 326b – S, 326a
al-Ḥuḍayn b. al-Mundhir (718) iii, **540a** – III, **558b**
Ḥudayr b. ʿAmr b. ʿAbd b. Kaʿb (VII) vi, 123a; vii, 123a – VI, 125a; VII, 125a
Ḥudayr b. Simāk (VII) i, 771b, 1283a; iv, 1187b; v, 995a; viii, 697b – I, 794b, 1322b; IV, 1220a; V, 990b; VIII, 717b
al-Ḥudayrī, Shaykh ʿUthmān b. al-Shaykh ʿAlī viii, 18b – VIII, 18b
Hudhalī i, 115a; iii, 540b – I, 118b; III, 559b
al-Hudhalī → Abū Dhuʾayb; Abū Kabīr; Abū Ṣakhr; Saʿīd b. Masʿūd
Ḥudhayfa b. ʿAbd b. Fuḳaym b. ʿAdī → al-Ḳalammas
Ḥudhayfa b. Badr al-Fazārī ii, 873a, 1023a; s, 177a, b, 178a – II, 893b, 1046b; S, 178a, b, 179a
Ḥudhayfa b. al-Yamān al-ʿAbsī (VII) i, 190a, 448b; iii, 512a, 1059b; v, 945b; vii, 189b – I, 194b, 461b; III, 529b, 1086a; V, 949a; VII, 190a
Hudhayl, Banū i, 149a, 545a; iii, 363b, **540a**; v, 763a; vi, 349a, 373b, 374a; ix, 908b; x, 3a – I, 153a, 562a; III, 375a, **559a**; V, 769a; VI, 333a, 358a; IX, 947a; X, 3a
Hudhayl b. ʿAbd al-Malik, Abū Muḥammad (1044) ix, 307b – IX, 316b
al-Hudhayl b. Hubayra x, 91b – X, 99a
al-Hudhayl b. ʿImrān al-Taghlibī (656) vi, 954a; x, 91b – VI, 946b; X, 99a
Ḥudhayra → ʿUyayna b. Ḥiṣn
Hudhud iii, **541b** – III, **560a**
Hūdid(e)s (Banū Hūd) i, 1040b; iii, **542a**, 849b; v, 683a; vi, 222b, 339b, 577a; vii, 1020b; viii, 690a; s, 80b, 81a, 381b – I, 1072a; III, **560b**, 873b; V, 688a; VI, 216a, 323b, 562a; VII, 1022b; VIII, 710a; S, 80b, 81a, 382a
Ḥudjarīyya i, 866a; ii, 507a, 1080a,b; iii, 545b, 902b; iv, 1091b, 1092a – I, 890b; II, 519b, 1105b; III, 564b, 926b; IV, 1122b, 1123a
al-Ḥudjāwī, Mūsā i, 949b; iii, 162a – I, 978b; III, 165b
Ḥudjaylān b. Ḥamad iv, 717b – IV, 746a
Ḥudjdja i, 832b; ii, 97b, 98a; iii, 254a, **543b**; iv, 203b – I, 855b; II, 99b, 100a; III, 261a, **562a**; IV, 212b
Ḥudjdjādj (Morocco/Maroc) iii, 339a – III, 349a
Ḥudjr, Banū vi, 649a – VI, 634b
Ḥudjr b. ʿAdī al-Kindī (VII) i, 693b; ii, 89b; iii, 242a, **545a**, 1265b; v, 349a, 499b; vii, 266b, 400b, 521b – I, 714b; II, 91a; III, 249a, **564a**, 1298a; V, 349b, 502b; VII, 268a, b, 401b, 521b

Ḥudjr b. al-Ḥāriṯẖ   i, 99a, 527a, 683b; ii, 785a; iii,
    1177a; v, 118b – I, 101b, 543a, 704a; II, 804a; III,
    1206a; V, 121a
Ḥudjr Ākil al-Murār   i, 526b, 548b; v, 118b, 119a – I,
    542b, 566a; V, 121a, b
Ḥudjra   iii, 545b – III, 564b
Ḥudjrat al-Aghawāt (Mecca)   vi, 166a – VI, 158b
Ḥudjriyya, Banū   iii, 545b; v, 895a – III, 564b; V, 901a
Ḥudjūr (Yemen)   vi, 436b – VI, 422a
al-Ḥudjwīrī, Abu 'l-Ḥasan ʿAlī (1072)   i, 794b; ii, 55a;
    iii, 84a,b, 435b, 546a, 570b; iv, 616b, 697a; vi, 225a,
    b –
    I, 818a; II, 56a; III, 86b, 87a, 449b, 565a, 590a; IV,
    641a, 725b; VI, 219a
Ḥudna (Hodna)   ii, 131a, 303a; iii, 546b; vi, 727a,
    728a, b – II, 134b, 311b; III, 565b; VI, 716a, b, 717b
Ḥudna   i, 749a; iii, 547b; iv, 478b; s, 144b –
    I, 771b; III, 566b; IV, 499b; S, 144b
Ḥudūd   iii, 548a – III, 567a
Ḥudūd al-ʿĀlam   i, 5a, 967a; ii, 581a, 799b; iii, 406a;
    iv, 223b, 342a, 1079b; v, 107b, 1011a; s, 376a –
    I, 5b, 996b; II, 595b, 818b; III, 418b; IV, 233a, 356b,
    1111a; V, 109b, 1007a; S, 376a
Ḥudūṯẖ   v, 96a, b – V, 98a, b
Ḥudūṯẖ al-ʿālam   iii, 548a – III, 567a
Huelva   → Walba
Huesca(r)   → Washḳa
Huete   → Wabḏẖa
Ḥufāsẖ   iii, 548b – III, 567b
al-Hufūf   iii, 237b, 548b; iv, 925b; vii, 282b; s, 234b –
    III, 244a, 567b; IV, 958b; VII, 284a; S, 234b
Hūglī   vii, 444a – VII, 445a
Hui   x, 629a – X,
al-Ḥukamāʾ   i, 95a – I, 97b
Ḥukaym b. Djabala   ii, 415a; iii, 583a – II, 425b; III,
    603a
Ḥukm   i, 257a, 1170b; ii, 273a, 294a; iii, 306b, 549a; v,
    241b – I, 265a, 1205b; II, 281b, 302a; III, 315b, 568a;
    V, 239b
Hukōm   i, 742b, 746b – I, 764b, 769a
Ḥuḳūḳ   iii, 551b – III, 570b
Ḥüküm   → Ḥukm
Ḥukūma   i, 384a; iii, 551b – I, 395a; III, 570b
Ḥükümet   i, 469a – I, 482b
Ḥulā (ornaments, ornements)   → Libās
al-Ḥūla (lake/lac)   iii, 568b – III, 588b
Ḥūla (town/ville)   iii, 568b – III, 588b
Hūlāgū b. Toluy b. Čingiz Khān (Mongol Īl-Khānid(e))
    (1265)   i, 21a, 190a, 329b, 353b, 665a, 787a, 902b,
    1086b, 1188a, 1314b; ii, 47a, 194a, 204b, 284b,
    376b, 606a, 966a, 1056b; iii, 208b, 569a, 1121a; iv,
    30b, 349b, 482a, 521a; v, 455b, 491a, 598a, 826b; vi,
    16a, 48b, 149b, 198a, 381b, 482a, b, 501a, b, 504b,
    505a, 540b, 601a; vii, 230a, 753b, 984a, 990b –
    I, 21b, 194b, 340a, 364b, 686a, 810a, 930a, 1119a,
    1223a, 1354b; II, 48a, 200a, 211a, 292b, 387a, 621a,
    987b, 1081a; III, 214b, 589a, 1148b; IV, 32b, 364b,
    503a, 544a; V, 458a, 494a, 601b, 833a; VI, 14a, 47a,
    148a, 182a, 365b, 468a, b, 479b, 480a, 486b, 489b,
    490b, 525a, 586a; VII, 232a, 754b, 984b, 992a
Hūlāgū (Lahore)   iii, 569b – III, 589b
al-Ḥulal al-Mawshiyya   iii, 570a – III, 589b
Hülegü, fief of/de   x, 44b – X, 46a
Ḥulm   → Taʿbīr al-Ruʾyā
Ḥulmāniyya   iii, 570b – III, 590a
Hultāna, Banū   vi, 742a – VI, 731b
Hulu Sungai   s, 150b – S, 150b
Ḥulūl   iii, 102b, 570b; iv, 283a – III, 104b, 590b; IV,
    295b
Ḥulwān (donative/ don)   → Inʿām; Māl al-bayʿa;
    Pīshkash

Ḥulwān (Egypt/-e)   iii, 572a – III, 591b
Ḥulwān (ʿIrāḳ)   iii, 571b; v, 89b, 460b; vi, 336a, 410b,
    539a; ix, 64b; s, 122b, 273a – III, 591a; V, 92a, 463b;
    VI, 320b, 395b, 523b; IX, 66a; S, 122a, 273a
Ḥulwān (tax, impôt)   ii, 148b – II, 152b
al-Ḥulwānī, Shīʿī (X)   vi, 727b – VI, 716b
al-Ḥulwānī, Abu 'l-Fatḥ   → Abu 'l-Fatḥ al-Ḥulwānī
Huma (Marāgha)   vi, 502b – VI, 488b
Humā (bearded vulture/gypaète)   iii, 572a – III, 592a
Humā (poet/poète) (1873)   iv, 70a – IV, 73b
Humāhim   i, 181a – I, 186a
Humai   iv, 567a – IV, 589b
Humām, Nāṣir al-Dīn   ii, 318a – II, 327b
Humām b. Yūsuf, Hawwāra Shaykh (XVIII)   i, 1029a; iii,
    300a; iv, 723a; vii, 179a, 420b, 445a – I, 1060b; III,
    309a; IV, 752a; VII, 181a, 422a, 446a
Humām al-Dīn b. ʿAlāʾ Tabrīzī (1314)   iii, 572b; vi,
    609a – III, 592b; VI, 593b
al-Humās b. Ḳubayb   iii, 125b – III, 128b
Humāy   iii, 572b; iv, 809b – III, 592a; IV, 842a
Ḥumayd, Banū   i, 862b; iv, 765a; s, 355b –
    I, 887a; IV, 795b; S, 355a
Ḥumayd b. ʿAbd al-Ḥamīd al-Ṭūsī (825)   i, 316a; iii,
    573a – I, 325b; III, 592b
Ḥumayd b. Ḥurayṯẖ al-Kalbī   ii, 1023b; iv, 493a – II,
    1047b; IV, 514b
Ḥumayd b. Ḳaḥṭaba (Marw al-Rūḏẖ) (777)   vi, 618a –
    VI, 602b
Ḥumayd b. Maḥmūd   ii, 484b – II, 497a
Ḥumayd b. al-Ṭawīl (759)   x, 29b – X, 30b
\Ḥumayd b. Ṯẖawr al-Hilālī (VII)   iii, 573a; iv, 744b;
    vii, 864b – III, 593a; IV, 774b; VII, 866a
Ḥumayd (Ḥamīd) b. Yaṣāl (X)   vii, 641b –
    VII, 641b
Ḥumayd b. Ziyād (922)   vii, 906a – VII, 906b
Ḥumayd al-Arḳaṭ (VIII)   i, 1297b; iii, 573b –
    I, 1337b; III, 593a
Ḥumayda, Amīr   iii, 952b – III, 977a
Ḥumayda b. Muḥammad   i, 1032b – I, 1064a
al-Ḥumaydī, ʿAbd Allāh b. al-Zubayr (834)   vii, 706a –
    VII, 707a
al-Ḥumaydī, Abū ʿAbd Allāh (1095)   i, 94b; ii, 72a; iii,
    573b, 790b – I, 97a; II, 73b; III, 593b
al-Ḥumayma   iii, 574a; vi, 427b; vii, 396a, 399b – III,
    594a; VI, 412b; VII, 397b, 401a
Ḥumaynī   i, 782a – I, 805b
Ḥumayr, Banū   vi, 263a – VI, 247b
Humāyūn (epithet/épithète)   iii, 572b, 574a –
    III, 592a, 594a
Humāyūn, Nāṣir al-Dīn (Mughal) (1556)   i, 80b, 228b,
    252b, 316a, 413a, 628a, 852b, 914b, 962a, 970a,
    1135b, 1192a, 1218b, 1323b; ii, 120b, 155a, 259a,
    264b, 271a, b, 494a, 498b, 973a; iii, 199b, 348a,
    422b, 423a, 449a, 455b, 485a, 492b, 575a, 633a; iv,
    475a, 523b, 533b, 537a, 1022a; v, 598a, 1217a; vi,
    47a, b, 52a, 126b, 128a, 131a, 310a, 407a, 410a,
    456b, 525b, 693a; vii, 130b, 138b, 314a, 316b, 319a,
    329a, 337b, 340b, 345a, 573b, 928b; s, 3a, 312a,
    313a, 325a –
    I, 82b, 235a, 260b, 326a, 443b, 648b, 876b, 942b,
    991b, 1000a, 1169b, 1227b, 1255a, 1364a; II, 123b,
    160a, 265b, 272b, 279b, 506b, 511a, 995b; III, 204b,
    358b, 436a, 437a, 464a, 471b, 502a, 509b, 595a,
    654a; IV, 496a, 546a, 557a, 560a, 1054a; V, 602a,
    1206b; VI, 45b, 46a, 50a, 124a, 126a, 129a, 295a,
    391b, 395a, 442a, 510a, 680b; VII, 132b, 141a, 316a,
    319a, 321a, 330b, 339a, 342a, 346b, 574a, 929a; S,
    2b, 312a, 313a, 324b
Humāyūn Shāh Bahmanī (1461)   iii, 421a, b, 577a; vi,
    66b – III, 434b, 435a, 597a; VI, 64b
Humāyūn-nāma   iv, 505a – IV, 527a

Ḥumlān (Yemen)   vi, 438b – VI, 424a
Hummām, Banū   viii, 866a – VIII, 896b
Ḥumrān b. Abān (Baṣra) (780)   i, 441a; vi, 878b, 920b
    – I, 453b; VI, 869b, 912b
Ḥumrīn   → Ḥamrīn, Djabal
Ḥums   iii, **577b** – III, **597b**
Ḥumūd b. ʿAzzān   s, 355b – S, 355b
Ḥumūm, Banū   vi, 473b, 474a, b, 475a –
    VI, 459b, 460a, b
Hūn   i, 120a – I, 123a
Ḥunayn (Mecca)   i, 9a, 12a; iii, 500a, **578a**; vi, 147a,
    266a; vii, 373a, 389a –
    I, 9a, 12a; III, 517a, **598a**; VI, 145b, 250b, 251a; VII,
    374b, 390a
Ḥunayn (seaport/port)   s, **376b** – S, **376b**
Ḥunayn b. Isḥāḳ al-ʿIbādī (873)   i, 213a, 234a, 235a,
    236a, 327a, 570a, 589a, 631b, 785b, 1014b, 1149b;
    ii, 60a, 300b, 349b, 358b, 402b; iii, **578b**, 977a; iv,
    110a, 254b; v, 133b, 701b; vi, 204a, 376a, 637a, b;
    vii, 403b, 538b, 539b, 559a; x, 453a; s, 52b, 375b –
    I, 219a, 241b, 242a, 243a, 337a, 588b, 608b, 652a,
    808b, 1045b, 1184a; II, 61a, 309a, 359a, 368a, 413a;
    III, **598b**, 1001b; IV, 115a, 266a; V, 136a, 706b; VI,
    188a, 360b, 622a, b; VII, 405a, 538b, 539b, 559b; X,
    485b; S, 53a, 375b
Hungary (Madjār, Madjāristān)   i, 267b, 291b, 398a,
    698a, 1075b, 1163b; ii, 562b, 716a; iii, 1001a; iv,
    591b; v, 373a, **1010b**
Huns (Khʷiyon/Hsiung-Nu   x, 691a – X, 733b
Hunza and/et Nagir   iii, **581a**; s, 158b, 367b –
    III, **601a**; S, 158b, 367b
Huppe, la   → Hudhud
Ḥūr   ii, 447b, 449a; iii, **581b** – II, 459b, 460b; III, **601b**
Ḥūrānī, Akram   iv, 125a – IV, 130b
Ḥurayḍa   s, 337b – S, 337a
Ḥurayfīsh al-Makkī   iv, 1006b – IV, 1038b
Ḥuraymilā   iii, **582b** – III, **602b**
Ḥurayriyya   iv, 838a; viii, 461b – IV, 871a; VIII, 477a
al-Hūrīnī, Naṣr   i, 596b – I, 616a
Ḥurḳūṣ b. Zuhayr al-Saʿdī (VII)   ii, 415a; iii, **582b** – II,
    426a, III, **603a**
Hurma Wuld ʿAbd al-Djalīl (1828)   vii, 624a – VII, 624a
Hurmuz   iii, **583b** – III, **604a**
Hurmuz I (Sāsānid(e)) (273)   iii, 584a, b – III, 604b
Hurmuz II (Sāsānid(e)) (309)   iii, 584a – III, 604b
Hurmuz III (Sāsānid(e)) (579)   iii, 584a – III, 604b
Hurmuz IV (Sāsānid(e)) (590)   iii, 584a; vi, 633a – III,
    604b – VI, 618a
Hurmuz (Hormuz)   i, 8a, 535b, 553a, 928a, 942b,
    1013a; iii, **584b**, 1121b; iv, 500b, 764b; v, 149a,
    150b, 183a, 671b, 673a, 675b; vi, 50b, 735a; s, 115a,
    129a, 234b –
    I, 8b, 552a, 570b, 956a, 971b, 1044b; III, **604b**,
    1149a; IV, 522a, 795a; V, 151b, 152b, 180b, 676b,
    677a, 678a, 680b; VI, 49a, 724a; S, 114b, 128a, 234a
Hurmuz , Bā, ʿAbd al-Raḥmān b. ʿUmar (1508)   iii,
    586a; vi, 132b – III, **606a**; VI, 130b
al-Hurmuzān (644)   iii, 582b, **586a**; iv, 97a; vi, 633b,
    920a – III, 603a, **606a**; IV, 101b; VI, 618a, 911b
Ḥurr   iii, **587b** – III, **607b**
al-Ḥurr b. ʿAbd al-Raḥmān al-Thaḳafī (VIII)   iii, **587b**;
    v, 510a; s, 81b – III, **607b**; V, 513b; S, 81b
al-Ḥurr b. Yazīd (680)   iii, **588a**, 609a – III, **608a**, 630a
al-Ḥurr b. Yūsuf   ii, 328a – II, 337b
al-Ḥurr al-ʿĀmilī, Shaykh al-Islam (1708)   vi, 550b –
    VII, 535a
al-Ḥurr al-ʿĀmilī, Shaykh Muḥammad b. al-Ḥasan
    (1693)   iii, **588a**, 1152a; iv, 165b; vii, 132a; s, 57a –
    III, **608b**, 1180a; IV, 172b; VII, 134a; S, 57b
Ḥurr Riyā b. Yazīd   iv, 638a – IV, 664a
Ḥurrāk   iv, 456b – IV, 476b

Ḥurra-yi Khuttalī   s, 125b – S, 125a
Ḥurriyya   iii, **589a**, 1062b, 1063b – III, **609a**, 1089a,
    1090a
Ḥürriyet we Iʿtilāf Fīrḳasī   ii, 104b; iii, 520a, **594b** – II,
    107a; III, 538a, **615a**
Ḥurūf, ʿIlm al-   ii, 376b, 734b; iii, **595b** –
    II, 386b, 753a; III, **616a**
Ḥurūf al-hidjāʿ   iii, 205a, **596b** – III, 210b, **617b**
Ḥurūfī   → Faḍl Allāh
Ḥurūfiyya   i, 193a, 260a, 720b, 1099b, 1162a, 1248a;
    ii, 733a, 924a, 1095a; iii, **600a**; iv, 48b, 721b; v,
    823a; vi, 226b, 228a, 549b –
    I, 199a, 268a, 742a, 1132b, 1196b, 1286a; II, 751b,
    945b, 1120b; III, **620b**; IV, 51b, 750b; V, 829a; VI,
    220a, 221b, 534a
Ḥusām, Fakhr al-Dīn   ii, 318a – II, 327b
al-Ḥusām b. Ḍirār   → Abu 'l-Khaṭṭār
Ḥusām al-Dawla   → Malik b. ʿAlī al-Barānī
Ḥusām al-Dawla Ardashīr b. Ḥasan   iii, 810a; v, 662b
    – III, 833b; V, 667b
Ḥusām al-Dawla Ardashīr b. Kīnakhwār   i, 1110a – I,
    1143b
Ḥusām al-Dawla al-Muḳallad (ʿUḳaylid(e)) (996)   vi,
    900b – VI, 891b
Ḥusām al-Dawla Shahriyār (Bāwandid(e))   s, 363b – S,
    363a
Ḥusām al-Dawla Tāsh   ii, 748b, 749a; iv, 358a – II,
    767a; IV, 373b
Ḥusām al-Dīn   → Timurtash
Ḥusām al-Dīn (Ḳapūdān)   ii, 26b – II, 26b
Ḥusām al-Dīn, Malāmī Shaykh (1553)   vi, 226b, 227a,
    b, 228a – VI, 220b, 221b, 222a
Ḥusām al-Dīn b. Abī ʿAlī   iii, 967a – III, 991b
Ḥusām al-Dīn b. ʿAlī Shīr   ii, 989a – II, 1012a
Ḥusām al-Dīn b. Abu 'l-Shawk   → Abu 'l-Shawk Fāris
Ḥusām al-Dīn Alp Yörük   vi, 738a – VI, 767b
Ḥusām al-Dīn Čelebi (1284)   ii, 19a, 394b, 395a; iii,
    602a – II, 19b, 405a, b; III, **623a**
Ḥusām al-Dīn Ghulām Ḥusayn (1938)   vi, 191a – VI,
    175a
Ḥusām al-Dīn Ḥasan (Marʿash) (1208)   vi, 507b – VI,
    492b
Ḥusām al-Dīn Khān   ii, 1124a – II, 1150b
Ḥusām al-Dīn Luʾluʾ   → Luʾluʾ
Ḥusām al-Dīn ʿUmar (XII)   viii, 749a – VIII, 779a
Ḥusām Girāy   i, 310b – I, 320b
Ḥusām Khān   v, 783a, b – V, 789b
Ḥusām Khān (Gudjarāt)   s, 335b – S, 335b
Ḥusām al-Salṭana (1848)   vi, 715a – VI, 704a
Ḥusām-Zāde Muṣṭafā Efendi (XV)   iii, 1243a; vii, 478b
    – III, 1275a; VII, 478b
al-Ḥusayma   v, 80a; s, **377a** – V, 82a; S, **377a**
al-Ḥusārī, Maḥmūd Khalīl Shaykh   x, 74a – X, 77a
Ḥusayn, a(d)miral   → Amīr Ḥusayn
Ḥusayn I b. Uways (Djalāyirid(e))) (1382)   i, 66b; ii,
    401b; iv, 584b; viii, 998a – I, 68b; II, 412a; IV, 608a;
    VIII, 1032b
Ḥusayn II (Djalāyitid(e))   ii, 401b – II, 412b
Ḥusayn I, Shāh (Ṣafawid(e)) (1722)   vii, 222b, 318b;
    viii, 771a – VII, 224b, 321a; VIII, 796b
Ḥusayn (Hidjāz)   → al-Ḥusayn b. ʿAlī, Sharīf
Ḥusayn Mawlāy (Fīlālī) (1794)   vi, 595b – VI, 580a
Ḥusayn, Mullā   i, 833a, 846b; v, 664a – I, 856a, 870a;
    V, 669a
Ḥusayn, Sharīf (1880)   vi, 151a – VI, 150a
Ḥusayn b. ʿAbd Allāh   → Ibn Sīnā
Ḥusayn b. ʿAbd al-Raḥmān al-Ahdal   → Ibn al-Ahdal
Ḥusayn b. ʿAbd Allāh Rawāḥī (1189)   viii, 459b – VIII,
    475a
Ḥusayn b. ʿAbd al-Wahhāb   ii, 845b, 849a –
    II, 865b, 869a

Ḥusayn b. Abī Bakr al-ʿAydarūs i, 782a – I, 805b
Ḥusayn b. Abī Manṣūr al-ʿIdjlī (VIII) vi, 441b – VI, 427a
Ḥusayn b. Aḥmad → Abū ʿAbd Allāh al-Shīʿī; Ibn Khālawayh
Ḥusayn b. Aḥmad al-Makramī (XX) vi, 190b – VI, 174b
Ḥusayn b. Aḥmad al-Shahīd ii, 730a – II, 748b
Ḥusayn b. ʿAlī → Ibn Mākūlā; al-Maghribī; al-Ṭughrāʾī
Ḥusayn b. ʿAlī (Abū ʿArīsh) (XIX) vii, 515a – VII, 515b
Ḥusayn b. ʿAlī (Ḥusaynid(e)) (1740) i, 1110b; iii, **604b**, 635b; iv, 828b – I, 1144a; III, **625b**, 657a; IV, 861b
Ḥusayn b. ʿAlī (Khayratīd(e)) ii, 518a – II, 530b
Ḥusayn b.ʿAlī, Ṣāḥib Fakhkh (786) i, 402b, 551a; ii, 745a; iii, **615b**; vii, 646a – I, 414a, 568b; II, 763b; III, **636b**; VII, 645b
al-Ḥusayn b. ʿAlī, Sharīf/King/Roi (1931) i, 39a, 98b, 555a, 709b; ii, 289b, 429b, 531b, 572b; iii, 263a, b, 363b, **605a**, 1065b, 1066b; iv, 782b, 947a; v, 62b, 63a, 998a, 1055a, b; vi, 45b, 151b, 152a, 154a, 160b, 161b, 166a, 262a, 304a, 615a, b; vii, 764b; s, 3b, 4b, 293b – I, 40a, 101a, 572b, 731a; II, 297b, 440b, 544b, 587a; III, 270b, 271a, 375a, **626a**, 1092a, 1093a; IV, 814a, 979b; V, 64b, 993a, b, 1051b, 1052a; VI, 44a, 150a, 151a, 152a, 154b, 155b, 158b, 246a, 289b, 600a; VII, 766b; S, 3a, b, 293a
Ḥusayn b. ʿAlī b. Abī Ṭālib (680) i, 44b, 55a, 113b, 385a, 430b, 508b, 550a, 711a; ii, 843a, 848b, 912a; iii, 119b, 164b, 242a, 588a, **607a**; iv, 637a; vi, 77b, 147b, 537a, 604a, 605b, 608a, 609a, 610b, 675b, 737a, 958b; vii, 267b, 470a, 478a, 688b, 689a; s, 94a, 128a, 352a, 401a – I, 45b, 56b, 116b, 396b, 443a, 524a, 567b, 732b; II, 863a, 868b, 933b; III, 122a, 168a, 249a,608a, **628a**; IV, 663b; VI, 75b, 146a, 522a, 589a, 590b, 592b, 594a, 595a, 662a, 726b, 951a; VII, 269b, 469b, 477b; S, 93b, 127a, 352a, 401b
Ḥusayn b. ʿAlī b. ʿAlī b. Muḥammad b. Djaʿfar al-Ḳurashī (1268) s, **62a** – S, **62b**
Ḥusayn b. ʿAlī b. Ḥanẓala → ʿAlī b. Ḥanẓala
Ḥusayn b. ʿAlī b. ʿĪsā b. Mahān (IX) i, 437b; vi, 333b – I, 450a; VI, 318a
Ḥusayn b. ʿAlī b. Luhrasp i, 237b – I, 244b
Ḥusayn b. ʿAlī al-Marwazī (amīr) i, 278a, 1003a; iv, 661b – I, 286b, 1034a; IV, 688a
Ḥusayn b. ʿAlī Pasha i, 236b, 554a, 1087a – I, 244a, 571b, 1119b
Ḥusayn b. Amīn al-Ṣayyād s, 209a – S, 208b
Ḥusayn b. Asad Allāh (Marʿashī) (XV) vi, 514a – VI, 499a
Ḥusayn b. Dadjn s, 81b – S, 81b
Ḥusayn b. al-Ḍaḥḥāk (864) iii, **617b**; iv, 1003a, 1004a, b; vii, 694b; s, 25a – III, **638b**; IV, 1035b, 1036a, 1037a; VII, 695a; S, 25a
Ḥusayn b. Djaʿfar s, 352a – S, 352a
Ḥusayn b. Djanbulāt ii, 443b – II, 455a
Ḥusayn b. Djawhar ii, 495b; iii, 79a, b; v, 623b – II, 508a; III, 81b, 82a; V, 627b
Ḥusayn b. al-Faḍl al-Badjalī s, 392a – S, 392b
Ḥusyn b. Fakhr al-Dīn ii, 635a, 751a – II, 651a, 769b
Ḥusayn b. Ḥamdān (918) iii, 126a, **619a**; iv, 493b, 494a – III, 129a, **639b**; IV, 515a
Ḥusayn b. Ḥamza iii, 156a – III, 159a
Ḥusaym b. al-Ḥusayn (1838) iii, **606b** – III, **627b**
Ḥusayn b. Ibrāhīm al-Natīli ii, 349b – II, 359a
Ḥusayn b. al-Imām al-Manṣūr bi-'llāh al-Ḳāsim (Zaydid(e)) (1640) vii, 270a – VII, 272a
Ḥusayn b. ʿImrān b. Shāhīn i, 212a; iii, 1176a – I, 218a; III, 1204b
Ḥusayn b. Iskandar-i Shaykhī (Marʿashī) (1402) vi, 512b – VI, 497b
Ḥusayn b. Ismāʿīl (IX) vii, 390a – VII, 391b
Ḥusayn b. al-Ḳāsim b. ʿUbayd Allāh (vizier) (932)) i, 387b; ii, 178a; iii, 768a; iv, 1094a; ix, 594b – I, 398b; II, 184a; III, 791b; IV, 1125a; IX, 617b
Ḥusayn b. Maḥmūd, Khʷādja (1339) vi, 505a – VI, 490a
Ḥusayn b. Manṣūr → al-Ḥallādj
Ḥusayn b. Manṣūr b. Bāyḳarā, Mīrzā (Tīmūrid(e)) (1506) i, 148a, 227b, 228a, 627b, 847b, 920a, 1082b; ii, 334a; iii, 177b, **603a**; iv, 34a, 48b, 536b; v, 59a, 389a; vi, 514b, 715b; vii, 90a; s, 423a – I, 152a, 234b, 648a, 871a, 948a, 1115a; II, 343b; III, 181b, **623b**; IV, 36b, 51b, 560a; V, 60b, 389b; VI, 499b, 704b; VII, 91b; S, 423b
Ḥusayn b. Muḥammad → al-Rāghib al-Iṣfahānī
Ḥusayn b. Muḥammad b. Nāṣir, Sharīf (1640) vi, 566a – VI, 551a
Ḥusayn b. Muḥammad Marʿashī, Abū Manṣūr (1030) vi, 517a – VI, 502a
Ḥusayn b. Muḥammad al-Marw al-Rūdhī i, 893a – I, 919b
Ḥusayn b. Numayr al-Sakūnī (686) i, 55a, 810a; iii, **620b**; v, 119b; vii, 521b; ix, 826b – I, 57a, 833a; III, **641a**; V, 122b; VII, 522a; IX, 861a
Ḥusayn b. al-Ruḳād iii, 153a – III, 156b
Ḥusayn b. Saʿīd (Djabrid(e)) s, 234b – S, 234b
Ḥusayn b. Saʿīd b. Ḥamdān iii, 127b, 129a; v, 923b – III, 130a, 131b; V, 929a
Ḥusayn b. Salāma i, 181b; ii, 517a – I, 186b; II, 530a
Ḥusayn b. al-Ṣiddīḳ al-Ahdal i, 255b, 781a – I, 263b, 804a
Ḥusayn b. Sulaymān (Ṣafawid(e)) (1726) i, 1068a; ii, 87b; iii, 348b, **603b**, 1102b, 1190b; iv, 37a, 104a, 1043b, 1092b; v, 493b, 494a, 1087a – I, 1100b; II, 89b; III, 359b, **624a**, 1129b, 1220a; IV, 39b, 108b, 1075a, 1123b; V, 496b, 497a, 1084b
Ḥusayn b. Ṭāhir al-Ṭāʾī iv, 188b – IV, 196b
Ḥusayn b. ʿUmar (Ibn Dirham) (X) s, **386a** – S, **386b**
Ḥusayn b. Ṭalāl b. Amīr ʿAbd Allāh (Hāshimite) (1999) ii, 674b; iii, 264b; x, 886b; s, 7b, 9a – II, 691b; III, 272a; X, S, 6b, 8b
Ḥusayn b. Uways → Ḥusayn I (Djalāyirid(e))
Ḥusayn b. Ẓāhir al-Wazzān iii, 79a – III, 81b
Ḥusayn b. Zikrawayh (Ḳarmaṭī) (X) iii, 619a; iv, 494a, 660b – III, 639b; IV, 515a, 687a
Ḥusayn Abū Muḥammad → Nāṣir al-Dawla Ḥusayn
Ḥusayn al-Afṭas (IX) vi, 148a – VI, 146b
Ḥusayn Aḥmad Madanī iii, 432a – III, 446a
Ḥusayn al-Ahwāzī iii, 123b – III, 126a
Ḥusayn Akhlāṭī i, 869a – I, 893b
Ḥusayn ʿAlā ii, 882b – II, 903a
Ḥusayn ʿAlī (Dakhan) (1718) vi, 535a – VI, 519b
Ḥusayn ʿAlī b. Fatḥ ʿAlī Shāh (Ḳādjār) (XVIII) vi, 484b – VI, 470b
Ḥusayn ʿAlī Khān Bārha i, 1015b, 1025b, 1026a, 1219b, 1330a, b; ii, 379b, 804a, 810a; iv, 279b, 392b, 393a, 507b; s, 126b – I, 1047a, 1057b, 1255b, 1370b, 1371a; II, 389b, 823a, 829a; IV, 292a, 409a,b, 529b; S, 125b
Ḥusayn ʿAlī Mīrzā Farmān-Farmā b. Fatḥ ʿAlī Shah (Ḳadjār) (1834) ii, 812b; iii, 1106b, 1107a; vii, 675a – II, 831b; III, 113b, 1134a; VII, 674b
Ḥusayn ʿAlī Nūrī, Mīrzā → Bahāʾ Allāh
Ḥusayn al-Asghar i, 552a – I, 569b
Ḥusayn ʿAwnī → Akagündüz
Ḥusayn ʿAwni Pasha (1876) i, 285b; iii, **621a**; vi, 68b, 372b; vii, 599b – I, 294a; III, **641b**; VI, 66b, 357a; VII, 599a

Ḥusayn Bādkūbaʾi, Sayyid   s, 23b – S, 24a
Ḥusayn Beg b. Tay Bug̲h̲a   iv, 584a, b – IV, 608a
Ḥusayn Bey (Egypt/e)   ii, 321b – II, 331a
Ḥusayn Bey (Tunis) (1835)   iii, 636a; iv, 828b; vii, 717b – III, 657a; IV, 861b; VII, 718b
Ḥusayn Djahānsūz   → Djahānsūz
Ḥusayn Djāhid (Yalçîn) (1957)   i, 287b; ii, 474b, 475a, b, 497b; iii, **621b**; iv, 872b; s, 98a – I, 296a; II, 486b, 487a, 488a, 510a; III, **642a**; IV, 906a; S, 97b
Ḥusayn Djajadiningrat   → Hoesein Djajadiningrat
Ḥusayn Djalīlī (1743)   vi, 901a – VI, 892b
Ḥusayn Djindji K̲h̲odja (1648)   iii, **623a**, 983a; iv, 720a – III, **643b**, 1007b; IV, 748b
Ḥusayn Dūst K̲h̲ān   i, 625a – I, 645b
Ḥusayn Fahmī Ṣādiḳ   s, 299b – S, 299a
Ḥusayn Hezārfenn (1678)   ii, 110a; iii, **623b** – II, 112b; III, **644a**
Ḥusayn Ḥilmī Pas̲h̲a (1922)   iii, **624a**; iv, 123b; vi, 74a – III, **645a**; IV, 128b; VI, 71b
Ḥusayn Ḳāʾinī   iv, 199b – IV, 208b
Ḥusayn Kāmil b. Ismāʿil Pas̲h̲a (1917)   i, 13b; iii, **624b**; vi, 166a; ix, 379a; s, 40b – I, 13b; III, **645b**; VI, 158b; IX, 391b; S, 41a
Ḥusayn Ḳaraʾunas, amīr (1369)   x, 510b – X, 547a
Ḥusayn al-K̲h̲aliʿ   → al-Ḥusayn b. al-Ḍaḥḥāk
Ḥusayn K̲h̲alīfa Pas̲h̲a   i, 2a, 1172a – I, 2a, 1207a
Ḥusayn K̲h̲ān (Āgra)   i, 856b – I, 880a
Ḥusayn K̲h̲ān (Kaytāḳī)   ii, 87a; v, 296b – II, 88b; V, 287b
Ḥusayn K̲h̲ān, Mīrzā (XIX)   vi, 291b; vii, 455b – VI, 276b; VII, 455b
Ḥusayn K̲h̲ān b. Aḥmad Sulṭān Bayat (1835)   vi, 202b – VI, 187a
Ḥusayn K̲h̲ān b. Mansūr Beg   v, 829b – V, 835b
Ḥusayn K̲h̲ān b. Riḍa Ḳulī K̲h̲ān (XIX)   v, 312a – V, 312a
Ḥusayn K̲h̲ān Ādjūdān-bās̲h̲ī   i, 833b – I, 856b
Ḥusayn K̲h̲ān Mus̲h̲īr al-Dawla, Mīrzā (XIX)   ii, 649b; iii, 555a; iv, 397b, 398a, 787a; v, 1086a; vi, 20b; vii, 1004a – II, 666a; III, 574a; IV, 415a, b, 819a; V, 1083a; VI, 18b; VII, 1006a
Ḥusayn K̲h̲armīl (Harā)   iii, 471b – III, 488b
Ḥusayn K̲h̲aznadār (XX)   vi, 177b – VI, 162b
Ḥusayn Kiyā, Sayyid (Marʿas̲h̲ī) (XV)   i, 237b; vi, 513a – I, 244b; VI, 498b
Ḥusayn Ḳulī K̲h̲ān (1655)   i, 1068a – I, 1100b
Ḥusayn Ḳulī K̲h̲ān (Ḳādjār) (XVIII)   iv, 104b, 391a, 392a; vi, 484a – IV, 109b, 407b, 408b; VI, 470a
Ḥusayn Ḳulī Mīrzā   ii, 838b – II, 858a
Ḥusayn al-Kurdī   i, 1032b; ii, 572a; iv, 552b – I, 1064a; II, 586b; IV, 576b
Ḥusayn Lawāsānī, Malik Sulṭān   v, 663a, b – V, 668b
Ḥusayn al-Mahdī, Imām   s, 22a – S, 22b
Ḥusayn al-Muṣaylihī   vi, 627a – VI, 612a
Ḥusayn al-Nadjdjār viii, 122b – VIII, 125b
Ḥusayn al-Nāṣir   s, 363a, b – S, 363a, b
Ḥusayn Niẓām S̲h̲āh I (1565)   iii, 426a, **625b**, 1160b; viii, 75a – III, 440a, **646b**, 1189a; VIII, 75a
Ḥusayn Niẓām S̲h̲āh II (1589)   ii, 921b; iii, 626a; viii, 75b – II, 943a; III, 647a; VIII, 75b
Ḥusayn Niẓām S̲h̲āh III (1633)   iii, 626a; viii, 76a – III, 647a; VIII, 76a
Ḥusayn Nūrī Ṭabarsī   iii, 588b – III, 608b
Ḥusayn Pas̲h̲a   → Ṣilaḥdār
Ḥusayn Pas̲h̲a, Ag̲h̲a (1849)   iii, **628a**, 999b; v, 36a – III, **649a**, 1024b; V, 37a
Ḥusayn Pas̲h̲a, ʿAmūdja-zāde (1702)   i, 481a; iii, **626b**; iv, 233b, 657b; vii, 708a – I, 495a; III, **648b**; IV,

244a, 684a; VII, 708b
Ḥusayn Pas̲h̲a, Deli (1659)   i, 904b; iii, **626a**; v, 258b – I, 932a; III, **647a**; V, 256b
Ḥusayn Pas̲h̲a, Hādjdj   ii, 402a – II, 412b
Ḥusayn Pas̲h̲a, Küčük (1803)   i, 948a; ii, 534b; iii, **627a**; v, 35b – I, 977a; II, 547b; III, **647b**; V, 36b
Ḥusayn Pas̲h̲a, S̲h̲arīf   v, 808b – V, 814a
Ḥusayn Pas̲h̲a b. Afrāsiyāb (1668)   i, 236b; vi, 112a – I, 244a; VI, 110a
Ḥusayn Pas̲h̲a Mezzomorto (1701)   iii, **629a** – III, **650a**
Ḥusayn Raḥmī (1944)   iii, 357b, 375a, 593a, **630a**; s, 64b – III, 368b, 387a, 613a, **651a**; S, 65a
Ḥusayn al-Rayyī   s, 252b – S, 252b
Ḥusayn Rus̲h̲dī Pas̲h̲a   iii, 625a – III, 646a
Ḥusayn Ṣāḥib al-S̲h̲āma   iii, 398a – III, 410b
Ḥusayn Sarḥān (XX)   vi, 177b – VI, 162b
Ḥusayn Sarrādj (XX)   vi, 177b – VI, 162b
Ḥusayn S̲h̲āh, ʿAlāʾ al-Dīn (Ḥusayn-S̲h̲āhī) (1519)   i, 719b, 1015a; ii, 32a; iii, 14b, 422a, **631b**, 632a, 634b; vi, 47a; ix, 85b – I, 741a, 1046b; II, 32b; III, 15b, 436a, **625b**, 653b, 655b; VI, 45b
Ḥusayn S̲h̲āh Arg̲h̲ūn (1555)   i, 627b, 962a; iii, 575b, **632b**, 634a – I, 648b, 991b; III, 595b, **654a**, 655a; IX, 89a
Ḥusayn S̲h̲ān Čak   s, 167a, 325a, 366b – S, 167a, 324b, 366a
Ḥusayn S̲h̲āh Langāh I (1502)   i, 1005b; ii, 47a; iii, **633b** – I, 1036b; II, 48a; III, **654b**
Ḥusayn S̲h̲āh Langāh II (XVI)   iii, 633a, **634a** – III, 654a, **655a**
Ḥusayn S̲h̲āh S̲h̲arḳī (Djawnpūr) (1495)   ii, 270b, 271a, 498b; iii, 419b, 420b, 453b, 631b, **632a**; iv, 1136a; v, 783b; vi, 694a; ix, 355a – II, 279a, 511a; III, 433a, 434a, 469a, 652b, **653a**; IV, 1167b; V, 789b; VI, 681b; IX, 366b
Ḥusayn S̲h̲āhīs (Bengal)   ix, 728a – IX, 759a
Ḥusayn Sirrī   iii, 515b; s, 300b, 301a – III, 533a; S, 300a, 301a
Ḥusayn Ṣūfī (K̲h̲ʷarazm) (XIV)   x, 89a – X, 96a
Ḥusayn -i Tabrīzī   i, 777a – I, 800a
Ḥusayn Wafā   ii, 433b – II, 445a
Ḥusayn Wāʿiz   → Kās̲h̲ifī
Ḥusaynābād   iii, **634b**, 1163a – III, **655b**, 1191b
al-Ḥusaynī, Mīr Ḥusayn (1499)   vi, 114a; viii, 543a – VI, 111b; VIII, 560b
al-Ḥusaynī, Muḥammad ʿAbd al-Ḥasīb (1654)   vii, 94b – VII, 96a
al-Ḥusaynī Dālān   iii, **634b** – III, **656a**
al-Ḥusaynī al-Ḥaḍramī, Abū Bakr (XVI)   vi, 112a – VI, 110a
al-Ḥusaynī Sādāt Amīr (1328)   iii, **635a**, iv, 474a; vi, 73a – III, **656a**; IV, 494b; VI, 71a
al-Ḥusaynī, Ṣadr al-Dīn (XIII)   s, **378a** – S, **378b**
Ḥusaynid(e)s (Medina)   i, 402a, 403a, 552a; vi, 148a, 627b – I, 412b, 414b, 569b; VI, 147a, 612b
Ḥusaynid(e)s (Tunisi/-e)   i, 281b, 863a, 1111a; ii, 463b; iii, 605a, **635b** – I, 290a, 887a, 1144a; II, 475b; III, 625b, **657a**
Ḥusaynīs   iii, 523b; s, 67a – III, 541b; S, 67b
Ḥusayniya-yi Irs̲h̲ād   iv, 167a – IV, 174a
al-Ḥusayniyya   → al-Ḥasaniyya
al-Ḥusayniyya (oasis/-e)   vi, 160b, 163a – VI, 154b, 156a
al-Ḥusayniyya (Mawālī)   → K̲h̲as̲h̲abiyya
al-Ḥusayniyya (Zaydī)   v, 1237b; vi, 441b; ix, 507a – V, 1228a; VI, 427a; IX, 526b
Ḥusayn-zāde ʿAlī   s, 47a – S, 47b
Hüseyin Aywansarayī (XVIII)   vii, 532a – VII, 532a
Huseyin Cahid   → Ḥusayn Djāhid

Huseyin Ra'ūf Bey (XX) iv, 297b; vii, 229a – IV, 310b; VII, 231a
Ḥüseyn Agha Ḳara ʿOthmān-oghlu iv, 593b – IV, 617a, b
Hüseyn Beg Ḥamīdoghlu ii, 692a; iii, 133b – II, 709a; III, 135b
Hüseyn Djāhid Yalčīn (XX) vi, 93a, 94b – VI, 91a, 92b
Hüseyn Ḥilmī Pasha (1910) vi, 983b; vii, 206b – VI, 975b; VII, 207b
Hüseyn-ii Lāmekānī (Malāmī) (1625) vi, 228a – VI, 221b
Hüseyin Pasha (beglerbeg) iv, 594b – IV, 618b
Ḥūsh iii, **637b**; s, 381b – III, **658b**; S, 382a
Hūshang (mythical king) iii, **637b**; iv, 445a; v, 377b; x, 110b; s, 263a, b – III, **658b**; IV, 464b; V, 378b; X, 119b; S, 263a
Hūshang b. Dilāwar Khān → Hushang Shāh Ghūrī
Hūshang Shāh Ghūrī (Mālwā) (1432) i, 924a; ii, 218b, 270b, 276b, 814b, 1125a; iii, 418a, **638a**, 1003a; iv, 219a, 513a; v, 1a; vi, 52b, 53a, 54a, 272a, 309b, 406b, 407a, b; vii, 278b, 279a, 957a – I, 952a; II, 225b, 278b, 285a, 833b, 1151b; III, 431b, **659a**, 1028a; IV, 228b, 535a; V, 1a; VI, 51a, b, 52a, 256b, 294b, 391b, 392a; VII, 280b, 958a
Hūshangābād vi, 309b – VI, 294b
Hushaym b. Bashīr al-Sulamī (799) i, 272b; iv, 149a; vii, 662b – I, 281a; IV, 155b; VII, 662b
al-Husnī, Muḥammad b. Abī 'l-Khayr (XVI) ix, 180a – IX, 185b
Ḥusn Djahān Khanum (Ḳādjār) (XVIII) vi, 484a – VI, 470a
Ḥusn al-Ghurāb iii, 52a, b – III, 54a, b
Ḥusn al-Khātima iii, 1246a — III, 1278b
al-Husnī, Muḥammad b. Abī 'l-Khayr (XVI) ix, 180a – IX, 185b
Ḥusnī al-ʿArabī, Maḥmūd iv, 125a – IV, 130a
Ḥusnī al-Zaʿīm → al-Zaʿīm
Ḥüsnü, Shefīḳ iv, 124a – IV, 129a,b
Hüsnümansur → Adiyaman
Husrev → Khusrev
al-Ḥuṣrī → Abū ʿAbd Allāh
al-Ḥuṣrī, Abu 'l-Ḥasan ʿAlī (1095) iii, **640a**; vii, 483b – III, **661b**; VII, 483b
al-Ḥuṣrī, Abū Isḥāḳ al-Ḳayrawānī (1022) i, 591a; iii, **639a**; vi, 108b, 109a, 438a, 606b; vii, 483b; s, 62b – I, 610a; III, **660a**; VI, 106a, 107a, 423b, 591a; VII, 483b; S, 63a
al-Ḥuṣrī, Abū Saʿīd (IX) vii, 785a – VII, 787a
al-Ḥuṣrī, Sāṭiʿ iv, 783a – IV, 814b
Ḥussāb i, 1145b – I, 1180a
Hussein Onn vi, 241b, 242a – VI, 212b, 213a
al-Ḥūt → Nudjūm; Yūnus; Zīdj
al-Ḥuṭam b. Ḍubayʿa iv, 764a – IV, 794b
al-Ḥuṭay'a (Djarwal b. Aws) (VII) i, 1297b; iii, 136b, 272a, 354a, **641a**, 941a; vi, 625b – I, 1337b; III, 139a, 280a, 365b, **662a**, 965b; VI, 610b
Hutaym, Banū i, 528b, 546a; iii, **641b; ix, 814b** – I, 544b, 563b; III, **663a; IX, 849b**
al-Ḥuṭaym (Ḥadjar Ismāʿīl, Mecca) vi, 165b – VI, 157b
Huwa Huwa iii, **642b** – III, **663b**
Huwala i, 941b, 942b; iv, 777b – I, 970b, 971b; IV, 808b
al-Huwaydira → al-Ḥādira
al-Ḥuwayrith b. Nuḳayẓ b. Wahb ii, 842b – II, 862a
al-Ḥuwayṭāt, Banū i, 315a; ii, 626a; iii, **642b**; iv, 335a; x, 885a – I, 324b; II, 641b; III, **664a**; IV, 349b; X,
al-Ḥuwayyiṭ → Fadak
Ḥuwayza → Ḥawīza
al-Ḥuwayzī, ʿAbd ʿAlī b. Djumʿa al-ʿArūsī s, 57a – S, 57b
Huwiyya iii, **644a** – III, **665a**
Ḥuwwārīn, Ḥawwārīn (Syria/-e) iii, **645b**; vii, 268a – III, **666b**; VII, 270a
Ḥuyyay b. Akhṭāb (VII) vii, 852b – VII, 854a
Hvar, island of/île de s, 185a – S, 186a
Hyderabad → Ḥaydarābād

I

Ibād → Naṣārā
ʿIbād Allāh Beg ii, 83b – II, 85b
Ibadan iii, **646a** – III, **667a**
ʿIbādāt i, 277a; iii, **647a**; iv, 154b – I, 285b; III, **668a**; IV, 161a
ʿIbādat Khāna s, **378a** – S, **378a**
al-Ibāḍiyya i, 57a, 120b, 121a, 125a, 134a, 139a, 140b, 141b, 166b, 167a, 171b, 188b, 249b, 250b, 371a, 736a, 759b, 770b, 810a, 813a, 1028a, 1043b, 1053b, 1175a; ii, 129a, 140b, 170a, 359b, 368b, 592b, 1010a; iii, 95a, **648a**, 924b, 927b, 1168a; iv, 78a, 1076a, 1077a; v, 697b, 997a, 1230a; vi, 38a, 84a, 311a, b, 637a, 945a, 948a; viii, 112b; ix, 425a, 766a, 775a; x, 99b; 816a; s, 15a, 88b, 90a, 225b, 337b, 338a, 355a, b – I, 58b, 124a, b, 128b, 138a, 143a, 145a, b, 171b, 176a, 194a, 257b, 258b, 382a, 758a, 782b, 793b, 833b, 836a, 1059b, 1075a, 1058a, 1210b; II, 132b, 144b, 175b, 369b, 378b, 607a, 1033b; III, 97b, **669a**, 949a, 951b, 1196b; IV, 82a, 1108a, b; V, 702b, 992b, 1220b; VI, 36b, 82a, 296a, b, 622a, 937a, 940b; VIII, 115a; IX, 438b, 799b, 868b; X, 107b, ;S, 15b, 88b, 89b, 225b, 337b, 355a, b
Ibʿādiyya (Abʿādiyya) s, **379a** – S, **379a**
Ibāḥa (I) iii, **660b** – III, **682a**
Ibāḥa (II) ii, 136b; iii, **662a**; iv, 997a – II, 140a; III, **683a**; IV, 1029b
Ibāḥatiya ii, 1031a; iii, 434a, **663a** – II, 1055a; III, 448a, **684b**
Ibāḥiyya → Ibāḥa (II)
ʿIbāra iv, 114a, b – IV, 119b
Ibb iii, **663b**; s, 236a – III, **685a**; S, 236a
Ibdāʿ iii, **663b**; iv, 986b, 987a – III, **685a**; IV, 1019a, b
Ibdāl iii, **665a** – III, **686b**
Ibil i, 541a, 880b, 882a; ii, 1055a; iii, 32b, **665b**; iv, 676b, 677a – I, 558a, 906a, 907b; II, 1079b; III, 34a, **687a**; IV, 704b
Ibkishtīn s, 159a, 161b – S, 159a, 161a
Iblīs i, 45b, 71b, 177a, b, 181a, 262a, 796a, 811b, 1093a; ii, 547a; iii, **668a**; vi, 217b, 218a; x, 1b; s, 136a – I, 47a, 73b, 181b, 182b, 186a, 270a, 819b, 834b, 1125b; II, 560a; III, **690a**; VI, 202a; X, 1b; S, 135b
Ibn iii, **669b** – III, **691b**
Ibn ʿAbbād → ʿAbbādids; al-Muʿtamid; Muḥammad b. Ismāʿīl
Ibn ʿAbbād (Ṣiḳilliyya) → Benavert
Ibnʿ Abbād al-Rundī (1390) iii, **670b**, 720a, 722b; viii, 616a; s, 404b – III, **692a**, 742a, 745a; VIII, 635a; S, 404b
Ibn ʿAbbād al-Ṣāḥib Ismāʿīl (995) i, 59b, 119b, 126b, 590b, 712b, 1352b, 1354a; ii, 570a, 749a, b; iii, 487a, **671a**, 677a, 704a, 764b; iv, 61a, 524b, 862b, 1069b; v, 1028b; vii, 273a, 312a, 495a, 560a, 771b; viii, 71a; s, 4a, 13a, b, 24a, 38a, 118b, 124a, 393a – I, 61b, 123a, 130b, 610a, 734a, 1392a, 1393a; II, 584b, 767a, b; III, 504a, **692b**, 698b, 726b, 787b; IV, 64a, 547a, 895b, 1101a; V, 1024b; VII, 275a, 314b,

495a, 561a, 773b; VIII, 72b S, 3b, 13b, 24a, 38a, 118a, 123a, 393b
Ibn ʿAbbāda (1310) viii, 157a – VIII, 159a
Ibn ʿAbbādī s, 416b – S, 416b
Ibn al-Abbār, Abū ʿAbd Allāh (1260) i, 594b, 602b; ii, 308a; iii, 66b, **673a**, 704b, 762b, 803b, 904a; iv, 468a; vi, 216b; vii, 569a; x, 585a; s, 382a, 388a – I, 614a, 622a; II, 316b; III, 69a, **694b**, 727a, 785b, 827a, 928a; IV, 489a; VI, 200b; VII, 569b; X, ; S, 382a, 388b
Ibn al-Abbār, Abū Djaʿfar Aḥmad (1041) iii, **673b** – III, **695b**
Ibn ʿAbbās → ʿAbd Allāh b. al-ʿAbbās
Ibn al-ʿAbbās (Belabbès) (XIX) vi, 250b – VI, 235a
Ibn al-ʿAbbās al-Ṣaghīr (XVI) ix, 21b – IX, 21b
Ibn ʿAbbūd al-Fāsī (XVI) vi, 248b – VI, 232b
Ibn ʿAbd Allāh → Ism
Ibn ʿAbd al-Barr al-Namarī, āl (1070) i, 108a, 600a; iii, **674a**; vi, 264b, 281b; vii, 293a, 553a; s, 26b – I, 111a, 619b; III, **695b**; VI, 249a, 266a; VII, 295a, 553b; S, 27a
Ibn ʿAbd al-Hādī → Yūsuf b. ʿAbd al-Hādī
Ibn ʿAbd al-Ḥakam, Abū ʿAbd Allāh (882) iii, **674b**; ix, 183a – III, **696a**; IX, 188b
Ibn ʿAbd al-Ḥakam, Abu ʾl-Ḳāsim (871) iii, **674b**, 775a, 1047b; vi, 411a, b, 412a, b, 413b, 944b; vii, 153b; viii, 829a; s, 88a – III, **696a**, 798b, 1074a; VI, 396a, 397a, 398b, 937a; VII, 155b; VIII, 857b; S, 87b
Ibn ʿAbd al-Ḥakam, Abū Muḥammad (882) iii, 674b; vi, 279a; x, 11b – III, 696a; VI, 264a; X, 11b
Ibn ʿAbd al-Haḳḳ i, 903a – I, 930a
Ibn ʿAbd Kān, Abū Djaʿfar ii, 305a, 328a – II, 313b, 337b
Ibn ʿAbd al-Karīm al-Ragrāgī ii, 1007b – II, 1031a
Ibn ʿAbd al-Malik al-Marrākushī (1301) iii, **675a**; s, 397a – III, **696b**; S, 397a
Ibn ʿAbd al-Munʿim al-Ḥimyarī i, 156b, 488a; iii, **675b**, 1033a; vi, 220b, 411b, 412b; s, 171a – I, 160b, 503a; III, **697a**, 1059a; VI, 214b, 396a, 397b; S, 171a
Ibn ʿAbd Rabbih (940) i, 590a, 600b, 601a, 667b; ii, 246a; iii, **676b**; iv, 1188a; vi, 603b, 904a; vii, 254b, 528b, 811b, 985b; viii, 376b, 499a; ix, 515a; s, 16b – I, 609b, 620a, 620b, 688b; II, 253a; III, **698a**; IV, 1220b; VI, 588a, 895b; VII, 256a, 528b, 813a, 986b; VIII, 389a, 516a; IX, 534b; S, 16b
Ibn ʿAbd Rabīhī viii, 873b – VIII, 903a
Ibn ʿAbd al-Raḥīm (1285) vi, 580a – VI, 565a
Ibn ʿAbd al-Raʾūf i, 157a; iii, 486b – I, 161b; III, 503n
Ibn ʿAbd al-Salām al-Marrākushī iv, 1134a – IV, 1165b
Ibn ʿAbd al-Ṣamad (XI) iii, **677a** – III, **699a**
Ibn ʿAbd al-Wahhāb (1792) i, 554a, 593a, 942b; ii, 176b, 320b, 321a, 569a; iii, 162a, 295a, 582b, **677b**; iv, 717b, 925a; vi, 462a; ix, 903b – I, 571b, 612b, 971b; II, 182a, 330a, b, 583b; III, 165b, 304a, 602b, **699a**; IV, 746a, 958a; VI, 448a; IX, 941a
Ibn ʿAbd al-Ẓāhir, Fatḥ al-Dīn iii, 679b, 680a – III, 701b, 702a
Ibn ʿAbd al-Ẓāhir, Muḥyi ʾl-Dīn (1292) iii, **679a**; iv, 464b, 965a; vi, 326a – III, **701a**; IV, 485a, 997b; VI, 310b
Ibn ʿAbdal → al-Ḥakam b. ʿAbdal
Ibn ʿAbdūn, Abū Muḥammad al-Fihrī (1134) i, 591a, 602a; iii, **680b**; vi, 606b; vii, 778b – I, 610a, 621b; III, **702a**; VI, 591a; VII, 780a
Ibn ʿAbdūn Muḥammad b. Aḥmad al-Ishbīlī (XII) i, 156a, 157a, 390b, 1148b; iii, 486b, **681a**; vi, 124a; vii, 587a, 778b – I, 160b, 161b, 401b, 1183a; III, 503b, **702b**; VI, 122a; VII, 587a, 780a
Ibn ʿAbdūs → al-Djahshiyārī
Ibn ʿAbdūs, Aḥmad (1079) iii, **681b**, 973b, 974a – III, **703a**, 998a, b
Ibn ʿAbdūs, Muḥammad (XII) iii, **681a** – III, **703a**
Ibn Abī ʿAbda (917) x, 851a – X,
Ibn Abi ʾl-ʿAḳb vi, 216b – VI, 200b
Ibn Abī ʿAḳīl (Tyre) (XI) vii, 731a – VII, 731b
Ibn Abī ʿĀmir → al-Mansūr bi-ʾllāh (Almanzor)
Ibn Abi ʾl-Ashʿath (X) s, 271b, **379b** – S, 271a, **379b**
Ibn Abi ʾl-ʿAshshār (X) ix, 846b – IX, 882b
Ibn Abī ʿAṣrūn, Sharaf al-Dīn al-Mawsilī (1189) i, 766a; iii, 120b, **681b**; vi, 380b – I, 788b; III, 123a, **703b**; VI, 364b
Ibn Abī ʿAtīḳ iii, **682a** – III, **703b**
Ibn Abi ʾl-ʿAwdjāʾ (772) i, 1081a; iii, **682b** – I, 1113a; III, **704a**
Ibn Abī ʿAwn (933) iii, **683a**; vii, 528a – III, **704b**; VII, 528b
Ibn Abī ʿAzafa → ʿAzafī
Ibn Abi ʾl-ʿAzāḳir → Muḥammad b. ʿAlī al-Shalmaghānī
Ibn Abi ʾl-Baghl → Muḥammad b. Yaḥyā
Ibn Abi ʾl-Bayān (1236) i, 1224b; iii, **683a**, 749b; v, 251b – I, 1261a; III, **705a**, 772b; V, 249b
Ibn Abī Dabbūs iii, 67a; iv, 338a – III, 69b; IV, 352b
Ibn Abī Dalīm (962) vi, 280a – VI, 265a
Ibn Abi ʾl-Dam iii, **683b**, 967a – III, **705a**, 991b
Ibn Abī Dāʾūd v, 406a, 804a – V, 407b, 809b
Ibn Abī Dīnār al-Ḳayrawānī (XVII) iii, **683b**; vi, 840b – III, **705b**; VI, 831b
Ibn Abi ʾl-Ḍiyāf (1874) iii, **684a** – III, **705b**
Ibn Abi ʾl-Djawād (ḳāḍī) (849) viii, 844b – VIII, 874a
Ibn Abī Djumʿa → Kuthayyir
Ibn Abī Djumhūr al-Aḥsāʾī (XV) s, **380a** – S, **380a**
Ibn Abī Duʾād → Aḥmad b. Abī Duʾād
Ibn Abi ʾl-Dumayna → al-Hamdānī
Ibn Abi ʾl-Dunyā, Abū Bakr al-Baghdādī (894) i, 326a, 590a; iii, **684a**, 922b; iv, 212a; vi, 214b; x, 33a – I, 336a, 609b; III, **706a**, 947a; IV, 221b; VI, 198b; X, 34b
Ibn Abi ʾl-Fawāris vi, 438b – VI, 424a
Ibn Abī Ghudda iv, 509b, 510b – IV, 531b, 532b
Ibn Abī Ḥadīd (1926) vi, 957a – VI, 949b
Ibn Abi ʾl-Ḥadīd (1257) iii, **684b**; vii, 784a, 904a; ix, 819a; s, 25b – III, **706b**; VII, 786a, 904b; IX, 854a; S, 25b
Ibn Abī Ḥadjala, Aḥmad b. Yaḥyā al-Tilimsānī (1375) iii, **686a**; vi, 111b – III, **707b**; VI, 109a
Ibn Abī Ḥaṣīna (1065) iii, **686b**; v, 935a – III, **708a**; V, 939a
Ibn Abī Ḥātim al-Rāzī → Abū Muḥammad al-Rāzī
Ibn Abi ʾl-Ḥawwārī (IX) vi, 569b – VI, 554b
Ibn Abī Ḥudhayfa → Muḥammad b. Abī Ḥudhayfa
Ibn Abī Hurayra (956) ix, 187b – IX, 193a
Ibn Abī Ḥuṣayna → Ibn Abī Ḥaṣīna
Ibn Abi ʾl-Iṣbaʿ (1256) vii, 491b; viii, 427a – VII, 491b; VIII, 441a
Ibn Abī Khālid s, 112a – S, 111a
Ibn Abi ʾl-Khayr → Abū Saʿīd b. Abi ʾl-Khayr
Ibn Abī Khaythama (892) iii, **687a**, 803b; vii, 649a – III, **708b**, 827a; VII, 648b
Ibn Abī Khāzim → Bishr b. Abī Khāzim
Ibn Abī Khinzīr, Āl (X) viii, 52b; ix, 585a – VIII, 53b; IX, 667b
Ibn Abi ʾl-Khiṣāl (XI) vii, 587a – VII, 587a
Ibn Abī Ḳuḥāfa → Abū Ḳuḥafa b. ʿĀmir
Ibn Abī Laylā, Muḥammad (ḳāḍī) (765) i, 123b; ii, 232a; iii, **687a**; viii, 388a – I, 127a; II, 239a; III,

709a; VIII, 401a
Ibn Abī Laylā al-Akbar (VII) iii, **687a** – III, **709a**
Ibn Abi 'l-Layth iv, 289b – IV, 302b
Ibn Abī Madyan (XVI) ix, 20b – IX, 21b
Ibn Abī Muslim → Yazīd b. Abī Muslim
Ibn Abi 'l-Rabīʾ ii, 743b, 744a; iii, 741a – II, 762a, b; III, 763b
Ibn Abī Rabīʿa → ʿUmar b. Abī Rabīʿa
Ibn Abī Randaḳa al-Ṭurṭūshī → al-Ṭurṭūshī
Ibn Abi 'l-Ridjāl, Abu 'l-Ḥasan ʿAlī al-Ḳayrawānī (XI) iii, **688a**, 902b; iv, 830b; vii, 483b; viii, 108b – III, **709b**, 927a; IV, 863b; VII, 483b; VIII, 110b—
Abi 'l-Ridjāl, Aḥmad (1092) iii, **688b** – III, **710a**
Ibn Abi 'l-Sādj → Muḥammad b. Abi 'l-Sadj
Ibn Abī Saʿīd ʿUthmān b. Saʿīd al-Mawṣilī (X) vi, 637b – VI, 622b
Ibn Abi 'l-Ṣaḳr → Muḥammad b. ʿAlī b. ʿUmar
Ibn Abi 'l-Ṣalt → Umayya b. Abi 'l-Ṣalt
Ibn Abi 'l-Samḥ → Mālik b. Abi 'l-Samḥ
Ibn Abī Sarḥ → ʿAbd Allāh b. Saʿd
Ibn Abī Shanab (1929) iii, **689a** – III, **711a**
Ibn Abī Sharīf, Kamāl al-Din v, 333a – V, 333b
Ibn Abi 'l-Shawārib iii, **691a** – III, **713a**
Ibn Abī Shayba (849) i, 758b; iii, **692a**; vii, 663a, 691b – I, 781a; III, **714a**; VII, 662b, 691b
Ibn Abi 'l-Surūr → al-Bakrī
Ibn Abī Ṭāhir Ṭayfūr (893) i, 108b, 591b, 751b, 1081a, 1082b; iii, **692b**, 757a, 820a; vii, 985b; viii, 537b; x, 14a; s, 122b –
I, 610b, 774a, 1113b, 1114b; III, **714b**, 780a, 843b; VII, 986a; VIII, 555a; X, 14b; S, 122a
Ibn Abī Ṭalḥa (737) x, 86a – X, 93a
Ibn Abī Ṭayyiʾ (1228) i, 150a, 823a; iii, **693b** – I, 154a, 846a; III, **715b**
Ibn Abī ʿUmāra, Aḥmad (1283) iii, 67a, 825b; iv, 338a, 416a, 828a; viii, 763b – III, 69b, 849a; IV, 352a, 434a, 861a; VIII, 788b
Ibn Abī Usāma iii, 922b – III, 947a
Ibn Abī Uṣaybiʿa, Muwaffar al-Dīn (1270) i, 213a, 214a, 235b, 247a, 571a, 594b, 803b; iii, 683a, **693b**, 737a; vi, 198a, 215a, 637b, 726b; viii, 103a; s, 25a, 45a, 154b, 290a, 313b, 379b, 391a, 397b –
I, 219b, 220a, 243a, 255a, 589b, 614a, 826b; III, 705a, **715b**, 760a; VI, 182a, 199a, 622b, 715b; VIII, 105b; S, 25b, 45b, 155a, 289b, 313b, 379b, 391a, 397b
Ibn Abī ʿUyayna the Elder/l'Ancien (819) vi, 333b – VI, 318a
Ibn Abī ʿUyayna the Younger/le Jeune (VIII) iii, **694a** – III, **716a**
Ibn Abī ʿUyayna → Muḥammad b. Abī ʿUyayna
Ibn Abī Yaʿlā → Abu 'l-Ḥusayn; Abū Khāzim
Ibn Abī Zamanayn (1009) iii, **694b**; vii, 538a – III, **716b**; VII, 538a
Ibn Abī Zarʿ (XIV) i, 290b; ii, 145b; iii, **694b**; v, 652b, 653a, 1209a; s, 27a, 376b –
I, 299b; II, 149b; III, **717a**; V, 657a, b, 1199b; S, 27a, 376b
Ibn Abi 'l-Zawāʾid → Sulaymān b. Yaḥyā
Ibn Abī Zayd al-Ḳayrawānī (996) i, 106a; iii, **695a**; iv, 341a, 830b; vi, 188b, 278b, 710a, 942b; vii, 387b, 473b, 538a; viii, 497b; s, 395a –
I, 109a; III, 717a; IV, 355b, 863a; VI, 172b, 263b, 698b, 935a; VII, 389a, 473a, 538a; VIII, 514b; S, 395a
Ibn Abi 'l-Zinād (790) s, 310b, **380a** – S, 310b, **380b**
Ibn ʿĀbidīn (1842) iii, 163b, **695b**; s, 172a – III, 167a, **717b**; S, 173a
Ibn al-Ādamī (920) iii, 1137a; vii, 210a – III, 1165b; VII, 211b
Ibn Aḍḥā, *ḳāḍī* (XI) vii, 563b – VII, 564a
Ibn Adham → Ibrāhīm b. Adham
Ibn ʿAdhārī → Ibn ʿIdhārī
Ibn ʿAdī s, 400b – S, 401a
Ibn al-ʿAdīm, Kamāl al-Dīn (1262) i, 594b, 823a; iii, 693b, **695b**; v, 927b; vii, 115b; viii, 498b – I, 614a, 846a; III, 715b, **717b**; V, 932b; VII, 117b; VIII, 515b
Ibn ʿAdjarrad, ʿAbd al-Karīm i, 207a – I, 213a
Ibn al-Adjdābī, Abū Isḥāḳ al-Ṭarābulusī (1251) iii, **696a**; vi, 183b, 374b; s, **380b** – III, **718a**; VI, 167a, 359a; S, **380b**
Ibn ʿAdjība (1809) iii, 262a, **696a**; s, 390b – III, 269b, **718a**; S, 391a
Ibn ʿAdjlān ii, 1031b – II, 1055b
Ibn Ādjurrūm (1323) iii, **697a**; vii, 392a – III, **719a**; VII, 393b
Ibn al-ʿAdjūz → Alīsaʿ
Ibn al-ʿAfīf al-Tilimsānī (1289) i, 596a; iii, **697b** – I, 615b; III, **719b**
Ibn al-Afṭas i, 242a – I, 249b
Ibn al-Ahdal i, 255b; iii, 711a – I, 263b; III, 733a
Ibn al-Aḥmar iii, **697b**; v, 1209a; vi, 310b, 311a, 604a; s, 112a – III, **719b**; V, 1199b; VI, 295b, 296a, 589a; S, 111b
Ibn al-Aḥnaf → ʿAbbās b. al-Aḥnaf
Ibn al-Ahtam → ʿAmr b. al-Ahtam; Khālid b. Ṣafwān
Ibn ʿĀʾidh (847) iii, **698a** – III, **720a**
Ibn ʿĀʾisha (Almoravid(e)) i, 389b, 1337b; ii, 526b; iv, 672b – I, 400b, 1377b; II, 539b; IV, 700a
Ibn ʿĀʾisha, Ibrāhīm b. Muḥammad (824) iii, **698b**; vi, 335a, 336a – III, **720b**; VI, 319b, 320b
Ibn ʿĀʾisha, Muḥammad (VIII) ii, 428b; iii, **698b** – II, 39b; III, **720b**
Ibn ʿĀʾisha, Muḥammad b. Ḥafṣ iii, **698b** – III, **720b**
Ibn Ibn Āʾisha, ʿUbayd Allāh iii, **698b** – III, **720b**
Ibn al-Akfānī al-Asadī, al-Ḳaḍī (1014) s, **381a** – S, **381a**
Ibn al-Akfānī, Hibat Allāh b. Aḥmad (1129) iii, 930b; s, **381a** – III, 955a; S, **381a**
Ibn al-Akfānī, Muḥammad b. Ibrāhīm (1348) vii, 30a; s, 45a, **381a** – VII, 30a; S, 45b, **381b**
Ibn Akhī Ḥizām i, 1149b – I, 1184a
Ibn ʿAḳīl (1071) iv, 215b – IV, 224b
Ibn ʿAḳīl, ʿAbd Allāh (1367) i, 126b, 1308b; iii, **698b**, 861b – I, 130a, 1348b; III, **720b**, 885b
Ibn ʿAḳīl, Abu 'l-Wafāʾ ʿAlī (1119) i, 69b, 273b, 276b; iii, 103a, 160a, **699a**, 751a, 843a; iv, 172b, 513b; v, 234b; vi, 637a; vii, 296b, 566a, 755a; s, 194b –
I, 71b, 282a, 285a; III, 105b, 163b, **721a**, 774a, 866b; IV, 180a, 535b; V, 232b; VI, 622a; VII, 298b, 566b, 756a; S, 193b
Ibn ʿAḳnīn, Yosēf iv, 304b, 306a – IV, 318b, 319b
Ibn Aktham → Yaḥya b. Aktham
Ibn al-Aʿlam i, 87a; vi, 600b – I, 89b; VI, 585a
Ibn ʿAlī → Muḥammad b. ʿAlī wuld/u Rzīn (Tāfīlālt)
Ibn ʿAlīwa (1934) iii, **700b**; iv, 95b, 326b – III, **722b**; IV, 99b, 340b
Ibn ʿAlḳama, Abū Ghālib Tammām (IX) iii, **701b** – III, **724a**
Ibn ʿAlḳama, Tammām b. ʿĀmir (896) i, 601a; iii, **702a** – I, 620b; III, **724a**
Ibn al-Alḳamī, Muʾayyad al-Dīn (1258) iii, 685a, **702a**; vi, 549b; vii, 727b – III, 706b, **724b**; VI, 534a; VII, 728a
Ibn al-ʿAllāf (930) iii, **702b** – III, **724b**
Ibn al-Aʿmā (1293) vi, 111a – VI, 109a
Ibn Amādjūr iii, **702b** – III, **725a**
Ibn/Wuld al-Aʿmash (1695) vii, 1052b – VII, 1054b
Ibn al-ʿAmīd → Ibn al-Kalānisī; al-Makīn

Ibn al-ʿAmīd, Abu ʾl-Faḍl (970) i, 212a, 434a, 590b, 1352b, 1354a; ii, 305a; iii, 258a, 671a, b, **703a**, 1242b; iv, 1182a; vi, 539a, 600b; vii, 144a, 196b, 656b, 771a; viii, 598a; s, 72b, 124a, 263b –
I, 218b, 446a, 610a, 1392a, 1393a; II, 313b; III, 265a, 692b, 693b, **725a**, 1274b; IV, 1215a; VI, 523b, 585a; VII, 146a, 196b, 656a, 772b; VIII, 617a; S, 72b, 123a, 263b
Ibn al-ʿAmīd, Abu ʾl-Fatḥ ʿAlī (976) i, 126b; iii, 258a, 671a, **704a**, 730a, 780b; v, 621a; s, 72b –
I, 130b; III, 265a, 692b, **726a**, 753a, 803b; V, 625a; S, 72b
Ibn al-Amīn Maḥmūd Kemāl → Inal
Ibn ʿĀmir, Abū ʿUmar (736) iii, **704b** – III, **726b**
Ibn Amīr Ḥādjib (Mali) (XIV) vi, 421b – VI, 407a
Ibn Amīra (1258) ii, 526b; iii, **704b** – II, 539b; III, **726b**
Ibn ʿAmmār → ʿAmmār, Banū; al-Ḥasan b. ʿAmmār; Ṭarābulus
Ibn ʿAmmār, Abu ʾl-Abbās Aḥmad (XIII) iii, **705a** – III, **727a**
Ibn ʿAmmār, Abū Bakr Muḥammad (1086) i, 6b, 7a, 602a; iii, 542b, **705b**, 904b, 963a; vi, 852b; vii, 633b, 766b, 768a –
I, 6b, 7a, 621b; III, 561a, **727b**, 929a, 987b; VI, 844a; VII, 633a, 768a, 770a
Ibn ʿAmmār Amīn al-Dawla, ḳāḍī (ʿAmmār, Banū) (1072) vii, 120b, 731a – VII, 122b, 731b
Ibn ʿAmmār al-Kutāmī → al-Ḥasan b. ʿAmmār
Ibn ʿAmr al-Ribāṭī (1822) s, **381b** – S, **381b**
Ibn al-Amsāyib (1768) ix, 20b – IX, 21b
Ibn al-Anbārī → al-Anbārī, Abū Bakr Muḥammad
Ibn al-ʿArabī, Abū Bakr Muḥammad, *ḳāḍī* (1148) iii, **707a**, 798b; iv, 290a; vi, 738a –
III, **729b**, 821b; IV, 302b; VI, 727a
Ibn al-Aʿrābī, Muḥammad b. Ziyād (845) ii, 248a; iii, **706b**; iv, 111a; vi, 821b; vii, 305b, 306b, 402a, 831b; s, 38b, 122a –
II, 255a; III, **728b**; IV, 116a; VI, 811b; VII, 307b, 308b, 403a, 833a; S, 39a, 121b
Ibn al-ʿArabī, Muḥyī ʾl-Dīn (al-Shaykh al-Akbar) (1240) i, 60a, 71a, b, 88b, 90a, 347a, 388b, 594a, 596a, 869a, 937a, 1092b, 1103a; ii, 296b, 376a, 377a, 450b; iii, 29a, 51b, 90a, 262a, 429b, **707b**, 798b, 871a, 910b, 952a, 1240a; iv, 49b, 114b, 813b; v, 166a, 433a, 544a, 614a, 1160b; vi, 73a, 216b, 247b, 280a, 351a, b, 354a, 570a, b; vii, 95b, 480b; viii, 715b, 753a; x, 317a; s, 93b, 208b, 293a, 313a, 363b, 364a, b, 380a –
I, 62a, 73a, b, 91a, 92b, 357b, 400a, 613b, 615a, 893b, 966a, 1125a, 1136a; II, 304b, 386b, 387b, 462a; III, 30a, 53a, 92b, 269b, 443b, **730a**, 821b, 895a, 934b, 976b, 1272a; IV, 52a, b, 119b, 846b; V, 163b, 435b, 548b, 618a, 1150a; VI, 71a, 200b, 231b, 265a, 335a, 336a, 338b, 555a, b; VII, 97a, 480a, b; VIII, 736a, 775a; X, 341a; S, 93a, 208a, 293a, 313a, 363b, 364a, 380b
Ibn ʿArabshāh, Aḥmad b. Muḥammad (1450) i, 137a, 595a; iii, 309a, **711b**; iv, 506b; vi, 316a, 632b, 971a –
I, 141a, 614b; III, 318b, **734a**; IV, 528b; VI, 301a, 617b, 963b
Ibn ʿArafa, Abū ʿAbd ʿAllāh al-Warghammī (1401) i, 1341a; iii, 68b, **712a**, 827b; vi, 281a, 728b – I, 1381a; III, 71a, **734b**, 851a; VI, 266a, 717b
Ibn Arfaʿ Raʾs v, 112a; s, 270a – V, 114b; S, 269b
Ibn Arfaʿ Rāsuh s, 23a – S, 23a
Ibn al-ʿArīf, Abu ʾl-Abbās Aḥmad (1141)
iii, **712a**, 732a, 816b – III, **734b**, 754b, 840a
Ibn al-ʿArīf, al-Ḥusayn iii, **713a** – III, **735b**
Ibn ʿArrām (Miṣr) (XIV) vii, 171a – VII, 173a
Ibn Arṭāṭ → Ibn Sayḥān
Ibn ʿArūs, Sīdī b. ʿArūs (1463) i, 679b; iii, 69a, **713b**; vi, 250a; s, 93a – I, 700a; III, 71b, **735b**; VI, 234a; S, 92b
Ibn ʿAsākir, Abu ʾl-Ḳāsim ʿAlī (1176) i, 150a, 594b; ii, 126a, 283b, 993b; iii, **713b**, 767a; vi, 122b, 353a; viii, 518a –
I, 154b, 614a; II, 129a, 291b, 1016b; III, **736a**, 790a; VI, 120a, 337b; VIII, 536a
Ibn ʿAsākir, Amīn al-Dawla (1288) vi, 350b – VI, 334b
Ibn ʿAsākir, al-Ḳāsim ii, 126a; iii, 714b –
II, 129a; III, 737a
Ibn Asbāṭ al-Gharrī (1520) viii, 986a –
VIII, 1020a
Ibn al-Ashʿath → Ḥamdān Ḳarmaṭ
Ibn al-Ashʿath, ʿAbd al-Raḥmān (704) i, 77a, 690b, 1086a, 1344b; ii, 197a; iii, 40b, 247b, **715a**, 841b; iv, 15a, 356b; v, 119b, 349a, 1231b; vi, 311b, 946a; vii, 114b, 359b, 408b, 606a; viii, 799b; x, 843b; s, 26a, 358a –
I, 79b, 711b, 1118a, 1384b; II, 203a; III, 42b, 254b, **737b**, 865b; IV, 16b, 372a; V, 122b, 350a, 1221b; VI, 296b, 938b; VII, 116b, 361b, 410a, 605b; VIII, 827a; X, S, 26b, 357b
Ibn al-Ashʿath, Muḥammad → Muḥammad b. al-Ashʿath al-Khuzāʿī
Ibn ʿĀshir, Abu ʾl-Abbās (1362) iii, 670b, 701b, **719b**; s, 390b – III, 692a, 723b, **742a**; S, 391a
Ibn ʿĀshir (1631) vi, 933a – VI, 924b
Ibn al-Ashtar → Ibrāhīm b. al-Ashtar
Ibn al-Ashtarkūwī (1143) vi, 110b – VI, 108b
Ibn ʿĀshūr (1698) iii, **720a** – III, **742b**
Ibn Āshūr, Muḥammad al-Fāḍil iii, 720b; iv, 159b, 924b – III, 743a; IV, 166a, 957b
Ibn ʿĀshūr, Muḥammad al-Ṭāhir (1868) i, 1314b; iii, **720b**; iv, 159b – I, 1355a; III, **743a**; IV, 166a
Ibn ʿĀṣim, Abū Bakr (1426) i, 427b, 602a; iii, **720b**, 948b; vi, 824b; vii, 392a – I, 440a, 622a; III, **743a**, 973a; VI, 814a; VII, 393b
Ibn ʿAsḳalādja (985) vi, 431b – VI, 417a
Ibn ʿAskar, Abū ʿAbd Allāh (1578) iii, **721a**; vi, 356a, b – III, **743b**; VI, 340b
Ibn ʿAskar, *ḳāḍī* (Málaga) (1239) vi, 220b, 221b, 222b – VI, 214b, 215b, 216a
Ibn ʿAskar, Muḥammad b. ʿAlī al-Ghassānī (1239) s, **381b** – S, **382a**
Ibn al-ʿAssāl iii, **721b**, 1205b; v, 92b; vi, 143b; s, 396a, b – III, **744a**, 1236a; V, 95a; VI, 142a; S, 396a, b
Ibn al-Aswad iii, 712b – III, 735a
Ibn ʿAṭāʾ (al-Ḥallādj) vi, 569b – VI, 554b
Ibn ʿAṭā Allāh (1104) vii, 538a – VII, 538a
Ibn ʿAṭāʾ Allāh (1215) vi, 279a – VI, 264a
Ibn ʿAṭāʾ Allāh al-Iskandarī (1309) i, 351b; ii, 225a, b; iii, 670b, **722b**, 952a; ix, 172a, b; s, 387a, 404a, b –
I, 362b; II, 231b, 232b; III, 692b, **745a**, 977a; IX, 177b, 178a; S, 387b, 404a, b
Ibn Aʿtham al-Kūfī (IX) i, 984b; iii, **723a**; viii, 873b – I, 1015b; III, **745b**; VIII, 903a
Ibn al-Athīr, ʿAlāʾ al-Dīn (1329) viii, 802a – VIII, 829a
Ibn al-Athīr, Ḍiyāʾ al-Dīn (1239) ii, 826a; iii, 221b, 487a, **724a**; iv, 252a, 755b; vii, 978b; s, 177b –
II, 845b; III, 228a, 504a, **746b**; IV, 263a, 786a; VII, 979b; S, 178b
Ibn al-Athīr, ʿIzz al-Dīn (1233) i, 594b, 595a, 683a, 794a, 1115b; iii, **724a**; v, 821a –
I, 614a, b, 703b, 817b, 1149a; III, **746b**; V, 827a
Ibn al-Athīr, Madjd al-Dīn (1210) iii, **723b**; vi, 350b; viii, 753b – III, **746a**; VI, 334b; VIII, 775b
Ibn ʿAṭiyya al-Muḥāribī ii, 744a – II, 762a

Ibn al-ʿAṭṭār al-Isrāʿīlī i, 344b – I, 355a
Ibn ʿAttāsh (XI) i, 353a; iii, 253b, **725a**; iv, 101b – I, 363b; III, 261a, **747b**; IV, 106a
Ibn Āwā iii, **725b** – III, **748a**
Ibn al-ʿAwdjā → Ibn Abi 'l-ʿAwdjāʾ
Ibn ʿAwn Allāh (988) x, 159a – X, 170b
Ibn ʿAwn al-Asadī vii, 312b – VII, 314b
Ibn al-ʿAwsadjī i, 762b – I, 785b
Ibn al-ʿAwwām (ḳāḍī) (1010) vi, 671a – VI, 657b
Ibn al-ʿAwwām (XIII) x, 147a – X, 158b
Ibn al-ʿAwwām al-Ishbīlī, Abū Zakariyyāʾ (1130) ii, 902a; iv, 1145b; vii, 202b, 203b, 906b; viii, 632b; s, 128b, 370b – II, 922b; IV, 1177a; VII, 203b, 204b, 907a; VIII, 671b; S, 128a, 370b
Ibn Ayās → Ibn Iyās
Ibn al-ʿAydarūs → ʿAbd al-Ḳādir al-ʿAydarūs; Abū Bakr al-ʿAydarūs
Ibn ʿAyshūn al-Sharrāṭ (1697) vi, 356b – VI, 340b
Ibn al-Azraḳ al-Fāriḳī (1154) iv, 348b; vi, 626b, 930a – IV, 363b; VI, 611b, 921b
Ibn ʿAzzūz, Sīdī Ballā (1789) vi, 354b; s, **382a** – VI, 338b; S, **382b**
Ibn Bābā al-Kāshānī → al-Ḳāshānī, Abu 'l-ʿAbbās
Ibn Bābashādh (1077) → Ṭāhir b. Aḥmad b. Bābashād
Ibn Bābawayh (1179) → Muntadjab al-Dīn
Ibn Bābawayh (I) (Bābūya), Abū Djaʿfar al-Ḳummī (991) i, 120a, 162b, 1216a, 1352a; ii, 848a; iii, 24b, **726b**, 1266a; iv, 182b; v, 363b, 370b; vi, 107a; vii, 312a, 758b, 786a; viii, 778a; s, 23b – I, 123b, 167a, 1252b, 1391b; II, 867b; III, 25b, **749a**, 1299a; IV, 190b; V, 364b, 371b; VI, 104b; VII, 314b, 760a, 788a; VIII, 804a; S, 24a
Ibn Bābshādh (XI) i, 131b – I, 135b
Ibn Bābūyā → Ibn Bābawayh
Ibn Bādīs, ʿAbd al-Ḥamīd (1940) iii, **727a**, 1003b; iv, 146b, 147b, 151a, 159a, 784b; v, 597a; viii, 765a, 902a – III, **750a**, 1028b; IV, 152b, 153b, 157b, 165b, 816b; V, 601a; VIII, 790b, 933a
Ibn Bādīs → Muʿizz b. Bādīs
Ibn Bādjdja (Avempace) (1139) i, 234b, 594a, 631b, 1250a; ii, 771a, 773b, 838a; iii, 302b, 542b, **728a**, 849b; v, 704a; vi, 87a, 204b; vii, 58a, 683b, 811b; viii, 534b – I, 242a, 613b, 652b, 1288a; II, 789b, 792a, 857b; III, 312a, 561b, **750b**, 873b; V, 709a; VI, 85a, 188b; VII, 58b, 683b, 813b; VIII, 552b
Ibn Badrūn (XII) iii, 680b; vi, 606b; vii, 778b – III, 702b; VI, 591a; VII, 780b
Ibn al-Baghdādī ii, 362a – II, 371b
Ibn al-Bāghandī (925) vii, 706b – VII, 707a
Ibn Baḥdal → Ḥassān b. Mālik al-Kalbī
Ibn Bahlūl → Abu 'l-Ḥasan b. Bahlūl
Ibn al-Bahlūl vi, 247a – VI, 231b
Ibn Bahmāniyār (XI) viii, 72a – VIII, 73b
Ibn Bahrīz vi, 204b – VI, 188b
Ibn al-Baʿīth (IX) vi, 504a, b; vii, 778a – VI, 489b, 490a; VII, 780a
Ibn Baḳī (1150) i, 595b, 602a; iii, **729b**, 851b; vii, 811b – I, 615a, 621b; III, **752a**, 875b; VII, 813b
Ibn al-Bāḳillānī → al-Bāḳillānī
Ibn Baḳiyya (X) i, 11b; iii, 704a, **730a**, 780b; s, 398a – I, 11b; III, 726b, **752b**, 803b; S, 398b
Ibn Bākūya i, 147a – I, 151a
Ibn al-Baladī (vizier) (1170) iii, **730b**, 950b; vii, 726b – III, **753a**, 975a; VII, 727a
Ibn Balʿām, Judah iv, 306a – IV, 319b
Ibn al-Balkhī (1116) iii, 1097a, b; vi, 493b; s, **382b** – III, 1124a, b; VI, 479b; S, **382b**
Ibn Bāna (Bānata) (891) ii, 1074a; iii, **730b** – II, 1098b; III, **753a**
Ibn Bāna, ʿAmr s, 64a – S, 64b
Ibn al-Bannāʾ al-Baghdādī (1079) iii, **730b**; s, 30a – III, **753b**; S, 30a
Ibn al-Bannāʾ al-Marrākushī (1321) iii, 339a, **731a**; iv, 477a, 725a; v, 1209b; vi, 375a; vii, 137a – III, 349a, **753b**; IV, 498a, 754b; V, 1200a; VI, 359b; VII, 139a
Ibn Baraka → Abū Muḥammad b. Baraka
Ibn Barhān (1126) x, 461b – X, 495a
Ibn Barniyya al-Kātib (X) viii, 811b – VIII, 839a
Ibn Barradjān (1141) iii, 712b, **732a**, 800b, 816b – III, 735a, **754b**, 823b, 840a
Ibn Barrī, Abu 'l-Ḥasan ʿAlī (1331) iii, **732b**, 733a – III, **755b**, 756a
Ibn Barri, Abū Muḥammad (1187) ii, 528a; iii, **733a** – II, 541a; III, **755b**
Ibn Bashkuwāl (1183) i, 156a, 594b, 602b, 1092b; iii, 673a, **733b**, 762b, 803b, 976a – I, 160a, 614a, 622a, 1125a; III, 694b, **756a**, 785b, 827a, 1000b
Ibn Bashrūh (1166) ix, 587a – IX, 609b
Ibn Baṣṣāl, Muḥammad b. Ibrāhīm (1105) ii, 901a; vii, 906b; x, 147a – II, 922a; VII, 907a; X, 158b
Ibn Bassām (IX) iii, **734b** – III, **757a**
Ibn Bassām al-Shantarīnī (1147) i, 602a; ii, 838a; iii, 354b, **734a**, 789b, 807b, 934b; vii, 528a, 811a; ix, 308b – I, 621b; II, 857b; III, 365b, **756b**, 813a, 831a, 959b; VII, 528a, 813a; IX. 318a, b
Ibn Baṭṭa al-ʿUkbarī (997) i, 1040a; iii, 159b, **734b**; iv, 172b, 183b, 469b; v, 10a; vi, 122b, 123a, 447a; viii, 497b; s, 17a, 362a – I, 1071b; III, 163a, **757b**; IV, 180a, 191b, 490b; V, 10b; VI, 120a, 121a, 432a; VIII, 514b; S, 17a, 362a
Ibn Baṭṭūṭa, Shams al-Dīn al-Ṭandjī (1368) i, 96b, 186b, 323a, 593b, 775a, 903a; ii, 391b, 586a; iii, **735b**; iv, 649a; v, 671a, 827a, 1126a; vi, 121b, 258a, b; s, 73b, 203b, 210b, 295b – I, 99a, 191b, 333a, 613a, 798a, 930b; II, 402a, 600b; III, **758a**; IV, 675b; V, 676b, 833b, 1122a; VI, 119b, 242b; S, 74a, 203a, 210a, 295a
Ibn al-Bawwāb, Abu 'l-Ḥasan ʿAlī Ibn al-Sitrī (1022) i, 1354a; iii, **736b**; iv, 1122b; vii, 281b, 728a; viii, 151a; x, 409a – I, 1393a; III, **759b**; IV, 1154a; VII, 283b, 728b; VIII, 153b; X, 437b
Ibn Bayhas (IX) vii, 279b – VII, 281a
Ibn al-Bayṭār (1248) i, 156a, 214b, 516a, 594b, 704a; ii, 349b, 1068a; iii, 267a, 693b, **737a**; iv, 627a; vii, 58a; s, 43a, 78a, 313b, 370b, 397a – I, 160b, 220b, 531b, 613b, 725a; II, 359a, 1092b; III, 274b, 715b, **759b**; IV, 652a; VII, 58b; S, 43b, 77b, 313b, 370b, 397a
Ibn al-Bazzāz al-Ardabīlī (1391) vi, 354b; s, **382b** – VI, 338b; S, **383a**
Ibn Bībī al-Munadjdjima (XIII) i, 1197b; iii, **737b**; viii, 972a – I, 1233a; III, **760a**; VIII, 1006a
Ibn Biklārish (1100) s, **383a** – S, **383b**
Ibn al-Birr (XI) iii, **738b**, 859b – III, **761a**, 884a
Ibn al-Birzālī → al-Birzālī
Ibn Bishr → ʿUthmān b. ʿAbd Allāh
Ibn Bishr i, 1312b; iii, 773a – I, 1353a; III, 796a
Ibn Bishr al-Ashʿarī (874) vi, 829a – VI, 819b
Ibn Bishrūn iii, 929a; v, 1109b – III, 953b; V, 1105b
Ibn al-Biṭrīḳ → Saʿīd b. al-Biṭrīḳ; Yaḥya b. al-Biṭrīḳ
Ibn Buhlūl (930) iii, **739a** – III, **761b**
Ibn Buḳayla i, 927b; iii, **739a** – I, 955b; III, **762a**
Ibn Bukhtīshūʿ ii, 894b; vii, 1040a – II, 915b; VII, 1042a

Ibn Bulbul → Ismāʿīl b. Bulbul

Ibn Burd → Bashshār b. Burd

Ibn Burd al-Akbar (1027) iii, **739b** – III, **762b**

Ibn Burd al-Aṣghar (1054) iii, **740a** – III, **762b**

Ibn Burghūth → Muḥammad b. ʿUmar

Ibn Buṭlān, al-Mukhtār (1068) i, 32b; iii, **740b**, 906b; v, 930b; vi, 110a, 638a – I, 33b; III, **763a**, 931a; V, 935a; VI, 108a, 623a

Ibn Crispin, Moses iv, 305a – IV, 318b

Ibn Daʾb (787) iii, **742a** – III, **764b**

Ibn al-Dabaythī → Ibn al-Dubaythī

Ibn Dabba → Yazīd b. Miḳsam

Ibn al-Ḍaḥḥāk → Ḥusayn b. al-Ḍaḥḥāk

Ibn Dāhir → Ḏjaysinh b. Dāhir

Ibn Daḳīḳ al-ʿĪd (1302) ix, 813aʾ s, **383b** – IX, 847b; S, **384a**

Ibn al-Daḳḳāḳ → Ibn al-Zaḳḳāḳ

Ibn al-Dāmād → al-Dāmād

Ibn Danān, Saʿdyā iv, 305b – IV, 319b

Ibn Dāniyāl, Shams al-Dīn al-Mawṣilī (1310) i, 570b, 595b; iii, **742a**; iv, 602b, 1136b; vi, 114b; vii, 495a – I, 589b, 615a; III, **765a**; IV, 627a, 1168a; VI, 112a; VII, 495a

Ibn Dāra → Ibn Sabʿīn

Ibn Darrāḏj i, 1094a – I, 1127a

Ibn Darrāḏj al-Ḳasṭallī (1030) i, 592b, 601b; iii, **742b** – I, 611b, 621a; III, **765b**

Ibn Darrāḏj al-Ṭufaylī → al-Ṭufaylī, Abū Saʿīd ʿUthmān

Ibn Dārust (1093) s, 29b, **383b** – S, 29b, **384a**

Ibn al-Dawādārī (XIV) iii, **744a** – III, **767a**

Ibn Dāwud, Abraham iv, 304b – IV, 318a

Ibn Dāwūd, Muḥammad (909) ii, 183a, 1032b; iii, 100b, 102a, **744b**, 762b, 792b, 949a, b; vii, 527b; viii, 14b – II, 188b, 1056a; III, 103a, 104b, **767b**, 785b, 816a, 974a; VII, 527b; VIII, 14b

Ibn al-Dāya (941) i, 1101b, 1156a; ii, 305a; iii, **745b** – I, 1134b, 1109b; II, 313b; III, **768a**

Ibn al-Dayba°, Abū ʿAbd Allāh al-Zabīdī (1537) iii, **746a**; vi, 474b, 897b – III, **769a**; VI, 460b; 889a

Ibn Dayṣān i, 48a; ii, 199a, b – I, 49b; II, 205a, b

Ibn Ḏhakwān, ʿAbd Allāh (1000) iii, **746b** – III, **769b**

Ibn Ḏhakwān, Abū ʾl-ʿAbbās Aḥmad (1022) iii, 739b, **746b** – III, 762b, **769b**

Ibn Ḏhakwān, Abū Bakr Muḥammad (1043) iii, **747a** – III, **769b**

Ibn Ḏhakwān, Abū Ḥātim Muḥammad (1023) iii, **747a** – III, **769b**

Ibn Ḏhī → al-Hamdānī

Ibn Diḥya, ʿUmar b. al-Ḥasan (1235) ii, 1038b; iii, 702a, **747a**; v, 1119b; vi, 896a – II, 1062b; III, 724a, **770a**; V, 1116b; VI, 887a

Ibn Dīnār → ʿĪsā b. Dīnār; Mālik b. Dīnār; Muḥammad b. al-Ḥasan b. Dīnār; Yazīd b. Dīnār

Ibn Dirham, al-Azdī s, **384a** – S, **384b**

Ibn Dirham, Ḏjaʿd (742) iii, **747b**, 1019a; iv, 926b; x, 343b – III, **770b**, 1045a; IV, 959b; X, 369a

Ibn Dirham ʿUmar b. Muḥammad (940) s, **386a** – S, **386a**

Ibn Dirham Yaʿḳūb b. Ismāʿīl b. Ḥammād (845) s, **384b** – S, **385a**

Ibn Dirham Yūsuf b. ʿUmar (967) s, **386a** – S, **386b**

Ibn Dirham Yūsuf b. Yaʿḳūb b. Ismāʿīl b. Ḥammād (910) s, **385a** – S, **385b**

Ibn al-Ḏjadd, Abū ʿĀmir Aḥmad (1155) iii, **748a** – III, **771a**

Ibn al-Ḏjadd, Abū Bakr Muḥammad (1190) iii, **748b** – III, **771a**

Ibn al-Ḏjadd, Abū ʾl-Ḥasan Yūsuf (XI) iii, **748a** – III, **771a**

Ibn al-Ḏjadd, Abū ʾl-Ḳāsim Muḥammad (1121) iii, **748a** – III, **771a**

Ibn Ḏjaʿfar (894) i, 141a; iii, **748b** – I, 145a; III, **771b**

Ibn Ḏjaḥdam → ʿAbd al-Raḥmān al- Fihrī

Ibn Ḏjahīr → Ḏjahīr, Banū

Ibn Ḏjahīr, ʿAmīd al-Dawla (1100) ii, 384a, b; vii, 755b – II, 394b, 395a; VII, 757a

Ibn Ḏjahīr, Fakhr al-Dawla → Fakhr al-Dawla Muḥammad

Ibn Ḏjahīr, Zaʿīm al-Ruʾasāʾ (1113) vii, 755b – VII, 757a

Ibn al-Ḏjahm → ʿAlī b. al-Ḏjahm; Muḥammad b. al-Ḏjahm

Ibn Ḏjahwar, Abī Ḥazm → Abū ʾl-Ḥazm Ḏjahwar

Ibn Ḏjahwar, Abū ʾl-Walīd i, 155b; ii, 389a; iii, 789a, 974a – I, 160a; II, 399b; III, 812b, 998b

Ibn al-Ḏjallāl (XI) vii, 413a – VII, 414a

Ibn Ḏjamāʿa (1416) vii, 537a – VII, 537a

Ibn Ḏjamāʿa, Āl (XIV) iii, **748b**; v, 333a – III, **771b**; V, 333a

Ibn Ḏjamāʿa, Badr al-Dīn (1333) i, 439b; iii, 711a, 748b, 952a; iv, 949b; v, 333a; vii, 168a – I, 452a; III, 733a, 771b, 977a; IV, 982a; V, 333b; VII, 169b

Ibn Ḏjamāʿa, Burhān al-Dīn Ibrāhīm (1388) iii, 748b, 749a; viii, 458B – III, 771b, 772a; VIII, 474A

Ibn Ḏjamāʿa, ʿIzz al-Dīn (1366) iii, 699a, 748b – III, 721a, 771b

Ibn Ḏjāmiʿ, ʿAbd al-Karīm s, 164a – S, 164a

Ibn Ḏjāmiʿ, Abū ʾl-Ḳāsim Ismāʿīl (IX) i, 118a; iii, **749b**, 996a; s, 26a, 116b – I, 121b; III, **772b**, 1021a; S, 26b, 116a

Ibn Ḏjāmiʿ, Hibat Allāh → Ibn Ḏjumayʾ Hibat Allāh al-Isrāʿīlī

Ibn Ḏjanāḥ (XI) iii, **750a** – III, **773a**

Ibn Ḏjarāda → Abū ʿAbd Allāh b. Ḏjarāda

Ibn Ḏjarrāḥ → Ḏjarrāḥid(e)s

Ibn al-Ḏjarrāḥ (1024) vii, 117a – VII, 119a

Ibn al-Ḏjarrāḥ, Muḥammad b. Dāwūd (908) i, 386b; ii, 197b; iii, 619b, **750a**; s, 24b, 284b – I, 397b; II, 203b; III, 640a, **773a**; S, 25a, 284b

Ibn al-Ḏjaṣṣāṣ, Ḥusayn (Ḥasan) (927) iii, **750b**; v, 49b – III, **773b**; V, 51a

Ibn al-Ḏjaṣṣāṣ, Isḥāḳ iii, 750b – III, 773b

Ibn al-Ḏjawālīḳī → al-Ḏjawālīḳī

Ibn al-Ḏjawzī, Abū ʾl-Faradj (1200) i, 69b, 70a, 274b, 275b, 594a, 595a, 802b; ii, 590b, 964a; iii, 160b, 700a, 735a, **751a**, 752b, 803a; vi, 105a, 266b, 350b, 351a, 352b, 353a, 354a, 634b; viii, 517a; s, 16b, 408a – I, 71b, 72a, 283a, 284a, 613b, 614b, 825b; II, 605a, 986a; III, 164a, 722a, 758a, **774a**, 775a, 826b; VI, 103a, 251b, 334b, 335b, 337a, 338a, b, 619b; VIII, 534b; S, 16b, 408a

Ibn al-Ḏjawzī, Muḥyi al-Dīn iii, 161a, 752a – III, 164b, 774b

Ibn al-Ḏjawzī, Sibṭ (1256) i, 150a, 595a; iii, 700b, **752b**; iv, 173a, 1099b; v, 1236b; vi, 243a, 354a; vii, 986a – I, 154b, 614b; III, 722b, **775a**; IV, 180b, 1130a; V, 1227a; VI, 227a, 338b; VII, 987a

Ibn al-Ḏjazarī, Abū ʾl-Khayr (1429) i, 594b; iii, **753a**; vii, 622a – I, 614a; III, **776a**; VII, 621b

Ibn al-Ḏjazarī, Shams al-Dīn → al-Ḏjazarī

Ibn Ḏjazla (1100) i, 1057a; iii, **754a**; iv, 331a – I, 1088b; III, **776b**; IV, 345b

Ibn al-Ḏjazzār al-Ḳayrawānī (1004) i, 803b; ii, 60a; iii, **754a**; iv, 830b; viii, 822a – I, 826b; II, 61a; III, **777a**; IV, 863b; VIII, 850b

Ibn al-Djiʿābī, Abū Bakr Muḥammad b. ʿUmar (966) vii, 312a – VII, 314b
Ibn al-Djīʿān (1480) vii, 174b; viii, 844b – VII, 176b; VIII, 925b
Ibn al-Djillīḳī, ʿAbd al-Raḥmān b. Marwān (889) i, **85b**, 494a, 1092a, 1339a; ii, 1009a; vi, 568a; vii, 808a – I, **88a**, 509a, 1124b, 1379a; II, 1032b; VI, 553a; VII, 810a
Ibn Djinnī (1002) i, 143b; ii, 774b, 802b; iii, **754b**, 934b, 1128b; iv, 122b, 123a, 182a; v, 242b, 804b, 840b; vii, 772a, 914b; s, 19a – I, 148a; II, 793a, 821b; III, **777b**, 959a, 1156b; IV, 127b, 128a, b, 190a; V, 240a, 810b, 847a; VII, 774a, 915a; S, 19a
Ibn al-Djiyāb (1150) vii, 137a – VII, 139a
Ibn al-Djuʿayd vii, 591b – VII, 591b
Ibn Djubayr, Abu 'l-Ḥusayn al-Kinānī (1217) i, 330a, 593b, 602b, 901a; ii, 143a, 228b; iii, 736a, **755a**; v, 1160b; vi, 106b, 148b, 195b, 380b; s, 205a – I, 340b, 613a, 622a, 928a; II, 147a, 235a; III, 759a, **777b**; V, 1150a; VI, 104b, 147b, 179b, 365a; S, 204b
Ibn Djudʿān → ʿAbd Allāh b. Djudʿān
Ibn Djuhayr → Ibn Djahīr
Ibn Djuldjul, Abū Dāwūd al-Andalusī (994) i, 214a, 600b; iii, **755b**; iv, 254b; vi, 641a; s, 52b, 59b, 309b, 397a – I, 220b, 620a; III, **778b**; IV, 266a; VI, 626a; S, 53a, 60a, 309b, 397a
Ibn Djumayʿ Hibat Allāh al-Isrāʾīlī (1198) iii, 683a, **749b**; v, 251b; s, 386a – III, 705a, **772b**; V, 249b; S, 386b
Ibn al-Djumayyil → Ibn Diḥya
Ibn Djuraydj al-Makkī (767) vi, 263b; vii, 398a, 662b, 758a; ix, 7a; x, 29a, 81a; s, 18a, **386a** – VI, 248b; VII, 399b, 662a, 759b; IX, 7b; X, 31a, 84b; S, 18a, **386b**
Ibn Djuzayy (1355) iii, 736a, 755a, **756a** – III, 758b, 778a, **779a**
Ibn Ḍubāra → ʿĀmir b. Ḍubāra
Ibn al-Dubaythī (1239) iii, **756a** – III, **779a**
Ibn Duḳmāḳ, Ṣārim al-Dīn al-Miṣrī (1406) iii, **756b**; vi, 411b, 653a; vii, 174b – III, **779b**; VI, 396b, 638b; VII, 176b
Ibn al-Dumayna (VIII) iii, **756b**; vi, 477a – III, **779b**; VI, 463a
Ibn Durayd, Abū Bakr al-Azdī (933) i, 125b, 564a, 590a; ii, 1093b; iii, 512a, **757a**; iv, 123a, 524b; v, 608a; vi, 108b, 195b, 196a, b, 199a, 347b, 604b, 634a; vii, 26a, 262a; viii, 14b, 376a; s, 361a, 388a – I, 129a, 582a, 609b; II, 1119a; III, 529b, **780a**; IV, 128a, 547a; V, 612a; VI, 106a, 180a, b, 183b, 332a, 589b, 619a; VII, 26a, 264a; VIII, 14b, 389a; S, 361a, 388b
Ibn Durustawayh (957) iii, **758a**; vii, 279b – III, **781a**; VII, 281b
Ibn Ezra, Moses iv, 307a – IV, 320b
Ibn Faḍl Allāh al-ʿUmarī (1349) i, 214a, 595a, 607a, 1139a, 1149a; ii, 303a, 305b, 732b; iii, 7a, 71b, **758a**, 1242b; iv, 431b, 510a, 742b; vi, 118b, 424a, 572a, 667b, 670a; ix, 869a; s, 395b – I, 220b, 614a, 627a, 1173b, 1183a; II, 311a, b, 314a, 751a; III, 7a, 74a, **781b**, 1274b; IV, 450a, 673b, 532a, 772a; VI, 116b, 409a, 557a, 653b, 656b, 660a; IX, 277a; S, 396a
Ibn Faḍlān (X) i, 1305a, 1306b, 1307a; ii, 1107b; iii, **759a**; iv, 753b, 1063b, 1066a; vi, 724b; s, 265a, b – I, 1345a, 1346b, 1347a; II, 1133b; III, **782a**; IV, 784a, 1095a, 1097b; VI, 713a; S, 264b, 265a
Ibn Fahd iii, **759b** – III, **782b**
Ibn Fahd, ʿIzz al-Dīn ʿAbd al-ʿAzīz (1515) iii, **760b** – III, **783b**
Ibn Fahd, Muḥibb al-Dīn Djār Allāh (1547) iii, **760b** – III, **783b**
Ibn Fahd, Nadjm al-Dīn ʿUmar (1480) iii, **760a** – III, **783b**
Ibn Fahd, Taḳī 'l-Dīn Muḥammad (1466) iii, **760a** – III, **783a**
Ibn al-Faḥḥām (1122) iii, **760b** – III, **784a**
Ibn al-Faḳīh (IX) i, 203b, 645b; ii, 580a, b; iii, 106a, **761b**, 1077b; iv, 131b, 1099a; vi, 640a; s, 56a, 265a – I, 209b, 666a; II, 594b, 595a; III, 108a, **784b**, 1104a; IV, 137a, 1130a; VI, 625a, b; S, 56b, 265a
Ibn Falīta, Aḥmad b, Muḥammad b. ʿAlī (1363) ix, 565b – IX, 588a
Ibn al-Fallāḥī ii, 858a – II, 878a
Ibn Fallūs → al-Mārdīnī, Abu 'l-Ṭāhir
Ibn al-Faraḍī (1013) i, 600b; iii, 733b, **762a**, 789b, 848a; vii, 400a; x, 585a – I, 620a; III, 756a, **785b**, 813a, 872a; VII, 401b; X,
Ibn Faradj al-Djayyānī (X) i, 601a; iii, 734a, **762b** – I, 620b; III, 756b, **785b**
Ibn Faraḥ al-Ishbīlī (1300) iii, **763a** – III, **786a**
Ibn Faraḥ al-Kurṭubī iii, 763a – III, 786a
Ibn Farḥūn, Burhān al-Dīn al-Yaʿmarī (1397) i, 280a, 594b; iii, **763b**; vi, 280a – I, 288b, 614a; III, **786b**; VI, 265a
Ibn al-Fāriḍ (1235) i, 60a, 89a, 596a, 816a, 1333a; ii, 363b; iii, **763b**; iv, 1006b – I, 62a, 91b, 615b, 839a, 1373b; II, 373b; III, **786b**; IV, 1038b
Ibn Farīghūn, Shaʿyā (X) s, 376a, **386b** – S, 376a, **387a**
Ibn Fāris, Abu 'l-Ḥusayn al-Lughawī (1004) i, 345b, 568a; iii, 111a, 672a, **764a**; iv, 524b; vi, 351a; vii, 914b; s, 346a – I, 356a, 586b; III, 113b, 693b, **787a**; IV, 547a; VI, 335a; VII, 915a; S, 346a
Ibn al-Farrāʾ → al-Baghawī
Ibn al-Farrāʾ, Abū Yaʿlā (1066) i, 273b, 435b, 1040a; iii, 159a, b, 512b, 699b, 730b, 735a, **765b**, 784b, 1165a; iv, 458b; vii, 927a; s, 195a – I, 282a, 447b, 1017b; III, 162b, 163a, 530a, 721b, 753b, 757b, **788b**, 808a, 1193b; IV, 478b; VII, 927b; S, 193b
Ibn Farrūkh v, 1159b – V, 1149a
Ibn Fasāndjus, Abu 'l-Faradj i, 11b; ii, 827a – I, 11b; II, 846b
Ibn Fatḥūn, Abu 'l-Ḳāsim (1114) viii, 635a – VIII, 654a
Ibn Fāṭima ii, 586a – II, 600b
Ibn Fattūḥ vi, 110a – VI, 107b
Ibn Fendīn → al-Ifrānī, Abū Ḳudāma Yazīd
Ibn Firishte → Firishte-oghlu
Ibn Firnās → ʿAbbās b. Firnās
Ibn al-Funduḳ (XII) ix, 617a – IX, 640a
Ibn al-Fūrak (1015) ii, 125b; iii, **766b** – II, 129a; III, **790a**
Ibn al-Furāt (828) vi, 278b – VI, 263b
Ibn al-Furāt, Abu 'l-ʿAbbās Aḥmad (904) i, 386b; iii, **767b** – I, 398a; III, **790b**
Ibn al-Furāt, Abu 'l-Faḍl Djaʿfar (1001) ii, 136a, 495a; iii, **768b**, 840b; v, 953b – II, 139b, 507b; III, **791b**, 864b; V, 957b
Ibn al-Furāt, Abu 'l-Fatḥ al-Faḍl (938) iii, 79a, **768a**; v, 953b; vi, 845b; ix, 584b – III, 81b, **791a**; V, 957b; VI, 836b; IX, 607a
Ibn al-Furāt, Abu 'l-Ḥasan ʿAlī b. Muḥammad, (vizier) (924) i, 386b, 835b; ii, 461b; iii, 100b, 133a, 619b, 739a, 750b, **767b**, 824a, 886b; iv, 265a, 1063b; v, 857a, 953a; vi, 352a, 498a, 518a; vii, 397a, 542a, b, 543a, 575b, 653a – I, 398a, 859a; II, 473b; III, 103a, 136a, 640a, b, 761b, 773b, **790b**, 848a, 910b; IV, 277a, 1094b; V, 864a, 957a; VI, 336a, 483b, 503a; VII, 398b, 542a, 543a, 576a, 652b

Ibn al-Furāt, Abu ’l-Khaṭṭāb Djaʿfar (909) iii, **768a** – III, **791a**
Ibn al-Furāt, Muḥammad (1405) iii, 693b, **768b** – III, 715b, **792a**
Ibn al-Furāt, ʿUmar (818) iii, **767a** – III, **790b**
Ibn Fūrradja (1141) vii, 772a – VII, 773b
Ibn al-Fuwaṭī (1323) iii, **769a** – III, **792a**
Ibn Gabirol (1058) iii, **770a**; iv, 304a – III, **793a**; IV, 318a
Ibn Ghalbūn iii, **770b** – III, **794a**
Ibn Ghalbūn → Muḥammad b. Khalīl
Ibn Ghālib al-Gharnāṭī (1175) iii, **771b** – III, **795a**
Ibn Ghānim i, 1186a; iii, **772a** – I, 1221a; III, **795a**
Ibn Ghāniya → ʿAlī b. Ghāniya; Yaḥyā b. Ghāniya
Ibn Ghannām (1294) iii, **772a** – III, **795b**
Ibn Ghannām, Shaykh (1810) iii, **772b** – III, **795b**
Ibn al-Gharābīlī → Ibn Ḳāsim al-Ghazzī
Ibn Gharsiya, Abū ʿAmir Aḥmad (XI) iii, **773a**; vii, 292b; ix, 515a – III, **796b**; VII, 294b; IX, 535a
Ibn al-Ghasīl → ʿAbd Allāh b. Ḥanẓala
Ibn al-Ghassāl vi, 606b – VI, 591a
Ibn Ghaybī (1435) vii, 190b, 191a, 207b, 208a, 209a, b; ix, 11b – VII, 191a, b, 208b, 209a, 210b; IX, 12a
Ibn Ghāzī, Abū ʿAbd Allāh (1513) iii, **773b** – III, **796b**
Ibn Ghāzī al-Ḳayrawānī vi, 712b – VI, 701b
Ibn Ghidhāhum (1867) vii, 452a, 718a, b; s, **387a** – VII, 453a, 719a, b; S, **387a**
Ibn Ghiyāth (Ghayyāth), Isaac iv, 306a – IV, 319b
Ibn Ghurāb (1406) iii, **773b**, 923a – III, **797a**, 947b
Ibn Giḳaṭilia, Moses iv, 306a – IV, 319b
Ibn Giṭūn Wulā al-Ṣaghīr vi, 251b – VI, 236a
Ibn al-Habbāriyya (1115) iii, 309a, 354b, **774a**, 799b, 1264b; iv, 504a, 506a; viii, 971b; s, 26b – III, 318b, 365b, **797b**, 823a, 1297a; IV, 526a, 528a; VIII, 1005b S, 26b
Ibn al-Ḥabḥāb → ʿUbayd Allāh b. al-Ḥabḥāb
Ibn Ḥabīb, Muḥammad → Muḥammad b. Ḥabīb
Ibn al-Ḥabīb al-Andalūsī (853) i, 600a, 718b; iii, 272b, **775a**; vi, 278b, 279a; x, 453b – I, 619b, 740a; III, 280b, **798a**; vi, 263b, 264a; X, 486a
Ibn Ḥabīb al-Dimashḳī (1377) i, 119a, 595a; iii, **775a**; vi, 351a – I, 122b, 614b; III, **798b**; VI, 335a
Ibn Ḥābiṭ → Aḥmad b. Ḥābiṭ
Ibn al-Ḥaddād (1088) iii, **775b** – III, **799a**
Ibn al-Ḥaddādiyya vi, 477a – VI, 463a
Ibn al-Hadhbānī, Naṣr al-Dīn (amīr) (1389) ii, 580b – VI, 565a
Ibn Ḥadjar al-ʿAsḳalānī (1449) i, 275b, 594b, 595a, 791a, 1297a; ii, 159a, 215a, 743b; iii, 25b, 730b, **776a**, 818b; iv, 142b, 642b; vi, 36a, 194a, 280b, 353a, 785a; vii, 212b, 576b, 581b; viii, 458b, 517a; x, 934b s, 88a, 388b – I, 284a, 614a, 614b, 814b, 1336b; II, 164a, 221b, 762a; III, 26b, 753b, **799a**, 842a; IV, 148a, 669a; VI, 34b, 178a, 265b, 337a, 775a; VII, 213b, 577a, 582; VIII, 474a, 534b; S, 88a, 389a
Ibn Ḥadjar al-Haytamī, Abu ’l-ʿAbbās (1567) iii, **778b**; iv, 451a, 741b; v, 1235a; vi, 88a, 133a, 352b; vii, 458a – III, **802a**; IV, 471a, 771a; V, 1225b; VI, 86a, 131a, 337a; VII, 458a
Ibn al-Ḥādjdj, Abū ʿAbd Allāh (1336) iii, **779b**; iv, 957b; vi, 214b, 654b – III, **803a**; IV, 991a; VI, 198b, 640a
Ibn al-Ḥādjdj, Abu ’l-ʿAbbās al-Ishbīlī (1249) iii, **779b** – III, **803a**
Ibn al-Ḥādjdj, Abu ’l-ʿAbbās al-Sulamī (1856) iii, **780a** – III, **803a**
Ibn al-Ḥādjdj, Abū ʿAbd Allāh al-Sulamī (1857) iii, **780a** – III, **803a**
Ibn al-Ḥādjdj, Abu ’l-Barakāt al-Balāfiḳī (1370) iii, **780a** – III, **803a**
Ibn al-Ḥādjdj, Abū Isḥāḳ Ibrāhīm iii, **780a** – III, **803a**
Ibn al-Ḥādjdj, Ḥamdūn b. ʿAbd al-Raḥmān al-Fāsī (1817) vi, 249b, 356b; s, **387b**, 390b – VI, 234a, 341a; S, **387b**, 391a
Ibn al-Ḥādjdj, Muḥammad al-Ṭālib iv, 774b; s, 387b – IV, 805b; S, 388a
Ibn al-Ḥādjdj, Shīth b. Ibrāhīm al-Ḳifṭī (1002) iii, **780a** – III, **803a**
Ibn al-Hadjdjādj, Abū ʿAbd ʿAllāh (1001) i, 133b, 858b; ii, 552a, 1032b; iii, 354b, **780a**, 1264a; vi, 468b; vii, 771a; s, 26a, 398b – I, 137b, 882b; II, 565b, 1056b; III, 365b, **803b**, 1297a; VI, 445b; VII, 772b; S, 26b, 398b
Ibn Ḥadjdjādj al-Ishbīlī ii, 901b – II, 922b
Ibn al-Ḥādjib, Djamāl al-Dīn al-Mālikī (1248) i, 721a; iii, **781a**, 861a; iv, 414b; vi, 278b, 279a; vii, 132a, 296b, 914b – I, 742b; III, **804a**, 885a; IV, 432b; VI, 263b, 264a; VII, 134a, 298b, 915a
Ibn Ḥādjib al-Nuʿmān (XI) iii, **781b** – III, **805a**
Ibn al-Ḥaḍramī, ʿAbd Allāh b. ʿAmr (658) ii, 480b; iii, **782a**; vii, 265b – II, 493a; III, **805a**; VII, 267a
Ibn al-Ḥāf (Bal-Ḥāf) vi, 81b – VI, 79b
Ibn Ḥafsh iv, 722b – IV, 751b
Ibn Ḥafṣūn → ʿUmar b. Ḥafṣūn
Ibn al-Ḥāʾik → al-Hamdānī
Ibn al-Hāʾim (1021) v, 333a; vi, 132b – V, 333a; VI, 130b
Ibn al-Hāʾim (Miṣr) (1412) vi, 543a – VI, 528a
Ibn al-Ḥakīm al-Rundī (1309) iii, 833b, 834a, 909a; vii, 1022b – III, 857b, 933b; VII, 1024b
Ibn Ḥamādu (1231) iii, **782b** – III, **805b**
Ibn Ḥamāma → Bilāl b. Rabāḥ
Ibn Ḥamdīn, Abu ’l-Ḳāsim Aḥmad iii, 850a, 851b, 958b – III, 874a, 875b, 983a
Ibn Ḥamdīn, Muḥammad iii, 849a, b; iv, 290a – III, 873a, b; IV, 302b
Ibn Ḥamdīs (1132) i, 592b, 602a, 1205a; ii, 1033a; iii, **782b**; iv, 1007a; v, 60b – I, 611b, 621b, 1241a; II, 1056b; III, **806a**; IV, 1039b; V, 62a
Ibn Ḥamdūn (Ismāʿīlī) vi, 439b – VI, 424b
Ibn Ḥamdūn, Abu ’l-Maʿālī (1166) iii, **784a**; vi, 108b; vii, 726b – III, **807a**; VI, 106b; VII, 727b
Ibn Ḥamdūn Aḥmad b. Ibrāhīm (IX) iii, **783b**; vi, 728a; s, 17b – III, **807a**; VI, 717a; S, 18a
Ibn Ḥāmid (1012) iii, 159a, b, 765b, **784b** – III, 162b, 163a, 789a, **807b**
Ibn Hammād → Ibn Hamādu
Ibn Ḥammādī (Relizane) (XIX) vi, 249b – VI, 233b
Ibn Ḥammūd iv, 733b – IV, 763a
Ibn Hamushk i, 161a; ii, 516a, 1014a; iii, 850b, 865a; iv, 116a, 665b – I, 165b; II, 528b, 1037b; III, 874b, 889a; IV, 121a, 692b
Ibn al-Ḥanafiyya → Muḥammad b. al-Ḥanafiyya
Ibn Ḥanbal → Aḥmad b. Ḥanbal
Ibn al-Ḥanbalī (1563) vii, 136a – VII, 138a
Ibn Hānī’ al-Andalūsī (973) i, 60b, 592a; ii, 855b, 861b; iii, **785a**; iv, 496b; vi, 728a; s, 62b – I, 62b, 611b; II, 875b, 881b; III, **808a**; IV, 518a; VI, 717a; S, 63a
Ibn Ḥānish (ḳāḍī) (1328) viii, 157b – VIII, 160a
Ibn al-Ḥannāṭ (1045) iii, **786a** – III, **809b**
Ibn al-Ḥanẓaliyya → Abū Djahl
Ibn Ḥarb → ʿAbd Allāh b. ʿAmr; ʿAbd Allāh b. Sabaʾ

Ibn Ḥarb → Muḥammad b. al-Mug̲h̲īra b. Ḥarb
Ibn al-Ḥārit̲h̲ (971) x, 585a – X,
Ibn Harma (VIII) iii, **786b**; iv, 1004b; v, 1156a – III, **809b**; IV, 1036b; V, 1145b
Ibn al-Ḥasan al-Nubāhī → al-Nubāhī
Ibn Ḥas̲h̲īs̲h̲ (ḳāḍī) (1328) viii, 157b – VIII, 160a
Ibn Ḥassūn, ḳāḍī (Mālaḳa) (1182) vi, 222b – VI, 216a
Ibn Ḥātim Badr al-Dīn (1295) s, **387b** – S, **388a**
Ibn Ḥawḳal (980) i, 96a, 488a, 1003a, 1041a; ii, 577b, 581a, 582a, 1002a; iii, 131a, 405b, **786b**; iv, 223a, b, 1079a, 1081a; v, 555a; vi, 120b, 313b, 639b, 640a; vii, 493a; s, 94b, 244b, 376b – I, 98b, 502b, 1034a, 1073a; II, 592a, 596a, b, 1025a; III, 133b, 418a, **810a**; IV, 232b, 233a, b, 1110b, 1112a; V, 560a; VI, 118b, 299a, 624b, 625a; VII, 493a; S, 93b, 244b, 376b
Ibn Ḥaws̲h̲ab → Manṣūr al-Yaman
Ibn al-Ḥawwās (XI) ii, 553a; iii, **788a**, 956a; iv,733b – II, 567a; III, **811a**, 980b; IV, 763a
Ibn al-Hayt̲h̲am (1039) i, 785b, 816a, 1102a; ii, 362a; iii, **788a**, 1135b; iv, 515b, 518a, 1059b; v, 397b, 536a, 703b, 1025b; vi, 376b, 377a, 450b, 637b; vii, 106b, 282b; viii, 102a, 560b; s, 412a, 413a, 414a – I, 809a, 839b, 1135a; II, 372a; III, **811b**, 1163b; IV, 537b, 540b, 1090b; V, 398b, 540b, 708b, 1021a; VI, 361a, b, 436a, 622b; VII, 108b, 284b; VIII, 104b, 578b; S, 412a, 413a, 414b
Ibn al-Hayt̲h̲amī i, 593a; iii, 856a – I, 612a; III, 880a
Ibn al-Ḥayy (1064) vii, 413a – VII, 414a
Ibn al-Hayyabān iv, 270a – IV, 282a
Ibn Ḥayyān, Abū Marwān (1076) i, 82b, 155b, 600b, 1040b; iii, **789a**; v, 1119b; vi, 221b, 431b; vii, 492b, 553a, 1042b – I, 85a, 160a, 620a, 1072a; III, **812b**; V, 1116a; VI, 215b, 417a; VII, 492a, 553b, 1044b
Ibn Ḥayyawayh iii, 922b – III, 947a
Ibn Ḥayyūs, Abu 'l-Fityān (1081) iii, **790a**; vi, 539a – III, **813b**; VI, 523b
Ibn Ḥāzim → Muḥammad b. Ḥāzim
Ibn Ḥazm, Āl iii, **790a** – III, **813b**
Ibn Ḥazm, Abū Bakr (1011) iii, **790a** – III, **813b**
Ibn Ḥazm, Abu 'l-Mug̲h̲īra (1046) iii, **790b**, 901b, 938b – III, **814a**, 926a, 936b
Ibn Ḥazm, Abū Muḥammad ʿAlī (1064) i, 84a, 147a, 265b, 414a, 427b, 497a, 590a, 600a, 601b, 865a; ii, 96b, 765a; iii, 308a, 744b, **790b**, 870b, 901b, 1019b, 1024a; iv, 113b, 142a, 272a; v, 703b, 704a; vi, 221b, 281b, 346b, 444b, 445a, b, 446a, b, 943b; vii, 55a, 293a, 553a; viii, 981a; s, 45a, 362b, 396b – I, 86b, 151a, 273b, 425b, 439b, 512a, 609a, 619b, 621a, 889a; II, 98b, 783b; III, 317a, 767b, **814a**, 894b, 926a, 1045a, 1050a; IV, 118b, 148a, 284a; V, 708b, 709a; VI, 215a, 266a, 330b, 430a, b, 431a, b, 432a, 935b; VII, 55b, 295a, 553b; VIII, 1015a,b; S, 45b, 362b, 397a
Ibn Ḥazm, Abū Rāfiʿ al-Faḍl b. ʿAlī (1068) iii, **790b** – III, **813b**
Ibn Ḥazm, Abū ʿUmar Aḥmad b. Saʿīd (1012) iii, **790a** – III, **813b**
Ibn Ḥibbān (965) i, 1348b; iii, **799a**; viii, 516b – I, 1388b; III, **822a**; VIII, 534a
Ibn Hibintā iv, 810a; vi, 711a; viii, 103b – IV, 842b; VI, 699b; VIII, 106a
Ibn Ḥid̲j̲d̲j̲a al-Ḥamawī (1434) i, 595b, 982b; iii, **799b**; vii, 1039b; x, 125a – I, 614b, 1013a; III, **823a**; VII, 1042a; X, 135a
Ibn Hilāl al-Ṣābiʾ → G̲h̲ars al-Niʿma Muḥammad
Ibn Hindū (1019) i, 236a; iii, **800a**; s, 72b – I, 243b; III, **823a**; S, 73a
Ibn Ḥinzāba → Ibn al-Furāt, al-Faḍl
Ibn Ḥirzihim, ʿAlī (1164) i, 137b; iii, 732a, **800a**; vii, 587b – I, 141b; III, 755a, **823b**; VII, 587b
Ibn His̲h̲ām, ʿAbd al-Malik (828) i, 158b; iii, 272b, **800b**; v, 41a, 1161b – I, 163a; III, 280b, **824a**; V, 42a, 1151b
Ibn His̲h̲ām, Abū Muḥammad ʿAbd al-Malik (833) vii, 361a; ix, 161a – VII, 363b; IX, 686b
Ibn His̲h̲ām, D̲j̲amāl al-Dīn (1360) i, 126b, 593a, 821b; iii, **801a**; iv, 414b; vii, 914b; s, 404b – I, 130a, 612b, 844b; III, **824b**; IV, 432b; VII, 914a; S, 404b
Ibn His̲h̲ām al-Lak̲h̲mī (1182) v, 608b, 609b; s, **388a** – V, 612b, 613b; S, **388b**
Ibn Ḥit̲h̲layn (XX) iii, 1067b, 1068a – III, 1094b
Ibn Hubal (1213) iii, **802a** – III, **825b**
Ibn Hubayra, ʿAwn al-Dīn al-S̲h̲aybānī (1165) vii, 406b, 679b, 726a; viii, 943b – VII, 408a, 679b, 727a; VIII, 976a
Ibn Hubayra, ʿUmar (VIII) iii, **802a**, 1157b – III, **825b**, 1186a
Ibn Hubayra, Yaḥyā al-S̲h̲aybānī (1165) i, 122b; ii, 1023b; iii, 160b, 751a, **802b**, 1157b; iv, 912a, 942b; v, 623a, 1016a – I, 126a; II, 1042b; III, 164a, 774a, **826a**, 1186a; IV, 945a, 975b; V, 627a, 1011b
Ibn Hubayra, Yazīd b. ʿUmar (VIII) i, 16a, 103a, 107b, 123a; iii, 266a, **802a**, 1255a; iv, 447b, 728b, 1132b; vi, 345a, 427b, 624a, b; vii, 388b; x, 844a, 845a – I, 16b, 106a, 110b, 126b; III, 273b, **825b**, 1287b; IV, 467a, b, 758a, 1164a; VI, 329a, 412b, 413a, 609a, b; VII, 389b; X,
Ibn Ḥubaysh (1188) iii, **803b** – III, **826b**
Ibn Hūd → Hūdid(e)s
Ibn Hūd al-Māssī ii, 1009b – II, 1033a
Ibn Ḥudayd̲j̲ → Muʿāwiya b. Ḥudayd̲j̲
Ibn Hud̲h̲ayl (XIV) i, 594a; ii, 786b; iii, **804a** – I, 613a; II, 805b; III, **827b**
Ibn Ḥudayr (al-Andalus) (X) vi, 431a – VI, 416a
Ibn al-Humām, Kamāl al-Dīn (1457) iii, 164a; vi, 848a – III, 167a; VI, 839a
Ibn Ḥumayd → Sulṭān b. Bid̲j̲ād
Ibn Ḥumayd → al-Rāzī, ʿAbd Allāh b. Ḥumayd
Ibn Ḥumayd al-Makkī iii, 162b – III, 166a
Ibn Hurmuz (VIII) vi, 263b – VI, 248a
Ibn Ḥusām (1470) iii, 114b; vi, 837a – III, 116b; VI, 827b
Ibn al-ʿIbrī (Bar Hebraeus) (1286) i, 214a; iii, **804b**; iv, 482a; vi, 231a, 502a; s, 314a – I, 220b; III, **828a**; IV, 503a; VI, 225a, 487b; S, 313b
Ibn ʿId̲h̲ārī al-Marrākus̲h̲ī (1312) i, 157a; iii, 789b, **805b**; iv, 830a; v, 1209a; vi, 311b; vii, 584a; s, 389b – I, 161a; III, 813a, **828b**; IV, 863a; V, 1199b; VI, 296b; VII, 584b; S, 390a
Ibn Idrīs (1201) vii, 297b – VII, 299b
Ibn Idrīs, Abu 'l-ʿAlāʾ (1879) iii, **806b** – III, **830a**
Ibn Idrīs, Abū ʿAbd Allāh Muḥammad (1847) iii, **806a** – III, **829b**
Ibn al-Iflīlī (1050) iii, **806b** – III, **830a**
Ibn Igit (XII) i, 1249a; ii, 744b – I, 1287a; II, 763a
Ibn al-Ik̲h̲s̲h̲īd, Abū Bakr Aḥmad (938) iii, **807a**; vii, 312a; x, 14b; s, 12b, 13a – III, **830b**; VII, 314b; X, 15a; S, 13a, b
Ibn Ilyās s, 327a – S, 326b
Ibn al-ʿImād al-Ḥanbalī (1679) i, 594b; iii, 162a, **807b**; s, 267b, 381a – I, 614a; III, 165b, **830b**; S, 267a, 381b
Ibn al-Imām (1155) viii, 819a – VIII, 847b
Ibn al-Imām al-S̲h̲ilbī (XII) iii, **807b** – III, **831a**
Ibn ʿInaba (1424) iii, **807b** – III, **831a**
Ibn ʿIrāḳ, Abū Naṣr Manṣūr b. ʿAlī (1036) i, 1236a, b, 1237a; iii, **808b**; iv, 1182a, b; vi, 543a – I, 1274a, b; III, **831a**; IV, 1215b; VI, 527

Ibn al-ʿIrāḳī   → Abū Zurʿa
Ibn ʿIrs   iii, **808b** – III, **832a**
Ibn ʿĪsā   → ʿAlī b. ʿĪsā b. al-Djarrāḥ
Ibn ʿĪsā   → Muḥammad b. ʿĪsā al-Ṣufyānī
Ibn ʿĪsā, Muḥammad (1607)   iii, **809b** – III, **833a**
Ibn ʿĪsā b. Maḏjd al-Dīn   i, 309b – I, 319b
Ibn-i Isfandiyār (XIII)   iii, **810a**; s, 357a –
    III, **833b**; S, 357a
Ibn Isḥāḳ. Muḥammad – b. Yasār (767)   i, 158b, 588a;
    iii, 23b, 272b, 800b, **810b**, 1205b; iv, 370a; v, 1161b,
    1162b, 1163a; vii, 283b, 361a; s, 87b, 358a –
    I, 163a, 607a; III, 25a, 280b, 824a, **834a**, 1236a; IV,
    386b; V, 1151b, 1152a, b; VII, 285b, 363b; S, 87b,
    358a
Ibn Isrāʾīl al-Dimaṣẖḳī (1278)   iii, **811b** – III, **835a**
Ibn al-Iṭnāba al-Ḵẖazradjī (VII)   iii, **812a** –
    III, **835b**
Ibn Iṭūwafat, Abū Ḥātim Yaʿḳūb b. Ḥabīb b. Midyan
    (XIV)   vi, 311b – VI, 296b
Ibn ʿIyāḍ (ḳāʾid) (XII)   x, 106a – X, 114a
Ibn Iyās (1524)   i, 571a, 595a; iii, **812a** – I, 590a, 614b;
    III, **835b**
Ibn Kabar, Abu ʾl-Barakāt (1320)   s, **388b**, 396a – S,
    389a, 396a
Ibn al-Ḳabisī   → al-Ḳābisī, Abu ʾl-Ḥasan ʿAlī
Ibn Ḳabṭūrnu (Ḳabṭūrna), Abū ʾl-Ḥasan   iii, **813b** – III,
    837a
Ibn Ḳabṭūrnu, Abū Bakr ʿAbd al-ʿAzīz (1126)
    iii, **813b** – III, **837a**
Ibn Ḳabṭūrnu, Abū Muḥammad Ṭalḥa (XII)   iii, **813b** –
    III, **837a**
Ibn al-Ḳaddāḥ   iii, 922b – III, 946b
Ibn al-Ḳāḍī, Ṣẖihāb al-Dīn al-Miknāsī (1616)
    i, 96b; iii, **814a**; vi, 351a; s, 223a –
    I, 99a; III, **837b**; VI, 335a; S, 223a
Ibn al-Ḳāḍī (Kabyle)   → Aḥmad b. al-Ḳāḍī
Ibn Ḳāḍī Samāwnā   → Badr al-Dīn b. Ḳāḍī Samāwnā
Ibn Ḳāḍī Ṣẖuhba, Badr al-Dīn (1470)   iii, **814b**; iv,
    641b; vi, 352a, 353a, 580b – III, **838a**; IV, 667b; VI,
    336a, 337a, 565a
Ibn Ḳaḍīb al-Bārī   iii, 1241a – III, 1273a
Ibn Ḳādūs   i, 440a – I, 452b
Ibn al-Kaʿḳāʿ al-Maḵẖzūmī   v, 997b – V, 993a
Ibn   Kākūya   →   ʿAlāʾ   al-Dawla   Muḥammad   b.
    Duṣẖmanziyār
Ibn Ḳalāḳis (1172)   iii, **814b**; viii, 42b – III, **838a**; VIII,
    43b
Ibn al-Ḳalānisī (1160)   iii, **815a**; iv, 181a; vi, 243a; vii,
    564a; s, 204b – III, **838b**; IV, 189a; VI, 227a; VII,
    564b; S, 204a
Ibn al-Ḳalānisī, vizier   s, 197a – S, 197a
Ibn al-Kalbī   → al-Kalbī
Ibn Kamāl   → Kemalpaṣẖa-zāde
Ibn Kamiʾa   → ʿAmr b. Kamiʾa
Ibn Kammūna (1284)   iii, **815b** – III, **839a**
Ibn Ḳanbar   → al-Ḥakam b. Ḳanbar
Ibn Karategin   iii, 703a – III, 725b
Ibn al-Kardabūs   vii, 286b – VII, 289a
Ibn Karib → Abū (Ibn) Karib
Ibn al-Ḳāriḥ   v, 933b, 934a; s, 37b – V, 937b, 938a; S, 38a
Ibn al-Karḵẖī, ʿImād al-Dīn (ḳāḍī) (XII)   viii, 439b –
    VIII, 454a
Ibn Karnas (1273)   vi, 111a – VI, 109a
Ibn Karrām   → Muḥammad b. Karrām
Ibn Ḳasī (Banū)   iii, **815b** – III, **839b**
Ibn Ḳasī, Aḥmad (1151)   i, 1339a; ii, 1009a, b; iii,
    712b, 732a, **816a**; v, 586b – I, 1379b; II, 1033a; III,
    755a, **839b**; V, 591b
Ibn Ḳāsim   → Muḥammad b. Ḥāzim
Ibn Ḳāsim al-Ghazzī (1512) i, 151a; iii, **817a** – I, 155a;
    III, **840b**

Ibn al-Ḳāsim Karīm iv, 362b, 363a – IV, 378b, 379a
Ibn al-Ḳāsim al-ʿUtāḳī (806)   ii, 889b; iii, **817a**; vi,
    264b, 278b, 279a, 280b; viii, 843b – II, 910a; III,
    840b; VI, 249b, 263b, 264a, 265a; VIII, 873a
Ibn al-Ḳasīra (XI)   vii, 587a – VII, 586b
Ibn al-Ḳāṣṣ (X)   vi, 183a – VI, 166b
Ibn Kathīr, Abū Maʿbad (VIII)   iii, **817b** – III, **841a**
Ibn Kathīr, ʿImād al-Dīn (1373)   i, 273b, 595b; iii,
    700a, **817b**, 927a, 954b; v, 571a; vi, 106b, 353a; vii,
    212b, 284a –
    I, 282a, 614b; III, 722b, **841a**, 951b, 979a; V, 575b;
    VI, 104b, 337a; VII, 213b, 285b
Ibn al-Ḳaṭṭāʿ, ʿAlī (1121)   iii, 738b, **818b**, 859b; iv,
    497b; vii, 528a, 772a; ix, 587a –
    III, 761b, **842a**, 884a; IV, 519a; VII, 528a, 773b; IX,
    609b
Ibn al-Ḳaṭṭāʿ, ʿĪsā (1006)   iii, **819a** – III, **842b**
Ibn al-Ḳaṭṭān, Abu ʾl-Ḳāsim (1163)   iii, 327b, **819b**; s,
    396b – III, 338a, **843a**; S, 397a
Ibn al-Ḳaṭṭān the Elder/lʾAncien (1231)   s, **389a** – S,
    389b
Ibn al-Ḳaṭṭān the Younger/le Jeune   i, 78a, 389a; s,
    389b – I, 80b, 400b; S, **389b**
Ibn al-Kattānī (1029)   vii, 528a – VII, 528b
Ibn al-Kawwāʾ   i, 382b – I, 393b
^bn Kays al-Ruḳayyāt (VII)   iii, 572a, **819b**; vii, 402a;
    viii, 42b – III, 592a, **843a**; VII, 403b; VIII, 43b
Ibn Kaysān, Abu ʾl-Ḥasan Muḥammad al-Naḥwī (911)
    iii, **820a**; v, 1131a; vii, 279b; viii, 14b; s, 389b – III,
    844a; V, 1127a; VII, 281b; VIII, 14bS, 390a
Ibn al-Ḳaysarānī (1174)   viii, 910b – VIII, 941b
Ibn al-Ḳaysarānī, Abu ʾl-Faḍl (1113)   iii, **821a**; vi,
    214b – III, **844b**; VI, 199a
Ibn al-Ḳaysarānī, Ṣẖaraf al-Dīn (1154)   iii, **821b** – III,
    845a
Ibn al-Kayyāl   → al-Kayyāl, Aḥmad b. Zakariyyaʾ (X)
Ibn al-Kayyāl (1532)   vi, 214b – VI, 198b
Ibn Ḳayyim al-Djawziyya (1350)   i, 273b, 274b, 276a,
    276b, 593a, 982b, 1114b, 1116b; ii, 449a; iii, 161b,
    513a, 745a, **821b**, 952b, 953a, 1020a; iv, 151b,
    1134a; v, 114a; vi, 217b; vii, 419b –
    I, 282a, 283a, 284b, 285a, 612b, 1013a, 1148a, 1150a;
    II, 461a; III, 165a, 530b, 768a, **845b**, 977a, b, 1045b;
    IV, 157b, 1165b; V, 116b; VI, 201b; VII, 421a
Ibn al-Kazzāz   vii, 400a – VII, 401b
Ibn Kemāl (XV)   vi, 1025b – VI, 1018a
Ibn Kerboghāʾ (Tatar) (XIV)   vi, 231a – VI, 225a
Ibn Ḵẖafādja, Abū Isḥāḳ (1139)   i, 602a; ii, 526b; iii,
    822b, 849b, 971a; iv, 1007a; vi, 606b; vii, 261b;
    1046b –
    I, 621b; II, 539b; III, **846a**, 873b, 995b; IV, 1039b;
    VI, 591a; VII, 263a, 1048b
Ibn Ḵẖafīf, al- Ṣẖayḵẖ al-Ṣẖīrāzī (al-Ṣẖayḵẖ al-Kabīr)
    (982)   iii, 103a, **823a**; iv, 46a; viii, 840b; ix, 432b –
    III, 105b, **846b**; IV, 49a; VIII, 870a; IX, 449a
Ibn Ḵẖākān (1134)   viii, 819a – VIII, 847b
Ibn Ḵẖāḳān (Ibn Ḵẖān) (1063)   vii, 120a – VII, 122a
Ibn Ḵẖāḳān, ʿAbd Allāh (926)   iii, **824b** –
    III, **848b**
Ibn Ḵẖāḳān, al-Fatḥ   → al-Fatḥ b. Ḵẖāḳān
Ibn Ḵẖāḳān, Muḥammad (924)   iii, **824a** –
    III, **848a**
Ibn Ḵẖāḳān, ʿUbayd Allāh b. Yaḥyā (vizier) (877)   i,
    1082b; iii, **824a**, 844b, 879b, 880a; vii, 583a, 766a,
    777b; s, 25a –
    I, 1114b; III, **848a**, 868b, 904a; VII, 583b, 767b,
    779b; S, 25a
Ibn Ḵẖāḳān, Yaḥyā (IX)   iii, **824a** – III, **847b**
Ibn al-Ḵẖāl (705)   ix, 101a – IX, 105b
Ibn Ḵẖalaf (Ibāḍī)   iv, 920a; v, 623b – IV, 953a; V,
    627b

Ibn Khalaf, Abū Ghālib Muḥammad b. ʿAlī (1016) s, 119a, b, **390a** – S, 118b, 119a, **390b**
Ibn Khalaf, Abū Shudjāʿ Muḥammad (1073) s, **390a** – S, **390b**
Ibn Khalaf, ʿAlī b. ʿAbd al-Wahhāb al-Kātib (XI) s, **390a, b** – S, **390b**
Ibn Khalaf al-Warrāḳ (XI) vi, 198a – VI, 182a
Ibn Khalās iii, 921b, 925a – III, 946a, 949b
Ibn Khālawayh (980) i, 120a, 258b; iii, 124b, **824b**, 874b, 880b; v, 927b; vi, 188b, 196a; viii, 14a; s, 37b, 361b –
I, 123a, 266b; III, 127b, **848a**, 898b, 904b; V, 933a; VI, 172a, 180a; VIII, 14b; S, 38a, 361a
Ibn Khaldūn, ʿAbd al-Raḥmān (1382) i, 15a, 286b, 376b, 579b, 593b, 595a, 659b, 681a, 816b, 858a, 959a, 1116b; ii, 285b, 308a, 586b, 767a, 774b; iii, 68b, 711a, **825a**, 1147a; iv, 260a; v, 782a, 1160b; vi, 188a, 194a, 199b, 216b, 220a, 248a, 255b, 258a, 280a, 310b, 311a, b, 348b, 728b; vii, 254b; s, 87b, 102b, 308a, 377a, 396a – I, 15b, 295a, 387b, 598a, 613a, 614b, 680b, 701b, 839b, 882a, 988a, 1150a; II, 293b, 316b, 601a, 785b, 793b; III, 71a, 733a, **849a**, 1175a; IV, 271b; V, 788a, 1150a; VI, 171b, 178a, 183b, 200b, 214a, 232a, 240a, 242b, 266a, 295b, 296a, b, 332b, 717b; VII, 256a; S, 87b, 102a, 307b, 377a, 396b
Ibn Khaldūn, Abū Zakariyaʾ Yaḥyā (1379) i, 123a; iii, 826b, **831b**; vi, 728b – I, 126b; III, 850a, **855a**; VI, 717b
Ibn al-Khalīlī (vizier) viii, 759a – VIII, 783b
Ibn al-Khallād → al-Rāmahurmuzī
Ibn Khallād (X) iii, **832a**; s, 12b, 32a – III, **856a**; S, 13a, 32a
Ibn Khallikān (1282) i, 72a, 594b, 669b, 1161a; ii, 285a; iii, 814a, **832b**, 934a; v, 481b; vi, 262b, 263a, b, 673b; s, 25b, 400a –
I, 74a, 614a, 690b, 1195b; II, 293a; III, 837b, **856a**, 958b; V, 484a; VI, 247a, b, 248a, 660a; S, 25b, 400b
Ibn Khamīs (1308) iii, **833a** – III, **857a**
Ibn Khamīs al-Mawṣilī al-Shāfiʿī (1157) vi, 354a – VI, 338a
Ibn al-Khammār iii, 895a – III, 919b
Ibn al-Kharrāṭ al-Ishbīlī (1180) viii, 635b – VIII, 654a
Ibn Kharūf al-Rundī al-Ishbīlī (1212) ix, 271a – IX, 383b
Ibn al-Khashshāb, ʿAbd Allāh (1172) iii, 803a, **834a** – III, 826b, **858a**
Ibn al-Khashshāb, Abu ʾl-Ḥasan i, 983b; iii, 87a – I, 1014a; III, 89a
Ibn al-Khaṣīb, Abū ʿAlī Aḥmad (IX) iii, **835a**; iv, 742b; vii, 722b; viii, 856a – III, **858b**; IV, 772a; VII, 723b; VIII, 885b
Ibn al-Khaṣīb, Abū Bakr (IX) iii, **835a** – III, **859a**
Ibn al-Khaṣīb, Aḥmad → al-Djardjarāʾī
Ibn al-Khaṣīb, Aḥmad b. ʿUbayd Allāh → al-Khaṣībī
Ibn al-Khaṭīb, Abū ʿAbd Allāh Lisān al-Dīn (1375) i, 594a, b, 602a; ii, 306a; iii, 756a, 826b, 827a, **835b**, 972b; v, 626a, 707b, 782a; vi, 111b, 187a, b, 220b, 221a; vii, 811b, 1024a; viii, 376b; s, 23a, 52b, 382a –
I, 613a, 614a, 621b; II, 314b; III, 779a, 850a, b, **859b**, 997a; V, 630a, 712b, 788a; VI, 109b, 170b, 171a, 214b; VII, 813b, 1025a; VIII, 389a; S, 23a, 53a, 382a
Ibn Khaṭīb Dārayyā i, 759a – I, 781b
Ibn Khātima (1369) iii, **837a**; v, 609a; s, 388b – III, **860b**; V, 613a; S, 389a
Ibn al-Khāṭir Masʿūd (XIII) viii, 15b – VIII, 15b
`ibn Khaṭṭāb → al-Khaṭṭābī
Ibn Khaṭṭāb al-Hawwārī ii, 875b – II, 896a
Ibn Khayr al-Ishbīlī (1179) i, 156a, 1198a; ii, 743b; iii, 221a, **837b**; vi, 111a; s, 88a – I, 160a, 1233a; II, 762a; III, 228a, **861b**; VI, 108b; S, 87b
Ibn al-Khayyār al-Djayyānī (Fès) (XII) vii, 679a – VII, 679a
Ibn al-Khayyāṭ, Abū Bakr Muḥammad (932) iii, **837b**; vi, 539a – III, **861b**; VI, 523b
Ibn al-Khayyāṭ, Abū al-Ḥasan ʿAlī (X) iii, **838a** – III, **862a**
Ibn Khayyāṭ al-ʿUṣfurī (854) iii, **838b**; vii, 265a, 268b – III, **862a**; VII, 267a, 270b
Ibn Khazar b. Ṣūlat iii, 1041b; v, 1175a, b, 1180b – III, 1067b; V, 1165a, b, 1170b
Ibn Khāzim → ʿAbd Allāh b. Khāzim
Ibn Khims al-Taghlibī s, 178a – S, 179a
Ibn Khurradādhbih (911) i, 32a, 589b, 761b; ii, 579a, 580a; iii, **839a**, 1077b; v, 319b; vi, 183a, 215b, 313b, 379b, 639b, 640a; s, 266a, 327a, 376b –
I, 33a, 608b, 784b; II, 593b, 594b; III, **863a**, 1104b; V, 319a; VI, 166b, 199b, 298b, 363a, 624b, 625a, b; S, 265b, 326b, 376b
Ibn Khuwayzmindād vi, 279a – VI, 264a
Ibn Khuzayma, Abū Bakr iii, 799a – III, 822b
Ibn al-Ḳifṭī, Djamāl al-Dīn (1248) i, 213a, 235b, 247a, 631a, 803b; ii, 770a, 771b; iii, **840a**; vi, 215a; viii, 103a; s, 17a, 25b, 32b, 45a, 289a, 362a –
I, 219b, 243a, 255a, 652a, 826b; II, 788b, 790a; III, **864a**; VI, 199a; VIII, 105b; S, 17a, 26a, 32b, 45b, 289a, 362a
Ibn Killis, Abū ʾl-Faradj Yaʿḳūb (991) i, 816a, 823b; ii, 127a, 169b, 483a, 857b, 859b, 860a; iii, 130a, 404b, **840b**; v, 623a, 1124a, 1125b; vi, 667b, 670a, 673b –
I, 839a, 846b; II, 130a, 174b, 495b, 877b, 879a, b; III, 132b, 417a, **864b**; V, 627a, 1120b, 1122a; VI, 653b, 656b, 660a
Ibn Kīrān, Abū ʿAbd Allāh (1812) s, **390b** – S, **391a**
Ibn Kīrān, Muḥammad b. ʿAbd al-Madjīd s, 390b – S, 391a
Ibn al-Ḳirriya (703) i, 1115a; iii, **841b** – I, 1148b; III, **865b**
Ibn al-Ḳiṭṭ (901) iii, **842a** – III, **865b**
Ibn Ḳiwām (XIII) vi, 354b – VI, 338b
Ibn Ḳubṭūrna → Ibn Ḳabṭūrnu
Ibn Ḳudāma al-Maḳdisī (1223) i, 273b, 277a, 949b; iii, 159a, 161a, 677b, 700a, 735a, 752a, 766b, **842b**; iv, 212a; v, 10a; vi, 122b, 123a, 353b, 636b; vii, 311b; viii, 497b; s, 322b –
I, 282a, 285b, 978b; III, 162b, 164b, 699b, 722a, 758a, 775a, 789b, **866a**; IV, 221b; V, 10a; VI, 120a, 121a, 337b, 621b; VII, 313b; VIII, 514b; S, 322b
Ibn Ḳudwa iv, 669a – IV, 696b
Ibn al-Ḳuff, Amīn al-Dawla (1286) ii, 481b; s, 130b, 271b, **391a** – II, 494a; S, 130a, 271b, **391a**
Ibn Kullāb al-Baṣrī (855) vii, 312b; s, **391b** – VII, 314b; S, **391b**
Ibn Kunāsa (823) iii, **843a** – III, **867a**
Ibn Kundādjīk → Isḥāḳ; Muḥammad b. Isḥāḳ
Ibn Ḳunfudh al-Ḳusanṭīnī (1407) iii, 339a, 719b, 731b, **843b**; vi, 356a – III, 349a, 742a, 754a, **867a**; VI, 340a
Ibn Kuraysh, Judah iv, 305a, b – IV, 319a
Ibn al-Kurdī ii, 633a – II, 648b
Ibn Ḳurhub ii, 853a; iv, 275b – II, 873a; IV, 287b
Ibn Kurr (XIV) vii, 685a – VII, 685b
Ibn al-Kushayrī iii, 160a, 1266a – III, 16b, 1299a
Ibn Ḳutayba, Abū Muḥammad ʿAbd Allāh al-Dīnawarī (889) i, 10b, 131a, 307a, 326b, 589a, 758b, 1092b; ii, 249a, 300a, 865a; iii, 28a, 512a, **844b**, 1263b; iv, 212a, 718a; v, 1026b; vi, 107b, 110b, 111b, 263a, 344b, 348a, 636a; vii, 254b, 978a, 985a; viii, 496a; s, 42b, 227a, 273a, 380b, 392b –
I, 10b, 134b, 316b, 336b, 608a, 781b, 1125a; II, 256a,

308b, 885a; III, 29a, 529b, **868b**, 1296a; IV, 221b, 746b; V, 1022b; VI, 105b, 108a, 109a, 247a, 328b, 332a, 620b; VII, 256a, 979a, 986b; VIII, 513a; S, 42b, 227a, 272b, 381a, 393a
Ibn Ḳutayba al-Marzūḳī vi, 374b – VI, 359a
Ibn Kut̲h̲ayyir al-Ahwāzī vi, 351b – VI, 336a
Ibn al-Ḳūṭiyya, Abū Bakr (977) i, 600a; iii, 702a, 789b, 845b, **847b**; vi, 430b – I, 619b; III, 724a, 813a, 869b, **871b**; VI, 416a
Ibn Ḳutlūbug̲h̲ā (1474) i, 594b; iii, 164a, **848b**; vi, 194a – I, 614a; III, 167b, **872b**; VI, 178a
Ibn Ḳuzmān, Abu 'l- Aṣbag̲h̲ ʿIsā (X) iii, **849a** – III, **873a**
Ibn Ḳuzmān, Abū Bakr Muḥammad b. ʿAbd al-Malik (al-Akbar) (1114) iii, **849a** – III, **873a**
Ibn Ḳuzmān, Abū Bakr Muḥammad b. ʿĪsā (al-Aṣg̲h̲ar) (1160) i, 501b, 595b, 602a; iii, **849b**; iv, 1007b; v, 744a, 1207a – I, 516b, 589b, 615a, 621b; III, **873b**; IV, 1040a; V, 749a, 1197b
Ibn Ḳuzmān, Abū 'l-Ḥusayn (1196) iii, **849b** – III, **873b**
Ibn Ḳuzmān, Abū Marwān ʿAbd al-Raḥmān (1169) iii, **849b** – III, **873a**
Ibn al-Labbād → ʿAbd al-Laṭīf al-Bag̲h̲dādī
Ibn al-Labbād, Abū Muḥammad s, 393a – S, 393b
Ibn al-Labbān (Mālikiyya) (1054) iii, 766b; vi, 279a – III, 789b; VI, 264a
Ibn al-Labbāna, Abū Bakr (1113) i, 602a; iii, 677b, **853a**; iv, 1007a; vi, 606b; vii, 811b – I, 621b; III, 699a, **877a**; IV, 1039b; VI, 591a; VII, 813b
Ibn Lad̲j̲aʾ (VII) iii, **853b** – III, **877b**
Ibn Lahīʿa, ʿAbd Allāh (790) iii, **853b**; vi, 412a – III, **877b**; VI, 397a
Ibn Lankak (970) iii, **854a**; v, 43b; s, 32a – III, **878a**; V, 44b; S, 32b
Ibn al-Layt̲h̲ (IX) x, 394a – X, 422b
Ibn al-Layt̲h̲ (XI) vii, 413a – VII, 414a
Ibn Lazza → Ibn Lizza
Ibn al-Liḥyānī (Ḥafṣid(e)) (1317) iii, 67b; x, 462b – III, 70a; X, 496a
Ibn Lisān al-Ḥummara iii, **854a** – III, **878a**
Ibn Lizza (Lirra) iii, **854b** – III, **878b**
Ibn Luʾayy, K̲h̲ālid iii, 1065b, 1066b, 1068a; v, 63a – III, 1092a, 1093b, 1095a; V, 64b
Ibn Lubb vi, 281b – VI, 266b
Ibn Luʾluʾ s, 119b – S, 119a
Ibn al-Lunḳuh ii, 901b – II, 922b
Ibn Luyūn, Abū ʿUt̲h̲mān al-Tud̲j̲ībī (1349) ii, 902a; iii, **855a**; vii, 200b – II, 923a; III, **879a**; VII, 201a
Ibn Māʾ al-Samāʾ, ʿUbāda (1030) iii, **855a**; vii, 492b, 811b – III, **879a**; VII, 498a, 813b
Ibn Maḍāʾ (1195) iii, **855b** – III, **879b**
Ibn Maʿdīkarib → ʿAmr b. Maʿdīkarib
Ibn al-Madīnī, ʿAlī b. ʿAbd Allāh (853) vii, 260b; viii, 515b – VII, 262b; VIII, 533a
Ibn Mād̲j̲a (887) ii, 108a; iii, 24a, 692b, **856a**; s, 232b – II, 110b; III, 25b, 714b, **880a**; S, 232b
Ibn al-Mad̲j̲dī (1506) vi, 543a – VI, 527b
Ibn Mād̲j̲id, S̲h̲ihāb al-Dīn Aḥmad (1500) i, 553b, 932a; ii, 517b, 583a, 586a; iii, **856a**; iv, 1082b, 1083a; v, 941a, 1025a; vi, 82b, 283a, 359a, 374b; vii, 51a, 245a; viii, 100a, 102b – I, 571a, 960b; II, 530b, 597b, 600b; III, **880a**; IV, 1114a; V, 944b, 1021a; VI, 80b, 268a, 343a, 359a; VII, 51a, 246b; VIII, 102b, 104b
Ibn al-Mād̲j̲is̲h̲ūn (829) iv, 87a; vi, 279a – IV, 91a; VI, 264a
Ibn Mād̲j̲ūr → Ibn Amād̲j̲ūr
Ibn al-Mag̲h̲āzilī iii, 367b – III, 379b
Ibn al-Mag̲h̲ribī → ʿAlī b. al-Ḥusayn al-Mag̲h̲ribī
Ibn Māhān, ʿAlī b. ʿĪsā (808) i, 437b; iii, 233b, 234a, 345b, **859a**, 1202a; iv, 16b, 645a, 718b; vi, 331b, 332a, b, 334a, 335a; viii, 385b – I, 450a; III, 240b, 241a, 356a, **883b**, 1232b; IV, 18a, 671b, 747a; VI, 316a, b, 317a, 318b, 319b; VIII, 399a
Ibn Maḥfūf → ʿAbd Allāh b. Maḥfūf
Ibn al-Maḥrūḳ (vizier) (1329) vii, 1023a – VII, 1025b
Ibn al-Māḥūz → ʿUbayd Allāh b. al-Māḥūz; Zubayr b. al-Māḥūz
Ibn Mak̲h̲lad, al-Ḥasan (882) ii, 197b; iii, **859b**; vii, 410b, 477a, 766a – II, 203b; III, **883b**; VII, 412a, 476b, 767b
Ibn Mak̲h̲lad, Sāʿid (889) iii, **859b**; ix, 594b; x, 826b – III, **883b**; IX, 617b; X,
Ibn Mak̲h̲lad, Sulaymān b. al-Ḥasan (X) i, 387b; iii, **859b** – I, 398b; III, **883b**
Ibn Mak̲h̲lūf → al-D̲j̲azūlī, Ibn Mak̲h̲lūf alNuwayrī
Ibn Makkī (Ḳābis) ii, 515a – II, 528a
Ibn al-Makkī (musicia(e)n) s, 64a – S, 64b
Ibn Makkī, Abū Ḥafṣ ʿUmar (XI) iii, 738b, **859b**; v, 608b; s, 388a – III, 761b, **884a**; V, 612b; S, 388b
Ibn al-Maklātī iii, 788a, 956a – III, 811b, 980b
Ibn Makram b. Sabāʾ b. Ḥimyar al-Aṣg̲h̲ar vi, 190b, 191a – VI, 174b, 175a
Ibn Mākūlā, Abū ʿAbd Allāh iii, 766a – III, 789a
Ibn Mākūlā, ʿAlī (XI) iii, **860b**; iv, 718b – III, **884b**; IV, 747b
Ibn Mākūlā, al-Ḥasan b. ʿAlī (1030) iii, **860a**; iv, 718b – III, **884a**; IV, 747b
Ibn Mākūlā, Hibat Allāh (XI) iii, **860a**; iv, 718b – III, **884a**; IV, 747b
Ibn Malak → Firis̲h̲te-og̲h̲lu, ʿAbd al-Laṭīf
Ibn Mālik, Abū ʿAbd Allāh al-D̲j̲ayyānī (1274) i, 126a, 602b; iii, 699a, **861a**, 966b; vi, 132b; vii, 388a, 914b; s, 404b – I, 130a, 622a; III, 721a, **885a**, 991a; VI, 130b; VII, 389a, 915a; S, 404b
Ibn Mālik, Badr al-Dīn (1287) v, 898a, 900b; viii, 894a – V, 904b, 907a; VIII, 825a
Ibn Mālik al-Yamanī (XI) iii, **862b** – III, **886b**
Ibn Malka → Abu 'l-Barakāt
Ibn Malka, Judah iv, 305a – IV, 318b
Ibn Mammātī, Abu 'l-Malīh (XI) iii, **862b** – III, **886b**
Ibn Mammātī, al-Asʿad b. Muhad̲h̲d̲h̲ab (1209) i, 800b, 801b; ii, 900a; iii, 734a, 747b, **862b**, 894b; iv, 135b, 613b, 1181b; v, 92a; vi, 118b, 141a; vii, 164a; viii, 913a; s, 408a – I, 824a, 824b; II, 921a; III, 757a, 770a, **887a**, 918b; IV, 141a, 638a, b, 1215a; V, 94a; VI, 116b, 139a; VII, 165b; VIII, 944b; S, 408a
Ibn Mammātī, al-Muhad̲h̲d̲h̲ab (1182) iii, **862b**; v, 92a – III, **886b**; V, 94a
Ibn al-Maʾmūn → al-Baṭāʾiḥī
Ibn Maʿn al-Andalusī (XVII) vi, 350a – VI, 334a
Ibn Manda iii, **863a** – III, **887b**
Ibn Manda, ʿAbd al-Raḥmān (1078) iii, 161a, **863b** – III, 164b, **888a**
Ibn Manda(h), Abū ʿAbd Allāh (1005) i, 142b; iii, 161a, **863b**; x, 10b – I, 146b; III, 164b, **887b**; X, 10b
Ibn Manda, Yaḥyā (1118) iii, **864a** – III, **888a**
Ibn Manglī, Muḥammad al-Nāṣirī (XIV) v, 1229b; vii, 43b, 885b, 948a; s, 175b, **392b** – V, 1219b; VII, 44a, 887a, 948b; S, 176b, **392b**
Ibn Mangud̲j̲ak i, 664b; ii, 110b – I, 684a; II, 113a
Ibn Manẓūr, Muḥammad b. Mukarram (1311) i, 822a; iii, **864b**; iv, 524b; vi, 349b, 351a, 374b, 906a; vii, 445a, 561b; x, 33a –

I, 845a; III, **888b**; IV, 547b; VI, 333b, 335a, 359a, 897b; VII, 446a, 562a; X, 34b
Ibn Mardanī<u>sh</u> (1172) i, 79b, 160b, 986a, 1288a, 1347a; ii, 115a, 516a, 526b, 1013b; iii, 850b, **864b**; iv, 116a; v, 392b; ix, 351b –
I, 81b, 165a, 1016b, 1327b, 1387b; II, 117b, 528b, 539b, 1037b; III, 847b, **889a**; IV, 121a; V, 393a; IX, 363a
Ibn al-Māristāniyya (1202) iii, 161a, 803a; vi, 430a – III, 164b, 826b; VI, 415b
Ibn Maʿrūf, Abū Muḥammad (ḳāḍī al-ḳuḍāt) vii, 358b; viii, 614b – VII, 361a; VIII, 634a
Ibn Marwān → Abū ʿAlī b. Marwān
Ibn Marwān, al-<u>Dj</u>illīḳī v, 498b – V, 501b
Ibn Maryam (1605) iii, **865b** – III, **889b**
Ibn al-Marzubān → Muḥammad b. <u>Kh</u>alaf
Ibn Marzūḳ → ʿUthmān b. Marzūḳ
Ibn Marzūḳ, Aḥmad b. Muḥammad s, 403a – S, 403b
Ibn Marzūḳ, Muḥammad VI al-Ḥafīd (1438) i, 1314b; iii, 720b, **866a** – I, 1355a; III, 743a, **890a**
Ibn Marzūḳ, <u>Sh</u>ams al-Dīn Abū ʿAbd Allāh al-Tilimsānī iii, **865b** – III, **890a**
Ibn Marzūḳ, <u>Sh</u>ams al-Dīn Muḥammad IV (1379) iii, **866b**; v, 1160b, 1209a; vi, 359a, 441a, 572a; s, 403a – III, **890b**; V, 1150a, 1199b; VI, 343a, 426b, 557a; S, 403a
Ibn Masʿada → ʿAmr b. Masʿada
Ibn Maṣāl (1150) i, 9a, 198b; ii, 858b; iii, **868a** – I, 9b, 204a; II, 878b; III, **892a**
Ibn Masarra, Muḥammad b. ʿAbd Allāh (931) i, 484a, 497a, 600a; ii, 774b; iii, 712b, 785a, 842a, **868b**; vi, 280a; vii, 570a; x, 453a –
I, 498a, 512a, 619b; II, 793a; III, 735a, 808b, 865b, **892b**; VI, 264b; VII, 570b; X, 486a
Ibn Māsawayh (857) i, 589b, 785b, 1223a; iii, 578b, **872a**; x, 453b; s, 271b, 303b, 314a –
I, 608b, 808b, 1259b; III, 599a, **896b**; X, 486a; S, 271a, 303b, 313b
Ibn Ma<u>sh</u>ī<u>sh</u> → ʿAbd al-Salām b. Ma<u>sh</u>ī<u>sh</u>
Ibn al-Mā<u>sh</u>iṭa (X) iii, **873a** – III, **897b**
Ibn Ma<u>sh</u>ṭūb (XIII) viii, 434a – VIII, 448b
Ibn Māssa s, 249b, 314a – S, 249b, 313b
Ibn Maṣṣāla al-Ibāḍī iii, 655b, 659b – III, 677a, 681a
Ibn Masʿūd, ʿAbd Allāh b. <u>Gh</u>āfil (VII) i, 114b, 687a; ii, 888b; iii, 41b, 540b, **873b**; iv, 378a; v, 127a, 350b, 406a, 407a, 409b; vi, 671a; vii, 187a, 258b; s, 227a, 311b –
I, 118a, 707b; II, 909a; III, 43a, 559b, **897b**; IV, 394b; V, 129b, 351a, 407b, 408a, 410b; VI, 657a; VII, 187b, 260a; S, 227a, 311a
Ibn Masʿūd al-<u>Kh</u>u<u>sh</u>anī ii, 743b; s, 306a – II, 762a; S, 306a
Ibn Masʿūd al-<u>Sh</u>īrāzī s, 271b – S, 271b
Ibn Maʿṣūm (1705) viii, 427a – VIII, 441a
Ibn Maṭrūḥ (1251) iii, **875b** – III, **899b**
Ibn Mattawayh (XI) i, 59b, 343a; iv, 615b; S, **393a** – I, 61b, 353b; IV, 640a; S, **393a**
Ibn Maʿtūḳ (XVII) vii, 673b – VII, 673b
Ibn al-Mawlā, Muḥammad b. ʿAbd Allāh (VIII) iii, **876a** – III, **900a**
Ibn al-Mawṣilī ii, 962a – II, 984a
Ibn Maymūn, Abū ʿImrān Mūsā (Maimonide(s)) (1204) i, 214b; iii, 267a, **876a**; iv, 304b, 306b; vii, 804b; viii, 96a, 538b; s, 52b –
I, 221a; III, 274b, **900a**; IV, 318a, b, 320a; VII, 806b; VIII, 98a, 556b; S, 53a
Ibn Mayyāda, Abū <u>Sh</u>arāḥīl (754) iii, **878a**; iv, 1003a; vi, 951a; vii, 629b – III, **902a**; IV, 1035b; VI, 946b; VII, 629a
Ibn Māza, Burhān al-Dīn iii, 163b – III, 167a
Ibn Mengüček → Ibn Mangu<u>dj</u>ak
Ibn Mīkāl iii, 757a, b – III, 780a, b
Ibn Miḳsam al-Naḥwī (965) s, **393a** – S, **393b**
Ibn al-Miʿmār (1244) ii, 964a, 965a, 966a; vii, 999b – II, 986a, 987a, 988a; VII, 1001a
Ibn Mis<u>dj</u>aḥ (VII) iii, **878b** – III, **902b**
Ibn Miskawayh → Miskawayh
Ibn Miskīn iv, 134b – IV, 140a
Ibn Mī<u>th</u>am al-Tammār (VIII) s, **393b** – S, **394a**
Ibn Muʿā<u>dh</u> s, 372a, 373b – S, 371b, 373b
Ibn al-Muʿa<u>dhdh</u>al, ʿAbd al-Ṣamad (854) iii, **878b**; viii, 378a; s, 352a – III, **902b**; VIII, 390b; S, 352a
Ibn al-Muʿa<u>dhdh</u>al, Aḥmad (IX) i, 1114b; iii, **879a** – I, 1148a; III, **903a**
Ibn al-Muʿallim → al-Mufīd
Ibn Muʿammar → Muḥammad b. Mu<u>sh</u>ārī
Ibn Muʿayyā iii, 808a – III, 831a
Ibn Mubārak (Maṣyad) vi, 790b – VI, 780a
Ibn al-Mubārak, ʿAbd Allāh (797) i, 124a, 1244a; iii, 512b, **879b**; vi, 263b; vii, 758a; viii, 498a; s, 87b, 386b –
I, 127b, 1282a; III, 530a, **903b**; VI, 248b; VII, 759b; VIII, 515a; S, 87b, 386b
Ibn al-Mubārak al-Lamaṭī → al-Lamaṭī
Ibn al-Mudabbir, Abu 'l-Ḥasan Aḥmad (884) i, 278b; ii, 144a, 328a; iii, **879b**; v, 91a; vi, 195a; vii, 161a – I, 287a; II, 148a, 337b; III, **903b**; V, 93b; VI, 179a; VII, 162b
Ibn al-Mudabbir, Ibrāhīm (892) iii, **879b**, 880a, 1242b; s, 35a, b – III, **903b**, 904a, 1274b; S, 35b
Ibn Mu<u>dj</u>āhid, Aḥmad b. Mūsā (936) i, 105b; iii, 101a, 817b, **880b**, 936a; v, 127b, 128a, 408b, 409a; vi, 188b; vii, 292b –
I, 108b; III, 103b, 841a, **904b**, 960b; V, 130a, b, 410a; VI, 172a; VII, 294b
Ibn al-Mu<u>dj</u>āwir, Yūsuf b. al-Ḥusayn al-<u>Sh</u>īrāzī (1204) iii, **881b** – III, **905b**
Ibn al-Mu<u>dj</u>āwir, Yūsuf b. Yaʿḳūb al-Dima<u>sh</u>ḳī (1291) i, 571a; iii, **880b**; vi, 81a, 474a –
I, 589b; III, **904b**; VI, 79a, 460a
Ibn al-Mufaḍḍal (VIII) viii, 387b – VIII, 400b
Ibn Mufarri<u>gh</u> (689) iii, 354a, 620b, **881b**, 1261b; iv, 536a – III, 365a, 641a, **906a**, 1294b; IV, 559a
Ibn Mufliḥ, Akmal al-Dīn (1602) iii, **882b** – III, **907a**
Ibn Mufliḥ, Burhān al-Dīn (1400) iii, 162a, **882b** – III, 165a, **907a**
—Mufliḥ, <u>Sh</u>ams al-Dīn (1362) iii, **882b** – III, **906b**
Ibn Mu<u>gh</u>ī<u>th</u> → ʿAbd al-Malik b. Mu<u>gh</u>ī<u>th</u>
Ibn al-Muhallab x, 844a – X,
Ibn Muḥammad (XIV) ix, 67a – IX, 70a
Ibn Muḥayṣin ii, 293a – II, 301a
Ibn Muḥriz (VIII) i, 828a; iii, **883a**; s, 273a – I, 851a; III, **907a**; S, 273a
Ibn Muḥriz (al-Marḳab) (XII) vi, 578a, b – VI, 563a
Ibn Muḥriz al-Wahrānī (1179) vi, 111a, 262a, 279a – VI, 108b, 246b, 264a
Ibn al-Muḳaddam, Amīr <u>Sh</u>ams al-Dawla (XII) ii, 283b; viii, 910b – II, 291b; VIII, 942a
Ibn al-Muḳaffaʿ, ʿAbd Allāh (756) i, 65b, 66a, 176a, 306b, 326b, 569b, 588a, 784b, 1216b; ii, 951a; iii, 113a, 313b, 372b, **883a**, 1019b, 1263a; iv, 92a, 503b, 504a, b, 755b, 948b, 1098a; vi, 109a, 204a, 539a; vii, 359b, 566a, 985a; viii, 107b, 996b; s, 85b, 88b, 263b –
I, 67b, 180b, 316a, 336b, 588a, 607a, 808a, 1252b; II, 973a; III, 115b, 323a, 384b, **907a**, 1045a, 1296a; IV, 96a, 525a, b, 526a, 786a, 981b, 1129a; VI, 107a, 188a, 523b; VII, 362a, 566b, 986a; VIII, 110a, 1031b; S, 85b, 88b, 263a

Ibn al-Muķaffaʿ, Sāwīrūs/Severus (X) iii, **885b**; vi, 144a; vii, 164a – III, **909b**; VI, 142b; VII, 165b
Ibn Mukarram → Ibn Manẓūr
Ibn Muķashshir iii, 81a – III, 83b
Ibn Muķbil, Abū Kaʿb al-ʿĀmirī (VII) vi, 403b; s, **394a** – VI, 388a; S, **394b**
Ibn al-Mukhtār (Timbuktu) (XVII) vi, 258b – VI, 243a
Ibn Muķla (940) i, 387b, 866a, b, 1040a, 1046b; ii, 305a, 388b; iii, 127a, 345a, 736b, **886b**, 902b, 936a, 1157a; iv, 423b, 1094a, 1122b; vii, 397a, 414a, 728a; viii, 151a – I, 398b, 890a, b, 1071b, 1078a; II, 313b, 399a; III, 130a, 355b, 759b, **910b**, 926b, 960b, 1185b; IV, 442a, 1125a, 1154a; VII, 398b, 415b, 728b; VIII, 153b
Ibn Mukram i, 132a – I, 136a; IV, 442a, 1125a, 1154a
Ibn Muldjam, ʿAbd al-Raḥmān al-Murādī (661) i, 385a; iii, **887a**; iv, 1075a; vii, 265b, 592a; s, 157a – I, 396a; III, **911a**; IV, 1107a; VII, 267b, 591b; S, 157a
Ibn Munādhir ii, 1011a; iii, **890a** – II, 1034b; III, **914a**
Ibn al-Munadjdjim → ʿAlī b. Yaḥyā; Yaḥyā b. ʿAlī
Ibn al-Mundhir (XIV) iii, **890b**; iv, 216a – III, **914b**; IV, 225b
Ibn Munīr → al-Ṭarābulusī al-Raffāʾ
Ibn al-Munķidh → Usāma; Munķidh, Banū
Ibn Munķidh, Abu ʾl-Ḥasan (1079) vii, 122a – VII, 124a
Ibn Munķidh, ʿAlī b. Mukallad (XI) vii, 121a – VII, 123a
Ibn al-Murābiʿ (1350) iii, **891a**; vi, 111b – III, **915a**; VI, 109a
Ibn Murrāna vi, 216b – VI, 200b
Ibn al-Murtaḍā → Muḥammad b. Yaḥyā al-Murtaḍā
Ibn al-Murtaḍā s, 25b, 225b – S, 26a, 225b
Ibn Musāfir → Muḥammad b. Musāfir
Ibn al-Musayyab (VII) viii, 645b – VIII, 665a
Ibn al-Muslima, Abū ʾl-Ķāsim ʿAlī (1058) i, 1073b, 1074b, 1356a; iii, 766a, 860b, **891a**; iv, 457b; v, 73b; vi, 272b – I, 1105b, 1106b, 1395a; III, 789a, 885a, **915a**; IV, 478a; V, 75b; VI, 257b
Ibn al-Mutawwadj (1330) vi, 653a – VI, 638b
Ibn Muṭayr (VIII) iii, **892a** – III, **916a**
Ibn al-Muʿtazz, Abu ʾl-ʿAbbās ʿAbd Allāh (ʿAbbāsid(e)) (908) i, 144a, 386b, 446a, 590a, 592a, 857b, 971b, 981b, 1132a; ii, 197b, 1032b; iii, 100b, 619b, 702b, 750b, **892a**, 955b, 1020a; iv, 90a, b, 491a, 1004a, 1005a; v, 319a, b, 321b; vi, 206a, 348a, 437b, 438a, 605a, 635b; vii, 277a, 541b, 963a, 1040a; viii, 376a, 378a; s, 25a, 31b, 35a, 122b, 385a, b – I, 148b, 398a, 458b, 609b, 611a, 881b, 1001b, 1012a, 1166b; II, 204a, 1056b; III, 103a, 640a, 724b, 773a, **916a**, 980a, 1045b; IV, 94b, 512a, 1036a, 1037b; V, 318b, 321a; VI, 190a, 332a, 423a, b, 589b, 620a; VII, 279a, 541b, 964b, 1042a; VIII, 389a, 390b; S, 25a, 32a, 35b, 122a, 386a
Ibn al-Muthannā iii, 1137a – III, 1165b
Ibn Muṭīʿ → ʿAbd Allāh b. Muṭīʿ
Ibn Muʿṭī, Abu ʾl-Ḥusayn Yaḥyā (1231) ii, 528b; iii, **893b**, 966b; vii, 914b – II, 541b; III, **917b**, 991a; VII, 915a
Ibn al-Muṭrān (1191) vi, 845a – VI, 836a
Ibn al-Muwakkit (1949) iii, **893b**; iv, 159b – III, **917b**; IV, 166b
Ibn Muyassar, Tādj al-Dīn (1278) iii, **894a**; vi, 144a – III, **918a**; VI, 142b
Ibn Muzāḥim → Naṣr b. Muzāḥim
Ibn al-Muzawwik → Ibn al-Sadīd
Ibn Muzayn (XI) ix, 308b – IX, 318a
Ibn al-Nabīh (1222) iii, **894b**; iv, 1006a – III, **918b**; IV, 1038a
Ibn al-Nadīm (995) i, 105a, 151b, 213a, 235a, 247b, 1081a, 1197b, 1354a; ii, 771b, 1093b; iii, 370b, **895a**, 1045a, 1151a; iv, 53b, 1119a; v, 207b; vi, 198b, 634b, 906a; s, 45a, 88b, 127b, 225b, 371b, 372b – I, 108b, 156a, 219b, 242a, 255a, 1113b, 1233a, 1393a; II, 790a, 1119a; III, 382b, **919a**, 1071a, 1179b; IV, 56b, 1150b; V, 205a; VI, 182b, 619b, 897b; S, 45b, 88b, 126b, 225b, 371b, 372a
Ibn al-Nadīm (1046) ix, 114a – IX, 118a
Ibn al-Nadjdjār, Muḥibb Allāh (1245) iii, 756a, **896b**; vi, 353a; vii, 728a – III, 779a, **920b**; VI, 337a; VII, 728b
Ibn al-Nadjdjār (1572) i, 949b – I, 978b
Ibn Nādjī, Abu ʾl-Ķasim (1435) vi, 353b, 355b; s, 173a, **394b** – VI, 337b, 339b; S, 173b, **395a**
Ibn al-Nafīs, ʿAlā al-Dīn (1288) i, 713b; iii, 694a, **897a**, 944b; vi, 354a; x, 355b – I, 735a; III, 716a, **921b**, 969b; VI, 338a; x, 381b
Ibn al-Naḥḥās (950) iii, **898b**; v, 121b; vii, 254b – III, **922b**; V, 124a; VII, 256a
Ibn al-Naḥwī (1119) iii, 800a, b; iv, 481a; x, 124b – III, 823b, 824a; IV, 502a; X, 114b
Ibn al-Nāķid iii, 683a – III, 705a
Ibn Nāķiyā, ʿAbd Allāh (1092) iii, **899a**; vi, 110a – III, **923a**; VI, 108a
Ibn al-Naķūr s, 195a – S, 193b
Ibn Nāṣir (al-Nāṣirī) s, **395a** – S, **395a**
Ibn Nāṣir, Aḥmad b. Maḥammad (1717) s, **395a** – S, **395b**
Ibn Nāṣir, al-Ḥusayn b. Muḥammad (1680) s, **395a** – S, **395b**
Ibn Nāṣir, Maḥammad b. Muḥammad (1674) s, **395a** – S, **395b**
Ibn al-Nāṣir, Muḥammad b. ʿAbd al-Salām (al-Kabīr) (1823) s, **395b** – S, **395b**
Ibn Nāṣir, Muḥammad (al-Makkī) (1729) s, **395a** – S, **395b**
Ibn Nāṣir al-Darʿī ii, 161a – II, 166a
Ibn Nasṭūrus → Isā b. Nasṭūrus
Ibn al-Naṭṭāḥ (866) iii, **899a** – III, **923b**
Ibn al-Naẓar (XII) iii, **900a** – III, **924a**
Ibn Nāẓir al-Djaysh iv, 510a; s, 395b – IV, 532b; S, 396a
Ibn Nubāta al Fāriķī (984) iii, **900a**; v, 75b – III, **924a**; V, 77b
Ibn Nubāta al-Miṣrī (1366) i, 1154a; iii, 781a, 799b, **900a**; iv, 471b, 864a – I, 1188a; III, 804a, 823a, **924b**; IV, 492b, 897a
Ibn Nubāta al-Saʿdī (1014) vi, 110a – VI, 107b
Ibn Nudjaym, Zayn al-Dīn al-Miṣrī (1562) i, 27a, 593a; ii, 163b; iii, 163b, **901a**; vi, 971b; vii, 969b – I, 28a, 612b; II, 168b; III, 167a, **925a**; VI, 964a; VII, 969b
Ibn Nūḥ → Muḥammad b. Nūḥ
Ibn Nuʿmān (al-mufīd) (1022) viii, 615a – VIII, 634a
Ibn Nusayr → al-Namīrī, Muàmmad b. Nuṣayr
Ibn Pakūdā, Baḥya iv, 303b, 304b – IV, 317b, 318a
Ibn Rabban → al-Ṭabarī
Ibn al-Rabīb (1038) iii, 790b, **901b** – III, 814a, **925b**
Ibn Radjab, ʿAbd al-Raḥmān (1392) iii, 161b, 700a, 803b, **901b**, 954b; iv, 990a; viii, 516a – III, 165a, 722b, 826b, **926a**, 979a; IV, 1022b; VIII, 533b
Ibn al-Rāhib (1290) vi, 143b; s, **396a** – VI, 142a; S, **396a**
Ibn Raḥīķ (XI) vi, 183a – VI, 167a
Ibn Raḥmūn vii, 282b – VII, 284b
Ibn Rāhwayh, Isḥāķ b. Ibrāhīm (853) iii, 844b, 846a, **902a**; vii, 691b, 706b – III, 868b, 870a, **926a**; VII, 691b, 707a
Ibn Rāʾiķ (amīr) (942) i, 19a, 20a, 446a, 866a, b, 870b,

1040a, 1046b; ii, 144a, 453b, 1080b; iii, 46a, 86a, 127b, 768b, 887a, **902b**, 1255b; iv, 215a; vii, 411b, 484a, 800a, 912b, 994b –
I, 20a, 20b, 458b, 890a, b, 894b, 1071b, 1078a; II, 148a, 465a, 1105b; III, 47b, 88a, 130a, 791b, 911a, **926b**, 1288a; IV, 224b; VII, 412b, 484a, 802a, 913b, 996a
Ibn al-Raḳā ii, 389a – II, 399b
Ibn al-Raḳīḳ, Abū Isḥāḳ Ibrāhīm al-Ḳayrawānī (1027) iii, **902b**; iv, 830b, 1007a; vii, 483b, 528b, 1040a – III, **927a**; IV, 863b, 1039a; VII, 483b, 528b, 1042a
Ibn al-Rakkāḍ i, 759b – I, 782b
Ibn al-Raḳḳāḳ → Ibn al-Zaḳḳāḳ
Ibn al-Ramāma → al-Ḳaysī, Abū ʿAbd Allāh Muḥammad
Ibn Rāmīn (VIII) viii, 996b – VIII, 1031a
Ibn al-Rashīḳ (Mālikiyya) (1234) vi, 279a – VI, 264a
Ibn Rashīḳ, Abū ʿAlī Ḥasan al-Kayrawānī (1063) i, 858a; iii, 354b, 640a, 688a, **903a**, 936a; iv, 250a, 867a; vi, 605a, 606b; vii, 254b, 277a, b, 309b, 483a, 661a, 978b; viii, 427a; s, 27a, 62b, 394b –
I, 882a; III, 365b, 661a, 709b, **927b**, 960b; IV, 260b, 900b; VI, 590a, 591a; VII, 256a, 279a, 312a, 483a, 660b, 979a; VIII, 441a; S, 27a, 63a, 395a
Ibn Rashīḳ, Abū Muḥammad (Murcia/-e) (XI) i, 6b; iii, 706a, **904b**; vii, 633b, 767a – I, 7a; III, 728a, **928b**; VII, 633a, 768b
Ibn Rawāḥa → ʿAbd Allāh b. Rawāḥa
Ibn al-Rāwandī (al-Rēwendī) (X) i, 129a, 130a; 373b, 780b; iii, **905a**, 1019b; iv, 1162b; v, 120b; vi, 458a; vii, 566a; s, 12b, 14a, 225b –
I, 132b, 133b; II, 383b, 799b; III, **929a**, 1045a; IV, 1194b; V, 123b; VI, 443b; VII, 566b; S, 13a, 14b, 225b
Ibn al-Rawwād (Tabrīz) vi, 504b – VI, 489b
Ibn Raysūn al-ʿAlamī (1645) vi, 356b – VI, 340b
Ibn Rayyān vi, 113b – VI, 111b
Ibn Razīḳ i, 1283a – I, 1322a
Ibn Rāzga → al-S͟hinḳīṭī, Sīdī ʿAbd Allāh b. Muḥammad b. al-Ḳāḍī
Ibn Razīn i, 1092b – I, 1125a
Ibn al-Razzāz al-D͟jazarī iii, 511a – III, 528b
Ibn al-Riḍā → Ḥasan al-ʿAskarī
Ibn Riḍwān, Abu 'l-Ḥasan (1061) iii, 740b, 741b, **906a**, 977a; vi, 638a; vii, 282b; viii, 42a; s, 30a – III, 763b, 764a, **930a**, 1001b; VI, 623a; VII, 284b; VIII, 43a; S, 30a
Ibn Rizām (951) i, 48a, 95b, 96a; iv, 662b; vi, 917b – I, 49b, 98b; IV, 689b; VI, 909a
Ibn Rubayʿān, ʿUmar ii, 354a; iii, 1068a – II, 363b; III, 1094b
Ibn Rūḥ, Abu 'l-Ḳāsim al-Nawbak͟htī (938) iii, 133a, **907a**; vii, 379b, 443b, 1043b – III, 136a, **931b**; VII, 398b, 444b, 1040a
Ibn Ruhayb → Ḳiṭfīr
Ibn al-Rūmī (896) i, 592a; iii, 354b, **907b**, 955b; iv, 1005a; vi, 253a, 603a, 605a, 625b, 955b; vii, 566b, 963b, 982a; viii, 376a, 377b; ix, 387a; s, 58b, 352b –
I, 611a; III, 365b, **931b**, 980a; IV, 1037b; VI, 237a, 588a, 589b, 610b, 948a; VII, 567b, 964b, 983a; VIII, 389a, 390a; IX, 394b; S, 59a, 352b
Ibn al-Rūmiyya, Abu 'l-ʿAbbās (1240) vi, 779a; s, 313b, **396b** – VI, 769a; S, 313b, **397a**
Ibn Rus͟hayd (1321) iii, **909a** – III, **933a**
Ibn Rus͟hd, Abū Ibn Rus͟hd al-Ḥafīd (1141) vii, 400a – VII, 401b
Ibn Rus͟hd, Abu 'l-Walīd al-Ḥafīd (Averroes) (1198) i, 162a, 179a, 209b, 214a, 234b, 327b, 342b, 350b, 415a, b, 594a, 630b, 982b, 1154b; ii, 96b, 765b, 766a, 771a, 773b; iii, 170a, 509b, 644b, 729a, 748b, **909b**, 978a, b, 1132a, 1149a; v, 704a, 843a; vi, 205a, 220a, 279a, 281b, 348b, 449a, b, 450a, 590b; vii, 288a, 387b, 539a, 805b; viii, 96a; s, 397b –
I, 166b, 183b, 215b, 220b, 241b, 337b, 353a, 361a, 427a, 613b, 651b, 1013a, 1188b; II, 98b, 784a, b, 789b, 792a; III, 173b, 527a, 666a, 751b, 771a, **934a**, 1002b, 1160a, 1177a; V, 709a, 849b; VI, 189a, 214a, 264a, 266b, 332b, 434b, 435a, 575b; VII, 290a, 389a, 539a, 807a; VIII, 98a; S, 398a
Ibn Rus͟hd, Abu 'l-Walīd Muḥammad al-D͟jadd (1126) vii, 247b; s, **397b** – VII, 249a; S, **398a**
Ibn Rusta, Abū ʿAlī Aḥmad (912) i, 100b, 775a; ii, 579b, 580a, b; iii, 232a, **920a**; vi, 640a, 656b – I, 103b, 798a; II, 594b, 595a; III, 239a, **944b**; VI, 625a, b, 642a
Ibn Rustam → ʿAbd al-Raḥmān b. Rustam
Ibn Saʿāda (1170) iii, **921a** – III, **945a**
Ibn al-Sāʿātī, Fak͟hr al-Dīn Riḍwān (1230) iii, **921a**, – III, **945b**
Ibn al-Sāʿātī, Muẓaffar al-Dīn Aḥmad (1295) iii, **921a**; vii, 969a – III, **945b**; VII, 969b
Ibn Sabaʾ, Bahāʾ al-Dīn (1207) → ʿAbd Allāh b. Sabaʾ
Ibn al-Ṣabbāg͟h (XI) s, 29b – S, 30a
Ibn Sabʿīn ʿAbd al-Ḥaḳḳ (1269) i, 594a, 772b; iii, **921b**; vi, 451b, 637b – I, 613b, 795b; III, **945**;VI, 436b, VI, 436b, 437a, 623a
Ibn Saʿd, Abū ʿAbd Allāh Muḥammad (845) i, 140a, 591a, 694a; iii, 838b, **922a**; vi, 262b, 263a; vii, 361b –
I, 144a, 610b, 715a; III, 862b, **946b**; VI, 247a, b; VII, 363b
Ibn al-Sābūnī (1320) viii, 156b – VIII, 158b
Ibn Ṣadaḳa iii, 221a – III, 228a
Ibn Saʿdān, Abū ʿAbd Allāh al-Ḥusayn b. Aḥmad (vizier) (984) i, 127a, 159a; vii, 304b; s, 119b, 361b, **398a** –
I, 130b, 163b; VII, 306b; S, 119a, 361a, **398b**
Ibn Ṣaddīḳ, Joseph iv, 304b – IV, 318a
Ibn al-Sadīd (1430) iii, **923a** – III, **947a**
Ibn al-Sadīd (1324) iii, **923a** – III, **947b**
Ibn Ṣadr al-Dīn al-S͟hirwānī i, 327a – I, 337a
Ibn Saʿdūn → Yaḥyā b. Saʿdūn
Ibn al-Ṣaffār, Abu 'l-Ḳāsim Aḥmad al-Andalusī (1035) iii, **924a**, 1137a; vii, 210b, 413a – III, **948b**, 1165b; VII, 212a, 414a
Ibn al-Ṣag͟hīr (902) iii, **924b**; vi, 841a, 947b – III, **949a**; VI, 832a, 940a
Ibn Ṣag͟hīr al-Barbarī al-Maṣmūdī iv, 920a – IV, 953a
Ibn Ṣāḥib al-Ṣalāt (XII) iii, **924b** – III, **949a**
Ibn Sahl al-Isrāʾīlī (1251) i, 602a; iii, **925a**, 1047a; iv, 1007b; vii, 811b; viii, 833b –
I, 621b; III, **949b**, 1073a; IV, 1039b; VII, 813b; VIII, 862a
Ibn Saḥnūn, Muḥammad iii, 681a; v, 503b – III, 703a; V, 507a
Ibn al-Sāʿī (1276) iii, **925b**; vii, 727b, 728a; s, 284b – III, **950a**; VII, 728a, b; S, 284a
Ibn Saʿīd → al-Mund͟hir b. Saʿīd
Ibn Sāʿid (Ḥawrān) iv, 552b – IV, 576b
Ibn Saʿīd, Abū D͟jaʿfar → Abū D͟jaʿfar Ibn Saʿīd
Ibn Saʿīd al-Mag͟hribī (1286) i, 119a, 602a, 602b; iii, 807b, **926a**; iv, 1081a; v, 1012a, 1020b; vi, 111a; vii, 186a, 528a, 824b; s, 86a, 266a –
I, 122b, 621b, 622a; III, 831a, **950b**; IV, 1112b; V, 1008a, 1016b; VI, 108b; VII, 186b, 528b, 826b S, 86a, 265b
Ibn al-Ṣāʾig͟h (1375) vi, 193b – VI, 177b
Ibn al-Ṣāʾig͟h (Ifrīḳiya) (XI) vi, 942b – VI, 934b
Ibn al-Ṣāʾig͟h al-ʿArūḍī (1322) iii, **926b** – III, **951a**

Ibn al-Saḳḳā' (1176) viii, 892a – VIII, 923a
Ibn al-Ṣalāḥ (1154) viii, 99b – VIII, 102a
Ibn al-Ṣalāḥ, Taḳī 'l-Dīn al-Shahrazūrī (1245) ii, 462a; iii, 25b, 27a, 818b, **927a,** 1108a; vi, 353a; vii, 631a; viii, 459b; x. 934b –
II, 474a; III, 26b, 28b, 842a, **951b**, 1139b; VI, 337a; VII, 631a; VIII, 475a; X,
Ibn Salām b. ʿUmar (ʿAmr) (XI) iii, **927a**; vi, 311a – III, **951b**; VI, 296a
Ibn Salama (Mālikiyya) vi, 263b – VI, 248b
Ibn al-Sal(l)ār → al-ʿĀdil b. al-Salār
Ibn Sālim iii, 570b – III, 590b
Ibn Sālim al-Kalāʿī → al-Kalāʿī, Abu 'l-Rabīʿ b. Sālim
Ibn Sallām → Abū ʿUbayd al-Ḳāsim b. Sallām
Ibn Sallām al-Djumaḥī (846) iii, 272b, 353b, 698a, **927b**, 1177b; vii, 580b, 978a; ix, 662b; s, 284a –
III, 280b, 365a, 720a, **952a**, 1206b; VII, 581a, 978b; IX, 688a; S, 284a
Ibn Sallāmī al-Maghribī, Abū ʿUthmān (983) vi, 280a – VI, 264b
Ibn al-Ṣalt, Aḥmad b. Muḥammad s, 400b – S, 401a
Ibn al-Salʿūs iv, 964b – IV, 997a
Ubn Samadjūn (XI) i, 214a; iii, **928a**; s, 313b, 314a – I, 220b; III, **952b**; S, 313b
Ibn al-Samāʿī (1275) vi, 352a – VI, 336a
Ibn Samʿān (Zandjī) (IX) vii, 526b – VII, 526b
Ibn al-Samḥ (1035) i, 600b; iii, **928b**, 1137a; s, 25a – I, 620a; III, **953a**, 1165b; S, 25b
Ibn Sammāk iii, 570a – III, 589b
Ibn Samʿun → Abu 'l-Ḥusayn
Ibn Samura → ʿUbayd Allāh Ibn Samura
Ibn Sanā' al-Mulk, Abu 'l-Ḳāsim (1211) i, 595b; ii, 1033a; iii, **929a**; vi, 255b; vii, 528a, 812a – I, 615a; II, 1057a; III, **953b**; VI, 240a; VII, 528b, 813b
Ibn al-Ṣāniʿ → Ibn Yaʿīsh, Muwaffaḳ al-Dīn
Ibn Sarābiyūn (X) iii, **929b** – III, **954a**
Ibn Sāra (1124) ix, 308a – IX, 318a
Ibn Ṣārah s, 352b – S, 352b
Ibn al-Sarāya → Ṣafī al-Dīn al-Hillī
Ibn al-Sarrādj → Ibn al-Ḳiṭṭ
Ibn al-Sarrādj (al-Ḥalabī) (1325) vii, 30a, 210b; viii, 575a – VII, 30a, 211b; VIII, 593b
Ibn al-Sarrādj, Abū ʿAlī iii, 842a – III, 866a
Ibn al-Sarrādj, Banū s, **398b** – S, **399a**
Ibn al-Sarrādj, Muḥammad b. ʿAlī (XIV) iii, **930a** – III, **954b**
Ibn al-Sarrādj, Abū Bakr Muḥammad al-Naḥwī al-Baghdādī (929) iii, **930a**, 1128a; vii, 279b, 914a; x, 4a – III, **945b**, 1156b; VII, 281b, 914b; X, 4a
Ibn al-Ṣarṣarī iii, 952a – III, 976b
Ibn Ṣaṣra, Ṣaṣarrā iii, **930b** – III, **955a**
Ibn Saʿūd → ʿAbd al-ʿAzīz Āl Suʿūd
Ibn al-Sawdā' → ʿAbd Allāh b. Saba'
Ibn Sawda → Ibn Sūda
Ibn Sawwār i, 1086b; ii, 127a; vi, 198a, b – I, 1118b; II, 130b; VI, 182a, b
Ibn Sayāba → Ibrāhim b. Sayāba
Ibn Sayf II iii, 604a – III, 624b
Ibn Sayḥān (VII) iii, **931b**; iv, 1002a – III, **956a**; IV, 1031b
Ibn al-Ṣaykal (1302) viii, 805b – VIII, 832b
Ibn al-Ṣayrafī, Abū Bakr Yaḥyā (1162) i, 389b; iii, **932b**; vii, 584a – I, 400b; III, **957a**; VII, 584b
Ibn al-Ṣayrafī, Tādj al-Ri'āsa (1147) ii, 80a, 304b, 305a; iii, **932a**, 1242b; vi, 423b –
II, 81b, 313a, b; III, **956b**, 1274b; VI, 408b
Ibn Sayyār al-Warrāk (X) ix, 93b, 576a – IX, 97b, 598a
Ibn al-Sayyid (995) i, 600a – I, 619b
Ibn Sayyid al-Nās, Fatḥ al-Dīn (1334) iii, **932b**; vi, 111b; vii, 388a; ix, 661a –
III, **957a**; VI, 109a; VII, 389a; IX, 687a
Ibn Shābāsh, Abu 'l-Ḥasan ʿAlī b. Faḍl (1052) ix, 159a – IX, 164a
Ibn al-Shabbāṭ iv, 403a – IV, 420b
Ibn Shaddād, ʿAbd al-ʿAzīz iii, **933a** – III, **957b**
Ibn Shaddād, Bahā' al-Dīn (1235) iii, **933b**; vi, 430a – III, **958a**; VI, 415a
Ibn Shaddād, ʿIzz al-Dīn al-Ḥalabī (1285) i, 946a; iii, **933b**, 938a; vi, 381a, 930a – I, 975a; III, **958a**, 962b; VI, 365a, 921b
Ibn Shaddād Yūsuf s, 197a – S, 197a
Ibn Shādhān (993) viii, 14a – VIII, 14a
Ibn Shādhān (1034) ix, 65a – IX, 66b
Ibn Shādhān al-Rāzī → al-Badjalī, Abū Bakr Muḥammad b. ʿAbd Allāh
Ibn al-Shadjarī al-Baghdādī (1148) i, 485b, 1241a; iii, 111a, **934b**; vii, 527a –
I, 500a, 1279a; III, 113b, **959a**; VII, 527b
Ibn Shahīd (Ḥafṣid(e)) s, 111b, 112a – S, 111a
Ubn al-Shahīd, Abū Ḥafs ʿUmar (XI) iii, **934b**; vi, 114b – III, **959b**; VI, 112b
Ibn Shāhīn → Nissīm ben Yaʿḳob Ibn Shāhīn
Ibn Shāhīn, ʿUmar b. Aḥmad (995) viii, 517a – VIII, 534b
Ibn Shāhīn al-Ẓāhirī (XV) iii, **935a** – III, **959b**
Ibn Shahrāshūb, Abū Djaʿfar (1192) i, 120a; ii, 848a; iii, **935a**, 1151b; vi, 351b – I, 123b; II, 867b; III, **960a**, 1180a; VI, 335b
Ibn Shākir → al-Kutubī
Ibn Shaḳīshaḳa s, 197a – S, 197a
Ibn Shakrūn al-Miknāsī (XVIII) s, 40a, **399b** – S, 40b, **400a**
Ibn Shālib al-Yahūdī (XI) viii, 813b – VIII, 841a
Ibn al-Shalmaghānī → Muḥammad b. ʿAlī al-Shalmaghānī
Ibn Shankā (1173) vii, 707a – VII, 708a
Ibn Shannabūdh (939) i, 1039b; iii, **935b**; v, 127b, 409a; s, 386a, 393b – I, 1071a; III, **960b**; V, 130a, 410a; S, 386b, 394a
Ibn Sharaf, Abu 'l-Faḍl (1139) i, 602a; iii, **936b** – I, 621b; III, **961b**
Ibn Sharaf al-Ḳayrawānī (1067) iii, 903b, **936a**; iv, 830b; v, 43b; vi, 108b, 109a, 110a, 606b; vii, 483a; s, 27a, 62b, 394b –
III, 927b, **960b**; IV, 863b; V, 44b; VI, 106a, 107a, b, 591a; VII, 483a; S, 27a, 63a, 395a
Ibn Sharāfī, Ṣafī al-Dīn v, 92a – V, 94b
Ibn al-Shārī (XIII) s, 388b – S, 389a
Ibn al-Sharīf al-Darḳāwī (XIX) ii, 160a; vii, 263a – II, 165b; VII, 265a
Ibn Sharya, ʿAbīd/ʿUbayd al-Djurhumī iii, 370a, **937a**; iv, 211b; vi, 197b – III, 382a, **961b**; IV, 221a; VI, 182a
Ibn al-Shāṭir (1375) iii, 1137b; iv, 518a, 810a; vi, 543a, 602a; vii, 30a, 210b; viii, 102a –
III, 1165b; IV, 540b, 843a; VI, 527b, 586a; VII, 30a, 212a; VIII, 104b
Ibn Shaykh (Nasraḥ) (XX) vi, 755a – VI, 744a
Ibn al-Shaykh al-Balawī i, 602a – I, 622a
Ibn Shaykh Ḥiṭṭīn → al-Dimashḳī
Ibn Shaykh al-Salāmiya → Ibn al-Ṣā'ī
Ibn Shibl (1080) iii, **937b**; iv, 1005b – III, **962a**; IV, 1038a
Ibn Shihāb i, 830a – I, 853a
Ibn Shihāb al-Zuhrī → al-Zuhrī
Ibn al-Shiḥna al-Ḥalabī, Muḥibb al-Dīn (1485) i, 119a; iii, **938a**; vi, 230a, 381b, 382a – I, 122b; III, **962b**; VI, 224a, 365b, 366a
Ubn Shīrzād (X) vii, 723b – VII, 724b
Ibn Shīth al-Kurashī ii, 329b – II, 339a

Ibn Shubruma (761) iii, 687b, **938a** – III, 709a, **962b**
Ibn Shudja' Farrukhshāh v, 76b – V, 78b
Ibn Shuhayd, Abū 'Āmir (1035) i, 591a, 601b; iii, 346b, 355a, 370b, 740a, 786a, 790a, b, **938b**; iv, 1007a; v, 114b, 778b; vi, 109b, 110a; ; vii, 495a; viii, 533b; ix, 455b; s, 250a –
I, 610a, 621a; III, 357b, 366a, 382b, 763a, 809b, 813b, 814a, **963a**; IV, 1039a; V, 117a, 784b; VI, 107b; VII, 495a; VIII, 551a; IX, 470b; S, 250a
Ibn Shukr i, 800b, 801b – I, 824a, b
Ibn al-Sīd al-Baṭalyawsī → al-Baṭalyawsī
Ibn Sīda (Sīduh), Abu 'l-Ḥasan (1066) i, 600a, 601a; ii, 300b; iii, **940a**; iv, 524b; vi, 374b; vii, 772a –
I, 620a, 621a; II, 308b; III, **964b**; IV, 547a; VI, 359a; VII, 773b
Ibn al-Sikkīt (858) i, 772a, 1241a; ii, 300a; iii, 803a, **940b**; iv, 1027b; vii, 831b, 841b; s, 15b, 394b –
I, 795a, 1279a; II, 308a; III, 826b, **965a**; IV, 1059b; VII, 833a, 842b, 843a; S, 16a, 395a
Ibn al-Simāṭ v, 1247b – V, 1238a
Ibn Sīmdjūr vi, 340a – VI, 324b
Ibn Sīnā, Abū 'Alī al-Ḥusayn (Avicenna) (1037) i, 74b, 112a, b, 147a, 179a, 213b, 234b, 327b, 342a,b, 350b, 415a, 427a, 434b, 589a, 630b, 772b, 784b, 785b, 839a, 926a, 1084a, 1236a, 1327a, 1354a; ii, 96a, 221a, 378b, 450a, 481b, 550a, 764b, 765a; iii, 30a, 170a, 329b, 330b, 333b, 509b, 543b, 897b, 916a, **941a**, 974b, 1028a, 1130b; iv, 120a, 331a, 358b, 366b, 466b, 615b; v, 842b, 1261b, 1262b; vi, 73b, 97b, 204b, 220a, 347a, 348b, 446b, 449b, 450a, b, 467a, 600b, 616b, 637a, 638a. 907a; vii, 200b, 682b, 683a; viii, 95a,b, 123b, 541a; x, 453b; s, 24a, 40b, 59b, 72b, 270a, 271b, 305b, 308a, 314a, 380a –
I, 76b, 115a, b, 151b, 183b, 220a, 242a, 338a, 352a, 353a, 361a, 426b, 439b, 446b, 608b, 651b, 795b, 808a, 809a, 862a, 954a, 1116b, 1274a, 1367b, 1393a; II, 98a, 228a, 388b, 462a, 494a, 564a, 783a, 784a; III, 31b, 174a, 339b, 341a, 343b, 527a, 562b, 921b, 940a, **965b**, 999a, 1054a, 1159a; IV, 125a, 345b, 374a, 382b, 487a, 640a; V, 849a, 1252b, 1253b; VI, 71b, 95b, 188b, 214a, 331a, 332b, 432a, 435a, b, 453a, 585b, 601b, 622a, 623a, 898b; VII, 201a, 682b, 683b; VIII, 97b, 126a, 558b; X, 486b; S, 24a, 40b, 60a, 73a, 269b, 271a, b, 305a, 308a, 313b, 380b
Ibn Sinān al-Khafādjī (1060) vii, 120a –
VII, 122a
Ibn Sīrīn, Abū Bakr Muḥammad (728) ii, 300b; iii, **947b**; v, 1232a; vi, 266b; viii, 374b, 645b – II, 309a; III, **972a**; V, 1222a; VI, 251b; VIII, 387b, 665a
Ibn al-Sitrī → Ibn al-Bawwāb
Ibn Sūda (Tāwdī, Fès) iii, **948a** – III, **973a**
Ibn Sūda, Abū 'Abd Allāh Muḥammad al-Tāw(u)dī (1795) iii, **948b**; vi, 356b –
III, **973a**; VI, 341a
Ibn Sūdūn i, 571a – I, 590a
Ibn al-Ṣūfī (IX) VIII, 863b – VIII, 894a
Ibn al-Ṣuḳā'ī al-Naṣrānī (1325) s, **400a** – S, **400b**
Ibn Sukkāra (995) ix, 342a, 453b; s, 352b –
IX, 353a, 468b; S, 352b
Ibn Ṣulayḥa (ḳāḍī) (XII) ii, 353b; vi, 578a –
II, 363a; VI, 563a
Ibn Sulaym al-Aswānī (X) iii, **949a** – III, **973b**
Ibn Ṣumādiḥ → al-Mu'taṣim Ibn Ṣumādiḥ
Ibn Sumayya → Ziyād b. Abīhi
Ibn Surāḳa (Damascus) i, 773a – I, 796b
Ibn Surāḳa al-'Āmirī, Muḥammad (1019)
vi, 106b, 183a, b – VI, 104b, 167a, b
Ibn Suraydj, Abu 'l-Abbās Aḥmad (918) iii, 100b, **949a**; ix, 36a, 893b – III, 103a, **974a**; IX, 36b, 929b
Ibn Suraydj, 'Ubayd Allāh (714) i, 118a, 828a; ii, 428b, 1011b; iii, **950a**; iv, 315b; vi, 262a, b; vii, 681b –
I, 121b, 851a; II, 439b, 1035a; III, **974b**; IV, 329b; VI, 246b, 247a; VII, 681b
Ibn al-Sūrī ii, 350a – II, 359b
Ibn Surūr al-Maḳdisī (XIII) vi, 637a – VI, 622a
Ibn Su'ūd → 'Abd al-'Azīz Āl Su'ūd
Ibn Suwār (1017) x, 360b – X, 387a
Ibn Suwār, 'Abd al-Ḳādir b. Muḥammad (1605) vi, 88a – VI, 86a
Ibn Suwār, Āl vi, 88a – VI, 86a
Ibn Suwayṭ ii, 77a – II, 78b
Ibn Swīkāt (Bessouiket) (XVIII) vi, 249b –
VI, 233b
Ibn al-Ta'āwīdhī (1188) i, 212b; iii, 891b, **950a** – I, 219a; III, 915b, **975a**
Ibn Ṭabāṭabā (934) vii, 277a – VII, 279a
Ibn Ṭabāṭabā, Muḥammad b. Ibrāhīm (815)
i, 149b, 402b; iii, 243b, **950b**; vi, 334a – I, 154a, 414a; III, 250b, **975b**; VI, 318b
Ibn Tafrāgīn iii, 49a, 68a, 826a, 867a; v, 1151a, 1247a – III, 50b, 70a, 849b, 891a; V, 1141b, 1237b
Ibn Taghrībirdī → Abu 'l-Maḥāsin
Ibn al-Ṭaḥḥān (XI) vii, 684a – VII, 684a
Ibn Ṭāhir → 'Abd Allāh b. Ṭāhir
Ibn Ṭāhir, Abū Bakr Aḥmad b. Isḥāḳ (Murcia/-e) (1119) vii, 633b – VII, 633a
Ibn Talḥa al-'Adawī al-Rādjī ii, 376a; v, 1236b – II, 386b; V, 1227a
Ibn Ṭālib (888) viii, 844a – VIII, 873b
Ibn Talīd (al-Mawṣil) (700) vi, 900a – VI, 891a
Ibn Ṭalūt iv, 459a – IV, 479b
Ibn al-Tammār → Ibn Mītham
Ibn Ṭarf → Sulaymān b. Ṭarf
Ibn al-Ṭathriyya vi, 477a – VI, 463a
Ibn Ṭayfūr (Mertola) i, 6a; vii, 761a – I, 6a; VII, 762b
Ibn Taymiyya, Madjd al-Dīn iii, 161a, 951a, 953b – III, 164b, 976a, 978a
Ibn Taymiyya, Taḳī al-Dīn Aḥmad (1328) i, 69b, 195a, 266b, 272b, 273b, 274b, 275b, 276a,b, 277a, 333a, 411b, 425a, 553a, 593a, 696a, 827b, 959a, 1238b; ii, 51a, 230a, 285b, 294a, 295a, 411b, 752b, 931a, 966a; iii, 161b, 162a, 429b, 512b, 700a, 711a, 722b, 752a, 821b, **951a**, 1148b, 1171b, 1207a; iv, 142a, 149b, 257b, 258b, 366a, 381b, 469b; v, 426a; vi, 34a, 122b, 176b, 353b, 360b, 447a, 452a, 651b; vii, 169b, 212a, 291b, 296b, 419b, 462a; viii, 125a, 147a, 156b, 534a, 759a; s, 354a –
I, 71b, 201a, 274b, 280b, 282a, 283a, 284a, b, 285a, b, 343a, 423b, 437a, 570b, 612b, 717b, 850b, 988a, 1276a; II, 52a, 236b, 293b, 302a, 303a, 422b, 771a, 953a, 988a; III, 164b, 165b, 443b, 530a, 722b, 733a, 745a, 775a, 845b, **976a**, 1176b, 1200b, 1237b; IV, 148a, 155b, 269a, 270a, 382a, 398a, 490b; V, 428b; VI, 32a, 120a, 337b, 344b, 432b, 437b, 637a; VII, 171a, 213b, 294a, 298b, 421a, 461b; VIII, 128a, 149b, 159a, 552a, 784a; S, 354a
Ibn al-Tayyām → Tammām b. Ghālib
Ibn al-Tayyānī i, 600a – I, 620a
Ibn al-Ṭayyib al-Baṣrī → Abu 'l-Ḥusayn
Ibn al-Ṭayyib al-'Irāḳī, Abu 'l-Faradj (1043)
i, 328a, 388a; ii, 780a, 929b, 948b; iii, 740b, **955a**, 1205b; vi, 204b, 637b, 638a; vii, 1031a; s, 25a, 396b –
I, 338a, 399a; II, 799a, 951b, 970b; III, 763b, **979b**, 1236a; VI, 188b, 622b, 623a; VII, 1033b; S, 25b, 397a
Ibn Thawāba (897) vii, 653a -VII, 652b
Ibn Thawāba, Abu 'l-'Abbās Ahmad (890) iii, **955a** – III, **979b**
Ibn Thawāba, Abu 'l-Ḥusayn Dja'far (897) iii, **955b**; vii, 653a – III, **979b**; VII, 652b

Ibn al-Thumna (1062) iii, 782b, 788a, **956a**; ix, 670a – III, 806a, 811b, **980b**; IX, 697a
Ibn Tifalwīt iii, 542b, 728a, 849b – III, 561b, 750b, 873b
Ibn al-Ṭiḳṭaḳā, Ṣafī al-Dīn (XII) i, 157b, 595b; iii, 702a, **956a**; vi, 627b – I, 162a, 614b; III, 724b, **980b**; VI, 612b
Ibn al-Tilmīdh, Abu 'l-Ḥasan, Amīn al-Dawla (1165) i, 111b, 344b, 858b, 1224a,b; iii, **956b**; vi, 726a – I, 115a, 355a, 882b, 1260b, 1261a; III, **981a**; VI, 716a
Ibn Ṭūbī, Mūsā iv, 307a – IV, 320b
Ibn Ṭufayl, Abū Bakr Muḥammad (1185) i, 162a, 594a, 1250a; ii, 773b, 1039b; iii, 330b, 333a, 729a, 910a, 911b, **957a**; vi, 590b; vii, 805b – I, 166b, 613a, 1288a; II, 792a, 1063b; III, 341a, 343a, 751b, 934a, 935b, **981b**; VI, 575b; VII, 807a
Ibn Ṭūlūn → Aḥmad b. Ṭūlūn
Ibn Ṭūlūn, Shams al-Dīn al-Ṣāliḥī (1546) i, 571a; iii, **957b**; iv, 1161b; vi, 352b, 354b, 359b, 685a; s, 195b – I, 590a; III, **982a**; IV, 1193b; VI, 337a, 338b, 343b, 685a; S, 195b
Ibn Tūmart al-Mahdī, Muḥammad (1130) i, 78a, 121b, 122a, 251a, 389b, 390a, 592b, 1129b, 1176a, 1186a, 1205a; ii, 307b; iii, 207a, **958b**; iv, 290a, 558a; v, 626a, 744b, 1160b, 1199b; vi, 281a, 339b, 592a, b, 597a, 742b, 743b; vii, 591a, 801b – I, 80a, 125a, b, 258b, 400b, 401b, 612a, 1163b, 1211a, 1221a, 1241a; II, 316b; III, 212b, **983a**; IV, 303a, 582a; V, 630a, 750a, 1150b, 1190a; VI, 265b, 324a, 576b, 577a, b, 581b, 732a, b, 733a; VII, 591a, 803b
Ibn Ṭumlūs (Alhagiag bin Thalmus) (1223) iii, **960a**; vi, 450b – III, **984b**; VI, 435b
Ibn Tūnārt → al-Kaysī, Abū ʿAbd Allāh Muḥammad
Ibn Turayk, Abu 'l-ʿAlāʾ iii, 782a – III, 805a
Ibn al-Ṭuwayr, Abū Muḥammad (1220) i, 801b; iii, **960b**; iv, 1145b; vii, 150b – I, 824b; III, **985a**; IV, 1177a; VII, 152b
Ibn ʿUbayya v, 333b – V, 333b
Ibn ʿUdjayl i, 1140b – I, 1175a
Ibn Udhayna → ʿUrwa b. Udhayna
Ibn ʿUkāsha (1078) i, 6b; vii, 766b – I, 6b; VII, 768b
Ibn ʿUḳba → Mūsā b. ʿUḳba
Ibn ʿUḳda, al-Hamdānī (944) s, **400b** – S, **401a**
Ibn al-Ukhuwwa, Ḍiyāʾ al-Dīn (1329) iii, **960b**; vii, 29a; s, 273b – III, **985a**; VII, 29b; S, 273a
Ibn ʿUlayya, Abū Isḥāḳ Ibrāhīm b. Ismāʿīl (832) vi, 263b; s, 90a – VI, 248b; S, 90a
Ibn ʿUmar → ʿAbd Allāh b. ʿUmar b. al-Khaṭṭāb; Yaʿḳūb b. ʿUmar al-Maghribī
Ibn ʿUmar, Djazīrat (Cizre) iii, **960b**; v, 447b, 458b; vi, 539b, 627a, 781a; s, 267a – III, **985a**; V, 450a, b, 461a; VI, 524a, 612a, 770b; S, 266b
Ibn ʿUmāra → al-Dīkdān
Ibn Umayl (X) ii, 358a,b; iii, 464b, **961b**; v, 112a; s, 270a – II, 367b, 368b; III, 481a, **986a**; V, 114b; S, 269b
Ibn ʿUmayr vi, 248a – VI, 232a
Ibn Umayya i, 1343a – I, 1383b
Ibn Umm Maktūm vi, 677a – VI, 663b, 664a
Ibn ʿUnayn (1233) iii, **962a**; vi, 539a – III, **986b**; VI, 523b
Ibn Unays vi, 646a – VI, 631b
Ibn ʿUrayba v, 1247b – V, 1238a
Ibn ʿUṣfūr (1271) iii, **962b**; vii, 914b; ix, 347a – III, **987a**; VII, 915a; 358a
Ibn al-ʿUshārī (1049) vi, 350b – VI, 334b
Ibn Ustādh-Hurmuz, Abū ʿAlī al-Ḥasan s, 118b, 119a – S, 118a
Ibn Uthāl (666) vi, 139b, 140a, 654b; x, 452b – VI, 138a, 640a; X, 485a
Ibn ʿUthmān al-Miknāsī (1799) vii, 387b; s, 308a, **401a** – VII, 388b; S, 307b, **401b**
Ibn ʿUyayna → Sufyān b. ʿUyayna
Ibn Wadʿān s, 83a – S, 82b
Ibn Wāfid (1074) i, 345a, 600b; ii, 901a; iii, **962b**; s, 314a – I, 355b, 620a; II, 922a; III, **987a**; S, 313b
Ibn Wahb → ʿAbd Allāh b. Sabaʾ
Ibn Wahb, ʿAbd Allāh al-Ḳurashī (813) iii, **963a**; iv, 87a; vi, 264b, 265a; vii, 691b – III, **987b**; IV, 91b; VI, 249a, b; VII, 691b
Ibn Wahb, Abu 'l-Ḥusayn (X) s, **402a** – S, **402b**
Ibn Wahb al-Kātib (X) viii, 427a – VIII, 441b
Ibn Wahbūn (1092) iii, **963a** – III, **987b**
Ibn Wahhās → al-Khazradjī, Muwaffaḳ al-Dīn
Ibn al-Waḥīd (1312) vii, 840a – VII, 841b
Ibn Waḥshiyya (IX) i, 247a; ii, 358a, 455b, 900a; iii, **963b**; iv, 120b, 659a; v, 112a, 222b, 997a; vii, 200a, 203b, 257b, 837a; viii, 677b; s, 59b, 310a, 392b – I, 255a; II, 367b, 467b, 920b; III, **988a**; IV, 126a, 685b; V, 114b, 220a, 1029b; VII, 200b, 204b, 259a, 838a; VIII, 697b; S, 60a, 309b, 393a
Ibn Waḳār, Joseph iv, 305a – IV, 318b
Ibn Walmiya iv, 337a, b, 339a – IV, 351b, 352a, 353a
Ibn al-Wannān (1773) i, 290b; iii, **965b**; vii, 388a; s, 381b – I, 299b; III, **990a**; VII, 389a; S, 382a
Ibn al-Wardī, Sirādj al-Dīn (1457) i, 594b; ii, 587b; iii, **966a**; iv, 1081b – I, 613b; II, 602a; III, **990b**; IV, 1112b
Ibn al-Wardī, Zayn al-Dīn (1349) i, 119a; iii, 772b, **966b**; iv, 471b; v, 548a; vi, 111b, 185b; vii, 537a – I, 122b; III, 795b, **991a**; IV, 492b; V, 552b; VI, 109a, 167b; VII, 537a
Ibn Warḳāʾ vi, 195b – VI, 180a
Ibn Warsand (IX) s, **402b** – S, **402b**
Ibn Waṣīf Shāh vi, 411b – VI, 396b
Ibn Wāṣil, Abū ʿAbd Allāh (1298) iii, 934a, **967a**; vi, 144a, 429b, 580a; s, 204b, 205a – III, 958b, **991b**; VI, 142a, 415a, 565a; S, 204a, b
Ubn Wāsūl (Midrārid(e))(X) vi, 1041a; vii, 486b – VI, 1034a, b; VII, 486b
Ibn Waththāb ii, 484b – II, 496b
Ibn Waṭwāṭ (1318) vii, 1040a – VII, 1042a
Ibn Wazīr → Sidrāy b. Wazīr
Ibn al-Wazīr, Ibrāhīm b. Muḥammad al-Ḥādawī (Zaydī) (1508) vi, 112a, VI, 110a
Ibn al-Wazzān s, 398a – S, 398a
Ibn Yaʿīsh, Muwaffaḳ al-Dīn (1245) i, 571a; ii, 896a; iii, 551a, **968a**; vi, 448b, 637b; vii, 914b – I, 589b; II, 917a; III, 570a, **992b**; VI, 343a, 622b; VII, 915a
Ibn Yaʿīsh, Solomo(n) (1603) iii, **967b** – III, **992a**
Ibn Yaʿīsh, Solomon (1345) iii, **967b** – III, **992a**
Ibn Yāḳūt → Muḥammad b. Yāḳūt
Ibn Yalbaḳ iii, 46a; iv, 423b – III, 47b; IV, 442a
Ibn Yallas, Muḥammad (1927) iii, 261b, **968a** – III, 269a, **992b**
Ibn Yāmīn (Benyāmīn) (1520) vi, 226b, 228a – VI, 220b, 221b
Ibn-i Yamīn, Amīr Fakhr al-Dīn Faryūmadī (1368) iii, **968a**; iv, 66a; viii, 448b; ix, 49a – III, **992b**; IV, 69b; VIII, 463b; IX, 50a
Ibn-i Yamīn Shiburghānī (1596) iii, 968b – III, 993a
Ibn Yāsīn → ʿAbd Allāh b. Yāsīn
Ibn al-Yasmīn (1204) vi, 543a – VI, 528a
Ibn Yūnus → Abu 'l-Muẓaffar b. Yūnus
Ibn Yūnus (1059) vi, 279a – VI, 264a
Ibn Yūnus (Yūnis), Abu 'l-Ḥasan ʿAlī al-Sadafī (1009) ii, 584a; iii, 9a, **969b**, 1137a; iv, 810a, 1079a; v, 85a, b; vi, 598a, 599b, 600b; vii, 202b; s, 115b, 413b –

II, 599a; III, 9b, **994a**, 1165a; IV, 843a, 1110b; V, 87b, 88a; VI, 583a, 584a, 585b; VII, 203a; S, 115a, 413b
Ibn Yūnus, Abū Saʿīd (958) iii, **969b** – III, **994a**
Ibn Yūnus, vizier (1188) x, 554b – X,
Ibn Zabāla vi, 666b – VI, 652b
Ibn al-Zabīr (698) iii, **970a** – III, **994b**
Ibn al-Zadjdjādj i, 942a – I, 971a
Ibn Ẓafar, Abū ʿAbd Allāh Ḥudjdjat al-Dīn (1170) iii, 309a, **970a**; iv, 506a; vii, 986a – III, 318b, **995a**; IV, 528a; VII, 987a
Ibn al-Zaʿfarānī, Abū ʿAbd Allāh vii, 868b – VII, 870a
Ibn Ẓāfir, Djamāl al-Dīn al-Azdī (1216) iii, **970b**; vii, 528a – III, **995a**; VII, 528b
Ibn Zāghū, Abu 'l-ʿAbbās Aḥmad (1441) ix, 247a – IX, 258a
Ibn Zāghū, Aḥmad b. Muḥammad s, 403a – S, 403a
Ibn Zāghū, Muḥammad b. Aḥmad iv, 477a – IV, 498a
Ibn Zakī iii, 708a – III, 730b
Ibn al-Zakkāk (1133) i, 602a; iii, 823a, **971a**; iv, 1007a; vii, 1046b – I, 621b; III, 846b, **995b**; IV, 1039b; VII, 1048b
Ibn Zakrawayh → Ḥusayn b. Zakrawayh; Yaḥyā b. Zakrawayh
Ibn Zakrī s, **402b** – S, **403a**
Ibn Zakrī al-Fāsī (1731) s, **403b** – S, **404a**
Ibn Zakrī al-Tilimsānī (1494) s, **402b** – S, **403a**
Ibn Zākūr (1708) iii, **971b** – III, **996a**
Ibn Zamrak (1393) i, 602a; iii, 836a, **972b**; vii, 811b, 1025a – I, 621b; III, 860a, **997a**; VII, 813b, 1027a, b
Ibn al-Zarkala → al-Zarkalī
Ibn Zarkūn iii, 680b, 798b – III, 702b, 821b
Ibn Zawlāk → Ibn Zūlāk
Ibn Zayd (1465) vi, 352b – VI, 337a
Ibn Zaydān, ʿAbd al-Raḥmān (1946) iii, **973a**; vi, 250a – III, **997b**; VI, 234a
Ibn Zaydūn, Abu 'l-Walīd (1070) i, 591a, 592b, 601b; ii, 1033a; iii, 681b, 706a, **973b**; v, 377a; vi, 751a; vii, 661a, 766b, 768a; viii, 533b – I, 610a, 611b, 621b; II, 1056b; III, 703a, 728a, **998a**; V, 377b; VI, 740b; VII, 661a, 768a, 769b; VIII, 551a
Ibn Zaylā, Abū Manṣūr al-Ḥusayn (1048) iii, **974b**; vi, 638a; vii, 207b, 683b; ix, 10a – III, **999a**; VI, 623a; VII, 208b, 683b; IX, 10a
Ibn al-Zayyāt, Abū Yaʿkūb al-Tādilī (1230) iii, **975a**; vi, 355b – III, **999b**; VI, 340a
Ibn al-Zayyāt, Muḥammad b. ʿAbd al-Malik (vizier) (847) iii, **974b**; vii, 191b, 652b, 776b, 777b; s, 106a – III, **999a**; VII, 192a, 652b, 778a, 779b; S, 105b
Ibn Zekri → al-Zawāwī, Muḥammad Saʿīd b. Aḥmad
Ibn al-Zibaʿrā, ʿAbd Allāh iii, **975a**; vi, 605a – III, **999b**; VI, 590a
Ibn Ziyād → ʿUbayd Allāh b. Ziyād
Ibn Ziyād (Zabīd) (IX) x, 481b; s, 338a – X, 517a; S 334b
Ibn Ziyād (Zabīd) (1568) iii, 779a – III, 802b
Ibn al-Zubayr → ʿAbd Allāh; ʿAmr; Muṣʿab
Ibn al-Zubayr, Abū ʿAbd Allāh (870) iii, **976b** – III, **1001a**
Ibn al-Zubayr, Abū Djaʿfar (1308) iii, 762b, **976a** – III, 785b, **1000b**
Ibn Zuhr iii, **976b**; iv, 289b; s, 392b – III, **1001a**; IV, 302b; S, 393a
Ibn Zuhr, Abu 'l-ʿAlāʾ (1130) iii, 850a, **976b** – III, 873b, **1001a**
Ibn Zuhr, Abū Bakr Muḥammad (1198) iii, **978b**; vii, 811b – III, **1003a**; VII, 813b
Ibn Zuhr, Abū Marwān (1161) i, 162a; ii, 481b; iii, 910b, **977b**; vi, 590b; viii, 652b – I, 166b; II, 494a; III, 935a, **1002a**; VI, 575b; VIII, 672a
Ibn Zuknūn i, 273b – I, 282a
Ibn Zūlāk (Zawlāk), Abū Muḥammad (996) iii, **979a**; vii, 164a, 487b; viii, 42b – III, **1003b**; VII, 165b, 487b; VIII, 43b
Ibn Zumruk → Ibn Zamrak
Ibn Zurʿa (1008) iii, **979b**; s, 398b – III, **1004a**; S, 398b
Ibnou-Zekri → Ibn Zakrī
Ibo → Nigeria/-e
ʿIbra iv, 557a, b, 1031b, 1038a – IV, 581b, 1063b, 1069b
Ibrā (ʿUmān) s, 355b, 356a – S, 355a, 356a
Ibrā (al-Sharkiyya) ix, 356b – IX, 358a
Ibrādism(e) iv, 739b – IV, 769b
Ibrāhīm (Abraham) i, 177a, 315b; ii, 280a, 1106a; iii, 37a, 165a, **980a**; iv, 184a, b, 318a, b, 956a, b, 959a-b; v, 20a, 421a, 423b, 550b; vi, 105b, 144b, 218b, 566a, 645a, 738a; ix, 383a, b; s, 317a – I, 182a, 325b; II, 288b, 1132a; III, 38b, 168b, **1004b**; IV, 192a, b, 332a, 333a, 989a, b, 988a-b; V, 20b, 423a, 425b, 555b; VI, 103b, 143a, 202b, 550b, 630a, 727a; IX, 386b; S, 316b
Ubrāhīm I (Aghlabid(e)) (812) i, 24a, 247b, 248a, 250a; iii, 233a, **981b**, 1032a; iv, 827a; vi, 133b, 295a; ix, 684a – I, 24b, 255b, 257b; III, 240a, **1006a**, 1058a; IV, 860a; VI, 131b, 280b; IX, 606b
Ibrāhīm II, Aḥmad b. Muḥammad (Aghlabid(e)) (902) i, 24a, 248b, 249a, 250b, 619b; iii, 297b, **892b**; iv, 275b, 337a; v, 105a, 777b; vii, 11a; s, 1a – I, 25a, 256a,b, 258a, 639b; III, 306b, **1006b**; IV, 287b, 351b; V, 107b, 783b; VII, 11b; S, 1a
Ibrāhīm (Ghaznavid(e)) → Ibrāhīm b. Masʿūd
Ibrāhīm (Karamānid(e)) (1451) vi, 978a – VI, 970b
Ibrāhīm (Ottoman) (1648) iii, 623a, **983a**; iv, 884b; v, 272b; vi, 202b, 345b – III, 643b, **1007b**; IV, 917b; V, 270b; VI, 186b, 330a
Ibrāhīm (Ṣafawid(e)) (1447) viii, 766a – VIII, 791b
Ibrāhīm (Umayyad(e)) i, 57b, 1244a – I, 59b, 1282a
Ibrāhtm, al-Malik al-Manṣūr → Ibrāhīm b. Shīrkūh
Ubrāhīm, Sultan, Dār Fūr → Ibrāhīm b. Muḥammad Ḥusayn
Ibrāhīm b. ʿAbd Allāh b. al-Ḥasan b. al-Ḥasan (ʿAlid(e)) (762) i, 45b, 103b, 123a, 402b, 952a, 1080a; iii, 616a, **983b**; vi, 263b, 334a, 428a; vii, 114b, 305b, 306a, 358b, 359b, 388b, 784a, 1043b; s, 48b, 130a – I, 46b, 106b, 126b, 414a, 981b, 1112b; III, 636b, **1008a**; VI, 248a, 318b, 413a; VII, 116b, 307b, 308a, 361a, 362a, 389b, 785b, 1046a; S, 48b, 129a
Ibrāhīm b. ʿAbd Allāh b. Yazīd b. al-Muhallab (IX) vii, 360a – VII, 362b
Ibrāhīm b. ʿAbd al-Djalīl (vizier) (XIV) vi, 441a – VI, 426b
Ibrāhīm b. ʿAbd al-Wāḥid iii, 843a – III, 866b
Ibrāhtm b. Abī Ḥātim Aḥmad al-ʿAzafī s, 112b – S, 112a
Ibrāhīm b. Abi 'l-Haytham (XI) vii, 773a – VII, 774b
Ibrāhīm b. Abī Salama s, 62a – S, 62b
Ibrāhīm b. Abi 'l-Khayr iv, 310a – IV, 324a
Ibrāhīm b. Adham (777) i, 274a; ii, 36b; iii, 843a, **985b**; viii, 892b – I, 282b; II, 37a; III, 867a, **1010a**; VIII, 923a
Ibrāhīm b. Aḥmad (Aghlabid amīr) (962) vi, 453a; vii, 76a; ix, 396a – VI, 438a; VII, 77a; IX, 408b
Ibrāhīm b. Aḥmad (Ṣamānid(e))(X) viii, 110a – VIII, 112a
Ibrāhīm b. ʿAlāʾ al-Dawla b. Bāysonghor i, 147b – I, 152a

Ibrāhīm b. ʿAlī → al-Shīrāzī
Ibrāhīm b. ʿAlī b. Ḥasan al-Saḳḳāʾ (1881) iii, 250a, **986b** – III, 257a, **1011a**
Ibrāhīm b. ʿAlī b. ʿĪsā i, 387b – I, 398b
Ibrāhīm b. al-Ashʿar → Ibn al-Sarrādj
Ibrāhīm b. al-Ashtar al-Naj (691) i, 50b, 76b; iii, 620b, **987a**; iv, 1186b; vi, 623a – I, 52a, 78b, 79a; III, 641a, **1011b**; IV, 1219a; VI, 608a
Ibrāhīm b. al-Ashtar al-Nakhaʿt (691) vii, 522a, 650b – VII, 522b, 650a
Ibrāhīm b. Ayyūb ii, 79b – II, 81a
Ibrāhīm b. Benyāmīn, Shaykh (Malāmī) (XVI) vi, 228a – VI, 222a
^brāhīm b. Bughāmardī iv, 494a – IV, 515a
Ibrāhīm b. Dhakwān al-Ḥarrānī (VIII) iii, **987b** – III, **1012a**
Inrāhīm b. Djalāl al-Dīn Aḥsan iii, 225a – III, 232a
Ibrāhīm b. Djibrīl iv, 356b – IV, 372a
Ibrāhīm b. al-Fakhkhār al-Yahūdī viii, 813b – VIII, 841a
Ibrāhīm b. Ghurāb (Miṣr) (XV) vii, 172a, 176b – VII, 174a, 178a
Ibrāhīm b. al-Ḥadjdjādj (911) iv, 822a; vi, 899a – IV, 855a; VI, 890a
Ibrāhīm b. Ḥammād (935) s, **385a** – S, **385b**
Ibrāhīm b. Haydar b. Djunayd (Ṣafawid(e)) (XV) viii, 766b – VIII, 792a
Ibrāhīm b. Hilāl → al-Ṣābīʾ
Ibrāhīm b. Hishām b. Ismāʿīl vi, 139b – VI, 137b
Ibrāhīm b. Ḥusām al-Dīn Ḥasan (Marʿash) (XIII) vi, 507b – VI, 492b
Ibrāhīm b. ʿĪsā Khān Tarkhān I (1558) vi, 189b, 190a – VI, 173b, 174a
—Ibrāhīm b. Ismāʿīl al-Aṭrash ii, 637a – II, 653a
Ibrāhīm b. Ismāʿīl b. Yasār iv, 190a – IV, 198a
Ibrāhīm b. Ḳarātakīn ii, 1110a – II, 1136a
Ibrāhīm b. Ḳays i, 1283a – I, 1321b
Ibrāhīm b. Khālid → Abū Thawr
Ibrāhīm b. al-Mahdī (ʿAbbāsid(e)) (839) i, 272a, 1312b; ii, 731a, 1072a; iii, 745b, 767b, 872b, **987b**, 996b; iv, 17a, 940a; v, 69b; vi, 205b, 335a, b, 336a; vii, 404a, 518b; s, 64a – I, 280a, 1352b; II, 749b, 1097a; III, 768a,b, 790b, 896b, **1012a**, 1021a; IV, 18b, 973a; V, 71b; VI, 190a, 319b, 320a; VII, 405a, 518b; S, 64b
Ibrāhīm b. Mālik → Ibrāhīm b. al-Ashtar
Ibrāhīm b. Marzubān (Musāfirid(e)) (983) ii, 680a; vi, 499b; vii, 636b; x, 897b – II, 697a; VI, 484b; VII, 656a; X,
Ibrāhīm b. Masʿūd II (Ghaznawid(e)) (1099) ii, 5a, 1052a, 1100a; iv, 942b; v, 622b; vi, 273b, 274a; vii, 193a; s, 21a – II, 5a, 1076a, 1126a; IV, 957b; V, 626b; VI, 258b; VII, 193b; S, 21a
Ibrāhīm b. al-Mudabbir → Ibn al-Mudabbir
Ibrāhīm b. Muhādjir iv, 667b – IV, 694b
Ibrāhīm b. Muḥammad (632) vi, 575a, 650b; vii, 374b – VI, 560a, 636a; VII, 376a
Ibrāhīm b. Muḥammad b. Abī ʿAwn (934) vii, 397b – VII, 398b
Ibrāhīm b. Muḥammad b. ʿAlī, al-Imām (749) i, 15b, 16a, 141a; iii, **988a**; iv, 446b; vi, 332b, 333a, 334b, 620b; vii, 396a – I, 16a, b, 145a; III, **1012b**; IV, 466b; VI, 317a, b, 319a, 605b; VII, 397b
Ibrāhīm b. Muḥammad b. Fahd al-Makramī iv, 201a – IV, 210a
Ibrāhīm b. Muḥammad b. Ṭalḥa (VII) vii, 522a – VII, 522a
Ibrāhīm b. Muḥammad ʿAlī Pasha (1848) vi, 541b; ix, 903b – VI, 526b; IX, 941b
Ibrāhīm b. Muḥammad al-Fazārī (804) ii, 36b – II, 37b
Ibrāhīm b. Muḥammad Ḥusayn i, 929b; ii, 123b – I, 957b; II, 126b
Ubrāhīm b. Muḥammad Ẓāfir al-Madanī v, 949a – V, 953a
Ibrāhīm b. Mūsā iii, 262b – III, 270a
Ibrāhīm b. Mūsā al-Kāẓim (IX) vi, 148a, 334b; s, 95a – VI, 146b, 319a; S, 94b
Ibrāhīm b. Muzayn i, 600a – I, 619b
Ibrāhīm b. Naṣr (X) vii, 477b – VII, 477a
Inrāhīm b. Sahl → Ibn Sahl
Ibrāhīm b. Sayāba (809) iii, **989a** – III, **1013b**
Ibrāhīm (Sayyid) b. Sayyid Muḥammad (Bayhaḳī) s, 131b – S, 131a
Ibrāhīm b. Shāhrukh (1435) iii, 337a, b, **989a**; iv, 221b – III, 347b, **1014a**; IV, 231a
Ibrāhīm b. Shīrkūh (1246) iii, 399b, **989b** – III, 412a, **1014a**
Ibrāhīm b. Sīmdjūr (X) viii, 110a, 1027b – VIII, 112a, 1062b
Ibrāhīm b. Sinān (X) vii, 405a; viii, 560b; x, 428b – VII, 406b; VIII, 578b; X, 459a
Ibrāhīm b. al-Sindī iii, **990a** – III, **1014b**
Ibrāhīm b. al-Sindī b. Shahāk (IX) vii, 259a – VII, 260b
Ibrāhīm b. Sulaymān al-Shāmī → al-Shāmī
Ibrāhīm b. ʿUmar al-Biḳāʿī al-Shāfiʿī iv, 92a – IV, 96a
Ibrāhīm b. al-Walīd I (Umayyad(e)) (750) iii, **990b**; vi, 623b, 624a – III, **1015a**; VI, 608b, 609a
Ibrāhīm b. Yaḥyā (800) ix, 182a – IX, 188a
Ibrāhīm b. Yaʿḳūb al-Isrāʾīlī al-Ṭurṭūshī (X) i, 157a; iii, **991a**, 1045a; v, 719a, 1012b, 1013a, 1014a; viii, 875a; s, 170b – I, 161b; III, **1015b**, 1071a; V, 724b, 1008a, 1009a, 1010a; VIII, 904b; S, 171a
Ibrāhīm b. Yūsuf b. Tāshufīn ii, 838a; iii, 728a, 822b, 977b – II, 857b; III, 750b, 846a, 1002a
Ibrāhīm ʿĀdil Shāh I i, 199a; iii, 15b, 426a, 626a, 1160b, 1161a; v, 1216a – I, 205a; III, 16a, 439b, 646b, 1189a,b; V, 1205b
Ibrāhīm ʿĀdil Shāh II (1627) i, 199b, 781b, 1200a, 1202b, 1203a,b, 1204a; ii, 921b, 922a; iii, 15b, 426b, 453b; v, 1216a; vi, 271b; vii, 341a – I, 205a, 804b, 1235b, 1238a,b, 1239b; II, 943a; III, 16a, 440b, 469b; V, 1205b; VI, 256a; VII, 343a
Ivrāhīm Agha → Kečiboynuzu Ibrāhīm Pasha
Ibrāhīm Āghā Mustaḥfiẓān iv, 431a – IV, 450a
Ibrāhīm Agha, Zurnazenbashî (XVII) vi, 1007b – VI, 999b
Ibrāhīm al-Aḥdab (1891) iii, **991b**; vi, 113b, 913b; s, 40a, 161a – III, **1016b**; VI, 111a, 905a; S, 40a, 160b
Ibrāhīm Aḥmad Barzānī (XX) vii, 714a – 715a
Inrāhīm al-ʿAwwānī (1320) vi, 353b; s, 172b – VI, 337b; S, 173b
Ibrāhīm al-Bādjūrī → Bādjūrī
Ibrāhīm Bahādur b. Meḥmed i, 783b; ii, 599a – I, 806b; II, 613b
Ibrāhīm Bayyūd (XX) viii, 902b – VIII, 933b
Ibrāhīm Beg (Tādjīk) (XX) iii, 483b – III, 500b
Ibrāhīm Beg b. Orkhān Beg (Menteshe) (1360) vi, 1018b – VI, 1011a
Ibrāhīm Beg Ḳarāmān-oghlu iv, 623b, 624a; v, 677a – IV, 648b; V, 682a
Ibrāhīm Bey (Faḳārī, Miṣr) (XVII) vii, 178b – VII, 180b
Ibrāhīm Bey (Tunis) iii, 605a; iv, 828b – III, 625b; IV, 861a
Ibrāhīm Bey Isfendiyār-oghlu iv, 108b – IV, 113b
Ibrāhīm Bey al-Kabīr (1816) iii, **992a**; iv, 853a; vi,

325b; vii, 179a, 420b – III, **1016b**; IV, 886a; VI, 310a; VII, 181a, 422a
Ibrāhīm al-Dasūḳī → al-Dasūḳī
Ibrāhīm Derwish Pasha (1896) ii, 878b; iii, **992b** – II, 899a; III, **1017b**
Ibrāhīm al-Djazzār i, 551a – I, 568b
Ibrāhīm Edhem Pasha (1893) i, 285b; iii, **993a** – I, 294b; III, **1017b**
Ibrāhīm Fūda (XX) vi, 175b – VI, 162a
Ibrāhīm Gulshenī → Gulshanī
Inrāhīm Ḥaḳḳī Pasha (1918) ii, 533b; iii, **993b**, 1188b; vi, 74a; vii, 547b – II, 546b; III, **1018b**, 1218b; VI, 72a; VII, 547b
Ibrāhīm al-Ḥalabī → al-Ḥalabī
Ibrāhīm al-Ḥāmidī → al-Ḥāmidī
Ibrāhīm al-Ḥarbī (898) i, 718a; iii, **994b**; s, 304b – I, 739b; III, **1019a**; S, 304a
Ibrāhīm al-Hāshīmī, Sharīf iv, 919b – IV, 952b
Ibrāhīm Ḥilmī Pasha → Kečiboynuzu Ibrāhīm Ḥilmī
Ibrāhīm Ḥusayn Mīrzā (Mirzās, Gudjarāt) iv, 666a; vii, 133a, 134a – IV, 693a; VII, 135a, 136a
Ibrāhīm al-Imām → Ibrāhīm b. Muḥammad b. ʿAlī
Ibrāhīm Ināl i, 420a, 512b, 1074a; ii, 5a; iii, 258b; iv, 26b, 466a, 807a; v, 388a, 454a, 489a – I, 432a, 528b, 1106a; II, 5a; III, 266a; IV, 28b, 486b, 839b; V, 389a, 456b, 492a
Ibrāhīm Kāhya → al-Ḳāzdughlī, Ibrāhīm
Ubrāhīm Karāma s, 162b – S, 162b
Ibrāhīm Ḳaṭārāghāsī iii, 88b – III, 90b
Ibrāhīm Katkhudā (1754) i, 391b – I, 402b
Ibrāhīm al-Khalīl → Ibrāhīm (Abraham)
Ibrāhīm Khalīl Khān iv, 573a – IV, 595b, 596a
Ibrāhīm Khān (1585) iii, **995a** – III, **1019b**
Ibrāhīm Khān (Ḳazān) iv, 849a – IV, 882a
Ibrāhīm Khān, Ẓahīr al-Dawla v, 155b, 164b – V, 156a, 162a
Ibrāhīm Khān b. Aḥmad iv, 581b – IV, 604b
Ibrāhīm Khān Avar i, 755b – I, 778a
Ibrājīm Khān Fatḥ Djang (Bihār) (1617) vi, 410a – VI, 395a
Ibrāhīm Khān Kākar (XVII) vi, 410a – VI, 395a
Ibrāhīm Khān Sūr (Bengal(e)) (1534) ii, 271b; vi, 47a-II, 279b; VI, 45b
Ibrāhīm Khan Zangana v, 169b – V, 167a
Ibrāhīm Khān-zāde iii, 995a – III, 1019b
Ibrāhīm Khāṣṣ Oda-Bashi̊ -→ Ibrāhīm Pasha (Maḳbul)
Ibrāhīm al-Khawwāṣ (963) x. 377b – X, 404b
Ibrāhīm Ḳuṭb Shāh v, 550a – V, 555a
Ibrāhīm Lōdī (Delhi) (1526) i, 252b, 848a, 1068b; ii, 271a; iii, 168a, 420b, **995a**; v, 784a; viii, 253b; s, 203a, 331b – I, 260b, 871b, 1101a; II, 279a; III, 172a, 434a, **1020a**; V, 790a; VIII, 255b; S, 202b, 331a
Ibrāhīm al-Mawṣilī (804) i, 10b, 107b, 108a, 118a; iii, 749b, 989a, **996a**; iv, 822a; vii, 518a, 563a; s, 17b, 64a, 116b, 128a, 183a –
I, 10b, 110b, 111a, 121b; III, 772b, 1013b, **1020b**; IV, 855a; VII, 518b, 564b; S, 18a, 64b, 116a, 127b, 184b
Ibrāhīm al-Māzinī s, 57b – S, 58a
Ibrāhīm Mīrzā b. Sulaymān Mīrzā (1560) vii, 135a – VII, 137a
Ibrāhīm Mīrzā (Ṣafawid(e)) (1517) viii, 1212a – VIII, 1248a
Ibrāhīm Mīrzā b. Bahrām Shāh (Ṣafawid(e)) (1568) viii, 775b – VIII, 801b
Ibrāhīm, Muḥammad al-Bashīr (1965) iii, **1003b**; iv, 158b – III, **1028b**; IV, 1661
Ibrāhīm al-Mūsawī s, 423a – S, 423b
Ibrāhīm Mussu → Karamoko Alfa
Ibrāhīm Müteferriḳa (1745) i, 63b, 270a, 1271b; ii, 589b, 704b; iii, **996b**; v, 641b; vi, 800a –
I, 65a, 278a,b, 1310b; II, 604a, 722b; III, **1021b**; V, 645b; VI, 790a
Ibrāhīm Naʿīm al-Dīn ii, 990b – II, 1013a
Ibrāhīm al-Nakhaʿī (714) ii, 888a,b; iii, 512a; v, 350b, 731a, b; vi, 925b; vii, 258b – II, 908b, 909b; III, 529b; V, 351b, 736a, b; VI, 917b; VII, 260a
Inrāhīm Nasir (Maldives) vi, 246a – VI, 230a
Ibrāhīm Pasha → Khodja; Shāḳshāḳī; Shayṭān
Ibrāhīm Pasha (Maḳbūl) (1536) i, 293b; ii, 400a, 722b, 884b, 1042b, 1136a; iii, **998a**, 1183b; iv, 333b, 1137b; v, 650a; vi, 759a; vii, 177b, 225a, 713a; viii, 202b; ix, 833b; s, 315b –
I, 302b; II, 410b, 741a, 904b, 1067a, 1163b; III, **1023a**, 1213a; IV, 348a, 1169a; V, 654a; VI, 748a; VII, 179a, 226b, 714a; VIII, 206a; IX, 818b; S, 315b
Ibrāhīm Pasha (al-Mawṣil) (XIX) vi, 542a – VI, 526b
Ibrāhīm Pasha, Ḥādjdjī iv, 594b – IV, 618b
IbrāhīmPasha, Ḳarā (1687) iii, **1001b** – III, **1026b**
Ibrāhīm Pasha b. Khalīl Djandarli̊ → Djandarli̊
Ibrāhīm Pasha b. Muḥammad ʿAlī Pasha (1848) i, 182b, 244a, 341b, 399a, 975a, 1079a, 1134a, 1138a, 1234a; ii, 38b, 108b, 288a,b, 321a,b, 514a, 636a, 912a; iii, 89a, 300a, 326b, 400a, 628b, **999a**; iv, 130b, 609b, 717b, 765a, 925b; v, 36a, 322b, 335a, 539b, 1253b; vi, 75a, 232a, 508b, 778a; vii, 182b, 217b, 241a, 515a; viii, 84b, 484b –
I, 188a, 251a, 352a, 410a, 1005b, 1111b, 1168b, 1172b, 1271a; II, 39a, 111a, 296a,b, 330b, 331a, 526b, 652a, 933b; III, 91b, 309a, 336b, 412b, 649b, **1024a**; IV, 136a, 634a, 746a, 795b, 958b; V, 37a, 321b, 335b, 543b, 1244b; VI, 73a, 226a, 494a, 767b; VII, 182b, 219a, 242a, 515b; VIII, 86b, 501a
Ibrāhīm Pasha al-ʿAẓm (XVI) v, 591b, 925b – V, 595b, 930b
Ibrāhīm Pasha Dāmād (1601) i, 270b, 826b; ii, 20a, 34a, 49a, 103b, 634b; iii, 342b, **1000b**; iv, 233b; vi, 800b – I, 279a, 849a; II, 20b, 35a, 50a, 105b, 651a; III, 352b, **1025b**; IV, 244a; VI, 790a
Ibrāhīm Pasha Katkhudā i, 68b – I, 70a
Ibrāhīm Pasha Millī v, 463a – V, 465b
Ibrāhīm Pasha Nevshehirli (1730) i, 269b, 270a, 836b, 1004b; ii, 20a; iii, 997b, **1002a**; iv, 969b; v, 641a, b, 642a, b, 643a, b; vi, 55b, 1005a; viii, 11a –
I, 277b, 278a, 859b, 1035a; II, 20a; III, 1022b, **1027a**; IV, 1001b; V, 645b, 646a, 647a, b; VI, 53b, 997b; VIII, 11b
Ibrāhīm Pasha Ṭawīl i, 236b; vi, 112b – I, 244a; VI, 110a
Ibrāhīm Pečewī → Pečewī
Ibrāhīm Pūr-i Dāwūd iv, 71a – IV, 75a
Ibrāhīm al-Rashīd al-Duwayḥī (1874) vii, 124a; viii, 990a; s, 279a – VII, 126a; VIII, 1024b; S, 278b
Ibrāhīm Rawḍa (Bīdjāpūr) vi, 126a – VI, 124a
Ibrāhīm al-Riyānī (1849) x, 468a – X, 498b
Ibrāhīm al-Ṣābiʾ s, 398b – S, 398b
Ibrāhīm al-Sadjīnī s, 44b – S, 44b
Ibrāhīm Sālār iii, 703b – III, 725b
Ibrāhīm Ṣāliḥ b. Yūnis al-Ḥusaynī (XX) x, 464b – X, 498b
Ibrāhīm Shāh Sharḳī (Djawnpūr) (1440) i, 702b, 859a, 1300a; ii, 51b, 180b, 499a; iii, 14b, 419a, **1003a**; iv, 513a; vi, 61b, 294b; vii, 278b, 279a; s, 206b –
I, 724a, 883a, 1340a; II, 52b, 186b, 511b; III, 15a, 432b, **1028a**; IV, 535a; VI, 59b, 279b; VII, 280b; S, 206a
Ibrāhīm al-Sharīf → Ibrāhīm Bey (Tunis)
Ibrāhīm Shāshī s, 50b – S, 51a
Ibrāhīm al-Shāṭibī iv, 381b – IV, 398b
Ibrāhīm Shināsī → Shināsī

Ibrāhīm Shīrāzī, Ḥādjdjī (1801) s, **405b** – S, **405b**
Ibrāhīm Sori Maudo ii, 942a, 960a, 1132a – II, 963b, 982a, 1159a
Ibrāhīm al-Ṣūlī (857) x, 129a – X, 139b
Ibrāhīm Tamghač Khān iii, 1114a,b, 1115b; iv, 200a – III, 1141b, 1142a, 1143a; IV, 209a
Ibrāhīm Temo ii, 430b – II, 441b
Ibrāhīm al-Yāzidjī → al-Yāzidjī
Ibrāhīm Yināl → Ibrāhīm Ināl
Ibrahimu Dabo iv, 549a – IV, 573a
Ibrail iii, **1004a** – III, **1029a**
ʿIbrī → Yahūd
ʿIbrī iii, **1004b** – III, **1029b**
Ibrīḳ v, 989a; s, **406a** – V, 984b; S, **406a**
Ibrīm → Ḳaṣr Ibrīm
Ibrīm (Piromi) s, 35b – S, 36a
Ibrishīm, Ibrisīm → Ḥarīr
ʿIbriyyūn iii, 1004b – III, 1029b
Ibruh i, 487b, 489a; iii, **1005a** – I, 502a, 503b; III, **1030a**
al-Ibshīhī, Aḥmad iii, 1006a – III, 1031a
al-Ibshīhī, Bahā al-Dīn (1446) ii, 536b; iii, 392a, **1005a**; vi, 115a, 823b, 904b; s, 350a – II, 549b; III, 404b, **1030b**; VI, 112b, 814a, 896a; S, 350a
al-Ibshīhī, Shihāb al-Dīn iii, 1006a – III, 1031a
Ibshīr Muṣṭafā Pasha → Ipshir Muṣṭafā Pasha
Ibtidāʾ iii, **1006a**; iv, 152a, 264a – III, **1031a**; IV, 158b, 276a
Ibuḳrāṭ(īs) → Buḳrāṭ
Ibyār (Djazīrat Banī Naṣr) vi, 453b – VI, 439a
Ič-oghlanî i, 394a, 395a; ii, 1087b, 1088b; iii, **1006b** – I, 405b, 406b; II, 1113a, 1114a; III, **1031b**
Ičil ii, 34b; iii, **1006b**; iv, 617a – II, 35b; III, **1031b**; IV, 641b
Içoglan → Ič-oghlanî
ʿĪd iii, **1007a**; v, 477a – III, **1032b**; V, 479b
ʿĪd al-aḍḥā i, 1b; iii, **1007b** – I, 1b; III, **1033a**
ʿĪd al-fiṭr iii, **1008a**; v, 714b – III, **1033a**; V, 720a
ʿĪd al-ghadīr iv, 1110b – IV, 1142a
ʿĪd al-kabīr → ʿĪd al-aḍḥā
ʿĪd-i Ḳurbān iv, 103b – IV, 108b
al-ʿĪd, Muḥammad iv, 159b – IV, 166b
al-ʿIdāda → al-Asturlāb
Iʿdādiyye i, 285b – I, 294a
al-Īdadjfaghī, Awfā b. Abū Bakr (1883) vii, 622b – VII, 622b
Iḍāfa → Nisba
Iḍāfa iii, **1008a** – III, **1033a**
Iḍam → Ḥamḍ, Wādī al-
Iʿdām → Ḳatl
Īdar ii, 1128a; iii, **1010a**; vi, 51a – II, 1154b; III, **1035a**; VI, 49a
ʿIdda i, 28a, 172b; iii, **1010b**; iv, 253b – I, 28b, 177b; III, **1036a**; IV, 265a
Iddī, Āl s, 269a – S, 268b
Iddighām → Idghām
Idfū → Adfū
Idghām iii, **1013a** – III, **1038b**
Idgish v, 254a – V, 251b
Idgü Bahādur Barlās v, 163b – V, 161a
Idhāʿa iii, **1014a** – III, **1039a**
Īdhadj (Māl-Amīr) iii, **1015b**; iv, 675b; v, 826b, 827a, 830b; vi, 494b – III, **1041a**; IV, 703a; V, 832b, 833b, 836b; VI, 480a
Idhkhir iv, 322a – IV, 336a
ʿIdī (Mahra) vi, 83b – VI, 81a
Idi Amin x, 780b – X,
Idil → Itil (river/rivière)
Idhn i, 429b; iii, **1016a**, 1181b – I, 442a; III, **1041b**, 1210b
Idhnnāme i, 679a – I, 700a
Idi Amin x, 780b
Idibaʾil i, 525a – I, 541a
Īdjāb i, 1111b; iii, **1017a** – I, 1145a; III, **1042b**
Idjār, idjāra iii, **1017a**; v, 126b – III, **1042b**; V, 129a
Idjāra iii, **1017b** – III, **1043a**
Iʿdjāz i, 858a, 958b, 981b; iii, **1018a**; v, 426b, 427a – I, 881b, 988a, 1012a; III, **1044a**; V, 428b, 429a
Idjāza i, 66a, 90b, 96a, 142b, 319b, 817a; ii, 304a; iii, 27a, 491a, **1020b**; iv, 412b, 634a, 950b, 1125b; v, 1125a, 1132b – I, 68a, 93b, 99a, 146b, 329a, 840a; II, 312b; III, 28b, 508a, **1046b**; IV, 430b, 660b, 983a, 1157a; V, 1121b, 1128a
Idjāza → Ḥadjdj
Idjdhāb iv, 95a – IV, 99a
al-Īdjī, ʿAḍud al-Dīn (1355) i, 342b, 593a, 715a, 715b; ii, 608a, 774a; iii, **1022a**, 1176a; iv, 737a; vi, 218a, 848a; vii, 480b; viii, 45a – I, 353a, 612a, 736b, 737a; II, 623a, 792b; III, **1047b**, 1205a; IV, 767a; VI, 202b, 839a; VII, 480a; VIII, 95b
Idjil i, 809a – I, 832a
ʿIdjl Banū i, 963b, 964b; iii, **1022b**; vi, 441b – I, 993b, 994a; III, **1048b**; VI, 427a
ʿIdjl b. Ludjaym s, 122a – S, 121b
al-ʿIdjlī → Abu ʾl-Nadjm; al-Aghlab; al-Ḳāsim b. ʿĪsā
al-ʿIdjlī, Abu ʾl-Aḥwaṣ ʿUmar b. al-Aḥwaṣ (759) vi, 946a – VI, 938b
al-ʿIdjlī, Abū Dulaf → al-Ḳāsim b. ʿĪsā
al-ʿIdjlī, Abū Manṣūr (738) i, 1099a; ii, 1094a; vi, **441b**; vii, 347b, 398b, 459b – I, 1132a; II, 1120a; VI, **427a**; VII, 349b, 400a, 459b
al-ʿIdjlī, Aḥmad b. ʿAbd Allāh (875) viii, 516a – VIII, 533b
al-ʿIdjlī, Asʿad b. Masʿūd b. Khalaf (1203) vi, 914a – VI, 905b
al-ʿIdjlī, Harūn b. Saʿīd ii, 377b; s, 130a – II, 387b; S, 129a
al-ʿIdjlī, al-Madhʿūr b. ʿAdī (VII) vii, 796b – VII, 798b
al-ʿIdjlī, al-Mughīra b. Saʿīd Ghālī (737) i, 141a, 1099a, 1116b; ii, 1094a; iv, 926b; vi, 441b; vii, 399a; s, 103b, 232b – I, 145a, 1132a, 1150b; II, 1120a; IV, 959b; VI, 427a; VII, 400a; S, 103a, 232b
ʿIdjliyya s, 130a – S, 129a
Idjmāʿ i, 259b, 1199b; ii, 182b, 411b, 888b; iii, **1023a**, 1061b; iv, 154a; v, 239a – I, 267b, 1235a; II, 188a, 422a, 909a; III, **1048b**, 1088a; IV, 160b; V, 237a
Idjnāwn ii, 369a – II, 379a
Idjtihād i, 259b, 276a; iii, 954a, 1025b, **1026a**; iv, 152b-154a, 1101a; v, 241a – I, 267b, 284b; III, 978b, 1051a, **1052a**; IV, 159a-160a, 1132a; V, 239a
Idjtimāʿ → Istiḳbāl
Idjtimāʿ iv, 259a; v, 577b – IV, 270b; V, 582a
al-Idkawī, ʿAbd Allāh (1770) vi, 112b – VI, 110b
Iḍmār iii, **1027b** – III, **1053b**
Idrāk iii, **1028a** – III, **1054a**
Idrākī Bēglārī (XVII) iii, **1029b** – III, **1055b**
Idrīs (the hidden/le caché) vi, 227b, 228a – VI, 221a, b, 222a
Idrīs (prophet(e)) iii, **1030b**; vi, 412b, 651a; viii, 387a – III, **1056b**; VI, 397a, 636b; VIII, 460b
Idrīs, Mawlāy → Idris II b. Idrīs
Idrīs (nāʾib) (Maṣawwaʿ) vi, 627b – VI, 628a
Idrīs, Suhayl v, 191b – V, 188b
Idrīs, Yūsuf v, 191a, b – V, 188b – I (al-Akbar) b. ʿAbd Allāh (Idrīsid(e)) (793) i, 402b, 1037a, 1175b; ii, 745a, 818a, 874a; iii, 616b, 617a, **1031a**; v, 1175a,

1189a; vi, 140b, 742b, 815b; vii, 389b; s, 103a –
I, 414a, 1068b, 1210b; II, 763b, 837b, 894a; III,
637b, **1057a**; V, 1165a, 1179a; VI, 138b, 731b, 805b;
VII, 390b; S, 102b

Idrīs II (al-Aṣg̲h̲ar) b. Idrīs I (Idrīsid(e)) (828) i,
1088a; ii, 818a, 874a; iii, **1031b**; v, 1189a, 1200a,
1201a; vi, 742b; s, 103a –
I, 1120a; II, 837b, 894a; III, **1057b**; V, 1179a, 1190a,
1191b; VI, 731b; S, 102b

Idrīs II al-ʿAlī (Ḥammūdid(e)) (1055) vi, 222a – VI,
216a

Idrīs I al-Sanūsī (1982) (Lybia/-e) i, 1049b, 1071b; ii,
667b; iv, 262a; v, 697a, 758a, b, 1066a; vi, 262a; ix,
24a –
I, 1081b, 1103b; II, 684a; IV, 274a; V, 701b, 764a,
1063b; VI, 246b; IX, 25b

Idrīs b. Abī Ḥafṣa vi, 625b – VI, 610b

Idrīs b. Aḥmad al-Ḥabūd̲ī s, 338b – S, 338a

Idrīs b. ʿAlī → al-Ḥans̲h̲

Idrīs b. ʿAlī b. Ḥammūd (Ḥammūdid(e)) (1039) vi,
222a – VI, 216a

Idrīs b. Bā Ḥmād s, 114a – S, 113b

Idis b. al-Ḥasan, ʿImād al-Dīn (1468) s, **407a** –
S, **407a**

Idrīs b. al-Ḥusayn, S̲h̲arīf (1625) s, **407b** –
S, **407b**

Idrīs b. Muḥammad al-Arbāb ii, 944a – II, 966a

Idrīs Alooma (Alawōma) iv, 567b; s, 164a –
IV, 589b; S, 163b

Idrīs Atuma i, 1259b – I, 1298a

Idrīs Bidlīsī → Bidlīsī

Idrīs ʿImād al-Dīn (1468) x, 403b – X, 432a

Idrīs al-Maʾmūn, Abu ʾl-ʿUlā (Almohad(e)) (1232) i,
1176b; iii, 207b; iv, 116a, 117b; vi, 592b, 593a,
595b –
I, 1211b; III, 213a; IV, 121b, 122b; VI, 577b, 580b

Idrīs al-Mutaʾayyid (Malaga) (1039) x, 144b – X, 155a

al-Idrīsī, Abū ʿAbd Allāh (1166) i, 157a, 168a, 214a,
488a, 594a, 602b, 1337b; ii, 578a, 582a, 585a; iii, 7a,
405a, **1032b**, 1077a; iv, 274b, 1080b; vi, 283a, 350b,
639b, 640a; vii, 245b; ix, 589b; s, 92a, 171a, 376b –
I, 161b, 172b, 220b, 503a, 613b, 622a, 1377b; II,
592b, 596b, 599b; III, 7a, 418a, **1058b**, 1103b; IV,
286b, 1111b; VI, 268a, 334b, 624b, 625a; VII, 247a;
IX, 612a; S, 91b, 171a, 376b

al-Idrīsī, Abū D̲jaʿfar, S̲h̲arīf (1251) vi, 411a, 412b;
viii, 428a, 895a; s, 123b – VI, 396a, 397b; VIII, 442a,
926a; S, 123a

al-Idrīsī, D̲jamāl al-Dīn s, **407b** – S, **407b**

al-Idrīsī, Muḥammad b. ʿAlī i, 98b, 277b, 709b; ii,
518a; v, 758a, 808b, 809a –
I, 101a, 286a, 731a; II, 531a; V, 763b, 814b, 815a

Idrīsid(e)s i, 156b, 403a, 1044a; ii, 145b, 818a, 821a,
853a, 1095b; iii, 30b, **1035b**; iv, 632a, b; vi, 134a,
712b –
I, 161a, 414b, 1076a; II, 149b, 837b, 840b, 872b,
1121b; III, 32a, **1061a**; IV, 657b; VI, 132a, 701a

Idrīsiyya i, 87b, 277b, 555a, 709b – I, 101a, 286a, 672b,
731a

Id̲tirār iii, **1037a** – III, **1063a**

Iduḵ Ḵut i, 1240a,b – I, 1278a

ʿIdwa s, 408a – S, 408b

al-ʿIdwī al-Ḥamzāwī, Ḥasan (1885) v, 1237a; s, **408a**
– V, 1228a; S, **408b**

Ifāḍa iii, 32a,b, 36a – III, 34a, 37b

al-ʿIfār ii, 631b; iii, **1037b** – II, 647a; III, **1063b**

Ifāt → Awfāt

ʿIffat b. Aḥmad Āl T̲h̲unayyān s, 305b – S, 305b

ʿIffatiyya vi, 485b – VI, 471b

Ifgan vii, 263a – VII, 265a

Iflāk → Eflāk

al-Iflīlī → Ibn al-Iflīlī

Iflīmūn → Aflīmūn

Ifni iii, **1038a** – III, **1064a**

Ifog̲h̲as i, 210b; iii, **1038b** – I, 216b; III, **1064b**

ʿIfrād iii, 35a, 53b – III, 37a, 55b

Ifrāg̲h̲a iii, **1038b** – III, **1064b**

Īfran, Banū (Īfrānid(e)s) i, 6a, 367a; iii, **1039a**; v,
1164b, 1175a, 1179a, 1245b; vi, 311b; vii, 761a – I,
6a, 378a; III, **1065a**; V, 1154b, 1165a, 1169a, 1236a;
VI, 296b; VII, 762b

al-Ifrand̲j i, 9b, 82b, 197a, 198b, 216a, 639b, 664a,
784a, 798a, 804a, 932b, 946a, 983a, 1017a, 1025a,
1054b, 1125b, 1332a; ii, 63b, 282b, 292b, 318b,
912a; iii, 325a, 398b, 503b, **1044a**, 1118b; iv, 520b,
642a, 779a; v, 921b, 924b; x, 81b; s, 205a –
I, 9b, 85a, 202b, 204b, 222a, 660a, 684a, 807a, 821b,
828a, 961a, 975b, 1013b, 1048b, 1056b, 1086b,
1159a, 1373a; II, 65a, 290b, 300b, 327b, 933b; III,
335a, 411a, 521a, **1070a**, 1146a; IV, 543a, 668b,
810b; V, 927a, 930a; X, 84b; S, 204b

al-Ifrānī (Īfrānī), Abū ʿAbd Allāh (1743) i, 315b; iii,
1046b; vi, 188a, 350b, 351a, 356b, 594b; s, 28b –
I, 325a; III, **1073a**; VI, 172a, 335a, 340b, 579a; X,
84b; S, 29a

al-Ifrānī, Abū Ḵudāma Yazīd b. Fendīn (803) iii,
1041b; viii, 112b – III, **1067b**; VIII, 115a

al-Ifrānī, Ayyūb b. Abī Yazīd (X) viii, 632a – VIII,
651a

al-Ifrānī, Yaʿlā b. Muḥammad b. Ṣāliḥ (X) vii, 263a –
VII, 265a

Ifrāṭ, Ifrāṭ fiʾl-Ṣifa → Mubālag̲h̲a

al-Ifrīḵī, ʿAbd al-Aʿlā b. Ḥudaydj (VIII) vi, 923a – VI,
915a

Ifrīḵiya i, 50a, 79a, 86a, 92b, 104a, 124b, 134b, 156b,
166a, 247b, 248a, 532b, 1321a; ii, 331b, 852b, 998a;
iii, 1032a, 1040b, **1047a**; iv, 175a, b, 176b, 177a; v,
503a, 723b, 877a; vi, 280a, 434a, 457a, 606a; vii,
70a; s, 1a, 62b, 306a –
I, 51b, 81b, 88b, 95a, 107a, 128a, 138a, 161a, 170b,
255b, 549a, 1361a; II, 341a, 872a, 1021a; III, 1058a,
1066b, **1073b**; IV, 182b, 183a, 184b; V, 506b, 728b,
882b; VII, 265a, 419b, 442b, 591a; VII, 70b; S, 1a,
63a, 306a

—language, literature/langues, littérature i, 568b – I,
587a

ʿIfrīt iii, **1050a**; s, 52b – III, **1076a**; S, 53a

Ifruḵlus → Buruḵlus

Iftāʾ ii, 866a,b – II, 886a,b

Iftik̲h̲ār al-Dīn Muḥammad al-Buk̲h̲ārī iv, 860a – IV,
893a

Iftik̲h̲ār K̲h̲ān (XVII) vii, 331b, 432b – VII, 333a, 433b

Īg ix, 158a → IX, 169a

Igal, Muḥammad Ḥād̲jd̲jī Ibrāhīm (Somalia/-e) (XX)
ix, 718b – IX, 749b

Igdir, Banū (Og̲h̲uz) vi, 416a, b; s, 168b, 169a – VI,
401a, b; S, 169a

Igerwān s, 113b – S, 113a

Ig̲h̲ār i, 1144b; iii, **1051a**; iv, 1032a – I, 1179a; III,
1077a; IV, 1064

Ig̲h̲arg̲h̲ar iii, **1051a** – III, **1077a**

Ig̲h̲lān s, 395a – S, 395b

Ig̲h̲rāḵ, Ig̲h̲rāḵ fiʾl-Ṣifa → Mubālag̲h̲a

Ig̲h̲raḵ, Sayf al-Dīn iv, 918a – IV, 951a

Igīlīz → Gīlīz

Igli vi, 743b, 744a – VI, 732b, 733a

Igliwa → Glāwa

Īhām → Tawriya

Iḥdāth iii, 664b, **1051a** – III, 686a, **1077b**

Ihlilad̲j iv, 357a – IV, 372b

Iḥrām iii, 35a, 36b, **1052b**; v, 329a – III, 36b, 38a,
1078b; V, 328b

Iḥsān → Muḥsan
Iḥsān, Aḥmad → Aḥmas Iḥsān
Iḥsān ʿAbd al-Ḳuddūs (XX) v, 190a; vi, 468b – V, 187b; VI, 454b
Iḥsān Allāh (Djudda) (XX) vi, 157b – VI, 153a
Iḥsān Allāh Khān ii, 445b; v, 310b – II, 457a; V, 310a
Iḥsās → Ḥiss
Iḥtisāb → Ḥisba
Iḥtishām al-Dawla s, 302a – S, 302a
Iḥyāʾ iii, **1053b** – III, **1079b**
Īḳāʿ s, **408b** – S, **409a**
ʿIḳāb (punishment/châtiment) → ʿAdhāb; ʿAdhāb al-Ḳabr; Djazāʾ; Ḥadd; Taʿzīr; ʿUḳūba
al-ʿIḳāb (battle/bataille, 1212) i, 495b; iii, **1055a**; vii, 989a – I, 510b; III, **1081a**; VII, 990a
ʿIkabb (VI) vii, 563a – VII, 563b
Iḳāla i, 319b; iii, **1056b** – I, 329b; III, **1082b**
Iḳāma i, 188b; iii, **1057a** – I, 194a; III, **1083a**
Iḳbāl, Āl s, 338a – S, 337b
Iḳbāl, Sir Muḥammad (1938) i, 327a; ii, 546b, 1036b; iii, 119b, 432a, **1057a**; iv, 170b; v, 601a; vi, 461b, 838b; vii, 297a, 422a – I, 337a; II, 560a, 1060b; III, 122a, 446a, **1083b**; IV, 178a; V, 605a; VI, 71a, 447a, 829a; VII, 299a, 423b
Iḳbāl b. Sābiḳ-i Sīstānī i, 347b – I, 358a
Iḳbāl al-Dawla → ʿAlī b. Mudjāhid al-Āmirī
Iḳbāl Khān → Mallū Iḳbāl Khān
Iḳbāl Khān (Mālwā) (XVI) vi, 54b – VI, 52b
Iḳbāl-nāma iv, 127b, 128b – IV, 133b, 134a
Iḳbāl al-Sharābī (XIII) vii, 727b – VII, 728a
Ikdjān vi, 727b – VI, 716b
Iḳfāʾ → Ḳāfiya
Ikhlāṣ iii, **1059b** – III, **1086a**
Ikhlāṣī, Shaykh Meḥmed iv, 761a – IV, 791a
Ikhmīm → Akhmīm
al-Ikhnāʾī, Taḳī al-Dīn iii, 953a – III, 977b
Ikhshīd (title/titre) iii, **1060b** – III, **1087a**
al-Ikhshīd → Kāfūr; Myḥammad b. Tughdj
Ikhshīdid(e)s i, 435b, 439b, 551b, 1042a; ii, 130a, 281b; iii, 129a, 768b, 979a, **1060b**; iv, 418a; s, 120b – I, 448a, 452a, 569a, 1073b; II, 133a, 289b; III, 131b, 791b, 1003b, **1087a**; IV, 436b; S, 120a
Ikhshīdiyya viii, 614b – VIII, 634a
Ikhshīn (river/gleuve) ix, 310a – IX, 329b
Ikhtilādj iii, **1061a** – III, **1087a**
Ikhtilāf i, 155a; iii, 160b, **1061b** – I, 159b; III, 164a, **1088a**
Ikhtisān, Muḥammad Ṣadr ʿAlāʾ (XIV) s, **409a** – S, **409b**
Ikhtiyār i, 413a; iii, 1037a, **1062b** – I, 424b; III, 1063a, **1089a**
Ikhtiyār al-Dīn Abu ʾl-Mudjāhid Ḳādir Khān (Kālpī) (1432) vi, 61b – VI, 59b
Ikhtiyār al-Dīn Aytak → Aytak
Ikhtiyār al-Dīn Ghāzī Shāh ii, 751b – II, 770a
Ikhtiyār al-Dīn Ḥusayn (XVI) vii, 988a – VII, 989a
Ikhtiyār al-Dīn Muḥammad Khāldjī → Muḥammad Bakhtiyār
Ikhtiyār al-Dīn Munshī iv, 1124a – IV, 1156a
Ikhtiyār al-Dīn Zangī (XIII) vii, 973b – VII, 974a
Ikhtiyār Heyʾeti i, 972b – I, 1002b
Ikhtiyār Khān (Dihlī) (XV) vi, 49b, 50a – VI, 48a, b
Ikhtiyār Khān Ṣiddīḳī (Gudjarāt) (XVI) vi, 52a – VI, 50b
Ikhtiyārāt (anthologies) → Mukhtārāt
Ikhtiyārāt (hemerology/-ie) iii, **1063b**; iv, 518b – III, **1090b**; IV, 541a
Ikhtiyāriyya s, **409b** – S, **409b**
al-Ikhwān (Wahhābīs) ii, 469a; iii, 361b, **1064a**; iv, 680b, 681a, 1133b; v, 574b, 998a, b; vi, 46a, 152b, 157b; ix, 904b; s, 3b – II, 480b; III, 373a, **1090b**; IV, 708b, 1165a; V, 579b, 993b, 994a; VI, 44b, 151a, 153a; IX, 942b; S, 2b
al-Ikhwān al-Djumhūriyyūn x, 96b – X, 104a
al-Ikhwān al-Muslimūn i, 416b, 1018b; ii, 429b, 882b; iii, 162b, 518a, 557b, **1068b**; iv, 161b, 206b; vi, 360b; viii, 717a; s, 6a, b, 7a, 300b – I, 428b, 1050a; II, 440b, 903a; III, 166a, 535b, 577a, **1095b**; IV, 168b, 216a; VI, 344b; S, 5a, 6a, 300a, b; VIII, 738a
Ikhwān al-Ṣafāʾ i, 247a, 350b, 589b, 659b, 737a, 772a, 1156a; ii, 93a, 358b, 361b, 554b, 579a, 765b, 766a, 774b; iii, 21b, 134a, 171a, 301a, 313a, 329a, 1059b, **1071a**, 1130a, 1139a, 1171b, 1207a; iv, 367a, 548a, 663a; v, 703a; vi, 99a, 450b, 905b; vii, 954b; s, 321a, 414a – I, 255a, 361b, 609a, 680b, 759a, 795b, 1190a; II, 95a, 368b, 371b, 568b, 593b, 784a, b, 793a; III,22b, 136b, 175a, 310a, 322b, 339a, 1086a, **1098a**, 1158a, 1167a, 1200b, 1237b; IV, 383a, 571b, 689b; V, 708a; VI, 96b, 436a, 897a; VII, 955a; S, 320b, 414a
Ikhwāniyyāt iv, 1005b – IV, 1037b
Ikhwat Yūsuf vii, 10b – VII, 11b
al-Iklīl → Nudjūm
Iklīl al-Malik s, **410a** – S, **410a**
Iḳlīme Khātūn (Marʿash) vi, 509b – VI, 495a
Iklān → Akli
Iḳlīm i, 489b, 988a; iii, **1076b**; iv, 223a, 273b; v, 398a – I, 504b, 1019a; III, **1103b**; IV, 233a, 285b; V, 399a
Iḳna → Ḳunā
ʿIkrāh i, 319a; s, **410b** – I, 329a; S, **410b**
Īḳrār iii, 511b, **1078a** – III, 529a, **1105a**
ʿIkrima b. Abī Djahl (VII) i, 115b, 151a, 690b, 812b; ii, 895b; iii, 653b, **1081b**; vi, 84a, 138a, b, 546b, 1038a; viii, 155a; ix, 6a; s, 232b, 386b – I, 119a, 155b, 711b, 835b; II, 916a; III, 675a, **1108b**; VI, 82a, 136b, 531a, 1031b; VIII, 157b; IX, 6a; S, 232b, 386b
Iḳrītish (Crete) i, 83a, 121b, 397b, 935b, 1249a; ii, 130a, 489b; iii, 621a, **1082a**; iv, 539a, 766a, 1054a, 1157b; v, 503a; vi, 58b; s, 120b, 186a – I, 85b, 125a, 409a, 964b, 1287a; II, 133b, 502a; III, 641b, **1109a**; IV, 562a, 796b, 1085a, 1189b; V, 506b; VI, 56b; S, 120a, 187a
al-Iḳrītishī iii, 1085b – III, 1112a
al-Iksīr iii, **1087b**; v, 113b – III, **1114a**; V, 116a
Iḳṭāʿ i, 533b, 802a, 1144a, b, 1146b, 1353a; ii, 187b, 508a; iii, **1088a**; iv, 18a, 26a, 32a, 323b, 975a, 1043b; v, 688a, 862b – I, 549b, 825a, 1178b, 1179a, 1180b, 1392b; II, 193b, 520b; III, **1115a**; IV, 19a-b, 28a, 34a, 337b, 1007b, 1075a; V, 693b, 869b
Iḳtibās iii, **1091b** – III, **1118a**
Iḳtiḍāb → Tadjnīs; Takhalluṣ
Iktisāb → Kasb
Iḳwāʾ → Ḳāfiya
Īl iii, **1092a** – III, **1118b**
Īl-Arslān iii, 1110b; iv, 29b, 658b, 1067b; s, 245b – III, 1138a; IV, 31b, 685b, 1099a; S, 245b
Īlāʿ → Ṭalāḳ
Īlāf iii, **1093a**; vi, 145b – III, **1119b**; VI, 143b
ʿIlāfī iv, 534b – IV, 558a
Ilāh iii, **1093b** – III, **1120a**
Ilāhābād → Allāhābād
Ilāhī iii, **1094a**; v, 275a – III, **1120b**; V, 273a
Ilāhī, Mullā ʿAbd Allāh (1490) vii, 754a, 936a; ix, 612a; x, 322a; s, 51b – VII, 775b, 936b; IX, 634a; X, 347a; S, 52a
Ilāhī Bakhsh "Maʿrūf" (1826) iii, **1095a** – III, **1121b**
Ilāhī Era s, **410b** – S, **411a**

Ilāhiyyāt   i, 343a, 415a; iii, 1147b – I, 353b, 426b; III, 1175b

Īlāk   s, **411a** – S, **411a**

Ilak Khān   → Ilek-Khāns

Īlāt   iii, **1095b** – III, **1122b**

Ilbarī   s, 124a – S, 123a

Ilbīra (Elvira)   i, 49a; ii, 1012a, 1014b; iii, **1110a**; iv, 739a; vi, 221b – I, 50b; II, 1036a, 1038b; III, **1137b**; IV, 769a; VI, 215b

al-Ilbīrī   → Abū Isḥāḳ al-Ilbīrī

Ilče   i, 469b; iii, 1092b – I, 483b; III, 1119a

Ilči   → Elči

Īlči, Mīrzā Abu 'l-Ḥasan Khān   s, 108b, 290a – S, 108a, 290a

Ildeñiz (Ildegiz, Eldigüz), Shams al-Dīn, atabeg (1175)   i, 190a, 300b; iii, **1110b**, 1112a; vi, 275b, 482a, 500a; vii, 406b, 730b, 922b; viii, 239a, 944a; ix, 270a, 195a – I, 194b, 310a; III, **1137b**, 1139b; VI, 260b, 468a, 485b; VII, 408a, 731a, 923a; VIII, 245a, 976a; IX, 175b, 199a

Ildeñizid(e)s (Eldigüzid(e)s, Ildigizid(e)s)   ii, 975b; iii, **1110b**; iv, 348b, 349a; vii, 922a – II, 998a; III, **1138a**; IV, 363b, 364a; VII, 922b

Ildjāʾ   ii, 188a; iii, 1113a – II, 194a; III, 1140a

Ilek-Khāns (Ḳarakhānid(e)s)   i, 236b, 421a, 987a, 1295a; ii, 1b, 4b, 791b, 893b, 1143b; iii, 345b, **1113a**; iv, 572b, 581a, 658b, 699a; v, 857b; vi, 340a, 809b; vii, 193a; x, 222b, 689a, 707b; s, 176b, 240a, 245b, 326a – I, 244a, 432b, 1017b, 1334b; II, 1b, 4b, 810b, 914b, 1170b; III, 356a, **1140a**; IV, 595b, 604b, 685a, 727a; V, 864a; VI, 324a, 800a; VII, 193b; X, 240b, 751b, 781b; S, 177b, 240a, 245b, 325b

Ileri, Djelāl Nūrī (1938)   iii, **1117a** – III, **1144b**

Ileri, Sedād Nūrī   iii, 1117a – III, 1144b

Ileri, Ṣubḥī Nūrī   iii, 1117a – III, 1144b

Îles Fortunées   → Djazāʾir al-Saʿādāt

Iletmish   → Iltutmish

Īlgaz   → Čankîrî

Ilghāz   → Muʿammā

Īlghāzī I Nadjm al-Dīn (Artuḳid(e)) (1184)   i, 664a, 665b, 983a, 1337a; iii, 87a, **1118a**; v, 124b; vi, 64b, 380a, 540b, 544a, 966a; vii, 578b, 725b, 733b, 983b – I, 683b, 684a, 686b, 1013b, 1377a; III, 89a, **1145b**; V, 127a; VI, 62a, 364a, 525a, 528b, 958b; VII, 579a, 726a, 734a, 984a

Ilghāzī II b. Nadjm al-Dīn Alpī (Artuḳid(e)) (1122)   iii, **1119a** – III, **1146b**

Ilḥād   → Mulḥid

Ilhām   iii, **1119b** – III, **1147a**

Ilhami Soysal (XX)   vi, 95b – VI, 93b

Īli   iii, **1120a**; iv, 512b; v, 363b – III, **1147b**; IV, 534b; V, 364b

Iličpur   → Eličpur

Ilîdja   iii, **1120b** – III, **1148b**

Ilig Naṣr (Karakhānid(e)) (X)   viii, 110a, 1028a – VIII, 112b, 1063a

Īlī   vi, 743a; viii, 440a; x, 405b – VI, 732b; VIII, 454b; X, 434a

Īlīen (Morocco/Maroc)   x, 405b – X, 434a

Īliyā   → al-Ḳuds

Īlīyā (metropolitan(e))   vi, 620a – VI, 605a

Īliyā Abū Māḍī (XX)   viii, 88a – VIII, 90a

Ilḳās Mīrzā   iv, 103a – IV, 107b

Īlkhānī   → Taʾrīkh

Īlkhāns   i, 227a, 329b, 346a, 467a, 468a, 470a, 510b, 666a, 703a, 861a, 872a, 902b, 1106b, 1128a; ii, 45a, 47a, 401a; iii, 122a, 473a, 569b, **1120b**, 1256a; iv, 31a, 48a-b, 349b; v, 58b, 455b, 677a; vi, 15a, b, 65a, 66a, 120a, 273b, 274a, 315b, 321b, 322a, 366a, 482b, 492b, 493a, 494a, 501b, 521b, 524a, b, 549b, 714a,

724b, 854b, 931b; viii, 168b, 175a, 443a,b; ix, 268b, 474b, 597a; x, 43a; s, 59a, 64b, 126b, 235b, 383a, 409b –

I, 234a, 339b, 356b, 481a,b, 484a, 526a, 687a, 724a, 885a, 896a, 930a, 1140a, 1162b; II, 46a, 48a, 411b; III, 124b, 489b, 589a, **1148b**, 1289a; IV, 33a, 51a, 364b; V, 60b, 458a, 682a; VI, 13a, b, 63a, b, 117b, 258a, b, 300b, 306a, 306b, 350a, 468b, 478b, 479b, 487a, 506a, 508b, 509a, 534a, 703a, 713b, 846a, 923b; VIII, 171b, 177b, 458a; IX, 276b, 493a, 620a; X, 44b; S, 59b, 65a, 125b, 235b, 383a

—administration   i, 1159a; ii, 81a, 83a, 311a, 313a, 334a, 903a; iii, 47b, 284a, 348a, 1089a; iv, 559b, 757a, 1045a, 1046a, b – I, 1193b; II, 82b, 84b, 320a, 322a, 343b, 924a; III, 49b, 292b, 358b, 1116a; IV, 582a, 787b, 1076b, 1077b

—art/architecture   iii, 1123a, 1127b; v, 1148a – III, 1151b, 1155b; V, 1139a

ʿIlla   i, 1327a; iii, **1127b** – I, 1367b; III, **1156a**

Illā   iv, 272b; v, 241b – IV, 284b; V, 239a

ʿIllaysh, Muḥammad b. Aḥmad (1882)   s, **411a** – S, **411b**

Illig agreement/accord   vii, 389b – VII, 391a

ʿIlliyyūn   iii, **1132b** – III, **1161a**

ʿIlm   iii, **1133a**; v, 1123b – III, **1161a**; V, 1120a

ʿIlm al-aktāf   → Katif

ʿIlm al-Dīn al-Anṣārī   → Wazir Khān

ʿIlm al-djamāl   iii, **1134a** – III, **1162a**

ʿIlm al-handasa   s, **411b** – S, **411b**

ʿIlm al-hayʾa   i, 1100b; ii, 586b; iii, 302a, 703a, 789a, **1135a**; iv, 491b, 1059a, 1182b; v, 46a, b, 83a-87b, 397a, 542b, 547a – I, 1133b; II, 601a; III, 311a, 725a, 812b, **1163a**; IV, 513a, 1090b, 1216a; V, 47b, 48a, 85b, 90a, 354b, 398a, 547a, 551b

ʿIlm al-ḥisāb   iii, **1138a**; iv, 1070a; v, 527b – III, **1166b**; IV, 1101b; V, 531a

ʿIlm al-ḥurūf   → Ḥurūf

ʿIlm al-kaff   → al-Kaff

ʿIlm al-kalām   ii, 605b, 608a, 618a, 898b, 931a; iii, 543b, 664b, 1132a, **1141b**; iv, 366b – II, 620b, 623a, 633b, 919b, 953a; III, 562b, 686a, 1160a, **1170a**; IV, 382b

ʿIlm al-manāẓir   → Manāẓir

ʿIlm al-mīḳāt   → Miḳāt

ʿIlm al-ridjāl   iii, **1150b**; vi, 312b – III, **1179a**; VI, 297b

ʿIlmiyye   iii, **1152a** – III, **1180b**

Ilsh   → Alsh

Ilsharaḥ Yaḥḍib (Yaḥṣib)   vi, 561b – VI, 546b

Iltizām   ii, 147b, 148a; iii, **1154a**; iv, 324a, 1096a; v, 93b; s, 238b – II, 152a,b; III, **1182b**; IV, 338b, 1127a; V, 95b; S, 238b

Iltizām (rhetoric, rhétorique)   → Luzūm mā lā yalzam

Iltutmish b. Ēlam Khān, Shams al-Dīn (Muʿizzī, Dihlī) (1236)   i, 208b, 432b, 764a, 856a, 912b, 1192a, 1209b, 1218b; ii, 50a, 120a, 153b, 260a, 266b, 267a, b, 274b, 609a, 1084a, 1143b; iii, 416a, 441a, 492a, **1155a**; iv, 533b; v, 549a, 597b, 629b, 883b, 1134b; vi, 48a, 189b, 309a, 368a, 406b, 488a, 532b, 691b; vii, 193b, 549a; viii, 81a; s, 124a, 284b, 353a, 360a – I, 214b, 444b, 787a, 880a, 940a, 1227a, 1245b, 1255a; II, 51a, 122b, 158b, 267b, 274b, 275b, 282b, 624a, 1109b, 1170b; III, 429a, 455b, 509a, **1183b**; IV, 556b; V, 553b, 601b, 633b, 890a, 1130a; VI, 46b, 173b, 294b, 352b, 391a, 474a, 516b, 679a; VII, 194a, 549a; VIII, 83a; S, 123a, 284b, 353a, 359b

Iltüzer Khān   iv, 1065a, 1068a; v, 24a – IV, 1096b, 1100a; V, 25a

ʿIlwa, Banū   → Muṭayr, Banū

Ilyās (Elijah) i, 404b, 1214b; iii, **1156a**; iv, 903a; v, 5a – I, 416a, 1250b; III, **1184b**; IV, 935b; V, 5a
Ilyās, Amīr (Ḳūm) (1428) vi, 513a – VI, 498b
Ilyās b. Aḥmad iv, 859a – IV, 892b
Ilyās b. Ḥabīb i, 86b – I, 89a
Ilyās b. Ḥamīd iii, 132b – III, 135b
Ilyās b. Ilyasaʿ s, 356b – S, 356b
Ilyās b. Isḥāḳ iv, 698b – IV, 727a
Ilyās b. Manṣūr al-Nafūsī (Ibāḍī) s, 1a – S, 1a
Ilyās b. Yuḥannā i, 593b – I, 613a
Ilyās Beg (Mirā<u>kh</u>or) v, 265a, b – V, 263a
Ilyās Beg b. Meḥmed Beg (Mente<u>sh</u>e) (1421) vi, 1018b – VI, 1011a
Ilyās Farḥāt vi, 308a – VI, 293a
Ilyās <u>Kh</u>ān s, 331b – S, 331a
Ilyās (Iliyyā) al-Naṣībī (Elia of/de Naṣībīn) (1046) vi, 118b, 119b, 120b; vii, 1031b – VI, 116b, 117a, 118b; VII, 1034a
Ilyās Pa<u>sh</u>a (XV) vii, 594b – VII,
Ilyās {a<u>sh</u>a (Anatolia/e) (XVII) s, 49a – S, 49b
Ilyās Pa<u>sh</u>a Umm Birayr (Kordofān) (XIX) v, 267b – V, 265b
Ilyās <u>Sh</u>āh, <u>Sh</u>ams al-Dīn (Bengal(e)) (1358) i, 1015a, 1168a; ii, 751b; iii, 202b, 416b; v, 638a; vi, 46b, 244b; viii, 5b, 258b – I, 1046a, 1203a; II, 770a; III, 208a, 430a; V, 642b; VI, 45a, 228b; VIII, 5b, 260b
Ilyās <u>Sh</u>āhīd(e)s (Bengal(e)) vi, 46b, 244b; viii, 258b, 373b; ix, 728a – VI, 45a, 228b; VIII, 260b, 386b; IX, 759a
Ilyas-og<u>h</u>lu ii, 207b – II, 214a
Ilyasaʿ iii, 1156b; v, 158b – III, 1185a; V, 157b
Ilyāsid(e)s iii, **1156b**; v, 158b – III, **1185a**; V, 157b
Īmāʾ → I<u>sh</u>āra
ʿImād, Mīr (XVI) vii, 442a – VII, 443a
ʿImād al-Dawla b. Hūd iii, 542b, 728a – III, 561b, 750b
ʿImād Abu ʾl-Ḳāsim (XII) vi, 608b – VI, 593a
ʿImād ʿAlī b. Būya (Buwayhid(e)) (949) i, 211b, 866b, 1046b, 1350a; ii, 178b; iii, 197a, **1157a**; iv, 23a, b, 100a, b, 222a; vi, 115b, 261b, 539a; vii, 484a, b – I, 217b, 890b, 1078b, 1390b; II, 184a; III, 202a, **1185b**; IV, 24b-25a, 104b, 232a; VI, 113b, 245b, 523b; VII, 484a, b
ʿImād Farāmarz iii, 1162a – III, 1190a
ʿImād Sāwtigin → Sāwtegin
ʿImād al-Dīn, Amīr (Astarābā<u>dh</u>) (XV) s, 380a – S, 380a
ʿImād al-Dīn, Mīr (Murtaḍāʾī) (XIV) vi, 512a – VI, 497a
ʿImād al-Dīn b. Arslān <u>Sh</u>āh v, 454b – V, 457a
ʿImād al-Dīn b. Ibrāhīm b. Ḥusām al-Dīn Ḥasan (Marʿa<u>sh</u>) (XIII) vi, 507b – VI, 492b
ʿImād al-Dīn b. Mawdūd Zangī II (1180) vi, 781a, b, 871a; viii, 131b – VI, 770b, 771a, 862a; VIII, 134a
ʿImād al-Dīn b. Ṣalāḥ al-Dīn → al-Malik al-ʿAzīz ʿImād al-Dīn
ʿImād al-Dīn b. Sayf al-Dīn ʿAlī Aḥmad b. al-Ma<u>sh</u>ṭūb (Manbi<u>dj</u>) (1202) vi, 381a – VI, 365b
ʿImād al-Dīn Abu ʾl-Fatḥ ʿUmar b. ʿAlī i, 765b – I, 788b
ʿImād al-Dīn ʿAlī, Faḳīh-i Kirmānī (773) iv, 1010a; s, **414b** – IV, 1042a; S, **415a**
ʿImād al-Dīn al-Bag<u>h</u>dādī (1335) vii, 135b, 136a, b – VII, 137b, 138a, b
ʿImād al-Dīn Darguzīnī (1150) vi, 782a – VI, 772a
ʿImād al-Dīn Ḥasan b. ʿAlī s, 83a – S, 82b
ʿImād al-Dīn Ismāʿīl → al-Ṣāliḥ ʿImād al-Dīn
ʿImād al-Dīn al-Kātib al-Iṣfahānī (1201) i, 150a, 523a, 594a, 595a, 801b, 1309b; iii, 222a, 834b, **1157b**; v, 528b; vi, 430a, 606a; vii, 527b, 726b; s, 123b, 205a, 326a, 378b – I, 154a, 538b, 613b, 614b, 825a, 1349b; III, 228b, 858a, **1186a**; V, 532b; VI, 415a, b, 590b; VII, 528a, 727b; S, 123a, 205a, 325b, 378b
ʿImād al-Dīn Kumal (Bal<u>kh</u>) (XII) ix, 16b – IX, 17a
ʿImād al-Dīn Muḥammad b. Aḥmad b. Ṣāʿid (ḳāḍī) vi, 14a – VI, 12b
ʿImād al-Dīn Rayḥān → Rayḥān
ʿImād al-Dīn ʿUmar al-<u>Sh</u>ay<u>kh</u> i, 766b – I, 789a
ʿImād al-Dīn Zangī I b. Aḳ Sunḳur (Zangid(e)) (1146) i, 426b, 1332a,; v, 332a, 454a, b, 922a; vi, 64a, 380a, 545b, 606a, 782a, 870a, 900b; vii, 543b; viii, 127a; ix, 68b – I, 439a, 1373a; V, 332a, 457a, 927b; VI, 62a, 364b, 530a, 590b, 772a, 861a, 891b; VII, 543b; VIII, 130a; IX, 71b
ʿImād al-Mulk (Multān) iii, 634a; s, 335b – III, 655a; S, 335a
ʿImād al-Mulk Fatḥ Allāh → Fatḥ Allāh
ʿImād al-Mulk Abu ʾl-Ḳāsim (XI) viii, 81b – VIII, 83b
ʿImād al-Mulk, <u>Gh</u>āzī al-Dīn (1746) i, 296a, 1024b; iii, 61a, **1158a**; v, 598b – I, 305a, 1056a; III, 63b, **1186b**; V, 602b
ʿImād <u>Sh</u>āh (Berār) (XVI) i, 1160a; vi, 51a – I, 1189a, VI, 49b
ʿImād <u>Sh</u>āhīs (Berār) i, 1170a; ii, 981b; iii, 425a, 447a, **1159a**; vi, 68a, 368a, 536b, 695b; s, 280a – I, 1205a; II, 1003b; III, 438b, 462a, **1187b**; VI, 66a, 352a, 521a, 683b; S, 279b
ʿImādī (<u>Sh</u>ahriyārī) (XII) iii, **1161b**; s, **416a** – III, **1190a**; S, **416a**
ʿImād-i Ḥasanī-i Sayfī iv, 1124b – IV, 1156a
ʿImādiyya → ʿAmādiya
Imāla iii, **1162a** – III, **1190b**
Imām → Imāma, Mas<u>dj</u>id
Imām al-Ḥaramayn → al-<u>D</u>juwaynī, ʿAbd al-Malik
Imām al-Hudā → Abu ʾl-Lay<u>th</u> al-Samarḳandī
Imām -bārā iii, **1163a**; v, 1033a – III, **1191b**; V, 1029b
Imām Ḳulī <u>Kh</u>ān (Fārs) (1632) i, 8b, 120b; ii, 446a, 812a, 975b; iv, 387b, 399a; v, 493a, 673a; vii, 673b; s, 340b – I, 8b, 124a; II, 458a, 831b, 998a; IV, 404a, 416b; V, 496a, 678a; VII, 673b; S, 340a
Imām Ḳulī Mīrzā b. ʿAbbās I (Ṣafawid(e)) (XVII) viii, 770b – VIII, 796b
Imām Ma (Yunnan) (XIX) viii, 260b – VIII, 265b
Imām <u>Sh</u>āh (1513) iii, **1163a**; iv, 202b; v, 26b – III, **1191b**; IV, 211b; V, 27a
Imām-<u>Sh</u>āhīs → Sat-panthīs
Imām al-Suhaylī → al-Suhaylī, Sīdī ʿAbd al-Raḥmān
Imām Yaḥyā iv, 296b – IV, 309b, 310a
Imāma i, 27a, 276b, 832b; ii, 660b, 931a, 1094a; iii, 547a, 954a, **1163b**; iv, 50a, 182b, 184a, 234b, 277b, 278b, 456b, 943b, 944a, 948a, 987b; v, 166b, 1236a; s, 327b – I, 28a, 285a, 855b; II, 677a, 953a, 1119b; III, 566a, 978b, **1192a**; IV, 52b, 190b, 192a, 245a, 289b, 290b, 477a, 976b, 977a, 981a, 1020a; V, 164a, 1226b; S, 327a
Imāmiyya i, 393a, 445b, 850a; iii, 497a, 1166b; iv, 610a; v, 1236a, b; s, 25b – I, 404a, 458b, 873b; III, 514a, 1195b; IV, 634b, 1226b, 1227a; S, 26a
Imāmzāda iii, 1124a, **1169b**; iv, 702a – III, 1152a, **1198b**; IV, 730a
Imāmzāda Abu ʾl-Faḍl wa-Yaḥyā (Maḥallat Bālā) (1300) vii, 12b – VII, 13b
Imāmzāda Karrār (Buzān) (1143) vii, 12b – VII, 13a

Imāmzāda Shāh Ḥusayn (Warāmīn) (1330) vii, 13a – VII, 13b
Imāmzāde (Shāh) ʿAbd al-ʿAẓīm → Shāh ʿAbd al-ʿAẓīm al-Ḥasanī
Īmān i, 276b, 335a, 1242a; ii, 294a; iii, **1170b**; iv, 171b, 172a, 173a, b – I, 285b, 345b, 1279b; II, 302a; III, **1199b**; IV, 179a, b, 180b, 181a
al-Imārāt al-ʿArabīyya al-Muttaḥida iv, 778b; v, 1058a; vii, 301b; s, 2b, 42a, **416b** – IV, 810a; V, 1055a; VII, 303b; S, 12b, 42a, **417a**
Imārat al-nubuwwa → Nubuwwa
ʿImāret → Khayr; Waḳf
Imazighen i, 433b, 1143a – I, 446a, 1208a
al-Imbābī, Muḥammad s, 411b – S, 411b
Imbros → Imroz
Imdād Allāh al-Hindī al-Makkī (1899) i, 701b; ii, 54b; iii, **1174a** – I, 723a; II, 55b; III, **1203a**
Imdād Ḥusayn Khān Nāṣir Djang ii, 808b – II, 828a
Imeretie → Kurdj
Imeum i, 741b – I, 763b
ʿImm vi, 871a – VI, 862a
Imraʾ al-Ḳays → Imruʾ al-Ḳays
Imrālī → Emreli
ʿImrān (ʿAmrām) i, 177a; iii, **1175a**; vi, 218b, 628b, 630a – I, 182a; III, **1204a**; VI, 202b, 613b, 615a
ʿImrān (Sind) iv, 535a – IV, 558a
ʿImrān b. al-Faḍl iii, 125b – III, 128a
ʿImrān b. Ḥiṭṭān (703) iii, 889b, **1175a**; iv, 1077a; s, 284a – III, 913b, **1204a**; IV, 1109a; S, 284a
ʿImrān b. Muḥammad b. Sabaʾ i, 181b – I, 186b
ʿImrān b. Mukhallad i, 248a – I, 255b
ʿImrān b. Mūsā (840) vi, 967b – VI, 959b
ʿImrān b. Mūsā al-Barmakī i, 1036a – I, 1067b
ʿImrān b. Shāhīn (979) i, 211b, 955a, 1096a; iii, 730a, **1175b**; vii, 358a, 484b, 818a – I, 218a, 984a, 1129a; III, 753a, **1204b**; VII, 360b, 484b, 820a
al-ʿImrānī, ʿAlī b. Aḥmad (955) viii, 108a – VIII, 110b
al-ʿImrānī, Muʿīn al-Dīn (XIV) i, 133a; iii, **1176a** – I, 137a; III, **1205a**
al-ʿImrānī al-Shīrāzī (XVI) iv, 309b – IV, 323b
ʿImrānid(e)/ʿImrāniyya ix, 507b – IX, 527a
Imroz i, 1280b; iii, **1176a**; v, 763b, 764b – I, 1320a; III, **1205a**; V, 769b, 770a
Imruʾ al-Ḳays iii, **1176b** – III, **1205b**
Imruʾ al-Ḳays (Lakhmid(e)) (328) i, 548b, 564b; v, 633a; vii, 871b, 945b – I, 566a, 582b; V, 637a; VII, 873a, 945b
Imruʾ al-Ḳays, Banū (Sulaym) ix, 817a – IX, 852a
Imruʾ al-Ḳays b. ʿĀbis al-Kindī (VII) iii, 1176b – III, 1205b
Imruʾ al-Ḳays b. ʿAwf v, 120a – V, 123a
Imruʾ al-Ḳays b. Ḥudjr (550) i, 99a, 405b, 452a, 527a, 583b, 1152a; ii, 241b, 550b, 785a, 1028b; iii, **1177a**; iv, 263b, 839a; v, 119a, 633a; vi, 261a, 477b; vii, 254b, 261a; x, 90a; s, 38a, 58b, 259a – I, 101b, 417a, 465a, 543a, 602a, 1186b; II, 248b, 564b, 804a, 1052a; III, **1205b**; IV, 275b, 872a; V, 121b, 637a; VI, 245b, 463b; VII, 256a, 263a; X, 97b; S, 38a, 59a, 258b
Imruʾ al-Ḳays ʿAdī b. Rabīʿa al-Taghlibī (al-Muhalhil) (VI) iii, 1176b, 1178a; vii, 580b, 581a, 979a – III, 1205, 1207a; VII, 581a,b, 979b
Imtiyāzāt ii, 912b; iii, **1178b**; iv, 38b – II, 934a; III, **1207b**; IV, 41a
Imẓad iii, **1195b** – III, **1225b**
In shāʾ Allāh iii, **1196a** – III, **1226b**
ʿInab → Khamr
İnaḳ iv, 1065a; v, 392a; s, **419a** – IV, 1096b; V, 392b; S, **419a**
Inaḳid(e)s s, 420a – S, 420a
Īnāl (kāshif) (Miṣr) (XVI) vi, 325a; vii, 177b – VI 309b; VII, 179b
İnal, Ibnülemin (1957) iii, **1199a** – III, **1229a**
Īnāl, Īnālid(e)s ii, 344a; iii, **1197b** – II, 354a; III, **1227b**
İnal, İnalčuḳ (1220) iii, **1198a** – III, **1228a**
Īnāl al-Adjrūd, al-Malik al-Ashraf Sayf al-Dīn (Mamlūk) (1461) i, 352a; iii, **1198a**; vii, 173b, 727a – I, 363a; III, **1228a**; VII, 175a, 727b
Īnālū → Abū ʿUmar Īnālū
Inʿām iii, 347b, **1200b** – III, 358a, **1231a**
Inʿām al-Ḥasan (1995) x, 38b – X, 39b
ʿInān (841) iii, **1202b** – III, **1232b**
Inanč Khātūn iii, 1111b – III, 1139a
Ināndj, Ḳiwām al-Dīn (Rayy) (1161) i, 300b; ii, 333b; iii, 1110b; vi, 500a, b – I, 310a; II, 343a; III, 1137b; VI, 485b
Inandj Bīghū, Amīr (Māzandarān) (1065) vi, 935b – VI, 927b
Ināndj (Inanč) Khātūn (Shāh-i Arman) (XII) iii, 1111b; ix, 183a – III, 1139a; IX, 199a
Īnānlū iv, 858b – IV, 891b
Inari Konte (Mali) (XIV) vi, 421b – VI, 407a
Iʿnāt → Luzūm mā lā yalzam
ʿĪnāt s, 337b, **420b** – S, 337a, **420b**
ʿInāya i, 90a, 415a; iii, **1203a** – I, 92b, 427a; III, **1233b**
ʿInāyat (India/-e) s, 292b, 293b – S, 292b, 293b
ʿInāyat Allāh (Afghānistān) s, 65b, 66b – S, 66a, 67a
ʿInāyat Allāh ʿAlī (1858) vii, 291a – VII, 293a
ʿInāyat Allāh Kan'bū (1671) iii, **1203b** – III, **1234a**
ʿInāyat Allāh Khān → al-Mashriḳī
ʿInāyat Allāh Khan (1726) vi, 131b; vii, 322a, 722b – VI, 130a; VII, 324a, 723b
ʿInāyat Allāh Khān (1681) s, **420b** – S, **420b**
ʿInāyat Allāh Khan (1682) s, **420b** – S, **421a**
ʿInāyat Allāh Khān b. Ḥāfiẓ Raḥmat iii, 61a – III, 63b
ʿInāyat Allāh Khān b. Ẓafar Aḥsan ii, 1004b – II, 1028a
India/-e → Hind
India, Muslim – ix, 800b – IX, 835a
Indian Congress Party s, 106b – S, 105b
Indian National Congress iii, **1204a**; vi, 78a; viii, 241a; s, 4b – III, **1234b**; VI, 76a; VIII, 247a; S, 3b
Indian Ocean → Baḥr al-Hind; Baḥr al-Zandj
Indjīl i, 264a; iii, **1205a** – I, 272a; III, **1235b**
Indjili Čavush iii, 375a – III, 387a
Īndjū iii, 55b, **1208a**; iv, 31b, 32a, 975b, 1094a; v, 163a; s, 235b – III, 58a, **1238b**; IV, 34a, b, 1008a, 1125a; V, 161a; S, 235b
Īndju Shīrāzī, Ḥusayn iv, 526a – IV, 549a
Indjūid(e)s → Indjū
Indochina/-e iii, **1208b** – III, **1239b**
Indonesia/-e iii, 502b, **1213a**; iv, 175b; v, 940b; s, 220a – III, 520a, **1243b**; IV, 183a; V, 944a; S, 220b
—administration i, 980b; iii, 566a; vi, 42b – I, 1010b; III, 586a; VI, 40b
—ethnography/-ie iii, 1214b – III, 1245a
—geography/-ie iii, 1213a – III, 1243b
—history/histoire ii, 19a, 595a, 662b; iii, 534a, 1218-1230 – II, 19a, 610a, 679a; III, 552b, 1249-1262
—institutions ii, 426b – II, 437b
—languages, literature/langues, littératures i, 88a, 92a; iii, 1215a, 1230b; iv, 1128a; v, 205a, 226b, 227a, 228b; vi, 239a; viii, 153a – I, 90b, 94b; III, 1245b, 1262b; IV, 1159b; V, 202b, 224a, b, 226a; VI, 204a; VIII, 155a

Indus → Mihrān
Inebakhtî → 'Aynabakhtî
Infi'āl → Fi'l
Infiṣāl → Waṣl
Infūsen → al-Nafūsa
Ingiliz Muṣṭafā ii, 511b – II, 524a
Ingush ii, 18a,b; iii, **1235b**; vii, 351b – II, 18a,b; III, **1267b**; VII, 353b
Inḥiṣār s, **421a** – S, **421a**
Inkār iii, **1236b** – III, **1268b**
Inḳilāb → Thawra
Innāyir → Yinnāyir
Innib (Mar'ash) vi, 507a – VI, 492a
Inniya v, 1262a, b, 1263b – V, 1253b, 1254b
Inönü → Iṣmet Inönü; Sultān Önü
Inönü, Erdal x, 696a – X,
Inos(z) → Enos
Inṣāf iii, **1236b** – III, **1268b**
Insān iii, **1237a** – III, **1269a**
al-Insān al-Kāmil i, 117b; iii, **1239a**; v, 543b – I, 121a; III, **1271a**; V, 548a
Inshā' i, 594a, 595a; ii, 306b; iii, **1241b**; iv, 705a, 760a – I, 613b, 614a; II, 315a; III, **1273b**; IV, 733a, 790b
Inshā Allāh Khān (1818) iii, 358b, 376b, 458a, **1244a**; v, 959a, 960b, 961b; vii, 669b – III, 370a, 388b, 474a, **1276a**; V, 963a, 964b, 965b; VII, 669a
Inshāṣ (Palace) s, 301a – S, 300b
Institut d'Egypte iii, **1245a** – III, **1277b**
Institut des Hautes Études Marocaines s, **421b** – S, **421b**
Institut des Hautes Études de Tunis s, **422a** – S, **422b**
Intī → Hintāta
al-Īntī (Hintāta), Abū Ḥafṣ 'Umar (XII) vi, 222b – VI, 216a
Intidāb → Mandate/Mandat
Intihā' iii, **1246a** – III, **1278a**
Intiḥār iii, **1246b** – III, **1278b**
Intiḳālī iv, 978a – IV, 1010b
Inzāl → Waḳf
Inzāl s, **423a** – S, **423a**
Ipsala (Kypsela) vi, 290b – VI, 276a
Ipshīr Muṣṭafā Pasha (1665) i, 4b; iii, 318a, 983b, **1248a**; v, 257a – I, 4b; III, 327b, 1008a, **1280b**; V, 254b, 255a
I'rāb i, 566a, 569b, 570a, 576b; iii, 697a, **1248b**; v, 567b – I, 584a, 588a,b, 595a; III, 719a, **1281a**; V, 571b
Irāde i, 414b; iii, **1250a** – I, 426b; III, **1282b**
Iradj Khān i, 702a – I, 723a
Īradj Mīrzā (1925) iv, 71b; vi, 609a; s, 84a – IV, 75b; VI, 594a; S, 83b
'Irāfa iv, 421b – IV, 440a
'Irāḳ iii, **1250a**; iv, 719a; v, 912a; vi, 16a, 28a, 45b, 82b, 119b, 225a, 337a, 345a, 387a, 467b, 469b, 470a, 517a, 624a, 797a; vii, 9a; ix, 87a; s, 179a, 198b, 259a – III, **1282b**; IV, 748a; V, 917b; VI, 14a, 26a, 44a, 80b, 117a, 219a, 321a, 329a, 371a, 453b, 455a, b, 502a, 609a, 786b; VII, 9a; IX, 90b; S, 180a, 198b, 258b
—art, architecture i, 609b, 1226a; iii, **1266b**; v, 292b, 293a, 1148a, – I, 629b, 1264a; III, **1299a**; V, 292a, b, 1139a
—ethnography/-ie i, 39a, 872b; iii, **1253a**; v, 440a, 466b – I, 40a, 896b; III, **1285b**; V, 442b, 469b
—geography/-ie i, 431a, 461a; iii, **1250a**; iv, 1b; v, 146a, 864b, 886b – I, 443a, 474a; III, **1283a**; IV, 1b; V, 148b, 871b, 893a
—history/histoire i, 16a, 18b, 21a, 33a, 46a, 53b, 76b, 77a, 111a, 140b, 211b, 383a,b, 388b, 400a, 549b, 1087a, 1350b; ii, 579b, 872b; iii, 263b, 521a, 558a, 560b, 1066a,b, **1254a**; iv, 15a, 16b-17b, 261b – I, 16b, 19a, 21b, 34a, 47b, 55a, 78b, 79b, 114a, 144b, 217b, 394a,b, 400a, 411b, 567a, 1119a, 1390b; II, 594a, 892b; III, 271b, 539a, 577b, 580a, 1093a, **1286b**; IV, 16a, 17b-18b, 273a
—institutions ii, 424b; v, 1044a, 1093b – II, 435b; V, 1040b, 1090b
—languages, literature/langues, litérature i, 568b, 576a; ii, 468b; iii, **1259a** – I, 586b, 595a; II, 480b; III, **1292a**
—sect(e)s i, 15a; iii, **1265a** – I, 15b; III, **1297b**
'Irāḳ-i 'Adjamī → Djibāl
al-'Irāḳī, 'Abd al-Raḥīm, Shaykh (XVI) iii, 817b, 927a; vii, 565a – III, 841a, 951b; VII, 565b
al-'Irāḳī, Fakhr al-Dīn (1289) iii, 635a, 710b, **1269a**; iv, 65b, 67b, 474a; vii, 480a; viii, 540a – III, 656b, 733a, **1302a**; IV, 69a, 71a, 494b; VII, 479b; VIII, 557b
al-'Irāḳī, Sayyid Shams al-Dīn (1526) s, **423a** – S, **423b**
al-'Irāḳī, Zayn al-Dīn (1404) vii, 290a; x, 934b – VII, 292a; X,
Irakli II v, 494b, 495a – V, 497b
Īraḳlīdis Abū Buḳrāṭ s, 154b – S, 155a
Iram i, 169b; iii, **1270a** – I, 174a; III, **1303a**
Iram Dhāt al 'Imād i, 169a, 181a; iii, **1270b** – I, 174a, 186a; III, **1303b**
Irān i, 38a, 62b, 270a, 291a, 406a; ii, 966b, 1135b; iv, **1a-75a**, 163b, 785a; vi, 11a, 119b, 291a, 471a, 491b, 517a, 521a, 761b, 803a, 825b, 853a; vii, 1a, 12a, 76a; s, 129a, 214b, 332b – I, 39a, 64b, 278b, 300a, 418a; II, 988b, 1162a; IV, **1a-79a**, 170b, 817a; S, 128a, 214a, 332b; VI, 11a, 117b, 276a, 456b, 477b, 502a, 505b, 750b, 792b, 815b, 844b; VII, 1a, 12b, 77a
—administration i, 978a; ii, 150a, 308b, 332b, 514b, 649b, 1081b; iii, 194b, 213b, 347b, 554a; iv, 1034a; v, 1042a – I, 1008b; II, 154b, 317a, 342a, 527a, 665b, 1106b; III, 199a, 219b, 358a, 573a; IV, 1066a; V, 1038a
—art, architecture iii, 501b; iv, 288a, b; v, 292b – III, 518b; IV, 301a; V, 292a, b
—demography/-ie s, **214b** – S, **214a**
—ethnography/-ie i, 36a; iv, 7a-11a; v, 439b, 466a – I, 37a; IV, 8a-12a; V, 442a, 468b
—geography/-ie ii, 902b; iv, 1a-8a; v, 865a – II, 923b; IV, 1a-8a; V, 872a
—institutions ii, 426a, 433a; iii, 527b; v, 919a, 1094b – II, 437a, 444b; III, 546a; V, 924a, 1091b
—languages, literature/langues, littérature i, 1132a; ii, 308b; iii, 355a, 372b; iv, 52b-75a, 308a, 714a; v, 228b – I, 1166a; II, 317a; III, 366a, 384b; IV, 55b-79a, 322a, 743a; V, 226b
—mythology/-ie iv, 12a-13a – IV, 12a-14a
—sect(e)s iv, 43a-52b – IV, 45b-55b
Īrānī → Mughals
Īrānshahr → Nīshāpūr
al-Irānshahrī → Abu 'l-Abbās al-Irānshahrī
Iraten iv, **75a** – IV, 79a
Irbid iv, **75b**; vi, 603a – IV, **79b**; VI, 588a
Irbil i, 1160b; iii, 1268a; iv, **76a**; v, 145b; vi, 781b – I, 1195b; III, 1301a; IV, **80a**; V, 148a; VI, 771a
al-Irbilī, 'Izz al-Dīn (1326) viii, 806a – VIII, 833a
—al-Irbilī, Ṣalāḥ al-Dīn (1234) viii, 583b – VIII, 602a
'Irḍ iv, **77a**; vi, 146a, 475a – IV, **81a**; VI, 144b, 461a
Irdānā Bī v, 29a – V, 30a
al-Irdjānī, Abū Yaḥyā Zakariyyā' (X) ii, 369a; iii, 656a; iv, **78a** – II, 379a; III, 677a; IV, **82a**

ʿIrfān Pas̲h̲a iv, 879a – IV, 911b
Irian Barat iii, 1213a,b, 1215a – III, 1243b, 1244b, 1246a
Irid̲j̲ S̲h̲āhnawāz K̲h̲ān i, 80b, 81b, 769a, 1331a – I, 83a, 83b, 792a, 1371b
al-ʿIrʿīr ii, 176a – II, 181b
ʿIrḳ, ʿurūḳ i, 537a; ii, 92a; iv, **78b** – I, 553b; II, 94a; IV, **82b**
ʿIrḳ → Ṣaḥrāʾ
ʿIrḳ al-Luʾluʾ → Ṣadaf
ʿIrḳa (Arḳa) iv, **79a**; vi, 579a – IV, **83a**; VI, 564a
Irmiyā iv, **79a**; v, 442b – IV, **83a**; V, 445a
Irōn → Ossets/Ossètes
Iron Gate → Bāb al-Abwāb; Dar-i āhanīn
Irsāliyye iv, **79b**, 435b; v, 35a – IV, **83b**, 454b; V, 36a
Irtid̲j̲āʿ → Rad̲j̲ʿiyya
Irtid̲j̲āl iv, **80b** – IV, **84b**
Irtifāʿ → Falak; ʿIlm al-Hayʾa
Irtys̲h̲ s, 245a – S, 245a
Īrwānī, Muḥammad s, 76a – S, 76a
al-ʿĪṣ iii, 152b – III, 156a
al-ʿĪṣ, Umayya b. ʿAbd S̲h̲ams s, 103b – S, 102b
ʿĪsā, Āl iv, 87b, 88a – IV, 91b, 92a
ʿĪsā, Nahr i, 897a; iv, **86b**, 88b – I, 924a; IV, **90b**, 92b
ʿĪsā, al-Ẓāhir i, 666b – I, 687b
ʿĪsā b. Abī His̲h̲ām (XII) viii, 653b – VIII, 672b
ʿĪsā b. Abī K̲h̲ālid (819) vi, 336a, 337a – VI, 320a, 321b
ʿĪsā b. Aḥmad al-Dawsarī v, 40a, b – V, 41a, b
ʿĪsā b. Aḥmad al-Rāzī i, 321a, 600b – I, 330b, 620a
ʿĪsā b. ʿAlī (ʿAbbāsid(e)) iii, 883a – III, 907b
ʿĪsā b. ʿAlī (Marʿas̲h̲) (778) vi, 506a – VI, 491b
ʿĪsā b. ʿAlī (physician/médecin) i, 388a – I, 399a
ʿĪsā b. ʿAlī b. ʿĪsā i, 387b; iii, 895a – I, 398b; III, 919a
ʿĪsā b. ʿAlī Āl K̲h̲alīfa iv, 953b – IV, 986a
ʿĪsā b. ʿAlī al-Ḥarrānī iv, 340b – IV, 355a
ʿĪsā b. Abān (836) ix, 392b – IX, 405b
ʿĪsā b. Bāyazīd I (Ottoman) vi, 974a – VI, 966b
ʿĪsā b. Dīnār al-G̲h̲āfiḳī (827) i, 600a; iv, **87a**; vi, 281a – I, 619b; IV, **91a**; VI, 266a
ʿĪsā b. D̲j̲ābir, faḳīh (XV) vii, 243a – VII, 244b
ʿĪsā b. D̲j̲aʿfar (IX) iii, 907b – III, 932a
ʿĪsā b. D̲j̲aʿfar b. Abi al-Manṣūr (Baṣra) (VIII) vii, 646a; ix, 775a – VII, 646a; IX, 808b
ʿĪsā b. D̲j̲aʿfar al-Ḥasanī (Mecca) (994) vi, 435b – VI, 421a
ʿĪsā b. Gümüs̲h̲tigin (XII) vi, 380a – VI, 364b
ʿĪsā b. al-Hayt̲h̲am al-Ṣūfī (860) iv, 1162a, b; vii, 785a – IV, 1194a, b; VII, 787a
ʿĪsā b. His̲h̲ām (mukaddī) vi, 108b, 109a; vii, 495a – VI, 106b; VII, 495a
ʿĪsā b. Idrīs II ii, 874a; iii, 1035b – II, 894a; III, 1061b
ʿĪsā b. Idrīs (Dulafid(e)) ii, 623a – II, 639a
ʿĪsā b. Ismāʿīl al-Aḳsarāʿī → al-Aḳsarāʿī
ʿĪsā b. K̲h̲alāt (ʿUkaylid(e)) (XI) viii, 394a – VIII, 407b
ʿĪsā b. K̲h̲alīd b. al-Walīd → Abū Saʿd al-Mak̲h̲zūmī
ʿĪsā b. Maʿdān (Makrān) (1030) vi, 193a – VI, 177a
ʿĪsā b. Maʿḳil i, 1293a – I, 1332b
ʿĪsā b. Maryam i, 177a, 265a, 272a, 1020b, 1141a; ii, 280a; iii, 1206a; iv, **81a**; v, 41a, 421a, 423b, 1231a; vi, 218b, 628b, 629b, 726a – I, 182a, 273a, 280a, 1052a, 1175b; II, 288b; III, 1236b; IV, **85a**; V, 42b, 423a, 425b, 1221b; VI, 202b, 613b, 614b, 715a
ʿĪsā b. Māsard̲j̲īs vi, 641a – VI, 626b
ʿĪsā b. Māssa vi, 637b – VI, 622b
ʿĪsā b. Mayzad al-Aswad (757) vi, 1038a – VI, 1031b
ʿĪsā b. Miskīn i, 249b – I, 257b
ʿĪsā b. Muḥammad b. Abī K̲h̲ālid (826) vi, 335b – VI, 320a
ʿĪsā b. Muḥammad b. Sulaymān i, 661b – I, 682a
ʿĪsā b. Muhannā (1284) iii, 403a; iv, **87b**; vii, 461b – III, 415a; IV, **91b**; VII, 461b
ʿĪsā b. Muhīn (Marʿas̲h̲) (1271) vi, 507b – VI, 493a
ʿĪsā b. Mūsā (ʿAbbāsid(e)) (783) i, 96a, 134a, 618b, 952a, 1033b; iii, 984a; iv, **88a**; v, 1238a; vi, 332a, 333a, 427b, 428a, b; vii, 389a; x, 791b; s, 31b – I, 98b, 137b, 637b, 981b, 1065a; III, 1008b; IV, **92b**; V, 1229a; VI, 316b, 317b, 412b, 413a, b; VII, 390a; X, ; S, 31b
ʿĪsā b. Mūsā (Ḳarmaṭī) i, 96a, 962b; iv, 198b, 662a, b, 838a – I, 98b, 992a; IV, 207a, 688b, 689a, 871a
ʿĪsā b. Mūsā al-Nūs̲h̲arī v, 327a – V, 327a
ʿĪsā b. Nasṭūrus i, 823b, 824b; ii, 858a; iii, 77a – I, 846b, 847b; II, 878a; III, 79b
ʿĪsā b. Rayʿān al-Azdī iii, 655b; v, 696a – III, 676b; V, 701a
ʿĪsā b. Ṣāliḥ (S̲h̲arḳiyya Hināwī, ʿUmān) (1896) s, 355b, 356a – S, 355a,b
ʿĪsā b. Ṣāliḥ (ʿUmān) (1946) i, 1283a; viii, 993a – I, 1321b; VIII, 1028a
ʿĪsā b. Salmān iv, 954a – IV, 986b
ʿĪsā b. al-S̲h̲ayk̲h̲ al-S̲h̲aybānī (882) ii, 344a; iv, **88b**; viii, 149a – II, 353b; IV, **92b**; VIII, 151a
ʿĪsā b. ʿUmar al-Hamdānī iv, 91a – IV, 95a
ʿĪsā b. ʿUmar al-T̲h̲aḳafī (766) i, 42b; iv, **91a**; vii, 815a; viii, 661a – I, 44a; IV, **95a**; VII, 816b; VIII, 680b
ʿĪsā b. ʿUt̲h̲mān b. Fūdī iii, 281b, 282a – III, 290a,b
ʿĪsā b. Yaḥyā i, 213a, 1236b – I, 219b, 1274a
ʿĪsā b. Yūsuf al-ʿIrāḳī iii, 1246b – III, 1279a
ʿĪsā b. Zakariyyāʾ ii, 140b – II, 144b
ʿĪsā b. Zayd b. ʿAlī s, 130a – S, 129a
ʿĪsā b. Zurʿa vi, 845b – VI, 836a
ʿĪsā Aydinog̲h̲lu i, 778a, 783b – I, 801a, 806b
ʿĪsā al-Asadī → al-Asadī, ʿĪsā
ʿĪsā Beg b. Evenros ii, 721a; iv, 139b – II, 739b; IV, 145b
ʿĪsā Beg b. Isḥāḳ (Bosnia/-e) (XV) vii, 244a – VII, 245b
ʿĪsā Bey i, 1263a, 1264b – I, 1301b, 1303a
ʿĪsā Čelebi i, 510b; ii, 599a – I, 526b; II, 614a
ʿĪsā al-ʿĪsā ii, 468a – II, 480a
ʿĪsā Ḳāʾimmaḳām (Īrān) s, 70b – S, 71a
ʿĪsā K̲h̲ān Iʿtimād al-Dawla iii, 554a – III, 573a
ʿĪsā K̲h̲ān Tark̲h̲ān I (1565) vi, 189b, 190a – VI, 173b
ʿĪsā K̲h̲ān Tark̲h̲ān II (1644) vi, 190a – VI, 174a
ʿĪsā al-K̲h̲aṭṭī (VII) vii, 546a – VII, 546a
ʿĪsā al-Kinānī al-Ḳayrawānī (1875) vi, 355b – VI, 339b
ʿĪsā al-Lag̲h̲wāṭī, al-Ḥād̲j̲d̲j̲ (1737) vi, 249a – VI, 233b
ʿĪsā al-Nūs̲h̲arī (908) vi, 674a; vii, 543a – VI, 660b; VII, 543a
ʿĪsā Sawād̲j̲ī (XV) viii, 750b – VIII, 770b
ʿĪsā al-Suktānī i, 428a – I, 440a
ʿĪsā ʿUbayd (1922) vi, 957a – VI, 949b
ʿĪsā al-Ẓāhir (Artuḳid(e)) (1406) vi, 540b, 541a – VI, 525a, b
Isaac → Isḥāḳ
Isaac b. Abraham iv, 605b – IV, 630a
Isāf wa-Nāʾila iv, **91a**; vi, 349a, 737a, 738b; viii, 756b; s, 133a – IV, **95b**; VI, 333b, 726a, 727b; VIII, 781aS, 132b
Īsāg̲h̲ūd̲j̲ī iv, **92a** – IV, **96a**

Isaiah/Isaïe → Shaʿyā
Isakča iv, **92a** – IV, **96a**
ʿIsām, Banū viii, 690a – VIII, 710a
ʿIsām al-Khawlānī (902) vi, 926b – VI, 918b
ʿIṣāmī, Fakhr al-Dīn (XIV) ii, 153b; iii, 1155b; iv, **92b**; vi, 48b, 532b; ix, 241b; s 105b – II, 158b; III, 1184a; IV, **96b**; VI, 47a, 516b; IX, 248a; S, 105a
ʿIsāmī, ʿIzz al-Dīn iv, 210b – IV, 220a
Īsānpur vi, 369a – VI, 353a
Īsar-dās (XVIII) iv, **93a** – IV, **97a**
ʿIsāwā, ʿĪsāwiyya i, 371a; iv, **93b**; vii, 36b; s, 325b, 350b, 351a – I, 382a; IV, **97b**; VII, 36b; S, 325b, 350b, 351a
ʿIsāwī → Naṣārā
al-ʿIsāwiyya (al-Iṣfahāniyya) i, 130a; iv, **96a**; ix, 73b – I, 133b; IV, **100a**; IX, 79a
Iṣbaʿ iv, **96b** – IV, **100b**
Iṣbahān → Iṣfahān
Isçehisar, Ischtschi Ḥiṣār → Īsdje Ḳarā Ḥiṣār
Īsdje Ḳarā Ḥiṣār iv, 578a – IV, 601b
Iṣfabadh b. Sāwtigīn al-Turkumānī iv, 208a – IV, 217b
Iṣfahān i, 142b, 643a; ii, 335a; iv, **97a**, 131b, 977b, 979a; v, 874a; vi, 17a, b, 18b, 20a, 198b, 274b, 275a, b, 332b, 365b, 366a, 486a, 494b, 515a, 516a, b, 523a, 525b, 526b, 527a, 539a, b, 552b, 633b; viii, 70a; ix, 46a; s, 23b, 43b, 54a, 75a, 95b, 140b, 141b, 142a, 157b, 169b, 257a, 274b, 275a, 308a, 326a, 336a, 363b, 365b, 380a, 384a – I, 146b, 663b; II, 345a; IV, **101b**, 137a, 1010a, 1011b; V, 880a; VI, 15a, b, 16b, 17b, 182b, 259b, 260a, b, 317a, 349b, 350a, 472a, 480a, 500b, 501a, b, 507b, 510a, 511a, b, 523b, 524a, 537a, 618b; VIII, 72a; IX, 47a; S, 23b, 44a, 54b, 75b, 95a, 140b, 141b, 142a, 158a, 169b, 256b, 274b, 275a, 308a, 325b, 335b, 363b, 365a, 380b, 384b
—history/histoire iii, 156a, 863b, 864a; iv, 7b, 37a, 97a-105b, 465a, b; v, 1157a – III, 159b, 887b, 888a; IV, 8a, 39b, 101b-110a, 486a, b; V, 1147a
—institutions ii, 426a; iii, 1124a; iv, 101b, 103a; s, 139a – II, 437a; III, 1152a; IV, 106a, 107b; S, 138b
—monuments i, 400b; iii, 1124b, 1125a; iv, 36b, 105b-107a, 1137a; v, 1148b, 1149a – I, 412a; III, 1152b, 1153a; IV, 39a, 110b-111b, 1132a; V, 1139b, 1140a
Iṣfahān b. Ḳarā Yūsuf iv, 587b, 588a – IV, 611a, b
al-Iṣfahānī → Abu 'l-Faradj; Abū Nuʿaym; ʿAlī b. Ḥamza; Djamāl al-Dīn Muḥammad; al-Djawād; Ḥamza; Ibn Dāwūd; ʿImād al-Dīn al-Kātib; al-Rāghib Rūkn al-Dīn
al-Iṣfahānī, Abū Mūsā Muḥammad iii, 821a – III, 845a
al-Iṣfahānī, Ḥādjdjī Āḳā Nūr Allāh s, 342b – S, 342a
al-Iṣfahānī, Ḥadjdjī Sayyid Abu 'l-Ḥasan Mūsawī (1946) vi, 552b, 553a; vii, 301a; s, 158a, 342a – VI, 537b; VII, 303a; S, 158a, 341b
al-Iṣfahānī, Mīrzā Abū Ṭālib s, 108a – S, 107b
al-Iṣfahānī, Niẓām al-Dīn (1281) viii, 583b – VIII, 602a
al-Iṣfahābī, Shams al-Dīn Abū ʿAbd Allāh Muḥammad b. Maḥmūd (ḳāḍī) (1289) vi, 381b – VI, 365b
al-Iṣfahānī, Shaykh Faḍl Allāh, Shaykh al-Sharīʿa (1920) vi, 552b; s, 342a – VI, 537a; S, 341b
Iṣfahāniyya → ʿĪsāwiyya
Isfandiyār Khān i, 120b; s, 91a – I, 124a; S, 90b
Isfandiyār b. Adharbād iv, 662a – IV, 689a
Isfandiyār b. Bishtāsb iv, 809b – IV, 842a
Isfandiyār Khān v, 24a; s, 281a – V, 25a; S, 281a
Isfarā'inī → al-Isfarāyīnī
Isfarāyīn iv, **107a** – IV, **112a**
al-Isfarāyīnī → Ṭāhir b. Muḥammad
al-Isfarāyīnī, Abu 'l-ʿAbbās al-Faḍl b. Aḥmad (vizier) (1013) vi, 915b – VI, 907a
al-Isfarāyīnī, Abū Ḥāmid (1015) ii, 136a; v, 345a; ix, 187b – II, 139b; V, 346a; IX, 193a
al-Isfarāyīnī, Abū Isḥāḳ Ibrāhīm (1027) iv, **107b**, 183a – IV, **112b**, 191a
al-Isfarāyīnī, Saʿd al-Dīn i, 827a – I, 850a
Isfendiyār, Mubāriz al-Dīn (Ḳasṭamuni) (1440) iv, 108b; vi, 974b – IV, 113a; VI, 966b
Isfendiyār-oghlu i, 1256a; iv, **108b**, 737b, 738a – I, 1294a; IV, **113a**, 767b, 768a
Isfendiyār-oghlu Ismāʿīl Beg (Sinop(e)) (1460) iv, 108b; vi, 71a; vii, 594b – IV, 113a; VI, 68b; VII, 594b
Isfendiyār-oghlu, Mubāriz al-Dīn (1440) vii, 644a – VII, 644a
Isfendiyār-oghlu Shemsī Aḥmed Pasha (Kïzïl Aḥmedlü) (1580) iv, 108b; vii, 595b – IV, 113a; VII, 595b
Isfīd Diz → Kalʿa-yi Safīd
Isfīdh (Safīdj/Sipih) → Nuṣratābād
Isfīdjāb v, 856a; ix, 557b, 659b – V, 863a; IX, 586a, 685a
Isfinṭ → Afsantīn
Isfizārī, Abū Ḥātim Muẓaffar (1100) viii, 542a – VIII, 559b
ʿIshāʾ → Ṣalāt
Isḥāḳ (Isaac) iii, 980a; iv, **109a**, 184a, b – III, 1004b; IV, **114a**, 192b
Isḥāḳ (Ḳarmaṭī) iv, 663b – IV, 690a, b
Isḥāḳ, Adīb (1885) ii, 417b, 429a, 466b, 467b; iv, **111b**; vii, 902b – II, 428a, 440a, 478a, 479a; IV, **116b**; VII, 903b
Isḥāḳ, Banū vii, 390a – VII, 391a
Isḥāḳ b. Abraham b. Ezra i, 111b – I, 115a
Isḥāḳ b. ʿAlī b. Yūsuf (Almoravid(e)) (1146) vi, 592a; vii, 585b – VI, 577a; VII, 586a
Isḥāḳ b. Alp Takīn (Ghaznawid(e)) i, 421b; vi, 433a – I, 433b, VI, 418a
Isḥāḳ b. Ayāz ii, 322a – II, 331b
Isḥāḳb. Ayyūb, Taghlibī (870) iv, 89b; vi, 900a – IV, 93b; VI, 891b
Isḥāḳ b. Aʿẓam Khān i, 88a – I, 90b
Isḥāḳ b. Ghāniya ii, 112a – II, 114b
Isḥāḳb. Ḥunayn (910) i, 234b, 589a, 631b, 784b, 1340a; ii, 362a; iii, 579a, 1045a, 1136b; iv, **110a**; vi, 204a, 347a; vii, 83a; s, 411b, 412a – I, 242a, 608b, 652a, 808a, 1380b; II, 372a; III, 599a, 1071a, 1165a; IV, **115a**; VI, 188a, 331a; VII, 84a; S, 412a
Isḥāḳ b. al-Ḥusayn (geographe(r)) iii, 1077a – III, 1103b
Isḥāḳ b. Ibrāhīm b. Ḥusayn b. Muṣʿab (Ṭāhirid(e)) Isḥāḳ b. Ibrāhīm B. Muṣʿab (Ṭāhirid(e)) (Ṣāhib al-Shurta) (849) i, 153b; vi, 336b, 337b; vii, 2b, 776b; x, 105a; s, 106a – I, 158a; VI, 320b, 322a; VII, 2b, 778a; X, 113a; S, 105b
Isḥāḳ b. Ibrāhīm b. Wahb al-Kātib (X) i, 982a, 1115a; vii, 661a – I, 1012b, 1148b; VII, 660b
Isḥāḳ b. Ibrāhīm Ḳarāmān-oghlu iv, 624a – IV, 649a
Isḥāḳ b. Ibrāhīm al-Mawṣilī (850) i, 118a, 718a; ii, 246a, 1011b; iii, 698b, 730b, 989a, 996b; iv, **110b**, 822a; v, 319b; vi, 97b, 103a, 262a; vii, 518b, 559a, 681b, 682a, 976a, 1042b; s, 64a, 128b, 183a – I, 121b, 739a; II, 253a, 1035a; III, 720b, 753a, 1013b, 1021a; IV, **115b**, 855a; V, 319a; VI, 95b, 101a, 246b; VII, 519a, 559b, 681b, 682a, 976a, 1044b; S, 64b, 127b, 184b
Isḥāḳ b. ʿImrān ii, 60a; iv, 627a, 829b; s, 303b, 314a – II, 61a; IV, 651b, 862b; S, 303b, 313b

Isḥāḳ b. Ismāʿīl, amīr   iv, 345a, 669b; v, 488a, b – IV, 359b, 697a; V, 491a, b
Isḥāḳ b. Ismāʿīl b. Ḥammād (860)   s, **384b** – S, **385a**
Isḥāḳ b. Kundādj(īḳ) (Mosul) (891)   i, 279a; ii, 524a; iv, 89b, 90a; v, 49a; vi, 900a; vii, 766a – I, 287b; II, 537a; IV, 93b, 94a; V, 50b; VI, 891b; VII, 767b
Isḥāḳ b. Maḥmaṣhādh   iv, 668a, 669a – IV, 695b, 696a
Isḥāḳ b. Muḥammad b. Ghāniya   ii, 1007a – II, 1030b
Isḥāḳ b. Muḥammad al-Aḥmar (IX)   vii, 517a – VII, 517b
Isḥāḳ b. Murād   iv, **111a** – IV, **116a**
Isḥāḳ b. Mūsā al-Hādī (IX)   vi, 335a – VI, 319b
Isḥāḳ b. Rāhwayh   → Ibn Rāhwayh
Isḥāḳ b. Sulaymān al-Isrāʾīlī (955)   i, 785b; ii, 60a; iv, **111b**, 304a, 829b; viii, 661b; s, 197b, 314a – I, 809a; II, 61a; IV, **116b**, 318a, 862b; VIII, 680b; S, 197b, 313b
Isḥāḳ b. Zayd b. al-Ḥārith al-Anṣārī   i, 49a; ii, 441a; iv, 838a – I, 50b; II, 453a; IV, 871a
Isḥāḳ Barbarossa   i, 678a,b – I, 698b, 699a
Isḥāḳ Efendi (1835)   iv, **112b** – IV, **117b**
Isḥāḳ Khān Karaʿī   iii, 1107b – III, 1135a
Isḥāḳ Khuttalānī   i, 392b; v, 301a – I, 404a; V, 300b
Isḥāḳ al-Mawṣilī   → Isḥāḳ b. Ibrāhīm al-Mawṣilī
Isḥāḳ Pasha (1453)   vi, 70a, 1025b – VI, 68a, 1018a
Isḥāḳ Pasha (Georgia) (1728)   v, 494a, b – V, 497a
Isḥāḳ al-Raffāʾ   iv, 797a, 800b – IV, 829b, 833a
Isḥāḳ Sükūtī (1903)   ii, 474b; iii, 393a; iv, **113a** – II, 487a; III, 405b; IV, **118a**
Isḥāḳ al-Turk   iv, 16b; v, 64a – IV, 17b; V, 65b
Isḥāḳābād   vi, 115b, VI, 113b
Isḥāḳid(e)s (Fūman)   viii, 450a – VIII, 465a
Isḥāḳiyya   → Kazarūniyya
Isḥāḳiyya (Karrāmiyya)   iv, 668a; v, 945b – IV, 695b; V, 949b
Ishakovič   → Üsküb
Isḥāḳzāy   ii, 629a – II, 644b
Isḥān   iv, **113a** – IV, **118a**
Īṣhāns   vi, 768a – VI, 757b
Isḥāra   iv, **113b** – IV, **118b**
Ishbāʿ (Elisabeth)   vi, 630a, VI, 615a
al-Ishbīli   → Abu ʾ-l-Khayr; al-Fatḥ b. Khāḳān; Ibn al-Kharrāṭ; Ibn Khayr; al-Ruʿaynī
Ishbīliya (Seville)   i, 5b, 6b, 7a,b, 83a, 162a, 491a, 493a; iii, 681a; iv, **114b**; vi, 361b, 364a, 431a, 597a; s, 388a – I, 5b, 6b, 7a,b, 85b, 166b, 506a, 508a; III, 702b; IV, **120a**; VI, 345b, 348a, 416a, 582a; S, 388b
—constructions   i, 499b, 501b, 1226b; iii, 498b; iv, 117a-118b – I, 514b, 516b, 1264a; III, 515b; IV, 122a-123b
Īshīk-āḳāsī   iv, **118b** – IV, **123b**
Ishim Khān   ii, 45a – II, 46a
ʿIshḳ   i, 416a; ii, 552a; iii, 103a; iv, **118b** – I, 428a; II, 565b; III, 105b; IV, **124a**
Ishkāshim   i, 853b – I, 877a
Ishkāshimī   i, 225a, 854a – I, 231b, 877b
ʿIshkhan   ii, 1118a – II, 1144b
ʿIshḳī, Muḥammad Riḍā Mīrzāda (1924)   iv, 789b; vi, 609a, 764a; vii, 662a, 754b; viii, 513a; s, 110a – IV, 821b; VI, 594a, 753a; VII, 661b, 756a; VIII, 530b; S, 109b
ʿIshḳiyya   x, 250b – X, 269a
Ishḳodra   i, 285a, 654a, 657a; iv, 588b; s, 281b, 359b – I, 293b, 674b, 677b; IV, 612a; S, 281b, 359b
Ishmael   → Ismāʿīl
Ishmaelite   v, 1014b, 1015b, 1019a – V, 1010b, 1011b, 1015a
Īshōʿdⁿnaḥ   vi, 648b – VI, 633b

Ishrāḳ   → al-Dāmād
Ishrāḳ   ii, 774a; iv, 50b, **119b** – II, 792b; IV, 53b, **125a**
Ishrāḳiyyūn   i, 234b, 351a, 416b, 596a; iv, **120b** – I, 242a, 362a, 428a, 615a; IV, **125b**
Ishtar   → Manāt
Ishtib (Štip)   iv, **121b**; vi, 89a – IV, **126b**; VI, 87a
Ishtiḳāḳ (etymology/-ie)   iv, **122a** – IV, **127a**
Ishtiḳāḳ (rhetoric/-que)   → Tadjnīs
Ishtirāk   → Tawriya
Ishtirākiyya   iv, **123b** – IV, **128b**
Īshūrūni   iv, 301b – IV, 315a
Īshwar-dās   → Īsar-dās
Īshwar Singh (Udjdjayn) (1455)   vi, 62a – VI, 60a
al-Isʿirdī, Nūr al-Dīn Muḥammad   iv, 1006a – IV, 1038a
al-Iskāfī, Abū ʿAlī Muḥammad b. Aḥmad b. al-Djunayd (X)   vii, 312b – VII, 314b, 315a
al-Iskāfī, Abū Djaʿfar Muḥammad (854)   iv, **126b**; vi, 636b; s, 13b – IV, **132a**; VI, 621b; S, 14a
al-Iskāfī, Abu ʾl-Faḍl Djaʿfar (IX)   iv, **126b** – IV, **132a**
al-Iskāfī, Abū Isḥāḳ Muḥammad (968)   iv, **127a** – IV, **132b**
al-Iskāfī, Abu ʾl-Ḳāsim Djaʿfar   iv, 127a – IV, 132b
Iskandar, Banū   vi, 938b – VI, 930b
Iskandar (Ḳarā-ḳoyunlu)   iv, 587a, b – IV, 609b, 611a
Iskandar b. Kayūmarth   iv, 898a; v, 663a – IV, 840b; V, 668b
Iskandar b. ʿUmar Shaykh (XV)   i, 1342a; ix, 667b – I, 1382b; IX, 683b
Iskandar, Dhu ʾl-Ḳarnayn   i, 935a, 1101a, 1206b; ii, 112b, 133a, 278b; iii, 181a; iv, **127b**, 131a, 498a; vi, 207b; viii, 79b – I, 963b, 1134a, 1242a; II, 115a, 136b, 286b; III, 185a; IV, **133a**, 136b, 519b; VI, 192a; VIII, 81b
Iskandar al-Afrūdīsī   i, 342a; ii, 550a, 771a; iii, 728b; iv, **129a** – I, 352b; II, 563b, 789b; III, 751b; IV, **134b**
Iskandar Agha b. Yaʿḳūb (Abkaryus) (1885)   iv, **130b**; vi, 352a – IV, **136a**; VI, 336b
Iskandar Beg   → Iskender Beg
Iskandar Beg al-Shahīr bi-Munshī (1632)   iv, **130b**; vi, 202a, 483a, 495a; viii, 787b – IV, **136a**; VI 186b, 469a, 480b; VIII, 814a
Iskandar al-Dimashkī   iv, 129a – IV, 134b
Iskandar Khān   i, 46b, 970a; ii, 44b; s, 340a – I, 47b, 1000a; II, 45b; S, 339b
Iskandar Muda (1636)   i, 743b; iii, 1220a; ix, 296a; s, 199b, 200b – I, 765b; III, 1251a; IX, 304b; S, 199b, 200b
Iskandar nāma   i, 299b, 325a; iii, 113a; iv, 62b, **127b**, 902b, 904a – I, 309a, 335a; III, 115b; IV, 66a, **133a**, 935b, 937a
Iskandar Pāsha   iv, 435b – IV, 455a
Iskandar-i Shaykhī b. Afrāsiyāb (1403)   i, 237a; vi, 511a, 512a, b – I, 244b; VI, 496b, 497a, b
Iskandar Shāh (Malacca) (XVI)   vi, 207b – VI, 192a
Iskandar Thānī   i, 743b – I, 765b
al-Iskandariyya (Egypt(e))   i, 13a, 32a, 121b, 396b, 531b, 947a, 976a, 1288a; ii, 65a; iii, 1082b, 1193b; iv, **132a**; vi, 45b, 140b, 324a, b, 358b, 359a, b, 378b; vii, 68a; s, 1a, 5a, 120b, 121b – I, 13a, 33a, 125a, 408a, 548a, 976a, 1006a, 1327b; II, 66a; III, 1109b, 1223b; IV, **137b**; VI, 44a, 139a, 308b, 342a, 343a, b, 363a; VII, 69a; S, 1a, 4a, 120a, 121a
—institutions   ii, 424a; v, 92a – II, 434b; V, 94a
al-Iskandariyya (towns/villes)   iv, **131a** – IV, **136b**

Iskandarūn (Alexandretta) i, 468b, 476b; ii, 35b; iv, **138a**; vi, 509b – I, 482b, 490b; II, 36b; IV, **143b**; VI, 494b
Iskandarūna iv, 131a – IV, 136b
Iskeče s, 330a – S, 330a
Iskender Beg (1468) i, 309b, 651b, 654b; ii, 721a; iv, **138b**, 574b; v, 724a, 725a; vii, 595a – I, 319a, 672a, 675b; II, 739b; IV, **144b**, 597b; V, 729b, 730a; VII, 594b
Iskender Čelebi i, 1083a; ii, 1042b; iii, 998b; vi, 610a – I, 1115a; II, 1067a; III, 1023b; VI, 594b
Iskender Pasha i, 268a; ii, 704b – I, 276a; II, 722a
Iṣlāḥ i, 383a; iv, **141a** – I, 394a; IV, **146b**
Islām ii, 294a; iv, 44a-52a, **171b** – II, 302a; IV, 46b-55a, **179a**
Islâm Ansiklopedisi s, 42a – S, 42a
Islām, encyclopaedias/-édies → Mawsūʿa
Islām Girāy I (Crimea/-ée) (1532) iv, **178a**; x, 811a – IV, **185a**; X,
Islām Girāy II (Crimea/-ée) (1588) ii, 1113b; iv, **178b** – II, 1139b; IV, **185a**
Islām Girāy III (Crimea/-ée) (1654) iv, **178b**; v, 139b, 719b; vi, 986b; vii, 62a; x, 811a – IV, **185b**; V, 142a, 724b; VI, 979a; VII, 62b; X,
Islām Khān i, 719b; ii, 216b, 797b – I, 741a; II, 223a, 816b
Islām Khān Sarwānī s, 203a – S, 202b
Islām Shāh Niʿmat Allāh Yazdī (XVI) vi, 483a – VI, 469a
Islām Shāh b. Shīr Shāh Sūr (Delhi) (1554) i, 432b; ii, 259a, 271a,b; iii, 199b, 423a, 492b; ix, 894a; s, 1b, 3a – I, 444b; II, 266a, 279a,b; III, 204b, 436b, 509b; IX, 930a; S, 1b, 2b
Islāmābād (India) ii, 32a; iv, **177b** – II, 32b; IV, **186a**
Islāmābād (Pakistan) iv, **177b** – IV, **186a**
Islāmī Djamāʿat vi, 78b – VI, 76b
Islāmī Djumhūrī Ittiḥād viii, 244a – VIII, 249b
Işlitan iii, 1040a – III, 1066a
Islambol → Istanbul
Isly (river/rivière) iv, **179a**; vii, 391a – IV , **186b**; VII, 392a
Ism (name/nom) ii, 302a; iv, **179a**; v, 396a – II, 310b; IV, **187a**; V, 397a
Ism (in grammar/en grammaire) iv, **181b** – IV, **189a**
ʿIṣma iii, 1024a; iv, **182b** – III, 1049b; IV, **190b**
ʿIsma Khātūn (XII) vii, 755b – VII, 757a
Ismaël → Ismāʿīl
Ismāʿīl (Ishmael) iii, 980a; iv, **184a**, 318a; v, 1014b; vi, 105b, 106a, 144b – III, 1004b; IV, **192a**, 332a; V, 1010b; VI, 103b, 143a
Ismāʿīl (engineer/ingénieur) (1272) vi, 406a – VI, 390b
Ismāʿīl (Izmail, town/ville) iv, **185a** – IV, **193b**
Ismāʿīl , Imām → Ismāʿīl b. Djaʿfar al-Ṣādiḳ
Ismāʿīl I , Abu 'l-Walīd (Naṣrid(e)) (1325) i, 1057b; vii, 1020, **1023a** – I, 1089b; VII, 1022a, **1025a**
Ismāʿīl II, Abu 'l-Walīd (Naṣrid(e)) (1360) vii, 1020b, **1024a** – VII, 1022b, **1026b**
Ismāʿīl (Noghay) (1563) viii, 86b – VIII, 88b
Ismāʿīl I (Rasūlid(e)) ii, 926a; iv, 1188b – II, 947b; IV, 1221b
Ismāʿīl I Shāh (Ṣafawid(e)) (1524) i, 193b, 228a, 237b, 262b, 311b, 625b, 627b, 903b, 920a, 1019a, 1030b, 1087a, 1120a,b, 1211b; ii, 8a, 44b, 254b, 310b, 344b, 374a, 812a, 937a, 967a; iii, 114a, 177b, 274a, 316a, 585a, 1101a; iv, 34b, 49b, 102b, **186a**, 389a, 610a, 855a; v, 457a, 492b, 603b; vi, 714b; vii, 176b, 300a, 316b, 672b; viii, 115b, 750b, 765b, 767a; ix, 128b; s, 94b, 95a, 138b, 147b, 382b – I, 199a, 235a, 244b, 270b, 321a, 646b, 648b, 931a, 948a, 1050b, 1062a, 1099a, 1119a, 1154a, 1247b; II, 8a, 45b, 262a, 319b, 354a, 384a, 831b, 959a, 989a; III, 116b, 181b, 282a, 325b, 605b, 1128a; IV, 37a, 52b, 107b, **194a**, 404b, 634b, 888b; V, 459b, 495b, 607b; VI, 703b; VII, 178b, 302a, 319a, 672b; VIII, 117b, 771a, 791a, 792b; IX, 133a; S, 94a, 94b, 138a, 147b, 383a
Ismāʿīl II Shāh (Ṣafawid(e)) (1577) i, 7b, 1208b; ii, 310b; iii, 157b; iv, **188a**; vii, 442a – I, 7b, 1244b; II, 319b; III, 161a; IV, **196a**; VII, 443a
Ismāʿīl III Shāh (Ṣafawid(e)) ii, 311a; iv, 104b, 390a, b, 639b – II, 319b; IV, 109a, 406b, 407a, 666a
Ismāʿīl I b. Aḥmad I (Sāmānid(e)) (907) i, 278a, 452b, 984b, 1001a, 1294a; iv, 21b, 22a, **188b**, 658b; v, 58a, 853a, 856a; vi, 365b; vii, 418a, 760a; viii, 63a, 500a, 796b, 1026b – I, 286b, 465b, 1015a, 1032a, 1333b; IV, 23b, **196b**, 685a; V, 59b, 859b, 863a; VI, 349b; VII, 419b, 761b; VIII, 64a, 517a, 823a, 1061a
Ismāʿīl II b. Nūḥ II (Sāmānid(e)) (1004) iv, **189b**; v, 622b; viii, 1028a; s, 176b – IV, **197b;** V, 626b; VIII, 1063a; S, 177b
Ismāʿīl, Abū 'l-Faḍl i, 1332a,b; ii, 282a; iii, 120a – I, 1372b, 1373a; II, 290a; III, 122b
Ismāʿīl, Mawlāy (ʿAlawid(e)) → Mawlāy Ismāʿīl
Ismāʿīl b. ʿAbbād → Ibn ʿAbbād al-Ṣāḥib
Ismāʿīl b. ʿAbbād al-Muʿtadid i, 6a – I, 6b
Ismāʿīl b. ʿAbbās → Ismāʿīl I (Rasūlid(e))
Ismāʿ īl b. ʿAbd al-Ḥaḳḳ v, 60a, b – V, 62a
Ismāʿīl b. ʿAbd al-Raḥmān b. Dhi 'l-Nūn ii, 243a – II, 250a
Ismāʿīl b. Abī Khālid (763) vii, 576a – VII, 576b
Ismāʿīl b. Abu 'l-Ḳāsim Djaʿfar b. al-Uṭrūsh i, 688a; iii, 255a – I, 688a; III, 262b
Ismāʿīlb. Abī Sahl al-Nawbakhtī i, 143b – I, 148a
Ismāʿīl b. Abī Uways (841) vii, 691b – VII, 691b
Ismāʿīl b. Aḥmad Ankarāwī (1631) iii, 711a; iv, **190a**; viii, 306a – III, 733b; IV, **198a**; VIII, 316a
Ismāʿīl b. ʿAlī b. ʿUthmān al-Thaḳafī s, 163a – S, 162b
Ismāʿīl b. ʿAmmār (VIII) viii, 996b – VIII, 1031a
Ismāʿīl b. Bulbul, vizier (892) iii, 739a, 767b, 955a; iv, **189a**; vii, 766a, 975a – III, 761b, 790b, 979b; IV, **197a**; VII, 767b, 975b
Ismāʿīl b. Djaʿfar b. Sulaymān b. ʿAlī (Baṣra) vi, 335a – VI, 319b
Ismāʿīl b. Djaʿfar al-Ṣādiḳ (VIII) i, 402b, 550b; ii, 851a; iv, 198a, 1133a; v, 1242b; vi, 333b; vii, 645b – I, 414b, 568b; II, 871a; IV, 206b, 1164b; V, 1233a; VI, 318a; VII, 645a
Ismāʿīl b. Djāmiʿ → Ibn Djāmiʿ, Ismāʿīl
Ismāʿīl b. Gīlākī (Ismāʿīlī, Ṭabas) (XII) vii, 489b, 535b – VII, 489a, 535b
Ismāʿīl b. Haydar b. Djunayd (Ṣafawid(e)) (XV) viii, 766b – VIII, 792a
Usmāʿīl b. Isḥāḳ b. Ismāʿīl b. Ḥammād → al-Azdī
—b. Ismāʿīl b. Ḥammād (910) s, **385a** – S, **385b**
Ismāʿīl b. al-Ḳāsim → Abu 'l-ʿAtāhiya
Ismāʿīl b. Khalaf (1065) ix, 587a – IX, 609a
Ismāʿīl b. Māzin iii, 299b – III, 309a
Ismāʿīl b. Muḥammad (amīr) (Kadmūs) (XIX) viii, 923a – VIII, 954b
Ismāʿīl b. Muḥammad b. ʿAlī Kurd Taymūr (XIX) vi, 75a – VI, 73a
Ismāʿīl b. Muḥammad al-Nīsābūrī iii, 738b – III, 761b
Ismāʿīl b. Mūsā b. Mūsā iv, 713a; v, 683a – IV, 741b; V, 688a
Ismāʿīl b. Mūsā al-Kāẓim s, 95a – S, 94b
Ismāʿīl b. Nūḥ (1004) iv, **189b**; v, 622b; s, 176b – IV, **197b**; V, 626b; S, 177b

Ismāʿīl b. Sebüktigin (X) ii, 799a, 1050b; iv, **189b**; vi, 65a – II, 818a, 1075a; IV, **197b**; VI, 63a
Ismāʿīl b. Ṣubayḥ al-Ḥarrānī, kātib al-sirr (VIII) vi, 333b – VI, 318a
Ismāʿīl b. ʿUbayd Allāh (Sūs) (VIII) vi, 923b – VI, 915a
Ismāʿīl b. Yāḳūtī i, 1051b, 1052a; iv, 28b – I, 1083a, b; IV, 30b
Ismāʿīl b. Yasār al-Nisāʾī (VIII) i, 206b; iv, 54a, **189b**; vii, 310a, 648b – I, 212b; IV, 57a, **198a**; VII, 312b; 648a
Ismāʿīl b. Yūsuf b. Ibrāhīm al-Saffāk (IX) vi, 106a, 148a; vii, 390b, 794a – VI, 104a, 146b; VII, 391b, 795b
Ismāʿīl b. Yūsuf al-Baṣrī iv, 1004a – IV, 1036b
Ismāʿīl b. Yūsuf al-Ukhayḍir i, 551a – I, 568b
Ismāʿīl b. Ziyād al-Nafūsī iii, 654a; iv, 336b – III, 675a; IV, 351a
Ismāʿīl ʿAdil Shāh iii, 425b, 1160a – III, 439b, 1188b
Ismāʿīl Agha Čengič (1840) viii, 520a,b – VIII, 537b, 538a
Ismāʿīl Agha Şīmḳo ʿAbdoy i, 1030b; v, 466a – I, 1062a; V, 468b
Ismāʿīl Allāh Bukhārī (XV) x, 83b – X,
Ismāʿīl ʿĀṣim Efendi → Čelebi-zade
Ismāʿīl al-Aṭrash ii, 636b, 637a – II, 653a
Ismāʿīl al-Azharī (Sudan) ix, 748b → IX, 781a
Ismāʿīl Bey (Miṣr) (1791) iii, 992a; iv, 853a; vii, 179b – III, 1016b; IV, 886a; VII, 181b
Ismāʿīl Bey (Serez) i, 778b, 1304a; ii, 640a – I, 801b, 1344a; II, 656b
Ismāʿīl Bey b. Īwāẓ Bey iv, 723a – IV, 752a
Ismāʿīl Bey Isfendiyār-oghlu iv, 108b – IV, 113b
Ismāʿīl Bey Ḳutḳashînlî ii, 217a – II, 223b
Ismāʿīl al-Dhabīḥ (engineer/ingénieur) (XX) vi,165b – VI, 158a
Ismāʿīl Djānbulāt iv, 284b, 285b – IV, 296b, 298a
Ismāʿīl Gasprinski → Gaspralî
Ismāʿīl Ghālib (1895) iii, 993b; iv, **190b** – III, 1018a; IV, **198b**
Ismāʿīl Ḥaḳḳi ʿĀlīshān (1944) ii, 637b; iv, **191a** – II, 653b; IV, **199b**
Ismāʿīl Ḥaḳḳī Baltadjîoghlu iv, 1126b – IV, 1158a
Ismāʿīl Ḥaḳḳī al-Brūsawī (1725) ii, 475a, 542b; iv, **191a** – II, 487a, 556a; IV, **199b**
Usmāʿīl Haḳḳī Pasha, Ḥāfiẓ (1911) ii, 698b, 699b; vi, 983b – II, 716a, 717b; VI, 975b
Ismāʿīl Husrev (XX) vi, 95a – VI, 93a
Ismāʿīl Kāmil Pasha ii, 351b, 615b, 874b, 1110b – II, 361a, 630b, 895a, 1137a
Ismāʿīl Kemāl i, 657b; iv, 195b – I, 678a; IV, 203b
Ismāʿīl Khān ii, 45b – II, 46b
Ismāʿīl Khān Ḳashḳāy iv, 706a – IV, 734b
Ismāʿīl Khandān i, 424b; iv, 1067a – I, 436b; IV, 1098b
Ismāʿīl al-Khashshāb ii, 356b – II, 366a
Ismāʿīl al-Manṣūr → al-Manṣūr (Fāṭimid(e))
Ismāʿīl Mīrzā b. Ṭahmāsp (Ṣafawid(e)) vi, 483a – VI, 469a
Ismāʿīl Mukh i, 923b; ii, 99b, 180a, 1124b – I, 951a; II, 101b, 185b, 1151a
Ismāʿīl al-Muntaṣir s, 245a – S, 245a
Ismāʿ^l Oghlan Shaykh (Malāmī) (1529) vi, 226b, 227a, b, 228a – VI, 220a, b, 221a, 222a
Ismāʿīl Pasha → Čerkes
Ismāʿīl Pasha b. al-ʿAẓm v, 925b – V, 930b
Ismāʿīl Pasha b. Bahrām i, 920a – I, 948a
Ismāʿīl Pasha b. Ibrāhīm Pasha, Khedive (1879) i, 37b, 142a, 825b, 929a, 1069b; ii, 149b, 167a, 423b, 514a, 642a, 647a, 728a, 892a, 934a; iii, 4b, 360a, 593a, 1000a, 1193b; iv, **192a**, 441b, 442a; v, 4a, 909a, 1060a, 1248a; vi, 23a, b, 25a, 68b, 75a, 192a, 197a, 342a, 643a, 794b; vii, 182b, 183b; viii, 40b, 58b; s, 40a, 179a, 296b, 299b, 379a, 408b – I, 38b, 146a, 848b, 957b, 1102a; II, 154a, 172b, 434b, 527a, 658a, 663b, 746b, 913a, 956a; III, 4b, 371a, 613b, 1025a, 1223b; IV, **200a**, 461b, 462a; V, 4a, 914b, 1057a, 1239a; VI, 20b, 21b, 22b, 66b, 73a, 175b, 181a, 326a, 628a, 784b; VII, 182b, 183b; VIII, 41b, 59b; S, 40a, 180a, 296a, 299a, 379a, 408b
Ismāʿīl Pasha b. Muḥammad ʿAlī Pasha (1822) vii, 425b; viii, 40b – VII, 427a; VIII, 41b
Ismāʿīl Pasha Ayyūb ii, 123b – II, 126b
Ismāʿīl Pasha Baghdādlî i, 905a – I, 932a
Ismāʿīl Pasha Nishāndjî (1690) iv, **193b**; v, 258b; vii, 239b – IV, **201b**; V, 256b; VII, 241a
Ismāʿīl Rūmī (1953) iv, 382a, b – IV, 398b, 399a
Ismāʿīl Ṣabrī (1953) iv, **194b** – IV, **202b**
Ismāʿīl Ṣabrī Pasha (1923) iv, **194b** – IV, **203a**
Ismāʿīl Ṣafā (1901) iv, **195a** – IV, **203b**
IsmāÚīl Shāh → Ismāʿīl I, II, III
Ismāʿīl Shahīd, Muḥammad (1831) ii, 735b; iii, 431a, 436a; iv, **196a**; vii, 442a – II, 754a; III, 445a, 450b; IV, **204b**; VII, 443a
Ismāʿīl Ṣidḳī (1948) ii, 934b; iii, 515b, 516a, 517a; iv, **197b**; s, 58a – II, 956a; III, 533a, 534a, 535a; IV, **206a**; S, 58b
Ismāʿīl al-Tamīmī ii, 633a – II, 649a
Ismāʿīlawayh (X) ix, 698b – IX, 727b
Ismāʿīlī, Banū (Maḳdishū) vi, 128b – VI, 126b
Ismāʿīlī (Shabānkāra) iii, 1097b – III, 1124b
Ismāʿīliyya i, 20a, 48a, 95b, 103b, 125a, 134a, 160a, 216b, 225b, 353a, 402b, 550b, 551a, 832b, 872a, 1052b, 1254b, 1332b, 1350b, 1358a; ii, 168b, 194a, 301a, 375a, 453b, 631b, 859a; iii, 80a, 123b, 253b, 254a, 411b, 433b, 862b, 1155b; iv, 28a, 29b, 30b, 46b-47a, **198a**, 660b, 859b, 887b, 910a; v, 25b, 1033a; vi, 65a, 190b, 191a, 219b, 274a, 322a, 438b, 499b, 500a, 791b; viii, 83a, 586b, 942a; s, 95b, 206b, 248b, 358b, 407a, 411a – I, 21a, 49b, 98b, 106b, 129a, 138a, 164b, 223a, 232a, 363b, 414b, 568b, 569a, 855b, 896a, 1084a, 1292b, 1373a, 1391a, 1398a; II, 174a, 200a, 309a, 385a, 465b, 647b, 879a; III, 82b, 126a, 261a, 424b, 447b, 886b, 1184a; IV, 30a, 31b, 32b, 49b-50a, **206b**, 687a, 892b, 920b, 943b; V, 26b, 1029a; VI, 63a, 174b, 175a, 203b, 258b, 306b, 424a, 485a, b, 781a; VIII, 85b, 605a, 974b; S, 95a, 206b, 248b, 358a, 407a, 411b
—doctrine i, 160b, 414b, 450a, 834b, 1098b, 1099b; ii, 97b, 136b, 848b, 1066a, 1070a; iii, 71b, 232a, 1071a, 1130a; iv, 183a, 203a; v, 167a, b, 1242b – I, 165a, 426a, 463a, 857b, 1131b, 1132b; II, 99b, 140a, 868b, 1091a, 1095a; III, 74a, 258b, 1098a, 1158b; IV, 190b, 212a; V, 164b, 165a, 1233b
Ismāʿīliyya (town/ville) iv, 193a, **206b**; s, 6a – IV, 201a, **215b**; S, 5b
ʿIsmān Adan Abdulla (Somalia/-e) (IX) ix, 718b – IX, 749b
ʿIsmat Allāh Bukhārāʾī (XV) x, 813b – X,
Ismat Chughtai (XX) vi, 489a – VI, 475a
ʿIṣmatiyya i, 903a – I, 930a
Iṣmet Inönü i, 734b, 1255b; ii, 6b, 26a, 432b, 595b, 596a; iii, 1199b; iv, 873b, 934a; s, 98b – I, 756b, 1294a; II, 6b, 21b, 443b, 610b, 611a; III, 1229b; IV, 907a, 967a; S, 98a
Isna iv, **206b**; vi, 366b – IV, **216a**; VI, 351a
Isnād i, 259a; ii, 302a; iii, 25a, 26a; iv, **207a**; v, 947a – I, 267a; II, 310b; III, 26a, 27b; IV, **216a**; V, 951a
Ispahbadh i, 1110a; iv, **207a**, 208b, 465a; v, 662a; s, 309a – I, 1143b; IV, **216b**, 217b, 486a; V, 667a; S, 309a

al-Ispadhiyyūn vii, 570a – VII, 571a
Ispahdūst al-Daylamī (X) vii, 485a – VII, 485a
Ispahsālār iv, **208a** – IV, **217b**
Ispand b. Ḳara Yūsuf (Ḳara Ḳoyunlu) (1444) vii, 672a – VII, 672a
Isparta iv, **210b** – IV, **220a**
Ispendje ii, 32a, 146b; iv, **211a**, 563a – II, 33a, 150b; IV, **220b**, 585b
Isperukh Khān i, 1305a – I, 1345a
Ispirīzāde Aḥmed Efendi v, 643b – V, 647b
Isrāʾ → Miʿrādj
Israel, Israël → Filasṭīn; Yaʿḳūb
Israel ha-Maʿārābī iv, 605b, 606a – IV, 630a, b
Isrāfīl i, 1093a; iv, **211a**; vi, 217a; s, 256a – I, 1125b; IV, **220b**; VI, 201a; S, 255b
Isrāʿīl, Banū i, 264b, **1020a**; vi, 737a,b – I, 272b, **1051b**; VI, 726a, 727a
al-Isrāʿīlī → Ibrāhīm b. Yaʿḳūb; Isḥāḳ b. Sulaymān
al-Isrāʿīlī, Abu 'l-Faḍl b. Abi 'l-Bayān (XI) i, 344b; viii, 108a – I, 355a; VIII, 110b
a'-Isrāʿīlī, Ibn al-ʿAṭṭār i, 344b – I, 355a
Isrāʿīliyyāt iv, **211b** – IV, **221a**
Issîk-kul iv, **212b** – IV, **222a**
Istabba (Estapa) vi, 221b – VI, 215a
Iṣṭabl iv, **213b**, 266a – IV, **233a**, 278a
Iṣṭakhr (town/ville) i, 43b, 1355b; ii, 925b; iv, **219b**; vi, 120a, 650a, 651a, 656a, 661a – I, 44b, 1394b; II, 947a; IV, **229a**; VI, 117b, 118a, 635a, 636b, 641b, 646b
Istakhr (cistern/citerne) v, 869b – V, 876a
al-Iṣṭakhrī → Abū ʿAmr; Abū Saʿīd
al-Iṣṭakhrī, Abū Isḥāḳ Ibrāhīm (950) i, 133a, 488a, 835b, 1003a, 1354a; ii, 581a,b, 582a; iii, 405b, 787a; iv, 220a, **222b**, 1079a; v, 1012a; vi, 313b, 639b, 640a; vii, 493a; s, 327a – I, 137a, 502b, 858b, 1034a, 1393a; II, 596a,b; III, 418a, 810b; IV, 229b, **232b**, 1110b; V, 1007b; VI, 298b, 624b, 625b; VII, 493a; S, 326b
al-Iṣṭakhrī, Abū Saʿīd (940) ii, 1099a – II, 1124b
Istami/ Ishtemi b. Bumîn (yabgu) (575) x, 687a, 691b – X, 729a, 734a
Istān → Ustān
Istanba → Abū Isḥāḳ Ibrāhīm al-Harawī
Istanbul i, 13b, 37a, 109a, 293b, 294a, 394a, 466b, 467a, 973a, 974b, 1334b; ii, 63b, 83b, 708b, 907b; iii, 216b; iv, **224a**; v, 694a, 882a; vi, 45b, 57a, 372b, 531b; s, 53b, 67b – I, 13b, 38a, 112a, 302b, 303a, 405b, 480b, 481a, 1003a, 1004b, 1374b; II, 65a, 85a, 726b, 928b; III, 223a; IV, **233b**; V, 698b, 888a; VI, 44a, 55a, 357a, 515b; S, 53b, 67b
—fires/incendies iv, 237a-238b – IV, 247b-248b
—institutions i, 1225b; ii, 425b; iii, 140a, 1137b; v, 366a – I, 1262a; II, 436b; III, 142b, 1166a; V, 367a
—monuments i, 774a, 830b, 1318a; iii, 143b; iv, 225b, 232a, 720a, 1159a; v, 67a, 243a, 261a, 533b – I, 797a, 853b, 1358b; III, 147a; IV, 235b, 242b, 749a, 1191a; V, 69a, 241a, 259a; 537b
—population iv, 238a-244b – IV, 248b-255a
—streets/rues iv, 235a-237a – IV, 245a-247a
Istanköy → On Iki Ada
Istār iv, **248b** – IV, **259b**
Istiʿāra iv, **248b** – IV, **259b**
Istibrāʾ i, 28a, 1027a; iv, **252b** – I, 29a, 1058b; IV, **263b**
Istibṣār, Kitāb al- ii, 874b; iv, **254a** – II, 894b; IV, **265a**
Istidja iv, **254a**, 355a – IV, **265b**, 370b
Iṣṭifan b. Basīl iv, **254b** – IV, **266a**
Iṣṭifān al-Duwayhī (1704) iv, **255a**; vi, 345b – IV, **266a**; VI, 330a
Istifhām iv, **255a** – IV, **266b**
Istiḥdār iv, 264b – IV, 276b
Istiḥsān ii, 164a; iii, 1237a; iv, **255b** – II, 169a; III, 1268b; IV, **267a**
Istiḳbāl iv, **259a** – IV, **270b**
Istikhāra iv, **259b** – IV, **271a**
Istikhdām → Tawriyya
Istiḳlāl iv, **260b**; v, 1194b, 1195a – IV, **272a**; V, 1194b, 1195a
Istiḳsām iv, **263a** – IV, **275a**
Iṣṭilāḥat ii, 765b; v, 805b – II, 784a; V, 811b
Istimṭār iii, 305b; iv, 270a – III, 315a; IV, 282a
Istiʾnāf iv, **264a** – IV, **276a**
Istinbāt → Māʾ; Rifāya
Istindjāʾ iv, **264b** – IV, **276a**
Istinshāḳ iv, **264b** – IV, **276b**
Istinzāl iv, **264b** – IV, **276b**
Istiʿrāḍ i, 810a; ii, 507b; iv, **269a**, 1076b; v, 19b – I, 833a; II, 520a; IV, **281a**, 1108b; V, 20a
Istiʿrāḍ, ʿarḍ iv, **265a** – IV, **276b**
Istiṣḥāb i, 276a; iv, **269b** – I, 284b; IV, **281b**
Istishrāḳ → Mustashriḳūn
Istisḳāʾ i, 109a; ii, 617b; iv, **269b**; v, 736a, 1202a – I, 112a; II, 633a; IV, **282a**; V, 741a, 1192b
Istiṣlāh → Istiḥsān
Istiṭāʿa i, 413b; iv, **271a** – I, 425b; IV, **283b**
Istithnāʾ i, 276b; ii, 302a; iii, 1079b, 1196a; iv, **272b** – I, 285b; II, 310b; III, 1106b, 1226b; IV, **284b**
Istiwāʾ, Khaṭṭ al- iv, **273a** – IV, **285a**
Istōnī (Istolnī) Belghrād ii, 208b; iv, **273b** – II, 215a; IV, **286a**
Īṭāʾ iv, 413a – IV, 431a
Iṭāʿa → Ṭāʿa
ʿItāb b. Warḳa iv, 99b – IV, 104a
Iʿtāḳ → ʿAbd
Italy/-ie → Īṭaliya
Īṭaliya i, 293a; iv, **274b**, 413b; v, 758a; – I, 302a; IV, **286b**, 487b; V, 763b
Iʿtarada iv, 269a – IV, 281a
Itāwa iv, **276a** – IV, **288a**
Ifāwā (Efājā) iv, **276a**; vi, 62a – IV, **288a**; VI, 60a
Itāy al-Bārūd s, 244a – S, 244a
Itbāʿ → Muzāwadja
ʿItbān b. Malik (VII) vi, 649a, 650a – VI, 634a, 635b
Itfīr → Ḳitfīr
Ithbāt iv, **277a** – IV, **289a**
Ithm iv, 1106b – IV, 1138a
Ithnā-ʿashariyya i, 134a, 765a, 1130a, 1142a, 1350b, 1352a; ii, 375a, 1093b; iii, 380a, 433b, 544b, 726b, 1021a, 1150b, 1166b; iv, 46b, 47b, 49b-50a, 186a, **277a**, 888a; vi, 16a, 312b; vii, 780a; ix, 507a; s, 56b, 134b, 248b – I, 138a, 787b, 1164a, 1176b, 1391a,b; II, 385a, 1119b; III, 392a, 447b, 563b, 749a, 1047a, 1179a, 1195b; IV, 49b, 50a, 52b, 194b, **289a**, 921a; VI, 14b, 297b; VII, 781b; IX, 526b; S, 57a, 134a, 248b
Iʿtibār Khān (1623) ii, 1085a; iii, 225b; iv, **279a** – II, 1110a; III, 232b; IV, **291a**
Iʿtiḳād iv, **279a** – IV, **291b**
Iʿtiḳād Khān (XVIII) iv, **279b**; s, 167b – IV, **292a**; S, 167b
Iʿtikāf iv, **280a** – IV, **292a**
Itil → Atil
Itil (river/rivière) iv, **280a**, 1175b – IV, **292b**, 1209a
Iʿtimād (al-Rumaykiyya) (XI) iii, 706a; vii, 766b; viii, 617b – III, 728a; VII, 768a; VIII, 636b
Iʿtimād al-Dawla → Shafīʿ Mazandarānī
Iʿtimād al-Dawla (Ibrāhīm Shīrāzī) s, 405b – S, 406a
Iʿtimād al-Dawla (Mīrzā Ghiyāth Beg) (1622) i, 253b; ii, 380b; iv, **282a**, 543b; vi, 369b; vii, 195a, 331b;

viii, 268a –
I, 261b; II, 390b; IV, **294a**, 567a; VI, 354a; VII, 195b, 333a; VIII, 275a
Iʿtimād al-Dawla (title/titre) iv, **281b**; v, 630a – IV, **294a**; V, 634a
Iʿtimād al-Dawla Ḳamar al-Dīn Khān (XVIII) vii, 446a – VII, 447a
Iʿtimād al-Ḥaram vi, 529a – VI, 513a
Iʿtimād Khān (Gudjārāt) (XVI) ii, 1129a; vii, 134a; s, 335b – II, 1155b; VII, 135b, 136a; S, 335a
Iʿtimād al-Salṭana → Muḥammad Ḥasan Khān Ṣaniʿ al-Dawla
Iʿtimādpur vi, 128a – VI, 126a
Iʿtimāzāda, Muḥammad iv, 73b – IV, 77a
Iʿtiṣām al-Dīn, Shaykh iii, 1046a; s, 108a – III, 1072a; S, 107a
ʿItḳ → ʿAbd
ʿItḳnāme iv, **282b** – IV, **295a**
al-Itlāḳiyya iii, 284a – III, 292b
ʿIṭr → ʿAnbar; Misk
Ittibāʿ iv, 152a – IV, 158b
Ittiḥād iv, **282b** – IV, **295a**
al-Ittiḥād al-ʿarabī ii, 674b – II, 691b
Ittiḥād-i Islām ii, 445b – II, 457a
Ittiḥād-i Muḥammedī Djemʿiyyeti iv, **283b** – IV, **296a**
al-Ittiḥād al-Lubnānī iii, 519b – III, 537b
al-Ittiḥād al-Sūrī iii, 520b – III, 538b
Ittiḥād we Teraḳḳī Djemʿiyyeti i, 734a; ii, 430b, 643b, 698b; iii, 204a, 251a, 526a, 994a; iv, 283b, **284a**, 611b, 872a, b, 873a; v, 905b, 1036a; vi, 74a; viii, 446b; s, 41b, 47b, 149b –
I, 756a; II, 441b, 660a, 716a; III, 209b, 258a, 544b, 1018b; IV, 296a, **296b**, 636a, 905b, 906a; V, 911a, 1032a; VI, 72a; VIII, 461bS, 42a, 47b, 149b
Ittiḥādiyya iii, 161b, 822a, 952a – III, 165a, 846a, 976b
Ittiṣāl → Ittiḥād
Ivanko → Yanko
Ivory Coast → Côte d'Ivoire
Iwā i, 919a – I, 947a
ʿIwaḍ iv, **286a** – IV, **298b**
ʿIwāḍ Beg (Kurd(e)) vi, 202a – VI, 186b
ʿIwāḍ Pasha, Ḥādjdjī, vizier (XV) vii, 594b – VII, 594a
ʿIwād Wadjīh (XVII) iv, **286b** – IV, **299a**
Īwān i, 950a, 1228b; ii, 114a, 115b; iv, **287a**, 1073b, 1137a, 1138b, 1141b, 1146b –
I, 979b, 1265a; II, 116b, 118a; IV, **299b**, 1105a, 1132a, b, 1134b, 1138a
Iwāẓ (ʿIwāḍ) Bey ii, 233b – II, 240a
Iwāẓ (Iwāḍ) Khaldjī, Ghiyāth al-Dīn ii, 267b; iii, 1155a – II, 275b; III, 1183b
Iwāẓ Khaldjī, Ḥusayn al-Dīn i, 393b – I, 405a
ʿIyād, Banū ii, 196b, 197b; iv, **289a**; v, 77a, b, 639b, 640a; x, 140b – II, 202b, 203a, b; IV, **301b**; V, 79b, 643b, 644a; X, 151b
ʿIyāḍ b. Ghānm (VII)) i, 329a, 635b, 679b, 695a, 1206b; ii, 344b, 523b, 624a, 625b; iii, 20a, 228a; iv, 841b; vi, 379a, 540a, 930a; vii, 983a; viii, 410a, 433b, 589b; ix, 68b –
I, 339b, 656b, 700b, 716b, 1242b; II, 354b, 536b, 639b, 641a; III, 21a, 234b; IV, 874b; VI, 363a, 524b, 921b; VII, 984a; VIII, 424a, 448a, 608a; IX, 71b
ʿIyāḍ b. Mūsā al-Sabtī al-Ḳāḍī (1149) i, 602b; ii, 743b; iii, 680b, 707b, 867b; iv, 183b, **289b**, 912b; v, 71b, 1208b; vi, 263a, 280a, b, 349b, 351a, 353b, 591a, 712a; vii, 584a, 625a, 691b; viii, 690b; x, 122a; s, 27a –
I, 622a; II, 762a; III, 702b, 729b, 891b; IV, 191b, **302b**, 945b; V, 73b, 1199a; VI, 247b, 265a, 334a, 335a, 337b, 576a, 701b; VII, 584b, 624b 692a; VIII, 711a; X, 131b; S, 27b
Iyāḍ b. Sūd, Banū iv, 289b – IV, 302b
al-Iyāḍī → Muḥammad al-Tūnisī
al-Iyāḍī, Abū Naṣr Aḥmad b. al-ʿAbbās (890) vi, 846a – VI, 836b
ʿIyāfa ii, 760a; iv, **290b** – II, 778b; IV, **303a**
ʿIyāl Manṣūr iii, 49b – III, 51b
ʿIyāl Zāyid ii, 175b – II, 181a
Iyāla → Eyālet
ʿIyān vi, 436a – VI, 421a, b
al-ʿIyānī, Djaʿfar b. al-Ḳāsim (XI) s, 22a – S, 22b
al-ʿIyānī, al-Ḥusayn b. al-Ḳāsim (Zaydī Imām) (1013) v, 1237b; vii, 773a; s, 22a – V, 1228a; VII, 774b; S, 22b
al-ʿIyānī, al-Manṣūr al-Ḳāsim (Zaydī Imām) vii, 773a – VII, 774b
ʿIyār → Sikka
ʿIyār-i Dānish → Kalīla wa-Dimna
Iyās b. Ḳabīṣa al-Ṭāʾī (VII) i, 689b, 690a; ii, 241a; v, 634a; x, 62a – I, 710b, 711a; II, 248a; V, 638a; X, 64a
Iyās b. Muʿāwiya (793) iv, **291a** – IV, **304a**
Iyās b. Muḍārib (VII) vii, 522b – VII, 522b
Izadyār b. Masʿūd i, 217b – I, 224a
Izâfet → Iḍāfa
Iʿzāz al-Dawla Marzubān b. ʿIzz al-Dawla Bakhtiyār (Būyid(e)) (X) vii, 358a – VII, 360b
Izhār al-Ḥasan b. Inʿām al-Ḥasan (1996) x, 38b – X, 39b
Izmail → Ismāʿīl (Izmail)
Izmīd/Izmit v, 250a; vi, 587b, 588b – V, 247b, 248a; VI, 572b, 573b
Izmīr i, 464a, 476a, 783b, 1335b; ii, 599a, b; iii, 210b, 214b; v, 505a, 1170a; vi, 68b; vii, 70b; s, 44b, 67b – I, 477b, 490b, 806b, 1375b; II, 613b, 614b; III, 216b, 220b; V, 508b, 1160a; VI, 66b; VII, 71b; S, 45a, 68a
—institutions ii, 425b – II, 436b
Izmir-oghlu → Djunayd (Aydïn-oghlu)
Iznīḳ i, 477a; ii, 746b; iv, **291b**, 702a, 1169a, b; v, 103b; vi, 366a; viii, 175b; s, 204a, 330b –
I, 491a; II, 765a; IV, **304b**, 730b, 1201b, 1202b; V, 105b; VI, 350a; VIII, 178a; S, 203b, 330a
—monuments iv, 291b, 292a – IV, 304b, 305a
al-Iznīḳī, Abu 'l-Faḍl Mūsā i, 137a – I, 141a
—, Ḳuṭb al-Dīn iii, 711a; v, 547a – III, 733b; V, 551b
Izraʿ v, 593b – V, 597a
ʿIzrāʾīl iv, **292b**; v, 210a; vi, 217a – IV, **305b**; V, 207b; VI, 201a
ʿIzz al-Dawla iv, **293b** – IV, **306b**
ʿIzz al-Dawla Bakhtiyār → Bakhtiyār
ʿIzz al-Dawla al-Bakrī → ʿAbd al-ʿAzīz al-Bakrī
ʿIzz al-Dīn b. ʿAbd b. al-Salām → ʿAbd al-Azīz b. ʿAbd al-Salām
ʿIzz al-Dīn b. al-Athīr → Ibn al-Athīr
ʿIzz al-Dīn b. ʿAwn al-Dīn Ibn Hubayra (XII) vii, 726b; viii, 943b – VII, 727a; VIII, 976a
ʿIzz al-Dīn b. Djahāndār ii, 379b; iii, 200a – II, 389b; III, 205a
ʿIzz al-Dīn b. Shudjaʿ al-Dīn v, 828b, 829a – V, 834b, 835a
ʿIzz al-Dīn Abu 'l-ʿAsākir Sulṭān (Shayzar) (1122) vi, 791a – VI, 780b
ʿIzz al-Dīn Abū Bakr al-Dubaysī (amīr) (al-Mawṣil) (1160) vi, 870b – VI, 861a
ʿIzz al-Dīn Aybak (Mamlūk) → Aybak, Muʿizz ʿIzz al-Dīn al-Muʿaẓẓamī (1248)
ʿIzz al-Dīn Aybak al-Turkumānī (1257) i, 732a, 804a, 944b; ix, 176a, b – I, 754a, 828b, 973b; IX, 181b, 182a
ʿIzz al-Dīn Aybak al-Turkī al-Ẓāhirī (Ḥimṣ) (1363) vi, 547b – VI, 532a

ʿIzz al-Dīn Aydamur al-ʿIzzī al-naḳīb (1303) vi, 547b – VI, 532a
ʿIzz al-Dīn Aydimur al-Ḥillī i, 814b – I, 837b
ʿIzz al-Dīn Farrukh-Shāh v, 1139b – V, 1133b
ʿIzz al-Dīn Ḥasanī Rikābī, Sayyid (Marʿashī) (1393) vi, 512b – VI, 497b
ʿIzz al-Dīn Ḥusayn ii, 1100a – II, 1126a
ʿIzz al-Dīn Ibrāhīm Ibn al-Muḳaddam (1181) vi, 380b, 381a – VI, 365a
ʿIzz al-Dīn Ibn Hubayra (XII) vii, 726b – VII, 727a
ʿIzz al-Dīn Kaykāwus → Kaykāʾūs I, II
ʿIzz al-Dīn Khān-i Ayāz s, 66b – S, 67a
ʿIzz al-Dīn Khaṭṭāb b. Maḥmūd b. Murtaʿish (1325) vi, 548a – VI, 532b
ʿIzz al-Dīn al-Maṣrī (XX) vi, 755a – VI, 744a
ʿIzz al-Dīn Masʿūd I (Zangid(e)) (1193) iii, 1119a; vi, 900b – III, 1147a; VI, 891b
ʿIzz al-Dīn Masʿūd II (Zangid (e)) (1218) iii, 1119a; viii, 127b – III, 1147a; VIII, 130a
ʿIzz al-Dīn Shīr iv, 586a – IV, 609a
ʿIzz al-Dīn Sūghandī, Sayyid vi, 511a – VI, 496b
ʿIzz al-Dīn al-Sulamī → al-Sulamī
ʿIzz al-Dīn Usāma (XII) i, 208a; iv, 779a; x, 884a – I, 214a; IV, 810b; X,
ʿIzz al-Dīn al-Wafāʾī (XV) x, 313a – X, 337a
ʿIzz al-Mulk i, 1052b – I, 1084a
ʿIzzat al-Dawla (Ḳādjār) (XIX) vii, 431b; s, 70b – VII, 432b; S, 71a
Izzat Sultan (XX) vi, 770b – VI, 760a
al-ʿIzzatī, Muḥammad b. Luṭf Allāh b. Bayrām (XVII) vii, 469b – VII, 469a
ʿIzzet ʿAbed Pasha i, 64a; iii, 364a – I, 66a; III, 375b
ʿIzzet Bey ii, 641a – II, 657a
ʿIzzet Efendi iv, 1126a – IV, 1158a
ʿIzzet Molla i, 558a; ii, 934b; iv, **295a**; v, 710b, 1083b – I, 576a; II, 956b; IV, **308a**; V, 715b, 1081a
ʿIzzet Muḥammad Pasha iii, 627b – III, 648a
ʿIzzet Pasha → Ḥasan ʿIzzet
ʿIzzet Pasha, Aḥmed Furgaç (1937) iv, 296a; vi, 984a; vii, 229a; s, 300a – IV, **309b**; VI, 976b; VII, 231a; S, 299b
ʿIzzī Süleymān Efendi (1755) iv, **298b** – IV, **311b**

J

Jacob → Isrāʿīl; Yaʿḳūb
Jacob ben Eleazar (Toledo) vi, 114b – VI, 112b
Jacob b. Reuben iv, 605b – IV, 629b
Jacob b. Simeon iv, 605b – IV, 629b
Jacobites → Yaʿkūbiyya
Jaén → Djayyān
Jaffa → Yāfā
Jagellons vii, 219a – VII, 220b
Jain → Djayn
Jaipur s, 140b, 142b – S, 140b, 142a
Jajce i, 1018a, 1263b; vi, 71b – I, 1049a, 1302a; VI, 69a
Jakarta → Djakarta
Jaleel, K.A. vi, 461a – VI, 446b
Jamna (river/-ière → Djamna
Janina → Yaniya
Janissaries/Janissaires → Yeñi Čeri
Japan/Japon → Yābān
Japara s, 201a, b – S, 201a, b
Japhet → Yāfith
Japheth b. Eli iv, 305b, 605a – IV, 319b, 629b
Japheth al-Barḳamānī iv, 605b – IV, 629b
Jassy → Yash
Jata (Mogholistān) x, 590b – X,
Játiva → Shāṭiba
Jatts → Zuṭṭ
Java i, 170b, 174a, 981a; ii, 352a, 497a; iii, 566b, 1213a, b, 1214b, 1218b, 1219b, 1222a, b, 1226a; iv, 1128a; v, 225b, 226b, 227b, 1154b; vi, 42b, 43b, 239a, 517a – I, 175a, 178b, 1011b; II, 362a, 509b; III, 586a, 1243b, 1244b, 1249b, 1250a, 1253a, b, 1257b; IV, 1159b; V, 223a, 224a, 225a, 1144a; VI, 41a, 42a, 204a, 502a
Jawnpur → Djawnpur
Jaxartes → Sīr Daryā
Jbala v, 1200b, 1203b – V, 1190b, 1194a
Jean le Baptiste → Yaḥyā b. Zakariyyāʾ
Jehlam (river/fleuve) s, 156a – S, 156a
Jellābas → Djallāb
Jenghiz Khan → Činghiz Khān
Jeremiah → Irmiyya
Jerez → Sharīsh
Jericho → Rīḥā
Jerusalem → al-Ḳuds
Jeshuah b. Judah (ʿAbu ʾl-Faradj Furkān) (XI) iv, 305a, 605a, 607a; vii, 539b – IV, 319a, 629b, 631a; VII, 539b
Jessore → Djassawr
Jesus/Jésus → ʿĪsā b. Maryam
Jethro → Shuʿayb
Jeunes Turcs → Yeni Othmanlîlar
Jews → Yahūd
Jimeno, Count/Comte i, 161a; iii, 771b – I, 165b; III, 794b
Jinnah → Djināh
Jnān al-ʿAfiya (Marrākush) vi, 596b – VI, 581b
Jnān Riḍwān (Marrākush) vi, 596b – VI, 581b
Job → Ayyūb
Jōʾēl, Rabbi iv, 505b – IV, 527b
John the Baptist → Yaḥyā b. Zakariyyāʾ
Johor vi, 116b, 208a, 232b, 235a, b, 236a, b, 239a; viii, 303a; s, 150b, 151b – VI, 114a, 192b, 206a, 208a, b, 209a, b, 204a; VIII, 312b; S, 150b, 152a
Jolo (island/île) viii, 303a – VIII, 312b
Jonah/Jonas → Yūnus
Jordan/-ie → Urdunn
Jordan/Jourdain → al-Urdunn
Joseph → Yūsuf
Joseph b. Noah → Yūsuf b. Nūḥ
Joseph ha-Rōʾeh → Yūsuf al-Baṣīr
Joshua/Josué → Yūshaʿ
Joshua ben Judah → Jeshuah b. Judah
Jou-Jan (Zhouan-Zhouan) (Asian Avars) x, 687a, 691a – X, 729a, 733b
Jo(u)mblatt → Djānbulāṭ
Jubba (river/fleuve) ix, 412a, 714b – IX, 425b, 745b
Judaeo-Arabic, Judéo-arabe i, 574b; iv, **299a**; v, 206b – I, 593b; IV, **312b**; V, 204a
Judaeo-Berber/Judéo-Berbère iv, **307b** – IV, **321a**
Judaeo-Persian/Judéo-Persan iv, **308a** – IV, **322a**

K

Ḳāʿa ii, 114b; iv, 428b – II, 117a; IV, 447a
Ḳaʿādi → al-Djarādatān[i]
Ḳaʾan → Khāḳān
Ḳāʿān (China/-e) vi, 501b – VI, 487a
Ḳāʾānčis iv, 30b – IV, 33a
Ḳaʾānī, Ḥabīb Allāh (1854) ii, 433b; iii, 373a; iv, 69b,

313a; vi, 609b; vii, 662a – II, 445a; III, 385a; IV, 73b, **327a**; VI, 594a; VII, 661b
Kaarta (Mali) iv, **313b**; vi, 259a – IV, **327b**; VI, 243b
Kaʿb, Banū i, 441a; iii, 1102b, 1107a;iv, **314b**, 740a, 765a; v, 81a; vii, 674b, 675a; ix, 898b – I, 454a; III, 1130a, 1134b; IV, **328b**, 770a, 795b; V, 83a; VII, 674b, 675a; IX, 935a
Kaʿb b. ʿAmr, Banū v, 78b, 79a – V, 81a
Kaʿb. Asad v, 436a – V, 438b
Kaʿb. al-As͟hraf (625) iv, **315a**; vi, 145a, 603b – IV, **329a**; VI, 143a, 588b
Kaʿb b. D͟juʿayl al-Tag͟hlabī (VII) iv, **315a** – IV, **329a**
Kaʿb b. Mālik, Abū ʿAbd Allāh (670) i, 50b; iii, 272b, 354a, 975b; iv, **315b**; vi, 604a – I, 52a; III, 280a, 365a, 1000a; IV, **329b**; VI, 588b
Kaʿb b. Māma i, 115b – I, 119a
Kaʿb b. Saʿd al-G͟hanawī vi, 817b – VI, 808a
Kaʿb b. Zuhayr (VII) i, 1011b, 1314b; iv, **316a**, 510a; v, 6b, 734a, 958b; vi, 467b, 896a; vii, 981a – I, 1042b, 1354b; IV, **330a**, 532a; V, 6b, 739b, 962b; VI, 453b, 887a; VII, 981b
Kaʿb al-Aḥbār, Abū Isḥāḳ (652) i, 926b; ii, 363; iii, 370a; iv, 212a, **316b**, 1135b; v, 324a, 1231b; vi, 247b – I, 955a; II, 373b; III, 382a; IV, 221b, 3**30b**, 1167a; V, 323b, 1222a; VI, 231b
Kaʿba i, 55b, 136a, 178a, 268a, 453a, 551b, 608b, 867a, 892b, 1054a; ii, 247a, 453a, 603b, 695b; iii, 33a, 40a, 101a, 980b; iv, 184a, b, 260a, **317a**; 926a; v, 77b, 78a, 434a, b, 435b, 520a, 990b; vi, 46a, 105b, 148a, 157b, **166b**, **180b**, 645a, b, 646b, 651a, 658b, 659a, 664a, 665a, 669b, 677b, 708b – I, 57a, 140a, 182b, 276a, 466a, 569a, 628b, 891b, 919a, 1086a; II, 254b, 465a, 618b, 713a; III, 34b, 42a, 103b, 1005a; IV, 192b, 271b, **331a**, 959a; V, 79b, 80a, 436b, 438a, 523b, 985b; VI, 44b, 103b, 146b, 153a, **158b**, **164b**, 630a, b, 632a, 636a, 644b, 650a, 651a, 652a, 655b, 664a, 697a, b
Kaʿba, Actes de la- VI, 316b, 317a
Ḳabā, ḳabāʾ v, 739b, 743b, 748a, b, 749a, b – V, 744b, 749a, 753b, 754a, b, 755a
al-Kaʿba al-Yamāniya ii, 241b – II, 248b
Ḳabača, Nāṣir al-Dīn → Nāṣir al-Dīn Ḳabača
Kabadian → Ḳubād͟hiyān
Ḳabādiyān ii, 1a, 2a – II, 1a, 2a
Ḳabad͟j K͟hātūn i, 1293b – I, 1333a
Kabāʾir iv, 1107b, 1108b – IV, 1139a, 1140a
Kabak → Kebek
Ḳabaḳbāzī → Laʿb
Ḳabaḳd͟jĭ-og͟hlu Muṣṭafā (Yamak) (1808) ii, 713a; iv, **322b**; vii, 710a – II, 731a; IV, **337a**; VII, 710b
Ḳabakulaḳ Ibrāhīm Ag͟ha (1730) vi, 55b – VI, 53b
Ḳabāla(t) i, 1144a; ii, 145b; iv, **323a**, 1032a, 1040a; ix, 253a – I, 1178b; II, 149b; IV, **337a**, 1064a, 1071b; IX, 261a, b
Ḳaban vi, 201a – VI, 185a
Ḳabard, Banū/Kabards i, 1000a, 1189b; ii, 21b, 22a, b; iii, 1235b; iv, **324b**, 596b; v, 288b; x, 920b – I, 1031a, 1224b; II, 22a, b, 23a; III, 1267b; IV, **339a**, 620b; V, 286b
Kabarega (Bunyoro) (1899) x. 779a – X,
Kabartay ii, 25a; vi, 56a – II, 25b; VI, 54a
Ḳabāṭiyya vi, 543b – VI, 528a
al-Ḳabbāb, Abū Muḥammad al-Tamgrūtī (1635) iv, **325b**; vi, 350a – IV, **339b**; VI, 334a
Ḳabbān → Mīzān
al-Ḳabbānī, D͟jamāl al-Dīn Abū ʿAlī al-Kaʿbī (1697) vi, 112a – VI, 110a
Ḳabḍ (contraction) i, 1088b; iii, 361a; iv, 326a – I, 1121a; III, 372b; IV, 340b
Ḳabḍ (possession) iii, 350a; iv, **325b** – III, 361a; IV, **340a**
Kabdān, Ahl vi, 1009a – VI, 1001b
Ḳabd͟jaḳ (Ḳipčaḳ) al-Manṣūrī (Ḥamāt) (1310) vii, 991b – VII, 993a
al-Kaʿbī, Abu ʾl-Ḳāsim al-Balk͟hī (932) i, 204b; ii, 518b; vi, 846b; s, 32a, 225b – I, 201b; II, 531b; VI, 837a; S, 32a, 225b
Kabid iv, **327a** – IV, **341a**
Ḳābiḍ, Mollā (1527) iv, **333b**, v, 41b; vi 227a – IV, **348a**; V, 42b; VI, 221a
Ḳabīḥa umm al-Muhtadī bi-ʾllāh (IX) viia – VII, 476b
Ḳabīḥa umm al-Muʿtazz (IX) s, 252b – S, 252b
Ḳābīl → Hābīl wa-Ḳābīl
al-Ḳābil (al-S͟harḳiyya) ix, 256v; s, 355b – IX, 368a; S, 355a
Ḳabil K͟hān iv, 760a – IV, 790a
Ḳabīla i, 700a; iv, **334a**, 362a – I, 721b; IV, **348b**, 377b
Ḳabīlīs (Yemen) vi, 491a – VI, 477a
Kabīr (poet/poète) i, 1166a; iii, 456b, 459b; v, 630b – I, 1200b; III, 472b, 475b; V, 634b
Kabīr K͟hān (Multān) (XIII) vi, 48a – VI, 46b
Ḳābis (Gabès) i, 950a; iv, **335b**; vi, 134a, 141a, 452b; s, 11a, 334a – I, 979b; IV, **350a**; VI, 132b, 139b, 438a; S, 10b, 334a
Ḳabīṣa b. Abī Ṣufra (VIII) vii, 359a – VII, 361b
al-Ḳabīṣī, ʿAbd al-ʿAzīz Abu ʾl-Ṣaḳr (X) iv, **340b** – IV, **355a**
al-Ḳābisī (Ibn-), Abu ʾl-Ḥasan al-Maʿāfirī (1012) iv, **341a**; vi, 188b, 353b; s, 26b – IV, **355b**; VI, 172b, 337b; S, 27a
Kābiya b. Ḥurḳūs (Māzin) vi, 954b – VI, 947a
Ḳabḳ i, 18a, 270b, 380a; iv, 324b, **341b**; v, 287b, 288b, 495b; vii, 351a; s, 136a, 143a, 169a, 218b – I, 18b, 279a, 391a; IV, 339a, **356a**; V, 286a, 287a, 498b; VII, 353a; S, 135b, 142b, 169a, 218b
Ḳablān al-Ḳāḍī al-Tanūk͟hī ii, 433b – II, 455b
Ḳablud͟ja → Ḳaplĭd͟ja
Kābora vi, 258b – VI, 243a
Kabou iv, **351b** – IV, **367a**
Kaboul → Kābul
Ḳabr iv, **352a**; v, 214b – IV, **367a**; V, 212a
Ḳabr Hūd i, 1045a; iii, 538a; s, 337b – I, 1076b; III, 556b; S, 337a
Ḳabra iv, **355a** – IV, **370b**
Kabs͟h → Badw (IIa); Silāḥ; Yürük; Zakāt
al-Kabs͟h (Miṣr) vii, 147b – VII, 149b
Kabs͟ha/Kubays͟ha s, 394a – S, 394b
al-Ḳabtawrī, Abu ʾl-Ḳāsim (1304) iv, **355b** – IV, **371a**
Kabūd D͟jāma vi, 494a – VI, 480a
Kabud͟hān s, 130b – S, 129b
Kābul i, 72a, 86a, 87b, 222a, b, 223a, 226b, 238a, b, 970a, 1347b; iii, 576a; iv, 175a, **356a**; v, 649a; vi, 86b, 122a, 342b, 419a; vii, 313b; s, 41a, 63a, 66a, b, 122a, 237a, b, 270a, 285a – I, 74a, 88b, 90a, 228b, 229a, b, 233b, 245a, b, 1000a, 1388a; III, 596a; IV, 182b, **371b**; V, 653a; VI, 84b, 120a, 327a, 404b; VII, 316a; S, 41b, 63b, 66a, 67a, 121a, 237a, b, 270a, 285a
—university/-é ii, 426a – II, 437a
Ḳabūl → Bayʿ
Ḳabūl Aḥmad ii, 1046a – II, 1070a
Kābul-S͟hāhs iv, 208a, 356b – IV, 217b, 371b, 372a
Ḳabūla al-Hindī iii, 104b – III, 107a
Kābulistān iv, **357b** – IV, **373a**
Ḳabūn vi, 547b – VI, 532a
Kabūn b. Taṣūla (Sūs) (946) vi, 434b – VI, 420a
Ḳābūs (Lak͟hmid(e)) (574) v, 633b; vii, 568b – V, 637b; VII, 569a

Ḳābūs b. Muṣʿab ii, 917b – II, 939a
Ḳābūs b. Saʿīd b. Taymūr (Āl Bū Saʿīd) (XX) vi, 735b ; x, 814b– VI, 725a; X,
Ḳābūs b. Wushm(a)gīr b. Ziyār (Ziyārid(e)) (1012) i, 211b, 591a, 1110a, 1236a; ii, 748b, 1139b; iv, **357b**; v, 1028a; vi, 632a; vii, 987b; viii, 383a; s, 13a, 361b – I, 218a, 610a, 1143b, 1274a; II, 767a, 1166b; IV, **373b**; V, 1024a; VI, 617a; VII, 988a; VIII, 396a; S, 13b, 361b
Ḳābūs-nāma iv, 815a – IV, 848a
Kabyle, language/langue i, 1184a, b; iv, 361a – I, 1219a, b; IV, 376b
Kabyles i, 371a, 371b, 372a, 374a, 1177b; ii, 537b, 603b; iii, 607a; iv, 360b-363a – I, 382a, 382b, 383a, 384b, 1212b; II, 551a, 618b; III, 627b; IV, 376a-379a
Kabylia/-e i, 171a, 365a, 369b, 433b; ii, 603b; iv, 75b, **358b**; vi, 427a, 475a, 586b; x, 118b; s, 190a – I, 176a, 376a, 380b, 446a; II, 618a; IV, 79b, **374a**; VI, 412b, 460b, 571a; X, 128a; S, 191a
Kačawča s, 74a – S, 74b
Kaččh(ī) Gandāwa iv, **364a**, 534b; v, 689b; vi, 50b – IV, **380a**, 557b; V, 694b; VI, 49a
Ḳaḍāʾ (divine decree/décret divin) i, 89b, 90a, 413a, 413b; ii, 618a; iv, **364b** – I, 92b, 424b, 425a; II, 633b; IV, **380b**
Ḳaḍāʿ (religious duty/service religieux) i, 169b – I, 174b
Ḳaḍā (region) i, 469a – I, 482b, 483a
al-Ḳaḍāʾ wa ʾl-Ḳadar iv, **365a** – IV, **381a**
Ḳadāḥ v, 989b – V, 984b
Ḳadam v, 95b – V, 98a
Ḳadam Sharīf iv, **367b**; vi, 126a – IV, **383b**; VI, 124a
Ḳādan, Ḳāḍī (Mahdawī) vii, 327b – VII, 329b
Ḳaʿdān al-Fāyiz, shaykh (XVIII) viii, 882b – VIII, 913a
Ḳadar i, 89b, 90a, 407a, 408b, 413a, 413b, 958b; ii, 365a, 374b, 618a; iii, 659a, 870b; iv, **365a**; v, 3b – I, 92b, 419a, 420b, 424b, 425a, 988a; II, 375a, 385a, 633b; III, 680b, 894b; IV, **381a**, b; V, 4a
Kadarbirt vi, 231a – VI, 225a
al-Ḳaḍārif iv, 686a, 687a – IV, 714a, 715a
Ḳadariyya i, 124a, 276b, 412b; iii, 248a, 494b, 990b, 1142b; iv, 366a, **368a**, 734b, 938a; v, 936a; vi, 279b; s, 358a – I, 127b, 285a, 424a; III, 255a, 511b, 1015a, 1170b; IV, 382a, **384b**, 764a, 971a; V, 940a; VI, 264b; S, 358a
Ḳadāsa iv, **372a** – IV, **388b**
Ḳaddāḥid(e)s i, 48b; ii, 851b – I, 50a; II, 871a
Ḳaḍḍām, Bā, Muḥammad b. ʿUmar (1544) vi, 132b – VI, 130b
Ḳaddūr al-ʿAlamī (Meknès) (1741) iv, **372b**; vi, 249b, 253a, 255a, b – IV, **389a**; VI, 234a, 237a, 239b
Ḳaddūr wuld Muḥammad al-Burdjī → Bū Ngāb
Ḳaddūra al-Djazāʾirī (1687) iv, **373a** – IV, **389b**
Ḳadhf i, 29b; iii, 20b; iv, **373a**; v, 730b – I, 30b; III, 21b; IV, **389b**; V, 735b
al-Ḳadhdhāfī, Muʿammar v, 758b, 1067a – V, 764b, 1064a
Ḳāḍī i, 491a, 741b; ii, 119a, 519b, 867a, 888a, 890b; iii, 487b, 492a, 1152b, 1153a; iv, 365a, **373b**, 941a; v, 631a, 1133a, b – I, 506a, 763b; II, 121b, 532b, 887a, 908b, 911a; III, 504b, 509a, 1180b, 1181b; IV, 381a, **390a**, 974a; V, 635a, 1128b, 1129a
Ḳāḍī b. Muḥammad b. Walmiya iv, 337a –IV, 351b
Ḳāḍī Aḥmad viii, 787b – VIII, 814a
Ḳāḍī ʿAskar i, 480b, 712a; iii, 1152b; iv, **375b**, 735b; vi, 1a – I, 495a, 733b; III, 1180b; IV, **392a**, 765b; VI, 1a
Ḳāḍī ʾl-djamāʿa iv, 374b – IV, 390b
Ḳāḍī Djihān Ḳazwīnī (XVI) viii, 775b; x, 109b – VIII, 801b; X, 118b
al-Ḳāḍī al-Fāḍil, Abū ʿAlī ʿAbd al-Raḥmān (1200) i, 150a, 594a, 801b; ii, 127a, 305b, 329b; iii, 679b, 863a, 901a; iv, **376a**, 613b, 614b; vi, 198a, 423b, 430a, 664a; vii, 164b; viii, 653b; s, 124a – I, 154a, 613a, 824b; II, 130a, 314a, 339a; III, 701a, 887a, 925a; IV, **392b**, 638a, 639a; VI, 182b, 409a, 415b, 650a; VII, 166a; VIII, 673a; S, 123a
Ḳāḍī al-Harawī → al-ʿAbbādī
Ḳāḍī Ismāʿīl (860) vi, 279a – VI, 264a
Ḳāḍī ʿIyāḍ → ʿIyāḍ b. Mūsā al-Sabtī
Ḳāḍī Khān, Fakhr al-Dīn (1196) iii, 163b; iv, **377**; vi, 558b – III, 167a; IV, **393b**; VI, 543a
Ḳāḍi ʾl-Ḳuḍāt i, 164b; iv, 374a – I, 169a; IV, 390a, b
Ḳāḍī Meḥmed → Lālezārī, Shaykh Meḥmed
Ḳāḍī Muḥammad (1947) ii, 88b; iii, 157a; iv, **377a**; v, 466a, b, 1213a, b – II, 90a; III, 160b; IV, **393b**; V, 469a, 1202b, 1203a
Ḳāḍī Nuʿmān → Nuʿmān
Ḳāḍī Nūr Allāh → Nūr Allāh al-Sayyid
Ḳāḍī al-Rashīd b. al-Zubayr s, 251b – S, 251b
Ḳāḍī al-Saʿīd → Ibn Sanāʾ al-Mulk
al-Ḳāḍī Ṣāʿid → Ṣāʿid al-Andalūsī
Ḳāḍī al-Tahartī → Ibn al-Rabīb
Ḳaḍīb iv, **377b**, 940a – IV, **394a**, 973a
Ḳadīm v, 96a, b – V, 98a, b
Ḳādimīs ii, 366b – II, 376b
Ḳadi̇n → Marʾa; Sarāy
al-Ḳādir → al-Asmāʾ al-ḥusnā
al-Ḳādir → Yaḥya al-Ḳādir
al-Ḳādir b. Dhi ʾl-Nūn (XI) vii, 288b, 633b – VII, 290b
al-Ḳādir bi-ʾllāh (ʿAbbāsid(e)) (1031) i, 1352b, 1353a, 1355a; iii, 159a, 255b, 256a, 735a, 860a; iv, **378a**, 940b, 942a; vi, 65a, 206a, 522a, b; vii, 312b; s, 14b, 118a, b, 119a, 253b, 361b – I, 1391b, 1392a, 1394a; III, 162b, 263a, 758a, 884a; IV, **394b**, 973b, 975a; VI, 63a, 190b, 507a; VII, 314b; S, 15a, 117b, 118a, 253b, 361b
ak-Ḳāḍir Khān → Ikhtiyār al-Dīn Abu ʾl-Mudjāhid Ḳādir Khān
al-Ḳādir Khān, Yūsuf (Ilek-khān) (1034) → Yūsuf Ḳādi̊r Khān
Ḳādir Shāh (Mallū Khān) (Mālwā) (XVI) iii, 421b, 422b, 426a; iv, 276b; vi, 310a, 407a – III, 435a, 436b, 439b; IV, 288b; VI, 295a, 391b
Ḳāḍir Walī → Shāh al-Ḥamīd ʿAbd al-Ḳādir
Ḳadirgha Limani̊ vi, 588a – VI, 572b
Ḳādirī, ʿAbd al-Madjīd s, 74a – S, 74b
Ḳādirī, ʿAbd al-Salām (1698) vi, 350a – VI, 334a
Ḳādirī, Abū ʿAbd Allāh (1773) iv, **379a**; s, 404b – IV, **395b**; S, 404b
Ḳādirī Čelebī iv, 333b; vii, 225a – IV, 348a; VII, 226b
Ḳādirī al-Ḥasanī, Abu ʾl-ʿAbbās (1721) iv, **379b** – IV, **396a**
Ḳādirī al-Ḥasanī, Abū ʿAbd Allāh (1695) iv, **380a** – IV, **396b**
Ḳādirī al-Ḥasanī, Abu ʾl-Faḍāʾil → al-Ḳādirī al-Ḥasanī, Abu ʾl-ʿAbbās
Ḳādirī al-Ḥasanī, Abū Muḥammad (1698) iv, **380a**, 382a, 1085a – IV, **396b**, 398b, 1116a
Ḳādiriyya i, 69a, 257b, 281a, 303a, 371a, 782a, 1009a, 1173a, 1260b; ii, 10a, 58b, 63b, 94b, 134b, 164a, 535b, 710a, 975a, 1003b, 1004a; iii, 103b, 160b, 176a, 646b; iv, **380b**, 549b, 951a; v, 287b, 393b, 475a; vi, 203b, 259b, 260a, 354b, 356b, 643b, 705a; vii, 246a, 620a; viii, 18b; x, 247b; s, 5a, 182b, 282b, 283a, 293a, 303a, 322a – I, 70b, 265b, 289b, 313a, 382a, 805a, 1040a, 1208a,

1298b; II, 10a, 59b, 64b, 96b, 138a, 169b, 549a, 729a, 997b, 1026b, 1027a; III, 106a, 164a, 180a, 667b; IV, **397a**, 573b, 983b; V, 286a, 394b, 478a; VI, 187b, 244a, b, 338b, 340b, 629a, 693b; VII, 248a, 619b; VIII, 18b; X, 266b; S, 4a, 182b, 282b, 292b, 303a, 321b
Ḳādiriyya Bakkāya ii, 1132a – II, 1158b
Ḳādis iv, **383a** – IV, **400a**
al-Ḳādisiyya (al-Kūfa) (635) ii, 893b; iii, 194b, 1254b; iv, 384b, **385b**, 775a; v, 634a; vi, 266b; viii, 112b – II, 914a; III, 199b, 1287a; IV, 401a, **401b**, 806b; V, 638a; VI, 251a; VIII, 114b
al-Ḳādisiyya (Sāmarrā) iv, **384a** – IV, **400b**
Kadiwala sayyids v, 26b – V, 27b
Ḳādiyānī → Aḥmadiyya
Ḳādī-zāde Aḥmed Shams al-Dīn v, 27b – V, 28b
Ḳādī-zāde ʿAlī i, 1284b – I, 1324a
Ḳādī-zāde Meḥmed Beg (XVI) i, 293b – I, 302b
Ḳādī-zāde Meḥmed Efendi (1635) vii, 598a – VII, 598a
Ḳādī-zāde-i Rūmī (1436) i, 393a, 869a; iv, 702b; vi, 601b; viii, 542a – I, 404b, 893a; IV, 731a; VI, 586b; VIII, 560a
Ḳādjārs i, 13b, 36a, 190b, 246b, 296a, 720b, 1250b; ii, 150a, b, 151a, 309a, 334b, 433b, 654b, 656a; iii, 554a, 1100a, 1101b, 1103b; iv, 38a, 51a, 294a, **387b**, 577b, 1052b; v, 371b, 461b, 630a; vi, 13b, 18b, 202b, 276b, 366a, 483b, 521b, 523a, b, 526a, 528a, b, 529a, b, 548b, 551b, 552b, 554b, 856b; vii, 440b, 678a; x, 47b; s, 70b, 71a, 104a, 257a, b, 260b, 302a, 336a, 405b –
I, 14a, 37a, 196a, 254a, 305a, 742a, 1288b; II, 154b, 155a, b, 318a, 344a, 444b, 671a, 672b; III, 573a, 1127a, 1129a, 1130b; IV, 40b, 53b, 307a, **404a**, 601a, 1084a; V, 372a, 464b, 634b; VI, 12a, 16b, 187a, 216b, 350a, 469b, 506a, 507b, 508a, 510b, 512a, b, 513a, b, 533a, 536a, 537a, 539a, 848a; VII, 441b, 678a; X, 49a; S, 71a, b, 103b, 256b, 257b, 260b, 302a, 335b, 405b
Ḳādjār, Banū iii, 1100a, 1101b, 1103b; iv, **387a** – III, 1127a, 1129a, 1130b; IV, **403b**
al-Kadjgharī → ʿAbd al-Ghāfir
Kadkhudā i, 978a; iv, 103b – I, 1008b; IV, 108a
Ḳadmūs iv, 200a; vi, 578a, b, 582a, 789b – IV, 209a; VI, 563a, b, 567a, 779b
Ḳadr → Ḳaḍā; Ramaḍān
Ḳadr Khān → Ḳādir Khān
Ḳadrī (XVII) iii, 114a; iv, **399a** – III, 116b; IV, **416b**
Ḳadrī Bey ii, 657b; iv, 853a – II, 674a; IV, 886b
Ḳāf (Mts) i, 926b; iii, 332a; iv, 342a, **400b**; ix, 101b – I, 955a; III, 342a; IV, 356a, b, **418a**; IX, 105a
al-Kāf (El-Kef) iv, **402b** – IV, **419b**
Kāf(k) iv, **399a** – IV, **416b**
Ḳāf(ḳ) iv, **400a** – IV, **417a**
Kafa → Kefe
Kafāʾa iv, **404a**, 1161b – IV, **421b**, 1193b
al-Kafādjī i, 1056b – I, 1088a
Kafāla iv, **404b** – IV, **422a**
Kafar Ṭāb vi, 378b, 381a; VII, 577b, 578a – VI, 363a, 365a; VII, 578a, b
Kafarbayya vi, 774b, 775a, b – VI, 764a, b, 765a
al-Kaff (ʿIlm-) iv, **405b** – IV, **423a**
Kaff → ʿArūḍ; Ḳuʿūd
Kaffa → Kefe
al-Ḳaffāl al-Shāsh (947) ix, 187b – IX, 193a
Kaffāra iv, **406b**, 688a, 768a – IV, **424a**, 716a, 798b
Kāfī → Ḥasan Kāfī
al-Kāfī Zaʿīm al-Ruʾasāʾ ii, 384b – II, 395a
Kafīl → Kafāla
Ḳāfila → Karwān; Tidjāra
Ḳāfilat al-Sūdān ii, 137b – II, 141a
Kāfir i, 224b, 225a; iv, **407b**, 410b; v, 649a – I, 231a, 231b; IV, **425a**, 428b; V, 653a
Kāfir (language/langue) ii, 138a, b; iv, 409b – II, 142a; IV, 427a
Kāfiristān i, 223b; ii, 140a; iv, **409a**; vi, 66a; s,237a, b – I, 230a; II, 143b; IV, **427a**; VI, 64a; S, 237a
Kāfirkūb(āt) iv, 44b, **411a** – IV, 47a, **429a**
Kāfirnihān ii, 2a – II, 2a
Ḳāfiya iv, **411b**; v, 320b – IV, **429b**; V, 320a
al-Kāfiyadjī (1447) iv, **414b**; vii, 491a – IV, **432b**; VII, 490b
Kāfiyya v, 740a – V, 745b
Ḳafīz → Makāyīl
Kafr ʿAwaḍ Allāh Ḥidjāzī s, 262b – S, 262a
Kafr al-Ḥiṣāfa s, 371a – S, 371a
Kafr Mandūr (Egypt) vi, 408a – VI, 393a
Ḳafsa (Gafsa) i, 161b; iv, **414b**; v, 1181b; vi, 355b – I, 166a; IV, **433a**; V, 1171b; VI, 339b
Ḳafṭān v, 737b, 739b, 752a – V, 743a, 745a, 757b
Kaftar s, 127a – S, 126a
Kāfūr (camphor/-re) iv, **417b** – IV, **435b**
Kāfūr, Abu ʾl-Misk (Ikhshīdid(e)) (968) i, 34a, 1042a; ii, 793b, 1080b; iii, 768b, 840b; iv, **418a**, 673b, 1091b; v, 327a, b, 619a; vi, 545a; vii, 147b, 161b, 411b, 488a, 770b –
I, 34b, 1073b; II, 812a, 1105b; III, 791b, 864b; IV, **436b**, 701a, 1122b; V, 327a, 623a; VI, 530a; VII, 149b, 163a, 413a, 487b, 772b
Kāfūr, Malik, Hazār-Dīnārī (1316) i, 444b; ii, 12b, 179b, 269a, 272a, 1084b, 1085a, 1124a; iv, **419a**, 921b, 922a, 923b, 1023a; v, 938a, 1258b; vi, 270b; vii, 289a, 457b; s, 105a –
I, 457b; II, 13a, 185a, 277a, 280b, 1109b, 1110b, 1150b; IV, **437a**, 954b, 955a, 956b, 1055a; V, 941b, 1249b; VI, 255b; VII, 291a, 457b; S, 104b
Ḳāf-zāde Fāʾidī (XVII) viii, 6b – VIII, 6b
Ḳāf-zāde Fayḍ Allāh Efendi (1611) viii, 6b – VIII, 6b
Kāghad (Kāghid) ii, 311a; iv, **419b**, 742a, 1114b; v, 854b; viii, 149b – II, 320a; IV, **437b**, 772a, 1146a; V, 861b; VIII, 152a
Kaghalgha → Ḳalghay
Ḳaghan → Khāḳān
Kāghitkhāne vi, 55b, 57a – VI, 53b, 55a
Kahar Muzakkar (Makassar) (XX) vi, 117a – VI, 114b
al-Kahf → Aṣḥāb al-Kahf
Kahf al-Dawla wa ʾl-Islām → Maḥmūd b. Sebüktigin
al-Ḳaḥḥāl → ʿAlī b. ʿĪsā
Kāhin i, 585b, 659b; iv, **420b**; v, 235a, 420a, 422a, 1101a – I, 604a, 680b; IV, **438b**; V, 233a, 422a, 424a, 1097a
al-Kāhina i, 367a, 770b, 1175a; iii, 271a, 296a, 1039b; iv, **422a**; vi, 751a, 753b –
I, 378a, 793b, 1210a; III, 279a, 305a, 1065b; IV, **440b**; VI, 740b, 743a
al-Ḳāhir bi-ʾllāh (ʿAbbāsid(e)) (950) i, 19a, 1039b; ii, 1080b; iii, 46a, 126b, 345a, 886b; iv, **423b**, 940a; vi, 206a, 539a; vii, 414a, 541b, 575b – I, 20a, 1071a; II, 1105b; III, 47b, 129b, 355b, 910b; IV, **442a**, 973a; VI, 190b, 523b; VII, 415b, 541b, 576a
Ḳāhir b. ʿAlī b. Ḳānit v, 926a – V, 931b
al-Ḳāhir al-Falak (Miṣr) vii, 148b – VII, 150b
al-Ḳāhira i, 9a, 396b, 451b, 551b, 832a, 976a; ii, 128a, 495a, 854a, 958b; iii, 81a, 756b, 813a; iv, 215b, **424a**; v, 993a; vi, 44b, 45a, 122b, 123a, 186a, 445a, 649b, 656b, 657a; ix, 791b –
I, 9b, 408a, 464b, 569b, 855b, 1006a; II, 131a, 507b, 873b, 980b; III, 83a, 779b, 836b; IV, 225a, **442b**; V, 988a; VI, 43b, 120b, 635a, 642a; VII, 825b
—fortifications iv, 428b, 429b, 430b, 436a; v, 92a – IV, 447a, 448b, 449b, 455b; V, 94b

—madrasas iv, 430a, 432a, 437a; v, 1125b, 1127b, 1140b, 1141a – IV, 449a, 451a, 456b; V, 1121b, 1124a, 1133b, 1134a
—modern city/ville moderne iv, 441b-444b – IV, 461b-464a
—monuments i, 620a, 621a-624, 813-821, 863a, b; iii, 81a, 190a; iv, 424a-428b, 438a, b, 439a, 440a – I, 640b, 641b-645, 837-844, 883a, b; III, 83a, 194b; IV, 442b-447a, 457b, 458a, 459a, b
—mosqu(é)es i, 620a, 814b; iv, 428b, 430a, 431a, 436b, 437b, 444b; v, 93a, 500b – I, 640b, 837b; IV, 447a, b, 449a, b, 455b, 457a, 464a; V, 95a, 503b
—population iv, 443a, b – IV, 463a, b
—tomb(e)s iv, 425a-428b, 429b, 430b, 434a – IV, 443b-447a, 448a, 449a, b, 453a
—university/-é i, 818a; ii, 132a, 424a; iv, 441b, 444a – I, 841a; II, 135a, 434b; IV, 461b, 464a
Kāhiya iv, 894b – IV, 927b
Ḳahḳaha iv, 188a – IV, 196a
al-Kaḥlaba Hubayra b. ʿAbd Hanāf ix, 864a – IX, 900a
Kahlān i, 544b; iv, 448a – I, 561b; IV, 468a
Kahlān b. Abī Lawā (Maṭmāṭī) (XI) vi, 842a – VI, 832b
Kahlās, Banū vi, 50b – VI, 49a
Kāhrabā' → Kahrubā
Kahramanmaraş vi, 509a, b – VI, 494b, 495a
Kahraman Mīrzā (1842) vii, 454a, b – VII, 454b, 455a
Ḳahramān-nāma i, 152b; iv, **444b** – I, 157a; IV, **464b**
Kahrubā iv, **445b** – IV, **465a**
Ḳahrūn b. Ghannūsh v, 59b – V, 61b
Ḳaḥṭaba b. Shabīb al-Ṭā'ī (749) i, 16a, 16b, 108b, 141a, 1033b; iii, 988b; iv, 99b, **445b**; vi, 332b, 333a, b, 345a; vii, 360a – I, 16b, 17a, 111b, 145b, 1065a; III, 1013a; IV, 104a, **465b**; VI, 317a, b, 318a, 329a; VII, 362b
Ḳaḥṭān i, 544b, 545b, 873b; ii, 176a; iii, 363b, 1065b; iv, **447b**; vi, 75a, 371b; s, 338a – I, 561b, 563a, 897b; II, 181b; III, 375a, 1092a; IV, **467b**; VI, 73a, 356a; S, 337b
al-Ḳaḥṭānī (Maḳdishū) vi, 128b, 472b – VI, 126b, 458b
al-Ḳaḥṭānī, Muḥammad b. ʿAbd Allāh (Mecca) (1979) vi, 157b, 158b – VI, 153a, b
Ḳahwa i, 540a, 1140b; ii, 1063a; iii, 179a; iv, **449a**; v, 109b – I, 557a, 1175a; II, 1078b; III, 183a; IV, **469a**; V, 112a
Kaḥyā → Ketkhudā
Kaḥyā (Djenāze) Ḥasan Pasha (1810) iv, **455b** – IV, **476a**
Ḳāʿid i, 977a; ii, 507b; iv, **456a**; v, 1198b – I, 1007b; II, 520a; IV, **476a**; V, 1188b
al-Ḳā'id b. Ḥammād (Ḥammādid(e)) (1054) iii, 137a; v, 623b, 1177b; vii, 482b – III, 140a; V, 627b, 1167b; VII, 482a
Ḳaïdes iv, 384b – IV, 401b
Ḳā'if → Ḳiyāfa
al-Ḳā'im, Ḳiyām al-Dīn (1793) ix, 214a – IX, 219b
al-Ḳā'im bi-Amr Allāh (ʿAbbāsid(e)) (1075) i, 132b, 420a, 461b, 1073b, 1074b, 1075a; ii, 384a; iii, 86b, 159b, 196a, 345b, 860b, 891a; iv, 26b, **457a**, 942a, b; v, 388b; vi, 243b, 272b, 275a, 674a; viii, 70a,b; s, 192a, b, 194a – I, 136a, 432a, 474b, 1105b, 1106b, 1107a; II, 394b; III, 88b, 163a, 200b, 356a, 885a, 915a; IV, 28b, **477b**, 975a; V, 389a; VI, 227b, 257b, 260a, 660b; VIII, 71b, 72aS, 193a, b
al-Ḳā'im bi-Amr Allāh (ʿAbbāsid(e)) (1455) iii, 1198b – III, 1228b
al-Ḳā'im bi-Amr Allāh (Fāṭimid(e)) (946) i, 699b, 1355b; ii, 491a, 851a, 853a; iv, **458b**; v, 1243b, 1246b; vi, 434b, 727b; vii, 642a; s, 62b, 236b – I, 720b, 1395a; II, 503b, 871a, 872b; IV, **478b**; V, 1234a, b, 1237a; VI, 419b, 716b; VII, 641b; S, 63a, 236b
al-Ḳā'im bi-Amr Allāh Āl Muḥammad (Mahdī) iv, 203b, 204a, **456b**; v, 1235b – IV, 212b, 213a, **477a**; V, 1226a, b
al-Ḳā'im bi-Amr Allāh Khān iii, 60a – III, 62b
Ḳā'im-maḳām ii, 444a; iv, **461b** – II, 455b; IV, **482a**
Ḳā'imi-maḳām-i Farāhānī, Abū 'l-Ḳāsim (1835) iv, 70b, 394a, **462a**; s, 73a – IV, 74a, 410b, **482b**; S, 73b
Ḳā'im-maḳām-i Farāhānī, ʿĪsā (1822) iv, **462a**; v, 919a – IV, **482b**; V, 924b
Ḳāïmāz i, 1160b – I, 1195a
Ḳā'ime i, 693a; iv, **460a** – I, 714a; IV, **480b**
Ḳā'in v, 354b, 355a, b – V, 356a, b, 357a
Kairowan/Kairovan → Ḳayrawān
Kaisos → Ḳays b. Salama
Ḳā'it Bāy, al-Malik al-Ashraf ʿAbd al-Naṣr (Mamlūk) (1496) i, 281a, 349a, 553a, 815a, 1060a, 1119b, 1190b, 1234a, 1281a, 1317b; ii, 166b, 286a, 529b, 530a; iii, 48b, 186b, 346a; iv, 133a, 429a, 432a, **462b**, 563a, 642b, 960a; v, 304a, 1143b; vi, 150a, 315a, 323b, 324a, b, 359b, 367b, 580a, 709a; vii, 61b, 173b, 175b, 295a, 727a; s, 208a, b – I, 289b, 360a, 571a, 838a, 1091b, 1153a, 1226a, 1270b, 1320a, 1358b; II, 172a, 294a, 542b, 543a; III, 50b, 190b, 357a; IV, 138b, 447b, 451a, **483a**, 585a, 669a, 992b; V, 303b, 1136a; VI, 148b, 300a, b, 308a, 309a, 343b, 351b, 565a, 697b; VII, 62a, 175a, 177a, b, 297a, 727b; S, 208a
Ḳā'it Bāy b. Muḥammad i, 1032b – I, 1064a
al-Ḳaʿḳāʿ iv, **463b** – IV, **484a**
al-Ḳaʿḳaʿ b. ʿAmr (VII) iv, **464a** – IV, **484b**
al-Ḳaʿḳāʿ b. Maʿbad al-Tamīmī iv, 463b – IV, 484b
Kākā'ī, Banū i, 262b; ix, 153a – I, 271a; IX, 158a
Kākudam (de(é)sert) vii, 584a – VII, 584a
Kākūyid(e)s/Kākwayhid(e)s i, 1356a; iv, **465a**; v, 824a; vi, 66a – I, 1395a; IV, **485b**; V, 830a; VI, 64a
K'akh ii, 22a – II, 22b
Kakheti v, 493a – V, 496a
Kakhtā (Kʸākhta) iv, **464a**; vi, 507a – IV, **485a**; VI, 492b
Kākī (Mānd) vi, 384b – VI, 369a
Kākī (Masraḥ) vi, 754a – VI, 743b
Kākī, Āl vi, 115b – VI, 113a
Kākī, Shams al-Dīn (XIII) vii, 274a – VII, 276a
Kāḳshāls iii, 423b – III, 437b
Ḳāḳūn iv, 842b – IV, 875b
Kākūyide)s x, 553a – X,
Kākwayhid(e)s → Kākūyid(e)s
Kalā (island/île) → Kalah
Ḳalʿa → Agadir; Burdj; Ḥiṣār; Ḥiṣn; Ḳaṣaba
Ḳalʿa i, 367a, 904a, b, 1319b; ii, 863b; iii, 137a – I, 378a, 931b, 932a, 1359b; II, 883b; III, 139b
al-Ḳalʿa (castle/château) iv, **467a** – IV, **488a**
al-Ḳalʿa (Ḥammād) → Ḳalʿat Banī Ḥammād
al-Ḳalʿa al-Bayḍā' → Ḳalʿe-i Sefīd
al-Ḳalʿa Kuhrūd v, 662a – V, 667b
Kalā-rustāḳ vi, 511b – VI, 497a
al-Kalābādhī (990) iii, 84a, 102b; iv, **467a**, 616b, 696b – III, 86a, 105a; IV, **488a**, 641a, 725a
Kalaband (Ottoman(e)) → Nafy
Ḳalafat ii, 61b – II, 62b
Kalah (Kalāh) ii, 105a; iv, **467b**, 502a; vi, 234a; vii, 71b – II, 107b; IV, **488a**, 524a; VI, 207a; VII, 72b
Kalāh-bār iv, 468a – IV, 488b

Ḳalaʿī (tin/étain) → Ḳalʿī
al-Kalāʿī → K̲h̲ālid b. Maʿdān
al-Kalāʿī, Abu 'l-Rabīʿ b. Sālim (1237) iii, 804a; iv, **468a**; vii, 388a – III, 827a; IV; **489a**; VII, 389a
al-Kalāʿī, Ibn al-G̲h̲afūr vii, 261a – VII, 263a
al-Kalāʿī, Muḥammad b. Ibrāhīm b. al-Maḥābī vi, 830b – VI, 821a
Ḳalʿa-i Duk̲h̲tār iv, 288al v, 657b – IV, 300b; V, 663a
Ḳalʿa-i Iṣṭak̲h̲r iv, 221b, 222a – IV, 231b
Ḳalʿa-i Sefīd → Ḳalʿe-i Sefīd
Ḳalʿa-i Sulṭāniyya → Ḳalʿe-i Sulṭaniyye
Ḳalʿa-yi Dabūs s, 176b – S, 177b
Ḳalāla vi, 435a – VI, 420b
Kalām i, 60b, 113a, 266a, 333a, 342b, 409b, 410a, 414a, 415b, 694b; ii, 95b, 449a, 608a, 618a, 824b; iii, 103b, 171b; iv, 46a, **468b**, 508b, 985a; v, 238a,b – I, 62b, 116b, 274a, 343a, 353a, 421b, 425b, 427a, 715b; II, 97b, 461a, 623a, 633b, 843b; III, 105b, 175a; IV, 48b, **489b**, 530b, 1017b; V, 236b
Ḳalam (pen/plume) iv, **471a**, 472a – IV, **491b**, 492b
Ḳalam (secretariat) iv, **471b** – IV, **492b**
Kalām (theology/-ie) → ʿIlm al-Kalām
Ḳalam al-Ṣāliḥiyya iv, 822b – IV, 855a
Ḳalama i, 1231a – I, 1268a
Kalaman i, 98a – I, 100b
Ḳalamdan → Ḳalam; Kitāba
Ḳalamdār iv, 471b; v, 988b – IV, 492a; V, 984a
Ḳalamkārī iv, **471b** – IV, **492b**
al-Ḳalammas iv, **472a** – IV, **493a**
Ḳalamūn vi, 544b – VI, 529a
Ḳalān iv, 31a, 1050a, b – IV, 33a, 1081b, 1082a
Kalān, Mīrzā i, 853a – I, 876b
Ḳalandar iv, 58b, **472b**; vi, 225b, 228b; s, 352b – IV, 62a, **493a**; VI, 219a, 222b; S, 352b
Kalandar Bak̲h̲s̲h̲ → D̲j̲urʾat
Ḳalandariyya i, 104b; ii, 165a, 395a; iv, **473a**; vi, 224a, 228b; viii, 3a; x, 250b –
I, 107b; II, 170a, 405b; IV, **493b**; VI, 217b, 222b; VIII, 3b; X. 269b
Ḳalandariyyāt → Ḳalandar
al-Ḳalānisī, Aḥmad b. ʿAbd al-Raḥmān s, 392a – S, 392b
al-Ḳalānisī, Muḥammad i, 344b – I, 355a
Ḳalānisiyya (Damas(cus)) vi, 193b; s, 197a – VI, 177b; S, 197a
Ḳalansuwa iv, 940a – IV, 973a
Kalāntar iv, 103b, **474a**; v, 155b; s, 275b, 405b – IV, 108a, **495a**; V, 156a; S, 275a, 405b
Kalāntar, Mīrzā Muḥammad s, 405b – S, 405b
Kalār s, 335a – S, 334b
Kalārud vi, 745b – VI, 734b
Kalas'a s, 242a – S, 242a
Kalaṣa ii, 31a, 138b – II, 31b, 142a
al-Ḳalaṣādī, Abu 'l-Ḥasan (XV) ix, 20a – IX, 21a
al-Ḳalaṣādī, ʿAlī (1846) iv, **476b**, 725b – IV, **497b**, 754b
Kalāt, Kilāt, Kelāt → Balūčistān
Kalāt (Kalʿat) Abī Sufyān i, 145b – I,, 150a
Kalāt Abī Ṭawil → Ḳalat Banī Ḥammād
Kalāt al-ʿAd̲j̲ād̲j̲ vi, 357b – VI, 342a
Kalāt Aḳd̲j̲a vi, 231a – VI, 225a
Kalāt al-Akrād vi, 231a – VI, 225a
Kalāt Ayyūb Calatayud) iv, **477b** – IV, **498b**
Kalāt al-Azraḳ i, 780b – I, 803b
Kalāt Banī ʿAbbās iv, **478a** – IV, **499a**
Kalāt Banī Ḥammād i, 367a, 1319b, ii, 863b; iii, 137a; iv, **478b**, 1166a; ix, 18a –
I, 378a, 1359b; II, 883b; III, 139b; IV, **499b**, 1198a; IX, 18b
La;āt Bayḍāʾ vi, 378a – VI, 362b
Kalāt Dawsar, Ḳalʿat D̲j̲aʿbar → D̲j̲aʿbar
Kalāt al-D̲j̲isr vii, 578a – VII, 578a
Kalāt Ḥammād → Ḳalʿa
Kalāt Huwwāra iv, **481b** – IV, **502b**
Kalāt K̲h̲ayrān vi, 576a – VI, 561a
Kalāt al-Muḍīk vi, 789a – VI, 779a
Kalāt al-Muhaylba → Balāṭunus
Kalāt al-Nad̲j̲m iv, **482a**; vi, 378a, 379a, 381a, 429a, 733a, b – IV, **502b**; VI, 362b, 363b, 365a, 414b, 722b
Kalāt Namrūd → al-Subayra
Kalāt Nawḥamām vi, 231a – VI, 225a
Kalāt al-Rabaḍ (ʿAd̲j̲lūn) vi, 547b – VI, 532a
Kalāt Rabāh (Calatrava) iii, 1055a, b; iv, **482b** – III, 1081a, 1082a; IV, **503b**
Kalāt al-Rūm → Rūm Ḳalʿesī
Kalāt al-S̲h̲aḳīf iv, **482b** – IV, **503b**
Kalāt S̲h̲arḳāt → At̲h̲ūr
Kalāt Yaḥmūr vi, 579a, 789b – VI, 564a, 779a
Ḳalaṭa → G̲h̲alaṭa
Ḳalʿat-i Nādirī iv, 38a; v, 59a, **102b** – IV, 40b; V, 61a, **105a**
Ḳalāʾun → Ḳalāwūn
al-Kalawd̲h̲ānī, Abū K̲h̲aṭṭāb (1117) x, 114a – X, 123b
Ḳalāwd̲h̲iya iv, **484a** – IV, **505a**
Ḳalawriya → Ḳillawriya
Ḳalāwūn, al-Malik al-Manṣūr (Mamlūk) (1290) i, 200b, 944b, 971a, 1016b, 1102b, 1127b, 1138a, 1224a, 1324b; ii, 38a, 285a, 305b, 353b; iii, 99a, 186b, 189a, 399b, 402b, 403a, 474b, 679b, 775b, 832b; iv, 464b, **484a**; v, 591a, 628a, 1140b; vi, 45a, 195a, 315b, 322b, 326b, 381b, 545b, 577b, 579b, 580a, 581b, 673b, 719a, 777b; viii, 90b, 147a; s, 205b, 389a –
I, 206b, 974a, 1001a, 1048a, 1135b, 1162a, 1172b, 1260b, 1365b; II, 38b, 293a, 314a, 363a; III, 101b, 191a, 193b, 412a, 415a, b, 491a, 701a, 798b, 856b; IV, 485a, **505a**; V, 595a, 632a, 1134a; VI, 43b, 179a, 300b, 306a, 307a, 311a, 365b, 530a, 562b, 564b, 566b, 660a, 708a, 767a; VIII, 92b, 149a; S, 205b, 389a
Kalaybar s, 116a – S, 115b
Ḳalʿa-yi Bāk̲h̲ta vi, 502a – VI, 487a
Ḳalʿa-yi S̲h̲ahriyār vi, 384b – VI, 368b
Ḳalʿa-yi Zohāk vi, 501a – VI, 486b
Ḳalaylîkoz Aḥmed Pas̲h̲a (1704) vi, 991a – VI, 983b
Ḳalb (heart/coeur) iv, **486a** – IV, **507a**
Kalb (dog/chien) iv, **489b** – IV, **510b**
Kalb, Banū i, 550a, 920a, 986b; ii, 90a, 553a; iii, 619a, 838a; iv, 370b, **492b**, **496a**, 820a; v, 105b, 1232a; vi, 221b, 333b, 379a, 435b, 544b, 545a, 546b, 622a, 623b, 624a, 717b; vii, 267b; s, 178a – I, 568a, 947b, 1017a; II, 91b, 567a; III, 639b, 862a; IV, 386b, **513b**, **517b**, 852b; V, 107b, 1222b; VI, 215b, 318a, 363b, 435b, 529b, 531a, 607a, 608b, 609a, 716b; VII, 269b; S, 179a
Kalb ʿAlī K̲h̲ān ii, 84a – II, 85b
Kalb b. Wabara iv, **492b**, 496a, 834a – IV, **513b**, 517b, 867a
Kalbāsī, Ḥād̲j̲d̲j̲ Muḥammad Ibrāhīm s, 76a, 135a – S, 76a, 134b
Kalb-i ʿAlī K̲h̲ān Afs̲h̲ār i, 240b – I, 247b
al-Kalbī, ʿAbbās b. His̲h̲ām (1609) iv, **496a** – IV, **517a**
al-Kalbī, Aḥmad b. Ḥasan (969) iv, 496b – IV, 518a
al-Kalbī, Aḥmad b. Yūsuf al-Akḥal (1030) iii, 788a; iv, 497a – III, 811a; IV, 518b
al-Kalbī, ʿAlī b. al-Ḥasan iv, 496b – IV, 518a
al-Kalbī, ʿAlī b. Abi 'l-Ḥusayn (938) iv, 496b – IV, 517b
al-Kalbī , His̲h̲ām b. Muḥammad (819) i, 210a, 758b; iii, 608a, 1047b; iv, 91b, **495a**; v, 350b; vi, 215b,

828b; vii, 402a, 967b; viii, 149b, 546a; s, 31b, 177a – I, 216b, 781b; III, 628b, 1074a; IV, 95b, **516b**; V, 351b; VI, 199a, 819a; VII, 403a, 968a; VIII, 151b, 564a; S, 31b, 178a
al-Kalbī, Khālid b. Arṭāṭ viii, 82b – VIII, 84b
a;-Kalbī, Muḥammad b. al-Sā'ib (763) iv, **495a**; viii, 983b; s, 90b – IV, **516a**; VIII, 1018a; S, 90a
al-Kalbī, al-Sā'ib b. Bishr iv, 494b – IV, 516a
al-Kalbī, Sulaymān b. Yakẓān s, 82a – S, 81b
Kalbīs (Syria/e) iii, 619a; iv, 370b – III, 639b; IV, 386b
Kalbid(e)s (Sicily/-e) i, 920a, 986b; ii, 553a; iv, **496a**; v, 105b; vii, 486b; ix, 585a – I, 947b, 1017a; II, 567a; IV, **517b**; V, 107b; VII, 486a, 487a; 607bb
Ḳalʿe → Ḳalʿa
Ḳalʿe-i Isfīd → Ḳalʿe-i Sefīd
Ḳalʿe-i Sefīd iv, **497b** – IV, **519a**
Ḳalʿe-i Sulṭāniyye ii, 11b – II, 11b
Kalembaina vii, 435b – VII, 436b
Ḳalender → Ḳalandar
Ḳalenderi → Ḳalandarīyya
Ḳalender-oghlï Meḥmed Pasha (1609) i, 267b, 510b, 826b, 1162b, 1334b; iii, 91b; iv, **499a**; viii, 197a; s, 239a – I, 276a, 526b, 849a, 1197a, 1347b; III, 94a; IV, **520b**; VIII, 200a; S, 239a
Ḳalghay ii, 1113b; iv, **499b**; vi, 734b, 735a – II, 1139b; IV, **521a**; VI, 723b, 724a
Ḳalhāt iv, **500b**; vi, 734b, 735a – IV, **522a**; VI, 723b, 724a
al-Ḳalhātī iii, 235b – III, 242a
Kalhōrā i, 229b, 230b; ii, 185a, b, 186a; iii, 323b; iv, 364b; ix, 440a, 634b – I, 236b, 237b; II, 191a, b; III, 333b; IV, 380b; IX, 457a, 659a
Kalhur v, 168b, 460b, 659a – V, 166a, 463b, 663b
Kali → Ḳāḍī
Ḳalʿī (Ḳalaʿī) (tin/étain) iv, 467b, **502a**; v, 964b, 967b – IV, 488a, **523b**; V, 969a
Ḳālī → Erzurūm
Ḳālī (carpet/tapis) → Bisāṭ
Ḳālī (pasture) vi, 493b – VI, 479b
al-Ḳālī, Abū ʿAlī al-Baghdādī (967) i, 156a, 590a, 600a; iii, 845a; iv, **501a**; vi, 344b, 430b, 713a, 822b, 916b; vii, 404a, 569b; viii, 14b – I, 160a, 609b, 619b; III, 868b; IV, **522b**; VI, 328b, 416a, 701b, 813a, 908a; VII, 405a, 570b; VIII, 14b
Kāl-i Shūr s, 235a – S, 234b
Ḳalīb i, 538b – I, 555a
Kalīdar s, 83b – S, 83a
Kālif iv, **502b**; s, 281a – IV, **524b**; S, 281a
Kalikat v, 360b; vi, 459a – V, 361b; VI, 444b
Ḳālīḳalā → Erzurūm
Kalikātā → Calcutta
Ḳālīḳūt vii, 71b – VII, 72a
Kalīla wa-Dimna i, 2b, 326b, 524b, 756a; ii, 758a, 951b; iii, 309a, 313b, 372b, 377a, 863a, 883b; iv, **503a**, 704a; s, 85b – I, 2b, 336b, 540a, 778b; II, 776a, 973b; III, 318b, 323a, 384b, 389a, 887a, 907b; IV, **524b**, 732b; S, 85b
Ḳalīm Abū Ṭālib (1651) iv, **506b**; vi, 271b; vii, 341a – IV, **528b**; VI, 256a; VII, 343a
Kalīm Allāh → Mūsā
Kalīm Allāh b. Maḥmūd Shihāb al-Dīn (Bahmānīd(e)) (1538) i, 923b, 1047a, 1200a; vi, 63b – I, 951b, 1079a, 1235b; VI, 61b
Kalīm Allāh Djahānābādī (1729) ii, 55a; iv, **507a** – II, 56a; IV, **529a**
Kalima iv, 83a, **508a** – IV, 87a, **530a**
Kalimantan i, 1258b; iii, 1213a, b, 1215b, 1225b; vi, 43a, b, 239a – I, 1297a; III, 1243b, 1244b, 1246a, 1257a; VI, 41b, 42a, 204a
Kalīmī → Yahūd
Kālindjār vi, 48a, 65b – VI, 46b, 63b
Kalinin → Porsï
Káliz → Khalisioi
Ḳalḳaliyyūn s, 302b – S, 302a
al-Ḳalḳashandī (nisba) iv, 511a – IV, 533a
al-Ḳalkashandī, Shihāb al-Dīn Aḥmad (1418) i, 119a, 239b, 430a, 595a, 761b; ii, 301b, 305b, 328a, 487a; iii, 344b, 487a, 1242b; iv, **509a**, 742b, 1119a; v, 627a; vi, 108b, 112a, 118b, 185b, 198a, 352a, 381b, 906b; vii, 257b; viii, 537a; s, 1a, 203b – I, 122b, 247a, 442a, 614a, 784a; II, 310a, 314a, 337b, 499b; III, 354b, 504a, 1275a; IV, **531a**, 772b, 1151a; V, 631a; VI, 106b, 109b, 116b, 167b, 182b, 336b, 366a, 898a; VII, 259a; VIII, 554b; S, 1a, 203a
Kalkhur iii, 1102b, 1109a – III, 1129b, 1136a
al-Kallā' i, 1086a; vii, 67b – I, 1118b; VII, 68a
Ḳallabāt i, 49b; iv, 686a, 687a – I, 51a; IV, 714a, 715a
Ḳallabāt (al-Matamma) i, 49b; vi, 643b – I, 51a; VI, 628a
Ḳallala iv, **511a** – IV, **533b**
Kalmuk i, 121a, 135a, 422a, 722a, 1002b, 1028a; ii, 21b, 25a, 39a, 47a; iii, 117a, 1120b; iv, 213b, **512a**, 584a; v, 134b; vi, 371a, 416b, 418a; x, 677a; s, 169a, 281a, 419b – I, 124b, 139a, 434a, 743b, 1033a, 1059b; II, 22a, 25a, 39b, 48a; III, 119b, 1148a; IV, 223a, **534a**, 607b; V, 137b; VI, 355b, 401b, 403a; X, ;S, 169a, 281a, 419b
Ḳalpak v, 751b – V, 757b
Kalpī iii, 443b, 638b; iv, **513a**; vi, 53b, 61b, 62a; vii, 278b, 279a; ix, 785b; s, 206b – III, 458a, 659b; IV, **535a**; VI, 51b, 59b, 60a; VII, 280b; S, 206a; IX, 819b
al-Ḳalshanī i, 863a – I, 887a
Ḳalūdiya → Ḳalawdhiya
Ḳalūniya iv, 578b – IV, 602a
al-Ḳalūṣ (Zandjī) (IX) vii, 526b – VII, 526b
Ḳālūsh s, 269a – S, 268b
Kalwādhā iv, **513a**; vi, 656b – IV, **535b**; VI, 642a
al-Kalwadhānī, Abū 'l-Khaṭṭāb (1116) iii, 160a, 766b; iv, **513b**; x, 114a; s, 193a – III, 163b, 789b; IV, **535b**; X, 123b; S, 194a
Ḳalyān, Ḳalyūn → Baḥriyya; Safīna
Kalyāni i, 1323b; iii, 426a, 626a, 1160a, 1161a; iv, **513b** – I, 1364a; III, 439b, 646b, 1188b, 1189b; IV, **536a**
Kalyar s, 313a – S, 312b
Ḳalyūb iv, **514a**; vi, 119a; s, 371a – IV, **536a**; VI, 116b; S, 371a
al-Ḳalyūbī, Shihāb al-Dīn (1596) iv, **515a** – IV, **537a**
al-Ḳalyūbiyya s, 121b – S, 121a
Kām Bakhsh i, 913b, 1202b – I, 941b, 1238b
Ḳamaʿa b. Khindif v, 76b, 77a – V, 79a
Kamadjas i, 1258a – I, 1296b
Ḳamaḥ → Kemākh
Kamāl → Kemāl
Kamāl, Shaykh s, 361a – S, 361a
Kamāl al-Dawla Shīrzād (Ghaznawid(e)) (1115) vi, 783a – VI, 773a
Kamāl al-Dīn b. Ḳawām al-Dīn (Marʿashī) (1358) vi, 511a, b, 512a, b, 513b – VI, 496b, 497a, b, 498a, b
Kamāl b. Arslan Khān Maḥmūd (Ḳarā-Khānid) s, 245b – S, 245b
Kamāl b. Mir-i Buzūrg (Marʿashī) vi, 516a – VI, 501a
Kamāl b. Muḥammad (Marʿashī) vi, 513b – VI, 498b
Kamāl b. Shams al-Dīn, Mīr (Marʿashī) (1502) vi, 514b – VI, 499b

Kamāl b. Yūnus (XIII) vi, 638a – VI, 623a
Kamāl Abu 'l-Faḍl Muḥammad al-Shahrazūrī (1160) vi, 870b – VI, 861a
Kamāl Abu 'l-Ma'ālī Muḥammad b. al-Amīr Naṣir al-Dīn Muḥammad (XV) vii, 295a – VII, 297a
Kamāl Aḥmad b. Ṣadr al-Dīn i, 766b – I, 789b
Kamāl al-Fārisī (XIV) iii, 1137a, 1139a; iv, **515b**, 804b; v, 397b, 547a; vi, 183b, 377a – III, 1165a, 1167b; IV, **537b**, 836b; V, 398b, 552b; VI, 167b, 361b
Kamāl Gurg ii, 405b, 1124a – II, 416b, 1150b
Kamāl Ḥusayn Beg i, 1191b – I, 1227a
Kamāl Ibn al-'Adīm → Ibn al-'Adīm
Kamāl Ismā'īl (Ismā'īl-i Iṣfahānī) (1237) iv, 62a, **515b**; vi, 609a; s, 235b, 239b – IV, 65b, **538a**; VI, 593b; S, 235b, 239b
Kamāl Ḳazwīnī ii, 54a – II, 55a
Kamāl Mar'ashī, Sayyid v, 663a – V, 668a
Kamāl Muḥammad, vizier (1150) vi, 782a – VI, 772a
Kamāl Shīr 'Alī → Bannā'ī
Kamāl al-Dunyā wa'l-Dīn al-Ḥasan b. Mas'ūd (Maṣyād) (XIII) vi, 790b – VI, 780a
Kamāl Ismā'īl-i Iṣfahānī → Kamāl al-Dīn Ismā'īl
Kamāl Khān Rustamī (1649) ii, 973b; vi, 837a – II, 995b; VI, 827b
Kamāl Khudjandī (1400) i, 1301a; iv, **516b** – I, 1341a; IV, **538b**
Kamāl al-Mulk b. 'Abd al-Raḥīm iii, 1201a – III, 1231b
Kamāl al-Mulk al-Simīrumī (1118) vi, 64a; vii, 754a – VI, 61b; VII, 755b
Kamāl al-Mulk Pasha-zāde → Kemāl Pasha-zāde
Kamāl al-Wizāra → Aḥmad Maḥmūdī
Kamālī (1611) viii, 776a – VIII, 802a
al-Kamāliyya iv, 991b – IV, 1024b
Kaman i, 606b – I, 626a
Kamanča → Malāhī
Ḳamāniča iv, **516b**; v, 260b – IV, **539a**; V, 258b
al-Ḳamar iv, **517a** – IV, **539b**
Ḳamar (singer/chanteuse) iv, 822a – IV, 855a
Ḳamar, Banū (Mahra) vi, 82b – VI, 80a
Ḳamar al-Dīn Čīn Ḳilič Khān → Āṣaf Djāh I, Niẓām al-Mulk
Ḳamar al-Dīn Dūghlāt ii, 622a – II, 637b
Ḳamar al-Dīn Khān i, 295b; iii, 59b – I, 304b; III, 62a
Ḳamarān i, 535b, 539a; iv, **519a**; vii, 514b – I, 551b, 556a; IV, **541b**; VII, 515a
Ḳambar Dīwāna iii, 482b – III, 499b
Kambayāt/Kanbāya vi, 271a – VI, 255b
Kamenetz Podolski → Ḳamāniča
Kāmfīrūz vi, 493b – VI, 479b
Kāmgār iv, 1018b – IV, 1050b
Ḳamḥ ii, 904a, 1062b; iv, **519b** – II, 924b, 1087b; IV, **542a**
Kamieniec → Ḳamāniča
Kāmil → 'Arūḍ
Kāmil → Sha'bān I
Kāmil, al-Malik, b. al-'Ādil (Ayyūbid(e)) (1238) → al-Malik al-Kāmil I b. al-'Ādil
Kāmil, al-Malik, b. al-Muẓaffar (Ayyūbid(e)) (1260) → al-Malik al-Kāmil II
Kāmil, Muṣṭafā → Muṣṭafā Kāmil
Kāmul 'Ayyād (XX) vi, 538b – VI, 523a
Kāmil Dāghistān (XX) vi, 538b – VI, 523a
Kāmil Ḥusayn iii, 1207b; iv, 85b – III, 1238a; IV,89b
Kāmil al-Ḥusaynī s, 67a, 68a – S, 67b, 68b
Kāmil Nu'manaw Yāshin (XX) vi, 768b – VI, 757b
Kāmil Pasha (1912) i, 286a; ii, 643b, 698b; iii, 520a, 595a, 605b, 624a; iv, 284a; vi, 983b – I, 294b; II, 659b, 716b; III, 538a, 615b, 626a, 645a; IV, 296a; VI, 976a
Kāmiliyya (Cairo/le Caire) (1225) vi, 320a; s, 197a – VI, 304b; S, 197a
Kamīn iii, 202b – III, 208a
Ḳamīs v, 733b, 748b, 749b – V, 738b, 754a, 755a
Kamkh → Kemākh
Ḳaml iv, **521b** – IV, **544a**
Ḳamlān, Banū vi, 434b, 435a, 727a – VI, 420a, b, 716a, b
al-Kammad (1704) iv, **522a** – IV, **545a**
al-Ḳammāṭ, Muḥammad (1479) vi, 132b – VI, 130b
Kammūn iv, **522a** – IV, **545a**
al-Kammūnī, Muḥammad (XI) iv, **523a** – IV, **546a**
Ḳammūniya → Ḳamūniya
Kāmrān, Mīrzā b. Bābur (Mughal) (1557) i, 228b; ii, 973a; iii, 422b, 423a, 455b, 485a, 575a, b, 576a, 633b, 634a; iv, **523b**, 537a; vii, 130b, 131a, 135a, 220a, 314a, 337b – I, 235a; II, 995b; III, 436b, 471b, 502a, 595a, b, 596a, 654b, 655b; IV, **546a**, 560a; VII, 132b, 133a, 137a, 222a, 316a, 339a
Kāmrān Mīrzā Nā'ib al-Salṭana (1860) iv, 393b; vi, 484b – IV, 410b; VI, 470b
Kāmrān Shāh Durrānī (1828) i, 230b; ii, 637b; iv, **523b** – I, 238a; II, 653b; IV, **546a**
Kāmrūp i, 719b; iv, **524a**; vi, 48a – I, 741a; IV, **546b**; VI, 46b
Ḳamṣar v, 869a – V, 875a
Ḳāmuhul vi, 967b – VI, 960a
Ḳamūniya iv, 825b, 826b – IV, 858b, 859b
Ḳāmūs ii, 585b, 801b, 926b; iii, 760a,b; iv, **524a**; v, 837a, 1093a – II, 660a, 820b, 948a; III, 783b; IV, **546b**; V, 843b, 1090a
Ḳān → Khān
Kān wa-kān iv, **528a**; v, 372b – IV, **551a**; V, 373b
Ḳanā → Ḳunā
Ḳanā'at Shāh Ataliḳ s, 98a – S, 97a
al-Ka'nabī, 'Abd al-Raḥmān (835) vi, 280b; vii, 691a – VI, 265b; VII, 691b
Kanaka (IX) viii, 106b – VIII, 109a
Kanākir vi, 546a – VI, 531a
Kānamī → Kānemī
Kan'ān iv, **528b**; v, 521b – IV, **551b**; V, 525a
Ḳanān b. Mattā (VII) viii, 535b – VIII, 553b
Kan'ān Pasha → Ken'ān Pasha
Kanarese → Kannada
Ḳanāt ii, 875b; iv, 8b, **528b**, 600b; v, 866a, b, 875b, 878b, 968b, 1108b – II, 896a; IV, 9a, **551b**, 624b; V, 872b, 873a, 881b, 884b, 971b, 1104b
Kanāta → Kunta
al-Ḳanāṭir iv, 555b; s, 230a – IV, 579b; S, 230a
Ḳanāṭir Fir'awn iv, 556b – IV, 580b
Ḳanawāt iv, **533a**; vi, 546b – IV, **556a**; VI, 531a
Kan(n)awdj ii, 808b; iv, 276a, **533b**; vi, 48a, 49b, 65b, 273a, 294b, 309a, 410a; vii, 407a; s, 21a, 312a – II, 827b; IV, 288a, **556b**; VI, 46b, 48a, 63b, 258a, 279b, 294b, 394b; VII, 408a; S, 21b, 312a
Ḳanbalū (island/île) vi, 784b; ix, 715b – VI, 774b; IX, 746b
Ḳanbāniya iv, **534a**; v, 509b – IV, **557a**; V, 513b
Ḳanbar Beg iv, 749b – IV, 779b
Kanbāya → Khambāyat
Kanbāya iii, 444b – III, 459b
Kanbōh → Supplement
Kanchandas i, 173a – I, 177b
Kānčī vi, 67b – VI, 65b

Ḳand → Sukkar
Kand b. Kharshbūn (Mohmand) vii, 220a – VII, 221b
Ḳandābīl iv, 364a, **534a** – IV, 380a, **557b**
Ḳandahār i, 5a, 8b, 72a, 80b, 95b, 222b, 223a, 768b, 1323b; ii, 134b, 628b; iv, 37b, **535a**; vi, 768a; vii, 130b, 131a, 313b, 318b, 438a, 854b; s, 63a, 66b, 367b, 423b – I, 5a, 8b, 74a, 83a, 98a, 229a, 230a, 791b, 1364a; II, 137b, 644b; IV, 40a, **558b**; VI, 757a; VII, 132b, 133a, 316a, 321a, 439a, 855b; S, 63b, 67a, 367b, 423b
Ḳandahār, Ḳandhār (Deccan) iv, **538a**; v, 579b – IV, **561b**; V, 584b
Kāndhalawīs x, 39a – X, 40a
Kandi iv, **538b** – IV, **561b**
Kandia Koulibali iii, 39a – III, 40b
Ḳandīl → Ḳindīl
Kandilli (Istanbul) vi, 57a – VI, 55a
Ḳandiya(e) iv, **539a**, 590b; v, 260a, 261a – IV, **562a**, 614b; V, 258a, 259a
Ḳandiya (al-Khandaḳ) → al-Khandaḳ
Kandj Pashā i, 1078b – I, 1110b
Kandūrī iv, **540a** – IV, **563b**
Kanem (Kānim) i, 1259b, 1260a; ii, 369a, 876a; iv, **540a**, 566b; vi, 281b; s, 163b, 164a, 165a – I, 1297b, 1298a; II, 379a, 896a; IV, **563b**, 589a; VI, 266b; S, 163a, b, 164b
Kanembu i, 1260a; iv, 540b, 566b; s, 163b – I, 1298b; IV, 564a, 589a; S, 163b
Kānemī (language/langue) ii, 441b; iii, 657b – II, 453a; III, 678b
al-Kāne(i)mī, ʿAbd Allāh (XIX) vii, 435b – VII, 436b
al-Kāne(i)mī, Shaykh Muḥammad al-Amīn (1837) i, 1260a; ii, 942a; iii, 38b; iv, 541a, **541b**, 567a; v, 357b; vii, 435b; x, 122b; s, 164b – I, 1298a; II, 963b; III, 40b; IV, 564b, **565a**, 589b; V, 359a; VII, 436b; X, 132a; S, 164a
Kanesh → Kültepe
Kangarid(e)s → Musāfirid(e)s
Kangāwar → Kinkiwar
Kangli̊ s, 420a – S, 420a
Ḳanghli, Ḳanḳli̊ iv, **542a**; s, 97b – IV, **565b**; S, 97a
Kāñgṛā iv, **542b** – IV, **566b**
Kānī, Abū Bakr (1791) iv, **544a**; vi, 826b – IV, **567b**; VI, 817a
Ḳāniʿ, Mir ʿAlī Sher (1788) iv, **544b** – IV, **568a**
Kānī, Muṣṭafā iv, 795b, 796a – IV, 828a
Kāniguram vi, 86a, b – VI, 84a, b
Ḳāniʿī, Aḥmad b. Maḥmūd al-Ṭūsī (XIII) vii, 1017a; viii, 971b – VII, 1019a; VIII, 1005b
Kanik, Orhan Veli (1950) iv, **545a** – IV, **568b**
Kanīsa iv, **545a**; vi, 649b – IV, **569a**; VI, 635a
Kanīsat al-Ghurāb i, 488b – I, 503a
Kanīsat al-Ḳiyāma iv, 545b – IV, 569a
Kanīsat al-Sawdāʾ vi, 775a – VI, 764b
Kān-i Zand vi, 384a – VI, 368a
Kanizsa, Kanizhe iv, **546b**, 878a – IV, **570a**, 910b
Kankan viii, 1049a – VIII, 1084b
Kankarides → Kurd(e)s
Kankiwar → Kinkiwar
Kankūt ii, 155b, 156a – II, 160a, 161a
Kannada (language/langue) v, 1258b – V, 1249b
Kannanūr (Cannanore) iv, **546b**; v, 587a; vi, 206b – IV, **570b**; V, 661b; VI, 191a
Kannās iv, **547b** – IV, **571a**
Kannudj → Kanawdj
al-Kannī, Abu ʾl-ʿAbbās s, 236a – S, 236a
Kano iii, 275b, 276a; iv, **548a**; v, 1165b; vi, 258b – III, 283b, 284a; IV, **572a**; V, 1155a; VI, 243a
Kānpur (Cawnpore) iv, **551b**; vi, 78a; s, 360b – IV, **575a**; VI, 76a; S, 360a
Ḳanṣ → Ṣayd
Ḳānṣawh Bey iv, 723a – IV, 752a
Ḳānṣawh al-Ghawrī (Ḳānṣūh al-Ghūrī) (Mamlūk) (1516) i, 315a, 815a, 1032b, 1057b, 1059a, 1060a; ii, 72b, 286a, 955a, 1127b, 1136b; iii, 346b, 760b, 813a; iv, 435a, b, 451a, **552a**; vi, 45a, 315a, 324b, 325a, 367b; vii, 175b, 176b; ix, 129a, b; s, 43b – I, 324b, 838a, 1064a, 1089b, 1091a, 1092a; II, 73b, 294a, 977a, 1154a, 1163b; III, 357a, 783b, 836b; IV, 454b, 471a, **575b**; VI, 43b, 300a, b, 309a, 351b; VII, 177b, 178b; IX, 134a, b; S, 43b
Ḳansāwuḳ Beg ii, 25a – II, 25b
Kansu iv, **553a**; v, 845a, b, 846a, 848a, b, 850b; x, 707a – IV, **577a**; V, 857a, b, 852b, 855a; X, 751b
Ḳānṣūh al-Ghūrī → Ḳānṣawh al-Ghawrī
Ḳānṣūh Pasha (Yemen) (XVII) vii, 270a – VII, 272a
Ḳanṭara (bridge/pont) ii, 555a, 716a; iv, **555a** – II, 569a, 734b; IV, **579a**
al-Ḳanṭara (Algeria, Spain, Egypt, Syria) i, 424a; iv, 555b; vi, 727a – I, 435b; IV, 579b; VI, 716a
Ḳanṭarat al-ʿĀshir (Wāsiṭ) vii, 348a – VII, 350a
Ḳanṭarat Umm Ḥakīm vi, 546b – VI, 531a
Ḳanṭarat Zaynab iv, 556a – IV, 580b
Ḳantimūr, Demetrius (XVIII) i, 269a, 271a – I, 277a, 279a
Ḳantimūr Pasha (Silistria) (XVII) i, 310b, 1287a – I, 320b, 1326b
Ḳāntū ix, 440b – IX, 457b
Ḳānūn i, 152a, 170a, 171a, 975b; ii, 79a, 81b, 147a, 519a; iv, **556b**, 946b – I, 156b, 174b, 176a, 1006a; II, 80b, 83a, 151a, 532a; IV, **580b**, 979a
Ḳānūn (music/musique) → Malāhī
Ḳānūnnāme i, 268a, 656b, 861b, 862a, 1147b, 1169b; ii, 83a; iv, 557a, **562a** – I, 276a, 677a, 885b, 886a, 1182a, 1204b; II, 84b; IV, 581a, **584b**
Ḳānūn Ṣanʿāʾ iv, 741b – IV, 771a
Ḳānūn al-Siyāsatnāma iii, 556b – III, 575b
Ḳānūngo ii, 156b – II, 161a
Ḳanūnī Süleymān → Süleymān I
Kanuri i, 179b, 809a, 1221b, 1259a, b; ii, 10b, 368b; iv, **566b** – I, 184a, 832a, 1258a, 1297a, b, 1298a; II, 10b, 378a; IV, **589a**
Kānwa s, 331b – S, 331a
Kanz, Banu ʾl- (Awlād al-Kanz) iv, **567b**; vi, 574b; viii, 90a,b, 863b – IV, **590a**; VI, 559b; VIII, 92b, 894b
Kaole vi, 370a – VI, 354a
Ḳapan ii, 147a; iii, 489b; iv, 226b, 228b – II, 151a; III, 506b; IV, 236b, 238b
Kāparbandj vi, 53b – VI, 51b
Kapgan Ḳaghan x, 687b – X,
Ḳapi̊ iv, **568a** – Iv, **590b**
Ḳapi̊-aghasi̊ → Ḳapu Aghasi̊
Kapi̊ daghi̊ vi, 587b, 588a – VI, 572b, 573a
Kapi̊ Kahyasi̊ → Sarāy
Kapi̊ ḳullari̊ i, 35b, 102a, 206b, 1256b; ii, 1090b, 1097b, 1120b; iv, 242b, 243a, 568a; v,249b; s, 269b – I, 36b, 105a, 212b, 1294b; II, 1116a, 1123b, 1147a; IV, 253a, b, 590b; V, 247b; S, 269a
Kapi̊ Ḳulu → Ordu
Ḳapi̊dji̊ iv, **568a** – IV, **590b**
Kapilendra (ca. 1467) x, 895a – X,
Kapilēshwar vi, 67a – VI, 65a
Ḳaplan Girāy I (Crimea/-ée) (1738) iv, **568b**; vi, 55b – IV, **591a**; VI, 53b
Faplan Girāy II (Crimea/-ée) (1771) iv, **569b** – IV, **592a**

Ḳaplan Muṣṭafā Pas̲h̲a → Muṣṭafā Pas̲h̲a Ḳaplan
Ḳaplîd̲j̲a iii, 1120b; iv, **569b** – III, 1148b; IV, **592a**
Ḳapu Ag̲h̲asî ii, 1088a; iv, **570b**, 1093a – II, 1113b; IV, **593a**, 1124a
Ḳapuča iv, **571b** – IV, **594a**
Ḳapudan Pas̲h̲a (Ḳaptan Pas̲h̲a) i, 269b, 948b, 1209a, 1266a, b, 1267b, 1268b; ii, 165b, 521b; iv, **571b**, 970b, 1158a; vi, 588b – I, 277b, 977b, 1245a, 1305a, b, 1306b, 1307b; II, 170b, 534b; IV, **594a**, 1002b, 1190a; VI, 573b
Kār Kiyā, Mirzā ʿAlī (XV) vi, 515b; viii, 767a – VI, 500b; VIII, 792b
Kār Kiyā Muḥammad (Marʿas̲h̲ī) (1474) vi, 514a – VI, 499a
Ḳarā iv, **572b** – IV, **595b**
Karā (province) s, 203a – S, 202b
al-Ḳarā, Banū i, 536a; vi, 80a, 83b, 84a, b, – I, 552b; VI, 78a, 81b, 82a, b
al-Ḳarā (Damas(cus)) vi, 734a – VI, 723b
Ḳara Ag̲h̲ač (Mand) vi, 384a – VI, 368a
Ḳara Ag̲h̲ač (Manisa) s, 282b – S, 282b
Ḳara Aḥmad → Aḥmad Pas̲h̲a
Ḳara Aḥmed S̲h̲ātîrog̲h̲lu s, 91b – S, 91a
Ḳara Āmid → Diyār Bakr
Ḳara Arslān, Fak̲h̲r al-Dīn (Artuḳid(e)) (1167) vi, 507a; vii, 579a – VI, 492b; VII, 579b
Ḳara ʿaynī → Čāldîrān
Ḳara Arslān Beg → Ḳāwurd b. Čag̲h̲rî Dāwūd
Ḳarāba iv, **595a** – IV, **619a**
Ḳarābād̲h̲īn → Aḳrābād̲h̲īn
Ḳarābā iv, 389a, **573a**; vi, 291a, 366a, 494a, b; vii, 498a; s, 47a, 139b, 143a – IV, 404b, **595b**; VI, 276b, 350a, 479b, 480a; VII, 498a; S, 47b, 139a, 142b, 143a
Ḳarā Bahādur s, 324b – S, 324a
Ḳarabās̲h̲ ʿAlī ʿAlā al-Dīn (1686) ix, 155b – IX, 160b
al-Ḳarābās̲h̲iyya iv, 991b, 993a – IV, 1024a, 1025b
Ḳarā Bayat i, 1117a; iii, 1101a – I, 1151a; III, 1128b
al-Karābīsī, Abū ʿAlī al-Ḥusayn b. ʿAlī (859) iv, **596a**; vii, 260b, 312b – IV, **620a**; VII, 262b, 314b
al-Karābīsī, Aḥmad b. ʿUmar iv, **596a** – IV, **620a**
al-Karābīsī, Asʿad b. Muḥammad (1174) iv, **596b** – IV, **620b**
Ḳarā Bîyîk-og̲h̲lū i, 396a – I, 407b
Ḳarā Bog̲h̲az s, 281a – S, 280b
Ḳarā Bog̲h̲dān → Bog̲h̲dān
Ḳaračay i, 1000b; ii, 23a; iv, **596b**; v, 288a; vii, 352a; x, 691a – I, 1031a; II, 24a; IV, **620b**; V, 286a, b; VII, 354a; X,
Karačelebi-zāde, Āl i, 915b; iv, 298b, **573a** – I, 943a; IV, 312a, **596a**
Karačī (Ad̲h̲arbāyd̲j̲ān) ii, 41a; v, 818a – II, 42a; V, 824a
Karāčī i, 1006a; ii, 426b; iv, **597a**; v, 356a, 1222b; s, 332b – I, 1037a; II, 437b; IV, **621a**; V, 357b, 1212b; S, 332a
Karāčī trial/procès de – vii, 421b – VII, 423b
Ḳarāčīl vii, 412a – VII, 413b
Ḳara-Ḍag̲h̲ (Montenegro) iii, 992b; iv, **574a**, 589a, 1054a; v, 263a; vi, 69a – III, 1017b; IV, **597a**, 612b, 1085b; V, 261a; VI, 67a
Ḳarā Dāwūd Pas̲h̲a → Dāwūd Pas̲h̲a (d./m. 1623)
Ḳarā Deniz iv, **575a**; vii, 70b – IV, **598a**; VII, 71a
Karadeniz Ereğlisi ii, 705a – II, 723a
Ḳara Dewlets̲h̲āh (1400) vi, 974a – VI, 966b
Ḳara D̲h̲u 'l-Ḳādir (XIV) vii, 462a – VII,461b
(al)-Karad̲j̲ (Karad̲j̲ Abī Dulaf) ii, 623b; vi, 493a, 495b; s, 17b, 122b – II, 639a; VI, 479a, 481a; S, 17b, 121b
Ḳarad̲j̲a (amīr) iii, 398b, 503b; iv, 210a – III, 411a, 521a; IV, 219b
Ḳara Beg → Zayn al-Dīn Ḳarad̲j̲a b. Dul-ḳādir (D̲h̲u 'l-Ḳadr)
Ḳara Beg (1445) i, 511a; – I, 526b
Ḳara Beg (1456) vi, 70a – VI, 68a
Ḳara Beg b. ʿAbd Allāh, G̲h̲āzī (1411) ii, 985b – II, 1008a
Ḳara Dag̲h̲ (Ad̲h̲arbāyd̲j̲ān) vi, 504a, 539b; s, 116a – VI, 489b, 524a; S, 115b
Ḳara Dag̲h̲ (al-D̲j̲azīra) vi, 539b – VI, 524a
al-Karad̲j̲ (Karad̲j̲ Abī Dulaf) iv, 598b – IV, 622b
Ḳarad̲j̲a Beg → Zayn al-Dīn Ḳarad̲j̲a b. Dulḳādir (D̲h̲u 'l-Ḳadr)
Ḳarad̲j̲a Ḥiṣār iv, **598b** – IV, **622b**
Ḳarad̲j̲a S̲h̲ehir iv, 580b – IV, 603b
al-Karād̲j̲akī (XI) vii, 313a – VII, 315b
Ḳarad̲j̲a-og̲h̲lan i, 677b; ii, 75b; s, 91b, 324a – I, 698b; II, 77a; S, 91a, 323b
al-Karad̲j̲ī, Abū Bakr Muḥammad (XI) i, 133b; iv, **600a**, 703a; s, 119b, 390a – I, 137a; IV, **624a**, 731a; S, 119a, 390b
Karad̲j̲-i Abū Dulaf vi, 494a – VI, 480a
Ḳarā Evlī iii, 1100a – III, 1127a
Ḳarā Faḍlī → Faḍlī, Meḥmed
al-Ḳarāfa → al-Ḳāhira
al-Ḳarāfa (cemetery/cimetière) s, 156a – S, 156b
Karaferye iv, **600b** – IV, **624b**
al-Karāfī (1285) vi, 279a, 280a, 638a; x, 112a – VI, 264a, 265a, 623a; X, 121a
Ḳaragan vi, 416b – VI, 401b
Ḳarag̲h̲ūl, Banū vi, 614a – VI, 599a
Ḳaragöz i, 152a, 792b, 1161b; iv, **601a**, 1136b; vi, 373a; vii, 657b – I, 156b, 815b, 1196a; IV, **625a**, 1168a; VI, 357b; VII, 657a
Ḳaragöz Meḥmed Beg (XVI) vii, 244b – VII, 246a
Ḳarā Gözlü iii, 1102b, 1109a; iv, **577b** – III, 1129b, 1136a; IV, **600b**
Ḳaragozlu, Muḥammad Ḥusayn K̲h̲ān (1825) vii, 453a – VII, 454a
Ḳarā Ḥasan iv, 1156a, b – IV, 1188a, b
Ḳarā Haydar-og̲h̲lu → Haydar-og̲h̲lu Meḥmed
Ḳarā Ḥiṣār iv, **578a** – IV, **601b**
Ḳarā Ḥiṣar Adalia → Ḳarā Ḥiṣār-i Teke
Ḳarā Ḥiṣar Develi iv, 843b – IV, 876b
Ḳarā Ḥiṣar-î Behrāms̲h̲āh (Bayrāms̲h̲āh) iv, 579b – IV, 602b
Ḳarā Ḥiṣar-î Demird̲j̲i iv, 579b – IV, 603a
Ḳarā Ḥiṣar-î Ṣāḥib → Afyūn Ḳarā Ḥiṣār
Ḳarā Ḥiṣar-î S̲h̲arḳī, S̲h̲abk̲h̲āne → S̲h̲ābīn Ḳarā Ḥiṣār
Ḳarā Ḥiṣar-i Teke iv, 579b – IV, 603a
Ḳarā Hülegü ii, 3a – II, 3a
Ḳarāʾī iii, 1107b; v, 154b – III, 1135a; V, 155b
Ḳarā Ibrāhīm Pas̲h̲a → Ibrāhīm Pas̲h̲a, Ḳarā
Ḳarāʾīm → Karaites
Karaites, Ḳarāʾiyyūn iv, 305a, b, **603b**; v, 136b, 326b; x, 697b – IV, 319a, **627b**; V, 139a, 326a; X,
al-Karak i, 804b; iv, **609a**; vi, 321b, 322a, b, 323a, 547b; vii, 989b, 991b, 992b; viii, 989a; s, 391a – I, 828b; IV, **633b**; VI, 306a, b, 307a, 532a; VII, 990b, 993a, 994a; VIII, 1023b; S, 391a
Karakalpak i, 1076b; ii, 971a; iii, 116b; iv, **610b**; vi, 418a, b; s, 97b – I, 1108b; II, 993a; III, 119a; IV, **635a**; VI, 403b; S, 97a
Karakalpak Literature x, **731a** -X, **777a**
Ḳarā Kemāl iv, 285b – IV, 298a
Ḳarā K̲h̲alīl D̲j̲andarlî → D̲j̲andarlî
Ḳarā K̲h̲alīlzade iv, 506a – IV, 528a
Ḳarā K̲h̲ān (1514) vi, 541b – VI, 526a
Ḳarā K̲h̲ān (Awliyā Ata) i, 767a – I, 790a
Karak̲h̲ iv, 347a – IV, 362a
Ḳarāk̲h̲ān → K̲h̲ayr K̲h̲ān

Ḳaraḵẖānid(e) (language/langue) iv, 700a – IV, 728a, b
Ḳaraḵẖānid(e)s → Ilek-ḵẖāns
Ḳara Ḵẖiṭāy i, 750a, 987a, 1001b, 1240a, 1295a, 1311a; ii, 43a, 67a, 607a, 1101b, 1109a; iii, 1114b; iv, 29a, b, 30a, 32a, 542b, **580b**, 1067b; v, 38b, 134b; vi, 481b, 557b; vii, 997b; viii, 943a; x, 543a –
I, 772b, 1017b, 1032a, 1278a, 1334b, 1351b; II, 43b, 68b, 622a, 1127b, 1135a; III, 1141b; IV, 31b, 32a, 34b, 566a, **604a**, 1099a, b; V, 39b, 137a; VI, 467b, 542a; VII, 999a; VIII, 975a; X,
al-Ḳarakī, Nūr al-Dīn ʿAlī (1534) iv, **610a**; vi, 550a,b; vii, 298a; viii, 777b – IV, **634b**; VI, 534b, 535aVII, 300a; VIII, 803b
Ḳarā Kirgiz → Kirgiz
Ḳarak Nūḥ iv, **609b** – IV, **634b**
Ḳarakol iv, **611a** – IV, **636a**
Ḳarā-köl i, 1135a; iv, 213b, **583b**; s, 97a, 227b, 318a – I, 1169b; IV, 223a, **607a**; S, 96b, 228a, 318a
Ḳarakol Djemʿiyyetī iv, **611b** – IV, **636a**
Ḳaraḳorum ii, 45b, 606b; iv, **612b**; vi, 482b; viii, 162b – II, 46b, 622a; IV, **637a**; VI, 468b; VIII, 165a
Ḳaraḳorum Mts iv, **611b**; s, 158b – IV, **636b**; S, 158b
Ḳaraköy s, 314b – S, 314a
Ḳarā Ḳoyunlu i, 190a, 311b, 508a, 666b, 903b, 919a; ii, 334a, 344b, 401b, 598b, 711b; iii, 1100b, 1256b; iv, 33b, 34a, **584a**; v, 456b; vi, 201a, 483a, 493a, 495a, 515b, 541a; vii, 271b; x, 45a, 963b – I, 194b, 321a, 523b, 687a, 930b, 947a; II, 344a, 354a, 412a, 613b, 730a; III, 1127b, 1289a; IV, 36a, b, **607b**; V, 459b; VI, 185b, 469a, 478b, 480a, 500b, 525b; VII, 273b; X, 46a,
Ḳarāḳul → Ḳarā-köl
Ḳaraḳum i, **613a**; vi, 416a, 621a – IV, **637b**; VI, 401a, 606a
Ḳarāḳum iv, 542b, 613a – IV, 566a, 637b
Ḳaraḳūna (island/île) ii, 235a – II, 242a
Ḳaraḳūsẖ, Bahāʾ al-Dīn al-Asadī (1201) iii, 173b; iv, **613a**; vi, 430a; vii, 151a, 816b –
III, 177a; IV, **638a**; VI, 415b; VII, 153a, 818a
Ḳaraḳūsẖ, Sẖaraf al-Dīn al-Armanī (1212) i, 161b, 165a, 533a, 797b, 798a; ii, 575a, 875b, 1007b, 1008a, 1110a; iii, 173b; iv, 210a, 337b, 424b, **614a**, 739b – I, 166a, 170a, 549b, 821a, b; II, 589b, 896a, 1031a, 1031b, 1136a; III, 177a; IV, 219b, 352a, 443a, **638b**, 769b
Ḳarā Maḥmūd → Medḥī, Maḥmūd Efendi (Gelibolu)
Ḳarā Maḥmūd Pasẖa, Isẖḳodralī Busẖatlī (1796) i, 657a; iv, **588a**; vii, 719b – I, 677b; IV, **612a**; 720b
Ḳarā Mambuche vi, 382a – VI, 366a
al-Ḳaram, Banū → Zurayʿid(e)s
Ḳaram, Yūsuf → Yūsuf Ḳaram
al-Ḳaram b. Yām i, 181b – I, 186b
Ḳaram Allāh Ḳurḳusāwī i, 929b; ii, 696b – I, 958a; II, 714a
Ḳarāma iv, **615a** – IV, **639b**
Ḳaramān i, 354b, 468a; iv, **616b**, 621a; v, 881b – I, 365b, 481b; IV, **641b**, 645b; V, 887b
Ḳaramān (town/ville) iv, 616b – IV, 641b
Ḳaramān b. Nūra Sūfī i, 467a, 468a; iv, 619b, 620a – I, 481a, 482a; IV, 643b, 644a
Ḳaramānī Aḵẖaweyn Meḥmed Čelebi (XVI) vi, 970b – VI, 963a
Ḳaramānī Meḥmed Pasẖa → Meḥmed Pasẖa Ḳaramānī
Ḳaramānī Meḥemmed Pasẖa (XV) ii, 529a – II, 542a
Ḳaramānī(e)s → Ḳaramān-oghullarî
Ḳaramānlī ii, 161b, 876a, 876b, 971b; iv, **617a** – II, 166b, 896a, 994a; IV, **641b**
Ḳaramānlī Aḥmad Bey iv, 617a – IV, 642a

Ḳaramān-oghlu, ʿAlāʾ al-Dīn ʿAlī (1379) i, 394a, 1118a; iv, 622b, 623a; v, 680a – I, 405b, 1151b; IV, 647b, 648a; V, 685b
Ḳaramān-oghlu Ibrāhim Beg (1468) vi, 71b – VI, 69b
Ḳaramān-oghlu Meḥmed (XV) vii, 644a – VII, 644a
Ḳaramān-oghullarî (Ḳaramānid(e)s) i, 240b, 244a, 292b, 1117b, 1118a; ii, 103b, 239b, 529b, 607b, 692a, 705b, 710b; iii, 1006b; iv, **619a**, 843a; v, 254a, 677a, b, 1144b; vi, 975a; vii, 271b, 479b; viii, 16a – I, 248a, 251a, 302a, 1151b; II, 105b, 246b, 542b, 622b, 709a, 723b, 727a; III, 1032a; IV, **643b**, 876b; V, 252a, 682a, b, 1137a; VI, 967a; VII, 273b, 479a; VIII, 16a
Ḳarāmat ʿAlī Djawnpūrī (1873) i, 952a; iv, 170a, **625b** – I, 981a; IV, 177b, **650b**
Karamba ii, 1132b – II, 1159a
Ḳarāmīd → Ḵẖazaf
Ḳarāmiṭa → Ḳarmaṭī
Karāmiyya → Karrāmiyya
Karamoko Alfa ii, 960a, 1132a – II, 982a, 1159a
Ḳarā Muḥammad i, 311b, 1051a; iv, 584b – I, 321a, 1082b; IV, 608a
Karamuk → Bolwadin
Ḳarā Murād Pasẖa iv, 766a – IV, 796b
Karamürsel vi, 587b – VI, 572b
Ḳarā Mūsā i, 293b – I, 302b
Ḳarā Muṣṭafā Pasẖa → Kemānkesẖ Ḳarā Muṣṭafā
Ḳarā Muṣṭafā Pasẖa Firārī i, 236b – I, 244a
Ḳarā Muṣṭafā Pasẖa Merzifonlu (1683) i, 948a, 1284b; ii, 522a, 572b; iv, **589b**; v, 261b, 272b, 720b; vi, 202b; viii, 4b –
I, 977a, 1324a; II, 535a, 587a; IV, **613a**; V, 259a, 270b, 726a; VI, 186b; VIII, 4b
Ḳarāmiṭa → Ḳarmaṭī
Karandal → Ḳalandar
Ḳaranful iv, **626b** – IV, **651b**
Ḳaranful b. Malik Sarwar (Djawnpūr) (XIV) vi, 273a – VI, 258a
Karanghu vi, 498b, 501a – VI, 483b, 486b
Karaosmanoğlu/Ḳarā ʿOthmān-Oghlî → Ḳarā ʿUthmān-oghullarî
Ḳarapapaḵẖ iv, **627a**; vii, 353a – IV, **652a**; VII, 355a
Ḳarā Pīrī Beg Ḳādjār iv, 387b, 389a – IV, 404b
Ḳarār → Mūsīḳī
al-Ḳarār i, 897a – I, 924a
Ḳarāra iii, 97b – III, 100b
Ḳarasaḳal i, 1076b – I, 1108b
Karasẖahr ix, 621b – IX, 641a
Ḳarāsẖams al-Din ix, 612a – IX, 634a
Ḳarasî i, 467b, 468a, 994a; ii, 686b; iv, **627b**; vi, 587b; viii, 176a – I, 481b, 482a, 1024b; II, 704a; IV, **652b**; VI, 572b; VIII, 178b
Ḳarasî-eli i, 468b – I, 482b
Ḳarā Sonḳor (atabeg) (1140) i, 1358a; ii, 975b – I, 1398a,b; II, 998a
Karasta i, 1205b – I, 1241b
al-Ḳaraṣṭūn iv, **629a** – IV, **653b**
Ḳarā-ṣū → al-Furāt
Ḳarā-ṣū → Ḵẖāsa
Ḳara-ṣu (Mākū) vi, 200b; vii, 498b – VI, 185a; VII, 498a
Ḳaraṣū-Bāzār iv, **629b** – IV, **654b**
Ḳarāsunḳur, Sẖams al-Dīn al-Manṣūrī (Alep(po)) (1328) iv, 432b; v, 1142b; vi, 501b; vii, 991b; viii, 157a – IV, 451b; V, 1135b; VI, 487a; VII, 993a
Ḳārat al-Kibrīt ii, 631a – II, 646b
Ḳarata, Banū i, 504a; iv, **630b** – I, 519b; IV, **655b**
Karataï, Banū i, 1338a – I, 1378a
Ḳarā Takīn → Ḳaratigin

Karatau vi, 415a – VI, 400a
Ḳaratāy → Djalāl al-Dīn
Ḳaratekin (Čanḳîrî) (XI) ii, 14a – II, 14a
Ḳaratigin iv, **631a**; s, 228a – IV, **656a**; S, 228a
Ḳaratigin Isfīdjābī i, 852a; ii, 1082a; s, 356b – I, 876a; II, 1107a; S, 356b
Ḳarātisa s, 42a – S, 42b
Ḳaraṭughan vi, 512a, 515b, 745b – VI, 497a, b, 500b, 734b
Ḳarā ʿOthmān-oghî i, 469a, 783a; ii, 206b, 207a; iv, **592b**; v, 1170b; vi, 541a, 931b – I, 483a, 806a; II, 213a, b; IV, **616b**; V, 1160a; VI, 525b, 923b
Ḳara Timurtash Pasha x, 698a – X,
Ḳara Ulus (nomad(e)s) vi, 242b – VI, 226b
Ḳaravul ' Karakol
Ḳarāvulān iv, 860a – IV, 893b
Ḳara Üweys Čelebi (XVI) vii, 596a – VII, 595b
Ḳarā Wāṣif iv, 611b – IV, 636a
Ḳarawī (language/langue) i, 575a – I, 593b
al-Ḳarawī, al-Shāʿir v, 1256b – V, 1247b
al-Ḳarawiyyīn → Masdjid al-Ḳarawiyyīn
Karawnas → Nīkūdārīs
Ḳarāwul vi, 20b – VI, 18a
Ḳaray, ḳaraylar iv, 608a – IV, 632b
Karay, Refīḳ Khālid (1965) iii, 357b; iv, **635b**, 812a; v, 194b, 196b; vi, 94b; s, 96a, 98b – III, 369a; IV, **661b**, 845a; V, 192a, 193b; VI, 92b; S, 95b, 98a
Ḳarā Yazîdjî (ʿAbd al-Ḥalīm) (1602) iv, 499a, **594a**, 843b; viii, 197a; s, 238b – IV, 520b, **618a**, 876b; VIII, 200a; S, 238b
Ḳarā Yülüḳ ʿUthmān (1435) i, 311b, 1054a, 1328a; ii, 614a; iii, 186a, 190a; iv, 586b, 587a, b, 871a; x,963b – I, 321a, 1085b, 1368b; II, 629a; III, 190b, 194a; IV, 609a, b, 611a, 904b; X,
Ḳarā Yūsuf Ḳaraḳoyunlu (1410) i, 311b, 666b, 791b, 1119a; ii, 401b, 614a; iv, 33b, 586a, b, 587a; vi, 202a, 541a, 976b; vii, 105b, 271b – I, 321a, 687b, 815a, 1152b; II, 412a, 629a; IV, 36a, 608b, 609a, b; VI, 186b, 525b, 969a; VII, 107b, 273b
Karak Nūḥ s, 380a – S, 380a
Karbalāʾ i, 1168b; ii, 938a; iii, 115a, 119b, 610a; iv, **637a**; v, 1033a; vi, 113a, 123b, 516b, 537a, 604a, 609b, 611a; vii, 456b, 690b, 778a; s, 74b, 75a, 94a, b, 134b, 231b – I, 1203b; II, 960a; III, 117b, 122a, 630b; IV, **663b**; V, 1029b; VI, 111a, 121a, 502a, 522a, 589a, 594a, 596a; VII, 456b, 691a, 780a; S, 75a, b, 93b, 94a, 134a, 231b
Karbalāʾī Ḳurbān s, 70b – S, 71a
Kārbān → Kārwān
Karbughā al-Mawṣilī (1098) i, 517a, 1052a; vi, 544a – I, 532b, 1084a; VI, 528b
Ḳardā Bāzabdā iv, **639a** – IV, **665b**
Kardan (steppe) vi, 56b – VI, 54b
Ḳarda iv, 76a – IV, 80a
al-Kardarī, Muḥammad b. Muḥammad (1424) vi, 352b – VI, 336b
al-Kardarī, Shams al-Aʾimma (1244) vii, 969a – VII, 969b
Kardj → Kerč
Ḳardū, Karduchoi v, 447b, 448a, b – V, 450a, b
al-Kardūdī, Abū ʿAbd Allāh (1849) iv, **639a** – IV, **665b**
Karghandede vi, 541b – VI, 526a
Karghawayh, Karghūyah i, 119b; iii, 129b; v, 923b – I, 123a; III, 132a; V, 929a
Kārgudhār iii, 1193a – III, 1222b
Ḳāriʾ → Ḳirāʾa; Ḳurʾān; Ḳurrāʾ
Ḳārī Yazd (XV) iv, 66a – IV, 69b
al-Ḳārī → ʿAlī
Ḳarība (singer/chanteuse) → Ḳurayba
Ḳarība (tax(e)) v, 259a – V, 257a
Karibʾil b. Dhamarʿalī vi, 561b, 562b – VI, 546b, 547a
Karubʾil Watar vi, 560b – VI, 545a
Karibʾil Yuhanʿim vi, 562a – VI, 547a
Karibīya → Kuraybiyya
Kārim iv, 640b – IV, 666b
Kārim al-Dīn al-Āmulī (1310) iii, 952a – III, 977a
Kārim al-Dīn al-Kabīr → Ibn al-Sadīd
Kārim Khān (Nagar) s, 327b – S, 327a
Kārim Khān Zand (Zands) (1779) i, 190a, 230a, 246b, 393b, 1341b; ii, 311a, 812a; iii, 1102b, 1103a, 1191a, 1257b; iv, 104b, 390a, b, **639b**, 695a, 1056b; v, 617a, 674a, 825b; vi, 495a, 551a, 715a; vii, 582b, 674b; s, 405b – I, 196a, 237a, 254b, 405a, 1382a; II, 319b, 831b; III, 1129b, 1130a, 1221a, 1290a; IV, 109a, 406b, 407a, **665b**, 723a, 1087b; V, 621a, 679a, 831b; VI, 480b, 535b, 703b; VII, 583a, 674b; S, 405b
Kārim Shāh → Agha Khān IV
Kārim Thābit s, 301a – S, 300b
Karīma vi, 434b – VI, 419b
Kārimī i, 800a; ii, 144b; iii, 776b; iv, 136a, b, 137a, **640a**; v, 514b; vi, 324a; s, 43a – I, 823b; II, 148b; III, 799b; IV, 141b, 142b, 143a, **666b**; V, 518a; VI, 308b; S, 43b
Karīmov, Islom z, 962a – X,
Ḳārin i, 47b; iv, 644a – I, 49a; IV, 670b
Ḳarīn iv, **643b** – IV, **670a**
Ḳarīn (Mts.) s, 298a – S, 297b
Ḳārin b. Shahriyār Bāwand i, 1110a; iv, 645b, 646b; s, 363b – I, 1143b; IV, 672a, 673a; S, 363a
Ḳārin b. Wandād-Hurmuzd iv, 645a – IV, 671b
Ḳārinid(e)s iv, 207b, **644a**; v, 661a; vi, 337b, 745a, 938b; s, 298a, 309a – IV, 217a, **670b**; V, 666b; VI, 321b, 734b, 930b; S, 297b, 308b
Karīnov, Islom x, 962a – X,
Karîshdîran Süleymān Beg iv, 225a – IV, 234b
Kāriyān v, 1110a, 1112a; vi, 384b – V, 1106a, 1108a; VI, 368b
Kārīz → Ḳanāt
Karkaddan iv, **647a** – IV, **673b**
Ḳarḳana iv, **650b** – IV, **676b**
Karkand → Karkaddan
Karkarn → Bisbarāy
Ḳarkashandī, Banū v, 333a – V, 333a
Ḳarḳastal s, 80a – S, 80a
al-Karkh (Baghdād; Sāmarrāʾ) i, 896a; iv, **652a**; vi, 428b, 613b; s, 13a, 172a, 192b, 193a – I, 921b; IV, **678b**; VI, 413b, 598b; S, 13b, 173a, 194a
Karkh Bādjaddā vi, 613b – VI, 598b
Karkha (river/rivière) iii, 1251a; iv, **653b**, 675a; v, 830a, 867b; vii, 674b, 675a – III, 1283b; IV, **680a**, 703a; V, 836a, 874a; VII, 674b
Karkhāyā iv, 652b – IV, 679a
al-Karkhī → al-Karadjī
al-Karkhī, Abū ʿAlī Muḥammad s, 25b – S, 26a
al-Karkhī, Abū ʾl-Ḥasan (952) ix, 36a; s, 12b, 13a, 14a – IX, 36a; S, 13a, b, 14a
al-Karkhī, Badr al-Dīn Muḥammad (1597) viii, 562a – VIII, 580a
al-Karkhī, Ḥasan Fatḥ (Malāmatī) (XIX) vi, 224a – VI, 218a
a;-Karkhī, Maʿrūf b. al-Fayzurān → Maʿrūf al-Karkhī
Karkhina → Kirkūk
Karkī s, 281a – S, 281a
Ḳarḳīsiyā iv, **654b**; s, 117a – IV, **681a**; S, 116b
Kārkiyā ii, 194a; v, 603a, b, 604a – II, 200a; V, 607a, b, 608a

Karkūr iv, **655b** – IV, **681b**
Karlî-Īli; Karlo-Īli iv, **656a**; v, 725b, 726a – IV, **682a**; V, 731a
Ḳarlofča iv, **657a**; v, 721a, 727b; vii, 708a; s, 187a – IV, **683b**; V, 726a, 732b; VII, 709a; S, 188b
Karlowitz → Ḳarlofča
Ḳarluḳ ii, 67a, 1107b; iii, 335b, 1113a, 1116b; iv, 188b, 213a, **658a**, 917a; v, 854b, 855b, 856a, 857a; x, 689b; s, 326b – II, 68a, 1133b; III, 345b, 1140b, 1144a; IV, 197a, 222b, **684b**, 950a; V, 861a, 862b, 863a, 864a; X, 781a; S, 326a
Karm iv, **659a** – IV, **685b**
Ḳarmāsīn → Kirmānshāh
Ḳarmaṭī (Ḳarāmiṭa) i, 11a, 19a, 73b, 95b, 194b, 387a, 551a, 822a, 824a, 867a, 942a, 1086a, 1276b, 1354b; ii, 98a, 168b, 281b, 385a, 452b, 482b, 495b, 854a, 1070a; iii, 123b, 126b, 238a, 246a, 255b, 380b, 619a, 799a; iv, 22b, 198a, 494a, **660b**, 764a; v, 327a, 348a, 923a; vi, 128a, 148a, 274b, 435b, 585a; vii, 484b, 543a, 652a, 760b, 769a, 770a; viii, 72a, 862b; s, 12b, 36b, 117b, 199a – I, 11a, 19b, 76a, 98b, 200a, 398a, 569a, 845a, 847a, 891b, 971a, 1118b, 1315b, 1394a; II, 100a, 174a, 289b, 368a, 464a, 495a, 508a, 874a, 1094b; III, 126a, 129b, 245a, 253a, 263a, 392b, 639b, 822b; IV, 24a, 206b, 515a, **687a**, 794b; V, 327a, 349a, 928b; VI, 126b, 146b, 259b, 420b, 570a; VII, 484b, 543a, 652a, 762a, 771a, b; VIII, 74a, 894a; S, 13a, 36b, 117a, 199a
Karmīniyya s, 176b – S, 177b
Karmisīn → Kirmānshāh
Ḳarmūna i, 6a, 1238a; iv, **665a** – I, 6a, 1275b; IV, **692a**
Ḳarn i, 1290b; iv, 825b; vii, 269b – I, 1330a; IV, 858b; VII, 271b
al-Karnabāʾī (Zandjī) (IX) vii, 526 – VII, 526b
Karnāl iv, **665b**; vi, 456b – IV, **692b**; VI, 442a
al-Karnarāʾī (Zandj) (IX) vii, 526b – VII, 526b
Karnāṭak i, 624b; iii, 316b; iv, **666b**; vi, 535a; vii, 459a – I, 645b; III, 326a; IV, **693b**; VI, 519b; VII, 459a
Ḳarnaw vi, 88b – VI, 86a
Karōfī ii, 156b – II, 161a
Karpenésion, Karpenisi → Kerbenesh
Karra vi, 48a – VI, 46b
Ḳarrād v, 132a, b – V, 135a, b
Karrāmiyya i, 187b, 411a, 714a; ii, 218b, 752a, 791a, 931b, 1103a; iii, 177b, 767a, 1145a, 1165a, 1173a; iv, 46a, 183b, 469a, **667a**, 1025b; v, 328b; vii, 577a; viii, 63a; s, 149a – I, 193a, 422b, 735b; II, 225a, 770b, 810a, 953a, 1129b; III, 181b, 790a, 1173a, 1193b, 1202a; IV, 48b, 191b, 490a, **694a**, 1057b; V, 328b; VII, 577b; VIII, 64a; S, 149a
Karranāy i, 1291b – I, 1331a
Ḳarrī → Ḳerrī
Ḳarrīṭa i, 206a – I, 212a
Kārrūn vi, 384a – VI, 368a
Karrūṣa i, 206a – I, 212a
Kars i, 468b, 637b, 638a, 640a, 641b; iv, **669b**; vi, 55b, 56a, 274a, 508a, b – I, 482b, 658b, 659a, 661a, 662a; IV, **696b**; VI, 53b, 54a, 259a, 493b, 494a
Ḳarṣana → Ḳurṣān
Karsh → Kerč
Ḳarshī i, 1019a; ii, 4a; iii, 1236b; iv, **671b**; v, 858b; vi, 418a; vii, 925a – I, 1050b; II, 4a; III, 1268b; IV, **699a**; V, 865b; VI, 403a; VII, 925b
Karshūnī iv, **671b** – IV, **699a**
Kart i, 227a, 1343a; iii, 177b, 1121b; iv, 32a, **672a**; v, 58b – I, 233b, 1383a; III, 181b, 1149a; IV, 34a, **699a**; V, 60b
Kart Maliks (Harāt) viii, 83a – VIII, 85b
Ḳarṭādjanna i, 51b, 77b; iii, 271a; iv, **672b**; v, 1188a – I, 53a, 79b; III, 279a; IV, **700a**; V, 1178a
al-Ḳarṭādjannī → Ḥāzim al-Ḳarṭādjannī
Ḳarṭas → Ḳirṭās
Ḳarṭasa ii, 105b – II, 108a
Kartasura ix, 892a – IX, 928a
Kartli v, 494a – V, 497a
Kartosoewirjo, S.H. vi, 731b – VI, 721a
Karūbiyya vi, 219b – VI, 203b
Kārūd → Ḳalʿa Kuhrūd
Karūkh iv, **673a** – IV, **700b**
Ḳārūn iv, **673a** – IV, **700b**
Kārūn (river/rivière) i, 8b; iii, 1251a; iv, 6a, 9a, 654a, **673b**; v, 65b, 80b, 867a, 869a – I, 8b; III, 1283b; IV, 6b, 9b, 680a, **701a**; V, 67b, 82b, 873b, 875b
Kārwa iii, 197b – III, 202a
Kārwān iv, **676a** – IV, **704a**
Ḳarwāsh b. al-Muḳallad b, al-Musayyab (ʿUkaylid(e)) (1050) i, 1073b; iii, 80b, 860a; iv, 378b, 911a; v, 896b; vi, 965b; vii, 118a; x, 787a; s, 119a – I, 1105b; III, 83a, 884b; IV, 395a, 944a; V, 903a; VI, 958a; VII, 120a; X, ; S, 118b
Ḳarwasha iv, **679b** – IV, **707b**
Ḳarya iv, **680a** – IV, **708a**
al-Ḳarya al-Ḥadītha → Djand
Ḳarya al-Suflā iv, **680b** – IV, **708b**
Ḳarya al-ʿUlyā iv, **680b** – IV, **708b**
Ḳaryat Djilyāna vi, 221b – VI, 215a
Ḳaryat al-Ḥaddādīn vi, 744b – VI, 733b
al-Karyatayn s, 117a – S, 116a
Kārzīn vi, 384a – VI, 368b
Karzūbī iii, 1097b – III, 1124b
al-Ḳaṣāb iv, **681a** – IV, **709a**
Ḳaṣab iv, **682a** – IV, **710a**
Ḳaṣāb, Teodor (1897) iv, **681b**; vi, 373a – IV, **709a**; VI, 357b
Ḳaṣab al-sukkar iv, **682b** – IV, **710b**
Ḳaṣaba (town/ville) i, 1320a; iii, 498b; iv, **684b**, 685b – I, 1360b; III, 515b; IV, **712b**, 713b
Ḳaṣaba (citadel) i, 974b; iv, **685a**; v, 654b – I, 1005a; IV, **713a**; V, 658b
Ḳaṣaba b. Kush s, 132a – S, 131b
Kasādī, Āl vii, 496a – VII, 496a
Kāsagarān Madrasa s, 23b – S, 23b
Ḳasak → Čerkes
Kasala i, 1158b; iv, **686a**; v, 1251a – I, 1193a; IV, **714a**; V, 1241b
Ḳasam iv, **687b**; v, 178b, 179b – IV, **715b**; V, 176a, 177a
Ḳasāma i, 1151a; ii, 342b; iv, 687b, **689b** – I, 1185b; II, 352a; IV, 715b, **717b**
Ḳāsān → Kāshān
al-Kāsānī, ʿAlāʾ al-Dīn (1189) iii, 163b; iv, **690a**; vii, 758b; viii, 532b; ix, 548a – III, 166b; IV, **718a**; VII, 760a: VIII, 550a; IX, 569b
Kasap → Ḳaṣāb
Ḳaṣaṣ → Ḳiṣṣa
Kasb i, 413b, 414a, 696b; ii, 365a; iii, 1037b; iv, **690b** – I, 425b, 717b; II, 375a; III, 1063a; IV, **718b**
Kasbah → Ḳaṣaba (town/ville)
Kasf → Kusūf
Kash (Shahr-i Sabz) iv, **694a**, 711b; v, 181a, 858b; ix, 46a; s, 97b – IV, **722a**, 740a; V, 178b, 865b; IX, 47a; S, 96b
Kashad al-Djuhanī v, 316a, b – V, 316a

Kashaf-Rūd vi, 495a, 713b; s, 83a – VI, 480b, 702b; S, 83a
Kashak (Kasak) → Čerkes
Kāshān i, 11a; ii, 746a; iii, 144b, 1125b; iv, **694b**, 1040a, 1047b, 1167a; v, 171a, 370a; vii, 72b, 960b; s, 71a, 75b, 139a, b, 141a, 142a – I, 11a; II, 764b; III, 147a, 1153b; IV, **722b**, 1071b, 1079a, 1199b; V, 168b, 371a; VII, 73b, 961b; S, 71b, 75b, 138b, 139a, 141a, b, 142a
Kashāna (Kashāta) (berber/-ère) vi, 310b – VI, 295b
al-Kashānī, ʿAbd al-Razzāk → ʿAbd al-Razzāk al-Kāshānī
al-Kashānī, Abu ʾl-ʿAbbās Aḥmad (1116) iv, **696a** – IV, **724b**
al-Kashānī, Abū Ṭālib → Ḳalīm Abū Ṭālib
al-Kashānī, Afḍal al-Dīn (1268) viii, 541a; x, 320b – VIII, 559a; X, 344b
al-Kashānī, Āḳā Muẓaffar s, 308b – S, 308b
al-Kashānī, Āyātullāh Abu ʾl-Ḳāsim (1962) ii, 882b; iii, 529b; iv, 165a, **695b**, 790a; vii, 300a, 446b, 654b – II, 903a; III, 548a; IV, 172b, **724a**, 822a; VII, 302a, 447b, 654a
al-Kashānī, Ghiyāth al-Dīn → al-Kāshī, Djamshīd
al-Kashānī, Ḥādjdjī Mīrzā Djānī (1852) iv, **696a** – IV, **724a**
al-Kashānī, ʿImād al-Dīn Yaḥyā (XIV) viii, 806b – VIII, 833b
al-Kashānī, ʿIzz al-Dīn Maḥmūd (1334) ix, 780b; s, 415b – IX, 814b; S, 415b
al-Kashānī, Maḳṣūd s, 139a – S, 138b
al-Kashānī, Mullā Muḥsin Fayḍ → Muḥsin-i Fayḍ-i Kāshānī
al-Kashānī, Taḳī al-Dīn Muḥammad (XVI) vii, 478a – VII, 478a
Kashf iv, **696b** – IV, **725a**
Kashfahān ii, 556a – II, 570a
Kashfī, Sayyid Djāʿfar (1850) vii, 298b – VII, 300b
Kashgān (river/rivière) v, 830a – V, 836a
Kashghāī → Ḳash-ḳaʾī
Kāshghar i, 46b; iii, 1114a; iv, **698b**; v, 38a, b, 846a; vi, 273b, 274a, 512b, 618b, 765b, 767a, 768b; x, 812a; s, 240a – I, 48a; III, 1141b; IV, 727a; V, 39a, b, 858a; VI, 258b, 259a, 498a, 603b, 755a, 756a, b, 757b; X, ;S, 240a
Kashghārī, Khʷādja Yūsuf (XIX) vii, 935b – VII, 936a
Kāshgh, Maḥmūd (XI) iii, 115b, 1114a, 1116a; iv, 525a, 527a, **699b**, 1080b; vi, 415b; vii, 567b; viii, 160b, 161a; s, 168b, 280b, 289b – III, 118a, 1141b, 1143b; IV, 547b, 549b, **727b**, 1111b; VI, 400b; VII, 568b; VIII, 163a; S, 168b, 280b, 289b
Kāshgh, Saʿd al-Dīn (1456) → Saʿd al-Dīn Kāshgharī
Kāshī → Benares/Bénarès
Kāshī iv, **701a**; v, 600a – IV, **729b**; V, 604a
al-Ḳāshī, Abu ʾl-ʿAbbās Aḥmad → al-Ḳāshānī
al-Kāshī (al-Kāshānī), Ghiyāth al-Dīn Djamshīd b. Masʿūd (1429) iii, 1137b, 1139b, 1140a; iv, **702b**, 725b, 726a; vi, 112b, 601a; vii, 136a; viii, 542a; x, 267b – III, 1166a, 1167b, 1168a; IV, **730b**, 754b, 755a; VI, 110a, 586a, b; VII, 138a; VIII, 559a; X, 287a
Kāshī, Ḥasan b. Maḥmūd (1310) viii, 423a – VIII, 437a
Kāshī, ʿImād al-Dīn b. Masʿūd (XVI) viii, 783b – VIII, 809b
Kāshī, Kāmāl al-Dīn Ḥusayn b. Masʿūd (1546) viii, 783b – VIII, 809b
Kāshī, Masʿūd b. Maḥmūd (1539) viii, 783b – VIII, 809b
Kāshī, Muḥammad Bāḳir b. ʿImād al-Dīn (XVI) viii, 783b – VIII, 809b
Kāshī, Nūr al-Dīn b. Kamāl al-Dīn (1561) viii, 783b – VIII, 809b
al-Ḳashīb (Mārib) vi, 561b – VI, 546b
Kāshif, Muḥammad Sharīf (1653) iv, **703a** – IV, **731b**
Kāshif al-Ghiṭāʾ, Āyatullāh (XX) vi, 553b – VI, 538a
Kāshif al-Ghiṭāʾ, Shaykh ʿAlī (1838) s, 75b – S, 76a
Kāshif al-Ghiṭāʾ, Shaykh Djaʿfar al-Nadjafī (1812) iv, **703b**; vii, 298b, 302b; s, 57a – IV, **731b**; VII, 300b, 304b; S, 57b
Kāshuf al-Ghiṭāʾ, Shaykh Mūsā s, 75a – S, 75b
Kāshifī, Kamāl al-Dīn Ḥusayn b. ʿAlī al-Wāʿiẓ (1504) i, 430b; iii, 274b, 351b, 372b, 490a; iv, 68a, 504b, **704a**, 1035a; vi, 609b, 761b, 762a; vii, 1017a; viii, 465a, 540b; s, 46b – I, 442b; III, 282b, 363a, 384b, 507a; IV, 71b, 526b, **732a**, 1067a; VI, 594a, 750b, 751b; VII, 1019a; VIII, 480b, 558b; S, 47a
Kashīnā, Kashnā → Katsina
al-Kashināwī, Muḥammad iv, 773b – IV, 805a
Kashīsh-Daghi → Ulu Dagh
Kāshḳāʾī, Ḳashḳāy ii, 925b; iii, 1105a, 1106a, 1110a; iv, 8a, 9a-b, **705b**; s, 142b, 146a, 147b – II, 947a; III, 1132a, 1133b, 1137a; IV, 8b, 9a, 10a, **734a**; S, 142a, 145b, 147b
Ḳashka-Daryā vi, 418a, 618a – VI, 403a, 604a
Ḳāshkār → Chitral
Kashkasha i, 709a – I, 729b
Kashkūl iv, **706b** – IV, **735a**
Kashlī Khān → Sayf al-Dīn Aybak b. Iltutmish
Kashmīr i, 71a, 231a, 392b, 856b; ii, 140a; iii, 317a, 420a; iv, **706b**; v, 588b; vi, 125b, 128a, 368a, 426a, 696b, 780a; viii, 68a; ix, 785b; s, 63a, 114b, 131b, 156a, 167a, 241a, 242a, 324b, 327b, 332a, 333a, 366a, b, 423a, b – I, 73a, 238a, 403b, 880b; II, 144a; III, 326b, 433b; IV, **735a**; V, 592a; VI, 123b, 126a, 352a, 411a, 684b, 770a; VIII, 64a; IX, 819b; S, 63b, 113b, 130b, 156a, 167a, 241b, 242a, 324a, 327a, 332a, b, 366a, 423b
—monuments i, 1347b, 1348a; iii, 448a – I, 1388a, b; III, 463b
Kashmīrī (language/langue) ii, 139a; iii, 413b; iv, 707a, **711b** – II, 142b; III, 426b; IV, 735b, **740a**
Kashmūla, Banū vi, 902a – VI, 893b
al-Kashnāwī, Muḥammad iv, 773b – IV, 805a
Kashshāfa iii, 185a – III, 189a
al-Kashshī, Abū ʿAmr Muḥammad b. ʿUmar (951) i, 134a, 794b; iii, 1151a; iv, **711b**; vi, 312b; viii, 517b – I, 137b, 818a; III, 1179b; IV, **740a**; VI, 297b; VIII, 535b
Ḳashtāla (Castile) iv, **712a**; v, 781b; s, 80b – IV, **740b**; V, 787b; S, 80a
al-Ḳashtālī, Aḥmad (XIV) vi, 356a – VI, 340a
Ḳasī, Banū i, 494a, 658a; iii, 815b; iv, 477b, **712b**; v, 683a; s, 80b, 82a – I, 509a, 679a; III, 839b; IV, 498b, **741**; V, 688a; S, 80b, 81b
Ḳāṣid → Safīr
Ḳasid Oghlu → Ḳāzdughliyya
Ḳaṣīda i, 583b, 586a, 592a, 601b, 668a, 671b, 676b, 677a, 1290a; ii, 293a, 1028b; iii, 1178a; iv, 57a-b, 59a-b, 65a, **713b**; v, 930b, 956a, 957a, 958b, 963a – I, 602a, 605a, 611b, 621a, 688b, 692b, 697a, 698a, 1329b; II, 301a, 1052b; III, 1207a; IV, 60b, 62b, 68b, **742a**; V, 935a, 960a, 961a, 962a, 967a
Ḳaṣīdat al-burda i, 1011b – I, 1042b
al-Ḳāsim (al-Muʾtamin, ʿAbbāsid(e)) (IX) vi, 331a, VI, 315b
al-Ḳaṣīm (Nadjd) i, 1312b, 1313a; iv, **717a**;; vi, 153a; viii, 613a; s, 3b, 304b, 305a –

I, 1352b, 1353a; IV, **745b**; VI, 151b; VIII, 632b; S, 2b, 304a, b
Ḳāsim, (Qassem) ʿAbd al-Karīm (1963) iii, 1259a; iv, **719a**; v, 468a, 1213b; vi, 29a; vii, 714a; viii, 446a – III, 1291b; IV, **747b**; V, 470b, 471a, 1203a; VI, 27a; VII, 715a; VIII, 461a
Ḳāsim, S.M. iv, 711a – IV, 739b
al-Ḳāsim b. ʿAbbād, ḳāḍī (XI) vi, 222a – VI, 216a
al-Ḳāsim b. Aḥmad I (1638) iv, **717a** – IV, **745b**
al-Kāsim b. Aḥmad b. Bāyazīd (1518) iv, **716b** – IV, **745b**
al-Ḳāsim b. ʿAlī b. ʿUmar s, 48b – S, 49a
al-Ḳāsim b. Aṣbagh (951) i, 600a, 1150a; iii, 845a; iv, **717b**; vii, 400a – I, 619b, 1184b; III, 868b; IV, **746b**; VII, 401b
al-Ḳāsim b. Djihāngīr (Aḳ-ḳoyunlu) (1445) i, 311b; vi, 542b – I, 321b; VI, 527a
al-Ḳāsim b. Djiryāl al-Dimashḳī s, 267a – S, 266b
al-Ḳāsim b. Ḥammūd (Ḥammūdid(e)) (1021) i, 6a; iii, 147a, 786a; vi, 222a; vii, 761a – I, 6b; 150a, b, 809b; VI, 216a; VII, 762b
al-Ḳāsim b. Ḥasan iii, 610b – III, 631b
al-Ḳāsim b. Ibrāhīm al-Rassī (Zaydī Imām, Yemen) (860) vi, 435b, 436b; vii, 546b, 773a, 786a; viii, 388a; viii, 453b, 980b; x, 111b – VI, 421a, b; VII, 546b, 774b, 787b; VIII, 401a, VIII, 468b, 1015a; X, 120b
al-Ḳāsim b. Idrīs II i, 1088a; iii, 1035b – I, 1120a; III, 1061b
al-Ḳāsim b. ʿĪsā al-Idjlī (840) i, 153b, 315b; ii, 623a; iv, **718a**; vii, 777a; s, 17b, 122a – I, 158a, 325b; II, 639a; IV, **747a**; VII, 779a; S, 17b, 121b
al-Ḳāsim b. Maḥfūẓ al-Baghdādī (XIII) vii, 29a – VII, 29a
al-Ḳāsim b. Muḥammad (Katar) → Djāsim b. Muḥammad
al-Ḳāsim b. Ḳuṭlubugha (1474) ix, 36a – IX, 35b
al-Ḳāsim b. Muḥammad, faḳīh (VII) vii, 393a – VII, 394a
al-Ḳāsim b. Muḥammad b. Abī Bakr s, **311b** – S, **311b**
al-Ḳāsim b. Muḥammad, al-Kabīr → al-Manṣūr bi-llāh al-Kāsim b. Muḥammad
al-Ḳāsim b. Muḥammad al-Muʾayyad v, 1242a – V, 1232b
al-Ḳāsim b. al-Rashīd iv, 859a – IV, 892a
al-Ḳāsim b. ʿUbayd Allāh b. Sulaymān (vizier) (904) ii, 178a; iii, 767b, 892b, 908a; iv, 110a, 293b; v, 621b; vii, 543a, 679a; ix, 594b; s, 118a – II, 184a; III, 790b, 916b, 932b; IV, 115a, 306b; V, 625b; VII, 543a, 678b; IX, 617b; S, 117b
al-Ḳāsim b. ʿUmar iii, 651b – III, 672b
al-Ḳāsim b. ʿUmar, Amīr ii, 635b – II, 651b
al-Ḳāsim b. Yūsuf b. al-Ḳāsim iii, 309a – III, 318b
al-Ḳāsim Agha (XVII) iv, **719b**; v, 257a – IV, **748b**; V, 255a
Ḳāsim ʿAlī (painter/peintrre) i, 1211b, 1213a – I, 1247b, 1249b
Ḳāsim ʿAlī, Mīr (1777) i, 1357b; ii, 1091b; iii, 61a – I, 1397b; II, 1117a; III, 63b
Ḳāsim Amīn (1908) i, 597a; ii, 423a; iii, 59a, 360a, 593a; iv, **720a**; vi, 220a, 470a, 957b; vii, 901a; s, 244b – I, 616b; II, 434a; III, 61b, 371a, 613b; IV, **749a**; VI, 213b, 456a, 949b; VII, 901b; S, 244b
Ḳāsim-i Anwar (1433) iv, 66a, **721a**, 1073b; viii, 540a – IV, 69b, **750a**, 1105a; VIII, 558a
Ḳāsim Barīd (Barīd Shāhī) (1504) i, 1047a, b, 1200a; iii, 15a, 421a; vi, 63a, b – I, 1078b, 1079a, 1235b; III, 16a, 434b; VI, 60b, 61a
Ḳāsim Beg ii, 529b; iv, 624a, b – II, 542b; IV, 649a
Ḳāsim Čelebi b. Bāyazīd (1417) iv, **716b** – IV, **745b**
Ḳāsim al-Dawla al-Bursuḳī → Āḳ Sunḳur al-Bursuḳī
Ḳāsim Djān, Munshī i, 72a – I, 74a
Ḳāsim Djānbulāt (Jumblat) → Djānbulāt
Ḳāsim Gannūn (Djannūn) iii, 1036b – III, 1062b
Ḳāsim Ghanī iii, 56b – III, 59a
Ḳāsim al-Ḳaysī (XX) vi, 614a – VI, 599a
Ḳāsim Khān (XVI) vii, 330a; s, 167b – VII, 331b; S, 167b
Ḳāsim Khān Mīr Baḥr (Afshar) i, 240a; iv, 709a; s, 132a – I, 247b; IV, 737b; S, 131a
Ḳāsim Khān (Tatar) i, 721b; iv, 723a, 849a – I, 743b; IV, 752a, 882a
Ḳāsim al-Khaṣāṣī → al-Khaṣāṣī
Ḳāsim Pasha ii, 813a – II, 832a
Ḳāsim Pasha Djazarī (1485) iv, **722a** – IV, **751a**
Ḳāsim Pasha Ewliyā (1485) iv, **722a** – IV, **751a**
Ḳāsim Pasha Güzeldje (1552) iv, 233a, **722b**; vii, 239b – IV, 243a, **751b**; VII, 241a
Ḳāsim al-Rassī b. Ṭabāṭabā vi, 433a – VI, 418b
Ḳāsim Shāh iv, 201b – IV, 210b
Ḳāsim al-Wāthiḳ iii, 147b – III, 150b
Ḳāsim Yughayta ii, 330b – II, 340b
Ḳāsim Yūsuf → Ḳāsim Čelebi
Ḳāsim al-Zarhūnī (1550) vi, 894a – VI, 885a, b
Ḳāsimī, Āl → Ḳawāsim
Ḳāsimī, Djamāl al-Dīn (1914) iv, 159a; vi, 360a,b; viii, 906b – IV, 166a; VI, 344a,b; VIII, 937b
Ḳāsimī, Shaykh Ṣaḳr b. Muḥammad s, 418a – S, 418a, b
Ḳāsimī, Shaykh Ṣaḳr b. Sulṭān s, 418a – S, 418b
Ḳāsimī Gunabādī (1574) iii, 114a; viii, 775a – III, 116b; VIII, 801a
Ḳāsimiyya (Egypt) ii, 233a;iii 300a; iv, **722b**; vi, 319a, 325a, b, 327b – II, 240a; III, 309a; IV, **751b**; VI, 303b, 309b, 314a
Ḳāsimiyya (Yemen) iii, 255a; vi, 436b – III, 262a; VI, 421b
Kasimov ii, 44b; iv, **723a**, 849a – II, 45a; IV, **752a**, 882a
Kāsimpasha (Istanbul) vi, 57a, 587b, 588a, b; s, 314b, 315b – VI, 55a, 572b, 573a; S, 314a, 315b
al-Ḳaṣīr, ʿAbd al-Raḥmān b. Aḥmad b. (1180) vi, 111a – VI, 108b
al-Kasirḳī → Nūr al-Dīn ʿAbd al-Raḥmān al-Kasirḳī
Ḳāsiyūn, Djabal iv, **724a**; vi, 599b; vii, 558b; s, 197a – IV, **753a**; VI, 584b; VII, 559a; S, 197a
Kaskar iv, **724b** – IV, **753b**
al-Kaskarī, Isrāʿīl (872) vii, 1031b – VII, 1034a
Kasr (fraction) iv, **725a**, 731b – IV, **754a**, 760b
Ḳaṣr (palace/palais) iv, 236b – IV, 247a
Ḳaṣr ʿAbd al-Karīm → al-Ḳaṣr al-Kabīr
Ḳaṣr Abī Dānis ii, 1009b – II, 1033a
Ḳaṣr al-Abyad → Khirbat al-Bayḍāʾ
Ḳaṣr Adjwad b. Zamīl s, 234b – S, 234a
Ḳaṣr al-Aghāliba → al-Abbāsiyya
Ḳaṣr al-Amīr vi, 455b – VI, 441a
Ḳaṣr al-ʿAynī s, 38a – S, 38b
Ḳaṣr Banī Muḳātil x, 791b – X,
Ḳaṣr Burḳuʿ s, 117a – S, 116b
Ḳaṣr Firʿawn → Walīlī
Ḳaṣr al-Ḥallābāt s, 117a – S, 116b
Ḳaṣr al-Ḥasanī i, 897b, 898a, 1312b; iii, 243b – I, 924a, b, 1352b; III, 250b
Ḳaṣr al-Ḥayr al-Gharbī i, 613a; ii, 557a, 1021a; iii, 71a, 141b, 310a, 494b; iv, **726a**; vi, 680a; viii, 452a; s, 117a – I, 633a; II, 571a, 1045a; III, 73b, 144b, 319b, 511b; IV, **755a**; VI, 667a; VIII, 467a; S, 116b
Ḳaṣr al-Ḥayr al-Sharḳi i, 613a, 613b, 831a; iii, 71a, 494b; iv, **727b**, 1011b; s, 117a –

I, 633b, 854a; III, 73b, 511b; IV, **756b**, 1045a; S, 116b
Ḳaṣr Hishām → Khirbat al-Mafdjar
Ḳaṣr Ibn Abī Aḥmad vi, 457a – VI, 442b
Ḳaṣr Ibn Hubayra iii, 265b, 266a; iv, **728b** – III, 273b; IV, **758a**
Ḳaṣr Ibrīm vi, 574b; vii, 545a; viii, 90a – VI, 559b; VII, 545a; VIII, 92a
Ḳaṣr al-Kabīr (Alcazarquivir) iv, **729a**; v, 1191a; vi, 741b, 743a – IV, **758a**; V, 1181a; VI, 731a, 732b
Ḳaṣr al-Ḳadīm → al-ʿAbbāsiyya
Ḳaṣr Kharāna → Kharāna
Ḳaṣr Kutāma → al-Ḳaṣr al-Kabīr
Ḳaṣr al-Luṣūṣ → Kinkiwar
Ḳaṣr al-Madjāz → al-Ḳaṣr al-Ṣaghīr
Ḳaṣr al-Mannār vi, 427a – VI, 412b
Ḳaṣr Maṣmūda → al-Ḳaṣr al-Ṣaghīr
Ḳaṣr al-Ṣaghīr i, 56a, 706b; iv, **729b**; vi, 741b – I, 57b, 728a; IV, **759a**; VI, 730b
Ḳaṣr al-Salām (al-Raḳḳa) viii, 411a – VIII, 425b
Ḳaṣr al-Shawḳ s, 44a – S, 44b
Ḳaṣr Yānī → Kaṣryānnih
Kasrā iii, 172b; iv, **731a**; x, 788b – III, 176b; IV, **760b**; X,
Ḳaṣrān v, 661b – V, 667a
Kasrānī i, 1007b – I, 1038b
Kasrawī Tabrīzī, Aḥmad (1946) ii, 882b; iii, 114a; iv, 166b, **732a**, 789b; v, 1097b, 1098a – II, 902b; III, 116b; IV, 173b, **761b**, 821b; V, 1093b, 1094a
al-Ḳasrī, Asad b. ʿAbd Allrh (VIII) viii, 1026a – VIII, 1060b
al-Ḳaṣrī, Khālid b. ʿAbd Allāh (vizier) (738) vii, 75b – VII, 76b
al-Ḳaṣrī, Muḥammad b. Khālid b. ʿAbd Allāh (VIII) vii, 798b – VII, 800a
Ḳaṣr-i Aḥnaf → Marw al-Rūdh
Ḳaṣr-i Shīrīn i, 624a, 1345b; ii, 793b, 794a; iv, **730b**; vi, 56b – I, 643b, 1386a; II, 812b; IV, **759b**; VI, 54b
Ḳaṣryānnih iv, **733a** – IV, **762b**
Ḳāṣṣ iv, **733b**; v, 186a, b, 187a, 951a; vi, 468a; ix, 552b – IV, **763a**; V, 183a, b, 184a, 954b; VI, 453b; IX, 574b
Ḳassāb, Ḥaydar-i (Sarbadārid(e)) (XIV) ix, 48b – IX, 49b
Kassāh → Kannās
Kassala → Kasala
Ḳassām i, 824a, b; ii, 483a; iii, 128b, 841a; iv, **735b**; vi, 4b – I, 847a, b; II, 495a; III, 131a, 864b **765a**; VI, 4b
Ḳassām (rebel) s, 37a – S, 37b
Ḳaṣṣār → Ghassāl
al-Ḳaṣṣār, Abū ʿAbd Allāh (1531) iv, **736a** – IV, **766a**
Ḳaṣṣāra, Abu ʾl-Ḥusayn ʿAlī (1843) iv, **736b** – IV, **766a**
al-Ḳaṣṣāriyya vi, 224b – VI, 218b
al-Ḳaṣṣāṣīn s, 300b – S, 300b
Ḳaṣṣārī iii, 132a – III, 134b
al-Ḳasṭal s, 230a – S, 230a
al-Ḳasṭallānī, Abu ʾl-ʿAbbās Aḥmad b. Muḥammad (1517) i, 1297a; iv, **736b**; vi, 87b, 112a – I, 1336b; IV, **766a**; VI, 85b, 110a
Ḳasṭallanī (Kestelī), Muṣliḥ al-Dīn Muṣṭafā (1495) iv, **737a**; vii, 272b – IV, **766b**; VII, 274b
al-Ḳasṭallī, Abū ʿAmr vi, 350a – VI, 334b
Kastamonu → Ḳasṭamūnī
Ḳasṭamūnī iv, 108b, **737a**; v, 693b, 966b, 977b, 1145b; vi, 69a, 120b; s, 274a – IV, 113a, **767a**; V, 698b, 970b, 977a, 1137b; VI, 67a, 118a; S, 273b
Ḳasṭīlya (Castille) → Ḳashtāla
Ḳasṭīliya (Ilbīra) iv, **739a** – IV, **769a**
Ḳasṭīliya (Tunisia/-e) ii, 462b, 463a; iv, **739b**; vi, 435a – II, 474b, 475a; IV, **769a**; VI, 420b
Kastoria → Kesriye
Kastriota, George → Iskender Beg
Ḳasṭūn vi, 507a – VI, 492b
Ḳaṣūr ii, 929a – II, 950b
Ḳāt iv, **741a** – IV, **770b**
Ḳaṭʿ iv, **741b** – IV, **771b**
Ḳaṭʿ al-Ṭarīḳ → Ḳatl; Sariḳa; Ṣuʿlūk
Ḳaṭā iv, **743a** – IV, **773a**
Ḳaṭā Sarāy iv, 579b – IV, 603a
Ḳaʿṭaba iv, **745b** – IV, **775a**
Ḳatabān i, 548a, 1132b; iii, 208a; iv, **746a**; vi, 560b, 561a – I, 565b, 1166b; III, 213b; IV, **775b**; VI, 545a, b
Katāda, Banū iii, 261b, 881a; ix. 507a – III, 276a, 905a; IX, 526b
Ḳatāda b. Diʿāma (735) i, 104b; iv, 370b, **748b**; v, 1232a – I, 107b; IV, 387a, **778b**; V, 1222a
Ḳatāda b. Idrīs, Sharīf (Abū ʿUzaiyyiz) (1221) i, 552b, 1032a; iii, 262b; iv, **748b**; vi, 433b; vii, 998b – I, 570b, 1064a; III, 270a; IV, **778b**; VI, 418b; VII, 1000a
Ḳatāda b. Mūsā II b. ʿAbd Allāh (Sharīf) vi, 149a – VI, 147b
Ḳatāda b. Salāma al-Ḥanafī iv, 832a – IV, 865a
Katahr iv, **749a**; s, 73b, 206b – IV, **779b**; S, 74a, 206a
Katahriyā vi, 48b – VI, 46b
Ḳaṭāʾiʿ ii, 187b; iv, 323a, b, **754b**, 973a, 1031a; v, 23a, 347a – II, 193b; IV, 337b, 338a, **785a**, 1005b, 1063a; V, 24a, 348a
al-Ḳaṭāʾiʿ i, 279a; ii, 958b, 959a – I, 287b; II, 980b, 981a
Katak → Orissa
Kataman v, 21b – V, 22a
Ḳaṭāmi bint al-Shidjna iii, 887a, 888a – III, 911a, 912a
Ḳaṭʿān b. Salma al-Zawāghī (811) vi, 840b – VI, 831a
Katanga iv, **749b** – IV, **780a**
Ḳataniya → Ṣiḳiliyya
Ḳaṭar i, 536a, 539b, 941a, 944a; ii, 177a; iv, **750b**, 953b; v, 1058a; vi, 37a, b, 358a; vii, 301b, 449b; s, 417a, b –
I, 552b, 556b, 969b, 971b; II, 182b; IV, **781a**, 985b; V, 1055a; VI, 35b, 342a; VII, 303b, 450b; S, 417a, b
Ḳaṭarī b. al-Fudjāʾa (Azraḳī) (697) i, 686b, 810b; iii, 40b; iv, 207b, 269a, **752b**, 938a, 1075b; v, 157b; vii, 357b; x, 124b –
I, 707b, 833b; III, 42b; IV, 217a, 281b, **783a**, 971a, 1107b; V, 157a; VII, 359b; X, 134a
Katavolenos, Thomas vi, 70b – VI, 68b
Katbughā → Kitbughā
Kateb Yacine (XX) vi, 754a – VI, 743b
al-Katf al-Buṣrī vi, 548a – VI, 532b
Kāth ii, 1142a; iv, **753b**, 1063b, 1064b, 1066b; vi, 340a – II, 1169a; IV, **784a**, 1095a, 1096a, 1098a; VI, 324a
Kathāwat s, 325a – S, 324b
Kathīr, Banū vi, 82b, 83b – VI, 80b, 81b
Kathīr al-Nawwāʾ s, 129b – S, 129a
Kathīr b. Saʿd v, 2a, b – V, 2a, b
Kathīrī, Āl iii, 291b; iv, 10a; v, 184a; vi, 132b; vii, 496a; s, 337b, 338b – III, 300b; IV, 11a; V, 181b; VI, 130b; VII, 496a; S, 337a, 338a
Ḳāṭhiyāwār → Djunagaṛh
Kathrā x, 788b – X,
Katī ii, 31a, 138b; iv, 409b, 410b – II, 32a, 142a; IV, 427a, 428b
Ḳatiʿ, ʿAlī Afḍal (XVI) viii, 784b – VIII, 810b

Kaʿti, Maḥmūd (Soninke) (1593) iv, **754a** – IV, **784b**
Ḳaṭiʿa → Ḳaṭāʾiʿ
Kātib i, 981b; ii, 324b; iii, 740a, 1242b; iv, **754b**; v, 1238b – I, 1012a; II, 334a; III, 762b, 1274b; IV, **785a**; V, 1229a
Kātib Čelebi (1657) i, 478b, 594b, 698a, 758a, 1198a; ii, 110a, 589a, 590a; iv, 168a, **760b**, 1082b; vi, 352b, 906a; vii, 48b, 917b; s, 171b, 289b – I, 492b, 614a, 719a, 781a, 1233a; II, 112b, 603b, 604b; IV, 175a, **791a**, 1114a; VI, 336b, 897b; VII, 48b, 918a; S, 171b, 289b
Kātib Ferdī (1537) vi, 542b – VI, 527a
Kātib al-Iṣfahānī → ʿImād al-Dīn
al-Katība iv, 1141a, b – IV, 1173a, b
al-Kātibī, Nadjm al-Dīn Dabīrān (1276) iv, **762a** – IV, **792b**
Kātibī, Shams al-Dīn (1435) iv, **762b** – IV, **793a**
Kātibī Rūmi ii, 588b, 589b – II, 603a, 604a
Kātib-i Rūnī → Sīdī Reʾīs
Kātibzāde Meḥmed Refīʿ iv, 1126a – IV, 1157b
al-Ḳaṭīf i, 73a, 942b; iv, **763b**; vi, 735a; vii, 301b, 859a; s, 234a – I, 75a, 971a; IV, **794a**; VI, 724a; VII, 303b, 860b; S, 234a
Katif, ʿIlm al- iv, **763a** – IV, **793b**
Ḳaṭīfe iii, 216b, 217b – III, 223a, b
al-Ḳaṭīfī, al-Nadjaf Ibrāhīm iv, 610a – IV, 635a
al-Ḳaṭīʿī → Abū Bakr
al-Ḳaṭīʿī al-Baghdādī iii, 756a – III, 779a
Ḳatīl, Mīrzā iii, 1244b – III, 1276b
Katīn → Khātūn
Ḳaṭirān → Ḳaṭrān
Ḳātir iii, 1105b, 1106a – III, 1132b, 1133b
Ḳāṭirdjī-oghlī Meḥmed Pasha (1668) i, 4b; iii, 317b; iv, **765b** – I, 4b; III, 327a; IV, **796a**
Ḳaṭʿiyya iv, 743a – IV, 772b
Katkhudā → Ketkhudā
Katkhudā Marzubān i, 955b – I, 984b
Katkhudā Pasha → Ibrāhīm Pasha
Ḳatl iv, **766b** – IV, **797a**
Ḳaṭlān, ʿAbd al-Fattāḥ (1931) viii, 907a – VIII, 938a
Kator → Kāfiristān
Katra Mīrānpūr iii, 61b – III, 64a
Katrabbul → Ḳuṭrabbul
Ḳaṭrān iv, **772b** – IV, **803b**
Ḳaṭrān, Ḥakīm (XI) iv, 61b, 525b, **773a** – IV, 65a, 548b, **804a**
Ḳaṭrāna x, 885a – X,
Katsina iii, 275a, 276a; iv, **773b** – III, 283a, 284a; IV, **804b**
Ḳatta-Kurghan vi, 418a – VI, 403a
Kattān iv, **774a** – IV, **805a**
al-Ḳaṭṭān, Yaḥyā b. Saʿīd (813) viii, 515a, 983b – VIII, 532b, 1018a
al-Kattānī, Āl iv, **774b** – IV, **805b**
al-Kattānī, Abū ʿAbd Allāh Djaʿfar b. Idrīs (1905) iv, 774b – IV, 805b
al-Kattānī, Muḥammad b. Djaʿfar (1927) iv, 774b; v, 1209b; s, 350b, 404a, b – IV, 805b; V, 1200a; S, 350b, 404b
al-Kattānt, Sharīf Muḥammad al-Kabīr b. ʿAbd al-Wahhāb (XX) viii, 905b – VIII, 936b
al-Kattānī, Shaykh Abu ʾl-Asʿad Muḥammad ʿAbd al-Ḥayy (1912) iv, 774b; viii, 905b – IV, 805b; VIII, 936b
al-Kattānī, ʿUmar b. Ṭāhir (1891) iv, 774b – IV, 805b
Kattāniyya viii, 905b – VIII, 936b
al-Ḳātūl iv, 384a – IV, 400b
Katum → Umay
Ḳaṭwān Steppe (battle/bataille) (1141) iii, 1114b; iv, 581b; ix, 16b; x, 543a – III, 1142a; IV, 604b, 605a; IX, 17a; X,
Katwar → Kāfiristān
Kavafoğlu → Atač, Nūr Allāh
Kavaklî → Čakmak, Mustafa Fevzi
Kavala → Ḳawāla
Kavala Shahīn → Shahīn Pasha
Kavas → Ḳawwās
Kāveh → Kāwah
Kavol ii, 41a – II, 42a
Ḳavuḳ v, 751a – V, 756b
Kāwa iv, 775a – IV, 806a
Ḳawad → Ḳiṣāṣ
Kawādh I (Sāsānid(e)) (531) vi, 378b; ix, 214a; s, 297b – VI, 363a; IX, 324a; S, 297a
al-Ḳawādhiyān ii, 577b – II, 592a
Kāwah (Kāveh) iv, **775a**; vi, 745b – IV, **806a**; VI, 735a
al-Kawākibī, ʿAbd al-Raḥmān (1902) i, 597b; iii, 593b; iv, 143b, 144a, 145b, 151a, 159a, 162b, **775b**, 782b; vi, 360a; vii, 764b; viii, 360a, 447a, 907a; ix, 517b – I, 617a; III, 614a; IV, 149b, 150a, 151b, 157b, 165b, 169b, **806b**, 814a; VI, 344a; VII, 766a; VIII, 373a, 461b, 938a; IX, 537b
al-Kawākibi, Nadjm al-Dīn (XVI) viii, 543a – VIII, 560b
Ḳawāla (Kavala) iv, **776a**; vii, 423a – IV, **807a**; VII, 424b
Ḳawām, Aḥmad Adharbāydjān (XX) i, 190b; ii, 653b; iii, 529a; v, 630b – I, 196a; II, 670a; III, 547b; V, 634b
Ḳawām al-Dīn I al-Marʿashī, Sayyid (Mīr-i Buzurg) vi, 510b, 511a, 512a, b, 515a, b – VI, 496a, b, 497a, b, 500b, 501a
Ḳawām al-Dīn II b. Riḍā al-Dīn (Marʿashī) (1407) vi, 512b, 513a, b – VI, 498a, b
Ḳawām al Dīn al-Mulk iii, 1106a; v, 674b – III, 1133b; V, 679b
Ḳawām al-Dīn Zawzanī iv, 1034b → IV, 1066b
Ḳawām al-Salṭana (XX) viii, 512a – VIII, 529b
Kawār i, 1221b; iv, **777a**; vi, 384a – I, 1258a; IV, **808a**; VI, 368a
al-Ḳawārīrī, ʿUbayd Allāh b. ʿAmr (849) vii, 691a – VII, 691b
al-Ḳawāsim, Āl i, 928a, 1282a; ii, 619a; iv, 751a, **777b**; v,70b, 183b, 507b, 508a, 765a; vi, 735a, b; viii, 435a, 436a; s, 42a – I, 956b, 1321a; II, 634b; IV, 781b, **808b**; V, 72b, 180b, 181a, 511a, b, 771a; VI, 724b; VIII, 449b, 450b S, 42b
Ḳawāsma, Banū viii, 91a – VIII, 93b
al-Kawfanī → al-Abīwardī
Kawīr s, 61a – S, 61b
Kawkab → Nudjūm
Kawkab al-Hawāʾ iv, **778b**; v, 120b – IV, **810a**; V, 123a
Kawkabān iii, 134a; iv, **779a**; vi, 433b, 434a, 436b – III, 137a; IV, **810b**; VI, 419a, b, 422a
Kawkaw → Gao
Ḳawlīs i, 323a; v, 818b – I, 333a; V, 824b
Ḳawm iii, 411a; iv, **780b**, 785b – III, 424a; IV, **812a**, 817a
Ḳawm (military/militaire) → Gūm
al-Ḳawmā → al-Ḳūmā
Ḳawmiyya iv, **781a**; vi, 586a – IV, **812b**; VI, 570b
Kawn wa-fasād iv, **794b** – IV, **827a**
Kawōm → Ḳawm
al-Kawr i, 536a, b – I, 552b, 553a
Ḳawriya → Ḳūriya
Ḳaws ii, 506b; iii, 469b, 470a, 476a; iv, **795b** – II, 519b; III, 486a, b, 492b; IV, **828a**
Ḳaws Ḳuzaḥ iv, **803a** – IV, **835b**

Ḳawṣara iv, **805a** – IV, **837a**
Ḳawṣūn (Miṣr) (1342) vi, 323a, b; vii, 170b – VI, 307b, 308a; VII, 172b
al-Kawthar ii, 448b; iii, 286a; iv, **805b**; x, 788b – II, 460b; III, 295a; IV, **838a**; X,
Kawtharī (Hamadān) (1606) viii, 776a – VIII, 802a
Kawthariyya viii, 46b – VIII, 47b
Ḳawuḳlu iv, **806a** – IV, **838b**
Ḳāwurd b. Čaghrî Beg Dāwūd (amīr) (Kirmān) (1074) i, 420a, 552a, 664b, 665a; iii, 195a, 507a, 1097b, 1098a; iv, 26b, 27b, 101a, **807a**; v, 158b, 353a; vi, 273b; vii, 193a; viii, 70a, 945b, 946a; s, 127a – I, 432a, 569b, 684b; III, 199b, 524b, 1124a, 1125a; IV, 28b, 29b, 105b, **839b**; V, 158a, 353b; VI, 258a; VII, 193b; VIII, 71b, 978a S, 126a
Kāwūs (Sassānid(e)) vi, 632a, 745a – VI, 617a, 734b
Kāwūs, Banū iv, **808a**; vi, 938b – IV, **840b**; VI, 930b
Kāwūs b. K(G)ayūmarth (1467) iv, 808a; v, 663a; vi, 513a – IV, 840b; V, 668b; VI, 498a
Ḳawwās iv, **808b** – IV, **841a**
al-Ḳawwāmī, Badr al-Dln (XII) viii, 582a – VIII, 600b
al-Ḳawwās (1591) vi, 112a – VI, 110a
Kay Khusraw → Kaykhusraw
Kaya → Ketkhudā
Kayalars v, 582a – V, 587a
Ḳayalîḳ iv, **808b** – IV, **841a**
Kayānīd(e)s iv, 12b, **809a**; ix, 75a, 76a – IV, 13a, **841b**; IX, 78a, 79a
Kaybar (battle/bataille) (1029) vii, 117a – VII, 119a
al-Kayd iv, **809b**, 1186a – IV, **842b**, 1219a
al-Ḳayd iii, 208a – III, 213b
Kaydaḳ → Ḳaytaḳ
Ḳaydū (Tīmūrid(e)) i, 1133b – I, 1168a
Ḳaydu Khān b. Ḳashi (Mongol) (1303) i, 504b, 1311b, 1312a; ii, 3a, 45a, b; iv, 808b, **811b**; v, 39a, 300a; vi, 420a, 782b; s, 240a – I, 520a, 1352a, b; II, 3b, 46a, b; IV, 841b, 8**44a**; V, 40a, 299b; VI, 405a, 772b; S, 240a
Ḳayghusuz Abdāl (1415) iv, **811b**; viii, 2b – IV, **844b**; VIII, 2b
Kaygîlî, ʿOthmān Djemāl (1945) iv, **812a**; s, 64b – IV, **845a**; S, 65a
Ḳāyî, Banū (Oghuz) iv, **812b**; x, 689b – IV, **845b**; X, 782a
Ḳayib Khān i, 1076b – I, 1108b
Ḳāyināt iv, 4a, b – IV, 4b
Kayîr Buḳu Khān s, 246a – S, 246a
Ḳayir Tigin → Ḳaratigin
Kayir Toḳu Khān (XII) ix, 558a – IX, 580a
Ḳayitbāy → Ḳāʾitbāy (Mamlūk)
Kaykāʾūs I b. Kaykhusraw I (Rūm Saldjūḳ) (1220) i, 313a, 336b, 467a, 510a; ii, 37b, 966b; iii, 708a; iv, 575b, **813b**; vi, 381a, 632a; viii, 949a – I, 323a, 343b, 480b, 525b; II, 38b, 988b; III, 730a; IV, 598b, **846a**; VI, 365b, 617a; VIII, 981b
Kaykāʾūs II ʿIzz al-Dīn (Rūm Saldjūḳ) (1279) i, 1188b, 1302b; ii, 204b, 610b, 971a; iv, 600b, **813b**; v, 104b, 254a, 286a; vi, 420b, 507b; vii, 479b; viii, 949b, 975a – I,1223b, 1342a; II, 210b, 625b, 993b; IV, 625a, **846b**; V, 106b, 252a, 284a; VI, 405b, 492b; VII, 479a; VIII, 982a, 1011b
Kaykaʾūs (Kayānid(e)) iv, 809a, **813a** – IV, 842a, **846a**
Kaykāʾūs b. Iskandar (Ziyārid(e)) (XI) iv, **815a**; vi, 761b; vii, 987b; s, 96b – IV, **847b**; VI, 751a; VII, 988a; S, 96a
Kaykāʾūs Shāh (Bengal(e)) (1301) ix, 83b – IX, 87b
Kay Khusraw (Kayānid(e)) i, 236b; iv, 809a, **815b**; ix, 696b – I, 244a; IV, 842a, **848b**; IX, 725a
Kay Khusraw I b. Ḳîlîdj Arslān II (Rūm Saldjūḳ) (1211) i, 346a, 466b, 517b; ii, 111a; iii, 708a; iv, **816a**, 1061b; vi, 507a – I, 356b, 480b, 533a; II, 113b; III, 730a; IV, **849a**, 1092b; VI, 492b
Kay Khusraw II b. Kayḳubād I, Ghiyāth al-Dīn (Rūm Saldjūḳ) (1245) i, 432a, 467a, 838b; ii, 38a; iv, **816b**; v, 271b, 286a, b; vi, 528a; vii, 193a, 479a, 990b; viii, 949a, 975a – I, 444b, 480b, 861b; II, 38b; IV, **849b**; V, 269b, 284a, b; VI, 512b; VII, 193b, 479a, 992b; VIII, 981b, 1011b
Kay Khusraw III b. Rukn al-Dīn Kîlîdj Arslān (Rūm Saldjūḳ) (1284) i, 703a; iv, 620b, **817a** – I, 724a; IV, 645a, b, **850a**
Kay-Khusraw b. Maḥmūd Shāh (Īndjūid(e)) (1338) iii, 1208a, b; vii, 820a – III, 1239a; VII, 822a
Kay Ḳubād (Kayānid(e)) iv, 809a – IV, 841b
Ḳayḳubād I ʿAlāʾ al-Dīn (Rūm Saldjūḳ) (1237) i, 329a, 354b, 355a, 424b, 467a, 510a, 665a, 799b, 1191b; ii, 38a, 444b, 692a, 710b, 711b; iii, 215b, 738a; iv, 521a, **817b**, 818b, 1084b; v, 255a, 285b; vi, 381a; vii, 273b, 871a; viii, 949a, 975a – I, 339b, 365b, 366a, 436a, 480b, 525b, 686a, 822b, 1226b; II, 38b, 456a, 709a, 727a, 729b; III, 222a, 760b; IV, 543b, **850a**, 851b, 1115b; V, 253a, 284a; VI, 365b; VII, 275b, 872b; VIII, 981b, 1011b
Kayḳubād II b. Kaykhusraw I (Rūm Saldjūḳ) (1257) iv, **818a**; ix, 12b – IV, **851a**; IX, 13a
Kayḳubād III (Rūm Saldjūḳ) (1303) ii, 201a; iv, **818a**; viii, 949b – II, 207b; IV, **851a**; VIII, 982a
Ḳayḳubād, Muʿizz al-Dīn (Dihlī) (1290) ii, 256b, 268a; iv, **818a**, 920b; s, 73b – II, 263b, 276b; IV, **851a**, 953b; S, 74a
Kayḳubādiyya iv, **818b** – IV, **851b**
Ḳayl iv, **818b** – IV, **851b**
Kayl → Makāyīl
Ḳayla, Banū i, 514a, 771a; v, 995a; vi, 477a – I, 529b, 794a; V, 990a; VI, 463a
Kaylif → Kālif
Kay-Luhrāsb → Kayānid(e)s
Kaylūkarī s, 243b – S, 243b
Kaymak → Kīmāk
Ḳaymāz, Ḳutb al-Dīn, amīr (1175) iii, 891b; vii, 707a, 726b – III, 915b; VII, 707b, 708a, 727a
Ḳaymaz Kāfūrī → Ṣārim al-Dīn
Ḳaymaz al-Zaynī, Mudjāhid al-Dīn (1198) viii, 127a – VIII, 130a
Ḳayn iv, **819a** – IV, **852a**
Ḳayn, Banu ʾl- i, 684b; iv, **819b** – I, 705b; IV, **852b**
Ḳayna i, 32b; ii, 551b, 1073b; iv, **820b**; vi, 468a; s, 247a – I, 33b; II, 565a, 1098a; IV, **853a**; VI, 453b; S, 247a
Ḳaynuḳāʿ, Banū i, 53a; iv, **824a**; v, 996a; vii, 367a, 370a, 561b – I, 55a; IV, **857a**; V, 991b; VII, 369b, 371b, 562a
Kayor, Kingdom of s, 179b – S, 180b
Kayra ii, 122a, b, 124b – II, 125a, b, 127b
al-Ḳayrawān i, 77b, 86b, 125a, 134b, 163b, 248a, 249a, 532b, 1175a; iii, 386a, 655a, 903b; iv, 479a, 532b, **824b**; v, 518a, 877b, 1159a; vi, 120b, 188b, 297b, 280b, 311b, 312a, 364a, 404b, 426b, 434b, 441a, 606a, 648b, 712b, 727a; viii, 843b; x, 790a; s, 26b, 62b, 103a, 144a, b, 145a, 172b, 274a, 303b, 306a, b, 394b – I, 79b, 89a, 128b, 138a, 168a, 255b, 257a, 548b, 1210a; III, 398b, 676a, 927b; IV, 501a, 555b, **857b**; V, 521b, 883b, 1149a; VI, 118b, 172b, 264a, 265b, 296b, 297a, 348a, 389a, 412a, 420a, 426b, 591a, 633b, 701a, 716a; VIII, 873a; X, ;S, 27a, 63a, 102b,

144a, b, 173b, 273b, 303b, 306a, 395a
—constructions i, 457b, 624a, 1346a; ii, 863a, iii, 287b; iv, 825b, 828b-831b – I, 472a, 645a, 1386b; II, 883a; III, 296a; IV, 858b, 861b-864a
—great mosque/la grande mosquée i, 248b, 619b, 621a, 950a; ii, 746a; iii, 271b; iv, 829b, 1165b; v, 220b – I, 256a, 639a, 641b, 979a; II, 764a; III, 279b; IV, 862b, 1198a; V, 218a
al-Ḳayrawānī → Ibn Abī Zayd
al-Ḳayrawānī, Abū Bakr Myḥammad b. al-Labbād (944) ix, 182a – IX, 188a
al-Ḳays → Ḳaws Ḳuzaḥ
al-Ḳays (island/île) → Kīsh
al-Ḳays, Djazīrat i, 942b – I, 971a, b
al-Ḳays, (ḳāḍī) (Fusṭāṭ) (643) vi, 671a – VI, 657b
al-Ḳays b. Abī Ḥāzim (703) vii, 576a – VII, 576b
al-Ḳays b. Abī Muslim al-Māṣir (VII) vii, 605b – VII, 605a
al-Ḳays b. ʿAmr al-Nadjāshī s, 10a – S, 9b
al-Ḳays b. ʿĀṣim iv, **832a** – IV, **865a**
al-Ḳays b. al-Haytham al-Sulamī i, 47b, 1001a; iv, 14b – I, 49a, 1031b; IV, 15b, 16a
al-Ḳays b. Hubayra b. ʿAbd Yaghūth (VII) vii, 592a – VII, 591b
Ḳays b. al-Ḥudādiyya ix, 864b – IX, 900b
al-Ḳays b. al-Ḥusayn iii, 223b – III, 230a
al-Ḳays b. al-Imām Aḥmad i, 1282a; s, 355b – I, 1321a; S, 355b
al-Ḳays b. al-Khaṭīm (620) iii, 941a; iv, **835b**; vi, 708a; vii, 65b – III, 965b; IV, **868b**; VI, 697a; VII, 66a
al-Ḳays b. Maʿdīkarib i, 689b, 696b; v, 119a – I, 7106, 718a; V, 122a
al-Ḳays b. al-Makshūḥ al-Murādī i, 110b, 728a; iv, 1134b – I, 113b, 750a; IV, 1166b
al-Ḳays b. Masʿūd al-Shaybānī i, 690a – I, 710b
al-Ḳays b. Muḥammad al-Ḥirāmī ii, 517b – II, 530b
al-Ḳays b. al-Mulawwaḥ (VII) viii, 78a – VIII, 80a
al-Ḳays b. al-Muntafiḳ vii, 582a – VII, 582b
al-Ḳays b. Saʿd i, 44a; iii, 241a, b, 242a – I, 45b; III, 248a, 249a
al-Ḳays b. Salāma b. al-Ḥārith i, 527a; iii, 1177b; v, 118b – I, 543a; III, 1206b; V, 121b
al-Ḳays b. Thaʿlaba, Banū i, 73a, 963b, 964a; x, 219a, 406b – I, 75b, 993b, 994a; X, 236b, 429a
al-Ḳays b. Yarwātiḳ (961) vii, 613a – VII, 612b
al-Ḳays b. Zuhayr b. Djadhīma al-ʿAbsī i, 115b; ii, 873a, 1023a; s, 177a, b, 178a – I, 119a; II, 893b, 1046b; S, 178a, b, 179a
al-Ḳays ʿAbd al-Rashīd i, 218b – I, 225a
Ḳays ʿAylān, Banū i, 76b, 329a, 529b 532a, 544b, 643a, 1241b; ii, 89a, 327b; iii, 1255a; iv, 314b, 493a, 494b, **833b**; vi, 221b, 265b, 266a, b, 303a, 333a, b, 334a, 345b, 544b, 545a, 546b, 620b, 622a; ix, 817a; x, 116a – I, 78b, 339b, 545b, 548a, 562a, 663b, 1279a; II, 91a, 337a; III, 1287b; IV, 328b, 514a, 515b, **866b**; VI, 215a, b, 250b, 251a, 288b, 317b, 318a, b, 329b, 529b, 531a, 605b, 607a; IX, 852a; X, 125b
Ḳaysaba b. Kulthūm s, 37b – S, 37b
Kaysān b. al-Muʿarraf al-Hudjaymī, Abū Sulaymān (VII) iii, 820b – III, 844b
Kaysān Abū ʿAmra (VII) iv, **836a**, b; vii, 523a; ix, 422a – IV, **869a**, b; VII, 523b; IX, 433a
Kaysāniyya i, 850b; ii, 1094b; iii, 1265b; iv, **836b**, 1086b; v, 350a, 433b, 552a, 1235b; s, 357b – I, 874a; II, 1120a; III, 1298b; IV, **869a**, 1117b; V, 350b, 435b, 557a, 1226a; S, 357b
Ḳayṣar iv, **839a** – IV, **871b**
Ḳayṣar, Banū i, 928a – I, 95a
Ḳayṣar Shāh b. Zamān i, 230b – I, 238a
al-Kaysarānī, Abu 'l-Faḍl b. Ṭāhir i, 100a; v, 330a – I, 103a; V, 330a
al-Ḳaysarī, Dāwūd b. Maḥmūd (1350) x, 322a; s, 364a, b – X, 346b; S, 364a
Ḳaysāriyya iv, **840a** – IV, **873a**
Ḳayṣariyya (Caesarea) iii, 475b; iv, **841a**; vi, 322a – III, 492a; IV, **874a**; VI, 306b
Ḳayṣariyya (Kayseri) iv, 623b, **842b**; v, 1145a, b; vi, 230b, 322a, 505b; s, 146a, 274a – IV, 648b, **876a**; V, 1137a, b; VI, 224b, 306b, 491a; S, 146a, 273b
Ḳaysar-nāma s, 41a – S, 41b
Kayseri → Ḳayṣariyya
al-Ḳaysī, Abū ʿAbd Allāh Muḥammad b. Djaʿfar (1172) x, 346a – X, 371b
Ḳaysī, Banū ii, 635a; iii, 42b; x, 843a; s, 82a – II, 651a; III, 44a; X, ; S, 81b
Kaysūm (Diyār Muḍar) vi, 334a, 336b, 506b, 507a – VI, 318b, 320b, 492a, b
Ḳaysūn i, 1190b – I, 1225b
Ḳayt al-Radjabī iv, 552a – IV, 576a
Ḳaytaḳ (Kaytagh) ii, 86b, 89a, 141b; iv, 345b, 350b, **846a**, 1176b – II, 88a, 90b, 145a; IV, 360a, 365b, **879b**, 1210a
Ḳaytās Bey i, 56a, 395a – I, 58a, 406b
Ḳāytbāy → Ḳāʾitbāy
Kayūmarth → Gayōmard), Shams al-Dīn
Kayūmarth b. Bīstutūn iv, 808a – IV, 840b
Kayūs b. Ḳubād i, 1110a – I, 1143b
Kayūsiyya (Bāwand) i, 1110a; viii, 383a – I, 1143b; VIII, 396a
al-Kayyāl, Aḥmad iv, **847a** – IV, **880a**
Ḳayyān iv, 822b – IV, 855b
Kayyarā s, 101b – S, 101a
Ḳayyim iv, **847b** – IV, **880b**
Ḳayyūm Nāṣirī (1902) iv, **848a** – IV, **881a**
Kāz → Ḳabḳ
Kaza → Ḳaḍāʾ
Kaza → Khāsa
Ḳazaghān iv, 32a – IV, 34b
Ḳazaḳ i, 120b, 135b, 268a, 418b, 481a, 722a, 1076b, 1077a, 1252a, 1287a; ii, 25a, 44b, 446a, 613a, 995b, 1066b; iii, 116b, 531b; iv, 40a, 178b-179a, 512b, 611a, **848a**; v, 134b, 135a; vi, 415a, 416b, 457a, 768b; vii, 353a; s, 169a – I, 124a, 139a, 276a, 430a, 495a, 743b, 1108b, 1109a, 1290a, 1326b; II, 25b, 45b, 458a, 628a, 1018a, 1091a; III, 119a, 550a; IV, 42b, 185b-186a, 534b, 635b, **881b**; V, 137b; VI, 400a, 401b, 442b, 757b; VII, 355b; S, 169a
Ḳazaḳ literature x, **729a** – X, **775a**
Kazākhstān ii, 44b; v, 135b; vi, 417a, 768b; x, 677b, 680b – II, 45b; V, 138a; VI, 402a, 758a; X,
Kazalinsk s, 244b – S, 244b
Ḳāzān i, 1075b, 1108a, 1308a; ii, 44b, 179a, 1113a; iv, 280b, 723b, **849a**; s, 82a, b, 96b – I, 1108a, 1141a, 1348a; II, 45a, 184b, 1139a; IV, 293a, 752b, **882a**; S, 82a, 96a
Ḳazan Khān (Čaghatay) (1347) ii, 4a; vii, 925a, 933b – II, 4a; VII, 925b, 934b
Kāzarān s, 73a – S, 73b
Kāzarūn (Kāzirūn) i, 240a; iv, **850b**; vi, 494a – I, 247b; IV, **883b**; VI, 480a
al-Kāzarūni, ʿAbd Allāh (Diyār Bakr) (XI) vi, 930b – VI, 922b
al-Kazarūnī, Shaykh Abū Isḥāḳ (1033) i, 147a, 162b, 1129a, 1245b; iv, **851a**; v, 1112a – I, 151a, 167a, 1163a, 1283b; IV, **884b**; V, 1108b

Kazarūniyya iv, 46b, 851a – IV, 49a, 884a, b
Ḳāzbēgī → Sikka
Kazbek → Ḳabḳ
al-Ḳāzdughlī, Ibrāhīm Kahyā (Miṣr) (1754) iv, 852a, b; vii, 179a – IV, 885a, b; VII, 181a
al-Ḳāzdughlī, Muṣṭafā iv, 852a – IV, 885a
Ḳāzdughliyya ii, 233b; iv, **852a**; vi, 325b; vii, 420a – II, 240b; IV, **885a**; VI, 309b; VII, 422a
Kāzh → Kāth
Kazi-asker → Ḳāḍī ʿAskar
Ḳāzī-Ḳūmuḳ → Lak
Kazi Mulla → Ghāzī Muḥammad
al-Kāẓim → Mūsā al-Kāẓim
Kāzim, Bā i, 767a – I, 790a
Kāzim Bey, Mīrzā s, 76a – S, 76a
Kāzim Ḳadrī, Ḥusayn (934) iv, **853a** – IV, **886b**
Kāzim Karabekir Pasha (1948) i, 641b; ii, 6b; iv, 671a, **853b** – I, 662a; II, 6b; IV, 698b, **887a**
Kāzim Rashtī, Sayyid (1843) iv, 51a, **854a**; vii, 422a, 440b, 454b – IV, 54a, **887b**; VII, 424a, 442a, 455a
al-Kāẓimayn (al-Kāẓimiyya) i, 903b; iv, **854b**; vi, 551a, 797a; vii, 397a, 485a; s, 57a, 77a, 94a, 95a – I, 931a; IV, **887b**; VI, 536a, 787a; VII, 398a, 485a; S, 57b, 76b, 93b, 94a
Kāẓimī → Sikka
al-Kāẓimī, ʿAbd al-Muḥsin (1935) iv, **856a** – IV, **889a**
al-Kāẓimī, ʿAbd al-Nabī b. ʿAlī (1840) iv, **856b** – IV, **889b**
al-Kāẓimī, Ḥaydar b. Ibrāhīm (1849) iv, **856b** – IV, **890a**
al-Kāẓimī, Meḥmed Sālim (1914) iv, **857a** – IV, **890a**
al-Kāẓimī, Murtaḍā Mushfiḳ iv, 72b; v, 198b – IV, 76b; V, 196a
Kāzimiyya → Kāzimayn
Kazimov → Ḳāsimov
Kazirūn → Kāzarūn
Ḳazwīn i, 8b, 688b; iv, 7b, **857b**; v, 875b; vi, 56b, 64a, 271a, b, 333a, 365a, 366a, 494a, 511b, 512b, 515a, b, 516a, 525b, 715a; viii, 115b, 389a; s, 43b, 83b, 84a, 139a, 336a, 423a – I, 8b, 709b; IV, 8b, **890b**; V, 881b; VI, 54b, 62a, 256a, 317b, 349a, 350a, 480a, 497a, 500a, b, 501b, 510a, 703b; VIII, 118a, 402b; S, 44a, 83b, 138b, 335b, 423b
—monuments iv, 862b – IV, 895b
al-Ḳazwīnī, ʿAbd al-Djalīl s, 56b – S, 57a
al-Ḳazwīnī, Abū Ḥātim Maḥmūd (XI) iv, **863a** – IV, **896a**
al-Ḳazwīnī, Djalāl al-Dīn Zakariyyāʾ (XV) vii, 988a – VII, 988b
al-Ḳazwīnī, Ḥamd Allāh → Ḥamd Allāh Mustawfī
al-Ḳazwīnī, Khalīl (1677) viii, 779a – VIII, 805b
al-Ḳazwīnī, Khaṭīb Dimashḳī (1338) i, 858a, 982b, 1116a; ii, 824a; iv, **863b**; v, 898a, b, 900b; vii, 277b, 388a, 537a; viii, 894a – I, 882a, 1013a, 1149b; II, 843a; IV, **896b**; V, 904a, b, 907a; VII, 279a, 389a, 537a; VIII, 925a
al-Ḳazwīnī, Nadjm al-Dīn ʿAbd al-Ghaffār (1266) iv, 509b, **864b** – IV, 532a, **898a**
al-Ḳazwīnī, Sayyid Mahdī s, 135a – S, 134b
al-Ḳazwīnī, Shāh Ṭāhir b. Shāh Raḍī al-Dīn (1549) vii, 300a; viii, 389a – VII, 302a; VIII, 402b
al-Ḳazwīnī, Zakariyyāʾ b. Muḥammad (1283) i, 157a, 204a, 419b, 571a, 594b, 836a; ii, 587b; iii, 30a, 313a, 991b; iv, **865a**, 1081b; vi, 185b, 218b, 374b, 501b, 904a; s, 128b – I, 161a, 209b, 431a, 589b, 613b, 859a; II, 602a; III, 31b, 322b, 1016a; IV, **898a**, 1112b; VI, 167b, 203a, 359a, 487a, 895a; S, 128a
al-Ḳazzāz, Abū ʿAbd Allāh Muḥammad b. ʿUbāda (1021) iv, **867a**; vii, 483b, 811b – IV, **900b**; VII, 483b, 813b
al-Ḳazzāz → Ḥakam b. Saʿīd
al-Ḳazzāz, Muḥammad b. ʿUbāda iii, 855b – III, 879b
al-Ḳbāb (Fès) vi, 123b – VI, 121b
Kebbawa ii, 1144b, 1146a – II, 1172a, 1173a
Kebbi (Nigeria) viii, 20a,b – VIII, 20a,b
Kebek Khān (Čaghatay) (1326) ii, 4a, 14b, 45a; iv, 419a, 671b, 921b; v, 858b; vii, 925a – II, 4a, 15a, 46a; IV, 437a, 699a, 954b; V, 865b; VII, 925b
Kebra Nagast i, 1220a – I, 1256b
Kēč → Kīdj (Kīz)
Kēč Makrān → Makrān
Keče → Libās
Kečedjīzāde → Fuʾād Pasha; ʿIzzet Mollā
Kechla i, 689a – I, 710a
Kēčī i, 1007a – I, 1038a
Kečiboynuzu Ibrāhīm Ḥilmī Pasha (1825) iv, 569b, **867b** – IV, 592a, **901a**
Kedah iii, 1218a, 1219b; iv, 467b; vi, 232b, 234a, 236b – III, 1249a, 1250b; IV, 488b; VI, 206a, 207a, 209a
Kediri s, 202a – S, 201b
Kědjuruns i, 740a – I, 762a
Kef, le → al-Kāf
Kefalia Shahīn → Shahīn Pasha
Kefe iii, 44a; iv, 576a, **868a**; v, 141a – III, 46a; IV, 599a, **901a**; V, 144a
Kel Ḥasan iv, 806b – IV, 839a
Kelantan vi, 232b, 236a, b, 241a – VI, 206a, 209a, 212a
Kelāt → Kalāt
Keldibek iii, 117a – III, 119b
Kelek iv, **870a** – IV, **903b**
Kelesh-beg (Prince/le prince) i, 101a – I, 104a
Kelek i, 424a, 476a – I, 436a, 490a
Kēlvē-Māhīm → Māhīm
Kemākh iv, **870b** – IV, **904a**
Kemāl, ʿAlī (1922) iv, **871b** – IV, **905a**
Kemāl, Meḥmed Nāmıḳ (1888) i, 61b, 62a, 74b, 630b; ii, 430b, 473b, 474a, 682a, 692b, 878a, 1047a; iii, 592a; iv, **875a**; v, 1172b; vi, 68b, 69a, 92b, 372b, 373a, 610a; vii, 599b; ix, 240b, 443b; s, 98a, 324b – I, 63b, 64a, 77a, 651a; II, 441b, 485b, 486a, 699a, 709b, 898b, 1071b; III, 612b; IV, **908b**; V, 1162b; VI, 66b, 90b, 357a, b, 595a; VII, 599a; IX, 247a, 461a; S, 97b, 324a
Kemāl al-Dīn → Kamāl al-Dīn
Kemāl Pasha-zāde (1534) i, 89a, 698a, 1208a; ii, 552b, 997b, 1137a; iii, 164a, 596b, 708b; iv, 333b, **879b**; vi, 227a, 609b, 724b; vii, 225a; viii, 44a; ix, 401b – I, 91b, 719b, 1244a; II, 566b, 1020b, 1163b; III, 167b, 617a, 730b; IV, 348a, **912a**; VI, 220b, 594b, 713b; VII, 227a; VIII, 45a; IX, 414b
Kemāl Reʾīs (1511) ii, 588a; iv, **881b**; v, 506b – II, 602b; IV, **914b**; V, 509b
Kemāl Tahir (Demir) (1973) iv, **882a**; v, 197a – IV, **915a**; V, 194a
Kemāl of/de Eğridir, Ḥādjdjī s, 50b – S, 51a
Kemāliye → Eğin
Kemānkesh ʿAlī Pasha (1624) iv, **884a**; vii, 597b, 707b – IV, **917a**; VII, 597b, 708b
Kemānkesh Ḳara Muṣṭafā Pasha (1643) ii, 804b; iii, 623a, 626b, 983a, 1001b; iv, 455b; v, 249a, vi, 1001a – II, 823b; III, 644a, 647a, 1007b, 1026b; IV, 476a; V, 246b; VI, 993b

Kemkhā iii, 216b – III, 223a
Ḳenā → Ḳunā
Kenʿān Pasha (1659) iv, **884b**; v, 258a – IV, **917a**; V, 256a
Keneges, Banū vi, 419a – VI, 404a
Kenèh → Ḳunā
Kenesarî Khān v, 135b – V, 138a
Kenya i, 38a; iv, **885a**; vi, 283a; s, 248a, b – I, 39a; IV, **918a**; VI, 268a; S, 248a, b
Kenz → Kanz, Banu 'l-
Kerala → Malabar
Kerala Muslim League vi, 460b – VI, 446a
al-Kerak → Karak
Kerasūn → Giresün
Kerbānsarāyî iv, 228a – IV, 238a
Kerbela → Karbalāʾ
Kerbenesh iv, **891b** – IV, **924a**
Kerboka i, 485a – I, 499b
Kerbughā → Karbughā
Kerč iv, **891b**; v, 141a – IV, **924a**; V, 143b
Keren i, 1163a; vi, 643a – I, 1197b; VI, 628a
Kerey → Giray
Kereyt, Kereit ii, 42a, b, 1112b – II, 42b, 43a, 1138b
Kerimba (islands/îles) iv, **892a** – IV, **925a**
Kerkenna → Ḳarḳana
Kerkha → Karkha
Kerkuk → Kirkūk
Kerkur → Karkūr
Kermān → Kirmān
Kermān Shāh → Kirmān Shāh
Kermiyān → Germiyān
Ḳerrī iv, **892b** – IV, **925b**
Kertch → Kerč
Kesh → Kash
Keshan vi, 290b – VI, 276a
Keskes → Kuskusu
Kesr-i mīzān ii, 83a – II, 85a
Kesriye (Kastoriá) iv, **893a** – IV, **926a**
Kesriyeli Aḥmed Pasha (1746) vi, 56b – VI, 54b
Kestelī, Kestellī → Ḳasṭallanī, Muṣṭafa
Ketāma → Kutāma
Ketapang s, 150b – S, 150b
Kētehr → Katahr
Ketendji ʿÖmer Pasha-zade Meḥmed iii, 318a – III, 327b
Ketkhudā ii, 1121a; iii, 1180a; iv, 8b, 476a, **893b** – II, 1147a; III, 1209a; IV, 9a, 497a, **926b**
Ketkhudā Ḥasan Pasha → Kahyā Ḥasan Pasha
Ketkhudā-zāde Süleymān (XIX) vi, 73b – VI, 71b
Kfar ʿAḳāb vi, 303a, 305a – VI, 288b, 290b
Khāʾ iv, **894b** – IV, **927b**
Khabar (information) iii, 369a; iv, **895a**; v, 1103a – III, 381a; IV, **928b**; V, 1099a
Khabar (grammar/grammaire) iv, **895b** – IV, **928a**
Khabar al-wāḥid iv, **896a** – IV, **928b**
Khabbāb b. al-Aratt (VII) iv, **896b** – IV, **929a**
Khabbāz v, 41b, 42a – V, 42b, 43a
Khabīr al-Mulk, Ḥasan Khān s, 53b – S, 54a
Khabīr al-Mulk, Rūḥī Khān s, 53b – S, 54a
al-Khabīth, ʿAlī Muḥammad v, 451b – V, 454a
Khabn → ʿArūḍ
Khabrāʾ iv, **879b** – IV, **930a**
Khābūr (rivers/rivières) i, 608a; iv, 655a, **897b**; vi, 378a, 379a, 539b, 733a – I, 628a; IV, 681b, **930b**; VI, 362a, 363b, 524a, 722b
Khābūr al-Ḥasaniya iv, 898a; s, 37a – IV, 931a; S, 37a
Khabūshān → Ḳūčān
al-Khabūshānī i, 197a – I, 203a
Khadāʿī (singer/chanteuse) (IX) vii, 413a – VII, 414b
al-Khaddām, ʿAbd Allāh b. Muḥammad iv, 515b – IV, 538a
Khaḍḍār i, 961a – I, 990b
Khaddāsh → Khidāsh
Khader, U.A. vi, 464b – VI, 450a
Khadīdja (Ibn Khaldūn) vi, 422a – VI, 407a
Khadīdja bint Khuwaylid (619) ii, 363b, 845b; iii, 152b; iv, **898b**; vi, 145b, 146a, 152b, 168b, 469a, 476b, 629a, 650b – II, 373a, 865b; III, 156a; IV, **931a**; VI, 144a, b, 151a, 159b, 455a, 462b, 614a, 636a
Khadīdja bint Ṭahmāsp vi, 483a – VI, 469b
Khadīdja bint al-Ḥasan s, 95a – S, 94b
Khadīdja Begum iv, 391a – IV, 407b
Khadīdje bint Aḥmed III (Ottoman) (1724) vi, 860b – VI, 851b
Khadīdje Sulṭān (1524) vi, 864b – VI, 855b
Khadīdje Sulṭān bint ʿAbd al-Ḥamīd I (Ottoman) (1775) vi, 859b – VI, 851a
Khadīdje Sulṭān bint Meḥemmed IV i, 96b; ii, 684b; iii, 216a, 252b – I, 99b; II, 701b; III, 222a, 259b
Khadīdje Sulṭān Turkhān iii, 998a, b; iv, 1100a – III, 1023a, b; IV, 1131a
Khadija Masroor (XX) vi, 489b – VI, 475b
Khādim i, 33a; iv, **899a**, 1087a – I, 34a; IV, **931b**, 1118a
Khādim al-Ḥaramayn iv, **899b**, 946a – IV, **932b**, 978b
Khādim Ḥasan Pasha Ṣoḳollî (1598) iv, **900b**, 1093a – IV, **933b**, 1124a
Khādim Pasha → ʿAlī Pasha; Sinān Pasha; Sulaymān Pasha
Khādim Süleymān Pasha (1547) iv, 435b, **901a**, 1093a; v, 35a, 534b, 1022b; vii, 779b; viii, 235a – IV, 455a, **934a**, 1124a; V, 36b, 539a, 1018a; VII, 781b; VIII, 240b
al-Khaḍir (al-Khiḍr) i, 117a, 347a, 1284a; ii, 1026a; iii, 1156a; iv, 674b, 810b, **902b**; v, 17b, 800b; vi, 123b – I, 120a, 357b, 1323b; II, 1049b; III, 1184b; IV, 702a, 843a, **935a**; V, 18a, 806b; VI, 121b
al-Khāḍir, Banū i, 546a; iv, **905b** – I, 563a; IV, **938b**
al-Khāḍir, Djazīrat iv, **906a** – IV, **939a**
al-Khaḍir Ghaylān (Tandja) (XVII) x, 184a – X, 198b
al-Khāḍir, Muḥammad b. al-Ḥusayn (1958) iv, **906a** – IV, **939a**
al-Khāḍir (Khiḍr) b. ʿAlī s, 263b – S, 263a
al-Khāḍir al-Mihrānī, Shaykh (Miṣr) (XIII) vii, 169b – VII, 171a
Khaḍiriyya i, 277b – I, 286a
Kh^{w}ādja (title/titre) iv, **907a**; v, 26a – IV, **940a**; V, 27a
Kh^{w}ādja ʿAbd al-Ṣamad (XVI) vii, 317a, 337b, 338a – VII, 319a, 339a, b
Kh^{w}ādja Aḥrar → ʿUbayd Allāh Aḥrar
Kh^{w}ādja ʿAlī (Sarbandārid(e)) (1386) ix, 48b – IX, 49b
Kh^{w}ādja ʿAlī b. Ṣadr al-Dīn (1429) ii, 350b; viii, 756a, 766a – II, 360a; VIII, 778a, 791b
Kh^{w}ādja Bāḳī bi-'llāh → Bāḳī bi-'llāh
Kh^{w}ādja Bāyazīd b. Bahlūl Lōdī (XV) vi, 62a – VI, 60a
Kh^{w}ādjā Djahān Sarwār (Sharḳī) x, 593a – X, 637b
Kh^{w}ādja Faḍl Allāh Abu 'l-Laythī (1460) vii, 90a – VII, 92a
Kh^{w}ādjā Ghulām Farīd iv, 302b – IV, 529b
Kh^{w}ādja Ghulām Turk (1463) iv, **908a**; vi, 66b, 67a – IV, **941a**; VI, 64b, 65a
Kh^{w}ādja Ḥusayn → Thanāʾī
Kh^{w}ādja Muḥammad b, Maḥmūd al-Hāfuẓī (1419) viii, 272b – VIII, 280a
Kh^{w}ādjagān (order/ordre) iv, 47b; vi, 72b; x, 256b – IV, 50b; VI, 70b; X, 269a
Kh^{w}ādjaganlîk i, 433a; iv, 908b – I, 445b; IV, 941b, 942a
Kh^{w}ādjagī, Kāʾānī Dakhbīdī, Mawlānā (1542) x, 250b; s, 122a – X, 269a; S, 121b

Khʷādja-i Djahān Aḥmad Ayāz (1351) i, 1036b, 1166a; ii, 814a; iii, 570a; iv, **907b** – I, 1068a, 1200b; II, 833b; III, 589b; IV, **940b**
Khʷādja-i Djahān Astarābādī (XV) iv, **908a** – IV, **941a**
Khʷādja-i Djahān Aʿẓam-i Humāyūn iv, **908a** – IV, **941a**
Khʷādja-i Djahān Dakhnī (XV) iv, **908a** – IV, **941a**
Khʷādja-i Djahān Malik Sarwar iv, **907b** – IV, **940b**
Khʷādja-i Djahān Nūr al-Dīn iv, **907b** – IV, **941a**
Khʷādja-i Djahān Surūr (XIV) iv, **907b** – IV, **941a**
Khʷādja-i Djahān Turk vi, 66b, 67a – VI, 64b, 65a
Khʷādja Kamāl al-Dīn (1932) i, 302b – I, 312a
Khʷādja Khiḍr iv, 905a, **908a** – IV, 938a, **941a**
Khʷādja Mīr Dard → Dard
Khʷādja Muʿīn al-Dīn Ḥasan Sidjzī → Čishtī
Khʷādja Muḥammad Islam Djūybārī (1563) x, 250b – X, 269a
Khʷādja Muʿīn al-Dīn Ḥasan Sidjzī (1236) x, 255b – X, 274b
Khʷādja Niyāz Ḥadjdjī ix, 649b – IX, 674b
Khʷādja Shams al-Dīn v, 827a – V, 833a
Khʷādjayev, Fayḍ Allāh (1937) x, 961a – X,
Khʷādja-zāde → Khōdja-zāde
Khʷādjegān-i Dīwān-i Hümāyūn iv, **908b**; vi, 340b; x, 250b – IV, **941b**; VI, 324b; X, 269a
Khadjkhadj (943) vi, 921a – VI, 913a
Khʷādjū Kamāl al-Dīn Kirmānī (1361) i, 1301a; iv, 66a, b, **909b**, 1010a; vi, 608b; vii, 662a, 754b, 821b; viii, 885a – I, 1340b; IV, 70a, **942b**, 1042a; VI, 593a; VII, 661b, 756a, 823a; VIII, 915b
Khadjuri Kač vi, 86a – VI, 84a
al-Khaḍrāʾ (palace) vii, 268b – VII, 270b
Kh(ʷ)āf iv, **910a**, 1073a; s, 57b, 420b – IV, **943a**, 1105a; S, 58a, 421a
Khafādja, Banū i, 528b; iv, **910b**; v, 348b; vii, 118a; s, 119a – I, 544b; IV, **943b**; V, 349a; VII, 120b; S, 118b
Khafādja b. Sufyān b. Sawādan (IX) ix, 670a – IX, 696a
al-Khafādjī (1073) ii, 824b; iv, 250a – II, 844a; IV, 261a
al-Khafādjī, Abū ʿAlī b. Thimāl (1008) viii, 394a – VIII, 407b
al-Khafādjī, Shihāb al-Dīn al-Miṣrī (1659) i, 68a, 594a, 1056a; iii, 222a; iv, **912a**; vii, 262a, 470a, 527b; viii, 736a – I, 70a, 613b, 1088a; III, 228b; IV, **945a**; VII, 264a, 469b, 528a; VIII, 757a
Khafāra ii, 143b; iii, 394a, 396b; iv, **913a** – II, 147a; III, 406b, 409a; IV, **945b**
Khafḍ (Khifāḍ) iv, **913a**; vi, 469b, 475b – IV, **946a**; VI, 455b, 461b
al-Khʷāfī, Abū Manṣūr ʿAbdallāh iv, 910a – IV, 943a
al-Khʷāfī, Faṣīḥ al-Dīn Aḥmad iv, 910b – IV, 943a
al-Khʷāfī, Niẓām al-Dīn ʿAbd al-Raḥīm v, 872b, 873b – V, 878b, 879b
al-Khʷāfī Khān (1732) i, 769b; iv, **914a** – I, 792b; IV, **947a**
Khafīf → ʿArūḍ
Khafiyye i, 64a – I, 66a
Khafr vi, 384a – VI, 368b
Khaibar → Khaybar
Khʷāharzāde, Badr al-Dīn (1253) vii, 969a – VII, 969b
Khāʾin Aḥmad → Aḥmad Pasha
Khāʾir Bey (1522) ii, 1042a; iv, 451a, 553a; vi, 325a, 327a; vii, 176b, 177a – II, 1066b; IV, 471a, 577a; VI, 309b, 311b; VII, 178b, 179a
Khāḳān (title/titre) iii, 335b; iv, 343b, **915a**, 1010b, 1174a, 1176b, 1177a; vi, 809b; viii, 621b; x, 688a – III, 345b; IV, 358a, **948a**, 1042b, 1207a, 1209b, 1210b; VI, 799b: VIII, 641a; X, 730a
Khāḳān → Fatḥ ʿAlī Shāh
Khāḳān, Ḳāḍī Nūr Allāh (XVII) vii, 988a – VII, 989a
Khāḳān, Muḥammad b. ʿUbayd Allāh (vizier) (X) vii, 397a, 653a – VII, 398b, 652b
Khāḳān, Mūsā b. ʿUbayd Allāh vi, 230a – VI, 224a
Khāḳān Meḥmed Bey (1606) iv, **916a**; s, 83a – IV, **949a**; S, 83a
Khāḳānī, Afḍal al-Dīn Ibrāhīm Shīrwānī (1199) i, 677a, 680a; iv, 62a, 63b, 348b, **915a**; v, 619b; vi, 608b, 1016b; s, 108a, 239b, 333b – I, 698a, 701a; IV, 65b, 66b, 363a, b, **948a**; V, 623b; VI, 593b, 1009b; S, 107a, 240a, 333a
Khāḳānid(e)s ’ Shirwān Shāh
Khāḳānīyān → Ilek-Khāns
Khakhay, Banū vii, 220a – VII, 221b
Khākhiṭ (Kakheti, Georgia/-e) viii, 873b – VIII, 903a
Khāksār (India/l'Inde) iv, **916b** – IV, **949b**
Khaksār (Iran) iv, 52a – IV, 54b
Khāl, akhwāl iv, **916b** – IV, **949b**
Khāl, Khayalān → Firāsa
Khalʿa → Khilʿa
Khalā iv, 272b, 273a – IV, 284b, 285a
Khaladj, Banū i, 99b, 217b; ii 1001a; iii, 1106b, 1108b; iv, 705b, **917a**; v, 369b; ix, 86a – I, 102a, 224a; II, 1024b; III, 1134a, 1136a; IV, 734a, **950a**; V, 370a; IX, 90a
Khaladjistān iv, 918a – IV, 951a
Khalaf, Banū ’l- ii, 463b – II, 475a
Khalaf b. ʿAbd al-Malik → Ibn Bashkuwāl
Khalaf b. Aḥmad (Sidjistān) (1008) i, 160a; ii, 1082a; iii, 471a, 502a; vi, 109a – I, 164b; II, 1107a; III, 487b, 519b; VI, 107a
Khalaf b. Ḥayyān al-Aḥmar, Abū Muḥriz (796) i, 105b, 115b, 143b, 718b, 1081a; ii, 248b; iii, 136a; iv, **919a** – I, 108b, 119a, 147b, 740a, 1113b; II, 255b; III, 139a; IV, **952a**
Khalaf b. Hishām iii, 155b – III, 158b
Khalaf b. Mubārak al-Ḳuṣayyir iii, 403b – III, 415b
Khalaf b. Mulāʿib al-Ashhabī (1106) i, 215a; iii, 398b; iv, **919a**; vii, 578a; viii, 922a – I, 221b; III, 411a; IV, **952a**; VII, 578b; VIII, 953b
Khalaf b. al-Samḥ (IX) i, 139a; ii, 441b; iii, 659b, 1040a; iv, 919b; v, 1230a; viii, 639a – I, 143a; II, 453a; III, 681a, 1066a; IV, 952b; V, 1220b; VIII, 658a
Khalaf al-Aḥmar (821) vi, 625b; viii, 545b; x, 3a – VI, 610b; VIII, 563b; X, 3a
Khalaf Allāh, Muḥammad Aḥmad i, 821a; ii, 452a; iv, 161b – I, 844a; II, 463b; IV, 168a
Khalafid(e)s viii, 797b – VIII, 824a
al-Khalafiyya iii, 659b, 1168a; iv, 47a, **919b**; viii, 639a – III, 681a, 1197a; IV, 49b, **952b**; VIII, 658a
Khalandj iv, 1085b; v, 107b – IV, 1116b; V, 110a
al-Khalandjī, ʿAbd Allāh b. Muḥammad b. Abī Yazīd (851) vii, 5a – VII, 5a
al-Khalaṣa iv, 263b – IV, 275b
Khaldī v, 448a – V, 450b
Khaldjī Samarkandī, ʿAbd al-Salām s, 121b – S, 121a

Khaldjīs (Mālwā) i, 393b; ii, 268a, 1084a; iii, 441b; iv, 268b, 818b, 918a, **920b**; v, 688b; vi, 52b-55a, 198b, 271a; vii, 193b; s, 124b, 280a, 352b, 353a, 409a – I, 405a; II, 276b, 1109b; III, 456a; IV, 280b, 851a, 951a, **953b**; V, 693b; VI, 50b-53a, 182b, 255b; VII, 194a; S, 123b, 280a, 352b, 409b
Khaldūn, Banū iv, 115b; s, 111b – IV, 120b; S, 111a
al-Khaldūniyya (alDjamʿiyya) iv, **924a** s IV,**957a**
Khalfūn, Amīr iv, 275a – IV, 287b
Khāliʿ Ḳasam i, 829a – I, 852a
Khālid, Banū i, 873b; ii, 77a, 108b; iii, 238a; iv, 765a, **925a**; v, 333a; vi, 334a, 336a; vii, 410a, 782b – I, 897b; II, 78b, 111a; III, 245a; IV, 795b, **958a**; V, 333a; VI, 318b, 320a; VII, 411b, 784b
Khālid b. ʿAbd Allāh b. Khālid b. Asīd (VII) vii, 650a – VII, 650a
Khālid b. ʿAbd Allāh al-Ḳasrī (743) i, 207a, 684b, 865b, 1094b, 1116b, 1242b; ii, 36a; iii, 42a, 493b, 650a, 715a, 747b, 802b, 1255a; iv, 913b, **925b**; v, 347a, 374a; vi, 441b, 665a, 666b, 667a, 669b; vii, 347b, 348a, 357a; s, 232b – I, 213a, 705b, 889b, 1127a, 1150b, 1280b; II, 36b; III, 43b, 510b, 671b, 737b, 770b, 826a, 1287b; IV, 946a, **958b**; V, 347b, 375a; VI, 427a, 651a, 652b, 653a, 655b; VII, 349b, 350a, 359b; S, 232b
Khālid b. ʿAbd al-ʿAzīz (Āl-Suʿūd) (1982) vi, 158a; ix, 915a – VI, 153b; IX, 942b
Khālid b. ʿAbd al-Malik al-Marwarrūdhī (831) vi, 600a – VI, 584b
Khālid b. ʿAbd al-Raḥmān al-Muhādjir (666) vi, 140a – VI, 138a
Khālid b. Abī Djaʿfar al-Barḳī s, 127b – S, 126b
ēālid b. Aḥmad al-Dhuhlī i, 1296b – I, 1336b
Khālid b. al-ʿĀsī b. Hishām (680) vi, 140a – VI, 138a
Khālid b. Asīd s, 267b, 386a – S, 267a, 386b
Khālid b. Barghash i, 1282b – I, 1321b
Khālid b. Barmak (767) i, **1033b**; vi, 745a, 941a – I, **1065a**; VI, 734a, 933a
Khālid b. Djaʿfar b. ʿĀmir ii, 1023a; iii, 812a – II, 1046b; III, 835b
Khālid b. Fayṣal b. ʿAbd al-ʿAzīz Āl Suʿūd s, 305b, 306a – S, 305b, 306a
Khālid b. Hamīd al-Zanātī v, 367a – V, 368a
Khālid b. Ibrāhīm, Abū Dāwūd v, 181b – V, 178b
Khālid b. Luʾayy (XX) vi, 152a, b, 153a, b – VI, 151a, b
Khālid b. Maʿdān al-Ṭāʾī iv, 446a; v, 19b – IV, 465b; V, 20a
Khālid b. Maʿdān b. Abī Kurayb al-Kalāʿī iv, 369a – IV, 385b
Khālid b. Manṣūr → Ibn Luʾayy
Khālid b. Muḥammad, Shaykh s, 418a – S, 418b
Khā;id b. Nazzār vi, 264b – VI, 249b
Khālid b. Ṣafwān b. al-Ahtam i, 1297b; iv, **927a**; v, 132a – I, 1337b; IV, **960a**; V, 135a
Khālid b. Saʿīd b. al-ʿĀṣ (635) iv, **927a**; vi, 546b; viii, 1051b – IV, **960a**; VI, 531a; VIII, 1087a
Khālid b. Shāhsuwār Bek i, 1157a – I, 1191b
Khālid b. Sinān al-ʿAbsī i, 509a; ii, 1024a; iii, 169a; iv, **928a**; vi, 381a – I, 524b; II, 1048a; III, 172b; IV, **961a**; VI, 365a
Khālid b. Suʿūd (Āl Suʿūd) (1841) ix, 904a – IX, 941b
Khālid b. al-Walīd b. al-Mughīra Makhzūmī (642) i, 110b, 111a, 145b, 208b, 484b, 549b, 788b, 964a, 1139a, 1215b, 1240b, 1343b, 1358b; ii, 279b, 366a, 625a, b, 1023b; iii, 85b, 223b, 397b, 578a, 739b, 1254b; iv, 13b, 289b, 407a, **928a**, 1106b; v, 458a; vi, 138a, b, 139a, 267b, 268a, 505b, 544b, 546b; vii, 356b, 370a, 372b, 549b, 756b; ix, 80a; x, 782b; s, 230b – I, 113b, 114a, 150a, 215a, 499a, 567a, 812a, 994a, 1173b, 1251b, 1278b, 1384a, 1398b; II, 288a, 376a, 640b, 641a, 1047a; III, 88a, 230a, 410a, 598b, 762a, 1287a; IV, 14a, b, 302a, 424b, **961a**, 1138a; V, 461a; VI, 136b, 137a, b, 252a, b, 491a, 529a, 531a; VII, 359a, 372a, 374a, 550a, 758a; IX, 83b; X, ; S, 230a
Khālid b. Yazīd (mukaddi) vii, 494a – VII, 494a
Khālid b. Yazīd b. Ḥātim iii, 694a – III, 716b
Khālid b. Yazīd b. Muʿāwiya (Umayyad(e)) (704) ii, 360b; iii, 271a, 398a; iv, **929a**; vi, 197b, 198a, 622a, b; vii, 268a; s, 270a – II, 370a; III, 278b, 410a; IV, **962a**; VI, 182a, b, 607a, b; VII, 270a; S, 269b
Khālid b. Yazīd b. Mazyad al-Shaybānī (IX) i, 154a; ii, 679a – I, 158a; II, 696a
Khālid b. Yazīd al-Kātib al-Tamīmī (883) iv, **929a** – IV, **962a**
Khākid al-ʿAbd (VIII) vii, 662b – VII, 662a
Khālid Baghdādī al-Kurdī, Mawlanā → Mawlānā Khālid Baghdādī al-Kurdī
Khālid al-Barmakī → al-Barāmika
Khālid Beklū i, 1157a – I, 1191b
Khālid Ḍiyā (Ziyā) (1945) i, 287b; iii, 260b; iv, **930a**; v, 194b, 195b – I, 296a; III, 267b; IV, **963a**; V, 191b, 192b
Khālid Fakhrī s, 168a – S, 168a
Khālid al-Ḳasrī → Khālid b. ʿAbd Allāh
Khālid Kurdī (XIX) vii, 939a – VII, 939b
Khālid al-Marwarrūdhī iv, 1182b – IV, 1215b
Khālid Muḥammad Khālid (XX) vi, 467a – VI, 453a
Khālid Muḥyī al-Dīn s, 6a – S, 5a
Khālid Pasha Ḳara ʿOthmān-oghlu iv, 593b – IV, 617b
Khālida (Djarīr) vi, 604b – VI, 589a
al-Khālidāt → al-Djazāʾir al-Khālida
Khālide Edīb (1964) iii, 622b; iv, **933a**; v, 194b, 196a; vi, 94a, 386a; s, 41b – III, 643a; IV, **966a**; V, 191b, 193b; VI, 92a, 370b; S, 42a
al-Khālidī (Muʿtazilī) vii, 312a – VII, 314b
al-Khālidī, Rūḥī (1913) iv, **936a** – IV, **969a**
al-Khālidiyyāni (X) iv, **936b**; vii, 935b, 936b – IV, **969b**; VII, 936a, 937a
al-Khalīdj vi, 587b, 667b – VI, 572a, 653b
Khalīdj Amīr al-Muʾminīn i, 932a; vii, 149a – I, 960b; VII, 151a
al-Khalīdj al-Banādiḳī i, 935b – I, 964a
Khālidj al-Ḥākimī → Khālidj Amīr al-Muʾminīn
Khalīdj al-Ḳusṭanṭīniyya i, 927a, 935b – I, 955a, 964a
Khalīdj al-Nāṣirī i, 1299b – I, 1339a
Khalīfa (caliph(e) iii, 344a; iv, **937a**, 1076b; v, 435a, b, 621a, 624a – III, 354b; IV, **970a**, 1108a; V, 437b, 625a, 628a
Khalīfa, Āl i, 233b, 540a, 554a, 942b; ii, 108b, 176b; iii, 23a; iv, 751a, **953a**; v, 508a, b, 573b; vi, 358a; vii, 464a; x, 956a – I, 241a, 556b, 572a, 917b; II, 111a, 181b; III, 24a; IV, 781a, **985b**; V, 511b, 512a, 578a; VI, 342a; VII, 463b; X,
Khalīfa, Shaykh (Māzandarān) (XIV) ix, 48a – IX, 48b
Khalīfa b. Abi ʾl-Maḥāsin (XIII) i, 388b; iv, **954a** – I, 399b; IV, **986b**
Khalīfa b. ʿAskar (XX) ii, 767b; iv, **954b** – II, 786a; IV, **986b**
Khalīfa b. Bahrām s, 309a – S, 309a
Khalīfa b. Khayyāṭ → Ibn Khayyāṭ al-ʿUṣfurī
Khalīfa b. Muḥammad iv, 953a – IV, 985b
Khalīfa b. Shakhbūṭ i, 166b – I, 171a
Khalīfa b. Warrū v, 1182b – V, 1172b
Khalīfa ʿAbd Allāh (1899) → ʿAbd Allāh b. Muḥammad al-Taʿāʿishī
Khalīfa al-Safṭī (1879) vi, 354b – VI, 339a

Khalīfa Shāh Muḥammad (XVIII) iv, **954b** – IV, **987a**
Khalīfa Sulṭān Ḥusayn b. Muḥammad b. Maḥmūd (Marʿashī) (1653) vi, 516b; viii, 780a – VI, 501b; VIII, 806a
Khalīfat al-Masīḥ i, 301b – I, 311a
Khālik Abū Anīs s, 74b – S, 75a
al-Khalīl → Ibrāhīm
al-Khalīl (Hebron) ii, 911b; iv, **954b**; vi, 654b, 662b, 675a – II, 933a; IV, **987a**; VI, 640a, 648b, 661b
Khalīl, Banū (Mārib) vi, 561b -VI, 546b
Khalīl, al-Malik al-Ashraf Ṣalāḥ al-Dīn (Mamlūk)(1293) i, 341b, 737b, 1127b, 1324b; ii, 912a, 966a; iii, 325a, 679b; iv, 485b, 964**b**; v, 595a – I, 351b, 759b, 1162a, 1365b; II, 933b, 988a; III, 335a, 701a; IV, 506b, **996b**; V, 598b
Khalīl b. Aḥmad (791) i, 11a, 106a, 587a, 588b, 668b, 669b, 670b, 674a, 675b; iii, 948b; iv, 412a, 524b, **962a**, 1187b; v, 711a, 806b; vi, 129b, 130a, 199a; vii, 262a, 560b, 569b; ix, 11a, 525b; s, 73b, 289b, 408b – I, 11b, 109a, 606a, 607b, 688b, 690a, 691a, 695a, 696a; III, 973a; IV, 429b, 547a, **994a**, 1220b; V, 716a, 812b; VI, 127b, 128b, 183b; VII, 263b, 561b, 570a; IX, 11b, 545b; S, 74a, 289a, 409a
Khalīl b. Alī Čandarli → Ḳara
Khalīl b. Badr b. Shudjāʿ v, 828a – V, 834b
Khalīl b. Isḥāḳ b. Ward (941) i, 163b; ii, 553a; iv, 459b, 979b; ix, 586a – I, 168a; II, 566b; IV, 479b, 480a, 1012a; IX, 607b
Khalīl b. Isḥāḳ, Ibn al-Djundī (1374) i, 1019b; iii, 781b; iv, **964a**; vi, 278b, 279a, 281b, 313b, 710a; vii, 387b, 538a, 1052b – I, 1051a; III, 805a; IV, **996a**; VI, 263b, 266b, 298b, 698b; VII, 389a, 537b, 1054b
Khalīl b. Ismāʿīl v, 801b – V, 807b
Khalīl b. Ḳalāwūn, al Malik al-Ashraf Ṣalāḥ al-Dīn (Mamlūk) (1293) vi, 195a, 322b, 507b; vii, 167b, 168b – VI, 179a, 307a, 493a; VII, 169a, 170a
Khalīl b. Ḳaradja ii, 239a – II, 246a
Khalīl b. Zayn al-Dīn Ḳaradja (Dhu 'l-Ḳadr) (XIV) vi, 507b – VI, 493a
Khalīl b. Uzun Ḥasan iv, 1048b – IV, 1080a
Khalīl Allāh (1884) → Shihāb al-Dīn al-Ḥusaynī
Khalīl Allāh, Shāh imām (1817) iv, 201b – IV, 210b
Khalīl Allāh b. Niʿmat Allāh Nūr al-Dīn (1456) viii, 45b, 46a, 48a – VIII, 46b, 49a
Khalīl Allāh b. Shāh Niʿmat Allāh Kirmānī → Khalīl Allāh But-Shikan
Khalīl Allāh But-Shikan b. Khalīl Allāh b. Shāh Niʿmat Allāh Kirmānī (1460) i, 1200b; iv, **965b**; vi, 63a – I, 1236b; IV, **998a**; VI, 61a
Khalīl Allāh Shīrvān-Shāh iv, 587b – IV, 611a
Khalīl Atā → Ḳazan Khān (Čaghatay)
Khalīl Bahādur iv, 621a – IV, 645b
Khalīl Beg (Ḳarāmān-oghlu) iv, 621b, 622a, b – IV, 646a, 647a
Khalīl Bey iv, 828a, b – IV, 861a
Khalīl Dede, Shaykh (XVIII) vii, 572b – VII, 573a
Khalīl Edhem → Eldem
Khalīl Efendi-zāde (1754) iv, **966a** – IV, **998b**
Khalīl Ghaffa i, 600a – I, 619b
Khalīl Ghānim (1903) ii, 471a; iii, 593a; iv, **966b** – II, 483a; III, 613b; IV, **998b**
Khalīl Gibran → Djabrān Khalīl Djabrān
Khalīl Ḥamīd Pasha i, 63a, 1064b; ii, 534a, 629b; iv, 211a – I, 65a, 1096b; II, 547a, 645b; IV, 220a
Khalīl Ḥilmī s, 98a – S, 97b
Khalīl al-Khūrī ii, 466a; x, 81b – II, 477b; X, 84b
Khalīl Mīrzā i, 1211b – I, 1247a
Khalīl Mīrzā (Tīmūrid(e)) → Khalīl Sulṭān
Khalīl Muṭrān (1949) iv, **966b**; vi, 414a; s, 34a – IV, **999a**; VI, 399a; S, 34b
Khalīl Naṣr (XX) vi, 797a – VI, 786b
Khalīl Nūrī Efendi iv, 544a – IV, 567b
Khalīl Pasha Djandarli (1453) ii, 445a, 721a; iv, **968b**; vi, 70a, 978a; viii, 194b – II, 456b, 739b; IV, **1000b**; VI, 68a, 970a; VIII, 197b
Khalīl Pasha Ḥādjdjī Arnawud (1733) iii, 1002a; iv, **969a** – III, 1027a; IV, **1001b**
Khalīl Pasha Ḳaiṣariyyeli (1629) i, 4a, 268a; iv, **970a**; vi, 999a; viii, 182a – I, 4a, 276a; IV, **1002a**; VI, 991b; VIII, 185a
Khalīl Pasha Kut → Enwer Pasha
Khalīl Ṣūfī → Niʿmat Allāh b. Aḥmad
Khalīl Sulṭān b. Mīrānshāh b. Tīmūr (Tīmūrid(e)) (1409) vii, 105b – VII, 107b
Khalīl Ṭūṭaḥ (XX) vi, 615b – VI, 600a
Khalīl Yakhshī Beg i, 309a; ii, 599b – I, 319a; II, 614b
Khalīl al-Ẓāhirī (XV) vi, 382a, 791a; vii, 286a – VI, 366a, 781a; VII, 288a
Khalīlī (1485) iv, **972b** – IV, **1004b**
al-Khalīlī, Imām Muḥammad b. ʿAbd Allāh (ʿUmān) (1954) viii, 993b; s, 356a – VIII, 1028b; S, 356a
Khalīlī, Shams al-Dīn (1365) v, 83b, 85a, 87a, b; vi, 543a – V, 85b, 87a, 89b, 90a; VI, 527b
Khāliṣ ii, 103a – II, 105b
Khāliṣa ii, 272b, 906b; iv, **972b**, 1035b; v, 688b; vi, 496a – II, 281a, 927b; IV, **1005a**, 1067b; V, 693b; VI, 481a
Khāliṣa (lady-in-waiting/dame de compagnie) s, 198b – S, 198b
al-Khāliṣa (citadel(le)) iv, **979b** – IV, **1012a**
Khāliṣī, Shaykh Mahdī s, 342a – S, 342a
Khalisioi v, 1015a, 1018b – V, 1011a, 1014a
Khalḳ iii, 663b, 664b; iv, **980a** – III, 685a, 686a, b; IV, **1012b**
Khalḳ Firḳasi i, 734b; ii, 432a, 595b – I, 756b; II, 443a, 610a
Khalḳevi iv, **988a**; v, 906b; vi, 95a – IV, **1020b**; V, 912b; VI, 93a
Khalkha (river/rivière) iv, **988b** – IV, **1021a**
Khalkhāl (Ādharbāydjān) iv, **989a**; vi, 494a – IV, **1021b**; VI, 480a
Khalkhālī, Muḥammad Ṣāliḥ s, 308b – S, 308b
Khallād b. ʿAmr b. al-Djamūḥ s, 230a – S, 230a
Khallād b. Khālid iii, 155b – III, 158b
Khallād b. al-Minḳarī (VIII) viii, 573a – VIII, 591b
al-Khallāl, Aḥmad b. Muḥammad Abū Bakr (923) i, 274a, b; ii, 1093a; iii, 158b; iv, **989b**; vi, 636a – I, 282b, 283a; II, 1118b; III, 162a; IV, **1022a**; VI, 621a
Khallukh → Ḳarluḳ
Khalwa iii, 1011a; iv, 381b, 383a, **990a**, 992b; v, 23a, 1201a, b – III, 1036b; IV, 398a, b, 399b, **1022b**, 1025a; V, 23b, 1191a, 1192a
Khalwatiyya i, 95a, 965b, 1137a; ii, 164b, 203b, 224a, 542b, 1137b; iv, 721b, **991a**; vi, 627a; viii, 19a; ix, 299a; x, 247b, 252a; s, 40b, 44a, 208a – I, 97b, 995b, 1171b; II, 169b, 209b, 231a, 556a, 1164b; IV, 750b, **1023b**; VI, 612a; VIII, 19a; IX, 307b; X, 266b, 270b; S, 41a, 44b, 207b
Khamāsa → Muzāraʿa
Khambāyat (Cambay) iii, 444b; iv, **993b**; vi, 233b, 283a, 369a, 694a; vii, 49a; s, 358b – III, 459b; IV, **1026a**; VI, 206b, 268a, 353a, 682a; VII, 49b; S, 358a
Khambhāt → Khambāyat
Khameneʾī vii, 300a – VII, 302a
Khamīs (Thursday/Jeudi) iv, 994a, 1009a – IV, 1026b, 1041b
Khamis b. Abdallah (Uganda) x, 779a – X,

Khamīs Mushayṭ iv, **994a**; vi, 158a – IV, **1026b**; VI, 153b
Khamlīdj ix, 620a – IX, 643b
Khamr ii, 1058b, 1059b, 1062a, 1069a; iii, 78b, 400b; iv, 135b, **994b** – II, 1083b, 1084b, 1086b, 1094a; III, 81a, 413a; IV, 141a, **1027a**
Khamrīyya i, 584b; iv, **998a** – I, 603b; IV, **1030b**
Khamsa (No. 5) i, 786a; iv, **1009a** – I, 809b; IV, **1041b**
Khamsa (poem/-e) iv, **1009b**; v, 1104a – IV, **1041b**; V, 1100a
Khamsa, Khamseh, Banū iii, 1106a, 1110a; iv, 9b; s, 146a, 147b – III, 1133b, 1137a; IV, 10a; S, 145b, 147b
Khamse → Wilāyāt-i Khamse
Khāmūsh Ḳîzîl Arslan b. Özbek (Ildeñizid(e)) (1191) i, 301a; iii, 1112a; vi, 501a; x, 554b – I, 310a; III, 1139b; VI, 486a; X,
Khān (title/titre) iii, 1113b; iv, **1010b**; v, 629b – III, 1140b; IV, **1042b**; V, 633b
Khān (staging-post/gîte d'étape) iv, 228a, b, 236a, 435a, 677b, **1010b**; v, 1124b – IV, 238a, b, 246b, 454b, 705a, **1043a**; V, 1121a
Khān Abdul Wali Khan (XX) vi, 489b – VI, 475b
Khān Aḥmad (Ardalān) v, 33b, 34a – V, 34b, 35a
Khān Aḥmad Khān i, 1208b – I, 1244b
Khān Ārzū (1739) vii, 96a – VII, 98a
Khān al-Asad vi, 384a – VI, 368a
Khān Ātash i, 262b – I, 270b
Khān ʿAyyāsh vi, 544b – VI, 529a
Khān Baba → Bayram Khānān
Khān Bahādur Khān i, 953b, 1043a – I, 983a, 1074b
Khān Balîḳ → Khānbalîḳ
Khān Begī Khānum i, 406a – I, 417b
Khān Danūn vi, 546b, 548a – VI, 531a, 532b
Khān Dawrān (XVIII) vii, 457a – VII, 457a
Khān Djahān ʿAlī (1459) → Khandjā ʿAlī
Khān Djahān Lōdī ii, 381a; iii, 424a; iv, **1017b** – II, 391a; III, 438a; IV, **1049b**
Khān Djahān Maḳbūl ii, 925a, 1084b; iv, **1019a** – II, 946b, 1109b; IV, **1051a**
Khān al-Khalīlī (al-Ḳāhira) s, 5a – S, 4b
Khān Khānān iv, 210b, **1019b**; v, 629b – IV, 220a, **1051b**; V, 633b
Khān Khānān Maḥmūd b. Fīrūz iv, 920b, 1019b – IV, 953b, 1052a
Khān al-Ḳuṣayr vi, 544b – VI, 529a
Khān Lādjīn vi, 544b – VI, 529a
Khān Shaykhūn vi, 455a – VI, 440b
Khān Sulṭānī, ʿAbd al-Rashīd (XIV) vi, 49a – VI, 47b
Khān Yakdas i, 1030b – I, 1062a
Khān Yūnis vi, 31a; ix, 630b – VI, 29b; IX, 654b
Khān Zamān ʿAlī Ḳulī Khān (1566) vii, 340b; ix, 196a – VII, 342b; IX, 301b
Khān al-Zayyāt vi, 548a – VI, 532b
Khāna Pasha i, 845a – I, 868b
Khanagāh, Khānaḳah → Khānḳāh
Khanāṣir → Khunāṣira
Khanāzir → Khinzīr
Khānbalîḳ iv, 420a, **1020a** – IV, 438b, **1052a**
Khʷand Mir ii, 500a – II, 512b
Khandaḳ i, 121b; ii, 130a; iii, 1083a, 1084a, b, 1086b; iv, **1020b**; vi, 604a; s, 351b – I, 125a; II, 133b; III, 1109b, 1111a, b, 1113a; IV, **1052b**; VI, 589a; S, 351a
Khandaḳ → Ḳandiya
al-Khandaḳ (al-Andalus) (939) vi, 431b – VI, 417a
Khandaḳ al-ʿAbīd (Miṣr) vii, 149b – VII, 151b
Khandaḳ Sābūr v, 634a – V, 638a
Khandaḳ Ṭāhir i, 897b – I, 924b
Khʷāndamīr (1535) i, 456a, 1211b, 1213a; iv, **1020b**; vii, 127a, 602b – I, 469a, 1247b, 1249b; IV, **1052b**; VII, 128b, 602a
Khande Rāo iii, 316b – III, 326a
Khāndēsh ii, 113a, 270b, 814a, 816a, 1125a; iii, 418b, 422a, 446b; iv, **1022a**; vi, 50b, 52a, 53a, 54a, b, 67b, 310a, 695a; s, 335b – II, 115b, 278b, 833b, 835b, 1151b; III, 432a, 435b, 461b; IV, **1054b**; VI, 48b, 50b, 51a, 52a, b, 65b, 295a, 683a; S, 335b
Khandjā ʿAlī (1459) ii, 486b; iii, 444a; ix, 877b – II, 498b; III, 459a; IX, 913a
Khandjara → Čankîrî
al-Khāndjī → Handžič
Khandwa vi, 53a – VI, 51a
Khāne iv, 243a, b – IV, 254a, b
Khānfū iv, **1024a**; vii, 72a – IV, **1056a**; 72b
Khān-i Ārzū (poet/e) (XVIII) ix, 90a – IX, 95b
Khān-i Djahān → Rao Mandalik Čudāsama
Khān-i Djahān Maḳbūl Tilangānī, Ḳiwām al-Mulk (1368) iv, 907b, **1019a**; vii, 795b – IV, 940b, **1051a**; VII, 797b
Khān-i Shahīd → Muḥammad b. Balban
Khan-i Zinyān vi, 384a – VI, 368a
Khāniḳīn iv, **1024b** – IV, **1056b**
al-Khanīnī vi, 113b – VI, 111b
Khānḳāh iv, 433a, **1025a**; v, 1129b; vi, 501b; s, 49b – IV, 452a, **1057a**; V, 1125b; VI, 486b; S, 50a
Khānlar Khān Iʿtiṣām al-Mulk iv, 787a – IV, 819a
Khānlarī, Parwīz Nātil iv, 71b, 72a – IV, 75b
Khannāb s, 327a – S, 326b
Khannās i, 262a – I, 270a
al-Khansāʾ (Tumāḍir bint ʿAmr) (644) i, 12a; ii, 627a; iii, 941a; iv, **1027a**; vi, 603a – I, 12a; II, 642b; III, 965b; IV, **1059a**; VI, 587b
Khansā (Khinsā) iv, **1026b** – IV, **1058b**
Khʷānsalār ii, 15a – II, 15a
Khʷānsārī, Aḳa Ḥusayn s, 308a – S, 308a
Khʷānsārī, Āyatullāh Aḥmad (1985) vi, 553b, VI, 538a
Khʷānsārī, Muḥammad Bāḳir (1895) iv, **1027b** – IV, **1059b**
al-Khʷānsarī, Muḥammad Riḍā al-Raḍawī s, 75a – S, 75b
Khʷānsārī, Muḥammad Taḳī Mūsawī (1952) iv, **1028b**; s, 157b – IV, **1060a**; S, 158a
Khanuwā iii, 202a; vii, 314a – III, 207a; vii, 316a
Khān-zāda Bēgum iv, **1029a** – IV, **1060b**
Khanzīt iv, **1029a** – IV, **1060b**
Khaput iv, **1029a**; v, 284b – IV, **1061a**; V, 282b
Khʷār iv, **1029b**; vi, 744b – IV, **1061a**; VI, 733b
Kharābshahr iii, 501b – III, 519a
Kharādj i, 861b, 969a, 990b, 1143b; ii, 116a, 131a, 142b, 146b, 154a, 187b, 559b, 561b, 562b, 566a, 869b; iii, 1088a; iv, 14a, b, 15b, 323a, b, 755a, 939a, 974a, **1030b**; v, 872a; vi, 496a – I, 885b, 999a, 1021a, 1178a; II, 118b, 134b, 146b, 150b, 159a, 193b, 573b, 575b, 576b, 580b, 890a; III, 1115a; IV, 15a, b, 16b, 337a, b, 785b, 972a, 1006a, **1062b**; V, 878a; VI, 481b
al-Kharadjī, Abū Bakr Muḥammad iv, 529b, 530a – IV, 552b, 553a
Khārag ii, 812b; iv, **1056a**; v, 81a, 507; vi, 619a – II, 831b; IV, **1087b**; V, 83b, 511a; VI, 604a
al-Kharāʾiṭ i, 1045b – I, 1077a
al-Kharāʾiṭī (939) i, 326a; iii, 745a; iv, **1057a** – I, 336a; III, 768a; IV, **1088b**
al-Kharaḳī, Aḥmad b. Isḥāḳ iv, 1004a – IV, 1036b
Kharaḳānī, Abu 'l-Ḥasan ʿAlī b. Aḥmad (1033) i, 147a, 515b, 780a; ii, 1078a; iv, **1057a**; x, 958a; s, 14b

– I, 151b, 531a, 803b; II, 1102b; IV, 1088b; X, ; S, 15a
Khara-Khula iv, 512a – IV, 534a, b
al-Kharaḳī, Abū Bakr Muḥammad (1138) iv, **1059a** – IV, **1090b**
Khārān iv, **1059b**; v, 102b, 684b; vi, 192b – IV, **1090b**; V, 104b, 690a; VI, 176b
Kharāna iv, **1060a** – IV, **1091a**
Kharāsūya bint Djustān III vii, 655b – VII, 655a
Khʷārazm i, 46b, 47a, 135a, 424b, 455b, 662b, 1131a; ii, 3a, 16a, 1141b; iii, 196a, 502a; iv, 753b, **1060b**; v, 24b, 542a, 857b; vi, 65b, 277b, 337a, 415b, 495a, 512a, 620a, 676a, 726b, 765a; ix, 428a; x, 708a; s, 168b, 169a, 245b, 279a, 289b, 420a –
I, 48a, 139a, 436b, 469a, 683a, 1165a; II, 3a, 16b, 1168b; III, 200b, 519b; IV, 784a, **1092a**; V, 25a, 546b, 864b; VI, 63b, 262b, 321a, 400b, 480b, 497b, 605a, 662b, 715b, 754a; IX, 444b; X, 752a; S, 169a, 245b, 279a, 289a, 420a
Khʷārazm-Shāhs i, 20b, 21a, 227a, 424b, 732a, 750a, 804a, 1132a; ii, 606b, 1053a, 1101a, b; iii, 471b, 1115a, 1155a; iv, 29a-30a, 349a, b, 542b, 583a, 817b, 1063b, **1065b**; v, 38b, 331a, 1014a, 1015b, 1018b; vi, 65b, 261b, 381b, 505a, 618a; viii, 63b; x, 743a; s, 245b, 279a –
I, 21b, 233b, 436b, 754a, 772b, 828a, 1166a; II, 621b, 1077b, 1127a, b; III, 488a, 1142b, 1183b; IV, 31b-32b, 364a, 566a, 606b, 850b, 1095a, **1097a**; V, 39b, 331b, 1009b, 1011a, 1014b; VI, 63b, 246a, 365b, 490a, 603a; VIII, 65a; X, ; S, 245b, 279a
al-Khʷārazmī, Abū ʿAbd Allāh Muḥammad (XI) iv, 1063a, **1068b**; vii, 913a; s, 130b, 371b, 387a –
IV, 1094b, **1100a**; VII, 913b; S, 129b, 371b, 387a
al-Khʷārazmī, Abū Bakr, Shaykh al-Ḥanafiyya (1012) vi, 634b – VI, 619b
al-Khʷārazmī, Abū Bakr Muḥammad b. al-ʿAbbās (993) i, 590b; ii, 78b; iii, 6b, 106b; iv, 1063a, **1069b**; vi, 108b, 905a –
I, 610a; II, 80a; III, 7a, 108b; IV, 1094b, **1101a**; VI, 106b, 896b
al-Khʷārazmī, Abū Djaʿfar Muḥammad b. Mūsā (847) i, 132b, 379b, 589b, 722b; ii, 360b, 577b, iii, 405a, 469a, 929b, 1137a, 1139a; iv, 1063a, **1070a**, 1078a, 1175b; vii, 210a; viii, 101b, 549b, 550a; s, 43a, 412b, 413b –
I, 136b, 390b, 608b, 744b; II, 370b, 592a; III, 418a, 485a, 954a, 1165b, 1167b; IV, 1094b, **1101b**, 1110a, 1208b; VII, 211b; VIII, 104a, 567b, 568a; S, 43a, 412b, 413b
al-Khʷārazmī, Abu 'l-Ḳāsim vi, 108b – VI, 106b
al-Khʷārazmī, Abu 'l-Muʾayyad al-Muwaffaḳ b. Aḥmad (1172) vi, 351b, 415b – VI, 335b, VI, 400b
al-Khʷarazmī, Aḥmad b. Muḥammad b. Isḥāḳ s, 343a – S, 343a
Khʷārazmī, Kamāl al-Dīn Ḥusayn (1551) x, 251a – X, 270a
al-Khʷārazmī, Tādj al-Dīn (1436) ix, 863a –IX, 899a
Khʷrazmians/-iens x, 696a – X, 732a
Khʷarazmia(e)n (language/langue) iv,1062b – IV, 1093b, 1094a
Kharbga iv, 1071b – IV, 1103b
Khārčinī → Khārṣīnī
Kharda vi, 535b – VI, 520a
al-Khardj i, 538b; iv, **1072b** – I, 555a; IV, **1104a**
al-Khārdj → Khārag
Khardja → Muwashshaḥ
Khārdje, Khārga → al-Wāḥāt
Khardjird → Khargird
Khardjlïḳ ii, 714b – II, 733a
Kharera vi, 294b – VI, 280a
Kharfūsh → Ḥarfūsh
Kharg → Khārag
Kharga iv, 529a – IV, 552a
Khargird iv, **1073a**; v, 1137b, 1148b – IV, **1105a**; V, 1132a, 1139b
al-Khargūshī, al-Wāʿiẓ (1015) iv, **1074a** – IV, **1105b**
al-Kharība al-Sawdāʾ → al-Sawdāʾ
Kharibtā vii, 394b – VII, 396a
al-Khārid, Wādī i, 538a; iv, **1074a** – I, 554b; IV, **1105b**
Kharid i, 829b – I, 852b
Khāridja b. Ḥiṣn al-Fazārī i, 690a; ii, 1023b; iii, 23b – I, 711a ; II, 1047a; III, 24b
Khāridja b. Ḥudhāfa i, 451b – I, 464b
Khāridja b. Zayd b. Thābit al-Anṣārī s, **311a** – S, **310b**
Khāridjites i, 16a, 40b, 49a, 54b, 55a, 77a,113a, 120a, 158a, 163a, 207a, 248a, 332b, 367a, 384a, b, 445b, 451b, 550b, 686b, 810a, 942a, 972a, 1044a, 1110b, 1178b, 1242b; ii, 90a, 166a, 416a, 523b, 524a, 978a, 1095b; iii, 153a, 233b, 583b, 648a, 651a, b, 652a, 715b, 1164a, 1265a; iv, 15a, 20b, 415b, 673a, 753a, 827a, **1074b**; v, 499a, 855a, 945b, 1189a; vi, 84a, 279b, 311b, 331a, 345a, 623b, 740a; vii, 265b, 266b, 562a; ix, 754a, 766a; x, 816a; s, 122b, 157a, 284a –
I, 16b, 41b, 50b, 56a, 57a, 79a, 116b, 123b, 162b, 167b, 213a, 255b, 343a, 395a, b, 458b, 464b, 478a, 568a, 707b, 833a, 971a, 1002a, 1075b, 1144a, 1213b, 1280b; II, 92a, 171a, 426b, 536b, 537a, 1000b, 1121a; III, 156b, 240a, 603b, 669a, 672b, 673b, 737b, 1192b, 1298a; IV, 16a, 22a, 433b, 700b, 783b, 860a, **1106a**; V, 502a, 862a, 949b, 1179a; VI, 82a, 264b, 296b, 316a, 329a, 608b, 729b; VII, 267a, 268b, 562b; IX, 787a, 799a; X, ; S, 122a, 157a, 284a
—doctrine i, 124a, 128b, 187b, 257b, 335a, 1027b; ii, 833b; iii, 19b, 235b, 658b, 661a, 1167b; iv, 938a, **1076a** –
I, 127b, 132b, 193a, 265b, 345b, 1059a; II, 853a; III, 20b,242a, 679b, 682b, 1196b; IV, 971a, **1108a**
Kharīṭa, Khārita iv, **1077b** – IV, **1109b**
Khʷārizm(ī) → Khʷārazm(i)
Kharḳ v, 878b, 879b, 880b – V, 884b, 885b, 886b
Kharkūshī → Khargūshī
al-Khwārizmī → Muḥammad b. Maḥmūd
Kharlukh → Ḳarluḳ
Kharm → ʿArūḍ
Kharpūt → Khart(a)pert
Kharrāna s, 229a – S, 229a
al-Kharrāz, Abū Saʿīd (899) iv, **1083a**; x, 314b – IV, **1114b**; X, 338b
Kharrūba → Makāyīl
al-Kharrūbī, Zakī al-Dīn iii, 776b; iv, 641b – III, 799b; IV, 668a
Kharshbūn (Mohmand) vii, 220a – VII, 221b
Khʷarshi ii, 251a – II, 258b
Khārṣīnī iv, **1084a** – IV, **1115a**
Khart(a)pert (al-Khartabirtī) i, 665a, 983a; iii, 128a; iv, 1029a, **1084a**; vi, 231a, 341b, 507a, b; vii, 999b; viii, 133a; s, 37a –
I, 686a, 1013b; III, 131a; IV, 1061a, **1115a**; VI, 224b, 325b, 492b, 493a; VII, 1001a; VIII, 136a; S, 37a
Kharṭūm i, 49b, 168b; v, **70a**, 1249b – I, 51a, 173b; V, **72a**, 1240b
—institutions i, 976a; ii, 424a – I, 1006a; II, 434b
Kharūṣ, Banū iv, **1084b** – IV, **1116a**
al-Kharūṣī, Salīm b. Rashīd viii, 85b – VIII, 87b
Khāṣ Pūlād-Khān ii, 88a – II, 89b
Khāsa (river/rivière) i, 184a; v, 441b – I, 189b; V, 444a
al-Khaṣāṣī, Abu'l-Faḍl Ḳāsim (1673) iv, 379a, 380a, **1085a** – IV, 396a, b, **1116a**
Khashab iv, **1085a**; v, 108b, 655b – IV, **1116b**; V, 110b, 659b

al-Khashabāt iv, **1086a**; vi, 359a – IV, **1117a**; VI, 343a
Khashabiyya iii, 987a; iv, 411b, 836b, **1086a**; vii, 357a – III, 1011b; IV, 429a, 869b, **1117b**; VII, 359b
Khashkhāsh i, 934b; ii, 522b – I, 963a; II, 535b
Khashm Djazra/- Khaṭma i, 536b – I, 553a
Khashm al-Girba viii, 92b – VIII, 94b
Khasht → Khōst
Khāṣī iv, **1087a**; vi, 317b – IV, **1118a**; VI, 302a
al-Khaṣīb → Ibn al-Khaṣīb
al-Khaṣīb b. ʿAbd al-Ḥamīd i, 143b; iii, 835a – I, 147b; III, 858b
al-Khaṣībī, Abū ʿAbd Allāh al-Ḥusayn b. Ḥamdān (957) viii, 146b – VIII, 148b
al-Khaṣībī, Abū ʿAlī Aḥmad → Ibn al Khaṣīb
al-Khaṣībī, Aḥmad b. ʿUbayd Allāh (940) iii, 835a; iv, **1094a** – III, 858b; IV, **1124b**
al-Khāsir → Salm al-Khāsir
Khāṣṣ i, 850a, 1080a, ii, 83a, 103b; iv, 238b, 972b, **1094a** – I, 873b, 1112a; II, 84b, 105b; IV, 249a, 1005a, **1125a**
Khāṣṣ, Khāṣṣa (Iran) → Khāliṣa
Khāṣṣ Aḥmed Beg ii, 985b – II, 1008a
Khāṣṣbek, al-Amīr al-Kabīr Niṣrat al-Dīn → Āḳ-Sunḳur al-Aḥmadīlī
Khāṣṣ Beg Arslān b. Balangirī (Palang-eri), amīr (1153) i, 300b; iv, **1097a**; vi, 275b, 782b; vii, 406b – I, 310a; IV, **1128a**; VI, 260b, 772a; VII, 407b
Khāṣṣ Murād Pasha (1473) vi, 72a – VI, 70a
Khāṣṣ Oda ii, 1088b, 1089b; iv, **1097a**; v, 18a, b, 938b – II, 1114a, 1115a; IV, **1128a**; V, 18b, 19a, 942b
Khāṣṣa i, 491a, 1099a; ii, 188a; iv, 36a, 972b, 976a, b, 977a, 1044a, 1094a – I, 506a, 1132a; II, 194a; IV, 38b, 1005a, 1009a, b, 1075a, 1125a
Khāṣṣa (occult(e)) iv, **1097b** – IV, **1128b**
Khāṣṣa ʿaskeri i, 1278b – I, 1317b
Khāṣṣa niwīs iv, 759a – IV, 789a
Khāṣṣa wa ʾl-ʿĀmma iv, **1098a**; v, 605b – IV, **1128b**; V, 609b
Khāṣṣadārs i, 238b; iv, 1143a – I, 246a; IV, 1175a
al-Khaṣṣāf i, 1113a; iii, 163a, 512b – I, 1146b; III, 166b, 530a
Khaṣṣakī i, 1225b – I, 1262a
al-Khāṣṣakī, Sayf al-Dīn Shaykh Ibn ʿAbd Allāh al-Ṣ afawī (1398) vi, 580b – VI, 565b
Khāṣṣakī Muḥammad Pasha i, 904b – I, 932a
Khāṣṣakiyya iv, **1100a** – IV, **1130b**
Khāṣṣekī i, 1225b; iv, **1100a**; v, 66b – I, 1262a; IV, **1131a**; V, 68b
Khāṣṣköy iv, 242a, 1096b; vi, 72a – IV, 252b, 1127b; VI, 70a
Khaṭaʾ iv, 768b, 769b, **1100b** – IV, 799b, 800b, **1131b**
al-Khatādjī, Shihāb al-Dīn s, 362a – S, 361b
Khaṭāʾī → Ismāʿīl (Ṣafawid(e))
Khaṭak i, 218b; iv, **1102a**; v, 72a, 250b – I, 224b; IV, **1133a**; V, 74a, 248b
Khātam, Khātim ii, 306a, 307a, 311b, 315a; iv, **1102b**; s, 256b – II, 314b, 316a, 320b, 324b; IV, **1133b**; S, 256a
Khathʿam, Banū (1071) i, 442a, 811b, 812a; iv, **1105b**; vi, 435b, 436a; viii, 82b; x, 3a – I, 455a, 835a; IV, **1137a**; VI, 421a; VIII, 84b; X, 3a
Khāthira, Day of/Journée de s, 177b – S, 179a
Khaṭīʾa iv, **1106b** – IV, **1138a**
Khaṭīb i, 981b; iv, **1109b**; v, 74a – I, 1012a; IV, **1141a**; V, 76a
Khaṭīb, Abū Bakr s, 195a – S, 193b
Khaṭīb al-Baghdādī (1071) i, 123b, 142b, 321b, 333a, 591b, 616b, 898a, 1309b; ii, 462a; iii, 27b, 512b, 735a, 754a, 860b; iv, **1111a**; v, 1129b; vi, 263a, 634b, 674a; viii, 518a; ix, 65a; s, 32b, 323a, 326a, 361a – I, 127a, 146b, 331b, 343a, 610b, 636b, 925a, 1349b; II, 474a; III, 29a, 530a, 758a, 777a, 884b; IV, **1142b**; V, 1126a; VI, 247b, 619b, 660b; VIII, 536a; IX, 66b; S, 32b, 322b, 325b, 361a
Khaṭīb Dimashḳ → al-Ḳazwīnī
Khaṭīb al-Iskāfī (1030) viii, 390a – VIII, 403b
Khaṭīb Muhammad Maulavi (1964) vi, 462a – VI, 448a
Khātim → Khātam
Khātima v, 960a – V, 964a
Khātimī → Muʾayyad-zāde (Müʾeyyed-zāde)
al-Khārimī, ʿAbd Allāh b. Yazīd (VII) vii, 522a VII, 522a
Khatlān → Khuttalān
al-Khatma, Khitma ii, 78b, 79b; iv, **1112b** – II, 80a, 81a; IV, **1144b**
al-Khaṭmī, ʿAbd Allāh b. Yazīd (VII) vii, 522a – VII, 522a
Khatmiyya i, 277b, 1029a, 1158b; ii, 710a; iii, 6a, 523b; iv, 686b; x, 249a – I, 286a, 1060b, 1193a; II, 729a; III, 6a, 542a; IV, 715a;X, 268a
Khaṭṭ i, 1354a; ii, 311a, 777b; iv, **1113a**; v, 210b-233b passim, 379b, 992a – I, 1393b; II, 320a, 796a; IV, **1144b**; V, 208b-231b passim, 380a, 987a
Khaṭṭ (geomancy/-ie) iv, **1128b** – IV, **1160a**
al-Khaṭṭ iv, 1123b, 1125a, **1130b**, 1155a, 1157a; v, 218a – IV, 1155a, 1157a. 1159a, **1162a**, V, 215b
Khaṭṭ al-Istiwāʾ → Istiwāʾ
Khaṭṭāb, Banū (Almeria) (XI) vi, 743a; x, 105b, 586a – VI, 732a; X, 113b,
al-Khaṭṭābī, ʿAbd al-Karīm iii, 701a – III, 723a
al-Khaṭṭābī, Ḥamd b. Muḥammad (996) iii, 1020a; iv, **1131b**; viii, 374b; ix, 887a – III, 1045b; IV, **1163a**; VIII, 387b; IX, 923a
Khaṭṭābiyya i, 486a, 1082a; iv, 203a, **1132a** – I, 500a, 1114b; IV, 212a, **1163b**
al-Khaṭṭār (Ḳurzul) s, 177b – S, 178b
Khaṭṭāra iv, 532b – IV, 556a
Khaṭṭ-i Humāyūn/Khaṭṭ-ī Sherīf i, 74b, 282a, 397a, 855a, 1090a; ii, 314a; iii, 553b; iv, **1131a**; v, 904b; x, 201a – I, 77a, 290b; 408b, 879a, 1122b; II, 323b; III, 572b; IV, **1162b**; V, 910b; X, 217a
Khaṭṭ-ī Sherīf → Khaṭṭ-i Humāyūn
Khatuḳāy ii, 25a – II, 25b
Khātūn (title/titre) iv, **1133a** – IV, **1164b**
Khātūn (Bukhārā) (VII) ix, 249b – IX, 257a
Khātūn al-ʿIsma bint Malik-Shāh (Saldjūḳ) (XII) vii, 408a – VII, 409b
Khātūnābādī, Mollā Muḥammad Bāḳir (XVIII) vii, 222b – VII, 224b
Khātūnī, Muwaffaḳ al-Dawla Abū Ṭāhir (XII) vii, 529b; s, 65a – VII, 530a; S. 65b
Khāwa iii, 643a; iv, **1133a** – III 664a; IV, **1164b**
Khawābī (fort(e)ress(e)) x, 310a – X, 333b
Khawand → Akhund
Khāwandagār i, 260b, 261b, 262a – I, 268b, 269b, 270a
Khāwarān/Khābarān vi, 914b – VI, 906a
Khawāridj → Khāridjites
Khawārizm(ī) → Khʷarazm(ī)
Khawarnaḳ i, 196b; iv, **1133b**; v, 633a – I, 202a; IV, **1165a**; V, 637a
Khawāṣṣ → Khāṣṣ, Khāṣṣa
Khawāṣṣ Khān (XVI) vi, 54b – VI, 52b
Khawāṣṣ al-Ḳurʾān iv, **1133b** – IV, **1165a**
Khawātūnābādi, Muḥammad Ṣāliḥ (1704) vii, 476a – VII, 475b
Khawbar → Khōbar

Khawla i, 400b – I, 412a
Khawla bint Ḥakīm i, 307b – I, 317a
Khawla bint al-Hudhayl b. Mubayra x, 91b – X, 99a
Khawla umm Muḥammad b. al-Ḥanafiyya vii, 402b – VII, 404a
Khawlān, Banū i, 881b; iv, **1134a**; vi, 436a; s, 22a – I, 907a; IV, **1165b**; VI, 421a; S, 22b
al-Khawlānī, Abū Idrīs (699) iv, **1135a** – IV, **1167a**, b
al-Khawlānī, Abū Muslim (682) iv, **1135b** – IV, **1167a**
Khawr i, 536a, 538b, 1094b, 1095a, b – I, 552b, 555b, 1127b, 1128a, b
Khawr Ḥasan v, 508a, b – V, 511b, 512a
Khayāl iii, 453b, 632b; iv, **1136a** – III, 469a, 653b; IV, **1167b**
Khayāl, Mīr Muḥammad Taḳī (1759) iv, **1136a** – IV, **1168a**
Khayāl al-ẓill iv, 602b, **1136b** – IV, 627a, **1168a**
Khayālī ii, 937a – II, 959a
Khayāli Bey (1556) iv, **1137a** – IV, **1168b**
Khaybar (629) i, 9a, 435a; ii, 725a, 844b; iv, **1137b**; v, 250b; vi, 150a, 738a; vii, 371b; viii, 299a,b; s, 351b – I, 9a, 447a; II, 744a, 864a; IV, **1169b**; V, 248a; VI, 148b, 727b; VII, 373b; VIII, 308bS, 351b
Khaybar (Khyber) Pass i, 238a, b; iv, **1143a**; vii, 220a; s, 329b – I, 245b, 246a; IV, **1174b**; VII, 222a; S, 329a
Khaydāḳ → Ḳaytāḳ
Khaydhār → al-Afshīn
Khāyir Bey al-ʿAlāʾī i, 315a – I, 324b
Khāyir Bey al-Djarkasī s, 38a – S, 38b
al-Khayl iv, 495b, **1143a**; v, 75b – IV, 517a, **1175a**; V, 78a
Khayma iv, **1146b**; v, 444a – IV, **1178a**; V, 446b
Khayr iv, **1151a** – IV, **1183a**
Khayr b. Muḥammad b. al-Khayr v, 1176a, b, 1179a – V, 1166a, b, 1169a
Khayr b. Muḥammad Ibn Khazar iii, 1042b; v, 1175b – III, 1068a; V, 1165b
Khayr b. Nuʿaym (ḳāḍī) (740) vi, 671a – VI, 657b
Khayr Allāh Efendi (1865) i, 61a; iv, **1153a**; vi, 758b, 759a – I, 63a; IV, **1185a**; VI, 748a
Khayr Bak (amīr) (1499) vi, 580b – VI, 565b
Khayr al-Bayān i, 1123a, b – I, 1157a
Khayr al-Dīn, Ustād iv, **1158b** – IV, **1190b**
Khayr al-Dīn Čandarli̊ → Djandarli̊
Khayr al-Dīn Pasha Barbarossa (1546) i, 367b, 368a, 512a, 678a, 947b, 1023b, 1300b; ii, 189b, 353a, 520a, 522a, 537b, 722b, 839b; iii, 69a, 94b, 245b, 1086a; iv, 361a, b, 572a, 656b, 828a, **1155a**; v, 268b, 270b, 504a, 1010b; vi, 141a, 529b; vii, 48a, 940a; viii, 569b; s, 80b – I, 378b, 527b, 698b, 699a, 977a, 1055a, 1340b; II, 195b, 362b, 533a, 535a, 550b, 741b, 859a; III, 71b, 97a, 252b, 1113a; IV, 377a, 594b, 683a, 861a, **1187b**; V, 266b, 268b, 507b, 1006a; VI, 139b, 514a; VII, 48b, 940b; VIII, 588a; S, 80a
Khayr al-Dīn Pasha al-Tūnusī (1890) i, 285b; ii, 436a; iii, 562a, 591b, 636b; iv, 924a, **1153b**; v, 949a; vi, 69a; vii, 433b, 434b, 451b, 452a, 901a – I, 294b; II, 447b; III, 581b, 612a, 657b; IV, 957a, **1185b**; V, 952b; VI, 67a; VII, 434b, 435b, 453a, b, 901b
Khayr al-Dīn Rāghib Pasha ii, 207b – II, 214a
Khayr al-Manāzil → M. Māham Anaga
Khayr Khān iii, 398b, 399a – III, 411a
Khayr al-Nassādj (914) ix, 432a – IX, 448b
Khayr Shāh, Sayyid iv, 1160b – IV, 1192b
Khayrābād (Indus) iv, **1159b** – IV, **1191b**
Khayrābād (Uttar Pradēsh) ii, 205a; iv, **1159b**; s, 420b – II, 211b; IV, **1191b**; S, 421a
Khayrān (ʿAmirid(e)) (1038) i, 84a; ii, 1012b; iii, 147a; vi, 576a, b; vii, 633a – I, 86b; II, 1036a; III, 150b; VI, 561a, b; VII, 633a
Khayrāt, Āl i, 709a, 709b; ii, 517b, 518a; vi, 191b; s, 30a – I, 729b, 731a; II, 530b; VI, 175a; S, 30b
Khayrat, Maḥmūd (XX) vii, 903a – VII, 903b
al-Khayrī, Rāshid v, 204a – V, 201b
Khayriyye Sulṭān bint Maḥmūd II (Ottoman) (1830) vi, 860a – VI, 851a
Khayrpūr ii, 258b, 263b, 264a, 669a; iii, 443a; iv, **1159b** – II, 265b, 271b, 272a, 685b; III, 457b; IV, **1191b**
Khayrullāh Efendi i, 61a – I, 63a
al-Khayrūn iii, 155b – III, 158b
Khaysh iv, **1160b** – IV, **1192b**
Khayshan iv, 553b – IV, 577b
Khaywān s, 335a – S, 334b
al-Khayyāmī, Abū Ḥafs ʿUmar vii, 196b, 199b – VII, 196b, 200a
Khayyāṭ iv, **1161a** – IV, **1193a**
al-Khayyāṭ, Abū ʿAlī Yaḥyā (835) viii, 107a – VIII, 109b
al-Khayyāt, Abu ʾl-Ḥusayn (913) i, 129a; ii, 386b, 1026b; iii, 905b, 1144a; iv, **1162a**; s, 12b, 225b – I, 132b; II, 397a, 1050a; III, 929b, 1172a; IV, **1194a**; S, 13a, 225b
al-Khayyāt, Abū ʿAlī Yaḥyā (835) iv, **1162a** – IV, **1194a**
al-Khayyāt, ʿUthmān v, 769a – V, 775a
al-Khayyāṭī, Sadīd b. Muḥammad (XII) viii, 893b – VIII, 924b
al-Khayzurān bint ʿAṭāʾ al-Djurashiyya (789) i, 633b, 1034a, 1035a, 1298a; iii, 22b, 231a, 232b; iv, **1164a**; v, 737b, 1239a; vi, 650b; s, 326b – I, 654b, 1065b, 1066b, 1338a; III, 23b, 238a, 239a; IV, **1196a**; V, 743a, 1229b; VI, 636a; S, 326a
Khazaf ii, 745a; iv, **1164b** – II, 763b; IV, **1196b**
Khazʿal Khan (1936) iv, **1171a**; viii, 512b – IV, **1204b**; VIII, 530a
Khazāʾil i, 1096b; ii, 339b – I, 1129b; II, 349b
Kharāʾil (King, le roi) i, 525b – I, 541b
Khazar i, 18a, 100b, 625b, 660a, 835b, 837a, 864a, 921b, 931a, 985a, 1000a, 1305a, b, 1307a, b; ii, 85b, 86a, 482b, 1107b; iii, 234a, 759a; iv, 280a, 343a, b, 344a, b, 346b, 608b, 891b, **1172a**; v, 382a, 488a, 1013b; vi, 415b, 428a, 623a, b, 740a; x, 690a, 692a; s, 106a, 297b – I, 18b, 103b, 646a, 681a, 858b, 860b, 888a, 949b, 959b, 1015b, 1031a, 1345a, b, 1347b, 1348a; II, 87a, b, 494b, 1133b; III, 241a, 782b; IV, 292b, 357b, 358a, b, 359a, 361b, 633a, 924b, **1205b**; V, 383a, 491a, 1009a; VI, 400b, 413b, 608b, 729b; X, 732a, 734a,b; S, 105b, 297a
—language/langue iv, 1178b – IV, 1212a
Khazar, Banū v, 1174b, 1175a, 1176b, 1179b – V, 1164b, 1165a, 1176b, 1169b
Khazar b. Ḥafṣ b. Maghrāw v, 1174b – V, 1164b
Khazarān i, 738b; iv, 1176a, 1178a – I, 760a; IV, 1209b, 1211a
Khazaria iv, 1176b, 1177b – IV, 1209b, 1211a
Khāzim b. Khuzayma (VIII) i, 550b; ii, 592b; iii, 652a; x, 816a, 927a – I, 568a; II, 607a; III, 673b; X,
Khāzim b. Muḥammad iii, 501b – III, 518b
Khāzin ii, 304b; iv, **1181b** – II, 313a; IV, **1214b**
al-Khāzin, Abū Djaʿfar (961) i, 1003a, 1100b; ii, 362a; iv, 629b, 1080a, **1182a**; vi, 600b; s, 412a – I, 1034a, 1133b; II, 372a; IV, 654b, 1111a, **1215a**; VI, 585a; S, 412a
Khazīne ii, 1088b; iv, **1183b** – II, 1114a; IV, **1216b**
Khazīne-i Enderūn i, 1147a; iv, 1183b, 1184a – I, 1181b; IV, 1216b, 1217a

Khazīne-i Ewrāḳ i, 75a, 1089b – I, 77a, 1122a
al-Khāzinī, Abu 'l-Fatḥ (XII) iii, 1137a; iv, **1186a**; vi, 601a; vii, 196b, 199b, 203b; viii, 655a; ix, 3a – III, 1165a; IV, **1218b**; VI, 585b; VII, 196b, 200a, 204b; VIII, 674b; IX, 3b
al-Khāzir (river/rivière) iv, 493a, **1186b**; vii, 523b – IV, 514b, **1219a**; VII, 523b
Khaznadār, Khāzindār iv, **1186b** – IV, **1219b**
Khaznadār, Muṣṭafā → Muṣṭafā Khaznadār
al-Khazradj, Banū i, 50b, 53b, 514a, 544b, 771a, 1283a; iii, 812a; iv, **1187a**; v, 995a; vi, 373b, 374a, 472a; vii, 367a, 852b; s, 229b, 230a –
I, 52a, 55a, 529b, 561b, 794a, 1322b; III, 835b; IV, **1220a**; V, 990a, b, 358a, 458a; VII, 369b, 854a; S, 229b, 230a
al-Khazradjī, Abū Dulaf (X) → Abū Dulaf
al-Khazradjī, Ḍiyā' al-Dīn (1410) iv, **1187b** – IV, **1220b**
al-Khazradjī, Muwaffaḳ al-Dīn (1410) ii, 441a; iv, **1188b** – II, 452b; IV, **1221a**
al-Khazradjiyya → al-Khazradjī, Ḍiyā' al-Dīn
Khazrūn, Banū v, 1182a, b, 1183a; vi, 404a, 946b – V, 1172a, b, 1173a; VI, 388b, 938b
Khazrūn b. Fulfūl b. Khazar (976) v, 1178a; vi, 404a, 1041a – V, 1168a; VI, 388b, 1034b
Khazrūn b. Sa'īd v, 1182b – V, 1172b
Khazz → Ḥarīr
Khedive → Khidiw
Khedive Ismā'īl → Ismā'īl Pasha
Khēma → Khayma
Khemshili, Khemshin v, **1a** – V, **1a**
Khenafsa s, 328a – S, 327b
Khērla v, **1a**; vi, 53a; s, 280a – V, **1a**; VI, 51a; S, 279b
Khettara iv, 529a – IV, 552a
Kheyūn b. Djenāh i, 684a – I, 705a
Khibā' iv, 1147a – IV, 1178b
Khiḍāb v, **1b**; – V, **1b**
Khidāsh (Khaddāsh) (736) i, 15b, 1293a; iv, 15b, 45a, 446a, 837b; v, **1b**, 63b; vii, 396a –
I, 16a, 1332b; IV, 17a, 47b, 466a, 870b; V, **1b**, 65b; VII, 397b
Khidāsh b. Zuhayr al-Aṣghar (VII) v, **3b**; vii, 581a; s, 394b – V, **3b**; VII, 581b; S, 395a
Khidhlān i, 413b; v, **3b**, 833b – I, 425b; V, **4a**, 839b
Khiḍir → Khayr al-Dīn Pasha Barbarossa
Khiḍir b. 'Abd Allāh (XV) vii, 685b – VII, 686a
Khidīw (Khedive) v, **4a** – V, 4a
Khiḍr iv, 1148a – IV, 1179b
al-Khiḍr → al-Khaḍir
al-Khiḍr b. Aḥmad, Taghlibī (875) vi, 900a – VI, 891b
Khiḍr Beg b. Ḳāḍī Djelāl al-Dīn (1459) ix, 630b – IX, 655b
Khiḍr Beg Aydinoghlu i, 778a, 783b; iii, 1183a; v, 506a – I, 801a, 806b; III, 1212a; V, 509b
Khiḍr Beg b. Ḳāḍī Djalāl al-Dīn (1458) iv, 225a; v, **4b** – IV, 234b; V, **4b**
Khiḍr Ghaylān (Morocco/Maroc) (1672) vi, 891b – VI, 883a
Khiḍr Ḥusayn → al-Khaḍir, Muḥammad b. al-Ḥusayn
Khiḍr-Ilyās v, **5a** – V, **5a**
Khiḍr Khwādja (Mongolistān) (1399) x, 677a – X,
Khiḍr Khān (Multān) (1395) vi, 49b, 50a, 294b; x, 593a; s, 206b – VI, 48a, b, 279b; X, 637b; S, 206a
Khiḍr Khān (Sayyids, Delhi) (1421) i, 444b; ii, 120b, 258b, 269a, 270b, 695a; iii, 417b, 418a, 485a; iv, 276b, 419a, 922b, 923b; v, **5b**, 598a, 782b, 783a; vii, 193b, 313a, 549a; ix, 118b; s, 73b –
I, 457b; II, 123b, 265a, 277b, 278b, 712b; III, 430b, 431a, 502a; IV, 288b, 437b, 955a, 956b; V, **6a**, 601b, 789a; VII, 194a, 316a, 549a; IX, 122b S, 74a
Khiḍr Khān b. Ibrāhīm (Ḳarakhānid(e)) (1081) iii, 1115b; vi, 274a; s, 65a – III, 1143a; VI, 258b; S, 65b
Khiḍrawayh, Aḥmad vi, 225a – VI, 219a
al-Khiḍrima x, 792a – X,
Khifāḍ → Khafḍ
Khil'a i, 24a; iii, 215b, 344b, 346b; v, **6a**, 620a, 737a, 752a – I, 25a; III, 222a, 355a, 357a; V, **6b**, 624a, 742a, 757b
Khilāfa → Khalīfa
Khilāfat movement i, 443a; ii, 255a; iii, 1204b; iv, 793b; v, **7a**; vi, 459b; vii, 421b, 678b; viii, 241b, 249a; s, 4b, 293b, 360a –
I, 456a; II, 262a; III, 1235a; IV, 825b; V, **7b**; VI, 445a; VII, 423a, 678b; VIII, 247a; S, 3b, 293a, 360a
Khilāt → Akhlāt
Khildjī → Khaldjī
Khillaut, Khilut v, 7a – V, 7a
Khimar iv, 10b – IV, 11b
Khinalug v, **8a** – V, **8a**
Khindif, Banū i, 545a; vi, 477a – I, 562a; VI, 463a
Khinsā → Khansā
Khinzīr v, **8a**; vi, 382b – V, **8b**; VI, 366b
al-Khiraḳī, Abu 'l-Ḳāsim (946) i, 277a; iii, 159a, b, 734b, 784b; v, **9b** – I, 285b; III, 162b, 163a, 757b, 808a; V, **10a**
Khirāsh b. Umayya s, 350a – S, 350a
Khirbat al-Bayḍā' v, **10a** – V, **10b**
Khirbat al-Mafdjar i, 613b; ii, 955b; iii, 71a, 142b, 310a, 494b; iv, 701b, 1164b; v, **10b**, 338a; s, 117a, 251a –
I, 633b; II, 977b; III, 73b, 145a, 319a, 511b; IV, 730a, 1197a; V, **11a**, 338b; S, 116b, 251a
Khirbat al-Minya ii, 955b; v, **17a**; s, 117a, 229a – II, 978a; V, **17b**; S, 116b, 229a
Khirḳa iv, 474a; v, **17b**, 737a – IV, 495a; V, **18a**, 742a
Khirḳa-yi Sa'ādet → Khirḳa-yi Sherīf
Khirḳa-yi Sherīf ii, 695b, 1088b; v, **18a**, 761b – II, 713a, 1114a; V, **18b**, 767b
Khīrkhān b. Ḳarādja iii, 120a, 1118b – III, 122b, 1146a
Khirkī → Awrangābād
al-Khirniḳ vi, 603a – VI, 587b
al-Khirrīt al-Nādjī (VII) v, **19b**, 451a – V, **20a**, 453b
al-Khirshī vi, 279a – VI, 263b
Khiṣā' iv, 1087b, 1090b – IV, 1119a, 1121b
Khiṣālī (Budin) (1651) vii, 531b – VII, 532a
Khīsh ii, 905b – II, 926b
Khiṭa → Ḳarā Khiṭāy
Khiṭā'ī → 'Alī Akbar
Khitān v, **20a**, 471a – V, **20b**, 473b
Khitans vii, 234b – VII, 236a
Khiṭaṭ v, **22b** – V, **23a**
Khiṭāy → Ḳarā Khiṭāy; al-Ṣīn
Khiṭba v, **22b** – V, **23b**
Khitma → Khatma
Khiṭṭa v, **23a** – V, **23b**
Khīwa i, 36a, 71a, 99b, 120b, 456a, 456b, 1296a; ii, 16a, 446a; iv, 611a, 1060b, 1064b, 1065a; v, **23b**, 859b; vi, 130b, 417a, 418a, 419a; s, 46a, 66a, 73a, 419b, 420a –
I, 37a, 73a, 102b, 124a, 469a, 469b, 1335b; II, 16b, 458a; IV, 635b, 1092a, 1096a, b; V, **24b**, 866b; VI, 128b, 402a, 403a, 404a; S, 46a, 66b, 73b, 420a
Khīwa Khānate iv, 1065a; v, 24a, 392a; s, 97b, 169a, 228a, 281a – IV, 1096b; V, 24b, 392b; S, 96b, 169a, 228a, 281a
Khiyābān (Mashhad) vi, 715b – VI, 704b
Khiyābān, Shaykh Muḥammad (1920) iv, 789b; v, **24b**; s, 110a, 365b, 366a – IV, 821b; V, **25a**; S, 109b, 365a, b
Khiyāla → Khayl

Khiyām → Khayma
al-Khiyāmī, Muḥammad iii, 812a – III, 835a
Khiyār v, **25a** – V, **26a**
Khiyār (theology/-ie) → Ikhtiyār
Khiyār b. Sālim al-Ṭaʿī iii, 652a – III, 673b
al-Khiyarī (1672) vi, 455a – VI, 440b
Khizāna i, 68a, 212b, 270a, 280a, 391a, 396b, 601a, 626a, 736a, 776a, 816b, 819a, 826b, 893b, 899a, 1018a, 1053a, 1139b, 1211b, 1272a, 1354a; ii, 7b, 126b, 127a, 132b, 290a, 714a, 837b, 871a, 885a; iii, 627a, 708b, 769a, 777b, 896a, 973a, 1200a, 1234b; –
I, 70a, 218b, 278a, 288b, 402a, 407b, 621a, 646b, 758a, 799a, 840a, 842a, 849b, 920a, 926a, 1049b, 1085a, 1174a, 1247b, 1311a, 1393a; II, 7b, 130a, 135b, 298a, 732b, 857b, 891b, 905b; III, 649a, 731a, 792b, 800b, 920b, 997b, 1230b, 1266b → Maktaba
Khizānadār → Khāzindār
Khizāne-i ʿāmire → Khazīne
Khizr, Khizir → Khiḍr
Khizrūn, Banū vii, 761a – VII, 762b
Khloṭ → Khulṭ
Khmelnitsky, Boghdan iv, 178b, 179a – IV, 185b, 186a
Khmer → Ḳimār
Khnīfra s, 223a – S, 223a
Kho ii, 31a, b – II, 31b, 32a
Khōdja(s) i, 36a, 172a, b, 246b, 552b, 1254a, 1333b; ii, 45b, 47b, 58b, 129a, 170b; iii, 381a, 434b, 545a; iv, 202b, 206a; v, **25b**, 942b; viii, 84a, 307a; s, 332a – I, 37a, 176b, 177a, 254a, 570a, 1272b, 1292a; II, 46b, 48b, 59b, 132b, 176a; III, 393a, 448b, 563b; IV, 211b, 215a; V, **26b**, 946a; VIII, 86b, 316b; S, 331b
Khodja Čelebi → Abu 'l-Suʿūd
Khodja Čiwizāde → Muḥyi al-Dīn Shaykh Muḥammad
Khodja Dāwūd Pasha → Dāwūd Pasha (1498)
Khodja Debhānī (XIII) viii, 210b – VIII, 215a
Khodja Efendi Saʿd al-Dīn (1599) i, 826a, 956a; ii, 713a; iii, 91b, 248b; iv, 900b; v, **27a**, 682b; vii, 596a, b –
I, 849a, 985b; II, 731b; III, 94a, 255b; IV, 933b; V, **28a**, 687b; VII, 595b, 596a
Khodja Eli → Ḳodja Eli
Khodja Ibrāhīm Pasha i, 395a – I, 406a
Khodja Kenʿān Pasha i, 843a; iv, 885a – I, 866a; IV, 917b
Khodja Muṣṭafā Pasha (1512) viii, 10a – VIII, 10a
Khodja Muṣṭafā Pasha (1529) iii, 341b; iv, 231a, 882a; vi, 1023a – III, 351b; IV, 241b, 914b; VI, 1016a
Khodja Rāghib Pasha → Rāghib Pasha
Khodja Sinān Pāshā (1486) → Sinān Pasha Khodja
Khodja Sinān Pasha (1595) → Sinān Pasha, Khodha
Khodja Ṭāhir Efendi (Prizren) (XIX) viii, 340b – VIII, 352a
Khodja Yūsuf Pasha i, 63a, 174b – I, 65a, 179b
Khodjaev (1938) v, **28a** – V, **29a**
Khodjand → Khudjand
Khōdjazāde iii, 1149a – III, 1177b
Khōī (Khūy) v, **28b**; vi, 120a, 200b, 201a, b, 202a, b, 243b, 494b, 502a, 504a; s, 365b – V, **29b**; VI, 117b, 185a, b, 186b, 187a, 227b, 480a, 487a, 489b; S, 365a
Khoḳand i, 71a, 504b, 1296a; ii, 45a, 67b, 440a, 792a; v, **29a**, 46a, 274a, 364a, 399b; vi, 371a, 419a, 557b; s, 97b, 98a, 228b, 420a –
I, 73a, 520a, 1335b; II, 46a, 68b, 458a, 811a; V, **30a**, 47a, 271b, 365a, 400b; VI, 355a, b, 404a, 542a; S, 97a, 228b, 420b
Khokars ii, 972b, 1053a; v, **31a**, 598a – II, 995a, 1077b; V, **32a**, 601b
Khomayr → Khumayr
Khomeinī → Khumaynī
Khōnās i, 243b; ii, 204b – I, 251a; II, 211a
Khorā vi, 53a – VI, 51a
Khorāsān → Khurāsān
Khorkhut s, 245a – S, 245a
Khorsābād vi, 365a – VI, 349a
Khosham s, 363a – S, 362b
Khoshḳadam → Khushḳadam, al-Malik al-Ẓāhir
Khosraw → Anūshirwān; Amīr Khusraw; Khosrew; Khusraw; Kisrā; Parwīz
Khosrew, Mollā (1480) iii, 163b, 164a; v, **32b**; vi, 980a; vii, 595a; ix, 401a –
III, 167a, b; V, **33b**; VI, 972b; VII, 594b; IX, 413b
Khosrew Beg Ghāzī (Bosnia) (1541) i, 1263b, 1270b, 1272a; ii, 201b; v, **31b**; ix, 29b; s, 185a – I, 1302a, 1209b, 1311a; II, 208a; V, **33a**; IX, 30a; S, 186a
Khosrew Pasha Bosniak (1632) v, **32b** – V, **33b**
Khosrew Pasha Deli (Dīvāne) (1544) iv, 902a; v, **35a**; vii, 911b – IV, 934b; V, **36a**; VII, 912a
Khosrew Pasha, Meḥmed (1855) v, **35b** – V, **36b**
Khōst v, **36b**, 1079b; vii, 438a, 573b; s, 66a – V, **37b**, 1076b; VII, 439a, 574b; S, 66b
Khotan iii, 1115b; v, **37a**; vi, 274a; ix, 617b; s, 98a – III, 1143a; V, **38a**; VI, 259a; IX, 641a; S, 97b
Khotin v, **39b**, 260b, 720a, 766a – V, **40b**, 258b, 725b, 772a
Khowár ii, 31a, 138b – II, 31b, 142a
Khoybūn i, 871a – I, 895b
al-Khubar v, **40a** – V, **41a**
Khubayb b. ʿAdī al-Anṣārī (VII) v, **40b** – V, **41b**
Khubayb b. Yasāf (VII) x, 839b – X,
Khūbmesīḥīs iv, 333b; v, **41a** – IV, 348a; V, **42b**
al-Khubūb i, 1312b, 1313a – I, 1352b, 1353a
Khubz ii, 1058a; v, **41b** – II, 1082b; V, **42b**
al-Khubza'aruzzī, Abu 'l-Ḳāsim (938) v, 42a, **43a**; vii, 114b; ix, 55b – V, 43a, **44b**; VII, 116b; IX, 58b
Khudā Bakhsh (1908) i, 1018a; v, **43b** – I, 1049b; V, **45a**
Khudā-Yār Khān → Yār Muḥammad Khān
Khudābanda → Muḥammad Khudābanda; Uldjaytū Khudābanda
Khudādād i, 359a – I, 370a
—b. Miḥrāb Khān v, 521a – V, 524b
Khudāwand v, **44a** – V, **45b**
Khudāwand Khān (Gudjarāt) (1526) iii, 1160a; vi, 51b – III, 1188b; VI, 50a
Khudāwand Khātūn (Saldjūḳ) (1332) viii, 15b – VIII, 16a
Khudāwand Muḥammad iv, 201b – IV, 210b
Khudāwendigār i, 468b; iv, 564a; v, **44b**; vii, 592b – I, 482b; IV, 586a; V, **45b**; VII, 592b
Khudāyār Biy (Mangit) (XVIII) vi, 418b – VI, 403b
Khudāya Khān (Khoḳand) (1875) v, 30a, b; vi, 769a – V, 31a, b; VI, 758a
Khudaybakhsh iv, 202b – IV, 211b
Khudāydād ii, 622a – II, 637b
Khudāynāma iii, 884a; iv, 11a, 809a – III, 908a; IV, 12a, 841b
Khudayr, Banū vi, 902a – VI, 893b
Khūdjān → Ḳūčān
Khudjand v, 30b, **45a**, 400a; vi, 77a – V, 31b, **46b**, 401a; VI, 75a
Khudjand, Āl-ī s, 239b – S, 239b
Khudjandī, Abu 'l-Ḳāsim iv, 101b – IV, 106a
Khudjandī, Abū Maḥmūd (1000) v, **46a**; vi, 600b – V, **47b**; VI, 585b
Khudjandī, Ḍiyā' al-Dīn ʿAlī Turka (1431) vi, 73a – VI, 71a

Khudjandī, Ḥāmid b. Khiḍr (X) viii, 574a –VIII, 593a
Khudjandī, Mu'ayyad al-Dīn s, 364b – S, 364a
Khūdjī → Khūzī
Khudjistān v, **47a** – V, **48b**
al-Khudjistānī → Aḥmad b. ʿAbd Allāh; Muḥammad b. ʿAbd Allāh
Khufāf b. Nudba ix, 864a – IX. 900a
Khugiyani s, 237b – S, 237a
Khū'ī (Khōī), Ayatullāh Ḥādjdjī Sayyid Abu 'l-Ḳāsim (1992) vi, 553b; vii, 301b, 919a – VI, 538a; VII, 303b, 919b
Khū'ī, Naṣīr (Nāṣir) al-Dīn x. 320b – X, 345a
Khuḳand → Khoḳand
Khulʿ → Ṭalāḳ
Khulafā' Sayyids (Iṣfahān) vi, 516b – VI, 501b
Khulayd b. ʿAbd Allāh al-Ḥanafī (VII) viii, 62b – VIII, 64a
Khulayd b. Ka's (VII) viii, 62b – VIII, 64a
Khulayd ʿAynayn ii, 569a – II, 583a
Khuld vi, 564b – VI, 549b
al-Khuld (Palace) i, 897a, b – I, 923b, 924a
Khuldābād i, 768a; v, **47a**; vi, 126a, b, 127a; vii, 315b – I, 791a; V, **48b**; VI, 123b, 124b, 125a; VII, 317b
Khulḳ → Akhlāḳ
Khulm v, **47b** – V, **49a**
Khulnā vi, 46b – VI, 45a
Khulṭ, Banū v, **48b**; vi, 592b, 741b, 743a – V, **49b**; VI, 577b, 730b, 732a
Khumār Beg i, 852a – I, 875b
Khumārawayh b. Aḥmad b. Ṭūlūn (Ṭūlūnid(e)) (896) i, 314b, 1290a; ii, 281b; iii, 745b, 750b; iv, 1090b; v, **49a**; vi, 657a, 676b; vii, 161a, 395a, 510a, 760a, 801b, 910b; x, 616b; s, 1a – I, 324b, 1329b; II, 289b; III, 768b, 773b; IV, 1121b; V, **50b**; VI, 643a, 663a; VII, 162b, 396a, 510a, 761b, 803a, 911a; X, 662b; S, 1a
Khumartāsh b. ʿAbd Allāh al-ʿImādī iv, 213b, 862b – IV, 211a, 895b
Khumaynī, Āyatollāh Ruḥollāh Mūsawī (1989) v, 372a; vi, 487a, 549a, 553b, 554a, b; vii, 298b, 300a, 301b, 448a, b, 449a, 450a, b, 762b, 860b; x, 61b; s, 95b, 104a, 342b – V, 372b; VI, 473a, b, 533b, 538a, b, 539a; VII, 300b, 302a, 303b, 449b, 450b, 451a, b, 764a, 862a; X, 63b; S, 95a, 103b, 342b
Khumayr v, **50b** – V, **52a**
Khumays b. Ḥudhāfa iii, 63b – III, 66a
Khumayyis, Āl ii, 631b – II, 647a
—Tarnān (1964) viii, 449a – VIII, 464a
Khumbara i, 1063a; iii, 478b – I, 1095a; III, 495a
Khumbaradjī i, 1062a; v, **52b** – I, 1093b; V, **54a**
Khumbaradjī Aḥmed Pasha → Aḥmad Pasha Bonneval
Khumm → Ghadīr al-Khumm
Khums i, 1085b, 1142a; ii, 146b, 156b, 869b – I, 1118a, 1176b; II, 150b, 160b, 889b
Khumurtāsh al-Ḥāfiẓī, Abū 'l-Muẓaffar (amīr) (1141) iii, 399a; viii, 832a – III, 411b; VIII, 860b
Khumurtāsh al-Sulaymānī i, 732a – I, 754a
Khūnadj (Khūna) iv, 420a – IV, 438a
al-Khunadjī ix, 20a – IX, 21a
Khunāṣira v, **53a** – V, **54b**
Khunātha bint Bakkār (1746) v, **53b** – V, **54b**
Khunayfghān vi, 384b – VI, 368b
Khunayḳ al-Ghirbān vi, 142a – VI, 140b
Khundj v, 670b, 671a; vi, 384b – V, 676a, b; VI, 368b
Khundj-ū-Fāl v, 671b – V, 676b
Khundjī, Faḍl Allah b. Rūzbihān (1521) iv, 1036b; v, **53b,** 873a; vi, 14a; vii, 928a, 988a – IV, 1068a, b; V, **55a,** 879a; VI, 12b; VII, 928b, 988b
al-Khunūs (Aljonós) vi, 221b – VI, 215a
Khunzal ii, 251a; v, **55b** – II, 258b; V, **57a**
Khūr iv, 6a – IV, 6b
Khurāfa iii, 369b – III, 381b
Khurāsān i, 3b, 16a, 18a, 19b, 43a, b, 52b, 59a, 77a, 99b, 108b, 141a, 147b, 149a, 228a, b, 230a, 246b, 278a, 296b, 437b, 529a, 684b, 964a, 1052a, 1293a, 1294a; ii, 4b, 43b, 1109a; iii, 163a; iv, 1051b; v, 2a, **55b**, 541a; 852b, 869a, 1238b; vi, 16a, 64b, 65a, 66a, 73a, 115b, 224b, 225a, 273b, 280b, 331a, b, 337a, 365b, 416a, 427b, 428a, 432b, 433a, 450a, 493a, 494b, 495a, 511a, 512a, 513b, 514b, 516b, 523a, 526b, 617b, 618a, 624b, 633b, 634a, 663b, 677a, 713b, 715b; vii, 266a, 396a, 409b, 410b, 440b, 453a, b, 477b; viii, 62b; s, 14b, 15a, 24a, 31b, 38a, 57b, 66b, 72b, 83a, 84a, 139b, 140a, 142a, 149a, 195a, 204a, 235a, 259a, 263a, 265a, 266a, 281a, 299a, 326a, b, 363b, 420b – I, 3b, 16b, 19a, 20b, 44b, 54a, 61a, 79a, 102a, 111b, 145a, 151b, 153a, 235a, 237a, 254b, 286b, 306a, 450a, 545a, 705b, 994a, 1083b, 1332b, 1333b; II, 4b, 44a, 1135a; III, 166b; IV, 1083a; V, 2a, **57b**, 545b, 859a, 875a, 1229b; VI, 14a, 62b, 63a, 64a, 71a, 113a, 218b, 219a, 258a, 265b, 315b, 316a, 321a, 349b, 401a, 413a, b, 418a, b, 435b, 479a, 480a, b, 496b, 497a, 498b, 499b, 501b, 508a, 511a, 602b, 603a, 609b, 618b, 619a, 649b, 663b, 702b, 704a; VII, 268a, 397b, 411a, 412a, 441b, 454a, 477a; VIII, 63b; S, 15a, 24a, 31b, 38a, 58a, 67a, 72b, 83a, b, 139a, b, 142a, 149a, 195a, 203b, 234b, 258b, 263a, 264b, 265b, 281a, 298b, 325b, 326a, 363b, 421a
—administration ii, 505a, 561a; v, 56b – II, 518a, 574b; V, 58a
—ethnology/-ie iii, 1107b; iv, 20a; v, 56a, b – III, 1135a; IV, 21b; V, 57b, 58a
—history/histoire ii, 978b; iv, 15a-b; v, 56b-59b – II, 1001a; IV, 16a-b; V, 58a-61a
Khurāsān, Banū v, **59b** – V, **61b**
Khurāsānī → Badr al-Dīn
Khurāsānī, Muḥammad Ḳāẓim (1911) v, 61a; vi, 552b, 553a; vii, 299b; ix, 479b; s, 76a, 95b – V, **63a**; VI, 537a, b; VII, 301b; IX, 497b; S, 76a, 95a
al-Khurayba v, 761b, 762a – V, 767b
Khuraym vi, 606a – VI, 591a
al-Khuraymī → Abū Yaʿḳūb al-Khuraymī
Khuraz Bek (Mangït) (XVIII) vi, 418a – VI, 403a
Khūrī i, 1006b – I, 1037b
al-Khūrī, Fāris (1962) v, **62a** – V, **63b**
al-Khūrī, Rashīd Salīm → al-Ḳarawī, al-Shāʿir
al-Khūrī, Shukrī ii, 471b – II, 483b
Khūriyā-Mūriyā → Khūryān-Mūryān
al-Khurma v, **62b** – V, **64a**
Khurram (Prince/le prince) → Shāh Djahān I (Mughal) (1666)
Khurramābād v, **63a**, 830a, 831b – V, **65a**, 836a, 837b
Khurramdīnī → Khurramiyya
Khurramiyya (Khurramdīniyya) i, 149b, 241a, 844a; iii, 234a; iv, 17a, 45a, 100a, 838b; v, **63b**, 243b, 823a; vi, 338b, 951b; vii, 664a – I, 153b, 248b, 867a; III, 241a; IV, 18b, 48a, 104a, 871b; V, **65a**, 241a, 829a; VI, 322b, 943b; VII, 664a
Khurramshahr i, 1342a; ii, 181a; iv, 6a; v, **65b**; s, 57a – I, 1382a; II, 187a; IV, 6b; V, **67b**; S, 57b
Khurrem Sulṭān (1558) i, 1225b; iii, 147b, 998b; iv, 232a, 1100a; v, **66a**, 333b, 720a, 802a; vii, 713a – I, 1262a; III, 150b, 1023b; IV, 242a, b, 1131a; V, **68a**, 334a, 725b, 807b; VII, 714a
Khursābād v, **67b** – V, **70a**
Khurshāh → Rukn al-Dīn Khurshāh
Khurshān b. Ḳubād al-Ḥusaynī → Niẓām-sāhī
Khurshīd (Dābūyid(e), Ṭabaristān) (761) ii, 74b; iii, 501b; v, **68b**; vi, 744b, 941a; s, 298b – II, 76a; III, 518b; V, **70b**; VI, 734a, 933a; S, 298a

Khurshīd, K.H. iv, 711a – IV, 739b
Khurshīd Aḥmed Pasha (Morea) (XIX) i, 399a, b; ii, 637a; iii, 88b; vii, 249b – I, 410b, 411a; II, 653a; III, 90b; VII, 242a
Khurshīd Silūrzī i, 513b – I, 529a
Khurshīdī v, 828a – V, 834a
al-Khurṭūm → Kharṭūm
Khurūdj iv, 412a – IV, 430a
Khūryān-Mūryān i, 535b, 540a, 1282b; v, **70a**; vi, 729b – I, 551b, 556b, 1321b; V, **72b**; VI, 718b
Khusdār → Kalāt; Ḳuṣdār
al-Khushanī, Abū ʿAbd Allāh (981) i, 600b; iii, 789b; v, **71a**; vi, 353b; vii, 400a; viii, 117b, 518a – I, 620a; III, 813a; V, **73a**; VI, 337b; VII, 401b; VIII, 120a, 536a
al-Khushanī → Ibn Masʿūd
al-Khushānī, Ibn ʿAbd al-Salām ix, 38a – IX, 38b
Khushḥāl Khān Khaṭak (1689) i, 218b, 221a; iv, 1102a; v, **72a** – I, 224b, 227b; IV, 1133b; V, **74a**
Khushaysh b. Aṣram (867) viii, 388a – VIII, 401a
Khushḳadam, ʿImād al-Mulk (Gudjarāt) (1526) vi, 51b, 52a – VI, 50a
Khushḳadam, al-Malik al-Ẓāhir (Mamlūk) (1467) ii, 239b; iii, 1198b; iv, 960a; v, **73a**; vi, 318b, 727a, 791a; s, 38a –
II, 246b; III, 1228b; IV, 992b; V, **74b**; VI, 303b, 727b, 781a; S, 38b
Khusraushāhī, Hādī iv, 167a – IV, 174a
Khusraw → Amīr Khusraw; Khosrew Beg; Kisrā I, II
Khusraw b. Djahāngīr → Khusraw Sulṭān
Khusraw Beg i, 1139b – I, 1174a
Khusraw Fīrūz, al-Malik al-Raḥīm (1057) i, 132a, 513a, 1073b, 1352b, 1356a; ii, 192b; iv, 457b; v, **73b** –
I, 136a, 528b, 1105b, 1106a, 1392a, 1395a; II, 199a; IV, 478a; V, **75b**
Khusraw Fīrūz (Djustānid) s, 357a – S, 356b
Khusraw Fīrūzān ii, 192a – II, 198a
Khusraw Khān Barwārī ii, 269a, 272a, 1076a, 1084a; iii, 416b; iv, 923b; s, 105b –
II, 277b, 280b, 1101a, 1109b; III, 429b; IV, 956b; S, 105a
Khusraw Malik, Tādj al-Dawla (Ghaznawid(e)) (1186) vii, 1016b – VII, 1018b
Khusraw Mīrzā iv, 787a; s, 70b, 108b – IV, 819a; S, 71b, 108a
Khusraw Parvīz → Kisrā II
Khusraw Pasha Bosniak (1632) i, 4a, 1159b, 1208b; ii, 1091a; iv, 971b; v, **32b**, 256b, 458a – I, 4b, 1194a, 1244b; II, 1116b; IV, 1004a; V, **33b**, 254b, 460b
Khusraw Pasha Dīvāne (Deli) → Khosrew Pasha Deli
Khusraw Shāh → Ghaznawid(e)s
Khusraw Shāh, Nāṣir al-Dīn → Khusraw Khān Barwārī
Khusraw Shāh b. Bahrām ii, 1052b – II, 1077a
Khusraw Sulṭān (Mughal) (1622) i, 686a; ii, 380a; iv, 282a; v, **74a**; vii, 131b, 315a, 331b –
I, 707a; II, 390b; IV, 294b; V, **76a**; VII, 133b, 317a, 333a
Khusrawānī v, 185a – V, 182b
Khusrawgird vi, 365b – VI, 349b
Khusrawī, Muḥammad Bāḳir Mīrzā (1950) iv, 72b; v, 198a; viii, 448a – IV, 76b; V, 195b; VIII, 463a
Khusraw-zāde v, 609b – V, 613a
Khusrew → Khosrew; Khusraw
Khusūf → Kusūf
al-Khuṣūṣ vi, 775a; viii, 874a – VI, 764b; VIII, 903b
al-Khuta'ītī, *ḳāḍī* (Alep(po)) (XI) vii, 693a – VII, 693a
Khuṭarniyya vi, 633b; vii, 521b – VI, 618b; VII, 522a
Khuṭba i, 20b, 132a, 261b; ii, 593a; iii, 35b; iv, 945a, 1110a; v, **74a**; vi, 657b, 668b – I, 21a, 135b, 136a, 269b; II, 607b; III, 37a; IV, 977b, 1141b; V, **76a**; VI, 643a, 654b
Khuttal → Khuttalān
Khuttalān v, **75b**; vii, 477b; s, 125a, b – V, **77b**; VII, 477a; S, 124a, b
Khuttalānī, Isḥāḳ (1423) viii, 134b – VIII, 137a
Khuttalī iv, 216a – IV, 225b
Khuwāra → Djand
al-Khuwārizmī → al-Kh(ʷ)ārazmī
Khūy → Khōī
al-Khūyī, ʿAbd al-Mu'min (painter/peintre) viii, 961a – VIII, 994b
al-Khūyī, Ḥasan b. ʿAbd al-Mu'min (XIV) viii, 544a – VIII, 561b
Khuzāʿa, Banū i, 453a, 1283b; v, **76b**, 434b; vi, 145a, 333a, 374a; vii, 356b – I, 466a, 1323a; V, **79a**, 436b; VI, 143a, 317b, 358a; VII, 359a
al-Khuzāʿī, ʿAbd Allāh b. al-Haytham (IX) vi, 333a – VI, 317b
al-Khuzāʿī, Abū ʿAlī Muḥammad b. ʿAlī b. Razīn → Diʿbil
al-Khuzāʿī, Abū Muḥammad i, 827a – I, 850a
al-Khuzāʿī, Aḥmad b. Naṣr (845) vii, 4b; viii, 1051b – VII, 4b; VIII, 1087b
al-Khuzāʿī, Ḥamza b. Mālik s, 326b – S, 326a
al-Khuzāʿī, Malik b. al-Haytham (IX) vi, 332a, b, 335a – VI, 316b, 317a, 319b
al-Khuzāʿī, Muḥammad b. al-Ashʿath (IX) vi, 333a – VI, 317b
al-Khuzāʿī, al-Muṭṭalib b. ʿAbd Allāh vi, 335a, b – VI, 319b, 320a
al-Khuzāmā v, **80a**; s, 377a – V, **82a**; S, 377a
Khuzayma b. Khāzim b. Khuzayma al-Tamīmī (IX) v, 488a; vi, 332b, 335b, 499a – V, 491a; VI, 317b, 320a, 484b
Khuzayma b. Thābit al-Anṣārī (VII) v, 621a; vi, 710a; ix, 555a – V, 625a; VI, 698b; IX, 577a
Khuzdar → Ḳuṣdār
Khūzistān i, 3a, 131b, 239b, 240a, 305b, 437b, 528b, 561b, 659a, 695a, 866b, 1350a; ii, 903a; iii, 291b; iv, 6a, 42b; v, 65b, **80a**, 824a, 831a, 866b, 867a; vi, 117b, 120a, 272b, 333b; vii, 672a, 675a; ix, 855b; s, 12b, 37b, 61a –
I, 3b, 135b, 247a, b, 315a, 450a, 544b, 579a, 679b, 716b, 890b, 1390b; II, 923b; III, 300b; IV, 6b, 45a; V, 67b, **82a**, 830a, 837a, 873a, b; VI, 115b, 117b, 257b, 318a; VII, 672a, 674b; IX, 891b; S, 13a, 38a, 61b
Khvarshi v, **81b** – V, **83b**
Khʷadāy-nāmak → Khudāynāma
Khʷaja Nizamuddin viii, 242a – VIII, 248a
Khʷāsh b. Yūsuf (1009) vii, 43b – VII, 44a
Khyber Pass → Khaybar
Kianghrī → Čankiri
Kiari, Muḥammad al-Amīn i, 1260a – I, 1298b
Kiaya → Ketkhudā
Kibar v, 868b – V, 875a
Ḳibla i, 609b; ii, 213b; iv, 318a; v, **82a**, 323b, 1140b, 1141a, 1169a – I, 629b; II, 220b; IV, 332a; V, 84a, 323a, 1134a, 1158b
Ḳibrisli Meḥmed Emīn Pasha (1860) i, 397a; vi, 1032a – I, 408b; VI, 1025a
al-Kibrīt v, **88b**, 706b – V, **91a**, 712a
Ḳibṭ i, 435b, 471a, 532a, 803a, 1146b; ii, 229b, 330a, 560b, 958a; iii, 4a, 721b, 886a; v, **90a** –
I, 448a, 485a, 548a, 826a, 1180b; II, 236b, 339b, 574b, 980b; III, 4a, 744a, 910a; V, **92b**
al-Ḳibṭī → Čingane
Ḳidāḥ iv, 488a – IV, 509a
Ḳidam v, **95a** – V, **97b**

Kidara i, 226a; iii, 303b – I, 232b; III, 313a
Kīdj/Kīz (Makrān) vi, 193a – VI, 177a
Ḳidjmās (amīr) (Damas(cus)) (1382) ii, 286a; vi, 580b – II, 294a; VI, 565a
Kifāyat Khān iv, 1128a – IV, 1159b
Ḳifṭ v, 90a, 92a, **99a**, 514a – V, 92b, 94a, **101a**, 517b
al-Ḳifṭī → Shīth b. Ibrāhīm
al-Ḳifṭī, ʿAlī b. Yūsuf → Ibn al-Ḳifṭī
al-Ḳifṭī, Yūsuf b. Ibrāhīm s, 289a – S, 289a
Kihāna ii, 322b; iv, 263b, 420b, 763a, 1128b; v, **99b**; vi, 247a –
II, 332a; IV, 275a, b, 438b, 793b, 1160a; V, **101b**; VI, 231a
Kihsan v, 1148b – V, 1139b
Kijumwa, Muhammad bin Abu Bakari (XX) vi, 612b – VI, 597b
Ḳīḳān, Kīkān → Kalāt
Kilā → Kalah
al-Ḳilāʿ → al-Ḳalʿa (castle/château)
Ḳilʿa Rāy Pithorā ii, 256a, b, 259a; v, 1214b – II, 263b, 264, 267a; V, 1204b
Kilāb b. Rabīʿa, Banū i, 441a, b, 442a; ii, 71b, 159b, 234a, 235a, 238a; v, **101b**, 459a, 923a; vi, 379a; vii, 115a, 693a; viii, 863b –
I, 454a, b; II, 73a, 164b, 240b, 242a, 244b; V, **103b**, 462a, 928b; VI, 363b; VII, 117a, 693a: VIII, 894b
Ḳilāba bint al-Ḥārith b. Kalada s, 355a – S, 354b
al-Kilābī (820) vii, 831b – VII, 833a
al-Kilābī, Abu 'l-ʿAbbās Aḥmad b. Saʿīd (939) vii, 115a – VII, 117a
al-ṭilābī, Abu 'l-Fatḥ ʿUthmān b. Saʿīd (944) vii, 115a – VII, 117a
al-ṭilābī, Safr b. ʿUbayd viii, 632a – VIII, 650b
al-Kilāʿī, ʿAyyād (ʿAbbād; ʿImād) b. Naṣr iv, 403a – IV, 420b
al-Kīlānī, Rashīd ʿAlī → Rashīd ʿAlī
Kilār ii, 1088b – II, 1114a
Kilāt (Kalāt, Kelāt) (Balūčistān) i, 39a, 99b, 230a, 1006a; iii, 564b; iv, 364b, 395a, 535a, 1059b; v, **101b**, 580a, 684b; vi, 192b, 193a, 502b; s, 22a, 332a –
I, 40a, 102b, 237a, 1037a; III, 584a; IV, 380b, 412a, 558a, 1091a; V, **103b**, 584b, 690a; VI, 176b, 177a, 488a; S, 222a, 331b
Kilāt-i Nādirī v, **102b** – V, **105a**
Ḳîlburun v, **103a** – V, **105a**
Kili i, 1253a – I, 1291a
Kilī, Banū v, 459b – V, 462b
Kilia i, 1119b – I, 1153a, b
Ḳîlîçzāde Ḥaḳḳī iv, 169a – IV, 176a
Kilīd al-Baḥr → Čanaḳ-ḳalʿe Boghazî
Ḳîlîdj Alayi → Taḳlīd-i Sayf
Ḳîlîdj ʿAlī Beg v, 48a – V, 49b
Ḳîlîdj ʿAlī Pasha → ʿUlūdj ʿAlī
Ḳîlîdj Arslan I b. Sulaymān b. Ḳutlumush (Rūm Saldjūḳ) (1107) i, 466a, b, 664a, 732a; ii, 110a, b; v, **103b**; vii, 408a; viii, 948a –
I, 480a, 684a, 754a; II, 112b, 113a; V, **105b**; VII, 409a; VIII, 980b
Ḳîlîdj Arslan II b. Masʿūd I (Rūm Saldjūḳ) (1192) i, 431b, 466b; ii, 111a; iv, 575b; v, **104a**, 254b; vi, 507a, 777a; vii, 816b; viii, 129b, 130a, 133a, 948b, 975a –
I, 444a, 480b; II, 113b; IV, 598b; V, **106a**, 252b; VI, 492b, 766b; VII, 818b; VIII, 132b, 135b, 981a, 1011a
Ḳîlîdj Arslan III b. Rukn al-Dīn (Rūm Saldjūḳ) (XIII) ii, 691b; v, **104b** – II, 709a; V, **106b**
Ḳilidj Arslan IV Rukn al-Dīn b. Khusraw II (Rūm Saldjūḳ) (1265) iv, 619b, 620a, 813b, 814a; v, **104b**, 254a; vii, 479a –
IV, 644a, b, 846b; V, **106b**, 252a; VII, 479a
Ḳîlîdj Arslān b. al-Malik al-Manṣūr (Ayyūbid(e)) (1220) vi, 429b – VI, 415a
Ḳîlîdj Bek i, 1157a – I, 1191b
Ḳilidjūrī v, 9a – V, 9b
Kilifi v, **105a** – V, **107a**
Ḳīlīḳiya → Cilicia/-ie
Killah → Kalah
Ḳillawriya iv, 496b; v, **105a** – IV, 518a; V, **107a**
Killigil ii, 701b, 702a – II, 719b
Killiz v, **105b** – V, **107b**
Kilmek Abiz i, 1076b – I, 1108b
Kilōgharī s, 352b – S, 352b
Kilwa iv, 886a, 892b; v, **106a**, 223b, 1157b; vi, 128a, b, 283a, b, 370a, 704a, 774a; ix, 700b – IV, 918b, 925a; V, **108b**, 221a, 1147b; VI, 126b, 268a, 354a, 692a, b, 763b; IX, 729b
al-Ḳily v, **107a** – V, **109a**
Kimäk v, **107b**, 126a; x, 690a; s, 245a – V, **109b**, 128b; X, 732b; S, 245a
Ḳimār i, 343a; v, **108b**, 616b, 768b – I, 353b; V, **111a**, 620b, 774b
Ḳimār (Khmer) ii, 9a; iii, 1208b; v, **108a**; 227a – II, 9a; III, 1239b; V, **110b**, 225a
al-Kīmāriyyūn (al-Ṣābi'a) vi, 921a – VI, 912b
al-Kīmiyāʾ iii, 965a; iv, 673b; v, **110a** –
III, 989b; IV, 701a; V, **112b**
Kinā v, 515b, 519b – V, 519a, 523a
Kinabalu, Mount s, 150a – S, 150a
al-Ḳināʾī, ʿAbd al-Raḥīm (1195) viii, 864b – VIII, 895a
Kīnakhwāriyya i, 1110a; s, 363b – I, 1143b; S, 363b
Kinalî ada vi, 588b – VI, 573a
Ḳinalîzāde ʿAlāʾ al-Dīn (1572) iv, 471b; v, **115a** – IV, 492b; V, **118a**
Ḳinalizāde (Ḥasan Čelebī of/de Bursa) (1604) v, **116a**; x, 55a – V, **118b**; X, 56b
Kināna b. Bishr (VII) vii, 269a – VII, 271a
Kināna b. Khuzayma, Banū i, 545a; ii, 625a, 627a, 883b; iv, 334a; v, **116a**; vi, 145a –
I, 562a; II, 640b, 642b, 904a; IV, 348b; V, **118b**; VI, 143a
Kināya v, **116b** – V, **119a**
Kinda, Banū i, 526b, 548b, 583b, 683b, 697a; ii, 354a; iii, 52b; v, 23a, **118a**; vi, 311a, 441b, 472a, 477b; ix, 77a; x, 90a; s, 326b, 337b –
I, 542a, 566a, 602b, 704a, 718a; II, 363b; III, 54b; V, 24a, **121a**; VI, 296a, 427a, 458a, 463a; IX. 80a; X, 97b; S, 326a, 337a
al-Kindī, ʿAbd al-Masīḥ v, **120b** – V, **123a**
al-Kindī, Abū ʿUmar (961) i, 153b; v, **121b**; vi, 412a – I, 157b; V, **124a**; VI, 397a
al-Kindī, Abū Yūsuf Yaʿḳūb b. Isḥāḳ (866) i, 154a, 234b, 235a, 327b, 328a, 344b, 589a, 631a, 1003b, 1100b; ii, 376b, 578b, 765b, 771b, 872a; iii, 169b, 303a, 664a; iv, 332b, 418a, 763b, 795a; v, 113b, **122a**, 237b, 398b, 702b, 950a; vi, 99a, 204b, 338b, 376b, 449a, 637a; vii, 681a, b, 682a, 1031b; viii, 108a, 302a; ix, 35a; s, 72b, 78a, 251b, 271b, 412a –
I, 158a, 242a, b, 338a, b, 355a, 608b, 652a, 1034a, 1134a; II, 387a, 593a, 784a, 790b, 892a; III, 173b, 312a, 685b; IV, 347a, 436a, 793b, 827a, b; V, 116a, **124b**, 235b, 400a, 707b, 954a; VI, 96b, 188b, 323a, 361a, 434b, 622a; VII, 681a, b, 682a, 1034a; VIII, 110b, 311a; IX, 25a; S, 73a, 77b, 252a, 271a, 412a
a;-Kindī, ʿAlī b. Muḥammad (VIII) viii, 573a – VIII, 591b
Ḳinîḳ, Banū x, 689b – X, 782a
Ḳindīl → Miṣbāḥ
Kinkiwar v, **123b**, 169a – V, **126a**, 166b
Ḳinnasrīn i, 761a; v, **124a**, 921a; vi, 338b, 379a, 380b, 506a, 544a, 623b –

I, 784a; V, **126b**, 926b; VI, 323a, 363b, 365a, 491a, 528b, 609a
Ḳinṭār → Makāyīl
Ḳîpčaḳ i, 135a, 927a, 1075b, 1105a, 1188b, 1302a; ii, 24a, 43a, 44b, 610a, 1108a, 1109a; iii, 1115a; iv, 32b, 349a, 350a, 527a, 542a, 892a; v, 30a, 108a, **125b**; vi, 321a, 325b; vii, 166a; x, 690b; s, 97b, 203b, 245b, 392b, 420a –
I, 139a, 955b, 1107b, 1138b, 1223b, 1342a; II, 24b, 44a, 45a, 625a, 1134a, 1135a; III, 1142b; IV, 35a, 363b, 364a, 365a, 549b, 565b, 924b; V, 31a, 110a, **128a**; VI, 305b, 310a; VII, 167b; X, 732b; S, 97a, 203a, 245b, 392b, 420a
Ḳîpčak, Sayf al-Dīn ii, 285b – II, 293b
Ḳîr S͟hehir → Kîrs͟hehir
Kirā᾽ v, **126b** – V, **129a**
Ḳirā᾽a → Tadrīs
Ḳirā᾽a(t) i, 114a, 565b, 567b; ii, 293a; iii, 434b, 704b, 761a, 817b; iv, 822a; v, **127a**; s, 393b –
I, 117a, 584a, 586a; II, 301a; III, 448b, 726b, 784a, 841a; IV, 855a; V, **129b**; S, 393b
Ḳirāḍ v, **129b** – V, **132a**
Ḳirān iii, 35a, 53b; iv, 259a; v, **130b** –
III, 37a, 55b; IV, 271a; V, **133a**
Ḳīrāt → Makāyīl
Ḳīrāṭ iii, 10b – III, 11a
Ḳiraynūn, Āl vi, 81b – VI, 79b
Ḳird v, **131a**; ix, 440b – V, **133b**; IX, 457b
Kirdi ii, 9b, 10a – II, 10a
Kirdî-Kalal → Ḳarata
Kîrd͟jalî i, 1304a – I, 1344a
Kiresun → Giresün
Ḳirg͟hiz/Ḳîrkîz → Ḳîrgîz
Ḳîrgîz i, 224a, 853b, 1076b, 1077a; ii, 66b, 67b, 571a; iii, 116a, 117a; iv, 10a, 213b, 631b; v, **134a**, 247a; vi, 370b, 371a, 770b; vii, 353b; viii, 178a; x, 688b –
I, 231a, 877a, 1108b, 1109a; II, 68a, b, 585b; III, 118b, 119b; IV, 10b, 223a, 656b; V, **137a**, 244b; VI, 355a, b, 760a; VII, 355b; VIII, 180b; X, 730b
Kîrgîz Literature x, **728a** – X, **774a**
Kirid → Ikrīts͟h
Ḳîrîm i, 4b, 62b, 270b, 293a, 893a, 1108a, 1119b; ii, 24b, 25a, 1112a; iii, 44b; iv, 499b, 568b, 608a, 891b; v, **136a**, 719b; s, 96b –
I, 4b, 64b, 279a, 302a, 919b, 1141a, 1153a; II, 25b, 26a, 1138a; III, 46a; IV, 521a, 591a, b, 632b, 924a; V, **138b**, 724b; S, 96a
Ḳîrîm K͟hānat(e) v, 141b, 142a, 312b – V, 144b, 145a, 312b
Ḳîrîmčaḳ x, 697b – X,
Ḳirimī, Diyā᾽ al-Dīn ʿAbd Allāh al-Ḳazwīnī x, 88b – X, 96a
Ḳirḳ-K͟hān vi, 538a – VI, 522b
Ḳîrḳ Kilise/Kinise v, **143b** – V, **146a**
Ḳirḳgöz (bridge/pont) vi, 230a, 231b – VI, 224a, 225b
al-Ḳirḳisānī, Abū Yaʿḳūb Yūsuf (Karaite) (X) iv, 306b; vii, 539b, 566a – IV, 320a; VII, 539b, 566b
Ḳirḳīsiya vi, 622b – VI, 607b
Ḳîrḳlareli → Ḳîrḳ Kilise
Ḳîrḳ Wezīr → S͟hayk͟h-zāde II
Kirkūk v, **144a**; vi, 55b, 56b, 614a; vii, 714b –
V, **146b**; VI, 53b, 54b, 599a; VII, 715b
Ḳîrk-yir iii, 44b – III, 46b
Kirmān i, 8a, 86a, 131b, 132a, 211b, 420a, 731b, 830b, 1005a, 1311a, 1350a; ii, 299a, 746b, 1051a; iii, 1156b; iv, 14b, 19b, 391b, 807a, 1046b, 1170a; v, **147a**, 294a, 835a, 1114a, 1116a; vi, 66a, b, 72b, 115b, 272b, 273b, 331b, 368b, 481b, 493b, 494a, 633b; s, 53a, 71b, 118b, 122b, 127a, 129a, 139b, 140b, 142a, 147b, 326a, 327a –
I, 8a, 88b, 135b, 136a, 217b, 432a, 753b, 853b, 1036a, 1351b, 1390b; II, 307a, 764b, 1075b; III, 1185a; IV, 15b, 21a, 408a, 839b, 1078a, 1203a; V, **149b**, 294a, 841b, 1110a, 1112a; VI, 64a, b, 70b, 113a, 257b, 258a, 316a, 352b, 467b, 479b, 480a, 618b; S, 53b, 72a, 117b, 122a, 126a, 128a, 139a, 140a, 142a, 147b, 325b, 326b
Kirmān (Karmān) b. Mentes͟he Beg (1300) vi, 1018a – VI, 1010b
Kirmānī, Awḥad al-Dīn (1238) v, **166a**; vi, 381b; viii, 753a – V, **163b**; VI, 365b; VIII, 775a
Kirmānī, ʿAlā᾽ al-Dīn (1870) viii, 542a – VIII, 559a
Kirmānī, Ḥād͟jd͟jī Muḥammad Karīm K͟hān (XIX) iv, 854b; vii, 303a, 440b; ix, 404a –
IV, 887b; VII, 305a, 442a; 417a
Kirmānī, Ḥamīd al-Dīn Aḥmad (1020) i, 450a; iii, 72a, 134a; iv, 204a; v, **166a**; vii, 968b, 1006b – I, 463a; III, 74b, 137a; IV, 213a; V, **164a**; VII, 1008b
Kirmānī, Kamāl al-Dīn → K͟h(ʷ)ād͟jū Kirmānī
Kirmānī, Mīrzā Āḳā K͟hān s, 109b – S, 108b
Kirmāns͟hāh iv, 7b; v, **167b**; vi, 491b, 493a, 495b, 498b; s, 73a, 84a, 135a, 142b –
IV, 8b; V, **165b**; VI, 477b, 479a, 480b, 483b; S, 73b, 83b, 134b, 142a
Kirmāsin → Kirmānshāh
Kirmāstī v, **171b** – V, **169a**
Ḳirmid v, 585b – V, 591a
Kirmīsīn → Ḳirmāns͟hāh
Ḳirmiz i, 645b; ii, 681a – I, 666a; II, 698a
Kirovabad → Gand͟ja
Ḳirs͟h → Sikka
Ḳîrs͟hehir v, **172a** – V, **169b**
Ḳirṭās i, 531b; ii, 307a; iv, 742a; v, **173b** – I, 547b; II, 315b; IV, 772a; V, **171a**
Ḳīr-wa-Kārzīn vi, 384a – VI, 368b
Ḳirwās͟h → Ḳarwās͟h
Kisā᾽ → Libās
al-Kisā᾽ī, Abū Bakr Muḥammad (XII) vii, 284a – VII, 285b
al-Kisā᾽ī, Abu ᾽l-Ḥasan ʿAlī b. Ḥamza (805) ii, 806b, 807b; iii, 155a; v, **174a**, 351a; vi, 331a; vii, 280a; viii, 573a; s, 22b, 128b –
II, 826a, b; III, 158b; V, **171b**, 351b; VI, 315b; VII, 281b; VIII, 591b; S, 22b, 127b
al-Kisā᾽ī, Mad͟jd al-Dīn (X) iv, 60b; v, **175b** –
IV, 64a; V, **172b**
al-Kisā᾽ī, Ṣāḥib Ḳiṣaṣ al-Anbiyā᾽ iii, 306a; v, **176a**, 180b – III, 315a; V, **173b**, 178a
Kisakürek, Necip Fazil ii, 432b – II, 444a
Kisangani v, **176b** – V, **174a**
Ḳiṣāṣ ii, 341a; iv, 770a; v, **177a** – II, 350b; IV, 800b; V, **174b**
Ḳiṣaṣ → Ḳiṣṣa
Ḳiṣaṣ al-anbiyā᾽ i, 169a; iv, 673b; v, 176a, **180a**, 186b, 193b, 197b, 205a –
I, 174a; IV, 700b; V, 173b, **177b**, 184a, 190b, 194b, 202b
Kīs͟h (Kays, D͟jabal) i, 552a, 942b, 1355a; iii, 881a; iv, 500b, **832a**; v, 670b, 671a; s, 222b –
I, 569b, 971a, b, 1394b; III, 905a; IV, 522a, **865a**; V, 676a; S, 222b
Kīs͟h (S͟hahr-i Sabz) i, 1066b; iv, 694a, 711b; v, **181a**, 858b; vii, 925a – I, 1098b; IV, 722a, 740a; V, **178b**, 865b; VII, 925b
Ḳîs͟hlaḳ iv, 1029b; v, **182b** – IV, 1061b; V, **180a**
Kis͟hlū K͟hān (Delhi) (XIII) iii, 202b; iv, 920b; vi, 48b – III, 207b; IV, 953b; VI, 47a
Kis͟hm, Badak͟hs͟hān i, 851b – I, 875b
Ḳis͟hm (island/île) iii, 653a; iv, 777b; v, **183a**, 675a, b – III, 674b; IV, 809a; V, **180b**, 680b
Ḳis͟hn v, **184a**; vi, 80a, 82a, b – V, **181a**; VI, 78a, 79b, 80b

Kishōr Singh, Maharao (1821) vi, 419b – VI, 404b
Ḳishr iv, 452a – IV, 472a
Kishsh → Kash; Kish
al-Kishshī, Abū Shakūr al-Sālimī (XI) vi, 847b – VI, 838b
Kishtwār s, 242a – S, 242a
Kishwar ii, 577a, 579b, 951b – II, 591b, 594a, 973b
Ḳisma, ḳismet v, **184a** – V, **181b**
Kisrā v, **184b** – V, **182a**
Kisrā (Ḳarmaṭī) iv, 663a, b – IV, 690a
Kisrā I Anūshirwān (Sāsānid(e)) (579) i, 102a, 516b, 522b, 549a, 835b, 1094a; ii, 114a, 190b, 740a; iii, 304a; iv, 14a, 265a, 839a; v, 184b; vi, 230b, 378b, 632a, 633a, 637b, 648a, 653b, 660b, 664b, 745a; vii, 912b; ix, 77b; s, 115b, 127a, 255b, 299a, 354b –
I, 105a, 532b, 538b, 566a, 858b, 1127a; II, 116b, 196b, 758b; III, 313a; IV, 14b, 277a, 872a; V, 182a; VI, 224b, 363a, 617a, 618a, 622b, 633b, 639a, 646a, 650b, 734b; VII, 913a; IX, 80b; S, 115a, 126a, 255b, 298b, 354a
Kisra II Parwīz b. Hormuzd II (Sasānid(e)) (628) i, 510a, 996a, 1094a; ii, 793b; iii, 219a; iv, 730b, 1133b; v, 184b, 633b; vi, 201b, 276a, 537a, 633a; vii, 841a; viii, 77b, 119b; ix, 79a; s, 298b –
I, 525b, 1026b, 1127a; II, 812b; III, 225b; IV, 759b, 1165a; V, 182b, 638a; VI, 186a, 261a, 521b, 618a; VII, 842b; VIII, 79b, 122a; S, 298a
Kisrawān vi, 343b, 344a; s, 33b – VI, 327b, 328a; IX, 82b; S, 33b
al-Kisrawī, Abu 'l-Ḥasan ʿAlī (IX) v, **185b** – V, **182b**
Kissa → Khāsa
Ḳiṣṣa, Ḳiṣaṣ ii, 306a; iii, 369a, 374a; v, **185b**, 951a – II, 182a; III, 381a, 386a; V, **183a**, 955a
Ḳiṣṣa Čahār Darwīsh i, 430b; iii, 373a – I, 442b; III, 384b
Ḳisṭ → Makāyīl
al-Kīsumī, Abū Riḍā s, 363a – S, 363a
Kiswa (town/ville) ii, 541a; iv, 317b, 319b; vi, 546b, 547a, 548a – II, 554b; IV, 331b, 333b; VI, 531a, b, 532b
Kiswa vi, **166a** – VI, **158b**
Ki-swahili → Swahili
Ḳiṭʿa → Muḳaṭṭaʿa
Kitāb i, 30a, 274a; ii, 214a, 302b; iii, 1127a; iv, 353b; v, **207a** – I, 31a, 282a; II, 221a, 310b; III, 1154b; IV, 368b; V, **204b**
Kitāb al-Djilwa v, **208b** – V, **206a**
Kitāb al-Istibṣār → Istibṣār
Kitābāt v, **210b**, 754b, 761b, 992b – V, **208a**, 760b, 767b, 988a
Kitābî Dede Ḳorḳud → Dede Ḳorḳud
Kitābkhāna → Maktaba
Kitai → Ḳarā Khiṭāy
Kitāmiyya → Shādhiliyya
K'i-tan vi, 456a – VI, 441b
Ḳitarā → Ḳithāra
Kitau vi, 385a – VI, 369a
Kitbugha al-Manṣūrī, al-Malik al-ʿĀdil (Mamlūk) (1297) i, 1126b, 1324b; ii, 285a; iii, 954b; iv, 965b; v, 595a; vi, 322b; vii, 168b, 169b, 991b; viii, 156b, 995b –
I, 1160b, 1365b; II, 293b; III, 979a; IV, 998a; V, 598b; VI, 307a; VII, 170a, 171a, 993a; VIII, 159a, 1030b
Kitbugha Noyon (XIII) i, 786b; vii, 167a – I, 810a; VII, 168b
Kitchener, Lord i, 13b, 46a; ii, 828a – I, 13b, 47a; II, 848a
Kiṭfīr i, 825b; v, **233b** – I, 848b; V, **231b**
Ḳithāra v, **234a** – V, **232a**
al-Kitmān → al-Ibāḍiyya; Khāridjites; Taḳiyya
Ḳiṭmīr → Aṣḥāb al-Kahf; Kalb
Ḳiṭrān → Ḳaṭrān
Kivar → Kibar
Kiwām al-Dawla → Bahā' al-Dawla Fīrūz
Kiwām al-Dīn Darguzīnī (Ansabādhī) (XII) vi, 64b – VI, 62b
Kiwām al-Dīn Shīrāzī iv, 910b, 1073b – IV, 943b, 1105a
Ḳiwāmī (Gandja) (XII) iv, 59b; vi, 609b; s, 416b – IV, 62b; VI, 594b; S, 416b
Kiyā Abu 'l-Faḍl (Thā'irid(e)) s, 363a – S, 363a
Kiyā Buzurg-Ummīd (XII) vi, 918a – VI, 909b
al-Kiyā al-Harrāsī, Shams al-Islām (1010) v, **234b**; vii, 562a, 755b; s, 347a – V, **232b**; VII, 562b, 756b; S, 347a
Ḳiyāfa ii, 211a, 916a, b; v, **234b** – II, 217b, 937b, 938a; V, **233a**
Kiyā-i Djalāl vi, 515b – VI, 500b
al-Ḳiyāma i, 186b; iv, 47a, 205a, b; v, **235b** – I, 192a; IV, 50a, 214a, b; V, **233b**
Ḳiyāmatābād vi, 501b – VI, 487a
Ḳiyān → Ḳayna
Kiyāna (Zāb) vi, 435a – VI, 420a
Ḳiyās i, 276a, 1199b, 1327a; ii, 102a, 182b; iii, 795a, 1025b, 1026a; iv, 153b, 256a; v, **238b** – I, 284b, 1235a, 1367b; II, 104b, 188a; III, 818b, 1051a, 1052a; IV, 160a, 267a; V, **236b**
Ḳiyāt s, 46a, 97b, 420a – S, 46a, 97a, 420a
Kiybad Çiftliği → Kayḳubadiyya
Ḳîz v, **242b** – V, **240b**
Ḳîz Kulesi vi, 359b – VI, 344a
Kizāma iv, 532b – IV, 555b
Ḳizduwān s, 246a – S, 246a
Ḳîzîl Adalar vi, 588b – VI, 573a
Ḳîzîl Aghač vii, 497b – VII, 497b
Ḳîzîl Ahmedlî → Isfendiyār Oghlu
Ḳîzîl Arslan Khāmūsh → Khāmūsh
Ḳîzîl Arslan ʿUthmān iii, 1111a, b, 1112a – III, 1138b, 1139b
Ḳîzîl-bāsh i, 1b, 224a, 262a, 1162a, 1229b; ii, 20b, 202b; iii, 253b, 316a, 1101a; iv, 34b, 35a, b, 36b, 186b, 188b; v, **243a**, 437b, 749a; vi, 483a; X, 108b – I, 1b, 230b, 270a, 1196b, 1266a, II, 21a, 209a; III, 260b, 325b, 1128a; IV, 37a, b, 38a, 39a, 194b, 196b; V, **241a**, 440a, 754b; VI, 469a; X, 118a
Ḳîzîl-elma (Ḳîzîl-alma) v, **245b** – V, **243b**
Ḳîzîl Irmāḳ v, 172a, **246b** – V, 169b, **244a**
Ḳîzîl Ḳum iv, 613a; v, **246b**; s, 244b – IV, 637b; V, **244b**; S, 244b
Ḳîzîl-üzen v, **247a**; vi, 502a; vii, 189b – V, **245a**; VI, 487a; VII, 189b
Kizimkazi v, **247b** – V, **245a**
Kīzkānān → Kilāt
Ḳîzlar Aghasî i, 295a; iii, 175b; v, 243a, 247b – I, 304a; III, 179a; V, 240b
Klementi i, 652a, 656b – I, 672b, 677b
Klis v, 774b, 775a – V, 780b, 781a
Ḳnīṭra iv, 556b – IV, 580b
Kōbad → Ḳubādh
Ḳobān iv, 674b, 675a – IV, 702a, b
Köbeči → Ḳubači
Kōč → Ḳufč
Ḳocaeli → Kodja-eli
Kocha i, 719b – I, 741a
Ḳoč Ḥiṣār v, **247b**; vi, 231b, 541b – V, **245b**; VI, 225a, 526a
Ḳočî Beg (XVII) i, 712a; iii, 983a; iv, 168a; v, **248b**, 266a; vii, 598a; viii, 184b –

I, 733b; III, 1007b; IV, 175a; V, **246b**, 264a; VII, 598a; VIII, 187b
Ḳočḳar (river/fleuve) iv, 212b – IV, 222a
Ḳočo x, 676a – X,
Ḳodja → Khodja
Ḳodja-eli i, 468b; v, **250a** – I, 482b; V, **247b**
Kogh Vasil (Kaysūm) (XII) vi, 776b – VI, 766a
Kōhāt i, 238b; v, **250b** – I, 246a; V, **248a**
al-Kōhēn al-ʿAṭṭār v, **251a** – V, **249a**
al-Kōhīn → al-Kūhīn
Kohinoor → Kūh-i Nūr
Kōhistān → Kuhistān
Kōh-rud → Ḳuhrūd
Kōʾil → ʿĀlīgarh
Ḳoḳan → Khoḳand
Kōkbürī → Gökbürī, Muẓaffar al-Dīn
Kokča → Badakhshān
Kokča (river/rivière) i, 851b – I, 875b
Kökîldāsh vi, 130b – VI, 128b
Kök-Türk (inscriptions) vi, 809b; viii, 178a – VI, 799b; VIII, 180b
Kökülü-oghlu ii, 207a – II, 213b
Kōlatirri Rādjās iv, 547a – IV, 570b
Kölbay Toghîs ulî vi, 767a – VI, 756a
Koléa v, 362a – V, 363a
Kolhāpur vi, 535a – VI, 519b
Ḳolonborna i, 1062b – I, 1094b
Köl Tegin x, 687b – X, 729b
Ḳomač iii, 47b – III, 49a
Ḳōmis → Ḳūmis
Komo vi, 422a – VI, 407a
Komoten → Gümüldjīne
Komul v, 846a; vi, 768a – V, 858a; VI, 757b
Konakry v, **252a** – V, **250a**
al-Konawi → al-Ḳūnawī
Kong ii, 63a; v, **252b** – II, 64b; V, **250b**
Ḳongrat → Ḳungrat
Konkan iii, 426a; vi, 50b, 269a, b; s, 246a – III, 440a; VI, 48b, 254a; S, 246a
Ḳonḳîrat ii, 41b; v, 391b – II, 42b; V, 392b
Ḳonya (Ḳūniya) i, 466b, 468a, 477b, 703a, 807a; ii, 202a, 746b; iv, 575b, 621a, b, 622a, 1167b; v, **253b**, 589a, 676b, 677b, 881a; vi, 59b, 71b, 120b, 275b, 366a, 710b; s, 83b, 137a, 146a, 280b – I, 480b, 481b, 491b, 724b, 830a; II, 208a, 765a; IV, 598b, 645b, 646b, 1200b; V, **251a**, 593a, 681b, 682b, 887b; VI, 57b, 69b, 118a, 260b, 350a, 699a; S, 83a, 136a, 146a, 280a
—monuments v, **254b**, 1145a, 1146a – V, **252b**, 1137a, b
Ḳonya (Ḳaramān) Ereğlisi ii, 705b – II, 723b
Kopak → Sikka
Köpek Khān → Kebek
Köpek, Saʿd al-Dīn iv, 816b; v, 285b – IV, 849b; V, 284a
Köprü → Vezīr Köprü
Köprü ḥaḳḳî ii, 147a – II, 151a
Köprü Ḥiṣārī v, **256a** – V, **254a**
Köprülü (viziers) i, 1064a; v, **256a** – I, 1096a; V, **254a**
Köprülü ʿAbd Allāh Pasha (1724) vi, 505a; vii, 854b – VI, 490b; VII, 855a
Köprülü Aḥmed Pasha s, 171a – S, 171b
Köprülü Fāḍil Aḥmed Pāsha (1676) i, 68b, 1032b; ii, 635a, 833a; iii, 477a, 1086b; iv, 516b, 539a, 590a, 591a; v, 258b, **259a**, 720b, 766a; vi, 982b; s, 171a – I, 70a, 1064a; II, 651a, 852b; III, 493b, 1113a; IV, 539a, 562a, 614a, b; V, 256b, **257a**, 726a, 772a; VI, 975a; S, 171b
Köprülü Fāḍil Muṣṭafā Pasha (1691) i, 268a; iv, 193b, 194a, 233b; v, **261a** – I, 276b; IV, 202a, b, 244a; V, **259a**
Köprülü Mehmed Fuad (1966) ii, 596a; v, **263b**; s, 82b – II, 611a; V, **261b**; S, 82a
Köprülü Meḥmed Pasha (1661) i, 4b; ii, 1090b; iii, 626b; iv, 233b, 589b, 720a; v, **256b**; vi, 345b, 982b; vii, 900a; ix, 697b – I, 4b; II, 1116b; III, 647b; IV, 244a, 613a, 749a; V, **254b**; VI, 329b, 330a, 974b; VII, 900b; IX, 726b
Köprülü Nuʿmān Pasha (1719) i, 268b, 269a, 395a; v, **262b** – I, 277a, 406a; V, **260b**
Köprülüzāde Meḥmed Fuʾād vi, 93b, 94a –VI, 91b, 92a
Ḳopuz → ʿŪd
Kōrā Djahānābād v, **264b** – V, **262b**
Korah → Ḳārūn
Koraltan, Refik ii, 596a; vi, 1011b – II, 611a; VI, 1004a
Korča v, **264b** – V, **262b**
Kordjāna ii, 235b – II, 242b
Kordofān i, 35a; ii, 123a; v, **266b**, 1249a, b; vii, 425b; s, 164a – I, 36a; II, 126a; V, **264a**, 1240a; VII, 427a; S, 164a
Ḳordos v, **268b** – V, **266a**
Korea/Corée → al-Shīla
Körfüz i, 395a; iv, 1157b; v, **268b**, 838a – I, 406b; IV, 1189b; V, **266b**, 844b
Körguz ii, 606a – II, 621a
Korîdjan (battle of/bataille de) vi, 55b – VI, 53b
Koritza → Korča
Ḳorḳmaz b. Fakhr al-Dīn Maʿn ii, 634b, 749b; iii, 205b – II, 651a, 768a; III, 211a
Ḳorḳud b. Bāyazīd (1513) i, 396a, 1120b; ii, 1042b; v, **269a** – I, 407b, 1154a; II, 1066b; V, **267a**
Ḳorḳud Dede → Dede Ḳorḳud
Köroghlu (XVI) i, 792b; ii, 75b; iii, 117a, 374b; v, **270a**; s, 239a – I, 816a; II, 77a; III, 119b, 386b; V, **267b**; S, 239a
Ḳoron v, **270b** – V, **268a**
Ḳoryürek, Enīs Behīdj (1949) v, **271a** – V, **269a**
Kôs → Ḳūṣ
Kōs Mīnārs vi, 368b – VI, 353a
Köse ʿAlī Pasha (XVII) vii, 899b – VII, 900b
Köse Da v, **271b**; vi, 231a; vii, 990b – V, **269b**; VI, 224b; VII, 992a
Köse Mikhāl ʿAbd Allāh (XIV) vii, 34a; viii, 192a – VII, 34a; VIII, 195b
Köse Mūsā Pasha iv, 322b – IV, 337a
Kösem Wālide/Kösem Sulṭān (Māhpaykar) (1651) iii, 623a, 983a; iv, 233b, 717a, 884b, 971b; v, **272a**; vii, 597b – III, 643b, 1007b; IV, 244a, 745b, 917b, 1003b; V, **270a**; VII, 597b
Ḳosh-begi v, **273a**; s, 97a, 419b – V, **271a**; S, 96b, 419b
Köshk v, **274a** – V, **272a**
Ḳoshma v, **274b** – V, **272b**
Ḳoshuḳ → Ḳoshma
Kosi (river/rivière) vi, 47a – VI, 45b
Ḳoṣowa, Kosovo v, **275b**; vi, 74a, 89a; vii, 593b, 595a; viii, 335b – V, **273b**; VI, 71b, 87a; VII, 593b, 595a; VIII, 347a
Kossaian v, 830b – V, 837a
Köstendil → Küstendil
Köstendje v, **277a** – V, **275a**
Kōt Kān'grā → Kān'grā
Kota kota v, **278a** – V, **276a**
Kota Tengah vi, 116b – VI, 114b
Kota Waringin s, 150b – S, 150b
Kotah vi, 419b, 536a – VI, 404b, 520b
Köten (ḲîpčaJ) (XIII) x, 693a – X, 735b
Koti iv, 1029b – IV, 1061b
Kotlā vi, 49b – VI, 48a

Kotlā Mubārakpur (Delhi) vi, 126b – VI, 124b
Kotoko ii, 10a; iii, 98a; v, **278a** – II, 10a; III, 100b; V, **276a**
Kotonou v, **279a** – V, **277a**
Kotumble → Kudummul
Ḳotur-čay vi, 200b, 201a, b, 202b, 504a – VI, 185a, b, 186b, 489b
Kötürüm → Djalāl al-Dīn Bāyazīd (Isfendiyar-oghlu)
Ḳotuz → Ḳuṭuz
Kōtwāl ii, 868a; iii, 199a, 493a; v, **279b**; s, 59a – II, 888a; III, 203b, 510a; V, **277b**; S, 59b
Kōtwālī Darwāza vi, 46b – VI, 45a
Kouandé v, **280b** – V, **278b**
Koulougli → Ḳul-oghlu
Koumiss → Kumis
Kounta → Kunta
Koweit → Kuwayt
Köy v, **281b** – V, **279b**
Köy enstitüleri v, **281b**; s, 283b – V, **279b**; S, 283b
Koyama vi, 370a – VI, 354b
Koyl v, **283a**; s, 331b – V, **281a**; S, 331a
Ḳoylu Ḥiṣār v, **283a** – V, **281a**
Ḳoyul Ḥiṣār v, **283b** – V, **281b**
Ḳoyun Baba v, **283b**; viii, 189b – V, **281b**; VIII, 192b
Ḳoyunlū iv, 389a – IV, 406a
Kozak → Kazakh
Ḳōzān i, 285a, b; v, **283b**; ix, 678a – I, 293b, 294b; V, **282a**; IX, 708a
Ḳozan-oghullari ii, 207a; v, **284a**; ix, 679a – II, 213b; V, **282b**; IX, 707b
Kozhikode vi, 206b – VI, 191a
Ḳožoñ v, 275b – V, 273b
Ḳrān → Sikka
Krawang s, 202a – S, 201b
Ḳrim → Ḳirim
Ḳriz iv, 1029a; v, **284b** – IV, 1061a; V, **282b**
Kroumir → Khumayr
Krujë iv, 139a, b, 140a; v, **284b** – IV, 144b, 145a, b, 146a; V, **282b**
Krum (Bulghar) (814) x, 692a – 734b
Krushevats → Aladja Ḥisār
Ksar, Ksour → Ḳaṣr; Ḳaṣaba
Ḳsentīnī → al-Ḳusanṭīnī
Ḳṣība → Ḳaṣaba (town/ville)
Kuala Lumpur i, 980a; ii, 426b; vi, 232b, 241a – I, 1010a; II, 437b; VI, 206a, 212a
Ḳuʿaytī, Āl i, 554b; vi, 81b; vii, 496a; s, 337b, 338b – I, 572a; VI, 79b; VII, 496a; S, 337a, 338b
al-Ḳuʿaytī, ʿUmar b. ʿAwadh (XIX) vii, 496a – VII, 496a
Ḳuba → Ḳubba
Ḳubā (Farghānā) ii, 791a – II, 810a
Kuba (al-Madīna) vi, 646b, 647a, 649a, 654a, 659b, 677a – VI, 632a, b, 634a, 639b, 645b, 663b
Ḳubači ii, 86b, 89a; iv, 1169a, 1170a; v, **285b** – II, 88a, 90b; IV, 1201b, 1203a; V, **283b**
Ḳubād b. Sulṭān Ḥusayn i, 920a – I, 948a
Ḳubādābād iv, 702a, 818a; v, **285b** – IV, 730b, 850b; V, **284a**
Ḳubādh II (Sāsānid(e)) (628) ix, 80a – IX, 83b
Ḳubādh b. Fīrūz (Sāsānid(e)) (531) i, 1041a, 1094a, 1134a; ii, 78a, 253a; iii, 571b; vi, 949a; ix, 76b; s, 127a – I, 1072b, 1127a, 1168b; II, 79a, 260b; III, 591b; VI, 941a; IX, 79b; S, 126a
Ḳubādh b. Yazīd iv, 347a – IV, 362a
Ḳubādhiyān v, **286b** – V, **285a**
Ḳubādja → Nāṣir al-Dīn Ḳabača
Ḳubād-oghlu (1400) vi, 974a – VI, 966b
Kubafolo v, **287a** – V, **285b**
Kuban i, 1305a – I, 1345a
Ḳuban (river/rivière) v, **287b** – V, **286a**
Kūbarā vi, 507b – VI, 493a
Ḳubāṭī iv, 774a – IV, 805a
Ḳubāwī, Abū Naṣr Aḥmad (XII) vii, 966a – VII, 966b
Kubayh ii, 137b – II, 141a
Kubaysha vi, 476b – VI, 462b
Ḳubba (Ḳuba) v, **296a**; s, 143a – V, **287b**; S, 143a
Kubba (palace) s, 301a – S, 300b
Kubba (tent/-e) iv, 1147a; vi, 651b – IV, 1179a; VI, 637a
Kubba (tomb/-eau) iv, 352b, 434a; v, 214b, **289a**, 1139b – IV, 367b, 453a; V, 212a, **288a**, 1133a
al-Ḳubba (Ḳubbat al-ʿAlam/al-Arḍ) v, **297a** – V, **296a**
Ḳubbat al-ʿĀlam → al-Ḳubba
Ḳubbat al-Bārūdiyyīn (Marrākush) vii, 587a – VII, 587a
Ḳubbat al-hawāʾ iii, 274a; v, **297b** – III, 282a; V, **297a**
Ḳubbat al-Ṣakhra i, 77b; ii, 911a, 978a; iii, 174b, 381a; v, **298a**; vi, 665b, 666a, 707a; vii, 8b – I, 80a; II, 932b, 978a; III, 178b, 393b; V, **297b**; VI, 652a, 695b; VII, 9a
Ḳubbe weziri v, **299b** – V, **299a**
Ḳūbčūr iii, 1099b; iv, 31a, 1042a, 1050a, 1051b; v, **299b**; vii, 233b – III, 1126b; IV, 33a, 1073b, 1081b, 1083a; V, **299a**; VII, 235b
Ḳubilāy b. Toluy b. Čingiz Khān (Mongol Great Khān) (1294) i, 1188a, 1311b; ii, 3a, 45b, 47a; iii, 472a; iv, 811b; v, 38b, 39a, **300a**; vi, 406a, 420a, 524a; vii, 230a – I, 1223a, 1352a; II, 3a, 46b; III, 488b; IV, 844b; V, 40a, **299b**; VI, 390b, 405a, 508b; VII, 232a
Kubilāy Noyon iv, 583b – IV, 607a
Kubrā, Shaykh Aḥmad b. ʿUmar Nadjm al-Dīn (1220) i, 754b; iv, 1064a; v, **300a**; vii, 870b; viii, 539b, 703a; ix, 110a, 784b; x, 251a; s, 423a – I, 777a; IV, 1095b; V, **299b**; VII, 872a; VIII, 557a, 723a; IX, 114a, 818b; X, 270a; S, 423b
Kubrat (Bulghar) (VII) x, 692a – X, 734b
Kubrāwiyya iv, 48a, 49a, 51b; v, 300a, 301a-b; vi, 549b; x, 251a, 328a; s, 353b – IV, 50b, 52a, 54b; V, 299b, 300b; VI, 534a; X, 251a, 269b, 353a; S, 353b
Ḳubrus i, 109a, 152a, 798b, 935b, 945b, 1054a; ii, 522a; iii, 186b, 189a, 1182b, 1198b; v, **301b**, 1077a, 1171a; vi, 324b; vii, 720b; s, 53a, 120b, 221b – I, 112a, 156b, 822a, 964b, 974b, 1085b; II, 535a; III, 190b, 193b, 1212a, 1228b; V, **301a**, 1074b, 1160b; VI, 309a; VII, 721b; S, 53b, 120a, 221b
Kubruslu → Ḳibrisli
Kubu i, 782a; v, **309b** – I, 805b; V, **309a**
Kūč → Ḳufč
Kuča ix, 617b; x, 348b – IX, 641a; 374a
Kūča-i Arg vi, 20b – VI, 18a
Kučak → Wisāl
Kūčak Khān Djangalī, Mīrzā (1921) ii, 445b; iv, 398b, 789b; v, **310a**; viii, 450a; s, 110a, 366a – II, 457a; IV, 416a, 821b; V, **309b**; VIII, 465a; S, 109b, 365b
Ḳūčān v, **311a**; vi, 495a; s, 83a – V, **311a**; VI, 480b; S, 83a
Kucha s, 136b – S, 136a
Küčlük i, 418b, 987b; ii, 42b, 43a, 791b; iii, 1114b; iv, 583a; v, 38b – I, 430b, 1018a; II, 43b, 810b; III, 1141b; IV, 606b; V, 39b
Küčük Aḥmad Pasha (1634) ii, 635a, 751a; vi, 345b – II, 651a, 769b; VI, 329b
Küčük ʿAlī-oghlu ii, 207b; s, 172b – II, 214a; S, 172b
Küčük Bālī Beg → Yaḥyā Pasha-zāde Küčük
Küčük Bostān i, 1279b – I, 1318b
Küčük Čelebi-zāde → Čelebi-zāde
Küčük Ḥasan Pasha i, 904b – I, 932a
Küčük Ḥusayn Pasha → Ḥusayn Pasha, Küčük

Küčük Ḳaynarča (treaty/uraité 1774) i, 56b, 62b, 311a, 470b, 893b; ii, 26b, 60b, 688b; iii, 589b, 1186a; v, 141a, **312b**, 495a; vii, 63a, 275b – I, 58a, 64b, 320b, 484b, 920a; II, 26b, 62a, 705b; III, 610a, 1216a; V, 143b, **312a**, 498a; VII, 63b, 277b
Küčük Köy s, 330a – S, 329b
Küčük Meḥmed (Janissary/-aire, Miṣr) (1694) iv, 852a; vii, 178b – IV, 885a; VII, 180b
Küčük Meḥmed Khān i, 721b; ii, 44a – I, 743b; II, 45a
Küčük Muṣṭafā → Muṣṭafā Čelebi
Küčük Saʿīd Pasha (1914) i, 285b; iii, 993b; v, **313b** – I, 294b; III, 1018a; V, **313b**
Küčük Suleymān Pasha i, 905b; iii, 91a – I, 933a; III, 93b
Küčük Sulṭān i, 1076a – I, 1108a,b
Kučum Khān (Sibir) (XVI) ii, 45a; v, **314b**; viii, 161a – II, 46a; V, **314a**; VIII, 163b
Küčümid(e)s i, 1076a – I, 1108a
Ḳuḍāʿa, Banū i, 1a, 545a, 563b, 962a; ii, 122a, 572a; iii, 363b; v, **315a**; vi, 145a, 649a; vii, 267b; viii, 91a; x, 788a, 842b – I, 1a, 562a, 581b, 991b; II, 125a, 586a; III, 375a; V, **314b**; VI, 143a, 634b; VII, 269b; VIII, 93a; X,
Ḳuḍāʿa b. Mālik b. Ḥimyar vi, 82a – VI, 80a
al-Ḳuḍāʿī, Muḥammad b. Salāma (ḳāḍī) (1062) vii, 164a; viii, 895a – VII, 165b; VIII, 926a
al-Ḳuḍāʿī, Yūsuf b. ʿAlī (XII) iii, 221a – III, 228a
Kūdakiyya v, 65a – V, 67a
Ḳudām b. Ḳādim (480) viii, 407b – VIII, 422a
Ḳudāma b. Djaʿfar al-Kātib al Baghdādī (932) i, 590b, 730a, 857b, 982a, b; ii, 579a, b, 580b; iii, 354b; iv, 249a; v, **318b**; vi, 313b, 348a, 605b, 640a; vii, 277a, 978b; viii, 496b; s, 266a, 402a – I, 609b, 752a, 881b, 1012b, 1013a; II, 593b, 594b, 595a; III, 365b; IV, 260a; V, **318a**; VI, 298b, 332a, 590a, 625a, b; VII, 279a, 979a; VIII, 513b, 514a; S, 265b, 402b
Ḳudār al-Aḥmar (Uḥaymir) i, 169b; iii, 1270a – I, 174a; III, 1303a
Ḳudayd vi, 373b, 374a; s, 312a – VI, 358a; S, 311b
Ḳuddūs → Muḥammad ʿAlī Bārfurūshī
Kudjuk (Küčük) b. al-Nāṣir Muḥammad (Mamlūk) (1341) vi, 323b – VI, 308a
Kudjūr iv, 808a; vi, 511b – IV, 840b; VI, 497a
Ḳudra iv, 271b, 272b; v, 576a, b – IV, 283b, 284b; V, 580b, 581a
Kudrī iv, 743b – IV, 773a
al-Ḳuds (Jerusalem) i, 215b, 352a, 549b, 797b, 799b, 975b, 1310a; ii, 63b, 911b; iii, 1158a; v, 82b, 92a, **322a**, 1127b; vi, 118b, 378b, 648a, 665a; vii, 274b; s, 154a – I, 222a, 363a, 567a, 821a, 823a, 1005b, 1350b; II, 65a, 932b; III, 1186a; V, 84b, 94b, **321b**, 1123b; VI, 116b, 363a, 633b, 651a; VII, 276a; S, 154b
—monuments ii, 911a; iii, 174a,b; v, 327b, **339a-344a**, 1143a, b – II, 932b; III, 178a,b; V, 327a, **340a-345a**, 1135b, 1136a
—population v, 328b, 329a, 334a, 336a, b – V, 328a, b, 334a, 336b, 337a
al-Ḳuds → al Masdjid al-Aḳṣā
Ḳudsī → Bakīkhānlī
al-Ḳudsī, Abū Ḥāmid Muḥammad (1483) iii, 772b; vi, 412b, 413b; vii, 141a, 165a, 175b, 176b – III, 795b; VI, 397b, 398a; VII, 143a, 166b, 177b, 178b
Ḳudsī, Muḥammad Djān (1646) v, **344b**; vii, 341a, b; viii, 776a; ix, 241b – V, **345b**; VII, 343a; VIII, 802a; IX, 247b
al-Ḳudsī, Nāẓim ii, 662a – II, 678b
Ḳudsiyya Bēgam i, 1195b, 1197a – I, 1231a, 1232b
Küdüdjin bint Tash Möngke (XIV) ix, 474b – IX, 493a
Kudummul v, **345a** – V, **345b**
al-Ḳudūrī, Abu ʾl-Ḥusayn/al-Ḥasan Aḥmad (1037) i, 310a, 791a; ii, 390a, 486a; iii, 163a; v, **345a**; vii, 310b; s, 192a – I, 319b, 814a; II, 400b, 498b; III, 166b; V, **346a**; VII, 312b; S, 193a
Kudyat al-ʿAbīd vi, 589a – VI, 574a
al-Kūfa i, 16a, 76b, 77a, 103a, 704a; ii, 196b, 415b, 453a; iii, 843a, 1252b, 1254b, 1255a; iv, 911a; v, 174a, **345b**, 945b; vi, 119b, 140b, 266b, 333b, 334b, 335b, 336b, 345a, 364b, 427b, 428a, b, 441b, 620a, 624a, 647b, 651a, 656b, 659b, 660a, b, 667a, 668a, 670b, 675b, 679a, b, 691a; vii, 396a, 769a, b; viii, 696b; ix, 826a; s, 15b, 16a, 19a, 48a, 198b, 225b, 230b, 304b, 357b, 358a, 389b, 393b, 400b, 401a – I, 16b, 78b, 79a, 106a, 725b; II, 203a, 426a, 465a; III, 867a, 1285a, 1287a,b; IV, 944a; V, 171b, **346b**, 949a; VI, 117b, 138b, 251b, 318a, b, 319b, 321a, 329a, 348b, 412b, 413a, b, 427a, 605a, 609a, 633a, 636b, 642a, 645b, 646a, 653a, 654a, 656b, 662a, 666a, b, 678b; VII, 397b, 770b, 771a; VIII, 716b; IX, 860b; S, 16a, b, 19a, 48b, 198b, 225b, 230a, 304b, 357b, 390a, 393b, 401a, b
—ethnography/-ie i, 529b, 568a; v, 346a, b – I, 545b, 586b; V, 347a, b
—literature/littérature ii, 729a, 806b; iv, 1003a; v, 350b – II, 747b, 826a; IV, 1035b; V, 351a, b
—monuments i, 610a; v, 347a, b, 348b – I, 629b; V, 347b, 348a, 349b
Kuffār → Kāfir (infidel/infidèle)
al-Kūfī, Abū Djaʿfar (931) vi, 351b – VI, 335b
al-Kūfī, Abu ʾl-Ḳāsim ʿAlī b. Aḥmad (963) vii, 517b – VII, 518a
al-Kūfī, ʿAlī b. Ḥāmid b. Abī Bakr s, 163a – S, 162a
al-Kūfī, Furāt b. Furāt (922) x, 86b – X, 93b
al-Kūfī, Muḥammad b. Sulaymān s, 335a – S, 335a
al-Kūfī, Shams al-Dīn Maḥmūd vi, 606a – VI, 591a
Kūfic ii, 67a, 91a, 260b, 372b, 709b; iv, 1121a, 1122a, 1123a, 1125a; v, 217a-221b, 229b-230b, 350b – II, 68a, 92b, 269a, 382b, 728b; IV, 1152b, 1154a, 1155a, 1156b; V, 214b-218b, 227b-228b, 351a
Ḳūfičīs → Ḳufṣ
Kufra ii, 492b; v, **351b**, 759b, 887a – II, 505a; V, **352b**, 765b, 893b
Ḳufṣ i, 1005a, b, 1354b; iii, 1098a; iv, 807a; v, 152b, **352b**; s, 129a – I, 1036a, b, 1393b; III, 1124b; IV, 839b; V, 154a, **353a**; S, 128b
Kūghūn s, 327a – S, 326b
Ḳuḥāfa x, 189a – X, 204b
Kūhak → Čopan Ata
Kūhandil Khān i, 231a, b; iv, 537b – I, 238a,b; IV, 561a
Kuḥaylat al-ʿAdjūz ii, 785b – II, 804a
Kūh-Gīlū (Kūh-Gālū) iii, 1107a; iv, 5b, 9a; v, 822a, 824b, 829b, 830b – III, 1134a; IV, 6a, 9b; V, 828b, 831a, 835b, 836a, b
Kūh-Gīlūya v, 826b, 827a; vi, 496a – V, 832b, 833a; VI, 481a
al-Kūhī, Abū Sahl s, – V, **453a**
Kūh-i Bābā i, 221b; v, **353a**; s, 367a – I, 228a; V, **354a**; S, 368a
Kūh-i Bāričī → Bāriz
Kūh-i Bazmān iv, 3b – IV, 3b
Kūh-i Binālūd s, 83a – S, 83a
Kūh-i Darang vi, 384a – VI, 368a
Kūh-i Hazār s, 127a – S, 126a
Kūh-i Iṣṭakhr iv, 221b – IV, 231b
Kūh-i Kalāt iv, 4a – IV, 4b
Kūh-i Ḳārin s, 309a – S, 309a
Kūh-i Lālazār s, 127a – S, 126a

Kūh-i Mānd vi, 384a – VI, 368a
Kūh-i Marrayi Shikaft vi, 384a – VI, 368a
Kūh-i Nār vi, 384a – VI, 368a
Kūh-i Nūḥ → Aghrî Dagh
Kūh-i Nūr iii, 348a; v, **353b**; vii, 854b – III, 358b; V, **354b**; VII, 856a
Kūh-i Raḥmat iv, 221a – IV, 230b
Kūh-i Rang v, 830a – V, 836a
Kūh-i Shāh Djahān s, 83a – S, 83a
Kūh-iSurkh iv, 4a – IV, 4b
Kūh-iTaftān iv, 3b – IV, 3b
al-Kūhin v, **353b**; s, 390b – V, **355a**; S, 391a
al-Kūhīn al-ʿAṭṭār → al-Kōhēn al-ʿAṭṭār
Ḳūhistān i, 1233a; v, 56a, **354a**; vi, 274a, 696b; s, 66b, 149a – I, 1270a; V, 57b, **355b**; VI, 258b, 684b; S, 67a, 149a
Kūhistanī (language/langue) ii, 138b; v, 356a – II, 142b; V, 357b
al-Ḳuhistānī (d./m. 1543) iii, 163b – III, 167a
Kūh-kamaraʾī, Ḥādjdj Sayyid Ḥusayn (1881) vii, 299b; s, 76a – VII, 301b; S, 76a
Kūh-kamarā, Ḥudjdjat (Āyatullāh) (XX) vii, 762b – VII, 764a
Kuḥl i, 1089a; v, **356a** – I, 1121b; V, **357b**
Kuḥlan vi, 436a – VI, 421a
Kuhna-Abīward i, 99b – I, 102b
Kuhna-Abīward Ḳahḳaha i, 99b – I, 102b
Ḳuhrūd (Kōh-rūd) v, **357a**, 869a; vi, 511b – V, **358b**, 875a; VI, 497a
Kūhyār Bāwand iv, 645b, 646b, 647a – IV, 672a, 673a, b
Kūka → Kūkawa
Kūkaltāsh, Khān Aʿẓam ʿAzīz Muḥammad (XVI) vii, 458a – VII, 458a
Kūkaltāsh, Khān-i Djahān (XVII) ii, 488b – II, 500b
Kūkawa (Kūka) i, 1260a, b; v, **357b**; s, 164b – I, 1298b, 1299a; V, **359a**; S, 164b
Ḳukli Meḥmed Beg v, 724b – V, 729b
Kūko iv, 361a, b – IV, 377a, b
Ḳul ii, 25b, 147b; v, **359a**, 630a – II, 26a, 151b; V, **360a**, 634a
Ḳul Muṣṭafā Ḳayîkdjî (XVII) v, **359b** – V, **360b**
Ḳul-Bābā Kökältāsh s, 340a – S, 339b
Ḳūla (town/ville) v, **359b** – V, **360b**
Kulāb → Khuttalān
Kulāčī ii, 975a; iv, 597a – II, 997b; IV, 621b
Kūlāh v, 751b – V, 757a
Kulāl (amīr) (1379) viii, 45a – VIII, 46a
Kūlam v, **360a**, 937b – V, **361a**, 941a
al-Ḳulayʿa v, **361a** – V, **362a**
Ḳulayʿat (Syria/-e) vi, 579a – VI, 564a
Kulayb vi, 490a – VI, 476a
Kulayb b. Rabīʿa al-Taghlibī i, 1089a; ii, 159b; iii, 393a; v, **362a**; s, 234b – I, 1121b; II, 164b; III, 405b; V, **363a**; S, 234a
Kulayb Wāʾil i, 526b – I, 542b
al-Kulaynī (al-Kulīnī), Abū Djaʿfar Muḥammad (939) i, 1352a; iii, 726b, 1266a; v, **362b**; vi, 12a, 549a, 552a; vii, 132a, 548a; s, 56b, 103b – I, 1391b; III, 749a, 1299a; V, **364a**; VI, 11b, 533b, 536b; VII, 134a, 548a; S, 57a, 103a
Kulbarga → Gulbarga
Ḳuldja (Ghuldja) iii, 1120b; v, **363b**; vi, 768b – III, 1148a; V, **364b**; VI, 758a
Külek Boghaz → Cilicia/Cilicie
Ḳulī Khān Maḥram i, 80b, 117b – I, 83a, 121a
Ḳulī Khān, Padshān (1682) s, 420b – S, 421a
Ḳulī Ḳuṭb al-Mulk, Sulṭān (Ḳuṭb Shāhī) (1518) ii, 922b, 1084b, 1118b, 1119a; iii, 15a, 421a; v, 549b, 1258a; vi, 63a, b, 696a – II, 944a, 1110a, 1145a,b; III, 16a, 435a; V, 554a, 1249a; VI, 61a, 684a
Ḳulī Shāh i, 1120b; v, 677b – I, 1154a,b; V, 682b
al-Kulīnī, Abū Djaʿfar Muḥammad → Kulaynī
Kullābiyya iii, 1164b; iv, 469a; s, 392a – III, 1193b; IV, 490a; S, 392b
Ḳullar-āḳāsī iv, 36b; v, 359b – IV, 39a; V, 360b
Ḳulliyya ii, 423a; iv, 435b; v, **364b** – II, 434a; IV, 455a; V, **366a**
Kulliyyat al-ādāb i, 176a – I, 181a
Külliyye v, **366a** – V, **366b**
Ḳulluḳ-aḳčasî → Čift-resmi
Ḳul-oghlu i, 369a, 371a, 1119a; ii, 173a, 520b; iii, 340a; iv, 481b; v, **366b**, 1010b, 1247b – I, 380a, 381b, 1152b; II, 178b, 534a; III, 350b; IV, 502b; V, **367b**, 1006b, 1238a
Ḳuloghlu (poet/poète) (XVII) v, **367a** – V, **367b**
Kūlsara vi, 498b, 501a – VI, 484a, 486b
Kulsāriʿ → Ḳuṭb al-Dīn
Kültepe s, 100b – S, 100a
Kulthūm (Ḳubāʾ) vi, 647a – VI, 632a
Kulthūm b. ʿIyāḍ al-Ḳushayrī (741) i, 86b, 990b, 1175a; iii, 169b, 494a; v, **367a** – I, 88b, 1021a, 1210a; III, 173a, 511a; V, **368a**
Kültigin (prince/le prince) iv, 583b; v, 854a – IV, 607b; V, 860b
Kulughlīs vii, 722a – VII, 723a
Ḳulumriya (Coïmbra/-e) i, 390a, 1338b; v, **367a** – I, 401b, 1379a; V, **368a**
al-Ḳulzum i, 931a, 932a; ii, 129b; v, **367b**; ix, 912a – I, 960a,b; II, 13a; V, **368b**; IX, 950a
Ḳum(m) (Ghom) i, 16b; iii, 1124b, 1169b; iv, 7b; v, 292b, 350a, **369a**; vi, 21a, 271a, 332b, 337b, 366a, 493a, 513a, 514a, 516b, 548b, 553a, b, 554a, b, 627b, 634b, 714b; viii, 387a; s, 56b, 104a, 127a, b, 139a, 157b, 158a, 305a, 342a – I, 17a; III, 1152b, 1198b; IV, 8b; V, 292a, 351a, **369b**; VI, 19a, 256a, 317a, 321b, 350a, 479a, 498b, 499a, 501b, 502a, 533a, 537b, 538a, b, 539a, 612b, 619b, 703b; VIII, 400b; S, 57a, 103b, 126b, 138b, 158a, 305a, 342a
Kuma (river/rivière) s, 169a – S, 169a
al-Ḳūmā/al-Ḳawmā v, **372b** – V, **373b**
Ḳumān ii, 202b; v, 126a, **373a**; x, 690b – II, 209a; V, 128b, **374a**; X, 732b
Ḳumān Ḳîpčaḳ Confederation x, 692b – X, 735a
Kumārī → Ḥasan, al-Malik al-Nāṣir Nāṣir al-Dīn (Mamlūk) (1362)
Ḳumāsh iii, 344b, 1126b; v, 151a, 216b, **373b**, 748a – III, 355a, 1154b; V, 153a, 214a, **374b**, 753b
Kumasi ii, 1003b – II, 1026b
Kumatgī iii, 287b – III, 296b
Kumayl b. Ziyād i, 89a – I, 91b
Ḳumayr, Banū viii, 1002b – VIII, 1037b
al-Kumayrī b. Zayd al-Asadī (743) viii, 83a, 122b – VIII, 85a, 125b
Kumayt b. Zayd al-Asadī (743) i, 402a; ii, 1011a; v, **374a**; viii, 83a, 122b – I, 412b; II, 1034b; V, **375a**; VIII, 85a, 125b
Ḳumbara → Khumbara
Kumbaradjī → Khumbaradjî
Kumbhalgaṛh vi, 53a – VI, 51b
Ḳumbi Ṣāliḥ → Kunbi Ṣāliḥ
Ḳumī → Malik Ḳumī
al-Ḳumī, Aḥmad b. Muḥammad b. al-Ḥasan b. al-Walīd (X) vii, 312a – VII, 314b
al-Ḳūmī, ʿAlī b. Ibrāhīm b. Hāshim (X) vi, 351b; vii, 399a – VI, 335b; VII, 400a
al-Ḳūmī, Ḥādjdjī Āḳā Ḥusayn s, 158a, 342b – S, 158a, 342a
al-Ḳūmī, Ḥasan b. Muḥammad iii, 1169b – III, 1198b

al-Ḳūmī, Ḳāḍī Aḥmad Ibrāhīm Ḥusaynī (XVI) v, **379a** – V, **379b**
al-Ḳūmī, Ḳāḍī Saʿīd (1692) vii, 476a – VII, 475b
al-Ḳūmī, Mīrzā Abū 'l-Ḳāsim (1817) vi, 551b; vii, 298b – VI, 536a; VII, 300b
al-Ḳūmī, Muḥammad (vizier) (XIII) vii, 727b – VII, 728a
al-Ḳūmī, Muḥammad b. ʿAbd Allāh (IX) viii, 89b – VIII, 92a
al-Ḳūmī, Muḥammad b. Aḥmad b. Dāwūd b. ʿAlī (978) vii, 312a – VII, 314b
al-Ḳūmī, Mullā Muḥammad Ṭāhir (1686) viii, 136a – VIII, 138b
al-Ḳūmī, Saʿd b. ʿAbd Allāh (911) iv, 661b; vii, 459b, 517a – IV, 688a; VII, 459b, 517b
al-Ḳūmt, Sayyid Muḥsin b. Muḥammad al-Ridawī s, 380a – S, 380a
al-Ḳūmī, Sayyid Ṣadr al-Dīn s, 134b – S, 134a
Kumīdjīs ii, 1a; iv, 631b; v, 75b, **375b** – II, 1a; IV, 656b; V, 78a, **376a**
Ḳumîḳ → Ḳumuḳ
Kumîs (Ḳîmîz) iv, 998a; v, **375b** – IV, 1030b; V, **376b**
Ḳūmis (Comes) i, 491a; v, **376a** – I, 506a; V, **376b**
Ḳūmis (Manf) vi, 411b – VI, 396b
Kūmis (province) v, **377a**; vi, 120a, 332b, 333a; s, 149a, 192a, 298a, 309b – V, **378a**; VI, 117b, 317a, b; S, 149a, 193a, 297b, 309a
Kūmis b. Antunyān v, 376b – V, 377a
al-Ḳūmisī, Daniel iv, 604a, b – IV, 628a, b, 629a
Kūmiya (berber/berbère) v, **378b**; vi, 310b – V, **379b**; VI, 295b
Ḳumḳum v, 988a – V, 983b
Ḳumr (Comoro Is.) i, 170a, 522a; v, **379b**, 939a, 940b; vi, 82b, 203b – I, 175a, 538a; V, **380b**, 943a, 944b; VI, 80b, 187b
al-Ḳūm-Ri<u>sh</u>ī, <u>Sh</u>ihāb al-Dīn iv, 810a – IV, 843a
Ḳumuḳ ii, 89a, 141b; v, **381b**, 617b; x, 691a, 920b – II, 90b, 145a; V, **382b**, 621b; X, 732b,
Ḳumuḳ (langu(ag)e, li(t)te(é)rature) v, 382b, 383a, 617b – V, 383b, 384a, 621b
Kumūn v, **384a**; s, 226a – V, **385a**; S, 226a
Ḳumū<u>sh</u> i, 767a – I, 790a
Kumzārī i, 575a – I, 593b
Ḳūn, Banū v, 373a, **385a**; x, 689b; s, 279a – V, 374a, **386b**; X, 781b; S, 279a
Ḳūn (Ḳumān)-Ḳîpčaḳ x, 690b – X, 732b
Kun Laszlo (Lászlo the Cuman) (1290) x, 693a – X, 735b
Ḳunā v, **385b**, 1161a – V, **387a**, 1150b
Kunar iv, 409b, 411a – IV, 427a, 429a
Kunāsa v, 347a, b – V, 348a, b
al-Ḳūnawī, 'Alāʾ al-Dīn i, 596a; iii, 953a – I, 615b; III, 977b
al-Kunawī, Ṣadr al-Dīn → Ṣadr al-Dīn
Ḳunayṭira → Ḳanṭara
Ḳunayṭra (Lubnān) vi, 31a, 455a – VI, 29a, 440b
Kunāz, Banū iv, 568a – IV, 590a
Ḳunbi Ṣāliḥ ii, 1002a; v, **386b** – II, 1025a; V, **387b**
Kund-Sūlḳān s, 423a – S, 423b
Kundar (river/rivière) s, 329b – S, 329a
Kun<u>dj</u>āh/Kan<u>dj</u>āh ii, 1006b; s, 322a – II, 1030a; S, 321b
Kun<u>dj</u>pura iv, 666b – IV, 693b
Kundur → Lubān
al-Kundurī, ʿAmīd al-Mulk (1064) i, 420a, 421a, 434a, 952b; ii, 192a, 605a; iii, 1148b, 1201a; iv, 458a; v, **387b**; vi, 523b; viii, 69b, 70a; s, 192a – I, 432a, 433a, 446a, 981b; II, 198a, 620a; III, 1176b, 1231b; IV, 478b; V, **389a**; VI, 508b; VIII, 71b; S, 193a
Ḳunduz i, 853a; v, **388b** – I, 876b; V, **389b**
Ḳunfu<u>dh</u>, Ḳunfa<u>dh</u> v, **389b** – V, **390a**
Kunfu<u>dh</u> b. ʿUmayr (VII) vii, 468b – VII, 468a
al-Ḳunfu<u>dh</u>a v, **391a**; vi, 154a – V, **391b**; VI, 152a
Kung v, 673a, b, 765a – V, 678a, b, 771a
Ḳungrāt i, 422a, 607b; ii, 45a; iv, 610b, 1065a; v, 24a, 273b, **391b**; vi, 418a; vii, 574b; s, 97b, 169a, 420a – I, 434a, 627b; II, 46a; IV, 635b, 1096b; V, 24b, 271b, **392b**; VI, 403a; VII, 575a; S, 97a, 169a, 420a
Kūnī ḳadar iv, 203a – IV, 212a
Ḳūniya (Ḳamūniya) iv, 826b – IV, 859b
Ḳuniya → Ḳonya
Ḳūnka v, **392a**; s, 143a – V, **393a**; S, 143a
Ḳunṣul → Consul
Ḳunṣul, Ilyās v, 1257a – V, 1248a
Ḳunsul, Zakī v, 1257a – V, 1248a
Kunta, Banū i, 809a; iv, 382a; v, **393a**, 889b, 1166a; vi, 259b, 357a; vii, 613b; ix, 756a – I, 832a; IV, 399a; V, **393b**, 896a, 1155b; VI, 244a, 341a; VII, 613b; IX, 791a
al-Kuntī, <u>Sh</u>ay<u>kh</u> Sīdī al-Mu<u>kh</u>tār (1811) vi, 259b; vii, 623a – VI, 244a; VII, 622b
Küntog<u>h</u>dî (Atabeg) (1119) vi, 64a, 500a; x, 42b – VI, 62a, 485a; X, 44a
Ḳunūt v, **395a** – V, **396a**
Kunūz i, 1028b – I, 1060a
Kunya ii, 302a; iv, 179a; v, 116b, **395b** – II, 310b; IV, 187a; V, 119a, **396b**
Kunya Urgenč → Urgenc
Kunyipakki Sahib, C.O.T. (XX) vi, 461a – VI, 446b
Kuominchün horde v, 845a, b – V, 857a, b
Kur (river/rivière) i, 634b; v, **396b**, 866a, 867b – I, 655b; V, **397b**, 872b, 874a
Ḳurʾ, Ḳurūʾ iii, 1011a; iv, 253b – III, 1036b; IV, 264b
Kūr Galdwan ii, 828a – II, 847b
Kūra i, 489b; v, **397b** – I, 504a; V, **399a**
Ḳurʿa iv, 259b; v, **398a** – IV, 271a; V, **399a**
al-Kura (sphe(è)re) v, **397a** – V, **398a**
Ḳura<u>kh</u> v, 729b, 730a – V, 734b, 735a
Kuram (river/rivière) → Kurram
Ḳurama v, **399b** – V, **400b**
Ḳuraʿān i, 1258a – I, 1296a
Ḳurād b. Ḥanīfa iii, 49a – III, 51a
Kuraibiya → Kuraybiyya
Ḳurʾān i, 55a, 77b, 107a, 383b, 549a, 565b, 567b, 585b, 922b, 1084b, 1199b, 1242a, 1345b; ii, 126a, 388b, 728b, 834b, 841a, 949b; iii, 24a, 41b, 65a, 152a, 369a, 513b, 874b, 1127a; iv, 81a-84b, 146a, b, 469b, 902b, 980b-986b, 1133b; v, 127a, **400a**; x, 72b –
I, 56b, 79b, 110a, 394b, 566b, 584a, 586a, 604b, 950b, 1117a, 1234b, 1279b, 1386a; II, 129b, 399a, 747a, 854a, 860b, 972a; III, 25a, 43a, 67b, 155b, 380b, 531a, 898b, 1155a; IV, 85b-88a, 152a, b, 490b, 935a, 1013a-1018b, 1165a; V, 129b, **401a**; X, 75b
—chronology(ie) v, **414b** – V, **416a**
—commentaries/-taires i, 89a, 104b, 117a, 120a, 126a, 143a, 152a, 302a, 310a, 352b, 425a, 701b, 958b, 1129a; iii, 696b, 753b, 845b, 880b; iv, 495a, 508a, 704b, 705a, 734b; v, 512b, 513b – I, 91b, 107b, 120b, 123b, 130a, 147a, 156b, 311b, 319b, 363a, 437a, 723a, 988a, 1163a; III, 718b, 776b, 869a, 904b; IV, 516a, 530a, 733a, b, 764a; V, 516a, 517a
—history/histoire v, **404a**, 426a – V, **405b**, 428a
—interpretations i, 24b, 38b, 90a, 128b, 158b, 204a, 257a, 264a, 267a, 272a, 275a, 325a, 338a, 561b, 603b, 691a, 788a, 935b, 968b, 1021a, 1026b, 1055a, 1071b, 1326b; ii, 71a, 95a, 128b, 219b,383b, 447a, 549b, 617a, 626b, 869b, 917a, 949b, 950a, 1025a; iii, 172a, 359a, 465a, 543b, 661a, 795a, 797a, 912a, 1091b, 1172a, 1205a; iv, 1106b –

I, 25a, 39b, 92b, 132b, 163a, 210a, 265a, 272a, 275a, 280a, 283b, 335a, 348b, 579b, 623b, 712a, 811a, 964a, 998a, 1052a, b, 1058a, 1087a, 1103b, 1367a; II, 72a, 97a, 132a, 226b, 394a, 459a, 563a, 632b, 642a, 889b, 938b, 972a, 1049a; III, 175b, 370b, 481a, 543b, 682a, 818a, 820b, 936b, 1118a, 1201a, 1235b; IV, 1138a
—language/langue v, **419a** – V, **420b**
—Muḥammad and/et v, **402b**, 415a, 1101a – V, **403b**, 416b, 1097a
—readings, readers/lectures, lecteurs v, **406a** – V, **407a**
—references/renvois i, 169a, 177a, 187a, 209a, 384a, 406-417, 448b, 453a, 514a, 680b, 714a, 773b, 795b, 850b, 922a, 940b, 1020a,b, 1032a, 1092b, 1150b, 1297b; ii, 168a, 182a, 214a, 223b, 293b, 363a, 447a, 536a, 551a, 576a, 848a, 1061a; iii, 13b, 53b, 165a, 209b, 235b, 295a, 302a, 377b, 379a, 537b, 668b, 980a, 1237a,b, 1239b; iv, 141a, 171b, 184a, b, 353b, 365b, 407a, b, 486b, 508b, 595a, 692a, 766b, 805b, 994b; v, 186a, 236a, b, 400b, 698a – I, 174a, 181b, 192b, 215a, 395a, 418-429, 461b, 466a, 529b, 701a, 735b, 796b, 819a, 874b, 949b, 969b, 1051b, 1063b, 1125b, 1185a, 1337a; II, 173a, 187b, 220b,230b, 301b, 373a, 459a, 549b, 564b, 590b, 867b, 1086a;III, 14b, 55b, 168b, 215a, 242b, 304b, 311a, b, 389b, 390b, 556a, 690a, 1004b, 1269a,b, 1271b; IV, 146b, 147a, 179a, 192a, b, 369a, 381b, 425a, b, 507a, 530b, 619a, 720a, 797a, 838a, 1027a; V, 183b, 234a, b, 402a, 703a
—scholars/savants i, 40a, 68b, 105a, 114a, 120a, 152a, 696a, 706b, 1129a; ii, 254a; iii, 155a, 753b, 880b, 936a, 1081b; iv, 1112b; v, 128a, 174a – I, 41a, 70b, 108a, 117a, 123b, 156a, 717a, 728a, 1163a; II, 261b; III, 158b, 776b, 904b, 960b, 1108b; IV, 1144b; V, 130b, 171b
—translations/traductions i, 68b, 88b, 404b; ii, 255a; iv, 891a, 1123a; v, **429a** – I, 70b, 91a, 416b, II, 262a; IV, 923b, 1155a; V, **431b**
al-Kūrānī, Ibrāhīm (1690) v, **432b**, 525b – V, **435a**, 529b
al-Kurānī, Shams al-Dīn → Gurānī
Kūrānkidj iv, 215a – IV, 224b
al-Ḳurashī → ʿAbd al-Ḳādir
al-Ḳurashī (Transoxania/-e) (XIII) viii, 582a – VIII, 600b
al-Ḳurashī, Abū Bakr b. Muʿāwiya (al-Andalus) (X) vi, 430b – VI, 416a
al-Ḳurashī, Abu 'l-Ḥasan → al-Kurshī
al-Ḳurashī, ʿAlī b. Ḥazm (1288) vii, 1040a – VII, 1042a
al-Ḳurashī, ʿAlī b. Muḥammad (1405) vi, 280a – VI, 265a
al-Ḳurashī, Djamāl iv, 525b – IV, 548b
Kurayb ii, 77b – II, 79a
Ḳurayba iv, 821a – IV, 854a
Kuraybiyya iii, 1265b; iv, 836b; v, **433b** – III, 1298b; IV, 869b; V, **435b**
al-Ḳurayniyya i, 628b – I, 649b
Ḳuraysh i, 80a, 382b, 545a, 549a, 565a, 890b, 891b, 1073b, 1074a, b, 1241b; ii, 128b, 348b, 627a, 883b; iii, 7b, 285b, 363b, 389a, 577b, 975b, 1093a; v, 116b, 316a, b, **434a**, 520a, b, 581a; vi, 137b, 145a, b, 267b, 349a, 422a, 439b; x, 841a; s, 284a – I, 82b, 393b, 562a, 566b, 583a, 916b, 918a, 1105b, 1106a, b, 1279a; II, 131b, 358a, 642b, 904a; III, 8a, 294b, 374b, 401b, 597b, 1000a, 1120a; V, 119a, 316a, **436a**, 523b, 524a, 586a; VI, 135b, 143a, 144a, 252a, 333a, 407a, 425a; X, ; S, 284a
Ḳuraysh b. Badrān (ʿUkaylid(e)) (1061) vi, 966a; vii, 693a – VI, 958a; VII, 693a
Ḳuraysh al-Biṭāḥ vi, 145a – VI, 143a
Ḳuraysh al-Ẓawāhir vi, 145a – VI, 143a
Ḳurayya (Baghdād) i, 901a, b – I, 928a, b
Ḳurayyāt (ʿUmān) vi, 734b – VI, 724a
Ḳurayyāt al-Milḥ v, **435b** – V, **438a**
Ḳurayẓa, Banū i, 381b; iv, 270a; v, **436a**, 996a; vi, 649a, 738b; vii, 367a, 370b, 561b, 852b – I, 392b; IV, 282a; V, **438b**, 991b; VI, 634a, 727b; VII, 369b, 372b, 562b, 854a
Kurāz b. Mālik al-Sulamī (695) vi, 620a – VI, 912a
al-Ḳuraẓī → Muḥammad b. Kaʿb
Ḳurba → Ḳarāba
Kurbāl v, 867b, 868a – V, 874a, b
Kurbālī, Shudjāʿ al-Dīn (1462) vi, 73a – VI, 71a
Ḳurbān v, **436b** – V, **439a**
Ḳurbat ii, 40b; v, 818a, b – II, 41b; V, 824a, b
Kurbuḳa, Kür-Bugha (1102) v, **437a** – V, **439b**
Ḳūrčī v, **437a** – V, **439b**
Ḳurčībāshī iii, 1102a; iv, 36b; v, 437b, 630a – III, 1129a; IV, 39a; V, 440a, 634a
Kurd ʿAlī, Muḥammad Farīd (1953) i, 598a, 990a, b; ii, 290a; iv, 159a; v, **437b**, 1090b; vii, 813b – I, 617b, 1020b, 1021a; II, 298a; IV, 166a; V, **440a**, 1088a; VII, 815a
Kurd Hamza ii, 750a – II, 768b
Kürd Sheykh Ḥasan (Čemishgezek) (XV) vi, 71a – VI, 69a
Kurdes I, 194b, 201a, 259a, 484b, 485b, 488a, 527b, 528b, 593b, 664b, 772b, 820a, 895a, 948a, 1062a, 1104a 1242b, 1244b, 1326b, 1393b, 1395a; II, 58b, 190b, 214b, 1136b, 1166b; III, 85b, 265a, 986a, 1123a, b, 1129b, 1136a, 1286b; IV, 6a, 8b, 9b, 10b, 394a; V, 147b, 149a, 311b, **441a**, 621a, 828a, 1202b, 1203a, b; VI, 185b, 366b, 368b; VIII, 176a; X, 50a; S, 118b
Kurdī (dog/chien) iv, 491a – IV, 512a
al-Kurdī, Muḥammad Amīn (1914) v, 475b, **486a** – V, 478b, **489a**
Kurdī, Shaykh ʿAlī (1519) vii, 935a – VII, 935b
Kurdish/Kurde (language/langue) i, 840a, 871b, 1006b; ii, 1139b; iii, 1b, 1260b; iv, 351a, b; v, 208b, 209a, b, **479a**, 1105a – I, 863b, 895b, 1037b; II, 1166b; III, 1b, 1293b; IV, 366a, b; V, 206a, 207a, **482a**, 1101a
Kurdistān i, 8a, 62b, 845a; ii, 8a; iv, 3a-b, 19b; v, **438b**; vi, 491b, 492b, 494a, 495a, 502a; ix, 829a, 831a; s, 72a, b – I, 8a, 64b, 868a; II, 8a; IV, 3b, 21a; V, **441a**; VI, 477b, 478b, 479b, 480b, 487a; IX, 865a, 866a; S, 72a
—economy(ie) v, **472b** – V, **475b**
—history/histoire v, **447b** – V, **450a**
—inhabitants/habitants v, **444a**, 456a, b – V, **446b**, 459a
—folklore/lit(t)erature v, **480b** – V, **483a**
—religion v, **474b** – V, **477b**
—society/-été v, **470a** – V, **472b**
Kurdistan Workers Party (PKK) x, 696a – X,
al-Kurdj (Gurdj, Gurdjistān (Georgia/-ie)) i, 8a, 100b, 420b, 636a, 642a, 644b; ii, 162b; iii, 1112b; iv, 342b, 347b, 348b, 349a, b, 351a,b. 391b, 476a, 670a, 1174b; v, **486b**; vi, 500a, b, 505a; vii, 352a;x, 966a – I, 8a, 103a, 432b, 657a, 663a, 665a; II, 168a; III, 1140a; IV, 357a, 362a, 363b, 364a, 366a,b, 408a, 497a, 697b, 1207b; V, **489b**; VI, 485b, 486a, 490a; VII, 354a; X,
—languages/langues iv, 350b; v, 486b – IV, 365b; V, 489b
Kurdjī Muḳaddam al-Burdjiyya i, 1325a – I, 1365b
Kurdoghlu Khiḍir Reis i, 743b – I, 765b

Kurds   i, 190a, 195b, 251a, 470b, 471b, 474a, 512a,
    513a, 575a,644a, 750a, 796b, 871a, 920a, 1030b,
    1072a, 1207a, 1208b, 1287a, 1354b, 1356a; ii, 57a,
    184b, 208a, 1110b, 1139b; iii, 83a, 258a, 961a,
    1096b, 1102b, 1109a, 1254a; iv, 5b, 8a, 9a, 10a,
    377b; v, 145a, 146b, 312a, **438b**, 617a, 822a, 1213a,
    b; vi, 201a, 382b, 384b; viii, 173bs, 71b, 119a; x, 48b;
    s, 118b
Kürdüdjin bint Abis̲h̲ K̲h̲ātūn (1319)   vi, 482a – VI,
    468a
Kurdufān   → Kordofān
Kürekčis   i, 760b; v, 880a, b – I, 783b; V, 886a, b
Ḳurḥ   v, **497b** – V, **500b**
Ḳurhub b. D̲j̲ābir al-K̲h̲uzāʿī   v, **498a** – V, **501a**
Kūri   iv, 540b – IV, 564a
Kuria Muria (islands/les îles-)   → K̲h̲ūryān-Mūryān
Ḳūrīltāy   iv, 499b; v, **498a**; vi, 482b – IV, 521b; V,
    501a; VI, 468b
Kürin   v, **498a**, 729b, 730a – V, **501b**, 734b, 735a
Kürin(K̲h̲ānat(e))   → Lezghin
Ḳūriya   v, **498b** – V, **501b**
Ḳurkī   s, 421a – S, 420b
Ḳurḳūb   v, **498b** – V, **501b**
Ḳurḳumāz b. Yūnis Maʿn (1516)   vi, 343a – VI, 327b
Ḳurḳūra   i, 325b – I, 335b
Kurr   → Kur (river/rivière)
Ḳurra   iv, 521b – IV, 544b
Ḳurrāʾ   v, 349b, 409a, **499a** – V, 350b, 410b, **502a**
Ḳurrāʾ, Banū   ii, 741a; iii, 79b; vii, 117a, 730a – II,
    759b; III, 82a; VII, 119a, 730b
Kurra, Muḥammad   ii, 123a; v, 267a – II, 126a; V,
    265a
Ḳurra b. S̲h̲arīk (714)   ii, 305a, 323b, 327b; iv, 742a,
    1103b; v, **500a**; vi, 648a, 662a; vii, 75a, 158b; viii,
    537b –
    II, 313b, 333b, 337a; IV, 772a, 1134b; V, **503a**; VI,
    633a, 647b; VII, 76a, 160a; VIII, 555b
Kurram (river/rivière)   v, **501a**; s, 329b –
    V, **504a**; S, 329a
Ḳurrat al-ʿAyn Ṭāhira, Fāṭima umm Salmā (1852)   i,
    834a, 846b, 847a; iv, 70b; v, **502a**; vi, 485a – I, 857a,
    870a, b; IV, 74b; V, **505a**; VI, 471a
Ḳurṣān   iv, 1056b; v, **502b** – IV, 1087b; V, **506a**
al-Kurs̲h̲ī, Abu ʾl-Ḥasan   iv, 729a – IV, 758a
Kursī   v, **509a**; vi, 663b – V, **512b**; VI, 649b
Ḳūrṣūl   → Bog̲h̲ā Tark̲h̲ān
Kurt   → Kart
Kürt Ḥāfiz̲ (1474)   vi, 72a – VI, 70a
Ḳurt Ḥasan b. D̲j̲unayd   ii, 599b – II, 614b
al-Ḳurtī, vizier   → G̲h̲iyāt̲h̲ al-Dīn Muḥammad (XII) i,
    361b; ii, 238a – I, 372b; II, 245a
Kürtigīn (Daylamī) (X)   vii, 800a – VII, 802a
Ḳurtuba (Córdoba/Cordoue)   i, 5b, 6b, 82a, 83a, 85b,
    390b, 491b, 493a, 494b; iii, 74a, 140a, 496a, 762a; v,
    318b, **509b**, 1008b, 1239b; vi, 186a, 279b, 364a,
    431a, 521a; vii, 766b; s, 152b, 397b –
    I, 6a, 6b, 84b, 85b, 88a, 401b, 506a, 508a, 509b; III,
    76b, 142b, 513a, 785b; V, 318a, **513a**, 1004b, 1230a,
    b; VI, 169b, 264a, 348a, 416b, 505b; VII, 768b; S,
    152b, 398a
—great mosque/la grande mosquée   i, 459a, 498b,
    500b, 618b, 950a, 1228a, 1319b; iii, 956a, b; iii, 495a;
    v, 510b – I, 472a, 513b, 516a, 637b, 979b, 1264b,
    1360a; II, 978a, b; III, 512a; V, 514a
Ḳurtuba, D̲j̲ibāl   i, 488b – I, 503b
al-Ḳurtubī   → ʿArib b. Saʿd; Ibn Faraḥ
al-Ḳurtubī, Abu ʾl-ʿAbbās   v, 512b – V, 516a
al-Ḳurtubī, Abū ʿAbd Allāh (1272)   v, **512b** – V, **516a**
al-Ḳurtubī, Abū Muḥammad (1092)   vi, 110a, 629a –
    VI, 108a, 614a
al-Ḳurtubī, Maslama b. al-Ḳāsim (924)   x, 12a – X, 12a

al-Ḳurtubī, Yaḥyā b. ʿUmar (1172)   v, **513b** – V, **517b**
Kurūʾ   → Ḳurʾ
Ḳūrū   s, 165a – S, 164b
Kuruca   vi, 70b – VI, 68b
Kuruks̲h̲etra   → T̲h̲ānesar
Ḳurūn Ḥamāt (battle/bataille) (1175)   vi, 781a – VI,
    771a
Kurūr   i, 272a – I, 280b
Kūrus   vi, 506a, 507a – VI, 491b, 492b
Ḳūrūs̲h̲ (Cyrrhus)   vi, 378a – VI, 362b
Ḳūṣ   v, 99b, **514a**, 519a; vi, 119a; viii, 864a; s, 383b –
    V, 101b, **517b**, 522b; VI, 116b; VIII, 894b; S, 384a
Kūs owasî   → Ḳoṣowaʾ
Ḳuṣadasî   vi, 1011b – VI, 1003b
Kūsān   vi, 745a, b – VI, 734b
Ḳusantīna   → Ḳustantīna
al-Ḳusantīnī, Ras̲h̲īd (1944)   v, **515b**; vi, 752a, 754b –
    V, **519b**; VI, 741b, 744a
al-Kūsawī al-D̲j̲āmī   i, 283a – I, 292a
Kusayla b. Lamzam   i, 367a, 1175a; iii, 296a; iv, 336b,
    827a; v, **517b**; s, 103a – I, 372b, 1210a; III, 305a; IV,
    351a, 860a; V, **521a**; S, 102a
al-Ḳusayr   → Abū Zaʿbal
al-Ḳusayr (al-Ḥira)   i, 450b – I, 463b
al-Ḳusayr (port)   v, 386a, **518b**; vi, 195a, 545b – V,
    387b, **522b**; VI, 179a, 530a
al-Ḳusayr ʿAmrā   i, **612a**; iii, 141b, 146b, 310a; vii,
    82a; s, 117b, 251a – I, **632a**; III, 144b, 150a, 319a;
    VII, 83b; S, 116b, 251a
Ḳuṣayy   ii, 128b; iii, 260a, 975b; iv, 320a, 421b; v,
    77b, 78a, 116b, 434b, **519b**, 581a, 692b; vi, 145a,
    349a –
    II, 131b; III, 267a, 1000a; IV, 334a, 440a; V, 80a,
    119a, 436b, **523a**, 586a, 697b; VI, 143a, 333a
Ḳuṣdār   v, 102a, **520b**; vi, 65b, 193a – V, 104a, **524a**;
    VI, 63b, 177a
Kūs̲h̲   v, **521a**; viii, 89a – V, **524b**; VIII, 91a
Ḳus̲h̲adalî, Ibrāhīm (1845)   ix, 145a – IX, 161a
Kus̲h̲adasī   i, 777b, 778a – I, 801a
Kus̲h̲ād̲j̲im, Maḥmūd b. al-Ḥusayn al-Sindī (961)   i,
    1153b; ii, 740b; iii, 809a; iv, 1005b; v, **525a**, 1229b;
    vi, 403b; vii, 646b, 851a, 949a; viii, 377b, 1022a; s,
    175b, 203b –
    I, 1188a; II, 759a; III, 832b; IV, 1037b; V, **529a**,
    1219b; VI, 388a; VII, 646a, 852a, 949b; VIII, 390b,
    1057a; S, 176b, 203a
Kus̲h̲an   i, 225b; s, 237a – I, 232b; S, 237a
Kus̲h̲āna   vi, 839a – VI, 829b
Kus̲h̲ānūs̲h̲ al-Burd̲j̲ān (Bulgar(e))   ii, 235a –
    II, 242a
al-Ḳus̲h̲ās̲h̲ī, Ṣafī al-Dīn (1661)   v, 433a, **525b** – V,
    435a, **529a**
Ḳus̲h̲ayr   i, 233b, 442a; v, **526a** – I, 240b, 454b; V,
    529b
al-Ḳus̲h̲ayrī, Abu ʾl-Ḳāsim (1073)   i, 146b; ii, 125b,
    605a; iii, 589a; iv, 697a; v, **526a**, vi, 225a, 569b,
    614a; vii, 100a; x, 314b; s, 14b, 15a –
    I, 151a; II, 129a, 620a; III, 609b; IV, 725a; V, **530a**;
    VI, 219a, 554b, 599a; VII, 102a; X, 338b; S, 15a
al-Ḳus̲h̲ayrī, Abū ʾl-Naṣr (1120)   v, **527a** –
    V, **531a**
al-Ḳus̲h̲ayrī, Muḥammad b. Saʿīd (945)   viii, 412b –
    VIII, 427a
al-Ḳus̲h̲ayrī, Sawwār b. Awfā (VII)   vii, 843a – VII,
    844a
Ḳus̲h̲-begi   → Ḳos̲h̲-begi
Ḳus̲h̲čī   v, 273a – V, 271a
Ḳūs̲h̲d̲j̲i   ii, 774a – II, 793a
al-Ḳūs̲h̲d̲j̲ī   → ʿAlī al-Ḳūs̲h̲d̲j̲ī
Kushitic   → Kūs̲h̲
Kūs̲h̲yār b. Labbān (XI)   iii, 1137a, 1139b; iv, 1071a; v,

527a; x, 267a – III, 1165a, 1167b; IV, 1102b; V, **531a**; X, 284b
Kushka vi, 621b – VI, 606b
Ḳushtemür iii, 197a – III, 202a
Kushterī, Shaykh iv, 601b – IV, 626a
al-Ḳushūrī → Naṣr
Ḳush-yalwa, Banū vi, 501a – VI, 486a
al-Ḳūṣī, ʿAbd al-Ghaffār b. Nūḥ (1307) viii, 458b – VIII, 473b
Ḳūsira → Ḳawṣara
Kuskusū v, **527b** – V, **531b**
Ḳuṣmān iv, 717a, b – IV, 746a, b
Ḳuss b. Sāʿida (VII?) i, 585b; v, **528b**; vii, 73b; x, 789a – I, 604a; V, **532b**; VII, 74b; X,
Ḳuṣṣās → Ḳāṣṣ, Ḳaṣṣa
Ḳuṣta (Maṣyad) vi, 790b – VI, 780a
Ḳusṭā b. Lūḳā al-Baʿlabakkī (912) i, 328a, 589a, 727a; ii, 771b, 900a; iii, 378a; iv, 329b, 600a; v, 397b, **529b**; vi, 637b; vii, 559a, b; s, 412a – I, 338a, 608b, 749a; II, 790a, 921a; III, 390a; IV, 344a, 624a; V, 398b, **533a**; VI, 622b; VII, 559b, 561a; S, 412b
Kustāndīl → Constantine III
Ḳusṭanṭīna i, 155a; v, **530a**; vi, 427a – I, 159a; V, **533b**; VI, 412a
Ḳusṭanṭīniyya iv, 224a; v, **532b**; x, 821b – IV, 234a; V, **536b**
Küstendil v, **534a** – V, **538a**
Ḳusṭūs al-Rūmī ii, 900a – II, 920b
Kusūf v, **535b** – V, **540a**
al-Ḳūṣūnī, Badr al-Dīn iv, 451b – IV, 471b
Ḳuṣūr i, 1321b – I, 1361b
Kūt al-ʿAmāra v, **537a**; vii, 582b – V, **541b**; VII, 583a
Kūtab vi, 499b, 501a – VI, 485a, 486b
Ḳutadghu Bilig i, 299a, 677b; iv, 700a; v, **538a**; x, 62b – I, 308a, 698a; IV, 728b; V, **542b**; X, 64b
Kütāhiya (Kütahya) i, 182b; ii, 747a; iv, 1169b; v, **539a**; vi, 59b, 525b; viii, 84b; s, 49a, 359b – I, 188a; II, 765b; IV, 1202b; V, **543b**; VI, 57b, 510a; VIII, 86b; S, 49b, 359a
Kütahya, Edict/Édit de vi, 496b – VI, 482a
Kutai v, **539b**; vi, 240a; s, 151a – V, **544a**; VI, 205a; S, 151a
Ḳutalmish → Ḳutlumush
Kutāma (Ketama) Banū i, 104a, 249a, 367a, 1037a, 1042a, 1175b, 1177b, 1178b, 1309b; ii, 852b; iii, 77a; iv, 199a, 827b, 830a; v, **540a**; 1160a, 1243a; vi, 435a, 727a, b, 728a; ix, 18a – I, 107a, 257a, 378a, 1068b, 1073b, 1210b, 1212b, 1213b, 1350a;II, 872b; III, 79a; IV, 208a, 860b, 862b; V, **544b**, 1150a, 1233b; VI, 420b, 716a, b, 717a; IX, 18b
al-Ḳutāmī, ʿAbd al-Karīm iv, 729a – IV, 758b
al-Ḳutāmī, Djaʿfar b. Kulayd (1038) vii, 120b – VII, 120b
al-Kutāmī, ʿUmayr b. Shuyaym (719) iv, 315b; v, **540b** – IV, 329b; V, **545a**
al-Kutāmī al-Fāsī, Abu 'l-Ḥasan ʿAlī → Ibn al-Ḳaṭṭān the Elder
Kutawaringin vi, 240a – VI, 205a
Ḳutayba i, 920b – I, 949a
Ḳutayba b. Muslim (715) i, 529b, 684b, 921a, 1001a, 1293b; ii, 1a, 601a, 790b; iii, 41a, 304a, 471a, 493b; iv, 1062a; v, 47b, 181a, 378a, **541a**, 853b, 854a, 1111a; vii, 359a, 1016a; viii, 67a; s, 299a – I, 545b, 705b, 949a, 1032a, 1333b; II, 1a, 615b, 809b; III, 43a, 313a, 487b, 510b; IV, 1093b; V, 49a, 178b, 379a, **545b**, 860a, b, 1107a; VII, 361a, 1017b; VIII, 68b; S, 298b
Ḳutayba b. Saʿīd (854) vii, 691a – VII, 691b
Ḳutayba b. Tughshāda i, 1294a, b – I, 1333b, 1334a
Ḳutaybid(e)s vi, 640b – VI, 625b
Ḳuṭayfa s, 117a – S, 116a
Kutayfāt → al-Afḍal Kutayfāt
Ḳutayla (musicia(e)n) (1330) viii, 806a – VIII, 833a
Ḳutayla bint ʿAbd al-ʿUzzā i, 109b – I, 112b
al-Ḳuṭb i, 95a, 280a; iv, 950a; v, **542b**; s, 323b – I, 97b, 289a; IV, 982b; V, **547a**; S, 323a
al-Ḳuṭb, Sayyid iii, 1069b, 1070a; iv, 160a, 166a – III, 1096b, 1097a; IV, 167a, 173a
al-Ḳuṭb ʿAlī, Shaykh iii, 456b – III, 472b
al-Ḳuṭb al-Awliyāʾ → ʿAbd al-Salām Khundjī
Ḳuṭb al-Dīn → al-Nahrawālī
Ḳuṭb al-Dīn I (Ḳutlugh-Khān) → Ḳuṭb al-Dīn Khān b. Burāḳ
Ḳuṭb al-Dīn II (Ḳutlugh-Khān) → Shāh Djahān b. Suyurghatmish
Ḳuṭb al-Dīn (Bengal) s, 366b – S, 366a
Ḳuṭb al-Dīn, Malik iv, 672a – IV, 699b
Ḳuṭb al-Dīn, Mullā i, 936b; ii, 132a; s, 292a, 293a – I, 965b; II, 135b; S, 291b, 293a
Ḳuṭb al-Dīn b. Tekish (Khʷārazm-shāh) → ʿAlāʾ al-Dīn Miḥammad b. Tekish
Ḳuṭb al-Dīn Abu 'l-Fatḥ Muḥammad Khān (Ḳutlugh-Khānid(e)) (1257) v, 161b, 162a, 553a, b; vi, 482b – V, 160a, 558a; VI, 468b
Ḳuṭb al-Dīn Aḥmad (Ḥekīm-bashi̊) iii, 340a – III, 350a
Ḳuṭb al-Dīn Aḥmad Shāh (Gudjarāt) (1451) vi, 53b – VI, 51b
Ḳuṭb al-Dīn Aybak (Muʿizzī, Delhi) (1210) i, 208b, 393b, 403b, 506b, 756b, 855b, 1209b, 1300a, 1321b; ii, 256a, 260a, 266b, 267a, 1084a, 1103a, 1123b; iii, 168a, 415b, 1155a; iv, 210a, 1127a; v, 283a, **546a**, 549a; vi, 368a, 691a, b; vii, 409b, 410a, 433a; viii, 81a; s, 284b, 359b, 360a – I, 214b, 404b, 415a, 522a, 779a, 879b, 1245b, 1339b, 1362a; II, 263b, 267b, 274b, 275a, b, 1109a, 1129a, 1150a; III, 171b, 429a, 1183b; IV, 219b, 1158b; V, 281a, **550b**, 553b; VI, 352b, 678b, 679a; VII, 411a, b, 434a; VIII, 83a; S, 284b, 359b
Ḳuṭb al-Dīn Bakhtiyār Kākī (1235) ii, 796b; v, **546b**, 549a; s, 353a – II, 815b; V, **551a**, 554a; S, 353a
Ḳuṭb al-Dīn Ḥabash ʿAmīd → Ḥabash ʿAmīd
Ḳuṭb al-Dīn Ḥasan al-Ghūrī ii, 1100a – II, 1126a
Ḳuṭb al-Dīn Il-Ghāzī (Mārdīn) (1183) vi, 781b – VI, 771a
Ḳuṭb al-Dīn Ināl b. Ḥassān (Manbidj) (1168) vi, 380b – VI, 364b
Ḳuṭb al-Dīn Ismāʿīl b. Yāḳūtī (XI) vi, 274b – VI, 259a
Ḳuṭb al-Dīn al-Iznīḳī (1418) v, **547a** – V, **551b**
Ḳuṭb al-Dīn Kulsāriʿ i, 731a – I, 753a
Ḳuṭb al-Dīn Mawdūd b. Zangī → Mawdūd b. ʿImād al-Dīn Zangī
Ḳuṭb al-Dīn Nayrīzī (1759) x, 328a – X, 353a
Ḳuṭb al-Dīn Mubārak → Mubārak Shāh I
Ḳuṭb al-Dīn Mubāriz (Shanānkāra) ix, 158a, 667b – IX, 163a, 698b
Ḳuṭb al-Dīn Muḥammad (Ghūrid(e)) i, 940a; ii, 382a, 928a, 1096b, 1100b – I, 968b; II, 392b, 950a, 1122b, 1126a
Ḳuṭb al-Dīn Muḥammad b. Anūshtigin (Khʷārazm-shāh) (1127) iv, 1067a; vi, 415b; viii, 943a; ix, 16a s, 279a – IV, 1099a; VI, 400b; VIII, 975a; IX, 16b; S, 279a
—al-Dīn Muḥammad b. ʿImād al-Dīn Zangī (XII) viii, 127a – VIII, 130a
Ḳuṭb al-Dīn al-Rāzī ii, 774a – II, 792b
Ḳuṭb al-Dīn Shīrāzī (1311) ii, 399a, b; iii, 1137b; iv, 1059b; v, **547a**; vi, 99a, 601a, 907b; vii, 204a, 684b; viii, 860b; ix, 481a –

II, 409b, 410a; III, 1165b; IV, 1090b; V, **551b**; VI,
97a, 586a, 899a; VII, 205a, 684b; VIII, 890b; IX,
500a
Ḳuṭb al-Dīn Yūsuf b. Yaʿḳūb, vizier (XII)   vii, 535b –
VII, 535a
Ḳuṭb al-Dīn-zāde Muḥammad (1480)   v, 547a, **548b** –
V, 551b, **553a**
Ḳuṭb K̲h̲ān (Monghyr) (1533)   vi, 47a – VI, 45b
Ḳuṭb K̲h̲ān Lōdī (XV)   iii, 632a; iv, 513a; v, 783a; vi,
62a, b – III, 653a; IV, 535a; V, 789b, VI, 60a
Ḳuṭb Mīnār   v, 546b, **548b**; vi, 361b, 368a, b, 369a,
691b – V, 551a, b, **553a**; VI, 345b, 352b, 353a, 679a
Ḳuṭb al-Mulk   → Ḳulī Ḳuṭb al-Mulk
Ḳuṭb S̲h̲āhīs (Golkonḍā)   i, 1048a; ii, 1119a; iii, 318b,
426a, 427a, 448a; v, **549b**; vi, 68a, 126b, 369a, 610b,
696a, 837b; vii, 80a, 300a; s, 302a – I, 1079b; II,
1145a; III, 328a, 440a, 441a, 463a; V, **554a**; VI, 66a,
124a, 353b, 595b, 684a, 828a; VII, 81b, 302a; S,
301b
Ḳuṭb al-Yaman al-Ahdal   i, 255b – I, 263b
Ḳuṭba b. Arus   → al-Ḥāḍira
Ḳuṭb-i ʿĀlam   → Burhān al-Dīn
Ḳuṭbid(e)s   ii, 517b – II, 530a
Kūthā   v, 550b – V, 555a
Ḳutham b. al-ʿAbbās (676)   v, **551a** – V, **555b**
Kuthayyir b. ʿAbd al-Raḥmān (Kuthayyir ʿAzza)
(723)   i, 402a; ii, 1029b; iv, 836b, 1086b; v, 433b,
551b; vi, 604a; vii, 978a –
I, 412b; II, 1053a; IV, 869b, 1118a; V, 436a, **556b**;
VI, 589a; VII, 979a
Kuthayyir b. Waslās b. S̲h̲amlāl (VIII)   vi, 744a – VI,
733a
Ḳutlu Beg   i, 311b – I, 321a
Ḳuṭlūdumūr, amīr   vi, 15a – VI, 13b
Ḳutlugh al-Aḥmadīlī   i, 300b – I, 310a
Ḳutlugh Inanč b. Pahlawān (1195)   iii, 1111b; vi, 921a;
viii, 945a – III, 1139a; VI, 913a; VIII, 977a
Ḳutlugh K̲h̲ān (XIII)   vi, 48a, b; s, 246a – VI, 46b, 47a;
S, 246a
Ḳutlugh K̲h̲ānid(e)s   i, 1311a; v, 161b, **553a** –
I, 1351b; V, 159b, 160a, **558a**
Ḳutlugh Murād K̲h̲ān   s, 46a, 420a – S, 46b, 420a
Ḳutlugh S̲h̲āh Noyan (1307)   v, **554a** – V, **559a**
Ḳutlugh Terken   → Turkān K̲h̲ātūn
Ḳutlugh Tīmūr   iv, 1064a – IV, 1095b
Ḳutlughtakin   i, 731b – I, 753b
Ḳutlumus̲h̲ b. Arslān Isrāʾīl (Saldjūḳ) (XI) i, 420a, 1074a;
iii, 195b; iv, 120a; vi, 274b; viii, 948a – I, 432a,
1106a; III, 200b; IV, 230a; VI, 259a; VIII, 980b
Ḳutlūs̲h̲āh   vi, 545b – VI, 530a
Ḳuṭn   v, **554b** – V, **559b**
Ḳuṭr   v, **566b** – V, **570b**
Ḳuṭrabbul   iii, 774a; v, **566b** – III, 797b; V, **571a**
Ḳuṭrub   v, **566b** – V, **571a**
Ḳuṭrub, Abū ʿAlī Muḥammad b. al-Mustanīr (821)   v,
567a; vii, 82b, 312b, 402a, 546b – V, **571b**; VII, 83b,
314b, 403a, 546b
Kuttāb   → Kātib
Kuttāb (school/école)   iv, 436a; v, **567b**, 909a, b, 911b,
1123a – IV, 455a, b; V, **572a**, 914b, 915b, 917a,
1119b
al-Kutubī, Abū ʿAbd Allāh al-Dimas̲h̲ḳī (1363)   v,
570b – V, **575a**
al-Kutubī, Muḥammad b. Ibrāhīm (1318)
vi, 945b – VI, 938b
al-Kutubiyya   → Marrākus̲h̲
Ḳutulmis̲h̲   → Ḳutlumus̲h̲
Kutun   i, 904b, 1009b – II, 925b, 1033b
Kütüphane   → Maktaba
Ḳuṭuz, al-Malik al-Muẓaffar (al-Muʿizzī Mamlūk)
(1260)   i, 786b, 1125a; ii, 284b; iii, 184b, 1121a; iv,

484b, 641a; v, **571a**; vi, 321b, 322a, 543b, 790b; VII,
166b, 167a, 729a –
I, 810a, 1158b; II, 293a; III, 189a, 1148b; IV, 505b,
667a; V, **575b**; VI, 306a, b, 528a, 780b; VII, 168a, b,
729b
al-Kuʿūb   → Kaʿb, Banū
Ḳuʿūd   v, **572a** – V, **576b**
Ḳuwā   iv, 330b – IV, 345a
Ḳuwād̲h̲iyān   → Ḳubād̲h̲iyān
Ḳuwait   → al-Kuwayt
Ḳuwayk, Banū   iv, 137a – IV, 143a
al-Kuwayt   i, 39b, 233b, 534a, 540a, 762a, 976a; ii,
176b, 469a, 673a; iii, 1066a, b; iv, 680b, 925a; v,
572a, 1057a; vi, 36b; vii, 449b; viii, 668b; s, 3b, 50a –
I, 40b, 241a, 550b, 556b, 785a, 1006b; II, 182a, 480b,
690a; III, 1092b, 1093a; IV, 708b, 958a; V, **576b**,
1054a; VI, 35a; VII, 450b; VIII, 688a; S, 2b, 50b
—university/-é   ii, 425a – II, 435b
Ḳuwwa   iv, 271b; v, **576a** – IV, 283b; V, **580b**
Ḳuwwat al-Islām (Delhi)   vi, 368a – VI, 352b
al-Ḳuwwatli   → S̲h̲ukrī
Kuybis̲h̲ev   iv, 281a – IV, 293a
Ḳuyud̲j̲u Murād Pas̲h̲a   → Murād Pas̲h̲a
Ḳūz (Agoz)   vi, 741b – VI, 731a
Kuzaḥ   iv, 803a – IV, 835b
Kūzakunānī, Ṣunʿ Allāh (1523)   vii, 935a – VII, 935b
Ḳuzdār   → Ḳuṣdār
Ḳuz-Ordu   → Balāsāg̲h̲ūn
Kwanadi   v, **579b** – V, **584a**
Kwararafas (Nigeria)   viii, 20b – VIII, 20b
Kwaffa   v, 102b, **579b** – V, 104b, **584b**
Kypsela   → Ipsala
Kythera   → Čoka Adasî

L

Laʿakat al-dam, Banū   v, **581a**; vi, 137b, 145a; vii,
783a; s, 189b – V, **586**; VI, 136a, 143b; VII, 785a; S,
190b
Laârba   → Arbāʾ
Laʿb   → Laʿib
Labāb   v, **581b** – V, **586b**
Labakī, Naʿʿūm   ii, 471b – II, 483b
Labbai   v, **582a**; vi, 206b, 503a, b – V, **587a**; VI, 191a,
488b
Labbayka   → Talbiya
Labbès   iv, 361a – IV, 377a
Labībī (XII)   v, **583a**; vi, 609a – V, **588a**; VI, 594a
Labīd b. Rabīʿa (660)   v, **583b**; vi, 603a; vii, 254b; viii,
377a; s, 178b – V, **588b**; VI, 588a; VII, 256a; VIII,
389b; S, 179b
al-Labīdī (1048)   vi, 354a – VI, 338a
Labin   v, **584b** – V, **590a**
Labla (Niebla)   i, 6a; ii, 1009a; iii, 748b; v, **586a**; vi,
431a – I, 6a; II, 1032b; III, 771b; V, **591a**; VI, 416a
Laccadives   i, 170b; iv, 547a, b; v, **587a**; vi, 206b – VI,
191a
Ladāk̲h̲   v, **588a**; s, 156a, 242a – V, **592a**; S, 156a,
242a
Lād̲h̲iḳ (Amasya)   v, **589a** – V, **593a**
Lād̲h̲iḳ (Denizli)   i, 204a; v, **589b** – I, 210b; V, **593b**
Lād̲h̲iḳ (Konya)   v, **589a** – V, **593a**
al-Lād̲h̲iḳī   vii, 685a – VII, 685a
al-Lād̲h̲iḳiyya   v, **589b**; vi, 322b, 379b, 577b, 578a,
579b, 582a; vii, 578a; viii, 128b; s, 133b – V, **593b**;
VI, 307a, 364a, 562b, 563a, 564b, 566b; VII, 578b;
VIII, 131a; S, 133a
Lād̲h̲ū S̲h̲āh, Mawlānā   s, 353a – S, 353a

Ladik vii, 272a – VII, 274a
Lādīḳ → Deñizli
Ladjā' v, **593a**; vi, 544b, 546a – V, **596b**; VI, 529a, 531a
Ladjāya s, 103a – S, 102b
Ladjdjūn (town/ville) v, **593b**; vii, 756b; x, 211b – V, **597b**; VII, 757b; X, 228b
Lādjīn, al-Malik al-Manṣūr Ḥusām al-Dīn (Mamlūk) (1299) i, 622b, 1126b, 1128a, 1325a; ii, 38a, 285a, 958b; iii, 286b, 951b; iv, 437b, 964b, 965b; v, **594b**; vi, 322b, 323a, 507b, 667a, 669b; vii, 169b – I, 643a, 1160b, 1162a, 1365b; II, 38b, 293a, 980b; III, 295b, 976a; IV, 457a, 997a, b; V, **598b**; VI, 307a, b, 493a, 653b, 656a; VII, 171a
Ladjnat al-fatwā i, 819b – I, 842b
Lafiyar Toga ii, 1146a – II, 1173b
Lafẓ v, 320b, 321b – V, 320a, b
La-Garde-Freinet → Fraxinetum
Laghîm, laghîmlar i, 1063a, 1064a; iii, 479b – I, 1095a, 1096a; III, 496a
Laghîmdjîlar i, 1062a – I, 1093b
Laghmān → Lamghān
Laghwāt, Banū v, 1181a – V, 1171a
Lagūṭ b. ʿAlī (Maghrāwī) (1057) vi, 742b – VI, 732a
Laḥad → Ḳabr
Laḥam (Mt.) vi, 576a – VI, 561a
Lahāna, Banū vii, 186a – VII, 186a
Lāharī, Bandar vi, 537a – VI, 521b
Lāhawr i, 1323a, 1324a, 1347b, 1348a; ii, 134b, 267b, 380a; iii, 450a; v, 31b, **597a**; vi, 47b, 48a, b, 49b, 65b, 190a, 369b, 488b, 516b, 535b, 691a; vii, 279a, 854b; s, 21a, 47a, 63a, 142b, 247a, 284b, 333a, 360a – I, 1363b, 1364b, 1388a, b; II, 137b, 275b, 390a; III, 465b; V, 32b, **601a**; VI, 46a, b, 47a, 48a, 63b, 173b, 353b, 354a, 474b, 501b, 520a, 678b; VII, 280b; 856a; S, 21a, 47b, 63b, 142a, 247a, 284b, 332b, 359b
—monuments v, 599b, 1217b, 1219b – V, 603a, 1207b, 1209b
—university/-é ii, 426a; iv, 1127a, b – II, 437a; IV, 1158b, 1159a
Lāhawri → ʿAbd al-Ḥamīd
Lahdj → Laḥidj
Lahdjat-i Sikandar Shāhī iii, 453b – III, 469a
al-Laḥdjī, Muslim s, 236a – S, 236a
Laḥidj i, 39b, 95b, 181a; ii, 192a, 193a, 675b; iii, 294a; v, **601b**, 604a; vi, 36a, b; vii, 779a; ix, 738b; x, 106b; s, 338a – I, 40b, 98a, 186a; II, 198a, 199a, 692a; III, 303a; V, **605b**, 608b; VI, 34b; VII, 781a; IX, 772a; X, 114b; S, 337b
Lāhīdjān ii, 192a, 193a; v, **602b**, 604b; vi, 502a, 513a, 514a, 515b; s, 363a, b – II, 199a; V, **606b**, 608b; VI, 487a, 498b, 499a, 500b; S, 363a
Lāhīdjī, ʿAbd al-Razzāḳ (1616) v, **605a**; vii, 548a – V, **609a**; VII, 548a
Lāhīdjī, Shams al-Dīn Muḥammad (1506) v, **604b**, 605b – V, **608b**, 609b
al-Lāḥiḳī → Abān b. ʿAbd al-Ḥamīd
Lahistan → Leh
Laḥn al-ʿāmma v, **605b**, 803b; vi, 248; s, 388b – V, **609b**, 809b; VI, 232a; S, 388b
Lahndā v, **610a** – V, **614a**
Lahore → Lāhawr
Lāhōrī, Ghulām Sarwar vi, 131b – VI, 129b
Lāhūt wa-Nāsūt i, 351a; v, **611b** – I, 361b; V, **615b**
Lāhūtī, Abu 'l-Ḳāsim (1957) iv, 71a; v, **614b**; vi, 608b; vii, 754b; s, 110a – IV, 75a; V, **618b**; VI, 593; VII, 756a; S, 109b
Laʿib v, 478b, **615a** – V, 481a, **619a**
al-Lā'iḥa al-Asāsiyya ii, 647b – II, 663b
Lā'iṭ → Liwāṭ
Lak (Kurd(e)s) i, 755b, 756a; ii, 86b, 87a, 141b; iii, 1102b, 1109a; iv, 344a, 351a; v, 154b, **616b**, 822b, 825b – I, 778a, b; II, 88a, 89a, 145a; III, 1129b, 1136a; IV, 358b, 366a; V, 155b, **620b**, 828b, 831b
Laḳ (Caucasus/-e) v, **617b** – V, **621b**
Laḳab ii, 302a; iv, 180a, 293b, 294a; v, **618b** – II, 310b; IV, 188a, 306b, 307a; V, **622b**
al-Laḳānī, ʿAbd al-Salām iv, 613b – IV, 638b
Laḳant v, **631b** – V, **635b**
Lakay, Ibrāhīm ii, 701a – II, 718b
Lakha, Banū vi, 741a – VI, 730b
Lakhdar Ben Khlouf (XVI) vi, 254b – VI, 238b
Lakhm, Banū ii, 573b; v, **632a**; X, 788a – II, 588a; V, **636a**
al-Lakhmī (1085) vi, 279a, 942b – VI, 264a, 934b
al-Lakhmī, Abu 'l-ʿAbbās → ʿAzafī, Banu 'l-
al-Lakhmī, Abū Ḥasan (1085) vii, 538a – VII, 538a
al-Lakhmī, Abu 'l-Ḳāsim → ʿAzafī, Banu 'l-
al-Lakhmī, ʿAlī b. Rabāḥ s, 81b – S, 81b
al-Lakhmī, Muḥammad → ʿAzafī, Banu 'l-
al-Lakhmī al-Sabtī, Muḥammad b. ʿAlī s, 388b – S, 389a
Lakhmid(e)s i, 73a, 405b, 450b, 451b, 526a, 532a, 548b, 684b, 890a; ii, 1021a; iii, 462b, 1254a; iv, 1144b; v, 632a, **632b**; vi, 97a, 221b; viii, 119b; s, 229b – I, 75b, 417a, 463b, 464b, 542a, 548b, 566a, 705b, 916b; II, 1044b; III, 479a, 1286b; IV, 1176b; V, 636a, **636b**; VI, 95a, 215a; VIII, 121b; S, 229b
Lakhnaw ii, 132a, b, 205a; iii, 451a; v, **634b**, 1033b; vi, 78a, 537a, 611a; s, 74a, b, 102a, 106a, 247a, 292b – II, 135b, 211b; III, 466b; V, **638b**, 1029b; VI, 75b, 521b, 595b, 596a; S, 74b, 75a, 101b, 105b, 247b, 292a
—monuments i, 66a; ii, 132a; v, 7a, **636a**, 1135b – I, 68a; II, 135b; V, 7b, **640a**, 1131a
Lakh(a)naw(a)tī (Gawr) i, 393b, 1015a; ii, 270a; v, **637b**; vi, 48a, 244b; x, 894b; s, 124a – I, 405a, 1046b; II, 278a; V, **642a**; VI, 46b, 228b; X, ; S, 123b
Laḳīṭ al-Iyādī v, **639a** – V, **643a**
Laḳīṭ b. ʿĀmir b. al-Muntafiḳ (VII) vii, 582a – VII, 582b
Laḳīṭ b. Bukayr b. al-Nadr (806) vii, 463b – VII, 463a
Laḳīṭ b. Mālik al-Ātikī i, 812b – I, 835b
Laḳīṭ b. Yaʿmur al-Iyādī (VI) iv, 289a; v, **639b** – IV, 302a; V, **643b**
Laḳīṭ b. Zurāra (VI) ii, 353b; iii, 168b; v, **640a**; vi, 603a; ix, 424b; s, 37b – II, 363b; III, 172b; V, **644b**; VI, 587b; IX, 419a; S, 37b
Laḳḳūt b. Yūsuf i, 251a – I, 258b
Lakshadweep → Laccadives/Laquedives
Lakshmaṇ Singh iii, 458a – III, 474a
Lakz → Lezgh
Lāl Kunwar ii, 379a – II, 389b
Lala iii, 340a; iv, 37a – III, 350a; IV, 39b
Lālā ʿAbla (Morocco/Maroc) vii, 415b – VII, 417a
Lālā ʿĀ'isha bint Muḥammad V b. Yūsuf (ʿAlawid(e)) (XX) vii, 415b – VII, 417a
Lālā Fāṭima Zahrā' bint Muḥammad V b. Yūsuf (ʿAlawid(e)) (XX) vii, 415b – VII, 417a
Lālā Mālika bint Muḥammad V b. Yūsuf (ʿAlawid(e)) (XX) vii, 415b – VII, 417a
Lala Meḥmed Pasha (1606) → Meḥmed Pasha, Lala, Shāhīnoghlu
Lālā Muṣṭafā Pasha → Muṣṭafā Pasha Lala
Lāla Ratan Čand s, 126b – S, 125b
Lala Shahīn Pasha (1388) .... i, 1159b, 1302b; ii, 683b,

722a, 914a; vi, 290b; vii, 593a – I, 1194b, 1342b; II, 700b, 740b, 935b; VI, 276a; VII, 593a....
Lālā Yāḳūt umm Muḥammad V b. Yūsuf (ʿAlawid(e)) (XX) vii, 415a – VII, 416b
Lāle v, 172b, 642a, 644a – V, 170a, 646a, 648a
Lāle dewrī i, 270a, 558a; iii, 1002b; v, **641a** – I, 278a, 575b; III, 1027b; V, **645a**
Lālezarī, Shaykh Meḥmed (XVIII) v, **644a** – V, **648a**
Lālezarī, Shaykh Meḥmed Ṭāhir (1789) v, **644a** – V, **648a**
Lālī → Shāh Sulṭān Muḥammad
Lālish v, **644a** – V, **648b**
Lalitpur v, **644b** – V, **648b**
Laʿlīzāde ʿAbd al-Bāḳī vi, 226a, 228a – VI, 219b, 221b
Lālkōṫ ii, 256a, b, 259a – II, 263a, b, 267a
Lālla Khadīdja i, 371b – I, 382a
Lālla Masʿūda (1557) vi, 597a – VI, 582a
Lallā ʿŪda vi, 591a – VI, 576a
Lallūdjī Lāl (1835) ii, 491a; iii, 458a; v, **644b** – II, 503a; III, 474a; V, **648b**
Lām v, **644b** – V, **649a**
Lām, Banū i, 431a, 528b, 1096a, b; iii, 1107b; iv, 10a, 552b; v, 81a, **645b**; vii, 582a, 673b – I, 443a, 544b, 1129a, b; III, 1134b; IV, 11a, 576b; V, 83a, **649b**; VII, 582b, 673b
Lamak (Lamech) v, **646b**; vi, 215b; vii, 681a – V, **650b**; VI, 199b; VII, 681a
Lamak b. Mālik, al-ḳāḍī (dāʿī) (XI) iv, 199b; vii, 271a, 732a – IV, 208a; VII, 273a, 732b
Lamās, Banū vi, 744a – VI, 733a
Lamasar → Lanbasar
Lamas-ṣū v, **647a**; s, 306b – V, **651a**; S, 306b
al-Lamaṭī, Abu ʾl-ʿAbbās b. al-Mubārak (1743) v, **647b**; vi, 356b – V, **651b**; VI, 340b
al-Lamaṭī, Aḥmad al-Ḥabīb (1751) v, **647b** – V, **651b**
Lamāya, Banū vi, 221b, 310b – VI, 215b, 295b
Lambadis v, **648a** – V, **652a**
Lamdiyya, Banū v, 1010b – V, 1006a
Lamech → Lamak
Lamghān iv, 409b, 411a; v, 649a, b – IV, 427a, 429a; V, 653a, b
Lamghānāt v, **648b**, 782a; s, 237a – V, **653a**, 788b; S, 237a
Lamghānī, Abū Yaʿḳūb Yūsuf (1209) vii, 785b – VII, 787b
Lāmiʿī, Abu ʾl-Ḥasan (1067) v, **649b** – V, **653b**
Lāmiʿī Čelebi, Shaykh Maḥmūd b. ʿOthmān (1531) ii, 869a; v, **649b**; vi, 354a, 609b; vii, 567b, 936a, 1018a – II, 889a; V, **654a**; VI, 338a, 594b; VII, 568b, 936b, 1020a
Lāmiʿī Gurgānī, Abū ʾl-Ḥasan (1067) viii, 970b – VIII, 1004b
Lamīn → al-Amīn b. Ḥamad, Shaykh
Lamine Bey → al-Amin Bey
Lamlam v, **651a** – V, **655b**
Lamṭ iii, 347a; v, **651b**, 1227b – III, 357b; V, **655b**, 1218a
Lamṭa, Banū v, 651b, **652a**; vii, 587a – V, 655b, **656b**; VII, 587a
Lamṭī, Wadjdjādj b. Zalwī (XI) vii, 583b, 584a, b – VII, 584a, b
Lamtūna, Banū i, 211a, 251a, 389b, 1176a, 1178b; ii, 1122a; v, **652b**; vi, 741a, 742a, b, 744a; vii, 584a, 613a, b; ix, 18a – I, 217a, 258b, 400b, 1211a, 1213b; II, 1148a; V, **656b**; VI, 730a, b, 731a, b, 733a; VII, 584b, 613a; IX, 18b
al-Lamtūnī, Abū Bakr b. ʿUmar (1075) i, 211a, 251a, 1176a; ii, 1002b, 1122a; iii, 288b; v, 653b, **654a**; vii, 584b, 585a, 613a – I, 217a, 258b, 1211a; II, 1025b, 1148a; III, 297b; V, 657b, **658b**; VII, 585a, b, 613a
al-Lamtūnī, Awbik b. Ačfagha (1674) vii, 614a – VII, 614a
al-Lamtūnī, Limtād (Limtān) b. Nafīr (XI) vii, 585a – VII, 585b
al-Lamtūnī, Yaḥyā b. ʿUmar (1055) vii, 584b – VII, 585a
Lamu v, **655a**, 963a; vi, 283a, 385a, 612b, 613a, 704a – V, **659a**, 967b; VI, 268a, 369a, 597b, 598a, 692b
al-Lān → Alān
Lanbasar iii, 501b; v, **656a** – III, 519a; V, **660b**
ʾlandjuya → Zanzibar
Langāh, Ḥusayn Shah → Ḥusayn Shāh Langāh
Langar iv, 1073b – IV, 1105a
Langaŕ Khān Langāh iii, 634a – III, 655a
Lankabālūs → Nicobar Islands/Îles -
Lankar Čak → Čaks
Lankoran v, **656b** – V, **661a**
Laodicaea → Lādhiḳ, Lādhiḳiyya
Laos iii, 1208b – III, 1239b
Laquedives I, 175a; IV, 570b, 571a; V, **661b**
Lār (island/île) v, **674b** – V, **680a**
Lār, Lārīdjān v, **657a**, 670b – V, **663a**, 675b
Lār, Lāristān v, 604b, **665a** – V, 608b, **670b**
Larache → al-ʿArāʾish
Lārak → Djāsak
Lāranda i, 468a; iv, 621a, b, 624a; v, **676b**, 1145b; vi, 71b – I, 481b; IV, 645b, 646b, 649a; V, **681b**, 1137b; VI, 69b
al-Lārī → Muṣliḥ al-Dīn
Lārī (coin/monnaie) → Lārīn
Lārī, ʿAbd al-Ghafūr (1507) vii, 935a – VII, 935b
al-Lārī, Muḥammad b. Ṣalāḥ (1572) v, **682a** – V, **687a**
al-Lārī, Muṣliḥ al-Dīn ii, 345b; v, **682a** – II, 355b; V, **687a**
Lârî, Yahuda iv, 309b – IV, 323b
Lārī Čelebi iii, 340a – III, 350a
Laribunder iv, 597b – IV, 621b
Laribus → al-Urbus
Lārida v, **682b** – V, **687b**
Lāridjān s, 357b – S, 356b
Lārīdjānī, Amīr-i Mukarram → Mīrzā Muḥammad Khān b. ʿAbbās
Larin ii, 120b; v, 672a, **683b** – II, 123b; V, 677a, **688b**
Larissa → Yenishehir
Lāriz v, 661a, 664b – V, 666b, 670a
Las Bēla v, **684a**; vi, 192b; s, 222b – V, **689a**; VI, 176b; S, 222b
Lascaris, Theodore iv, 816a, b – IV, 849a
Lāsh ii, 605a – II, 620a
Lāshārīs s, 332a – S, 331b
Lashgarniwīs iv, 757b – IV, 788a
Lāshīn, Maḥmud Ṭāhir v, 189a – V, 186a
Lashkar → ʿAskar Mukram
Lashkar (army/-ée) v, **685a** – V, **690a**
Lashkarī (Daylamī) iv, 100a – IV, 104b
Lashkarī, ʿAlī b. Mūsa iv, 347b, 773a – IV, 362b, 804a
Lashkarī b. Mardī (Ziyārid(e)) (X) vii, 498a, 656a; x. 42b – VII, 497b, 655b; X, 43b
Lashkar-i Bāzār i, 1345a; ii, 1054a, 1082b, 1083a; v, **690b**; vi, 65b; ix, 45a – I, 1385b; II, 1078b, 1107b, 1108a; V, **695b**; VI, 63a; IX, 45b
Lāshōn iv, 301b – IV, 315a
al-Lāt i, 151b; iv, 321b; v, **692a**; vi, 373b, 374a, 645b; vii, 347a – I, 155b; IV, 336a; V, **697a**; V, 358, b, 630b; VII, 349a
al-Lāt, Banū x, 116a – X, 125b

Latakia/Lataquié → al-Lād̲h̲iḳiyya
Laṭīf b. Muẓaffar S̲h̲āh (Gud̲j̲arāt) vi, 51b, 52a – VI, 50a
Laṭīfī, ʿAbd al-Laṭīf Čelebi (1582) v, 116a, **693a**; x, 55a – V, 118b, **698a**; X, 56b
Lawandar vi, 511b – VI, 497a
Lawāsān vi, 511b – VI, 497a
Lawāta, Banū i, 207b, 440a, 1049a, 1174b, 1349b; iii, 1040a; v, **694b**; vi, 435a, 591b, 943b – I, 213b, 452b, 1081a, 1209b, 1390a; III, 1066a; V, **699b**; VI, 420b, 576b, 935b
al-Lawātī, Abū Muḥammad (1133) v, **697b** – V, **702a**
Lawei s, 150b – S, 150b
Lawḥ i, 90a, 851a; 911b; iv, 354a; v, **698a**; s, 93a, 231a – I, 92b, 874b, 939a; IV, 369b; V, **703a**; S, 93a, 230b
al-Lawḥ al-maḥfūẓ → Lawḥ
Lawn v, **698b** – V, **703b**
Laws̲h̲a v, **707b** – V, **712b**
Lâye s, 182b – S, 182b
Layl and/et Nahār v, **707b** – V, **712b**
Laylā bint al-D̲j̲ūdī ii, 625b – VI, 641a
Laylā bint Masʿūd i, 400b – I, 412a
Laylā bint Nuʿmān iii, 255a; iv, 23a, 1066a – III, 262a; IV, 24b, 1097b
Layla al-Ak̲h̲yaliyya (VII) iv, 912a; v, **710a**; vi, 477b, 603a; vii, 843a – IV, 945a; V, **715a**; VI, 463b, 587b; VII, 844a
Laylā K̲h̲ānïm (1847) v, **710a** – V, **715a**
Laylā K̲h̲ānïm (1936) iii, 1117a; v, **710b** – III, 1144b; V, **715b**
Laylā-u Mad̲j̲nūn → Mad̲j̲nūn wa-Laylā
Laylān vi, 498b, 502a – VI, 483b, 487a
Laylat al-barāʾa i, 1027b – I, 1059a → Ramaḍān
Laylat al-Ḳadr iv, 280a – IV, 292a → Ramaḍān
Laylī ii, 191a – II, 197a
Laylī b. Nuʿmān → Laylā b. Nuʿmān
Layt̲h̲, Banū vii, 392b – VII, 394a
al-Layt̲h̲ b. Faḍl (802) vi, 119a – VI, 116b
Layt̲h̲ b. Mahaṭṭa (Tanūk̲h̲) x, 190b – X,207a
al-Layt̲h̲ b. al-Muẓaffar (784) iv, 963a; v, **711a**; vii, 190a – IV, 995a; V, **716a**; VII, 190b
al-Layt̲h̲ b. Saʿd (791) v, **711b**; vi, 263b; s, 87b – V, **716b**; VI, 248b; S, 87b
Layt̲h̲ b. ʿAlī iii, 619b – III, 640a
Layt̲h̲ b. Kahlān iii, 856b, 857b – III, 880b, 881b
al-Layt̲h̲ī, Naṣr b. S̲h̲abat̲h̲ vi, 334a – VI, 318b
al-Layt̲h̲ī, Yaḥyā b. Yaḥyā (848) i, 83a; vi, 279a, 281a; 165a – I, 85b; VI, 264a, 266a; 170b
Lāyzān iv, 343a – IV, 357b
Laz i, 100b, 469b, 471b, 474b; iv, 350a, 351a, 576b; v, **712a** – I, 103b, 483b, 485b, 488b; IV, 365a, 366a, 599b; V, **717a**
Lazarus/Lazare v, **714b** – V, **719b**
Lazistān v, 712a, 713a, b – V, 717a, 718a, b
Lazz, Āl i, 759b – I, 782b
League of Arab States → Arab League
Lebanon → Lubnān
Lĕbaran v, **714b** – V, **720a**
Lebna Dengel vi, 642a – VI, 627a
Lebou/Lebu v, 694b, 753b – V, 699b, 759b
Leff i, 1179b; v, **715a** – I, 1214b; V, **720a**
Lefḳos̲h̲a v, **716a** – V, **721a**
Légion arabe, la I, 47b; III, 272a, 1291b
Leh (Poland/Pologne) i, 4a, 1119b; iv, 178b, 179a, 516b, 590b; v, 139b, 140a, b, 260b,**719a**, 766a, b – I, 4b, 1153b; IV, 185b, 186a, 539a, 614b; V, 142b, 143a, 258b, **724a**, 772a, b
Lēk → Lakz
Lekë Dukagjin i, 170b, 652a – I, 175a, 672b
Lemdiya → al-Madiyya
Lemnos → Limni
Lenkoran → Lankoran
Leninabad → K̲h̲ud̲j̲and
Leo Africanus/Léon l'Africain (XVI) iv, 339b; v, **723a** – IV, 354a; V, **728a**
Leo(n) I (Armenia/-énie) i, 182b; ii, 37a – I, 187b; II, 38a
Leo(n) II (Armenia/-énie) ii, 37b – II, 38a
Leo(n) III (Armenia/-énie) iv, 1174a; vi, 381b, 580a – IV, 1207a; VI, 365b, 565a
Leo(n) IV (Armenia/-énie) iv, 1174a – IV, 1207a
Leo(n) V (Armenia/-énie) i, 790a; ii, 38b – I, 813a; II, 39a
Leon → Liyūn
Lepanto/-e → Aynabak̲h̲tï
Lérida → Lārida
Lesbos → Midilli
Les̲h̲ v, **724a** – V, **729a**
Leskofd̲j̲alï G̲h̲ālib ii, 878a; iii, 1200b; s, 324b – II, 898b; III, 1230b; S, 324a
Letur s, 143a – S, 143a
Leucas → Levkas
Levante → S̲h̲arḳ al-Andalus
Levend → Lewend
Levi b. Japheth iv, 605a – IV, 629b
Levice s, 171a – S, 171b
Levkas (island/île) iv, 656a; v, **725b** – IV, 682a; V, **730b**
Lévrier → Salūḳī
Lewend iii, 317b; v, 506b, **728a**; vi, 56b; vciii, 185a – III, 327b; V, 510a, **733a**; VI, 54b; VIII, 188a
Lewnī (painter/peintre) vii, 603a – VII, 602b
Leylā Saz → Laylā K̲h̲ānïm (1936)
Lez ii, 86a, 89a; iii, 604a; iv, 343a; v, 494a, 498a, 617b, 713a, **729b** – II, 87b, 90b; III, 624b; IV, 357b; V, 497a, 501b, 621b, 718a, **734b**
Lezgi → Lezg̲h̲
Liʿān i, 1150b; iv, 689a; v, **730a** – I, 1185a; IV, 717a; V, **735b**
Liʿb → Laʿib
Libān → Lubnān
Libās ii, 206b; v, 6a, 476a, **732a** – II, 213a; V, 6b, 479a, **737b**
Liberia v, **753a** – V, **758b**
Lībiyā i, 39b, 1071a, 1177a; ii, 94a, 667a, 676a; iii, 385a, 1049a; iv, 262a; v, 696a, **753b**, 1066a; vi, 467b, 1043b; s, 216a – I, 40b, 1103a, 1212a; II, 96a, 684a, 693a; III, 397b, 1075b; IV, 274a; V, 700b, **759b**, 1063b; VI, 453b, 1037a; S, 216a
—demography/-ie s, **216a** – S, **216a**
—inscriptions v, 221b, **754b** – V, 219a, **760b**
—lit(t)erature ii, 470b – II, 482b
—university/-é ii, 425a; v, 912a – II, 436a; V, 917b
Libn → Labin
Libya/Libye → Lībiyā
Libyan/Libyque i, 1180b, 1185a; v, 694b – I, 1215b, 1220a; V, 699b
Lifard̲j̲ān vi, 384a – VI, 368b
Ligue des États arabes → al-D̲j̲āmiʿa al-ʿArabiyya
Ligue islamique → al-Rābita al-Islāmiyya
Liḥyān, Banū i, 562b; v, **761b**; vi, 349a; vii, 371a – I, 580b; V, **767b**; VI, 333a; VII, 372b
al-Liḥyānī, ʿAlī b. Ḥāzim v, 763a – V, 769a
Liḥyānite → Liḥyān
Liḥya-yi S̲h̲erīf v, **761a** – V, **767a**
Likaylik, Muḥammad Abū – ix, 651a – IX, 676a
Li Xun (Persian) (X) x, 460a – X, 493b
Līlī b. al-Nuʿmān s, 356b, 357a – S, 356b
Līm, Līmūn → Muḥammadāt

Limassol → Ḳubruṣ
Limbang Valley s, 152b – S, 152b
Limni v, 257b, **763b** – V, 255a, b, **769b**
Linga v, 507b, 674b, **765a** – V, 511a, 679b, **770b**
Liongo s, 351a, b – S, 351a, b
Liparit (Georgian) vi, 626b – VI, 611b
Lipḳa v, **765b** – V, **771a**
Liptako ii, 942a – II, 964a
Lisān v, 803a, 805a – V, 809a, 811a
Lisān al-ʿArab → Ibn Manẓūr
Lisān al-Dīn Ibn al-Khaṭīb → Ibn al-Khaṭīb
Lisān al-Ḥummara → Ibn Lisān al-Ḥummara
Lisānī (1533) iv, 68b; VIII, 775a – IV, 72a; VIII, 801a
Lisbon/Lisbonne → al-Ushbūna
Lishbūna i, 1338b – I, 1379a
Liṣṣ v, **767b** – V, **773b**
Līṭānī, Nahr al- iv, 483a – IV, 504a
al-Līth vi, 153b, 154a – VI, 152a
Lithām v, 744a, b, 745a, **769a** – V, 749b, 750a, b, **775a**
Lithuania/Lithuanie v, 137b, 140a, 765b – V, 140b, 142b, 771b
Little, Malcolm → Malcolm X
Liu (T)Chiai-lien → Liu (T)Chih
Liu (T)Chih (XVIII) v, **770a** – V, **776a**
Livadya v, **772a** – V, **778a**
Livno v, **774a** – V, **780a**
Liwāʾ i, 349a; ii, 507b; iii, 383b, 384b; v, **776a** – I, 359b; II, 520a; III, 396a, 397a; V, **782a**
Līwā → al-Djiwāʾ
Liwāʾ-i Sherīf → Sandjaḳ-i Sherīf
Līwān → Īwān
Liwāṭ v, **776b**; vi, 317b – V, **782b**; VI, 302b
Liyāḳat ʿAlī Khān (1951) iii, 532b; v, **779b**; vi, 489b; viii, 242a – III, 551a; V, **785b**; VI, 475b; VIII, 248a
Liyāḳat al-Lāh iii, 119b – III, 122a
Liyūn (Léon) v, **781a** – V, **787b**
Liyya (Ṭāʾif) vi, 266a – VI, 251a
Lobbo → Aḥmadu Lobbo; Ba Lobbo
Lob Nor (lake/lac) x, 302a – X, 325a
Lōdī, ʿAlam Khān (XVI) i, 848a; ii, 271a, 1129a; iii, 420b – I, 871b; II, 279a, 1155b; III, 434a
Lōdīs (Delhi) i, 756b; ii, 258b, 263b, 264a, 270b, 274b; iii, 442b; iv, 513a; v, **782a**; vi, 46b, 49a, 126a, 127b, 369a, 488a; vii, 795b; s, 1b, 313a – I, 779a; II, 265a, 271b, 272a, 279a, 283a; III, 457b; IV, 535a; V, **788b**; VI, 45a, 47b, 123b, 125b, 353a, 474a; VII, 797b; S, 1b, 313a
Loe Djirga s, 66a – S, 66b
Logone v, 278b – V, 276b
Loja → Lawsha
Loḳmān, Seyyid → Luḳmān b. Sayyid Ḥusayn
Lombardy/Lombardie → Īṭaliya
Lombok i, 1219b, 1226a; v, **785a** – I, 1250b, 1257b; V, **791b**
Lop Nor → Lob Nor
Lope b. Musa → Lubb b. Mūsā
Lor, Lorī → Lur, Lurī
Loralai district (Balūčistān) s, 331b – S, 331b
Lorca → Lurḳa
Los Pedroches → Faḥṣ al-Ballūṭ
Lot/Loth → Lūṭ
Lōtōn → Khotan
Louxor → al-Uḳṣur
Lowarāʿī ii, 29a – II, 29b
Lōya Djirga i, 232b; ii, 657b – I, 239b; II, 674a
Luarsab I (al-Kurdjī) (XVI) v, 492b, 493a – V, 495b, 496a
Luʿba v, 616a – V, 620a
Lubān (incense/encens) v, **786a**; vi, 83b, 666a – V, **792a**; VI, 81b, 652a
Lubb b. Muḥammad iv, 713a – IV, 742a
Lubb b. Mūsā b. Ḳāsī (863) vii, 288b – VII, 290b
Lubb b. Mūsā b. Mūsā iv, 713a – IV, 741b
Lubka → Lipḳa
Lubnān (Lebanon/Liban) i, 975b, 1078a, b; ii, 185a, 403b, 443b, 444a, 595a, 661a; iii, 559a; iv, 834b; v, **787a**, 1253a; vi, 26b, 387b, 467b, 470a, 796b; x, 117a – I, 1006a, 1110b; II, 190b, 414a, 455a, b, 610a, 677b; III, 578b; IV, 867b; V, **793b**, 1244a; VI, 24b, 371b, 453b, 455b, 786a; X, 126b
—history/-oire iv, 261b – IV, 273b
—industries iii, 211a; v, 791b, 795b – III, 217a; V, 798a, 801b
—institutions ii, 424a; iii, 523a; v, 912a, b, 1051a – II, 435a; III, 541a; V, 917b, 918b, 1047b
—langu(ag)e, lit(t)e(é)rature i, 575a; ii, 467a – I, 594a; II, 479a
Lubūd v, **798a** – V, **804a**
al-Lubūdī s, 267b, 341b – S, 267b, 341a
Lucena → al-Yussāna
Lucera → Lūshīra
Lucknow → Lakhnaw
Ludd v, **798b** – V, **804b**
Lūdhiāna v, **803a** – V, **809a**
Lūdjāra → Lūshīra
al-Ludjdj i, 1083b – I, 1115b
Lugha iv, 122a, b, 524a; v, **803a** – IV, 127b, 128a, 546b; V, **809a**
Lugha, ʿIlm al- → Lugha
Lughat-nāma → Dehkhudā
al-Lughawī → Abu ʾl-Ṭayyib
Lughz v, **806b** – V, **812b**
Luhayfa bint Abū Safyān i, 145b – I, 150a
al-Luḥayya v, **807a**; vi, 192a; s, 30b – V, **813a**; VI, 175b; S, 30b
Luhrāsb iv, 809a – IV, 842a
al-Lukām → al-Lukkām, Djabal
Luḳaṭa v, **809b** – V, **815b**
al-Lukkām, Djabal ii, 982a; v, **810a**, b; vi, 778a – II, 1004b; V, **816a**, b; VI, 767b
al-Luḳaymī → Asʿad
Lukayz i, 73a – I, 75a
Luḳmān b. ʿĀd i, 146a, 984a; ii, 112b; iii, 309a; v, **811a**; vi, 235a, 565b – I, 150a, 1014b; II, 115a; III, 318b; V, **817a**; VI, 207b, 550b
Luḳmān b. Sayyid Ḥusayn (1601) v, **813b** – V, **820a**
Luḳmāndji b. Ḥabīb Allāh (1760) v, **814b** – V, **821a**
Lüleburgaz v, **815a** – V, **821a**
Lūlī ii, 40b, 41a; v, **816b**; ix, 64b – II, 41b, 42a; V, **822b**; IX, 66a
Lulon → Luʾluʾa
Luʾluʾ (pearl/perle) v, **819a**, 969b – V, **825b**, 972b
Luʾluʾ (eunuch(e), Aleppo) (1116) i, 1337a; iii, 86b, 1118b; vi, 578a – I, 1377a; III, 89a, 1146a; VI, 563a
Luʾluʾ (amīr) iii, 398a – III, 410b
Luʾluʾ, Badr al-Dīn (Zangid(e)) (1259) i, 195b, 1161a; ii, 348b; iii, 961a; iv, 76b; v, **821a**; vi, 321b, 352a, 900b; vii,727b, 728b, 990b; ix, 45b – I, 201a, 1195b; II, 358b; III, 985b; IV, 80b; V, **827a**; vi, 306a, 336a, 892a; vii, 728a, 729a, 992a; IX, 46b
Luʾluʾ, Ḥusām al-Dīn i, 784a, 932b; v, 368b – I, 807a, 961a; V, 369b
Luʾluʾ al-Kabīr al-Djarrāḥī (1009) iii, 130b; v, **820a**, 923b; vii, 116a – III, 133a; V, **826a**, 929a; VII, 118a
Luʾluʾa (fort(e)ress(e) ii, 36a, b, 37b; vi, 3338a – II, 37a, 38b; VI, 322b
al-Luʾluʾī, al-Ḥasan b. Ziyād (819) vi, 331a; vii, 758a – VI, 315b; VII, 759b
Lummān b. Yūsuf (930) ix, 586b – IX, 609a

Lummasar i, 1359b – I, 1399b
Lūnī (river/fleuve) s, 329b – S, 329a
Lur(s) i, 513a, 955b; iii, 1096b, 1097b, 1102b; iv, 5b, 8a, 9a; v, 616b, 817a, **821a**; s, 147b – I, 528b, 985a; III, 1123a, 1124b, 1129b; IV, 6a, 8b, 9b; V, 621a, 823b, **827b**; S, 147b
Lūrā v, 234a – V, 232a
Lūrī v, 816b, 817a – V, 823a
Lūrī → Lūlī
Lurī (langu(ag)e) iii, 1261a; v, 818a, 823a, b – III, 1293b; V, 824b, 829b
Lur-i Buzurg iii, 1097b; v, **826a** – III, 1124b; V, **832b**
Lur-i Kūčik iii, 1106a; v, 821b, 824b, 826a, **828a**, 829b – III, 1133a, b; V, 828a, 830b, 832a, **834a**, 835b
Luristān i, 8a, 732a, 840a; iii, 337a, 1102a; v, 63a, 617a, 817b, 824a, 828a, **829b**; vi, 491b, 494b, 495a, b – I, 8a, 754a, 863a; II, 347a, 1129a; V, 65a, 621a, 823b, 830b, 834a, **835b**; VI, 477b, 480a, b
Lūrḳa v, **832b** – V, **839a**
Lūs̲h̲ira iv, 274b – IV, 287a
Lusignan v, 303a – V, 302b
Lustre iv, 1167a – IV, 1199b
Lūṭ (Lot) v, 421a, 776b, **832b**; vi, 495b – V, 423a, 782b, **839a**; VI, 481a
Lūṭ b. Yaḥyā → Abū Mik̲h̲naf
Luṭf (grace/grâce) v, **833b** – V, **839b**
Luṭf → Amān; Mīr
Luṭf ʿAlī Beg Ād̲h̲ar (1781) iv, 69b; v, **834a**; vii, 530a – IV, 73a; V, **840a**; VII, 530b
Luṭf ʿAlī K̲h̲ān iii, 604a – III, 624b
Luṭf ʿAlī K̲h̲ān Zand (1794) i, 246b, 1008b; ii, 812a; iv, 391a, b, 476a; v, 156a, 164b, **835a**; viii, 665b; s, 336a, 405b – I, 254b, 1039b; II, 831b; IV, 408a, 497a; V, 162a, **841a**; VIII, 685a; S, 335b, 405b
Luṭf Allāh, Mullā s, 353b – S, 353b
Luṭf Allāh b. Wād̲j̲īh al-Dīn Masʿūd (Sarbadārid(e) (XIV) ix, 48b → IX. 49b
Luṭf Allāh K̲h̲ān s, 76a, b – S, 76b
Luṭfī (1463) ii, 1133a; v, **835b** – II, 1160a; V, **841b**
Luṭfī, ʿAbd al-Mad̲j̲īd v, 189b – V, 186b
Luṭfī, Mollā iv, 880a – IV, 912b
Luṭfī, Muṣṭafā → al-Manfalūṭī
Luṭfī Beg → Luṭfī Pas̲h̲a
Luṭfī Efendi (1907) i, 286a, 972b, 974a; ii, 714a; iii, 515a, 593b; v, **836b** – I, 295a, 1002b, 1004a; II, 732b; III, 532b, 614a; V, **843a**
Luṭfī Pas̲h̲a (1562) v, 268b, **837b** – V, 266b, **844a**
Luṭfī al-Sayyid, Aḥmad (1963) v, **838b**, 1092a; vi, 955b; vii, 441b, 901a – V, **845a**, 1089a; VI, 948a; VII, 442b, 901b
Luṭfiyya → S̲h̲ād̲h̲iliyya
Lūṭī iv, 99b; v, 776b, **839a** – IV, 103b; V, 782b, **846a**
Lutpulla Mutällip (1945) vi, 768a – VI, 757b
Luwāta → Lawāta
Luxor → al-Uḳṣūr
Luzon s, 152a – S, 152a
Luzūm mā lā yalzam v, **839b**, 931a, 932a – V, **846a**, 935b, 936a
Lydda → Ludd

M

Māʾ i, 1029b, 1094-7; ii, 343b; v, **859b**, 1007a, 1108b – I, 1061a, 1127-30; II, 353a; V, **866b**, 1002b, 1104a
Maʿabiyat → al-Mabyāt
Mā al-ʿAynayn al-Ḳalḳamī, S̲h̲ayk̲h̲ (1910) i, 734a; v, **889b**; ix, 446a; s, 47b – I, 755b; V, **896a**; IX, 463a; S, 48a
Maʿād v, **892b** – V, **899a**
Maʿadd i, 102b, 544b, 549a; iv, 448a, b; v, **894b** – I, 105b, 562a, 566a; IV, 468a, b; V, **901a**
Maʿadd (amīr) → al-Muʿizz li-Dīn Allāh (Fāṭimid(e))
Maʿadd b. ʿAdnān v, 315a, 894b – V, 314b, 901a
Maʿādī, Banū i, 1097a; vii, 672a – I, 1130a; VII, 672a
Maadid s, 144b – S, 144b
Maʿāfir v, **895a** – V, **901a**
al-Maʿāfirī, Abu ʾl-Ḥasan ʿAlī (1208) v, **895b** – V, **902a**
al-Maʿāfirī, Abu ʾl-K̲h̲aṭṭāb ʿAbd al-Aʿlā (Imām) (761) vi, 311b, 312a, 946a – VI, 296b, 297a, 938a
al-Maʿāfirī, ʿAmr (Miṣr) (VIII) vii, 160b – VII, 162a
al-Maʿāfirī, Muḥammad b. K̲h̲ayrūn iv, 825b – IV, 858b
al-Maʿāfirī, Saʿīd b. ʿAbd Allāh (VIII) vi, 280b – VI, 265a
Maʿalt̲h̲āyā v, **896a** – V, **902b**
al-Maʿāmirī, Suʿūd b. Baʿīd (1878) vii, 227a – VII, 229a
Maʿān v, **897a** – V, **903a**
al-Maʿānī i, 784b, 858a; ii, 550a – I, 808a, 882a; II, 563b
Maʿānī ʾl-s̲h̲iʿr iii, 110b – III, 113a
al-Maʿānī wa ʾl-bayān v, **898a** – V, **904a**
Maʿārif v, **902b** – V, **908b**
Maʿarrat Maṣrīn (Miṣrīn) v, **921a** – V, **926b**
Maʿarrat al-Nuʿmān i, 1289a; v, **922a**; vi, 429a; viii, 119a – I, 1328b; V, **927b**; VI, 414b; VIII, 121b
al-Maʿarrī, Abu ʾl-ʿAlāʾ (1058) i, 108a, 131a, 591a, 592b, 1092b, 1290b; ii, 127b; iii, 640b, 686b, 1019b; v, 840a, 922b, 926b, **927a**, 1211a, 1212b; vi, 616b; vii, 261a; viii, 470b; s, 32b, 37b, 119b, 289a – I, 111a, 134b, 610a, 611b, 1125a, 1330a; II, 130b; III, 662a, 708b, 1045b; V, 846b, 928a, 932a, **932b**, 1201a, 1202a; VI, 601b; VII, 263a; VIII, 486b; S, 32b, 38a, 119a, 289a
al-Maʿarrī, Abū G̲h̲ālib Ḥumām b. al-Faḍl al-Muhad̲h̲d̲h̲ib vi, 578a – VI, 563a
Maʾāṣir ii, 143a – II, 147a
Maʾāt̲h̲ir al-Umarāʾ i, 241b, 808a; iii, 340b; iv, 814b; v, **935b** – I, 248a, 831a; III, 331b; IV, 946a;; V, **939b**
Maʿazza, Banū viii, 866a – VIII, 896b
Maba s, 164a – S, 164a
Maʿbad b. Wahb (singer/chanteur) (743) i, 118a; ii, 428b; iii, 698b; iv, 821b; v, **936b**; vi, 262a, b – I, 121b; II, 439b; III, 720b; IV, 854b; V, **940a**; VI, 246b, 247a
Maʿbad b. al-ʿAbbās b. ʿAbd al-Muṭṭalib i, 862b – I, 886b
Maʿbad al-D̲j̲uhanī (703) ii, 1026b; iii, 1142a; iv, 370a, 371a, b; v, **935b**; vii, 567a – II, 1050a; III, 1170b; IV, 386a, 387b; V, **939b**; VII, 568a
Maʿbad Mūsā vi, 651a – VI, 636b
Mā baʿd al-ṭabīʿa v, **841a** – V, **848a**
Ma Chʾao-ching → Ma Hua-lung
Ma Chung-ying (XX) v, **844b** – V, **856b**
Ma Hu-shan v, 846b – V, 858b
Ma Hua-lung (1871) iv, 554b; v, **847a**, 850b; viii, 240a – IV, 578b; V, **851a**, 855a; VIII, 245b
Ma Huan (XV) v, **849a**; vi, 212a – V, **853b**; VI, 196a
Ma Ming-hsin (XVIII) iv, 554b; v, 847b, **850b** – IV, 578a; V, 851b, **854b**
Mā warāʾ al-Nahr i, 8a, 103b, 147b, 454b, 1188a, 1294a, 1312a; ii, 3b, 45a, 587a, 1108a; iv, 175a, 188b; v, **852b**; vi, 77a, b, 274a, 331b, 418a, 432b, 512a, b, 656a; s, 50b, 97a, b, 122a, 176b, 192b, 228a, 244b, 326b, 340a, 411a –

I, 8a, 106b, 152a, 467b, 1223a, 1333b, 1352a; II, 3b, 46a, 601b, 1134a; IV, 182b, 197a; V, **859a**; VI, 75a, 259a, 316a, 403a, 418a, 497b, 498a, 641b; S, 51a, 96b, 121a, 177b, 194a, 228a, 244b, 326a, 339b, 411a
Ma Yüan-chʾang iv, 554b – IV, 578b
Maʿbar (Coromandel) iii, 407a; v, **937a**, 1122a; vi, 271a – III, 419b; V, **940b**, 1118b; VI, 256a
al-Maʿbarī, Shaykh Zayn al-Dīn (XVI) v, **938a** – V, **942a**
Mābeyn i, 64a; v, **938b** – I, 66a; V, **942b**
Mabkhara → Mibkhara
Mablaḳa iv, 747a, b – IV, 777a, b
Mabnā al-Ḥashradj vi, 563b, VI, 548a
Mabramān (IX) vii, 279b – VII, 281b
al-Mabyāt v, 498a – V, 501a
Măčar iv, 350a – IV, 365a
Macassar → Makassar
Macedonia/-ie → Māḳadūnyā
Macina → Masīna
Macoraba → Makka
Ma-chu (Mazhu) (1710) ix, 623b – IX, 647a
Mad Mullah → Muḥammad b. ʿAbd Allāh Ḥassān al-Mahdī
Mādaba x, 884b – X,
Madagascar v, **939a**; vi, 774a – V, **943a**; VI, 763b
—language/langue v, 942b, 943b – V, 946b, 947a
al-Madāʾin i, 77a, 810b; iii, 241b; iv, 386a; v, **945a**; vi, 333b, 335b, 427b, 648a, 653b, 664b; s, 118a, 263b – I, 79a, 833b; III, 248b; IV, 402b; V, **948b**; VI, 318a, 320a, 413a, 633a, 639a, 650b; S, 117b, 263a
Madāʾin Ṣāliḥ → al-Ḥidjr
al-Madāʾinī, Abu ʾl-Ḥasan (830) i, 758b, 760a; ii, 1097a; iii, 682a, 723a, 1263a; iv, 291a, 927a, v, **946b**; vi, 350b; vii, 281a –
I, 781b, 782b; II, 1123a; III, 704a, 745b, 1296a; IV, 304a, 960a; V, **950b**; VI, 334b; VII, 283a
Madalī i, 504b – I, 520a
Madali Khān → Muḥammad ʿAlī Khān (Khōkand)
Maʿdān vi, 193a; s, 243a – VI, 177a; S, 243a
al-Madanī, Aḥmad Tawfīḳ iv, 159b – IV, 166a
al-Madanī, Ibn Maʿṣūm (1692) vii, 527b – VII, 528a
al-Madanī, Shaykh Muḥammad i, 808a; iii, 28b; v, 948b, 949a – I, 831a; III, 30a; V, 952b
Madaniyya v, **948b**; vi, 454b; s, 371a – V, **952b**; VI, 440a; S, 371a
Madār, Shāh → Badīʿ al-Dīn
Madārī i, 859a – I, 883a
Mādar-i Shāh iv, 1015a, 1016b – IV, 1046-7a, 1048b
al-Madd wa ʾl-djazr v, **949b** – V, **953b**
Mādda iii, 328b, 329b – III, 338b, 339b
Maddāḥ iii, 368a; iv, 735a; v, **951a**; vi, 373a – III, 379b; IV, 765a; V, **954b**; VI, 357b
Maḍḍar, Shaykh iii, 206b – III, 212a
Māddiyya ii, 97b – II, 99b
Maʿden ii, 707a – II, 725a
Madghalīs iii, 852a – III, 876a
Mādghīs i, 1349b – I, 1390a
Madḥ → Madīḥ
Madhāb iii, 52a; vi, 436a – III, 54a; VI, 421b
al-Madhār/Maysān vi, 633b, 920a – VI, 618b, 911b
al-Madhār vi, 921b – VI, 913a
al-Mādharāʾī, Āl (884) iii, 979a; v, 50a, **953a**; vi, 670a, 671b; vii, 161b – III, 1003b; V, 51b, **957a**; VI, 656b, 658a; VII, 163a
al-Mādharāʾī, Abū Bakr Muḥammad (956) v, 953b – V, 957a
al-Mādharāʾī, Abū Zunbur al-Ḥusayn (929) v, 953a – VII, 957a
al-Mādharāʾī, ʿAlī b. Aḥmad (897) v, 953a – V, 957a
al-Madhārī, Abu ʾl-Ḥasan (1189) vi, 921a – VI, 913a
Madhav Rāo iii, 316b; vi, 535b – III, 326a; VI, 520a
Madhhab v, 1129a, 1141b, 1150b – V, 1125a, 1134b, 1141a
Madhḥidj, Banū i, 544b, 728a; v, 120b, **953b**; vi, 141b, 472a; vii, 777a ; viii, 94a –
I, 561b, 750a; V, 123a, **957b**; VI, 140a, 458a; VII, 778b; VIII, 96a
Madḥiyya → Madīḥ
Mādhō Lāl Ḥusayn (XVI) vii, 327b – VII, 329b
Maʾdhūn 1, 29a; ii, 97b; iii, 50b – I, 29b; II, 99b; III, 52a
Māḍī v, **954b** – V, **958b**
Madīḥ/Madḥ iv, 714b; v, 931a, **955a**; vi, 351a – IV, 743b; V, 935b, **959a**; VI, 335a
al-Madjḥidjī, Muḥammed b. al-Ḥasan i, 600b; iii, 791b – I, 620a; III, 815a
Maʿdīkarib Yaʿfur (Tubbaʿ) (ca. 520) ii, 244a; v, 118b; x, 576a – II, 251a; V, 121a; X,
Maʿdin ii, 29b, 924a; v, **963b** – II, 29b, 945b; V, **968a**
al-Maʿdin v, **993b** – V, **989a**
Maʿdin Banī Sulaym s, 198b – S, 198b
Maʿdin al-Naḳira s, 198b – S, 198b
al-Madīna i, 45a, 50b, 53a, 110b, 609a; ii, 592b, 854a; iii, 362a, 1067a; v, **994a**; vi, 1a, 33a, b, 34a, b, 45b, 118a, 139b, 140b, 147a, 148a, 157a, 190b, 191a, 263b, 264a, 280b, 344a, 621b, 645b, 666b, 668a; s, 198b, 267b, 335a, 337b; –
I, 46b, 51b, 54b, 113b, 629a; II, 607b, 874a; III, 373b, 1093b; V, **989a**; VI, 1a, 31b, 32a, b, 44a, 116a, 137b, 138b, 145b, 146b, 152b,174b, 175a, 248a, b, 265a, 328b, 606b, 630b, 652b, 654a; S, 198b, 267a, 334b, 337a
—city/ville v, 1000-1007 – V, 996b-1003a
—constitution of/de v, 995b – V, 991a
—history/histoire iii, 896b; iv, 335b; v, 994a – III, 921a; IV, 350a; V, 989b
—population v, 999a, b, 1003a – V, 994b, 995a, 998b
—university/-é v, 1005b – V, 1001b
al-Madīna al-Zāhira v, **1007b**, 1239b; vi, 431a, 455b – V, **1003b**, 1230a; VI, 416b, 441a
Madīnat Fās ii, 818a; iii, 1031b, 1032a – II, 838a; III, 1057b, 1058a
Madīnat Ibn Hubayra iii, 266a – III, 273b
Madīnat ʿIzz al-Islam → Ṣabra (al-Manṣūtiyya)
Madīnat al-Manṣūr → Baghdād
Madīnat al-Salām i, 894b; viii, 974b – I, 921b; VIII, 1010b
Madīnat Sālim (Medinaceli) ii, 998a; v, **1008a** – II, 1021a; V, **1004a**
Madīnat al-Zahrāʾ i, 84a, b, 202a, 459a, 498a, 950a; ii, 745b, 747b, 957a; iii, 498b; iv, 1165b; v, 510b, **1008b**; vi, 431a –
I, 86a, b, 208a, 472a, 513a, 979a; II, 764a, 766a, 979a; III, 516a; IV, 1198a; V, 514b, **1004a**; VI, 416b
Madīnat Zāwī i, 511b – I, 527a
al-Madīnī → Abū Ayyūb; Muḥammad b. ʿUmar
Maḍīra v, **1010a** – V, **1005b**
al-Madiyya (Médéa) v, **1010a**; vi, 404a, b – V, **1006a**; VI, 388b, 389a
Madjabra i, 763b – I, 786a
Madjādhīb ii, 944b; iv, 686b – II, 966b; IV, 714b
Madjālis → Madjlis
Madjalla → Medjelle
Madjallat al-Azhar i, 819a, 820b – I, 842b, 844a
Mādjān (canal) vi, 619b – VI, 604b
Madjanna x, 789a – X,
Madjānīḳ i, 1057a, 1059a – I, 1089a, 1090b
Madjapahit iii, 1219a, 1221b; s, 201a, 202a – III, 1249b, 1252b; S, 201a, b

Madjar, Madjaristān v, **1010b** – V, **1006b**
al-Madjarra v, **1024b** – V, **1020b**
al-Mādjashūn (781) vi, 264a – VI, 248b
Madjāz i, 158b; iii, 898b; v, **1025b** – I, 163a; III, 923a; V, **1021b**
Madjbūb iv, 1087a – IV, 1118b
Madjd al-Dawla, Abū Ṭālib Rustam b. Fakhr al-Dawla (Būyid(e)) (1029) iii, 764b; iv, 100b, 465a; v, **1028a**; vi, 66a; s, 118b – III, 787b; IV, 105a, 486a; V, **1024a**; VI, 63b, 64a; S, 118a
Madjd al-Dīn → Hibat Allāh b. Muḥammad
Madjd al-Dīn b. Abī Ṭālib b. Niʿma (Balkh) vi, 608b – VI, 593a
Madjd al-Dīn b. al-Athīr → Ibn al-Athīr
Madjd al-Dīn b. al-Dāya (Munḳidh, Banū) (XII) vii, 578b – VII, 579a
Madjd al-Dīn Abū Bakr (1168) vi, 380b – VI, 364b
Madjd al-Dīn Baghdādī (1209) i, 347a, 764a; vii, 870b; viii, 703a – I, 357b, 787a; VII, 872a; VIII, 723b
Madjd al-Dīn Barāwistanī al-Ḳummī (vizier) ix, 181b – IX, 197b
Madjd al-Dīn Isḥāḳ iii, 708a – III, 730a
Madjd al-Dīn Muḥammad, ḳāḍī (Gulpāyagān) vi, 14a – VI, 12b
Madjd al-Dīn Muḥammad al-Ḥusaynī al-Madjdī (XVII) viii, 893b – VIII, 924a
Madjd al-Mulk al-Balāsānī (1099) i, 1052b, 1336b; ii, 333b; v, **1028b**; vii, 754a ; viii, 81b – I, 1084a, 1377a; II, 343a; V, **1024b**; VII, 755b; VIII, 83b
Madjd al-Mulk Sīnakī iv, 787b – IV, 819b
Madjd al-Mulk Yazdī ii, 334a, 607b – II, 343b, 622b
al-Madjdal i, 846a – I, 869b
Madjdalyābā (fort(e)ress(e)) vii, 910b – VII, 911a
Madjdhūb, Abū Zayd ʿAbd al-Raḥmān (1569) v, **1029a**; vi, 248b, 356b, 756a – V, **1025a**; VI, 232b, 340b, 745a
al-Madjdhūb (1569) v, **1029a** – V, **1025a**
Madjdhūbī → Madjādhīb
Madjdī b. ʿAmr v, 316b – V, 316a
Madjd-i Hamgar s, 235b – S, 235a
al-Madjdjāsī, Muḥammad b. al-Ḥasan s, 126a – S, 125a
al-Madjdjāwī, ʿAbd al-Ḳādir (1913) v, **1029b** – V, **1025b**
Madjdūd b. Masʿūd b. Maḥmūd (Ghaznawid(e)) (1041) iii, 168a; vi, 780b – III, 171b; VI, 770a
Madjghariyya → Madjar
Madjhūl ii, 897a; iii, 26b – II, 918a; III, 27b
Madjīd, Banū ix, 739b – IX, 772a
Mādjid b. Saʿīd b. Sulṭān (Āl Bū Saʾīd) (1870) i, 1282b; ii, 129a; v, **1030a**; x, 817a; s, 355b, 356a – I, 1321b; II, 132a; V, **1026a**; X, ; S, 355b
Mādjid b. ʿUrayʿir iv, 925b – IV, 958b
Mādjid al-Kurdī (XX) vi, 157a – VI, 153a
Madjid Ṭūbiyā vi, 469a – VI, 454b
Madjīdiyya → Ḥāfiẓiyya
Madjīdiyya library (Mecca) vi, 175b
Mādjir (tribe/tribu) s, 387a – S, 387a
al-Mādjishūn, ʿAbd al-Malik (828) vi, 280b – VI, 265b
al-Madjisṭī → Baṭlamiyūs
Madjkasa Berbers s, 111b – S, 110b
Madjlis i, 891b, 974a, b, 975a, 976a, 979b, 1035b; ii, 87a; iii, 528a, 529a; v, 920a, **1031a** – I, 918a, 1004a, b, 1005b, 1006a, 1010a, 1067a; II, 88b; III, 546a, 547a; V, 925b, **1027a**
Madjlis al-Aʿyān ii, 658b, 659b; iii, 528a; v, 262b, 1035b, 1044a, 1054a – II, 675a, 676a; III, 546b; V, 260a, 1031b, 1040b, 1051a
Madjlis Ḳiyādat al-Thawra s, 6b – S, 6a
Madjlis-niwīs iv, 758a – IV, 788a
Madjlis al-nuwwāb v, 1044a, 1051b, 1054a, 1060b, 1061a, 1064a, 1066b – V, 1040b, 1048a, 1050b, 1057b, 1058a, 1061b, 1063b
Madjlis al-shaʿb v, 1049a, 1059b, 1061b, 1065a – V, 1045b, 1056b, 1058b, 1062a
al-Madjlis al-Sharʿī al-Islāmī al-Aʿlā s, 68a – S, 68b
Madjlis ul-Islam il-Aʿlā Indonesia iii, 1229b – III, 1261b
Madjlis-i Khāṣṣ iii, 553a – III, 572a
Madjlis Ḳuṭub ii, 797b – II, 816b
Madjlis al-Nuẓẓār ii, 647a; iii, 557a – II, 663b; III, 576a
Madjlis-i shūrā ii, 658b, 660a; v, 1042a, 1058a, 1059a, **1082b** – II, 675a, 767b; V, 1038a, 1055a, 1056a, **1080a**
Madjlis Shūrā al-Nuwwāb ii, 647a, 659b – II, 663b, 676a
Madjlis al-umma v, 1044a, 1054a, 1057a, 1061a, 1066b, 1068b – V, 1040b, 1050b, 1054a, 1058a, 1063b, 1066a
Madjlis-i ʿumūmī ii, 643a; v, 1035a, b, 1085b – II, 659a; V, 1031b, 1082b
Madjlis-i wālā v, 1084b, 1085a – V, 1082a
Madjlis-i wükelā ii, 643a – II, 659a
al-Madjlisī, Muḥammad Taḳī → Madjlisī-yi Awwal
Madjlisī-yi Awwal, Muḥammad Taḳī (1659) v, 1087a, **1088b**; vi, 550b; vii, 94a – V, 1084a, **1086a**; VI, 535a; VII, 96a
Madjlisī-yi Thānī, Muḥammad Bāḳir (1698) i, 593a; iii, 588b, 1169b; iv, 278a; v, **1086b**, 1087a, 1089b; vi, 550b, 551a; vii, 94a, 132a, 298a, 935b; viii, 136a, 779a; ix, 854a; s, 134b – I, 612b; III, 608b, 1198b; IV, 290a; V, **1084a**, 1086b; VI, 535a, b; VII, 96a, 134a, 300a, 936a; VIII, 138b; 805b; IX, 889b; S, 134a
Madjmaʿ al-baḥrayn i, 935b, 940b; iv, 903a, b – I, 964a, 969b; IV, 936a, b
al-Madjmaʿ ʿIlmī i, 572b; v, 438a, **1090a**; s, 11b – I, 591a; V, 440b, **1087a**; S, 11a
al-Madjmaʿ al-ʿIlmī al-ʿArabī i, 572a; ii, 290a – I, 591a; II, 298a
al-Madjmaʿ al-ʿIlmī al-Miṣrī → Institut d'Égypte
Madjmaʿ al-Lughat al-ʿArabiyya i, 572b; s, 11b – I, 591a; S, 10b
Madjmaʿ-i Ukhuwwat ii, 434a – II, 445a
Madjnūn ii, 1031a; iii, 273a, 841b; v, **1101a**; vi, 468b – II, 1055a; III, 281a, 865b; V, **1097a**; VI, 454b
Madjnūn Banī ʿĀmir → Madjnūn Laylā
Madjnūn Laylā v, **1102b** – V, **1098b**
Madjrā iv, 412a, b – IV, 430a, b
Madjrīṭ iv, 533a; v, **1107a** – IV, 556a; V, **1103a**
al-Madjrīṭī, Abu al-Ḳāsim Maslama (1007) i, 600b, 1101a; iii, 924a, 1072b; v, **1109a**; vi, 412a, 413b, 601a, 711b; viii, 52b, 677b; ix, 568b – I, 620a, 1134b; III, 948b, 1099a; V, **1105a**; VI, 396b, 398b, 585b, 700b; VIII, 53b, 697b; IX, 591a
Māʾdjūdj → Yāʾdjūdj wa-Māʾdjūdj
Madjūs (Norsemen/Nordiques) i, 83a, 494a, 864b; ii, 525a; iii, 74b; iv, 115b; v, 503b, 586a, 1013a, **1118a** – I, 85b, 509a, 888b; II, 538a; III, 77a; IV, 120b; V, 506b, 591b, 1008b, **1114b**
Madjūs (Zoroastrians) i, 15b, 83a, 264a, 626a, 1354b; ii, 638a, 970b, 1035b, 1124a; iv, 43a, 54a, 910a, 1063a; v, 157a, 370b, **1110a**, 1121b; vi, 337a, 633b, 675a; x, 439b – I, 16a, 85a, 272b, 647a, 1393b; II, 654b, 993a, 1059b,

1150b; IV, 45b, 56b, 943a, 1094b; V, 156b, 371a, **1105b**, 1118a; VI, 321a, 618b, 661b; X, 471b
al-Madjūsī → ʿAlī b. al-ʿAbbās al-Madjūsī
Madjūsiyān ii, 162b – II, 167b
Madjzūʾ i, 671a – I, 691b
Madmūn v, **1121b** – V, **1118b**
Madras i, 979a; ii, 426a; v, **1122a**; s, 47a, 247a – I, 1009a; II, 437a; V, **1118b**; S, 47b, 247a
Madrasa i, 20b, 593a, 899a, 1272a; iii, 1124a, 1227b, 1255b, 1264a; iv, 28a, 167b, 288b, 1025b; v, 255b, 907b, **1123a**, 1200a – I, 21b, 612a, 926a, 1311a; III, 1152a, 1259a, 1288a, 1297a; IV, 29b-30a, 174b, 301a, 1057b; V, 253b, 913a, **1119b**, 1190a
Madrasa Abū ʿInāniyya (Fès) s, 223b – S, 223b
Madrasa ʿĀdiliyya (Damas(cus)) vi, 671b; vii, 274a – VI, 657b; VII, 276a
Madrasa Ashrafiyya (Damas(cus)) v, 1143a, b, 1144a; vi, 193b, 664a – V, 1136a,b; VI, 177b, 650a
Madrasa Ashrafiyya (Alep(po)) (1210) vii, 10a – VII, 10b
Madrasa Čakmaḳiyya (Damas(cus)) vi, 187a – VI, 171a
Madrasa Dammāghiyya (Damas(cus)) vi, 664a – VI, 650a
Madrasa Dār al-siyādat (Kirmān) vii, 480b – VII, 480a
Madrasa Djamāl al-Dīn vi, 674b – VI, 661a
Madrasa Djamāliyya (Cairo/le Caire) vi, 672b, 673a – VI, 659a, b
Madrasa Fāḍiliyya (Cairo/le Caire) vi, 198a, 664a – VI, 182b, 650a
Madrasa al-Falāḥ (Mecca) vi, 173b – VI, 161b
Madrasa al-Firdaws (Alep(po)) (1235) vii, 10a – VII, 10b
Madrasa al-Ḥākim (Cairo/le Caire) vi, 193b – VI, 177b
Madrasa Halawiyya (Alep(po)) (1245) vii, 14a – VII, 15a
Madrasa al-Ḥasan (Cairo/le Caire) vi, 193b – VI, 177b
Madrasa Ḥaydariyya (Ḳazwīn) (1220) vii, 12b – VII, 13b
Madrasa Iḳbāliyya (Damas(cus)) vi, 193b – VI, 177b
Madrasa Ḳalawūn (1285) vii, 11a – VII, 11b
Madrasa Ḳalender-Khāne (Istanbul) vii, 272a – VII, 274b
Madrasa Khāniyya (Bukhārā) vi, 782b – VI, 772b
Madrasa Khātūniyya (Mārdīn) vi, 542b – VI, 527a
Madrasa Khōdja Bedr al-Dīn (Mīlās) vii, 56a – VII, 56b
Madrasa al-Ḳuḍāʿiyya (Damas(cus)) vii, 469a – VII, 468b
Madrasa al-Ḳumḥiyya (Cairo/-e) viii, 913b – VIII, 945a
Madrasa al-Madjdiyya vi, 677b – VI, 664b
Madrasa Maḥmūd Gawan (Bīdar) vi, 695b – VI, 683b
Madrasa al-Maḥmūdiyya (Cairo/le Caire) vi, 199b – VI, 184a
Madrasa Masʿūdiyya (Diyār Bakr) vii, 13a – VII, 14a
Madrasa Mustanṣiriyya (Baghdād) (1234) i, 902a, b, 903a; v, 1127a; vi, 198a; vii, 727b, 728a, b – I, 929a, b, 930a; V, 1123b; VI, 182a; VII, 728b, 729a
Madrasa Niẓāmiyya (Baghdād) (1067) i, 901b, 902a; iv, 458a; v, 1126a, 1127a; vi, 198a, 635a, 657b; vii, 728a; viii, 71b, **82a**; s, 4b, 29b, 192a, b, 326a – I, 928b, 929a; IV, 478b; V, 1122b, 1123b; VI, 182a, 620a, 643a; VII, 728b; VIII, 73a, **84a**; S, 4a, 30a, 193a, b, 325b
Madrasa Niẓ (Čishtiyya) ii, 55a – II, 56a
Madrasa Niẓ (Damascus) s, 197a – S, 197a
Madrasa Niẓ (Marw) s, 326a – S, 325b
Madrasa Niẓ (Farangī Maḥall) s, 4b, 292a, 293a – S, 4a, 292a, 293a
Madrasa Paṫnā (1630) vi, 697b – VI, 685b
Madrasa al-Rāḳiya (Mecca) vi, 173b – VI, 161b
Madrasa Ṣāḥibiyya vi, 672b, 673a – VI, 659a, b
Madrasa al-Ṣāliḥiyya (Cairo/le Caire) vi, 671b; vii, 565a – VI, 657b; VII, 566a
Madrasa Shādbakhtiyya (Alep(po)) vii, 10a – VII, 10b
Madrasa Shīrghāzī (Khīwa) vi, 130b – VI, 128b
Madrasa Sitt Ridwiyya (Mārdīn) vi, 542b – VI, 527a
Madrasa Sulṭāniyya (Alep(po)) (1223) vii, 10a – VII, 10b
Madrasa Tādjiyya (Baghdād) s, 384a – S, 384b
Madrasa al-Ẓāhiriyya (Damas(cus)) ii, 286a, 290a; vi, 671b – II, 294a, 298a; VI, 657b
Madrasa Zindjīriyya (Mārdīn) vi, 542b – VI, 527a
Maḍraṭān s, 352a – S, 352a
Madrid → Madjrīṭ
Madura ii, 391b; iii, 1213b, 1219a, 1226a; v, **1154b**; vi, 43b; s, 202b – II, 402a; III, 1244b, 1249b, 1257b; V, **1144a**; VI, 42a; S, 202a
al-Madya → al-Madiyya
Madyan Shuʿayb v, **1155b** – V, **1145b**
Māf, Manāfa → Manf
Mafākhir i, 892a – I, 918b
Mafākhir al-Barbar iii, 782b; v, **1156b** – III, 805b; V, **1146b**
al-Māfarrūkhī, Mufaḍḍal b. Saʿd (XI) v, **1157a** – V, **1147a**
Mafia (island/île) v, **1157b**; vi, 370a – V, **1147a**; VI, 354b
Mafḥaḳ iii, 327a – III, 337a
Mafḳūd ii, 995b – II, 1018b
Mafraḳ s, 157a – S, 157b
Mafrūshāt v, **1158a** – V, **1148a**
Mafṣūl v, **1159a** – V, **1149a**
Ma Fu-ch"u (XIX) x, 575a – X,
Magal s, 182a – S, 182b
Magan (Makkan) vi, 192b; ix,774b – VI, 176b; IX, 808a
Magas iv, 345b, 349b – IV, 360a, 364b
Maggan b. Kāmil b. Djāmiʿ iii, 386b – III, 398b
Magh i, 952a – I, 981a
Maghā (Muḥammad) b. Mansa Mūsā (Mali) (XIV) vi, 421b – VI, 406b
Maghāfir iii, 64b – III, 67a
Maghāghā (Egypt/Égypte) s, 408a – S, 408b
Maghāgha (tribe/-u) v, 695a, b, 697a – V, 700a, b, 702a
Maghāʾir Shuʿayb v, 1156a – V, 1146a
al-Maghāmī (900) vi, 352b – VI, 336b
Maghāra ii, 14a – II, 14a
Maghāriba v, **1159a** – V, **1149a**
Maghazberd vi, 202b – VI, 186b
al-Maghāzī iii, 698a; v, 996a, **1161b** – III, 720a; V, 991b, **1151a**
Maghīla, Banū iii, 1040b, 1041a; v, **1164a**; vi, 221b, 310b, 311b, 815a – III, 1066b, 1067a; V, **1154a**; VI, 215b, 295b, 296b, 805a
al-Maghīlī, Muḥammad b. ʿAbd al-Karīm (1503) ii, 977b; iii, 276a; iv, 548b, 549b, 550a; v, **1165a**; vii, 394a; viii, 18a; x, 122a – II, 1000a; III, 284a; IV, 572b, 573b; V, **1155a**; VII, 395b; VIII, 18a; X, 131b

Maghlova ix, 630a – IX, 654a
Maghmadās i, 125a; iii, 654a – I, 128b; III, 675a
Maghnāṭīs v, **1166b** – V, **1156a**
Maghnisa i, 1225b; iv, 593b; v, **1169b** – I, 1262a; IV, 617b; V, **1159b**
Maghōsha (Famagusta) v, **1171a**; vi, 372b – V, **1160b**; VI, 357a
Maghrāwa, Banū i, 122b, 1246b; ii, 821b; iii, 1041b, 1042a; v, 596a, **1173b**; vi, 404a, b, 435a, 728b, 742b; vii, 722a – I, 126a, 1284b; II, 841a; III, 1067a, 1068a; V, 599b, **1163b**; VI, 388b, 389a, 420b, 717a, 731b; VII, 722b
al-Maghrāwī, Abū Fāris ʿAbd al-ʿAzīz (1605) vi, 248b, 249a, 254b, 607a – VI, 233a, 238b, 591b
al-Maghrāwī, Sīdī ʿAbd Allāh i, 1127a – I, 1161a
al-Maghrāwī, ʿUbayd Allāh Aḥmad b. Bū Djumʿa (XVI) vii, 243a – VII, 244b
al-Maghrib (North Africa/Afrique du Nord) v, **1183b**; ix, 789bb – V, **1173b**; IX, 826b
al-Maghrib (al-Mamlaka al-Maghribiyya Morocco/Maroc) i, 18a, 47a, 50a, 57b, 78b, 84b, 92a, 162a, 288b, 355a-357b, 366b, 1058a, 1231b, 1321a; ii, 130b, 619b, 748a; iii, 38a, 66a, 163a, 204a, 251b, 256b, 1038a, 1041a, 1049b; iv, 262b; v, 742b, 1149b, 1150a, 1159a, 1175a, b, **1184a**; vi, 38a, 123b, 248a, 439a, 606a, 750a, 798b, 841b, 1036b; vii, 11a, 70a, 587a; viii, 61b, 794a, 905a; ix, 820a; s, 103a, 190b, 215a, 223a – I, 18b, 48b, 51b, 59b, 81a, 87a, 95a, 166b, 297b, 366a-368b, 377b, 1089b, 1268a, 1361b; II, 133b, 635a, 766a; III, 39b, 68b, 166b, 247a, 258b, 263b, 1064a, 1067a, 1075b; IV, 274b; V, 748a, 1140b, 1149a, 1165a, b, **1174a**; VI, 36b, 121b, 424a, 739b, 832a; VII, 11b, 70b, 586b; VIII, 62b, 821a, 936a; IX, 855a; S, 102b, 191b, 214b, 215a, 223a
—administration i, 171a, 428a, 917b, 1148b; ii, 145a, 307b, 413a, 673b, 676a; iii, 395b, 561b, 562a, 563b, 564a; iv, 784b; v, 1072a, **1198b** – I, 176a, 440a, 1007b, 1183a; II, 149a, 316a, 423b, 690a, 693a; III, 408a, 581a, b, 582b, 583a; IV, 816a; V, 1069b, **1188b**
—demography/-ie s, **215a** – S, **214b**
—ethnography/-ie i, 34b, 39a, b, 533b, 1177b; ii, 160a; iii, 298b; iv, 329b, 331b, 332b; v, 696b, 1164b, **1196a**, 1207b – I, 35b, 40a,b, 549b, 1212b; II, 165a; III, 307b; IV, 343b, 346a, b; V, 701b, 1154b, **1186a**
—geography/-ie v, **1184a** – V, **1174a**
—history/histoire v, **1188a** – V, **1178a**
—institutions ii, 425b; iii, 525a; v, 917b, 1094a, 1150b – II, 436a; III, 543a; V, 922b, 1091a, 1141a
—langu(ag)es, lit(t)erature i, 96a, b, 156b, 315b, 571b, 578b; ii, 469b; iii, 806b, 814a, 902b; v, 757a, **1203a**, 1159a; vi, 248a, 606a, 798b, 1036b – I, 99a, 161a, 232a, 325a, 590a, 591b, 597b, 1036a; II, 481b; III, 829b, 830a, 837b, 927a; V, 762b, **1193b**, 1149a; VI, 232a, 591b, 1036a
—monuments v, 289b, 1152a, 1153b, 1201a – V, 289a, 1142a, 1143a, 1191b
—religion v, 1199a – V, 1189b
al-Maghrib al-Akṣā vi, 141a – VI, 139b
al-Maghribī → ʿAbd al-Ḳādir; Abu ʾl-ʿAbbās; Muḥammad Shīrīn
al-Maghribī, Abu ʾl-Ḥasan ʿAlī b. al-Ḥusayn (1009) i, 824b; iii, 79a; v, 928a, **1210b** – I, 847b; III, 81b; V, 933b, **1201a**
al-Maghribī, Abu ʾl-Ḳāsim al-Ḥusayn b. ʿAlī (1027) ii, 483b; iii, 80a, 896b; v, 929b, **1211b**; vii, 1017a, 1031b – II, 82a, 920b; V, 934b, **1201a**; VII, 1019b, 1034a
Maghribī, Aḥmad Khattū (1446) i, 1329b; ii, 1125b; v, **1209b**; s, 10b – I, 1370a; II, 1153a; V, **1200b**; S, 10a
al-Maghribī, ʿAlī b. ʿĪsā (1835) viii, 399b – VIII, 413b
al-Maghribī, Banū v, **1210a** – V, **1200b**
al-Maghribī, al-Ḥusayn b. ʿAlī (965) v, **1210b** – V, **1200b**
al-Maghribī, Muḥyi ʾl-Dīn (1281) vi, 601a, b – VI, 586a
al-Maghribī, Saʿīd vii, 613a – VII, 613a
Maghribī al-Shanḳītī (XX) vi, 75b – VI, 73b
Maghumi i, 1259b; iv, 566b – I, 1297b; IV, 589a
Māghūs, Banū vi, 742a, 743b – VI, 731a, 732b
Māgir, Banū vi, 741b – VI, 731a
Māgiriyyūn iii, 339a – III, 349a
Māgres s, 167a – S, 167a
Māh al-Baṣra iv, 13b; v, **1212b** – IV, 14b; V, **1202a**
Māh al-Kūfa → Dīnawar
Māh-Peyker ii, 183b – II, 189b
Maha i, 1028b – I, 1060a
Mahābād v, 466a, **1213a**; vi, 502a; vii, 714a – V, 469a, **1202b**; VI, 487a; VII, 715a
Mahābat Khān (Mughal) (1634) i, 81a, 686a; ii, 180a, 381a; iv, 1018a, b, 1020a; v, 250b, **1214a**; vi, 488a; viii, 125a – I, 83b, 707a; II, 185b, 391a; IV, 1050a, b, 1052a; V, 248b, **1203b**; VI, 474b; VIII, 127b
Mahābat Khān II (Mughal) v, 1214b – V, 1204a
Mahābat Khān (Shīr) → Muḥammad Mahābat Khān
Maḥabba ii, 55b; iii, 103a; iv, 94b, 119b – II, 56b; III, 105b; IV, 98b, 124b
Maḥabbat Khān (Bareilly) ii, 602a; iii, 61b – II, 617a; III, 64a
Mahābhārata i, 856b – I, 880b
al-Maʿhad al-ʿIlmī al-Suʿūdī vi, 173b – VI, 161b
Maʿhad al-Nūr (Mecca) vi, 174a – VI, 161b
Maʿhad al-Ṭibbī al-ʿArabī (Damas(cus)) vi, 304a – VI, 289b
Mahadba s, 144b – S, 144a, b
Mahādila → al-Ahdal
al-Maḥādjir i, 766b – I, 789b
Mahāʾimī, ʿAlāʾ al-Dīn b. Aḥmad (1431) vii, 920a – VII, 920b
Maḥall i, 317a; v, **1214b** – I, 326b; V, **1204a**
al-Maḥalla v, **1220b**; vi, 119a – V, **1211a**; VI, 116b
Maḥalla Daḳalā v, 1221b – V, 1212a
al-Maḥalla al-Kubrā ii, 1009b; v, **1221a** – II, 1033b; V, **1211b**
Maḥalla Sharḳiyūn v, 1221b – V, 1212a
Maḥallat Abū ʿAlī s, 18a – S, 18a
Maḥallātī, Āghā Khān I, Sayyid Ḥasan ʿAlī Shāh (1881) i, 246a, b, 1008b; iv, 201b; v, 27a, 164b, **1221b**; vii, 454b – I, 254a, 1039b; IV, 210b; V, 27b, 162b, **1212a**; VII, 455a
Maḥalle iv, 229b-231b, 234a, 238a, 239b; v, **1222b** – IV, 239b-241b, 244b, 248b, 250a; V, **1213a**
al-Maḥallī, Djalāl al-Dīn (1459) v, **1223a**; viii, 42b – V, **1213b**; VIII, 43b
Maham → Mahīm
Māham iii, 455b – III, 471b
Māham Anga (XVI) i, 1136b; vii, 330b – I, 1170b; VII, 332a
Maḥāmīd, Banū i, 1299a; vi, 251a – I, 1339a; VI, 235a
Maḥammad b. Abī Bakr (1636) vi, 187a, 188a; s, 223a – VI, 171a, b; S, 223a
Maḥammad b. Muḥammad al-Ḥafīd (al-Aṣghar) (1731) vi, 933a – VI, 925a
Maḥammad b. al-Sharīf, Mawlāy (ʿAlawid(e)) (1664) i, 355b; vi, 250a – I, 366b; VI, 234a
Maḥammad ʿAbdille → Muḥammad b, ʿAbd Allāh Ḥassān al-Mahdī
Maḥammad al-Ḥādjdj → al-Dilāʾ
Maḥammad al-Shaykh (Saʿdid(e)) (1557) vi, 594a, b, 597b – VI, 579a, 582a

Maḥammad al-Shaykh al-Aṣghar (Saʿdid(e)) (1655) vi, 595a – VI, 579b
Māhānasar vi, 512a – VI, 497b
Maḥanḍ Bāba b. ʿUbayd (1860) vii, 622b – VII, 622b
al-Māhānī → Muḥammad b. ʿĪsā b. Aḥmad
Māhānī, Ustādh Muʾmin b. Ḳuṭb al-Dīn s, 139a – S, 138b
Mahārashtrā vi, 63a, 536b; s, 246b – VI, 61a, 521a; S, 246b
Mahari → Kotoko
Maḥārim → Ḥarīm
Maḥasī i, 1029a – I, 1060b
Maḥāsin i, 981b – I, 1012a
al-Maḥāsin wa-ʾl-masāwī v, **1223b** – V, **1214a**
Mahāt v, 651b, **1227a** – V, 655b, **1217b**
Mahathir Mohamad, Datuk Seri (XX) vi, 241b, 242a – VI, 212b, 213a
Maḥbūb b. al-Raḥīl al-ʿAbdī, Abū Sufyān (VIII) iii, 651a; v, **1230a** – III, 672a; V, **1220b**
Maḥbūb ʿAlī Khān ii, 84a; iii, 322b – II, 85b; III, 332a, b
Maḥbūba (singer/chanteuse) iv, 821b, 822b – IV, 854b, 855a
Maḥbūbī, Āl-i v, 858a; viii, 749a – V, 865a; VIII, 779b
al-Maḥbūbī, Aḥmad b. ʿUbayd Allāh (1232) viii, 749a – VIII, 779b
al-Maḥbūbī, Maḥmūd iii, 163b – III, 167a
al-Maḥbūbī, Shams al-Dīn Muḥammad b. Aḥmad (XII) viii, 749a – VIII, 779b
al-Maḥbūbī, ʿUbayd Allāh b. Masʿūd (1346) vi, 848a; viii, 749a – VI, 839a; VIII, 779b
al-Maḥbūbiyyūn iii, 659b – III, 680b
Mahd Awliyāʾ Khayr al-Nisāʾ Begum (XIX) vi, 483a, 515a; s, 71a – VI, 469a, 500a; S, 71b
Mahdawīs ii, 500a; iii, 492b; v, **1230b**; s, 222a – II, 512b; III, 509b; V, **1221a**; S, 222a
Mahdī → al-Djawnpūrī; Ibn Tūmart al-Mahdī; Muḥammad b. ʿAbd Allāh Ḥassān
al-Mahdī (restorer/restaurateur) ii, 851a; iii, 1167a; iv, 203b, 204a, 278b, 456b, 662a; v, **1230b**; vi, 216a, 247b – II, 871a; III, 1195b; IV, 212b, 213a, 291a, 477a, 688b; V, **1221a**; VI, 200b, 231b
al-Mahdī (Fāṭimid(e)) → al-Mahdī ʿUbayd Allāh
al-Mahdī, Abū ʿAbd Allāh Muḥammad (ʿAbbāsid(e)) (785) i, 59b, 103b, 107b, 402b, 550b, 710b, 897a; ii, 143b, 159b, 234b, 281b, 305a; iii, 20a, 22a, 232b, 265b, 616a, 749b, 876a, 996a, 1015b; iv, 88b, 645a, 838a, 939b, 940b, 1164a; v, 69b, 1233a, **1238a**; vi, 106a, 139b, 140a, 147b, 205b, 263b, 334b, 428a, b, 493a, 506a, 625a, 636b, 673a, 707b, 708b, 744b, 745a, 821b; vii, 306b, 507a, 645b; x, 227a; s, 17b, 35a, 48b, 89a, 94a, 199a, 225b, 304b, 326b, 352a – I, 61a,106b, 110b, 414a, 568a, 732a, 923b; II, 147b, 164b, 241b, 289b, 313b; III, 21a, 23a, 239b, 273a, 636b, 772b, 900a, 1021a, 1041a; IV, 92b, 671b, 871a, 972b, 973b, 1196a; V, 71b, 1223b, **1228b**; VI, 104a, 137b, 138b, 146a, 190a, 248a, 319a, 413b, 479a, 491b, 610a, 621b, 659b, 696a, 697a, 734a, 811b; VII, 308b, 507a, 645b; X, 245a; S, 17b, 35b, 49a, 89a, 93b, 199a, 225b, 304a, 326a, 352a
al-Mahdī, Muḥammad b. Hishām b. ʿAbd al-Djabbār (Umayyad(e)) (1010) i, 84b; ii, 485b; iii, 495b; v, 1107b, **1239a**; s, 153a – I, 86b; II, 498a; III, 512b; V, 1103b, **1230a**; S, 153a
al-Mahdī (Sudanese/Soudanais) → Muḥammad Aḥmad b. ʿAbd Allāh
al-Mahdī b. Abī ʾl-Faḍl Djaʿfar, al-Thāʾir fī ʾllāh vi, 941b – VI, 933b
Mahdī b. ʿAlwān al-Sharī (al-Ḥarūrī) (IX) vi, 335b – VI, 320a
Mahdī b. Sayyid Riḍā Ḥusaynī, Sayyid (XVII) vii, 132a – VII, 134a
Mahdī b. Tawālā ii, 874a – II, 894b
al-Mahdī Aḥmad (Zaydid(e)) (1681) vii, 270a – VII, 272a
Mahdī ʿAlī Khān (XIX) iv, 170b; v, **1240a** – IV, 178a; V, **1230b**
Mahdī Baḥr al-ʿUlūm, Sayyid s, 157b – S, 158a
Mahdī Khān Astarābādī (XVIII) iv, 69b; v, **1240a**; s, 46b – IV, 73a; V, **1231a**; S, 47a
Mahdī Ḳulī Hidāyat v, 24b – V, 25b
Mahdī Ḳulī Khān iv, 573a – IV, 596a
Mahdī Ḳuli Sulṭān i, 240a – I, 247b
al-Mahdī li-Dīn Allāh Aḥmad b. al-Ḥasan b. al-Ḳāsim (Zaydī Imām) (1681) i, 554a; v, **1241b**; vii, 779a – I, 571b; V, 1233a; VII, 781a
al-Mahdī li-Dīn Allāh Aḥmad b. al-Ḥusayn (Zaydī Imām) (1258) v, **1241a** – V, **1231b**
al-Mahdī li-Dīn Allāh Aḥmad b. Yaḥyā b. al-Murtaḍā (Zaydī Imām) (1437) v, **1241a**; vii, 55a – V, **1232a**; VII, 55b
Mahdī al-Mniaï (XX) vi, 755a – VI, 744a
al-Mahdī ʿUbayd Allāh (Fāṭimid(e)) (934) i, 48a, 104a, 249a, 1175b, 1178b, 1238a; ii, 168b, 453a, b, 850b, 852a, b, 860b, 861b; iii, 123b, 785a; iv, 198a, b, 204a, 458b, 660b; v, 1175a, 1237b, **1242a**, 1246a; vi, 434b, 439a, 712b, 727a, 1039b; vii, 575b, 641a, 941b; viii, 922a; s, 236b – I, 49b, 107a, 257a, 1210b, 1213b, 1275b; II, 174a, 464b, 465b, 870b, 872a, b, 880a, 881b; III, 126b, 808b; IV, 207a, 213a, 479a, 687a; V, 1165a, 1228a, **1233a**, 1236b; VI, 419b, 424b, 701b, 716a, 1033a; VII, 576a, 641a, 942a; VIII, 953b; S, 236b
Mahdī ʿUlyā bint ʿAbd Allāh → Mahd Awliyāʾ Khayr al-Nisāʾ Begum
Mahd-i ʿUlyā umm ʿAbbās I (1600) vi, 939a – VI, 931a
Mahdid(e)s i, 552b; iii, 125b; v, **1244a**; vii, 861b – I, 570a; III, 128b; V, **1235a**; VII, 863a
al-Mahdiyya (S(o)udan) ii, 63b, 124a; iii, 5a; iv, 952b; v, 267b, **1247b**; vii, 124b – II, 64b, 127a; III, 5a; IV, 985a; V, 265b, **1238b**; VII, 126a
al-Mahdiyya (town/ville Morocco/Maroc) i, 356a; iii, 500a; v, **1245a**; s, 144b – I, 367a; III, 517a; V, **1236a**; S, 144a
al-Mahdiyya (Tunisia/-e) i, 163b, 700a, 830a, 1319b; ii, 853a, 862b, 956a; iii, 138b, 470b; iv, 460a; v, 1243a, **1246a**; vi, 427a, 434b, 455b, 712b, 727b; s, 11a – I, 168a, 721a, 853a, 1359b; II, 873a, 882b, 978a; III, 141a, 486b; IV, 480a; V, 1234a, **1236b**; VI, 412a, 419b, 441a, 701a, 716b; S, 10b
al-Mahdjar v, **1253a** – V, **1244a**
Maḥdjūr iii, 50a – III, 52a
Maheskar vi, 53b – VI, 52a
Maḥfūr iv, 897b – IV, 930b
Maḥfūz iii, 26b – III, 27b
Maḥfūz ʿAlī al-Bārūnī s, 15b – S, 15b
Maḥfūz, Nadjib v, 190b, 191a, b – V, 187b, 188b
Māh-i Mulk Khātūn s, 65a – S, 65b
Māhī Sawār ii, 32a – II, 32b
Mahīm (Maham) v, **1257b**; vii, 919b – V, **1248b**; VII, 920a
Māhīm v, **1258a** – V, **1249a**
Mahisūr (Mysore) iii, 428a; v, 1216a, **1258b**; vi, 459b, 535b; x, 532b – III, 442a; V, 1206a, **1249a**; VI, 445a, 520a; X,
—monuments v, 1259b – V, 1250b
Māhiyya i, 513b, 514a, 785a; v, **1261a** – I, 529b, 808a; V, **1252a**
Maḥkama vi, **1a** – VI, **1a**

Maḥlūl vi, **44b** – VI, **43a**
Maḥmadīl vi, 499b – VI, 485a
Maḥmal iii, 34a; vi, **44b** – III, 35b; VI, **43a**
Mahmand → Mohmand
Maḥmashādh iv, 669a – IV, 696a
Maḥmūd (Samarḳand) s, 65a – S, 65b
al-Maḥmūd, Āl (Yemen) vii, 779b – VII, 781a
Maḥmūd, Sayyid (Nīshāpūr) s, 360a – S, 360a
Mahmud, sultan (Malacca) vi, 209a, 212b, 213a – VI, 193a, 196b, 197a
Maḥmūd I Nāṣir al-Dīn b. Ilyās Shāh (Bengal(e)) (1459) vi, **46b** – VI, **45a**
Maḥmūd II Nāṣir al-Dīn (Bengal(e)) (XV) ii, 486b; vi, **46b** – II, 498b; VI, **45a**
Maḥmūd III Ghiyāth al-Dīn (Bengal(e)) (1538) iii, 422b; vi, **47a** – III, 436a; VI, **45b**
Maḥmūd I, Nāṣir al-Dīn b. Iltutmish (Delhi) (1266) i, 1194b, 1300a, 1322b; ii, 260a, 267b, 268a, 274b, 609b, 973a, 1047b; iv, 749b; v, 546a; vi, **47b**, 127b, 273a, 368b; s, 124a –
I, 1229b, 1340a, 1363a; II, 269a, 275b, 276a, 283a, 624b, 995a, 1072a; IV, 779b; V, 551a; VI, **46a**, 125b, 258a, 352b; S, 123a
Maḥmud II Nāsir al-Dīn b. Sulṭān Muḥammad Shāh Tughluḳ (Delhi) (1412) i, 1068b; ii, 218b, 270a, 276b, 498b, 1125a; iii, 417b; iv, 533b, 543a; vi, **49a**, 294a, b, 406b; vii, 313b; s, 206b – I, 1101a; II, 225b, 278b, 284b, 511a, 1151b; III, 430b; IV, 557a, 566b; VI, **47b**, 279b, 391a; VII, 316a; S, 206a
Maḥmud I Sayf al-Dīn, Begaṙhā (Begṙā, Gudjarāt) (1511) i, 924a, 1068b, 1200a; ii, 10b, 54a, 597b, 678a, 814b, 1127a; iii, 421b; v, 26b, 1216b; vi, **50a**, 53b, 54a, 269b, 270a –
I, 952a, 1101a, 1235b; II, 11a, 55a, 612a, 695a, 834a, 1153b; III, 435b; V, 27a, 1206b; VI, **48b**, 52a, 254b
Maḥmūd II b. Muẓaffar Shāh I (Gudjarāt) (1526) vi, **51b** – VI, **50a**
Maḥmūd III Abu 'l-Futūḥāt Saʿd al-Dīn (Gudjarāt) (1554) i, 1135b; ii, 1128b; iv, 901b; vi, **52a** – I, 1170a; II, 1155a; IV, 934b; VI, **50a**
Maḥmūd II b. Muḥammad Khān (Ḳarakhānid(e) (1164) ix, 16b – IX, 17a
Maḥmūd I Ghāzī (Ottoman) (1754) i, 56a, 776a; iv, 900b; v, 643b; vi, **55a**; vii, 319a –
I, 58a, 799a; IV, 933a; V, 647b; VI, **53a**; VII, 321b
Maḥmūd II (Ottoman) (1839) i, 61a, 399a, 790b, 836b, 948a; ii, 209b, 684a, 714a; iii, 91a, 628b; iv, 295b; v, 19a, 36a, 816a, 903b, 1084b; vi, **58a**, 196b, 284b, 341a, 508b, 531a, 541b; vii, 425b, 547a, 677b; viii, 59a, 84b; s, 168a, 211b –
I, 63a, 410b, 814a, 859b, 977b; II, 216a, 701b, 732b; III, 93b, 649b; IV, 308b; V, 19b, 37a, 822a, 909b, 1082a; VI, **56a**, 181a, 269b, 325a, 494a, 515b, 526a; VII, 427a, 547a, 677a, b; VIII, 60a, 86bS, 168a, 211b
—reform(e)s i, 469a, 657a, 778b, 783a, 837b, 838a, 905b, 972b, 1226a, 1304a; ii, 202a, 207a, 339a, 512b, 513b, 519b, 563a, 615a, 641b, 724a, 907b, 1091a; iii, 203b, 384b, 552b, 1153b, 1257b – I, 483a, 678a, 801b, 806a, 861a, b, 933a, 1002b, 1262b, 1344a; II, 208b, 213b, 349a, 525b, 526b, 532b, 577a, 630a, 657b, 742b, 929a, 1116b; III, 209a, 397a, 571b, 1182a, 1290b
Maḥmūd I b. Turkān Khātūn (Saldjūḳ) (1094) i, 1051b, 1070b; vi, 275a; vii, 541a; viii, 81b, 942a; s, 384a –
I, 1083a, 1103a; VI, 260a; VII, 541a; VIII, 83b, 974a; S, 384a
Maḥmūd II b. Muḥammad b. Malik-Shāh (Saldjūḳ) (1131) i, 300a, 353b, 858b; ii, 894a; iii, 195a, 345a, 1118b, 1255b; iv, 29a, 466a; vi, **63b**, 500a, 782a; vii, 733b; viii, 81b, 943b; s, 3a – I, 309b, 364a, 882b; II, 914b; III, 200a, 355b, 1146b, 1288b; IV, 31a, 487a; VI, **61b**, 485a, 771b; VII, 734a; VIII, 83b, 975b S, 2a
Maḥmūd (Mirdāsid(e)) (1074) vi, 544a – VI, 528b
Maḥmūd b. ʿAbd al-Djabbār i, 82b – I, 85a
Maḥmūd b. Abī Saʿīd i, 148a, 852b; iii, 483b; iv, 410a; v, 389a – I, 152b, 876a; III, 500b; IV, 428a; V, 389b
Mahmūd b. Aḥmad of/de Ḳalhāt (XIII) iv, 500b – IV, 522a
Maḥmūd b. ʿAlī (XIV) s, 83a – S, 83a
Maḥmūd b. Amīr Walī vii, 849a – VII, 851a
Maḥmūd b. Bābur (Tīmūrid(e))(XV) vi, 513b, 514b – VI, 499a, 500a
Maḥmūd b. Būrī → Shihāb al-Dīn Maḥmūd
Maḥmūd b. Ghiyāth al-Dīn (Ghūrid(e)) (XIII) vii, 410a – VII, 411b
Maḥmūd b. Ghulām Muḥammad Ṭarzī iii, 13b – III, 14a
Maḥmūd b. Ḥamza al-Hamzāwī ii, 182b – II, 188b
Maḥmūd b. Ismāʿīl → Luʾluʾ, Badr al-Dīn
Maḥmūd b. Iltutmish (Muʿizzī, Delhi) vii, 193b – VII, 194a
Maḥmūd b. Ismāʿīl → Luʾluʾ, Badr al-Dīn
Maḥmūd b. Maḥmūd b. Bābur (Tīmūrid(e)) vi, 513b – VI, 499a
Maḥmūd b. al-Malāḥimī s, 393a – S, 393b
Maḥmūd b. Malikshāh → Maḥmud I (Saldjūḳ)
Maḥmūd b. Mīr Ways (Ghalzay) (XVIII) i, 229a, b, 1008b; ii, 1001a; iii, 604a, b; iv, 37a, 537a; viii, 771a –
I, 236a, b, 1039b; II, 1024b; III, 624b, 625a; IV, 39b, 560b; VIII, 797a
Maḥmūd b. Muḥammad → Mīrem Čelebi
Maḥmūd b. Nāṣir Raʾīsiyya ii, 29b – II, 30a
Maḥmūd b. Naṣr → Rashīd al-Dawla Maḥmūd
Maḥmūd b. Sebüktigin (Ghaznawid(e)) (1030) i, 217b, 226b, 424b, 506b, 662a, 780a, 1020a, 1036b, 1068b, 1130b, 1194a, 1218b, 1300a, 1356a; ii, 119b, 308b, 488b, 597a, 730a, 799a, 809b, 919a, 972b, 1043b, 1049a, 1050b, 1099b, 1123b; iii, 195a, 196b, 197b, 255b, 347b, 415b, 1113b; iv, 24b, 189b, 294b, 410a, 543a, 1066b, 1150b; v, 956b, 1028b; vi, **65a**, 193a, 276a, 406b, 410a, 440a, 517a, 600b, 606a, 691a, 715b; vii, 407a, 549a; viii, 110a, 253a, 1028a; ix, 45a; x, 869b; s, 125b, 252b, 253b, 280a, 284b, 305a –
I, 223b, 233b, 436b, 522a, 683a, 803a, 1051a, 1068a, 1100b, 1164b, 1229b, 1255a, 1339b, 1395a; II, 122b, 317b, 500b, 612a, 749a, 818a, 828b, 940a, 994b, 1068a, 1073b, 1075a, 1125b, 1150a; III, 199b, 201a, 202b, 263a, 358b, 428b, 1141a; IV, 26a, b, 197b, 307b, 427b, 566b, 1098a, 1182b; V, 960b, 1024b; VI, **62b**, 177a, 261a, 391a, 394b, 425b, 502a, 585b, 593a, 678b, 715b; VII, 408a, 549a; VIII, 112b, 255a, 1063a; IX, 46a; S, 124b, 252b, 253b, 280a, 284b, 304b
Maḥmūd b. Turghut Oghlu iv, 624b – IV, 649a
Maḥmūd b. ʿUmar b. Muḥammad Aḳit (Timbuktu) (XV) vii, 394a – VII, 395a
Maḥmūd b. Walī s, 227b, 419b – S, 227b, 419b
Maḥmūd b. Zangī b. Aḳ Sunḳūr (Zangid(e)) (XII) vii, 10a – VII, 10b
Maḥmūd b. Zangī, Nūr al-Dīn → Nūr al-Dīn Maḥmūd b. ʿImād al-Dīn Zangī
Maḥmūd Aḥmad i, 735a, 765a, 929b; ii, 124a; v, 267b, 268a, 1250b, 1251a, b – I, 757a, 788a, 958a; II, 127a; V, 265b, 1241a, 1242a
Maḥmūd Ālūsī-zāde → Maḥmūd Shukrī
Maḥmūd ʿAyyād iv, 1153b – IV, 1185b
Maḥmūd ʿAẓmī Pasha, amir al-Ḥadjdj (XX) vi, 155a – VI, 152a

Maḥmūd Beg (Ḳarāmān-og͟hlu) iv, 621b – IV, 646a
Maḥmūd of/de Betl-Kak͟hab rosso i, 765a – I, 778b
Maḥmūd Bey iii, 636a – III, 657a
Maḥmūd Čelebi (XVII) vii, 472b – VII, 472a
Maḥmūd D̲j̲alāl al-Dīn iv, 1125b – IV, 1157a
Maḥmūd Ekrem Bey → Ekrem Bey
Maḥmūd Esʿad vi, 94b – VI, 92b
Maḥmūd Gāwān, K͟hʷād̲j̲ā ʿImād al-Dīn (1482) i, 199a, 924a, b, 925a, 1200a, 1323a; iii, 15a, 421a, 577a, 1159b; v, 1135a; vi, 53b, 62b, **66b**, 269a, 369a; vii, 459a – I, 204b, 952a, b, 953a, 1235b, 1363b; III, 15b, 434b, 597a, 1187b; V, 1130b; VI, 52a, 60b, **64b**, 253b, 353b; VII, 459a
Maḥmūd G͟halzai → Maḥmūd b. Mīrways
Maḥmūd G͟hazān → G͟hazān K͟hān
Maḥmūd of/de G͟hazna → Maḥmūd b. Sebüktigin
Maḥmūd G͟hilzay b. Mīr Ways (XVIII) ix, 854b – IX, 890a
Maḥmūd G͟hiz͟hduwānī s, 46b – S, 47a
Maḥmūd G͟hūrī → G͟hiyāt͟h al-Dīn Muḥammad b. Sām
Maḥmūd Gokaldās͟h i, 628a, 1192a – I, 648b, 1227b
Maḥmūd Ḥamdī Ḥamūda, dr. vi, 178a
Maḥmūd al-Hamzāwī iii, 156a – III, 159b
Maḥmūd Ḥasan ii, 437a; v, 7a – II, 448b; V, 7b
Maḥmūd Ḳābādū iv, 1153b – IV, 1185b
Maḥmūd Karantao ii, 1003b – II, 1027a
Maḥmūd Kārī i, 1342b; iii, 355b – I, 1382b; III, 366b
Maḥmūd Kemāl → Īnal
Maḥmūd K͟hald̲j̲i I b. Malik Mug͟hīt͟h (Mālwā) (1469) i, 924a, 1200a; ii, 12b, 219a, b, 1125b; iii, 418b, 638b; v, 1a; vi, 50b, 51a, **52b**, 62a, 67a, 87a, 272a, 309b, 406b, 407b; s, 280a – I, 942a, 1235b; II, 13a, 226a, 1153a; III, 431b, 660a; V, 1a; VI, 48b, 49a, **51a**, 60a, 65a, 85a, 256b, 294b, 391b, 392a; S, 279b
Maḥmūd K͟hald̲j̲ī II b. Nāṣir al-Dīn S͟hāh (Mālwā) (1531) i, 914b; ii, 12b, 1128a; iii, 421b; vi, **54b**, 309b, 310a, 407a, 970a – I, 942b; II, 13a, 1154b; III, 435a; VI, **52b**, 295a, 391b, 962a
Maḥmud II K͟hān (Ḳarāk͟hānid(e)) (1141) iii, 1114b, 1116b; iv, 581b; v, 45b – III, 1142a, 1144a; IV, 604b; V, 47a
Maḥmūd K͟hān, Naṣīr al-Dīn (Kālpī) (XV) vi, **61b** – VI, **59b**
Maḥmūd K͟hān, Nawwāb (Mug͟hals) vi, 77b – VI, 75b
Maḥmūd K͟hān b. Laṭīf b. Muẓaffar S͟hāh (Gud̲j̲arāt) vi, 52a – VI, 50b
Maḥmūd K͟hān b. Nāṣir i, 1006a – I, 1037a
Maḥmūd K͟hān b. Yūnus (XVI) x, 349a – X, 375a
Maḥmūd K͟hān Lōdī, Masnad-i ʿAlī s, 73b – S, 74a
Maḥmūd K͟hān Māzandarānī, Mus͟hīr al-Wizāra s, 23b – S, 24a
Maḥmūd K͟hān Rohillā i, 1206a – I, 1242a
Maḥmūd al-K͟hʷārazmī → Maḥmūd Yalawač
Maḥmūd K͟hayrām (Aḳs͟hehir) (1269) ix, 61a – IX, 62b
Maḥmūd K͟hōd̲j̲a Behbudiy (1919) vi, 767a, 769a, b – VI, 756a, 758a, b
Maḥmūd Kokaltās͟h → Maḥmūd Gokaldās͟h
Maḥmūd Langāh iii, 633a, 634a – III, 654a, 655a
Maḥmūd al-Malāḥimī s, 25b – S, 25b
Maḥmūd al-Masʿadī (XX) vi, 750b – VI, 739b
Maḥmūd Muk͟htār Pas͟ha (XX) iv, 284a; vii, 525b – IV, 296a; VII, 526a
Maḥmūd Nedīm Pas͟ha (1883) i, 56b, 285b; iii, 250b, 621a; iv, 681b; vi, **68a** – I, 58a, 294a; III, 257b, 641b; IV, 709b; VI, **66a**
Maḥmūd Pas͟ha → al-Falakī; Ḳara Maḥmūd; Ṭayyār
Maḥmūd Pas͟ha (Yemen) (1567) vi, **72a**; vii, 600a – VI, **70a**; VII, 600a
Maḥmūd Pas͟ha Welī (1474) ii, 691a, 722b; iv, 230a, 1017a; vi, **69b**; s, 282b – II, 708b, 741a; IV, 240b, 1049a; VI, **67b**; S, 282b
Maḥmūd Pasīk͟hānī iii, 600b; viii, 114b – III, 621b; VIII, 117a
Maḥmūd Raʾīf (XIX) vi, 725a – VI, 714a
Maḥmūd Ras͟hīd Efendi vi, 113b – VI, 111a
Maḥmūd Riyāḍ s, 240b – S, 241a
Maḥmūd Samarḳandī, Mawlānā (XV) ii, 678a; vi, 50b – II, 695a; VI, 49a
Maḥmūd S͟habistarī (S͟habustarī) (1318) iv, 67b; vi, **72b**; viii, 540a – IV, 71a; VI, **70b**; VIII, 558a
Maḥmūd S͟hāh (Bahmanī) i, 923b, 1047a; iii, 15a, 421a, 1159b – I, 951b, 1078b; III, 16a, 434b, 1188a
Maḥmūd S͟hāh (Özbeg) i, 853a; ii, 30b – I, 876b; II, 31a
Maḥmūd S͟hāh, K͟hʷād̲j̲ā vii, 271a – VII, 273a
Maḥmūd S͟hāh Durrāni i, 230b; ii, 637b, 839a – I, 237b; II, 635b, 858b
Maḥmūd S͟hāh Īnd̲j̲ū iii, 1208a – III, 1239a
Maḥmūd S͟hāh K͟hald̲j̲ī → Maḥmūd I K͟hald̲j̲ī
Maḥmūd S͟hāh, Nāṣir al-Dīn (Tug͟hluḳid(e) (1412) x, 593a – X, 637a
Maḥmūd S͟hāh S͟harḳī (D̲j̲awnpūr) (1458) ii, 270b, 499a; iii, 419b; vi, **61b**; ix, 355a – II, 279a, 511b; III, 433a, VI, **59b**; IX, 366b
Maḥmūd S͟hewḳat Pas͟ha (1913) i, 64a; ii, 15b, 431a, 531a, 682b, 698b; iii, 204a, 595a, 994a; iv, 296b, 297a; vi, **73b**, 614b, 983b – I, 65b; II, 15b, 422b, 544a, 699b, 716b; III, 209b, 615b, 1018b; IV, 310a; VI, **71b**, 599b, 976a
Maḥmūd S͟hihāb al-Dīn (Bahmanī) (1518) vi, **62b** – VI, **60b**
Maḥmud S͟hukri al-Alūsī → al-Alūsī, Maḥmūd S͟hukrī
Maḥmūd Ṭarābī (1238) i, 1295a; v, 858a; vi, 77a – I, 1335a; V, 865a; VI, 75a
Maḥmūd Tard̲j̲umān (1575) vi, **74b** – VI, **72b**
Maḥmūd Ṭarzī s, 65b, 109b – S, 66a, 109a
Maḥmūd Taymūr (1973) i, 597b, 598a, b; v, 187b, 189a, b, 192a; vi, **75a**, 414b – I, 617a, b, 618a; V, 181a, 184b, 187a, 189a; VI, **73a**, 399b
Maḥmūd Ṭayyār → Ṭayyār Maḥmūd Pas͟ha
Maḥmūd Ṭog͟hrïl Ḳara K͟hān b. Yūsuf Ḳadïr K͟hān (Marg͟hīnān) (1075) vi, 557b – VI, 542a
Maḥmūd Tug͟hluḳ → Maḥmūd II (Dihlī)
Maḥmūd Urmewī ii, 345b; v, 5a – II, 355a; V, 5a
Maḥmūd Yalawač (XIII) ii, 2b, 791b; iv, 1020a; v, 38b, 858a; vi, **77a** – II, 2b, 810b; IV, 1052a; V, 39b, 865a; VI, **75a**
Maḥmūd Zarkūn i, 280a, 289a – I, 288b, 298a
Maḥmūdabād (Mug͟hān) ii, 1127a, 1129a; iii, 445b; vi, 494a – II, 1153b, 1155b; III, 460a; VI, 479b
Maḥmūdābād, Āl vi, **77b** – VI, **75b**
Maḥmūdek K͟hān iv, 723a, 849a – IV, 752a, 882a
Maḥmūdī, Banū v, 460a – V, 462b
Maḥmūdī Beg (Mākū) (1639) vi, 202b – VI, 186b
Maḥmūd-i Kutubī (1402) vii, 481a – VII, 480b
al-Maḥmūdiyya viii, 114b; s, 371a – VIII, 117a; S, 371a
Maḥmūdpūr vi, 691a – VI, 678b
Mahmut Makal (XX) vi, 96a – VI, 93b
Māhpaykar → Kösem
Mahr i, 172b, 174a, 209a; vi, **78b**, 476a – I, 177b, 179a, 215b; VI, **76b**, 462a
Mahra i, 110b, 543b; iii, 9a, 652a; v, 184a; s, 339b – I, 113b, 560b; III, 9b, 673a; V, 181b; S, 339a
Mahra, Banū vi, **80a** – VI, **78a**
Mahra b. Ḥaydān b. ʿAmr b. al-Ḥāf vi, 81b; ix, 403a – VI, 79b; IX, 415b

Maḥram Bilḳīs vi, 84a, 561b, 562a – VI, 82a, 546b
Mahrattās → Marāthās
Mahrī i, 575a; iii, 176b; vi, **84a**; s, 339b – I, 593b; III, 180b; VI, **82a**; S, 339a
Mahriyya iii, 666a, 667b – III, 678b, 689b
Māhrū iv, 758b – IV, 789a
Mahsatī iv, 62a; vi, **85b** – IV, 65b; VI, **83b**
Mahsūd, Banū vi, **86a**; s, 285a – VI, **84a**; S, 285a
Maḥsūsāt vi, **87a** – VI, **85a**
Māhūī Sūrī, Marzbān vi, 620a – VI, 605a
Māhūr vi, **87a**, 269a – VI, **85a**, 254a
Maḥw iv, 277a – IV, 289a
Maḥyā i, 1040a; vi, **87b** – I, 1071b; VI, **85b**
Mā'i Daya Kawr i, 432b – I, 445a
Maimonides, Abraham iv, 305a, 306a, b – IV, 318b, 319b, 320a
Maimonides, Moses → Ibn Maymūn
Ma-in (town/ville) vi, 283a – VI, 268a
Maʿīn, Banū i, 525a, 548a; v, 183b; vi, **88b**, 561a; ix, 91a – I, 540b, 565b; V, 180b, 181a; VI, **86b**, 545b; IX, 94a
Maʿīn al-Din i, 803a – I, 826a
Maʿīn al-Djawf vi, 433a; ix, 91a – VI, 418b; IX, 94a
Mainu Kano, Malam iv, 549b – IV, 573b
Majorca/Majorque → Mayurḳa
Maḳābir Ḳuraysh → Kāẓimayn
Maḳʿad ii, 114b – II, 117a
Māḳadūnyā vi, **88b** – VI, **86b**
Maḳāla ii, 802a; vi, **90a** – II, 821a; VI, **88a**
Makalla → al-Mukallā
Maḳām (music/musique) iii, 83b; vi, **96b** – III, 86a; VI, **94b**
Maḳām ʿAbd al-ʿAzīz (al-Gharrā) vii, 10a – VII, 10a
Makām al-Ḥanafī vi, 165b – VI, 157b
Maḳām Ibrāhīm iv, 317b, 318a, b; vi, **104b**, 165b, 708b – IV, 331b, 332a, 333a; VI, **102b**, 157b, 697a
Maḳām-i Aʿlā i, 918a – I, 946a
Maḳāma iii, 106b, 221b, 373a; iv, 64a; vi, **107a**; s, 267a – III, 109a, 228a, 384b; IV, 67a; VI, **105a**; S, 266b
Maḳāmāt ii, 246a; iii, 899a – II, 253a; III, 923a
Mākān b. Kākī, Abū Manṣūr (940) i, 688a, 866a, 867a, 1350a; ii, 928a; iii, 255a, 1157a; iv, 23a; v, 158a; vi, **115b**, 539a; s, 357a – I, 709a, 890a, 891a, 1390b; II, 949b; III, 262b, 1185b; IV, 24b; V, 157b; VI, **113a**, 523b; S, 357a
Makanpur s, 358b – S, 358b
Makanta Jigi (Fajigi) vi, 422a – VI, 407a
Makarfi, Malam Shuʾaibu iii, 283a – III, 291b
Makāri → Kotoko
Makassar iii, 1219b; v, 1155a; vi, **116a**; ix, 877a; s, 151a, 199b, 201b – III, 1250b; V, 1145a; VI, **113b**; IX, 759b; S, 151a, 199b, 201b
Makāyīl vi, **117a** – VI, **115a**
Maḳbara vi, **122a** – VI, **120a**
Maḳbūl Ibrāhīm Pasha → Ibrāhīm Pasha (Maḳbūl)
Maḳdishū iii, 3a; iv, 885b; v, 131b; vi, **128a**, 370a, 704a – III, 3b; IV, 918a; V, 134a; VI, **126a**, 354a, 692b
al-Maḳdisī (966) vii, 284a – VII, 285b
al-Maḳdisī, ʿAbd al-Ghanī (1203) iii, 161a, 735a, 752a, 842b; vi, 350b – III, 164b, 758a, 775a, 866b; VI, 334b
al-Maḳdisī, ʿAbd al-Karīm b. ʿAbd al-Raḥmān iv, 511a – IV, 533a
al-Maḳdisī, Abū ʿAbd Allāh (1000) → al-Muḳaddasī
al-Maḳdisī, Abū ʿAbd Allāh (1343) iii, 763a – III, 786b
al-Maḳdisī, Abū Bakr b. Muḥammad iv, 511a – IV, 533a
al-Maḳdisī, Abu 'l-Ḥasan al-Rabʿī (1137) vi, 713a – VI, 701b
al-Maḳdisī, Abū Sulayman Muḥammad iii, 1071b; v, 330a – III, 1098a; V, 330a
al-Maḳdisī, Ḍiyāʾ al-Dīn (1245) vi, 350b; s, 195b – VI, 334b; VI, 334b; S, 195b
al-Maḳdisī, Ibrāhim b. ʿAlī iv, 511a – IV, 533a
al-Maḳdisī, Muḥammad b. ʿAlī i, 949b – I, 979a
al-Maḳdisī, Shihāb al-Dīn vii, 295a – VII, 297a
al-Maḳdisī, Naṣr b. Ibrāhīm s, 326a – S, 325b
Makhač-ḳalʿe VI, **129b** – VI, **127b**
al-Makhaḍīb → al-Mukhaḍḍaba
al-Makhāʾī → ʿAlī b. ʿUmar al-Shādhilī
Makhāridj al-Ḥurūf iii, 598a; vi, **129b** – III, 618b; VI, **127b**
Makhāziniyya iv, 456b – IV, 477a
al-Makhdūm → Sharīf Awliyā Karīm
Makhdūm, Shaykh (Mappila) vi, 461b – VI, 447b
Makhdūm Djahāniyān s, 10b – S, 10b
Makhdūm Ḥāmid Gandj Bakhsh ii, 186b – II, 192b
Makhdūm Ḳuli (Firāḳī) (1782) vi, **130b**; iv, 853b; v, 859b – IV, 886b; V, 866b; VI, **128b**
Makhdūm al-Mulk, Sharaf al-Dīn (ʿAbd Allāh Sulṭānpūrī) (1582) vi, **131a** – VI, **129a**
Makhdūm al-Mulk Manīrī (Manērī) (1381) vi, **131a**, 410a – VI, **129b**, 395a
Makhdūm Shāh Dawlat (Abū Yazīd) (1608) vi, 410a, b; vii, 331b – VI, 395a; VII, 333a
Makhdūma-yi Djahān Nargis Bēgam vi, 66b, 488b – VI, 64b, 474b
Makhdūm-i ʿĀlam (Bihār) vi, 47a – VI, 45b
Makhdūm-i Aʿẓam → Khʷādjagī, Mawlānā
Makhdūm-i Djahāniyān → Djalāl al-Dīn Ḥusayn al-Bukhārī
Makhfī (Zīb al-Nisāʾ Begum) (1702) vi, **131b**, 488b; vii, 341b – VI, **129b**, 474b; VII, 343b
Makhiwal s, 361a – S, 360b
Makhkhan Singh iii, 336a – III, 346a
Makhlad, Banū vi, **132a** – VI, **130a**
Makhlad b. Kaydād al-Nukkārī → Abū Yazīd al-Nukkārī
Makhlad b. Yazīd, ḳaḍī vi, 132a – VI, 130a
Makhlaṣ → Takhalluṣ
Makhlūf, Muḥammad (XX) vi, 280a – VI, 265a
Makhrama, Abū Muḥammad al-Ṭayyib (1540) vi, **132b** – VI, **130b**
Makhrama, ʿAfīf al-Dīn ʿAbd Allāh (1565) vi, **132b** – VI, **131a**
Makhrama, ʿAfīf al-Dīn Abu 'l-Ṭayyib (1497) vi, **132b** – VI, **130b**
Makhrama, Bā (Abū) i, 255b; iii, 881a; vi, **132b** – I, 263b; III, 905a; VI, **130b**
Makhrama, ʿUmar b. ʿAbd Allāh (1545) vi, 132b – VI, 130b
Makhredj vi, **133a** – VI, **131a**
Mākhūkh (Banū Wamānū, XI) iii, 138a; vi, 427a – III, 141a; VI, 412a
Makḥūl b. Abī Muslim al-Dimashḳī (730) iv, 356b, 369a; vii, 631b; viii, 713a – IV, 372a, 385b; VII, 613a; VIII, 733b
Makhzan i, 79b, 288b, 355b, 368b, 369a, 1145b, 1191a; ii, 146a, 326b, 510a, b; v, 48b, 1191a, 1192b, 1193a, 1198b; vi, **133b**; s, 336b – I, 82a, 297b, 366a, 379b, 380a, 1180a, 1226b; II, 150a, 336b, 522b, 523a; V, 50a, 1181a, 1182b, 1183a, 1188b; VI, **131b**; S, 336a
Makhzen → Makhzan
Makhzen, Banū vi, 589b, 590b – VI, 574a, 575b
Makhzūm, Banū i, 9a, 115b; iii, 3b, 975b; vi, **137b**,

145a, 262b, 649a; vii, 362a; s, 32b –
I, 9a, 118b; III, 3b, 1000a; VI, **135b**, 143a, 246b, 634b; VII, 364a; S, 33a
al-Makhzūmī, ʿAbd al-Raḥmān b. Zayd b. Muḥammad b. Ḥanzala (852) vii, 5a – VII, 5a
al-Makhzūmī, Abu ʾl-Ḥasan al-Ḳurashī (1189) v, 863a; vi, **140b**; vii, 164a – V, 870a, VI, **139a**; VII, 165b
al-Makhzūmī, Hāniʾ ix, 84b – IX, 88a
al-Maʿḳil, Banū i, 93b, 211a, 355b, 356a, 374b, 533a; ii, 134a; iii, 256b, 288b, 300b; v, 1196b; vi, 134a, b, **141a**, 741a, b; vii, 613b –
I, 95b, 217a, 366b, 385b, 549b; II, 137a; III, 265a, 297b, 310a; V, 1187a; VI, 132b, 133a, **139a**, 730b; VII, 613a
Maʿḳil b. Ḍirār → al-Shammākh b. Ḍirār
Maʿḳil b. ʿĪsā iv, 718b; s, 122b – IV, 747b; S, 122a
Maʿḳil b. Ḳays al-Riyāḥī v, 19b – V, 20a
Maʿḳil b. Sinān al-Ashdjaʿī iii, 226b, 227a –
III, 233b, 234a
Makīn vi, 86a – VI, 84a
al-Makīn b. al-ʿAmīd, Djirdjis (1273) vi, **143b**, 629b; s, 396a, 400a – VI, **141b**, 614b; S, 396b, 400b
Makīna (Fès) vi, 136a – VI, 134b
Mākisīn iv, 898a – IV, 930b
Makk i, 1171b; ii, 615a – I, 1206b; II, 630b
Makka (Mecca) i, 12a, 35a, 55a, 77a, 80a, 136a, 151b, 549a, 551b, 552b, 890b, 976a, 1032b, 1232b; ii, 453a, 854a; iii, 33b, 260a, 362a; iv, 318b, 321b, 335b; v, 77a; vi, 33a, b, 34b, 44b, 45a, 118a, 137b, 139b, 140b, **144b**, 320a; s, 3b, 106a, 198b, 267b, 278b
—geographical description vi, 144b, 720a
1. Pre-Islamic/early Islamic periods vi, 144b, 405b, 644b
—Pre-Islamic Mecca vi, 144b
—Mecca and the beginnings of Islam vi, 146a
—Mecca 632 – 750 vi, 147a
2. ʿAbbāsid – modern period vi, 147b
i. Mecca 750-961 vi, 147b, 663a
ii. ca. 960-1200) vi, 148a, 617a, 672b, 674b, 676a, 677b
iii. ca.1200-1788) vi, 149a
iv. The Sharīfate/ The Kingdom vi, 150b
3. The Modern City vi, 152a
—communications vi, 178b
—economy vi, 162b
—education and cultural life vi, 173a
—floods vi, 179b
—health care vi, 178a
—libraries vi, 175a
—literature i, 826b, 965b; ii, 91b, 590a, 757a, 829a; iii, 760a; v, 850a; vi, 177a
—al-Masdjid al-Ḥarām/other religious buildings vi, 164b
—the physical city vi, 161b
—pilgrimage vi, 169a
—politics and administration vi, 152a
—population and society vi, 159a
—press vi, 176a
—seizure of the Ḥarām vi, 157b
—water supply vi, 179a
4. Mecca the centre of the world vi, 180b
— determination of the sacred direction vi, 181b
—Islamic sacred geography vi, 183a
— orientation of Islamic religious architecture vi, 185b
— orientation of the Kaʿba vi, 181a
Makka (La Mekke/La Mecque) I, 12a, 36a, 57a, 79a, 82b, 140a, 155b, 566b, 569a, 570b, 916b, 1006a, 1064a, 1269b; II, 465a, 874a; III, 35a, 267a, 373b; IV, 332b, 335b, 350a; V, 79b; VI, 31b, 32a, b, 43a, 44a, 116a, 135b, 137b, 138b, **142b**, 304a; S, 3a, 105a, 198b, 267a, 278b
—description géographique VI, 142b, 709a, 661a, 663a, 664a
I. période pré-islamique/début de l'Islam VI, 143a
—La Mekke pré-islamique 143a
—La Mekke au début de l'Islam VI, 144b, 629b
—La Mekke de 632 à 750 VI, 145b, 390a
II. Des ʿAbbāsides à l'époque moderne
1. 750-961 VI, 146a, 649a
2. 960-1200 VI, 146b, 657b, 659a
3. environ 1200-1788) VI, 147b
4. Le chérifat/les Wahhābites/le royaume VI, 149a
III. La ville moderne VI, 151a
—administration VI, 151a
—approvisionnement en eau VI, 163b
—bibliothèques VI, 162a
—communications VI, 163b
—économie VI, 156a
—enseignement/ vie culturelle VI, 161a
—inondations VI, 163b
—littérature I, 849b, 995b; II, 93a, 604b, 775b, 848b; III, 783b; V, 854b; VI, 162b
—al-Masdjid al-Ḥarām et autres édifices religieux VI, 157b
—le pèlerinage VI, 160a
—population et société VI, 154a
—presse VI, 162a
—la prise du Ḥarām VI, 153a
—santé VI, 163a
—topographie VI, 155a
IV. La Mekke centre du monde VI, 164b
—détermination de l'orientation sacrée VI, 166a
—géographique islamique sacrée VI, 166b
—orientation de l'architecture islamique VI, 169b
—orientation de la Kaʿba VI, 165a
Maḳḳara vi, 187a – VI, 170b
al-Maḳḳarī, Muḥammad b. Muḥammad vi, 187a – VI, 170b
al-Maḳḳarī, Shihāb al-Dīn Abu ʾl-ʿAbbās al-Tilimsānī (1632) i, 157a, 595a; iii, 814a; v, 1159b, 1160b; vi, 112a, **187a**, 247b; 1042b; s, 223a, 381a –
I, 161a, 614b; III, 837b; V, 1149b, 1150a; VI, 109b, **170b**, 231b, 1044b; S, 223a, 381b
al-Makkarī, al-Djadd (1357) ix, 364 – IX. 376a
Makkhourēbi → Maghrāwa
al-Makkī → ʿAbd al-Wahhāb; Abū Ṭālib; Ibn Ḥumayd
Makkī, Abū Muḥammad al-Ḳurṭubī (1045)
vi, **188b** – VI, **172a**
Makkī, Banū v, 696a; viii, 763b – V, 701a; VIII, 781b
al-Makkī, al-Muwaffak b. Aḥmad vi, 352b – VI, 336b
Makkī b. Kāmil b. Djāmiʿ iv, 337b – IV, 351b
al-Makkiyya al-Fāsiyya → Madaniyya
al-Maklātī, Muḥammad b. Aḥmad (1631) iii, 468b; vi, 112b – III, 484b; VI, 110a
Maklī vi, **189b** – VI, **173a**
Maḳlūb iii, 26a – III, 27b
Makna (port) vii, 373b – VII, 374b
Makramat Khān i, 254a – I, 261b
al-Makramī, ʿAbd Allāh b. Aḥmad b. Ismāʿīl (dāʿī) vi, 191a – VI, 175a
al-Makramī, ʿAbd Allāh b. ʿAlī (dāʿī) vi, 191b – VI, 175b
al-Makramī, Aḥmad b. Ḥasan b. Ismāʿīl vi, 192a – VI, 176a
al-Makramī, ʿAlī b. Muḥsin āl Shibām (1936) vi, 192a – VI, 176a

al-Makramī, Ḍiyāʾ al-Dīn Ismāʿīl (1770) vi, 191b – VI, 175b
al-Makramī, Djābir b. al-Fahd (XVII) vi, 191a – VI, 175a
al-Makramī, Ḥasan b. Ismāʿīl b. Muḥsin āl Shibām (1872) vi, 192a – VI, 175b, 176a
al-Makramī, Ibrāhīm b. Ṣafī al-Dīn (1683) vi, 191a – VI, 175a
al-Makramī, Ṣafī al-Dīn Muḥammad (1633) vi, **190b**, 191a; ix, 829a -VI, **174b**, 175a; IX, 864a
Makramid(e)s i, 552b; ii, 517b; iii, 179b; iv, 201a; vi, **191a**; ix, 829a – I, 570a; II, 530b, III, 183b; IV, 210a; VI, **174b**; 864a
Makrān i, 211b, 1005a; iii, 1121b; iv, 3b; v, 684a; vi, 65b, **192b**, 780a; vii, 405b; s, 129a, 222a, 332a, b – I, 217b, 1036a; III, 1149a; IV, 4a; V, 689a; VI, 63b, **176a**, 770a; VII, 407a; S, 128a, 222a, 331b, 332a
Makrand Ray i, 1042b – I, 1074a
Makrānī i, 1005a, 1007a – I, 1036a, 1038a
Makrīn b. Muḥammad al-Bughṭūrī → al-Bughṭūrī
al-Maḳrīzi, Tāḳī al-Dīn Abu ʾl-ʿAbbās (1442) i, 138b, 594b, 595a, 791a, 965b; ii, 107b, 327a, 328a; iii, 268b, 488b, 676a, 679b, 756b; v, 29b, 863a; vi, 119a, 122b, 143b, **193b**, 317b, 353a, 363a; s, 210b, 273b, 295a, 388b, 396a – I, 142b, 614a, 814b, 995a; II, 110a, 337a, 338a; III, 276a, 505b, 698a, 701a, 779b; V, 23a, 870a; VI, 117a, 120b, 141b, **177b**, 302a, 337a, 347a; S, 210a, 273a, 294b, 389a, 396b
Makrūh vi, **194b** – VI, **178b**
Maks (Mukūs) i, 170a, 1144a; ii, 142b, 146a; iii, 1182b; iv, 134b, 323a, b, 324a; vi, **194b**, 323a, 573b – I, 174b, 1178b; II, 146b, 150a; III, 1211b; IV, 140b, 337a, b, 338b; VI, **178b**, 307b, 558b
al-Maks (Miṣr) vii, 150a; s, 120b – VII, 152a; S, 120a
al-Maksī (vizier) (XIII) vi, 672b – VI, 659a
al-Maksī, Shihāb al-Dīn (XIII) vii, 29b – VII, 29b
Maḳṣūra → Masdjid
Maḳṣūra i, 240a; ii, 115b; vi, **195b** – I, 24b; II, 118a, VI, **180a**
Maktab vi, **196b** – VI, **181a**
Maktaba iv, 635a; v, 38a, 43b, 159a, 261a, 338a, 371b, 641b, 890b, 1005a, 1125a, 1212b; vi, **197b** – IV, 661a; V, 33a, 45a, 158a, 259a, 338b, 372a, b, 646a, 897a, 1000b, 1001a, 1121b, 1202a; VI, **181b**
al-Maktaba al-Ahliyya vi, 614b – VI, 599b
Maktabdār, ʿAlāʾ al-Dīn (1486) vii, 935a – VII, 935b
Maktabī al-Shīrāzī (XV) iv, 1010a; v, 1105a; vi, 833a – IV, 1042b; V, 1100b; VI, 823b
Maḳtal iii, 374a – III, 386a
Maḳṭūʿ ii, 563b; iii, 25b – II, 577b; III, 27a
Maktūbāt ii, 55b, 56a – II, 56b, 57a
al-Maktūbiyya (Marʿash) vi, 509b – VI, 495a
al-Maḳtūl → al-Suhrawardī
Maktūm b. Baṭī b. Suhayl ii, 619a – II, 634b
Mākū vi, **200b**, 504a – VI, **184b**, 489b
Makua vi, **203b** – VI, 187b
al-Maḳūlāt vi, **203b** – VI, **188a**
Maḳurra i, 425a, 1029a – I, 1060b
al-Maḳwa s, 50a – S, 50b
Māl ii, 148a, 150b; iv, 1034a; vi, **205a** – II, 152b, 155a; IV, 1066a; VI, **189a**
Māl al-bayʿa iii, 1201b; vi, **205b** – III, 1231b; VI, **190a**
Māl Khātūn i, 348a – I, 358b
Māla ii, 905b – II, 926b
al-Maʿlā (Maḳbara, Mecca) vi, 160a, 168b, 179b – VI, 154b, 159b, 163b
Malabar iv, 547; v, 360a, 937a; vi, **206a**, 234a, 245a, 458a, b, 459a, b, 463a – IV, 570b; V, 361a, 941a; VI, **190b**, 207a, 229b, 443b, 444a, b, 445a, 448b
Malacca i, 979a, b; iii, 1218b, 1219b, 1225b; iv, 467b; vi, 116b, **207a**, 232b, 233b, 234a, 235a, b, 237a, 240b; s, 199b – I, 1009b, 1010a; III, 1249a, 1250b, 1257a; IV, 488b; VI, 114a, **191b**, 206a, b, 208a, b, 210a, 211b; S, 199b
Malāfita ii, 235b – II, 242b
Málaga → Mālaḳa
Malāhī vi, **214a** – VI, **198a**
Malāḥim ii, 377a; vi, **216a** – II, 387a; VI, **200a**
Malāʾika vi, **216b** – VI, **200b**
Malak, Malʾak → Malāʾika
Malak Ḥifnī Nāṣif (1918) vi, **219b**, 470a – VI, **213b**, 456a
Malak Ṭāʾūs i, 263a – I, 271a
Malaka vi, **220a** – VI, **214a**
Mālaḳa (Málaga) i, 6a, 43b, 1321a; ii, 747b; iii, 498b, 500a, 681a; vi, **220b**, 339b; vii, 1028b; s, 381b – I, 6a, 6b, 45a, 1361a; II, 766a; III, 515b, 517a, 703a; VI, **214a**, 323b; VII, 1030b, 1031a; S, 382a
Malal → Mali
Malam vi, **223a** – VI, **217a**
Malāmatiyya i, 313a, 794b, 1137a, 1239b, 1245a; ii, 395a, 963b; iii, 132a, 662b, 899a; iv, 46a, 472b, 473a, 1109b; vi, **223b**; s, 361a – I, 322b, 818a, 1171b, 1277b, 1283a; II, 405b, 985b; III, 134b, 684a, 923b; IV, 49a, 493a, 494a, 1141a; VI, **217a**; S, 361a
Mālamīr → Īdhadj
Mālān → Mālīn
Malang vi, **228b** – VI, **222b**
Malāryā (Malaria) v, 867a; vi, **229a** – V, 873b; VI, **223a**
al-Malaṭī, Abu ʾl-Ḥusayn (987) vi, **230a** – VI, **224a**
Malaṭya ii, 234b; vi, **230a**, 507a, b, 508b, 541a, 544a, 740a – II,241a; VI, **224a**, 492a, 493a, 494a, 526a, 528b, 728a
al-Malaṭyawī (Malaṭī), Muḥammad b. Ghāzī (1202) vi, 632a – VI, 617a
Mālawās vi, 309a – VI, 294b
Malay language/Malais i, 41b, 88a, 92a; ii, 27b, 549b; iii, 377a, 1215b, 1216a, 1220a, 1231a, 1234a; iv, 1128a; v, 205a; vi, 239a – I, 42b, 90b, 94b; II, 28a, 563b; III, 388b, 1246b, 1247a, 1251a, 1263a, 1266a; IV, 1159b; V, 202b; VI, 204a
Malay peninsula vi, 207a, **232b**
Malays/Malais (people) vi, **239a**; s, 150b – VI, **204a**; S, 150b
Malaysia/Malaisie i, 41b, 979a; iii, 377a, 385a, 502b, 1214b, 1219b; v, 226a, b, 227a, 228a, b; vi, 239a, **240b**; s, 220b – I, 42b, 1009b; III, 388b, 397b, 520a, 1245a, 1250b; V, 224a, b, 225b, 226a, b; VI, 204a, **211b**; S, 220b
Malāzgird (1071) i, 420b, 465b, 510a; v, 539a; vi, **242b**, 379b; viii, 70a – I, 432b, 479b, 525b; V, 543b; VI, **226b**, 364a; VIII, 71b
Malcolm X (1965) vii, 703a – VII, 703b
Mālda (Māldah, Māldaha) vi, **244b**, 368b – VI, **228b**, 353a
Maldives iii, 385a, 407a; iv, 547a, 1085b; v, 587a; vi, **245a** – III, 397b, 419b; IV, 570b, 1116b; V, 661b; VI, **229a**
Malé (Maldives) vi, 245a, b – VI, 229a, 230a
Malḥam b. Ḥaydar ii, 635b – II, 651b
Malḥam b. Maʿn ii, 635a – II, 651a
Malḥama vi, **247a** – VI, **231a**
Malḥūn i, 571b; v, 1207a; vi, **247b** – I, 590a; V, 1197b; VI, **232a**
Mali ii, 63a, 94a; iii, 276a, 657a; iv, 313b; vi, **257b**, 281b, 401a, 421b, 572b; viii, 1049a; ix, 121b, 756a; s, 218a, 295b –

II, 64a, 96a; III, 284a, 678b; IV, 327b; VI, **242a**, 266b, 385b, 406b, 557b; VIII, 1084b; IX, 225a, 789a S, 217b, 295a
Māli-Amīr → Īdhadj
Māl-i Irsāliyye → Irsāliyye
Malībār → Malabar
al-Malīdjī, Muḥammad Muḥyi ʾlDīn (XVII) ix, 316a – IX, 326a
Malifattan vi, 503a – VI, 488b
Malīḥ (Mleh) vi, 230b – VI, 224b
Malik (title/titre) ii, 858a; iv, 818b; v, 627b; vi, **261a** – II, 877b; IV, 851a; V, 631b; VI, **245b**
Mālik b. Abi ʾl-Samḥ al-Ṭāʾī (754) iii, 698b; vi, **262a** – III, 720b; VI, **246b**
Malik b. Adham al-Bāhilī iv, 447a – IV, 467a
Mālik b. al-ʿAdjlān i, 771a; iv, 1187b; v, 995a – I, 794a; IV, 1220a; V, 990a
Malik b. ʿAli al-Baranī, Shāh (Djand) s, 245b – S, 245b
Mālik b. ʿAlī al-Ḳaṭanī i, 600a – I, 619b
Mālik b. ʿAlī al-Khuzāʿī s, 122b – S, 122a
Mālik b. ʿAmr al-Ḥimyarī v, 315a – V, 314b
Mālik b. Anas (796) i, 164a, 280a, 338b, 412a, 550b, 588b, 685a, 773b,957b, 966b, 1244b; ii, 889b; iii, 23b, 24a, 763b,811a, 817a, 963a; iv, 146a, 257a, 718a; v, 711b, 712a, 731b, 997b; vi, **262b**, 278a, 337a, 352b, 366a, 658a, 739a; vii, 649a; s, 384b – I, 169a, 288b, 349a, 424a, 568a, 607b, 706a, 796b, 987a, 996a, 1282a; II, 910a; III, 25a, 786b, 834a, 840b, 987b; IV, 152a, 268b, 747a; V, 716b, 717a, 736b, 993a; VI, **247a**, 263a, 321a, 336b, 337a, 621a, 643b, 728a; VII, 648b; S, 385a
Mālik b. Asmāʾ b. Khāridja iv, 1002b – IV, 1035a
Mālik b. ʿAwf b. Saʿd b. Rabīʿa al-Naṣrī (VII) ii, 627a; iii, 286a, 578a; vi, **265b** – II, 643a; III, 294b, 598a; VI, **250b**
Mālik b. Badr al-Fazārī s, 177b – S, 178b
Mālik b. Baḥdal vii, 267b – VII, 269b
Malik b. Dīnār al-Sāmī (748) i, 1080b; vi, **266b**, 459a; viii, 354b; x, 394b –
I, 1113a; VI, **251b**, 444b; VIII, 367a; X, 423a
Mālik b. Fahm, Banū iv, 500b; x, 191a, 816a – IV, 522a; X, 206a
Mālik b. Ḥimyar vi, 82a – VI, 80a
Mālik b. al-Ḥārith al-Nakhaʿī → al-Ashtar
Mālik b. Ḥudhayfa b. Badr al-Fazārī s, 178b – S, 179b
Mālik b. Mismaʿ (691) i, 964b; iii, 540a; vi, 640b – I, 994a; III, 559a; VI, 625b
Mālik b. Nuwayra b. Djamra, Abu ʾl-Mighwār (632) vi, **267a**; vii, 768b – VI, **251b**; VII, 770a
Mālik b. Rabīʿa b. Riyāḥ al-Hilālī s, 92b – S, 92b
Mālik b. al-Rayb (714) vi, 954b – VI, 947a
Mālik b. Ṭawḳ i, 751b, 1289b; s, 122b – I, 773b, 1329a; S, 122a
Mālik b. Zuhayr s, 177b – S, 178b
al-Malik al-ʿĀdil I, Abū Bakr Muḥammad b. Ayyūb, Sayf al-Dīn (Ayyūbid(e)) (Alep(po), Damas(cus)/ Egypt(e), Diyār Bakr) (1218) i, **197b**, 665a, 798b, 799b, 800a, b, 803b, 996a, 1316b; ii, 283b, 284a, 347b; iii, 87b, 228b, 504a; iv, 430a, 483b, 520a, 568a, 609a, 613b; vi, 261b, 380b, 381a, 429a, b, 434a, 540b, 547b, 781b; vii, 164b, 273a, 461b, 989b; viii, 127a –
I, **203a**, 684b, 822a, 823a, 824a, b, 828a, 1026b, 1356b; II, 292a, 357b; III, 89b, 235b, 521a; IV, 448b, 504b, 543a, 590a, 634a, 638a; VI, 246a, 365a, 414b, 419b, 525a, 532a, 771b; VII, 166b, 275a, 461b, 990b; VIII, 130a
al-Malik al-ʿĀdil II, Abū Bakr Sayf al-Dīn b. al-Malik al-Kāmil (Ayyūbid(e)) (1248) i, **198b**, 766a, b – I, **204a**, 789a
al-Malik al-Afḍal b. Ṣalāḥ al-Dīn (Ayyūbid(e)) (1225) i, 197b, 198a, **215a**, 732a, 798b, 1017a; ii, 283b; iii, 724a, 876b; iv, 376b; vi, 380b, 381a, 547b; vii, 998b; viii, 995a –
I, 203b, **221b**, 754a, 822a, 1048b; II, 291b; III, 747a, 900b; IV, 393a; VI, 365a, b, 532a; VII, 1000a; VIII, 1030a
Malik Aḥmad b. Malik Ḥasan Niẓām al-Mulk (1496) vi, 63a – VI, 61a
Malik Aḥmad Baḥrī (Niẓām Shāhī) (1510) i, 295a, 303a; ii, 814b, 1048b; iii, 15b, 1159b; vi, 51a, 63a, **269a**; viii, 73b; s, 246a –
I, 304a, 312b; II, 834a, 1110a; III, 16b, 1188a; VI, 49a, 61a; **253b**; VIII, 75a; S, 246a
Malik Aḥmad Ghāzī → Dānishmend
Malik Aḥmad Pasha v, 461a – V, 463b
Malik Alṭūniya i, 1194a; ii, 973a – I, 1229b; II, 995a
Malik ʿAmbar (ʿAnbar) (1626) i, 81a, 768a, 781b, 1204a; ii, 158b; iii, 15b, 202b, 424a, 426b; iv, 1018a, 1023a; vi, **269a**, 534b; vii, 204b, 957a; viii, 74a –
I, 83b, 791a, 804b, 1239b; II, 163b; III, 16a, 208a, 437b, 440b; IV, 1050a, 1055a; VI, **254a**, 519a; VII, 205b, 957b; VIII, 76a
al-Malik al-Amdja → Bahrām Shāh (Ayyūbid(e))
Malik Andīl → Fīrūz Shāh, Sayf al-Dīn
Malik ʿArab (Anḳara) (XII) ii, 110b – II, 113a
Malik Arslan (Dhu ʾl-Ḳadr) (1465) vi, 507b – VI, 493a
Malik Arslān b. Masʿūd → Arslān Shāh b. Masʿūd (Ghaznawid(e))
Malik Arslan b. Sulaymān ii, 239b – II, 246b
al-Malik al-Ashraf I Muẓaffar al-Dīn (Ayyūbid(e)) (Damas(cus), Diyār Bakr) (1220) vii, 989b, 990b – VII, 990a, 992b
al-Malik al-Ashraf I Muẓaffar al-Dīn b. al-Malik al-ʿĀdil (Ayyūbid(e)) (Damas(cus), Diyār Bakr) (1237) vi, 540b, 665b, 931a; vii, 989b, 990b, 998b – VI, 525a, 651b, 923a, 990a, 992b; VII, 1000a
Malik Ashraf b. Amīr Čūbān (Čūbānid(e)) (1357) i, 325a; ii, 401a; iii, 1208b; vi, 501a; viii, 753a, 766a – I, 335a; II, 411b; III, 1239a; VI, 486b; VIII, 774b, 791b
al-Malik al-Ashraf b. al-ʿĀdil (Ayyūbid(e)) (1198) vii, 998b – VII, 1000a
Malik Ashraf Shaʿbān → Shaʿban II
al-Malik al-Ashraf ʿUmar (Rasūlid(e)) (1296) x, 147a – X, 158b
al-Malik al-Awḥad Nadjm al-Dīn b. al-Malik al-ʿĀdil (Ayyūbid(e), Diyār Bakr) (1210) i, 198a, 329a, 799a; vi, 931a – I, 203b, 339b, 822b; VI, 923a
Malik Ayāz (1522) ii, 322a, 1127b, 1128a; vi, **269b** – II, 331b, 1154a, b; VI, **254b**
al-Malik al-ʿAzīz b. Djalāl al-Dawla Shīrzīl, Abū Manṣūr (Būyid(e)) (1049) i, 132a; ii, 391a; iii, 1201b; vi, **270b**; vii, 1018a –
I, 136a;, II, 401b; III, 1232a; VI, **255b**; VII, 1020a
al-Malik al-ʿAzīz Ghiyāth al-Dīn Muḥammad (Ayyūbid(e), Alep(po)) (1237) iii, 934a; vi, 381a, b – III, 958b; VI, 365b
al-Malik al-ʿAzīz Muḥammad (Ayyūbid(e)) (1237) vi, 381a – VI, 365b
al-Malik al-ʿAzīz Ṭughtigin B. hyyūb cayyūbid(e) (yemen) (1197) x, 303a – X, 326a
al-Malik al-ʿAzīz ʿUthmān b. al-Malik al-ʿĀdil (Ayyūbid(e)) (1237) vii, 274a – VII, 276a
al-Malik al-ʿAzīz ʿUthmān ʿImād al-Dīn b. Ṣalāḥ al-Dīn (Ayyūbid(e), Egypt(e)) (1198) i, 197b, 198a, 798b, 1214b; ii, 283b; iv, 376b, 613b; vi, 381a, b; vii, 165a – I, 203b, 822a, 1250b; II, 292a; IV, 393a, 638a; VI, 365b; VII, 166b
al-Malik al-ʿAzīz Yūsuf → Yūsuf b. Barsbāy
al-Malik al-ʿAzīz Ẓahīr al-Dīn Tughtigīn b. Ayyūb

(Ayyūbid(e), Yemen) (1197) i, 664a, 731b, 1332a, 1337a; ii, 282a, 353b, 458a; iii, 120a, 398b, 503b, 1118b; iv, 200a; vi, 433b –
I, 684a, 753b, 1372b, 1377a; II, 290a, 363a, 469b; III, 122b, 411a, 521a, 1146a; IV, 208b; VI, 418b
Malik Bahrām v, 782b – V, 789a
Malik Dīnār (1195) → Dīnār, Malik
Malik Dīnār (1319) → Ẓafar Khān (Gudjarāt)
Malik Djahān Khānum bint Muḥammad Ḳāsim Ḳādjār (XIX) vii, 453a – VII, 454a
al-Malik al-Djawād Yūnus (Ayyūbid(e))
vii, 989b – VII, 990b
Malik Djuwān i, 769a; ii, 134b – I, 792a; II, 138a
Malik Firūz v, 782b, 783a – V, 789a, b
Malik Ghāzī (Ḳîrshehir) v, 172b – V, 170a
Malik Ghāzī Shaḥna (architect(e)) vi, 692a –
VI, 680a
Malik Gopī vi, 51b, 270a – VI, 49b, 255a
Malik Ḥasan Niẓām Baḥrī al-Mulk (1481)
vi, 62b, 63a, 67a, b, 269a; vii, 459a – VI, 60b, 65a, b, 253b; VII, 459a
Malik Ḥifnī Nāṣif → Nāṣif, Malik Ḥifnī
Malik Kāfūr → Kāfūr Hazārdīnārī
Malik Kālā v, 782b, 783a – V, 789a
Malik al-Kalām → Malik Ḳummi
al-Malik al-Kāmil I Nāṣir al-Dīn b. al-ʿĀdil (Ayyūbid(e), Egypt(e)) (1238) i, 14b, 198a, 665a, 765b, 766a, 798b, 799a, b, 800b, 803a, 804a, 940b; ii, 65b, 126a, 292b, 347b, 911b; iii, 504a, 747a; iv, 200b, **520a**, 818a; v, 331a; vi, 359b, 381a, 413a, 429b, 440a, 547b; vii, 147b, 273a, b, 727b, 989b, 998b; viii, 127a; ix, 167b; s, 197a, 392b, 407b –
I, 15a, 203b, 684b, 788b, 789a, 822a, b, 824a, 826a, 828a, 969a; II, 66b, 129a, 300b, 357b, 933a; III, 521a, 770a; IV, 209b, **543a**, 850b; V, 331a; VI, 343b, 365b, 398a, 415a, 425b, 532a; VII, 149b, 275a, b, 728b, 990a, 1000a; VIII, 130a; IX, 176a S, 197a, 393a, 407b
al-Malik al-Kāmil II b. al-Muẓaffar (Ayyūbid(e), Mayyāfāriḳīn) (1260) iv, **521a**; vi, 931b –
IV, **544a**; VI, 923a
Malik Kardī (Marāgha) vi, 502b – VI, 488a
Malik Karib Yuʾmin vi, 563b – VI, 548b
Malik Khātūn bint Malikshāh I (XI) vii, 540b – VII, 540b
Malik Khurram ii, 405b – II, 416b
Malik Khushnūd (1646) vi, 837b – VI, 828a
Malik Ḳummi (1616) i, 1203a; vi, **271a**; vii, 340b, 341a – I, 1238b; VI, **256a**; VII, 342b, 343a
Malik Maḥmūd (Mengüček) (XII) iv, 871a – IV, 904b
Malik Maḥmūd (Sīstān) (XVIII) vii, 853a –
VII, 854b
al-Malik al-Manṣūr → Nadjm al-Dīn Ghāzī Ḳalawūn (Mamlūk)
al-Malik al-Manṣūr Muḥammad b. ʿUmar (Ayyūbid(e), Ḥamāt) (1220) iii, 697b; vi, 380b, 381b, **429a**, 777b, 816b, 999a; s, 205b –
III, 719b; VI, 365a, b, **414a**, 767a, 818a, 1000b; S, 205a
al-Malik al-Manṣūr ʿUmar (Rasūlid(e)) s, 338b – S, 338a
Malik Masʿūd (amīr al-Mawsil) (1120) vi, 500a – VI, 485a
al-Malik al-Masʿūd (Arṭuḳid(e)) s, 250a –
S, 250a
al-Malik al-Masʿūd Yūsuf (Ayyūbid(e), Yemen) (1229) i, 552b – I, 570b
al-Malik al-Muʾayyad → Abu ʾl-Fidā (Ayyūbid(e))
al-Malik al-Muʾayyad Shaykh (Mamlūk) (1421) ii, 24a, 781b; iii, 48a, 99b, 186a, 187a; iv, 431b, 586a, 623b; vi, 580b; vii, 168a, 169a, 172b, **271a** –
II, 24b, 800b; III, 50a, 102a, 190b; IV, 450b, 608b, 609a, b, 648a; VI, 565b; VII, 169b, 170b, 174a, b, **273a**
al-Malik al-Muʿaẓẓam Shams al-Dīn Tūrān-Shāh (Ayyūbid(e) (Yemen) _ *Tur®n%®h b. Ayy,b*
al-Malik al-Muʿaẓẓam Sharaf al-Dīn ʿĪsā b. al-Malik al-ʿĀdil I (Ayyūbid(e), Damas(cus)) (1227) i, 198a, 434b, 780b, 799a, b, 804a, 1124b; ii, 284a; iii, 399b, 747a, 962a, 967a; iv, 520b, 779a, 842a; v, 331a, 925a; vii, 273a, 989b; viii, 987b –
I, 203b, 446b, 803b, 822b, 823a, 828a, 1158b; II, 292a; III, 412a, 770a, 991b; IV, 543a, 810b, 875a; V, 331a, 930b; VII, **275a**, 990b; VIII, 1022b
al-Malik al-Muʿaẓẓam Sharaf al-Dīn Tūrān-Shah (Ayyūbid(e), Damas(cus), Diyār Bakr, Egypt(e)/ Damascus/Ḥiṣn Kayfa, Āmid) (1249) i, 198a, 434b, 780b, 799a, b, 804a, 1124b; ii, 284a; iii, 399b, 747a, 962a, 967a; iv, 520b, 779a, 842a; v, 331a, 925a; vi, 321a, 326a, 381a, b, 440b; vii, 166a; viii, 988b –
I, 203b, 446b, 803b, 822b, 823a, 828a, 1158a; II, 292a; III, 412a, 770a, 991b; IV, 543a, 810b, 875a; V, 331a, 930b; VI, 305b, 310b, 365b, 425b; VII, 167b; VIII, 1023b
Malik Mubārak Shāh Karanfal (Sharkī) (1461)
iii, 14b, 419b; ix, 355a – III, 15a, 432b; ix, 366b
al-Malik al-Mughīth (Karak) (XIII) vii, 167b – VII, 169a
Malik Mughīth (Mālwā) (1443) vi, 52b, **271b**, 406b, 407b, 695a – VI, 51a, **256b**, 391b, 392a, 682b
Malik Muḥammad b. Ghāzī (Malaṭya) (1141) iv, 506b, vi, 507a – IV, 528a; VI, 492a
al-Malik Muḥammad b. Muʿixx al-Dīn → Kart
Malik Muḥammad Djāyasī (Djāysī) (1542)
iii, 457a, vi, **272a** – III, 472b; VI, **257a**
Malik Muḥammad Nādjī s, 366a – S, 366a
al-Malik al-Muʿizz ʿIzz al-Dīn Aybak (Mamlūk) (1257) i, 732a, 804a, 944b; vi, 668b – I, 754a, 828b, 973b; VI, 655a
Malik al-Mutakallimīn iv, 789a – IV, 820b
Malik Muẓaffar b. Bahrāmshāh → Malik Ghāzī Shaḥna
al-Malik al-Muẓaffar Shihāb al-Dīn Ghāzī b. al-Malik al-ʿĀdil (Ayyūbid(e), Diyār Bakr) (1244) i, 197b, 798b, 1160b; ii, 347b; iii, 120a, 683b; iv, 614a, 640b; vi, 931a; vii, 273b, 974a – I, 203b, 822a, 1195b; II, 357b; III, 122b, 705a; IV, 638b, 667a; VI, 923a; VII, 275b, 974b
al-Malik al-Muẓaffar Taḳī al-Dīn ʿUmar b. Nūr al-Dawla (Ayyūbid(e), Ḥamāt) (1191) vi, 380b, 381a, b, 429a, 430a; vii, **816a** – VI, 365a, b, 414a, 415a; VII, **818a**
Malik Nāʾib → Kāfūr Hazārdīnārī
al-Malik al-Nāṣir I Ṣalāḥ al-Dīn Yūsuf b. Ayyūb (Saladin) (Ayyūbid(e), Egypt(e)) (1193)
i, 96b, 150a, 197b, 353b, 517a, 552b, 662b, 665a, 711a, 797a, 814b, 832a, 932b, 971a, 989b, 1016b, 1138a, 1140a, 1358a; ii, 64b, 127a, 144a, 163a, 283b, 292b, 344b, 353b, 461b, 501b, 556a, 856b, 959a, 1056a; iii, 87a, 99a, 120a, 208b, 228b, 399b, 474a, 510b, 693b, 751b, 933b, 120a, 208b, 228b, 399b, 474a, 510b, 693b, 751b, 933b, 934a, 1157b, 1158a, 1201a; iv, 137a, 376b, 429b, 613a, 640b, 877b, 899b, 944a; v, 92a, 330b, 455a, 800b, 924b, 1127b; vi, 143b, 149a, 195a, b, 261b, 320a, 380b, 429a, 430a, 540b, 543b, 547a, 578b, 579a, 606a, 656a, 657a, 667b, 668a, 671b, 673b, 676a, b, 708a, 733b, 780b; viii, 131b, **910a**; ix, 267b; s, 121a, 123b, 154a, 205a –
I, 99a, 154a, 202b, 364b, 532b, 570a, 683b, 684b, 732b, 820b, 837b, 855b, 961a, 1001a, 1020a, 1048a, 1172a, 1174b, 1398a; II, 66a, 130a, 148a, 168a,

291b, 300b, 354a, 363a, 473a, 514a, 570a, 876b, 981a, 1081a; III, 89b, 101b, 122b, 214b, 235a, 411b, 490b, 528a, 715b, 774a, 958b, 1186a, b, 1231b; IV, 142b, 392b, 448b, 638a, 667a, 910b, 932b, 977a; V, 94a, b, 330b, 457b, 806b, 930a, 1123b; VI, 142a, 147b, 179a, b, 246a, 304b, 364b, 414a, 415b, 525a, 528a, 532a, 563b, 590b, 641b, 643a, 653b, 654b, 658a, 660a, 662b, 663a, 696b, 722b, 770b; VIII, 134a, **941a**; IX, 375b; S, 120b, 123a, 154b, 205a

al-Malik al-Nāṣir II Ṣalāḥ al-Dīn Dāwūd b. al-Malik al-Muʿaẓẓam (Ayyūbid(e), Alep(po), Damas(cus)) (1259) i, 804b; ii, 284a, b, 348a; iii, 87b, 186b, 187b, 399b, 933b, 989b; iv, 521a; vi, 321b; vii, 166b, 274a, 727b, 728b, **989b**; s, 197a, 391a – I, 828b; II, 292a, b, 357b; III, 90a, 191a, b, 412a, 958a, 1014b; IV, 544a; VI, 305b, 306a; VII, 168a, 276a, 728b, 729a, **990a**; S, 197a, 391b

al-Malik al-Nāṣir, Ṣalāḥ al-Dīn Yūsuf (al-Nāṣir Yūsuf) (Ayyūbid(e), Alep(po), Damas(cus)) (1260) vii, 321b, 989b, **990a** – VII, 305b, 306a, 990b, **991a**

Malik of/de Nimrūz ix, 683b – IX, 712a

Malik al-Nuḥāt → al-Ḥasan b. Ṣafī

Malik Rādjā Fārūkī ii, 814a; iii, 417a; iv, 1023a – II, 833b; III, 430a; IV, 1055a

al-Malik al-Raḥīm, Abū Naṣr (Būyid(e)) (1058) vi, **272b** – VI, **257b**

Malik al-Sādāt Ghāzī → Sayyid Masʿūd

al-Malik al-Saʿīd (Artukid(e)) → Ghāzī I (Artukid(e))

al-Malik al-Saʿīd (Mamlūk(e)) → al-Saʿīd Baraka Khān

al-Malik al-Ṣāliḥ (Samudra-Pasè) (1297) i, 742b; iii, 1218b, 1225b; viii, 279a – I, 764b; III, 1249a, 1257a; VIII, 287a

al-Malik al-Ṣāliḥ ʿImād al-Dīn Ismāʿīl (Ayyūbid(e), Damas(cus), Egypt(e)) (1245) i, 711a, 766b, 799a, 804a; ii, 284a; iii, 989b; iv, 483b; vii, 990b; viii, 464a, **987b**; s, 255b – I, 732b, 789b, 822b, 828a; II, 292a; III, 1014a; IV, 504b; VII, 992a; VIII, 479b, **1022b**; S, 255a

al-Malik al-Ṣāliḥ Nadjm al-Dīn Ayyūb → al-Ṣāliḥ Nadjm al-Dīn Ayyūb

al-Malik al-Ṣāliḥ Nūr al-Dīn → Nūr al-Dīn Maḥmūd b. ʿImād Zangī

al-Malik al-Ṣāliḥ Shams al-Dīn → al-Malik al-Muʿaẓẓam Shams al-Dīn

Malik Sandjas → Alp Khān

Malik Sārang vi, 270a – VI, 255a

Malik Sarwar (Sharkī) (1399) ii, 270b, 498b, 1084b; iii, 14b, 417a, 419b; iv, 276b, 533b, 907b; vi, 49a, **273a**; ix, 352a – II, 278b, 511a, 1110a; III, 15a, 430b, 432b; IV, 288b, 556b, 940b; VI, 47b, **257b**; 366b

Malik Shaʿbān vi, 50a – VI, 48b

Malik Shāh → Kh(ʷ)ādja-i Djahān Turk

Malik-Shāh I b. Alp Arslan (Saldjūḳ) (1092) i, 243b, 353a, 421a, 465b, 517a, 552a, 639b, 662b, 664a, 731a, 750b, 780b, 870a, 901a, 1051b, 1336b; ii, 282a, 344a, 347b, 384b, 397b, 406a; iii, 86b, 195a, 208b, 471b, 1114b, 1202a; iv, 27a, b, 28a, 101a, 458a, 807b; v, 159b; vi, 13b, 16a, 63b, **273a**, 379b, 482a, 523b, 524a, 540b, 600a, 618a, b, 620b, 627a, 628a; vii, 15b, 489a, 540b, 679b, 693a, b; viii, 69b, 941a; x. 267a; s, 14b, 73b, 94b, 383b – I, 250b, 363b, 432b, 479b, 532b, 569b, 660a, 683a, b, 753a, 773a, 803b, 894a, 928a, 1083a, b, 1376b; II, 290a, 354a, 357a, 394b, 408a, 417a; III, 89a, 199b, 214a, 488a, 1142a, 1232b; IV, 29a, b, 30a, 105b, 478b, 840a; V, 158b; VI, 12b, 14a, 61b, **258a**, 364a, 468a, 508a, b, 525a, 585b, 603a, b, 605b, 611a, 613a; VII, 15b, 489a, 540b, 679a, 693a, b; 71a, 973a; X, 287a; S, 15a, 74a, 94a, 384a

Malik-Shāh II b. Barkyārūḳ (Saldjūḳ) (1105) vi, **275b** – VI, **260b**

Malik-Shāh III b. Maḥmūd b. Muḥammad (Saldjūḳ) (1152) iv, 1097a; vi, 64a, **275b**; viii, 944a – IV, 1128a; VI, 62a, **260b**; 976b

Malik-Shāh b. Ḳilidj Arslan I (Saldjūḳ) (1107) vi, **275b**, 578a – VI, **260b**, 578b

Malik-Shāh b. Ḳilidj Arslan II (Saldjūḳ) (1192) vi, **275b** – VI, **260b**

Malik-Shāh b. Tekish (Khʷārazm-Shāh) (1197) viii, 63b; s, 246a – VIII, 65a; S, 246a

al-Malik Shahānshāh b. al-Muẓaffar, Taḳī al-Dīn (Ayyūbid(e)) (XII) vii, 816b – VII, 818a

Malik al-Sharḳ → Malik Sarwar

Malik Shīr Khān i, 1194b – I, 1229b

Malik al-Shuʿarāʾ iv, 56a; vi, **276a** – IV, 59a; VI, **261a**

Malik Sy, Cheikh El-Hadji vi, 705b – VI, 694a

Mālik al-Ṭāʾī → Mālik b. Abi ʾl-Samḥ al-Ṭāʾī

Malik Tādj al-Dīn s, 105b – S, 105a

Malik al-Tudjdjār ii, 602a, 814b; v, 1258a; vi, **276b** – II, 616b, 834a; V, 1249a; VI, **261b**

Malik Ṭuḥfa vi, 50a – VI, 48b

Malik Yak Lakhī s, 105b – S, 105a

Malik Yāḳūt Sulṭānī iii, 16a – III, 17a

Malik Yūz Beg vii, 193b – VII, 194a

al-Malik al-Ẓāhir Ghāzī b. Ṣalāḥ al-Dīn (Ayyūbid(e), Alep(po)) (1216) i, 197b, 798b, 803a, 989b, 996a, 1316b; ii, 37b, 353b, 556b; iii, 87b, 178a, 208b, 399b, 693b, 863a; iv, 482a; v, 924b; vi, 380b, 381a, 429a, b, 507a, 540b, 544a, 547b, 579a – I, 203b, 822a, 826a, 1020a, 1026b, 1356b; II, 38b, 363a, 570a; III, 89b, 182a, 214b, 412a, 715b, 887a; IV, 503a; V, 930a; VI, 365a, 414b, 492b, 525a, 528b, 532a, 564a

al-Malika al-Sayyida al-Ḥurra (Sulayhid(e)) (1138) vii, 725b; x, 403a – VII, 726b; X, 432a

Mālikāne i, 728a; iv, 1096a; vi, **277b** – I, 801b; IV, 1127a; VI, **262b**

al-Mālikī s, 306b – S, 306a

Al-Mālikī, Abū ʿAbd Allāh Muḥammad (1046) vi, 353b – VI, 337b

Malikī, Khalīl iii, 529a, b; s, 60b – III, 547b, 548a; S, 61a

Malikī b. Muḥammad ii, 1146b – II, 1173b

Mālikiyya i, 249b, 338b, 339a, 494a; ii, 618b, 828b, 859b, 1010a; iii, 6b, 17a, 308b, 350b, 695a; iv, 87a-b, 290a, 341a, 404b; v, 895b; vi, 2a, **278a**; s, 113a – I, 257a, 349a, b, 508b; II, 634a, 848a, 879b, 1033b; III, 6b, 18a, 318a, 361b, 717a; IV, 91a-b, 303a, 355b, 422a; V, 902a; VI, 2a, **263a**; S, 112b

Malikī → Djalālī

Malik-nāma i, 421a – I, 433a

Malikpur i, 1322b; ii, 260a – I, 1363a; II, 269a

Malik-yi Djahān vi, 488a – VI, 474a

Malikzāda Fīrūz b. Tādj al-Dīn Turk (1389) vi, 61b – VI, 59b

Malīla i, 356b; iii, 298b; s, 325b – I, 367a; III, 308a; S, 325a

Mālīn i, 952b – I, 981b

Malindi iv, 887a, b, 888b; vi, **283a**, 385a; vii, 226a – IV, 920a, b, 921b; VI, **268a**, 369a; VII, 228a

Malinké ii, 63a; v, 252b; vi, 257b; s, 295b – II, 64a, b; V, 250b; VI, 242a; S, 295a

Māliyyāt → Māl

Māliyye i, 1090b; ii, 83b; vi, **283b** – I, 1123a; II, 85a; VI, **268b**

Malḳara vi, **290b**; ix, 631b – VI, **275b**; IX, 655b

Malkoč-oghullarī (XIV) i, 340b; vii, 34a – I, 351a; VII, 34b

Malkom Khān, Mīrzā Nāẓim al-Dawla (1908) ii, 650a; iii, 554b; iv, 72a, 73b, 164a, 397b, 788a; v,

919b, 1086a; vi, **291a**, 763b; vii, 438b, 1003b; s, 23b, 53b, 71b, 108b, 109a, 290b –
II, 666a; III, 573b; IV, 76a, 77b, 171a, 415a, 820a; V, 925a, 1083b; VI, **276a**, 752b; VII, 440a, 1005b; S, 24a, 54a, 72a, 108a, b, 290b
Malla Khān iv, 631b; v, 30a – IV, 656b; V, 31a
Mallāḥ i, 181a; i, 230a; vi, **292b**, 591b – I, 186a; II, 237a; VI, **278a**, 576b
Mallal vi, 401a, b – VI, 385b, 386a
Mallālī (XVI) ix, 29b – IX, 21a
Mallel → Mālī
Malloum, General s, 166b – S, 166b
Mallū Iḳbāl Khān (1405) i, 1300a; iii, 417b; iv, 533b; vi, 49a, b, **294a**; s, 206a – I, 1340a; III, 430b; IV, 557a; VI, 47b, 48a, **279b**; S, 206a
Mallū Khān → Ḳādir Shāh
Malta/Malte/Māl(i)ṭa i, 250b, 936a; ii, 801b; iii, 251b; vi, **295a**; s, 47b, 55a, 120b – I, 258b, 965a; II, 820b; III, 258b; VI, **280a**; S, 48a, 55b, 120a
Maltais, le VI, 281a
Maltaise, littérature VI, 284b
Maltese language vi, 295b
Maltese literature vi, 298b – VI, 284b
Malthai → Maʿalthāyā
al-Maʿlūf, Āl vi, **303a** – VI, **288b**
al-Maʿlūf, Amīn Fahd (1943) vi, **304a** – VI, **289b**
al-Maʿlūf, Djamīl (1950) vi, **304b** – VI, **290a**
al-Maʿlūf, Djurdj Ḥassūn (1965) vi, **307b** – VI, **293a**
al-Maʿlūf, Fawzī (1930) iii, 112a; v, 1257a; vi, **306b** – III, 114b; V, 1248a; VI, **291b**
al-Maʿlūf, Ibrāhīm (Abū Natiḥ) (XV) vi, 303a – VI, 288b
al-Maʿlūf, ʿĪsā Iskandar (1956) vi, 303a, **305a** – VI, 288b, **290b**
al-Maʿlūf, Kayṣar Ibrāhīm (1961) vi, **304b** – VI, **289b**
Maʿlūf, Lūwīs (Louis) (1947) iv, 525a; vi, **303b** – IV, 547b; VI, **289a**
al-Maʿlūf, Mīshāl (Michel) (1942) v, 1256a; vi, **305a** – V, 1247a; VI, **290a**
al-Maʿlūf, Nāṣīf (1865) vi, **303b** – VI, **288b**
al-Maʿlūf, Shafīk (1976) v, 1256b, 1257a; vi, **306a** – V, 1247b, 1248a; VI, **291a**
al-Maʿlūf, Shaykh Aḥmad vi, 303a – VI, 288b
al-Maʿlūf, Yūsuf Nuʿmān (1956) vi, **304a** – VI, **289a**
Maʿlūlā vi, **308a** – VI, **293a**
Mālwā i, 208a, 923b, 924a, 1026a, 1155a; ii, 219a, 276a, 1125a; iii, 421a, b, 446a, 481b, 638a; v, 1216a; vi, 50b, 51a, 52a, 53a, 54a, 55a, 61b, 270a, 272a, **309a**, 342b, 368a, 406b, 407b, 533b, 536a, 694b, 953a, 970a, 1027b; vii, 79b, 314a; viii, 68a; s, 105a, 280a, 331b –
I, 214b, 951b, 952a, 1057b, 1189b; II, 225b, 284b, 1151b; III, 434b, 435a, 460b, 498a, 659b; V, 1206a; VI, 48b, 49a, 50b, 51a, b, 52a, 53a, 59b, 254b, 256b, **294b**, 327a, 352a, 391a, 392a, 517b, 519a, b, 682b, 945b, 962a, 1020b; VII, 80b, 316b; VIII, 69b; S, 104b, 279b, 331a
Malwiyya (Moulouya) v, 1185a, 1187a; vi, 141a, b – V, 1175a, 1177a; VI, 139b
Malzūza, Banū vi, **310b** – VI, **295b**
al-Malzūzī → Abū Ḥātim al-Malzūzī
Mama Bonfoh iv, 352a – IV, 367a
Mamadjān (ḳun) vi, 493a – VI, 479a
Mamadu Djoue ii, 960a, 1132b – II, 982b, 1159a
Mamadu Mustafa Mbacké (1945) vii, 609b – VII, 609a
al-Māmaḳānī, ʿAbd Allāh b. Muḥammad al-Nadjafī (1933) vi, **312b** – VI, **297b**
Mamaḳānī, Shaykh Muḥammad Ḥasan b. ʿAbd Allāh (1905) vi, 553a – VI, 537b
Mamālīk iv, 36a, 976b, 977b, 1044a – IV, 38b, 1009a, 1010a, 1075a
al-Mamālik, Mīrzā Yūsuf Mustawfī (XIX) vii, 1004a, b – VII, 1005b, 1006a
Mamand, Banū vii, 220a – VII, 222a
Maʿmar b. al-Muthannā → Abū ʿUbayda
Maʿmar b. Rashīd (770) vii, 662b; ix, 7a, b, 661a – VII, 662a; IX, 7b, 286b
Maʿmar Abu 'l-Ashʿath s, 88b – S, 88b
Māmash i, 1217b – I, 1254a
Mamassanī, Banū iii, 1102b, 1106b; iv, 9a, 498b; v, 822a, 825a, 829b; vii, 453b; s, 147b –
III, 1129b, 1134a; IV, 10a, 520a; V, 828a, 831a, 835b; VII, 454b; S, 147b
Mamay (Tatar(e)) i, 1107b – I, 1141a
Māmāy Bey iv, 723a – IV, 752a
al-Mambassī, Muḥammad b. Aḥmad b. Shaykh (1890) vii, 227a – VII, 229a
Mamdūḥ v, 956a, 959b – V, 960a, 963b
al-Māmī, al-Shaykh Muḥammad (1865) vi, **313a**; vii, 619a, 624b, 626a – VI, **298a**; VII, 619a, 624a, 625b
Mamikonians i, 636b; ii, 679a; vi, 623b – I, 657b; II, 696a; VI, 608b
Māmiya al-Rūmī iv, 451b – IV, 471b
Mamlaka vi, **313b** – VI, **298b**
Mamlān i, 638a – I, 658b
Mamlūk i, 34a; ii, 506b; vi, **314a** – I, 34b; II, 519a; VI, **299a**
Mamlūks i, 33a, 34a, 63a, 182b, 468a, 666b, 786b, 804a, 905b, 910a, 971a, 1119b, 1138a, 1190b, 1288b; ii, 38a, 65b, 284b, 292b, 340a, 348a, 572a, 1043b, 1056b; iii, 120b, 402b; iv, 31b; v, 373b, 739b; vi, 194a, 195a, 261b, **321a**, 530a, 545b, 580b, 668b, 669b, 671b, 673b, 674a, 724b, 979b; vii, 165a; ix, 129a, 168a, 596b; x, 966b; s, 205b, 395b –
I, 33b, 34b, 65a, 187b, 482a, 687a, 810a, 828b, 932b, 937b, 1001a, 1153a, 1172b, 1225b, 1328a; II, 38b, 66b, 292b, 300b, 350a, 357b, 586b, 1067b, 1081a; III, 123a, 415a; IV, 33b; V, 374b, 744b; VI, 178a, 179a, 246a, **305b**, 514a, 530a, 565a, 655a, 656a, 657b, 660a, b, 713b, 972a; VII, 166b; IX, 134a, 276b, 618b; X, ; S, 205b, 396a
—administration i, 34a, 102a, 435b, 444a, 765a, 816b, 1046a, 1349a; ii, 23b, 102b, 172b, 230a, 301b, 330a, 414a, 421b, 508b; iii, 48a, 346a, 758b, 773b; iv, 210a, 267b; v, 332a, b, 627b, 628a; s, 138a, 393a – I, 34b, 105a, 448a, 456b, 788a, 839b, 1077b, 1389b; II, 24b, 105a, 177b, 236b, 309b, 339b, 424b, 432b, 521a; III, 49b, 356b, 781b, 797a; IV, 219b, 279b; V, 332b, 631b, 632a; S, 137b, 393a
—art, architecture i, 1316b; iv, 430b; v, 218a, 1140b – I, 1358a; IV, 449b; V, 215b, 1133b
—history/histoire i, 1128a; iii, 775b, 813a; iv, 462b – I, 1162a; III, 798b, 836b; IV, 483a
—military/militaire i, 445b, 944b, 945b, 1058b, 1324b; ii, 130a, 444b; iii, 99a, 184a, 472b – I, 458b, 973b, 974b, 1090b, 1365b; II, 135b, 456a; III, 101b, 188a, 489a
al-Mammasī (944) vi, 353b; s, 306b – VI, 338a; S, 306a
Mammeri, faḳīh (XX) vii, 415b – VII, 417a
Mams vi, 434b – VI, 420a
Mamūḳ b. Ibāḳ iv, 849a – IV, 882a
al-Ma'mūn → al-Baṭā'iḥī
al-Ma'mūn b. Hārūn al-Rashīd (ʿAbbāsid(e)) (833) i, 18a, 78a, 271a, b, 272b, 279a, 316a, 399b, 400a, 402b, 437a, 844a, 1280a; ii, 235a, 281b, 505b, 726b, 730b, 731a, 911a; iii, 173a, 228a, 231b, 234a, 243b, 618a, 987b, 1148a; iv, 17a, 45b, 645a, b, 939b, 940b; vi, 148a, 198a, 205b, **331a**, 340a, 411a, 438a, 499a, 599b, 606a, 619b, 620b, 635b, 649b, 662a, 665a,

668b, 710b, 714a; vii, 147b, 358b; x, 227a; s, 15a, 22b, 26a, 32b, 35a, 88b, 144a, 252b, 263a, 338a, 384b, 408a –
I, 18b, 80a, 279b, 280a, 281a, 288a, 325b, 411a, b, 414a, 449b, 867b, 1319a; II, 241b, 289b, 518b, 745a, 749b, 750a, 932b; III, 177a, 235a, 238a, 241a, 250b, 638b, 1012a, 1176b; IV, 18a-b, 48a, 671b, 972b, 973b; VI, 146b, 182a, 190a, **315b**, 324b, 395b, 423b, 484b, 584a, 591a, 604a, 605b, 610b, 635a, 647b, 651a, 654b, 699b, 702b; VII, 149b, 361a; X, 245a; S, 15b, 23a, 26b, 33a, 35b, 88b, 144a, 252b, 263a, 337b, 385a, 408a
—reforms/réformes i, 589a, 114a; ii, 198a, 232a, 578a – I, 608a, 1175b; II, 204b, 238b, 592b
al-Ma'mūn, Abu 'l-ʿAlā' (Almohad(e)) (1232) i, 1176a; iii, 207b; iv, 116a, 117b; vi, **339b** – I, 1211a; III, 213a; IV, 121b, 122b; VI, **323b**
Ma'mūn I Khwarazmshāh ii, 1142a; iv, 1066b – II, 1169a; IV, 1098a
Ma'mūn II Khwarazmshāh i, 1236b; iv, 1066b – I, 1274a; IV, 1098a, b
al-Ma'mūn b. al-Baṭā'iḥī → al-Baṭā'iḥī
al-Ma'mūn b. Dhu 'l-Nūn (Toledo/Tolède) (1075) i, 6b, 986a; ii, 243a, 901a; iv, 665b; vii, 766b; viii, 867b – I, 6b, 1016b; II, 250a, 922a; IV, 692b; VII, 768b; VIII, 889a
Ma'mūn b. Muḥammad, Abu 'l-ʿAbbās (Maʿmūnid Khwārazm-Shāh) (997) vi, **340a** – VI, **324a**
al-Ma'mūn b. Muḥammad al-Shaykh al-Mahdī i, 55b, 56a – I, 57b
al-Maʿmūnī, Abū Ṭālib ʿAbd al-Salām (993) vi, **340a** – VI, **324b**
Ma'mūnid(e)s → Khwarazm-Shāhs
Ma'mūniyya (Marrākush) vi, 596b – VI, 581b
Ma'mūr vi, **340b** – VI, **324b**
Maʿmūr Khān, ʿAbd al-Karīm v, 600a – V, 603b
al-Maʿmūra → al-Mahdiyya (town/ville, Morocco/Maroc)
al-Maʿmūra (al-Maṣṣīṣa) vi, 778b – VI, 768a
Maʿmūrat al-ʿAzīz (Elaziğ) iv, 1084b; vi, **341b**, 539b – IV, 1115b; VI, **325b**, 524a
Maʿmūriyye Ḳalʿesi i, 481a – I, 495b
Maʿn, Banū i, 181b, 552a, 767a; ii, 634b, 635a, 749b; iv, 834b; v, 259a, 602a, 792b; vi, **343a**; ix, 439a; s, 49b, 338a –
I, 186b, 569b, 789b; II, 650b, 651a, 768a; IV, 867b; V, 257a, 606a; VI, **327b**; IX, 456a; S, 50a, 337b
Maʿn b. Aws al-Muzanī (VII) vi, **344a**, 477a – VI, **328b**, 463a
Maʿn b. Ḥātim iii, 125b – III, 128a
Maʿn b. Muḥammad b. Ṣumādiḥ al-Tudjībī (1052) iii, 740a; vi, **344b,** 576b – III, 763a; VI, **329a**, 561b
Maʿn b. Zā'ida, Abu 'l-Walīd al-Shaybānī (769) i, 364a, 964b; iii, 892a; vi, 344b, 576b; vi, **345a**, 625a; viii, 462a, 996b; ix, 391b; s, 338a, 386b –
I, 375a, 994a; III, 916a; VI, **329a**, 610a; VIII, 477b, 1031b; IX, 404b; S, 337b, 386b
Mān Singh (1614) ii, 1144a; iii, 632a; vi, **342b**; vii, 129b, 131b – II, 1171a; III, 653a; VI, **326b**; VII, 131b, 133b
Maʿna vi, **346a** – VI, **330b**
Maʿnā v, 320b, 321b – V, 320a, b
Manād b. Manḳūs (X) ix, 18a – IX, 18b
Manāf vi, **349a** – VI, **333a**
Manāhil, Banū vi, 83b – VI, 81b
al-Manākha iii, 179a, 327a; vi, 192a – III, 183a, 337a; VI, 175b
al-Manākhī, Djaʿfar b. Ismāʿīl (905) vi, 439a – VI, 424b
Manāḳib v, 1209a; vi, 263a, **349a** – V, 1199b; VI, 247b, **333b**
al-Manāma i, 540a, 941a, b, 942b; vi, **357b**; vii, 464a; s, 42a – I, 556b, 970a, b, 971b; VI, **341b**; VII, 463b; S, 42b
Manāniyya (Mānawiyya) vi, 421b – VI, 406b
Manār, Manāra (lighthouse/phare) iv, 132b, 383b; vi, **358b** – IV, 138b, 400a; VI, **342b**
al-Manār vi, **360a** – VI, **344a**
Manāra, Manār (Minaret) vi, **361b** – VI, **345b**
Manāra (Marrākush) vi, 596b – VI, 581b
Manārat al-ʿAbd iv, 638a, b – IV, 664a, 665a
Manārat al-ʿArūs (Damas(cus)) vi, 362b – VI, 346b
Manārat al-Mudjīda vi, 364b – VI, 348b
Manas iii, 116a; vi, **370b** – III, 118b; VI, **355a**
Manashshā i, 823b – I,846b
al-Manāṣir, Banū i, 371a, 372a; vi, **371b** – I, 382a, 383a; VI, **356a**
Manāstir → Monastir
Manāstir (Bitola) vi, 371b – VI, 356a
Manāstirli Meḥmed Rifʿat (1907) vi, **372b**; s, 359b – VI, **356b**; S, 359a
Manāt iii, 540b; iv, 322a; v, 692a, b, 995b; vi, **373b**, 645b – III, 559a; IV, 336a; V, 697a, b, 990b; VI, **358a**, 630b
Manāwa, Banū vi, 435a – VI, 420b
Manāzdjird/Manāzgerd → Malāzgird
al-Manāzī → Malāzgird
al-Manāzī, Shaykh Abū Naṣr (1050) vi, 930b – VI, 922b
al-Manāzil (lunar mansions/-lunaires) i, 1225a; iii, 83b; iv, 517a; vi, **374a** – I, 1261b; III, 86a; IV, 539b; VI, **358b**
Manāẓir i, 98a; vi, **376a** – I, 101a; VI, **360b**
Manbasa → Mombasa
Manbidj i, 119b; vi, **377b**, 429a, 505b, 506b – I, 123a; VI, **362a**, 414b, 491a, 492a
al-Manbidjī, Naṣr al-Dīn iii, 952a – III, 976b
Manbik → Manbidj
Mancus ii, 298b – II, 306b
Mānd (Fārs) vi, **383b** – VI, **367b**
Manda iv, 885b; v, 655a; vi, **385a** – IV, 918a; V, 659a; VI, **369a**
Mandaeans/Mandéens → Ṣābi'a; Ṣubba
Mandakhā vi, 385a – VI, 369a
Mandalgaṙh vi, 53a, b – VI, 51b
Mandalī vi, 614a – VI, 599a
Mandān vi, 744b – VI, 733b
Mandara ii, 114b – II, 117a
Mandasor vi, 53a, 55a, 270a, 272a, 310a – VI, 51b, 53a, 255a, 256b, 295a
Mandat(e)s vi, **385b** – VI, **370a**
Mande vi, **400b** – VI, **385a**
Mandesh ii, 1099b – II, 1125b
Mandīl (cloth) v, 735a, 749b; vi, **402b** – V, 740b, 755a; VI, **387a**
Mandīl, Awlād/Banū v, 1180a; vi, **404a** – V, 1170a; VI, **388b**
Mandil b. ʿAbd al-Raḥmān b. Abī Nās (XIII) v, 1180a; vi, 404a – V, 1169b; VI, 388b
Mandīl al-amān iii, 188a – iii, 192b
Mandīlsar vi, 498b – VI, 483b
Mandingos, Mande ii, 1132a; iii, 275b; vi, **400b**, 401a, 422a; viii, 20b; s, 295b – II, 1159a; III, 283b; VI, **385a, b,** 407a; VIII, 20b; S, 295a
Mandīsh (Ghūr) vii, 407a – VII, 408b
Māndistān vi, 383b, 384b, 385a – VI, 367b, 368b, 369a
Mandjak al-Nāṣirī iii, 775b, 818a – III, 798b, 841b
Mandjaḳ Pasha (1669) vii, 469b – VII, 469a
Mandjak al-Yūsufī iv, 425b – IV, 446a
Mandjanīḳ i, 658b; ii, 188a; iii, 201b, 469b, 472b,

482a; vi, **405a** – I, 679b; II, 194a; III, 207a, 486a, 489a, 499a; VI, **389b**
Mandjar (river/rivière) vi, 53b – VI, 52a
Māndjhan, Mīr Sayyid iii, 457a – III, 472b
al-Mandjūr, Abu 'l-ʿAbbās Aḥmad al-Fāsī (1587) vi, **406a** – VI, **390b**
Mandsore s, 331b – S, 331a
Māndū ii, 219a, 276b, 1128a; iii, 421b, 446a, 638a, b; v, 1216a; vi, 52b, 53a, 54a, b, 272a, 309b, 310a, **406b**; vii, 314a, b – II, 226a, 285a, 1154b; III, 435a, 461a, 659a; V, 1206; VI, 51a, b, 52a, b, 256b, 294b, 295a, **391a**; VII, 316a, b
Mandūb vi, **408a** – VI, **393a**
Mandūr, Muḥammad b. ʿAbd al-Ḥamīd Mūsā (1965) v, 1257b; vi, **408a**; viii, 88a; s, 58b – V, 1248a; VI, **393a**; VIII, 90b; S, 59a
Manēr (Manīr) vi, 131a, **409b** – VI, 129b, **394b**
Manērī, Sharaf al-Dīn Aḥmad → Makhdūm al-Mulk
Manērī, Shaykh Yaḥyā (1291) vi, 410a – VI, 395a
Manf (Minf, Munf, Munayf) vi, **410b** – VI, **395b**
al-Manfalūṭ vi, 119a, 414a; viii, 865a; s, 40b, 383b – VI, 116b, 399a; VIII, 895b; S, 41a, 384a
al-Manfalūṭī, Muṣṭafā Luṭfī (1924) i, 597a; iv, 159b; v, 188a; vi, 75b, **414a**, 956a; vii, 901b – I, 616b; IV, 166b; V, 185b; VI, 73b, **399a**, 948b; VII, 902a
Manfāʾūs b. ʿAdīm (king/le roi) vi, 412a – VI, 396b
Manfish → Manf
Manfiyya → Mafia
Manfūḥa i, 628b – I, 649b
Mangat Rai i, 606b – I, 626a
Manghir/Mangir → Sikka
Mangishlak vi, **415a**; s, 168b, 169a, 245b, 280b, 281a – VI, **400a**; S, 168b, 169a, 245b, 280b, 281a
Mangistau Mts vi, 415a – VI, 400a
Mangit (tribe(u)s Özbek) i, 1295b; ii, 44b, 446a; v, 182a, 273b; vi, 416b, **417b**; s, 97a, b, 228a, 281a, 419b, 420a – I, 1335b; II, 45b, 458a; V, 179b, 271b; VI, 401b, **402b**; S, 96b, 97a, 228a, 281a, 420a
Mangits (dynasty/-ie) Bukhārā) vi, **418b**, 621a – VI, **403b**, 606a
Mangkūt → Mangit
al-Manglī, Muhammad → Muḥammad al-Manglī
Mangrol vi, **419b** – VI, **404b**
Mangū → Möngke
Mangū-Tīmūr, Khān (Mongol) (1280) vi, **419b** – VI, **404b**
Mangubars → Mengubars
Mangudjak → Mengüček
Mangūr i, 1217b – I, 1254a
Mangūtakīn (991) i, 824b, 1042a; ii, 483b, 855a; iii, 77a, 130a; v, 820a, b, 928a; vi, 545b – I, 847b, 1073b; II, 495b, 875a; III, 79b, 133a; V, 826b, 933b; VI, 530a
Manhūk i, 671a – I, 692a
Manīʿ (Numayrid(e)) iii, 228a – III, 235a
Mānī vi, **420b**; x, 227a – VI, **405b**; 245a
al-Maʿnī, Aḥmad (amīr) (XVII) vi, 346a – VI, 330a
Mānī b. Fāttik (Fātik) (274) vi, **421a**; viii, 675b – VI, **406b**; VIII, 695b
Manīʿ b. Ḥassān, Abu 'l-Fityān (1026) iv, 911a – IV, 944a
Māniʿ b. Rabīʿa al-Muraydī (XV) i, 553a; ii, 320b, 321a – I, 571a; II, 330a
Manič (river/rivière) s, 169a – S, 169a
Manichaeism/Manichéisme i, 130a; iii, 885a; iv, 43b, 1025a; v, 853a; vi, 421a; viii, 672a, 676a – I, 134a; III, 909a; IV, 46a, 1057b; V, 859bl; VI, 406b; VIII, 692a, 696a
Maʿnid(e)s (peace/paix) s, 159a – S, 159a
Maʿnid(e)s → Maʿn, Banū
al-Manīʿī, Abū ʿAlī Ḥassān (1089) viii, 403a – VIII, 417a
Manīka vi, 578b – VI, 563a
Mānikpūr vi, 48a; s, 203a – VI, 46b; S, 202b
Manila s, 152a – S, 152a
Manisa → Maghnisa
Mankalī-Bughā iii, 818a – III, 841b
Mankashlā vi, 415b – VI, 400b
Mānkdīm Shashdiw (1034) vii, 786a, 787a – VII, 787b, 788b
Mankit → Mangit
Mankubirnī → Djalāl al-Dīn Khʷārazm-Shāh
Mankurūs b. Khumātigin (XII) viii, 851a – VIII, 880b
Manna (Soninke) x, 142a – X, 152a
Männan Uyghur (1955) vi, 768b, 769b – VI, 758a, b
al-Mannāwī, Aḥmad b. Muḥammad s, 403a – S, 403b
al-Mannūbiyya i, 309a – I, 318b
Manōhar (painter/peintre) (XVII) vi, 425b; vii, 339a – VI, 410b; VII, 340b
Manōhar, Manōhargaṛh (fortress, forteresse) vi, **421b** – VI, **406b**
Mān-rūd v, 821b, 831b – V, 827b, 837b
Mansa Mūsā (Mali) (1337) iii, 275b; iv, 641a; vi, 258a, b, 402a, **421b**; vii, 588a; viii, 847b – III, 283b; IV, 667b; VI, 242b, 243a, 386b, **406b**; VII, 588a; VIII, 877a
Mansā Sulaymān (Mali) vi, 258a – VI, 242b
Mansā Ulī (Walī) (Mali) vi, 258a – VI, 242b
Manṣab, Manṣabdār v, 685b, 688b; vi, **422b** – V, 691a, 694a; VI, **407b**
Mansārām i, 1166a – I, 1200b
Manshiya (palace, Marrākush) vii, 387a – VII, 388b
Manshūr ii, 303a, 309a; vi, **423a** – II, 311b, 317b; VI, **408b**
Mansūkh → Nāsikh
Manṣūr (Moghol Khān) (1545) x, 677a – X,
Manṣūr (painter/peintre) (1624) vi, 424b; vii, 339a – VI, 410a; VII, 340b
Manṣūr (Moghol Khān) (1545) x, 677a – X,
al-Manṣūr Abū Djaʿfar ʿAbd Allāh (ʿAbbāsid(e)) (775) i, 12b, 17a, 23b, 43a, 45b, 59b, 86b, 103b, 123a, 141b, 212b, 402b, 454a, 485a, 952a, 1030a, 1033b, 1080b, 1232b, ii, 178a, 576b; iii, 135b, 266a, 984a; iv, 939a, b, 940b; v, 69b, 326a, 620b, 1160a, 1233a, 1238a; vi, 140a, 147b, 230b, 263b, 278a, 311b, 331a, 333a, 345a, **427a**, 439b, 506a, 540a, 625a, 659b, 691a, 707b, 710b, 744b, 821b; vii, 113b, 388b, 396a, 628a, 645b; viii, 462a; s, 17b, 31b, 267b, 304b, 306b, 384b, 385b, 386b – I, 12b, 17b, 24a, 44a, b, 61a, 89a, 106b, 126b, 145b, 219a, 414a, 467a, 499b, 981b, 1061b, 1065a, 1112b, 1269b, II, 183b, 591a; III, 138a, 273b, 1008b; IV, 972a, b, 973b; V, 71b, 325b, 624b, 1149b, 1223b, 1228b; VI, 138b, 146a, 224b, 248a, 263a, 296b, 315b, 318a, 329a, **412b**, 425a, 491b, 524b, 610a, 645a, 678b, 696a, 699b, 734a, 812a; VII, 116a, 389b, 397a, 628a, 645b; VIII, 477b; S, 17b, 31b, 267b, 304b, 306a, 385b, 386a, b
—foundation of/fondation de Baghdād i, 616a, 895a, 896a, 897a – I, 636b, 921b, 922b, 923b
al-Manṣūr (Afṭasid(e)) → Ibn al-Afṭas; ʿAbd Allāh b. Muḥammad b. Maslama
al-Manṣūr (Almohad(e)) → Abū Yūsuf Yaʿkūb
al-Manṣūr (Ḥammādid(e)) → al-Manṣūr b. al-Nāṣir
al-Manṣūr (Marīnid(e)) → Yaʿkūb al-Manṣūr

al-Manṣūr (Marwānid(e), Diyār Bakr) (1096) vi, 627a – VI, 612a
al-Manṣūr (Zīrid(e)) s, 62b – S, 63a
al-Manṣūr, Madīnat → Baghdād
al-Manṣūr, Muḥammad b. Abī Djaʿfar (777) vii, 76a – VII, 77a
Mansur, Sultan (Malacca) (XV) vi, 209a, 212b – VI, 193a, 196b
al-Manṣūr b. Abī ʿĀmir al-Maʿāfirī → al-Manṣūr bi-'llāh (Almanzor, al-Andalus)
Manṣur b. Abī Mālik (al-Maʿkil) (1287) vi, 142a – VI, 140a
al-Manṣūr, Aḥmad (Saʿdid(e)) → Aḥmad al-Manṣūr
Manṣur b. ʿAbdūn ii, 858a; iii, 79a; v, 1211a – II, 878a; III, 81b; V, 1201a
al-Manṣūr b. A'lāʿ al-Nās → al-Manṣūr b. al-Nāṣir
Manṣūr b. ʿAlī b. ʿIrāḳ Djīlānī → Ibn ʿIrāḳ
Manṣūr b. Bādja (IX) vi, 437b – VI, 423a
al-Manṣūr b. Buluggīn (Zīrid(e)) (996) i, 824a, 1309a; iii, 137a; s, 62b – I, 847a, 1349b; III, 139b; S, 63a
Manṣūr b. Djumhūr (744) vi, 439b; s, 232b – VI, 425a; S, 232b
Mansūr b. Dubays I (Mazyadid(e)) (1086) i, 684a; vi, 966a – I, 705a; VI, 958a
Manṣūr b. Fakhr al-Dīn b. Ḳurḳumāz Maʿn (1635) vi, 343b – VI, 328a
Manṣūr b. Ḳarātegīn iv, 100b; viii, 110a – IV, 104b; VIII, 112a
Manṣūr b. Kutlumush b. Arslān Isrāʾīl (Saldjūḳ) (1078) i, 1336b; vi, 274b; viii, 948a – I, 1376b; VI, 259a; VIII, 980b
Manṣūr b. Luʾluʾ iii, 80b, 130b; v, 623b, 820b – III, 83a, 133a; V, 627b, 826b
al-Manṣūr b. al-Mahdī (ʿAbbāsid(e)) (817) vi, 335a, b, 650a – VI, 319b, 320a, 635a
Manṣūr b. Maymūn iv, 346b, 347a – IV, 361a, 362a
Manṣūr b. Muḥammad b. Aḥmad b. Yūsuf b. Ilyās(XV) viii, 542b; x, 355a – VIII, 560a; X,
Manṣūr Muḥammad b. Aḥmad b. Yūsuf b. Ilyās (XV) x, 355a – X,
Manṣūr b. Muḥammad al-Azdī al-Harawī (ḳāḍī) (1048) vi, 913b – VI, 905a
al-Manṣūr b. al-Mutawakkil i, 242b – I, 250a
al-Manṣūr b. al-Nāṣir (Ḥammādid(e)) (1105) i, 1205a; iii, 138a, 753a; iv, 479a; vi, 140a, **426b** – I, 1240b; III, 141a, 806b; IV, 501a; VI, 139b, **412a**
Manṣūr b. Naṣr al-Tunbudhī i, 248a; iv, 827b – I, 256a; IV, 860a
Manṣūr b. Nūḥ I, Abū Ṣāliḥ (Sāmānid(e)) (976) i, 421b, 984b, 1294b; ii, 100a; v, 430a; vi, **432b**; s, 259a, 265b – I, 433b, 1015a, 1334b; II, 102a; V, 432b; VI, **418a**; S, 258b, 265a
Manṣūr b. Nūḥ II, Abu 'l-Ḥārith (Samānid(e)) (999) i, 1236a; vi, 65a, **433a**; s, 259a – I, 1274a; VI, 63a, **418a**; S, 258b
Manṣūr b. Saʿīd (Marwānid(e)) (1085) v, 453a; vii, 693b – V, 455b; VII, 693b
Manṣūr b. Yazīd al-Ḥimyarī vii, 694b – VII, 694b
Manṣūr b. Yūnus Buzurg (IX) vii, 647b – VII, 647b
al-Manṣūr ʿAbd Allāh b. Ḥamza (Zaydī Imām) (XIII) vii, 773a – VII, 774b
al-Manṣūr ʿAlā al-Dīn ʿAlī (Mamlūk) (1382) ii, 159a – II, 164a
al-Manṣūr ʿAlī b. al-Mahdī ʿAbd Allāh (Zaydī Imām) (XIX) vii, 515a – VII, 515b
Manṣūr Ata i, 299a – I, 308a
Manṣūr al-Bahūtī → al-Bahūtī al-Miṣrī
al-Manṣūr bi-'llāh (Almanzor) (al-Andalus) (1002) i, 75b, 446a, 489b, 494a, 499a, 601b, 628a, 1055a, 1238a, 1338b; ii, 373a, 485b, 542a, 998a; iii, 46a, 74b, 495b, 713a, 743a, 746b; iv, 216b, 712b; v, 133a, 511a, 626a, 781a, b, 1007b, 1008a, 1107b, 1177b; vi, **430b**, 520b, 842a, 852a;570a, 942b; viii, 632a; ix, 740b; ix, 852b; x, 852b; s, 92b, 125a – I, 77b, 459a, 504a, 509a, 514a, 621a, 649a, 1086b, 1275b, 1379a; II, 383a, 498a, 555b, 1021a; III, 48a, 77a, 512b, 735a, 765b, 769b; IV, 226a, 741a; V, 135b, 514b, 630a, 787b, 788a, 1003b, 1004a, 1103b, 1167b; VI, **416a**, 505b, 832b, 844a; VII, 571a, 942b; VIII, 651a; IX, 773a; X, ;S, 92a, 124a
al-Manṣūr bi-'llāh (Zaydī Imām) (XVIII) vii, 515a – VII, 515a
al-Manṣūr bi-'llāh, Ismāʿīl (Fāṭimid(e)) (953) i, 163b, 1238a; ii, 491b, 861b; iv, 460a; v, 1246b; vi, **434a**, 728a; vii, 485b; s, 144b, 236b – I, 168a, 1275b; II, 503b, 881b; IV, 480a; V, 1237b; VI, **419b**, 716b; VII, 485a; S, 144a, 236b
al-Manṣūr bi-'llāh ʿAbd Allāh b. Ḥamza (Zaydī Imām) (1217) v, 1240b; vi, **433b**; s, 236b, 363b – V, 1231b; VI, **418b**; S, 236a, 363a
al-Manṣūr bi-'llāh ʿAlī (Imām) (1809) s, 30b – S, 30b
al-Manṣūr bi-'llāh al-Ḳāsim b. ʿAlī al-ʿIyānī (Zaydī Imām) (1003) vi, **435b** – VI, **421a**
al-Manṣūr bi-'llāh al-Ḳāsim b. Muḥammad (Zaydī Imām) (1620) v, 1241b; vi, **436a**, **b**; vii, 996a; ix, 2a; s, 30b – V, 1233a; VI, **421b**; VII, 995a; IX, 2a; S, 30b
al-Manṣūr al-Dhahabī (Saʿdid(e)) (1603) vi, 406a, 607a, 933a – VI, 390b, 391a, 591b, 924b
al-Manṣūr Ḥādjdjī (Mamlūk) (1390) vi, 548a – VI, 532b
al-Manṣūr al-Ḥusayn b. al-Mutawakkil (Zaydī Imām) (1747) vi, 191a – VI, 175a
Manṣūr al-Namarī (805) vi, **437b**, 625a – VI, **432a**, 610a
al-Manṣūr Ṣalāh al-Dīn Muḥammad s, 395b – S, 396a
Mansūr al-Shihābī ii, 444a, 635b – II, 455b, 651b
al-Manṣūr ʿUmar (Rasūlid(e) (1249) viii, 436a – VIII, 471b
al-Manṣūr ʿUthmān b. Djaḳmaḳ (Mamlūk) (1453) vii, 727a – VII, 728a
Manṣūr Ushurma, Shaykh ii, 18a, 88a – II, 18b, 89b
Manṣūr al-Yaman al-Nadjdjār al-Kūfī (Ibn Ḥawshab) (914) i, 103b, 551b; ii, 852a; iv, 198a, b, 661a; vi, **438b**; s, 236b – I, 106b, 569a; II, 872a; IV, 206b, 207a, 687b; VI, **424a**; S, 236b
Manṣūr Zalzal vi, 97b, 103a; s, 128b – VI, 95b, 101a; S 127b
al-Manṣūra (Miṣr) vi, 314b, **440a**; vii, 166a – VI, 299b, **440b**; VII, 167b
al-Manṣūra (Sind) vi, **439b**, 691a – VI, **425a**; 678b
al-Manṣūra (Tilimsān) iii, 470b; vi, **440b**, 572a – III, 487a; VI, **426a**, 557a
al-Manṣūrī → al-Manāṣīr, Banū
al-Manṣūriyya → Ṣabra
al-Manṣūriyya (Ifrīḳiyya) iv, 479a; s, 62b, 236b – IV, 501a; S, **426a**, 557a
Manṣūriyya (Mamlūk) vi, 316a, 322b – VI, 301a, 307a
al-Manṣūriyya (Miṣr) vii, 162a; s, 62b, 236b – VII, 163b; S, 63a, 236b
Manṣūriyya (Shīʿī) i, 258a; vi, **441b** – I, 266a; VI, **427a**
Manṭiḳ, ʿIlm al- vi, **442a** – VI, **427b**
al-Manṭiḳī → Abū Sulaymān al-Manṭiḳī
Mantzikert → Malāzgird
Mānū, Ḳaṣr vi, **452b** – VI, **438a**
Mānū Djān Khānum bint Āghā Muṭahhar (XVIII) vii, 444a – VII, 445a
Manūčihr I b. Yazīd iv, 347a – IV, 361b

Manučihr II b. Faridūn ii, 764a, 798a; iv, 348b, 915a – II, 782b, 817a; IV, 363a, 948a
Manūčihr b. Ḳābūs (Ziyārid(e)) (1029) iv, 100b, 358a, 465a; v, 662a; vi, 66a; s, 235a – IV, 105a, 373b, 486a; V, 667b; VI, 64a; S, 235a
Manūčihr Iḳbāl (1977) vii, 450b – VII, 452a
Manūčihr Khān (Luristān) (XVII) vii, 674a – VII, 673b
Manūčihr Khān Muʿtamid al-Dawla (1847) i, 833b; iv, 1091b; v, 825b; vi, 803b; vii, 557a, 675a – I, 856b; IV, 1123a; V, 831b; VI, 793b; VII, 557a, 675a
Manūčihrī, Abu 'l-Nadjm Dāmghānī (1041) i, 1301a; iv, 61a; v, 1104a; vi, **453a**; vii, 661b; s, 35a – I, 1341a; IV, 64b; V, 1099b; VI, **438b**; VII, 661a; S, 35b
Manūf al-Suflā vi, **453b** – VI, **439a**
Manūf al-ʿUlyā vi, **453b** – VI, **439a**
al-Manūfī, ʿAbd Allāh – al-Mālikī (1347) vi, **454a** – VI, **439b**
al-Manūfī, ʿAbd al-Djawwād b. Muḥammad (1658) vi, **454a** – VI, **439b**
al-Manūfī, Abu 'l-ʿAbbās Aḥmad b. Muḥammad (1521) vi, **454a** – VI, **439b**
al-Manūfī, Abu 'l-Ḥasan ʿAlī (1532) vi, **454a** – VI, **439b**
al-Manūfī, Maḥmūd Abu 'l-Fayḍ (1972) vi, **454b** – VI, **440a**
al-Manūfī Manṣūr b. ʿAlī (1722) vi, **454b** – VI, **439b**
al-Manūfī, Muḥammad b. Ismāʿīl (1452) vi, **454a** – VI, **439b**
al-Manūfī, Ramaḍān al-Ashʿath vi, 454a – VI, 439b
al-Manūfiyya al-Aḥmadiyya vi, 454a – VI, 439b
Maʿn-zāda, Ḥusayn b. Fakhr al-Dīn II al-Maʿnī (1690) vi, 343b, **345a** – VI, 328a, **329b**
Manzah Bint al-Sulṭān i, 699b, 700a – I, 721a
Mantzikert → Malāzgird
Manzil (lunar mansion/- lunaire) → Manāzil
Manzil (stage/halte) vi, **454b** – VI, **440a**
Manzil Bashshū (Ifrīḳiya) vi, 455b, **457a** – VI, 441a, **442b**
al-Manzila Bayn al-Manzilatayn vi, **457b** – VI, **443a**
Manẓūr ʿAlī Khān ii, 1092b – II, 1118a
Mao (Kānim) s, 165a, b, 166a – S, 165a, b, 166a
Mappila i, 172a; iii, 411b; iv, 547a; v, 587a; vi, 206b, 245a, **458a**; vii, 49a – I, 176b; III, 424a; IV, 570b; V, 661b; VI, 191a, 229b, **443b**; VII, 49b
Mār ghat (Margat) → al-Marḳab
Mār Ghātūm (Margathum) → al-Marḳab
Mār Kābān (Marckapan) → al-Marḳab
Mār Kābūs (Markappos) → al-Marḳab
Mār Sābā v, 330a – V, 330a
al-Mar'a (woman/la femme) iv, 720a, b; v, 587b, 895b; vi, **466a** – IV, 749a, b; V, 662a, 902a; VI, **452a**
—education v, 905a, b, 907a, 909a – V, 911a, 913a, 915a
Marʿā (pasture/pâturage) vi, **490a** – VI, **476a**
Marādjiʿ al-taḳlīd iii, 491a, b – III, 508a, b
Marādjil umm al-Ma'mūn (ʿAbbāsid(e)) vi, 331a – VI, 315b
Marāfiḳ ii, 325a; vi, **498a** – II, 335a; VI, **483a**
Marāgha i, 300a, 301a; vi, 494a, **498a**, 504b, 601a, b; vii, 395a – I, 309b, 310a; VI, 479b, **483b**, 490a, 586a, b; VII, 396a
—observatory/observatoire iii, 1125a, 1135b, 1137b – III, 1153a, 1164a, 1165b
Marāgha'ī, Zayn al-ʿĀbidīn (1910) iv, 72a, 164b, 789a; s, 109b – IV, 76a, 171b, 821a; S, 108b
al-Marāghī, ʿAbd al-Ḳādir (1435) vii, 684b, 1042b; s, 409a – VII, 685a, 1044b; S, 409a
al-Marāghī, Muṣṭafā iv, 159b; v, 429b – IV, 166a; V, 432a
al-Marāghī, Ṣadr al-Dīn iv, 862b – IV, 895b
Marah Rusli (XX) vi, 240b – VI, 205b
Mārahrawī → Aḥsan Mārahrawī
Marāʿī iv, 1042a, b – IV, 1073b, 1074a
Maraḳiyya iii, 474b; v, 582a – III, 491a; V, 587a
Marakkayar vi, **503a** – VI, **488b**
Marand iii, 1125a; vi, **504a**; s, 365b – III, 1153a; VI, **489a**; S, 365a
Marandj vi, 783a – VI, 773a
Marandjiṣa iii, 1040b, 1041a – III, 1066b, 1067a
Marʿash i, 4a, b, 1190b; vi, 380a, **505b** – I, 4a, b, 1225b; VI, 364b, **490b**
al-Marʿashī → al-Shushtarī, Sayyid Nūr Allāh b. Sharīf Marʿashī
Marʿashī, Ḳawām al-Dīn (Mīr-i Buzurg) i, 237a – I, 244b
Marʿashī-Nadjafī, Āyatallāh Shihāb al-Dīn vi, 516b, 517a, 553b – VI, 502a, 538a
Marʿashīs vi, **510b**, 549b; vii, 672b – VI, **496a**, 534a; VII, 672b
Marāṣid ii, 143a – II, 147a
Marāsim vi, **518a** – VI, **502b**
Marāt (Wādī Rahyū) vi, 404a – VI, 388b
Marāthās i, 208b, 230a, 253a, 296a, 400b, 403b, 418a, 625a, 757a, 796b, 808a, 952a, 1170a, 1202b, 1300a, 1330a, 1331a; ii, 99a, 219a, 808b, 1092b, 1130a; iii, 15b, 60b, 202b, 316b, 320a, 424b, 427b; iv, 1023b; v, 1259a; vi, 269a, b, 310a, 407a, **534a**; vii, 315b, 443b, 457a, 899a; viii, 74a, 253b, 300b, 382b; s, 55b, 246b – I, 214b, 237a, 261a, 305a, 412a, 415a, 429b, 645b, 779b, 792b, 831b, 981a, 1205a, 1238b, 1340a, 1371a, 1372a; II, 101a, 225b, 828a, 1118a, 1156b; III, 16b, 63a, 208a, 326a, 330b, 438a, 441b; IV, 1055b; V, 1250a; VI, 254a, b, 295a, 392a, **518b**; VII, 317b, 445a, 457a, 899b; VIII, 76a, 255b, 309b, 395bS, 56a, 246b
Marāthī vi, **536b** – VI, **521a**
Marātib vi, **536b** – VI, **521a**
Marāzīg vii, 897a, b – VII, 897b, 898a
Marāziḳa → Ibn Marzūḳ, Muḥammad VI
Marbaṭ (Marbiṭ) vi, **537b** – VI, **522a**
Marbat al-Dimm vi, 563b – VI, 548a
Marcuella → Marḳwīz
Mardam, ʿAdnān b. Khalīl (XX) vi, 538b – VI, 523b
Mardam, Djamīl (1961) vi, **538a** – VI, **522b**
Mardam, Khalīl (1959) vi, **538b** – VI, **523a**
Mardān-shāh (Maṣmughān) (VII) vi, 744b – VI, 733b
Mardanīsh → Ibn Mardanīsh
Mardanīsh, Banū s, 80b – S, 80b
al-Mardāwī, 'Alāʿ al-Dīn (1480) iii, 162a, 766b – III, 165a, 789b
Mardāwidj b. Ziyār (Ziyārid(e), 935) i, 125b, 688a, b, 866a, 1350a, b, 1354a; ii, 192b, 299b, 454a, 1082a, 1141b; iii, 105b, 195b, 255a, 1157a; iv, 19a, 23a, 100a, 661b; vi, 115b, 521b, 523a, **539a**; viii, 597b; s, 357a – I, 129a, 709a, b, 890a, 1390b, 1391a, 1393b; II, 198b, 307b, 465b, 1107a, 1168b; III, 180a, 200a, 262a, 1185b; IV, 20b, 24b-25a, 104b, 688b; VI, 113a, 506b, 507b, **523b**; VIII, 616b; S, 357a
Marḍī (Murḍā) Ibn al-Ṭarsūsī (XIII) vii, 885b – VII, 887a
Mārdīn (Māridīn) i, 311b, 664a, 665b, 666b; ii, 344b; iii, 1118a; iv, 898a; v, 248a, 457b, 1145a; vi, 111b, **539b**; x, 527a; s, 36a – I, 321b, 684a, 686b, 687a; II, 354a; III, 1146a; IV, 930b; V, 246a, 460a, 1137a; VI, 109a, **524a**; X, ;S, 36b

al-Mārdīnī (1591) vi, 112a – VI, 110a
al-Mārdīnī, ʿAbd Allāh b. Khalīl (1406) vi, **542b** – VI, **527b**
al-Mārdīnī, Abu ʾl-Ṭāhir Ibn Fallūs (1252) vi, **542b** – VI, **527b**
al-Mārdīnī, Muḥammad b. Muḥammad, Sibṭ al-Mardīnī (1506) vi, **543a** – VI, **527b**
Mardj (Shūf) s, 159a, 160b – S, 159a, 160b
al-Mardj → Barḳa
Mardj ʿAdhrāʾ vi, 544b, 545b; VI, 529a, 530b
Mardj al-Aṭrākhūn vi, 778b – VI, 768b
Mardj Banī ʿĀmir vi, **543b** – VI, **528a**
Mardj Dābiḳ iv, 553a; vi, 231b, 325a, **544a** – IV, 577a; VI, 225a, 309a, **528b**
Mardj al-Dībādj vi, 776b – VI, 766a
Mardj al-Ḳassāb vi, 545b – VI, 530a
Mardj Rāhiṭ i, 5a, 920a, b; ii, 90a, 1106a; iv, 493a; vi, **544a**, 622a; vii, 268b; viii, 756b – I, 5a, 947b, 949a; II, 91b, 1132a; IV, 514b; VI, **529a**, 607a; VII, 270a; VIII, 781a
Mardj al-Shaḥm vi, 774b – VI, 763b
Mardj al-Ṣuffar vi, 544b, 545a, **546a**; vii, 462a; viii, 756b – VI, 529a, b, **530b**; VII, 462a; VIII, 781a
Mardj ʿUyūn ii, 234b; vi, 430a – II, 241b; VI, 415a
Mardjaʿ-i Taḳlīd v, 371b; vi, **548b**; s, 75b, 76a, 103b, 158a – V, 372b; VI, **533a**; S, 76a, 103a, 158a
Mardjān (amīr) (1521) 1, 938a – I, 967a
Mardjān (amīr) (Zabīd) (1022) vii, 861a – VII, 862b
M. Mardjān (Baghdād) i, 903b – I, 930b
Mardjān (coral/corail) vi, **556a** – VI, **541a**
Mardjanī i, 1307 – I, 1347b
Mardjumak Aḥmad → Merdjümek, Aḥmed b. Ilyās
Mardūd iii, 26b – III, 28a
Marea → Māryā
Mār Ghāt (Margat) → al-Marḳab
Mār Kābān (Marckapan) → al-Marḳab
Mār Kābūs (Markappos) → al-Marḳab
Marghelān → Marghīnān
Marghīnān (Marghelān) ii, 792a; v, 29a, b; vi, **557a** – II, 811a; V, 30a; VI, **542a**
al-Marghīnānī, ʿAbd al-ʿAzīz b. ʿAbd al-Razzāk (1084) vi, **558b** – VI, **543a**
al-Marghīnānī, Abu ʾl-Fatḥ Zayn al-Dīn vi, **558b** – VI, **543a**
al-Marghīnānī, Abu ʾl-Ḥasan Naṣr b. al-Ḥasan viii, 383b – VIII, 396b
al-Marghīnānī, Abu ʾl-Ḥasan Ẓahīr al-Dīn (1112) vi, 558b – VI, 543a
al-Marghīnānī, Bahāʾ al-Dīn ii, 3b – II, 3b
al-Marghīnānī, Burhān al-Dīn Abu ʾl-Ḥasan (1197) iii, 163b; vi, **557b**, 558b; ix, 36a – III, 167a; VI, **542b**, 543a; IX, 36b
al-Marghīnānī, al-Ḥasan b. ʿAlī vi, 558a – VI, 542b
al-Marghīnānī, ʿImād al-Dīn al-Farghānī vi, 558b – VI, 543a
al-Marghīnānī, Muḥammad Abu ʾl-Fatḥ Djalāl al-Dīn al-Farghānī → al-Marghīnānī, ʿImād al-Dīn al-Farghānī
al-Marghīnānī, ʿUmar Niẓām al-Dīn al-Farghānī vi, **558b** – VI, **543a**
al-Marghīnānī, Ẓahīr al-Dīn al-Ḥasan (XII) vi, 558b – VI, 543a
Marḥala vi, **558b** – VI, **543b**
Mari → Čeremiss(es)
Mari → Ḳayyim
al-Marʿī iii, 954b – III, 979a
Mārī Hills s, 331b – S, 331b
Mārī Ilyās Ziyāda → Mayy Ziyāda
Mārī Jāta (Sunjata, Mali) vi, 421b – VI, 406b
Mariamites vi, 629b – VI, 614b
Mārib (Maʾrib) i, 102b, 549a, 890b; ii, 785a, 1060b; iii, 223a; v, 811a; vi, 474b, **559a**; viii, 663a; s, 336b, 337a – I, 105b, 566a, 916b, II, 804a, 1085b; III, 230a; V, 817a; VI, 460a, **543b**; VIII, 682bS, 336b
Mārida (Mérida) i, 493a, 1319b; ii, 1009a; iii, 74a, 288a, 498b, 499b; vi, **567b** – I, 508a, 1360a; II, 1032b; III, 67b, 296b, 515b, 516b; VI, **552b**
al-Māridānī, ʿAlī iii, 818a – III, 841b
Māridīn → Mārdīn
al-Māridīnī, Sibṭ iii, 1141a – III, 1169b
Maʿrifa ii, 358a; iii, 262a, 1133a; iv, 847a; vi, **568b** – II, 368a; III, 269b, 1161b; IV, 880a; VI, **553b**
al-Mārighnī, Abū ʿAmr ʿUthmān b. Khalīfa (XII) viii, 113a – VIII, 115a
Mārīkala vi, 780b – VI, 770a
Marīnā x, 79b – X, 82b
Marindja → Bahčekent
Marīnid(e)s (Banū Marīn) i, 92b, 93a, 122b, 124b, 129b, 155a, 167b, 290b, 367b, 445b, 495b, 1148b, 1176b, 1346b; ii, 146a, 353a, 819a, 822a, 979a, 1095b; iii, 49a, 68a, 386b, 462a, 825b; iv, 116b, 338a, 633b; v, 531a, 626b, 1128a, 1150a, 1190a, 1208a; vi, 134a, b, 142a, 222b, 281a, 293a, 310b, 404a, 440b, 441a, **571a**, 593a, 741b, 742b, 743a; vii, 37a, 613b, 803a, 1021b, 1022a, b; ix, 545b; s, 45b, 103a, 112a, 113b, 318a, 336b – I, 95a, b, 126a, 128a, 133b, 159a, 172b, 299b, 378a, 458a, 510b, 1183a, 1211b, 1387a; II, 150a, 362b, 838b, 841b, 1001b, 1121b; III, 51a, 70b, 399a, 478a, 849b; IV, 121b, 352b, 659b; V, 535a, 630b, 1124a, 1140b, 1180a, 1198b; VI, 132b, 133a, 140a, b, 216b, 266a, 278b, 295b, 388b, 426a, b, **556a**, 577b, 730b, 732a; VII, 37a, 613b, 805a, 1023b, 1024a, b; IX, 567a; S, 46a, 102b, 111b, 113a, 317b, 336a
al-Marīs (Nobatia) vi, **574b**; viii, 88b, 89b – VI, **559b**; VIII, 91a, b
al-Marīsī → Bishr b. Ghiyāth
al-Marīsiyya i, 1242a – I, 1279b
Māristān → Bīmāristān
Maritsa → Merič
Māriya (the Copt/la Copte) (637) iii, 64a; vi, **575a**, 650b; vii, 372a, 396b – III, 66b; VI, **560a**, 636a; VII, 373b, 397b
Mariya ulfa (XX) x, 77a – X, 77a
al-Mariyya (Almería) i, 32a, 489a, 864b; iii, 135a, 498b, 712b; v, 219a; vi, 344b, **575b**; vii, 70a; s, 383a – I, 33a, 504a, 888b; III, 137b, 515b, 734b; V, 216b; VI, 329a, **560b**; VII, 71a; S, 383b
Māriya bint al-Ḥārith b. Djulhum umm al-Aswad (Lakhmid(e)) (VI) vii, 568b – VII, 569b
Mariyyat Badjdjāna → al-Mariyya (Almería)
Māriz s, 129a – S, 128a
Marka vi, 258b – VI, 243a
al-Marḳab (Margat) i, 118b, 1016b; iv, 485a; vi, 345b, **577a** – I, 122a, 1048a; IV, 506a; VI, 329b, **562a**
Marḳab (observatory/observatoire) → Marṣad
Markha, Wādī iv, 747a – IV, 777a
Markhassa i, 640b – I, 661a
Mārk(i)siyya (Marxism(e)) vi, **583a** – VI, **568a**
Markwīz s, 80a – S, 80a
Marmara Deñīzī i, 463a; vi, **587a** – I, 476b; VI, **572a**
al-Marmarāwī, Aḥmad Shams al-Dīn b. ʿĪsā (1504) iv, 992a, b – IV, 1024b, 1025a
Marmoucha s, 145a – S, 144b
Marnīsa, Banū vi, 1009a – VI, 1001b
Maroc → al-Maghrib, al-Mamlaka al-Maghribiyya
Maronites i, 1280b, 1281a; ii, 65b, 467b, 637a, 750a,

795a; iii, 523a; iv, 255a; v, 791a, b, 792a; s, 268b, 269a – I, 1320a; II, 67a, 479b, 653a, 768a, 814a; III, 541a; IV, 266a; V, 797a, b, 798a; S, 268b
Marrakesh/Marrakech → Marrākush
Marrākush i, 79a, 251a, 289a; ii, 818b, 819a, b, 1116b; iii, 148b, 462a, 501a, 675a, 975a; iv, 533a; v, 654a, b, 1186b, 1208a; vi, 38b, 124a, 142b, 187a, 250a, 293b, 339b, 340a, 350a, 351a, 364a, 406a, 521a, 571b, 573a, 572b, **588b**, 742b; vii, 391a; ix, 47a; s, 29a, 48a, 103a, 114a, 124b, 389a, 397b, 401b – I, 81a, 258b, 298a; II, 838a, b, 839a, 1142b; III, 152a, 478a, 518a, 697a, 999b; IV, 556a; V, 658b, 1176b, 1198b; VI, 37a, 122a, 141a, 170b, 234b, 278b, 324a, 334b, 335a, 348a, 390b, 505b, 556b, 557b, 558a, **573b**, 732a; VII, 392a; IX, 47b; S, 29a, 48b, 102b, 113b, 382b, 389b, 398a, 402a
—Djāmiʿ al-Kutubiyyīn → Masdjud al-Kutubiyya
—lit(t)erature i, 1224b; iii, 806b – I, 1261a; III, 829b
—monuments i, 56a, 58b, 85a, 161b, 289a, 459a, 499b, 1320b, 1346b, 1347a; v, 1153b; vii, 391a – I, 57b, 60a, 87b, 166a, 298a, 472a, 514b, 1361a, 1357a, b; V, 1143b; VII, 392a
al-Marrākushī → ʿAbd al-Wāḥid; al-Ḥasan b. ʿAlī ʿUmar; Ibn ʿAbd al-Malik; Ibn al-Bannāʾ
al-Marrrākushī, Abū ʿAlī al-Ḥasan b, ʿAlī (1280) i, 727a; ii, 586b; v, 1209b; vi, **598a**; vii, 201b, 210b; viii, 575a; s, 413b – I, 749a; II, 601a; V, 1200a; VI, **582b**; VII, 202a, 211b; VIII, 593b; S, 414a
Marrāsh, ʿAbd Allāh (XIX) vi, 598b – VI, 583b
Marrāsh, Fatḥ Allāh (XIX) vi, 598b – VI, 583b
Marrāsh, Fransīs b. Fatḥ Allāh (1874) iii, 591b; vi, **598b** – III, 612a; VI, **583a**
Marrāsh, Maryāna vi, 598b, 599a – VI, 583b, 584a
Marrīs s, 332a – S, 331b
Mars (planet/-ère) → al-Mirrīkh
Marsā → Mīnāʾ
Marsā ʿAlī → Ṣikilliyya
Marsā ʾl-Kharaz vi, 556b – VI, 541a
Marsā Mūsā s, 125a – S, 124a
Marsā Zafran → Maghmadās
Marṣad (observatory/observatoire) i, 1141a; iv, 702b; vi, **599b** – I, 1175b; IV, 731a; V, 354b; VI, **584a**
Marṣafā vi, 602a – VI, 587a
al-Marṣafī, al-Ḥusayn (1890) iii, 593b; iv, 1098a; vi, **602a** – III, 614a; IV, 1129a; VI, **587a**
Marsūm ii, 303a, b, – II, 311a, b
Martapura s, 151a – S, 151a
Martel, Charles i, 86b, 493a, 988b – I, 89a, 508a, 1019a
Marthiya i, 508b, 584b; ii, 73a; iv, 1027a; v, 611b, 635b, 1033b; vi, **602b** – I, 524a, 603a; II, 74b; IV, 1059a; V, 615a, 639b, 1029b; VI, **587b**
Martolos i, 1164a; vi, **613a**; viii, 609a – I, 1198b; VI, **598a**; VIII, 628b
Marūčak → Marw-i Kūčik
Maʿrūf → Ilāhī Bakhsh
Maʿrūf, Banū i, 1096a – I, 1129a
Maʿrūf al-Karkhī, Abū Maḥfūẓ b. Fīrūz (815) iv, 653a; vi, 354a, **613b**, 614a; vii, 647a, 871a – IV, 679b; VI, 338b, **598b**, 599a; VII, 647a, 872b
Maʿrūf al-Ruṣāfī (1945) i, 597b; iii, 1264b; vi, **614a**; ix, 230a – I, 617a; III, 1297b; VI, **599a**; IX, 235b
Mārūn s, 269a – S, 268b
Mārūn, Yūḥannā v, 791a – V, 797b
Mārūn al-Nakkāsh → al-Nakkāsh
Mārūt → Hārūt wa-Mārūt
Marw al-Rūdh vi, 334a, **617b**, 627b – VI, 318b, **602b**, 612a
al-Marw al-Rūdī → Ḥusayn b. ʿAlī; Ḥusayn b. Muḥammad
Marw al-Shāhidjān (Marw) i, 16a, 18a, 47b, 750a, 1007a, 1067a, 1293b, 1294a; ii, 4b, 43b; iv, 131b; v, 56b, 58b, 293a, 554b, 868b; vi, 199b, 205b, 331b, 332b, 333b, 334b, 335b, 337b, 419a, 427b, 493b, 600a, 617b, **618a**, 627b, 628a, 633b, 656a; s, 89a, 195a, 240a, 281a, 326a, 357a – I, 16b, 19a, 49a, 772b, 1038a, 1099a, 1333a, b; II, 4b, 44a; IV, 137a; V, 58b, 60b, 293a, 559b, 874b; VI, 183b, 190a, 316a, 317a, 318a, 319a, b, 321b, 404a, 413a, 479b, 585b, 602b, **603a**, 612b, 613a, 618b, 641b; S, 88b, 195a, 240a, 281a, 325b, 356b
al-Marwa → al-Ṣafā
Marwān I b. al-Ḥakam b. Abi ʾl-ʿĀṣ (Umayyad(e)) (684) i, 453b, 1242b; ii, 89b, 360b, 415b, 416a, 726a; iii, 65a, 227a, 242b, 270b, 607b, 620b, 932a; iv, 493a, 929b, 938b; v, 74b, 451a; vi, 544b, 545a, 546b, **621b**, 623a, 625a, 626a, 641a, 653b, 659a, 661b, 671b; vii, 269a; s, 10a, 52b, 230b – I, 466b, 1280a; II, 91a, 370a, 426b, 744b; III, 67b, 233b, 249b, 278b, 628b, 641a, 956b; IV, 514a, 962b, 971b; V, 76b, 453b; VI, 529b, 531a, **606b**, 608a, 610a, 611a, 626a, 639a, 645a, 647b, 657a; VII, 270b; S, 9b, 53a, 230b
Marwān II b. Muḥammad b. Marwān b. al-Ḥakam (Umayyad(e)) (750) i, 43a, 53b, 57b, 65b, 100b, 103a, 108b, 354a, 660b, 787b, 835b, 837a, 1244a, 1343b; ii, 130a, 505a, 523b, 958a; iii, 29a, 228a, 229b, 398a, 493b, 651b, 802b, 990b; iv, 344a, b, 370b, 447b, 1174a; vi, 147b, 506a, **623a**, 626a, 641b, 656a; vii, 497b, 910b; x, 844b – I, 44a, 55a, 59b, 67b, 103b, 106a, 111b, 365a, 681a, 811a, 858b, 860b, 1282a, 1383b; II, 133a, 518a, 536b, 980b; III, 30b, 234b, 236b, 410a, 510b, 673a, 826a, 1015a; IV, 358b, 387a, 467a, 1207a; VI, 146a, 491a, **608a**, 611a, 627a, 641b; VII, 497b, 911a; X,
Marwān (miller/meunier) (X) vi, 626a – VI, 611a
Marwān, ḳāḍī vi, 670b – VI, 657a
Marwān b. ʿĀbid al-Mutaʿāl (1911) vi, 627a – VI, 612a
Marwān b. Ḥafsa (VIII) ix, 665b – IX, 691b
Marwān b. al-Ḥakam → Marwān I
Marwān b. al-Haytham al-Sulaymī ii, 234a – II, 241a
Marwān b. Muḥammad → Marwān II
Marwān b. Yazīd b. al-Muhallab (VIII) vii, 359b; s, 41a – VII, 362a; S, 41a
Marwān al-Akbar b. Abī Ḥafṣa (797) ii, 248b; iii, 1202b; vi, 345a, 437b, **625a** – II, 255b; III, 1233a; VI, 329b, 423a, **610a**
Marwān al-Aṣghar b. Abi ʾl-Djanūb vi, **625a** – VI, **610a**
Marwān al-Khalfāwī (1329) vi, 627a – VI, 612a
Marwānid(e)s (Diyār Bakr) i, 13a, 81b, 82b, 95b, 118a, 493b, 1206b; ii, 344a; iii, 676b; iv, 27b; v, 453a; vi, 270b, 274b, 540b, **626a**, 930a; viii, 70b; s, 103b – I, 13a, 84a, 84b, 98b, 121b, 508b, 1242b; II, 353b; III, 698a; IV, 29b; V, 455b; VI, 255b, 259b, **611a**, 922a; VIII, 72a; S, 103a
Marwānid(e)s (Umayyad(e)s) i, 13a, 118a; vi, **626a**; s, 103b – I, 13a, 121b; VI, **611a**; S, 103a
Marwānid(e)s (Umayyad(e)s, al-Andalus) i, 81b, 493b; iii, 676b – I, 84a, 508b; III, 698a
Marwāniyya vi, **627a** – VI, **612a**
Mārwāṙ → Djōdhpur
Marwārīdī (XVI) vii, 473a – VII, 472b
al-Marwarrūdhī, al-Ḥusayn (1070) vii, 781a – VII, 783a
al-Marwarrūdhī, Khālid b. ʿAbd al-Malik (831) iv, 1182b; vi, 600a – IV, 1215b; VI, 584b
al-Marwazī → Abū Saʿīd; Abū Yaḥyā; Ḥabash al-Ḥāsib

al-Marwazī, Abu 'l-Abbās   iv, 55a – IV, 57b
al-Marwazī, Abū Bakr (888)   i, 274a, b, 1039a; iii, 159a; vi, **627b** – I, 282b, 283a, 1070b; III, 162b; VI, **612a**
al-Marwazī, Abu 'l-Faḍl (XI)   vi, **627b** – VI, **612b**
al-Marwazī, Abū Isḥāḳ (951) ix, 187b – IX, 198a
al-Marwazī, Abu 'l-Ḳāsim al-Fūrānī (1079)   vii, 781a – VII, 783a
al-Marwazī, Abū Ṭālib ʿAzīz al-Dīn (XIII)   vi, **627b** – VI, **612b**
al-Marwazī, Aḥmad b. ʿAlī (905)   vii, 706b – VII, 707a
al-Marwazī, Aḥmad b. Bis̲h̲r (973)   vii, 538a – VII, 538a
al-Marwazī, G̲h̲assān b. Muḥammad (849)   vii, 5a – VII, 5a
al-Marwazī, Ibrāhīm b. Aḥmad (951)   vii, 538a – VII, 538a
al-Marwazī, S̲h̲araf al-Dīn Masʿūdī (XIII)   viii, 542a VIII, 560a
al-Marwazī, S̲h̲araf al-Zamān Ṭāhir (1120)   v, 385b, 1011a, b; vi, **628a** – V, 386b, 1006b, 1007a; VI, **613a**
Marw-i Kūčik   vi, 617b; s, 281a – VI, 602b; S, 281a
Mary   → Maryam
Mārya (Marea)   vi, **628a** – VI, **613a**
Maryab   vi, 565a – VI, 550a
Maryam (Mary/Marie)   ii, 848a; iii, 1175a, 1206a; iv, 81b, 82a; v, 90a; vi, **628b** – II, 868a; III, 1204a, 1236b; IV, 85b, 86a; V, 92b; VI, **613b**
Maryam Begum (XVIII)   vi, 483b – VI, 469b
Maryam K̲h̲ānum (XIX)   vi, 484a – VI, 470a
Maryam Umīd Muzayyin al-Sulṭān (XX)   vi, 486a – VI, 472a
Marzbān (Ṭamis̲h̲a)   v, 661b; s, 298a – V, 667a; S, 297b
Marzbān b. S̲h̲arwīn (X)   vi, 632a, b – VI, 617a, b
Marz(u)bān-nāma   iv, 63b, 506b; v, 1028a; vi, **632a** – IV, 67a; 528a; V, 1024a; VI, **617a**
Marzpān (Marzubān)   vi, **633a** – VI, **618a**
Marzubān (Daylamī) (X)   vi, 499b – VI, 484b
Marzubān b. Bak̲h̲tiyār   → Ṣamṣam al-Dawla (Būyid(e))
Marzubān b. Dj̲ustān   ii, 191a – II, 197a
Marzubān I b. Muḥammad (Musāfirid(e)) (957)   i, 190a, 660b, 1041b; ii, 680a; iii, 703b; iv, 345b, 346a, 662b; v, 452a; vii, 655b; viii, 998b – I, 194b, 681b, 1073a; II, 697a; III, 725b; IV, 360b, 689b; V, 454b; VII, 655b; VIII, 1033b
Marzubān b. Rustam b. S̲h̲ahriyār   iii, 372b; iv, 506a; v, 1028a – III, 384b; IV, 528a; V, 1024a
al-Marzubān b. Rustam b. S̲h̲arwīn   → Marzbān b. S̲h̲arwīn
Marzubān b. Wahriz (Yemen) (VI)   vi, 633b – VI, 618b
al-Marzubānī, Abū ʿUbayd Allāh al-Bag̲h̲dādī (994)   i, 154b, 758b; iii, 879a; vi, **634a**, 709b; vii, 312a; viii, 14a; s, 24b, 33a, 400b – I, 158b, 781b; III, 903a; VI, **619a**, 698a; VII, 314b; VIII, 14a; S, 25a, 33a, 401a
Marzban (Marzubān)-nāma   iv, 63b, 506b; v, 1028a; vi, **632a** – IV, 67a; 528a; V, 1024a; VI, **617a**
Marzūḳ b. Maẓlūm   ii, 234b – II, 241a
al-Marzūḳī, Abū ʿAlī Aḥmad b. Muḥammad (1030)   i, 154a; vi, **635b**; vii, 307a – I, 158b; VI, **620b**; VII, 309b
al-Masʿā   vi, 165b, 167a – VI, 158a, 159a
Maṣāff   iii, 156b – III, 191a
Maṣāffiyya   ii, 1080b; iii, 45b – II, 1105b; III, 47b

Masāḥa   iv, 1037b, 1038a – IV, 1069a, b
Masāʾil wa-adj̲wiba   i, 274a, 320a; vi, **636a** – I, 282b, 330a; VI, **621a**
Masākira   s, 356a – S, 356a
al-Masʾala al-minbariyya   i, 765a – I, 787b
al-Masʾala al-Suraydj̲iyya   iii, 949b – III, 974a
Masāliḥ   i, 761a – I, 784a
al-Masālik wa 'l-Mamālik   i, 488a; vi, **639b** – I, 502b; VI, **624b**
Masāmiʿa, Āl   vi, **640b** – VI, **625b**
Maṣāmida   → Masmūda, Banū
Masardj̲asān   vi, 620a – VI, 605a
Māsardj̲awayh (Māsardj̲īs)   vi, **640b**; s, 52b – VI, **626a**; S, 53a
Māsarm   vi, 384a – VI, 368a
al-Masāwī   → al Maḥāsin wa 'l-Masāwī
Maṣawwaʿ   i, 932a, 976a; ii, 91a; iv, 687a; vi, **641b**; viii, 184a, 235b – I, 1006b; II, 92b; IV, 715a; VI, **626b**; 186b, 241a
Mascara (Algeria/-ie)   → al-Muʿaskar
Mascate   → Maskaṭ
Masculin(e)   (in grammar/en grammaire)   → Mud̲h̲akkar
Masd̲j̲id (mosque/-ée))   i, 497-500, 608-624, 830a, 1200b; ii, 777b; iii, 1124a; iv, 229b; v, 366a, 1123b, 1124a, b; vi, **644b** – I, 512-516, 628-645, 853a, 1236a; II, 796a; III, 1152a; IV, 240a; V, 367a, 1120a, b, 1121a; VI, **629b**

Masd̲j̲id/ Masd̲j̲id-i (A)

Abarḳūh (1415)   vi, 685a – VI, 672b
al-ʿAbbās (Yemen) (XIII)   vi, 683b – VI, 670b, 671a
ʿAbdallāhābād (K̲h̲urāsān) (XII)   vi, 684b – VI, 671b
Abī Bakr (Mecca)   vi, 651a – VI, 636a
Abī Dulaf (Sāmarrāʾ)   vi, 364b, 365a; vii, 9a – VI, 348b, 349a; VII, 9b
Abī Hurayra (al-Madīna, Dj̲īza, al-Ramla, Yubnā)   vi, 652a, b – VI, 637b, 638a
ʿAdī b. Ḥātim   vi, 653a – VI, 638b
Ādīna (Ḥaḍrat Pānd̲ū̲a) (1374)   vi, 693b; vii, 79a; ix, 575b – VI, 681a; VII, 80b; IX, 598a
Ādīna (Sabzawār) (879)   vii, 76b – VII, 77b
Afḍal K̲h̲ān (Bidj̲āpur) (1653)   vi, 689b, 696a – VI, 677b, 684a
Afḍal K̲h̲ān (Gulbargā)   vi, 698b – VI, 687a
Afyon (1273)   vi, 682b – VI, 669b
Ag̲h̲māt (704)   vi, 743b – VI, 733a
Aḥmad S̲h̲āh (Aḥmadābād) (1414)   vii, 79b – VII, 80b
Aḥmad Yasawī (Turkestan) (1394)   vi, 685a –VI, 672b
al-Aḥmadī (Ṭanṭā)   x, 189a – X, 204b
Aḥmed G̲h̲āzī (Mīlās) (1378)   vii, 56a – VII, 56b
Aḥmed Pas̲h̲a (Istanbul) (1562)   vi, 687a – VI, 674b
ʿĀʾis̲h̲a (Mecca)   vi, 650b – VI, 636a
Akbae (Adj̲mēr) (1570)   viii, 315b – VIII, 326a
Āḳbug̲h̲awiyya (Cairo/le Caire)   vi, 672b – VI, 659a
Ak̲h̲ī Elvān (Ankara) (1382)   vi, 683a; vii, 78b – VI, 670a; VII, 79b
ʿAkk (ʿAkka)   vi, 652b – VI, 638a
al-Aḳmar (Cairo/le Caire) (1125)   vi, 657a, 667b, 683a; vii, 150b, 504a; viii, 314b – VI, 642b, 654a, 670a; VII, 152b, 504a; VIII, 324b
al-Aḳṣā (Jerusalem) (VII)   i, 3a, 201a, 610a, 618b; ii, 263a, 911a; iv, 367b, 1169b; v, 298a, 299a, 323b, 325a, 340b, 342b, 343a; vi, 31b, 362a, 655a, 657a, 659b, 662a, 677b, 680a, **707a**; s, 205a –

I, 3a, 206b, 630b, 637b; II, 271a, 932b; IV, 383b, 1202a; V, 297b, 298b, 322, 324b, 341a, b, 343b, 344a; VI, 30a, 346a, 640b, 643a, 645a, 648a, 664a, 666b, 667a, **695b**; S, 204b
al-Aḳṣā (Ḳudus, Java) vi, 708a – VI, 696b
Āḳsarāy (Shahr-i Sabz) (1396) viii, 315b – VIII, 325b
Āḳsunḳur (Miṣr) (1412) vi, 654a, 667b; vii, 78b – VI, 639b, 653b; VII, 79b
ʿAlāʾ al-Dīn (Bursa) (1335) vi, 686a – VI, 673b
ʿAlāʾ al-Dīn (Ḳonya) (1135) vi, 366a, 682b, 683a; vii, 78a – VI, 350a, 669b, 670a; VII, 79a
ʿAlāʾ al-Dīn (Niğde) (1223) vi, 682b, 686a; vii, 13a, 79a; viii, 15b – VI, 669b, 673b; VII, 14a, 80a; VIII, 15b
Aladja ʿImāret (Selānīk) (1486) ix, 124a – IX, 128b
Alaeddin (Ankara) (1197) vii, 78b – VII, 79b
ʿAlī → al-Nadjaf
ʿAlī (Iṣfahān) (1522) vi, 685b; viii, 787b – VI, 673a; VIII, 814a
ʿAlī (Ḳuhrūd) vii, 13a – VII, 14a
ʿAlī b. Yūsuf (Marrākush) vi, 590b, 597a – VI, 575b, 581b
ʿAlī Barīd (Bīdar) (1576) vi, 695b – VI, 683b
ʿAlī Ḳulī Agha (Iṣfahān) vi, 686a – VI, 673a
ʿAlī Shāh (Tabrīz) (1310) vi, 685a; viii, 315b – VI, 672a; VIII, 325b
ʿAlī Shahīd Pīr (Bīdjāpūr) vi, 696a – VI, 684a
Alif Khān (Dhōlkā) iii, 445a – III, 460a
ʿAmādiyya (1153) vii, 77b – VII, 78b
al-ʿAmr (al-Fusṭāṭ) (641) vi, 193b, 362a, 363a, 653b, 654a, 656b, 657a, b, 658b, 659a, 660b, 661b, 662a, 663a, b, 664a, b, 665b, 666a, 667b, 668a, 670a, b, 671a, 672b, 673a, b, 674a, 675a, 679a, 740b; vii, 8b, 159a –
VI, 177b, 346a, 347a, 639a, b, 642a, b, 643a, 644a, 645a, 646b, 647b, 648a, 649a, b, 650a, b, 651b, 652a, 653b, 654b, 656b, 657b, 658b, 659b, 660a, b, 661b, 666a, 730a: VII, 8b, 160b
ʿAmr (Ḳūs) (1155) vii, 77b – VII, 78b
Anḍā (Bīdjāpur) vi, 689b, 696a – VI, 677b, 684a
Arbaʿ Rukūn (Maḳdishū) (1268) vi, 128b, 370a – VI, 126b, 354a
Ardabīl vi, 684b – VI, 671b
Ardahāl vii, 19a – VII, 19a
Aŕhāʾī-Dinkā Djhōńpŕā (Adjmēr (1236) vi, 691b; vii, 13b; viii, 267a, 315b – VI, 679a; VII, 14b; VIII, 274b, 325b
Aŕhāʾī Kangūra (Kāshī, Benares) vi, 689b, 694a; vii, 79b – VI, 677a, 681b; VII, 80b
al-Arḳam b. al-Arḳam (Mecca) vi, 168a – VI, 159b
Arslānhane Cami (Ankara) (1290) vii, 13b – VII, 14a
al-Ashʿath vi, 653a – VI, 638b
Ashrafiyya (Taʿizz) (XIV) vi, 683b; x, 118a – VI, 671a; X, 127b
Ashtardjān (1315) vi, 684b, 685a – VI, 672a
al-ʿAskar (Cairo/le Caire) (785) vi, 662a, 668a – VI, 648a, 654b
al-ʿAssālī (Damas(cus)) (XVII) s, 49b – S, 50a
Atabegī (naw) (Shīrāz) (XIII) viii, 701b – VIII, 721b
Aŧalā (Djawnpur) (1376) vi, 689a, 693b, 697a; viii, 315b – VI, 676b, 681b, 685a; VIII, 326a
ʿAtīḳ Djāmiʿ (Prizren) viii, 338a – VIII, 340b
ʿAtīḳ Djāmiʿ (Tarabzun) (1461) viii, 338a; x. 217a – VIII, 349b; X, 234b
Ayazma Djāmiʿi (Üsküdar/Scutari) (1758) vii, 709b;x, 924a – VII, 710b; X,
al-ʿĀyin (1240) i, 780b – I, 804a
Ayodhya (1528) vii, 329a – VII, 330b
al-Azhar (Cairo/le Caire) (1085) vi, 654a, 662a, b, 663b, 665a, b, 667b, 668a, 671b, 672b, 673a, b, 677b, 679b, 680a, b; vii, 10b, 150a –
VI, 639b, 648a, b, 649b, 651a, b, 653b, 654b, 658a, 659a, 660a, 664a, b, 666b, 667a, b; VII, 11a, 152a
Azirān (1325) vi, 685a – VI, 672a

Masdjid (B)

Bāb Aylān (Marrākush) vi, 590b – VI, 575b
Bāb Dukkāla (Marrākush) vi, 590b, 597a; viii, 725a – VI, 575b, 582a; VIII, 745b
Bādal Maḥall Darwāza (Čandērī) vi, 695b – VI, 683b
Badjistān (XV) vi, 685a – VI, 672b
al-Badriyya (Jerusalem) vi, 672b – VI, 659a
Bādshāhī (Lāhawr) (1673) vi, 369b, 698a; vii, 333b – VI, 354a, 686a; VII, 335b
al-Baghla (al-Madina) vi, 650b – VI, 636a
Baʿlabakk (XII) vi, 679b, 680a – VI, 666b, 667a
Balkh (X) vi, 680a – VI, 667a
Banābashî (Sofya) ix, 705b – IX, 734a
Baŕā Gumbad (Delhi) vii, 79a – VII, 80a
Baŕā Sōnā (Gawŕ) (1526) vi, 693b – VI, 681b
al-Barātha (Kalwādhā) (940) vi, 656b – VI, 642a
Baŕī (Čhōŧā Panḍuʾā) (XIV) vi, 368b; vii, 79a – VI, 352b; VII, 80b
Barḳūḳ (Cairo/le Caire) (1410) vii, 78b – VII, 79b
Barūdjird (Burūdjird) vi, 365a – VI, 349a
Bashan (X) vi, 684b – VI, 671b
Basṭām vi, 684b – VI, 672a
al-Bayʿa (al-Madina) vi, 650b – VI, 636a
Bayraḳlî (Prizren) (1573) viii, 339a – VIII, 350b
Bāyazīd II (Amasya) (1486) vii, 79a; ix, 629b – VII, 80a; IX, 653b
Bāyazīd II (Istanbul) (1506) vi, 687a – VI, 674b
Baybars (Cairo/le Caire) (1269) vi, 683a; viii, 315a – VI, 670b; VIII, 325a
Bēgam Shāhī → Masdjid Maryam Zamānī
Begampur (Delhi) (1325) vi, 692a, 693b; viii, 315b – VI, 679b, 681b; VIII, 325b
Berrīma (Marrākush) vi, 590b – VI, 575b
Beyşehir (1296) vi, 682b – VI, 669b
Bhadreshwar (Gudjarāt) (X) vi, 689a, 691a – VI, 676b, 678b
Bharoč (XIV) vi, 692a – VI, 679b
Bībī Khānum (Samarḳand) (1399) vi, 685a, b – VI, 672b, 673a
Bībī Kī (Burhānpur) vi, 695a – VI, 683a
Bilāl (Mecca) vi, 651a – VI, 636a
Birrābād vi, 684b – VI, 671b
Bīshāpūr vi, 683b – VI, 671a
Blād al-Ḥaḍar (Tozeur) vii, 12a – VII, 12b
Bū Fatātā (Susa) (838) vii, 11a – VII, 11b
Bū ʿInāniyya (Maghrib) vi, 663a – VI, 649a
Bukhārā vi, 684a – VI, 671a
Büyük (Sofya) (XV) ix, 704b – IX, 733a

Masdjid (Č)

Čamkatta (Gawŕ) (1475) vi, 693b – VI, 681a
Čār Sutūn (Tirmidh) (XI) vi, 684b – VI, 671b
Careva Dzamiya (Sarajevo) (1566) ix, 30a – IX, 30a
Čashum vi, 686a – VI, 673a
Čelebi Sulṭān Meḥemmed (Dimetoḳa) vi, 686b – VI, 674a
Čhōŧa Panḍuā vi, 693a – VI, 681a
Čhōŧa Sōnā (Gawr) (1493) vi, 693b – VI, 681b)

Čihil Sutūn (Ziyāratgāh) (1485) vi, 685a – VI, 672b
Čīnili (Üsküdar/Scutaru) (1640) x, 924a – X,

Masdjid (D)

Dābgīr (Ṭhaṭṭā) (1588) vi, 698b; ix, 638b – VI, 686b; IX, 662b
Dā'ī Angā (Lāhawr) (1635) vi, 697b, 698b – VI, 685b, 687a
Dakar vi, 705a – VI, 693b
Damrī (Aḥmadnagar) vi, 695b – VI, 683b
Dandānḳān (XI) vi, 684b – VI, 671b
Dār al-ʿIlm (Cairo/le Caire) vi, 671b – VI, 658a
Dashtī (1325) vi, 685a – VI, 672a
Dawlatābād (XIV) vi, 692a – VI, 679b
Dāwūd vi, 645a – VI, 630a
Defterdār Kapîsî (Istanbul) vi, 57a – VI, 55a
Dhamār (Yemen) (XIII) vi, 683b – VI, 671a
Dhibin (1250) vi, 683b – VI, 670b
Dhū Ashraḳ (1019) vi, 683b – VI, 671a
Dhu 'l-Kifl b. Ayyūb vi, 652b – VI, 638a
Dialmath (Senegal) vi, 705a – VI, 693b
al-Dibs s, 234b – S, 234b
Diggaron (Hazāra) vi, 684b – VI, 671b
Dilāwar Khān (Khed) vi, 695b – VI, 683b
Dilāwar Khān (Māndū) (1405) vi, 695a – VI, 682b
Divriği (1180) vi, 682b, 683a – VI, 669b, 670a
Diyārbakir (1091) vi, 682b – VI, 669b
Dizdār Naṣūḥ (Mostar) (XVI) vii, 244b – VII, 246a

Masdjid (Dj)

Djālōr (XIV) vi, 692a – VI, 679b
Djamāʿat Khāna (Delhi) (1325) vi, 691b; vii, 79a – VI, 679a; VII, 80a
Djamāl ʿAbd al-Nāṣir (Tripoli) (1970) x, 214b – X, 231b
Djamālī (Delhi) (1536) vi, 693a, 697a – VI, 680b, 685a
Djāmiʿ (Abyāna) (1077) vii, 77a – VII, 78a
Djāmiʿ (Āgrā) (1648) vi, 697b; vii, 80a, 333a; viii, 268b, 316a – VI, 685b; VII, 81a, 335a; VIII, 276a, 326b
Djāmiʿ (Aḥmadābād) (1423) vi, 694b; viii, 267b – VI, 682a; VIII, 274b
Djāmiʿ (Ardistān) (1158) vii, 12b; viii, 314b – VII, 13a; VIII, 324b
Djāmiʿ (Ashtardjān (1315) viii, 315a – VIII, 325b
Djāmiʿ (Badā'ūn) (1223) vi, 691b – VI, 679a
Djāmiʿ (al-Baṣra) → Masdjidī
Djāmiʿ (Benares) vii, 334a – VII, 335b
Djāmiʿ (Bīdar, – Solah Khamba) (1423) vi, 695b – VI, 683a, b
Djāmiʿ (Bīdjāpūr, – Ibrāhīm) (1550) vi, 696a – VI, 684
Djāmiʿ (Burhānpur) (1589) vi, 695a – VI, 683a
Djāmiʿ (Čāmpānēr) (1518) vi, 694b – VI, 682a
Djāmiʿ (Čandērī) vi, 695a; vii, 79b – VI, 683a; VII, 81a
Djāmiʿ (Delhi) vii, 80a, 452b; viii, 268a, 316a – VII, 81a, 454a; VIII, 276a, 326b
Djāmiʿ (Djawnpur) (1438) vi, 694a – VI, 681b
Djāmiʿ (Fahradj) (IX) vii, 12a – VII, 12b
Djāmiʿ (Fatḥpur Sikrī) (1574) vi, 690a, 697a; vii, 14a, 80a, 330b, 331a, 333b – VI, 677b, 685a; VII, 14b, 81a, 332a, b, 335a
Djāmiʿ (Fīrūzshāh Kōṭlā) (1354) vi, 692b – VI, 680a
Djāmiʿ (Gāwilgaṛh) (1488) vi, 695b – VI, 683b
Djāmiʿ (Golkonḍā) (1518) vi, 696a – VI, 684a
Djāmiʿ (Gulbargā) (1367) vi, 690a, 695a; vii, 80a VI, 677b, 683a; VII, 81a
Djāmiʿ (Harāt) vii, 78b; viii, 314b – VII, 80a; VIII, 324b
Djāmiʿ (Ḥaydarābād) (1597) vi, 696b – VI, 684b
Djāmiʿ (Irič) (1412) vi, 692b; vii, 79a – VI, 680a; VII, 80b
Djāmiʿ (Iṣfahān) (1314) vii, 12b; viii, 314b – VII, 13b; VIII, 324b
Djāmiʿ (Iṭāwā) vi, 694a; vii, 79b – VI, 682a; VII, 80b
Djāmiʿ (Khambāyat) (1325) vi, 692a – VI, 679b
Djāmiʿ (Khudābād) vi, 698b – VI, 686b
Djāmiʿ (Kirmān) (1550) vi, 698b; vii, 13a – VI, 686b; VII, 13b
Djāmiʿ (Lahore) (1673) viii, 316a – VIII, 326b
Djāmiʿ (Lamu) (1511) vii, 80a – VII, 81b
Djāmiʿ (Lāṭ-, Dhār) (1404) vii, 79b – VII, 81a
Djāmʿ (Mahdiyya) (920) viii, 314b – VIII, 324b
Djāmiʿ (Māndū) (1454) vi, 406b, 407a, b, 695a; vii, 79b – VI, 391b, 392a, 682b; VII, 81a
Djāmiʿ (Manṣūra, Sind) vi, 691a – VI, 678b
Djāmiʿ (Mathurā) (1660) vi, 839a; vii, 334a – VI, 829b; VII, 335b
Djāmiʿ al-Miḥyās s, 38a – S, 38a
Djāmiʿ (Mīraṭh) (1556) vii, 113a – VII, 115a
Djāmiʿ (Monastir, Tunisia/-e) (1000) vii, 228b – VII, 230b
Djāmiʿ (Muḥammadiyya) vii, 77a – VII, 78a
Djāmiʿ (Murādābād) (1632) vii, 601b – VII, 601a
Djāmiʿ (Nāyin/Na'in) (1311) vii, 12a, 78a; viii, 314a – VII, 13a, 78a; VIII, 324a
Djāmīʿ (Plewna) (XVI) viii, 318b – VIII, 329a
Djāmīʿ (al-Rāfiḳa/al-Raḳḳa) (VIII) viii, 411a – VIII, 425a
Djāmiʿ (Reza'iye/Riḍā'iyya) (1277) vii, 12b – VII, 13b
Djāmiʿ (Rhohankhed) (1582) vi, 695b – VI, 683b
Djāmīʿ (Samarḳand) (1403) viii, 315b, 1036b – VIII, 325b, 1072a
Djāmīʿ (Sāmarrā') (852) viii, 314a, 1039b – VIII, 324a, 1075b
Djāmiʿ (Shāhdjahānābād) (1656) vi, 689a; vii, 333a – VI, 676b; VII, 335a
Djāmiʿ (Shīrāz) (IX) vii, 12a – VII, 13a
Djāmiʿ (Shushtar) vii, 76b – VII, 77b
Djāmiʿ (Solah Khamba, Bīdar) (1423) vi, 695b – VI, 683a, b
Djāmiʿ (Srīrangapaṭṭana) vi, 369b – VI, 353b
Djāmiʿ (Sūsa) (851) ix, 901b – IX, 938a
Djāmiʿ (Suryān) vii, 78a – VII, 79a
Djāmi' (Thaffā) (1657) vii, 333a – VII, 335a
Djāmiʿ (Tūnis) i, 950a, 1228a – I, 979a, 1264b
Djāmiʿ (Ungwana, Kenya) (1500) vii, 80a – VII, 81b
Djāmīʿ (Warāmīn) (1326) viii, 314b – VIII, 325a
Djāmiʿ (Yazd) (1375) vii, 13a – VII, 13b
Djāmiʿ (Zawāra) (1156) vii, 12b; viii, 314b – VII, 13a; VIII, 324b
Djāmīʿ al-abyaḍ (al-Ramla(viii, 424a – VIII, 438a
Djāmiʿ Ibrāhīm (Bīdjāpūr) (1550) vi, 696a – VI, 684a
Djāmīʿ al-kabīr (al-Ramla) viii, 424a – VIII, 438a
Djāmīʿ al-Muẓaffar (Taʿizz) viii, 456b – VIII, 472a
Djāmiʿ al-Sulṭān (Rawḍa) (1481) viii, 464b – VIII, 480a
Djāmiʿ Yūsuf (Bīdjāpur) (1512) vi, 696a – VI, 683b, 684a

al-Djanad (Yemen) vi, 683b – VI, 670b
Djenne (Mali) vi, 705a – VI, 693b
Djibla (Yemen) (1087) vi, 683b – VI, 671a
al-Djilā' (Ṣan'ā') vi, 683b – VI, 670b
al-Djinn (m. al-Bay'a, m. al-Ḥaras) (Mecca) vi, 168b, 650b – VI, 159b, 636a
Djirdjis (Mosul) vi, 652a – VI, 637a
Djum'a (Iṣfahān) vi, 719b – VI, 708b
Djuyūshī (Cairo/le Caire) (1085) vii, 150b – VII, 152b
al-Dulāmiyya (Damas(cus)) vi, 672b – VI, 659a
Dunaysir (1204) vi, 682b, 683a – VI, 669b, 670a

Masdjid (E)

Ek Mīnār kī (Rāyčūr) (1513) vi, 695b – VI, 683b
Emīn Pasha (Prizren) (1831) viii, 339b – VIII, 351b
Erzurum (1135) vi, 682b – VI, 669b
Eşrefoğlu (Beyşehir) (1297) vii, 78a – VII, 79a
al-Faḍīkh (al-Madina) (625) vi, 650b – VI, 635b, 636a

Masdjid (F)

Fahradj (IX) vi, 679b – VI, 666b
Fakhr al-Dīn (Maḳdishū) vi, 704b – VI, 693a
Faryumad (XIII) vi, 684b – VI, 671b
al-Fatḥ (Medina) vi, 650b – VI, 636a
Fatḥpurī (Āgra) vi, 697b – VI, 685b
Fātiḥ (Istanbul) (1463) vi, 57a, 687a, b; viii, 842b – VI, 55a, 674b, 675a; VIII, 872a
Firdaws (1201) vi, 684b – VI, 671b
Fīrūzshāh (Turbat-i Djām) (1442) vi, 684b; viii, 315a – VI, 672a; VIII, 325b

Masdjid (G)

Gawhar Shād (Harāt) (1418) vi, 685a – VI, 672b
Gawhar Shād (Mashhad) (1418) vi, 685a – VI, 672a
Gaz (1315) vi, 685a – VI, 672a
al-Ghamurī (Cairo/le Caire) vi, 88a – VI, 86a
Ghāzī al-Dīn Khān (Delhi) vii, 334a – VII, 335b
Girgā viii, 865b – VIII, 896a
Gök (Amasya) (1266) vi, 686a – VI, 673b
Guédé (Senegal) vi, 705a – VI, 693b
Gulbarga vii, 458b – VII, 458b
Gulpāyagān (1116) vi, 684a – VI, 671b
Gunbād (Ziyāratgāh) (1483) vi, 685b – VI, 672b
Gunmant (Gawṛ) (1484) vi, 693b – VI, 681b

Masdjid (H)

al-Ḥadjdjādj b. Yūsuf al-Thaḳafī (Wāsiṭ) vii, 8b – VII, 9a
Ḥadjdjī Khātūn (Samsun) (1694) viii, 1053a – VIII, 1088b
Ḥafṣa Khatun (Selānīk) (1467) ix, 124a – IX, 118b
Hafshūya (XIV) vi, 684b – VI, 672a
al-Ḥākim (Cairo/le Caire) (991) vi, 656b, 663b, 667b, 670a, 671b, 679b, 680a, b; viii, 314b; x, 103b – VI, 642a, 649b, 653b, 656a, 658a, 666a, 667a, b; VIII, 324b; X, 111b
Ḥakim (Iṣfahān) (1656) vi, 686a; viii, 789a – VI, 673a; VIII, 815a
Halwar (Senegal) vi, 705a – VI, 693b
al-Ḥarām (Mecca) vi, 164b, 659b, 675a, **708a** – VI, 157b, 645a, 661b, **697a**
Ḥarrān vi, 679b, 680a – VI, 666b
Ḥasan (Rabat) (1195) vi, 682a – VI, 669a
Hilāl Khān Ḳāḍī (Dhōlkā) (1333) vi, 369a, 694a – VI, 353a, 682a
Hūd ('Akka, Damas(cus), Ḥaḍramawt) vi, 652b – VI, 638a
Hüdavendigār Cami (Bursa) vi, 366a – VI, 350a
al-Ḥuddān vi, 670b – VI, 656b
al-Ḥusayn → Karbalā'
Ḥusayniyya (Farīzhand) vii, 77a – VII, 78a
Hūshang (Māndū) vii, 79b – VII, 81a

Masdjid (I)

Ibb (Yemen) vi, 683b – VI, 671a
Ibn Ṣāliḥ (Marrākush) (1331) vi, 597a – VI, 582a
Ibn Ṭūlūn (Cairo/le Caire) (878) vi, 651a, 656b, 662a, b, 663a, b, 664b, 665a, 667a, 668a, 670a, 671b, 672b, 673a, 674b, 679b, 680a; vii, 10a, 510a – VI, 636b, 642a, 648a, b, 649a, b, 650a, b, 651a, 653a, b, 654b, 656b, 658a, 659a, b, 661a, 666b, 667a; VII, 10b, 510a
Ibn Yūsuf (Marrākush) vi, 38b, 590a, 591a, 594b, 597b – VI, 37a, 575a, b, 579a, 582a
Ibrāhīm (m. Bilāl, Mecca) vi, 168b, 651a – VI, 160a, 636a
Ibrāhīm (Munyat Ibn al-Khaṣīb) vi, 651a – VI, 636b
Ibrāhīm Rawḍa (Bīdjāpūr) (1626) vi, 696a – VI, 684a
al-Idjāba (Medina) vi, 650b – VI, 636a
Ikhlāṣ Khān (Bīdjāpūr) (1560) vi, 696a – VI, 684a
Ilyās Bey (Miletus/Milète) (1404) vi, 366a – VI, 350a
Imām (Iṣfahān) (1637) viii, 789a – VIII, 815b
Imām 'Alī al-Riḍā (Mashhad) (1215) vii, 13a, 78a – VII, 14a, 79a
Imām al-Hādī Yaḥyā (Ṣa'da) (X) vi, 683b – VI, 671a
Imām Ḥasan (Ardistān) (1158) vi, 684b; viii, 314b – VI, 672a; VIII, 324b
Imāmzāda Ismā'īl (Barz) vii, 77a – VII, 78a
'Imāret (Ankara) (1427) i, 511a – I, 526b
'Īsā Bey (Selcuk) (1374) vi, 366a, 683a – VI, 350a, 670a
Iṣfahān vi, 685a – VI, 672a, b
Ishbīliya (1175) vi, 682a – VI, 669a
Iṣṭakhr vi, 679b – VI, 666b
Istiḳlāl (Jakarta) vi, 700b – VI, 688b

Masdjid (K, Kh)

Kābulī Bāgh (1526) vi, 693a – VI, 680b
Kačpura (1530) vii, 329a – VII, 330b
Kadj (1325) vi, 685a – VI, 672a
Kafarbayya vi, 774b – VI, 764a
al-Kāfūrī vi, 661b – VI, 647b
Ḳā'it Bāy vi, 454a; s, 44a – VI, 439b; S, 44b
al-Ḳal'a (Cairo/le Caire) vi, 662a – VI, 648a
Kalān (1387) vi, 692b – VI, 680a
Kālī (Bīdar) (1694) vi, 695b – VI, 683b
al-Kallāsa (Damas(cus)) vi, 666b – VI, 653a
Kamāl Mawlā (Dhār) (1392) viii, 267b – VIII, 274b
al-Ḳamḥiyya (Cairo/le Caire) vi, 671b – VI, 658a
Kānpūr vii, 421b – VII, 423a
al-Ḳarāfa vi, 657b – VI, 643b
al-Ḳarakhāniyya (Samarḳand) (XI) vi, 679b – VI, 666b

al-Ḳarāsunḳuriyya (Cairo/le Caire) vi, 672b – VI, 659a
al-Ḳarawiyyīn (Fès) (859) ii, 821-3; iv, **632a**; v, 1152a, 1190a, 1208a; vi, 38b, 136a, 187a, 199b, 406a, 591a, 681b; vii, 504b, 587a; s, 126a, 303a – II, 840-2; IV, **657a**; V, 1142a, 1180a, 1198b; VI, 36b, 37a, 134b, 171a, 183b, 390b, 575b, 668b; VII, 504b, 587a; S, 125a, 302b
Karīm al-Dīn (Bīdjāpur) (1320) vi, 695b – VI, 683a
al-Ḳaṣaba (Tunis) (1232) vi, 457a – VI, 442b
al-Ḳaṣba (Marrākush) (1185) vi, 682a – VI, 669a
Kāshān (1462) vi, 685a – VI, 672b
Ḳāsīmiyye (Sekānīkī) (1492) ix, 124a – IX, 128b
Ḳayrawān (836) iv, 828b; vi, 679a, b, 680a, b; vii, 11a, 76a – IV, 861b; VI, 666a, b, 667a, b; VII, 11b, 77a
Kayseri (1140) vi, 682b – VI, 669b, 670a
Kemayoran (Surabaya) vi, 700b – VI, 688b
Khadīdja (Mecca) vi, 650b – VI, 636a
al-Khāḍir (Damas(cus)) vi, 652b – VI, 638a
Khʷādja Siyāh Pūsh (Sistān) vi, 691b – VI, 679a
Khān Muḥammad Mirdha (Ḍhākā) (1706) vi, 698a – VI, 686b
Khāṭirī (Cairo/le Caire) vii, 78b – VII, 79b
Khaybar (628) vi, 650b – VI, 635b
al-Khayf (Minā) (1467) vi, 168b, 650b, 654a; vii, 65a – VI, 160a, 636a, 639b; VII, 65b
Khayr al-Manāzil (Delhi) vi, 690a; vii, 330b, 331a – VI, 677b; VII, 332a, b
Khayr al-Manāzil (Māham Anaga) (1561) vi, 696b – VI, 684b
Khirkī (Delhi) vi, 690a, 692b; vii, 195a – VI, 677b, 680a; VII, 195b
Khishtī (Maḥmūdpūr) (1021) vi, 691a – VI, 678b
Khudāwendigār (Čekirge) (XIV) vii, 594a – VII, 593b
Khünkär (Üsküb) (1436) x, 922b – X,
Ḳila-yi Kuhna (Delhi) (1542) vii, 13b – VII, 14b
Kilwa vi, 704b – VI, 693a
Ḳîrḳ Ḳîz (Termez) vi, 691b – VI, 679b
Kisimkazi (Zanzibar) (1107) vi, 704a; vii, 80a – VI, 692b; VII, 81b
Kubbeli Djāmiʿ (Afyūn Ḳaraḥiṣār) (1341) viii, 831b – VIII, 860a
Kūča Mīr (Nāṭanz) (XII) vi, 684b – VI, 671b
Ku-ch'ie Lou Djāmiʿ (Ch'eng-t'u(ix, 919b – IX, 958a
Kuhna (Purāna Ḳilʿa. Delhi) (1535) vi, 693a; viii, 267b, 315b – VI, 681a; VIII, 274b, 326a
Kukli Meḥmed Bey (Prizren) (1538) viii, 338b – VIII, 350b
Ḳum(m) vi, 684b – VI, 672a
Ḳurtuba (787) vi, 679a, b, 680a, 682a – VI, 666a, b, 669a
Ḳurwa (Irān) vi, 684a – VI, 671a
Kuṭa Deḍé (Java) vi, 701a – VI, 689a
Ḳuṭb Shāhī (1585) vii, 79b – VII, 80b
al-Kutubiyya (Marrākush) (XII) i, 79a, 166a, 1226b; vi, 589b, 590b, 596a, 597a, 682a; vii, 11b, 504b – I, 81a, 170b, 1264a; VI, 574b, 575b, 580b, 581a, 582a, 669a; VII, 12b, 504b
Ḳuwwat al-Islām (Dihlī) (1199) ii, 256a; vi, 689a, b, 691a; viii, 315b – II, 263b; VI, 676b, 677a, 678b; VIII, 325b

Masdjid (L)

Lāl Darwāza (Djawnpur) (1447) vi, 62b, 694a – VI, 60b, 681b
Lālbāgh (Ḍhākā) (1678) vi, 698a – VI, 686b
Lāleli vii, 709b – VII, 710b
Langar kī (Gulbargā) (1435) vi, 695b – VI, 683b
Lāṭ (- Djāmiʿ) (Dhār) (1404) viii, 267b – VIII, 274b
Lattan (Gawṛ) (1475) vi, 693b – VI, 681a
Lindjān (XIV) vi, 684b – VI, 672a
Liyya (Ṭāʾif) (629) vi, 650b – VI, 635b
Lōdī (Khayrpur) (1494) vi, 692b, 693a; viii, 315b – VI, 680b; VIII, 326a

Masdjid (M)

Madrasa (Paṭnā) (1630) vi, 697b – VI, 685b
Magogoni (Dār es-Salaam) vii, 80b – VII, 81b
Magribija (Sarajevo) (XVI) ix, 31a – IX, 31a
Mahābat Khān (Peshāwar) viii, 300a – VIII, 309b
al-Mahdiyya (Tunisia/-e) (X) vi, 367a – VI, 351a
Maḥmūd Pasha (Prizren) (1821) viii, 339b – VIII, 351b
Makkā (Bīdjāpur) vi, 689b – VI, 677a
Makka (Ḥaydarābād) (1617) vi, 696b – VI, 684b
al-Maḳs (Cairo/le Caire) vi, 656b, 671b, 672b – VI, 642a, 658a, 659a
Malatya (1237) vi, 682b – VI, 669b
Malik ʿĀlam (Aḥmadābād) (1422) vi, 694b – VI, 682a
Malik Mughīth (Māndū) (1432) vi, 272a; vii, 79b – VI, 256b; VII, 80b
Malika Djahān Bēgam (Harāt) (1586) vi, 696a – VI, 684a
Manisa (1376) vi, 683a – VI, 670a
al-Manṣūr (Baghdād) vi, 671b, 674a – VI, 658a, 660b
Mardjān (Baghdād) i, 903b – I, 930b
Maribud (1462) vi, 685a – VI, 672b
al-Māridānī (Cairo/le Caire) (1340) vi, 719a – VI, 708a
Maryam Zamānī (Lahore) (1614) vi, 697a; vii, 331b – VI, 685a; VII, 333b
Mashhad vi, 684b – VI, 672a
Masīla (M'sila) Zāb) vi, 187a, 435a, **727a** – VI, 170b, 420b, **716a**
Maydān (Abyāna) (1103) vii, 14a – VII, 15a
Maydān (Kāshān) (XV) vii, 78b – VII, 79b
Mayyāfāriḳīn (1155) vi, 682b, 683a – VI, 669b, 670a
Medina (al-Rawḍa) vi, 677a – VI, 663b
Meḥmed Pasha (Amasya) (1486) vii, 79a – VII, 80a
Merām (Ḳonya) (1402) vi, 682b – VI, 670a
Mihrimah (Istanbul) (1568) vi, 687a; ix, 630a – VI, 674b; IX, 654a
Mihtar-i Maḥall (Bīdjāpūr) vi, 696a – VI, 684a
Miḳyās (al-Djazīra) vi, 656b – VI, 642a
Mīnā (Āgra) vi, 697b – VI, 685b
Minyā (1154) viii, 864a – VIII, 895a
Mīr Čaḳinaḳ (Yazd) (1436) vi, 685a – VI, 672b
Miṣriyān (XI) vi, 684b; vii, 12b – VI, 671b; VII, 13a
Mopti (Mali) vi, 705a – VI, 693b
Mostar (1474) vii, 244b – VII, 246a
Mōth kī (Khayrpur) (1505) vi, 693a – VI, 680b
Mōtī (Āgra) (1653) vi, 698a; viii, 269a – VI, 686a; VIII, 276a
Mōtī (Lahore) (1645) vi, 697b – VI, 685b
al-Muʾayyad (Cairo/le Caire) vi, 657a, 665b, 671b, 672b, 674b; vii, 272a – VI, 642b, 651b, 658a, 659a, 661a; VII, 274a
Mudjarrad Kamāl (Gulbargā) (1400) vi, 695b – VI, 683a
Muḥāfiẓ Khān (Aḥmadābād) (1492) vi, 694b – VI, 682b

Muḥammad b. Tipū Sulṭān (1842) vii, 79b – VII, 80b
Muḥammad ʿAlī (Cairo/le Caire) (1857) vii, 151b, 427b – VII, 153b, 428b
Mungēr (Bihar) vii, 129b – VII, 131b
Murādiyye (Manisa) (1583) vii, 597a; ix, 69b – VII, 597a; IX, 72b
al-Mustanṣiriyya (Baghdād) vi, 663a – VI, 649a
Mutʿa (Cordoba/Cordoue) x, 159a – X, 170b
al-Muṭahhar (Cairo/le Caire) s, 244a – S, 244a
al-Muẓaffar (Taʿizz) (XIII) vi, 683b; x, 118a – VI, 671a; X, 127b
al-Mwāsīn (Marrākūsh) vi, 590a, b, 591b, 594b, 597a – VI, 575a, b, 576a, 579a, 582a

Masdjid (N)

al-Nabī (Medina) vi, 659b, 660b, 666a, 677b, 680b – VI, 645a, 646b, 652a, 664a, 667b
Nagīna (Āgra) (1630) vi, 697b; viii, 316a – VI, 685b; VIII, 326b
Nāʾīn/Nāyin (Irān) (X) vi, 365a, 679b, 684a –VI, 349a, 666b, 671a
Nakhčivān (1186) vi, 684b – VI, 672a
Namāzgāh (Ḳarshī) vii, 329a – VII, 330b
Namira (Ibrāhīm al-Khalīl) (Arafa) vi, 154a, 168b – VI, 152a, 160a
al-Nāṣir Muḥammad b. Ḳalawūn (Cairo/le Caire) (1318) vi, 683a – VI, 670b
al-Nāṣiriyya (Cairo/le Caire) vi, 671b, 672b – VI, 658a, 659a
Nawwāb Sardār Khān (Aḥmadābād) (1660) vi, 698b – VI, 687a
Ndioum (Senegal) vi, 705a – VI, 693b
Niksar (1145) vi, 682b – VI, 669b
Nīlūfer ʿImāreti (Iznīḳ) (XIV) vii, 594a – VII, 593b
Nīrīz (Irān) (973) vi, 684a – VI, 671a
Nīshāpūr (XV) vi, 685a – VI, 672b
Niẓāmiyya (Abarḳūh) (1325) viii, 315a – VIII, 325b
al-Nukhayla (Cordova) vi, 188b – VI, 172b
Nūr-i ʿOthmāniyye (Istanbul) vi, 56b, 57a – VI, 54b, 55a

Masdjid (O)

Orhan Gazi (Bilecik) vi, 686a – VI, 673b

Masdjid (P)

Pādshāhī (Lāhawr) (1673) viii, 269a – VIII, 276b
Pāʾīn (Farīzhand) vii, 77a – VII, 78a
Pānīpat (1528) vi, 693a; vii, 329a – VI, 680b; VII, 330b
Pāfan (XIV) vi, 692a – VI, 679b
Patthar (Srīnagar) (1620) vii, 331b – VII, 333a
Pīrī Meḥmed Pasha (Istanbul) viii, 307b – VIII, 317b

Masdjid (R)

Rabba (Ṭāʾif) vi, 655b – VI, 641a
Rada (Yemen) (XIII) vi, 683b – VI, 671a
Raḳḳa (IX) vi, 680a – VI, 667a
Ramazan Efendi (Khodjamustafapasha) (1585) vi, 687a – VI, 674b
Rānī Rūpawātī (Aḥmadābād) (1510) vi, 694b, 695a – VI, 682b, 683a
Rānī Siprī (Sabarī) (Aḥmadābād) (1514) vi, 369a, 694b – VI, 353a, 682b
Ras Mkumbuu (Pemba) vi, 370a – VI, 354a
Rāshida (Cairo/le Caire) vi, 649a, 650a, 656b, 671b – VI, 634b, 635a, 642a, 658a
Rasūlid(e)s (Taʿizz) vi, 683b – VI, 671a
al-Rawḍa (Yemen) (XIII) vi, 683b – VI, 670b
al-Raʾya (Mecca) vi, 650b – VI, 636a
al-Rifāʿī (Cairo/-e) (XIX) viii, 526a – VIII, 543b
Rīgistān (Samarḳand) (1417) vi, 685a – VI, 672b
Rūm Meḥmed Pasha (Üsküdar/Scutari) (1473) x, 924a
Rushkhar (1454) vi, 685b – VI, 672b
Rüstem Pasha (Istanbul) (1561) ix, 630a – IX, 654a

Masdjid (S)

Sadrettin Konevi (Ḳonya) (1274) vii, 13b – VII, 14a
Sahib Ata (Konya) (1358) viii, 315a – VIII, 325a
al-Ṣāḥibiyya (Cairo/le Caire) vi, 672b – VI, 659a
Sāla (1232) i, 780b – I, 804a
Ṣalāḥ al-Dīn (Mīlās) (1330) vii, 56a – VII,56b
Ṣāliḥ (ʿAkka) vi, 652b – VI, 638a
al-Ṣāliḥ Nadjm al-Dīn (Cairo/le Caire) (1250) vii, 504a – VII, 504a
al-Ṣāliḥ Ṭalāʾiʿ (Cairo/le Caire) (1160) vi, 674a, 719a – VI, 661a, 708a
Salik (Basīrhāt) (1305) vi, 693a – VI, 681a
Ṣalkhad (1232) i, 780b; viii, 995b – I, 804a; VIII, 1030a
Sāmarrāʾ (852) vi, 679b, 681a; vii, 9a – VI, 666a, b, 668a; VII, 9b
Sambhal (1526) vi, 693a; vii, 329a – VI, 680b; VII, 330b
Ṣanʿāʾ (VII) vi, 681a – VI, 668a
Sandjar (Kālī) (Delhi) vi, 690a – VI, 677b
Sandjar (Niẓam al-Dīn) (1370) vi, 692b – VI, 680a
Sangān-i Pāʾīn (1140) vi, 684b – VI, 671b
al-Ṣarghitmishiyya vi, 674b – VI, 661a
Sar-i Rīg (1424) vi, 685a – VI, 672b
Sarkhēdj (1451) vi, 694b – VI, 682a
Sarm vi, 686a – VI, 673a
Sātgunbadh (Ḍhākā) vi, 698a – VI, 686b
al-Ṣawmaʿa (Hūt, Yemen) (XIII) vi, 683b – VI, 670b
Sayyid ʿĀlam (Aḥmadābād) (1412) vi, 694b – VI, 682a
Sayyida Ruḳayya (Cairo/le Caire) (1133) vii, 504a – VII, 504a
Şehzade (Istanbul) (1548) vi, 687a – VI, 674b
Selimiye (Edirne) (1576) vi, 687b; vii, 79a; ix, 619b – VI, 675a; VII, 80a; IX, 653b
Sfax (849) vi, 680a; vii, 76b – VI, 667a; VII, 77b
Shāh (Iṣfahān) (1612) vi, 685b – VI, 673a
Shāh (Mashhad) (1451) vi, 190b, 366a, 685b – VI, 174a, 350a, 672b
Shāh ʿĀlam vi, 692b – VI, 680a
Shāh Bāzār (Gulbargā) (1360) vi, 695a – VI, 683a
Shāhdjahān (Ṭhaṭṭā) (1647) vi, 698b – VI, 686b
Shāh Djahānī (Adjmēr) (1638) vi, 697b – VI, 685b
Shāh Hamadān (Shrinagar) vi, 696b – VI, 684b
Shāh Muḥyī ʾl-Dīn (Čarkh) (XII) vii, 14a – VII, 15a
Shāh-i (Ghardjistān) (1175) vi, 691b – VI, 679a
Shāh-i Djāmiʿ (Bari Khatu) (XIII) vi, 691b – VI, 679a
al-Shams (Karbalāʾ) vi, 650a, b – VI, 635a, 636a
Shaykh ʿAbd al-Nabī (Delhi) (1575) vii, 330b – VII, 332a

Shaykh Bārha (Ẓafarābād) (1311) vi, 694a – VI, 681b
Shaykh Ḥasan Muḥammad Čishtī (Aḥmadābād) (1565) vi, 694b – VI, 682b
Shaykh Luṭf Allāh (Iṣfahān) (1602) vi, 685b, 719b; viii, 789a – VI, 673a, 708b; VIII, 815b
Shaykh Muʿīn al-Dīn Čishtī (Adjmēr) (1570) vii, 330b – VII, 332a
Shaykhū (Cairo/le Caire) vii, 78b – VII, 79b
Shehzāde (Istanbul) ix, 629b – IX, 653b
Shem b. Nūḥ (Ṣanʿāʾ) vi, 651a – VI, 636b
Shibām (X) vi, 683b – VI, 671a
Shīrāz (XVI) vi, 684b, 685a – VI, 672a, b
Shuʿayb vi, 652b – VI, 638a
al-Shuhadāʾ (Yogyakarta) vi, 700b – VI, 688b
–Shūnīziyya (Baghdād) ix, 65b – IX, 67a
Sīdī ʿAbd Allāh al-Ḥadjdjām vi, 891a – VI, 882a
Sīdī Bel ʿAbbās (Marrākūsh) vi, 590b – VI, 575b
Sīdī Bū Marwān (ʿAnnāba) (1033) s, 156a – S, 156b
Sīdī Saʿīd al-Ḥabshī (Aḥmadābād) (1572) vi, 694b – VI, 682b
Sīdī ʿUḳba (al-Ḳayrawān) vi, 364a – VI, 348a
Simāk (al-Kūfa) vi, 653a – VI, 638b
Simnān (XI) vi, 684b – VI, 671b, 672a
Sīn (1136) vi, 684b – VI, 671b
Sīrāf (Irān) (VIII) vi, 683b; vii, 12a – VI, 671a; VII, 12b
Sirha (Yemen) vi, 683b – VI, 671a
Siu (Kenya) (1523) vii, 80b – VII, 81b
Sivas vi, 682b – VI, 669b
Ṣofu Sinān Pasha (Prizren) (1613) viii, 339a, 340a – VIII, 351a, 352a
Sokollu (Istanbul) (1572) vii, 79a – VII, 80a
Sonahrī (Delhi) (1751) vi, 698a – VI, 686b
–Srīnagar ix, 734b, 735a – IX, 767a
Sulaymān (Iṣṭakhr) vi, 650a – VI, 635a
Sūlaymāniyye (Istanbul) (1557) vi, 687a, b; ix, 629b – VI, 674b, 675a; IX, 653b
al-Sulṭān (Baghdād) (XI) vi, 275a – VI, 260a
Sultan Ahmed (Istanbul) (1616) iv, 233a; vi, 687b – IV, 243b; VI, 675a
Sulṭān Ḥasan (Cairo/le Caire) (1356) vi, 683a; vii, 78b, 151b; viii, 315a – VI, 670b; VII, 79b, 153b; VIII, 325a
Sultan Meḥemmed (Prizren) viii, 338b – VIII, 350b
Sulṭān Muḥammad (Merzifon) vii, 480a – VII, 479b
Sūsa (850) vi, 679b, 680a, 683b – VI, 666a, 667a, 671a

Masdjid (T)

Tabrīz (1465) vi, 685b – VI, 672b, 673a
Tādj Maḥall vi, 697b – VI, 685b
Takhlatan Baba (Khurāsān) (XII) vi, 684b – VI, 671b
Tamur (Yemen) (XI) vi, 683b – VI, 670b
Ṭarābulus al-Gharb (XIV) vi, 683b – VI, 670b
Tārīkhāna (Dāmghān) (X) vi, 679b, 684a; vii, 12a, 78b; viii, 314a – VI, 666b, 671a; VII, 12b, 79b; VIII, 324a
al-Ṭaybarsiyya (Cairo/le Caire) vi, 672b – VI, 659a
Tekkeci Ibrāhīm Agha (Istanbul) (1590) vi, 687a – VI, 674b
Thāntipāra (Gawṛ) (1480) vi, 693b – VI, 681b
Tīla (Lakhnaw) s, 292a – S, 292a
Tilimsān vii, 11b, 587a – VII, 12a, 587a
Timbuktu vi, 705a – VI, 693b
Tinmāl (1153) vii, 12a, 504b – VII, 12b, 504b
Tithid (Yemen) (XIII) vi, 683b – VI, 670b
Tivaouane (Senegal) vi, 706b – VI, 695a
Tolī (Golkonḍā) (1633) vi, 369b, 696b – VI, 353b, 684b
Tulaytula (Toledo) (X) vi, 680a – VI, 667a
Tunis (864) vi, 679a, 680a, b – VI, 666a, b, 667b

Masdjid (U)

Uç Şerefeli (Edirne) (1447) vi, 686b; ix, 629a – VI, 674a; IX, 653a
Ūkha (Bayāna) (1316) vi, 692a – VI, 679b
Ulu Cami (Birgi) (1312) vi, 683a – VI, 670a
Ulu Cami (Bitlis) (1160) vi, 686a – VI, 673b
Ulu Cami (Bursa) (1394) vi, 686b; vii, 594a – VI, 673b; VII, 593b
Ulu Cami (Divriği) (1228) vi, 366a; vii, 79b; viii, 315a – VI, 350a; VII, 79b; VIII, 325a
Ulu Cami (Edirne) (1403) vi, 686b – VI, 674a
Ulu Cami (Erzurum) (1179) vii, 13a – VII, 14a
Ulu Cami (Kïzïltepe) (1204) vii, 13a – VII, 14a
Ulu Cami (Malaṭya) vi, 231a – VI, 225a
Ulu Cami (Siirt) vii, 78a – VII, 79a
Ulu Cami (Şivrihisar) (1272) vii, 78a – VII, 79a
Ulu Djāmiʿ (Afyūn Ḳaraḥiṣār) viii, 831b – VIII, 860a
Ulu Djāmʿ (SīwRs) (XII) ix, 689a – IX, 718b
ʿUmar → al-Ḳuds
ʿUmar (Boṣrā) vii, 9a – VII, 9a
ʿUmariyya (Mosul) vii, 9b – VII, 9b
Umayyad(e)s (Damas(cus)) (710) vi, 662b, 663a, 664a, 666b, 670b, 671a, 674a, 677a; vii, 9a, 10a – VI, 648b, 650a, 653a, 657a, b, 660b, 664a; VII, 9a, 10a
Umm Kulthūm (1122) vii, 10b – VII, 11a
al-ʿUmra (Mecca) vi, 168b – VI, 160a
Urfa (XII) vi, 682b – VI, 669b
Urmiya/Riḍāʾiyya (XIII) vi, 684b – VI, 671b

Masdjid (W)

Wālādjāhī (Madras) s, 292b, 293a – S, 292a, 293a
Walide Djāmiʿ (Üsküdar/Scutari) (1708) x, ; X,
Warāmīn (1322) vi, 685a – VI, 672a
al-Wazīr (Baghdād) vi, 614b – VI, 599b
Wazīr (Kāshān) vi, 686a – VI, 673a
Wazīr Khān (Lahore) (1634) vi, 697a; vii, 333a – VI, 685a; VII, 335a

Masdjid (Y)

Yaḥyā al-Shabīh (Cairo/le Caire) (1150) vii, 504a – VII, 504a
Yaʿḳūb Bey (Prizren) viii, 338b – VIII, 350b
Yaʿḳūb al-Manṣūr (Marrākūsh) (1195) vii, 12a – VII, 12b
Yaʿḳūb wa-Yūsuf (Cairo/le Caire) vi, 651a – VI, 636b
Yazd (1330) vi, 683b, 684b, 685a; viii, 315a – VI, 671a, 672a, b; VIII, 325b
Yazd-i Khāsī vi, 684a – VI, 671a
Yeñi Djāmiʿ (Tarābazun) (1500) x, 217a – X, 224b
Yeşil Cami (Bursa) (1413) vi, 686b; vii, 13b – VI, 673b; VII, 14b
Yeşil Cami (Iznīḳ) (1378) vi, 686a – VI, 673b
Yïldïrïm Bāyazīd (Bursa) (1390) vi, 686b – VI, 673b
Yïldïz-Dede (Istanbul) vi, 57a – VI, 55a
Yivli Minare (Antalya) (1373) vi, 683a – VI, 670a
Yūnis (Niniveh) vi, 662b – VI, 648b

Yūsuf Agha al-Ḥīn (Cairo/le Caire) (1625) vi, 719a – VI, 708a

Masdjid (Z)

Ẓafār Dhibin (Yemen) vi, 683b – VI, 671a
al-Ẓāhir (Cairo/le Caire) vii, 151b – VII, 153b
al-Ẓahiriyya (Cairo/le Caire) vi, 674b – VI, 661a
Zawāra (1133) vi, 684b – VI, 672a
Ziyāratgāh (Harāt) (1482) vi, 685a – VI, 672b
Masdjidī (Baṣra) vi, **709a** – VI, **698a**
Masdjumi, Mashumi iii, 534a, b, 1230a – III, 553a, 1262a
Maṣfiwa, Banū vi, 742a – VI, 731a
Masfūt s, 42a – S, 42b
al-Masḥ ʿAlā ʾl-Khuffayn vi, **709b** – VI, **698a**
Māshāʾ Allāh i, 722b, 1101b; iii, 8b; v, 130b; vi, **710b** – I, 744b, 1135a; III, 9a; V, 133b; VI, **699a**
Māshaʾ Allāh b. Atharī (IX) vi, **710b**;viii, 106b – VI, **699b**; VIII, 109a
Maṣḥaf → Muṣḥaf
Maṣḥaf-räsh v, 208b, 209a, b, 210a – V, 206a, b, 207a, b
Mashaʾiyya iv, 120b – IV, 126a
Mashāḳa, Mīkhāʾil (1888) vi, **712a** – VI, **700b**
Mashāriḳa v, 1159a; vi, **712a** – V, 1149a; VI, **701a**
Mashawasha vi, 943b – VI, 935b
Mashāwiriyya iv, 456a – IV, 476b
Mashāyikh iv, 167b – IV, 175a
Mashāyikh, Pīr v, 27a – V, 27b
Mashdūf iii, 289a – III, 298a
Mashhad (town/ville) i, 8a, 400b, 1067a; ii, 173b; iv, 7b, 38a; v, 59a, b, 289a, 1149a; vi, 190b, 336a, 418b, 484a, 495b, 510b, 516a, 526b, 550b, 553b, **713b**; s, 53a, 71a, 73a, 75a, b, 139b, 365a, b, 380a, 423b – I, 8a, 412a, 1099a; II, 178b; IV, 8b, 40b; V, 61a, 288b, 1140a; VI, 174a, 320a, 350a, 403b, 470a, 480b, 496b, 501a, 511a, 535a, 538a, **702b**; S, 53b, 71b, 73b, 75b, 76a, 139a, 365a, 380a, 423b
—university/-é ii, 426a – II, 437a
Mashhad (shrine/tombeau) vi, **713b** – VI, **702a**
Mashhad Abī Hurayra vi, 652a – VI, 637b
Mashhad ʿAkk (ʿAkka) vi, 652b – VI, 638a
Mashhad ʿAlī → al-Nadjaf
Mashhad Dhu ʾl-Kifl b. Ayyūb vi, 652b – VI, 638a
Mashhad Djirdjis (Mosul) vi, 652a – VI, 637a
Mashhad al-Ḥāʾir s, 94a – S, 93b
Mashhad Hūd (ʿAkka, Damas(cus), Ḥadramawt) vi, 652b – VI, 638a
Mashhad al-Ḥusayn → Karbalāʾ
lashhad al-Kāẓimī → Kāẓimayn
Mashhad al-Khaḍir (Damas(cus)) vi, 652b – VI, 638a
Mashhad Rabba (Ṭāʾif) vi, 655b – VI, 641a
Mashhad Ṣāliḥ (ʿAkkā) vi, 652b – VI, 638a
Mashhad Shāh-i (Ghardjistān) (1175) vi, 691b – VI, 679a
Mashhad Shuʿayb vi, 652b – VI, 638a
al-Mashhadān → Karbalāʾ
Mashhadī, Mīr Sayyid Aḥmad (XVI) vii, 442a – VII, 443a
Mashhad-i Miṣriyān (XI) ii, 253b; vi, **716b** – II, 260b; VI, **705b**
Mashad-i Murghāb vi, 383b – VI, 368a
Mashhūr vi, **717a** – VI, **706a**
Mashīʾa i, 414b – I, 426b
Mashkēl (valley/-ée, Balūčistān) vi, 192b – VI, 176a
Mashrabiyya (turned wood/bois tourné) v, 1153a; vi, **717b** – V, 1143a; VI, **706a**
Mashriḳ v, 1159a; vi, **720a** – V, 1149a; VI, **708b**
Mashriḳ al-Adhkār i, 918a; vi, **720** – I, 945b; VI, **709a**
al-Mashriḳī, ʿInāyat Allāh iv, 916b – IV, 949b
Mashrūʿ ii, 390a – II, 400b
Mashrūbāt vi, **720b** – VI, **709b**
Mashrūṭiyya → Dustūr
Mashṭūr i, 671a – I, 692a
al-Maʿshūḳ (Takrīt) vii, 414a – VII, 415b
Mashʾūm ii, 759a – II, 777b
Mashwara (Mashūra) ii, 641b; vi, **724a** – II, 658a; VI, **712b**
Mashyakha (Mashīkha) vi, **725b** – VI, **714b**
al-Masīḥ (Messiah/Messie) iv, 82b; vi, **726a** – IV, 86b; VI, **715a**
Masīḥ b. Ḥakam iv, 329a – IV, 343b
Masīḥ al-Dimashḳī s, 314a – S, 313b
al-Masīḥī al-Djurdjānī, ʿIsā b. Yaḥyā (1010) vi, **726b** – VI, **715b**
Masik → al-Ḥārith, Djabal
Māsikha iv, 796b – IV, 828b
al-Masīla, wādī i, 538b; s, 337a – I, 555a; S, 337a
Masīla (Mʾsila) (Zāb) iv, 479a, b; vi, 187a, 435a, **727a**; s, 62b – IV, 501a, b; VI, 170b, 420b, **716a**; S, 63a
Masina (Fulbe) i, 303a, b; ii, 941b; iii, 39b; vi, 259b, 281b – I, 312b, 313a, II, 963b; III, 41a; VI, 244a, 266b
Maʾṣir vi, **728b** – VI, **717b**
Maṣīra i, 535b; vi, **729a** – I, 552a; VI, **718a**
Masjumi vi, **730a** – VI, **719a**
Maṣḳala b. Hubayra v, 19b – V, 20a
Maskana vi, **733a** – VI, **722a**
Masḳaṭ i, 536a, 539a, 554b, 942b, 1071b, 1098b, 1282b, 1283a, 1314a; iv, 500b; v, 183b; vi, 38a, 729b, **734a**; s, 332b, 355b, 356a – I, 552a, 556a, 572a, 971b, 1103b, 1131b, 1321b, 1354a; IV, 522b; V, 181a; VI, 36a, 718b, **723b**; S, 331b, 355b
Maskh ii, 95b; iii, 305b, 306a; v, 131a; vi, **736b** – II, 97b; III, 315a, b; V, 134a; VI, **725b**
Maskin ii, 197a; vii, 359b – II, 203a; VII, 361b
Maṣlaḥa i, 276a, 276b; ii, 254b; iii, 954a; iv, 257a, b, 258a; vi, **738b** – I, 284b, 285a; II, 262a; III, 978b; IV, 268a, b, 269b; VI, **727b**
Maslama, Banū → Afṭasid(e)s
Maslama b. ʿAbd al-Malik b. Marwān (Umayyad(e)) (738) i, 12b, 449b, 835b, 837a, 996a, 1033b, 1094b, 1102b, 1187a; ii, 85b, 234a, 236b, 237a; iii, 493b, 1255a; iv, 343b, 344a, 843a, 870b, 938b, 973b, 1173b; v, 533a; vi, 363a, 623a, b, **740a**; vii, 359a, 408b; viii, 6b; s, 31b – I, 12b, 462b, 858b, 860a, 1026b, 1065a, 1127a, 1136a, 1222a; II, 87a, 241a, 243b; III, 510b, 1287b; IV, 358a, b, 876a, 904a, 971b, 1005b, 1207a; V, 537a; VI, 347a, 60b, **729a**; VII, 361b, 410a; VIII, 6b; S, 31b
Maslama b. Mukhallad (Makhlad/Mukhlid) b. al-Ṣāmit al-Anṣārī(682) ii, 327b; vi, 660b, 661b, 663a, 664b, 676b, 677a, **740b**; vii, 266b; x, 790a – II, 337a; II, 337a; VI, 646b, 647b, 649a, 650b, 663a, b, **729b**; VII, 268b; X,
Maslama al-Madjrīṭī → al-Masjrīṭī
Maṣmūda, Banū i, 1176a, 1177b, 1178b, 1350a; ii, 623a; iii, 69b, 207a, 959a; iv, 730a; vi, 590b, 592a, 593b, **741a**, 802a – I, 1211a, 1212b, 1213b, 1390a; II, 638b; III, 72a, 213a, 984a; IV, 759a; VI, 575a, 576b, 578a, **730a**, 804a
al-Maṣmūdī (Shāʿir) (XVII) vi, 249a – VI, 233a
al-Maṣmūdī, Yaḥyā b. Yaḥyā (848) vi, 264a, b – VI, 249a

Maṣmughān (Damāwand) v, 661b; vi, 335a, **744a** – V, 667a; VI, 319b, **733b**
Maṣmughān b. Wandā-Ummīd (864) vi, 745b – VI, 734b
Masnad-i ʿAlī → Daryā Khān Noḥānī
al-Masnāwī, Abū ʿAbd Allāh (1724) s, 223b, 403b, 404a – S, 223b, 404a
Mason Bey (XIX) vi, 643a – VI, 628a
Maṣr al-ʿAtīḳa ii, 958a – II, 980a
Maṣraf Defteri vi, **745b** – VI, **735a**
Masraḥ (theatre) vi, **746a** – VI, **735a**
Masraḥī v, 516b – V, 520a
Masraḥiyya iv, 73b – IV, 77b
Masruḳ vii, 258b – VII, 260a
Masrūḳ b. Abraha s, 115b – S, 115a
Masruḳān i, 711b; iv, 674a – I, 733a; IV, 701b
Masrūr (eunuch/-que) (IX) ii, 1079b; vi, 752b – II, 1104b; VI, 742a
Masrūr b. al-Walīd i, 1244a; iii, 990b – I, 1282a; III, 1015a
Māssa, Banū vi, **773b** – VI, **763a**
Massāḥ iv, 1041b – IV, 1073a
al-Massāḥ, Aḥmad al-Faḍl vii, 196b – VII, 196b
Massalajem (Madagascar) vi, **774a** – VI, **763b**
Maṣṣālī Ḥādjdj iv, 362b – IV, 378b
Massar i, 1166b; iv, 275a – I, 1201a; IV, 287a
Massassi → Bambara
Massenya i, 910a, b – I, 937b, 938a
al-Māssī → Ibn Hūd
al-Maṣṣīṣa (Mopsuestia) i, 42b; ii, 35b; vi, 338a, 505b, 506a, 650a, **774a**; vii, 777a; viii, 874a – I, 43b; II, 36b; VI, 322a, 491a, b, 635a, **763b**; VII, 779a; VIII, 903b
Massūfa i, 389b – I, 400b
Massūfa, Banū vii, 584b – VII, 585a
al-Massūfī → Barrāz
al-Massūfī, Muḥammad b. ʿAbd b. Yanūmar (XIV) vii, 625a – VII, 625a
al-Massūfī, Yaḥyā b. Ghāniya (1148) vii, 586a – VII, 586a
Mast ʿAlī Shāh (Niʿmat-Allāhī) (XIX) viii, 46b – VIII, 47b
Masṭawa, Banū vi, 743a – VI, 731b
Mastūdj vi, **779b** – VI, **769b**
Mashrabiyya vi, **717b** – VI, **706a**
Mashriḳ v, 1159a; vi, **720a** – V, 1149a; VI, **708b**
Mashriḳ al-Adhkār i, 918a; vi, **720a** – I, 945b; VI, **709a**
al-Mashriḳī, ʿInāyat Allāh iv, 916b – IV, 949b
Mashruʿ ii, 390a – II, 400b
Mashrubāt vi, **720b** – VI, **709b**
Mashrūtiyya → Dustūr
Mashṭūr i, 671a – I, 692a
al-Maʿshūḳ (Takrīt) vii, 414a – VII, 415b
Mashʾūm ii, 759a – II, 777b
Mashwara (Mashūra) ii, 641b; vi, **724a** – II, 658a; VI, **712b**
Mashyakha (Mashīkha) vi, **725b** – VI, **714b**
al-Masīḥ (Messiah/-ie) iv, 82b; vi, **726a** – IV, 86b; VI, **715a**
Masīḥ b. Ḥakam iv, 329a – IV, 343b
Masīḥ al-Dimashḳī s, 314a – S, 313b
al-Masīḥī al-Djurdjānī, ʿĪsā b. Yaḥyā (1010) vi, **726b** – VI, **715b**
Masik → al-Ḥārith, Djabal
Māsikha iv, 796b – IV, 828b
al-Masīla, wādī i, 538b; s, 337a – I, 555a; S, 337a
Masīla (Mʾsila) (Zāb) vi, 187a, 435a, **727a**; VI, 170b, 420b, **716a**
Māsina (Fulbe) i, 303a, b; ii, 941b; iii, 39b; vi, 259b, 281b – I, 312b, 313a; II, 963b; III, 41a; VI, 244a, 266b
Maʾṣir vi, **728b** – VI, **717b**
Maṣīra i, 535b; vi, **729a** – I, 552a; VI, **718a**
Masjumi vi, **730a** – VI, **719a**
Maṣḳala b. Hubayra v, 19b – V, 20a
Maskana vi, **733a** – VI, **722a**
Masḳaṭ i, 536a, 539a, 554b, 942b, 1071b, 1098b, 1282b, 1283a, 1314a; iv, 500b; v, 183b; vi, 38a, 729b, **734a**; s, 332b, 355b, 356a – I, 552a, 556a, 572a, 971b, 1103b, 1131b, 1321b, 1354a; IV, 522b; V, 181a; VI, 36a, 718b, **723b**; S, 331b, 355b
Maskh ii, 95b; iii, 305b, 306a; v, 131a; vi, **736b** – II, 97b; III, 315a, b; V, 134a; VI, **725b**
Maskin ii, 197a; vii, 359b – II, 203a; VII, 361b
Maṣlaḥa i, 276a, b; ii, 254b; iii, 954a; iv, 257a, b, 258a; vi, **738b** – I, 284b, 285a; II, 262a; III, 978b; IV, 268a, b, 269b; VI, **727b**
Maslama, Banū → Afṭasid(e)s
Maslama b. ʿAbd al-Malik b. Marwān (Umayyad(e)) (738) i, 12b, 449b, 835b, 837a, 996a, 1033b, 1094b, 1102b, 1187a; ii, 85b, 234a, 236b; iii, 493b, 1255a; iv, 343b, 344a, 843a, 870b, 938b, 973b, 1173b; v, 533a; vi, 363a, 623a, b, **740a**; vii, 359a, 408b; s, 31b – I, 12b, 462b, 858b, 860a, 1026b, 1065a, 1127a, 1136a, 1222a; II, 87a, 241a, 243b; III, 510b, 1287b; IV, 358a, b, 876a, 904a, 971b, 1005b, 1207a; V, 537a; VI, 347a, 609b, **729a**; VII, 361b, 410a; S, 31b
Maslama b. Mukhallad (Mukhlid) b. al-Ṣāmit (682) ii, 327b; vi, 660b, 661b, 663a, 664b, 676b, 677a, **740b**; vii, 266b – II, 337a; VI, 646b, 647b, 649a, 650b, 663a, b, **729b**; VII, 268b
Maslama al-Madjrīṭī → al-Madjrīṭī
Maṣmūda, Banū i, 1176a, 1177b, 1178b, 1350a; iii, 69b, 207a, 959a; iv, 730a; vi, 590b, 593b, **741a**, 802a – I, 1211a, 1212b, 1213b, 1390a; III, 72a, 213a, 984a; IV, 759a; VI, 575a, 576b, 578a, **730a**; 804a
al-Maṣmūdī (shāʿir) (XVII) vi, 249a – VI, 233a
al-Maṣmūdī, Yaḥyā b. Yaḥyā (848) vi, 264a, b – VI, 249a
Maṣmughān (Damāwand) v, 661b; vi, 335a, **744a** – V, 667a; 319b, **733b**
Maṣmughān b. Wandā-Ummīd (864) vi, 745b – VI, 734b
Masnad-i ʿAlī → Daryā Khān Noḥānī
al-Masnāwī, Abū ʿAbd Allāh s, 403b, 404a – S, 404a
Mason Bey (XIX) vi, 643a – VI, 628a
Maṣr al-ʿAtīḳa ii, 958a – II, 980a
Maṣraf Defteri vi, **745b** – VI, **735a**
Masraḥ (theatre) vi, **746a** – VI, **735a**
Masraḥī v, 516b – V, 520a
Masraḥiyya iv, 73b – IV, 77b
Masrūḳ vii, 258b – VII, 260a
Masrūḳ b. Abraha s, 115b – S, 115a
Masrūḳān i, 711b; iv, 674a – I, 733a; IV, 701b
Masrūr (IX) vi, 752b – VI, 742a
Masrūr b. al-Walīd i, 1244a; iii, 990b – I, 1282a; III, 1015a
Māssa, Banū vi, **773b** – VI, **763a**
Massāḥ iv, 1041b – IV, 1073a
al-Massāḥ, Aḥmad al-Faḍl vii, 196b – VII, 196b
Massalajem (Madagascar) vi, **774a** – VI, **763b**
Maṣṣālī Ḥādjdj iv, 362b – IV, 378b
Massar i, 1166b; iv, 275a – I, 1201a; IV, 287a
Massassi → Bambara
Massenya i, 910a, b – I, 937b, 938a
al-Māssī → Ibn Hūd

al-Maṣṣīṣa i, 42b; vi, 338a, 505b, 506a, 650a, **774a**; vii, 777a –
I, 43b; VI, 322a, 491a, b, 635a, **763b**; 779a
Massūfa, Banū i, 389b; vii, 584b – I, 400b; VII, 585a
al-Massūfī, Barrāz (XI) ii, 1009b; iii, 771b; iv, 116a; v, 586b – II, 1033a; III, 794b; IV, 121a; V, 591b
al-Massūfī, Muḥammad b. ʿAbd b. Yanūmar (XIV) vii, 625a – VII, 625a
al-Massūfī, Yaḥyā b. Ghāniya (1148) vii, 586a – VII, 586a
Maṣṭawa, Banū vi, 742a – VI, 731b
Mastūdj vi, **779b** – VI, **769b**
Masʿūd, Badr al-Dīn Khurshīdī v, 828b – V, 834b
Masʿūd, Sayyid Salār Ghāzī → Ghāzī Mīyān, Sālār Masʿūd
Masʿūd, Sīdī (Marrakūsh) vi, 501b – VI, 570a
Masʿūd I b. Maḥmūd b. Sebüktigin (Ghaznawid(e)) (1040) i, 147a, 217b, 278a, 424b, 459a, 1005b, 1130b, 1236b, 1344b, 1356a; ii, 4b, 1049a, 1051a, 1053a, 1083a, 1100a; iii, 167b, 195b, 255b, 345a, 482b, 1201b; iv, 25a, 100b, 1067a; v, 624a; vi, 65b, 66a, 193a, 453a, 521b, 522a, b, 523a, 524a, 714b, **780a**; vii, 19a, 257a, 477b; viii, 69b; s, 195a, 235a, 245b –
I, 151b, 224a, 286b, 436b, 472b, 1036b, 1164b, 1274a, 1385a, 1395a; II, 4b, 1073b, 1075b, 1077b, 1108a, 1125b; III, 171b, 200a, 263a, 355b, 499b, 1232a; IV, 26b, 105a, 1098b; V, 628a; VI, 63b, 64a, 177a, 438b, 506a, b, 507a, b, 508b, 703b, **769b**, VII, 18b, 259a, 477a; VIII, 71aS, 195a, 235a, 245b
Masʿūd II (Ghaznawid(e) (1049) ii, 1051b – II, 1075b
Masʿūd III ʿAlāʾ al-Dawla (Ghaznawid(e)) (1115) ii, 1052a, 1100a; vi, 783a; vii, 535a, 783a; s, 21a, b – II, 1076b, 1126a; VI, 773a; VII, 535a, 773a; S, 21a, b
Masʿūd I b. Muḥammad b. Malik-Shāh (Rūm Saldjūḳ) (1152) i, 181b, 182b, 300a, 466b, 684a, 731b; ii, 37b, 110b, 1083a; iii, 20a, 196b, 345a, 731b, 1255b; v, 253b; vi, 64a, 275b, 500a, 506b, 507a, **782a**, 870b; vii, 496b, 543b, 733b, 734b; viii, 439a, 943b, 974b – I, 186b, 187b, 309b, 480b, 538b, 705a, 753b; II, 38a, 113a, 1108b; III, 21a, 201b, 355b, 1137b1288b; V, 251b; VI, 61b, 260b, 485b, 492a, 492a, **771b**, 861b; VII, 407b, 543b, 734a, b; VIII, 454a, 976a, 1011a
Masʿūd II (Rūm Saldjūḳ) (1305) i, 703a; iv, 620b, 621a, 817b; vi, 231a – I, 724a; IV, 645b, 850a; VI, 225a
Masʿūd I (Zangid(e)) iii, 1119a – III, 1147a
Masʿūd b. ʿAmr al-Atakī (683) i, 304a, 810a; vii, 114b, 877b – I, 313b, 833b; VII, 116b, 879a
Masʿūd b. Ibrāhīm → Masʿūd III (Ghaznawid(e))
Masʿūd b. ʿIzz al-Dīn Kaykaʾūs II (Rum Saldjūḳ) (XIII) vi, 420b – VI, 405b
Masʿūd b. al-Kāmil (Ayyūbid(e)) (XIII) vi, 149b, 433b – VI, 148a, 419a
Masʿūd b. Mawdūd → Masʿūd II (Ghaznawid(e))
Masʿūd b. Mawdūd b. Zangi (Zangid(e), al-Mawṣil) (1193) vi, **780b** – VI, **770b**
Masʿūd b. Menteshe Beg (1319) vi, 1018b – VI, 1010b
Masʿūd b. Saʿd b. Salmān → Masʿūd-i Saʿd-i Salmān
Masʿūd Bakk ii, 55a, 1115a; iii, 429b – II, 56a, 1141a; III, 443b
Masʿūd Beg b. Maḥmūd Yalawač (1289) i, 1240b, 1312a; ii, 2b, 3a, 791b; iv, 808b; v, 38b, 858a; vi, 77a, b, **782b** –
I, 1278a, 1352a; II, 2b, 3a, 810b; IV, 841b; V, 39b, 865a; VI, 75a, **772b**
Masʿūd Bilālī iii, 197a – III, 201b
Maʿūd Khān b. Muḥammad Shāh Ghūrī (XV) vi, 52b, 309b – VI, 51a, 295a
Masʿūd al-Khurāsānī vi, 524a – VI, 508b
Masʿūd Mīrzā Ẓill al-Sulṭān (XIX) vi, 291b – VI, 277a
Masʿūd Rukn al-Dīn Mawdūd (Artuḳid(e)) (1232) iv, 521a – IV, 543b
Masʿūd Shāh, ʿAlāʾ al-Dīn ii, 267b – II, 276a
Masʿūd-Shāh Īndjū iii, 1208a, b; iv, 498b – III, 1239a; IV, 520a
Masʿūd al-Tāhirī al-Djūṭī s, 404a – S, 404a
Masʿūd Yalavač → Masʿud Beg b. Maḥmūd Yalavač
Masʿūd I (Zangid(e)) ʾ ʿIzz al-Dīn
Masʿūd b. Muṣṭafā Barzānī (XX) vii, 715a – VII, 715b
Masʿūd b. al-Nāṣir (XVI) vii, 37b – VII, 37b
Masʿūd Shāh Īndjū iii, 1208a, b; iv, 498b – III, 1239a; IV, 520a
al-Masʿūdī, Abu ʾl-Ḥasan ʿAlī b. al-Ḥusayn (956) ii, 361a, 591b, 837a, 851b; ii, 579b, 580b, 583b, 865a; iii,166a, 405b, 739b, 1206b; iv, 345b; v, 950a, 1012a; vi, 107b, 195b, 640a, **784a**, 905a; vii, 187b, 245b; s, 42b, 56a, 295a – I, 371b, 610b, 860a, 875a; II, 594a, 595a, 598a, 885a; III, 170a, 418a, 762a, 1237a; IV, 360a; V, 954a, 1007b; VI, 105b, 180b, 625b, **773b**, 896b; VII, 188a, 247a; S, 43a, 56b, 294b
Masʿūd-i Rāzī (1039) vii, 19a – VII, 19a
Masʿūd-i Saʿd-i Salmān (1121) i, 252b; iii, 456b; iv, 61b; vi, 608a, b, 762a, **783a**; vii, 535a, 754b; S, 333a, b, 334a –
I, 260a; III, 472a; IV, 64b; VI, 593a, b, 751a, **772b**; VII, 535a, 755b; S, 332b, 333a, b
Masʿūdiyya Madrasa vi, 782b – VI, 772b
Maʿṣūm (title/titre) ii, 86b, 88a – II, 88b, 90a
Maʿṣūm, Khwādja Muḥammad Murād (XVIII) vii, 936b, 938a – VII, 937a, 938b
Maʿṣūm Khān (Mangit) → Murād b. Dāniyāl Biy Atalik
Maʿṣūm ʿAlī Shāh Dakkanī (Niʿmat Allāhī) (1797) i, 283b; iv, 51a; viii, 46a,b; s, 23b – I, 292a; IV, 53b; VIII, 47a; S, 24a
Maʿṣūm Beg —afawī iv, 188a – IV, 196b
Maʿṣūm Nāmī → Mīr Muḥammad Maʿṣūm, Nāmī
al-Maʿṣūmī, Abū Saʿīd (XI) vi, 638a – VI, 623a
Maʿṣūm-i pāk i, 1162a – I, 1196b
Māsūniyya → Farāmush-Khāna; Farmāsūniyya
Masūsa (tribe/tribu) v, 695b – V, 700b
Maṣyād iv, 200a; vi, 577b, **789a**; vii, 578b – IV, 209a; VI, 562b, **778b**; VII, 579a
Maṣyāf → Maṣyād
Maṭābikh Kisrā i, 685b – I, 706b
Maṭāf iv, 318a – IV, 332a, b
al-Maṭāliʿ (ascensions) vi, **792b** – VI, **782b**
al-Maṭāmīr → Maṭmūra
al-Matamma v, 1251a; vi, **794b** – V, 1242a; VI, **784a**
Matan s, 150b – S, 150b
Maṭar (Mawālī) s, 17b – S, 17b
Mataram iii, 1219b, 1221b; v, 1155a, b; ix, 852b, 892a; s, 150b, 199b, 201a, 202a –
III, 1250a, b, 125a, b; V, 1145a; IX, 888a, 928a; S, 150b, 199b, 201a, b
Maṭariyya vi, 631b – VI, 616b
Maṭbaʿa i, 282a, 289b, 640b, 641a, 906b, 907b, 1071a, 1299b; ii, 464b, 472b, 533a, 589b, 682b; iii, 136, 993b, 997b; iv, 70a-b, 143a, 310a, 311a, 607b; v, 190a, 641b, 1254b; vi, **794b** –
I, 290b, 298b, 661b, 934a, 935a, 1103a, 1339b; II, 476a, 484b, 546a, 604a, 699b; III, 14a, 1018a, 1022b; IV, 74a, 149a, 324a, 325a, 632a; V, 187a, 645b, 1245b; VI, **784b**
al-Maṭbaʿa al-Kāstiliyya s, 408a – S, 408b
Maṭbaʿa al-Madīna al-Munawwara s, 18a – S, 18b
Maṭbaʿa-i ʿĀmire v, 313b – V, 313b
Maṭbakh vi, **807a** – VI, **797a**

Matdjar al-Sulṭānī iv, 136a, b – IV, 142a
Mātem gedjeleri i, 1162a – I, 1196b
Matghara, Banū vi, 310b, **815a**, 923a – VI, 295b, **805a**, 915a
Mathal ii, 102a; iii, 369b; iv, 248b; v, 424b; vi, **815b** – II, 104a; III, 381a; IV, 259b; V, 426b; VI, **805b**
Mathālib i, 892a; vi, 349b, **828a** – I, 918b; VI, 333b, **818b**
al-Mathāmina i, 195a; vi, **829b** – I, 200b; VI, **819b**
Mathānī → al-Ḳurʾan
Mathnawī (in Arabic/en Arabe) → Muzdawidj
Mathnawī (in Persian, Turkish, Urdu/en Persan, Turc, Ourdou) i, 677a; ii, 395a, 396a; iv, 58a, b, 62a-63a, 66b-67a; v, 201b, 650b, 1106a; vi, **832a**; s, 324a – I, 698a; II, 405b, 406b, IV, 61a, b, 65b-66b, 70a-b; V, 198b, 654b, 1102a; VI, **822b**; S, 323b
Mathurā iv, 177b; vi, 343a, 369b, 602a, **839a** – IV, 186a; VI, 327a, 354a, 586b, **829b**
al-Maṭlaʿ vi, **839a** – VI, **830a**
Maṭmāṭa, Banū vi, 251a, 310b, **840a**, 1009a – VI, 235a, 295b, **831a**, 1001b
Maṭmūra vi, 338a, **842a** – VI, 322a, **833a**
Matn vi, **843a** – VI, **833b**
Matn (Durūz district) vi, 343b, 344a – VI, 328a
Maṭraḥ vi, 734b, 735b, **843a** – VI, 723b, 724b, 725a, **834a**
Maṭraḳčî, Nasūḥ al-Silāhī (1564) vi, **843b** – VI, **834b**
Maṭrān, Khalīl → Muṭrān
Matruh iv, 529a – IV, 552a
Matrūk → Marʿa (Turkey/Turquie)
Mattā b. Yūnus (Yūnān) al Ḳunnāʾī Abū Bishr (940) i, 151b, 631b, 737a, 982b; ii, 779a; iii, 112a, 368a; iv, 252b; vi, 204a, 443b, 444a, **844b**; vii, 1031a; viii, 614b – I, 156a, 652a, 759a, 1013a; II, 797b; III, 114a, 380a; IV, 263b; VI, 188b, 429a, b, **835a**; VII, 1033b; VIII, 634a
Matthias Corvinus (1490) vii, 219a – VII, 220b
Matun (Khōst) vi, 86b – VI, 84b
al-Māturīdī, Abū Manṣūr (944) i, 124a, 589b; iii, 1145a; iv, 272a; vi, **846a**; s, 90b – I, 127b, 609a; III, 1173b; IV, 284a; VI, **836b**; S, 90a
Māturīdiyya i, 334a, b, 343a, 410b, 411a, b, 413b, 696a; ii, 834a; iii, 330a, 465b; iv, 183b, 365b; vi, **847a** – I, 344b, 345a, 353b, 422a, 423a, b, 425a, 717a; II, 853b; III, 340a, 482a; IV, 191b, 381b; VI, **838a**
Maulavi, E.K. (XX) vi, 462b – VI, 448a
Maulavi, Khatib Muḥammad (1964) vi, 462a – VI, 448a
Maulavi Abussabah Ahmedali (Mappila) (1971) vi, 461a – VI, 446b
Maumoon Abdul Gayoom (Maldives) (XX) vi, 246a – VI, 230a
Maʿūna vi, **848b** – VI, **839b**
Maures I, 32b; II, 27a; VI, **839b**
Mauritania/-ie → Mūrītāniya
Mauritius/Maurice vi, **848b** – VI, **840b**
Mawākib vi, **849b** – VI, **841a**
Mawāl, mawāliya i, 404a; iii, 289b – I, 415b; III, 298b
Mawālī → Mawlā
Mawāliyā vi, **867b** – VI, **858b**
al-Māwardī, Abu ʾl-Ḥasan ʿAlī (1058) i, 119a, 328b, 435b, 439b, 982b, 1356a; ii, 116a, 131a; iii, 159b, 486a, 766a, 1165a, 1237a; iv, 173a, 457b, 458b, 949b; vi, 11a, 496a, 820a, **869a**; vii, 296b, 506b; viii, 95a; x, 918a; s, 192a – I, 122b, 338b, 447b, 452a, 1013a, 1395a; II, 118b, 134b; III, 163a, 503a, 789a, 1193b, 1269a; IV, 180b, 477b, 478b, 982a; VI, 11a, 481b, 811b, **859b**; VII, 298b, 507a; VIII, 97a; X, ;S, 193a
Mawāt iii, 1053b; iv, 1036a; vi, **869b** – III, 1079b; IV, 1067b; VI, **860b**
Mawāzīn vi, **117a** – VI, **115a**
Mawḍūʿ iii, 26b – III, 28a
Mawdūd b. Altuntakin (amīr, Mosul) (1113) i, 1332b; ii, 282a; vii, 983b – I, 1373a; II, 290a; VII, 984a
Mawdūd b. ʿImād al-Dīn Zankī, Ḳuṭb al-Dīn (Zangid(e), Mosul) (1170) i, 1160b; ii, 489b; iii, 961a; vi, **870a**; vii, 406b; viii, 127b – I, 1195a; II, 501b; III, 985b; VI, **861a**; VII, 408a; VIII, 130b
Mawdūd b. Masʿūd b. Maḥmūd (Ghaznawid(e)) (1048) i, 278a; ii, 5a, 1051b; iv, 815a; vi, 780b, **871b**; vii, 407a – I, 286b; II, 5a, 1075b; IV, 848a; VI, 770a, **862b**; VII, 408b
Mawdūdī → Abu ʾl-ʿAlāʾ Mawdūdī
Mawdūdī (Mawdoodi), Sayyid Abu ʾl-ʿAlāʾ (1979) vi, **872a**; viii, 242b – VI, **863a**; VIII, 248ab
Māwiya vi, 474b – VI, 460b
Mawḳif vi, **874a** – VI, **865a**
Mawlā i, 30b, 569a, b, 890b; ii, 324a, 951a; iii, 388b, 412a, 719a, 1152b; iv, 44a-b, v, 925b, vi, **874a** – I, 31b, 587b, 588a, 917a; II, 333b, 973a; III, 401a, 424b, 741b, 1181a; IV, 47a; V, 931a; VI, **865a**
Mawla ʿAlī b. Muḥammad b. Falāḥ (XV) vii, 672a – VII, 672a
Mawlā (Mūl) ʾl-Ḳṣūr → al-Ghazwānī, Sīdī ʿAbd Allāh
Mawkā Ṣandalī → Muḥammad b, Ḥurmuz
Mawlāʾīs iv, 202b – IV, 211b
Mawlānā v, 627a – V, 631a
Mawlānā ʿAbd Allāh → Makhdūm al-Mulk
Mawlānā ʿAlī Aḥmad (Delhi) vii, 473b – VII, 473a
Mawlānā Darwīsh Muḥammad (XVI) vii, 337b – VII, 339a
Mawlānā Dūst (Kābul) (XVI) vii, 337b, 473b – VII, 339a, 473a
Mawlānā Ḥasan Kawkabī (XVI) vii, 676b – VII, 676b
Mawlānā Ibrāhīm (Delhi) vii, 473b – VII, 473a
Mawlānā Khālid Baghdādī al-Kurdī (1867) v, 475a, 486a; X, 250b – V, 478a, 489a; X, 269b
Mawlānā Khūnkār vi, **882b** – VI, **874b**
Mawlānā Maḳṣūd (Herat) vii, 473b – VII, 473a
Mawlānā Muḥammad ʿAlī (1951) i, 302b; v, 7a, b – I, 312a; V, 7a, b
Mawlānā Rūmī → Djalal al-Dīn Rūmī
Mawlānā Yūsuf (painter/peintre) (XVI) vii, 337b – VII, 339a
Mawlawī → Djalāl al-Dīn Rūmī
Mawlawī, Mullā ʿAbd al-Rahīm Taydjawzī (1883) vi, **883a** – VI, **874b**
Mawlawiyya i, 234a, 1161b; ii, 164b, 224a, 226b, 393b; iv, 48a, 65b, 190b; vi, 354b, 530b, **883a**; ix, 858a; x, 251b; s, 83b, 283a – I, 241a, 1196b; II, 170a, 231a, 233a, 404a; IV, 50b, 68b, 198b; VI, 338b, 515a, **883a**; IX, 844a; X, 270a; S, 83a, 283a
Mawlāy (ʿAlawī/Saʿdī title) v, 627a; vi, **888b** – V, 631a; VI, **880a**
Mawlāy → ʿAlawid(e)s: al-Rashīd b. al-Sharīf; ʿAbd Allāh b. Ismāʿīl; Muḥammad III b. ʿAbd Allāh; Sulaymān, Abū ʾl-Rabīʿ b. Muḥammad; ʿAbd al-Raḥmān b. Hishām; Muḥammad IV b. ʿAbd al-Raḥmān; ʿAbd al-ʿAzīz b. al-Ḥasan; ʿAbd al-Ḥāfiẓ (→ al-Ḥāfiẓ); Yūsuf b. al-Ḥasan; Muḥammad V b. Yūsuf Saʿdid(e)s: ʿAbd Allāh al-Ghālib bi-ʾllāh; Aḥmad al-Manṣūr al-Dhahabī
Mawlāy ʿAbd Allāh b. Muḥammad b. Yūsuf (ʿAlawid(e)) (XX) vii, 415b – VII, 417a

Mawlāy Bū ʿAlī (Marrākus͟h) (XV) vi, 594a – VI, 578b
Mawlāy al-Ḥarrānī (Tāfilālt) (1672) vi, 891b – VI, 883a
Mawlāy al-Ḥasan → al-Ḥasan I, Mawlāy
Mawlāy Ḥasan b. Muḥammad V b. Yūsuf (ʿAlawid(e)) (XX) vii, 415b – VII, 417a
Mawlāy Ḥasan b. Yūsuf (ʿAlawid(e)) (XX) vii, 415a – VII, 416b
Mawlāy Idrīs (Fès) vi, 124b – VI, 122b
Mawlāy Idrīs b. Yūsuf (ʿAlawid(e)) (XX) vii, 415a – VII, 416b
Mawlāy Idrīs, Zāwiyat (town/ville) v, 1188b; vi, **889a** – V, 1178b; VI, **880b**
Mawlāy Ismāʿīl b. al-S͟harīf (ʿAlawid(e)) (1727) i, 34b, 47a, 159b, 289a, 365a; ii, 17b, 173a, 367b, 510a, 819b, 823a, 1022a; iii, 231a, 499b, 1047a; iv, 214a; v, 49a, 53b, 1191b, 1245b; vi, 135a, 142b, 250a, 293b, 591a, 595a, 596b, **891b**; vii, 37b; s, 40a, 113b, 114a, 125b, 126a, 132a, 223b, 399b – I, 35b, 48b, 164a, 298a, 366b; II, 17b, 178a, 377b, 523a, 839a, 842b, 1045b; III, 237b, 516b, 1073a; IV, 223b; V, 50a, 54b, 1181b, 1236b; VI, 133a, 141a, 234a, 278b, 575b, 579b, 581b, **882b**; VII, 38a; S, 40b, 113a, b, 125a, 131b, 223b, 400a
Mawlāy Maḥammad al-S͟haykh I, Abū ʿAbd Allāh al-Mahdī (al-Imām) (Saʿdid(e)) (1557) vi, **893** – VI, **884a**
Mawlāy Maḥammad al-S͟hayk͟h II, al-Maʾmūn (Saʿdid(e)) (1613) vi, **894b** – VI, **885b**
Mawlāy Maḥammad al-S͟hayk͟h III b. Mawlāy Zaydān al-Ṣag͟hīr (Saʿdid(e)) (1655) vi, **894b** – VI, **886a**
Mawlāy al-Saḥlī (XVI) ix, 758a – IX, 791a
Mawlāy Yūsuf b. al-Ḥasan (ʿAlawid(e)) (1926) i, 357b; ii, 160a; iv, 634b; vii, 415a; s, 48a – I, 368b; II, 165a; IV, 660b; VII, 416b; S, 48a
Mawlāy Zīdān (Saʿdī) (1628) ix, 545b – IX, 567a
Mawlid/Mawlūd i, 281a, 1004a, 1161a; v, 1200b; vi, **895a** – I, 289b, 1035a, 1195b; V, 1190b; VI, **886a**
Mawlid al-Nabī (Mecca) vi, 168a – VI, 159b
Mawlid Sayyidatnā Fāṭima (Mecca) vi, 168a, 650b – VI, 159b, 636a
Mawlidiyya (Mawli(ū)diyyāt i, 58b; vi, 248a, **897b** – I, 60a; VI, 232b, **889a**
Mawrūr (Morón) i, 6a; vi, **898b** – I, 6a; VI, **890a**
al-Mawrūrī → D͟jūdī
Mawsids͟h (Maws͟hid) vii, 513b – VII, 513b
al-Mawṣil i, 731b, 732a, 866b, 907a, 975b, 1074a; ii, 90b, 348a, 385a; iii, 127a, 218a, 1256b, 1258a, 1267b; iv, 584b; v, 145b, 437a, 451a, b, 454a, 463b, 821a; vi, 55b, 56b, 69a, 75a, 198a, 243b, 270b, 378b, 379b, 380a, b, 387a, 471a, 500a, 502b, 539b, 541a, 624a, 626a, 648a, 652a, 667a, 733b, 780b, 870a, **899a**; viii, 131b; s, 36a, b, 37a, 49b, 100a, 192b, 379b – I, 753b, 754a, 890b, 934a, 1005b, 1106b; II, 92a, 358a, 395a; III, 130a, 224b, 1289a, 1290b, 1300b; IV, 608a; V, 148a, 439b, 453b, 454a, 457a, 466a, 827a; VI, 53b, 54b, 67a, 73a, 182a, 227b, 255b, 300b, 362b, 364a, b, 371b, 456b, 485a, 487b, 524b, 525b, 609a, 611a, 633a, 637a, 653a, 722b, 770b, 861a, **890b**; VIII, 134a; S, 36a, b, 37a, 50a, 99b, 193b, 379b
al-Mawṣilī, ʿAbd Allāh b. Muṣṭafā al-Fayḍī (XIX) vi, 113b – VI, 111a
al-Mawṣilī, Bakr b. al-Ḳāsim b. Abī T͟hawr (X) vi, **902b** – VI, **894a**
al-Mawṣilī, Ibn Abī Saʿīd vi, 902b – VI, 894a
al-Mawṣilī, Muʿāfa b. ʿImrān (800) x. 8b – X, 8b
al-Mawṣilī, Muḥammad b. Yaḥyā b. Abī Manṣūr (IX) vi, 215a – VI, 199a
al-Mawṣilī, Murr b. ʿAlī viii, 53a – VIII, 53b
al-Mawṣilī, Tād͟j al-Dīn b. Muḥammad (1361) vii, 257b – VII, 259a
al-Mawṣilī, Ubayy b. Kaʿb vii, 494a – VII, 494a
al-Mawṣilī, ʿUt͟hmān b. ʿAlī al-ʿUmarī (1770) vi, 112b, 114a – VI, 110b, 111b
Mawsim vi, 233a, **903a**; s, 53a – VI, 206a, **894b**; S, 53b
Mawsūʿa vi, **903b** – VI, **894b**
Mawt vi, **910b** – VI, **902a**
al-Mawwāḳ vi, 279a – VI, 264a
Mawwāl → Mawāliyā
al-Mawzaʿī, S͟hams al-Dīn ʿAbd al-Ṣamad (1621) vi, **911b** – VI, **903a**
Mawzūna → Sikka
Maybūʿ ix, 673a → IX, 700b
Maybud vi, **912a** – VI, **903b**
al-Maybudī, K͟haṭīr al-Mulk (vizier) (1119) i, 1052b; vi, **912a** – I, 1084a; VI, **903b**
al-Maybudī, Mīr Ḥusayn al-Manṭiḳī (XVI) vi, **912a** – VI, **903b**
al-Maybudī, Ras͟hīd al-Dīn (XII) vi, **912a** – VI, **903b**
Maydān ii, 954b; vi, **912b** – II, 976b; VI, **904a**
Maydān-i Mas͟hḳ vi, 529a – VI, 513a
al-Maydānī, Abū ʾl-Faḍl Aḥmad al-Naysābūrī (1124) i, 794a; ii, 590b; iii, 992a; iv, 525b; vi, 478a, 823b, **913a** – I, 817b; II, 605a; III, 1016b; IV, 548b; VI, 464a, 813b, **904b**
al-Maydānī, S͟hayk͟h ʿAbd al-G͟hānī (1881) viii, 908a – VIII, 939a
al-Maydī v, 808b – V, 814b
Mayfaʿ i, 538a; s, 337a – I, 555a; S, 337a
Mayhana, Mīhana i, 147a; vi, **914b** – I, 151b; VI, **906a**
al-Mayhanī (XII) iii, 1243a – III, 1275a
Mayhanī, Muḥammad b. ʿAbd al-K͟hāliḳ (XI) vii, 679b – VII, 679b
al-Mayhanī, S͟hayk͟h Abū Saʿīd s, 154a – S, 154b
al-Mayl vi, **914b** – VI, **906a**
Maylāʾ vi, 442a – VI, 427b
Maylī (Harāt) (1576) viii, 775b – VIII, 801b
Maymad s, 116a – S, 115b
Maymana ii, 608b, 609a; vi, **915a**; ix, 431a – II, 623b, 624a; VI, **906b**; IX, 447b
Maymandī, Abu ʾl-Ḳāsim Aḥmad b. Ḥasan (S͟hams al-Kufāt) (1032) i, 278a; iii, 255b, 345a; vi, 453a, 522a, **915b**; vii, 653a, 679a – I, 286b; III, 263a, 355b; VI, 438b, 507a, **907a**; VII, 652b, 679a
Maymandī, Manṣūr b. Saʿīd s, 21a – S, 21b
al-Maymandī i, 278a; iii, 255b, 345a – I, 286b; III, 263a, 355b
al-Maymanī al-Rād͟j(a)kūtī, ʿAbd al-ʿAzīz (1978) vi, **916a** – VI, **907b**
Maymūn iii, 574b; v, 132b – III, 594b; V, 135a
Maymūn b. Aḥmad ii, 1082b; iv, 347a – II, 1108a; IV, 361b
Maymūn b. ʿAmr (928) ix, 586b – IX, 609a
Maymūn b. al-Aswad al-Ḳaddāḥ (765) i, 48a; ii, 851b; v, 1242b; vi, **917b** – I, 49b; II, 871a; V, 1233a; VI, **909a**
Maymūn b. D͟jaddār (Yiddar) (1155) ii, 1013b; vii, 591a – II, 1037a; VII, 591a
Maymūn b. Mihrān, Abū Ayyūb (735) vi, 878a, **916b** – VI, 869a, **908a**
Maymūn b. Yiddar → Maymūn b. D͟jaddār
Maymūna (Malta/e) iii, 362b; vi, 295b; s, 311a – III, 374a; VI, 280b; S, 311a
Maymūna bint al-Ḥārit͟h (681) vi, **918a**; vii, 372b – VI, **909b**; VII, 374a
Maymūn-Diz i, 1359b; iii, 501b; vi, **917b** – I, 1399b; III, 519a; VI, **909b**

al-Maymūnī, Abu 'l-Malīḥ (VIII) vi, 917a – VI, 908b
al-Maymūnī, ʿAmr b. Maymūn b. Mihrān (VIII) vi, 917a – VI, 908b
al-Maymūnī, Dja'far b. Burḳān (VIII) vi, 917a – VI, 908b
Maymūniyya i, 48a – I, 49b
Mayo ii, 464a – II, 475b
Maysalūn (battle/bataille, 1920)- vi, **918a**; viii, 141a – VI, **910a**; VIII, 143b
Maysān vi, **918b** – VI, **910a**
Maysara al-ʿAbdī i, 1292b – I, 1332b
Maysara al-Maṭgharī (740) i, 1175a; v, 1189a; vi, 815a, **923a**; viii, 638a; ix, 767b – I, 1210a; V, 1179a; VI, 805b, **915a**; VIII, 657a; IX, 801a
al-Maysī, Luṭf Allāh (1622) viii, 779a – VIII, 805a
al-Maysir i, 1111b; iv, 263b; v, 108b; vi, **923b**; s, 394b – I, 1145a; IV, 275a; V, 111a; VI, **915b**; S, 394b
Maysūn bint Baḥdal b. Unayf al-Kalbiyya (680) i, 920a; vi, **924b**; vii, 267b; x, 867b – I, 947b; VI, **916a**; VII, 269b; X,
Maysūr (936) i, 163b; iii, 1036b; iv, 459a, b –I, 168a; III, 1062a; IV, 479a, 480a
Maysūr (Mysore) → Mahisur
Mayta ii, 1069a; vi, **924b** – II, 1093b; **916b**
al-Maʿyūf, Banū vi, 303a – VI, 288b
Mayūrḳa i, 490a, 1055a; ii, 111b, 1007a; iii, 704b; iv, 1157a; vi, 457a, **926a**, 989a; s, 120b, 307a – I, 504b, 1086b; II, 114a, 1030b; III, 727a; IV, 1189a; VI, 442b, **918a**, 990a; S, 120a, 307a
al-Mayūrḳī → al-Ḥumaydī, Abū ʿAbd Allāh
al-Mayūrḳī, Abū Bakr Muḥammad (1142) iii, 712b, 732a – III, 735a, 754b
al-Mayūrḳī, Abu 'l-Ḥasan ʿAlī (1082) vi, **927a** – VI, **919a**
Maywātīs iii, 433b – III, 447b
Mayy Ziyāda (Mārī Ilyās Ziyāda) (1941) vi, **927a** – VI, **919a**
Mayyāfāriḳīn i, 665a, 679b; ii, 344b; iii, 129b, 900a; iv, 521a; vi, 119b, 270b, 540a, 626a, b, **928a**, 1017a; s, 36b, 37a – I, 684b, 700b; II, 354a; III, 132a, 924a; IV, 544a; VI, 117a, 255b, 525a, 611a, b, **920a**, 1019a; S, 36b, 37a
Mayyāra, Abū ʿAbd Allāh Maḥammad al-Akbar (1662) vi, 406b, **932b**; s, 404a – VI, 391a, **924b**; S, 405a
Mayyūn i, 535b, 539a, 837b; vi, **933a** – I, 551b, 556a, 860b; VI, **925a**
Maʿz → Ghanam
Māza, Banū iii, 163a – III, 166b
Mazagan → al-Djadīda
Mazagran vi, 248b – VI, 232b
Mazāḳī v, 261a – V, 259a
Maẓālim i, 209a, 387b; ii, 145b, 519b; vi, **933b** – I, 215b, 398b; II, 149b, 532b; VI, **925b**
Māzandarān i, 8a, b, 147b, 148a, 237a; ii, 903b; iv, 808a; v, 663a, b, 664a; vi, 202b, 415b, 510b, 511b, 512a, b, 513a, b, 514a, b, 515a, b, 516a, 632b, 726b, **935b**; viii, 650b; s, 239b – I, 8a, b, 152a, b, 244a; II, 924b; IV, 840b; V, 668a, 669a, b; VI, 187a, 400b, 496a, 497a, 498a, b, 499a, b, 500a, b, 501b, 617b, 715b, **927a**; VIII, 668a; S, 239b
al-Māzandarānī, ʿAbd Allāh b. Muḥammad b. Kiyā (1363) ii, 81a – II, 82b
Māzandarānī, Mullā Muḥammad Ṣūfī (XI) i, 840b – I, 864a
Māzandarānī, Saʿīd al-ʿUlamāʾ (XIX) vi, 552a; s, 95b – VI, 536b; S, 95a
Mazandjān v, 456b – V, 459a
Mazang ii, 41a – II, 42a
Māzar → Ṣiḳiliyya
Mazār → Maḳbara; Ziyāra
Mazār-čub vi, 936a – VI, 928a
al-Māzarī, Abū ʿAbd Allāh (al-Imām) (1141) vi, **942b**; vii, 228a – VI, **934b**; VII, 230a
al-Māzarī, Abū ʿAbd Allāh Muḥammad al-Iskandarānī (1135) vi, **943a** – VI, 935b
al-Māzarī, Abū ʿAbd Allāh (al-Zakī) (1118) vi, **943a**; ix, 587a – VI, **935b**; IX, 609a
Mazārīʿ, Āl v, 223b; s, 355b – V, 221a; S, 355b
Mazār-i Sharīf i, 530b, 1001b; vi, 765a, **942a**; s, 94a, 281a – I, 546b, 1032a; VI, 754a, **934a**; S, 93b, 281a
Mazāta, Banū vi, 310b, 311a, **943b** – VI, 296a, **935b**
al-Mazātī, Abu 'l-Rabīʿ Sulaymān b. Yakhlaf (1078) vi, 946b, **948a** – VI, 938b, **940a**
al-Mazātī, Dūnās b. al-Khayr (XII) vi, 946b – VI, 938b
Mazdaeans/Mazdéens iv, 11a-12b, 43a; vi, 337a, 949a – IV, 12a-13b, 45b; VI, 321a, 941a
Mazdak (Mazdaḳ) (531) i, 2b; v, 63b; vi, **949a** – I, 2b; V, 65a; VI, **941a**
Mazdakites i, 844a; ii, 228a; v, 63b, 64a, 853a; x, 440a – I, 867a; II, 235a; V, 65b, 66a, 859b; X, 471b
Mazdalī b. Sulankān i, 986a; ii, 1013a – I, 1016b; II, 1036b
Maẓhar (theophany/-ie) vi, **952a** – VI, **944b**
Maẓhar, Ismāʿīl iv, 125a – IV, 130a
Maẓhar, Maryam (XX) vii, 903a – VII, 903b
Maẓhar, Mīrzā Djāndjānān (1781) iii, 430b; iv, 507a; vi, **953a**; vii, 327b, 533a, 938b – III, 444b; IV, 529a; VI, **945b**; VII, 329a, 533a, 939a
Maẓhar al-Dīn Ibn Nishāṭī (XVII) vi, 837b – VI, 828a
al-Mazimma s, 377b – S, 377b
Māzin, Banū vi, **953b** – VI, **946a**
al-Māzinī, Abū ʿUthmān Bakr b. Muḥammad (863) iv, 122b, 822a; vi, 954a, **954b**; vii, 279b, 281a – IV, 127b, 855a; VI, 946b, **947a**; VII, 281b, 282b
al-Māzinī, Ibrāhīm ʿAbd al-Ḳādir (1949) i, 597b; v, 189a, b; vi, 91a, 414b, 415a, **955b**; vii, 441a – I, 617b; V, 186b; VI, 89a, 399b, 400a, **947b**; VII, 442a
al-Māzinī, Muḥammad b. ʿAbd Allāh vii, 538a – VII, 538a
Maẓlūm vi, **958b** – VI, **950b**
Mazouna → Māzūna
Mazraa → Mezere
Mazraʿa vi, **959a** – VI, **951b**
Mazrūʿī, Banū iv, 887a, b, 889b; vi, **961b**; vii, 227a – IV, 919b, 920a, 922a; VI, **954a**; VII, 228b
al-Mazrūʿī, Shaykh al-Amīn b. ʿAlī (1947) iv, 890b; vi, 962b; x, 195b; s, 248a – IV, 923b; VI, 954b; X, 211a; S, 248a
Māzūn ix, 775a – IX, 808b
Māzūna (Dahra) vi, 404a, b; vii, 263a – VI, 388b, 389a; VII, 265a
Mazyad, Banū (Mazyadid(e)s) i, 300b, 512a, 684a, 1052b, 1086a, 1096a; iv, 27b; vi, 64a, 270b, 380a, 500a, **965a**; vii, 726b; viii, 71b, 716a; s, 119a, 326a – I, 309b, 527b, 704b, 1084a, 11118b, 1129a; IV, 29b; VI, 62a, 255b, 364a, 485b, **957b**; VII, 727a; VIII, 73a, 736b S, 118b, 325b
al-Māzyār b. Ḳārin b. Wandā(d)hurmuz (Ḳārinid(e)) (841) i, 52b, 241a; iv, 20b, 207b, 645b, 646a, b; v, 64b; vi, 337b, 338b, 745a, b; vii, 776a; x, 17b; s, 309a – I, 54b, 248b; IV, 22a, 217a, 672a, b, 673a; V, 66b; VI, 321b, 323a, 734b; VII, 778a; X, 18a; S, 308b
Mazyata s, 103a – S, 102b
Mbacké, Āl → Amadu Bamba; Falilu; Mamadu Mustafa
Mbārak b. Gharīb (1696) vi, 962a – VI, 955a
Mbārak al-Mazrūʿī iv, 889b – IV, 922a

Mboamaji (Tanzania/-e) vi, 370a – VI, 354b
Mbweni vi, **966b** – VI, **959a**
Meʾālī (1535) vi, 610a, **967a** – VI, 594b, **959a**
Mecca → Makka
Mecelle → Medjelle
Mech(h)ed → Mashhad
Mechitar i, 640b – I, 661b
Meclis → Madjlis
Mecque, La → Makka
Mēd vi, 385a, **967a** – VI, 369a, **959b**
Medan vi, 239a – VI, 204a
Meddāḥ → Maddāḥ
Médéa → al-Madiyya
Medeniyyet vi, **968a** – VI, **960b**
Medḥī, Dervīsh Ḥasan (XVII) vi, **969b** – VI, **961b**
Medḥī, Maḥmūd Efendi, Ḳara Maḥmūd (Gelibolu) (1597) vi, **969a** – VI, **961b**
Medḥī, Nūh-zāde Seyyid Muṣṭafā Čelebi (1680) vi, **969a** – VI, **961b**
Medīḥī, Meḥmed (Istanbul) (1672) vi, **969b** – VI, **962a**
Medīḥī, Muṣṭafā Čelebi (Sīrōz) (XVI) vi, **696b** – VI, **962a**
Medina/Médine (Saudi Arabia/Arabie Séoudite → al-Madīna
Medina/Médina (Maghrib) v, 347b, 348a, 1108a; vi, **969b** – V, 348b, 1104a; VI, **962a**
Medina Sidonia → Shadūna
Medinaceli → Madīnat Sālim
Medinī Rāʾī (Rādjpūt) (1527) ii, 13a, 1128a; iii, 421b; vi, **970a** – II, 13a, 1154b; III, 435a; VI, **962a**
Mediouna s, 144b, 145a – S, 144a, b
Mediterranean Sea/Méditerranée, La → Baḥr al-Rūm
Medjdī, Meḥmed Čelebi (1591) vi, **970b** – VI, **963a**
Medjelle i, 285a; iii, 164a, 250a, 661a; iv, 168b; vi, **971a** – I, 294a; III, 167b, 257b, 682a; IV, 175b; VI, **963b**
Medjerda (river/rivière) vi, 727b – VI, 716b
Medjīdiyye → Sikka
Medjīdiyye (Medgidia) ii, 28b, 119b; vi, **972b** – II, 29a, 122b; VI, **965a**
Medjlis → Madjlis
Medjlis-i Wālā vi, **972b** – VI, **965a**
Medrese → Madrasa
Meerut → Mīrath
Mefkhari → ʿAṭāʾ Bey, Meḥmed
Meguiden s, 328a – S, 327b
Méhari/-ste vi, 83b – VI, 81b
Meharza s, 328a – S, 327b
Mehedak → al-Mahdiyya
Meḥemmed (turkish form of/forme turque de "Muḥammad") vi, **973b** – VI, **966a**
Meḥemmed I Čelebī b. Bāyazīd I (Ottoman) (1421) i, 299b, 394a, 432a, 468a, 510b, 869b, 988a; ii, 98a, b, 239b, 599a, 611b, 684a, 984b, 990a; iii, 356b, 711b; iv, 623b; vi, 531a, **973b**; viii, 193b – I, 309a, 405b, 444a, 482a, 526a, 893b, 1018b; II, 100b, 246b, 614a, 626b, 701a, 1007a, 1013a; III, 368a, 734a; IV, 648a; VI, 515a, **966a**; VIII, 196b
Meḥemmed II Fātiḥ (Ottoman) (1481)) i, 312b, 468a, 739a, 767b, 777a, 992b, 999a, 1007b, 1061a, 1062a, 1119a, 1163b, 1253a, 1334b; ii, 239b, 291b, 374a, 529a, 612a, 684a, 691a, 839b, 982b, 1140b; iii, 190b, 213a; iv, 140a, 224b, 225a, 576a, 624a, 969a; vi, 70a, 71a, 291a, 507b, 530a, b, 588a, 724b, 800a, 913b, **978a**; vii, 465b, 550b, 739b; viii, 194a; x, 965b; s, 257a, 283a, 315b – I, 322a, 482a, 760b, 790b, 800a, 1023a, 1029b, 1038b, 1092b, 1094a, 1153a, 1198a, 1290b, 1374b; II, 246b, 299b, 384a, 542a, 627a, 701a, 708b, 859b, 1005a, 1167b; III, 195a, 219a; IV, 146a, 234b, 235a, 599a, 649a, 1001a; VI, 68a, 69a, 276a, 493a, 514a, b, 572b, 713b, 790a, 904a, **970a**; VII, 465a, 551a, 740a; VIII, 197a; X, ; S, 257a, 282b, 315a
—administration i, 310b, 470a, 640b, 655b, 1256a, 1265b; ii, 82b, 118b, 211b, 337b, 338a, 687a, 715a, 907a, 1086b; iii, 1181a, 1183a; iv, 225a, 238a, 376a, 560a, 563a, 564b, 900a; v, 850a, 882a – I, 320a, 484a, 661a, 676a, 1294b, 1304b; II, 84a, 121a, 218a, 347b, 704a, 733a, 928a, 1112a; III, 1210a, 1212b; IV, 235a, 248b, 392a, 582b, 585a, 587a, 933a; V, 886a, 888a
—constructions i, 481a, 775b, 836b, 1078a, 1225b, 1251b; ii, 11b, 684b; iv, 225a, b, 226a, 228a-230b – I, 495a, 798b, 860a, 1110a, 1262a, 1289b; II, 11b, 701b; IV, 234b, 235b, 238a-240b
Meḥemmed III (Ottoman) (1603) i, 310a, 380b, 956a; ii, 34a, 690a, 880b; iii, 1185a; iv, 900b; v, 19a, 27b; vi, 202a, **981a**; x,, 679a – I, 319b, 391b, 985b; II, 34b, 707a, 901a; III, 1214b; IV, 933b; V, 19b, 28a; VI, 186b, **973a**
Meḥemmed IV Awdjī (Ottoman) (1687)) i, 1278b; ii, 345b, 684a, b; iii, 983b, 1185a; iv, 590a, b; v, 260a, b, 261b, 272b, 720b; vi, 56b, 295b, 345b, **982a**; vii, 89a; x, 679a; s, 257b – I, 1318a; II, 355a, 701a, b; III, 1008a, 1214b; IV, 613b, 614a, b; V, 258a, b, 259b, 270b, 725b; VI, 54b, 280b, 329b, 330a, **974b**; vii, 90b; S, 257b
Meḥemmed V Reshād (Ottoman) (1918) i, 64a; vi, 166a, **983a**; vii, 525b; viii, 59b – I, 65b; VI, 158b, **975b**; VII, 525b; VIII, 61a
Meḥemmed VI Waḥīd al-Dīn (Ottoman) (1926) i, 734a; ii, 104b; iv, 873a, b, 946b; vi, 530b, 531b, **984a** – I, 756a; II, 107a; IV, 906b, 907a, 979b; VI, 514b, 516a, 976b
Mehkeme → Maḥkama
Meḥmed, Mehmet → Meḥemmed
Meḥmed II (Ḳaramānid(e)) (1413) vi, 975b –VI, 968a
Meḥmed b. ʿAlāʾ al-Dawla Bozḳurd (Dhu 'l-Ḳadr) (1515) vi, 509b – VI, 495a
Meḥmed Beg b. Yaʿḳūb I (Ermiyān-oghullarî) (XIV) ii, 989b; ix, 418b; – II, 1012b ; IX, 432a
Meḥmed Agha (XV) vi, 69b, 70a – VI, 67b
Meḥmed Agha (Ḳule Aghasî) (XIX) s, 281b – S, 281b
Meḥmed ʿĀkif (1936) vi, **985a** – VI, **977b**
Meḥmed ʿAlī Pasha → Muḥammad ʿAlī Pasha
Meḥmed ʿĀshîḳ → ʿĀshîḳ
Meḥmed ʿAtāʾ (1919) s, 96a – S, 95b
Meḥmed Baghčesarāyī (1651) vi, **986b** – VI, **979a**
Meḥmed Balṭadjî → Meḥmed Pasha Balṭadjî
Meḥmed Beg b. Ibrāhīm Beg (Menteshe) (1370) vi, 1018b – VI, 1011a
Meḥmed Čelebi → Ghazālī, Meḥmed; Meḥemmed I
Meḥmed Djelāl (XIX) vii, 532a – VII, 532b
Meḥmed Edīb (XVII) vi, 778a – VI, 768a
Meḥmed Emīn ʿAlī Pasha → ʿAlī Pasha Muḥammad Amīn
Meḥmed Emīn Pasha (XVIII) vii, 709a – VII, 710a
Meḥmed Emīn al-Toḳadī (1745) vii, 724b – VII, 725b
Meḥmed Emīn Yurdakul (1944) vi, **986b**; viii, 251a; s, 47b, 149b – VI, **979a**; VIII, 267b S, 48a, 149b
Meḥmed Emnī Beyefendi (XVIII) vi, 56a – VI, 54a
Meḥmed Esʿad → Esʿad Efendi; Ghālib Dede
Meḥmed Farrūkh Pasha (XVI) s, 234b – S, 234b
Meḥmed Girāy I (Crimea/-ée) (1523) vi, **989a** – VI, **981b**
Meḥmed Girāy II (Criema/-ée) (1584) viii, 184b – VIII, 187a

Meḥmed Girāy, Derwīsh (XVIII) vi, **989a** – VI, **981b**
Meḥmed Ḥafīd (XIX) vii, 257b – VII, 259b
Meḥmed Ḥākim Efendi (1770) ii, 26b; vi, **989b** – II, 26b; VI, **982a**
Meḥmed Khalīfe b. Ḥüseyn (1687) vi, **990b** – VI, **983a**
Meḥmed Khusrew, Defterdār (Miṣr) (XIX) vii, 425b – VII, 427a
Meḥmed Lala Pasha → Meḥmed Pasha, Lala
Meḥmed Lālezārī → Lālezārī
Meḥmed Nedjātī (XVII) s, 171b – S, 171b
Meḥmed Pasha (wālī Erzerūm) (1647) vi, 202b – VI, 187a
Meḥmed Pasha (Yemen) (XVII) vi, 437a; vii, 270a – VI, 422b; VII, 272a
Meḥmed Pasha, Aydînlî (XVI) vii, 514a – VII, 514a
Meḥmed Pasha, Balṭadjî (1712) i, 269a, 395a, 1004b; vi, **991a**; vii, 839a – I, 277a, 406a, 1035a; VI, **983b**; VII, 840b
Meḥmed Pasha, Bîyîklî (1521) ii, 345a, b; v, 248b, 457b; vi, 541b, **992b** – II, 355a; V, 246a, 460a; VI, 526a, **985a**
Meḥmed Pasha, Bushatlî i, 675a; iv, 588b – I, 677b; IV, 612a
Meḥmed Pasha, Čerkes (1625) i, 174b; v, 33a; vi, **993a** – I, 179b; V, 34a; VI, **985b**
Meḥmed Pasha, Dalṭaban (XVIII) vii, 708a – VII, 709a
Meḥmed Pasha, Djalīlī ii, 402a – II, 423a
Meḥmed Pasha, Djerrāḥ (XVI) vi, 981a – VI, 973b
Meḥmed Pasha, Elmās (1697) vi, **993a**; vii, 708a – VI, **985b**; VII, 708b
Meḥmed Pasha, Gürdjü (I) (Khādim) (1626) vi, **994a**; vii, 707b – VI, **986a**; VII, 708b
Meḥmed Pasha, Gürdjü (II) (1666) vi, **994b** – VI, **987a**
Meḥmed Pasha, ʿIwaḍ (1743) vi, **995a** – VI, **987b**
Meḥmed Pasha, Ḳaramānī (1481) vi, **995b** – VI, **988a**
Meḥmed Pasha, Kōra i, 920a – I, 948a
Meḥmed Pasha, Lālā, Melek-Nihād (II) (1595) vi, **996b** – VI, **989a**
Meḥmed Pasha, Lālā, Shāhīnoghlu (1606) i, 267b, 1284b; ii, 716b; iv, 499a; v, **640b**; vi, **996b** – I, 275b, 1324b; II, 735a; IV, 520b; V, **640b**; VI, **989a**
Meḥmed Pasha, Melek, Dāmād (1802) vi, **997b** – VI, **990a**
Meḥmed Pasha, Muḥsin-zāde (1774) i, 56b, 62b; iii, 158a, 253a; vi, **998a**; vii, 708b – I, 58a, 64b; III, 161b, 260a; VI, **990b**; VII, 709b
Meḥmed Pasha, Öküz (1620) ii, 635a; iv, 970b; vi, **998b**; viii, 182a – II, 651a; IV, 1002b; VI, **991a**; VIII, 185a
Meḥmed Pasha Rāmī (1707) i, 349b; iv, 657b; vi, **999b**; ix, 60a – I, 406a; IV, 684a; VI, **992a**; IX, 57b
Meḥmed Pasha, Rūm(ī) (1478) vi, 71b, 72a, **1000a** – VI, 69b, **992b**
Meḥmed Pasha Saḳîzî (XVII) x, 214a – X, 231a
Meḥmed Pasha Ṣarī → Ṣarī Meḥmed Pasha
Meḥmed Pasha, Ṣilāḥdār iv, 437b – IV, 457b
Meḥmed Pasha Ṣoḳollī → Ṣoḳollī, Ṣoḳollu
Meḥmed Pasha, Sulṭān-zāde (1646) iii, 623a, 983a; vi, **1000b** – III, 644a, 1007b; VI, **993a**
Meḥmed Pasha, Tabanîyassî (1639) vi, **1001a** – VI, **993b**
Meḥmed Pasha, Tiryāḳī (1751) i, 267b; iv, 546b, 878a;vi, **1001b**; ix, 557b – I, 275b; IV, 570a,910b; VI, **994a**; IX, 579b
Meḥmed Pasha Yegen (Gümrükčü) (1745) i, 56b, 292a; ii, 534a; iv, 544a; v, 729a; vi, 995a, **1002b** – I, 58a, 301a; II, 547a; IV, 567b; V, 734a; VI, 987b, **995a**
Meḥmed Pasha Yegen, Ḥādjdjī Seyyid (1787) i, 56b; ii, 534a; iv, 544a; vi, **1003a** – I, 58a; II, 547a; IV, 567b; VI, **995a**
Meḥmed Radīf Pasha i, 709b – I, 731a
Meḥmed Rāshid → Rāshid, Meḥmed
Meḥmed Rashīd (wālī Syria/-e) (XIX) s, 296a – S, 296a
Meḥmed Raʾūf (1931) vi, **1003a** – VI **995b**
Meḥmed Reʾīs, Ibn Menemenli (XVII) vi, **1003b** – VI, **995b**
Meḥmed Rüshdī Pasha (XIX) vii, 599b – VII, 599a
Memed Ṣādiḳ iv, 284b – IV, 297a
Meḥmed Saʿīd Ghālib Pasha (1829) iv, 295b; vi, **1003b** – IV, 308b; VI, **996a**
Meḥmed Saʿīd Pasha (XIX) vi, 69a – VI, 67a
Meḥmed Ṣāliḥ Efendi (Ḥekimbashî) (XIX) i, 973a – I, 1003a
Meḥmed Ṣāliḥ Efendi, Shaykh al-Islām (1762) vi, **1004a** – VI, **996b**
Meḥmed Shākir Pasha (1914) s, 348b – S, 348b
Meḥmed Sherīf (XIX) s, 63a – S, 63b
Meḥmed Tewfīḳ Efendi, Khodja (XIX) s, 149b – S, 149b
Meḥmed Yîrmîsekiz Çelebi Efendi (1732) iii, 997b, 1002a; v, 641b, 642a; vi, **1004b**; viii, 859b – III, 1022b, 1027b; V, 645b, 646a; VI, **997a; VIII, 891a**
Meḥmed Zaʿīm (XVI) vi, **1006b** – VI, **999a**
Meḥmet ʿĀkif Ersoy iv, 169a – IV, 176a
Mehri → Mahrī
Mehtar ii, 30b – II, 31a
Mehter vi, **1007a** – VI, **999b**
Mekke, La → Makka
Meknes/Meknès → Miknās
Melāmīlik x, 252a – X, 270b
Melazo vi, 560a – VI, 545a
Melek Aḥmed Pasha ii, 718a – II, 736b
Melek Meḥmed Pasha iv, 455b – IV, 476a
Melek Ṭāwūs → ʿIzrāʾīl
Melilla (Malīla) i, 356b; iii, 298b; vi, 120b, **1008b**; vii, 387a, 391b, 641b; s, 325b – I, 367a; III, 308a; VI, 118b, **1001a**; VII, 388b, 392b, 641a; S, 325a
Melilot/Mélilot → Iklīl al-Malik
Melitene i, 1103a, b, 1104a; ii, 110a, b, 238a; iv, 484a – I, 1137a, b; II, 112b, 113a, 245a; IV, 505a
Melkites → Rūm
Mellāḥ → Mallāḥ
Mellita iv, 650b, 651b – IV, 676b, 678a
Melukhkha vi, 192b – VI, 176b
Memdūḥ Pasha (XIX) i, 825b – I, 848b
Memdūḥ Şevket Esendal → Esendal
Memek Čelebi (1600) iii, 175b – III, 179b
Memi Shāh → Āteshīzāde Memi
Memish Beg (XVI) ii, 1046a – II, 1070b
Memon → al-Maymanī al-Rādj(a)kūtī
Memon (Gudjarāt) i, 172a; vi, **1009b** – I, 176b; VI, **1002a**
Memphis → Manf
Menangkabau → Minangkabau
Menderes, Adnan (1961) ii, 204a, 432b, 596a; iii, 527a; vi, **1011b** – II, 210b, 444a, 611a; III, 545a; VI, **1004a**
Menderes, Büyük- vi, **1010a** – VI, **1002b**
Menderes, Eski- vi, **1011b** – VI, **1003b**
Menderes, Küçük- vi, **1011a** – VI, **1003b**
Menekshe (Monemvasia) vi, **1013b** – VI, **1005b**
Menelik II (Ethiopia/-e) (1913) viii, 161b – VIII, 164a
Menemen vi, **1015b** – VI, **1008a**
Menemendji-oghlu ii, 207a – II, 213b
Menemenli-zāde Meḥmed Ṭāhir (1902) vi, **1016a** – VI, **1008b**

Mêng-Kuan iv, 554b – IV, 578b
Mengli Girāy I (Crimea/-ée) (1515) i, 293a, 843a, 893a, 1166b; ii, 1112b, 1113a; v, 137a, 138a, 719b; vi, **1016a**; viii, 236a – I, 302a, 866b, 920a, 1201b; II, 1139a; V, 140a, b, 724b; VI, **1008b**; VIII, 241b
Mengü-Bars b. Böri-Bars (Saldjūḳ) (XII) i, 1336b, 1358a; vii, 408a – I, 1377a, 1398a; VII, 409a
Mengüček (Mangūdjak) (Mengüčekid(e)s) (Erzindjān) (XII) i, 466a, b, 467a, 639a, 983a; ii, 340a, 711b; iv, 578b, 871a; vi, 231a, **1016b** – I, 480a, b, 659b, 1013b; II, 350a, 729b; IV, 602a, 904a; VI, 224b, **1009a**
Mensūkhāt vi, **1017a** – VI, **1009b**
Menteshe-eli i, 467b, 988a, 1250b; ii, 204b, 599a; v, 505b, 506a; vi, **1017a** – I, 481b, 1018b, 1288b; II, 211a, 614a; V, 509a, b; VI, **1009b**
Menteshe Beg (1296) vi, 1018a – VI, 1010b
Menteshe-Oghullari̊ vi, **1018a**; vii, 56a, 348b – VI, **1010b**; VII, 56b, 350b
Menūtum → Manāt
Mē'ō vi, 48a, **1019a**; s, 124a – VI, 46b, **1011b**; S, 123b
Mer d'Aral → Aral
Mer d'Azov → Baḥr Māyuṭis
Mer Baltique → Baḥr al-Warank
Mer Caspienne → Baḥr al-Khazar
Mer de Marmara → Marmara Deñizi
Mer Morte → Baḥr Lūṭ
Mer Noire → Baḥr Bunṭus
Mer Rouge → Baḥr al-Ḳulzum
Merca (Somalia/-ie) vi, 129a, 170a – VI, 127a, 134a
Mercimek Ahmet → Merdjümek
Mercury/Mercure → ʿUṭārid
Merdjān, beglerbegi (XVI) iv, 571a – IV, 593b
Merdjümek, Aḥmed b. Ilyās (XV) vi, **1019a** – VI, **1012a**
Mere Ḥuseyn Pasha (XVII) vii, 707b – VII, 708b
Merguez → Mirkās
Mergui (Burma/Birmanie) vi, **1020a** – VI, **1012b**
Merič (river/fleuve) vi, **1022a** – VI, **1014b**
Merida/Mérida → Mārida
Me(é)rinid(e)s → Marīnid(e)s
Merka vi, 127a, 354a, **1022b** – VI, 129a, 370a, **1015b**
Merkez, Shaykh Muṣliḥ al-Dīn (1552) vi, **1023a** – VI, **1015b**
Merkez Ḳalʿesi vi, 778a – VI, 768a
Merkit ii, 42a, 43a, 571a – II, 43a, 44a, 585b
Mersin i, 476b; vi, **1023b** – I, 490b; VI, **1016a**
Mersiye → Marthiya
Mertola → Mīrtula
Mertvi̊y Kultuk (bay/baie) vi, 417a – VI, 402a
Merv → Marw al-Shāhidjān
Merv-Rūd → Marw al-Rūdh
Merwāŕā → Rādjāsthān
Merzifūn (Mārsiwān, Merzifon) iv, 589b; v, 1147a; vi, **1023b** – IV, 613a, b; V, 1138b; VI, **1016a**
Mesdjid → Masdjid
Mesfiwa vi, 590b – VI, 575a
Meshʿale vi, **1024a** – VI, **1017a**
Mesh(h)ed → Mashhad
Mesh(h)ed ʿAlī → al-Nadjaf
Mesh(h)ed Ḥusayn → Karbalāʾ
Meshrūṭa, Meshrūṭiyyet → Dustūr
Mesīḥ Meḥmed Pasha, Khādim (1589) vi, **1024b** – VI, **1017b**
Mesīḥ Pasha (1501) vi, **1025a** – VI, **1017b**
Mesīḥī (1512) vi, **1026a** – VI, **1019a**
Mesopotamia/Mésopotamie → al-Djazīra; Irāḳ
Messahallah → Māshāʾ Allāh
Meṣṣālī al-Hādjdj iii, 524b; iv, 785a – III, 542b; IV, 816b
Messiah/Messie → al-Masīḥ
Mesta (river/fleuve) vi, 89a – VI, 87a
Mesue → Ibn Masāwayh
Mevlānā Yūsuf Sinān Germiāni → Sheykhī Čelebi
Mēwāŕ vi, 53a, b, 54a, **1027a** – VI, 51b, 52a, **1019b**
Mēwāt vi, 48a, 49b, **1028b**; vii, 278b – VI, 46b, 48a, **1021a**; VII, 280b
Mēwātī → Mēʾō
Mewḳūfātčî, Mewḳūfātī vi, **1029a** – VI, **1022a**
Mewlānā ʿĪsā vi, 836a – VI, 826b
Mewlānā Khūnkār → Mawlānā Khūnkār
Mewlānā Saʿd al-Dīn (ḳāḍī) (XVI) vii, 225a – VII, 227a
Mewlewiyyet, Mollali̊ḳ iv, 375a; vi, 133b, **1029b** – IV, 391b; VI, 131b, **1022b**
Mewlūd → Mawlid
Meydān Česhmesi vi, 57a – VI, 55a
Mezere → Maʿmūrat al-ʿAzīz
Mezīd Beg (1400) vi, 974a – VI, 966b
Mezö-Keresztes (Battle of/Bataille de) (1596) iv, 499a; v, 27b; vi, **1030a**; s, 238b – IV, 520b; V, 28b; VI, **1023a**; S, 238b
Mezzomorto → Ḥusayn Pasha Mezzomorto
Mgīld, Bānū s, 113b, 145a – S, 113a, 144b
Mḥammad b. al-Khayr (Belkheīr) (XIX) vi, 252a – VI, 236b
M'ḥammad Bey (Tunis) (1859) vii, 717b – VII, 718b
Miʾān Bhuʾā, Masnad-i ʿAlī (XVI) vi, **1030b** – VI **1023b**
Mibkhara v, 987b – V, 983a
Michael → Mīkāl
Michael b. Sefer Beg (Abkhāz) (1864) i, 101a – I, 104a
Michael of/de Tinnīs (XI) vii, 164a – VII, 165b
Midād ii, 307a, 311a; vi, **1031b** – II, 315b, 320a; VI, **1024b**
Miʿdān → Maʿādī, Banū
Miʾdhana → Manār, Manāra
Midḥat, Aḥmed → Aḥmad Midḥat
Midḥat Djemāl Kuntay (1951) v, 197a – V, 194b
Midḥat Pasha (1884) i, 63b, 285b, 286a, 289b, 906b, 907b, 1096a, 1097a, 1304a; ii, 288b, 289a, 468b, 642a, 909a, 935b; iii, 621b, 1257b; iv, 638a, 765b, 876b; v, 904b; vi, 69a, 372b, 797a, **1031b**; vii, 599b – I, 65b, 294a, 298a, 934a, 935a, 1129a, 1130a, 1344a; II,296b, 297a, 480b, 658a, 930a, 957b; III, 642a, 1290b; IV, 664b, 796a, 909b; V, 910b; VI, 67a, 357a, 787a, **1025a**; VII, 599a
Midianite → Madyan Shuʿayb
Midilli (Mytile(è)ne) vi, 69a, 71a, b, **1035b** – VI, 67a, 69a, b, **1028b**
Midjmar s, 23b – S, 23b
Miḍrab iv, 1147a – IV, 1179a
Midrār, Banū (Midrārid(e)s) i, 83a, 1175b; ii, 495a; vi, **1038a** – I, 85b, 1210b; II, 507a; VI, **1031a**
Midyān Ḥaḍrat (Shaykh ʿAbd Allāh) (XVII) vii, 432b – VII, 433b
Midyāt vi, 539b, 542a – VI, 524a, 526b
Midyūna (Madyūna), Banū vi, 310b, **1042a** – VI, 295b, **1035b**
al-Midyūnī, ʿIsā b. Ḥandūn (XI) vi, 1043b – VI, 1036b
Mifrash (Mafrash; Mifresh) vii, **1a** – VII, **1a**
Miftāḥ v, 990a – V, 985a
Miftāḥ al-Ḥikma i, 995b – I, 1026b
Miftāḥ al-Mulk → Mīrzā Maḥmūd b. Yūsuf
Miftāḥ al-ʿUlūm i, 594a, 858a, 982a – I, 613b, 882a, 1012b
Mihdī Bāzargān vi, 549a – VI, 533b
Mihir Bhodja Pratīhāra ii, 1122b, 1123a – II, 1148b, 1149a

Mihmindār iv, 1043a; vii, **2a** – IV, 1074b; VII, **2a**
Miḥna i, 811a; ii, 931a; iii, 1148a; v, 426a, 1124a; vi, 338a; vii, **2b** – I, 834a; II, 953a; III, 1176b; V, 428b, 1121a; VI, 322b; VII, **2b**
Mihnī, Banū (Kirmān) v, 153b – V, 154b
Mihr → Taʾrīkh
Mihr Āfrūz vi, 488a – VI, 474a
Mihr ʿAlī (painter/peintre) vii, 603a – VII, 602b
Miḥr al-Nisāʾ → Nūrdjahān
Miḥrāb vii, **7a** – VII, **7a**
Miḥrāb Khān i, 1006a; v, 102a – I, 1037a; V, 104a, b
Mihrabānid(e)s ix, 183b – IX, 712a
Mihragān (Mihradjān) ii, 798b; vi, 523a; vii, **15a** – II, 817a; VI, 507b; VII, **15a**
Mihragān (Mihradjān) b. Rūzbih vii, 19b – VII, 19b
Mihrān (Indus) i, 222a; iii, 408a; iv, 597b; v, 872b; vii, **20b** – I, 228b; III, 420b, 421a; IV, 621b; V, 878b; VII, **20b**
Mihrān Efendi (XIX) ii, 474b, 475a; iv, 872b – II, 486b, 487a; IV, 906a
Miḥrāth vii, **21b** – VII, **21b**
Mihrawlī ii, 259a, 266a – II, 266b, 274b
Mihrgān → Mihragān
Mihribān (river/fleuve) vi, 745b – VI, 734b
Mihrī Khātūn (1512) vii, **23b** – VII, **23b**
Mihrī Māh Sulṭān bint Sulaymān II (Ottoman) (1578) iii, 147b; v, 66b; vi, 862a; vii, **6b** – III, 150b; V, 68b; VI, 853a; VII, **6b**
Mihrishāh Sulṭān iv, 233b – IV, 244a
Mihrumāh Sulṭān iv, 231b – IV, 241b
Mihtar → Mehter
Mihyār b. Marzawayh (Marzōye) al-Daylamī (1037) i, 592b; vi, 603a, 605b; vii, **24b**, 982b; s, 119b – I, 611b; VI, 588a, 590b; VII, **24b**, 983a; S, 119a
Mihzam, Banū s, 24b – S, 25a
Mīkāʿīl b. Djaʿfar i, 1306b, 1307b – I, 1346b, 1348a
Mīkāl (Mīkaʾīl) (archangel/archange) ii, 363b, 846b; vi, 217a, 219b; vii, **25a** – II, 373a, 866a; VI, 201a, 203b; VII, **25a**
Miʿkāl (al-Riyāḍ) s, 234b – S, 234b
al-Mīkālī, Abu ʾl-Faḍl (amīr, XI) vii, 527b; s, 343a – VII, 527b; S, 343a
Mīkālīs (Khurāsān) vi, 196a; vii, **25b**; x, 426a – VI, 180a; VII, **25b**; X, 456b
Miḳāt iii, 362b, 1052b; vii, **26b** – III, 373b, 1079a; VII, **26b**
Miḳdād b. ʿAmr (653) ii, 846b; iii, 873b; vii, **32a**, 517b – II, 866b; III, 897b; VII, **32b**, 518a
Miḳdād Aḥmed Pasha (1791) ii, 207b – II, 214a
al-Miḳdādī, Muṭahhar b. Muḥammad (1650) vii, 94b – VII, 96b
al-Miḳdām → Yaḥyā III (Idrīsid(e))
Mīkhāʾīl Mushāka → Mushāka, Mīkhāʾīl b. Djirdjīs
Mīkhāʾīl Nuʿayma ix, **229a** – IX, **235a**
Mīkhāʾīl al-Ṣabbāgh (1816) vii, **33a** – VII, **33b**
Mīkhāl-oghlu i, 340b; vii, **34a** – I, 351a; VII, **34a**
Mikhāl-oghlu Ghāzī ʿAlī Bewy (1507) viii, 318a – VIII, 328b
Mīkhāl-oghlu Meḥemmed (XV) vii, 644b – VII, 644b
Mīkhāl-oghlu Mīkhāl Beg (XV) vii, 712b – VII, 713b
Mikhdham (sword/épée) vi, 374a – VI, 358b
Mikhlāf/Makhālīf ii, 517a, b; vii, **35a** – II, 530a, b; VII, **35a**
Mikhlāf al-Sulaymānī ii, 517a; vi, 191b; s, 30a – II, 530a; VI, 175a; S, 30b
Mikindani (port) vii, **35a** – VII, **35a**
Miḳlama iv, 471b – IV, 492a
Miknās (al-Zaytūn) (Meknès) i, 85a, 356a, 134b; ii, 819b; iii, 973a; v, 1192a; vi, 141b, 293a, 356a, 406a, 571b, 572a, 595a; vii, **35b**, 387a; ix, 47a; s, 53a, 103a, 350b, 397b, 399b – I, 87b, 366b, 1387a; II, 839b; III, 997b; V, 1182a; VI, 140a, 278a, 340a, 390b, 556b, 557a, 580a; VII, **35b**, 388a; IX, 47b; S, 53b, 102b, 350b, 398a, 400a
Miknāsa, Banū i, 1349b; vi, 741a, 923a; vii, 36b – I, 1390a; VI, 730a, 915a; VII, 37a
al-Miknāsī, Abū Allāh Muḥammad b. Ḥamza (XIX) vi, 356b – VI, 340b
al-Miknāsī, Masāla b. Ḥabūs (924) ii, 853a; iii, 1036a; vii, 641a, b, 941b – II, 872b; III, 1062a; VII, 641a, b, 942a
Miḳyās (Nilometer/-mètre) iii, 572a; v, 91b, 862b; vi, 413a, 618b; vii, **39b**; viii, 41b – III, 591b; V, 93b, 869b; VI, 397b, 603b; VII, **40a**; VIII, 42a
Mīlād vii, **40b** – VII, **40b**
Milāḥa (Navigation) ii, 583a, 586a; iii, 856b, 627b; vii, **40b** – II, 597b, 600b; III, 880b, 648a; VII, **40b**
al-Milal wa ʾl-Niḥal vii, **54a** – VII, **54b**
Milān, Banū vi, 201b – VI, 185b
Mīlānī, Āyatullāh Muḥammad (1975) iv, 165b; vi, 553b – IV, 172b; VI, 538a
Mīlās (Milas) vii, **55a**; s, 138a – VII, **56a**; S, 137b
Miletus/Milète → Balāṭ
Milḥ v, 250b, 435b, 965a, 967b, 976a, 981b; vii, **57a** – V, 248b, 438a, 969a; VII, **57b**
al-Mīlī, Mubārak iv, 157a, 159b – IV, 163b, 166a
Mīl-i Nādirī vi, 365b – VI, 349b
Mīl-i Rādkān (Gurgān) vi, 713b – VI, 702a
Miliana → Milyāna
Milk (ownership/propriété) i, 28b, 661a; iv, 1035b; vii, **60b** – I, 29b, 682a; IV, 1067a; VII, **61a**
Milkān vi, 562b – VI, 547a
Milla (religion, sect(e)) ii, 294b; iv, 174a; vii, 54b, **61a** – II, 302b; IV, 181b; VII, 55a, **61b**
Millat → Millet
Millet (religion, religious community/ communauté religieuse, nation) i, 470a; ii, 6b; iii, 1180b; iv, 785b, 790b; vii, **61b** – I, 484a; II, 6b; III, 1209b; IV, 817a, 822b; VII, **61b**
Millī, Banū vi, 541b – VI, 526a, b
Millī Kongre ii, 431b – II, 442b
Milliyyat iv, 785b – IV, 817b
Milyāna, Miliana vi, 404a, b; vii, **64a** – VI, 388b, 389a, b; VII, **64b**
Mīm vii, **64b** – VII, **65a**
Miʿmār-bashi̊ iv, 235a, b – IV, 245b, 246a
Mīmiyya → Muḥammadiyya
Minā (Mecca) iii, 32b, 36a; vi, 140b, 169b; vii, **65a**; viii, 379a,bs, 33a, 317a, 350a, 357b – III, 34a, 38a; VI, 138b, 160b; VII, **65b**; VIII, 392a,bS, 33b, 316b, 350a, 357a
Mīnāʾ (port) vii, **66a** – VII, **66b**
Mīna, Ḥannā v, 190b, 191a – V, 188a
Mīnāʾ al-Aḥmadī s, 50a – S, 50b
Mīnāʾ al-Fahl vi, 735b – VI, 725a
Mīnaʾ Ḳābūs vi, 736a – VI, 725a
al-Mīna (Mīnās) ii, 1056a – II, 1080b
Mīnāb s, 129a – S, 128a
Minaeans/Minéens → Maʿīn
Mināʾī i, 201b; iv, 1167a; vii, **72b** – I, 207a; IV, 1199b; VII, **73b**
Minangkabau i, 170b, 173b, 174a; iii, 1214b, 1222b, 1225b, 1228a; vii, **73b**; viii, 237b; s, 151a – I, 175a, 178b; III, 1245a, 1253a, 1253b, 1257a, 1259b; VII, **74a**; VIII, 243a S, 151a
Mīnār, Minaret → Manāra
Minbar i, 202b, 776a; vii, **73b** – I, 208b, 799a; VII, **74b**
Miñbashi̊ i, 1229a – I, 1265b

Mindanao → Phillippines
Mindū, Shaykh (XIV) vi, 231a – VI, 225a
Minglī Girāy Khān → Menglī Girāy I
Minhādj-i Sirādj → al-Djūzdjānī
Minicoy vi, 206b; vii, **80b** – VI, 191a; VII, **82a**
Minḳād, Wādī s, 157a – S, 157b
al-Minkarī → Naṣr b. Muzāḥim
Minnet Beg-Oghlu Meḥmed Beg (XV) vi, 70b – VI, 68b
Minorca/Minorque → Minūrḳa
Minṭaḳat al-Burūdj vii, **81b** – VII, **83a**
Minṭāsh (Mamlūk) (1390) i, 1050b, 1051a; ii, 239b; iii, 187a; vi, 231b; vii, 170b, 462a – I, 1082b; II, 246a; III, 191a; VI, 225a; VII, 172b, 462a
Minṭāsh (Türkmen; amīr) (1321) vi, 381b – VI, 366a
Minūčihrī → Manūčihrī
Minūf, Minūfī → Manūf, Manūfī
Minūfiyya s, 44a – S, 44b
Minūrḳa iv, 1157a; iv, 1157a; vii, **87a** – IV, 1189a; VII, **88b**
al-Minyā (province) s, 18a, 408a – S, 18b, 408b
Minyā al-Ḳamḥ vi, 408a – VI, 393a
Minyat ʿAfīf s, 44a – S, 44b
Mīnyo, Nahr i, 489a – I, 503b
Mīr (title/titre) vii, **87b** – VII, **89b**
Mir ʿAbd Allāh Khān Marʿashī (XVI) iv, 364b; vi, 515b – IV, 380b; VI, 501a
Mīr Aḥmad b. Ramaḍān (Ramaḍān-oghlu) (1416) viii, 418b – VIII, 433
Mīr Ākhūr vii, **88a** – VII, **89b**
Mīr ʿAlāʾ al-Mulk Marʿash (XVI) vi, 516b – VI, 501b
Mīr ʿAlī Khān (Mīr Taymūr) (Marʿashī) (XVI) vi, 515a – VI, 500b
Mīr ʿAlī Shīr Nawāʾī, Niẓām al-Dīn (1501) i, 292b, 504b, 813b, 1019a, 1082b, 1211b, 1212b; ii, 179a, 421b, 422a, 792a; iii, 177b, 358a, 603a; iv, 66a-b, 1010a, 1020b; v, 835b; vi, 768a; vii, **90a**, 473a, 530a, 567b, 935a; s, 83a, 324a – I, 301b, 520a, 837a, 1050a, 1115a, 1247b, 1248b; II, 185a, 432b, 811a; III, 181b, 369a, 624a; IV, 70a, 1042a, 1052b; V, 842a; VI, 757a; VII, **91b**, 472a, 530b, 568b, 935b; VIII, 581b, 600a; S, 83a, 323b
Mīr ʿAlī Tabrīzī iv, 1124b – IV, 1156a
Mīr Amman → Amān, Mīr
Mīr Athar (1794) vi, 837b – VI, 828b
Mīr ʿAzīz Khān b. ʿAbd Allāh (Marʿashī) (XVI) vi, 515a – VI, 500a
Mīr Babar ʿAlī → Anīs
Mīr-i Buzurg → Marʿashī, Ḳawām al-Dīn
Mīr-i Dāmād Astarābādī → al-Dāmād
Mīr Damīr (XIX) vi, 611a, b – VI, 596a
Mīr Dard (XVIII) vii, 328a – VII, 329b
Mīr Djaʿfar → Djaʿfar, Mīr Muḥammad
Mīr Djaʿfar ʿAlī (1713) vi, 612a – VI, 596b
Mīr Djumla, Muḥammad Saʿīd (1663) i, 719b, 769a; ii, 216b, 1135a; iii, 318b, 427a; iv, 1020a; vi, 63a; vii, **93b** – I, 741b, 792a; II, 223a, 1162a; III, 328a, 440b; IV, 1052a; VI, 60b; VII, **95a**
Mīr Ghulām Ḥasan → Ḥasan, Mīr Ghulām
Mīr Ḥusayn Khān (Marʿashī) (XVII) vi, 515a, – VI, 500b
Mīr Ḳāsim ʿAlī (1777) vii, **93b** – VII, **95b**
Mīr Ḳawām al-Dīn (Marʿashī) (XV) vi, 514a – VI, 499a
Mīr Khalīḳ Abū Babar ʿAlī Anīs (XIX) vi, 611a – VI, 596a
Mīr Khudādād v, 102b – V, 104b
Mīr Lawḥī, Sayyid Muḥammad (XVII) v, 1088a; vii, **94a** – V, 1085a; VII, **96a**
Mīr Maʿsūm → Mīr Muḥammad Maʿsūm, Nāmī
Mīr Mīrān Ghiyāth al-Dīn (Yad) (XVI) viii, 775b – VIII, 801b
Mīr Mithar ʿAlī (1831) vii, 291a – VII, 293a
Mīr Muḥammad b. Ḳāḍī Kalandar (Ṣūfī) → Miyān Mīr
Mīr Muḥammad Ḥusayn Shahristānī (XIX) vi, 516b – VI, 502a
Mīr Muḥammad Maʿṣūm, Nāmī (1606) i, 962a, 1192b; iii, 245b; vii, **96a**, 317b – I, 991b, 1227b; III, 252b; VII, **97b**, 320a
Mīr Muḥammad Taḳī Mīr (1810) ii, 1036b; iii, 119a, 358b, 376a; v, 961b; vi, 611a, 837b; vii, **96a**, 533a; x, 878a – II, 1060b; III, 121b, 370a, 388a; V, 965b; VI, 595b, 828b; VII, **98a**, 533a; X,
Mīr Muhannā (Khār(a)g) iv, 1056b – IV, 1087b
Mīr Munnū → Muʿīn al-Mulk b. Ḳamar al-Dīn
Mīr Muṣawwir Abū Mīr Sayyid ʿAlī (XVI) vii, 337b – VII, 339a
Mīr Nadjm al-Dīn b. Aḥmad (Marʿashī) vi, 516a – VI, 501b
Mīr Nūr Allāh (naḳīb, Ṣafawid(e)) (XVI) vi, 516a – VI, 501b
Mīr Sāmān i, 316b – I, 326b
Mīr Sayyid ʿAlī b. Amīr Asad Allāh Marʿashī (XVI) vi, 516b; vii, 317a, 337b, 338a – VI, 501b; VII, 319a, 339a, b
Mīr Shams al-Dīn iv, 709a – IV, 737a
Mīr Shīr ʿAli → Afsūs
Mīr Taymūr → ʿAbd al-Karīm b. ʿAbd Allāh (Marʿashī)
Mīr Turāb → Sālār Djang
Mīr Ways (Ghalzay) (XVIII) i, 218b, 226b, 229a; ii, 1011a; iii, 603b; iv, 537a; vii, 318b; viii, 771a; ix, 854b – I, 224b, 233a, 236a; II, 1024b; III, 624b; IV, 560b; VII, 321a; VIII, 797a; IX, 890a
Mīrāb → Māʾ, Irān
Miʿrādj i, 1310b; ii, 448b; vii, **97b** – I, 1350b; II, 460a; VII, **99b**
Mīrafāb i, 1171b, 1172a – I, 1206b, 1207a
Mīrak Ḥusayn Yazdī s, 204a – S, 203b
Mīrak Naḳḳāsh i, 1211a, b – I, 1247a, b
Mīrān Ṣāḥib → Shāh al-Ḥāmid ʿAbd al-Ḳādir
Mīrān Muḥammad Shāh I (Fārūḳī; Khāndēsh) (1537) ii, 815a, 1128b; iii, 422a, 1160a; vi, 52a; vii, **105a** – II, 834a, 1155a; III, 435b, 1188b; VI, 50a, b; VII, **107a**
Mīrān Muḥammad Shāh II (Fārūḳī; Khāndēsh) (1576) ii, 815a; iii, 1161a, b; vii, 134a – II, 834b; III, 1189b, 1190a; VII, 136a
Mīrān Ṣāḥib → Shāh al-Ḥamīd ʿAbd al-Ḳādir
Mīrān Shāh ʿAlī (Aḥmadnagar, XVI) iii, 626a – III, 646b
Mīrān Shāh Ḥaydar (XVI) iii, 625b – III,646b
Mīrāndjī → Miyān Mīr, Miyāndjī
Mīrānī (ʿUmān) vi, 735a – VI, 724a
Mīrānīs (Balūčī) ii, 185b – II, 191b
Mīrānshāh b. Tīmūr Lang (Tīmūrid(e)) (1408) i, 66b; ii, 733a, b; iii, 600b; iv, 914b, 1029a; vi, 714b; vii, **105b** – I, 68b; II, 751b, 752b; III, 621a; IV, 947b, 1060b; VI, 703a; VII, **107b**
Mirʾāt (mirror/miroir) v, 988a; vii, **105b** – V, 984a; VII, **108a**
Mirʿāt al-Aḥwāl ii, 466a, 471a – II, 477b, 483a
Mīrāth i, 1142b; vii, **106b** – I, 1177a; VII, **108b**
Mīrath (Meerut) vii, **113a** – VII, **115a**
Mīrāthī, ʿImād al-Dīn iv, 1041a – IV, 1072b
al-Mirbad (al-Baṣra) i, 1080a, 1086a; vi, 709b; vii,

113b, 843a, 873a; s, 172a – I, 1112b, 1118b; VI, 698a; VII, **115b**, 844a, 874b; S, 173a
al-Mirbāṭ iii, 270a; vi, 83b; vii, 53a, **114b** – III, 277b; VI, 81b; VII, 53b, **116b**
Mirčea ii, 611a – II, 626b
Mirdās, Banū (Mirdāsid(e)s) i, 442a, 1349a; iii, 86a, 686b; v, 459a; vi, 626b; vii, **115a** – I, 454b, 1389b; III, 88b, 708a; V, 461b; VI, 611a; VII, **117a**
Mirdās b. Udayya, Abū Bilāl (680) iii, 169a, 648a, 1175b; iv, 1075b; vii, **123a**; ix, 766a – III, 172b, 669b, 1204b; IV, 1107a; VII, **125a**; 799b
Mīrem Čelebi (1525) iv, 810a; viii, 541b – II, 842b; VIII, 559b
al-Mīrghanī, Ḥasan b. Muḥammad iv, 686b – IV, 715a
al-Mīrghanī, Muḥammad ʿUthmān (1851) i, 1029a; vii, 124a; s, 278b – I, 1060b; VII, 125b; S, 278b
Mīrghaniyya/Khatmiyya i, 277b, 1029a, 1158b; ii, 710a; iii, 6a, 523b; iv, 686b; vii, **124a**; viii, 92b – I, 286a, 1060b, 1193a; II, 729a; III, 6a, 542a; IV, 715a; VII, **125b**; VIII, 94b
Mīrī (Amīrī) i, 1147b; ii, 148a; vii, **125a** – I, 1181b; II, 152b; VII, **126b**
Mīrī, Shaykh ii, 768a – II, 786b
Mīr-i Buzurg → Ḳawām al-Dīn I al-Marʿashī, Sayyid
Mīr-i Khātūn bint Arghu Āḳā (XIV) viii, 999a – VIII, 1034a
Mīr-i Mīrān vii, **95b** – VII, **97b**
Miriamiyya vi, 631b – VI, 616b
Mirim Kösbesi (1550) ix, 209a – IX, 215a
Mirkās (Mirḳās/Merguez) vii, **126b** – VII, **127b**
Mirkhwānd, Muḥammad b. Khwāndshāh (1498) iv, 1020b; vii, **128b**; s, 46b – IV, 1052b; VII, **126b**; S, 46b
Mīrmīran i, 1160a – I, 1194b
al-Mirrīkh (Mars) vii, **127a** – VII, **129a**
Mirsaid Mirshakar (1993) x, 65b – X, 68a
Mīrtula (Mārtula/Mertola) i, 6a; ii, 1009b; vii, **127b** – I, 6a, II, 1033a; VII, **129a**
Mirwaḥa vii, **127b** – VII, **129b**
Mirwāt → Čeh
Miryam → Maryam
Mīrzā (Mirzā) (title/titre) vii, **129a** – VII, **131a**
Mīrzā ʿAbd Allāh → Burton, Sir Richard
Mīrzā ʿAbd Allāh Khān → Shihāb Turghīzī
Mīrzā Abū Ṭālib (Ṣadr) vi, 18a – VI, 16a
Mīrzā Aḥmad Khān (XVIII) vii, **129b** – VII, **131b**
Mīrzā Āḳā Tabrīzī (XIX) vi, 763b – VI, 752b
Mīrzā ʿAskarī b. Bābūr (Mughal) (1558) vii, **130b** – VII, **132b**
Mīrzā ʿAzīz Kūka (Kōka) b. Shams al-Dīn Aḥmad Ghaznawī (1624) i, 80b, 507a; ii, 815a; vii, 129b, **131a**, 134a, 331b, 938a, 1055a – I, 83a, 522a; II, 834b; VII, 131b, **133a**, 136a, 333a, 938b, 1057a
Mīrzā Buzurg → Ḳāʾim-maḳām-i Farāhāni, ʿIsā
Mīrzā Djaʿfar Ḳarādjadāghī (XIX) vi, 763a – VI, 752b
Mīrzā Ghālib → Ghālib, Mīrzā Asad Allāh
Mīrzā Ghulām Aḥmad Ḳādiyānī → Aḥmadiyya
Mīrzā Ḥaydar Dūghlāt → Ḥaydar Dūghlāt, Mīrzā
Mīrzā Hindāl → Hindāl, Mīrzā, Abū Nāṣir Muḥammad
Mīrzā Ḥusayn Khān Sipahsālār (XIX) vi, 763a; s, 109a – VI, 752b; S, 108a
Mīrčā Ḥusayn Khān b. Ṣabā (1848) viii, 665b – VIII, 685b
Mīrzā Ibrāhīm Adham (XVII) vii, 132b – VII, 134a
Mīrzā ʿĪsā Ḳāʾimmaḳām (XIX) vi, 551b – VI, 536a
Mīrzā Iskandar (1415) v, 163b – V, 161b
Mīrzā Kalič Beg (1929) ix, 627a – IX, 661b
Mīrzā Kāmrān → Kamrān, Mīrzā b. Bābur
Mīrzā Khān (Aḥmadnagar, 1600) ii, 921b; iii, 626a; s, 327b – II, 943a; III, 647a; S, 327a
Mīrzā Khān (Badakhshān, 1520) i, 852b – I, 876b
Mīrzā Khān Sulṭān Maḥmūd (Marʿashī) (XVI) vi, 515a – VI, 500a
Mīrzā Maḥmūd b. Yūsuf (XX) vii, 257b – VII, 259b
Mīrzā Meḥemmed Isfendiyār-oghlu iv, 108b – IV, 113b
Mīrzā Muḥammad Ḥakīm → Muḥammad Ḥakīm, Mīrzā
Mīrzā Muḥammad Khalīl Marʿashī Ṣafawī (1805) vi, 516b – VI, 501b
Mīrzā Muḥammad Khān b. ʿAbbās Ḳulī Khān (XX) v, 664a, b – V, 699b
Mīrzā Muḥammad Mukīmī (1665) vi, 837a – VI, 827b
Mīrzā Muḥammad Taḳī Kashānī → Sipihr
Mīrzā Muḥammad Zamān → Muḥammad Zamān, Mīrzā
Mīrzā Muḳīm Abu ʾl-Manṣur Khān → Ṣafdar Djang
Mīrzā Naṣr → Shihāb Isfahānī
Mīrzā Rafīʿ al-Dīn, ṣadr → Nāʾinī, Mīrzā
Mīrzā Rafīʿā (XVIII) vi, 17a, 18a, b – VI, 15a, b, 16a, b
Mīrzā Rafīʿā, Muḥammad b. Ḥaydar, Ḥusaynī Ṭabāṭabāʾī Nāʾinī (1673) vii, **132a** – VII, **134a**
Mīrzā Ṣādiḳ Khān → Amīrī
Mīrzā Ṣāliḥ (XIX) ii, 649b – II, 665b
Mīrzā Sayyid Djaʿfar Khān Tabrīzī, Muhandis Bashī (1862) vii, 678a – VII, 678a
Mīrzā Sayyid Muḥammad Mutawallī (Marʿashī) → Shāh Sulaymān II (Ṣafawid(e))
Mīrzā Shādmān b. Mīrzā ʿAzīz Kōka (XVII) vii, 131b – VII, 133b
Mīrzā Shams al-Dīn b. Mīrzā ʿAzīz Kōka (XVII) vii, 131b – VII, 133b
Mīrzā Taḳī Khān → Amīr Kabīr
Mīrzā Yaḥyā Dawlatābādī (XX) ix, 741b – IX, 774a
Mīrzā Yaḥyā Nūrī → Subḥ-i Azal
Mīrzā Yaʿḳūb Abū Malkom Khan (XIX) vi, 291a – VI, 276b
Mīrzā Zakī (XVIII) vi, 527b – VI, 512a
Mīrzāʾī → Aḥmadiyya
Mīrzāpur vii, **132b** – VII, **134b**
Mīrzās (Gudjarāt, Badakhshān ii, 1129a, b; iii, 422a, 423b; vi, 342b; vii, 131a, b, **133a**, 314b – II, 1156a; III, 435b, 437a; VI, 326b; VII, 133a, **135a**, 316b
Mīrzā-yi Shīrāzī-yi Buzurg → Shīrāzī, Mīrzā Muḥammad Ḥasan
Mīrzā-yi Shīrāzī-yu Kūčik → Shīrāzī, Muḥammad Taḳī b. Muḥibb ʿAlī Ḥāʾirī
Mīrzā-zāde Meḥmed Emīn → Sālim
Mirzo Tursunzoda (1977) x, 65b – X, 68a
Misāḥa (survey/arpentage) vii, **137b** – VII, **139b**
Misāḥa, ʿIlm al- vii, **135a** – VII, **137a**
Misalla (obelisk/obélisque) vii, **140b** – VII, **142b**
Misʿar b. Fadakī iv, 269a – IV, 281a
Misʿar b. Muhalhil → Abū Dulaf
Miṣbāḥ → Sirādj
Misbāḥa → Subḥa
Misher vi, 420b – VI, 406a
Mishkān vi, 494a – VI, 480a
Mishmast iii, 1103a – III, 1130a
Mishmish vii, **141b** – VII, **144a**
Mishowda vi, 504a – VI, 489b
Misis → al-Maṣṣīṣa
Misiṭṭāsa i, 1037a – I, 1068b
Misk vii, **142a** – VII, **144b**

Miskawayh (Ibn), Abū ʿAlī Aḥmad (1030) i, 127a, 234b, 326b, 327b, 328a, 328b, 590a, 1353b, 1354a; ii, 80a, 174a; iii, 703b, 955a, 1237a; vi, 199a, b, 571a, 638a; vii, **143a**; s, 72b, 119b, 263b, 398b – I, 130b, 241b, 337a, 337b, 338a, 339a, 609a, 1392b, 1393a; II, 81b, 179b; III, 725b, 979b, 1269a; VI, 183b, 184a, 556a, 623a; VII, **145a**; S, 73a, 119a, 263a, 398b
Miskīn ii, 757b; vii, **144b** – II, 776a; VII, **146b**
Miskīn al-Dārimī (708) vii, 145a – VII, 147a
al-Mislaḥ s, 198b – S, 198b
Mismaʿ b. Shihāb vi, 640b – VI, 625b
al-Mismaʿī, ʿAbd Allāh b. Ibrāhīm (X) iii, 1015b; iv, 100a – III, 1041a; IV, 104b
Miṣr (Egypt/Égypte) i, 13b, 21a, 215b, 396a, 451a, 531b, 638b, 750b, 797b, 800a, 801a, 870a, 1054a, 1107a; ii, 495a, 668a, 853b, 854a, 914a; iii, 4b, 264a, 384b, 395a, 653b, 1259a; v, 556b, 558b, 1060a; vi, 22b, 82b, 118b, 288b, 337b, 366b, 467b, 469b, 471a; vii, 10a, **146a**; viii, 906b; s, 120b, 216a – I, 13b, 22a, 222a, 407b, 464a, 547b, 659b, 773a, 821a, 823b, 824b, 894b, 1085b, 1140a; II, 507b, 684b, 873b, 935a; III, 4b, 272a, 397a, 407b, 675a, 1291b; V, 561a, 563b, 1057a; VI, 20b, 80b, 116b, 273b, 321b, 350b, 453b, 455a, 456b; VII, 10b, **148a**; VIII, 937b S, 120a, 216a
—administration i, 976a; ii, 148a, 327a, 595a, 647a; iii, 556a, 1154a, 1185b, 1193b; iv, 192b, 193a, 323b, 1033b – I, 1006a; II, 152b, 336b, 610a, 663a; III, 575a, 1182b, 1215a, 1223b; IV, 200b, 201a, b, 337b, 338a, 1065a
—agriculture iii, 625a, 1154a – III, 645b, 1182b
—demography/-ie s, 216a – S, 216a
—education v, 907b, 1091b – V, 913a, 1088b
—ethnography/-ie i, 35a, 37b, 39a; iii, 299b; v, 317b – I, 36a, 38b, 40a; III, 309a; V, 317a
—history/histoire i, 138b, 965a; ii, 355b; iii, 675a, 756b, 813a, 894b; v, 121b – I, 142b, 995a; II, 365a; III, 696b, 779b, 836b, 918b; V, 124a
—institutions ii, 126b, 128a, 129b, 132a, 423b; iii, 1068b; iv, 192b – II, 130a, 131a, 133a, 135a, 434b; III, 1095b; IV, 201a
—langu(ag)e, lit(t)e(é)rature i, 74b, 142a, 568b, 575a; ii, 465a, 466a, 764a; iii, 935a – I, 76b, 146a, 587a, 594a; II, 477a, 478a, 782b; III, 959b
—monuments v, 290a – V, 289b
—statesmen/hommes d'état i, 51b, 58a, 293b, 391b, 1069b; ii, 764a – I, 53a, 60a, 302b, 402b, 1101b; II, 782b
Miṣr Bay iv, 552a – IV, 576a
Miṣr(īm/āyim) b. Bayṣar b. Ḥām vi, 411b – VI, 396b
Miṣr al-fatāt (Young Egypt/Jeune Égypte) ii, 429a; iii, 518a; s, 5b – II, 440a; III, 535b; S, 4b
Misrāḳlî → Sulaymān Pasha
Misrāta (Miṣrāta/Mesrāta), Banū iii, 1040a; v, 948b; vii, **186a** – III, 1066a; V, 952b; VII, **186a**
al-Miṣrī, ʿAzīz ʿAlī (XX) viii, 140b, 141a – VIII, 143a
al-Miṣrī, ʿAbd Allāh b. ʿAbd al-Ḥakam vi, 264b – VI, 249a
Miṣrī Efendi → Niyāzī
Miṣṣīs/Miṣṣīṣa (Mopsuestia) → Maṣṣīṣa
Missolonghi vi, 59a – VI, 56b
Mistra vi, 70b – VI, 68b
Mistāwa → al-Nukkār
Misurata → Misrāta
Miswāk vii, **187a** – VII, **187a**
al-Miswar b. Hāniʾ (XII) vi, 312a – VI, 297a
Mīthāḳ vii, **187b** – VII, **187b**
Mīthāḳ-i Millī vii, **188a** – VII, **188a**
Mithāliyya iv, 507a – IV, 529a
Mithḳāl → Dīnār; Ḥabba; Istār
Mithḳāl, Amīr v, 1141b, 1142a – V, 1134b, 1135a
Mitīdja → Bulayda
Mitwālī s, 268b, 269a – S, 268b
Miʿwadh → Ḥamāʾil
al-Miyādīn → al-Raḥba
Miyān-duʾāb vi, 502b – VI, 488a
Miyān-du-rūd iv, 645a; vi, 745b; s, 298a – IV, 671b; VI, 734b; S, 297b
Miyān Gul Djān (XX) ii, 317a – II, 326a
Miyān Gul Gul Shāhzāda (XX) ii, 317a – II, 326b
Miyān Ḥasan Khān Sūrī (XV) ii, 271a – II, 279b
Miyān Mīr, Miyādjī, Bālā Pīr (1635) ii, 134b; vii, **189a**, 327b – II, 138a; VII, **189b**, 329b
Miyān Muṣṭafā Gudjarātī (1575) ii, 500a – II, 512b
Miyān Rādjū (1607) vi, 269b – VI, 254a
Miyāna (Miyānidj) vii, **189b** – VII, **189b**
Miyānābād iv, 107b – IV, 112b
Mizāb iv, 318a – IV, 332a
Miʿzaf(a) vii, **189b** – VII, **190a**
Mizʿal Khān iv, 1171a – IV, 1204b
Miẓalla iv, 214a, 1147a; vi, 521a; vii, **191b** – IV, 223b, 1178b; VI, 506a; VII, **192a**
al-Mīzān → Minṭaḳat al-Burūdj
al-Mīzān (balance) ii, 358b; iii, 212b, 465b; iv, 600a, 1186a; vii, **195b** – II, 368b; III, 218b, 482a; IV, 624b, 1219a; VII, **196a**
Mīzān (Ottoman weekly/hebdomadaire) vii, **204b** – VII, **205b**
Mīzāndjî Meḥmed Murād Bey (1917) ii, 474b; iv, 871b; vii, 204b, **205a** – II, 486b; IV, 905a; VII, 205b, **206a**
Mizhar → Mazhar
Mizmār vii, **206b** – VII, **207b**
Mizwala (sundial/cadran solaire) vii, **210a** – VII, **211a**
Mizwār i, 687b; vii, **211b** – I, 708b; VII, **213a**
al-Mizza (Mezzé) vi, 624a; vii, **212a** – VI, 609a; VII, **213a**
al-Mizzī, Djamāl al-Dīn Abu 'l-Ḥadjdjādj al-Kalbī (1341) iii, 817b, 818a, 952a, 954b; vii, 30a, **212a**, 576b, 692a; viii, 517a – III, 841a, 842a, 976b, 979a; VII, 30a, **213b**, 577a, 692a; VIII, 534b
al-Mizzī, Muḥammad b. Aḥmad (XIV) viii, 575a – VIII, 593b
Mkwaja vi, 370a; vii, **213a** – VI, 354b; VII, **214b**
Mleh i, 182b, 639a; ii, 37b – I, 187b, 660a; II, 38a
Moa (Tanzania/-e) vi, 370a – VI, 354b
Moab s, 190b, 191a – S, 191b, 192a
Mōbadh vii, **213b** – VII, **215a**
Mocha/Mokhā → al-Mukhā
Modibbo Adama (1848) i, 179b, 180a; ii, 9b, 942b – I, 184b; II, 9b, 964a
Modibo Muḥammad (XV) vi, 258b – VI, 243a
Modon v, 270b, 271a; vii, **216b** – V, 268b; VII, **218b**
Mö'etüken b. Čaghatay i, 1010a; ii, 2a – I, 1041a; II, 2a
Mogadishu → Maḳdishū
Mogador → al-Suwayra
Mogholistān ii, 45a, b, 622a; v, 858a; vi, 77a, b; vii, **218a**; s, 96b – II, 46a, b, 637b; V, 865a; VI, 75a; VII, **219b**; S, 96a
Moghols vii, **218b** – VII, **220a**
Mogul → Mughal
Moḥā u Aḥmad al-Ahansalī iii, 167a – III, 170b
Mohács (Mihāč) vi, 74b; vii, **218b**; viii, 185a; s, 171a – VI, 72b; VII, **220b**; VIII, 188a; S, 171a
Mohamed bin Nasor Shaksi (XX) vi, 612b – VI, 597b
Mohamman ii, 1145b – II, 1173a

Mohammed Racim (Rāsim) (XX) s, 224b – S, 224b
Mohān s, 360a – S, 359b
Moḥand u l-Hādj iv, 363a – IV, 379a
Mohmand vii, **220a**, 548b; s, 237b – VII, **221b**, 548b; S, 237a
Mohur vii, **221a** – VII, **222b**
Moidu Moulavi, E. (Mappila) (XX) vi, 460a – VI, 445b
Moidu Padiyath (Mappila) (XX) vi, 464b – VI, 450a
Mois Dibra iv, 139b, 140a – IV, 145b, 146a
Moïse → Mūsā
Mokhā → al-Mukhā
Moḳrānī i, 369b, 1197a; iv, 478b – I, 380b, 1232b; IV, 499b
Moktar Ould Daddah (al-Mukhtār Wuld Dāddāh) vii, 615b – VII, 615a, b
Moldavia → Boghdān
Molesalam Grasias i, 172a – I, 176b
Mollā (title/titre) vii, **221a** – VII, **223a**
Mollā Arab (Muftī) (1483) ix, 400b – IX, 413b
Mollā Bādjī (Bāshī, Bāshīgarī) → Mollā
Mollā Bilāl (XIX) x, 221a – X, 239a
Mollā Čelebi → Muḥyi ʾl-Dīn Meḥmed al-Djamālī
Mollā Ḳābid (1527) vii, **225a** – VII, **226b**
Mollā Khusraw → Khusraw, Mollā
Mollā Kurānī → Gurānī, Sharaf al-Dīn
Mollā Naṣr al-Dīn → Naṣr al-Dīn Khodja
Mollā Ṣadra → Mullā Ṣadra
Moluccas iii, 1219a, 1226a
Moluques, les III, 1250a, 1257b
Mombasa i, 1282a; iv, 886a; v, 655b; vi, 129a, 283b, 370a; vii, **225a**; s, 248a, 355b – I, 1321b; IV, 918b; V, 659b; VI, 127a, 268a, 354b; VII, **227a**; S, 248a, 355b
Mōmnas → Satpanthīs
Monastir (Tunisia/-e) i, 1319a; vii, **227b** – I, 1359b; VII, **229b**
Monastir (Yugoslavia/-e) → Manāstir
Moncef Bey → Munṣif Bey
Mondros (Mudros) vii, **229a** – VII, **231a**
Monemvasia → Menekshe
Monghyr → Mungīr
Möngke b. Toluy b. Čingiz Khān (Mongol Great Khān) (1260) i, 1105b, 1106a, 1187b, 1240b, 1311b; ii, 3a, 45b; iii, 1121a; iv, 814a; v, 299b, 300a; vi, 77b; vii, **230a** – I, 1139a, 1223a, 1278a, 1352a; II, 3a, 46b; III, 1148b; IV, 847a; V, 299a, b; VI, 75a; VII, **231b**
Möngke-Temür (Batuʾid(e), 1280) i, 1188b; ii, 812a, 1112a – I, 1223b; II, 831a, 1138a
Mongolia/-ie iv, 988b; vii, **230b**; x, 687a – IV, 1021a; VII, **232a**
Mongols i, 21a, 121a, 190a, 227a, 329b, 353b, 354b, 508a, 639b, 660b, 786b, 791b, 804b, 872a, 879b, 902b, 1105a, 1240b, 1295a, 1308a; ii, 3b, 38a, 41b, 67b, 194a, 229b, 285b, 344b, 393a, 707b, 746a, 928b, 1142a; iii, 87b, 105b, 177b, 402b, 702b, 1121a; iv, 30a-32a, 48a-b, 349a, 485a, 512a, 562b, 612b, 817a, 921b, 1049b-1051b; v, 58b, 456a, 748b; vi, 48a, b, 77a, 198b, 314b, 482b, 492b, 493b, 494a, 500b, 501a, 540b, 545b, 547b, 606a; vii, **230b**; viii, 472b; ix, 474a, 811b; x, 690b; s, 184a, 246a, 256a, b – I, 21b, 124b, 194b, 233b, 339b, 364b, 365a, 523a, 660a, 681b, 810a, 815a, 828b, 896a, 905a, 929b, 1138b, 1278a, 1335a, 1348a; II, 3b, 38b, 42a, 68b, 200a, 236b, 293b, 354a, 403a, b, 726a, 764b, 950a, 1169a; III, 90a, 108a, 181b, 415a, 724b, 1148b; IV, 32a-34b, 50b-51a, 364a, 506a, 534a, 584b, 637a, 850a, 954b, 1081a-1083a; V, 60b, 458b, 754a; VI, 46b, 75a, 182b, 299b, 468b, 478b, 479b, 486a, 486b, 525a, 530a, 532a, 591a; VII, **232b**; VIII, 488a; IX, 492b, 866b; X, 733a; S, 185b, 246a, 255b, 256a
—art iii, 1125b, 1126a, – III, 1153b, 1154a, b
—histories/histoires ii, 606b; iii, 114a – II, 621b; III, 116b
—warfare/en guerre ii, 1083b; iii, 183b, 188a, 197b, 472a, 1099b – II, 1108b; III, 188a, 192b, 202b, 488b, 1126b
Montenegro → Ḳaradagh
Moors i, 31b; ii, 27a; vii, **235b**
Mopla(stan) → Māpilla
Mora (game/jeu) iv, 114a – IV, 119a
Mora (Morea/Morée) ii, 534a, 691a, 985a; iii, 91a, 212a; iv, 241a; v, 268b, 270b, 717b; vi, 58b, 59a, b, 71b; vii, **236b**; s, 149b – II, 547a, 708b, 1007b; III, 93b, 217b; IV, 251b; V, 266b, 268b, 723a; VI, 56b, 57a, b, 69a; VII, **237b**; S, 149b
Morādābād → Murādābād
Moravia → Čeh
Mordve i, 1338a – I, 1378a
Mordves/Mordvins → Burtās
Morea/Morée → Mora
Morikubala Dore ii, 1132a – II, 1158b
Moriscos/-ques i, 55b, 404b, 496a, 496b, 502a, 1343a; iv, 239a, 673a; v, 504b; vii, **241b**; s, 81a – I, 57b, 416b, 511a, 511b, 517a, 1383b; IV, 249b, 700b; V, 507b; VII, **243a**; S, 81a
Moro National Liberation Front (MNLF) viii, 304b, 305a – VIII, 314a, b
Morocco → al-Maghrib, al-Mamlaka al-Maghribiyya
Moron → Mawrūr
Mor(r)a → Mukhāradja
Moros (Philippines) viii, 303b, 304a – VIII, 313a,b
Moses → Mūsā
Moses of Khoren s, 274b – S, 274b
Mossadegh → Muṣaddiḳ, Muḥammad
Mossi vi, 402b – VI, 387a
Mostaganem → Mustaghānim
Mostar vii, **244a** – VII, **245b**
Mosul/Mossoul → al-Mawṣil
Moudros → Mondros
Moulay → Mawlāy
Moulay Hafid → Ḥāfiẓ, ʿAbd al-
Moulouya → Malwiyya
Mourre → Mora
Moyinkutty Vaidyar (1891) vi, 464a – VI, 450a
Mozambique vi, 203b, 283a; vii, **245a**; ix, 698b – VI, 187b, 268a; VII, **246b**; IX, 727a
Mozarab i, 82b, 491a, 494a, 1339a; v, 367b, 376a; vii, **246b**; s, 92a, 397b – I, 85a, 506a, 509a, 1379a; V, 368b, 376b; VII, **248b**; S, 92a, 398a
Mrābṭīn i, 1049b – I, 1081a
Mshatta → al-Mushattā
Msīd → Kuttāb
Msīla → Masīla
Mt. Dʾeli vi, 207a – VI, 191a
Mtambwe Mkuu vii, **249b** – VII, **251a**
Mʾtir, Banū s, 145a – S, 144b
Mtugga, Banū vi, 743a – VI, 732b
al-Muʿābada (Mecca) vi, 154a, b, 161b, 170a – VI, 152a, 156a, 160b
Muʾaddib v, 568a – V, 572b
Muʿādh b. ʿAfrāʾ vi, 645b – VI, 631a
Muʿādh b. Djabal (VII) i, 460b, 694a, 695a; ii, 372a; iv, 771a; v, 241a; vii, 635b – I, 474a, 715a, 716a; II, 382a; IV, 802a; V, 238b; VII, 635a
Muʿādh b. al-Nuʿmān i, 771b; iii, 812a – I, 794b; III, 835b
Muʿādh al-Harrāʾ (802) viii, 573a; x, 361a – VIII, 541b; X, 387a

Muʿādha al-ʿAdawiyya (VII) viii, 354b – VIII, 367a
Muʿadhdhin → Adhān; Masdjid
Muʿadhdhinzāde ʿAlī Pasha iii, 251b; iv, 571b – III, 258b; IV, 594b
Muʿadjdjal i, 172b – I, 177b
al-Muʿāfa b. Ṭāwūs vi, 900a – VI, 891a
al-Muʿāfā b. Zakariyyāʾ (1000) i, 154a; iii, 42a, 824b; viii, 546a – I, 158b; III, 44a, 848b; VIII, 564a
Muʿāfī iv, 1045a – IV, 1076b
Muʿāhada (earlier times/époque ancienne) → ʿAhd; Bakṭ; Imtiyāzāt
Muʿāhada (modern times/époque moderne) vii, **250a** – VII, **251b**
Muʿāhidūn v, 376a – V, 376b
Muʾākhāt vii, **253b** – VII, **255b**
al-Muʾallafa Ḳulūbuhum i, 12a, 266b; vii, **254a** – I, 12a, 274b; VII, **255b**
Muʿallaḳ iii, 26a – III, 27a
al-Muʿallaḳāt iii, 136a, 222b, 1178a; vii, **254a** – III, 138b, 229a, 1207a; VII, **256a**
Muʿallal iii, 26a – III, 27a
Muʿallim v, 568a – V, 572b
Muʿallim Nādjī (1893) ii, 474b; iv, 195b, 874b, 930b; vii, **255a** – II, 486b; IV, 204a, 908a, 963b; VII, **257a**
al-Muʿallim al-Thālith → al-Dāmād
Muʿāmalāt i, 277a; iv, 560b; vii, **255b** – I, 285b; IV, 583a; VII, **257b**
Muʿamma v, 806b; vii, **257a** – V, 812b; VII, **259a**
Muʿammāʿī → al-Ḥusaynī, Mīr Ḥusayn
Muʿammar i, 117a, 519b; vii, **258a** – I, 120a, 535b; VII, **259b**
Muʿammar, Āl (Tamīm) ii, 321a; iii, 678a – II, 330b; III, 700a
Muʿammar b. ʿAbbād al-Sulamī, Abū ʿAmr (830) i, 1243a; iii, 1143a; vii, **259a**; s, 88b, 226a – I, 1281a; III, 1171b; VII, **260b**; S, 88b, 226a
Muʿammar b. al-Aḥmar iv, 1132b; v, 702a – IV, 1164a; V, 707a
al-Muʿammarī → Abū Manṣūr al-Maʿmarī
al-Muʿammar al-Maghribī → Abu ʾl-Dunyā
Muʿammir → Muʿammar
al-Muʿammariyya → al-Khaṭṭābiyya
Muʿanʿan iii, 26a; vii, **260a** – III, 27a; VII, **262a**
Muʾannath → Mudhakkar
Muʿanṣar b. Ḥammad v, 1179b – V, 1169b
Muar (Malacca) vi, 207b – VI, 192a
Muʿāraḍa (collation) → Muḳābala
Muʿāraḍa (opposition) vii, **261a** – VII, **262b**
Muʿarrab vii, **261b** – VII, **263b**
Muʾarridj, Abū Fayd al-Sadūsī (819) vi, 138b, 821b, 822a; vii, 967b; s, 73b – VI, 137a, 811b, 812b; VII, 968a; S, 74a
Muʾarrikh → Kh(ʷ)āndamīr
al-Muʿaskar (Mascara) vii, **262b** – VII, **264b**
Muʿaṭṭib, Banū vii, 347a – VII, 349a
Muʿaṭṭib ibn Ḳushayr iv, 839b – IV, 872b
Muʿaṭṭila → Taʿṭīl
Muʿāwada vii, **263b** – VII, **265a**
Muʿāwiya, Banū v, 118b; vi, 473a – V, 121a; VI, 459a
Muʿāwiya I b. Abī Sufyān b. Ḥarb (Umayyad(e)) (680) i, 40b, 43b, 85b, 194b, 275b, 710b, 760a, 1137b; ii, 35b, 89b, 116a, 128b, 129b, 280b, 323b, 343b, 456b, 911a, 931a, 1093b; iii, 20a, 241a, b, 391b, 397b, 455a, 545a, 607b, 1163b; iv, 315a, 493a, 734a, 841b, 938a, 973a, 1074b; v, 302a, 324b, 1123a; vi, 139a, b, 140a, 147a, 193a, 197b, 230b, 247b, 336b, 334b, 362a, 363a, 505b, 547b, 621b, 622a, 626a, 650b, 654b, 657b, 660b, 661b, 662a, 665a, 666a, 668b, 669b, 670a, 774a; vii, 254a, **263b**, 269a, 347a, b, 358b, 393b, 689a; ix, 584a; x, 841b; s, 10a, 88a, 89b, 103b, 133b, 157a, 221b, 230b, 243a, 394a – I, 41b, 44b, 87b, 200b, 284b, 732a, 782b, 1172a; II, 36b, 91a, 118b, 131b, 133a, 288b, 333a, 353b, 468a, 932b, 952b, 1119a; III, 21a, 248a, b, 404a, 410a, 471a, 564a, 628a, 1192a; IV, 329a, 514a, 763b, 874b, 971a, 1005b, 1106a; V, 301b, 324a, 1119b; VI, 137b, 138a, 145b, 177a, 182a, 224b, 231b, 320b, 328b, 346a, 347a, 491a, 531b, 606b, 607a, 611a, 636a, 640a, 643a, 646a, 647b, 651a, 652a, 654b, 655b, 656b, 763b; VII, 255b, **265b**, 271a, 349a, 360b, 394b, 689a; IX, 606b, 853a; X, ;S, 9b, 87b, 89b, 103a, 133a, 157a, 221b, 230b, 243a, 394b
—conflict with ʿAlī/conflit avec ʿAlī i, 383a, b, 384a, 451b, 549b, 636b, 704b, 1343b; ii, 480b, 625b; iii, 12b, 889b – I, 394a, b, 395a, 464b, 567a, 657a, 725b, 1384a; II, 493a, 641a; III, 13a, 913b
Muʿāwiya II b. Yazīd b. Muʿāwiya I (Umayyad(e)) (684) ii, 89b; iii, 270b; iv, 369b; vi, 544b, 545a, 546b, 622a, 626a; vii, **268a** – II, 91a; III, 278b; IV, 385b; VI, 529b, 531a, 607a, 611a; VII, **270a**
Muʿāwiya, Banū v, 118b – V, 121a
Muʿāwiya b. al-ʿĀṣ s, 103b – S, 103a
Muʿāwiya b. Bakr al-ʿImlāḳī iv, 820b; s, 246b – IV, 853b; S, 246b
Muʿāwiya b. al-Ḥārith al-Ṣimma ii, 627a – II, 642b
Muʿāwiya b. Ḥudaydj (672) x, 212b – X, 229b
Muʿāwiya b. Hishām (Umayyad(e), al-Andalus) (735) i, 1103a; iii, 494b; vii, **269a** – I, 1136a; III, 511b; VII, **271a**
Muʿāwiya b. Ḥudaydj b. Djafna al-Sakūnī al-Tudjībī (672) iv, 825b, 826a; vi, 740b; vii, **269a**, 393b – IV, 858b, 859a; VI, 729b, 730a; VII, **271a**, 394b
Muʿāwiya b. al-Mughīra s, 103b – S, 103a
Muʿāwiya b. Ṣāliḥ vi, 221a – VI, 215a
Muʿāwiya b. ʿUbayd Allāh → Abū ʿUbayd Allāh
Muʿāwiya b. ʿUḳayl vii, 582a – VII, 582b
Muʿawwidhatānⁱ vii, **269b** – VII, **271b**
Muʿayn, Banū → Maʿīn, Banū
al-Muʿayṭī, al-Muntaṣir bi-ʾllāh (Denia) (XI) ii, 111b; vii, 292b – II, 114a; VII, 294b
al-Muʾayyad (Rasūlid(e)) (1322) vii, 30a – VII, 30a
al-Muʾayyad (Ṣāliḥid(e)) (X) vii, 641b – VII, 641a
al-Muʾayyad, Āl (Yemen) vii, 779b – VII, 781a
al-Muʾayyad, Shafīḳ iii, 519b – III, 537a
al-Muʾayyad b. al-Mutawakkil ʿalā ʾllāh (ʿAbbāsid(e)) (IX) vii, 777b – VII, 779b
al-Muʾayyad Aḥmad b. Īnāl (Mamlūk) (1461) v, 73a; vii, 727a – V, 75a; VII, 727b
al-Muʾayyad bi-ʾllāh → Hishām II (Umayyad(e), al-Andalus)
al-Muʾayyad bi-ʾllāh, Aḥmad b. al-Ḥusayn (Imām) (1020) vii, 786a; s, 13a, 335b, 363a – VII, 787b; S, 13b, 335a; 363a
al-Muʾayyad bi-ʾllāh Muḥammad, Ibn al-Imām al-Mutawakkil ʿalā ʾllāh Ismāʿīl (1668) vii, **270a** – VII, **272a**
al-Muʾayyad bi-ʾllāh Muḥammad (Zaydid(e)) (1644) i, 553b; vi, 436b, 437a; vii, **270a**, 514b, 779a – I, 571b; VI, 422a, b; VII, **272a**, 514b, 780b
Muʾayyad al-Dawla (Būyid(e)) vi, 659a – VI, 645a
Muʿayyad Dāwūd (Rasūlid(e)) (XIV) ix, 338a – IX, 349a
al-Muʾayyad fi ʾl-Dīn Allāh Abū Naṣr al-Shīrāzī (dāʿī) (1077) i, 132b, 832b, 1074a; ii, 98a, 169a, 855b, 856a; iii, 905b; iv, 47a; v, 930a; vii, **270b**, 732a; ix, 221a – I, 136a, 855b, 1106a; II, 100a, 174a, 875b, 876a; III, 929b; IV, 49b; V, 934b; VII, **272b**, 732b; IX, 227a

Mu'ayyad al-Mulk b. Niẓām al-Mulk (XII) i, 1052a, b; vii, 408a, 489b – I, 1083b, 1084a; VII, 409a, 489a
al-Mu'ayyadiyya (Mamlūk) vi, 303b – VI, 303b
Mu'ayyadzāde (Ḳāḍī ʿasker) (1507) i, 1082b – I, 1115a
Mu'ayyad-zāde (Mü'eyyed-zāde), ʿAbd al-Raḥmān b. ʿAlī Čelebi (1516) vii, 23b, **272a**; viii, 1b – VII, 23b, **274a**; VIII, 1b
Mu'ayyid al-Dawla, Abū Manṣūr Būya (Būyid(e)) (984) i, 211b, 1350b; ii, 748b; iii, 258a, 671a, 704a; iv, 100b. 358a; vii, **272b**; s, 13a – I, 218a, 1390b; II, 767a; III, 265b, 692b, 726a; IV, 104b, 373b; VII, **274b**; S, 13b
Mu'ayyid al-Dīn, vizier (1195) iv, 974b – IV, 1007a
Mu'ayyid al-Dīn al-ʿArḍī (al-ʿUrḍī) (1266) vi, 501b, 601a – VI, 486b, 586a
Mu'ayyad al-Dīn Djandī (1300) viii, 753b – VIII, 775a
Mu'ayyid al-Mulk ʿUbayd Allāh b. Niẓām al-Mulk (XI) i, 1036a; viii, 70b, 81b – I, 1067b; VIII, 72a, 83b
Muʿayyir al-Mamālik, Dūst ʿAlī (XIX) vi, 481b, 484a, b – VI, 467b, 470a, b
Muʿaẓẓam, Prince → Bahādur Shāh I
al-Muʿaẓẓam Sharaf al-Dīn, ʿĪsā, al-Malik → al-Malik al-Muʿaẓẓam Sharaf al-Dīn
al-Muʿaẓẓam Sulaymān (Ayyūbid(e), Sanʿā') (XIII) vi, 433b – VI, 419a
Muʿazzaz Khān (Nawwāb) (XVIII) vii, 129b – VII, 131b
Mūbad Shāh ii, 74a – II, 75a
Mübādele (exchange/échange) vii, **275a** – VII, **276b**
Mubāḥ → Aḥkām; Sharīʿa
Mubāhala (Mulāʿana) i, 265a; ii, 848b, 849b; vii, **276a** – I, 273a; II, 868b, 869b; VII, **278a**
Mubālagha vii, **277a** – VII, **279a**
Muballi → Dikka; Masdjid
Mubāra'a i, 1027a – I, 1058b
Mubārak, Āl iii, 582b – II, 602b
Mubārak (Āl Ṣabaḥ) (1915) viii, 668b – VIII, 688b
Mubārak (Āmirid(e)) i, 446b, 985b – I, 459a, 1016a
al-Mubārak b. Kāmil b. ʿAlī (Munḳidh, Banū) (1193) vii, 579b – VII, 580a
Mubārak Abu 'l-Aṭbāḳ (Mbārk Bū Leṭbāḳ) vi, 250a – VI, 234a
Mubārak Āl Ṣabbāh ii, 673a; v, 574a, b – II, 690a; V, 578ba
Mubārak Ghāzī (Bengal/-e) vii, **278b** – VII, **280a**
Mubārak Khān (Khāndēsh) (XVI) vi, 310a – VI, 295a
Mubārak Khān ʿAbbāsī ii, 186b – II, 192a
Mubārak Khān I Dāwūdpōtrā ii, 185b, 186a – II, 191b, 192a
Mubārak Khān II Dāwūdpōtrā ii, 186a – II, 192a
Mubārak Khān Fārūkī ii, 814b – II, 834a
Mubārak Khān Lūḥānī i, 1136b – I, 1171a
Mubārak Khān Noḥānī s, 203a – S, 202b
Mubārak al-Maghribī al-Bukhārī i, 449a – I, 462a
Mubārak Nāgawri (al-Mahdawī) i, 117a; ii, 870b, – I, 120b; II, 891a
Mubārak Shāh (Badakhshan) i, 852b – I, 876a
Mubārak Shāh II (Farūḳī) (1566) ii, 815a, 816a; iii, 422a; vi, 52a – II, 834b, 835b; III, 435b; VI, 50b
Mubārak Shāh I Ḳuṭb al-Dīn (Khaldjī) (1320) i, 444b; ii, 120a, 179b, 258b, 269a, 1084b, 1085b; iii, 416b; iv, 419b, 923b; vi, 62a, 126b, 692a; vii, 457b; s, 105b – I, 457b; II, 123a, 185b, 265a, 277b, 1109b, 1110b; III, 429b; IV, 437b, 956b; VI, 60a, 124b, VI, 679b; VII, 457b; S, 104b
Mubārak Shāh II b. Khiḍr Khān, Muʿizz al-Dīn (Sayyid, Delhi) (1434) i, 1323a; ii, 270b; iii, 638b; iv, 513a; vii, 195a, **278b**; ix, 118b, 119a – I, 1363b; II, 278b; III, 659b; IV, 535a; VII, 195b, **280b**; IX. 123a
Mubārak Shāh b. Ḳara Hölegü i, 1311b; II, 3a, b – I, 1352a; II, 3a, b
Mubārak Shāh al-Marwarrūdhī (XIII) viii, 581b; s, 285a – VIII, 600b; S, 284b
Mubārak (Sayyid) b. Sayyid Ibrāhīm (Bayhaḳī) s, 131b – S, 131a
Mubārakābād i, 1323a; ii, 258b; vii, 279a – I, 1363b; II, 265a; VII, 280b
Mubārakpur ii, 258b, 263b – II, 265a, 271b
Mubārakshāh (1375) viii, 806b – VIII, 833b
al-Mubāriz Aḳdjā (amīr) (XIII) vi, 381a – VI, 365a
Mubāriz al-Dīn Čawlī ii, 693b – II, 711a
Mubāriz al-Dīn Muḥammad (Muẓaffarid(e)) (1364) ii, 737a, 812a; iii, 56a, 1022a; iv, 498b, 672a; v, 163a, 554a; vii, 480b, 820a, b; ix, 198b; s, 415a – II, 755b, 831b; III, 58a, 1048a; IV, 520a, 699b; V, 161a, 559a; VII, 480a, 822a; IX, 204b; S, 415a
Mubāriz al-Dīn Muḥammad Bey i, 703a – I, 724b
Mubāriz Khān (Deccan) ii, 99b; iii, 318b, 320a – II, 101b; III, 328a, 330b
Mubāriz Khān (Delhi) → Muḥammad Shāh V
Mubāriz al-Mulk (XVI) vi, 270a – VI, 255a
al-Mubarḳaʿ (Sufyānid(e)) (841) vi, 338b; vii, **279a** – VI, 323; VII, **281a**
al-Mubarrad, Abū 'l-ʿAbbās Muḥammad b. Yazīd al-Azdī (900) i, 97b, 125b, 321b, 590a, 1223b; ii, 300a; iii, 930a, 1263b; iv, 122b; v, 948a; vi, 348a; vii, **279b**, 390b, 914a; ix, 317b, 387b; x, 4a, 433a; s, 25a, 27b, 352a, 389b – I, 100b, 129a, 331b, 609b, 1260a; II, 308a; III, 954b, 1296b; IV, 128a; V, 951b; VI, 332a; VII, **281b**, 392a, 914b; IX, 327b, 400a; X, 4a, 464b; S, 25a, 27b, 352a, 390a
al-Mubarraz vii, **282b** – VII, **284a**
Mubashshir b. Fātik, Abu 'l-Wafā' (XI) i, 235b, 236a, 247a; iii, 463b, 906b; vii, **282b** – I, 243a, b, 255a; III, 480a, 930b; VII, **284b**
Mubashshir b. Sulaymān iii, 853a – III, 877a
Mubashshir wa-Bashīr vi, 219b – VI, 203b
al-Mubayyiḍa → al-Muḳannaʿ
Mubham iii, 26a – III, 27b
Mūbiḳāt iv, 1107b, 1109a – IV, 1139a, 1140b
Mubīn, Mullā (Farangī Maḥall) s, 292b – S, 292a
Mubtada' vii, **283a** – VII, **285a**
Mudabbadj iii, 26a – III, 27b
Mudallas iii, 26a – III, 27a
Mudanya vi, 587b; vii, **284a** – VI, 572b; VII, **286a**
Mudar → Rabīʿa
Muḍar, Banū iv, 832b, 833b; v, 76b, 77a; vi, 727b; vii, 266a, viii, **352b** – IV, 865b, 866b; V, 79a; VI, 716b; VII, 268a; VIII, **365a**
Muḍāraba vii, **284b** – VII, **286b**
Muḍāriʿ i, 108a; v, 954b; vii, **285b** – I, 111a; V, 958b; VII, **287b**
Muḍarites i, 529b, 544b, 684b; iii, 233a – I, 545b, 562a, 705b; II, 239b
Mudarris, Sayyid Ḥasan (1936) vii, 300a – VII, 302a
Mudarrisī, Taḳī iv, 73b; v, 200b – IV, 77a; V, 198a
Muḍarriṭ al-Ḥidjāra → Amr b. Hind
al-Mudawwana (Ibāḍī) → Abū Ghānim
al-Mudawwana (Mālikī) → Saḥnūn
al-Mudawwar (Almodovar) vii, **286a** – VII, **288a**
Mudawwar, Djamīl v, 188a – V, 185b

Mudawwara vii, **286a**; x, 885a – VII, **288a**; X,
al-Mudayna → Surt
al-Muddaththir/al-Muzzammil vii, **286a** – VII, **288a**
al-Muḍayrib s, 355b – S, 355a
Mudéjar iv, 118a; vii, 242a, 249a, **286a**; s, 81a – IV, 123b; VII, 243b, 250b, **288b**; S, 80b
Mudgal vii, **289a**, 458b- VII, **291a**, 458b
Mudhakkar vii, **289b** – VII, **291b**
al-Mudhaykhira vi,439a – VI, 424b
Mudghalīs (1181) viii, 804a – VIII, 831a
Mudīr vii, **290a** – VII, **292a**
Mudīriyya ii, 828a – II, 847b
Mudjaddid vii, **290a**, 296b – VII, **292a**, 298b
Mudjaddid-i Alf-i Thānī → Aḥmad Sirhindī. Shaykh
Mudjaddidīs i, 297b; vii, 936b – I, 307a; VII, 937a
Mudjāhid → Rasūl, Banū
Mudjāhid, al-Muwaffak b. ʿAbd Allāh al-ʿĀmirī (Denia) (1044) i, 446b; ii, 111b, 112a, 837a; iii, 743b, 773a; vii, **292a**; viii, 880a,b – I, 459a; II, 114a, 856b; III, 766a, 796b; VII, **294a**; VIII, 910a,b
Mudjāhid, Sayyid Muḥammad s, 75a – S, 75b
Mudjāhid b. Djabr al-Makkī, Abu ʾl-Ḥadjdjādj (718) vii, **293a**, 758a; viii, 1014b s, 386b – VII, **295a**, 759b; VIII, 1050aS, 386b
Mudjāhid al-Dīn Ḳāʾimāz, amīr (1199) i, 798b; vi, 781a – I, 822a; VI, 771a
Mudjāhid(e)s (Denia) vi, 926b – VI, 918b
Mudjāhidin-i islām iv, 52a – IV, 55a
Mudjāhidūn i, 1333b; ii, 140b, 316b; iii, 335b, 1068a; iv, 196b, 729b – I, 1273a; II, 144a, 326a; III, 345b, 1095a; IV, 205a, 258b
Muʿdjam → Ḳāmūs
Mudjannada i, 490a – I, 504b
Mudjāshiʿ b. Masʿūd al-Sulamī v, 157b – V, 157a
Mudjassima → Tashbīh
Mudjāwir v, 1134a; vii, **293b** – V, 1129b; VII, **295b**
Mudjawwaza → Tülbend
Mudjbira → Djabriyya
Mudjdjāʿa b. Siʿr iii, 41a; iv, 534b – III, 43a; IV, 558a
Mudjdjān iv, 1002b, 1003a, 1004a – IV, 1035a, b, 1036b
Mudjīb al-Raḥmān v, 1082a – V, 1079b
Mudjīr al-Dīn Abak → Abu Saʿīd Abak
Mudjīr al-Dīn Amīrshāh iv, 738a; s, 59a – IV, 767b; S, 59b
Mudjīr al-Dīn Aybak viii, 128a – VIII, 131a
Mudjīr al-Dīn al-ʿUlaymī, Abu ʾl-Yumn (1522) iii, 161b, 954b; iv, 958a; v, 322b; vi, 658b; vii, **294b** – III, 165a, 979a; IV, 991a; V, 321b; VI, 644b; VII, **296b**
Mudjīr-i Baylaḳānī iv, 62a; s, 239b – IV, 65b; S, 240a
Muʿdjiza iv, 615a, b, 616a, b; vii, **295b** – IV, 639b, 640a, b, 641a; VII, **297b**
Mudjrā → Madjrā
Mudjtabā Mīrlawḥī → Nawwāb-i Safawī
Mudjtahid iii, 1025b, 1026b; iv, 278a, 1101a; vii, **295b**; ix, 914a; s, 103b – III, 1051b, 1052b; IV, 290b, 1132a; VII, **298a**; IX, 952a; S, 103a
Mudjtathth vii, **304a** – VII, **306a**
Mudjūn vii, **304a** – VII, **306a**
Mudlidj b. Muhannā (XV) vii, 462b – VII, 462a
al-Mudlidjī, Abū ʾl-Ḳāsim (X) i, 127a – I, 130b
al-Mudlidjī, ʿAlḳama b. Mudjazzaz (VII) vii, 863a – VII, 864b
Mudmar vii, **304b** – VII, **306b**
Mudradj iii, 26a – III, 27b
Mudros → Mondros
Mudṭarib iii, 26a – III, 27b
Muezzin → Muʾadhdhin
Mufādana iv, 324a – IV, 338a
Mufaḍḍal s, 38b – S, 39a
al-Mufaḍḍal b. Abī Faḍāʾil (XIV) vii, **305a**; s, 388b – VII, **307a**; S, 389a
al-Mufaḍḍal b. Maʿshar vii, 581a – VII, 581b
al-Mufaḍḍal b. Muḥammad b. Yaʿlā al-Ḍabbī (781) → al-Ḍabbī
al-Mufaḍḍal (II) b. Salama b. ʿĀsim al-Ḍabbī (903) → al-Ḍabbī
Mufaddal b. Ṣāliḥ s, 233a – S, 232b
al-Mufaḍḍal b. ʿUmar al-Djuʿfī iv, 1132b, 1133a – IV, 1164a, b
al-Mufaḍḍal b. Yazīd b. al-Muhallab vii, 359a; s, 41a – VII, 361a; S, 41a
Mufaḍḍaliyya → al-Khaṭṭābiyya
al-Mufaḍḍaliyyāt vii, **306b** – VII, **308b**
Mufākhara i, 584b, 586b; iv, 77b, 448b; v, 1223b; vii, **308b** – I, 603a, 605a; IV, 81b, 468b; V, 1214a; VII, **311a**
al-Mufarradj b. Sallām iv, 275a – IV, 287b
Mufarridj b. Daghfal al-Ṭāʾī (Djarrāḥid(e)) i, 824a, b; ii, 482b, 483a, 854b; iii, 77a, 79b, 128b, 841a; iv, 841b; s, 37a – I, 847a, b; II, 495a, b, 874a; III, 79b, 82a, 131a, 864b; IV, 874b; S, 37b
Mufarridj b. al-Djarrāh v, 327b – V, 327b
Mufāwaḍa vii, **310a** – VII, **312b**
al-Mufawwaḍ, Djaʿfar b. al-Muʿtamid (ʿAbbāsid(e)) (IX) i, 278b; vii, 766a – I, 287a; VII, 767b
al-Mufīd, Shaykh Abū ʿAbd Allāh al-ʿUkbarī (1022) iii, 1266a; iv, 182b; vi, 219a, 549a; vii, **312a**, 758b; viii, 372b; s, 56b, 89b – III, 1299a; IV, 190b; VI, 203b, 533b; VII, **314a**, 760a; VIII, 385b; S, 57a, 89b
Mufliḥ →Abū Sāliḥ Mufliḥ
Mufrad i, 95a, 1083b; vii, **313a** – I, 97b, 1116a; VII, **315b**
al-Muftari → Ḥā-mīm
Muftī → Fatwa; Shaykh al-Islām
Müftī-zāde (Müftüoghlu) Aḥmed → Aḥmad Ḥikmet
Mugan Kaghan (572) x, 687a – X, 729a
Mughals i, 81a, 117b, 199a, 228b, 229a, b, 238a, 252b, 316a, 768a, 769a, 1069a, 1159a, 1161a, 1168b, 1347b; ii, 120b, 155a, 157a, 265a, 336b, 806a, 815a, 868a, 1084b, 1129b; iii, 199a, 201a, b, 411a, 422b, 424b, 448b; iv, 268b, 563a, 709a, 759b, 1056a; v, 72a, 629b; vi, 77b, 198b, 310a, 422b, 424b, 488a, 533b, 534a, b, 696b, 813b; vii, 80a, 129b, 194a, **313b**, 795b, 943b; ix, 598a; s, 131b, 167b, 246b, 252b, 253a, 257b, 258b, 280a, 335b – I, 83b, 121a, 204b, 235b, 236a, b, 245a, 260a, 326a, 791a, 792a, 1101a, 1193b, 1195b, 1203a, 1387b; II, 123b, 160a, 162a, 273a, 346a, 825a, 834b, 888a, 1110a, 1156a; III, 204a, 206a, b, 423b, 436b, 438a, 464a; IV, 280b, 585a, 737b, 789b, 1087a; V, 74a, 633b; VI, 75b, 182b, 295a, 407b, 410a, 474b, 517b, 518a, b, 684b, 803b; VII, 81a, 131a, 194b, **315b**, 797b, 944a; IX, 621a; S, 130b, 167b, 246b, 252b, 257b, 258a, 279b, 335a
—constructions v, 888b, 889a, 1215a, 1216b – V, 895a, b, 1204b, 1206b
Mughalānī Bēgam i, 296a; iii, 1158b – I, 305a; III, 1187a
al-Mughallis, Abū ʿAbd Allāh al-Ḥusayn s, 119b – S, 119a
al-Mughammas (Mecca) vii, **346b** – VII, **348a**
Mūghān s, 143a – S, 143a
Mūghān steppe vi, 56a, 492b, 494a, 495b, 527b – VI, 54a, 478b, 479b, 480b, 512a
Mughanni ii, 1073a, b – II, 1098a, b
Mughārasa vii, **346b** – VII, **348b**

al-Mughāwir → Almogávares
al-Mughayyabāt al-Khams vii, **346b** – VII, **348b**
Mughīra, Banū i, 98a; vi, 138a, 139a – I, 101a; VI, 136b, 137a
al-Mughīra b. ʿAbd Allāh → al-Uḳayshir al-Asadī
al-Mughīra b. ʿAbd Allāh b. ʿUmar b. Makhzūm vi, 137b – VI, 135b
al-Mughīra b. ʿAbd al-Raḥmān b. Makhzūm vi, 139a, 140b – VI, 137b, 138b
al-Mughīra b. ʿAbd Allāh b. al-Aswad → al-Ukayshir
al-Mughīra b. ʿAbd al-Raḥmān III (al-Andalus) (X) vi, 431a – VI, 416b
al-Mughīra b. Abī Burda al-Ḳurashī (VIII) v, 1160a – V, 1149b
al-Mughīra b. Abī Ṣufra (VIII) vii, 359a – VII, 361b
al-Mughīra b. Khālid b. Makhzūm vi, 140a – VI, 138b
al-Mughīra b. Saʿīd al-Badjalī → al-Mughīriyya
al-Mughīra b. Saʿīd al-ʿIdjlī, Ghālī (737) i, 141a, 1099a, 1116b; ii, 1094a; iv, 926b; vi, 441b; vii, 388b, 459b; s, 103b, 232b – I, 145a, 1132a, 1150b; II, 1120a; IV, 959b; VI, 427a; VII, 389b, 459b; S, 103a, 232b
al-Mughīra b. Shuʿba, Abū ʿAbd Allāh al-Thaḳafī (668) i, 111a, 382b, 695a, 714a; iii, 40a, 545a, 1265b; iv, 385a; v, 346b; vi, 710a, 920a; vii, 27a, **347a**; ix, 421a – I, 114b, 393b, 716a, 735b; III, 41b, 564a, 1298a; IV, 402a; V, 347b; VI, 698b, 911b; VII, 27a, **349a**; 435a
Mughīra b. Sunyer (X) x, 303b – X, 317a
al-Mughīriyya i, 1116b; vii, **347b**, 459b – I, 1150b; VII, **349b**, 459b
al-Mughīth, al-Malik (Ḥims) (XIII) vi, 381a – VI, 365b
Mughīth, Malik (Hind) (XV) iii, 418b, 638b – III, 431b, 660a
Mughīth al-Rūmī i, 493a; v, 510a – I, 508a; V, 513b
al-Mughīth ʿUmar b. Ayyūb (1244) iv, 609a; viii, 989a – IV, 634a; VIII, 1023b
Mughla (Muğla) vii, **348b** – VII, **350b**
Mughniyya, Muḥammad Djawād (1979) vii, 780b – VII, 782b
Mughrāna, Banū vi, 742a – VI, 731b
Mughulistān → Mogholistān
Mughuliyya iv, 420a – IV, 438a
Mughultāy (1290) ix, 661a – IX, 687a
Mughulṭāy b. Ḳilīdj b. ʿAbd Allāh (1361) vii, **350a**; viii, 156b – VII, **352a**; VIII, 159a
Mughulṭāy ʿAlā' al-Dīn (1307) viii, 158a – VIII, 160a
Muḥāḍara iv, 697a, b – IV, 725a, b
Muḥaddith → Ḥadīth
al-Muhadhdhab, al-Ḳāḍī iv, 214b – IV, 224a
Muhadhdhab al-Dīn v, 272a – V, 269b
al-Muhadhdhab b. Mammātī → Ibn Mammātī
Muhadhdhib al-Dawla ʿAlī b. Naṣr s, 118b, 119a – S, 118a, b
Muhādjarat movement/mouvement v, 171a – V, 168b
Muhādjir vii, **350b** – VII, **352a**
Muhādjir, Banu ʾl- i, 65b; ii, 305a; iv, 478a; s, 82a – I, 67b; II, 313b; IV, 498b; S, 81b
al-Muhādjir b. ʿAbd Allāh al-Kilābī s, 31b – S, 32a
al-Muhādjir b. Abī Umayya b. al-Mughīra Makhzūmī (VII) i, 110b; vi, 138b, 139b; viii, 97a – I, 113b; VI, 137a, 138a; VIII, 99b
al-Muhādjirūn i, 54b, 515a; iii, 226b, 366b, 874a; v, 995b; vii, **356a** – I, 56b, 530b; III, 233b, 378b, 898a; V, 991a; VII, **358b**
Muḥāfiẓ Khān (XVI) ii, 1127a; vi, 52a, 54b – II, 1153b; VI, 50b, 52b
Muḥaḳḳak iv, 1123a, 1125a – IV, 1155a, 1157a
al-Muḥaḳḳiḳ (1277) vii, 297b – VII, 299b
Muḥaḳḳlḳ-i Awwal → al-Ḥilmī, Nadjm al-Dīn
Muḥaḳḳiḳ-i Ṭūṣī → al-Ṭūṣī, Nāṣir al-Dīn
Muḥakkima → Khawāridj; Taḥkīm
al-Muḥakkima al-ūlā → Harūrites
Muḥāl → Manṭiḳ
al-Muhalhil b. Muḥammad i, 512b, 513a – I, 528a, b
al-Muhalhil b. Rabīʿa → Imruʾ al-Ḳays ʿAdī b. Rabīʿa al-Taghlibī
al-Muhallab b. Abī Ṣufrā, Abū Saʿīd al-Azdī (702) i, 55a, 76b, 77a, 304a, 810b, 1242b; iii, 40b; iv, 15a, 752b, 1075b, 1145b; v, 57a; vii, **357a**, 523b; s, 357b – I, 57a, 77a, 79a, 313b, 833b, 1280b; III, 42a; IV, 16a, 783a, 1107b, 1177a; V, 58b; VII, **359a**, 524a; S, 357b
al-Muhallabī → Yazīd b. Ḥātim
al-Muhallabī (1246) vii, 772a – VII, 774a
al-Muhallabī, Abu ʾl-Ghanāʾim al-Mufaḍḍal (X) vii, 358a – VII, 360b
al-Muhallabī, Abu ʾl-Ḥusayn al-Ḥasan b. Aḥmad (990) vii, **357b**; viii, 16b – VII, **360a**; VIII, 16b
al-Muhallabī, Abū Muḥammad al-Ḥasan b. Muḥammad (vizier) (963) i, 118a, 126b, 1352b; iii, 780a, 854a; vi, 965b; vii, **358a**, 771a; s, 13a, 32b, 362a, b – I, 121b, 130b, 1392a; III, 803b, 878a; VI, 957b; VII, **360b**, 772b; S, 13a, 32b, 361b, 362a
Muhallabid(e)s i, 158a, 305a; iii, 649b, 981b; vi, 428a, 640b; vii, **358b**, 1016a; viii, 465b; x, 541b; s, 352a – I, 162b, 314b; III, 670b, 1006a; VI, 413b, 625b; VII, **361a**, 1018a; VIII, 481a; X, ; S, 352a
al-Muḥallī, Ḥamīd b. Aḥmmad vi, 433b, 434a – VI, 419a, b
Muḥallil v, 109b – V, 112a
Muḥammad, the Prophet (632) i, 453a, 514a, 728a, 959a, 1020b, 1021a, 1092b, 1283b; ii, 168a, 227a, 363a, 538b, 593a, 758b, 932a, 1061a; iii, 32a, 33a, 90b, 435a, 800b, 933a, 1231b, 1240b; iv, 316a, 356a, 994b, 996b; v, 75a, 402b, 734a; vi, 146a, 652a; vii, **360b**, 570b
—beliefs concerning the Prophet i, 178a, 187b, 264a, 266a, 267a, 306b, 314b, 333a, 336b, 337a, 349a, 443a, 1310a, b, 1314b; ii, 363b, 376a, 847a, 883b, 950a, 993a, 1005b, 1058b, 1098b; iii, 94b, 256a, 462a, 607a, 1018b; iv, 270a, 319a, 367b, 821a, 1074a; v, 82a
—companions i, 114b, 129a, 343b, 881b, 405a, 448b, 514a, 695a, 1077b, 1313a; ii, 728b; iii, 582b, 873b, 1024a; iv, 896b, 927a; v, 406a
—history iv, 736b; v, 415a, 771a
—life events i, 12a, 53a, 109b, 110a, 115b, 136b, 151a, 152b, 307b, 381b, 442b, 451a, 509b, 549a, 609a, 633b, 771b, 868a, 922a, 1011b; ii, 113b, 372a, 461b, 625a, 725a, 842b, 846b, 873b, 953a, 993b, 1023b; iii, 33a, 64a, 94a, 223a, 240b, 286a, 366b, 539a, 578a, 975b; iv, 320a, b, 771a, 824a, 832b, 898b, 927b, 928b, 1020b, 1103a, 1138b; v, 78b, 79a, 316a, b, 317a, 436b, 995b, 1161b
—relics i, 109a, 736a, 1314b; ii, 695b; iv, 367b, 368a; v, 761a
Muḥammad, le Prophète (632) I, 466a, 530a, 750a, 988b, 1051b, 1053a, 1125b, 1322b; II, 173b, 234a, 373a, 552a, 607b, 777a, 953b, 1085b; III, 33b, 34b, 93a, 449a, 824a, 957b, 1263b, 1272b; IV, 330a, b, 371a, 1027a, 1029a; V, 77a, 403b, 739b; VI, 144b, 637a; VII, **363a**, 571a
—compagnons I, 118a, 133a, 354a, 392a, 416b, 461b, 529b, 716a, 1109b, 1353b; II, 747a; III, 603a, 897b, 1050a; IV, 929a, 960a; V, 407a
—croyances à l'égard du Prophète I, 183a, 193a, 272a, 274a, 275a, 316a, 324b, 343b, 347a, b, 359b, 455b, 1350a, b, 1354b; II, 373b, 386a, 867a, 904a, 972b, 1016a, 1029a, 1083a, 1124b; III, 94b, 295a, 478b,

628a, 1044a; IV, 282a, 333a, 383b, 854a, 1105b; V, 84a, b
—évènements de sa vie   I, 12a, 55a, 112b, 113a, 118b, 140b, 155b, 157a, 317a, 392b, 455a, 464a, 524b, 566b, 629a, 654b, 794b, 892a, 922a, 1042b; II, 116a, 382a, 473a, 640b, 743b, 862b, 866a, 893b, 975b, 1016b, 1047a; III, 33a, 66b, 94a, 230a, 247b, 294b, 378a, 557b, 598a, 1000a; IV, 334b, 802a, 857a, 865b, 931a, 960b, 961b, 1052b, 1134b, 1170b; V, 80b, 81a, 315b, 316a, b, 438b, 991a, 1151a
—histoire IV, 766b; V, 416b, 777a
—reliques I, 112a, 758a, 1354b; II, 712b; IV, 383b, 384a; V, 767a
Muhammad, K.T. (Mappila)   vi, 464b – VI, 450a
Muhammad, N.P. (Mappila)   vi, 464b – VI, 450a
Muḥammad II b. Muḥammad I al-Sẖarīf, Mawlāy (ʿAlawid(e), 1664)   vi, 142b – VI, 141a
Muḥammad, Sultan of/de Brunei   s, 151b – S, 152a
Muḥammad (Bayhaḳī Sayyid)   s, 131b – S, 130b
Muḥammad I (ʿAbbādid(e))   i, 5b, 242a; iv, 115b – I, 5b, 249b; IV, 121a
Muḥammad II (ʿAbbādid(e))   → al-Muʿtamid
Muḥammad I (Aghlabid(e))   i, 248b, 250b – I, 256a, 258a
Muḥammad II (Aghlabid(e))   i, 249a, 250b, 1152a – I, 256b, 258a, 1186b
Muḥammad I (ʿAlawid(e))   i, 355b; s, 113b – I, 366b; S, 113a
Muḥammad II b. Muḥammad I al-Sẖarīf, Mawlāy (ʿAlawid(e)) (1664)   i, 355b; v, 1191b; vi, 142b – I, 366b; V, 1181b; VI, 141a
Muḥammad III b. ʿAbd Allāh, Sīdī (ʿAlawid(e)) (1790)   i, 47b, 356a, 506b; ii, 116b, 146a, 308a, 367b, 510b, 727a, 820a; iii, 339b, 395b, 966a; iv, 634a, 635b; v, 1192a; vi, 249a, 250a, 293b, 589a, 597a, 842b; vii, 39a, 387a, 391a; viii, 507b; s, 40b, 325b, 401a, b – I, 49a, 367a, 521b; II, 119a, 150a, 317a, 377b, 523a, 745b, 839b; III, 349b, 408a, 990b; IV, 660a, 661b; V, 1182a; VI, 233a, 234b, 279a, 573b, 582a, 833a; VII, 39a, 388a, 392a; VIII, 525a; S, 40b, 325a, 401b, 402a
Muḥammad IV b. Abd al-Raḥmān, Sīdī (ʿAlawid(e)) (1873)   i, 315b, 356b, 357a; ii, 332a, 510b; iii, 562a, 806b; vi, 249a, 250b, 595b, 798b; vii, 391a; s, 114a, 303a – I, 325a, 367b, 368a; II, 341b, 523a; III, 581b, 830a; VI, 233a, 234b, 580a, 788b; VII, 392a; S, 113b, 303a
Muḥammad V b. Yūsuf (ʿAlawid(e)) (1961)   i, 357b, 358a; ii, 673b, 1116b; iii, 564a; iv, 634b, 635b, 775a; v, 1072a, 1194b; vi, 262a; vii, 415a – I, 368b, 369a; II, 690a, 1142b; III, 583a; IV, 660b, 661b, 806a; V, 1069b, 1184b; VI, 246b; VII, 416b
Muḥammad I (Bahmanid(e)) (1375)   vi, 67a; vii, 458a – VI, 65a; VII, 458a
Muḥammad II (Bahmanid(e)) (1397)   vii, 458b – VII, 458b
Muḥammad III, Sẖams al-Dīn Lasẖkarī (Bahmānid(e)) (1482)   vi, 67a, b; vii, 458b – VI, 64b, 65b; VII, 459a
Muḥammad I (Ḥafṣid(e))   → al-Mustanṣir
Muḥammad II (Ḥafṣid(e))   → Abū ʿAṣida
Muḥammad III (Ḥafṣid(e))   → Abū Darba
Muḥammad IV (Ḥafṣid(e))   → al-Muntaṣir
Muḥammad V (Ḥafṣid(e))   → Abu ʿAbd Allāh Muḥammad V
Muḥammad I b. al-Ḳāsim b. Ḥammūd al-Mahdī (Ḥammūdid(e)) (1048)   iii, 147b – III, 150b
Muḥammad III (Ḥammūdid(e))   iii, 147b – III, 150b
Muḥammad I (Ismaʿīlī)   i, 353b, 1359b; iv, 859b – I, 364a, 1399b; IV, 893a

Muḥammad II (Ismaʿīlī)   i, 353b; iv, 205a – I, 364b; IV, 214a
Muḥammad III, ʿAlāʾ al-Dīn (Ismaʿīlī, Alamūt) (1255)   i, 353b; iv, 205b; vi, 790b – I, 364b; IV, 214b; VI, 780a
Muḥammad I (Ḳarakẖānid(e))   iii, 1114a – III, 1141b
Muḥammad II b. Sulaymān Bughrā Khān (Ḳarakẖānid(e)) (1130)   i, 1294b; iii, 1114b, 1115a; vii, 535b; x, 689a – I, 1334a; III, 1142a, b; VII, 535b; X,
Muḥammad I (Ḳarāmānid(e))   → Muḥammad b. Ḳaramān
Muḥammad II (Ḳarāmānid(e))   iv, 623b – IV, 648a, b
Muḥammad IV (Marinid(e))   iii, 832a, 836a – III, 855b, 859b
Muḥammad I b. Naṣr al-Gẖālib (Naṣrid(e)) (1273)   i, 495b, 1089a; ii, 307b, 1014a, 1015b, 1016b; iii, 826b; vi, 222b, 577a; vii, 1020a, 1021b; s, 381b – I, 510b, 1121b; II, 316b, 1038a, 1039a, 1040a; III, 850a; VI, 216b, 562a; VII, 1022a, 1022b; S, 382a
Muḥammad II al-Faḳīḥ (Naṣrid(e)) (1302)   ii, 1016b; vi, 222b, 521a; vii, 1020a, 1021b – II, 1040b; VI, 216b, 505b; VII, 1022a, 1023b
Muḥammad III al-Maghlūʿ (Naṣrid(e)) (1309)   iii, 833b; vii, 563b, 1020a, 1022a – III, 857b; VII, 564a, 1022a, 1024b
Muḥammad IV, Abū ʿAbd Allāh (Naṣrid(e)) (1333)   iv, 355b; vii, 1020b, 1023a – IV, 370b; VII, 1020b, 1025b
Muḥammad V al-Gẖānī bi-ʾllāh, Abū ʿAbd Allāh (Naṣrid(e)) (1359)   i, 1225a; ii, 115a, 1017a; iii, 804a, 835b, 972b; vii, 1020b, 1024a – I, 1261b; II, 117a, 1040b; III, 827b, 859b, 997a; VII, 1022b, 1026a
Muḥammad VI al-Gẖālib bi-ʾllāh, Abū ʿAbd Allāh (El Bermejo) (Naṣride(e)) (1362)   vii, 1020b, 1024a – VII, 1022b, 1026b
Muḥammad VII, Abū ʿAbd Allāh (Naṣrid(e))(1408)   iii, 804a, 972b; vii, 1020b, 1025a – III, 827b, 997a; VII, 1022b, 1027a
Muḥammad VIII al-Mutamassik (El Pequeño) (Naṣrid(e)) (1429)   vii, 1020b, 1025b, 1026a; s, 399a – VII, 1022b, 1028a; S, 399a
Muḥammad IX al-Gẖālib bi-ʾllāh (El Zurdo) (Naṣrid(e)) (1453)   vii, 1020b, 1025b, 1026a; s, 399a – VII, 1022b, 1028a, b; S, 399a
Muḥammad X, Abū ʿAbd Allāh (al-Aḥnaf/El Cojo) (Naṣrid(e)) (1447)   vii, 1020b, 1026a; s, 399a – VII, 1022b, 1028a; S, 399b
Muḥammad XI (El Chiquito) (Naṣrid(e)) (1455)   vii, 1020b, 1026a – VII, 1022b, 1028b
Muḥammad XII, Abū ʿAbd Allāh (Boabdil) (Naṣrid(e)) (1492)   i, 501b; vi, 222b; vii, 1020b, 1026b; s, 399a – I, 516b; VI, 216b; VII, 1022b, 1029b; S, 399b
Muḥammad XIII b. Saʿd (al-Zagẖal) (Naṣride(e)) (1489)   vii, 1020b, 1026b, 1027b – VII, 1022b, 1029b, 1030a
Muḥammad I-VI (Ottoman)   → Meḥemmed I-VI
Muḥammad I (Āl Ṣabāḥ) (1896)   viii, 669a – VIII, 688b
Muḥammad I Ghiyāth al-Dīn b. Malik Sẖāh (Saldjūḳ) (1118)   i, 522b, 664a, 684a, 780a, 1052a, 1336b; ii, 975b; iii, 47a, 196a, 197b, 254a, 1097b; iv, 28b, 29a, 101b, 102a; v, 159a, b, 662a; vi, 64a, 275a, b, 493b, 499b; vii, 408a, 529b; viii, 81b, 716a, 942b; s, 382b – I, 538b, 683b, 705a, 803b, 1083b, 1377a; II, 998a; III, 49a, 201a, 202a, 261a, 1124a; IV, 30b, 31a, 106a, b; V, 158a, b, 667a; VI, 61b, 260a, b, 479b, 485a; VII, 409a, 530a; VIII, 83b, 737a, 974b S, 383a
Muḥammad I Mugẖīth al-Dīn b. Arslan Sẖāh (Saldjūḳ) (1156)   vi, 853a – VI, 844b

Muḥammad II b. Maḥmūd b. Muḥammad b. Malik-Shāh (Saldjūḳ) (1159) i, 684a, 865b; iv, 1097a; v, 160b; vi, 64a, 500a, 871a; vii, **406a**; viii, 944a – I, 705a, 890a; IV, 1128a; V, 159a; VI, 62a, 485b, 861b; VII, **407b**; VIII, 976b
Muḥammad I b. ʿAbd al-Raḥmān II (Umayyad(e), al-Andalus) (886) i, 11a, 83a, 85b, 494a, 498a, 957a; iii, 816a; iv, 713a; v, 510b, 1107b; vi, 926b; vii, 248a; x, 850b – I, 11a, 85a, 88a, 509a, 513a, 956a; III, 839b; IV, 741b; V, 514a, 1103b; VI, 918b; VII, 249b, 250a; X,
Muḥammad II b. Hishām al-Mahdī(Umayyad(e)) (1010) → al-Mahdī (Umayyad(e))
Muḥammad III b. ʿAbd al-Raḥmān al-Mustakfī (Umayyad(e)) → al-Andalus, Umayyad(e)s of Spain/ d'Espagne
Muḥammad II al-Burtuḳālī (Waṭṭāsid(e)) (1525) i, 706b; vii, 37b – I, 727b; VII, 37b
Muḥammad, al-ʿĀlim b. Ismāʿīl (ʿAlawid(e)) (XVIII) iii, 49b; vi, 595a – III, 51b; VI, 580a
Muḥammad, Awlād ii, 876a – II, 896a
Muḥammad b. ʿAbbād → Muḥammad I (ʿAbbādid(e))
Muḥammad b. ʿAbbād i, 1166b – I, 1201b
Muḥammad b. ʿAbbās (Ḳādjār) → Ḳādjār
Muḥammad b. al-ʿAbbās b. al-Baṣrī → Ṣāḥib al-Rākūba
Muḥammad b. al-ʿAbbās b. Mandīl vi, 404a – VI, 388b
Muḥammad b. al-ʿAbbās al-Yazīdī iii, 23b – III, 24b
Muḥammad b. ʿAbd Allāh → Ibn al-Abbār, Abū ʿAbd Allāh (1260); Ibn al-Khaṭīb Abū ʿAbdallāh, Lisān al-Dīn (1375); Ibn Mālik, Abū ʿAbdallāh al-Djayyānī (1274)
Muḥammad b. ʿAbd Allāh → Muḥammad III (ʿAlawid(e))
Muḥammad b. ʿAbd Allāh (Ḥamāliyya) → al-Sharīf al-Akhḍar
Muḥammad b. ʿAbd Allāh (Ḥasanid(e)) s, 232b – S, 232b
Muḥammad b. ʿAbd Allāh b. ʿAbd al-Ḥakam (882) → Ibn ʿAbd al-Ḥakam, Abū ʿAbd Allāh
Muḥammad b. ʿAbd Allāh b. ʿAbd al-Ḥakam (Mālikī) (845) vii, 4b – VII, 4b
Muḥammad b. ʿAbd Allāh b. al-Ḥasan b. al-Ḥasan, al-Nafs al-Zakiyya (ʿAlid(e)) (762) i, 45b, 103b, 123a, 402a, b, 550b; ii, 485a, 745a; iii, 256b, 616a; v, 1233a, b; vi, 263a, b, 332a, 334a, 427b; vii, 348a, 358b, 359b, **388a**, 459b, 645b; ix, 423b, 761b – I, 46b, 106b, 126b, 412b, 414a, 568a; II, 497b, 763b; III, 265a, 636b; V, 1223b, 1224a; VI, 248a, 316b, 318b, 413a; VII, 349b, 350a, 361a, 362a, **389b**, 459b, 645a; IX, 417b, 794b
Muḥammad b. ʿAbd Allāh b. Khāzim i, 1293a – I, 1332b
Muḥammad b. ʿAbd Allāh b. al-Muḳaffaʿ i, 631a; iii, 883b – I, 652a; III, 907b
Muḥammad b. ʿAbd Allāh b. Saʿīd al-Yaharī iii, 124a – III, 127a
Muḥammad b. ʿAbd Allāh b. Ṭāhir Dhī 'l-Yamīnayn (867) vii, **390a**, 722b; viii, 856a – VII, **390b**, 723b; VIII, 885b
Muḥammad b. ʿAbd Alllāh b. Yūnus (1059) ix, 586b – IX, 609a
Muḥammad b. ʿAbd Allāh b. Ẓafar al-Ṣaḳalī → Ibn Ẓafar
Muḥammad b. ʿAbd Allāh b. Ziyād → Muḥammad al-Ziyādī
Muḥammad b. ʿAbd Allāh Āl Khalīfa iv, 953b – IV, 986a
Muḥammad b. ʿAbd Allāh al-Ghālib → Muḥammad al-Maslūkh
Muḥammad b. ʿAbd Allāh Ḥassān al-Mahdī (1920) i, 1172b; vii, **389b**; viii, 162a, 990a – I, 1208a; VII, **390b**; VIII, 164b, 1024b
Muḥammad b. ʿAbd Allāh al-Kharūṣī iv, 1085a – IV, 1116a
Muḥammad b. ʿAbd Allāh al-Khudjistānī iii, 254b – III, 261b
Muḥammad b. ʿAbd Allāh al-Sāmarrī iii, 161a – III, 164b
Muḥammad b. ʿAbd Allāh al-Shintināwī vi, 627a – VI, 612a
Muḥammad b. ʿAbd Allāh Yumn al-Dawla i, 1310a – I, 1350a
Muḥammad b. ʿAbd al-ʿAziz b. Saʿūd v, 998b – V, 993b, 994a
Muḥammad b. ʿAbd al-Bāḳī (1583) ix, 101b – IX, 105b
Muḥammad b. ʿAbd al-Djabbār (XI) x, 853a
Muḥammad b. ʿAbd al-Ḥalīm (1681) vii, 469b – VII, 469a
Muḥammad b. ʿAbd al-Ḳādir al-Kardūdī → al-Kardūdī
Muḥammad b. ʿAbd al-Karīm (Rīf) (XX) viii, 523a, 905b – VIII, 540b, 936b
Muḥammad b. ʿAbd al-Malik → Ibn Ṭufayl; Ibn al-Zayyāt; Ibn Zuhr
Muḥammad b. ʿAbd al-Malik (Umayyad(e)) (700) vi, 900a – VI, 891a
Muḥammad b. ʿAbd al-Malik b. Ayman i, 600a – I, 619b
Muḥammad b. ʿAbd al-Malik al-Ṭawīl s, 80a – S, 79b
Muḥammad b. ʿAbd al-Malik al-Zayyāt ii, 385b – II, 396a
Muḥammad b. ʿAbd al-Muʿīn b. ʿAwn, Sharīf iii, 263a, 605b; vi, 150b, 151a – III, 270b, 626a; VI, 149b
Muḥammad b. ʿAbd al-Muʾmin i, 79b, 160b; iii, 386b – I, 82a, 165a; III, 399a
Muḥammad b. ʿAbd al-Raḥīm → Ibn al-Furāt
Muḥammad b. ʿAbd al-Raḥmān → Muḥammad IV (Alawid(e))
Muḥammad b. ʿAbd al-Raḥmān (886) x, 824a – X,
Muḥammad b. ʿAbd al-Raḥmān b. Abi 'l-Baḳāʾ (XIII) vi, 824b – VI, 814b
Muḥammad b. ʿAbd al-Raḥmān al-ʿAṭawī (864) vii, **392b** – VII, **394a**
Muḥammad b. ʿAbd al-Raḥmān al-Gashtulī (1793) viii, 399a – VIII, 413a
Muḥammad b. ʿAbd al-Raḥmān al-Ḳāʾim bi-amr Allāh (Saʿdid(e)) (1517) vi, 893a – VI, 884b
Muḥammad b. ʿAbd al-Razzāḳ (X) vi, 499b; vii, 656a; viii, 1028b; x, 232a – VI, 484b; VII, 655b; VIII, 1063b; X, 250a
Muḥammad b. ʿAbd al-Ṣamad iv, 381a – IV, 397b
Muḥammad b. ʿAbd al-Wahhāb → Ibn ʿAbd al-Wahhāb
Muḥammad b. ʿAbdūn vi, 450a – VI, 435b
Muḥammad b. Abi 'l-ʿAbbās iii, 135b – III, 138a
Muḥammad b. Abī ʿAffān. imām (IX) x, 816b – X,
Muḥammad b. Abī ʿĀmir → al-Manṣūr b. Abī ʿĀmir
Muḥammad b. Abī Bakr → Ibn Ḳayyim al-Djawziyya; Ibn Sayyid al-Nās
Muḥammad b. Abī Bakr (al-Ṣiddīḳ) (VII) i, 44a, 109b, 451b; iii, 241a; vi, 740b; vii, 269a, **393a**; s, 92b – I, 45b, 112b, 464b; III, 247b; VI, 729b; VII, 271a, **394a**; S, 92b
Muḥammad b. Abī Bakr (Songhay) (1538) ii, 977b; vii, **393b**; ix, 756b – II, 1000a; VII, **395a**; IX, 789b

Muḥammad b. Abī ʾl-Djawarī (IX) ix, 670a – IX, 696b
Muḥammad b. Abī Ḥudhayfa (657) vii, 393a, **394b** – VII, 394a, **395b**
Muḥammad b. Abī ʾl-Ḳāsim → Ibn Abī Dīnār
Muḥammad b. Abī Muḥammad → Ibn Ẓafar
Muḥammad b. Abī Muḥammad Ibn Abi ʾl-Zinād (VIII) s, 380b – S, 380b
Muḥammad b. Abī Rawḥ Luṭf Allāh b. Abī Saʿīd i, 145b – I, 150a
Muḥammad b. Abi ʾl-Sādj al-Afshīn (Sādjid(e)) (901) i, 145b; ii, 524a, 679b; v, 49a; vii, **395a**; viii, 745a – I, 149b; II, 537a, 696b; V, 50b; VII, **396a**; 766b
Muḥammad b. Abī Tawādjīn al-Kutāmī i, 91b – I, 94a
Muḥammad b. Abī ʿUyayna b. al-Muhallab (VIII) vii, 359b, **395a** – VII, 362a, **396b**
Muḥammad b. Abī Yūsuf Yaʿḳūb (al-Nāṣir) → al-Nāṣir, Muḥammad b. Abī Yūsuf
Muḥammad b. Abī Zaynab → Abu ʾl-Khaṭṭāb
Muḥammad b. ʿAffān iii, 652b – III, 673b
Muḥammad b. Afrāsiyāb vi, 511a – VI, 496b
Muḥammad b. al-Aghlab → Muḥammad I (Aghlabid(e))
Muḥammad b. Aḥmad → Muḥammad II (Aghlabid(e)); Abu ʾl-Muṭahhar al-Azdī; Ibn al-ʿAlḳamī; Ibn Iyās; Ibn Rushd
Muḥammad b. Aḥmad (Āl-i Burhān) (1219) viii, 749a – VIII, 779b
Muḥammad b. Aḥmad, Abu ʾl-Shalaʿlaʿ ii, 851a – II, 871a
Muḥammad b. Aḥmad b, Ḳarīm al-Dīn (1578) ix, 316a – IX, 326a
Muḥammad b. Aḥmad b. Khayrāt vi, 191b – VI, 175a
Muḥammad b. Aḥmad b. Rushd vii, 538a – VII, 538a
Muḥammad b. Aḥmad b. Sālim (909) viii, 993b – VIII, 1028b
Muḥammad b. Aḥmad Abī ʿAwn iii, 683a – III, 704b
Muḥammad b. Aḥmad al-Andalūsī (XI) vii, 413a – VII, 414a
Muḥammad b. Aḥmad al-Ḥabūḍī s, 338b – S, 338a
Muḥammad b. Aḥmad al-Ḥudīgī ii, 527a – II, 540a
Muḥammad b. Aḥmad Ibn Ṭāhir (Mursiya) (XI) vii, 767a – VII, 768b
Muḥammad b. Aḥmad al-Iskandarānī (XIX) vii, **395b** – VII, **397a**
Muḥammad b. Aḥmad al-Manṣūrī vi, 665a – VI, 651a
Muḥammad b. Aḥmad Mayyāra i, 428a; iii, 721a – I, 440a; III, 743b
Muḥammad b. Aḥmad (Sharwān-Shāh) iv, 346b – IV, 361a
Muḥammad b. Aḥmad al-Shaybānī iv, 90b – IV, 94b
Muḥammad b. Aḥmad Ṭāhāzāde iii, 88a – III, 90b
Muḥammad b. al-Aḥmar → Muḥammad I (Naṣrid(e))
Muḥammad b. ʿĀʾid i, 98b, 106b, 709b; v, 808b – I, 101a, 109b, 731a; V, 814b
Muḥammad b. Āḳā Rustam Rūzafzūn vi, 514b – VI, 499b
Muḥammad b. ʿAḳīl (1806) vii, 115a – VII, 117a
Muḥammad b. ʿAlī → Ibn ʿArabī; Ibn ʿAskar (1239); Ibn Bābawayh; Ibn Djawād al-Iṣfahānī; Ibn Muḳla; Ibn al-Ṭiḳṭaḳā; Ibn Waḥshiyya
Muḥammad b. ʿAlī, Sayyid (1600) viii, 778b – VIII, 804b
Muḥammad b. ʿAlī b. ʿAbd Allāh al-ʿAbbās (743) i, 15a, 48b, 124b, 381a; ii, 168b; iii, 1265b; iv, 15b, 837a; v, 2a, 3a; vii, **396a**, 399a – I, 15b, 50a, 128b, 392a; II, 173b; III, 1298b; IV, 16b-17a, 870a; V, 2b, 3a; VII, **397a**, 400b
Muḥammad b. ʿAlī al-Layth (Ṣaffarid(e)) (911) viii, 796a – VIII, 823a
Muḥammad b. ʿAlī b. Muḥallī (Marrākush) vi, 593a – VI, 578a
Muḥammad b. ʿAlī b. Yūsuf ii, 1007a – II, 1030b
Muḥammad b. ʿAlī b. ʿUmar (1105) vii, **397a** – VII, **398a**
Muḥammad b. ʿAlī al-Baḥrānī iii, 588b – III, 609a
Muḥammad b. ʿAlī al-Barḳī s, 127a – S, 126b
Muḥammad b. ʿAlī al-Fenārī iv, 244b – IV, 255b
Muḥammad b. ʿAlī al-Hamadānī i, 392b – I, 404a
Muḥammad b. ʿAlī al-Idrīsī → al-Idrīsī, Muḥammad b. ʿAlī
Muḥammad b. ʿAlī al-Idrīsī (ʿAsīr) vi, 192a – VI, 176a
Muḥammad b. ʿAlī al-Riḍā (835) i, 713a; vii, **396b** – I, 734b; VII, **397b**
Muḥammad b. ʿAlī al-Shalmaghānī (934) ii, 218a, 1094b; iii, 101a, 683a; vii, **397a**, 812a – II, 225a, 1120b; III, 103b, 704b; VII, **395b**, 839a
Muḥammad b. ʿAlī Sipāhīzāde i, 119a; ii, 587b – I, 122b; II, 602a
Muḥammad b. ʿAlī wuld/u Rzīn (Tāfīlālt) vi, 249b – VI, 233b
Muḥammad b. ʿAlī Zayn al-ʿAbidīn al-Bāḳir (V. Imām) (735) vi, 441b, 917b; vii, 95a, 348a, 388b, **397b**, 459b; ix, 168a, 422b; s, 129b, 231a, 232b, 233a – vi, 427a, 909a; VII, 96b, 349b, 389b, **399a**, 459b; IX, 173a, 436b; S, 128b, 230b, 232b
Muḥammad b. ʿĀmir Abū Nuḳṭa al-Rufaydī i, 709a – I, 729b
Muḥammad b. Amīr Ghāzī (Dānish mendid(e)) vi, 506b – VI, 492a
Muḥammad b. ʿAmmār b. Yāsir i, 448b – I, 461b
Muḥammad b. Āmsāyb (Ben Msayeb) vi, 249a, 253b – VI, 233b, 237a
Muḥammad b. ʿAnnāz i, 512a; iii, 258b, 571b – I, 528a; III, 266a, 591b
Muḥammad b. al-ʿArabi → Ibn al-ʿArabī
Muḥammad b. al-ʿArabiyya i, 47b – I, 48b
Muḥammad b. ʿArafa i, 357b, 358a; v, 1194b – I, 368b, 369a; V, 1184b
Muḥammad b. ʿĀrif b. Aḥmad ʿAbd al-Ḥaḳḳ s, 313a – S, 312b
Muḥammad b. Aṣbagh (Bayyāna) (915) vii, **400a** – VII, **401b**
Muḥammad b. Aṣbagh b. Labīb (938) vii, **400a** – VII, **401b**
Muḥammad b. Aṣbagh b. Muḥammad (918) vii, **400a** –VII, **401b**
Muḥammad b. Aṣbagh al-Azdī vii, 400a – VII, 401b
Muḥammad b. al-Ashʿath b. Kays al-Kindī (686) iii, 715a; vii, **400b**, 523a, 689b – III, 737b; VII, **401b**, 523b, 690a
Muḥammad b. al-Ashʿath al-Khuzāʿī (761) i, 134b; iii, 654b, 981b, 1040b, 1041b; iv, 827a; vi, 841a – I, 138a; III, 675b, 1006a, 1066b, 1067b; IV, 860a; VI, 831b
Muḥammad b. Arslan → Muḥammad I (Saldjūḳ)
Muḥammad b. ʿAshūr al-Kindī → Ibn ʿĀshūr
Muḥammad b. ʿĀṣim i, 600a – I, 619b
Muḥammad b. ʿAttāb v, 488a – V, 491a
Muḥammad b. ʿAṭṭū al-Djānātī (Marrakush) vi, 593a – VI, 578a
Muḥammad b. ʿAwaḍ b. Lādin al-Ḥaḍramī vi, 166b, 167b – VI, 158b, 159a
Muḥammad b. ʿĀyid → Muḥammad b. ʾĀʿid
Muḥammad b. ʿAyshūn al-Sharrāṭ iv, 380a – IV, 396b
Muḥammad b. ʿAyyāsh ii, 1014b – II, 1038a
Muḥammad b. Aẓhar i, 1212b – I, 1249a

Muḥammad b. Badr al-Dīn al-Munshiʾ (1592) i, 310a – I, 319b
Muḥammad b. al-Baʿīth (Buʿayth) (IX) iv, 88b; vi, 504b; x, 42a – IV, 92b; VI, 489b; X, 43b
Muḥammad b. Bakhtiyār → Muḥammad Bakhtiyār Khaldjī
Muḥammad b. Baḳiyya b. ʿAlī → Ibn Baḳiyya
Muḥammad b. Balban ii, 268a; s, 67a, 124b – II, 276a; S, 67a, 123b
Muḥammad b. Bānī iii, 326b – III, 336b
Muḥammad b. Barakāt i, 553a, 1032b; ii, 517b – I, 571a, 1064a; II, 530a
Muḥammad b. Barakāt I b. Ḥasan b. ʿAdjlān, Sharīf (1497) i, 553a, 1032b; ii, 517b; vi, 150a – I, 571a, 1064a; II, 530a; VI, 148b
Muḥammad b. Bashīr → Muḥammad b. Yasīr
Muḥammad b. Bashīr (Bushayr) (IX) vii, 460a, 517a, 647b – VII, 460b, 517b, 647b
Muḥammad b. Bashshār Bundār (866) vii, 691b; x, 11b – VII, 691b; X, 11b
Muḥammad b. Bilāl, Kurd(e) (906) vi, 900b – VI, 891b
Muḥammad b. Bughā (IX) vii, 477a – IV, 476b
Muḥammad b. Buzurg-Ummīd → Muḥammad I (Ismaʿīlī)
Muḥammad b. Dāwūd → Ibn Ādjurrūmī; Ibn Dāwūd, Muḥammad
Muḥammad b. Dāwūd b. al-Djarrāḥ → Ibn al-Djarrāḥ
Muḥammad b. al-Djabbār ii, 1009a – II, 1032b
Muḥammad b. Djābir b. ʿAbd Allāh s, 231a – S, 230b
Muḥammad b. Djaʿfar → Djaʿfar b. Abī Ṭālib; al-Kattānī; al-Ḳazzāz; al-Kharāʾiṭī; al-Muntaṣir bi-'llāh; al-Rāḍī
Muḥammad b. Djaʿfar al-Azkawī → Ibn Djaʿfar
Muḥammad b. Djaʿfar al-Ṣādiḳ al-Dībādj (IX) i, 145a, 402b, 551a; vi, 334b – I, 149b, 414a, 568b; VI, 319a
Muḥammad b. al-Djahm al-Barmakī i, 153b, 1036a; iii, 355a; vii, **401a** – I, 157b, 1067b; III, 366a; VII, **402a**
Muḥammad b. Djarīr ii, 790b – II, 809b
Muḥammad b. al-Djazarī → Ibn al-Djazarī, Abu 'l-Khayr
Muḥammad b. Dumlādj (1075) vii, 121b – VII, 123a
Muḥammad b. Dushmanziyār → ʾAlāʾ al-Dawla
Muḥammad b. Eretna → Ghiyāth al-Dīn Muḥammad
Muḥammad b. al-Faḍl b. Māhān (Sind) (IX) vi, 967b – VI, 960a
Muḥammad b. Faḍl Allāh iii, 155b – III, 159a
Muḥammad b. al-Faḍl al-Djardjarāʾī → al-Djardjarāʾī
Muḥammad b. Fakhr al-Dīn Muḥammad iii, 457b – III, 473b
Muḥammad b. Falāḥ iv, 49a – IV, 52a
Muḥammad b. Farāmarz → Khosrew Mollā
Muḥammad b. Farīd (Dihlī Sayyid) (1443) ix, 118b, 119a – IX, 122b, 126a
Muḥammad b. Farīghūn → Abu'l-Ḥārith
Muḥammad b. Fayṣal b. ʿAbd al-ʿAzīz Āl Suʿūd s, 305b – S, 305b
Muḥammad b. Fuḍayl viii, 486a – VIII, 513a
Muḥammad b. al-Furāt → Ibn al-Furāt, Muḥammad
Muḥammad b. Ghāzī (Dānishmend) ii, 110b; iv, 843a – II, 113a; IV, 876a
Muḥammad b. Ghāzī → Malik Muḥammad b. Ghāzī (Malaṭya)
Muḥammad b. Gümüshtigin (Dānishmendid(e)) (1142) viii, 948b – VIII, 981a
Muḥammad b. Habbāriyya (1115) viii, 376ab – VIII, 389a
Muḥammad b. Ḥabīb Abū Djaʿfar (860) i, 158b; ii, 480a; iii, 820a, 907b; vi, 822b; vii, **401b**; x, 2b; s, 177a – I, 162b; II, 492a; III, 843b, 931b; VI, 812b; VII, **403a**; X, 2b; S, 178a
Muḥammad b. al-Ḥādjdj ii, 1013a; iii, 542b – II, 1036b; III, 561b
Muḥammad b. Hādjdjādj iv, 665b – IV, 692b
Muḥammad b. al-Hadjdjām ii, 1009b – II, 1033a
Muḥammad b. Ḥamad al-Sharḳi ii, 936b – II, 958b
Muḥammad b. Ḥammād b. Isḥāḳ Ibn Dirham s, **385a** – S, **385b**
Muḥammad b. al-Ḥanafiyya b. ʿAlī b. Abī Ṭālib (700) i, 15a, 41a, 48b, 55b, 124b, 381a, 402a, 959a, 1116b; ii, 168b, 1026a, 1094b; iii, 608b, 1232b, 1265b; iv, 836b, 1086b; v, 433b, 552a, 1231a, 1235b; vi, 240a, 350b; vii, **402b**, 521a; ix, 421b; s, 48b, 343a, 357b, 401a – I, 15b, 42a, 50a, 57a, 128b, 392a, 412b, 1150a; II, 173b, 1049b, 1120a; III, 629a, 1264a, 1298b; IV, 869b, 1117b; V, 435b, 557a, 1221b, 1226a; VI, 205a, 334b; VII, **404a**, 521b; IX, 425b; S, 49a, 342b, 357b, 401b
Muḥammad b. al-Ḥanash iv, 552b – IV, 576a
Muḥammad b. Ḥanbal i, 272b – I, 280b
Muḥammad b. Hāniʾ → Ibn Hāniʾ
Muḥammad b. al-Ḥārith b. Bashkīr (IX) vii, 190a – VII, 190b
Muḥammad b. al-Ḥarsh → Bū Dalī
Muḥammad b. Hārūn (IX) iii, 254b; vii, 418a – III, 261b; VII, 419b
Muḥammad b. Hārūn (Rasūl) (XII) viii, 455a – VIII, 470b
Muḥammad b. Ḥasan → Muḥammad II, III (Ismaʿīlī)
Muḥammad b. al-Ḥasan → Ibn Durayd; Ibn Ḥamdūn; al-Shaybānī, Abū ʿAbū Allāh
Muḥammad b. Ḥasan (Sayyid Bayhaḳī) s, 131b – S, 131a
Muḥammad b. al-Ḥasan b. ʿAlī → al-Ḥurr al-ʿĀmilī
Muḥammad b. al-Ḥasan b. Dīnār (864) vii, **403b** – VII, **405a**
Muḥmmad b. Ḥasan b. Idrīs (Dāʿī Muṭlaḳ) s, 358b – S, 358b
Muḥammad b. Ḥasan al-Sarakhsī i, 146a – I, 150a
Muḥammad b. al-Hayṣam iv, 668a – IV, 695b
Muḥammad b. al-Haytham i, 154a – I, 158a
Muḥammad b. Ḥāzim b. ʿAmr al-Bāhilī (IX) vii, **404a** – VII, **405a**
Muḥammad b. Hazzaʿ b. Zaʿal ii, 619a – II, 634b
Muḥammad b. Hilāl b. al-Muḥassin al-Ṣābi' viii, 103a – VIII, 105b
Muḥammad b. Hindū-shāh Nakhčiwānī (XIV) vii, **404b** – VII, **405b**
Muḥammad b. Hishām b. Ismāʿīl (VIII) i, 627a; vi, 139b – I, 647b; VI, 137b
Muḥammad b. Hishām b. ʿAbd al-Djabbār → al-Mahdī (Umayyad(e))
Muḥammad b. al-Hudhayl → Abu 'l-Hudhayl al-ʿAllāf
Muḥammad b. Ḥumayd al-Ṭūsī iii, 573a – III, 593a
Muḥammad b.Hurmuz (X) viii, 797a – VIII, 824a
Muḥammad b. Ḥusām iv, 68a – IV, 71b
Muḥammad b. Ḥusayn → Meḥmed Khalīfe; al-Sharīf al-Rāḍī
Muḥammad b. Ḥusayn (Ḥusaynid(e)) iii, 635b; iv, 828b – III, 657a; IV, 861b
Muḥammad b. Ḥusayn b. al-Astarābādī → Ghiyāth al-Dīn Muḥammad

Muḥammad b. Ibrāhīm → Simdjūr, Banū
Muḥammad b. Ibrāhīm II b. Ṭahmāsp (ʿĀdil-Shāhi) (1656) vii, **404b** – VII, **406a**
Muḥammad b. Ibrāhīm b. Ḥadjdjādj iv, 115b – IV, 120b
Muḥammad b. Ibrāhīm b. Ṭabāṭabā → Ibn Ṭabāṭabā
Muḥammad b. Idrīs → Ibn Idrīs
Muḥammad b. Idrīs II (Idrīsid(e), 836) i, 1088a; ii, 874a; iii, 1035b – I, 1120a; II, 894a; III, 1061b
Muḥammad b. Idrīs b. ʿAlī b. Ḥammūd (Mālaḳa) (1048) vi, 222b – VI, 216a
Muḥammad b. Ilyās → Abū ʿAlī
Muḥammad b. ʿĪsā (1582) vi, 112b; viii, 526a – VI, 110a; VIII, 543b
Muḥammad b. ʿĪsā (Burghūth) (IX) i, 1326b; iii, 1037a; iv, 692b; vii, 867a, 868b – I, 1367a; III, 1063a; IV, 721a; VII, 868b, 870a
Muḥammad b. ʿĪsā b. Aḥmad al-Māhānī (866) ii, 362a; iv, 1182b; vi, 600b; vii, **405a**; s, 412a, 413b – II, 372a; IV, 1215b; VI, 585a; VII, **406a**; S, 412a, 413b
Muḥammad b. ʿĪsa al-Ṣufyānī al-Mukhtārī iv, 93b – IV, 97b
Muḥammad b. Isḥāḳ → Abu 'l-ʿAnbas al-Ṣaymarī; Ibn Isḥāḳ, Muḥammad; Ibn al-Nadīm
Muḥammad b. Isḥāḳ b. Ghāniya ii, 112a, 1007a – II, 114b, 1030b
Muḥammad b. Isḥāḳ b. Kundādj(īk) iv, 90a, 494a; vi, 540a, 900a – IV, 94a, 515a; VI, 524b, 891b
Muḥammad b. Isḥāḳ b. Manda → Ibn Manda, Abū ʿAbd Allāh
Muḥammad b. Isḥāḳ b. Miḥmashādh i, 146b; iv, 668b – I, 151a; IV, 695b
Muḥammad b. Ismāʿīl b. Djaʿfar i, 48a; ii, 375a; iii, 123b, 1072a, 1167b; iv, 198a, 203b, 204a, 1133a – I, 49b; II, 385a; III, 126b, 1099a, 1196a; IV, 207a, 212b, 213a, 1164b
Muḥammad b. Ismāʿīl Ibn ʿAbbād iii, 740a – III, 763a
Muḥammad b. Kaʿb al-Ḳuraẓī i, 140a; v, 436a, b – I, 144a; V, 438b, 439a
Muḥammad b. Ḳāʾitbāy (Mamlūk) (1499) vii, 175b – VII, 177b
Muḥammad b. Ḳalaʾun → al-Nāṣir Muḥammad
Muḥammad b. al-Ḳalḳashandī → Ibn Abī Ghudda
Muḥammad b. Ḳara Arslan i, 665a; iii, 507a – I, 684b; III, 524b
Muḥammad b. Ḳaramān i, 467a; ii, 204b, 989a; iv, 620a, b – I, 481a; II, 211a, 1012a; IV, 644b, 645a
Muḥammad b. Ḳārin → al-Māziyār
Muḥammad b. Karrām ii, 1011a; iv, 183b, 667a – II, 1034b; IV, 191b, 694a
Muḥammad b. al-Ḳāsim → al-Anbārī
Muḥammad b. al-Ḳāsim (ʿAlid(e)) (IX) i, 52b; ii, 485a; iii, 74a; vii, 776a – I, 54a; II, 497b; III, 76b; VII, 777b
Muḥammad b. al-Ḳāsim (al-Djazīra al-Khaḍrāʾ) (XI) vi, 222b – VI, 216a
Muḥammad b. Ḳāsim (Sind) (710) vi, 206b, 439b, 691a, 967b – VI, 191a, 425a, 678b, 959b
Muḥammad b. al-Ḳāsim b. Hammūd iii, 786a; iv, 115b – III, 809b; IV, 120b
Muḥammad b. Ḳāsim al-Thaḳafī (715) i, 679a, 1005b, 1068b, 1192a; ii, 27a, 154a, 188a, 488a, 1123a; iii, 41a, 323b, 482a; iv, 533b; vi, 206b, 439b, 691a, 967b; vii, **405b**, 548b; viii, 253a; s, 163a, 243a – I, 699b, 1036b, 1100b, 1227a; II, 27a, 158b, 194a, 500b, 1149a; III, 43a, 333b, 499a; IV, 556b; VI, 191a, 425a, 678b, 959b; VII, **406b**, 548b; VIII, 255a; S, 162a, 243a
Muḥammad b. al-Ḳāsim b. ʿUbayd Allāh iv, 424a – IV, 442a
Muḥammad b. Khalaf b. al-Marzubān (921) iii, 111a, 820a; vii, **406a** – III, 113b, 843b; VII, **407b**
Muḥammad b. Khālid i, 1034b, 1035a, 1036a – I, 1066a,b, 1067a
Muḥammad b. Khalīfa b. Salmān (XIX) II, 108b; iv, 953a, b – II, 111a; IV, 985b, 986a
Muḥammad b. Khalīl iv, 535a – IV, 558a
Muḥammad b. Khalīl Ibn Ghalbūn iv, 617b – IV, 642a
Muḥammad b. Khaṭīb (Ḳuṣdār) (XII) vii, 535a, 536a – VII, 535a, 536a
Muḥammad b. al-Khayr Ibn Khazar iii, 1042b; v, 1176a – III, 1086b; V, 1166a
Muḥammad b. al-Khayr b. Muḥammad v, 1176b, 1177a – V, 1166b, 1167a
Muḥammad b. Khazar b. Ḥafṣ v, 1174a – V, 1165a
Muḥammad b. Khazar al-Maghrāwī (X) vii, 486a – VII, 486a
Muḥammad Ibn Khazar al-Zanātī → Ibn Khazar b. Ṣūlāt
Muḥammad b. Khunays i, 1293a – I, 1332b
Muḥammad b. Khuzāʿī (VI) ix, 817b – IX, 852b
Muḥammad b. Lope (Lubb) Ibn Ḳasī iii, 816a; iv, 713a – III, 839b; IV, 741b
Muḥammad b. Maḥammad b. Abī Bakr al-Murābiṭ s, 223b – S, 223b
Muḥammad (al-Mahdī) b. al-Manṣūr s, 31b – S, 31b
Muḥammad b. Maḥmūd (Saldjūḳ) → Muḥammad II (Saldjūk)
Muḥammad b. Maḥmūd b. Sebüktigin (Ghaznawīd(e)) (1041) ii, 1051a; iii, 1201b; vii, **407a** – II, 1075b; III, 1232a; VII, **408a**
Muḥammad b. Maḥmūd al-Khʷārazmī i, 124a – I, 128a
Muḥammad b. Maḥmūd al-Ḳabrī → Muḳaddam b. Muʿāfa al-Ḳabrī
Muḥammad b. al-Makkī vi, 354b – VI, 338b
Muḥammad b. Makkī al-ʿAmilī (1384) vi, 13a; vii, **407a** – VI, 12a; VII, **408b**
Muḥammad b. Malikshāh → Muḥammad I (Saldjūk)
Muḥammad b. Maʿn b. Ṣumādiḥ al-Tudjībī (Abū Yaḥyā) (Almeria) (1097) iii, 775b, 934b; vi, 576b – III, 799a, 959b; VI, 561b
Muḥammad b. Manṣūr → Sayf al-Ḥaḳḳ Abu ʾl-Mafākhir
Muḥammad b. Manṣūt (Sarakhs) (XII) ix, 5a – IX, 5a
Muḥammad b. al-Manṣūr bi-'llāh al-Ḳāsim b. Muḥammad (Ḳāsimī Zaydī) (XVII) vi, 436b – VI, 422a
Muḥammad b. Marwān I b. al-Ḥakam (Umayyad(e)) (719) i, 42a, 77a, 100b, 1041a; ii, 523b; iii, 29a; vi, 505b, 740a, 917a; vii, **408b** – I, 43b, 79b, 103b, 1072b; II, 537a; III, 30b; VI, 491a, 729a, 908b; VII, **409b**
Muḥammad b. Marwān al-Aṣghar b. Abi 'l-Djanūb vi, 625b – VI, 610b
Muḥammad b. Marzūḳ → Ibn Marzūḳ
Muḥammad b. Maslama al-Awsī al-Anṣārī (VII) i, 382b; iv, 315a; vii, 852b – I, 393b; IV, 329a; VII, 854a
Muḥammad b. Masʿūd i, 1132a – I, 1166a
Muḥammad b. Mawlāy ʿArafa (ʿAlawid(e)) (XX) vii, 416b – VII, 418a
Muḥammad b. Mawlāy Ismāʿīl (ʿAlawid(e)) (1706) vii, 38b – VII, 39a
Muḥammad b. al-Miʿmār → Ibn al-Miʿmār
Muḥammad b. Mīrānshāh b. Tīmūr (Timūrid(e)) vii, 104b, 105b – VII, 106b, 107b
Muḥammad b. Muʿaykil ii, 492b – II, 504b
Muḥammad b. al-Mubārak b. Maymūn (1201) viii, 401a – VIII, 415a

Muḥammad b. al-Mubāriz ii, 736b – II, 755a
Muḥammad b. al-Mughīra b. Ḥarb s, 352a – S, 352a
Muḥammad b. Muḥammad → Abu 'l-Wafā'; al-Ghazālī; Ibn ʿAṣim; Ibn Djahīr; Ibn al-Habbāriyya; Ibn Nubāta al-Miṣrī; ʿImād al-Dīn al-Kātib al-Iṣfahānī; Simdjūr, Banū
Muḥammad b. Muḥammad b. Abi 'l-Luṭf i, 759a – I, 782a
Muḥammad b. Muḥammad b. Zayd i, 149b; iii, 951a – I, 154a; III, 976a
Muḥammad b. Muḥammad Čiwizāde ii, 56b – II, 57b
Muḥammad b. Muḥammad al-Djayhānī → al-Djayhānī
Muḥammad b. Muḥammad b. al-Shiḥna (1485) vii, 537a – VII, 537a
Muḥammad b. Muḥammad al-Shīrāzī → Ibn Khafīf
Muḥammad b. Muhannā → Nuʿayr
Muḥammad b. Mukarram → Ibn Manẓūr
Muḥammad b. Mukaththir iv, 748b – IV, 778b
Muḥammad b. al-Munkadir vi, 263a – VI, 247b
Muḥammad b. Murād (XV) vii, 207b – VII, 208b
Muḥammad b. Murtaḍā → Fayḍ-i Kāshānī
Muḥammad b. Mūsā (ʿAbd al-Wādid(e)) → Abū Zayyān II
Muḥammad b. Mūsā b. Shākir → Mūsā, Banū
Muḥammad b. Mūsā b. Shākir (IX) vi, 600a – VI, 585a
Muḥammad b. Mūsā al-Khʷārazmī → al-Khʷārazmī
Muḥammad b. Mūsā Kudatlī i, 756a – I, 778b
Muḥammad b. Musāfir (Musāfirid(e)) (941) vi, 539a – VI, 523b
Muḥammad b. Musāfir Kangarī (Ṭārum) (X) ii, 192a; vi, 539a – II, 198a; VI, 523b
Muḥammad b. Musallam al-Bālisī iv, 641a – IV, 667a
Muḥammad b. Mushārī ii, 321b – II, 331a
Muḥammad b. al-Mustanīr → Ḳuṭrub
Muḥammad b. Muṭarrif vi, 264b – VI, 249b
Muḥammad b. al-Muthannā (866) vii, 691a – VII, 691b
Muḥammad b. al-Muwallad iv, 89a – IV, 93a
Muḥammad b. al-Muẓaffar (Muẓaffarid(e)) (XIV) ii, 401b; iv, 221b – II, 412a; IV, 231a
Muḥammad b. Nāṣir (Bū Shenṭūf) (Marrākūsh) (1525) vi, 594a – VI, 579a
Muḥammad b. Nāṣir (1674) x, 170b – X, 183b
Muḥammad b. Nūḥ (890) viii, 85a – VIII, 87a
Muḥammad b. Nūḥ al-ʿIdjlī (833) i, 272b; vii, 3a – I, 281a; VII, 3a
Muḥammad b. al-Nuʿmān → Shayṭān al-Ṭāḳ
Muḥammad b. al-Nuʿmān, ḳāḍī (X) i, 823b; ii, 169b; iii, 76b – I, 846b; II, 174 b; III, 79a
Muḥammad b. Nūr (Baḥrayn) (IX) i, 813a, 942a; iii, 652b; ix, 775a; x, 816b – I, 836a, 971a; III, 674a; IX, 808b, 809a; X,
Muḥammad b. Nuṣayr al-Namīrī i, 713a – I, 734b
Muḥammad b. Rāfiʿ (859) vii, 691a – VII, 691b
Muḥammad b. Rāʾiḳ → Ibn Rāʾiḳ
Muḥammad b. Ramiya, Shaykh (XX) x, 196a – X, 211b
Muḥamad b. Rashīd → Rashīd, Āl
Muḥammad b. Razīn → Abu 'l-Shīṣ al-Khuzāʿī
Muḥammad b. Rushayd iv, 337a, b – IV, 351b, 352a
Muḥammad b. Sabaʾ i, 181b, 1214b, 1215a; iv, 200b; v, 1244b – I, 186b, 1251a; IV, 209a; V, 1235a
Muḥammad b. Saʿd → Ibn Mardanīsh
Muḥammad b. Saʿd b. Abī Waḳḳās iii, 717a – III, 739b
Muḥammad b. Saʿd al-Awfī iii, 922b – III, 947a
Muḥammad b. Saʿdān s, 177a – S, 178a
Muḥammad b. Sahla (XVIII) vi, 250b – VI, 235a
Muḥammad b. Saḥnūn al-Tanūkhī (870) iii, 681a; v, 503b; vii, 409a, 1052b – III, 703a; V, 507a; VII, 410a, 1054b
Muḥammad b. Saʿīd b. Hārūn (Ukhshūnūba) (XI) i, 6a; ii, 1009a; vii, 761a, 766b – I, 6a; II, 1032b; VII, 762b, 768a
Muḥammad b. Ṣāliḥ (1909) vii, 389b; s, 279a – VII, 390b; S, 278b
Muḥammad b. Ṣāliḥ (Suʿūd, Āl) (al-Dirʿiyya) (1765) i, 554a; ii, 321a; iii, 162a, 678b – I, 571b; II, 330b; III, 165b, 700a
Muḥammad b. Ṣāliḥ al-Īfranī (1767) iii, 1042a – III, 1068a
Muḥammad b. Sālim → Ibn Wāṣil
Muḥammad b. al-Salīm, Ḳādī al-Ḳurtuba (X) vi, 430b – VI, 416a
Muḥammad b. Sālim al-Ḥifnī (1767) iv, 992a – IV, 1024b
Muḥammad b. Ṣaʿlūḳ iii, 254b, 255a – III, 261b, 262a
Muḥammad b. Sām I, Ghiyāth al-Dīn (Ghūrid(e)) (1203) i, 208b, 217b, 1165b, 1192b, 1194a, 1300a; ii, 119b, 266b, 752a, 922b, 972b, 1049b, 1052b, 1101a, b, 1122b, 1123b; iii, 414b, 433b; iv, 666b, 669a; v, 501a, 782b; vi, 65b, 365b, 618a; vii, 409b; viii, 63b, 81a, 253a; s, 242a, 284b, 360a – I, 214b, 224a, 1200b, 1228a, 1229b, 1339b; II, 122b, 274b, 770a, 943b, 994b, 1074a, 1077b, 1127a, b, 1148b, 1150a; III, 428b, 448a; IV, 693b, 696b; V, 504b, 788b; VI, 63b, 349b, 603a; VII, 411a; VIII, 65a, 83a, 255b; S, 242a, 284b, 359b
Muḥammad b. Sām I, Muʿizz al-Dīn Muḥammad (Ghūrid(e)) (1206) vii, **409b**, 433a, 549a; viii, 63b – VII, **411a**, 434a, 549a; VIII, 65a
Muḥammad b. Shabīb vii, 606b, 784b – VII, 606b, 786b
Muḥammad b. Shādān iii, 856b, 857b – III, 880b, 881b
Muḥammad b. Shaddād (Shaddādid(e)s) (VIII) ii, 680a; ix, 169a; x, 827a – II, 697a; IX, 164b; X,
Muḥammad b. Shahriyār, Ispahbad s, 356b – S, 356b
Muḥammad b. al-Shiḥna (1412) vii, 469a – VII, 469a
Muḥammad b. Shīrkūh iii, 399b – III, 411b
Muḥammad b. Sīrīn → Ibn Sīrīn
Muḥammad b. Slīmān al-Djazūlī, Sīdī vi, 597b – VI, 582a
Muḥammad b. Subayyil, Shaykh (XX) vi, 157b – VI, 153a
Muḥammad b. Sulaymān (Ḥasanid(e)) i, 551a; iii, 135b, 617a, 682b – I, 568b; III, 138a, 637b, 704b
Muḥammad b. Sulaymān b. ʿAbd Allāh b. al-Ḥasan (Idrīsid(e)) (IX) iii, 1032a, 1035b; vi, 841b – III, 1058a, 1061b; VI, 832a
Muḥammad b. Sulaymān Kāshgharī Yïghan Beg (vizier) (1124) ix, 16b – IX, 17a
Muḥammad b. Sulaymān al-Kātib (X) ii, 281b; iii, 126a, 345a, 759a; vii, 543a – II, 289b; III, 129a, 355b, 782a; VII, 543a
Muḥammad b. Sulaymān al-Rūdānī (XVII) i, 1032b – I, 1064a
Muḥammad b. Sulaymān al-Tanakabunī (XIX) i, 113a; v, 197b – I, 116a; V, 195a
Muḥammad b. Sūrī ii, 1096b, 1099b – II, 1122b, 1125b
Muḥammad b. Surūr al-Ṣabbān b. al-Ḳunfudha (1899) vi, 177b – VI, 163a
Muḥammad b. Suʿūd (Āl Suʿūd) (1765) vii, **410a** – VII, **411b**

Muḥammad b. Tādjīt al-Maṣmūdī v, 498b – V, 501b
Muḥammad b. Ṭāhir → Ibn al-Ḳaysarānī, Abū 'l-Faḍl
Muḥammad b. Ṭāhir II b. ʿAbd Allāh (Ṭāhirid(e)) (Khurāsān) (884) ii, 1082b; iv, 20b, 21a, 667b; vii, 390b, **410b**; x, 105a – II, 1107b; IV, 22a, b, 694b; VII, 391b, **412a**; X, 113a
Muḥammad b. Ṭāhir al-Ahdal i, 255b – I, 263b
Muḥammad b. Ṭāhir al-Ḥārithī (1188) vii, **410b** – VII, **412a**
Muḥammad b. al-Ṭayyār (VIII) vii, 398b – VII, 400a
Muḥammad b. al-Ṭayyib, Sīdī i, 303a, 367b; iv, 383a – I, 312b, 377b; IV, 400a
Muḥammad b. al-Ṭayyib al-ʿAlamī → al-ʿAlamī
Muḥammad b. Tekish → ʿAlāʾ al-Dīn Muḥammad
Muḥammad b. Thābit b. al-ʿAbbās b. Mandīl b. ʿAmmār (XIV) vi, 404b; x, 213b – VI, 389a; X, 230b
Muḥammad b. Thānī ii, 177a; iv, 751b – II, 183a; IV, 782a
Muḥammad b. Tughdj al-Ikhshīd (Ikhshīdid(e)) (946) i, 870b; ii, 36b, 281b, 305a, 1080b; iii, 86a, 129a, 768b; iv, 418a, 459a; v, 91b, 327a, 953b; vi, 379a; vii, 115a, 148a, 161a, b, **411a**, 800a; viii, 464a; s, 120b – I, 895a; II, 37b, 289b, 313b, 1105b; III, 88a, 131b, 791b; IV, 436b, 479b; V, 94a, 327a, 957b; VI, 363b; VII, 117a, 150a, 162b, 163a, **412b**, 802a; VIII, 479b; S, 120a
Muḥammad b. Tughluḳ (Tughluḳid(e)) (1351) i, 756b, 855b, 868b, 923b, 1036a, b, 1165b, 1192a, 1199b, 1300a, 1322a, 1329a; ii, 48a, 50a, 51a, 99b, 120a, 154b, 179b, 218b, 220a, 258a, 269b, 276b, 597a, 924b, 1076b, 1084b, 1124b, 1135a; iii, 202b, 416b, 428b, 442a, 453a, 492a; iv, 218b, 514a, 538a, 907b, 923b, 1019a; v, 598a; vi, 131b, 532b, 692a, 837b, 867a, 1027b; vii, 194a, 221a, 345b, **411b**, 473a; x, 591a; s, 73b, 105b, 117b, 352b, 409a, b – I, 779a, 879b, 893a, 951a, 1067b, 1068a, 1200b, 1227a, 1235a, 1340a, 1362b, 1369b; II, 49a, 51a, 52a, 101b, 123a, 159b, 185b, 225b, 226b, 264a, 277b, 284b, 612a, 946a, 1101b, 1109b, 1150b, 1162a; III, 207b, 429b, 442b, 456b, 469a, 509a; IV, 228a, 536a, 561b, 940b, 956b, 1051a; V, 601b; VI, 129b, 516b, 679b, 828a, 858a, 1020b; VII, 194b, 222b, 347b, **413a**, 472b; X, 635a; S, 74a, 105a, 117a, 352b, 409b
Muḥammad b. Tūmart → Ibn Tūmart
Muḥammad b. ʿUbayd Allāh → Abu 'l-Maʿālī
Muḥammad b. ʿUmar b. ʿAbd al-Raḥmān b. al-Ḥārith (VIII) vi, 140b – VI, 138b
Muḥammad b. ʿUmar b. Lubāba i, 600a – I, 619b
Muḥammad b. ʿUmar al-Aṣamm ii, 100b – II, 102b
Muḥammad b. ʿUmar Ibn Burghūth (1056) vii, **412b** – VII, **414a**
Muḥammad b. ʿUmar al-Kashshī → al-Kashshī, Abū ʿAmr
Muḥammad b. ʿUmar al-Madīnī iv, 742a – IV, 772a
Muḥammad b. ʿUmar al-Tūnusī → al-Tūnusī
Muḥammad b. Umayya b. Abī Umayya (IX) vii, **413a** – VII, **414b**
Muḥammad b. ʿUrayʿir (XVIII) iv, 925a – IV, 958a
Muḥammad b. ʿUthmān (ʿAbd al-Wādid) → Abū Zayyān I
Muḥammad b. ʿUthmān al-ʿAmrī (916) i, 713a; vii, 443b – I, 734b; VII, 444b
Muḥammad b. Waḍḍāḥ (IX) vii, 400a – VII, 401b
Muḥammad b. al-Walīd → al-Ṭurṭushī
Muḥammad b. Wandarīn, Abū Djaʿfar (Bāwandid(e)) (XI) v, 230a; vi, 713b; viii, 383a – V, 227b; VI, 702a; VIII, 396a
Muḥammad b. Wānūdīn ii, 744b – II, 763a
Muḥammad Ibn Warsand b. al-Ḥasan s, 402b – S, 403a
Muḥammad b. Wāsiʿ i, 959b – I, 989a
Muḥammad b. Waṣīf (X) vii, **413b**; viii, 797b – VII, **415a**; VIII, 824b
Muḥammad b. Wasīl al-Tamīmī v, 158a – V, 157b
Muḥammad b. Yaḥyā → Ibn Bādjdja
Muḥammad b. Yaḥyā b. Abī Ṭālib → ʿAzafī
Muḥammad b. Yaḥya al-Barmākī ii, 1036a – I, 1067b
Muḥammad b. Yaḥyā al-Dhuhlī i, 1296b – I, 1336b
Muḥammad b. Yaḥyā al-Yaḥṣubī i, 6a; ii, 1009a; v, 586b – I, 6a; II, 1033a; V, 591b
Muḥammad b. Yaʿḳūb al-Nīsābūrī → al-Aṣamm, Muḥammad
Muḥammad b. Yāḳūt, Abū Bakr (935) ii, 453b; iii, 46a; iv, 100a, 127a; vii, **413b**, 542a – II, 465a; III, 47b; IV, 104b, 132b; VII, **415a**, 542a
Muḥammad b. Yallas → Ibn Yallas, Muḥammad
Muḥammad b. Yasār iv, 190a – IV, 198a
Muḥammad b. Yasīr al-Riyāshī, Abū Djaʿfar (IX) iii, 309a; vii, **414a** – III, 318b; VII, **415b**
Muḥammad b. Yazīd → Ibn Mādja; al-Mubarrad
Muḥammad b. Yazīd (wālī, Ḳayrawān) (VIII) i, 50a; iii, 587b – I, 51b; III, 607b
Muḥammad b. Yazīd (Sharwān-Shāh) iv, 345b – IV, 360a
Muḥammad b. Yazīd b. Ḥātim (Muhallabid(e)) (IX) vi, 333b – VI, 318a
Muḥammad b. Yināl al-Tardjumān (X) x, 236a – X, 254b
Muḥammad b. Yūsuf → Abū Ḥayyān; Muḥammad V (ʿAlawīd(e))
Muḥammad b. Yūsuf b. Aḥmad → Muḥammad I (Naṣrid(e))
Muḥammad b. Yūsuf b. Hūd (XII) ii, 1014a; iii, 543a; iv, 116a, 254b; vi, 339b – II, 1037b; III, 562a; IV, 121b, 265b; VI, 323b
Muḥammad b. Yūsuf b. Ibrāhīm (Ḥasanid(e)) (IX) vi, 148a – VI, 146b
Muḥammad b. Yūsuf b. al-Sarrādj → Ibn al-Sarrādj
Muḥammad b. Yūsuf b. Yaʿḳūb → Ibn Dirham, Muḥammad b. Yūsuf b. Yaʿḳūb
Muḥammad b. Yūsuf al-ʿĀmirī → al-ʿĀmirī, Abū 'l-Ḥasan Muḥammad b. Yūsuf
Muḥammad b. Yūsuf al-Sanūsī → al-Sanūsī
Muḥammad b. Zakariyya (XVII) vii, 469b – VII, 469a
Muḥammad b. Zayd b. Muḥammad (Zaydī) (900) ii, 191b; iii, 245a, 254b; iv, 189a; v, 662a; vii, **417b**, 1015b; s, 335a – II, 197b; III, 252a, 261b; IV, 197a; V, 667a; VII, **419a**, 1017b; S, 334b
Muḥammad b. Ẓufar (XII) viii, 749a – VIII, 779a
Muḥammad ʿAbābsa (1953) vi, 251a – VI, 235b
Muḥammad ʿAbbās Shāh (Ḳādjār) (1848) vi, 276b, 484a, 715a – VI, 261b, 470a, 704a
Muḥammad ʿAbd Allāh al-ʿĀdil s, 389a – S, 389b
Muḥammad ʿAbd al-Ḥayy al-Kattānī iv, 774b – IV, 806a
Muḥammad ʿAbd al-Karīm ʿAlawī → ʿAbd al-Karīm Munshi
Muḥammad ʿAbd al-Karīm Ṣābūn ii, 123b – II, 126b
Muḥammad ʿAbd al-Munʿim i, 13b – I, 14a
Muḥammad ʿAbdīlle Ḥassān → Muḥammad b. ʿAbd Allāh Ḥassān

Muḥammad ʿAbduh (1905) i, 38b, 327a, 414a, 416a, 597a, 817b; ii, 97a, 417b, 429a, 451b, 465b, 471a, 1065b;III, 59a, 1020a, 1145b, 1149b; iv, 112a, 143b, 144a, 146b, 149b, 151a, 159a, 162b, 321b, 471a, 720b, 856a; v, 187a; vi, 23a, 24b, 25a, 41b, 75b, 219b, 237b, 238a, 360a, 361a, 414a, 462a, 607a, 739b; vii, **418a**, 421a, 434b, 713b, 716a, 813a, 900b, 901a; viii, 446b, 698b, 900b, 902b, 906b; s, 64a, 121b, 123a, 244b, 248a, 296a – I, 39b, 337a, 426a, 427b, 616b, 841a; II, 99a, 428a, 440a, 463a, 477a, 483a, 1090b; III, 61b, 1046a, 1174a, 1178a; IV, 117a, 149b, 150a, 152b, 155b, 157b, 165b, 169b, 335b, 491b, 749a, 889b; V, 184b; VI, 21a, 22b, 23a, 40a, 73b, 213b, 210a, 211a, 344a, b, 345a, 399a, 448a, 592a, 729a; VII, **419b**, 422b, 435b, 714b, 717a, 815a, 901a, b; VIII, 461b, 718b, 931b, 932b, 937bS, 64b, 121a, 122b, 244b, 248a, 296a
Muḥammad Abdurrahiman Sahib (Mappila) (XX) vi, 460a – VI, 445b
Muḥammad ʿĀbid Khān Bitlīs (XVIII) vi, 505a – VI, 490b
Muḥammad ʿAbid Ḥusayn, Ḥādjdjī (XIX) ii, 205a – II, 211b
Muḥammad Abu ʾl-Dhahab (1775) vii, **420a** – VII, **422a**
Muḥammad Abū Ḥatīm i, 940a – I, 968b
Muḥammad Abū Likaylik (XIX) ii, 944b – II, 966b
Muḥammad Abū Madyan b. ʿAbd al-Raḥmān (Dār Fūr) (XIX) ii, 123b – II, 126b
Muḥammad Abū Numayy, Sharīf (1566) vi, 150a – VI, 148b
Muḥammad Abū Raʾs al-Nāṣirī (1822) vi, 250a – VI, 234a
Muḥammad Abū Samḥ ʿAbd al-Ẓāhir, Shaykh (XX) vi, 173b – VI, 161b
Muḥammad Abū Zayd (XX) vii, **420b** – VII, **422b**
Muḥammad ʿĀdil-Shāh (1656) i, 199b, 1202b, 1204a, b – I, 205a, 1238a, 1240a
Muḥammad V ʿĀdil-Shāh → Muḥammad Shāh V
Muḥammad Afḍal Khān → Afḍal Khān Barakzay
Muḥammad al-Afshīn → Muḥammad b. Abi ʾl-Sādj
Muḥammad Afshīn b. Dīwdād (Sādjid(e)) (IX) vi, 499a – VI, 484b
Muḥammad Aghā (Turkče Bilmez) (XIX) vii, 515a – VII, 515b
Muḥammad Aḥmad b. ʿAbd Allāh al-Mahdī (1885) i, 49b, 50a, 168b, 735a, 765a, 929b, 962a, 1172a; ii, 123b, 828a; iv, 687a, 952b; v, 70a, 267b, 1247b, **1248b**; vi, 281a; viii, 170b – I, 50b, 51b, 173b, 757a, 788a, 957b, 991b, 1207a; II, 126b, 847b; IV, 715a, 985a; V, 72a, 265b, 1238b, **1239a**; VI, 266b; VIII, 173a
Muḥammad Akbar Ḥusaynī ii, 56a – II, 56b
Muḥammad Akbar Khān i, 231b; ii, 638a; s, 237b – I, 238b; II, 654a; S, 237b
Muḥammad ʿAkī vii, 220b – VII, 222a
Muḥammad ʿĀkif Pasha (1845) vi, 610a – VI, 595a
Muḥammad Akmal, Mullā s, 134b – S, 134a
Muḥammad Āl Khalīfa → Muḥammad b. Khalīfa b. Salman
Muḥammad al-ʿAlamī i, 352a – I, 363a
Muḥammad ʿAlī (Andjumān) v, 7a; s, 5a, 74a, 247b, 293b, 360a – S, 4a, 74b, 75a, 247b, 293a, 360a
Muḥammad ʿAlī (Lahore) vii, 422a – VII, 423b
Muḥammad ʿAlī (Mustaʿlī) i, 1254b – I, 1292b
Muḥammad ʿAlī, Prince/le prince iii, 1199b; s, 300a – III, 1230a; S, 299b
Muḥammad ʿAlī (Rāmpūr) (1931) vii, **421a**; viii, 249a – VII, **422b**; VIII, 263a
Muḥammad ʿAlī b. Muẓaffar al-Dīn → Muḥammad ʿAlī Shāh Ḳādjār
Muḥammad ʿAlī b. Tawfīḳ i, 13b – I, 13b
Muḥammad ʿAlī Bahāʿī i, 915b – I, 943b
Muḥammad ʿAlī Bārfurūshī Ḳuddūs, Mullā (1849) i, 833b, 847a; vii, **422a** – I, 856b, 870a; VII, **424a**
Muḥammad ʿAlī Furūghī (XX) ii, 952a; v, 1095b, 1096a, b, 1097a; vii, 446b – II, 974b; V, 1092b, 1093a, b; VII, 447b
Muḥammad ʿAlī Ḥaīn (1766) viii, 542a – VIII, 560a
Muḥammad ʿAlī Ḥudjdjat-i Zandjānī, Mullā (1851) vii, **422b** – VII, **424a**
Muḥammad ʿAlī Kānpūrī ii, 132b – II, 135b
Muḥammad ʿAlī Khān, Nawwāb i, 625a; iv, 666b – I, 645b; IV, 693b
Muḥammad ʿAlī Khān Ḳāshḳāy iii, 1106b; iv, 706a – III, 1133b; IV, 734b
Muḥammad ʿAli Khān (Khōkand) iv, 631b; v, 30a – IV, 656b; V, 31a
Muḥammad ʿAlī Khān al-Bukhārī → al-Bukhārī
Muḥammad ʿAlī Maghribī (XX) vi, 176b – VI, 162b
Muḥammad ʿAlī Māhir ii, 1004b – II, 1028a
Muḥammad ʿAlī Mīrzā b. Fatḥ ʿAlī Shāh (Ḳādjār) (1823) iv, 394b, 861b; v, 170a – IV, 409a, 894b; V, 167b
Muḥammad ʿAlī Muḥammad Khān (XX) vi, 78a – VI, 75b
Muḥammad ʿAlī Nāṣiḥ iv, 71b – IV, 75b
Muḥammad ʿAlī Pasha (1849) i, 13a, 35a, 182b, 404a, 554b, 571b, 755a, 1078b, 1172a, 1288b, 1299a, b; ii, 123b, 128a, 148b, 149a, 288b, 356a, 423b, 465a, 514a, 647a; iii, 218b, 238a, 556a, 999a, 1086b, 1154a, 1193b; iv, 442a, 490a; v, 267a, b, 907b, 1085b, 1248a; vi, 22b, 24b, 58b, 59b, 60b, 75a, 150b, 151a, 197a, 232a, 325b, 327a, 330a, 341a, 453b, 469b, 602b, 643a, 718a, 719a; vii, 151b, 241a, **423a**, 720a; viii, 484b, 485a; ix, 903b; s, 30a, b, 38a, 179a, 301b, 379a – I, 13a, 136a, 188a, 415b, 572a, 590b, 777b, 1111a, 1207a, 1328a, 1339a, b; II, 126b, 131a, 152b, 153a, 296b, 365b, 434b, 477a, 526b, 663b; III, 224b, 245a, 575a, 1024a, 1113b, 1182b, 1223b; IV, 462a, 511a; V, 265a, 913a, 1082b, 1238b; VI, 20b, 24b, 56b, 57b, 58b, 73a, 149b, 181a, 226a, 310a, 311b, 314b, 325b, 439a, 455b, 587a, 628a, 706b, 708a; VII, 153b, 242b, **424b**, 721a; VIII, 501a,b; IX, 941b; S, 30b, 38b, 180a, 301b, 379a
Muḥammad ʿAlī Riḍā (XX) vi, 176b – VI, 162b
Muḥammad ʿAlī Shāh b. Muẓaffar al-Dīn (Ḳādjār) (1925) ii, 650b, 651b, 652a; iv, 39b, 392a, 398b, 789b; vi, 502b, 553a, 715a; vii, **431b**, 918b; viii, 140a; ix, 191b; s, 53b, 72a, 91b, 291a, 365b – II, 667a, 668a; IV, 42a, 408b, 411b, 415b, 821a; VI, 488a, 537b, 704a; VII, **432b**, 919b; VIII, 142b; IX, 198a; S, 54a, 72a, 91b, 290b, 365a
Muḥammad ʿAlī Zaynal Riḍā (XX) vi, 173b, 176b, 178a – VI, 161b, 162b
Muḥammad ʿAlī-i Zandjānī i, 847a – I, 870a
Muḥammad al-ʿĀlim b. Mawlāy Ismāʿīl (ʿAlawid(e)) (XVIII) vi, 595a; s, 126a – VI, 580a; S, 125a
Muḥammad Amīn (Amīna Kazwīnī) (XVII) vii, 443b – VII, 444b
Muḥammad Amīn (China/la Chine) → Ma Ming-hsin
Muḥammad Amīn (Shāmil) (XIX) i, 1190a – I, 1225a
Muḥammad Amīn, Inaḳ (XVIII) iv, 1065a; v, 24a; s, 420a – IV, 1096b; V, 25a; S, 420a
Muḥammad Amīn, Shaykh (Tokat) (1745) vii, 936b – VII, 937a
Muḥammad Amīn Badakhshī i, 1023a – I, 1054b

Muḥammad al-Amīn Bey iv, 262b – IV, 274b
Muḥammad Amīn Bukhārī s, 419b – S, 419b
Muḥammad Amīn Dīdī (Maldives) (XX) vi, 246a, b – VI, 230a, 231a
Muḥammad al-Amīn al-Kānemī → al-Kānemī, Muḥammad al-Amīn
Muḥammad Amīn Khān (1518) iv, 849a – IV, 882a
Muḥammad Amīn Khān (1855) s, 46a – S, 46b
Muḥammad Amīn al-Kurdī → al-Kurdī
Muḥammad Amīr Aḥmad Khān, Rādjā (1973) vi, 78a – VI, 76a
Muḥammad Amīr Pandja Kash ii, 83b – II, 85b
Muḥammad Anūsha iv, 1064b, 1068a – IV, 1096a, 1100a
Muḥammad Anwar Shāh al-Kashmīrī al-Hindī iv, 84b – IV, 88b
Muḥammad ʿĀrif i, 287b; ii, 391b – I, 296a; II, 402a
Muḥammad al-Aṣghar b. al-Maʾmūn (ʿAbbāsid(e)) (IX) vi, 331b – VI, 316a
Muḥammad ʿAshi̊k → ʿAshi̊k, Muḥammad
Muḥammad al-ʿAṭṭār, Shaykh (XIX) vii, 670b – VII, 670b
Muḥammad al-Awḳaṣ b. ʿAbd al-Raḥmān, Ḳāḍī (VIII) vi, 140b – VI, 138b
Muḥammad ʿAyn al-Dawla iii, 1114a – III, 1141b
Muḥammad Aytīmur (Sarbadārid(e)) (1346) ix, 48a – IX, 49a
Muḥammad Aʿẓam b. Awrangzīb i, 913b, 1201b; ii, 216b; iii, 457b – I, 941a, 1237a; II, 223a; III, 473b
Muḥammad Aʿẓam b. Dūst Muḥammad i, 232a; ii, 417a, 638a – I, 239a; II, 428a, 654a
Muḥammad Aʿẓam b. Pāyinda Khān i, 231a; ii, 637b; v, 501b – I, 238a; II, 653b; V, 504b
Muḥammad Bā Faḍl (1497) vi, 132b – VI, 130b
Muḥammad Badāʾūnī → Shaykh Niẓām al-Dīn Awliyāʿ
Muḥammad al-Badr iv, 745b – IV, 775b
Muḥammad Bahāwal Khān → Bahāwal Khān
Muḥammad Baḥrī Pasha ii, 990b – II, 1013a
Muḥammad Baḳāʾ b. Ghulām Muḥammad Sahāranpūrī (1685) vii, **432b** – VII, **433b**
Muḥammad Bakhtiyār Khaldjī (1206) i, 393b, 1209b; ii, 267b, 297a, 1103a; v, 638a; vi, 244b; vii, **433a**, 573a – I, 404b, 1245b; II, 275b, 305a, 1129a; V, 642a; VI, 228b; VII, **434a**, 573b
Muḥammad Bāḳī b. ʿĪsā Khān Tarkhān, Mīrzā (1585) i, 628a; vi, 190a – I, 648b; VI, 173b
Muḥammad Bāḳī Naḳshbandī → Bāḳī bi-ʾllāh
Muḥammad al-Bāḳir, Abū Djaʿfar → Muḥammad b. ʿAlī Zayn al-ʿĀbidīn al-Bāḳir
Muḥammad Bāḳir b. Muḥammad Taḳī al-Madjlisī → Madjlisi-yi Thānī
Muḥammad al-Bākir, Abū Djaʿfar → MuZammad b. ʿAlī Zayn al-ʿAbidīn
Muḥammad al-Bāḳir, Amīr (Imām Muḥammad-Shāhī) (1796) iv, 202a – IV, 210b, 211a
Muḥammad Bāḳir Iṣfahānī, Hājjī Shaykh (1883) vii, 918b – VII, 919a
Muḥammad Bāḳir al-Madjlisī → al-Madjlisī
Muḥammad Bāḳir Mīrzā b. ʿAbbās I (Ṣafawid(e)) (1614) viii, 770b – VIII, 796a
Muḥammad Bāḳir Mīrzā Khusrawī (XX) ix, 402b – IX, 415b
Muḥammad Bāḳir Nadjm-i Thānī (1637) i, 848a, 1019a; vii, **433a**, 988a – I, 871a, 1050b; VII, **434a**, 989a
Muḥammad Bāḳir Shaftī s, 75a – S, 75b
Muḥammad Bāḳir-i Bihbihānī iv, 51a – IV, 53b
Muḥammad al-Balʿamī → al-Balʿamī
Muḥammad al-Baṭāʾiḥī (Ḳādiriyya) iv, 381a – IV, 397b
Muḥammad al-Baṭāʾihī (Rifāʿiyya) iv, 350a – IV, 365a
Muḥammad Bayram I (1800) vii, 433b – VII, 434b
Muḥammad Bayram II (1831) vii, 433b – VII, 434b
Muḥammad Bayram III (1843) vii, 433b – VII, 434b
Muḥammad Bayram IV (1861) vii, 433b – VII, 434b
Muḥammad Bayram al-Khāmis iv, 1154a; vii, **433b**, 901a – IV, 1186a; VII, **434b**, 901b
Muḥammad Beg (Turcoman) ii, 204b – II, 211a
Muḥammad Beg Aydinoghlu i, 783a; ii, 989a, 1044b – I, 806a, b; II, 1012a, 1069a
Muḥammad Beg Ḳarāmānid(e) → Muḥammad b. Ḳarāmān; Muḥammad II (Ḳarāmānid(e))
Muḥammad Beg Ustādjlū i, 1067a – I, 1099a
Muḥammad Behdjet iv, 195a – IV, 203b
Muḥammad Bello b. Shaykh ʿUthmān b. Fūdī (1837) vii, **435b**; viii, 356b; x, 122b – VII, **436a**; VIII, 369b; X, 132a
Muḥammad Bey (Ḥusaynid(e)) (1859) i, 977a; ii, 638b; iii, 561b, 636a; vi, 798b; vii, **436b** – I, 1007a; II, 654b; III, 581a, 657b; VI, 788a; VII, **437b**
Muḥammad Bey b. Aḥmad Bey Mirzā (XVII) i, 1208b – I, 1244b
Muḥammad Bey b. Maḥmūd (Tunisia/Tunésie) (1663) i, 1049a; ii, 161a; vi, 840b – I, 1081a; II, 166a; VI, 831b
Muḥammad Bey b. Yaḥya i, 1164a, b – I, 1198 b, 1199a
Muḥammad Bey Abu ʾl-Dhahab → Abu ʾl-Dhahab, Muḥammad Bey
Muḥammad Bey Abu ʾl-Dhahab → Muḥammad Abu ʾl-Dhahab
Muḥammad Bey al-Alfī (1807) i, 1288b; iv, 853a; vii, 423b – I, 1328a; IV, 886a; VII, 425a
Muḥammad Bey Khālid → Muḥammad Khālid Zuḳal
Muḥammad Bey Khusraw ii, 123b, 351b; iv, 686b; v, 267a – II, 126b, 361a; IV, 714b; V, 265a
Muḥammad Bey Minnet-oghlu i, 1263b – I, 1302a
Muḥammad Bey ʿUthmān Djalāl (1898) vii, **437a** – VII, **438b**
Muḥammad Boḍu Takurufānu (Maldives) (XVI) vi, 245b – VI, 230a
Muḥammad al-Bukhārī → al-Bukhārī
Muḥammad al-Bulālī i, 929a – I, 957b
Muḥammad Burhān al-Dīn b. Ṭāhir Sayf al-Dīn x, 103b – X, 111b
Muḥammad al-Burtuḳālī → Muḥammad II (Waṭṭāsid(e))
Muḥammad Čavush iv, 592b – IV, 616b
Muḥammad Čelebī (Ottoman) → Meḥemmed I
Muḥammad Čelebi b. Burhān al-Dīn i, 1328a – I, 1368b
Muḥammad Čelebi Efendi → Yirmisekiz Čelebi Meḥmed
Muḥammad Čelebi Üsküdarī ii, 442b – II, 454b
Muḥammad Čurbak vii, 410a – VII, 411a
Muḥammad Dāʾim ii, 28b – II, 29a
Muḥammad Dāwūd Khān (1978) v, 1079b; vii, **438a** – V, 1077a; VII, **439a**
Muḥammad Dāwūd Shāh (Atjèh) (1903) i, 744a – I, 766a
Muḥammad Demirdāsh al-Muḥammadī s, 208a – S, 207b
Muḥammad al-Dībādj → Muḥammad b. Djaʿfar

Muḥammad Djaʿfar Ḳaraḍja-Dāg̲h̲ī Muns̲h̲ī (XIX) i, 332a; vii, **438b** – I, 342b; VII, **439b**

Muḥammad Djaʿfar K̲h̲ān → Djaʿfar Mīr

Muḥamad Djamāl al-Dīn Huvadu (Maldives) (XVI) vi, 245b – VI, 230a

Muḥammad Djamālī ii, 420a – II, 431a

Muḥammad Djān i, 232a – I, 239a

Muḥammad al-Djawād ʿAlī al-Riḍā al-Taḳī (IX. Imām) (835) iii, 1167a; iv, 855a; vii, 313a; s, 95a, 127b – III, 1195b; IV, 888a; VII, 315b; S, 94a, 126b

Muḥammad Djawād al-Djazāʾirī s, 28a – S, 28b

Muḥammad al-Djawnpūrī → al-Djawnpūrī, Sayyid Muḥammad

Muḥammad Djayāsī → Malik Muḥammad Djayāsī

Muḥammad Djūkī i, 135a, 148a; s, 51a – I, 139a, 152a; S, 51b

Muḥammad al-Durrī (XX) vi, 755a – VI, 744a

Muḥammad Edīb ii, 590a – II, 604b

Muḥammad Efendī Aḳ Kirmānī i, 310b – I, 320a

Muḥammad Efendī Čiwizāde ii, 57a – II, 57b

Muḥammad Emīn (Crimea/-ée) (1519) viii, 832a – VIII, 860b

Muḥammad Emīn b. Haḏjḏji Meḥmed i, 295a – I, 304a

Muḥammad Emīn b. Muṣṭafā Feyḍī Ḥayātī-zāde (XII) iii, 303b – III, 312b

Muḥammad Emīn Pas̲h̲a iii, 1199a – III, 1229a

Muḥammad-Enweri Kadić i, 1271b – I, 1310b

Muḥammad Eretna → G̲h̲iyāt̲h̲ al-Dīn Muḥammad

Muḥammad Es̲h̲ref iii, 357b – III, 368b

Muḥammad Faḍl b. ʿAbd al-Raḥmān (Dār Fūr) (1838) ii, 123b – II, 126b

Muḥammad al-Fāḍil b. Ās̲h̲ūr → Ibn Ās̲h̲ūr, Muḥammad al-Fāḍil

Muḥammad Fāḍil al-Ḳalkamī v, 889b, 890a – V, 896a, b

Muḥammad al-Fahhām iv, 165b – IV, 172b

Muḥammad al-Faḳīh → Muḥammad II (Naṣrid(e))

Muḥammad Farīd → Abū Ḥadīd

Muḥammad Farīd Bey b. Aḥmad Farīd Pas̲h̲a (1919) iii, 515a; vii, **439a**, 716a – III, 533a; VII, **440a**, 717a

Muḥammad Farīd Waḏjdī (1954) vii, **439b** – VII, **440b**

Muḥammad Fasanḏjus → Abu ʾl-Faraḏj Muḥammad Fasanḏjus

Muḥammad Fatḥ Allāh Barakāt iii, 516a – III, 534a

Muḥammad Ferīd → Dāmād Ferīd Pas̲h̲a

Muḥammad al-G̲h̲ālib bi-ʿllāh → Muḥammad I (Naṣrid(e))

Muḥammad al-G̲h̲ānī → Muḥammad V (Naṣrid(e))

Muḥammad G̲h̲arḏjistānī i, 227a – I, 234a

Muḥammad G̲h̲awt̲h̲ Gwālidyār (1562) ii, 1144a; iii, 430a, 436a; vi, 127b; vii, **439b** – II, 1171a; III, 444a, 450a; VI, 125b; VII, **441a**

Muḥammad G̲h̲uri → Muḥammad b. Sām, G̲h̲iyāt̲h̲ al-Dīn; – Muʿizz al-Dīn; Muḥammad S̲h̲āh G̲h̲ūrī

Muḥammad Girāy I ii, 1046a, 1113a; iv, 849b – II, 1070b, 1139b; IV, 882b

Muḥammad Girāy II iv, 178b; v, 138b – IV, 185b; V, 141a, b

Muḥammad Girāy III i, 310b; v, 719b – I, 320b; V, 724b

Muḥammad Girāy IV ii, 25a; v, 139b, 719b – II, 25b; V, 142b, 725a

Muḥammad Gīsū Darāz → Gīsū Darāz

Muḥammad Gulandām iii, 56a – III, 58b

Muḥammad Gūlēd, S̲h̲ayk̲h̲ (1918) ix, 722b – IX, 754a

Muḥammad al-Ḥabīb Bey (Ḥusaynid(e)) (1929) iii, 636b – III, 658a

Muḥammad al-Ḥabīb (Mauritania/-) (1860)

vii, 614b – VII, 614a

Muḥammad Hādī b. al-Lawḥī (XVII) vii, 95b – VII, 97b

Muḥammad al-Hādī Bey (Ḥusaynid(e)) (1906) iii, 636b – III, 658a

Muḥammad al-Ḥādjdj b. Maḥmūd b. Abī Bakr (XVII) vi, 187a – VI, 171a

Muḥammad Ḥāfiẓ Ibrāhīm → Ḥāfiẓ Ibrāhīm

Muḥammad Ḥakīm, Mīrzā (1585) i, 316a, 733a, 1122b; iii, 423b; iv, 410b; v, 649b; vi, 342b; vii, 573b; s, 122a – I, 326a, 755a, 1156b; III, 437b; IV, 428a; V, 653b; VI, 327a; VII, 574b; S, 121a

Muḥammad Ḥakīm Biy (Mangȋt) (XVIII) vi, 418b – VI, 403b

Muḥammad Ḥāmid al-Faḳī (XX) vi, 176b – VI, 162b

Muḥammad Ḥāmid K̲h̲ān ii, 597b – II, 612b

Muḥammad Harsānī, S̲h̲ayk̲h̲ (XX) vi, 171b – VI, 161a

Muḥammad Ḥasab Allāh ii, 91b – II, 93a

Muḥammad Ḥasan (Zarrin ḳalam) s, 167b – S, 167b

Muḥammad Ḥasan ʿAwwād (XX) vi, 176b – VI, 162b

Muḥammad Ḥasan Faḳī (XX) vi, 177b – VI, 163a

Muḥammad Ḥasan Gīlānī s, 23b – S, 23b

Muḥammad Ḥasan K̲h̲ān Ḳādjār i, 701b; iii, 1103a; iv, 389b, 390a, b, 639b – I, 722b; III, 1130a; IV, 406b, 407a, 666a

Muḥammad Ḥasan K̲h̲ān S̲h̲anīʿ al-Dawla (1896) ii, 433b, 952a; iv, 70b; vii, **440a**; x, 233b; s, 71b, 75b – II, 445a, 974a; IV, 74b; VII, **441a**; X, 252a; S, 72a, 76a

Muḥammad Ḥasan Kutubī (XX) vi, 178a – VI, 163a

Muḥammad Ḥasan Mīrzā i, 262b – I, 270b

Muḥammad Ḥasan Wazzānī (Morocco/Maroc) (XX) vii, 416a – VII, 417b

Muḥammad Hās̲h̲im Āṣaf Rustam al-Ḥukamāʾ vi, 483b – VI, 469b

Muḥammad al-Hās̲h̲imī → al-Hās̲h̲imī

Muḥammad Ḥasan Nūrī, Mīrzā s, 23b – S, 23b

Muḥammad al-Ḥāsib (861) vii, 39b – VII, 40a

Muḥammad Ḥaydar Dug̲h̲lāt → Ḥaydar Mīrzā

Muḥammad al-Ḥifnī (XVIII) ii, 167a; vi, 627a – II, 172a; VI, 612a

Muḥammad al-Hilālī → Muḥammad al-Bulālī

Muḥammad Ḥusayn b. Bahrām b. S̲h̲āh Ismāʿīl I, Mīrzā (Ṣafawid(e)) (XVI) vii, 129b – VII, 131b

Muḥammad Ḥusayn b. Muḥammad Faḍl ii, 123b, 124b – II, 126b, 127b

Muḥammad Ḥusayn ʿAṭā K̲h̲ān iii, 376a – III, 388a

Muḥammad Ḥusayn Āzād (1910) vii, 668a – VII, 668a

Muḥammad Ḥusayn Bus̲h̲rūʾī, Mullā (1849) vii, 422a, **440b** – VII, 424a, **441b**

Muḥammad Ḥusayn Dūg̲h̲lāt ii, 622b; iii, 317a – II, 638a; III, 326b

Muḥammad Ḥusayn Haykal (1956) vi, 176b; vii, **441a**, 713b – VI, 162b; VII, **442a**, 714b

Muḥammad Ḥusayn K̲h̲ān Develū iv, 390a, b – IV, 406b, 407a

Muḥammad Ḥusayn K̲h̲ān Nāẓim al-Dawla iv, 104b, 578a – IV, 109b, 601a

Muḥammad Ḥusayn S̲h̲ahriyār iv, 71b – IV, 75b

Muḥammad Ḥusayn Tabrīzī (XVI) vii, **442a** – VII, **443a**

Muḥammad al-Ḥusaynī al-Buk̲h̲ārī s, 10b – S, 10a

Muḥammad Ibn Gīṭūn vi, 607a – VI, 591b

Muḥammad Ibn al-Zayn viii, 886b – VIII, 916b

Muḥammad Ibrāhīm Dhawḳ → Dhawḳ
Muḥammad Ibrāhīm al-Ghazzāwī (XX) vi, 175b – VI, 162a
Muḥammad Ibrāhim al-Zarben x, 71b – X, 74a
Muḥammad al-Idrīsī → al-Idrīsī
Muḥammad Iḳbāl → Iḳbāl, Muḥammad
Muḥammad al-Ilkhān ii, 401a – II, 411b
Muḥammad al-Ikhshīd → Muḥammad b. Ṭughdj al-Ikhshīd
Muḥammad ʿIllīsh ii, 167a – II, 172b
Muḥammad Ilyās (1944) iii, 433b; x, 38a – III, 447b; X, 39b
Muḥammad Īndjū iii, 1208b – III, 1239a
Muḥammad ʿĪsā Tarkhān i, 628a, 1192a; iii, 1030a – I, 648b, 1227b; III, 1056a
Muḥammad Isfandiyārī → Nīmā Yūshīdj
Muḥammad Ismāʿīl b. ʿAbd al-Ghānī al-Shahīd → Ismāʿīl Shahīd, Muḥammad
Muḥammad Ismāʿīl Khān Nūrī v, 155b, 165a – V, 156a, 162b
Muḥammad Ismāʿīl Mēraṭhī (1917) vi, 838b – VI, 829a
Muḥammad ʿIṣmatī (XVII) vii, 469b – VII, 469a
Muḥammad ʿIzzat Darwaza (Darwazeh) (1984) vii, **442b** – VII, **443b**
Muḥammad Ḳāḍī s, 51b – S, 52a
Muḥammad Ḳādirī (XVII) vii, 925b – VII, 926a
Muḥammad Ḳadrī Pasha (XIX) iii, 164a; vi, 23b, 27a, 29b – III, 167b; VI, 21b, 25a, 27b
Muḥammad al-Ḳāʾim al-Mahdī (XII. Imām) (940) i, 402b; iii, 247a; vii, **443a**; s, 95a – I, 414b; III, 254a; VII, **444a**; S, 94b
Muḥammad Kāshānī, ḳaḍī (ṣadr) (XVI) vi, 18a – VI, 16a
Muḥammad al-Ḳāʾim bi-Amr Allāh i, 245a – I, 252b
Muḥammad Kāmil Pasha v, 314a – V, 313b
Muḥammad Ḳaramānlī iv, 617b – IV, 642a
Muḥammad Ḳāsim (painter/peintre) (XVII) vii, 603a – VII, 602b
Muḥammad Ḳāsim, Mawlawī (XIX) ii, 205a; iii, 431a – II, 211b; III, 445b
Muḥammad Ḳāsim Khān b. Sulaymān Ḳādjār (XIX) vi, 484b – VI, 470b
Muḥammad Ḳāsim Khān Mīr-i Baḥr (XVI) i, 253a – I, 261a
Muḥammad Kāẓim, Munshī (1681) vii, 342b, **443b** – VII, 344b, **444b**
Muḥammad Kāzim Khurāsānī (XX) s, 54a – S, 54b
Muḥammad al-Khāḍir b. al-Ḥusayn → al-Khāḍir, Muḥammad b. al-Ḥusayn
Muḥammad Khʷadja i, 808b – I, 831b
Muḥammad Khālid Zuḳal ii, 123b,124a, 827b; v, 1250a – II, 127a, 847b; V, 1240b
Muḥammad Khān, Dashtī (1881) vi, 384b – VI, 369a
Muḥammad Khān, Sayyid (1864) s, 46a – S, 46b
Muḥammad Khān (Ḳarakhānid(e)) → Muḥammad I, II, III; Muḥammad b. Sulaymān
Muḥammad Khān (Turcoman) iv, 389b – IV, 406a
Muḥammad Khān b. Aḥmad Shāh (Gudjarāt) (XV) vi, 52b – VI, 51a
Muḥammad Khān b. Balban s, 124a – S, 123b
Muḥammad Khān b. Ḥadjdjī Muḥammad Kirmānī (1906) ix, 409b – IX, 417b
Muḥammad Khān Awḥadī (Bayāna) (XV) vi, 53b; vii, 278b, 279a – VI, 51b; VII, 280b
Muḥammad Khān Bangash Karlānī, Nawwāb (1743) ii, 808a, 1085a; vii, **443b** – II, 827b, 1110b; VII, **444b**
Muḥammad Khān Ḳoyunlū iv, 390b – IV, 407b
Muḥammad Khān Madjd al-Mulk Sinakī iv, 397b – IV, 415a
Muḥammad Khʷarizmshāh → ʿAlā al-Dīn Muḥammad Khʷarizm Shāh
Muḥammad al-Khayrātī, amīr (XVIII) vi, 191b – VI, 175b
Muḥammad al-Khiḍr Ḥusayn (XX) vii, 439b – VII, 440b
Muḥammad Khodja iii, 605a – III, 625b
Muḥammad Khor (XIX) viii, 463b – VIII, 479a
Muḥammad Khudābanda (XVI) vii, 478a – VII, 477b
Muḥammad Khusraw Pasha (XIX) ii, 292b; vi, 285a – II, 300b; VI, 270a
Muhammad Koya, C.H. (Mappila) (XX) vi, 460a – VI, 446a
Muḥammad Ḳulī Khān Ḳāshḳāy iv, 706a – IV, 734b
Muḥammad Ḳulī Ḳuṭb Shāh, Sultan (1611) iii, 318b, 319a, 426b; v, 550a, 630a, 961a; vi, 610b, 837b – III, 328a, 440b; V, 555a, 634a, 965a; VI, 595b, 828a
Muḥammad Ḳuṭb Shah iii, 427a – III, 440b
Muḥammad Lārī → Lārī, Muḥammad Salāḥ
Muḥammad Lashkarī → Muḥammad Shāh III (Bahmanī)
Muḥammad Lārī → Lārī, Muḥammad b. Ṣalāḥ
Muḥammad al-Liḥyānī → Muḥammad III (Ḥafṣīd(e))
Muḥammad Māḍī → Abu ʾl-ʿAzāʾim
Muḥammad Mādjid al-Kurdī, Shaykh (XX) vi, 175b, 176a – VI, 162a
Muḥammad Mahābat Khān I (1770) ii, 597b – II, 612b
Muḥammad Mahābat Khān (1960) ii, 598a – II, 613a
Muḥammad Mahdī (Djawnpūr) v, 1230b; s, 222a – V, 1221a; S, 222a
Muḥammad al-Mahdī (Ḥammūdid(e)) → Muḥammad I (Ḥammūdid(e))
Muḥammad al-Mahdī (Saʿdid(e)) v, 1191a – V, 1181a
Muḥammad al-Mahdī (Sanūsī) ii, 493a; s, 165a – II, 505a; S, 164b
Muḥammad al-Mahdī (Umayyad(e)) → Muḥammad II (Umayyad(e))
Muḥammad al-Mahdī b. Muḥammad ʿAlī al-Sanūsī (1902) ix, 25b – IX, 27a
Muḥammad Mahdī Khān → Mahdī Khān Astarābādī
Muḥammad Maḥmūd ii, 934b; iii, 516a, 517a, 518b; s, 18a – II, 956a; III, 534a, b, 536b; S, 18b
Muḥammad al-Makhlūʿ → Muḥammad II (Naṣrid(e))
Muḥammad al-Makkī (IX) vii, 401a – VII, 402b
Muḥammad al-Māmī, Shaykh v, 891b, 892a – V, 898a, b
Muḥammad al-Manglī i, 1154a; ii, 740b – I, 1188a; II, 759a
Muḥammad al-Mānṣālī (XX) vi, 752a – VI, 741a
Muḥammad al-Maslūkh i, 56a, 706b; ii, 367b; iii, 721a – I, 57b, II, 377b; III, 743b
Muḥammad Masʿūd (Miṣr) (XX) vi, 602b – VI, 587b
Muḥammad Masʿūd, Dihātī (1947) iv, 72b; v, 199a – IV, 76b; V, 196a
Muḥammad Mīrāb, Shīr → Muʾnis (Khīwa)
Muḥammad Mīrzā → Muḥammad Shāh (Ḳādjār)
Muḥammad Muʿazzam Bahādur Shāh b. Awrangzīb → Bahādur Shāh I (Mughal) (1712)
Muḥammad Mubārak Khān → Mubārak Khān
Muḥammad Mufīd (XVII) iii, 490b – III, 507a
Muḥammad Muḥsin (XX) iv, 626a – IV, 650b
Muḥammad Muḥsin al-Ḥādjdj (1812) vii, **444a** – VII, **445a**

Muḥammad Muḳīm Khān → Muḳīm Khān
Muḥammad Muʾmin Khān Muʾmin (1851) vi, 838a – VI, 828b
Muḥammad al-Mundhir ii, 1009a – II, 1033a
Muḥammad al-Muntaṣir → Muḥammad b. Idrīs II
Muḥammad Murād Beg → Murād Beg
Muḥammad al-Murtaḍā li-Dīn Allāh b. al-Hādī, Abu 'l-Ḳāsim (Rassī Zaydī) (922) vii, **444b**, 773a; s, 335b – VII, **445b**, 774b; S, 335a
Muḥammad Murtaḍā al-Zabīdī (1791) i, 596b, 782a; ii, 355b, 927a, 948b; iv, 524b; vii, **445a**; viii, 728b – I, 615b, 805a; II, 365b, 948b, 973a; IV, 547b; VII, **446a**; VIII, 749b
Muḥammad Mūsā Kudatlī ii, 87b – II, 89a
Muḥammad al-Mustaʿīn → Muḥammad VII (Naṣrid(e))
Muḥammad al-Mustakfī → Muḥammad III (Umayyad(e))
Muḥammad al-Mustaʿlī → Muḥammad III (Ḥammūdid(e))
Muḥammad al-Muʿtamid → al-Muʿtamid
Muḥammad al-Mutawakkil al-Maslūkh → Muḥammad al-Maslūkh
Muḥammad al-Muẓaffar → al-Muẓaffar (Afṭasid(e))
Muḥammad Muzammil Allāh Khān, Sir (1938) vi, 165b – VI, 157b
Muḥammad al-Nadjdjār, al-Ḥādjdj (Marrākush) (XIX) vi, 249b, 250b – VI, 233b, 234b
Muḥammad Nadjīb (Neguib) (1984) ii, 648b; vii, **445b**; s, 6a, 7a, 301a – II, 665a; VII, **446b**; S, 5a, b, 6a, 301a
Muḥammad al-Nafs al-Zakiyya → Muḥammad b. ʿAbd Allāh b. al-Ḥasan b. al-Ḥasan, (ʿAlid(e))
Muḥammad al-Nasawī ii, 962a – II, 984a
Muḥammad al-Nāṣir (Almohad(e)) → al-Nāṣir, Muḥammad b. Abī Yūsuf Yaʿḳūb
Muḥammad al-Nāṣir (Naceur Bey, Ḥusaynid(e)) (1922) iii, 636b; vi, 750a – III, 658a; VI, 739b
Muḥammad Naẓīm iii, 581a – III, 601b
Muḥammad Nergisi i, 1271a – I, 1310b
Muḥammad Nuṣrat Nuṣratī (1684) vi, 837a – VI, 827b
Muḥammad Pāʿīzī iii, 114a – III, 116b
Muḥammad Panāh, Mīr (Ghāzī al-Dīn Khān, Fīrūz Djang II) (1752) iii, 1158a; vii, **446a** – III, 1186b; VII, **447a**
Muḥammad Pasha → Meḥmed Pasha; Derwīsh Meḥmed Pasha; Duče Meḥmed Pasha; Kalenderoghlū Meḥmed Pasha; Khāṣṣakī Meḥmed Pasha; Köprülü Meḥmed Pasha; Ṣofu Meḥmed Pasha; Soḳollu Meḥmed Pasha
Muḥammad Rabaḍān i, 404b – I, 416b
Muḥammad Rafīʿ Bādhil iii, 114b – III, 116b
Muḥammad Raḥīm Biy (Mangit) (XVIII) vi, 418b – VI, 403b
Muḥammad Raḥīm Khān Atalïk (Khīwa) (1825) i, 1295b; ii, 116a; iv, 610b, 1065a; v, 24a, 29a; vii, 574b; s, 46a, 97a, 420a – I, 1335b; II, 118b; IV, 635b, 1096b, 1097a; v, 25a, 30a; VII, 575a; S, 46b, 96b, 420a
Muḥammad Raḥīm Khān II, Sayyid (1872) s, 46a, 228b – S, 46b, 228b
Muḥammad Rashād → Meḥemmed V
Muḥammad al-Rashīd → Muḥammad b. Ḥusayn (Ḥusaynid(e))
Muḥammad al-Rashīd, Bey (1759) viii, 448a – VIII, 463b
Muḥammad Rashīd Pasha (XIX) i, 906b; iii, 628b, 999b; v, 36a, 462a – I, 933b; III, 649b, 1024b; V, 37a, b, 464b
Muḥammad Rashīd Riḍā → Rashīd Riḍā
Muḥammad Rasūl Khān ii, 598a – II, 612b
Muḥammad Raʾūf iii, 622b – III, 643a
Muḥammad Rezā Shāh → Muḥammad Riḍā Shāh Pahlawī
Muḥammad Riḍāʾ b. Sangīn ʿAlī ii, 29b – II, 30a
Muḥammad Riḍā Aḥsan Allāh → Ẓafar Khān
Muḥammad Riḍā ʿIshḳī → ʿIshḳī, Muḥammad Riḍā
Muḥammad Riḍā Khān iii, 1106b – III, 1134a
Muḥammad Riḍā Mīrāb b. Er Niyāz Bek → Āgahī
Muḥammad Riḍā al-Shabībī v, 1093b – V, 1090b, 1091a
Muḥammad Riḍā Shāh Pahlawī (1980) ii, 653a; iii, 454a; iv, 40b-42b, 165a; v, 721b, 920b, 1042b, 1098a; vi, 21b, 22a; vii, 300a, **446a**, 715a – II, 669b; III, 469b; IV, 43a-45b, 172a; V, 726b, 926a, 1039a, 1094a; VI, 19b; VII, 302a, **447b**, 715b
Muḥammad Rinānī iv, 104b; v, 834a – IV, 109a; V, 840b
Muḥammad al-Ṣādiḳ Bey (Tunis) (1882) i, 37a; ii, 638b; iii, 562a, 636b; iv, 1154a; vii, 434b, 437a, **451b**, 717b, 718a; viii, 61a – I, 38a; II, 654b; III, 581a, 657b; IV, 1186b; VII, 435b, 438a, **453a**, 718b, 719a; VIII, 62a
Muḥammad Ṣafī al-Dīn (Sukadana, Borneo) viii, 1042a – VIII, 1078a
Muḥammad al-Ṣaghīr s, 208b – S, 208a
Muḥammad al-Ṣaghīr b. Yūsuf i, 863a – I, 887a
Muḥammad Saʿīd → Khalīl Efendi-zāde; Marīnid(e)s
Muḥammad Saʿīd (Mīr Djumlā) → Mīr Djumla, Muḥammad Saʿīd
Muḥammad Saʿīd b. Muḥammad ʿAlī Pasha (1863) vii, 182b – VII, 182b
Muḥammad Saʿīd Abu 'l-Khayr (XX) vi, 157a – VI, 153a
Muḥammad Saʿīd ʿAbd al-Maḳsūd (XX) vi, 176b, 177b – VI, 162b
Muḥammad Saʿīd Ashraf (1708) vi, 131b – VI, 130a
Muḥammad Saʿīd Bābasēl ii, 91b – II, 93b
Muḥammad Saʿīd Sarmad (1659) ii, 134b; iii, 492b; vii, **452b** – II, 138a; III, 509b; VII, **453b**
Muḥammad Sāḳī Mustaʿidd Khān → Mustaʿidd Khān
Muḥammad Ṣāliḥ Beg (Kalāntar) (1621) iv, 476a – IV, 497a
Muḥammad Ṣāliḥ Kan'bū (XVII) iii, 1203b; v, 600b; vi, 418a; vii, 342b – III, 1234a; V, 604b; VI, 403a; VII, 344b
Muḥammad Ṣāliḥ Naṣīf, Shaykh (XX) vi, 176a, b – VI, 162a
Muḥammad Ṣāliḥ Shīrāzī iv, 787a – IV, 818b
Muḥammad Sālim, ḳāḍī iv, 410b – IV, 428a
Muḥammad al-Sammān i, 92a – I, 94b
Muḥammad Shāh I (Bahmānid(e)) i, 924b, 925b, 1068b; ii, 1119a – I, 952a, 953b, 1101a; II, 1145a
Muḥammad Shāh II (Bahmānid(e)) i, 925b, 1200a; iii, 417b – I, 953b, 1235b; III, 431a
Muḥammad Shāh III Lashkarī (Bahmānid(e) 1, 923b, 1047a, 1200a, 1323a; iii, 1159a; s, 280a – I, 951b, 1078b, 1235b, 1363b; III, 1187b; S, 279b
Muḥammad Shāh (Ḳādjār) (1848) i, 246b; ii, 812b, 839a; iii, 554a; iv, 38b, 105a, 392a, 393a; vi, 804a; vii, 299a, 422b, **452b**; viii, 58a; s, 71a, 94b, 108b – I, 254a; II, 831b, 858b; III, 573a; IV, 41a, 109b, 408b, 409b; VI, 794a; VII, 301a, 424b, **454a**; VIII, 59a; S, 71b, 94a, 108a
Muḥammad Shāh I ʿAlāʾ al-Dīn (Khaldjī, Delhi) (1316) i, 444b, 506b, 710a, 1036a, b, 1068b, 1202b, 1322a; ii, 99b, 120a, 154b, 179b, 256b, 260b, 268b, 272b, 405a, 1084b, 1124a; iii, 201a, 416a, 434a, 492a; iv, 218b, 419a, 921a-923b; v, 883b; vi, 121b, 406b; vii, **457b**; s, 73b, 105a, 176a, 279b, 325a –
I, 457a, 522a, 731b, 1067b, 1068a, 1100b, 1238a,

1362a; II, 101b, 123a, 159b, 185a, 263b, 269a, 276b, 281a, 416a, 1109b, 1150b; III, 206a, 429b, 448a, 509a; IV, 228a, 437a, 954a-956b; V, 890a; VI, 119b, 391a; VII, **457b**; S, 74a, 104b, 177b, 279b, 324b

Muḥammad S̲h̲āh I b. Djahān-S̲h̲āh Nāṣir al-Dīn (Mug̲h̲al) (1748)   i, 229b, 295b, 834a, 1026a, 1042b, 1166a, 1330a; iii, 59b, 520a, 454a; iv, 666a; vi, 310a, 456b, 535a, 602a; vii, 316a, 319a, 339b, 443b, 446a, **457a**, 854b –
I, 236b, 305a, 857a, 1057b, 1074b, 1200b, 1371a; III, 62a, 330b, 469b; IV, 693a; VI, 295a, 442a, 519b, 586b; VII, 318a, 321b, 341a, 445a, 447a, **457a**, 856a

Muḥammad S̲h̲āh IV (Sayyid, Delhi) (1443)   ii, 270b; v, 598a, 783a, b; vi, 53a – II, 278b; V, 602a, 789b; VI, 51a

Muḥammad S̲h̲āh V (Delhi)   ii, 271b, 1144a; iii, 423a – II, 279a, 1160b; III, 436b

Muḥammad S̲h̲āh (S̲h̲arḳī) (1458) ix, 355a – IX, 366b

Muḥammad S̲h̲āh II b. Tug̲h̲luḳ S̲h̲āh I (Tug̲h̲luḳid(e), Delhi) (1351)   → Muḥammad b. Tug̲h̲luḳ

Muḥammad S̲h̲āh III b. Fīrūz S̲h̲āh (Tug̲h̲luḳid(e), Delhi) (1393)   iv, 276a; vi, 273a – IV, 288b; VI, 258a

Muḥammad S̲h̲āh (Djawnpūr)   → Muḥammad b. Fīrūz S̲h̲āh III (Tug̲h̲luḳ)

Muḥammad S̲h̲āh, Sultan (Malacca) (XV)   vi, 210b – VI, 195a

Muḥammad S̲h̲āh b. Ḥadjdjādj   v, 162b, 163a, 554a – V, 160b, 161a, 558b

Muḥammad S̲h̲āh b. Ḥasan S̲h̲āh (Kas̲h̲mīr)   s, 131b – S, 130b, 131a

Muḥammad S̲h̲āh b. Malik S̲h̲āh (Kirmān) (Saldjūḳ) (1156)   viii, 945b – VIII, 978a

Muḥammad S̲h̲āh Djahān K̲h̲ān   ii, 317a – II, 326b

Muḥammad S̲h̲āh Fārūḳī   → Mīrān Muḥammad I, II

Muḥammad S̲h̲āh Gaṇeśa   ii, 797b; iii, 419a; viii, 259b – II, 816b; III, 432b; VIII, 260b

Muḥammad S̲h̲āh G̲h̲ūrī   → G̲h̲aznī K̲h̲ān b. Hus̲h̲ang S̲h̲āh G̲h̲ūrī (Mālwā)

Muḥammad S̲h̲āh Karīm (Gudjarāt) (1451)   ii, 1125b; iii, 1010a; vi, 50a, 53b – II, 1153a; III, 1035b; VI, 48b, 51b

Muḥammad S̲h̲āh (Kas̲h̲mīr)   s, 324b, 423b – S, 324a, 423b

Muḥammad S̲h̲āh K̲h̲udābanda b. Tahmāsp I (Ṣafawid(e)) (1588)   i, 7b, 8b; iii, 157b; vi, 17b, 483a, 515a, 526a – I, 7b, 8b; III, 161a; VI, 15b, 469a, 500a, 510b

Muḥammad S̲h̲āh K̲h̲usraw   ii, 316b, 317a – II, 326a, b

Muḥammad S̲h̲āh Özbeg   i, 853a – I, 876b

Muḥammad S̲h̲āh Sayyid   → Muḥammad S̲h̲āh IV (Dihlī)

Muḥammad S̲h̲āh Tangal (Mappila) (XVIII) vi, 463a – VI, 449a

Muḥammad S̲h̲āhī imāms   iv, 201b, 202a – IV, 210b, 211a

Muḥammad S̲h̲ākir Efendi   iv, 618a – IV, 642b

Muḥammad S̲h̲ams al-Dīn S̲h̲āhī (1894)   x, 65a – X, 67b

Muḥammad al-S̲h̲arīf   → Muḥammad I (ʿAlawid(e))

Muḥammad S̲h̲arīf, K̲h̲alīfa   i, 765a; v, 1249a, 1250a, b, 1251b – I, 788a; V, 1239b, 1240b, 1241b, 1242b

Muḥammad S̲h̲arīf b. Dūst Muḥammad   → Muʿtamad K̲h̲ān

Muḥammad S̲h̲arīf b. Iʿtimād al-Dawla   iv, 282a – IV, 294b

Muḥammad S̲h̲arīf al-Adhamī (XI)   vi, 379b – VI, 364a

Muḥammad S̲h̲arīf Ḳābil   → Ḳābil K̲h̲ān

Muḥammad S̲h̲arīf K̲h̲ān   ii, 316b, 317a – II, 326a

Muḥammad S̲h̲arīf al-Nadjafī (XVII)   vii, **457b** – VII, **457b**

Muḥammad S̲h̲arīf Pas̲h̲a   → S̲h̲arīf Pas̲h̲a

Muḥammad S̲h̲arīf al-ʿUlamāʾ, Mullā   s, 75a – S, 75b

Muḥammad al-S̲h̲arīf al-Wadāʾī   s, 164b – S, 164b

Muḥammad S̲h̲arḳī   iii, 419b – III, 433a

Muḥammad al-S̲h̲aṭṭī   → al-S̲h̲aṭṭī, Muḥammad

Muḥammad S̲h̲aybānī   → S̲h̲ībānī K̲h̲ān Muḥammad (Özbeg)

Muḥammad al-S̲h̲aybānī   → al-S̲h̲aybānī

Muḥammad al-S̲h̲ayk̲h̲ (Saʿdid(e)) (1557)   vii, 37b – VII, 37b

Muḥammad al-S̲h̲ayk̲h̲ al-Mahdī   i, 245a; iii, 251a – I, 252b; III, 258b

Muḥammad al-S̲h̲ayk̲h̲ II al-Maʾmūn   i, 605a, 1058a; iii, 810a; s, 29a – I, 624b, 1089b; III, 833a; S, 29a

Muḥammad S̲h̲īrān   i, 393b – I, 404b

Muḥammad S̲h̲īrīn Mag̲h̲ribī (1406) i, 1301a; iv, 66a – I, 1341a; IV, 69b

Muḥammad al-Ṣūfī, S̲h̲ayk̲h̲   s, 353b – S, 353a

Muḥammad Ṣūfī Māzandarānī   → Māzandarānī, Mullā Muḥammad Ṣūfī

Muḥammad Sug̲h̲rā   i, 1218b – I, 1255a

Muḥammad Sulṭān (1834)   iv, 197a – IV, 205b

Muḥammad Sulṭān Bayātī   iii, 1101a – III, 1128b

Muḥammad Sulṭān Pas̲h̲a (Miṣr) (XIX)   vii, 184b – VII, 184b

Muḥammad Sulṭān Rūmī   i, 1168a – I, 1202b

Muḥammad Surūr al-Ṣabbān (XX)   vi, 166a, 175b – VI, 158a

Muḥammad Ṭāhir   → Pīr ʿAlī

Muḥammad al-Ṭāhir   → Ibn ʿĀs̲h̲ūr

Muḥammad Ṭāhir (1672)   iv, 286b; vii, 139b – IV, 299b; VII, 141b

Muḥammad Ṭāhir b. ʿAlī Paťani Gudjarātī (1578)   vii, **458a** – VII, **458a**

Muḥammad Ṭāhir As̲h̲aʾī   → G̲h̲anī

Muḥammad Ṭāhir al-Kurdī (XX)   vi, 176b, 177a, 178a – VI, 163a

Muḥammad Ṭāhir al-S̲h̲ikillī al-Ḥusaynī   iv, 736a – IV, 766a

Muḥammad al-Taḳī   → Muḥammad al-Djawād

Muḥammad Taḳī, Mīrzā   v, 169b – V, 192b

Muḥammad Taḳī ʿAlī Ābādī   ii, 433b – II, 445a

Muḥammad Taḳī Bahār   → Bahār

Muḥammad Taḳī Iṣfahānī, S̲h̲ayk̲h̲   → Āḳā Nadjafī

Muḥammad Taḳī K̲h̲ān (Fārs) (XVIII)   vi, 735a – VI, 724a

Muḥammad Taḳī K̲h̲ān, Mīrzā   → Taḳī K̲h̲ān, Mīrzā Muḥammad (Amīr Kabīr)

Muḥammad Taḳī K̲h̲ān Pisyān (XX)   s, 110a, 366a – S, 109b, 365b

Muḥammad Tāḳī Ḳummī (1990)   x, 139b – X, 151a

Muḥammad Taḳī Madjlisī   → Madjlisī-yi Awwal

Muḥammad Taḳī Mīr   → Mīr Taḳī Mīr

Muḥammad Taḳī Siphir (1880)   iv, 70a – IV, 73b

Muḥammad Ṭalʿat   → Ṭalʿat, Meḥmed

Muḥammad al-Tawdī   → Ibn Sūda, Abī ʿAbd Allāh

Muḥammad Tawfīḳ   → Tawfīḳ Pas̲h̲a

Muḥammad Tawfīḳ Makkī (XX)   vi, 176a

Muḥammad al-Ṭawīl (XX)   vi, 153a – VI, 151b

Muḥammad Taymūr (1921)   vi, 75a, b – VI, 73a, b

Muḥammad Tayrāb   ii, 123a; v, 267a – II, 126a; V, 265a

Muḥammad Ṭayyib   ii, 205b – II, 212a

Muḥammad al-Ṭayyib al-Anṣārī   v, 998b – V, 994a

Muḥammad Tewfīḳ   → Tewfīḳ Meḥmed; Čerkes Meḥmed Tewfīḳ

Muḥammad Tīmūr i, 1019a – I, 1050b
Muḥammad Ture/Touré → Muḥammad b. Abī Bakr (Songhay)
Muḥammad Tughluḳ → Muḥammad Shāh II, III (Dihlī)
Muḥammad Ture/Touré → Muḥammad b. Abī Bakr (Songhay)
Muḥammad al-Tūnisī s, 306a – S, 306a
Muḥammad ʿUbayd Allāh b. Hazārmard v, 451b – V, 454a
Muḥammad Ulugh Khān s, 335b – S, 335a
Muḥammad ʿUmar b. ʿAbd al-Raḥmān iii, 13a – II, 14a
Muḥammad ʿUmar al-Tūnisī ii, 137a – II, 141a
Muḥammad ʿUthmān Djalāl (1898) i, 597a; vi, 746a; vii, 901b, 902b – I, 616b; VI, 735b; VII, 902a, 903a
Muḥammad ʿUthmān al-Mīrghānī → al-Mīrghānī
Muḥammad Walī Khān ii, 435b, 652b – II, 447a, 668b
Muḥammad Wārith s, 46b – S, 47a
Muḥammad wuld Ahmad Yūra (1921) vii, 622b – VII, 622b
Muḥammad wuld Tulba al-Yaʿḳūbī (1856) vii, 625b – VII, 625b
Muḥammad Yādgār (Tīmūrid(e)) (1470) vii, 90b – VII, 92a
Muḥammad al-Yaḥṣubī → Muḥammad b. Yaḥyā
Muḥammad Yaḥyā, Khʷādja s, 51b – S, 52a
Muḥammad al-Yālūshī (XIX) vii, 407b – VII, 409a
Muḥammad Yūsuf al-Kāzarūnī i, 1218b – I, 1255a
Muḥammad Ẓāhir Shāh i, 232b – I, 240a
Muḥammad al-Zākī ʿUthmān i, 1172a – I, 1207a
Muḥammad Zamān Khan → Abū Ridjāʾ
Muḥammad Zamān Khān b. Asʿad Khān (Djalālābād) (XIX) s, 237b – S, 237b
Muḥammad Zamān Mīrzā (XVI) vii, 314a – VII, 316a
Muḥammad Zanjina ii, 1003b – II, 1026b
Muḥammad al-Ẓāfir iv, 1154b – IV, 1186b
Muḥammad Zayd al-Ibyānī (XIX) vi, 23b – VI, 21b
Muḥammad al-Ziyadī i, 551a; v, 602a – I, 568b; V, 606a
Muḥammada vii, 361b – VII, 364a
Muḥammadābād → Bīdar; Čāmpāner; Ghāzīpūr; Gudjarāt; Kālpī
Muḥammadan Union → Ittiḥād-i Muḥammedī Djemʿiyyeti
al-Muḥammadī, Ḳānī-Bay b. ʿAbd Allāh (amīr) (XV) vi, 580b – VI, 565b
Muḥammadī Harawī (XVI) vii, 603a; viii, 514a – VII, 602b; VIII, 531b
Muḥammad-i Khaṭībī s, 333b – S, 333a
Muḥammad-i Waṣīf iv, 55a – IV, 58a
Muḥammad-i Zamān, Mīrzā (XVI) i, 914b; ii, 322b, 1128b; iii, 422b; iv, 1021a; vi, 52a – I, 942b; II, 332a, 1155a; III, 436b; IV, 1053a; VI, 50a
Muḥammadī b. Djahangīr v, 829a – V, 835a
al-Muḥammadiyya → Faḍāla
Muḥammadiyya (ʿĀlid(e)s) vii, **459a** – VII, **459b**
Muḥammadiyya (al-Ḳāhira) iii, 992a – III, 1016b
Muḥammadiyya (Manṣūriyya) ii, 1094b; vi, 441b; vii, 459b – II, 1120b; VI, 427a; VII, 459b
Muḥammadiyyah (Indonesia/Indonésie) i, 745b, 746a; iii, 534a, 1229a; vi, 730a; s, 151a – I, 768a; III, 552b, 1261a; VI, 719a; S, 151a
Muḥammadnagar → Golkondā
Muhammadu Bello ii, 942a, 1145a; iii, 38b, 276b – II, 964a, 1172a; III, 40b, 284b
Muhammadu dan Amu iv, 550b, 551a – IV, 574b
Muḥammadzays → ʿAbd al-Raḥmān Khān (Bārakzay); Afghānistān; Amān Allāh Khān; Ḥabīb Allāh Khān
Muhamman Alwali iv, 549a – IV, 573a
Muhamman Rumfa (1499) iv, 549a, 550a – IV, 572b, 573b
Muḥammara iv, 675a, b; v, 66a; vii, **461a** – IV, 702b, 703a; V, 67b; VII, **461a**
Muḥammira v, 64a, 65a – V, 66a, 67a
Muhandis-khāne → Muhendiskhāne
Muhannā, Banū i, 403a, 1313a; iv, 88a; vii, **461a**; viii, 986b; ix, 507a – I, 414b, 1353a; IV, 92a; VII, **461a**; VIII, 1021a; IX, 526b
Muhannā b. ʿĪsā b. Muhannā (1334) iii, 952a; iv, 88a; vii, 461b – III, 976b; IV, 92a; VII, 461b
Muḥanna b. Naṣīr, Mir v, 507a, b – V, 510b
Muḥārib, Banū vi, 145a; vii, **463a** – VI, 143a; VII, **462b**
Muḥārib b. Mūsā vi, 878b – VI, 869b
al-Muḥāribī → Ibn ʿAṭiyya
Muhārish i, 1074b; 1075a – I, 1106b, 1107a
Muḥarraf iii, 26a – III, 27b
al-Muḥarraḳ (island/île) i, 941a; vi, 357b, 358a; vii, **464a** – I, 970a; VI, 341b, 342a; VII, **463b**
al-Muḥarram vii, **464a** – VII, **463b**
Muḥarram, Aḥmad iii, 112a – III, 114b
Muḥarriḳ → Amr b. Hind
Muḥarrirān iv, 757b – IV, 787b
Muḥāsaba ii, 81a; vii, **465a** – II, 82b; VII, **464a**
Muḥasayn, Āl iv, 1171a – IV, 1204b
al-Muḥāsibī, Abū ʿAbd Allāh al-Ḥārith b. Asad (857) i, 277a, 326b, 694b, 1245b; ii, 242b, 450b; iii, 83b, 466a, 720a; iv, 212a; vii, 101a, 465a, **466b**; viii, 547a; x, 314b; s, 125b, 392a – I, 285b, 336b, 716a, 1283b; II, 249b, 462a; III, 85b, 482b, 742a; IV, 221b; VII, 103a, 464b, **466b**; VIII, 565a; X, 338b; S, 124b, 392b
Muḥaṣṣil vii, **467b** – VII, **467a**
al-Muḥassin (Muḥsin) b. ʿAlī b. Abī Ṭālib (VII) vii, **468b** – VII, **468a**
al-Muḥassin Ibn al-Furāt (X) i, 387a; iii, 702b, 767b; vii, 397a, 653a – I, 398b; III, 725a, 791a; VII, 398b, 652b
al-Muḥassin al-Tanūkhī → al-Tanūkhī
Muḥaṣṣiṣ-i mamlakat iv, 475a – IV, 495b
Muḥāwere iv, 602a – IV, 626a
al-Muḥaydatha vi, 303a; s, 27b – VI, 288b; S, 28a
Muḥaysīn iv, 10a – IV, 11a
Muḥdath ii, 96b; iii, 1051b; v, 96b – II, 98b; III, 1077b; V, 99a
Muhendiskhāne i, 63a, ii, 425b; v, 903a, 908a – I, 65a; II, 436b; V, 909b, 914a
Muḥibb Aḥmed "Diranas" (1980) vii, **469a** – VII, **468b**
Muḥibb Allāh Allāhābādī ii, 54b, 55a, 134b; s, 293a – II, 55b, 56a, 138a; S, 293a
Muḥibb Allāh Bihārī → al-Bihārī
Muḥibb al-Dīn → al-Ṭabarī
Muḥibb al-Dīn al-Khāṭib iii, 519a; iv, 160a – III, 537a; IV, 166b
Muḥibbī → Sulaymān I
al-Muḥibbī, Faḍl Allāh (1671) vii, **469b** – VII, **469a**
al-Muḥibbī, Muḥammad al-Amīn (1699) i, 68b, 594b; vii, **469b**, 527b, 772a – I, 70a, 614a; VII, **469a**, 528a, 773b
al-Muḥibbī, Muḥibb al-Dīn Abu 'l-Faḍl (1608) vii, **469a** – VII, **468b**
al-Muḥillūn vii, **470a** – VII, **469b**
Mühimme Defterleri i, 1090b; vii, **470a** – I, 1123a; VII, **470a**
al-Muḥīṭ → al-Baḥr al-Muḥīṭ

Muḥkam (XIX) vi, 611a – VI, 596a
Muḥkam Čand s, 332a – S, 331b
Muhr ii, 121a, 311b, 806a; vii, **472a**; s, 256b – II, 124a, 320b, 825b; VII, **471b**; S, 256a
Muhrdār iv, 1104a – IV, 1135b
Muḥrim iii, 1052b, 1053a – III, 1078b, 1079a
Muḥriz, Banū vi, 578a – VI, 563a
Muḥriz b. Khalaf, (Sīdī Maḥrez) (1022) iii, 695a; iv, 341a; vi, 354a; vii, **473b** – III, 717a; IV, 355b; VI, 338a; VII, **473a**
Muḥriz b. Ziyād iii, 386a, b; iv, 827b; v, 59b, 60b – III, 398b, 399a; IV, 860b; V, 61b, 62b
al-Muḥrizā iv, 674b – IV, 702a
Muḥṣan vii, **474b** – VII, **474a**
Muḥsin, Ḥādjdjī Āḳā s, 342a – S, 341b
Muḥsin, Mawlā → Fayḍ-i Kāshānī
Muḥsin b. Farīd i, 181b, 767a – I, 186b, 790a
Muḥsin b. al-Ḳāʾid iii, 137b – III, 140a
Muḥsin b. Sālim iii, 294a – III, 303a
Muḥsin ʿAlī Muḥsin (XIX) vii, **475a** – VII, **474b**
Muḥsin al-Amīn (1952) vii, 780b – VII, 782a
Muḥsin Fānī ii, 74a – II, 75a
Muḥsin al-Ḥakīm, Āyatullāh Shaykh (1970) vi, 553a, b; vii, 301b – VI, 537b, 538a; VII, 303b
Muḥsin Khān Ghāzī i, 1123a – I, 1156b
Muḥsine iii, 998b – III, 1023b
Muḥsin-i Fayḍ-i Kāshānī, Muḥammad b. Murtaḍā → Fayḍ-i Kāshānī
Muḥsin-zāde → ʿAbd Allāh Pasha Muḥsin-zāde; Meḥmed Pasha Muḥsin-zāde
al-Muhtadī bi-'llāh (ʿAbbāsid(e)) (870) iv, 89a; vi, 670a; vii, **476b**; s, 402a – IV, 93a; VI, 656a; VII, **476a**; S, 402b
Muḥtādj, Abū ʿAlī Aḥmad Čaghānī (Muḥtadjid(e)) (955) ii, 1b; iv, 60b – II, 1b; IV, 64a
Muḥtādj, Abū Bakr Muḥammad b. Muẓaffar b. – (Muḥtadjid(e)) (941) vii, 477b – VII, 477a
Muḥtadjid(e)s vii, **477b** – VII, **477a**
Muḥtaram Shāh I ii, 29b – II, 30a
Muḥtaram Shāh II ii, 30a – II, 30b
Muḥtaram Shāh III ii, 30a – II, 30b
Muḥtasham-i Kāshānī (1587) iv, 68a; vi, 271a, 608b, 609a, b, 610b; vii, **477b**; viii, 775a,b – IV, 71b; VI, 256a, 593a, 594a, 595a; VII, **477b**; VIII, 801a,b
Muḥtasib i, 26b, 344b, 477a, 629b, 752a, 898b, 977b; ii, 228b, 519b; iii, 485b, 487a, 490a, 492a; v, 280a, 876a –
I, 27b, 355a, 491b, 650a, 774b, 925b, 1008a; II, 235b, 532b; III, 503a, 504a, 507a, 509a; V, 278a, 882a
al-Muḥtasib → Abū ʿAbd Allāh al-Shīʿī
Muḥyī 'l-Dīn, Shaykh (Čishtī) (XVI) vi, 272a – VI, 257a
Muḥyī 'l-Dīn b. ʿAbd al-Ẓāhir (XIII) vi, 424a – VI, 409b
Muḥyī 'l-Dīn b. al-ʿArabī → Ibn al-ʿArabī
Muḥyī 'l-Dīn Khaṭīb (XX) vi, 176a – VI, 162a
Muḥyī 'l-Dīn Khayyāṭ (XX) vi, 614b – VI, 599b
Muḥyī 'l-Dīn Lārī (1526) vii, **478b** – VII, **478a**
Muḥyī 'l-Dīn Masʿūd b. Ḳîlîdj Arslan II i, 510a – I, 525b
Muḥyī 'l-Dīn Meḥmed al-Djamālī (XVI) vii, 478b – VII, 478b
Muḥyī 'l-Dīn Muḥammad b. Aḥmad al-Walīd (Yemen) vi, 433b – VI, 419a
Muḥyī 'l-Dīn Muḥammad Čiwi-zāde ii, 56b – II, 57b
Muḥyi 'l-Dīn Shāh Meḥmed Fenārī-zāde ii, 879b; iv, 333b – II, 899b, 900a; IV, 348a
Muḥyī 'l-Dīn Yaḥya b. Faḍl Allāh ii, 732a; iii, 758b – II, 750b; III, 781b
Muḥyī-i Gülshenī ii, 1136a – II, 1162b
Muʿīd → Mustamlī
al-Muʿīd li-dīn Allāh (XI) vi, 566a – VI, 551a
Muʿīn (painter/peintre) (XVII) vii, 603a – VII, 602b
Muʿīn al-Dīn b. Sharaf al-Dīn Farāhī → Mullā Miskīn
Muʿīn al-Dīn ʿAlī → Ḳāsim-i Anwār
Muʿīn al-Dīn Djāmī, Shaykh (XIV) viii, 749b – VIII, 770a
Muʿīn al-Dīn Ḥasan b. Ṣadr al-Dīn i, 766a, b –I, 789a, b
Muʿīn al-Dīn Ḥasan Čishtī → Čishtī
Muʿīn al-Dīn Ḳattāl (XV) vii, 440a – VII, 441a
Muʿīn al-Dīn Mukhtaṣṣ al-Mulk (vizier) (1127) ix, 15b – IX, 16a
Muʿīn al-Dīn Natanzī (XV) vi, 483a, 494b – VI, 469a, 480a
Muʿīn al-Dīn Sulaymān Parwāna (1277) iii, 1269a; iv, 619b, 814a, 817a; vii, **479a**; viii, 15b, 949b – III, 1302a; IV, 644a, 846b, 850a; VII, **478b**; VIII, 15b, 982a
Muʿīn al-Dīn Unur (Anar) (XII) i, 1332a; ii, 282a; iii, 399a; vii, 579a; viii, 128a – I, 1372b; II, 290b; III, 411b; VII, 579b; VIII, 130b
Muʿīn al-Dīn Yazdī (1387) vii, **480b** – VII, **480a**
Muʿīn al-Fuḳarāʾ → Aḥmad b. Muḥammad (Maḥmūd)
Muʿīn al-Miskīn (1501) vii, **481b** – VII, **481a**
Muʿīn al-Mulk b. Ḳamar al-Dīn i, 295b, 296a; iii, 1158b – I, 304b, 305a; III, 1187a
Muʿīn al-Mulk Abu 'l-Maḥāsin, Sayyid al-Ruʾasāʾ (XI) vii, 489b – VII, 489b
al-Muʿizz (Mamlūk) → ʿIzz al-Dīn Aybak (Mamlūk)
al-Muʿizz b. Bādīs (Zīrid(e)) (1062) i, 533a, 860a, 1023b; iii, 137a, 324b, 385b, 386a, 688a, 695a, 903a, 936a; iv, 199a, 497a, 805a, 827b; v, 59b, 530b, 1182b, 1246b; vii, 474a, **481b**, 731a, 994a; s, 26b, 62b –
I, 549a, 884a, 1055a; III, 140a, 334b, 398a, b, 709b, 717b, 927b, 960b; IV, 207b, 208a, 518b, 837b, 860b; V, 61b, 534b, 1172b, 1237b; VII, 473b, **481a**, 732a, 995b; S, 27a, 63a
al-Muʿizz b. Muḥammad b. Walmiya iv, 337a – IV, 351b
al-Muʿizz b. Zīrī b. ʿAtiyya v, 1177b, 1178b, 1179a – V, 1167b, 1168b, 1169a
Muʿizz al-Dawla, Aḥmad b. Būya (Būyid(e)) (967) i, 11b, 19b, 20a, 419a, 711b, 866b, 899b, 1047a, 1352a; ii, 178b, 994a, 1082b; iii, 127b, 195b, 1156b, 1157a, 1175b, 1202a; iv, 23a, b, 266a, 855a; vi, 539a; vii, 358a, **484a**, 723b, 799a, 995a; s, 13a, b, 36b, 127a, 259a, 362a –
I, 11b, 20a, 21a, 431a, 733a, 890b, 926b, 1078b, 1391b; II, 184a, 1017a, 1108a; III, 130a, 200a, 1185a, b, 1204b, 1232b; IV, 25a-b, 278a, 888b; VI, 523b; VII, 360b, **484a**, 724b, 801a, 996b; S, 13a, 14a, 36b, 126a, 258b, 361b
Muʿizz al-Dīn al-Kurtī iv, 672a – IV, 699b
al-Muʿizz li-Dīn Allāh, Maʿadd (Fāṭimid(e)) (975) i, 592a, 814a, 823a, 1175b; ii, 195a, 329a, 491b, 494b, 495a, 853a, b, 855a, 860a, b, 861b, 963a, 994a, 1099a; iii, 246a, 298b, 785b, 840b, 886a, 1084a; iv, 198b, 662b, 663b; v, 862b; vi, 673b, 727b, 728a, 1040b; vii, 162a, **485a**; viii, 117a; ix, 45a; s, 62b, 236b, 252b –
I, 611b, 837b, 846a, 1210b; II, 201a, 338b, 503b, 507a, b, 873a, b, 875a, 879b, 880b, 881b, 985a, 1017a, 1125a; III, 253a, 307b,808b, 864b, 910a, 1111a; IV, 207b, 689b, 690a; V, 869b; VI, 659b, 716b, 717a, 1034a; VII, 163b, **485a**; VIII, 119b; IX, 45b; S, 63a, 236b, 252b
Muʿizz al-Dīn Ḥusayn ii, 1049b – II, 1074a
Muʿizz alDīn Kart (Harāt) → Kart

Muʿizz al-Dīn (Shihāb al-Dīn) Muḥammad b. Sām (Ghūrid(e)) → Muḥammad b. Sām I, Ghiyāth al-Dīn
Muʿizz al-Dīn Sandjar (Marw) iii, 603a – III, 623b
Muʿizz al-Dīn Sandjar Shāh b. Sayf al-Dīn Ghāzī II (Zangid(e)) (XII) vi, 781a – VI, 770b
al-Muʿizz Ismāʿīl b. Ṭughtakīn (Ayyūbid(e)) (XIII) vi, 433b, 434a – VI, 418b, 419b
Muʿizzī, Amīr Abū ʿAbd Allāh (1147) iii, 356a; vi, 275b, 276a, b, 609a – III, 367a; VI, 260b, 261a, 594a
Muʿizzī b. Burhānī iv, 61b, 466b; s, 384a – IV, 65a, 487b; S, 384b
Muʿizzī Naysabūrī, Muḥammad b. ʿAbd al-Malik (1125) vii, **489a**; viii, 71b, 76a, 970b – VII, **489a**; VIII, 73a, 78a, 1005a
Muʿizziyya ii, 1083a; vi, 321b – II, 1108b; VI, 305b
Muʿizziyya (Sicily/-e) → Taormina
Mujibur Raḥman (XX) viii, 243a – VIII, 248b
Muḳābal iii, 84a; iv, 259a – III, 86b; IV, 271a
Muḳābala (law/loi) iv, 193a – IV, 201a
Muḳābala (opposition/collation) vii, **490a** – VII, **489b**
al-Mukaʿbar (Baḥrayn) (VI) vii, 763b – VII, 765a
Muḳaddam vii, **492a** – VII, **491b**
Muḳaddam, Aḥmad Khān (XIX) vi, 502b – VI, 488a
al-Muḳaddam, Banū vi, 381a, 502b – VI, 365a, 488a
Muḳaddam, Dr. Muḥammad (XX) v, 1098a – V, 1094a
Muḳaddam b. Muʿāfā al-Ḳabrī (911) i, 601a; iv, 355a; vii, **492a**, 811a – I, 620b; IV, 370b; VII, **492a**, 813a
Muḳaddas Khurāsānī, Bābī vii, 303a – VII, 305a
al-Muḳaddasī, Shams al-Dīn Abū ʿAbd Allāh Muḥammad (X) i, 488a, 570b; ii, 127a, 581a, 582a; iii, 761b, 1078a, 1252b; iv, 45b, 220a, 223a, 1079a, 1088a; v, 328b, 330a; vi, 119a, b, 120b, 144b, 199a, 313b, 359a, 378a; vii, **492b**; s, 266a, 363a, 392a – I, 502b, 589a; II, 130b, 596a, b; III, 784b, 1104b, 1285a; IV, 48b, 229b, 233a, 1110b, 1119a; V, 328a, 330a; VI, 117a, 118b, 143a, 183a, 299a, 343a, 362b; VII, **492b**; S, 265b, 362b, 392b
Mukaddī iv, 735a; vii, **493b** – IV, 765a; VII, **493b**
Muḳaddima vii, **495b** – VII, **495a**
al-Mukaḥḥal → ʿAmr b. al-Ahtam
Muḳāʿis, Banū iv, 832a – IV, 865a
Muḳali ii, 43a – II, 43b
al-Mukallā i, 182a, 554b; ii, 173b; vi, 81b, 84a, 177a; vii, **496a**; s, 338b – I, 187a,, 572a; II, 179a; VI, 79b, 82a; VII, **495b**; S, 338a
al-Muḳallad b. al-Musayyib, Ḥusām al-Dawla (ʿUḳaylid(e)) (1000) vi, 900b; vii, **497a** – VI, 891b; VII, **497a**
Muḳallad b. Naṣr b. Munḳidh (1059) vii, 577b – VII, 578a
Mukallafa ii, 79b – II, 81a
Muḳallid → Ḳaṣṣ; Maddāḥ; Taḳlīd
al-Muḳammiṣ iv, 304a – IV, 317b
Mūḳān (Mūghān) vi, 499a; vii, **497b**; ix, 221a – VI, 484b; VII, **497a**; IX, 227a
Mūḳān b. Dalūla (X) vii, 498a – VII, 497b
al-Muḳannaʿ (VIII) i, 141b, 1294a; ii, 1107a; iii, 617a; iv, 16b, 45b; v, 64a, 181b, 855a, 1238b; vii, **500a**, 664a; s, 411a – I, 145b, 1333b; II, 1133a; III, 637b; IV, 17b, 48a; V, 66a, 179a, 862a, 1229b; VII, **499b**, 664a; S, 411b
Muḳannī iv, 529b – IV, 552b
Muḳanṭarāt vii, **500b** – VII, **500a**
Muḳāraʿa → Mukhāradja
Muḳāraḍa → Ḳirāḍ
Muḳarbaṣ(s) vii, **500b** – VII, **500b**
Mukārī vii, **501b** – VII, **501a**
Muḳarnas i, 1229a; ii, 777b, 864a; iv, 481a; vi, 366b; vii, **501b** – I, 1265b; II, 796a, 884a; IV, 502a; VI, 350b; VII, **501b**
Muḳarrab Khān (Delhi) (XIV) vi, 49a, b, 294a, b – VI, 47b, 48a, 279b
Muḳarrab Khān Gakkhaŕ (XVIII) ii, 973b, 1131b – II, 996a, 1158a
Mukarram b. Yām → al-Karam b. Yām
al-Muḳarram Aḥmad b. ʿAlī al-Ṣulayḥī i, 181b, 552a; iii, 125b – I, 186b, 570a; III, 128a
al-Muḳarrariyya iii, 284a – III, 292b
Mukarrib i, 547b; vi, 562b, 563a – I, 565a; VI, 547b
Mukarzal, Naʿʿūm ii, 471a – II, 483a
Mukarzal, Sallūm ii, 471b – II, 483b
Muḳāsama ii, 158a; iv, 1032a, 1037b, 1038a, 1055b; vii, **506b** – II, 163a; IV, 1063b, 1069a, b, 1087a; VII, **506b**
Mukāshafa iv, 696b, 697a, b – IV, 725a, b
Mukāsir ii, 97b – II, 99b
Muḳāṭaʿa i, 642b, 651b, 1080a, 1144b; ii, 33b, 118b, 147b, 188a, 907b; iii, 284a; iv, 225b, 323b, 1038a, 1046a; v, 792a, b; vii, **508a** – I, 663a, 672a, 1112a, 1179a; II, 34a, 121b, 151b, 193b, 929a; III, 293a; IV, 235b, 337b, 1070a, 1077b; V, 798b; VII, **508a**
Mukātaba i, 30a; ii, 302b, 328b; iii, 27a – I, 31a; II, 310b, 338a; III, 28b
Muḳātil b. ʿAṭiyya al-Maghrāwī (X) v, 1176b, 1177a, 1178b; vi, 605b – V, 1166b, 1167a, 1168b; VI, 590a
Muḳātil b. Mismaʿ (VIII) vi, 640b – VI, 625b
Muḳātil b. Sulaymān b. Bashīr al-Azdī (767) vii, **508b**, 571a, 607a; x, 160b, 391a; s, 90b – VII, **508b**, 571b, 607a; X, 172a, 419a; S, 90a
Muḳaṭṭaʿāt iv, 58a; vii, **509a** – IV, 61a; **509a**
al-Muḳaṭṭam ii, 288b, 403b, 466b; vi, 122b, 123a, 413a; vii, **509a** – II, 296b, 414b, 478b; VI, 120b, 398a; VII, **509b**
al-Muḳawḳis (VII) i, 1016a; v, 90b; vi, 413a, 575a; vii, 154b, 372a, 509b, **511a** – I, 1047a; V, 92b; VI, 398a, 560a; VII, 156b, 373b, 509b, **511a**
Muḳayyin iv, 822b – IV, 855b
al-Mukhā i, 932b, 1140b; iv, 449b, 450a; vii, **513b**; s, 30b – I, 961a, 1175a; IV, 470a; VII, **513b**; S, 30b
al-Mukhabbal b. Rabīʿa s, 394b – S, 395a
al-Mukhaḍḍaba iii, 49b – III, 51b
Mukhaddirāt → Afyūn; Bandj
Mukhaḍram i, 12a, 140a; vii, **516a** – I, 12a, 144b; VII, **516a**
Mukhallefāt i, 1147b, 1148a; vii, **517a** – I, 1181b, 1182a; VII, **517a**
al-Mukhammis → al-Musammaṭ
Mukhammisa iv, 1132b, 1133a; vii, 459b, 468b, **517a** – IV, 1164b; VII, 460a, 468a, **517a**
Mukhāradja vii, **518a** – VII, **518a**
Mukhāriḳ, Abu 'l-Muhannāʾ b. Yaḥyā (844) vii, **518a**; s, 64a – VII, **518b**; S, 64b
Mukhāriḳ b. Shihāb (620) vi, 954a – VI, 946b
Mukharrim i, 897b, 900a, 901a – I, 924b, 927a, 928a
al-Mukharrimī → Abū Saʿd al-Mubārak
Mukhāṭara vii, **518b** – VII, **519a**
Mukhattam vii, **519a** – VII, **519a**
Mukhayriḳ (VII) ii, 844b – II, 864a
Mukhbir al-Saltana → Mahdī Ḳulī Hidāyat
Mukhlisī → Muṣṭafā b. Süleymān I
Mukhtār vii, **519a** – VII, **519b**
Mukhtār (al-Maʿḳil) vi, 141b – VI, 140a
al-Mukhtār, Muḥammad b. ʿĪsā (1524) x, 248a – X, 266b

al-Mukhtār b. Abī ʿUbayd al-Thakafī (687) i, 5a, 15a, 41a, 45a, 50b, 55a, 76b, 304a, 850b; ii,198b, 523b; iii, 236a, 715a, 718a, 987a, 1255a, 1265b; iv, 44b, 836a, b; v, 349b, 350a; vi, 640b; vii, 357a, 400b, 403a, 470a, **521a**, 605b, 650a, 689a; ix, 421b; x, 843a; s, 357b –
I, 5a, 15b, 42a, 46a, 52a, 57a, 78b, 313b, 874a; II, 204b, 536b; III, 243a, 737b, 740b, 1011b, 1287b, 1298b; IV, 47a, 869a, b; V, 350b; VI, 625b; VII, 359b, 402a, 404a, 470a, **521b**, 605a, 649b, 689b; IX, 435b; X, ; S, 357b
al-Mukhtār b. ʿAwf al-Azdī, Abū Ḥamza (748) i, 550b; ii, 141a; iii, 651b, 658a; iv, 1076a; vi, 147b; vii, **524b**; x, 845a; s, 337b, 338a –
I, 568a; II, 145a; III, 673a, 679b; IV, 1108a; VI, 146a; VII, **524b**; X, ;S, 337b
Mukhtār b. Maḥmūd al-Zāhidī iv, 1062b – IV, 1094a
Mukhtar b. ʿUmar Tal i, 297a – I, 306a
Mukhtar Auez Ulï (1961)) vi, 768b – VI, 757b
Mukhtār al-Bakkālī, al-Ḥādjdj (1839) vi, 249a, b, 250b, 255b – VI, 233a, b, 234b, 239b
Mukhtār Bey (Maṣawwaʿ) (XIX) vi, 643a – VI, 628a
al-Mukhtār al-Kabīr, Sīdī v, 393b, 394a –
V, 394b
Mukhtār Pasha, Ghāzī Aḥmed (1919) vi, 372b; vii, **525a** – VI, 357a; VII, **525a**
Mukhtār Pasha Tepedelenli (XIX) i, 398b, 399a – I, 410a, b
al-Mukhtār al-Ṣaghīr, Sīdī v, 394a – V, 395a
al-Mukhtāra i, 133b, 389a; ii, 4441; vii, **526a** –
I, 137b, 400a; II, 455b; VII, **526a**
Mukhtārāt vii, **526b** – VII, **527a**
Mukhtārī, Sirādj al-Dīn (1159) s, 416a – S, 416b
Mukhtārī Ghaznawī, Abū ʿUmar ʿUthmān b. ʿUmar (1118) vii, **535a** – VII, **535a**
Mukhtāriyya v, 393b, 394a – V, 394b, 395a
al-Mukhtārūn v, 50a – V, 51b
Mukhtaṣar vii, **536a** – VII, **536a**
Mukhtaṣṣ Khān (XVI) iv, 276b; vi, 546 – IV, 288b; VI, 52b
Muḳīm b. Arghūn Khān i, 227b, 627b; ii, 1049b; iv, 357a, 536b – I, 234b, 648a; II, 1074a; IV, 372b, 560a
Muḳīm Abu 'l-Manṣūr Khān, Mīrzā (Ṣafdar Djang) vii, 195a – VII, 195b
Muḳīm Khān Sārawī v, 663b – V, 669a
Muḳḳrān, ūlād iv, 478b – IV, 499b
Muḳrā vii, **540a** – VII, **540a**
Mukram i, 711b – I, 733a
Mukrān → Makrān
Muḳrānī → Moḳrānī
Mukrī, Banū iii, 1102b, 1109a; v, 460b; vi, 128b; viii, 895b – III, 1129b, 1136b; V, 463a; VI, 126b; VIII, 926b
al-Mukrī (Morocco/Maroc) vii, 415a – VII, 416b
al-Muḳrīʾ, Muḥammad vi, 374b – VI, 359a
Mukrī Kurd(e)s (amīrs) vi, 502b; ix. 92b –
VI, 487b; IX, 16b
al-Mukrī al-Rāzī, ʿAbd sl-Djabbār b. ʿAbd Allāh (XII) x, 40a – X, 41b
Mukrianī, Ḥusayn Ḥuznī v, 483b – V, 486b
Muḳrim i, 553b, 942b; iv, 764b – I, 571a, 971b; IV, 795a
Mukrin b. Adjwad s, 234b – S, 234a
Muḳtaʿ ii, 272b, 273a, 508a; v, 862b – II, 280b, 281a, 520b; V, 869b
al-Muḳtabis i, 82b, 600b – I, 85a, 620a
Muḳtaḍab vii, **540a** – VII, **540a**
al-Muḳtadī bi-Amr Allāh (ʿAbbāsid(e)) (1094)
i, 901a; iv, 458a, 942b; vi, 274b, 275a, 379b, 523b; vii, **540a**; viii, 70b; ix, 481b; s, 192b, 194a – I, 928a; IV, 478b, 975b; VI, 259b, 260a, 364a, 508a; VII, **540a**; VIII, 72`; IX, 500b; S, 193a, b
al-Muḳtadir bi-'llāh (ʿAbbāsid(e)) (932) i, 19a, 387a, 446a, 688b, 867a, 898a, 899a, 936a; ii, 344b, 383b, 388b, 462a, 1080b; iii, 100b, 126b, 344b, 388a, 619b, 691b, 692a, 739a, 750b, 757b, 767b, 768a, 886b, 892b, 1201b; iv, 214b; v, 132a, 737b; vi, 206a, 498a, 518a, 539a; vii, 414a, **541b**, 575b; s, 118a, 192a, 199a, 372a, 385b –
I, 20a, 398b, 458b, 709b, 891b, 925a, b, 965a; II, 354b, 393a, 399a, 473b, 1105b; III, 103a, 129b, 355a, 400b, 640a, 713b, 714a, 761b, 773b, 780b, 790b, 791a, 910b, 916b, 1232a; IV, 224a; V, 135a, 743a; VI, 190a, 483b, 503a, 523b; VII, 415b, **541b**, 576a; S, 117a, 193a, 199a, 372a, 386a
al-Muḳtadir b. Hūd → Aḥmad I (Hūdid(e))
al-Muḳtafī bi-'llāh(ʿAbbāsid(e)) (908) i, 11a, 19a, 898a; ii, 461b; iii, 345a, 892b, 1044b; iv, 494a, 940a; vi, 275a; vii, **542b**; s, 118a, 304b –
I, 11a, 19b, 924b; II, 473b; III, 355b, 916b, 1070b; IV, 515a, 973a; VI, 260a; VII, **542b**; S, 117b, 304b
al-Muḳtafī li-Amr Allāh (ʿAbbāsid(e)) (1160) i, 865b; iii, 160b, 197a, 1255b; vi, 275b, 870b; vii, **543b**; s, 193b – I, 890a; III, 164a, 201b, 1288b; VI, 260b, 861b; VII, **543b**; S, 194a
Muktagīrī s, 280a – S, 280a
al-Muḳtanā, Bahāʾ al-Dīn (XI) i, 552a; ii, 632b; iii, 154b; vii, **544a** – I, 569b; II, 648b; III, 158a; VII, **544a**
al-Muḳtaṭaf ii, 288b, 403b, 428a, 466b – II, 296b, 414a, 439a, 478b
al-Muḳurra (al-Maḳurra) iv, 568a; vi, 574b; vii, **544b**; viii, 89b – IV, 590a; VI, 559b; VII, **544b**; VIII, 91b
Mukūs → Maks
al-Mulāʿī · → Abū Nuʿaym
Muladī → Muwallad
Mulalhil ii, 1028b – II, 1052b
Mulāṭafa, mulaṭṭifāt ii, 304a – II, 312b
Mulaththamūn v, 652b, 744a, 769b – V, 656b, 749b, 775b
Mūlāy → Mawlāy
Mūlāy ʿAlī Bū Ghālem iv, 729a – IV, 758a
Mūlāy Būʿazzā i, 159b – I, 164a
Mulāy Bushʿīb → Abū Shuʿayb
al-Mulayda (battle/bataille) (1891) viii,439a; s, 3b – VIII, 453b; S, 2b
Mulayḥ b. al-Ḥakam viii, 377a – VIII, 390a
Mülāzemet vii, **545a** – VII, **545a**
Mulāzim vii, **545b** – VII, **545b**
Mulāzimiyya v, 1252a, b – V, 1242b, 1243a, b
Mulham, Dirghām Nāṣir al-Muslimīn (XII) ii, 318a, b – II, 327b
Mulḥid vii, **546a** – VII, **546a**
Mulḥim (Maʿn) (XVII) vi, 343b – VI, 328a
Mūlid → Mawlid
Mulk v, 623a; vii, **546b** – V, 627a; **546b**
Mulk Amān (Chitral) (XIX) ii, 30a – II, 30b
Mulk-ārā (Ḳādjār) (XIX) vi, 484a – VI, 470a
Mulkiyya(e) ii, 425b, 692a; iv, 909a; v, 904a; vii, **547a** – II, 436b, 709b; IV, 942b; V, 910a; VII, **547a**
Mullā → Molla
Mullā Apāḳ s, 331b – S, 331a
Mullā Ilāhī, ʿAbd Allāh (1490) → Ilāhī, Mullā ʿAbd Allāh
Mullā Miskīn (1501) i, 423b – I, 435b
Mullā Muḥsin → Muḥsin-i Fayḍ-i Kāshānī
Mullā Ṣadrā Shīrāzī, Ṣadr al-Dīn (1640) i, 596a; ii, 104a, 774a; iii, 103b, 664a, 1130b; iv, 50b, 121a, 509a; v, 605a; vii, 132a, 452b, 475b, **547b**; viii, 541b, 782a; s, 24a, 305a, 308a, b –
I, 615b; II, 106b, 792b; III, 106a, 685b, 1158b; IV, 53b, 126b, 531a; V, 609a; VII, 134a, 453b, 475a,

547b; VIII, 559a, 808a; S, 24a, 305a, 308a, b
Mullā Shāh Badakhshī (1661) ii, 134b; vii, 189a; ix, **196a** – II, 138a; VII, 189b; IX, **201b**
Mullā Shaydā → Shaydā, Mullā
Mullā Wadjhī (1609) vi, 837b – VI, 828a
Mullagorī, Banū vii, **548b** – VII, **548b**
Mullāʾī i, 225b; iii, 1102b – I, 232a; III, 1130a
Multān i, 218a, 230b, 628a, 912a; iii, 419b, 433b, 441b, 443b, 633a, b, 634a, 1155b; iv, 199a; v, 26a, 782b, 783a, 885a; vi, 48a, b, 49b, 50a, 65a, b, 112a, 127b, 131a, 294b, 691a, 695b; vii, 405b, 409b, 412a, **548b**; viii, 68a, 253a; s, 10b, 66b, 105a, 284b, 329b, 332a, 423b – I, 224a, 237b, 648b, 939b; III, 433a, 447b, 456a, 458b, 654a, b, 655a, 1184a; IV, 207b; V, 27a, 788b, 789a, 891b; VI, 46b, 47a, 48a, 63a, b, 110a, 125b, 129a, 279b, 678b, 683b; VII, 407a, 411a, 413b, **548b**; VIII, 69b, 255a; S, 10a, 67a, 104b, 284b, 329a, 331b, 423b
Multān Mall i, 218a – I, 224a
al-Multazam iv, 318a – IV, 332a
Mültezim (Multazim) ii, 147b, 148a, b; iii, 1154a; vii, **550b** – II, 151b, 152a, b; III, 1182b; VII, **550b**
Mulūk al-Ṭawāʾif (Persia/la Perse) vii, **551a** – VII, **551a**
Mulūk al-Ṭawāʾif (Reyes de Taifas) i, 6a, b, 94b, 130b, 155b, 242a, 495a, 865a, 1320a; ii, 331b; iii, 496a, 640a, 791b; vii, **552a** – I, 6a, 97a, 134a, 160a, 249b, 510a, 889a, 1360b; II, 341a; III, 513a, 661b, 814b; VII, **552b**
Mulūya, Wādī s, 113b – S, 113a
Mumahhid al-Dawla Saʿīd Abū Manṣūr (Marwānid(e)) (Diyār Bakr) (1011) i, 1298b; iii, 130b; v, 453a; vi, 626a, 930b; vii, 116a – I, 1338a; III, 133a; V, 455b; VI, 611a, 922a; VII, 118a
Mumayyiz → Bāligh
al-Mumazzaḳ i, 74a – I, 76a
Muʾmin vii, **554b** – VII, **555a**
Muʾmin (Mōmin), Ḥakīm Muḥammad Khān (1851) vii, **555a** – VII, **555b**
Muʾmin b. Aḥmad i, 1306b, 1307b – I, 1346b, 1348a
Muʾmin b. al-Ḥasan i, 1306b, 1307b – I, 1346b, 1348a
Muʾmin ʿĀrif (Yamanī) vi, 410a – VI, 394b
Muʾmin Khān (Gudjarāt) i, 1053a; ii, 1130a; – I, 1084b; II, 1156b
Mūʾmin Khān (poet/poète) (1851) iii, 119b; v, 961b – III, 122a; V, 966a
Muʾmina Khatūn iii, 1110b – III, 1137b
Muʾminid(e)s → al-Muwaḥḥidūn
Mūmiyāʾ vii, **556a** – VII, **556b**
Mumtaḥin al-Ḍawla s, 109a – S, 108b
Mumtāz, Barkhwurdār b. Maḥmūd Turkmān (XVIII) vii, **557a** – VII, **557a**
Mumtāz Efendi (1871) iv, 1126a – IV, 1158a
Mumtāz Khan → Iʿtibar Khān
Mumtāz Maḥall (1631) i, 253b, 686a, 1161a, 1331a; vii, **557a**; x, 58b – I, 261b, 707a, 1196a, 1371b; VII, **557b**; X, 60b
Munā vi, 154a, 155a, 162a – VI, 152a, 156a
Munabbāt, Banū vi, 142a, b – VI, 140a, 141a
Munādī vii, **557a** – VII, **557b**
Munādjāt vii, **557b** – VII, **558a**
Munadjdjim vii, **557b** – VII, **558a**
al-Munadjdjim (IX) vi, 99a – VI, 96b
Munadjdjim, Abu ʾl-ʿAbbās Hibat Allāh (X) vii, 561a – VII, 561b
Munadjdjim, Abū ʿAbd Allāh Hārūn (901) vii, 561a, 559b – VII, 560b, 561b
Munadjdjim, Abū Aḥmad Yaḥyā (912) vii, 559a – VII, 559b
Munadjdjim, Abū ʿAlī Yaḥyā (830) vii, 558b – VII, 559a
Munadjdjim, Abu ʾl-Ḥasan Aḥmad (939) vii, 559b – VII, 561a
Munadjdjim, Abu ʾl-Ḥasan ʿAlī (888) vii, 559a – VII, 555a
Munadjdjim, Abu ʾl-Ḥasan ʿAlī (963) vii, 560a – VII, 561a
Munadjdjim, Abū ʿĪsā Aḥmad (X) vii, 559b – VII, 561a
Munadjdjim, Abu ʾl-Ḳāsim Yūsuf (X) vii, 560a – VII, 561a
Munadjdjim, Abū Manṣūr Abān (VIII) vii, 558b – VII, 559a
al-Munadjdjim, ʿAlī b. Hārūn (X) s, 362b – S, 362a
Munadjdjim, Banu ʾl- i, 1141a; vii, 358b, **558b**; s, 375b – I, 1175b; VII, 361a, **559a**; S, 375b
al-Munadjdjim, Kanka al-Hindī vi, 412a – VI, 396b
al-Munadjdjim, Yaḥyā b. ʿAlī (913) iv, 111a; v, 516b; vii, 681b – IV, 116a; V, 517a; VII, 681b
Munadjdjim Bāshī → Münedjdjim-bashî
Munāfara iv, 77b – IV, 81b
Munaffidh i, 1148b; ii, 146a – I, 1183a; II, 150a
al-Munāfiḳūn i, 53b; v, 996a, b; vii, **561a**, 852b – I, 55a; V, 991b; VII, **561b**, 854a
Munāhada → Mukhāradja
Munakhkhal b. Djamīl s, 233a – S, 232b
al-Munakhkhal al-Yashkurī vii, **562b**, 841a – VII, **563b**, 842b
al-Munakkab vii, **563b** – VII, **564a**
Munāsafa vii, **564a** – VII, **564b**
Munāshada vii, 564b – VII, 565a
al-Munāwī, ʿAbd al-Raʾūf (1621) iii, 29a; vii, **565a** – III, 30b; VII, **565b**
al-Munāwī, Yaḥyā (Shaykh al-Islām) (XVI) vii, 565a – VII, 565b
al-Munawwar, Muḥammad b. s, 154a – S, 154b
al-Munawwar ʿAlī Shāh (1884) iv, 51a – IV, 54b
al-Munayyir vi, 114a – VI, 111b
al-Munayzila s, 234b – S, 234a
Munāẓara iii, 431b; v, 1130b, 1223b; vii, **565b** – III, 445b; V, 1126b, 1214a; VII, **566a**
al-Munāzī, Abū Naṣr Aḥmad v, 929b – V, 934b
Munāzil, ʿAbd Allāh (Malāmatiyya) vi, 225a – VI, 218b
Mundā iii, 412a – III, 425a
al-Mundhir I (Lakhmid(e)) i, 939a; v, 633a – I, 967b; V, 637a
al-Mundhir III Ibn al-Nuʿmān (Lakhmid(e)) (554) i, 99a, 115b, 451b, 526b, 527a, 548b; ii, 1021a; iii, 94a, 222a, 462b; v, 633a, 640a; vi, 951a; ix, 77a – I, 101b, 119a, 464b, 542b, 543a, 566a; II, 1044b; III, 96b, 229a, 479a; V, 637a, 644b; VI, 943b; IX, 80a
al-Mundhir IV (Lakhmid(e)) (580) v, 633b; vii, **568b** – V, 637b; VII, **569a**
al-Mundhir b. al-Ḥārith b. Djabala (Ghassānid(e)) (582) i, 1249b; ii, 244b, 1021a, b; v, 633b; vii, 568b; viii, 630a – I, 1287b; II, 251b, 1044b, 1045a; V, 637b; VII, 569b; VIII, 648b
al-Mundhir b. Ḥasān al-ʿAbdī vi, 677a – VI, 664a
al-Mundhir b. Māʾ al-Samāʾ → al-Mundhir III
al-Mundhir b. Muḥammad (Umayyad(e), al-Andalus) (888) i, 49a, 85b; vi, 222a; vii, **568b**; s, 92a, 153a – I, 50b, 88a; VI, 215b; VII, **569b**; S, 92a, 153a
al-Mundhir b. al-Muḳtadir ii, 112a – II, 114b
al-Mundhir b. al-Nuʿmān (VII) vii, 671a – VII, 671a
Mundhir b. Saʿīd al-Ballūṭī (966) i, 497a, 600a; ii, 744b; vii, **569a** – I, 512a, 619b; II, 763a; VII, **570a**

al-Mundhir b. Sāwā (Sāwī) (VII) vii, **570a** – VII, **571a**
al-Mundhir b. Yaḥyā al-Tudjībī iii, 147a, 743a – III, 150b, 766a
al-Mundhirī, Abū Muḥammad al-Ḳawī s, 194a – S, 195a
al-Mundhirī, Muḥammad b. Dja'far i, 114b, 822a – I, 117b, 845a
Mundjī i, 225a – I, 231b
Münedjdjim Bashî (1702) i, 836a; ii, 110a; iii, 392b; iv, 1175a; vii, **572b**; viii, 1a; s, 59a – I, 859a, II, 112b; III, 405a; IV, 1208b; VII, **573a**; VIII, 1a; S, 59b
Mungi Śivgaon (treaty/traité) vi, 535a – VI, 519b
Mungīr i, 1209b, 1210a; vi, 47a; vii, **573a** – I, 1245b, 1246a; VI, 45b; VII, **573b**
Municipality/-é → Baladiyya
Münīf (1733) s, 83a – S, 83a
Münīf Muṣṭafā Efendi (XVIII) vi, 56b – VI, 54b
Münīf Pasha (1910) ii, 473b, 532a, 682b; vi, 92b; vii, **573a**, 813b – II, 485b, 545a, 699b; VI, 90b; VII, **573b**, 815a
Mun'im Khān (Mun'im Beg) (1575) i, 1136b; ii, 183b, 498b, 499b; iv, 1020a; v, 638b; vii, 133b, 330b, **573b**; ix, 196a – I, 1170b; II, 189a, 511a, 512a; IV, 1052a; V, 642b; VII, 135b, 332b, **574a**; IX, 201b
Munīr al-Dawla (XIX) vi, 484b – VI, 470b
Munīr al-Khādim (X) vi, 545b – VI, 530a
Munīr Lāhawrī (1644) vii, **574a** – VII, **574b**
Munīra al-Mahdiyya (1965) x, 144a – X, 154b
Münīrī Belghrādī i, 324b; ii, 968b – I, 334b; II, 990b
Mu'nis (Khīwa) (1829) vii, **574b** – VII, **575a**
Mu'nis (Lakhnaw) (XIX) vi, 611b – VI, 596b
Mu'nis 'Alī Shāh, Ḥādjdj Mīrzā 'Abd al-Ḥusayn (Ni'mat Allāhī (1953) viii, 47b – VIII, 48b
Mu'nis Dede Derwīsh (1732) vii, **575a** – VII, **575b**
Mu'nis al-Faḥl (- al-Khāzin) (914) vii, **575a** – VII, **575b**
Mu'nis al-Khādim → Mu'nis al-Muẓaffar
Mu'nis al-Muẓaffar, Abu 'l-Ḥasan, al-Khādim (933) i, 11a, 19a, 34a, 386b, 387a, 446a; ii, 191b, 325b; iii, 46a, 126b, 619b, 620a; iv, 22b, 423b; v, 1243b; vii, 192a, 414a, 541b, **575a**, 994b – I, 11a, 20a, 34b, 398a, b, 458b; II, 198a, 335b; III, 47b, 129a, 640a, b; IV, 24a, 442a; V, 1234a; VII, 192a, 415a, 541b, **575b**, 996a
Mu'nis b. Yaḥyā al-Mirdāsī iii, 386a; iv, 337a – III, 398b; IV, 351b
Mu'nisa (Kayna) s, 252b – S, 252b
Munkar (Ḥadīth) vii, **575b** – VII, **576b**
Munkar wa-Nakīr i, 187a, 334b; iii, 1231b; iv, 667b; vi, 217b, 219b; vii, **576b** – I, 192a, 345a; III, 1263b; IV, 694b; VI, 210b, 203b; VII, **577a**
Munḳidh, Banū vi, 789b; vii, **577b**; ix, 410a – VI, 779b; VII, **578a**; IX, 424a
Munsariḥ → 'Arūḍ
Munshī vii, **580b** – VII, **580b**
Munshi Abdullah (1854) vi, 240b – VI, 205b
Munshī 'Aṭa Muḥammad (1855) ix, 440a – IX, 457a
Munshī Harkaran (XVII) vii, 343a – VII, 345a
Munshī Mawlawī → 'Abd al-Karīm Munshī
Munshī Nawal Kishōr (1895) x, 879a – X,
Munshī Nawbat Rā'e Naẓar (XIX) vi, 612a – VI, 597a
Munṣif vii, **580b** – VII, **581a**
Munṣif Bey iii, 636b – III, 658a
Munṣifa (Munṣifāt) vii, **580b** – VII, **581a**
Muntadjab al-Dīn (1179) vii, **581a** – VII, **581b**
Muntadjab al-Dīn Abu 'l-Ḥasan 'Alī al-Ḳum(m)ī) (XII) iii, 1151b – III, 1179b
Muntadjib al-Dīn, "Zar Bakhsh" (Khuldābād) vi, 127a – VI, 125a
al-Muntafiḳ, Banū i, 270b, 684a, 873a, 942a, 1086a, 1087a, 1096a, b; ii, 77a; iii, 1107b, 1257b; v, 81a; vii, **582a**, 674a; ix, 801b; s, 119a, 234b – I, 279a, 705a, 897a, 971a, 1118b, 1119b, 1129a, b; II, 78b; III, 1134b, 1290a; V, 83a; VII, **582a**, 673b; IX, 836a; S, 118b, 234b
al-Muntafiḳ b. 'Āmir b. 'Ukayl, Banū vii, 582a – VII, 582a
Muntafiḳ district ('Irāḳ) vi, 615a; vii, **582a** – VI, 600a; VII, **582b**
Munṭaḳa i, 297a – I, 306b
al-Muntakhab → Abū Zakariyyā' Yaḥyā III
Muntakhab al-Dawla iv, 842a – IV, 875a
al-Muntaṣir (Ḥafṣid(e)) iii, 69a; iv, 416a – III, 71a; IV, 434a
al-Muntaṣir bi-'llāh (Abbāsid(e)) (862) i, 402b; ii, 461b, 837b; vi, 625b; vii, **583a**, 777b – I, 414a; II, 473b, 857b; VI, 610b; VII, **583b**, 779b
al-Muntaṣir b. Abi 'l-'Abbās (Marīnid(e)) (XIV) vi, 594a – VI, 578b
al-Muntaṣir b. Abī Liḥya (Gafsa) (XI) vi, 355b – VI, 339b
al-Muntaṣir b. Khazrūn v, 1181a, 1182b – V, 1171a, 1172b, 1173a
Muntazah (palace/palais) s, 301a – S, 300b
Muntaẓirī, Āyatullāh (XX) vi, 554a; vii, 300a – VI, 538b; VII, 302a
Munūf → Manūf
Munyat al-Aṣbagh (Miṣr) vii, 149a – VII, 151a
Munyat Ibn al-Khaṣīb vi, 651a – VI, 636b
Murabba' → Musammaṭ
Murabbīh Rabbuh b. Mā' al-'Aynayn, Shaykh (1942) vii, 621a – VII, 621a
al-Murābī, Abu 'l-'Abbās iv, 736a – IV, 766a
Murābiṭ → Ribāṭ
al-Murābiṭūn (Almoravid(e)s) i, 7a, 78b, 165a, 242b, 251a, 367a, 389a, 495a, 602a, 986a, 1092a, 1176a; ii, 134a, 1007a; iii, 207a, 800a, 959a, 1043a; v, 744a, 1178b, 1189b; vi, 134a, 216b, 259a, 279b, 281a, 427a, 520b, 571b, 576b, 590b, 592a; vii, **583b**, 613a; viii, 616b; ix, 754b, 899b; s, 27a, 80b – I, 7a, 81a, 170a, 250a, 258b, 378a, 400b, 510a, 621b, 1016b, 1124b, 1211a; II, 137a, 1030b; III, 213a, 823b, 984a, 1069a; V, 749b, 1168b, 1179b; VI, 132b, 200b, 243a, 264b, 265b, 412a, b, 505b, 556b, 561b, 575a, 576b, 577a; VII, **584a**, 612b; VIII, 636a; IX, 787b, 935b; S, 27b, 80b
—administration i, 445b, 1148b; ii, 145b, 230a; v, 626a – I, 458b, 1183a; II, 149b, 237a; V, 630a
—constructions i, 499a, 1320b; ii, 818b, 821b, 1015a; iii, 300b; iv, 633a; v, 1150a – I, 514b, 1361a; II, 838a, 841a, 1039a; III, 309b; IV, 659a; V, 1140b
—history/histoire i, 44a, 156b; iii, 932b; v, 653b – I, 45a, 161a; III, 957a; V, 657b
Murād I (Ottoman) (1389) i, 322b, 394a, 468a, b, 481a, 510b, 1117b, 1191b, 1263a, 1302b, 1325b; ii, 15b, 210b, 291b, 444b, 684b, 983b; iv, 376a, 623a, 945a; v, 44b, 276a; vi, 89a, 290b, 530b; vii, **592b**; viii, 193a; s, 314b, 331a – I, 332b, 405b, 482a, b, 495a, 526a, 1151b, 1227a, 1301b, 1342b, 1366b; II, 15b, 217a, 299b, 456b, 701b, 1006a; IV, 392a, 648a, 978a; V, 46a, 274a; VI, 87a, 275b, 514b; VII, **592a**; VIII, 196a; S, 314b, 329b
Murād II (Ottoman) (1451) i, 199a, 468a, 654b, 655b, 992a, 1061a, 1225b, 1248a, 1252b, 1334a; ii, 82b, 98a, 210b, 443a, 599b, 684a,b, 685a, 697a, 703a, 721a, 984b, 990a, 1086a; iv, 139b, 624a, 656a, 968b, 1093a; v, 1170a; vi, 70a, 73a, 530a, b; vii, **594b**; viii,

193b; s, 274a, 315a –
I, 204b, 482a, 675a, 676a, 1023a, 1093a, 1262a, 1286a, 1290b, 1374b; II, 84a, 100b, 217a, 454b, 614b, 701a, b, 702a, 714b, 721a, 739b, 1007b, 1013a, 1111b; IV, 145a, 648b, 682b, 1001a, 1124a; V, 1159b; VI, 68a, 71a, 514a, b; VII, **594a**; VIII, 196b; S, 273b, 314b
Murād III (Ottoman) (1595) i, 775b, 1017b, 1208b; ii, 82b, 208a, 442b, 615a, 881a; iv, 638a; v, 27b, 766a, 814b, 1170a; vi, 377a, 505a, 601b, 799a; vii, **595b**, 601a; s, 138a –
I, 798b, 1049a, 1244b; II, 84a, 214b, 454b, 630b, 901b; IV, 664a; V, 28a, 772a, 820b, 1160a; VI, 361b, 490b, 586b, 789a; VII, **595b**, 600b; S, 137b
Murād IV (Ottoman) (1640) i, 4a, 310b, 424a, 468b, 475a, 481a, 775b, 826a, 904a; ii, 49a, 119b, 345b, 718a; iii, 91b, 352a, 357a, 626a, 1257a; iv, 451b, 574a, 717a, 728b; v, 18b, 34b, 272b, 493b; vi, 150a, 202b, 232a, 345b; vii, 319a, **597b**; s, 49a, b, 94b, 171b, 315b –
I, 4b, 320b, 436a, 482b, 489a, 495a, 799a, 849a, 931b; II, 50a, 122a, 355a, 736b; III, 94a, 363a, 368a,647a, 1290a; IV, 472a, 596b, 745b, 757b; V, 19a, 35b, 270a, 496b; VI, 149a, 186b, 225b, 329b; VII, 321b, **597a**; S, 49b, 50a, 94a, 172a, 315a
Murād V (Ottoman) (1904) i, 63b; ii, 49a, 642a; iv, 876a, b; vii, **599a**; S, 63a – I, 65b; II, 50a, 658a; IV, 909a, b; VII, **599a**; S, 63b
Murād b. Amīr Shāhī, Sulṭān (Marʿashī) (XVI) vi, 514b, 515a – VI, 500a
Murād II b. Mīrza Khān, Mīr Sulṭān (Marʿashī) (XVI) vi, 515a – VI, 515a
Murād, Banū iii, 223a; v, 954a; vi, 472a; vii, **591b** – III, 229b; V, 958a; VI, 458a; VII, **591a**
Murād, Ḥadjdjī → Shāmil
Murād, Muḥammad (Mat-Murad, Dīwān-begi) (XIX) s, 228b – S, 228b
Murād b. Aḥmad b. Bāyazīd iv, 716b – IV, 745b
Murād (Shāh –) b. Akbar (Pahari) (Mughal) (1599) i, 81a; ii, 981b; vi, 814b; vii, **592a**; viii, 74a – I, 83a; II, 1003b; VI, 805a; VII, **592a**; VIII, 75b
Murād b. Dāniyāl Biy Atalïḳ, Shāh (Mangït) (1785) vi, 418b, 419a, 621a; s, 97a – VI, 403b, 404a, 606a; S, 96b
Murād b. Djem (1523) ii, 530b; viii, 570a – II, 543b; VIII, 588b
Murād b. Mālik b. Udad vii, 591b – VII, 591a
Murād b. Yaʿḳūb i, 311b, 312a – I, 321b
Murād Bakhsh b. Shāh Djahān (1661) i, 768b; ii, 134b; iv, 914b; vi, 345b; vii, **599b**, 601b –
I, 791b; II, 138a; IV, 947b; VI, 329b; VII, **599b**, 601a
Murād Agha (1556) x, 213b – X, 230b
Murād Beg (Tardjumān) (XVI) x, 237a – X, 255b
Murād Beg (Ḳunduz) (1838) i, 853a; ii, 638a – I, 876b; II, 654a
Murād Beg Tardić v, 774b – V, 780b
Murād Bey, Muḥammad (neo-Mamlūk) (1801) iii, 992a; iv, 853a; vi, 325b; vii, 179a, 180b, 420b; ix, 229a; s, 38b –
III, 1016b; IV, 886a; VI, 310a; VII, 181a, 182a, 422a; IX, 234b; S, 38b
Murād Bey Abū Bālā (1702) iv, 828a – IV, 861a
Murād Bey Sulaymān (XX) vi, 93a, 614b – VI, 91a, 599b
Murād Girāy (Crimea/-ée) (1683) iv, 178b; v, 140a; vi, 989a – IV, 185b; V, 142b; VI, 981b
Murād Ḥādjdjī → Shāmil
Murād Khān b. Ismāʿīl Pasha i, 920a – I, 948a
Murād Khān (Kashmīr) → Iʿtiḳād Khān
Murād Pasha (1473) iv, 230a – IV, 240b
Murād Pasha Ḳuyudju (1611) i, 267b, 511a, 904a; ii, 635a, 750a; iv, 499a, 970a; vii, 275b, **600a**; viii, 237a; s, 239a –
I, 275b, 526b, 931a; II, 651a, 768a; IV, 520b, 1002a; VII, 277b, **600a**; VIII, 242b; S, 239a
Murād Raʾīs v, 504a – V, 507b
Murād Sulṭān i, 1076b – I, 1108b
Murād-suyu (Murat Su) → al-Furāt
Murādābād iv, 749b; vi, 48a, 49a, 50a vii, **601b**; s, 73b, 74a, 321b – IV, 779b; VI, 46b, 47b, 48a; VII, **601a**; S, 74a, b, 331a
Murādī → Murād III; Murād IV
al-Murādī, ʿAbd al-Raḥmān (1803) vii, **602a** – VII, **602a**
al-Murādī, Abū Bakr Muḥammad b. al-Ḥasan al-Ḥaḍramī, Imām (1096) vii, 613a – VII, 613a
al-Murādī, ʿAlī (1771) vii, **602a** – VII, **601b**
al-Murādī, Ḥusayn (1774) vii, **602a** – VII, **601b**
al-Murādī, Muḥammad (1755) vii, **602a** – VII, **601b**
al-Murādī, Muḥammad Khalīl al-Ḥusaynī (1791) i, 594b; ii, 355b, 839b; vi, 345b; vii, **602a** – I, 614a; II, 365b, 859a; VI, 330a; VII, **601b**
al-Murādī, Muḥammad b. Manṣūr (IX) s, 48b – S, 49a
al-Murādī, Murād b. ʿAlī al-Ḥusaynī al-Bukhārī (1720) vii, **602a** – VII, **601b**
al-Mutādī, al-Rablʿ (884) ix, 182a, 187a – IX, 188a, 192b
al-Murādī, ʿUmar b. ʿAbd Allāh (VIII) vi, 923a – VI, 915a
Murāḳaba → Muḥāsaba
Muraḳḳaʿ vii, **602b** – VII, **602a**
Murakkab i, 1083b – I, 1116a
Muraḳḳish al-Akbar (VI) vii, 306a, **603a** – VII, 308b, **602b**
Muraḳḳish al-Aṣghar i, 963b; iv, 998a, b; vii, **604a** – I, 993a; IV, 1030b, 1031a; VII, **603b**
al-Muraysīʿ vii, 356b; viii, 820a – VII, 359a; VIII, 848a
Murcia/-e → Mursiya
Murḍā b. ʿAlī i, 798a; vi, 406a – I, 821b; VI, 390b
Murdādh → Taʾrīkh
al-Murdār, Abū Mūsā (840) iii, 1019b, 1266a; vi, 636b; vii, 546b, **604a** – III, 1045a, 1299a; VI, 621b; VII, 546b, **603b**
Murdi-čay (river/rivière) vi, 498b – VI, 483b
Murdjān i, 781a – I, 804a
Murdjiʾa i, 123b, 124a, 249b, 276b, 1241b; ii, 833b, 931a, 1022a; iii, 807b, 1142b, 1164a, 1171a; iv, 408a; vi, 457b; vii, 508b, **605b**; s, 358a –
I, 127a,b, 257b, 285a, 1279b; II, 853a, 952b, 1046a; III, 830b, 1171a, 1192b, 1200a; IV, 425b; VI, 443a; VII, 509a, **605a**; S, 357b
Murdjiʾābād (Balkh) vii, 606b – VII, 606a
al-Murdjibī, Ḥāmid b. Muḥammad (Tippu Tip) (1905) iv, 750a, b; V, 176b; vii, **607b** – IV, 780a, b; V, 174a; VII, **607b**
al-Murdjibī, Muḥammad b. Djuma (1881) x, 194b – X, 210a
Murghāb (river/fleuve) i, 222b, 313b, 853b; v, 868b, 873b; vi, 617b, 618a, b, 621a; vii, **608b** – I, 229a, 323a, 877a; V, 874b, 879b; VI, 602b, 603a, 606a, b; VII, **608a**
Murīd vii, **608b** s VII, **608b**
Murīdiyya (Murīdism(e)) (Senegal) ii, 63b; iii, 157a; vii, **609a**; ix, 146a; s, 182a –
II, 64b; III, 160b; VII, **608b**; IX, 151a; S, 182a
Mūrisṭus (Mūrṭus/Mīrisṭus) (868) vii, **610a** – VII, **609b**
Mūrītāniyā i, 211a, 1177b; ii, 672a, 676a, 1122a; iii, 231a, 288b, 385a; v, 697a, 1074a; vi, 142a; vii, **611a**;

ix, 445b; s, 182b, 218a –
I, 217a, 1212b; II, 689a, 693a, 1148a; III, 237b, 297b, 397b; V, 702a, 1071b; VI, 140b; VII, **610b**; IX, 463a; S, 182b, 217b
al-Mūriyānī, Abū Ayyūb Sulaymān b. Makhlad (771) vii, **628a** – VII, **628a**
Murra, Banū (Āl -) i, 545b, 873b; ii, 176b, 725b, 1023b; vi, 371b; vii, 461b, 488a, **628b**, 630a, 840b; s, 5a –
I, 563a, 897b; II, 182a, 744a, 1047a; VI, 356a; VII, 629b; VII, 461b, 488a, **628a**, 629b, 842a; S, 4a
al-Murrī, al-Djunayd iii, 223b – III, 230b
al-Murrī, Ṣāliḥ iv, 734b – IV, 764a
Mursal iii, 26a; vii, **631a** – III, 27a; VII, **630b**
Murshid vii, **631b** – VII, **631b**
Murshid Ḳulī Khān (1658) i, 7b, 786b; ii, 157b, 488b, 810a; iv, 976b; vii, **632a** – I, 7b, 791b; II, 162b, 500b, 829a; IV, 1009a; VII, **631b**
Murshidābād (Bengal(e)) vi, 369b; vii, 444a, **632b** – VI, 354a; VII, 445a, **632a**
Murshidī → ʿAbd al-Raḥmān b. ʿĪsā
Murshidiyya → Kāzarūniyya
al-Mursī → Yāḳūt
al-Mursī, Abu 'l-ʿAbbās (1287) v, 17b; ix, 172a, b; x, 247a; s, 159a – V, 18a; IX, 177b, 178a; X, 266a: S, 159a
Mursiya (Murcia/-e) i, 6b, 58b, 82b, 489a, 1320a, 1347a; ii, 115a; iii, 706a, 904b; iv, 672b; vi, 339b, 521a; vii, **633a**; x, 105b; s, 144b –
I, 7a, 60b, 85a, 504a, 1360b, 1387b; II, 117b; III, 728a, 929a; IV, 700a; VI, 324a, 505b; VII, **632a**; X, 113b; S, 144a
al-Murtaḍā → ʿAbd al-Raḥmān IV (Umayyad(e), al-Andalus)
Murtaḍā I Niẓām Shāh (1588) ii, 815a, 921b; iii, 426b, 1161a; vi, 271b; viii, 73b – II, 834b, 943a; III, 440a, 1189b; VI, 256a; VIII, 75a
Murtaḍā II Niẓām Shāh (1610) iii, 15b; iv, 1018b; vi, 269b; viii, 74a – III, 16a; IV, 1050b; VI, 254a; VIII, 76a
al-Murtaḍā (Almohad(e)) (1266) s, 112a, 389a, b – S, 111a, 389b,
Murtaḍā (Hind) s, 329b – S, 329a, 390a
al-Murtaḍā, al-Sharīf Abu 'l-Ḳāsim, ʿAlam al-Hudā (1044) i, 130a, 154b, 1352a; ii, 127b; iii, 1266a; iv, 182b; v, 363a; vi, 458a, 549a, b, 634b; vii, 313a, **634a**, 786a, 903b; viii, 462b; s, 23a, 25b, 56b, 95a –
I, 133b, 158b, 1391b; II, 130b; III, 1299a; IV, 190b; V, 364a; VI, 443b, 533b, 534a, 619b; VII, 315b, **633b**, 788a, 904a; VIII, 478a; S, 23b, 25b, 57a, 94b
(al-)Murtaḍā b. al-ʿAfīf (XIII) vii, **634b** – VII, **634b**
Murtaḍā b. ʿAlī Sārī b. Kamāl al-Dīn (Marʿashī) (XV) v, 663a; vi, 513a – V, 668a; VI, 498a
Murtaḍā b. Kamāl al-Dīn (Marʿashī) (XV) vi, 512b, 513a – VI, 498a
Murtaḍā b. Riḍā al-Dīn (Marʿashī) (XV) vi, 513b – VI, 498b
Murtaḍa ʿAlī ii, 88a – II, 89b
Murtaḍā Anṣārī, Shaykh (1864) vii, 299a – VII, 301a
Murtaḍā Baktāshī ii, 735a,b – II, 754a
Murtaḍā al-Dawla Manṣūr b. Luʾluʾ al-Kabīr (1010) vii, 116a – VII, 118a
Murtaḍā Ḥusayn i, 1219a – I, 1255a
Murtaḍā Ḳulī Khān Iḳbāl al-Salṭana (Mākū) (1923) vi, 203a – VI, 187a
Murtaḍā Ḳulī Khān Shamlu (XVII) iv, 390b, 391a, 1124b; viii, 784a – IV, 407b, 1156a; VIII, 810a
Murtaḍā Kulī Khān Wākil al-Mulk (XIX) v, 165a – V, 162b
Murtaḍā Pasha (XVII) i, 4b, 236b; v, 34b, 258a, b, 1023a; viii, 7a – I, 4b, 244a; V, 35b, 256a, 1018b; VIII, 7a
Murtaḍāʾid(e)s vi, 512a – VI, 497a
Murtadd iv, 408a, 771a, 1076b; v, 179a; vii, **635a** – IV, 426a, 801b, 1108a; V, 176b; VII, **634b**
Murtadi fils du Gaphiphe → (al-)Murtaḍā b. al-ʿAfīf
Murtahin iv, 488b – IV, 509b
Murūʾa (Muruwwa) ii, 961a; vii, **636b** – II, 983a; VII, **636a**
Murud s, 246b – S, 246b
Murwan-Ḳru i, 100b; v, 487b, 488a – I, 103b; V, 490b
Murzuḳ (Libya/Libie) i, 38a; ii, 876a; vii, **638a** – I, 39a; II, 896a; VII, **638a**
Muş vi, 242b – VI, 226b
Mūsā (Moses/Moïse) ii, 280a, 917b; iii, 231b, 1175a; iv, 293a, 903a, b, 904a; v, 421a, 423b; vii, **638b** – II, 288b, 939a; III, 238b, 1204a; IV, 306a, 935b, 936b; V, 423a, 425b; VII, **638b**
Mūsā, Aḥmad (IX) vii, 640a, b – VII, 639b, 640b
Mūsā, Banū i, 84b, 403a; vi, 600a; vii, **640a**; viii, 559b; x, 428b; s, 267a, 371b, 372b, 373a, 412b –
I, 87a, 414b; VI, 585a; VII, **639b**; VIII, 577b; X, 459a; S, 266b, 371b, 372a, 373a, 412b
Mūsā, Muḥammad (873) vii, 640a – VII, 639b
Mūsā, Salāma iv, 125a – IV, 130a
Mūsā I al-Djawn iii, 262b, 984b – III, 270a, 1009a
Mūsā II b. ʿAbd Allāh (Mūsāwīd(e)) iii, 262b; vi, 148b – III, 270a; VI, 147a
Mūsā b. ʿAbd Allāh b. Ḥasan → Mūsā I al-Djawn
Mūsā b. ʿAbd Allāh b. Khāzim (Tirmīdh (705) i, 48a, 529b; iii, 304a, 542a, 576b; x, 542a, 576b – I, 49a, 546a; III, 313a; X,
Mūsā b. Abi 'l-ʿĀfiya (938) ii, 853a, 979a; iii, 1036a; iv, 459a; vi, 1008b; vii, **641a**, 942a –
II, 872b, 1001a; III, 1062a; IV, 479a; VI, 1001a; VII, **640b**, 942b
Mūsā b. Abī Djābir al-Azkānī iii, 652a –
III, 673b
Mūsā b. al-Amīn (ʿAbbāsid(e)) (IX) vi, 332b – VI, 317a
Mūsā b. al-ʿĀzār (Moses b. Eleazar) (X) i, 344b – I, 355a
Mūsā b. ʿAzra (1135) vii, **642a** – VII, **642a**
Mūsā b. Bughā (877) i, 278b, 1287b; ii, 191a; iii, 29a, 245a; iv, 493b, 859a; vii, 477a, 801a –
I, 287a, 1327a; II, 197b; III, 30b, 252a; IV, 515a, 892a; VII, 476b, 803a
Mūsā b. Djaʿfar → Mūsā al-Ḳāẓim
Mūsā b. Fortūn iv, 712b – IV, 741b
Mūsā b. Ḥafṣ iv, 645b – IV, 672a
Mūsā b. al-Ḥārith (Kinda) vii, 671a – VII, 671a
Mūsā b. Ḥudayr i, 600a – I, 619b
Mūsā b. Ibrāhīm b. Shīrkūh → al-Ashraf Mūsā
Mūsā b. ʿImrān (prophet/prophète) vi, 412b – VI, 397a
Mūsā b. ʿĪsā (ʿAbbāsid(e)) (799) i, 162b; x, 810b – I, 166b; X,
Mūsā b. Kaʿb al-Tamīmī (VIII) vi, 332b, 744b – VI, 317a, 734a
Mūsā b. Maḥmūd Ḳāḍīzāda Rūmī, Ṣalāḥ al-Dīn (XV) x, 813b – X,
Mūsā b. Maymūn → Ibn Maymūn
Mūsā b. Muḥammad b. Abī Bakr (Songhay) (XVI) vii, 394a – VII, 395b
Mūsā b. Mūsā Ibn Ḳasī i, 1012a; iii, 815b; iv, 712b; s, 82a – I, 1043a; III, 839b; IV, 741b; S, 81b
Mūsā b. Nuṣayr (716) i, 58b, 492b, 1079b, 1242b, 1338b; ii, 1009a, 1095b; iii, 271b;
iv, 115a, 494b, 665a; v, 1189a; vi, 134a, 568a, 742a; vii, **643a**; s, 81b, 125a –

I, 60b, 507b, 1111b, 1280b, 1378b; II, 1032b, 1121a; III, 279a; IV, 120a, 515b, 692a; V, 1179a; VI, 132a, 553a, 731b; VII, **643a**; S, 81b, 124a
Mūsā b. Rabīʿa b. Māniʿ al-Muraydī ii, 569a – II, 583b
Mūsā b. Shākir (IX) vii, 640a – VII, 639b
Mūsā b. Shākir, Banū vii, 559a, s, 413b, 414a – VII, 559a; S, 414a
Mūsā b. Ṭalḥa v, 1231a – V, 1221b
Mūsā b. ʿUḳba al-Asadī (758) v, 1162a, 1163a; vii, **644a** – V, 1151b, 1152b; VII, **643b**
Mūsā b. ʿUmar b. ʿĀmir b. Kunnu (XVII) vi, 642b – VI, 627b
Mūsā b. Yaḥyā (Barmakid(e)) (835) i, 1036a; vi, 332a – I, 1067b; VI, 316b
Mūsā ag Amāstan i, 255a – I, 263a
Mūsā Aydînoghlu i, 783b; ii, 599a – I, 806b; II, 614a
Mūsā Beg (Ḳarāmān-oghlu) iv, 621b, 622a – IV, 646b, 647a
Mūsā Beg b. Ibrāhīm Beg (Menteshe) (1375) vi, 1018b – VI, 1011a
Mūsā Čelebi b. Bāyazīd I (Ottoman) (1413) ii, 291b, 599a, 611b, 684a; vi, 973b; vii, **644a** – II, 299b, 614a, 626b, 701a; VI, 966a; VII, **643b**
Mūsā al-Hādī → al-Hādī ilā ʾl-Ḥaḳḳ (ʿAbbāsid(e))
Mūsā Ḥarfūsh ii, 750a; iii, 205b – II, 768a; III, 211a
Mūsā al-Kāẓim (VII. Imām) (799) i, 108a, 402b, 550b, 850b; ii, 374b, 375a; iii, 233b, 497a, 616b; iv, 855a, b, 1132b; v, 1236a; vi, 921b; vii, 396b, **645b**, 672a; s, 95a, 383a, 402b – I, 111a, 414a, 414b, 568b, 874a; II, 385a; III, 240b, 514a, 637a; IV, 888a, b, 1164a; V, 1226b; VI, 913a; VII, 397b, **645a**, 672a; S, 94a, b, 383a, 403a
Mūsā Khān Pūlādī i, 1136b – I, 1171a
Mūsā Mzurī (1861) x, 194b – X, 210a
Mūsā Pasha, Ḳāʾim-Maḳām (XVIII) vii, 709b – VII, 710b
Mūsā Rayna s, 423b – S, 423b
Mūsā al-Ṣadr, Imām (1978) vii, 301b; viii, 388a; ix, 315a, 884a – VII, 303b; VIII, 401b; IX, 325a, 920a
Mūsā Shahawāt^{in}, Abū Muḥammad (VIII) iv, 190a; vii, **648b** – IV, 198a; VII, **648a**
Mūsā Sulaymān iii, 370b – III, 382a
Muṣʿab (Miṣr) (785) vii, 160b – VII, 162a
Muṣʿab b. ʿAbd Allāh al-Zubayrī (851) vii, **649a** – VII, **648b**
Muṣʿab b. ʿUmayr (625) vii, **649b** – VII, **649a**
Muṣʿab b. al-Zubayr, Abū ʿAbd Allāh (691) i, 55a, 76b, 304a, 453b, 810b, 1242b, 1243a, 1349a; ii, 197a; iii, 40a, 715a, 970a, 1255a, 1265b; iv, 494b; v, 731a; vi, 139a, b, 622a, 623a, 640b; vii, 357a, 400b, 408b, 523b, **649b**; ix, 421b; s, 357b, 380b – I, 57a, 79a, 313b, 466b, 833b, 1280b, 1389a; II, 203b; III, 41b, 737b, 994b, 1287b, 1298b; IV, 516a; V, 736a; VI, 137a, 138a, 607b, 608a, 625b; VII, 359b, 402a, 409b, 524a, **649b**; IX, 435b; S, 357b, 381a
Musābaḳa → Maydān
al-Muṣʿabayn i, 1133a – I, 1167b
Musabbaʿāt ii, 122a,b; v, 267a – II, 125a,b; V, 265a
al-Musabbiḥāt vii, **650b** – VII, **650a**
al-Musabbiḥī (1030) iii, 81a, 894b; vii, 115b, 163b, **650b** – III, 83a, 918b; VII, 117b, 165a, **650b**
al-Muṣʿabī, Abā Yazmū (XIII) iii, 96b, 97a – III, 99a, 100a
al-Muṣʿabī, Abu ʾl-Ṭayyib (X) vii, **652a** – VII, **651b**
Muṣādara i, 1144a; ii, 152b; iv, 463b; vii, **652b** – I, 1178b; II, 157a; IV, 484a; VII, **652a**
Musaddas → Musammaṭ
Muṣaddiḳ, Muḥammad (1967) i, 978b; ii, 653a, 882b; iii, 529b; iv, 41b, 695b, 790a, 1028b; v, 630b, 1042b; vii, 447a, **653b**; s, 60b, 110b, 158a – I, 1009a; II, 669b, 903a; III, 547b, 548a; IV, 44a, 724a, 822a, 1060b; V, 634b, 1039a; VII, 448a, **653a**; S, 61a, 109b, 158a
al-Muṣaffāt → Ḥamīda bint Ṣaʿīd al-Barbariyya
Musāfirid(e)s i, 98b, 637b, 638a, 1041b; ii, 192a, 680a; iv, 345a, 346a; vi, 66a, 499a, b; vii, **655b**; ix, 169b – I, 101b, 658b, 1073a; II, 198a, 697a; IV, 360a, b; VI, 64a, 484b; VII, **655a**; IX, 174b
Musāhama → Mukhāradja
Muṣaḥḥaf iii, 26a – III, 27b
Muṣāḥib vii, **657b** – VII, **657a**
Muṣāḥib Muṣṭafā Pasha (1686) i, 96b; ii, 684b; vii, 839a – I, 99b; II, 701b; VII, 840b
Muṣāḥib-Zāde Djelāl (Musahip-zade Celal) (1959) vii, **657b** – VII, **657a**
Musāʿid (al-Matamma) (1820) vi, 794b – VI, 784b
Musāḳāt v, 871b; vii, **658b** – V, 878a; VII, **658a**
Musālima i, 491a – I, 505b
al-Muṣallā i, 482a; v, 1141a, 1147a; vi, 653b; vii, **658b** – I, 496b; V, 1134a, 1138b; VI, 639a; VII, **658b**
al-Muṣallā al-ʿAtīḳ (Baghdād) vi, 653b – VI, 639a
al-Muṣallā al-Ḳadīm (Cairo/le Caire) vi, 654a – VI, 639a
Muṣallā Khawlān (Cairo/le Caire) vi, 653b – VI, 639a
Musallamī iv, 1045a – IV, 1076b
Musallim al-Tardjāwī v, 267a, b – V, 265a
Musalmānī i, 952a – I, 981a
Musalmānī Bānglā i, 1167a – I, 1202a
Musalsal iii, 26a; iv, 1124a, 1125b – III, 27a; IV, 1155b, 1157a
Musāmaḥat ii, 303a – II, 311b
Musammaṭ i, 677b; iv, 715a; vii, **660b** – I, 698a; IV, 743b; VII, **660a**
Musandam i, 536a; v, 508a – I, 552a; V, 511b
Muṣannaf vii, **662b** – VII, **662a**
al-Musannāt vii, 393b – VII, 394b
Muṣannifak, ʿAlā al-Dīn ʿAlī al-Bisṭāmī al- Ṣiddīḳī (1470) i, 867b; vi, 995b, **663a** – I, 891b; VI, 988a, **662b**
Muṣarrif-zāde → Shefīḳ Meḥmed Effendi
Musāwāt iii, 530b; vii, **663a** – III, 549a; VII, **663a**
al-Mūsawī i, 256a – I, 263b
al-Mūsawī, Sayyid Sharaf al-Dīn → Bulbul Shāh
Mūsawī Shīʿa s, 402b – S, 403a
Mūsāwid(e)s i, 552a; iii, 262b – I, 569b; III, 270a
Musāwir (Khāridjī) (IX) ii, 524a; vi, 900a – II, 537a; VI, 891a
Musāwir b. Sawwār al-Warrāḳ (VIII) vii, **663b** – VII, **663b**
Mūsāwīs (Ḥasanid(e)s) (Mecca) vi, 148a, b ; ix, 507a – VI, 146b, 147a; IX, 526b
Mūsāwīs (Persia/la Perse) → Mūsā al-Kāẓim
Muṣawwaʿ → Maṣawwaʿ
Musawwida iii, 617a; vii, **664a** – III, 637b; VII, **663b**
Musaylima b. Ḥabīb, Abū Thumāna al-Kadhdhāb (633) i, 110b, 964a; ii, 1060a; vi, 138b, 675b; vii, **664b**; viii, 52a, 739a – I, 113b, 993b; II, 1084b; VI, 137a, 662a; VII, **664a**; VIII, 53a, 760a
al-Musayyab b. ʿAlas (VI) vii, 306b, 764a – VII, 308b, 765b
al-Musayyab b. Nadjaba (685) ix, 826b – IX, 861a
al-Musayyab b. Zuhayr al-Ḍabbī → al-Ḍabbī
Muscat → Masḳaṭ

Müsellem (müsellim) i, 1268b; ii, 33a; vii, **665a** – I, 1307b; II, 33b; VII, **665a**
Museveni x, 781a – X,
Mūsh (Muş) i, 644a; vi, 242b; vii, **665b** – I, 664b; VI, 226b; VII, **665b**
Mushā' i, 661a; vii, **666b** – I, 682a; VII, **665b**
Mushā'ara vii, **667b**; ix, 434a – VII, **667b**; IX, 450b
Mushabbiha → Tashbīh
Muṣḥaf v, 207a; vii, **668b** – V, 204b; VII, **668a**
al-Muṣḥafī, Dja'far b. 'Uthmān (982) i, 601b, 628a; iii, 346b; vi, 431a, 926b; viii, 833b – I, 621a, 649a; III, 357b; VI, 416b, 918b; VIII, 862b
Muṣḥafī, Shaykh Ghulām Hamadānī (1824) iii, 358b, 1244a; vii, 475b, **669b**; s, 102a – III, 370a, 1276b; VII, 474b, **669a**; S, 101b
Mushāhada iv, 697a – IV, 725a
Mushāḳa, Mīkhā'īl b. Djirdjīs (1888) vi, 99a; vii, **670b**, 686a – VI, 97a; VII, **670a**, 686a
al-Mushaḳḳar (port) vii, 570b, **671a**, 859b – VII, 571a, **671a**, 860b
al-Mushallal (Ḳudayd) vi, 373b; vii, 694a – VI, 358a; VII, 694a
Mūshār/Minshār vi, 231a – VI, 225a
Mushāraka vii, **671b** – VII, **671a**
Mushārī b. Sa'ūd (1821) ii, 321b – II, 331a
Mushārī b. Sa'ūd b. Djalwī (XX) vi, 155b – VI, 152a
al-Musharraf b. Muradjdja' v, 330a, 332a – V, 330a, 332a
Musharrif al-Dawla (1025) i, 131b; ii, 391a; iv, 378b; viii, 595b – I, 135b; II, 401a; IV, 395a; VIII, 614b
Musha'sha' i, 1096a; iii, 1256b; iv, 49a; v, 80b; vi, 549b; vii, **672a**; viii, 777b; ix, 856a – I, 1129a; III, 1289a; IV, 52a; V, 82b; VI, 534a; VII, **672a**; VIII, 803b; IX, 891b
Mushāt iii, 187a – III, 191a
al-Mushattā (al-Mshattā) i, 613b, 615a, 616a; iii, 310a; v, 183a; vii, **675b**; s, 117a – I, 634b, 635b, 636a; III, 319a; V, 180a; VII, **675b**; S, 116b
Mushfiḳī, 'Abd al-Raḥmān (1588) vii, **676b** – VII, **676b**
Mushidd i, 802a – I, 825a
Mushīr vii, **677a** – VII, **677a**
Mushīr al-Dawla, Mīrzā Sayyid Dja'far Khān (1862) iv, 787a, 788a; vii, **678a**; s, 108b – IV, 818b, 820a; VII, **678a**; S, 108a
Mushīr Ḥusayn Ḳidwā'ī vii, **678b**; s, 4b, 74a – VII, **678b**; S, 3b, 74b
Müshīr, müshīriyyet i, 1111a; ii, 724a – I, 1144b; II, 742b
Mushk-i 'Ālam i, 232a – I, 239a
Mushkān → Abū Naṣr Mushkān
Mushrif ii, 146a; iv, 759a; vii, **678b** – II, 149b; IV, 789a; VII, **678b**
Mushrif al-Kurdī, Ḥusayn (amīr) (XVI) vii, 514a – VII, 514a
Mushrik → Shirk
Mushtāḳ ii, 433b; iv, 69b – II, 444b; IV, 73a
Mushtāḳī s, 1b – S, 1b
Mushtarī (planet/planète Jupiter) vii, **680a** – VII, **680a**
al-Mushtarik (Mushtarak) i, 184b; vii, **680b** – I, 190a; VII, **680b**
Mūsī i, 261a – I, 269a
Mūsīḳī/Mūsīḳā i, 1124a; iii, 974b; v, 477b; vii, **681a**; viii, 448b – I, 1158a; III, 999a; V, 480a; VII, **681a**; VIII, 463b
Muṣlī Čawush i, 267b – I, 276a
Muṣliḥ iv, 141a – IV, 147a
Muṣliḥ al-Dīn Lārī → al-Lārī, Muṣliḥ al-Dīn
Muṣliḥ al-Dīn Muṣṭafā b. Sha'bān (1561) vi, 991a – VI, 983b
Muṣliḥ al-Dīn Muṣṭafā al-Ḳarāḥiṣārī → Akhtarī
Muṣliḥ al-Zandjī (IX) vii, 526b – VII, 526b
Muslim iv, 171b, 173a, b, 176a, b, 177a; v, 1015a, 1019a; vii, **688b** – IV, 179a, 180b, 181a, 183b, 184a, b; V, 1010b, 1014b; VII, **689a**
Muslim, non-arab(e) → Mawlā
Muslim b. 'Aḳīl b. Abī Ṭālib (680) i, 337b; iii, 164b, 608a, 609a, 620b, 715a; vi, 438b; vii, 400b, 521b, 592a, **688b**; viii, 119a; ix, 421b – I, 348a; III, 168a, 629a,b, 641a, 737b; VI, 424a; VII, 401b, 521b, 592a, **689a**; VIII, 121a; IX, 435a
Muslim b. 'Awsadja al-Asadī (VII) vii, 689a – VII, 689b
Muslim b. al-Ḥadjdjādj (875) i, 114b, 1297a; ii, 159a; iii, 24a, 708b, 803a, 909b; vii, 260a, 361b, 631a, **691a**, 706a; viii, 516a; s, 232b – I, 117b, 1336b; II, 164a; III, 25b, 731a, 826b, 933b; VII, 262a, 363b, 630b, **691b**, 706b; VIII, 533b; S, 232b
Muslim b. Ḳuraysh, Sharaf al-Dawla ('Uḳaylid(e)) (1085) i, 517a, 664a; ii, 282a, 347b, 348b, 384b; iii, 86b, 686b, 790a; vi, 274b, 546b; vii, 120b, 577b, **692b**; viii, 947a; x, 787a – I, 532b, 683b; II, 290a, 357a, 358a, 394b; III, 89a, 708b, 813b; VI, 259b, 531a; VII, 122b, 578a, **693a**; VIII, 979b; X,
Muslim b. Ḳutayba vi, 604a – VI, 589a
Muslim b. Sa'īd al-Kilābī (VIII) vi, 633b; vii, 1016a – VI, 618b; VII, 1018a
Muslim b. 'Ubays (VII) i, 810a; vii, 858b, 877b – I, 833b; VII, 860a, 879a
Muslim b. 'Uḳba al-Murrī (VII) i, 45a, 55a, 76b; ii, 89b, 1023b; iii, 226b, 227a, 620b; v, 997a; vi, 622a; vii, 629b, **693b** – I, 46b, 57a, 78b; II, 91a, 1047b; III, 233b, 234a, 641a; V, 992a; VI, 607a; VII, 629b, **694a**
Muslim b. al-Walīd al-Anṣārī (823) i, 10a, 587b, 857b; ii, 248b; iii, 73a, 1264a; iv, 1004b; vi, 437b, 604b; vii, 413a, **694a**, 982a – I, 10a, 606b, 881a; II, 255b; III, 75b, 1297a; IV, 1037a; VI, 423a, 589b; VII, 414b, **694b**, 982b
Muslim Educational Society vi, 461a – VI, 446b
Muslimiyya vi, 544a – VI, 528b
Muslimūn vii, **695a** – VII, **695b**
Muslin → al-Mawṣil
Muslu Čawush (1608) vii, 600b; s, 239a – VII, 600b; S, 239a
Musnad i, 273b, 275b; iii, 25b; vii, **704b** – I, 281b, 284a; III, 27a; VII, **705b**
Mussoorie s, 66a – S, 66a
Mustacaplioğlu, Esat Adil iv, 124b – IV, 129b
al-Mustaḍī, Mawlāy ('Alawid(e)) (1740) i, 47b; vi, 595a – I, 48b; VI, 580a
al-Mustaḍī' bi-Amr Allāh ('Abbāsid(e)) (1180) i, 212b, 273a; iii, 751a; vii, **707a**; s, 193b – I, 219a, 281b; III, 774a; VII, **707b**; S, 194b
Mustadjāb Khān Bahādur, Nawwāb (1774) vii, **707a** – VII, **708a**
Mustadrika vii, 868b – VII, 870a
Muṣṭafā I (Ottoman) (1638) ii, 183b, 713a; iv, 884a; v, 272a; vii, **707b** – II, 189b, 731b; IV, 917a; V, 270a; VII, **708a**
Muṣṭafā II (Ottoman) (1703) i, 96b, 398a; ii, 684a; iv, 1104b; v, 18b, 262b; vi, 5a, 55a; vii, **707b** – I, 99b, 409b; II, 701a; IV, 1136a; V, 19a, 260b; VI, 5a, 53a; VII, **708b**
Muṣṭafā III (Ottoman) (1773) i, 1004a; ii, 49a; iii, 158a, 269a; iv, 892a; vii, **708b** – I, 1035a; II, 50a; III, 161b, 277a; IV, 925a; VII, **709b**
Muṣṭafā IV (Ottoman) (1808) iv, 322b; vi, 58a; vii, **709b**; viii, 75b – IV, 337a; VI, 56a; VII, **710b**; VIII, 77b

Muṣṭafā (walī, Ḳonya) (XV) i, 244a; ii, 184a – I, 251a; II, 190a
Muṣṭafā b. Ḥādjdjī Āḳā Muḥsin, Sayyid s, 342a – S, 341b
Muṣṭafā b. Ibrāhīm (Mēṣṭfa bēn Bṛāhīm) (XIX) vi, 250b, 253b, 255b – VI, 235a, 237b, 240a
Muṣṭafā b. Idrīs (amīr) (1788) vi, 791b – VI, 781a
Muṣṭafā b. Ismāʿīl (1843) ii, 173a; vii, 434a, b, 452a – II, 178a; VII, 435a, b, 453b
Muṣṭafā b. al-Ḳāḍī Ṭāhā (XIX) vii, 205a – VII, 206a
Muṣṭafā b. Meḥemmed I (Ottoman) (1425) vii, 594a – VII, 594b
Muṣṭafā b. Sülaymān Ḳānūnī (Ottoman) (1553) i, 1301b; ii, 737b, 738a; iii, 147b; vii, 713a; viii, 641a – I, 1341b; II, 756a,b; III, 150b; VII, 714a; VIII, 660a
Muṣṭafā b. Umūr II ii, 599b – II, 614b
Muṣṭafā ʿAbd al-Rāziḳ (1947) vii, **713a** – VII, **714a**
Muṣṭafā Abū Muḥammad Bayram al-Khāmis vii, 433b – VII, 434b
Muṣṭafā Abū Ṭāhir al-Ḥusaynī s, 67a – S, 67b
Muṣṭafā Agha (Dār al-Saʿāda Aghasi̊) (XVII) iv, 194a, 590b – IV, 202b, 614b
Muṣṭafā Agha, Dede (XIX) vii, 519a – VII, 519b
Muṣṭafā Agha ʿOthmān-oghlu iv, 593a – IV, 617a
Muṣṭafā ʿAlī → ʿAlī, Muṣṭafā b. Aḥmad Čelebi
Muṣṭafā ʿAṣim s, 328b – S, 328a
Muṣṭafā al-Baghdādī (1148) vii, 9b – VII, 10a
Muṣṭafā Barzānī, Mullā (1979) i, 1072a; v, 467a, b, 468a, b, 469a, b, 1213b, 1214a; vii, **714a** – I, 1104a,b; V, 470a, b, 471a, b, 472a, 1203a, b; VII, **714b**
Muṣṭafā Beg (Shūshīk) (XVII) vi, 202b – VI, 187a
Muṣṭafā Beg b. Iwaḍ Beg al-Maḥmūdī (Mākū) (XVI) vi, 202a – VI, 186b
Muṣṭafā Behdjet Efendi → Bahdjat Muṣṭafā
Muṣṭafā Bey Čapan-oghlu ii, 207b – II, 214a
Muṣṭafā Čalabi Ṣābūndjī (Mosul) (XX) vi, 901b – VI, 893a
Muṣṭafā Čelebi → Bičaḳdji-zāde; Djalālzāde
Muṣṭafā Čelebī (Küčük Muṣṭafā) b. Meḥemmed I (1423) ii, 990a; vii, **712b** – II, 1013a; VII, **713a**
Muṣṭafā Čelebi, Düzme, b. Bāyazīd I (1422) i, 783b, 899b; ii, 599b, 684a, 697a, 721a; v, 763b; vii, 237a, 594b, **710a** – I, 806b, 893b; II, 614a, b, 701a, 714b. 739b; V, 769b; VII, 238b, 594a, **711a**
Muṣṭafā Dāʿī, Shaykh v, 952a – V, 956a
Muṣṭafā Davidovič ii, 979b, 980a – II, 1002a,b
Muṣṭafā li-Dīn Allāh → Nizār b. al-Mustanṣir
Muṣṭafā Djinānī (1585) viii, 213b, 215a – VIII, 218a, 219b
Muṣṭafā Efendi (Masraḥ) (XIX) vi, 759a – VI, 748a
Muṣṭafā Efendi b. Sahrab (XVII) vi, 247b – VI, 231b
Muṣṭafā Fāḍil Pasha → Fāḍil Pasha
Muṣṭafā Feyḍī iii, 303a – III, 312b
Muṣṭafā ʿIzzet Efendi i, 776a – I, 799a
Muṣṭafā Kabakči̊ → Kabakči̊
Muṣṭafā Kāmil Pasha (1908) i, 597a; iii, 59a, 515a; iv, 967a; vii, 439a, **715a**; viii, 49a; ix, 151b – I, 616b; III, 61b, 532b; IV, 999b; VII, 440a, **716a**; VIII, 50a; IX, 156b
Muṣṭafā Kʸahyā al-Ḳazdughlī (Miṣr) (XVII) vii, 178b – VII, 180b
Mustafā Kemāl Pāsha → Atatürk
Muṣṭafā Kemāl Pasha (town/ville) → Kirmāstī
Muṣṭafā Khān i, 1155a – I, 1189b
Muṣṭafā Khayrī Efendi, Ürgüplü (1921) vii, **716b** – VII, **717b**
Muṣṭafā Khaznadār (1878) i, 282a; iii, 636a, b; iv, 1153b, 1154a; vii, 436b, 451b, 452a, **717b**; s, 387a – I, 290b; III, 657b; IV, 1185b, 1186a; VII, 437b, 453a, **718a**; S, 387b
Muṣṭafā Khodja iii, 636a – III, 657a
Muṣṭafā al-Manṣūrī ix, 517a – IX, 537a
Muṣṭafā al-Marāghī, Shaykh s, 300a – S, 299b
Muṣṭafā Nadjīb Pasha iv, 618a – IV, 643a
Muṣṭafā al-Naḥḥās Pasha ii, 934b; iii, 515b, 516a, 517a; s, 5b, 300a, b – II, 956a; III, 533a, 534a, b; S, 4b, 5a, 299b, 300a
Muṣṭafā Nāʾilī Pasha (XIX) i, 397a; vi, 68b – I, 408b; VI, 66a
Muṣṭafā Naẓīf Efendi (XVIII) vi, 56b – VI, 54b
Muṣṭafā Nihat Özön (1980) vii, 658a – VII, 658a
Muṣṭafā Nūrī Pasha ii, 636b – II, 652b
Mustafa Oğulcuk → Esendal
Muṣṭafā Pasha → Ḳara; Khodja; Köprülüzāde; Muṣāḥib; Soḳollu
Muṣṭafā Pasha (XIII) vii, 11a – VII, 11b
Muṣṭafā Pasha (1623) ii, 751a – II, 769a
Muṣṭafā Pasha (1760) i, 1152a – I, 1186a
Muṣṭafā Pasha (Sūria) (1850) vi, 308a – VI, 293b
Muṣṭafā Pasha, Bayraḳdār (ʿAlemdār) (1808) i, 778b, 1304a; ii, 207a, 512b, 640a, 641b, 713a; iv, 322b; vi, 58a; vii, 710a, **719a** – I, 801b, 1344a; II, 213b, 525b, 656a, 657b, 731a; IV, 337a; VI, 56a; VII, 710b, **720a**
Muṣṭafā Pasha, Bushatli̊ (1860) i, 657a; v, 276b; vii, **719b** – I, 678a; V, 274b; VII, **720b**
Muṣṭafā Pasha, Čelebi (XIX) vii, 710a, 719a – VII, 710b, 720a
Muṣṭafā Pasha, Ipshīr → Ipshīr
Muṣṭafā Pasha, Isfendiyār-oghlu iv, 108b – IV, 113b
Muṣṭafā Pasha, Ḳara Shāhīn (1564) vii, **720a**; viii, 521a – VII, **721a**; VIII, 539a
Muṣṭafā Pasha, Köprülü → Köprülü
Muṣṭafā Pasha, Lala (1580) i, 380a, 468b; iv, 670b; v, 305a, 493a; vi, 455a; vii, **720b**; viii, 184a – I, 391a, 482b; IV, 697b; V, 304b, 496a; VI, 440b; VII, **721b**; VIII, 187a
Muṣṭafā Pasha Ḳaplan i, 905a – I, 932a
Muṣṭafā Pasha al-Nashshār (1555) vii, **721a** – VII, **722a**
Muṣṭafā Pasha Ṭūḳān al-Nābulusī s, 20b – S, 20b
Muṣṭafā Rāḳim iv, 1125b – IV, 1157a
Muṣṭafā Reshid Pasha → Reshīd Pasha, Muṣṭafā
Muṣṭafā Riyāḍ Pasha (Miṣr) (XIX) iii, 514b, 515a; vii, 184a – III, 532b; VII, 184a
Muṣṭafā Ṣafī Efendi v, 18a – V, 19a
Mustafa Yali̊nkat → Esendal
Muṣṭafā Zühdi s, 171b – S, 171b
Muṣṭafābād ii, 597b, 1127a; vi, 50b, 53a, 55a – II, 612b, 1153b; VI, 49a, 51b, 53a
Muṣṭafānagar vi, 67b – VI, 65b
Mustafīd iii, 25b – III, 26b
Mustaghānim (Mostaganem) vi, 754a; vii, **721b** – VI, 743b; **722b**
Mustaḥabb vii, **722b** – VII, **722b**
Mustaʿidd Khān, Muḥammad Sāḳī (1723) i, 954a; vii, 342b, **722b** – I, 983b; VII, 344b; **723b**
al-Mustaʿīn bi-'llāh, Abū 'l-ʿAbbās Aḥmad b. Muḥammad (ʿAbbāsid(e)) (866) i, 21b, 145a, 278b, 897b, 1287b; v, 1160a; vii, 390b, **722b** – I, 22a, 149b, 287a, 924b, 1327a; V, 1149b; VII, 391b, **723b**
al-Mustaʿīn bi-'llāh, Abu 'l-Faḍl (ʿAbbāsid(e)) (1430)

ii, 781b; vii, 168a, **723a** – II, 800a; VII, 169b, **724a**
al-Mustaʿīn (Hūdid(e)) → Aḥmad II; Sulāyman b. Hūd
al-Mustaʿīn (Umayyad(e)) → Sulaymān al-Mustaʿīn
al-Mustakfī bi-'llāh (ʿAbbāsid(e) (949) i, 20a, 1352b; vii, 484b, **723b** – I, 21a, 1391b; VII, 484a, **724b**
Mustakhīrūn iv, 259b – IV, 271a
Mustakhridj v, 376a; vii, **724a** – V, 377a; VII, **725a**
Müstaḳīm-zāde, Saʿd al-Dīn Sulaymān (1788) vii, **724a**, 936b – VII, **725a**, 937a
Muṣṭalaḥat i, 572a – I, 590b
Mustaʿlī bi-'llāh, Abu 'l-Ḳāsim Aḥmad (Fāṭimid(e)) (1101) i, 215b, 353a, 1254a; ii, 170b, 857a; iv, 200a; vii, **725a**; viii, 83a – I, 221b, 364a, 1292a; II, 176b, 877a; IV, 208b; VII, **726a**; VIII, 85a
Mustaʿlī-Ṭayyibī Ismāʿīlis vii, 411a, 725a; ix, 824b, 829a; s, 61b, 62a, 70b, 358b, 407a – VII, 412a, 726a; IX, 859a, 864a; S, 62a, b, 71a, 358a, 407a
Muṣṭaliḳ, Banu 'l- vi, 648b; vii, 371a; viii, 820a – VI, 634a; VII, 372b; VIII, 848a
Muṣṭalik v, 78b – V, 80b
Mustaʾmin → Amān
Mustamlī v, 1133b; vii, **725b** – V, 1129a; VII, **726b**
al-Mustamsik (ʿAbbāsid(e)) (1517) vii, 394a – VII, 395a
al-Mustandjid (I) bi-'llāh (ʿAbbāssid(e)) (1170) i, 212b, 684a; iii, 160b, 730b, 751a; vi, 54a; vii, 707a, **726a**; s, 193b – I, 219a, 705a; III, 164a, 753a, 774a; VI, 52a; VII, 707b, **727a**; S, 194a
al-Mustandjid (II) bi-'llāh (ʿAbbāsid(e)) (1479) iii, 1198b; vii, **727a** – III, 1228b; VII, **727b**
al-Mustanīr → al-ʿIdjlī, Abū Manṣūr
al-Mustanṣir (I) bi-'llāh, Abu Djaʿfar (ʿAbbāsid(e)) (1242) i, 21b; iii, 203b, 219b; vi, 322a; vii, **727a** – I, 22b; III, 209a, 226b; VI, 306b; VII, **728a**
al-Mustanṣir (II) bi-'llāh, Abu 'l-Ḳāsim (ʿAbbāsid(e), Cairo/le Caire) (1261) i, 21b; ii, 966a; iv, 944b; vii, 167b, **729a** – I, 22a; II, 988a; IV, 977b; VII, 169a, **729b**
al-Mustanṣir, Abū Yaʿḳūb Yūsuf (Almohad(e)) s, 389a – S, 389b
al-Mustanṣir bi-'llāh, Abū Tamīm (Fāṭimid(e)) (1094) i, 200b, 215a, 814b, 832b, 869b, 901b, 1073b, 1074b; ii, 169a, 855b, 856a, 857b, 859a, 861b, 958b; iii, 686b; vi, 453b, 626b, 707b; vii, 162b, 271a, 282b, 483a, **729b**; s, 260b, 390a – I, 206a, 221b, 837b, 855b, 894a, 929a, 1105b, 1106b; II, 174b, 875b, 876a, 877b, 878b, 881a, 981a; III, 708a; VI, 439a, 611b, 696b; VII, 164a, 273a, 284b, 482b, **730a**; S, 260a, 390b
al-Mustanṣir, Abū Muḥammad (Ḥafṣid(e)) (1277) i, 21a, 1152a, 1346b; iii, 66b, 338a, 673a, 705a; iv, 179a; vi, 196b, 404a – I, 22a, 1186b, 1386b; III, 69a, 348a, 695a, 727a; IV, 186b; VI, 180b, 388b
al-Mustanṣir (Hūdid(e)) → Aḥmad III
al-Mustanṣir II (Nizārī Imām) iv, 206a; v, 26b – IV, 215a; V, 27b
Mustapha Kateb (Masraḥ) (XX) vi, 754a – VI, 743a
Mustaʿrib → Mozarab
Mustaʿriba vii, **732b** – VII, **733a**
al-Mustarshid bi-'llāh, Abū Manṣūr al-Faḍl (ʿAbbāsid(e)) (1135) i, 353b, 522b, 858b, 901a; iii, 345a, 1255b; iv, 29b, 942b; vi, 64a, b; vii, **733a**; s, 194a – I, 364a, 538b, 882b, 928a; III, 355b, 1288b; IV, 31b, 975b; VI, 62a; VII, **733b**; S, 193b
Mustashār vii, **732b** – VII, **733b**
Mustashar al-Dawla Tabrīzī iv, 787b; s, 53b – IV, 819b; S, 54a
Mustashriḳūn vii, **735b** – VII, **736a**
al-Mustaʿṣim bi-'llāh, Abū Aḥmad ʿAbd Allāh (ʿAbbāsid(e)) (1258) i, 21a, 902b, 919a; iv, 30b; vi, 606a; vii, 166b, **753b**; s, 199a, 252b – I, 21b, 929b, 947a; IV, 32b; VI, 591a; VII, 168a, **754b**; S, 199a, 252b
al-Mustaʿṣimī → Yāḳūt
Mustawdaʿ ii, 851b – II, 871b
Mustawfī ii, 83a, 333b; iv, 977b; vii, **753b** – II, 84b, 343a; IV, 1010a; VII, **755a**
Mustawfī, Abū Naṣr Muḥammad (XI) vii, 535a – VII, 535a
Mustawfī, Ḥamd Allāh → Ḥamd Allāh Mustawfī al-Ḳazwīnī
Mustawfī al-mamālik ii, 335a, b – II, 344b, 345a
al-Mustawrid b. ʿUllafa (663) iii, 1265b; vi, 920a; vii, 347b – III, 1298a; VI, 912a; VII, 349a
Mustazād i, 677b; vii, **754b** – I, 698a; VII, **755b**
al-Mustaẓhir bi-'llāh (ʿAbbāsid(e)) (1118) i, 659b, 901a; ii, 385a; iii, 351b; vi, 275a; vii, 408a, **755a**; s, 194a, b, 326a – I, 680a, 928a; II, 395a; III, 362b; VI, 260a; VII, 409b, **756a**; S, 193b, 325b
al-Mustaẓhir bi-'llāh → ʿAbd al-Raḥmān V
Müstethna Eyāletler vii, **756a** – VII, **757b**
Muʾta (town/ville) ii, 372b; vi, 604a; vii, 372b, **756a** – II, 382b; VI, 588b; VII, 374a, **757b**
Mutʿa i, 209a; ii, 551b; vii, **757a**; s, 133a – I, 215b; II, 565a; VII, **758b**; S, 132b
Mūtā ii, 190b – II, 196b
al-Muṭāʿ v, 544a – V, 548b
Mutaʿarriba vii, **759b** – VII, **761a**
Mutadārik iv, 412b; vii, **759b** – IV, 430b; VII, **761a**
al-Muʿtadd → Hishām III
al-Muʿtaḍid bi-'llāh, Abu 'l-ʿAbbās b. al-Muwaffaḳ (ʿAbbāsid(e)) (902) i, 11a, 14b, 19a, 249a, 592a, 637a, 896a, 897b, 898a, 964b, 1141a; ii, 128b, 325b, 344b, 524a, 1080a; iii, 344b, 761b, 767b, 818a, 892b, 908a; iv, 21b, 22a, 42b, 90a, b, 189a, 265b, 940b, 49b; vi, 540a, 658a, 669b, 671a, 673a, 729a, 807b; vii, 395a, **759b**, 910b; s, 117b, 284a – I, 11a, 14b, 19b, 256b, 611b, 658a, 922b, 924b, 994b, 1175b; II, 131b, 335b, 354b, 537a, 1105a; III, 355a, 784b, 790b, 841b, 916b, 932a; IV, 23a, b, 51a, 94a, b, 197b, 277b, 973b, 51a; VI, 524b, 643b, 655b, 657b, 659b, 717b, 797b; VII, 396a, b, **761b**, 911a; S, 117a, 284a
al-Muʿtaḍid bi-'llāh, Abū ʿAmr b. ʿAbbād (ʿAbbādid(e)) (1069) i, 5b, 155b, 242a, 1040b, 1339a; ii, 389a, 1009a; iii, 496a, 640a, 705b; iv, 115b; v, 586b; vii, 249a, **760b** – I, 6a, 160a, 249b, 1072a, 1379a; II, 399b, 1032b; III, 513a, 661b, 728a; IV, 121a; V, 591b; VII, 250b, **762a**
al-Mutadjarrida vii, 563a, 841a – VII, 563b, 842b
Mutafarriḳa, Ibrāhīm → Ibrāhīm Müteferriḳa
al-Muṭahhar b. al-Mutawakkil ʿalā 'llāh (Yemen) (1572) vii, 721b, **761b**, 779b; viii, 235b – VII, 722a, **763a**, 781a; VIII, 240b
al-Muṭahhar b. Sharaf al-Dīn iv, 201a – IV, 210a
al-Muṭahhar b. Ṭāhir al-Maḳdisī, Abū Naṣr (X) v, 65a, 330a; vii, **762a** – V, 67a, 330a; VII, **763b**
Muṭahhar of/de Kara (XIV) x, 593a – X, 637b
al-Muṭahhar al-Hillī 1, 593a – I, 612b
Muṭahharī, Āyatullāh Murtaḍā (1979) iv, 166a; vii, **762b** – IV, 173a; VII, **764a**
Muṭahharten Bey i, 1119a; iv, 871a – I, 1152b; IV, 904b

Muʿtaḳ i, 30b – I, 31b
Mutaḳārib vii, **763a** – VII, **765a**
Mutakāwis → Ḳāfiya
al-Mutalammis (580) i, 451b; vii, **763a** – I, 464b; VII, **765a**
Muʿtamad Khān, Muḥammad Sharīf (1639) vii, 342b, 343a, **764a** – VII, 344b, **766a**
Muʾtaman al-Dawla Isḥāḳ Khān i, 680a – I, 701a
Muʾtaman al-Khilāfa iv, 613a – IV, 638a
al-Muʾtaman al-Sādjī i, 515b; iii, 730b – I, 531b; III, 753b Muʾtamar vii, **764b** – VII, **766a**
Muʾtamar vii, **764b** – VII, **766a**
al-Muʿtamid Ibn ʿAbbād (Muḥammad b. ʿAbbād al-Muʿtaḍid) (ʿAbbādid(e)) (1095) i, 6a, b, 251a, 592b, 601b; ii, 389b, 874a; iii, 677a, 706a, 783a, 853a, 905a, 963a, 973b; iv, 115b, 1007a; vi, 215b, 216a, 606b, 669b; vii, 553a, 633b, 761a, **766a**, 775b; s, 1a – I, 6b, 258b, 611b, 621b; II, 399b, 894b; III, 699a, 728a, 806a, 877a, 929a, 987b, 998a; IV, 121a, 1039b; VI, 200a, 591a, 655b; VII, 553a, 633a, 763a, **768a**, 777b; S, 1a
al-Muʿtamid ʿalā ʾllāh (ʿAbbāsid(e)) (892) i, 18b, 279a, 637a, 897b; ii, 389b; iii, 247a, 839b; vi, 215b, 216a, 606b, 669b; vii, 390b, **765b**; s, 16a, 402a – I, 19a, 287b, 658a, 924b; II, 400a; III, 254a, 863a; VI, 200a, 591a, 655b; VII, 391b, **767b**; S, 16b, 402b
al-Muʿtamīd (Zīrid(e)) iv, 117a – IV, 122a
al-Muʿtamid b. Abī ʿInān (Marrākush) (XIV) vi, 593b – VI, 578b
Muʿtamid al-Dawla → Ḳarwāsh b. al-Muḳallad
Muʿtamid al-Dawla iii, 1105b; v, 646a – III, 1133a; V, 650a
al-Muʾtamin b. Hārūn al-Rashīd (IX) vi, 332a – VI, 317a
al-Muʾtamin Ibn Hūd, Yūsuf b. Aḥmad (Hūdid(e)) (1083) vii, **768a** – VII, **770a**
Mutammim b. Nuwayra (VII) vi, 267a, 603a; vii, 308a; **768b** – VI, 251b, 588a; VII, 310a, b, **770a**
al-Mutanabbī, Abū ʾl-Ṭayyib Aḥmad (955) i, 119b, 212b, 592a, 601a, 827b, 845b, 1249b; ii, 802b; iii, 338a, 672a, 738b, 743b, 754b, 780a, 807a, 1264a; iv, 418b, 867b, 1069b; v, 927b, 934b; vi, 253a, 605b, 616b, 956b; vii, 261a, **769a**, 982b; s, 24a, 27b, 32b, 58b, 277b, 361b – I, 123a, 218b, 611b, 620b, 850b, 869a, 1287b; II, 821b; III, 348a, 693b, 761b, 766b, 777b, 803b, 830b, 1297a; IV, 437a, 900b, 1101a; V, 933a, 938b; VI, 237a, 590b, 601b, 949a; VII, 263a, **770b**, 983a; S, 24b, 27b, 32b, 59a, 277a, 361b
Mutanabbī al-Gharb viii, 420a – VIII, 434b
Mutarādif → Ḳāfiya
al-Muṭarrif (835) vi, 279a – VI, 264a
Muṭarrif b. ʿAbd Allāh al-Marwānī (894) vi, 899a; s, 153a – VI, 890a; S, 153a
al-Muṭarrif b. al-Mughīra b. Shuʿba (Mandāʾin) (VII) iii, 40b – III, 42b
Muṭarrif b. Shihāb b. ʿAmr al-Shihābī (1067) vii, 772b – VII, 774b
Muṭarrifiyya vii, **772b**; s, 22b, 236a – VII, **774b**; S, 22b, 236a
al-Muṭarrizī, Burhān al-Dīn Abu ʾl-Fatḥ Nāṣir (1213) v, 319a, b, 320b; vii, 190a, **773b**, 914b – V, 318a, b, 319b; VII, 190a, **775b**, 915a
Mutaṣarrif vii, **774a** – VII, **776a**
Mutaṣarrifiyya iv, 794a; v, 1253a, b – IV, 800a; V, 1244a, b
Mutashābih i, 275a, 409a, 412a – I, 283b, 421a, 423b
al-Muʿtaṣim biʾllāh → Yaḥyā b. al-Nāṣir b. al-Manṣūr
al-Muʿtaṣim bi-ʾllāh b. Hārūn al-Rashīd (ʿAbbāsid(e)) (842) i, 11b, 16b, 18b, 52b, 153b, 241a, 271a, 273a, 279b, 437b, 449b, 510a, 844a, b, 897b, 1096a, 1287b, 1346a; ii, 235b, 328a, 505b, 730b, 1079b; iii, 618a; iv, 97b, 215a, 646b; vi, 198a, 206a, 319b, 335a, b, 337b, 338a, b, 379a, 504b, 625b, 666a; vii, 279a, b, **776a**; s, 106a, 127b, 243a, 252b, 384b – I, 12a, 17a, 19a, 54a, 157b, 248b, 279b, 281a, 288a, 449b, 462b, 525b, 867b, 924a, 1129a, 1327a, 1386a; II, 242a, 337b, 518b, 749a, 1104b; III, 639a; IV, 101b, 224b, 673a; VI, 182a, 189a, 304a, 319b, 320a, 321b, 322a, b, 363b, 489b, 610b, 652a; VII, 281a, **777b**; S, 105b, 127a, 243a, 252b, 385a
al-Muʿtaṣim, Muḥammad b. Maʿn b. Ṣumādiḥ al-Tudjībī (Tudjībid(e)) (1091) iii, 775b, 934b; vii, 501a, **775b** – III, 799a, 959b; VII, 500b, **777b**
al-Muʿtaṣim bi-ʾllāh → Yaḥyā b. al-Nāṣir b. al-Manṣūr
Mutaṭawwiʿa (Muṭṭawiʿa) vii, **776b** – VII, **778b**
al-Mutawakkil ʿalā ʾllāh, Abu ʾl-Faḍl (ʿAbbāsid(e)) (861) i, 18b, 271b, 273a, 386a, 620b, 637a, 713a, 1287b, 1289b; ii, 130a, 281b, 292b, 324b, 385b, 437b, 837b, 1080a; iii, 579a, 618a, 691a, 824a, 940b; iv, 637b, 940b; v, 1111a; vi, 106a, 206a, 504b, 625b, 656b, 660a, 663a, 667a; vii, 279b, 280b, **777b**; s, 16b, 26a, 35a, 48a, 64a, 94b, 106a, 117b, 199a, 252a, b, 384b, 392a – I, 19a, 279b, 281a, 397b, 640b, 659b, 734b, 1327a, 1329a; II, 133a, 289b, 300a, 334a, 396a, 449a, 857a, 1105a; III, 599a, 639a, 713a, 848a, 965b; IV, 663b, 973b; V, 1107a; VI, 104a, 190a, 489b, 490a, 610b, 642a, 645b, 649a, 653a; VII, 281b, 282b, **779b**; S, 16b, 26b, 35b, 49a, 64b, 93b, 105b, 117a, 199a, 252a, b, 385a, 392b
al-Mutawakkil I (ʿAbbāsid(e), Cairo/le Caire) (1406) vi, 548a – VI, 532b
al-Mutawakkil III, Muḥammad (ʿAbbāsid(e), Cairo/le Caire) (1517, d. 1543) i, 21b; iv, 945b; vii, 911b – I, 22b; IV, 978b; VII, 912a
al-Mutawakkil ʿalā ʾllāh (Afṭasid(e)) (1095) vii, **778a** – VII, **780a**
al-Mutawakkil (Hūdid(e)) → Muḥammad b. Yūsuf b. Hūd
al-Mutawakkil Aḥmad b. Sulaymān iii, 125b; v, 1240b; s, 236a – III, 128b; V, 1231b; S, 236a
al-Mutawakkil ʿalā ʾllāh Aḥmad b. Sulaymān (Zaydī) (XII) vi, 433a – VI, 418b
al-Mutawakkil ʿalā ʾllāh Ismāʿīl b. al-Ḳāsim, Imām (Zaydī) (1676) ii, 517b; iii, 688b; v, 1241b; vi, 437a; vii, 514b, **778b** – II, 530b; III, 710b; V, 1233a; VI, 422b; VII, 515a, **780b**
al-Mutawakkil ʿalā ʾllāh Sharaf al-Dīn Yaḥyā, Imām (Zaydī) (1555) vi, 436b; vii, **779b** – VI, 422a; VII, **781a**
al-Mutawakkil Muḥammad b. Yaḥyā b. Muḥammad, Imām (Zaydī) (XIX) i, 555a; vii, 515a – I, 572b; VII, 515a
Mutawālī (Métoualis) vii, **780a** – VII, **781b**
al-Mutawallī, Abū Saʿd (1086) vii, **781a** – VII, **783a**
al-Mutawassiṭ → ʿAbd al-Raḥmān II
Mutawātir iii, 25b; iv, 412b; vii, **781b** – III, 26b; IV, 430b; VII, **783a**
Muṭawwif vii, **782a** – VII, **783b**
Muṭayr, Banū i, 545b; ii, 77a; iii, 1065b, 1068a; iv, 680b; vii, **782b** – I, 563a; II, 78b; III, 1092a, 1094; IV, 708b; VII, **784a**
Muṭayyabūn → Laʿaḳat al-Dam
Muṭayyabūn, Banū i, 151a;v, 581a, b; vi, 137b, 145a – I, 155a; V, 586a, b; VI, 136a, 143b
Mutayyam al-Hāshimiyya iv, 821b; s, 116b, 252b – IV, 854b; S, 116a, 252b
Mutayyan, Muḥammad b. ʿAbd Allāh b. Sulaymān al-Ḥaḍramī (909) viii, 517b – VIII, 535a

Mutazawwidjāt i, 308b – I, 318a
Muʿtazila i, 4b, 59b, 127b, 266a, 271a, 272a, 326a, 454a, 694a, 1002b, 1243a; ii, 365a, 373a, 388a, 449a, 569b; iii, 496b, 658b, 699a, 1142b, 1143a, 1148a, 1150a, 1165b, 1266a; iv, 46a, 366a, 379a, 1162a; vi, 218b, 331b, 336a, b, 337a, b, 338a, 376a, 448a, 457b, 458a, 467a; vii, **783a**; s, 12b, 16b, 17a, 23a, 25a, b, 30a, 31b, 56b, 88b, 103a, 225b, 306a, 335b, 343a, b, 344a, 391b, 392a, 393a –
I, 5a, 61b, 131a, 274a, 279b, 280a, 336b, 467a, 715a, 1033b, 1281a; II, 375a, 383a, 398b, 461a, 584a; III, 513b, 680a, 721b, 1171a, b, 1176b, 1178a, 1194a, 1298b; IV, 48b, 382a, 395b, 1194a; VI, 202b, 316a, 320b, 321a, b, 322b, 360b, 433b, 443a, b, 453a; VII, **785a**; S, 13a, 17a, 23b, 25b, 30a, 32a, 57a, 88a, b, 102b, 225b, 306a, 335a, 342b, 343b, 344a, 391b, 392b, 393b
—doctrine i, 17b, 128a, 178b, 187b, 204b, 209a, 334a, 410a-415b, 713b, 714a, 1092b; ii, 518a, 618a, 772a, 833b; iii, 171b, 465b, 661a, 672a, 1063a, 1146a; iv, 126b, 172a, 183a, 271b, 408a, 469a; v, 576b, 702a –
I, 18b, 131b, 183b, 193a, 210b, 215b, 344b, 422a-427b, 735a, b, 1125a; II, 531a, 633b, 790b, 853a; III, 175b, 481b, 682b, 693b, 1089b, 1174a; IV, 132a, 179b, 190b, 283b, 425b, 490a; V, 581a, 707a
al-Muʿtazila (Shiʿites) vii, **793b** – VII, **795a**
al-Muʿtazz bi-'llāh b. Djāfar (ʿAbbāsid(e)) (869) i, 273a, 278b, 897b, 1287b; ii, 36b, 1079b; iv, 89a, 126b; v, 1160a; vii, 390b, 477b, 777b, **793b** –
I, 281b, 287a, 924b, 1327a; II, 37a, 1104b; IV, 93a, 132a; V, 1150a; VII, 391b, 476b, 779b, **795b**
Müteferriḳa vii, **794a** – VII, **796a**
Müteferriḳa, Ibrāhīm → Ibrāhīm Müteferriḳa
Müterdjim Meḥmed Rüshdī (XIX) vi, 69a – VI, 67a
Mutesa (Uganda) (1884) x, 779a – X,
al-Muthaḳḳib al-ʿAbdī (590) i, 74a; viii, 421b – I, 76a; VIII, 436a
Muthallath (triangle) vii, **794b** – VII, **796a**
Muthamman vi, 127b; vii, **795a** – VI, 125b; VII, **796b**
al-Muthannā, Muḥammad b. ʿAbd Allāh (IX) vii, 649a – VII, 648b
al-Muthannā b. Ḥāritha (635) i, 111a, 964a; ii, 241a; iii, 194b, 1254b; iv, 13b, 385a; vi, 920a; vii, **796b** –
I, 114a, 994a; II, 248a; III, 199b, 1287a; IV, 14a, b, 401b, 402a; VI, 911b; VII, **798b**
Muthbita → Ahl al-ithbāt
Muṭīʿ b. Iyās al-Kinānī (785) i, 160a; ii, 1031b; iii, 135b; iv, 1003b; vii, **797b**; viii, 884a, 996b; ix, 387a –
I, 164b; II, 1055b; III, 138b; IV, 1036a; VII, **799b**; VIII, 914b, 1031b; IX, 394b
al-Muṭīʿ li 'llāh (ʿAbbāsid(e)) (974) i, 211b, 1352b; iii, 128a; vi, 786a; vii, 358a, 724a, **799a**; s, 36a –
I, 217b, 1391b; III, 130b; VI, 776a; VII, 360b, 724b, **801a**; S, 36b
al-Muṭīʿa s, 121b – S, 121a
Muṭʿim b. ʿAdī (VII) vii, 366a, 1045a – VII, 368b, 1047a
Muṭʿim al-Ṭayr iv, 91b – IV, 95b
Muṭlaḳ vii, **799b** – VII, **801b**
Muṭrān, Khalīl → Khalīl Muṭrān
al-Muttaḳī li 'llāh b. al-Muḳtadir (Abbāsid(e)) (968) i, 867a; iii, 127b; vi, 206a; vii, 723b, **800a**; s, 386a –
I, 891a; III, 130a; VI, 190b; VII, 724b, **801b**; S, 386b
al-Muttaḳī, ʿAlī b. Ḥusām al-Dīn (1567) vi, 247b; vii, 458a – VI, 231b; VII, 458a
al-Muttaḳī al-Hindī, ʿAlī (1567) i, 593a; ii, 500b; iii, 435a; vii, **800b** – I, 612a; II, 513a; III, 449a; VII, **802b**
Muṭṭalib, Banū i, 258a; vi, 145a; vii, 361b –
I, 266a; VI, 143a; VII, 364a
al-Muṭṭalib b. ʿAbd Manāf i, 80a, 115b; iii, 1093a – I, 82a, 118b; III, 1120a
Muttaṣil iii, 25b – III, 27a
al-Muṭṭawī, Tamīm b. Baḥr (IX) viii, 178a – VIII, 180b
Mütügen → Möeʿtüken
Muwāḍaʿa iv, 253b; vii, **801a** – IV, 264b; VII, **802b**
al-Muwāfaḳa wa 'l-djamāʿa ii, 78b – II, 80a
al-Muwaffaḳ b. al-Mutawakkil (ʿAbbāsid(e)) (880) i, 18b, 145a, 278b, 279a, 389a, 898a; ii, 196a, 1080a; iii, 859b, 908a, 976b; iv, 189a, 655a, 940b; v, 49a, b; vi, 673a, 921a; vii, 766a, **801a**; viii, 796as, 117b, 384b, 385a, 402a –
I, 19b, 149b, 287a, b, 400a, 925a; II, 202a, 1105a; III, 883b, 932a, 1001a; IV, 197a, b, 681a, 973b; V, 50b, 51a; VI, 659b, 912b; VII, 767b, **803a**; VIII, 823aS, 117a, 385b, 402b
al-Muwaffaḳ, Abū ʿAlī b. Ismāʿīl (X) s, 118b – S, 118a
Muwaffaḳ b. ʿAlī al-Harawī, Abū Manṣūr i, 213b, 686a, 1014b; iii, 267a; iv, 1123b – I, 220a, 707a, 1045b; III, 274b; IV, 1155a
Muwaffaḳ al-Dīn b. Ḳudāma → Ibn Ḳudāma
Muwaffaḳ al-Dīn Abu 'l-Maʿālī Aḥmad iii, 684b, 685a – III, 706b, 707a
Muwaffaḳ al-Dīn Yaʿḳūb s, 391a – S, 391a
al-Muwaffaḳiyya vi, 921a – VI, 912b
Muwaffiḳ al-Mulk → Ibn al-Tilmīdh
al-Muwaḥḥidūn (Almohad(e)s) i, 78a, 92b, 94b, 122a, 160b, 165a, 367a, 495b, 602a, 1176a, 1205b, 1339b; ii, 112a, 527a, 818b, 1007b, 1009b, 1110b; iii, 207a, 300b, 461b, 771b, 864b, 959b; v, 744b, 1189b, 1199b; vi, 134a, b, 141b, 216b, 404a, 520b, 521a, 571b, 572b, 573b, 577a, 589a, 596b, 597a, 741a, 742b, 852b; vii, 585b, **801b**; viii, 616b; x, 213a; s, 103a, 111b, 113b, 153a, 336b –
I, 80a, 95a, 125b, 165a, 169b, 378a, 510b, 621b, 1211a, 1241b, 1379b; II, 114b, 540a, 838a, 1031a, 1033a, 1136b; III, 212b, 309b, 478a, 794b, 889a, 984a; V, 750a, 1179b, 1190a; VI, 132a, b, 133a, 140a, 200b, 388b, 505b, 556b, 557b, 558b, 562a, 573b, 576b, 577a, 581a, b, 730b, 732a, 844a; VII, 586a, **803b**; VIII, 636aS, 102b, 111a, 113a, 153a, 336a; X, 230b
—administration i, 1148b; ii, 145b, 230a, 307b; iv, 943b; v, 626a – I, 1183a; II, 149b, 237a, 316b; IV, 976b; V, 630a
—constructions i, 1320b; ii, 822a; iii, 499b; iv, 633b – I, 1361a; II, 841bb; III, 516b; IV, 659b
—history/histoire i, 94b; iii, 570a, 924b; iv, 337b; v, 530b – I, 97a; III, 590a, 949a; IV, 352a; V, 534b
al-Muwaḳḳar vii, **807a** – VII, **808b**
Muwaḳḳit → Mīḳāt
Muwallad vii, **807a** – VII, **809a**
Muwalladūn i, 49a, 491a, 494a; iii, 770b – I, 50b, 505b, 508b; III, 794a
Muwāraba vii, **808b** – VII, **810b**
al-Muwāṣafa ii, 79a – II, 80b
Muwashshaḥ i, 426b, 595b, 601a, 602a; ii, 1033a, 1074a; iii, 729b, 851b, 855b, 929a; vii, **809a** – I, 438b, 615a, 620b, 621b; II, 1057a, 1098b; III, 752b, 875b, 879b, 953b; VII, **811a**
Muwāṭin vii, **812b** – VII, **814b**
al-Muwayliḥī, Ibrāhīm (1906) vii, **813a**, 902b – VII, **815a**, 903a
al-Muwayliḥī, Muḥammad (1930) i, 597a; iii, 59b; vi, 113b, 114b; vii, **814a**, 902a; viii, 736b – I, 616b; III, 62a; VI, 111a, 112a; VII, **815b**, 902b; VIII, 757b
Muways b. ʿImrān b. Djumayʿ (VIII) vii, 414b, 784b, **815a** – VII, 416a, 786b, **816b**
Muwaẓẓaf ii, 158a – II, 163a

Muyaka b. Mwinyi Haji al-Ghassaniy (1837) iv, 887a; vi, 612b; vii, 227a – IV, 919b; VI, 597b; VII, 229a
Muzabbid al-Madanī vii, 857a – VII, 858b
al-Muẓaffar (1008) → ʿAbd al-Malik b. Abī al-Maʿāfirī
Muzafar, sultan (Malacca) (XV) vi, 209a, 212a, b – VI, 193a, 196b
al-Muẓaffar (Afṭasid(e)) → ʿAbd al-Malik al-Muẓaffar
al-Muẓaffar (Artukid(e)) i, 665a – I, 686a
al-Muẓaffar (Ayyūbid(e)) → al-Malik al-Muẓaffar ʿUmar
Muẓaffar (Balansīya) i, 446b, 985b – I, 459a, 1016a
Muẓaffar (Maḳdishū) (XVI) vi, 128b – VI, 126b
al-Muẓaffar, Abu ʾl-Fatḥ ii, 1142b – II, 1169b
al-Muẓaffar b. ʿAlī (986) iii, 1176a; vii, **818a** – III, 1204b; VII, **820a**
Muẓaffar b. Kaydur (834) vii, 3b – VII, 3b
Muẓaffar II b. Maḥmūd Shāh (Gudjarāt) (1526) vii, 478b; viii, 64b – VII, 478a; VIII, 66a
al-Muẓaffar b. al-Malik al-Manṣūr (XIII) vi, 429b – VI, 415a
al-Muẓaffar b. al-Manṣūr → ʿAbd al-Malik b. Abī ʿĀmir al-Maʿāfirī
Muẓaffar b. Muḥammad Ḳāsim Muẓaffar Djunābadī (1596) x, 146a – X, 157b
Muẓaffar b. Nadjm al-Dīn Ghāzī I, Saʿīd (Artuḳid(e), Mārdīn) (XIII) vi, 540b – VI, 525a
Muẓaffar Aḥmad (XX) vii, 848a – VII, 849b
al-Muẓaffar Aḥmad b. al-Muʾayyad Shaykh (Mamlūk) (1421) iii, 1198a; vii, 272a – III, 1228a; VII, 274a
Muẓaffar ʿAlī (painter/peintre) (XVI) viii, 787b – VIII, 813b
Muẓaffar Barlās vii, 90b – VII, 92a
Muẓaffar Beg Turkamān (XVI) vi, 514b – VI, 500a
Muẓaffar al-Dīn b. ʿAlī Shīr ii, 989a – II, 1012a
Muẓaffar al-Dīn b. Naṣr Allāh Mangït (Bukhāra) (1885) v, 30b; vi, 419a – V, 31b; VI, 404a
Muẓaffar al-Dīn b. Nuṣrat al-Dīn (Marʿash) (XIII) vi, 507b – VI, 492b
Muẓaffar al-Dīn Gök-büri (Irbil) (1207) i, 300b, 1160b, 1161a; iii, 228b; iv, 76a-b; v, 477a; vi, 500b, 895b; vii, 273b, 727b, 817b; viii, 127b – I, 310a, 1195a, b; III, 235a; IV, 80a; V, 479b; VI, 485b, 886b; VII, 275b, 728b, 819a; VIII, 130a
Muẓaffar al-Dīn Muḥammad Shāh → Muḥammad Shāh b. Ḥadjdjādj
Muẓaffar al-Dīn Shāh (Ḳādjār) (1907) i, 1088b, 1296a; ii, 310b, 650a, b; iii, 555b; iv, 392a, 393b; vi, 276b, 291b, 529b; vii, 431b, **818a**; viii, 58b; s, 72a, 84a – I, 1120b, 1335b; II, 319b, 666b, 667a, 668a; III, 574b; IV, 408b, 410b; VI, 261b, 277a, 513b; VII, 432b, **820a**; VIII, 59bS, 72a, 83b
Muẓaffar al-Dīn Yuluḳ (Yavlaḳ) Arslan (1292) iv, 738a; viii, 544a – IV, 767b; VIII, 562a
Muẓaffar Djang i, 153a; iii, 320b – I, 157b; III, 331a
Muẓaffar Ḥusayn → Fidāʾī Khān Kōka
Muẓaffar Khān (Shāh) iv, 631b – IV, 656b
Muẓaffar Muḥammad (Shabānkāra) (1260) ix, 158a – IX, 163b
Muẓaffar al-Mulk ii, 31a – II, 31b
Muẓaffar Murtaḍāʾī, Sayyid (Hazārdjarīb) (1596) vi, 515a, b – VI, 500b, 501a
Muẓaffar Sayf al-Dīn Ḥādjdjī I (Mamlūk) (1347) ii, 24a; iii, 48a, 239b – II, 24b; III, 50a, 246b
Muẓaffar Shāh I Gudjarātī (1411) i, 506b, 1193a, 1300a, 1329b; ii, 218b, 270b, 276b, 322a, 405b, 597b, 1124b, 1125a; iii, 417a, 638a; vi, 50a – I, 522a, 1228b, 1340a, 1370a; II, 225b, 278b, 285a, 331b, 416b, 612a, 1151a, 1151b; III, 430b, 659b; VI, 48a
Muẓaffar Shāh II (Gudjarātī) (1526) ii, 322a, 405b, 1128a; iii, 422a, 1010a; vi, 54b, 55a, 269b, 270a – II, 331b, 416b, 1154b; III, 435b, 1035b; VI, 52b, 53a, 254b, 295a
Muẓaffar Shāh III (Gudjarātī) (1593) i, 80b, 156a, 938b; ii, 678a, 815a, 1129a; vi, 52b; vii, 131b – I, 83a, 161a, 967a; II, 695a, 834b, 1156a; VI, 50b; VII, 133b
Muẓaffar Shāh (Malacca) (1459) ix, 852a – X, 887b
Muẓaffar Shāh Shams al-Dīn Ḥabshī, Dīwāna (1493) ii, 1084b; iii, 14b, 631b; vi, 47a – II, 1110a; III, 15b, 652b; VI, 45b
Muẓaffar Shams Balkhī (1400) vii, **819b** – VII, **821b**
al-Muẓaffar Yūsuf (Rasūlid(e)) (1295) viii, 456a, 457a; s, 338b, 387b, 388a – VIII, 471b, 472b; S, 338a, 388a
Muẓaffarid(e)s i, 3b; ii, 401b; iii, 56a, 57b, 1208b; iv, 32a, 102b, 498b; v, 163b; vi, 493a; vii, 480b, **820a**; s, 327a, 335b, 415a – I, 3b; II, 412a; III, 58a, 60a, 1239a; IV, 34b, 107a, 520a; V, 161a; VI, 478b; VII, 480a, **821b**; S, 326b, 335a, 415a
Muzaffarnagar s, 126b – S, 125b
Muẓaffarpur vii, **822a** – VII, **823b**
al-Muzanī, Abū Ibrāhīm (878) i, 686b; vii, 409a, **822a**, 824b; viii, 497b – I, 707b; VII, 410b, **823b**, 826a; VIII, 514b
Muzāraʿa ii, 187b, 905b; iv, 1154a; v, 871b; vii, **822b** – II, 193b, 926b; IV, 1186a; V, 878a; VII, **824a**
al-Muzarrid (VI) ix, 11a – IX, 11b
Muzāta, Banū vi, 727a – VI, 716a
Muzāwadja vii, **823a** – VII, **824b**
Muzawwir v, 1004a – V, 1000a
al-Muzayḳiyāʾ → ʿAmr b. ʿĀmir
Muzayna (Muzayyin), Banū (Shilb) i, 6a; ii, 1009a; vi, 344a; vii, 356b, 761a, **824a** – I, 6a; II, 1032b; VI, 328b; VII, 359a, 762b, **825b**
Muzdalifa iii, 32b, 36a; vi, 105b, 162a, 169b; vii, **825a**; s, 33a – III, 34a, 37b; VI, 103a, 156a, 160b; VII, **826b**; S, 33b
Muzdawidj i, 2b, 587a; iv, 58a; vii, **825b** – I, 2b, 606a; IV, 61a; VII, **827a**
Muẓhir al-Shāwī (1958) vi, 616b – VI, 601a
Muzn (Māzandarān) vi, 937b – VI, 929b
Muznī, Banū i, 1247a – I, 1284b
Mwana Mkisi (Mombasa) vii, 226a – VII, 227b
Mwanga (Uganda) (1888) x, 779b – X,
Mwengo b. Athumani, Bwana s, 351b – S, 351b
Mysia iv, 627b, 628a – IV, 652b, 653a
Mysore → Mahisūr
Mytilene/Mytilène → Midilli
Mzāb i, 171b, 687a; ii, 1010a; iii, 96a, 97b, 98b, 656b; vi, 364b; vii, **826a**; s, 15b – I, 176a, 708a; II, 1033b; III, 98b, 100a, 101a, 677b; VI, 348b; VII, **827b**; S, 15b
Mzabites i, 371a; ii, 1010a; iii, 95a, 97a, b, 145a – I, 382a; II, 1033b; III, 97b, 100a, 148a

N

Naʿām vii, **828a** – VII, **830a**
al-Naʿāʾim s, 320b – S, 320a
Nabʿ iv, 797b – IV, 830a
Nabaʾ iii, 369a – III, 381a
Nābal i, 936a – I, 965a
al-Nabarāwī, ʿAbd Allāh (1859) vii, **831a** – VII, **832b**
Nabāt i, 213a; ii, 908b, 1038a, 1058b; vii, **831a** – I, 219a; II, 929b, 1062b, 1083a; VII, **833a**

Nabaṭ (Nabīṭ) (Nabataeans/Nabatéens) i, 528a, 548a, 563a, 564b, 1096a; ii, 246b, 278b, 1060a; iii, 366a; iv, 995a; v, 762a, 1156a; vi, 230b, 373b; vii, **834a** – I, 544a, 565b, 581a, 582b, 1129a; II, 253b, 287a, 1084b; III, 377b; IV, 1027b; V, 768a, 1146a; VI, 224b, 358a; VII, **835b**
Nabaṭī (poetry/poésie) vi, 230b, 373b; vii, **838a** – VI, 224b, 358a; VII, **839a**
al-Nabātī → Abu 'l-ʿAbbās
Nabaṭiyya (Djabal ʿĀmil) vii, 407b – VII, 409a
Nabawiyya ii, 964a – II, 986a
Nabaz iv, 180a – IV, 188a
Nabeul s, 11a, 145a – S, 10b, 144b
Nabhān (Ṭayyiʾ) s, 305a – S, 304b
Nabhān, Banū i, 553b; iv, 885b, 886b; vii, **838b**; viii, 85a, 287a – I, 571a; IV, 918b, 919b; VII, **839a**; VIII, 87a, 245b
al-Nabhānī, Ḥimyar b. Nāṣir (ʿUmān) (1920) viii, 993b – VIII, 1028a
al-Nabhānī → Taḳī al-Dīn al-Nabhānī
Nabī v, 423b – V, 425b
Nabī Djirdjīs → Djirdjīs
Nabī Yūnus → Nīnawā
Nābī Yūsuf (poet/poète) (1712) vi, 826b, 886b, 991b, 999b; vii, **839a**; s, 83a, 324a – VI, 817a, 877b, 984a, 992a; VII, **840a**; S, 83a, 323b
Nabīdh iv, 996a; vii, **840a** – IV, 1028b; VII, **841a**
Nābigha al-Dhubyānī (VI) i, 196a, 1149a, 1241b; ii, 1020b; iii, 1261a; vii, 254b, 563a, **840b**; viii, 119b; s, 178b – I, 202a, 1183b, 1279b; II, 1044b; III, 1294a; VII, 256a, 563b, **841b**; VIII, 122a; S, 179b
al-Nābla al-Djaʿdī, Ḳays b. ʿAbd Allāh (698) i, 115b; iv, 315b; v, 710a; vi, 625a; vii, **842b** – I, 119a; IV, 329b; V, 715a; VI, 610a; VII, **844a**
al-Nabīt i, 771b – I, 794b
Nābita ii, 386b; vii, **843b** – II, 397a; VII, **845a**
Nabl iv, 799a – IV, 831b
Nabob → Nawwāb
Nabtāb i, 440b; ii, 252b – I, 453a, II, 260a
Nabuchodonosor → Bukht-naṣar
Nābulus iv, 834b, 835a; vi, 543b; vii, **844a** – IV, 867b, 868a; VI, 528a; VII, **845a**
al-Nābulūsī → ʿAbd al-Ghānī b. Ismāʿīl
al-Nābulusī, Shams al-Dīn (1394) v, 9b – V, 10a
al-Nābulusī, ʿUthmān b. Ibrāhīm i, 800b, 801b; ii, 329b; v, 862b – I, 824a, b; II, 339a; V, 869b
Naceur Bey → Muḥammad al-Nāṣir
Nacir Ed Dine → Dinet, Alphonse
Nadhīr vii, **845a** – VII, **846b**
Nadhīr Aḥmad Dihlawī (1912) iii, 359a; v, 203a; vii, **845b**; x, 879b – III, 370a; V, 200b; VII, **846b**; X,
Nadhīr Ḥusayn → Sayyid Nadhīr Ḥusayn
Nadhr iv, 688a; vii, **846a**; s, 221b – IV, 716b; VII, **847b**; S, 221b
Nadhr al-Islām, Ḳāḍī (1976) i, 1169a; vii, **847b** – I, 1204a; VII, **849a**
Nadhr Muḥammad b. Dīn, Khān (Djānid(e)) (1651) i, 1195b, 1197a; vii, **849b**; ix, 411b – I, 1230b, 1232b; VII, **851a**; ix, 448a
Nadīm vii, **849b** – VII, **851a**
al-Nadīm → Ibn al-Nadīm
Nadīm, ʿAbd Allāh (1896) i, 597a; ii, 429a; v, 909b – I, 616b; II, 440a; V, 915a
Nadīm, Aḥmad → Nedīm, Aḥmed
al-Nadīm, al-Sayyid ʿAbd Allāh (1896) vii, 716a, **852a** – VII, 717a, **853a**
Nadir → Naẓīr al-Samt
Naḍīr, Banu 'l- i, 53a; ii, 869b; iv, 1139a, 1140b; v, 436a, 996a; vi, 647a, 650b; vii, 367a, 370a, **852b** – I, 55a; II, 889b; IV, 1170b, 1172a; V, 438b, 991b; VI, 632a, 635b; VII, 369b, 372a, **853b**
Nādir Khān (Gakkhar) (1853) ii, 973b – II, 996a
Nādir Khān (Mahsūd) (XX) vi, 86b – VI, 84b
Nādir Mīrzā b. Shāh Rukh (Afshārid(e)) (XVIII) vi, 715a – VI, 704a
Nādir Shāh Afshār (Afshārid(e)) (1747) i, 71b, 95a, 190a, 229a, b, 240b, 270a, 291a, 295a, 395b, 431b, 460a, 625b, 701b, 905a, 928a, 970b, 1001b, 1005b, 1008b, 1020a, 1087a, 1217b, 1281b, 1295b, 1330a, 1341b; ii, 88a, 186a, 206a, 265b, 310b, 350b, 1049b, 1114b, 1131b; iii, 106a, 177b, 427b, 485a, 1103a, 1257b; iv, 37b-38a, 50b, 104a, 357a, 389b, 390a, 537a, 638a, 666a, 978a, 1048b; v, 103a, 164a, 312a, 461a, 494a, 643a, 1240a; vi, 55b, 56a, b, 202b, 310a, 418b, 495a, 502b, 527b, 528b, 529a, 535b, 551a, b, 715a, 939b; vii, 222b, 299a, 316a, 457a, 674b, **853a**; viii, 9a, 253b, 771b; x, 47a; s, 94b, 97b, 237b, 251b, 259a, 260b, 276a, 281a, 336a, 358b, 420a –
I, 73b, 98a, 196a, 236a, b, 248a, 278b, 300a, 304b, 407a, 443b, 473a, 646b,722b, 932b, 956b, 1000a, 1032a, 1036b, 1039b, 1051b, 1119b, 1254a, 1321a, 1335b, 1371a, 1381b;II, 89b, 192a, 212b, 273b, 319b, 360a, 1074a, 1140b, 1158a; III, 108b, 182a, 441b, 502a, 1130a, 1290a; IV, 39b-40b, 53b, 109a, 372b, 406a, b, 560b, 664a, 693a, 1010b, 1080a; V, 105a, 162a, 311b, 464a, 497a, 647a, 1231a; VI, 53b, 54a, 187a, 295a, 403b, 480b, 488a, 511b, 512a, 513a, 520a, 535b, 536a, 703b, 931b; VII, 224b, 301a, 318b, 457a, 674a, **854a**; VIII, 9b, 255b, 797a; X, 48b; S, 94a, 97a, 237a, 251b, 259a, 260a, 275b, 281a, 335b, 358b, 420a
Nādir Shāh Bārakzay (1933) ii, 232b, 658b; v, 1079a; vii, 438a – II, 239b, 675a; V, 1076b; VII, 439a
Nādira ii, 536b; iii, 369b; vii, **856b** – II, 550a; III, 381b; VII, **858a**
al-Naḍīra bint al-Ḍayzan iii, 51a – III, 53a
Nādira Begam (XVII) ii, 135a – II, 138b
Nādira Khānim (1842) vi, 768a – VI, 757a
Nadīr-i Nādirpūr iv, 72a – IV, 75b
Nādiya (Nabadwip) vii, 433a – VII, 434a
Nadjadāt iii, 1167b; vii, 562a, **858b** – III, 1196b; VII, 562b, **860a**
al-Nadjaf i, 385a; iv, 703b; vi, 88a, 351b, 516a, b, 552b; vii, **859b**; s, 54b, 75b, 76a, 91b, 94a, b, 104a, 119a, 157b, 342a, 380a –
I, 396a; IV, 732a; VII, **861a**; S, 54b, 76a, 91b, 93b, 94a, 103b, 118b, 158a, 341b, 380a; VI, 86a, 335b, 501a, b, 537a
Nadjaf Khān i, 253a, 403a; iv, 666a; v, 283a – I, 261a, 415a; IV, 693a; V, 281a
Nadjaf-Ḳulī (Ḳādjār) s, 290b – S, 290a
al-Nadjafī, Fakhr al-Dīn al-Ṭurayḥī (1674) vii, 528a – VII, 528b
Nadjafī, Hādjdjī Shaykh Muḥammad Ḥasan Iṣfahānī (1849) vi, 552a, b; s, 75b – VI, 536b, 537a; S, 76a
Nadjafī, Shaykh Djaʿfar (1812) s, 134b, 135a – S, 134a, b
Nadjāḥ (Tihāma) (XI) s, 22b – S, 22b
Nadjāḥ b. Salama (IX) vii, 653a – VII, 652b
Nadjaḥid(e)s i, 552a, 552b; v, 1244a, b; vii, **861b** – I, 569b, 570a; V, 1235a; VII, **862b**
Nadjāsa, Banū vi, 311a – VI, 296a
al-Nadjāshī (negus) i, 482a; iii, 10a; vi, 145b, 653b; vii, 372a, **862a** – I, 496b; III, 10b; VI, 143b, 639a; VII, 373b, **863b**
al-Nadjāshī, Aḥmad b. ʿAlī (1063) iii, 1151b; vi, 785a; vii, 313a; ix, 114a; s, 233a – III, 1179b; VI, 775a; VII, 315b; IX, 118s; S, 233a
al-Nadjāshī (poet/poète) → Ḳays b. ʿAmr
Nadjāt, Mīr ʿAbd al-ʿĀl (1714) vii, **864a** – VII, **865a**
Nadjātī → Nedjātī

Nadjd i, 233a, 539a, 554a; ii, 159b, 320b, 660a; iii, 362b, 1066b, 1067b; iv, 717a, 1143b; vi, 9a, 33a, b, 34a, 56b, 81a, 84a, 150a, 156b, 191b, 266a, 267b; vii, **864a**; s, 3b, 234b, 304b, 318a – I, 240a, 555b, 571b; II, 164b, 330a, 676b; III, 373b, 1093a, 1094a; IV, 746a, 1175b; VI, 9a, 31b, 32a, b, 54b, 79a, 82a, 148b, 152b, 175b, 251a, 252b; VII, **865b**; S, 2b, 234a, 304a, 318a
—dialect i, 573b – I, 592b
Nadjd b. Muslim iv, 1103b – IV, 1134b
Nadjd al-Djāh s, 22b – S, 22b
Nadjda b. ʿĀmir al-Ḥanafī al-Ḥarūrī (691) i, 55a, 120a, 550a, 810a, 942a; iii, 661a; iv, 764a, 1076a; vii, 858b; s, 338a – I, 57a, 123b, 567b, 833a, 971a; III, 682b; IV, 794b, 1107b; VII, 860a; S, 337b
al-Nadjdī → ʿAbd Allāh b. Ibrāhīm
al-Nadjdjād, Abū Bakr iii, 159a, 734b – III, 162b, 757b
al-Nadjdjār → Balīnūs (of Perge/de Perga)
Nadjdjār, Banū vi, 474b, 645b – VI, 460b, 630b
al-Nadjdjār, ʿAbd al-Wahhāb v, 180b – V, 178a
al-Nadjdjār, Abū Ḥāmid Aḥmad b. Muḥammad s, 343a – S, 342b
al-Nadjdjār, al-Ḥusayn b. Muḥammad Abū ʿAbdallāh (IX) i, 204b, 1242a; iv, 271b, 692b, 1187b; vii, 392b, 546b, 604a, **866b** – I, 210b, 1280a; IV, 284a, 720b, 1220a; VII, 394a, 546b, 604a, **868a**
al-Nadjdjāriyya i, 1326a; vii, **868a** – I, 1367a; VII, **869b**
Nadjdjārzāda, ʿAbd al-Raḥīm → Ṭālibov
Nadjdiyya i, 77a; s, 338a – I, 79a; S, 337b
Nādjī, Ibrāhīm (1953) vii, **868b** – VII, **870a**
Nadjīb (Neguib) → Muḥammad Nadjīb
al-Nadjīb b. Muḥammad (1600) viii, 18b – VIII, 18b
Nadjīb b. Sulaymān al-Ḥaddād (1899) vi, 746a, 751b, 755a; vii, **869a** – VI, 735b, 741a, 744a; VII, **870b**
Nadjīb Allāh Khān iii, 336a – III, 346a
Nadjīb ʿAzūrī (XX) iii, 519a – III, 537a
Nadjīb al-Dawla (Rohilla) (1770) i, 296a, 1042b, 1206a; iii, 61a, 1158b; vii, **869b**; viii, 572a,b – I,305a, 1074b, 1242a; III, 63b, 1187a; VII, **871a**; VIII, 590b, 541a
Nadjīb al-Dīn ʿAlī b. Buzghush (1279) viii, 860a – VIII, 890a
Nadjīb al-Dīn Firdawsī (1291) vi, 131a, 410a – VI, 129b, 395a
Nadjīb Diyāb s, 28a – S, 28a
Nadjīb Muḥammad Surūr (1978) vii, **869b** – VII, **871a**
Nadjīb Pasha iv, 638a – IV, 664b
Nadjīb al-Rīḥānī (1949) ii, 39b; vi, 746b, 750b – II, 40b; VI, 735b, 739b
Nadjīb Ziyāb (XX) ii, 471a – II, 483a
Nadjībābād vii, **870a** – VII, **871b**
Nadjiram vi, 384b – VI, 368b
Nadjis vii, **870a** – VII, **871b**
Nādjiya, Banū v, 19b – V, 20a
Nadjm al-Dawla Khumārtigin s, 382b – S, 382b
Nadjm al-Dīn, Adda Mullā (Paṭhān) vii, 220b – VII, 222a
Nadjm al-Dīn Ayyūb Abū Ṣalāḥ al-Dīn (1173) viii, 132b – VIII, 135a
Nadjm al-Dīn Ibn Abī Asrūn iii, 681b, 682a – III, 703b
Nadjm al-Dīn Alpī (Artuḳid(e), Mārdīn) (1176) vi, 930b – VI, 922b
Nadjm al-Dīn-i Dāya (1256) s, 364a, b – S, 364 a, b
Nadjm al-Dīn Il Ghāzī I (Artukid(e)) (1122) ix, 11b – IX, 12a
Nadjm al-Dīn Ghāzī II, al-Malik al-Manṣūr (Artuḳid(e)) (1312) viii, 802a – VIII, 829a
Nadjm al-Dīn al-Ḥarrānī (XIV viii, 624a – VIII, 643a)
Nadjm al-Dīn Ismāʿīl vi, 790b – VI, 780b
Nadjm al-Dīn Ḳārin → Ḳārin b. Shahriyār Bāwand
Nadjm al-Dīn Kubrā → Kubrā, Shaykh Aḥmad b. ʿUmar Nadjm al-Dīn
Nadjm al-Dīn al-Miṣrī (XIII) vii, 29b – VII, 30a
Nadjm al-Dīn Muḥammad (vizier) (1335) ix, 191b – IX, 197b
Nadjm al-Dīn Rāzī Dāya (1256) vi, 15a; vii, **870b**; viii, 539b; 972a; ix, 862a – VI, 13a; VII, **872a**; VIII, 557b, 1006b; IX, 897b
Nadjm-i Thānī → Muḥammad Bāḳir Nadjm-i Thānī (1637)
Nadjrān i, 151b, 538a, 555a; ii, 127b, 131a, 244b; iii, 223a; vi, 190b, 191a, 192a, 371b, 433a, 436a, 559b; vii, 373b, **871b**; ix, 729a; s, 335a – I, 155b, 554b, 572b; II, 131a, 134b, 251b; III, 229b; VI, 174b, 175a, 176a, 356a, 418b, 421a, b, 544a; VII, 375a, **873a**; IX, 864a; S, 334b
al-Nadjrānī, ʿAlī b. ʿAbd Allāh b. ʿUtba s, 393a – S, 393b
Nadjwā iii, 81a – III, 83b
al-Naḍr b. al-Ḥārith b. ʿAlḳama (VII) i, 358b; iii, 370a; vii, 369b, **872b**; s, 91a – I, 369b; III, 382a; VII, 371b, **874a**; S, 90b
Naḍr b. Kināna i, 1021b – I, 1053a
al-Naḍr b. Saʿīd al-Ḥarashī, Ḳaysī (VIII) i, 53b; ii, 90a; vi, 624a – I, 55b; II, 92a; VI, 609a
al-Naḍr b. Shumayl al-Māzinī (820) iii, 155a; vi, 954b; vii, **873a**; s, 317b – III, 158b; VI, 947a; VII, **874b**; S, 317b
Nadrūma (Nedroma) v, 397a; vii, **873b**; s, 144b – V, 379b; VII, **875a**; S, 144a
Nadvat ul-Mujahideen (Mappila) vi, 462b – VI, 448a
Nadwa → Dār al-Nadwa
Nadwat al-ʿUlamāʾ (Lakhnaw) ii, 132b; iii, 433a; vii, **874b** – II, 135b; III, 447a; VII, **876a**
Nadwī, Sayyid Sulaymān (1953) ii, 132b; iii, 435a, 1174a; vii, **875b** – II, 136a; III, 449a, 1203a; VII, **877a**
Nafādh iv, 412a – IV, 430a
Nafaḳa iii, 1011b – III, 1037a
Nafaḳat al-safar iii, 184a, 186a – III, 188b, 190b
Nafal → Ghanīma
Nafar iv, 9b – IV, 10a
Nafas → Nafs; Nefes
al-Nafāthiyya iii, 659b – III, 680b
Naffātī → Nafāthiyya
Naffīs (river/fleuve) vi, 742a, b, 743b – VI, 731a, b, 732b
Nāfiʿ (ḥadīth) (735) i, 140a; vi, 278b; vii, **876a** – I, 144a VI, 263b; VII, **877b**
Nāfiʿ b. ʿAlḳama ii, 1011b – II, 1035a
Nāfiʿ b. ʿAbd al-Ḳays al-Fihrī (VII) vii, 154a – VII, 156a
Nāfiʿ b. Abd al-Raḥmān al-Laythī (785) i, 718a; iii, 155b, 732b; v, 127b, 997b; vi, 263a; vii, **878a** – I, 739b; III, 158b, 755b; V, 130b, 993a; VI, 247b; VII, **878b**
Nāfiʿ b. al-Azraḳ al-Ḥanafī al-Ḥanẓalī (683) i, 120a, 810a; iii, 367a, 648b; vi, 457b, 636a; vii, 858b, **877a** – I, 123b, 833a; III, 378b, 669b; VI, 443a, 621a; VII, 860a, **878b**
Nāfiʿ b. al-Ḥārith b. Kalada s, 354b – S, 354b
Nāfiʿ b. Kalada s, 354b – S, 354b
Nāfiʿ b. ʿUmar (735) x, 29a – X, 30a
Nāfidh, Aḥmed iv, 877b, 878a – IV, 910b

Nāfidh, Fārūk (XX) viii, 221a – VIII, 225b
Nāfila vii, **878a** – VII, **879a**
Nafīr → Nefīr
Nafīs b. ʿIwaḍ s, 271b – S, 271b
Nafīsa, al-Sayyida (mausoleum/-ée) vii, **879a** – VII, **880a**
Nafīsa bint al-Ḥasan b. Zayd b. al-Ḥasan (824) vii, 879a – VII, 880a
Nafīsī, Saʿīd (1966) vii, **879b** – VII, **880b**
Nafs iv, 487a; vii, **880a** – IV, 508a; VII, **881a**
al-Nafs al-Zakiyya → Muḥammad b. ʿAbd Allāh b. al-Ḥasan b. al-Ḥasan (ʿAlid(e)) (762)
Nafṭ i, 967a, 1055b, 1056a, 1059a, 1068b; ii, 507a; iii, 470a, 475b; vii, **884a** – I, 996b, 997a, 1087a, b, 1090b, 1100b; II, 519b; III, 486a, 492a; VII, **885a**
Nafṭa (Nefṭa) (Tunisia/-ie) vii, **890b** – VII, **891a**
Nafṭa (Ḳasṭīliya) s, 402b – S, 403a
Nafūd i, 537a, 1312b; ii, 92a; vii, **891a** – I, 553b, 1352b; II, 93b; VII, **891b**
al-Nafūsa, Banū (Infūsen) i, 1349b; iii, 654a, 655b; vi, 452b, 453a; vii, **892a** – I, 1390a; III, 675a, 677a; VI, 438a; VII, **892b**
Nafūsa, Djabal → Djabal –
al-Nafūsī, Abū Sahl al-Fārisī (Rustamid(e)) (VIII) vii, **895a** – VII, **896a**
Nafy vii, **895b** – VII, **896b**
Nafza, Banū vii, **896b** – VII, **897a**
Nafzāwa, Banū i, 1349b; vii, **896b** – I, 1390a; VII, **897a**
al-Nafzāwī, Muḥammad ii, 552b – II, 566b
Nagar vii, **897b**; s, 327b – VII, **898b**; S, 327a
Nagarkōt → Kāṅgrā
Nagawr iii, 441b; v, 884a; vi, 48b; vii, 134b, **898a**; s, 353a, b – III, 455b; V, 890a; VI, 47a; VII, 136b, **898b**; S, 353a, b
Nāgawrī, Shaykh Ḥamīd al-Dīn Suwali (1274) vii, 898a – VII, 899a
Nāgawrī, Shaykh Mubārak (1593) vii, 898a – VII, 899a
Naghmī, Naghamī v, 951b – V, 955b
Naghrallā, Banū ’l- i, 491b – I, 506a
Nagir → Hunza and/et Nagir
Nagīsa vi, 742a – VI, 731a
Nāgōshias i, 1255a – I, 1293a
Nagpur vi, 535b; vii, **898b** – VI, 520a; VII, **899a**
Nagyvárad vii, **899b** – VII, **900a**
Nahār → Layl and/et Nahār
Nahāwandī → ʿAbd al-Bāḳī
al-Nahāwandī, Benjamin iv, 604a, b, 606b – IV, 628a, 629a, 630b
Nahḍa iv, 142b, 143b; v, 794b; vii, **900a** – IV, 148b, 149a; V, 800b; VII, **901a**
al-Nahḍa (al-Ḳāhira) s, 5b – S, 4b
Nahdat al-ʿUlamāʾ iii, 534a, b, 1229b, 1230b – III, 552b, 553a, 1261a, 1262a
Nahdatul Ulama vi, 730a; s, 151a – VI, 719a; S, 151a
al-Nahdayn ix, 1a – IX, 1a
Nahdī, Banū vi, 221b – VI, 215a
Nahdj al-Balāgha vii, **903b** – VII, **904a**
al-Naḥḥās, Abū Djaʿfar (950) vii, 569b; viii, 14a; x, 84b – VII, 570a; VIII, 14b; X, 91b
al-Naḥḥās, Muṣṭafā (1965) vii, **904b** – VII, **905a**
al-Naḥḥāsīn (al-Ḳāhira) s, 5a – S, 4b
Naḥīfī, Süleymān (1739) vii, **905a** – VII, **906a**
Nahīk Mudjāwid al-Rīḥ iv, 91b – IV, 95b
al-Nahīkī, ʿAbd Allāh b. Muḥammad (X) vii, 460a, 905b – VII, 460a, 906a
al-Nahīkī, Abu ’l-ʿAbbās ʿUbayd Allāh (IX) vii, 906a – VII, 906b
Nāḥiye iv, 229b, 230a, b; vii, **906a** – IV, 239b, 240a, b; VII, **906b**
Nāḥiyy Tūnb iv, 778a, b; s, 417b – IV, 809b, 810a; S, 418a
Naḥl vii, **906a** – VII, **906b**
Nahr i, 52b, 1029b, 1094b; ii, 438a; iv, 133b, 193a; v, 368a, 885a, 886a; vii, **909b** – I, 54a, 1061a, 1127a; II, 449b; IV, 139a, 201a; V, 369a, 891b, 892a; VII, **910a**
Nahr Abī Fuṭrus i, 103a; vii, **910a** – I, 106a; VII, **910b**
Nahr al-ʿĀṣī → al-ʿAṣī
Nahr al-Aʿwadj vi, 546a, 547b – VI, 530b, 532a
Nahr al-ʿAwdjāʾ → Nahr Abī Fuṭrus
Nahr Bāniyās vi, 577b – VI, 562b
Nahr Baradān → Ṭarsūs
Nahr Ḥūrīth → Aḳ-Ṣū
Nahr ʿĪsā ibn ʿAlī → ʿĪsā, Nahr
Nahr al-Isḥāḳī x, 141a – X, 152a
Nahr Ḳadīsha (Tripoli in Syria) x, 214b – X, 231b
Nahr al-Kalb vi, 343b – VI, 327b
Nahr al-Khawṣar vi, 900b – VI, 892a
Nahr al-Ḳubāḳib vi, 230a – VI, 224a
Nahr al-Ḳuwayḳ vi, 544a – VI, 528b
Nahr al-Maʿḳil vii, 67a; s, 16a – VII, 68a; S, 16b
Nahr al-Malik → Didjla
Nahr Markiya vi, 577b – VI, 562b
Nahr al-Ratīn → Shāpūr (river/fleuve)
Nahr Ṣughd → Zarafshān
Nahr Tīrā s, 352a – S, 352a
Nahr al-Ubulla vii, 67a – VII, 68a
Nahr Yazīd s, 197a – S, 197a
Nahr Zubayda vi, 900b – VI, 892a
Nahr al-Zuṭṭ s, 243a – S, 243a
al-Nahradjūrī, Abū Aḥmad iii, 1071b – III, 1098a
al-Nahradjūrī, Abū Yaʿḳūb (X) vi, 224a – VI, 217b
al-Nahrawālī, Ḳuṭb al-Dīn Muḥammad (1582) vii, **911b** – VII, **912a**
al-Nahrawān i, 40b, 384b; ii, 250a, 343b; iii, 236b; iv, 1075a; vii, **912b** – I, 41b, 395b; II, 257a, 353a; III, 243a; IV, 1106b; VII, **913a**
al-Nahrawānī, Abū Ḥakīm (1161) iii, 751a – III, 774a
Nahray ben Nissim ii, 988b – II, 1011b
Nahrwāl → Anhalwāra; Pātan
Naḥw iv, 122a; v, 804a; vii, **913a** – IV, 127b; V, 810a; VII, **913b**
Naḥwī v, 1133b – V, 1129b
Nāʾib vii, **915a** – VII, **915b**
Naʾib ʿĀlim Khān (1866) vi, 942a – VI, 934b
Nāʾif b. ʿAbd al-ʿAzīz (Āl Saʿūd) (XX) vi, 158a – VI, 153b
Naïl, Awlād i, 371b – I, 382b
Nāʾila → Isāf
Nāʾilī (1634) i, 1302a – I, 1341b
Nāʾilī (Pīrī-zāde) (Nāʾilī-yi Ḳadīm) (1666) ii, 1000a; vii, **916a**; s, 324a – II, 1023a; VII, **916b**; S, 323b
Nāʾilī, Ṣāliḥ (1876) vii, 916a – VII, 916b
Naʿīm, Aḥmed s, 83a – S, 83a
Naʿīm, Āl iv, 752a; s, 42a – IV, 782a; S, 42b
Naʿīm al-Dīn (Naʿīmī) (XVIII) vii, **917a** – VII, **917b**
Naʿīmā, Muṣṭafā (1716) vi, 343b, 345b, 725a, 990b; vii, **917a** – VI, 328a, 329b, 714a, 983b; VII, **917b**
Nāʾīn (Nāyin) vii, **918a** – VII, **918b**
Nāʾīnī, Mīrzā Muḥammad Ḥusayn Gharawī (1936) iv, 164b; vi, 553a; vii, 301a, **918b**; s, 109b, 342a – IV, 171b; VI, 537b; VII, 303a, **919a**; S, 109a, 341b
Nāʾīnī, Mīrzā Rāfīʿ al-Dīn (1688) vi, 516b; viii, 779a – VI, 501b; VIII, 805a
Nāʿiṭ vi, 566a – VI, 551a
Naitias (Naʾitas) vii, **919b** – VII, **920a**

Najāra, Israel iv, 310a – IV, 324a
Naḳā vii, **920a** – VII, **920b**
Nakad i, 1078a – I, 1110b
Naḳā'iḍ vii, **920a** – VII, **920b**
al-Naḳb vii, **920b** – VII, **921a**
Naḳd vii, **921a** – VII, **921b**
Naḳd al-Mīthāḳ vii, **921a** – VII, **921b**
al-Nakhaʿī al-Aḥmar al-Kūfī, Isḥāḳ b. Muḥammad (899) vii, 460a – VII, 460a
al-Nakhaʿī, Ḥafṣ b. Ghiyāth (809) viii, 388a – VIII, 401a
al-Nakhaʿī, Ibrāhīm b. Yazīd (717) vii, **921b** – VII, **922a**
Nakhāwila v, 998b, 999b – V, 994a, 995a
Nakhčiwān i, 8a, 191b; vi, 200b, 202b, 365b; vii, **922a**; viii, 175a – I, 8a, 197a; VI, 185a, 187a, 349b; VII, **922b**; VIII, 177b
Nakhdjawānī, Muḥammad b. Hindūshāh (XIV) iii, 284a, 1243a; iv, 526a; v, 872b; vi, 15a, 456a; ix, 5a – III, 293a, 1275a; IV, 548b; V, 878b; VI, 13b, 441b; IX, 5b
Nakhidjevan s, 275a – S, 274b
Nakhkhās i, 32b – I, 33a
Nakhl vii, **923a**; ix, 763b – VII, **923b**; IX, 797a
Nakhla i, 540a; ii, 1058a; iii, 237b; iv, 995b; v, 595b; vi, 146b; vii, 356b, 369b, **924b** – I, 557a; II, 1082b; III, 244b; IV, 1028a; V, 599b; VI, 145a; VII, 358b, 371a, **925a**
Nakhla al-Mudawwar s, 161a – S, 161a
Nakhlī → Ḥāfiẓ Tanish
Nakhshab vii, **925a** – VII, **925b**
Nakhshabī, Shaykh Ḍiyā' al-Dīn (1350) iv, 69a; vii, **925a** – IV, 73a; VII, **925b**
al-Naḳīʿ iv, 1144a – IV, 1175b
Naḳīb iii, 184a; iv, 267a; v, 1131b; vii, **926a**; s, 208b – III, 188b; IV, 279a; V, 1127b; VII, **926b**; S, 208a
al-Naḳīb, ʿAbd al-Raḥmān iii, 521a – III, 539a
Naḳīb al-Ashrāf iii, 1152b; iv, 103b, 474b; vii, **926b**; s, 122b, 132b – III, 1181a; IV, 108a, 495b; VII, **927a**; S, 122a, 132a
Naḳībī → Mīr Lawḥī
Naḳīḍa → Naḳā'iḍ
Nakīr → Munkar wa-Nakīr
Naḳīr (drink/boisson) iv, 995b – IV, 1028b
Nakiye, Elgün (Khanim) iv, 933b – IV, 966b
Naḳḳāra-khāna vii, **927b** – VII, **928a**
Nakkārī → Yazīdīs
Naḳḳāsh → Ghiyāth al-Dīn
al-Naḳḳāsh, Mārūn b. Ilyās (1855) i, 597a; vi, 746a; vii, **930a** – I, 616b; VI, 735a, b; VII, **930b**
Naḳḳāsh, Muḥammad → Darwīsh Muḥammad
al-Naḳḳāsh, Salīm → Salīm b. Khalīl
Naḳḳāsh ʿAlī Pasha v, 649b – V, 654a
Naḳḳāsh Ḥasan Pasha (1622) vii, **931a** – VII, **931b**
Naḳḳāsh-khāna iv, 1169a; vii, **931a** – IV, 1202a; VII, **931b**
Naḳl vii, **932a** – VII, **932b**
Naḳsh → Kitābāt
Naḳshband, Muḥammad b. Muḥammad Bahā' al-Dīn al-Bukhārī (1389) vi, 354b; vii, **933a**; viii, 539b, 704a; x, 250b; s, 50b, 364b – VI, 338b; VII, **933b**; VIII, 557b, 724a; X, 268aS, 51b, 364b
al-Naḳshabandī, ʿAbd al-Ḥaḳḳ (XX) v, 1005b – V, 1001a
Naḳshbandiyya i, 755b, 782a, 1072a, 1137a, 1295b; ii, 18a, 88a, 91b, 137b, 293a, 296b, 711b, 879a, 1078a; iii, 38a, 432b, 662b; iv, 48b; v, 53b, 475a, 486a, 851a, 859a; vi, 224a, 225b, 354b, 408a, 953a; vii, **934b**; viii, 237b; s, 50b, 51b, 71a – I, 778a, 805a, 1104a, 1171b, 1335a; II, 18a, 90a, 93a, 141b, 301a, 304b, 730a, 899a, 1103a; III, 39b, 446b, 684a; IV, 51b; V, 55a, 478a, 489a, 855b, 866a; VI, 218a, 219a, 338b, 393a, 945b; VII, 9**35a**; VIII, 243aS, 51a, 52a, 72a
Naḳshdjam vii, 124a – VII, 126a
Naḳshe (Naxos) vii, **939b**; ix, 483b – VII, **940a**; IX, 502a
Naḳsh-i Djahān (palace/palais, Iṣfahān) vi, 525b, 526b – V, 510a, 511a
Naḳsh-i Radjab iv, 220b – IV, 230b
Naḳsh-i Rustam (Shāpūr) ii, 135b; iv, 220b, 221a, b – II, 139a; IV, 230b, 231a
Nakūk → Abu 'l-ʿAlā' b. Yaʿḳūb
Nakūr (Nukūr) v, 1119a; vi, 120b; vii, 641b, **941a**; s, 377a – V, 1115b; VI, 118b; VII, 641b, **941b**; S, 377a
Nāḳūs i, 188a; vii, **943a** – I, 193a; VII, **943a**
Naʿl v, 733a, 735b, 736a, 752b – V, 738a, 740b, 741a, 758a
Naldrug iii, 448a; vii, **943a** – III, 463a; VII, **943b**
Nalgunda vi, 66b – VI, 64b
Nāma vii, **943b** – VII, **944a**
al-Namalī, Muḥammad b. Ḥassān ii, 552a – II, 566a
Namāra vi, 261a; vii, **944a** – VI, 245b; VII, **944b**
Namā-rustāḳ vi, 513a – VI, 498a
Namāz → Ṣalāt
Namāzgāh vii, **947a** – VII, **947b**
Nāmdār Khān b. Ṣalābat Djang s, 280a – S, 280a
Nāmdjīn → Bāḥmīn
Nāmī → Mīr Muḥammad Maʿṣūm
Nāmiḳ Kemāl → Kemāl, Meḥmed Nāmiḳ
Nāmiḳ Pasha i, 906b – I, 933b
Namir/Nimr vii, **947b** – VII, **948a**
Namir b. Ḳāsiṭ, Banū i, 545a; vi, 437b – I, 562a; VI, 423a
al-Namir (Namr) b. Tawlab al-ʿUklī (644) vii, 563a, **950b** – VII, 563b, **951a**
Nāmir al-Hawā' → Namāra
al-Namīrī, Muḥammad b. Nuṣayr (IX) viii, 146a – VIII, 148b
Naml vii, **951a** – VII, **951b**
Namrūd vii, **952b**;viii, 49a; s, 101a – VII, **953a**; VIII, 50a; S, 100b
Nāmūs ii, 486b; vii, **953b** – II, 499a; VII, **954a**
Nānā Ṣāḥib i, 822b; iv, 551b – I, 845b; IV, 575a
Nānak (Gurū –, Sikh)) (1538) iii, 456b; vii, **956b**; viii, 253b; ix, 576b – III, 472b; VII, **957a**; VIII, 255b; IX, 598b
Nanda → Djām Nanda
Nānder vii, **957a** – VII, **957b**
Nandjarādj iii, 316b – III, 326a
Nandurbār vii, **957a** – VII, **958a**
Nangrahār (Ningrahār) vii, **957b**; s, 237a, b – VII, **958b**; S, 237a, b
Naples → Nābal
Nār iii, 78a; iv, 237a; vii, **957b** – III, 80a; IV, 247b; VII, **958b**
Nār al-ḥarratayn iv, 928a; v, 1110a, 1111a, 1112a, 1113a, 1115b – IV, 961a; V, 1106a, 1107a, 1108a, 1109a, 1112a
Narāḳ (Nirāḳ) vii, **960b** – VII, **961a**
Narāḳī, Muḥammad Mahdī b. Abī Dharr (1794) vii, 960b – VII, 961a
Narāḳī, Mullā Aḥmad (1829) vi, 552a; vii, **960b**; s, 75b – VI, 536b; VII, **961b**; S, 75b
Narameikhla, King/le roi i, 606a, 1333a – I, 625b, 1272b
Nārandj vii, **961b** – VII, **962b**
Narāyan Singh ii, 47b – II, 48b
Narbadā/Narmadā (river/rivière) vi, 310a, 535a, 536a – VI, 295a, 519b, 520b
Narbonne → Arbūna

Nārbūta Beg (Khān) v, 29a – V, 30a
Nard v, 109a, 110a; vii, **963a** – V, 111b, 112b; VII, **963b**
Nardjis vii, **963b** – VII, **964b**
Naré-Famaghan vi, 401b – VI, 386a
Narela vi, 62a – VI, 60a
Narghīla → Tütün
Nargūnd ii, 220a – II, 227a
Nariman Narimanov s, 365a – S, 365a
Nārimān Ṣādiḳ s, 299b – S, 299a
Narin/Naryn (river/fleuve) ix, 659a – IX, 684a
Narkh iii, 489a; vii, **964a** – III, 506a; VII, **965a**
Narmāshīr (Narmāsīr) vii, **965a** – VII, **965b**
Narnāla iii, 1161b; vii, 314b, **965a** – III, 1189b; VII, 317a, **966a**
Nārnawl vi, 128a; vii, **965b** – VI, 126a; VII, **966a**
Nars (Kūfa) vi, 438b – VI, 424a
Narseh (Sāsānid(e)) iv, 753b; ix, 73a – IV, 784a; IX, 76a
Narshakhī, Abū Bakr Muḥammad (X) i, 1294a, b; v, 856b; vii, **966a**; viii, 749a, 1027a; s, 125b, 326b, 327a – I, 1334a; V, 863b; VII, **966b**; VIII, 779a, 1062a; S, 124b, 326b
Narsingh Ray s, 206b – S, 206a
Narwar s, 10b – S, 10a
Nasā (Nisā) i, 320b, 701a; vii, **966b**; x, 88b – I, 330b, 722a; VII, **967a**; X, 95b
Nasab iii, 238b; iv, 179b, 495b; vii, **967a** – III, 245b; IV, 187b, 516b; VII, **967b**
Naṣaf → Nakhshab
al-Nasafī, Abū ʿAbd Allāh i, 125b, 160b, 414b; iv, 198a, 203b, 661b, 662b; v, 167a – I, 129a, 165a, 426a; IV, 206b, 212b, 688b, 689b; V, 164b
al-Nasafī, Abū Ḥafṣ ʿUmar Nadjm al-Dīn (1142) i, 333a; 593a; iii, 901b; iv, 737a; vi, 47b, 218b, 558a, 848a; vii, 781b, **969a** – I, 343a; 612a; III, 925b; IV, 767a; VI, 202b, 542b, 838b; VII, 783b, **969b**
al-Nasafī, Abu 'l-Ḥasan Muḥammad b. Aḥmad al-Bazdawī (943) i, 125b, 160b, 414b; iv, 198a, 203b, 661b, 662b; v, 167a; vi, 846b; vii, **968b** – I, 129a, 165a, 426a; IV, 206b, 212b, 688b, 689b; V, 164b; VI, 837a; S, 131a
al-Nasafī, Abu 'l-Muʿīn al-Makḥūlī (1114) vi, 846a, 847b; vii, 546b, **968b** – VI, 837a, 838b; VII, 546b, **969a**
Nasafī, ʿAzīz al-Dīn (1300) viii, 703b; x, 321a – VIII, 723b; X, 345a
al-Nasafī, Ḥāfiẓ al-Dīn Abu 'l-Barakāt (1310) iii, 163b; vi, 848a; vii, **969a** – III, 167a; VI, 839a; VII, **969b**
al-Nasāʾī Abū ʿAbd al-Raḥmān (915) iii, 24a; vi, 132b; vii, **969b**; s, 87b – III, 25b; VI, 130b; VII, **970a**; S, 87b
al-Nasāʾī al-Madlidjī, Aḥmad iv, 509b – IV, 531b
Nasaḳ ii, 156a, 157a, 158a – II, 161a, 162a, b
Naṣārā i,31b, 264b, 265a, b, 470a, 1020a, 1040b; ii, 229a, b, 230a, 459a, 637a, 859b; iii, 77b, 1206a, b; iv, 43b, 76b, 241a, 243b; v, 141b, 265a, 326b, 330b, 334a, 335b, 793b, 795b, 799a, 1020a; vii, **970a**; x, 248a– I, 32b, 272b, 273a, b, 484a, 1051b, 1072a; II, 236a, b, 237a, 471a, 653a, 879b; III, 80a, 1236b, 1237a; IV, 46a, 80b, 252a, 254b; V, 144a, 263a, 326a, 330b, 334a, 336a, 799b, 801b, 805a, 1016a; VII, **970b**; X, 266b
al-Nasawī, Abū Naṣr Muḥammad b. ʿAbd al-Raḥīm (XI) vi, 638a – VI, 623a
al-Nasawī, Shihāb al-Dīn Muḥammad (1249) vii, **973b** – VII, **974a**
Naṣb vii, **974b** – VII, **975a**
Nasdj → Bisāṭ; Ḥarīr; Ḳuṭn; Libās; Ṣūf
Nashaʾkarib ix, 675b – IX, 763b
Nashāshībī, Isʿāf (XX) vi, 615b – VI, 600a
Nashāshībī, Rāghib (XX) vi, 615b – VI, 600b
Nashāshībīs iii, 523b – III, 541b
Nashāṭ, Mīrzā ʿAbd al-Wahhāb (1828) vii, **975a** – VII, **975b**
Nashawā → Nakhčiwān
al-Nāshiʾ al-Akbar, Abu 'l-ʿAbbās (906) vii, 605a, **975a**; viii, 886a; ix, 454a; s, 89b, 225b, 265a – VII, 604b, **975b**; VIII, 916a; IX, 469a; S, 89b, 225b, 264b
Nashīd vii, **975b** – VII, **976a**
Nāshira al-Yarbūʿī s, 26a – S, 26b
Nashīṭ i, 828a; iii, 878b; vii, **976a** – I, 851a; III, 902b; VII, **976b**
Nashk, Banū iv, 335b – IV, 350a
Nashshān → al-Sawdāʾ
Nashtakin → al-Darazī
Nashwān b. Saʿīd al-Ḥimyarī (1177) i, 564a; iii, 124a; vi, 565a, b, 829b; vii, **976b**; x, 147a; s, 225b, 289b, 339b – I, 582a; III, 127a; VI, 550a, 820a; VII, **976b**; X, 158b; S, 225b, 289b, 339a
Nasīʾ (intercalation) vii, **977a** – VII, **977b**
Nasīʾ (title/titre) iv, 472a; vii, **977b** – IV, 493a; VII, **978b**
Nasīb i, 583b, 584a; ii, 1028a, b; iv, 488a, 714a, 715a; v, 930b, 956a; vii, **978a** – I, 602a, II, 1052a, b; IV, 509a, 742b, 744a; VII, **978b**; S, 935a, 960a
Nasīb ʿArīḍa (XX) viii, 88a – VIII, 90a
Nasīb Djanbulāṭ ii, 444a – II, 455b
al-Naṣībī, Abū Isḥāḳ Ibrāhīm b. ʿAlī vii, 312a; s, 13b – VII, 314b; S, 13b
Naṣībīn iv, 898a; vi, 427b, 539b, 542a, 626a, b, 633a, 667a; vii, **983a**; s, 36a, 37a – IV, 930b; VI, 413a, 524a, 526b, 611a, 618a, 653a; VII, **983b**; S, 36b, 37a
Nāṣif, Malik Ḥifnī i, 597b; iii, 360a; iv, 720b – I, 617a; III, 371a; IV, 749b
Nāṣif al-Yāzidjī → al-Yāzidjī
Naṣīḥat al-Mulūk vii, **984b** – VII, **985a**
al-Nāṣiḥī, Abū Muḥammad s, 343a – S, 343a
Nāsikh → Naskh
Nāsikh, Shaykh Imām Bakhsh (1838) ii, 84b; vii, **988b**; s, 102a – II, 86a; VII, **989a**; S, 101b
al-Nāsikh wa 'l-Mansūkh → Naskh
Nasīm, Dayā Shankar Ḳawl (1832) vii, **989a** – VII, **989b**
Nasīm Oghlu Aḥmad b. Ḥasan (XVIII) i, 310a – I, 319b
al-Nāṣir (ʿAbbāsid(e)) → al-Nāṣir li-Dīn Allāh
al-Nāṣir (Fīlālī) (1745) vi, 595a – VI, 580a
al-Nāṣir (Mamlūk) → Ḥasan, al-Malik al-Nāṣir Nāṣir al-Dīn; al-Nāṣir Muḥammad
al-Nāṣir (Marrākush) (1514) vi, 594a – VI, 579a
al-Nāṣir (Umayyad(e)) → ʿAbd al-Raḥmān III
al-Nāṣir, Abu 'l-Saʿādāt Muḥammad i, 1060a – I, 1092a
Nāṣir, Banū vii, 675a; s, 395a – VII, 675a; S, 395b
al-Nāṣir, Ibrāhīm al-Malīḥ b. Muḥammad (Yemen) (XI) vi, 436a – VI, 421b
Nāṣir, Khʷādja Mīr (1758) vii, 939a – VII, 939b
al-Nāṣir, al-Malik al-Nāṣir Nāṣir al-Dīn → Ḥasan, al-Malik al-Nāṣir (Mamlūk)
al-Nāṣir, Mawlāy i, 605a – I, 624b
al-Nāṣir, Muḥammad b. Abī Yūsuf Yaʿḳūb al-Manṣūr (Almohad(e)) (1213) i, 166a; ii, 819a, 1007b; iii, 1055a; iv, 337b; vii, **989a** – I, 170b; II, 838b, 1031b; III, 1081a; IV, 352a; VII, **990a**

al-Nāṣir, Yūsuf b. Yaḥyā b. Aḥmad (Yemen) (XI) vi, 436a – VI, 421b
al-Nāṣir b. ʿAlennās (ʿAlnās) (Ḥammādid(e)) (1089) i, 1205a; iii, 137b, 386a; iv, 479a; v, 59b; vi, 427a; vii, **993b** –
I, 1240b; III, 140b, 398b; IV, 501a; V, 61b; VI, 412a; VII, **995a**
al-Nāṣir b. Barḳūḳ (Mamlūk) (XV) vi, 193b – VI, 177b
Nāṣir b. Faradj Allāh, amīr (XV) vii, 672b – VII, 672a
al-Nāsir b. al-Ghālib bi-'llāh (Saʿdī) (1595) vi, 1009b – VI, 1001b
Nāṣir b. Khalīfat al-Bāʿūnī i, 1109a – I, 1142b
Nāṣir b. Mubārak iv, 752a – IV, 782b
Nāṣir b. Muhannā (XVII) vii, 462b – VII, 462a
Nāṣir b. Murshid (Yaʿrūbid(e)) (XVII) i, 554a; viii, 435b; x, 816b – I, 571b; VIII, 450a; X,
al-Nāṣir ʿAbd Allāh b. Ḥasan, Imām (Yemen) (1840) vii, 996a – VII, 998a
al-Nāṣir Aḥmad (Rasūlid(e)) → Aḥmad b. Ismāʿīl
al-Nāṣir Aḥmad b. al-Nāṣir Muḥammad (Mamlūk) (1344) vii, **992b** – VII, **994a**
Nāṣir ʿAlī Shāh Malik-niyā (Niʿmat-Allāhī) (XX) viii, 46b – VIII, 47b
Nāṣir ʿAlī Sirhindī (1697) vii, **1005b** – VII, **1007b**
Nāṣir al-Dawla → Ibn Baḳiyya
Nāṣir al-Dawla (Kirmān) s, 53a – S, 53b
Nāṣir al-Dawla (Labla) v, 586b – V, 591b
Nāṣir al-Dawla, Abū Muḥammad al-Ḥasan (Ḥamdānid(e)) (968) i, 119b, 866b, 870b, 1352b; ii, 178b, 524b; iii, 126b, 127a, 346a, 902b; vi, 930a; vii, 397a, 983b, **994b**; s, 36b, 379b –
I, 123a, 890b, 895a, 1391b, 1392a; II, 184a, 537b; III, 129b, 130a, 356b, 926b; VI, 922a; VII, 398b, 984a, **996a**; S, 36b, 379b
Nāṣir al-Dawla b. Sikandar iii, 322a – III, 332a
Nāṣir al-Dawla Badr → Badr b. Ḥasan(a)wayh
Nāṣir al-Dawla Ḥusayn ii, 856a, 857b, 858b; iii, 129a – II, 876a, 877b, 878b; III, 131b
Nāṣir al-Dawla Ibn Ḥamdān, Sulṭān al-Dawla (Miṣr) (1073) vii, 730a, b – VII, 730b, 731a
Nāṣir al-Dawla Manṣūr b. Niẓām al-Dīn (Marwānid(e), Diyār Bakr) (1085) vi, 626b – VI, 611b
Nāṣir al-Dīn → Čirāgh-i Dihlī; Humayūn; Maḥmūd I, II (Bengal(e))
Naṣīr al-Dīn, Shaykh (XIV) s, 352b – S, 352b
Nāṣir al-Dīn b. Ḥasan Karlu i, 227a – I, 234a
Nāṣir al-Dīn b. Kamāl al-Dīn (Marʿashī) (XV) vi, 513a – VI, 498a
Nāṣir al-Dīn b. Kawām al-Dīn (Marʿashī) (XV) vi, 512b – VI, 498a
Naṣīr al-Dīn b. Muḥammad b. al-Naḳīd (XIII) vii, 727b – VII, 728a
Nāṣir al-Dīn b. Musallam (1373) iv, 643a – IV, 669b
Nāṣir al-Dīn b. al-Muẓaffar Taḳī 'l-Dīn ʿUmar (Ayyūbid(e)) (Manbidj) (XII) vi, 380b – VI, 365a
Nāṣir al-Dīn b. Sayyid-i Adjall (1292) ix, 623a – IX, 647a
al-Nāṣir li-Dīn Allāh (Zaydī Imāms) vii, **995b** – VII, **997b**
al-Nāṣir li-Dīn Allāh, Abu 'l-ʿAbbās Aḥmad (ʿAbbāsid(e)) (1225) i, 20a, b, 322b, 1150a; ii, 327a, 964a, 1044a; iii, 109b, 160b, 488b, 1256a; iv, 29b, 749a, 942b; vi, 429b, 430a, 433b, 434a; vii, 728b, **996b**; viii, 111a; s, 193b, 378b –
I, 20b, 21b, 332a, 1184b; II, 336b, 986a, 1068b; III, 112a, 164a, 505a, 1288b; IV, 32a, 779a, 975b; VI, 415a, b, 419a, b; VII, 729a, **998b**; VIII, 113b; S, 194b, 378b
al-Nāṣir li-Dīn Allāh, Aḥmad Abu 'l-Ḥasan b. Yaḥyā al-Hādī ila 'l-Ḥaḳḳ, Imām (Yemen) (937) vii, 995b, **996b** – VII, 997b, **998a**
Nāṣir al-Dīn al-Asad iv, 820b, 821a – IV, 853b, 854a
Nāṣir al-Dīn Awbik b. Ačfagha → al-Lamtūnī, Awbik b. Ačfagha
Naṣīr al-Dīn Djaḳar (XII) vii, 734a – VII, 734b
al-Nāṣir al-Dīn Faradj (Mamlūk) (1412) vii, 271b, 723a – VII, 273b, 724a
Nāṣir al-Dīn Ḳabāča (Kubādja) (XIII) i, 764a, 1192a, 1194a; ii, 267b, 393a, 609a, 1103a; iii, 416a, 1155a; v, 597b; vii, 410a, 549a; s, 360a – I, 787a, 1227a, 1229b; II, 275b, 403b, 624a, 1129a; III, 429a, 1183b; V, 601b; VII, 411a, 549a; S, 359b
Nāṣir al-Dīn al-Kaymarī iv, 842b – IV, 875b
Nāṣir al-Din Khaldjī ii, 381a – II, 391b
Nāṣir al-Dīn Maḥmūd (Artūḳid(e), Diyār Bakr) (1222) s, 266b – S, 266a
Nāṣir al-Dīn Maḥmūd b. Iltutmish → Maḥmūd I (Delhi)
Nāṣir al-Dīn Maḥmūd b. Yaḥyā → Čirāgh-i Dihlī
Nāṣir al-Dīn Meḥmed Beg (Ḳaramānid(e)) (XV) vii, 271b – VII, 273b
Nāṣir al-Dīn Muḥammad b. Dhu 'l-Karnayn ii, 111a – II, 113b
Nāṣir al-Dīn Muḥammad b. Khalīl ii, 239b – II, 246a
Nāṣir al-Dīn Muḥammad b. Muḥammad (1462) vi, 193b – VI, 177b
Nāṣir al-Dīn Muḥammad Shāh (Tughluḳid(e)) (1393) x, 593a; s, 126b – X, 637a; S, 125b
Nāṣir al-Dīn Muḥammad al-Zurayḳ iii, 155b – III, 159a
Nāṣir al-Dīn Mukram b. ʿAlāʾ s, 326a – S, 325b
Nāṣir al-Dīn Munshī (XIV) vi, 481b – VI, 467b
Nāṣir al-Dīn Shāh (Ḳādjār) (1896) i, 626b, 833b, 846b, 847a, 916a, 1088b; ii, 152b, 418a, 433b, 649b, 650a; iii, 554a, 1103b; iv, 39a, 72a, 392a, 393a, 696a, 788a, 855b; v, 659a, 919b, 1085b; vi, 19a, 20a, b, 21a, 277a, 291b, 481b, 484a, b, 485b, 528b, 529b, 551b, 715a, 763a, 804a; vii, 440a, b, 573b, 918b, **1003a**; viii, 58a; s, 23b, 41a, 70b, 71a, 94b, 108b, 260b, 290b, 302a –
I, 647a, 856b, 870a, 944a, 1120b; II, 157a, 429a, 445a, 666a, b; III, 573a, 1130b; IV, 41b, 76a, 408b, 410a, 724b, 819b, 888b; V, 663b, 925a, 1083a; VI, 17a, b, 18b, 19a, 262a, 276b, 467b, 470a, b, 471b, 513a, b, 536a, 704a, 752a, 794a; VII, 441a, b, 574a, 919a, **1004b**; VIII, 59a; S, 24a, 41b, 71a, b, 94a, 108a, 260a, 290b, 301b
Nāṣir al-Dīn Shāh b. Ghiyāth al-Dīn (Mālwā) (1510) vi, 54b, 309b, 407a – VI, 52b, 295a, 391b
Nāṣir al-Dīn al-Ṣūrī (amīr) (XII) vi, 870a – VI, 861a
Nāṣir al-Dīn Ṭāhir b. Fakhr al-Mulk al-Muẓaffar (1153) viii, 81b – VIII, 83b
Naṣīr al-Dīn al-Ṭūsī (1274) i, 113a, 326b, 328b, 353b, 393a, 450a, 594a, 721a, 839a, 1198a; ii, 362a, 399b, 607b, 765b, 774a; iii, 24b, 103b, 390a, 726b, 1122a, 1137b, 1151b, 1266a; iv, 48b, 121a, 205b, 976a, 1028a, 1036a; v, 547a; vi, 450a, 501a, b, 549b, 601a, b; vii, 143b; viii, 135a; s, 412a, 413a, 414a –
I, 116a, 337a, 339a, 364b, 404b, 463a, 613b, 743a, 862a, 1233b; II, 372a, 410a, 622b, 784a, 792b; III, 25b, 106a, 402b, 749a, 1149b, 1165b, 1179b, 1299a; IV, 51a, 126a, 214b, 1008a, 1060a, 1067b; V, 552a; VI, 435b, 486b, 487a, 534a, 586a; VII, 145b; VIII, 137b; S, 412a, 413a, 414b
Nāṣir Djang (Farrukhābād) → Imdād Ḥusayn Khān
Nāṣir Djang (Ḥaydarābād) iii, 320a, b – III, 331a

al-Nāṣir Faradj b. Barḳūḳ → Faradj, al-Malik al-Nāṣir Zayn al-Dīn (Mamlūk, 1412)
al-Nāṣir al-Fattāh vi, 112b – VI, 110a
Nāṣir al-Ḥaḳḳ Abū Muḥammad iv, 19a – IV, 20b
al-Nāṣir li-'l-Ḥaḳḳ → Ḥasan al-Uṭrūsh
al-Nāṣir al-Ḥasan b. ʿAlī b. Dāwūd, Imām (Yemen) (1596) vii, 996a – VII, 997b
al-Nāṣir al-Ḥasan b. ʿIzz al-Dīn, Imām (Yemen) (1523) vii, 996a – VII, 997b
al-Nāṣir Ḥasan b. al-Nāṣir Muḥammad (Mamlūk) (1361) viii, **992b** – VIII, **994b**
al-Nāṣir al-Kabīr → Ḥasan al-Uṭrūsh
Nāṣir Khān (Bengal(e)) (1442) vi, 46b – VI, 45a
Nāṣir Khān (Kālpī) (XV) vi, 53b, 61b – VI, 51b, 59b
Naṣīr Khān II b. Miḥrāb Khān (Balūčistān) (1857) i, 1006a – I, 1037a
Naṣīr Khān b. Muẓaffar Shāh → Maḥmūd II b. Muẓaffar Shāh (Gudjarāt)
Nāṣir Khān Brahūʾī (1795) i, 230a, 296a, 1006a, 1010b; iv, 1059b; v, 102a, 580a; s, 222a, 332b – I, 237a, 305b, 1036b, 1037a, 1041b; IV, 1091a; V, 104a, 584b; S, 222a, 331b
Nāṣir Khān Fārūkī (Khāndēsh, 1437) i, 710a, 1329a, 1331a; ii, 814b, 1125a; iii, 419a, 638a – I, 731b, 1369b, 1371b; II, 833b, 1151b; III, 432a, 659b
Nāṣir Khān Ḳāshḳāy iv, 706b – IV, 734b
Naṣīr Khān Lārī (XVIII) v, 673b, 674a – V, 679a
Naṣīr Khān Lārī (XIX) v, 674a – V, 679a
Nāṣir Khān Noḥānī s, 203a – S, 202b
Nāṣir-i Khusraw (1060) i, 137a, 233b, 450a, 552a, 852a, 1220b; ii, 584b, 861a, 997b; iii, 328b, 1130b; iv, 61b, 63a, 199b; v, 175b, 930a, 956b; vi, 119b, 626b, 652b, 672b; s, 108a, 203b, 208a – I, 141b, 240b, 463a, 569b, 876a, 1257a; II, 599a, 881a, 1020b; III, 338b, 1158b; IV, 65a, 66b, 208a; V, 173a, 934b, 960b; VI, 117a, 611b, 638a, 658b; S, 107a, 203a, 207b
Nāṣir Mīrzā i, 228a, 852b – I, 234b, 876a
al-Nāṣir Muḥammad (Ṣāḥib al-Mawākib), Imām (Yemen) (XVII) vii, 515a – VII, 515a
al-Nāṣir Muḥammad b. Isḥāḳ b. al-Mahdī Aḥmad, Imām (Yemen) (1753) vii, 996a – VII, 997b
al-Nāṣir Muḥammad b. Ḳāʾit Bāy (Mamlūk) (1498) vi, 324b, 501b; vii, 172b, **993a** – VI, 309a, 487a; VII, 174a, **994b**
al-Nāṣir Muḥammad b. Ḳalāwūn (Mamlūk) (1341) i, 118b, 610b, 779a, 1126b, 1127b, 1128a, 1299b, 1324b; ii, 38a, 68a, 285a, b, 330a; iii, 99a, 189b, 220a, 346b, 744b, 890b, 923b, 952b; iv, 136b, 424b, 430b, 464b, 609a, 834b, 864a, 965b; v, 373b, 595a, 1140b; vi, 195a, 231a, 258a, 314b, 315b, 318a, 322a, b, 323a, 324a, 326a, b, 367a, b, 381a, 424a, 455a, 545b, 547b, 662a; vii, 168b, 169b, 170a, 176a, **991a**; viii, 90b, 156b, 157a, 864b; s, 395b – I, 122a, 631b, 802a, 1160b, 1162a, 1339b, 1365b; II, 39a, 69b, 293a, b, 339b; III, 101b, 194a, 226b, 357a, 767a, 914b, 947b, 977a; IV, 142a, 443a, 449b, 485a, 634a, 867b, 897a, 998a; V, 374b, 598b, 1134a; VI, 179a, 225a, 242b, 299b, 300b, 302b, 306a, 307a, b, 308b, 310b, 311a, 351b, 365b, 409b, 440b, 530a, 532a, 648a; VII, 170a, 171b, 177b, **993a**; VIII, 92b, 159a,b, 895b; S, 396a
Nāṣir al-Mulk (Čitrāl) ii, 31a – II, 31b
Nāṣir al-Mulk (Irān) (XX) ii, 652a, b; vii, 432a – II, 668b, 669a; VII, 433a
al-Nāṣir al-Ṣaghīr al-Ḥusayn b. al-Ḥasan (Caspian Zaydī/Zaydī Caspien) (1083) vii, **995b** – VII, **997b**
al-Nāṣir Salāḥ al-Dīn, Imām (Yemen) (1391) vii, 996a – VII, 997b
al-Nāṣir Ṣalāḥ al-Dīn Yūsuf (Ayyūbid(e)) (1259) → al-Malik al-Nāṣir II
al-Nāṣir(ī) al-Salāwī, Shihāb al-Dīn (1897) → Aḥmad al-Nāṣirī
al-Nāṣir b. Yūsuf → al-Malik al-Nāṣir Ṣalāḥ al-Dīn Yūsuf (Ayyūbid(e))
Nāṣira (Damas(cus)) vi, 545a – VI, 530a
Nāṣira (Nazareth) vi, 631a; vii, **1008a** – VI, 616a; VII, **1009a**
Nāṣirābād → Sīstān
Nāṣirābādī, Mawlānā Sayyid Dildār ʿAlī (Ghufrān Maʿāb) (1820) vii, 300b – VII, 302b
Nāṣirābādī, Sayyid ʿAlī Akbar (1909) vii, 301a – VII, 303a
Nāṣirābādī, Sayyid Ḥusayn b. Dildar ʿAlī (1856) vii, 300b – VII, 303a
Nāṣirābādī, Sayyid Muḥammad b. Dildar ʿAlī (1867) vii, 300b – VII, 303a
Nāṣirābādī, Sayyid Muḥammad Taḳī (1872) vii, 301a – VII, 303a
al-Nāṣirī → Ibn Nāṣir; Aḥmad al-Nāṣirī al-Salāwī
Nāsir-i Khusraw, Abū Muʿīn al-Ḳubādhiyānī (1060) iv, 61b, 63a, 199b; v, 175b, 930a, 956b; vi, 119b, 626b, 652b, 672b; vii, 141a, 163a, 535b, 730a, 732a, **1006a**; s, 108a, 203b, 208a – IV, 65a, 66b, 208a; V, 173a, 934b, 960b; VI, 117a, 611b, 638a, 658b; VII, 143a, 164b, 535b, 730b, 732b, **1007b**; S, 107a, 203a, 207b
al-Nāṣirī, Muḥammad Makkī (XX) viii, 906a – VIII, 937a
al-Nāṣiriyya → Bidjāya
Nāṣiriyya (Caspian region/région caspienne) s, 363a – S, 363a
Nāṣiriyya (Damas(cus)) s, 197a – S, 197a
Nāṣiriyya (Faradj) vi, 316b – VI, 301a
Nāṣiriyya (Morocco/Maroc) i, 290a, b; ii, 134a; vi, 713a; s, 395a – I, 299a, b; II, 137b; VI, 701b; S, 395b
Nāṣiriyya (Yemen/Yémen) iii, 255a – III, 262a
al-Nāṣiriyya (order/ordre) vii, **1009a** – VII, **1011a**
al-Nāṣiriyya (town/ville) vii, **1009a** – VII, **1011a**
Nāṣirwand v, 603a – V, 607a
Naskh/al-Nāsikh wa 'l-Mansūkh i, 265b, 850b; iii, 28a, 898b; iv, 170a; v, 415b; vii, **1009b** – I, 273b, 874b; III, 29b, 923a; IV, 177b; V, 417a; VII, **1011a**
Naskhī → Khaṭṭ; Kitābāt
Nasnās/Nisnās → Ḳird
Nasr (deity) vii, **1012a** – VII, **1016b**
Nasr (vulture/vautour) vii, **1012b** – VII, **1014a**
Naṣr I b. Tamghač Khān (Ḳarakhānid(e)) (1080) i, 1295a; iii, 1114b, 1115a; iv, 217b; vi, 273b, 275b; viii, 748b – I, 1334b; III, 1142a, b; IV, 227a; VI, 258b, 260b; VIII, 779a
Naṣr I b. Aḥmad I b. Sāmān-ghudā (Sāmānid(e)) (892) i, 1294a; iv, 21b, 188b; viii, 1026b; s, 265b – I, 1333b; IV, 23b, 196b, 197a; VIII, 1061a S, 265a
Naṣr II b. Aḥmad b. Ismāʿīl, amīr (Sāmānid(e)) (943) i, 278a, 1294b; ii, 1082b; iii, 254b, 759a, 1156b; iv, 22b; v, 856b; vi, 115b, 539a, 608b, 853a; vii, 397b, 652a, **1015a**; viii, 110a, 1027a; s, 265a, 411a – I, 286b, 1334b; II, 1107b; III, 262a, 782a, 1185a; IV, 24a; V, 863b; VI, 113a, 523b, 593a, 844b; VII, 398b, 651b, **1017a**; VIII, 112a, 1062a; S, 264b, 411b
Naṣr (Mosul) (IX) vi, 900a – VI, 891b
Naṣr b. ʿAbbās b. Abi 'l-Futūḥ i, 9b, 198b; ii, 318a; iv, 514a – I, 9b, 204b; II, 327a; IV, 536b
Naṣr b. Abī Layth → al-Aṣamm, Abū Bakr (Miṣr)
Naṣr b. Aḥmad → al-Khubzaʾaruzzī
Naṣr b. ʿAlī, Ilig Khān (Özkend) (XI) iii, 1113b; vi, 65a; viii, 242b – III, 1141a; VI, 63a; VIII, 242b
Naṣr b. ʿĀṣim iv, 731b – IV, 761a
Naṣr b. Ibrāhīm (Ilek-Khān) s, 65a – S, 65b
Naṣr b. Khalaf (Sīstān) (XII) vii, 535b – VII, 535a

Naṣr b. Maḥmūd iii, 790a – III, 813b
Naṣr b. Marzūḳ s, 88a – S, 87b
Naṣr b. Muʿāwiya, Banū vi, 265b, 266a – VI, 250b
Naṣr b. Muḥammad, Abu 'l-Djuyūsh (Naṣrid(e)) (1314) iii, 833b; vii, 1020a, **1022b** – III, 857b; VII, 1022a, **1024b**
Naṣr b. Muḥammad al-Samarḳandī → Abu 'l-Layth
Naṣr b. Murshid, Imām (Yaʿrubid(e)) (XVII) vi, 735a – VI, 724a
Naṣr b. Muzāḥim, Abu 'l-Faḍl al-Minkarī (827) i, 383b; vii, **1015b**; x, 107b; s, 233a – I, 394b; VII, **1017b**; X, 115b; S, 233a
Naṣr b. Nuṣayr al-Ḥulwānī (X) vi, 195b; vii, 418a, **1015a** – VI, 180a; VII, 419b, **1017b**
Naṣr b. Sadīd al-Mulk ʿAlī (Munkidh, Banū) (1098) vii, 578a – VII, 578b
Naṣr b. Ṣāliḥ b. Mirdās (Mirdāsid(e)) (1029) vii, 117a – VII, 119a
Naṣr b. Sayyār al-Laythī (748) i, 16a, 206b, 529b, 1293b; ii, 561a; iii, 224a, 471a, 493b, 802b, 988a; iv, 15b, 446b; v, 57a, b, 711a, 854a; vi, 331b, 620b; vii, **1015b**; x, 845a – I, 16b, 212b, 545b, 1333b; II, 575a; III, 230b, 231a, 487b, 510b, 826a, 1013a; IV, 16b, 466b; V, 59a, 716a, 861a; VI, 316b, 605b; VII, **1017b**; X, 845a
Naṣr b. Sebüktigin iv, 189b; v, 1126b – IV, 197b; V, 1123a
Naṣr b. Shabath al-ʿUḳaylī (IX) i, 52b; ii, 524a; iii, 950b; vi, 336b, 337a; vii, **1016b** – I, 54a; II, 537a; III, 975b; VI, 320b, 321b; VII, **1018b**
Naṣr Āl Madhkūr i, 942b – I, 971b
Naṣr Allāh (Afghānistān) s, 65b, 237b – S, 66a, 237b
Naṣr Allāh, ḳāḍī (Baghdād) (XIII) vi, 77b – VI, 75b
Naṣr Allāh (Mangit) (1860) vi, 419a – VI, 404a
Naṣr Allāh (amīr) (Bukhārā) i, 1296a; iv, 694b; v, 30a, 46a – I, 1335b; IV, 722b; V, 31a, 47a
Naṣr Allāh b. ʿAbd al-Ḥamīd iii, 372b; iv, 504b – III, 384b; IV, 526a
Naṣr Allāh b. ʿAbd al-Raḥmān i, 232b; iii, 13a – I, 239b; III, 14a
Naṣr Allāh b. al-Djazarī s, 267a – S, 266b
Naṣr Allāh b. Muḥammad b. ʿAbd al-Ḥamīd (Naṣr Allāh Munshī) (XII) iv, 64a; vii, **1016b**; s, 21b – IV, 67b; VII, **1018b**; S, 22a
Naṣr Allāh Iṣfahānī, Mīrzā (XIX) iv, 164a – IV, 171a
Naṣr Allāh Mīrzā b. Nādir Shāh (Afshārid(e)) vii, 457a – VII, 457a
Naṣr al-Dawla, Abū Naṣr Aḥmad b. Marwān (Marwānid(e)) (Diyār Bakr) (1061) ii, 384a, 484b; iii, 344b; v, 453a; vi, 626a, b, 930b; vii, **1017a** – II, 394b, 496b; III, 355a; V, 455b; VI, 611a, b, 922a; VII, **1019a**
Naṣr al-Dīn (Berber) (XIX) i, 1172a – I, 1207a
Naṣr al-Dīn Ibrāhīm (XII) vii, 816b – VII, 818a
Naṣr al-Dīn Khodja (Nasreddin Hoca) i, 313a; ii, 591a; iii, 375a; vii, **1018a**; s, 170b – I, 323a; II, 605b; III, 387a; VII, **1020a**; S, 170b
Naṣr Khān → Naṣr I (Ḳarakhanid(e))
Naṣr al-Ḳushūrī iii, 45b, 101a, 886b – III, 47b, 103b, 910b
Naṣr al-Mulk Ḳaragözlū iv, 578a – IV, 601a
Naṣrābādī, Muḥammad Ṭāhir (XVII) vii, 530a; s, 340b – VII, 530b; S, 340a
Naṣrat Shāh ii, 218b – II, 225b
Naṣrawī → Naṣārā
Naṣrid Maliks (Sīstān) ix, 683b – IX, 712a
Naṣrid(e)s (Banū Naṣr/Banu 'l-Aḥmar) i, 495b, 500a; ii, 307b, 1015b, 1016b; iii, 499a; v, 625b; vii, **1020a**; s, 112b, 256b, 307a, 398b; vi, 221a, 222b, 521b, 572a – I, 510b, 515a; II, 316b, 1039a, 1040a; III, 516a; V, 629b; VI, 215a, 216b, 505b, 557a; VII, **1022a**; S, 112a, 256b, 307a, 399a
Nāṣriyya (Yūsuf) (Ayyūbid(e)) vi, 320a – VI, 304b
Naṣṣ vii, **1029a** – VII, **1031b**
al-Nassādj vii, **1029b** – VII, **1032a**
Nassādjī iv, 1042b – IV, 1074a
Nassads vii, **1029b** – VII, **1032a**
Naṣṣār, Nadjīb ii, 468a – II, 480a
Nasser, Colonel → ʿAbd al-Nāṣir, Djamāl
Nastaʿlīḳ → Khaṭṭ
Nasṭūr vii, 362a – VII, 364b
Nasṭūriyyūn (Naṣāṭira) ii, 67a, b, 1120a; iii, 886a, 1122a, 1206a; v, 121a, 896b; vi, 542a; vii, **1030a**; viii, 173b – II, 68b, 1146b; III, 910a, 1149b, 1236b; V, 123b, 902b; VI, 527a; VII, **1032b**; VIII, 176a
Naṣūḥ Pasha (1614) i, 268a; ii, 443b, 750a, b; vi, 999a; vii, **1033a**; s, 238b – I, 276a; II, 455a 768b, 769a; VI, 991a; VII, **1035b**; S, 238b
Naṣūḥ Pasha ʿOthmān-oghlu i, 395a – I, 406b
Naṣūḥ al-Ṣilāḥī i, 904b – I, 931b
al-Naṣūḥiyya iv, 991b – IV, 1024a
Naṣūmī, Muḥammad (1718) ix, 155b – IX, 161a
Nāsūt v, 611b, 612a – V, 615b, 616a
Naʿt ii, 302a; iv, 715b; vii, **1034a** – II, 310b; IV, 744b; VII, **1036b**
Naṭanz iii, 1124b; vii, **1034a** – III, 1152b; VII, **1036b**
Naṭanzī, Ḥusayn (XV) iv, 525b; ix, 42a – IV, 548b; IX, 42b
Nathrī, Shaykh Mūsā iv, 72b; v, 198a – IV, 76b; V, 195b
Natīdja vii, **1034b** – VII, **1037a**
Nāṭiḳ bi-'l-Ḥaḳḳ (Mūsā b. al-Amīn) (ʿAbbāsid(e)) (IX) iv, 203a, b; vii, **1034b** – IV, 212b; VII, **1037a**
al-Nāṭiḳ bi-'l-Ḥaḳḳ, Abū Ṭālib iii, 832a; s, 13a, 343a – III, 856a; S, 13b, 343a
Nātil-Rustāḳ (Rustamdār) vi, 511b, 513a – VI, 497a, 498b
al-Natīlī → al-Ḥusayn b. Ibrāhīm
National Front (Iran) iv, 41a, b, 42a
Naṭrūn i, 1068b; v, 965a, 979b; vii, **1035a**; s, 130b – I, 1100b; V, 969b; VII, **1037b**; S, 130a
Natsir, Mohammed (XX) vi, 731b, 732a – VI, 720b, 721a
Naṭṭāḥa → Ibn al-Khāṣīb, Abū ʿAlī
Nauplion vii, **1035a** – VII, **1037b**
Nāʿūra i, 492a, 1232a; iii, 29b; v, 860b, 861a, 863b, 864a, 969a; vii, **1037a** – I, 507a, 1269a; III, 31a; V, 867b, 868a, 870b, 871a, 972a; VII, **1039a**
Navarino vii, 426a, **1037b** – VII, 427a, **1039b**
Navarra vii, **1039b** – VII, **1041b**
Navas de Tolosa, Las → al-ʿIḳāb
Naw' → Anwā'
Naw Bahār i, 1033a; vii, **1039a** – I, 1064b; VII, **1041b**
al-Nawādjī, Shams al-Dīn Muḥammad (1455) vii, **1039b** – VII, **1042a**
Nawā'ī, ʿAlī Shīr → Mīr ʿAlī Shīr Nawā'ī
Nawālī → Naṣūḥ aḳ Hiṣārī
Nawār (bint ʿamm al-Farazdaḳ) vi, 476a – VI, 462a
Nawār → Čingāne; Lūlī; Zuṭṭ
al-Nawāwī, Muḥammad b. ʿUmar al-Djāwī (XIX) vii, **1040b** – VII, **1042b**
al-Nawawī, Muḥyi al-Dīn Abū Zakariyyā' (1277) iii, 25b, 763a, 779a, 860b, 927a; iv, 1108a; v, 20a; vi, 133a, 263a, 353a, 651b; vii, 691b, **1041a**; viii, 425a; s, 83a, 390b – III, 27a, 786b, 802b, 885a, 951b; IV, 1139b; V, 20b; VI, 131a, 247b, 337a, 637a; VII, 692a, **1043b**; VIII, 439a; S, 82b, 391a

Nawba iii, 453b; vi, 521a; vii, 927b, **1042a** – III, 469b; VI, 506a; VII, 928a, **1044a**
Nawbakht vi, 710b, 834b; vii, **1043b** – VI, 699b, 825a; VII, **1045b**
al-Nawbakhtī, Abu 'l-Ḳāsim al-Ḥusayn (938) vii, 542b; viii, **812a** – VII, 542b; VIII, **839a**
al-Nawbakhtī, Abū Sahl Tīmādh (924) vii, 312a, b, 786a, 1043b, 1044a – VII, 314a, 315a, 788a, 1046a
al-Nawbakhtī, al-Faḍl b. Abī Sahl (IX) vii, 1044a – VII, 1046a
al-Nawbakhtī, Ḥasan (786) vii, 1043b – VII, 1046a
al-Nawbakhtī, al-Ḥasan b. Mūsā (922) iii, 497b; vii, 786a, **1044a**; s, 225b, 393b – III, 514b; VII, 788a, **1046a**; S, 225b, 394a
al-Nawbakhtī, Ḥusayn b. Rūḥ → Ibn Rūḥ
al-Nawbakhtī, Ibrāhīm b. Isḥāḳ b. Abī Sahl (X) vii, 1043b – VII, 1046a
al-Nawbakhtī, Isḥāḳ b. Ismāʿīl (X) vii, 542a – VII, 542a
Nawbandadjān vii, **1044b** – VII, **1047a**
Nawf, Banū ix, 90b – IX, 93a
Nawfal, Banū v, 435a; vi, 145a; vii, **1045a** – V, 437a; VI, 143a; VII, **1047a**
Nawfal, Hind (XX) vii, 903a – VII, 903b
Nawfal b. Asad b. ʿAbd al-ʿUzza x, 2b – X, 2b
al-Nawfalī, Āl vii, **1045a** – VII, **1047b**
Nawʿī, Muḥammad Riḍā (1610) vii, **1046b** – VII, **1048a**
Nawr al-Ward v, 827b – V, 833b
Nawriyya vii, **1046a** – VII, **1048b**
Nawrōdjī, Dādābhā'ī ii, 545b – II, 559a
Nawrūz iv, 8b, 477a; vi, 521b, 523a, 526b, 527a, 528b, 529a, 857a; vii, 15b, **1047a** – IV, 9b, 479b; VI, 506b, 507b, 511a, 512b, 513b, 848b; VII, 15b, **1049a**
Nawrūz, Amīr (Marāgha) (XIII) i, 1130a; ii, 1043a; iv, 878a; v, 554a; vi, 502a – I, 1164a; II, 1067b; IV, 910b; V, 559a; VI, 487b
Nawrūz Aḥmed Khān i, 46b; iv, 512a – I, 48a; IV, 534a
Nawrūz al-Ḥāfiẓī al-Ẓāhirī (1414) ii, 781b; iii, 186a; vii, 271b, 723a – II, 800a; III, 190b; VII, 273b, 724a
Nawrūznāma iv, 64a – IV, 67b
Nawshahr s, 131b – S, 131a
Nāwūsiyya ii, 375a; vii, 645b, **1048a** – II, 385a; VII, 645a, **1050a**
Nawwāb/Nawāb (title/titre) vii, **1048a** – VII, **1050b**
Nawwāb Islām Khān vi, 690a – VI, 677b
Nawwāb Mīrzā Dā → Dāgh, Nawwāb Mīrzā Khān
Nawwāb Mīrzā Shawḳ (1871) vi, 838a – VI, 828b
Nawwāb Sayyid Ṣiddīḳ Ḥasan Khān (1890) i, 259b, 827b, 1196a; vii, **1048b**; s. 293a – I, 267b, 850b, 1231b; VII, **1050b**; S, 292b
Nawwāb Shāh Djahān Begum (XX) vii, 1048b – VII, 1051a
Nawwāb Wazīr Khān vii, 189b – VII, 189b
Nawwāb Wazīrs (Awadh) s, 74b, 325b – S, 75a, 325a
Nawwāb-i Ṣafawī ii, 882b; iii, 529b; iv, 165a – II, 902b; III, 548a; IV, 172b
Nawwāf b. Nūrī Shaʿlān (1921) viii, 644a – VIII, 663a
Naxos → Naḳshe
Nāy (Ghazna) vi, 783a – VI, 773a
Nayčari ii, 97a – II, 99a
Nayman ii, 42a; s, 97b, 420a – II, 43a; S, 97a, 420a
Nayrab iv, 724a – IV, 753a
Nayrīz (Nīrīz) vii, **1049b** – VII, **1051b**
al-Nayrizī, Abu 'l-ʿAbbās al-Faḍl (X) i, 727a; vii, **1050a** – I, 749a; VII, **1052a**
al-Nayrizī, Abū Manṣūr (900) iii, 1137a; V, 85b; vii, 199b – III, 1165b; V, 88a; VII, 200a
Naysābūr → Nīshāpūr
al-Naysābūrī → al-Nīsābūrī
al-Naysābūrī, al-Ḥasan b. al-Muẓaffar s, 289b – S, 289a
Nayzak iv, 811a – IV, 843b
Naẓar i, 949a; vii, **1050a** – I, 978b; VII, **1052b**
Nazar Beg b. Ghāzī Beg (Somāy) (1669) ix, 727b – IX, 758b
Naẓar Muḥammad Khān i, 768b – I, 791b
Nazareth → al-Nāṣira
Nazhūn iii, 850a – III, 874a
Nāzila vii, **1052a** – VII, **1054a**
Nāẓim, Dr iv, 284b, 285a – IV, 297a, b
Nāẓim, Muṣṭafā (1696) vii, **1054a** – VII, **1056a**
Nāẓim, Nabī-zāde i, 287b; ii, 699b, 700b – I, 296a; II, 717b, 718a
Nāẓim, Yaḥyā (1726) vii, **1054a** – VII, **1056b**
Nāẓim Farrūkh Ḥusayn (1670) vii, **1052b** – VII, **1055a**
Nāẓim Ḥikmet (Ran) (Nāẓim Hikmet Borzecki) (1963) iv, 882b; vii, **1053a** – IV, 915a; VII, **1055a**
Nāẓim Pasha (Baghdād) (XX) i, 906b; ii, 624a, 698b; iii, 402a; iv, 296b, 297a; vi, 614b – I, 934a; II, 639b, 716b; III, 414a; IV, 310a; VI, 599b
Naẓīr (- al-Samt) vii, **1054b** – VII, **1057a**
Nāẓir al-maẓālim → Maẓālim
Naẓīrī, Muḥammad Ḥusayn (1612) vii, 340b, 341a, **1054b**; ix, 241a – VII, 342b, **1057a**; IX, 247b
Nāẓir-zāde iii, 538a – III, 557a
Nazlī (queen/reine) s, 299a – S, 299a
Nazli Ilicak (XX) vi, 95b – VI, 93b
Naẓmī, Meḥmed Edirneli (1555) vii, 531b, **1055b** – VII, 531b, **1058a**
Naẓmī, Sheykh Meḥmed b. Ramaḍān (1701) vii, **1055b** – VII, **1058a**
Naẓmī-zāde Murtaḍā (1705) vi, 1019b – VI, 1012b
Nāzūk (X) iii, 768a; vii, 542a – III, 791a; VII, 542a
al-Nāẓūr vii, **1056a** – VII, **1058b**
Nazwā → Nizwā
al-Nazwī, Abū Bakr Aḥmad b. ʿAbd Allāh al-Kindī al-Samdī (1161) viii, 800a – VIII, 827a
al-Naẓẓām, Abū Isḥāḳ Ibrāhīm b. Sayyār (835) i, 128b, 272a, 713b, 737a; ii, 386a, 518b, 569b; iii, 302b, 1143a, 1266a; iv, 183a, 615a; v, 240b, 384a, b, 893b; vi, 335a, 336b, 636b, 737b; vii, 259a, b, 401a, 546b, 567a, 604a, 784b, **1057a**; x, 83b; s, 90b, 226a, 393b – I, 132b, 280a, 735a, 759a; II, 396a, 531b, 584a; III, 312a, 1171b, 1299a; IV, 190b, 640a; V, 238b, 385a, b, 899b; VI, 319b, 321a, 621b, 726b; VII, 261a, b, 402b, 546b, 568a, 604a, 786b, **1059b**; X, 90b; S, 90a, 226a, 394a
Ndiassâne s, 182b – S, 182b
Ndjamena s, 166b – S, 166b
Nebuchadnezzar → Bukht-Naṣar
Nečari → Nayčari
Necdet Sancar (1975) viii, 251b – VIII, 268b
Necip Fazil Kısakürek (XX) vi, 95b – VI, 93b
Nedīm → Nadīm
Nedīm, Aḥmed (1730) i, 270a, 1302a; ii, 1000a; iii, 1002b; iv, 574a, 715b; v, 641a, b, 642a; vi, 198b; viii, **1a**; s, 324a – I, 278a, 1341b; II, 1023a; III, 1027b; IV, 597a, 744b; V, 645b, 646a; VI, 183a;viii, **1a**; S, 323b
Nedjātī, Muṣṭafā v, 282a – V, 280a
Nedjātī Bey, ʿĪsā (1509) i, 292b; ii, 221a; vi, 609b, 610a; vii, 24a; viii, **1b**; s, 324a – I, 301b; II, 227b; VI,

594b; VII, 24a; VIII, **1b**; S, 323b
Nedjīb ʿAsim (1935) iv, 791a – IV, 823a
Nefes v, 275a; viii, **2b** – V, 273a; VIII, **2b**
Nefʿī, ʿOmar Efendi (1635) iii, 357a; iv, 715b; vi, 886b; viii, **3a**; s, 282b, 324a – III, 368a; IV, 744a; VI, 877b; VIII, **3a**; S, 282b, 323b
Nefīr (trumpet/trompette) i, 1291a, b; viii, **3b** – I, 1330b, 1331a; VIII, **3b**
Nefīrī Behrān (XVI) vi, 1007b – VI, 999b
Nefṭa ii, 463a, 464a – II, 475a, 476a
Negara Dār ul-Islām iii, 1228b; vi, 731b – III, 1260b; VI, 720b
Negev → al-Naḳb
Negri Sembilan vi, 232b – VI, 206a
Negroponte → Eğriboz
Neguib, Muḥammad → Muḥammad Nadjīb
Negübey → Nīkpāy
Negus → al-Nadjāshī
Nellur vi, 67b – VI, 65b
Nemče viii, **4a** – VIII, **4a**
Nememcha i, 371b; ii, 464a; s, 144b – I, 382b; II, 476a; S, 144a, b
Nepal viii, **5a** – VIII, **5b**
Nergisī (Nergisī-zāde), Meḥmed Efendi (1635) viii, **6b** – VIII, **6b**
Neshaī (1520) viii, **7b** – VIII, **7b**
Nesh'et Khōdja Süleymān (1807) viii, 7a – VIII, 7a
Nesīmī, Sayyid ʿImād al-Dīn (1417) iii, 600b; vi, 226b; viii, **8a**; s, 324a – III, 621b; VI, 220b; VIII, **8a**S, 323b
Nesin, Aziz iii, 357b; iv, 882b; v, 195a – III, 369a; IV, 915b; V, 192a
Nestoria(e)ns → Nasṭūriyyūn
Nevruz, Emīr → Nawruz, Amīr
Nevzāt, Refīḳ iv, 123b – IV, 129a
Newābād vi, 57a – VI, 55a
Newāʾī → Navāʾī
Newʿī, Yaḥyā b. Pīr ʿAlī (1599) vii, 597a; viii, **8b**, 581b; s, 83a – VIII, **8b**, 600a; S, 83a
New Saray i, 1188b – I, 1223b
Newʿī-zāde ʿAṭāʾī → ʿAṭāʾī
Newres, ʿAbd al-Razzāḳ (Newres-i Ḳadīm) (1762) viii, **9a** – VIII, **9a**
Newres-i Djedīd (1876) viii, **9a** – VIII, **9b**
Newrokop viii, **9b** – VIII, **9b**
Newshehir viii, **11a** – VIII, **11b**
Newshehirli Ibrāhīm Pasha → Ibrāhīm Pasha Newshehirli
Newzād, Tewfik iv, 930b – IV, 963b
Nēzak Ṭarkhān → Nīzak Ṭarkhān
N'gaous → Niḳaws
Niani (Mali) vi, 258b – VI, 243a
Niassenes s, 182b – S, 182b
Nibrāwī → al-Nabarāwī
Nicaea/Nicée → Iznīḳ
Nicander s, 59b – S, 60a
Niccolò II Gattilusio (Lesbos) (XV) vi, 71a – VI, 69a
Niccolò da Canale (Euboea) (XV) vi, 72a – VI, 69b
Nicephorus Phocas (X) i, 789b; iii, 86a, 120a, 398a, 1084a, b; v, 921b, 923b; vii, 487a, b – I, 813a; III, 88b, 122b, 410b, 1111a, b; V, 927a, 929a; VII, 486b, 487a
Nicobars Islands/Îles - iii, 407a; viii, **12a** – III, 419b; VIII, **12a**
Nic(k)opolis → Niḳbūlī
Nicosia/Nicosie → Lefḳosha
Nidjābat Khān iv, 666b, IV, 693b
Niebla → Labla
Niffar (Nuffar) viii, **12b** – VIII, **12b**
al-Niffarī, Muḥammad b. ʿAbd al-Djabbār (976) viii, **13b** – VIII, **13b**
Nifṭawayh, Abū ʿAbd Allāh (935) i, 822a; vi, 634a; vii, 279b, 403b; viii, **14a**; x, 386a – I, 845a; VI, 619a; VII, 281b, 405a; VIII, **14a**; X, 414a
Niğde vi, 366a, 508b; viii, **15b** – VI, 350a, 494a; VIII, **15b**
Nigde, Ḳāḍī Aḥmad of/de s, 59a – S, 59b
Niger (river/fleuve) viii, **16b** – VIII, **16b**
Niger(state/état) vi, 281b, 401a; viii,**17b**; s, 218a – VI, 266b, 385b;VIII, **17b**; S, 217b
Nigeria/Nigérie i, 39a, 179a; ii, 10a, 942a; iii, 275a; vi, 281b; viii, **19b**; s, 217a – I, 40a, 184a; II, 10b, 963b; III, 283a; VI, 266b; VIII, **19b**; S, 217a
Nigīsa iv, 53b – IV, 56b
Nihāl Čand Lāhawrī (XIX) viii, **23a** – VIII, **23a**
Nihāwand i, 16a; iv, 13b, 447a, 653b; v, 1212b, 1213a; vi, 332b, 493a; vii, 853b; viii. **23a**; s, 297b – I, 16b; IV, 14b, 467a, 680a; V, 1202a, b; VI, 317a, 479a; VII, 854b; VIII, **23b**; S, 297b
al-Nihāwandī, ʿAbd al-Baḳī (1632) vii, 343a; viii, **24a** – VII, 344b; VIII, **24a**
al-Nihāwandī, Aḥmad b. Muḥammad (790) vi, 599b – VI, 584a
Nihāya viii, **24a** – VIII, **24a**
Nihḍat-i Āzādī iv, 166a – IV, 173b
Nīk ʿĀlam Khān i, 1193a – I, 1228b
Nikāba viii, **25b** – VIII, **25b**
Nikāḥ viii, **26b** – VIII, **26b**
Nikāpur vi, 269a – VI, 254a
Niḳaws s, 103a – S, 102b
Nībūlī (Nicopolis) viii, **35a** – VIII, **35b**
Nīkpāy ii, 3a – II, 3b
Niksar (Neo-Caesarea, Bythynia/-e) viii, **36a**; s, 154a – VIII, **36b**; S, 154b
Nīkūdārīs (Negüderis) vii, 218b, 233a – VII, 220a, 235a
Niḳūlāʾūs (Nicola(u)s of/de Damas(cus) viii, **36b** – VIII, **37a**
al-Nīl (river/fleuve) i, 735a, 929a; iii, 71b; iv, 133b, 424b, 442b; v, 862a, 863a, 1249b; vi, 401a; viii, **37b**; s, 413a – I, 757a, 957a; III, 74a; IV, 139a, 443a, 462b; V, 869a, 870a, 1240a, b; VI, 385b; VIII, **38a**; S, 413a
Nīl Kanth (Māndū) vi, 407a – VI, 392a
Nīlambar i, 719b – I, 741a
Nīlūfer Khātūn (XIV) viii, **43a** – VIII, **43b**
Nīm-dih vi, 384b – VI, 368b
Nīmā Yūshīdj iv, 71b; viii, **43a** – IV, 75a; VIII, **44a**
Niʿmat Allāh, Hadjdjī i, 261b – I, 269b
Niʿmat Allāh b. Aḥmad b. Mubārak al-Rūmī (1561) i, 776b; iv, 526a; viii, **44a** – I, 799b; IV, 549a; VIII, **45a**
Niʿmat Allāh b. Ḥabīb Allāh Harawī (XVII) vii, 220a; viii, **44b** – VII, 221b; VIII, **45a**
Niʿmat Allāh Harawī s, 1b – S, 1b
Niʿmat Allāh Nūr al-Dīn Walī al-Kirmānī (1431) → Niʿmat-Allāhiyya
Niʿmat Allāh Walī → Niʿmat-Allāhiyya
Niʿmat Khān, ʿAlī (1710) viii, **48a** – VIII, **49a**
Niʿmat-Allāhiyya i, 925b, 1342a; iv, 49b, 51b, 66a, 951b, 961b; v, 157a, 1222a; vi, 66b, 549b, 551a; viii, **44b**; x, 326a, 327b; s, 134b, 156a – I, 953b, 1382b; IV, 52a, 54b, 69b, 984a, 994a; V, 156b, 1212b; VI, 64b, 534a, 535b; VIII, **45b**; X, 351a, 352b; S, 134a, 156a
Niʿmatīs iv, 99a, 860b – IV, 103b, 893b
Nimr (Shandī) (XIX) vi, 794b – VI, 784a
Nimr, Banū iv, 834b – IV, 867b
Nimr, Fāris (1951)ii, 467a; v, 1090b; vii, 902b; viii, **48b** – II, 479a; V, 1087b; VII, 903b; VIII, **49b**
al-Nimr b. Ḳāsit iv, 493b – IV, 515a

Nimr Muḥammad ii, 351b – II, 361a
Nimrān i, 1239b – I, 1277a
Nimrūd → Namrūd
Nimrūz → Sīstān
Nims (mongoose/mangouste) viii, **49b** – VIII, **50b**
Nimzat s, 182b – S, 182b
Nīnawā viii, **50b** – VIII, **51b**
Nindru s, 74a – S, 74a
Ninive(h) → Nīnawā
Ning-Hsia viii, **51a** – VIII, **52a**
Nioro iii, 289a – III, 298a
Nippur → Niffar
Nirandj viii, **51b** – VIII, **52b**
Nīrīz i, 954b; viii, **52b** – I, 984a; VIII, **53b**
Nirīz (Fārs) → Nayrīz
Nirun (Mongols) vi, 417b – VI, 402b
Nisā → Nasā
Niṣāb (Yemen) vi, 81a – VI, 79a
Nīsābūr → Nīshāpūr
al-Nisābūrī → Ismāʿīl b. Muḥammed; al-Ḥākim
al-Nīsābūrī (1327) ix, 887a – IX, 923a
al-Nīsābūrī, Aḥmad b. Ibrāhīm (dāʿī) (XI) vii, 732a – VII, 732b
al-Nīsābūrī, al-Faḍl b. Shādhān (873) vii, 460b – VII, 460b
al-Nīsābūrī, al-Ḥasan b. Muḥammad, Abu 'l-Ḳāsim (1052) viii, **53a** – VIII, **54a**
al-Nīsābūrī. al-Ḥasan b. al-Muẓaffar (1050) s, 289b – S, 289a
al-Nīsābūrī, Muḥammad b. al-Mundhir vii, 569b – VII, 570a
al-Nīsābūrī, Sahl b. ʿUthmān (XII) vi, 713a – VI, 701b
al-Nīsābūrī, Salama b. Shabīb (IX) vii, 409a – VII, 410b
al-Nīsābūrī, Yaḥyā b. Yaḥyā (839) vii, 691a – VII, 691b
Nīsān (month/mois) viii, **53b** – VIII, **54b**
Nīsān, Banū i, 256a; iii, 1197b; viii, **53b** – I, 264a; III, 1228a; VIII, **54b**
Nīsānid(e)s → Nīsān, Banū
Nisba iv, 180a; viii, **53b** – IV, 187b; VIII, **54b**
Niṣf al-Nahār viii, **56b** – VIII, **57a**
Nish vi, 56a, b, 70b; viii, **56b** – VI, 54a, b, 68b; VIII, **57b**
Nishān i, 1170b; ii, 309a; vi, 537a; viii, **57b;** – I, 1205b; II, 317b; VI, 521b; VIII, **58b**
Nishāndjî iv, 560b, 561a; viii, **62a** – IV, 583a, b; VIII, **63a**
Nishāndjî, Khodja → Djalālzāde Muṣṭafā Čelebi
Nīshāpūr i, 3b, 452b, 750a; ii, 4b, 43b, 746b; iii, 472a; iv, 669a; v, 58a, 354a, 526b, 1126b; vi, 14a, 115b, 120a, 128b, 223b, 224b, 273b, 340a, 523a, 600a, 620b, 627b, 633b, 657a, 661a, 670b, 671a, 715a, b, 780b; viii, **62b**; s, 14b, 21a, 32a, 72b, 149a, 204a, 235a, 251a, 253a, 254b, 259b, 263b, 299a, 343a, 357a, 359b, 392a – I, 3b, 465b, 772b; II, 4b, 44a, 764b; III, 488b; IV, 696a; V, 60a, 355b, 530b, 1122b; VI, 12b, 113a, 118a, 126b, 217a, 218b, 258a, 324b, 508a, 585a, 605b, 612b, 618b, 642a, 646b, 657a, 657b, 703b, 704a, 770a; VIII, **63b**; S, 15a, 21a, 32a, 73a, 149a, 203b, 234b, 251a, 253a, 254a, 259a, 263a, 298b, 343a, 356b, 359b, 392b
Nīshāpūrī, Ẓāhīr al-Dīn (1184) viii, **64a** – VIII, **65b**
Nishāt ii, 433b – II, 444b
Nishdān iv, 488a – IV, 509a
Nishtār, Sardār ʿAbd al-Rabb iii, 532b – III, 551a
Niṣībīn/Nisibis → Naṣībīn
Nisnās → Nasnās
Nissīm ben Yaʿḳob Ibn Shāhīn iv, 306b – IV, 320a, b
Nīṭas → Baḥr Bunṭus
Nithār viii, **64a** – VIII, **65b**
Nitra s, 171a – S, 171b
Niyāḥa viii, **64b** – VIII, **66a**
Niyāzi, Banū iii, 423a – III, 436b
Niyāzī, Shams al-Dīn Meḥmed (Miṣrī Efendi) (1694) viii, **65a** – VIII, **66b**
Niyāzi Bey (XX) i, 63b; ii, 698b; viii, **65b** – I, 65b; II, 716a; VIII, **67a**
Niyya viii, **661** – VIII, **67b**
Nīzak, Ṭarkhān (Hephtalite) (710) i, 857a, 1001a; iii, 304a; iv, 208a; v, 57a, 541b; viii, **67a**; ix, 80b – I, 881a, 1031b; III, 313a; IV, 217a; V, 58b, 546a; VIII, **68b**; IX, 84a
Niẓām (title/titre) viii, **67a** – VIII, **68b**
Niẓām ʿAlī Khān (Ḥaydarābād) (1802) iii, 320b; viii, 67b – III, 331b; VIII, 69a
Niẓām Badakhshī (1584) viii, **67b** – VIII, **69a**
Niẓām Burhānpūrī i, 1331a; ii, 837b – I, 1372a; II, 857a
Niẓām al-Dawla b. Marwān v, 453a – V, 455b
Niẓām al-Dīn (amīr-i dād) iv, 818a – IV, 851a
Niẓām al-Dīn, Mullā Muḥammad (1748) i, 936b; ii, 132a; v, 1135b; vi, 354b; viii, **68b**; s, 292a, b, 293a – I, 965b; II, 135b; V, 1131a; VI, 339a; VIII, **70a**; S, 292a, b
Niẓām al-Dīn b. al-Ḥakīm (1358) viii, 806a – VIII, 833a
Niẓām al-Dīn Aḥmad b. Muḥammad Muḳīm al-Harawī (1594) i, 60b, 856b, 857a; ii, 922a; vii, 342a; viii, **67b**; s, 302a – I, 62b, 880b; II, 943b; VII, 344a; VIII, **69a**; S, 301b
Niẓām al-Dīn Awliyāʾ, Shaykh (Čishtī) (1325) i, 444b, 856a, 1024a, b, 1036b, 1328b; ii, 48a, 50a, 51a, 55a, b, 1076b; iii, 249a; iv, 921b; v, 884b; vi, 126b, 131a, 198b, 691b; viii, **68a**; x, 255b; s, 352b, 353a – I, 457b, 879b, 1055b, 1068a, 1369b; II, 48b, 51a, 52a, 56a, b, 1101a; III, 256a; IV, 954b; V, 891a; VI, 124b, 129b, 182b, 679a; VIII, **69b**; X, 274b; S, 352b, 353a
Niẓām al-Dīn Awrangābādī ii, 55a; iv, 507b – II, 56a; IV, 529b
Niẓām al-Dīn Maḥmūd (Shabānkāra) (XIII) ix, 158a; s, 414b – IX, 163a; S, 415a
Niẓām al-Dīn Naṣr b. Naṣr al-Dawla (Marwānid(e)) (Diyār bakr) (1079) vi, 626b – VI, 611b
Niẓām al-Dīn Thānesarī → Thānesarī
Niẓām al-Dīn ʿUmar s, 197a – S, 197a
Niẓām al-Islām, Ḥadjdjī (XIX) vi, 529a – VI, 513a
Niẓam Khān (prince) → Sikandar Shāh Lōdī
Niẓām al-Milla → Malik b. ʿAlī al-Barānī
Niẓām al-Mulk → Ibn Rāwal Djay Singh
Niẓām al-Mulk (Dōʾāb) s, 126b – S, 125b
Niẓām al-Mulk b. Abī Saʿd al-Djunaydī i, 764a – I, 787a
Niẓām al-Mulk Āṣaf Djāh → Āṣaf Djāh I
Niẓām al-Mulk Čīn Ḳilič Khān, Ḳamar al-Dīn (1748) i, 710a, 1026a, 1170a, 1193a, 1200a, 1201b, 1330b. 1331a; ii, 99b, 981b; iii, 318b, 320a, 427b; iv, 1023b; vi, 535a, b; vii, 446a; viii, 67a, **73a**; ix, 246b; s, 280a – I, 731b, 1057b, 1205a, 1228b, 1235b, 1237a, 1371a, b, 1372a; II, 101b, 1004a; III, 328a, 330b, 441a; IV, 1055b; VI, 519b, 520a; VII, 447a; VIII, 69a, **74b**; IX, 254a; S, 279b
Niẓām al-Mulk Dakhnī iii, 1159b – III, 1188a
Niẓām al-Mulk Ḍiyāʾ al-Mulk Aḥmad (XII) vii, 408b – VII, 409b
Niẓām al-Mulk Ḥasan (vizier) (XII) ix, 16b – IX, 17a
Niẓām al-Mulk al-Ṭūsī (1092) i, 353a, 421a, 552a,

593a, 696a, 731a, 1051b, 1130a; ii, 5a, 344a, 384b, 605a, 963b, 1083a; iii, 253b, 347b, 774b, 1088b, 1099a; iv, 25b, 26a, 27b, 807b, 942b, 1073b; v, 387b, 388b, 625a, 1126b, 1127a, 1128b, 1137b; vi, 13b, 14a, 16a, 20b, 66a, 273b, 274b, 275a, 521b, 523b, 605b, 608b, 627a, 949a; vii, 408a, b, 540b, 679a, 987a, b; viii, **69b**, 971b; s, 14b, 29b, 30a, 384a – I, 364a, 433a, 569b, 612a, 717a, 753a, 1083a, 1164a; II, 5a, 354a, 394b, 620a, 985b, 1108b; III, 261a, 358a, 797b, 1115b, 1126a; IV, 27b, 28a, 29b, 840a, 975a, 1105a; V, 389a, b, 629a, 1123a, 1125a, 1132a; VI, 12b, 14a, 18b, 64a, 258a, 259b, 260a, 506b, 508a, 590a, 593a, 611b, 941b; VII, 409b, 540b, 679a, 988a, b; VIII, **71a**, 1006a; S, 15a, 29b, 30a, 384a

Niẓām Shāh (Bahmanid(e)) (1463) ii, 1127a; vi, 50b, 53b, 488b – II, 1153b; VI, 48b, 52a, 474b

Niẓām-Shāhī (1565) viii, **73a** – VIII, **74b**

Niẓām-Shāhīs i, 303a, 768a, 1170a; ii, 180a; iii, 425a, 426a, 447a, 1161a; vi, 63a, 67a, 368a, 536b, 695b; vii, 943a; viii, **73b**; s, 246a, 259a – I, 312b, 791a, 1205a; II, 185b; III, 439a, 440a, 462a, 1189b; VI, 61a, 65a, 352a, 521a, 683b; VII, 943b; VIII, **75a**; S, 246b, 259a

Niẓāmī, Ḥasan (XIII) viii, **81a** – VIII, **81a**

Nizāmī, Niẓām al-Dīn Abū Muḥammad (1202) i, 680a, 1213a; ii, 794a, 966b, 1143a; iii, 114a, 1112a; iv, 62b, 63a, 66b, 92b, 127b, 128a, 1009b; v, 1104a; vi, 1016b; s, 46b, 415a – I, 701a, 1249a; II, 813a, 988b, 1170a; III, 116b, 1139b; IV, 66a, b, 70a, 97a, 133a, b, 1041b; V, 1100a; VI, 1009b; S, 47a, 415b

Niẓāmī, Shāh Ḳudrat Allāh s, 293a – S, 293a

Niẓāmī ʿArūḍī Samarḳandī, Aḥmad b. ʿUmar b. ʿAlī (1156) vi, 91b, 276a, 726b, 833a; viii, **76b**; s, 333a, 359b – VI, 89b, 261a, 715b, 823a; VIII, **77b**; S, 332b, 359b

Niẓām-i Djedīd ii, 207a, 511b, 512a, b, 713a; iv, 322b; v, 35b, 907b; viii, **75a** – II, 213b, 524b, 525a, 731a; IV, 337a; V, 36b, 913a; VIII, **76b**

Niẓāmī Gandjawī, Djamāl al-Dīn (XIII) viii, **76b** – VIII, **78b**

Niẓām-i Shāmī → Shāmī. Niẓām- al-Dīn

Niẓām-i Wafā iv, 71b – IV, 75b

Niẓāmiyya (Āl Niẓām al-Mulk) i, 1051b, 1052b; ii, 1083a; vi, 275a; viii, **81b** – I, 1083a, 1084a; II, 1108b; VI, 260a; VIII, **83b**

Niẓāmiyya → Madrasa

Niẓāms (Ḥaydarabād) vii, 316a – VII, 318a

Nizamuddin ii, 262b, 263a; iii, 442b – II, 270a, 271a; III, 457a

Nizār b. Maʿadd i, 544b; v, 894b; viii, **82a**; ix, 554a – I, 562a; V, 901a; VIII, **84a**; IX, 576a

Nizār b. al-Mustanṣir (Fāṭimid(e)) (1095) i, 215b, 353a, 552b; ii, 170b, 857a, 858b; iv, 28a, 200a; vii, 725a; viii, **83a**, 84a – I, 222a, 364a, 570a; II, 175b, 877a, 878a; IV, 30a, 208b; VII, 726a; VIII, **85a**, 86a

Nizārī Kuhistānī, Ḥakīm Saʿd al-Dīn (1320) i, 1233a; iv, 67b; viii, **83b** – I, 1270a; IV, 71a; VIII, **85b**

Nizārīs i, 20b, 215b, 246a, b, 352b, 353a, 440a, 552b, 659a, 853b, 1052b, 1099b, 1126a, 1233a, 1254a, 1359b; ii, 64b, 98a, 170b, 859b, 882a, 1039a, 1040b; iii, 72a, 254a, 267b, 268a, 544b, 1169a; iv, 47a, 200a, 201b, 202a, b, 944a; v, 25b; vii, 578a, b, 755a; viii, **84a**, 126a, 133b, 442a, 598b; s, 95b – I, 21b, 222a, 254a, 363b, 452b, 570a, 680a, 877b, 1084a, 1132b, 1160a, 1270a, 1292a, 1399b; II, 66a, 100a, 176a, 879a, 902b, 1063a, 1065a; III, 74b, 261a, 275b, 563b, 1197b; IV, 50a, 208b, 210a, b, 211a, b, 976b; V, 26b; VII, 578b, 579a, 756a; VIII, **86a**, 128b, 136a, 456b, 617b; S, 95a

—doctrine iv, 205a – IV, 214a

Nizhād iv, 785b – IV, 817a

Nizīb vi, 60b, 541b; viii, **84b** – VI, 58b, 526b; VIII, **86b**

Nizwā (Oman) i, 1071b; iii, 652b; vii, 838b; viii, **85a**; ix, 775a – I, 1103b; III, 673b; VII, 840a; VIII, **87a**; IX, 808b

Noah → Nūḥ

Nobatia → al-Marīs

Noghait, Noḳāy (amīr) (1299) i, 1107a, 1188b; ii, 44b, 610a; iii, 117a; vi, 420a; x, 690b – I, 1140b, 1223b; II, 45b, 625b; III, 119b; VI, 405a; X, 733a

Noghay (Tatar(e)s) i, 721b, 1000a, 1075b, 1189b, 1287a; ii, 25a, 44b, 89a; iv, 569b; v, 140b, 141a, 314b; vi, 371a, 415a, 416b, 417b, 418a, 457a; vii, 351a; viii, **85b** – I, 743b, 1031a, 1108a, 1224b, 1326b; II, 25b, 45b, 90b; IV, 592a; V, 143a, 144a, 314b; VI, 355b, 400a, 401b, 402b, 403a, 442b; VII, 352b; VIII, **87b**

Nógrad s, 171a – S, 171a

Nokra ii, 91a – II, 92b

Nomadism(e) i, 872-892; iii, 1096a; iv, 263b, 1177b; v, 472b, 648a, 658a, 659a, 1197b – I, 896b-919a; III, 1122b; IV, 275b, 1211a; V, 475b, 652a, 663b, 1187b

Nonhera s, 325a – S, 324b

Noradin (prince, Mākū) vi, 202a – VI, 186a

Noria → Nāʿūra

Nouakchott vii, 615b; viii, **86b** – VII, 615a; VIII, **89a**

Nové Zámky v, 259b, 260a, 261a; s, 171a – V, 257b, 259a; S, 171b

Noyan (title/titre) viii, **87a** – VIII, **89b**

Nuʿaym → Naʿīm, Āl

Nuʿaym b. Ḥammād (840) ii, 388a; vii, 4a; viii, **87b** – II, 398b; VII, 4a; VIII, **89b**

Nuʿaym b. Khāzim b. Khuzayma al-Tamīmī (IX) vi, 335a – VI, 319b

Nuʿaym b. Muḳarrin (VII) vi, 744a, b – VI, 733b

Nuʿayma, Mikhāʾīl i, 598a; v, 188b, 189b, 1254b, 1255a, b, 1256b; vi, 91a, 409a; viii, **88a** – I, 617b; V, 186a, 187a, 1245b, 1246a, b, 1247b; VI, 89a, 394a; VIII, **90a**

al-Nuʿaymī, ʿAbd al-Ḳādir (1521) ii, 585b; viii, 504b; s, 195b – II, 600a; VIII, 521b; S, 195b

Nuʿayr b. Ḥiyār b. Muḥannā, amīr (1400) ii, 614a; iv, 88a; vii, 462a – II, 629a; IV, 92a; VII, 462a

Nūba, Banū i, 966a; ii, 127b, 131a, 940a; iv, 485b; v, 266b; 268a, 521b; vi, 281b; s, 19b – I, 996a; II, 131a, 134b, 962a; IV, 506b; V, 264b, 265b, 525a; VI, 266b; S, 19b

Nūba (Nubia/-e) viii, **88b** – VIII, **90b**

Nūba languages/langues viii, **91b** – VIII, **93b**

al-Nubāhī (Mālaḳa) (XIV) vi, 112a, 221b, 222b – VI, 109b, 215a, 216a

Nūbār Pasha (1899) ii, 696b; iii, 1194b; viii, **91a** – II, 714a; III, 1224b; VIII, **95a**

Nubāta, Banū i, 665a – I, 686a

Nubāta b. ʿAbd Allāh al-Ḥimnānī (IX) viii, **93b** – VIII, **95b**

Nubāta b. Ḥanẓala al-Kilābī iv, 447a – IV, 467a

Nubia/-e → Nūba

Nubuwwa viii, **93b** – VIII, **95b**

al-Nudjabāʾ i, 95a; v, 995b – I, 97b; V, 991a

al-Nudjayr viii, **97a** – VIII, **99b**

Nudjūm iv, 492a; v, 100b, 1024b; viii, **97b** – IV, 513a; V, 103a, 1020b; VIII, **99b**

Nudjūm, Aḥkām al- i, 1101a; iii, 1063b; viii, **105b** – I, 1134b; III, 1090b; VIII, **108a**

Nufayʿ b. Masrūḥ → Abū Bakra

Nufayla → Ibn Buḳayla

Nuffār i, 382b, 383a – I, 393b, 394a
Nūḥ → Djuḥā
Nūḥ (prophet/prophète) i, 177a; iv, 528b; 609b; v, 421a; vi, 106a, 218b; viii, **108b** – I, 182a; IV, 551b, 634b; V, 423a; VI, 103b, 202b; VIII, **111a**
Nūḥ, Banū vi, 899a – VI, 890b
Nūḥ I b. Naṣr b. Aḥmad (Sāmānid(e)) (954) iv, 22b, 23a, 24b; vi, 261b, 608b; vii, 477b; viii, **109b**, 1027b; s, 35a –
IV, 24b, 26a; VI, 246a, 593a; VII, 477a; VIII, **112a**, 1062b; S, 35a
Nūḥ II b. Manṣūrr b. Nūḥ I (Sāmānid(e)) (997) i, 985a; ii, 100a, 799a; vi, 65a, 340a, 915b; viii, **110a**, 1028a; s, 265b – I, 1015b; II, 102a, 817b; VI, 63a, 324a, 907a; VIII, **112b**, 1063a; S, 265a
Nūḥ b. Asad ii, 791a; iii, 1113b; viii, 1026a – II, 810a; III, 1140b; VIII, 1061a
Nūḥ b. Muṣṭafā (1659) viii, **110b** – VIII, **112b**
Nūḥ b. Shaybān b. Mālik b. Misma' (VIII) vi, 640b – VI, 625b
Nuḥām viii, **110b** – VIII, **113a**
Nūhānīs (Bihār) vi, 47a – VI, 45b
Nuḥās v, 964b, 966a, 967b, 970b, 977b; viii, **111b** – V, 968b, 970b, 973a, 977a; VIII, **113b**
Nuhu Mbogo (1921) x, 780a – X,
al-Nukabā' → al-Nudjabā'
Nūḳān vi, 714a – VI, 702b, 703a
al-Nukayr vi, 507b – VI, 493a
al-Nukhayla viii, **112b** – VIII, **114b**
Nukhayridjan ii, 197b – II, 203b
al-Nukkār (al-Nakkāra) viii, **112b**, 639a – VIII, **115a**, 658a
al-Nukkārī → Abū Yazīd
Nukkāriyya (Ibāḍī) vi, 840b – VI, 831b
Nukkawī iv, 860b – IV, 893b
al-Nuḳra viii, **114a** – VIII, **116b**
al-Nuḳrāshī iii, 1069a; s, 58a – III, 1095b; S, 58b
Nuḳṭat al-Kāf viii, **114a** – VIII, **116b**
Nuḳṭawiyya iii, 600b; iv, 50a; vi, 433b; viii, **114b** – III, 621b; IV, 52b; VI, 419a; VIII, **117a**
Nuku Mbogo (1921) x, 780a – X,
Nukūr s, 103a – S, 102b
Nukuz, Banū vi, 418a; s, 97b, 420a – VI, 403a; S, 97a, 420a
Nūl al-Aḳṣā v, 652a, b, 654a – V, 656a, b, 658a
al-Nu'mān I (Lakhmid(e)) i, 196b; iv, 1133b; v, 633a – I, 202a; IV, 1165a; V, 637a
al-Nu'mān II (Lakhmid(e)) v, 633a – V, 637a
al-Nu'mān III b. al-Mundhir IV (Lakhmid(e)) (601) i, 73a, 196a, 452a, 728b, 1241a; ii, 241a, 354a; iii, 812a; iv, 1024b; v, 583b, 633b; vii, 563a, 568b, 840b, 841a; viii, **119b**, 278a, 918b; ix, 79b –
I, 75a, 202a, 465a, 750a, 1279a; II, 248a, 363b; III, 835b; IV, 1056b; V, 588b, 637b; VII, 563b, 569a, 842a, b; VIII, **121b**, 286a, 949b; IX, 82b
al-Nu'mān b. Abī 'Abd Allāh Muḥammad al-Maghribī, *ḳāḍī* (974) ii, 859a, 861b; iii, 308a, 1084b; vi, 438b; viii, **117a**; s, 70b, 402b –
II, 879a, 881b; III, 317b, 1111a; VI, 424a; VIII, **119b**; S, 71a, 403a
al-Nu'mān b. 'Abd al-'Azīz iii, 1085a, b – III, 1111b, 1112a
al-Nu'mān b. 'Adi (VII) vi, 920a – VI, 911b
al-Nu'mān b. Bashīr al-Anṣārī (684) i, 952b, 1078a; iii, 226b, 272b, 398a, 608b; iv, 1187b; v, 922b; vii, 689a; viii, **118b** –
I, 982a, 1110a; III, 233a, 280a, 410a, 629a; IV, 1220b; V, 928a; VII, 689b; VIII, **121a**
al-Nu'mān b. Djasr iv, 820a – IV, 852b
al-Nu'mān b. al-Ḥārith b. al-Ayham (Ghassānid(e)) (VI) viii, 630a – VIII, 649a
al-Nu'mān b. Muḥammad (957) viii, 715b – VIII, 736a
al-Nu'mān b. al-Muḳarrin (VII) viii, 23b – VIII, 23b
al-Nu'mān b. al-Mundhir → al-Nu'man III (Lakhmid(e))
al-Nu'mān b. Mundhir (Ghassānid(e)) ii,1021a, b – II, 1045a
al-Nu'mān b. Thābit → Abū Ḥanīfa
al-Nu'man al-Gharūr v, 634a – V, 638a
Nu'mān Pasha → Köprülüzāde
al-Nu'mānī, Muḥammad b. Ibrāhīm (956) viii, 811b – VIII, 839a
Numāyish → Masraḥiyya
Numayr (IX) i, 551a – I, 568b
Numayr, Banū ii, 347b; iii, 228a; vi, 379a, 546b; vii, 117b – II, 357a; III, 235a; VI, 363b, 531a; VII, 119b
Numayr b. 'Āmir b. Ṣa'ṣa'a, Banū viii, **120a** – VIII, **122b**
al-Numayrī, Abū Ḥayya → Abū Ḥayya
al-Numayrī, Dja'far Muḥammad (1985) v, 1065a; viii, 92b; ix, 748b – V, 1062a; VIII, 94b; IX, 782b
Numidian v, 754b, 755a – V, 760b, 761a
Nūniyya iv, 668a – IV, 695b
Nūn viii, **120b** – VIII, **123a**
Nupe (Nigeria) viii, 20b – VIII, 20b
Nūr viii, **121b** – VIII, **124a**
Nūr Afzā (garden/jardin) s, 366b – S, 366a
Nūr 'Alī Shāh b. Ḥadjdjī Ni'mat Allāh (1895) i, 261b – I, 269b
Nūr Allāh b. Aḥmad al-Mi'mār, ustādh (XVII)# iv, 507a – IV, 529a
Nūr Allāh Beg v, 462a – V, 465a
Nūr Allāh al-Sayyid Sharīf al-Mar'ashī al-Shushtarī (1610) i, 721a; ii, 380b; iii, 434a, 1152a; vi, 54b, 516a; vii, 132a, 300a, 672a,b; viii, **123b** –
I, 742b; II, 391a; III, 448a, 1180a; VI, 55b, 501b; VII, 134a, 302b, 672b; VIII, **126b**
Nūr Bānū Wālide Sulṭān (Murād III) (1583) vii, 595b; viii, **124a**, 818a – VII, 595b; VIII, **126b**, 846a
al-Nūr Bey Muḥammad 'Anḳara i, 1156b; ii, 123b – I, 1191a; II, 126b
Nūr al-Dawla Balak b. Bahrām b. Artuḳ (Artuḳid(e)) (XII) vi, 380a – VI, 364a
Nūr Dawlat Girāy Khān iv, 723b – IV, 752b
Nūr al-Dīn (deputy/représentant) iv, 500a – IV, 521b
Nūr al-Dīn (Khōdja) (dā'ī) → Satgur Nūr
Nūr al-Dīn, 'Abd al-Ḳādir (1987) viii, **126a** – VIII, **129a**
Nūr al-Dīn b. Edigü (Noghay) (1440) viii, 86a – VIII, 88a
Nūr al-Dīn Arslān Shāh I b. Mas'ūd b. Mawdūd b. Zangī (Zangid(e), Mosul) (1211) vi, 781b; vii, 9b, ,728b; viii, **127a** – VI, 771b; VII, 10a, 729a; VIII, **130a**
Nūr al-Dīn Djibrā'īl b. Bahā al-Dīn Djadja (XIII) v, 172a, b – V, 169b, 170a
Nūr al-Dīn Maḥmūd b. Zangī (Zangid(e) (1174) i, 150a, 197a, 198b, 215a, 446b, 639a, 664b, 791b, 797a, 971a, 1017a, 1025a, 1224a, 1332a, b, 1349a; ii, 64b, 111a, 126a, 283a, 318a, b, 347b, 354b, 856b; iii, 87a, 109b, 208b, 228b, 399a, 504a, 681b, 714a; iv, 482a, 1088a; v, 104a, 924b, 1129a; vi, 380a, b, 507a, 545b, 547a, 606a, 663a, 708a, 733b, 780b, 870a, b; vii, 163b, 578b, 579a, 726b, 816a; viii, **127b**; ix, 486a; s, 195a – I, 154a, 202b, 204b, 221b, 459b, 660a, 684b, 815a, 820b, 1001a, 1048b, 1056b, 1260b, 1372b, 1373a, 1389b; II, 66a, 113b, 129a, 291a, 327b, 357b, 364a, 876b; III, 89b, 112a, 214a, 235a, 411b, 521a, 703b, 736b; IV, 503a, 1191a; V,

106a, 930a, 1125a; VI, 364b, 492b, 530a, 532a, 590b, 648b, 696b, 722b, 770b, 860a, b; VII, 165a, 579a, b, 727a, 818a; VIII, **130b**; IX, 595a; S, 195a
Nūr al-Dīn Muḥammad II (Nizārī) (1210) viii, **133b**, 442b – VIII, **136a**, 457b
Nūr al-Dīn Mun<u>sh</u>ī (XIII) vii, 974a – VII, 974b
Nūr al-Dīn Pa<u>sh</u>a iv, 873b – IV, 907a
Nūr-<u>Dj</u>ahān (Miḥr al-Nisāʾ) (1645) i, 253b, 686a, 1161a; ii, 380b; iv, 282a, 709a, 914b; v, 600b, 601a; vi, 488b; vii, 327b; viii, **124b**; s, 366a – I, 261b, 707a, 1196a; II, 390b; IV, 294a, b, 737b, 947b; V, 604b, 605a; VI, 474b; VII, 329a; VIII, **127b**; S, 366a
Nūr al-Ḥaḳḳ b. ʿAbd al-Ḥaḳḳ Dihlawī (XVII) vii, 432b; viii, **134a** – VII, 433b; VIII, **136b**
Nūr Ḳuṭb al-ʿĀlam, Sayyid (1416) i, 1168a; ii, 51b; iii, 1003a; viii, **125a** – I, 1203a; II, 52b; III, 1028a; VIII, **128a**
Nūr Muḥammad Alīzay i, 295b – I, 305a
Nūr Muḥammad (Kalhorā) (1754) i, 431b, 1192a; ix, 440a – I, 443b, 1227b; IX, 457a
Nūr Muḥammad <u>Sh</u>āh iv, 202b; v, 26b – IV, 211b; V, 27a
Nūr Muḥammadī iii, 1240a; viii, **125a**; s, 411b – III, 1272a; VIII, **128a**; S, 411b
Nūr Satgur (1094) viii, **125b** – VIII, **128b**
Nur Sutan Iskandar (XX) vi, 240b – VI, 205b
Nūr Turk iii, 433b – III, 448a
Nūrba<u>kh</u>sh, Sayyid Muḥammad b, Muḥammad b. ʿAbd Allāh (1464) i, 392b; iv, 48b; v, 301a; vi, 73a; viii, **134a**; s, 423a – I, 404a; IV, 51b; V, 300b; VI, 71a; VIII, **137a**; S, 423b
Nūrba<u>kh</u>shī, <u>Sh</u>ams al-Dīn Muḥammad b. Yaḥyā al-Lāhiğī (1515) viii, 135b – VIII, 138a
Nūrba<u>kh</u>shiyya i, 392b; v, 301a, 604b; vi, 549b; vii, 300b; viii, **134a**; s, 366b, 423a, b – I, 404a; V, 300b, 608b; VI, 534a; VII, 302b; VIII, **136b**; S, 366a, 423b
Nurculuk viii, **136b** – VIII, **139b**
Nūrī (gypsies/tziganes) viii, **138a**- VIII, **140b**
al-Nūrī (932) vi, 569b – VI, 554b
al-Nūrī, Abu ʾl-Ḥusayn Aḥmad al-Ba<u>gh</u>awī (907) iii, 1247a; iv, 990b; viii, **139b**; x, 314b – III, 1279a; IV, 1023a; VIII, **141b**; X, 338b
Nūrī, Mīrzā → Bahāʾ Allāh; Ṣubḥ-i Azal
Nūrī, Mīrzā Āḳā <u>Kh</u>ān, Iʿtimād al-Dawla (XIX) vii, 1003b – VII, 1005a
Nūrī, <u>Sh</u>ay<u>kh</u> Faḍl Allāh (1909) vii, 918b; viii, **140a**; ix, 192b; s, 110a – VII, 919a; VIII, **142b**; IX, 198a; S, 109a
al-Nūrī b. <u>Sh</u>aʿlān (XX) i, 483a; ii, 492b, 626a – I, 497b; II, 505a, 641b
Nūrī Bīmāristān (Damas(cus)) vi, 193b – VI, 177b
Nuri Killičil → Enwer Pa<u>sh</u>a
Nūrī Pa<u>sh</u>a (Killigil) i, 191b, 1071a; ii, 701b – I, 197a, 1103a, b; II, 719b
Nūrī al-Saʿīd (1958) ii, 872b; iii, 521b, 522a; v, 1045a; vi, 615a, 616a; viii, **140b**, 246a, 445b; s, 7a – II, 893a; III, 539b, 540a; V, 1041b; VI, 600a, 601a; VIII, **143a**, 252a, 460b; S, 6b
Nūrī <u>Sh</u>aʿlān (XX) viii, 644a – VIII, 663a
Nūrīn vi, 504b – VI, 490a
Nūristān → Kāfiristān
Nūriyya (Cairo/le Caire) s, 197a – S, 197a
Nursī, <u>Sh</u>ey<u>kh</u> Badīʿ al-Zamān (Bediuzzaman Said Riza-nursî) (1960) viii, **143a** – VIII, **145b**
Nurullah Ataç (1957) vi, 95b – VI, 93b
Nūrzāy ii, 629a – II, 644b
Nuṣayb ii, 1029b – II, 1053a
Nuṣayb al-Akbar b. Rabāḥ, Abū Miḥ<u>dj</u>ān (730) viii, **145a** – VIII, **147a**
Nuṣayb al-Aṣ<u>gh</u>ar, Abu ʾl-Ḥa<u>dj</u>nāʾ (IX) viii, **144b** – VIII, **147a**
Nuṣaybīn → Naṣībīn
Nuṣayr b. Ṣāliḥ al-Ibāḍī iii, 655a – III, 676a
Nuṣayrīyya (Nuṣayrīs) i, 134a, 470b, 471b, 688a, 832b, 1082a, 1098b, 1099b; ii, 358b, 994a, 1070b, 1094b; iv, 202a, 1133a; vi, 582a, 791b; viii, **145b**; s, 207a, 364b – I, 138a, 484b, 485b, 709a, 856a, 1114b, 1131b, 1132b; II, 368a, 1017a, 1095a, 1120b; IV, 211a, 1164b; VI, 567a, 781a; VIII, **148a**; S, 206b, 364b
al-Nu<u>sh</u>ādir viii, **148a** – VIII, **150b**
al-Nū<u>sh</u>a<u>dj</u>ān b. Wahrīz s, 354b – S, 354b
al-Nū<u>sh</u>arī (al-Naw<u>sh</u>arī), Abū Mūsa (IX) viii, **149a** – VIII, **151a**
al-Nū<u>sh</u>arī, wālī (X) iv, 89a; vi, 670b – IV, 93a; VI, 656b
Nū<u>sh</u>irwān → Anūshi(a)rwān
Nu<u>sh</u><u>sh</u>āb iv, 799a – IV, 831b
Nū<u>sh</u>tagin → Anū<u>sh</u>tigin
al-Nu<u>sh</u>ūʾ Abū <u>Sh</u>ākir s, 396a – S, 396b
Nu<u>sh</u>ūr → Ḳiyāma
Nus<u>kh</u>a viii, **149a** – VIII, **151a**
Nuṣrat Allāh, ḳāḍī (XIV) vi, 77b – VI, 75b
Nuṣrat Bībī vi, 488a – VI, 474a
Nuṣrat al-Dīn b. Ibrāhim b. Ḥusām al-Dīn Ḥasan (Marʿa<u>sh</u>) (XIII) vi, 507b – VI, 492b
Nuṣrat al-Dīn b. <u>Kh</u>āmū<u>sh</u> (Atabeg) (1210) i, 301a; vi, 501a – I, 310b; VI, 486a
Nuṣrat al-Dīn b. Ṣāḥib ʿAṭāʾ i, 243b – I, 250b
Nuṣrat al-Dīn Abū Bakr → Abū Bakr b. Pahlawān Muḥammad
Nuṣrat al-Dīn Aḥmad Ibn Hazārasp iii, 337a, b, 1016a; v, 827a – III, 347a, b, 1041b; V, 833a
Nuṣrat al-Dīn Amīr-Amīran b. ʿImād al-Dīn Zangī (XII) vi, 870a, b; viii, 127b – VI, 861a, b; VIII, 130b
Nuṣrat al-Dīn Arslān Āba → Aḳ-Sunḳūr II
Nuṣrat al-Dīn <u>Kh</u>āṣṣ-bek → Arslan Abīhī
Nuṣrat al-Dīn Muḥammad b. ʿAlāʾ al-Dīn (Marā<u>gh</u>a) (XIII) vi, 500b – VI, 486a
Nuṣrat al-Dīn Yaḥyā (Muẓaffarid(e)) (1393) vii, 480b – VII, 480b
Nuṣrat <u>Kh</u>ān (Delhi) (XIV) i, 506b, 1192a; ii, 1124a; iv, 922a; vi, 49a, b – I, 522a, 1227a; II, 1150b; IV, 955a; VI, 47b
Nuṣrat <u>Kh</u>ātūn vi, 488a – VI, 474a
Nuṣrat <u>Sh</u>āh (Bengal(e)) (1532) iii, 422b, 632a; v, 638b; vi, 47a – III, 436a, 653a; V, 643a; VI, 45b
Nuṣrat <u>Sh</u>āh (Delhi) ii, 270a – II, 278b
Nuṣrat <u>Sh</u>āh II (Tu<u>gh</u>luḳid(e)) (1399) vi, 294a, b – VI, 279b
Nuṣratābād viii, **154a** – VIII, **156b**
Nuṣratī, Muḥammad Nuṣrat (XVII) iii, 119a; viii, **154b** – III, 121b; VIII, **156b**
Nuṣub viii, **154b** – VIII, **157a**
al-Nuwayrī, ʿImād al-Dīn (1317) viii, 157b – VIII, 159b
al-Nuwayrī, Muḥammad b. al-Ḳāsim al-Iskandarānī (1374) vii, 171b; viii, **155b** – VII, 173a; VIII, **158a**
al-Nuwayrī, <u>Sh</u>ihāb al-Dīn Aḥmad (1332) i, 595a, 794a, 1116b; iv, 334a, b, 485b; vi, 144a, 311b, 340b, 906b; viii, **156a**; s, 43a, 128b – I, 614a, 817b, 1150a; IV, 349a, 506b; VI, 142b, 296b, 324b, 898a; VIII, **158a**; S, 43a, 128a
Nuzha → Miʿzaf
Nyitas i, 173a – I, 177b

O

Ob (river/fleuve) viii, **160a** – VIII, **163a**
Oba v, 472a – V, 475a
Obat iv, 648b – IV, 675a
ʿObhadya, ʿObhedel → ʿĪsāwiyya
Oblučica → Isakča
Océan Atlantique → al-Baḥr al-Muḥīṭ
Océan Indien → Baḥr al-Hind; Baḥr al-Zandj
Ochialy → ʿUlūdj ʿAlī
Ochrida → Okhri
Ocsónoba → Ukshūnuba
Oczakov → Özi
Odenatus II (267) → Udhayna b. Hayrān b. Wahb Allāt
Odjaḳ i, 947b, 1256a, b, 1267a, 1277b; ii, 1091a; iv, 167b; viii, **161a**; s, 409b – I, 977a, 1294a, b, 1305b, 1317a; II, 1116b; IV, 174b; VIII, **163b**; S, 409b
Odjaḳlïḳ → Odjaḳ
Odon → Khotan
Ofen viii, **161b** – VIII, **164a**
Ogādēn vii, 389b; viii, **161b** – VII, 390b; VIII, **164a**
Ögedey (Mongol) (1241) i, 227a, 1105a, b; ii, 2a, b, 3a, 43a, 44a, 45b, 606a, 928b; iv, 584a, 612b; v, 38b, 858a; vi, 77a, b, 482b; vii, 230a, 234a; viii, **162a** – I, 233b, 1138b; II, 2a, b, 3a, 44a, 45a, 46b, 621a, 950a; IV, 607b, 637a; V, 39b, 865a; VI, 75a, 468b; VII, 231b, 236a; VIII, **164b**
Oghlan → Ghulām(iv)
Oghul viii, **163a** VIII, **165b**
Oghul Ḳaymish ii, 45b – II, 46b
Oghur iv, 1172a, b; x, 691b – IV, 1205b; X, 734a
Oghurdjik Alp s, 280b – S, 280b
Oghuz → Ghuzz
Oghuz-Khān (Kaghan) ii, 1109a; iii, 115b, 314b; v, 125b – II, 1135a; III, 118a, 324a; V, 128a
Oghuznāma iii, 115a; viii, **163a** – III, 117a; VIII, **165b**
Ohrid → Okhrl
Oirats ii, 44b; v, 595a – II, 45b; V, 598b
Oḳču-zāde, Meḥmed Shāh Beg (1630) viii, **164a** – VIII, **166b**
Okhrī (Ohrid) viii, **164b** – VIII, **167a**
Oktay → Ögedey
Oktay Rifat (Horozcu) (1988) viii, **168a** – VIII, **170b**
Öküz Meḥmed Pasha ii, 635a; iv, 970b; viii, 182a – II, 651a; IV, 1002b; VIII, 185a
Okyar, ʿAlī Fethi ii, 432a; iv, 297b, 872b; viii, **168b** – II, 443b; IV, 310b, 906a; VIII, **171a**
ʿÖlah → ʿUlah
Oläng-i Ḳurūḳ vi, 541b – VI, 526a
Old Man of the Mountain, The → Rāshid al-Dīn Sinān
Öldjeytü, Ghiyāth al-Dīn Muḥammad Khār-(Khudā)banda (Mongol Īlkhān) (1316) i, 162a, 347a, 903a, 1031b; ii, 14b, 194a, 1111b; iii, 57b, 390a, 952b, 1122b, 1124b, 1127a; iv, 32a, 48b; v, 554b, 630a; vi, 13a, 323a, 494b, 501b, 502b, 540b, 549b; vii, 13a, 462a, 992a; viii, **168b**; s, 83b – I, 166b, 357b, 930a, 1063a; II, 15a, 200a, 1137b; III, 60a, 402b, 977a, 1150b, 1152b, 1155a; IV, 34a, 51a; V, 559a, 634a; VI, 12a, 307b, 479b, 487a,b,525a, 534a; VII, 13b, 461b, 993b; VIII, **171b**; S, 83b
Olendirek viii, **169b** – VIII, **172a**
Olghun, Meḥmed Ṭāhir (Tahir Olgun) (1951) viii, **170a** – VIII, **172b**
Oman → ʿUmān
Omar, Sultan (Terengganu) (1876) x, 419a – X, 448b
Omar Ali Saifuddin, Sultan Sir s, 152a – S, 152a
Omar, Ömer → ʿUmar
Omar Khayyām → ʿUmar al-Khayyām
Omdurman (Umm Durmān) i, 50a, 976a; v, 70a, 1249b, 1250b, 1251b; viii, **170b** – I, 51a, 1006a; V, 72a, 1240b, 1241b, 1242a; VIII, **173a**
ʿÖmer b. Mezīd (XV) vii, 531b – VII, 531b
ʿÖmer ʿĀshïḳ (1707) viii, **171a** – VIII, **173b**
ʿÖmer Beg (Mora) (XV) vii, 237a – VII, 238b
ʿÖmer Beg (Naḳshe) (XIV) vii, 940a – VII, 940a
ʿÖmer Ḍiyāʾ al-Dīn s, 83a – S, 83a
ʿÖmer Efendi (XVIII) viii, **171b** – VIII, **174a**
ʿÖmer Fuʾādī (1636) ix, 155b – IX, 160b
ʿÖmer Seyf ül-Dīn (Ömer Seufeddin/Seyfettin) (1920) ii, 440a; iii, 357b; iv, 636b; vi, 93b; viii, **172a**, 251a; s, 55a, 98b, 282a – II, 451b; III, 368b; IV, 662b; VI, 91b; VIII, **174b**; 267b; S, 55b, 98a, 282a
Omo v, 522a, 523b – V, 526a, 527b
On Iki Ada (Dodecanese) viii, **172b** – VIII, **175a**
On Oḳ Union (VII) x, 691b – X, 734a
Oner, amīr (XI) vii, 541a – VII, 541a
Ong Khān i, 418b; ii, 42a, 571a, 1112b – I, 430b; II, 42b, 585b, 1138b
Oporto → Burtuḳāl
Orakzay Paṭhāns vi, 127a – VI, 125a
Orāmār (Oramar) viii, **173a** – VIII, **175b**
Oran → Wahrān
Orbay, Ḥüseyin Raʾūf (1964) iv, 297b; vii, 229a; viii, **174a** – IV, 310b; VII, 231a; VIII, **176b**
Orda b. Djuči (XIII) x, 560b – X,
Ordu viii, **174a** – VIII, **177a**
Ordūbād vii, 922a; viii, **174b** – VII, 922b; VIII, **177b**
Orenburg s, 245a – S, 245a
Öreng Timur → Urang Temür
Oreto → Urīt
Orfa → al-Ruhā
Orgiba Djadīda vi, 590a – VI, 575a
Orihuela → Uryula
Orik, Nahīd Ṣïrrï (Nahit Sirri Örik) (1960) viii, **175a** – VIII, **177b**
Orissa → Uṛīsā
Orkhān (pretender/prétendant) (XV) vi, 978a – VI, 970a
Orkhān b. ʿOthmān I Ghāzī (Ottoman) (1362) i, 175a, 318a, 348a, 468a, 468b, 994a, 1187a, 1229a, 1334a; ii, 337b, 443a, 686b, 722a, 982b, 1045a; iii, 212a; iv, 291b, 628a, 969a; v, 248b, 283b; viii, **175a**, 192b – I, 180a, 327b, 358b, 482a, 482b, 1024b, 1222b, 1265b, 1374a; II, 347b, 454b, 704a, 740b, 1005a, 1069a; III, 218a; IV, 304b, 653a, 1001a; V, 246b, 281b; VIII, **178a**, 195a
Orkhān b. Sulaymān Čelebi (XV) vii, 644b, 645a – VII, 644a, b
Orkhān Beg b. Masʿūd b. Menteshe Beg, Shudjāʿ al-Dīn (1344) vi, 1017b – VI, 1010a
Orkhān Kemāl, Mezmed Rāshid (Orhan Kemâl Ögütçü) (1970) viii, **177a** – VIII, **179b**
Orkhan Seyfī (Orhan Seyfi Orhon) (1972) viii, **177b**; s, 168a – VIII, **180a**; S, 168a
Orkhan Welī Kanik s, 150a – S, 150a
Orkhon (river/rivière) i, 1240a; viii, **177b** – I, 1277b; VIII, **180b**
Orkïna Khātūn i, 418b; ii, 3a, b – I, 430b; II, 3a,b
Ōmuṛī i, 225a, 1006b – I, 231b, 1037b
Ōrmuṛs i, 217a, 224a – I, 223b, 230b
Oromo (Galla) i, 176b; ii, 545a,b,974a; iii, 5b, 6a; iv, 88b; V, 522a, 524a; viii, **178a** – I, 181b; II, 558b, **996b**; III, 6a,b; IV, 921b; V, 525b, 527b; VIII, **180b**
Oronte(s) → al-ʿĀṣī
Orta viii, **178b** – VIII, **181a**

Orta oyunu iv, 806b; vi, 373a; viii, **178b** – IV, 839a; VI, 357b; VIII, **181b**
Ortač, Yūsuf Ḍiyā (Yusuf Ziyā Ortaç) (1968) viii, **179a** – VIII, **182a**
Ortaḳčï-ḳul ii, 1090b – II, 1116a
Oruč Owasï s, 239a – S, 239a
Orudj b. Timurtash ii, 599b – II, 614b
Örüg-Temür b. Ananda iv, 553b – IV, 577b
Ösek → Eszék
Ösh → Uččh
Osman → ʿUthmān
Osman dan Fodio → ʿUthmān Ibn Fūdī
Osman Digna → ʿUthmān Abū Bakr Digna
Osman Nūrī → Ergin, Osman Nūrī
Osmanov Muḥammad v, 383a – V, 384a
Osrushana → Usrushana
Ossetes/Ossètes i, 354a, 837a, 1000a; viii, **179b** – I, 365a, 860a, 1031a; VIII, **182b**
Ossetia/Ossétie iv, 349b – IV, 364b
Ossetic/Ossète (language/langue) iv, 351a, b – IV, 365b, 366b
Ostādh → Ustādh
Ostādsīs → Ustādhsīs
Ostrovica vi, 70b – VI, 68b
ʿOtba (ʿOtūb), Banū → ʿUtba, Banū
Otčigin ii, 2b – II, 2b
Ötemish iv, 849b – IV, 882b
ʿOthmān, Āl-i – → ʿOthmānlï
ʿOthmān I, Ghāzī (Ottoman) (1326) i, 467b, 1191a; II, 710b, 715b; iv, 375a; vi, 724b; viii, **180b**; ix, 12b – I, 481b, 1226a; II, 727b, 734a; IV, 391a; VI, 713b; VIII, **183a**; IX. 13a
ʿOthmān II b. Aḥmad I (Ottoman) (1622) i, 395b, 1253b; ii, 183b, 277a, 713a; iv, 971a; vii, 707b; viii, **182a** – I, 406b, 1291b; II, 189b, 285b, 731b; IV, 1003a, b; VII, 708b; VIII, **185a**
ʿOthmān III b. Muṣṭafā II (Ottoman) (1757) i, 395b; vi, 56b, 57a; viii, **182b** – I, 407a; VI, 54b, 55a; VIII, **185b**
ʿOthmān b. Ertoghrul (XIII) v, 256a – V, 254a
ʿOthman Agha (Tardjumān) (XVII) x, 237a – X, 255b
ʿOthmān Efendi (XVIII) vii, 709a; viii, 709a – VII, 710a; VIII, 710a
ʿOthmān Faḍlī, Shaykh (XVII) iv, 191a – IV, 199b
ʿOthmān Ḥamdi Bey (1910) ii, 210a, 694b; iii, 993b; viii, **183a** – II, 216b, 712a; III, 1018a; VIII, **186a**
ʿOthmān Khodja (Bukhārā) (XX) ii, 700b – II, 718b
ʿOthmān Nūrī → Ergin, Osman
ʿOthmān Nūrī Pasha (Ḥidjāz) (XIX) vi, 151a, 176a – VI, 150a, 162
ʿOthmān Pasha (Ghāzī) (Plewna) (1877) viii, 319a – VIII, 329b
ʿOthmān Pasha (Rumeli) (XVIII) vi, 613b – VI, 598b
ʿOthmān Pasha al-Kurdjī (XVIII) iii, 325a; v, 925b – III, 335a; V, 931a
ʿOthmān Pasha Özdemir-oghlu (1585) i, 697b; ii, 880b, 1046b; v, 249a, 270a; vii, 600b; viii, **183b**, 235b – I, 719a; II, 901a, 1070b; V, 247a, 267b; VII, 600a; VIII, **186b**, 241a
ʿOthmān Pasha al-Ṣādiḳ (Damas(cus)) (XVIII) vii, 420b; s, 20b – VII, 422a; S, 20b
ʿOthmān Pasha, Yegen (1689) iv, 194a; viii, **185a** – IV, 202a,b; VIII, **188a**
ʿOthmān Pazar (Osman Pazar) viii, **185a** – VIII, **188b**
ʿOthmān Pāsha Yegen → Yegen ʿOthmān Pāsha
ʿOthmāniyya → Ergani
ʿOthmānlï i, 8a, 21b, 190a, 467a-468b, 640a, 767b, 791b, 808b, 942b, 998b, 1060b-1064b, 1119b, 1128b, 1218b, 1250b, 1252a, 1321a; ii, 286b, 345a, 634b, 710b, 989b, 1056b; iii, 88a, 1086b, 1183a; iv, 35a, b, 36b, 37b, 1156a; v, 493a, 494a, 716a, 726a, 739b, 974a; vi, 134b, 529b, 541b, 566a; ix, 269b – I, 8a, 122a, 194b, 481a-482b, 661a, 790b, 815a, 831b, 971b, 1029b, 1092b-1096b, 1153a, 1162b, 1254b, 1288b, 1290a, 1361b; II, 294b, 355a, 650b, 727b, 1012b, 1081a; III, 90b, 1113a, 1212a; IV, 37b, 38b, 40a, 1188a; V, 496a, 497a, 721a, 731a, 745a, 975b; VI, 132b, 513b, 526a, 551a; IX, 277b
—administration i, 435b, 1159a, 1225b; ii, 118a, 146b, 230b, 313b-316a, 429b-433a, 562b-565b, 1085b-1091a; iii, 164a, 190b-193b, 211b-215b, 349a, 476a-480b, 489a, 552b, 997a; iv, 268a, 560a, 562b, 678b, 893b, 945b-947a, 1053b, 1094b; v, 249a, 334a, b, 878b, 1035a, 1082b; vi, 1b, 3a, 529b, 858a – I, 448a, 1194a, 1262a; II, 121a, 150b, 237a, 323a-325b, 440b-444a, 576b-580a, 1111a-1117a; III 167b, 195a-198a, 217b-221b, 360a, 492b-497a, 505b, 571b, 1022a; IV, 280a, 582b, 585a, 706b, 926b, 978a-979b, 1085a, 1125a; V, 247a, 334a, b, 884b, 1031b, 1080; VI, 1b, 3a, 513b, 849b
—architecture iv, 236a, 570a; v, 292a, b – IV, 246b, 593a; V, 292a
—education v, 902b – V, 908b
—history/histoire v, 814a – V, 820a
—literature/littérature ii, 587b; iii, 352a; iv, 527a, 877b, 878a, 1153a; v, 28a – II, 602a; III, 363a; IV, 550a, 910b, 1185a; V, 28b
—in Egypt/en Égypte vii, 177a – VII, 179a
ʿOthmānlï Ḥürriyet Djemʿiyyeti iv, 284a – IV, 296b
ʿOthmānlï Ikhtilāl Fïrḳasï iii, 393a – III, 405b
ʿOthmānlï Ittiḥād we Teraḳḳī Djemʿiyyeti → Ittiḥād we Teraḳḳī Djemʿiyyeti
ʿOthmānlï Sosyalist Fïrḳasï iv, 123b – IV, 128b
ʿOthmān-zāde Aḥmad Tāʾib (1724) vi, 69b; viii, **188a**; s, 83a – VI, 67b; VIII, **191a**; S, 83a
ʿOthmāndjïk (Osmancik) viii, **189a** – VIII, **192a**
ʿOthmānlï viii, **190a** – VIII, **192b**
Otranto/Otrante i, 293a – I, 302a
Otrār → Utrār
Ottomans → ʿOthmānlï
Ötüken viii, **231a**; x, 688a – VIII, **236a**; X, 730a
Ouarou Ouari v, 281a – V, 279a
Ouarsenis → Wansharīs
Oubangui-Chari s, 165b – S, 165a
Oudh → Awadh
Oued Nīnī iv, 422b – IV, 441a
Oued Saoura s, 328a – S, 327b
El-Oudiane ii, 464a – II, 476a
Oued → Wādī
Oudjda → Wadjda
Ould Dādda, Mukhtār v, 1074b, 1075a – V, 1072a, b
Ouled → Awlād
Ouolof → Djolof
Ourdou → Urdu
Oxus → Āmū Daryā
Ōy iv, 1150b – IV, 1182b
Oymāḳ v, 243b, 245a – V, 241b, 242b
Oyo (Nigeria) viii, 20b, **231b** – VIII, 20b, **236b**
Oyrat → Kalmuks
Özal, Turgut (1993) x, 695a – X,
Ozan i, 697b; viii, **232a** – I, 718b; VIII, **237a**
Özbeg(r) i, 8a, 46b, 47a, 135a, 148a, 224a, 227b, 228b, 406a, 530b, 839b, 847b, 852b, 1001b, 1066b, 1067b, 1107b, 1295b; ii, 44b, 792a; iii, 116b, 177b; iv, 35a, b, 36b, 186b, 1064b; v, 55a, 389a, 859a; vi,

416b, 418b, 419a, 557b, 621a, 714b, 715a, 942a; vii, 91b, 316b; viii, **232a**s, 46a, 51a, 66a, 97a, b, 168b, 169a, 340a, 419b; x, 109a, 690b –
I, 8a, 48a, 138b, 152a, 230b, 234b, 235a, 417b, 547a, 862b, 871a, 876b, 1032a, 1098b, 1100a, 1140b, 1335a; II, 45b, 811a; III, 119a, 181b; IV, 37a-b, 38b, 194b, 1096a; V, 56b, 390a, 866a; VI, 401a, 403b, 542a, 606a, 703b, 934a; VII, 93b, 318b, 319a; VIII, **237a**; X, 118a, ;S, 46b, 51b, 66b, 96b, 97a, 169a, 339b, 419b
Özbeg b. Muḥammad Pahlawān (Ildeñizid(e)) (1225) vi, 501a, 632a; viii, **234b** – VI, 486a, 617a; VIII, **240a**
Özbeg b. Pahlawān i, 353b; ii, 393a, 975b; iii, 1112a; s, 378b – I, 364b; II, 403b, 998a; III, 1139a; S, 378b
Özbeg Khān (Batu'id(e)) (1341) i, 908b, 1107a; v, 136b; ix, 42a; s, 203b – I, 936a, 1140b; V, 139a; IX, 42b; S, 203a
Özbegistan → Uzbekistan
Özbeg Literature x, **721a** – X,
Özbeg (Mongol) x, 690b – X, 733a
Özbeg-Tatars vii, 353a – VII, 355a
Özdemir-oghlî ʿOthmān Pasha → ʿOthmān Pasha
Özdemir Pasha (1560) iii, 4b, 11b; iv, 450a; v, 628a; vi, 642a; vii, 721b, 761b; viii, **235a**; ix, 2a – III, 4b, 12a; IV, 470a; V, 632a; VI, 627b; VII, 722a, 763b; VIII, **240b**; IX, 2a
Özdemir-zāde ʿOthmān Pasha (1585) x, 46a – X, 47b
Özî (Özü) i, 1287a; iii, 252a; v, 103a; vi, 56a; viii, **236a** – I, 1326b; III, 259a; V, 105a, b; VI, 54a; VIII, **241a**
Özkend (Uzkend) ii, 791b; viii, **236b** – II, 810b; VIII, **242a**
Özü → Özî

P

Pā' (Bā'-i farsī) viii, **237a** – VIII, **242a**
Pādhūspān → Rūyān
Pādhūspānid(e)s → Bādūsbānid(e)s
Pādishāh viii, **237a** – VIII, **242b**
Pādishāh Khātūn bint Terken Khātūn (XIII) v, 162a, b, 553b; vi, 482b – V, 160a, b, 558b; VI, 468b
Padri iii, 1222b; viii, **237b** – III, 1253b; VIII, **243a**
Pādshāh Bēgam i, 1161a; ii, 378b – I, 1195b; II, 389a
Paghmān (Kābul) vi, 768a; s, 65b – VI, 757a; S, 66a
Pahang vi, 232b – VI, 206a
Pahārpūr vi, 62a – VI, 60a
Pahlawān viii, **238b** – VIII, **244b**
Pahlawān Bahādur (XIX) ii, 30b – II, 31a
Pahlawān Maḥmūd Pūryār Khʷārazmī vi, 73b – VI, 71b
Pahlawān Muḥammad b. Ildeñiz, Nuṣrat al-Dīn (Ildeñizid(e), 1186) vi, 500a, b, 781b; vii, 922b; viii, **239b**, 944b – VI, 485b, 771a; VII, 923a; VIII, 244b, **245a,** 977a
Pahlawi (Pahlavi) ii, 1142b; iii, 113a, 1136b; iv, 40a; viii, 38b, **239b** – II, 1169b; III, 115b, 1164b; IV, 42b; VIII, 59b, **245b**
Pahlawi (language/langue) v, 229a, 660b, 1112a – V, 226b, 666a, 1108a
Pā'ī viii, **239b** – VIII, **245b**
Pai Yen-hu (Muḥammad Ayyūb) (1882) v, 848a; viii, **240a** – V, 852a; VIII, **245b**
Paisā → Paysā
Pāk Pātan (Pākistān) viii, **240a** – VIII, **246a**
Pakhtūn → Pashto
Pakistan ii, 29b, 132a, 437a, 545b, 595a, 598a, 668b, 676a, b; iii, 385a, 409b, 440a, 532a, 564b; iv, 1b, 171a, 711a; v, 501a, 599a, 780b, 1081a; vi, 489a, 772a; vii, 355a-356a; viii, **240b**; s, 220a, 327b, 331b, 332a –
II, 30a, 135b, 448b, 559a, 610a, 613a, 685b, 693a, b; III, 397a, 422a, 454a, 550b, 584a; IV, 1b, 178b, 739b; V, 504a, 602b, 786a, 1078b; VI, 475a, 761b; VII, 357a-358a; VIII, **246a**; S, 220a, 327a, 331a, b
Paku Buwono → Surakarta
Pālāhang viii, **244a** – VIII, **250a**
Palam (Delhi) s, 206b – S, 206a
Palamāw (Palamū) i, 1210a; viii, **244b** – I, 1246a; VIII, **250a**
Palangka Raya s, 150a – S, 150b
Pālānpur viii, **244b** – VIII, **250b**
Palembang vi, 207b, 236b, 239a; viii, **245a**; s, 150b, 200a, 201a – VI, 191b, 209b, 204a; VIII, **250b**; S, 150b, 200a; 201a
Palermo → Balarm
Palestine → Filasṭīn
Palghat/Palkheo vi, 206b, 535a – VI, 191a, 519b
al-Palimbānī → ʿAbd al-Ṣamad
Palmyra/-e → Tadmur
Palmyrena → al-Bakhrā'
Pambak → Panbuk
Pamir Agreement/Accord de – (1919) i, 87b – I, 90a
Pamir language/langue → Ghalča
Pāmirs i, 454b, 853a, b; ii, 997b; vi, 419a; viii, **245a** – I, 467b, 877a; II, 1020b; VI, 404a; VIII, **251a**
Pamplona → Banbalūna
Pāmpūr s, 332a – S, 332a
Pamuk-ova → Aḳ Ḥiṣār
Pan-Arabism(e) viii, **245b,** 447a – VIII, **251b**, 461b
Pan-Islamism(e) viii, 143b, **248a**, 359b, 360a,b – VIII, 146a, **261a**, 372a,b, 373a,b
Pan-Turkism(e)/Panturquisme viii, **250a** – VIII, **266b**
Panāh ʿAlī Khān iv, 573a – IV, 595b
Panāhī i, 955b – I, 984b
Panbuk v, 557a – V, 561b, 562a
Pānč Pīr i, 868b – I, 892b
Panča Sila ii, 663a; iii, 534b, 1230a; vi, 731a – II, 679b; III, 553b, 1261b; VI, 720a
Pančatantra i, 42a, 1359b; iii, 313b; iv, 503a, 506a – I, 43a, 1399b; III, 323a; IV, 525a, 528a
Pančāyat i, 758a, 978b; v, 1114b, 1115a – I, 780b, 1009a; V, 1111a
Pandačuk s, 333a – S, 332a
Pandārī ii, 156a – II, 160b
Pandit Dayā Shankar Nasīm (1843) vi, 838a – VI, 828b
Pandj (river/fleuve) i, 454b – I, 467b
Pandj Pīr (Pačpiriyā) viii, **252a** – VIII, **254a**
Pandja ʿAlī (al-Mawṣil) vii, 9b – VII, 10a
Pandjāb i, 72a, b, 230a; ii, 426a, 1050b; iii, 443b; v, 886a; vi, 48a, b, 368a, 532b, 535b; viii, 240b, **252b**; s, 21a, 63a, 66b, 203a, 241a, 367a –
I, 74b, 237a; II, 437a, 1075a; III, 458a; V, 892a; VI, 46b, 47a, 352a, 516b, 520a; VIII, 246b, **254b**; S, 21a, 63b, 67a, 202b, 241b, 368a
Pandjābī iii, 1b; v, 610a; viii, **255a** – III, 1b; V, 614a; VIII, **257b**
Pandjdih i, 87b; vi, 618a; viii, **257a** – I, 90a; VI, 603a; VIII, **259b**
Pandjhīr, Pandjshīr i, 504a; v, 968b; viii, **258a**; s, 125b – I, 519a; V, 971b; VIII, **260b**; S, 124b
Pāndu'ā (Pāndvā) iii, 4441; viii, **258b** – III, 458b; VIII, **260b**
Pandjwāy → Ḳandahār
Pāndū (Čak) s, 167a – S, 167a

Pangulu → Penghulu
Pānīpat i, 296b, 1053a; iii, 61a; vi, 535b; vii, 313b, 314a, 316a; viii, 253b, **258b,** 430b – I, 305b, 1084b; III, 63b; VI, 520a; VII, 316a, b, 318b; VIII, 255b, **261a**, 445a
Pānīpāt (battle/bataille) (1526) i, 848a, 1068b; iii, 199b, 200a, 995b; v, 784a; s, 312a, 313a, 325a, 331b – I, 871b, 1101a; III, 204b, 205b, 1020b; V, 790a; S, 312a, 324b, 331a
Pānīpatī, Ḳāḍī Thanā᾿ Allāh (1810) vii, 938b – VII, 939a
Pānipātī, Niẓām al-Dīn s, 308b – S, 308b
Panjgūrī i, 1007a – I, 1038a
Pānka iv, 1160b – IV, 1193a
Pantelleria → Ḳawṣara (Ḳūsira)
Panthay viii, **259b** – VIII, **264a**
Paon, thrône en forme de → Takht-i Ṭāwūs
Papyrus i, 531b; ii, 307a; iv, 742a; v, 173b; viii, 149b, **261b** – I, 547b; II, 315b; IV, 772a; V, 171a; VIII, 152a, **268b**
Para ii, 119b; s, 325a – II, 122a; S, 324b
Para (Paros) (island/île) viii, **265b** – VIII, **272a**
Pāra (coin/monnaie) ii, 119b; viii, **266b** – II,122a; VIII, **273b**
Parāčī i, 224a, 225a; v, 649a – I, 230b, 231b; V, 653a
Parakou ii, 94b – II, 96b
Paramāra ii, 218b – II, 225a
Parameśvara (Malacca) (XV) ix, 852a – IX, 887b
Parasang → Farsakh
Parasramdēv s, 242a – S, 242a
Parčin-Kārī viii, **267a** – VIII, **274a**
Parda-dār iii, 46b; viii, **270b** – III, 50b; VIII, **278a**
Parendā i, 1323b; vi, 67b; viii, **270b** – I, 1364a; VI, 65b; VIII, **278a**
Pargana i, 317a; ii, 156b; viii, **270b** – I, 326b; II, 161a, VIII, **278a**
Parī (Peri) viii, **271a** – VIII, **278b**
Parī Khān Khānum bint Ṭahmāsp vi, 483a – VI, 469a
Parias (al-Andalus) viii, **272a** – VIII, **279b**
Pariyān (river/rivière) v, 868a – V, 874b
Parkent → Fārkat
Parmaḳ ḥisābi̊ i, 677b – I, 698b
Paropamisus (Mountains/Monts) i, 221b; s, 367b – I, 228a; S, 367a
Pārs → Fārs
Pārsā, Khʷādja Muḥammad (1420) vi, 225b; vii, 934a, b ; viii, 458b, 539b – VI, 219a; VII, 934b, 935b; VIII, 474a, 557b
Pārsā᾿iyya viii, **272b** – VIII, **280a**
Pārsīs ii, 1124a; v, 1114a, b, 1115a, 1116a, 1117a; vii, 222b; viii, **273a** – II, 1150b; V, 1110b, 1111a, b, 1112b, 1113b; VII, 224b; VIII, **280b**
Parsiyā → Bīr Sāl
Partai Islam Se Malaysia viii, **275b** – VIII, **283a**
Partai Nasional Indonesia vi, 731a – VI, 720a
Partai Sarekat (Serikat) Islam Indonesia iii, 1229b, 1230a; vi, 731a – III, 1261b, 1262a; VI, 720a
Parwān → Farwān
Parwāna → Muʿīn al-Dīn Sulaymān Parwāna
Parwāna-Oghullari̊ vii, 480a – VII, 479b
Parwānačī viii, **276b** – VIII, **284b**
Parwīn Iʿtiṣāmī (1941) iv, 71b; vi, 486a, 609a; viii, **285a**; s, 110a – IV, 75b; VI, 472a, 594a; VIII, **285a**; S, 109b
Parwīs (Mughal) (1626) viii, 74a – VIII, 76a
Parwīz → Kisrā II
Parwīz (Parwez), Ghulām Aḥmad (XX) iv, 171a – IV, 178b
Parwīz, Khusraw (II) (Sāsānid(e)) (628) viii, **277b**, 918b – VIII, **285b**, 949b
Parwiz b. Djahangīr i, 81a, 1331a; v, 1214a – I, 83b, 1371b; V, 1204a
Parwīz al-Rūmī (1579) vii, 537a – VII, 537a
Paryāb → Faryāb
Pasai, Pasè i, 742b; iii, 1218b; vi, 234b, 240a; s, 199b – I, 764b; III, 1249b; VI, 207b, 205a; S, 199b
Pasak vi, 202a – VI, 186b
Pasantren → Pesantren
Pasargadae s, 129a – S, 128b
Pasarofča (Passarowitz) i, 269b; iii, 1002a; v, 641b; vi, 56a; viii, **278a** – I, 277b; III, 1027a; V, 645b; VI, 54a; VIII, **286a**
Pasè viii, **279a** – VIII, **287a**
Pasha (title/titre) i, 368a; viii, **279b** – I, 379a; VIII, **287b**
Pashaī (language/langue) i, 225a; ii, 138b – I, 231b; II, 142b
Pasha Djūdar (XVI) (Tinbuktu) ix, 756b – IX, 789b
Pasha Ḳapusu (Wezīr Ḳapusu) viii, **281b** – VIII, **290a**
Pashaīs i, 224b; iv, 410a; v, 356a, 649a – I, 231a; IV, 427b; V, 357b, 653a
Pashali̊ḳ viii, **282a** – VIII, **290a**
Pashalimani̊ vi, 588a – VI, 573a
Pasha-Yigit i, 654a, 1118a, b, – I, 674b, 1151b, 1152a
Pashang b. Yūsuf Shāh II v, 827b – V, 833b
Pashmaḳlik iv, 1095a – IV, 1125b
Pashto i, 217a, **220a**, b, 1124a; ii, 31b, 101b, 1103b; iii, 1b; iv, 538a, 1102a; v, 72a, 356a; s, 41b – I, 223b, **226b**, 227a, 1158a; II, 32a, 103b, 1129b; III, 1b; IV, 561a, 1133a; V, 74b, 357b; S, 41b
Pashtūn v, 72a; s, 367a – V, 74a; S, 368a
Pashtūnistan vii, 220b; viii, **282a** – VII, 222b; VIII, **290a**
Pashtūnistān Movement s, 285b – S, 285a
Pasir s, 151a – S, 151a
Pasir (Kalimantan Timur) viii, **283a** – VIII, **291a**
Pasisir (Java) viii, **284a** – VIII, **292b**
Passarowitz → Pasarofča
Paswan-oghlu ʿOthmān (1807) i, 398b, 778b, 1304a; ii, 971b; iii, 628a; viii, **284b** – I, 410a, 801b, 1344a; II, 994a; III, 648a; VIII, **292b**
Paswē vi, 502a – VI, 487a
Paṫan i, 80b, 506b; ii, 1124a; iii, 444b – I, 83a, 522a; II, 1150b; III, 459b
Pāṫan viii, **285a** – VIII, **293b**
Patani (Thailand) viii, **285b** – VIII, **294a**
Pate (island/île) iv, 885b, 886a, b; v, 655a, b; vi, 385a, 612b, 963a; vii, 838b; viii, **286b**; ix, 686a; s, 351b, 355b – IV, 918b, 919b; V, 659a, 660a; VI, 369a, b, 597b, 955b; VII,840a; VIII, **295a**; IX, 714b; S, 351b, 355b
Paṫhāns i, 216b, 218a, 769a, 864a; iii, 411a; vi, 86a; viii, 244b; ix, 440a; s, 270a, 285a, 329b – I, 223a, 224b, 792a, 888b; III, 423b; VI, 84a; VIII, 250b; IX, 457a; S, 270a, 285a, 329a
Patiālā i, 1194b; ii, 488b; s, 66b – I, 1229b; II 501a; S, 67a
Patih Yūnus iii, 1219a – III, 1250a
Paṫnā i, 1018a; vi, 198b, 409b; viii, **287a** – I, 1049b; VI, 183a, 394b; VIII, **295b**
Pátrai, Patras → Baliabadra
Paṭrīk (patriarch(e)) viii, **287b** – VIII, **296a**
Patrona Khalīl (1731) i, 97a, 270b; iii, 1002b; v, 643a; vi, 55b, 995a; viii, **287b** – I, 99b, 278b; III, 1027b; V, 647a; VI, 53b, 987b; VIII, **296a**
Patta → Pate
Paulus of/de Aigina s, 52a – S, 52b
Pavagaṙh vi, 51a, 270a – VI, 49a, 254b
Pawan (river/rivière) s, 150b – S, 150b

Pawlā viii, **288a** – VIII, **296b**
Payag (painter/peintre) (XVII) vi, 426b – VI, 412a
Payās vii, 69b; viii, **288a** – VII, 70b; VIII, **296b**
Pāygāh iv, 218a, b – IV, 227b, 228a
Payghū viii, **288b** – VIII, **297a**
Pā-yi Bābān vi, 620a – VI, 605a
Payinda Khan i, 12b, 230b, 231a; ii, 637b – I, 14b, 237b, 238a; II, 653b
Paykand v, 853b ; viii, 500a – V, 860a, b; VIII, 517a
Paylāwa s, 331b – S, 331b
Paysā (Pice) viii, **288b** – VIII, **297a**
Pʿaytarakan s, 116a – S, 115b
Pazārdjïḳ vi, 508b, 509a – VI, 494a, b
Pāzavārīs vi, 514a, 515b – VI, 499a, 500b
al-Pazdawī, Abu 'l-Yusr → al-Bazdawi
Pāzūkī → Bāzūkiyyūn
Pāzvandoghlu → Paswan-oghlu
Pazyryk s, 136b, 145a, 146a, 148a – S, 136a, 145a, b, 148a
Peacock Throne → Takht-i Ṭāwūs
Pečeneg i, 607b, 1305b, 1307b; ii, 237a; iv, 1175b, 1176b; v, 1011a, 1013b, 1014a, 1015b, 1016b, 1017a, b, 1018a; viii, **289a**, 875a; x, 689b, 690b, 692b – I, 627a, 1345b, 1348a; II, 244a; IV, 1208b, 1210a; V, 1006b, 1009b, 1011a, 1012b, 1013b, 1014a; VIII, **297b**, 904b; X, 732a, b, 735a
Pečewī, Ibrāhīm (1649) i, 1286a; viii, **291a**; s, 171a – I, 1325b; VIII, **299b**; S, 171b
Pechina → Badjdjāna
Pécs viii, **291b** – VIII, **300a**
Pedjīn vi, 1017b – VI, 1010a
Pedro de Alfonso (Moses Sefardi) (1110) vii, 737a – VII, 738a
Pedroche → Biṭrawsh
Pégon iii, 1234b – III, 1266b
Pehlewān → Pahlawān
Pekin → Khānbalïḳ
Peloponnesus/-èse → Mora
Pemba Island/Île de- vi, 370a; viii, **292a** – VI, 354a; VIII, **301a**
Pembela Tanah Air vi, 730b – VI, 719b
Pemuda Pusa i, 745b – I, 768a
Pen name → Takhalluṣ
Penang i, 979b; vi, 232b, 237a, 240b ; viii, **292b** – I, 1009b, 1010a; VI, 206a, 210a, 211b; VIII, **301b**
Penbe v, 558b, 559a – V, 563b, 564a
Penče i, 1357b; ii, 314b ; viii, **293b** – I, 1397b; II, 323b, VIII, **302b**
Pendjik ii, 210b, 1087a; viii, **293b** – II, 217a, 1112b; VIII, **302b**
Pengangā (river/rivière) vi, 87a – VI, 85a
Penghulu viii, **294a** – VIII, **302b**
Péninsule Arabique → ʿArab, Djazīrat al-
Péninsule Malaise VI, 191b, **206a**
Peñon iv, 1156b – IV, 1188b
Penyengat (island/île) vi, 237a – VI, 209b
Pera → Beyoghlu
Perak vi, 232b, 235a, 236a, b; viii, **295a** – VI, 206a, 207b, 208b, 209b; VIII, **304a**
Pérez, Ivan → Ibrahim Taybilī
Pergamon → Bergama
Perim → Mayyūn
Perlak vi, 210b, 234b – VI, 195a, 207a
Perlis vi, 232b, 236b – VI, 206a, 209a
Perovsk → Ak Masdjid
Persatuan Islam vi, 731b – VI, 720b
Persatuan Ulama-ulama Seluruh Atjèh i, 745b, 746b, 747b – I, 768a, 769a, 769b
Persepolis iv, 221a, b, 535b – IV, 230b, 231a, 558b
Persia/Perse → Irān
Persian Gulf → Baḥr Fāris
Persian Tobacco Concession s, 53b, 54b
Pertew Erdhem Pasha (1873) iv, 112b; viii, 296a – IV, 117b; VIII, 305a
Pertew Meḥmed Pasha (XVI) viii, **295b** – VIII, **304b**
Pertew Meḥmed Saʿīd Pasha (1837) viii, **295b** – VIII, **304b**
Pērūz Shāpūr → al-Anbār
Perwāne b. ʿAbd Allāh (XVI) vii, 531b – VII, 532a
Perzerin → Prizren
Pesantren viii, **296a** – VIII, **305a**
Peshāwar i, 223a, 238b, 282b, 970a; ii, 426b; iv, 196b; v, 251a; viii, **299a**; s, 41a, 237a – I, 229b, 245b, 291a, 1000a; II, 437b; IV, 205a; V, 248b; VIII, **308b**; S, 41b, 237a
Pēshdādī iv, 12b – IV, 13a
Pēshwā viii, **300b**, 342a; s, 246b – VIII, **309b**, 354a; S, 246b
Pest viii, **301b** – VIII, **310b**
Petančić, Feliks (Petancius) s, 185b – S, 186b
Peter the Venerable (1156) vii, 737b – VII, 738a
Petro Varadin → Waradīn
Petroleum/Pétrole
—Gulf/Golfe iv, 752a, 778b, 1057a, 1171b; v, 40b, 573a – IV, 782b, 809b, 1088a, 1205a; V, 41b, 577b
—Irāḳ v, 146a – V, 148b
—Iran iv, 41b, 42b; v, 81a, 831b – IV, 44a, 45a; V, 83a, 837b
—Lībiyā v, 758b, 760b – V, 764b, 766b
Pétrolière, Industrie → Nadjd; Nafṭ
Petrus Alfonsi (1130) viii, **302a** – VIII, **311a**
Peul → Fulbe
Peyāmī Ṣafā v, 196b; vi, 95b – V, 193b; VI, 93a
Phanariot (e) → Fener
Pharos iv, 132b, 133a – IV, 138b
Philadelphia (Anatolia/Anatolie) → Alashehir
Philby, Harry St. John Bridger (1960) viii, **302a** – VIII, **311b**
Philippines iii, 1219b; vii, 236b; viii, **303a**; s, 152a – III, 1250b; VI, 840a; VIII, **312b**; S, 152a
Philopon(us), John/Jean → Yaḥyā al-Naḥwī
Pickthall, Mohammed Marmaduke William (1936) viii, **305b** – VIII, **315a**
Pie → Pāʾī
Pierre le Grand I, 277a, 278b, 406a, 832a; III, 624b; IV, 1096b
Pierre noire → Kaʿba
Pihānī, Mīr Ṣar-i Djahān (XVI) viii, **749b** – VIII, **770a**
Pīl → Fīl
Pīlakhna s, 331b – S, 331a
Pīlībhīt iii, 60b – III, 63a
Pīlkhāna iv, 218b, 219b – IV, 228a, 229a
Pīlkhāne → Fīl
Pindārī i, 1195b; vi, 536a – I, 1230b; VI, 520b
Pīr iii, 411b; iv, 202b, 206a; viii, **306a** – III, 424b; IV, 211b, 215b; VIII, **315b**
Pīr Aḥmad b. Ibrāhīm Beg (Ḳarāmān-oghlu) (1475) iv, 624a, b; vi, 71b – IV, 649a; VI, 69b
Pīr Aḥmad b. Pashang (Hazāraspid(e)) (1408) iii, 337a, b; v, 827b – III, 347b; V, 833b
Pīr ʿAlī (Kart) → Ghiyāth al-Dīn Pīr ʿAlī
Pīr Budaḳ iv, 586b – IV, 609a, b
Pīr Dede Sulṭān (XIII) vi, 1023b – VI, 1016b
Pīr Ḥasan Beg iv, 584b, 586a – IV, 608a, b
Pīr Ḥusayn iii, 1208b – III, 1239a
Pīr Ḥusayn b. Sahat iv, 670a – IV, 697b
Pīr Ilyās vii, 23b – VII, 23b
Pīr Meḥmed Wehbī Khayyāṭ (1848) ii, 878b – II, 898b
Pīr Muḥammad b, Djihāngīr b. Khalil b. Tīmūr (1406) i, 227a; ii, 1049b; iii, 417a; iv, 536b; vi, 49b, 524a,

525a; vii, 313b; ix, 197a –
I, 234a; II, 1074a; III, 430b; IV, 560a; VI, 48a, 508b, 509b; VII, 316a; IX, 202b
Pīr Muḥammad Khān (Mālwa) (1561) i, 1155a; ii, 815a; iii, 576a; vi, 310a – I, 1189b; II, 834b; III, 596a; VI, 295a
Pīr Pandjāl Pass vii, 332a – VII, 334a
Pīr Ṣadr al-Din (XV) viii, **307a**; ix, 637a – VIII, **316b**; IX, 661b
Pīr-Shāh → Ghiyāth al-Dīn
Pīr Shams (al-Dīn) viii, **307a** – VIII, **317a**
Pīr Tārīk → Bāyazid Anṣārī
Pīr ʿUmar iv, 871a – IV, 904b
Pīrāk vi, 512a, b – VI, 497a, b, 498a
Pīrān i, 1217b – I, 1254a
Pirate Coast → al-Sāḥil
Pîremêrd → Tewfîq, Hacî
Pīrī Beg b. Kalb ʿAlī Beg iv, 1045a – IV, 1076b
Pīr-i Kāmil i, 1121b, 1122a – I, 1155b, 1156a
Pīrī Meḥmed Pasha (1532) i, 293b; ii, 400a; iii, 341b; iv, 232a, 566a; viii, **307b** –
I, 302b; II, 410b; III, 351b; IV, 242a, 588a; VIII, **317a**
Pīrī Pasha (Istanbul) s, 168b – S, 168b
Pīrī Reʾis b. Hādjdjī Meḥmed Muḥyi ʾl-Dīn (1553) i, 936b; ii, 588a, 590a; iv, 882a, 1082b; vi, 588a, 735a; vii, 47b; viii, **308a** –
I, 965b; II, 602b, 604b; IV, 914b, 1113b; VI, 572b, 724a; VII, 48a; VIII, **317b**
Pīrī-zāde Meḥmed Ṣāʾib i, 286b; viii, **309b** – I, 295a; VIII, **319b**
Pirlepe (Prilep) vi, 89a; viii, **310a** – VI, 87a; VIII, **319b**
Pīrpanthis i, 173a – I, 177b
Pīrūzābād → Firūzābād
Pisar-i Kākū → ʿAlāʾ al-Dawla Muḥammad b. Dushmanziyār
Pīshāwarī, Adīb iv, 789b – IV, 821b
Pīshdādid(e)s iv, 809a; viii, **312a**; ix, 54b –
IV, 841b; VIII, **322a**; IX, 55b
Pīshīn v, 579b, 580b – V, 584b, 585a
Pishkān (cap(e)) s, 332a – S, 331b
Pīshkash ii, 150b, 152b; iii, 347b; viii, **312b** – II, 155a, 157a; III, 358a; VIII, **322b**
Pīshkūh iii, 1106a; v, 826a, 829b, 830a, b – III, 1133a; V, 832a, 835b, 836a, 837a
Pīshpek ii, 67b; viii, **313a** – II, 68b; VIII, **323a**
Pīshtāḳ v, 599b, 600a; viii, **313b** –
V, 603b, 604a; VIII, **323b**
Pīshyān ii, 106b – II, 109a
Pisḳopiye v, 265b – V, 263a
Pist viii, **316b** – VIII, **327a**
Pithorā Rāy → Prithvī Rādj
Piyāle Pasha (1578)) ii, 461a; iv, 233a, 571b; v, 304b; vii, 940a; viii, **316b** – II, 473a; IV, 243a, 594b; V, 304a; VII, 940b; VIII, **327a**
Piyārē, Shaykh s, 313a – S, 312b
Plato(n) → Aflāṭūn
Pleven → Plewna
Plewna viii, **317a** – VIII, **327b**
Plotin(us) → al-Shaykh al-Yūnānī
Plovdiv → Filibe
Poitiers → Balāṭ al-Shuhadāʾ
Poland → Leh
Polemon al-Kāhin (Manf) vi, 411b – VI, 396b
Polemon of/de Laodicea → Aflīmūn
Poley → Bulāy
Pologne →Leh
Polnyi Wakuf → Aḳ Ḥiṣār
Pomaks i, 1000a, 1304a; viii, **320a** – I, 1030b, 1344a; VIII, **330b**
Pondok → Pesantren
Ponnani vi, 206b, 461b, 462a, 463a – VI, 191a, 447b, 449a
Pontianak viii, **324a**; s, 150a, b, 151a, 199b – VIII, **334b**; S, 150b, 151a, 199b
Poole, E. → Elijah Muhammad
Poona → Pūna
Popalzāy i, 95b; ii, 629a – I, 98a; II, 645a
Pornäk (Türkmen) vi, 201a – VI, 185b
Port Said viii, **324b**; s, 7b – VIII, **335b**; S, 7a
Port Sudan/Soudan iv, 687b – IV, 715b
Portal → Pīshṭāḳ
Porte de Fer → Bāb al-Abwāb; Dar-i Āhanīn
Porto-Novo ii, 93b, 94a, b; v, 279b – II, 95b, 96a, b; V, 277b
Portugal → Burtuḳāl
Posta (Postage stamps/Timbres-poste) viii, **325b** – VIII, **336b**
Posta (Postal services/Services postaux) viii, **325b** – VIII, **336a**
Pōthōhārī v, 611a – V, 614b
Potiphar → Ḳiṭfīr
Powinda, Mullā (1913) vi, 86a, b, – VI, 84a, b
Pozanti → Bozanti
Prang Sabil i, 747a; viii, **333a** – I, 769a; VIII, **344b**
Pratap Singh i, 426b; iv, 709b – I, 438b; IV, 738a
Pratīhāra ii, 1122b – II, 1148b
Prawiranegara, Sjafruddin vi, 731b, 732b –
VI, 720b, 721b
Prayāg → Allāhābād
Prēm Čand (1936) iii, 458b; v, 204a; viii, **333b** – III, 474b; V, 201b; VIII, **345b**
Prester John/Prêtre Jean ii, 42a, 1143b; iv, 581b – II, 42b, 1170b; IV, 605a
Preveze (Prevesa) viii, **334b** – VIII, **346b**
Prilep → Pirlepe
Printemps en Littérature Arabe → Zahriyyāt
Printemps en Littérature Ottomane → Rabīʿiyyat
Prishtina viii, **335b** – VIII, **347a**
Prithvī Rādj i, 217b, 1194a; ii, 50a, 256a, 1122b; iii, 168a – I, 224a, 1229b; II, 51a, 263b, 1148b; III, 171b
Prizren viii, **349a** – VIII, **349a**
Proclus → Buruḳlus
Proto-Ismāʿīliyya → Ismāʿīl b. Djaʿfar al-Ṣādiḳ
Prūmīyon iii, 963b – III, 988b
Pseudo-al-Wāḥidī vi, 823b – VI, 813b
Ptolémée → Baṭlamiyūs
Pʾu Shou-keng (XIII) viii, **341a** – VIII, **353a**
Pukkoya Tangal P.M.S.A. (1975) vi, 460a, b – VI, 446a
Pul → Fulbe
Pular → Fula
Pulūr v, 657b, 659b – V, 663a, 665a
Pulwar iv, 220b, 221b – IV, 230b, 231b
Pūna vi, 534b, 535b; viii, **341b** – VI, 519a, 520a; VIII, **353b**
Punč-Bārāmūla s, 423b – S, 423b
Pundja ii, 1125a – II, 1151b
Puniāl vi, 127a; s, 327b – VI, 125a; S, 327a
Punjab → Pandjāb
Pūr Dāʾūd iv, 789b – IV, 821b
Purānā Ḳilʿa vi, 126a – VI, 123b
Pūr-i Bahāʾ-i Djāmī (XIII) viii, **342a** – VIII, **354a**
Pūr-i Dāwūd, Ibrāhīm (1968) viii, **343a** –
VIII, **355a**
Purnā (river/rivière) s, 279b – S, 279b
P.U.S.A. → Persatuan Ulama
Pusht-i Kūh iii, 1106a; v, 646b, 829b, 830a; vi, 491b – III, 1133a; V, 650b, 835b, 836a; VI, 477b
Pushto → Pashto

Pushtūn s, 237b – S, 237a
Pushtūnistān → Pashtūnistān
Pūst viii, **343b** – VIII, **355b**
Pūst-neshīn viii, **343b** – VIII, **355b**
Putiphar → Ḳiṭfīr
Pythagoras/-e → Fīthāghūras

Q

Qasr → Ḳaṣr
Qassem → Ḳāsim, ʿAbd al-Karīm
Qatar → Ḳaṭar
Qena → Ḳunā
Qìltu iii, 1259b – III, 1292a
Qom → Ḳumm
Quedah → Kĕdah
Queen of Sheba → Bilḳīs
Quetta → Kwaṭṭa
Quiloa → Kilwa
Quilon → Kūlam
Quinsai → Khansā
Qurat ul-Ain Hyder (XX) vi, 489b – VI, 475b
Qwl → Ḳayl

R

Rāʾ (letter/lettre) viii, **343a** – VIII, **356a**
Raʿamsās (Raʿamsīs) vii, 140b – VII, 142b
Rabʿ viii, **344a** – VIII, **356a**
Rabāb i, 1124a; viii, **346a** – I, 1158a; VIII, **359a**
Rabaḍ viii, **348b** – VIII, **361b**
al-Rabadha iv, 1144a; vi, 622b; viii, **349a**; s, 198b – IV, 1175b; VI, 607b; VIII, **362a**; S, 198b
al-Rabaḍiyyūn iii, 1082b – III, 1109b
Rabāḥ b. ʿAdjala i, 659b – I, 680b
Rabāḥ b. ʿAmr al-Kaysī (796) x, 60b – X, 62b
Rabāḥ b. Djanbulāt ii, 443b – II, 455b
Rabāḥ al-Ḳaysī (VIII) viii, 354b – VIII, 367a
al-Rabāḥī ii, 575a – II, 589b
al-Rabaḥī, Yūsuf b. Sulaymān (1056) viii, **349b** – VIII, **362a**
al-Rabaʿī, Abu 'l-Ḥasan (1029) viii, **349b** – VIII, **362a**
Raʿbān vi, 506b, 507a – VI, 491b, 492a, b
Rabat → Ribāṭ al-Fatḥ
Rabb viii, **350a** – VIII, **362b**
Rabbath, Edmund iv, 783a – IV, 814b
Rabeh i, 910b, 1260a; v, 358b – I, 938a, 1298b; V, 359b
Rabghūzī, Nāṣir al-Dīn (1310) vii, 193a; viii, **350a** – VII, 193b; VIII, **362b**
Rabīʿ (month/mois) viii, **350b** – VIII, **363a**
al-Rabīʿ b. Dāʾūd (VIII) i, 157b – I, 162a
al-Rabīʿ b. Ḥabīb al-Baṣrī (791) iii, 651a; vii, 663a; viii, 836a – III, 672a; VII, 662b; VIII, 865a
al-Rabīʿ b. al-Ḳaṭṭān (946) vi, 353b – VI, 338a
al-Rabīʿ b. Ṣabīḥ (777) vii, 662b – VII, 662a
al-Rabīʿ b. Sulaymān vi, 674b – VI, 661a
al-Rabīʿ b. Yūnus, Ḥādjib (785) iii, 45b; iv, 1164a; viii, **350b** – III, 47a; IV, 1196a; VIII, **363b**
Rabīʿ b. Zayd (Recemundus) (X) i, 628b; vii, 248b; viii, **351a** – I, 649a; VII, 250a; VIII, **364a**
al-Rabīʿ b. Ziyād al-ʿAbsī s, 177b, 178a, b – S, 178b, 179a, b
al-Rabīʿ b. Ziyād al-Ḥārithī (VII) i, 1313a; iv, 14b, 356b; v, 57a, 157b; vi, 620a – I, 1353b; IV, 15b, 372a; V, 58b, 157a; VI, 605a
Rabīʿa, Banū i, 1a, 72b, 526b, 529b, 544b, 545b, 964b, 1029a, 1096b, 1158a; v, 537a; vi, 333b, 504a, b, 540a; vii, 266a, 461a, 675a; viii, 90b, 91a, **352b**, 863a; s, 122a – I, 1a, 74b, 542b, 545b, 562a, b, 994a, 1060b, 1129b, 1192b; V, 541b; VI, 318a, 489b, 490a, 524b; VII, 268a, 461a; 675a; VIII, 92b, 93a, **365a**, 894a; S, 121b
Rabīʿa b. Abī ʿAbd al-Raḥmān ii, 888b, 1067b – II, 909a, 1092b
Rabīʿa b. ʿAmr al-Djarashī (VII) vi, 545a – VI, 529a
Rabīʿa b. Farrukh (Rabīʿat al-Raʾy) (749) vi, 263a, 278b – VI, 247b, 263b
Rabīʿa b. Ḥāritha b. ʿAmr b. ʿĀmir v, 77a – V, 79b
Rabīʿa b. Kaʿb (al-Aratt) b. Rabīʿa vi, 141b – VI, 140a
Rabīʿa b. Kaʿb al-Aslamī i, 266b – I, 274b
Rabīʿa b. Muḳaddam i, 520a – I, 535b
Rabīʿa b. Mukhāshin vii, 74a – VII, 75a
Rabīʿa b. Naṣr ix, 84b – IX, 83a
Rabīʿa b. Nizār vi, 437b – VI, 423a
Rabīʿa b. Riyāḥ al-Hilālī s, 92b – S, 92b
Rabīʿa b. Rufayʿ ii, 627a – II, 643a
Rābiʿa al-ʿAdawiyya al-Ḳaysiyya (801) vi, 266b; viii, **354b** – VI, 251b; VIII, **367a**
Rābiʿa Dawrānī (Awrangābād) vi, 369b; vii, 333b – VI, 354a; VII, 335a
Rābiʿa Ḳuzdārī iv, 61a – IV, 64b
Rabīʿat al-Raʿy → Rabīʿa b. Farrukh
Rabīb al-Dawla Abū Manṣūr (1119) viii, **356a** – VIII, **369a**
Rābigh (Bandar) iii, 362b; vi, 153b, 154a, 166a; viii, **356b** – III, 374a; VI, 152a, 158b; VIII, **369a**
Rābiḥ (Bornu) → Rabeh
Rābiḥ b. Faḍl Allāh (1900) i, 1157a; v, 278b; viii, **356b**; s, 164b – I, 1191a; V, 276b; VIII, **369b**; S, 164b
Rabīʿiyyāt viii, **357a** – VIII, **369b**
al-Rābiṭa (al-Mariyya) vi, 576a; viii, **359a** – VI, 561a; VIII, **372a**
al-Rābiṭa al-Islāmiyya ii, 132a, 546a; iii, 532b, 534a, 1204b; iv, 793a; vi, 461a; viii, **359b**; ix, 905a – II, 135b, 559b; III, 551a, 552b, 1235a; IV, 825b; VI, 447a; VIII, **372a**; IX, 942b
al-Rābiṭa al-Ḳalamiyya ii, 364a – II, 374a
al-Rābiṭa al-Sharḳiyya s, 121b – S, 121a
Rabwah i, 302a – I, 311b
Rachel → Rāḥīl
Raḍāʿ (Riḍāʿ) viii, **361a**, 824a – VIII, **373b**, 852b
Radawlī → Rudawlī
Radd viii, **362b** – VIII, **375b**
Raḍḍiya Sulṭāna i, 1194a; ii, 120a, 267b, 973a, 1143b; iii, 14a, 433b, 1156a – I, 1229b; II, 123a, 276a, 995a, 1170b; III, 15a, 448a, 1184a
Raden Patah iii, 1219a – III, 1250a
Raden Raḥmat → Sunan Ampel
Raden Trenggana iii, 1219b – III, 1250a
Rādhān, Nahr i, 184a – I, 189b
al-Rādhāniyya i, 32a; ii, 817a; iii, 1044b; iv, 1088b; vii, 43a, 69b; viii, **363b** – I, 33a; II, 836b; III, 1070b; IV, 1119b; VII, 43b, 70a; VIII, **376a**
Rādhanpūr viii, **367b** – VIII, **380b**
al-Rādī → al-Rundī, Abū Khālid Yazīd
al-Rāḍī, al-Sharīf → al-Sharīf al-Rāḍī
al-Rāḍī bi-'llāh, Abu 'l-ʿAbbās Aḥmad b. al-Muḳtadir (ʿAbbāsid(e)) (940) i, 19a, 866a, b, 1038a, 1298b; ii, 453b; iii, 46a, 127a, 159a, 345a, 346a, 902b; iv, 424a, 940b; vii, 994b; viii, **368a**; s, 386a – I, 20a, 890a, b, 1069b, 1338b; II, 465a; III, 47b, 130a, 162b, 355b, 356b, 926b; IV, 442b, 973b; VII, 996a; VIII, **380b**; S, 386a, b

Raḍī al-Dīn Abū Saʿīd al-ʿIrāḳī (1166) vi, 824a – VI, 814a
Raḍī al-Dīn al-Hanbalī (1563) v, 609b – V, 613a
Rāḍī al-Dīn Ḥasan al-Ṣaghānī → al-Ṣaghānī
Rāḍī al-Dīn, shaykh (Bhāgalpūr) i, 954a – I. 983b
Rādī Kiyā, Sayyid ii, 194a; v, 603b; s, 363b – II, 200a; V, 607a; S, 363a
Radīf iv, 57a; v, 836a; viii, **368b** – IV, 60b; V, 842a; VIII, **381b**
Rāḍiye Kalfa (XVI) vii, 596a – VII, 595b
Raḍiyya Begum → Raḍḍiya Sulṭāna
Raḍiyya Sulṭān Bēgum (1722) iv, 638a – IV, 664a
Raḍiyyat al-Dunyā wa-'l-Dīn bint Iltutmish (Dihlī, 1240) vi, 261b, 488a; viii, **371a** – VI, 246a, 474a; VIII, **384a**
Radjʿā i, 51a; i, 79a; iv, 457a, 837a; v, 236a, 433b; viii, **371b** – I, 52b; II, 80a; IV, 477a, 870a; V, 234a, 436a; VIII, **384b**
Radjāʾ b. Ayyūb al-Ḥiḍārī (IX) ii, 198a; vii, 279a, b – II, 204b; VII, 281a
Rādjā Aḥmad (Farukī) → Malik Rādjā
Rādjā ʿAlī Khān → ʿĀdil Shāh IV
Rādjā Bhādj → Bhōdja
Rādjā Bīrbal i, 229a; ii, 296b; iii, 457b – I, 236a; II, 304b; III, 473b
Rādjā Chait Singh i, 757a – I, 779b
Rādjā Dāhir i, 1068b; ii, 188a – I, 1100b ; II, 194a
Rādjā Djay Singh I, II → Djay Singh Sawāʾī
Rādjā Ganēsh (Bengal(e)) (1418) iii, 417b, 1003a; vi, 46b; viii, **373b** – III, 430b, 1028a; VI, 45a; VIII, **386b**
Rādjā Mān Singh i, 229a, 1210a, 1254a; ii, 296b; s, 333a – I, 236a, 1245b, 1292a; II, 304b; S, 332a
Rādjā Prithiwīrādj s, 325a – S, 324b
Rādjā Rām iii, 424b – III, 438b
Rādjā Shitāb Rāyʾ i, 702a – I, 723b
Rādjā Srī i, 1218b – I, 1255a
Rādjā Suhādeva s, 156a, 366a – S, 156a, 366a
Rādjā Ṭodar Mall (XVII) vi, 269b; viii, 74a – VI, 254b; VIII, 76a
Radjaʿa v, 892b, 894b – V, 899a, 900b
Radjab (month/mois) viii, **373b** – VIII, **386b**
Radjab ʿAlī Beg Surūr, Mīrzā v, 202a – V, 199b
Radjab Dīwān-Begi s, 228b – S, 228b
Radjab Pasha v, 34b – V, 35b
Radjabiyya iii, 35a – III, 36b
al-Radjabiyyūn i, 95a – I, 97b
Rādjāma(u)nd(a)rī vi, 67a, 269a – VI, 65a, 254a
Rādjarām b. S'ivādjī (XVII) vi, 535a – VI, 519a
Rādjāsthān vi, 49b, 1027a – VI, 48a, 1019b
Radjaurī s, 324b – S, 324a
Radjaz i, 142a, 673b; ii, 246a, 1073a; iv, 80b, 714a; viii, **375b**, 733a – I, 146a, 694a; II, 253a, 1097b; IV, 84b, 742b; VIII, **388b**, 754a
al-Radjdjāf v, 1250b, 1251a – V, 1241b, 1242a
Radjdjāla iii, 187a – III, 191a
Rādjgīr vi, 131a – VI, 129b
Rādjī iii, 114b – III, 117a
Radjʿiyya (Irtidjāʿ) viii, 379a – VIII, 392a
Radjm viii, **379a** – VIII, **392a**
Rādjmahal vi, 343a; viii, **381a** – VI, 327a; VIII, **394a**
Rādjpūts i, 208b, 252b, 413a, 913b; ii, 271b, 272a, 567a, 597b, 1122a; iii, 202a, 423b; v, 264b; vi, 50b, 52a, 54b, 127b, 309a, 342b, 1019a, 1027a; vii, 315b; viii, **381b**; s, 55b, 73b, 126b, 332a, 353b – I, 214b, 260b, 443b, 941b; II, 280a, 581a, 612a, 1148b; III, 207b, 437a; V, 262b; VI, 49a, 50b, 52b, 125b, 294b, 326b, 1011b, 1020a; VII, 318a; VIII, **394b**; S, 56a, 74a, 125b, 331b, 353b
Radjrādja (Regraga) viii, 671b – VIII, 691a
Rādjshāhī ii, 426b – II, 437b
Rādkān vi, 495b; viii, **383a** – VI, 480b; VIII, **396a**
Radloff iii, 116b – III, 119a
Radmān s, 22b – S, 22b
al-Rādūyānī, Muḥammad b. ʿUmar (1114) iv, 59b; viii, **383a** – IV, 62b; VIII, **396b**
Raḍwā i, 536a; v, 433b; vii, 388b; viii, **383b** – I, 552b; V, 436a; VII, 389b; VIII, **396b**
Rafʿ → Ṭalāḳ
Rafʿ (grammar/grammaire; tradition) viii, **383b** – VIII, **397a**
Rafaḥ vi, 31b; viii, **385a** – VI, 29b; VIII, **398a**
Rafanea vi, 578a – VI, 563a
al-Raffāʾ, Muḥammad b. ʿAlī (XII) ix, 4b – IX, 4b
al-Raffāʾ, al-Sarī al-Mawṣilī (X) iv, 936b; viii, 633a – IV, 969b; VIII, 652a
Rāfiʿ b. Harthama (896) i, 452b; ii, 191b; iv, 21a, b; vii, 418a; viii, 63a, **385b** – I, 465b; II, 197b; IV, 23a; VII, 419a; VIII, 64a, **398b**
Rāfiʿ b. al-Layth b. Naṣr b. Sayyār (IX) ii, 1b; iii, 233b, 234a, 859b; iv, 16b, 17a, 658b; v, 45a, 711a, 855b; vi, 331b, 333a – II, 1b; III, 240b, 241a, 859b; IV, 18a, 685a; V, 46b, 716a, 862a, b; VI, 316a, 317b
Rāfiʿ b. Makkī b. Djāmiʿ iv, 337a, b – IV, 351b, 352a
Rafīʿ al-Daradjāt (Pādshāh) (XVIII) i, 1026a; ii, 810b; vi, 535a; vii, 457a – I, 1057b; II, 829b; VI, 519b; VII, 457a
Rafīʿ al-Dawla Shāh Djahān II (Mughal) → Shāh Djahān, Rafīʿ al-Dawla
Rafīʿ al-Dīn, Mawlānā Shāh Muḥammad b. Shāh Walī Allāh (1818) viii, **386a** – VIII, **399a**
Rafīʿ al-Dīn Nāʾinī s, 23b – S, 23b
Rafīʿ al-Shān i, 914a, 1210a; ii, 379a – I, 941b, 1246a; II, 389b
Rāfiʿ al-Ṭahṭāwī → al-Ṭahṭāwī
al-Rāfiḍa (al-Rawāfiḍ) iii, 308a; iv, 46b; v, 236a; vi, 744a, 916b; viii, **386b**; s, 86a – III, 317b; IV, 49a; V, 234a; VI, 733a, 908a; VIII, **400a**; S, 86a
al-Rāfiʿī, ʿAbd al-Karīm (1226) viii, **389a** – VIII, **402a**
al-Rāfiʿī, Muṣṭafā Ṣādiḳ i, 598a; iii, 1018b – I, 617b; III, 1044a
Rafīḳ, Aḥmad → Aḥmad Rafīḳ
Rafīḳ Khān i, 87b – I, 90a
al-Rāfiḳa vi, 331b; viii, 410b; s, 48b – VI, 316a; VIII, 425a; S, 49a
Rafsandjān viii, **389b** – VIII, **402b**
Rafsandjānī, ʿAlī Akbar Hāshimī, Ḥudjdjat al-Islām (XX) vi, 554a; viii, 389b – VI, 538b; VIII, 402b
al-Raghāma vi, 153b – VI, 151b
al-Rāghib al-Iṣfahānī, Abū 'l-Ḳāsim (XI) ii, 125b; vii, 561b; viii, **389b**; s, 172a – II, 129a; VII, 562a; VIII, **403a**; S, 173a
Rāghib Pasha, Khodja Meḥmed (1763) i, 965b; iii, 157a, 269a; vi, 826b; vii, 708b, 839a; viii, 183a, **390b** – I, 995b; III, 160b, 277a; VI, 817a; VII, 709b, 840b; VIII, 185b, **404a**
Raghiwa s, 103a – S, 102b
Raghunnāth Bādjī, Rād (Marāṭha) (XVIII) vi, 535b – VI, 520a
Ragrāga, Banū ii, 623a; vi, 591a, 741b, 742b, 743a, 744a – II, 638b; VI, 575b, 731a, b, 732a, 733a
Raghūsa (Ragusa/-e) i, 999a, 1266a; iv, 1055a; viii, **391a**; s, 183b, 184a, b – I, 1030a, 1305a; IV, 1086a; VIII, **404b**; S, 185a, b
Raḥā → Ṭāḥūn
Raḥābum vi, 562b, 563a, b – VI, 547b, 548a, b
Raḥāmina, Banū iii, 300b; vi, 741b; vii, 391a – III, 310a; VI, 730b; VII, 392b
al-Raḥba (Raḥbat Mālik b. Ṭawḳ) vii, 271a; viii, 168b, **393b**; s, 36a – VII, 273a; VIII, 171b, **407a**; S, 36b
Rahbāniyya viii, **396b** – VIII, **410b**

al-Raḥbī iii, 693b – III, 715b
Raḥbiyyān s, 356a – S, 356a
Rahdj al-ghār iv, 482b – IV, 503b
Raḥḥāl (Nahār al-Radjdjāl) b. ʿUnfuwa (VIII) vii, 664b – VII, 664b
Raḥḥāṣiyya ii, 964a – II, 986a
Rāhib viii, **397a** – VIII, **411a**
al-Rāhib Anbā Buṭrus → al-Sanā al-Rāhib
Rāhib Ḳuraysh → Abū Bakr b. al-Mughīra al-Makhzūmī
Rāḥīl viii, **397a** – VIII, **411a**
Raḥīl viii, **397b** – VIII, **411b**
Raḥīm → Allāh; Basmala; al-Ḳurʾān; Raḥma
Raḥīm Bakhsh ii, 187a – II, 193a
Raḥīm Ḳulī Khān s, 46a – S, 46b
Raḥīm Yār Khān → Bahāwal Khān
Raḥma iv, 488a; viii, **398a** – IV, 509a; VIII, **412a**
Raḥma b. Djābir (1826) i, 928a; ii, 108b; iv, 751a, 765a; v, 508a, b – I, 956b; II, 110b; IV, 781b, 795b; V, 511b, 512a
Raḥmān → Allāh; Basmala; al-Ḳurʾān; Raḥma
Raḥmān Bābā (XVIII) vii, 328a – VII, 329a
Raḥmāniyya i, 371a; ii, 224a; iv, 362b, 993b; viii, **399a**; x, 247b – I, 382a; II, 231a; IV, 378a, 1026a; VIII, **413a**; X, 266b
Raḥmat Allāh, Shaykh ii, 54a – II, 55a
Raḥmat Allāh Khān ii, 316b – II, 326a
Raḥmat al-Nisāʾ Nawāb Bāʿī i, 913b – I, 941a
Raḥmat ʿAlī Shāh, Zayn al-ʿĀbidīn (Niʿmat-Allāhī) (1861) viii, 47a, b – VIII, 47b, 48a
Rähmätullā Atäḳoziyew Uyghun (XX) vi, 770b – VI, 760a
Raḥmī, Hüseyin iv, 284b, 285a, b, 932a; v, 195b – IV, 296b, 297b, 298a, 964b; V, 193a
Rahn viii, **400a** – VIII, **414a**
Rahnamā, Zayn al-ʿĀbidīn iv, 166b – IV, 173b
Raḥraḥān v, 640a, b; vi, 268a – V, 644b; VI, 253a
Rāhu ii, 502a – II, 514b
al-Rāʾī i, 196a; ii, 245a; s, 24b – I, 201b; II, 252a; S, 24b
Rāʾī Čand Pūrbīya → Mēdinī Rāʾī
al-Rāʿī al-Numayrī (714) viii, 120b, **400b** – VIII, 123a, **414b**
al-Rāʾid al-Tūnusī viii, **401a** – VIII, **415a**
Rāʿiḳ (VII) viii, **402a** – VIII, **416a**
Rainder (port) vi, 53b – VI, 51b
Raïs (XX) vi, 754a – VI, 743b
Raʾīs (chief/chef) iv, 474b; v, 1131b; viii, **402a** – IV, 495b; V, 1127b; VIII, **416a**
Raʾīs Ahl Naghd → Adjwad b. Zāmil
Raʾīs Ḥāmid i, 928a – I, 956a
Raʾīs al-Kuttāb → Reʾīs ül-Küttāb
Raʾīsiyya ii, 29b; v, 154a – II, 30a; V, 155a
Raʿiyya (Reʿāyā) i, 712a, 999b, 1169b, 1266b; iv, 563a, 564a, 565a, 1096a; v, 262a, 880b; viii, **403b** – I, 733b, 1030a, 1204b, 1305b; IV, 585a, 586b, 587b, 1126b; V, 260a, 886b, 887a; VIII, **417b**
Rajāʾ b. Ḥaywa v, 325b – V, 325a
Raja Muda (Penyengat) vi, 237a – VI, 209b
Rajputana iv, 922a – IV, 955a
Rakʿa viii, **406b** – VIII, **420b**
Raḳāsh, Banū i, 2b – I, 2b
al-Raḳāshī → Abān b. ʿAbd al-Ḥamīd
Raḳāshīs iv, 734b – IV, 764a
Rakhīk, Awlād iv, 637b – IV, 664a
Rakhshān (valley/vallée de) vi, 192b – VI, 176a
Raḳīb viii, **406b** – VIII, **420b**
Rāḳid viii, **407a** – VIII, **421a**
al-Raḳīḳ al-Ḳayrawānī → Ibn al-Raḳīḳ
al-Raḳīm → Aṣḥāb al-Kahf
Raḳḳ (Riḳḳ) viii, **407b** – VIII, **422a**
Raḳḳa (ceramic/céramique) iv, 1167b, 1168a – IV, 1200a, 1201a
al-Raḳḳa i, 11a, 457b, 831b; iii, 1268a; vi, 336a, 378b, 379b, 381b, 428a, b, 599b, 600b, 622b, 733b; viii, 131b, **410a**; s, 36a, 413b – I, 11a, 472a, 854b; III, 1301a; VI, 320b, 362b, 364a, 365b, 413b, 584b, 585a, 607b, 722b; VIII, 134a, **424a**; S, 36b, 414a
Raḳḳāda i, 24a, 250b, 1346a; ii, 955b; iv, 829a, 830b; vi, 434b, 727b; viii, **414b**; s, 144a – I, 25a, 258a, 1386b; II, 978a; IV, 862a, 863b; VI, 419b, 716b; VIII, **428b**; S, 144a
Raḳḳāṣ viii, **415a** – VIII, **429b**
al-Raḳḳī → Aḥmad al-Raḳḳī; al-Muḳammiṣ
al-Raḳḳī, Sulaymān b. Djarīr s, 130a – S, 129a
Rákoczy, George (II) v, 257b, 258a, b – V, 255b, 256b
Raḳṣ viii, **415b** – VIII, **429b**
Rām-Hurmuz vi, 198a, b; viii, **416b**; s, 90a – VI, 182a, b; VIII, **431a**; S, 90a
Rām Narāyan ii, 1091b – II, 1117a
Rām Rāy i, 1047a; iii, 626a – I, 1079a; III, 646b
Rama Čandra iv, 922a, b – IV, 955a, b
Ramad viii, **417a** – VIII, **431b**
Ramaḍān (month/mois) viii, **417b** – VIII, **432a**
Ramaḍān, Saʿīd (XX) iv, 160a – IV, 167a
Ramadān Efendi → Bihishtī
Ramaḍān-oghullarï i, 182b, 183a, 468b, 790a; ii, 38b; iv, 623a; vii, 271b; viii, **418a** – I, 187b, 188a, 482a, 813a; II, 39a; IV, 647b; VII, 273b; VIII, **432b**
Ramaḍān-zāde Meḥmed Čelebi Pasha Yeshildje (1571) vi, 70a; viii, **419a** – VI, 68a; VIII, **434a**
Rāmadeva, Rādja iv, 419a, b – IV, 437a, b
al-Ramādī (1013) i, 601b; v, 744a, 779a; viii, **419b** – I, 621a; V, 749a, 785b; VIII, **434a**
al-Rāmahurmuzī, Abū Muḥammad al-Ḥasan Ibn Khallād (971) iii, 27a; vi, 821a; vii, 491a; viii, **420b**; x, 934a – III, 28a; VI, 811a; VII, 490b; VIII, **435a**; X,
Ramal iii, 883a; viii, **421a** – III, 907a; VIII, **435b**
Rāmčandra s, 366a – S, 366a
Ramdan Aban iv, 362b – IV, 378b
Rāmdjird v, 868a – V, 874b
Rāmī Meḥmed Pasha (1707) → Meḥmed Ramī Pasha
Rāmī Tabrīzī, Sharaf al-Dīn (XIV) viii, **422a** – VIII, **436a**
al-Ramīmī (al-Rumaymī), Muḥammad b. Yaḥyā(XI) vi, 577a – VI, 562a
Ramiro III (Léon) (X) vi, 431b – VI, 416b
Rāmisht → Abu ʾl-Ḳāsim Rāmisht
Ramiya of/de Bagamoyo, Shaykh (XX) x, 196a – X, 211b
Raml ii, 220b, 761b; iv, 1128b; v, 943a; viii, **423b** – II, 227b, 780a; IV, 1160a; V, 947a; VIII, **437b**
al-Ramla i, 618b, 1030a; ii, 483b, 911a; iii, 287b; v, 326a, 328a, 329a, 799b, 800b; vi, 506a, 652b, 661b, 668a; viii, **423b**; s, 20b, 37a – I, 637b, 1061b; II, 495b, 932b; III, 296b; V, 325b, 327b, 329a, 805b, 806b; VI, 491b, 638a, 647b, 654b; VIII, **437b**; S, 20b, 37b
al-Ramlī, Malik (Karaite) iv, 604a – IV, 628a
al-Ramlī, Muḥammad b. Aḥmad (1595) iii, 779a; viii, **424b** – III, 802b; VIII, **438b**
al-Rammāl → Aḥmad b. ʿAlī b. Zunbul
Rāmpūr i, 218a; vi, 198b, 611b; vii, 421a; viii, **425b**; s, 73b, 292a, b – I, 224b; VI, 183a, 596b; VII, 422b; VIII, **439b**; S, 74a, 292a
Ramz viii, **426b** – VIII, **440b**
Ran → Nāẓim Ḥikmet
Rānā Kumbha iii, 418b – III, 431b
Raʿna Muṣṭafā Efendi (1832) viii, 11a – VIII, 11a
Rānā Sāngā (Mēwāṛ) (1528) vi, 270a; vii, 314a;

viii, 382b, **430b** – VI, 254b; VII, 316a; VIII, 395b, **444b**
Ranbīr Singh iv, 709b – IV, 738a
Rančī s, 106b – S, 106a
Rand, Banu 'l- iv, 415b, 416b; v, 1181b – IV, 434a, b; V, 1171b
Randjit-dēv s, 242a – S, 242a
Randjīt Singh (1839) i, 230b, 432b, 454b, 1020a, 1347b; ii, 47b, 186b, 929a, 1131a; iii, 336a; iv, 196b, 709b; v, 353b, 599a; viii, 253b: ix, 693b; s, 242a, 332a – I, 237b, 445a, 467b; 1051b, 1388a; II, 48b, 192b, 950b, 1157b; III, 346a; IV, 205a, 738a; V, 354b, 602b; VIII, 255b; IX, 722a; S, 242a, 331b
Rangīn, Saʿādat Yār Khān (1835) viii, **431a** – VIII, **445a**
Rangoon/Rangoun viii, **431a** – VIII, **445b**
Rānikūh vi, 115b – VI, 113a
al-Rānīrī, Nūr al-Dīn (1666) i, 88a, 742a; iii, 1220a, 1233a, 1234a; vi, 235b, 240a; viii, 294a – I, 91a, 764a; III, 1251a, 1265a, 1266a; VI, 208a, 205a; VIII, 303a
al-Ranisūl vi, 221b – VI, 215a
Rank viii, **431b** – VIII, **445b**
Rann (river/rivière) vi, 50b – VI, 49a
Ranthambor vi, 48a, 53a – VI, 46b, 51b
Rāo Mandalik Čudāsama (Djūnāgaŕh) (XV) vi, 50b – VI, 49a
Rāo Pahāŕ Singh iii, 61b – III, 64a
Rapak viii, **433a** – VIII, **447b**
Raprī vi, 62a – VI, 60a
Ra's viii, **433b** – VIII, **447b**
Ra's al-ʿĀm viii, **433b** – VIII, **448a**
Ra's Asīr → Guardafui
Ra's al-ʿAyn (ʿAyn Warda) i, 789a; iv, 898a; vi, 437b, 539b ; viii, **433b** – I, 812b; IV, 930b; VI, 423a, 524b; VIII, **448a**
Ra's Burūm vii, 496b – VII, 496a
Ra's ḍarbat ʿAlī vi, 81a – VI, 79a
Ra's al-Djibāl → Musandam
Ra's al-Djufayr vi, 358a – VI, 342a
Ra's al-Ḥadd vi, 729a – VI, 718a
Ra's Ḥāfūn vi, 128a – VI, 126a
Ra's Kalbuh vi, 735b – VI, 725a
āa's al-Khayma i, 928a; iv, 777b; v, 508a, 765a; vi, 38a; viii, **435a**; s, 416b – I, 956b; IV, 808b; V, 511b, 771a; VI, 36a; VIII, **449b**; S, 417a
Ra's al-Khums → Ra's al-Rubʿ
Ra's al-Māʾ vi, 547b – VI, 532a
Ra's Mkumbuu (Pemba) vi, 370a – VI, 354a
Ra's Musandam viii, **436b** – VIII, **451a**
Ra's (al-)Tannūra viii, **437b** – VIII, **452a**
Ra's al-tīn (palace/palais) s, 301a – S, 300b
Ra's al-Wādī i, 1171b – I, 1207a
Rasāʾil al- Ḥikma ii, 633a – II, 649a
al-Rasʿanī vi, 114a – VI, 111b
Raṣāṣ v, 964b, 967a – V, 969a
Rashāʾida, Banū viii, **437b** – VIII, **452a**
Rashāyida, Banū (Arabia/-ie) iii, 642a – III, 663b
Rāshayyā vi, 28a – VI, 26a
Rasheed Jahan (XX) vi, 489a – VI, 475a
Rashīd (1734) vii, 839a – VII, 840b
Rashīd (Rosetta) vii, 69b; viii, **438a**; s, 18a, 120b – VII, 70a; VIII, **452b**; S, 18a, 120a
al-Rashīd (ʿAbbāsid(e)) (809) → Hārūn al-Rashīd
Rāshid (freedman/affranchi) (VIII) iii, 1031a – III, 1057a
Rashīd, Āl i, 554b, 1313a; ii, 176b, 492b; iii, 1066a; iv, 481b; 717b, 1073a, 1142b; v, 574b; vi, 83b, 985b; viii, **438b**; ix, 904a; s, 3b, 145a, 350a,b – I, 572b, 1353a; II, 182a, 505a; III, 1092b; IV, 502b; 746a, 1104b, 1174a; V, 579a; VI, 81b, 978a; VIII, **453a**; IX, 942a; S, 144b, 305a,b
Rāshid, Meḥmed (1735) viii, **441a** – VIII, **455b**
Rāshid, N.M. (1975) viii, **441b** – VIII, **456a**
Rāshid b. ʿAmr al-Djudaydī (675) vi, 967b – VI, 959b
Rashīd b. Ḥumayd (ʿAdjmān) (XX) s, 42a – S, 42b
Rāshid b. Iyās b. Muḍārib (685) vii, 522b – VII, 523a
al-Rashīd b. Maʾmūn (Almohad(e)) → ʿAbd al-Wāḥid II al-Rashīd
Rāshid b. Maṭar al-Ḳāsimī Raʾs al-Khayma (XVIII) iv, 777b – IV, 809a
Rāshid b. Mughāmis (Baṣra) (XVI) iii, 1257a; iv, 764b; s, 234b – III, 1289b; IV, 795a; S, 234b
Rāshid b. Muḥammad (Mandīl) (XIV) vi, 404b – VI, 389a
Rashīd b. al-Naḍr (ʿUmān) (890) iii, 757a – III, 780a
Rāshid b. Saʿīd (ʿUmān) (XI) iii, 653b – III, 674b
Rāshid b. Saʿīd al-Maktum, Shaykh (Dubbai) (XX) s, 418b – S, 418b
al-Rashīd (Mawlāy) b. al-Sharīf (Filālī) (1672) i, 355b; ii, 510a, 819b, 823a; iv, 729b; v, 1191b; vi, 142b, 250a, 595a, 743a; viii, **440a**; s, 223b, 377b – I, 366b; II, 522b, 839a, 842b; IV, 758b; V, 1181b; VI, 141a, 234a, 579a, 732b; VIII, **454b**; S, 223b, 377b
Rashīd ʿAlī al-Gaylānī (al-Djīlānī) 1965) iii, 264a, 521b, 522a, b, 1258b; vi, 616a; viii, 141b, **445a**; ix, 831a; s, 69a – III, 271b, 539b, 540a, b, 1291b; VI, 601a; VIII, 144a, **460a**; IX, 866b; S, 69b
Rashīd Ayyūb (XX) viii, 88a – VIII, 90a
al-Rāshid bi-'llāh, Abū Djaʿfar al-Manṣūr (ʿAbbāsid(e)) (1138) i, 353b; iii, 1255b; viii, **439a** – I, 364a; III, 1288b; VIII, **454a**
Rashīd al-Dawla Maḥmūd b. Naṣr (Mirdāsid(e)) (1074) iii, 86a, 790a; v, 924a; vi, 379b, 578a – III, 88b, 813b; V, 929b; VI, 364a, 563a
Rashīd al-Dīn b. Khāḳānī Shirwānī (1175) vi, 608b – VI, 593b
Rāshid al-Dīn Sinān b. Salmān b. Muḥammad al-Baṣrī (1193) i, 353b; iv, 206a; vi, 578a, 790a; viii, 134a, **442a** – I, 364b; IV, 215a; VI, 563a, 779b; VIII, 136b, **456b**
Rashīd al-Dīn Ṭabīb, Faḍl Allāh (1318) i, 595a, 1011a; ii, 334a, 1043b, 1109b; iii, 57b, 122a, 215b, 1045a, 1089b, 1122b; iv, 31b, 975b, 1035b, 1037a; vi, 15b, 16a, 457a, 481b; viii, 163b, 169a, **443a**; ix, 870a; s, 280b – I, 614b, 1042a; II, 343b, 1067b, 1135b; III, 60a, 124b, 221b, 1071a, 1116a, 1150a; IV, 34a, 1008a, 1067a, 1069a; VI, 14a, 442b, 467b; VIII, 166a, 171b, **458a**; IX, 906a; S, 280b
Rashīd al-Dīn Waṭwāṭ (1177) iv, 62a, 267b; v, 902b; viii, 383b, **444b**, 543a, 971a; ix, 297b; s, 240a – IV, 65a, 279b; V, 908b; VIII, 396b, **459b**, 560b, 1005a; IX, 306b; S, 240a
Rāshid Efendi iv, 845a, 874a – IV, 878b, 907b
Rashīd Karāma b. ʿAbd al-Ḥamīd (Tripoli) x, 216b – X, 233b
Rashīd Khān i, 1124a – I, 1158a
Rashīd Muḥammad Pasha → Meḥmed Rashīd Pasha
Rashīd Pasha (Kurdistān) (1837) vi, 541b – VI, 526a
Rashīd Pasha, Muṣṭafā (1859) i, 284b, 309b; 396b, 397b, 505b, 1089b; ii, 693a, 934b; iii, 592a, 993a; v, 36a, b; vi, 68a, b, 285a, b; vii, 468b, 532a, 720a; viii, 59a; ix, 443a; s, 168a – I, 293a, 319a, 408a, b, 520b, 1122a; II, 710b, 956b; III, 612a, 1017b; V, 37b; VI, 66a, b, 270a, 965a; VII, 468a, 532b, 721a; VIII, 60b; IX, 460a; S, 168a
Rashīd Riḍā, Sayyid Muḥammad (1935) i, 46a, 598a;

ii, 170b, 294b, 295b, 451b, 466b; iii, 162b, 520b, 1168b; iv, 142a, b, 143b-149a, 159a, 162b, 775b, 782b, 947a; vi, 360a, b, 361a, 462a, 739b, 897a; vii, 419a, 764b; viii, **446a**, 901a; s, 151a, 248a –
I, 47a, 617b; II, 176a, 302b, 303a; 463a, 478b; III, 166a, 538b, 1197b; IV, 148a, 149b-155a, 165b, 169b, 807a, 814a, 979b; VI, 344a, b, 345a, 448a, 729a, 888a; VII, 420b, 766a; VIII, **461a**, 932a; S, 151a, 248a
Rāshid Rustum s, 224b – S, 224b
Rashīd Yāsimī (1951) viii, **448a** – VIII, **463a**
Rashīdī (XI) vi, 276b; s, 65a – VI, 261b; S, 65b
al-Rashīdī, Muḥammad Gūlēd s, 279a – S, 278b
al-Rashīdiyya (al-Djamʿiyya) (order/ordre) viii, **448b**; x, 249a; s, 279a – VIII, **463b**; X, 268a; S, 278b
Rāshidūn iii, 1164a, 1168b; iv, 937b; vi, 875b – III, 1193a, 1197b; IV, 970b; VI, 866b
Rashmaya vi, 712a – VI, 700b
Rasht ii, 1111a; iv, 7b, 631a; viii, **449b**; s, 91b – II, 1137a; IV, 8b, 656b; VIII, **464b**; S, 91b
Rasht, treaty of/ traité de (1732) viii, 771b – VIII, 797b
Rashtī, Ḥabīb Allāh s, 76a – S, 76a
Rashtī, Sayyid Kāẓim (1844) viii, **450b**; ix, 404a – VIII, **465b**; IX, 416b
Rāshtrakūṭa → Balharā
Rashwa iii, 343b; viii, **451a** – III, 354a; VIII, **466a**
Rāsim, Aḥmad → Aḥmad Rāsim
Raslān, Banū vi, 791b – VI, 781a, b
Rasm viii, **451b** – VIII, **467a**
Rasmī → Aḥmad Rasmī
al-Rass (Araxes) i, 252a, 634b; v, 397a, 441b; vi, 200b, 201a, b, 504a; viii, **453a**; s, 116a, 274b –
I, 259b, 655a; V, 398a, 444a; VI, 185a, b, 489b; VIII, **468a**; S, 115b, 274b
al-Rass → Aṣḥāb al-Rass
al-Rassī, al-Ḳāsim b. Ibrāhīm (Zaydī) (860) → al-Ḳāsim B. Ibrāhīm
Rassid(e)s i, 403a; vi, 436b; viii, **454b**; ix, 507a – I, 414b; VI, 421b; VIII, **469b**; IX, 526b
Rasūb (sword/épée) vi, 374a – VI, 358b
Rasūl v, 423b; viii, **454b** – V, 425b; VIII, **470a**
Rasūlid(e)s i, 552b, 553a, 803b; iv, 1188b; v, 895b, 1241a; vi, 81b, 433b, 434a; vii, 996a; viii, **455a**; x, 118a; s, 338a, 387b –
I, 570b, 828a; IV, 1221b; V, 901b, 1231b; VI, 79b, 418b, 419b; VII, 997b; VIII, **470b**; X, 127b; S, 338a, 388a
Ratan, Bābā Ḥādjdjī i, 1194b; vii, 258b; viii, **457b** – I, 1230a; VII, 260b; VIII, **473a**
Ratan Nāth Sarshār (1903) x, 879a – X,
Ratanpūr vi, 53a – VI, 51a
Raṭhors i, 769a; ii, 567a; iv, 93a; vi, 53a; s, 55b, 420b – I, 792a; II, 581a; IV, 97a; VI, 51b; S, 56a, 421a
Rātib viii, **459a** – VIII, **474b**
Raṭl → Makāyil
Ra'ūf, Muḥammad → Muḥammad Ra'ūf
Rauf Bey i, 836b; ii, 6b – I, 859b; II, 6b
Ra'ūf Pasha iii, 4b; v, 36b – III, 5a; V, 37b
Ravi s, 63a – S, 63b
Ravza → Khuldābād
Rawāfiḍ i, 257b, 864a; ii, 605a – I, 265b, 888a; II, 620a
Rawāḥa, Banū viii, **459a** – VIII, **474b**
Rāwal Djay Singh (Čāmpāner) (XV) vi, 51a – VI, 49a
Rāwal Rāy Singh (Djaysalmēr) (XVIII) ii, 186a – II, 192a
Rāwalpindi viii, **460a** – VIII, **475b**
Rāwalpindi (treaty/traité) (1919) s, 66a – S, 66a
Rawān iv, 732b – IV, 762a
Rāwandān i, 239a; viii, **460a** – I, 246b; VIII, **475b**
al-Rawandī, ʿAbd Allāh (VIII) viii, 461a – VIII, 476b
al-Rawandī, Abū 'l-Ḥusayn (864) viii, 95a – VIII, 97b
al-Rāwandī, Abū Hurayra (VIII) iv, 838a; viii, 461b – IV, 871a; VIII, 477a
al-Rāwandī, Ḥarb b. ʿAbd Allāh (764) viii, 461a – VIII, 476b
al-Rāwandī, Maḥmūd b. Muḥammad iv, 1074a – IV, 1105b
Rāwandī, Muḥammad b. ʿAlī (XIII) vi, 275b; viii, **460b** – VI, 260b, VIII, **476a**
Rāwandiyya i, 15b, 17b; iv, 45b, 837b; vi, 345a, 428a, b, 744b, 853a; viii, **461a** – I, 15b, 18a; IV, 48a, 870b; VI, 329a, 413a, b, 734a, 844b; VIII, **476b**
Rawāndiz viii, **463a** – VIII, **478b**
Rāwar vi, 493b – VI, 479b
Rawḍa (Khuldābād) vi, 126a – VI, 123b
al-Rawḍa (Roda, island/île) i, 944b; iv, 424b, 430a; vii, 147a, 148a; viii, **463b**; s, 120b –
I, 973b; IV, 443a, 448b; VII, 149a, 150a; VIII, **479a**; S, 120a
Rawḍa-Khʷānī viii, **465a** – VIII, **480b**
Rawḍakhwān iv, 50b – IV, 53a
Rawḥ b. Ḥātim b. Ḳabīṣa b. al-Muhallab (791) iii, 655a; v, 69b; vii, 360a; viii, **465b**, 996b – III, 676a; V, 71b; VII, 362b; VIII, **481a**, 1031b
Rawḥ b. Zinbāʿ al-Djudhāmī (703) i, 436a, 1242b; ii, 360b, 573b; iii, 270b, 1175b; vi, 622a; vii, 694a; viii, **466a** –
I, 448b, 1280b; II, 370a, 588a; III, 278b, 1204a; VI, 607a; VII, 694a; VIII, **481b**
Rāwī (reciter/raconteur) i, 566b, 584b; iv, 735a; viii, **466b** – I, 584b, 603b; IV, 765a; VIII, **482a**
Rawī (rhyme letter/lettre de la rime) iv, 412a, 413a – IV, 430a, 431a
Rāwīnī s, 83a – S, 83a
Rawk viii, **467b** – VIII, **483a**
Rawḳ iii, 99a, 863a, 1090a; iv, 557b – III, 101b, 887a, 1116b; IV, 581b
Rāwnīr s, 83a – S, 83a
al-Rawshan i, 1239b – I, 1277a
Rawshaniyya i, 1123b; vi, 342b ; vii, 220a; viii, **468a** – I, 1157b; VI, 327a; VII, 222a; VIII, **484a**
Rawther v, 582a; viii, **469a** – V, 587a; VIII, **485a**
al-Rawwād b. al-Muthannā (VIII) viii, 469b – VIII, 485b
al-Rawwād al-Azdī (IX) (Ādharbāydjān) vi, 499b; x, 42a – VI, 484b; X, 43b
al-Rawwādī, Abū Manṣūr b. Muḥammad al-Amīr (Tabrīz) (XI) x, 42b – X, 44a
Rawwādid(e)s (Banū Rawwād) (XI) i, 190a, 300a, 638a; iv, 346a; vi, 499b; vii, 656b; viii, **469b**; x, 42b –
I, 194b, 309b, 658b; IV, 360b; VI, 484b; VII, 656b; VIII, **485b**; X, 43b
Ray → Rayy
Ray Čand Pūrbiya vi, 54b, 407a – VI, 52b, 391b
Ray Rayān vi, 50b – VI, 49a
Rāya → Liwā'
Rāyčūr iii, 425a, b; vi, 368b, 369a; vii, 289a; viii, **470a** – III, 438b, 439a; VI, 353a, b; VII, 291a; VIII, **486a**
Rayda (Rīda) viii, **470a** – VIII, **486a**
Raydan (Ḥimyar) viii, 664a – VIII, 683b
Raydān al-Saḳlabī i, 1042a; iv, 1091b – I, 1073b; IV, 1122b
al-Raydāniyya iii, 184b; vi, 325a; ix, 630b –
III, 189a; VI, 309b; IX, 654b
Raydūn iii, 31a – III, 32b
Rayḥān, ʿImād al-Dīn (XIII) ii, 609b, 1084a; vi, 47b, 48a, b – II, 624b, 1109b; VI, 46a, b, 47a
Rayḥān, Mu'ayyid al-Dīn (atabeg) (XII) v, 159a, 160a; viii, 946a – V, 158a, b; VIII, 978b

Rayḥāna v, 436b – V, 439a
al-Rayḥānī, Amīn (1940) i, 597a; viii, **470b** – I, 616b; VIII, **486b**
Rāyin s, 327a – S, 326b
Raymānites vi, 80b – VI, 78b
Raymond II of/de Tripoli s, 204b – S, 204b
Raymond Lull (1315) vii, 737b – VII, 738b
Raymond Martin (1286) vii, 737b – VII, 738b
Rayna vi, 511b, 744b – VI, 497a, 733b
Raypūr vi, 53a – VI, 51a
Raysūt vi, 83b; vii, 53a; viii, 914b – VI, 81b; VII, 53b; VIII, 946a
Rayṭa (ʿAbbāsid(e)) (VIII) i, 107b; iv, 1164a – I, 110b; IV, 1196a
Rayṭa bint Abi ʾl-ʿAbbās al-Saffāḥ (VIII) vi, 139b – VI, 137b
al-Rayy i, 125b, 1356a; ii, 127a, 190a, 191a, 192b, 746a; iii, 219b, 287a; iv, 465b, 1167a; v, 661b, 662a, 1028b, 1137b, 1238a; vi, 14b, 64a, b, 66a, 115b, 117b, 120a, 198b, 199a, 273a, 332a, b, 333a, 340a, 428a, 500a, b, 522b, 524a, 539a, 600b, 627b, 633b, 744b, 745a; viii, **471a**; s, 13a, 15a, 23b, 32a, 33a, 56b, 72b, 118b, 236a, 297b, 309a, 356b, 357a, 416a, 423b –
I, 129a, 1395a; II, 130b, 196a, 197b, 198b, 764b; III, 226a, 296a; IV, 486a, 1199b; V, 667a, 1024b, 1132a, 1229a; VI, 13a, 62a, b, 63b, 113a, 115b, 117b, 182b, 183b, 257b, 316b, 317a, b, 324b, 413b, 485b, 507a, 508b, 523b, 585a, 612b, 618b, 733b, 734a; VIII, **487a**; S, 13b, 15a, 24a, 32a, 33a, 57a, 72b, 118a, 236a, 297b, 309a, 356b, 357a, 416a, 423b
Rayya (Reyyo) vi, 221b, 222a; viii, **473b** – VI, 215a, b; VIII, **489b**
Rayyān b. al-Aslaʿ s, 178b – S, 179b
al-Rayyān b. al-Walīd ii, 917b – II, 939a
Razgrad → Hezārg͟hrad
al-Rāzī → Abū Ḥātim; Abū Muhammad; Fak͟hr al-Dīn; Ḳuṭb al-Dīn
al-Rāzī, ʿAbd Allāh b. Humayd (862) x, 11a – X, 11b
al-Rāzī, ʿAbd al-Raḥmān Ibn Abī Ḥātim (938) ii, 462a; viii, 516b – II, 474a; VIII, 534a
al-Rāzī, Abū Bakr Muḥammad b. Zakariyyāʾ (935) i, 112a, 125b, 213b, 235a, 327b, 328a, 344b, 381a, 387b, 486a, 589b, 1223b, 1224a, 1340b; ii, 359a, 780b, 1068a; iii, 328b, 944b; iv, 329b, 847a; v, 112a, 167b; vi, 204b, 247a, 347a, 449a, 616b, 629a; vii, 196b; viii, 123a, **474a**; x, 453a; s,14a, 52b, 271b, 314a, 392b –
I, 115a, 129a, 220a, 242a, 337b, 338a, 355a, 392a, 399a, 500b, 608b, 1260a, b, 1380b; II, 368b, 799b, 1092b; III, 338b, 969a; IV, 344a, 880b; V, 114b, 165a; VI, 188b, 231b, 331b, 434b, 601b, 614a; VII, 196b; VIII, 125b, **490a**; X, 486b; S, 14b, 53a, 271a, 313b, 393a
al-Rāzī, Abū Ḥātim Muḥammad b. Idrīs (890) viii, 516b, 998a – VIII, 534a, 1033a
al-Rāzī, Abu ʾl-Ḥusayn (958) vi, 353a – VI, 337a
al-Rāzī, Abū Zurʿa ʿUbayd Allāh b. ʿAbd al-Karīm (878) viii, 516a – VIII, 533b
al-Rāzī, Aḥmad b. ʿAbd Allāh (1068) viii, **477b**, 518a – VIII, **493b**, 535b
al-Rāzī, Aḥmad b. Muḥammad b. Mūsā (955) i, 156b, 488a, b, 489b, 600b; iii, 771b; iv, 718a; x, 585b – I, 160b, 502b, 503a, 504a, 620a; III, 795a; IV, 747a; X,
Rāzī, Amīn Aḥmad (XVII) viii, **478a** – VIII, **494b**
Rāzī, D̲jamāl al-Dīn Abu ʾl-Futūḥ K̲h̲uzāʿī (XII) viii, 541a – VIII, 558b
al-Rāzī, Ibn al-Muʿaẓẓam (XIII) vi, 111b – VI, 109a
Rāzī, Ḳuṭb al-Dīn (1364) ii, 774a; viii, 514a, b – II, 792b; VIII, 559a
Rāzī, Mīr ʿAskar ʿĀdil K̲h̲ān (1696) vii, 1006a – VII, 1007b
al-Rāzī, Muḥammad b. Muḳātil (841) vi, 846a – VI, 837a
Rāzī, Nad̲j̲m al-Dīn "Dāya" (1256) → Nad̲j̲m al-Dīn Rāzī
Razīḳ (canal) vi, 619a, b – VI, 604a
Razīn, Banū viii, **478b**; ix, 307a; s, 80b – VIII, **495a**; IX, 316b; S, 80b
Razīn b. Muʿāwiya al-Saraḳusṭī, Abū ʾl-Ḥasan (1129/1140) viii, **479a** – VIII, **495b**
Razmak s, 285a – S, 285a
Razmārā, General Ḥād̲j̲d̲j̲ī ʿAlī (1951) ii, 882b; iv, 41a; vii, 447a – II, 903a; IV, 43b-44a; VII, 448b
Rbīʿ → Rabiʿ
Reʿāyā → Raʿiyya
Reconquista i, 494a, 495a, 496a; v, 367b – I, 508b, 510a, 511a; V, 368b
Red Sea → Baḥr al-Ḳulzum
Redīf Pas̲h̲a (Yemen) (XIX) vii, 525a – VII, 525b
Red̲j̲āʾī-zāde Aḥmed D̲j̲ewdet (XIX) vii, 532a – VII, 532b
Red̲j̲āʾī-zāde Maḥmūd Ekrem → Ekrem Bey
Red̲j̲āʾī-zāde Meḥmed D̲j̲elāl Bey (1882) viii, **480a** – VIII, **496a**
Red̲j̲eb Pas̲h̲a, Topal (1632) iii, 252a; vii, 598a; viii, **480a** – III, 259a; VII, 597b; VIII, **496b**
Refet Pas̲h̲a i, 836b; iv, 636a – I, 859b; IV, 662a
Refīʿ D̲j̲ewād iv, 873b – IV, 907a
Refīʿī (XV) viii, 8a, **480b** – VIII, 8b, **497a**
Refīḳ K̲h̲ālid Ḳaray → Karay, Refīḳ K̲h̲ālid
Reg viii, **481a** – VIII, **497a**
Rehanina → Raḥāmina
Reine de Saba → Bilḳīs
Reʾīs Efendi Rāmī (XVIII) vii, 708a – VII, 709a
Reʾīs ül-Küttāb (Reʾīs Efendi) viii, **481b** – VIII, **497b**
Reji iv, 930b – IV, 963b
Relizane (region/région) vi, 249b – VI, 233b
Rembau (Rumbow) viii, **483b** – VIII, **500a**
Remmāl K̲h̲ʷād̲j̲a (XVI) viii, 833a – VIII, 861b
République Arabe Unie → al-D̲j̲umhūriyya al-ʿarabiyya al-muttaḥida
Rēr Faḳīh → Muḳrī
Rēr S̲h̲ēk̲h̲ → ʿAḳabī
Resava vi, 70b – VI, 68b
Res̲h̲ād Nūrī (Reşad Nuri Güntekin) (1956) v, 196b; viii, **483b**; s, 96a – V, 193b; VIII, **500a**; S, 95b
Res̲h̲īd → Ras̲h̲īd
Res̲h̲īd Efendi (XIX) vi, 372b – VI, 356b
Res̲h̲īd Pas̲h̲a, Muṣṭafā (1858) viii, **484b**, 726b – VIII, **501a**, 747a
Res̲h̲t → Ras̲h̲t
Resm viii, **486a** – VIII, **502b**
Resmī → Aḥmad Rasmī
Révolte Arabe I, 47a; II, 297b, 892b; III, 271a, 664b
Rewān (Eriwān) i, 8a, 640a, 643a, 644a, 645a, b; vi, 202b; viii, **487a;** s, 365a – I, 8a, 661a, 664a, b, 665b, 666a; VI, 187a; VIII, **503b**; S, 365a
Rewān Ḳaṣr vi, 55b, 56b – VI, 53b, 54b
Rēwand b. Bēwarāsp Ad̲j̲dahāk (al-Mawṣil)) vi, 899b – VI, 890b
Rewānī (1524) viii, **489b** – VIII, **506a**
Rey Lobo → Ibn Mardanīs̲h̲
Reyes de Taifas → Mulūk al-Ṭawāʾif
Rezā S̲h̲āh → Muḥammad Riḍā S̲h̲āh Pahlawī
Rezzou → G̲h̲azw
Rḥama b. D̲j̲ābir b. ʿAd̲h̲bī (D̲j̲alāhima) x, 956b – X,
Rḥāmma, Banū vi, 590b, 595b – VI, 575a, 580a
Rhodes → Rodos

Rhodope vi, 89a – VI, 87a
Riau Archipel(ago) vi, 208a, 236b, 237a, 239a; viii, **490b** – VI, 192b, 209b, 204a; VIII, **507a**
Riʿāyat Shāh → ʿAlāʾ al-Dīn
Ribā i, 693b, 1111b, 1112b; iv, 691b – I, 715a, 1145a, 1146a; IV, 719b
al-Ribāb (Ḳayna) s, 247a – S, 247a
Ribāṭ i, 5a, 248b, 901b, 1023b; ii, 36a, 71b, 539b; iii, 499a; iv, 380b, 434a, 677a, 1026a; v, 856a, 1129b, 1150a, 1200b; vi, 359a; viii, **493b** – I, 5b, 256a, 929a, 1055a; II, 36b, 72b, 553a; III, 516a; IV, 397a, 453a, 705a, 1058a; V, 863a, 1125b, 1140b, 1191a; VI, 343a; VIII, **510b**
Ribāṭ al-Fatḥ (Rabat) i, 34b, 35a, 79b, 832b, 1225a, 1226b, 1228a, 1320b; iii, 143b, 499a; v, 504b, 1245b; vi, 39a, 40a, 142b, 293b, 294a, 364a, 521a, 597a; viii, **506b**; s, 144b, 223b – I, 35b, 81b, 855b, 1261b, 1264a, 1265a, 1361a; III, 146a, 516b; V, 507b, 1236b; VI, 37a, 38b, 140b, 279a, 348a, 505b, 582a; VIII, **524a**; S, 144a, 223b
—university/-é ii, 425b – II, 436b
Ribāṭ Sayyidī Shikar (Tansift) vi, 743b – VI, 733a
Ribāṭ-i Sharaf vi, 691b; viii, **508b** – VI, 679a; VIII, **526a**
Riḍāʿ → Raḍāʿ
Riḍā (mysticism(e)) viii, **509a** – VIII, **526b**
Riḍā, Meḥmed b. Meḥmed (1671) viii, **509b** – VIII, **526b**
Riḍā ʿAbbāsī (artist(e)) (XVII) i, 1213b, viii, **509b**, 788a – I, 1249b; VIII, **527a**, 814b
Riḍā Čelebi (XVII) vii, 472b – VII, 472a
Riḍā al-Dīn b. Ḳawām al-Dīn al-Marʿashī (XIV) vi, 511b, 512a, b, 513a, 515b, 516b – VI, 497a, 498a, 500b, 501b
Riḍā al-Dīn Abu 'l-Maʿālī (XIII) vi, 790b – VI, 780b
Riḍā Khān → Riḍā Shāh Pahlawī
Riḍā Kirmānī, Mīrzā (XIX) s, 53b – S, 54a
Riḍā Kiyā, Sayyid (Gīlān) (XV) vi, 513a – VI, 498a
Riḍā Ḳulī b. Nādir Shāh (Afshārid(e)) (1747) v, 103a – V, 105a
Riḍā Ḳulī Khān b. Muḥammad Hādī (1871) iv, 70a, 526b, 1065a; vii, 530a; viii, **510a**; ix, 658a; s, 46b – IV, 73b, 549b, 1096b; VII, 530b; VIII, **527a**; IX, 683a; S, 47a
Riḍā Ḳulī Khān Ḳādjār (XVIII) iv, 391a; v, 663b – IV, 407b, 408a; V, 669a
Riḍā Ḳulī Mīrzā b. Ḥusayn ʿAlī Mīrzā Farmān-Farma (XIX) iv, 393a; s, 290b – IV, 409b; S, 290a
Riḍā (Rizā) Nūr (1942) iii, 595a; iv, 113a, 791b, 872b; viii, **511a** – III, 615b; IV, 118a, 823b, 906a; VIII, **528a**
Riḍā Shāh (Pahlawī) (1941) i, 5b, 190b, 720b, 978a, b, 1014a; ii, 445b, 514b, 654a, 903a, 1112a; iii, 528b, 1110a, 1193a; iv, 40a, b, 52a, 398b, 789b, 1172a; v, 826a, 920a, 1042b, 1095a, b; vi, 203a, 486a, b; vii, 223a, 299b, 447a, 654a; viii, **511a**; s, 84a, 91b, 110a, 207b, 342b – I, 5b, 196a, 742a, 1008b, 1045a; II, 457b, 527b, 670b, 924a, 1138a; III, 547a, 1137a, 1223a; IV, 42b, 43a, 55a, 416a, 821b, 1205a; V, 832b, 925b, 1038b, 1092a; VI, 187a, 472a, b; VII, 225a, 301b, 448a, 653b; VIII, **528b**; S, 83b, 91b, 109b, 207b, 342a
Rîḍā Tewfīḳ → Bölük-bashî, Rîḍā Tewfīḳ
Riḍāʾī, Āḳā (XVII) viii, **514a** – VIII, **531b**
Riḍāʾiyya (Rezaiyyeh) → Urumiyya
Riḍiyya → Raḍiyyat al-Dunyā bint Iltutmish
Ridjāl iv, 711b; viii, **514b** – IV, 740a; VIII, **523a**
Ridjāl al-ghayb i, 94b, 772a; ii, 1025b – I, 97b, 795a; II, 1049b
Riḍwān (angel/l'ange) ii, 846a, b – II, 866a, b
Riḍwān (ḥādjib) (1359) iii, 836a; vii, 1023b, 1024a – III, 859b; VII, 1025b, 1026a
Riḍwān (Paradis(e)) viii, **519a** – VIII, **536b**
Riḍwān b. Muḥammad al-Sāʿātī (XIII) viii, 654b; s, 371b, 372b – VIII, 674a; S, 371b, 372a
Riḍwān (Ruḍwān) b. Tutush (Saldjūḳ, Alep(po)) (1113) i, 664a, 1052a; ii, 169b, 282a; iii, 86b, 398b; v, 921b, 924a, b; vi, 380a, 546b; vii, 725b; viii, **519a**, 947a; x, 167b, 600a – I, 683b, 1083b; II, 175a, 290a; III, 89a, 411a; V, 927a, 929b, 930a; VI, 364a, 531b; VII, 726a; VIII, **536b**, 979b; X, 180a, 644b
Riḍwān b. Walakhashī (vizier) (XII) i, 939b; ii, 858a, b; iii, 55a; iv, 137a; v, 627b; viii, 831b; ix, 372b – I, 968a; II, 877b, 878b; III, 57a; IV, 142b; V, 631b; VIII, 860b; IX, 384b
Riḍwān Bannigash (Banegas) s, 399a – S, 399a
Riḍwān (Rizvān) Begovič, ʿAlī Pasha (1851) i, 1268b; vii, 244b; viii, **519b** – I, 1307b; VII, 246a; VIII, **537a**
Riḍwān Bey (amīr al-ḥadjdj) (Miṣr) (1656) ii, 233a; iv, 723a; vi, 325a; vii, 178b – II, 240a; IV, 752a; VI, 309b; VII, 180a
Riḍwān Kāhya al-Djulfī iv, 852b – IV, 885b
Riḍwān Pasha (1585) viii, **521a** – VIII, **539a**
Rīf i, 749b, 859b; ii, 820b; iii, 499b; v, 1184b, 1185b, 1194a; vi, 356a, 361a; viii, 440b, **521b**; s,191a, 377b – I, 771b, 883b; II, 840a; III, 516b; V, 1174b, 1175b, 1184b; VI, 340a, 345a; VIII, 455a, **539a**; S, 192a, 377b
Rifāʿa, Banū vi, 649a – VI, 634b
Rifāʿa Bey al-Ṭahṭāwī (1873) i, 571b, 596b, 755a; ii, 641b, 801a; iii, 590b; iv, 1155a; v, 907b, 908a, b, 909a; vi, 725a, b; vii, 427a, 901b, 902a, b, 915b – I, 590b, 616a, 777b; II, 658a, 820a; III, 610b; IV, 1187a; V, 913b, 914a, b; VI, 714a, b; VII, 428b, 902a, b, 903a, 916a
Rifāda i, 9a, 80a – I, 9a, 82b
al-Rifāʿī, Abu 'l-ʿAbbās Aḥmad b. ʿAlī (1183) vi, 354b, 463a – VI, 338b, 449a
al-Rifāʿī, Aḥmad b. ʿAlī (1183) viii, **524b** – VIII, **542a**
al-Rifāʿī, Aḥmad b. Sulaymān (1291) vii, 11a – VII, 11b
Rifāʿī Bey al-Ṭahṭāwī (1873) viii, **523b**; x, 252a – VIII, **541a**
Rifāʿiyya i, 281a; ii, 16a, 164b, 1134a; iii, 122b, 291a, 952a; vi, 88a; viii, 340b, **525b**; x, 252a – I, 289b; II, 16b, 170a, 1160b; III, 125b, 300a, 976b; VI, 86a; VIII, 352b, **543a**; X, 271a
Rifat, Oktay iv, 545a – IV, 568b
Rifʿat, Ṣādiḳ → Ṣādiḳ Rifʿat Pasha
al-Rīfī → Aḥmad al-Rīfī
Righa, Banū v, 1181a, b – V, 1171a, b
Rīgistān i, 1294b – I, 1334a, b
Rīḥ (wind/vent) viii, **526b** – VIII, **544a**
Rīḥā (Alep(po)) viii, **527b** – VIII, **545b**
Rīḥā (Jericho) viii, **527a** – VIII, **545a**
al-Rīḥānī, Amīn (1940) v, 1254b, 1255b, 1256b; vi, 113b, 614b – V, 1245b, 1246b, 1247b; VI, 111b, 599b
Riḥla viii, **528a** – VIII, **545b**
al-Rijeby, Mādjid b. Djābir (1808) vii, 227a – VII, 229a
Rikʿa → Khaṭṭ
Rikāb (stirrup/étrier) viii, **528b** – VIII, **546b**
Rikābdār (Rikībdār) viii, **529b** – VIII, **547b**
Rikḳ → Raḳḳ
Rimm (Druze) s, 135b – S, 135b
Rinčana s, 156a – S, 156a
Rind viii, **531a** – VIII, **549a**

Rinds, Banū i, 1005b; s, 332a – I, 1036b; s, 331b
Risāla viii, **532a** – VIII, **549b**
Rīshahr (battle, 637) i, 1341a; ix, 311a – I, 1381b; IX, 320b
Rishīs s, 114b – S, 114a
Rissani x, 82b – X, 86a
Riwāḳ (Ruwāḳ) viii, **544b** – VIII, **562b**
Riwāya viii, **545b** – VIII, **563a**
Riyāʾ (Riʾāʾ) viii, **547a** – VIII, **565a**
al-Riyāḍ i, 628b, 1231a; ii, 425a, 569b; iv, 1073a; vi, 33a, 34b, 151a, 152b; viii, **547b**; ix, 904a; s, 3b – I, 649b, 1267b; II, 435b, 583b; IV, 1104b; VI, 31b, 32b, 149b, 151a; VIII, **565b**; IX, 941b; S, 2b
Riyāḍ al-ʿArūs (Marrākush) vi, 597b – VI, 582a
Riyād Pasha (Miṣr) → Muṣṭafā Riyād Pasha
Riyāḍ al-Ṣulḥ (Lubnān) (XX) v, 787b, 794b – V, 793b, 801a
Riyādī (Mollā Meḥmed) (1644) viii, **548b** – VIII, **566b**
al-Riyāḍiyyāt (al-Riyāḍa) viii, **549b** – VIII, **567b**
Riyāfa viii, **562a** – VIII, **580a**
Riyāḥ, Banū i, 161b, 533a; ii, 463b; iii, 66b, 137b, 386a; iv, 337a; v, 48b; vi, 728b, 741b; viii, **562b** – I, 166a, 549b; II, 475a; III, 69a, 140b, 398b; IV, 351b; V, 50a; VI, 717b, 730b; VIII, **580b**
Riyāḥ b. ʿUthmān b. Ḥayyān al-Murrī (VIII) vii, 388b, 629b – VII, 390a, 629a
al-Riyāḥī → Abu ʾl-Hindī; Maʿḳil b. Ḳays
al-Riyāḥī, Muḥammad b. Yaḥyā i, 600a – I, 619b
Riyāḥiyya iv, 837a – IV, 870a
Riyāl viii, **563b** – VIII, **581b**
Riyāla (Bey) viii, **564a** – VIII, **582b**
Riyām, Banū vi, 82b; viii, **566a** – VI, 80a; VIII, **584b**
al-Riyāshī, Abu ʾl-Faradj (871) vii, 279b, 281a; ix, 652b – VII, 281b, 282b; IX, 677b
Rizā → Riḍā
al-Rizaḳ al-aḥbāsiyya ii, 148b – II, 153a
Rizām b. Sābiḳ iv, 838a – IV, 870b
Rizāmiyya v, 63b – V, 65b
Rizayḳāt Baḳḳāra i, 929a, 962a; ii, 122a, 123b – I, 957b, 991b; II, 125a, 126b
Rize ii, 62a; viii, **566b** – II, 63b; VIII, **584b**
Rizḳ i, 204b; viii, **567b** – I, 210b; VIII, **586a**
Rizḳ Allāh Ḥassūn → Ḥassūn
Rizwan → Riḍwān
Rodos i, 293a, 935b, 945b, 1250b; ii, 6a; iv, 1169b; v, 506b; viii, **568b**; s, 222a – I, 302b, 964b, 974b, 1288b; II, 6a; IV, 1202b; V, 510a; VIII, **587a**; S, 222a
Rodosto → Tekirdagh
Roem, Mohammed (XX) vi, 731b, 732b – VI, 720b, 721b
Roger II (Sicily/-e) i, 79a; ii, 585a, 855a; iii, 1032b; iv, 337b, 651a; v, 1246b; ix, 585b – I, 81b; II, 599b, 875a; III, 1058b; IV, 352a, 677b; V, 1237b; IX, 608a
Rōh viii, **571a**; s, 1b- VIII, **589b**; S, 1b
Rohilkhand i, 218a; iv, 749b; viii, **571a** – I, 224b; IV, 779b; VIII, **589b**
Rohillas (Rohilas) i, 253a, 856a, 953b, 1042b, 1206a; iii, 59b, 61b, 427b; viii, 462a, **572b** – I, 261a, 879b, 982b, 1074a, 1242a; III, 62a, 64a, 441b; VIII, 444a, **591a**
Rohtak v, 1258a; vi, 49a, 50a – V, 1248b; VI, 47b, 48b
Rōhtās ii, 1091b; iii, 449a; vi, 343a; viii, **573a** – II, 1117b; III, 464b; VI, 327a; VIII, **591b**
Rōhtāsgaṙh viii, **573a** – VIII, **591b**
Romanus IV Diogenes (XI) vi, 242b, 243a – VI, 226b, 227a
Rome → Rūmiya
Ronda → Runda
Rosetta → Rashīd
Rōshān, Pīr Bāyezīd i, 853b, 854a; vii, 220a – I, 877a, b; VII, 222a
Roshānārā (1671) vii, 333b – VII, 335a
Rōshānī i, 225a – I, 231b
Rōshāniyya → Rawshaniyya
Rostom (Kay Khusraw, Georgia/e) (1658) v, 493b – V, 496b
Rotulla dynasty/-ie (Prizren) viii, 339b – VIII, 351a, b
Rouiched vi, 754a – VI, 743b
Roumélie → Rūm-eli
Roupéniens → Rubenides
Rouzathul-Uloom (Feroke, Mappila) vi, 462a – VI, 447b
Roxelana/-e → Khurrem Sulṭān
Rozagī → Rūzagī
al-Ruʾāsī i, 105b; ii, 806b; vii, 280a – I, 108b; II, 826a; VII, 282a
al-Ruʾāsī, Muḥammad b. Abī Sāra al-Nahwī (VIII) viii, **573a** – VIII, **591b**
al-Ruʾāsī, ʿUthmān b. ʿĪsā al-ʿĀmirī (IX) vii, 647b – VII, 647b
al-Ruʿaynī, Abu ʾl-Ḥasan al-Ishbīlī (1267) ii, 743b; iv, 468a; viii, **573b** – II, 762a; IV, 489a; VIII, **592a**
Rubʿ viii, **574a** – VIII, **592b**
al-Rubʿ al-Khālī i, 537a, b, 539a, 759b, 1231a; vi, 371b; viii, **575b** – I, 553b, 554a, 555b, 782a, 1268a; VI, 356a; VIII, **594a**
Ruʾba b. al-ʿAdjdjādj al-Tamīmī (762) i, 142a, 207b, 1154b; iii, 73a, 573b, 1262a; vii, 208b, 546a; viii, 377a, **577a**; x, 71b; s, 31b, 286b – I, 146b, 214a, 1188b; III, 75b, 593b, 1294b; VII, 210a, 546a; VIII, 390a, **595b**; X, 71a; S, 31b, 286b
Rubāʿī (pl. Rubāʿiyyāt) i, 677a; iv, 58a, 62a; v, 166a; viii, **578b** – I, 698a; IV, 61a, 65b; V, 163b; VIII, **597a**
Rūbandj vi, 937b – VI, 929b
Rubāṭ I (Sinnār) (1644) ix, 650b – IX, 675b
Rubayyiʿ b. Zayd ii, 176b – II, 182a
Rubenid(e)s i, 182a, 466a, 639a, 790a – I, 187b, 479b, 660a, 813a
Rubghūzī → Rabghūzī
al-Ruburtayr (Reverter) (1145) i, 78b, 390a – I, 81a, 401b
Rūdakī, Abū ʿAbd Allāh Djaʿfar (940) i, 1216a; iv, 53a, 60b, 63a, 504b, 773b; v, 956a; vi, 276a, 609a, b; viii, 76a, **585a**; s, 35a – I, 1252b; IV, 56a, 64a, 66a, 526a, 804b; V, 959b; VI, 261a, 594a; VIII, 78a, **603b**; S, 35b
al-Rudānī (1693) vi, 264a – VI, 249a
Rudawlawī, Aḥmad ʿAbd al-Ḥaḳḳ s, 312b, 313a – S, 312b, 313a
Rudawlī ii, 54b; s, 293a, 312b – II, 55b; S, 293a, 312b
Rudaynī, Banū x, 42a – X, 43b
Rūdhbār (Rūdbār) iii, 254a; iv, 859b; v, 149a, b, 247a; vi, 493b; viii, **586a** – III, 261a; IV, 893a; V, 151a, 152a, 245a; VI, 479b; VIII, **604b**
al-Rūdh(a)bārī (X) vii, 164a – VII, 165b
Rūdhrāwar viii, 586b – VIII, 605a
Rūdhrawārī, Abū Shudjāʿ Muḥammad b. al-Ḥusayn (1095) ii, 384b; iii, 258b; vii, 294a; viii, 70b, **586b**; s, 398a – II, 394b; III, 256b; VII, 296a; VIII, 72a, **605b**; S, 398b
Rūd-i Shahr s, 97a – S, 96b
Rūdisar → Hawsam
Rūdj vi, 578b – VI, 563b
Rūdjūʿ viii, **587a** – VIII, **605b**
Rudwān → Riḍwān
Rufāʿa x, 96b – X, 104a
Rūfus al-Afsīsī viii, **588a** – VIII, **606b**
Rufus of Ephesus/-d'Éphèse → Rūfus al-Afsīsī
Rūḥ → Nafs

Rūḥ Allāh → Khumaynī, Āyatollāh
Rūḥ al-Amīn Khān al-ʿUthmānī i, 1219a – I, 1255a
al-Ruhā (al-Ruhāʾ) i, 466a, 639b, 1054a; ii, 63b, 347b; vi, 243b, 378b, 379b, 381b, 507b, 626b; viii, 127b, **569a** – I, 480a, 660a, 1085b; II, 65a, 357a; VI, 227b, 362b, 364a, 365b, 492b, 611a; VIII, 130b, **607b**
Rūhānī → Amīr Rūḥānī
Rūḥānī (XX) iv, 71b – IV, 75b
Rūḥāniyya viii, **593b** – VIII, **612b**
Rūḥī (1511) iii, 91b; viii, **594a** – III, 94a; VIII, **613a**
Rūḥī, Shaykh Aḥmad (XIX) s, 53a – S, 53b
Rūhī Fāḍil Efendi (1528) viii, 594a – VIII, 613a
Rūhiyyè Khānum (Mary Maxwell, XX) i, 916a – I, 943b
Ruhmī viii, **594b** – VIII, **613b**
al-Ruhūnī, Muḥammad (1815) vi, 356b – VI, 340b
al-Ruḳabāʾ → Abdāl
Ruḳayya bint Hāshim b. ʿAbd Manāf i, 80a – I, 82a
Ruḳayya bint Muḥammad (624) i, 136b; ii, 845a; viii, **594b** – I, 140b; II, 865a; VIII, **613b**
Ruḳayya Bēgam bint Mīrzā Hindāl (1626) iii, 456a – III, 471b
al-Rukhkh viii, **595a** – VIII, **614a**
al-Rukhkhadj i, 86a; viii, **595a** – I, 88b; VIII, **614a**
al-Rukhkhadjī, Abū ʾl-Faradj (IX) viii, **595b** – VIII, **614b**
al-Rukhkhadjī, Muʾayyid al-Mulk (XI) viii, 595b – VIII, 614b
Rukhṣa viii, **595b** – VIII, **614b**
Rukhṣatī s, 91b – S, 91a
al-Ruḳʿī, al-Ḥādjdj al-Khayyāṭ (1703) s, 403b, 404a – S, 404a, b
Rukn (pl. arkān) viii, **596b** – VIII, **615b**
Rukn al-Dawla, Atabeg (Fārs) s, 382b – S, 382b
Rukn al-Dawla, Abū ʿAlī al-Ḥasan b. Būya (Buwayhid(e)) (976) i, 211b, 419a, 955a; ii, 178b, 680a, 928a; iii, 258a, 703a, 704a, 1157a; iv, 23a, b, 100b, 859b; v, 452b; vi, 499b, 539a, 600b; vii, 656b, 777a; viii, **597b**; s, 36b, 259a – I, 217b, 431a, 984a; II, 184a, 697a, 949b; III, 265a, 725b, 726a, 1185b; IV, 25a, 104b, 892b; V, 455a; VI, 484b, 523a, 585a; VII, 656a, 779a; VIII, **616b**; S, 37a, 258b
Rukn al-Dawla Khān → Iʿtiḳād Khān
Rukn al-Dīn → Ḳîlîdj Arslan IV
Rukn al-Dīn b. ʿAbd al-Ḳādir al-Djīlī iii, 751b – III, 774b
Rukn al-Dīn b. Burāḳ (Kutlugh- Khānid(e)) i, 1311b; v, 161b, 162a, 553b – I, 1351b; V, 159b, 160a, 558a
Rukn al-Dīn b. Ēlam Khān (Dihli) (XIII) vii, 193b – VII, 194a
Rukn al-Dīn Aḥmadīlī i, 300b – I, 310a
Rukn al-Dīn ʿAlāʾ al-Dawla → ʿAlāʾ al-Dawla al Simnānī
Rukn al-Dīn Bārbak b. Maḥmūd I (Bengal(e)) (1474) vi, 46b; viii, **598b** – VI, 45a; VIII, **617b**
Rukn al-Dīn Čanda ii, 1077a – II, 1102a
Rukn al-Dīn al-Iṣfahānī ii, 125b – II, 129a
Rukn al-Dīn Kart (1283) iv, 672a – IV, 699b
Rukn al-Dīn Khur-Shāh (Nizārī) (1257) i, 354a; ii, 606a; iv, 201b; vi, 918a; viii, **598b** – I, 364b; II, 621b; IV, 210a; VI, 909b; VIII, **617b**
Rukn al-Dīn Kilidj Arslān → Kilidj Arslān IV
Rukn al-Dīn Masʿūd I b. Ḳîlîč Arslan I (Rūm Saldjūḳ) (1156) viii, 128a – VIII, 131a
Rukn al-Dīn Mawdūd, shaykh ii, 54a – II, 55a
Rukn al-Dīn Sām b. Lankar iv, 466b – IV, 487a
Rukn al-Dīn al-Samarḳandī → al-ʿAmīdī
Rukn al-Dīn Sulaymān II Shāh (Rūm Saldjūḳ) (1204) i, 431b, 510a; iv, 575b, 816a; vi, 632a – I, 444a, 525b; IV, 598b, 849a; VI, 617a
Rukn al-Dīn Ṭughrïl II → Ṭughrïl II, Rukn al-Dīn
Rukn al-Dīn Ṭughrïl III → Ṭughrïl III b. Arslān Rukn al-Dīn
Rukn al-Dīn Yūsuf → Yūsuf Shāh II
Ruknā Masīḥ al-Kāshānī (1655) iv, 1128a; viii, 776a, 851a – IV, 1159b; VIII, 802a, 880b
Ruknābād (Āb-i Ruknī) viii, **599b** – VIII, **618b**
al-Ruknī, ʿAlāʾ al-Dīn Ayoughdī, Amīr (XIII) iv, 960a – IV, 992a
Ruḳya viii, **600a** – VIII, **619a**
Rūm i, 18a, 54b, 76b, 77a, 83a, 121b, 182b, 346a, 420b, 465b, 468a, 470a, 517a, 637b, 638b, 639a, 679b, 789b, 1128a, 1319a; ii, 14a, 81a, 345a, 347b, 456a, 712a, 853a; iii, 77a, 128b, 129b, 233b, 271a, 344b, 1046a, 1083b, 1089a; iv, 175a, 839a; v, 104a, b, 124b; vi, 97a, 316b, 379b; viii, **601a** – I, 18b. 56b, 78b, 79b, 85b, 125a, 187b, 356b, 432a,b, 479a, 482a, 484a, 532b, 658b, 659a, b, 700b, 813a, 1162b, 1359b; II, 14a, 82b, 354b, 357a, 468a, 730b, 873a, 875a; III, 79b, 131a, 132a, 240b, 279a, 354b, 1072b, 1110b, 1115b; IV, 182b, 817b; V, 106a,b, 127a; VI, 95a, 301b, 363b; VIII, **620a**
Rūm Ḳalʿesi (Ḳalʿat al-Rūm) vi, 322b; viii, **606b** – VI, 307a; VIII, **625b**
Rūm Meḥmed Pasha (XV) → Meḥmed Rūm(ī) Pasha
Rūm Saldjūks → Saldjūks
Rūma → Rūmiya
Rumania ii, 688a, b
Rūmelī i, 97a, 396a, 398a, b, 469a, 697b, 998b, 1160a, 1304b; ii, 83a, 443a, 722a; iv, 232b; v, 261a, 881a; vi, 89a, 372a; viii, 606a, **607b**; s, 268b – I, 99b, 407a, 409b, 410a, 482b, 719a, 1029a, 1194b, 1344b; II, 85a, 455a, 741a; IV, 242b; V, 258b, 887b; VI, 87a, 356b; VIII, 625a, **627a**; S, 268a
Rumeli Ḥiṣārî i, 1251b, 1318a; iii, 483a; viii, **611b** – I, 1289b, 1358b; III, 500a; VIII, **631a**
Rumeli Kavaghî i, 481a, 1252a – I, 495a, 1290a
Rūmeli Pāyeli Ibrāhīm Efendi (XVIII) vi, 55a – VI, 53a
Rūmī viii, **612a** – VIII, **631a**
al-Rūmī → Ashraf; Djalāl al-Dīn; Ḳusṭūs
Rūmī Khān i, 1062a, 1068b; iii,482a – I, 1094a, 1101a; III, 499a
Rūmiya (Rome) iv, 274b, 275a; v, 945a, b; viii, **612b** – IV, 286b, 287a; V, 949a, b; VIII, **631b**
Rūmlū, Banū iii, 1101b – III, 1128b
Rūmlū, Nūr ʿAlī Khalīfa (XVI) viii, 768a – VIII, 793b
Rumman, Banū i, 1246b – I, 1284b
al-Rummānī, Abū ʾl-Ḥasan ʿAlī b. ʿĪsā (994) i, 126b, 858a, 1115b; iii, 1020a; iv, 249a; v, 242b, 426b; vii, 312a, 914a; viii, **614a**; ix, 317b; s, 13a, 27b, 362b – I, 130a, 881b, 1149a; III, 1045b; IV, 260a; V, 240a, 429a; VII, 314a, b, 915a; VIII, **633a**; IX, 327b; S, 13b, 27b, 362a
Rūna s, 21a – S, 21a
Runda i, 6a, 11b; vii, 1022a, b; viii, **615b** – I, 6a, 11b; VII, 1024a, b; VIII, **635a**
al-Rundī → Ibn al-Ḥakīm
al-Rundī, Abū Khālid Yazīd (1091) viii, **617b** – VIII, **636b**
Rupenians → Rubenid(e)s
Rūnī, Abū ʾl-Faradj → Abū ʾl-Faradj b. Masʿūd Rūnī
Rūpiyya (rupee) ii, 121a; viii, **618a** – II, 123b; VIII, **637a**
Rūpmātī i, 1155a; vi, 407a, b – I, 1189b; VI, 391b, 392b
Rūs i, 4a, 625b, 738b, 836a; iii, 759a; iv, 346b, 347a, 348b, 1175b, 1176a; v, 1120a, b, 1121b; viii, **618b**; ix, 169a –

I, 4a, 646b, 760b, 859a; III, 782b; IV, 361a, b, 363b, 1209a; V, 1116b, 1117a, 1118a; VIII, **638a**; IX, 174b
al-Ruṣāfa viii, **629b** – VIII, **648a**
al-Ruṣāfa (al-ʿAbbāsiyya) i, 24a, 1320a – I, 25a, 1360b
al-Ruṣāfa (al-Andalus) vi, 431a; viii, **631b** – VI, 416a; VIII, **650b**
al-Ruṣāfa (Baghdād) i, 897a, b, 898b, 901a, 902b; viii, **629b**; s, 193b, 386a, 400b – I, 923b, 924b, 925a, 928a, 929b; VIII, **648a**; S, 194b, 386b, 401a
Ruṣāfa (al-Nuʿmān) vi, 378a, 624a; s, 117a – VI, 362b, 609a; S, 116b
al-Ruṣāfa (Syria/-e) vi, 378a, 624a; viii, **630a**; s, 117a – VI, 362b, 609a; VIII, **648b**; S, 116b
al-Ruṣāfī, Abū ʿAbd Allāh Muḥammad b. Ghālib (1177) i, 602a; vi, 111a; viii, 632b, **633a** – I, 621b; VI, 108b; VIII, 651b, **652a**
al-Ruṣāfī, Maʿrūf → Maʿrūf al-Ruṣāfī
Rusčuk (Ruse) viii, **633b** – VIII, **652a**
Rūshanī → ʿUmar Rūshanī
al-Rushāṭī, Abū Muḥammad (1147) viii, **635a** – VIII, **654a**
Rushayd b. Kāmil b. Djāmiʿ iv, 337a, b – IV, 351b, 352a
Rushayd al-Daḥdāḥ ii, 795b – II, 814b
Rushdī, Fāṭima (XX) vi, 750b – VI, 739b
Rushdī Malḥaṣ (XX) vi, 176b – VI, 162a
Rushdī Pāshā → ʿAbd al-Raḥmān; Ḥusayn Rushdī Pasha; Shirwānī-zāde
Rüshdiyye i, 285b, 1272a; v, 904a, b, 905a – I, 294a, 1311a; V, 910a, b, 911b
Russians/Russes → Rūs
Russo-Persian wars/guerres x,, 48a – X, 49a
Russo-Turkish wars (1769-1774) i, 4b, 294b, 948a; iii, 193a, 253a
—(1877-1878) ii, 88b, 613b; iii, 993a
Rustāḳ viii, **636a** – VIII, **654b**
al-Rustāḳ (ʿUmān) iv, 1085a; viii, **636a**; s, 355b – IV, 1116a; VIII, **655a;** S, 355b
Rustaḳubādh i, 711b – I, 733a
Rustam (Shāh-nāma) iii, 113a, 114a, 153b; iv, 809a,b, 813a; viii, **636b** – III, 115b, 116b, 156b; IV, 842a, 846a; VIII, **655a**
Rustam I, Shāh Ghāzī (Bāwandid(e), Ispahbadiyya) (1163) v, 662a; vi, 938b – V, 667b; VI, 931a
Rustam II (Bāwandid(e)), Kāʾūsiyya b. Sharwīn II (980) s, 309a – S, 309a
Rustam II, Shams al-Mulūk Shāh Ghāzī (Bāwandid(e), Ispahbadiyya) (1209) i, 1110a; iii, 810a; vi, 938b – I, 1143b; III, 833b; VI, 931a
Rustam b. Bahram b. Shāh Ismāʿīl I, Mīrzā (Ṣafawid(e)) (1641) vii, 129b – VII, 131b
Rustam b. Farrukh Hurmuzd (637) viii, **638a** – VIII, **656b**
Rustam b. Maḳṣūd (Aḳ Ḳoyunlu) (1497) i, 312a; iv, 186b, 387a, b; viii, **766b** – I, 321b; IV, 194b, 404a, b; VIII, **792a**
Rustam b. Nūr al-Dīn Khurshīdī (Luristān) (XIII) v, 828a – V, 834b
Rustam Khān (Ḳaytaḳ) → Rustum Khān
Rustam Khān, Mīr (Khayrpūr) (XVIII) i, 1192b – I, 1227b
Rustam Khān b. Karagözlu (XIX) vii, 453a – VII, 454a
Rustamdār iv, 808a; v, 663a, b; vi, 511a, b, 512a, b, 513a, b, 514a, b, 515a; viii, 650b – IV, 840b; V, 668b; VI, 496b, 497a, 498a, b, 499a, b, 500a; VIII, 668b
Rustamdārī, Banū vi, 515b – VI, 500b
Rustamdārī, Ḥusayn ʿAḳīlī (1571) vi, 908b – VI, 900a
al-Rustamī, Ḥusayn b. ʿAmr (IX) vii, 215a – VII, 216b
Rustamid(e)s (Rustumid(e)s) i, 83a, 167a, 445b; ii, 141a, 145b, 852b; iii, 655a, 658b, 924b; vi, 452b; viii, **638a**; x, 99b – I, 85b, 172a, 458b; II, 144b, 149b, 872a; III, 676b, 679b, 949a; VI, 438a; VIII, **657a**; X, 107b
Rustem Pasha (1561) i, 291b, 1279b; ii, 685a; iii, 147b; iv, 232a; v, 35b, 67a; vi, 228b; vii, 6b, 713a, 720b; viii, 202b, **640b** – I, 300b, 1318b; II, 702b; III, 150b; IV, 242a; V, 36b, 69a; VI, 222a; VII, 6b, 714a, 721b; VIII, 206a, **659b**
al-Rustughfanī, Abu ʾl-Ḥasan (X) vi, 846a – VI, 837a
Rustum and/et Isfandiyār s, 91a – S, 90b
Rustum (Ḳādisiyya) ii, 893b; iii, 195a, 1254b; iv, 385b – II, 914a; III, 199b, 1287a; IV, 402a
Rustum-Khān (Ḳaytaḳ) (XVII) ii, 87b; iv, 846b; vii, 601b – II, 89a; IV, 879b; VII, 601a
Rusudan (Queen/la reine, Georgia/-e) (1247) v, 490b – V, 493a, b
Rusūkhī, Ismāʿīl s, 83a – S, 83a
Ruswā, Mirzā Muḥammad Hādī (1931) v, 203b, 1106b; viii, **641b**; ix, 161a; x, 879b – V, 201a, 1102b; VIII, **660b**; IX. 166b; X,
Ruṭaynā iv, 679b – IV, 707b
Rutbīl → Zunbīl
Rutul (Dāghistān) viii, **642b** – VIII, **661b**
Ruwād → Arwād; Ṭarṭūs
Ruwāla, Banū i, 483a, 873b, 1093b; ii, 492b; iii, 1018a; vi, 46a, 490b; viii, **643a** – I, 497a, 897b, 1126a; II, 505a; III, 1043b; VI, 44b, 476b; VIII, **662a**
Ruwāndiz → Rawāndiz
Ruwaydjān vi, 384a – VI, 368a
Ruwaym (410) iii, 823b; vi, 570a; x, 377a – III, 847a; VI, 555a; X, 404b
Ruʾyā iii, 600a; iv, 259b, 260a; viii, **645a** – III, 621a; IV, 271b; VIII, **664a**
Ruʾyā-i ṣādiḳa iv, 72b – IV, 76b
Rūyān ii, 74b; iv, 808a; v, 661b; vi, 337b, 539a; viii, **650b**; s, 297b – II, 76a; IV, 840b; V, 666b; VI, 321b, 523b; VIII, **668a**; S, 297a
Rūyānī, Abu ʾl-Maḥāsin iv, 859b – IV, 892b
Ruʾyat Allāh i, 411b; viii, **649a** – I, 423b; VIII, **669a**
Ruʾyat al-Hilāl viii, **649b** – VIII, **669b**
Rūyīn-diz i, 300b, 301a; vi, 500a-501b – I, 310a; VI, 485b, 486a, 487a
Rūzafzūn (Sawādkūh) (1517) vi, 515b, 938b – VI, 500b, 930b
Rūzafzūn, Aḳā Rustam (sipahsālār) (XVI) vi, 514b – VI, 499b
Rūzafzūn, ʿAlī b. Iskandar (sipahsālār) (XV) vi, 513b, 514a – VI, 499a
Rūzafzūn, Bahrām (sipahsālār) (XV) vi, 513b – VI, 498b, 499a
Rūzafzūn, Iskandar (sipahsālār) (XV) vi, 513a – VI, 498b
Rūzafzūn, Muḥammad (XVI) vi, 514b, 515a – VI, 500a
Rūzakī (Rozagī), Banū v, 458b, 459a – V, 461b
Rūzakī, Sayyid Aḥmad Beg (XVI) vi, 931b – VI, 923b
Rūzbahān b. Windād-Khūrshīd iii, 703a, 1202a – III, 725b, 1232b
Rūzbahān Baḳlī → Rūzbihān al-Baḳlī
Rūzbih b. Buzurdjmihr vi, 660a – VI, 646a
Rūzbihān al-Baḳlī al-Shīrāzī (1209) iii, 823a; iv, 851b; v, 53b; viii, 429a, **651b**; x, 320b – III, 847a; IV, 885a; V, 55a; VIII, 443a, **670b**; X, 345a
Rūzbihan al-Wazzān al-Miṣrī v, 300b – V, 299b, 300a

Ruzhekī → Ruzāgī
Rūznāma viii, **652a** – VIII, **671a**
al-Rūznāmadj ii, 78b, 79b, 81a – II, 80a, 81a, 82b
Rūznāmedji viii, **652a** – VIII, **671b**
al-Ruzz ii, 904a, 907a, 1062b; iv, 519b; v, 879b; viii, **652b** – II, 925a, 928b, 1087a; IV, 542a; V, 885b; VIII, **671b**
Ruzzīk b. Ṭalāʾiʿ, Abū Shudjāʿ (vizier) (1163) i, 197a; ii, 318a; iv, 376a; viii, **653b** – I, 202b; II, 327a; IV, 392b; VIII, **672b**
Rzewuski, Wenceslas Severin (1831) viii, **654a** – VIII, **673a**

S

Ṣaʿ viii, **654a** – VIII, **673a**
Sāʿa iii, 921a; v, 708b; viii, **654b** – III, 945b; V, 713b; VIII, **674a**
Saʿāda viii, **657b** – VIII, **677a**
Saʿāda, Antūn iii, 523a, b; iv, 125a – III, 541b; IV, 130b
Saʿāda, Banū viii, 708a – VIII, 728a
Saʿādat b. Muḥammad Girāy II iv, 178b – IV, 185b
Saʿādat ʿAlī Khān, Nawāb (Awadh) (1814) i, 757b, 809a; iii, 1244a; v, 637a; viii, **660b** – I, 780a, 832b; III, 1276b; V, 641a, b; VIII, **680a**
Saʿādat Allāh Khān i, 624b – I, 645b
Saʿādat Girāy Khān I ii, 179a, 1046a, 1113b; iv, 178a – II, 184b, 1070b, 1139b; IV, 185a
Saʿādat Ḥasan Mantō (1955) x, 886a – X,
Saʿādat Khān → Burhān al-Mulk, Nawwāb
Saʿādat Khān Bahādur → Burhān al-Mulk, Mīr Muḥammad Amīn, Nawwāb
Saʿādat Khān Swātī iii, 335b – III, 346a
Saʿādat Yār Khān → Ṣādiḳ Muḥammad Khān III
Saʿādatābād Square (Iṣfahān) vi, 526b – VI, 511a
Saadia Gaon → Saʿadyā al-Fayyūmī
Saʿadyā ben Yōsēf, Saʿīd Yaʿḳūb Yūsuf al-Fayyūmī (942) i, 343a; ii, 95b; iv, 304a, 305b, 306a, 604a; vii, 786a; viii, **661a**; ix, 10a – I, 353b; II, 97b; IV, 317b, 319a, 320a, 628b; VII, 788a; VIII, **680b**; IX, 10b
Saʿālīk → Suʿlūk
al-Sāʿātī, Muḥammad s, 371b, 373a, b – S, 371b, 373a, b
Sabʿ, Sabʿa viii, **662b** – VIII, **681b**
Ṣaʿb Dhu ʾl-Ḳarnayn al-Ḥimyarī vi, 565b – VI, 550b
Ṣabā, Fatḥ ʿAlī Khān (1822) iii, 114a; iv, 69b; vi, 276b – III, 116b; IV, 73a; VI, 261b
Saba (Queen/la reine) → Bilḳīs
Sabaʾ (Sabeans/Sabéens) i, 548a, b; iii, 9a; vi, 88b, 560a, 561a, 562a, 831b; viii, **663a**; ix, 91a; s, 337a – I, 565b, 566a; III, 9b; VI, 86b, 544b, 545b, 547a, 822a; VIII, **682b**; IX, 93b; S, 336b
Ṣabā (zephyr) ii, 1035a – II, 1059a
Sabāʾ b. Abī ʾl-Suʿūd i, 1214b; iii, 134a; v, 954a – I, 1251a; III, 136b; V, 958a
Sabaʾ b. Aḥmad (Ṣulayhid(e)) (1098) vii, 773a; ix, 1b – VII, 774b; IX, 1b
Sabaʾ b. Managhfād ii, 1095b – II, 1121b
Sabaʾ b. Yashdjub b. Yaʿrub b. Ḳaḥṭān vi, 560a – VI, 544b
Sabaʾ al-Aṣghar s, 337b – S, 337a
Sabab i, 671b, 672a; iii, 1129b; viii, **666b** – I, 692a, b; III, 1157b; VIII, **686a**
Sabaea → al-Ṣābiʾa
Sabah (Borneo) vi, 232b, 241a, 242a; viii, **668a**; s, 150a – VI, 206a, 212a, 213a; VIII, **687b**; S, 150a
Ṣabāh (jeweller/bijoutier) s, 251b – 252a
Ṣabāḥ, Āl i, 233b, 540a; ii, 176b; v, 573b, 574a; viii, **668b** – I, 241a, 556b; II 181b; V, 578a, b; VIII, **688a**
Ṣabāḥ I (Ṣabāḥ, Āl) (1756) viii, 668b – VIII, 688a
Sabāḥ al-Dīn ("Prens" Sabahattin) (1948) ii, 430b, 474b, 475a; iii, 593a; viii, **669a** – II, 442a, 487a; III, 613b; VIII, **688b**
Ṣabāḥ al-Dīn ʿAlī v, 195a, 197a – V, 192a, 194a
Sabahattin Ali (1948) vi, 95b; viii, **669b** – VI, 93b; VIII, **689a**
Sabahattin (Raḥmī) Eyuboğlu → Eyyūboghlu, Ṣabāḥ al-Dīn Raḥmī
al-Sabāʾī (966) vi, 353b – VI, 338a
Sabaeans → Sabaʾ
Sabaʾiyya i, 382b; iii, 1265a; s, 357b – I, 393b; III, 1298a; S, 357b
Ṣabandja viii, **670b** – VIII, **690a**
Sabarta → Isparta
Sabasṭiyya viii, **670b** – VIII, **690b**
Sabʿat Khawātim v, 222b – V, 220b
Sabʿatayn s, 337a – S, 336b
Sabʿatu Ridjāl (Marrākush) vi, 591a; viii, **671b** – VI, 575b; VIII, **691a**
Ṣabbā viii, **671b** – VIII, **691b**
al-Ṣabbāgh, Aḥmad b. Muṣṭafā al-Sikandarānī s, 44a – S, 44b
Sabéens → Sabaʾ; Sābiʾ
Ṣābiʾ (Sabians/Sabéens: Ḳurʾān, ʿIrāḳ, Ḥarrān) viii, **672a** – VIII, **692a**
al-Ṣābiʾ, Abū Isḥāḳ Ibrāhīm b. Ḥilāl b. al-Huḥass (994) i, 591b, 955a, 1354a; ii, 305a; iii, 258a, 387b, 671b, 703b, 780a; iv, 756b; viii, 674a; x, 14a; s, 4a, 19a, 398a – I, 611a, 984b, 1393a; II, 313b; III, 265b, 400a, 693a, 726a, 803b; IV, 786b; VIII, 693b; X, 14b; S, 3b, 19a, 398b
al-Ṣābiʿ, Ghars al-Niʿma b. Hilal (X) x, 14a – X, 14b
Ṣābiʾa (Mandaeans/Mandéens) i, 264a, 527b; iii, 9b, 52a, 166a, 228a, 1075b; v, 120a, 895a; vi, 247a, 337a, 338a, 413b, 559a, 613b, 950b; viii, **675a**; ix, 801b; s, 336b – I, 272a, 543b; III, 10a, 54a, 169b, 170a, 235a, 1102b; V, 122b, 901b; VI, 231b, 321a, 322a, 398b, 543b, 598b, 943a; VIII, **694b**; IX, 836a; S, 336b
Sabians → Ṣābiʾ
Ṣābiʾat al-Baṭāʾiḥ → Ṣābiʾa
Ṣābiʾat Ḥarrān → Ṣābiʾa
Ṣabīḥ s, 251b – S, 251b
al-Sabīʿī, Abū Isḥāḳ (745) vii, 398b – VII, 399b
al-Sabīʿī al-Hamdānī s, 400b – S, 401a
Sābiḳ b. Maḥmūd b. Ṣāliḥ (Mirdāsid(e)) (1079) iii, 790a; vii, 577b – III, 813b; VII, 578a
Sābiḳ b. Sulaymān b. Harāth b. Mūlāt, Ibn Dūnās vi, 842a; vii, 186a – VI, 832b; VII, 186a
Sabīka umm Muḥammad b. ʿAlī al-Riḍā vii, 396b – VII, 397b
al-Sābiḳūn viii, **678b** – VIII, **698b**
Sabīl iv, 435b; viii, **679a** – IV, 455a; VIII, **699a**
Ṣābir (Lombardia) iv, 275b; v, 1244a – IV, 287b; V, 1234b
Sābir b. Ismāʿīl al-Tirmidhī (Adīb Ṣābir) (1142) viii, **683a**, 971a – VIII, **702b,** 1005a
al-Ṣābir, ʿAlāʾ al-Dīn ʿAlī b. Aḥmad s, 313a – S, 312b
Ṣābir, Mīrzā ʿAlī Akbar (1911) viii, **683b** – VIII, **703a**
Ṣābiriyya ii, 54a; s, 313a – II, 55a; S, 312b
Sabirs (Central Asia/Asie Centrale) iv, 1172a, b, 1178b – IV, 1205b, 1212a
Sabʿiyya i, 178b; iv, 203a, b; viii, **683b** – I, 183a; IV, 212b; VIII, **703a**

Sabk (Shibl) al-Daylamī (902) viii, 631a – VIII, 650a
Sabkatī → Maḥmūd I Ghāzī (Ottoman)
Sabkha ii, 877b; viii, **685a** – II, 897b; VIII, **705a**
Sabk-i Hindī ii, 999b, 1034a; iv, 60a, 68b-69a; viii, **683b** – II, 1023a, 1058a; IV, 63a-b, 72b; VIII, **703b**
Sabk-i ʿIrāḳī iv, 60a; viii, 683b – IV, 63a; VIII, 703b
Sabk-i Khurāsānī iv, 60a; viii, 683b – IV, 63a; VIII, 703b
Sabk-i Turkistānī iv, 60a; viii, 683b – IV, 63a; VIII, 703b
Sābla iv, 674a, 675a – IV, 702a, b
Ṣabr (patience) viii, **685b** – VIII, **705b**
Ṣabr (aloe(ès)) viii, 687b – VIII, 707b
Ṣabra (al-Manṣūriyya) ii, 114b, 861b, 863a; iv, 830a,b; vi, 435a; viii, **688b** – II, 117a, 881b, 883a; IV, 862b, 863b; VI, 420a; VIII, **708a**
Ṣabra (Sabratha) vi, 452b; viii, **687b** – VI, 438a; VIII, **707b**
Sabra b. Maʿbad vii, 757b – VII, 759a
Sabra b. Nakhf b. Abī Ṣufra (VIII) vii, 359b – VII, 361b
Sabt (Sabbath) viii, **689a** – VIII, **709a**
Sabta (Ceuta) i, 83b, 356b; iv, 355b; v, 1192a; vi, 216b, 431b, 572a, 573a, 574a, 593b, 594a, 595a, 596a; vii, 387a, 391b, 641b; viii, **689b**; s, 111b, 124b, 125a –
I, 86a, 367a; IV, 371a; V, 1182a; VI, 200b, 417a, 557a, 558a, 559a, 577b, 578b, 580a, b; VII, 388b, 392b, 641b; VIII, **709b**; S, 110b, 124a
al-Sabtī b. Hārūn al-Rashīd i, 1289a – I, 1328b
al-Sabtī, Aḥmad b. Djaʿfar al-Khazradjī, Abū ’l-ʿAbbās (1205) viii, 690b, **691a**, 715b – VIII, 710b, **711a**, 736a
al-Sabtī, Abu ’l-ʿAbbās (1205) iii, 893b, 975a – III, 917b, 999b
al-Sabtī, Abu ’l-Ḳāsim (1358) vi, 196b – VI, 180b
al-Sabtī, Ḳāḍī Abu ’l-Faḍl ʿIyāḍ b. Mūsā(1149) vii, 625a – VII, 624b
al-Sabtī, Muḥammad b. ʿIyāḍ vi, 111a, 355a – VI, 108b, 339a
Sabuktakīn/Sabuktigīn → Sebüktegin
Ṣābūn viii, **693a** – VIII, **713a**
al-Ṣābūndjī, Ḥusayn iv, 852b – IV, 885b
Ṣābundjī, Louis (1931) viii, **693b** – VIII, **713b**
Sābūr, Dhu ’l-Aktāf → Shāpūr II
Sābūr b. Abī Ṭāhir iv, 664a – IV, 691a
Sābūr b. Ardashīr, Abū Naṣr (1025) i, 242a, 899a, 1352b; ii, 127a; vi, 199a; viii, **694a**; x, 915a; s, 119b, 361b –
I, 249b, 926a, 1391b; II, 130b; VI, 183a; VIII, **713b**; X, ;S, 119a, 361b
Sābūr b. Sahl i, 344b, 1224a – I, 355a, 1260b
Sābūr b. Sahl b. Sābūr (869) i, 344b, 1224a; viii, 694a – I, 355a, 1260b; VIII, 714a
Sābūr al-Djunūd → Shāpūr I
Ṣabūrī, Abū Muḥammad Taḳī Bahār (XIX) vi, 276b – VI, 261b
Ṣabyā s, 278b – S, 278b
Sabz ʿAlī (Ramaḍān ʿAlī) (1938) viii, **694b** – VIII, **714a**
Sabzawār (Harāt; Khurāsān) iii, 968b; vi, 13a; vii, 76b, 90a; viii, **694b**; ix, 47b; s, 41a –
III, 993a; VI, 12a; VII, 77b, 91b; VIII, **714b**; IX, 48b; S, 41b
al-Sabzawārī, Abū Saʿīd al-Ḥasan b. al-Ḥusayn (1450) iv, 704b – IV, 733a
Sabzawārī, Ḥadjdj Mullā Hādī (1878) iv, 50b; viii, **695a**; s, 41a – IV, 53b; VIII, **715a**; S, 41b
Sabzawārī, Muḥammad ʿAlāʾ al-Dīn (XV) viii, 542b – VIII, 560a
Sabzawārī, Muḥammad Bāḳir (1679) viii, 779a; s, 308a – VIII, 805a; S, 308a
Sabzawārī, Shāh Riḍā (XVII) vii, 1052b – VII, 1055a
Sabzawārī, Shams al-Dīn (1300) ii, 394a; v, 26a; vii, 550a – II, 404b; V, 26b; VII, 550a
Saččal Sarmast (1827) ix, 637a s IX, 661b
Ṣād viii, **695b** – VIII, **715b**
Saʿd (atabeg Fārs) (XIII) vi, 482a – VI, 468a
Saʿd (Mamlūks) vi, 327b – VI, 314a
Saʿd b. Zangī (Salghurid(e)) (1260) vi, 608b; viii, 720a – VI, 593a; VIII, 740b
Saʿd b. Abī Waḳḳās (671) i, 140a, 336b, 382b, 445a, 485a, 697a; iii, 260a, 587a, 739b, 874a, 1254b; iv, 385a, b, 775b, 796a; v, 345b, 451a, 945a; vi, 647b, 648a, 649a, 653b, 659a, 660a, 664b, 702a; vii, 75a, 364a, 394b, 783b; viii, **696a**; ix, 44b, 618a, 661b –
I, 144a, 347a, 393b, 458a, 499a, 718a; III, 267b, 607a, 762a, 898a, 1287a; IV, 402a, b, 806b, 828b; V, 346b, 453b, 949a; VI, 633a, b, 634b, 639a, 644b, 646a, 650b, 690b; VII, 76a, 366b, 395b, 785b; VIII, **716a**; IX, 45a, 641b, 687a
Saʿd b. ʿĀʾidh al-Ḳaraẓ s, 172a – S, 173a
Saʿd b. al-ʿĀs iv, 858b – IV, 891b
Saʿd b. Bakr, Banū iii, 94a, 363b; vi, 648b; viii, **697b** – III, 96b, 375a; VI, 634a; VIII, **717a**
Saʿd b. Fahm, Banū x, 2b – X, 2b
Saʿd b. Fayṣal b. ʿAbd al-ʿAzīz Āl Suʿūd s, 305b – S, 305b
Saʿd b. Mardanīsh → Ibn Mardanīsh
Saʿd b. Masʿūd (VII) vii, 521a; ix, 421b ; x, 431a– VII, 521b; IX, 435b; X, 462a
Saʿd b. Muʿādh b. al-Nuʿmān al-Ashhalī (627) i, 514b, 771b; v, 436b; vi, 374a, 645a, 646b; vii, 370b, 371a; viii, **697b** –
I, 530a, 794b; V, 439a; VI, 358b, 630b, 631b; VII, 372b; VIII, **717b**
Saʿd b. Muḥammad → Ḥayṣa Bayṣa
Saʿd b. Rabīʿ (VII) vii, 254a – VII, 255b
Saʿd b. ʿUbāda (634) i, 514b; v, 996b; vii, 356b, 1020a; viii, **698a** – I, 530b; V, 992a; VII, 359a, 1022a; VIII, **717b**
Saʿd (I) b. Zangī Abū Shudjāʿ ʿIzz al-Dīn (Salghurid(e)) (1226) i, 434a; iv, 1037a, 1041a; v, 161a; viii, **701a**, 978b – I, 446b; IV, 1068b, 1072b; V, 159b; VIII, **721a**, 1013a
Saʿd b. Zayd Manāt al-Fizr, Banū i, 102a; ii, 71b; viii, **701b**; s, 31a, 178a – I, 104b; II, 72b; VIII, **721b**; S, 31b, 179a
Saʿd Allāh Khān (XVII) vii, 321b – VII, 323b
Saʿd Allāh Khān, Mullā (Sartōr Faḳīr, Bunēr) (XIX) ii, 317a – II, 326a
Saʿd Allāh Khān ʿAllāmī al-Tamīmī ii, 47b; iv, 759b – II, 48b; IV, 790a
Saʿd Allāh Khān Rohilla iii, 60a, b – III, 62b, 63a
Saʿd Allāh Lāhorī iii, 634a – III, 655b
Saʿd Allāh Pasha (Diyār Bakr) (XIX) vi, 542a – VI, 526b
Saʿd al-ʿAshīra, Banū vii, 591b – VII, 591a
Saʿd al-Aysar v, 49a, 50a – V, 50b, 51b
Saʿd Buh s, 182b – S, 182b
Saʿd al-Dawla, (Jew/Juif, Baghdād) (1291) i, 903a; iii, 1122a; iv, 48a; vii, 234b – I, 930a; III, 1150a; IV, 51a; VII, 236b
Saʿd al-Dawla b. al-Ṣafī al-Abharī (1291) viii, **702a** – VIII, **722b**
Saʿd al-Dawla Sharīf I, Abu ’l-Maʿālī (Ḥamdānid(e)) (991) i, 119b; iii, 86a, 128a, b, 129b; v, 820a, 923b; s, 37a – I, 123a; III, 88b, 130b, 131a, 132a; V, 826b, 929a; S, 37a
Saʿd al-Dawla al-Ṭawāshī → al-Ṭawāshī
Saʿd al-Dīn (1599) → Khodja Efendi
Saʿd al-Dīn (Rūyin-diz) vi, 501a – VI, 486a

Saʿd al-Dīn (Ethiopia/-e) i, 176b, 763b – I, 181b, 786b
Saʿd al-Dīn Hammūʾī (1252) viii, 135a, **703a**; s, 235b, 364b – VIII, 137b, **723a**; S, 235a, 364a
Saʿd al-Dīn Ibn al-ʿArabī viii, 753b – VIII, 775a
Saʿd al-Dīn Khiḍr i, 766b – I, 789b
Saʿd al-Dīn Köpek b. Muḥammad (1240) viii, **704b** – VIII, **725a**
Saʿd al-Dīn Muḥammad al-Kāshgharī (1456) ii, 421b, vii, 935a; viii, **704a** – II, 432b; VII, 935b; VIII, **724a**
Saʿd al-Dīn al-Shaybānī al-Djibāwī (XIII) viii, 728b – VIII, 749a
Saʿd al-Dīn Taftāzānī → al-Taftāzānī
Saʿd al-Dīn al-Warāwīnī (1246) iv, 506b; vi, 632a, b, 658b – IV, 528b; VI, 617a, b, 644a
Saʿd al-Ḳaraẓ vi, 677a – VI, 663b
Saʿd (Saʿīd) al-Khayr b. ʿAbd al-Malik (Umayyad(e)) (VIII) vii, 398a – VII, 399b
Saʿd al-Mulk Abu ʾl-Maḥāsin, vizier (XII) vi, 275b; vii, 754a; x, 42b – VI, 260b; VII, 755b' X, 44a
Saʿd wa-Naḥs viii, **705a** – VIII, **725b**
Saʿd Zaghlūl Pasha (1927) ii, 417b, 423a, 467a, 934a; iii, 59a, 516a; iv, 197b, 856a; v, 910a; vi, 607a; vii, 439a, 904b; viii, **698a**; s, 58a – II, 428a, 434a, 478b, 956a; III, 61b, 533b; IV, 206a, 889b; V, 915b; VI, 592a; VII, 440b, 905a; VIII, **718a**; S, 58b
Sada (festival/fête) vi, 523a – VI, 507b
Ṣaʿda (Yemen) vi, 433a, b, 435b, 436a, 437a, 566a; viii, **705b**; s, 22a, 236a, 335a, 407a – VI, 418b, 421a, 422a, 551a; VIII, **725b**; S, 22b, 236a, 334b, 407a
Ṣadā viii, **706b** – VIII, **726b**
Saʿdābād i, 232b; v, 642a – I, 240a; V, 646a
Ṣadaf v, 819b; viii, **707a** – V, 825b; VIII, **727a**
al-Ṣadafī, Abū ʿAlī Ḥusayn b. Muḥammad (1120) iv, 290a; viii, 635a, **707b** – IV, 302b; VIII, 654a, **727b**
Ṣadāḳ viii, **708b** – VIII, **728b**
Ṣadaḳa i, 1142a, 1144a; iii, 350a; iv, 1151b; v, 424b; viii, **708b** – I, 1176b, 1178b; III, 361a; IV, 1183b; V, 426b; VIII, **729a**
Ṣadaḳa, Banū, viii, **716a** – VIII, **736b**
Ṣadaḳa I b. Manṣūr (Mazyadid(e)) (1108) i, 684a; iii, 197b, 389b, 774b; iv, 27b, 29a, 911b; vi, 380a, 966a; vii, 408a, 755b; viii, **716a**, 942b – I, 705a; III, 202a, 402a, 797b; IV, 29b, 31a, 944b; VI, 364a, 958a; VII, 409b, 757a; VIII, **736b**, 974b
Ṣadaḳa II b. Dubays II (Mazyadid(e)) (1138) vi, 966a – VI, 958b
Ṣadaḳa b. Abi ʾl-Ḳāsim Shirāzī iii, 373a; iv, 63b – III, 385a; IV, 67a
Ṣadaka b. ʿAlī (VII) x, 897a – X,
Ṣadaḳa b. ʿAlī al-Azdī (IX) vi, 337a – VI, 321b
Ṣadaḳa b. Yūsuf al-Falāḥī (1048) vii, 118b – VII, 121b
al-Saʿdānī viii, **716b** – VIII, **737a**
Saʿdaniyya iii, 291a – III, 300a
al-Sadārā → Sudayrī
Sadaśiv Rāo (Marāṭhās) (XVIII) vi, 535b – VI, 520a
al-Sādāt, Anwar (1981) v, 1062a; vii, 291b, 451a; viii, **716b**; s, 5b, 6a, 306a – V, 1059a; VII, 293b, 452a; VIII, **737b**; S, 4b, 5a, 305b
Sādāt-i Marʿashī iv, 48b – IV, 51a
Sadd al-Dharāʾiʿ viii, **718a** – VIII, **739a**
Ṣaddām Ḥusayn (XX) vii, 715a; viii, 247a – VII, 715b; VIII, 253a
Saddūm (XVIII) vii, 616a – VII, 616a
Sadekov s, 365b – S, 365b
al-Saʿdī, ʿAbd al-Malik b. Muḥammad b. ʿAṭiyya (VIII) vii, 524b – VII, 525a
al-Saʿdī, ʿAbd al-Raḥmān b. ʿAbd Allāh (Timbuktu) (1656) i, 595a; vi, 258b; viii, **718b** – I, 614b; VI, 243a; VIII, **739b**
Saʿdī, Abū ʿAbd Allāh Musharrif al-Dīn b. Muṣliḥ (1292) viii, 540a, **719a**, 892a – VIII, 557b, **740a**, 922b
al-Saʿdī, Abū Shudjāʿ Shāwar b. Mudjīr (XII) viii, 653b – VIII, 673a
Saʿdī, Shaykh Muṣliḥ al-Dīn (1292) i, 241b, 680a, 780a, 1301a, 1345b; ii, 1034a, 1035a, b; iii, 93b, 373a, 573a; iv, 65b, 67b; vi, 608b, 609a, 825b, 833a; vii, 480b; s, 46b, 415a – I, 249a, 701a, 803a, 1341a, 1385b; II, 1058a, 1059a, b; III, 96a, 385a, 592b; IV, 69a, 71a; VI, 593a, b, 815b, 823b; VII, 480b; S, 47a, 415a
Saʿdī b. Abi ʾl-Shawk i, 513a – I, 528b
Saʿdī Čelebi iii, 90a; iv, 333b – III, 92b; IV, 348a
Sadīd al-Mulk ʿAlī (Munḳidh, Banū) (1082) vii, 577b – VII, 578a
Saʿdid(e)s (Saʿdians/Saʿdiens) i, 55b, 56a, 58b, 93a, 245a, 288b, 355a, 403a, 496b, 689a, 1058a, 1149a; ii, 134a, 146a, 164b, 181b, 510a, 819b, 823a; iii, 70a, 251b, 257a, 426a, 1047a; v, 627a, 1191a, b; vi, 134b, 142b, 187b, 248b, 594a, 596a, 741b, 743a, 888b; vii, 37b; viii, **723a**; ix, 545b; s, 28b, 29a, 223b, 336b – I, 57b, 60a, 96a, 252b, 297b, 366a, 414b, 511b, 710a, 1089b, 1183a; II, 137a, 150a, 170a, 187a, 522b, 839a, 842a; III, 72b, 258b, 264a, 478b, 1073a; V, 631a, 1181a, b; VI, 132b, 133a, 140b, 141a, 171a, 232b, 579a, 580b, 730b, 732a, 880a; VII, 37b; VIII, **743b**; IX, 567a; S, 29a, 223b, 336a
Ṣādiḳ, Colonel iii, 595a – III, 615b
Ṣādik, G.M. iv, 711a – IV, 739b
Ṣādiḳ Beg iv, 593b – IV, 617b
Ṣādiḳ Ḥalwāʾī, Mawlānā s, 122a – S, 121a
Ṣādiḳ Hidāyat → Hidāyat, Ṣādiḳ
Ṣādik Khān Shakākī i, 1030b; ii, 838b; iii, 1109a – I, 1062a; II, 858a; III, 1136b
Ṣādiḳ Khān Zand i, 1087a; iv, 104b; v, 674a – I, 1119b; IV, 109a; V, 679a
Ṣādiḳ al-Mahdī (Sūdān) (XX) ix, 749b s IX, 782b
Ṣādiḳ Muḥammad Khān I (Dāwūdpōtrā) (1746) ii, 185b, 186a – II, 191b, 192a
Ṣādiḳ Muḥammad Khān II (1825) ii, 186b – II, 192b
Ṣādiḳ Muḥammad Khān III ii, 186b – II, 192b
Ṣadiḳ Muḥammad Khān IV (1899) ii, 187a – II, 193a
Ṣādiḳ Muḥammad Khān V (1956) ii, 187a – II, 193a
Ṣādiḳ Muṭṭalibī i, 432b – I, 445a
Ṣādiḳ Rifʿat Pasha, Meḥmed (1857) iii, 552a, 591a; viii, **726a** – III, 571a, 611a; VIII, **746b**
Ṣādiḳī (coin/monnaie) viii, **726b** – VIII, **747a**
Ṣādiḳī Bēg (painter/peintre) vii, 603a; viii, 776b, 787b – VII, 602b; VIII, 802b, 814a
al-Ṣādiḳiyya, al-Madrasa v, 915a; viii, **726b** – V, 920b; VIII, **747b**
Sādin iv, 421b; viii, **728a** – IV, 439b; VIII, **749a**
Ṣadīna, Banū vi, 310b – VI, 295b
Sadīr, A. (XX) vi, 768b – VI, 758a
Ṣādirāt ii, 152a; iv, 1041a, 1042a – II, 156b; IV, 1072b, 1073a, b
Sadīrī, Muḥammad Muʾmin (XVII) vii, 475b – VII, 475a
Saʿdiyya viii, **728b** – VIII, **749a**
Sādj viii, **732b** – VIII, **753a**
Sadjʿ i, 591a, 594a, 673b; ii, 307a; iii, 1242b; v, 420a, 839b; viii, **732b** – I, 610a, 613b, 694b; II, 315b; III, 1274b; V, 422a, 846a; VIII, **753a**
Sadjāḥ, Umm Ṣādir bint Aws b. Ḥikk (VII) i, 110b, 247b, 451a; iii, 169a, 224b; iv, 463b; vi, 267b, 268a,

675b; vii, 665a; viii, **738b** – I, 113b, 255a, 463b; III, 172b, 231b; IV, 484b; VI, 252b, 662a; VII, 664b; VIII, **759b**
Sadjāḥī → Sadjāḥ
al-Sadjāwandī, Abū ʿAbd Allāh (1165) viii, **739a** – VIII, **760a**
al-Sadjāwandī, Sirādj al-Dīn (XIII) iii, 163b; viii, 739b – III, 167a; VIII, 760b
Sadjda viii, **740a** – VIII, **760b**
Sadjdjād Ḥusayn, Ḥusayn iii, 359a – III, 370a
Sadjdjāda iv, 950a; viii, **740b** – IV, 982b; VIII, **761b**
al-Sādjī, Abū Yaḥyā Zakariyyāʾ (909) viii, 840b – VIII, 869b
Sādjid(e)s i, 145a, 190a, 637a, 660b; ii, 679b; iv, 22a, b; v, 489a; vi, 539a; vii, 922a; viii, **745a** – I, 149b, 194b, 658a, 681b; II, 696b; IV, 23b, 24a; V, 491b; VI, 523b; VII, 922b; VIII, **766a**
Sādjiyya i, 866a; ii, 1080b – I, 890b; II, 1105b
Sadjsin v, 1016a, b – V, 1011b, 1012a
Sādjūr (river/rivière) vi, 377b, 378a, 379a, b, 382a – VI, 362a, 364a, 366a
Sadok Bey (1860) vi, 798b – VI, 788a
Sadōzays i, 229a, 230a, 295a – I, 236a, 237a, 304b
Ṣadr (chest, poitrine) viii, **746a** – VIII, **767b**
Ṣadr (eminent person/homme éminent) viii, **748a** – VIII, **769b**
Ṣadr (Ḳumm) s, 157b – S, 158a
al-Ṣadr, Muḥammad Bāḳir (Āyatullāh) (1980) vii, 301b – VII, 303b
Ṣadr al-Dīn → Rinčana
Ṣadr al-Dīn (Kashmīr) iv, 708a – IV, 736b
Ṣadr al-Dīn (vizier) (Gaykhātū b. Abaḳa) (XIII) vii, 232a – VII, 234a
Ṣadr al-Dīn, Pīr iv, 202b – IV, 211b
Ṣadr al-Dīn Ardabīlī b. Ṣafī al-Dīn Ardabīlī (1391) viii, **752b**; s, 382b – VIII, **774b**; S, 383a
Ṣadr al-Dīn ʿAynī (1954) viii, **753a**; x, 65b – VIII, **774b**; X, 67b
Ṣadr al-Dīn Azurda → Āzurda, Ṣadr al-Dīn
Ṣadr al-Dīn al-Baṣrī (XIII) vi, 352a – VI, 336a
Ṣadr al-Dīn Ḳūnawī (1274) iii, 708a, b, 710b, 1269a; vi, 247b ; viii, 210b, 703b, **753a**, 860a – III, 730b, 731a, 733a, 1302a; VI, 231b; VIII, 214b, 723b, **775a**, 890a
Ṣadr al-Dīn Muḥammad b. Ghiyāth al-Dīn Manṣūr (1498) viii, 543a – VIII, 560b
Ṣadr al-Dīn Muḥammad Shīrāzī → Mulla Ṣadrā Shīrāzī
Ṣadr al-Dīn Mūsā, Shaykh iv, 721a – IV, 750a
Ṣadr al-Dīn Mūsā b. Ṣafī al-Dīn Ardabīlī (1391) iv, 721a; viii, **755a**, 766a – IV, 750a; VIII, **777a**, 791b
Ṣadr al-Dīn Ṣadr (Āyatullāh) (XX) vii, 762b – VII, 764a
Ṣadr al-Dīn Sheykhoghlu (XIV) vi, 632b – VI, 617b
Ṣadr al-Dīn Shīrāzī → al-Shīrāzī, Ṣadr al-Dīn
al-Ṣadr al-Shahīd Ḥusām al-Dīn ʿUmar (1141) vi, 558a – VI, 542b
Ṣadr al-Sharīʿa al-Thānī iii, 163b – III, 167a
Ṣadr al-Ṣudūr i, 316b, 1327b – I, 326b, 1368a
Ṣadrā Shīrāzī → al-Shīrāzī, Ṣadr al-Dīn
Sadrata viii, **756a** – VIII, **780b**
Sadrātā i, 1246b; v, 697b – I, 1284b; V, 702b
al-Sadrātī → ʿĀṣim; Abū Yaʿḳūb
Sadrettin Celal (Ṣadr al-Dīn Djelāl) (XX) iv, 124a; vi, 94b, 95b – IV, 129b; VI, 92b, 93b
Ṣadr-i Aʿẓam i, 1091a; ii, 333a, 335b; iii, 554a, 555a; iv, 393b; v, 631a; viii, **751b** – I, 1123b; II, 343a, 345a; III, 573a, 574a; IV, 410b; V, 635a; VIII, **773a**
Ṣadūk, Shaykh-i → Ibn Bābawayh
Saʿdullāh Pasha iii, 592b – III, 613a
al-Saʿdūn, ʿAbd al-Muḥsin (XX) vii, 582b – VII, 583a
Saʿdūn, Āl → al-Muntafiḳ
Saʿdūn, Banū → al-Muntafiḳ, Banū
Saʿdūn, Nāṣir Pasha (XIX) vii, 582b – VII, 583a
Saʿdūn, Shaykh Manīʿ (XVIII) iii, 1191a; vii, 582a – III, 1221a; VII, 582b
al-Saʿdūn, Shaykh Manṣūr (XIX) vii, 582b – VII, 583a
Saʿdūn b. Manṣūr (Muntafiḳ, Banū) (1911) vii, 582b – VII, 583a
Saʿdūn b. Muḥammad Āl Ghurayr ii, 321a; iv, 925a – II, 330b; IV, 958a
Saʿdūn al-Surunbāḳī i, 85b – I, 88a
al-Ṣafā vi, 544b, 546a; viii, **756b** – VI, 529a, 531a; VIII, **781a**
al-Ṣafā (Mecca) ii, 71a; vi, 162a, 165b, 167a, 178a; viii, **756a**; s, 175a – II, 72b; VI, 156a, 158a, 159a, 163a; VIII, **781a**; S, 176a
Ṣafā, Bābā Ḥadjdjī (1740) x, 251a – X, 269b
Ṣafā Girāy (Ḳazan) (1531) viii, 832a – VIII, 861a
Ṣafāʾ Khān iv, 849b – IV, 882b
Ṣafad vi, 343b; viii, **757a** – VI, 327b; VIII, **781b**
al-Ṣafadī, al-Ḥasan b. Abī Muḥammad (XIV) viii, **759a** – VIII, **783b**
Ṣafadī, Muṭaʿ v, 191a – V, 188a
al-Ṣafadī, Ṣalāḥ al-Dīn Khalīl b. Aybak (1363) i, 594b; ii, 285b; iv, 863b; v, 609a; vi, 112a, 143b, 196a, 198b, 247b; vii, 170b, 306b, 390b; viii, 458b, 672a, **759a**; x, 68b, 395a; s, 48b, 381a, 388a, b, 400a – I, 614a; II, 293b; IV, 896b; V, 613a; VI, 109b, 141b, 180a, 182b, 231b; VII, 172b, 309a, 392a; VIII, 474a, 691b, **783b**; X, 71a, 423b; S, 49a, 381b, 388b, 389a, 400b
Ṣafāʾī (1725) viii, 991a – VIII, 1025b
Ṣafaitic/ṣafaitique vi, 349a; viii, **760b** – VI, 333a; VIII, **785b**
Safāḳus (Sfax) viii, **762b** – VIII, **787b**
al-Ṣafāḳusī, ʿAlī al-Sharafī (XVI) vi, 185b; vii, 47b – VI, 169a; VII, 46b
al-Safāḳusī, Maḥmūd b. Saʿīd Maḳdīsh (1813) viii, 763a – VIII, 788a
Ṣaʿfān vi, 191b – VI, 175b
Ṣafar (month/mois) viii, **764b** – VIII, **790a**
Ṣafar (Sfar), Muḥammad al-Bashīr (1917) viii, **765a** – VIII, **790b**
Safar (journey/voyage) viii, **764b** – VIII, **789b**
Ṣafarov, ʿAlī Ḳulī s, 71b – S, 72a
Ṣafātene/Ṣafāite i, 562b – I, 580b
Ṣafawid(e)s, Ṣafawiyya i, 190a, 311b, 1066a-1068b, 1120a; ii, 7b, 598b; iii, 177b, 220a, 315b, 1100a; iv, 34a-37b, 49a, 68b, 103a-104a, 118b, 130b, 186a, b, 187a, 387b, 537a, 670b; v, 33b, 34a, 59a, 379a, 603b, 749a; vi, 11a, 18b, 226a, 271a, 483a, b, 493a, 495a, 510b, 515b, 521b, 522b, 523a, 525a, 548b, 549b, 550a, b, 724b, 855a, 931b; viii, 755a, **765b**; ix, 475b; x, 45b; s, 51b, 71a, 139a, 227b, 257a, 308a, 327a – I, 194b, 321a, 452a, 1098a-1100b, 1154a; II, 7b, 613b; III, 181b, 226b, 325a, 1127a; IV, 36b-40a, 51b, 72a, b, 107b-108b, 123b, 136a-b, 194a, b, 195a, 404a, 560a, 697b; V, 34b, 35a, 60b, 380a, 607b, 754b; VI, 11a, 16b, 220a, 256a, 469a, b, 478b, 480a, 496a, 500b, 506a, 507a, b, 509b, 533a, 534a, b, 535a, 713b, 846b, 923b; VIII, 777a, **791a**; IX, 493b; X, 47a; S, 52a, 71b, 138b, 227b, 256b, 308a, 326b
—administration i, 36a, 240a, 1088a, 1159a, 1346a; ii, 150a, b, 162b, 311b, 334a, 967a, 1083b; iii, 47b, 198b, 490b, 1257a; iv, 474b, 757b, 860b, 951b, 976b, 1048b, 1052b, 1092b; v, 244a, 630a, 869a; x, 45b – I, 37a, 247b, 1120b, 1193b, 1386b; II, 154b, 155a, b,

167b, 320b, 344a, 989a, 1108b; III, 49b, 203a, 507b, 1289b; IV, 495b, 788a, 893b, 984a, 1009a, 1080a, 1084a, 1123b; V, 242a, 634a, 875b; 47a
Ṣafawiyya (order/ordre) s, 382b, 383a – S, 383a
Ṣafdar ʿAlī b. Ghazan Khān iii, 581a – III, 601b
Ṣafdar ʿAlī b. Saʿādat Allāh i, 625a – I, 645b
Ṣafdar Djang (Awadh (Oudh), 1754) i, 757a; ii, 808b, 870a; iii, 60a, b, 1158b, 1163a; vi, 128a, 369b, 353b, 537a; vii, 316a, 334a; viii, **793b** – I, 779b; II, 827b, 890b; III, 62a, 63a, 1186b, 1191b; VI, 126a, 354a, 520a, 521b; VII, 318b, 335b; VIII, **820b**
Ṣaff iv, 334b; viii, **793b** – IV, 349a; VIII, **820b**
al-Saffāḥ → Abū 'l-ʿAbbās al-Saffāḥ
al-Ṣaffār, Ismāʿīl b. Abī Naṣr (1069) viii, 748b – VIII, 779a
al-Ṣaffārī, Abū Isḥāḳ Ibrāhīm (XII) viii, 749a – VIII, 779a
Ṣaffārid(e)s i, 18b, 23b, 226b, 439b, 452b, 1354b; ii, 191b, 962b, 1082b; iii, 346a; iv, 20b-21b, 188b, 208b; vi, 65b, 193a, 274a, 620b, 872a; vii, 766a; viii, **795a**; s, 113a – I, 19b, 24a, 233b, 452a, 465b, 1393b; II, 197b, 984b, 1107b; III, 356b; IV, 22a-23a, 197a, 218a; VI, 63b, 177a, 258b, 605b, 863a; VII, 767b; VIII, **822a**; S, 112b
al-Ṣāffāt viii, **798a** – VIII, **825a**
Saffet Bey (XIX) vi, 758b – VI, 747b
Ṣafī (Fakhr al-Dīn ʿAlī Kāshifī) (1532) iv, 69a, 704a; vii, 1019a; viii, **800b** – IV, 73a, 732a; VII, 1021a; VIII, **827b**
Safi (port) → Aṣfī
Ṣafī/Ṣawāfī i, 1144a; iv, 972b, 973a; viii, **798b** – I, 1178b; IV, 1005a; VIII, **825b**
Ṣafī I, Shāh (Ṣafawid(e)) (1642) i, 228b; ii, 104a, 335a; iii, 220b, 348b, 1190a; iv, 977a; v, 1089b; vi, 516b, 550b; vii, 318a, 476a; viii, 770b; s, 63a, 83b, 276a – I, 235b; II, 106b, 345a; III, 227a, 359b, 1220a; IV, 1009b; V, 1086b; VI, 501b, 535b; VII, 320a, 475b; VIII, 796a; S, 63b, 83a, 275b
Ṣafī II, Shāh (Ṣafawid(e)) (1694) → Sulaymān Shāh
Safi, Banū s, 237b – S, 237a
Ṣafī-ʿAlī-Shāhiyya ii, 434a; iv, 52a; viii, 47a; x, 327b – II, 445a; IV, 54b; VIII, 48a; X, 352a
Ṣafī Amīr al-Muʾminīn → Bahāʾ al-Dawla Fīrūz
Ṣafī (Sofi)-Čay vi, 498b, 501a, b – VI, 483b, 486b
Ṣafī al-Dīn ʿAbd Allāh b. Shukr iii, 863a – III, 887a
Ṣafī al-Dīn ʿAbd al-Muʾmin (1294) ii, 1074a; vii, 191a, 209a – II, 1098b; VII, 191b, 210a
Ṣafī al-Dīn al-Ardabīlī (Ṣafawid(e)) (1334) i, 625b, 1197b; ii, 967a; vi, 131b, 354b; viii, 766a, **801a**; s, 139a, 382b – I, 646b, 1233a; II, 989a; VI, 130a, 338b; VIII, 791b, **828a**; S, 138b, 383a
Ṣafī al-Dīn al-Ḥillī (1351) i, 595b, 666b, 858a, 982b; ii, 1033a; iii, 852a, 1264b; iv, 1006a; vi, 248a; vii, 495a, 661a, 812a; viii, 111a, 376a, 378a, **801b**; ix, 70b – I, 614b, 687a, 882a, 1013a; II, 1057a; III, 876a, 1297b; IV, 1038b; VI, 232a; VII, 494b, 661a, 813b; VIII, 113b, 389a, 391a, **828b**; IX, 73a
Ṣafī al-Dīn al-Urmawī, ʿAbd al-Muʾmin (1294) vi, 99a, 102b; vii, 683b, 684a, 1042b; viii, **805b**; s, 408b, 409a – VI, 97a, 100b; VII, 683b, 684a,1044b; VIII, **832b**; S, 409a
Ṣafī Ḳuli Khān i, 229b, 904a – I, 236a, 931b
Ṣafī Mīrzā b. Shāh Sultān Ḥusayn (Ṣafawid(e)) (XVIII) vi, 56b; viii, 771b – VI, 54b; VIII, 797a
Ṣafiābād i, 701b – I, 722b
Ṣafī Sayf Khān, Mīrzā (XVII) vii, 574a – VII, 574b
Safīd Kūh i, 222a; viii, **807b**; s, 237b – I, 228b; VIII, **834b**; S, 237a
Safīd Rūd ii, 189b; iv, 6b; v, 602b, 866a; vi, 498b, 500a; viii, **807b**; s, 356b, 363a – II, 195b; IV, 7a; V, 606b, 872b; VI, 483b, 485b; VIII, **835a**; S, 356a, 362b
Safīdpūsh iv, 409b – IV, 427a
Safīna vii, 53a; viii, **808a** – VII, 53b; VIII, **835a**
Ṣafīnāz Dhu 'l-Fiḳār s, 299b – S, 299a
Ṣafīpur s, 293a – S, 293a
Safīr ii, 590a; iii, 590a; viii, **811b** – II, 604b; III, 610a; VIII, **838b**
Safīrī (XX) vi, 754a – VI, 743b
Sāfīthā (chastel blanc) vi, 579a; viii, **815b** – VI, 564a; VIII, **843a**
Ṣafiyat al-Nīsāʾ bint Muḥammad Akbar b. Awranzīb (XVII) iv, 93a – IV, 97a
Ṣafiyya bint Amīr Abū ʿAbd Allāh b. Mardanīsh (Martinez) (XII) vi, 339b – VI, 323b
Ṣafiyya bint Ḥuyayy b. Akhṭab (670) i, 55b, 1022a; ii, 275a; iv, 1140a; v, 619b; vi, 658b; vii, 852b; viii, **817a** – I, 57a, 1053b; II, 283a; IV, 1171b; V, 623b; VI, 644a; VII, 853b; VIII, **845a**
Ṣafiyye Wālide Sulṭān (Cecilia Baffo) (1605) i, 267b; iv, 233b, 900b; vii, 595b; viii, 124a, **817b** – I, 275b; IV, 243b, 933b; VII, 595b; VIII, 127a, **846a**
Ṣafḳa viii, **818a** – VIII, **846a**
Safvet-bey Başagič i, 1271b – I, 1311a
Ṣafwān b. Idrīs (1201) viii, **819a** – VIII, **847a**
Ṣafwān b. al-Muʿaṭṭal al-Sulamī (638) i, 307b; iii, 272a; iv, 870b; viii, **819b** – I, 317a; III, 280a; IV, 904a; VIII, **848a**
Ṣafwān b. Ṣafwān al-Anṣarī i, 1080b; viii, **818b** – I, 1113a; viii, **846b**
Ṣafwān b. Umayya i, 115b, 151a – I, 119a, 155b
Ṣafwat Pasha (XIX) vi, 151b – VI, 150a
Ṣafwat al-Mulk iii, 399a – III, 411b
Sagartians v, 448b – V, 451a
Sagbāns ii, 512b – II, 525b
Sagh Gharībler → Ghurabāʾ
al-Ṣaghānī, Aḥmad b. Muḥammad (X) vi, 600b – VI, 585b
al-Ṣaghānī, Raḍiyy al-Dīn Ḥasan (1252) i, 856a; iii, 435a, 1155b; iv, 504a; vi, 113b; vii, 190a, 637b; viii, **820a** – I, 879b; III, 449a, 1183b; IV, 526a; VI, 111b; VII, 190a, 637a; VIII, **848b**
Ṣaghāniyān → Čaghāniyān
Ṣaghīr (child/enfant) viii, **821b** – VIII, **849b**
Saghīr Aḥmed-zāde Meḥmed Bey (XIX) vi, 68b – VI, 66b
Saghrouchen, Aït s, 145a – S, 144b
Sagrajas → al-Zallāḳa
Saguiet-el-Hamra s, 294a – S, 294a
Ṣaḥāba viii, **827b** – VIII, **856b**
Saḥabī al Astarābādhī, Kamāl al-Dīn (1601) iv, 68b; viii, **829a** – IV, 72a; VIII, **857b**
Sahand vi, 494a, 498a, b, 499b, 500b – VI, 479b, 483b, 485a, b
Sāhādjī (Marātha) s, 246b – S, 246b
Sahara → al-Ṣaḥrāʾ; Takidda
Sahāranpūr district viii, **829b**; s, 312b – VIII, **858a**; S, 312b
al-Sahbāʾ i, 538b; iv, 1072b; viii, **830a** – I, 555a; IV, 1104a; VIII, **858b**
al-Ṣahbāʾ → Umm Ḥabīb
Saḥbān Wāʾil viii, **830a** – VIII, **859a**
Ṣaḥḥāflar-Sheykhī-zāde Esʿad Meḥmed Efendi (1848) viii, 564b – VIII, 582b
Ṣāḥib viii, **830b** – VIII, **859a**
Ṣāḥib b. ʿAbbād → Ibn ʿAbbād

Ṣāḥib ʿAṭāʾ Fakhr al-Dīn ʿAlī (XIII) i, 243b, 313a; ii, 81a; iv, 620a, b, 817a; vii, 479b – I, 250b, 323a; II, 82b; IV, 644b, 645a, 850a; VII, 479b
Ṣāḥib Atā Oghullarī viii, **831a** – VIII, **860a**
Ṣāḥib al-Bāb viii, **831b** – VIII, **860b**
Ṣāḥib al-Djawāhir → Nadjafī, Hadjdjī Shaykh Muḥammad Ḥasan Iṣfahānī
Ṣāḥib Fakhkh → al-Ḥusayn b. ʿAlī
Ṣāḥib al-Fuṣūl, Shaykh Muḥammad Ḥusayn s, 75b – S, 76a
Ṣāḥib Girāy Khān I (Crimea/-ée, 1551) i, 1075b; ii, 25a, 1113a; iv, 178a, 849b; v, 138a; viii, **832a** – I, 1108a; II, 25b, 1139a; IV, 185a, 882b; V, 140b; VIII, **860b**
Ṣāḥib al-Ḥamrāʾ i, 829a – I, 852a
Ṣāḥib al-ḥimār → Abū Yazīd al-Nukkārī
Ṣāḥib Ismāʿīl b. ʿAbbād → Ibn ʿAbbād
Ṣāḥib al-Khabar iv, 895b – IV, 928b
Ṣāḥib Khān b. Nāṣir al-Dīn Shāh (Khaldjī, Mālwā) (XVI) ii, 12b, 1128a; vi, 54b – II, 13a, 1154b; VI, 52b
Ṣāḥib Ḳirān viii, **833a** – VIII, **862a**
Ṣāḥib-Ḳirān-nāma (1062) iii, 114b, 153b – III, 116b, 157a
Ṣāḥib al-Madīna viii, **833b** – VIII, **862a**
Ṣāḥib al-Nāḳa → Yaḥyā b. Zikrawayh
Ṣāḥib al-Rākūba iv, 1005b – IV, 1038a
Ṣāḥib al-Shāma →Abū ʿAlī al-Muḥassin (Ṣābiʾ); Ḥusayn b. Zikrawayh
Ṣāḥib al-Zandj → ʿAlī b. Muḥammad al-Zandjī
Ṣaḥīfa viii, **834b** – VIII, **863b**
Ṣaḥīḥ i, 791a, 1297a; ii, 389b; iii, 25a; viii, **835b** – I, 814b, 1336b; II, 400a; III, 26b; VIII, **865a**
al-Sāḥil (Sahel) i, 539b; ii, 619a, 936b; iv, 778a; viii, **836b** – I, 556b; II, 634b, 958b; IV, 809b; VIII, **866a**
al-Sāḥilī, Abū Isḥāḳ al-Gharnāṭī (1346) ix, 757b – IX, 790b
Sāhir, Djelāl (Celal Sahir Erozan) (1935) viii, **838a** – VIII, **867b**
Sahl b. Abān iii, 856b, 857b – III, 880b, 881b
Sahl b. Bishr i, 1100b, 1102a; viii, 107a, 108a – I, 1133b, 1135a; VIII, 109b, 110a
Sahl b. Hārūn b. Rāhawayh (830) i, 1141a; iii, 309a, 1263a; vi, 108b, 920b; viii, **838b** – I, 1175b; III, 318b, 1296a; VI, 106b, 912b; VIII, **868a**
Sahl b. Maṣlīaḥ, Abū ʾl-Surrī (Karaite) iv, 605a – IV, 629b
Sahl b. Muḥammad al-Ṣuʿlukī i, 686b – I, 707b
Sahl b. Saʿd vi, 79a, 645b – VI, 77a, 631a
Sahl b. Salāma al-Anṣārī (IX) vi, 335a, b, 336a – VI, 319b, 320a
Sahl b. Sunbāṭ (IX) i, 660b, 844b; iv, 344b; ix, 254a – I, 681b, 867b; IV, 359b' IX, 261b
Sahl al-Dīn al-Kūhī ii, 362a – II, 372a
Sahl al-Tustarī, Abū Muḥammad b. ʿAbd Allāh (896) i, 1039a; ii, 858a; iii, 106a, 159a; vi, 225a, 570a, 672b; viii, 123a, **840a**; ix, 548b; x, 60b, 86b – I, 1070b; II, 878a; III, 102b, 162b; VI, 218b, 555a, 659a; VIII, 125b, **869b**; IX, 570b; X, 62b, 93b
Sahl al-Warrāḳ s, 306b – S, 306b
Sahla bint Suhayl b. ʿAmr (VII) vii, 394b – VII, 395b
Sahlān b. Musāfir iii, 258a – III, 265a
al-Sahlī, Abu ʾl-Ḥusayn (XI) vi, 638a – VI, 623a
Sahl-i Sumbatian → Sahl b. Sunbāṭ
Sahlid(e)s vi, 334b – VI, 319a
Sahm → Ashām
al-Sahm viii, **841b** – VIII, **871a**
Sahm, Banū vi, 137b, 145a – VI, 136a, 143a
al-Sahmī, Ḥamza b. Yūsuf (1038) viii, 518a, **842b** – VIII, 536a, **872a**
Ṣaḥna viii, **843a** – VIII, **872b**
Ṣaḥn-i Thamān (Medāris-i Thamāniyye) viii, 842b – VIII, 872a
Saḥnūn, ʿAbd al-Salām b. Saʿīd al-Tanūkhī (854) i, 249b, 250b, 685a; iii, 681a, 817a; v, 503b; vi, 265a, 278b, 279a, 352b, 353b, 739a; vii, 387b, 409a, 1052b; viii, 638a, **843a** – I, 257b, 258a, 706a; III, 703a, 840b; V, 507a; VI, 249b, 263b, 264a, 336b, 337b, 728a; VII, 389a, 410a, 1054b; VIII, 657a, **872b**
Saho iii, 6a; v, 522a; vi, 628a – III, 6b; V, 525b; VI, 613a
al-Saḥrāʾ i, 307a, 748b, 770a, 1177b, 1231b; iii, 288b; v, 653a, 755b, 757b, 890a, 1187b; vi, 83b; viii, **845b**; s, 328a – I, 316b, 771a, 793a, 1212b, 1268a; III, 297b; V, 657a, 761a, 763a, 896b, 1177b; VI, 81b; VIII, **875a**; S, 327b
Ṣaḥrāwīs (Morocco/Maroc) vii, 584a – VII, 584a
al-Ṣaḥṣāḥ b. Djandaba ii, 234a, 237b – II, 241a, 244b
Sahsārām iii, 449a; vi, 127b; viii, **850a** – III, 464a; VI, 126a; VIII, **879b**
al-Saḥūl viii, **850b** – VIII, **880a**
Saḥūr v, 372b – V, 373b
Ṣahyūn vi, 322b; viii, **850b** – VI, 307a; VIII, **880a**
Ṣāʾib, Mīrzā Muḥammad ʿAlī (1676) iv, 69a; vii, 341a, b; viii, 776a, **851a** – IV, 72b; VII, 343a; VIII, 802a, **880b**
al-Sāʾib b. Abi ʾl-Sāʾib al-Makhzūmī (VIII) iv, 898b; vii, 293a – IV, 931a; VII, 295a
al-Sāʾib b. Bishr → al-Kalbī, al-Sāʾib
Sāʾib Khāthir (683) i, 828a; ii, 428b, 878b; viii, **852b** – I, 851a; II, 439b, 902b; VIII, **882a**
Ṣaʿīd (Mawālī) s, 17a – S, 17b
al-Ṣaʿīd/ Ṣaʿīd Miṣr vii, 156b; viii, **861b** – VII, 158a; VIII, **892b**
Ṣāʿid, Āl-i s, 239b – S, 239a
Saʿīd, Banū (Alcalá) s, 382a – S, 382b
Saʿīd, Banū (Mānbidj) vi, 382a – VI, 366b
Saʿīd b. ʿAbd Allāh (VIII) viii, 985a – VIII, 1019b
Saʿīd b. ʿAbd Allāh (Ḳishn) (XVI) vi, 82b – VI, 80b
Saʿīd b. ʿAbd al-Malik (Umayyad(e)) (VIII) vi, 900a – VI, 891a
Saʿīd b. ʿAbd al-Raḥmān b. al-Ḥakam s, 10a – S, 9b
Saʿīd b. Abī ʿArūba (773) vii, 662b; viii, **853a**; s, 386b – VII, 662a; VIII, **882b**; S, 386b
Saʿīd b. Abīb (XIX) vii, 608a – VII, 607b
Saʿīd b. Aḥmad, Imām (Āl Bū Saʿīd) (1811) i, 1281b; x, 817a – I, 1321a; X,
Saʿīd b. ʿAmr al-Ḥarashī (VIII) i, 864a, 1134a; iii, 493b, 802b; v, 45a, 854a; vi, 623b, 820a – I, 888a, 1168b; III, 510b, 825b; V, 46b, 860b; VI, 608b, 810b
Saʿīd b. al-ʿĀṣ b. Saʿīd b. al-ʿAṣ b. Umayya (678) i, 695b, 704a; ii, 1141b; v, 56b, 499b; vi, 344b, 621b; viii, **853a**; ix, 826a; s, 103b, 298a – I, 716b, 725b; II, 1168b; V, 58a, 502b; VI, 328b, 606b; VIII, **882b**; IX, 860bS, 103a, 297b
Saʿīd b. Asad b. Mūsā b. Ibrāhīm s, 88a – S, 88a
Saʿīd b. al-ʿĀṣī (VII) vii, 497b – VII, 497b
Saʿīd b. Bā Ḥmād s, 114a – S, 113b
Saʿīd b. Bahdal al-Shaybānī ii, 90a; ix, 766b – II, 92a; IX, 800a
Saʿīd b. Barakāt i, 1032b – I, 1064b
Saʿīd b. Bashīr iv, 748b – IV, 778b
Saʿīd b. al-Biṭrīḳ (Eutychius) (940) vi, 143b; viii, **853b** – VI, 142a; VIII, **883a**
Saʿīd b. al-Djubayr (713) iv, 926a; vi, 107a; vii, 758a; ix, 555a – IV, 959a; VI, 105a; VII, 759b; IX, 577a
Saʿīd b. al-Ḥakam (1282) vii, 87a – VII, 88b
Saʿīd b. Ḥamdān vii, 414a – VII, 415b
Saʿīd b. Ḥibat Allāh i, 111b; iii, 754a – I, 114b; III, 777a

Saʿīd b. Ḥumayd (871) viii, **856a**; s, 25a, 284b, 352a – VIII, **885b**; S, 25a, 284b, 352a
Saʿīd b. al-Ḥusayn al-Anṣarī iv, 712b – IV, 741b
Saʿīd b. Idrīs b. Ṣāliḥ (VIII) vii, 941a – VII, 941b
Saʿīd b. ʿĪsā, Shaykh ii, 173b – II, 179a
Saʿīd b. Ḳays al-Hamdanī iii, 123b, 241b – III, 126a, 248a
Saʿīd b. Khafīf al-Samarḳandī vii, 210a – VII, 211b
Saʿīd b. Khalfān al-Khalīlī iv, 1085a; s, 355b, 356a – IV, 1116a; S, 355b
Saʿīd b. Khālid b. ʿAbd Allāh al-ʿUthmānī (VIII) vii, 648b – VII, 648b
Saʿīd b. Khazrūn b. Fulful v, 1180b – V, 1170b
Sāʿid b. Makhlad → Ibn Makhlad, Sāʿid
Saʿīd b. Manṣūr (842) vii, 663a, 691b; ix, 874a – VII, 662b, 691b; IX, 910b
Saʿīd b. Masʿūd I i, 424b – I, 436b
Saʿīd b. Masʿūd al-Hudhalī iii, 950a – III, 975a
Ṣāʿid b. Muḥammad al-Ustuwāʾī i, 146b – I, 151a
Saʿīd b. Mukhallad v, 621a – V, 625a
Saʿīd b. al-Musayyab al-Makhzūmī (712) ii, 888a; iii, 948a; v, 1124a, 1231b; vi, 140a; vii, 631b; ix, 204a; x, 29a. 821a; s, **311b** – II, 908b; III, 972b; V, 1120b, 1222a; VI, 138b; VII, 631a; IX, 210a; X, 30a, ; S, **311b**
Saʿīd b. Naṣr al-Dawla (Marwānid(e), Diyār Bakr) (1079) vi, 626b – VI, 611b
Saʿīd b. Muslat i, 709b – I, 729b
Saʿīd b. Sabandād s, 352a – S, 352a
Saʿīd b. Saʿīd b. al-ʿĀṣ (VII) ix, 787a – IX, 821b
Saʿīd b. Salm b. Kutayba (IX) ix, 487a – IX, 506a
Saʿīd b. Sulṭān, Sayyid (Āl Bū Saʿīd) (1856) i, 37b, 554b; iv, 887b; v, 183b; vi, 129a, 735b, 962a; vii, 227a; viii, **856b**; x, 194b, 818b; s, 355b – I, 38b, 572a; IV, 920a; V, 181a; VI, 127a, 724b, 954a; VII, 229a; VIII, **886a**; X, 210a, S, 355b
Saʿīd b. Taymūr b. Fayṣal (Āl Bū Saʿīd, ʿUmān) (1970) i, 1071b; iii, 1005a; vi, 735b; viii, 85b; x, 817a – I, 1103b; III, 1030a; VI, 725a; VIII, 87b; X,
Saʿīd b. ʿUthmān b. ʿAffān (VII) v, 181a, 551a; vii, 357a – V, 178b, 556a; VII, 359b
Saʿīd b. Yaʿḳūb al-Dimashḳī, Abū ʿUthmān (950) i, 1223b, 1340a; ii, 948b; vi 902b; viii, **858b** – I, 1259b, 1380b; II, 970b; VI, 894a; VIII, **887a**
Saʿīd b. Yarbūʿ Makhzūmī (VII) vi, 138b – VI, 136b
Saʿīd b. Yūsuf al-Ahansalī iii, 167a – III, 170b
Saʿīd b. Zayd (670) viii, **857a** – VIII, **887b**
Saʿīd Abū Bakr (1948) viii, **857b** – VIII, **888a**
Saʿīd Abu ʾl-Faḍāʾil Saʿīd al-Dawla al-Mawṣilī (Ḥamdānid(e), Alep(po)) (1002) iii, 130a; v, 928a; vi, 230b – III, 133a; V, 933b; VI, 224b
Saʿīd al-Aḥwal (Nadjāhid(e)) (1089) ix, 816a – IX, 851a
Saʿīd ʿĀlimkhān (amīr) (Bukhārā) vi, 771a – VI, 760a
Ṣāʿid al-Andalusī (1070) i, 235b; ii, 951b; vii, 55a, 413a, 551b, 553a; viii, **867b** – I, 243a; II, 973b; VII, 55b, 414a, 552a, 553b; VIII, **889a**
Saʿīd Atā (1218) i, 299a; x, 250a – I, 308a; X, 269a
Said Atba i, 371b – I, 382b
Ṣāʿid al-Baghdādī, Abū ʾl-ʿAlāʾ (1026) i, 601b; iii, 713a; vi, 713a; viii, **868a** – I, 621a; III, 735b; VI, 702a; VIII, **889b**
Saʿīd al-Bānī, Shaykh (XX) vi, 538b – VI, 523a
al-Saʿīd Baraka Khān i, 1234a; ii, 285a; iii, 679a; iv, 484b – I, 1270b; II, 293a; III, 701a; IV, 505b
Saʿīd al-Dīn Farghānī (Saʿīd-i Farghānī) (1292) viii, **860a**; x, 320b – VIII, **890a**; X, 345a
Saʿīd Djanbulāṭ ii, 444a; iii, 991b – II, 455b; III, 1016b
Saʿīd al-Djīlānī (Shāmī Pīr) (XX) vi, 86b – VI, 84b
Saʿīd Efendi/Pasha, Meḥmed Čelebi-zāde (1761) iii, 997b; vi, 1005a; viii, **859a** – III, 1022b; VI, 997b; VIII, **891a**
Saʿīd al-Fayyūmī iv, 111b – IV, 116b
Saʿīd al-Ḥabshī iii, 16a – III, 16b
Saʿīd Ḥalīm Pasha (1917) ii, 698b, 699a; vi, 983b; vii, 717a – II, 716b; VI, 976a; VII, 718a
Saʿīd Imām-zāde iii, 269a – III, 277a
Saʿīd Khān i, 852b; iii, 317a – I, 876b; III, 326b
al-Saʿīd al-Muʿtaḍid Abu ʾl-Ḥasan ʿAlī (Almohad(e)) (1248) v, 48b; vi, 593a – V, 50a; VI, 577b
al-Saʿīd Nāsir al-Dīn Baraka (Berke) b. Baybars (Mamlūk) (1280) vi, 322b, 326b – VI, 306b, 311a
Saʿīd of/de Palu, Shaykh (XX) vi, 888a – VI, 879b
Saʿīd Pasha (khedive) (1863) ii, 149b, 423b; iii, 1193b, 1194a; iv, 192a, 442a; v, 908b; vi, 23b, 25a, 75a; vii, 182b, 290a, 428b; viii, **859b**; s, 379a – II, 153b, 434b; III, 1223b, 1224a; IV, 200a, 462a; V, 914b; VI, 21b, 22b, 73a; VII, 182b, 292a, 429b; VIII, **891a**; S, 379b
Saʿīd Pasha, vizier (1912) ii, 643b; iii, 595a; vi, 983b; vii, 525b – II, 659b; III, 615b; VI, 976a; VII, 526a
Saʿīd Pasha Küčük → Küčük Saʿīd Pasha
Saʿīd al-Suʿadāʾ (Khānaḳāh) iv, 433a; vi, 454a; viii, **861a** – IV, 452a; VI, 439b; VIII, **891b**
Saʿīd al-Yaḥṣubī al-Maṭarī iv, 115a – IV, 120b
Saïda → Saʿīda
Saʿīda (town/ville) viii, **868b** – VIII, **898a**
Sāʿida b. Djuʾayya i, 115a; vii, 980b – I, 118a; VII, 981b
Saʿīdā Gīlānī (XVII) viii, **869a** – VIII, **898b**
Saʿīdābād → al-Sīradjān
Ṣaʿīdī s, 9b – S, 9a
Saʿīdī, Āl ii, 167b – II, 173a
Sāʿidī, Ghulām Ḥusayn v, 200b – V, 198a
Saʿīdov, Hārūn v, 618b – V, 622b
Saʿīdpūr s, 325a – S, 324b
Ṣāʾifa viii, **869b** – VIII, **899a**
Saifa Arʾad iii, 3b – III, 4a
Saifawa i, 1259b; s, 164a – I, 1297b; S, 163b
Ṣāʾl viii, **871a** – VIII, **900b**
Ṣāʾin al-Dīn Turka (1432) viii, 540a – VIII, 558a
Ṣāʾīn Ḳalʿa viii, **871b** – VIII, **901b**
Ṣāʾin Khānī, Banū (Türkmen) vi, 495a – VI, 480a
Saʿir viii, **872a** – VIII, **902a**
Saʿīr → Suʿayr
Saʾis iv, 215b – IV, 255a
Sāʾis s, 113b – S, 113a
al-Sāḳ viii, **872a** – VIII, **902a**
Saḳa v, 882b – V, 889a
Saka (language/langue) v, 37a, b – V, 38b, 39a
Saka, Banū v, 375b – V, 376b
al-Sakākīnī, Ḥasan b. Muḥammad (1342) vi, 279b – VI, 264b
Sakākīnī, Khalīl (XX) vi, 615b – VI, 600a
Saḳal v, 761a, 768a – V, 767a, 774a
Saḳal-ĭ Sherīf → Liḥya-yi Sherīf
Ṣaḳāliba i, 32a, 76a, 490b, 909b; iv, 344a, 1088b; v, 1120b; vii, 941b; viii, 623a, **872b**; s, 297b – I, 33a, 78a, 505b, 937a; IV, 359a, 1119b; V, 1117a; VII, 942a; VIII, 642a, **902a**; S, 297a
Sakan b. Saʿīd i, 600b – I, 620a
Saḳar viii, **881a** – VIII, **911a**
Saḳar, Banū v, 582a – V, 587a
Saḳarya (river/rivière) v, 880b; viii, 191a, 192a, **881a**; ix, 653b – V, 887a; VIII, 194a, 195a, **911b**; IX, 678b

Sakata → Sokoto
al-Saḳaṭī i, 32b, 157a; iii, 486b, 681a – I, 33b, 161b; III, 503b, 703a
al-Sakhāwī → ʿAlam al-Dīn al-Sakhāwī
al-Sakhāwī (1378) vi, 280a – VI, 265a
al-Sakhāwī, Shams al-Dīn (1497) i, 594b, 595a, 1109b, 1110a, 1309a; iii, 746a, 777b, 814b; iv, 509a; v, 54a; vi, 194a; vii, 296b; viii, **881b**; ix, 913b – I, 614a, 614b, 1142b, 1143a, 1349a; III, 769a, 801a, 838a; IV, 531b; V, 55b; VI, 178a; VII, 299a; VIII, **913a**; IX, 952a
Ṣakhr → Abū Sufyān
Ṣakhr (demon/démon) ii, 106b – II, 109a
Ṣakhr, Banū i, 528b; iv, 335a; viii, **882b** – I, 544b; IV, 349b; VIII, **912b**
al-Sakhtiyānī, Ayyūb (VIII) vii, 607a – VII, 607a
Sāḳī viii, **883b** – VIII, **913b**
al-Saḳīfa, Saḳīfat Banī Sāʿida viii, **887b** – VIII, **918a**
Sakīna viii, **888b** – VIII, **918b**
Sāḳī-nāma iv, 59a – IV, 62a
Sakīna bint Ḥusayn b. ʿAlī b. Abī Ṭālib vi, 611a – VI, 596a
Sāḳiya al-Ḥamrāʾ i, 1176b; v, 890a, 892a; vi, 142a; vii, 584a – I, 1211b; V, 896b, 898b; VI, 140b; VII, 584b
Saḳîz (Chios) i, 268b; iii, 210b, 252b, 629b; v, 557a; vi, 69a; viii, **889b**; s, 281b – I, 276b; III, 216b, 259b, 650b; V, 562a; VI, 67a; VIII, **920a**; S, 281b
Saḳîzlî Aḥmad Asʿad iv, 966b – IV, 998b
Saḳîzlî Edhem Pasha → Ibrāhīm Edhem Pasha
Saḳîzlî Ohannes Pasha (XIX) ii, 473b – II, 485b
al-Ṣakk ii, 79a, 382b – II, 80b, 393a
Saḳḳā → Saḳa
Saḳḳāʾ viii, **892a** – VIII, **922b**
al-Saḳḳāʾ → Ibrāhīm b. ʿAlī b. Ḥasan
Sakkākī (1400) viii, **892b** – VIII, **923a**
al-Sakkākī, Abū Yaʿḳūb Yūsuf (1229) i, 594a, 858a, 982a, 1116a; iv, 251b, 864a; v, 898a, 899b, 900b, 902b, 1026a; vii, 537a; viii, 427a, **893b** – I, 613b, 882a, 1012b, 1149b; IV, 262b, 897b; V, 904a, 906a, 907a, 908b, 1021b; VII, 537a; VIII, 441a, **924a**
Sakkākiyya iii, 660a – III, 681a
Sakkān, Ṣayḥkān → Mānd
Saḳḳāra viii, **894b** – VIII, **925a**
Saḳḳīz viii, **895b** – VIII, **926b**
al-Saḳlāwiyya, Nahr i, 485b – I, 499b
Ṣaḳr b. Muḥammad b. Sālim al-Kasīmī iv, 778b – IV, 810a
Ṣaḳr b. Rāshid al-Kāsimī iv, 778a – IV, 809a
Saḳr b. Sulṭān i, 1314a – I, 1354b
Sakrūdj s, 269a – S, 268b
Saksāwa/Saksīwa, Banū vi, 742a, 743a – VI, 731a, 732a, b
Saḳsīn vi, 415b; viii, **895b** – VI, 400b; VIII, **926b**
Saktāna, Banū vi, 742a – VI, 731a
Sakūn v, 119b – V, 122a, b
Sakūra vi, 258a – VI, 242b
Salā (town/ville) i, 85a, 780b, 1224b; iii, 500a, 1043a; v, 290a, 504a, b; vi, 124a, 293a, b, 294a, 356a, 572a, 573a, 592a, b, 741a, 742b; viii, **898b**; s, 63b, 145a, 397b – I, 87b, 804a, 1261b; III, 517a, 1069a; V, 289a, 507b; VI, 122a, 278a, b, 279a, 340a, 557a, 558a, 577a, 730b, 731b; VIII, **929b**; S, 64a, 144b, 398a
Ṣalābat Djang (XVIII) ii, 180a; iii, 320b; iv, 1023b; s, 280a – II, 185b; III, 331a, b; IV, 1055b; S, 280a
Ṣalābat Khān II (XVII) vi, 456b; viii, 74b – VI, 442a; VIII, 76b
Saladin → al-Malik al-Nāṣir I Ṣalāḥ al-Dīn (Ayyūbid(e))
Salādjiḳa v, 154a – V, 155a
Salaf i, 1112b; viii, **899b** – I, 1146a; VIII, **930b**
al-Salaf wa ʾl-Khalaf viii, **910a** – VIII, **931a**
Salafiyya i, 272b, 416b, 425b; ii, 295a, 412a; iii, 701a, 727b, 1145b; iv, 142b, 145b-160b; v, 595b, 597a; vii, 387b, 415b; viii, 447b, **900b**; s, 63b – I, 280b, 428b, 437b; II, 303a, 423a; III, 723a, 750a, 1174a; IV, 148b, 151b-167b; V, 599a, 601a; VII, 388b, 417a; VIII, 462b, **931b**; S, 64a
Ṣalāḥ (Shādhilī) (1645) i, 352b – I, 363a
Ṣalāḥ ʿAbd al-Ṣabūr (1981) viii, **909a** – VIII, **940a**
Salāḥ Bey (Constantine) (XVIII) i, 1247a – I, 1285a
Salah Birsel (XX) vi, 96a – VI, 93b
Ṣalāḥ al-Dīn, al-Malik al-Nāṣir Abū ʾl-Muẓaffar Yūsuf b. Ayyūb (Saladin) → al-Malik al-Nāṣir I Ṣalāḥ al-Dīn
Ṣalāḥ al-Dīn b. Mubārak al-Bukhārī iv, 298b – IV, 312a
Ṣalāḥ al-Dīn Abū Fāṭima Khātun s, 83b – S, 83a
Ṣalāḥ al-Dīn Khudā Bakhsh v, 44a – V, 45a
Ṣalāḥ al-Dīn, Shaykh (Maldives) (1950) vi, 247a – VI, 231a
Ṣalāḥ al-Dīn Mūsā → Ḳāḍī-zāde-i Rūmī
Ṣalāḥ al-Dīn al-Ṣafadī → al-Safadī
Ṣalāḥ al-Dīn, al-Malik al-Nāṣir Abū ʾl-Muẓaffar Yūsuf b. Ayyūb (Saladin) → al-Malik al-Nāṣir I Ṣalāḥ al-Dīn (Ayyūbid(e))
Ṣalāḥ al-Dīn Zarkūb ii, 394b, 397a – II, 405a, 407b
Ṣalāḥ Reʾīs (XVI) i, 1247a; v, 506b; x, 589b – I, 1285a; V, 519a; X,
Salakta vi, 364a – VI, 348a
Ṣalāla vi, 735b, 736a; viii, **914b**; s, 337a – VI, 725a; VIII, **946a**; S, 336b
Salam iv, 326a; v, 559a; viii, **914b** – IV, 340a; V, 564a; VIII, **946a**
Salām viii, **915b** – VIII, **947a**
Salāma, Banū → Tudjībid
Salāma, Būlus iii, 112a – III, 114b
Salāma b. al-Akwaʿ vii, 757b – VII, 759a
Salāma b. ʿĀṣim (854) i, 10b; ii, 807a; vi, 822a; x, 423b – I, 10b; II, 826a; VI, 812a; X, 464b
Salāma b. Budjayr ix, 422b – IX, 436b
Salama b. Dīnār (757) viii, **918a** – VIII, **949b**
Salāma b. Djandal (VI) viii, **918a** – VIII, **949b**
Salām b. al-Faḍl (805) x, 11b – X, 11b
Salāma b. al-Ḥārith i, 527a; v, 118b – I, 543a; V, 121a
Salāma b. Kuhayl s, 129b – S, 129a
Salāma b. Saʿīd iii, 653b – III, 675a
Salāma b. Ẓarib iv, 832b – IV, 865a
Salāma al-Ḥidjāzī (XX) vi, 75b, 750a; vii, 438a – VI, 73b, 739b;VII, 439a
Salāma al-Khayr v, 526a – V, 530a
Salāma Mūsā (1958) vi, 584a; viii, **919a**; ix, 517a – VI, 568b; VIII, **950a**; IX. 537a
Salamān and/et Absāl viii, **920a** – VIII, **951b**
Salamanca → Shalamanḳa
Salāmat ʿAlī → Dabīr
Salāmat Allāh s, 293b – S, 293b
al-Salāmī, Muḥammad iii, 821a – III, 844b
Salāmish (Süleymish) b. Baybars, Badr al-Dīn (Mamlūk) (1279) iv, 484b; vi, 322b – IV, 505b; VI, 307a
al-Salāmiyya iv, 202a; vi, 429a, 546b; viii, **921**a; s, 93b, 101a – IV, 211a; VI, 414b, 531b; VIII, **952b**; S, 93a, 100b
Sālār (military chief/chef militaire) viii, **924a** – VIII, **955b**
Salar (N-W. China) viii, **923b** – VIII, **955a**
Salār (XIV) i, 1126b, 1139a, 1325a; iii, 952a; vi, 323a – I, 1160b, 1173b, 1365b; III, 976b; VI, 307b

Salar (tribe/tribu) iv, 553b, 554b; v, 850b, 851a – IV, 577b, 578b; V, 855a
Sālār al-Dawla b. Muḥammad ʿAlī Shāh (Ḳādjār) (XX) ii, 652b; iv, 393b; v, 171a, 466a, 826a; vii, 432a, b – II, 669a; IV, 410b; V, 168b, 468b, 832a; VII, 433a, b
Sālār al-Dawla (Ḳādjār) iv, 393b – IV, 410a
Sālār al-Daylamī (XI) vii, 313a – VII, 315b
Sālār al-Dīn, Shaykh (XV) s, 114a – S, 113b
Sālār Djang (1883) ii, 158b; iii, 322b; viii, **924b** – II, 163b; III, 332a; VIII, **956a**
Sālār Khalīl (Andkhoy) v, 230a – V, 228a
Sālār al-Manṣūrī (XIV) vii, 991b – VII, 993a
Sālār Masʿūd Ghāzī → Ghāzī Miyān
Ṣalāt i, 188a; ii, 593b, 617a; iii, 1057a; iv, 321a, 771b; v, 74a, b, 75a, 82a, b, 395a, 424b, 709a; viii, **925a** – I, 193b; II, 608a, 632b; III, 1083a; IV, 335a, 802b; V, 76a, b, 77a, 84b, 85a, 396a, 426b, 714a; VIII, **956b**
Sālāt (Zāb) vi, 435a – VI, 420a
Ṣalāt al-Khawf viii, **934a** – VIII, **965b**
al-Ṣalatān i, 74a – I, 76a
Ṣalāt-i Maʿkūsa s, 313a – S, 313a
Ṣalawāt → Taṣliya
al-Salawī, ʿAbd al-Ḳādir b. ʿAbd al-Raḥmān (1897) vi, 351b – VI, 336a
Ṣalb viii, **935a** – VIII, **967a**
Saldjūḳ b. Duḳāḳ s, 245a – S, 245a
Saldjūḳid(e)s i, 20b, 98b, 236b, 465b, 510a, 639a, 661b, 799b, 900b, 1001a, 1336b, 1356a; ii, 4a, 344a, 855b, 1051a, 1108a; iii, 471b, 891b, 1255b; iv, 18b, 20a, 25a-29b, 208b, 294b, 347a, 1067a; v, 58a, 159b, 623a, 739a, 748a; vi, 64a, 148b, 198a, 231a, 261b, 274a, 327a, 366a, 379b, 453a, 482a, 493b, 499b, 523a, b, 524a, 530a, 540b, 549b, 550b, 620b, 809b, 854a, 872a, 900b; vii, 163b; viii, 163a, 472a, **936a**; ix, 266b; x, 42b, 690a; s, 29b, 59a, 119a, 146a, 149a, 154a, b, 168b, 192a, 195a, 205a, 245b, 279a, 326a, 378a – I, 21a, 101b, 244a, 479a, 525b, 659b, 682b, 822b, 927b, 1032a, 1376b, 1395a; II, 4a, 353b, 875b, 1075b, 1134a; III, 488a, 915b, 1288a; IV, 20a, 21b, 27a-32a, 218a, 307b, 362a, 1098b; V, 60a, 158b, 627a, 744b, 753b; VI, 61b, 147a, 182a, 224b, 246a, 258b, 311b, 350a, 364a, 438b, 468a, 479a, 484b, 508a, b, 514b, 525a, 534a, 535a, 605b, 799b, 845b, 862b, 891b; VII, 165a; VIII, 165b, 488a, **967b**; IX, 274b; X, 44a, 732b; S, 29b, 59b, 118b, 146a, 149a, 154a, b, 168b, 193a, 195a, 205a, 245b, 279a, 325b, 378b
—administration i, 256a, 318a, 340a, 420a, 434a, 439b, 731a, 1045b, 1159a; ii, 80b, 229b, 506a, 1083a; iii, 47a, 1088b, 1098b; iv, 267a, b, 807a, 975a; v, 159a; vii, 679b – I, 264a, 327b, 350b, 431b, 446a, 452a, 753a, 1077b, 1193b; II, 82b, 236b, 519a, 1108a; III, 49a, 1115b, 1125b; IV, 279a, b, 839b, 1007b; V, 158a; VII, 679b
—art, architecture v, 217b, 1144b – V, 215a, 1137a
—literature/littérature i, 570b; iii, 1158a – I, 589a; III, 1186b
Saldjūḳid)e)s Rūm i, 215a, 346a, 466b, 467b, 477a, 510a, 702b, 843b, 1107a, 1159b, 1190b; ii, 13b, 344b, 444b, 712a, 989a; iii, 215b, 737b; iv, 294b, 464b, 813b; v, 103b, 104a, 271b; viii, **948a** – I, 221b, 356b, 480a, 481b, 491a, 525b, 724a, 866b, 1140a, 1194a, 1225b; II, 13b, 354a, 456a, 730b, 1012a; III, 221b, 760a; IV, 307b, 485a, 846a; V, 106a, b, 269b; VIII, **980b**
Saldjūḳ-Shāh b. Muḥammad b. Malik-Shāh (Saldjūḳ) (1131) vi, 64a, 782a; viii, 943b – VI, 61b, 771b; VIII, 975b
Saldjūḳ-Shāh b. Salghur-Shāh b. Saʿd (Salghūrid(e)) (1263) i, 1358a; iv, 498a; vi, 482a – I, 1398b; IV, 519b; VI, 468a
Salé → Shāl(l)a
Saleha Abid Husain (XX) vi, 489a – VI, 475a
Salghīr → Salur, Banū
Salghūrid(e)s ii, 812a; iii, 337a, 1099b; iv, 29b; viii, **978b**; ix, 474a – II, 831a; III, 347a, 1126b; IV, 31b; VIII, **1012b**; IX, 492a
Salḥīn (Salḥum/Silḥīn) vi, 561b, 562a; viii, **979b** – VI, 546b, 547a; VIII, **1013b**
Sali Bahādur (Mongol, XIII) vi, 48b – VI, 47a
al-Ṣalīb viii, **980a** – VIII, **1014b**
Salifu bi Hama ii, 942a – II, 964a
Ṣāliḥ (adj.) viii, **982b** – VIII, **1017a**
Ṣāliḥ (prophet/-è) v, 124b, 421a; vi, 106a, 652b; viii, **984a** – V, 127b, 423a; VI, 103b, 638a; VIII, **1019a**
Ṣāliḥ (rāwī) (IX) i, 154a, 274b – I, 158a, 282b
al-Ṣāliḥ (Artuḳid(e), Mārdīn) (1408) vi, 540b, 541a – VI, 525b
Salīḥ, Banū i, 14b, 403a, 526a; viii, **981b**; ix, 507a – I, 15a, 414b, 542a; VIII, **1016a**; 526b
Ṣāliḥ b. ʿAbd al-Ḳuddūs (783) i, 128a; ii, 1072a; iv, 1004a; vi, 820b; viii, **984b** – I, 131b; II, 1097a; IV, 1036b; VI, 811a; VIII, **1019a**
Ṣāliḥ b. ʿAbd al-Raḥmān (VIII) vii, 359a – VII, 361b
Ṣāliḥ b. Aḥmad b. Ḥanbal i, 273b; iii, 158b – I, 281b; III, 162a
Salīḥ b. ʿAlī (Sharḳiyya Hināwī) (XIX) s, 355b – S, 355b
Ṣāliḥ b. ʿAlī b. ʿAbd Allāh b. al-ʿAbbās (769) i, 108b; iii, 398a; iv, 375b; vi, 428a, 506a, 775a; viii, 921b, **985a** – I, 111b; III, 410b; IV, 392a; VI, 413b, 491b, 764b; VIII, 953a, **1019b**
Ṣāliḥ b. Djanāḥ vii, 637b – VII, 637a
Ṣāliḥ b. Ḥusayn Djibil i, 762b – I, 785b
Ṣāliḥ b. Kuthayr iii, 659a – III, 680b
Ṣāliḥ b. Manṣūr (Artuḳide(e), Mārdīn, 1367) vi, 540b – VI, 525a
Ṣāliḥ b. Mirdās, Asad al-Dawla (Mirdāsid(e)) (1029) ii, 484a; iii, 86a, 130b, 398b; v, 921b, 929a, 933a; vi, 379b; vii, 116a, 577b – II, 496a; III, 88b, 133b, 411a; V, 927a, 934a, 937a; VI, 364a; VII, 118a, 578a
Ṣāliḥ b. Muḥammad Sharīf al-Adhamī (XI) vi, 379b – VI, 364a
Ṣāliḥ b. Musarriḥ (VII) ix, 766b s IX, 799b
Ṣāliḥ b. al-Naḍr (ʿayyār) (IX) viii, 795b – VIII, 822b
Ṣāliḥ b. Rashīd iii, 234a, 618a – III, 241a, 638b
Ṣāliḥ b. Saʿīd al-Ḥimyarī (864) vii, 941b – VII, 942a
Ṣāliḥ b. Ṭarīf (al-Bar(a)ghwāṭī) (795) i, 1044a, b, 1178b, 1186a; v, 1199b; vi, 743b; viii, **985a** – I, 1076a, 1213b, 1221a; V, 1190a; VI, 733a; VIII, **1019b**
Ṣāliḥ b. Wasīf (870) vii, 477a, 794a – VII, 476b, 795b
Ṣāliḥ b. Yaḥyā b. Ṣāliḥ b. Ḥusayn (1436) i, 946b; v, 791b; viii, **985b** – I, 976a; V, 797b; VIII, **1020a**
al-Ṣāliḥ ʿAlī b. Ḳalāwūn (Mamlūk) (1290) vi, 322b, 367b – VI, 307a, 351b
al-Ṣāliḥ Ayyūb → al-Ṣāliḥ Nadjm al-Dīn
Ṣāliḥ Bey (Ḳāsimī) iv, 723a – IV, 752a
Ṣāliḥ Bey (Algeria/Algérie) iii, 300a; v, 531b, 532a – III, 309a; V, 536a
Ṣāliḥ Čelebi → Djalālzāde
Ṣāliḥ Efendī (XVIII) vii, 30b – VII, 30b
Ṣāliḥ al-Fallāḥ (1748) vi, 327b – VI, 314a
al-Ṣāliḥ ʿImād al-Dīn Ismāʿīl, al-Malik (Mamlūk) (1345) vii, 992b; viii, **986a**; s, 255b – VII, 994a; VIII, **1020b**; S, 255a
al-Ṣāliḥ Ismaʿīl b. Badr al-Dīn Luʾluʾ, al-Malik (1261) vi, 900b; viii, **988a** – VI, 892a; VIII, **1023a**

al-Ṣāliḥ Ismāʿīl b. al-Malik al-ʿĀdil (Ayyūbid(e)) (XIII) vii, 274a – VII, 276a
al-Ṣāliḥ Ismāʿīl b. Nūr al-Dīn Maḥmūd (Zangid(e)) (1180) i, 1358a; ii, 283b; iii, 87a; vi, 781a; viii, 910b – I, 1398a; II, 291b; III, 89b; VI, 770b, 771a; VIII, 941b
Ṣāliḥ ʿItirdjī, Shaykh (XIX) vi, 175b – VI, 162a
Sāliḥ Muḥammad Djamāl (XX) vi, 176a – VI, 162a
al-Ṣāliḥ Nadjm al-Dīn Ayyūb, al-Malik (Ayyūbid(e)) (1249) i, 198b, 711a, 766a, b, 801a, 802b, 804a, 912b, 944b, 1124b; ii, 284a, 347b; iii, 184b, 875b, 967a, 989b; iv, 430a, b, 521a; v, 628a, 922a; vi, 143b, 314a, b, 320a, 321a, 325b, 326a, 507b; vii, 147b, 148a, 164b, 666a, 990a; viii, **988b** – I, 204a, 732b, 789a, b, 824b, 826a, 828a, 940a, 973b, 1158b; II, 292a, 357b; III, 188b, 899b, 991b, 1014a; IV, 448b, 449a, 543b; V, 632a, 927b; VI, 142a, 299a, b, 304b, 305b, 310a, b, 492b; VII, 149b, 150a, 166a, 665b, 990b; VIII, **1023a**
al-Ṣāliḥ Naṣir al-Dīn Muḥammad, al-Malik (Mamlūk) (1421) viii, **987b** – VIII, **1022b**
al-Ṣāliḥ Nūr al-Dīn, al-Malik → Nūr al-Dīn Maḥmūd b. ʿImād al-Dīn Zangī
Ṣāliḥ Pasha (1919) vi, 984b; vii, 188b – VI, 977a; VII, 188b
Ṣāliḥ Reʾīs → Ṣalāḥ Reʾīs
al-Ṣāliḥ, al-Malik b. al-Malik al-Ashraf Shaʿbān II (Mamlūk) (1389) i, 1050b, 1051a; ii, 159a – I, 1082a, b; II, 164a
al-Ṣāliḥ Ṣalāḥ al-Dīn Ḥādjdjī, al-Malik (Mamlūk) (1412) viii, **987a** – VIII, **1021b**
al-Ṣāliḥ Ṣalāḥ al-Dīn Ṣāliḥ, al-Malik (Mamlūk) (1360) iii, 239b; viii, **986b** – III, 246b; VIII, **1021a**
Ṣāliḥ Ṣidḳī Ef. Hadžihusejnović i, 1271b – I, 1310b
al-Ṣāliḥ Ṭalāʾiʿ ->Ṭalāʾiʿ b. Ruzzīk
Ṣāliḥ al-Yamanī, Shaykh (1696) ii, 87b – II, 89a
Ṣāliḥa Sulṭān bint Aḥmed III (Ottoman) (XVIII) vi, 862a – VI, 853a
Ṣāliḥa Sulṭān bint Maḥmūd II (Ottoman) (XIX) vi, 860a – VI, 851a
al-Ṣāliḥī, Abu ʾl-Ḥusayn iv, 986a; vii, 606b – IV, 1018b; VII, 606b
Ṣāliḥī, Muḥammad b. Muslim iv, 1163a; v, 806a – IV, 1195a; V, 811b
Ṣāliḥī, Muḥammad b. Yūsuf (1536) ix, 661a – IX, 687a
al-Ṣāliḥī al-Ḥadjdjār (1329) viii, 156a – VIII, 158b
Ṣāliḥid(e)s vii, 941a, b, 942a, b – VII, 941b, 942a, b
Ṣāliḥiyya (cemetery/cimetière, Damas(cus)) vi, 123a – VI, 120b
al-Ṣāliḥiyya (al-Djazīra) viii, **989b** – VIII, **1024b**
al-Ṣāliḥiyya (Miṣr) iii, 184b; vi, 325b – III, 188b; VI, 310a
al-Ṣāliḥiyya (Syria/-e) iv, 532b; viii, **989b**; s, 20b – IV, 555b; VIII, **1024b**; S, 20b
Ṣāliḥiyya (regiment/régiment) i, 1325a – I, 1365b
Ṣāliḥiyya (ṭarīḳa) viii, **990a**; s, 279a – VIII, **1024b**; S, 278b
Ṣāliḥiyya (Zaydī) iii, 244a – III, 251a
al-Ṣāliḥūn viii, **990a** – VIII, **1025a**
Ṣāliḥ-zāde Meḥmed Emīn (XVIII) vii, 724b – VII, 725b
Sālik v, 1029a – V, 1025a
Sālim viii, **990b** – VIII, **1025a**
Sālim (Mirzā-zāde Meḥmed Emīn) (1743) viii, **990b** – VIII, **1025a**
Sālim, Abu ʾl-ʿAlāʾ (mawlā) (VIII) iv, 755b; vii, 985a; x, 226a – IV, 785b; VII, 985b; X, 244a
Sālim, Banū vi, 647a, 650a – VI, 632b, 635b
Salīm, Muḥammad Ḳulī (1647) viii, **991b** – VIII, **1026b**
Salīm b. ʿAbd Allāh, Jumbe v, 278a – V, 276a
Sālim b. ʿAbd al-Raḥmān (XIII) viii, 631a – VIII, 650a
Sālim b. ʿAbdallāh i, 277b – I, 286a
Sālim b. Abī Ḥafṣa s, 129b – S, 129a
Sālim b. Aḥmad al-Nafrawī s, 44a – S, 44b
Salīm b. Akbar → Djahāngīr
Sālim b. Dhakwān vii, 562a – VII, 562b
Sālim b. Ghalbūn i, 250b – I, 258a
Sālim b. Idrīs al-Ḥabūḍī s, 338b – S, 338a
Sālim b. Ḳāsim iv, 749a – IV, 779a
Salīm b. Khalīl al-Nakḳāsh (1884) iv, 112a; vii, 902b; viii, **992b** – IV, 117a; VII, 903b; VIII, **1027a**
Sālim b. Mālik ii, 354b – II, 364a
Sālim b. Mubārak Āl Ṣabāh iii, 1066a; iv, 680b; v, 574b – III, 1092b; IV, 708b; V, 579b
Sālim b. Muḥammad, ʿIzz al-Dīn (1606) viii, **991b** – VIII, **1026a**
Sālim b. Mustafād (1024) vii, 116b – VII, 118b
Sālim b. Rāshid (ʿUmān) (1920) viii, 993b – VIII, 1028a
Sālim b. Rashīd (937) ix, 585a – IX, 607b
Sālim b. Sulṭān i, 1282a; viii, 856b – I, 1321a; VIII, 886a
Sālim b. Thuwaynī s, 355b – S, 355b
Sālim al-ʿAydūdī vi, 251a – VI, 235b
Sālim Abū ʾl-ʿAlāʾ (VIII) viii, 532b, 533a – VIII, 550b
Salīm Bābān i, 291a, 1217b – I, 300a, 1254a
Salīm al-Bishrī s, 132b – S, 132a
Sālim of/de Burullus (VIII) vi, 775a – VI, 764b
Salīm Čishtī, Shaykh (XVI) ii, 379b, 840a, b; vi, 127a, b, 690a; viii, 514a – II, 390a, 860a; VI, 125a, b, 677b; VIII, 531b
Salīm Fāris ii, 801a; iii, 593a – II, 820a; III, 613b
Sālim Isḥāḳ (1948) ix, 370a – IX, 382a
Salīm Ḳabūdān i, 929a – I, 957b
Sālim al-Kharūsī i, 1283a – I, 1321b
Sālim al-Maghribī i, 280b – I, 289a
Salīm al-Nakḳāsh iv, 112a – IV, 117a
Salīm Shāh → Islām Shāh Sūrī
Sālim al-Tūmī i, 678a; ii, 520a – I, 699a; II, 533a
Salīma, Banū iv, 500b; vi, 645a, 647b, 649a, 653b; s, 131a – IV, 522a; VI, 630b, 632b, 634a, 639a; S, 130b
Salīma Sulṭāna Bēgum (XVI) i, 1136a, b; ii, 380a; vi, 488b – I, 1170b, 1171a; II, 390b; VI, 474b
Salīmgaṛh vi, 132a – VI, 130a
al-Sālimī (XIV) iii, 935a – III, 959b
al-Sālimī → ʿAbd Allāh b. Ḥumayyid
al-Sālimī, Abū Muḥammad ʿAbd Allāh b. Ḥumayd (1914) i, 736a; viii, **993a**; s, 356a – I, 758a; VIII, **1028a**; S, 356a
Sālimiyya (Baṣra) i, 153a; iii, 269b; viii, 840b, **993b**; x, 60b – I, 157a; III, 277b, 590b; VIII, 870a, **1028b**; X, 62b
Salimu, al-Ḥādjdj → Karamba
Sāliyāne (Salyāne) viii, **994a** – VIII, **1029a**
Ṣalkhad (Ṣarkhad) (town/ville) i, 780b; iii, 293a; vii, 274a; viii, **994b**; s, 391a – I, 804a; III, 302a; VII, 276a; VIII, **1029b**; S, 391b
al-Sallāl, ʿAbd Allāh (Yemen) (XX) ix, 2a – IX, 2a
Sallām, Āl i, 95b – I, 98a
Sallām al-Tardjumān (IX) x, 236a – X, 254b
Sallāma Umm al-Manṣūr (Abbāsid(e)) (VIII) vi, 427b – VI, 412b
Sallāma al-Zarḳāʾ ii, 428b; iii, 2b, 682a; iv, 821b; viii, **996b** – II, 439b; III, 2b, 704a; IV, 854b; VIII, **1031a**

Sallāmat al-Ḳass   viii, 996b – VIII, 1031b
al-Sallāmī   s, 326b – S, 326a
al-Sallāmī, Abū ʿAlī al-Ḥusayn b. Aḥmad al-Bayhaḳī (X)
    viii, 996b – VIII, 1031b
al-Sallāmī, Madjd al-Dīn Ismāʿīl (XIV)   vi, 315b; vii,
    170a, 176a – VI, 300b; VII, 171b, 178a
Sallārid(e)s   → Musāfirid(e)s
Salm b. ʿAmr al-Khāsir (802)   i, 1081b; vi, 437b; viii,
    997a – I, 1114a; VI, 423a; VIII, 1032a
Salm b. Ḳutayba (776)   iv, 493b; vii, 798b –
    IV, 514b; VII, 800a
Salm b. Ziyād b. Abīhī, Abū Ḥarb (692)   i, 5a, 47b; v,
    853b; vii, 357a; viii, 997b; s, 26a – I, 5a, 49a; V,
    860a; VII, 359b; VIII, 1032a; S, 26a
Salmā   → Adjaʾwa-Salmā
Salma bint ʿAmr Umm ʿAbd al-Muṭṭalib b. Hāshim (VI)
    i, 80a; iii, 260a; vi, 474b; vii, 757a – I, 82a; III, 267b;
    VI, 460b; VII, 758b
Salma b. Saʿd   → Salāma b. Saʿīd
Salma bint al-Ṣāʾigh umm al-Nuʿmān III (Lakhmid(e))
    (VI)   vii, 568b – VII, 569b
Salmān, Banū   vi, 436a – VI, 421a
Salmān, Masūd-i Saʿd-i (1121)   viii, 448b; s, 21a –
    VIII, 463b; S, 21b
Salmān, Shaykh   ii, 181a; iv, 314b, 675a – II, 187a; IV,
    328b, 702b
Salmān b. Ḥamad   i, 944a; iv, 954a – I, 973b; IV, 986b
Salmān b. Rabīʿa al-Bāhilī (VII)   i, 635b, 636a, 660a,
    921b, 1041a; iv, 343b; ix, 254a, 488a –
    I, 656b, 681a, 949b, 1072b; IV, 358a; IX, 261a, 507a
Salmān al-Fārisī (VII)   i, 114a, 258a, 922b; ii, 846a, b,
    847a, 850a, 1094b; iii, 470b; v, 430a, 945b, 946a; vi,
    225b; vii, 370b, 460a, 517a, b; viii, 711b, 998a; ix,
    819b –
    I, 117a, 266a, 950a; II, 866a, b, 867a, 870a, 1120b;
    III, 487a; V, 432b, 949a, b; VI, 219b; VII, 372b,
    460a, 517b, 518a; VIII, 731b, 1033a; IX, 854b
Salmān Pāk   → Salmān al-Fārisī
Salmān Sāwadji (1376)   i, 300a, 764b; ii, 439b; iv, 66a,
    67a; viii, 448b, 997b – I, 309a, 787b; II, 451a; IV,
    69b, 70b; VIII, 463b, 1032b
Salmāniyya   viii, 998a – VIII, 1033a
Salmās (Irān)   viii, 998a – VIII, 1033a
Salmās (Mākū)   vi, 203a – VI, 187a
Salmon b. Jeroham   → Sulaymān b. Ruhaym
Sāl-nāme   i, 75a, 975a; viii, 898a – I, 77a, 1005b; VIII,
    928b
Salomon   → Sulaymān
Salonica   → Selānīk
Salor, Banū   vi, 416a, b – VI, 401a, b
Salsabīl   viii, 999a – VIII, 1034a
Ṣalṣāl (giant/géant)   viii, 972b – VIII, 1006b
al-Salṭ (al-Salt) (town/ville)   viii, 999b –
    VIII, 1034b
al-Ṣalt b. Mālik (IX)   i, 140b, 141b; iii, 748b, 757a – I,
    145a, b; III, 771b, 780a
Salṭana   viii, 1000b – VIII, 1035b
Saltes   → Shalṭīsh
Saltuḳ-oghullarī (Erzurum)   i, 639a; ii, 712a; iv, 578b,
    670a; viii, 1001b –
    I, 659b; II, 730b; IV, 602a, 697a; VIII, 1036a
Saltūḳid(e)s   → Saltuḳ-oghullarī
Salūḳī   iv, 491a; viii, 1001b – IV, 512a;
    VIII, 1037a
Salūḳiyyīn   ii, 352a, 1122b – II, 361b, 1148b
Salūl, Banū   viii, 1002a – VIII, 1037b
Salur, Banū   v, 582a; viii, 1005a; s, 146b, 280b, 281a –
    V, 587a; VIII, 1040a; S, 146b, 280b
Salur Ḳazan   s, 280b – S, 280b
Salvatierra → Shalbatarra
Salwā   viii, 1006a – VIII, 1041a

Salwān (Morocco/Maroc)   vi, 892a – VI, 883b
Sālyāne   ii, 83a, 723a – II, 85a, 741b
Sām (Shem)   viii, 1007a – VIII, 1042a
Sām (Sīstān)   viii, 1011a – VIII, 1046a
Sām Mīrzā b. Shāh Ismāʿīl I (1566)   i, 228b;
    iv, 68b; vii, 530a; viii, 775b, 1012a- I, 235a; IV, 72a;
    VII, 530b; VIII, 801b, 1047a
Samāʾ (heaven/ciel)   viii, 1041a – VIII, 1049a
Samāʿ   viii, 1018a – VIII, 1052b
Sāma b. Luʾayy, Banū   vi, 266b – VI, 251b
Samāʾ al-Dawla (Ayyūbid(e)) (1028)   iii, 331a – III,
    341a
al-Samad, al-Ḥusayn b. ʿAbd (1576)   viii, 777b – VIII,
    803b
Ṣamad Khān (Marāgha) (XX)   vi, 502b – VI, 488a
Samāḥa, Masʿūd   v, 1255b – V, 1246b
Samak   viii, 1020b – VIII, 1055a
Samakatān   → al-Nudjūm
Samālū (al-Maṣṣīṣa)   vi, 778b – VI, 768b
Sāmāna   vi, 47b, 48b, 50a, 294b, 664b – VI, 46a, 47a,
    48b, 279b, 650b
Samandağ → al-Suwaydiyya
Samandal   viii, 1023b – VIII, 1058b
Samandar   ii, 86a; iv, 1173a – II, 87b; IV, 1206b
al-Samʿānī, ʿAbd al-Karīm b. Muḥammad Tādj al-Dīn
    (1166)   i, 146b, 594b; iii, 327b, 756a; vi, 263a,
    846a; vii, 776b; viii, 1024b; s, 195a, 246a, 304a,
    326a, b –
    I, 151a, 614a; III, 337b, 779a; VI, 247b, 836b; VII,
    778b; VIII, 1059a; S, 195a, 246a, 304a, 325b, 326a
al-Samʿānī, Abū ʾl-Ḳāsim (1140)   viii, 1024a – VIII,
    1059a
al-Samʿānī, Abū Saʿīd (XII)   ix, 847b – IX, 883a
Sāmānid(e)s   i, 33a, 125b, 278a, 421b, 434a, 439b,
    570b, 662a, 688a, 1001a, 1294a, 1344b, 1354b; ii,
    192b, 253b, 748b, 791a, 1050b, 1082b; iii, 46b,
    1113b, 1116a; iv, 18b, 21b-22b, 60b, 188b, 189a,
    266b, 1066a; v, 622b, 856a, b; vi, 65a, b, 66a, 115b,
    261b, 276a, 340a, 432b, 433a, 522a, 557b, 620b,
    720a, 832b, 941b; vii, 193a, 477b, 1015a; viii, 472a,
    1025b; x, 741b; s, 21b, 35a, 72b, 149a, 204a, 245a,
    356b, 411a –
    I, 33b, 129a, 286b, 433a, 446a, 452a, 589a, 682b,
    709a, 1032a, 1333b, 1384b, 1393b; II, 198b, 261a,
    767a, 810a, 1075a, 1107b; III, 48a, 1141a, 1143b;
    IV, 20a, 23a-24a, 63b-64a, 197a, 278b, 1097b; V,
    626b, 862b, 863a; VI, 62b, 63a, b, 113a, b, 246a,
    261a, 324a, 418a, 506b, 542a, 605b, 709a, 823a,
    933b; VII, 193a, 477a, 1017a; VIII, 487b, 1060b; S,
    21b, 35a, 73a, 149a, 203b, 245a, 356a, 411a; X,
Sāmānkhudāt   i, 685a – I, 706a
Samannūd   vi, 119a; viii, 1031a – VI, 116b;
    VIII, 1066b
Ṣamanto   vi, 508a – VI, 493b
Samar   iii, 369b – III, 381b
Samara   → Kuybishev
Samarinda   s, 150a, 151a – S, 150b, 151a
Samarita(i)ns   → al-Sāmira
Samarḳand   i, 32a, 46b, 135a, 147b, 148a, 848a; ii,
    43a, 61b, 746a; iii, 711b, 799a, 1137b; iv, 33a; v,
    541b, 551a, 853b, 1149a; vi, 16a, 186a, 273b, 418a,
    419a, 494b, 513a, 524b, 525a, 601b, 618b, 633b,
    720a, 765a, 767a, 769a; vii, 313b; viii, 1031b; ix,
    427a; s, 50b, 97a, 125b, 340a –
    I, 33a, 48a, 139a, 151b, 152a, 871a; II, 44a, 62b,
    764b; III, 734a, 822b, 1166a; IV, 35b; V, 545b, 556a,
    860b, 1140a; VI, 14b, 169b, 258b, 403a, 404a, 480a,
    509a, b, 586a, b, 603b, 618b, 709a, 754a, 756a, 758a;
    VII, 316a; VIII, 1067a; IX, 443a; S, 51a, 96b, 124b,
    339b
al-Samarḳandī   → ʿAbd al-Razzāḳ; Abu ʾl-Layth; Abū

Muḳātil; al-Hāfiẓ; Djahm b. Ṣafwān; al-Hāfiẓ; Nīẓāmī ʿArūḍī
al-Samarḳandī, ʿAlāʾ al-Dīn Abū Bakr Muḥammad (1145) iv, 690a; vi, 846a – IV, 718a; VI, 837a
Samarḳandī, Bābā Ḥaydar (1550) vii, 936a – VII, 936b
Samarḳandīʾ, Badr al-Dīn v, 301a – V, 300a
al-Samarḳandī, Nāṣir al-Dīn (1258) vii, 969b – VII, 969b
al-Samarḳandī, Shams al-Dīn Muḥammad Ashraf (1303) vii, 566a; viii, **1038a** – VII, 567a; VIII, **1074a**
Samarḳandī, Sharaf al-Dīn Ḥusayn b. Ḥasan (XIII) viii, 542a – VIII, 560a
Sāmarrāʾ i, 18b, 211b, 897b; ii, 745b; iii, 1255a; iv, 215a, 384a, 653b, 1166a; v, 293a; vi, 198a, 338b, 364a, b, 504b, 552b, 600a, 656b, 660a, 667a; vii, 776b; viii, **1039a**; ix, 44b; s, 94a, 95a, 106a, 251a, 256a, b, 342a – I, 19a, 218a, 924b; II, 764a; III, 1288a; IV, 224b, 400b, 679b, 1198a; V, 292b; VI, 182a, 322b, 348a, b, 489b, 537a, 585a, 642a, 645b, 653a; VII, 778a; VIII, **1074b**; IX, 45b; S, 93b, 94a, b, 105b, 251a, 255b, 256a, 341b
—dams/barrages ii, 948a; iii, 1251a – II, 969b; III, 1283b
—great mosque/la grande mosquée i, 620a, b, 622b, 830a, 1228a, 1315b; iii, 287a – I, 639b, 640b, 643a, 853b, 1264b, 1356a; III, 295b
—monuments i, 457b, 1346a; ii, 114a; iii, 1267b – I, 472a, 1386a; II, 116b; III, 1300b
al-Sāmarrī → ʿAlī b. Muḥammad; Muḥammad b. ʿAbd Allāh
al-Samarrī → al-Simmārī
Samastha Kerala Jamiat-ul-Ulema (Mappila) vi, 460b – VI, 446a
al-Samaṭrānī → Shams al-Dīn
Samāwa (ʿIrāḳ) vii, 582b, 769a; viii, **1041a** – VII, 583a, 771a; VIII, **1076b**
al-Samawʾal b. ʿĀdiyāʾ (VI) i, 565a, 690a; iii, 1177a; iv, 303a; viii, **1041a** – I, 583a, 711a; III, 1206a; IV, 316b; VIII, **1077a**
Samawʾal b. Yaḥyā al-Maghribī (1175) i, 520b; ii, 238a, 552b; iv, 600a; x, 112a, 960b – I, 536b; II, 245a, 566a; IV, 624a; X, 121a
Sambas viii, 1042a; s, 150a, b, 151a – VIII, **1077b**; S, 150b, 151a
Sambāṭ I i, 507a, 637a; ii, 679b – I, 522b, 658a; II, 696b
Sambāṭ II i, 507b, 637b, 638a – I, 522b, 658b
Śambhadjī (Marāṭha) (1689) i, 769b; iv, 1023b; vi, 535a; s, 246b – I, 792b; IV, 1055b; VI, 519a; S, 246b
Śambhadjī II b. Rādjarām (Marāṭha) (1760) vi, 535a, b – VI, 519b, 520a
Sambhal → Murādābād
Ṣam viii, **1042b** – VIII, **1078a**
al-Samḥ b. Mālik al-Khawlānī i, 608b; iii, 587b; v, 510a; s, 81b – I, 628a; III, 608a; V, 514a; S, 81b
Samhar vi, 641b, 642b – VI, 626b, 627b
al-Samhūdī, Nūr al-Dīn Abu ʾl-Ḥasan ʿAlī (1506) vi, 653a, 658b; viii, **1043a**; s, 234b, 304b, 350a – VI, 638b, 644a; VIII, **1078b**; S, 234a, 304a, 350a
Sāmī (1733) vii, 839a – VII, 840b
al-Samī (Azimuth) viii, **1054a** – VIII, **1089b**
al-Sāmī, ʿAbd al-Aʿlā b. ʿAbd al-Aʿlā (805) viii, 853a – VIII, 882b
Sāmī, Shems ül-Dīn (1904) viii, **1043b** – VIII, **1079a**
Sāmī al-Bārūdī iii, 59a – III, 61b
Sāmī Bey → Shams al-Dīn Sāmī
Sāmī Pasha (XX) ii, 637b – II, 653b
al-Sāmira viii, **1044a** – VIII, **1080a**
Samīrān → Shamīrān
al-Sāmirī viii, **1046a** – VIII, **1082a**
Samīṣād vi, 508b – VI, 494a
al-Ṣāmit viii, **1046b** – VIII, **1082b**
al-Samlālī, Aḥmad b. Mūsā (1564) vi, 350a – VI, 334a
al-Samlālī, al-Sayyida Maryam bint Masʿūd al-Sūsī (1751) vi, 357a – VI, 341a
al-Samlālī, Yibūrk vi, 350a – VI, 334b
Samlis ii, 770b – II, 789a
Sammā (dynasty, Sind) i, 627b; iii, 419b; vi, 189b; viii, **1047a** – I, 648b; III, 433a; VI, 173a; VIII, **1082b**
Sammād → Kannās
al-Sammāk, Abū Djaʿfar (IX) ix, 47a – IX, 60a
al-Ṣammān i, 536b; ii, 92a; viii, **1048a** – I, 553a; II, 93b; VIII, **1084a**
al-Sammān, Muḥammad b. ʿAbd al-Karīm (1775) x, 248b – X, 267b
al-Sammāniyya iv, 991b, 993a; x, 4b, 248b – IV, 1024b, 1026a; X, 4b, 267b
Sammāsī, Khwādja Muḥammad (XIV) vii, 933b – VII, 934a
Sammūr → Fanak; Farw
Sammūra iii, 842a – III, 865b
Ğal-Samn i, 541a; ii, 1057b; viii, **1048b** – I, 558a; II, 1082a; VIII, **1084a**
Sāmogaṙh iii, 202a, b – III, 207b
Samori Turé (1900) i, 297a; ii, 63a, 1003b, 1132b; v, 253a; viii, **1048b** – I, 306b; II, 64a, 1027a, 1159b; V, 251a; VIII, **1084b**
Samos → Sīsām
Sampit s, 150b – S, 150b
Samrū (Sumrū), Bēgam (1836) viii, **1049b** – VIII, **1085b**
al-Ṣamṣām, Ḥasan i, 986b; iii, 788a; iv, 497a – I, 1017a; III, 811a; IV, 518b
Ṣamṣām al-Dawla (Iran) (XX) iii, 1193a – III, 1223a
Ṣamṣām al-Dawla, Abū Kālīdjār (Būyid(e)) (998) viii, **1050a** -VIII, **1086a**
Ṣamṣām al-Dawla, Shāh Nawāz Khān (1758) → Maʾāthir al-Umarāʾ
Ṣamṣām al-Dawla Marzubān (Būyid(e)) (998) i, 1351a; ii, 749a; iii, 128b, 244b; iv, 220a; v, 452b; s, 4a, 118a, 119b, 398a – I, 1396a; II, 767b; III, 131b, 251b; IV, 230a; V, 455b; S, 3b, 117b, 119a, 398b
Ṣamṣām al-Dawla Shāhnawāz ->Maʾāthir al-Umarāʾ
Ṣamṣām al-Salṭana, Nadjaf Ḳulī Khān (1930) viii, **1050b** – VIII, **1086b**
al-Ṣamṣāma i, 453a; viii, **1051b** – I, 466a; VIII, **1087a**
Samsat → Sumaysāṭ
Ṣāmsūn (Samsun) i, 476b; ii, 20b, 446b; iv, 575b; viii, **1052a** – I, 490b; II, 20b, 458a; IV, 598b; VIII, **1087b**
Samudra, Pangeran s, 150b – S, 150b
Samudra-pasai (Sumatra) vi, 210b, 702a – VI, 195a, 690a
Samuel → Ushmūʾīl
Samuel ben Ḥofni (1034) iv, 305b; vii, 539b – IV, 320b; VII, 539b
Samuel b. Moses al-Maghribī iv, 306b, 605b – IV, 320b, 630a
Samuel b. Nagrēlla i,130b; ii, 1012b, 1016b – I, 134a; II, 1036b, 1040a
Samūʾīl b. Yaḥyā b. ʿAbbās al-Maghribī al-Andalusī (1174) vii, 199b – VII, 200a
Samūm viii, **1056a** – VIII, **1091b**
Ṣanʿāʾ i, 102b, 440b, 551a, 554b; ii, 1096a; iii, 125a; v, 808b; vi, 36a, 138b, 433b, 436a, b, 437a, 438b, 439a, 559a, 566a, 651a, 667a, 677a; vii, 270a; viii, 184a, 235b; ix, **1a**; s, 22a, b, 61b, 62a, 115b, 236a, 335a,

337b, 338a, 387b –
I, 105b, 453b, 568b, 572b; II, 1121b; III, 128a; V, 814b; VII, 272a; VI, 34a, 137a, 418b, 419a, 421a, b, 422a, b, 424a, b, 543b, 551a, 636b, 653a, 663b; VII, 272a; VIII, 186b, 240b; IX, **1a**; S, 22b, 62a, b, 115a, 236a, 334b, 337a, 338a, 388a
Ṣanāʿ (near/près de Ṣanʿāʾ) s, 236a – S, 236a
Sanāʾ al-Mulk al-Ḥusayn i, 440a – I, 452b
al-Sanā al-Rāhib s, 396a – S, 396b
Sānabād(h) vi, 335b, 714a – VI, 320a, 702b
Sanābira iv, 664b – IV, 691a
Sanad (Sind) b. ʿAlī (864) vi, 600a; vii, 196b, 199b – VI, 584b; VII, 196b, 200a
Sanadjāt ix, **3a** – IX, **3a**
al-Sanādjiḳ iii, 186b – III, 191a
al-Ṣanāfīrī iii, 776a – III, 799b
Sanāʾī, Abu ʾl-Madjd Madjdūd b. Ādam (1180) i, 764b, 1019a; iv, 57b, 61b, 63a; vi, 609a; vii, 535b; ix, **3b**; s, 240a, 334a, 416b –
I, 787b, 1050b; IV, 61a, 65a, 66b; VI, 594a; VII, 535b; IX, **3b**; S, 240a, 333b, 416b
Ṣanam ix, **5b** – IX, **5b**
al-Ṣanam iv, 384a – IV, 401a
Ṣanam ḳādis ix, **6a** – IX, **6b**
Sanamayn vi, 548a – VI, 532b
Sanandadj ix, **6b**; s, 136b, 145b – IX, **6b**; S, 136a, 145a
al-Ṣanʿānī, ʿAbd al-Razzāḳ b. Ḥammām (827) v, 1162a; vii, 571b, 663a; viii, 374a; ix, **7a**; x, 86a – V, 1151b; VII, 572a, 662b; VIII, 387a; IX, **7b**; X, 93b
al-Ṣanʿānī, Abū Firās Daghtham (Duʿaym) (XII) vi, 433b – VI, 419a
al-Ṣanʿānī, Ḍiyāʾ al-Dīn Shaʿbān (1736) ix, **8a** – IX, **8a**
al-Ṣanʿānī, Ḥanash b. ʿAbd Allāh (VIII) s, 81b – S, 81b
al-Ṣanʿānī, Muḥammad b. ʿAbd al-Aʿlā (869) x, 11b – X, 11b
Ṣanāriyya iv, 345a; v, 487b, 488a – IV, 359b; V, 490b, 491a
Ṣanʿatī (1644) vi, 837a – VI, 828a
Ṣanʿatīzāda, ʿAbd al-Ḥusayn iv, 72b; v, 198a – IV, 76b; V, 195b
Ṣanāw vi, 80a – VI, 78a
Sanāwa-Shumba vi, 384b – VI, 368b
al-Ṣanawbarī, Abū Bakr Muḥammad b. Aḥmad (945) iv, 55b; vi, 604b; vii, 566b; ix, **8a**, 652b – IV, 58b; VI, 589a; VII, 567b; IX, **8b**, 677bb
Sanbar b. al-Ḥasan iv, 664a – IV, 691a
Sanbāt → Sambāṭ
Sancho Garcès Abarca (Navarra) (X) vi, 431b – VI, 417a
Sancho Garcia (Castille) (XI) i, 75b, 76a – I, 78a
Sancho Gimeno → Jimeno
Sanchuelo → ʿAbd al-Raḥmān b. Muḥammad b. ʿAbī ʿĀmir
Sand Seas, Arabian → Nafūd
Sandābil i, 116a; ix, **9a** – I, 119b; IX, **9b**
Ṣandal (X) iv, 459a – IV, 479b
Ṣandal (sandal/santal) ix, **9a** s IX, **9a**
Ṣandal al-Ḥalabī (X) vi, 1040a – VI, 1033b
Ṣandj (sindj) ix, **9b** – IX, **10a**
Sandjābī, Karīm (XX) vii, 451a – VII, 452b
Sandjaḳ i, 468b, 469a, 652a, 655b, 1263b, 1264a; ii, 722b, 723b; iv, 563b, 1094b; v, 776a; ix. **11b** – I, 482b, 483a, 672b, 676a, 1302a, b; II, 741a, 742a; IV, 586a, 1125b; V, 782a; IX, **12a**
Ṣandjaḳ Beyi → Sandjaḳ
Sandjaḳdār i, 1135a – I, 1169a
Sandjaḳ-i Sherif v, 19a; ix, **13b** – V, 19b; IX, **14a**
Sandjan v, 1113a, b – V, 1109b
Sandjar b. Malik-Shāh Nāṣir al-Dīn (Saldjūḳ) (1157) i, 94b, 283a, 353b, 504a, 524a, 662a, 687a, 750a, 940a, 1001b, 1052a, 1132a; ii, 81a, 333b, 382a, 893b, 1052a, 1100a, 1101a, 1109a, 1143b; iii, 196a, b, 336b, 345a, 1099a, b, 1114b; iv, 18b, 29a, b, 217b, 466a, 581b, 1067a, 1186a; v, 58b, 439a, 454a; vi, 14a, b, 64a, b, 85b, 493b, 524a, 600a, 620a, b, 628a, 782a, 966a; vii, 408a, 489b, 543b, 733b, 755a, b; viii, 76a, 81b, 942b; ix, **15a**; s, 65a, 245b, 279a, 326a, 333b –
I, 97a, 291b, 364a, 519a, 540a, 683a, 708a, 772b, 968b, 1032a, 1083b, 1084a, 1166a; II, 82b, 343b, 392b, 914b, 1076b, 1126a, 1127a, 1135a, 1170b; III, 200b, 201b, 346b, 355b, 1126a, b, 1142a; IV, 20a, 31a, b, 227a, 487a, 604b, 1099a, 1219a; V, 60a, 441b, 456b; VI, 12b, 13a, 61b, 62a, b, 83b, 479a, b, 508b, 585b, 605a, b, 613a, 771b, 958b; VII, 409a, 489a, 543b, 734b, 756b, 757a; VIII, 78a, 83b, 974b; IX, **15b**; S, 65b, 245b, 279a, 325b, 333b
Sandjar Abū Shudjāʿī i, 1138a, 1324b – I, 1172b, 1365b
Sandjar al-Ḥalabī (XIII) vi, 322a, b – VI, 306b, 307a
Sandjar Shāh b. Sayf al-Dīn Ghāzī II (Zangid(e)) (XII) vi, 781a, b – VI, 771a, b
Sandjar Shāh b. Ṭughān Shāh (Saldjūḳ, Harāt) (1187) viii, 63b – VIII, 64b
Sandjar Sihwastânī (XIII) vi, 48a – VI, 46b
Sandjīl (Mons Peregrinus) x, 215a – X, 232b
Ṣandūḳ iv, 227b – IV, 237b
Ṣanf (Champa) ii, 8b; iii, 1209a; v, 227a; vi, 234a; ix, **17a** – II, 8b; III, 1239b; V, 225a; VI, 207a; IX, **17b**
Sangamēshwar vi, 67a – VI, 65a
Sangat Sin i, 432b – I, 445a
Sang-i Maghribī i, 1068b – I, 1100b
Sangīn ʿAlī I ii, 29b – II, 30a
Sangīn ʿAlī II ii, 30a – II, 30a
Sāngrām, Mahārānā ii, 1128a; iii, 1010a – II, 1154b; III, 1035b
Ṣanhādja, Banū Ḥammād i, 699a, 700a, 762a, 1174b, 1175b, 1309a, 1319b, 1350a; ii, 115a, 873b, 1121b; iv, 199a, 479b; v, 652b, 653a, 769b, 1177b, 1204a, b; vi, 221b, 259b, 404b, 427a, 728a, 741a, 742a, b, 744a, 1009a; vii, 486a, 583b, 585b, 612b, 994a; viii, 18b; IX, **18a**; s, 113b –
I, 720b, 721a, 785a, 1209b, 1210b, 1349b, 1359b, 1390a; II, 117b, 894a, 1148a; IV, 208a, 501b; V, 656b, 657a, 775b, 1167b, 1194b, 1195a; VI, 215b, 244a, 389a, 412a, b, 717a, 730a, 731a, b, 733a, 1001a; VII, 486a, 584a, 586a, 612a, 995b; VIII, 18b; IX, **18b**; S, 113a
al-Sanhādjī, Ibrāhīm b. ʿAbd Allāh (1597) x, 346a – X, 371b
al-Ṣanhādjī, Sīdī Yūsuf b. ʿAlī (1196) vi, 591a – VI, 576a
Ṣanhādjiyyūn iii, 339a – III, 349a
Sanḥān (Yemen) vi, 436b – VI, 422a
al-Sanhūrī, ʿAbd al-Razzāḳ (1971) vi, 739b; ix, **18b** – VI, 729a; IX. **19a**
al-Sanhūrī, Abu ʾl-Ḥasan (1484) ix, **19a** – IX, **19b**
al-Sanhūrī, Abu ʾl-Nadja → Sālim b. Muḥammad
al-Sanhūrī, ʿAlī (XVI) vi, 454a – VI, 439b
Ṣāniʿ i, 898b; iv, 819a – I, 925b; IV, 852a
Ṣāniʿ al-Dawla → Muḥammad Ḥasan Khān
al-Sāniḥ iv, 290b – IV, 303b
Sanīn Ḥusayn ii, 124a – II, 127a
Sāniya → Nāʾūra
Saniyya Lands s, 179a – S, 180a
Sankarani vi, 258b – VI, 243a
Sankhodhar → Bet
Ṣannādj al-ʿArab → Ibn Muḥriz
Saʿnōnī i, 531a – I, 547a

Sansār Čand   iv, 543b – IV, 567a
Sanskrit/Sanscrit   iii, 412b, 1136a, 1215b, 1216a; v,
540a – III, 425b, 1164a, 1246a, 1247a; V, 544a
Santa Cruz   i, 245a – I, 252b
Santa Maria de Alarcos   → al-Arak
Santa Maria de Algarve   → S̲h̲antamariyat al-g̲h̲arb
Santa Maura   → Levkas
Santarem   → S̲h̲antarīn
Santaver   → S̲h̲antabariyya
Sante Bennur   vi, 696a – VI, 684a
Santiago de Compostela   → S̲h̲ant Yāḳub
Sanṭūr   ix, 19b s IX, 20a
Santurin Adasi̊   ix, 20a IX, 20b
Ṣanūʿ, Yaʿḳūb (XIX)   vii, 902b – VII, 903b
Sanua, James/Jacques   → Abū Naḍḍāra
Sanūb   → Sinob
al-Sanūsī, Abū ʿAbd Allāh Maḥammad b. Yūsuf (1490)
i, 333a, 334a, 593a, 696a, 867b, 1019b; iii, 780a; ix,
20a; s, 403a, b –
I, 343a, 344a, 612a, 717b, 891b, 1051a; III, 803a; IX,
20b; S, 403a, b
al-Sanūsī, al-Mahdī b. Muḥammad   v, 352b – V, 353a
Sanūsī, S̲h̲ayk̲h̲ Sayyid Aḥmad (1933)   vi, 530b; ix,
23b – VI, 514b; IX, 25a
al-Sanūsī, Sīdī Muḥammad b. ʿAlī (1859)   ii, 224a,
378a, 492b; iv, 952b; v, 760a; vi, 355b; vii, 434a; ix,
22b; s, 164b, 278b –
II, 231a, 388a, 505a; IV, 985a; V, 766a; VI, 339b;
VII, 434b; IX, 24a; S, 164b, 278b
Sanusi, Sir Muhammadu, amīr (Kano) (XX)   iv, 550a –
IV, 573b
Sanūsiyya   i, 136a, 277b, 763a, 1049b, 1071a, 1258b,
1260b; ii, 161b, 165a, 224a, 378a; iv, 541b, 777a,
952a, 954b; v, 352a, 760a; viii, 19a; ix, 24b; x, 249a;
s, 164b –
I, 140a, 286a, 786a, 1081a, 1103a, 1296b, 1298b; II,
166b, 170a, 231a, 388a; IV, 564b, 808b, 984b, 986b;
V, 353a, 766a; VIII, 19a; IX, 26a; X, 268a; S, 164b
Saphadin   → al-Malik al-ʿĀdil I Abū Bakr Muḥammad
b. Ayyūb, Sayf al-Dīn
Sār, Banū (Ḥaḍramawt)   vi, 82a – VI, 79b
Šar Planina   vi, 89a – VI, 87a
Sāra (Bible)   ix, 26b – IX, 28a
Sarā   → Sarāy
Sāra (singer/chanteuse)   iv, 821a – IV, 854a
Sara, Banū   s, 163b, 165b, 166a, b – S, 163b, 165a,
166a, b
Sāra b. Aḥmad al-Sudayrī   s, 3b – S, 2b
Sarāb   ix, 27a – IX, 28b
Saracens/Sarrasins   v, 1014b, 1019a; ix, 27b –
V, 1010b, 1015a; IX, 28a
Sarāfīl, Sarāfīn   → Isrāfīl
Saragossa/-e   → Saraḳusta
Sarajevo   i, 1263a, b, 1265b, 1266b, 1267a, b, 1268a,
b, 1270b, 1273a; v, 32a; ix, 28b –   I, 1301b,
1302a, 1304a, 1305a, 1306a, 1307a, b, 1309b, 1312a;
V, 33a; IX, 29a
Sarakata   i, 741a, b – I, 763a, b
Sarak̲h̲s   i, 47b; v, 293b; vi, 335b, 495a, 620b, 633b; ix,
5a, 34a; x, 89a; s, 195a –
I, 49a; V, 293a, b; VI, 320a, 480b, 605b, 618b; IX, 5a,
34b; X, 96a; S, 195a
al-Sarak̲h̲sī, ʿAbd al-Raḥmān b. ʿAbd al-Karīm (XII)   ii,
752a – II, 770a
al-Sarak̲h̲sī, Abu ʾl-ʿAbbās Aḥmad b. al-Ṭayyib
(899)   i, 339a, 590a, 1003b; ii, 578b; vi, 204b; vii,
683b, 1031b; ix, 35a –
I, 349b, 609a, 1034a; II, 593a; VI, 188b; VII, 684a,
1034a; IX, 35a
al-Sarak̲h̲sī, Muḥammad b. Aḥmad S̲h̲ams al-Aʾimma
(1096)   iii, 163a, b, 1024a; v, 130a; vi, 215a, 452a,

558a, 640a; ix, 35b – III, 166b, 167a, 1050a; V, 133a;
VI, 199a, 437b, 542b, 625a; IX, 36a
al-Sarak̲h̲sī, Lukmān (s̲h̲ayk̲h̲)   ix, 34b – IX, 35a
Sarāḳūdj   iii, 186a – III, 190b
Saraḳusṭa (Saragossa)   i, 82a, 390a, 493a, 495b; iii,
542a, b, 728a, 1093a; v, 219a; vi, 520b; vii, 768a; ix,
36a; s, 81b, 82a, 383a –
I, 84b, 401a, 508a, 510a; III, 560b, 561a, 750b,
1064b; V, 216b; VI, 505b; VII, 770a; IX, 36b; S, 81b,
383b
—monuments   i, 497b, 499a – I, 512b, 514a
al-Saraḳusṭī, Abu ʾl-Ḳāsim T̲h̲ābit (925)   ix, 38a – IX,
38b
al-Saraḳusṭī, Abū Muḥammad ḲRsim b. T̲h̲ābit (914)
ix, 38a – IX, 38b
al-Saraḳusṭī, Muḥammad (XV)   vi, 281b – VI, 266b
Sarāna   iv, 1042b – IV, 1074a
Sarandīb (Sri Lanka/Ceylo(a)n)   ix, 39a – IX, 39a
Sarandjām   i, 260b, 262a – I, 268b, 270a
Sārang K̲h̲ān   v, 31b – V, 32b
Sārang K̲h̲ān Lōdī (Tug̲h̲lukid(e)) (XV)   vi, 49a, b, 294a
– VI, 47b, 48a, 279b
Sārangpūr   vi, 53a; ix, 39a – VI, 51a; IX, 39b
Sarāparda   ix, 39b – IX, 40a
al-Sarāt   i, 536a, 707b, 811b; iii, 362a; vi, 144b, 266a;
ix, 39b – I, 552b, 729a, 834b; III, 373a; VI, 143a,
250b; IX, 40a
Saraṭan   ix, 40a – IX, 40b
Sarawak   vi, 232b, 241a; ix, 40b; s, 150a, 151a, 152a –
VI, 206a, 212a; IX, 41a; S, 150a, 151a, 152a
Sarāy ix, 44a – IX, 44b
Saray (Astrak̲h̲ān)   i, 1106a, b, 1108a; iv, 349b, 350a;
vi, 420a; ix, 41b; s, 203b –
I, 1139b, 1141a; IV, 364b, 365a; VI, 405a; IX, 42a;
S, 203a
Sarāy (Bag̲h̲dād)   i, 904b, 906a – I, 932a, 933a
Sarāy-ag̲h̲asi̊   ii, 1088a, 1089a; iv, 571a –
II, 1113b, 1114b; IV, 593b
Saray Bosna   s, 354a – S, 354a
Sarāy-Mulk K̲h̲ātūn (XV)   vii, 193b – VII, 194a
Saray Ovasi̊   → Sarajevo
Sarbadārid(e)s   iii, 968b, 1123a; iv, 32a, 48b; v, 59a;
vi, 13a, 511a, 515b, 549b; ix, 47b, 158b; x, 552b –
III, 993a, 1150b; IV, 34b, 51a; V, 60b: VI, 12a, 496b,
500b, 534a; IX, 48b, 164a; X,
Sarbandī   iv, 10b – IV, 11b
Sarbuland K̲h̲ān   i, 1053a, 1330a – I, 1084b, 1370b
Sarčam   iii, 1125a – III, 1153a
Sardāb   ii, 114a; ix, 49b – II, 116b; IX, 50b
Sardāniya   i, 86b; ix, 49b; s, 86b. 120b –
I, 89a; IX, 50b; S, 89a, 120a
Sardār (Sirdār)   ix, 50b – IX, 51b
Sardar, Amīr K̲h̲ān (1826)   vii, 453a – VII, 454a
Sardār Muḥammad ʿAzīz (XX)   vii, 438a –
VII, 439a
Sardār Muḥammad Hās̲h̲im K̲h̲ān   i, 232b –
I, 240a
Sardār Muḥammad Ibrāhīm   iv, 711a – IV, 739b
Sardhana   ix, 50b – IX, 51b
Sardinia/Sardaigne   → Sardāniya
Sardj   ix, 51a – IX, 52a
Sardjūn b. Manṣūr al-rūmī (VIII)   iv, 755a; vii, 268a; x,
226a – IV, 785b; VII, 270a; X, 244a
Sardsir   → Kis̲h̲lak
Sarekat Islam   viii, 534a, 1223b, 1229a; ix, 51b – III,
552b, 1254b, 1261a; IX, 52b
Ṣarf   iv, 326a; ix, 53a – IV, 340a; IX, 54a
Sarfrāz K̲h̲ān   i, 400b; ii, 371a – I, 412a; II, 381a
Sarg̲h̲atmus̲h̲ (Sarg̲h̲itmis̲h̲) al-Nāṣirī (1358)   iii, 239b,
699a; iv, 424a; vi, 323b, 367b; vii, 170b – III, 246b,
721a; IV, 442b; VI, 308a, 351b; VII, 172b

Sargūdjā vi, 53a – VI, 51a
Sarghūn II v, 68a, b – V, 70a, b
Sarhadd ix, **54a** – IX, **55a**
Sarhang ix, **54a** – IX, **55b**
Sārī (Ḳumān) v, 373a – V, 374a
Sārīʿ/Sāriya (town/ville, Māzandarān) vi, 511a, b, 512a, b, 513a, b, 514a, b, 515b, 517a, 745b; ix, **54b**; s, 298a, 309a, 356b, 357a – VI, 497a, b, 498a, 499a, b, 500b, 502a, 502b, 734b; IX, **56a**; S, 297b, 308b, 356b, 357a
al-Sarī b. al-Ḥakam b. Yūsuf al-Balkhī (820) vii, 160b; ix, **55a** – VII, 162a; IX, **56b**
al-Sarī b. Manṣūr → Abu ʾl-Sarāya
Ṣarï ʿAbd Allāh Effendī (1661) iii, 711a; ix, **59a** – III, 733b; IX, **56b**
al-Sarī al-Aḳṣam iv, 1132b – IV, 1164a
Ṣarï Beyoghlï Muṣṭafā iv, 593a – IV, 617a
Ṣarï-čay vi, 201a – VI, 185a
Sarï Demir Tash Pashā iv, 623a – IV, 648a
Sarï Kenʿān Pasha → Kenʿān Pasha
Sarï Kürz (Görez) (1521) ix, **59b** – IX, **57a**
Sarï Meḥmed Pasha (1717) ix, **60a** – IX, **57b**
Sarï Muṣṭafa Pasha iv, 969b – IV, 1001b
Sar-i Pul ix, **26b**, 431a – IX, **28a**, 447b
al-Sarī al-Raffāʾ ix, **55b** – IX, **58a**
al-Sarī al-Saḳaṭī, Abu ʾl-Ḥasan (867) i, 1245b; ii, 600a; vi, 613b; vii, 467b; ix, **56b** – I, 1283b; II, 615a; VI, 598b; VII, 467a; IX, **59b**
Ṣarï Ṣalṭuḳ Dede (XII) i, 299a, 838b, 842b, 843a, 993a, 998b, 1031b; ii, 610b, 612a; iii, 115a; iv, 628a, 885a; ix, **61a** – I, 308a, 862a, 865b, 866b, 1023b, 1029b, 1063a; II, 625b, 627a; III, 117a; IV, 653a, 917b; IX, **62a**
Sarif (Mecca) vi, 918a – VI, 909b
Ṣarīfa i, 1097a – I, 1130a
al-Ṣarīfīnī s, 195a – S, 193a
al-Ṣarīfīnī, Shuʿayb b. Ayyūb (875) viii, 14a – VIII, 14a
Sarighshin iv, 1178a – IV, 1211a, b
Sarïḳ (tribe/tribu) s, 143b, 146b, 281a – S, 143a, 146b, 281a
Sarika ix, **62b** – IX, **63b**
Sarikat → Shirka
Ṣārim b. Sayf al-Dīn (Mukrī) (XVI) ix, 92b s IX, 96b
Ṣārim al-Dīn (al-Ṣārimī) Ibrāhīm b. al-Muʾayyad Shaykh (Mamlūk) (1420) vii, 271b – VII, 273b
Ṣārim al-Dīn Ḳaymaz Kāfūrī al-Manbidjī (XIII) iv, 483b; vi, 381a – IV, 504b; VI, 365b
Ṣārim al-Dīn Mubārak (Alamūt) vi, 790b – VI, 780b
Sar-i-mūsh iv, 811a – IV, 843b
Ṣarï-ṣu vi, 200b, 201a – VI, 185a
Sarīr (Avaristān) ii, 86a; iv, 343a, 346a – II, 87b; IV, 357b, 361a
Sarï-Tash (mountain/montagne) vi, 416b – VI, 401b
Sāriya → Sārīʿ
Sarkan Bashkurt i, 1075b – I, 1107b
Sarkār Āḳā ix, **63b**; 404b – IX, **65a**; 417b
Sarkārs i, 316b; iii, 320b – I, 326b; III, 331b
Sarkash iv, 53b; vi, 276a – IV, 56b; VI, 261a
Sarkel → Sharkil
Ṣarkhad → Ṣalkhad
Sarkhāstān iv, 646b, 647a – IV, 673a, b
Sarkhēdj (Aḥmadābād) iii, 445a, b; vi, 51a; ix, **64a** – III, 460a, b; VI, 49b; IX, **65b**
Sarkīs, Khalīl ii, 467b – II, 479a
Sārliyya ix, **64a** – IX, **65b**
Sarmad → Muḥammad Saʿīd Sarmad
Sarmada vi, 578b – VI, 563b
Sarmast, Saččal v, 611a – V, 615a
Ṣarmis → Čeremiss(es)
Sārōē → Sārūya
Sarpul-i Dhuhāb ix, **64b** – IX, **66a**
Sarrādj → Sardj
Sarrādj, ʿAbd al-Ḥamīd s, 8a – S, 7a
al-Sarrādj, Abū ʿAlī → Ibn al-Sarrādj, Abū ʿAlī
al-Sarrādj, Abū Muḥammad Djaʿfar b. Aḥmad (1106) i, 69a, 516al vi, 263b; ix, **65a**; – I, 71a, 531b; VI, 248a; IX, **66b**
al-Sarrādj, Abū Naṣr (988) iii, 546b, 589a; viii, 429a, 579b, 583b, 994a; ix, **65b** – III, 565b, 609b; VIII, 443a, 598a, 602a, 1028b; IX, **67a**
al-Sarrādj, Banū → Ibn al-Sarrādj
al-Sarrādj, Djaʿfar b. Aḥmad vi, 263b – VI, 248a
al-Sarrādj, Yaḥyā iii, 670b – III, 692b
al-Sarrādj al-Baghdād → al-Sarrādj, Abū Muḥammad
al-Ṣarrāf, Aḥmad (XIX) vii, 903a – VII, 903b
Sarrasins → Saraceni
Ṣarrūf, Yaʿḳūb (1912) i, 597a; vii, 902b, 903a; ix, **66b** – I, 616b; VII, 903b; IX, **69a**
Ṣarṣar x, 588a – X,
al-Ṣarṣarī (1160) vi, 898a – VI, 889a
Sarshār, Ratan Nāth iii, 359a, 376a; v, 202b – III, 370a, 388a; V, 200a
Sar-shumārī iv, 1042b – IV, 1074a
Sārt (Tādjīks) v, 30a, 273b; vi, 557b; ix, 66b – V, 31a, 271b; VI, 542a; IX, 69a
Sart (Sardes) ix, **68a**; x, 63a, b, 66b – IX, **71a**; X, 65a, b, 68b
Sartak i, 1106a, 1187b – I, 1139a, 1223a
Saru, Banū vi, 474a – VI, 460a
Ṣaru Ṣaltuḳ → Ṣarï Ṣaltïḳ
Sarūdj ix, **68b** – IX, **71b**
Sarudja (Sarïdja) iii, 317b – III, 327b
Ṣarudja Pasha ii, 985b – II, 1008a
al-Sarūdjī, Abū Zayd vi, 115a; ix, 68b – VI, 112b; IX, 71b
Sāruḳ (town/ville) s, 142b – S, 142a
Sārūḳ (river/rivière) vi, 502b – VI, 487b
Ṣarūkhān (dynasty/-ie) i, 467b, 654a; v, 505b, 506a, 1169b; vi, 975a, 1015b, 1018b; ix, **69a** – I, 481b, 674b; V, 509a, b, 1159b; VI, 967a, 1008a, 1011a; IX, **72a**
Ṣarūkhān-oghullarï → Ṣarūkhān
Sarūkhānī → Gulshanī
Saru-ḳurghan vi, 502b – VI, 487b
Sarūr iii, 376a – III, 388a
Sārūya ii, 74b – II, 76a
Sarvantikʿar vi, 776b – VI, 766a
Sarwār Khān (Tank) (XIX) s, 329b – S, 329a
Sarwar al-Mulk (XV) vii, 279a – VII, 281a
Sarwistān ix, **69b**; s, 327a – IX, **72b**; S, 326b
Sasa Beg (1308) i, 783a – I, 806b
Ṣaʿṣaʿa i, 382b – I, 393b
Sasaks (Lombok) v, 785a, b – V, 791b, 792a
Sāsān (Kayānid(e)) iv, 809b – IV, 842b
Sāsān, Banū vii, 495a; ix, **70a**; s, 250a – VII, 494b; IX, **72b**; S, 250a
Sāsānid(e)s i, 66a, 226a, 938b, 1041a, 1094a; ii, 77b, 190a, 951a; iii, 50b, 113a, 177a, 304a, 470b, 884a; iv, 13a-b, 219b, 850b; v, 56b, 184b, 634a, 831a, 1110a; vi, 11a, 97a, 261a; ix, **70b**; s, 116a, 251a, 297b – I, 67b, 232b, 967b, 1072b, 1126b; II, 79a, 196a, 973a; III, 52b, 115b, 181a, 313a, 487a, 908a; IV, 14a-b, 229b, 883b; V, 58a, 182a, 638a, 837a, 1106a; VI, 11a, 95a, 245b; IX, **73a**; S, 115a, 251a, 297a
—art, architecture ii, 742b, 743a – II, 761a, b
Sasarām → Sahsarām
Sāsī b. Muḥammad (XX) vi, 251a – VI, 235a
Sasï Buḳa (Özbeg) s, 246a – S, 246a
Sastroamidjojo, Ali (XX) vi, 732a – VI, 721a
Ṣāṣūn v, 459a – V, 461b

Satalia → Antalya
Sātgā'on (Bengal(e)) ix, **83b** – IX, **87a**
Satgur Nūr iv, 202b; v, 26a – IV, 211b; V, 26b
Sati-Beg (Il-Khānid(e)) (1319) ii, 68a, b, 401a; vi, 482b – II, 69a, b, 411b; VI, 468b
Sāṭiʿ al-Huṣrī ii, 1117b; v, 905b – II, 1143b; V, 910b
Saṭīḥ b. Rabīʿa iii, 739b; ix, **84a**, 440b – III, 762a; IX, **87b**; 457b
Satpanth iv, 206a – IV, 215a
Satpanthīs i, 173a; iii, 1163a; iv, 202b; ix, **85a** – I, 177b; III, 1191b; IV, 211b; IX, **88b**
Sattār Khān s, 365b – S, 365a
Satuḳ Bughra Khān → ʿAbd al-Karīm Khān
Saturdjī Meḥmed Pasha v, 27b – V, 28b
Saturiḳ iii, 1125a – III, 1153a
Satya Pīr Bengal(e)) iii, 422b; ix, **85a** – III, 436a; IX, **88b**
Saʿūd → Suʿūd
Saudi Arabia → al-Suʿūdiyya
Sa'udj-Bulāḳ → Āwdj-Bulāḳ
Saul/Saül → Ṭālūt
Sava (river/rivière, Bosnia(e)) vi, 56a – VI, 54a
Sava (town/ville, Afghānistān) ii, 746a – II, 764b
Savak iv, 41b – IV, 44a
Sarak (Savaz) ii, 70a – II, 71a
Sāwa (Sāva) (Persia/-se) ii, 746a; v, 868b; vi, 64a; ix, **85b** – II, 764b; V, 868b; VI, 62a; IX, **89a**
al-Sawād (Malaṭya) i, 382b; ii, 577a; iv, 1140b; v, 345b, 347b; vi, 230b, 633b, 738b; ix, **87a**; s, 59a – I, 393b; II, 591b; IV, 1172b; V, 346b, 348b; VI, 224a, 618a, 727b, 728a; IX, **90b**; S, 59b
Sawād b. Ghanm b. Kaʿb b. Salima, Banū vi, 649a – VI, 634b
Sāwadjī, Saʿd al-Dīn (1312) viii, 169a; ix, 86b – VIII, 171b; IX, 90a
al-Sāwadjī, ʿUmar b. Sahlān (1145) ix, 782a – IX, 816a
Sawādkūh vi, 511b, 513a, 514a, b, 515a; vii, 440b – VI, 497a, 498b, 499b, 500a; VII, 441b
Sawādkūhīs vi, 512a – VI, 497b
Ṣawāfī → Safī
Sawāʿī → Djay Singh
Sawākin i, 782b, 1158a, 1172a; iv, 643a, 687a; v, 1249b, 1251a; vi, 642b, 643a; viii, 235b; ix, **87b** – I, 806a, 1192b, 1207a; IV, 669b, 715a; V, 1240a, 1241b; VI, 627b, 628a; VIII, 240b; IX, **91a**
Sawalān vi, 501a, 504a – VI, 486b, 489b
Sawār (amīr) (Alep(po)) (XII) v, 124b, 125b, 922a; vi, 380a – V, 127a, 128a, 927b; VI, 364b
Ṣawda (Zawda), Banū vi, 742a – VI, 731a
al-Sawdā' (al-Kharibat -) ix, **90b** s IX, **92a**
al-Sawdā' (Khūriyā Mūriyā) i, 535b – I, 551b
Sawdā, Mīrzā Muḥammad Rafīʿ (poet/poète)(1781) i, 241b; iii, 119a, 358b; iv, 716b; v, 959a, b, 961a; vi, 611a; vii, 669b, 998b; ix, **90a;** x, 878a; s, 109b, 358b –
I, 249a; III, 121b, 369b; IV, 745a; V, 963a, b, 965a; VI, 595b; VII, 669a, 989a; IX, **95b;** X, ;S, 109a, 358b
Sawdā' bint Zamʿa b. Ḳays (674) i, 307b; vi, 646a; ix, **89b**; s, 172a – I, 317a; VI, 631a; IX, **95a**; S, 173a
Sawdān i, 1166b; iv, 275b; ix, **92a** – I, 1201a; IV, 287b; IX, **96b**
Sāwdj-Bulāḳ v, 1213a; vi, 498b, 502a, b – V, 1202b; VI, 483b, 487a, 488a
Sawdjī, Sawdjī ix, **93a** – IX, **97a**
Sawdjī Beg b. Ertoghrul ix, 93a – IX, 97a
Sawdūb, amīr (nāẓir al-Azhar) (XV) vi, 672b –VI, 659a
al-Sāwī, Djamāl al-Dīn (1232) iv, 473a, b; x,251a – IV, 494a; X, 269b
Sāwī (Sāwadjī), Zayn al-Dīn ʿUmar b. Sahlān (XII) viii, 542a – VIII, 559b
Sawīḳ ix, **93b** – IX, **97b**
al-Ṣawīra (Mogador) → al-Ṣuwayra
Ṣawlat al-Dawla Khān iv, 706b – IV, 734b
Ṣawlat Djang ii, 1091b – II, 1117a
Sawm ix, **93b** – IX, **98a**
Ṣawm v, 424b; ix, **94a** – V, 426b; IX, **98a**
al-Ṣawmaʿī → Aḥmad b. Abi 'l-Ḳāsim
Sāwra (valley/vallée) s, 28b – S, 29a
Sawra b. Ḥurr al-Tamīmī ii, 600b – II, 615b
Sawrān s, 245a, b – S, 245a, b
Sawrāshtra ii, 1123b, 1130b – II, 1149b, 1157b
Sawsanī, Abū Sahl iii, 256a – III, 263a
Sawte(i)gin, ʿImād al-Dīn (Ghulām) (XI) i, 660b; ii, 1082b; iii, 471b; iv, 348a; vi, 274a; x, 480b; s, 383b – I, 681b; II, 1107b; III, 488a; IV, 363a; VI, 259a; X, 515b; S, 384a
Ṣawtiyya ix, **95b** – IX, **100a**
Sāwudjbulā s, 73a – S, 73b
Sawuran Ḳalʿe → Sarvantikʿar
Sawwār b. ʿAbd Allāh s, 113a – S, 112b
Sawwār b. Ḥamdūn ii, 1012b – II, 1036a
Saʿy iii, 35a, 36b; iv, 185a; ix, **97b** – III, 37a, 38a; IV, 193a; IX, **101b**
Sayābidja i, 761b; ix, **97b** – I, 784b; IX, **102a**
Sayābiga → Sayābidja
Sayd ix, **98b** – IX, **102b**
Ṣaydā (Sidon) iii, 474b; iv, 483a, 484a; ix, **99a**; s, 49a, 120b, 268a – III, 491a; IV, 504a, b; IX, **103a**; S, 49b, 120a, 267b
al-Ṣaydana/al-Ṣaydala ix, **100a** – IX, **104b**
al-Ṣaydawī, Shams al-Dīn Muḥammad (1506) ix, **101a** – IX, **105a**
Saydnāyā (Maʿlūlā) vi, 308a – VI, 293b
Sayf (sword/épée) ii, 1122a; iv, 502b; v, 972b, 973a – II, 1148b; IV, 524a; V, 974b, 975a
Sayf b. ʿAbd Allāh (893) (Usrūshana) x, 925a – X,
Sayf b. Dhī Yazan (Sīrat) i, 102a; ii, 1096a; iv, 566b; vi, 830a; ix, **101b**; s, 115b, 164a – I, 105a; II, 1122a; IV, 589a; VI, 820b; IX, **105b**; S, 115a, 163b
Sayf b. Sulṭān I (Yaʿrubid(e)) (1649) v, 507a; vi, 735a; viii, 85a – V, 510b; VI, 724a; VIII, 87b
Sayf b. Sulṭān (Yaʿrūbid(e) (1711) x, 816b – X,
Sayf b. Sulṭān II (Yaʿrūbid(e)) (1737) i, 1281b; vi, 735a – I, 1321a; VI, 724a
Sayf b. ʿUmar al-Tamīmī (809) i, 51a, 629a; iv, 385a; v, 324a; vi, 267b; viii, 638a; ix, **102a** – I, 52b, 650a; IV, 401b; V, 323b; VI, 252b; VIII, 657a; IX. **106b**
Sayf b. Zāmil b. Djabr s, 234a – S, 234a
Sayf ʿAlī Beg i, 1135a – I, 1169b
Sayf ʿAyn al-Mulk iii, 1161a – III, 1189b
Sayf al-Dawla Abū 'l-Ḥasan ʿAlī (Ḥamdānid(e)) (967) i, 118a, 119b, 329a, 517a, 679b, 789b, 791b, 845b; ii, 36b, 178b, 344a, 693b; iii, 20a, 86a, 127a, b, 129a, b, 398a, 404b, 507a, 824b, 900a; v, 124b, 525a, 923b; vi, 242b, 379a, 506b, 545a, 775b, 930a; vii, 115b, 411b, 770a, b, 983b, 995a, b; ix, **103a** s, 12b, 36a, 37b, 361b, 362a –
I, 121b, 123a, 339b, 532b, 700b, 813a, 815a, 869a; II, 37b, 184a, 353b, 710b; III, 21a, 88a, 129b, 130a, 131b, 132a, 410b, 416b, 524a, 848b, 924a; V, 127a, 529a, 929a; VI, 226b, 363b, 491b, 530a, 765a, 922a; VII, 117b, 413a, 772a, 984a, 996b, 997a; IX, **107b**; S, 13a, 36b, 38a, 361a, b
Sayf al-Dawla Aḥmad b. Hūd → Aḥmad III (Hūdid(e))
Sayf al-Dawla Maḥmūd b. Ẓahīr al-Dawla (Ghaznawid(e)) (1076) ii, 1052a; vi, 783a; s, 21a, 24a – II, 1076b; VI, 772b; S, 21a, 24a
Sayf al-Dawla Ṣadaḳa s, 326a – S, 325b
Sayf al-Dīn → al-ʿĀdil I

Sayf al-Dīn (Alep(po)) (XII) vi, 380b – VI, 364b
Sayf al-Dīn (Shansabānid(e) /Ghūrid(e)) ix, **110a** – IX, **114a**
Sayf al-Dīn b. Afrāsiyāb (Marʿashī) (XIV) vi, 511a – VI, 496b
Sayf al-Dīn Aybak b. Iltutmish (XIII) vi, 47b – VI, 46a
Sayf al-Dīn ʿAzāz al-Ṣāliḥī, amīr (1298) vi, 777b – VI, 767b
Sayf al-Dīn Bākharzī, Abu ʾl-Maʿālī (1261) i, 347b; v, 301a; viii, 539a; ix, **110a**, 862b; x, 251a – I, 358a; V, 300a; VIII, 557b; ix, **114a**; X, 270a
Sayf al-Dīn Balabān al-Djukāndār (1306) viii, 158a – VIII, 160a
Sayf al-Dīn Bizlār al-Manṣūrī, amīr (1298) vi, 777b – VI, 767b
Sayf al-Dīn Dengiz (XIV) vi, 231a – VI, 225a
Sayf al-Dīn Fīrūz → Fīrūz Shāh (Bengal(e))
Sayf al-Dīn Ghāzī I b. ʿImād al-Dīn (Zangid(e)) (1149) i, 1160b; ii, 489b, 1045a; iii, 327b; vi, 870b; viii, 127b; ix, 12b – I, 1195a; II, 501b, 1069b; III, 337b; VI, 861a; VIII, 130b; IX, 13a
Sayf al-Dīn Ghāzī II (Zangid(e)) (1160) ii, 1045a; vi, 781a, 871b – II, 1069b; VI, 861a
Sayf al-Dīn ʿImād al-Dīn Farāmurz s, 416a – S, 416b
Sayf al-Dīn Ḳïpčaḳ al-Manṣūrī (1298) vi, 545b, 777b – VI, 530a, 767b
Sayf al-Dīn al-Malik al-Nāṣirī ii, 126a – II, 129a
Sayf al-Dīn Muḥammad ii, 1101a, 1103a – II, 1127a, 1129b
Sayf al-Dīn-oghlu (Tripoli) (XVII) vii, 707b – VII, 708b
Sayf al-Dīn Sunḳur, atābeg (XIII) vi, 434a – VI, 419a
Sayf al-Dīn Sūrī i, 940a; ii, 382a, 1100a – I, 968b; II, 392b, 1126a
Sayf al-Dīn Tungur (XIV) vi, 544a – VI, 528b
Sayf al-Ḥaḳḳ Abu ʾl-Mafākhir Muḥammad b. Manṣūr (XII) ix, 4a – IX, 4a
Sayf al-Islām Badr ii, 674b – II, 691b
Sayf al-Mulk Ibn ʿAmrūn (al-Kahf) (XII) vi, 789b – VI, 779b
Sayf al-Mulūk (Khāndesh) s, 335b – S, 335b
Sayf al-Raḥmān ii, 31a – II, 31b
Sayfī (XVI) i, 323a; v, 314b – I, 333a; V, 314a
Sayfī ʿArūdī Bukhārī (XV) ix, **111b** – IX, **115b**
Sayfī Harawī (XIV) ix, **112a** – IX, **116a**
Saygun, Adnan iii, 1094b – III, 1121a
al-Sayḥ i, 233a – I, 240b
Ṣayhad (desert) vi, 566a; s, 337a – VI, 551a; S, 336b
Sayḥān (Saros) i, 184a; ii, 35a, 502b; ix, 112a – I, 189a; II, 36a, 515b; IX. **116a**
Sayḥūn → Sïr Daryā
Sayhūt s, 337a – S, 337a
Ṣāyigh, Fatḥ Allāh (XIX) ix, **113a** – IX, **117a**
Ṣāyigh, Tawfīḳ (1971) ix, **113b** – IX, **117b**
Sāyin Bulāt iv, 723b – IV, 752b
Saymara (town/ville) ix, **113b** – IX, **117b**
al-Ṣaymarī, Abu ʾl-ʿAbbas Yaʿḳūbī ii, 552a; ix, **114a** – II, 566a; IX, **118a**
al-Ṣaymarī, Abū ʿAbd Allāh Muḥammad (XI) ix, 668b; s, 25a – IX, 694b; S, 25b
al-Ṣaymarī, Abu ʾl-ʿAnbas → Abu ʾl-ʿAnbas al-Ṣaymarī
al-Ṣaymarī, Muḥammad b. ʿUmar (927) vii, 785b – VII, 787b
Saymūr vii, 919b – VII, 920a
Sayr b. ʿAbd Allāh (Usrūshana) (1893) x, 925a – X,
al-Ṣayrafī, Muḥammad b. Badr (942) ix, **114a** – IX, **118a**
al-Ṣayrafī, Shihāb al-Dīn ʿAbd Allāh (XIV) viii, 806b – VIII, 833b
Sayrām (town/ville) ii, 39a, 45b; ix, **114b**, 621b – II, 39b, 46a; IX, **118b**, 645a
Sayʾūn, Saywūn (Ḥaḍramawt) vi, 132b; vii, 496b; ix, **115a**; s, 337b, 338b – VI, 130b; VII, 496a; IX, **119a**; S, 337a, 338b
Sayūna ix, 699a, b s IX, 728a, b
Ṣayyād, Banū iv, 10b – IV, 11b
al-Ṣayyād, ʿIzz al-Dīn Aḥmad (1271) viii, 525b – VIII, 543b
al-Ṣayyādī, Muḥammad Abu ʾl-Hudā (1909) vi, 88a; viii, 526a – VI, 86a; VIII, 544a
Sayyāḥ, Ḥādjdj s, 109b – S, 108b
Sayyiʾa iv, 1106b – IV, 1138a
Sayyid (Saʾid) (title/titre) i, 1022b; ii, 687b; iii, 411a; v, 627a; ix, **115a** – I, 1054a; II, 705a; III, 423b; V, 631a; IX, **119b**
Sayyid ʿAbd al-ʿAẓīm Mīrzā → Aghā-bakhsh
Sayyid Abū Bakr iii, 1218b – III, 1249b
Sayyid Abū Bakr (Sharīf al-Hāshim) (Sulu) (XV) viii, 303b – VIII, 312a
Sayyid Āghā Ḥasan → Amānat
Sayyid Aḥmad b. ʿAbd al-Raḥmān iv, 780a – IV, 811b
Sayyid Aḥmad b. ʿAlawī Marʿashī (1144) vi, 517a – VI, 502a
Sayyid Aḥmad b. Muḥammad b. ʿAlī Mūsāwī Marʿashī (XIX) vi, 516b – VI, 502a
Sayyid Aḥmad Brēlwī → Aḥmad Brēlwī
Sayyid Aḥmad Khān → Aḥmad Khān, Sir Sayyid
Sayyid Aḥmad Shāh, Mīrzā v, 164a – V, 162a
Sayyid Akbar i, 238b; iv, 1143a – I, 246a; IV, 1174b
Sayyid ʿAlī Dūghlāt ii, 622a – II, 637b
Sayyid ʿAlī Hamadānī (1384) viii, 134b – VIII, 137a
Sayyid ʿAlī Khān ii, 47b – II, 48a
Sayyid ʿAlī Muḥammad → Bāb
Sayyid ʿAlī Muḥammad Shād ʿAẓīmābādī (1927) vi, 838b – VI, 829a
Sayyid ʿAlī Naṣr (1961) vi, 764a – VI, 753a
Sayyid ʿĀlim Khān, amīr (Mangït) (1920) vi, 419a – VI, 404a
Sayyid Awlād ʿAlī Khān (1803) vii, 1048b – VII, 1050b
Sayyid al-Awwal i, 606b – I, 626a
Sayyid ʿAẓīm i, 193b – I, 199b
Sayyid Badrān b. Falāḥ (Mushaʿshaʿ) (XVI) vii, 673a – VII, 673a
Sayyid Baṭṭāl → al-Baṭṭāl
Sayyid Burhān Khān iv, 724a – IV, 753a
Sayyid Darwīsh (1923) x, 144a – X, 154b
Sayyid Ḍiyāʾ al-Dīn (XX) vii, 654a; s, 84a – VII, 653b; S, 83b
Sayyid Djaʿfar b. Nūrbakhsh (XVI) viii, 135b – VIII, 138a
Sayyid Djalāl al-Dīn Bukhārī (XIV) ix, 673 – IX, 701a
Sayyid Dūst Muḥammad b. Sayyid Ḳuṭb al-Dīn s, 325a – S, 324b
Sayyid Falāh b. Muḥsin (Mushaʿshaʿ) (1514) vii, 673a – VII, 672b, 673a
Sayyid Fatḥī (XVIII) vi, 56b – VI, 54b
Sayyid Fayyāḍ (Mushaʿshaʿ) (XVI) vii, 673a – VII, 672b
Sayyid Ḥasan b. Ḥamza b. ʿAlī Marʿash (968) vi, 517a – VI, 502a
Sayyid Ḥasan Beg (XVIII) iv, 201b – IV, 210b
Sayyid Ḥasan Ghaznawī (1161) ix, **116a** – IX, **120a**
Sayyid Ḥasan Mudarris (1938) vii, 223b – VII, 225a
al-Sayyid al-Ḥimyarī, Abū Hāshim (789) i, 431b; ii, 136a; iii, 882a; iv, 836b; v, 552b; vi, 604a, 635b; ix,

116b, 454a –
I, 443b; II, 139b; III, 906a; IV, 869b; V, 557a; VI, 589a, 620b; IX, **121a**, 469a
Sayyid Ḥusayn / – Sirdān → Tirmidhī, Sayyid Burhān
Sayyid Isḥāḳ ii, 733a – II, 751b
Sayyid Kāẓim Rashtī → Ḳāẓim Rashtī
Sayyid Khān ii, 973b – II, 995b
Sayyid Ḳuṭb (1966) viii, 907b; ix, **117a** – VIII, 939a; IX, **121b**
Sayyid Ḳuṭb al-Dīn b. Sayyid Masʿūd (XIV) s, 325a – S, 324b
Sayyid Maḥmūd Djawnpūrī ii, 500a – II, 512b
Sayyid Mansab (1922) iv, 887a – IV, 919b
Sayyid Masʿūd s, 325a – S, 324b
Sayyid Mīrān Hāshimī (1697) vi, 837b – VI, 828a
Sayyid Mubārak b. Muṭṭalib b. Badrān (Mushaʿshaʿ) (1616) vii, 672a, b – VII, 673a
Sayyid Muḥammad, Mīr s, 340a – S, 339b
Sayyid Muḥammad, Mīrzā (XIX) s, 23b, 74a – S, 23b, 74a
Sayyid Muḥammad b. ʿAlī → al-Idrīsī
Sayyid Muḥammad b. Falāḥ (Mushaʿshaʿ) (1465) vii, 672a – VII, 672a
Sayyid Muḥammad b. Sayyid ʿAlāʾ al-Dīn ii, 967b – II, 989b
Sayyid Muḥammad b. Sayyid ʿAlī al-Hamdānī iv, 708b – IV, 736b
Sayyid Muḥammad Buzurg-Sawār i, 262a; ii, 194a – I, 270a; II, 200b
Sayyid Muḥammad Dāmād (Āyatullāh) (XX) vii, 762b – VII, 764a
Sayyid Muḥammad Djawnpūrī → al-Djawnpūrī
Sayyid Muḥammad Khān (Awadh) (XIX) ii, 1046a – II, 1070a
Sayyid Muḥammad Khān (Delhi) s, 247a – S, 247a
Sayyid Muḥammad Mīrzā Dughlāt ii, 622b – II, 638a
Sayyid Muḥsin (Mushaʿshaʿ) (1499) vii, 672b – VII, 672b
Sayyid Murād iv, 1158a – IV, 1190a
al-Sayyid Murtaḍā i, 266a,b – I, 274b
Sayyid Murtaḍā Efendi, Shaykh al-Islām (1750) vi, 1004b – VI, 996b
Sayyid Nadhīr Ḥusayn i, 259b – I, 267b
Sayyid Nūḥ ii, 588b – II, 603a
Sayyid al-Ruʾasāʾ Ibn Kamāl al-Mulk (1083) viii, 72a – VIII, 73b
Sayyid Sadjdjād b. Badrān (Muʿshaʾshaʿ) (XVI) vii, 673a – VII, 673a
Sayyid Shams al-Dīn (XV) vi, 62a – VI, 60a
Sayyid Ṣiddīḳ Ḥasan → Nawwāb Sayyid Siddīḳ
Sayyid al-Tābiʿīn → Saʿīd b. al-Musayyab
Sayyid Ṭālib al-Rifāʿī al-Naḳīb iii, 520a – III, 538a
Sayyid Yaḥyā b. Sayyid Ḳuṭb al-Dīn s, 325a – S, 324b
al-Sayyida → ʿĀʾisha al-Mannūbiyya
Sayyida ʿĀtiḳa vii, 10b – VII, 11a
Sayyida Ḥurra bint Aḥmad i, 181b, 552a; ii, 856a; iii, 134a; iv, 200b – I, 186b, 570a; II, 876a; III, 136b; IV, 209a
al-Sayyida al-Kubrāʾ → Ṣubḥ
Sayyida Ruḳayya vii, 10b – VII, 11a
Sayyida umm Fakhr al-Dawla iv, 465a; v, 1028a, b – IV, 486a; V, 1024a
Sayyida Zaynab bint Muḥammad al-Shahāriyya (1702) vii, 879a; ix, 201b – VIII, 880a; IX, 207b
Sayyid(e)s (Delhi) vi, 50a, 692b; vii, 795b; ix, **118b** – VI, 48b, 680a; VII, 797b; IX, **122b**
Sayyidī Abū Saʿīd i, 863b – I, 887b
Sāz ix, **120a**; s, 91b – IX, **124a**; S, 91a
Sbīṭla → Subayṭila
Sbuk → Subuk
Scanderbeg → Iskender Beg
Scenites i, 527b
Schnitzer, Carl → Emīn Pasha
Scutari → Üsküdār
Sea → Baḥr
Sea of Azov → Baḥr Māyuṭis
Sea of Marmara → Marmara Deñizi
Seʿādet Giray Khān I (Crimea/-ee) (1532) viii, 832a – VIII, 861a
Seʿadya → Saʿīd
Sebastiyya → Sabastiyya
Sebeos (bishop/l'évêque) i, 635b, 636b – I, 656b, 657b
Sebḥa → Sabkha
Sebou (river/rivière) → Sabū, Wādī
Sebük-eri (X) viii, 796b – VIII, 823a
Sebüktegin, Abū Manṣūr Nāṣir al-Dawla (Ghaznawid(e)) (977) i, 11b, 142b, 226b, 421b, 424b, 899b, 1348b; ii, 799a, 978a, 1049a, 1050b; iii, 46b, 197a, 415b; iv, 24b, 208b, 917b; v, 622b, 649a; vi, 65a, 193a; vii, 193a, 987a; viii, 67b, 110a, 797b, 1028a; ix, **121a**; s, 284b –
I, 11b, 147a, 233b, 433b, 436b, 926b, 1388b; II, 818a, 1000b, 1073a, 1075a; III, 48b, 202a, 428b; IV, 26a, 218a, 950b; V, 626b, 653a; VI, 62b, 177a; VII, 193b, 987b; VIII, 69a, 112b, 824a, 1063a; IX, **125b**; S, 284b
Secuna (Cordova) → Shaḳunda
Secunderabad → Sikandarābād
Sedrata ii, 115a – II, 117b
Seethi Sahib, K.M. (1960) vi, 460a, 462a – VI, 445b, 448a
Sefāretnāme → Safīr
Sefawa iv, 566b – IV, 589a
Sefer-beg i, 101a – I, 104a
Sefer Ghāzī (Agha) iv, 178b, 630a – IV, 185b, 655a
Sefrou → Sufrūy
Segestan → Sīstān
Segovia → Shaḳūbiyya
Segu, Segou i, 297a; iii, 39a; vi, 259a, b, 402b; ix, **121b** – I, 306a; III, 41a; VI, 243b, 244a, 387a; IX, **126a**
Segura → Shaḳūra
Seh Nurullah (Shaykh Nūr Allāh) (XVI) ix, 852b – IX, 888a
Sehī Bey (Edirne) (1548) ix, **122a**; x, 55a – IX, **126b**; X, 56b
Sekou Ouattara v, 252b – V, 250b
Sekou Touré ii, 1133a – II, 1159b
Seku Hamadu → Aḥmadu
Selāmlïḳ ii, 114b; ix, **123a** – II, 117a; IX, **127b**
Selangor vi, 232b, 236b, 242a – VI, 206a, 209b, 213a
Selānīk vi, 69a, 74a, 89a, 150b; ix, **123a**; s, 63a, 269b – VI, 67a, 71b, 87a, 149b; IX, **127b**; S, 63b, 269a
Selānīkī, Muṣṭafā Efendi (1600) ix, **126b** –IX, **131b**
Selayar vi, 116a – VI, 113b
Selčuk → Aya Solūk
Selčük b. Toḳaḳ Temir Yalïgh x, 690a – X, 732b
Seldjen-oghlu iii, 1199a – III, 1229a
Seldjuks/Seldjukides → Saldjūḳid(e)s
Selīm I (Yavuz) (Ottoman) (1520) i, 21b, 182b, 310b, 329b, 362a, 396a, 441a, 468a, 475a, 477a, 553b, 1032b, 1120b, 1207b, 1208a, 1234a; ii, 7b, 38b, 72b, 240a, 286a, b, 291b, 340a, 373b, 374a, 400a, 420b, 634b, 684a, 722b, 968a, 1042a; iii, 213b, 216a, 341b, 708b, 1183b; iv, 376a, 553a, 716b, 868b, 880a, 899b, 900a, 945b, 1156a; v, 269b; vi, 150a, 231b, 315a, 325a, 530a, b, 531a, 544a, 588a, 795a; vii, 176b, 272b, 319a; viii, 195b; ix, **127a**; s, 274a –

I, 22b, 187b, 320b, 340a, 373a, 407b, 453b, 482a, 489a, 491a, 571a, 1064a, 1154a, b, 1243b, 1244a, 1271a; II, 7b, 39a, 73b, 246b, 294a,b, 299b, 350a, 384a, 410b, 431a, 650b, 701a, 741a, 1066b; III, 219b, 222a, 351b, 730b, 1212b; IV, 392b, 576b, 745b, 902a, 912b, 932b, 933a, 978b, 1188a; V, 267b; VI, 148b, 225a, 300a, 309a, 514b, 515a, 528b, 572b, 785a; VII, 178b, 274b, 321a; VIII, 198b; VII, **131b**; S, 273b
Selīm II (Ottoman) (1574) i, 152a, 329b, 380a, 775b; ii, 25a, 82b, 737b; iii, 1183b; v, 67a, 138b, 814a; vi, 708b; viii, 124a, 195b, 770b; ix, **131b** – I, 156a, 340a, 391a, 798b; II, 25b, 84a, 756a; III, 1213a; V, 69a, 141a, 820b; VI, 697a; VIII, 126b, 199a, 796a; IX, **136a**
Selīm III (Ottoman) (1807) i, 63a, 790b, 948a, 1064b, 1165a, 1171b, 1252a, 1268a, 1278a; ii, 12a, 83b, 206b, 339a, 511b, 512a, 684a, 694a, 697a, 712b, 999a; iii, 384b, 627b; iv, 168a, 322b, 589a, 900b; v, 725a; vi, 6a, 58a, 284b, 725a, 757b, 801b, 912b; vii, 275a, 424a, 709b; viii, 59a, 75a; ix, **132b** – I, 65a, 814a, 977a, 1096b, 1199b, 1206b, 1290a, 1307a, 1317b; II, 12a, 85a, 213a, 349a, 524b, 525a, 701a, 711b, 715a, 731a, 1022a; III, 397a, 647b; IV, 175b, 337a, 612b, 933a; V, 730a; VI, 6a, 56a, 269b, 714a, 747a, 791b, 904a; VII, 277a, 425a, 710b; VIII, 60a, 76b; IX, **137b**
Selīm Giray I (Crimea/-ée) (1704) i, 893b; ii, 990b, 1047a; iv, 569a; v, 140a; ix, **134b** – I, 920a; II, 1013a, 1071b; IV, 591b; V, 142b, 143a; IX, **139b**
Selīm Giray II (Crimea/-ée) (1748) vi, 1002b – VI, 995a
Selīm Giray III (Crimea/-ée) (1771) i, 4b; v, 141a – I, 4b; V, 143b
Selīm Meḥmed Pas̲h̲a v, 36a – V, 37a
Selīm Pas̲h̲a ii, 636a – II, 652b
Selmān Reʾīs (1527) iv, 552b; ix, **135a** – IV, 576b; IX, **140a**
Selwī (Sevlievo) ix, **136a** – IX, **141a**
Semāʿ K̲h̲āne → Samāʿ
Semarang s, 201a – S, 201a
Semaun s, 151b – S, 152a
Sembat Bagratuni (Armenia/-ie, 914) iv, 90a; vii, 395a – IV, 94a; VII, 396a
Semedirek/Semadirek (Samothrace) ix, **137a** – IX, **142a**
Semendria → Smederovo
Semetey b. Manas (Ḳirg̲h̲iz) vi, 371a – VI, 355b
Semey (Semipalatinsk) vi, 768b – VI, 757b
Semīr Aḥmed Pas̲h̲a (XVI) vii, 7a – VII, 7a
Semireč(i)ye ii, 43a; iii, 1120a; v, 858b; vi, 274a, 618b; vii, 218a; ix, 659a; x, 689a – II, 43b; III, 1148a; V, 865b; VI, 259a, 603b; VII, 219b; IX, 684b; X,
Şemo, Ereb v, 484a – V, 487a
Sencer Divitçioğlu (XX) vi, 96a – VI, 94a
Sened-i Ittifāḳ ii, 640a,b – II, 656a,b
Senegal ii, 94a, 567a; vi, 281b; vii, 609a; ix, 137b; x, 465a, 575a; s, 179a, 182a, 218a – II, 95b, 581b; VI, 266b; VII, 608b; ix, **142b**; X, 499a, ; S, 180b, 182a, 218a
Senghor Léopold Sédar ix, 144b – IX, 149b
Senkere (Sankara) ix, **148b** – IX, **153b**
Senna → Sanandad̲j̲
Sennār → Sinnār
Senneh s, 136b, 142b, 145a – S, 136a, 142a, 145a
Senoufo ii, 63a; v, 252b – II, 64b; V, 250b
Şenyurt vi, 542a – VI, 526b
Sepoy → Sipāhī
Sepoy Mutiny (1857) s, 325b – S, 325a
"Septimains" → Sabʿiyya
Serajévo → Sarajevo
Serʿasker → Bāb-i Serʿasker
Serbest Firka s, 47b – S, 48a
Serbest(iyyet) iii, 589b – III, 610a
Serbia/-e → Ṣirb
Serçe Liman vii, 45b – VII, 45b
Seringapatam → S̲h̲rīrangapaṭṭanam
Serḳīn, Awlād v, 596a, b – V, 600a
Serres (Serrai) → Siroz
Servet → Ṭāhir Bey
Seth → S̲h̲īt̲h̲
Sétif vi, 435a; s, 145a – VI, 420b; S, 144b
Sevan → Gökče-Tengiz
Sevdalinka i, 1271a – I, 1310a
"Seveners" → Sabʿiyya
Severus/Sévère → Ibn al-Muḳaffaʿ
Sèves, Colonel → Sulaymān Pas̲h̲a al-Faransawī
Sevilla/-e → Is̲h̲bīliya
Sevin Beg → K̲h̲ān-zāda Bēgum
Sevind̲j̲ b. Būrī iii, 120a – III, 122b
Şevket Süreyya Aydemir (XX) vi, 95a – VI, 93a
Sewind̲j̲ (amīr, Türkmen) (XIII) vi, 501a – VI, 486a
Seychelles ix, **149a** – IX, **154a**
Seydī Aḥmed Pas̲h̲a v, 258b – V, 256b
Seydī ʿAlī Pas̲h̲a v, 764a – V, 770a
Seyf el-Dīn, Ömer v, 194b – V, 191b
Seyfī (1590) ix. **149b** – IX, **154a**
Seyhan → Sayḥān
Seyrānī (XIX) vi, 826b – VI, 817a
Seyrek-zāde vi, 971a – VI, 963b
Seytek (Ḳirg̲h̲iz) vi, 371a – VI, 355b
Seyyid → Sayyid
Sezāʾī Ḥasan Dede (1738) ii, 686a; ix, **150a** – II, 703b; IX, **154b**
Sezāʾī, Sāmī Pas̲h̲a-zāde (1936) v, 194a, 195a; ix, **150a** – V, 191b, 192b; IX, **155a**
Ṣfar, Bas̲h̲īr iv, 159b – IV, 166b
Sfax v, 220b – V, 218a-b
Sgrafiatto iv, 1166b – IV, 1199a
S̲h̲aaban Robert (1962) vi, 612b, 613a; ix, **150b** – VI, 597b, 598a; IX, **155b**
S̲h̲aʿanba v, 361b, 362a – V, 362b, 363a
S̲h̲aʿb i, 535a; iv, 334a, 746a, 819a; ix, **150b** – I, 551b; IV, 348b, 776a, 851b; IX, **155b**
S̲h̲aba → Katanga
S̲h̲aʿbad̲h̲a (S̲h̲aʿwad̲h̲a) ix, **152b** – IX, **157b**
S̲h̲abak, Banū i, 990a; iv, 187b; ix, **152b** – I, 1020b; IV, 196a; IX, **157b**
S̲h̲abak̲h̲tān ix, **153b** – IX, **158b**
S̲h̲aʿbān (month/mois) ix, **154a** – IX, **159a**
S̲h̲aʿbān I, al-Malik al-Kāmil (Mamlūk) (1345) iii, 48a; v, 1141a; ix, **154b** – III, 50a; V, 1134a; IX, **159b**
S̲h̲aʿbān II, al-Malik al-As̲h̲raf Nāṣir al-Dīn (Mamlūk) (1377) i, 790a, 1050b; ii, 970a; iii, 346b; vii, 171a; ix, **154b**; s, 395b – I, 813a, 1082a; II, 992a; III, 357a; VII, 172b; IX, **160a**; S, 396a
S̲h̲aʿbān Welī (1568) ix, 155b – IX, 160b
al-S̲h̲ābandar, ʿAbd al-Raḥmān iii, 522b – III, 540b
al-Shaʿbāniyya i, 426b; iv, 991b, 992a; ix, **155a** – I, 439a; IV, 1024a, b; IX, **160b**
S̲h̲abānkāra, Banū iii, 1097a; v, 161a, 450b, 454a, 671a; vii, 408a; viii, 701b; ix, **156b**; s, 326a, 382b – III, 1124a; V, 159b, 453a, 456b, 676a; VII, 409b; VIII, 721b; IX, **161b**; S, 325b, 383a
S̲h̲abānkāraʾī, Muḥammad b. ʿAlī (1358) i, 1131a; vii, 987a; ix, **158b** – I, 1165b; VII, 987b; IX, **163b**
S̲h̲ābarān ix, 488b – IX, 507a
S̲h̲ābās̲h̲iyya ix, **159a** – IX, **164a**

Shabath b. Ribʿī (VII) vii, 522b – VII, 523a
al-Shābb al-Ẓarīf → Ibn al-ʿAfīf al-Tilimsānī
Shabbānāt, Banū vi, 141b, 142a, b, 294a, 595a – VI, 139b, 140a, 141a, 279a, 579b
al-Shabbās (1052) iv, 663b – IV, 690b
Shabbatay Ṣebī (1676) ix, **159a** – IX, **164b**
Shabbaz → Kāth
Shabbetai Ṣebi ii, 615b, 987a – II, 631a, 1009b
al-Shābbī, Abu 'l-Ḳāsim (1934) i, 598b; ix, **160a** – I, 618a; IX, **165b**
al-Shābbī, Muḥammad al-Masʿūdī (XVII) vi, 355b – VI, 339b
Shabeelle → Shebelle
Shābbī Sīdī ʿArfa viii, 763a – VIII, 788b
Shabbīr Ḥasan Khān Djosh (1982) ix, **161a** – IX, **166b**
Shābbiyya iii, 69b; iv, 828a – III, 71b; IV, 861a
al-Shaʿbī, ʿĀmir b. Sharāḥīl (722) ix, **162b** – IX, **167b**
al-Shaʿbī, al-ḳāḍī al-Kūfī (721) vi, 670b; vii, 631b; viii, 387a; s, 232b – VI, 657a; VII, 631a; VIII, 400a; S, 232b
Shabīb b. Badjara iii, 887a, 889a – III, 911a, 912b
Shabīb b. al-Barṣāʾ vii, 629b – VII, 629a
Shabīb b. Shayba, Abū Maʿmar (VIII) ix, **163b** – IX, **169a**
Shabīb b. Waththāb (Numayrī) (1038) vii, 118a – VII, 120b
Shabīb b. Yazīd b. Nuʿaym al-Shaybānī (697) i, 77a, 693b; iii, 40b, 203b, 649b, 715b, 1168a; iv, 369b, 1075b; ix, 164a, 766b –
I, 79a, 714b; III, 42b, 209a, 670b, 737b, 1196b; IV, 385b, 1107b; ix, **169b**, 799b
Shabīb al-Nadjrānī iv, 369b – IV, 385b
Shabībiyya iv, 369b – IV, 385b
Shābīn Ḳarā Ḥiṣār iv, 578b – IV, 601b
Shabistar vi, 72b, 73a – VI, 70b
Shabistarī, Maḥmūd-i → Maḥmūd Shabistarī
Shabistarī, Mudjtahid (XX) iv, 166b – IV, 173b
Shaʿbiyya → al-Nukkār
Shābkhāne iv, 579a – IV, 602b
Shabrīṭ b. al-Ṭawīl, Banū s, 82a – S, 81b
Shabṭūn (819) ix, **165a** – IX, **170a**
al-Shābush(t)ī, Abū 'l-Ḥasan ʿAlī (988) ii, 127a, 195a; vi, 199b; vii, 390b; ix, **165b** –
II, 130a, 201a; VI, 183b; VII, 391b; IX, **170b**
Shabwa iii, 52a,b; vi, 80b, 559a, 560b; ix, **165b**; s, 336b, 337a, b – III, 54a,b; VI, 78b, 544a, 545a; IX,, **171a**; S, 336b, 337a
Shādagān ii, 181a – II, 187a
Shadd ix, **166b** – IX, **172a**
Shaddād b. ʿĀd i, 181a; iii, 173b, 1270b; ix, **169a** – I, 186a; III, 177b, 1303b; IX, **174b**
Shaddād Abū ʿAntara s, 178a – S, 179a
Shaddād b. ʿAmr (VII) i, 44b; ix, **169a** – I, 46a; IX, **174b**
Shaddādid(e)s i, 420b, 421a, 507b, 639a, 660b, 796b; iv, 345a, 347a, b, 670a; v, 452a, 489a; vi, 64b, 274a; ix, **169a** –
I, 432b, 433a, 523a, 659b, 681b, 820a; IV, 360a, 361b, 362a, 697b; V, 454b, 492a; VI, 62b, 259a; IX, **174b**
Shādgeldī → Ḥadjdjī Shādgeldī
Shādhdh iii, 25b, 26b – III, 27a,b
Shadhfarī vi, 384a – VI, 368a
Shādhī iii, 115a – III, 117b
Shādhī Ayyūb → Ayyūb b. Shādhī
al-Shādhilī, Abu 'l-Ḥasan ʿAlī b. ʿAbd Allāh al-Djabbār al-Zarwīlī (1258) i, 1b, 91b, 309a, 1019b; iii, 513b, 722b; iv, 449b; vi, 280a, 355a, b, 356a; ix, **170b**; x, 247a; s, 350b –
I, 1b, 94a, 318b, 1050b; III, 531a, 745a; IV, 469b; VI, 264b, 339a, 340a; IX, **176a**; X, 266a; S, 350b
al-Shādhilī, ʿAlī b. ʿUmar (1418) i, 781a; iv, 449b, 450a, b, 741a; vii, 513b –
I, 804b; IV, 469b, 470a, b, 771a; VII, 513b
al-Shādhilī, Shams al-Dīn Abu 'l-Fatḥ b. Wafāʾ al-Iskandarī (1358) vi, 112a – VI, 109b
al-Shādhiliyya i, 70b, 371a, 596b, 679b, 966a, 1260b; ii, 160a, 224a,b; iii, 339b, 535b, 670b; iv, 992b; v, 948b; vi, 88a, 203b, 454b; vii, 246a; viii, 18b; ix, **172b**, 507b; x, 247a; s, 18a, 44a, 93a, 208b, 223a, 244a, 278b, 408a, 411a –
I, 72b, 382a, 615b, 700a, 996a, 1298b; II, 165a, 231a,b; III, 349b, 554b, 692b; IV, 1025a; V, 952b; VI, 86a, 187b, 440a; VII, 248a; VIII, 18b; IX, **178a**, 527a; X, 266a; S, 18b, 44b, 93a, 208a, 223a, 244a, 278b, 408b, 411b
Shadhkān → Shāpūr
Shādī Khān (Bengal(e)) (1442) vi, 46b – VI, 45a
Shādiābād → Māndū
Shadirwān iv, 481a; v, 1146a; ix, **175a** –
IV, 502a; V, 1137b; IX, **180a**
Shadjāʿat Khān (Gudjarāt) (1701) iv, 93a – IV, 97a
Shadjāʿat Khān (Mālwā) (1554) vi, 310a, 407a – VI, 295a, 391b
Shadjar(at) al-Durr, umm Khalīl (1257) i, 732a, 766a; vi, 45a, 261b, 321a,b, 327a; vii, 166b, 990a; viii, 989a; ix, **176a** – I, 754a, 789a; VI, 43b, 246a, 305b, 306a, 311b; VII, 168a, 991a; VIII, 1024a; IX, **181b**
al-Shadjdjār i, 704a – I, 725a
Shadūna (Media Sidonia) ix, **176b** – IX, **182a**
Shādyākh vi, 854a – VI, 845b
Shafāʿa i, 334b, 958b; ii, 306b; ix, **177b** – I, 345a, 988a; II, 315a; IX, **183a**
al-Shafaḳ ix, **179b** – IX, **185a**
Shāfiʿ b. ʿAlī al-ʿAskalānī (1330) vi, 144a, 352a; vii, 167a; ix, **180b** – VI, 142b, 336a; VII, 169a; ix, **186b**
Shafīʿ Māzandarānī, Mīrzā s, 336a, 406b –
S, 335b, 406a
Shafīʿa Yazdī (1670) iv, 1124b; ix, **186a** –
IV, 1156a; IX, **187a**
al-Shāfiʿī, al-Imām Abū ʿAbd Allāh Muḥammad b. Idrīs (820) i, 123b, 155a, 259a, 272b, 551a, 588b, 773a, 1130b, 1199a, 1242a; ii, 102b, 889b; iii, 24a, 63b, 162b, 674b, 1024a; iv, 256a, 425a, 430a, 896a; v, 240a, 731b, 1131a, 1142a; vi, 113b, 263b, 265b, 352b, 353a, 451b, 452a, 605a, 652b, 739a; vii, 691b; viii, 497b; ix, **181a** –
I, 127a, 159a, 267a, 281a, 568b, 607b, 796a, 1164b, 1234b, 1280a; II, 104b, 910a; III, 25a, 66a, 166a, 696a, 1049b; IV, 267b, 443b, 449a, 928b; V, 237b, 736b, 1127a, 1135a; VI, 111b, 248b, 250a, 336b, 337a, 437a, 589b, 637b, 728a; VII, 691b; VIII, 514b; ix, **187a**
al-Shāfiʿī, Muḥammad b. al-Ḥasan (1277) vi, 354a – VI, 338a
Shāfiʿiyya i, 150b, 338a, 339a; ii, 559a; iii, 6b, 17a, 512b, 687b; iv, 46a, 47b, 172b, 269b; v, 109b; vi, 2a, 3a; ix, **185a** –
I, 155a, 349a, b; II, 573a; III, 6b, 17b, 530a, 709b; IV, 48b, 50a, 180a, 281b; V, 112a; VI, 2a, 3a; IX, **191a**
Shafiḳ Manṣūr (1925) viii, 360a – VIII, 372b
Shāfil (Yemen) i, 446a – I, 459a
Shafshawa(ān)/Shīshāwa i, 55b; vi, 742b, 743b; ix, 189b – I, 57b; VI, 731b, 732b; IX, **195b**
Shaftī, Sayyid Muḥammad Bāḳir (1844) vii, 302b, 453b; s, 75b, 135a – VII, 304b, 454b; S, 76a, 134b
Shafūniyya vi, 544b – VI, 529a
Shāgirds iii, 217b – III, 224a
Shāh/Shāhanshāh (titles/titres) v, 630a, b; ix, **190b** – V, 634a, b; IX, **196a**

Shāh b. Mīkāl (Mīkālī) (914) vii, 26a – VII, 26a
Shāh ʿAbbās I, II, III (Ṣafawid(e)) → ʿAbbās
Shāh ʿAbd Allāh (1485) ix, 269b; x, 256a – IX, 381b; X, 274b
Shāh ʿAbd al-ʿAẓīm al-Ḥasanī (864) ii, 650b; vi, 21a; ix, **191a** – II, 667a; VI, 19a; IX, **197a**
Shāh ʿAbd al-ʿAzīz al-Dihlawī → ʿAbd al-ʿAzīz al-Dihlawī
Shāh ʿAbd al-Ḳādir Dihlawī → ʿAbd al-Ḳādir Dihlawī
Shāh ʿAbd al-Laṭīf → Bhitāʾī
Shāh ʿAbd al-Raḥīm al-ʿUmarī i, 1023a; ii, 254a; v, 1135b – I, 1054b; II, 261b; V, 1131a
Shāh Abu ʾl-Ḳāsim Sulṭān → Bēglār
Shāh Afḍal (Chitral) (1795) ii, 30a – II, 30b
Shāh Afḍal II b. Muḥtaram Shāh II (Chitral) (1853) ii, 30a – II, 30b
Shāh ʿĀlam I Bahādur Shāh (Mughal) → Bahādur Shāh
Shāh ʿĀlam II, Djalāl al-Dīn ʿAlī Dhawhar (Mughal) (1806) i, 813b; ii, 121b, 186a, 808b, 1092b; iii, 428a; vi, 535b, 536a, 537a; vii, 94a, 316a, 346a; viii, 5b; ix, **192b** – I, 836b; II, 124a, 192a, 827b, 1118a; III, 441b; VI, 520a, b, 521b; VII, 95b, 318b, 348a; VIII, 6a; IX, **198b**
Shāh ʿĀlam b. Burhān al-Dīn Ḳuṭbi-i ʿĀlam (XV) i, 1329b; vi, 781b – I, 1370a; VI, 771a
Shāh ʿĀlam Khān iii, 59b – III, 62a
Shāh ʿAlī Khān iv, 723b, 849b – IV, 752b, 882b
Shāh-i Arman (Turconans, Akhlāṭ) i, 329a; vi, 781b; ix, **193a** – I, 339b; VI, 771a; IX, **198b**
Shāh Bandar ix, **193b** – IX, **199b**
Shāh Beg Arghūn i, 227b, 228a, 627b, 961b, 1192a; iii, 420a, 632b; iv, 535a, 536b – I, 234b, 235a, 648a, 991b, 1227b; III, 433b, 654a; IV, 558a, 560a
Shāh Bēgam (1605) vii, 331b – VII, 333a
Shāh Budāgh Khān, amīr (XVII) vi, 407a – VI, 392a
Shāh Dāʿī Shīrāzī (poet/poète) (XV) viii, 45b – VIII, 46a
Shāh Dawla, pīr (1713) ii, 1131b – II, 1158a
Shāh Djahān I (Mughal) (1666) i, 60b, 66a, 81a, 199b, 208a, 228b, 252b, 253a, 686b, 710a, 856a, 1161a, 1200a, 1324a, 1329b, 1331a, 1347b; ii, 99b, 121a, 157b, 162a, 180a, 380a, 446a, 598b; iii, 424a, 450a, 492b, 1204a; iv, 507a, 543a, 914b, 1018a, b; v, 74a, 598a, 600a, 688a, 1135b, 1214a; vi, 126b, 131b, 345b, 407a, 426a, 456b, 533b; vii, 139b, 189a, 194a, 204a, b, 315a, 318a, 332a, 339a, 346a, 404b, 443b; viii, 74a, b; ix, **195a**; x, 58b; s, 63a, 142b, 167b, 258a, b, 313b, 366b, 420b – I, 62b, 68a, 83b, 205a, 214b, 235b, 260b, 261a, 707b, 731b, 879b, 1196a, 1235b, 1364b, 1370b, 1371b, 1387b; II, 101b, 124a, 162a, 167a, 185b, 458a, 613b; III, 438a, 465b, 509b, 1234b; IV, 529a, 566b, 947b, 1050a, b; V, 76a, 602a, 603b, 693a, 1131a, 1203b; VI, 124b, 129b, 329b, 392a, 411b, 442a, 518a; VII, 141b, 189b, 194b, 205a, b, 317b, 320a, 333b, 334a, 341a, 347b, 406a, 444b; VIII, 76a; IX, **200b**; X, 60b; S, 63b, 142a, 167b, 258a, 313a, 366b, 421a
Shāh Djahān II, Rafīʿ al-Dawla (Mughal) (1719) i, 914a, 1026a; vii, 457a – I, 914b, 1057b; VII, 457a
Shāh Djahān III (Mughal) (1760) vii, 316a – VII, 318b
Shāh Djahān b. Suyurghatmïsh (1306) v, 163a, 554a – V, 161a, 558b
Shāh Djalāl Mudjarrad Kūnyāʾī (XIV) ix, 611a – IX, 634a
Shāh Dūst → Fatḥ Khān
Shāh Fāḍil ii, 30a – II, 30b
Shāh Faḳīr ʿAlwī (1780) ix, 440a – IX, 457a
Shāh Fakhr al-Dīn ii, 55a, 56a; iii, 436a, 1158b – II, 56a, 57a; III, 450a, 1187a
Shāh Fulādī (peak/sommet) i, 221b – I, 228a
Shāh Ghāzī Rustam I iv, 266a – IV, 278a
Shāh al-Ḥamīd ʿAbd al-Ḳādir (Marakkayar) (1600) vi, 503b – VI, 489a
Shāh Ḥātim Dihlawī iii, 119a – III, 121b
Shāh Ḥusayn Abbāsī v, 829a – V, 835a
Shāh Ḥusayn Khān i, 1219a – I, 1255b
Shāh-i Djangal Bash ii, 205a – II, 211b
Shāh Ismāʿīl I, II, III (Ṣafawid(e)s) → Ismāʿīl I, II, III
Shāh Ismāʿīl Ghāzī ʿArabī (XV) ii, 297a; viii, 598b – II, 305a; VIII, 617b
Shāh Kābulī i, 1201a – I, 1237a
Shāh Ḳādān (Khalīfa) (XVI) vii, 440a – VII, 441a
Shāh Ḳādirī, Mullā ii, 134b, 378b – II, 138a, 389a
Shāh Kalīm Allāh Djahānābadī ii, 551; iii, 432b – II, 56a; III, 446b
Shāh Ḳāsim b. Muḥammad Nūr Bakhsh s, 423b – S, 423b
Shāh Ḳāsim Fayḍbakhsh b. Nūrbakhsh (1511) viii, 135b – VIII, 138a
Shāh Ḳāsim Huwaʾllāhī i, 1201a – I, 1237a
Shāh Ḳāsim Sulaymānī (1606) vii, 132b – VII, 134b
Shāh Katōr → Muḥtaram Shāh II
Shāh Khāmūsh iv, 202b – IV, 211b
Shāh Ḳulī Ḳādjār iv, 389a – IV, 404b
Shāh Ḳulī Sulṭān iv, 476a – IV, 496b
Shāh Madār → Badīʿ al-Dīn
Shāh Maḥmūd (Muẓaffarid(e)) (1375) ii, 401b – II, 412a
Shāh Mālang iv, 202b – IV, 211b
Shāh Malik b. ʿAlī Yabghu (Ghuzz) (XI) ii, 4b, 1108a; iv, 1067a; vi, 416a; ix, **195b** – II, 4b, 1134a; IV, 1098b; VI, 401a; IX, **201a**
Shāh Manṣūr Shīrāzī (1581) ix, **195b** – IX, **201b**
Shāh-i Mashhad v, 1147b, 1148a – V, 1139a
Shāh Meḥmed b. Ḳarā Yūsuf iv, 586b, 587b – IV, 609a, 611a
Shāh Mīnā v, 634b, 636a – V, 639a, 640a
Shāh Mīr (Mīrzā) → Shams al-Dīn Shāh Mīrzā
Shāh Mīr b. Mīr Ḳawām al-Dīn (Marʿashī) (XVII) vi, 516a – VI, 501b
Shāh Mīrs s, 167b – S, 167b
Shāh Mīrzā Zarkash vii, 95b – VII, 97a
Shāh Muḥammad b. ʿAbd Aḥmad (1661) ix, **196a** – IX, **201b**
Shāh Muḥammad ʿAlī (Ḳādjār) (1909) v, 24b; vi, 21b – V, 25a; VI, 19a
Shāh Muḥibb Allāh b. Khalīl Allāh (XV) vi, 63a – VI, 61a
Shāh Muḥibb Allāh b. Shāh Niʿmat Allāh (Kirmān) (XV) vi, 66b – VI, 64b
Shāh Muḥibb Allāh Ilāhābādī (XVII) viii, 69a – VIII, 69a
Shāh Murād (Bukhārā) (1800) vi, 766a – VI, 755b
Shāh Muẓaffar (Muẓaffarid(e)) (1353) i, 1211b; vii, 820b – I, 1247b; VII, 822a
Shāh Muẓaffar al-Dīn (Ḳādjār) (1907) vi, 21a – VI, 19a
Shāh Naṣīr (XVIII) ii, 221b – II, 228b
Shāh Nawāz I (Vakhtang, Georgia/-e) (XVII) v, 493b – V, 496b
Shāh Nawāz II (Giorgi XI, Georgia/-e) (1688) v, 493b – V, 496b
Shāh Nawāz Khān → Gurgīn Khān
Shāh Nawāz Khān → Ṣamṣām al-Dawla Khān
Shāh Nawāz Khān (1758) vii, 343a – VII, 344b
Shāh Nawāz Khān (Chitral) ii, 30a – II, 30b

Shāh Nawāz Khān (Iridj) → Iridj Shāhnawāz Khān
Shāh Nawāz Khān Awrangābādī v, 935b – V, 939b
Shāh Niʿmat Allāh → Niʿmat Allāhiyya
Shāh Niyaz Aḥmad ii, 55a – II, 56a
Shāh Nizām al-Dīn i, 853a – I,876b
Shāh Nizār iv, 201b – IV, 210b
Shāh Nūr Muḥammad ii, 55a – II, 56a
Shāh Raḍī al-Dīn i, 852b; iv, 202b – I, 876b; IV, 211b
Shāh Rafīʿ al-Dīn i, 69a; iii, 430b, 431a; iv, 196a – I, 70b; III, 444b, 445a; IV, 204b
Shāh Rūd v, 656b; ix, **196b**; s, 149a – V, 660b; IX, **202a**; S, 149a
Shāh Rūkh (Afshārid(e)) (1795) vi, 715a – VI, 704a
Shāh Rūkh (Čaghatayid(e) → Shāh Rūkh Mīrzā b. Tīmūr
Shāh Rūkh I (Khoḳand) (XVIII) ii, 45a; v, 29a – II, 46a; V, 30a
Shāh Rūkh Mīrzā b. Ibrāhīm Mīrzā (Badakhshān Mīrzās) (1607) i, 230a, b, 246b, 295b; v, 59a; vii, 135a; s, 43b – I, 237a, b, 254b, 305a; VII, 137a; S, 44a
Shāh Rūkh Mīrzā b. Tīmūr Lang (Tīmūrid(e))(1447) i, 66b, 90b, 227a, 230a, b, 246b, 295b, 1001b, 1054a, 1133b; ii, 6a, 270b, 792a; iii, 57b, 58a, 114a, 346b, 778a; iv, 33a, b, 34a, 102b, 586b, 587a, b, 642b, 721b, 945a, 1020a, 1040b; v, 59a, 858b; vi, 16a, 61b, 324b, 505a, 512b, 513a, b, 619a, 621a, 714b, 976b; vii, 173a, 313b, 928a; viii, 750a; ix, **197a**; x, 513b, 812a; s, 43b, 49a, 84a – I, 68b, 93b, 234a, 237a, b, 254b, 305a, 1032a, 1086a, 1168a; II, 6a, 278b, 811a; III, 60a, b, 116b, 357a, 801b; IV, 35b, 36a, 107a, 609a, b, 611a, 669a, 750b, 978a, 1052a, 1072a; V, 30a, 59b, 490b, 703b, 865b; VII, 14b, 174b, 309a, 316a, 498a, b, 604a, 606a, 928b, 968b; VIII, 770b; IX, **202b**; X, 550a, ; S, 49b, 84a, 97a
Shāh Rustam v, 829a – V, 835a
Shāh Ṣafī I → Ṣafī I Shāh
Shāh Shudjāʿ (Afghānistān) → Shudjāʿ al-Mulk Durrānī
Shāh Shudjāʿ (Bengal(e)) i, 229a, 606a, 768b, 769a, 1333a; ii, 216b, 813b – I, 236a, 625b, 791b, 792a, 1272b; II, 223a, 832b
Shāh Shudjāʿ b. Mubāriz al-Dīn (Muẓaffarid(e)) (1384) ii, 401b; iii, 56a; iv, 498b; v, 827b, 828b; vii, 480b, 481a, 820b; ix, **198b**; s, 415a – II, 412a; III, 58a; IV, 520a; V, 833b, 835a; VII, 480a, b, 822b; IX, **204a**; S, 415a
Shāh Sulaymān I (Ṣafawid(e)) (1694) → Sulaymān Shāh
Shāh Sulaymān II (Ṣafawid(e)) (1763) vi, 18a, 483b, 516b – VI, 16a, 469b, 501b
Shāh Sulaymān (Taunsa, Čishtiyya) ii, 56a – II, 57a
Shāh Sulṭān bint Selīm I (1575) ix, **199b** – IX, **205a**
Shāh Sulṭān bint Selīm II (1580) ix, **200b** – IX, **206a**
Shāh Sulṭān Ḥusayn I (Ṣafawid(e)) (1722) vi, 16b, 18a, 483b, 525a, 551a, 856a; vii, 62a; viii, 771b – VI, 14b, 16a, 469b, 510a, 535b, 847b; VII, 62a; VIII, 797a
Shāh Sulṭān Muḥammad Badakhshī i, 852b – I, 876a
Shāh Ṭāhir al-Ḥusaynī (Muḥammad Shāhī) (1545) ix, **200b** – IX, **206b**
Shāh Ṭahmāsp I, II (Ṣafawid(e)s) → Ṭahmāsp I, II
Shāh-Temir (fortress/forteresse) vi, 418a – VI, 403a
Shāh Turkān umm Fīrūz Shāh I Rukn al-Dīn (Delhi) (XIII) vi, 488a – VI, 474a
Shāh Walī Allāh al-Dihlawī → al-Dihlawī
Shāh Walī Khān i, 232b – I, 239b
Shāh Wilāyat (XII) vii, 965b – VII, 966a
Shāhābād ii, 1120a; s, 313a – II, 1146a; S, 312b
Shahāda i, 332b, 407b; iii, 269b; ix, **201a** – I, 342b, 419a; III, 277a; IX, **207a**
Shāhanshāh (title/titre) → Shāh
Shaḥāra, Banū vi, 80a – VI, 78a
Shaḥāra (Yemen) vi, 436b; ix, **201b** – VI, 422a; IX, **207a**
Shahāridja ix, **202a** – IX, **207b**
Shāh-bandar i, 1013a; vi, 209b; s, 199b, 200a – I, 1044a; VI, 194a; S, 200a
Shahbander-zāde → Ḥilmī, Aḥmed
Shahbāz Girāy ii, 25b, 1114a – II, 26a, 1140a
Shāhbāz Ḳalandar iv, 474a – IV, 494b
Shahdānadj ix, 202a – IX, 208a
Shāhdiz iii, 725b; iv, 200a – III, 748a; IV, 208b
Shāhdjahān Bēgam i, 1196a, 1197a – I, 1231a, b, 1232b
Shāhdjahānābād i, 253a; ii, 258a, 259a; iii, 450b; v, 889a; vii, 332b, 333b – I, 260b; II, 266a; III, 466a; V, 895b; VII, 334b, 335a
Shāhdjahānpūr s, 292b – S, 292a
Shāhdjī Bhōnslē (XVII) i, 769a, 1202b; vi, 534b; viii, 74b – I, 792a, 1238a; VI, 519a; VIII, 76b
Shāhgarh → Kanawdj
al-Shaḥḥām, Abū Yaʿḳūb Yūsuf (IX) i, 128b; ii, 569b; iv, 1163a; vii, 604a; ix, **202b**; s, 226b – I, 132b, II, 584a; IV, 1195a; VII, 604a; IX, **208a**; S, 226b
Shāhī (coinage/monnaie) ix, **203a** – IX, **208b**
Shāhī (island/île) vi, 501b, 504b – VI, 486b, 489b
Shāh-i Zinda (Tīmūrid) s, 154b – S, 154b
Shāhid iv, 354a; ix, **207a** – IV, 369b; IX, **212a**
Shahīd ix, **203b** – IX, **209b**
Shahīd (Shuhayd) b. al-Ḥusayn al-Balkhī (927) vi, 609a; ix, **208b**; s, 35a – VI, 594a; IX, **214b**; S, 35a
al-Shahīd al-Awwal → Muḥammad b. Makkī
Shahīd Balkhī → Shahīd (Shuhayd) b. al-Ḥusayn
Shahīd Muḥammad Pasha iv, 970a – IV, 1002a
al-Shahīd al-Thānī, Zayn al-Dīn b. ʿAlī (1557) vi, 13a; viii, 777b; ix, **209a**; s, 56b – VI, 12a; VIII, 803b; IX, **215a**; S, 57a
Shāhidbāzī v, 166a – V, 163b
Shāhidī (1550) vii, 349a – VII, 351a
Shāhīn (XX) s, 109b – S, 109a
Shahīn (Spāhbed) (VII) ix, 79b – IX, 82b
Shahīn, Āl ix, **210a** – IX, **216a**
Shāhīn, Banū → ʿImrān b. Shāhīn
Shāhīn, Dizh → Sāʾīn Ḳalʿa
Shāhīn, Lala (1388) i, 653b, 1159b, 1302b; ii, 683b, 722a, 914a, 1086a; iv, 1093a; vi, 290b; vii, 593a; ix, 211a – I, 674b, 1194b, 1342b; II, 700b, 740b, 935b, 1111b; IV, 1124a; VI, 276a; VII, 593a; IX, **217a**
Shāhīn, Mawlānā (XVI) iv, 309a, b; vii, 510b – IV, 323a, b; VII, 510b
Shāhīn b. ʿAbd Allāh (XIV) ix, 211a – IX, 217a
Shāhīn Girāy i, 310b – I, 320b
Shāhīn Girāy Khān i, 63a; ii, 447a; v, 141a, b – I, 64b; II, 458b; V, 143b, 144a
Shāhīn-i Shīrāzī (XIV) ix, **211a** – IX, **217a**
Shahmār vi, 937b – VI, 930a
Shahmardān b. Abi 'l-Khayr al-Rāzī (1120) vi, 908a; x, 146a – VI, 899b; X, 157b
Shāhnāmedjī ix, **211b** – IX, **217a**
Shāhnawāz Khān (1659) vi, 131b – VI, 129b
Shahnāz Āzād (XX) vi, 486a – VI, 472a
Shahnāz bint Muḥammad Riḍā Shāh Pahlawī (XX) vii, 447a – VII, 448a
Shāhpur vi, 62a – VI, 59b
Shahr ("town/ville") ix, **212a** – IX, **217b**

Shahr b. Bādhām i, 728a; s, 116a – I, 750a; S, 115b
Shahr b. Ḥawshab (718) vii, 576a – VII, 576b
al-Shahrāfī vi, 247b – VI, 231b
Shahrān iv, 994a – IV, 1026b
Shahrangīz (Shahrashūb) ix, **212a** – IX, **218a**
Shahrashūb → Shahrangīz
Shahrastān vi, 663b, 664b; viii, 439b – VI, 649b, 650b; VIII, 454b
al-Shahrastānī, Abu ʾl-Fatḥ Muḥammad b. ʿAbd al-Karīm (1153) i, 129a, 130a, 151b, 234b, 247a, 450a, 483b, 1340b; ii, 96b, 764b, 767a, 930a; iii, 328b, 496b; iv, 847a; vi, 347a, 476a; vii, 55a; ix, **214b**; s, 25b, 43b, 343b, 345a – I, 132b, 133b, 156a, 242a, 255a, 463a, 498a, 1380b; II, 98b, 783a, 785b, 951b; III, 339a, 513b; IV, 880a, b; VI, 331b, 462a; VII, 55b; IX, **220b**; S, 26a, 44a, 343b, 344b
al-Shahrastānī, Muʿīn al-Dīn iii, 600a – III, 620b
al-Shahrastānī, Sayyid Muḥammad ʿAlī (1967) ix, **216b** – IX, **222b**
Shahrazād i, 361a, 362a, b; ix, **217b** – I, 372a, 373a; IX, **223b**
Shahrazūr (Shahrizūr) ix, **218a** – IX, **223b**
al-Shahrazūrī, Kamāl al-Dīn Abū ʾl-Faḍl Muḥammad (XII) viii, 132a – VIII, 134b
al-Shahrazūrī, Muḥyī ʾl-Dīn (ḳāḍī) (1190) vi, 111a; ix, **219b** – VI, 109a; IX, **225a**
al-Shahrazūrī, Shams al-Dīn (XIII) i, 236a; iv, 121a; ix, **219b** – I, 243a; IV, 126a; IX, **225b**
al-Shahrazūrī, Ṭaḳī ʾl-Dīn Ibn al-Ṣalāḥ → Ibn al-Ṣalāḥ
al-Shahrazūrī (vizier) (XII) iii, 1157b – III, 1186a
Shahrbarāz (630) iv, 342b; ix, 79b, 80a – IV, 357a; IX, 82b, 83b
Shahrdārī i, 978b – I, 1009a
Shahr-i Bābak v, 152a, b – V, 154a
Shahr-i Bilḳīs iv, 107b – IV, 112b
Shahr-i Khān v, 30a – V, 30b
Shahr-i Kurd vi, 719b – VI, 708b
Shahr-i Naw i, 952b; vi, 53a – I, 981b; VI, 51a
Shahr-i Sabz → Kash; Kish
Shāhrikī iv, 10b – IV, 11b
Shahrīr → Taʾrīkh
Shahristān i, 320b; iv, 98b; ix, **220a**; s, 406b – I, 330b; IV, 103a; IX, **226a**; S, 406b
Shahriyār I (Kāʾūsiyya, Bāwandid(e)) (825) i, 871b; iv, 645b – I, 896a; VI, 672a
Shahriyār II (Kaʾūsiyya, Bāwandid(e)) (930) s, 356b – S, 356b
Shahriyār III b. Dārā (Kāʾūsiyya, Bāwandid(e)) (1006) i, 1110a; ii, 919b; s, 309a – I, 1143b; II, 940b; S, 309a
Shahriyār, Sayyid Muḥammad (1988) ix, **220b** – IX, **226b**
Shahriyār b. Djahāngīr i, 686b; ii, 381a; iv, 1018a – I, 707b; II, 391a; IV, 1050b
Shahriyār b. al-Ḥasan (XI) ix, **221a** – IX, **227a**
Shahriyār b. Khusraw b. Djahāngīr (XVII) vii, 315a – VII, 317b
Shāriyār b. al-Maṣmughān → al-Māzyār b. Ḳārin
Shahrizūr i, 16a, 261a; v, 33b, 34a, 144b, 145b, 455b; viii, 463a – I, 16b, 269a; V, 34b, 35a, 147a, 148a, 458a; VIII, 479a
Shahr-kent → Djand
Shāhrūkh → Shāh Rūkh
Shāhrukh, Mīrzā i, 230a, b, 246b, 295b; v, 59a; s, 43b – I, 237a, b, 254b, 305a; V, 61a; S, 44a
Shāhrukh Bī v, 29a; s, 97b – V, 30a; S, 97a
Shāhrukhī ii, 120b – II, 123b
Shahrwīn b. Rustam Bāwand i, 871b; s, 356b – I, 896a; S, 356b
Shāhsivan (Shāhsewen), Banū iii, 1102a, 1108b, 1109a, 1110a; iv, 9b, 858b; vii, 498a; ix, **221a** – III, 1129a, 1136a, b, 1137a; IV, 10b, 891b; VII, 498a; **227a**
Shāhsuwār (Dhu ʾl-Ḳadr) (1472) i, 182b; ii, 38b, 239b; iii, 186b; iv, 462b; vi, 778a – I, 187b; II, 39a, 246b; III, 190b; IV, 483a, b; VI, 767b
Shāh-Takhtī (Araxes) vi, 203a – VI, 187a
Shāhū b. Sʾambhadjī (Marāṭhā) (1749) i, 913b; ii, 219a; iv, 1023b; vi, 535a, b, 536a – I, 941b; II, 225b; IV, 1055b; VI, 519b, 520a, b
Shahu Misham (Mombasa) vii, 226a – VII, 228a
Shāhwardī b. Muḥammadī v, 829a, b – V, 835b
Shāh-zāda → Miyān Gul Gul Shāhzada
Shāh-zāda (Bīdjāpūr) ii, 1084b – II, 1110a
Shāh-zāda Aḥmad v, 823a – V, 829a
Shāh-zāda Shāhrukh b. Muḥammad Bāḳī Tarkhān (Tarkhānid(e), Maklī) (1584) vi, 190a – VI, 173b
Shāʾiḳiyya, Banū vi, 794b; s, 278b – VI, 784b; S, 278b
Shaʿīr ix, 225a – IX, 252a
Shāʿir ix, **225a** – IX, **231a**
Shāʾista Khān iv, 177b – IV, 186a
Shakāk, Banū ix, **245a** – IX, **252b**
Shaḳāḳī (Shikaghī), Banū iii, 1102b, 1109a; ix, **246b** – III, 1129b, 1136b; IX, **253b**
Shakānī iii, 1097b – III, 1124b
Shakar Gandj → Farīd al-Dīn Masʿūd
Shakarkheldā ix, **246b** – IX, **254a**
Shaḳāwa ix, **246a** – IX, **254a**
Shaker Beklū i, 1157a – I, 1191b
Shaḳhab, Tell al- iii, 189a; vi, 545b, 546b, 547a, b, 548a – III, 193b; VI, 530a, 531a, b, 532a, b
Shakhbūṭ b. Dhiyāb i, 166b – I, 171a
Shakhbūṭ b. Sulṭān i, 166b; iv, 778b – I, 171a; IV, 809b
Shakhṣ i, 409b, 785a; ix, **247a** – I, 421a, 808a; IX, **254b**
Shakīb Arslān, Shaykh (1946) iii, 524b, 525a; iv, 159a; v, 794b; vii, 415b, 765a; ix, **248a**; s, 159b – III, 542b, 543a; IV, 166a; V, 800b; VII, 417a, 766b; IX, **255b**; S, 159b
Shaḳīf ʿArnūn → Ḳalʿat al-Shaḳīf
Shaḳīḳat al-Nuʿmān ix, **248b** – IX, **256a**
Shākir (ʿUḳba b. Nāfiʿ) (VII) vi, 743b – VI, 733a
Shākir (Zāb) vi, 435a – VI 420a
Shākir, Aḥmad Muḥammad (1958) ix, **249a** – IX, **256b**
Shākir, Banū → Mūsā b. Shākir, Banū
Shākir Pasha v, 462b – V, 465b
al-Shākiriyya ix, **249b** – IX, **257a**
Shaḳīshaḳiyya s, 197a – S, 197a
Shakk ix, **250a** – IX, **257b**
Shakkāf s, 111b, 112a – S, 111a
Shakkāziyya ix, **251b** – IX, **259a**
Shakkī iv, 350a; ix, **253b** – IV, 365a; **260b**
Shakla bint al-Maṣmughān (Damāwand) (IX) vi, 335a – VI, 319b
Shakshāk ii, 621a – II, 636b
Shāḳshāḳī Ibrāhīm Pasha i, 268a – I, 276a
Shakūbiyya ix, 255a – IX, 263a
Shakunda ix, 255b – IX, 263a
al-Shaḳundī, Abu ʾl-Walīd (1231) vi, 221a; vii, 191a, 207a, 209a; ix, **256a** – VI, 214b; VII, 191b, 208a, 210a; IX, **263b**
Shaḳūra i, 7a; ix, **256a** – I, 7a; IX, **264a**
Shaḳyā b. ʿAbd al-Wāḥid al-Miknāsī i, 82a, 634a – I, 84b, 654b
Shāl, Shālkot → Kwaṭṭa
Shāl(l)a → Salā
Shalla (Chella) ix, **258b** – IX, **267a**
al-Shalāḥī (XIV) vi, 215b; vii, 190a, b – VI, 199b; VII, 190a, b
Shalamanḳa (Shalamantiḳa) ix, **256b** s IX, **264a**

Sha'lān (Ruwala, Banū) viii, 644a – VIII, 663a
Shalanba (Dunbāwand) vi, 744b – VI, 733b
al-Shalawbīn, Abū 'Alī 'Umar (1247) iii, 338a; ix, **257b** – III, 348a; IX, **265b**
Shalbaṭarra ix, **258b** – IX, **266b**
Shālīmār i, 1347b, 1348a; vii, 332a, 333a; s, 63a – I, 1388a, b; VII, 333b, 334b; S, 63b
Shallāl, Banū vi, 902a – VI, 893b
al-Shalmaghānī, Abū Muḥammad → Muḥammad b. 'Alī al-Shalmaghānī
Shalṭīsh (Saltés) i, 6a, 155b; ix, **259a** – I, 6a, 160a; IX, **267b**
Shaltūt, Maḥmūd (1963) iv, 159b; ix, **260b**; s, 158a – IV, 166a; IX, **268b**; S, 158a
al-Shalūbīnī ii, 528b – II, 541b
Shālūs iii, 254b; s, 356b – III, 261b; S, 356a
Sham (Balučistān) s, 331b – S, 331b
Sham (Tabrīz) vi, 601b – VI, 586a
al-Shām/al-Sha'm (Syria/-e) i, 4b, 17a, 19a, 46a, 103a, 111a, 145a, 279a, 383b; ii, 595a, 661a, b, 676a, 854a; iii, 85a, 184a, 233a, 263b, 521a, 522b, 559a, 560b, 1254b; iv, 206a; vi, 25b, 59b, 60b, 64b, 273b, 364a, 378b, 387b, 467b, 469b, 470a, 796b; vii, 9b, 69b; viii, 906b; ix, **261b** – I, 4b, 17b, 19b, 47b, 106a, 114a, 149b, 287b, 394b; II, 610a, 677b, 678a, 693a, 874a; III, 87a, 188a, 239b, 271a, 539a, 540b, 578a, 580a, 1287a; IV, 215a; VI, 23b, 57b, 58b, 62b, 258a, 347b, 363a, 371b, 453a, b, 455a, b, 786b; VII, 10a, 70b; VIII, 937b; IX, **269b**
—art, architecture i, 609b, 1226a; v, 291a, b – I, 629a, 1262b; V, 290b
—demography/démographie s, 212a – S, 212b
—ethnography/ethnographie v, 440a, 469b, 1253b – V, 442b, 472b, 1244b
—history/histoire iv, 261b; v, 438a – IV, 273b; V, 440b
—institutions ii, 125b, 424a; iii, 99b, 521a; v, 912a, b, 1046b, 1090b – II, 128b, 435a; III, 102a, 538b; V, 918a, 1043a, 1088a
—language, literature/langue, littérature i, 568b, 575a; ii, 468a – I, 586b, 594a; II, 479b
—products/produits iii, 211a, 218b; ix, **261b** – III, 217a, 225a; IX, **269b**
Shāma ix, **281a** – IX, **289b**
Sham'a ix, **281b** – IX, **290a**
Shamākha → Shīrwān
Shamākhī ii, 87b; iii, 604a; iv, 350a; vi, 320a – II, 89b; III, 625a; IV, 365a; VI, 304b
Shamāmūn (Nubia/nubie) iv, 485b – IV, 506b
Shaman ix, **282a** – IX, **290b**
Shaman Khēl, Banū (Paṭhān) vi, 86a – VI, 84a
al-Shamardal b. Sharīk al-Yarbū'ī (VIII) viii, 377b; ix, **282b** – VIII, 390b; IX, **291a**
Shamash ('Irāḳ) vi, 650a – VI, 635a
Shāmāt s, 327a – S, 326b
Shambhadjī s, 55b – S, 56a
Sham'dānī-zāde iv, 761a – IV, 791b
Shamdīnān i, 427a; ix, **262b** – I, 439a; IX, **291a**
Sham'ī (XVII) i, 1208b, 1345b – I, 1244b, 1386a
al-Shāmī (1585) vi, 214b, 352b – VI, 199a, 337a
al-Shāmī, Abū Bakr (1095) s, 194a – S, 193b
al-Shāmī, Ibrāhīm b. Sulaymān (IX) i, 83a – I, 85b
Shāmī, Niẓām al-Dīn (XV) iii, 57b, 58a; ix, **283b** – III, 60a, b; IX, **292a**
Shāmil (Dāghistān) (1871) i, 755b, 756a; ii, 18a, 87b, 88b; iii, 157a; iv, 631a; v, 618a; ix, **283b** – I, 778a, 778b; II, 18b, 89a, 90a; III, 160b; IV, 656a; V, 622a; IX, **292a**
Shāmil-ḳal'e → Makhač-ḳal'e
Shamir b. Dhi 'l-Djawshan iii, 609b, 610b; iv, 836a – III, 630b, 631a; IV, 869a
Shamīrān → Tārom
Shamkh, Banū s, 37b – S, 37b
Shāmkhāl ii, 87a; v, 382a, b, 618a – II, 88b; V, 383a, b, 622a
Shāmlū i, 1159b; iii, 1100a, 1109b; iv, 577b; v, 243b – I, 1194a; III, 1127a, 1136b; IV, 601a; V, 241b
Shāmlū-Ustadjlū iii, 157b – III, 161a
Shammā' ix, **288a** – IX. **296b**
al-Shammākh b. Ḍirār al-Ghaṭafānī (643) i, 1154b; vii, 843b; viii, 377a; ix, **288b**; s, 304b – I, 1188b; VII, 844b; VIII, 389b; IX, **297a**; S, 304b
al-Shammākh b. Shudjā' (Shirwān) (IX) ix, 487a – IX, 506a
Shammākha (town/ville) ix, **289b**, 487a – IX, **298a**, 508a
al-Shammākhī al-Ifrānī, Abu 'l-'Abbās Aḥmad (1522) i, 121a, 125a, 167a, 1186a, 1287b; iii, 656b, 927b; vi, 311a, 840b; ix, **289b** – I, 124b, 128b, 171b, 1221a, 1327a; III, 678a, 952a: VI, 296a, 831a; IX, **298a**
al-Shammākhī, Abū Sākin 'Āmir i, 1053b – I, 1085a
Shammār, Banū i, 528b, 873b; ii, 77a, 492b; iii, 180a, 326b, 1065b, 1253b; v, 348a; vi, 371b, 614a, 733b, 902a; vii, 582a; ix, **290a**; s, 101b – I, 544b, 897b; II, 78b, 505a; III, 184a, 336b, 1092a, 1286a; V, 349a; VI, 356a, 599a, 722b, 893b; VII, 582b; IX, **298b**; S, 101a
Shammar Yuhar'ish (Yur'ish) (300) i, 548b; iii, 10a; x, 575b – I, 566a; III, 10b; X,
Shammās (monk/moine) viii, 234a – VIII, 241a
Shammās b. 'Uthmān, Makhzūmī (VII) vi, 138a – VI, 136b
al-Shammāsiyya (Baghdād) i, 897b, 899b; vi, 599b – I, 924b, 926a; VI, 584b
Shampa → Ṣanf
Shamrīn vi, 230b – VI, 224a
Shams (sun/soleil) ix, **291a** – IX, **299b**
Shams bint Riḍa Shāh Pahlawī (XX) vi, 486b – VI, 472b
Shams al-'Amāra (palace/palais, Tehran/ Téhéran) vi, 529b – VI, 513b
Shams Badrān s, 8b, 9a – S, 8a, b
Shams al-Dawla Abū Ṭāhir (Būyid(e)) (1021) i, 512b, 1354a; iii, 671b; v, 1028a; ix, **295b**; s, 118b – I, 528a, 1393a; III, 693a; V, 1024a; IX, **303b**; S, 118a
Shams al-Dawla Sulaymān i, 664b – I, 684a
Shams al-Dīn → al-Dimashḳī; Djuwaynī; Ildeñiz; al-Ṣaydāwī; Shams-i Tabrīzī
Shams al-Dīn (Bahmanid(e)) i, 1200a – I, 1235b
Shams al-Dīn (Bengal(e)) (1442) → Ilyās Shāh
Shams al-Dīn (Malaysia/-e) vi, 235b – VI, 208a
Shams al-Dīn (Mi'mār, Khwārazm) (XII) vi, 14b – VI, 13a
Shams al-Dīn, Pīr iv, 202b; v, 26a – IV, 211b; V, 26b
Shams al-Dīn Kurt I (Kart, Harāt) (1285) iii, 177b; iv, 672a – III, 181b; IV, 699b
Shams al-Dīn II b. Rukn al-Dīn Kurt (Kart, Harāt) (1329) iv, 536b, 672a – IV, 560a, 699b
Shams al-Dīn b. 'Abd al-Malik, amīr (Sindjār) (1149) vi, 870b – VI, 861b
Shams al-Dīn b. Djamshīd Ḳārīn (Mar'ashī) (XV) vi, 512b – VI, 497b
Shams al-Dīn b. Nadjm al-Dīn Ismā'īl (Maṣyād) (XIII) vi, 790b – VI, 780b
Shams al-Dīn b. Kamāl al-Dīn (Mar'ashī) (XV) vi, 514a, b, 516a – VI, 499b, 501a
Shams al-Dīn b. Murtaḍā (Mar'ashī) (XV) vi, 513b – VI, 499a
Shams al-Dīn b. Taman Djāndār iv, 108b – IV, 113a
Shams al-Dīn (Ḳarāmān-oghlu) iv, 622b – IV, 647a

Shams al-Dīn ʿAbd al-Malik (1200) vi, 381a – VI, 365a
Shams al-Dīn Abū Rādjāʾ ii, 597b – II, 612a
Shams al-Dīn ʿAlī Shāh Kart (Kurt) (Harāt) (1308) viii, 83b – VIII, 85b
Shams al-Dīn Āmulī (1307) vi, 908a – VI, 899b
Shams al-Dīn al-Ānī (XIV) vi, 13a – VI, 12a
Shams al-Dīn Dandānī (1457) vi, 1027b – VI, 1020b
Shams al-Dīn al-Dimashḳī (1327) vi, 111b – VI, 109a
Shams al-Dīn Dīv (XVI) vi, 515a – VI, 500a
Shams al-Dīn Ibrāhīm Shāh (Sharḳī) (1440) ix, 355a – IX, 366b
Shams al-Dīn Īletmish → Īltutmish
Shams al-Dīn ʿIrāḳī, Mīr s, 353b, 366b – S, 353b, 366a
Shams al-Dīn ʿItāḳī (XVIII) x, 356a – X, 382a
Shams al-Dīn Ḳara-Sunḳur (amīr) Ārdharbāydjān) vi, 501b – VI, 487a
Shams al-Dīn Ḳārin Ghawrī (Marʿashī) (XV) vi, 512b – VI, 498a
Shams al-Dīn Khān (1835) ii, 83b – II, 85a
Shams al-Dīn Lāhidjī (Gīlānī) (XVI) vi, 18a – VI, 16a
Shams al-Dīn Māhūnī iii, 633a, 634a – III, 654a, 655b
Shams al-Dīn Muḥammad III Lashkarī (Bahmānid(e)) (1482) vi, 62b, 407a – VI, 60b, 391b
Shams al-Dīn Muḥammad b. Ḳays al-Rāzī → Shams-i Ḳays
Shams al-Dīn Muḥammad b. Rukn al-Dīn Khur-Shāh (Nizārī) (1310) ix, **285b** – IX, **304a**
Shams al-Dīn Muḥammad b. Murtaḍā (Marʿashī) (1452) vi, 513a – VI, 498b
Shams al-Dīn Muḥammad al-Babāwī ii, 330b – II, 340a
Shams al-Dīn Muḥammad al-Dimashḳī i, 775a, 1327b – I, 798a, 1368b
Shams al-Dīn Muḥammad Ghūrī (1203) ii, 1101a – II, 1127a
Shams al-Dīn Muḥammad Tabrīzī → Shams-i Tabrīzī
Shams al-Dīn Ṣāliḥ, al-Malik al-Ṣāliḥ (Artuḳid(e), Mārdīn) (1364) vi, 111b; viii, 802a – VI, 109a; VIII, 829a
Shams al-Dīn al-Samarḳandī s, 413a – S, 413b
Shams al-Dīn al-Samaṭrānī (1630) i, 742a; iii, 1220a, 1233a; viii, 294a; ix, **296a** – I, 764a; III, 1251a, 1265a; VIII, 303a; IX, **304b**
Shams al-Dīn Sāmī Bey Frasherī (XIX) i, 298b; ii, 474a; v, 195a; vi, 92b, 373a – I, 307b; II, 486a; V, 192b; VI, 90b, 357b
Shams al-Dīn Shāh Mīrzā Swātī iv, 708a; s, 167a – IV, 736b; S, 167a
Shams al-Dīn Sulṭānpūrī, Shaykh (XVI) vi, 131a; s, 3a – VI, 129a; S, 2a
Shams al-Dīn-i Sīrādj ʿArīf (XIV) ix, **296b**; s, 105b – IX, **305a**; S, 105b
Shams al-Maʿālī → Ḳābūs b. Wushmagīr b. Ziyār
Shams-Māh Khātūn (Dhu ʾl-Ḳadr) (X) vi, 509b – VI, 495a
Shams al-Mulk ʿUthmān b. Niẓām al-Mulk (XII) i, 522b, 902a; vi, 64b; viii, 81b – I, 538b, 929a; VI, 62a; VIII, 83b
Shams al-Mulk Naṣr → Naṣr I (Ḳarakhānid(e))
Shams al-Mulūk → Duḳaḳ; Rustam
Shams al-ʿUrafāʾ, Sayyid Ḥusayn Ḥusaynī (1935) viii, 46b – VIII, 47b
Shamsa ix, **298b** – IX, **307a**
Shamsābād vi, 62a, b – VI, 60a
Shamsān i, 98b – I, 101a
Shamshān i, 180b – I, 185b
Shams-i Fakhrī → Fakhrī Shams al-Dīn Muḥammad
Shams-i Ḳays (XIII) i, 982b; iv, 59b, 64b, 714a; v, 1027a; viii, 578b; ix, **297a**; s, 21b – I, 1013a; IV, 62b, 68a, 743a; V, 1022b; VIII, 597b; IX, **305b**; S, 22a
Shamsī Khān v, 33b – V, 34b
Shams-i Munshī → Nakhdjawānī, Muḥammad
Shams-i Tabrīz(ī) (1247) ii, 394a; v, 26a; ix, **298a** – II, 404v; V, 26b; IX, **306b**
Shamsī Pasha iv, 108b – IV, 113b
Shamsī-yi Aʿradj Bukhārī (XIII) viii, 749a – VIII, 779b
Shamshīr b. Azar s, 327b – S, 327a
Shamshīr Bahādur i, 1012b – I, 1043b
Shämsiddin Shäräfiddinaw Khurshid (1960) vi, 768b – VI, 757b
Shamsīyān iv, 473b – IV, 494b
Shamsiyya ii, 1070b; iv, 203a, 473b, 991b; v, 26a; vi, 542a; ix, **299a** – II, 1095a; IV, 212a, 494b, 1024a; V, 27a; VI, 526b; IX, **307b**
Shamsūn (Samson) ix, **300a** – IX, **308b**
Shamʿūn vi, 575a – VI, 560a
Shamwīl (Samuel) ix, **301b** – IX, **309a**
al-Shanāwī, Aḥmad i, 829b – I, 852b
Shanbal i, 829a – I, 852a
Shandī ii, 351b; ix, **301b** – II, 361a; IX, **309a**
Shandjwilo, Shandjūl → ʿAbd al-Raḥmān b. Abī ʿAmīr
Shandūr ii, 29a – II, 29b
al-Shanfarā iv, 744b, 919a; vii, 308a, 309a; ix, **301a**; s, 176a – IV, 774b, 952a; VII, 310a, 311b; **309b**; S, 177a
Shangānī (Mogadisciu) vi, 129a – VI, 127a
Shānī (XVII) viii, 776a – VIII, 802a
Shanish vi, 576a – VI, 561a
Shānī-zāde Meḥmed ʿAṭāʾ Allāh Efendi (1826) ii, 713a; iii, 590a; v, 1083b; vi, 725a; ix, **303a** – II, 731a; III, 610b; V, 1081a; VI, 714a; IX, **311b**
Shanḳīr s, 295a – S, 294b
Shann, Banū i, 73a, 74a – I, 75a, 76a
Shans adāsi → Ada Ḳalʿe
Shansabanī ii, 1099a, 1100a, 1101a – II, 1125a, b, 1127a
Shanshiya → Djidʿatī
Shansi (Shan-hsi) ix, **303b** – IX, **312a**
Shant Mānkash (Simancas) ix, **304a** – IX, **312b**
Shant Yāḳub (Santiago de Compostela) i, 494b; ix, **304b** – I, 509a; IX, **313b**
Shantabariyya (Santaver) ii, 243a; iii, 299a; ix, **305b** – II, 250a; III, 308a; IX, **314b**
al-Shantamarī, Abu ʾl-Ḥadjdjādj (1083) i, 521b, 601a; iii, 111a, 807a, 963a; ix, **306a** – I, 537b, 620b; III, 113b, 830b, 987b; IX, **315a**
Shantamariyyat al-Gharb (Faro) i, 6a; ix, **306a** – I, 6a; IX, **315a**
Shantamariyyat al-Sharḳ (Albarracin) ix, **307a** – IX, **316b**
Shantarīn (Santarem) i, 161b, 1338b; ix, **308a** – I, 166a, 1379a; IX, **317b**
Shanūʾa i, 812a; ix, 775a – I, 835a; IX, 808b
Shāpūr (river/fleuve) vi, 383b; ix, **309b** – VI, 368a; IX, **319n**
Shāpūr (town/ville) iv, 850b; ix, **310b** – IV, 883b; IX, **320a**
Shāpūr (Sābūr) I b. Ardashīr (Sāsānid(e)) (270) i, 484b, 516b, 788b; ii, 1119b; iii, 50b; iv, 675b; v, 573b; ix, **309b** – I, 499a, 532a, 812a; II, 1146a; III, 52b; IV, 703b; V, 578a; IX, **319a**
Shāpūr II b. Hormizd II (Sāsānid(e)) (379) i, 225b, 484b, 548b; iii, 303b; v, 640a; vi, 633a; ix, 73b, **309b** – I, 232b, 499a, 566a; III, 312b; V, 644a; VI, 618a; IX, 76b, **319a**
Shāpūr III (Sāsānid(e)) ix, 75a, 309b – IX, 78a, 319a
Shāpūr b. Shahriyār Bāwand iv, 645b – IV, 672a

Shāpūr al-Djunūd → Shāpūr I
Shāpūr-Kh(ʷ)āst v, 831b – V, 837b
Shāpūr Mīrzā Iʿtiḳād Khān (1650) vii, 574a – VII, 574b
Shār ix, **311a** – IX, **321a**
Shaʿr ix, **311b** – IX, **321a**
Sharāb → Mashrūbāt
Sharabyānī, Mullā Muḥammad Ḳāẓim Fāḍil (1904) vi, 553a – VI, 537b
Sharaf ix, **313b** – IX, **323b**
al-Sharaf (Aljarafe) i, 7a, 135b; iv, 115a – I, 7a, 139b; IV, 120a
al-Sharaf (Yemen) vi, 436b – VI, 422a
Sharaf al-Dawla Muslim b. Ḳuraysh (ʿUḳaylid(e)) (1085) iii, 228a; vi, 379b – III, 235a; VI, 364a
Sharaf al-Dawla, Abu ʾl-Fawārīs Shīrdhīl (Būyid(e)) (989) i, 1354a; iii, 244b; vi, 600b; ix, **314a**; s, 118a, 398a – I, 1393a; III, 251b; VI, 585a; IX, **324a**; S, 117b, 398b
Sharaf al-Dīn, ʿAbd al-Ḥusayn b. al-Sayyid Yūsuf al-Mūsāwī al-ʿĀmilī (1957) vii, 301b; ix, **314b** – VII, 303b; IX, **324b**
Sharaf al-Dīn, Ḥasan Rāmī → Rāmī Tabrīzī
Sharaf al-Dīn, Mawlānā s, 353a – S, 353a
Sharaf al-Dīn b. Ḳawām al-Dīn al-Marʿashī (XIV) vi, 512a, b, – VI, 497a, 498a
Sharaf al-Dīn Abū Tawwāma ii, 216a – II, 223a
Sharaf al-Dīn ʿAlī Yazdī (1454) vii, 343b; ix, **315b** – VII, 345a; IX, **325b**
Sharaf al-Dīn Husām al-Dīn al-Bulghārī i, 1307b – I, 1347b
Sharaf al-Dīn ʿĪsā → al-Muʿaẓẓam ʿĪsā
Sharaf al-Dīn Khān → Bidlīsī
Sharaf al-Dīn Mawdūd al-Mawṣilī, amīr (XII) vi, 547a – VI, 531b
Sharaf al-Dīn Saʿd Allāh i, 322b, 346b, 510b – I, 332b, 357a, 526a
Sharaf al-Dīn Shāh Wilāyāt vii, 601b – VII, 601b
Sharaf al-Dīn Yaḥyā Manerī (1371) i, 868b; x, 255b – I, 893a; X, 274b
Sharaf Djihān (1560) viii, 775b – VIII, 801b
Sharaf Khʷādja, Shaykh s, 280b – S, 280b
Sharaf al-Maʿālī i, 440a – I, 452b
Sharaf al-Mulk (vizier) (1227) i, 301a; vi, 500b, 501a, 505a; s, 359b – I, 310a; VI, 486a, 490a; S, 359b
Sharaf al-Mulk b. Ḳuraysh (ʿUḳaylid(e)) (1080) vii, 122a – VII, 124a
Sharaf-nāma iv, 127b, 128a, b – IV, 133a, b, 134a
Sharaf Rashīdov (1983) x, 961b – X,
al-Sharafa s, 335a – S, 334b
al-Sharafī, ʿAlī b. Aḥmad iv, 1082a – IV, 1113b
Sharīfī, Mīrzā Makhdūm iv, 860b – IV, 893b
al-Sharafī, Muḥammad b. ʿAlī iv, 1082b – IV, 1113b
Sharafshāh b. Djaʿfarī iv, 859b – IV, 892b
Sharāḥīl Dhū Yazan ii, 244b – II, 251b
Sharahim Shaumar (XX) vi, 768b – VI, 757b
al-Shaʿrānī, ʿAbd al-Wahhāb b. Aḥmad (1565) i, 596a; iii, 901a; v, 1237a; vi, 87b, 88a, 821a; vii, 565a; viii, 425a; ix, **316a**, 914a – I, 615b; III, 925b; V, 1227b; VI, 85b, 86a, 811b; VII, 565b; VIII, 439a; IX, **325b**, 952a
al-Shaʿrānī, Sulaymān b. Mūsā (IX) vii, 526a – VII, 526b
al-Shaʿrāniyya vi, 88a – VI, 86a
Sharar, ʿAbd al-Halīm v, 203b – V, 201a
Sharāra, ʿAbd al-Laṭīf iv, 783a – IV, 814b
al-Sharārāt i, 546a, 873a; iii, 642a; ix, **316b** – I, 563b, 897a; III, 663a; IX, **326b**
al-Sharāt ii, 535a; ix, **317a** – II, 548b; IX, **327a**
Sharāwiḥ, Banū vi, 82a – VI, 79b
Sharbithāt vi, 84b – VI, 82b
Shardja s, 42a – S, 42b
al-Shardja → al-Shāriḳa
Shārekī → Shāhrikī
Sharḥ ix, **317a** – IX, **327a**
Shari (river/rivière) s, 164b – S, 164a
Shārlʿ ix, **320b** – IX, **330a**
Sharīʿa i, 152a, 170a, 173b, 260b, 353b, 1099b, 1142b, 1143a; ii, 146b, 660a, b, 668a; iii, 76a, 164a, 662b; iv, 156b, 556b, 559a; v, 860a, 870b; ix, **321a** – I, 156b, 174b, 178a, 268b, 364b, 1132b, 1177a, b; II, 150b, 676b, 677a, 685a; III, 78b, 167b, 684a; IV, 163a, 580b; V, 867a, 876b; IX, **331a**
Shariat Act (1937) i, 172a, b – I, 176b, 177b
Sharīʿat Allāh, Ḥādjdjī (1839) i, 952a; ii, 783b; iv, 625b; vii, 291a – I, 981a; II, 802b; IV, 650b; VII, 293a
Sharīʿatī, ʿAlī (1977) vii, 451a; ix, **328a** – VII, 452b; IX, **338b**
Sharīʿatī, Muḥammad Taḳī iv, 166a – IV, 173b
Sharīʿatmādarī (Āyatullāh, Ḳum) (1986) vi, 553b; vii, 300a; ix, **329a** – VI, 538a; VII, 302a; IX, **339a**
Sharīf (pen-name/nom de plume) ix, **337b** – IX, **348b**
Sharīf (title/titre) ix, **329b** – IX, **340a**
al-Sharīf, Mawlāy → Muḥammad I (ʿAlawid(e))
Sharīf ʿAbd al-Raḥmān (Pontianak) (1808) viii, 324a – VIII, 335a
al-Sharīf Abū Muḥammad Idrīs (1314) ix, **338a** – IX, **349a**
Sharīf Aḥmad (Abū ʿArīsh) s, 30b – S, 30b
al-Sharīf al-Akhḍar iii, 107a, 289a – III, 109b, 298a
al-Sharīf al-ʿAḳīlī (XI) ix, **338b** – IX, **349b**
al-Sharīf Āmulī (XVI) ix, **339a** – IX, **350a**
Sharīf Awliyā Karīm al-Makhdūm (Jolo) (XIV) iii, 1218b; viii, 303a – III, 1249b; VIII, 312b
al-Sharīf al-Djurdjānī → al-Djurdjānī
al-Sharīf al-Gharnāṭī (1359) ix, **339b** – IX, **350b**
al-Sharīf al-Ḥusaynī (1374) vi, 353a – VI, 337a
al-Sharīf al-Idrīsī → al-Idrīsī
Sharīf Muḥammad Kabungsuwan (XVI) viii, 303b – VIII, 313a
al-Sharīf al-Murtaḍā → al-Murtaḍā al-Shārīf Abu ʾl-Ḳāsim
Sharīf Pasha, Muḥammad (Miṣr) (1887) i, 1070a; iii, 515a; vii, 184b; ix, **340a** – I, 1102a; III, 532b; VII, 184b; IX, **351a**
Sharīf Pasha Ṣabrī s, 300a – S, 299b
al-Sharīf al-Rāḍī (1016) i, 592b, 1352a; iii, 244b, 463a, 780b, 1266a; iv, 277b; vi, 603a, 604b, 605b; vii, 24b, 313a, 634a, 903b; ix, **340b**; s, 23a, 95a – I, 611b, 1391b; III, 251b, 479a, 804a, 1299a; IV, 290a; VI, 588a, 589a, 590b; VII, 24b, 315b, 633b, 904a; IX, **351b**; S, 23b, 94b
al-Sharīf al-Rundī (1285) vi, 606b – VI, 591a
al-Sharīf al-Talīḳ (1005) ix, **343a** – IX, **354a**
al-Sharīf al-Tilimsānī (Ahl) iii, 670b, 866b; ix, **343b** – III, 692a, 890b; IX, **354b**
Sharīfīs (Irān) iv, 51b – IV, 54b
Sharīfī-zāde (1630) vi, 354a – VI, 338a
Sharīfs (Mecca) i, 552a; vi, 148a; vii, 319b – I, 569b; VI, 147a; VII, 321b
Sharīfs (Morocco/Maroc) → Shurafāʾ
Sharifu Badruddini (Lamu) vi, 613a – VI, 598a
Shāriḥ ül-Menār-zāde Aḥmed (1641) ii, 751a; vii, 917b; ix, **348a** – II, 769b; VII, 918a; IX, **359a**
Sharīḳ b. al-Aʿwar al-Ḥārithī (VII) vii, 689b – VII, 689b
Sharīḳ b. Shaykh al-Mahrī i, 1294a; iv, 16a – I, 1333b; IV, 17b

Sharīk al-ʿAbsī ii, 525b – II, 538b
Sharika ix, **348a** – IX, **359a**
al-Shāriḳa (Shardjah) i, 166b, 928b; ii, 619a, 936b; iv, 777b; vi, 37b; ix, **349a**; s, 42a, 416b, 418a – I, 171a, 956b; II, 634b, 958b; IV, 808b; VI, 36a; IX, **360a**; S, 42b, 417a, 418a
Sharīsh (Jerez) ix, **349b** – IX, **361a**
al-Sharīshī, Abu ʾl-ʿAbbās (1222) i, 602a; iii, 221b; vi, 110b; ix, **350a** – I, 622a; III, 228a; VI, 108b; IX, **361b**
Shāriya (singer/chanteuse) ix, **350b** – IX, **362a**
Sharḳ al-Andalus i, 82b; ix, **351a** – I, 85a; IX, **362a**
Sharḳāt s, 101b – S, 100b
Sharḳawa (Sherkāwa) ix, **352b** – IX, **364a**
al-Sharḳāwī, ʿAbd al-Raḥmān (1987) i, 819b; ix, **353a** – I, 842b; IX, **364b**
Sharḳāwiyya s, 40b – S, 41a
Sharkhā i, 176b; iii, 3b – I, 181a; III, 3b
Sharkhub vi, 547a – VI, 531b
Sharḳī ix, **353b** – IX, **365a**
al-Sharḳī b. al-Kutāmī (767) ix, **354a** – IX, **365b**
Sharḳī, Ibrāhīm (XV) vi, 49b, 50a – VI, 48a
Sharkil iv, 1175a, 1176a, 1178a; vi, 384a – IV, 1208b, 1209b, 1211b; VI, 368b
Sharḳīs (Djawnpūr) i, 756b; iii, 632a; iv, 533b, 534a; vi, 46b, 53b, 61b, 294b, 693b; viii, 68a, 125a; ix, **355a**; s, 203a, 325a – I, 779a; III, 653a; IV, 557a; VI, 45a, 51b, 59b, 279b, 681b; VIII, 69b, 128a; IX, **366a**; S, 202b, 324b
Sharḳīshla s, 91b – S, 91a
al-Sharḳiyya (Baghdād) i, 901b, 1011a; s, 385b – I, 928b, 1042a; S, 386a
al-Sharḳiyya (Miṣr) vi, 408a, 411b; ix. **356b** – VI, 393a, 396b; IX, **368a**
al-Sharḳiyya (ʿUmān) vi, 84b; ix, **356b** – VI, 82b; IX, **368a**
Sharm al-Shaykh s, 8b – S, 8a
al-Shārrāṭ i, 487a, 489a; ix, **357b** – I, 501b, 503b; IX, **369a**
Sharshal (Cherchell) iv, 1156a; vi, 371b, 404a, b; ix, **357b**; s, 145a – IV, 1188a, b; VI, 356a, 388b, 389b; IX, **369a**; S, 144b
Sharṭ ix, **358b** – IX, **370a**
Sharūr iv, 186b – IV, 194b
Sharūr (plain(e)) viii, 767a – VIII, 792b
Sharvashidze i, 101a; v, 496a – I, 103b; V, 499a
Sharwān → Shirwān
Sharwīn I (Kāʾūsiyya, Bāwandid(e)) (797) vi, 745b – VI, 734b
Sharwīn Mts iv, 645b, 646b; s, 298a – IV, 672a, 673a; S, 297b
Shāsh → Tashkent
al-Shāshī → ʿAbd Allāh b. Maḥmūd; Abū Bakr
al-Shāshī, Abū Bakr Muḥammad al-Ḳaffāl (975) x, 349a – X, 374b
Shashmaḳom vi, 768b; ix, **360b** – VI, 757b; IX, **372b**
al-Shāshshī, Aḥmad b. Muḥammad (955) ix, 36a – IX, 36a
Shaṭā ix, **361a** – IX, **372b**
Shaṭḥ (Shaṭḥiyya) ix, **361b** – IX, **373a**
Shāṭiba ix, **362b** – IX, **374a**
al-Shāṭibī, Abū Isḥāḳ (1388) iv, 149b; vi, 739b; ix, **364a** – IV, 155b; VI, 728b; IX, **376a**
al-Shāṭibī, Abu ʾl-Ḳāsim (1194) iv, 736b; vi, 130b; vii, 622a; ix, **365a** – IV, 766b; VI, 128b; VII, 621b; IX, **376b**
al-Shātibī, Muḥammad b. Sulaymān iv, 137a – IV, 143a
Shāṭir Djalāl (XVI) vii, 478a – VII, 477b
Shāṭir Beg Muḥammad i, 840b – I, 864a
Shaṭnīl s, 135b, 136a – S, 135b
Shatrandj i, 1359a, b; ii, 955a, 1038b; iii, 775a; v, 110a, 478b; ix, **366b** – I, 1399a, b; II, 977a, 1062b, 1399a, b; III, 798a; V, 112b, 481a; IX, **378a**
Shaṭṭ ix, **368a** – IX, **379b**
Shaṭṭ al-Amaya (Aʿmā) iv, 674a, b – IV, 702a, b
Shaṭṭ al-ʿArab i, 5a, 133b, 1086b, 1087b; ii, 175b; iii, 1251b; iv, 6a, 674b, 675a; v, 65b, 66a; vii, 449b, 582b, 675a; ix, **368a** – I, 5a, 137b, 1119a, 1120a; II, 181a; III, 1284a; IV, 6b, 702a, b; V, 67b, 68a; VII, 451a, 583a, 675a; IX, **380a**
Shaṭṭ Bamishīr (Behemshīr) iv, 674b, 675a – IV, 702a, b
Shaṭṭ al-Ḳadīmī iv, 674a – IV, 702a
Shaṭṭ Ḳobān (Goban) → Shaṭṭ al-Amaya
Shaṭṭ al-Nīl viii, 13b – VIII, 13b
al-Shaṭṭanawfī, Nūr al-Dīn (1314) i, 70a, 596a; iii, 160b; viii, 525a – I, 72a, 615b; III, 164a; VIII, 543a
Shaṭṭārī, Shaykh ʿAbd Allāh (XVI) vii, 440a – VII, 441a
Shaṭṭāriyya i, 88a, 1284a; iii, 1233b; vii, 440a; viii, 237b; ix, **369b** – I, 90b, 1323b; III, 1265b; VII, 441a; VIII, 243a; IX, **381b**
al-Shaṭṭī, Muḥammad Djamīl ii, 182b; iii, 161b – II, 188b; III, 165a
Shāʾul, Anwar v, 189b; ix, **370a** – V, 186b; IX, **382a**
Shawādhdh v, 128a – V, 130b
Shawāhid ix, **370b** – IX, **382b**
Shawānkāra → Faḍlawayh, Banū; Shabānkāra
Shāwar, Abū Shudjāʿ (vizier) (1169) i, 197a, 797a; ii, 318a, b, 856b, 858b, 959a; iv, 376a ; viii, 130b; ix, **372b** – I, 202b, 820b; II, 327b, 876b, 878b, 981a; IV, 392b; VIII, 133a; IX, **384b**
al-Shawāribī iv, 514b – IV, 536b
al-Shawbak vii, 989b; ix, **373a** – VII, 990a; IX, **385a**
Shawdhab (Bistam) al-Yashkurī (VIII) iii, 650a; x, 821b – III, 671b; X,
Shāwiya (Chaouia) x, 169b – X, 182a
Shāwl dialects ix, 376a – IX, 388b
al-Shāwī, Abu ʾl-ʿAbbās (1605) ix, **374a** – IX, **386a**
al-Shāwirī, ʿAbd Allāh b. al-ʿAbbās (dāʿī) (IX) vi, 439a – VI, 424a
Shāwish → Čāʾūsh
al-Shawīsh (al-Djawīsh), ʿAbd al-ʿAzīz (XX) vii, 716a – VII, 717a
Shāwiya, Banū i, 371a, 372a, 770a; ii, 117a; viii, 794b; ix, **374b**; x, 169b – I, 382a, 383a, 793a; II, 119b; VIII, 821a; IX, **386b**; X, 182a
Shawḳ ix, **376b** – IX, **389a**
Shawḳ, Taṣadduḳ Ḥusayn (1871) ix, **377b** – IX, **390a**
Shawḳa vii, 672a – VII, 672a
Shawḳal ii, 86b, 87a – II, 88a, b
al-Shawkānī, Muḥammad b. ʿAlī (1839) iv, 142b; vii, 297a; ix, **378a** – IV, 148a; VII, 299a; IX, **390b**
Shawḳat ʿAlī (1938) vi, 78a, 459b; viii, 249a; ix, **378a**; s, 5a, 74a, b, 293b, 360a – VI, 76a, 445a; VIII, 263a; IX, **390b**; S, 4a, 74b, 293a, 360a
Shawkat Bukhārī (1695) i, 1301b; ix, **378b** – I, 1341a; IX, **391a**
Shawkat Djang ii, 371b, 1091b – II, 381b, 1117a
Shawḳī, Aḥmad (1932) i, 597b, 598a; iv, 856a; vi, 307a, 409a, 414a, 607a, 956a; vii, 422a, 903a; ix, 229b, **379a**; s, 34a, 57b – I, 617a, 618a; IV, 889b; VI, 292a, 393b, 399a, 592a, 948b; VII, 423b, 903b; IX, 235b, **391b**; S, 34b, 58a
Shawḳī Efendī Rabbānī (1957) i, 916a, 917b; vii, 921b; ix, **380a** – I, 943b, 945b; VII, 922a; IX, **392b**
al-Shawshāwī vii, 622a – VII, 621b
al-Shawwāf, ʿAbd al-Wahhāb iv, 719a – IV, 748a
Shawwāl ix, **380b** – IX, **393a**
Shay → Čay
Shayʾ ix, **380b** – IX, **393a**

Shay' al-Ḳawm ix, **382b** – IX, **395a**
Shaʿyā ix, **382b** – IX, **395a**
Shayāḍima vi, 744a – VI, 732a
al-Shayb wa'l- shabāb ix, **383a** – IX, **395b**
Shayba, Banū iv, 317a, b, 318a, 320b; vi, 148b, 168a; vii, 362a; ix, **389b** – IV, 331b, 332a, 334b; VI, 147a, 159b; VII, 364b; IX, **402a**
Shayba b. ʿUthmān → Shayba, Banū
Shaybak Khān Uzbek (XVI) vi, 514b – VI, 499b
Shaybān, Banū iii, 1103a; iv, 88b-90b; v, 362b; vi, 345a, 546b, 624a, 640b, 900a, 930a; ix,**391a**; s, 15b – III, 1130a; IV, 92b-94b; V, 363b; VI, 329a, 531a, 609a, 625b, 891b, 922a; IX, **403b**; S, 16a
Shaybān b. Djoči (Batu'id(e)) ii, 44b, 67b; x, 560b – II, 45b, 68b; X,
Shaybān al-Ṣaghīr iii, 988b; iv, 447a – III, 1013a; IV, 467a
al-Shaybānī → al-Daḥḥāk b. Ḳays; ʿĪsā b. al-Shaykh; Yazīd b. Mazyad
al-Shaybānī, Abū ʿAbd Allāh Muḥammad b. al-Ḥasan (805) i, 123a, 124a, 164b, 588b; iii, 162b, 512b; iv, 377a, 691a; vi, 24a, 264b; vii, 310b, 537b, 662b; ix, 35b, **392b** – I, 126b, 127b, 169a, 607b; III, 166a, 529b; IV, 393b, 719a; VI, 21b, 249a; VII, 313a, 537b, 662b; IX, 36a, **405a**
al-Shaybānī, Abū ʿAmr Isḥāḳ b. Mirār (820) iv, 524b; vi, 197b; vii, 831b, 841a, 843a; ix, **394b**; s, **15b**, 394b – VI, 181b; IV, 547a; VII, 833a, 842b, 844b; IX, **407a**; S, **16a**, 395a
al-Shaybānī, Abū Dāwūd Khālid b. Ibrāhīm al-Dhuhlī (XI) vi, 332b – VI, 317a
al-Shaybānī, Abu 'l-Ḳāsim Hibat Allāh s, 193a – S, 194a
al-Shaybānī, Abū Naṣr Fatḥ Allāh (1890) iv, 70a; ix, **395b** – IV, 73b; IX, **408a**
al-Shaybānī, Abu 'l-Sarāyā al-Sirrī b. Manṣūr (IX) vi, 334a – VI, 318b
al-Shaybānī, Aḥmad b. ʿĪsā b. Shaykh (IX) i, 145a; iv, 903a, b; vi, 540a; vii, 760a – I, 149b; IV, 94a, b; VI, 524b; VII, 761b
al-Shaybānī, Aḥmad b. Mazyad (Ḳaysī) (IX) vi, 333b – VI, 318a
al-Shaybānī, Ibrāhīm b. Muḥammad (911) ix, **396a** – IX, **408b**
Shaybānī Khān (Shaybānid(e)) (1510) → Shībānī Khān
Shaybānid(e)s – Shībānid(e)s)
al-Shaybī, ʿAbd Allāh b. ʿAbd al-Ḳādir (XX) vi, 160b, 165b – VI, 154b, 157b
Shaydā, Mullā ix, **396b** – IX, **400b**
Shayfta, Muṣṭafā Khān iii, 93b – III, 96a
Shāyista Khān i, 606a, 769a; ii, 32a, 216b – I, 626a, 792a; II, 32b, 223a
Shaykh (title/titre) iii, 411a, 721a; iv, 335a, 678a; v, 1131a, 1133a; ix, **397a** – III, 423b, 743b; IV, 349b, 706a; V, 1127a, 1129a; IX, **410a**
Shaykh (Mamlūk) → al-Mu'ayyad Shaykh
Shaykh b. ʿAbd Allāh b. Shaykh (1) i, 781a – I, 804b
Shaykh b. ʿAbd Allāh b. Shaykh (2) i, 781b – I, 804b
Shaykh b. Muḥammad b. Ṣāliḥ (1919) viii, 990a – VIII, 1024b
Shaykh ʿAbd Allāh (Kashmīr) iv, 710a, b – IV, 738b, 739a
Shaykh ʿAbduh i, 1070a; v, 188a – I, 1102a; V, 185b
Shaykh Abū Isḥāḳ (Īndjūid(e)) (1356) vii, 820a – VII, 822a
Shaykh Ādam, Safī al-Dīn (1621) ix, **398a** – IX, **410b**
Shaykh ʿAdī → ʿAdī b. Musāfir
Shaykh Aḥmad (Durban) (1886) ix, 730b – IX, 762b
Shaykh al-Aḳl i, 1078b – I, 1110b
Shaykh ʿAlī b. Uways ii, 401b; iv, 584b – II, 412a; IV, 608a
Shaykh ʿAlī Āghā b. Fatḥ ʿAlī Khān (Ḳādjār) v, 296b – V, 288a
Shaykh ʿAlī Khān Zand iv, 390b – IV, 407a
Shaykh Badr al-Dīn (XV) vii, 645a – VII, 645a
Shaykh al-Bakrī i, 966a; ii, 165a, 181b – I, 995b; II, 170a, 187a
Shaykh al-balad ix, 398b – IX, 411a
Shaykh Dāwūd Kirmānī (1574) x, 255b – X, 274b
Shaykh Ghālib → Ghālib Dede, Shaykh
Shaykh al-Ḥāra → Ismāʿīl Pāshā
Shaykh Ḥasan-i Buzurg (Djalāyirid(e)) x, 552b – X,
Shaykh Ḥusayn (Ethiopia/-e) (1200) ix, **398b** – IX, **411b**
Shaykh Ibrāhīm (Sharwan-Shāh) iv, 350a, 586b – IV, 364b, 609a
Shaykh al-Islām i, 837b; ii, 420b, 867a, b; iii, 250a, 552b, 1152a; iv, 168a, 573b; v, 1083b; vi, 6b; ix, **399b** – I, 861a; II, 431a, 887a, b; III, 257a, 571b, 1180b; IV, 175b, 596b; V, 1080b; VI, 6b; IX, **412b**
Shaykh al-Islām Yaḥyā iii, 1200b; s, 324a – III, 1230b; S, 323b
al-Shaykh al-Kabīr → Ibn Khafīf
al-Shaykh al-Kāmil iv, 93b – IV, 97b
Shaykh Khiḍr (1586) vii, 189a – VII, 189b
Shaykh Maḥmūd i, 262b – I, 271a
Shaykh al-Maḥmūdī (Alep(po)) (XV) vii, 723a, b – VII, 724a, b
Shaykh Manṣūr ii, 25b – II, 26a
Shaykh Mīrzā ʿAlī Shahristānī, Ḥādjdj (Marʿashī) vi, 516b – VI, 502a
Shaykh Mu'ayyad i, 1328a – I, 1368b
Shaykh Muḥammad (painter/peintre) vii, 603a – VII, 602b
Shaykh Mūsā Barāhima ii, 166b – II, 171b
Shaykh Mūsā Nathrī (1968) ix, **402a** – IX, **415a**
Shaykh al-Ra'īs Abu 'l-Ḥasan Mīrzā (Ḳādjār) vi, 292a – VI, 277a
Shaykh Rifāʿa → al-Taḥtāwī
Shaykh Rukn al-Dīn Abu l-Fatḥ (1334) x, 255b – X, 274b
Shaykh Saʿd vi, 650a – VI, 635b
Shaykh Saʿdī → Saʿdī, Abū ʿAbd Allāh
al-Shaykh Saʿīd (Bāb al-Mandab) vi, 933a; ix, **402b** – VI, 925a; IX, **415b**
Shaykh Saʿīd → Safī al-Dīn Ardabīlī
Shaykh Saʿīd Nakshbandī v, 463b, 464b – V, 466b, 467b
Shaykh Saʿīd Shaʿbān (Tripoli) (XX) x, 216a – X, 233b
Shaykh Ṣāliḥ (XX) vi, 791b – VI, 781b
al-Shaykh al-Ṣāliḥ → ʿAbd Allāh al-Shaykh
Shaykh Saʿūd iv, 638a – IV, 664b
al-Shaykh al-Shīrāzī → Ibn Khafīf
Shaykh al-Ṭā'ifa → al-Ṭūsī, Muḥammad b. al-Ḥasan
Shaykh al-Ṭayyib al-Madjdhūb ii, 122b; iv, 687a – II, 125b; IV, 715a
al-Shaykh al-Yūnānī i, 234b; ii, 765a; iii, 942b; ix, **403a** – I, 241b; II, 783b; III, 967b; IX, **416a**
Shaykh Yūnus → Küčik Khān Djangalī
Shaykh Yūsuf → Abidin Tadia Tjoessoep
Shaykh Ẓāhir i, 341b – I, 352a
Shaykh Zayn i, 849a, b – I, 872b, 873a
Shaykha → Shīkha
Shaykhā Khokar (XIV) v, 31b; vi, 49b – V, 32b; VI, 48a
Shaykhān (river/rivière) vi, 539b – VI, 524a

Shaykhiyya (theology/-ie) i, 304b, 850b; iv, 51a, 854a, b; vi, 551b; vii, 422a, 440b; ix, **403b**; s, 305a – I, 314a, 874a; IV, 54a, 887b; VI, 563a; VII, 424a, 442a; IX, **416b**; S, 305a
Shaykhī (poets/poètes) ii, 990a; iii, 43b – II, 1013a; III, 45a
Shaykhiyān vi, 384b – VI, 369a
Shaykhiyya-Djūriyya (ṭarīḳa) iv, 48b; vi, 511a – IV, 51a; VI, 496b
Shaykhū, amīr (XIV) vi, 413b – VI, 398b
Shaykhū, Luwīs (L. Cheikho) (1927) ix, **405b** – IX, **418b**
Shaykhū al-ʿUmarī → Ibn Faḍl Allāh al-ʿUmarī
Shaykhūn al-ʿUmarī (1357) i, 444a; iii, 239b; vi, 327a, 367b; vii, 993a – I, 456b; III, 246b; VI, 311b, 351b; VII, 994b
al-Shaykhūniyya vi, 454a – VI, 439b
Shaykhūpūra vi, 368b – VI, 353a
Shayḳiyya ii, 351a, 615b, 944b; ix, **406a** – II, 360b, 630b, 966b; IX, **420a**
Shaymāʾ bint Ḥalīma (VII) viii, 697b – VIII, 717a
al-Shayṭān i, 177a; iii, 668b, 1050a; iv, 643b; ix, **406b** – I, 181b; III, 690a, 1076a; IV, 670a; IX, **420a**
Shayṭān Ibrāhīm Pasha i, 1284b – I, 1324a
Shayṭan al-Ṭāḳ (Muḥammad b. al-Nuʿmān) (VIII) ii, 374b; ix, **409a** – II, 385a; IX, **422b**
Shayyād ix, **409b** – IX, **423a**
Shayzar (town/ville) vi, 118b, 606a; vii, 577b, 578a; ix, **410a** – VI, 116a, 590b; VII, 578a, b; IX, **423b**
al-Shayzarī, ʿAbd al-Raḥmān b. Naṣr (1193) i, 800b; ii, 482a; iii, 486b – I, 823b; II, 494a; III, 503b
al-Shayzarī, Abu ʾl-Ḥasan ʿAlī iii, 761a – III, 784b
al-Shayzarī, Amīn al-Dīn (XIII) ix, **411a** – IX, **425a**
Sheba, Queen of/Reine de → Bilḳīs
Shebek → Shabak
Shebelle (river/fleuve) ix, **412a**, 714b – IX, **425b**, 745b
Shebīn Ḳarā Ḥiṣār → Ḳarā Ḥiṣār
Shebsefa Kadîn (1805) ix, **412b** – IX, **426a**
Shefīḳ Ḥüsnü (XX) vi, 94b – VI, 92b
Shefīḳ Meḥmed Efendi (1715) ix, **412b** – IX, **426a**
Shefḳatī, ʿAlī iv, 681b – IV, 709b
Shehe Mvita (Mombasa) vii, 226a – VII, 227b
Shehīd ʿAlī Pasha → Dāmād ʿAlī Pasha
Shehir Emāneti ix, **413a** – IX, **426b**
Shehir Emīni → Shehir Emāneti
Shehir Ketkhudasî i, 974a; ix, **414a** – I, 1004b; IX, **427b**
Shehr → Shahr
Shehremānet i, 972b, 974b, 975a – I, 1003a, 1004b, 1005b
Shehremīni i, 972b, 974a – I, 1002b, 1004a
Shehr-i Sebz → Kash
Shehzāde (title/titre) ix, **414a** – IX, **427b**
Shehrīzāde Aḥmed b. Müdhehhib ii, 589b – II, 604a
Shehu-s (Bornū) i, 1260a, b; v, 359a – I, 1298a, b, 1299a; V, 360a
Sheikh → Shaykh
Sheker Bayramî → ʿĪd al-Fiṭr
Shekhu Aḥmadu (Shaykh Aḥmad, Mali) (XIX) vi, 259b – VI, 244a
Shekib Efendi ii, 636b – II, 652b
Shela (Lamu) vi, 385a – VI, 370a
Shemʿdānī-zāde Süleymān Efendi (1779) ix, **414a** – IX, **428a**
Shemʿī (XVI) ix, **414b** – IX, **428b**
Shems al-Dīn Günaltay (1961) ix, **415b** – IX, **429a**
Shemsiyya vi, 886a – VI, 877b
Shenlik ix, **416b** – IX, **430a**
Shen-si (Shaanxi) v, 848a; ix, **415b** – V, 852a, b; IX, **429b**
Shepherd, the (astronomy) s, 321a
Shēr Aḥmad Khān iv, 711a – IV, 739b
Shēr Shāh Sūr → Shīr Shāh Sūrī
Shēr Singh → Shīr Singh
Sherāga ii, 510a, b – II, 522b, 523b
Sherārda ii, 510a – II, 523a
Sherbet ix, 417a – IX, 430b
Sheref, ʿAbd al-Raḥmān (1925) ix, **417a** – IX, **431a**
Sherefli Ḳočhisar v, 247b – V, 245b
Ṡherí → Djibbālī
Shērs (Shārs) (Ghardjistān) ii, 1010b; vi, 65b – II, 1034a; VI, 63b
Shērzād b. Masʿūd ii, 1052a; s, 21a – II, 1076b; S, 21b
Shesh Bolūḳī Reshkūlī s, 148a – S, 148a
Shetiyya iv, 401b – IV, 419a
Shewkī Beg (Şevki Bey) (1896) ix, **417b** – IX, **431b**
Sheykh Badr al-Dīn (Samāwnā) x. 253b – X, 272b
Sheykh Ḥasan Efendi → Sezāʾī
Sheykhī Čelebi (Germiāni) (1429) iii, 356b; vi, 609b, 835b; viii, 211a; ix, 240a – III, 367b; VI, 594b, 826a; VIII, 215a; IX, 246b
Sheykh-oghlu, Ṣadr al-Dīn 1401) viii, 211a; ix, **418a** – VIII, 215a; IX, **431b**
Sheykh-zāde → Sheykh-oghlu
Sheykh-zāde Aḥmed (Aḥmed-i Miṣrī) (XV) ix, **419a** – IX, **433a**
Sheytānlïḳ (island/île) ix, **419a** – IX, **433a**
Sheyyād Ḥamza (XIII) viii, 972b; ix, **419b** – VIII, 1007a; IX, **433a**
Shīʿa i, 15a, 16b, 20a, 51a, 124b, 130a, 149b, 224a, 347a, 382a, 399b, 402a, 589b, 713a, 794b, 832b, 941b, 1040a, 1120a, 1162a, 1198a, 1254a; iii, 411b, 434a, 1265a; iv, 34b, 46b, 277b, 855a; v, 1033a; vi, 11a, 272b, 476a, 548b; vii, 854a, 921b; viii, 777a; x, 496b; s, 342a, 367b, 402a, b, 423b, 496b – I, 15b, 17a, 21a, 52b, 128a, 134a, 153b, 231a, 357b, 392b, 411a, 412b, 608b, 734b, 818a, 855b, 970b, 1071b, 1154a, 1196b, 1233b, 1292a; III, 424b, 448a, 1298a; IV, 37a, 49a, 289b, 290a, 888a; V, 1029b; VI, 11a, 257b, 462a, 533a; VII, 855b, 922a; VIII, 803a; X, 532a; S, 341b, 367b, 402b, 424a
—doctrine i, 188a, 258a, 334a, 339b, 402a, 1026b, 1098b, 1113b, 1352a; ii, 374b, 539a, 834a; iii, 78b, 242b, 544b, 664a, 1130a; iv, 19a, 278b, 698a; v, 1235b; ix, **420a**, 819a; s, 305a – I, 193b. 266a, 344b, 350a, 412b, 1058a, 1131b, 1147a, 1391a, b; II, 384b, 552a, 853b; III, 81a, 249b, 563b, 685b, 1158a; IV, 20b, 290b, 726a; V, 1226a; IX, **433b**, 854a; S, 305a
Shiʿar ix, **424a** – IX, **438b**
Shiʿb ʿAlī (Mecca) vi, 168a – VI, 159b
Shiʿb Djabala vi, 603a; vii, 582a; ix, **424b**; s, 177a, 178a – VI, 587b; VII, 582b; IX, **439a**; S, 178a, 179a
Shibām vi, 132b, 439a; vii, 496a; ix, **425a**; s, 337b, 338a, 407a – VI, 130b, 424b; VII, 496a; IX, **439a**; S, 337a, b, 407a
Shibām Aḳyān vi, 436a – VI, 421a
Shibām al-Ghirās → Shibām
Shibām Ḥaḍramawt → Shibām
Shibām Ḥarāz → Shibām
Shibām Kawkabān → Shibām

Shiban (Aḳ Orda) s, 96b – S, 96a
Shibān → Shaybān
Shībānī Khān Muḥammad (Özbeg) (1510) i, 627b, 847b, 849a, 1001b, 1019a, 1211b, 1295b; iii, 198a, 1101a; iv, 1036b; v, 54b, 55a, 59a, 859a; vi, 418a, 714b; vii, 928a; viii, 768a; ix, **426a**, 684a; x, 681a, 722a; s, 51b –
I, 648a, 871a, 872a, 1032a, 1050b, 1247b, 1335a; III, 203a, 1128a; IV, 1068a; V, 56a, b, 60b, 866a; VI, 403a, 703b; VII, 928b; VIII, 793b; IX, **442b**, 712b; X, 767b; S, 52a
Shībānid(e)s i, 8a, 46b, 120b, 121a, 228b, 637a, 690a, 963b, 964b, 1110b; ii, 44b, 72a, 792a; iv, 9b, 1064b; v, 859a, b; viii, 232a; ix, **428a**; s, 96b, 227b, 340a, b –
I, 8a, 47b, 124a, 125a, 235a, 658a, 711a, 993b, 994a, 1144a; II, 45b, 73a, 811a; IV, 10a, 1096a; V, 866a, b; VIII, 237a; IX, **444b**; S, 96a, 227b, 339b, 340a
Shibarghān (town/ville) ix, **431a** – IX, **447b**
Shibīn al-Kūm vi, 453b – VI, 439a
Shibiththth ix, **431b** – IX, **448b**
Shibl al-Dawla → Mirdās, Banū
Shiblī (Sārī) (XV) vi, 514a – VI, 499a
al-Shiblī → Ibn Shibl
al-Shiblī → al-Hindī, Sirādj al-Dīn al-Ḥanafī
al-Shiblī, Abū Ḥafs (1372) ix, **433a** – IX, **449b**
al-Shiblī, Abu 'l-Ḳāsim (Abū Bakr) Dulaf b. Djaḥdar (945) i, 387b; iv, 990a; vi, 280a, 569a; ix, **432a** – I, 399a; IV, 1023a; VI, 264b, 554a; IX, **448b**
al-Shiblī, Badr al-Dīn al-Dimashḳī (1367) i, 758b, 759a – I, 781a, b
Shiblī, Shaykh (945) viii, 8a – VIII, 8a
Shiblī academy/-ie → Dār al-Muṣannifīn
Shiblī al-Aṭrash ii, 637a – II, 653b
Shiblī al-Mallāṭ s, 159b – S, 159b
Shiblī Nuʿmānī, Muḥammad (1914) ii, 132b, 489a; iii, 433a; v, 960a, 1136a; vi, 612a; vii, 875b; ix, **433b**; x, 839b; s, 106a, b, 293a –
II, 135b, 501a; III, 447a; V, 964a, 1131a; VI, 597a; VII, 877a; IX, **450a**; X, ;S, 105b, 292b
Shīdān vi, 494a – VI, 480a
al-Shidyāḳ ' Asʿad al-Shidyāḳ; Fāris al-Shidyāḳ
al-Shidyāḳ, Āl vi, 712a – VI, 700b
Shifāʿī, Muẓaffar b. Muḥammad al-Ḥusaynī (1556) viii, 783b – VIII, 810a
Shifāʿī, Sharaf al-Dīn (1627) iv, 69a, viii, 776a, 851a – IV, 72b; VIII, 802a, 880b
Shifāʾī Iṣfahānī, Ḥakīm Sharaf al-Dīn (1628) iv, 69a; ix, **434a** – IV, 72b; IX, **450b**
Shigaley → Shāh ʿAlī
Shighnān → Shughnān
Shīḥ ix, **434b** – IX, **451a**
Shihāb, Banū ix, **435a** – IX, **452a**
Shihāb al-Dawla → Mawdūd b. Masʿūd
Shihāb al-Dīn → Muḥammad b. Sām I, Muʿizz al-Dīn
Shihāb al-Dīn, Pīr v, 26a – V, 27a
Shihāb al-Dīn b. ʿAlāʾ al-Dīn, Sayyid iii, 155b – III, 159a
Shihāb al-Dīn b. Nāṣir al-Dīn Shāh (Mālwā) (XVI) vi, 54b – VI, 52b
Shihāb al-Dīn Aḥmad b. Mādjid → Ibn Mādjid
Shihāb al-Dīn Aḥmad b. ʿAbd al-Ḳādir (XVII) vii, 290b – VII, 292b
Shihāb al-Dīn Aḥmad b. Abū Bakr Marʿashī (1467) vi, 517b – VI, 502a
Shihāb-al-Dīn Aḥmad b. Faḍl Allāh → Ibn Faḍl Allāh al-ʿUmarī
Shihāb al-Dīn Dawlatābādī → al-Dawlatābādī
Shihāb al-Dīn al-Ḥusaynī, Shāh (1884) ix, **435b** – IX, **453a**
Shihāb al-Dīn al-Ḳarāfī (1285) vi, 185a; ix, **436a** – VI, 167b; IX, **453b**
Shihāb al-Dīn al-Ḳūṣī (1255) vi, 429b – VI, 415a
Shihāb al-Dīn Maḥmūd (Bahmānid(e)) (1518) vii, 289a – VII, 291a
Shihāb al-Dīn Maḥmūd b. Būrī i, 1332a; ii, 282a; iii, 399a – I, 1372b; II, 290b; III, 411b
Shihāb al-Dīn Maḥmūd b. Ḳarādja iii, 120a – III, 122b
Shihāb al-Dīn Maḥmūd b. Takash al-Ḥārimī (Ḥamāt) (1176) vi, 790a – VI, 780a
Shihāb al-Dīn Mālik ii, 354b – II, 364a
Shihāb al-Dīn al-Maḳsī (XIII) vii, 210b – VII, 211b
Shihāb al-Dīn al-Miṣrī al-Ḥanafī → al-Khafādjī
Shihāb al-Dīn Muḥammad Ghūrī → Muʿizz al-Dīn Muḥammad b. Sām
Shihāb al-Dīn Shāhīn Pasha → Shāhīn Pasha
Shihāb al-Dīn Shīrāshāmak iii, 420a; iv, 708a – III, 433b; IV, 736b
Shihāb al-Dīn ʿUmar → ʿUmar Shāh
Shihāb al-Dīn ʿUmar b. Muʿīn al-Dīn Djāmī (XIV) viii, 749b – VIII, 770a
Shihāb Iṣfahānī (1874) ix, **436a** – IX, **452a**
Shihāb Mahmrā s, 66b – S, 67a
Shihāb Turshīzī (1800) ix, **436b** – IX, **452b**
al-Shihābī (1800) iv, 69b – IV, 73a
al-Shihābī → ʿAbd al-Khāliḳ; Aḥmad; Ḥaydar; Manṣūr
Shihābid(e)s i, 1078a; ii, 634b, 635a; iv, 834b; v, 259a; s, 268a, b, 269a – I, 1110b; II, 650b, 651a; IV, 867b; V, 257a; S, 268a, b
Shiḥna ix, **437a** – IX, **454a**
al-Shiḥr i, 554b; iv, 901b; v, 656a, 786a, b; vi, 81b, 133a, 385b; vii, 51a, 496a; ix, **438b**; s,337b, 338a, b –
I, 572a; IV, 934b; V, 660a, 792b; VI, 79a, 131a, b, 369b; VII, 51b, 496a; IX, **455b**; S, 337b, 338a
Shiḥrī (Shaḥrī) ix, **439a** – IX, **456a**
Shiḳāḳ, Banū i, 1031a – I, 1062b
Shikār aghalarï ii, 6a – II, 6a
Shikārī ix, **439a** – IX, **456b**
Shikārpūr ii, 185b, 186a; ix, **440a** – II, 191b, 192a; IX, **457a**
Shikasta → Khaṭṭ
Shiḳḳ ix, **440b** – IX, **457b**
Shīkha iv, 823b – IV, 856b
Shiḳḳa Banāriya → al-Kāf
Shiḳḳdār ii, 273a, 868a – II, 281a, 888a
al-Shīla (al-Sīla) (Korea) ix, **440b** – IX, **457b**
Shilb (Silves) i, 6a, 165b, 862a, 1339a; ii, 1009a; iii, 816b; ix, **441a** – I, 6a, 170a, 886b, 1379a; II, 1032b; III, 840a; IX, **458a**
al-Shilbī → Ibn al-Imām
al-Shilbī, Maryam bint Abī Yaʿḳūb (XI) ix, 441b – IX, 458b
al-Shilbiyya (XII) ix, 441b – IX, 458b
al-Shillī, Abū ʿAlawī Muḥammad b. Abū Bakr(1682) i, 828b; vi, 352a; ix, **441b** – I, 851b; VI, 336a; IX, **459a**
Shilluk ii, 828a, 944a – II, 847b, 966a
Shīmā bint Ḥalīma (VI) viii, 362b – VIII, 375b
Shimr (Ḥusayn b. ʿAlī) vi, 737a – VI, 726b
Shimrān vi, 20b – VI, 18a
Shimshāṭ ix, **442a** – IX, **459a**
al-Shimshaṭī, Abu 'l-Ḥasan ix, **442a** – IX, **459b**
Shimʿūn vi, 631b – VI, 616b
Shīn → Sīn
Shīnā, Salmān (1978) ix, **442b** – IX, **459b**
Shinās vii, 53a – VII, 53b
Shināsī, Ibrāhīm Efendi (1871) i, 61b, 294a, 298a, 973a; ii, 466a, 473b, 682a; iii, 591b; iv, 875b; vi,92a,

373a, 758a, b; ix, **443a** –
I, 63b, 303a, 307b, 1003a; II, 478a, 485b, 699a; III, 612a; IV, 908b; VI, 90a, 357b, 747b; IX, **460a**
Shīnī (Shīniyya. Shānī) ix, **444a** – IX, **461b**
Shinḳīṭ/Shindjīṭ i, 211a, 733b; vii, 611a, 623b, 624a; ix, **445a** – I, 217a, 755b; VII, 610b, 623a, b; IX, **462a**
al-Shinḳīṭī, Aḥmad b. al-Amīn (1913) v, 892a; vii, 624a; ix, **445b**; s, 123a –
V, 898b; VII, 624a; IX, **463a**; S, 122b
al-Shinḳīṭī, Muḥammad b. al-Mukhtār (1882) x, 249a – X, 267b
al-Shinḳīṭī, Sīdī ʿAbd Allāh b. al-Ḥādjdj Ibrāhīm (1878) vii, 624a – VII, 623b
al-Shinḳīṭī, Sīdī ʿAbd Allāh b. Muḥammad b. al-Ḳāḍī (Ibn Rāzga) (1730) vii, 624a – VII, 624a
al-Shinḳīṭī, al-Ṭālib Abū ʿAbd Allāh (Bilaʿmash) (1695) vii, 624a – VII, 624a
Shintara (Cintra) ix, **446b** – IX, **463b**
Shinwārīs i, 238a; s, 66b, 237b – I, 245b; S, 67a, 237a
al-Shinshawrī, ʿAbd Allāh (1590) vii, 135a –
VII, 137a
Shiʿr ix, **448b** – IX, **464a**
Shīr → Asad
Shīr Afdal ii, 30b, 317a – II, 31a, 326a
Shīr Afkan → ʿAlī Ḳulī Khān Istadjlū
Shīr ʿAlī (vizier, Mashhad) (XV) vi, 715b – VI, 704b
Shīr ʿAlī Khān b. Dōst Muḥammad (Afghānistān) (1879) i, 87a, 231b, 232a, 796b; ii, 417a, 638a; iv, 537b; vi, 807a; ix, **446b** –
I, 89b, 239a, 819b; II, 428a, 654a; IV, 561a; VI, 796a; IX, **486b**
Shīr ʿAlī Khān (Khōkand) (1845) v, 30a – V, 31a
Shīr Khān → Shīr Shāh Sūrī (Delhi)
Shīr Khān (Bengal(e)) (1272) i, 1254a – I, 1292a
Shīr Khān Bābī ii, 597b – II, 612b
Shīr Khān Lōdī (XVII) vii, 530b – VII, 530b
Shīr Shāh Sūrī (Afghān, Delhi) (1545) i, 218a, 228b, 252b, 316a, 1015a, 1135b, 1155a, 1209b, 1218b, 1323b; ii, 13a, 121a, 154b, 155b, 259a, 271a, 272b, 498b, 973a, 1122b, 1144a; iii, 199b, 201b, 422b, 423a, 449a, 575b; iv, 276b, 1127b; v, 598a, 687b; vi, 47a, b, 48b, 127b, 131a, 272a, 310a, 407a; vii, 131a, 138b, 195a, 314a, 317a, 325a, 344b, 680a, 965b; ix, **448a**, 894a; s, 1b, 3a, 176b, 203a, 312a, 325a –
I, 224b, 235b, 260b, 326a, 1046b, 1169b, 1189b, 1245b, 1255a, 1364b; II, 13a, 123b, 159b., 160a, 266a, 279a, 281a, 511a, 995b, 1149a, 1171a; III, 205a, 206b, 436a, b, 464a, 595b; IV, 288b, 1159a; V, 602a, 693a; VI, 45b, 46a, 47a, 125b, 129a, 257a, 294a, 391b; VII, 132b, 141a, 195b, 316a, 319a, 326b, 346b, 679b, 966a; IX, **488a**, 930a; S, 1b, 2b, 177b, 203a, 312a, 324b
Shīr Singh ii, 140b; iii, 336a; iv, 196b – II, 144a; III, 346a; IV, 205a
Shīr wa-Khurshīd → Nishān
Shīrāʾ ix, **470b** – IX, **489b**
al-Shiʿrā (Sirius) ix, **471b**; s, 320b – IX, **488b**; 320a
Shīrāshāmak → Shihāb al-Dīn Shīrāshāmak
Shīrawayh, Abū Shudjāʿ (1115) iii, 105b; ix, **472a** – III, 108a; IX, **498a**
Shīrāz i, 36a, 132a, 1341b; ii, 812a; iii, 55b, 1208b; iv, 7b, 220a; v, 835a; vi, 120a, 128b, 198b, 199a, 272b, 283a, 383b, 384a, 408a, 484b, 516a, 517a, 551a, 627b, 671b, 764a; vii, 820a, b; ix, **472b**; s, 38a, 118b, 119b, 142b, 147b, 291a, 302a, 305a, 336a –
I, 37a, 136a, 1382a; II, 831b; III, 58a, 1239a; IV, 8b, 229b; V, 841a, b; VI, 117b, 126b, 182b, 183a, 257b, 268a, 368a, 392b, 470b, 501a, 502a, 535b, 612b, 657b, 753b; VII, 822a, b; IX, **491a**; S, 38a, 117b, 118a, 119a, 142a, 147b, 290b, 301b, 305a, 335b
—institutions i, 212b; ii, 426a – I, 218b; II, 437a
—monuments i, 127a; iii, 1124b – I, 131a; III, 1152b
Shīrāzī (Kilwa) ix, **489a** – IX, **499a**
al-Shīrāzī → al-ʿAbbās b. al-Ḥusayn; Ḳuṭb al-Dīn
Shīrāzī, ʿAbd al-Hādī (Āyatullāh) (1962) vi, 553b; ix, **480a** – VI, 538a; IX, **498a**
al-Shīrāzī, Abū ʿAbd Allāh iv, 1074a – IV, 1105b
al-Shīrāzī, Abu ʾl-Faradj iii, 161a, 766b –
III, 164b, 789b
al-Shīrāzī, Abu ʾl-Ḥasan ii, 649b; iv, 787a; v, 61a – II, 666a; IV, 819a; V, 63a
al-Shīrāzī, Abu ʾl-Ḥusayn (XII) ix, **481a** –
IX, **499b**
al-Shīrāzī, Abū Isḥāḳ (1083) iii, 899a; vi, 655a; vii, 397a, 540b; viii, 71b; ix, 65a, **481a**; s, 29b, 192a –
III, 923a; VI, 640b; VII, 398a, 540b; VIII, 73a; IX, 66b, **500a**; S, 30a, 193a
Shīrāzī, Elwān (XV) vi, 73a – VI, 71a
Shīrāzī, Ḥasan al-Mahdī al-Ḥusaynī (Āyatullāh) (1980) ix, **481a** – IX, **498b**
Shīrāzī, Mahdī b. al-Sayyid Ḥabīb Allāh al-Ḥusaynī (1960) ix, **480a** – IX, **498a**
Shīrāzī, Mīrzā ʿAlī Agha (1936) ix, **480a** –
IX, **498a**
Shīrāzī, Mīrzā Muḥammad Ḥasan (1895) vi, 552b; vii, 299a, 918b; ix, **479b**; s, 76a, 77a – VI, 537a; VII, 301b, 919a; IX, **497a**; S, 76a, 77a
Shīrāzī, Mīrzā Muḥammad Taḳī b. Muḥibb ʿAlī Ḥāʾirī (1920) vi, 552b; ix, **480b** – VI, 537a; IX, **498b**
Shīrāzī, Mīrzā Ṣāliḥ (XIX) s, 108a, 290b – S, 107b, 290a
Shīrāzī, Mīrzā al-Sayyid Ismāʿīl (1888) ix, **480a** – IX, **498a**
al-Shīrāzī, Muḥammad b. lyās i, 344b – I, 355a
al-Shīrāzī, Nūr al-Dīn Muḥammad b. Abi ʾl-Ṭayyib (XIV) vi, 847b – VI, 838b
Shīrāzī, Rafiʿ al-Dīn (1620) ix, **483a** – IX, **499b**
al-Shīrāzī, Ṣadr al-Dīn → Mullā Ṣadrā Shīrāzī
Shīrāzī, Shaykh Hāshimī (XIX) vii, 440b –
VII, 441b
Shīrbaz vi, 506b – VI, 492a
al-Shirbīnī, Yūsuf b. Muḥammad (XIII) i, 571b, 595b; ix, **483a** – I, 590a, 615a; IX, **501b**
Shire (Syros) ix, **483b** – IX, **502a**
Shīrgīr → Anūshtigin Shīrgīr
Shīrī → ʿAlī Beg Hersek-zāde
Shīrīn → Farhād wa-Shīrīn
Shirin Begī ii, 1113b; iv, 630a – II, 1139b; IV, 654b
Shīrīn Bika Āḳā bint Ṭaraghay (Tīmūrid(e)) (1385) viii, 1036a – VIII, 1071a
Shīrīn Maghribī, Muḥammad ix, **484a** – IX, **502b**
Shirk ix, **484b** – IX, **503**
Shīrkūh, al-Mudjāhid (Ḥims) (XIII) viii, 988b – VIII, 1023b
Shīrkūh, Abu 'l-Ḥārith b. Shādī (1169) i, 197a, 197b, 797a; ii, 318b, 856b, 858a; iii, 399a, 862b; iv, 210a; vi, 320a, 322a, 380b, 547b, 871a; vii, 163b, 726b; viii, 127b, 130a, b, 131a; ix, **486a** – I, 202b, 203a, 820b; II, 328a, 876b, 878a; III, 411b, 886b; IV, 219b; VI, 304b, 306b, 364b, 532a, 862a; VII, 165a, 727a; VIII, 130b, 132b, 133a, b; IX, **504b**
Shīrkūh II, Asad al-Dīn iii, 399b – III, 412a
Shirmake, ʿAbd al-Rashīd (Somalia/-e) (1969) ix, 718b, 719b – IX, 749b, 751a
Shīrpūr i, 1254a – I, 1292a
Shirriz vi, 744a, b – VI, 733b
Shīr-rūd-dūhazār vi, 512b – VI, 497b
Shīrwān (Sharwān, Shirwān) i, 8a, 191b, 406a, 958a; ii, 86a, 193a; iii, 211a; iv, 343a, 344b, 346a-350a; v, 296a, 458b; vi, 55b, 56b, 64b, 320a, 416b, 500a, 516b; ix, **487a**; s, 139b, 143a, 326a, 333b –
I, 8a, 197a, 417b, 987b; II, 87b, 199a; III, 216b; IV,

357b, 359a, 361a-365a; V, 287b, 461a; VI, 53b, 54b, 62b, 304b, 401b, 485a, 501b; IX, **505b**; S, 139a, 142b, 143a, 325b, 333a
Shirwān (river/rivière) → Diyālā
Shīrwān-Shāh iv, 348a; vi, 274b; ix, **488a** – IV, 363a; VI, 259al IX, **506b**
Shīrwān Shāhs i, 835b, 967b; ii, 1082b; iv, 345a, b, 348a, 350a – I, 859a, 997a; II, 1108a; IV, 360a, 363a, 365a
al-Shirwānī, Fatḥ Allāh al-Mu'min (1453) vii, 685a, 976a – VII, 685a, 976b
al-Shirwānī, Meḥmed/Muḥammad Rushdī Pasha (1875) vi, 175b; vii, 205b – VI, 162a; VII, 206b
Shirwānī, Yaḥyā (1463) x, 252a – X, 270b
Shirwānī, Zayn al-ʿĀbidīn (1837) viii, 117a – VIII, 119a
Shirwānī-zāde Rüshdi Pasha (1874) i, 285a; iii, 621a; vii, 205b – I, 294a; III, 642a; VII, 206b
Shīrzādiyān iv, 860a – IV, 893a
Shishaklī, Adīb al- ii, 662a; v, 1048a – II, 678b; V, 1044b, 1045a
Shishāwa vi, 142a, 743b – VI, 140b, 733a
Shishman i, 1118b, 1302b, 1303a; ii, 611a – I, 1152a, 1342b, 1343a; II, 626a
Shishmanid(e)s i, 1302b – I, 1342b
Shīth b. Ādam (Seth) i, 178a, 247a; vi, 901a; ix, **489b** – I, 183a, 255a; VI, 892b; IX, **508b**
Shīth b. Bahrām ii, 1099b – II, 1125a
Shīth b. Ibrāhīm al-Ḳifṭī iii, 780a – III, 803a
Shīthānī ii, 1100a, 1101a – II, 1125b, 1127a
Shitrandj → Shatrandj
Shīv(w)ādjī b. Shādjī Bhōnsle (Marāṭhā) (1680) i, 199b, 769a, 1202b; ii, 99b, 602a, 1129b; iii, 15b, 202b, 424b, 427a; iv, 1023a; vi, 269b, 534b, 535a, 536a; vii, 315b, 404b; viii, 74b; s, 246b – I, 205a, 792a, 1238a; II, 101b, 616b, 1156b; III, 16b, 208a, 438a, 440b; IV, 1055b; VI, 254b, 519a, 520b; VII, 317b, 406a; VIII, 76b; S, 246b
Shivādjī II b. Rādjarām (Marāṭhā) (XVIII) vi, 535a – VI, 519b
Shiw Prasād iii, 458a – III, 474a
Shīz v, 1110a, 1112a; ix, **490b** – V, 1106a, 1108a; IX, **509a**
Shkarawa i, 1189b, 1190a – I, 1224b, 1225a
Shkodra → Ishkodra
Shlūḥ → Tashelhīt
Shoa i, 763b; ii, 10a, b; iii, 3b; iv, 540b – I, 786b; II, 10a, b; III, 3b; IV, 564a
Shodhi Efendi → Shawkī Efendi Rabbānī
Shoghi → Shawḳī
Shoghi Efendi → Shawḳī Efendi
Shōlāpūr iii, 426a, 626a, 1160a, 1161a; ix, **490b** – III, 439b, 646b, 1188b, 1189b; **509a**
Shor Bazaar s, 66b – S, 67a
Shorfā → Sharīf; Shurafā'
Shrārda (rebel(le)) (XIX) i, 84b; vi, 595b – I, 87a; VI, 580a
Shrīnagar → Srīnagar
Shrīrangapaṭṭanam iii, 451a; v, 1259a, 1260a, b – III, 466b; V, 1250a, 1251a, b
Shriwardhan s, 246b – S, 246b
Shu → Ču
Shuʿāʿ al-Salṭana (Ḳādjār) (XX) ii, 652b; iv, 393b; vii, 432a, b – II, 669a; IV, 410b; VII, 433a, b
Shuʿayb (prophet/-ète) ix, 491a – IX, 510a
Shuʿayb I b. ʿUmar (880) i, 680b; v, 421a, 1156a, b; vi, 1035b – I, 701b; V, 423a, 1146a; VI, 1029a
Shuʿayb b. Djalāl al-Dīn Manīrī (XV) vi, 354a – VI, 338a
Shuʿayb b. al-Ḥabḥāb al-Azdī i, 104b – I, 107b
Shuʿayb b. Mahdam iii, 53a – III, 55a
Shuʿayb b. al-Muʿarrif viii, 112b – VIII, 115a
Shuʿayb b. Muḥammad b. ʿAbd Allāh (VIII) vii, 576b – VII, 577a
Shuʿayb b. Sahl (842) vii, 4a – VII, 4a
Shuʿayb b. Ṣāliḥ viii, 657b – VIII, 676b
al-Shuʿayba vi, 144b; s, 50a – VI, 143a; S, 51a
Shuʿaybiyyūn iii, 339a – III, 349a
Shuʿba b. ʿAyyāsh (808) i, 105b; iii, 63a; vi, 263b; s, 18a, 232b – I, 108b; III, 65b; VI, 248b; S, 18a, 232b
Shuʿba b. al-Hadjdjādj (777) i, 445b; vii, 260a; viii, 515a; ix, **491b** – I, 458b; VII, 262a; VIII, 532b; IX, **510a**
Shubāṭ → Ta'rīkh
Shubayl b. ʿAzra al-Dubāʿī (757) ix, 766b – IX, 800a
Shubha ii, 831b; iii, 21b; ix, **492b** – II, 851b; III, 21b; IX, **511b**
Shubrā al-Khayma (Damanhūr) ii, 105b; vi, 303a – II, 107b; VI, 288b
Shubrāwī, Shaykh ʿAbd Allāh i, 819b, 1152a – I, 842b, 1186a
Shubruma b. al-Ṭufayl iii, 938a – III, 963a
Shudjāʿ, Shaykh (Khalwatī) (1588) vii, 596a; ix, 155b – VII, 595b; IX, 160b
Shudjāʿ b. al-Ḳāsim (IX) vii, 723a – VII, 724a
Shudjāʿ b. Shāh Djahān iii, 634b; s, 258b – III, 656a; S, 258a
Shudjāʿ al-Dawla, Mīrzā Djalāl al-Dīn Nawāb, Awadh) (1775) i, 680a, 702a, 757a, 1042b, 1357b; ii, 870b; iii, 61a, b, 1158b, 1244a; v, 637a; viii, 426a; ix, 90a, **493a** – I, 701a, 723b, 779b, 1074b, 1397b; II, 890b; III, 63b, 64a, 1187a, 1276a; V, 641a; VIII, 440a; IX, 95b, **512a**
Shudjāʿ al-Dīn Khurshīd v, 828a – V, 834a
Shudjāʿ al-Dīn Orkhan b. Menteshe vii, 56a – VII, 56b
Shudjāʿ al-Dīn Sulaymān Pasha iv, 108b – IV, 113a-b
Shudjāʿ Khān (Mālwā) (1554) i, 1155a; vi, 407a – I, 1189b; VI, 391b
Shudjāʿ al-Mulk, Nawwāb (Awadh) (XVIII) vii, 707a – VII, 708a
Shudjāʿ al-Mulk b. ʿAmān al-Mulk ii, 30b – II, 31a
Shudjāʿ al-Mulk Bukhārī iii, 634a – III, 655b
Shudjāʿ al-Mulk Durrānī (Afghanistān) (1839) i, 72b, 230b, 231a, b; ii, 186b, 638a, 1001a; iv, 537b; v, 102a; vi, 806b; s, 270a – I, 74b, 237b, 238a, b; II, 192b, 654a, 1024b; IV, 561a; V, 104a, b; VI, 796b; S, 270a
Shudjāʿ al-Salṭana → Ḥasan ʿAlī Mīrzā
Shudjāʿī, Shams al-Dīn (XIV) ix, **493b** – IX, **512a**
al-Shūf ii, 749b; vi, 343a, 344a; ix, **494a**; s, 159a – II, 768a; VI, 327b, 328a; IX, **513a**; S, 159a
Shufʿa i, 172b; v, 878b; ix, **494b** – I, 177a; V, 884b; IX, **513b**
Shufurwa, Sharaf al-Dīn (XII) iv, 62a; viii, 971b; ix, **495a** – IV, 65b; VIII, 1005b; IX, **514a**
Shughnān (Shighnān) i, 851b, 853b, 854a; iv, 202b; ix, **495b** – I, 875a, 877b; IV, 211b; IX, **514b**
Shughnī (language/langue i, 225a – I, 231b
Shughr ii, 556a – II, 570a
al-Shuhadā' (Mecca) ii, 744b; vi, 147b, 153a – II, 763a; VI, 146a, 151b
Shuhāra → Shahāra
Shuhaym, Banū s, 356a – S, 356a
Shuhūd → Shāhid
Shuḥūra (pass/col) vi, 546a – VI, 531a
Shukāʿa (Shukāʿ) ix, **496b** – IX, **545b**
Shukr ix, **496b** – IX, **515b**
Shukr b. Abi 'l-Futūḥ (Musāwī) (1061) vi, 148b – VI, 147a

Shukr Allāh, Mīrzā (XVI) vii, 442a – VII, 443a
Shükr Allāh Efendī (XVII) v, 19a – V, 19b
Shukrān, Banū vii, 263a – VII, 264b
Shukrī, ʿAbd al-Raḥmān (1958) vi, 955b; ix, **998a**; s, 58a – VI, 948a; IX, **517b** S, 58a
Shukrī al-Khūrī → al-Khūrī
Shukrī al-Ḳuwwatlī ii, 290a – II, 298a
Shukrī Muṣṭafā (1978) vii, 291b; x, 61b, 121b – VII, 293b; X, 63b, 132b
Shukriyya iv, 686a, b, 687a – IV, 714a, b, 715a
Shükrü, Midḥat iv, 284b – IV, 296b
Shükrü (Shükrī) Bey, Aḥmed (1926) iii, 1199a; ix, **499a** – III, 1229b; IX, **518a**
Shükūfe ii, 908b – II, 929b
Shūl (China/-e) ix, **499a** – IX, **518b**
Shūl (amīrs) (XIII) v, 826b; vi, 482a – V, 832b; VI, 468a
Shuʿla iv, 69b – IV, 73a
Shulayr, Djabal i, 489a – I, 503b
Shūlistān iv, 498a; v, 824a, 829b; ix, **499b** – IV, 519b; V, 830b, 835b; IX, **518b**
Sh(u)lūḥ (Marrākush) i, 1181b, 1182a, b, 1183a, b, 1350a; vi, 590b, 591b, 743b – I, 1216b, 1217a, b, 1218a, b, 1390a; VI, 575a, 576b, 732b
Shūmān ix, **500b** – IX, **520a**
Shumaym, Abu ʾl-Ḥasan ʿAlī (1204) ix, **501a** – IX, **520a**
al-Shumayn al-Ḥillī iii, 111a, 221b – III, 113b, 228a
Shumayṭiyya (Sumaytiyya) i, 509a; ix, **501b** – I, 524b; IX, **520b**
al-Shumaysī (Mecca) vi, 154b – VI, 152a
Shumayyil, Shiblī b. Ibrāhīm (1917) iv, 125a; **501b**, 517a – IV, 130a; **521a**, 537a
Shumen → Shumnu
Shumla (Khūzistān) (XII) i, 239b, 513b; vi, 58b, 59b; vii, 707a, 726b – I, 247a, 529a; VI, 56b, 57a; VII, 708a, 727a
Shumnu ix, **502a**, 702b – IX, **521a**, 731a
Shungwaya (Somalia/-e) ix, **504a** – IX, **523b**
al-Shūnī, Nūr al-Dīn (1537) vi, 87b, 88a – VI, 85b, 86a
al-Shūnīzī → Kāẓimayn
Shunḳub ix, **504b** – IX, **524a**
Shūrā i, 84b; ii, 866a; v, 1084a; ix, **504b** – I, 87a; II, 886a; V, 1081b; IX, **524a**
Shurafāʾ (Shorfāʾ) i, 355a, b, 368b, 371b, 403a; iii, 1037a; v, 1187b, 1191a, b, 1200a, 1201b; vii, 36a; viii, 440a; ix, **507a**, 899b – I, 366a, b, 379b, 382a, 414b; III, 1062b; V, 1177b, 1181a, b, 1190a, 1192a; VII, 36a; VIII, 454b; IX, **526b**, 936a
Shuraḥbīl b. ʿĀmir (684) vi, 677a – VI, 663b
Shuraḥbīl b. al-Ḥārith (al-Mathāmina) i, 527a; v, 118b; vi, 829b – I, 543a; V, 121a; VI, 820a
Shuraḥbīl b. Ḥasana (639) i, 111a, 341a, 1139a, 1149a; ii, 498a; iii, 397b, 569a; iv, 927b; v, 119b; vi, 546b; ix, 262b, **508b** – I, 114a, 351b, 1173b, 1183b; II, 510b; III, 410a, 589a; IV, 960b; V, 122a; VI, 531a; IX, 271a, **528a**
Shuraḥbīl b. al-Simṭ al-Kindī (VII) i, 1343b; iii, 168b; ix, 553b – I, 1384a; III, 172b; IX, 575b
Shuraḥbīl b. Yaḥṣib (Mārib) vi, 561b – VI, 546b
Shuraḥbiʾil Yaʿfur (Mārib) vi, 561b, 563b – VI, 546b, 548b
Shurāt → Khāridjites
Shurayḥ b. al-Ḥārith b. Ḳays (ḳāḍī) (695) vi, 670b; ix, **508b** – VI, 657a; IX, **528b**
Shurbubba vii, 614a – VII, 613b
Shurīda, Muḥammad Taḳī (1826) ix, **509b** – IX, **529b**
Shurṭa ii, 505a, 507a, 510a; iii, 487b; iv, 373b; ix, **510a** – II, 517b, 520a, 522b; III, 504b; IV, 390a; IX, **529b**
Shūsh → al-Sūs
Shūsha iv, 573a; s, 47a – IV, 595b; S, 47b
Shushānī → Shwāshna
Shūshtar (Shūshtar, Tustar) i, 695a, 711b; ii, 350b; iv, 674a, 675b; v, 451b, 867a; vi, 494b, 516a, 627b, 672b; vii, 673a, b; ix, **512a** – I, 716b, 733a; II, 360b; IV, 701b, 703a, b; V, 454a, 873b; VI, 480a, 501a, 612b, 659a; VII, 673a, b; IX, **531b**
al-Shūshtarī, ʿAbd al-Laṭīf Mūsawī Djazāʾirī s, 108a, 290a – S, 107b, 289b
al-Shushtarī, Abu ʾl-Ḥasan ʿAlī (1269) i, 501b; iii, 921b; iv, 1006b; vii, 56b, 812a; ix, **513a**; x, 320b; s, 264a – I, 516b; III, 946a; IV, 1039a; VII, 57a, 813b; IX, **533a**; X, 345a; S, 263b
al-Shushtarī, Sayyid ʿAbd al-Ḥusayn Marʿashī(XIX) vi, 517a – VI, 502a
al-Shushtarī, Sayyid Niʿmat Allāh al-Djazāʾirī s, 57a – S, 57b
al-Shushtarī, Sayyid Nūr Allāh → Nūr Allāh al-Sayyid Sharīf al-Marʿashī
Shustar → Shushtar
Shuʿūb iv, 334a – IV, 348b
Shuʿūbiyya i, 16b, 158a, 206b, 276a, 1080b; ii, 729a, 951b; iii, 353b, 773b, 846a, 885a; iv, 16a, 54b, 190a, 786a; vi, 215a, 313b, 880b; viii, 880b; ix, **513b**; s, 17b, 404b – I, 17a, 162b, 212b, 284b, 1113a; II, 748a, 973b; III, 364b, 796b, 870a, 909a; IV, 17a, 57b, 198a, 817b; VI, 199a, 298b, 872a; VIII, 910b; IX, **533b**; S, 18a, 405a
Shuʿurī Ḥasan Efendī iv, 526b – IV, 549a
Shuwa i, 1259b; ix, **516a**; s, 164a – I, 1297b; IX, **536a**; S, 164a
Shuwaymiyya vi, 84b – VI, 82b
al-Shuwayr vi, 305a, 307b – VI, 290b, 293a
al-Shwayfāt vi, 304a – VI, 289b
Shuyūʿiyya ix, **517a** – IX, **537a**
Shyāḍma, Banū vi, 591a – VI, 576a
Sī ʿAbd al-Ḥayy al-Kettānī (XX) vii, 416b, 417a – VII, 418a, b
Sī Aḥmad al-Bakkāy iii, 39a – III, 40b
Sī Faṭmī ben Slīmān (XX) vii, 417a – VII, 418b
Si Mohand (Mhand) x, 119a – X, 128b
Siak Sri Infrapura → Sumatra
Sialkōt → Siyālkūt
Al-Sīb (Damā) vi, 735b – VI, 725a
Ṣibā iv, 488b – IV, 509b
Sibāʿ b. ʿAbd al-ʿUzzā al-Khuzāʿī iv, 896b – IV, 929a
Sibāʿ b. Nuʿmān iv, 16a – IV, 17b
al-Sibāʿī, Muṣṭafā iii, 1069b, 1070a; iv, 160a; viii, 906b – III, 1096b, 1097a; IV, 167a; VIII, 939a
Sibāʿī, Yūsuf v, 190a – V, 187b
Sibāḳ → Faras
Sībawayh(ī), Abū Bishr ʿAmr b. ʿUthmān (796) i, 321b, 588b; ii, 896a; iii, 204b. 205a, 1162a; iv, 122b, 255a, 399b; v, 174b, 803b; vi, 130a, 346b, 443b, 635b; vii, 262a, 277a, 281b, 914a; ix, **524a**; s, 22b – I, 331b, 607b; II, 916b; III, 210a, b, 1190b; IV, 127b, 266b, 417a; V, 172a, 809b; VI, 128a, b, 330b, 429a, 620b; VII, 264a, 279a, 283b, 914b; IX, **544a**; S, 23a
Sībāy iii, 400a; iv, 552a, b, 553a – III, 412b; IV, 576a, b
Siberia → Sibir
Siberia – Turkic languages x, **732b** – X, **778b**
Sībī (Sīwī) ix, **531a**; s, 270b – IX, **551b**; S, 270a

Sibir ix, **531b** – IX, **552a**
Sibir, Khān of (XV) ii, 45a – II, 46a
Sibṭ → Ibn al-Djawzī; Ibn al-Taʿāwīdhī; al-Mārdīnī, Muḥammad b. Muḥammad
Sicily/-e → Ṣiḳilliyya
al-Sīd i, 986a; ii, 526b; iii, 542b, 770b; ix, **533a**; s, 81a – I, 1016b; II, 539b; III, 561b, 794a; IX, **553b**; S, 80b
Sidama iii, 6a – III, 6b
Sidamo v, 524b – V, 527b
Siddi Lebbe ii, 28a – II, 28a
al-Ṣiddīḳ ix, **534b** s̲ IX, **555a**
Ṣiddīḳ Ḥasan Khān al-Kannawdjī → Nawwāb Sayyid Ṣiddiḳ Ḥasan Khān
Ṣiddīḳa Dawlatābādī (XX) vi, 486a, b, – VI, 472a, b
al-Siddīḳī → al-Firūzābādī
al-Ṣiddīḳī (Bakriyya) ix, **535a** s̲ IX, **555b**
Ṣiddīḳī, Shāh Ghulām Muḥammad Ṣūfī (XX) ix, 730b s̲ IX, 762b
Ṣiddīḳī Shaykhs (Maḥmūdābād) vi, 77b – VI, 75b
Sidḥ vi, 84a – VI, 82a
Sidhpūr ix, **535a** – IX, **555b**
Sidi ix, **535b** – IX, **556a**
Sīdī ʿAbd Allāh al-Khayyāṭ (Talaghza) vi, 891a – VI, 882a
Sīdī Abu ʾl-Ḥasan ʿAlī b. Ḥamdūsh (1718) vi, 891a; s, 350b – VI, 882a, b; S, 350b
Sīdī Aḥmad (Banū ʿAbbās) iv, 478a, b – IV, 499a, b
Sīdī Aḥmad b. ʿAlī iv, 350a – IV, 365a
Sīdī Aḥmad u-Mūsā → Ḥmad u-Mūsā
Sīdī Aḥmad b. Yūsuf → Aḥmad b. Yūsuf
Sīdī Aḥmad al-Bakkāy (1514) ix, 758a – IX, 791a
Sīdī Aḥmad Dghughī → Sīdī Abu ʾl-Ḥasan ʿAlī b. Ḥamdush
Sīdī ʿAlī → Sīdī Abu ʾl-Ḥasan ʿAlī b. Ḥamdush
Sīdī ʿAlī b. Khlef b. Ghālib → Mūlāy ʿAlī Bū Ghālem
Sīdī ʿAlī Arulatī iv, 349b – IV, 364b
Sīdī ʿAlī Čelebi (1554) vii, 51a – VII, 51b
Sīdī ʿAlī Ḥarzūz (1549) vi, 894a – VI, 885b
Sīdī ʿAlī al-Mzālī (Fès) vi, 124a – VI, 121b
Sīdī ʿAlī Reʾīs (1562) vii, 319a; ix, **535b** – VII, 321a; IX, **556a**
Sīdī Badr → Muẓaffar Shāh Ḥabshī
Sīdī Bel-ʿAbbās al-Sabtī iv, 729a; vi, 589b, 590b, 591a, 596a – IV, 758a; VI, 574a, 575b, 576a, 581a
Sīdī Bel-Abbès → Sīdī Bu ʾl- ʿAbbās
Sīdī Ben Aḥmed iv, 729a – IV, 758a
Sīdī Ben ʿAmmār → Ibn ʿAmmār, Abu ʾl-ʿAbbās
Sīdī Ben ʿArūs → Ibn ʿArūs
Sīdī Ben Slīmān → al-Djazūlī
Sīdī Berridjāl → Ibn Barradjān
Sīdī Bou Said → Sayyidī Abū Saʿīd
Sīdī Bū ʿAzzā → Abū Yaʿzā
Sīdī Bu ʾl-ʿAbbās ix, **536b** – IX, **557a**
Sīdī Bū Madyan → Abū Madyan
Sīdī Bū ʿUthmān vi, 595b; s, 48a – VI, 580b; S, 48b
Sīdī Bū Yaʿḳūb → Abū Yaʿḳūb Yūsuf al-Bādisī
Sīdī Būshta (Abu ʾl-Shitāʾ) s, 405b – S, 405b
Sīdī ʾl-Ḥādjdj v, 596a – V, 600a
Sīdī Ḥammū i, 1186a – I, 1221a
Sīdī Ḥarāzam (Fès) vi, 123b – VI, 121b
Sīdī Lakhdar Bakhkhlūf (al-Akhḍar) (XVI) vi, 248b, 249a, 253b – VI, 232b, 233b, 237b
Sīdī Khalīl → Khalīl b. Isḥāḳ al-Djundī
Sīdī Lahsen Lyūsī (1691) ix, 769b – IX, 803a
Sīdī Maḥmūd al-Baghdādī (XVI) ix, 758b – IX, 791a
Sīdī Maḥrez → Muḥriz b. Khalaf
Sīdī Muḥammad → Muḥammad I-V (ʿAlawid(e))
Sīdī Muḥammad b. ʿĪsā (XV) vii, 36b – VII, 36b
Sīdī Muḥammad b. al-Mukhtār v, 394a – V, 395a
Sīdī Muḥammad b. al-Ṭayyib → Muḥammad b. al-Ṭayyib
Sīdī Muḥammad ʿAbd Allāh (Ḥamāliyya) → al-Sharīf al-Akhḍar
Sīdī Muḥammad al-ʿAyyāshī ii, 367b – II, 377b
Sīdī al-Mukhtār (1811) ix, 758a – IX, 791a
Sīdī al-Muntaṣir al-Muḥammad (XIV) vii, 638a – VII, 638a
Sīdī Muwallih iv, 921a – IV, 953b
Sīdī (ʿAlī) Reʿīs ii, 588b, 589b; iii, 856b – II, 603a, 604a; III, 880b
Sīdī al-Ṣāḥib → al-Balawī, Abū Zamʿa
Sīdī ʿUḳba → ʿUḳba b. Nāfiʿ
Sīdī Yāḳūt (Ḥabshī) s, 246a – S, 246b
Sidiḳ Zälili (XVIII) vi, 768a – VI, 757b
Sīdiyya Bābā, Shaykh (XIX) vii, 609a – VII, 609a
Sīdiyya al-Kabīr (1868) vii, 623a – VII, 622b
Sidjādī, ʿAlāʾ al-Dīn v, 481b – V, 484b
Sidjdjīn iii, 1132b; ix, **538a** – III, 1161a; IX, **559b**
Sidjill i, 9b, 1090a; ii, 79a, 302b, 308b; ix, **538a** – I, 9b, 1123b; II, 80b, 310b, 317b; IX, **559b**
Sidjilmās(s)a ii, 885a; iii, 149a, 256b; v, 1175a, 1177a, 1178a; vi, 142a, b, 571b, 573a, 593a, 727b, 743b, 815a, 1038a; vii, 585a; viii, 440a; ix, **545a**; s, 28b, 29a, 295b, 370a, 389b – II, 905b; III, 152b, 263b; V, 1165a, 1167a, 1168a; VI, 140a, b, 556b, 558a, 577b, 716b, 732b, 805b, 1031a; VII, 585b; VIII, 454a; IX, **566b**; S, 29a, 295a, 370a, 389b
al-Sidjilmāsī, Abū Muḥammad al-Ḳāsim (XIV) vii, 277a; viii, 427a; ix, **546a** – VII, 279a; VIII, 441a; IX, **568a**
al-Sidjilmāsī, ʿAlī (1647) vii, 626b – VII, 626b
Sidjistān → Sīstān
al-Sidjistānī → Abū Bakr; Abū Dāwūd; Abū Ḥātim; Abū Sulaymān
al-Sidjistānī, ʿAbd Allāh (1929) ix, **546b** – IX, **568b**
Sidjn ix, **547a** – IX, **568b**
Sidjzī → Čishti
al-Sidjzī → Abū Yaʿḳūb; Aḥmad; Amīr Ḥasan
al-Sidjzī, ʿAbd Allāh (IX) vii, 410b – VII, 412a
al-Sidjzī, Abū Saʿīd viii, 108a – VIII, 110b
Ṣidḳ iv, 487b; ix, **548b** – IV, 508b; IX, **570a**
Ṣidḳa Kaʿkī (XX) vi, 163b – VI, 156a
Ṣidḳī → Bakr Ṣidḳī; al-Zahāwī
Ṣidḳī, Muḥammad iv, 148b; v, 191a – IV, 154b; V, 188a
Sidon → Ṣaydā
Sidona → Shadūna
Sidr ix, **549a** – IX, **571a**
Sidrat al-Muntahā ix. **550a** – IX, **572a**
Sidrāy b. Wazīr i, 1339a; ii, 1009a; iii, 816b – I, 1379b; II, 1033a; III, 840a
al-Sidrī s, 35b – S, 35b
Sīduh → Ibn Sīda
Sierra Leone ix, **550b**; s, 217b – IX, **572b**; S, 217a
Sīf al-Naṣr ii, 876a – II, 896b
Sīf ʿUmāra s, 222b, 223a – S, 222b, 223a
Ṣifa/Ṣifāt i, 333b, 410b; ii, 550b; iv, 182a; ix, **551a** – I, 344a, 422b; II, 564a; IV, 190a; IX. **573a**
Ṣifātiyya i, 334a – I, 344a
Sīfawayh al-Ḳāṣṣ (VIII) ix, **552b** s̲ IX, **574b**
Ṣiffīn i, 40b, 51b, 304a, 383b, 448b, 451b, 697a; iii, 12b; v, 936a; vi, 139a, 378b; vii, 693b; ix, **552b**; X, 107a; s, 89b, 230b – I, 41b, 53b, 313b, 394b, 461b, 464b, 718a; III, 13a; V, 939b; VI, 138a, 362b; VII, 694a; IX, **574b**; X, 115b; S, 89b, 230b
al-Ṣifr ix, **556b** – IX, **578b**

Sigetwār ix, **557b** – IX, **579b**
Sïghnāḳ (Sughnāḳ) (town/ville) ix, **557b**; x, 561a; s, 245a, 246a – IX, **580a**; X, ; S, 245a, 246a
al-Sïghnāḳī, Ḥusām al-Dīn (1314) vii, 969a; x, 561a – VII, 969b; X,
Ṣiḥāfa ix, **558a** – IX, **580a**
Siḥāḳ v, 777b; ix, **565b** – V, 783b; IX, **588a**
Sihālī s, 292a – S, 291b
Sihām al-Mulk s, 365a – S, 365a
Siḥr i, 1084b; iv, 770a; v, 100b; ix, **567b** – I, 1117a; IV, 801a; V, 102b; IX, **590a**
Ṣihrīdj → Ḳanāt
Ṣihyawn (Sion) ix, **571b** – IX, **593b**
Siʿird (Siʿirt) ix, **573b** – IX, **596a**
Sīkān vi, 493b – VI, 479b
Sikandar → Iskandar
Sikandar (Gudjarāt) ii, 1128b – II, 1155a
Sikandar b. ʿAlī ʿĀdil-Shāh (ʿĀdil-Shāhs) (1700) i, 199b, 769b, 12102b; vi, 837a – I, 205a, 792b, 1238a; VI, 828a
Sikandar b. Muẓaffar Shāh I (Gudjarāt) (1526) vi, 51b – VI, 50a
Sikandar b. Sulṭān Fatḥ Shāh (Kashmīr) (XVI) s, 324b – S, 324a
Sikandar Bēgam i, 1195b, 1197a – I, 1231a, 1232b
Sikandar b. Ḳuṭb al-Dīn, But-Shikān (Kashmīr) (1410) iii, 420a; iv, 708a, b; ix, **575b**; s, 131b – III, 433b; IV, 736b, 737a; IX, **597b**; S, 130b
Sikandar Djāh (Ḥaydarābād) (XIX) iii, 322a; vi, 806a – III, 332a; VI, 796a
Sikandar Khān (Satwas) (XVI) vi, 54b, 55a – VI, 52b, 53a
Sikandar Shāh I, ʿAlāʾ al-Dīn (Tughlukid(e), Delhi) (1393) vi, 49a – VI, 47b
Sikandar Shāh I (Bengal(e)) (1390) i, 719b; viii, 258b; ix, **575b** – I, 741a; VIII, 261a; IX, **598a**
Sikandar Shāh II Lōdī (Lōdīs, Delhi)) (1517) i, 252b, 914b, 1323a; ii, 12b, 155a, 205a, 271a, 421a, 498b, 1048a, 1114a; iii, 420b, 439a, 453b, 492a, 631b, 632a; v, 784a, b, 1135a; vi, 51b, 126a, 410a, 970a, 1030b; vii, 139a; s, 10b, 73b, 203a, 312a, 313a, b – I, 260b, 942a, 1363b; II, 13a, 160a, 211b, 279a, 431b, 511a, 1072b, 1171a; III, 434a, 453b, 469a, 509a, 653a, 653b; V, 790a, b, 1130b; VI, 49b, 124a, 395a, 962b, 1023b; VII, 141a; S, 10a, 74a, 202b, 312a, b, 313a
Sikandar Shāh III Aḥmad Khān Sūr (Sūrīs, Delhi) (1555) i, 316a, 1135b; ii, 271b; iii, 423b, 576a – I, 326a, 1170a; II, 279b; III, 437a, 596a
Sikand(a)ra iv, 131b; vi, 369b – IV, 137b; VI, 353b
Sikandarābād/Secundarabad → Ḥaydarābād iii, 318b; – III, 328b
Siḳāya i, 9a, 80a – I, 9a, 82b
Sikbādj ix, **576a** – IX, **598a**
Sikhs i, 72a, 230a, b, 231a, 282b, 296a, b, 454a, 913b, 970b, 1020a; ii, 28b, 637b, 929a, 973b; iii, 63a, 225b, 245b, 335b, 336a, 435b; iv, 666a, 709b; v, 597b, 598b; viii, 253b, 254b; ix, **576b**; s, 242a, 332a – I, 74b, 237a, b, 238b, 291a, 305a, 467b, 941b, 1000b, 1051b; II, 29a, 654a, 950b, 996a; III, 65b, 232b, 252b, 345b, 346a, 450a; IV, 693a, 738a; V, 601a, 602a, b; VIII, 255b, 256b; IX, **598b**; S, 242a, 331b
Ṣiḳilliyya i, 86a, b, 248b, 250a, 935b; ii, 130b, 853a; iii, 220a, 299a, 657b, 788a; iv, 274b, 275b, 459b, 496a, b, 805a; v, 697a, 1243b; vi, 337b, 435b, 455b, 1043b; ix, 507b, **582a**; s, 120b, 303a – I, 88b, 89a, 256a, 258a, 964b; II, 133b, 873a; III, 226b, 308a, 679a, 811a; IV, 286b, 287b, 479b, 517b, 837b; V, 702a, 1234b; VI, 322a, 420b, 441a, 1037b; IX, 527a, **604b**; S, 120a, 303a
Sikka ii, 117b; iii, 256a, 384a; iv, 190b, 220a, 467a, 945a, 1177b; v, 965b, 966a; ix, **591b** – II, 120a; III, 263b, 396b; IV, 199a, 230a, 487b, 977b, 1211a; V, 969b, 970a; IX, **614b**
Sikkat al-Ḥadīd ix, **600b** – IX, **624a**
al-Sikkīn (XI) ii, 858b; vii, 732a – II, 878a; VII, 732b
al-Sikkīt ii, 300a; iii, 940b – II, 308a; III, 965a
al-Ṣiḳlabī, ʿAbd al-Raḥmān iv, 672b – IV, 700a
Sīkūl iv, 213a – IV, 222b
Sila ix, **603a**; x, 11a – IX, **626a**; X, 11a
al-Silafī, al-Ḥāfiẓ Abū Ṭāhir Ḥāfiẓ (1180) iv, 137a; vi, 429a; ix, 65a, **607b** – IV, 142b; VI, 414a; IX, 66b, **630b**
Silāḥ i, 1055b; ii, 506b; v, 973a – I, 1087b; II, 519b; V, 975a
Silāḥdār ix, **609b** – IX, **632b**
Silāḥdār ʿAlī Pasha → ʿAlī Pasha Silāḥdār
Silāḥdār Findïḳlïlï Meḥmed Agha (1726) v, 18b; ix, **610b** – V, 19a; IX, **633b**
Silāḥdār Dāmād ʿAlī Pasha → ʿAlī Pasha Dāmād
Ṣilāḥdār Ḥusayn Pasha i, 905a – I, 932a
Silāḥdār Muṣṭafā Pasha (XVII) vi, 232a – VI, 225b
Sile s, 136a – S, 135b
Silhādī i, 914b – I, 942b
Silhet (Sylhet) ix, 610b – IX, 634a
Silifke (Seleucia) iii, 1007a; ix, **611a** – III, 1032a; IX, **634a**
Silistre i, 4b; ii, 611b; iii, 253a; iv, 878a; viii, 236a – I, 4b; II, 626b; III, 260a; IV, 910b; VIII, 241a, b
Silivri Kapïsï iv, 232b – IV, 243a
Siliwan → Mayyāfāriḳīn
Silm, Āl i, 759b – I, 782b
Silsila ix, **611a** – IX, **634b**
Silsilat al-Dhahab s, 173a – S, 173b
Silves → Shilb
al-Sīm, lughat ix, **611b** – IX, **634b**
Silwān vi, 629a – VI, 614a
Simāk b. Makhrama (VII) ix, 553b – IX, 575b
Simancas → Shant Mānkash
Simāṭ iv, 957a, b – IV, 990b
Sīmāvī, Sedād ii, 475a, b – II, 487b
Simaw (Simav) ix, **612a**; s, 359b – IX, **635a**; S, 359a
Simawne → Badr al-Dīn (Simawne)
al-Sīmāwī → Abu 'l-Ḳāsim Muḥammad al-ʿIrāḳī
Simdjūr, Banū i, 1354b – I, 1393b
Sīmdjūr al-Dawātī s, 357a – S, 357a
Sīmdjūrī, Abū ʿAlī b. Abī 'l-Ḥasan (994) v, 624b; vi, 65a, 340a; viii, 110a, 1027b – V, 628b; VI, 63a, 324a; VIII, 112b, 1062b
Sīmdjūrī, Abū 'l-Ḥasan Muḥammad b. Ibāhīm (X) viii, 110a, 1028a; x, 945a – VIII, 112b, 1063a; X,
Sīmdjūrid(e)s ix. **612a** – IX, **635a**
Simferopol i, 312a – I, 322a
Simḥah Isaac b. Moses iv, 606a – IV, 630a
Sīmīn Dānishwar (XX) vi, 486a – VI, 472a
Sīmiyāʾ iv, 264b; ix, **612a** s IV, 276b; IX, **635b**
Ṣimkān vi, 384a – VI, 368b
Ṣimḳo → Ismāʿīl Agha Ṣīmḳo
al-Simmarī, Abū 'l-Ḥasan ʿAlī b. Muḥammad (941) viii, **812a** – VIII, **839a**
Simnān (town/ville) vi, 366a, 492a; ix, **613b**; s, 73a, 309b – VI, 350a, 478a; IX, **636b**; S, 73b, 309a
al-Simnānī → ʿAlāʾ al-Dawla; Ṭāʾūs
al-Simnānī, Abū Djaʿfar Muḥammad (1052) ix, **614b** – IX, **637b**
al-Simnānī, Abu 'l-Ḥasan Aḥmad s, 194a – S, 193b
Simoom/Simoun → Samūm
Simplicius → Samlis

Simsār → Dallāl
Simsim   ix, **614b** – IX, **638a**
al-Simṭ b. al-Aswad   v, 119b – V, 122a
Sīmur   i, 509a, 753a; ii, 106b, 1099b, 1138a; iii, 112b;
    iv, 402a; ix, **615a** –
    I, 524b, 775b; II, 109a, 1125b, 1165a; III, 115a; IV,
    419b; IX, **638b**
Sīn/S̲h̲īn (letters/lettres)   ix, **615b** – IX, **639a**
al-Ṣīn (China/-e)   i, 91a, 390b, 927b; ii, 42b, 45b, 477b,
    583a, 1076a; iii, 653b, 1115b; iv, 553a; v, 364a,
    770a, 854b; ix, **616b**; x, 460b, 475b –
    I, 93b, 402a, 956a; II, 43b, 46b, 490a, 597b, 1101a;
    III, 674b, 1143a; IV, 577a; V, 365a, 776a, 861a; IX,
    640a; X, 493b, 510b
Ṣīn/Čīn Kalān (K̲h̲ānfū/Canton)   ix, **626b** –
    IX, **640a**
Ṣiṇā (language/langue)   ii, 139a – II, 142b
Sīnāʾ (Sinai)   ix, **625a** – IX, **649a**
Sīnāʿa   ix, **625b** – IX, **649b**
Sīnād   iv, 412b – IV, 430b
Sinai, Mount/Mont   → Sīnāʾ; al-Tīh; al-Ṭūr
Sinān (architect(e)) (1588)   i, 511a, 768a, 843b, 1256b;
    ii, 685b, 686a, 705b; iii, 144b; iv, 232a, b, 233a,
    1017a, 1158a; v, 67a, 815b, 837b, 882a; vi, 868b,
    687a; ix, **629a** –
    I, 526b, 791a, 866b, 1295a; II, 702b, 703a, 723b; III,
    147a; IV, 242a, 243a, 1049a, 1190a; V, 69a, 821b,
    844a, 888b; VI, 674a, b; IX, **653a**
Sinān (685)   iv, 534b; s, 131a – IV, 558a; S, 130b
Sinān (ketk̲h̲udā) (XVI)   vi, 436b – VI, 422a
Sinān, Rās̲h̲id al-Dīn   → Rās̲h̲id al-Dīn Sinān
Sinān b. Salama b. al-Muḥabbiḳ al-Hud̲h̲alī (VII)   vi,
    193a – VI, 177a
Sinān b. Sulaymān   ii, 484a – II, 496a
Sinān b. T̲h̲ābit   i, 387b, 867a, 899a – I, 399a, 891a,
    925b
Sinān b. ʿUlayyān al-Kalbī (1024)   vii, 117a – VII, 118b
Sinān Pas̲h̲a   → Člālazāde; K̲h̲od̲j̲a
Sinān Pas̲h̲a (grand vizier) (1596)   vii, 912a – VII,
    912b
Sinān Pas̲h̲a (Tunis) (XVI)   vii, 433b – VII, 434b
Sinān Pas̲h̲a, K̲h̲ādim (1517)   ii, 1042a; iii, 341b; iv,
    1093a; ix, 14b, **630b** – II, 1066b; III, 351b, 352a; IV,
    1124a; IX, 15a, **654b**
Sinān Pas̲h̲a, K̲h̲od̲j̲a (1486)   ix, **630b** – IX, **655a**
Sinān Pas̲h̲a, K̲h̲od̲j̲a (1596)   i, 340b, 697b, 1298b,
    1303b; ii, 34a, 287b, 688a, 880b; iii, 94b; v, 1023a;
    vi, 996b; vii, 433b, 762a; viii, 184a; ix, **631a** –
    I, 351a, 719a, 1338b, 1343b; II, 34b, 295b, 705b,
    901a; III, 97a; V, 1018b; VI, 989a; VII, 434b, 763b;
    IX, **655a**
Sinān Pas̲h̲a Dāmād   i, 292b; ii, 985b; iv, 230b – I,
    301b; II, 1008a; IV, 240b
Sinān Pas̲h̲a al-Kayk̲h̲iyā (Yemen) (1608)   vi, 436b;
    vii, 514a; viii, 339a – VI, 422a; VII, 514a; VIII, 351a
Sinān Pas̲h̲azāde Meḥmed Pas̲h̲a   iv, 594b – IV, 618b
Sinandad̲j̲ → Sanandad̲j̲
Sinbādnāma   iii, 313b, 373a – III, 323a, 384b
Sind   i, 43b, 228a, 229b, 230b, 246b, 627b, 962a,
    1194b; ii, 74a, 153b, 185a; iii, 323b, 404b, 415a,
    419b, 448b; iv, 199b, 202b, 597b, 793a, 1160a; vi,
    48a, 50b, 193a, 368a, 439a, 489a, 640b, 689a, 691a;
    vii, 388b; viii, 68a, 240b; ix, **632a**; s, 252a – I, 44b,
    235a, 236b, 237b, 254a, 648b, 991b, 1230a; II, 75a,
    158b, 191a; III, 333b, 417a, 428b, 433a, 463b; IV,
    208a, 211b, 621b, 825b, 1192a; VI, 46b, 49a, 177a,
    352a, 424a, 475b, 625b, 676b, 678b; VII, 389a; VIII,
    69b, 246b; IX, **856b**; S, 252a
Ṣindābūr (Sandabur)   ii, 1127b; ix, **638b** – II, 1154a;
    IX, **663a**
Sindān (Sandān)   ix, **638b** – IX, **663a**

Sindbād   ix, **638b** – IX, **663a**
Sindbād al-Ḥakīm (Syntipas)   ix, **640a** – IX, **664b**
Sindh   vii, 314a – VII, 316b
Sindhī (langu(ag)e   i, 1007b; ii, 101b; ix, 636a – I,
    1038b; II, 103b; 660b
Sindhia   ii, 1144a – II, 1171a
Sindhind   i, 11a; iii, 1137a; ix, **640b** – I, 11b; III,
    1165a; IX, **665a**
S̲h̲īndhīyā, D̲j̲ayappa (Marāt̲h̲ā) (XVIII)   vi, 535b – VI,
    520a
S̲h̲īndhīyā, Mahādad̲j̲ī Rāo (Marāt̲h̲ā) (1794)   ii, 1092b;
    vi, 535b, 536a – II, 1118a; VI, 520a, b
al-Sindī   → Abū ʿAṭāʾ; Abū ʿAlī; Abū Maʿs̲h̲ar
Sindī, Banū   i, 1246b – I, 1284b
al-Sindī, Raḥmat Allāh b. ʿAbd Allāh (1585)
    vii, 294a – VII, 296a
al-Sindī b. S̲h̲āhik (IX)   iii, 990a; vi, 332a, 335a; vii,
    259a, 646b – III, 1014b; VI, 316b, 319b; VII, 260b,
    646a
Sind̲j̲ābī (Send̲j̲āwī), Banū   ix, **641b** – IX, **666a**
Sind̲j̲ār (town/ville)   iii, 1268a; vi, 539b, 599b, 781a,
    870b; vii, 9a; s, 381a, 413b –
    III, 1301a; VI, 524a, 584b, 770b, 861b; VII, 10a; S,
    381b, 414a
Sind̲j̲ār, D̲j̲abal   viii, 147a; ix, **643a** – VIII, 149a; IX,
    667b
al-Sind̲j̲ārī, Ḥasan al-Mak̲h̲zūn (amīr) (XIII)   viii, 147a –
    VIII, 149a
Sind̲j̲as, Banū   v, 1179a, b, 1181a, b, 1182a –
    V, 1169a, b, 1171a, b, 1172a
Sind-Rūd̲h̲   vii, 20b; s, 366b – VII, 20b; S, 366a
Sinet   → K̲h̲itān
Ṣinf   i, 477a; ii, 967a; iii, 217b; iv, 894a; ix, **644a** – I,
    491b; II, 989a; III, 223b; IV, 927a; IX, **668b**
Singapore   i, 979a; ii, 426b; vi, 207b, 236b, 237a, 241a;
    ix, **646b**; s, 220b –
    I, 1009b; II, 437b; VI, 192a, 209a, 210a, 212a; IX,
    671b; S, 220b
Singkawang   s, 151a – S, 151b
Ṣinhād̲j̲a   i, 79a, 84a, 355b, 356a, b, 367a; ii, 623a – I,
    81b, 86b, 366b, 367a, 378a; II, 638b
Ṣīnī (porcelain(e)   iv, 1168b, 1169a, 1170a; v, 857a; ix,
    647a – IV, 1201b, 1202a, 1203a; V, 864a; IX, **672a**
Sīnimā   → Cinema/Cinématographe
Sinkāt   iv, 686b, 687a – IV, 714b, 715a
Sinkiang   ii, 43a; v, 846a, b; ix, **648b** – II, 43b; V,
    857b, 858a; IX, **673b**
Sinna (senna)   → Sanandad̲j̲
al-Sinnabra   vi, 547a, 622b; viii, 423a; s, 117a – VI,
    531b, 607b; VIII, 437b; S, 116b
Sinnār   i, 35a; ii, 943b; v, 267a; vii, 425b;
    ix, **650b** – I, 36a; II, 965b; V, 265a; VII, 427a; IX,
    675b
Sinnawr   ix, **651b** – IX, **676b**
Siounik (Arrān)   vi, 337a – VI, 321b
Sinūb (Sinop(e))   i, 476b; iv, 575b, 577a, 813b; v,
    505b; vi, 70b, 71a; ix, **653b** –
    I, 490b; IV, 598b, 600a, 846b; V, 509a; VI, 68b, 69a;
    IX, **678b**
Sipāhī   i, 1264b, 1265a, 1268b; iii, 191a, b, 192b; iv,
    565a, 1095b; ix, **656a** –
    I, 1303a, b, 1307b; III, 195b, 196a, 197b; IV, 587b,
    1126b; IX, **681b**
Sipāhī Meḥmed   v, 775a – V, 781a
Sipāhī og̲h̲lanlarî   i, 102a, 1004a – I, 105a, 1034b
Sipahsālār   → Ispahsālār
Sipihr S̲h̲ukōh   ii, 134b II, 138a
Sipihrī, Suhrāb (1880)   iv, 70a; ix, 658a – IV, 73b; IX,
    683a
Sīr b. Abī Bakr   i, 7a, 242b; ii, 1013a; iv, 116a – I, 7b,
    250a; II, 1036b; IV, 121a

Ṣīr Banī Yās, Ḏjazīrat   i, 535b; ix, **658b** –
   I, 552a; IX, **684a**

Sîr Daryā (Jaxartes)   i, 135a, 607a; ii, 778a, 790a,
   791a; v, 30b, 45a, 46a; vi, 557a; ix, **659a**; s, 244b,
   245a, b –
   I, 139a, 627a; II, 797a, 809a, 810a; V, 31b, 46b, 47a;
   VI, 542a; IX, **684a**; S, 244b, 245a, b

Sir Sayyid   → Aḥmad Ḳẖān

Sīra   iii, 369b, 374a; v, 1161b, 1163b; ix, **660b** – III,
   381a, 386a; V, 1151b, 1153a; IX, **686a**

Sīra Shaʿbiyya   ix, **664a** – IX, **689b**

Sirādj   v, 986b; ix, **665a** – V, 982b; IX, **691a**

Sirādj ʿAfīf, Shams al-Dīn-i   → Shams al-Dīn-i Sīrādj
   ʿAfīf

Sirādj al-Dawla Mīrzā Maḥmūd (Nawwāb) (1757)   i,
   400b; ii, 7a, 371a, 1091b; ix, **666b** –
   I, 412a; II, 7a, 381b, 1117a; IX, **692a**

Sirādj al-Dīn al-Awrangābādī (1763)   vi, 837b – VI,
   828a

Sirādj al-Dīn Djunaydī, Shaykh   vi, 369a –
   VI, 353b

Sirādj al-Dīn al-Ḥanafī   → al-Hindī

Sirādj al-Dīn Muẓaffar b. al-Ḥusayn (1237)   vi, 790b –
   VI, 780a

Sirādj al-Dīn ʿUthmān   → Akẖī Sirādj al-Dīn ʿUtẖmān,
   Shaykh

Sirādj al-Ḳuṭrub   ix, **667a** – IX, **692b**

al-Sīradjān (town/ville)   ix, **667a** – IX, **693a**

Sīrāf (port)   i, 550b, 552a, 927b, 1355a; ii, 130b; iv,
   500b, 1085b; v, 670b; vi, 365a, 385b; vii, 52a, 66b;
   ix, **667b**; s, 118a –
   I, 568a, 569b, 956a, 1394a; II, 134a; IV, 522a, 1116b;
   V, 676a; VI, 349a, 369b; VII, 52b, 67a; IX, **693b**; S,
   117b

al-Sīrāfī, Abū Muḥammad Yūsuf (995)   ix, **689b** – IX,
   696a

al-Sīrāfī, Abū Saʿīd (979)   i, 97b, 126b; ii, 896b; vi,
   443b, 444a, b, 845b; vii, 281a, 490b, 914a; viii, 614b;
   ix, 327b, **668b**; s, 362b –
   I, 100b, 130a; II, 917a; VI, 429a, 429b, 430a, 836b;
   VII, 283a, 490b, 915a; VIII, 634a; IX, 327b, **694a**; S,
   362a

al-Sīrāfī, Aḥmad b. ʿAlī b. al-ʿAbbās b. Nūḥ
   (1022)   viii, 811b – VIII, 839a

Sirāikī   → Lahnda; Sind, Langu(ag)e

Sirakūsa (Syracuse)   ix, **669b** – IX, **696a**

Ṣirāṭ   ix, **670b** – IX, **697b**

Sīrat al-Amīr Ḥamza   iii, 153b, 376a, 1207a – III,
   156b, 387b, 1237b

Sīrat ʿAntar   → ʿAntar

Sīrat Banī Hilāl   iii, 387a – III, 399b

Sīrat al-Baṭṭāl   → Dhu ʾl-Himma

Sīrat al-Dalhama   → Dhu ʾl-Himma

Sīrat Sayf b. Dẖī Yazān   → Sayf Ibn Dẖī Yazān

Ṣirb (Serbia/-e)   i, 1163b, 1165a; v, 276a; vi, 70a; **671a**
   – I, 1198b, 1199b; V, 274a; VI, 68a; IX, **698b**

Sirdāb   v, 12b – V, 11b

Sirdār   → Sardār

Sīrdjān   v, 150a, 151a, 152a, b; s, 327a – V, 152a, b,
   154a; S, 326b

Sirfandakār   vi, 507b – VI, 493a

Sirhān b. Saʿīd b. Sirhān (XVIII)   vii, 838b – VII, 840a

Sirhind   i, 1194a; vi, 50a, 62a; ix, **673b**; s, 126b, 313a –
   I, 1229a; VI, 48b, 60a; IX, **700b**; S, 125b, 312b

Sirhindī, Mawlānā ʿAbd al-Ḳādir (XVI)   vi, 131a; s, 3a –
   VI, 129a; S, 2b

Sirhindī, Shaykh Aḥmad al-Farūḳī (1624)   → Aḥmad
   Sirhindī

Sirhindī, Yaḥyā (XV)   s, 105a – S, 104b

Siri   s, 206b – S, 206a

Sīrī   i, 1322a; ii, 256b, 269a; iii, 481b; iv, 921b; vi, 49a,

50a, 294a – I, 1362a; II, 263b, 277a; III, 498a; IV,
   954b; VI, 47b, 48b, 279b

Sīrīn bint Shamʿūn (VII)   vi, 575a – VI, 560a

Sirʿīn (Lebanon/Liban)   vi, 303a – VI, 288b

Sirius   → al-Shiʿra

Sirkap   s, 259b – S, 259b

Siroz (Serres/Serrai)   ix, **673b**; s, 330a –
   IX, **701a**; S, 329b

Sirrī Pasha (XIX)   i, 907b – I, 935a

Sīrwā(n)   vi, 742a – VI, 731a

Ṣirwāḥ   vi, 80b, 560b, 562b, 831a; ix, **675b** – VI, 78b,
   545a, 547a, 821b; IX, **703a**

Sirwāl   ix, **676a** – IX, **704b**

Siryāḳūs (Cairo(e))   vi, 454a – VI, 439b

Sīs   i, 8a; ii, 36a, 38a; v, 283b; vi, 507b, 508b, 724b; ix,
   678a –
   I, 8a; II, 36b, 38b; V, 282a; VI, 493a, 494a, 713b; IX,
   706a

Sisak   → Sisḳa

Sīsām (Samos)   ix, **679b** – IX, **708b**

Sīsar   ix, **680a** – IX, **709b**

Sisḳa (Sisak)   ix, **681a** – IX, **708a**

Sisodiās   vi, 53a – VI, 51b

Sīstān   i, 5a, 43b, 86a, 147b, 211b, 222b, 223a, 452b,
   1344a; ii, 5a, 49b, 903b; iv, 4b, 19a-b, 54a, b, 55a; v,
   57a, 390a, 868a; vi, 65b, 331b, 333a, 337b, 345a,
   368b, 640b; viii, 795a; ix, **681b**; s, 21a, 26a, 326b –
   I, 5a, 44b, 88b, 152a, 217b, 229a, b, 230a, 465b,
   1384b; II, 5a, 50b, 924b; IV, 5a, 20b, 57a, b, 58a; V,
   58b, 391a, 874b; VI, 63b, 316a, 317b, 322a, 329a,
   352b, 625b; VIII, 822a; **708b**; S, 21a, 26a, 326a

Sīstānī   → Farruḳẖī-i Sīstānī

Sistova   → Zistova

Sitāra   iii, 360a; iv, 823b – III, 371b; IV, 856b

Siti binti Saad (1950)   ix, **685a** – IX, **713b**

Sitr   ix, **685a** – IX, **714a**

Sitt al-Mulk bint al-ʿAzīz (Fāṭimid(e) (1023)   ii, 484a,
   855b, 857a; iii, 80b; iv, 944a; vii, 116b, 482b; ix,
   685b –
   II, 496a, 875a, 877a; III, 83a; IV, 976b; VII, 118b,
   482b; IX, **714a**

Sitt al-Nisāʾ   vi, 488b – VI, 474b

Sitt al-Tudjdjār   iv, 136a – IV, 142a

Sittī Ḳẖātūn (Dẖu ʾl-Ḳadr) (XV)   ii, 895a; vi, 507b, 978a
   – II, 916a; VI, 493a, 970b

Siu (Siyu)   ix, **686a**; s, 355b – IX, **714b**; S, 355b

Sivas   → Sīwās

Sivāsiyya   iv, 991b – IV, 1024a

Sīwa   ix, **686b** – IX, **715a**

Sīwādjī (Marāt̲ha)   → Shiv(w)ādjī

Siwāk   → Miswāk

Siwāl   s, 353b – S, 353b

Sīwās   i, 511a; iv, 1167b; v, 248a; vi, 72a, 120b, 231a,
   232a, 275b, 315b; ix, **689b**; s, 146a, 274a – I, 526b;
   IV, 1200a; V, 246a; VI, 70a, 118a, 224b, 225b, 260b,
   300b; IX, **718a**; S, 146a, 273b

Sīwāsī, ʿAbd al-Aḥad Nūrī (1651)   vi, 227b; ix, 299b –
   VI, 221b; IX, 308a

Sīwāsī, ʿAbd al-Madjīd (1639)   ix, 299b – IX, 308a

Sīwāsī, Ḳara Aḥmad Shams a-Dīn (1597)   ix, 299a –
   IX, 307b

Sīwistān (Sind)   vii, 189a, 412a – VII, 189b, 413b

Siwri Ḥiṣār   ix, **681b** – IX, **720a**

Siyāg̲h̲a   → Sāʾig̲h̲

Siyāḥčas̲h̲m   iv, 661b – IV, 688b

Siyāh-Ḳalem (XV)   ix, **692a** – IX, **720b**

Siyāh-Kūh   vi, 415a, b – VI, 400a, b

Siyāh-pūsh   iv, 409b, 410b – IV, 427a, 428b

Siyāḳat   ii, 128a, 332b, 952a; iv, 1124a, 1125b; ix,
   692b – II, 131a, 342a, 974a; IV, 1155b, 1157a; IX,
   721a

Siyākh vi, 384a, b – VI, 368a, b
Siyālkūt (Sialkot) ix, **693a**; s, 241b – IX, **721b**; S, 241b
al-Siyālkūtī, ʿAbd al-Ḥākim (1657) i, 297b, 1022b; ix, **693b** – I, 307a, 1054a; IX, **722a**
Siyārwardiyya iv, 342b – IV, 357a
Siyāsa ix, **693b** – IX, **722a**
Siyāsat-nāma → Naṣīḥat al-Mulūk
Siyāwakhsh b. Mihrān b. Bahrām-Čubīn (VIII) vi, 744b – VI, 733b
Siyāwush (b. Kay Ḳāʾūs II) i, 703a; iv, 620a, b, 813b, 815b, 1061b; v, 274b; ix, **696b** – I, 724a; IV, 645a; 846a, 848b, 1092b; V, 272b; IX, **725a**
Siyāwush Pasha, Abāza (1688) i, 380b, 1284b; iv, 193b; vi, 983a; vii, 275b; viii, 185a; ix, **697b** – I, 391b, 1324a; IV, 202a; VI, 975a; VII, 277b; VIII, 188a; IX, **726a**
Siyāwush Pasha Kanizheli (1602) ix, **697a** – IV, **726a**
Siyer → Sīra
Sjahrir ii, 664a, b – II, 681a
Skandelion → Iskandaruna
Skanderbeg → Iskender Beg
Skārdū i, 1004b – I, 1035b
Sḳīfa ii, 115b – II, 118a
Skiros vi, 71b – VI, 69b
Sklēros s, 37a – S, 37a
Skopje → Üsküb
Skutari → Ishkodra
Slavs → Saḳāliba
al-Slāwī → al-Nāṣir al-Salāwī
Slēmān, Awlād ii, 876a – II, 896b
Slīmān → Sulaymān
Sliman ben Ibrahim s, 224a, b – S, 224a, b
Slīmān Benaissa (XX) vi, 754a – VI, 743b
Slovakia → Čeh
Smacid(e)s i, 733b, 734a – I, 755b
Smala → Zmāla
Ṣmara v, 890a, b – V, 896b, 897a
Smbat → Sambāṭ
Smederovo vi, 70a, b, 71a – VI, 67b, 68b, 69a
Ṣmyr (Shakla) bint Khurshīd (Ṭabaristān) (VIII) vi, 745a – VI, 734a
Smyrna/-e → Izmīr
Soaïtou Mamadou v, 279b – V, 277b
Sōba (town/ville) i, 425b; iv, 892b; ix, **698a** – I, 437b; IV, 925b; IX, **727a**
Socotra → Suḳuṭrā
Socrate(s) → Suḳrāṭ
Sodom(e) v, 833a – V, 839a
Soekarno → Sukarno
Soekiman, Dr. → Sukiman, Dr.
Sofāla vi, 128a; ix, **698b** – VI, 126b; IX, **727a**
So-fei-er, Sayyid ix, 622b, 623a – IX, 646b
Sofia → Ṣofya
Ṣofta (Sukayn) ix, **702a** s IX, **734b**
Ṣofu Meḥmed Pasha (XVII) iii, 983b – III, 1008a
Ṣofu Sinān Pāsha (1615) viii, 339a – VIII, 351a
Ṣofya (Sofia) vi, 70b; ix, **702b** – VI, 68a; IX, **731a**
Sogguen ii, 1095b – II, 1121b
Soghdia/-ir → Ṣughd
Sögman-āwā vi, 201a – VI, 185a
Sögüd (Sögüt) ix, **706a** – IX, **735a**
Sögüdjuk i, 63a – I, 65a
Sōhāg ii, 1114b – II, 1140b
Sohar → Ṣuḥār
Sohrān, amīr (Barādūst) i, 1031a – I, 1062b
Sohrān, Banū v, 460b – V, 463a
Soḳḳar vi, 200b, 201a, b, 202b – VI, 185a, 185b, 187a
Sökmen → Alp; Artuḳid(e)s; Shāh-i Arman
Sokna ii, 575b – II, 590a
Ṣoḳollī-zade Ḥasan Pasha iv, 594b, 901a – IV, 618b, 933b
Ṣoḳollu Meḥmed Pasha (1579) i, 291b, 1018a, 1264b; ii, 56b, 103b, 704a, 881a; iii, 995a; v, 815b; vi, 72b; vii, 595b, 596a, 720b; ix, **706b**; x, 959a – I, 300b, 1049a, 1303a; II, 57b, 105b, 722a, 901b; III, 1019b; V, 821b; VI, 70b; VII, 595b, 721b; IX, **735b**; X,
Ṣoḳollu Muṣṭafā Pasha i, 1285b, 1286a; ii, 880b; v, 775a – I, 1324b, 1325b; II, 901a; V, 781a
Sokolović → Ṣoḳollu
Sokoto ii, 1145a; iii, 277a; iv, 549b; vi, 281b; vii, 435b, 436a; viii, 20b; ix, **711a** – II, 1172b; III, 285a; IV, 573a, b; VI, 266b; VII, 436b, 437a; VIII, 20b; IX, **742a**
Soḳoṭra, Soḳoṭrī → Suḳuṭra
Sol Gharībler → Ghurabāʾ
Ṣolaḳ ix, **712a** – IX, **743a**
Solaḳ-zāde. Meḥmed Hemdemī (1658) iii, 249a; ix, **712b** – III, 256a; IX, **743b**
Soldaïa → Sudak
Solomon → Sulaymān
Somali/Somalia/(-e) Somaliland i, 176b, 553a, 1038a, 1172b; ii, 113b, 535b; iii, 4a, 5b; v, 522a, 524a; vi, 128a, 283a; viii, 162a; ix, **713a** – I, 181a, 571a, 1069b, 1207b; II, 116a, 549a; III, 4a, 6a; V, 525b, 527b; VI, 126a; IX, **744a**
Sōmāy ix, **727a** – IX, **758b**
Sōmnāth → Sūmanāt
Somniani bay/baie vi, 192b – VI, 176a
Sonārgā'on i, 868b; ii, 216a, 751b; ix, **728a** – I, 893a; II, 223a, 770a; IX, **759a**
Sonde, îles de la – III, 1243b, 1257b; V, 791b; IX, **759b**
Songaṙh vi, 407a – VI, 391b
Songhay i, 1259b; ii, 94a, 252a, 977a; iii, 1038b; iv, 549a, 754b; vi, 258b, 259a, b, 281b, 402b; vii, 393b; viii, 724a; ix, **728a**, 756b; x, 89b, 122a – I, 1298a; II, 96a, 259a, 999b; III, 1064b; IV, 572b, 784b; VI, 243a, b, 266b, 387a; VII, 395a; VIII, 745a; IX, **760a**, 789b; X, 96b, 131b
Songo Mnara Island/Île de- vi, 370b – VI, 354b
Soninké iii, 288b; iv, 314a; vi, 258a, 401a – III, 297b; IV, 328a; VI, 242a, 385b
Sonḳor (Sunḳur) ix, **730a** – IX, **762a**
Sonnī ʿAlī (Songhay) (1492) ii, 252a, 977a; ix, 756b; x, 122a – II, 259a, 999b; IX, 789b; X, 131b
Soofie Saheb → Ṣiddīḳī, Shāh Ghulām Muḥammad Ṣūfī
Sōpūr iv, 707b – IV, 736a
Soraya → Thurayya
Sorgatmix → Suyurghatmīsh b. Noradin
Sorguč → Tulband
Sori ii, 942b – II, 964a
Sorḳoḳtani umm Möngke (XIII) vi, 782b; vii, 230a; ix, 110b – VI, 772b; VII, 231b; IX, 114b
Sosso vi, 401b – VI, 386a
Soudan → Sūdān
Souf s, 145a – S, 144b
Soumangourou (Sosso, Mande) vi, 402a – VI, 386b
Soundiata vi, 402a – VI, 386b
Sousse → Sūsa
South Africa, Islam in ix, **730a** – IX, **762a**
Soy iii, 374a – III, 385b
Soyinadji (Soyin Ḥādjī), Banū vi, 416b; s, 168b, 169a – VI, 401b; S, 169a
Soyūrghāl ix, **731b** – IX, **764a**

Soyurghatmi̲s̲h̲ → Suyūrg̲h̲atmi̲s̲h̲
Spahi → Sipāhī
Spahpat → Ispahbad̲h̲
Spain → al-Andalus
Spartel (Morocco/Maroc) ix, **734a** – IX, **766a**
Sphinx → Abū 'l-Hawl
Split i, 1267a; v, 774b; s, 186a – I, 1306a;
V, 780b; S, 187b
Sri Lanka → Ceylon; Sarandīb
Srīnagar iii, 448a; iv, 707b; ix, **734a**; s, 114a, 131b,
156a, 332a, 333a, 353b, 366a, b, 423b – III, 463b; IV,
735b; IX, **766b**; S, 113b, 131a, 156a, 332a, 353b,
366a, 423b
Śrīrangapatttanam ix, **736b** – IX, **769a**
Śrīvijaya vi, 207b, 234a – VI, 191b, 207a
Stenka Razin (1671) viii, 450a – VIII, 465a
Stephanos → Is̲t̲ifan b. Basīl
S̲t̲ip → Is̲h̲tib
Stuhlweissenburg → Székesfehérvár
Su (water/eau) ix, **736b** – IX, **769a**
Sū (G̲h̲azna) vi, 783a – VI, 773a
Su-Lu i, 684b; iii, 493b – I, 705b; III, 510b
Su-ssu-shi-san v, 851b – V, 855b, 856a
Suakin → Sawākin
al-Suʾālātī, Muḥammad b. Muḥammad (XVII)
vii, 470a – VII, 469b
Suʿāwī, ʿAlī (1878) ix. **737b** s̲ IX, **770a**
Suʿayr ix, **738a** s̲ IX, **770b**
Sūba i, 316b; ix, **738a** s̲ I, 326b; IX, **770b**
Sūbadār ii, 337a; ix, **738b** s̲ II, 346b; IX, **771a**
Sūbāḥ, Āl x, 956a – X,
Su Bas̲h̲ī ix, **736b** s̲ IX, **769a**
Ṣubas̲h̲ī Tigin (ḥād̲j̲ib) (XI) iii, 47a; vi, 523a; vii, 928a
– III, 49a; VI, 508a; VII, 928b
Subayʿ (Sabayʿ), Banū i, 628b; iii, 363b; v, 62b; ix,
738b – I, 649b; III, 375a; V, 64a; IX, **771a**
Subayʿa bint ʿAbd S̲h̲ams (VI) vi, 477b – VI, 463b
al-Subayba ix, **739a** s̲ IX, **771b**
Subayḥī. Banū ix, **739b** s̲ IX, **772a**
Subayta (Isbayta) ix, **739b** s̲ IX, **772a**
Subayt̲ila (Sufetula) ix, **740a** s̲ IX, **772b**
Ṣubba (Mandaeans/Mandéens) i, 1096a; iii, 1254a; vi,
247a; viii, 672a, 675a – I, 1129a; III, 1286b; VI,
231b; VIII, 692a, 694b
Sübetey i, 836a; ii, 43a; iv, 107b; v, 311b – I, 859a; II,
44a; IV, 112a; V, 311b
Ṣubḥ → Ṣalāt
Ṣubḥ (sultana) (X) vi, 430b, 431a – VI, 416a, b
Ṣubḥ al-Bas̲h̲kunsiyya ix, **740b** – IX, **773a**
Ṣubḥa ix, **741b** – IX, **774a**
Subḥān ix, **742b** – IX, **775a**
Subḥān-Ḳulī K̲h̲ān s, 419b – S, 419b
Subḥān Werdī K̲h̲ān (XIX) ix, 6b s̲ IX, 7a
Ṣubḥī, Muṣṭafā iv, 124a – IV, 129a
Ṣubḥ-i Azal Mīrzā Yaḥyā Nūrī (Bābī) (1912) i, 809a,
833b, 847a, 911b; iv, 51b, 696a; viii, 114a; ix, **741a**;
s, 53b –
I, 832a, 856b, 870b, 939a; IV, 54b, 724a; VIII, 116b;
IX, **773b**; S, 53b
Ṣubḥī Meḥmed Efendi (1769) ix, **743a** s̲ IX, **775b**
al-Subkī (town/ville) ix, **743b** – IX, **776b**
al-Subkī, Bahā al-Dīn Abū Ḥāmid Aḥmad (1371) ii,
107b; iv, 863b – II, 110a; IV, 897a
al-Subkī, S̲h̲āfiʿī ʿulamā ix, **744a** – IX, **776b**
al-Subkī, S̲h̲ayk̲h̲ Maḥmūd b. Muḥammad (1933) vi,
897a; ix, 745b; s, 244b – VI, 888a; IX, 778a; S, 244b
al-Subkī, Tād̲j̲ al-Dīn Abū Naṣr ʿAbd al-Wahhāb (1370)
i, 593a, 594b, 1308b; ii, 215a; iii, 818a, 954b; vi,
353a, 847b, 869a; vii, 212b, 296b –
I, 612b, 614a, 1348b; II, 221b; III, 841b, 979a; VI,
337a, 838b, 860a; VII, 213b, 298b

al-Subkī, Taḳī al-Dīn Abu 'l-Ḥasan, S̲h̲ayk̲h̲ al-Islām
ʿAlī (1355) ii, 215a, 926a; iii, 822a, 954b; viii, 125b
– II, 221b, 947b; III, 845b, 979a; VIII, 128a
al-Subkī Taḳī al-Dīn Abu 'l-Fatḥ Muḥammad
(1344) iii, 711a – III, 733a
al-Subkiyyūn ix, **745b**; s, 244b – IX, **778a**;
S, 244b
al-Subūʿī, al-Subūʿī b. Muḥammad iv, 828b – IV, 861b
Subuk i, 637b; ii, 679b – I, 658a; II, 696b
Subuktigîn → Sebuktegin
Subutāi → Sübetey
Suchow iv, 553b, 554a; v, 848a – IV, 577a, 578a; V,
852a
Suʿdā, Sūdābeh iv, 813a – IV, 846a
Sūdāḳ (Crimea/-ée) → Sug̲h̲dāḳ
Sūdān i, 49a, 279b, 289a, 297a, 1058a; ii, 121b; iii,
657b; iv, 262a; v, 70a, 1248a, b; vi, 467b, 594b,
646b; viii, 724a; ix, 698a, **746a**; x, 96b; s, 217b –
I, 50b, 51a, 288b, 297b, 306a, 1089b; II, 124b; III, 678b;
IV, 274a; V, 72a, 1238b, 1239a; VI, 453b, 579a,
631b; VIII, 745a; IX, 727a, **778b**; X, 104a; S, 217b
—administration i, 976a, 1156b; ii, 595a, 668a; iii,
385a; v, 1063b – I, 1006a, 1191a; II, 610a, 684b; III,
397b; V, 1061a
—ethnography/-ie i, 1a, 37b, 39a, 1058a; ii, 767b,
1110b; iii, 300a; v, 317b, 318b –
I, 1a, 35b, 40a, 1089b; II, 786a, 1136b; III, 309b; V,
317a, 318a
—institutions ii, 425a; iii, 523b – II, 436a;
III, 541b
—language, literature/langue, littérature i, 575b; ii,
467a; iii, 949a – II, 594a; II, 479a; III, 973b
Sūdān, Banū vii, 672a – VII, 672a
Sūdān, Bilād al- ix, 752b – IX, **785b**
Sudayf b. Maymūn (764) vi, 724a; ix, **762a** – VI,
713a; IX, **794b**
Sudayrī (al-Sadārā) i, 748a; ii, 175a; ix, **762a** – I,
770a; II, 181a; IX, **795a**
al-Suddī, Ismāʿīl b. ʿAbd al-Raḥmān (745) vii, 758a;
viii, 387a; ix, **762a** – VII, 759b; VIII, 400a; IX, **795a**
al-Sūdī, Aḥmad b. ʿAbd Allāh b. Sālim (1634) ii, 730a
– II, 748b
Sūdī, Aḥmed (1596) ix, **762a** – IX, **795b**
Sud̲j̲ān Rāy Bhandārī (XVIII) i, 241b; ix, **762b** – I,
249a; IX, **796a**
Sud̲j̲d̲j̲ā ix, **763a** – IX, **796a**
al-Suds al-fak̲h̲rī v, 46b – V, 47b, 48a
Suez → al-Suways
Sūf → Wādī Sūf
Ṣūf (wool/laine) ix, **764b** – IX, **797b**
Sufāla (ʿUmān) viii, 85a – VIII, 87b
Sufayna s, 198b – S, 198b
Sufetula → Subayt̲ila
Ṣuffa → Ahl al-Ṣuffa
Ṣūfī → Taṣawwuf
al-Ṣūfī → ʿAbd al-Raḥmān al-Ṣūfī
al-Ṣūfī, Abū 'l-Ḥusayn viii, 102b – VIII, 104b
Ṣūfī Islām (1807) vii, 935b – VII, 936a
Sūfid(e)s iv, 1064a – IV, 1095b
Ṣūfigarī v, 244a – V, 242a
al-Ṣūfisṭāʾiyyūn (Sophist(e)s) ix, **765a** – IX, **798b**
Ṣūfiyāna ix, **765b** – IX, **799a**
al-Ṣūfiyya (Damas(cus)) vi, 122b – VI, 120b
Ṣufriyya iii, 648a, 654b, 657b, 1040b, 1175a; vi, 311b;
vii, 123b, 815a; viii, 638a, b; ix, **766a** – III, 669b,
675b, 679a, 1066b, 1204a; VI, 296b; VII, 125b, 817a;
VIII, 657a, b; ix, **799a**
Ṣufrūy (Sefrou) (town/ville) vi, 142b, 242b; ix, **769a**;
s, 191a – VI, 140b, 240b; IX, **802b**; S, 192a
Suftad̲j̲a ii, 382b; iii, 283b; ix, **769b** –
II, 393a; III, 292a; IX, **803a**

Sufyān, Banū v, 48b; vi, 741b, 743a – V, 50a; VI, 730b, 732a
Sufyān b. ʿAwf al-Ghāmidī (VII) vi, 505b – VI, 491a
Sufyān b. Khālid al-Liḥyānī v, 763a – V, 769a
Sufyān b. Muʿāwiya al-Muhallabī (VIII) iii, 883b; vii, 360a – III, 907b; VII, 362b
Sufyān b. Mudjīb al-Azdī (VII) x, 215a – X, 232a
Sufyān b. ʿUyayna (811) i, 272b, 827a, 960b; vi, 263b; vii, 662b; ix, 7a, 182a, **772a**; s, 386b – I, 281a, 850a, 990a; VI, 248b; VII, 662a; IX, 7b, 187b, **805b**; S, 386b
Sufyān b. Yazīd b. al-Muhallab (VIII) vii, 359b – VII, 362a
Sufyān al-ʿAbdī, Abū ʿAbd Allāh (739/794) ix, **776a** – IX, **803b**
Sufyān al-Hudhalī (VII) vi, 646a – VI, 631b
Sufyān al-Thawrī (778) ii, 538b, 889b; iii, 155a, 687b, 843a; vi, 263b, 353a, 671b; vii, 607a, 662b, 758a; viii, 354b, 983b; ix, 7a, **770b**; s, 232b, 384b – II, 552a, 910a; III, 158b, 709a, 867a; VI, 248b, 337b, 658a; VII, 607a, 662a, 759b; VIII, 367a, 1018a; IX, 7b, **804a**; S, 232b, 385a
Sufyān al-Yamanī i, 829a – I, 852a
Sufyānid(e)s i, 17a; ii, 281b; iv, 457a, 494a; v, 1232a; vi, 139b, 333b; vii, 693b; ix, 772b; s, 103b – I, 17b; II, 289b; IV, 477a, 515a; V, 1222b; VI, 138a, 318a; VII, 694a; IX,, **806a**; S, 103a
al-Ṣughd (Soghdia/-e) ii, 67a, 790b; iii, 1060b; v, 181a, 541b, 542a, 852b, 854a; viii, 1031b; ix, **772b**; s, 64a, 65a, 176b – II, 68a, 80b; III, 1087a; V, 178b, 546a, b, 859a, 860b; VIII, 1067a;IX, **806a**; S, 64b, 65a, 177b
Sughdāḳ iv, 575b, 576a, 817b; vi, 575, 576a; ix, **773b** – IV, 508b 850b; VI, 598b; IX, **807a**
al-Sughdī → Abū Ḥafṣ Sughdī
Sughnāk → Suḳnāḳ
Sughundjak Noyan iv, 1046b – IV, 1078a
Sūhādj → Sōhāg
Ṣuḥār (ʿUmān) i, 563b, 1098a, 1281b; iv, 500b; vi, 385b, 734b, 735a; vii, 66b, 67a, 838b; viii, 85a; ix, **774b**; s, 234b – I, 581b, 1131a, 1321a; IV, 522a; VI, 369b, 723b, 724a; VII, 67a, b, 840a; VIII, 87a; IX, **808a**; S, 234b
Ṣuḥār al-ʿAbdī iii, 650a – III, 671a
Ṣuhayb (VII) iii, 587a – III, 607a
Ṣuhayb, Banū vi, 878b – VI, 869b
Suhayl vi, 645b – VI, 631a
Suhayl b. ʿAmr (ʿĀmir, VII) i, 115b, 151a – I, 119a, 155b
Suhayl b. Bayḍāʾ (VII) vi, 659a – VI, 645a
Suhayl, Saʿd b. ʿAbd Allāh (XIX) vi, 352a – VI, 336a
al-Suhaylī, Sīdī ʿAbd al-Raḥmān (Imām al-Suhaylī) (1185) vi, 591a; vii, 538a; ix, 661a; s, 382a – VI, 576a; VII, 538a; IX, 686b; S, 382b
Suḥaym (ʿAbd Banī ʾl-Ḥasḥās (657) ix, 776b – IX, 810a
Suḥaym b. Wathīl al-Riyāḥī (VII) ii, 998b; ix, 227a, 776b – II, 1021b; IX, 232b, 810a
Ṣuḥbatiyya i, 195b – I, 201b
Suhrāb (al-Ḥīra) (574) v, 633b; vii, 568b – V, 637b; VII, 569b
Suhrāb b. Āḳā Rustam Rūzafzūn (Marʿashī) (XVI) vi, 514b – VI, 499b
Suhrāb Khān, Mir (Khayrpūr) (1830) iv, 1160a – IV, 1192a
Suhraward (town/ville) ix, **777b** – IX, **811b**
Suhrawardī, Abu ʾl-Nadjīb ʿAbd al-Ḳāhir b. ʿAbd Allāh (1168) vi, 131b; vii, 608b; ix, **778a** – VI, 129b; VII, 608b; IX, **811b**
Suhrawardī, Ḥusayn Shahīd iii, 533a, b – III, 552a
al-Suhrawardī, Shams al-Dīn (1340) viii, 805b – VIII, 832b
Suhrawardī, Shaykh ʿAbd Allah (XV) s, 10b, 11a – S, 10a
Suhrawardī, Shaykh Bahāʾ al-Dīn → Bahāʾ al-Dīn Zakariyyāʾ Suhrawardī
al-Suhrawardī, Shihāb al-Dīn Abū Ḥafṣ ʿUmar (1234) i, 347a, 596a; ii, 55a, 964b, 966b; iv, 516a, 990b; vi, 111a, 224a, 225a, b, 468b, 571a; vii, 480b, 608b, 728b, 871a, 997b, 998b, 999b; viii, 506a; ix, **778b**; x, 255b; s, 313a, 353a, 380a, 414b, 415b – I, 357b, 615a; II, 56a, 986b, 988b; IV, 538a, 1023a; VI, 108b, 217b, 219a, 454a, 555b; VII, 480b, 608b, 729a, 872b, 999a, 1000a, 1001b; VIII, 523a; IX, **812b**; X, 274b; S, 312b, 353a, 380b, 415a, b
al-Suhrawardī, Shihāb al-Dīn Yaḥyā b. Ḥabash al-Maḳtūl (1191) i, 234b, 351b, 416b, 595b, 803a; ii, 774a; iii, 1131b; iv, 64a, 119b, 120b, 943a; vi, 111a; vii, 548a; ix, **782a**; s, 41a, 67a – I, 242a, 362b, 428a, 615a, 826a; II, 792b; III, 1160a; IV, 67b, 125a, b, 975b; VI, 108b; VII, 548a; IX, **816a**; S, 41b, 67b
Suhrawardiyya i, 912a; ii, 421a; iii, 823a; iv, 48a, 1026b; vi, 225b; ix, 780b, **784b**; s, 10b, 156a, 312a, 353a – I, 939b; II, 431b; III, 847a; IV, 50b, 1058b; VI, 219b; IX, 814a, **818b**; S, 10a, 156a, 312a, 353a
al-Suhūl i, 628b – I, 649b
Sūḳ i, 898b; ii, 959a, 962a; iii, 486b; iv, 136a; v, 665b; ix, **786b** – I, 925a; II, 981a, 984a; III, 503b; IV, 141b; V, 671a; IX, **820b**
al-Sūḳ (Sahara) → Tādemekket
Sūḳ al-Ahwāz → al-Ahwāz
Sūḳ al-ʿAṭṭārīn s, 422b – S, 422b
Sūḳ al-Gharb (Bairūt) s, 162a – S, 162a
Sūḳ Ḥamza iv, 479a, b – IV, 501a, b
Sūk al-Khamīs vi, 595b – VI, 580a
Sūḳ Kutāma iv, 729b – IV, 758b
Sūḳ al-Shuyūkh (town/ville) ix, **801b** – IX, **836a**
Sūḳ al-Thalāthāʾ i, 899b, 900a; s, 381a – I, 926b, 927a; S, 381a
Sukadana s, 150b, 201a – S, 150b, 201a
al-Suḳāʿī vi, 143b – VI, 141b
Sukarno ii, 663a, 664a, 665a, 666a; iii, 534a; vi, 731a, 732a, b, 733a – II, 679b, 680b, 682a, 683a; III, 552b; VI, 720a, 721a, b, 722a
Sukayn → Sofya
Sukayna bint al-Ḥusayn b. ʿAlī (VII) i, 305a; ii, 1011b; vii, 650b; ix, **802a** – I, 314b; II, 1035a; VII, 650a; IX, **836b**
Sukhf ii, 552a; iii, 354b, 780b; ix, **804a** – II, 565b; III, 365b, 804a; IX, **833b**
Sūkhrā (Kārinid(e)) iv, 644a; vi, 745b – IV, 670b; VI, 735a
Sūkhrāniyyān → Ḳārinid(e)s
Sukhum (Iskhum) i, 100b, 101a, b – I, 103b, 104a
Sukiman, Dr. vi, 731b, 732a, b – VI, 720b, 721a, b
Sukkar i, 305b; ii, 904a, 1062b, 1064b; iv, 682b; ix, **804b** – I, 315a; II, 925a, 1087a, 1089a; IV, 710b; IX, **839a**
al-Sukkarī, Abū Saʿid al-Ḥasan b. al-Ḥusayn (888) i, 107a, 154b, 158b, 331a, 718b; ii, 245b; iii, 820a; v, 768a; vii, 402b; ix, **805a**; s, 37b, 394b – I, 110a, 158b, 162b, 341b, 740a; II, 252b; III, 843b; V, 774a; VII, 403b; IX, **840a**; S, 37b, 395a
al-Sukkarī, Aḥmad (XX) s, 371a – S, 371a
Suḳmān b. Artuḳ al-Ḳuṭbī (amīr) (Akhlāṭ) (1104) i, 300a, 329a, 639a, 664a, 666a, 983a, 1052a; iii, 507a, 1118a; v, 454a; vi, 499b, 500a, 540b, 546b, 930b; vii, 726a; ix, 68b –

I, 309b, 339b, 659b, 684a, 686b, 1013b, 1084a; III, 524a, 1145b; V, 456b; VI, 485a, b, 525a, 531b, 922b; VII, 726a; IX, 71b
Suḳmān II (S͟hāh-i Arman) (1185) iii, 1119a; ix, 193a – III, 1147a; IX, 199a
Suḳmān al-Ḳuṭbī (S͟hāh-i Arman) (1112) ix, 193a; x, 42b – IX, 198b; X, 44a
Sukmāniyya iv, 483b – IV, 504b
Suknā ix, 805b – IX, 840b
Suḳnāk Tigin i, 418b – I, 430b
Suḳrāṭ i, 235b; ix, **805a**; s, 154b – I, 243a; IX, **840b**; S, 155a
al-Suktānī → ʿĪsā al-Suktānī
Sukūn → al-Ḥaraka wa 'l-sukūn
Sukūt ix, **806b** – IX, **841a**
Sükūtī, Isḥāḳ → Isḥāḳ Sükūtī
Suḳuṭrā i, 535b; iii, 270a, 652a; v, 184a; vi, 82a, b; ix, **806b** – I, 551b; III, 277b, 673a; V, 181b; VI, 80a, b; IX, **841a**
al-Ṣulaba i, 546a, 873a, b – I, 563b, 897a, 898a
Sulaḥfā ix, **811a** – IX, **845b**
Sulāma, Banū vii, 266a, 672a – VII, 268a, 672a
al-Sulamī → Abu 'l-Aʿwar; Yazīd b. Usayd
al-Sulamī, ʿAbd Allāh b. K͟hāzim (VII) vii, 357a – VII, 359b
al-Sulamī, ʿAbd al-Raḥmān Muḥammad b. al-Ḥusayn (1021) vi, 223b, 821a; viii, 579b, 583b; ix, **811b**; x, 86b – VI, 217a, 811b; VIII, 598b, 602b; IX, **846a**; X, 93b
Sulamī, Abū 'l-Faḍl Muḥammad (X) viii, 110a – VIII, 112a
al-Sulāmī, Abū ʿAbd al-Raḥmān i, 146a, 266b; s, 343a – I, 150b, 274b; S, 343a
al-Sulamī, al-As͟hras b. ʿAbd Allāh (VIII) ii, 600b; iii, 493b; x, 894b – II, 615b; III, 510b; X,
al-Sulamī, ʿĀsim b. Ḳays (640) vi, 920b – VI, 912a
al-Sulamī, ʿIzz al-Dīn ʿAbd al-ʿAzīz b. ʿAbd al-Salām (1262) vi, 351a; ix, **812b** – VI, 335a; IX, **847a**
al-Sulāmī, D̲jamāl al-Islām iii, 714a – III, 736a
al-Sulamī, Ḳays b. al-Hayt͟ham (VII) viii, 62b – VIII, 64a
al-Sulamī, Muʿammar b. ʿAbbād vi, 347a – VI, 331a
al-Sulamī, Yazīd b. Usayd (VIII) ix, 488a – IX, 507a
Sulawesi ii, 19a; iii, 1213a, 1214b, 1219b, 1220, 1226a; vii, 71b; ix, **813b**; s, 151a – II, 19a; III, 1243b, 1244a, 1245a, 1250b, 1251a, 1257a; VII, 72b; IX, **848b;** S, 151a
Sulawesi Selatan vi, 116a – VI, 113b
Ṣulayb, Banū iii, 642a; ix, **814b** – III, 663a; IX, **840b**
al-Ṣulayḥī, ʿAlī b. Muḥammad (Ṣulayḥid(e)) (1066) iv, 199b, 664a; vi, 148b; vii, 730b; ix, 816a; s, 22a, 62a – IV, 208a, 691a; VI, 147a; VII, 731b; IX, 851a; S, 22b, 62b
Ṣulayḥid(e)s i, 552a; ii, 170b, 856a; iii, 125a, 259b; iv, 199b; vii, 163a, 731a; viii, 706a; ix, **815b**; s, 62a, 236a, 338a, 407a – I, 569b; II, 175b, 876a; III, 128a, 266b; IV, 208a; VII, 164b, 731b; VIII, 726a; IX, **850b**; S, 62b, 236a, 337b, 407b
Sulayk b. al-Sulaka iv, 1106b; vi, 477a, b; ix. 864a – IV, 1138a; VI, 463a, b; IX, 900a
Sulaym, Banū i, 12a, 108a, 374b, 532b, 533a, 544b, 1049a, 1232b, 1240b; ii, 234a, 235a, 741a; iii, 66b; iv, 1144a; v, 760a; vi, 145b, 712b; vii, 372b; viii, 863b; ix, **817a**; s, 199a – I, 12a, 111a, 385b, 548b, 549a, 562a, 1081a, 1269a, 1278b; II, 240b, 242a, 759b; III, 69a; IV, 1175b; V, 766a; VI, 144a, 701a; VII, 374a; VIII, 894b; IX, **862a**; S, 199a
Sulaym b. Ayyūb al-Rāzī (1055) x, 461b – X, 494b
Sulaym b. Ḳays al-Ḥilālī (714) ix, **818b** – IX, **854a**
Sulaymā bint ʿAṣar al-ʿUḳaylī s, 394a – S, 394b
Sulaymān Mountains/Montagnes ii, 205b; ix, **819b**; s, 329b, 331b – IX, **854b**; S, 329a, 331b
Sulaymān (Ottoman) (1421) vi, 531a – VI, 515b
Sulaymān the Magnificent/le Magnifique (1566) → Süleymān
Sulaymān S͟hāh I (Ṣafī II) (Ṣafawid(e)) (1694) iv, 1092b; v, 1087a; vi, 256a, 257a, b, 855b; viii, 771a; ix, **820b** – IV, 1123b; V, 1084b; VI, 510b, 511a, b, 847a; VIII, 796b; IX, **863b**
Sulaymān S͟hāh II (Ṣafawid(e)) (1750) iv, 390a; s, 276a – IV, 406b; S, 275b
Sulaymān, Awlād i, 1258b – I, 1296b
Sulaymān, Banū v, 927a – V, 932b
Sulaymān, King/le roi i, 686a; iii, 236b, 541b; iv, 221a; v, 423b – I, 707a; III, 243b, 560b; IV, 230b, 231a; V, 425b
Sulaymān, Mawlāy, Abu 'l-Rabīʿ b. Muḥammad (ʿAlawid(e)) (1822) i, 315a, 356b; ii, 117a, 160b, 308a, 510b, 820a, 885b; iv, 634a; v, 1192a; vi, 113a, 250b, 293a, b, 595b, 596b, 597a; vii, 39a; ix, **819b**; s, 113b, 114a, 132a, 390b, 401b – I, 325a, 367b; II, 119b, 165b, 317a, 523a, 839b, 905b; IV, 660a; V, 1182b; VI, 110b, 234b, 278a, b, 580a, 581b; VII, 39b; IX, **855a**; S, 113a, b, 131b, 391a, 402a
Sulaymān, S͟hayk͟h (Kaʿb) → Salmān, S͟hayk͟h
Sulaymān (traveller/voyageur) ii, 583b, 1123b – II, 598a, 1150a
Sulaymān b. ʿAbd Allāh b. Ṭāhir (Ṭāhirid(e) (IX) vii, 390b; x, 105a – VII, 391b; X, 113a
Sulaymān b. ʿAbd al-Malik (Umayyad(e)) (717) i, 50a, 58a, b, 77b, 124b, 305a, 1030a; ii, 72b, 327b, 911a; iii, 42a, 85b, 155a; v, 533a, 799b, 1231a; vi, 544a, 666b, 668a, 669b; vii, 148a, 359a; ix, **821a**; s, 311b – I, 51b, 60a, b, 80a, 128a, 314b, 1061b; II, 73b, 337b, 932b; III, 43b, 88a, 158b; V, 537a, 805b, 1221b; VI, 528b, 652b, 654b, 655b; VII, 150a, 361a; IX, **855b**; S, 311b
Sulaymān b. ʿAbd al-Raḥmān I al-Dāk͟hil (Umayyad(e)), al-Andalus) (VIII) ii, 1009a; iii, 74a, 495a; iv, 254b, 672b – II, 1032b; III, 76b, 512a; IV, 265b, 700a
Sulaymān b. ʿAbd al-Raḥmān al-Ṣanīʿ (1969) vi, 175b – VI, 162a
Sulaymān b. ʿAbd al-Wahhāb iii, 678b – III, 700b
Sulaymān b. ʿAddū (Murābiṭ) (1060) vii, 585a – VII, 585b
Sulaymān b. Aḥmad vi, 637b – VI, 622b
Sulaymān b. Aḥmad (Brunei) s, 152a – S, 152a
Sulaymān b. ʿAlī b. ʿAbd Allāh (ʿAbbāsid(e)) (789) i, 43a, 105a, 1080b; iii, 883a; iv, 495a; vii, 414b; ix, **822b**; s, 352a – I, 44b, 108a, 1112b; III, 907b; IV, 516a; VII, 416a; IX, **856b**; S, 352a
Sulaymān b. ʿAlī al-ʿAbbāsī (al-ʿAbsī) → Sulaymān b. ʿAlī b. ʿAbd Allāh
Sulaymān b. ʿAlī al-Hās͟himī (786) vi, 262b, 428a; vii, 114a – VI, 247a, 413b; VII, 116a
Sulaymān b. al-As͟hʿat͟h → Abū Dā'ūd al-Sid̲jistānī
Sulaymān b. Bāyazīd I (Ottoman) (1411) vi, 973b – VI, 966a
Sulaymān b. Čag͟hrî Beg Dā'ūd i, 420a; ii, 5a; iii, 1201a; iv, 27a – I, 432a; II, 5a; III, 1231b; IV, 29a

Sulaymān b. Dā'ūd b. al-ʿĀḍid iv, 200b – IV, 209b
Sulaymān b. Dāwūd (King Solomon/ le roi Salomon) iii, 836a; iv, 1104b; ix, **832b** – III, 860a; IV, 1135b; IX, **857a**
Sulaymān b. Djaʿfar b. Fallāḥ i, 1042a; ii, 483b; iii, 77a – I, 1073b; II, 495b; III, 79b
Sulaymān b. Djāmiʿ (Zandjī) (IX) vii, 526a, b – VII, 526b
Sulaymān b. Djarīr al-Raḳḳī (Zaydī) (VIII) i, 851a; vii, 787b; viii, 387a; ix, **824a**; s, 225b, 392a – I, 875a; VII, 789b; VIII, 400a; IX, **858b**; S, 225b, 392b
Sulaymān b. Ghālib (IX) ix, 55a – IX, 56b
Sulaymān b. Ghāzī iii, 507b – III, 524b
Sulaymān b. Ḥabīb b. al-Muhallab (VIII) vii, 359b – VII, 362a
Sulaymān b. al-Ḥakam → Sulaymān al-Mustaʿīn
Sulaymān b. Ḥasan al-Hindī (1597) iv, 201a; vi, 190b, 191a; ix, **824b**, 829a – IV, 210a; VI, 174b, 175a; IX, **859a**, 864a
Sulaymān b. al-Ḥasan b. Makhlad → Ibn Makhlad, Sulaymān b. al-Ḥasan
Sulaymān b. Ḥassān → Ibn Djuldjul
Sulaymān b. Hishām b. ʿAbd al-Malik (Umayyad(e)) (VIII) i, 787b, 1103a; ii, 90b; iii, 398a, 990b; vi, 623b, 624a; s, 183a – I, 811a, 1136a; II, 92a; III, 410a, 1015a; VI, 609a, b; S, 184b
Sulaymān b. Hūd al-Mustaʿīn ii, 243a; iii, 496a, 542a; iv, 478a – II, 250a; III, 513a, 561a; IV, 499a
Sulaymān b. Kathīr al-Khuzāʿī (750) i, 15b, 16a, 103b, 141a, 1293a; iii, 988a; v, 3a; vi, 620b; vii, 396a; ix, **825a** – I, 16a, 106b, 145a, 1332b; III, 1012b; V, 3a; VI, 605b; VII, 397b; IX, **859b**
Sulaymān b. Ḳatta vi, 604a – VI, 589a
Sulaymān b. Ḳîlîdj Arslan II → Rukn al-Dīn Sulaymān II
Sulaymān b. Ḳutulmîsh b. Arslan Isrāʿīl (Saldjūḳ) (1086) i, 182b, 346a, 465b, 517a, 909b, 1336b; ii, 354b; iii, 86b, 195b, 208b; iv, 291b; v, 103b; vi, 274b; vii, 693b; viii, 947a; ix, **825b** – I, 187b, 356b, 479b, 532b, 937b, 1376b; II, 364b; III, 89a, 200b, 214a; IV, 304b; V, 105b; VI, 259a; VII, 693b; VIII, 979b; IX, **860a**
Sulaymān b. Mihrān → al-Aʿmash
Sulaymān b. al-Mundhir ii, 112a – II, 114b
Sulaymān b. Mūsā II (Mūsāwīd(e)) (737) iii, 262b; vi, 148b, 917a – III, 270a; VI, 147a, 908b
Sulaymān b. Orkhān (XIV) vi, 887b – VI, 879a
Sulaymān b. Ruhaym iv, 305b, 605a – IV, 319a, b, 629a
Sulaymān b. Shihāb s, 81b – S, 81b
Sulaymān b. Ṣurad al-Khuzāʿī (685) ii, 196b, 523b; iii, 608a, 620b; iv, 637b; vii, 521b; ix, 431b, **826a**; x, 398a – II, 202b, 536b; III, 629a, 641a; IV, 663b; VII, 522a; IX, 435b, **860b**; X, 426b
Sulaymān b. Ṭarf i, 709a, 737b; ii, 517a – I, 729b, 759b; II, 529b
Sulaymān b. Ṭawḳ (XI) vii, 116b – VII, 118b
Sulaymān b. ʿUfayṣān iv, 1072b – IV, 1104b
Sulaymān b. Wahb al-Kātib (vizier) (905) vii, 477a, 766a; viii, 427a; s, 402a – VII, 476b, 767b; VIII, 441b; S, 402b
Sulaymān b. al-Walīd (Umayyad(e)) (717) vi, 740a; vii, 643b; s, 183a – VI, 729a; VII, 643a; S, 184b
Sulaymān b. Yaḥyā (VIII) ix, **827a** – IX, **861b**
Sulaymān b. Yaʿḳūb b. Aflaḥ iii, 660a – III, 681a
Sulaymān b. Yasar → Fuḳahā al-Madīna
Sulaymān b. al-Zubayr Raḥma i, 929b, 1157a; ii, 123b – I, 957b, 1191a; II, 126b
Sulaymān Abū Ghaliyya (XX) vi, 171b – VI, 161a
Sulaymān ʿAskerī ii, 699b – II, 717a
Sulaymān Azhar (XX) vi, 165b – VI, 157b
Sulaymān al-Balansī → Sulaymān b. ʿAbd al-Raḥmān I
Sulaymān Beg b. Nāṣir al-Dīn Muḥammad (Dhu 'l-Ḳadr) (1454) vi, 509b – VI, 495a
Sulaymān Beg Bābān (XVII) i, 845a – I, 868a
Sulaymān Beg Bālṭa-oghlū → Bālṭa-oghlū
Sulaymān Beg b. Khalīl Beg Ḳarāmān-oghlu (1361) iv, 622b – IV, 647a, b
Sulaymān Bek b. Muhammad Bek iv, 506b – IV, 528b
Sulaymān Bey Ashraf-oghlu i, 703a; iv, 620b, 621a – I, 724a; IV, 645b
Sulaymān Bey Čapen-oghlu ii, 207b – II, 214a
Sulaymān Bey Isfendiyār-oghlu iv, 108b – IV, 113b
Sulaymān Čelebi (Ḳadiʿasker) (XV) i, 312b; ii, 98a; iii, 132a – I, 322b; II, 100b; III, 134b
Sulaymān Čelebi b. Bāyazīd (Ottoman) (1411) i, 394a, 654a; ii, 98a, 159a, 599a, 611b, 684a, 984b; iii, 1183a; vii, 644a, b – I, 405b, 674b; II, 100b, 164a, 614a, 626b, 701a, 1007a; III, 1212b; VII, 644a
Sulaymān Djāndārid(e) i, 1117b, 1118a – I, 1151b
Sulaymān al-Ḥarīrī al-Tūnisī s, 40a – S, 40b
Sulaymān Kāhya v, 532a – V, 536a
Sulaymān Kararanī i, 316a; ii, 183a – I, 326a; II, 189a
Sulaymān al-Ḳardāhī (XX) vi, 750a – VI, 739b
Sulaymān Khān (XVI) vi, 541b – VI, 526a
Sulaymān Khān (wālī) (XIX) vii, 440a; ix, 6b – VII, 441a; IX, 7a
Sulaymān Khān al-Thānī → Bihrūz Khān
Sulaymān al-Mahrī (1553) ii, 586a; iii, 856b; iv, 97a, 1082b, 1083a; v, 941a, b; vi, 82b, 359a; vii, 51a; viii, 100a, 102b; ix, **827b** – II, 600b; III, 880b; IV, 101a, 1114a; V, 945a, b; VI, 80b, 343a; VII, 51b; VIII, 102b, 104b; IX, **862a**
Sulaymān Mīrzā b. Khān Mirzā (Badakhshān Mīrzās) (1589) i, 228b, 852b, 1123b; iii, 528a, b; vii, 135a – I, 235a, 876b, 1157b; III, 546b, 547a; VII, 136b
Sulaymān Mountains/Montagnes ii, 205b; ix, **819b**; s, 329b, 331b – II, 212a; IX, **854b**; S, 329a, 331b
Sulaymān al-Mustaʿīn (Umayyad(e), Andalus,1016) ii, 243a, 516a, 1012a; iii, 147a, 495b, 1043b; v, 1239b; x, 853a – II, 250a, 528b, 1035b; III, 150a, 512b, 1069b; V, 1230b; X,
Sulaymān al-Naḥwī al-Ḥalabī ii, 795a – II, 814a
Sulaymān Pasha → Kücük Suleyman Pasha
Sulaymān Pasha (1819) i, 1078b; ii, 635b – I, 1110b; II, 652a
Sulaymān Pasha (1932) iv, 791a – IV, 822b
Sulaymān Pasha b. Orkhan (Ottoman) (1359) i, 510b; ii, 683b, 983b; vi, 290b, 291a; vii, 592b – I, 526a; II, 700b, 1006a; VI, 276a; VII, 592b
Sulaymān Pāsha Babān (1754) i, 845a – I, 868b
Sulaymān Pasha Büyük (1802) i, 62b, 905b, 1087a; ii, 184b; iii, 1257b – I, 64b, 932b, 1119b; II, 190a; III, 1290a
Sulaymān Pasha al-Faransāwī (Colonel Joseph Sève) (1860) ii, 514a; iii, 999b, 1000a; iv, 428a; v, 907b, 908a; vii, 425b; ix, **828b** – II, 526b; III, 1024b, 1025a; IV, 447a; V, 913b, 914a; VII, 427a; IX, **863a**
Sulaymān Pasha Isfendiyār-oghlu (XIV) iv, 738a – IV, 768a
Sulaymān Pasha Khādim → Khādim Süleymān Pasha
Sulaymān Pasha Mis(z)rāḳlî, Abu Laylā (1749) i, 199a, 905a, 1087a; iii, 1110b – I, 204b, 932b, 1119b; III, 1137b

Sulaymān Shafīḳ Kamālī Pasha (XX) i, 98b, 709b – I, 101a, 731a
Sulaymān Shāh b. Muḥammad b. Malik-Shāh (Saldjuḳ) (1161) vi, 64a, 871a; vii, 406b, 543b; viii, 943b, 944b, 975a – VI, 61b, 861b; VII, 407b, 543b; VIII, 976a, 977a, 1011b
Sulaymān Shukōh b. Dara i, 768b; ii, 134b – I, 791b; II, 138a
Sulaymān Shukōh b. Shāh ʿĀlam (XVIII) ii, 602a; iii, 1095a; vii, 669b – II, 617a; III, 1122a; VII, 669a
Sulaymān Solong ii, 122b – II, 125b
Sulaymān al-Tādjir s, 56a – S, 56b
Sulaymānān iv, 674b – IV, 702b
al-Sulaymānī iii, 799a – III, 822b
Sulaymānī, Payraw (1933) x, 65b – X, 67b
Sulaymānī Kurds v, 459b – V, 462a
Sulaymānīs (Mecca/Yemen) i, 403a, 709a; ii, 517a; v, 1244b; vi, 148b; ix, 507a, **829a** – I, 414b, 729b; II, 530a; V, 210a, 1235a; VI, 147a; IX, 526b, **864a**
Sulaymānis (Hind) i, 552b, 1255a; ii, 98a; iv, 201a – I, 570a, 1293a; II, 100a; IV, 210a
Sulaymāniyya (town/district, ʿIrāḳ) v, 467b; vi, 614a; viii, 199a; ix, **829b** – V, 470a, b; VI, 599a; VIII, 202b, IX, **865a**
Sulayman-nāme ii, 921a – II, 942b
Sulaymān-shāh b. Parčam Īwāʾī i, 919a – I, 947a
Sulaymanu iv, 549a – IV, 573a
Sulduz (Süldüz), Banū (Mongol) ix, **831b** – IX, **866b**
Suldūz (Ādharbāydjān) ix, **832a** – IX, **867a**
Sülemish iv, 621a – IV, 646a
Süleymān (Sulayman the Magnificent/le Magnifique) (Ottoman) (1566) i, 152a, 293a, 398a, 406a, 432a, 468b, 553b, 557b, 842b, 956a, 1117b, 1128b, 1163b, 1250b, 1253b; ii, 612a, 715b; iii, 147b; iv, 638a, 1157a; v, 630b; vi, 3a, b, 4b, 5a, 228b, 496b, 508a, b, 510a, 609b, 893b; vii, 225a, 239a, 319a; viii, 4a, 195b; ix, **832b**; x, 109a; s, 94b, 95a, 154a, 238a, 274a, 315b – I, 156a, 302a, 409b, 417b, 444a, 482b, 571a, 575b, 866a, 985b, 1151a, 1162b, 1198b, 1288b, 1291b; II, 627a, 734a; III, 150b; IV, 664a, 1189b; V, 635a; VI, 3a, b, 4b, 5a, 222b, 482a, 493b, 494a, 495a, 594b, 885a; VII, 226b, 240b, 321a; VIII, 4b, 198b; IX, **858a**; X, 118a; S, 94a, b, 154b, 238a, 273b, 315b
—administration i, 712a, 469a, 1266a; ii, 103b, 118b, 287a, 907a; iii, 213b, 1183a; iv, 565a, b, 900a; v, 882a – I, 733b, 483a, 1304b; II, 105b, 121a, 295a, 928b; III, 220a, 1212b; IV, 587b, 933a; V, 888b
—constructions i, 768a, 1134a, 1166b, 1225b; ii, 12a, 345b; iv, 232a; v, 333b – I, 791a, 1168b, 1201b, 1262a; II, 12a, 355a; IV, 242a, b; V, 334a
—literature/littérature ii, 400a, 588b, 869a; iv, 574a – II, 410b, 603a, 889a; IV, 596b
Süleymān II (Ottoman) (1691) v, 262a; vii, 319a – V, 260a; VII, 321b
Süleymān II (Ottoman) (1691) vii, 319a; ix, **842a** – VII, 321b; IX, **877a**
Süleymān Čelebi b. Bāyazīd (Ottoman) (1411) i, 394a, 654a; ii, 98a, 159a, 599a, 611b, 684a, 984b; iii, 1183a; vii, 644a, b; ix, **843a** – I, 405b, 674b; II, 100b, 164a, 614a, 626b, 701a, 1007a; III, 1212b; VII, 644a; IX, **878a**
Süleymān Čelebi, Dede (1422) ix, **843a** – IX, **878b**
Süleymān Efendi → ʿIzzī Süleymān Efendi
Süleymān Pasha, Malaṭyalí (1687) ix. **844b** – IX, **879b**
Süleymān Pasha (Mohács) vii, 219b – VII, 221b
Süleymān Pasha b. Orkhan (1357) viii, 175b, 176a; ix, **843b** – VIII, 178a, b; IX, **879a**
Süleymān Pasha Berkīn-zade (Bargjini) (1616) x, 533a – X,
Süleymān Shāh Germiyān-oghlu (1387) i, 299b; ii, 98a, 989b; v, 359b, 539a; ix, 418b – I, 309a; II, 100b; V, 360b, 543b; 432a
Süleymaniyye (Istanbul) iv, 232a; vi, 366b – IV, 242b; VI, 350b
Süleymanlí (Zeytūn) vi, 508b, 509a – VI, 494a, b
Ṣulḥ i, 1143b; ii, 131a; iv, 14b; ix, **845a** – I, 1178a; II, 134b; IV, 15b; IX, **880b**
Ṣulḥ-i-ḳull i, 117b, 317a; ix, **846a** – I, 120b, 327b; IX, **881b**
al-Ṣūlī, Abū Bakr Muḥammad b. Yaḥyā (946) i, 10a, 144b, 154a, 590a, 867a; iii, 466b, 893a, 908b; vi, 198b, 352a, 634a; vii, 279b, 559a; ix, 8b, **846b**; s, 24b, 35b, 37b, 118a, 386a – I, 10a, 148b, 158b, 609b, 891a; III, 483a, 917a, 932b; VI, 182b, 336a, 619a; VII, 281b, 559b; IX, 8b, **882a**; S, 25a, 35b, 38a, 117a, 386a
Sūlī b. Ḳaradja ii, 239b – II, 246a
Sullam ix, **848b**; s, 396b – IX, **883b**; S, 396b
Sulṭān (title/titre) iv, 942a, b; v, 628a; ix, **849a** – IV, 975a, b; V, 632a; IX, **884b**
Sulṭān I b. Sayf (Yaʿrubid(e)) (1679) v, 507a; vi, 735a, 843a – V, 510b; VI, 724a, 834a
Sulṭān II b. Sayf (Yaʿrūbid(e)) (1719) v, 507a; vi, 735a; ix, 775b – V, 510b; VI, 724a; IX, 809b
Sulṭān b. ʿAbd al-ʿAzīz (Āl-Suʿūd) (XX) vi, 158a, b – VI, 153b
Sulṭān b. Aḥmad (Bū Saʿīd) (1804) i, 1282a; v, 183b; vi, 735b; s, 332b – I, 1321a; V, 180b; VI, 724b; S, 331b
Sulṭān b. Bidjād (Āl Ḥumayd) (XX) ii, 354a; iii, 1065b, 1066b, 1067b; vi, 152a, b – II, 363b; III, 1092a, 1093b, 1094a; VI, 151a
Sulṭān b. Ḥāmid al-Ḳaysī iv, 925a – IV, 958a
Sulṭān b. Muḥammad b. Ṣaḳr iv, 778b – IV, 810a
Sulṭān b. Ṣaḳr i, 928a; ii, 619a; iv, 778a – I, 956b; II, 634b; IV, 809a, b
Sulṭān b. Salāmah iv, 752a – IV, 782b
Sulṭān b. Sayf (Yaʿrūbid(e)) (XVII) vi, 735a; x, 816b – VI, 724a; X,
Sulṭān b. Thumāl iv, 911a – IV, 944a
Sulṭān Ādam Gakkhaŕ ii, 973a; iii, 576a – II, 995b; III, 596a
Sultan Agung ii, 390b; iii, 1221b; s, 201a, b – II, 400b; III, 1252b; S, 201a, b
Sultan Aḥmad (Djalāyirid(e)) → Aḥmad b. Uways
Sulṭān Aḥmad Khān Avar i, 755b – I, 778a
Sulṭān Aḥmad Mīrzā i, 227b, 847b – I, 234b, 870b
Sulṭān ʿAlī (calligraphe(r)) (XVI) viii, 787b – VIII, 814a
Sulṭān ʿAlī Kātib i, 1212a, b – I, 1248a, b
Sulṭān ʿAlī Oghlu → Sulṭān Galiev
Sulṭān ʿAlī Sadōzay i, 231a – I, 238a
Sulṭān al-Aṭrash ii, 290a, 637b – II, 297b, 653b
Sulṭān Bāhū (Jhang) (1691) vii, 328a; viii, 256a – VII, 329b; VIII, 258b
Sulṭān-Band (Marw) vi, 621a, b – VI, 606a, b
Sulṭān Bāyazid Dūrī iv, 1127b – IV, 1159a
Sulṭān Begādā → Maḥmūd I Begŕā (Gudjarāt)
Sulṭān al-Dawla Abū Shudjāʿ (Būyid(e)) (1024) i, 131b; ii, 391a; iv, 378b; vi, 626a; ix, **854a**; s, 119a, b – I, 135b; II, 401a; IV, 395a; VI, 611a; IX, **889b**; S, 118b, 119a
Sulṭān al-Dawla Arslān Shāh (Ghaznawid(e)) (1115) vi, 783a – VI, 773a
Sulṭān Djahān Bēgum (XX) i, 1195b, 1196a, 1197a; vii, 1049a – I, 1231a, b, 1232b; VII, 1051a
Sulṭān Galiev iii, 532a; iv, 792b – III, 550b; IV, 824b

Sulṭān G̲h̲ārī (Delhi) vii, 195a – VII, 195b
Sulṭān G̲h̲āzī S̲h̲āh Čak → G̲h̲āzī K̲h̲ān Čak
al-Sulṭān al-Ḥanafī s, 18b – S, 18b
Sulṭān Ḥasan Mīrzā Nayyir al-Dawla (XIX) s, 23b – S, 24a
Sulṭān Ḥusayn, S̲h̲āh (Ṣafawid(e)) (1726) vi, 16b, 18a, 483b, 525a, 551a, 856a; vii, 62a; viii, 771b; ix, **854a** –
VI, 14b, 16a, 469b, 510a, 535b, 847b; VII, 62a; VIII, 797a; IX, **889b**
Sulṭān Ḥusayn Bayḳara → Ḥusayn Bayḳara
Sulṭān Ḥusayn Lingāh → Ḥusayn S̲h̲āh Langāh I
Sulṭān Ḥusayn Mīrzā → Ḥusayn I (Ṣafawid(e))
Sulṭān Ibrāhīm (Fārs) (XVI) vi, 17b – VI, 15b
Sultan Ibrāhīm Nūr al-Dīn (Maldives) (XIX) vi, 246a – VI, 230a
Sulṭān Isḥāḳ → Sulṭān Ṣohāk
Sulṭān Ismāʿīl S̲h̲āh (Čak) s, 324b – S, 324a
Sulṭān-Ḳalʿa vi, 619a, b, 620a, 621a – VI, 604a, b, 605a, 606a
Sulṭān K̲h̲alīl b. Uzun Ḥasan iv, 267b – IV, 279b
Sulṭān K̲h̲ātūn i, 1117b; v, 679b – I, 1151b; V, 684b
Sulṭān Ḳulī → Ḳulī Ḳuṭb al-Mulk
Sulṭān Maḥmūd Māhīsawār i, 1168a – I, 1202b
Sulṭān Muḥammad (painter/peintre) viii, 788a – VIII, 814b
Sulṭān Muḥammad b. Awrangzīb vii, 315b – VII, 318a
Sulṭān Muḥammad b. Muḥammad b. Falāḥ (Mus̲h̲aʿs̲h̲aʿ) (XV) vii, 672b – VII, 672b
Sulṭān Muḥammad al-ʿĀdil (Maldives) (XII) vi, 245b – VI, 229b
Sulṭān Muḥammad K̲h̲ān (Bārakzay) i, 231a; ii, 637b – I, 238b; II, 654a
Sulṭān Muḥammad K̲h̲ān Kās̲h̲ḳāy iv, 706a – IV, 734b
Sulṭān Muḥammad Mīrzā b. ʿAbbās I (Ṣafawid(e)) (XVII) viii, 770b – VIII, 796b
Sulṭān Muḥammad S̲h̲āh → Maḥallatī, Ag̲h̲a K̲h̲ān
Sulṭān Naṣir al-Dīn G̲h̲āzī Čak → G̲h̲āzī K̲h̲ān Čak
Sulṭān Nit̲h̲ār Bēgum (1624) vii, 331b – VII, 333a
Sulṭān Öñü (Eskis̲h̲ehir) ix, **855a** – IX, **890b**
Sulṭān Saʿīd (S̲h̲aybānid(e)) (1572) vii, 677a – VII, 676b
Sulṭān Sand̲j̲ar (Tīmūrīd(e)) (XV) i, 147b – I, 152a
Sulṭān Ṣārang ii, 973a – II, 995b
Sulṭān Sehāk (XV) ix, **855a** – IX, **891a**
Sulṭān S̲h̲āh (G̲h̲ūrīd(e)) (XII) vi, 618a – VI, 603a
Sulṭān S̲h̲āh b. Īl Arslan (K̲h̲ʷārazmī) (XII) ii, 253a, 1101b; iv, 583a, 1067b; ix, 34b – II, 260b, 1127b; IV, 606b, 1099a; ix, 35a
Sulṭān-S̲h̲āh b. Ḳāwurd (Saldjūḳ, Kirmān) (1085) iii, 86b, 87a; v, 159b; vi, 273b – III, 89a; V, 158b; VI, 258b
Sulṭān S̲h̲āh b. Riḍwān (Saldjūḳ) (1123) viii, 947b – VIII, 980a
Sulṭān S̲h̲āh Lōdī b. Malik Bahrām (1431) v, 782b, 783a – V, 789a
Sulṭān S̲h̲āhzāda → Bārbak S̲h̲āh Ḥabshi
Sulṭān Ṣohāk i, 260b, 261b, 262a, b – I, 269a, 269b, 270a, b
Sultan Sulaymān (Tu Wen-Hsiu) (XIX) viii, 260b – VIII, 265b
Sulṭān Taḳi Sulṭān (Sōmāy) (XVII) ix, 727b – IX, 758b
Sulṭān al-Ṭalaba (festival) ix, **857b** – IX, **893b**
Sulṭān Uways b. Idgü v, 163b – V, 161b
Sulṭān Walad b. D̲j̲alāl al-Dīn Rūmī (1312) i, 147a; ii, 394a; iv, 67a; vi, 833a, 835a, 883a, 886b; viii, 972b; ix, 298a, **858a** ′ s, 49b, 83b –
I, 151b; II, 404b; IV, 71a; VI, 823a, 826a, 875a, 878a; VIII, 1006b; IX, 306b, **894a**; S, 50a, 83a

Sulṭān Ways Mīrzā i, 852b – I, 876a
Sulṭān Yaʿḳūb (Aḳ-Ḳoyunlu) → Yaʿḳūb b. Uzun Ḥasan
Sulṭāna bint Aḥmad al-Sudayrī s, 305b – S, 305b
Sulṭāna Čand Bībī (Aḥmadnagar) vi, 488b – VI, 474b
Sulṭānābād (towns/villes) ix, **859a**; s, 73a – IX, **895a**; S, 73b
Sulṭānābād-i Čamčamāl vi, 494a – VI, 479b
Sulṭāniyya (D̲j̲ibāl) i, 261a; iii, 1124b; iv, 1167b; v, 294a; vi, 494a, 495b, 528b, 540b; viii, 169a; ix, **859b**; s, 83b –
I, 269a; III, 1152b; IV, 1200b; V, 293b; VI, 479b, 480a, b, 512b, 525b; VIII, 171b; IX, **895b**; S, 83b
Sulṭāniyya (Maklī) vi, 189b – VI, 173b
Sulṭānpūr vi, 131a – VI, 129a
Sulṭānpūrī, ʿAbd Allāh (Mak̲h̲dūm al-Mulk) (1584) v, 1235b; s, **3a** – V, 1226a; S, **2a**
Sultansky, Mordecai vi, 606a – IV, 630b
Sulṭānzāde Isḥāḳ Bey iv, 112b – IV, 117b
Sulṭānzāde Muḥammad Pas̲h̲a → Muḥammad Pas̲h̲a Sulṭānzāde
Su-lu (Türges̲h̲ Kaghan) (738) x, 560a – X, 601b
Sulu archipel(ago) → Philippines
Sulūk ix, **861b** ṣ IX, **897b**
S̲h̲ulūḳ → Wādī ʾl-ʿArab
Ṣuʿlūk v, 768a; ix, **863b**; s, 37a – V, 774a; IX, **899b**; S, 37b
al-Ṣuʿlūkī, Abū Sahl Muḥammad (980) ix, **868a** ṣ IX, **904a**
al-Ṣuʿlūkī, Abu ʾl-Ṭayyib (1611) ix, **868b** – IX, **904b**
Ṣumādiḥ, Banū vi, 576b – VI, 561b
Sumak s, 136a – S, 135b
Sumāmī, Muḥammad ʿĀbid (XVIII) vi, 953a – VI, 945b
Sūmanāt (Somnāth) ii, 597a, 598a, 1123b, 1125a; vi, 63b; viii, 1047a; ix, **868b** –
II, 612a. b, 1150a, 1151a; VI, 63b; VIII, 1083a; IX, **904b**
Sumaniyya (Buddhists/Bouddhistes) i, 15b, 17b, 953a, 1031a, 1092b, 1284a, 1333b; ii, 972b; iii, 335b, 1122a; iv, 43b, 356a, 512b; v, 37b, 853a; ix, **869a** –
I, 16a, 18a, 982a, 1062b, 1125a, 1273a, 1323a; II, 994b; III, 345b, 1150a; IV, 46a, 371b, 534b; V, 38b, 859b; IX, **905a**
Sumatra iii, 1213a, b, 1214b, 1215b, 1218a, 1219a, 1225b; v, 226a, b; 227b, 228a, b; vi, 43a; vii, 73b; ix, **870b** –
III, 1243b, 1244b, 1245a, 1246a, 1249a, 1250a, 1257a; V, 223b, 224a, 225a, 226a, b; VI, 41b; VII, 74a; IX, **906a**
al—umayl b. Ḥātim Abū D̲j̲aws̲h̲ān al-Kilābī (Cordoba/Cordoue) (759) i, 135a; iii, 602a; iv, 494b; ix, **870b**; x, 848b; s, 81b, 82a –
I, 138b; III, 622b; IV, 515b, 516a; IX, **906b; X,** ;S, 81b
Sumayr iii, 41b – III, 43a
Sumaysāṭ vi, 230b, 505b; ix, **871b** – VI, 224b, 491a; IX, **907b**
al-Sumaysāṭī → al-S̲h̲ims̲h̲āṭī
Sumayṭiyya vii, 645b – VII, 645a
Sumayya umm ʿAmmār b. Yāsir (VII) ix, 295b; s, 354b – IX, 211b; S, 354b
Sumbar (river/fleuve) vi, 716b – VI, 705b
Sumbawa (Sunda/Sonde) i, 1219b, 1226a; ix, 887a – I, 1250b, 1257b; ix, 759b
Sumerā/Sumrā (Sind) viii, 1047a; ix, **872a** – VIII, 1083a; IX, **908a**
Sumhuʿalī Yanūf b. D̲h̲amarʿalī vi, 562b – VI, 547b
Sumhuʿalī Yanūf b. Yadaʿ°il D̲h̲arīḥ vi, 559b, 560a, b, 562b – VI, 544b, 545a, 547b

Summ (samm) ix, **872a** – IX, **908a**
al-Ṣummān → al-Ṣammān
Summaya bint Khubāṭ s, 354b – S, 354b
al-Sumnānī, Abū Dja'far iii, 544a, 1146b – III, 563a, 1174b
Sumnūn (Samnūn) b. Ḥamza (910) ix, **873a** – IX, **909a**
Ṣun' Allāh b. Dja'far al-'Imādī (1612) ix, **873b** – IX, **910a**
Suna II, Kabaka (1856) x, 778b – X,
Sūnām s, 66b – S, 67a
Sunan ix, **874a** – IX, **910a**
Sunan Ampel (1467) iii, 1219a – III, 1249b
Sunan Bonang iii, 1218b, 1219a – III, 1249b
Sunan Giri iii, 1218b, 1219a; v, 1155a – III, 1249b; V, 1144b
Sunaq-qurghan (Sïghnāk) s, 245a – S, 245a
Sunargaon vi, 131a – VI, 129b
Sunbādh (Khurāsān) vi, 427b, 744b; ix, **874b** – VI, 413a, 734a; IX, **910b**
al-Sunbāṭī, Aḥmad b. 'Abd al-Hakk iv, 451a – IV, 471a
Sunbūk → Milāha; Safīna
Sunbul Khānum (XVIII) vi, 484a – VI, 470a
Sünbül Sinān Efendi (1500) vi, 1023a – VI, 1015b
al-Sunbula → Minṭakat al-Burūdj
Sunbuliyya/Sünbüliyye iv, 991b, 992a; vi, 1023a; ix, **875a** – IV, 1024a, b; VI, 1015b; IX, **911a**
Sünbül-zāde Wehbī (1809) ix, **876a** – IX, **912a**
Sūndā islands iii, 1213a, 1226a; v, 785a; ix, **877a**
Sundarban ix, **872b** – IX, **913a**
Su(ou)ndjata Keita (XIII) vi, 258a; ix, 756a – VI, 242a; IX, 789a
Sungur Bey Shamsī Pasha → Shams al-Dīn b. Taman
Sunkur/Sonkor (town/ville) ix. **877b** – IX, **913a**
Sunkur b. Mawdūd Muẓaffar al-Dīn (Salghurid(e)) (1161) ii, 812a; iii, 1097b; v, 826b; viii, 978b – II, 831a; III, 1124b; V, 832b; VIII, 1013a
Sunkur Agha (Niğde) (XIV) viii, 15b – VIII, 15b
Sunkur al-Ashkar (Damas(cus)) (XIII) ii, 285a; iii, 403a, 832b; iv, 88a, 485a; v, 594b; vi, 322b; vii, 461b; viii, 851a – II, 293a; III, 415a, 856b; IV, 92a, 506a; V, 598b; VI, 307a; VII, 461b; VIII, 880b
Sunna i, 175b, 258b, 275b, 325b, 773a, 1039b, 1199a; ii, 859a, 888b; iii, 953b, 994b; iv, 142a-b, 147b, 148a; ix, **878a** – I, 180a, 266b, 284a, 335b, 796a, 1071a, 1234b; II, 879a, 909b; III, 978a, 1019b; IV, 148a-b, 153b, 154a; IX, **913b**
Sünnet Odasi̊ vi, 55b – VI, 53b
Sunnī i, 1254a; ii, 64b, 283a, 290a, 859b, 931b; iii, 87a, 411b, 1168b – I, 1292b; II, 65b, 291a, 298a, 879a, 953a; III, 89b, 424b, 1197a
Sunni 'Alī → Songhay
Sun'ullāh Efendi (XVII) vii, 600b – VII, 600a
Suphi Ezgi (1962) ix, 418a s IX, 431b
Sūr ix, **881b** – IX, **917b**
Ṣūr (Tyr(e)) i, 215b; iv, 129b; v, 789a; ix, **883a**; s, 120b – I, 222a; II, 133a; V, 796a; IX, **919a**; S, 120a
Ṣūr ('Umān) vi, 729b; vii, 53a; ix, 356b – VI, 718b; VII, 53b; IX, 368a
Sūr, Afghān i, 228b; iii, 423a; s, 1b – I, 235b; III, 436b; S, 1b
Sūr Dās iii, 457a – III, 473a
Sur (Kaṣr) al-Ḥadjar (Marrākush) vi, 596b – VI, 581a
Sūra (Kur'ān) v, 409b; ix, **885b** – V, 411a; IX, **921a**
Ṣūra (image) i, 1084a; ix, **889a** – I, 1116a; IX, **925a**
Ṣūra Ma'mūniyya i, 1003b; ii, 578b – I, 1034a; II, 593a
Surabaya s, 150b, 202b – S, 150b, 202a
Surādik iv, 1147a – IV, 1178b
Sūradj Kund ii, 255b – II, 263a
Sūradj Mal Djāt i, 1193a; ii, 488b; iii, 1158b – I, 1228a; II, 501a; III, 1187a
Suradjgaṙh vi, 47a – VI, 45b
Surākā b. 'Amr i, 921b; iv, 342b – I, 949a; IV, 357a
Surāka b. Bukayr (VII) vii, 497b – VII, 497b
Surāka b. Mirdās al-Asghar (699) ix, **892a** – IX, **928a**
Surakarta vi, 43a; ix, **892a** – VI, 41b; IX, **928a**
Sūrat (India) v, 1114a, b; vi, 53b, 233b, 534b; vii, 71b; ix, **893a** – V, 1110b; VI, 51b, 206b, 519a; VII, 72a; ix, **929a**
Ṣurat al-arḍ ix, **893b** – IX, **929b**
Sūrat Singh s, 361a – S, 360b
al-Suraydjiyya, al-Mas'ala ix, **893b** s IX. **929b**
Ṣuraym ii, 71b – II, 73a
Sūrghān Shīra ii, 67b – II, 69a
Sürgün iv, 225a, 238a, 239a; v, 305b – IV, 235a, 248b, 249b; V, 305a
Surhāb-mat vi, 515a – VI, 500a
Surḥūbiyya → al-Djārūdiyya
Sūrī → Sūrs
Sūrīd (king/le roi) vi, 411b – VI, 396b
Surkhāb i, 512b, 513a – I, 528a, b
Surkhāb b. 'Annāz i, 513b; v, 824b, 828a – I, 529a; V, 830b, 834a
Surkhāb b. Badr i, 513a; v, 454a – I, 529a; V, 456b
Surkhāb b. Bāw iv, 644b – IV, 671a
Surkhāb Beg i, 406a – I, 418a
Ṣurkhābiyya iv, 1086b – IV, 1118a
Surkhay Khān → Čulāk-Sūrkhay
Sūrkhāy-Mīrzā ii, 87a – II, 89a
Surkh-rag vi, 384a – VI, 368a
Sürmeli 'Alī Pasha → 'Alī Pasha Sürmeli
Ṣurna s, 136a – S, 135b
Ṣurra i, 483b; iv, 1133b; ix, **894a** – I, 497b; IV, 1165a; ix, **930a**
Ṣurrat al-Ḥaramayn iv, 1133b – IV, 1165a
Sūrs (Afghans, Delhi) vii, 795b; ix, **894a** – VII, 797b; IX, **930a**
Sursuk vi, 543b – VI, 528a
Surt (town/ville) vi, 946a; ix, **894b** – VI, 938a; IX, **930b**
Surūmī, bā, 'Abd Allāh b. Aḥmad al-Shiḥrī (1536) vi, 133a – VI, 131a
Surūr, Mīrzā Radjab 'Alī Beg (1867) ix, **895a** – IX, **931b**
Surūr al-Fātikī (XII) v, 1244b – V, 1235a
Surūr, Nadjīb → Nadjīb Muḥammad Surūr
Surūrī, Muḥammad (XVI) i, 380a; iv, 526a – I, 391a; IV, 549a
Surūrī, Muṣliḥ al-Dīn (1562) ix, **895b** – IX, **932a**
Surūrī, Seyyid 'Othmān (1814) ix, **896b** – IX, **932b**
Surūrī Kashānī (XVII) ix, **896b** – IX, **933a**
Surūsh, Muḥammad 'Alī Khān (1868) iv, 70a; ix, **897a** – IV, 73b; IX, **933b**
Sūrya (Syria/-e) → al-Shām
Sūryānūs ii, 770b – II, 789a
Sūs (licorice/réglisse) ix, **897b** – IX, **934a**
al-Sūs (Sūsa, Shūsh) (Khūzistān) i, 86a, 245a; ii, 527a; v, 1178b, 1187b; vi, 494b, 589a, b; 590b, 591b, 594a, b, 595a, 633b, 741a, 742b, 743b; vii, 643b; ix, **898a**; s, 29a, 40a, 47b, 133b, 336b, 402b – I, 88b, 252;b; II, 540a; V, 1168b, 1177b; VI, 480a, 573b, 574b, 575a, 576b, 579a, b, 618b, 730a, 731b,

732b; VII, 643a; IX, **934b**; S, 29b, 40b, 48a, 133a, 336a, 403a
al-Sūs al-Aḳṣā (Morocco/Maroc) ix, **899a** – IX, **935a**
Sūsa (Sousse, Tunisia/Tunésie) i, 248b, 620a, 1319a; ii, 130a; iii, 499b; iv, 654a; v, 830a; vi, 113b, 141b, 142a, b, 143a, 295a, 434b; ix, **901a** – I, 256a, 640a, 1359b; II, 133b; III, 517a; IV, 680b; V, 836b; VI, 113aa, 139b, 140b, 141a,b, 280b, 420a; IX, **937b**
Sūsan (Sawsan) ix, **902b** – IX, **940a**
Sūsandjird v, 498b – V, 502a
Sūsū, Banū i, 762b; vi, 258a – I, 785a; VI, 242a
Sūsūn iv, 1042b – IV, 1074a
Sutan Takdir Alisjahbana vi, 240b – VI, 205b
Sūtānuti ii, 7a – II, 7a
Sutaylī iv, 584a – IV, 607b
Sutledj v, 885b – V, 891b
Sütlüdje iv, 233a; s, 168b – IV, 243a; S, 168b
Sutra ix, **902b** – IX, **940a**
Sutūda, Manūčihr s, 376a – S, 376a
Suṭūḥiyya i, 280b; x, 189a – I, 289a; X, 204a
Suʿūd, Āl (dynasty/-ie) i, 98b, 554b, 942b, 1313a; ii, 176b, 320b, 573a; iii, 363b; iv, 717b, 765a, 778a, 953a, 1072b; v, 574b, 575a; ix. **903a**; s, 30a – I, 101b, 572a, 971b, 1353a; II, 182a, 330a, 587a; III, 375a; IV, 746a, 795b, 809b, 985b, 1104b; V, 579a, b; IX, **941a**; S, 30b
Suʿūd b. ʿAbd al-ʿAzīz Āl Suʿūd) (1814) ii, 321a; iv, 765a, 925b; vi, 150b, 191b; ix, 903b – II, 330b; IV, 795b, 958b; VI, 149a, 175b; IX, 941b
Suʿūd b. ʿAbd al-ʿAzīz (Āl Suʿūd) (1964) i, 555a, 958a; ii, 660b; vi, 156a, 169b; ix, 904b – I, 572b, 987b; II, 677a; VI, 152b, 160b; IX, 942b
Suʿūd b. ʿAzzān b. Ḳays s, 356a – S, 356a
Suʿūd b. Fayṣal b.ʿAbd al-ʿAzīz (Āl Suʿūd) (1860) ii, 176b; iv, 1073a; s, 305b – II, 182a; IV, 1104b; S, 305b
Suʿūd b. Fayṣal b. Turkī (Āl Suʿūd) (1874) ix, 904a – IX, 941b
Suʿūd b. Muḥammad b. Muḳrin (1724) vii, 410a – VII, 411b
Suʿūd al-Kabīr iv, 1073a – IV, 1104b
Suʿūdī, Abu ʾl-Faḍl al-Mālikī (XVI) ix, **905a** – IX, **943a**
Suʿūdī (Abu ʾl-Suʿūdī) b. Yaḥyā al-Dimashḳī (1715) ix, **905b** – IX, **943b**
Suʿūdī, Sayf al-Dīn (1335) ix, **905b** – IX, **943b**
al-Suʿūdiyya, al-Mamlaka al-ʿArabiyya (Saudi Arabia/ Arabie Séoudite) Saʿūdi Arabia i, 39a, b, 534a, 539a, 1314a; ii, 425a, 557b, 660a; iii, 363a; v, 1056b; vi, 33a, 144b; ix, **905b**; s, 417b – I, 40a, b, 55 a, b, 555b, 1354a; II, 435b, 571b, 676b; III, 374a; V, 1053b; VI, 31a, 142b; IX, **943b**; S, 417b
Suut Kemal Yetkin (XX) vi, 95b – VI, 93b
Suwāʿ iii, 540b; **908b** – III, 559a; **947a**
Suwār (Sawar) i, 1305b, 1306b; v, 686a; ix, **909a** – I, 1345b, 1346b; V, 691a; IX, **947b**
al-Suwārī → al-Ḥadjdj Sālim
Suwayd b. al-Khadhdhāk i, 74a – I, 76a
Suwayd b. Muḳarrin i, 1247a; iv, 207b, 644a; v, 378a; s, 297b – I, 1285a; IV, 217a, 670b; V, 378b; S, 297b
Suwayd al-Haranī s, 366b – S, 366b
Suwaydān iv, 751b – IV, 781b
Suwaydī, Banū v, 459a – V, 461b
al-Suwaydī, ʿAbd Allāh b. al-Ḥusayn al-Baghdādī (1760) vi, 112b – VI, 110a
al-Suwaydī, ʿAbd al-Raḥmān b. ʿAbd Allāh (1786) vi, 113a – VI, 110b
al-Suwaydī (Ibn al-), ʿIzz al-Dīn (1292) ix, **909b** – IX, **947b**
Suwaydiyya vi, 579a; ix, **916a** – VI, 564a; IX, **948a**
Suwayf, Banū s, 371a – S, 371a
Suwayḳat Ibn Mathkūd vii, 186b – VII, 186b
al-Suwayra (Morocco/Maroc) vi, 589a; vii, 391b; ix, **920a** – VI, 573b; VII, 393a; IX, **940b**
al-Suways (Suez) i, 13a, 315a, 554b; iv, 206b; v, 368b; vi, 195a; ix, **912a**; s, 6b – I, 13a, 324b, 572b; IV, 215b; V, 369b; VI, 179a; IX, **950a**; S, 5b
Sūyāb ii, 67a; ix, **913a**; x, 560a, 689a – II, 68a; IX, **951b**; X, , 781b
Sūyūmbigi, Princess(e) iv, 850a – IV, 883a
Suyūrghāls ii, 150b, 152a; iv, 1043b – II, 155a, 156b; IV, 1075a
Suyūrghatmish b. Ḳuṭb al-Dīn, Djalāl al-Dīn Abū Muẓaffar (1294) v, 162a, b, 553b, 554a; vi, 482a – V, 160a, b, 558b, 559a; VI, 468a
Suyūrghatmīsh b. Noradin (XV) vi, 202a – VI, 186a
Suyurghatmīsh b. Terken Khātūn (Kirmān) (XIII) vi, 482b – VI, 468b
Suyūrsāt ii, 152a; iv, 1043a – II, 157a; IV, 1074b
Suyūṭ → Asyūṭ
al-Suyūṭī, Djalāl al-Dīn (1505) i, 27a, 72a, 429a, 594b, 595a, 721a, 729a, 759a, 1110a, 1198a, 1309a; ii, 826b; iii, 90a, 435a, 697a, 711a, 957b; iv, 550a, 863b; v, 419b, 1223a, 1235a; vi, 112a, 181a, 194b, 262b, 263a, b, 264b, 351b, 352b, 353a, 354a, 454a, 907a; vii, 175a, 254b, 261b, 262a, 290b, 296b, 394a; ix, 757b, **913a**; s, 352b, 388a – I, 28a, 74a, 441a, 614a, b, 742b, 751a, 782a, 1143a, 1233b, 1349a; II, 846b; III, 92b, 449a, 719a, 733a, 982a; IV, 574a, 897a; V, 421b, 1213b, 1225b; VI, 109b, 165a, 178b, 247a, 247b, 248a, b, 249a, 335b, 336b, 337a, 338b, 439b, 898a; VII, 177a, 256a, 263b, 264a, 292a, 298b, 395a; IX, 790b, **951b**; S, 352b, 388b
Sūz, Sayyid Muḥammad Mīr (1798) ix, **916a** – IX, **954b**
Sūzanī (Sozanī). Muḥamma ʿAlī al-Ṣamarḳandī (1166) iii, 355b; iv, 62a; viii, 749a, 971a; ix, **916b**; s, 65a – III, 366b; IV, 65a; VIII, 779b, 1005a; IX, **954b**; S, 65a
Sūzī Čelebi (1524) vii, 34b; viii, 338a; ix, **916b** – VII, 34b; VIII, 350a; IX, **955a**
Sūzmanī, Banū → Lūlī
Svatopluk → Čeh
Svištov → Zishtowa
Swahili ii, 59a, 129a; iv, 886b, 888b; v, 177a, 205b, 223a, 655b, 962b; vi, 612b, 827b; ix, **917a** – II, 60a, 132a; IV, 919a, 921a; V, 174a, 203a, 221a, 659b, 967b; VI, 597a, 818a; IX, **955b**
Swāt (Pakistan)) i, 864a; v, 356a; vi, 127a; ix, **918b** – I, 888b; V, 357b; VI, 125a; IX, **956b**
Swimon I b. Luarsab (al-Kurdjī) (1600) v, 493a – V, 495b, 496a
Sy, el-Hadji Abdoul Aziz s, 182a – S, 182a
Sy, el-Hadji Malick s, 182a – S, 182a
Sylla → Fodié; Yaʿḳūba
Sylhet → Silhet
Syntipas → Sinbād al-Ḥakīm
Syr Darya → Sīr Daryā
Syros (Syra) → Shire
Syria/-e → Shām
Syrianus → Sūryānūs
Szechuan (Ssū-ch'uan, Si-chuan) ix, **919a** – IX, **957b**
Szécsény s, 171a – S, 171a
Szeged ix, **920a** – IX, **958b**
Székesfehérvár ix, **920b** – IX, **958b**
Szigetrar ii, 881b – II, 902a

T

Tāʾ x, **1a** – X, **1a**
Ṭā" x, **1a** – X, **1a**
Ṭā-hā x, **1b** – X, **1b**
Ṭāʿa x, **1b** – X, **1b**
Taʾabbaṭa Sharr^{an} i, 130b; ii, 1079a; iii, 540b; vii, 308a, 309b; x, **2b** – I, 134b; I, 1104a; III, 559a; VII, 310a, 311b; X, **2b**
Taʿaddī x, **3b** – X, **3b**
Taʿadjdjub x, **4a** – X, **4a**
Taʿāʾīsha i, 49b; ii, 122a, 124a; v, 1250a, b; x, **4b** – I, 50b; II, 125a, 127a; V, 1241a, b; X, **4b**
Ṭaʿām x, **4b** – X, **4b**
Taʿarrub x, **5a** – X, **5a**
Taʿāsīf → ʿAlam al-Dīn Ḳayṣar
Taʿaṣṣub → ʿAsabiyya
Taʿāwīdh → Ibn al-Taʿāwīdhī
Taʿāwun x, **5b** – X, **5b**
Taʿāwwudh x, **7a** – X, **7a**
Ṭābaʿ iv, 1105b – IV, 1137a
Tabac → Tūtūn
Ṭabaḳa x, **7a** – X, **7a**
al-Ṭabaḳa al-Khāmisa i, 1060a – I, 1092a
Ṭabakāt i, 106a, b, 274b; ii, 922a; x, **7b** – I, 109a, b, 282b; II, 943b; X, **7b**
Tabāla x, **10b** – X, **10b**
Tabārakallāh i, 1032a; v, 425b – I, 1063b; V, 427b
Ṭābarān → Ṭūs
al-Ṭabarānī, Abu ʾl-Ḳāsim (971) i, 273b; iii, 159a, 864a; x, **10b**; s, 400b – I, 282a; III, 162b, 888a; X, **10b**; S, 401a
al-Ṭabarānī, Abū Kathīr Yaḥyā al-Kātib (932) viii, 661b – VIII, 680b
al-Ṭabarānī, Surūr al-Ḳāsim (1034) viii, 146b – VIII, 149a
Ṭabarī (language/langue) i, 872a – I, 896a
al-Ṭabarī, Abū Djaʿfar Muḥammad b. Djarīr (923) i, 51a, 140a, 459a, 567b, 591a, 628a, 760a, 984b; ii, 133a, 215a, 793a, 1111b; iii, 57b, 608a, 1062a, 1206b; v, 1130b; vi, 199a, 262b, 265a, 403b, 605a, 905a; ix, 547a; x, **11a** – I, 52b, 144a, 472b, 585b, 610b, 649a, 782b, 1015a; II, 136b, 222a, 812a, 1138a; III, 60a, 628b, 1088b, 1237a; V, 1126b; VI, 183b, 247a, 249b, 388a, 589b, 896b; IX, 568b; X, **11a**
al-Ṭabarī, Abu ʾl-Ṭayyib (al-ḳāḍī, al-imām) (1058) i, 459a, 773a, 1039b; ii, 412a; iii, 302a; x. **15b**; s, 192a – I, 472b, 796a, 1071a; II, 422b; III, 311a; X, **16a**; S, 193a
al-Ṭabarī, Aḥmad b. ʿAbd Allāh (1295) iv, 797a; x, **16a** – IV, 829a; X, **16b**
al-Ṭabarī, ʿAlī b. Rabban (IX) i, 213b, 265b; iii, 378a; v, 701b; viii, 148b; x, 12a, **17a**, 453a; s, 314a – I, 220a, 273b; III, 389b; V, 706b; VIII, 151a; X, 12a, **17b**, 486a; S, 313b
al-Ṭabarī, Muḥibb al-Dīn (1251) vi, 106b, 350a, b, 351b – VI, 104b, 334a, b, 335b
al-Ṭabarī, ʿUmar b. Farrukhān (VIII) vi, 710b; viii, 107a, 108a – VI, 699b; VIII, 109a, 110a
Ṭabarīs s, 335a – S, 335a
Ṭabaristān i, 40a, 52b, 688a, 760a, 871b, 1110a, 1350a; iii, 233b, 245a, 810a; iv, 644a, b; v, 68b, 69b, 661a; vi, 66a, 115b, 120a, 148a, 335a, 337a, b, 511a, 517a, 527a, 539a, 744b, 780a, 935b; x, **18b**; s, 13a, 235a, 297b, 298a, 299a, 356b, 357a, 363a, b – I, 41b, 54a, 709a, 782b, 896a, 1143a, 1390b; III, 240a, 252a, 833b; IV, 670b, 671a; V, 70b, 71b, 666b; VI, 64a, 113a, 117b, 146b, 319b, 321a, b, 496b, 502a, 511a, b, 523b, 733b, 770a, 927b; X, **19a**; S, 13b, 235a, 297a, b, 298b, 356a, 357a, 362b, 363a
Ṭabariyya (Tiberias) vi, 652b; x, **18b** – VI, 638a; X, **19a**
Tabarḳa (Tabarca) v, 50b, 51b; x, **19b** – V, 52a, 53a; X, **20a**
Tabarruʾ x, **20b** – X, **21b**
Ṭabarsarān ii, 85b, 87b, 89a; iv, 343a, 345b; x, **22b** – II, 87a, 89a, 90b; IV, 357b, 360a; X, **23a**
Ṭabarsī → Ḥusayn Nūrī
al-Ṭabarsī → al-Ṭabrīsī
al-Ṭabarsī, Shaykh Abū ʿAlī al-Faḍl (1154) i, 326a; vii, 422b, 441a – I, 336a; VII, 424a, 442a
Ṭabas i, 1052b; v, 354b; 868b; x, **22b** – I, 1084a; V, 356a, 875a; X, **23a**
Ṭabāshīr x, **23a** – X, **23b**
Ṭabāṭabāʾī, ʿAlīm Allāh (1743) ii, 1092a – II, 1117b
Ṭabāṭabāʾī, Āyatullāh Muḥsin Ḥakīm (1970) s, 104a – S, 103b
Ṭabāṭabāʾī, Ḥudjdjat al-Islām Sayyid Muḥammad Ḳāzim Yazdī (1919) vi, 552b – VI, 537a
Ṭabāṭabāʾī, Sayyid Ḍiyāʾ al-Dīn (1969) i, 978a; iii, 529a; v, 310b; viii, 511b; x, **23b** – I, 1008b; II, 547b; V, 310a; VIII, 529a; X, **24a**
Ṭabāṭabāʾī, Sayyid Muḥammad Ḥusayn b. Muḥammad (Āyatullāh) (1947) iv, 166a, b; vi, 553a; vii, 762b – IV, 173a, b; VI, 537b; VII, 764a
Ṭabāṭabāʾī, Sayyid Muḥammad Mahdī (baḥr al-ʿulūm) (1797) vi, 552a – VI, 536b
Ṭabāṭabāʾī, Sayyid Ṣādiḳ Abū Sayyid Muḥammad Ṭabāṭabāʾī (XX) iv, 164a – IV, 171a
Tabattul → Zuhd
Ṭabbākh x, **23b** – X, **24b**
Ṭabbāl x, **24a** – X, **25a**
Tābiʾ → Posta
Ṭabʿī (1670) vi, 837b – VI, 828a
Ṭabīʿa x, **25a** – X, **25b**
Ṭabīb → Ṭibb
al-Ṭabīb, ʿImād al-Dīn Maḥmūd b. Masʿūd (XVI) viii, 542b – VIII, 560a
Ṭābīnān v, 686a, b, 689a – V, 691b, 694a
Ṭabīʿiyyūn ii, 96a – II, 98a
Taʿbīr → Ruʾyā
Tabissa/Tébessa i, 163a – I, 167b
Ṭābiʿūn i, 276a; iv, 149a; x, **28b** – I, 284b; IV, 155b; **29b**
Tabḳa vi, 382b – VI, 367a
Ṭabkh x, **30a** – X, **31a**
Ṭabl ii, 621a; x, **32b** – II, 636b; X, **34a**
Tablī iv, 166b – IV, 174a
Ṭabl-khāna x, **34b** – X, **36a**
Tabriʾa i, 1026b – I, 1058b
Tablīgh → Daʿwa
Tablīghī Djamāʿat x, **38a** – X, **34a**
al-Ṭabrisī (al-Ṭabarsī), Abū Manṣūr (XII) vii, 312b; x, **39b**, 85a – VII, 314b; X, **41a**; 92a
al-Ṭabrīsī (Ṭabarsī), Amīn al-Dīn Abū ʿAlī al-Faḍl (1154) vii, 422b, 441a; x, **40a**, 85a – VII, 424a, 442a; X, **41a**, 92a
Ṭabrīsī (Ṭabarsī), Ḥadjdjī Mīrzā Ḥusayn b. Muḥammad (1902) x, **41a** – X, **42b**
Tabrīz i, 190b, 325a; ii, 8a, 435b; iii, 157b, 212b; iv, 7b, 33a, 392a; vi, 18b, 55b, 72b, 120a, 315b, 484b, 494a, 498a, b, 499a, b, 501b, 502a, b, 504a, b, 505a, 514a, 523b, 526b, 584a; viii, 184b; s, 73a, 110a, 135a, 138b, 139a, b, 140a, 142a, 208a, 275a, 289a, 365b; x, **41b** – I, 196a, 335a; II, 8a, 447a; III, 161a, 218a; IV, 8a, 35b, 409a; VI, 16b, 53b, 70b, 117b, 300b, 470b, 479b, 483b, 484b, 485a, 487a, b, 488a, 489a, b, 490a, 499b, 508b, 511a, 568b; VIII, 187b; X, **42b**; S, 73b,

109a, 134b, 138a, b, 139a, b, 142a, 208a, 274b, 289a, 365a
—institutions ii, 426a, 1043a – II, 437a, 1067b
—monuments i, 1124a, 1125a; iv, 702a – III, 1152a, 1153a; IV, 730a
Tabrīzī (nisba) x, **50a** – X, **51b**
al-Tabrīzī, Abū Zakariyyā' Yaḥyā (1109) i, 69a, 154b, 593a, 794a; iii, 111a; v, 930a; vi, 824a; vii, 307b, 978b –
I, 71a, 159a, 612a, 817a; III, 113b; V, 934b; VI, 814a; VII, 309b, 979b
Tabrīzī, Aḥmad Kasrawī → Kasrawī Tabrīzī
Tabrīzī, Bahā' al-Dīn Ya'ḳūb (XIII) vi, 73a – VI, 70b
Tabrīzī, Fak͟hr al-Dīn 'Alī → Ṣāḥib 'Aṭā'
Tabrīzī, Ḳāsim-i Anwār → Ḳāsim-i Anwār
Tabrīzī, Ibn K͟halaf → Burhān
Tabrīzī, Muḥammad 'Aṣṣār → 'Aṣṣār
al-Tabrīzī, Muḥammad Ḥusayn → Muḥammad Ḥusayn Tabrīzī
Tabrīzī, Rad͟jab 'Alī s, 308a – S, 308a
Tabrīzī, S͟hams-i S͟hams-i Tabrīz(ī)
Tabūk i, 9a; vi, 158a, 455a, 647a, b, 650a; vii, 373b; x, **50b**; s, 351b –
I, 9a; VI, 153b, 440b, 632b, 635b; VII, 374b; X, **51b**; S, 351b
Ṭabūr x, **51a** – X, **52b**
Tabūs͟hkān iii, 224a – III, 230b
Tābūt v, 864a – V, 871a
Tacapas → Ḳābis
Tadallīs (Dellys) x, **51b** – X, **53a**
'tadbīr x, **52b** – X, **53b**
Taddart i, 372a – I, 383a
Tādemmeket, Tādmekka iii, 657a – III, 678b
Tad͟hkira ii, 80a, 179a, 304a; v, 193a; x, **53b** – II, 81b, 185a, 312b; V, 190b; X, **54b**
al-Ta'dīl x, **55a** – X, **56b**
al-Ta'dīl bayn al-Saṭrayn x, **55b** – X, **57a**
Ta'dīl al-Zamān x, **55b** – X, **57a**
al-Tādilī (XIII) vi, 741b – VI, 731a
al-Tādilī, Ibrāhīm b. Muḥammad (1894) x, **55b** – X, **57b**
al-Tādilī, Yūsuf b. Yaḥyā Ibn al-Zayyāt → Ibn al-Zayyāt
Tād͟j v, 634a, 748a, 749a; x, **57a** – V, 638a, 753b, 754b; X, **58b**
Tād͟j al-'Ad͟jam (XII) i, 440a – I, 452b
Tād͟j al-Dawla → Tutus͟h
Tād͟j al-Dawla (Labla) (1041) ii, 1009a; v, 586b – II, 1033a; V, 591b
Tād͟j al-Dawla Muḥammad (Munḳid͟h, Banū) (1157) vii, 578b – VII, 579a
Tād͟j al-Dawla Ṭāwūs K͟hānum Iṣfahānī (XVIII) vi, 484a – VI, 470a
Tād͟j al-Dīn → Abū Muḥammad 'Abd Allāh b. 'Umar; Altîntas͟h; Fīrūz S͟hāh (Bahmānī); al-Subkī
Tād͟j al-Dīn, Ḳāḍī 'l-Ḳuḍāt (1262) vi, 667b – VI, 653b
Tād͟j al-Dīn, Mawlanā s, 352b – S, 352b
Tād͟j al-Dīn, Pīr v, 26b – V, 27a
Tād͟j al-Dīn 'Abd al-Mad͟jid (1343) ix, 666a – IX, 692a
Tād͟j al-Dīn Abū Bakr s, 66b – S, 67a
Tād͟j al-Dīn (I) Abu 'l-Faḍl Naṣr (Sīstān) (1073) ix, 683b – IX, 712a
Tād͟j al-Dīn (II) Abu 'l-Faḍl Naṣr (Sīstān) (1164) ix, 683b – IX, 712a
Tād͟j al-Dīn Abu 'l-Futūḥ (Alamut, Maṣyad) (1239) vi, 790b – VI, 780a
Tād͟j al-Dīn 'Alī-S͟hāh (1318) viii, 169a, 443b – VIII, 171b, 458b
Tād͟j al-Dīn Ḥarb b. Muḥammad (Nīmrūz) (1213) ix, 682b – IX, 711a
Tād͟j al-Dīn Ḥusayn b. Fak͟hr al-Dīn 'Alī i, 243b – I, 250b
Tād͟j al-Dīn Inaltigin (1235) ix, 683b – IX, 712a
Tād͟j al-Dīn K͟handgāh (G͟haznawid(e)) (XI) vi, 410a – VI, 394b
Tād͟j al-Dīn Muk͟htaṣ (1289) iv, 76b; vi, 653b – IV, 80b; VI, 639a
Tād͟j al-Dīn Mu'tazz iv, 738a – IV, 767b
Tād͟j al-Dīn Yïldïz Mu'izzī (1215) x, **60a** – X, **62a**
Tād͟j K͟hān Narpalī (XVI) vi, 52a – VI, 50a
Tād͟j K͟hātūn bint Muḥammad Bayhaḳī s, 131b – S, 130b
Tād͟j Maḥall i, 253b; ii, 47b, 287a; iii, 450b; vi, 126a, 127a, 1289a, 369b; vii, 332b; viii, 268b; x, **58b** – I, 261b; II, 48b, 296a; III, 466a; VI, 124a, 125a, 126a, 353b; VII, 334a; VIII, 275b; X, **60b**
Tād͟j al-Mulk (Delhi) v, 61 – V, 6a
Tād͟j al-Mulk Abu 'l-G͟hanā'im (1093) i, 1051b; iii, 774b; vi, 275a; vii, 541a; viii, 72a, 81b –
I, 1083a; III, 797b; VI, 260a; VII, 541a; VIII, 73b, 74a, 83b
Tād͟j al-Mulūk bint Tīmūr K͟hān (XX) vii, 446a – VII, 447b
Tād͟j al-Mulūk Būrī (Būrid(e)) (1132) i, 1017a, 1332a, b; ii, 282a; iii, 120a; vi, 547a – I, 1048b, 1372b, 1373a; II, 290a; III, 122b; VI, 531b
Tād͟j al-Salṭana bint Nāṣir al-Dīn S͟hāh (Ḳād͟jār)(XX) vi, 481b – VI, 467b
Tad͟jallī x, **60b** – X, **62b**
Tad͟jammul Ḥusayn K͟hān ii, 809a – II, 828a
Tad͟jdīd x, **61b** – X, **63a**
Tād͟jīk i, 224a, 530b, 853b, 854a, 857a, 1010a; iv, 310a, b, 313b; v, 244b, 614b, 857b, 858a; vi, 371a, 557b; ix, 682b; x, **62a**; s, 98a, 237b, 367b –
I, 230b, 547a, 877b, 881a, 1041a; IV, 324a, b, 327b; V, 242b, 618b, 864b; VI, 355a, 542a; IX, 711a; X, **64a**; S, 97a, 237a, 367a
Tad͟jīkī x, **64b** – X, **66b**
Tād͟jīkistān i, 531a; x, **66a** – I, 547a; X, **68b**
Tād͟jir x, **67a** – X, **69a**
Tād͟jī-zāde D͟ja'fer Čelebi (1516) vi, 967a; viii, 212a – VI, 959b; VIII, 216a
Tad͟jmīr x, **67a** – X, **69b**
Tad͟jnīs x, **67b** – X, **70a**
al-Tad͟jrīs͟hī, al-Amīr Muṣṭafā iv, 856b – IV, 890a
Tād͟juh (Tagus/-e) x, **70b** – X, **73a**
Tad͟jur(r)a x, **71a** – X, **74a**
Tad͟jwīd x, **72b** – X, **75a**
Tādlā vi, 141b, 592a, 741a, 742a, b; x, **75a**; s, 132a, 223a – VI, 140a, 577a, 730b, 731b; X, **78a**; S, 131b, 223a
Tadlīs x, **77a** – X, **80b**
Tadmait s, 328a – S, 327b
Tādmakkat x, **78a** – X, **81a**
Tadmīn x, **78b** – **82a**
Tadmur i, 563a; vi, 373b, 544b, 622a; x, **79a;** s, 117a – I, 581a; VI, 358a, 529b, 607a; X, **82b**; S, 116b
Tadrīs x, **80a** – X, **83b**
Tādrus b. al-Ḥasan (1029) vii, 117a – VII, 119a
Tadūra vi, 412b – VI, 397b
Tadwān vi, 384a – VI, 368b
Taswīn x, **81a** – X, **84b**
Tafaḍḍul Ḥusayn K͟hān ii, 809a – II, 828a
Tafarrud͟j x, **81b** – X, **84b**
Tafḍīl x, **82a** – X, **85a**
al-Ṭaff (steppe) iv, 384b; x, **82a** – IV, 401a; X, **85b**
Tafīla x, 884b – X,
Tāfīlāl(e)t i, 355b; iii, 256b; v, 1187b; vi, 135a, 141b, 142b, 143a, 248b, 249a, 590b, 742a; viii, 440a; ix, 545b; x, **82b**; s, 223b, 370a –
I, 366b; III, 263b; V, 1177b; VI, 133a, b, 139b, 140b, 141b, 233a, 575b, 731b; VIII, 454b; IX, 567a; X, **86a**; S, 223b, 370a

Tafīsh vi, 562b – VI, 547a
Tafkhīm x, **83a** – X, **90a**
Ṭafra x, **83a** – X, **96a**
Tafsīr i, 40a, 60b, 274b, 410a; ii, 363a; iii, 172a, 434b; iv, 147a, 984b; x, **83b** –
I, 41a, 62b, 283a, 422a; II, 373a; III, 175b, 449a; IV, 153a, 1017a; X, **90b**
Tāfta iii, 216b; x, **88a** – III, 223a; **95a**
Taftāzān (Khurāsān) x, 88b – X, 95b
al-Taftāzānī, Saʿd al-Dīn Masʿūd (1390) i, 342b, 858a, 982b, 1019b, 1116a, 1345b; ii, 174a, 602b, 774b; iii, 163b, 711a, 1168a; iv, 414b; vi, 218b, 848a; vii, 388a; x, **88b** –
I, 353a, 882a, 1013a, 1051a, 1149b, 1386a; II, 179b, 617b, 793a; III, 167a, 733b, 1197a; IV, 432b; VI, 202b, 839a; VII, 389a; X, **95b**
Tagdaoust → Awdaghust
Tagh Boyu → Akhāl Tekke
Taghā → Tughā
Taghāliba ii, 175b, 176a – II, 181a, b
Taghāza x, **89a** – X, **96b**
Ṭaghī ii, 1124b – II, 1151a
Ṭaghiya vi, 374a – VI, 358b
Taghlib b. Wāʾil, Banū i, 526b, 527a, 528a, 545a, 963a, 1240b, 1241a; iii, 222b, 1254a; iv, 1143b; v, 362a; vi, 378a, 379a, 490a; vii, 373b; x, **89b**; s, 178a –
I, 542b, 543a, 544a, 562a, 993a, 1278b; III, 229a, 1287a; IV, 1175b; V, 363a; VI, 362a, 363a, 476a; VII, 375a; X, **97a**; S, 179a
Taghlib b. Wāʾil ii, 176a – II, 181b
al-Taghlibī, al-Ḥakam b. ʿAmr vi, 193a – VI, 177a
Taghlibiyya viii, 730b – VIII, 751b
Taghrībirdī al-Bashbughāwī ii, 781a, b, 782a – II, 800a, b
Taghrībirdī al-Ẓāhirī ii, 286a – II, 294a
Taghrīr x, **93a** – X, **100b**
Tāghūt x, **93b** – X, **101a**
Tagmut vi, 590b – VI, 575a
Tagore, Rabindranath s, 162a – S, 162a
Tagus/-e → Wādī Tadjū
Tah, Shaykh Abū ʿUbayd Allāh (XIX) vii, 454b – VII, 455a
Ṭāha, ʿAlī Maḥmūd (1949) x, **95a** – X, **102b**
Ṭāhā Ḥusayn (1973) i, 565b, 598a, 890a; iv, 906b; v, 189a, b, 1092a; vi, 91a, 408a, 409a, 461a, 956a; vii, 441a, 713b; x, **95a**; s, 58a –
I, 584a, 617b, 916a; IV, 939b; V, 186b, 187a, 1089a; VI, 89a, 393a, b, 446b, 948b; VII, 442a, 714a; X, **103a;** S, 58b
Ṭāhā, Maḥmūd Muḥammad (1985) x, **96b** – X, **104a**
Tahadjdjud x, **97b** – X, **105a**
Tahamtan, Ḳuṭb al-Dīn i, 942b; iii, 585a; iv, 764b – I, 971b; III, 605a; IV, 795a
al-Tahānawī, Muḥammad Aʿlā (XVIII) i, 595a; iii, 170b, 1238b, 1241b; vi, 219a, 442a, b, 443a, b, 451a; x, **98a** –
I, 614a; III, 174a, 1270b, 1273b; VI, 203a, 427b, 428a, b, 429a, 436b; X, **105b**
Taḥannuf iii, 165b, 166a – III, 169a, b
Tahannuth x, **98b** – X, **106a**
Ṭahār, Ṭahāra iv, 372b; v, 20b; x, **99a** – IV, 389a; V, 21a; X, **106b**
Tāhart i, 1175b; iii, 654b, 655a, 657a; v, 696b, 1164b; vi, 312a, b, 435a, 452b, 727b, 840b; vii, 263a; z, **99b** –
I, 1210b; III, 676a, 678a; V, 701b, 1154a; VI, 297a, b, 420b, 438a, 716b, 831a; VII, 265a; X, **107b**
al-Ṭaḥāwī, ʿAḥmad b. Muḥammad (933) i, 123b, 310a; iii, 163a; vi, 352b; vii, 822a; x, **101a**; s, 156a, 310b –
I, 127a, 319b; III, 166b; VI, 337a; VII, 824a; X, **108b**; S, 156b, 310b
Tahawwur Khān s, 420b – S, 420b
Taḥayyur iv, 95a – IV, 99a
Taḥdjīr iii, 1054a – III, 1080a
Ṭaḥḥān x, **102a** – X, **110a**
Ṭāhir I → Ṭāhir b. al-Ḥusayn
Ṭāhir II iv, 20b – IV, 22a
Ṭāhir, Banū (Murcia) x, **105b** – X, **113b**
al-Ṭāhir, ʿAlī Nāṣūḥ v, 412b – V, 413b
Ṭāhir b. Abū Ṭayyib iii, 107a – III, 109b
Ṭāhir b. Aḥmad b. Bābashādh, Abū Ḥasan (1077) iii, 733a, 761a; x, **103b** –
III, 755b, 784a; X, **110b**
Ṭāhir b. Ghalbūn b. Abi ʾl-Ṭayyib al-Ḥalabī (1008) vi, 188b – VI, 172a
Ṭāhir b. Hilāl b. Badr (XI) i, 512b; iii, 258b; ix, 295b – I, 528a; III, 266a; IX, 304a
Ṭāhir (I) b. al-Ḥusayn al-Būshandjī (Ṭāhirid(e)) (822) i, 18a, 52b, 271b, 437b, 751b, 897b; ii, 524a; iii, 231b, 694b; iv, 17a, 20a, b, 645a; v, 57b, 621a; vi, 333a, b, 334a, 336a, b, 337b, 438a; vii, 985b, 1016b; x, **103a**; s, 15a –
I, 19a, 54a, 280a, 450a, 773b, 924a; II, 537a; III, iv, 238a, 716b; IV, 18a, b, 22a, 671b; V, 59a, 625a; VI, 317b, 318a, b, 320b, 321b, 423a; VII, 986a, 1018b; X, **110b**; S, 15a
Ṭāhir (II) b. ʿAbd Allāh (Ṭāhirid(e)) (859) iv, 20b; x, 105a – IV, 22a; X, 113a
Ṭāhir b. Ḥusayn al-Ahdal, Sayyid i, 255b – I, 263b
Ṭāhir b. Khalaf iii, 502a; s, 118b – III, 519b; S, 118a
Ṭāhir b. Muḥammad b. ʿAbd Allāh (999) x, **103b** – X, **111a**
Ṭāhir b. Muḥammad b. ʿAmr (Ṣaffārid(e)) (X) viii, 796b – VIII, 823a
Ṭāhir b. Muḥammad al-Isfarāʾinī iv, 107b – IV, 112a
Ṭāhir b. Zayn al-ʿAbidīn s, 95a – S, 94b
Tahir Alangu (XX) vi, 95b – VI, 93b
Ṭāhir ʿAlī Sharīf (XX) vi, 751b – VI, 741a
Ṭāhir al-Balkhī iv, 797a, 800b – IV, 829b, 833a
Ṭāhir Dhu ʾl-Yaminayn (VIII) viii, 590a; x, 14a – VIII, 608b; X, 14b
Ṭāhir Efendi iv, 882b – IV, 915a
al-Ṭāhir al-Ḥaddād iv, 720b; viii, 858a – IV, 749b; VIII, 888b
Ṭāhir al-Ḥawwa (XIX) vi, 252a – VI, 236a
Ṭāhir al-Ḥusaynī s, 67a – S, 67b
Ṭāhir Ḥusaynī Dakkanī iv, 202a – IV, 210b
Ṭāhir Pasha (Miṣr) (1803) i, 1269a; v, 35b; vii, 423b – I, 1308a; V, 36b; VII, 425a
al-Ṭāhir Raḥāb (XX) vi, 251b – VI, 235b
Ṭāhir Sayf al-Dīn, Abū Muḥammad (1965) x, **103b** – X, **111b**
Ṭāhir Selām i, 630a – I, 651a
Ṭāhir Waḥīd, Mīrzā Muḥammad (1698) x, **104a** – X, **112a**
Ṭāhira → Ḳurrat al-ʿAyn
Ṭāhirid(e)s (Khurāsān) i, 52b, 439b, 440b, 441a, 553a, 1008b, 1342b; ii, 253b, 505b, 1081b; iii, 245a, 746a; iv, 18b, 20a, b, 646a; v, 57b; vi, 336b, 338b, 620b; vii, 777b, 867a, 996a; x, **104b**; s, 338b –
I, 54a, 452a, 453b, 571a, 1039b, 1383a; II, 261a, 518b, 1107a;III, 252a, 769a; IV, 20a, 21b-22a, 672b; V, 59a, b; VI, 320b, 323a, 605b; VII, 779b, 868b, 997b; X, **112b**; S, 338a
Ṭāhirid(e)s (al-Andalus) x, **105b** – X, **113b**
Ṭāhirid(e)s (South Arabia) x, **106 b** – X, **114b**
Taḥkīm x, **107a** – X, **115a**
Tahlīl x, **108a** – X, **117a**

Tahmān b. ʿAmr al-Kilābī x, **108b** – X, **117b**
Ṭahmāsibī, Khalīl ii, 882b; s, 158a – II, 903a; S, 158b
Ṭahmāsp I, Abu 'l-Fatḥ, Shāh (Ṣafawid(e)) (1576) i, 228b, 291a, 329b, 406a, 967b, 1066b, 1068a, 1135b, 1208b, 1211a, b; ii, 310b, 334b; iii, 214a, 253b, 575b, 1101a, 1189b, 1191a, 1257a; iv, 35a, b, 102b, 103a, 188a, 537a, 610a; v, 244b, 492b; vi, 16b, 17b, 18b, 456b, 483a, b, 495a, 514b, 515a, 516b, 525b, 550a, b, 608b, 714b, 715a; vii, 314a, 316b, 317a, 440b, 478a, 928b; viii, 73a, 115b, 766a, 768b, 775b; ix, 834b; x, **108b**; s, 43b, 140a, 383a – I, 235a, 300a, 340a, 417b, 997a, 1098b, 1100a, 1170a, 1244b, 1247a, b; II, 319b, 344a; III, 220a, 260b, 595b, 1128a, 1219b, 1220b, 1289b; IV, 37b, 38a, 107b, 196a, 560a, 634b; V, 242b, 495b; VI, 14b, 16a, b, 442a, 469a, b, 480a, 499b, 500a, 501b, 510a, 534b, 535a, 593a, 703b; VII, 316b, 319a, b, 441b, 477b, 929a; VIII, 75a, 118a, 791b, 794a, 801b; IX, 869b; X, **117b**; S, 44a, 139b, 383b
Ṭahmāsp II, Shāh (Ṣafawid(e)) (1740) i, 395b; iii, 604b, 1002b; iv, 37a, 389b, 390a; v, 663b; vi, 55b, 715a; vii, 853a; x, **110b** – I, 407a; III, 625a, 1027b; IV, 39b, 406a, b; V, 669a; VI, 53b, 703b; VII, 854b; X, **119b**
Tahmāsp b. ʿAbbās I (Ṣafawid(e)) (XVII) ii, 1083b – II, 1108b
Ṭahmāsp b. Muḥammad Khudābanda (Ṣafawid(e)) (XVI) i, 8b; iii, 157b; iv, 860b, 861a – I, 8b; III, 161a; IV, 893b, 894a
Ṭahmāsp Ḳulī Khān → Nādir Shāh
Ṭahmasp Mīrzā b. Shāh Sulṭān Ḥusayn (Ṣafawid(e)) (XVIII) viii, 771b – VIII, 797a
Ṭahmūrath (Pīshdādid(e)) i, 459a; v, 494b;ix, 54b; x, **110b**, 111a – I, 472a; V, 497b; IX, 55b; X, **119b**, 120a
Tahnīṭ x, **111a** – X, **120a**
Taḥrīf x, **111a** – X, **120a**
Taḥrīr x, **112b** – X, **121b**
Taḥṣīl x, **113a** – X, **122b**
Taḥsīn Efendī (Pasha) i, 61b, 64a; iii, 1199a – I, 63a, 66a; III, 1229a
Taḥsīn, Mīr Muḥammad Ḥusayn (XVIII) x, **113b** – X, **122b**
Taḥsīn wa-Taḳbīḥ x, **114a** – X, **123a**
Taḥt al-Ḳalʿa (Damas(cus)) vi, 455a – VI, 440b
Taḥt al-Ḳalʿa (Istanbul) iv, 228a – IV, 238a
al-Ṭahṭāwī, Rifāʿa Bey (1873) → Rifāʿa Bey
Tahūda iv, 827a – IV, 860a
Ṭāḥūn x, **114b** – X, **123b**
al-Ṭāʾī → Abū Tammām; Budjayr b. ʿAws; Dāwūd; Djundab b. Khāridja; Ḥātim
al-Ṭāʾī (1778) vii, 969b – VII, 969b
al-Ṭāʾī (al-Ṭūsī), Muḥammad b. Ḥumayd (IX) vi, 337a, b – VI, 321b, 322a
Ṭāʾī, Banū viii, 53a – VIII, 53b
al-Ṭāʾiʿ li-Amr Allāh (ʿAbbāsid(e)) (1003) i, 212a, 955a, 1352b; ii, 195a; iii, 345a; vi, 522a, 667a, 669b; x, **115a**; s, 23a, 118b – I, 218b, 984a, 1391b; II, 201b; III, 355a; VI, 506b, 653b, 656a; X, **124a**; S, 23b, 118a
Taičiʿut ii, 41b – II, 42b
al-Ṭāʾif i, 9a, 55a, 609a; iii, 363a; v, 434b, 692b; vi, 145b, 147b, 151b, 152a, 157a, 160b, 162b, 224a, 266a, b, 405a, 650a, b; vii, 366a, 373a; x, **115a**; s, 3b, 133b, 134a, 152a, 318a, 354a, b – I, 9a, 57a, 629a; III, 374b; V, 436b, 697b; VI, 144a, 146a, 150a, 151a, 152b, 154b, 156a, 218a, 251a, 389b, 635b; VII, 368b, 374b; X, **124b**; S, 3a, 133a, b, 152a, 318a, 354a, b
Ṭāʾifa x, **116a** – X, **125b**
Ṭāʾifiyya x, **117a** – X, **126b**
Ṭāʾir v, 184b – V, 181b
al-Ṭāʾir / al-Ṭayr x, **117b** – X, **127a**
Taʿizz vi, 474b, 911b; vii, 270a, 761b; viii, 184a, 235b, 456a; x, **118a**; s, 338b – VI, 460a, 903a; VII, 272a, 763b; VIII, 187a, 240b, 471b; X, **127b**; S, 338a
Ṭāḳ iii, 501b, 502a; v, 69b – III, 518b, 519b; V, 71b
Ṭāḳa (Ḥaḍramawt) vi, 83b – VI, 81b
al-Ṭāḳā (Sudān) → Kasala
Takafūr (Nicephorus Phocas) ii, 236a – II, 243a
Taḳalī v, 267a – V, 264b
al-Taʿkar (Ibb) ix, 816a – IX, 851a
Takash → Tekish
Taḳbaylīt x, **118b** – X, **128a**
Takbīr x, **119b** – X, **129a**
Taḳdīr x, **119b** – X, **129b**
Takfīr x, **122a** – X, **131b**
al-Takfīr wa 'l-Hidjra x, **122b** – X, **132a**
Takhalluṣ x, **123a** – X, **132b**
Takhmīs x, **123b** – X, **133b**
Takht-i Djamshīd → Iṣtakhr
Takhtadjī x, **125b** – X, **135b**
Takht-i Fūlād (Iṣfahān) vii, 132a; s, 308a – VII, 134a; S, 308a
Takht-i Rustam (Iṣtakhr) iv, 221b – IV, 231b
Takht-i Sulaymān Shīz iii, 1125a; iv, 1166a, 1167b; vi, 499a; x, 896b – III, 1153a; IV, 1198a, 1200a; VI, 484a; X,
Takht-i Ṭāwūs (Peacock Throne) vi, 528a; viii, 869a; x, **125a** – VI, 512a; VIII, 898b; X, **135a**
Takhṭīṭ al-Ḥudūd x, **126b** – X, **136b**
Takhyīl x, **129a** – X, **139a**
Taḳī Arānī (1939) s, 110a – S, 109b
Taḳī Awḥadī (1632) vii, 530a; x, **132a** – VII, 530b; X, **142b**
Taḳ-i Bustān (Kirmānishāh) v, 169a – V, 166b
Taḳī Bāfḳī, Shaykh Muḥammad s, 342b – S, 342a
Taḳī al-Dīn → al-Muẓaffar
Taḳī al-Dīn, Ḳāḍī al-Ḳuḍāt (1280) vi, 673b – VI, 660a
Taḳī al-Dīn b. Muḥammad Maʿrūf (1585) v, 27b; vi, 377a, 601b; vii, 30b; viii, 555b; x, **132b;** s, 372a – V, 28b; VI, 361b, 586b; VII, 30b; VIII, 573a; X, **143a;** S, 371b
Taḳī al-Dīn al-Futūḥī → Ibn al-Nadjdjār
Taḳī al-Dīn ʿIrāḳī, Kh(ʷ)ādja s, 415b – S, 415a, b – VII, 530b; S, 415a, 416b
Taḳī al-Dīn Muḥammad b. Sharaf al-Dīn (XVII) vii, 530a; x, **133a** – VII, X, **143b**
Taḳī al-Dīn al-Nabhānī (1977) x, **133b** – X, **144a**
Taḳī al-Dīn ʿUmar → al-Malik al-Muẓaffar ʿUmar
Taḳī al-Dīn ʿUmar b. Turān Shāh (Ayyūbid(e)) (XII) vi, 380b – VI, 365a
Taḳī Kāshī → Taḳī al-Dīn MuThammad b. Sharaf
Taḳī Khān, Amīr Kabīr, Mīrzā (1852) → Amīr Kabīr
Taḳī Shīrāzī, Mīrzā Muḥammad s, 342a – S, 341b
``takidda (Takedda) x, **133b** – X, **144b**
Taḳīmir, Mīr (XVIII) vii, 669b – VII, 669a
Takīn b. Tutush (Saldjūḳ) (XII) viii, 995a – VIII, 1030a
Takirwan iv, 826a – IV, 859a
Taḳiyya i, 402a, 811a, 1099a; v, 375a; x, **134b**; s, 230b – I, 414a, 834a, 1132a, b; V, 375b; X, **145a**; S, 230b
Taḳī-zāda, Sayyid Ḥasan (1970) v, 1097b; x, **136a;** s, 365b – V, 1093b; X, **146b**; S, 365b
Takkalū, Banū v, 245a; x, 109a, **136b** – V, 242b; X, 118a, **147b**
Taklā, Bishāra and/et Salīm ii, 466b; iv, 967a; vii, 902b – II, 478a; IV, 999a; VII, 903b
Takla b. Hazārasp iii, 337a, b – 347a, b

Taklamakan → Tarim
Taḳlīd i, 1039a; II, 182b, 303a, 890a; iii, 1026b, 1173b; iv, 152a' x, **137a** – I, 1070b; II, 188b, 311a, 910b; III, 1052b, 1202b; IV, 158a; X, **148a**
Taklīd-i Sayf → Marāsim. 4
Taklīf x, **138b** – X, **149b**
Takrīb x, **139b** – X, **150b**
Takrīt (Tikrīt) iii, 1252b, 1268a; iv, 289a; vi, 143b, 966a; vii, 396b, 400b, 543b; viii, 716a; x, **140b**; s, 36b –
III, 1285a, 1301a; IV, 302a; VI, 142a, 958b; VII, 398a, 402a, 543b; VIII, 737a; X, **151b**; S, 37a
al-Takrītī, ʿAbd al-Laṭīf b. Rus̲h̲ayd iv, 137a – IV, 143a
Taḳrīẓ ii, 304a – II, 312b
Takrūna x, **141b** – X, **152b**
Takrūr i, 297a; ii, 941b, 970a; iii, 657a; vi, 87b, 258a, 259b, 281b, 320a; vii, 612b; ix, 138b, 139a, 752b; x, **142a** –
I, 306a; II, 963a, b, 992a; III, 678b; VI, 85b, 242b, 244a, 266b, 304b; VII, 612a; IX, 143b, 144a, 785b; X, **152a**
al-Takrūrī, Abū Muḥammad b. ʿAbd Allāh (X) vii, 612b – VII, 612b
Taks̲h̲īf iv, 678a – IV, 705b
Taksīm vi, 57a; x, **143a** – VI, 55a; X, **154a**
Taḳsīṭ x, **144a** – X, **154b**
Taḳtūḳa x, **144a** – X, **154b**
Takūdār → Aḥmad Takūdār
Tākurunnā viii, 615b, 616a; x, **144b** – VIII, 635a; X, **154b**
Takwa Milinga (Manda) vi, 385a, b – VI, 369a, b
Taḳwīm x, **145a** – X, **156b**
Taḳwīm-i Weḳāʾiʿ i, 285a; ii, 465b; v, 313b – I, 293b; II, 477a; V, 313b
Takwīn x, **147b** – X, **159a**
Ṭalab al-ʿIlm → ʿIlm
Ṭalaba (Ṭullāb) iii, 97b, 98a, b; v, 1134a; x, **148b** – III, 100a, b, 101a; V, 1129b; X, **160b**
Ṭalabānī, D̲j̲alāl (XX) vii, 714b, 715a – VII, 715a, b
Ṭalabānī, S̲h̲ayk̲h̲ Riḍā v, 147a – V, 149b
Ṭalabīra (Talavera) x, **149a** – X, **160b**
Ṭalāʾiʿ b. Ruzzīk (vizier) (1161) i, 9b, 196b; ii, 318a, 855b, 856b, 858a; iv, 429a, 944a; v, 514b; vii, 61b; viii, 130a, 864a; x, **149a**; s, 115b –
I, 9b, 202b; II, 327a, 875b, 876b, 878a; IV, 448a, 976b; V, 518a; VII, 62a; VIII, 133a, 895a; X, **161a**; S, 115a
Ṭalāʾīʿ b. Ruzzīḳ (vizier) (1164)
Ṭalāḳ i, 27b, 28b, 172b, 173b, 174a, 177a, 178a, 179a; ii, 836b; iii, 19a, 949b, 952b; iv, 286a, 689a; x, **151a** –
I, 28b, 177a, 178a, 179a; II, 856a; III, 19b, 974b, 977b; IV, 298b, 717a; X, **162b**
Ṭālaḳān ii, 43b; vi, 618a; x, **157a** – II, 44a; VI, 602b; X, **168b**
al-Ṭāl(a)ḳānī, Abu 'l-Ḥasan (995) vi, 820b, 823a – VI, 811a, 813b
Ṭālaḳānī (Ṭāliḳānī), Āyatullāh Sayyid Maḥmūd (1979) iv, 166a; vi, 549a, 553b; vii, 762b; x, **158a** – IV, 173b; VI, 533b, 538a; VII, 764a; X, **169b**
Ṭalāl b. ʿAbdallāh b. al-Ḥusayn (1972) iii, 264b; x, 886b – III, 272a; X,
Ṭalāl b. ʿAbd Allāh b. Ras̲h̲īd → Ras̲h̲īd, Āl
Ṭalāl b. ʿAbd al-ʿAzīz ii, 660b; iv, 1142b – II, 677a; IV, 1174a
al-Ṭalamanḳī, Abū ʿUmar Aḥmad (1037) x, **159a** – X, **170b**
Talas →Ṭarāz
Ṭalʿat, Meḥmed → Ṭalʿat Pas̲h̲ā Ḥarb
Ṭalʿat Bey (Pas̲h̲a) Meḥmed (1921) ii, 431a, b, 497b, 698b, 699a, b; iii, 360a, 622b; iv, 284b, 285a, b, 636a, 720b; v, 1003b; vi, 615a, 983b; vii, 229a; x, **159b**; s, 98a, 296b –
II, 442a, 443a, 510a, 716a, b, 717b; III, 371a, 643b; IV, 296b, 297b, 298a, 662a, 749b; V, 999b; VI, 600a, 976a; VII, 231a; X, **171a**; S, 97b, 296a
Ṭalbiya iii, 37a; v, 582a; x, **160a** – III, 38b; V, 587a; X, **172a**
Ṭald̲j̲iʾa → Ḥimāya
Talfīḳ x, **161a** – X, **173b**
Ṭalḥa b. Ṭāhir (I) b. al-Ḥusayn (Ṭāhirid(e) (828) i, 52b, 272a; iv, 20b; vi, 337b; x, 104b – I, 54a, 280a; IV, 22a; VI, 322a; X, 112b
Ṭalḥa b. ʿUbayd Allāh al-Taymī (656) i, 43b, 110a, 308a, 381b, 382a, 383a; ii, 414b, 415b; iii, 1165b; iv, 316a; v, 316a; vi, 139b, 621b; vii, 364a; x, **161b**; s, 89b –
I, 44b, 112b, 317b, 392b, 393a, 394a; II, 425a, 426b; III, 1194a; IV, 330a; V, 316a; VI, 138a, 606b; VII, 366b; X, **174a**; S, 89b
Ṭalḥa b. Yaḥyā s, 113b – S, 113a
Ṭalḥa al-Naḍrī al-Layt̲h̲ī i, 266b – I, 274b
Ṭalḥa al-Ṭalaḥāt s, 26a – S, 26a
Ṭalḥāt al-Ṭalaḥāt (684) x, **162b** – X, **175a**
al-Ṭāliʿ x, **163a** – X, **175a**
Ṭalīʿa x, **164a** – X, **176b**
Ṭālib → Ṭalaba
Ṭālib b. Abī Ṭālib i, 152b – I, 157a
Ṭālib b. Aḥmad i, 1306b, 1307b – I, 1346b, 1348a
Ṭālib Āmulī (1626) vii, 341a; ix, 241a; x, **164b** – VII, 343a; IX, 247b; X, **177a**
Ṭālib al-Ḥaḳḳ (ʿAbd Allāh b. Yaḥyā) (VIII) i, 550b; ii, 592b; iii, 651b, 658a; iv, 1076a; v, 1230a; vii, 524b; s, 337b, 338a –
I, 568a; II, 607a; III, 672b, 679b; IV, 1108a; V, 1220b; VII, 525a; S, 337b
Ṭālib Pas̲h̲a al-Naḳīb (XX) vi, 615b – VI, 600b
Ṭālibid(e)s → ʿAlid(e)s
Ṭālibiyya s, 401a – S, 401a
Ṭālibūf (Talibov), Mīrzā ʿAbd al-Raḥīm, Nad̲j̲d̲j̲ārzāda (1911) iv, 72a, 164b, 789a; x, **164b**; s, 109b – IV, 76a, 171b, 821a; X, **177b**; S, 108b
Ṭālibzada → Ṭālibov
Ṭalīḳ → Ṭulaḳāʾ
Taʿlīḳ (Taʿlīḳa) x, **165a** – X, **178a**
Ṭāliḳān vi, 511b, 512a- VI, 497a
Ṭāliḳānī, Āyatullāh → Ṭālaḳānī
Talʿiḳī-zāde, Meḥmed b. Meḥmed el-Fenārī (1603) vii, 931a; x, **165b** – VII, 931b; X, **178b**
Tālīkōtā viii, 252a; x, **166a** – VIII, 254b; X, **178b**
Taʿlimiyya → Ismāʿīliyya
Ṭālis̲h̲ vii, 497b, 498b, 935b; x, **166a**; s, 143a – VII, 497b, 498a, 936a; X, **179a**; S, 143a
Talḳāta, Banū ix, 18a – IX, 18b
Talk̲h̲īṣ → Muk̲h̲taṣar
Tall (Tell) x, **167a** – X, **179b**
Tall, el-Had̲j̲i Omar s, 182a – S, 182b
Tall, el-Had̲j̲i Seydou Nourou s, 182a – S, 182b
Tall Bās̲h̲ir vi, 380a, 381b, 499b, 506b, 507a, 544a; x, **167a** –
VI, 364a, 365b, 485a, 492a,b; 528b; X, **180a**
Tall Ibn Maʿs̲h̲ar vii, 578b – VII, 579a
al-Tall al-Kabīr x, **167b** – X, **180b**
Tall al-Sulṭān vi, 781a – VI, 771a
al-Tallaʿfarī, S̲h̲ihāb al-Dīn (1277) v, 110a; x, **168a** – V, 112a; X, **180b**
al-Tallaʿukbarī, Hārūn b. Mūsā s, 400b – S, 401a
Talman (XVIII) vi, 56a – VI, 54a
Tālpūrs i, 230b; ii, 168a; iii, 323b; iv, 1160a; ix, 440a, 635a –
I, 237b; II, 191b; III, 333b; IV, 1192a; 457a, 659a

Talsindah vi, 48a – VI, 46b
Ṭālūt (Saul) i, 404b; x, **168b** – I, 416a; X, **181a**
Ṭālūt b. al-Ḥusayn (Kilwa) (XIV) vi, 370a – VI, 354b
al-Talūṭī ʿAlī ix, 20a – IX, 21a
Tam, Banū i, 1190a – I, 1225a
Tāmag͟hilt → Mag͟hīla
Tamahak → Ṭawārik. 2
al-Ṭamāmī (al-Ẓamāmī), Abū Zakariyyāʾ (dāʿī) (IX) vi, 439a – VI, 424a
Taman Siswa i, 746a – I, 768a
Tamanrasset i, 255a – I, 263a
Tamar (Georgian queen/reine) v, 490a – V, 493a
Tamarurt vi, 743b – VI, 732b
Tāmasnā (Berber) ii, 623a; vi, 741b, 742b; x, **169a** – II, 638b; VI, 730b, 731a, b; X, **182a**
Tamas͟hek → Ṭawārik. 2
Tamattuʿ → Iḥrām; Mutʿa
Tamazig͟ht x, 118b, **169b**; s, 113b – X, 128a. **182a**; S, 113a
Tāmdalī vi, 742b – VI, 731b
Tamerlane → Tīmūr Lang
Tamg͟ha i, 861b; ii, 147a, 310a; iii, 489b; iv, 31a, 1050a; x, **170a** – I, 885b; II, 151a, 319a; III, 506b; IV, 33a, 1081b; X, **182b**
Tamg͟hāč K͟hān → Muḥammad II b. Sulaymān Bug͟hrā K͟hān (Ḳarak͟hānid(e))
Tamgrūt i, 290b; vi, 350a; x, **170b**; s, 395a – I, 299b; VI, 334a; X, **183b**; S, 395b
al-Tamgrūtī, Abū 'l-Ḥasan (1594) i, 593b; x, **171a** – I, 613a; X, **184a**
Ṭāmī b. S͟huʿayb al-Rufaydī ii, 518a – II, 530b
Tamil → Labbai; Marakkayar; Rawt͟her
Tamīm (poet/poète) (985) vii, 661a – VII, 660b
Taʾmīm x, **176b** – X, **189a**
Tamīm, Banū i, 47b, 304a, 343b, 528b, 529b, 545a, 963b, 1247b, 1293a; ii, 70a, 181a, 353b, 480b; iii, 49a, 295a, 1254a; iv, 717a, 832b; v, 346a; vi, 267a, b, 349a, 640b, 646a; vii, 123a, 266a, 373b; s, 177a, 243a – I, 49a, 313b, 354a, 544b, 545b, 562a, 993a, 1285b, 1332b; II, 71a, 187a, 363b, 493a; III, 51a, 304a, 1287a; IV, 746a, 865b; V, 347a; VI, 251b, 252b, 333a, 625b, 631b; VII, 125a, 268a, 375a; S, 178a, 243a
Tamīm b. Baḥr al-Muṭṭawwiʿ (IX) x, **171a** – X, **184a**
Tamīm b. Buluggīn b. Bādīs (Mālaḳa) (1090) i, 43b; vi, 222b – I, 45a; VI, 216a
Tamīm b. al-Muʿizz li-Dīn Allāh, Abū ʿAlī (Fāṭimid(e)) (985) ii, 852b, 857a, 861b; iii, 903b; viii, 42b; x, **171b** – II, 872b, 877a, 881b; III, 927b; VIII, 43b; X, **184a**
Tamīm b. al-Muʿizz, Abū Yaḥyā (Zīrid(e)) (1107) vii, 731b, 994a; x, **172a** – VII, 732a, 995b; X, **185a**
Tamīm b. al-Muʿizz b. Bādīs iii, 137b, 138a, 386a, b; v, 60a – III, 140b, 398b; V, 62a
Tamīm b. Murr, Banū x, **172b**; s, 305a – X, **185b**; S, 305a
Tamīm b. Naṣr b. Sayyār iv, 447a – IV, 467a
Tamīm b. Yūsuf b. Tās͟h(u)fīn (amīr) (Almoravid(e)) (XII) i, 389b, 390a; ii, 516a, 901b, 1013a; vi, 110b, 742b; s, 397b – I, 401a; II, 528b, 922b, 1036b; VI, 108b, 732a; S, 398a
Tamīm b. Zīrī → Abu 'l-Kamāl
Tamīm al-Dārī (VII) i, 405a; ii, 306b, 486b; iv, 734a, 956a; vi, 657b ; viii, 1043a; ix, **176a** – I, 416b; II, 315a, 498b; IV, 763b, 989b; VI, 643a; VIII, 1079a; X, **188b**
Tamīma x, **177b** – X, **190b**
al-Tamīmī, Abu 'l-Ḥasan v, 10a – V, 10b
al-Tamīmī, Abū K͟huzayma s, 309a – S, 309a
al-Tamīmī, Abū ʿUbayda Muslim b. Abī Karīma (Ibāḍī Imām) (VIII) viii, 113a – VIII, 115b
al-Tamīmī, al-Aswad b. Sarīʿ (635) vi, 671a – VI, 657a
al-Tamīmī, Ismāʿīl (1832) vi, 113a – VI, 110b
Tamīmīs → Tamīm b. Murr, Banū
Tamir-Bug͟ha al-As͟hrafī → Minṭās͟h (Mamlūk)
Tamir K͟hān S͟hūra (Bunaksk) x, 164b – X, 177b
Ṭamīs͟ha s, 298a, 356b, 357a – S, 298a, 356b, 357a
al-Ṭamiyya (mountain/montagne) vii, 348a – VII, 349b
Tamkīn (Kābul) iii, 84b; vii, 473b – III, 87a; VII, 473a
Tammām b. ʿAlḳama → Ibn ʿAlkama
Tammām b. ʿĀmir → Ibn ʿAlḳama
Tammām b. G͟hālib (1044) x, **178a** – X, **191a**
Tammām b. G͟hālib → al-Farazdaḳ
Tammām al Tamīmī iii, 982a – III, 1006b
Tammār x, **179a** – X, **192b**
Tammūz x, **179b** – X, **192b**
Tamr → Nak͟hl
Tamt͟hīl x, **179b** – X, **192a**
Tānā S͟hāh → Abu 'l-Ḥasan Ḳuṭb S͟hāh
al-Tanakabunī → Muḥammad b. Sulaymān
Tanas i, 678b; vi, 120b, 371b, 404a, b, 576a; x, **180a** – I, 699a; VI, 118b, 356a, 388b, 389a, b, 561a; X, **193b**
al-Tanasī, Muḥammad (1494) x, **181b;** s, 403b – X, **196a**; S, 403b
Tanāsuk͟h ii, 136b; iv, 45a; x, **181b** – II, 140a; IV, 48a; X, **196a**
Tanawlī iii, 336a – III, 346a
al-Tanāwutī (ʿIbāḍīs) (XI) x, **183a** – X, **197b**
Tanbūr → Ṭunbūr
al-Tandag͟hī, Muḥammad Fāl b. Muttāliyya (XIX) vii, 623a – VII, 622b
Ṭand͟ja (Tangier) i, 85a, 356a, 706b; vi, 39a, b, 40a, 135a, 136b; x, **183b**; s, 112a – I, 87a, 367a, 727b; VI, 37a, 38a, b, 133b, 134b; X, **198a**; S, 111b
Tand͟ja Bāliya iii, 500a – III, 517a
Tand͟jūr vi, 535a, b – VI, 519a, 520a
Tanfīd͟ha ii, 308a – II, 317a
T'ang v, 38a – V, 39a
Tanga/Tanka vi, 612b; x, **185a** – VI, 597b; X, **200a**
Tanganyika → Tanzania
Tanger → Ṭand͟ja
Tang͟hiz → Tankiz
Tang-i Ḳas͟hḳay vi, 384a – VI, 368b
Tangier → Ṭand͟ja
Tangistān s, 336a – S, 335b
Tangri Ḳag͟han (741) x, 687b – X, 730a
Tangut ii, 2a, 42b, 43b; iii, 115b; iv, 553b – II, 2a, 43b, 44b; III, 118a; IV, 577b
Tanḥūm ben Yōsēf ha-Yerus͟halmī iv, 306a – IV, 319b
Tanibak, Sayf al-Dīn ii, 285b – II, 293b
al-Tanʿīm vi, 168b – VI, 160a
Tank vi, 86a; s, 329b – VI, 84a; S, 329a
Tanka ii, 119b, 120a; v, 785a – II, 122b, 123a; V, 791a
Tankalūs͟hā al-Bābilī (I) viii, 103b, 106b – VIII, 105b, 108b
Tankiz al-Ḥusāmī al-Nāṣirī (vizier) (1340) i, 119a, 1138a, 1214a; ii, 285b, 354b; iii, 952b; iv, 960a; vi, 323a, 455a, 548a; vii, 170b, 992a; x, **185b** – I, 122a, 1172b, 1250b; II, 293b, 364a; III, 977a; IV, 992b; VI, 307b, 440b, 532b; VII, 172a, 993b; X, **201a**
Tankizbug͟hā (amīr) iv, 432b – IV, 451b
Tannūr → Maṭbak͟h
Ṭannūs al-S͟hidyāḳ vi, 346a – VI, 330a
Tanpinar, Aḥmed Ḥamdī (1962) v, 195a; x, **186a** – V, 192a; X, **201b**
Tañrı̊ x, **186b**, 688a – X, **201b**, 730a

Tansar, Kitāb　x, **188a** – X, **203b**
Tānsin (Tānsin) Mīrzā (1589)　ii, 1144a; iii, 453b; x, **188b** – II, 1171a; III, 469b; X, **203b**
Tansift　vi, 741b, 742a – VI, 731a
Ṭanṭā　i, 281a, 404a; ii, 1009b; iv, 367b; vi, 87b, 408a, 453b, 499a, 652b; x, **188b**; s, 40b –
I, 289b, 415b; II, 1033b; IV, 384a; VI, 85b, 393a, 439a, 484a, 637b; X, **204a**; S, 41a
al-Ṭanṭarānī, Aḥmad b. ʿAbd al-Razzāḳ (XI)　viii, 970b – VIII, 1005a
al-Ṭanṭāwī, Muḥammad Ayyād (1861)　x, **190a** – X, **205a**
Ṭanṭāwī Djawharī (1940)　vii, 439b – VII, 440b
Tanūḵh, Āl　i, 528a; ii, 634b, 751a; iii, 85b; iv, 289a; x, **190b**; s, 284a – I, 544a; II, 650b, 769b; III, 88a; IV, 302a; X, **206a**; S, 284a
al-Tanūḵhī, ʿAbd Allāh (1480)　ii, 633a; vii, 544a – II, 649a; VII, 544a
al-Tanūḵhī, Abū ʿAlī al-Muḥassin b. ʿAlī (994)　i, 176a, 764a, 1249b; iii, 373a, 1263b; iv, 703a; v, 768b; vi, 108a; vii, 358b; viii, 579b, 583b; x, **192b**; s, 32b, 361a, 398a –
I, 180b, 787a, 1287b; III, 385a, 1296b; IV, 731b; V, 774b; VI, 106a; VII, 361a; VIII, 598b, 602a; X, **208a**; S, 32b, 361a, 398b
al-Tanūḵhī, Abu 'l-Ḳāsim ʿAlī b. Muḥammad (ḳāḍī) (1271)　vi, 169a; vii, 358b; ix, 433a; s, 361a – VI, 180a; VII, 360b; IX, 449b; S, 361a
al-Tanūḵhī, Djamāl al-Dīn (1479)　x, **192b** – X, **207b**
al-Tanūḵhī, Naṣr Allāh b. ʿAbd al-Munʿim (1274)　viii, 87b – VIII, 90a
al-Tanwādjiwī, Sayyid ʿAbd Allāh (1732)　vii, 622a – VII, 621b
Tanwīn　iv, 413a, b; x, **193b** – IV, 431b; X, **208b**
Ṭanyūs Shāhin (1895)　ii, 595a; iii, 591b; x, **193b** – II, 609b; III, 612a; X, **209a**
Tanzania/-ie, Muslims in/en　i, 39a; iv, 890a; x, 104a, **194a**; s, 248b – I, 40a; IV, 923a; X, 112a, **209a**; S, 248b
Tanzil　→ Waḥy
Tanẓīm al-Nasl, Tanẓīm al-Usra　x, **197a** – X, **212b**
Tanẓīmāt　i, 13a, 37a, 56b, 286a, 318a, 397a, 469a, 652a, 657a, 693a, 972b, 1090b, 1304a; ii, 33b, 682b, 936a; iii, 285a, 592b, 1188a; iv, 168a, 560b; v, 36b, 631a, 904a, 1084b; vi, 285b, 469b; viii, 198b, 200a, 206b; x, **201a** –
I, 13a, 38a, 58b, 294b, 328a, 408b, 483a, 673a, 678a, 714a, 1002b, 1123a, 1344a; II, 34a, 699b, 957b; III, 293b, 613a, 1217b; IV, 175b, 583a; V, 37b, 635a, 910a, 1081b; VI, 270b, 455b; VIII, 202a, 203a, b, 210a; X, **216b**
Taormina　iv, 496b – IV, 518a
Taoudenni　i, 809a; x, 89b – I, 832a; X, 97a
Taourirt　vi, 141b – VI, 139b
Tapanta, Banū　i, 1189b, 1190a – I, 1224b, 1225a
Tapar, Muḥammad (Saldjūḳ) (XII)　i, 353a, 1359b; VII, 755a – I, 364a, 1399b; VII, 756b
Tappa Ḥiṣār　ii, 107a – II, 109b
Tāptī (river/rivière)　iv, 1022b; s, 279b – IV, 1054b; S, 279b
Tapu　i, 1090b; ii, 147a; x, **209b** – I, 1123a; II, 151a; X, **226a**
Ṭarab (emotion)　x, **210b** – IV, 856a; X, **227b**
Ṭārāb/Tārāb (Buḵhārā)　x, 211b – X, 228b
Taraba　→ Wādī Turaba
Tarabai umm Shivādjī II (Marāṭha) (1700)　vi, 535a – VI, 519b
Ṭarabāy, Banū　iii, 325a; v, 594a; x, **211b** – III, 335a; V, 597b, 598a; X, **228b**
Ṭarabī, Maḥmūd (1238)　vii, 749a; x, **211b** – VIII, 779b; X, **228b**
Tarābīn, Banū　vii, 921a – VII, 921b

al-Ṭarābulsī, Abū Saʿīd Ḵhalīfa b, Farhūn　iv, 1130a – IV, 1161b
Ṭarābulus al-gharb (Tripoli, Libya/-ie)　i, 1317a; v, 759b, 760b, 1183a; vi, 3a, 58b, 60b, 68b, 404a, 452b; x, **212a**; s, 1a, 163b – I, 1358a; V, 765a, b, 766b, 1173a; VI, 3a, 56b, 58b, 66b, 388b, 438a; X, **229a**; S, 1a, 163b
Ṭarābulus (Aṭrābulus) al-shām (Tripolis)　i, 125a, 448a, 946b; iii, 474b; iv, 485a; v, 591a; vi, 118b, 322b, 323a, 345a, 360a, 580a; vii, 62b; x, **214b** – I, 128b, 461a, 976a; III, 491b; IV, 506a; V, 595a; VI, 116b, 307a, 329b, 344a, 565a; VII, 63a; X, **221b**
al-Ṭarābulusī, Muḥammad b. Shaʿbān (1611)　vi, 355b – VI, 339b
al-Ṭarābulusī al-Raffā (1153)　iii, 821b; x, **216b** – III, 845a; X, **233b**
Tarabzun　i, 468b, 476b, 645a; v, 712b; vi, 69a, 70b, 71a; x, **216b**; s, 328b – I, 482a, 490b, 665b; V, 717b; VI, 67a, 68b; X, **234a**; S, 328a
Ṭaradiyyāt　I, 587a, 1154b; iii, 309a – I, 606b, 1189a; III, 318b
Ṭarafa b. al-ʿAbd al-Bakrī (VI)　i, 451b; ii, 1028b; iii, 666b; iv, 998b; vi, 603a; vii, 254b, 604a, 763b; x, **219a** –
I, 464b; II, 1052a; III, 688a; IV, 1031a; VI, 587b; VII, 256a, 603b, 765a; X, **236a**
al-Ṭaraʾifī, Aḥmad b. ʿAbdūs　iv, 668a – IV, 695b
Ṭaraʾifiyya　iv, 668a – IV, 695b
Tārā Ḵhān　s, 327b – S, 327a
Tarakzay Mohmands　vii, 220a – VII, 222a
`tarančis (Kāshghar)　x, **220b** – X, **238b**
Tarannum　iv, 413b – IV, 431b
Taranto/Tarante　→ Iṭāliya
Tārāpūr (Māndū)　vi, 407a – VI, 391b, 392a
Tārashni (1023)　vii, 613a – VII, 612b
Ṭarāwīḥ　x, **222a** – X, **239b**
Ṭarāz (Talas)　iv, 188b; vi, 420a; ix, 621b, 622a; x, **222a** – IV, 197a; VI, 405a; IX, 645a, b; X, **240a**
Tarbiya (education)　x, **223a** – X, **241a**
Tarbiyat Ḵhān (XVII)　vii, 318b – VII, 320b
Ṭard　→ Ṣayd
Tardī Beg　i, 1135b, 1136a – I, 1170a
Ṭardiyya　x, **223a** – X, **241a**
Tardj (Ḵhathʿam)　vi, 435b, 436a – VI, 421a
Tardjama　x, **224a** – X, **242b**
Tardjiʿ-band/Tarkīb-band　i, 677b; iii, 273b; iv, 715a; x, **235b** – I, 698a; III, 281b; IV, 743b; X, **253b**
Tardjumān (Turdjumān)　ii, 476b, 980a; x, **236a** – II, 488b, 1002b; X, **254b**
al-Tardjumān al-Mayūrḳī, ʿAbd Allāh (Fray Anselmo Turmeda)　vi, 927a – VI, 919a
Tardu b. Isṭami (603)　x, 687a , 691b- X, 729b, 734a
Ṭarfīd(e)s　i, 709a – I, 729b
Ṭarghī　ii, 268b; iv, 921b – II, 277a; IV, 954b
Ṭarī (gold coin)　x, **238b** – X, **257b**
Tari Taghāʿī　iii, 968b – III, 993a
Taʿrīb　x, **240a** – X, **258b**
Ṭarīf (VIII)　i, 493a, 1044a – I, 507b, 1075b
Taʿrīf　x, **241a** – X, **259b**
Ṭarīf, Āl (Yemen)　vi, 30b; s, 335a – VI, 28b; S, 334b
Ṭarīf, Djazīrat　→ Ṭarīfa
Ṭarīfa　i, 7a, 493a; vi, 573a; x, **241b**; I, 7a, 507b; VI, 558a; x, **260a**
Tarifiyt　x, **242a** – X, **260b**
Ṭarīfiyya (Ibāḍī)　iii, 659a – III, 680b
Ṭāriḳ b. Suwayd al-Haḍramī　iv, 995b – IV, 1028a
Ṭāriḳ b. Ziyād b. ʿAbd Allāh (VIII)　i, 50a, 493a, 985b, 1175a; ii, 352b, 524b, 786a; iii, 298b; iv, 665a; vi, 221b, 744a; vii, 643b; x, **242a**; s, 92a –
I, 51b, 507b, 1016a, 1210a; II, 362b, 537b, 805a; III,

307b; IV, 692a; VI, 215b, 733a; VII, 643a; X, **261a**; S, 91b
al-Ṭarīḳ al-S̲h̲arḳi iii, 362b – III, 374a
al-Ṭarīḳ al-Sulṭānī iii, 362b – III, 373b, 374a
Ṭarīḳa ii, 164a, 224a; iv, 47b, 167b, 168a; v, 1200a; vi, 87b; x, **243b** – II, 169a, 231a; IV, 50b, 174b, 175a, b; V, 1190b; VI, 85b; X, **262b**
Taʾrīk̲h̲ ii, 307a, 315a; iii, 468a, 838b; x, **257b** – II, 315b, 324a; III, 484a, 862b; X, **276b**
Taʾrīk̲h̲ al-Bāb i, 836a; iv, 346a – I, 859a; IV, 360b
Taʾrīk̲h̲ al-Hind al-G̲h̲arbī iii, 1045b – III, 1071b
Taʾrīk̲h̲ al-Islām ii, 215a, b – II, 222a, b
Taʾrīk̲h̲ al-Mustabṣir iii, 881a – III, 905a
Taʾrīk̲h̲ al-Sūdān ii, 251b, 252a – II, 259a
Tāʾrīk̲h̲-i D̲j̲alālī → D̲j̲alālī
Taʾrīk̲h̲-i Ilāhī → Ilāhī Era
Taʾrīk̲h̲-i ʿOt̲h̲mānī End̲j̲ümeni i, 505b, 1089b; ii, 475a – I, 520b, 1122a; II, 487a
Tarim (Basin) (Sinkiang) ix, 648a, 649b; x, **302a**, 707a – IX, 673b, 674b; X, **325a**. 751b
Tarīm (Yemen) vi, 82b, 132b, 490a; x, **302b**; s, 337b, 338a, 339a, 420b – VI, 80b, 130b, 476a; X, **326a**; S, 337a, 337b, 338b, 420b
Tarīm b. Ḥaḍramawt b. Saba' al-Asg̲h̲ar x, 303a – X, 326a
Tarīm al-Sukūn b. al-As̲h̲ras b. Kinda x, 303a – X, 326a
Tarīn iii, 335b, 336a – III, 345b, 346a
Tarisapally vi, 458b – VI, 444a
Tariverdiov → Ḥaydar K̲h̲ān ʿAmū Ug̲h̲lī
al-Ṭarḳ bi 'l-Ḥasā K̲h̲aṭṭ
Ṭarḳala (Sūs) vi, 741a – VI, 730a
Tarkan K̲h̲ātūn bint ʿIzz al-Dīn Masʿūd b. Ḳuṭb al-Dīn Mawdūd (1242) vi, 871b – VI, 862a
Ṭark̲h̲ān (title/titre) x, **303a – X, 326a**
Tark̲h̲ān, al-K̲h̲(ʷ)arizmī Ras (VIII) iv, 1174a – IV, 1207b
Ṭark̲h̲ān Nīzak → Nīzak Ṭark̲h̲ān
Tark̲h̲āns vi, 189b; ix, 634b – VI, 173a; IX, 659a
Ṭarkī (Tārk̲h̲ū) ii, 86a, 87a – II, 87b, 89a
Tarkīb-band → Tard̲j̲īʿ-Band
Tarma ii, 114a – II, 116b
Tarmas̲h̲īrīn (Mongol) (1326) i, 418b; ii, 4a, 45a, 922b; v, 598a; vii, 113a, 412a – I, 430b; II, 4a, 46a, 944a; V, 601b; VII, 115a, 413b
Ṭarom → Ṭarum
Ṭarrakūna (Tarragona/-e) x, **303b** – X, **326b**
Ṭarrār x, **304a** – X, **327a**
Ṭars̲h̲ x, **304b** – X, **327b**
Tarsīʿ x, **394b** – X, **328a**
Ṭarsūs (Tarsus/-e) i, 183a; ii, 35b, 36b, 129b; vi, 338a, 506a, 775a; x, **306a**; s, 120b – I, 188a; II, 36b, 37a, 133a; VI, 322a, 491b, 764b; X, **329a**; S, 120a
Ṭarsūsī, Abū Ṭāhir → Abū Ṭāhir Ṭarsūsī
al-Ṭarsūsī, Abū ʿAma ʿUt̲h̲mān x, 307a – X, 330b
al-Ṭarsūsī, Mardī (Murdā) b. ʿAlī b. Mardī (XII) x, **307a** – X, **330b**
al-Tarsūsī, Nad̲j̲m al-Dīn (1348) ix, 539a – IX, 560b
al-Ṭarsūsī, ʿUt̲h̲mān b. ʿAbd Allāh (X) viii, 498b – VIII, 515b
Tartar → Tatar
Tārtāra vii, 548b – VII, 548b
Tartīb x, **307b** – X, **331a**
Tartiya-rustāḳ vi, 513a – VI, 498a
Tarṭūs (Tortosa/-e) i, 825a; vi, 538a, 577b, 578b, 579a, b, 581b; ix, 268a; x, **309b** – I, 848a; VI, 522b, 562b, 563b, 564a, b, 566a; IX, 276b; X, **333a**
Tārūdānt/Taroudant vi, 742a, 743b, 893a; ix, 900b; x, **310b**; s, 48a, 402b – VI, 721a, 733b, 884b; IX, 936b; X, **334b**; S, 48b, 403a
Ṭārum/Ṭārom (Daylam) ii, 192a; vi, 515b, 539a; vii, 497b, 655b, 657a; x, **311a** – II, 198a; VI, 500b, 523b; VII, 497b, 655a, 656b; X, **334b**
Tārūt iv, 763b; vii, 142b – IV, 794a; VII, 144b
Tarwiya x, **312b** – X, **336a**
al-Ṭāsa x, **312b** – X, **336b**
Taṣadduḳ Ḥusayn → Nawwāb Mīrzā S̲h̲awḳ
Taṣawwuf i, 60a, 69a, 70b, 89a, 92a, 96a, 138b, 142b, 146a, 195a, 234b, 266b, 280a, 283a, 297b, 298b, 326a, 346b, 352a, 392b, 416a, 441a, 515b, 592b, 701b, 717a, 765b, 794b, 829a, 951a, 957a, 960b, 1088b, 1239b, 1244a; ii, 165a, 166b, 220b, 223b, 242b, 422b, 450a, 1025b, 1041a; iii, 75b, 83b, 103b, 262a, 363a, 662a, 697a, 707b, 752a, 763b; iv, 35a, 46a-b, 47b, 49a, 51b, 64b-65a, 114a, 183b, 467a, 508a, 554b, 616a, 950a, 1074a; v, 333a, 698b, 1235b; x, **313b** – I, 62a, 71a, 72b, 91b, 94b, 98b, 143a, 146b, 147a, 150b, 201a, 242a, 275a, 289a, 291b, 306b, 308a, 336b, 357a, 363a, 403b, 427b, 453b, 531a, 612a, 723a, 738b, 788b, 817b, 852a, 980a, 986b, 990a, 1121a, 1277a, 1282a; II, 170a, 172a, 227b, 230b, 249b, 433b, 462a, 1049b, 1065a; III, 78a, 86a, 105b, 269b, 683b, 719a, 729b, 775a, 787a; IV, 37b, 49a, 50a-b, 52a, 54b, 68a-b, 119a, 191b, 488a, 530a, 578a, 641a, 982b, 1105b; V, 333b, 703b, 1226a; X, **337b**
Tasbīḥ → Subḥa
Taṣdīḳ i, 1242a; iv, 279a – I, 1279b; IV, 291b
Tās̲h̲ Farrās̲h̲ (XI) iii, 1097b; vi, 523a; ix, 157a – III, 1124b; VI, 508a; IX, 162a
Tas̲h̲ Möngke (Mangū) b. Hūlāgū (Mongol) (1252) iv, 1047a; vi, 482a – IV, 1078b; VI, 468a
Tas̲h̲ahhud x, **340b** – X, **366a**
Tas̲h̲an vi, 974a – VI, 966b
Tas̲h̲bīb ii, 1028b; iii, 1006a; iv, 714b; v, 958b – II, 1052a; III, 1031a; IV, 743b; V, 962b
Tas̲h̲bīh i, 275a, 333b, 410b, 414b; iii, 160a; iv, 249b; x, **341a** – I, 283b, 343b, 422b, 426b; III, 163b; IV, 260b; X, **366a**
Tas̲h̲bīh wa-Tanzīh i, 257b, 334a; ii, 388b; x, **341b** – I, 256b, 344a; II, 399a; X, **367a**
Tas̲h̲elḥīt i, 433b, 1181b, 1186a; ii, 116b; ix, 900b; x, **344a** – I, 446a, 1216b, 1221a; II, 119a; IX, 937a; X, **369b**
Tās̲h̲fīn b. ʿAlī b. Yūsuf → Tās̲h̲ufīn
Tās̲h̲fīn b. Tīnʿamer (XII) i, 699b; vi, 427a – I, 720b; VI, 412b
Taṣḥīf x, **347a** – X, **373a**
Tās̲h̲kent i, 46b, 47a; ii, 45b; iii, 224a; v, 30a, b, 399b; vi, 767a, b; s, 50b, 51a, 98a, 228b, 245a, b, 411a; x, **348a** – I, 48a; II, 46a; III, 230b; V, 31a, b, 400b; VI, 756a, b; S, 51a, b, 97a, 228b, 245a, b, 411a; X, **373b**
Tās̲h̲k̲h̲ūd̲j̲a Asīrī (K̲h̲odjand) (1916) x, 65a – X, 67b
Tas̲h̲köprüzāde, ʿIṣām al-Dīn (1561) x, **351b** – X, **377a**
Tas̲h̲köprüzāde, Kemāl al-Dīn (1621) i, 89a, 594b, 698a, 732b; iii, 164a, 467b; iv, 704b; vi, 907a, 971a; x, **352a**; s, 381b, 383b – I, 91b, 614a, 719b, 745b; III, 167b, 483b; IV, 733a; VI, 898b, 963a; X, **377b**; S, 381b, 384a
Tas̲h̲köprüzāde, Muṣliḥ al-Dīn Muṣṭafā (1529)
i, 89a, 594b, 698a, 732b; iii, 164a, 467b; iv, 704b; vi, 907a, 971a; x, **351a**; s, 381b, 383b – I, 91b, 614a, 719b, 745b; III, 167b, 483b; IV, 733a; VI, 898b, 963a; X, **377a**; S, 381b, 384a
Tas̲h̲kun Og̲h̲ullarî i, 1159b – I, 1194a
Tas̲h̲lîd̲j̲alî Yaḥyā (Taşlîcalî) (1582) ii, 937a; iv, 1137b; vi, 610a; vii, 531a; viii, 213a; x, **352a** – II, 959a; IV, 1169a; VI, 594b; VII, 531b; VIII, 217b; X, **378a**

Tashmūt b. Hūlāgū iv, 521a – IV, 544a
Ṭashöz (Thasos) v, 763b; x. **352b** – V, 769b; X, **378b**
Tashrīʿ x, **353a** – X, **378b**
Tashrīfāt → Marāsim I; Nīshān
Tashrīḥ x, **354b** – X, **380b**
Tashrīḳ vii, 65b; x, **356b** – VII, 66b; X, **382b**
Ṭashtamur al-ʿAlāʾī ii, 24a, 1112a – II, 25a, 1138a
Ṭashtikīn (amīr al-ḥadjdj) vi, 434a – VI, 419a
Tashtimur vi, 718b – VI, 707b
Tāshufīn b. ʿAlī (Almoravid(e)) (1145) i, 78b, 390b; ii, 100b, 744b, 1013b; iii, 850b; iv, 290a; x, **357a** – I, 81a, 401b; II, 102b, 763a, 1037a; III, 874b; IV, 303a; X, **388a**
Tasili (Tassili) x, **357b** – X, **383b**
Ṭasinī (Banū Yazīdī) v, 460a – V, 463a
Tasʿīr x, **358b** – X, **384b**
Taṣliya vi, 87b; x, **358b** – VI, 85b; X, **385a**
Tasm, Banū x, **359a** – X, **385a**
Tasmiya → Basmala
Taṣnīf x, **360a** – X, **386a**
Tasnīm x, **360b** – X, **386a**
Taṣrīf x, **360a** – X, **386b**
Tassūdj vi, 504a; x, **361a** – VI, 489b; X, **387b**
Tasūdj-i Dashtī vi, 384b – VI, 368b
Ṭasūdjī, ʿAbd al-Laṭīf iv, 72a – IV, 76a
Taṣwīr x, **361b** – X, **387b**
al-Tasyīr x, **366a** – X, **393a**
Tāt ii, 89a; iv, 313b; v, 604b; x, **368a** – II, 90b; IV, 327b; V, 608b; X, **395a**
iii, 455b; s, 331b – II, 1171a; III, 471b; S, 331a
Tatar i, 32b, 269a, 721b, 722a, 808b, 893b, 1028a, 1106b, 1107a, 1108a, 1188b, 1287a, 1297a, 1302b; ii, 41b, 42b, 68b, 70a, 610b, 995b; iii, 403a; iv, 179a, 280b, 848a, 850a; vi, 378a, 381b, 420a, b, 544a, 547b; vii, 350b; viii, 250b; x, **370a**, 699b; s, 171b – I, 33b, 277a, 743b, 831b, 920a, 1059b, 1139b, 1140b, 1141a, 1223b, 1326b, 1337a, 1342b; II, 42a, b, 43a, 69b, 71b, 625b, 1018b; III, 415b; IV, 186a, 293a, 881a, 883a; VI, 362b, 365b, 405a, 406a, 528b, 532a; VII, 352b; VIII, 267a; X, **397b**, 743a; S, 171b
Tatar (Crimea/-ée) i, 722a, 893b, 894a, 983b, 1000a, 1252a, 1286b; ii, 24b, 88a, 612b; iii, 531b; iv, 500a, 630a, b, 849b; v, 136a, 137b, 139a, b, 720a, **765b** – I, 743b, 920a, b, 1014b, 1031a, 1290a, 1326a; II, 25b, 89b, 627b; III, 550a; IV, 521b, 655a, b, 882b; V, 139a, 140a, 141b, 142b, 725a, **771b**
Tatar (Ḳazan) i, 1188b, 1307b; ii, 366a, 980a – I, 1224a, 1347b; II, 376a, 1002b
Tatar Literature x, **730a** – X, **775b**
Ṭāṭār, al-Ẓāhir Sayf al-Dīn b. al-Muẓaffar Aḥmad (Mamlūk) (1421) i, 1053b; iii, 186a; vii, 172b; s, 39a – I, 1085b; III, 190a; VII, 174b; S, 39b
Tātār Khān b. Muẓaffar Khān (Gudjarāt) (1403) ii, 1125a; vi, 49b – II, 1151b; VI, 47b
Tatār Khān (Lāhawr) (XIV) ii, 973a; iii, 570a – II, 995b; III, 589b
Tatar Khān Lūdī (XV) s, 242a – S, 242a
Tātār Khān Sarang Khānī (XVI) ii, 1144a;
Tatar Pazarcîk x, **371b** – X, **398b**
Taṭarruf x, **372a** – X, **399a**
Tatawlalî Maḥremī (1535) viii, 213a – VIII, 217b
Taṭbīḳ ii, 254b – II, 261b
Tathlīth x, **373b** – X, **400b**
Tathr, Banū vii, 582a – VII, 582b
Tātī iv, 858b; x. **369b** – IV, 891b; X, **396b**
Taʿṭīl → Tashbīh wa-Tanzīh
Tatmīn → Taḍmīn
Tattaʿ vi, 590b – VI, 575b
al-Tattawī → ʿAbd al-Rashīd al-Tattawī
Ṭāʾūḳ → Daḳūḳāʾ
Ṭāʿūn iii, 240a – III, 246b
Taurus → Toros
Ṭāʾūs b. Kaysān (724) i, 1245a; v, 1131b; s, 232b – I, 1283a; V, 1222a; S, 232b
Ṭāʾūs Sīmnānī, Ḳuṭb al-Dīn (XV) i, 91a, 148a – I, 93b, 152b
Tavī (Djamnū) s, 241b – S, 242a
Ṭavīla iv, 219a – IV, 228b
Tavium ii, 62b – II, 63b
Tawābil → Afāwīh
Tawaddud x, **375b** – X, **402b**
Ṭawāf x, **376a** – X, **403a**
Ṭawāʾif →Mulūk al-Ṭawāʾif
Tawakkul x, **376b** – X, **403b**
Tawakkul b. Bazzāz → Ibn al-Bazzāz al-Ardabīlī
Tawakkul b. Tūlak-Beg (XVII) vii, 529b – VII, 530a
Tawakkul Khān, (Kazakh) (XVI) iv, 512a; v, 135a – IV, 534a; V, 138a
Tawallud x, **378a** – X, **405a**
Tawallulī, Farīdūn iv, 72a – IV, 75b
al-Tawʾamān → Minṭaḳat al-Burūdj
Tawargha vi, 311b – VI, 296b
Ṭawāriḳ (Touareg) i, 36b, 39b, 170b, 210b, 254b, 307a, 371a, b, 433b, 809a, 1179b, 1221b, 1259b; ii, 368b, 509b, 740a, 977b, 1022b; iii, 726a, 1038b, 1195b; iv, 777a, 1150a; v, 221b, 754b, 759b, 769b; vi, 258b, 259b, 402b; x, **379a**; s, 164b – I, 37a, 40b, 175a, 217a, 262b, 316b, 382a, b, 446a, 832a, 1214b, 1258a, 1297b; II, 378b, 522a, 758b, 1000a, 1046a; III, 749a, 1064a, 1225b; IV, 808a, 1181b; V, 219a, 760b, 765b, 775b; VI, 243a, b, 387a; X, **406b**; S, 164b
Tawārik (Touareg/Twāreg) Language/-e i, 792a, 1180b, 1182a, b, 1183a, b, 1185a; x, **380b** – I, 815b, 1216a, b, 1217a, b, 1218a, b, 1220a; X, **408a**
Tawārīkh-i Ḳosṭanṭiniyya i, 776b – I, 799b
Tawāshī →Khāṣī I
al-Ṭawāshī, Bahādur al-Shihābī (amīr) (XIV) vi, 580b – VI, 565b
al-Ṭawāshī, Saʿd al-Dawla i, 440a – I, 452b
Ṭawāshī Shudjāʿ al-Dīn ʿAnbar al-Lālā (1324) viii, 156b, 157b – VIII, 159a, 160a
Ṭawāshin i, 33a; iv, 1088a – I, 34a; IV, 1119b
Tawāt → Tuwāt
al-Ṭawāhīn (Palestine) ix, 35a – IX, 35a
Tawātur x, **381b** – X, **409a**
Tawāyiha, Banū iii, 643a – III, 664b
Tawāzun al-Sulutāt, Faṣl al-Sulutāt x, **382a** – X, **410a**
Tawba iv, 1108a, b; x, **385a** – IV, 1139b, 1140a; X, **413a**
Tawba b. al-Ḥumayyir, Abū Ḥarb (674) iv, 912a; v, 710a; vi, 477b, 603a; x, **386a** – IV, 945a; V, 715a; VI, 463b, 588a; X, **413b**
Tawba b. Namir al-Ḥaḍramī (ḳāḍī) vi, 673a –VI, 659b
al-Ṭawfī, Nadjm al-Dīn →al-Ṭūfī
Tawfīḳ x, **386b** – X, **414b**
Tawfīḳ, Sulaymān iv, 857a – IV, 890a
Tawfīḳ Aḥmad s, 224b – S, 224b
Tawfīḳ al-Ḥakīm (1987) vi, 76b, 409a, 746b; x, **386b** – VI, 74b, 393b, 735b; X, **414b**
Tawfīḳ al-Madanī (XX) vi, 753b – VI, 743a
Tawfīḳ Pasha, Aḥmad (Khedive) (1892) i, 13b, 142a, 815a, 1069b; ii, 181b, 514a, 647b; iii, 557a; v, 94a; vi, 531b, 984a; vii, 184a, 434b, 437b; x, **388a**; s, 40a, 408b – I, 13b, 146a, 838b, 1102a; II, 187b, 527a, 663b; III, 576b; V, 96b; VI, 516a, 976b; VII, 184a, 435b, 438b; X, **416b**; S, 40a, 408b
Tawfīḳ Rifʿat Pasha v, 1092a – V, 1089a
Tawḥīd x, **389a** – X, **417a**
al-Tawḥīdī → Abū Ḥayyān al-Tawḥīdī

Ṭawīl (metre) x, **389b** – X, **417b**
Ṭawīl → Ibrāhīm Pa<u>sh</u>a Ṭawīl
Ṭaʾwīl x, **390b** – X **418b**
Ṭawīl, Banu x, **390a** ; s, 80b, 82a – X, **418b**; S, 80b, 81b
al-Ṭawīl, Muḥammad Amīn <u>Gh</u>ālib (XX) viii, 147b – VIII, 149b
al-Ṭawīl, Tād<u>j</u> al-Dīn (1311) viii, 157a – VIII, 159b
Ṭawīl <u>Kh</u>ālīl (<u>D</u>jalālī) s, 238b – S, 238b
Tawīl-og<u>h</u>lu Muṣṭafā (1608) vii, 601a – VII, 600b
Tawīla → Larin
al-Ṭawīla x, **392a** – X, **420b**
Tawke (Kaza<u>kh</u> <u>Kh</u>ān) (XVIII) x, 681b – X,
Tawḳīʿ x, **392b** – X, **420b**
Tawḳīt → Mīkāt
Tawlūd (island/île) vi, 641b – VI, 626b
Tawliyat, Abu ʾl-Faḍl s, 158a – S, 158a
Tawrāt x, **393b** – X, **421b**
Tawrīḳ x, **395a** – X, **423b**
Tawriya x, **395a** – X, **423b**
al-Tawrīzī, Nūr al-Dīn ʿAlī (1429) iv, 642b – IV, 669a
Ṭāwūs → Ṭāʾūs
Ṭāwūs (peacock) x, **396a** – X, **424b**
Ṭāwūs al-ʿUrafāʾ, Saʿādat ʿAlī <u>Sh</u>āh (1876) viii, 47a – VIII, 47b
Ṭawūsiyya x, **397b** – X, **426a**
Tawwābūn ix, 826a; x, **398a** – IX, 850b; X, **426b**
Tawwa<u>dj</u> (Tawwaz) vi, 383b; vii, 357a; x, **398b** – VI, 368a; VII, 359a; X, **427a**
al-Tawwātī, Aḥmad al-Tihāmī (1715) s, 44a – S, 44b
al-Tawwazī (847) vii, 279b, 281a – VII, 281b, 282b
Tawzar/Tūzar ii, 463a, 464a; vii, 897a – II, 475a, 476a; VII, 898a
Tawzīʿ ii, 145b – II, 149b
Taxila s, 259b – S, 259b
al-Ṭayālisī, Abū Dāwūd (819) iii, 24a; vii, 706a; x. **398b** – III, 25a; VII, 707a; X, **427a**
al-Ṭayālisī. <u>D</u>jaʿfar b. Muḥammad (X) x, **399a** – X, **427b**
Ṭayammum x, **395b** – X, **428a**
Ṭayba → al-Madīna
Ṭaybād viii, 267a – VIII, 274a
Ṭaybarṣ al-Wazīrī, ʿAlāʾ al-Dīn (XIII) i, 814b; iii, 228b; vi, 507b – I, 838a; III, 235b; VI, 493a
Ṭaybug<u>h</u>ā al-A<u>sh</u>rafī al-Bi(a)klimi<u>sh</u>ī al-Yūnānī iv, 797a; vi, 543a – IV, 829b; VI, 527b
Ṭaybug<u>h</u>ā al-ṭawīl (1366) ix, 54b – IX, 160a
Tayčiʾut, Banū vi, 417b – VI, 402b
Ṭayf al-<u>Kh</u>ayāl x, **400a** – X, **428b**
Ṭayfūr iv, 811a – IV, 843b
Ṭayfūr b. ʿĪsā → Abū Yazīd al-Biṣṭāmī
Ṭayfūr al-Dīn i, 859a – I, 882b
Ṭayfūrid(e)s i, 862a – I, 886b
al-Taylasān → Tāli<u>sh</u>
Taym b. Murra, Banū (Taym Ḳuray<u>sh</u>) vi, 145a, 263a; vii, 393a; x, **401a** – VI, 143a, 247b; VII, 394a; X, **430a**
Taym Allāh b. <u>Th</u>aʿlaba, Banū x, **400b** – X, **429a**
Taymāʾ i, 547b, 1231a; x, **401b**; s, 117a – I, 565a, 1267b; X, **430a**; S, 116b
Taymallāt b. <u>Th</u>aʿlaba i, 963b – I, 993b
Taymannīs i, 224b; ii, 5b; s, 367b – I, 231a; II, 5b; S, 367a
al-Taymī → Abū Ḥanīfat al-Nuʿmān
al-Taymī, Hilāl b. ʿUllafa (VII) viii, 638a – VIII, 657a
Taymūr, Maḥmūd → Maḥmūd Taymūr
Taymūr, Muḥammad (1921) i, 597b, 598a; v, 189a – I, 617a, b; V, 186a
Taymūr Muḥammad b. ʿAlī Kurd (XIX) vi, 75a – VI, 73a
Taymūr b. Fayṣal (Bū Saʿīd) (1932) i, 1283a; vi, 735b – I, 1322a; VI, 724b
Taymūr Ba<u>kh</u>tiyār (1970) vii, 448b – VII, 450a
Taymūr Mīrzā iv, 393a; s, 290b – IV, 409b; S, 290a
Taymūrī i, 224b; ii, 5b; iii, 1107b – I, 231a; II, 5b; III, 1135a
al-Taymūriyya, ʿĀʾi<u>sh</u>a (1902) i, 597b; vii, 903a – I, 617a; VII, 903b
al-Ṭayr → al-Ṭāʾir
Tayrāb → Muḥammad Tayrāb
Ṭayyār al-Furāt → al-Ḳaʿkaʿ b. Maʿbad
Ṭayyār Maḥmūd Pa<u>sh</u>a (1807) ii, 207b; iv, 322b; vii, 719a – II, 214a; IV, 337a; VII, 720a
Ṭayyār Pa<u>sh</u>a-zāde Aḥmed Pa<u>sh</u>a v, 258a – V, 256a
al-Ṭayyāriyya → al-<u>D</u>janāḥiyya
Ṭayyiʾ/Tayy, Banū i, 528a, b, 544b, 563b, 683a; 1241a; ii, 262a, 482b; v, 348a; vi, 472a, 474b; vii, 116b, 461a, b, 672a; viii, 865a; x, 62a, **402b**; s, 37b, 304b – I, 544a, b, 561b, 581b, 704a, 1279a; II, 241a 495a; V, 349a; VI, 246b; 458a, 460b; VII, 118b, 461a, b, 672a; VIII, 895b; X, 64a, **431a**; S, 37b, 304a, b
Ṭayyiʾ, <u>D</u>jabala i, 203a; ii, 482b – I, 209a; II, 495a
al-Ṭayyib, Mawlāy (1679) s, 404a – S, 404b
al-Ṭayyib b. al-Āmir (Faṭimid(e)) (XII) i, 440a; ii, 170b, 858b; iii, 1168b; iv, 200a; vi, 191a – I, 452b; II, 175b, 878b; III, 1197b; IV, 209a; VI, 175a
al-Ṭayyib al-Sāsī (XX) vi, 176b – VI, 162a
al-Ṭayyib al-Ṣiddīḳī (XX) vi, 114b, 755b, 756a – VI, 112a, 745a
Ṭayyib<u>dj</u>ī, Badr al-Dīn iii, 1204a – III, 1234b
Ṭayyibī, Banū iii, 1107a – III, 1134a
Ṭayyibī Ismāʿīliyya → Ismāʿīliyya
Ṭayyibiyya i, 371a; ii, 98a; iii, 71b, 134a, 1168b; iv, 200b, 201a, 204a, b; v, 166b; x, 247b, **403a**; s, 44à, 61b – I, 382a; II, 100a; III, 74a, 136b, 1197b; IV, 209a, b, 210a, 213a, b; V, 164b; X, 266a, **431b**; S, 44b, 62a
Ṭayyib<u>sh</u>āh → <u>D</u>jalāl al-Dīn Ṭayyib<u>sh</u>āh
Ṭāz (amīr) → al-Ẓāhirī, Sūdūn min ʿAlī Bak
Tāzā i, 355b; iii, 499a; vi, 141b, 572a, 592a, 681b, 741a; x, **404a**; s, 63b, 377b – I, 366b; III, 516a; VI, 140a, 557a, 577a, 668b, 669a, 730a; X, **433a**; S, 64a, 377b
Tāzarwālt/Tāzerwālt iii, 535b; vi, 589b, 743a, 744a, 774a; x, **405a** – III, 554a, b; VI, 574b, 732b, 733a, 763a; X, **434a**
al-Tāzī (1831) vi, 356b – VI, 340b
al-Tāzī, Ibrāhīm b. Muḥammad (XV) ix, 20b – IX, 21a
Taʿzīr ii, 519a; ix, 547b, 548b; x, **406a** – II, 532a; IX, 569b; X, **484b**
Taʿziya ii, 848b; iv, 50b, 73b, 857a; v, 636b; x, **406b** – II, 868a; IV, 53a, 77b, 890a; V, 640b; X, **435a**
Tazwīr x, **408b** – X, **432b**
Tazyīf x, **409b** – X, **438b**
Tbilisi → Tiflīs
Tchad → Čad
Teba s, 152b – S, 153a
Tebessa x, **410b**; s, 144b, 145a, 387a – X, **439b**; S, 144a, b, 387b
Tebou ii, 875a, 876a, 877a; v, 760a – II, 895b, 896b, 897b; V, 766a
Teda → Tūbū
Te<u>dj</u>en (river/rivière) vi, 494b – VI, 480a
Tegüder (Takudar) (Īl-<u>kh</u>ān) (1284) i, 903a; ii, 606b, 607b; iii, 1122a; iv, 31a, 620b, 817b, 975b; v, 827a; x, **411b** - I, 930a; II, 621b, 622b; III,1250a; IV, 33b, 645b, 850a, 1008a; V, 833a; X, **441a**
Tehran/Teheran → Tihrān

Tʿeimuraz → Tahmūrath
Tekālif x, **412a** – X, **441b**
Teke-eli x, **412a** – X, **441b**
Tekele b. Muẓaffar al-Dīn (Salghurid(e)) (1198) viii, 978b – VIII, 1013a
Teke-oghullarî (Türkmen) i, 517b; x, **412b** – I, 533a; X, **442b**
Tekfur (Bursa) i, 1333b; x, **413b** – I, 1374a; X, **443a**
Tekīn (933) v, 329b – V, 329b
Tekin Alp (Moïse Cohen) (XX) vi, 94a; viii, 251a – VI, 91b; VIII, 267b
Tekine Mirza (XV) iii, 44a – III, 46a
Tekirdagh vi, 290b, 588b; x, **414a** – VI, 275b, 573b; X, **443b**
Tekish, b. Il Arslan ʿAlā ʾl-Dīn (Khwārazmshāh) (1200) ii, 253a, 606a, 1101b; iii, 1111b; iv, 29b, 102a, 583a, 1067b; vi, 482a, 908a, 997a, b; viii, 63b, 749a; x, **414b**; s, 245b – II, 260b, 621a, 1127b; III, 1139a; IV, 32a, 106b, 606b, 1099a; VI, 468b, 899b, 998b, 999a; VIII, 65a, 779a; X, **444b**; S, 245b
Tekish b. Alp Arslān (Saldjūḳ) (XI) iv, 27b; vi, 273b – IV, 29b; VI, 258b
Tekke i, 467b; ii, 695a; v, 269b; x. **415a** – I, 481b; II, 712b; V, 267a; X, **445a**
Tekke (Türkmen) s, 143b, 145a, 146b, 147a, 281a – S, 143a, 145a, 146b, 147a, 281a
Tekkelū iii, 1105a – III, 1132b
Tekedji-zāde Ibrāhīm Efendi i, 776a – I, 799a
Teleorman → Deli-Orman
Telingāna vi, 269a; vii, 412a, 459a; x, **416b** – VI, 254a; VII, 413a, 459a; X, **446a**
Teliyāgaṛhī pass/défilé de - vi, 47a – VI, 45b
Telkhīṣ x, **416b** – X, **446b**
Telkhīṣdjı x, **416b** – X, **446a**
Tell → Tall
Tell Abū Sēfe iv, 556a; vi, 378a – IV, 580a; VI, 362b
Tell ʿAdjāba → ʿArbān
Tell al-Aḥmar → Tell Abū Sēfe
Tell ʿArān vi, 380a – VI, 364b
Tell Bāshir Tall Bāshir
Tell Espī iv, 498b – IV, 520a
Tell Ḥamdūn vi, 507b – VI, 493a
Tell Kawkab vi, 539b – VI, 524a
Tell Khālid vi, 544a – VI, 528b
Tell el-Kheleyife i, 558b – I, 576a
Tell Muraybat vi, 733a – VI, 722b
Telugu v, 648a – V, 652a
Temeshwár i, 291b; v, 1023a; vii, 708a; x, **417a** – I, 300b; V, 1019a; VII, 708b; X, **446b**
Temirboghā → Timurbugha
Temīr-Khān-Shūrā → Makhač-ḳalʿe
Templiers → Dāwiyya et Isbitāriyya
Temučin/Temüdjin → Čingiz Khān
Temürtash → Timurtash
Tenedos → Bozdja-ada
Ténès → Tanas
Tenggarong s, 151a – S, 151a
Tengku Abdul Rahman s, 152a – S, 152a
Tenovajib iii, 289a – III, 298a
Tepebashî vi, 57a – VI, 55a
Tepedelen ʿAlī Pasha → ʿAlī Pasha Tepedelenli
Teptyar x, **417b** – X, **447a**
Teraḳḳī-perver Djumhūriyyet Fîrkasî ii, 432a, 596a; iv, 854a, 934b; x, **417b**; s, 41b – II, 433b, 610b; IV, 887a, 967b; X, **447b**; S, 42a
Terdjān x, **418a** – X, **448a**
Terdjümān (in mysticism) x, **418b** – X, **448b**
Terdjümān-i Aḥwāl ii, 466a, 473b – II, 478a, 485b
Terdjüme Odasî iii, 553b – III, 572b
Terek x, **418b** – X, **448b**
Terengganu vi, 232b, 236b, 239b; x, **419a** – VI, 206a, 209a, 214b; X, **448b**
Ierengganu (Demak) (1546) ix, 852b – IX, 888a
Terengganu Stone/Pierre de vi, 210b, 234a – VI, 195a, 207a
Terken Khātūn x, **419a** – X, **449a**
Terken Khātūn (Kutlugh Khanid(e) (1281) v, 162a, 553b, 554a; vi, 482b; ix, 110b – V, 160a, 558b, 559a; VI, 468b; IX, 115a
Terken Khātūn (wife of/épouse de Malik Shāh, Saldjūḳ) (1094) i, 1051b, 1071b; iv, 28b, 101b; vi, 274a, 275a, 482a; vii, 541a; viii, 72a; x, 419b; s, 384a - I, 1083a, 1103a; IV, 30b, 106a; VI, 259a, 260a, 468a, b; VII, 541a; VIII, 74a; X, 449a; S, 384b
Terken Khātūn (wife of/épouse de Tekish, Saldjūḳ) (1232) iv, 30a; vi, 482a – IV, 32a; VI, 468a,b
Ternate x, **419b**; s, 199b – X, **449b**; S, 199b
Tersāne x, **420a** – X, **450a**
Terter I i, 1302b – I, 1342a
Terter II i, 1302b – I, 1342a
Tesalya (Thessaly) x, **420b** – X, **450b**
Teshrifāt → Marāsim. 4
Teshrīfātdji ii, 338b – II, 348b
Tetouan → Tiṭṭāwīn
Teukos the Babylonian/de Babylone → Tankalūshā al-Bābilī
Teuku Muḥammad Ḥasan i, 745a, 746a, 746b – I, 767a, 768b
Teuku Njaʿ Arif i, 745a, 746a, 746b – I, 767a, 768b, 769a
Teuku Panglima Pōlém Muḥammad Dāwūd i, 744a, 746a – I, 766a, 768b
Teungku Andjōng i, 742a – I, 764b
Teungku di-Kuala → ʿAbd al-Raʾūf al-Sinkilī
Teungku Muḥammad Dāwūd Bevereuʾéh i, 746a, 747a – I, 768b, 769b
Tewfik Bey → Ebüziya Tevfik
Tewfīk Fikret (1915) i, 287b; ii, 440a, 474b, 475a; iii, 357b; iv, 169a, 195b, 931a; vi, 93a, 614b; vii, 469a; ix, 240b; x, **422b**; s, 98a, 149b – I, 296a; II, 451b, 486b, 487a; III, 368b; IV, 176a, 204a, 964a; VI, 91a, 599b; VII, 468b; IX, 247a; x, **452b**; S, 97b, 150a
Tewfīḳ Meḥmed → Čaylaḳ Tewfīḳ
Tewfīḳ Pasha → Tawfīḳ Pasha
Tewfîq, Hacî v, 482b – V, 485b
Tewḳiʿī ʿAbd ul-Raḥmān Pasha (1676) viii, 752b – VIII, 774a
Teyran, Feqiyê v, 482a – V, 485a
Thāʾ x, **423b** – X, **453b**
Thaʿāliba, Banū vi, 141a – VI, 139b
al-Thaʿālibī, ʿAbd al-ʿAzīz (1944) viii, 901a; x, **424b** – VIII, 931b; X, **454b**
al-Thaʿālibī, ʿAbd al-Raḥmān b. Muḥammad b. Makhlūf (1468) vi, 143a; ix, 20b; x, **425b**, 427b – VI, 141a; IX, 21a; X, **456a**, 458a
al-Thaʿālibī, Abū Manṣūr (XI) x, **425b** – X, **456a**
al-Thaʿālibī, Abū Manṣūr ʿAbd al-Malik b. Muḥammad b. Ismāʿīl (1038) i, 321b, 590a, 591a, 845b, 952b, 1348b; ii, 918b; iii, 1157b; iv, 54b, 1066b; v, 619a, 1226b; vi, 109a, 340a; vii, 262a, 470a, 527b, 986a; viii, 1028b; x, 68a, **426a**; s, 119b – I, 331b, 609b, 610a, 869a, 981b, 1389a; II, 940a; III, 1186a; IV, 57b, 1098a; V, 623a, 1216b; VI, 107a, 324b; VII, 264a, 469b, 527b, 528a, 986b; VIII, 1063b; X, 90b, **456b**; S, 119a
al-Thaʿālibī, Abū Manṣūr al-Ḥusayn al-Marghanī (XI) ii, 133b; iii, 114a – II, 136b, III, 116a
al-Thaʿālibī, al-Shaykh (XX) v, 1161a – V, 1151a
al-Thaʿālibī, Sīdī ʿAbd al-Raḥmān ii, 520a – II, 533a

Thabāba b. Salāma al-Djudhāmī iv, 494b – IV, 516a
Thabīr, Djabal viii, 383b; x, **428a** – VIII, 396b; X, **458b**
al-Thabīr (well/source) vi, 666b; vii, 65a – VI, 652b; VII, 65b
Thābit, ʿAlā al-Dīn ʿAlī (1712) vi, 826b; x, **428a** – VI, 817a; X, **458b**
Thābit, Banū → ʿAmmār, Banū
Thābit b. al-ʿAbbās b. Mandīl (XIII) vi, 404a, b – VI, 388b, 389a
Thābit b. Arkān (VII) vii, 756b – VII, 758a
Thābit b. Djābir b. Sufyān → Taʾabbaṭa Sharran
Thābit b. Ḳays iii, 403b – III, 416a
Thābit b. Ḳurra, Abū 'l-Ḥasan b. Zahrūh al- Ḥarrānī (Ṣābiʾ) (901) i, 235b, 589b, 1100b, 1101a; iii, 166a, 228a, 1135a, 1136b, 1138b; iv, 110b, 629a, 804b, 1078b; vi, 204a, 215a, 600b; vii, 83a, 210a, 559a; viii, 558a, 560a, 672b, 677b; x, **428b**; s, 59b, 271b, 411b, 412a, 414a –
I, 242b, 608b, 1113b, 1134a; III, 169b, 235a, 1163b, 1165a, 1167a; IV, 115b, 654a, 836b, 1110a; VI, 188b, 199a, 585a; VII, 84a, 211b, 559b; VIII, 576a, 578a, 693a, 697a; X, **459a**' S, 60a, 271a, 412a, 414a
Thābit b. Ḳuṭba (Bukhāra) (VII) ix, 250a – IX, 257a
Thābit b. Naṣr al-Khuzāʿī (VIII) vi, 332a, 775a – VI, 316b, 764b
Thābit b. Nuʿaym (VIII) vi, 623b, 624a – VI, 608b, 609a
Thābit b. Sinān i, 1223b, 1353b; iii, 387b, 388a – I, 1260a, 1392b; III, 400a, b
Thābit al-Ḥaddād, Abu 'l-Miḳdād s, 129b – S, 129a
Thābit Ḳuṭna, Abū 'l-ʿAlāʾ Thābit b. Kaʿb Djābir (728) vii, 606a; x, **429b** – VII, 606a; X, **460a**
Thabraca → Tabarka
Thaddarth iv, 359a, 361b – IV, 375a, 377b
Thādj x, **429b** – X, **460a**
Thaghr → al-Thughūr
Thaghr al-Aʿlā (Araghūn) s, 80b – S, 80b
al-Thaghrī, Abū ʿAbd Allāh Muḥammad b. Yūsuf (XIV) ix, 347a – IX, 358a
al-Thaghrī, Abū Saʿīd Yūsuf b. Muḥammad al-Ṭāʾī (IX) i, 1289a; x,**430a** – I, 1328b; X, **461a**
al-Thaghrī, Aḥmad (XV) vi, 222b – VI, 216b
Thailand, Islam in - v, 227a; x, **430a** – V, 224b; X, **461a**
al-Thāʾir fī ʾllāh, Abu 'l-Faḍl Djaʿfar b. Muḥammad (961) iii, 255a; vi, 941b; x, **430b**; s, 363a – III, 262b; VI, 933b; X, **461b**; S, 363a
Thāʾirid(e)s s, 363a – S, 363a
al Thaḳafī → Abū ʿUbayd; ʿĪsā b. ʿUmar; Ismāʿīl b. ʿAlī b. ʿUthmān
al-Thaḳafī, Ahmad b. ʿUbayd Allāh (926) vi, 829a – VI, 819b
al-Thaḳafī, al-ʿAlāʾ b. Djāriya vii, 570b – VII, 571b
al-Thaḳafī, Ibrāhīm b. Muḥammad (896) x, **431a** – X, **462a**
al-Thaḳafī, al-Mughīra b. Shuʿba (VII) vi, 499a – VI, 484b
al-Thaḳafī, Muḥammad b. Ḳāsim → Muḥammad b. Ḳāsim al-Thaḳafī
al-Thaḳafī, Tammām b. ʿĀmir (vizier) (IX) vii, 569a – VII, 569b
al-Thaḳafī, Yūsuf b. ʿUmar b. Muḥammad (744) iii, 493b; iv, 926a, 927a; v, 374b; vi, 139b, 140a, 441b; vii, 629b; x, **431b**; s, 127a, 232b, 251b – III, 510b; IV, 959a, 960a; V, 375a; VI, 137b, 138b, 427a; VII, 629b; X, **462b**; S, 126b, 232b, 251b
al-Thaḳafī, Yūsuf al-Barm (VIII) vi, 618a – VI, 602b
Thaḳafīs vi, 266a, b, 646a, 657a – VI, 250b, 251a, 631b, 642b
Thaḳīf, Banū i, 145a, 544b; iii, 286a, 363b; v, 520b; vi, 266a, 677a; vii, 347a; x, 115a, **432a** – I, 149a, 562a; III, 294b, 375a; V, 524a; VI, 250b, 664a; VII, 349a; X, 124b, **463a**
Thala s, 387a – S, 387a
Thaʿlab (fox/renard) x, **432b** – X, **464a**
Thaʿlab, Abu 'l-ʿAbbās Aḥmad (1904) x, **433a** – X. **464b**
Thaʿlab, Aḥmad b. Yaḥyā (904) i, 321b, 485b, 590a, 718b, 971b; ii, 245b, 806b, 1093b; iii, 758a, 820b; iv, 249a; v, 320a, 351a, 607b, 1033a; vi, 348a; vii, 277a, 280a, 282a, 312b, 390b, 914a; viii, 546a; ix, 318a; x, 69a; s, 15b, 25a, 388a, 389b –
I, 331b, 500a, 609b, 740a, 1001b; II, 252b, 826a, 1119a; III, 781a, 844a; IV, 260a; V, 319a, 351b, 611b, 1029a; VI, 332a; VII, 279a, 281b, 283b, 314b, 392a, 914b; VIII, 564a; IX, 328a; X, 71b; S, 16a, 25a, 388b, 390a
Thaʿlab, Sharīf Ḥisn al-Dīn (XIII) viii, 864b – VIII, 895a
Thaʿlaba, Banū (Sulaym) ix, 817a; x, **433b** – IX, 852a; X, **465a**
Thaʿlaba b. ʿUkūba, Banū i, 962b; ii, 71b – I, 992b; II, 73a
Thaʿlaba b. Salāma al-ʿĀmilī i, 134b; ii, 1009a; iii, 602a – I, 138b; II, 1032b; III, 622b
Thaʿlaba b. Yarbūʿ, Banū vi, 267a, b, 268a – VI, 251b, 252a, 253a
al-Thaʿlabī, Abū Isḥāḳ Aḥmad v, 180b – V, 178a
al-Thaʿlabī (al-Taghlibī), Muḥammad b. al-Ḥārith (IX) x, **434a** – X, **465b**
al-Thaʿlabī/al-Taghlibī, al-Amīr al-Ḥamdānī → Mihmindār
al-Thaʿlabī al-Nīshābūrī, Aḥmad b. Muḥammad (1035) vii, 283b; x, **434a**; s, 90b – VII, 285b; X, **465a**; S, 90a
al-Thaʿlabiyya x, **434b**; s, 198b – X, **466a**; S, 198b
Thaldj, Banū x, 435a – X, 466b
Thallādj x, **435a** – X, **466b**
Thālnēr iii, 446b; vi, 51a, 127b; x, **435b** – III, 461b; VI, 49b, 125b; X, **467b**
Thamādi → al-Djarādatān[i]
Thamal, amīr i, 449b – I, 462b
al-Thamara iii, 746a – III, 768b
Thāmir iv, 314b – IV, 328b
Thamisṭiyus (Themistius) (388) x, **435b** – X, **467b**
Thamūd, Banū i, 145a, 169b, 548a; iii, 366a, 1270a; v, 763a; x, **436a** – I, 149a, 174a, 565a; III, 377b, 1303a; V, 769a; X, **469b**
Thamudic/Thamoudéen i, 562b, 564b; vi, 349a, 373b; x, **436b** – I, 580b, 582b; VI, 333a, 358a; X, **467b**
Thānā (ville/town) iii, 418b; x, **438b** – III, 432a; X, **470b**
Thanāʾ Allāh, Mawlānā (XIX) iii, 431b – III, 445b
Thanāʾī (1587) viii, 775b; x, **439a** – VIII, 801b; X, **470b**
Thanawiyya (Dualist(e)) x, **439b** – X, **471a**
Thānesar (Thāneswar) x, **441b** – X, **473b**
Thānesarī, Mawlānā Aḥmad (1412) x, **442a** – X, **474a**
Thānēsarī, Djalāl al-Dīn Muḥammad b. Maḥmūd (1582) x, **442a**;s, 313a – X, **474a**; S, 312b
Thānesarī, Niẓām al-Dīn (1626) ii, 55a; x, **442b** – II, 56a; X, **474a**
Thānī, Āl i, 539b; ii, 177b; iv, 751b – I, 556b; II, 183a; IV, 782a
Thaniyyat al-aḥīsa x, 959b – X,
Thaniyyat al-ʿUḳāb vi, 544b, 545a, 778b – VI, 529a, b, 768b
Thānkawālā vi, 131a – VI, 129a
Thannuris s, 229b – S, 229b

Thar (desert) vi, 65b – VI, 63b
Tha'r x, **442b** – X, **474b**
Tha'rān b. Dhamar'alī Yuhabirr vi, 563b – VI, 548b
Tha'rān Yuhan'im vi, 563b – VI, 548b
al-Tharwānī, Muḥammad b. 'Abd al-Raḥmān iv, 1003a – IV, 1035a
Tharwat 'Ukāsha s, 6a – S, 5a
Thasos → Ṭashöz
Thathul (Armenian/-ien) vi, 506b – VI, 492a
Thaffā i, 80b; iii, 448b, 633a; vi, 189b; viii, 1047b; x, **443b** – I, 83a; III, 463b, 654a; VI, 173a; VIII, 1083a; X, **475b**
Thawāba b. Salāma i, 135a; iii, 602a – I, 138b; III, 622b
al-Thawr → Minṭaḳat al-Burūdj
Thawr b. Yazīd v, 329b – V, 329b
Thawra x, **444a** – X, **476a**
Thawrān b. Ibrāhīm → Dhu'l-Nūn, Abu 'l-Fayḍ
al-Thawrī → Sufyān al-Thawrī
Thawriyya iv, 46a – IV, 48b
Theodemir Tudmīr
Theodosia/-ie → Kefe
Theophrastus/-te i, 736b, 737b; s, 59b – I, 758b, 759a; S, 60a
Therwet-i Fünūn i, 287a; ii, 439b,440a, 474b, 692b, 877b; iii, 261a; iv, 931a; v, 194b, 195b; x, **445b** – I, 296a; II, 451a, b, 486b, 710a, 898a; III, 268a; IV, 964a; V, 191b, 192b; X, **477b**
Thessaly/-ie vi, 58b – VI, 56b
Thiḳa x, **446a** – X, **478a**
Thiḳat al-Mulk Tāhir b. 'Alī ix, 41 – IX, 4a
Thimāl b. Ṣāliḥ b. Mirdās (Mirdāsid(e)) (1062) iii, 686b, 740b; v, 924a; vii, 117a – III, 708a, 763b; V, 929b; VII, 119a
Thomas the Slav/le Slave (IX) vi, 336a – VI, 320b
al-Thughūr i, 465b, 761a, b, 789b; ii, 36a, 503a; vi, 230b, 775b; x, **446b**; s, 120a – I, 479a, 783b, 784a, 813a; II, 36b, 37a, 515b; VI, 224b, 765a; X, **478a**; S, 119b
Thulā x, **449a** – X, **481b**
Thuluth → Khaṭṭ
Thumāl (amīr) iv, 911a – IV, 944a
Thumāma b. Ashras, Abū Ma'n al-Numayrī (828) i, 271b; ii, 386a; iii, 1266a; vii, 604a, 784b; x, **449b**; s, 48b, 89a – I, 280a; II, 396a; III, 1299a; VII, 604a, 786b; X, **482a**; S, 49a, 88b
Thumāma b. Uthāl i, 964a; iii, 167a; vii, 664b – I, 993b; III, 170b; VII, 664b
Thurayya ('Abalāt, Mecca) (VIII) ii, 1011b – II, 1035a
al-Thurayyā (Baghdād) i, 898a – I, 924b
Thurayyā bint Maḥmūd Ṭarzī (1968) s, 65b – S, 66a
Thurayyā (Sorayya) Isfadiyyārī (XX) vii, 447a – VII, 448a
Thüreyya, Meḥmed (1909) x, **450a** – X, **482b**
Thuwaynī b. Sa'īd b. Sulṭān (Āl Bū Sa'īd) (1866) i, 1282b; v, 1030b; x, 817a – I, 1321b; V, 1026a, b; X,
Ṭibā'a → Maṭba'a
Ṭibāḳ x, **450b** – X, **483a**
Ṭibb ii, 1120a; x, **452a** – II, 1146b; X, **484b**
Tibbat al-Khurd → Baltistān
Ṭibbiyye-i 'adliyye-i Shāhāne ii, 996b – II, 1019b
Tibbu → Tubu
Tibesti x, **461a**; s, 163b, 165a, 166a – X, **494a**; S, 163b, 165a, 166a
Tibet → Tubbat
Ṭībī i, 942b – I, 971b
Tibrīz → Tabrīz
al-Tibrīzī, Abū Zakariyyā' Yaḥyā (1109) x, **461a** – X, **494b**
Tibrīzī, Shams al-Dīn → Sabzawārī, Shams al-Dīn
al-Tidjānī (Māsina) (1887) i, 297a; ii, 941b; ix, 853a – I, 306a; II, 963b;
al-Tidjānī, Abū Muḥammad (XIV) x, **462a** – X, **495b**
al-Tidjānī, Muḥammad b. Aḥmad (1309) i, 207a; ii, 552b; iv, 339b; vi, 574a, 840b; ix, 853a – I, 213b; II, 566b; IV, 354a; VI, 442b, 831a; IX, 889a
al-Tidjānī, Sī Aḥmad b. Maḥmad (1815) i, 297a; ii, 941b; iii, 107b; iv, 550b; vi, 706b; vii, 263a; ix, 22b; x, 248a, 249a, **463a** – I, 306a; II, 963b; III, 110a; IV, 574b; VI, 695a; VII, 265a; IX, 24a; X, 266b, 267b. **496b**
Tidjāniyya i, 297a, 315b, 371a, 1009a, 1260b; ii, 10a, 63a, 94b, 432b, 975a, 1004a; iii, 38b, 107a, 289a, 646b; iv, 549b; v, 287b; vi, 259b, 260a, 356b, 705a, 706b; vii, 620a; x, **464a**; s, 165a, 182a, 371a, 387a – I, 306a, 325a, 382a, 1040a, 1298b; II, 10a, 64b, 96b, 444a, 997b, 1027a; III, 40a, 109b, 298a, 667b; IV, 573b; V, 286a; VI, 244a, b, 340b, 693b, 695a; VII, 619b; x, **497b**; S, 165a, 182a, 371a, 387b
Tidjāra x. **466b** – X, **499b**
Tidjīn-Rūd s, 309b – S, 309a
Tidore x. **475a**; s, 199b – X, **510a**; S, 199b
T'ieh-le (Timg-ling) x, 691b – X, 734a
T'ien Wu (1784) v, 851b; x, **475b** – V, 856a; X, **510b**
al-Tifāshī, Sharaf al-Dīn Aḥmad b. Yūsuf (1253) i, 419b, 1220b; ii, 93b; iv, 881b; vi, 374b; vii, 82b, 1042b; x, **476a** – I, 431a, 1257a; II, 95a; IV, 914a; VI, 359a; VII, 84a, 1044b; X, **511a**
Tifinagh i, 1185a; v, 221b, 222a, 754b-757b; x, **476b** – I, 1220a; V, 219a, b, 760a-763a; X, **511b**
Ṭiflī Aḥmed Čelebi (1660) v, 952a; x, **478a** – V, 955b; X, **513b**
Tiflīs (Tbilisi) i, 644a; iv, 346b, 349a, 391b; v, 487a-489b, 493a, 495a, 497a; vi, 55b, 64b, 203a; vii, 453a; x, **478b**; s, 47a, 275a – I, 664b; IV, 361a, 364a, 408a; V, 490a-492b, 496a, 498a, 500a; VI, 53b, 62b, 187a; VII, 454a; X, **514a**; S, 47b, 274b
Tiflīsī, Abu 'l-Faḍl Ḥubaysh iv, 525b – IV, 548b
al-Tiflīsī, Abū 'Imrān iv, 604a – IV, 628a
al-Ṭighnārī, Abū 'Abd Allāh (XII) ii, 901b; vii, 201a, 203b; x, **479b** – II, 922b; 202a, 204b; X, **515a**
Tighnît vi, 201a – VI, 185a
Tighremt i, 1321b – I, 1361b
Tigin (Takīn) (title/titre) x, **480b** – X, **515b**
Tigīnābād iv, 536b – IV, 537a
Tigre (Tigrinya) → Djabart
Tigris/-e → Didjla
al-Tīh (Faḥs al-Tīh) x. **480b** – X, **516a**
Tihāma (al-Tahā'im) i, 536b, 539a; ii, 1025a; v, 808a, 809a, 1244a, b; vi, 35b, 191b; ix, 815b; x, **481a**; s, 22b, 236, 335a – I, 553a, 555b; II, 1048b; V, 814a, 815a, 1235a; VI, 34a, 175a; IX, 851a; X, **516b**; S, 22b, 236a, 334b
al-Tihāmī, Abu 'l-Ḥasan (1025) vi, 626b; x, **482a** – VI, 611b; X, **517b**
Tihbat-i khurd → Baltistān
Ṭihrān (Teh(e)ran) i, 978a, 1088b; ii, 426a; iv, 7b, 391a; v, 876a; vi, 19b, 20b, 277a, 366a, 484b, 493a, 495b, 528b; x, **482b**; s, 23b, 41a, 73a, 142a, 291a, 423a – I, 1008b, 1121a; II, 437a; IV, 8a, 408a; V, 882a; VI, 17b, 18a, 262a, 350a, 470b, 478b, 481a, 512b; X, **518a**; S, 23b, 41b, 73b, 142a, 290b, 423b
Ṭihran (Iṣfahān) x, **496a** – X, **513b**
al-Ṭihrānī, Āghā Buzurg (1970) x, **496a** – X, **532a**
Ṭihrānī, Ḥadjdjī Mīrzā Ḥusayn Khalīlī (1908) vi, 553a; x, **497b**; s, 95b – VI, 537b; X, **533a**; S, 95a
Tik wa-Tum x, **498a** – X, **533b**
Tikiya-yi Dawlat vi, 485a – VI, 471a

Tikla b. Hazārasp v, 826b – V, 832b
Tikrīt Takrīt
Tilangāna vi, 68a – VI, 66a
Tilangānī, Khān-i Djahān Maḳbūl → Khān-i Djahān Maḳbūl
Tilimsān (Tlemcem) i, 92a, 93a, 122b, 124b, 155a, 168a, 367a, 678b; ii, 173a, 1008a; iii, 251a, 339b, 470a, 1041a, 1042b; v, 518a, 1175a, 1179a; vi, 141a, b, 142a, 187a, 249a, 281a, 311b, 404a, b, 405b, 427a, 440b, 441a, 572a, 573a, 592a, 593a, b, 681b; ix, 20b; x, **498b**; s, 29a, 145a, 376b, 403a – I, 95a, b, 126a, 128a, 159a, 172b, 378a, 699a; II, 178a, 1032a; III, 258b, 349b, 486b, 1067a, 1068b; V, 521b, 1165a, 1169a; VI, 139b, 140a, 170b, 233a, 266a, 296b, 388b, 389a, 390b, 412a, b, 426a, b, 557a, 558a, 577a, 578a, 668b; IX, 21a; X, **534a**; S, 29a, 144b, 376b, 403a
—literature/littérature iii, 832a, 865b – III, 855b, 889b
—monuments i, 499b; iii, 144a; v, 290a, 1151b – I, 514b; III, 145b; V, 289a, b, 1141b
al-Tilimsānī → al-Sharīf
al-Tilimsānī, ʿAbd Allāh b. Muḥammad, Sharīf (1390) ix, **346b** – IX, **357b**
al-Tilimsānī, Abu ʾl-ʿAbbās Aḥmad (1490) ix, **347a** – IX, **358a**
al-Tilimsānī, Abū ʿAbd Allāh al-Sharīf (1369) ix, 364b – IX, 376a
al-Tilimsānī, Abu ʾl-Faradj (1463) ix, **347a** – IX, **358b**
al-Tilimsānī, Abū Yaḥyā , Sharīf (1423) ix, **346b** – IX, **357b**
al-Tilimsānī, ʿAfīf al-Dīn (XIII) i, 569a; viii, 13b, 755a – I, 615b; VIII, 13b, 776a
al-Tilimsānī, Ibn Saʿd (XVI) ix, 20b – IX, 21b
al-Tilimsānī. Ibn Zāghū Aḥmad b. Muḥammad (1441) x, **499b** – X, **535b**
al-Tilimsānī, Ibrāhīm b. Abī Bakr (1291) x, **500a** – X, **535b**
al-Tilimsānī, Muḥammad b. Aḥmad, Sharīf (1369) ix, **343b** – IX, **354b**
al-Tilimsānī, Muḥammad b. Sulaymān (1289) x, **500a** – X, **536a**
al-Tilimsānī, Sulaymān b. ʿAlī (1291) x, **500a** – X, **535b**
Tilsām x, **500a** – X, **536a**
Tilūtān (Tayalūthān) (837) vii, 613a – VII, 612b
Tīmār i, 652b, 654a, 655b, 656b, 999b, 1147b, 1264a, 1266b; ii, 32b, 33b, 82a, 147a, b; iii, 284b, 1089a; iv, 1094b; v, 249a, 880b, 881a; x, **502a**; s, 238b – I, 673a, 674b, 675a, 676a, 677b, 1030a, 1182a, 1302b, 1305a; II, 33a, 34a, 83b, 151a, b; III, 293a, 1116a; IV, 1125a; V, 247a, 886b, 887a; X, **538a**; S, 238a
Timāwī b. Ayyūb al-Millī (1838) vi, 541b – VI, 526b
Timbuktu (Tinbuktu) i, 35a, 280a; ii, 252a; v, 394a; vi, 258b, 259a, b, 281b, 364b, 421b, 589b; viii, 718b; ix, 756b, 757a; x, **508a**; s, 29a, 295b – I, 35b, 288b; II, 259b; V, 395a; VI, 243a, 244a, 266b, 348b, 407a, 574b; VIII, 739b; IX, 789b, 790b; X, **544a**; S, 29a, 295a
Timimoun s, 328a, b – S, 327b, 328a
Timm s, 135b – S, 135b
Timnaʿ i, 1132b; iv, 746b, 747a; vi, 88b, 559a, 560b – I, 1167a; IV, 776b, 777a; VI, 86b, 544a, 545a
Timothy I (patriarch(e)) (VIII) x, 227a – X, 245a
Timsāḥ x, **510a** – X, **546a**
Timsāḥ (lake/lac) x, **510b** – X, **546a**
Timthāl → Ṣanam
Tīmūr Lang (Tīmūrid(e)) (1405) i, 66b, 227a, 237a, 244a, 311b, 468a, 470a, 530b, 721b, 852b, 903b, 999a, 1046a, 1051a, 1107b, 1119a; ii, 45a, 86b, 120b, 204b, 239b, 270a, 285b, 697a, 781b, 990a; iii, 187b, 189b, 198a, 199b,417a, 827b, 1100b; iv, 32b-33a, 102b, 349b, 410a, 586a, 670a, 871a, 1104b; v, 182a, 457a, 491b, 858b; vi, 16a, 49b, 50a, 61b, 202a, 231b, 273b, 294b, 309b, 324a, 381b, 406b, 417b, 483a, 493a, 494b, 502b, 512a, b, 515b, 524b, 525a, 537a, 540b, 541a, 692b, 974a; vii, 171b, 172a, 498a, 644a, 666a, 710b, 821a; viii, 193a; ix, 46a. 597a; x, 44b, **510b**, 560b, 593a, 898a; s, 49a, 94b, 242a, 327a – I, 68b, 234a, 244b, 251a, 321a, 482a, 484a, 546b, 743a, 876a, 930b, 1029b, 1077b, 1082b, 1141a, 1152b; II, 46a, 88a, 123b, 211a, 246a, 278b, 293b, 714b, 800b, 1012b; III, 192a, 194a, 202b, 204b, 430b, 851b, 1127b; IV, 34b-35b, 107a, 364b, 428a, 608b, 697b, 904b, 1136a; V, 179b, 459b, 494a, 865b; VI, 14b, 48a, 59b, 186a, 225a, 258a, 279b, 294b, 308b, 366a, 391a, 402b, 469a, 478b, 480a, 487b, 497a, b, 500b, 509a, 521b, 525a, b, 680b, 966b; VII, 173a, 174a, 498a, 643b, 665b, 711a, 822b; VIII, 196a; IX, 47a, 620a; X, 46a, **546a**. 602a, 637a, ; S, 49b, 94a, 242a, 326b
—literature/littérature ii, 591b; iii, 58a, 274a, 711b – II, 606a; III, 60a, 281b, 734a
Timūr Malik b. Urus Khān (XIV) x, 561a – X,
Tīmūr Pasha Khān b. ʿAlī Khān Bayat (1895) vi, 203a – VI, 187a
Tīmūr Shāh Durrānī (1793) i, 230a, b, 296a, 970b; ii, 186a, 628b, 952a; iii, 1158b; vi, 715a – I, 237a, b, 305a, 1000a; II, 192a, 644b, 974a; III, 1187a; VI, 704a
Tīmūrbughā, al-Ẓāhir (Mamlūk) (1468) iv, 462b – IV, 483a
Tīmūrbughā al-Afdalī Minṭāsh (XIV) vi, 548a, 580b; vii, 170b, 462a; viii, 987b – VI, 532b, 565a; VII, 462a; VIII, 1022a
Tīmūrid(e)s i, 135a, 147b, 227a, b, 1001b; ii, 45b, 309a, 334a, 792a; iii, 483b, 1256b; iv, 33a, 66a, 350a; v, 59a, 824b; vi, 17b, 366a, 483a, 515b, 521b, 522b, 524b, 557b; vii, 90a, 170b, 193b; 462a; viii, 987b; x, **513a**; s, 71a, 138b, 227b, 256a, b, 313a – I, 139a, 151b, 234a, 1032a; II, 46a, 317b, 343b, 810b; III, 500b, 1289a; IV, 35a, b, 69b, 364b; V, 60b, 830b; VI, 15b, 350a, 469a, 500b, 507a, 509a, 542a; VII, 91b, 172b, 194a, 462a; VIII, 1022a; X, **549b**; S, 71b, 138a, 227b, 255b, 256a, 313a
—history/histoire iv, 914b; s, 96b – IV, 947a; S, 96a
Tīmūrtāsh b. Amīr Čūbān (1328) i, 468a, 703a; ii, 68a, 706a; iv, 622a; vi, 315b, 372a – I, 481b, 724b; II, 69b, 724a; IV, 646b; VI, 300b, 356a
Tīmūrtāsh b. Ḳara ʿAlī Bey (XIV) i, 738b, 1159b, 1302b; ii, 722a – I, 760b, 1194b, 1342b; II, 741a
Tīmūrtash b. Nadjm al-Dīn Il-Ghāzī I (Artuḳid(e)) (1154) i, 664b; vi, 380a, 544a, 871b, 930b; x, **527a** – I, 684a; VI, 364a, 528b, 862a, 922b; X, **565a**
Tīmūrtāsh b. Ḳara ʿAlī Beg (1404) x, **528a** – X, **566a**
Tīmūrtāsh Oghullari̊ x, **528a** – X, **566a**
Timzought → Tīmzūghat
Tīmzūghat vi, 405a – VI, 389b
Tīn x, **529a** – X, **567b**
Ṭīn x, **529b** – X, **568a**
Ṭīna x, **530a** – X, **568a**
al-Tinbuktī → Aḥmad Bābā
Tinbuktū → Timbuktu
Tindarma vii, 394a – VII, 395a
Tindi, Banū i, 504a; iv, 630b – I, 519b; IV, 655b
Tindūf (Tindouf) x, **530b** – X, **568b**
Tinerkouk s, 328b – S, 328a
Tingitana vi, 591b – VI, 576b
Tingiz s, 195b – S, 195b
Tinkalūs → Tankalūshā al-Bābilī
Tīnmāl, Tīnmallal i, 459a; iii, 207b, 959a; vi, 592b,

682a, 742a, 743b; x, **530b** – I, 472a; III, 213a, 984a; VI, 577b, 669a, 731a, 732b; X, **568b**

al-Tinnīn (Draco)   x, **531a**; s, 191a – X, **569b**; S, 192b

Tinnīs   ii, 72b; vii, 69b; x, **531b** – II, 74a; VII, 70a; X, **570a**

Tippu Tip   → al-Murd̲j̲ibī

Tipū Mastān Awliyā   i, 625a – I, 645b

Tipū Sulṭān (1799)   i, 625a, 1015b; ii, 220a; iii, 119b, 316b, 322a; iv, 547b; v, 648a, 884b, 886a, 1259a, 1260a, b; vi, 459b, 735a; x, **532b** – I, 645b, 1047a; II, 227a; III, 122a, 326b, 331b; IV, 571a; V, 652b, 890b, 892a, 1250a, 1251a, b; VI, 445a, 724b; X, **571b**

Ṭīra   ii, 758b, 759b, 760a, 1097a; iv, 290b – II, 777a, b, 778b, 1123a; IV, 303b

Tīrāh   i, 238a, b – I, 245b, 246a

Tīrāhi   i, 237b – I, 245a

Tīrān   → Tihrān. II

Tiran/-a   x, **533a** – X, **572a**

Tīrān, Straits of/Détroits de   s, 8b – S, 8a

Tirana   → Tiran

Ṭirāz   i, 501a; ii, 301b, 302a; iii, 218a, 219a; v, 498b, 736b, 857a; x, **534b**' s, 144a, 341a – I, 516a; II, 310a; III, 224b, 225b; V, 502a, 741b, 864a; X, **573b**; S, 144a, 340b

al-Ṭirāz   iii, 863a – III, 887a

Tīre (Tire)   x, **538b** – X, **578b**

Tirebolu   x, **539a** – X, **579a**

Tirhāla (Trik(k)ala)   x, **539b** – X, **579b**

al-Tīrhānī, Abū 'l-Ḥasan b. Bahlūl   i, 737b – I, 759a

Tirhut (Bihar)   x, **540b**; s, 409a – X, **581a**; S, 409b

al-Ṭirimmāḥ, 'Adī b. 'Abd Allāh al-D̲j̲ubayr (al-Ṭirimmāḥ al-Akbar) (**VII**)   x, **541a** – X, **581b**

al-Ṭirimmāḥ b. D̲j̲ahm al-Ṭā'ī al-Sinbisī   x, **541a** – X, **581b**

al-Ṭirimmāḥ b. Ḥakīm al-Ṭā'ī (**VIII**)   x, **541b** – X, **581b**

al-Ṭirimmāḥ al-Akbar (Ka'ka' b. Nafr/Ibn Ḳays al-Ṭā'ī (**VII**)   ii, 1011a; vii, 402a; x, **541a** – II, 1034b; VII, 403a; X, **581b**

Tīris al-G̲h̲arbiyya   vii, 625b – VII, 625b

Tirmid̲h̲ (Termez)   ii, 1a, 4b, 43a; vi, 273b, 764b; x, **542b** – II, 1a, 4b, 44a; VI, 258b, 754a; X, **582b**

al-Tirmid̲h̲ī, Abū 'Abd Allāh Muḥammad b. 'Alī al-Ḥakīm (936)   viii, 404a; x, 314b. **544a** – VIII, 418a; X, 338b. **584b**

al-Tirmid̲h̲ī, Abū 'l-Ḥasan 'Alī al-Muzayyin (939)   viii, 840b – VIII, 869b

al-Tirmid̲h̲ī, Abū 'Īsā Muḥammad b. 'Īsā b. Sawra (892)   i, 114b; iii, 24a, 25a, 27b, 707a; vi, 351a; viii, 123a, 516a; x, **546b**; s, 232b – I, 117b; III, 25b, 26a, 29a, 729b; VI, 335a; VIII, 125b, 533b; X, **587a**; S, 232b

al-Tirmid̲h̲ī, Muḥammad b. 'Alī al-Ḥakīm (**X**)   viii, 404a – VIII, 418a

Tirmid̲h̲ī, Sayyid Burhān al-Dīn Ḥusayn Muḥaḳḳiḳī (1240)   x, **546b** – X, **587a**

Tīrnowa (Tarnovo)   x, **547a** – X, **587b**

Ṭirs   → Raḳḳ. I

Tīryāḳī Ḥasan Pas̲h̲a   → Meḥmed Pas̲h̲a,Tīryāḳī

Tirza   vi, 384b – VI, 368b

Tis̲h̲īt (Mauritania/-e)   vii, 624b – VII, 624b

al-Tīs̲h̲ītī, Abū 'Abd Allāh Muḥammad (1711)   vii, 625a – VII, 624b

Tis̲h̲rīn   x, **548a** – X, **588a**

Ṭiṭ (Ṭiṭṭ an Fiṭr/'Ayn al-Fiṭr)   vi, 741b; x, **548a** – VI, 731a; X, **588b**

Ṭiṭarī, Ṭiṭerī   i, 368a, 699b; vi, 141a, 405a, 728a – I, 379a, 721a; VI, 139b, 389b, 717a

Tiṭṭāwīn (Tétouan)   vi, 39a, 40a, 293a, b, 294a, 574a; vii, 391b; x, **549a** – VI, 37a, 38b, 278a, 279a, 559a; VII, 392b; X, **589b**

Tītū Mīr/Miyān, Sayyid Mīr Nit̲h̲ār 'Alī (1831)   vii, 291a; x, **550a** – VII, 293a; X, **590b**

Tivaouane   s, 182a – S, 182a

Tiyāhā, Banū   vii, 921a – VII, 921b

Tiyek   s, 171b, 172a – S, 172a, b

Tiyūl (Tuyūl)   ii, 150b, 152a, 153a; v, 244b; x. **550b** – II, 155a, 156b, 158a; V, 242a; X, **591a**

Tiyūywin   s, 402b – S, 403a

Tīz   vi, 193a – VI, 177a

Tīzī n'Ma's̲h̲ū   s, 48a – S, 48b

Tizi n-Test   vi, 743b – VI, 732b

Tizi Ouzou   iv, 359b – IV, 375a, b

Tizi-Telwet   vi, 742a – VI, 731a

Tīznit   vii, 583b; ix, 900b; s, 47b, 48a – VII, 584a; IX, 936b; S, 48a, b

Tlemcen   → Tilimsān

Tobacco (pipe –)   → Tutun

Tobacco Régie Concession   vi, 20b, 485a, b; viii, 140a; ix, 479b; s, 71b, 77a, 104a – VI, 18b, 471a, b; VIII, 142b; IX, 497b; S, 72a, 77a, 103b

Tobiah b. Moses   iv, 605b – IV, 629b

Tobīrčiḳog̲h̲lū Ḳayib K̲h̲ān   → Ḳayib K̲h̲ān

Tobna   vi, 727b – VI, 716b

Tobol (river)   x, **551b** – X, **592a**

Tobol Tatar   x, 551b – X, 592b

Toči   vi, 86a – VI, 84a

Ṭōḍar Mal, Rād̲j̲ā (Gud̲j̲arāt) (1589)   ii, 156a, 183b; iii, 457b; vii, 131a, 134b; x, **552a** – II, 161a, 189a; III, 473b; VII, 133a, 136b; X, **592b**

Ṭodg̲h̲a   vi, 590b – VI, 575b

Togan, Zeki Welidi   i, 1077a; ii, 700b – I, 1109a; II, 718b

Tog̲h̲a, Tog̲h̲an   → Tug̲h̲a, Tug̲h̲an

Tog̲h̲a Temür (Īl-K̲h̲ān) (1353)   x, **552a** – X, **593a**

Tog̲h̲ḍī beg (1033)   vi, 853b – VI, 845b

Tog̲h̲luk   → Tug̲h̲luk

Ṭog̲h̲rïl/ (personal name)   x, **552b** – X, **593b**

Tog̲h̲ril   → Ṭug̲h̲ril

Tog̲h̲uzg̲h̲uz   i, 1240a; x, **555b**, 687b, 691b – I, 1278a; X, **596b**, 729b, 734a, 736a

Togo, Islam in/au –   iv, 351b; vi, 281b; x, **557b** – IV, 367a; VI, 266b; X, **598b**

Tohāna   x, 98a – X, 105b

Tok Kenali (1933)   viii, 286a – VIII, 294a

Tokar   → Tūkar

Toḳat (Tokat)   iii, 212b; v, 557b; x, **558b** – III, 218b; V, 562b; X, **600a**

Tokat Kös̲h̲kü   vi, 57a – VI, 55a

Toḳay Tīmūr b. D̲j̲oči b. Čingiz K̲h̲ān   x, 560b – X, 602a

Toker, Samuel (**XVII**)   x, 214a – X, 231a

Tokhma Ṣuyu   vi, 232a – VI, 225b

Toḳhtu K̲h̲ān   ii, 610b – II, 625b

Toḳmaḳ   ii, 67b; x, **560a** – II, 68b; X, **601b**

Tokolors   → Tukulors

Toḳtamîs̲h̲ (Tok̲h̲tamîs̲h̲) K̲h̲ān (Golden Horde) (1406)   x, 511a, **560b** – X, 547b, **602a**

Toḳtamis̲h̲ Girāy (Cremea/Crimée) (1608)   ii, 1047a, 1113b; iv, 1064a; v, 765b – II, 1071a, 1139b; IV, 1095b; V, 771b

Toḳtamîs̲h̲ K̲h̲ān, G̲h̲iyāt̲h̲ al-Dīn (Batu'id(e)) (1395)   i, 1107b; ii, 44a, b, 86b, 1112a; vi, 417b – I, 1141a; II, 45a, b, 88a, 1138b; VI, 402b

Toḳto'a   ii, 42b – II, 43b

Toḳūkān (Tog̲h̲on) Abū Mangū-Tīmūr (Batu'id(e)) (**XIII**)   vi, 419b – VI, 405a

Töküs̲h̲   i, 664a – I, 683b

Tōlä   x, 185a, **563b** – X, 200a, **605b**

Tolba   → Sulṭān al-Ṭalaba

Toledo/Tolède   → Ṭulayṭula

Tolobey   i, 808b – I, 831b

Toluy/Tuluy b. Čingiz K̲h̲ān (1332)   i, 227a, 1105a; ii,

43b, 45b; iv, 542b; vi, 621a; x, **564a** – I, 233b, 1138b; II, 44a, 46b; IV, 566a; VI, 606a; X, **605b**
Tomārā vi, 49a – VI, 47b
Tomašević, Stjepan (XV) vi, 71a – VI, 69a
Tombalabaye, François s, 166a, b – S, 166a, b
Tombouctou → Timbuktū
Tong Yabgu (Western Türk) (630) x, 687b – 729b
Tonguç, Ismail Hakki v, 281b, 282a, b – V, 280a, b
Tonk i, 444a, 1195b; x, **564b** – I, 457a, 1230b; X, **606a**
Ṭoñuzlu → Deñizli
Tonyukuk (691) x, 687b – X, 729b
Ṭop x, **564b** – X, **606b**
Ṭop ʿArabadjïlarï i, 1061b – I, 1093b
Ṭopal Meḥmed Pasha v, 257b, 764a – V, 255a, 770a
Ṭopal ʿOthmān Pasha (1733) i, 292a; v, 144b, 461b, 494a; vii, 853b; x, **564b** – I, 301a; V, 147a, 464a, 497a; VII, 855a; X, **606b**
Ṭopal ʿOthmān Pasha (1874) i, 1268b, 1272a; x, **565b** – I, 1307b, 1311a; X. **607a**
Ṭopal Redjeb Pasha (1632) vii, 898a – VII, 597b
Ṭopčïbashï, ʿAlī Merdān s, 47a – S, 47b
Ṭopdju → Ṭop
Ṭopkapï Sarāyï i, 836b, 1091a; ii, 694b, 996b; iv, 231b, 232b, 233a, 368a; v, 67a, b, 274a; vi, 198b; ix, 46b; x, **566a** – I, 860a, 1123b; II, 712a, 1019b; IV, 241b, 243a, b, 384a; V, 69a, b, 272a; VI, 183a; IX, 47b; X, **608a**
Ṭopkhāne → Bārūd; Ṭop
Ṭoprak Ḳalʿe → Athūr
Ṭōr → al-Ṭūr
Torah → al-Tawrāt
Ṭorānī (dialect(e)) vi, 542a – VI, 526b
Töregene Khātūn (Tūrākīnā) (Mongol) (1246) ii, 45b; vi, 482b; x, **569a** – II, 46b; VI, 468b; X, **611b**
Ṭorghud → Turghud
Ṭorghud (commander) (XIV) x, **570a** – X, **612b**
Ṭorghud, Banū x, **569b** – X. **612a**
Ṭorghud ʿAlī (1565) x, 213b – X, 230b
Ṭorghud Eli x, **570b** – X, **612b**
Ṭorghid Re'īs (1565) x, **570b** – X, **615a**
Torī Khēl s, 285a – S, 285a
Torlaḳ Hū Kemāl i, 869b – I, 893b
Toros Dağları (Taurus Mts.) i, 463a; ii, 35a; x, **571a** – I, 476b; II, 36a; X, **613b**
Tortosa → Ṭurṭūsha
Tortum s, 308a – S, 307b
Tosḳ → Arnawutluḳ
Touareg → Ṭawāriḳ
Touareg (language/langue) → Ṭawārikitwāreg
Touat → Tuwāt
Toucouleurs X, **647a**
Touggourt →Tuggurt
Tourkopo(u)loi (Turcoples) x, **571b** – X, **614a**
Tozeur → Tūzar
Trabzon → Tarabzun
Trabzonlu Hüseyn Rüshdī Pasha ii, 200a – II, 206b
Trahgām s, 167a – S, 167a
Tralleis → Aydïn
Transcaspia/-e vi, 716b – VI, 705b
Transcaucasia/-e iv, 349a, b; v, 440a, 495b, 496b – IV, 364a; V, 442b, 498b, 499b
Transjordan/-ie → al-Urdunn
Transoxania/-e → Mā warāʾ al-Nahr
Transylvania/-e → Erdel
Trāra i, 372a; v, 379a – I, 383a; V, 379b
Travnik (Bosnia/e) i, 1270b; x, **572b** – I, 1309b; X, **615b**
Trebizond/Trébizonde → Tarabzun
Trengganu → Terenganu
Trestenik-oghlu Ismāʿīl → Ismāʿīl Bey (Serez)
Tribeni (Fīrūzābād) vi, 693a; x, **574a** – VI, 681a; X, **616b**
Triločanpāl vi, 65b – VI, 63b
Tripoli (Lībiya) → Ṭarābulus al-gharb
Tripolis → Ṭarābulus al-shām
Tripolitania/-taine i, 134b, 139a, 1071a; ii, 595a; iii, 296b, 654b, 655a, 1040a; iv, 617a, 919b; v, 758a, b, 759b, 760a, 1182a; vi, 248a, 310b, 312a, 361a, 945b – I, 138a, 143a, 1103b; II, 609b; III, 305b, 675b, 676b, 1066a; IV, 641b, 952b; V, 763b, 764a, 765a, 766a, 1172a; VI, 232a, 295b, 297a, 345a, 938a
Troc → Muʿāwada
Troki iv, 608a, b – IV, 632b, 633a
Trucial Coast → al-Sāḥil; ʿumān
Trucial States → al-Imārāt al-ʿArabiyya al-Muttaḥida
Trūd, Banū ix, 763b – IX, 796b
Truna Jaya v, 1155a, b – V, 1145a
Tsakhur x, **574b** – X, **617a**
Tskhum → Sukhum
Tu Wen-Hsiu (1873) x, **574b** – X. **617a**
Tuʿām → al-Buraymī
Tuan Guru → Abdullah Kadi Abdus Salaam
Tuanku Imam Bonjol (Padri) (XIX) viii, 238b – VIII, 244b
Tuanku Maḥmūd i, 745b – I, 767b
Tuanku Radja Keumala i, 745a – I, 767b
Tuāreg → Ṭawāriḳ
Ṭūb v, 585b – V, 590b
Ṭūbā (Touba) x, **575a**; s, 182a – X, **617b**; S, 182a
Tubal b. Lamak ii, 620a; x, 32b – II, 635b; X, 34a
Tuban s, 201b – S, 201b
Tubbaʿ (pl. Tabābiʿa) iii, 882a; viii, 979a; x, **575b** – III, 906b; VIII, 1014a; X, **618b**
Tubbat (Tibet) i, 71a, 1004b; x, **576a** – I, 73a, 1035b; X, **618b**
Tuberon, Ludovik Crijević s, 185b – S, 186b
Ṭubna (Tobna) i, 125a, 1246b; iii, 1041b; vi, 311b, 312a; ix, 768b; x, **580a** – I, 128b, 1284b; III, 1067b; VI, 296b; IX, 801b; X, **623a**
Tūbū (Tūbū) (Tibesti) i, 1221b; 1258a; ii, 368b; iv514a; v, 352a; x, **580b**; s, 163b, 164b, 165a, 166a – I, 1258a, 1296a; II, 378b; IV, 564a; V, 353a; X, **623b**; S, 163b, 164b, 165a, 166a
Tūda → Tudeh
Tudeh party/parti iii, 529a,b, 530a; iv, 40b-41a, 41b, 790a; s, 60b – III, 547a,b, 548a; IV, 43a-b, 44a, 822a; S, 61a
Tudela → Tuṭīla
Tūdjī vi, 511a, b – VI, 497a
Tudjīb, Banū iii, 816a; iv, 478a, 713a; v, 119b, 120a, 683a; vi, 344b; x, **582b**; s, 80b, 82a – III, 839b; IV, 499a, 741b; V, 122a, b, 688a; VI, 329a; X, **626a**; S, 80a, 81b
al-Tudjībī, ʿAbd Allāh b. Masʿūd (VIII) iii, 653b – III, 675a
al-Tudjībī, ʿAlam al-Dīn (1329) x, **584b** – X, **628b**
al-Tudjībī, ʿAtīḳ (1030) vi, 353b – VI, 337b
al-Tudjībī, al-Ḥasan b. Muḥammad b. al-Ḥusayn (XI) vii, 413a – VII, 414a
al-Tudjībī, Muḥammad b. Hāshim (938) vi, 852a; vii, 248b – VI, 843b; VII, 250a
al-Tudjībī, Sulaym b. ʿItr (ḳāṣṣ, ḳāḍī) (VII) vi, 657b – VI, 643a
al-Tudjībī, Sulaymān b. Khalaf (1081) vii, 537b – VII, 537b
Tudjībid(e)s → Tudjīb, Banū
Tūdjīn, Banū i, 122b, 167b; vi, 404a – I, 125a, 172b – VI, 388b

Tudmīr (al-Andalus) vi, 576b; vii, 633a; x, **585a** – VI, 561b; VII, 632b; X, **628b**
Tudmīr b. ʿAbdūs i, 58b; iii, 706a; iv, 672b; s, 81b – I, 60b; III, 728a; IV, 700a; S, 81b
Tufāl Khān Dakhnī ii, 815a; iii, 425a, 1161a – I, 834b; III, 439a, 1189b
Tūfān → Nūḥ
Tufang → Bārūd. V
Tufangčī-āḳāsī iv, 36b – IV, 39a
Ṭufayl b. ʿAwf al-Ghanawī (ca. 608) i, 115b, 772a; ii, 1005a; x, **586a** – I, 119a, 795a; II, 1028b; X, **630a**
Ṭufaylī x, **586b** – X, **630a**
al-Ṭufaylī, Abū Saʿīd ʿUthmān (IX) x, **587a** – X, **631a**
Tuffāḥ x, **587a** – X, **631a**
al-Ṭūfī, Nadjm al-Dīn (1316) iii, 700a; iv, 259a,b; vi, 739b; x, **588a** – III, 722a; IV, 269b, 270a; VI, 728b; X, **631b**
Tūfīḳ iv, 359a – IV, 375a
Tuggurt (Touggourt) x, **589a** – X, **633a**
Tūgh iii, 191b; v, 766b; x, **590a** – III, 196a; V, 772b; X, **634a**
Ṭughā Tīmūr (Čaghatayid(e)) (1291) ii, 3b, 44a, 401a; v, 663a; vi, 502b; ix, 48a – II, 3b, 45a, 411b; V, 668a; VI, 487b; IX, 48b
Tughalčin iii, 417b – III, 431a
Ṭughān (amīr) (XV) vi, 667b – VI, 653b
Tūghān b. Malik Ayāz (Diū) (XVI) ii, 322a – II, 331b
Tughān Arslān (Bidlīs) (1138) ii, 680b, 764b – II, 697b, 783a
Tughan Khān (Balāsāghūn) (XI) i, 987a – I, 1017b
Ṭughān Shāh Abū Bakr b. Alp Arslan II (Saldjūḳ, Harāt) (1185) i, 827a; ii, 552a; viii, 63b, 970b – I, 850a; II, 566a; VIII, 64b, 1004b
Tughāy (XIV) vii, 412b – VII, 413b
Ṭughdj b. Djuff ii, 281b; iv, 493b – II, 289b; IV, 515a
Tughluḳ, Malik → Ghiyath al-Dīn Tughluḳ I
Tughluḳ Shah → Ghiyāth al-Dīn Tughluḳ I
Tughluḳ Temūr (Čaghatayid(e)) (1363) ii, 45a, 622a; iv, 32b; ix, 649a; x, 510b, **590b** – II, 46a, 637b; IV, 34b; IX, 674a; X, 547a. **634b**
Tughluḳābād i, 1322a; ii, 257b, 262a; iii, 441b, 481b; v, 888a, 1215a; vi, 126a – I, 1362b; II, 263b, 265a, 269b; III, 456a, 498a; V, 894b, 1204b; VI, 124a
Tughluḳid(e)s (Delhi) v, 884a; vi, 198b, 369a, 488a, 692a; vii, 193b; x, **591a**; s, 206b – V, 890a; VI, 182b, 353a, 474a, 679b; VII, 194b; X, **635a**; S, 206a
Ṭughrā ii, 310a, 311b, 314b, 804a, b; iv, 796b, 1104b; v, 232b; x, **595a** – II, 319a, 320b, 323b, 823a, b; IV, 829a, 1136a; V, 230b; X, **639a**
Tughrā. Mullā (1667) x, **598b** – X, **643a**
al-Ṭughrāʾī, Abū Ismāʿīl al-Ḥusayn s, 326b – S, 326a
al-Ṭughrāʾī, Muʾayyid al-Dīn al-Ḥasan (al-Ḥusayn) b. ʿAlī al-Iṣfahānī (1121) i, 206b; iii, 1264b; v, 112a, 114a; vi, 64a, 275b, 606a; viii, 971a; x, **599a** – I, 212b; III, 1297a; V, 114b, 116b; VI, 62a, 260b, 590b; VIII, 1005a; X, **643b**
Ṭughrïl (Ṭoghrïl) I (Ṭughril Beg), Abū Ṭālib Muḥammad b. Mīkāʾīl (Great Saldjūḳ) (1063) i, 20b, 132a, 420a, 512b, 513a, 627a, 839b, 900b, 1073b, 1074b, 1075a, 1336b, 1356a; ii, 4b, 5a, 192b, 348b, 680b, 855b, 856a, 1051a, 1108b; iii, 159b, 344b, 345b,471b, 891b, 1098b; iv, 25a, 26b-27a, 101a, 347b, 457b, 458a, 465b, 942a; v, 388a, b, 623a; vi, 64a, 242b, 272b, 274b, 482a, 500a, 521b, 523a, b, 626b, 847b, 966a; vii, 193a, 271a, 983a, 1017a, b; viii, 63b, 69b, 938b; x, **553a**; s, 14b, 29b, 192a, 195a – I, 21a, 136a, 432a, 528b, 647b, 863a, 927b, 1105b, 1106b, 1107a, 1376b, 1395a; II, 4b, 5a, 199a, 358a, 697b, 875b, 876a, 1075b, 1134b; III, 163a, 355a, 356a, 488a, 915b, 1125b; IV, 26b, 28b-29a, 105a, 362b, 478a, b, 486b, 975a; V, 389a, b, 627a; VI, 61b, 226b, 257b, 259b, 468a, 485a, b, 506b, 508a, 611b, 838b, 958a; VII, 193b, 273a, 984a, 1019a, b; VIII, 64b, 71a, 970a; X, **593b**; S, 15a, 29b, 193a, 195a
Ṭughrïl (Ṭoghrïl) II, Rukn al-Dīn b. Muḥammad b. Malik-Shāh (Great Saldjūḳ) (1134) i, 300b; iii, 196b; iv, 860a, vi, 64a, b, 782a, 809b; vii, 733b, 734a; viii, 943b; x, **554a**; s, 416a – I, 309b; III, 201b; IV, 893a; VI, 61b, 62a, 771b, 799b; VII, 734a, b; VIII, 976a; X, **595a**; S, 416b
Ṭughrïl (Ṭoghrïl) III b. Arslān b. Ṭughrïl (II). Rukn al-Dīn (Great Saldjūḳ) (1194) ii, 894a; iii, 1111a, b; iv, 948b, 1067b; vii, 997a; viii, 64a, 78a, 239b, 944a, b; x, **554b**; s, 378b, 416a – II, 915a; III, 1138b, 1139a; IV, 981a, 1099b; VII, 998b; VIII, 65b, 80a, 245a, 976b, 977b; X, **595b**; S, 378b, 416b
Ṭughrïl b. Sunḳur Ḳuṭb al-Dīn (Salghurid(e)) (1181) viii, 978b – VIII, 1013a
Ṭughrïl-Arslan (Malaṭya) (XII) i, 983a; ii, 110b – I, 1013b; II, 113a
Ṭughrïl Birār i, 1130b; ii, 1052a – I, 1165a; II, 1076a
Ṭughrïl Khān (governor/gouverneur Bengal) s, 124a – S, 123b
Ṭughrïl Khān (Ḳarakhānid(e)) i, 987a – I, 1017b
Ṭughrïl Khān (Kereyt) → Ong Khān
Ṭughrïl Shāh b. Ḳïlïdj Arslān II (Rūm Saldjūḳ) (1225) x, **555a** – X, **596a**
Ṭughrïl-tigin b. Ekinči b. Ḳočḳar (XII) vi, 415b; s, 279a – VI, 400b; S, 279a
Ṭughshāda i, 1293b – I, 1333b
Ṭughtakīn → Ṭughtigin
Ṭughtakīn, Sayf al-Dīn (Ayyūbid(e)) (XII) vii, 579b – VII, 580a
Ṭughtigin, Ẓāhir al-Dīn Atabeg (Būrid(e)) (1128) iii, 398b; vi, 547a, 578a, 789b; vii, 461b, 578b; viii, 947a, 999b; x, **600a** – VI, 531b, 563a, 779a; VII, 461b, 579a; VIII, 979b, 1034b; X, **644b**
Tuhāmī Glawi, al-Ḥādjdj (Marrakesh) (XX) vii, 416b, 417a – VII, 418a, b
Tuhāmī Ḥabābū vii, 415a – VII, 416b
Tuhāmī al-Madghari (1856) vi, 249a, 250b, 253a – VI, 233a, 234b, 237a
Tukal Bogha ii, 610b – II, 625b
Ṭūḳān iv, 834b – IV, 867b
Tūkar iv, 680b, 687a – IV, 714b, 715a
Tukarōʿī iii, 202b – III, 208a
al-Tuḳatī (1495) vii, 537a – VII, 537a
Ṭukhāristān i, 852a; vi, 273b; vii, 477b; x, **600b**; s, 125a – I, 875b; VI, 258b; VII, 477a; X, **645b**; S, 124a
al-Tukhāwī, Muḥammad Aḥmad s, 371a – S, 371a
al-Tukhāwiyya s, 371a – S, 371a
Ṭūkhī, ʿAbd Allāh v, 190a – V, 187b
Tukhorghan → Dih-i Khʷāraḳān
Tuktamīr (892) vi, 900a – VI, 891b
Tukulor (toucouleur) x, **602a** – X, **647a**
Tūlak (Khurasān) s, 66b – S, 67a
Ṭulaḳāʾ (sing. Ṭaliḳ) x, **603a** – X, **648a**
Tūlakī, Malik Ḍiyā al-Dīn i, 1194a – I, 1229b
al-Tūlawī → Buṭrus
Ṭulayḥa b. Khuwaylid al-Asadī (642) i, 110b, 683b, 1358b; iv, 385b, 858b; x. **603a** – I, 113b, 704b, 1398b; IV, 402b, 891b; X, **648a**
Ṭulayṭula (Toledo/Tolède) i, 6b, 7a, 82b, 83a, 242b, 493a; iii, 12a, 74a, 702a; vii, 778b; x, **604a**, 849a,b ; s, 23a – I, 6b, 7a, 85a, 86a, 250a, 508a; III, 12b, 76b, 724a;

VII, 780b; X, **649a**; S, 23a
al-Ṭulayṭulī, Abū 'l-Ḥasan (X) x, **607b** – X, **653a**
Ṭulb iii, 185b; x. **608a** – III, 190a; X, **653a**
Tulband x, **608a** – X, **653b**
Tulkarm x, **615b** – X, **661b**
Tulsī Dās iii, 457a – III, 473a
Tulumbadjî i, 270a; iv, 234b, 237b; vi, 57a; x, **616a** – I, 278a; IV, 245a, 248a; VI, 55a; X, **662a**
Ṭūlūnid(e)s i, 14b, 18b, 278a, 435b, 439b, 1346a; ii, 36b, 281b; vi, 373a; x, **616b**; s, 120b – I, 15a, 19b, 287a, 448a, 452a, 1386b; II, 37a, 289b; VI, 357b; X, **662b**; S, 120a
Tulūy → Toluy
Tum Tik wa-Tum
Tuʿma, Ilyās Abū Faḍl (XX) x, **618b** – X, **665a**
Tūmān (tümen) x, **619a** – X, **665a**
Tūmān, Amīr (XX) iv, 578a – IV, 601a
Tūmān Bāy, al-Ashraf (Mamlūk) (1517) i, 779a; ii, 172b, 1042a; iii, 188a, 813a; iv, 552a, 553a; vi, 325a; vii, 174a, 176b; x, 621b – I, 802b; II, 178a, 1066b; III, 192b, 836b; IV, 576a, 577a; VI, 309b; VII, 176a, 178b; X, 668a
Ṭūmār iv, 742a; v, 873b – IV, 772a; V, 879b
Tūmārī i, 260b – I, 268b
Tumbāk → Tutun
Tumbatu x, **622a** – X, **669a**
Tumbine Khān (Mongol) vi, 417b – VI, 402b
Tümen x, **622b** – X, **669a**
Tumenggung, Pangeran s, 150b – S, 150b
Tūn (Ḳūhistān) v, 355a; x, **623a** – V, 356a; X, **670a**
Tun Abdul Razak (XX) vi, 241b – VI, 212b
Ṭuna x, **623b** – X, **670a**
Tunakābun vi, 936a – VI, 928a
Tunb, Greater and Lesser/la Grande et la Petite iv, 778a, b; vii, 449b; viii, 435a; x. **624b**; s, 417b – IV, 809b, 810a; VII, 450b; VIII, 449b; X, **671a**; S, 418a
al-Tunbudhī → Manṣūr b. Naṣr al-Tunbudhī
Tunbūr x, **624b** – X, **671b**
Tundjeli (Tunceli) ii, 208a; v, 465a; x, **628a** – II, 214b; V, 468a; X, **675a**
Tundjur, Banū i, 1258a; ii, 122a; iv, 541a; s, 164a – I, 1296a; II, 125a; IV, 564b; S, 164a
Tunganistan v, 846b; x, **628b** – V, 858b; X, **675b**
Tungans (Dungans, Chin. T'ung-kan)) x, **629a** – X, **676a**
Tunggang Parangan, Tuan s, 151a – S, 151a
al-Tūnī, ʿAbd al-Muʾmin b. Khalaf al-Dimyāṭī → al-Dimyāṭī
Ṭūnī, Ḳuṭb al-Dīn Ḥaydar (1426) x, 251a – X, 269b
Tūnis i, 86b, 163b, 248b, 281b, 1225a; ii, 130a, 189b, 1008b; iii, 94b, 145a, 605a; v, 1127b, 1151a; vi, 404b, 573a, 676b; x, **629b**; s, 133b, 145a – I, 89a, 168a, 256b, 290a, 1261b; II, 133b, 195b, 1032a; III, 97a, 148a, 625b; V, 1124a, 1141b; VI, 389a, 558a, 663a; X, **676b**; S, 133a, 144b
al-Tūnisī (1051) vi, 279a – VI, 264a
al-Tūnisī. Maḥmūd Bayram (1961) x, **639b** – X, **686b**
al-Tūnisī, Muḥammad b. ʿUmar (1857) x, **640a** – X, **687b**
al-Tūnisī, Shaykh Zayn al-ʿĀbidīn (XIX) x, **641a** – X, **688a**
Tunisia/Tunésie i, 18a, 19a, 34b, 35a, 37a, 79a, 171a, 977a, 1177a, 1321a; ii, 413a, 526a, 595a, 638b, 676a, 748a; iii, 297a, 384b, 395b, 561b, 563a, b, 605a, 635b, 683b, 684a, 927b; iv, 175a, 262b, 403a, 824b, 954b, 1157a; v, 59b, 696a, 915a, 1067b; vi, 58b, 60b, 248a, 251b, 467b, 840a, 946b, 1043b; viii, 60b, 794b, 900b; x, **641a**; s, 11a, 215b, 254b – I, 18b, 20a, 35b, 36a, 38a, 81b, 176a, 1007a, 1212a, 1361b; II, 424a, 539a, 610a, 654b, 693a, 766b; III, 306b, 397a, 408a, 581a, 582b, 583a, 625b, 657a, 705b, 952a; IV, 182b, 274a, 420b, 857b, 986b, 1189a; V, 61b, 701a, 920b, 1065a; VI, 56b, 58b, 232a, 235b, 273b, 453b, 831a, 938b, 1036b; VIII, 62a, 821b, 931b; X, **688b**; S, 10b, 215b, 254a
—demography/-ie s, 215b – S, 215b
—institutions ii, 425a, 436a; iii, 524a – II, 436a, 447b; III, 542a
—language/-e. literature/littérature ii, 470a – II, 482a
—population v, 1181b – V, 1171b
Tūnk iv, 213a – IV, 222b
Tūnkath vi, 557b; s, 411a – VI, 542a; S, 411a
Tunku Abdul Rahman (XX) vi, 241a, b, 242a – VI, 212a, 213a
Tunukābun vi, 513a, b, 514b – VI, 498a, b, 499b
al-Tūnusī → Khayr al-Dīn
al-Tūnusī, Muḥammad b. ʿUmar (XIX) ii, 122b, 827b – II, 125b, 847a
Tūpčiyān i, 1066a, 1068a, b, 1069a – I, 1098a, 1100a, 1101a
Tüp-Karagan, cap(e) vi, 417a – VI, 402a
al-Ṭūr (Tōr) vi, 195a; viii, 865a; x, **663a** – VI, 179a; VIII, 896a; X, **715a**
Tur, ʿAbd al-Raḥmān Aḥmad (Somalia/-ie) ix, 722a – IX, 753a
Ṭūr ʿAbdīn vi, 539b, 540a, 542a; x, **665a** – VI, 524a, b, 526b; X, **717b**
Tura Khāns i, 135a, 1075b – I, 139a, 1108a
Turaba → Wādī Turaba
Ṭurābāy, Banū ii, 912a; vi, 543b – II, 933b; VI, 528a
Turakhan Beg (1456)) vii, 237a; x, **670b** – VII, 238b; X, **723a**
Ṭūrān (Shāh-nāma) i, 236a; v, 314b; vi, 193a, 492a; x, **672a** – I, 243b; V, 314a; VI, 177a, 478a; **725a**
Ṭūrān (Ḳuṣdār) x, **679b** – X, **725b**
Tūrān-čar (Turīsha) s, 299a – S, 298b
Turanism/Touranisme viii, 250a – VIII, 266b
Tūrān-Shāh I b. Ḳāwurd (Saldjūḳ, Kirmān) (1097) vi, 273b – VI, 258b
Tūrān Shāh II b. Tughrïl (Saldjūḳ) (Kirmān) (1183) v, 160a, b – V, 158b, 159a
Tūrānshāh of/de Hurmuz (XIV) i, 942b – I, 971b
Tūrānshāh b. Ayyūb, al-Malik al-Muʿaẓẓam (Ayyūbid(e)) (1180) i, 181b, 552b, 709a; iii, 125b; v, 895b, 1244b; vi, 433b; vii, 577b, 731a; viii, 90a; x, **673a**; s, 338a - I, 186b, 570b, 729b; III, 128b; V, 901b, 1235a; VI, 417b; VII, 580a, 732a; VIII, 92b; X, **726a**; S, 337b
al-Ṭurayf ii, 320b, 321a – II, 330a, b
Turayhīb b. Bandar b. Shuḳayr iv, 680b, 681a – IV, 708b
Turba x, **673b** – X, **726b**
Turban → Tulband
Turbatī, Khʷādjā Abū 'l-Ḥasan (1633) viii, 851b – VIII, 881a
Turbat-i Ḥaydarīyya → Zawa
Turbat-i Shaykh-i Djām i, 283a; iii, 1125a; x, 675b; s, 41a, 367b – I, 292a; III, 1152b; X, 728b; S, 41b, 367a
Turbe → Turba
Turcoman → Türkmen
Turcs I, 19a, 20b, 21a, 32a, 33b, 57b, 96a, 172b, 179b, 188b, 378a, 920a, 518b; II, 615b, 1003a, 1133a; IV, 698b; X, **728b**
Turcs -Dobrudja X, **742b**
Turcs – Eurasie/Europe Centrale X, **733b**
Turcs – folklore X, **780b**
Turcs – Grèce X, **742a**
Turcs – histoire X, **729a**
Turcs – histoire tribale en Asie Centrale X, **781a**
Turcs – langues X, **744b**
Turcs – littérature X, **759b**

Turcs – musique   X, **779a**
Turcs – ex-Yougoslavie   X, **740b**
Ṭurfa Āl al-S̲h̲ayk̲h̲   s, 305b – S, 305b
Turfān/Turpan   ii, 45b; iv, 529a; vi, 768a; x, **675b**; s,
    136b – II, 46b; IV, 552a; VI, 757b; X, **782b**; S, 136a
Turgay   x, **677b** – X, **784a**
Türges̲h̲, Banū   i, 684b; iii, 224a; iv, 583b;
    v, 854a, b, 855b; ix, 413a; x, 560a, 590a, 687b, 689a –
    I, 705b; III, 230b; IV, 607b; V, 860b, 861a, 862a; IX,
    951b; X, 601b, 634a, 729b, 730a, 781a
Ṭurg̲h̲ūd ʿAlī Pas̲h̲a   ii, 459b, 461a; iii, 69b; iv, 416a,
    656b, 828a; v, 504a, 1247a – II, 471b, 473a; III, 72a;
    IV, 434a, 683a, 861a; V, 507b, 1237b
Turg̲h̲ut Og̲h̲lu Ḥasan Beg   iv, 624a – IV, 648b
Tūrī, Banū   v, 501b – V, 504b
al-Ṭūrī, Muḥammad b. ʿAlī   iii, 901b – III, 925b
Turis̲h̲a   → Tūrān-čar
Turk, Aträk   vi, 316a – VI, 301a
al-Turk, Nikūlā b. Yūsuf (1828)   z, **678b** – X,
Türk Odjag̲h̲î (Odjaklarî)   ii, 431a, 432a; iv, 791a,
    933b; x, **678a**; s, 47b – II, 442a, 443b; IV, 823a,
    966b; X, **784b**; S, 48a
Türk yurdu   → Maḳāla. 3
Turk b. Yāfit   iv, 914b – IV, 947b
Turkān   → Yerken
Turkān Āḳā (Tīmūrid(e)) (1383)   viii, 1035a – VIII,
    1070b
Turkče Bilmez   i, 709b; v, 391a, 808a – I, 731a; V,
    392a, 814a
Türkčülük   → Pan-Turkism
Türkeli   → Avs̲h̲a
Türkeş, Alparslan (XX)   iv, 791b; viii, 251b –
    IV, 823b; VIII, 268a
Turkey   i, 13b, 37b, 39a, 62b, 74b, 238b, 281b, 462a,
    734a, 871a, 972b; ii, 594b, 595a, 640a, 966b; iii,
    213b; iv, 1b, 790b; v, 464b, 505a; vi, 366a, 470a,
    496b, 757a, 799a, 809a, 826a; vii, 13a, 70b, 76a; x,
    684b; s, 214a
Turkey – demography   s, 214a
Turkey – education   v, 906a, 1099b
Turkey – ethnography   v, 439b, 750b
Turkey – institutions   i, 972b, 1225b; ii, 425b, 429b,
    708b; iii, 526a; iv, 167b; v, 1037b
Turkey – Republic of –   x, **693b**
Turk̲h̲ān Sulṭān (1683)   iv, 233b; v, 273a; x, 679a; s,
    257b – IV, 243b; V, 270b; X, S, 257b
Ṭurk̲h̲ān-og̲h̲lu ʿÖmer Beg (XV)   v, 772a; vi, 71b – V,
    778a, b; VI, 69a
Turk̲h̲ān-og̲h̲ullarî   i, 340b – I, 351a
Turk̲h̲ān Sulṭān (1683)   x, **679a – X,**
Turkī b. ʿAbd Allāh b. Suʿūd (Āl Suʿūd) (1834)   i,
    554b; ii, 176b, 321b; iv, 765a, 953a, 1073a; vii, 782b;
    ix, 904a –
    I, 572a; II, 182a, 331a; IV, 795b, 985b, 1104b; VII,
    784b; IX. 941b
Turkī b. Fayṣal b. ʿAbd al-ʿAzīz (Āl Suʿūd) (XX)   vi,
    158a; s, 305b – VI, 153b; S, 305b
Turkī b. Saʿīd (Bū Saʿīd) (1888)   i, 1283a; v, 183b,
    1030b; s, 356a – I, 1321b; V, 181a, 1026a; S, 355b
Turkistān   i, 36a, 72b, 147b, 223b; ii, 477a; iv, 175a;
    792a; v, 858a, 859a; vi, 483b; x, **679a**; s, 51b, 66a,
    125a, 143b, 240a –
    I, 37a, 74b, 152a, 230a; II, 489a; IV, 182b, 824b; V,
    865a, 866a; VI, 469b; X,   ;S, 52a, 66b, 124a, 143a,
    240a
Turkistanis   vii, 353a – VII, 355a
Türkiye Büyük Millet Meclisi   v, 1037b, 1040a – V,
    1034a, 1036a
Türkiye Işçi Partisi   iv, 124b – IV, 130a
Türkiye Işçi ve Čiftči Sosyalist Fîrkasî   iv, 123b, 124a
    – IV, 129a

Türkiye Komünist Partisi   iv, 124a – IV, 129a
Türkmen   i, 4a, 120b, 224a, 311a, 340a, 420b, 460a,
    467a, 470b, 639a, 665b, 666b, 700b, 750b, 843b,
    1133b; ii, 1108b, 1117a; iii, 1098b, 1108a, 1110a,
    1256b; iv, 10a, 25b, 28b, 1065a; v, 24a, 104a, 145b;
    vi, 148b, 230b, 231a, 317a, 416a, b, 482a, 492b,
    493b, 502b, 541a, 580b, 620b, 715a, 780b; ix, 826a;
    x, 126b, **682a**, 690a, ʾ6-98a, s, 49a, 75b, 143b, 146b,
    147a, 168b, 280b –
    I, 4a, 124a, 231a, 320b, 350b, 432b, 473a, 481a,
    484b, 659b, 686a, 687a, 722a, 773a, 866b, 1168a; II,
    1134b, 1143a; III, 1125a, 1135a, 1137a, 1289b; IV,
    10b, 27a, 30b, 1096b; V, 25a, 106b, 148a; VI, 147a,
    224b, 225a, 301b, 401a, 468a, 478b, 479a, 487b,
    525b, 565b, 605b, 704a, 770a; IX, 860b; X, 135b,
    732b, 741a; S, 49b, 76a, 143a, 146a, 147a, 168b, 280b
Türkmen Literature   x, **727b** – X, **773a**
Türkmen (Turg̲h̲udlu)   vi, 71b – VI, 69b
Türkmen čāy (I)   ii, 152a; iii, 1191b; iv, 38b, 394b; v,
    495b; vi, 19b, 21a; x, **685b** – II, 156b; III, 1221b; IV,
    41a, 411b; V, 498b; VI, 17b, 19a; X,
Turkmenistan   x, **686a** – X,
Türkoğlu   vi, 509a – VI, 494b
Turkoman chai   → Türkmen čāy (I)
Turkomānī, S̲h̲ayk̲h̲ Süleymān   v, 173a – V, 170b
Turkopoloi   ix, 268a – IX, 276a
Turks   i, 18b, 19b, 20b, 31b, 33a, 55b, 93a, 168a, 174b,
    183b, 367b, 893b, 505b; ii, 601a, 980b, 1107a; iv,
    671a; x, **686b**
Turks – Dobrudja   x, **699b**
Turks – folklore   x, **734b**
Turks – Greece   x, **699a**
Turks – history   x, **687a**
Turks – languages   ii, 473b; iii, 373b, 1115b; iv, 699b,
    715a, 853b; v, 193a, 223b, 538a, 1100a, 1101a; x, **701a**
Turks – literature   x, **715a**
Turks – music   x. **733a**
Turks – outside Turkey   x, **697a**
Turks – tribal history in Central Asia   x, **689a**
Turks – Western Asia /Central Europe   x, **691a**
Turks – former Yugoslavia   x, **697b**
Türkü   x, **736a** – X,
al-Turkumānī (amīr) (XIV)   viii, 156b – VIII, 159a
al-Turkumānī, al-Madanī (1886)   vi, 250b –
    VI, 234b
Turla (Dnestr)   vi, 56a – VI, 54a
Turpan   → Turfan
Turquie   I, 14a, 38b, 40a, 64b, 77a, 246a, 290b, 475b,
    756a, 895a, 1002b; II, 609a, b, 656a, 988b; III, 219b;
    IV, 1b, 822b; V, 467b, 508b; VI, 350a, 456a, 482a,
    746a, 789a, 799b, 816b; VII, 14a, 70b, 76a; S, 213b
Turquie – démographie   s, 213b
Turquie – éducation   V, 911b, 1095a
Turquie – ethnographie   V, 442a, 756a
Turquie – institutions   I, 1002b, 1262a; II, 436b, 440b,
    708b; III, 544a; IV, 174b; V, 1034a
Turquie – langues, littérature   II, 485b; III, 385b,
    1143a; IV, 727b, 744a, 886b; V, 190a, 221b, 542b,
    1096a, 1101a
Turquie – République   x, **736a**
Turs   →Rank; Silāḥ (in Suppl.)
Turs̲h̲īz (Ḳūhistān)   x, **727a**; s, 149a – S, 149a
Ṭūrsūn Beg (XV)   x, **737b** – X,
Ṭursun Faḳīr   x, **738a** – X,
Tursun Yunus (Uyg̲h̲ur)   vi, 768a – VI, 757b
al-Ṭurṭūs̲h̲ī, Ibn Abī Randaḳa Abū Bakr (1126)   i,
    594a, 602a; iv, 136b; v, 1160b; vi, 279a; vii, 986a –
    I, 613a, 621b; IV, 136b; V, 1150a; VI, 264a; VII, 986b
Ṭuruf, Banū   iii, 1107b; vii, 675a – III, 1134b; VII,
    675a
Ṭuruḳ (Tanzania-/e)   x, 195b – X, 219b

Ṭūs v, 293b; vi, 331b, 335b, 633b, 714a, b; x, **740b**; s, 14b, 357a –
V, 293b; VI, 316a, 320a, 618b, 702b, 703a; X, ; S, 15a, 356b
Ṭūs, Malik (XIV) vi, 512a – VI, 497a, b
Tus̲h̲tarī, S̲h̲ams al-Dīn Muḥammad i, 703b – I, 725a
al-Ṭūsī → ʿAlī b. ʿAbd Allāh; Asʿadī; Naṣīr al-Dīn; al-Sarrād̲j̲
al-Ṭūsī, Abu ʾl-ʿAbbās Aḥmad b. Masrūḳ (911) viii, 583b – VIII, 602b
al-Ṭūsī, Abū D̲j̲aʿfar Muḥammad b. al-Ḥasan (S̲h̲ayk̲h̲ al-Ṭāʾifa) (1067) iv, 711b; vi, 12a, 312b, 549a, 906a; vii, 297b, 313a, 459b, 581b, 634a; viii, 372b, 517b, 713b, 811b; x, 40a, 85a, **745a**, 935b; s, 56b, 233a – IV, 740b; VI, 11a, 297b, 533b, 897b; VII, 299b, 315b, 460a, 582a, 633b; VIII, 385b, 535b, 734a, 839a; X, 41b, 92a, ; S, 57a, 233a
al-Ṭūsī, Abu ʾl-Ḥasan (786) vi, 821b, 822a – VI, 811b, 812b
al-Ṭūsī Ḳāniʿī, Aḥmad b. Maḥmūd iv, 504b, 1081a – IV, 526b, 1112a
Ṭūsī, Muḥammad (XII) vi, 907b – VI, 899a
Ṭūsī, Muḥammad b. Ḥamīd (IX) viii, 53a – VIII, 54a
al-Ṭūsī, al-Muẓaffar i, 727a – I, 748b
al-Ṭūsī, Naṣīr al-Dīn Abū D̲j̲aʿfar Muḥammad (1274) vii, 132a; viii, 540b, 541a, 542a, 754a; x, **746a** – VII, 134a; VIII, 558b, 559a, b, 560a, 775b
al-Ṭūsī, S̲h̲araf al-Dīn viii, 553a – VIII, 570b
Tustar → S̲h̲us̲h̲tar
al-Tustarī, Ḥasan b. Ibrāhīm b. Sahl (XI) ii, 858a – II, 878a
al-Tustarī, Sahl b. ʿAbd Allāh → Sahl al-Tustarī
Ṭūsūn b. Muḥammad ʿAlī Pas̲h̲a (1816) iii, 362b, 999a; v, 997b; vi, 150b; vii, 424a, 425b – III, 374a, 1024a; V, 993a; VI, 149b; VII, 425b, 427a
Tūt x, **752a** – X,
Tutak x, **752b** – X,
Tuṭīla iii, 816a; x, **752b**; s, 80a, 81a, 82a – III, 839b; X, ; S, 80a, b, 81b
al-Tuṭīlī, al-Aʿmā → al-Aʿmā al-Tuṭīlī
Tūtiyā v, 965a, 967b, 970b – V, 969a, 973a
Tutun x, **753a** – X,
Tütünsüz Aḥmed Beg → Aḥmad Riḍwān
Tutus̲h̲ (I) b. Alp Arslān, Tād̲j̲ al-Dawla (Sald̲j̲ūḳ) (1095) i, 314a, 466a, 517a, 664a, 731a, 751a, 971a, 1051b, 1332a, 1349a; ii, 282a, 347b, 1039a; iii, 86b, 1118a; iv, 27b, 28b; v, 328a, 437a, 924a; vi, 274b, 379b, 540b, 546b, 930b; vii, 121b, 693a, 731a, 755a; viii, 81b, 519a, 947a; x, **756b** – I, 324a, 479b, 532b, 683b, 753b,773a, 1001a, 1083a, 1372b, 1389b; II, 290a, 357a, 1063a; III, 89a, 1145b; IV, 29b, 30b; V, 328a, 364a, 439b, 929b; VI, 259b, 525a, 531a, 922b; VII, 123b, 693a, 731b, 756b; VIII, 83b, 536b, 979a, b
Tutus̲h̲ b. Duḳāḳ (XII) viii, 519a – VIII, 537a
Ṭuwāna (Tyana/-e) i, 11b, 12b; vi, 338a, 740a – I, 12a, 13a; VI, 322b, 729a
Tuwāt (Touat) i, 210b; v, 1165a, b; vi, 141a; viii, 794b; x, **757a**; s, 328a – I, 216b; V, 1155a, b; VI, 139b; VIII, 821b; S, 327b
al-Ṭuwayḳ (Tuēḳ), D̲j̲abal i, 536b, 628b, 747b; vii, 865a; viii, 675b; x, **758b** – I, 553a, 649b, 770a; VII, 866b; VIII, 594a; X,
Ṭuways, Abū ʿAbd al-Munʿim (711) ii, 620b, 1073b; iii, 878b; x, **759a**; s, 183a – II, 636a, 1098b; III, 902b; X, ;S, 184b
Tuyūl iv, 1044a, 1045b – IV, 1075a, 1076b
Tuz Gölü x, **759b** – X,
Tūzar Tozeur) ii, 463a, 464a; iv, 740a; vii, 897a; x, **759b** – II, 475a, 476a; IV, 769b; VII, 898a; X,
Ṭuzd̲j̲u-og̲h̲ullarï viii, 567a – VIII, 585a
Tūzīn, Banū s, 113b – S, 113a
Tūzūk x, **760b** – X,
Tūzūn al-Turkī (945) iii, 127b; vii, 723b, 800a, 995a – III, 130a; VII, 724b, 802a, 996a
Twelvers → It̲h̲nā-ʿas̲h̲ariyya
Tyana/-e → Ṭuwāna
Tyawka K̲h̲ān v, 135a – V, 138a
Tyr(e) → Ṣūr
Tzachas → Čaka

U

U Nu i, 1333b; v, 431a – I, 1273a; V, 433a
ʿUbād, Banū (Ṭayyiʾ) iv, 911b; vi, 649a – IV, 944b; VI, 634b
ʿUbāda b. Māʾ al-Samāʾ → Ibn Mā" al-Samāʾ
ʿUbāda b. Ṣāmit v, 324b, 590a – V, 324a, 594a
Ubāg̲h̲ (ʿAyn Ubāg̲h̲) **761a** – X,
ʿUbar → Wabar
ʿUbayd, Banū vii, 582a – VII, 582b
ʿUbayd b. Ayyūb al-ʿAnbarī (VIII) x, 2b – X, 2b
ʿUbayd b. Maʿālī iv, 430a – IV, 449a
ʿUbayd b. S̲h̲arya → Ibn S̲h̲arya
ʿUbayd Abū Ziyād s, 355a – S, 354b
ʿUbayd Allāh (Fāṭimid(e)) → al-Mahdī ʿUbayd Allāh
Ubayd Allāh, S̲h̲ayk̲h̲ (Kurd(e)) (XIX) v, 462b; vi, 203a, 502b; vii, 935b; s, 71a – V, 465a; VI, 187a, 488a; VII, 936a; S, 72a
ʿUbayd Allāh b. al-ʿAbbās b. ʿAbd al-Muṭṭalib (704) i, 41a; iii, 241a, 242a, 617a; vi, 344b; x, **761a** – I, 42a; III, 248a, 249a, 637b; VI, 328b; X,
ʿUbayd Allāh b. ʿAbd Allāh b. Ṭāhir (Ṭāhirid(e)) (850) vii, 18b, 410b; x, 105a, 435a – VII, 18b, 412a; X, 113a, 466b
ʿUbayd Allāh b. ʿAbd Allāh al-Hud̲h̲alī → al-Fuḳahāʾ al-Madīna al-Sabʿa
ʿUbayd Allāh b. Abī Bakra, Abū Ḥātim (698) iv, 356b; vii, 777a; x, **761b** – IV, 372a; VII, 778b; X,
ʿUbayd Allāh b. Aḥmad b. Abī Ṭāhir (925) iii, 693a; iv, 21a; x, **761b** – III, 715a; IV, 22b; X,
ʿUbayd Allāh b. Aḥmad b. G̲h̲ālib (848) vii, 5a – VII, 5a
ʿUbayd Allāh b. Arṭāh i, 399b – I, 411a
ʿUbayd Allāh b. Bās̲h̲īr x, **762b** – X,
ʿUbayd Allāh b. D̲j̲aḥs̲h̲ (VII) vii, 862b – VII, 864a
ʿUbayd Allāh b. D̲j̲ibrīl (1058) vi, 351b – VI, 336a
ʿUbayd Allāh b. al-Ḥabḥāb (ca. 741) i, 439a, 1157b; ii, 328a; iii, 494a; vi, 742b; vii, 159b, 613a; ix, 584a; x, **762b** – I, 451b, 1192a; II, 337b; III, 511a; VI, 731b; VII, 161a, 612b; IX, 606b; X,
ʿUbayd Allāh b. al-Ḥurr (VII) vii, 650a; ix, 866b – VII, 650a; IX, 902b
ʿUbayd Allāh b. Idrīs II (Idrīsid(e)) → ʿAbd Allāh b. Idrīs II (Idrīsid(e))
ʿUbayd Allāh b. Maḥmūd S̲h̲aybānid(e) (1539) i, 1295b – I, 1335a
ʿUbayd Allāh b. al-Māḥūz i, 810b – I, 833b
ʿUbayd Allāh b. Nabhān ii, 188a – II, 194a
ʿUbayd Allāh b. Samura iii, 717a, b – III, 739b, 740a
ʿUbayd Allāh b. al-Sarī b. al-Ḥakam (IX) vii, 160b – VII, 162a
ʿUbayd Allāh b. Sulaymān b. Wahb (901) iii, 750a, 892b, 955b; iv, 90b; vii, 760a – III, 773a, 916b, 980a; IV, 94b; VII, 761b, 762a

ʿUbayd Allāh b. ʿUmar b. al-Khaṭṭāb (657) iii, 65a, 587a; ix, 554a; x, **763a** – III, 67b, 607a; IX, 576a; X,
ʿUbayd Allāh b. ʿUthmān x, 848b – X,
ʿUbayd Allāh b. Yaḥyā → Ibn Khāḳān, ʿUbayd Allāh
ʿUbayd Allāh b. Ẓabyān (VII) vii, 650b – VII, 650a
ʿUbayd Allāh b. Ziyād b. Abīhi (686) i, 3b, 76b, 304a, 337b, 1086a, 1293b; ii, 89b, 759b, 788a; iii, 164b, 226b, 270b, 588a, 608b, 609a, 715a, 882a, 987a, 1254b; iv, 1186b; v, 853b; vi, 622a, b, 665a, 675b, 677a; vii, 114b, 123b, 400b, 523a, b, 689b, 690a, b, 1045a; viii, 119a; ix, 411b, 826a; x, **763a**, 842b – I, 4a, 78b, 313b, 348a, 1118a, 1333a; II, 91b, 778a, 807a; III, 168a, 233b, 278b, 608a, 629a, b, 737b, 906a, 1011b, 1287b; IV, 1219a; V, 860a; VI, 607a, b, 651a, 662b, 664a; VII, 116b, 125a, 402a, 523b, 689b, 690a, b, 1047b; VIII, 121b; IX, 435a, 860b; X,
ʿUbayd Allāh Aḥrār, Kh(w)ādja → Aḥrār, Khʷādja ʿUbayd Allāh
ʿUbayd Allāh Khān Özbeg (1540) i, 228b, 1067b; iii, 388a; v, 55a; x, 109a; s, 51b, 340a – I, 235b, 1100a; III, 400b; V, 56b; X, 118a; S, 52a, 339b
ʿUbayd Allāh Khān Özbeg (1711) v, 273b; s, 97a, 419b – V, 271b; S, 96b, 419b
ʿUbayd Allāh Khān Shībānī ix, 34b – IX, 35a
ʿUbayd Allāh al-Mahdī → al-Mahdī ʿUbayd Allāh
ʿUbayd Allāh Sindhī s, 360a – S, 360a
ʿUbayd al-Ḥarfūsh (Ḥurayfīsh) iii, 206a – III, 212a
ʿUbayda (VIII) vi, 544a – VI, 528b
ʿUbayda b. al-Djarrāh → Abū ʿUbayda ʿĀmir b. ʿAbd Allāh b. al-Djarrāḥ
ʿUbayda b. al-Ḥārith (623) vii, 32b – VII, 32b
ʿUbayda b. Hilāl (680) vii, 123b – VII, 125b
al-ʿUbaydalī, Sharīf Tādj al-Sharaf Muḥammad al-Ḥusaynī al-Ḥalabī (1267) viii, 895b – VIII, 926a
al-ʿUbaydī, Muḥammad b. ʿAbd al-Raḥmān (VIII) vi, 440a; vii, 527b – VI, 425b; VII, 527b
ʿUbayd-i Zākāni al-Kazwīnī (1369) iii, 355b, 373a, 1208b; iv, 66a, 67b; vii, 572b, 1019a; x, **764a** – III, 366b, 385a, 1239a; IV, 69b, 71a; VII, 573a, 1021a
ʿUbaydid(e)s iii, 782b; s, 306b – III, 805b; S, 306a
Ubayy b. Kaʿb (ca. 650) i, 104b; iv, 1112b; v, 127b, 406a, 407b; x, **764b**; s, 227a – I, 107b; IV, 1144b; V, 130a, 407b, 408b; X, ; S, 227a
al-Ubayyiḍ (el-Obeid) v, 267b, 1249b; x, **765a** – V, 265a, b, 1240a; X,
al-ʿUbbād i, 137b; iii, 866a; vi, 572a; ix, 20b; s, 403a – I, 141b; III, 890a; VI, 557a; IX, 21a; S, 403a
Ubbadha (Ubeda) x, **765a** – X,
al-ʿUbbādī, Abū ʿAbd Allāh Muḥammad s, 403a – S, 403b
ʿUbey s, 161a – S, 160b
Ubna (Khān al-Zayt) x, 713a – X,
al-Ubrūḳ ii, 340b – II, 350a
al-Ubulla i, 43b, 1085a; ii, 143a; iii, 1252b; vi, 773b, 920a; vii, 66b; x, **765b** – I, 44b, 1117b; II, 147a; III, 1285a; VI, 763a, 911b; VII, 67a; X,
Ubykh x, **766b** –
Uččh ii, 791b; iii, 443b, 633a; v, 26a, b; vi, 48a, b, 49b, 127b; vii, 409b; ix, 785b; x, **766b**; s, 10b, 66b – II, 810a; III, 458b, 654a; V, 27a; VI, 46b, 47a, 48a, 125b; VII, 411a; IX, 819b; X, ; S, 10a, 67a
Ucciali → Wuchali
Uclés → Uklīdj
ʿŪd x, **767b** – X,
ʿŪda, ʿAbd al-Ḳādir iii, 1069b – III, 1096a
ʿUdār ii, 1078b – II, 1103b
Ūdāya, Banū i, 47a; ii, 510b, 820a; vi, 142b, 590a, b, 741b – I, 48b; II, 523a, 839b; VI, 141a, 575a, 730b
al-ʿUdayd x, **773b** – X,
Udaypur (Nēwar) vi, 127b, 342b; x, **773b** – VI, 125b, 327a; X,
Udfu → Adfū
al-Udfuwī, Abū Bakr (998) vi, 188b – VI, 172a
Udgīr x, **773b** – X,
Udhayna b. Hayrān b. Wahb Allāt (Odenatus II) (267) x, 79b – X, 82b
ʿUdhra, Banū ii, 427b, 1031b; v, 317b, 497b; vi, 415a, 472a, 477b; x, **773b** – II, 438b, 1055b; V, 317a, 500b; VI, 400a, 458a, 463a; X,
ʿUdhrī x, **774b** – X,
al-ʿUdhrī, Abū 'l-ʿAbbās Aḥmad (1085) i, 157a; iii, 991b; vi, 431b, 576a; vii, 501a; x, **776a**; s, 80a, 92a – I, 161a; III, 1016a; VI, 416b, 561a; VII, 500b; X, ; S, 80a, 91b
Udhruḥ → Adhruḥ
Udj ii, 611a, 613a, 1044b, 1118a; ii, 1044b; x, **777a** – I, 1152a; II, 626b, 628a, 1068b; X,
ʿUdj/ʿĀdj b. ʿAnak (ʿŌg) x, **777b** – X,
Udj-beyi → Udj
Udjak i, 1217b – I, 1254a
Ūdjān vi, 494a, b, 524a – VI, 479b, 480a, 509a
ʿUdjayf b. ʿAnbasa (838) i, 11b; x, **778a** – I, 12a; X,
ʿUdjayr b. ʿAbd Allāh al-Salūlī iv, 1002b – IV, 1035a
Udjda → Wadjda
Udjdjayn ii, 577a; iii, 1155b; v, 297a; vi, 54b, 62a, 65b, 309a, 602a; x, **778b**; s, 105a – II, 591b; III, 1184a; V, 296b; VI, 52b, 60a, 63b, 294b, 586b; X, ; S, 104b
al-Udjhūrī (1656) viii, 479b – VIII, 496a
ʿUdjam → ʿAdjam
al-ʿUdjmān i, 545b, 873b; iii, 238b, 1065b – I, 563a, 897b; III, 245a, 1092a
ʿUdūl → ʿAdl
ʿUdwat al-Andalus iii, 1032a – III, 1058a
al-Ufrānī → al-Ifrānī
Uftāde, Muḥyī al-Dīn ii, 542b, 543a; iii, 538b – I, 556a; III, 557a
Uganda, Muslims in - x, **778b** – X,
Uggʷag → Wadjdjādj
Ughānān v, 163a – V, 161a
Ughurlu Muḥammad b. Uzun Ḥasan (Aḳ Ḳoyunlu) (XV) iv, 588a; vi, 72a – IV, 611b; VI, 70a
Uguday → Ögedey
Uḥayḥa b. al-Djulāḥ, al-Awsī x, **782a** – X,
al-Uḥaymir al-Saʿdī ix, 866a – IX, 902a
ʿUhda → Darība. 4
Uhdjiyya v, 807a – V, 812b
Uḥud (625) vii, 370a; x, **782a** – VII, 372a; X,
Ujiji ii, 58b – II, 59b
ʿUḳāb x, **783b** – X,
ʿUḳār (Mahra) vi, 82b – VI, 80a
ʿUkāsha → ʿUkkāsha
Ukawafī s, 351a – S, 351a
Ukaydir b. ʿAbd al-Malik al-Sakūnī (VII) ii, 625a; v, 119b; x, **784a** – II, 640b; V, 122a; X,
ʿUḳayl, Banū i, 421a, 442a, 512a, 942a, 1073a, 1356a; ii, 348b; iii, 129a; iv, 27b, 764a, b, 911a; vi, 379a, 546b; vii, 488a, 582a; x, **784b**; s, 37a, 119a – I, 433a, 454b, 527b, 971a, 1105b, 1395a; II, 358a; III, 131b; IV, 29b, 794b, 795a, 944a; VI, 363b, 531a; VII, 488a, 582a, b; X, ;S, 37b, 118b
ʿUḳayl al-ʿUkbarī i, 116a – I, 119b
al-ʿUḳaylī, ʿAsar (VII) s, 394a – S, 394b
al-ʿUḳaylī, Isḥāḳ b. Muslim (VIII) vi, 427b; viii, 589b – VI, 412b; VIII, 608b
al-ʿUḳaylī, Muḥammad b. ʿAmr (934) vii, 576b; viii, 516a – VII, 577a; VIII, 534a

ʿUḳaylid(e)s vi, 270b, 274b, 379b, 626a, b, 900b; vii, 1017a; viii, 71b; x, **786b** – VI, 255b, 259b, 364a, 611a, 891b; VII, 1019a; VIII, 73a; X,
al-Uḳays̲h̲ir (al-Mug̲h̲īra b. ʿAbd Allāh) (699) iv, 1002b; x, **787a** – IV, 1035a; X,
al-Uḳayṣir ii, 1024a; x, **788a** – II, 1047b; X,
ʿUkāẓ i, 343a; iii, 760b; vi, 251b, 477b; vii, 309b; ix, 817b; x, **789a** – I, 353b; III, 783b; VI, 235b, 463b; VII, 312a; IX, 852b; X,
ʿUḳba b. Abī Muʿayṭ (624) i, 115b, 136b; ii, 842b; vii, 369b – I, 118b, 140b; II, 862a; VII, 371b
ʿUḳba b. ʿAmir al-Dj̲uhanī (VII) vi, 740b; vii, 394b – VI, 730a; VII, 395b
ʿUḳba b. al-As̲h̲ʿat̲h̲ i, 150b – I, 154b
ʿUḳba b. al-Azraḳ (VII) vi, 665a – VI, 651a
ʿUḳba b. al-Ḥadj̲dj̲ādj̲ al-Salūlī (VIII) i, 76a, 1011b, 1079b; vi, 923a – I, 78a, 1043a, 1111b; VI, 915a
ʿUḳba b. Nāfiʿ b. ʿAbd al-Ḳays (683) i, 248b, 367a, 532b, 770a, 1175a, 1221b, 1259b; ii, 575a, 875b, 992a; iii, 667b; iv, 415b, 567a, 739b, 777a, 826a, b, 827a; v, 393a, 518a, 1189a; vi, 134a, 740b, 742a, 743b, 773b, 944b; viii, 18a; x, **789a**, 848a; s, 81b – I, 256a, 377b, 548b, 793a, 1210a, 1258a, 1297b; II, 589b, 896a, 1014b; III, 689a; IV, 433b, 589b, 769b, 808b, 859a, b, 860a; V, 393b, 521b, 1179a; VI, 132a, 730a, 731b, 733a, 763a, 937a; VIII, 18a; X, ; S, 81b
ʿUḳba b. Ruʾba i, 1080b – I, 1113a
ʿUḳba b. Salm (VIII) i, 45b, 1080b; vi, 820a – I, 46b, 1112b; VI, 810b
ʿUḳba al-Sulaymī (faḳīh, ḳāḍī) ii, 234b, 235a, 236a – II, 241b, 242a, b
ʿUkbānī, Āl s, 403a – S, 403a
al-ʿUḳbānī, al-Ḳāsim b. Saʿīd iv, 477a; s, 403a – IV, 498a; S, 403b
ʿUḳbār (Zāb) vi, 435a – VI, 420a
al-ʿUkbarī → Ibn Baṭṭa
al-ʿUkbarī, ʿAbd Allāh b. al-Ḥusayn (1219) vi, 438a, 824b; vii, 772a; x, **790b** – VI, 423b, 815a; VII, 773b; X,
al-ʿUkbarī, al-Aḥnaf (X) vii, 495a – VII, 494b
al-Ukbarī, Ismāʿīl iv, 604a – IV, 628a
al-ʿUkbarī, Mīs̲h̲awayh iv, 604a – IV, 628a
al-ʿUkbarī, Muḥammad b. ʿAbd al-Raḥmān (1267) viii, 428a – VIII, 442a
ʿUḳbī (XX) viii, 903a – VIII, 934a
al-ʿUḳbī, Ṭayyib iv, 159b – IV, 166a
al-Uḳḥuwāna vii, 117a – VII, 119a
al-Uk̲h̲ayḍir (castle/château) x, **791a** – X,
al-Uk̲h̲ayḍir, Banū i, 403a. 551a, 618a, 831b, 1226b, 1315b; ii, 114b; iii, 262b, 1267b; iv, 88b, 384b; vi, 364b; ix, 507a; x, **792a**; s, 115b – I, 414b, 568b. 637a, 855a, 1264a, 1356a; II, 116b; III, 270a, 1300b; IV, 92b, 401a; VI, 348b; IX, 526b; X, ; S, 114b
al-Uḳḥuwāna vii, 117a – VII, 119a
Ukiyānūs → al-Baḥr al-Muḥīṭ
ʿUḳḳāl → ʿĀḳil
ʿUkkās̲h̲a b. ʿAbd al-Ṣamad iv, 1004a – IV, 1036b
ʿUkkās̲h̲a b. Ayyūb al-Fazārī (742) iii, 169b; iv, 336b, 826a – III, 173a; IV, 351a, 859a
ʿUkkāz, Bu i, 1247a – I, 1285a
al-ʿUḳla (S̲h̲abwa) vi, 80b – VI, 78b
al-ʿUklī, Abu 'l-Wadj̲īh s, 85b – S, 85a
Uḳlīdis (Euclid(e)) iv, 596a, 600a, 1182a; v, 123a; x, **792b** – IV, 620a, 624b, 1215b; V, 126a; X,
al-Uḳlīdīsī, Abu 'l-Ḥasan ʿIlm al-Ḥisāb
al-Uḳlidīsī, Aḥmad b. Ibrāhīm iii, 1139b – III, 1168a
Uklīs̲h̲ (Ucclès) x, **794a** – X,
Ukraine v, 260b – V, 258b
Uks̲h̲ūnūba (Oesonoba) i, 1339a; ii, 1009a; x, **794b** – I, 1379a; II, 1032b; X,
al-Uḳṣūr (Luxor) vi, 366b; x, **795a** – VI, 351a; X,
Uḳṣūṣa x, **796b** – X,
ʿUḳūba x, **799a** – X,
al-ʿUlā v, 497b, 761b; x, **800a** – V, 501a, 767b; X,
Ūlād Slīmān iv, 540b, 541a – IV, 564a, b
Ula → Ulug̲h̲
Ulag̲h̲či K̲h̲ān i, 1187b – I, 1223a
al-ʿUlah, Banū ii, 167b – II, 173a
Ulaḳ x, **800a** – X,
ʿUlamāʾ x, **801b** – X,
al-ʿUlaymī, Mudj̲īr al-Dīn → Mudj̲īr al-Dīn al-ʿōlaymī
Ulays, Banu 'l- iv, 494a – IV, 515a
ʿUlayya bint al-Mahdī (825) x, **810b** – X,
ʿUlayyān, Āl i, 1312b – I, 1353a
Uldj̲aytū K̲h̲udābanda → Öldj̲eytü
Ulèëbalangs i, 741a, 742a, 744a, 744b, 745b, 747a – I, 763a, 764b, 766a, 766b, 768a, 769b
ʿUl(l)ayka vi, 578b, 791a – VI, 563b, 781a
Ulema → ʿUlamāʾ
al-ʿUlt̲h̲ī, Isḥāḳ b. Aḥmad iii, 161a – III, 164b
Ulu da x, **810b** – X,
ʿUlūdj̲ ʿAlī (1587) iii, 94b; v, 726b; x, 213b, **810b** – III, 97a; V, 731b; X, 230b,
ʿUlūfe x, 811b – X,
Ulug̲h̲ Beg, Muḥammad Ṭarag̲h̲ay (1449) x, **812a** – X,
Ulug̲h̲ Beg b. Abī Saʿīd iv, 357a – IV, 372b
Ulūg̲h̲ Beg b. S̲h̲āh Ruk̲h̲ (Tīmūrid(e)) (1449) i, 227b, 393a, 1295b; ii, 399a, 586b; iii, 1137b; iv, 584a, 702b; v, 858b; vi, 540b, 601b, 602a, 768a – I, 234a, 404b, 1335a; II, 409b, 601a; III, 1166a; IV, 607b, 731a; V, 865b; VI, 525b, 586a, b, 757a
Ulug̲h̲ Bilge Iḳbāl K̲h̲ān i, 767a – I, 790a
Ulug̲h̲ K̲h̲ān (title/titre) x, **814a** – X,
Ulug̲h̲ K̲h̲ān, Almās Beg (K̲h̲aldj̲ī, Delhi) (XIV) i, 506b, 1193a; ii, 597a, 1124a; iv, 922a – I, 522a, 1228b; II, 612a, 1150b; IV, 955a
Ulug̲h̲-K̲h̲ānī al-Āṣafī → Ḥadj̲dj̲ī al-Dabīr
Ulug̲h̲ K̲h̲ān-i Aʿẓam (XIII) i, 217b; ii, 609b – I, 224a; II, 624b
Ulug̲h̲ Muḥammad (Crimea/-ée) (1438) viii, 832a – VIII, 860b
Ulug̲h̲ Muḥammad (Meḥmed) K̲h̲ān (Golden Horde/ Horde blanche) (1446) i, 1252b, 1308a; ii, 44b; iii, 44a; iv, 849a – I, 1290b, 1348b; II, 45a; III, 46a; IV, 882a
Ulug̲h̲ Noyon i, 1010b – I, 1042a
Ulus x, 513a, **814a** – X, 550a,
ʿUlyā Ḥaḍrat (1965) s, 65b – S, 66a
ʿUlyāʾiyya i, 1082a, 1096a; x, **814b** – I, 1114b, 1129a; X,
Umāma bint Abi 'l-ʿĀs (VII) i, 400b – I, 412a
ʿUmān (Oman) i, 73a, 110b, 132a, 140b, 141b, 211b, 535a, 539b, 545a, 551b, 552a, 555a, 811b, 928a, 1013b, 1281b, 1283a, 1354b; ii, 592b; iii, 652a; iv, 500b, 777b, 807b, 1130b; v, 507a, 1059a; vi, 38a, 80b, 82b, 84b, 118a, 272b, 333b, 358a, 371b, 385b, 843a; vii, 301b, 449b, 514b, 838b; x, **814b**; s, 42a, 118b, 178a, 222b, 234b, 332a, b, 338a, 355a, 417a – I, 75a, 113b, 136a, 145a, b, 217b, 551b, 556a, 562a, 569a, b, 572b, 834b, 956a, 1044b, 1321a, b, 1393b; II, 607a; III, 673a; IV, 522a, 809a, 840a, 1162a; V, 510b, 1055b; VI, 36a, 79a, 80a, 82b, 116a, 257b, 318a, 342a, 356a, 369b, 834a; VII, 303b, 451a, 515a, 839b; X, ; S, 42b, 118a, 178a, 223a, 234a, 331b, 332a, b, 337b, 355a, 417b
al-ʿUmānī → al-Fuḳaymī, Muḥammad b. D̲h̲uʾayb
ʿUmānīs vi, 129a – VI, 127a

ʿUmar (I) b. al-Khaṭṭāb (644) i, 9a, 12a, 52a, 104b, 110a, 129a, 145b, 158b, 188a, 337b, 343b, 381b, 382a, 445a, 545b, 549b, 687a, 718a, 729a, 738a, 932a, 1085a, 1141a, b, 1143b, 1215b, 1343b; ii, 77b, 159b, 190b, 232a, 304b, 323b, 360a, 454b, 725b, 842b, 888b, 1006a, 1056a; iii, 64a, 65a, 586b; iv, 14a, 270b, 316b, 320b, 365a, 386a, 927b, 928b, 937b, 995b, 1140b, 1142a; v, 324a; vi, 1a, 105a, 138b, 139a, 140b, 147a, 168a, 193a, 350b, 351a, 362a, 379a, 467a, 476a, b, 575a, 604a, 636a, 645a, b, 647a, 648a, b, 650b, 651b, 652a, 654b, 658a, b, 659a, 660a, 661a, 665a, 666a, 668b, 671a, 675a, b, 724a, 737a, 738b; vii, 295a, 509b, 1030b; viii, 93b, 835a, b; ix, 504b; x, **818b**; s, 48b, 89b, 129b, 130a, 198b, 343a –
I, 9a, 12a, 53b, 107b, 113a, 133a, 150a, 163a, 193b, 348a, 354a, 392b, 393a, 458a, 562b, 567a, 707b, 739b, 751a, 760a, 960b, 1117b, 1175b, 1176a, 1178a, 1251b, 1384a; II, 79a, 164b, 196b, 239a, 313a, 333a, 370a, 466a, b, 744b, 862a, 909b, 1029b, 1080b; III, 66b, 67b, 606b; IV, 15a, 282b, 330b, 335a, 381a, 403a, 960b, 961b, 970b, 1028a, 1172b, 1173b; V, 323b; VI, 1a, 103a, 137a, 138b, 145b, 159b, 177a, 335a, b, 346a, 363a, 453a, 461b, 462b, 560a, 588b, 621a, 630b, 632a, 633a, b, 636a, b, 637a, b, 640a, 643b, 644a, 645a, b, 647a, 651a, 652a, 654b, 657a, b, 661b, 662a, 713a, 726b, 727b; VII, 297a, 510a, 1033a; VIII, 96a, 864a, b; IX, 524a S, 49a, 89a, 129a, 198b, 343a; X,
ʿUmar (II) b. ʿAbd al-ʿAzīz b. Marwān (Umayyad(e)) (720) i, 53b, 117a, 181b, 257b, 305a, 435a, 729b, 966b; ii, 36a, 72b, 198a, 227b, 304b, 327b, 480a, 561a, 622b, 726a; iii, 228a, 428b, 650a, 674b; iv, 369b, 742a, 939a, 997a; v, 53a, 590b, 923a, 1124a, 1231b; vi, 107b, 197b, 350b, 351a, 457b, 626a, 641a, 652a, 659a, 662a, 665a, 712b, 740a, 774b, 917a; vii, 8b, 27a, 157b, 398a; x, **821a**, 842a; s, 41a, 52b, 311b, 358a –
I, 55a, 120b, 186b, 265b, 314b, 447b, 751b, 996a; II, 36b, 73b, 204b, 234b, 313a, 337b, 492a, 575a, 638a, 145a; III, 234b, 442b, 671a, 696a; IV, 386a, 772a, 972a, 1029b; V, 54b, 594a, 928b, 1120b, 1222a; VI, 105b, 182a, 334b, 335b, 443a, 611a, 626a, 637b, 645a, 647b, 651a, 701a, 729b, 764a, 908b; VII, 9a, 27a, 159b, 399a; X, ; S, 41a, 53a, 311a, 358a
ʿUmar, Banū iii, 299b – III, 309a
ʿUmar, al-Ḥādjdj (Tukulor) (XIX) vi, 281b – VI, 266b
ʿUmar (marabout, Marrākush) (1766) vi, 595a – VI, 580a
ʿUmar b. al-ʿAbbās b. Mandīl (1277) vi, 404a – VI, 388b, 389a
ʿUmar b. ʿAbd Allāh b. Abī Rabīʿa (712) i, 10b, 305a, 566a; ii, 427b, 428b, 1011b, 1029b, 1030b; iii, 682a; iv, 488b, 1008b; vi, 140b, 468a, 477b; vii, 694b, 981b; x, **822b**; s, 10a –
I, 10b, 314b, 584a; II, 438b, 439b, 1035a, 1053a, 1054b; III, 704a; IV, 509b, 1040b; VI, 139a, 453b, 463b; VII, 694b, 982b; X, S, 9b
ʿUmar b. ʿAbd Allāh al-Aḳṭaʿ (amīr) (Malaṭya) vi, 230b – VI, 224b
ʿUmar b. ʿAbd al-ʿAzīz → ʿUmar (II) (Umayyad(e))
ʿUmar b. ʿAbd al-ʿAzīz (Dulafid(e)) (IX) vii, 395a – VII, 396a
ʿUmar b. ʿAbd al-Muʾmin, vizier (XII) i, 160b – I, 165a
ʿUmar b. Abī Bakr (Songhay) (XV) vii, 394a – VII, 395a
ʿUmar b. Abī Bakr, al-Ḥādjdj (Ghana) (1934) ii, 1004a – II, 1027b
ʿUmar b. Abi ʾl-Ṣalt (Rayy) (VII) iv, 207b; v, 541a – IV, 217a; V, 545b
ʿUmar b. Aḥmad b. ʿAbd al-ʿAzīz (Dulafid(e)) (896) vii, 760a – VII, 761b
ʿUmar b. ʿAlāʾ (VIII) vi, 744b, 941a; viii, 650b – VI, 734a, 933a; VIII, 668a
ʿUmar b. ʿAlī, al-Malik al-Manṣūr Nūr al-dīn (Rasūlid(e)) (1250) i, 553a; v, 1241a – I, 570b; V, 1231b
ʿUmar b. ʿAlī b. al-Ḥasan vi, 334b – VI, 319a
ʿUmar b. ʿAlī (Sharaf al-Dīn) → Ibn al-Fāriḍ
ʿUmar b. Arghūn Shāh (XIV) viii, 894b – VIII, 925b
ʿōmar b. Ayyūb → al-Muẓaffar
ʿUmar b. Bāyazīd Anṣārī i, 1123a, b – I, 1157a, b
ʿUmar b. al-Fāriḍ → Ibn al-Fāriḍ
ʿUmar b. Ḥaddū (XIII) vi, 743a – VI, 732a
ʿUmar b. Ḥafṣ → Muhallabid(e)s. IV
ʿUmar b. Ḥafṣ b. ʿUthmān b. Ḳabīṣa b. Abī Ṣufra (Hazārmard) (768) i, 125a; vi, 311b, 312a, 1042b; vii, 359b – I, 128b; VI, 296b, 297a, 1035b; VII, 362a
ʿUmar b. Ḥafṣ al-Ballūṭī → Abū Ḥafṣ ʿUmar al-Ballūṭī
ʿUmar b. Ḥafṣūn (muwallad) (918) i, 83b, 494a, 997a, 1150a, 1300b, 1343a; ii, 516a, 915b, 1012b; iii, 785a, 842a; iv, 254b, 534a; v, 376b, 1243b; vi, 222a; vii, 248b, 563b, 569a, 808a, 941b; x, **823b**, 850b; s, 152b –
I, 86a, 509a, 1027b, 1184a, b, 1340a, 1383b; II, 528b, 937a, 1036a; III, 808b, 865b; IV, 265b, 557b; V, 377a, 1234a; VI, 215b; VII, 250a, 564a, 569b, 810a, 942a; X, ; S, 152b
ʿUmar b. Hāniʾ al-ʿAnsī iv, 370a – IV, 386a
ʿUmar b. Ḥanẓala vi, 12a, b – VI, 11b
ʿUmar b. Hubayra al-Fazārī → Ibn Hubayra, ʿUmar
ʿUmar b. Ibrāhīm al-Khayyām → ʿUmar Khayyām
ʿUmar b. Idrīs II (Idrīsid(e)) (IX) ii, 874a; iii, 1035b – II, 894a; III, 1061b
ʿUmar b. Īmkaten (Ibāḍī) (VIII) iii, 654a – III, 675a
ʿUmar b. Ismāʿīl al-Hawwārī (1396) iii, 299b – III, 309a
ʿUmar b. al-Ḳāsim al-Nashshār i, 105b – I, 108b
ʿUmar b. al-Khaṭṭāb → ʿUmar (I) (Umayyad(e))
ʿUmar b. Khuraym al-Murrī (VIII) vii, 629b – VII, 629a
ʿUmar b. al-Malik al-ʿĀdil Abū Bakr (Ayyūbid(e)) (XIII) x, 884a – X,
ʿUmar b. Mihrān (Miṣr) (VIII) vii, 160b – VII, 162a
ʿUmar b. Mīrānshāh b. Tīmūr (Tīmūrid(e)) (XV) vii, 105b – VII, 107b
ʿUmar b. Muḥammad al-Kanemī i, 1260a; v, 357b, 358a – I, 1298a; V, 359a
ʿUmar b. al-Nuʿmān i, 361b, 363a; ii, 238a – I, 372b, 374a; II, 245a
ʿUmar b. Ramaḍān al-Thalātī i, 121b – I, 125a
ʿUmar b. Rasūl (XIII) vi, 433b – VI, 419a
ʿUmar b. Riyāḥ s, 129b – S, 129a
ʿUmar b. Rubayʿān → Ibn Rubayʿān
ʿUmar b. Saʿd b. Abī Waḳḳās (VII) iii, 588a, 609b, 611a; iv, 836a; vii, 523a, 690a – III, 608a, 630a, 632a; IV, 869a; VII, 523b, 690b
ʿUmar b. Saʿīd al-Fūtī (1864) x, 122b, 464a, **825b** – X, 132a, 497b
ʿUmar b. Saʿīd al-Ḥādjdj (Malī) (XIX) vi, 259b; vii, 436a – VI, 244a; VII, 437a
ʿUmar b. Shabba b. ʿAbīda (878) i, 158b; v, 607b; x, **826b**; s, 38b – I, 163a; V, 611b; X, ; S, 39a
ʿUmar b. Sulaymān al-Shayẓamī → ʿUmar al-Sayyāf
ʿUmar b. ʿUbayd Allāh b. Maʿmar (VII) i, 120a, 810a, 1242b; vii, 671a – I, 123b, 833b, 1280b; VII, 671a
ʿUmar b. Wīghran b. Mandīl (XIV) vi, 404b – VI, 389a
ʿUmar b. Yūsuf b. Rasūl, al-Malik al-Ashraf (Rasūlid(e)) (1297) iii, 267a; vi, 829b –

III, 274b; VI, 820a
ʿUmar Agha Ḳara ʿOthmān-oghlu iv, 593a, b – IV, 617a, b
ʿUmar ʿArab (XX) vi, 177b – VI, 163a
ʿUmar Bā Makhrama Makhrama
ʿUmar the Cutler/le Coutelier (1475) vi, 226a, b, 228b – VI, 219b, 220b, 222a
ʿUmar Djaghāraʾī, Bahā al-Dīn (XV) vii, 126b – VII, 128b
ʿUmar Djibrīl, Shaykh (Niger) viii, 18a – VIII, 18a
ʿUmar Efendi (XVIII) i, 1271b; ii, 20a; vi, 227b – I, 1310b; II, 20a; VI, 221b
ʿUmar Fākhūrī s, 224b – S, 224b
ʿUmar Fatḥī s, 301a – S, 300b
ʿUmar al-Ḥusaynī (faḳīh) (1530) vi, 143a – VI, 141a
ʿUmar Khān (Khokand) (1822) vi, 765b, 768a – VI, 755a, 757a
ʿUmar Khān b. Aḥmad Shāh (Gudjarāt) (1438) vi, 52b, 53a – VI, 51a, b
ʿUmar Khān b. Nārbūta v, 29b – V, 30a, b
ʿUmar Khān Avar i, 755b – I, 778a
ʿUmar Khān Kāsī ii, 54b; s, 313a – II, 55b; S, 312b
ʿUmar Khān Sarwānī → ʿAbbās Sarwānī
ʿUmar Khayyām (1133) i, 113a, 839a, 841a, 1132a; ii, 362a, 397b, 533b; iii, 1139a; iv, 54a, 62a, 64a; vi, 275b, 600a, 638a; viii, 76a, 552b, 580a, 971b; x, **827b**; s, 35a, 235b, 412a, 413a, b, 414a – I, 116a, 862b, 864a, 1166a; II, 371b, 408b, 546b; III, 1167a; IV, 57a, 65b, 67b; VI, 260b, 585b, 623a; VIII, 78a, 570a, 598b, 1006a; X, ; S, 35a, 235b, 412a, 413a, b, 414b
ʿUmar Luṭfī (XX) x, 5b – X, 5b
ʿUmar Makram, al-Sayyid (1822) vii, 424a, 429b; x, **834a** – VII, 425b, 430b; X,
ʿUmar al-Mālaḳī al-Zadjdjal (XV) vi, 112a –VI, 109b
ʿUmar Mīrzā (Tīmūrid(e)) (XV) iv, 586a; vi, 202a – IV, 609a; VI, 186a
ʿUmar al-Mukhtār v, 758a – V, 764a
ʿUmar al-Murtaḍā, Abū Ḥafṣ (Almohad(e)) (1266) vi, 593a – VI, 577b
ʿUmar al-Mutawakkil i, 242b; iii, 680b, 813b – I, 250a; III, 702a, 837a
ʿUmar Nasuhī Bilmen → Bilmen
ʿUmar al-Nuʿmān ii, 234a; x, **834b** – II, 241a; X,
ʿUmar Pasha (Baghdād) (XVIII) i, 199a, 905a; vi, 551a, 811b – I, 204b, 932a; VI, 535b, 801b
ʿUmar Pasha Latas i, 1268b – I, 1307b
ʿUmar al-Rūshanī ii, 1136b, 1137a, b; iv, 991b; s, 208a – II, 1163a, 1164a, b; IV, 1024a; S, 208a
Umar Said Tall, al-Hajj ix, 853b – IX, 889a
ʿUmar al-Saḳḳāf (XX) vi, 154a – VI, 152a
ʿUmar Ṣayrafī (XX) ii, 527b; vi, 177b – VI, 163a
ʿUmar al-Sayyāf (1485) ii, 527b – II, 540b
ʿUmar Seyf al-Dīn (Omer Seyfettin) → ʿÖmer Seyf ül-Dīn
ʿUmar Shaykh Mīrzā I b. Tīmūr (Tīmūrid(e)) (1394) vii, 133a; ix, 667b; x, **835a** – VII, 135a; IX, 683b; X,
ʿUmar Shaykh Mīrzā II Kürägän b. Abī Saʿīd b. Tīmūr (Tīmūrid(e)) (1494) i, 148a, 847b; ii, 792a; x, **835b** – I, 152b, 870b; II, 810b; X,
ʿUmar Tal → al-Ḥādjdj ʿUmar
ʿUmar Ṭughrïl Tigin b. Maḥmūd Ṭughrïl Ḳara Khān (Ḳarakhānid(e)) (1074) vi, 557b – VI, 542a
ʿUmar al-Ẓāhir → Ẓāhir al-ʿUmar
ʿUmāra, Banū s, 222b – S, 222b
ʿUmāra b. ʿAkīl x, 69a – X, 71b
ʿUmāra b.ʿAlī al-Ḥakamī i, 197a, 552b, 593b – I, 202b, 570a, 613a
ʿUmāra b. ʿAmr i, 113b – I, 116b
ʿUmāra b. Khuraym al-Murrī (VIII) vii, 629b – VII, 629a
ʿUmāra b. Wathīma (902) x, **835b** – X,
ʿUmāra al-Yamanī (1174) ii, 861b; iii, 814b; v, 1244a; x, **836a** – II, 881b; III, 838b; V, 1235a; X,
al-ʿUmarī (Medina) (VIII) iii, 616a, 617a – III, 636b, 637b
al-ʿUmarī, ʿAbd al-Raḥmān (IX) i, 1158a; viii, 863a – I, 1192b; VIII, 894a
al-ʿUmarī, Aḥmad → Ibn Faḍl Allāh al-ʿUmarī
al-ʿUmarī, Amīn b. Khayr Allāh (1789) vii, 1040a – VII, 1042b
al-ʿUmarī, ʿIṣām al-Dīn ʿUthmān b. ʿAlī (XVIII) vii, 528a – VII, 528a
al-ʿUmariyya i, 1009a; iii, 659b – I, 1040a; III, 681a
Umaru Bakatara ii, 1146b – II, 1173b
Umaru Salaga iv, 550b – IV, 574a
al-Umawī, Yaʿīsh b. Ibrāhīm (1490) vii, 136a – VII, 138a
Umay (wife of/épouse de Tañrï) x, 688a – X,
ʿUmayr b. Bayān al-ʿIdjlī iv, 1132b – IV, 1164a
ʿUmayr b. Ḥubāb al-Sulamī ii, 1023b; iii, 819b; iv, 493a, 870b, 1186b; viii, 433b – II, 1047b; III, 843a; IV, 514b, 904a, 1219a; VIII, 448a
ʿUmayr b. Saʿd al-Anṣārī (VII) vii, 264b; viii, 433b – VII, 266a; VIII, 448a
ʿUmayr b. Shuhaym → al-Ḳuṭāmī
ʿUmayr b. Sinān al-Māzinī vi, 954b – VI, 946b
Umayya, Banū vii, 362a – VII, 364a
Umayya b. ʿAbd Allāh b. Khālid i, 148b, 1293a – I, 153a, 1333a
Umayya b. ʿAbd al-ʿAzīz, Abū 'l-Ṣalt (1134) i, **149a**; x, **836b** – I, **153b**; X,
Umayya b. ʿAbd Shams (VII) x, **837b** – X,
Umayya b. Abi 'l-—alt (VII) i, 44b, 149a, 418a, 565a, 584b; iii, 165b, 541b, 975b, 1206a; v, 180b; vi, 603b; vii, 363a; x, **839a**; s, 247a – I, 46a, **153b**, 429b, 583a, 603b; III, 169a, 560a, 1000a, 1236b; V, 178a; VI, 588b; VII, 365b; X, ;S, 247a
Umayya b. Khalaf (VII) i, 1215a; x. **839b** – I, 1251a; X,
Umayyad(e)s (Banū Umayya) i, 16a, 43a, 45a, 49a, 51b, 55b, 76a, 103a, 439b, 550a, 920a; ii, 360a; iv, 15b-16a; v, 736a; vi, 1b, 118b, 194a, 379a, 518a, 519a, 669b, 676a, 875b; vii, 42b; ix, 263b, 264a, b, 491a; x, **840a**; s, 103b, 116b, 396b – I, 16b, 44a, 46b, 50b, 53a, 57a, 78b, 106a, 452a, 567b, 947b; II, 370a; IV, 16b-17a; V, 741b; VI, 1b, 116b, 178a, 363a, 503a, 504a, 655b, 656a, 662b, 866b; VII, 42b; IX, 272a, b, 273a, 315b; X, ; S, 102b, 116a, 397a
Umayyad(e)s – administration ii, 304b, 323b; iv, 755b, 938a – II, 313a, 333a; IV, 785b, 971a
Umayyad(e)s – constructions i, 609b, 612b; ii, 280b, 821b; v, 10b-16b, 17a, 216b, 325b – I, 629b, 632b; II, 288b, 841a; V, 11a-17a, 17b, 214a, 325a, b
Umayyad(e)s – literature/littérature i, 118a, 760a – I, 121b, 782b
Umayyad(e)s in Spain/en Espagne vi, 2a, 221a, 331a, 712b; x, **847b** – VI, 2a, 215a, 316a, 701a; X,
Umbay İnaḳ s, 420a – S, 420a
ʿUmdat al-mulk iv, 758b – IV, 789a
Umīdī iv, 68b – IV, 72a
Umm ʿĀṣim i, 58b – I, 60b
Umm al-Banīn bint al-Mughīra b. ʿAbd al-Raḥmān (VII) i, 400b; ii, 1023b; vi, 139a – I, 412a; II, 1047a; VI, 137b
Umm Djaʿfar viii, 884a – VIII, 914b
Umm Djundad vii, 261a – VII, 263a

Umm Dubaykarāt (Sudān) i, 50a – I, 51b
Umm Dunayn (Maks) vi, 195a – VI, 179a
Umm al-Faḍl bint al-Maʾmūn (IX) i, 713a; vii, 396b – I, 734b; VII, 397b
Umm Farwa bint Abī Ḳuḥāfa (VII) vii, 400b – VII, 401b
Umm Gharayāt i, 418a – I, 430a
Umm Ḥabīb bint al-Maʾmūn (IX) i, 400b; vii, 396b – I, 412a; VII, 397b
Umm Ḥabība bint Abī Sufyān (VII) i, 151a; iv, 927b; vii, 264a, 862b – I, 155b; IV, 960b; VII, 266a, 864a
Umm Ḥakīm bint al-Ḥārith b. Hishām b. al-Mughīra (VII) vi, 139a, 546b, 547b – VI, 137a, 531a, 532a
Umm al-Ḥasan Sitt al-Mashāyikh Fāṭima (XIV) vii, 407b – VII, 408b
Umm Hāshim Fākhita bint Abī Hāshim b. ʿUtba(VII) vi, 622a; vii, 268a – VI, 607a; VII, 270a
Umm al-Ḥasan Fāṭima bint al-Ḥasan (IX) s, 334b – S, 334b
Umm Hishām (VIII) vi, 139b – VI, 137b
Umm ʿĪsā bint Mūsā al-Hādī (VIII) vi, 331b – VI, 316a
Umm al-Ḳaywayn vi, 38a; x, **853b**; s, 416b – VI, 36a; X, ;S, 417a
Umm al-Khaḳān bint Amīr Kabīr Mīrzā Muḥammad Taḳī Khān vii, 431b – VII, 432b
Umm Khalīl Shadjar al-Durr → Shadjar al-Durr
Umm Khāridja vi, 478a – VI, 464a
Umm al-Kitāb i, 89b; ii, 849a; iv, 203a; x, **854a** – I, 92a; II, 869a; IV, 212a; X,
Umm Kulthūm (singer/chanteuse) (1975) x, **855b** – X,
Ümm Külthūm bint Aḥmed III (Ottoman) (1724) vi, 860b – VI, 851b
Umm Kulthūm bint ʿAlī i, 109b, 136b, 308b; ii, 843a; iii, 889a; s, 13b – I, 112b, 140b, 318a; II, 863a; III, 913a; S, 14a
Umm Kulthūm bint Muḥammad (VII) x, **855a** – X,
Umm al-Ḳurā x, **856a** – X,
Umm al-Ḳuṣūr vi, 546a – VI, 531a
Umm al-Ḳuwayn viii, 435a – VIII, 449b
Umm Mūsā iv, 637b; s, 94a – IV, 663b; S, 93b
Umm al-Rabīʿ (Marrākush) vi, 593a, b – VI, 577b, 578a
Umm Rūmān bint ʿĀmir i, 109b, 110a, 307b – I, 112b, 113a, 317a
Umm al-Raṣāṣ x, **856a** – X,
Umm Salāma (VII) i, 258a, 308a; ii, 846a; iii, 64a, 612b; iv, 927a; vi, 650b; s, 230b – I, 266a, 317b; II, 866a; III, 66b, 633b; IV, 960a; VI, 635b; S, 230b
Umm Salama bint Mūsā al-Kāẓim (IX) vii, 647a – VII, 647a
Umm Salāma bint Yaʿḳūb b. Salama (VIII) vi, 139b – VI, 137b
Umm Salāma Hind bint Abī Umayya (679) x, **856b** – X,
Umm Sharīḳ bint ʿAṣar al-ʿUḳaylī s, 394a – S, 394b
Umm ʿUthmān → Sallāma al-Zarḳāʾ
Umm al-Walad x, **857a** – X,
Umm al-Walīd x, **859b** – X,
Umm Zaynab iii, 954b – III, 979a
Umma x, **859b** – X,
Umma Khān Avar i, 755b; ii, 87b – I, 778a; II, 89a
ʿUmmāl → ʿĀmil
Ummarār i, 1158b, 1239b – I, 1193a, 1277b
Ummī vii, 364b; x, **863b** – VII, 367a; X,
Umm-i Sinān, Shaykh (1658) viii, 65a – VIII, 66b
Ummīdī (1519) viii, 775a – VIII, 801a
ʿUmra x, **864b** – X,
ʿUmrā Khān ii, 30b, 317a – II, 31a, 326a
ʿUmūm wa-Khuṣūṣ x, **866b** – X,
Ümur I Pasha, Bahāʾ al-Dīn (Aydïnoghlu) (1348) i, 346a, 653b, 783a, 1302b; ii, 683b, 983b; iii, 115a, 1086a; v, 505b, 506a; vi, 1036a; vii, 47b; viii, 890a; x, **867a**; s, 330a – I, 356b, 674a, 806b, 1342b; II, 700b, 1006a; III, 117b, 1113a; V, 509a; VI, 1029a; VII, 47b; VIII, 920b; X, ; S, 329b
Ümür II (Aydïnoghlu) i, 783b; ii, 599a – I, 806b; II, 614a
Ümür Beg/Pasha → Ümür I (Aydïnoghlu)
Ümür Beg Timūrtāshoghlu v, 250a – V, 248a
Una (Gudjarāt) vi, 270b – VI, 255a
Unayf b. Daldja (VII) x, **867b** – X,
Unayza x, **867b**
ʿUnāza (ʿUnayza) i, 534a, 1312b; iv, 717a; vi, 153a; vii, 782b – I, 550a, 1352b; IV, 746a; VI, 151b; VII, 784b
al-Ungudja → Zandjibār
United Arab Emirates → al-Imārāt al-ʿArabiyya al-Muttaḥida
United Arab Republic → al-Djumhūriyya al-ʿarabiyya al-muttaḥida
al-Unḳalī/Unḳūriyya → Madjar
Unḳaliyyīn, Unḳūriyya → Madjar
ʿUnnāb x, **868a** – X,
Ūnsa II (Sinnār) (1692) ii, 944a, b; ix, 650b – II, 965b, 966a; IX, 675b
al-ʿUnṣulayn vi, 820b – VI, 811a
ʿUnṣur x, **868b** – X,
ʿUnṣur al'Maʿālī Kay Kāʾūs → Kay Kāʾūs
ʿUnṣurī, Abu ʾl-Ḳāsim Ḥasan (1039 (1049)) iv, 61a, 62b; vi, 66a, 276a, 453a, 609a; vii, 19a; x, **869a**; s, 21b – IV, 64b, 66a; VI, 64a, 261a, 438b, 594a; VII, 19a; X, ; S, 22a
Unūdjūr b. Muḥammad b. Ṭughdj (Ikhshīdid(e)) (961) iii, 129a; iv, 418a, b; vii, 161b, 411b; ix, 99b – III, 132a; IV, 436b; VII, 163a, 412b; IX, 307b
ʿUnwān x, **870b** – X,
ʿUnwān, Muḥammad Riḍa (1667) x, **872a** – X,
Ūparkōt ii, 597b, 598a; vi, 50b – II, 612b, 613a; VI, 49a
Ura Tübe v, 29b, 30a; vi, 419a; s, 228a – V, 30b, 31a; VI, 404a; S, 228a
ʿUrābī Pasha, Aḥmad (Miṣr) (1911) i, 141b, 142a, 815a, 1070a; ii, 28a, 417b, 514b; iii, 514a, 515a; vi, 586b, 602b, 643a; vii, 184a, b, 418b, 852a; x, 388b, **872a**; s, 132b, 408b, 411b – I, 146a, 838b, 1102a; II, 28a, 428b, 527a; III, 531b, 532b; VI, 571a, 587a, 628a; VII, 184b, 420a, 853b; X, 416b, ; S, 132a, 408b, 411b
ʿUrābī Sidjīnī (XX) vi, 157a – VI, 152b
ʿUrāʿir, Day of/Journée de s, 178a – S, 179a
Ural river → Yayïḳ
Urang Temür ii, 1112a; iv, 868a – II, 1138a; IV, 901b
ʿUrayʿir, Banū iv, 925a, b – IV, 958a, b
ʿUrayʿir (al-Aḥsāʾ) (XVIII) vi, 191b – VI, 175b
ʿUrayma vi, 579a – VI, 564a
Uraz Muḥammad Khān iv, 724a – IV, 753a
al-Urbus i, 104a, 163a, 250b; iv, 403a – I, 107a, 168a, 258b; IV, 420b
al-ʿUrḍī vii, 201a – VII, 201b
Urdjudhūna (Archidona) vii, 569a; x, **873a** – VII, 570a; X,
Urdjūza Radjaz
Urdū i, 430b, 505b, 807b, 827b; ii, 101a, 490b, 797a, 1036a; iii, 1b, 93b, 119a, 358b, 375b, 413a, 460b, 536b, 1057a, 1244b; iv, 716b; v, 201a, 635b, 958a, 1106a; vi, 62b; x, **873b**; s, 247a, 358b –

I, 442b, 521a, 830b, 850b; II, 103b, 503a, 815b, 1060a; III, 1b, 96a, 121b, 369b, 387b, 426a, 477a, 555a, 1083b, 1276b; IV, 745a; V, 198b, 639b, 962a, 1102a; VI, 60b; S, 247a, 358b
Urdū – literature/littérature vi, 610b, 827a, 837a; vii, 667b; x, **877b** – VI, 595a, 817b, 827b; VII, 667b
Urdumāniyyūn i, 83a, 494a; v, 1119b – I, 85b, 509a; V, 1116a
al-Urdunn (Jordan/-ie; Jordan/Jourdain) i, 39a, 46a, 534a, 975b, 1017a; ii, 555a, 662b; iii, 264a, 560a, b; iv, 262a; v, 337b, 912a, 1053b; vi, 31b, 32a, 388a, 797a; x, **881a**; s, 251b –
I, 40a, 47a, b, 550a, 1005b, 1048a; II, 569a, 679a; III, 272a, 579b, 580a; IV, 273b; V, 338a, 917b, 1050b; VI, 29b, 30a, 372b, 786b; X, ; S, 251b
—West Bank/Rive occidentale v, 1054b, 1055a – V, 1051a, 1052a
ʿUrf x, **887b** – X,
Urfa ’ al-Ruhā
Urfalï Nüzhet ʿÜmer Efendi (1778) vi, 632b – VI, 617b
ʿUrfī Shīrāzī, Djamāl al-Dīn (1591) i, 680a; ii, 794b, 878a; iv, 69a; v, 958a; vi, 608b; vii, 340b, 341a; viii, 775b; ix, 241b; x, **892a** –
I, 701a; II, 813a, 898b; IV, 72b; V, 962a; VI, 593a; VII, 342b; VIII, 801b; IX, 247b
Ürgenč (Urgenč, Urgandj) x, **892b** – X,
Urghan (Urghanūn) (organ/orgue) x, **893a** – X,
Uṙīsā (Orissa) vi, 67a, b, 343a, 406b, 535b; vii, 459a; x, **894b** – VI, 64b, 65a, 327a, 391b, 519b; VII, 459a; X,
Urīṭ iv, 482b – IV, 503b
ʿUrḳūb vi, 817a – VI, 807b
Urm x, **896a** – X,
Urmar → Orāmār
al-Urmawī, Ṣafī al-Dīn → Ṣafī al-Dīn
Urmiyā (Jeremiah/Jérémie) → Irmiyā
Urṃiya (Lake/Lac) i, 191a; iii, 569b; v, 442b vi, 72b, 120a, 498b, 500b, 502b, 504a, b; x, **896a** –
I, 196b; III, 589a; V, 445a; VI, 70b, 117b. 483b, 487b, 489b
ʿUrr ʿAdan → ʿAdan
ʿUrs (ʿUrus) x, **899b** – X,
ʿUrūba x, **907b** – X,
Urtuḳid(e)s → Artuḳid(e)s
Urudj b. ʿĀdil (XVI) x, **908a** – X,
ʿUrūḳ al-Rumayla ii, 92a – II, 93b, 94a
Urumči v, 846a, b; vi, 767a, 768a – V, 858a; VI, 756a, 757b
Urumiyya (Riḍā’iyya) vi, 203a – VI, 187b
Urus Khān (Tokay Tīmūrid(e)) (XIV) ii, 44a; x, 560b – II, 45a; X,
Urus Mīrzā i, 1075b – I, 1108a
Uruzgān s, 367a – S, 367b
ʿUrwa b. Ḥizām b. Muhāṣir al-ʿUdhrī (ca. 650)x, **908b** – X,
ʿUrwa b. Masʿūd b. Muʿattib al-Thaḳafī (630) iv, 839a; vii, 347a; x, **909a** – IV, 872a; VII, 349a; X,
ʿUrwa b. Udayya (658) iii, 169a; vii, 123a –
III, 172b; VII, 125a
ʿōrwa b. Udhayna (VIII) x, **909b** – X,
ʿUrwa b. al-Ward al-ʿAbsī (VII) i, 518b; ii, 1072b; iii, 941a; vii, 309b; ix, 864a; x, 2b, **910a** – I, 534a; II, 1097a; III, 965b; VII, 311b; IX, 900a; X, 2b,
ʿUrwa b. al-Zubayr b. al-ʿAwwām (710) i, 867b; iii, 24a; iv, 189b; v, 997b, 1161b; vii, 27a, 361a; viii, 533a; x, **910b**; s, 311a –
I, 892a; III, 25a; IV, 198a; V, 993a, 1151b; VII, 27a, 363b; VIII, 551a; X, ; S, 311a
ʿUrwa al-Raḥḥāl ii, 883b; iii, 285b; v, 101b – II, 904a; III, 294b; V, 103b
al-ʿUrwa al-wuthḳā ii, 429a – II, 440b
Uryūla x, **913a** – X,
Uşak s, 137b – S, 137a
al-Usāma i, 682b – I, 703b
Usāma b. Munḳidh (b. Murshīd) b. ʿAlī (1188) i, 9b, 570b, 593b, 665b, 680b, 1153b; ii, 64b, 318a, 739a, 740b, 1037a, 1065b; iii, 809a; iv, 514a; v, 9a, 330b; vi, 469b, 606a, 790a; vii, 577b, **578b**, 733b; viii, 133b, 913b; ix, 410b; s, 205a, 362a –
I, 9b, 589b, 613a, 686a, 701b, 1188a; II, 65b, 327a, 757b, 759a, 1061b, 1090b; III, 832b; IV, 536b; V, 9b, 330b; VI, 455a, 590b, 779b; VII, 578a, **579a**, 734b; VIII, 136a, 944b; IX, 424a; S, 204b, 362a
Usāma b. Zayd b. Ḥāritha al-Kalbī al-Salīḥī (674) i, 110b, 382b; ii, 327b; v, 1161b; vi, 877a; vii, 374b; x, **913a** –
I, 113b, 393b; II, 337b; V, 1151a; VI, 868b; VII, 376a; X,
Usāma b. Zayd al-Tanūkhī (720) ii, 327b; vi, 423b, 670b; viii, 41b – II, 337b; VI, 408b, 656b; VIII, 42b
Usayd b. Ḥuḍayr i, 514b; viii, 697b – I, 530b; VIII, 717b
Usays s, 117a, 229a – S, 116a, 229a
al-Usayyidī, ʿUmar b. Yazīd (727) ix, 282b – IX, 291a
al-Uṣba al-Andalusiyya → al-Mahdjar
ʿUṣfūr al-Azdī iv, 796b – IV, 828b
ʿUṣfūrid(e)s i, 553a, 942b; iv, 764b; x, **913b** – I, 570b, 971b; IV, 795a; X,
ʿUshāḳ (Uşak) x, **913b** – X,
Ushāḳī-zāde iv, 930a – IV, 963a
(al-)Ushbūna (Lisbon(ne)) i, 1338b; x, **914b** – I, 1379a; X,
al-Ūshī, ʿAlī b. ʿUthmān (1179 (?)) vi, 848a; x, **916a** – VI, 838b; X,
Ushmūm (idol(e) i, 126a – I, 129b
Ushmūm Ṭannāḥ (Miṣr) vi, 440a, b – VI, 425b, 426a
Ushmūnayn vi, 624b; x, **916a** – VI, 609b; X,
al-Ushnāndānī, Abū ʿUthmān Saʿīd (900)
iii, 757a; vi, 347b – III, 780a; VI, 332a
Ushnū (Ushnuh) vi, 494a, b, 500b; x, **916b** – VI, 479b, 480a, 486a; X,
ʿUshr x, **917a** – X,
Ushrūsana (Usrūshana) i, 241a; vi, 337b, 338b; vii, 395a; x, 924b; s, 406b – I, 248b; VI, 321b, 323a; VII, 396a; X, ; S, 406b
ʿUshshāḳī, Ḥasan Ḥusām al-Dīn (1592) x, 919a, 920a – X,
ʿUshshāḳiyya vi, 1004a; x, **920a** – VI, 996b; X,
ʿUshshāḳī-zāde x, **919a** – X,
ʿUshshāḳī-zāde, Ibrāhīm b. al-Seyyid (1724) x, **919b** – X,
Ushurma, Manṣūr (1794) x, **920b** – X,
Uskāf Banī Djunayd iii, 1267a – III, 1300a
Üsküb i, 698a, 1263a; vi, 70b, 89a; x, **922a** – I, 719b, 1301b; VI, 68b, 87a; X,
Üsküdār iii, 216b, 220a, 623a; iv, 233a, 244a, 720a, 1017a; v, 273a; vi, 3a, 57a, 227b, 529b; **x, 923b;** s, 315a – III, 223a, 226b, 644a; IV, 243a, 255a, 749a, 1049a; V, 271a; VI, 3a, 55a, 221a, 514a; X, ; S, 315a
Uslūdj b. al-Ḥasan ii, 860a; iii, 840b – II, 879b; III, 864b
Usman, Faqih (XX) vi, 732a – VI, 721a
Usman dan Fodio → ʿUthmān b. Fūdī
Ūsmī ii, 87a, 88a, 141b; iv, 846b – II, 88b, 90a, 145b; IV, 879b
Ustādār i, 33a, 801b; x, **925a** – I, 34a, 825a; X,
Ustādh x, **925b** – X,
al-Ustādh al-aʿẓam → Bā ʿAlawī, Muḥammad b. ʿAlī (1255)
Ustādh-Hurmuz iii, 244b – III, 251b
Ustādhsīs iii, 177b; iv, 16b; v, 1111b; vi, 428a; x, **926b**

– III, 181b; IV, 17b; V, 1107b; VI, 413b; X,
Ustadjlū, Aḥmad Beg (1576) vi, 16b – VI, 15a
Ustādjlū, Banū ii, 1101b, 1105a; viii, 769a – III, 1128b, 1132b; VIII, 794b
Ustadjlū, Muḥammad (1507) vi, 541a – VI, 526a
Ustān x, **927a** – X,
Ustāndār x, **927b** – X,
Usṭāth (Asṭath) (IX) x, **927b** – X,
Ustolnī Belghrād → Istōnī (Istolnī) Belghrād
Usṭūl x, **928a** – X,
Ustūnāwand (Djarhud) vi, 744b – VI, 733b
Usṭūra iii, 369a – III, 381a
Ustuwā vi, 869a; x, **928b** – VI, 860a; X,
Üst-Yurt Plateau vi, 415a, 416b – VI, 400a, 401b
Uṣūl x, **928b** – X,
Uṣūl al-Dīn x, **930b** – X,
Uṣūl al-Fiḳh x, **931b** – X
Uṣūl al-Ḥadīth x, **934a** – X,
Uṣūlī (1538) viii, 212b; s, 83a – VIII, 216b; S, 83a
Uṣūlīs iv, 50a; s, 103b – IV, 53a; S, 103a
Uṣūliyya vi, 549a, 550b, 551a; vii, 297b; viii, 779b; x, **935a**; s, 56b, 95b – VI, 533b, 535a, b; VII, 299b; VIII, 805b; X, ; S, 57a, 95a
Usuman iv, 550a – IV, 574a
Usuoghullarï s, 282b – S, 282a
Uswān (Aswan) v, 514b, 887a; vi, 366b; viii, 863b; x, **938a**; s, 7a, 8b, 35b, 36a, 57b – V, 518a, 893a; VI, 351a; VIII, 894a; X, ; S, 6b, 8a, 36a, 58a
al-Uswārī, Abū ʿAlī (IX) iv, 734b; vii, 401a – IV, 764a; VII, 402b
al-Uswārī, Mūsā b. Sayyār iv, 734b – IV, 764a
Ūsya iii, 1154b – III, 1183a
Usyūṭ → Asyūṭ
al-ʿUtab, Banū x, 91a – X, 98b
Uṭāmish (vizier) (863) vii, 390a, 722b, 723a – VII, 391b, 723b, 724a
ʿUṭārid (Mercury/-e) x, **940b** – X,
ʿUṭārid b. Ḥādjib iii, 49a – III, 51a
ʿUṭārid b. Muḥammad al-Ḥāsib (IX) i, 87a; x, **942b** – I, 89b; X,
al-ʿUṭayba, Baḥr (Damas(cus)) vi, 544b; x, **944a** – VI, 529a; X,
ʿUtayba, Banū i, 545b; ii, 354a; iii, 1065b; vi, 159a, 177b; vii, 782b; x, **942b** – I, 563a; II, 363b; III, 1092a; VI, 154a; VII, 784b; X,
ʿUtayba b. Abū Lahab i, 136b – I, 140b
ʿUtayba b. al-Ḥārith i, 1247b – I, 1285b
al-ʿUtaybī, Djuhaymān b. Muḥammad (XX) vi, 157b, 158a, b – VI, 153a, 153b
ʿUṭayf b. Niʿma iv, 493b – IV, 515a
ʿUtba (slave girl/esclave) (VIII) i, 107b; iv, 1164b – I, 110b; IV, 1196b
ʿUtba (ʿUtūb), Banū i, 482b – I, 497a
ʿUtba b. Abī Sufyān (VII) vi, 740b – VI, 730a
ʿUtba b. Abū Lahab i, 136b – I, 140b
ʿUtba b. Farḳad al-Sulamī (VII) v, 896b; vi, 899b; ix, 818a; x. 897a – V, 903a; VI, 891a; IX, 853a; X,
ʿUtba b. Ghazwān (635) i, 1085a; iii, 583a; v, 80b; vi, 647b, 920a; s, 354b – I, 1117b; III, 603a; V, 82b; VI, 633a, 911b; S, 354b
ʿUtba b. Ḳays b. Zuhayr al-ʿAbsī s, 177b – S, 178b
ʿUtba b. Rabīʿa b. ʿAbd Shams (624) x, **944b** – X,
al-ʿUtbī (1035) i, 591b – I, 611a
al-ʿUtbī, Abū ʿAbd Allāh Muḥammad (868) i, 600a; x, **945b** – I, 619b; X,
al-ʿUtbī, Abū ʿAbd al-Raḥmān Muḥammad (842) i, 591b; x, **945b** – I, 611a; X,
al-ʿUtbī, Abū Djaʿfar (vizier) (958) vii, 26a; x, 945a – VII, 26a; X.
al-ʿUtbī, Abu ʾl-Ḥusayn (vizier) (982) vi, 340a; viii, 110a, 1027b, 1028a; x, 945a; s, 72b, 265b – VI, 324b; VIII, 112b, 1062a, 1063a; X, ; S, 73a, 265b
al-ʿUtbī, Abū Naṣr (vizier) (X) vi, 340a – VI, 324b
al-ʿUtbī, Abu ʾl-Naṣr Muḥammad b. ʿAbd al-Djabbār (1036) vi, 278b; vii, 21a; x, 945a – VI, 263b; VII, 21a; X,
al-ʿUtbī, Āl x, **945a** – X,
al-Uthāl (al-Athal) x, **946a** – X,
ʿUthmān I, II, III (Ottoman) → ʿOthmān I, II, III
ʿUthmān II Abū Saʿīd (Marīnid(e)) (1331) iii, 909a; vi, 124a, 572b, 593b, 594a; s, 112b – III, 933b; VI, 122a, 557b, 578a, b; S, 112a
ʿUthmān, Abū ʿUmar i, 1152b; ii,540a; iii, 69a – I, 1186b; II, 553b; III, 71b
ʿUthmān, Banū (Maʿḳil) vi, 141b – VI, 140a
ʿUthmān, Sayyid iii, 457a – III, 473a
ʿUthmān b. ʿAbd Allāh b. Bishr iii, 103a – III, 105b
ʿUthmān b. Abi ʾl-ʿĀṣ i, 695b; ii, 811b, 823b; iv, 14b – I, 716b; II, 831a, 843a; IV, 15b
ʿUthmān b. Abī Bakr → ʿUthmān Digna
ʿUthmān b. Abī Bakr (Gidadd dan Laima) (XIX) vii, 435b – VII, 436b
ʿUthmān b. Abī Shayba (853) vii, 691a – VII, 691b
ʿUthmān b. Abi ʾl-ʿUlā, vizier (XIV) vii, 1023a, b – VII, 1025a, b
ʿUthmān b. Abī Yūsuf → ʿUthmān II (Marīnid(e))
ʿUthmān b. ʿAffān (656) i, 43b, 51b, 52a, 92b, 93a, 114b, 195a, 308a, 336b, 381b, 382a, 451b, 549b, 704a, 957b; ii, 414a, 1023b; iii, 240b, 272a, 539a, 583a, 587a, 1163b; iv, 937b; v, 405a, 996b; vi, 138b, 139a, 147a, 279b, 379a, 603a, 604a, 621b, 660a, 661b, 663b, 664a, 665b, 668b, 670a, 671a, 676a, 677a; vii, 263b, 394b; ix. 505a;x, **946a**; s, 10a, 89b, 129b, 130a, 131a, 198b, 221b, 230b, 304b, 343a – I, 44b, 53a, 53b, 95b, 118a, 200b, 317b, 347a, 392b, 393a, 464b, 567a, 725b, 987a; II, 425a, 1047a; III, 247b, 279b, 558a, 603a, 607a, 1192a; IV, 970b; V, 406b, 992a; VI, 137a, b, 138a, 145b, 264b, 363a, 588a, b, 606b, 646a, 647b, 649b, 650a, 651b, 654b, 656a, 657a, 662b, 663b, 664a; VII, 265b, 395b; IX, 524b; X, ; S, 9b, 89b, 129a, 130a, 198b, 221b, 230b, 304b, 343a
ʿUthmān b. Aḥmad → ʿUthmān b. Muʿammar
ʿUthmān b. ʿAnbasa b. Abī Sufyān (VII) vii, 268b – VII, 270b
ʿUthmān b. al-ʿAṣ (VII) iv, 220a; viii, 435b – IV, 229b; VIII, 450a
ʿUthmān b. Čaghrï Beg Dāwūd (Saldjūḳ) (XI) vi, 273b – VI, 258b
ʿUthmān b. Čaḳmaḳ ii, 6b; iii, 1198a – II, 6b; III, 1228b
ʿUthmān b. Fūdī (Ibn Fūdī/Usman dan Fodio, Tukulor, Sokoto) (1817) i, 179b, 303a; ii, 941b, 942a, 1003b, 1144b; iii, 276b; iv, 549b; v, 394b, 1166a; vi, 281b; vii, 435b; viii, 18a, b; x, 122a, **949b** – I, 184b, 312b; II, 963b, 1027a, 1172a; III, 284b; IV, 573b; V, 395b, 1155b; VI, 266b; VII,436b; VIII, 18a, b; X, 132a.
ʿUthmān b. Ḥayyān al-Murrī (VIII) i, 113a; vii, 629b; ix, 821b – I, 116b; VII, 629a; IX, 856a
ʿUthmān b. Ḥunayf ii, 415a; iii, 583a – II, 425b; III, 603a
ʿUthmān b. al-Ḥuwayrith (VI) vi, 146a – VI, 144a
ʿUthmān b. Ḳaṭan iii, 715b – III, 738a
ʿUthmān b. Khalīfa ʿAbd Allāh (Shaykh al-Dīn) (1900) v, 1250b, 1251b, 1252a – V, 1241b, 1242b, 1242b
ʿUthmān b. Marzūḳ (1169) x, **951b** – X,

ʿUthmān b. Maẓʿūn b. Ḥabīb (625) i, 957b; ii, 1060a; iii, 1017b; iv, 1089a; viii, 396b; x, **951b** – I, 987a; II, 1084b; III, 1043a; IV, 1120b; VIII, 410b; X,
ʿUthmān b. Muʿammar ii, 321a; iii, 678a; iv, 925a – II, 330b; III, 700a; IV, 958a
ʿUthmān b. Muḥammad Fodiye – ʿUthmān b. Fūdī
ʿUthmān b. Niẓām al-Mulk, vizier (XII) vii, 735a – VII, 735b
ʿUthmān b. Saʿīd al-ʿAmrī (IX) i, 713a; iii, 247a; vii, 443b – I, 734b; III, 254a; VII, 444b
ʿUthmān b. Ṣāliḥ (832) vi, 413b; viii, 854a – VI, 398b; VIII, 883b
ʿUthmān b. Ṭalḥa iii, 975b; iv, 320b – III, 1000a; IV, 334b
ʿUthmān b. ʿUmāra b. Khuraym al-Murrī (VIII) vii, 629b – VII, 629a
ʿUthmān b. al-Walīd II iii, 990b – III, 1015a
ʿUthmān b. Yaghamrāsan (Mandīl) (XIII) vi, 404a, b – VI, 389a
ʿUthmān Ādam (Djānū) (XIX) v, 267b, 1250b – V, 265b, 1241a
ʿUthmān Āghā Mustaḥfiẓān iv, 438a – IV, 457b
ʿUthmān ʿAlī Khān ii, 99b; iii, 323a – II, 101b; III, 332b
ʿUthmān al-Battī v, 731a – V, 736a
ʿUthmān Batūr (1943) ix, 649b – IX, 674b
ʿUthmān Bey al-Bardīsī (1807) ii, 292b; iv, 853a; vii, 423b – II, 300b; IV, 886a; VII, 425a
ʿUthmān Bey Dhu 'l-Faḳār iv, 852a, b – IV, 885b
ʿUthmān Dāy (Dayi̊/Dey, Tunis) (1610) i, 496a, b; ii, 161a; iv, 338b; vii, 243a – I, 511a; II, 166a; IV, 352b; VII, 244b
ʿUthmān Diḳna (Osman Digna) b. Abī Bakr (XIX) i, 49b, 1158b, 1239b; iv, 687a; v, 1249b, 1250a, 1251a; x, **952a** – I, 51a, 1193a, 1277b; IV, 715a; V, 1240a, 1241a, b; X,
ʿUthmān al-Djāzānī ii, 517b – II, 530b
ʿUthmān dan Fodio → ʿUthmān b. Fūdī
ʿUthmān al-Ḥaddād v, 51a – V, 52b
ʿUthmān Katkhudā al-Kazdughlī i, 815a – I, 838a
ʿUthmān Khān (Djālor) ii, 1127a – II, 1153b
ʿUthmān Khān b. Ibrāhīm (Ḳarakhānid(e)) (1212) iii, 1115a; iv, 583a, 1067b, 1068a; viii, 1033b – III, 1142b; IV, 607a, 1099b; VIII, 1069a
ʿUthmān al-Muḍāʾifī iii, 363b – III, 375a
ʿUthmān al-Nābalusī → al-Nābalūsī
ʿUthmān Pasha → ʿOthmān Pasha
ʿUthmān Sirādj al-Dīn (XIX) vii, 935b – VII, 936a
ʿUthmān Ulīdī (Bizerta) (XIX) vi, 251a – VI, 235a
ʿUthmān al-Zandjīlī i, 181b; s, 338a – I, 186b; S, 337b
ʿUthmān al-Zindjārī x, 303a – X, 326a
ʿUthmān-i Marandī → Shāhbāz Ḳalandar
ʿUthmānid(e)s iv, 89b – IV, 93b
ʿUthmāniyya x, **952a** – X,
ʿUthmānzāde iv, 505a – IV, 527a
ʿUthmānzay s, 285a – S, 285a
Uthūlūdjiyā (theology/ie) x. **954b** – X,
Utrār (Otrār) ii, 43a, 778b; x, **955a** – II, 44a, 797a; X,
al-ʿUtrūsh → Ḥasan al-Uṭrūsh
Utsmi → Ḳaytaḳ
Uttar Pradesh vi, 489a; s, 74a, 325a, 360a – VI, 475a; S, 74b, 324b, 359b
al-ʿUtūb (sing. ʿUtbī) iv, 751a; vi, 358a, 735a, b; viii, 668b; x, **955b** – IV, 781a; VI, 342a, 724b; VIII, 688a; X,
Uwāl iv, 664a, b – IV, 690b, 691a
Uwaym b. Lāwudh (Lud) iii, 1270a – III, 1303a
ʿUwaymir b. Ḥārith v, 730b – V, 736a
ʿUwayṣ → Aʿyāṣ
Uways I b. Ḥasan-i Buzurg (Djalāyirid(e)) (1374) i, 325a, 720a, 1096a; ii, 401a, 733b; iv, 584b; vii, 189a; x, **957a** – I, 335a, 741b, 1129a; II, 411b, 752a; IV, 608a; VII, 189b; X,
Uways II b. Shāh Walad (Djalāyirid(e)) (1421) x, **957b** – X,
Uways b. Muḥammad b. Baykarā (Tīmūrid(e) (XV) i, 148a – I, 152a
Uways al-Ḳaranī (657) vi, 354a; vii, 472b, 592a; x, **958a** – VI, 338a; VII, 472a, 592a; X,
Uways Muḥammad, Shaykh (1909) ix, 722b – IX, 754a
Uways Pasha (Yemen) (XVI) viii, 235b – VIII, 240b
Uwaysiyya x, **958a** – X,
Üweys, Ḳara (1591) x, **958b** – X,
al-ʿUyayna i, 628b; ii, 321a; iii, 677b, 678a; x, **959a** – I, 649b; II, 330b; III, 699a, 700a; X,
ʿUyayna b. Ḥiṣn al-Fazārī (VII) i, 690a, 1077b, 1358b; ii, 873b, 1023a; v, 79b; ix, 115b; x, **959b** – I, 711a, 1110a, 1398b; II, 893b, 1047a; V, 81b; IX, 120a; X,
Uyghur i, 1240a; ii, 2b, 311a, 315b, 840a, 1106b; iii, 115b, 116a, 217a, 1116a; iv, 699b; v, 846a, b; vi, 421b, 768a; vii, 353a; viii, 178a; x, 687b, 688a; s, 97b, 419a, 420a – I, 1278a; II, 2b, 320a, 324b, 859b, 1133a; III, 118a, 223b, 1143a; IV, 727b, 728a; V, 858a; VI, 406b, 757b; VII, 355b; VIII, 180b; X, 730a, 751b; S, 97a, 419b, 420a
Uyghur Khān (XVII) vii, 220a – VII, 222a
Uyghur Literature x, **725b** – X,
Uyghur, On x, 687b – X, 730a
Uyrat → Kalmuks
ʿUyūn Dāwūdiyya vi, 230a – VI, 224a
ʿUyūn Mūsā → ʿAyn Mūsā
ʿUyūn Sīdī Mallūk vi, 892a – VI, 883b
ʿUyūnid(e)s i, 73b, 552a, 553a, 942a; iii, 238a; iv, 764b; vii, 628b; x, **960a** – I, 76a, 570a, b, 971a; III, 245a; IV, 795a; VII, 628b; X,
Uyvar s, 171a – S, 171b
Ūzār → Ong Khān
ʿUzayr (Ezra) x, **960a** – X,
ʿUzayr (ʿIrāḳ) i, 265a; vii, 582b; s, 33b – I, 273a; VII, 583a; S, 33b
al-ʿUẓayyim → al-ʿAḍaym
ʿUzayyiz b. Fayṣal iii, 1067b, 1068a – III, 1094b
Uzbek, Uzbak, Uzbīk → Özbeg
Uzbek Literature x, **721a** – X, **766b**
Uzbekistan i, 531a; vi, 770a; x, **960b** – I, 547a; VI, 759a; X,
Uze → Ghuzz
Uzganī, Aḥmad b. Saʿd al-Dīn (X) x. 958a – X,
Uzgend, Uzkend → Özkend
Uzuk ii, 806a – II, 825b
Uzun Ḥasan (Ḥasan al-Ṭawīl) (Aḳ-Ḳoyunlu) (1478) i, 148b, 244a, 293a, 311b, 340a, 393a, 468b, 861b, 1067a, 1234a, 1252b; ii, 150a, 151a, 174a, 598b, 839b, 1136a; iii, 212b, 315b, 1101a; iv, 34a, 463a, 474a, 562b, 588a, 871a, 945a, 1048a; v, 492a; vi, 71a, 72a, 117b, 120a, 495a, 514a, 541a, 979a; vii, 173b, 666b, 727a; viii, 766b; x, 45b, **963b**; s, 208a – I, 152b, 251a, 302a, 321a, 350b, 404b, 482a, 885b, 1099a, 1270b, 1290b; II, 154b, 155b, 179b, 613b, 859b, 1163a; III, 218b, 325a, 1128a; IV, 36b, 483b, 495a, 585a, 611b, 904b, 978a, 1079b; V, 495a; VI, 69a, b, 115a, 118a, 480a, 499a, 525b, 971a; VII, 175b, 665b, 727b; VIII, 792a; X, 47a, ; S, 208a
Uzun Khalīl i, 1257a – I, 1295a
al-ʿUzzā iv, 321b; v, 692a, b; vi, 373b, 374a, 645b; x, **967b** – IV, 336a; V, 697a, b; VI, 358a, b, 630b; X,

V

Vahrām → Bahrām
Vaikom Muhammad Basheer (XX) vi, 464b – VI, 450a
Vakf-Mearif i, 1274b – I, 1313b
Vakhtang (1676) → Shāh Nawāz I
Vakhtang (1724) v, 493b, 494a – V, 496b
Valachie → Eflāḳ
Valencia/-ce → Balansiya
Valenia → Bāniyās
Vālide Djāmiʿi → Yeni Djāmiʿ
Valona → Awlonya
Vambéry, Arminius (XIX) viii, 250b – VIII, 267a
Van (lake/lac) → Wān
Van Ḳaraḥiṣārî iv, 580b – IV, 604a
Van Kulu ii, 497a – II, 509a
Vardar → Wardar
Varna → Warna
Varvar ʿAlī Pasha iii, 318a, 983b; v, 257a – III, 327b, 1008a; V, 254b
Vasak i, 939b – I, 968a
Vaspurakan i, 637b, 638a – I, 658a, 658b
Vasvár, treaty of/traité de v, 259b – V, 257b
Vāvār (Mappila) vi, 463b – VI, 449b
Veda iii, 112b; iv, 206a – III, 115a; IV, 215b
Vedat Nedim Tör (XX) vi, 95a – VI, 93a
Velez/Vélez → Bālish
Venice/Venise x, 966a – X,
Vermudo II (Léon) (X) vi, 431b – VI, 417a
Vernāg s, 366b – S, 366a, b
Verne s, 136a – S, 135b
Vérria → Karaferye
Veysel → ʿĀshîḳ Weysel; Uways al-Ḳaranī
Vezīr Köprü v, 256a – V, 254a
Vidin → Widin
Vidjāyanagara i, 199b; ii, 981a; iii, 147b, 417a, b, 421a, 425a, 426a, 1160b; v, 549b, 938a, 1258b – I, 205a; II, 1003b; III, 151a, 430b, 431a, 434b, 438b, 440a, 1189a; V, 554b, 942a, 1249b
Vidyāpati i, 1168a – I, 1203a
Vienna/-e → Viyana
Vietnam ii, 9a; iii, 1208b – II, 9a; III, 1239b
Vikram → Bikrami
Vilayet → Wilāyāt
Vilches → Bildj
Vishtāsp → Bishtāsb
Viyana i, 294b, 1157b, 1285b; iv, 591b – I, 303b, 1191b, 1325a; IV, 615b
Vizier → Wazīr
Vlad Drakul (XV) vi, 71a – VI, 69a
Vlora → Awlonya
Volga → Itil
Volodimir I (Rūs) (1015) x, 692b – X, 735a
Volubilis → Walīlā/Walīlī
Voyvoda i, 1253a; iv, 1095b – I, 1291a; IV, 1126b
Vrančić, Antun (Verantius) s, 185b – S, 186b

W

Waba' iii, 240a – III, 246b
Wabar viii, 576a – VIII, 595a
Wabdha (Huete) i, 161a – I, 165b
Wād Bū Regreg vi, 135a – VI, 133b
Wādaʿa (Yemen) vi, 436a – VI, 421a, b
Wadāʿi (Wādāy, Čad) i, 98a, 910b, 1260a; ii, 123a, b, 124a; v, 357b; s, 164a, b, 165b, 166a – I, 100b, 938a, 1298a, b; II, 126a, b, 127b; V, 359a; S, 164a, b, 165b, 166a
Waḍḍāḥ al-Yaman x, 124b; s, 272b – X, 134a; S, 272a
Wad(d)ān ii, 575a, b; vi, 742b, 945b; vii, 623b – II, 589b, 590a; VI, 731b, 938a; VII, 623a
Wadhārī s, 176b – S, 177b
Wādī ʿAbadān vi, 81a – VI, 79a
Wādī 'l-ʿAbīd vi, 340a, 742a; s, 223b – VI, 324a, 731a; S, 223b
Wādī Abū Ḍabʿa s, 173b – S, 174b
Wādī Abū Rakrāk viii, 506b – VIII, 524a
Wādī 'l-Abyaḍ v, 1156a – V, 1145b
Wādī Adhana (Dhana) vi, 559a, 560a, 561b, 562a, b, 564a, 565b – VI, 543b, 544b, 546b, 547a, 549a, 550b
Wādī al-Aḥḳāf vi, 81a – VI, 79a
Wādī ʿAkl s, 159b – S, 159b
Wādī ʿAllāḳī → al-ʿAllāḳī, Wādī
Wādī ʿAllāla x, **180a** – X, **193b**
Wādī Ānā i, 489a – I, 503b
Wādī 'l-ʿArab (Cyrenaica/Cyrénaïque) vi, 455b – VI, 441a
Wādī ʿAraba (Jordan/-ie) i, **558b**; s, 117a – I, **576a**; S, 116b
Wādī Arīgha → Wādī Rīgh
Wādī Āsh (Guadix) vi, 575b; s, 399a – VI, 560b; S, 399a
Wādī Badr vi, 191a, b – VI, 174b, 175b
Wādī Barhūt → Barhūt
Wādī 'l-Baṭn viii, 613b – VIII, 632b, 633a
Wādī Bayhān → Bayhān, wādī
Wādī Buṭnān → Buṭnān
Wādī Ḍahr vi, 191a – VI, 175a
Wādī Damā s, 356a – S, 356a
Wādī Darʿa (Dra) vi, 134b; x, 170b – VI, 132b; X, 183b
Wādī Dawʿan → Dawʿan
Wādī 'l-Dawāsir i, 337a, 341a, 538a; ii, 177a – I, 347b, 351a, 554b; II, 182b
Wādī 'l-Djarīr vii, 865b – VII, 867a
Wādī Djayzān i, 109a; ii, **516a** – I, 129b; II, **529a**
Wādī Duwayro i, 489a – I, 503b
Wādī Farsān vi, 167a – VI, 159a
Wādī Fāṭima vi, 162b, 167a, 179b – VI, 156a, 159a, 163b
Wādī Fā'w ii, **867b** – II, **887b**
Wādī Ḥadjar i, 538a; vii, 496b – I, 555a; VII, 496b
Wādī Ḥaḍramawt i, 538a; iii, 51b, 52a; vi, 80a; x, 303a – I, 555a; III, 53b; VI, 78a; X, 326a
Wādī Ḥalfayn vi, 84b – VI, 82b
Wādī 'l-Ḥamḍ → Ḥamḍ, Wādī al-
Wādī Ḥanīfa i, 538b, 628b; ii, 92a – I, 555a, 649b; II, 94a
Wādī Ḥarīb → Ḥarīb
Wādī Ḥibawnā vi, 191a – VI, 175a
Wādī Ibrāhīm vi, 179b – VI, 163b
Wādī Ibro → Ibruh
Wādī Issīl vi, 589a – VI, 574a
Wādī 'l-Kabīr i, 487b, 489a; iv, 116a – I, 502a, 503b; IV, 121a
Wādī 'l-Ḳilt s, 173b – S, 174b
Wādī Ksob vi, 727b – VI, 716b
Wādī 'l-Ḳurā v, 317b, 497b; vi, 344a, 875a; vii, 265a, 371b, 694a – V, 317a, 500b; VI, 328b, 866a; VII, 266b, 373b, 694a
Wādī Madhāb vi, 436a – VI, 421a
Wādī 'l-Madīna vi, 220b – VI, 214a
Wādī Madraka vi, 167a – VI, 159a
Wādī 'l-Makhāzin i, 288b, 1058a; iii, 721a; v, 48b; vi, 894b – I, 297b, 1098b; III, 743b; V, 50a; VI, 886a
Wādī Masīla vi, 80a, 83a; x, 303a – VI, 78a, 81a; X, 326a

Wādī Mellegue vi, 727a – VI, 716a
Wādī Miskyana vi, 727a – VI, 716a
Wādī Nabhān iv, 779b – IV, 811a
Wādī Naʿmān vi, 179b – VI, 163b
Wādī al-Naṭrūn → Naṭrūn; Dayr al-Suryānī
Wādī Nūn vi, 134a – VI, 132b
Wādī Radjil vii, 865a – VII, 866a
Wādī Rahyū vi, 404a – VI, 388b
Wādī Ramāʾ vi, 80a – VI, 78a
Wādī 'l-Raml v, 530a – V, 534a
Wādī Rī v, 1181b – V, 1171b
Wādī Rimaʿ i, 1140b – I, 1175a
Wādī 'l-Rumah i, 538a, 1097b – I, 554b, 1130b
Wādī 'l-Rumma vii, 865b; viii, **613a** – VII, 867a; VIII, **632b**
Wādī Sabū v, 1185b, 1245a, b; vi, 741a – V, 1175b, 1236a; VI, 730b
Wādī 'l-Sadīr → Wādī Tūmīlāt
Wādī al-Sahbāʾ i, 538b; ii, 92a; iv, 1072b – I,555a, II, 94a; IV, 1104a
Wādī Ṣaḥr vi, 727b – VI, 716b
Wādī Salīṭ vii, 808a – VII, 810a
Wādī Sarīr viii, 613a – VIII, 632b
Wādī Shaḳūra i, 489a – I, 503b
Wādī Shalīf (Chélif) vi, 923b – VI, 915a
Wādī Shanīl vi, 221b – VI, 215a
Wādī Sīdī Tūdjimān vii, 263a – VII, 264b
Wādī Sirḥān i, 538a; vi, 490b; vii, 865a; ix, **673a** – I, 554b; VI, 476b; VII, 866a; IX, **700b**
Wādī Sūf ix, **763b** – IX, **796b**
Wādī Sūs vi, 742a – VI, 731a
Wādī Tadghat s, 132a – S, 132a
Wādī Tadjū i, 489a – I, 503b
Wādī Tansift vi, 589a – VI, 574a
Wādī 'l-Taym vi, 344a – VI, 328a
Wādī Thawba vi, 81a – VI, 79a
Wādī Tifālfalt vi, 594b – VI, 579b
Wādī al-Tīh ix, 912a – IX, 950b
Wādī Tūmī(ay)lāt i, 14b; x, 167b – I, 14b; X, 180b
Wādī Turaba i, 1299a; v, 62a; x, **670a** – I, 1339a; 64a, X, **722b**
Wādī Umm Rabīʿ vi, 589a, 741a, b – VI, 573b, 730b, 731a
Wādī Wargha s, 103a – S, 102b
Wādī Zabīd i, 1140b – I, 1175a
Wādī 'l-Zāhir vi, 179b – VI, 163b
Wādī Zīz x, 82b – X, 86a
al-Wādī Āshī (1158) vi, 111a – VI, 108b
Wādiḥ (Ṭulayṭulā) (XI) i, 1044b; iii, 495b, 791a; viii, 880a – I, 1076a; III, 512b, 814b; VIII, 910a
Wādīs (Tihāma) x, 482a – X, 517b
al-Wādiyāshī, Muḥammad b. Djābir ii, 744a – II, 762b
Wadjda i, 357b, 1281b; v, 1177a, 1187a; vi, 142b; viii, 440a – I, 368a, 1320b; V, 1167a, 1177a; VI, 141a; VIII, 455a
Wadjdī, Muḥammad Farīd (1954) i, 598a; iv, 159b, 720b; vi, 113b – I, 617b; IV, 166a, 749b; VI, 111a
Wadjdjādj b. Zallū (Zalw) (XI) vi, 744a; vii, 613a; s, 27a – VI, 733a; VII, 612b; S, 27a
Wadjh al-Ḳamar i, 280b – I, 289a
Wadjhī, Mullā ii, 865b; iii, 375b – II, 885b; III, 387b
Wādjid ʿAlī Khān (XIX) vi, 908b – VI, 900a
Wādjid ʿAlī Shāh, Nawwāb (Awadh) (1856) i, 757b; ii, 7b, 73a; v, 635a; vi, 611b, 772b, 806a – I, 780a; II, 7b, 74b; V, 639a; VI, 596b, 762a, 795b
Wadjīh al-Dīn Gudjarātī, Shaykh (XIV) i, 764b; vii, 440a – I, 787b; VII, 441a
Wadjīh al-Dīn Masʿūd (Sabzawār) (1343) ix, 47b – IX, 48b
Wadjīh al-Dīn Zangī b. al-Faryūmādī (1287) viii, 342b – VIII, 354b
Wadjīhid(e)s (ʿUmān) vii, 484b – VII, 484b
al-Wādjikā → Abū Aḥmad ʿAbd al-Salām
al-Wadjnāʾ b. Rawwād al-Azdī (Tabrīz) (IX) vi, 499a; x, 42a – VI, 484b; X, 43b
Wafāʾī → Aḥmad Ḥādjdjī Beg
al-Wafāʾī, ʿAbd al-ʿAzīz (1450) ix, 252b – IX, 260a
Wafāʾiyya ix, 173a – IX, 178b
Wafd ii, 467a, 934a; iii, 516a, 1069a; iv, 197b, 261a; vii, 904b, 905a; viii, 700a, b; s, 5b, 58a, 300b – II, 478b, 956a; III, 533b, 1095b; IV, 206a, 272b; VII, 905b; VIII, 720a, b; S, 4b, 58b, 300a
al-Wāfī, Shaykh Aḥmad (1921) viii, 449a – VIII, 464a
Wāfidiyya i, 946b, 1324b – I, 975b, 1365b
Wafīk Pasha → Aḥmad Wafīk Pasha
Wafḳ ii, 370a; v, 222b – II, 380a; V, 220a
Wahb, Banū vii, 477a; viii, 535b – VII, 476b; VIII, 553b
Wahb b. Baḳiyya i, 949a – I, 978a
Wahb b. al-Munabbih, Abū ʿAbd Allāh (728) ii, 363b; iii, 14a, 370a, 538a; iv, 212a, 369a; v, 811b; vii, 283b; viii, 478a; s, 88a, 116a – II, 373b; III, 14b, 382a, 556b; IV, 221b, 385b; V, 817b; VII, 285b; VIII, 494a; S, 87b, 115b
al-Wahbiyya ii, 459b, 460a; iii, 659a; vii, 893a – II, 471a, 472a; III, 680a; VII, 893b
Waḥdetī → Derwīsh Wāḥdetī
Wahhābīs/-iyya i, 38b, 98b, 106b, 166b, 233b, 277a, 528b, 554a, 628b, 748a, 1282a; ii, 10a, 63b, 254b, 517b, 572b, 625b, 783b; iii, 162b, 238a, 291b, 431a, 433a, 606a, 677b, 954b, 999a, 1064b; iv, 626a, 778a, 1073a; v, 62b, 507b, 808a, 997b, 998b; vi, 35a, 45b, 56b, 58b, 150b, 238a, 260a, 651b, 665a, 735b; vii, 425b; viii, 238a, 447a; x, 943b; s, 3b, 30b, 94b, 244b, 355b – I, 39b, 101a, 109b, 171a, 241a, 286a, 544b, 571b, 649b, 770b, 1321a; II, 10a, 64b, 262a, 530b, 587a, 641b, 802b; III, 166a, 245a, 300b, 445a, 447a, 627a, 699a, 979b, 1024a, 1091a; IV, 651a, 809a, 1104b; V, 64b, 511a, 814a, 993a, 994a; VI, 33b, 44a, 54b, 56b, 149a, 211a, 244b, 637a, 651a, 724b; VII, 427a; VIII, 243b, 462a; X, ; S, 2b, 30b, 94a, 244a, 355b
Wahhābī doctrine i, 188b, 259b, 416b, 714b, 1199b; iii, 679a; iv, 142b – I, 194a, 267b, 428b, 736a, 1235a; III, 700b; IV, 148b
Wahhābī literature/littérature i, 796b; ii, 91b; iii, 773a – I, 820a; II, 93a; III, 796a
Wahhās b. Ghānim v, 1244b – V, 1235a
Waḥīd → Yaḥyā-i Dārābī
Wahid Hasjim, K.H. (XX) vi, 731a, b – VI, 720a, b
Wāḥidī (1535) iv, 472b, 473b; viii, 775b – IV, 493b, 494bl VIII, 801a
al-Wāḥidī, Abu 'l-Ḥasan (1076) v, 415b; vi, 476b, 913a; vii, 771a, b – V, 417a; VI, 462b, 904b; VII, 773a, b
Wāhidī, Banū ii, 222b – II, 229b
Wahīd-i Dastgardī iv, 71b – IV, 75b
Wāḥidiyya iv, 668a – IV, 695b
Wahm i, 112a; iii, 509b – I, 115a; III, 527a
Wahrān (Oran) i, 270b; ii, 160b, 173a; vi, 592a; s, 376b – I, 279a; II, 165b, 178a; VI, 577a; S, 376b
Wahrīz (VI) ii, 190b, 193a; vii, 513b; s, 115b – II, 196b, 199a; VII, 514a; S, 115a
Wahriz Boēs (Bōya) i, 102a, 102b; ii, 190 – I, 105a, 105b; II, 196a
Waḥshī (VII) iv, 68b; vii, 665a – IV, 72b; VII, 664b
Waḥshī (Bāfḳ) (1583) viii, 775b – VIII, 801b
Wahsūdān (Rawwādī) (989) vii, 498a – VII, 497b
Wahsūdān b. Djustān (IX) ii, 191a; iii, 245a; v, 602b – II, 197a; III, 252a; V, 606b

Wahsūdān b. Mahlān b. Abī 'l-Haydja (Rawwādī) (1054) iv, 347b, 453b; vi, 499b; viii, 470a; x, 42b – IV, 362b, 456a; VI, 484b, 485a; VIII, 485b; X, 43b
Wahsūdān b. Muḥammad (Musāfirid(e)/ Sallārid(e)) (957) iv, 662b; vii, 656b – IV, 689b; VII, 656a
Wahsūdānid(e)s ii, 192a; iv, 773a – II, 198a; IV, 804a
Wā'il, Banū i, 920b; vi, 649a – I, 949a; VI, 634a
Wā'il b. Ḥadjr (VII) s, 337b – S, 337a
Wā'iẓ b. Isḥāḳ, 'Ubayd Allāh (XVIII) v, 1106a, b – V, 1102a, b
Wakāla → Wikāla
Waḳ'anuwīs i, 317a; ii, 338b – I, 326b; II, 348b
Waḳār vii, 478a – VII, 477b
Waḳash s, 236a – S, 236a
Waḳ'at al-Shi'b ii, 600b – II, 615b
Wakhān i, 223b – I, 230a
Wakhī i, 225a; ii, 31b – I, 231b; II, 32a
Wakhsh v, 75b; s, 125a – V, 77b; S, 124b
Wakhushtū Sulṭān (Georgia/-ie) (XVII) vii, 673b – VII, 673b
Wakī' i, 693b, 694a; s, 386b – I, 714b, 715a; S, 386b
Wakī' b. al-Djarrāḥ (812) i, 272b; vii, 607a; x, 29b – I, 281a; VII, 607a; X, 30b
Wāḳi'a nuwīs → Waḳ'anuwīs
Wāḳid b. Djunaydib s, 177b – S, 178b
al-Wāḳidī, Abū 'Abd Allāh Muḥammad (822) i, 140a; ii, 159a, 922bl; v, 1161b; vi, 262b, 263b, 411a; vii, 361a; viii, 515a; s, 263a – I, 144a; II, 164a, 946b; V, 1151a; VI, 247a, 248a, 369a; VII, 363b; VIII, 532b; S, 263a
Wāḳif, Mollā Panāh i, 193b; ii, 217a – I, 199a; II, 223b
Wāḳifiyya (Shī'a) i, 275a; v, 1236a; vii, 647b – I, 283b; V, 1226b; VII, 647a
Wakīl al-Dawla, 'Abd al-Raḥīm v, 171a – V, 168b
Wakīl al-Ra'āyā, Ḥādjdjī (XX) vi, 485b – VI, 471b
Wāḳim (al-Madīna) vii, 694a – VII, 694a
Waḳḳās, Sayyid v, 771a – V, 777b
Waḳḳāṣ Biy (Mangit) (XV) vi, 417b – VI, 402b
al-Waḳḳashī (al-Waḳshī), Abu 'l-Walīd (1096) i, 149a; vi, 606b; vii, 280b – I, 153b; VI, 591a; VII, 282b
Wakkom Muhammad Abdul Khader Maulavi (Mappila) (1932) vi, 462a – VI, 447b
Wāḳ-wāḳ v, 939b, 940a; vii, 245b; ix, 440b, 698b – V, 943b, 944a; IX, 457b, 727b
Walad Djalal (Zibane) vi, 364b – VI, 348b
Wālādjāh Muḥammad 'Alī Khān i, 937a – I, 965b
Walāsh → Adhur-Walāsh
Walasma' i, 763b; iii, 3b, 4a, 176a – I, 786b; III, 3b, 4a, 180a
Wālāta (Mauritania/-e) ii, 1002b; vii, 624b – II, 1026a; VII, 624b
al-Walātī, Muḥammad 'Abd Allāh (1805) vii, 625b – VII, 625a
Walba (Huelva) i, 6a, 155b – I, 6a, 160a
Walcott, Louis Eugene → Farrakhan
Wald 'Alī i, 483a – I, 497b
Wald Sulaymān (Bishr) i, 483a – I, 497b
Waldiyān vi, 504a – VI, 489b
Walī, Amīr (Astarābādī) (XIV) ii, 401b – II, 412a
Walī, Shaykh (1549) i, 1284b – I, 1323b
Walī Allāh (Farangī Maḥall) (1853) s, 292b – S, 292a
Walī Awrangābādī (1707) x, 878a – X,
Walī Dasht-Bayāḍī (1592) viii, 775b – VIII, 801b
Walī al-Dīn (1342) i, 893a; iii, 24b – I, 919b; III, 25b
Walī al-Dīn Efendī iii, 158a – III, 161b
Walī al-Dīn Yakan iii, 593b – III, 614a
Walī Khān Bakash iii, 1106b; iv, 498b – III, 1134a; IV, 520a
Walī Mīrzā iv, 393a – IV, 409b
Walī Muḥammad Khān ii, 638a – II, 654a
Walī Wēlūrī (XVIII) vi, 611a – VI, 596a
Wāliba b. al-Ḥubāb (VIII) i, 107b, 143b; iv, 1003b; vii, 798b; viii, 884a – I, 110b, 147b; IV, 1036a; VII, 800b; VIII, 914b
al-Walīd I b. 'Abd al-Malik (Umayyad(e)) (715) i, 45a, 58a, b, 77b, 196a, 305a, 381a, 493a, 610b, 612a, 761b, 787b, 1223a; ii, 198a, 280b, 304b, 788b, 956a, 957a; iii, 41a, 42a, 85b; iv, 712b, 742a, 973a; vi, 147a, 359b, 363b, 625a, 649b, 652a, 660b, 661a, 670a, 680b, 683b, 707b, 740a; s, 10a, 229a, 243a, 273a, b, 311a, b – I, 46a, 60a, 60b, 80a, 201b, 392a, 508a, 631b, 632a, 784b, 811a, 1259b; II, 204a, 289a, 313a, 807a, 978a, 979a; III, 43a, b, 88a; IV, 741a, 772a, 1005b; VI, 145b, 343b, 347b, 610a, 635a, 637a, 646b, 656a, 667b, 670b, 696a, 729a; S, 9b, 229a, 243a, 273a, 310b, 311b
al-Walīd II b. Yazīd (Umayyad(e)) (744) i, 12b, 57b, 196b, 587a, 613a, 952b; ii, 198a, 427b; iii, 136a, 494b, 878a; iv, 1003a; v, 936b; vi, 139b, 623b, 624a, 740a; vii, 676a; s, 117a, 243a – I, 12b, 59a, 202a, 606a, 633a, 982a; II, 204b, 439a; III, 139a, 511b, 902a; IV, 1035b; V, 940b; VI, 137b, 608b, 609a, 729b; VII, 676a; S, 116b, 243a
al-Walīd b. 'Abd al-Malik b. Zaydān (Sa'did(e)) (1636) vi, 595a – VI, 579a
Walīd b. Hishām → Abu Rakwa
al-Walīd b. al-Ḥusayn → al-Sharḳī b. al-Ḳuṭāmī
Wālid b. Khālunā (1798) vii, 614a, 622b – VII, 613b, 622a
Walīd b. Khayzurān (X) vii, 248b – VII, 250a
al-Walīd b. al-Mughīra (VII) i, 115b; iii, 1017b; vi, 137b, 138a, 139a, 140a; viii, 1002b – I, 118b; III, 1043a; VI, 136a, b, 137b, 138a; VIII, 1037b
al-Walīd b. Muslim (810) vii, 662b – VII, 662a
al-Walīd b. Ṭarīf ii, 524a; iii, 233b – II, 537a; III, 240a
al-Walīd b. 'Uḳba b. Abī Mu'ayṭ (VII) i, 382a; iii, 874a; vii, 497b; x, 166b – I, 393a; III, 898a; VII, 497b; X, 179a
al-Walīd b. 'Utba b. Abī Sufyān (VII) iii, 607b, 608a; vi, 621b, 622a; vii, 268b – III, 628b; VI, 606b, 607a; VII, 270a, b
al-Walīd b. al-Walīd b. al-Mughīra vi, 139a, b – VI, 137b
al-Walīd b. Yazīd → al-Walīd II
al-Walīd al-'Abdī iii, 648b – III, 669b
al-Walīd al-Ḳurayshī, Āl s, 62a – S, 62b
Walīdād Khān i, 1300a – I, 1340a
Wālide Ṣāliḥa Sulṭān (XVIII) vi, 55a, b – VI, 53a, b
Wālide Sulṭān Bezm-i 'Alem (XIX) i, 74b, 1226a; iv, 720a; v, 257a, 261b – I, 77a, 1262b; IV, 749a; V, 255a, 259a
Wālide Sulṭān Ṣafiyye → Ṣafiyye Sultān Baffa
Wālide Turkhan Khadīdje Sulṭān vi, 56b – VI, 54b
Walikota i, 981a – I, 1011b
Walīla/Walīlī (Volubilis) iii, 1031b, 1032a; vi, 889a, b; s, 103a – III, 1057a, 1058a; VI, 880b; S, 102b
Wallachia → Eflāḳ
Wallāda bint al-Mustakfī i, 601b; iii, 681b, 973b; vi, 751a – I, 621b; III, 703a, 998b; VI, 740b
Walwal incident (1934) ix, 717b – IX, 748b
Wamānū, Banū vi, 427a – VI, 412a, b
Wāmiḳ wa-'Adhrā i, 1301a – I, 1341a
Wān (lake/lac) i, 627a, 634b, 637b, 638a,644a, 1207a; ii, 34a; v, 441a, 442a, b; s, 130b - I, 647b, 655b, 658a, b, 664b, 1242b; II, 34b; V, 443b, 444b; S, 129b
Wandād-Hurmuzd (Ḳarinid(e)) (780) iv, 645a; vi,

745b, 937b – IV, 671b; VI, 734b, 929b
Wandād-Safān iv, 645a – IV, 671b
Wandād Ummīd (Ḳarinid(e)) (IX) vi, 745b – VI, 734b
Wang Daiyu (1657) x, 321b – X, 346a
Wangara iv, 548b, 773b; vi, 258b – IV, 572a, 804b; VI, 243a
al-Wānī, Muḥammad b. Muṣṭafā i, 310a – I, 319b
al-Wanisī, Ḥamdān (XX) viii, 902a – VIII, 933a
Wansharī (Ouarsenis) i, 371a, 372a; vi, 404a; s, 103a – I, 382a, 383a; VI, 388b; S, 102b
al-Wansharīsī, Abu 'l-ʿAbbās Aḥmad (1509) i, 1341a; vii, 287a, 288b, 1052b; s, 27a, 403a – I, 1381b; VII, 289a, 290a, 1054b; S, 27b, 403b
al-Wansharīsī, Shaykh al-Bashīr (1130) iii, 959b; vi, 592a – III, 984a; VI, 577a
Wānūdīn b. Khazrūn b. Khazar v, 1178a, b – V, 1168a, b
Wanzamār, Banū v, 1174a, b, 1179a, 1180b – V, 1164a, b, 1169a, 1170b
Wanzamār b. ʿArīf ii, 979a – 1001b
Wara (Čad) i, 98a; s, 164a – I, 100b; S, 164a
Wāra Dyābi (Takrūr) ix, 753b – IX, 786b
Warād → Nagyvárad
Warād, Banū s, 350b – S, 350b
Waraḳa b. Nawfal (VII) iii, 1206a; iv, 898b; vii, 363a; viii, 676a – III, 1236b; IV, 931b; VII, 365a; VIII, 695b
Warangal v, 1216b – V, 1206b
Warayn, Banū vi, 815a; s, 145a – VI, 805a; S, 144b
Ward (Byzantin(e)) (X) vi, 519b – VI, 504b
Ward, Banu 'l- i, 1023b; iii, 386b – I, 1055a; III, 398b
al-Ward al-Lakhmī i, 1023b – I, 1055a
Warda → al-DjarādatānI
Wardak s, 367a – S, 367b
Wardān iii, 887a, 889a – III, 911a, 913a
al-Wardānī, Ibrāhīm Nāṣif (1910) viii, 360a – VIII, 372b
al-Wardī, ʿUmar b. Muẓaffar al-Maʿarrī Zayn al-Dīn (1348) iv, 864b; vi, 381b – IV, 898a; VI, 366a
Wardjābī b. Rābīs vii, 584b – VII, 585a
Wardjalān(Wardjlān → Wargla
al-Wardjalānī → Abū Zakariyyāʿ Yaḥyā b. al-Khayr al-Wardjalānī
al-Wardjalānī, Abū Yaʿḳūb Yūsuf b. Ibrāhīm (XI) x, 183a – X, 197b
Warfadjdjūma, Banū ix, 768a – IX, 801b
Wargha vi, 741a – VI, 730a, b
al-Warghī (1776) vi, 112b – VI, 110b
Wargla iii, 656b, 657b, 1041a; s, 15b – III, 677b, 678b, 1067a; S, 15b
Warīka, Banū vi, 742a – VI, 731a
al-Wārith b. Kaʿb al-Kharūṣī (IX) iii, 652b; iv, 1085a; ix, 775a – III, 673b; IV, 1116a; IX, 808b
Wārith Shāh (1766) viii, 256b – VIII, 258b
Warithuddin Muhammad (Wallace Deen Muhammad) (XX) vii, 703a, b – VII, 704a
Warḳāʾ al-Nakhaʿī iv, 495a – IV, 516a
Wārkū, Banū iii, 1040b – III, 1066b
Warrā, Banū v, 1178b, 1179a – V, 1168b
al-Warrāḳ, Abū ʿĪsā → Abū ʿĪsā Muḥammad al-Warrāḳ
Warrāḳ, Ibn Sayyār → Ibn Sayyār
al-Warrāḳ, Muḥammad b. Yūsuf (X) i, 156b – I, 161a
Warrū b. Saʿīd v, 1182a, b – V, 1172a, b
Warsheikh vi, 129a – VI, 127a
Warsifān, Banū v, 1179a, b, 1183a – V, 1169a, b, 1173a
Wartadī, Banū vi, 1009a – VI, 1001a
al-Warthīlānī (1779) ii, 161a; ix, 20b; s, 403a – II, 166a; IX, 21b; S, 403a
Warwar ʿAlī Pasha → Varvar ʿAlī
Waryāghal, Banū s, 377a – S, 377a
Warzamār, Banū → Wanzamār, Banū
Warzarāt vi, 590b – VI, 575b
Washka i, 1057b; vi, 345a – I, 1089a; VI, 329a
Washmagīr b. Ziyār (Ziyārid(e)) (967) iii, 255a; iv, 23a, 100a, b; vi, 115b, 539a, b, 941b; viii, 597b – III, 262b; IV, 25a, 104b; VI, 113a, 524a, 933b; VIII, 616b
al-Washshāʿ ii, 1032b; iii, 1263b; iv, 822b; v, 737a – II, 1056a; III, 1296b; IV, 855b; V, 742b
Wāsiʿ Alīsī iv, 505a; vi, 900a – IV, 527a; VI, 891b
Wāṣif, Aḥmed (1806) vi, 340b – VI, 325a
Waṣīf b. Ṣuwārtigin al-Khazarī (amīr al-Ḥadjdj) (X) vii, 543a; s, 304b – VII, 543a; S, 304b
Waṣīf al-Turkī (ḥādjib) (IX) i, 271b, 273a, 789b; ii, 26b; vi, 900a; vii, 390a, 395a, 583a, 722b, 777b, 793b – I, 279b, 281b, 813a; II, 27a; VI, 891b; VII, 391b, 396a, 583b, 723b, 779b, 795b
Wāṣifī vii, 92b; s, 46b – VII, 94a; S, 47a
Wāṣil, Banū viii, 866a – VIII, 896b
Wāṣil b. ʿAṭāʾ (748) i, 127b, 454a, 1080b; ii, 833b; iii, 985a, 1025b, 1142b; iv, 142a; vi, 457b, 458a; vii, 260a, 783a; x, 440a; s, 225b, 227a – I, 131b, 467a, 1113a; II, 853a; III, 1009b, 1051b, 1171a; IV, 148a; VI, 443a, b; VII, 261b, 785a; X, 471b; S, 225b, 227a
Wasīm-Awsīm vi, 411a – VI, 396a
Wasīn, Banū → Wisyān, Banū
Wāsiṭ i, 77a, 103a, 132a, 867a, 949a, 1094b; ii, 248a, 319b; iii, 41a, 1252b, 1255a, 1267a; iv, 724b; vi, 119b, 247a, 270b, 335b, 345a, 427b, 613b, 661a, 679b, 691b, 740a; vii, 672a; s, 41a, 118a, 119a, 126b, 193a, 243a, 385a – I, 79b, 106a, 135b, 891a, 978a, 1127a; II, 255a, 328b; III, 42b, 1285a, 1287b, 1300a; IV, 753b; VI, 117b, 231b, 255b, 319b, 329a, 412b, 598b, 646b, 666b, 678b, 729b; VII, 672a; S, 41b, 117b, 118b, 125b, 193b, 243a, 385b
Wāsiṭa ii, 857b – II, 877b
al-Wāsiṭī, Abū Bakr (Khaṭīb) (931) v, 332a; x, 314b, 377b – V, 332a; X, 338b, 404b
al-Wāsiṭī, Abu 'l-Fatḥ (1194) ii, 166b; vi, 354b – II, 171b; VI, 338b
al-Wāsiṭī, Abū Ghālib Muḥammad b. ʿAlī (XI) vii, 270b – VII, 272b
al-Wāsiṭī, Abu 'l-Ḳāsim ʿAlī b. Muḥammad (932) vi, 569b; vii, 312a; s, 13b – VI, 554b; VII, 314b; S, 13b
al-Wāsiṭī, Aḥmad b. Ibrāhīm (1311) iii, 954b – III, 979a
al-Wāsiṭī, Aḥmad b. Muḥammad, vizier (IX) v, 49a; s, 1a – V, 50b; S, 1a
al-Wāsiṭī, Djamāl al-Dīn (XIII) viii, 806a – VIII, 833a
al-Wāsiṭī, Ghāzī vii, 305a – VII, 307a
Waṣṣāf, ʿAbd Allāh b. Faḍl Allāh al-Shīrāzī (1334) iv, 67b; vi, 15b; vii, 343b, 481a – IV, 71b; VI, 13b; VII, 345a, 480b
Wasūṭ iv, 1147a – IV, 1178b
Waṭan i, 64a; iv, 785b, 790b – I, 66a; IV, 817a, 822b
Waṭaniyya iv, 784b, 785a – IV, 816a, b
al-Wāthiḳ bi-'llāh (ʿAbbāsid(e)) (847) i, 10b, 18b, 271a, 551a, 1298b; ii, 188b, 198a, 236a; iii, 618a; iv, 138a; vi, 206a, 625b; vii, 4a, 279b, 518a, 776b, 777b; ix, 205b; s, 33a, 106a, 199a – I, 10b, 19a, 279b, 568b, 1338a; II, 194b, 204b, 243a; III, 639a; IV, 143b; VI, 190a, 610b; VII, 4a, 281a, 518b, 776b, 779b; IX, 211b; S, 33a, 105b, 199a
al-Wāthiḳ (Almohad(e)) → Abū Dabbūs
al-Wāthiḳ (Ḥafṣid(e)) iii, 67a – III, 69a
Wāthila b. al-Askaʿ i, 266b – I, 274b

Wat͟hīma b. Mirsāl (IX) vii, 768b – VII, 770b
Wat͟ht͟hāb iii, 228a – III, 235a
Watid i, 670b, 671b, 674b – I, 691b, 692b, 695a
Waṭṭār, Ṭāhir al- v, 190a, 191a – V, 187b, 188a
Waṭṭāsid(e)s i, 706a, 1057b; ii, 463a, 510a, 819b; iv, 94a; v, 1190b, 1200a; vi, 134b, 248b, 574a, 741b, 1009a; vii, 37b; viii, 723a; ix, 507b – I, 727b, 1089b; II, 475a, 522b, 839a; IV, 98a; V, 1180b, 1190a; VI, 132b, 133a, 232b, 559a, 730b, 1001b; VII, 37b; VIII, 744a; IX, 527a
Waṭwāṭ → Ras͟hīd al-Dīn
al-Waṭwāṭ, D̲jamāl al-Dīn (1318) ii, 900a; v, 1227a; vii, 897a; viii, 158b – II, 921a; V, 1217a; VII, 897b; VIII, 161a
al-Waʾwāʾ al-Dimas͟hḳī (X) ix, 55b – IX, 58b
Wāwazgīt, Banū i, 161b; vi, 742a; s, 144b – I, 166a; VI, 731a; S, 144b
Wayhind vi, 65b – VI, 63a
Ways K͟hān iv, 512a – IV, 534a
Ways K͟hān Zand v, 664a – V, 669a
Wāziʿ, Āl i, 1299a – I, 1339a
Waẓīfa iv, 1055b – IV, 1087a
Wazīr Begam → Çhoṭi Begam
Wazīr al-Dawla, Nawāb iv, 197a – IV, 205b
Wazīr Ḥasan, Sayyid (XX) vi, 78a – VI, 76a
Wazīr K͟hān (ʿIlm al-Dīn al-Anṣārī, Lāhawr, 1710) i, 914a; ii, 47b; v, 600a – I, 941b; II, 48b; V, 604a
Wazīr K͟hān Harawī i, 80b – I, 83a
al-Wazīr al-Mag͟hribī (XI) vii, 651a – VII, 650b
Wazīr Muḥammad K͟hān i, 1195b – I, 1230b
al-Wazīr al-Ṣāḥib Ṣafāʾ al-Dīn (XIII) vi, 111a – VI, 109a
Wazīr Singh ii, 797b – II, 816b
Wazīra bint Munad̲jd̲jā (1316) viii, 156a – VIII, 158b
Wazīrābād v, 888a – V, 894b
Wazīrīstān vi, 86a, b; s, 285a, 329b – VI, 84a, b; S, 285a, 329a
Wazzān (Morocco/Maroc) i, 687b; vi, 356b, 890b; s, 404a – I, 708b; VI, 340b, 881b; S, 404b
al-Wazzānī, Muḥammad Ḥasa iii, 525a, b; s, 10a – III, 543a, b; S, 9b
Wēbi S͟habēllā vi, 128b – VI, 126b
Wed Bou Regreg → Wādī Abū Raḳrāḳ
Wed̲jīhī Pas͟ha ii, 636b – II, 652b
Wefāʾ, S͟hayk͟h (1490) vii, 30b, 349a – VII, 30b, 351a
Wehbī → Pīr Meḥmed
Wehbī, Seyyid (1736) vii, 839a – VII, 840b
Welī Maḥmūd → Maḥmūd Pas͟ha Welī
Welī Pas͟ha i, 175a, 398b, 399a – I, 179b, 410a, 410b
Wenceslaus → Čeh
Werčikwār s, 158b – S, 158b
Whēbyōt s, 339b – S, 339b
White Horde i, 1106b; ii, 44a, b
Wibisono, Jusuf vi, 731b – VI, 720b
Widādī i, 193b – I, 199a
Widin iii, 628a, 629b; vi, 56a; viii, 284b, 287b – III, 648a, 650b; VI, 54a; VIII, 293a, 296a
Wid̲jaʾ iv, 1088a, 1089b – IV, 1119a, 1120b
Wid̲jāda iii, 27b – III, 28b
al-Widyān i, 538b – I, 555a
Wikāla ii, 148b; iv, 435a, b, 840b, 1015b – II, 152b; IV, 454b, 873b, 1047b
Wiḳār al-Mulk s, 74a – S, 74b
Wilāyat ʿAlī, Mawlawī (1853) vii, 291a – VII, 293a
Wilāyet → Eyālet
William of Rubruck vii, 230a – VII, 232a
Wīmā (Dunbāwand) vi, 744b – VI, 733b
Wirān, Ḥāfiẓ G͟hulām ii, 222a – II, 228b
Wird ii, 224a; iv, 94b; s, 93a – II, 231a; IV, 99a; S, 93a
Wīs u-Rāmīn ii, 1142b – II, 1169b
Wiṣāl, Kučak ii, 433b; IV, 69b – II, 445a; IV, 73b
Wīsū i, 1305a, 1306a – I, 1345b, 1346b
Wisyān, Banū iii, 1041a – III, 1066b
al-Wisyānī, Abū Mūsā iii, 657a – III, 678b
al-Wisyānī, S͟hayk͟h Abū K͟hazar (X) vi, 947a – VI, 939b
Witu Sultanate iv, 889a, b – IV, 921b, 922a
Wizāra → Wazīr
Wizr b. D̲jābir Asad al-Rahīṣ i, 519a – I, 534b
Wolof → D̲jolof
Wu Ma v, 844b – V, 856b
Wuchali, Treaty of/Traité de- vi, 643b – VI, 628a
Wuhayb b. ʿAbd Manāf i, 438b – I, 450b
Wuḥaydāt, Banū vii, 921a – VII, 921b
Wurukas͟ha, lake/lac iv, 400b – IV, 418a
Wus͟hmgīr → Was͟hmagīr
Wut͟hūḳ al-Dawla (XX) v, 24b; viii, 512a – V, 25b; VIII, 529b

X

Xanî, Ehmedê v, 482a – V, 485a
Xativa → S͟hāṭiba

Y

Yaʿāḳīb, Banū iii, 1004b – III, 1030a
Yaʿāriba → Yaʿrubid(e)s
Yabāku, Banū x, 689b – X, 781b
Yabdar s, 402b – S, 403a
Yabg͟hu i, 420a, 661b, 852a; ii, 1107b; iv, 658b; x, 689b; s, 244b, 245a – I, 432a, 682b, 875b; II, 1133b; IV, 685a; X, 782a; S, 244b, 245a
Yabrīn (oasis) viii, 1048a – VIII, 1084a
Yābura (Evora) ix, 441a – IX, 458a
Yaʿburī iii, 134a – III, 137a
Yacoub → Yaʿḳūb
Yadaʿʾil D̲harīḥ b. Sumhūʿalī vi, 562a; ix, 675b – VI, 547a; IX, 703b
Yadaʿʾil Watar b. Sumhūʿalī Yanūf vi, 561a – VI, 545b, 546a
Yadaʿʾil Yanūf vi, 559b – VI, 544b
Yadālī, S͟hayk͟h Muḥammad Saʿīd b. al-Muk͟htār (1752) vii, 614a, 622b – VII, 613b, 622a
Yaddar, Banū ii, 527a; vi, 743a – II, 540a; VI, 732a
Yaddū b. Yaʿlā iii, 1042b, 1043b; v, 1177a – III, 1068b, 1069b; V, 1167a
Yādgār, Aḥmad s, 1b – S, 1b
Yādgar Nāṣir Mīrzā (XVI) iii, 633a – III, 654a
Yādigār Muḥammad (Astrakhan K͟hān) (XVI) iv, 849b – IV, 882b
Yādigār Muḥammad (Tīmūrid(e)) (1470) i, 148b; vii, 928a – I, 152b; VII, 928b
Yāfaʿ (sultanat(e)) ii, 675b – II, 692a
Yāfā (Jaffa) vi, 32b, 322a; vii, 168b; s, 20b – VI, 30b, 306b; VII, 170a; S, 21a
Yāfiʿ (Yemen) vii, 779a – VII, 781a
al-Yāfiʿī (1464) vi, 353a – VI, 337b
al-Yāfiʿī, ʿAbd Allāh b. Asʿad al-Yamanī (1367) i, 255b; ii, 392a; vi, 354b; viii, 45a – I, 263b; II, 402b; VI, 338b; VIII, 45b
Yāfiʿī, Banū iv, 745b; vii, 496a; s, 338b – IV, 775b; VII, 496a; S, 338a

Yafran iii, 1039b, 1040a; vi, 435a – III, 1065b, 1066a; VI, 420b
al-Yafrānī, Hilāl b. Abī Ḳurra (1657) x, 144b – X, 155a
al-Yaftalī, Abū 'l-Fatḥ (951) i, 852a – I, 876a
Yaʿfur → Yuʿfir
Yaʿfūr ii, 624a; iii, 393b – II, 639b; III, 406a
Yaʿfurid(e)s i, 551a, b; vi, 438b, 439a – I, 568b, 569a; VI, 424a, b
Yag̲h̲ma, Banū x, 689a – X, 781b
Yag̲h̲amrāsan/Yag̲h̲murāsa(e)n (Zayyānid(e), Tlemcen) (XIII) i, 92b; iii, 866a; v, 1180a; vi, 404a, 593a, 815b; vii, 722a – I, 95a; III, 890a; V, 1170a; VI, 388b, 389a, 578a, 805b; VII, 723a
Yag̲h̲ī-basan b. G̲h̲āzī, Malik Niẓām al-Dīn (Dānishmendid(e) (1166) ii, 110b; viii, 36a; s, 154a – II, 113a; VIII, 36b; S, 154b
Yag̲h̲ī-bastī (Īnd̲j̲ū) (XIV) iii, 1208b – III, 1239a
Yāg̲h̲isiyān, Amīr (Anṭakiya) (XI) i, 517a; v, 921b, 924a; viii, 947a – I, 532b; V, 927a, 929b; VIII, 979b
al-Yag̲h̲īsiyānī, Ṣalāḥ al-Dīn Muḥammad, (amīr, Ḥamāt) (XII) vi, 870a; viii, 127b – VI, 861a; VIII, 130b
Yāg̲h̲istān ii, 140a – II, 143b
Yag̲h̲līkčī Emīr iv, 193b – IV, 202a
Yag̲h̲mā D̲j̲andaḳī, Abu 'l-Ḥasan (1859) iii, 355b; iv, 69b; vii, 754b – III, 366b; IV, 73b; VII, 756a
Yag̲h̲māʾī, Ḥabīb-i iv, 71b – IV, 75b
al-Yag̲h̲mūrī, S̲h̲ihāb al-Dīn iv, 960a – IV, 992b
Yag̲h̲nōbī → al-Sug̲h̲d
Yag̲h̲ūt̲h̲ (idol) iii, 223a; vi, 651a; vii, 591b, 592a – III, 229b; VI, 636b; VII, 591b
Yagma, Banū x, 689a – X,
al-Yaḥīrī, Yaḥyā b. al-Ḥusayn s, 236a – S, 236a
Yaḥmad, Āl i, 813a; iv, 1084b; ix, 775a – I, 836a; IV, 1116a; IX, 808b
Yaḥmūm vi, 653b – VI, 639a
Yaḥṣib → Ils̲h̲araḥ Yaḥḍib
Yahūd i, 264b, 265a, b, 491b, 546b, 565a, 1020-22, 1178a; ii, 85b, 145b, 229a, 230a, 563b, 620a, 725b, 835b, 859b, 912b, 913a, 1010a; iii, 80a, 147b, 324b, 326a; iv, 8a, 43b, 98b, 99a, 133b, 239a, 241b, 299a-313b, 603b, 824a, 1138a-1142a, 1174b; v, 326b, 334a, b, 337a, 436a, 668b, 994b; vi, 591b – I, 272b, 273a, b, 506a, 563b, 583a, 1051-53, 1213a; II, 87a, 149b, 236a, 237a, 577b, 635b, 744b, 855a, 879b, 934a, b, 1033b; III, 80a, 150b, 334b, 336a; IV, 8b, 46a, 103a, 139a, b, 249b, 252b, 312b-327b, 627b, 857a, 1170a-1173b, 1208a; V, 326a, 334a, b, 337b, 438b, 673b, 990a; VI, 576a
Yahūdā b. Ḳuraysh̲ (900) viii, 1008a – VIII, 1043a
al-Yahūdī → Māsard̲j̲awayh
Yahūdī, Yūsuf iv, 310a – IV, 324a
al-Yahūdiyya (Afg̲h̲ānistān) vi, 915a – VI, 906b
Yahūdiyya (Iṣfahān) iv, 98b, 106a – IV, 103a, 110b
Yaḥyā (Banū G̲h̲āniya) (XIII) vi, 404a – VI, 388b
Yaḥyā (John the Baptist/St. Jean-Baptiste) vi, 630a – VI, 615a
Yaḥyā, Banū (Málaga) vi, 221a – VI, 215a
Yaḥyā, Imām (Yemen) (XX) vi, 262a – VI, 146b
Yaḥyā, S̲h̲ayk̲h̲ al-Islām (1644) ix, 240a – IX, 246b
Yaḥyā I al-Muʿtalī (Ḥammūdid(e)) (1036) i, 5b; iii, 147a; vi, 222a – I, 5b; III, 150b; VI, 216a
Yaḥyā II b. Idrīs b. ʿAlī (Ḥammūdid(e)) (1039) vi, 222a – VI, 216a
Yaḥyā I (Idrīsid(e)) iii, 1035b; iv, 632a – III, 1061b; IV, 657b
Yaḥyā II (Idrīsid(e)) iii, 1035b – III, 1061b
Yaḥyā III al-Miḳdām (Idrīsid(e)) (905) iii, 1036a; vii, 641a – III, 1062a; VII, 640b
Yaḥyā IV (Idrīsid(e)) (922) iii, 1036a; vi, 742b; vii, 641a; s, 132a – III, 1062a; VI, 731b; VII, 641a; S, 131b
Yaḥyā b. ʿAbd Allāh (marabout) (Sūs) (XVII) vi, 594b – VI, 579b
Yaḥyā b. ʿAbd Allāh b. al-Ḥasan (al-Daylamī) (VIII) i, 271b, 402b, 1034b; ii, 191a; iii, 233b, 616a, 617a; vii, 389a; s, 130a – I, 280a, 414a, 1066a; II, 197a; III, 240a, 637a, b; VII, 390b; S, 129a
Yaḥyā b. ʿAbd Allāh b. Saʿīd al-Ḥaḥī (XVII) s, 29a – S, 29b
Yaḥyā b. ʿAbd al-Azīm al-D̲j̲azzār (1270) x, 5a – X, 5a
Yaḥya b. ʿAbd al-Malik b. Makkī (1393) iv, 338a – IV, 352b
Yaḥyā b. Abī Bakr b. Yūsuf b. Tās̲h̲ufīn i, 389b; iii, 728a – I, 401a; III, 751a
Yaḥyā b. Abī Ḥafṣa Yazīd (VII) vi, 625a – VI, 610a
Yaḥyā b. Abī Ḥās̲h̲id b. al-Ḍaḥḥāk s, 22a – S, 22b
Yaḥyā b. Abī Manṣūr al-Munad̲j̲d̲j̲im (830) iii, 8b, 1136b; vi, 599b, 600a – III, 9a, 1165a; VI, 584b, 585a
Yaḥyā b. Abī Ṭālib (ʿAzafī, Ceuta) (XIV) vii, 1023a – VII, 1025a
Yaḥyā b. Abī Yaḥyā, S̲h̲ams al-Dīn s, 236a – S, 236a
Yaḥyā b. Ādam (818) iv, 1141b; x, 917b – IV, 1173a; X,
Yaḥyā b. ʿAdī (974) i, 126b, 130a, 151b, 234b, 235a, 328a, 631b, 737a; ii, 779a; iii, 895b, 980a; v, 121a; vi, 204a, 637b, 845a; viii, 615a; s, 25a, 398b – I, 130b, 134a, 156a, 241b, 242a, 338b, 652a, 759a; II, 797b; III, 919b, 1004b; V, 123b; VI, 188b, 622b, 836a; VIII, 634b; S, 25b, 398b
Yaḥyā b. Akt̲h̲am (IX) i, 271a, 273a; iii, 879a; vii, 778a – I, 279b, 281b; III, 903b; VII, 780a
Yaḥyā b. ʿAlī b. Abī Ṭālib (VII) s, 92b – S, 92b
Yaḥyā b. ʿAlī b. G̲h̲āniya (XII) i, 390a; ii, 1007a – I, 401b; II, 1030b
Yaḥyā b. ʿAlī b. Ḥammūd → Yaḥyā I (Ḥammūdid(e))
Yaḥyā b. al-ʿAzīz iii, 138b; iv, 479b – III, 141a; IV, 501a
Yaḥyā b. al-Biṭrīḳ i, 235a, 589b, 736b; iii, 311b – I, 242a, 608b, 758b; III, 321a
Yaḥyā b. G̲h̲āniya (1148) i, 165b; ii, 463b, 575a, 1007b; iii, 66b, 1039a; iv, 337b, 614b, 828a; viii, 763b – I, 170a; II, 475a, 589b, 1031a; III, 69a, 1064b; IV, 352a, 639a, 860b; VIII, 788b
Yaḥyā b. al-Ḥakam (696) vi, 139a, 774b – VI, 137b, 763b
Yaḥyā b. Ḥamdūn i, 1088a – I, 1120b
Yaḥyā b. Ḥamza al-ʿAlawī iv, 252a; v, 901a – IV, 263a; V, 907a
Yaḥyā b. al-Ḥārit̲h̲ al-D̲h̲imārī iii, 704b – III, 726b
Yaḥyā b. Hart̲h̲ama iv, 100a – IV, 104a
Yaḥyā b. al-Ḥasan b. D̲j̲aʿfar s, 401a – S, 401b
Yaḥyā b. Ḥātim Ipnā vi, 247a – VI, 231b
Yaḥyā b. Hubayra → Ibn Hubayra, Yaḥyā
Yaḥyā b. Ḥurayt̲h̲ al-D̲j̲ud̲h̲āmī (Mālaḳa) (747) vi, 221b – VI, 215b
Yaḥyā b. al-Ḥusayn → Yaḥyā al-Hādī
Yaḥyā b. Ibrāhīm al-Gudālī (XI) ii, 1121b; v, 653b; vi, 744a; s, 27a – II, 1148a; V, 657b; VI, 733a; S, 27a
Yaḥyā b. Idrīs → Yaḥyā IV (Idrīsid(e))
Yaḥyā b. al-Ḳāsim → Yaḥyā III (Idrīsid(e))
Yaḥyā b. Ḳāsim (ʿIrāḳ) vii, 9b – VII, 10a
Yaḥyā b. Ḳawām al-Dīn al-Marʿas̲h̲ī (XV) vi, 512b – VI, 498a
Yaḥyā b. Ḳays al-Māribī vi, 566b – VI, 551b

Yaḥyā b. Khaldūn → Ibn Khaldūn, Yaḥyā
Yaḥyā b. Khālid al-Barmakī (805) i, 936a, 1033a, 1034a, b, 1223a; ii, 79b, 305a; iii, 232b, 989a; iv, 16b, 119a, 1164a; v, 1238b; vi, 599b; vii, 215a, 646a; s, 48b, 225b, 393b – I, 964b, 1065a, b, 1066a, 1259b; II, 81a, 313b; III, 239b, 1014a; IV, 18a, 124a, 1196a; V, 1229b; VI, 584a; VII, 216b, 645b; S, 49a, 225b, 394a
Yaḥyā b. Maḥmūd (XIII) vi, 199a – VI, 183a
Yaḥya b. Maḥmūd al-Gudjarātī (1689) iv, 507a – IV, 529a
Yaḥyā b. Maʿīn (847) viii, 515b; ix, 7b – VIII, 533a; IX, 7b
Yaḥyā b. Manda s, 193a – S, 194a
Yaḥyā b. al-Mansūr Ḥamīd al-Dīn (Zaydī) (Maḥmūd al-Mutawakkil ʿalā Allāh (1948) v, 809a; vi, 192a, 262a – V, 815a, VI, 176a, 246b
Yaḥyā b. Meḥmed ül-Kātib (XV) vii, 531b; viii, 544b – VII, 532a; VIII, 562a
Yaḥyā b. Muʿādh → Bābak al-Khurramī
Yaḥyā b. Muʿādh (Nīshāpūr) (872) vi, 570a – VI, 554b
Yaḥyā b. Muʿādh b. Muslim (Dhuhl, Banū) (IX) vi, 333a, 336b – VI, 317b, 320b
Yaḥya b. Muḍar (al-Andalus) (IX) vi, 281a – VI, 266a
Yaḥyā b. Muḥammad → Yaḥyā I (Idrīsid(e))
Yaḥyā b. Muḥammad Ḥamīd al-Dīn iv, 745b – IV, 775b
Yaḥyā b. Muḥammad al-Mutawakkil (1948) viii, 564a – VIII, 582a
Yaḥyā b. al-Mundhir iii, 743a – III, 766a
Yaḥyā b. al-Nāṣir b. al-Manṣūr al-Muʿtasim bi-'llāh (Almohad(e)) (1229) vi, 339b, 592b – VI, 323b, 577b
Yaḥyā b. Saʿdūn (1092) vi, 353b – VI, 337b
Yaḥyā b. Saʿīd → al-Antākī
Yaḥyā b. Saʿīd (760) iii, 24b; vi, 263a, b; x, 29b – III, 26a; VI, 247b, 248b; X, 30b
Yaḥyā b. Sāʿid (930) s, 400b – S, 401a
Yaḥyā b. Saʿīd (1034) vii, 115b – VII, 117b
Yaḥyā b. Saʿīd al-Ḳaṭṭān → al-Ḳaṭṭān
Yaḥyā b. Sallām al-Baṣrī iv, 829b – IV, 862b
Yaḥyā b. al-Samīna i, 600a – I, 619b
Yaḥyā b. Sarūr, Sharīf vi, 150b – VI, 149b
Yaḥyā b. al-Shāṭir iii, 228a – III, 235a
Yaḥyā b. Sulaymān (875) vi, 900a – VI, 891b
Yaḥyā b. Taʿfūft i, 689a – I, 710a
Yaḥyā b. Tamīm i, 149a – I, 153b
Yaḥyā b. ʿUmar (Almoravid(e)) (1056) ii, 1002b, 1122a; iii, 288b; v, 653b, 654a, b; vii, 613a – II, 1025b, 1148a; III, 297b; V, 657b, 658b; VII, 613a
Yaḥyā b. ʿUmar (Ifrīḳiya) (902) iii, 486a; viii, 844a; ix, 586b – III, 503a; VIII, 873b; IX, 609a
Yaḥyā b. ʿUmar (Kūfa) (IX) vii, 390a – VII, 391b
Yaḥyā b. ʿUmar al Ṭālibī ii, 485a; iii, 908a, 1022b – II, 497b; III, 932a, 1048b
Yaḥyā b. ʿUthmān b. Ṣāliḥ (895) viii, 895a – VIII, 926a
Yaḥyā b. Wasīnū ii, 1013a – II, 1036b
Yaḥyā b. Yaghmūr (1150) vii, 37a – VII, 37a
Yaḥyā b. Yaḥyā → Yaḥyā II (Idrīsid(e))
Yaḥyā b. Yaḥyā (Mālikī) (848) iv, 87a; vi, 744a – IV, 91a; VI, 733a
Yaḥyā b. Yaʿmar (ḳāḍī) vi, 670b – VI, 657a
Yaḥyā b. Yaʿmur (Baṣra) iv, 731b – IV, 761a
Yaḥyā b. Zakariyyāʾ ii, 279b, 281a; iii, 613b, 1175a, 1206a; iv, 724a, 912b; v, 421a; vii, 551b – II, 287b, 289a; III, 634b, 1204a, 1236b; IV, 753a, 945b; V, 423a; VII, 552a
Yaḥyā b. Zayd b. ʿAlī (743) i, 402b; ii, 608b, 1139b; iii, 1265b; iv, 446b; v, 3a, 230a; vii, 396a; ix, 433b – I, 414a; II, 623b, 1166b; III, 1298b; IV, 466a; V, 3a, 228a; VII, 397b; IX, 437b
Yaḥyā b. Zikrawayh ii, 850b; iv, 493b, 660b – II, 870a; IV, 515a, 687a
Yaḥyā b. Ziyād al-Ḥārithī (VIII) iv, 1003b; vii, 798b; ix, 387a – IV, 1036a; VII, 800b; IX, 399b
Yaḥyā al-Anṭakī (1065) vii, 164a – VII, 165b
Yaḥyā al-Aṭrash ii, 637b – II, 653b
Yaḥyā al-Barmākī → Yaḥyā b. Khālid
Yaḥyā Efendī iv, 505a – IV, 527a
Yaḥyā al-Ghazāl → al-Ghazāl
Yaḥyā al-Hādī ila 'l-Ḥaḳḳ iv, 944b – IV, 977a
Yaḥyā Ḥaḳḳī (XX) vi, 91a – VI, 89a
Yaḥyā Ḥamīd al-Dīn (Zaydī) (1904) vi, 192a; ix, 201b – VI, 176a; IX, 207a
Yaḥyā al-Ḳādir i, 446b, 986a; ii, 243a; s, 23a – I, 459a, 1016b; II, 250a; S, 23b
Yaḥyā Karāwī (sarbadār) (XIV) x, 552b – X,
Yaḥyā al-Kātib iii, 1243a – III, 1275a
Yaḥyā Kemāl Beyatlı̊ v, 195a; s, 167b, 324b – V, 192a; S, 168a, 324a
Yaḥyā Khān (XX) iv, 177b; v, 1081b; viii, 242b – IV, 186a; V, 1079a; VIII, 248b
Yaḥyā al-Laythī i, 83a – I, 85b
Yaḥyā al-Maghribī → Abū Zakariyyāʾ al Maghribī
Yaḥyā Manērī, Shaykh (1291) vi, 410a – VI, 395a
Yaḥyā al-Naḥwī ii, 771b, 780b – II, 790a, 799b
Yaḥyā Nūrī, Mīrzā (Ṣubḥ-i Azal) (bābī) i, 809a, 833b, 847a, 911b; iv, 51b, 696a; viii, 114a; s, 53b – I, 832a, 856b, 870b, 939a; IV, 54b, 724a; VIII, 116b; S, 53b
Yaḥyā Pāsha-zāde Küčük Bālī Beg (1566) iv, 657a; x, 213b – IV, 683b; X, 230b
Yaḥyā-i Dārābī i, 847a – I, 870a
Yaḥyā-i Shirwanī ii, 1136b; iv, 991a, 992b; s, 208a – II, 1163a; IV, 1024a, 1025b; s, 208a
Yakhshı̊ Khān b. Maḥmūd Beg (Ḳaramān-oghulları̊) (XIV) iv, 621b, 622a, b – IV, 646a, b, 647a
Yakhshī Khān b. Ḳarasi̊ (Bergama) (XIV) iv, 628a – IV, 653a
Yakhshī b. Tīmurtash i, 1303a; ii, 611a – I, 1342b; II, 626a
Yaḳīnī vii, 567b – VII, 568b
Yaḳtan iv, 448a – IV, 468a
Yaḳṭīb (tree/arbre) vi, 651a, 901a – VI, 636b, 892a
Yaʿḳūb (Jacob) iii, 980a – III, 1004b
Yaʿḳūb, Shaykh (Malāmī) (1581) vi, 228a, b – VI, 222a
Yaʿḳūb, Sīdī vi, 591a – VI, 576a
Yaʿḳūb I (Germiyān-oghlu) i, 346a, 510b; ii, 989a, b – I, 356b, 526a; II, 1012a
Yaʿḳūb II (Germiyān-oghlu) (1428) i, 1118a; ii, 990a; vii, 644a; viii, 210b – I, 1151b; II, 1012b; VII, 644a; VIII, 215a
Yaʿḳūb, Abū Yūsuf → Abū Yūsuf Yaʿḳūb
Yaʿḳūb b. Aḥmad al-Kurdī (1078) vi, 913a – VI, 904b
Yaʿḳūb b. ʿAlī Shīr → Yaʿḳūb I (Germiyān-oghlu)
Yaʿḳūb b. Dāʾūd → Abū ʿAbd Allāh Yaʿḳūb b. Dāʾūd
Yaʿḳūb b. Ḥumayd b. Kāsib (IX) vii, 409a – VII, 410b
Yaʿḳūb b. Isḥāḳ b. al-Ward iv, 275b, 459b – IV, 287b, 479b
Yaʿḳūb b. Killis → Ibn Killis
Yaʿḳūb b. Layth al-Ṣaffār (Ṣaffārid(e)) (879) i, 145a, 452b, 1001a, 1008b, 1009b, 1294a, 1344b; ii, 196a, 553b, 812a, 978a, 1048b, 1082b, 1120a; iii, 195b, 245a; iv, 20b, 21a, b, 356b, 673a, 917b; v, 58a, 158a, 451b; vii, 410b, 413b, 777b, 794a, 801b; viii, 63a, 595b, 795b; ix, 683a; x, 105a; s, 125b, 127a – I, 149b, 465b, 1032a, 1039b, 1041a, 1333b, 1384b; II, 202a, 567b, 831a, 1000b, 1073a, 1107b, 1146a;

III, 200b, 252a; IV, 22a, b, 23a, 372a, 700b, 950b; V, 59b, 157b, 454a; VII, 412a, 415a, 779a, 795b, 803a; VIII, 64a, 614b, 822a, b; IX, 711b; X, 113a; S, 124b, 126a
Yaʿḳūb b. Muḥammad al-Taʿāʾishī i, 49b; v, 1250b, 1251b, 1252b – I, 51a; V, 1241b, 1242a, 1243a
Yaʿḳūb b. Mūsā s, 199a – S, 199a
Yaʿḳūb b. Nuʿmān al-Bulghārī i, 1307b – I, 1347b
Yaʿḳūb b. Shayba (875) vii, 706a – VII, 707a
Yaʿḳūb b. Sulaymān → Yaʿḳūb II (Germiyān-oghlu)
Yaʿḳūb b. Sulṭān Shāh iv, 1159a – IV, 1191a
Yaʿḳūb b. Ṭāriḳ iii, 1136a – III, 1164b
Yaʿḳūb b. Tāsh(u)fīn (Almoravid(e)) (XI) vi, 134a – VI, 132a
Yaʿḳūb al-ʿAwdāt (XX) vi, 307b – VI, 293a
Yaʿḳūb Beg (Kāshghar) (1877) i, 314a, 733b; iii, 1120b; v, 30b, 364a; vi, 766a; viii, 240a; ix, 649b; x, 677a; s, 98a –
I, 323b, 751a; III, 1148a; V, 31b, 365a; VI, 755a; VIII, 245b; IX, 674b; X, ; S, 97b
Yaʿḳūb Beg b. Uzun Ḥasan (Aḳ Ḳoyunlu) (1490) i, 293a, 311b, 1019a, 1067a; ii, 884a, 1136b, iii, 316a; iv, 1048b; v, 54a, 243b, 492b; vi, 514a, 541a; vii, 104b, 173b; viii, 750a, 766b – I, 302a, 321a, 1050a, 1099a; II, 905a, 1163a; III, 325b; IV, 1080a; V, 55b, 241b, 495a; VI, 499b, 525b; VII, 106b, 175b; VIII, 770b, 792a
Yaʿḳūb Čarkhī s, 50b – S, 51b
Yaʿḳūb al-Dibsī (XVIII) ii, 795a – II, 814a
Yaʿḳūb Efendi ii, 203b – II, 209b
Yaʿḳūb Ḥanna, Muʿallim v, 93b, 94a – V, 96a
Yaʿḳūb Ḳadrī ʿOthmān-oghlu iv, 593b; v, 196a – IV, 617b; V, 193b
Yaʿḳūb Khān Barakhzay i, 87b, 232a, 796b – I, 90a, 239a, 819b
Yaʿḳūb al-Madjishūn (780) x, 32b – X, 34a
Yaʿḳūb al-Manṣūr (Almohad(e)) → Abū Yūsuf Yaʿḳūb al-Manṣūr
Yaʿḳūb Pasha (1500) vi, 1025b; vii, 239a – VI, 1018b; VII, 240b
Yaʿḳūb Pasha (Ḥekīm-Bashî) iii, 340a – III, 350a
Yaʿḳūb Pasha Ḳarā ʿOthmān-oghlu (XIX) iv, 593b – IV, 617b
Yaʿḳūb Ṣanūʿ (XIX) vii, 438a – VII, 439a
Yaʿḳūb Ṣarfī, Shaykh iv, 709a; s, 167b – IV, 737b; S, 167b
Yaʿḳūb Shāh (Kashmīr) iv, 709a – IV, 737b
Yaʿḳūb Shāh Čak b. Yūsuf Shāh s, 132a, 167a – S, 131a, 167b
Yaʿḳūb al-Tammār s, 25a – S, 25a
Yakūba Sylla ii, 63b; iii, 107b, 180a – II, 64b; III, 110a, b
al-Yaʿḳūbī, Aḥmad b. Abī Yaʿḳūb (897) i, 591b; ii, 579b, 580a; iii, 1077b, 1206b; vi, 639b, 640a, 905a – I, 610b; II, 594a, b; III, 1104a, 1237a; VI, 624b, 625a, b, 896a
Yaʿḳūbiyya v, 121a, 896b – V, 123b, 902b
Yakun, Walī al-Dīn i, 597a – I, 616b
Yakup Kadri Karaosmanoğlu (XX) vi, 95a – VI, 93a
Yakut literature x, **732a** – X, **778a**
Yāḳūt (ḥādjib) (X) i, 1046b; iii, 46a, 197a, 1157a – I, 1078a; III, 47b, 202a, 1185b
Yāḳūt al-Ḥabshī → Djamāl al-Dīn Yaḳūt
Yāḳūt Khān iii, 15b – III, 16b
Yāḳūt al-Mawṣilī ii, 496b – II, 509a
Yāḳūt al-Mursī i, 1070a – I, 1102b
Yāḳūt al-Mustaʿṣimī iii, 736b; iv, 1122b; viii, 805b, 806b – III, 759b; IV, 1154b; VIII, 832b, 833b
Yāḳūt al-Rūmī, Shihāb al-Dīn al-Ḥamawī (1229) i, 456b, 488a, 571a, 594b, 712b; ii, 585b; iii, 724a, 840a; iv, 131b, 132a, 223b; v, 1012a, 1019a, b; vi, 185b; s, 195a –
I, 470a, 502b, 589b, 614a, 734a; II, 600a; III, 746b, 864a; IV, 137a, b, 233a; V, 1008a, 1015a, b; VI, 167b; S, 195a
Yāḳūtī (Artuḳid(e)) (XII) vi, 540b – VI, 525a
Yāḳūtī b. Čaghrî (XI) ii, 5a – II, 5a
Yaʿlā b. al-Futūḥ al-Azdādjī (Orania) (XI) vii, 942b – VII, 942b
Yaʿlā b. Muḥammad al-Ifranī ii, 494b; iii, 1042a – II, 507a; III, 1068a
Yaʿlā b. Muḥammad b. al-Khayr v, 1179a – V, 1169a
Yaʿlā b. Munya iv, 1134b – IV, 1166b
Yalangtush Biy s, 97a – S, 96b
Yalbaḳ (X) vii, 414a – VII, 415b
Yalbughā Nāṣirī Aḥmad (amīr) (XIV) vi, 667b; vii, 170b; viii, 987b; ix, 154b; s, 409a – VI, 654a; VII, 172b; VIII, 1022a; IX, 159b; S, 409b
Yalbughā al-ʿUmarī (1366) vi, 231b, 323b; vii, 171a; ix, 154b – VI, 225a, 308a; VII, 172b; IX, 159b
Yalbughā al-Yaḥyawī (Damas(cus)) (XII) ix, 154b – IX, 159b
Yalçin → Ḥusayn Djāhid
Yālī ii, 1119b – II, 1145b
Yalī Köshku vi, 57a – VI, 55a
Yaliṭ vi, 562b – VI, 547a
Yaltakīn i, 824b – I, 847b
Yam (pass/col) vi, 504a – VI, 489b
Yām, Banū i, 545b; ii, 517b; iii, 179b, 259b, 327b; iv, 201a; vi, 190b, 191a, b, 566a; ix, 1b, 829a; s, 387b – I, 563a; II, 530b; III, 183b, 266b, 337b; IV, 210a; VI, 174b, 175a, 551a; IX, 1b, 864a; S, 388a
Yām b. Nūḥ iv, 528b – IV, 551b
Yamak iv, 322b – IV, 337a
al-Yamāma i, 110b; ii, 126b, 569a; iv, 1072b; vi, 138b, 268a, 333b, 439a, 625b, 640b; s, 32a, 178a – I, 113b; II, 129b, 583b; IV, 1104a; VI, 137a, 252b, 318a, 424b, 610b, 625b; S, 32b, 179a
al-Yamāmī, Muḥammad b. ʿAbd al-Waḥīd iv, 89b – IV, 93b
Yaman (Yemen) i, 98b, 102a, 110b, 441a, 535a, 539a, 543b, 549a, 551b, 728a, 803b; ii, 660b; iii, 294a, 651b; iv, 198a, 199b, 448a, 519a, 745b, 834a, b, 902a; v, 807a, 895a, 1059a; vi, 9a, 35b, 40b, 45b, 72a, 74a, 84a, 118a, 137b, 138a, 140b, 141a, 144b, 145b, 149b, 151a, 178b, 190b, 191a, 221b, 266a, 280b, 293a, 320a, 321b, 334b, 337b, 345a, 371b, 436a, 473b, 559a, 561a, 720a, 911b; ix, 1a, 829a; x, 94a, 481b; s, 3b, 8b, 22a, 32b, 115b, 318a, 335a, 343b –
I, 101a, 105a, 113b, 453b, 551b, 556a, 560b, 566b, 569a, 749b, 826b; II, 677a; III, 303a, 672b; IV, 206b, 208a, 467b, 541b, 775a, 867a, b, 934b; V, 813a, 901a, 1056a; VI, 9a, 34a, 38b, 39a, 44a, 70a, 72a, 82a, 116a, 136a, 136b, 139a, b, 143a, 144a, 148a, 150a, 163a, 174b, 175a, 215a, 251a, 265b, 278b, 304b, 305b, 319a, 321b, 329a, 356a, 421a, 459a, 543b, 546a, 709a, 903a; IX, 1a, 864a; X, 101b, 517a; S, 3a, 8a, 22b, 32b, 115a, 317b, 334b, 343a
Yaman – ethnography/-ie i, 39b, 194b; v, 346a, 953b – I, 40b, 200b; V, 347a, 957b
Yaman – literature/littérature ii, 441a; iii, 124b, 688b, 746b; iv, 1188b – II, 452b; III, 127a, 710b, 769b; IV, 1221a
Yama -South/Sud v, 1059b – V, 1056b
Yaman, Banū ii, 635a; iii, 233a; vi, 303a, 620b; s, 338a – II, 651a; III, 239b; VI, 288b, 605b; S, 338a
Yamanī, ʿAbd Allāh (VII) vii, 472b – VII, 472a
al-Yamanī, Ḥasan b. Aḥmad vi, 352a – VI, 336b
Yaʿmar (Ḥazn) b. Zāʾida b. Laḳīṭ → Abū Nukhayla

Yāmid s, 61b – S, 62a
Yamīn al-Dawla → Maḥmūd b. Sebüktigin
Yamīniyān vi, 65a – VI, 63a
Yamlūl, Banū ii, 463b; iv, 739b – II, 475a; IV, 769b
Yamut, Banū iii, 1108a; vi, 495a – III, 1135a; VI, 480b
Yanāltegīn i, 1130a – I, 1164a
Yanbuʿ iv, 748b; vi, 35a, 149a, 157a, 320a; ix, 908a, b; s, 383b – IV, 778b; VI, 33a, 147b, 152b, 304a; IX, 946a; S, 384a
Yanbuḳ (Ḥaḍramawt) vi, 81a – VI, 79a
Yancî Kent (Diḥ-i Naw/al-Madīna al-Djadīda) x, 690a – X, 732a
Yang Dipertuan Agung s, 152a – S, 152a
Yanidj Beg ii, 984a – II, 1006b
Yānis al-Rūmī (1132) i, 939a; ii, 858a; iii, 54b; viii, 831a – I, 968a; II, 878a; III, 56b; VIII, 860a
Yānis al-Mutaʿarrab ii, 234b, 237a – II, 241b, 244a
Yanko b. Dobrotič ii, 611a, 971b – II, 626a, 993b
Yannaḳo b. Yanniḳo iv, 713a – IV, 741b
Yānnū b. ʿUmar al-Ḥādjdj (XI) vii, 587b – VII, 587b
Yanosh → Sigismund, John
Yanova v, 258a, 259a – V, 255b, 257a
Yanya i, 398b – I, 410a
Yao (Mozambique) vi, 203b – VI, 187b
Yār Aḥmad Khūzānī → Nadjm-i Thānī
Yār Beg i, 853a – I, 876b
Yār Muḥammad (Kalhōra) (1718) ix, 440a – IX, 457a
Yār Muḥammad Khān i, 231b, 282b, 1195a; ii, 185b, 186a; iv, 523b – I, 238b, 291a, 1230b; II, 191b, 192a; IV, 546b
Yarbay iv, 461b – IV, 482b
Yarbūʿ, Banū vi, 267a, b, 268a – VI, 251b, 252a, 253a
Yardjūkh i, 278b – I, 287a
Yarghu vi, 482b – VI, 468b
Yarī Beg i, 1068a – I, 1100a
Yārī Mudhahhib i, 1211b, 1212a – I, 1247b, 1248a
Yārkand i, 46b; ix, 617b; s, 98a – I, 48a; IX, 641a; S, 97b
Yārkandī Turks s, 327b – S, 327a
Yarkon (river/fleuve) → Nahr Abi Fuṭrus
Yarll ii, 303b, 309a – II, 312a, 318a
Yarpūz vi, 505b – VI, 491a
Yaʿrūbī, Nāṣir b. Murshid ix, 775b – IX, 804b
Yaʿrubid(e)s i, 554a, 1282a; vi, 735a, 843a, 963a; vii, 227a; viii, 636a, 856b; s, 355a – I, 571b, 1321a; VI, 724a, 834a, 955a; VII, 228b; VIII, 655a, 886a; S, 355a
Yārūkh ii, 483b – II, 496a
Yās, Banū i, 166a; ii, 557b, 618b, 619a; iv, 751b, 752a; v, 508b; vi, 961b; viii, 576b; s, 419a – I, 171a; II, 571b, 634a, b; IV, 781b, 782b; V, 512a; VI, 954a; VIII, 595a; S, 419a
Yasār Abū Ḥasan al-Baṣrī (VII) vi, 920a – VI, 911b
Yasārīzāde Muṣṭafā ʿIzzet iv, 1126a – IV, 1157b
Yasawī, Khwādja Aḥmad → Aḥmad Yasawī
Yasawiyya i, 299a; iii, 1115a; iv, 48a; x, 250a – I, 308a; III, 1142b; IV, 50b; X, 268b
Yashbak al-Shaʿbānī ii, 781b; iv, 210a – II, 800a; IV, 219b
Yashbak al-Ẓāhirī, Dawādār (Miṣr) (XV) vii, 173b, 174a, 175b – VII, 175a, 176a, 177b
Yashdjub b. Yaʿrub vi, 565b – VI, 550b
Yashīr i, 700a – I, 721a
al-Yashkūrī → Shirḳ
Yashkurī (Kaskar) s, 354b – S, 354b
Yashmut b. Hūlāgū (XIII) vi, 540b, 931b – VI, 525a, 923a
Yashruṭiyya ix, 174a – IX, 179a
al-Yaṣhūbī, Muḥammad b. Yaḥyā (Labla) (XI) vii, 761a – VII, 762b
Yasî (Ḥaḍrat) (Kazakhistān) x, 250a – X, 268b
Yasî (Turkistān) i, 147b, 299a; v, 859a – I, 152a, 308a; V, 866a
Yāsīn (valley/vallée) ii, 30b; s, 158b, 327b – II, 31a; S, 158b, 327a
Yāsīn al-Hāshimi (XX) iii, 521b; viii, 445b – III, 539a, b; VIII, 460a
Yāsir ʿArafat s, 9a – S, 8b
Yaṣlitan → Īslitan
Yasrān (oasis/-e) vi, 562a, b, 563a – VI, 546b, 547a, b, 548a
Yassî Čimen vi, 71a – VI, 69a
Yatenga vii, 394a – VII, 395a
Yathill vi, 88b – VI, 86b
Yathrib i, 429a; iv, 824a, 835b; v, 436a, 994b; vi, 373b, 374a – I, 441a; IV, 857a, 868b; V, 438b, 989b; VI, 358a
Yāṭib s, 407b – S, 407b
Yatīm Aḥmad vi, 610b – VI, 595b
al-Yatīma (pearl/perle) s, 253a – S, 252b
Yaʿūḳ vi, 651a – VI, 636b
Yaurawa (Nigeria) viii, 20b – VIII, 20b
Yavlaḳ Arslan → Muẓaffar al-Dīn Yavlaḳ
Yawm al-Djawnayn → Shiʿb Djabala
Yawm al-Liwā ix, 777a – IX, 810b
Yawm al-Rashāʾ ix, 777a – IX, 810b
Yawm Taḥlāḳ al-Limam x, 90a – X, 97a
Yawrawa (Nigeria) viii, 20b – VIII, 20b
Yaxartes → Sīr Daryā
Yaya i, 348a; ii, 33a, 444b – I, 358b; II, 33b, 456b
Yayče v, 32a – V, 33a
Yaylak v, 182b – V, 180a
Yazanīs iv, 541a – IV, 564a
Yazbak ii, 444a – II, 455b
Yazd i, 3b; iii, 216a, 502a; iv, 7b, 465b, 466a, b; v, 152a, 171a, 871a, 1115b, 1116a, 1148b; vi, 366a, 494a, 627b; s, 54b, 61a, 73a, 115a, 139b, 342a, 386a – I, 3b; III, 222a, 519a; IV, 8b, 486a, b, 487a, b; V, 154a, 168b, 877b, 1112a, b, 1139b; VI, 350a, 480a, 612b; S, 55a, 61b, 73b, 114b, 139a, 341b, 386b
Yazdadjird I (Sāsānid(e)) (420) ix, 75a – IX, 78a
Yazdadjird II (Sāsānid(e)) (457) v, 144b; ix, 76a – V, 147a; IX, 79a
Yazdadjird III (Sāsānid(e)) (651) iii, 571b, 586a; iv, 13b, 14b, 207b, 385a, b, 386a; v, 56b; vi, 620a, 745a; ix, 80a; s, 298a, 312a – III, 591b, 606b; IV, 14b, 15b, 216b, 402a, b; V, 58a; VI, 605a, 734b; IX, 83b; S, 297b, 311b
Yazdān iii, 584a – III, 604a
Yazdānfādhār vi, 493a – VI, 479a
Yazdānkhwāst → Māshāʾ Allāh b. Atharī
Yazdī → Madjd al-Mulk
al-Yazdī, ʿAbd Allāh (1573) viii, 778b – VIII, 804b
Yazdī, Djalāl al-Dīn Muḥammad (XVII) viii, 786a – VIII, 812a
Yazdī, Mrs. (XX) vi, 485b – VI, 471b
Yazdī, Sayyid Kāẓim (XX) vi, 553a – VI, 537b
Yazdī, Sharaf al-Dīn (1454) viii, 542b; s, 46b – VIII, 560a; S, 47a
Yazdigird → Yazdadjird
Yazīd I b. Muʿāwiya (Umayyad(e)) (683) i, 5a, 40a, 45a, 50a, 54a, 55a, 109a, 453b, 550a, 920a, 1029b, 1152a; ii, 89b, 198a, 280b, 541a, 739b; iii, 226a, 227a, 270b, 607b, 620b, 645b, 976a; iv, 938b; v, 132a, 997a; vi, 140a, 147a, 216a, 379a, 505b, 622a, 634b, 640b; vii, 267b, 268a; viii, 119a; s, 10a, 26a, 230b, 231b – I, 5a, 41b, 46b, 51b, 56a, b, 112a, 466b, 567b, 947b,

1061a, 1186b; II, 91a, 204a, 289a, 554a, 758a; III, 233a, 234a, 278a, 628b, 641a, 666b, 1000b; IV, 971b; V, 134b, 992a; VI, 138a, 145b, 200a, 363b, 491a, 607a, 619b, 625b; VII, 269b, 270a; VIII, 121a; S, 9b, 26a, 230b, 231b

Yazīd II b. ʿAbd al-Malik (Umayyad(e)) (724) i, 50a, 305a, 1149a; ii, 228b, 726b, 788b; iii, 2b, 42a, 650a, 802a; iv, 75b-76a; v, 590b; vi, 140b, 740a; vii, 359a; s, 10a, 52a, 243a – I, 51b, 314b, 1183b; II, 235b, 745a, 807a; III, 2b, 43b, 671b, 825b; IV, 79b; V, 594a; VI, 139a, 729b; VII, 361b; S, 9b, 52b, 243a

Yazīd III b. al-Walīd II (Umayyad(e)) (744) i, 53b, 57a; iii, 224a, 990b; iv, 370b; vi, 623b; x, 842a – I, 55a, 59a; III, 230b, 1015a; IV, 386b; VI, 608b; X,

Yazīd, Banū iv, 345a, 347a, 348a – IV, 359b, 362a, 363a

al-Yazīd, Mawlāy → al-Yazīd b. Muḥammad b. ʿAbd Allāh

Yazīd b. ʿAbd Allāh (Mālikī) vi, 263b – VI, 248b

Yazīd b. ʿAbd al-Malik → Yazīd II

Yazīd b. Abī Anīsa iv, 1076b – IV, 1108b

Yazīd b. Abī Ḥabīb (746) v, 1124a; vi, 944b – V, 1120b; VI, 937a

Yazīd b. Abī Muslim i, 50a; ii, 145b; iii, 42a – I, 51b, II, 149b; III, 43b

Yazīd b. Abī Sufyān (639) i, 111a, 151b, 447a, 460b, 997b; ii, 280a, b, 535a, 911a; vii, 254a, 264a; ix, 99a, 263a, b – I, 114a, 155b, 460a, 474a, 1028b; II, 288b, 548b, 932b; VII, 255b, 266a; IX, 103b. 271a, 272a

Yazīd b. Aḥmad iv, 346b – IV, 361a

Yazīd b. Anīsa (Ibāḍī) viii, 112b – VIII, 115a

Yazīd b. Djubayr vi, 774b – VI, 764a

Yazīd b. Ḥammād b. Zayd s, 384b – S, 385a

Yazīd b. Hārūn s, 89a – S, 88b

Yazīd b. Ḥātim b. Ḳabīsa b. al-Muhallabī (786) i, 18a, 125a; iii, 233a, 654b, 785a, 876a; iv, 336b, 827a, 829a; vi, 310b, 312a, 428a; vii, 160b, 189b, 229b, 360a; viii, 638b, 873b; ix, 901b – I, 18b, 128b; III, 240a, 676a, 808a, 900a; IV, 351a, 860a, 862a; VI, 295b, 297a, 413b; VII, 162a, 190a, 229b, 362a; VIII, 657b, 873a; IX, 938a

Yazīd Ibn Hubayra → Ibn Hubayra

Yazīd b. Ilyās iii, 1032a – III, 1058a

Yazīd b. Khālid al-Ḳasrī (745) vi, 624a – VI, 609a

Yazīd b. Maysara i, 959b – I, 989a

Yazīd b. Mazyad al-Shaybānī (801) i, 149b; iii, 233b, 234a; iv, 645a; vi, 345a, 438a; vii, 694a; ix, 392a, 488a – I, 153b; III, 240a, 241a; IV, 671b; VI, 329a, 423b; VII, 694b; IX, 904b, 507a

Yazīd b. Miḳsam Ibn Dabba iv, 1003a – IV, 1035b

Yazīd b. Muʿāwiya (Umayyd(e)) x, 841b – X,

Yazīd b. Mufarrl iv, 54b – IV, 57b

Yazīd b. al-Muḥallab b. Abī Ṣufra (720) i, 12b, 77a, 550a, 720a; ii, 809a, 1141b; iii, 41a, 42a, 177a, 649b, 650a, 717b, 1255a; iv, 15a-b, 644b, 926b, 1098b; v, 157b; vi, 140b, 740a, 920b, 954b; vii, 357b, 359a, 777a; viii, 873b; ix, 821b; x, 429b, 828b, 844a; s, 41a, 299a, 350a – I, 13a, 79b, 567b, 742a; II, 828b, 1168b; III, 42b, 43b, 181b, 670b, 671a, 740a, 1287b; IV, 16b, 671a, 959b, 1129a; V, 157a; VI, 139a, 729b, 912b, 946b; VII, 359b, 361a, 778b; VIII, 903a; IX, 855b; X, 460a, ;S, 41a, 298b, 350a

al-Yazīd b. Muḥammad b. ʿAbd Allāh, Mawlāy (ʿAlawid(e)) (1792) i, 356b; ii, 510b, 835b; v, 1192a; vi, 595a; vii, 39a, 387a; s, 401b – I, 367b; II, 523a, 855a; V, 1182b; VI, 580a; VII, 39a, 388a; S, 402a

Yazīd b. ʿUmar b. Hubayra → Ibn Hubayra, Yazīd

Yazīd b. Usayd al-Sulamī i, 837a; iv, 344b, 578b, 1174a – I, 860b; IV, 359a, 602a, 1207b

Yazīd b. al-Walīd → Yazīd III

Yazīd b. Yazīd b. al-Muhallab s, 41a – S, 41a

Yazīd b. Zurayʿ iii, 838b – III, 862a

Yazīd al-Rāḍī iii, 748a – III, 771a

al-Yazīdī → Muḥammad b. al-ʿAbbās

al-Yazīdī, Abū ʿAlī (IX) vi, 821b – VI, 811b

al-Yazīdī, Faḍl (IX) vii, 282a – VII, 283b

al-Yazīdī, Yaḥyā (al-Baṣra) ii, 293a; v, 174b; vii, 403b – II, 301a; V, 172a; VII, 405a

Yazīdī, Yazīdiyya i, 195b, 471b, 571a, 770b; ii, 16a, 184b, 459b, 526a, 1042a, 1070a; iii, 95b, 656a, b, 1040a, 1253b; v, 462a, 475b, 644a; vi, 201b – I, 201b, 485b, 589b, 793b; II, 16b, 190b, 471a, 539a, 1066a, 1095a; III, 98a, 677a, b, 680a. b. 1066a; V, 464b, 478b, 648b; VI, 185b

al-Yazīdī al-Naḥwī (925) vi, 352a – VI, 336a

Yazīdī (Mazyadī) Shāhs vi, 201b; ix, 488a – VI, 185a; IX, 507a

Yazīdīs/Yazīdiyya (Shārwān) → Yazīd, Banū

Yazīdiyya (sub-sect) iii, 660a; iv, 1076b; v, 208b, 210b – III, 681a; IV, 1108b; V, 206a, 208a

al-Yāzidjī, Ibrāhīm (1906) i, 572a, 596b; ii, 428a; iv, 967a; vi, 90b – I, 590b, 616a; II, 439a; IV, 999a; VI, 88b

al-Yāzidjī, Nāṣīf (1871) i, 596b; ii, 428b; vi, 113a, 114b, 303b; vii, 901b; viii, 736a; s, 40a, 159b, 161a, b – I, 616a; II, 440a; VI, 111a, 112a, 288b; VII, 902a; VIII, 757a; S, 40a, 159b, 160b, 161a

Yāzi̊djı̊-oghlu Aḥmed → Bīdjān, Aḥmed

Yazi̊dji̊-oghlu ʿAlī (XV) i, 21b, 419b; ii, 81a; iii, 738a; iv, 813a; viii, 163b – I, 22b, 431b; II, 82b; III, 760b, 761a; IV, 845b; VIII, 166a

Yazi̊dji̊-oghlu Meḥmed Čelebi (1451) i, 1202a; ii, 985b; iii, 43b, 711a; ix, 62a – I, 1237b; II, 1008a; III, 45a, 733b; IX, 63a

Yazi̊dji̊ Ṣalāḥ al-Dīn vi, 836a – VI, 826b

Yazi̊r, Banū vi, 416a – VI, 401a

al-Yāzūrī, Abū Muḥammad al-Ḥasan (XI) i, 533a, 1074a, b; ii, 495b, 856a, 858a, 860b; iii, 385b; v, 623b; vii, 730a, 731b – I, 549a, 1106a, b; II, 507b, 876a, 878a, 880b; III, 398a; V, 627b; VII, 730b, 732a

Yedigey → Edigü

Yedikule iv, 225a, 233a – IV, 234b, 243b

Yefet ben Eli → Japheth b. Eli

Yefremoy, Filipp v, 29a – V, 30a

Yegen Meḥmed Pasha → Meḥmed Pasha Yegen

Yegen ʿOthmān Pasha → ʿOthmān Pasha Yegen

Yeha vi, 560a – VI, 545a

Yeh-lü Ta-shih iv, 581a, b, 583a – IV, 604b, 605a, 606b

Yehūdā ben Shlomo Ḥarīzī (1225) vi, 114b – VI, 112b

Yemen/Yémen → Yaman

Yengikent → Djand

Yenibaghče iv, 232b – IV, 243a

Yeni-Čeri (Janissaries/Janissaires) i, 4a, 36a, 199a, 206b, 268b, 270b, 293b, 904a, 1061a, b, 1119a, 1120b, 1147b, 1162b, 1165a, 1256a, b, 1268a, 1277b; ii, 16a, 33b, 184b, 189b, 210b, 212a, 287a, 374a, 443a, 512b, 532b, 684a, 687a, 880b, 1086a, 1089b, 1135a; iii, 88a, 192a, b, 341b, 552b, 628b, 636a; iv, 237b, 242b, 867b; v, 32b, 275b, 359b, 642b, 643a; vi, 58a, 59a, 125a, 325a, 505a; viii, 176b, 178b, 182b, 193a, 196a, 198a, b; ix, 133a; s, 269b – I, 4a, 36b, 204b, 213a, 276b, 278b, 302b, 931a,

1093a, b, 1153a, 1154b, 1182a, 1197a, 1199b, 1294a, b, 1307a, 1317a; II, 16b, 34a, 190b, 195b, 217a, 218b, 295a, 384a, 454b, 525a, 545b, 701a, 704b, 901a, 1111a, 1115a, 1161b; III, 90b, 197a, 351b, 571b, 649b, 657a; IV, 248a, 253a, b, 901a; V, 34a, 273b, 360b, 647a, b; VI, 56a, 57a, 123a, 309b, 490b; VIII, 179a, 181b, 185a, 196a, 199b, 201b; IX, 137b; S, 269a
Yeničeri Aghasî i, 658b, 687a, 838a, 1256a; ii, 34a, 212b, 723b; iv, 232a – I, 679a, 708a, 861b, 1294b; II, 34b, 219a, 742a; IV, 242b
Yeni Il i, 241a – I, 248b
Yeni Djāmiʿ iv, 233b – IV, 243b
Yeñi Ḳale iv, 892a; v, 140a, 141a – IV, 925a; V, 143a, b
Yeni Kapî iv, 233a – IV, 243b
Yeni Odalar iv, 228b, 229b – IV, 238b, 239b
Yeni Othmanlîlar i, 13b, 37b, 61b, 63b, 64a, 210a, 641b, 657a, 974b; ii, 430b, 642a, 643b, 728a, 876a; iii, 553b, 592a; iv, 872a; vi, 6b, 9a, b, 68b, 89b – I, 13b, 38b, 63b, 65b, 216a, 662a, 678a, 1004b; II, 441b, 658a, 659b, 746b, 896b; III, 572b, 612a; IV, 905b; VI, 6b, 9b, 66b, 87b
Yeñishehirli ʿAbd Allāh Efendi, Shaykh al-Islām (1730) vi, 1004a – VI, 996b
Yeñishehirli ʿAwnī (XIX) s, 324b – S, 324a
Yeprim Khān iv, 862b – IV, 895b
Yĕrāḳā, Afdah, Shabbethai iv, 607b – IV, 632a
Yesḥaḳ (Ḥabash) (1429) iii, 4a – III, 4a
Yeshbek (XV) iv, 463a – IV, 483b
Yeshbum (ʿAwlaḳī) i, 767a – I, 789b, 790a
Yeşil Hisar iv, 580a – IV, 603b
Yesü Möngke (Mongol, 1260) ii, 3a, b – II, 3a, b
Yesügei Abū Čingiz-Khān (1176) ii, 41b – II, 42a
Yesün-Toʾa i, 1311b – I, 1352a
Yeti Ṣu → Semirečye
Yetīm ʿAli Čelebi iv, 1158b – IV, 1190b
Yidghā ii, 31b – II, 32a
Yigit i, 322b – I, 332b
Yigit Pasha i, 1263a; v, 276b – I, 1301b; V, 274b
Yîlandäräsi vi, 201a – VI, 185a
Yîlanlî-oghlu ii, 207b – II, 214a
Yilbughā → Yalbughā
Yilbughā Nāṣirī (XIV) i, 1050b; ii, 285b, 286a – I, 1082b; II, 293b, 294a
Yilbughā al-Sālimī iv, 437b – IV, 457a
Yilbughā al-ʿUmarī (1366) i, 1050b; iii, 239b; vi, 231b, 323b – I, 1082a; III, 246b; VI, 225a, 308a
Yîldîz Palace/palais de vi, 74b, 372b, 531b – VI, 72b, 357a, 515b
Yîldîz, Tādj al-Dīn i, 64a, 393b, 855b; ii, 120a, 267a, 1049b, 1101b, 1103a; iii, 1155a; v, 501a, 546a; s, 360a – I, 66a, 404b, 879b; II, 122b, 275b, 1074a, 1127b, 1129a; III, 1183b; V, 504b, 551a; S, 359b
Yîltuwar i, 1305b – I, 1345b
Yima → Djamshīd
Yimāk → Kipčak
Yināl → Ināl
Yintān b. ʿUmar iii, 959a – III, 983b
al-Yīnūḳ al-Farghānī vii, 191b – VII, 192a
Yisḥāk (baḥr nagāš) vi, 642b – VI, 627b
Ylbughā → Yalbugha/Yilbughā
Yithaʿʾamar Bayyin b. Sumhuʿalī Yanūf vi, 559b, 560a, 563a – VI, 544b, 548a
Yithaʿʾamar Watar vi, 560b – VI, 545b
Yoḳlama iv, 268a – IV, 280a
Yol parasî i, 475b – I, 489b
Yola i, 180a; ii, 942b – I, 185a; II, 964a
Yomut Türkmen iv, 1065a; v, 24a; s, 143b, 146b, 281a – IV, 1096b; V, 24b; S, 143a, 146b, 281a
Yoruba (Nigeria) iii, 646a; viii, 20b – III, 667a; VIII, 20b
Yörük x, 698a – X, 741a
Yōsēf ben Abraham → Yūsuf al-Baṣīr
Yotḳan v, 37a – V, 38a
Young Egypt Society → Djamʿiyyat Ittiḥād Miṣr al-Fatāt
Young Turks viii, 200a – VIII, 203b
Youssi, Aīt s, 145a – S, 144b
Yubnā vi, 652b – VI, 638a
Yücel, Ḥasan ʿAlī iii, 1199b, 1200b; v, 281b, 282a, b; s, 42a, 283b – III, 1230a, 1231a; V, 280a, b; S, 42a, 283b
Yūdāsaf → Bilawhar wa-Yūdāsaf
Yūdghān iv, 96a, b, 603b – IV, 100a, b, 628a
Yuʿfir, Āl s, 335a – S, 334b
Yuʿfirid(e)s vii, 444b; viii, 706a – VII, 445b; VIII, 726a
Yugoslavia/Yougoslavie i, 1275a; iv, 574a, b; v, 32a, 277a – I, 1314b; IV, 597a; V, 33a, 275a
Yuḥābir b. Madhḥidj vii, 591b – VII, 591a
al-Yuḥānisī, Abū Marwān ʿAbd al-Malik b. Ibrāhīm al-Ḳaysī (XIII) vi, 356a – VI, 340a
Yuḥannā (Ayla) vii, 373b – VII, 374b
Yuḥannā b. Haylān ii, 778b – II, 797b
Yuḥannā b. Sarābiyūn i, 213b; s, 271b – I, 219b; S, 271a
Yuḥannā b. Yaʿḳūb b. Abkār iv, 130b – IV, 136a
Yuḥannā b. Yūsuf (980) vii, 196b, 199b – VII, 196b, 200a
Yuḥannā al-Kaṣīr v, 368a – V, 369a
Yük iii, 212b – III, 218b
Yukhārībāsh iv, 387b, 389b, 390b – IV, 404a, 406a, 407a
Yuknakī → Aḥmad Yuknakī
Yulbars Khān v, 846a – V, 858a
Yuldash-oghlu Fazyl → Fāḍil Yuldash
Yulūḳ Arslān iii, 1119b – III, 1147a
Yumgān iv, 199b – IV, 208a
Yumugul-oghlu → Togan, Z.V.
Yūnānī College (Delhi) vi, 488b – VI, 474b
Yund Adalarî i, 792a – I, 815b
al-Yūnīnī, Ḳuṭb al-Dīn (1326) iii, 752b; vi, 354a; s, 400a – III, 775b; VI, 338b; S, 400b
al-Yūnīnī, Sharaf al-Dīn iii, 861b – III, 885b
Yūnis b. Ḳurḳumāz Maʿn (XVII) vi, 343b – VI, 327b
Yūnis Maʿn b. Fakhr al-Dīn ʿUthmān (1511) vi, 343a – VI, 327b
Yünnan v, 869a; viii, 259b – V, 875a; VIII, 264a
Yūnus (prophet/prophète) vi, 901a; viii, 51a – VI, 892a; VIII, 52a
Yūnus, Ḳapudān iii, 1176b – III, 1205a
Yūnus, Mongol khān (1478) x, 349a – X, 375a
Yūnus, Shaykh ii, 181b; iv, 428a – II, 187b; IV, 446b
Yšnus b. ʿAbd al-Aʿlā (877) x, 11b – X, 11b
Yūnus b. ʿAbd Rabbih vi, 879a – VI, 870b
Yūnus b. ʿAbd al-Raḥmān iii, 497b – III, 514b
Yūnus b. (Abī) Farwa (zindīḳ) vi, 829a – VI, 819a
Yūnus b. ʿAlī Bey iii, 605a, 635b – III, 625b, 657a
Yūnus b. Bukayr (814) vii, 361a; ix, 661a – VII, 363b; IX, 686b
Yūnus b. Ḥabīb (VIII) i, 105b, 158a; vi, 625b, 821b – I, 108b, 162b; VI, 610b, 811b
Yūnus b. Ilyās → Yūnus b. al-Yasaʿ
Yūnus b. al-Yasaʿ i, 1044a; v, 1160b – I, 1076a; V, 1150a
Yūnus al-Aṣṭurlābī s, 267a, 372a – S, 266b, 372a
Yūnus Beg (Tardjumān) (1541) x, 237a – X, 255b

Yūnus al-Dawādār iv, 425b – IV, 446a
Yūnus Emre (1320) iii, 1094a; iv, 812a; v, 264a, 677a, 681b; viii, 2b, 972b; s, 283a – III, 1121a; IV, 844b; V, 262a, 682a, 686b; VIII, 2b, 1007a; S, 282b
Yūnus al-Kātib (VIII) vii, 528a; s, 183a – VII, 528b; S, 184b
Yūnus Khān (Mongol) (1487) i, 148a; ii, 45b, 622a; x, 349a – I, 152a; II, 46a, 637b; X, 375a
Yūnus Khodja (Tashkent) (XIX) x, 349b – X, 375a
Yūnus Maʿn ii, 443b, 750b – II, 455b, 769a
Yūnus Nādī (XX) ii, 475b; iii, 1117a; vi, 94b, 95b – II, 487b; III, 1144b; VI, 92b, 93b
Yūnus Pasha (1517) ii, 1042a; viii, 307b – II, 1066b; VIII, 317a
Yūra viii, 160a – VIII, 163a
Yüregir-oghlu Ramaḍān i, 182b; ii, 38b – I, 187b; II, 39a
Yürkedj Pasha (XV) vii, 594b – VII, 594b
Yürük i, 470b, 651b, 1302b; ii, 40b, 612b; iv, 563a – I, 484b, 672a, 1342b; II, 41b, 627b; IV, 585b
Yürün-Ḳüsh (XII) vii, 733b – VII, 734a
Yūshā (Istanbul) vi, 57a – VI, 55a
Yūshaʿ b. Nūn (Joshua/Josué) v, 926b; vi, 412b – V, 931b; VI, 397a
al-Yūsī, Abū ʿAlī al-Ḥasan (XVII) vi, 607a; viii, 671b; s, 28b, 223a – VI, 591b; VIII, 691a; S, 29a, 223a
al-Yussāna i, 491b – I, 506a
Yūsuf (Ḥimyar) → Dhū Nuwās, Yūsuf Ashʿar
Yūsuf (Sādjid(e)) (926) vii, 656a – VII, 655b
Yūsuf I (Almohad(e)) → Abū Yaʿḳūb Yūsuf
Yūsuf I al-Muʾayyad bi-'llāh, Abu 'l-Ḥadjdjādj (Naṣrid(e)) (1354) i, 1339b; ii, 115a, 1017a; iii, 835b; v, 1128a, 1149b; vii, 1020b, **1023b** – I, 1379b; II, 117b, 1040b; III, 859b; V, 1124b, 1140b; VII, 1022b, **1025b**
Yūsuf II al-Mustaghnī bi-'llāh (Naṣrid(e)) (1392) iii, 972b; vii, 1020b, **1025a** – III, 997a; VII, 1022b, **1027a**
Yūsuf III al-Nāṣir li-Dīn Allāh, Abu 'l-Ḥadjdjādj (Naṣrid(e)), 1417) ii, 353a; vii, 1020b, **1025b** – II, 362b; VII, 1022b, **1027b**
Yūsuf IV Abu 'l-Ḥadjādjdj (Ibn al-Mawl/Abenalmao) (Naṣrid(e)) (1432) vii, 1020b, 1026a; s, 399a – VII, 1022b, 1028a; S, 399b
Yūsuf V Ibn Aḥmad/Ibn Ismāʿīl (Aben Ismael) (Naṣrid(e)) (1462) vii, 1020b, 1026a, b; s, 399a – VII, 1022b, 1028a, b; S, 399b
Yūsuf I al-Malik al-Muẓaffar Shams al-Dīn (Rasūlid(e)) (1295) i, 553a; v, 1241a – I, 570b; V, 1231b
Yūsuf, Abū 'l-Ḳāsim (Sādjid(e)) (928) vii, 656a; viii, 745b – VII, 655b; VIII, 767a
Yūsuf, Abū Yaʿḳūb → Abū Yaʿḳūb Yūsuf
Yūsuf, Mawlāy → Mawlāy Yūsuf
Yūsuf b. al-Abbār iv, 338a – IV, 352b
Yūsuf b. ʿAbd Allāh → Abu 'l-Futūḥ Yūsuf
Yūsuf b. ʿAbd al-Hādī (1503) iii, 486b, 842b; vi, 350b, 353b – III, 503b, 866b; VI, 334b, 337b
Yūsuf b. ʿAbd al-Muʾmin → Abū Yaʿḳūb Yūsuf
Yūsuf b. ʿAbd al-Raḥmān al-Fihrī (wālī al-Andalus) (VIII) i, 82a, 493b, 608b, 1079b; iv, 494b; v, 510b; vi, 221b, 568a; vii, 563b; ix, 870b; s, 81b – I, 84b, 508b, 628a, 1111b; IV, 515b; V, 514a; VI, 215b, 553a; VII, 564a; IX, 906b; S, 81b
Yūsuf b. ʿAbd al-Wahhāb s, 11a – S, 10b
Yūsuf b. Abi 'l-Sādj (X) i, 205a, 387a, 507a, 642b; ii, 191b, 453a, 679b; iii, 126b, 236a, 619b; iv, 22b; vii, 541b – I, 211a, 398a, 522b, 663b; II, 198a, 465a, 696b; III, 129b, 243a, 640b; IV, 24a; VII, 541b
Yūsuf b. Abī Saʿīd Muḥammad al-Marwanī (852) ii, 679a; vii, 666a – II, 696a; VII, 665b
Yūsuf b. Aḥmad → Yūsuf al-Muʿtamin
Yūsuf b. ʿAlī Küčük i, 1160b – I, 1195a
Yūsuf b. Bābak i, 153b – I, 158a
Yūsuf b. Barsbāy ii, 6a – II, 6a
Yūsuf b. Dīwdād (Marāgha) (X) vi, 499a – VI, 484b
Yūsuf b. Djihānshāh iv, 588a – IV, 611b
Yūsuf b. al-Ḥasan b. Aḥmad "Shīrāzī" (Mombasa) (XVII) vii, 226a, b – VII, 228a, b
Yūsuf b. Ḥasdāy i, 1091b – I, 1124a
Yūsuf b. Ibrāhīm, Sulṭān ii, 124a – II, 127a
Yūsuf b. Ibrāhīm al-Dāya iii, 745b – III, 768a, b
Yūsuf b. Ḳādis iii, 1055b – III, 1082a
Yūsuf b. Kaʾus i, 637a – I, 658a
Yūsuf b. Khalīl iv, 244b – IV, 255b
Yūsuf b. Muḥammad (Harāt) (XVI) viii, 784b – VIII, 810b
Yūsuf b. Muhammad b. Abī ʿIyāḍ b. ʿAbd al-Ḥakk (Marīnid(e)) (XIV) vi, 593b – VI, 578a
Yūsuf b. Nagralla i, 130b – I, 134a
Yūsuf b. Nūḥ iv, 605a – IV, 629b
Yūsuf b. Saʿīd al-Ahansalī iii, 167a – III, 170b
Yūsuf b. al-Sarrādj, Abu 'l-Ḥadjdjādj (1427) s, 399a – S, 399a
Yūsuf b. al-Sarrādj (1460) s, 399a – S, 399b
Yūsuf b. Sulaymān (dāʿī muṭlaḳ) s, 358b – S, 358b
Yūsuf b. Sulaymān (Gharnāṭa) ii, 1014a – II, 1037b
Yūsuf b. Ṭāhir al-Khuwayyī (Khūwī) (1137) vi, 913b – VI, 905a
Yūsuf b. Tāsh(u)fīn (Almoravid(e)) (1106) i, 7a, 43b, 251a, 389b, 495a, 1148b, 1176a; ii, 525a, 818b, 821b, 874a, 1013a; iii, 138a, 542b, 771a, 904b, 977a; iv, 672b, 943a; v, 654b, 655a, 1178a, 1179a, 1189b; vi, 222b, 592a, 596a, 597a, 742b, 743b; vii, 585a, 589b, 613a, 721b, 767a, b – I, 7a, 45a, 258b, 401a, 510a, 1183a, 1211a; II, 538a, 838a, 841a, 894b, 1036b; III, 141a, 561b, 794a, 929a, 1001b; IV, 700a, 976a; V, 658b, 659a, 1168a, 1169a, 1179b; VI, 216a, 576b, 581a, b, 732a, b; VII, 585b, 589b, 613a, 722b, 769a
Yūsuf b. ʿUmar → Yūsuf I (Rasūlid(e))
Yūsuf b. ʿUmar al-Thaḳafī → al-Fihrī
Yūsuf b. Uzun Hasan → Ḳarā Yūsuf
Yūsuf b. Wadjīh (ʿUmān) (X) vii, 358a – VII, 360b
Yūsuf b. Yaʿḳūb (prophet/prophète) i, 1229b; ii, 873a; v, 193b, 233b, 423b; vi, 412b – I, 1266b; II, 893a; V, 190b, 231b, 425b; VI, 397a
Yūsuf b. Yaʿḳūb (Imāmī) s, 233a – S, 232b
Yūsuf (Sanūsī) s, 165a – S, 164b
Yūsuf ʿĀdil-Shāh (-Khān) (ʿĀdil-Shāh, Bīdjāpūr) (1510) i, 199a, 1202b; ii, 922b, 1084b; iii, 15a, 1159b; vi, 62b, 63a, b; vii, 459a – I, 204b, 1238a; II, 944a, 1110a; III, 16a, 1187b, 1188a; VI, 60b, 61a; VII, 459a
Yūsuf Āghā, (Rikābdār) (1646) iii, 623a, 983a, 1086a – III, 644a, 1007b, 1113a
Yūsuf Āghā Efendi (XVIII) vii, 276a – VII, 277b
Yūsuf Akčura (Simbirsk) (XX) vi, 584a; s, 47b – VI, 568b, 569a; S, 48a
Yūsuf ʿAlī Khān i, 827b; ii, 83b – I, 850b; II, 85a
Yūsuf Amīrī (XV) vii, 567b – VII, 568b
Yūsuf Asʿar → Dhū Nuwās
Yūsuf al-Athīr s, 159b, 161a, b – S, 159b, 160b, 161a
Yūsuf al-ʿAẓm (XX) vi, 918b – VI, 910a
Yūsuf al-Badīʿī s, 362a – S, 361b
Yūsuf al-Barm iv, 16b; v, 855a – IV, 17b; V, 862a

Yūsuf al-Baṣīr (XI) iv, 305a, 306b, 605a; vii, 540a, 786a – IV, 319a, 320b, 629b; VII, 540a, 788a
Yūsuf Beg i, 354b – I, 365b
Yūsuf al-Bitrūdjī ii, 1009a; v, 586b – II, 1033a; V, 591b
Yūsuf Buluggīn → Buluggīn b. Zīrī
Yūsuf al-Dāʿī (Yemen) (XI) vi, 436a, b – VI, 421b, 422a
Yūsuf Ḍiyāʾ s, 168a – S, 168a
Yūsuf Ḍiyā Pasha ii, 202a, 635b – II, 208a, 652a
Yūsuf al-Fihrī → Yūsuf b. ʿAbd al-Raḥmān
Yūsuf Hamadhānī, Shaykh (XII) i, 299a, 515b; ii, 1078a; ix, 4a – I, 308a, 531b; II, 1103a; IX, 4b
Yūsuf Ḥubaysh ii, 801a – II, 819b
Yūsuf al-Ḥusaynī (XIX) vii, 437a – VII, 438b
Yūsuf ʿIzz al-Dīn (Ottoman) (XIX) vii, 525a – VII, 525a
Yūsuf Ḳādir Khān b. Hārūn Bughra Khān (Ilek-khān) (1034) i, 662a; ii, 4b; iii, 347b, 1114a; v; 38b; vi, 853b; vii, 407a; viii, 236b; ix, 649a – I, 683a; II, 4b; III, 358b, 1141b; V, 39b; VI, 845a; VII, 408a; VIII, 242b; IX, 674a
Yūsuf Kāmil Pasha (1876) iii, 1199a; vi, 69b – III, 1229a; VI, 67b
Yūsuf Ḳaramanli ii, 161b; iv, 617b, 618a – II, 166b; IV, 642b
Yūsuf Khān (Harāt) (XX) vi, 715a, b – VI, 704a
Yūsuf Khān Čak (Kashmīr) (1586) → Yūsuf Shāh Čak
Yūsuf Khān Mustashār al-Dawla, Mīrzā (XIX) iv, 164a, 397b; vi, 291b; s, 71b, 109a – IV, 171a, 415a; VI, 277a; S, 72a, 108a
Yūsuf Khān Riḍwī (Raḍawī) Mīrzā (Kashmīr) (XVI) iv, 709a; vii, 129b; s, 132a, 167b – IV, 737b; VII, 131b; S, 131a, 167b
Yūsuf Khāṣṣ Ḥādjib (XI) i, 299a, 987a; iii, 1114a, 1116a; iv, 699a; v, 538a; ix, 239a; x, 368b – I, 308b, 1017b; III, 1141b, 1143a; IV, 727a; V, 542b; IX, 245b; X, 395a
Yūsuf Khayl, Tatār Khān s, 203a – S, 202b
Yūsuf Ḳurayshī, Shaykh iii, 633b, 634a – III, 654b, 655a
Yūsuf al-Makassarī (1699) x, 257a – X, 276a
Yūsuf al-Manṣūr (1105) vii, 501a – VII, 501a
Yūsuf Muḥammad (1965) x, 38b – X, 39b
Yūsuf Mukhliṣ Pasha i, 992b – I, 1023b
Yūsuf al-Muʿtamin i, 7a; iii, 542b, 706a – I, 7a; III, 561b, 728a
Yūsuf al-Muẓaffar v, 683a – V, 688a
Yūsuf Pasha (1646) → Yūsuf Agha
Yūsuf Pasha (1838) → Yūsuf Ḳaramānli
Yūsuf Pasha Khodja → Khodja Yūsuf Pasha
Yūsuf Pasha Sayfā (Sayf-oghlu) (1624) ii, 443b, 635a, 749b, 750b; vi, 345a, 580b – II, 455a, 651a, 768a, 769a; VI, 329b, 565b
Yūsuf Shāh, Shams al-Dīn (Bengal(e)) (1481) i, 1168a – I, 1203a
Yūsuf Shāh I b. Alp Arghūn (Lur-i Buzurg) (XIII) v, 826b – V, 833a
Yūsuf Shāh II, Rukn al-Dīn (1340) v, 827a – V, 833b
Yūsuf Shāh Čak (Kashmīr) (1568) iv, 709a; s, 131b, 132a, 167a, 332b; 366b – IV, 737b; S, 131a, 167a, 332a; 366a
Yūsuf Shams al-Dīn Tabrīzī, Shaykh vi, 245b – VI, 229b
Yūsuf Shihāb i, 1078a; ii, 444a, 635b; s, 268b – I, 1110b; II, 455b, 651b; S, 268a
Yūsuf al-Sibāʿī vi, 468b – VI, 454b
Yūsuf Sinān b. ʿAlī b. Ḳayā Bey → Sunbuliyya
Yūsuf Sinān b. Yaʿḳūb Efendi (XVI) ii, 203b – II, 210a
Yūsuf al-Thaḳafī s, 354b – S, 354b
Yūsuf Wahbī (1981) ii, 39b; vi, 746b, 750b – II, 40a; VI, 735b, 739b
Yūsuf Yāsīn, Shaykh (XX) vi, 172b, 176b – VI, 161a, 162b
Yūsuf u Zalīkhā (Zulaykhā) iv, 62b; s, 65a – IV, 66a; S, 65b
Yūsufzays i, 218b, 220a, 229a, 229b, 769a, 864b; iv, 1102a; vi, 127a, 342b; vii, 220a – I, 224b, 226a, 236a, 792a, 888b; IV, 1133a; VI, 125a, 327a; VII, 221b
Yu-t'ien → Khotan
Yüz, Banū s, 46a – S, 46b
Yüz Āsaf i, 1217a – I, 1253b
Yuzbekī, ʿIzz al-Dīn Balban-i (1259) vi, 48a – VI, 46b
Yuzbek-i Tughrïl (Ḳïpčaḳ, Lakhnawti) (1257) vi, 48a – VI, 46b
Yüzellilikler s, 149b – S, 149b

Z

Zāb i, 16a, 43a, 424a, 426b; ii, 249b; iii, 982a; iv, 1186b; v, 442a, 1180b; vi, 311b, 434b, 435a, 624b, 727a, b; s, 103a – I, 16b, 44a, 436a, 439a; II, 256b; III, 1006b; IV, 1219a; V, 444b, 1170b; VI, 296b, 419b, 420a, 609b, 716a, b; S, 102b
al-Zabādī, ʿAbd al-Madjīd (1750) vi, 250a, 350a – VI, 234b, 334a
al-Zabādī, Abu 'l-Ḥasan al-Manālī s, 404a – S, 404a
Zābadj Zābag (Śrivijāya) vi, 207b, 234a; – VI, 181b, 207a
al-Zabāniyya vi, 217a – VI, 201a
Zabbā, Banū ix, 898b – IX, 935a
al-Zabbāʾ (Zenobia) i, 450b, 548b; iv, 556b; vi, 468a; x, 79b – I, 463b, 566a; IV, 580b; VI, 453b; X, 82b
Zabbāl → Kannās
Zabbān b. Sayyār al-Fazārī i, 690a; iii, 23a – I, 711a; III, 24b
Zabibē i, 525a – I, 541a
Zabīd ii, 91a, 996a; iii, 746a; iv, 1188b; v, 1244a, b; vi, 192a, 246a, 433a, 474b, 720a; vii, 270a, 514b, 579b; viii, 184a, 235b; x, 106b, 481b; s, 30b, 289a, 338a – II, 92b, 1019a; III, 769a; IV, 1221b; V, 1235a; VI, 175b, 230a, 418b, 460b, 709a; VII, 272a, 515a, 580a; VIII, 187a, 240b; X, 114b, 516b; S, 30b, 289a, 337b
al-Zabīdī (1791) viii, 458b – VIII, 474a
al-Zabīdī, Muḥammad b. Yaḥyā (1160) vii, 546b – VII, 546b
al-Zabīdī, Shaykh Abū ʿAbd Allāh → Ibn al-Daybaʿ
Zabita → Ḍābiṭ
Zābita Khān → Ḍābiṭa Khān
Zabtiyye → Ḍabṭiyya
Zābulistān i, 86a, 147b, 226b; ii, 1048b; iii, 304a, 715b; iv, 356b; v, 1166b; vi, 65a; vii, 777a; viii, 67a; s, 125b, 263a – I, 88b, 152a, 233b; II, 1073a; III, 313a, 738a; IV, 372a; V, 1156b; VI, 62b; VII, 778b; VIII, 68b; S, 124b, 263a
Zabuls/Zabols i, 226a – I, 232b
al-Zabūr i, 264a – I, 272a
Ẓabya (Ḳayna) s, 247a – S, 247a
Zād al-Rākib ii, 785a; iv, 1143b – II, 804a; IV, 1175b
Zādawaih i, 451b – I, 464b
Zadjal i, 501b, 574b, 595b, 602a; ii, 1033a; iii, 849b, 851a; v, 1207a; vi, 248a – I, 516b, 593a, 615a, 621b; II, 1057a; III, 873b, 875a; V, 1197b; VI, 232a
al-Zadjdjādj, Abū Isḥāk Ibrāhīm (923) iii, 838a; iv, 181b; viii, 14b; ix, 347a; x, 15b, 84b – III, 861b; IV,

189b; VIII, 14b; IX, 358a; X, 358a; X, 16a, 91b
al-Zadjdjādjī, Abu 'l-Ḳāsim ʿabd al-Raḥmān (949) iii, 597a, 838a, 1128a; vi, 224a; vii, 279b, 914a; x 15b – III, 617b, 861b, 1156a; VI, 217b; VII, 281b, 914b; X, 16a
al-Zadjdjādjī, Abu 'l-Ḳāsim iii, 597a, 838a, 1128a – III, 617b, 861b, 1156a
al-Zadjdjādjī, Abū ʿUmar (949) vi, 224a; vii, 279b, 914a – VI, 217b; VII, 281b, 914b
Zafadola → Aḥmad III (Hūdid(e))
Ẓafār → Ẓufār
Ẓafar, Banū vi, 649a – VI, 634a
Ẓafar ʿAlī Khān iii, 359a; s, 247b – III, 370a; S, 247b
Ẓafar Djang → Tadjammul Ḥusayn Khān
Ẓafar Khān (1663) viii, 851b – VIII, 881a
Ẓafar Khān (Bahmānid(e)) → ʿAlāʾ al-Dīn Ḥasan Bahman
Ẓafar Khān (Gudjarāt) (1403) x, 593a – X, 637b
Ẓafar Khān (Kashmīr) (XVII) iv, 709a – IV, 737b
Ẓafar Khān Ghāzī (Sātgāʾon) (XIII) ix, 83b – IX, 87b
Ẓafar Khān Lodī II (Daryā Khān) (XIV) vi, 62a, 294a, 407b – VI, 60a, 279b, 392b
Ẓafar Khān Malik Dīnār, nāẓim (Gudjarāt) (1319) ii, 1124a, b; x, 593a – II, 1150b, 1151a; X, 637b
Zafarabad ii, 498b, 499b – II, 510b, 512a
al-Zaʿfarānī, Mūsā → al-Tiflīsī, Abū ʿImrān
Zaʿfarāniya vii, 868b – VII, 870a
Zaʿfarānlū iii, 1104a, 1108a; v, 312a – III, 1131a, 1135a; V, 311b
al-Zafayān viii, 377a – VIII, 390a
Zafīr → Ḍafīr
al-Zāfir (Fāṭimid(e)) (1154) i, 9a, 198b; iii, 868a; vii, 579a; x, 149b – I, 9b, 204a; III, 892b; VII, 579b; X, 161a
Zāfir b. Sulaymān iv, 289b – IV, 302b
al-Ẓafra i, 166a; ii, 557b – I, 171a; II, 571a
Zafrullah Khān i, 302a – I, 311b
Zaganos Pasha (XV) iv, 969a; vi, 70a; vii, 237a – IV, 1001a; VI, 68a; VII, 238b
Zaggan, Banū vi, 741a – VI, 730b
al-Zaghall → Muḥammad XII (Naṣrid(e))
Zaghārī (dog/chien) iv, 491a – IV, 512a
Zaghāwa s, 190a, b – S, 191a, b
Zaghlūl → Saʿd Zaghlūl
Zaghra s, 330a – S, 329b
Zagros iii, 1253a; iv, 1a, 2b, 5a, b, 8a; v, 865b; vi, 200b; s, 147b – III, 1285b; IV, 1a, 2b, 5b, 6a, 8b; V, 872a; VI, 184b; S, 147b
al-Zahāwī, Djamīl Ṣidḳī (1936) i, 597b; iii, 1264b; iv, 145a, 720b; vi, 607a, 614a, 615a – I, 617a; III, 1297b; IV, 151a, 749b; VI, 592a, 599a, 600a
Zahel → Sahl b. Bishr
Zāhid Gīlānī, Shaykh (1301) viii, 755a, 801a – VIII, 777a, 828a
Zāhid al-ʿUlamāʾ al-Fāriḳī i, 1224a – I, 1260b
Zāhida Khātūn (Shīrāz) (XII) vi, 482a; ix, 473b – VI, 468a; IX, 492a
Zāhidī, Faḍl Allāh (general/général) (XX) iv, 41b; vii, 447a – IV, 44a; VII, 448b
al-Zāhidī, Mukhtār b. Muḥammad (1260) viii, 893b – VIII, 924b
Zāhidiyya → Ṣafawid(e)s
al-Ẓāhir (Mamlūk title/tître mamlūk) → under following name/sous le nom suivant
al-Ẓāhir (ʿAbbāsid(e)) (1226) i, 198a, 227a – I, 203b, 234a
al-Ẓāhir (Fāṭimid(e)) (1036) ii, 855a, b, 856a, 859a; iv, 514a; vi, 707b; vii, 162b, 482b – II, 874b, 875a, b, 878b; IV, 536b; VI, 696a; VII, 164a, 482b
al-Ẓāhir (Yemen) vi, 433a – VI, 418b
al-Ẓāhir, al-Malik → al-Ẓāhir Ghāzī
Zāhir Bouzrar (XX) vi, 754a – VI, 743b
Ẓāhir al-Dawla, ʿAlī Khān ii, 434a – II, 445a
Ẓāhir al-Dawla Ibrāhīm (Ghaznawid(e)) (1099) vi, 783a – VI, 772b
Ẓāhir al-Dīn b. al-ʿAṭṭār (XII) vii, 707a – VII, 708a
Ẓāhir al-Dīn b. Naṣīr al-Dīn (Marʿashī) vi, 513b, 514a, 516a – VI, 498b, 499b, 501a
Ẓahīr al-Dīn Marʿashī s, 363b – S, 363a
Ẓāhir al-Dīn Muḥammad Bābur Pādishāh (Tīmūrid(e)) (1530) vi, 768a – VI, 757a
Ẓāhir al-Dīn Mukhtār al-Manṣūrī (1316) viii, 158a – VIII, 160a
al-Ẓāhir Ghāzī b. Ṣalāh al-Dīn, al-Malik (Ayyūbid(e), Alep(po)) (1216) i, 197b, 798b, 803a, 989b, 996a, 1316b; ii, 37b, 353b, 556b; iii, 87b, 178a, 208b, 399b, 693b, 863a; iv, 482a; v, 924b; vi, 380b, 381a, 429a, b, 507a, 540b, 544a, 547b, 579a – I, 203b, 822a, 826a, 1020a, 1026b, 1356b; II, 38b, 363a, 570a; III, 89b, 182a, 214b, 412a, 715b, 887a; IV, 503a; V, 930a; VI, 365a, 414b, 492b, 525a, 528b, 532a, 564a
Ẓāhir Hamdān (region) s, 22a – S, 22b
al-Ẓahīr Ḳānsawh, al-Malik (Mamlūk) (1500) vi, 580b – VI, 565b
Ẓahīr al-Kāzarūnī (1298) vi, 111a – VI, 109a
Ẓāhir Shāh Bārakzay (XX) vii, 438b – VII, 439b
Ẓāhir al-ʿUmar al-Zaydānī, Shaykh (ʿAkkā) (1776) i, 63a, 391b; ii, 534a, 635b, 912a; iii, 325a, 992a; vi, 325b; vii, 33a, 179a, 420b; viii, 738b; ix, 270a; s, 20b, 268a, b, 269a – I, 65a, 403a; II, 547a, 651b, 933b; III, 335a, 1016b; VI, 310a; VII, 33b, 181a, 422a; VIII, 783a; IX, 278b; S, 20b, 268a, b
al-Ẓāhira i, 1098a; iii, 1004b – I, 1131a; III, 1029b
al-Ẓāhirī → ʿAbd Allāh b. Ḳāsim; Ibn Dāwūd; Ibn Ḥazm, ʿAlī
Zahīr-i Fāryābī iv, 62a; s, 108a, 239b – IV, 65a; S, 107a, 240a
al-Ẓāhirī, Īnāl Bay b. Ḳidjmās (XV) vi, 580b – VI, 565b
al-Ẓāhirī, Sayf al-Dīn Baktimur Djillak (XV) vi, 580b – VI, 565b
al-Ẓahirī, Sūdūn min ʿAlī Bak (amīr) (Ṭāz) (XV) iii, 239b; vi, 580b – III, 246b; VI, 565b
Ẓāhīrī Samarḳandī (1161) x, 232a – X, 250b
Ẓāhiriyya i, 414a, 1325a; ii, 182b, 890a; iii, 308a, 744b, 790b, 1149a; iv, 46a; v, 73a; vi, 193b; vii, 271b, 570a; s, 386a, 396b – I, 425b, 1365b; II, 188a, 910b; III, 317a, 767b, 814a, 1177b; IV, 48b; V, 75a; VI, 177b; VII, 273b, 570b; S, 386b, 397a
Zaḥla vi, 303a, 304a, b, 305a, 306a, b – VI, 288b, 289a, b, 290a, 291a, b
al-Ẓahr s, 50a – S, 50b
Ẓahrān i, 73a, 811b; ii, 108b; iii, 363b – I, 75a, 835a; II, 111a; III, 375a
al-Zahrāwī, ʿAbd al-Ḥamīd (1916) viii, 908a – VIII, 939a
al-Zahrāwī, Abu 'l-Ḳāsim (1009) i, 214a, 600b; ii, 482a, 901a; x, 454b; s, 271b, 272a – I, 220b, 620a; II, 494a, 922a; X, 487a; S, 271b
al-Zaʿīm, Ḥusnī (colonel) (1949) ii, 662a; v, 1047b; vi, 538a – II, 678b; V, 1044a; VI, 522b
al-Zaʿīm b. Yaḥyā (Zayyān, Banū) (XIII) vii, 722a – VII, 723a
Zaʿīr (Zaër), Banū vi, 142b – VI, 140b
Zaïre iv, 749b – IV, 780a
al-Zaʿīrī, Muḥammad b. Mubārik s, 28b – S, 29a

Zakandar v, 969a – V, 972a
Zākānī → ʿUbayd-i Zākānī
Zakarawayh vii, 192a – VII, 192a
Zakʿarid(e)s i, 507b, 508a – I, 523a
Zakariyyāʾ (Zacharias/-ie) vi, 630a; s, 402b – VI, 615a; S, 403a
Zakariyyāʾ b. Mammatī → Ibn Mammātī, Muhadhdhab
Zakariyya Aḥmad (1961) x, 144a – X, 154b
Zakāriyyāʾ al-Anṣārī iii, 779a; viii, 425a – III, 802a; VIII, 439a
Zakariyya Khān v, 598b – V, 602b
Zakariyyā Muḥyī al-Dīn s, 5b, 6a – S, 4b, 5a
Zakariyyā Tāmir vi, 469a – VI, 454b
Zakariyyā-zāde Yaḥyā Efendi (XVII) iv, 884a; vii, 597b – IV, 917a; VII, 597b
Zakāt i, 968b, 1099b, 1142a, 1144a, 1146a; ii, 142b, 154a; iv, 485b, 1151b, 1152b; v, 424b, 1252a – I, 998b, 1132b, 1176b, 1178b, 1180b; II, 146a, 158b; IV, 506b, 1183b, 1185a; V, 426b, 1243a
al-Zaḳāzīḳ s, 262b – S, 262a
Zakhūr Rāhib, Raphaël Anṭūn iii, 1245a – III, 1277b
Zakī, Aḥmad → Abū Shādī
Zaki al-Dīn Muḥammad al-Birzālī i, 1238a – I, 1276a
Zakī Nadjīb Maḥmūd (1993) x, 61b – X, 63b
al-Zākī Ṭamal ii, 828a – II, 847b
Zakī Ṭulaymāt (XX) vi, 750b, 751a – VI, 740a
Zakiya vi, 546a – VI, 531a
al-Zakiyya, Muḥammad b. ʿAbd Allāh al-Nafs(762) vi, 441b – VI, 427a
Zakka Khēls Afrīdī i, 238a, b; vii, 220b – I, 245b, 246a; VII, 222a
al-Zaḳḳāḳ (1549) vi, 894a – VI, 885b
al-Zaḳḳāḳ, ʿAlī (1507) i, 428a; iii, 948b – I, 440a; III, 973a
Zakrī → Ibn Zakrī
Zalīkhā/Zulaykhā vi, 412b – VI, 397a
Ẓālim b. al-Ṣaḥṣāḥ ii, 234a – II, 241a
Ẓālim Singh (fawdjdār) (1826) vi, 419b – VI, 404b
Zallāḥ ix, 774b – IX, 808a
al-Zallāḳa i, 7a, 43b, 242b; v, 1189b; vii, 553b, 590a, 775b, 778b – I, 7a, 45a, 250a; V, 1179b; VII, 554a, 590a, 777b, 780b
Zallīdj ii, 748a – II, 766a
Zām iv, 96b – IV, 101a
al-Zamakhsharī, Abu ʾl-Ḳāsim Maḥmūd (1144) i, 120a, 412a, 594a, 709a, 1129a; ii, 896a, 1079a; iii, 249a, 302a, 368b, 968a; iv, 524b, 525a, b, 527a, 615a; vi, 110b, 346b, 352b, 448b, 816a, 823b; vii, 469b, 914b; ix, 887a; x, 85a, 131b; s, 343a – I, 123b, 424a, 613a, 729b, 1163a; II, 917a, 1104a; III, 256a, 311a, 380b, 992b; IV, 547a, b, 548b, 550a, 640a; VI, 108a, 330b, 337a, 434a, 806a, 814a; VII, 469a, 915a; IX, 923a; X, 92a, 142a; S, 343a
Zamān, Mīr Muḥammad (XVI) viii, 783b – VIII, 809b
Zamān Khān (Kūh Gilūya) (XVII) vii, 674a – VII, 673b
Zamān Shāh Durrānī (Durranī) (1800) i, 72b, 230b; ii, 838b; iii, 1158b; iv, 391b; v, 599a – I, 74b, 237b; II, 858b; III, 1187a; IV, 408b; V, 602b
Zamāna Beg → Mahābat Khān
Zamān-i Yazdī i, 1301a – I, 1341a
Zamāniyya s, 325a – S, 324b
Zamfara (Nigeria) viii, 20a – VIII, 20a
Zāmil b. Djabr ii, 176a – II, 181b
Zamīn Dāwar i, 86a; ii, 1100b; viii, 595b –I, 88b; II, 1126b; VIII, 614b
Zamīndārī ii, 158b, 784b; v, 686b – II, 163b, 803a; V, 691b
Zamīndāwar iv, 536a, b; v, 691a; viii, 595b – IV, 559b; V, 695b; VIII, 614b
Zammūr (X) iii, 1043b – III, 1069a
Zammūr, Banū iv, 78a – IV, 82a
Zamora → Sammūra
Zamorins (Calicut) iv, 547a; vi, 459a – IV, 570b, 571a; VI, 444b
Zamrāwa, Banū vi, 742a – VI, 731b
Zamzam iv, 91b, 185a, 318a, 321a; vi, 144b, 151b, 165b, 166a, 167b, 171b, 665a, 666a, b, 676a, b, 677b, 708b – IV, 95b, 193a, 332b, 335a; VI, 143a, 150b, 157b, 158a, 159b, 161a, 651a, 652a, b, 663a, b, 664a, 697a
Zanādiḳa ii, 96a, 770b – II, 98a, 789a
Ẓanāga → —anhādja
Zanāna Rawḍa (Fatḥpur Sikrī) vi, 690a – VI, 677b
Zanāra v, 695a, 697a – V, 700a, 702a
Zanāta, Banū i, 92a, 367a, 533a, 699b, 762b, 860a, 1174b, 1175b, 1177b, 1309a; ii, 818b, 821a, 852b; iii, 137b, 138a, 654a, 1036a, 1039a; v, 1174a, b, 1179a, 1182b; vi, 221b, 310b, 427a, 434b, 435b, 571a, b, 572a, 573b, 727a, 728a, b, 741a, 742b, 943b; vii, 802b, 994a; x, 100b; s, 328b – I, 95a, 378a, 549b, 720b, 785a, 884a, 1209b, 1210b, 1212b, 1349b; II, 838a, 840b, 872b; III, 140b, 141a, 675a, 1062a, 1065a; V, 1164a, b, 1169a, 1172b; VI, 215b, 295b, 412a, b, 420a, b, 556a, b, 557a, 558b, 716a, 717a, 730a, 731b, 935b; VII, 804b, 995b; X, 108b; S, 328a
al-Zanātī, Abū ʿAbd Allāh Muḥammad iv, 1129b – IV, 1161a
al-Zanātī, Khālid b. Ḥamīd/Ḥumayd (740) vi, 923b – VI, 915a
al-Zanātī, Masʿūd b. Wānūdīn (XI) vii, 585a – VII, 585b
Zand iii, 1102b; iv, 38a; v, 461b, 617a, 663b; s, 405b – III, 1129b; IV, 40b; V, 464a, 621a, 669a; S, 405b
Žanda Pīl → Aḥmad-i Djām
Zandādj (Zandāk), Banū v, 1181a – V, 1171a
Zandaḳa → Zindīḳ
Zanda-rūd → Zāyanda-rūd
Zandaward s, 354b – S, 354b
Zandj i, 18b, 23b, 33b, 36a, 73b, 133b, 388b, 551a, 921a, 937b, 1086a, 1096a; iii,880a; iv, 567a; v, 940b, 941b; vi, 606a, 920b; vii, 650a, 760a, 766a, 801b; ix, 698b; s, 49a – I, 19a, 24a, 34a, 37a, 76a, 137b, 400a, 569a, 949a, 966b, 1118b, 1129a; III, 904a; IV, 589b; V, 944a, 945a; VI, 591a, 912b; VII, 650a, 761b, 767b, 803a; IX, 727b; S, 49b
Zandj, sea of/mer des → Baḥr al-Zandj
al-Zandj → ʿAlī b. Muḥammad
Zandjān vi, 498b, 502a; vii, 422b; s, 71a – VI, 483b, 487a; VII, 424a; S, 72a
al-Zandjānī, Abu ʾl-Ḥasan ʿAlī iii, 1071b – III, 1098a
Zandjānī, Ṣadr al-Dīn Aḥmad Khālidī (XIII) viii, 749b – VIII, 770a
al-Zandjī. Muslim b. Khālid (795) ix, 182a – IX, 187b
Zandjibār (Zanzibar) i, 36a, 554b, 1043b, 1282a, b; iv, 885b, 887b, 888a, 889a; v, 106b, 1030a; vi, 129a, 370a, 517a, 735b; vii, 53a; viii, 292b, 564a; ix, 699a; x, 194b, 622a; 816b; x, 816b; s, 351b – I, 37a, 572a, 1075a, 1321a, b; IV, 920a, b, 921b; V, 109a, 1026a; VI, 127a, 354a, 502a, 724b; VII, 53b; VIII, 301a, 582a; IX, 727b; X, 210a, 669a, ; S, 351b
Zands (Irān) vi, 202b, 551a; s, 71a – VI, 187a, 535b; S, 71b
Zangana, Banū iii, 1109a; v, 169b, 461a – III, 1136a; V, 167a, 463b

Zangī, Mullā   i, 1121b – I, 1155a
Zangī b. Mawdūd, Muẓaffar al-Dīn (Salg̲h̲urid(e)) (XII)
    viii, 978b – VIII, 1013a
Zangid(e)s/Zankid(e)s   i, 665b, 1161a; ii, 282b; vi,
    327a; vii, 998b; ix, 597a; s, 205a –   I,   686a,
    1195b; II, 290b; VI, 311b; VII, 1000a; IX, 619b; S,
    205a
Zängimār (river/rivière)   vi, 200b, 201a –
    VI, 185a
Zankī, ʿImād al-Dīn b. Arslan S̲h̲āh I (Zangid(e), Mosul)
    (XIII)   v, 454b – V, 457a
Zankī, Nūr al-Dīn Maḥmūd (Zangid(e), Damas(cus)/
    Alep(po), 1174)   → Nūr al-Dīn Maḥmūd b. Zangī
Zankī b. Aḳ-Sunḳur, ʿImād al-Dīn (Zangid(e), Mosul)
    (1146)   i, 314a, b, 426b, 466b, 664b, 797a, 971a,
    1160b, 1358a; ii, 64b, 347b, 348b, 354b, 489a,
    1082a; iii, 87a, 120a, 228b, 399a; v, 332a, 454a, b,
    922a, 924b; vii, 578b, 733b, 734a – I, 324a, 439a,
    480a, 684b, 820a, 1001a, 1195a, 1398a; II, 66a,
    357b, 358a, 364a, 501b, 1107b; III, 89b, 122b, 235a,
    411a; V, 332a, 457a, 927b, 930a; VII, 579b, 734b
Zankī b. Čökermis̲h̲ (XII)   vii, 408a – VII, 409b
Zankid(e)s   → Zangid(e)s
Ẓanna, Banū   vi, 82b – VI, 80b
Zanzibar   → Zand̲j̲ibār
Zar   v, 676a – V, 681a
Zarāfa   iii, 346b, 666a – III, 357a, 687b
Zarafs̲h̲ān (river/rivière)   iii, 483a; v, 247a; vi, 419a,
    619a; viii, 1031b; s, 97a – III, 500a; V, 245a; VI,
    404a, 604a; VIII, 1067a; S, 96b
Zarah   iii, 150a – III, 153b
Zarand(-g)(-dj)/Sid̲j̲istān   v, 151a, 868a; vi, 368b,
    633b, 667a – V, 152b, 874b; VI, 352b, 618b, 653a
al-Zarānīḳ   i, 1140b – I, 1175a
Zarda Kūh   vi, 494b – VI, 480a
Zarhūn   s, 103a, 350b – S, 102b, 350b
Ẓarib   vi, 562b – VI, 547a
Zarībiyya   iv, 668a – IV, 695b
Ẓarīfa   vi, 564b – VI, 549b
Zarīr(-ān)   iii, 113a – III, 115b
al-Zarḳāʾ (Jordan/ie)   x, 885a – X,
al-Zarḳāʾ (singer/chanteuse)   viii, 996b – VIII, 1031b
Zarḳāʾ bint al-Ḥasan al-Yamāma (VII)   iii, 455a; v,
    777b; ix, 565b; x, 359b – III, 470b; V, 783b; IX,
    588a; X, 386a
al-Zarḳalī (Azarquiel) (1100)   i, 600b, 725b, 726a,
    727a; ii, 243b; iii, 1137a; vi, 601a –
    I, 620a, 747b, 748a, b; II, 250b; III, 1165b; VI, 585a
al-Zarḳālluh (XI)   vi, 543a – VI, 527b
al-Zarkas̲h̲ī (1391)   ix, 887a – IX, 923a
al-Zarḳawī, Aḥmad Mūsā   s, 153a – S, 153b
Zarmihr b. Sūk̲h̲rā (K̲ārinid(e)) (VI)   iv, 644a; vi, 745b;
    s, 298a – IV, 670b; VI, 734b; S, 297b
Zarmihrid(e)s   vi, 745b – VI, 735a
Zarrūḳ, Aḥmad b. Aḥmad al-Fāsī   s, 404b –
    S, 404b
Zarrūḳ, Aḥmad b. Muḥammad al-Fāsī   s, 44a, 403a –
    S, 44b, 403b
Zarrūḳī   iv, 380a – IV, 396b
Zarrūḳiyya   ix, 173a – IX, 178b
Zarūd   s, 198b – S, 198b
Zarwāl, Banū   i, 84b – I, 87a
Zarzā, Banū   x, 916b – X,
Zattallī   → Dd̲j̲aʿfar
al-Zawāḥ̣ī, Sulaymān b. ʿAbd Allāh (XI)   ix, 816a – IX,
    851a
Zawāḥid(e)s   vi, 831b – VI, 822a
al-Ẓawāhir   i, 1313b, 1314a – I, 1354a
al-Zawāwī   → Ibn Muʿṭī
al-Zawāwī, Abu ʾl-Ḳāsim (XVI)   ix, 20b – IX, 21b
al-Zawāwī, ʿAlī (XVII)   iii, 720a – III, 742b

al-Zawāwī, ʿĪsā b. Maḥmūd (Mālikī)   vi, 263a, b, 353a
    – VI, 247b, 248a, 337a
al-Zawāwī, Muḥammad Saʿīd b. Aḥmad (XX)   viii, 902a
    – VIII, 933a
al-Zāwayī, Ḳuṭb al-Dīn Haydar (1221)   x, 251a – X,
    269b
Zawda, Banū   vi, 742b – VI, 731b
Zāwī b. Zīrī (Zīrid(e)) (XI)   i, 84a; ii, 1012a; iii, 1110a;
    vii, 563b; ix, 18a – I, 86b; II, 1035b; III, 1137b; VII,
    564a; IX, 18b
Zawīla   ii, 875b; iii, 657b; iv, 567a; x, 789b – II, 896a;
    III, 678b; IV, 589b; X,
Zawīlat Ibn K̲h̲aṭṭāb (Zouila)   vii, 186b – VII, 186b
Zāwiya   i, 139a, 290b, 1225a; iv, 380b, 383a, 433a; v,
    1129b, 1201b, 1208b; s, 223a –
    I, 143a, 299b, 1261b; IV, 397a, 399b, 452a; V,
    1126a, 1191b, 1199a; S, 223a
al-Zawrāʾ   vi, 676a – VI, 662b
al-Zawzan   iv, 910a; v, 450b – IV, 943a; V, 453a
Zawzanī (980)   vii, 772a – VII, 774a
al-Zawzanī, Abū ʿAbd-Allāh al-Ḥusayn (1093)   iv,
    910a; s, 289b – IV, 943a; S, 289b
al-Zawzanī, Abū Muḥammad ʿAbd Allāh al-
    ʿAbdalakānī (1030)   vii, 527a – VII, 527b
Zawzanī, Aṣīl al-Dīn   s, 363a – S, 362b
Zawzanī, Ḥusayn   iv, 525b – IV, 548b
Zāyanda-rūd   iv, 98a, 674a; v, 869a, 872b, 873b, 874a;
    vi, 17b; s, 275a –
    IV, 102b, 701b; V, 875b, 878b, 879b, 880a; VI, 15b; S,
    275a
al-Zayānī   → al-Zayyānī
Zayānid(e)s   → ʿAbd al-Wādid(e)s
Zayd, S̲h̲arīf (1666)   vi, 150a – VI, 149a
Zayd b. ʿAlī b. Ḥusayn (740)   i, 402b; ii, 889a; iii,
    493b, 617b, 1265b; iv, 371b, 446b, 1086b, 1161a; v,
    3a; vi, 264a, 649b; vii, 396a, 662b; ix, 423a; x, 41b; s,
    19a, 48b, 127a, 130a, 401a –
    I, 414a; II, 910a; III, 510b, 638a, 1298b; IV, 387b,
    466a, 1117b, 1193a; V, 3a; VI, 248b, 635a; VII,
    397b, 662b; IX, 437a; X, 43a; S, 19a, 49a, 126b,
    129a, 401b
Zayd b. ʿAmr b. Nufayl   ii, 1060a; iii, 1206a – II,
    1084b; III, 1236b
Zayd b. al-Dd̲j̲abal al-Ṭāʾī   iv, 858b – IV, 891b
Zayd b. Ḥammād (VI)   i, 565a; vii, 568b – I, 583a; VII,
    569b
Zayd b. Ḥāritha (VII)   i, 25a, 50b, 109b; ii, 275a, 372a,
    573b, 842b, 873b; iv, 492b, 898b; vii, 364a, 372b,
    374b, 756b; viii, 677a –
    I, 25b, 52a, 112b; II, 283b, 382a, 588a, 862a, 893b;
    IV, 514a, 931b; VII, 366b, 374a, 376a, 757b; VIII,
    696b
Zayd b. ʿĪsā   s, 48b – S, 49a
Zayd b. K̲h̲ālid   vii, 187a – VII, 187a
Zayd b. K̲h̲alifa   i, 928b – I, 956b
Zayd b. al-K̲h̲aṭṭāb   i, 1241b; ii, 569b – I, 1279b; II,
    583b
Zayd b. Mūsā al-Kāẓim (Ḥusaynid(e)) (IX)   vi, 334a –
    VI, 318b
Zayd b. Rifāʿa (1010)   i, 127a; iii, 1071b; vi, 823a – I,
    130b; III, 1098b; VI, 813b
Zayd b. T̲h̲ābit   ii, 540b, 886b; iii, 65a; v, 404b, 405a –
    II, 554a, 907a; III, 67b; V, 406a, b
Zayd b. Zāmil   iii, 1072b – IV, 1104b
Zayd b. K̲h̲ayl al-Ṭāʾī   ii, 1005a; iii, 812a; iv, 832b; s,
    304b – II, 1028b; III, 835b; IV, 865b; S, 304a
Zayd al-K̲h̲ayr   → Zayd al-K̲h̲ayl al-Ṭāʾī
Zayd al-Nār (IX)   vi, 334b – VI, 319a
Zaydān, Dd̲j̲irdjī (1914)   i, 597a; ii, 466b; v, 188a; vii,
    900b, 902b; s, 161a, 263a – I, 616b; II, 478a; V,
    185b; VII, 901a, 903b; S, 161a, 262b

Zaydān b. Mawlāy Ismāʿīl (ʿAlawid(e)) (1707) vi, 595a; vii, 38b – VI, 580a; VII, 39a
Zaydān al-Nāṣir b. Aḥmad al-Manṣūr, Mawlāy (Saʿdid(e)) (1627) i, 280a; iii, 256b; iv, 970b; v, 1191b; vi, 594b; viii, 724b; s, 29a – I, 288b; III, 265a; IV, 1002b, 1003a; V, 1181b; VI, 579a; VIII, 745b; S, 29a
Zaydāni → Saʿdid
al-Zaydī, al-Ḳāsim b. Ḥusayn (1003) vi, 436a – VI, 421b
Zaydiyya i, 48b, 106b, 402b, 403a, 551b, 552a, 553b, 554a, 1350a, b; ii, 218a, 1111b; iii, 125b, 254a, 688b, 984b; iv, 44a, 46b, 944b; v, 1240b; vi, 36a, 149a, b, 150a, 334a, 338a, 433a, 435b; vii, 508b; ix, 423a, 507a; s, 13a, b, 19a, 25b, 32a, 48a, b, 129b, 334b, 338a, 343a, 356b, 363a, 401a – I, 50a, 109b, 414a, b, 569a, b, 571a, b, 1390b, 1391a; II, 224b, 1137b; III, 128b, 261b, 710b, 1009a; IV, 47a, 49a-b, 977a; V, 1231b; VI, 34a, 147b, 148a, 149a, 318b, 322a, 418b, 421a; VII, 509a; IX, 437a, 526b; S, 13a, 14a, 19a, 26a, 32b, 48b, 49a, 128b, 334b, 338a, 342b, 356a, 363a, 401a
Zaydiyya – doctrine i, 445b, 1113b; iii, 486b, 1166a, 1265b; iv, 183a, 944b; v, 1237b; s, 236a – I, 458b, 1147a; III, 503b, 1194b, 1298b; IV, 190b, 977a; V, 1228a; S, 236a
Zāyid b. Khalīfa i, 166b; iv, 778a – I, 171a; IV, 809b
Zāyid al-Malṭūm ii, 175b, 176a – II, 181a
Zāyid b. Sulṭān al-Nihayyān, Shaykh s, 418b – S, 418b
Zaylaʿ i, 176b, 763b; iii, 3a, 5b; vi, 82b; vii, 515a; ix, 715a, b – I, 181a, 786b; III, 3b, 5b; VI, 80b; VII, 515a; IX, 746a, 747a
al-Zaylaʿī (1342) iii, 163b; vii, 969b – III, 167a; VII, 969b
al-Zaylāʿī, Shaykh ʿAbd al-Raḥmān (1882) ix, 722b – IX, 754a
Zayn, Sultan Aḥmad b. Muḥammad (Patani) (1906) viii, 1042b – VIII, 1078a
Zayn al-ʿĀbidīn (Kashmīr) iii, 420a, 453a; iv, 707a, 708b; s, 131b, 167a – III, 433b, 469a; IV, 735b, 736b; S, 130b, 167a
Zayn al-ʿĀbidīn, Sayyid (Mīrzāpūr) vii, 132b – VII, 134b
Zayn al-ʿĀbidīn b. Ghiyāth al-Dīn al-Marʿashī (XV) vi, 513a – VI, 498a
Zayn al-ʿĀbidīn b. Ismaʿīl i, 47b – I, 48b
Zayn al-ʿAbidīn b. Kaicil Gapi Baouna (Ternate) (1500) x, 419b – X, 449b
Zayn al-ʿAbidīn b. Mīr-i Buzurg (Marʿashī) (XV) vi, 512b, 514a, 516a – VI, 499a, b, 501a
Zayn al-ʿĀbidīn ʿAlī b. al-Ḥusayn (714) iii, 227b, 611b; iv, 277b; vi, 663a; vii, 398a; s, 231b, 401a – III, 234a, 632a; IV, 289b; VI, 649a; VII, 399a; S, 231b, 401b
Zayn al-ʿĀbidīn al-Kuntī v, 394a – V, 395a
Zayn al-ʿĀbidīn Pasha iv, 194a – IV, 202b
Zayn al-ʿAbidīn Sharīf iv, 1123a – IV, 1155a
Zayn al-Aṣnām i, 359a – I, 370a
Zayn al-Dīn, Shaykh (XVII) iii, 588b – III, 608b
Zayn al-Dīn b. ʿAlī al-ʿĀmilī → al-Shahīd al-Thānī
Zayn al-Dīn b. Shaykh ʿAlī, Shaykh (Mappila) (1521) vi, 461b – VI, 447b
Zayn al-Dīn ʿAbd al-Salām Kamūyī s, 414b – S, 415a
Zayn al-Dīn ʿAlī Kücük (XII) vi, 870b; viii, 129b – VI, 861a; VIII, 132b
Zayn al-Dīn Barakāt → Barakāt b. Mūsā
Zayn al-Dīn Bashāra, Amīr-i Ākhūr (XIII) viii, 15b – VIII, 15b
Zayn al-Dīn Ḳaradja b. Dulḳādir (Dhu 'l-Ḳadr) (1353) ii, 239a; vi, 507b – II, 246a; VI, 493a
Zayn al-Dīn Maʿn (XVI) vi, 343a – VI, 327b
Zaynab (Zenobia) → al-Zabbāʾ
Zaynab Begum bint Ṭahmāsp (Ṣafawid(e)) (XVI) vi, 483a – VI, 469a
Zaynab bint ʿAbd Allāh iii, 616a – III, 636b
Zaynab bint ʿAlī ii, 843a; iii, 609b – II, 863a; III, 630b
Zaynab bint Djaḥsh i, 44b; vi, 650b – I, 45b; VI, 635b
Zaynab bint al-Ḥārith (VII) ix, 205b – IX, 211a
Zaynab bint Isḥāḳ v, 1178b – V, 1168b
Zaynab bint Maẓʿūn iii, 63b, 1017b – III, 66a, 1043a
Zaynab bint Muḥammad vii, 879a – VII, 880a
Zaynab bint Ṭahmāsp iv, 977a – IV, 1009a
Zaynab bint Yaḥyā b. ʿAbd al-Salām (1334) viii, 156a – VIII, 158b
Zaynab al-Nafzāwiyya (XI) i, 251a, 389b; v, 654b, 655a; vi, 742b; vii, 585a – I, 258b, 401a; V, 658b, 659a; VI, 732a; VII, 585b
Zaynābād i, 1331a – I, 1371b
al-Zaynabī b. Ḳūla (VII) vi, 745a – VI, 734a
al-Zaynabī, Abu 'l-Ḳāsim ʿAlī b. al-Ḥusayn (ḳāḍī al-ḳuḍāt) (1149) s, 193a – S, 194a
al-Zaynabī, Abu 'l-Ḳāsim ʿAlī b. Ṭarrād (Ṭirād) (vizier) (XII) iii, 327b; vii, 735a; viii, 356a – III, 337b; VII, 735b; VIII, 369a
Zaynabī ʿAlawī (1031) vii, 19a – VII, 19a
Zaynal Khān v, 33b – V, 34b
Zayniyya x, 251a – X, 270a
Zaytūn (port) vii, 72a – VII, 72b
Zaytūna s, 334a – S, 334a
al-Zayyādī, Nūr al-Dīn ʿAlī b. Yaḥyā (1615) viii, 425a – VIII, 439a
Zayyān, Banū → ʿAbd al-Wādid(e)s
Zayyān b. Mardanīsh iv, 673a – IV, 700b
al-Zayyānī, Abu 'l-Ḳāsim (1833) i, 315b, 593b; ii, 874b; iii, 806a; vi, 113a; vii, 387b; s, 401b – I, 325a, 613a; II, 895a; III, 829b; VI, 110b; VII, 388b; S, 402a
Zayyānid(e)s → Zayānid(e)s
al-Zayyāt, Abū Ṭālib iii, 963b; vii, 203b – III, 988a; VII, 204b
Zāzā, Banū ii, 193a, 1139b – II, 199a, 1166b
Zēbākī i, 225a – I, 231b
Zehrā Khanīm ii, 980a – II, 1002b
Zeila → Ẓaylaʿ
Zekeriya Sertel (XX) vi, 95b – VI, 93b
Zekī Welīdī → Togan, Zekī
Zemmūr i, 84b, 171b; s, 144b – I, 87a, 176a; S, 144b
Zenāga → Ṣanhādja
Zenāta → Zanāta
Zenghī b. Bursuḳ i, 1336b – I, 1377a
Zengi ʿImād al-Dīn → Zankī
Zenkid(e)s → Zangid(e)s
Zenobia → al-Zabbāʾ
Zenta iii, 193b – III, 198a
Zerdabi, Ḥasan Bey Melikov ii, 476b – II, 488b
Zerzāya iii, 139a – III, 142a
Zeyrek-zāde Rukn al-Dīn Efendi (XVI) vi, 967a – VI, 959b
Zeytūn vi, 508b – VI, 494a
Ẓha → Djuḥā
Zhana ii, 25a – II, 25b
Zhōb (river/rivière) s, 329b – S, 329a
Zhouan-zhouan (Juan-juan) x, 687a – X, 729a
Zhukotin i, 1305b – I, 1345b
Zhūpīn iii, 197a – III, 202a
Zia-ul Haqq (Ḍiyāʾ al-Haḳḳ), Muḥammad (1988) v, 1082a; viii, 243a – V, 1079b; VIII, 249a
Zīb al-Nisāʾ Begum bint Awrangzīb → Makhfī
Zibane vi, 364b – VI, 348b
Zibaṭra vi, 231a, 505b, 775b – VI, 225a, 491a, 765a
Zibel → Djabala
al-Zibriḳān b. Badr i, 343b; iii, 641a; iv, 832b – I, 354a; III, 662b; IV, 865b